Safety Symbols

These symbols appear in laboratory activities to alert you to possible dangers and to remind you to work carefully.

Safety Goggles Always wear safety goggles to protect your eyes during any activity involving chemicals, flames or heating, or the possibility of flying objects, particles, or substances.

Lab Apron Wear a laboratory apron to protect your skin and clothing from injury.

Breakage Handle breakable materials such as thermometers and glassware with care. Do not touch broken glass.

Heat-Resistant Gloves Use an oven mitt or other hand protection when handling hot materials. Heating plates, hot water, and glassware can cause burns. Never touch hot objects with your bare hands.

Plastic Gloves Wear disposable plastic gloves to protect yourself from contact with chemicals or organisms that could be harmful. Keep your hands away from your face, and dispose of the gloves according to your teacher's instructions at the end of the activity.

Heating Use a clamp or tongs to hold hot objects. Do not touch hot objects with your bare hands.

Sharp Object Scissors, scalpels, pins, and knives are sharp. They can cut or puncture your skin. Always direct sharp edges and points away from yourself and others. Use sharp instruments only as directed.

Electric Shock Avoid the possibility of electric shock. Never use electrical equipment around water, or when the equipment or your hands are wet. Be sure cords are untangled and cannot trip anyone. Disconnect equipment when it is not in use.

Corrosive Chemical This symbol indicates the presence of an acid or other corrosive chemical. Avoid getting the chemical on your skin or clothing, or in your eyes. Do not inhale the vapors. Wash your hands when you are finished with the activity.

Poison Do not let any poisonous chemical get on your skin, and do not inhale its vapor. Wash your hands when you are finished with the activity.

Physical Safety This activity involves physical activity. Use caution to avoid injuring yourself or others. Follow instructions from your teacher. Alert your teacher if there is any reason that you should not participate in the activity.

Animal Safety Treat live animals with care to avoid injuring the animals or yourself. Working with animal parts or preserved animals may also require caution. Wash your hands when you are finished with the activity.

Plant Safety Handle plants only as your teacher directs. If you are allergic to any plants used in an activity, tell your teacher before the activity begins. Avoid touching poisonous plants and plants with thorns.

Flames Tie back loose hair and clothing, and put on safety goggles before working with fire. Follow instructions from your teacher about lighting and extinguishing flames.

No Flames Flammable materials may be present. Make sure there are no flames, sparks, or exposed sources of heat present.

Fumes Poisonous or unpleasant vapors may be produced. Work in a ventilated area. Avoid inhaling a vapor directly. Test an odor only when directed to do so by your teacher, using a wafting motion to direct the vapor toward your nose.

Disposal Chemicals and other materials used in the activity must be disposed of safely. Follow the instructions from your teacher.

Hand Washing Wash your hands thoroughly when finished with the activity. Use antibacterial soap and warm water. Lather both sides of your hands and between your fingers. Rinse well.

General Safety Awareness You may see this symbol when none of the symbols described earlier applies. In this case, follow the specific instructions provided. You may also see this symbol when you are asked to design your own experiment. Do not start your experiment until your teacher has approved your plan.

CALIFORNIA TEACHER'S EDITION

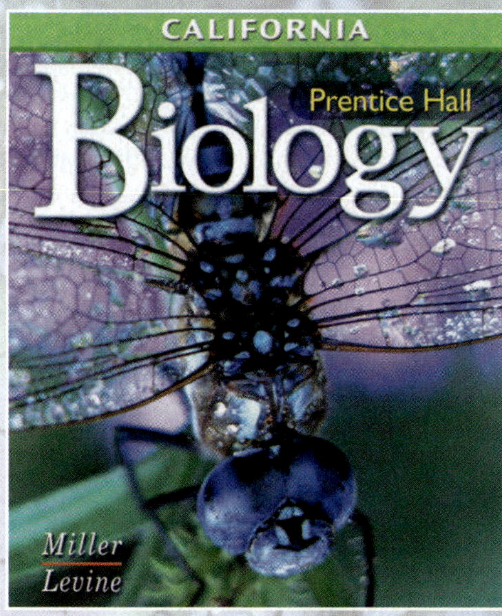

Kenneth R. Miller, Ph.D.
Professor of Biology
Brown University
Providence, Rhode Island

Joseph Levine, Ph.D.
Science Writer and Producer
Concord, Massachusetts

Overview of Teacher's Edition

Upper Saddle River, New Jersey
Boston, Massachusetts

ISBN 0-13-201353-3
1 2 3 4 5 6 7 8 9 10 10 09 08 07 06

Contents in Brief

A Science Program Backed by Research

In developing Prentice Hall *Biology*, we used research studies as a central, guiding element. Research on *Biology* indicated key elements of a textbook program that ensure students' success: support for reading and mathematics in science, consistent opportunities for inquiry, and an ongoing assessment strand. This research was conducted in phases and continues today.

Prentice Hall Research Cycle

1. Exploratory: Needs Assessment

Along with periodic surveys concerning state and national standards as well as curriculum issues and challenges, we conducted specific product development research, which included discussions with teachers and advisory panels, focus groups, and quantitative surveys. We explored the specific needs of teachers, students, and other educators regarding each book we developed in Prentice Hall *Biology*.

2. Formative: Prototype Development and Field-Testing

During this phase of research, we worked to develop prototype materials. Then, we tested the materials by field-testing with students and teachers and by performing qualitative and quantitative surveys. In our early prototype testing, we received feedback about our lesson structure. Results were channeled back into the program development for improvement.

3. Summative: Validation Research

Finally, we conducted and continue to conduct long-term research based on scientific, experimental designs under actual classroom conditions. This research identifies what works and what can be improved in the next revision of Prentice Hall *Biology*. We also continue to monitor the program in the market. We talk to our users about what works, and then we begin the cycle over again. The next section contains highlights of this research.

4. Preparing for NCLB

Because NCLB mandates science assessment in 2007, Pearson Prentice Hall is committed to providing scientific research to support the efficacy of our science programs in the classroom. Our study designs will follow closely the criteria of NCLB. Since NCLB specifies a minimum level of improvement that students must achieve each year, actual adequate yearly progress (AYP) will be reflected in the research used to validate the program.

Foundational Research: Inquiry in the Science Classroom

"How do I know if my students are inquiring?" "If students are busy doing lots of hands-on activities, are they using inquiry?" "What is inquiry, anyway?" If you're confused, you are not alone. Inquiry is the heart and soul of science education, with most of us in continuous pursuit of achieving it with our students!

Defining Science Inquiry

What is it? Simply put, inquiry is the intellectual side of science. It is thinking like a scientist—being inquisitive, asking why, and searching for answers. The National Science Education Content Standards define inquiry as the process in which students begin with a question, design an investigation, gather evidence, formulate an answer to the original question, and communicate the investigative process and results.

Michael J. Padilla, Ph.D.
President NSTA, 2004–2005
Professor of Science Education
University of Georgia
Athens, Georgia

"Because inquiry is an intellectual pursuit, it cannot merely be characterized by keeping students busy and active."

Understanding Inquiry

The National Research Council in Inquiry and the National Science Education Standards (2000) identified several "essential features" of classroom inquiry. We have modified these essential features into questions to guide you in your quest for enhanced and more thoughtful student inquiry.

1. ***Who asks the questions?*** In most curricula, these focusing questions are an element given in the materials. As a teacher you can look for labs that, at least on a periodic basis, allow students to pursue their own questions.
2. ***Who designs the procedures?*** To gain experience with the logic underlying experimentation, students need continuous practice with designing procedures. Some labs in which the primary target is content acquisition designate procedures. But others should ask students to do so.
3. ***Who decides what data to collect?*** Students need practice in determining the data to collect.
4. ***Who formulates explanations based upon the data?*** Students should be challenged to think—to analyze and draw conclusions based on their data, not just copy answers from the text materials.
5. ***Who communicates and justifies the results?*** Activities should push students to not only communicate but justify their answers. Activities also should be thoughtfully designed and interesting so that students want to share their results and argue about conclusions.

Making Time for Inquiry

One last question—Must each and every activity have students do all of this? The answer is an obvious and emphatic No. Some activities focus on content acquisition, and thus they specify the questions and most of the procedures. But many others stress in-depth inquiry from start to finish.

Evaluator's Checklist

Does your science program promote inquiry by—

- ✔ Enabling students to pursue their own questions?
- ✔ Allowing students to design their own procedures?
- ✔ Letting students determine what data are best to collect?
- ✔ Challenging students to think critically?
- ✔ Pushing students to justify their answers?

Reading Comprehension in the Science Classroom

Q&A

Q: Why are science texts often difficult for students to read and comprehend?

A: In general, science texts make complex literacy and knowledge demands on learners. They have a more technical vocabulary, a more demanding syntax, and place a greater emphasis on inferential reasoning.

Q: What does research say about facilitating comprehension?

A: Studies comparing novices and experts show that the conceptual organization of experts' knowledge is very different from that of novices. For example, experts emphasize core concepts when organizing knowledge, while novices focus on superficial details. To facilitate comprehension, effective teaching strategies should support and scaffold students as they build an understanding of the key concepts and concept relationships within a text unit.

Q: What strategies can teachers use to facilitate comprehension?

A: Three complementary strategies are very important in facilitating student comprehension of science texts. First, guide student interaction with the text using the built-in strategies. Second, organize the curriculum in terms of core concepts (e.g., the **Key Concepts** in each section). Third, develop visual representations of the relationships among the key concepts and vocabulary that can be referred to during instruction.

Nancy Romance, Ph.D.
Professor of Science Education
Florida Atlantic University
Fort Lauderdale, Florida

"Effective teaching strategies should support and scaffold students as they build an understanding of the key concepts and concept relationships within a text unit."

Evaluator's Checklist

Does your science program promote reading comprehension with—

- ✔ Text structured in an outline format and key concepts highlighted in boldface type?
- ✔ Real-world applications to activate prior knowledge?
- ✔ Key concepts, critical vocabulary, and a reading skill for every section?
- ✔ Relevant photos and carefully constructed graphics with questions?
- ✔ Reading checkpoints that appear in each section?

Built-in Reading Support in the Student Edition

During the section—

- Boldface sentences identify each Key Concept and encourage students to focus on the big ideas of science.
- Reading checkpoints reinforce students' understanding by slowing them down to review after concepts are discussed.
- Caption questions draw students into the art and photos, helping them connect the content to the images.

After students read—

- Section Assessments revisit the Key Concepts, use critical-thinking skills, and extend learning.

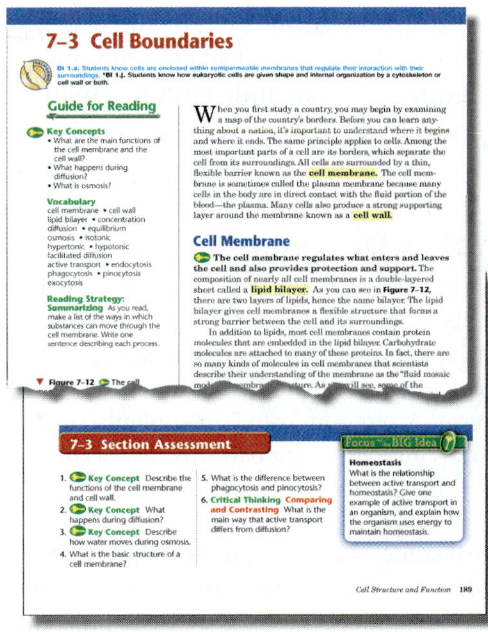

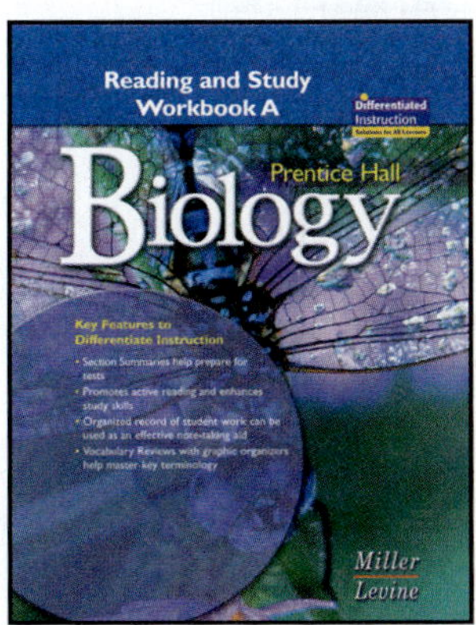

Reading and Study Workbook A

Key Features

- Section Summaries help students prepare for tests.
- Study worksheets for each section make students active and engage readers.
- Note-taking skills are developed as students read the text and complete the worksheets.
- Vocabulary Reviews with graphic organizers help students master key terminology.

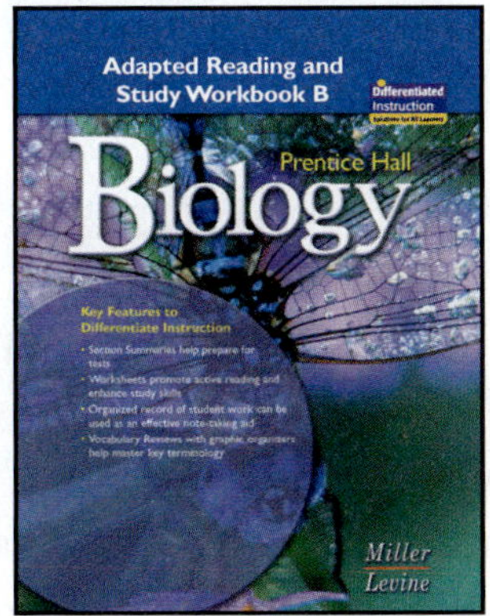

Adapted Reading and Study Workbook B

Key Features

- Section Summaries, written at a lower reading level, are appropriate for use with special needs students.
- Study worksheets employ tested strategies to engage special needs students and build understanding.
- Activities for less proficient learners make content accessible.
- Vocabulary Reviews are adapted to make key terminology accessible to special needs students.

Universal Access in the Science Classroom

What's different about each of the students in your classroom? Just about everything. A typical classroom is composed of students whose differences include culture, language, interest, motivation, and knowledge.

What is Universal Access?

When you begin your school year, you quickly observe the spectrum of your students—limited science background to nearly science experts, basic English skills to English proficiency, independent workers to "fidgets and roamers," and a host of others. How can the needs of all of these students be met? The simple answer is: *Universal Access*—focusing on students' individual needs and providing varied materials and grouping patterns that accommodate individual learning differences. Universal access emphasizes these principles:

1. All students are unique, and their strengths and needs change as their literacy develops and as they grow in their knowledge of science.
2. Instruction that attempts to meet the needs of all students must be flexible and adaptable for each individual.
3. Assessment of students' strengths and needs must be continuous to ensure that each student learns all he or she can.
4. Instruction must be multisensory with learning opportunities that rely on all of the senses, and it must be scaffolded for each student's learning level.
5. Instruction with multimedia enhances the probability of each student's learning.

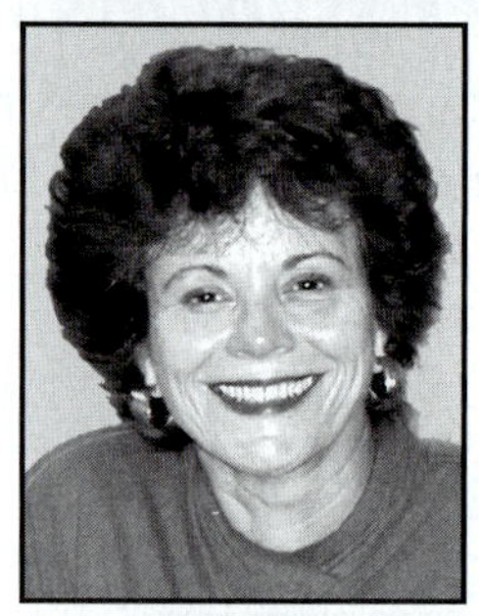

James Flood
Diane Lapp
School of Teacher Education
San Diego State University
San Diego, California

What techniques help universal access?

Whenever possible, enhance learning with **one-to-one teaching episodes,** conferring individually with one student while other students are working independently. In addition, **small group instruction** of students with similar instructional needs—where you are in close proximity with students so that quick, supportive responses can be immediate and exact—is very effective.

A wide array of materials written at different levels makes information accessible to students. This range of materials should include:

- **Print materials** that are written at many different reading levels and exhibit many different genres and formats (textbooks, magazines, newspaper articles, computer messages, reference materials)
- **Media** including videos, computer programs, multimedia productions, and virtual reality explorations
- **Artifacts** or realia that make information accessible to students, for example, pictures and videos, music, and objects that can be touched and studied

Depending upon prior content knowledge, students require **different levels of pacing.** Universal access requires that some lessons be accelerated for some students and decelerated for others, and it often requires the repetition of a lesson.

Evaluator's Checklist

Does your science program promote universal access by—

- ✔ Reinforcing reading skills throughout the Student Edition?
- ✔ Integrating varied learning experiences into the program resources?
- ✔ Providing teaching suggestions for differentiating instruction?
- ✔ Labeling resources according to student ability levels?
- ✔ Guiding lesson pacing for varied ability levels?

Universal Access in the *Biology* Program

Universal access does not mean that the teacher offers each and every student in the class a "different" lesson. Rather, it means that multiple methods of instruction are used to maximize each student's likelihood of understanding the material. The Prentice Hall *Biology* program provides a variety of support and instructional materials to meet the learning needs of all students.

Support for Students

Highlights among the materials that support universal access for students include:

- **Key Concept** icons in the Student Edition identify key ideas and focus on the main concepts in *Biology*.
- A strong **visual learning strand** plays a large role in the Student Edition where graphs, charts, illustrations, and photos work hand-in-hand with the text to clarify complex topics.
- Go Online **Web resources** from NSTA SciLinks and **PHSchool.com** give students opportunities to master concepts outside the text.
- The **Reading and Study Workbook A** and **Adapted Reading and Study Workbook B** support every section of the Student Edition, guiding students through the content and providing practice for reading and math skills.
- Laboratory Manuals A and B give students **hands-on experiences with the content** while challenging students according to their ability levels.
- **Discovery Channel DVD** makes the content accessible through dynamic footage and high-impact stories.
- The **Interactive Textbook** contains the complete Student Edition online and on CD-ROM for an interactive visual experience with the content in which they get reading support, activities, and assessment feedback.

Support for Teachers

- The **Univeral Access** teaching notes within each section differentiate instruction for less proficient readers, advanced readers, English Language Learners, and inclusion/special needs students.
- **Leveling of the student resources and teaching notes** on the planning guide, at point-of-use, and in the lesson plans aids planning for all students.
- **Chapter Tests A and B** assess students with a level of rigor appropriate to their ability levels.
- **TeacherExpress™** allows teachers to print out lesson plans to customize for universal access.

Universal Access Inclusion/Special Needs

To engage students' interest in feeding relationships and ecological pyramids, ask them about feeding relationships with which they may have some familiarity. For example, most students will know birds in their neighborhood feed on either seeds and berries or animals such as worms and insects. Elicit from students ideas about relative numbers at different trophic levels, energy transfer, and biomass comparisons.

PLANNING KEY

Ability Levels
for students performing . . .
below grade level L1
at grade level L2
above grade level L3

Print Compone
SE Student Edition
TE Teacher's Edition
RSW Reading & Study W
ARSW Adapted Reading &
Workbook B
TR Teaching Resources
IF Investigations in Fi

Program Resources

TR: Lesson Plan 1–1, Section Summary, p. 5 L1, p. 13 L2, Worksheets, p. 8 L1, pp. 15–16 L2
RSW: Section 1–1 L2

TR: Lesson Plan 1–2, Section Summary, p. 5 L1, p. 13 L2, Worksheets, pp. 9–10 L1, pp. 17–19 L2, Enrichment L2 L3
RSW: Section 1–2 L2
ARSW: Section 1–2 L1
IDM: Issues and Decisions 2 L2 L3

Assessment in the Science Curriculum

No Child Left Behind clearly challenges school districts across the nation to raise expectations for all students with testing of student achievement in science beginning in 2007–2008.

A primary goal of NCLB is to provide classroom teachers with better data from scientifically valid assessments in order to inform instructional planning and to identify students who are at risk and require intervention. It has been a common practice to teach a science lesson, administer a test, grade it, and move on. This practice is a thing of the past. With the spotlight now on improving student performance, it is essential to use assessment results as a way to identify student strengths and challenges. Providing student feedback and obtaining student input is a valuable, essential part of the assessment process.

Assessment is a never-ending cycle, as is shown in the following diagram. Although you may begin at any point in the assessment cycle, the basic process is the same.

ASSESS: Use a variety of assessment tools to gain information and strengthen student understanding.

ANALYZE: Analyze assessment results to create a picture of student strengths and challenges.

TARGET: Choose a target to create a focused path on which to proceed.

STRATEGIZE: Identify strategies to achieve the target, create a plan for implementation, and choose assessment tools.

IMPLEMENT: Implement the plan with a focus on gathering and using assessment information throughout.

An important assessment strategy is to ensure that students have ample opportunities to check their understanding of skills and concepts before moving on to the next topic. Checking for understanding also includes asking appropriate, probing questions with each example presented. This enables students and teachers to know whether the skills or concepts being introduced are actually understood.

Eileen Depka
Supervisor of Standards and Assessment
Waukesha, Wisconsin

"Meeting the NCLB challenge will necessitate an integrated approach to assessment with a variety of assessment tools."

Evaluator's Checklist

Does your science program include assessments that—

- ✔ Are embedded before, during, and after lesson instruction?
- ✔ Align to standards and to the instructional program?
- ✔ Assess both skill acquisition and understanding?
- ✔ Mirror the various formats of standardized tests?

Assessment in Prentice Hall *Biology*

Prentice Hall *Biology*'s range of strategies for monitoring progress will help teachers find the right opportunity for reaching all their students. The assessment strategies in Prentice Hall *Biology* ensure student success in content mastery as well as high-stakes test performance.

In the Student Edition

Caption Questions enhance critical-thinking skills and maximize the effectiveness of art, graphics, and narrative.

Reading Checkpoints assess students' understanding at key points during a lesson.

Section Assessment Questions review and assess the understanding of the Key Concepts.

Comprehensive Chapter Reviews and ***Assessment*** provide opportunities for students to check their own understanding and practice valuable high-stakes test-taking skills.

In the Program Resources

***ExamView® Computer Test Bank* CD-ROM** provides teachers access to thousands of modifiable test questions.

Diagnostic Tests and ***Standardized Test Preparation Workbook*** include diagnostic and prescription tools, progress-monitoring aids, and practice tests that help teachers focus on improving test scores.

Interactive Textbook provides a wealth of assessment tools. Students can monitor their progress at point of use with ongoing assessment, help tutorials, and instant feedback.

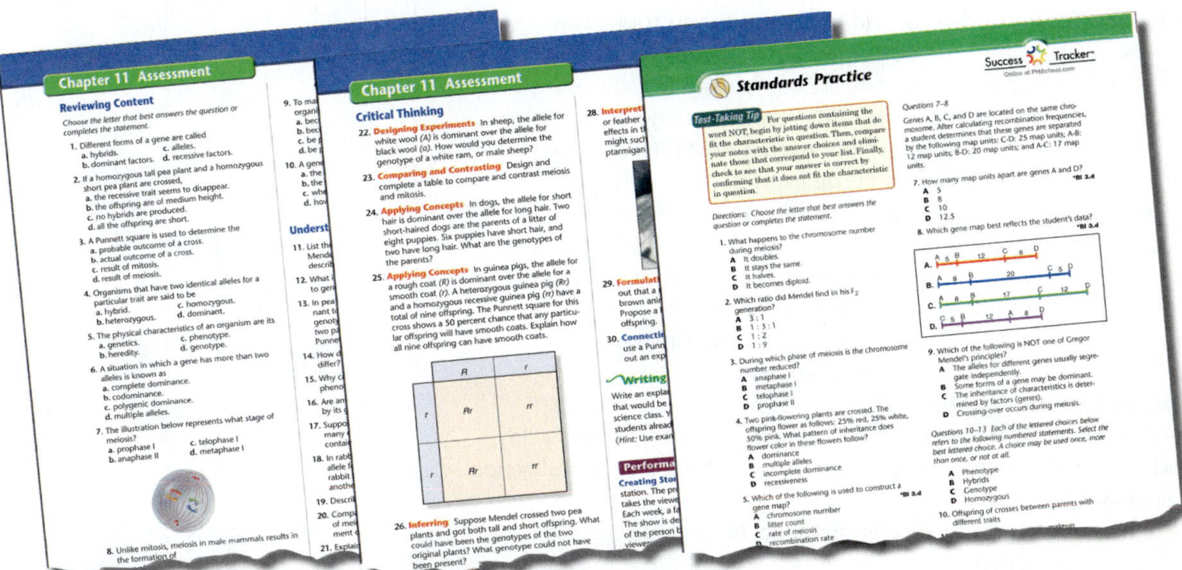

Standard Course of Study for Biology: Year-at-a-Glance

Use this organizational chart for a long-range view of where the California Content Standards for Biology/Life Sciences are covered in Prentice Hall *Biology*. (Note that standards in blue type address the NCLB High School standards as well as the Biology standards.)

California Content Standards	PRENTICE HALL BIOLOGY CHAPTERS 1	2	3	4	5	6	7	8	9	10	11
Cell Biology											
Grade 7											
1. All living organisms are composed of cells, from just one to many trillions, whose details usually are visible only through a microscope. As a basis for understanding this concept:											
7 1.c. *Students know* the nucleus is the repository for genetic information in plant and animal cells.							●				
7 1.d. *Students know* that mitochondria liberate energy for the work that cells do and that chloroplasts capture sunlight energy for photosynthesis.								●	●		
7 1.e. *Students know* cells divide to increase their numbers through a process of mitosis, which results in two daughter cells with identical sets of chromosomes.										●	
Grade 8											
6. Principles of chemistry underlie the functioning of biological systems. As a basis for understanding this concept:											
8 6.b. *Students know* that living organisms are made of molecules consisting largely of carbon, hydrogen, nitrogen, oxygen, phosphorus, and sulfur.		●									
8 6.c. *Students know* that living organisms have many different kinds of molecules, including small ones, such as water and salt, and very large ones, such as carbohydrates, fats, proteins, and DNA.		●									
Biology/Life Science											
1. The fundamental life processes of plants and animals depend on a variety of chemical reactions that occur in specialized areas of the organism's cells. As a basis for understanding this concept:											
BI 1.a. *Students know* cells are enclosed within semipermeable membranes that regulate their interaction with their surroundings.							●				
BI 1.b. *Students know* enzymes are proteins that catalyze biochemical reactions without altering the reaction equilibrium and the activities of enzymes depend on the temperature, ionic conditions, and the pH of the surroundings.		●									
BI 1.c. *Students know* how prokaryotic cells, eukaryotic cells (including those from plants and animals), and viruses differ in complexity and general structure.							●				
BI 1.d. *Students know* the central dogma of molecular biology outlines the flow of information from transcription of ribonucleic acid (RNA) in the nucleus to translation of proteins on ribosomes in the cytoplasm.											
BI 1.e. *Students know* the role of the endoplasmic reticulum and Golgi apparatus in the secretion of proteins.							●				
BI 1.f. *Students know* usable energy is captured from sunlight by chloroplasts and is stored through the synthesis of sugar from carbon dioxide.								●			
BI 1.g. *Students know* the role of the mitochondria in making stored chemical-bond energy available to cells by completing the breakdown of glucose to carbon dioxide.									●		
BI 1.h. *Students know* most macromolecules (polysaccharides, nucleic acids, proteins, lipids) in cells and organisms are synthesized from a small collection of simple precursors.		●									
*BI 1.i. *Students know* how chemiosmotic gradients in the mitochondria and chloroplast store energy for ATP production.								●	●		
*BI 1.j. *Students know* how eukaryotic cells are given shape and internal organization by a cytoskeleton or cell wall or both.							●				

Standards identified with an asterisk (*) are not tested on the California Standards Test. However, they are important to the comprehension of the strand, and all students should have the opportunity to learn them.

PRENTICE HALL BIOLOGY CHAPTERS

12 13 14 15 16 17 18 19 20 21 22 23 24 25 26 27 28 29 30 31 32 33 34 35 36 37 38 39 40

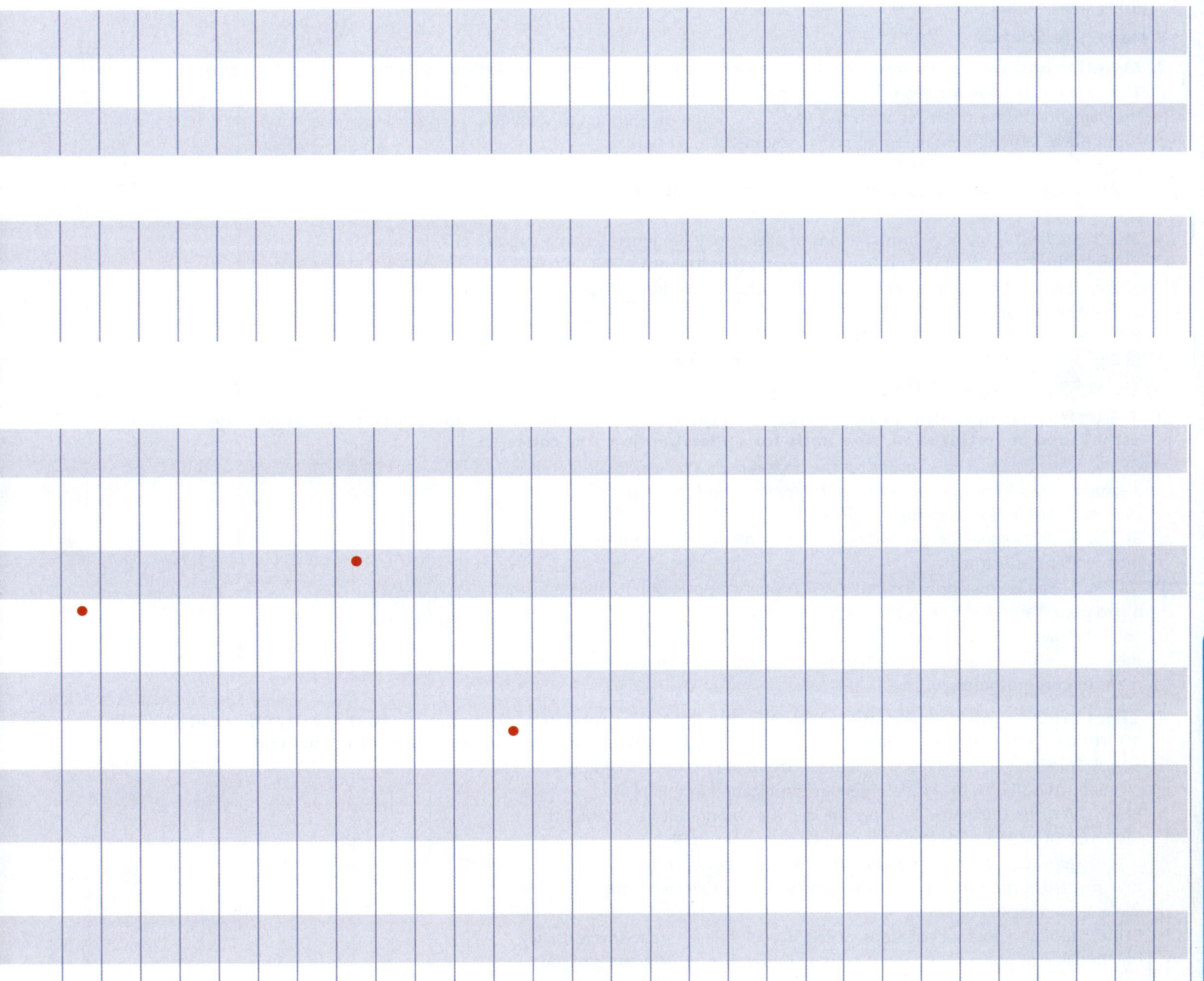

California Content Standards

PRENTICE HALL BIOLOGY CHAPTERS

Genetics

Grade 7

2. A typical cell of any organism contains genetic instructions that specify its traits. Those traits may be modified by environmental influences. As a basis for understanding this concept:

California Content Standards	1	2	3	4	5	6	7	8	9	10	11
7 2.a. *Students know* the differences between the life cycles and reproduction methods of sexual and asexual organisms.											
7 2.c. *Students know* an inherited trait can be determined by one or more genes.											•
7 2.d. *Students know* plant and animal cells contain many thousands of different genes and typically have two copies of every gene. The two copies (or alleles) of the gene may or may not be identical, and one may be dominant in determining the phenotype while the other is recessive.											•
7 2.e. *Students know* DNA (deoxyribonucleic acid) is the genetic material of living organisms and is located in the chromosomes of each cell.											

Biology/Life Science

2. Mutation and sexual reproduction lead to genetic variation in a population. As a basis for understanding this concept:

California Content Standards	1	2	3	4	5	6	7	8	9	10	11
BI 2.a. *Students know* meiosis is an early step in sexual reproduction in which the pairs of chromosomes separate and segregate randomly during cell division to produce gametes containing one chromosome of each type.											•
BI 2.b. *Students know* only certain cells in a multicellular organism undergo meiosis.											•
BI 2.c. *Students know* how random chromosome segregation explains the probability that a particular allele will be in a gamete.											•
BI 2.d. *Students know* new combinations of alleles may be generated in a zygote through the fusion of male and female gametes (fertilization).											•
BI 2.e. *Students know* why approximately half of an individual's DNA sequence comes from each parent.											•
BI 2.f. *Students know* the role of chromosomes in determining an individual's sex.											
BI 2.g. *Students know* how to predict possible combinations of alleles in a zygote from the genetic makeup of the parents.											•

3. A multicellular organism develops from a single zygote, and its phenotype depends on its genotype, which is established at fertilization. As a basis for understanding this concept:

California Content Standards	1	2	3	4	5	6	7	8	9	10	11
BI 3.a. *Students know* how to predict the probable outcome of phenotypes in a genetic cross from the genotypes of the parents and mode of inheritance (autosomal or X-linked, dominant or recessive).											•
BI 3.b. *Students know* the genetic basis for Mendel's laws of segregation and independent assortment.											•
*BI 3.c. *Students know* how to predict the probable mode of inheritance from a pedigree diagram showing phenotypes.											
*BI 3.d. *Students know* how to use data on frequency of recombination at meiosis to estimate genetic distances between loci and to interpret genetic maps of chromosomes.											•

4. Genes are a set of instructions encoded in the DNA sequence of each organism that specify the sequence of amino acids in proteins characteristic of that organism. As a basis for understanding this concept:

California Content Standards	1	2	3	4	5	6	7	8	9	10	11
BI 4.a. *Students know* the general pathway by which ribosomes synthesize proteins, using tRNA to translate genetic information in mRNA.											
BI 4.b. *Students know* how to apply the genetic coding rules to predict the sequence of amino acids from a sequence of codons in RNA.											
BI 4.c. *Students know* how mutations in the DNA sequence of a gene may or may not affect the expression of the gene or the sequence of amino acids in the encoded protein.											
BI 4.d. Students know specialization of cells in multicellular organisms is usually due to different patterns of gene expression rather than to differences of the genes themselves.											

Standards identified with an asterisk (*) are not tested on the California Standards Test. However, they are important to the comprehension of the strand, and all students should have the opportunity to learn them.

PRENTICE HALL BIOLOGY CHAPTERS

12 13 14 15 16 17 18 19 20 21 22 23 24 25 26 27 28 29 30 31 32 33 34 35 36 37 38 39 40

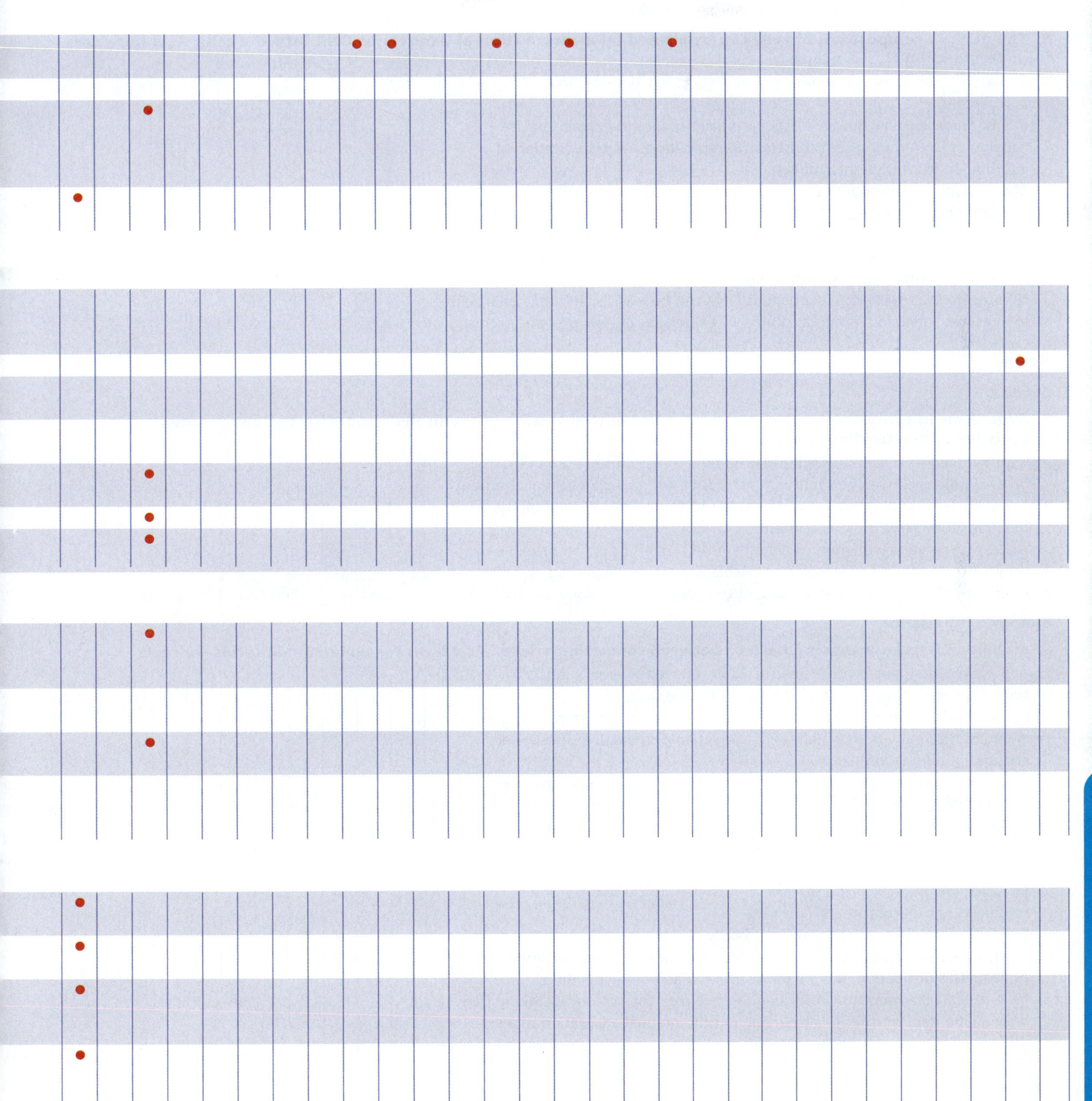

California Content Standards	PRENTICE HALL BIOLOGY CHAPTERS										
	1	2	3	4	5	6	7	8	9	10	11
BI 4.e. *Students know* proteins can differ from one another in the number and sequence of amino acids.		●									
*BI 4.f. *Students know* why proteins having different amino acid sequences typically have different shapes and chemical properties.		●									

5. The genetic composition of cells can be altered by incorporation of exogenous DNA into the cells. As a basis for understanding this concept:

California Content Standards	1	2	3	4	5	6	7	8	9	10	11
BI 5.a. *Students know* the general structures and functions of DNA, RNA, and protein.											
BI 5.b. *Students know* how to apply base-pairing rules to explain precise copying of DNA during semiconservative replication and transcription of information from DNA into mRNA.											
BI 5.c. *Students know* how genetic engineering (biotechnology) is used to produce novel biomedical and agricultural products.											
*BI 5.d. *Students know* how basic DNA technology (restriction digestion by endonucleases, gel electrophoresis, ligation, and transformation) is used to construct recombinant DNA molecules.											
*BI 5.e. *Students know* how exogenous DNA can be inserted into bacterial cells to alter their genetic makeup and support expression of new protein products.											

Ecology

Grade 6

5. Organisms in ecosystems exchange energy and nutrients among themselves and with the environment. As a basis for understanding this concept:

California Content Standards	1	2	3	4	5	6	7	8	9	10	11
6 5.b. *Students know* matter is transferred over time from one organism to others in the food web and between organisms and the physical environment.			●								
6 5.c. *Students know* populations of organisms can be categorized by the functions they serve in an ecosystem.				●							
6 5.e. *Students know* the number and types of organisms an ecosystem can support depends on the resources available and on abiotic factors, such as quantities of light and water, a range of temperatures, and soil composition.				●							

Biology/Life Science

6. Stability in an ecosystem is a balance between competing effects. As a basis for understanding this concept:

California Content Standards	1	2	3	4	5	6	7	8	9	10	11
BI 6.a. *Students know* biodiversity is the sum total of different kinds of organisms and is affected by alterations of habitats.						●					
BI 6.b. *Students know* how to analyze changes in an ecosystem resulting from changes in climate, human activity, introduction of nonnative species, or changes in population size.					●	●					
BI 6.c. *Students know* how fluctuations in population size in an ecosystem are determined by the relative rates of birth, immigration, emigration, and death.					●						
BI 6.d. *Students know* how water, carbon, and nitrogen cycle between abiotic resources and organic matter in the ecosystem and how oxygen cycles through photosynthesis and respiration.			●								
BI 6.e. *Students know* a vital part of an ecosystem is the stability of its producers and decomposers.			●								
BI 6.f. *Students know* at each link in a food web some energy is stored in newly made structures but much energy is dissipated into the environment as heat. This dissipation may be represented in an energy pyramid.			●								
*BI 6.g. *Students know* how to distinguish between the accommodation of an individual organism to its environment and the gradual adaptation of a lineage of organisms through genetic change.						●					

Standards identified with an asterisk (*) are not tested on the California Standards Test. However, they are important to the comprehension of the strand, and all students should have the opportunity to learn them.

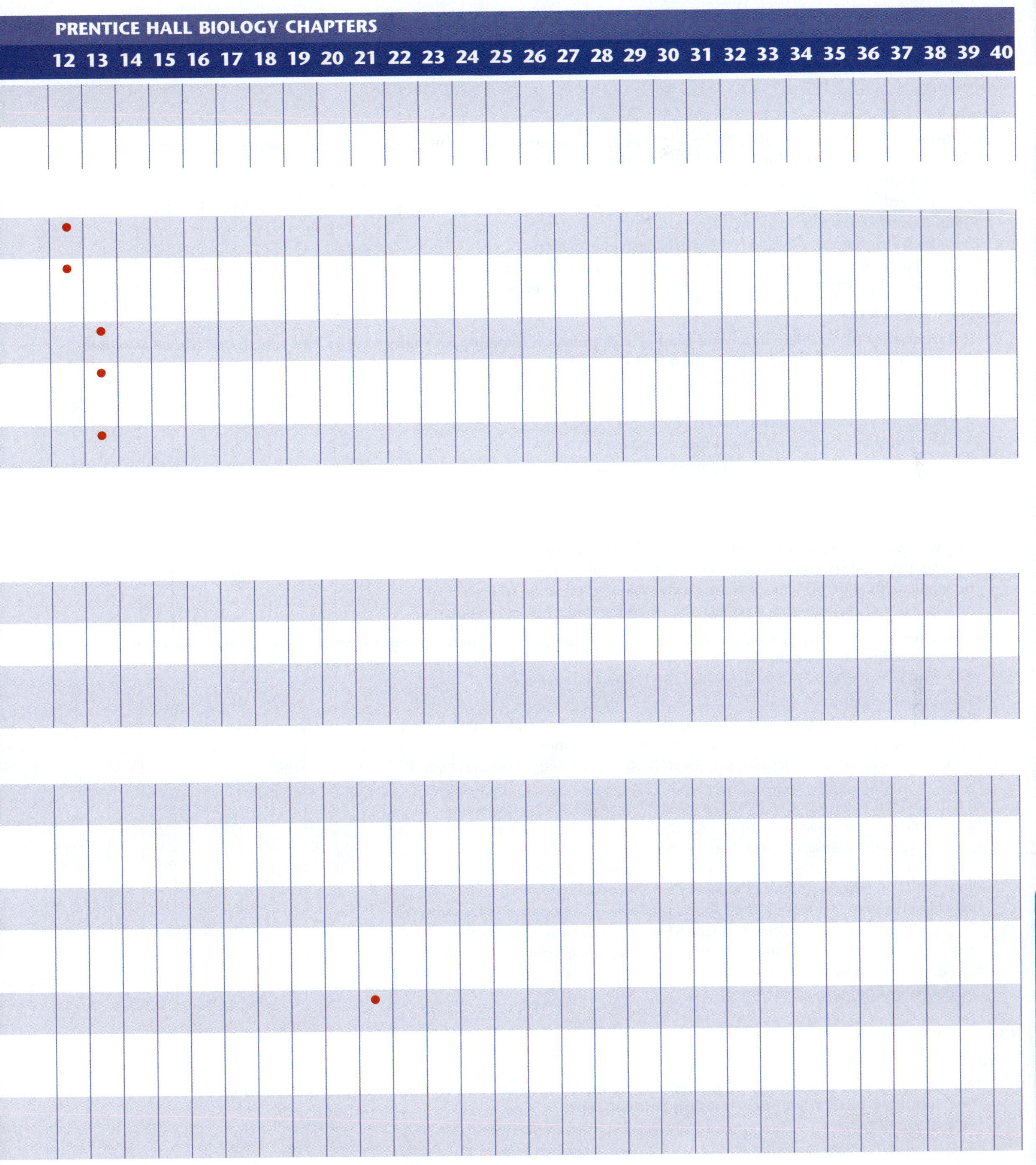

PRENTICE HALL BIOLOGY CHAPTERS

12	13	14	15	16	17	18	19	20	21	22	23	24	25	26	27	28	29	30	31	32	33	34	35	36	37	38	39	40
•																												
•																												
	•																											
	•																											
	•																											
									•																			

California Content Standards	PRENTICE HALL BIOLOGY CHAPTERS										
	1	2	3	4	5	6	7	8	9	10	11
Evolution											
Grade 7											
3. Biological evolution accounts for the diversity of species developed through gradual processes over many generations. As a basis for understanding this concept:											
7 3.a. *Students know* both genetic variation and environmental factors are causes of evolution and diversity of organisms.											
7 3.b. *Students know* the reasoning used by Charles Darwin in reaching his conclusion that natural selection is the mechanism of evolution.											
7 3.c. *Students know* how independent lines of evidence from geology, fossils, and comparative anatomy provide the bases for the theory of evolution.											
Biology/Life Science											
7. The frequency of an allele in a gene pool of a population depends on many factors and may be stable or unstable over time. As a basis for understanding this concept:											
BI 7.a. *Students know* why natural selection acts on the phenotype rather than the genotype of an organism.											
BI 7.b. *Students know* why alleles that are lethal in a homozygous individual may be carried in a heterozygote and thus maintained in a gene pool.											
BI 7.c. *Students know* new mutations are constantly being generated in a gene pool.											
BI 7.d. *Students know* variation within a species increases the likelihood that at least some members of a species will survive under changed environmental conditions.											
*BI 7.e. *Students know* the conditions for Hardy-Weinberg equilibrium in a population and why these conditions are not likely to appear in nature.											
*BI 7.f. *Students know* how to solve the Hardy-Weinberg equation to predict the frequency of genotypes in a population, given the frequency of phenotypes.											
8. Evolution is the result of genetic changes that occur in constantly changing environments. As a basis for understanding this concept:											
BI 8.a. *Students know* how natural selection determines the differential survival of groups of organisms.											
BI 8.b. *Students know* a great diversity of species increases the chance that at least some organisms survive major changes in the environment.											
BI 8.c. *Students know* the effects of genetic drift on the diversity of organisms in a population.											
BI 8.d. *Students know* reproductive or geographic isolation affects speciation.											
BI 8.e. *Students know* how to analyze fossil evidence with regard to biological diversity, episodic speciation, and mass extinction.											
*BI 8.f. *Students know* how to use comparative embryology, DNA or protein sequence comparisons, and other independent sources of data to create a branching diagram (cladogram) that shows probable evolutionary relationships.											
*BI 8.g. *Students know* how several independent molecular clocks, calibrated against one another and combined with evidence from the fossil record, can help to estimate how long ago various groups or organisms diverged evolutionarily from one another.											
Physiology											
Grade 7											
5. The anatomy and physiology of plants and animals illustrate the complementary nature of structure and function. As a basis for understanding this concept:											
7 5.a. *Students know* plants and animals have levels of organization for structure and function, including cells, tissues, organs, organ systems, and the whole organism.							●				

Standards identified with an asterisk (*) are not tested on the California Standards Test. However, they are important to the comprehension of the strand, and all students should have the opportunity to learn them.

PRENTICE HALL BIOLOGY CHAPTERS

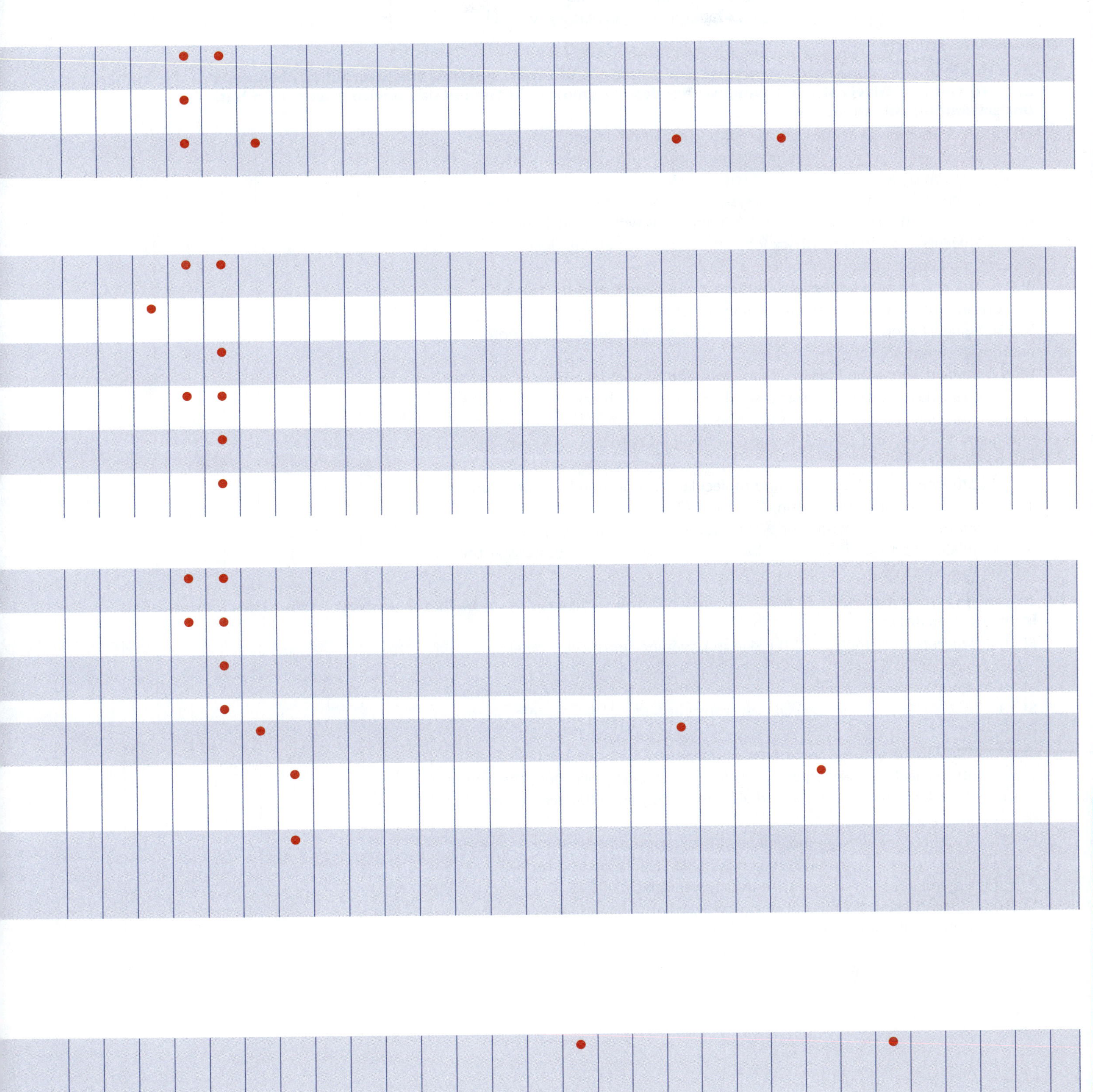

	12	13	14	15	16	17	18	19	20	21	22	23	24	25	26	27	28	29	30	31	32	33	34	35	36	37	38	39	40
				•	•																								
				•																									
				•		•												•			•								
				•	•																								
			•																										
					•																								
				•	•																								
					•																								
					•																								
				•	•																								
				•	•																								
					•																								
					•																								
						•												•											
							•															•							
							•																						
															•									•					

Year-at-a-Glance

California Content Standards	PRENTICE HALL BIOLOGY CHAPTERS										
	1	2	3	4	5	6	7	8	9	10	11
7 5.c. *Students know* how bones and muscles work together to provide a structural framework for movement.											
7 6.j. *Students know* that contractions of the heart generate blood pressure and that heart valves prevent backflow of blood in the circulatory system.											
Biology/Life Science											
9. As a result of the coordinated structures and functions of organ systems, the internal environment of the human body remains relatively stable (homeostatic) despite changes in the outside environment. As a basis for understanding this concept:											
BI 9.a. *Students know* how the complementary activity of major body systems provides cells with oxygen and nutrients and removes toxic waste products such as carbon dioxide.											
BI 9.b. *Students know* how the nervous system mediates communication between different parts of the body and the body's interactions with the environment.											
BI 9.c. *Students know* how feedback loops in the nervous and endocrine systems regulate conditions in the body.											
BI 9.d. *Students know* the functions of the nervous system and the role of neurons in transmitting electrochemical impulses.											
BI 9.e. *Students know* the roles of sensory neurons, interneurons, and motor neurons in sensation, thought, and response.											
*BI 9.f. *Students know* the individual functions and sites of secretions of digestive enzymes (amylases, proteases, nucleases, lipases), stomach acid, and bile salts.											
*BI 9.g. *Students know* the homeostatic role of the kidneys in the removal of nitrogenous wastes and the role of the liver in blood detoxification and glucose balance.											
*BI 9.h. *Students know* the cellular and molecular basis of muscle contraction, including the roles of actin, myosin, Ca^{+2}, and ATP.											
*BI 9.i. *Students know* how hormones (including digestive, reproductive, osmoregulatory) provide internal feedback mechanisms for homeostasis at the cellular level and in whole organisms.											
10. Organisms have a variety of mechanisms to combat disease. As a basis for understanding the human immune response:											
BI 10.a. *Students know* the role of the skin in providing nonspecific defenses against infection.											
BI 10.b. *Students know* the role of antibodies in the body's response to infection.											
BI 10.c. *Students know* how vaccinations protect an individual from infectious diseases.											
BI 10.d. *Students know* there are important differences between bacteria and viruses with respect to their requirements for growth and replication, the body's primary defenses against bacterial and viral infections, and effective treatments of these infections.											
BI 10.e. *Students know* why an individual with a compromised immune system (for example, a person with AIDS) may be unable to fight off and survive infections by microorganisms that are usually benign.											
*BI 10.f. *Students know* the roles of phagocytes, B-lymphocytes, and T-lymphocytes in the immune system.											

Standards identified with an asterisk (*) are not tested on the California Standards Test. However, they are important to the comprehension of the strand, and all students should have the opportunity to learn them.

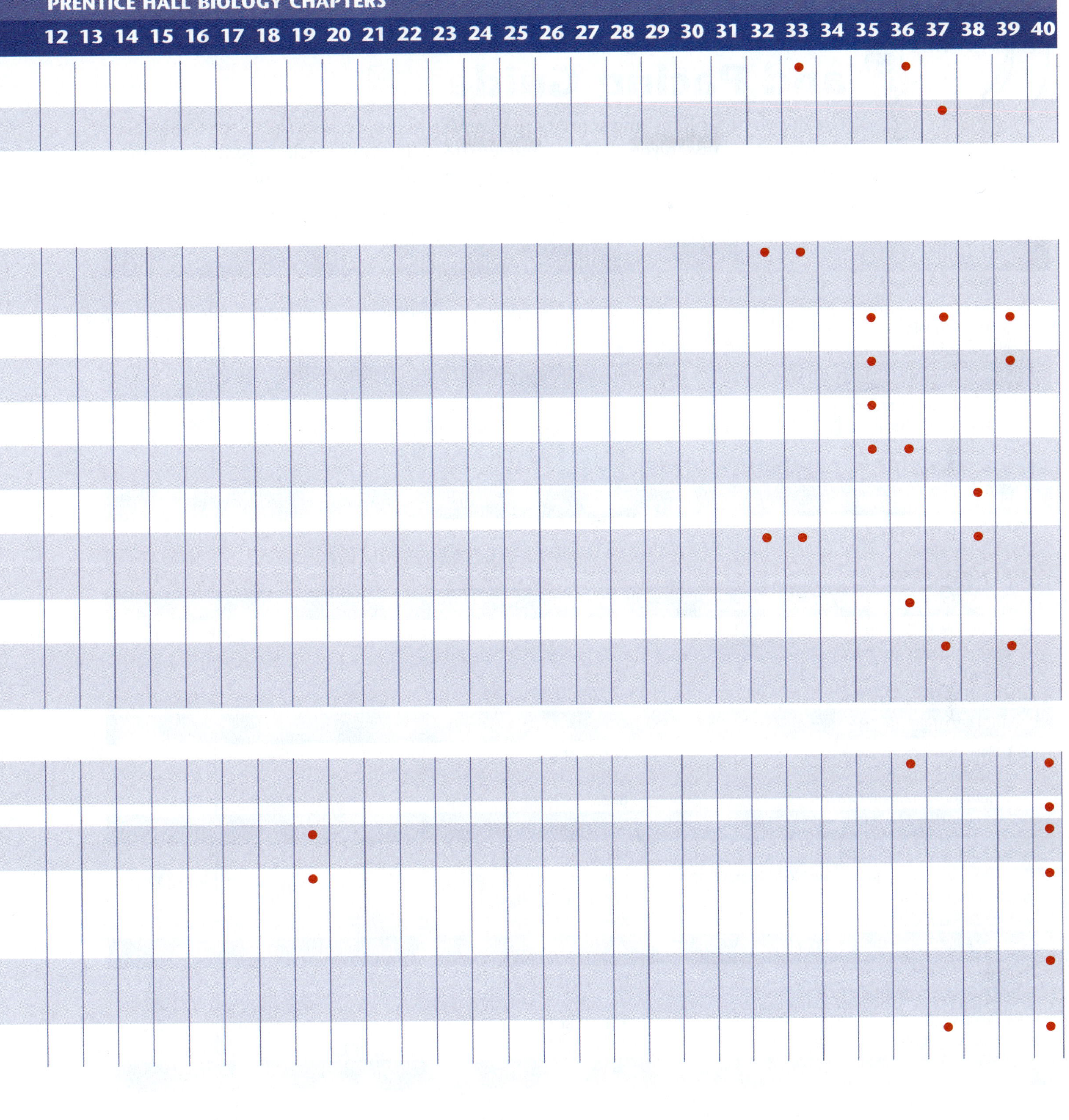
PRENTICE HALL BIOLOGY CHAPTERS
12 13 14 15 16 17 18 19 20 21 22 23 24 25 26 27 28 29 30 31 32 33 34 35 36 37 38 39 40

Section-by-Section Correlation and Pacing Guide

Use this chart for long- and short-term planning to ensure coverage of the California Content Standards in your biology course. The Pacing Guide reflects general times in single periods and can be modified to meet the needs of your students.

Chapter 1 The Science of Biology	California Content Standards	Periods
1–1 What Is Science?	BIIE 1.f	1
1–2 How Scientists Work	7IIE 7.c, 8IIE 9.c, BIIE 1.f, BIIE 1.j, BIIE 1.n	1
1–3 Studying Life		2
1–4 Tools and Procedures	BIIE 1.a	1
Chapter 2 The Chemistry of Life		
2–1 The Nature of Matter		1
2–2 Properties of Water		1
2–3 Carbon Compounds	8 6.b, 8 6.c, BI 1.h, BI 4.e, *BI 4.f	1
2–4 Chemical Reactions and Enzymes	BI 1.b	1
Chapter 3 The Biosphere		
3–1 What Is Ecology?		1
3–2 Energy Flow	6 5.b, BI 6.d, BI 6.e, BI 6.f	2
3–3 Cycles of Matter	BI 6.d	1
Chapter 4 Ecosystems and Communities		
4–1 The Role of Climate		1
4–2 What Shapes an Ecosystem?	6 5.c, 6 5.e	2
4–3 Biomes	6 5.e	2
4–4 Aquatic Ecosystems	6 5.e	2
Chapter 5 Populations		
5–1 How Populations Grow	BI 6.b, BI 6.c	1
5–2 Limits to Growth	BI 6.c	1
5–3 Human Population Growth	BI 6.c	1
Chapter 6 Humans in the Biosphere		
6–1 A Changing Landscape	BI 6.b	1
6–2 Renewable and Nonrenewable Resources	BI 6.b	1
6–3 Biodiversity	BI 6.a, BI 6.b, *BI 6.g	2
6–4 Charting a Course for the Future	BI 6.b	1
Chapter 7 Cell Structure and Function		
7–1 Life Is Cellular	BI 1.c, BIIE 1.k	1
7–2 Eukaryotic Cell Structure	7 1.c, BI 1.c, BI 1.e, *BI 1.j	2
7–3 Cell Boundaries	BI 1.a, *BI 1.j	2
7–4 The Diversity of Cellular Life	7 5.a	1
Chapter 8 Photosynthesis		
8–1 Energy and Life		1
8–2 Photosynthesis: An Overview	7 1.d, BIIE 1.k	1
8–3 The Reactions of Photosynthesis	BI 1.f, *BI 1.i	2
Chapter 9 Cellular Respiration		
9–1 Chemical Pathways	BI 1.g	2
9–2 The Krebs Cycle and Electron Transport	7 1.d, *BI 1.i	2

Chapter 10 Cell Growth and Division	California Content Standards	Periods
10–1 Cell Growth		1
10–2 Cell Division	7 1.e	2
10–3 Regulating the Cell Cycle		1
Chapter 11 Introduction to Genetics		
11–1 The Work of Gregor Mendel	7 2.d, BI 2.d, BI 3.b	1
11–2 Probability and Punnett Squares	7 2.d, BI 2.g, BI 3.a, BI 3.b	1
11–3 Exploring Mendelian Genetics	7 2.d, BI 2.g, BI 3.b	2
11–4 Meiosis	BI 2.a, BI 2.b, BI 2.d, BI 2.e	2
11–5 Linkage and Gene Maps	BI 3.b, *BI 3.d	1
Chapter 12 DNA and RNA		
12–1 DNA	7 2.e, BI 5.a, BIIE 1.k	2
12–2 Chromosomes and DNA Replication	7 2.e, BI 5.b	1
12–3 RNA and Protein Synthesis	BI 1.d, BI 4.a, BI 4.b, BI 5.a	2
12–4 Mutations	BI 4.c	1
12–5 Gene Regulation	BI 4.d	1
Chapter 13 Genetic Engineering		
13–1 Changing the Living World	BI 5.c	1
13–2 Manipulating DNA	BI 5.c, *BI 5.d	1
13–3 Cell Transformation	BI 5.c, *BI 5.e	1
13–4 Applications of Genetic Engineering	BI 5.c	1
Chapter 14 The Human Genome		
14–1 Human Heredity	7 2.d, BI 2.e, BI 2.f, BI 2.g, BI 3.a, *BI 3.c	3
14–2 Human Chromosomes	BI 2.g, BI 3.a, BI 7.b	2
14–3 Human Molecular Genetics		1
Chapter 15 Darwin's Theory of Evolution		
15–1 The Puzzle of Life's Diversity	BIIE 1.f	1
15–2 Ideas That Shaped Darwin's Thinking	7 3.b, BIIE 1.n	1
15–3 Darwin Presents His Case	7 3.a, 7 3.b, 7 3.c, BI 7.a, BI 7.d, BI 8.a, BI 8.b	2
Chapter 16 Evolution of Populations		
16–1 Genes and Variation	7 3.a, BI 7.c, BI 7.d	1
16–2 Evolution as Genetic Change	BI 7.a, *BI 7.e, *BI 7.f, BI 8.e	1
16–3 The Process of Speciation	BI 8.a, BI 8.b, BI 8.d, BIIE 1.f	2
Chapter 17 The History of Life		
17–1 The Fossil Record	BI 8.e, BIIE 1.i	1
17–2 Earth's Early History		1
17–3 Evolution of Multicellular Life	7 3.c, BI 8.e	1
17–4 Patterns of Evolution	7 3.c, BI 8.e	1
Chapter 18 Classification		
18–1 Finding Order in Diversity		1
18–2 Modern Evolutionary Classification	*BI 8.f, *BI 8.g	1
18–3 Kingdoms and Domains		1
Chapter 19 Bacteria and Viruses		
19–1 Bacteria	BI 10.d	2
19–2 Viruses	BI 1.c, BI 10.d	1
19–3 Diseases Caused by Bacteria and Viruses	BI 10.c, BI 10.d	1
Chapter 23 Roots, Stems, and Leaves		
23–4 Leaves	BI 1.f	1
23–5 Transport in Plants		1

California

Chapter 26 Sponges and Cnidarians	California Content Standards	Periods
26–1 Introduction to the Animal Kingdom	7 5.a	1
26–2 Sponges	7 2.a	1
26–3 Cnidarians	7 2.a	1
Chapter 27 Worms and Mollusks		
27–1 Flatworms		1
27–2 Roundworms		1
27–3 Annelids		1
27–4 Mollusks		2
Chapter 28 Arthropods and Echinoderms		
28–1 Introduction to the Arthropods		1
28–2 Groups of Arthropods		2
28–3 Insects		1
28–4 Echinoderms		1
Chapter 30 Nonvertebrate Chordates, Fishes and Amphibians		
30–1 The Chordates		1
30–2 Fishes		2
30–3 Amphibians		1
Chapter 32 Mammals		
32–1 Introduction to the Mammals	BI 9.a, *BI 9.g	2
32–2 Diversity of Mammals		1
32–3 Primates and Human Origins	7 3.c	1
Chapter 35 Nervous System		
35–1 Human Body Systems	7 5.a, BI 9.c	1
35–2 The Nervous System	BI 9.b, BI 9.d, BI 9.e	1
35–3 Divisions of the Nervous System	BI 9.b, BI 9.e	1
Chapter 36 Skeletal, Muscular, and Integumentary Systems		
36–1 The Skeletal System	7 5.c	1
36–2 The Muscular System	7 5.c, BI 9.e, *BI 9.h	1
36–3 The Integumentary System	BI 10.a	1
Chapter 37 Circulatory and Respiratory Systems		
37–1 The Circulatory System	7 6.j, BI 9.b, *BI 9.i	1
37–2 Blood and the Lymphatic System	*BI 10.f	1
37–3 The Respiratory System	BI 9.b	2
Chapter 38 Digestive and Excretory Systems		
38–1 Food and Nutrition		1
38–2 The Process of Digestion	*BI 9.f	2
38–3 The Excretory System	*BI 9.g	1
Chapter 39 Endocrine and Reproductive Systems		
39–1 The Endocrine System	BI 9.c, *BI 9.i	1
39–2 Human Endocrine Glands	BI 9.b, *BI 9.i	2
39–3 The Reproductive System	BI 2.b, *BI 9.i	2
39–4 Fertilization and Development		2
Chapter 40 The Immune System and Disease		
40–1 Infectious Disease	BI 10.d	1
40–2 The Immune System	BI 10.a, BI 10.b, BI 10.c, *BI 10.f	2
40–3 Immune System Disorders	BI 10.e	1
40–4 The Environment and Your Health		1

California Content Standards—Investigation and Experimentation

Use this chart to see where the Investigation and Experimentation standards are covered in the student book. Standards listed in blue are tested on the NCLB High School Life Science Test. Standards in black are part of the Biology/Life Science Standards Test.

Standard	Pages in Student Edition where practiced
Scientific progress is made by asking meaningful questions and conducting careful investigations. As a basis for understanding this concept and addressing the content in the other strands, students should develop their own questions and perform investigations. Students will:	
Grade 6	
6IIE 7c. Construct appropriate graphs from data and develop qualitative statements about the relationships between variables.	27, 51, 54, 111, 113, 118, 123, 249, 254, 420, 707, 709, 875, 935, 1053
6IIE 7e. Recognize whether evidence is consistent with a proposed explanation.	158, 161, 213, 254, 313, 340, 361, 411, 905
Grade 7	
7IIE 7.c. Communicate the logical connections among hypotheses, science concepts, tests conducted, data collected, and conclusions drawn from the scientific evidence.	8–14, 19, 79, 81, 111, 133, 158, 161, 249, 334, 462, 603, 620, 739, 870, 960, 1053, 1055
Grade 8	
8IIE 9.b. Evaluate the accuracy and reproducibility of data.	81, 313, 340, 351, 411, 491, 905
8IIE 9.c. Distinguish between variable and controlled parameters in a test.	8–14, 27, 51, 54, 161, 334, 508, 739, 990
Biology/Life Science	
BIIE 1.a. Select and use appropriate tools and technology to perform tests, collect data, analyze relationships, and display data.	24–28, 42, 54, 113, 118, 161, 231, 234, 334, 368, 420, 521, 627, 709, 739, 759, 883, 942
BIIE 1.b. Identify and communicate sources of unavoidable experimental errors.	54, 234, 334, 491, 648, 964
BIIE 1.c. Identify possible reasons for inconsistent results, such as sources of error or uncontrolled conditions.	54, 231, 340, 411, 759, 815, 842, 883
BIIE 1.d. Formulate explanations by using logic and evidence.	53, 118, 187, 194, 213, 215, 361, 387, 441, 531, 541, 543, 573, 608, 637, 640, 674, 709, 753, 787, 799, 815, 834, 875, 879, 905, 915, 937
BIIE 1.e. Solve scientific problems by using quadratic equations and simple trigonometric, exponential, and logarithmic functions.	133, 180, 368, 387, 420
BIIE 1.f. Distinguish between hypothesis and theory as scientific terms.	3–14, 369–372, 404–410
BIIE 1.g. Recognize the usefulness and limitations of models and theories as scientific representations of reality.	153, 180, 187, 242, 254, 281, 313, 326, 351, 361, 387, 441, 482, 790, 799, 811, 865, 905, 915, 937, 964, 982, 1005
BIIE 1.h. Read and interpret topographic and geologic maps.	Appendix G (pp. 1084–1085)
BIIE 1.i. Analyze the locations, sequences, or time intervals that are characteristic of natural phenomena.	113, 133, 416, 417–422
BIIE 1.j. Recognize the issues of statistical variability and the need for controlled tests.	8–14, 161, 224, 392, 521
BIIE 1.k. Recognize the cumulative nature of scientific evidence.	169–173, 204–207, 287–299, 368, 374–375, 438, 486–487, 836–837
BIIE 1.l. Analyze situations and solve problems that require combining and applying concepts from more than one area of science.	79, 709, 750, 932
BIIE 1.m. Investigate a science-based societal issue by researching the literature, analyzing data, and communicating the findings.	23, 128, 233, 330, 354, 403, 484, 647, 700, 853, 1048
BIIE 1.n. Know that when an observation does not agree with an accepted scientific theory, the observation is sometimes mistaken or fraudulent and that the theory is sometimes wrong.	8–14, 373–377

Master Materials List

Item	*Quantity	Chapter
Adhesive notes: white, red, yellow	1 of each color	40-2 QL
Agar plate, sterile	1 2 3	16 Lab 19 IA 19 Lab
Alcohol, isopropyl 70%	10 mL 200 mL	32 Lab 16 Lab
Aluminum foil	strip	5 Lab, 8 IA, 26 Lab
Amylase solution, 1%	20 mL	37 Lab, 38 Lab
Annatto coloring (achiote seed extract)	2–5 drops	39 IA
Antacid tablet, carbonated	1	37-3 QL
Antibiotic paper disks	4	16 Lab
Ants, live from 3 different colonies from same species	 15 10	 28 Lab 28 Lab
Aphids, pea	20	3-2 QL
Apples (different varieties)	5	13 IA
Apron, lab	1 per student	For all appropriate labs
Aquarium net	1 1	34 Lab p. 1081 FT
Aquarium with live fish	1	4 IA, 30-2 QL
Arthropod specimens or pictures	4–5	28 IA
Arthropod exoskeleton	2–3	29 IA
Artichoke	1	23 IA
Balance	1	30 Lab, 31 Lab
Ball-and-socket joint	1	36 IA
Balloon large, round large, round small, round red, yellow, blue	 6 1 1 3 of each color	 31-2 QL 37 Lab 37 Lab 40-2 QL
Battery (6V) and wires with alligator clips	1	35 Lab
Beads pop, 4 colors	12 16 (4 of each color)	6-2 QL 12 IA
red black	33 67	16 IA 16 IA
Beaker, 50-mL 100-mL 100-mL 150-mL 250-mL 400-mL 500-mL 1000-mL	 5 1 3 1 1 1 1 1	 2 Lab 5 Lab, 6 Lab 17 Lab 10–1 QL, 23 Lab 17–1 QL, 17 Lab, 23–4 QL, 28–4 QL, 37–3 QL, 39 IA 8 Lab 7–3 QL 4 Lab, 6-2 QL, 16 IA, 30 Lab
Beans lima red seedlings white	 2 10 15 2 5	 5 Lab 15 IA 14-2 QL 3-2 QL 14-2 QL
Beetles, ladybird (ladybug)	4	3-2 QL
Benedict's solution	25 mL	38 Lab
Biuret reagent	50 mL	32 Lab
Bleach	50 mL	36-2 QL
Blocks plastic building wooden	 20 4	 1 IA 28-3 QL
Blood, animal (sterile heparinized)	1–3 drops	7 Lab
Bologna, slice	1/2 slice	29 Lab
Bone bird breastbone bird leg bird (cut section) bird wing mammal (cut section) mammal (whole)	 1 1 1 1 1 1	 31 Lab 31 Lab 31 Lab 31 Lab 31 Lab 31 Lab
Bottle, plastic, 1-L	1	37 Lab
Box, clear/plastic	1	34 Lab
Brassica plant with flower	1	24 Lab
Bread, moldy	1 piece	21-2 QL
Brine shrimp	1	29 Lab
Brine shrimp eggs	1 bottle per class	1-3 QL

Key: **IA**=Inquiry Activity **QL**=Quick Lab **Lab**=End-of-Chapter Lab **FT**=Field Trip *=Quantities per group

Item	*Quantity	Chapter
Broccoli	1	15-3 QL
Bromthymol blue solution	2–5 drops	8 Lab, 9-2 QL
Brussels sprouts	1	15-3 QL
Butter	1 tablespoon	2 IA
Cabbage		
common	1	15-3 QL
Chinese, chopped	1 cup	9 Lab
Calcium chloride solution, concentrated	50 mL	24 Lab
Calculator	1	11-2 QL, 31 Lab, 37 Lab
Camera (optional)	1	p. 1079 FT, p. 1081 FT, p. 1084 FT
Candle	1	9 IA
Cardboard box	1	25-2 QL
box dividers	2	25-2 QL
Cardboard tubes	2	38-2 QL
Carmine dye	a few granules	20-2 QL
Cauliflower	1	15-3 QL
Celery, raw with leaves	3 stalks	23-5 QL
Cellophane, blue, red, and green	1 sheet of each	8 Lab
Cheesecloth	1	p. 1081 FT
Chicken, neck, disinfected	1	33 IA
wing, raw bleached		36-2 QL
Chlorophyll solution	1	8-2 QL
Clam, live	1 test tube	29-2 QL
Coin	1	15 Lab
Coleus plant	1	25 Lab
Container, airtight	1	21 Lab
plastic, small	2	29-2 QL
Cotton		
balls	1	20 Lab
swab	1	23-5 QL
swab, sterile	3	16 Lab, 19 Lab
Coverslips	1 box per class	1 Lab, 4 Lab, 5 Lab, 7 Lab, 20 IA, 20-2 QL, 20 Lab, 21 Lab, 22-4 QL, 22 Lab, 24-1 QL, 24 Lab, 32 Lab, p. 1078 FT, p. 1081 FT, p. 1084 FT
Craft materials (clay, Styrofoam™, etc.)	See investigation.	7-2 QL, 19-3 QL
Crayfish, live	1	28 IA, 29-2 QL, 29 Lab
Cricket, live	1	28-3 QL
Culture		
bacterial	1 per class	16 Lab, 19 Lab
Chlorella	1 per class	3 Lab, 20-2 QL
Euglena, concentrated	1 per class	8 IA
hydra	1 per class	29 Lab
hydra, brown	1 per class	26 Lab
hydra, green	1 per class	26 Lab
Paramecium caudatum	See Investigation.	20-2 QL, 20 Lab
Cups		
paper (small)	3	6-3 QL
	4	4-2 QL
paper (medium)	1	6-3 QL, 17-1 QL
	12	25 Lab
	2	5-2 QL
paper (large)	1	6-3 QL
plastic	1–2	14-2 QL, 30-2 QL, 36 Lab, 37-2 QL, 38-2 QL, p. 1081 FT
Dialysis tubing, 1-inch diameter	15 cm	36 Lab
Dissecting probe	1	24 Lab, 31 Lab, 33 IA
Dissecting tray	1	27 Lab, p. 1081 FT
Dowel, wooden	1	19 Lab
Dropper pipette	1	1 Lab, 2 Lab, 20 IA, 22-4 QL, 22 Lab, 24-1 QL, 24 Lab, 27-3 QL, 27 Lab, 28-4 QL, 30-2 QL, 32 Lab, 36 Lab, 39-4 QL, p. 1079 FT, p. 1081 FT, p. 1084 FT
	2	3 Lab, 5 Lab, 20-2 QL, 20 Lab, 21 Lab, 26 Lab, 29 Lab
	4	2-2 QL, 4 Lab, 20 Lab
Earthworm, live	1	27-3 QL, 28 IA, 29 Lab
Ecosystem (aquarium or terrarium)	1	4 IA
Eggs		
raw	1	31 IA, 37 Lab
hard-boiled and peeled	2	10-2 QL

Key: **IA**=Inquiry Activity **QL**=Quick Lab **Lab**=End-of-Chapter Lab **FT**=Field Trip *=Quantities per group

Item	*Quantity	Chapter
white, cooked	1	38 Lab
yolk, cooked	1	29 Lab
Fern plant, living	1	22 IA, 22 Lab
Fern frond with sori	1	22-4 QL
Fibers, various	10	32 Lab
Field guide, insects	1	28 Lab
Field guides	3–5	p. 1079 FT
Filter paper		
circles	2	30 Lab
disks	1 box per class	2 Lab, 6 Lab, 36 Lab
square	1	36 Lab
Fish		
betta, male	1	34 Lab
dissected	1	30 IA
freshwater (flesh)	5 grams	30 Lab
live	1	30 IA, 30–2 QL
saltwater (flesh)	5 grams	30 Lab
Fish food	1 teaspoon	30-2 QL
Flashlight	1	9 IA
Flower	1	24-1 QL
Flowering plant, living	1	22 IA, 24 Lab
Fluorescein, dilute or Glo Germ oil	1 pkg. per class	40 IA
Food coloring		
any color	5 drops	23-5 QL, 29-2 QL, 30-2 QL
green, red, yellow, blue	10 drops	10-1 QL
Food, unrefrigerated		p. 1081 FT
Forceps		
long	1	17 Lab
normal size	1	2 Lab, 7 Lab, 8 Lab, 16 Lab, 17 Lab, 20 Lab, 21 Lab, 22 Lab, 24-1 QL, 24 Lab, 32 Lab, 36-2 QL
Frog		
early embryos	2–4	39-4 QL
egg	2–4	31 IA
Fruit, different kinds	5	18 IA, 24 IA
Funnel	2	30 Lab, p. 1081 FT

Item	*Quantity	Chapter
Glass rod	2	30 Lab
	4	32 Lab
Gloves		
heat-resistant	1 pr. per student	38 Lab
plastic, disposable	1 pr. per student	For all appropiate labs
Glue	1	10 Lab, 19-3 QL, 19 Lab
Graduated cylinder		
10-mL	1	5 Lab, 9-2 QL, 30 Lab
25-mL	1	2 Lab
25-mL	3	17 Lab
50-mL	1	3 Lab, 7-3 QL, 36 Lab
100-mL	1	5 Lab, 6 Lab
250-mL	1	31 Lab
Grass clippings	1 cup	4 Lab
Grasshopper, live or photo	1	28 IA
Hand lens	1	1 IA, 1-3 QL, 6 Lab, 16 IA, 17 IA, 19 Lab, 22 IA, 22-3 QL, 22 Lab, 28 IA, 28 Lab, 30 IA, 33 IA
Hinge	1	36 IA
Hose clamp	1	p. 1081 FT
Hot plate	1	37 Lab
Hydrochloric acid solution, 0.2%	20 mL	38 Lab
Hydrogen peroxide solution, 1%	30 mL	2 Lab
Ice bath	1	2 Lab
Incubator	1 per class	19 Lab
Index card, white unruled	1	7-2 QL, 35 Lab
	3	33 QL
	25	11 Lab
Ink, India	1 drop	23 Lab
Iodine solution	15 drops	7-3 QL
	1–2 drops	7 Lab
	25 mL	8 Lab
Iron ring and ring stand	1	p. 1081 FT
Jar, wide-mouth, large	2	3-2 QL
with lids	2	p. 1079 FT, p. 1081 FT, p. 1084 FT

Key: **IA**=Inquiry Activity **QL**=Quick Lab **Lab**=End-of-Chapter Lab **FT**=Field Trip *=Quantities per group

Item	*Quantity	Chapter
Joints	See investigation.	
ball-and-socket example		36 IA
hinge example		36 IA
Juice		
apple	10 mL	2-2 QL
lemon	10 mL	2-2 QL
Knife, paring	1	18 IA
Lamp, desk, 40 watt	1	27 Lab
Lancelet		
dissected	1	30 IA
preserved	1	30 IA
Leaves		
dried	1 cup	4 Lab
freshly collected	5–10	18 IA, 18 Lab
Lenses		
concave	1	35 Lab
convex	2	35 Lab
Light bulb (6V) and socket	1	35 Lab
Light, ultraviolet (battery-operated)	1	40 IA
Litmus paper, blue	2 1″ strips	30 Lab
Liver		
puree	1 oz	2 Lab
raw	1 oz	2 Lab
Magnifying glass	1	p. 1079 FT, p. 1081 FT, p. 1084 FT
Marker, felt-tip	1	11 Lab
Measuring spoons 1.25-mL (1/4 teaspoon)	1	9 Lab
Meterstick	1	35 Lab
Methyl cellulose	1	20 IA
Microorganisms chart or book	1	4 Lab
Microscope		
compound	1	1 Lab, 4 Lab, 5 Lab, 7 IA, 7 Lab, 10 IA, 10 Lab, 20-2 QL, 20 IA, 20 Lab, 21-2 QL, 21 Lab, 22-3 QL, 22 Lab, 24-2 QL, 32 Lab, p. 1079 FT, p. 1081 FT, p. 1084 FT
dissecting	1	27-1 QL, 27-3 QL, 27 Lab, 28 Lab, 29 Lab, 39-4 QL
Millipede, live or photo	1	28 IA

Item	*Quantity	Chapter
Mirror, small	1	34 Lab
Modeling clay	1 package	19 Lab, 26-1 QL, 33 Lab, 35 Lab
Moss plant, living	1	22 IA, 22 Lab
Mousetrap, plastic	3	35-3 QL
Mushroom	1	21 IA
Newspaper	1	1 Lab
Noisemaker (bell or clicker)	1	34 IA
Oil, vegetable	20 mL	39 IA
Onion		
raw	1	7 Lab, 23 IA
red	1	7 Lab
Organisms, diverse specimens	3–5	26 IA, 28 IA
Paintbrush, small	1	24 Lab
Paper bag, brown	1	24-4 QL
Paper, construction		
assorted colors	2–4 sheets	13-2 QL, 16-2 QL, 19 Lab, 34 Lab, 39 Lab
black	1 sheet	8 Lab, 19 Lab, 27 IA, 27 Lab, 35 Lab
green, gray, purple, red, tan, and yellow	1 sheet of each color	12 Lab
graph	1 sheet	5 IA, 14 Lab, 15 IA, 17-1 QL
loose-leaf	1–2 sheets	32-3 QL, 34-2 QL
scrap	1 sheet	35-3 QL
white, unlined	2 sheets	17-1 QL, p. 1081 FT
Paper towels		
brown	2 sheets	38 IA
white	1 roll per class	2 QL, 7 Lab, 8 Lab, 10-1 QL,13 Lab, 21 Lab, 23 Lab, 27 Lab, 30 Lab, 36-2 QL, 36 Lab, 38-2 QL
Pen, marking	3	p. 1081 FT
Pencils		
colored	2	3 Lab, 4 Lab, 8-2 QL, 14 Lab,35 IA,
glass-marking	1	2 IA, 2 Lab, 3 Lab, 6 Lab, 8 Lab, 9-2 QL, 13 Lab, 16 Lab, 19 IA, 19 Lab, 26 Lab, 30 Lab, 32 Lab, 38 Lab
with eraser	1	27 IA

Key: IA=Inquiry Activity **QL**=Quick Lab **Lab**=End-of-Chapter Lab **FT**=Field Trip *=Quantities per group

Master Materials List *(continued)*

Item	*Quantity	Chapter
Pepsin solution 1%	20 mL	38 Lab
Petri dish	1	2 Lab, 23 Lab, 27 IA, 27 Lab, 28 Lab, 29 Lab
	2	6 Lab
	4	13 Lab
	5	8 Lab, 28 Lab
Petroleum jelly	1	23-5 QL, p. 1081 FT
pH paper	1 pkg. per class	2-2 QL, 6 Lab, 9 Lab
Phenolphthalein indicator solution	20 mL	36 Lab
Photograph easels, cardboard	2	35 Lab
Pins, dissecting	1	40-2 QL
Pipe cleaners	1 pkg. per class	10 Lab, 19 Lab
Planarian	1	27 IA, 27-1 QL, 28 IA, 29 Lab
Plants		
desert (cactus or succulent)	1	25 IA
rain forest (African violet or orchid)	2–4 per class	25 IA
small, in dark, opaque container	1	9 IA
Plastic box, clear	1	31 IA
Plastic foam ball	1	19 Lab
Plate, disposable	1	9 IA
Plastic sandwich bag	1	7-3 QL
Plastic sandwich bags, resealable	2	9 Lab
	10	p. 1079 FT, p. 1081 FT, p. 1084 FT
Pollen nutrient solution,		
with calcium	20 mL	24 Lab
without calcium	20 mL	24 Lab
Potato chip		
baked	1 chip	38 IA
regular	1 chip	38 IA
Potato		
cooked	1/2	38 Lab
raw	1	23 IA
Pots, plant, empty	2	3-2 QL, 13 Lab
Pot with soil	1	25-2 QL
Potted plant	1	8 Lab
Probe, blunt metal	1	29 Lab
Pump, balloon (hand-powered)	1	31-2 QL
Razor blade, single-edged	1	27-1 QL, 36-2 QL, 38 Lab
Red chili pepper, chopped	2 per class	9 Lab
Rooting compound (auxin powder)	1 jar per class	25 Lab
Rubber bands	2	3-2 QL
	1	27 IA
Rubber cement	1	32 Lab
Rubber stopper		
no hole	6	2 IA, 38 Lab
	2	3 Lab
one hole, #3	1	2 IA, 37 Lab
Rubber tubing, 10 cm	1	p. 1081 FT
Ruler, metric		
15 cm	1	16-2 QL, 16 Lab
30 cm	1	10-1 QL, 12 Lab, 16 Lab, 19-3 QL, 23-4 QL, 23 Lab, 25 Lab, 27 Lab, 34-2 QL, 35-3 QL, 36 Lab, 37 Lab, 38-2 QL, 38 Lab
transparent, 15 cm, plastic	1	1 Lab, 17 IA
Rutabaga	1	15-3 QL, 15 Lab
Safety goggles	1 pair per student	For all appropriate labs
Salt, noniodized	2.5 mL (1/2 tsp.)	9 Lab
Salt solution, concentrated		
25%	1–5 drops	7 Lab
0.5%	10 mL	20 Lab
1.0%	10 mL	20 Lab
Sand	2 cups	4-1 QL, 6-2 QL
Scalpel	1	2-2 QL, 7 Lab, 10-1 QL, 18 IA, 21 Lab, 22-3 QL, 23-4 QL, 24-2 QL, 25 Lab, 36-2 QL, 38 Lab

Key: **IA**=Inquiry Activity **QL**=Quick Lab **Lab**=End-of-Chapter Lab **FT**=Field Trip *=Quantities per group

Item	*Quantity	Chapter
Scissors	1	1 Lab, 8 Lab, 10 Lab, 11 Lab, 12 Lab, 13-2 QL, 14 Lab,16-2 QL, 19-3 QL, 19 Lab, 21 Lab, 25-2 QL, 30 Lab, 33 Lab, 34-2 QL, 35-3 QL, 36-2 QL, 36 Lab, 37 Lab, 38-2 QL, 38 Lab
Screening, flexible	2 pieces	3-2 QL
Seeds		
apple or orange	1	24 IA
burr type	1	24 IA
bean	20	5-2 QL
	4	23 Lab, 25-2 QL
	10	21 Lab
	100	17 Lab
corn	10	21 Lab
dandelion	1	24 IA
gymnosperm cones	1	24 IA
irradiated	10	13 Lab
maple	1	24 IA
nonirradiated	10	13 Lab
peas	200	17 Lab
radish or mustard	100	6 Lab
rice	20	4-1 QL
rye	10	4-1 QL
wheat	10	21 Lab
Shale billets from Green River, CO	1	17 IA
Shells, mollusk	2–3	29 IA
Shower-head arm mount	1	36 IA
Silver nitrate solution	10 mL	30 Lab
Slides		
microscope	1	1 Lab, 39 IA, p. 1079 FT, p. 1081 FT, p. 1084 FT
depression glass	4	7 Lab
	1 box per class	1 Lab, 4 Lab, 7 Lab, 20 IA, 20-2 QL, 20 Lab, 21-2 QL, 21 Lab, 22-2 QL, 22 Lab, 24-2 QL, 24 Lab, 27 Lab, 32 Lab, p. 1081 FT

Item	*Quantity	Chapter
Slides, prepared		
bacteria	1	1 Lab, 7 IA
crossed fibers	1	1 Lab
frog embryos	1	39-4 QL
frog muscle	1	10 IA
grass leaf	1	10 IA
human cheek cells	1	7 Lab
human muscle	1	10 IA
leaf cross section	1	7 IA
nerve cells	1	7 IA
onion root tip	1	10 Lab
paramecium	1	1 Lab
root cross section	1	1 Lab
Spirillium volutans	1	1 Lab
stem cross section	1	1 Lab, 10 IA
tree leaf, whole-mount	1	10 IA
Snail, live, land	1	27 Lab
Soap, liquid	1 mL	2 IA
Sodium bicarbonate (baking soda)	10 mL	30 Lab, 36 Lab
Soil, potting	1 large bag per class	4-1 QL, 4 Lab, 5-2 QL, 13 Lab, 25 Lab
Soy sauce	10 mL	2 IA
Specimens for classification	1 set	18 Lab
Spectroscope	1	8-2 QL
Spider, live	1	28 IA
Spoon, tea	1	10-1 QL, 17 Lab
Stain		
aniline blue	1–2 drops	21 Lab
methylene blue	1	5 Lab
Starch	10 mL	2-2 QL, 7-3 QL
Starfish, live or photo	1	28 IA
Sticks, ice cream	2–4	34 Lab
Straw		
large, clear plastic	1	27-3 QL
small	2	9-2 QL
soda	2	33 Lab
Strep A diagnostic kit	1	40 Lab
String	30 cm	8 Lab, 30 Lab, 35-3 QL
Sugar	10 grams	2 IA

Key: **IA**=Inquiry Activity **QL**=Quick Lab **Lab**=End-of-Chapter Lab **FT**=Field Trip *=Quantities per group

Item	*Quantity	Chapter
Sulfuric acid, dilute (0.1 N)	10 mL	6 Lab
Sunflower seeds, in shell	1	22-4 QL
Tape		
duct	See investigation.	29 Lab, 35-3 QL
masking		6-2 QL, 14-2 QL, 19 IA, 25-2 QL, 31-2 QL, 33 Lab
packing	See investigation.	35-3 QL
transparent		8 Lab, 10 Lab, 11 Lab, 12 Lab, 13-2 QL, 16-2 QL, 16 Lab, 19-3 QL, 19 Lab, 21-2 QL, 26 Lab, 27 IA, 30 Lab, 34 Lab, 35 Lab
Teeth, mammal (incisors, canines, molars)	1–5	32 IA
Telephone-book page	1	11-2 QL
Terrarium	1	4 IA, 28-3 QL
Test tube		
150-mm, with stopper	8	2 IA, 5 Lab, 8 Lab, 9-3 QL
	4	30 Lab
large, with stopper	2	3 Lab, 39 IA
	8	8 Lab, 38 Lab, 39 IA
small	2	9-2 QL
	4	32 Lab
small, with screw cap	8	8 IA, 26 Lab
Test-tube holder	1	38 Lab
Test-tube rack	1	3 Lab, 5 Lab, 8 IA, 26 Lab, 32 Lab, 38 Lab
Thermometers	3	2 Lab
	1	9 Lab, 19 Lab
Tissues, facial	1 box per class	32 Lab
Tofu	1 tsp.	2 IA
Toothpicks	1 box per class	19 Lab, 20 IA, 20-2 QL, 23 Lab, 25 Lab,
		33 Lab, 40-2 QL
Trisodium phosphate, 10% solution	10 mL	3 Lab
Trowel or spade	1	p. 1081 FT
Twist tie	1	7-3 QL
Tub, plastic	2	2 Lab
Vinegar	100 mL	30 Lab
Watch or clock with a second hand	1	2 Lab, 9-2 QL, 16-2 QL, 17 Lab, 20 Lab, 27 Lab, 28 Lab, 31-2 QL, 34 Lab, 37 IA
Watch glass	1	29 Lab
Water		
distilled	600 mL	30 Lab
	50 mL	7 Lab
nonchlorinated (aged)	600 mL	4 Lab
	1 gal	30–2 QL
	2–5 drops	27–3 QL
pond	50 mL	3 Lab, 26 Lab
	1–2 drops	20 IA
spring	10 mL–50 mL	27 IA, 29-2 QL
sterile	10 mL	40 Lab
Water bath		
boiling water	1 per class	38 Lab
hot	1	32 Lab
warm	1 per class	2 Lab
Yarn		
any color	30 cm	10 Lab
2 shades of red, 2 shades of green	80 cm of each color	11 Lab

Key: **IA**=Inquiry Activity **QL**=Quick Lab **Lab**=End-of-Chapter Lab **FT**=Field Trip *=Quantities per group

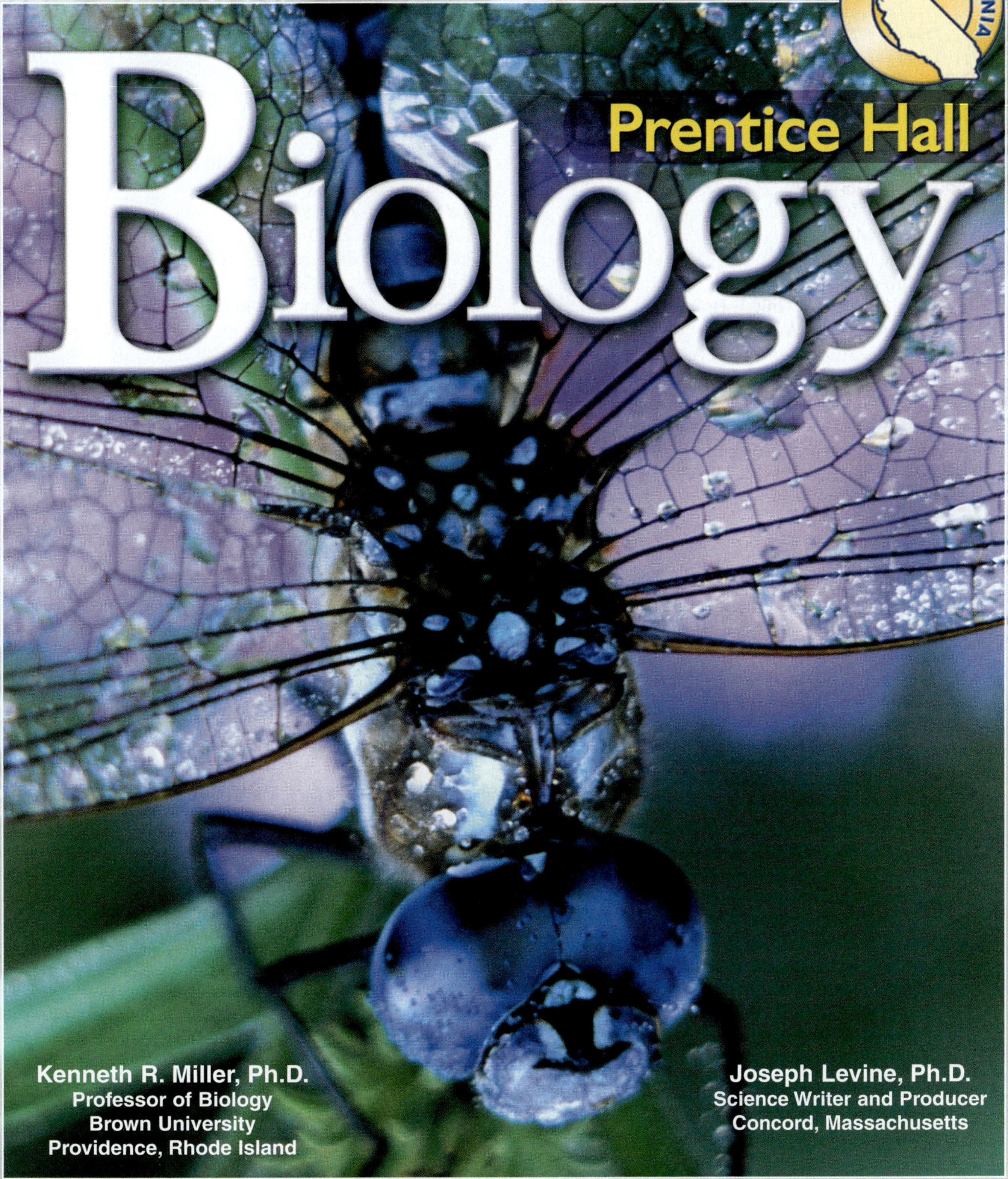

Prentice Hall Biology

CALIFORNIA

Kenneth R. Miller, Ph.D.
Professor of Biology
Brown University
Providence, Rhode Island

Joseph Levine, Ph.D.
Science Writer and Producer
Concord, Massachusetts

PEARSON
Prentice Hall

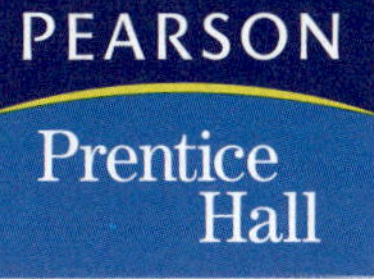

Upper Saddle River, New Jersey
Boston, Massachusetts

Print Components

California Student Edition
California Teacher's Edition
Laboratory Manual A
Laboratory Manual A, Annotated Teacher's Edition
Laboratory Manual B
Laboratory Manual B, Annotated Teacher's Edition
Teaching Resources, Unit 1–Unit 10
Reading and Study Workbook A
Reading and Study Workbook A, Annotated Teacher's Edition
Adapted Reading and Study Workbook B
Adapted Reading and Study Workbook B, Annotated Teacher's Edition
Biotechnology Manual
Laboratory Assessment With Scoring Guide
Issues and Decision Making
Investigations in Forensics
Probeware Lab Manual
Teacher's ELL Handbook
Lab Worksheets

Technology

Transparencies Plus Transparencies
PresentationExpress™ CD-ROM
StudentExpress™ CD-ROM
Biology iText Web Site
BioDetectives DVD
Prentice Hall *Biology* Web Site
TeacherExpress™ CD-ROM
Computer Test Bank CD-ROM
Animated Biological Concepts DVD
Lab Simulations CD-ROM
Virtual Labs CD-ROM

Spanish Components

Student Edition
Teacher's Guide
Chapter Tests: Levels A and B
Section Summaries with Vocabulary Review
Section Summaries Audio CD-ROM
Animated Biological Concepts Videotape Library

ISBN 0-13-201352-5
1 2 3 4 5 6 7 8 9 10 10 09 08 07 06

About the Authors

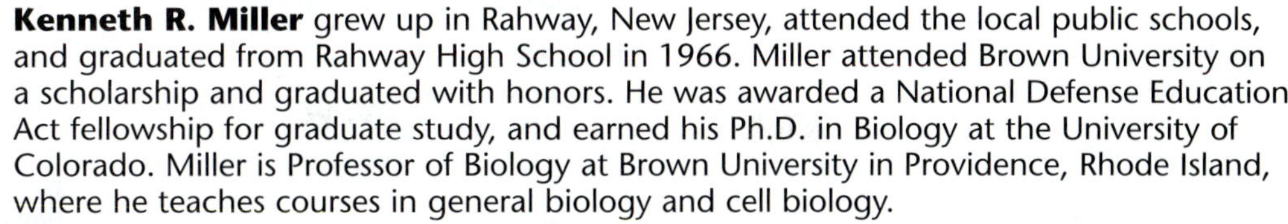

Kenneth R. Miller grew up in Rahway, New Jersey, attended the local public schools, and graduated from Rahway High School in 1966. Miller attended Brown University on a scholarship and graduated with honors. He was awarded a National Defense Education Act fellowship for graduate study, and earned his Ph.D. in Biology at the University of Colorado. Miller is Professor of Biology at Brown University in Providence, Rhode Island, where he teaches courses in general biology and cell biology.

Miller's research specialty is the structure of biological membranes. He has published more than 70 research papers in journals such as *CELL, Nature,* and *Scientific American.* In 1999, he wrote the popular trade book *Finding Darwin's God.*

Miller lives with his wife, Jody, on a small farm in Rehoboth, Massachusetts. He is the father of two daughters, one of whom is a wildlife biologist. He swims competitively in the masters' swimming program and umpires high school and collegiate softball.

Joseph S. Levine was born in Mount Vernon, New York, where he attended public schools. He earned a B.S. in Biology at Tufts University, a master's degree from the Boston University Marine Program, and a Ph.D. at Harvard University. His research has been published in scientific journals ranging from *Science* to *Scientific American*, and in several academic books. He taught introductory biology, marine ecology, and neurobiology for six years at Boston College.

After receiving a Macy Fellowship in Science Broadcast Journalism at WGBH-TV, Levine dedicated himself to improving public understanding of science. His popular scientific writing has appeared in five trade books and in magazines such as *Smithsonian*, *GEO*, and *Natural History*. He has produced science features for National Public Radio and has designed exhibit programs for state aquarium projects in Texas, New Jersey, and Florida.

Since 1987, Levine has served as scientific advisor at WGBH, where he worked on *NOVA* programs and on projects including the film *Cocos: Island of Sharks* and the series *The Secret of Life*. Most recently, he served as Science Editor for *The Evolution Project*.

Levine and his family live in Concord, Massachusetts, a short distance from Thoreau's Walden Pond.

Consultants

California Advisory Board

Luz Castillo
Prairie Vista Middle School
Hawthorne, CA

Laura Finco
Stone Valley Middle School
Alamo, CA

Ron Michelotti
Savanna High School
Anaheim, CA

Reading Consultant

Bonnie Armbruster, Ph.D.
Department of Curriculum and Instruction
University of Illinois
Champaign, IL

ESL Consultant

Nancy Montgomery, Ed.D.
Senior Consultant
Language and Literacy
Dallas, TX

Safety Consultant

Douglas Mandt
Lab Safety Consultant
Edgewood, WA

Lab Activity Consultant

Paul C. Johnson
University of New Hampshire
Durham, NH

Activity Writers and Testers

Diane Clark
Monticello High School
Charlottesville, VA

Lucy M. Fern
Ridgewood High School
Ridgewood, NJ

Laine Gurley, Ph.D.
Rolling Meadows High School
Rolling Meadows, IL

Patricia Anne Johnson
Ridgewood High School
Ridgewood, NJ

Kathy Laney
Hicksville High School
Hicksville, OH

Wade Mercer
Fairhill School
Dallas, TX

Neo/SCI
Rochester, NY

Patsye Peebles
Louisiana State University Lab School
Baton Rouge, LA

Herbert L. Saxon, Ed.D.
Ball State University
Muncie, IN

Evan P. Silberstein
Spring Valley High School
Spring Valley, NY

Dwight Taylor
Goldenview Middle School
Anchorage, AK

Consultants

Content Reviewers

J. David Archibald, Ph.D.
Professor of Biology
Curator of Mammals
San Diego State University
San Diego, CA

David M. Armstrong
Professor
Environmental, Population, and Organismic Biology
University of Colorado
Boulder, CO

Gary M. Aron
Professor of Biology
Southwest Texas State University
San Marcos, TX

Katharine Atkinson
Associate Professor of Cell Biology
Department of Cell Biology and Neuroscience
University of California, Riverside
Riverside, CA

David L. Brautigan
Director, Center for Cell Signaling
Professor, Microbiology and Medicine (Endocrinology)
University of Virginia
Charlottesville, VA

Kent D. Chapman, Ph.D.
Associate Professor
Department of Biological Sciences
University of North Texas
Denton, TX

Elizabeth Coolidge-Stolz, MD
Medical Writer
North Reading, MA

Dr. Darleen A. DeMason
Botany and Plant Sciences
University of California, Riverside
Riverside, CA

Elizabeth De Stasio
Raymond H. Herzog Professor of Science and Associate Professor of Biology
Lawrence University
Appleton, WI

Richard E. Duhrkopf
Associate Professor of Biology
Biology Department
Baylor University
Waco, TX

Betsey Dyer
Professor of Biology
Wheaton College
Norton, MA

Milton Fingerman
Professor of Biology
Department of Ecology and Evolutionary Biology
Tulane University
New Orleans, LA

Katherine Glew
Assistant Professor
University of Puget Sound
Tacoma, WA

Michael T. Griffin
Instructor of Biology
Department of Biology
Angelo State University
San Angelo, TX

Linda A. Guarino
Professor
Department of Biology, Entomology & Biochemistry
Texas A&M University
College Station, TX

Deborah L. Gumucio, Ph.D.
Associate Professor
Department of Cell and Developmental Biology
University of Michigan Medical School
Ann Arbor, MI

Paul R. Haberstroh, Ph.D.
Assistant Professor of Chemical Oceanography
Department of Marine Science
University of Hawaii at Hilo
Hilo, HI

Arthur H. Harris
Professor
Laboratory for Environmental Biology
University of Texas at El Paso
El Paso, TX

Evan B. Hazard, Ph.D.
Professor Emeritus of Biology
Bemidji State University
Bemidji, MN

Marilyn A. Houck
Associate Professor of Biological Sciences
Texas Tech University
Lubbock, TX

Joan E. N. Hudson
Associate Professor of Biology
Department of Biological Sciences
Sam Houston State University
Huntsville, TX

Donald C. Jackson
Professor of Physiology
Brown University
Providence, RI

Bonnie F. Jacobs
Assistant Professor and Chair
Environmental Science Program
Southern Methodist University
Dallas, TX

Jeremiah N. Jarrett
Assistant Professor
Department of Biological Sciences
Central Connecticut State University
New Britain, CT

Kirk Johnson
Curator of Paleontology
Denver Museum of Nature and Science
Denver, CO

Ted Johnson, Ph.D.
Professor of Biology
St. Olaf College
Northfield, MN

Donald E. Keith
Professor
Department of Biological Sciences
Tarleton State University
Stephenville, TX

David E. Lemke
Professor of Biology
Department of Biology
Southwest Texas State University
San Marcos, TX

Joe Leverich, Ph.D.
Professor
Biology Department
St. Louis University
St. Louis, MO

Martin K. Nickels, Ph.D.
Professor of Physical Anthropology
Illinois State University
Normal, IL

Paul F. Nicoletto
Associate Professor
Biology Department
Lamar University
Beaumont, TX

Richard Puzdrowski, Ph.D.
Assistant Professor of Biology
School of Science and Computer Engineering
University of Houston, Clear Lake
Houston, TX

Connie P. Russell
Assistant Professor
Department of Biology
Angelo State University
San Angelo, TX

Gerald P. Sanders, Sr.
Biology Publishing Consultant
Former Biology Instructor at Grossmont College
El Cajon, CA

Ronald L. Sass, Ph.D.
Professor of Biology, Chemistry, and Education
Department of Ecology and Evolutionary Biology
Rice University
Houston, TX

Eric S. Schmitt, Ph.D., M.S.
Certified Genetic Counselor
DNA Diagnostic Laboratory
Baylor College of Medicine
Houston, TX

David Scholnick
Assistant Professor
Eckerd College
St. Petersburg, FL

Dr. Dilbagh Singh
Professor of Biology
Blackburn College
Carlinville, IL

Bruce A. Wilcox
Affiliate Faculty
University of Hawaii
Kailua, HI

Alan C. Yen
Research Fellow
Harvard University
Cambridge, MA

Bruce A. Young
Professor of Biology
Department of Biology
Lafayette College
Easton, PA

Edward J. Zalisko
Professor of Biology
Illinois Professor of the Year, 2000
Blackburn College
Carlinville, IL

High-School Reviewers and Contributing Writers

Dr. William C. Alexander
South Carolina Governor's School for Science and Mathematics
Hartsville, SC

John Bartsch
Amsterdam High School (retired)
Amsterdam, NY

Myron E. Blosser
Harrisonburg High School
Harrisonburg, VA

James Boal
Natrona County High School
Casper, WY

Jan Bowersox
Nathan Hale High School
Seattle, WA

LouEllen Parker Brademan
Potomac Senior High School
Dumfries, VA

Heidi Busa
Marcellus High School
Marcellus, NY

Dr. Charles E. Campbell
Burbank High School
Burbank, CA

Robert Campbell
Wilson Classical High School
Long Beach, CA

Beverly Cea
Grimsley High School
Greensboro, NC

Mary P. Colvard
Cobleskill-Richmondville High School
Cobleskill, NY

Bob Culler
Avon Lake High School
Avon Lake, Ohio

Don Morris Curry
Silverado High School
Las Vegas, NV

Liz Dann
Phoenix Country Day School
Paradise Valley, AZ

Bob Demmink
East Kentwood High School
Kentwood, MI

Eloise Farmer
Torrington High School
Torrington, CT

Dale Faughn
Caldwell County High School
Princeton, KY

Steve Ferguson
Lee's Summit High School
Lee's Summit, MO

Diedre Galvin
Ridgewood High School
Ridgewood, NJ

Dennis Glasgow
Little Rock School District
Little Rock, AR

Ruth Gleicher
Niles West High School
Skokie, IL

John E. Gonzales
Temescal Canyon High School
Lake Elsinore, CA

Betsy Halpern
South Eugene High School
Eugene, OR

Dick Jordan
Timberline High School
Boise, ID

Marion LaFemina
Ridgewood High School
Ridgewood, NJ

Janice Lagatol
Fort Lee High School
Fort Lee, NJ

Leon Lange
Fort Campbell High School
Fort Campbell, KY

Michael I. Lopatka
Edgewater High School
Orlando, FL

Sue Madden
Chippewa Valley High School
Clinton Township, MI

Lora L. Marschall
Nathan Hale High School
Tulsa, OK

Gregory W. McCurdy
Salem High School
Salem, IN

Lynne M. McElhaney
LeFlore High School
Mobile, AL

Tamsen Knowlton Meyer
Boulder High School
Boulder, CO

Francis K. Mustapha
Snider High School
Fort Wayne, IN

Duane Nichols
Alhambra High School
Alhambra, CA

Joe E. Nunley, Jr.
Riverdale High School
Murfreesboro, TN

Richard K. Orgeron
Carencro High School
Lafayette, LA

Charlotte M. Parnell
Lakeside High School
Hot Springs, AR

Wendy Peterson
Velva High School
Velva, ND

Amelia Quillen
Smyrna High School
Smyrna, DE

Tracy Rader
Fulton Jr. High School
Indianapolis, IN

Debbie Richards
Bryan High School
Bryan, TX

Kathey A. Roberts
Lakeside High School
Hot Springs, AR

Dr. Thomas P. Rooney
Father Judge High School
Philadelphia, PA

Linda S. Samuels
Dana Hall School
Wellesley, MA

Jorge E. Sanchez
Green Valley High School
Henderson, NV

Sheila Smith
Terry High School
Terry, MS

Bob Sprang
Mitchell Public High School
Mitchell, SD

Tracy Swedlund
Medford Area Senior High
Medford, WI

Frank Tworek
Omaha North High School
Omaha, NE

Brenda Waldon
Clayton County Public Schools
Morrow, GA

Adam Weiss
Essex High School
Essex Junction, VT

Audra J. Williams
Sprayberry High School
Marietta, GA

Contents

UNIT 4 Genetics 260–365

UNIT 5 Evolution 366–467

UNIT 6 Microorganisms and Fungi 468–547

UNIT 7 Plants 548–653

UNIT 8 Invertebrates 654–763

UNIT 9 Chordates 764–887

UNIT 10 The Human Body 888–1059

Labs and Activities

Inquiry Activity

Quick Lab

Real-World Lab

Design an Experiment

Exploration

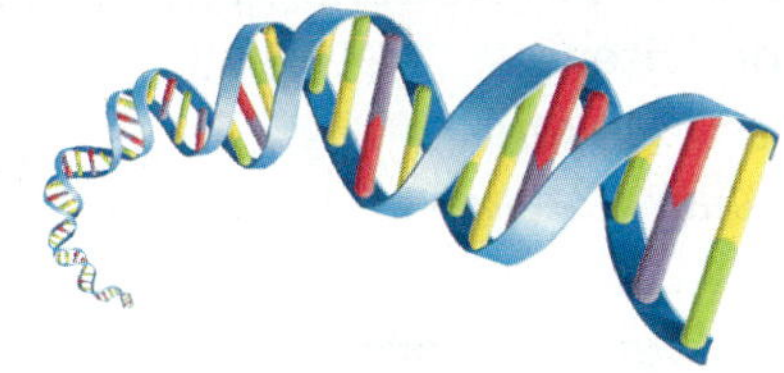

Analyzing Data

Problem Solving

Features

Biology and History

Careers in Biology

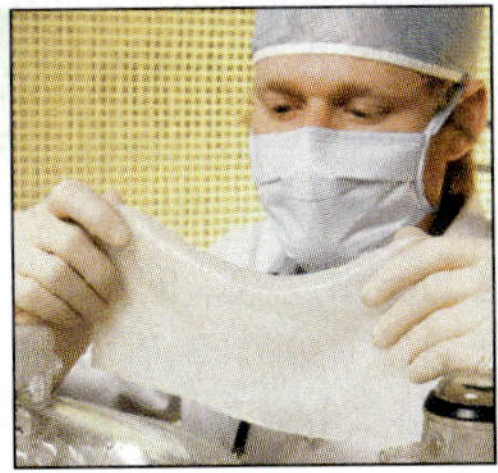

Go Online active art

Dear Student

Joe Levine and I wrote this book for a very simple reason: We wanted to let you in on a secret. Biology isn't just a "subject" in school. Biology is the science of life itself. Biology is the study of what makes an eagle fly, a flower bloom, or a caterpillar turn into a butterfly. It's the study of ourselves—of how our bodies grow and change and respond to the outside world, and it's the study of our planet, a world transformed by the actions of living things. Of course, you might have known some of this already. So, what's the secret?

The secret is that you've come along at just the right time. In all of human history, there has never been a moment like the present, a time when we stood so close to the threshold of answering the most fundamental questions about the nature of life. You belong to the first generation of students who can read the human genome almost as your parents might have read a book or a newspaper. You are the first students who will grow up in a world that has a chance to use that information for the benefit of humanity, and you are the very first to bear the burden of using that knowledge wisely.

If all of this seems like heavy stuff, it is. But there is another reason we wrote this book, and we hope that is not a secret at all. Science is fun! Biologists aren't a bunch of serious, grim-faced, middle-aged folks in lab coats who think of nothing but work. In fact, most of the people we know in science would tell you honestly, with broad grins on their faces, that they have the best jobs in the world. They would say there's nothing that compares to the excitement of doing scientific work, and that the beauty and variety of life make every day a new adventure.

We agree, and we hope that you'll keep something in mind as you begin the study of biology. You don't need a lab coat or a degree or a laboratory to be a scientist. What you do need is an inquiring mind, the patience to look at nature carefully, and the willingness to figure things out. We've filled this book with some of the latest and most important discoveries about living things, but we hope we've also filled it with something else: our wonder, our amazement, and our sheer delight in the variety of life itself. Come on in, and enjoy the journey!

Sincerely,

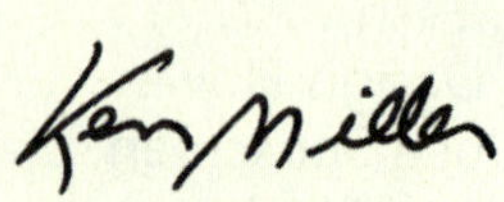

What do you think about biology? Are you interested in the natural world and the workings of your body? Or could you care less, and do you find yourself wondering "What's in it for me?" However you think, Ken and I wrote this book to convince you that biology is exciting, fascinating—and important to you. In fact, biology is more important to the daily lives of all humans today than it has ever been.

Why? You could answer in three words: "We are one." Now, this is a science text, so this statement isn't meant in any kind of "touchy-feely" or "New Age" way. "We" means all living things on earth. And "are one" means that all of us are tied together more tightly, in more different ways, than anyone ever dreamed of until recently. That's what biology tells us.

All forms of life—from bacteria to palm trees to humans are based on information written in a single, universal code carried in our genes. As biologists "read" those genes, they find nearly identical instructions directing life's processes in all of us. That's why medical researchers can learn about human diseases—diseases that may strike you or your family—by studying yeast. We are one on the molecular level.

All organisms interact with one another and with the environment in ways that create our planet's web of life. Organisms make tropical rain forests and coral reefs, prairies and swamps—and farms and cities. Our interactions involve not only each other—but also the winds and ocean currents that tie our planet together. Human activity can change, and is changing, local and global environments in ways that alter our ability to produce food and protect ourselves from diseases. We are one on the global ecological level.

All organisms change over time as they adapt to their surroundings. If humans alter the environment, we encourage other organisms to change. When we deploy antibiotics against bacteria, they develop resistance to our drugs. If we use pesticides against insects, they become immune to our poisons. We are one in our ability to evolve over time.

Those are the kinds of connections you will find in this book. Microscopic. Enormous. Amusing. Threatening. But always fascinating. That's why—no matter where you start off in your attitude about biology—we think you are in for some surprises!

Sincerely,

Joe Levine

Biology/Life Science Content Standards

The *Science Content Standards for California Public Schools* was adopted in 1998. The California Biology/Life Science strand is organized into 11 general standard sets. The standard sets are Cell Biology, Genetics (Meiosis and Fertilization), Genetics (Mendel's Laws), Genetics (Molecular Biology), Genetics (Biotechnology), Ecology, Evolution (Population Genetics), Evolution (Speciation), Physiology (Homeostasis), Physiology (Infection and Immunity), and Investigation and Experimentation. Each standard set is divided into a series of specific topic standards. Use this section as a preview for your Biology course and as a review guide when you study for exams. In each of the Practice Problems, the correct answer is marked with an asterisk. If a standard has an asterisk, it means that you won't be tested on the item.

Standard Set 1. Cell Biology

1. **The fundamental life processes of plants and animals depend on a variety of chemical reactions that occur in specialized areas of the organism's cells. As a basis for understanding this concept:**

1.a. ***Students know*** **cells are enclosed within semipermeable membranes that regulate their interaction with their surroundings.**

What It Means to You

All cells are surrounded by a cell membrane. The cell membrane controls what enters and leaves the cell. It also protects and supports the cell. Materials move in and out of the cell by diffusion, osmosis, and active transport.

Where You Will Learn It

Section 7–3

PRACTICE PROBLEM

A substance that moves across a cell membrane without using the cell's energy tends to move

A away from the area of equilibrium.
B away from the area where it is less concentrated.
C* away from the area where it is more concentrated.
D toward the area where it is more concentrated.

1.b. ***Students know*** **enzymes are proteins that catalyze biochemical reactions without altering the reaction equilibrium and the activities of enzymes depend on the temperature, ionic conditions, and the pH of the surroundings.**

What It Means to You

Enzymes are proteins that act as biological catalysts. They speed up chemical reactions in cells. Like other catalysts, enzymes work by lowering the activation energy of a reaction. Enzymes provide a site where reactants are brought together but do not participate in the reaction themselves.

Where You Will Learn It

Section 2–4

PRACTICE PROBLEM

At what temperature do most enzymes in the human body function best?

A 0°C
B* 37°C
C 98°C
D 100°C

1.c. *Students know* how prokaryotic cells, eukaryotic cells (including those from plants and animals), and viruses differ in complexity and general structure.

What It Means to You

The student understands that all cells are surrounded by a cell membrane. All cells contain DNA at some point in their lives. However, eukaryotic cells are usually larger than prokaryotic cells and have a nucleus that contains their genetic material. The student also knows that viruses are much smaller and simpler than cells. They do not have cell membranes or nuclei. Unlike cells, viruses cannot reproduce by themselves.

Where You Will Learn It

Section 7–1, Section 7–2, Section 19–2

PRACTICE PROBLEM

How is a eukaryotic cell different from a prokaryotic cell?

A It has a cell membrane.
B It contains DNA.
C* It has a nucleus.
D It carries out functions necessary for life.

1.d. *Students know* the central dogma of molecular biology outlines the flow of information from transcription of ribonucleic acid (RNA) in the nucleus to translation of proteins on ribosomes in the cytoplasm.

What It Means to You

DNA stores the information needed to make proteins. This information is copied, or transcribed, from DNA into messenger RNA (mRNA), which carries the message out of the nucleus to the ribosomes. The mRNA is then used as a template to assemble proteins.

Where You Will Learn It

Section 12–3

PRACTICE PROBLEM

From which DNA template was this mRNA strand transcribed?

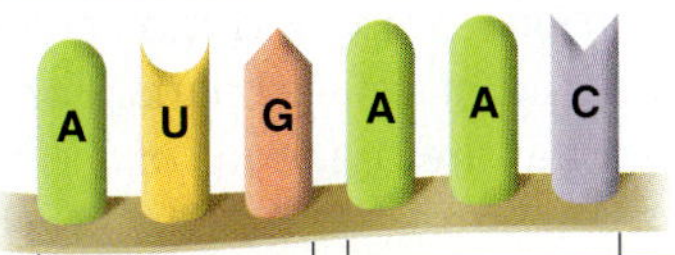

A* TACTTG
B ATGAAC
C AUGAAC
D UACUUG

1.e. *Students know* the role of the endoplasmic reticulum and Golgi apparatus in the secretion of proteins.

What It Means to You

There are two types of endoplasmic reticulum (ER)—rough and smooth. Rough ER makes proteins. Smooth ER makes membrane lipids. Proteins produced in the rough ER move into the Golgi apparatus, where they are modified. The Golgi apparatus then sorts and packages the proteins for storage or secretion outside the cell.

Where You Will Learn It

Section 7–2

PRACTICE PROBLEM

Which of these is the correct sequence in the processing of proteins?

A ribosomes to Golgi apparatus to rough endoplasmic reticulum
B Golgi apparatus to ribosomes to rough endoplasmic reticulum
C* ribosomes to rough endoplasmic reticulum to Golgi apparatus
D rough endoplasmic reticulum to Golgi apparatus to ribosomes

California

1.f. *Students know* **usable energy is captured from sunlight by chloroplasts and is stored through the synthesis of sugar from carbon dioxide.**

1.g. *Students know* **the role of the mitochondria in making stored chemical-bond energy available to cells by completing the breakdown of glucose to carbon dioxide.**

What It Means to You

Photosynthesis uses the energy of sunlight to convert water and carbon dioxide into high-energy sugars and oxygen. Plants gather the sun's energy with chlorophyll—a light-absorbing molecule found in chloroplasts. Mitochondria are organelles within eukaryotic cells that release energy by breaking down food molecules in the presence of oxygen. This process is called cellular respiration.

Where You Will Learn It

Section 7–2, Section 8–2, Section 8–3, Section 9–1, Section 9–2

PRACTICE PROBLEM

Living things store energy in the chemical bonds of compounds. One of the principal chemical compounds that living things use to store energy is

A DNA.
B* sugar.
C water.
D carbon dioxide.

1.h. *Students know* **most macromolecules (polysaccharides, nucleic acids, proteins, lipids) in cells and organisms are synthesized from a small collection of simple precursors.**

What It Means to You

Many of the large carbon compound molecules in living things are made up of smaller parts. For example, polysaccharides are made up of monosaccharides.

Where You Will Learn It

Section 2–3

PRACTICE PROBLEM

A polymer is a large molecule made up of smaller units called monomers. Proteins are polymers. What monomer makes up proteins?

A lipids
B carbohydrates
C* amino acids
D nucleic acids

***1.i.** *Students know* **how chemiosmotic gradients in the mitochondria and chloroplast store energy for ATP production.**

What It Means to You

You will learn that, in the light-dependent reactions of photosynthesis, energy from the sun is used to move hydrogen ions through the thylakoid membrane. As the ions pass back through the membrane, their energy is used to make ATP. A similar process occurs in the electron transport chain of cellular respiration. Energy from NADH is used to move hydrogen ions through the inner mitochondrial membrane. The ions pass back through the membrane, creating energy to make ATP.

Where You Will Learn It

Section 8–3, Section 9–2

PRACTICE PROBLEM

The light-dependent reactions and the Calvin cycle together make up the process

A* photosynthesis.
B cellular respiration.
C glycolysis.
D fermentation.

1.j.** ***Students know **how eukaryotic cells are given shape and internal organization by a cytoskeleton or cell wall or both.**

What It Means to You

Eukaryotic cells have a network of protein filaments, called the cytoskeleton, that helps support the cell and is also involved in movement. Many organisms also have cell walls, tough layers outside the cell membrane that protect and support the cell.

Where You Will Learn It

Section 7–2, Section 7–3

PRACTICE PROBLEM

Which groups of organisms have cells with cell walls?

A eukaryotes only
B plants only
C* plants, algae, fungi, and many prokaryotes
D algae and fungi only

Standard Set 2. Genetics (Meiosis and Fertilization)

2. **Mutation and sexual reproduction lead to genetic variation in a population. As a basis for understanding this concept:**

2.a. ***Students know*** **meiosis is an early step in sexual reproduction in which the pairs of chromosomes separate and segregate randomly during cell division to produce gametes containing one chromosome of each type.**

2.b. ***Students know*** **only certain cells in a multicellular organism undergo meiosis.**

What It Means to You

Meiosis is the process in which cells divide in two twice, cutting the number of cells in half through the separation of homologous chromosomes in a diploid cell. Unlike mitosis, meiosis occurs only in the sex cells of sexually reproducing organisms. The end result of meiosis is gametes: sperm and eggs.

Where You Will Learn It

Section 11–4

Practice Problem

Meiosis begins with a single diploid cell and produces

A two diploid cells.
B two haploid cells.
C four diploid cells.
D* four haploid cells.

2.c. ***Students know*** **how random chromosome segregation explains the probability that a particular allele will be in a gamete.**

2.d. ***Students know*** **new combinations of alleles may be generated in a zygote through the fusion of male and female gametes (fertilization).**

What It Means to You

You will learn that during meiosis, homologous chromosomes separate and different alleles are segregated from one another. You will also learn that when male and female gametes combine during fertilization, new combinations of alleles form.

Where You Will Learn It

Section 11–1, Section 11–2, Section 11–4

PRACTICE PROBLEM

If two plants with *Tt* alleles for height are crossed, what are the possible gametes that can form?

A* *T, t*
B *tt, Tt*
C *T*
D *tt, Tt, TT*

California

2.e. *Students know* **why approximately half of an individual's DNA sequence comes from each parent.**

2.f. *Students know* **the role of chromosomes in determining an individual's sex.**

What It Means to You

Individuals get half of their chromosomes from each parent. Because chromosomes carry the DNA, half of the DNA comes from each parent. Humans have 46 chromosomes: 44 are autosomes and 2 are sex chromosomes. The sex chromosomes determine whether a person is male or female. Each person gets an X chromosome from his or her mother and either a Y or an X chromosome from his or her father. People with XX are female; those with XY are male.

Where You Will Learn It

Section 11–4, Section 14–1

PRACTICE PROBLEM

An individual's sex is determined by the chromosome(s) received from his or her

A mother.
B* father.
C both mother and father.
D siblings.

2.g. *Students know* **how to predict possible combinations of alleles in a zygote from the genetic makeup of the parents.**

What It Means to You

The gene combinations that might result from a genetic cross can be determined by using a Punnett square. The types of gametes from each of the F_1 parents are shown along the left and top sides of the square. The possible gene combinations of the F_2 offspring are filled into the boxes that make up the square.

Where You Will Learn It

Section 11–1, Section 11–2, Section 11–3, Section 14–1, Section 14–2

PRACTICE PROBLEM

For the flowers of a particular plant species, yellow (*Y*) is the dominant allele and white (*y*) is the recessive allele. Suppose that a yellow-flowered plant (*YY*) is crossed with a white-flowered plant (*yy*). Which statement best describes the phenotypes and genotypes of their offspring?

A* all yellow-flowered (*Yy*)
B all white-flowered (*yy*)
C half yellow-flowered (*YY* or *Yy*) and half white-flowered (*yy*)
D three-quarters yellow-flowered (*YY* or *Yy*) and one-quarter white-flowered (*yy*)

Standard Set 3. Genetics (Mendel's Laws)

3. A multicellular organism develops from a single zygote, and its phenotype depends on its genotype, which is established at fertilization. As a basis for understanding this concept:

3.a. *Students know* how to predict the probable outcome of phenotypes in a genetic cross from the genotypes of the parents and mode of inheritance (autosomal or X-linked, dominant or recessive).

3.b. *Students know* the genetic basis for Mendel's laws of segregation and independent assortment.

What It Means to You

The genotypes of offspring shown in a Punnett square can be used to determine the phenotypes of the offspring. X-linked alleles are carried on the X chromosome. A trait controlled by an X-linked recessive allele will be shown in males even if only one recessive allele is present. You will learn that Mendel's laws of segregation and independent assortment are a result of the segregation of alleles during gamete formation.

Where You Will Learn It

Section 11–1, Section 11–2, Section 11–3, Section 14–1, Section 14–2

PRACTICE PROBLEM

Colorblindness is a recessive, sex-linked trait. If a colorblind man has children with a woman who has only the dominant alleles for this trait, which of the following statements could be true?

A Their daughters may be colorblind.
B Their sons may be colorblind.
C* None of their children will be colorblind.
D All of their children will be colorblind.

***3.c.** *Students know* how to predict the probable mode of inheritance from a pedigree diagram showing phenotypes.

What It Means to You

A pedigree is a diagram that can be used to predict genotypes. A pedigree shows the relationships within a family and which members express a particular trait. These phenotypes can be used to infer probable genotypes and the way alleles for traits are inherited within the family.

Where You Will Learn It

Section 14–1

PRACTICE PROBLEM

The blue squares on the diagram indicate a person with hemophilia, a sex-linked disorder.

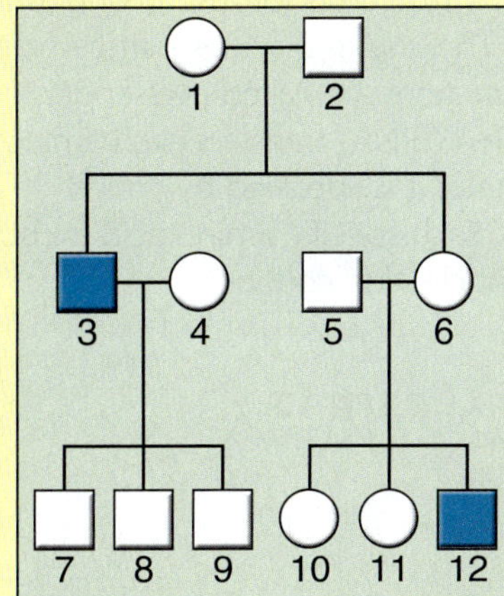

Which person is a carrier of the disease?

A person 2
B person 5
C* person 6
D person 9

California

***3.d.** *Students know* **how to use data on frequency of recombination at meiosis to estimate genetic distances between loci and to interpret genetic maps of chromosomes.**

What It Means to You

You will learn that chromosomes, not genes, assort independently. The closer together that genes are on a chromosome, the less likely they are to be separated during crossing-over. You will also learn that rates of crossing-over can be used to construct gene maps.

Where You Will Learn It

Section 11–5

PRACTICE PROBLEM

Here are the locations and names of some genes on chromosome 2 of the fruit fly:

13.0	dumpy wing
51.0	reduced bristles
75.5	curved wing
104.5	brown eye

Which two genes would most likely be separated during crossing-over?

A dumpy wing and curved wing
B reduced bristles and curved wing
C* dumpy wing and brown eye
D brown eye and reduced bristles

Standard Set 4. Genetics (Molecular Biology)

4. **Genes are a set of instructions encoded in the DNA sequence of each organism that specify the sequence of amino acids in proteins characteristic of that organism. As a basis for understanding this concept:**

4.a. *Students know* **the general pathway by which ribosomes synthesize proteins, using tRNA to translate genetic information in mRNA.**

4.b. *Students know* **how to apply the genetic coding rules to predict the sequence of amino acids from a sequence of codons in RNA.**

What It Means to You

Most genes contain instructions for assembling amino acids into proteins. The RNA molecules that carry copies of these instructions are called messenger RNA (mRNA). Transfer RNA (tRNA) transfers each amino acid to the ribosome as it is specified by coded messages in mRNA. Each specific amino acid is coded by a specific three-nucleotide codon.

Where You Will Learn It

Section 12–3

PRACTICE PROBLEM

In messenger RNA, each codon specifies a particular

A nucleotide.
B purine.
C pyrimidine.
D* amino acid.

4.c. ***Students know*** **how mutations in the DNA sequence of a gene may or may not affect the expression of the gene or the sequence of amino acids in the encoded protein.**

What It Means to You

Mutations, or changes to the genetic code, can involve single nucleotides or whole chromosomes. Many mutations have little or no effect on an organism. Other mutations can cause dramatic changes in protein structure or gene activity and are harmful.

Where You Will Learn It

Section 12–4, Section 14–2, Section 40–1

PRACTICE PROBLEM

What is a mutation?

A any change that is harmful to an organism
B* any change in a gene or chromosome
C any change that is helpful to an organism
D any change in the phenotype of a cell

4.d. ***Students know*** **specialization of cells in multicellular organisms is usually due to different patterns of gene expression rather than to differences of the genes themselves.**

What It Means to You

Only a fraction of the genes in a cell are expressed at a given time. An expressed gene is a gene that is transcribed into RNA. Nearly all cells in an organism contain the same DNA, but each gene can be turned on or off and expressed in different ways. This results in different patterns of development in different organisms.

Where You Will Learn It

Section 12–5

PRACTICE PROBLEM

During the development of a multicellular organism, many different types of cells can arise from a single cell. Which process allows for this to occur?

A* cell specialization
B binary fission
C fertilization
D respiration

4.e. ***Students know*** **proteins can differ from one another in the number and sequence of amino acids.**

4.f.** ***Students know **why proteins having different amino acid sequences typically have different shapes and chemical properties.**

What It Means to You

Proteins are polymers made up of long chains of amino acids. The chains can be folded in various ways and combined with other chains to determine the type of protein. There are more than 20 different amino acids, but they all have the same basic structure. The part of the amino acid that is different is called the R-group. The different R-groups give the different amino acids different chemical properties.

Where You Will Learn It

Section 2–3, Section 2–4

PRACTICE PROBLEM

Which of the following best describes the structure of proteins?

A simple chains of identical amino acids
B complex, folded chains of identical amino acids
C simple chains of different amino acids
D* complex, folded chains of different amino acids

California

Standard Set 5. Genetics (Biotechnology)

5. **The genetic composition of cells can be altered by incorporation of exogenous DNA into the cells. As a basis for understanding this concept:**

5.a. ***Students know*** **the general structures and functions of DNA, RNA, and protein.**

5.b. ***Students know*** **how to apply base-pairing rules to explain precise copying of DNA during semiconservative replication and transcription of information from DNA to mRNA.**

What It Means to You

Both DNA and RNA are made up of nucleotides. Each nucleotide is made up of a 5-carbon sugar, a phosphate, and a nitrogenous base. The differences between DNA and RNA are (1) the sugar in DNA is deoxyribose and the sugar in RNA is ribose; (2) RNA is generally single-stranded; (3) RNA contains uracil instead of thymine. During DNA replication, the two strands of the double helix are separated. As each new strand forms, new bases are added following the rules of base pairing. During transcription, one strand of DNA is used as a template from which nucleotides are assembled into a strand of RNA.

Where You Will Learn It

Section 12–1, Section 12–2, Section 12–3

PRACTICE PROBLEM

Which type of molecule is shown?

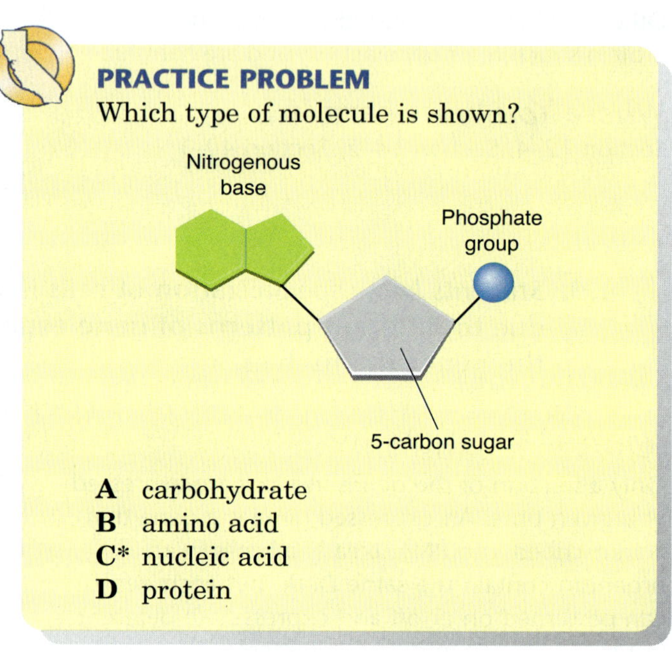

A carbohydrate
B amino acid
C* nucleic acid
D protein

5.c. ***Students know*** **how genetic engineering (biotechnology) is used to produce novel biomedical and agricultural products.**

5.d.** ***Students know **how basic DNA technology (restriction digestion by endonucleases, gel electrophoresis, ligation, and transformation) is used to construct recombinant DNA molecules.**

5.e.** ***Students know **how exogenous DNA can be inserted into bacterial cells to alter their genetic makeup and support expression of new protein products.**

What It Means to You

You will learn that segments of DNA can be removed from the chromosomes of one organism and inserted into the chromosomes of another organism. This organism may then express the trait coded by the DNA. One use of this technique is to mass-produce desired products such as human proteins.

Where You Will Learn It

Section 13–2, Section 13–3, Section 13–4

PRACTICE PROBLEM

DNA fragments are separated and analyzed using a technique called

A polymerase chain reaction.
B* gel electrophoresis.
C cloning.
D transformation.

Standard Set 6. Ecology

6. Stability in an ecosystem is a balance between competing effects. As a basis for understanding this concept:

6.a. *Students know* biodiversity is the sum total of different kinds of organisms and is affected by alterations of habitats.

6.b. *Students know* how to analyze changes in an ecosystem resulting from changes in climate, human activity, introduction of nonnative species, or changes in population size.

What It Means to You

Biodiversity is the sum total of the genetically based variety of all organisms in the biosphere. Biodiversity can be threatened by changes to habitats, hunting of wildlife, pollution, and invasive species. Any of these factors can also affect whole ecosystems.

Where You Will Learn It

Section 6–3, Section 6–4

PRACTICE PROBLEM

A construction company clear-cuts a forest to build a new mall. Which of the following is most likely an effect of this action?

A increase in biodiversity
B decrease in erosion
C increase in habitats for native species
D* decrease in food sources for native species

6.c. *Students know* how fluctuations in population size in an ecosystem are determined by the relative rates of birth, immigration, emigration, and death.

What It Means to You

A population will grow when birthrates exceed death rates and will shrink when death rates exceed birthrates. Immigration, or movement of individuals into an area, will increase a population, whereas emigration, or movement of individuals out of an area, will decrease it.

Where You Will Learn It

Section 5–1, Section 5–3

PRACTICE PROBLEM

If a population grows larger than the carrying capacity of its environment, the

A* death rate may rise.
B birthrate may rise.
C death rate may fall.
D immigration rate may increase.

California

6.d. *Students know* **how water, carbon, and nitrogen cycle between abiotic resources and organic matter in the ecosystem and how oxygen cycles through photosynthesis and respiration.**

6.e. *Students know* **a vital part of an ecosystem is the stability of its producers and decomposers.**

6.f. *Students know* **at each link in a food web some energy is stored in newly made structures but much energy is dissipated into the environment as heat. This dissipation may be represented in an energy pyramid.**

What It Means to You

Matter and energy move between organisms and their environment. The original source of energy is the sun, and producers convert this light energy into chemical energy. As organisms feed on one another, matter and energy move to successively higher trophic levels. About 90 percent of the energy is lost at each level. Matter is released back into the environment when organisms die and decay, as well as through various processes such as cellular respiration.

Where You Will Learn It

Section 3–2, Section 3–3, Section 9–2

PRACTICE PROBLEM

Photosynthesis is a major process involved in which of the following cycles?

A nitrogen cycle
B* carbon cycle
C sodium cycle
D phosphorus cycle

***6.g.** *Students know* **how to distinguish between the accommodation of an individual organism to its environment and the gradual adaptation of a lineage of organisms through genetic change.**

What It Means to You

Over time, populations and not individual organisms evolve. Individual organisms may be able to adapt to changes in their environment, but they cannot change their traits to do so. Different individuals within a population may be better adapted to changed environments than others. Over time, their traits will be selected for and become more common in the population.

Where You Will Learn It

Section 16–2

PRACTICE PROBLEM

Which of the following best explains the effect an adaptation has on an organism?

A* It increases the organism's chance to survive.
B It decreases the organism's chance to reproduce.
C It does not affect an organism's chance to survive.
D It decreases the organism's ability to eat.

Standard Set 7. Evolution (Population Genetics)

7. **The frequency of an allele in a gene pool of a population depends on many factors and may be stable or unstable over time. As a basis for understanding this concept:**

7.a. ***Students know*** **why natural selection acts on the phenotype rather than the genotype of an organism.**

What It Means to You

Some organisms survive and reproduce; others die without reproducing. Natural selection operates on the physical traits, or phenotype, of the organism, not on its genotype.

Where You Will Learn It

Section 16–2

PRACTICE PROBLEM

The process of natural selection is based on the assumption that

A environmental changes will cause changes in body structure in individuals.
B most changes from generation to generation are the result of mutations.
C part of the population of organisms always remains stable.
D* different traits inherited by offspring have different survival value.

7.b. ***Students know*** **why alleles that are lethal in a homozygous individual may be carried in a heterozygote and thus maintained in a gene pool.**

What It Means to You

Recessive lethal alleles will cause death only in a homozygous individual. A person who is heterozygous for a trait will either not have the trait or have only a weak version of the trait. The heterozygous person will contribute the lethal recessive allele to a population's gene pool. Being heterozygous for a trait may provide an evolutionary advantage such as resistance to disease.

Where You Will Learn It

Section 14–1, Section 14–2

PRACTICE PROBLEM

Which of these is a fatal genetic disorder caused by a recessive allele?

A albinism
B* Tay-Sachs disease
C Huntington disease
D sickle cell disease

7.c. ***Students know*** **new mutations are constantly being generated in a gene pool.**

What It Means to You

Mutations are the source of genetic variation in a species. Mutations can affect single genes or can produce changes in entire chromosomes.

Where You Will Learn It

Section 12–4

PRACTICE PROBLEM

A mutation that adds or deletes a nucleotide and shifts the reading frame of the codons that follow is known as a

A point mutation.
B* frameshift mutation.
C duplication.
D inversion.

7.d. ***Students know*** **variation within a species increases the likelihood that at least some members of a species will survive under changed environmental conditions.**

What It Means to You

Individual members of a species have slightly different traits. This genetic diversity promotes survival if environmental conditions change.

Where You Will Learn It

Section 15–3, Section 16–1

PRACTICE PROBLEM

Differences among individuals of a species are referred to as

A* natural variation.
B fitness.
C natural selection.
D adaptation.

7.e.** ***Students know **the conditions for Hardy-Weinberg equilibrium in a population and why these conditions are not likely to appear in nature.**

7.f.** ***Students know **how to solve the Hardy-Weinberg equation to predict the frequency of genotypes in a population, given the frequency of phenotypes.**

What It Means to You

The Hardy-Weinberg principle states that allele frequencies in a population will remain constant unless one or more factors cause these frequencies to change. The Hardy-Weinberg principle holds only if: there is random mating, the population is very large, there is no movement into or out of the population, there are no mutations, and there is no natural selection.

Where You Will Learn It

Section 16–2

PRACTICE PROBLEM

Wolves select mates according to desired characteristics such as size. What condition of the Hardy-Weinberg principle does this violate?

A* random mating
B large population
C no mutations
D no natural selection

Standard Set 8. Evolution (Speciation)

8. **Evolution is the result of genetic changes that occur in constantly changing environments. As a basis for understanding this concept:**

8.a. ***Students know*** **how natural selection determines the differential survival of groups of organisms.**

8.b. ***Students know*** **a great diversity of species increases the chance that at least some organisms survive major changes in the environment.**

What It Means to You

Natural selection favors organisms that are well adapted to their environment. Organisms that are less suited to the environment may die off before passing on their traits. Natural selection can be used to explain adaptation and its effects on the number and types of species that currently exist. When a species is unable to adapt to meet its needs, it may die out completely.

Where You Will Learn It

Section 15–3, Section 16–3

PRACTICE PROBLEM

The evolution of the many finch species observed by Darwin from a single finch species is an example of

A convergent evolution.
B coevolution.
C* natural selection.
D mutualism.

8.c. *Students know* **the effects of genetic drift on the diversity of organisms in a population.**

8.d. *Students know* **reproductive or geographic isolation affects speciation.**

What It Means to You

Genetic drift is the change in allele frequency in a population due to random change. If a small subgroup of a population is separated from the larger population, the subgroup may have fewer different alleles than the main population. Populations become reproductively isolated when they can no longer interbreed and produce fertile offspring.

Where You Will Learn It

Section 16–2, Section 16–3

PRACTICE PROBLEM

A small population of a species becomes separated from the rest of the species. By chance, this population has different allele frequencies than the rest of the species. Over time, the population evolves into a new species. This is an example of

A* genetic drift.
B spontaneous generation.
C inheritance of acquired traits.
D coevolution.

8.e. *Students know* **how to analyze fossil evidence with regard to biological diversity, episodic speciation, and mass extinction.**

What It Means to You

The fossil record can tell scientists a great deal about past life. The fossil record shows that there have been periods when the number of species expanded rapidly, as well as periods when many species suddenly died off.

Where You Will Learn It

Section 15–1, Section 15–3, Section 17–3, Section 17–4

PRACTICE PROBLEM

Which of the following provides evidence that living things have been evolving for millions of years?

A* fossil record
B natural variation within a species
C superficial similarities
D mutations

***8.f.** *Students know* **how to use comparative embryology, DNA or protein sequence comparisons, and other independent sources of data to create a branching diagram (cladogram) that shows probable evolutionary relationships.**

***8.g.** *Students know* **how several independent molecular clocks, calibrated against each other and combined with evidence from the fossil record, can help to estimate how long ago various groups or organisms diverged evolutionarily from one another.**

What It Means to You

A cladogram shows how closely related different species are. The closer together two organisms' branches are, the more recently they shared a common ancestor. Many different types of evidence can be used to determine evolutionary relationships, including comparative embryology, anatomy, and DNA. A scientist examines changes in DNA due to random neutral mutations. The more different mutations there are in two strands of DNA, the farther back they had a common ancestor.

Where You Will Learn It

Section 18–2

PRACTICE PROBLEM

If species A and B have very similar genes and proteins, what is probably true?

A* Species A and B shared a relatively recent common ancestor.
B Species A and B are the same species.
C Species A is older than species B.
D Species B is older than species A.

Standard Set 9. Physiology (Homeostasis)

9. As a result of the coordinated structures and functions of organ systems, the internal environment of the human body remains relatively stable (homeostatic) despite changes in the outside environment. As a basis for understanding this concept:

9.a. *Students know* how the complementary activity of major body systems provides cells with oxygen and nutrients and removes toxic waste products such as carbon dioxide.

What It Means to You

Each body system is only one small part of the total organism. The systems work together for optimal functioning of the body as a whole. The respiratory system brings oxygen into the body and removes carbon dioxide. The digestive system breaks down food and transfers nutrients to the bloodstream. The circulatory system transports oxygen and nutrients to cells and carries away wastes.

Where You Will Learn It

Section 35–1, Section 37–1, Section 37–3, Section 38–2

PRACTICE PROBLEM

In which part of the body are oxygen and carbon dioxide exchanged between the air and the blood?

A heart
B* lungs
C stomach
D small intestine

9.b. *Students know* how the nervous system mediates communication between different parts of the body and the body's interactions with the environment.

9.c. *Students know* how feedback loops in the nervous and endocrine systems regulate conditions in the body.

What It Means to You

Organisms maintain a constant internal environment, even when conditions outside the body change. The nervous system monitors body conditions, such as temperature, and signals endocrine glands, such as the hypothalamus, to release chemicals that help keep internal conditions constant.

Where You Will Learn It

Section 35–1, Section 35–2, Section 39–1, Section 39–2

PRACTICE PROBLEM

How would the hypothalamus respond if the nervous system detected that your body temperature had dropped below 37°C?

A It would not do anything.
B It would produce heat to warm the body.
C* It would produce chemicals that would speed up cellular activity.
D It would produce chemicals that would slow down cellular activity.

9.d. ***Students know*** **the functions of the nervous system and the role of neurons in transmitting electrochemical impulses.**

9.e. ***Students know*** **the roles of sensory neurons, interneurons, and motor neurons in sensation, thought, and response.**

What It Means to You

The nervous system controls and coordinates functions throughout the body and responds to internal and external stimuli. Neurons transmit electrochemical impulses throughout the body. Sensory neurons carry impulses from the sense organs to the spinal cord. Motor neurons carry impulses from the brain and spinal cord to muscles and glands. Interneurons connect sensory and motor neurons and carry impulses between them.

PRACTICE PROBLEM

What part of the nervous system would carry an impulse from your eyes to the spinal cord?

A* sensory nervous system
B cerebral nervous system
C autonomic nervous system
D somatic nervous system

Where You Will Learn It

Section 35–2, Section 35–3

9.f.** ***Students know **the individual functions and sites of secretions of digestive enzymes (amylases, proteases, nucleases, lipases), stomach acid, and bile salts.**

9.g.** ***Students know **the homeostatic role of the kidneys in the removal of nitrogenous wastes and the role of the liver in blood detoxification and glucose balance.**

What It Means to You

Many different enzymes contribute to the chemical digestion of food. Saliva in the mouth contains amylase, which breaks down starch into sugar. Glands in the stomach produce pepsin and hydrochloric acid, which begin the breakdown of protein. The pancreas and liver produce substances that aid in digestion, especially in the digestion of fat. Nephrons within the kidneys remove wastes from the blood. Blood is first filtered, and then most of the liquid is reabsorbed. The liver also helps break down toxins such as alcohol.

PRACTICE PROBLEM

The digestive enzyme lipase is produced by the

A* pancreas.
B small intestine.
C stomach.
D mouth.

Where You Will Learn It

Section 38–2, Section 35–5, Section 38–3

California

9.h.** ***Students know **the cellular and molecular basis of muscle contraction, including the roles of actin, myosin, Ca^{2+}, and ATP.**

What It Means to You

Muscle fibers contain overlapping filaments made up of proteins called myosin and actin. Energy supplied by ATP causes the filaments to slide over each other, contracting the muscle. Calcium ions (Ca^{2+}) are also involved in the process that controls muscle contraction.

Where You Will Learn It

Section 36–2

PRACTICE PROBLEM

The regions that move together when muscles contract are called

A* Z lines.
B sarcomeres.
C cross-bridges.
D myofibrils.

9.i.** ***Students know **how hormones (including digestive, reproductive, osmoregulatory) provide internal feedback mechanisms for homeostasis at the cellular level and in whole organisms.**

What It Means to You

Hormones are chemicals that are released in one part of the body and affect another part of the body. Hormones control body conditions such as temperature, and thus they help organisms maintain a constant internal environment. Feedback mechanisms work to regulate the activity of the body and help maintain homeostasis.

Where You Will Learn It

Section 35–1, Section 39–1, Section 39–2

PRACTICE PROBLEM

You are outside for an extended period of time on a cold day. How does your body react?

A* Cells throughout the body speed up their activities.
B Cells throughout the body slow down their activities.
C Your body produces sweat.
D Heat evaporates from the body surface.

Standard Set 10. Physiology (Infection and Immunity)

10. **Organisms have a variety of mechanisms to combat disease. As a basis for understanding the human immune response:**

10.a. ***Students know*** **the role of the skin in providing nonspecific defenses against infection.**

What It Means to You

The most important function of the skin is to physically block pathogens from entering the body. Glands in the skin also produce acidic oil and sweat that kill many bacteria.

Where You Will Learn It

Section 36–3, Section 40–2

PRACTICE PROBLEM

The skin is considered to be a nonspecific defense because it

A* does not discriminate among different pathogens.
B does not block pathogens.
C always blocks all pathogens.
D blocks only specific pathogens.

10.b. *Students know* **the role of antibodies in the body's response to infection.**
10.c. *Students know* **how vaccinations protect an individual from infectious diseases.**

What It Means to You

Antibodies are proteins that recognize and bind to antigens. When the antibodies bind to antigens on pathogens, the pathogens are destroyed. Vaccines are injections of weakened or mild forms of a pathogen to produce immunity. Vaccinations stimulate the production of antigens, preventing bacterial and viral infections.

PRACTICE PROBLEM

A vaccine produces

A an inactive response.
B a secondary immune response.
C passive immunity.
D* active immunity.

Where You Will Learn It

Section 19–3, Section 40–2

10.d. *Students know* **there are important differences between bacteria and viruses with respect to their requirements for growth and replication, the body's primary defenses against bacterial and viral infections, and effective treatments of these infections.**
10.e. *Students know* **why an individual with a compromised immune system (for example, a person with AIDS) may be unable to fight off and survive infections by microorganisms that are usually benign.**
***10.f.** *Students know* **the roles of phagocytes, B-lymphocytes, and T-lymphocytes in the immune system.**

What It Means to You

A virus is simpler than a cell and cannot reproduce on its own. However, many viruses harm their host organism by destroying its cell structures. The skin and immune system are the main defenses against viruses and bacteria. Bacterial diseases can be treated with antibiotics. For most viruses, only the symptoms can be treated, not the specific virus. Phagocytes are white blood cells that engulf and destroy bacteria. B lymphocytes provide immunity against antigens and pathogens in body fluids. T lymphocytes defend against pathogens and abnormal cells inside cells. The HIV virus destroys helper T cells, allowing minor infections to become serious and often fatal.

PRACTICE PROBLEM

If a person is exposed to a pathogen to which he or she had previously been exposed, what type of cells would produce antibodies specific to that pathogen?

A B lymphocytes
B T lymphocytes
C* memory B cells
D memory T cells

Where You Will Learn It

Section 19–1, Section 19–2, Section 19–3, Section 40–1, Section 40–2, Section 40–3

UNIT 1

Dear Colleague,

"Want to write a textbook?" That was the starting point of a conversation between the two of us that went on for months. Did we really want to do this? Did we have the time? And, finally, would it make a difference? You can guess, we're sure, how we answered those questions.

Trying to cover the enormous scope of the biological sciences in a single textbook is at once a terrifying and an exhilarating experience. More than once, we felt the task was beyond us. From time to time, we had to seek out fellow scientists to point the way, to help us identify key concepts, and even to encourage us with assurances that the task was worth completing.

More often, however, we felt a sense of amazement. Like you, we have chosen careers as biologists, and perhaps like you, we emerged from our formal educations with a sense that we had mastered the field. We were wrong about that, of course, and continuing to discover just how wrong we were has been one of the delights of our lives.

Students can be overwhelmed by the sheer amount of information presented in any biology course, and it's easy to see why. From ecology to systematics, from genetics to the nervous system, there's just so much to learn. The false impression students can get from such studies, of course, is that biology has pretty much come to an end, that just about everything has been figured out. Scientists, they might be tempted to conclude, are very smart people who are proud of what they know and are embarrassed by ignorance. Scientists, a student once told us, are ashamed to admit there's anything they don't know.

That student's assertion couldn't have been more wrong. What really turns a scientist on isn't knowledge,

UNIT 1 The Nature of Life

Yosemite National Park in California is home to many different organisms.

but ignorance. A field that is pretty well figured out is the last thing that most scientists want to hear about. What's exciting is what we don't know, the unsolved problem, the inexplicable observation, the unexplored territory. We wrote this book, in large measure, to make this clear.

Scientists are, by nature, optimists. They believe that nature, ultimately, can be understood, and that helping to achieve such understanding is one of the most important things a human being can do in life. We members of the scientific community—you and we—also carry around a little trade secret that the general public never quite seems to notice: namely, that biology is fun. There's no point in keeping that a secret from your students, and this is a second reason we wrote this book.

We hope that you will view this book as a resource, as something that you can draw upon to enlighten, to excite, and even to amuse your students. If you find the book useful, we'll be happy. But, we hope you will go well beyond that. We live in remarkable times, and your students are growing up in what historians may come to regard as the most exciting decades in the history of biology. We spared no effort in trying to make that clear, and we know you will do the same.

In the final analysis, teachers are not only part of the scientific community—you are the most important part of it. You are the nurturers of new talent, the caretakers of youthful curiosity; you are the inspirations that fill the scientific enterprise with hope, energy, and vigor. We regard ourselves as your partners in that effort, and we hope you'll feel the same way. We hope you'll share your thoughts, suggestions, and criticisms of this textbook with us, because we know we'll learn from them. And we thank you most especially for the honor of sharing your classroom with us.

Go Online
PHSchool.com

Students can research the nature of life on the site developed by authors Ken Miller and Joe Levine.

Sincerely,

Ken Miller

Joe Levine

Chapter Planner 1 The Science of Biology

Section and Section Objectives	Time	STANDARDS NCLB	STANDARDS Biology	Activities and Labs
1–1 What Is Science?, pp. 3–7 **1.1.1** ***Explain*** what the goal of science is. **1.1.2** ***Explain*** what a hypothesis is.	1 period (1/2 block)	BIIE 1.f		**SE:** ***Inquiry Activity,*** Can your procedure be replicated?, p. 2 L2 **TE:** ***Build Science Skills,*** p. 4 L2 **TE:** ***Build Science Skills,*** p. 5 L2 L3 **BTM:** Concept 1 L2 L3
1–2 How Scientists Work, pp. 8–14 **1.2.1** ***Describe*** how scientists test hypotheses. **1.2.2** ***Explain*** how a scientific theory develops.	2 periods (1 block)	7IIE 7.c, 8IIE 9.c, BIIE 1.f, BIIE 1.j	BIIE 1.n	**SE:** ***Biology and History,*** Major Discoveries, pp. 12–13 L2 L3 **TE:** ***Address Misconceptions,*** p. 12 L1
1–3 Studying Life, pp. 15–22 **1.3.1** ***Describe*** some characteristics of living things. **1.3.2** ***Explain*** how life can be studied at different levels.	2 periods (1 block)			**TE:** ***Build Science Skills,*** p. 15 L2 **SE:** ***Quick Lab,*** What are the characteristics of living things?, p. 18 L2 **SE:** ***Issues in Biology,*** When Scientists Have a Conflict of Interest, p. 23 L2 L3
1–4 Tools and Procedures, pp. 24–28 **1.4.1** ***Describe*** the measurement system most scientists use. **1.4.2** ***Explain*** how light microscopes and electron microscopes are similar and different. **1.4.3** ***Describe*** two common laboratory techniques. **1.4.4** ***Explain*** why it is important to work safely in biology.	1 period (1/2 block)		BIIE 1.a	**TE:** ***Build Science Skills,*** p. 25 L1 L2 **SE:** ***Analyzing Data,*** Bacterial Reproduction, p. 27 L2 **SE:** ***Exploration,*** Using a Compound Microscope, p. 29 L2 **LMA:** Chapter 1 Lab L2 L3 **LMB:** Chapter 1 Lab L1 L2 **IF:** Investigation 1 L1 L2 L3
Chapter Assessment, pp. 30–33	1 period (1/2 block)			

ACTIVITY PLANNER

SE: *Inquiry Activity,* p. 2; 15 min.; sets of 10 interlocking blocks, cardboard screen

TE: *Build Science Skills,* p. 4; 10 min.; moldy piece of bread or slice of cheese in a sealed plastic bag

TE: *Build Science Skills,* p. 5; 15 min.; boxes with different arrangements of partitions, marbles

TE: *Address Misconceptions,* p. 12; 10 min.; index cards

TE: *Build Science Skills,* p. 15; 15 min.; watch or clock with second hand, living animal

SE: *Quick Lab,* p. 18; 15 min.; hand lens, dormant brine shrimp eggs, water, hatched brine shrimp eggs, covered bowls

TE: *Build Science Skills,* p. 25; 15 min.; microscope

SE: *Exploration,* p. 29; 45 min.; compound microscope, microscope slide, newspaper or other small-print text, scissors, dropper pipette, prepared slide of bacteria, coverslips, prepared slide of crossed fibers, transparent 15-cm plastic ruler, prepared slide of root or stem

PLANNING KEY

Ability Levels

for students performing . . .

below grade level L1

at grade level L2

above grade level L3

Print Components

SE	Student Edition	LA	Lab Assessment
TE	Teacher's Edition	BTM	Biotechnology Manual
RSW	Reading & Study Workbook A	IDM	Issues and Decision Making
ARSW	Adapted Reading & Study Workbook B	LW	Lab Worksheets
TR	Teaching Resources	LMA	Laboratory Manual A
IF	Investigations in Forensics	LMB	Laboratory Manual B

Tech Components

CTB	Computer Test Bank
BD	BioDetectives DVD
TP	Transparencies Plus
PLM	Probeware Lab Manual
ABC	ABC DVD Library
LS	Lab Simulations
VL	Virtual Labs

Interactive textbook with assessment at PHSchool.com

Program Resources	Assessment	Media and Technology
TR: Lesson Plan 1–1, Section Summary, p. 5 L1, p. 13 L2, Worksheets, p. 8 L1, pp. 15–16 L2 **RSW:** Section 1–1 L2	**SE:** 1–1 Section Assessment, p. 7 **TR:** Section Review 1–1	**iText:** Section 1–1 **TP:** 1–1 Interest Grabber, Section Outline, Observation and Inference
TR: Lesson Plan 1–2, Section Summary, p. 5 L1, p. 13 L2, Worksheets, pp. 9–10 L1, pp. 17–19 L2, Enrichment L2 L3 **RSW:** Section 1–2 L2 **ARSW:** Section 1–2 L1 **IDM:** Issues and Decisions 2 L2 L3	**SE:** 1–2 Section Assessment, p. 14 **TR:** Section Review 1–2	**iText:** Section 1–2 **TP:** 1–2 Interest Grabber, Section Outline, Flowchart, Figure 1–8, Figure 1–10, Figure 1–11
TR: Lesson Plan 1–3, Section Summary, p. 6 L1, p. 13 L2, Worksheets, p. 11 L1, pp. 20–21 L2 **RSW:** Section 1–3 L2 **ARSW:** Section 1–3 L1	**SE:** 1–3 Section Assessment, p. 22 **TR:** Section Review 1–3	**iText:** Section 1–3 **TP:** 1–3 Interest Grabber, Section Outline, Characteristics of Living Things, Figure 1–21
TR: Lesson Plan 1–4, Section Summary, p. 7 L1, p. 14 L2, Worksheets, pp. 22–23 L2 **LW:** Chapter 1 Exploration L1 L2 L3 **RSW:** Section 1–4 L2 **ARSW:** Section 1–4 L1	**SE:** 1–4 Section Assessment, p. 28 **TR:** Section Review 1–4	**iText:** Section 1–4 **TP:** 1–4 Interest Grabber, Section Outline, Making a Graph From a Data Table
	SE: Chapter 1 Assessment, pp. 30–33 **TR:** Chapter Vocabulary Review, Graphic Organizer, Chapter 1 Test	**iText:** Chapter 1 Assessment **CTB:** Chapter 1 Test

Go Online
Students can do research, share data, and test their knowledge online.

TIME SAVER

PRESSED FOR TIME?

To Preview the Chapter
- Introduce students to Key Concepts and Vocabulary terms in each section.
- Assign the Reading Strategies for each section.

To Cover the Chapter Quickly
- Have students read all of Section 1–1, Designing an Experiment in Section 1–2, Characteristics of Living Things in Section 1–3, and all of Section 1–4.
- Assign Section Reviews 1–1 and 1–4, questions 1–6 and 8–10 in Chapter 1 Assessment, and questions 1–6 in Chapter 1 Standards Practice.

To Review the Chapter
- Assign Sections 1–1 through 1–4 in the Reading and Study Workbook or the Adapted Reading and Study Workbook.
- Assign Section Reviews for 1–1 through 1–4 and the Chapter Vocabulary Review for Chapter 1 in the Teaching Resources.

CHAPTER 1

ENGAGE/EXPLORE

Inquiry Activity

Objective Students will be able to infer that a scientific procedure should be written in such a way that it can be replicated by other scientists. L2

Skill Focus **Inferring, Evaluating and Revising**

Materials sets of 10 interlocking blocks, cardboard screen

Time 15 minutes

Advance Prep Divide the class into teams, and provide teams with identical sets of 10 interlocking blocks.

Strategies

- Make sure each team contains students with a variety of abilities.
- Check to see that each team is writing its directions without being observed by any other teams.

Expected Outcomes Most teams will write some directions that are unclear or misleading. Students will infer that directions should be carefully written so that other people can understand and replicate the procedure.

Think About It

1. A typical response might suggest that the writer of the directions should assume that the reader has never seen what is being described. The writer should describe each step in precise, specific language to avoid confusion.

2. Writing procedures that can be replicated allows other scientists to repeat the experiment to see if the same results occur every time.

Assess Prior Knowledge

Display several pictures of natural environments that show a variety of organisms, including various plants and animals. These pictures might be of a rain forest or a wetland, which are environments that contain a diversity of life. Ask students to choose one of the pictures to examine closely. Then, have each student compile a list of 20 questions a biologist might ask about the organisms in the picture.

CHAPTER 1

The Science of Biology

Researchers paired this wood ant and microchip to show their relative sizes. A scanning electron microscope was used to make this image, which has been artificially colored.

Inquiry Activity

Can your procedure be replicated?

Procedure

1. Behind a screen, assemble 10 blocks into an unusual structure. Write directions that others can use to replicate that structure without seeing it.
2. Exchange directions with another team. Replicate the team's structure by using its directions.
3. Compare each replicated and original structure. Identify which parts of the directions were clear and accurate, and which were unclear or misleading.

Think About It

1. **Evaluating and Revising** How could you have written better directions?
2. **Inferring** Why is it important that scientists write procedures that can be replicated?

HISTORY OF SCIENCE

The science of biology in ancient Greece
Although the word *biology* was not used until the early nineteenth century, the science of life has a history of thousands of years. Alcmaeon, a Greek physician born in about 535 BC, is one of the first persons to have studied human anatomy. He discovered the optic nerve, and he speculated that the brain was the center of intellectual activity. The Greek philosopher Aristotle, born in 384 BC, was a meticulous observer of living things, and he classified over 500 animal species in a strict hierarchy. He even proposed a theory of progressive change among animals—an early suggestion of evolution.

1–1 What Is Science?

BIIE 1.f. Distinguish between hypothesis and theory as scientific terms.

One ancient evening, lost in the mists of time, someone looked into the sky and wondered for the first time: What are those lights? Where did plants and animals come from? How did I come to be? Since then, humans have tried to answer those questions. At first, the answers our ancestors came up with involved tales of magic or legends like the one that accounted for the eye-like markings on the peacock's tail in **Figure 1–1.** Then, slowly, humans began to explore the natural world using a scientific approach.

What Science Is and Is Not

What does it mean to say that an approach to a problem is scientific?  **The goal of science is to investigate and understand the natural world, to explain events in the natural world, and to use those explanations to make useful predictions.**

Science has several features that make it different from other human endeavors. First, science deals only with the natural world. Second, scientists collect and organize information in a careful, orderly way, looking for patterns and connections between events. Third, scientists propose explanations that can be tested by examining evidence. In other words, **science** is an organized way of using evidence to learn about the natural world. The word *science* also refers to the body of knowledge that scientists have built up after years of using this process.

Guide for Reading

 **Key Concept**
- What is the goal of science?

Vocabulary
science
observation
data
inference
hypothesis

Reading Strategy: Making Comparisons As you read, list steps that scientists use to solve problems. After you read, compare the methods you use to solve problems with those used by scientists.

◀ **Figure 1–1** Male peacocks have markings on their tails that resemble giant eyes. According to an ancient Greek myth, the peacock's "eyes" once belonged to Argus, a giant with 100 eyes. An angry goddess had Argus killed, but she transferred the giant's eyes to the tail of the peacock.

TIME SAVER — SECTION RESOURCES

Print:
- ***Teaching Resources,*** Lesson Plan 1–1, Adapted Section Summary 1–1, Adapted Worksheets 1–1, Section Summary 1–1, Worksheets 1–1, Section Review 1–1
- ***Reading and Study Workbook A,*** Section 1–1
- ***Adapted Reading and Study Workbook B,*** Section 1–1
- ***Biotechnology Manual,*** Concept 1

Technology:
- ***iText,*** Section 1–1
- ***Transparencies Plus,*** Section 1–1

Section 1–1

1 FOCUS

Objectives

1.1.1 ***Explain*** what the goal of science is.
1.1.2 ***Explain*** what a hypothesis is.

Guide for Reading

Vocabulary Preview

Have students write the Vocabulary words, dividing each into its separate syllables as best they can. Remind students that each syllable usually has only one vowel sound. The correct syllabications are: sci•ence, ob•ser•va•tion, da•ta, in•fer•ence, hy•poth•e•sis.

Reading Strategy

Tell students that they should write at least one phrase about how a scientist works for each of the blue heads in the section.

2 INSTRUCT

What Science Is and Is Not

Build Science Skills

Applying Concepts Divide the class into small groups, and ask each group to propose an explanation for why it rains, without including any scientific thinking in their explanation. Groups might propose that clouds are crying, that there is an invisible river in the sky, or that an invisible rain god pours water on Earth when angry. Once each group has agreed upon an explanation, have a member from each present it to the class. Then, ask: **Suppose someone does not believe your explanation. Could you supply evidence to support your explanation?** *(For almost all explanations, the answer will be no.)* **Why not?** *(There is no way to gather evidence, there is no way to observe a cloud that is "crying," and so on.)* Emphasize that scientists propose explanations that can be tested by examining evidence.  

1–1 (continued)

Thinking Like a Scientist

Build Science Skills

Observing Place moldy bread or cheese in a sealed plastic bag. Show it to the class and ask: **Can you describe in detail what you see?** *(Observations should include the color and texture of the mold, the extent to which it covers the bread or cheese, and whether the mold is in solid patches or small spots.)* **What questions would you as a biologist ask after seeing the mold?** *(Possible questions: What caused the mold? Will the mold cover more of the bread or cheese? Does all bread or cheese get moldy?)* L2

Build Science Skills

Inferring Explain to students that some scientists use the following method when confronted with a problem to be solved: organize, analyze, evaluate, make inferences, and predict trends from data. Explain what each of these skills involves. For example, scientists often organize data into tables and graphs. They analyze the data through processes such as noting how manipulated variables affect responding variables. They evaluate data by checking its accuracy and reliability, including any measurements. Scientists make logical interpretations, or inferences, based on observations and knowledge. They predict trends by looking at trends shown in the data they already have. Also refer students to Appendix A in their textbooks. After you have explained and discussed science process skills, have students apply them to a real-world situation. For example, students might analyze newspaper weather data and predict trends based on the data. L2 L3

▲ **Figure 1–2** **The goal of science is to investigate and understand nature.** The first step in this process is making observations. This researcher is observing the behavior of a manatee in Florida.

Thinking Like a Scientist

Suppose a car won't start. Is the car out of gas? A glance at the fuel gauge tests that idea. Perhaps the battery is dead. An auto mechanic can use an instrument to test that idea. To figure out what is wrong with the car, people perform tests and observe the results of the tests.

This familiar activity uses the approach scientists take in research. Scientific thinking usually begins with **observation,** the process of gathering information about events or processes in a careful, orderly way. Observation generally involves using the senses, particularly sight and hearing. The information gathered from observations is called **data.**

There are two main categories of data. Quantitative data are expressed as numbers, obtained by counting or measuring. The researcher in **Figure 1–2,** for example, might note that the manatee "has one scar on its back." Qualitative data are descriptive and involve characteristics that can't usually be counted. The researcher might make the qualitative observations that "the scar appears old" and "the animal seems healthy and alert."

Scientists may use data to make inferences. An **inference** is a logical interpretation based on prior knowledge or experience. The researcher in **Figure 1–3,** for example, is testing water in a reservoir. Because she cannot test *all* the water, she collects water samples from several different parts of the reservoir. If all the samples are clean enough to drink, she may infer that all the water is safe to drink.

◀ **Figure 1–3** Researchers testing water for lead pollution cannot test every drop, so they check small amounts, called samples. **Inferring** *How might a local community use such scientific information?*

ESL SUPPORT FOR ENGLISH LANGUAGE LEARNERS

Vocabulary: Writing

Beginning Write the word *observation* on the board. Ask English-proficient and ESL students to make observations about the classroom. Using single words or short phrases, write their responses on the board under the word *observation.* Then, have your ESL students write the word *observation* on their papers. Have them use single words or pictures to name several things they observe in the classroom. L1

Intermediate Extend the Beginning activity by recording observations on the board using complete sentences. Then, when the ESL students prepare their own list, have them speak complete sentences to describe their observations instead of single words or pictures. Students who need assistance with their sentences can be paired with an English-proficient student. L2

Explaining and Interpreting Evidence

Scientists try to explain events in the natural world by interpreting evidence logically and analytically. Suppose, for example, that many people contract an unknown disease after attending a public event. Public health researchers will use scientific methods to try to determine how those people became ill.

After initial observations, the researchers will propose one or more hypotheses. A **hypothesis** is a proposed scientific explanation for a set of observations. Scientists generate hypotheses using prior knowledge, or what they already know; logical inference; and informed, creative imagination. For the unknown disease, there might be several competing hypotheses, such as these: (1) The disease was spread from person to person by contact. (2) The disease was spread through insect bites. (3) The disease was spread through air, water, or food.

CA (a)  BIIE 1.f

Scientific hypotheses must be proposed in a way that enables them to be tested. Some hypotheses are tested by performing controlled experiments, as you will learn in the next section. Other hypotheses are tested by gathering more data. In the case of the mystery illness, data would be collected by studying the location of the event; by examining air, water, and food people were exposed to; and by questioning people about their actions before falling ill. Some hypotheses would be ruled out. Others might be supported and eventually confirmed.

Researchers working on complex questions often collaborate in teams like the one in **Figure 1–4.** These groups have regular meetings at which the members analyze, review, and critique one another's data and hypotheses. This review process helps ensure that their conclusions are valid. To be valid, a conclusion must be based on logical interpretation of reliable data. To learn about sources of error in scientific investigations, see Appendix A.

CHECKPOINT *How do scientists develop hypotheses?*

◀ **Figure 1–4** Researchers often collaborate by working in teams, combining imagination and logic to develop and test hypotheses. **Applying Concepts** *How do scientists decide whether to accept or reject a hypothesis?*

Explaining and Interpreting Evidence

Build Science Skills

Formulating Hypotheses Divide the class into small groups, and give each group a "mystery box." Prepare each box ahead of time, each with a different arrangement of partitions and each containing one or more marbles. Explain to groups what the boxes contain, in general terms. Tell students their task is to formulate a hypothesis about the specific arrangement of partitions in their group's box. Have them tilt, turn, and tap the box to move the marbles inside so that sounds and sensations will provide clues about the internal arrangement. Each group should make a sketch of its hypothesis of how the partitions are arranged inside its mystery box. Then, groups should make a list of what further tests could be performed to support or refute the hypothesis, short of opening the box. (Students may have the misconception that hypotheses are always confirmed, because the activities they have done in science classes were usually designed to support a hypothesis.) L2 L3

BIO INSIGHTS

FACTS AND FIGURES

Evidence can be misused

There have been times in human history when scientific evidence or apparent evidence has been misused to serve the ends of racial prejudice and sexual bias. For example, the Swiss-American biologist Louis Agassiz (1807–1873) expressed the racist belief that non-European peoples were inferior to Europeans. Other scientists at the turn of the nineteenth century shared his view. They accepted unsubstantiated or inaccurate data to try to support their ideas. In the late nineteenth century, a group of scientists called craniologists made measurements of brain and skull size to prove that women were intellectually inferior to men. These "scientific studies" were cited in attempts to deny women equal rights. Today, scientists know that among humans, brain size has nothing to do with intelligence.

Answers to . . .

CHECKPOINT *Hypotheses may arise from prior knowledge; logical inference; and informed, creative imagination.*

Figure 1–3 *The leaders of a community might use the test results to warn residents about water pollution, take steps to prevent or remedy pollution problems, or assure residents that the water is safe to drink.*

Figure 1–4 *Scientists accept or reject a hypothesis by evaluating the outcome of a controlled experiment or by gathering more data.*

1–1 (continued)

Science as a Way of Knowing

Use Community Resources

Scientists from the community can provide students with firsthand knowledge about careers in science. Invite a local scientist to speak to the class about his or her career and about looking at the world with a scientific view. Also, identify some local people with careers related to science. As much as possible, mention women and individuals of different ethnicities and backgrounds with whom students can relate. These neighbors will help students see that they too can enter careers in science. Keep in mind that some findings of modern science as well as some types of scientific experiments may be incompatible with the beliefs of certain ethnic or religious groups. The support of respected members of the community of different cultural backgrounds may help promote understanding. L1 L2

Use Visuals

Figure 1–5 Lead a discussion about differences in the way the hikers who discovered the corpse might have thought about the body and the way the scientists who removed the corpse probably thought about the body. Then, ask: **After the initial observations, what are some ways that scientists could find out more about this ancient corpse?** *(Accept any reasonable response. Students might suggest X-raying the body or even dissecting it.)* L2

Science and Human Values

Use Community Resources

Invite a university biologist and a member of the local clergy to address the class on an issue related to science, such as cloning, research using stem cells, or laws about endangered species. Ask the speakers to talk about how people who agree with their viewpoints might confront such an issue. L1 L2

Science as a Way of Knowing

This book contains lots of facts, but don't think biological science is a set of truths that never change. Instead, science is a way of knowing. This means that rather than unchanging knowledge, science is an ongoing *process*—a process that involves asking questions, observing, making inferences, and testing hypotheses. You can learn more about these and other science skills in Appendix A.

Because of new tools, techniques, and discoveries, such as the discovery of the iceman shown in **Figure 1–5**, scientific understanding is always changing. Research can have a profound impact on scientific thought. For example, the discovery of cells revolutionized understanding of the structure of living things. Without doubt, some things you learn from this book will soon be revised because of new information. But this doesn't mean that science has failed. On the contrary, it means that science continues to succeed in advancing understanding.

Good scientists are skeptics, which means that they question both existing ideas and new hypotheses. Scientists continually evaluate the strengths and weaknesses of hypotheses. Scientists must be open-minded and consider new hypotheses if data demand it. And despite the power of science, it has definite limits. For example, science cannot help you decide whether a painting is beautiful or whether school sports teams should be limited to only the best athletes.

The scientific way of knowing includes the view that the whole physical universe is a system, or a collection of parts and processes that interact. In the universe, basic natural laws govern all events and objects, large or small. The physical universe consists of many smaller systems. Biologists focus on living systems, which range from invisibly small to the size of our entire planet.

▼ **Figure 1–5** In 1991, hikers in the Italian Alps discovered a well-preserved corpse that was about 5000 years old. Scientists might have asked how the corpse could be so well preserved, but they already knew the answer. Sub-zero temperatures keep the organisms that cause decomposition from doing their job. **Asking Questions** ***What are some other scientific questions that might be asked about this discovery?***

FACTS AND FIGURES

Ötzi the Ice Man

The human remains shown in Figure 1–5 were discovered at the end of a warm summer in a barren Alpine pass near the Italian-Austrian border. Carbon-14 testing showed that the man had died some 5300 years earlier, during the Neolithic Age. He was named Ötzi the Ice Man because he was found in the Ötzal Alps and he had been preserved in glacial ice since his death. The unusually warm summer of 1991 had melted ice on the pass and exposed the body to view. Ötzi now lies on display at the South Tyrol Museum of Archaeology in Bolzano, Italy. Researchers have done many studies on Ötzi, including some using X-rays and CAT scans. Chemical analysis of a tiny clump at the top of his colon showed that he had eaten food from a nearby valley just eight hours before he died. His last meal had been a cracker-hard, unleavened bread made from einkorn wheat.

Science and Human Values

Because of new knowledge gained through research, scientists continually revise and reevaluate their ideas. The importance of science, however, reaches far beyond the scientific world. Today, scientists contribute information to discussions about health and disease, and about the relationship between human beings and the living and nonliving environment.

Make a list of things that you need to understand to protect your life and the lives of others close to you. Chances are that your list will include drugs and alcohol, smoking and lung disease, AIDS, cancer, and heart disease. Other questions focus on public health and the environment. How can we best use antibiotics to make sure that those "wonder drugs" keep working for a long time? How much of the information in your genes should you be able to keep private? Should communities produce electricity using fossil fuels, nuclear power, or hydroelectric dams? How should chemical wastes be disposed of? Who should be responsible for their disposal?

All of these questions involve scientific information. For that reason, an understanding of science and the scientific approach is essential to making intelligent decisions about them. None of these questions, however, can be answered by science alone. They involve the society in which we live and the economy that provides jobs, food, and shelter. They may require us to consider laws and moral principles. In our society, scientists alone do not make final decisions—they make recommendations. Who makes the decisions? We, the citizens of our democracy do—when we vote to express our opinions to elected officials. That is why it is more important than ever that everyone understand what science is, what it can do, and what it cannot do.

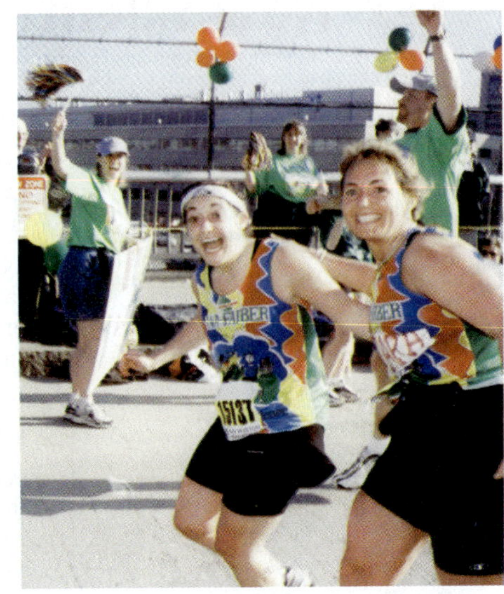

▲ **Figure 1–6** Scientific research has an impact on many aspects of our lives. These racers are raising money to help support research directed at preventing and treating cancer. **Applying Concepts** *Identify three ways in which science affects your life.*

1–1 Section Assessment

1. **Key Concept** What does science study?
2. What does it mean to describe a scientist as skeptical? Why is skepticism considered a valuable quality in a scientist?
3. What is the main difference between qualitative and quantitative observations?
4. What is a scientific hypothesis? In what two ways can a hypothesis be tested?
5. Is a scientific hypothesis accepted if there is no way to demonstrate that the hypothesis is wrong? Explain your answer.
6. **Critical Thinking Making Judgments** Suppose a community proposes a law to require the wearing of seatbelts in all moving vehicles. How could scientific research have an impact on the decision?

Thinking Visually

Making a Table
List the five main senses—vision, hearing, smell, taste, and touch—and give an example of an observation that you have made using each sense. Then, add at least one inference that could be made based on each observation.

3 ASSESS

Evaluate Understanding

Have students write an explanation in their own words of what a hypothesis is and the three ways in which a hypothesis may arise.

Reteach

Direct students' attention to the manatee pictured in Figure 1–2, and ask students at random to explain what quantitative and qualitative observations a biologist might make about this animal.

Thinking Visually

Students should list an observation and a logical inference for each sense. For example, if you see wet pavement, it may have rained or someone may have washed a car in that location. If you hear a bird sing, it may be singing to mark a territory or attract a mate. If a tabletop feels sticky, someone may have spilled syrup on the table.

If your class subscribes to the iText, use it to review the Key Concepts in Section 1–1.

1–1 Section Assessment

1. Science is the study of the natural world, the search for patterns and connections between events.
2. Skeptics question both existing ideas and new hypotheses. Skepticism is valuable because scientific understanding is always changing.
3. Qualitative observations involve characteristics that cannot be measured or counted.
4. A hypothesis is a proposed scientific explanation for a set of observations. One can be tested by performing a controlled experiment or by gathering more data.
5. No. Scientific hypotheses must be proposed in a way that enables them to be tested.
6. Answers will vary. A typical response might suggest that research could determine whether seatbelts would reduce accident fatalities.

Answers to . . .

Figure 1–5 *Typical answers might include: Was the corpse male or female? How did the person die? How old was the person? Where might the person have been going at the time that he or she died?*

Figure 1–6 *Answers will vary. A typical answer might suggest how science affects a student's life in the areas of health care, environment, and communication.*

Section 1–2

7IIE 7.c, 8IIE 9.c, BIIE 1.f, BIIE 1.j, BIIE 1.n

1 FOCUS

Objectives

1.2.1 ***Describe*** how scientists test hypotheses.

1.2.2 ***Explain*** how a scientific theory develops.

Guide for Reading

Vocabulary Preview

Have students preview the section's Vocabulary terms by skimming the text, finding the highlighted, boldface terms, and writing down the definitions of each in their notebooks.

Reading Strategy

Have students make an outline of the section, using the blue heads as the first level of the outline and the green heads as the second level. Explain that the third and possibly fourth levels of the outline should be supporting details of the topics suggested by the heads.

2 INSTRUCT

Designing an Experiment

Build Science Skills

Applying Concepts Drawing from the green headings in the students' text, write the steps for designing an experiment on the board:

1. Ask a question
2. Form a hypothesis
3. Set up a controlled experiment
4. Record and analyze results
5. Draw a conclusion

Then, have students recall a common superstition, such as the one that proposes that a black cat crossing your path brings bad luck. Ask students how they would use an experiment to verify or disprove this superstition, using the steps written on the board. L2

1–2 How Scientists Work

7IIE 7.c. Communicate the logical connections among hypotheses, science concepts, tests conducted, data collected, and conclusions drawn from the scientific evidence. **8IIE 9.c.** Distinguish between variable and controlled parameters in a test. **BIIE 1.f.** Distinguish between hypothesis and theory as scientific terms. **BIIE 1.j.** Recognize the issues of statistical variability and the need for controlled tests. **BIIE 1.n.** Know that when an observation does not agree with an accepted scientific theory, the observation is sometimes mistaken or fraudulent (e.g. the Piltdown Man fossil or unidentified flying objects) and that the theory is sometimes wrong (e.g. the Ptolemaic model of the movement of the Sun, Moon, and planets).

Guide for Reading

Key Concepts
- How do scientists test hypotheses?
- How does a scientific theory develop?

Vocabulary
spontaneous generation
controlled experiment
manipulated variable
responding variable
theory

Reading Strategy: Outlining As you read, make an outline of the main steps in a controlled experiment.

Have you ever noticed what happens to food that is left in an open trash can for a few days in summer? Creatures that look like worms appear on the discarded food. These creatures are called maggots. For thousands of years people have been observing maggots on food that is not protected. The maggots seem to suddenly appear out of nowhere. Where do they come from?

Designing an Experiment

People's ideas about where some living things come from have changed over the centuries. Exploring this change can help show how science works. Remember that what might seem obvious today was not so obvious thousands of years ago.

About 2300 years ago, the Greek philosopher Aristotle made extensive observations of the natural world. He tried to explain his observations through reasoning. During and after his lifetime, people thought that living things followed a set of natural rules that were different from those for nonliving things. They also thought that special "vital" forces brought some living things into being from nonliving material. These ideas, exemplified by the directions in **Figure 1–7**, persisted for many centuries. About 400 years ago, some people began to challenge these established ideas. They also began to use experiments to answer their questions about life.

▼ **Figure 1–7** About 2000 years ago, a Roman poet wrote these directions for producing bees. **Inferring** *Why do you think reasonable individuals once accepted the ideas behind this recipe?*

Recipe for Bees

1. Kill a bull during the first thaw of winter.
2. Build a shed.
3. Place the dead bull on branches and herbs inside the shed.
4. Wait for summer. The decaying body of the bull will produce bees.

Asking a Question For many years, observations seemed to indicate that some living things could just suddenly appear: Maggots showed up on meat; mice were found on grain; and beetles turned up on cow dung. People wondered how these events happened. They were, in their own everyday way, identifying a problem to be solved by asking a question: How do new living things, or organisms, come into being?

Forming a Hypothesis For centuries, people accepted the prevailing explanation for the sudden appearance of some organisms, that some life somehow "arose" from nonliving matter. The maggots arose from the meat, the mice from the grain, and the beetles from the dung. Scholars of the day even gave a name to the idea that life could arise from nonliving matter—**spontaneous generation.** In today's terms, the idea of spontaneous generation can be considered a hypothesis.

In 1668, Francesco Redi, an Italian physician, proposed a different hypothesis for the appearance of maggots. Redi had observed that these organisms appeared on meat a few days after flies were present. He considered it likely that the flies laid eggs too small for people to see. Thus, Redi was proposing a new hypothesis—flies produce maggots. Redi's next step was to test his hypothesis.

TIME SAVER — SECTION RESOURCES

Print:
- ***Teaching Resources,*** Lesson Plan 1–2, Adapted Section Summary 1–2, Adapted Worksheets 1–2, Section Summary 1–2, Worksheets 1–2, Section Review 1–2, Enrichment
- ***Reading and Study Workbook A,*** Section 1–2
- ***Adapted Reading and Study Workbook B,*** Section 1–2
- ***Issues and Decision Making,*** Issues and Decisions 2

Technology:
- ***iText,*** Section 1–2
- ***Transparencies Plus,*** Section 1–2

Setting Up a Controlled Experiment In science, testing a hypothesis often involves designing an experiment. The factors in an experiment that can change are called variables. Examples of variables include equipment used, type of material, amount of material, temperature, light, and time.

Suppose you want to know whether an increase in water, light, or fertilizer can speed up plant growth. If you change all three variables at once, you will not be able to tell which variable is responsible for the observed results. **Whenever possible, a hypothesis should be tested by an experiment in which only one variable is changed at a time. All other variables should be kept unchanged, or controlled.** This type of experiment is called a **controlled experiment.** The variable that is deliberately changed is called the **manipulated variable.** The variable that is observed and that changes in response to the manipulated variable is called the **responding variable.**

Based on his hypothesis, Redi made a prediction that keeping flies away from meat would prevent the appearance of maggots. To test this hypothesis, he planned the experiment shown in **Figure 1–8.** Notice that Redi controlled all variables except one—whether or not there was gauze over each jar. The gauze was important because it kept flies off the meat.

CHECKPOINT *What was the responding variable in Redi's experiment?*

CA (a) BIIE 1.j, 8IIE 9.c

For: Redi's Experiment activity
Visit: PHSchool.com
Web Code: cbp-1012

▼ **Figure 1–8** **In a controlled experiment, only one variable is tested at a time.** Redi designed an experiment to determine what caused the sudden appearance of maggots. In his experiment, the manipulated variable was the presence or absence of the gauze covering. The results of this experiment helped disprove the hypothesis of spontaneous generation.

Redi's Experiment on Spontaneous Generation

OBSERVATIONS: Flies land on meat that is left uncovered. Later, maggots appear on the meat.

HYPOTHESIS: Flies produce maggots.

PROCEDURE

Controlled Variables: jars, type of meat, location, temperature, time

Manipulated Variable: gauze covering that keeps flies away from meat

Responding Variable: whether maggots appear

Uncovered jars

Maggots appear.

Several days pass.

Covered jars

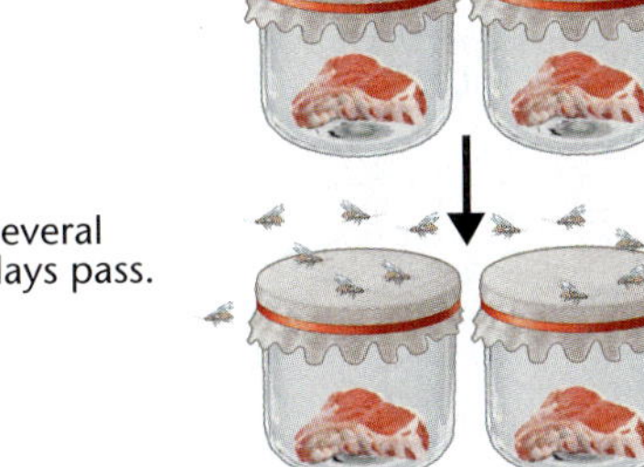

No maggots appear.

CONCLUSION: Maggots form only when flies come in contact with meat. Spontaneous generation of maggots did not occur.

Go Online active art

For: Redi's Experiment activity
Visit: PHSchool.com
Web Code: cbe-1012
Students can interact online with the art of Redi's experiment.

Use Visuals

Figure 1–8 Ask students: **What was Redi's hypothesis?** *(Flies produce maggots.)* **Why did he design an experiment that tested only one variable?** *(He designed such an experiment to make sure that any differences he observed during the experiment were caused by that single variable.)* **What was the manipulated variable in Redi's experiment?** *(Whether or not there was gauze over each jar)* **What is the difference that you can see between the two setups?** *(After several days, maggots appear on the meat in the uncovered jars, but no maggots appear on the meat in the covered jars.)* L2

Build Science Skills

Designing Experiments Show students an example or photo of moldy bread. Explain that mold will grow on bread that is exposed to air at room temperature. Then, ask each student to design an experiment to test the effects of water and sunlight on the growth of bread mold. Tell students that they may use up to four slices of bread and any materials available in the classroom. Ask that they ask a question, formulate a hypothesis, and identify the manipulated variable and the control in the proposed experiment. Discuss various experimental designs as a class. Students should take any safety precautions necessary to prevent exposure to mold or mold spores.

UNIVERSAL ACCESS

Less Proficient Readers
For students who have trouble understanding the three experiments discussed in the section, spend time orally comparing and contrasting the illustrations in Figures 1–8, 1–10, and 1–11. Make sure students can identify the controlled, manipulated, and responding variables in each experiment. L1

English Language Learners
Explain to students that the word *generation* in the term *spontaneous generation* is related to the verb *to generate*, or "to bring into existence." Then, discuss what it means to be "spontaneous" and how the common meaning of the word is related to the meaning used in science. L1 L2

Advanced Learners
Encourage students who need a challenge to investigate how college science textbooks present a systematic approach to problem solving, often called the scientific method. Details will vary, though the basic principles will be the same in all sources. Have these students make a presentation to the class. L3

Answers to . . .

The responding variable was whether maggots appeared.

Figure 1–7 *A typical response might suggest that without controlled experiments such a recipe could seem logical based on prior observations.*

1–2 (continued)

Build Science Skills

Designing Experiments Divide the class into small groups, and have each group consider this question: Does the amount of sleep a student gets affect how well the student does in school? Ask each group to design an experiment that would address that question. Point out that they should ask a question, form a hypothesis, describe a controlled experiment, and describe how the results could be recorded and analyzed. L2

Repeating Investigations

Demonstration

Display a number of periodicals and science journals for students to study, including issues of *Science* and *Nature.* Go over two or three of the experiments described, pointing out the hypothesis, the manipulated variable, the responding variable, the control, the results, and the conclusion for each experiment. Then, divide the class into small groups and assign each group an experiment in one of the journals to analyze according to the experimental process described in their textbook. L2 L3

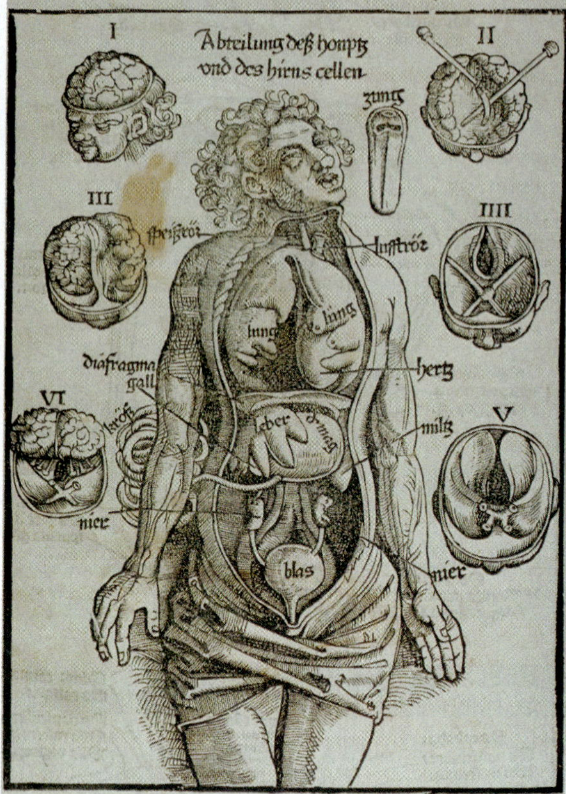

▲ **Figure 1–9** For centuries, the workings of the human body remained a mystery. Gradually, scientists observed the body's structures and recorded their work in drawings like this. This diagram dates back to fifteenth-century Austria. **Comparing and Contrasting** *How does this drawing compare with the modern illustrations in Unit 10?*

Recording and Analyzing Results Scientists usually keep written records of their observations, or data. In the past, data were usually recorded by hand, often in notebooks or personal journals. Sometimes, drawings such as **Figure 1–9** recorded certain kinds of observations more completely and accurately than a verbal description could. Today, researchers may record their work on computers. Online storage often makes it easier for researchers to review the data at any time and, if necessary, offer a new explanation for the data. Scientists know that Redi recorded his data because copies of his work were available to later generations of scientists. His investigation showed that maggots appeared on the meat in the control jars. No maggots appeared in the jars covered with gauze.

Drawing a Conclusion Scientists use the data from an experiment to evaluate the hypothesis and draw a valid conclusion. That is, they use the evidence to determine whether the hypothesis was supported or refuted. Redi's results supported his hypothesis. He therefore concluded that the maggots were indeed produced by flies. CA a

As scientists look for explanations for specific observations, they assume that the patterns in nature are consistent. Thus, Redi's results could be viewed not only as an explanation about maggots and flies but also as a refutation of the hypothesis of spontaneous generation.

CHECKPOINT *What did Redi conclude?*

a 7IIE 7.c

Repeating Investigations

A key assumption in science is that experimental results can be reproduced because nature behaves in a consistent manner. When one particular variable is manipulated in a given set of variables, the result should always be the same. In keeping with this assumption, scientists expect to test one another's investigations. Thus, communicating a description of an experiment is an essential part of science. Today's researchers often publish a report of their work in a scientific journal. Other scientists review the experimental procedures to make sure that the design was without flaws. They often repeat experiments to be sure that the results match those already obtained. In Redi's day, scientific journals were not common, but he communicated his conclusion in a book that included a description of his investigation and its results.

HISTORY OF SCIENCE

An emphasis on experimentation

Galileo Galilei (1564–1642) is generally considered to have established the modern scientific method, as demonstrated in his investigations. Some stories about Galileo cannot be verified, including the one about the Leaning Tower of Pisa, but his approach to the study of nature is beyond question. He challenged Aristotle's view that the natural state of a body was at rest, a view accepted for 2000 years. Galileo's discovery of Jupiter's moons supported the Copernican model of the solar system. His emphasis on experimentation as the way to prove the validity of ideas was part of the broader movement of free thought and skepticism that was characteristic of the European Renaissance.

Needham's Test of Redi's Findings Some later tests of Redi's work were influenced by an unexpected discovery. About the time Redi was carrying out his experiment, Anton van Leeuwenhoek (LAY-vun-hook) of the Netherlands discovered a world of tiny moving objects in rainwater, pond water, and dust. Inferring that these objects were alive, he called them "animalcules," or tiny animals. He made drawings of his observations and shared them with other scientists. For the next 200 years or so, scientists could not agree on whether the animalcules were alive or how they came to exist.

In the mid-1700s, John Needham, an English scientist, used an experiment involving animalcules to attack Redi's work. Needham claimed that spontaneous generation could occur under the right conditions. To prove his claim, he sealed a bottle of gravy and heated it. He claimed that the heat had killed any living things that might be in the gravy. After several days, he examined the contents of the bottle and found it swarming with activity. "These little animals," he inferred, "can only have come from juice of the gravy."

Spallanzani's Test of Redi's Findings An Italian scholar, Lazzaro Spallanzani, read about Redi's and Needham's work. Spallanzani thought that Needham had not heated his samples enough and decided to improve upon Needham's experiment. **Figure 1–10** shows that Spallanzani boiled two containers of gravy, assuming that the boiling would kill any tiny living things, or microorganisms, that were present. He sealed one jar immediately and left the other jar open. After a few days, the gravy in the open jar was teeming with microorganisms. The sealed jar remained free of microorganisms.

Spallanzani concluded that nonliving gravy did not produce living things. The microorganisms in the unsealed jar were offspring of microorganisms that had entered the jar through the air. This experiment and Redi's work supported the hypothesis that new organisms are produced only by existing organisms.

CHECKPOINT *How did Spallanzani's investigative procedures improve upon Needham's work?*

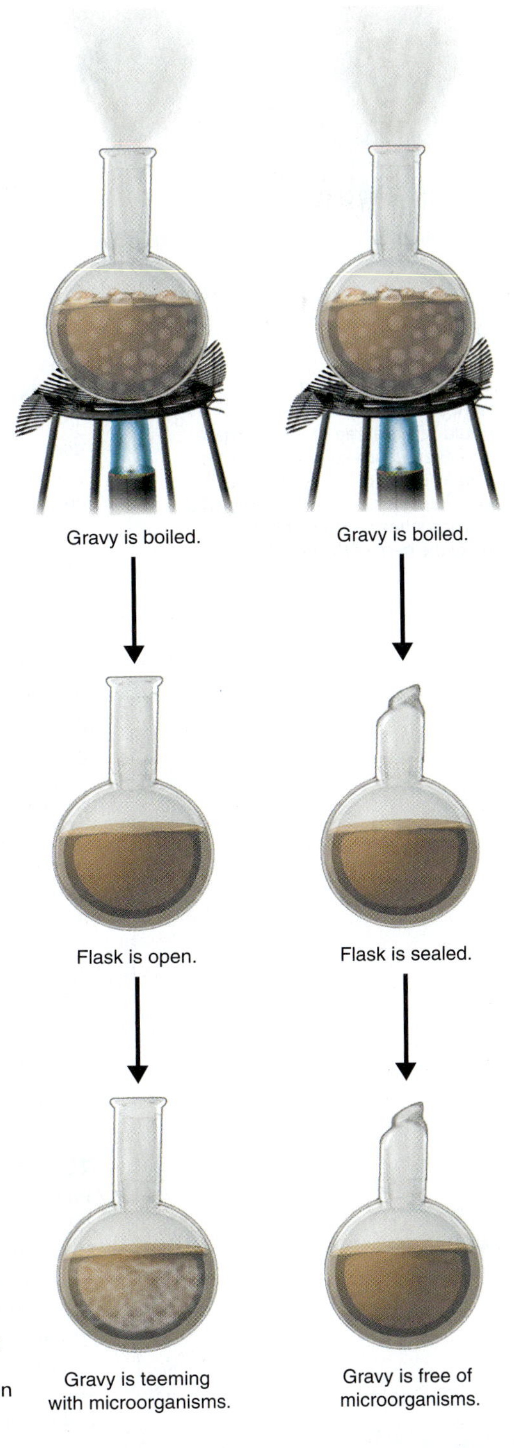

▶ **Figure 1–10** Spallanzani's experiment showed that microorganisms will not grow in boiled gravy that has been sealed but will grow in boiled gravy that is left open to the air. **Interpreting Graphics** *What variable was controlled in this experiment?*

Build Science Skills

Applying Concepts After students have read about Needham's test of Redi's findings, ask: **What was Needham's hypothesis in his experiment?** *(Spontaneous generation could occur under the right conditions.)* **In what way did he change Redi's experiment?** *(Needham heated a sealed bottle of gravy. Redi never used heat in his experiment.)* **What assumption did Needham make that made his results invalid?** *(He assumed that heating the gravy killed all the "animalcules." That assumption was wrong.)* **What is the result when a scientist draws a conclusion from data that are derived from an invalid assumption?** *(The conclusion is flawed.)* L2

Use Visuals

Figure 1–10 Ask students: **What was Spallanzani's hypothesis?** *(Boiling would kill any tiny living things in gravy, and no growth of organisms would occur in a sealed flask.)* **Is boiling the manipulated variable in Spallanzani's experiment? If not, what is?** *(Boiling was not the manipulated variable; the manipulated variable was whether or not the flask was sealed.)* **What variables were kept the same, or controlled, in his experiment?** *(Same gravy, same boiling, same flasks, same time)* L2

BIO INSIGHTS

HISTORY OF SCIENCE

Water teeming with "animalcules"
Anton van Leeuwenhoek had a passion for tiny things. During a lifetime of investigation, he studied the structure of muscle, skin, hair, tooth scrapings, and various small insects. His famous discovery of "animalcules" occurred late in the summer of 1674 when he returned home from boating on a local lake with a sample of the water. That water was cloudy, and most people at the time thought that such cloudiness was caused by a heavy dew. But, when Leeuwenhoek used one of the lenses he had mounted as a microscope, he was surprised to see that the water was teeming with tiny organisms, so many that it was cloudy with them. This and other discoveries made him world-famous. Perhaps his most remarkable discovery was made in 1676 when he described tiny organisms that are now known to have been bacteria.

Answers to . . .

CHECKPOINT *Redi concluded that maggots were produced by flies.*

CHECKPOINT *Spallanzani boiled the gravy, assuming that boiling would kill any microorganisms.*

Figure 1–9 *Students' answers will vary. A typical comparison might suggest that modern illustrations are much more realistic and accurate.*

Figure 1–10 *The controlled variable was the boiling of the gravy.*

1–2 (continued)

Address Misconceptions

After reading about the experiments of Redi, Spallanzani, and Pasteur, some students may be confused about the steps a scientist takes in carrying out an experiment. To review these steps, use the following activity. Write the steps on a set of index cards. Place the cards face down on a desk or table. Have each student pick a card at random. Ask the students to line themselves up so that the steps they have drawn are in the correct order. Then, have students take turns describing each step. L1

Build Science Skills

Applying Concepts Point out that a jar of pasta sauce is kept on a grocery store shelf or in a cupboard at home unrefrigerated. But, once the top is opened, the jar must be kept in a refrigerator to keep the contents from spoiling. Ask students: **What can you infer from Pasteur's work about why an opened jar must be kept in a refrigerator?** *(Pasteur showed that all living things come from other living things, and opening the jar exposes the contents to organisms in the air, just as breaking the neck of the flask did in his experiment.)* Have students write a description of a controlled experiment they might carry out that would test the hypothesis that organisms would grow in an opened jar of food. L2 L3

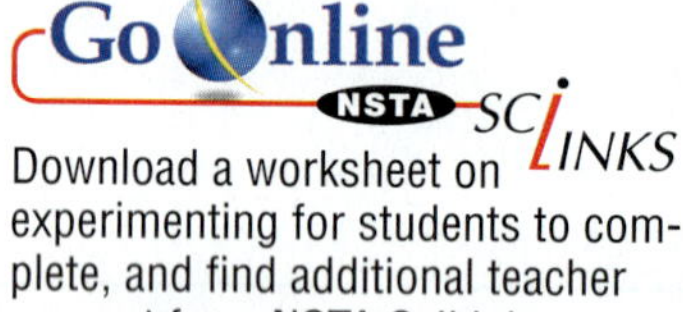

Download a worksheet on experimenting for students to complete, and find additional teacher support from NSTA SciLinks.

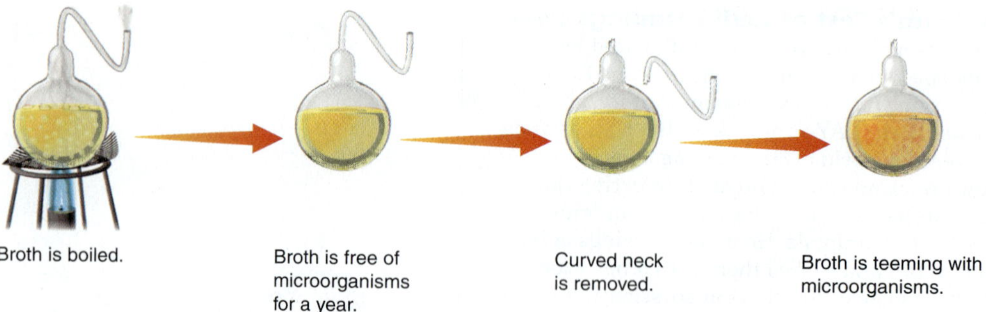

▲ **Figure 1–11** Pasteur's experiment showed that boiled broth would remain free of microorganisms even if air was allowed in, as long as dust and other particles were kept out. **Inferring** *Why did microorganisms grow after Pasteur broke the neck of the flask?*

Pasteur's Test of Spontaneous Generation Well into the 1800s, some scientists continued to support the spontaneous generation hypothesis. Some of them argued that air was a necessary factor in the process of generating life because air contained the "life force" needed to produce new life. They pointed out that Spallanzani's experiment was not a fair test because air had been excluded from the sealed jar.

In 1864, French scientist, Louis Pasteur, found a way to finally disprove the hypothesis of spontaneous generation. He designed a flask that had a long curved neck, as shown in **Figure 1–11.** The flask remained open to the air, but microorganisms from the air did not make their way through the neck into the flask. Pasteur boiled the flask thoroughly to kill any microorganisms it might contain. Pasteur waited an entire year. In that time, no microorganisms could be found in the flask.

About a year after the experiment began, Pasteur broke the neck of the flask, allowing air dust and other particles to enter the broth. In just one day, the flask was clouded from the growth of microorganisms. Pasteur had clearly shown that microorganisms had entered the flask with particles from the air. His work convinced other scientists that the hypothesis of spontaneous generation was not correct. In other words, Pasteur showed that all living things come from other living things. This change in thinking represented a major shift in the way scientists viewed living things.

CHECKPOINT *What improvement did Pasteur make to Redi's experiment?*

The Impact of Pasteur's Work During his lifetime, Pasteur made many discoveries related to microorganisms. His research had an impact on society as well as on scientific thought. He saved the French wine industry, which was troubled by unexplained souring of wine, and the silk industry, which was endangered by a silkworm disease. Moreover, he began to uncover the very nature of infectious diseases, showing that they were the result of microorganisms entering the bodies of the victims. Pasteur is considered one of biology's most remarkable problem solvers.

BIO INSIGHTS

HISTORY OF SCIENCE

The dawn of modern science

Andreas Vesalius (1514–1564) was a physician from Brussels, Belgium. Because dissection of human cadavers was forbidden in northern Europe, Vesalius moved to Italy in the 1530s, where he taught anatomy at universities and performed numerous dissections. One of his achievements was to demonstrate that men and women had the same number of ribs—the common belief had been that men had one fewer rib than women, because Eve was created from Adam's rib. In 1543, Vesalius published his book on human anatomy. It contained outstanding illustrations, many of which were done by a student of the great Italian painter Titian. In this groundbreaking work, Vesalius showed the human body in natural positions. It ended the influence of the Greek physician Galen, whose works on anatomy had dominated scientific thinking since the second century.

◀ **Figure 1–12** In some animal field studies, scientists observe the animals from a distance. In other studies, researchers make measurements and attach tracking devices to learn more about the animal.

When Experiments Are Not Possible

It is not always possible to do an experiment to test a hypothesis. For example, to learn how animals in the wild interact with others in their group, researchers carry out field studies. It is necessary to observe the animals without disturbing them. Ethical considerations prevent certain experiments, such as determining the effect on people of a chemical suspected of causing cancer. In such cases, medical researchers may choose volunteers who have already been exposed to the chemical. For comparison, they would study a group of people who have not been exposed to the chemical.

When researchers design such alternative investigations, they try to maintain the rigorous thinking associated with a controlled experiment. They often study large groups of subjects so that small differences do not produce misleading results. They try to identify as many relevant variables as possible so that most variables are controlled. For example, in a study of a cancer-causing chemical, they might exclude volunteers who have other serious health problems. By exerting great care in planning these kinds of investigations, scientists can discover reliable patterns that add to scientific knowledge.

CHECKPOINT *Why are controlled experiments sometimes impossible?*

How a Theory Develops

As evidence from numerous investigations builds up, a particular hypothesis may become so well supported that scientists consider it a **theory.** That is what happened with the hypothesis that new organisms come from existing organisms. This idea is now considered one of the major ideas in science. It is called biogenesis, meaning "generating from life."

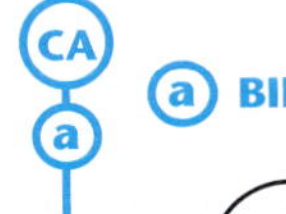

a BIIE 1.f

You may have heard the word *theory* used in everyday conversations as people discuss ideas. Someone might say, "Oh, that's just a theory," to criticize an idea that is not supported by evidence. **In science, the word *theory* applies to a well-tested explanation that unifies a broad range of observations.** A theory enables scientists to make accurate predictions about new situations.

For: Links on experimenting
Visit: www.SciLinks.org
Web Code: cbn-1012

When Experiments Are Not Possible

Build Science Skills

Classifying Have each student write down two topics related to biology that he or she would like to investigate and develop one hypothesis related to each topic. Divide the class into small groups, and ask each group to classify the hypotheses of each of its members according to whether a controlled experiment could be used in testing them. If the answer is no, challenge groups to explain how each hypothesis could be investigated in a way in which scientists could discover reliable patterns that could add to scientific knowledge. L2

How a Theory Develops

Address Misconceptions

Discuss with students how the word *theory* is used in everyday speech. One dictionary definition of the word lists *conjecture* and *speculation* as synonyms. Point out that people often use the word *theory* when they are really referring to a hypothesis—for example, "I have a theory about why the washing machine doesn't work." L1

Build Science Skills

Comparing and Contrasting Ask students to look for examples from the print or electronic media where the term *theory* is used. Have them determine for each example whether the usage represents the scientific meaning of theory or its meaning in everyday speech. L2

TEACHER TO TEACHER

Before introducing Pasteur's test of spontaneous generation, I have students carry out a simulation of his experiment. Students fill three precleaned test tubes with 5–10 mL of nutrient broth. Tube A is left open. Tube B is loosely fitted with an autoclaved rubber stopper, which is always handled with an alcohol-cleaned forceps. Tube C is fitted with a rubber stopper pierced with a bent piece of glass tubing that has also been autoclaved. The three tubes are heated in a boiling-water bath for at least 30–40 minutes and then observed daily for about one week. Students look for signs of turbidity. Tube A will show growth within a day or two. Tubes B and C will stay sterile.

—*Gregory W. McCurdy*
Biology Teacher
Salem High School
Salem, IN

Answers to . . .

CHECKPOINT *He used a flask with a long curved neck to allow air, but not microorganisms, to enter the flask.*

CHECKPOINT *Answers may include ethical reasons. However, accept all logical responses.*

Figure 1–11 *The curved neck prevented microorganisms from making their way into the flask. Once the neck of the flask was broken, microorganisms could get to the broth, where the microorganisms multiplied.*

1–2 (continued)

3 ASSESS

Evaluate Understanding

Have students focus on Pasteur's experiment. Then, call on students at random to state the question Pasteur asked, explain what his hypothesis was, describe his controlled experiment, analyze the results of that experiment, and explain what conclusion he drew.

Reteach

Review Redi's experiment by having students revisit Figure 1–8. Then, have students write a description of the experiment as if they were Redi writing to a colleague. Emphasize that they should ask a question, write a hypothesis, explain how a controlled experiment was set up, analyze the results, and draw a conclusion.

Writing in Science

Students' answers will vary. A good response will describe the hypothesis of spontaneous generation as the idea that life could arise from nonliving matter. Students should explain that this hypothesis seemed valid in light of people's everyday observations—that some living things could just suddenly appear. Any alternative scientific exploration is acceptable. For example, eggs were laid in rotting meat, resulting in maggots.

If your class subscribes to the iText, use it to review the Key Concepts in Section 1–2.

Figure 1–13 **A theory is a well-tested explanation that unifies a broad range of observations.** The theories of plate tectonics and evolution help explain why marsupials such as the koala (top) and kangaroo (below) can be found only in Australia and some nearby islands.

Sometimes, more than one theory is needed to explain a particular circumstance. For example, why are the marsupial mammals in **Figure 1–13** found only in Australia and some nearby islands? An answer lies with the theories of plate tectonics and evolution. Millions of years ago, when marsupials were evolving, Australia, Antarctica, and South America were joined as a single landmass. That landmass began to break apart, and Australia became a separate continent. Its marsupials were thus separated from other kinds of mammals, and they evolved as a unique group.

A useful theory may become the dominant view among the majority of scientists, but no theory is considered absolute truth. Scientists analyze and critique the strengths and weaknesses of theories. As new evidence is uncovered, a theory may be revised or replaced by a more useful explanation. Sometimes, scientists resist a new way of looking at nature, but over time new evidence determines which ideas survive and which are replaced. Thus, science is characterized by both continuity and change.

 BIIE 1.f

1–2 Section Assessment

1. **Key Concept** Why is Redi's experiment on spontaneous generation considered a controlled experiment?
2. **Key Concept** How does a scientific theory compare with a scientific hypothesis?
3. How do scientists today usually communicate their results and conclusions?
4. How did the design of Pasteur's flask help him successfully refute the hypothesis of spontaneous generation?
5. **Critical Thinking** **Making Judgments** Evaluate the impact of Pasteur's research on both scientific thought and society. What was the effect of Pasteur's investigations on scientists' ideas and people's lives?

Writing in Science

Critique a Hypothesis

Write a paragraph in which you analyze the spontaneous generation hypothesis. *Hint:* In preparation, ask yourself questions such as these: What observations did the hypothesis account for? Why did it seem logical at that time? What evidence was overlooked or ignored?

1–2 Section Assessment

1. Redi controlled all variables but one—whether or not there was gauze over each jar.
2. A hypothesis is a proposed scientific explanation for a set of observations, whereas a theory is a well-tested explanation that unifies a broad range of observations.
3. They often publish a report of their work in a scientific journal.
4. The curved neck of Pasteur's flask prevented microorganisms from the air from getting into the broth, keeping the broth free of microorganisms. He showed that all living things come from other living things.
5. Pasteur's work represented a major shift in the way scientists viewed living things. He showed that infectious diseases were the result of microorganisms entering bodies, and therefore this discovery set the stage for medical advances that have protected people from diseases.

1–3 Studying Life

Guide for Reading

Key Concepts
- What are some characteristics of living things?
- How can life be studied at different levels?

Vocabulary
biology
cell
homeostasis
sexual reproduction
asexual reproduction
metabolism
stimulus

Reading Strategy: Summarizing As you read, make a list of the properties of living things. Write one sentence describing each property.

Deep in the skull of a British teenager, an invisible invader eats away at brain tissue until it resembles a sponge. In a Costa Rican rain forest, a chameleon crawls past a bright red tree frog whose blue legs look like a pair of blue jeans, while a toucan uses its rainbow-colored bill to slice into a wild avocado. These scenes all involve biology—the study of life. (The Greek word *bios* means "life," and *-logy* means "study of.") **Biology** is the science that employs the scientific method to study living things.

The scientific study of life has never been more exciting than it is today. Why? Think about headline news stories you may have heard about over the last couple of years—and even over the last couple of days. Hantavirus crops up in Southwestern states. Dengue fever threatens the Gulf Coast. Mice, sheep, and even dogs have been cloned. Genetically-engineered crop plants are designed to resist insect pests. The stories behind these and many other headlines come from the study of living things.

Characteristics of Living Things

Are the firefly and the fire in **Figure 1–14** alive? They are both giving off energy. Describing what makes something alive is not easy. No single characteristic is enough to describe a living thing. Also, some nonliving things share one or more traits with living things. Mechanical toys, automobiles, and clouds move around, for example, whereas mushrooms and trees live their lives in one spot. Other things, such as viruses, exist at the border between organisms and nonliving things.

Despite these difficulties, it is possible to describe what most living things have in common. **Living things share the following characteristics:**

- **Living things are made up of units called cells.**
- **Living things reproduce.**
- **Living things are based on a universal genetic code.**
- **Living things grow and develop.**
- **Living things obtain and use materials and energy.**
- **Living things respond to their environment.**
- **Living things maintain a stable internal environment.**
- **Taken as a group, living things change over time.**

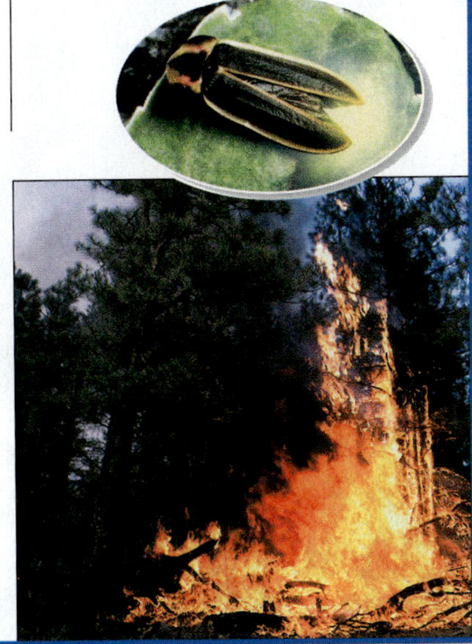

Figure 1–14 A Colorado firefly beetle (top) has all of the characteristics of living things. Even though fire (bottom) uses materials and can grow as living things do, fire is not alive because it does not have other characteristics of living things.

Section 1–3

1 FOCUS

Objectives

1.3.1 ***Describe*** some characteristics of living things.
1.3.2 ***Explain*** how life can be studied at different levels.

Guide for Reading

Vocabulary Preview

Pronounce each of the Vocabulary words for the class, and have students repeat the pronunciation in unison. Note any words that English language learners have trouble pronouncing, and work with them to correct their problems.

Reading Strategy

Students should write one sentence describing each of the eight characteristics listed on page 15. You might have students rewrite the items in the list and revise their sentences as they read the section.

2 INSTRUCT

Characteristics of Living Things

Build Science Skills

Comparing and Contrasting Divide the class into small groups, and allow each group to examine two objects: a watch or clock with a working second hand and an active, living animal such as a fish or an insect. Ask groups to compare the two, noting similarities and differences. Have group members collaborate on writing a paragraph explaining what makes one object a living thing and the other object not. 

SECTION RESOURCES

Print:
- ***Teaching Resources,*** Lesson Plan 1–3, Adapted Section Summary 1–3, Adapted Worksheets 1–3, Section Summary 1–3, Worksheets 1–3, Section Review 1–3
- ***Reading and Study Workbook A,*** Section 1–3
- ***Adapted Reading and Study Workbook B,*** Section 1–3

Technology:
- ***iText,*** Section 1–3
- ***Transparencies Plus,*** Section 1–3

1–3 (continued)

Build Science Skills

Comparing and Contrasting Ask students to compare the bear and the salamander shown in Figure 1–15. Ask students: **What characteristics of life do both of these organisms exhibit?** *(Both exhibit all the eight characteristics of life. Students should note that they are made of cells and that they both reproduce. Allow students to speculate about how each animal exhibits the other characteristics.)* **How are these two living things similar, and how are they different?** *(They are similar in that they are both animals. They are different in size, shape, structure, and habitat, among many other ways.)* L2

FIGURE 1–15 THE CHARACTERISTICS OF LIVING THINGS

All living things share certain characteristics as is evident in this redwood forest.

Living things are based on a universal genetic code. All organisms store the complex information they need to live, grow, and reproduce in a genetic code written in a molecule called DNA.

Living things are made up of cells. A **cell** is the smallest unit of an organism that can be considered alive.

Living things maintain a stable internal environment. Although conditions outside an organism may change dramatically, most organisms need to keep conditions inside their bodies as constant as possible. This process is called **homeostasis.**

Taken as a group, living things evolve. The basic traits individual organisms inherit from their parents usually do not change. Over many generations, however, given groups of organisms typically evolve, or change over time.

UNIVERSAL ACCESS

Less Proficient Readers
Make sure students grasp the difference between sexual and asexual reproduction, because this distinction will be important in chapters to come. Point out that the prefix *a-* simply means "not," and thus *asexual reproduction* literally means "not sexual reproduction." To help students compare and contrast the two, have them make a Venn diagram that notes how the two processes are alike and different. L1

English Language Learners
Help students create a personal science glossary that can be added to as they learn new terms in reading each chapter of this text. Encourage these students to dedicate a small notebook for this purpose or to devise another way to keep an organized glossary. Students can keep an alphabetized list, or they might simply make a list for each chapter. For each term, students should write a definition and note its pronunciation. L1 L2

Living things grow and develop. Every organism has a particular pattern of growth and development. During development, a single fertilized egg divides again and again. As these cells divide, they undergo differentiation, which means that the cells begin to look different from one another and to perform different functions.

Living things respond to their environment. Organisms detect and respond to **stimuli** from their environment. A stimulus is a signal to which an organism responds.

Living things reproduce. All organisms reproduce, which means that they produce new organisms. Most plants and animals, including this black bear, engage in sexual reproduction. In **sexual reproduction,** cells from two different parents unite to form the first cell of the new organism. Other organisms reproduce using **asexual reproduction,** in which a single parent produces offspring that are identical to itself.

Living things obtain and use material and energy. All organisms, including this Pacific salamander, must take in materials and energy to grow, develop, and reproduce. The combination of chemical reactions through which an organism builds up or breaks down materials is called **metabolism.**

Build Science Skills

Comparing and Contrasting Emphasize to students the difference between growth in living and growth in nonliving things. A good comparison to make is the growth of a child compared with that of a garbage heap. Point out that as a child eats food—pasta, fruits, vegetables, meat—he or she grows. In contrast, if you were to throw the same foods into a pile, the garbage heap would also grow. Ask: **Based on the example given, how would you compare the growth of living and nonliving things?** *(Answers may include the concepts of assimilation and organization, development of specific structures, and/or organized growth rather than a "pile.")* **Do organisms always grow and develop at the same rate?** *(Most students will know that organisms don't.)* **When do organisms stop growing and developing?** *(The process goes on at different rates but does not completely stop until death.)*

Use Visuals

Figure 1–15 Ask students: **How does the salamander obtain the energy it needs to live?** *(It eats other organisms for the energy stored in their bodies.)* **Where do the giant redwoods and other plants obtain the energy they need to live?** *(From the sun through the process of photosynthesis)* Point out that all the living things on Earth ultimately obtain the energy they need from the energy of sunlight, as students will learn in greater detail in subsequent chapters.

TEACHER TO TEACHER

To get students to think about the characteristics of life, I give them the following scenario:

You are a member of a local research laboratory. One afternoon, you receive a shoebox marked "Handle with care." In it, you find three gelatinous, orange-colored masses of material. Each mass is approximately 5 cm in diameter. You also find a message from a local resident: "I found these things along the roadside at the bridge near a creek. Can you tell me if they are alive and what I should do with them? They started showing up right after the spring rains this year and seem to be growing fast."

Have students answer the following questions: (1) As you observe the masses, what evidence would make you think they are living things? (2) List the questions that you would ask as you begin your investigation.

—Debbie Richards
Biology Teacher
Bryan High School
Bryan, TX

1–3 (continued)

Quick Lab

 7IIE 7.c

Objective Students will be able to infer some characteristics of living things. L2

Skill Focus **Formulating Hypotheses, Evaluating, Inferring**

Materials hand lens, dormant brine shrimp eggs, water, hatched brine shrimp eggs, bowls covered with fabric

Time 15 minutes

Advance Prep Obtain dormant brine shrimp eggs—also called "sea monkeys"—from a biological supply house. A day, or at least several hours, before the activity begins, put some of the dormant eggs in water so that students can observe live hatchlings in step 3.

Safety Make sure students wash their hands with soap and warm water after handling the dormant eggs or live shrimp.

Strategy Have the hatchlings in bowls covered with fabric and stationed around the classroom. After students have written their predictions, uncover the bowls and invite students to observe.

Expected Outcomes Students will recognize that the line between living and nonliving is not as clear as they might have thought.

Analyze and Conclude

1. Answers will depend on students' predictions. Most students will not have predicted that the objects they observed in step 1 would become live shrimp or anything else alive.
2. Students should recognize that the objects they observed in step 3 were alive and infer that the objects they observed in step 1 were also alive.
3. Accept any reasonable response, provided that the arguments are logical and based on observation.

Quick Lab

 7IIE 7.c

What are the characteristics of living things?

Materials hand lens, unknown objects (dry), same objects soaked in water

Procedure 

1. Examine the dry unknown object your teacher provides. Record your observations.
2. **Predicting** In step 3, you will observe the same kind of object after it has been soaked in water. Write a prediction describing what you expect to see.
3. Examine one of the objects that has been soaking in water for a period of time. Record your observations. Wash your hands when you have finished.

Analyze and Conclude

1. **Evaluating** Was the prediction you made in step 2 correct? Explain your answer.
2. **Inferring** Were the objects you observed in step 1 living or nonliving? Were the objects you observed in step 3 living or nonliving? Use the observations you made as supporting evidence for your answers.
3. **Formulating Hypotheses** Suggest one or more ways to explain the differences between the dry and wet objects.

Big Ideas in Biology

The units of this book seem to cover different subjects. But we'll let you in on a secret: That's not how biology works. All biological sciences are tied together by themes and methods of study that cut across disciplines. Some of these "big ideas" may sound familiar because they overlap with the characteristics of life or the nature of science. You will see that these big ideas themselves overlap and interlock with one another. All of them crop up again and again in the chapters that follow.

Science as a Way of Knowing Science is not a list of "facts," but "a way of knowing." The job of science is to use observations, questions, and experiments to explain the natural world in terms of natural forces and events. Successful scientific research reveals rules and patterns that can explain and predict at least some events in nature. Science therefore enables us to take actions that affect events in the world around us. Making certain that scientific knowledge is used for the benefit of society requires an understanding of the nature of science—its strengths, its limitations, and its interactions with our culture.

Interdependence in Nature All forms of life on Earth are connected together into a biosphere, which literally means "living planet." Within the biosphere, organisms are linked to one another and to the land, water, and air around them. The relationships between organisms and their environment depend on two processes—the flow of energy and the cycling of matter. Human life and the economies of human societies also require matter and energy, so human life depends directly on the economy of nature.

▼ **Figure 1–16** Over time, as life has evolved into many different forms, organisms have entered into a variety of relationships. Interactions between predators and prey (including those between insect-eating plants and insects) and between hosts and parasites often play important roles in regulating the sizes of both plant and animal populations.

Matter and Energy Life's most basic requirements are matter that serves as nutrients to build body structures and energy to fuel the processes of life. Some organisms, such as plants, obtain energy from sunlight and take up the nutrients they need from air, water, and soil. Other organisms, including most animals, must eat plants or other animals to obtain both nutrients and energy. These requirements are the basis of the interdependence of all living things in the biosphere.

Cellular Basis of Life Organisms are composed of one or more cells, which are the smallest units that can be considered fully alive. Cells can grow, respond to their surroundings, and reproduce. Despite their small size, cells are complex and highly organized.

Many living things consist of only a single cell and are called unicellular organisms. The organisms you are most familiar with—for example, animals and plants—are multicellular. The cells in multicellular organisms are often remarkably diverse, existing in a variety of sizes and shapes. In some multicellular organisms, each type of cell is specialized to perform a different function. The human body, for example, contains at least 85 different cell types.

Information and Heredity Life's processes are directed by information carried in a genetic code that is common, with minor variations, to every organism on Earth. That information, carried in DNA, is copied and passed from parent to offspring. The information coded in DNA forms an unbroken chain that stretches back roughly three and a half billion years. Yet, the DNA inside your cells right now can influence your risk of getting cancer, the amount of cholesterol in your blood, and the color of your children's hair.

Unity and Diversity of Life The remarkable thing about the living world is that all living things are fundamentally alike at the molecular level, even though life takes an almost unbelievable variety of forms. All organisms are composed of a common set of carbon-based molecules, all use proteins to build their structures and carry out their functions, and all store information in a common genetic code. One great contribution of evolutionary theory is that it explains both this unity of life and its diversity.

Evolution In biology, evolution, or changes in living things through time, explains the inherited similarities as well as the diversity of life. Evolution is the unifying theme of biology. Evolutionary theory tells us that all forms of life on Earth are related because we all trace our ancestry back to a common origin more than 3.5 billion years ago. Evidence of this shared history is found in all aspects of living and fossil organisms, from physical features to structures of proteins to sequences of biological information found in DNA and RNA.

▲ **Figure 1–17** Certain types of sulphur-eating bacteria, which last shared common ancestors with humans more than 3.5 billion years ago, share surprising amounts of DNA with us. These unicellular organisms are poisoned by the oxygen we breathe, yet live in water that would boil us alive. They can literally "eat" sulphur but contain stretches of DNA that look remarkably like certain genes in our cells.

Big Ideas in Biology

Build Science Skills

Applying Concepts Explain to students that the "big ideas" in biology are themes, not facts, theories, or hypotheses. Although the big ideas are similar to the characteristics of life, they are more general, unifying concepts found in all sciences—biology, chemistry, earth science, and physics. The big ideas are the major ideas that link conceptual organization of the various scientific disciplines. The big ideas in this program include the following: science as a way of knowing; interdependence in nature; matter and energy; cellular basis of life; information and heredity; unity and diversity of life; evolution; structure and function; homeostasis; and science, technology and society.

HISTORY OF SCIENCE

A constant "internal milieu"

In 1851, French physiologist Claude Bernard (1813–1878) discovered that nerves in an animal's body control the dilation and constriction of blood vessels. He observed that on hot days the blood vessels of the skin become dilated, whereas on cold days those same blood vessels become constricted. Bernard concluded that the function of these changes has to do with regulating the body's internal temperature. On hot days, dilated, blood-filled vessels radiate heat away from the body. On cold days, constricted, blood-depleted vessels conserve body heat. Thus, even when the external environment changes, an animal has a way of maintaining a constant "internal milieu." His concept of the maintenance of an internal balance within an animal is incorporated in the modern concept of homeostasis, which literally means "same condition."

1–3 (continued)

Branches of Biology

Build Science Skills

Asking Questions To introduce the topic of branches of biology to students, play a game of 20 questions with the class. Think of a familiar plant or animal, such as a dandelion, an ant, or a sparrow. Tell students that you are thinking of a certain organism and that they are allowed 20 yes-or-no questions to determine what this organism is. As the game progresses, you might suggest questions to the class; do not let them stray too far from the correct answer. Tell students that whether they realized it or not, they were conducting a scientific investigation. They were presented with a problem, and they needed to ask the right questions to reach a solution. Emphasize that in science, answers are often available—it's figuring out the right questions that is difficult. Explain that scientists from different branches of biology ask different questions-—approaching living things at different levels of organization. L1 L2

▲ **Figure 1–18** Despite the cold temperatures of this robin's environment, its body temperature remains fairly constant, partly because its feathers provide a layer of insulation and partly because of the body heat it produces.

Structure and Function The structures of wings enable birds and insects to fly. The structures of legs enable horses to gallop and kangaroos to hop. When organisms need to do anything—from capturing food to digesting it and from reproducing to breathing—they use some kind of structure that has evolved in ways that make a particular function possible. Each major group of organisms has evolved its own particular body part, or "tool kit," that evolves into different forms as various species adapt to the challenges of life in a wide range of environments.

Homeostasis All living organisms expend energy to keep conditions inside their cells within certain limits. An organism's ability to maintain a tolerable internal environment in the face of changing external conditions is vital to its survival. Any breakdown of that stability may have serious or even fatal consequences. The robin shown in **Figure 1–18** is maintaining homeostasis by puffing up its feathers to stay warm.

Science, Technology, and Society Science seeks to provide useful information. But many discoveries raise ethical questions. Just because we can use scientific information in a particular way, should we do so? How should we use genetic engineering? Should cloning of humans be banned? Should cloning of any animals and plants be prohibited? How can we use our growing understanding of how human activity affects our world? Should we take action to stop global warming? What's the best way to protect our food and water supplies? In our democracy, these questions can only be answered by a public that truly understands what science is and how it works.

Branches of Biology

Living things come in an astonishing variety of shapes, sizes, and habits. Living systems also range in size from groups of molecules that make up structures inside cells to the collections of organisms that make up the biosphere. No single biologist could study all this diversity, so biology is divided into different fields. Some fields are based on the types of organisms being studied. Zoologists study animals. Botanists study plants. Other fields study life from a particular perspective. For example, paleontologists study ancient life.

Some fields focus on the study of living systems at different levels of organization, as shown in **Figure 1–19.** **Some of the levels at which life can be studied include molecules, cells, organisms, populations of a single kind of organism, communities of different organisms in an area, and the biosphere. At all these levels, smaller living systems are found within larger systems.** Molecular biologists and cell biologists study some of the smallest living systems. Population biologists and ecologists study some of the largest systems in nature. Studies at all these levels make important contributions to the quality of human life.

FACTS AND FIGURES

Branches of biology

The branches of biology are too numerous to list. Zoologists, botanists, paleontologists, and ethologists are just a few of the great variety of biologists. Biochemists study the chemistry of living things. Geneticists study heredity and variation among organisms. Cytologists, or cell biologists, study the structure and function of cells. Ecologists study the interaction of organisms in ecosystems. Microbiologists study the structure and function of microorganisms. The list goes on, and those mentioned are just the biologists who pursue knowledge in what is sometimes called theoretical science. There are also many biologists who work in applied or practical science, including physicians, medical researchers, wildlife managers, foresters, and agricultural researchers, to name just a few.

Levels of Organization		
Biosphere	The part of Earth that contains all ecosystems	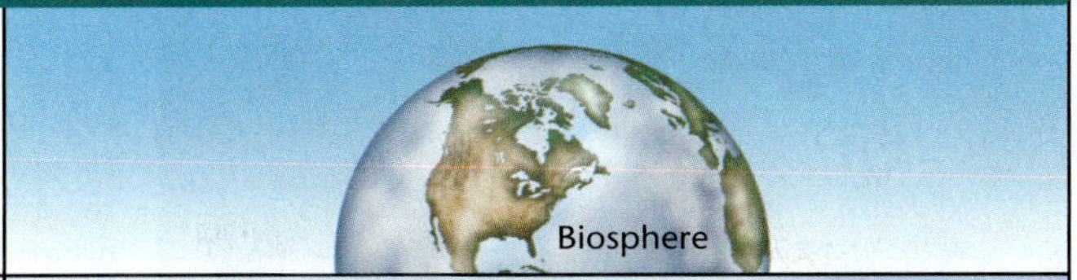 Biosphere
Ecosystem	Community and its nonliving surroundings	 Hawk, snake, bison, prairie dog, grass, stream, rocks, air
Community	Populations that live together in a defined area	 Hawk, snake, bison, prairie dog, grass
Population	Group of organisms of one type that live in the same area	 Bison herd
Organism	Individual living thing	 Bison
Groups of Cells	Tissues, organs, and organ systems	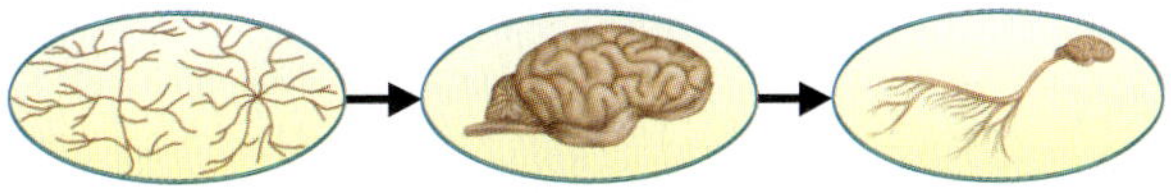 Nervous tissue → Brain → Nervous system
Cells	Smallest functional unit of life	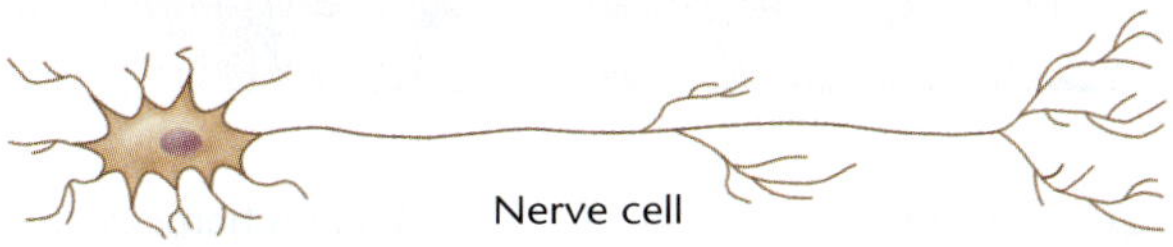 Nerve cell
Molecules	Groups of atoms; smallest unit of most chemical compounds	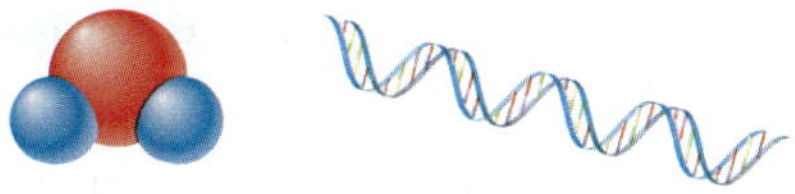 Water, DNA

Figure 1–19 **Living things may be studied on many different levels.** The largest and most complex level is the biosphere. The smallest level is the molecules that make up living things.

Use Visuals

Figure 1–19 Make sure students understand the hierarchy implied in the figure: molecular, cellular, multicellular, organism, population, community, ecosystem, and biosphere. Have students use a dictionary to clarify the meaning of these terms. Then, ask students to make a graphic organizer that could represent relationships among the terms, such as a series of larger and larger circles. L1 L2

Build Science Skills

Asking Questions Display the same pictures of natural environments that students examined for the Assess Prior Knowledge activity on page 2. Ask students again to choose one of the pictures to examine closely and to compile a list of 20 questions a biologist might ask about the organisms in the picture. Explain that these questions could concern anything from the molecular level to the biosphere level. Have students compare the 20 questions they wrote after having read these sections with the 20 questions they wrote previously. L2

1–3 (continued)

Biology in Everyday Life

Build Science Skills

Applying Concepts Ask students to choose a commercial product that they use every day, such as a certain soap, type of makeup, kind of chewing gum, or brand of deodorant. Ask them to explain in a paragraph how they could use what they have learned so far in this chapter to find out how the product affects their bodies and whether it could be harmful in some way. L2

3 ASSESS

Evaluate Understanding

Have students explain in writing how a living thing, such as the Venus' flytrap shown in Figure 1–16, exhibits all of the characteristics of living things.

Reteach

Point out a living thing and a nonliving thing in the classroom, such as a computer and a fish in an aquarium. Have students compare and contrast the two using the eight characteristics of living things.

Focus on the BIG Idea

Students could observe whether the object ingests or excretes materials, whether it increases in size over time, and whether it responds to stimuli from the environment.

If your class subscribes to the iText, use it to review the Key Concepts in Section 1–3.

Answer to . . .

Figure 1–20 *A typical response might suggest that researchers will find cures for many diseases.*

▲ **Figure 1–20** Progress in biology has meant huge improvements in health not just for you and your family but, in some societies, for pets as well. **Predicting** *How do you expect advances in biology to change healthcare during your lifetime?*

Biology in Everyday Life

As you begin studying biology, you may be thinking of it as just another course, with a textbook to read plus labs, homework, and tests. It's also a *science* course, so you may worry that it will be too difficult. But you will see that more than any other area of study, biology touches your life every day. In fact, it's hard to think of anything you do that isn't affected by it. It helps you understand and appreciate every other form of life, from pets such as the dog in **Figure 1–20** to dinosaurs no longer present on Earth. It provides information about the food you need and the methods for sustaining the world's food supplies. It describes the conditions of good health and the behaviors and diseases that can harm you. It is used to diagnose and treat medical problems. It identifies environmental factors that might threaten you, such as disposal of wastes from human activities. More than any other science, biology helps you understand what affects the quality of your life.

Biologists do not make the decisions about most matters affecting human society or the natural world; citizens and governments do. In just a few years, you will be able to exercise the rights of a voting citizen, influencing public policy by the ballots you cast and the messages you send public officials. With others, you will make decisions based on many factors, including customs, values, ethical standards, and scientific knowledge. Biology can provide decision makers with useful information and analytical skills. It can help them envision the possible effects of their decisions. Biology can help people understand that humans are capable of predicting and trying to control their future and that of the planet.

1–3 Section Assessment

1. **Key Concept** Describe five characteristics of living things.
2. **Key Concept** What topics might biologists study at the community level of organization?
3. Compare sexual reproduction and asexual reproduction.
4. What biological process includes chemical reactions that break down materials?
5. What is homeostasis? Give an example of how it is maintained.
6. **Critical Thinking Applying Concepts** Suppose you feel hungry, so you reach for a peach you see in a fruit bowl. Explain how both external and internal stimuli are involved in your action.

Focus on the BIG Idea

Science as a Way of Knowing List some observations that could be made to determine whether an object that is not moving is living or nonliving. Refer to Section 1–1 to help yourself recall what an observation is.

1–3 Section Assessment

1. Students should describe any five of the eight characteristics listed on page 15.
2. Students should describe topics about populations that live in an area, such as interactions among different populations and changes in size or habits.
3. In sexual reproduction, cells from two different parents unite to produce the first cell of a new organism. In asexual reproduction, the new organism has a single parent.
4. Metabolism
5. Homeostasis is the process by which organisms keep internal conditions fairly constant. Examples will vary, though most students will describe an internal feedback mechanism, such as temperature regulation.
6. External stimuli might include the sight and smell of the peach. Internal stimuli might include feeling hungry or the thought that this food would be good to eat.

BIIE 1.m

When Scientists Have a Conflict of Interest

Scientists are expected to be completely honest about their investigations. Doctors are expected to place the welfare of their patients first. Yet, conflicts of interest can often threaten the credibility of a researcher. A conflict of interest exists when a person's work can be influenced by personal factors such as financial gain, fame, future work, or favoritism. For example, suppose scientists have received funds to test a potential anti-cancer drug. If experiments show that the drug is not very effective, the researchers may be tempted to conceal the results in order to avoid losing their funding.

The Viewpoints

Regulation Is Necessary

Some scientists argue that, because the public must be able to trust the work of science, some rules are essential for preserving scientific integrity. Every profession should regulate its members, and every science publication should have strict rules about avoiding conflicts of interest. In any published work, announcements of potential conflicts should be required. In some cases, scientists should avoid or be forbidden to do work that involves personal gain in addition to the usual payment for doing the work. Some form of government regulation may be needed.

Regulation Is Unnecessary

Other scientists insist that conflict-of-interest regulations are unnecessary for the majority of researchers, who are honest and objective about their work. It is unfair to assume that a researcher's discoveries would be different because of the nature of the financial support for the research. In fact, without the opportunity for scientists to get additional funding for successful work, many new drugs or new techniques would never have been developed. So it is important that scientists be allowed to investigate any topic, even those in which they have the opportunity for personal gain.

Research and Decide

1. **Analyzing the Viewpoints** To make an informed decision, learn more about this issue by consulting library or Internet sources. Then answer the following question: How might the views about a possible conflict of interest differ among a group of scientists, the company employing a scientist, and people seeking information from a scientist?
2. **Forming Your Opinion** How should this problem of possible conflicts of interest be decided? Include information or reasoning that answers people with the opposite view.
3. **Role-Playing** Suppose doctors who own a company developing a new medicine want their patients to help test the medicine. Let one person represent a doctor, a second person a patient, and a third person a medical reporter asking: Should the patients take part in the tests?

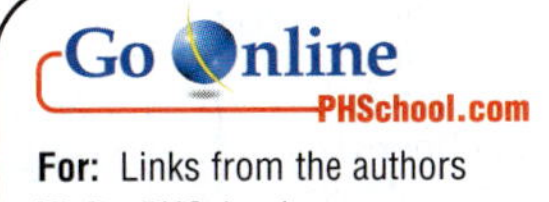

For: Links from the authors
Visit: PHSchool.com
Web Code: cbe-1013

BACKGROUND

Reasons to be concerned
There are no sciencewide rules about reporting conflicts of interest, nor is there government regulation requiring biologists to do so. Various publications and professional organizations have their own code of ethics. In recent years, there has been a growing concern about how such conflicts might be affecting scientific research, especially the great amount of research done in universities. By 1997, U.S. companies were spending $1.7 billion a year on university-based science and engineering research. By the late 1990s, more than 90 percent of companies connected to the life sciences had some kind of relationship with university scientists. Yet, in a survey of science journals, 142 of 210 did not publish a single disclosure of conflict of interest in 1997. Some observers also worry about scientists' skewing their work toward government interests, because federal funding of research is common.

BIIE 1.m

After students respond to question 3 in Research and Decide, have student volunteers role-play the situation for the class. Follow that by a class discussion of the issue. Then, ask each student to write a statement about his or her own assessment of such a conflict of interest.

Research and Decide

1. Students might find a variety of viewpoints about this issue in books, periodicals, or Internet sites about current affairs. Answers to the question will vary. A typical response might suggest that the group of scientists might be dedicated to pursuing scientific truth but also be intent on satisfying those who have funded the research. Additionally, the company employing the scientists might want both the truth and results that will help its profit. People seeking information from a scientist may simply want unbiased data, though they might not want results that somehow upset their view of the world.

2. A typical response might suggest that journals and professional organizations should adopt strict guidelines about conflicts of interest and that there should even be some government regulation. Students should back their positions with logical arguments.

3. Have students write a dialogue that includes viewpoints from the doctor and the patient, with the reporter questioning each. The reporter might press the doctor on whether owning the company is a conflict of interest that would invalidate the test. The reporter might ask the patient whether the doctor can be trusted and whether the test will be conducted in a safe way.

Students can research conflicts of interest on the site developed by authors Ken Miller and Joe Levine.

Section 1–4

BIIE 1.a

1 FOCUS

Objectives

1.4.1 ***Describe*** the measurement system most scientists use.

1.4.2 ***Explain*** how light microscopes and electron microscopes are similar and different.

1.4.3 ***Describe*** two common laboratory techniques.

1.4.4 ***Explain*** why it is important to work safely in biology.

Guide for Reading

Vocabulary Preview

Have students write a preliminary definition of each of the Vocabulary terms. As they read the section, they should revise their definitions.

Reading Strategy

Before students read, have them skim the section to identify the main ideas. As they read the section, have them make a list of the supporting details for each main idea.

2 INSTRUCT

Find a worksheet on microscopes for students and additional teacher support from NSTA SciLinks.

A Common Measurement System

Addressing Misconceptions

To reinforce students' ability to make and use metric measurements, prepare a set of flashcards that students can use to learn equivalent units of metric measure. For example:

- 1 kilometer = *(1000)* meters
- 0.45 liter = *(450)* milliliters
- 5000 milligrams = *(5)* grams
- 130 meters = *(0.13)* kilometer
- 2500 milliliters = *(2.5)* liters
- 0.017 grams = *(17)* milligrams

L1

1–4 Tools and Procedures

BIIE 1.a. Select and use appropriate tools and technology (such as computer-linked probes, spreadsheets, and graphing calculators) to perform tests, collect data, analyze relationships, and display data.

Guide for Reading

Key Concepts
- What measurement system do most scientists use?
- How are light microscopes and electron microscopes similar? How are they different?

Vocabulary
metric system
microscope
compound light microscope
electron microscope
cell culture
cell fractionation

Reading Strategy: Using Graphic Organizers As you read, create a table that lists the equipment and techniques discussed in this section. List one example of what biologists can accomplish using each piece of equipment or procedure.

For: Links on microscopes
Visit: www.SciLinks.org
Web Code: cbn-1014

Imagine being one of the first people to see living things through a magnifying glass. How surprised you would have been to discover a whole new realm of life! Could there still be other types of life that remain undiscovered today because the right tools are not available?

Scientists select and use equipment, which sometimes includes technology such as computers, for their investigations. Electronic balances measure the mass of objects with great precision. Microscopes and telescopes make it possible to observe objects that are very small or very far away. With powerful computers, scientists can store and analyze vast collections of data. Biologists have even devised procedures that help them unlock the information stored in the DNA of different organisms.

A Common Measurement System

Because researchers need to replicate one another's experiments and most experiments involve measurements, scientists need a common system of measurement. **Most scientists use the metric system when collecting data and performing experiments.** The **metric system** is a decimal system of measurement whose units are based on certain physical standards and are scaled on multiples of 10. A revised version of the original metric system is called the International System of Units, or SI. The abbreviation SI comes from the French *Le Système International d'Unités.*

Because the metric system is based on multiples of 10, it is easy to use. Notice in **Figure 1–21** how the basic unit of length, the meter, can be multiplied or divided to measure objects and distances much larger or smaller than a meter. The same process can be used when measuring volume and mass. You can learn more about the metric system in Appendix C.

Common Metric Units

Length	Mass
1 meter (m) = 100 centimeters (cm) 1 meter = 1000 millimeters (mm) 1000 meters = 1 kilometer (km)	1 kilogram (kg) = 1000 grams (g) 1 gram = 1000 milligrams (mg) 1000 kilograms = 1 metric ton (t)
Volume	**Temperature**
1 liter (L) = 1000 milliliters (mL) 1 liter = 1000 cubic centimeters (cm^3)	0°C = freezing point of water 100°C = boiling point of water

▶ **Figure 1–21** **Scientists usually use the metric system in their work.** This system is easy to use because it is based on multiples of 10.

SECTION RESOURCES

Print:
- ***Laboratory Manual A,*** Chapter 1 Lab
- ***Laboratory Manual B,*** Chapter 1 Lab
- ***Teaching Resources,*** Lesson Plan 1–4, Adapted Section Summary 1–4, Section Summary 1–4, Worksheets 1–4, Section Review 1–4
- ***Reading and Study Workbook A,*** Section 1–4
- ***Adapted Reading and Study Workbook B,*** Section 1–4
- ***Investigations in Forensics,*** Investigation 1
- ***Lab Worksheets,*** Chapter 1 Exploration

Technology:
- ***iText,*** Section 1–4
- ***Transparencies Plus,*** Section 1–4

Water Released and Absorbed by Tree

Time	Absorbed by Roots (g/h)	Released by Leaves (g/h)
8 AM	1	2
10 AM	1	5
12 PM	4	12
2 PM	6	17
4 PM	9	16
6 PM	14	10
8 PM	10	3

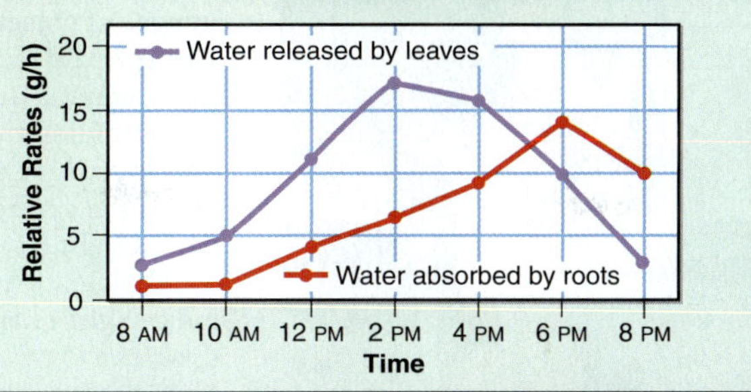

Analyzing Biological Data

When scientists collect data, they are often trying to find out whether certain factors changed or remained the same. Often, the simplest way to do that is to record the data in a table and then make a graph. Although you may be able to detect a pattern of change from a data table like the one in **Figure 1–22,** a graph of the data can make a pattern much easier to recognize and understand.

The amount of data produced by biologists today is so huge that no individual can look at more than a tiny fraction of it. To make sense of the data, biologists often turn to computers. For example, computers help determine the structure of molecules. They also allow biologists to search through a DNA molecule, find significant regions of the molecule, and discover how organisms are affected by those regions. At the opposite end of the scale, computers are essential to gathering data by satellite, analyzing the data, and presenting the results. Analyses of satellite data are used to make predictions about complex phenomena such as global climate changes.

CHECKPOINT *How can a graph help biologists analyze data?*

▲ **Figure 1–22** One way to record data from an experiment is by using a data table. Then, the data may be plotted on a graph to make it easier to interpret. **Using Tables and Graphs** *At what time of day is the rate of water released by leaves equal to the rate of water absorbed by roots?*

Microscopes

When people think of scientific equipment, one of the first tools that comes to mind is the microscope. **Microscopes,** such as the light microscope in **Figure 1–23,** are devices that produce magnified images of structures that are too small to see with the unaided eye. **Light microscopes produce magnified images by focusing visible light rays. Electron microscopes produce magnified images by focusing beams of electrons.** Since the first microscope was invented, microscope manufacturers have had to deal with two problems: What is the instrument's magnification—that is, how much larger can it make an object appear compared to the object's real size? And how sharp an image can the instrument produce?

▲ **Figure 1–23** **Light microscopes produce magnified images by focusing visible light rays.**

Analyzing Biological Data

Use Visuals

Figure 1–22 Direct students' attention to the graph. Then, ask: **On which axis is time recorded?** *(On the horizontal axis, or x-axis)* **On which axis are the relative rates recorded?** *(On the vertical axis, or y-axis)* **What pattern does the graph show at a glance about water given off and taken in by a tree?** *(The water released by leaves peaks at 2 PM; the water absorbed by roots peaks at 6 PM.)* L1 L2

Microscopes

Build Science Skills

Applying Concepts Most students will remember some things about microscopes from previous science courses, but there is likely to be a wide range of proficiencies in the class. This is the time to get out the light microscopes and have a hands-on review of the parts and their functions. Have students work with partners to practice naming parts, describing functions, and demonstrating proper handling and use. 

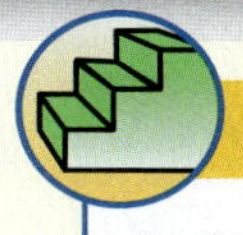

UNIVERSAL ACCESS

Inclusion/Special Needs
Make sure all students can make a graph from data. Before students study Figure 1–22, give them graph paper and the data in the figure's table, and ask them to graph the data. Work with students who have difficulty with this task. L1

English Language Learners
Explain that the term *microscope* is derived from the Greek words *micro-*, meaning "small," and *skop-*, meaning "see." Thus, *microscope* means an instrument for seeing small objects. Then, ask students what *microorganism* means. Students should infer that it means a "small living thing." L1 L2

Advanced Learners
Challenge interested students to find out if a local university science department has an electron microscope. If one is available, encourage students to make an appointment to observe the instrument and learn how it works. L3

Answers to . . .

CHECKPOINT *A graph helps make patterns easier to recognize and understand.*

Figure 1–22 *The rate of water released by leaves is equal to the rate of water absorbed by roots at around 5 PM.*

1–4 (continued)

Build Science Skills

Making Judgments Point out that all microscopes have limits of resolution. Explain that as the magnifying power of a light microscope is increased, more and more detail can be seen, at least up to a certain point. Detail is lost and objects get blurry beyond that point, which is called the limit of resolution. Resolution is the capability to distinguish the individual parts of an object. Ask students: **If you are looking at feathers or insect legs under a microscope, how important is excellent resolution?** *(Not very important, because you are looking at overall structure)* **What if you are looking at slides of plant or animal cells?** *(Resolution is now very important, because detail is important.)* **Name some obvious advantages to looking at living rather than dead specimens under the microscope.** *(Advantages include the ability to observe living color, movement, and reactions to stimuli.)* L2

Build Science Skills

Applying Concepts Give students a list of the following topics, and ask them which kind of microscope, if any, would best serve the topic's investigation, with an explanation of why that kind would serve best:

- **The feeding habits of unicellular protozoa** *(A light microscope, because the organisms are small and would need to be studied alive)*
- **The surface of a red blood cell** *(A scanning electron microscope, because it would be best for looking at surfaces)*
- **The feeding habits of a house cat** *(No microscope is necessary to observe the behavior of an animal as large as a cat.)*
- **The interior structures of a cell** *(A transmission electron microscope, because of the need for high resolution to view the fine structure of cell organelles)* L1 L2

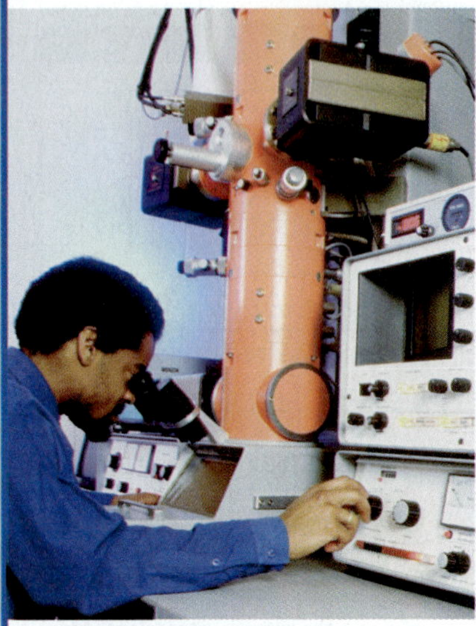

▲ **Figure 1–24** This scientist is using an electron microscope to make observations. **Electron microscopes produce images by focusing beams of electrons.**

Light Microscopes The most commonly used microscope is the light microscope. Light microscopes can produce clear images of objects at a magnification of about 1000 times. **Compound light microscopes** allow light to pass through the specimen and use two lenses to form an image. Light microscopes make it possible to study dead organisms and their parts, and to observe some tiny organisms and cells while they are still alive. You can refer to Appendix D to learn how to use a compound light microscope.

Biologists have developed techniques and procedures to make light microscopes more useful. Chemical stains, also called dyes, can show specific structures in the cell. Fluorescent dyes have been combined with video cameras and computer processing to produce moving three-dimensional images of processes such as cell movement.

Electron Microscopes All microscopes are limited in what they reveal, and light microscopes cannot produce clear images of objects smaller than 0.2 micrometers, or about one-fiftieth the diameter of a typical cell. To study even smaller objects, scientists use electron microscopes. **Electron microscopes,** such as the one shown in **Figure 1–24,** use beams of electrons, rather than light, to produce images. The best electron microscopes can produce images almost 1000 times more detailed than light microscopes can.

Biologists use two main types of electron microscopes. Transmission electron microscopes (TEMs) shine a beam of electrons through a thin specimen. Scanning electron microscopes (SEMs) scan a narrow beam of electrons back and forth across the surface of a specimen. TEMs can reveal a wealth of detail inside the cell. SEMs produce realistic, and often dramatic, three-dimensional images of the surfaces of objects. Because electron microscopes require a vacuum to operate, samples for both TEM and SEM work must be preserved and dehydrated before they are placed inside the microscope. This means that living cells cannot be observed with electron microscopes, only with the light microscope. **Figure 1–25** shows images taken with a light microscope, a transmission electron microscope, and a scanning electron microscope.

▼ **Figure 1–25** Observe the images of pollen grains as seen with a light microscope (left), transmission electron microscope (center), and scanning electron microscope (right). **Interpreting Graphics** ***In which image can you see the most detail on the pollen grain's surface?***

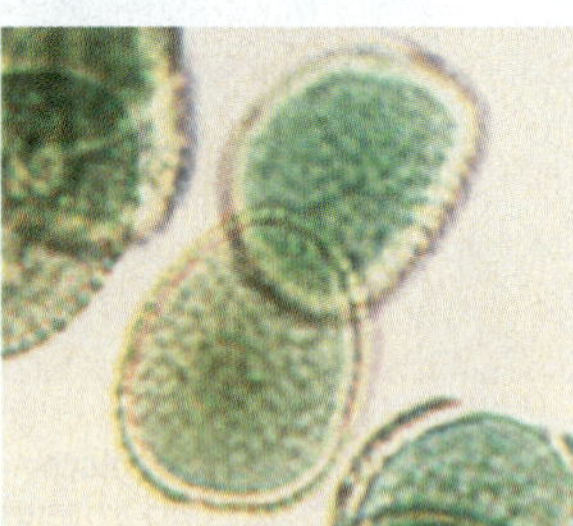

(magnification: about 400×)

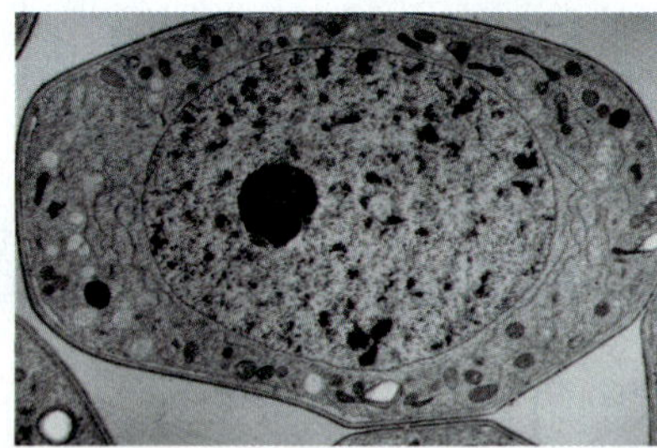

(magnification: about 2200×)

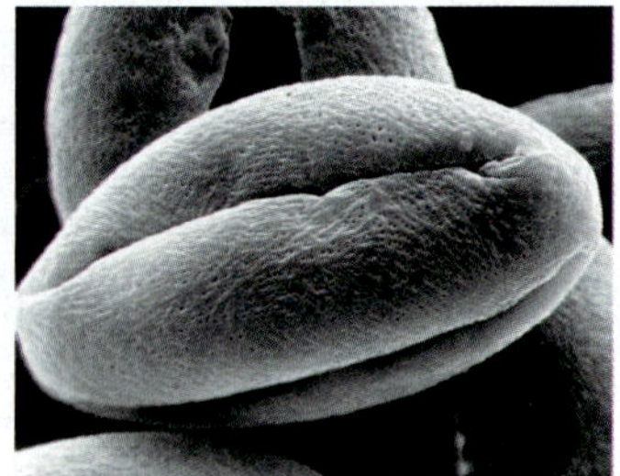

(magnification: about 1000×)

FACTS AND FIGURES

Electron microscopes

In both transmission electron microscopes and scanning electron microscopes, the lenses are made of electromagnets, which gather and focus the beam of electrons. The beam of electrons is produced by heating a filament. For an image to be produced, the path of the electrons must be unobstructed. Therefore, the samples are placed in a vacuum instead of in air. Objects must be extremely thin—less than 0.1 micron—to be examined by a TEM, because the TEM produces an image by passing a beam of electrons through an object. The electrons then either produce an image on a fluorescent screen or produce a permanent image on photographic film. Objects examined by an SEM need not be thin, because the electrons are picked up by detectors after bouncing off the specimen, and the detectors provide the data necessary to form an image on a monitor.

Analyzing Data

6IIE 7.c, 8IIE 9.c

Bacterial Reproduction

Bacteria are microorganisms that can reproduce by dividing into two. The graph shows the results of an experiment on the effect of temperature on bacterial reproduction. At the beginning, three populations of bacteria, all of the same type, were of equal size. Each population was kept at a different temperature for 4 days.

Bacterial Growth and Temperature

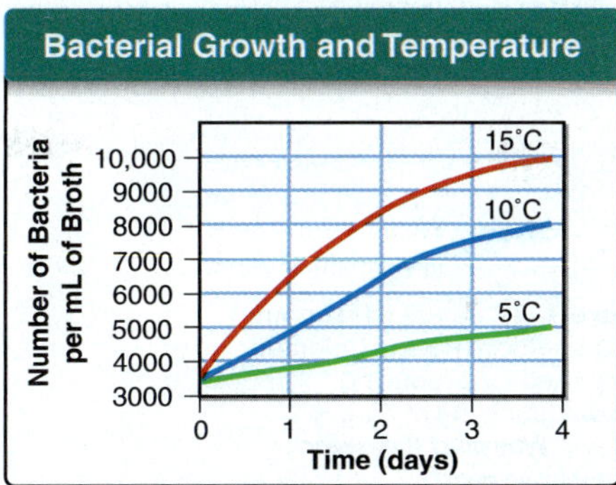

1. **Classifying** What variable did the researcher change during this experiment?
2. **Inferring** What do the shapes of the curves tell you about the changes in population size?
3. **Calculating** For the bacteria kept at 15°C, how did population size change during the experiment?
4. **Drawing Conclusions** What effect did the different temperatures have on the growth of the bacterial populations?
5. **Predicting** Suppose some bacteria used in this experiment were kept at a temperature of 100°C (the temperature of boiling water). Would you expect the population sizes to increase even faster than at 15°C? Explain your reasoning.

Laboratory Techniques

Biologists use a variety of techniques to study cells. Two common laboratory techniques are cell culturing and cell fractionation.

Cell Cultures To obtain enough material to study, biologists like the one in **Figure 1–26** sometimes place a single cell into a dish containing a nutrient solution. The cell is able to reproduce so that a group of cells, called a **cell culture,** develops from the single original cell. Cell cultures can be used to test cell responses under controlled conditions, to study interactions between cells, and to select specific cells for further study.

Cell Fractionation Suppose you want to study just one part of a cell. How could you separate that one part from the rest of the cell? Biologists often use a technique known as **cell fractionation** to separate the different cell parts. First, the cells are broken into pieces in a special blender. Then, the broken cell bits are added to a liquid and placed in a tube. The tube is inserted into a centrifuge, which is an instrument that can spin the tube. Spinning causes the cell parts to separate, with the most dense parts settling near the bottom of the tube. A biologist can then remove the specific part of the cell to be studied by selecting the appropriate layer.

CHECKPOINT *What is a cell culture?*

▼ **Figure 1–26** This researcher is transferring bacteria to a solid that contains nutrients, which will enable the bacteria to reproduce. **Comparing and Contrasting** *How do the results of a cell culture differ from the products of cell fractionation?*

Laboratory Techniques

Analyzing Data

6IIE 7.c, 8IIE 9.c

The experiment is typical of how cell cultures of bacteria and other microorganisms are studied to test responses under controlled conditions. The specific range of temperatures in which bacteria can grow varies among species. Some species, called psychrophiles, can grow at temperatures below 0°C. Other species, called thermophiles, grow at temperatures approaching the boiling point of water and are incapable of growth below 45°C. Most bacteria, called mesophiles, have an optimal growth temperature between 10°C and 50°C. L2

Answers

1. Temperature

2. The population of bacteria at 5°C grew slowly and steadily. At 10°C, the population grew rapidly at first; the rate of growth decreased after about two days. The population at 15°C grew most rapidly at first; the rate of growth slowed steadily after a day, and the population appears to have leveled off at about four days.

3. The population size grew from about 3500/mL of broth at the start to 10,000/mL at the end.

4. The bacterial population grew most at the highest temperature and grew least at the lowest temperature.

5. Students might suggest that population size would increase even faster than at 15°C, because the graph shows that the higher the temperature, the more the bacterial growth. Because 100°C is the boiling point of water, students may say that the bacteria would not survive at 100°C.

BIO INSIGHTS — HISTORY OF SCIENCE

From the kitchen to the lab

The ability to study bacteria in a laboratory is crucial for understanding their structure and function. Robert Koch (1843–1910), a German bacteriologist, was one of the first scientists to perfect a method of doing so. The growth medium he first used was beef broth. The addition of the protein gelatin to the broth solidified the medium, but a problem remained. Many bacteria could digest the gelatin, and the result was the formation of little puddles in the medium, making it difficult to study the bacteria. The answer came in 1881 when the wife of one of Koch's coworkers told Koch about the agar-agar she used in cooking as a solidifying agent. Koch discovered that this substance, produced by the red alga *Gelidium,* could not be digested by bacteria. Agar—the current term for agar-agar—has been used in laboratories as a culture medium ever since.

Answers to . . .

CHECKPOINT *A group of cells that develops from a single cell placed into a dish containing nutrient solution*

Figure 1–25 *In the image from the scanning electron microscope*

Figure 1–26 *A cell culture is a group of cells that develops from a single original cell. Cell fractionation separates cell parts.*

1–4 (continued)

Working Safely in Biology

Demonstration

To acquaint students with the laboratory in which they will be working, point out the location of the water, the nearest fire extinguisher, and the first-aid equipment. Explain the procedures to follow in case of fire, accident, or injury. You may wish to make instructions for display in the lab. Show how to use safety goggles and heat-resistant gloves. Show some of the equipment students will use in the lab, including glassware, microscopes, heating devices, chemicals, knives, and scalpels. For each piece of equipment, ask: **What is the safety symbol associated with this item?** *(Some students may be familiar with common safety symbols.)* Point out and discuss the safety symbols used in their textbook and laboratory manuals. L1 L2

3 ASSESS

Evaluate Understanding

Call on students at random to explain the differences in structure and image obtained from a compound light microscope, a TEM, and an SEM.

Reteach

Have students look at the image on page 2. Ask them to tell how they know, without reading the caption, that the image was made by an SEM and not a light microscope or a TEM.

You & Your Community

Students' products should include any five of the science safety rules detailed in Appendix B. A typical poster might include one rule from five different categories. Most students will organize their posters as suggested in the directions, though some may develop more imaginative designs.

If your class subscribes to the iText, use it to review the Key Concepts in Section 1–4.

Answer to . . .

Figure 1–27 *To protect themselves from exposure to nuclear wastes*

Working Safely in Biology

Scientists working in a laboratory or in the field like those in **Figure 1–27** are trained to use safe procedures when carrying out investigations. Laboratory work may involve flames or heating elements, electricity, chemicals, hot liquids, sharp instruments, and breakable glassware. Laboratory or field work may involve contact with living or dead organisms—not just the plants, animals, and other living things you can see but other organisms you cannot see without a microscope.

Whenever you work in your biology laboratory, it's important for you to follow safe practices as well. Before performing any activity in this course, study the safety rules in Appendix B. Before you start any activity, read all the steps, and make sure that you understand the entire procedure, including any safety precautions that must be followed.

The single most important rule for your safety is simple: Always follow your teacher's instructions and the textbook directions exactly. If you are in doubt about any part of an activity, always ask your teacher for an explanation. And, because you may be in contact with organisms you cannot see, it is essential that you wash your hands thoroughly after every scientific activity. Remember, you are responsible for your own safety and that of your teacher and classmates. If you are handling live animals, you are responsible for their safety as well.

▼ **Figure 1–27** These workers are cleaning up Rocky Flats, a Colorado site once used for producing nuclear weapons. **Applying Concepts** *Why must they wear heavy protective gear?*

1–4 Section Assessment

1. **Key Concept** Why do scientists use a common system of measurement?
2. **Key Concept** What is the difference in the way light microscopes and electron microscopes produce images?
3. What types of objects can be studied with a light microscope? What types can be studied with an electron microscope?
4. Describe the technique and purpose of cell fractionation.
5. **Critical Thinking Applying Concepts** It has been said that many great discoveries lie in wait for the tools needed to make them. What does this statement mean to you? If possible, include an example in your answer.

You & Your Community

Safety Poster

After reading the safety guidelines in Appendix B, prepare a poster on lab safety to display in your school in which you describe at least five safety rules. You might organize your poster or brochure in two columns labeled *Dangerous Way* and *Safe Way*, and contrast unsafe behaviors with their safe alternatives.

1–4 Section Assessment

1. They need to replicate one another's experiments, which often involve measurements.
2. Light microscopes produce images by focusing visible light rays, whereas electron microscopes produce images by focusing beams of electrons.
3. Light microscopes and electron microscopes can be used to study dead and preserved specimens. Only light microscopes can be used to study living organisms or cells.
4. In cell fractionation, cells are broken into pieces, added to a liquid, and placed in a tube. The tube is spun in a centrifuge, where the cell parts are separated into layers according to density. This technique is done to study specific parts of a cell.
5. Sample answer: More advanced tools might reveal parts of living things never observed before. Students may list discoveries that required the development of microscopes.

Using a Compound Microscope

In this investigation, you will use a compound microscope to determine the positions and sizes of objects. Before you begin, read the safety rules described in Appendix B. Then, read Appendix D to learn how to use a microscope.

Problem

What kinds of information can a compound microscope provide?

Materials

- compound microscope
- microscope slide
- newspaper or other small-print text
- scissors
- dropper pipette
- coverslips
- prepared slide of crossed fibers
- transparent 15-cm plastic ruler
- prepared slide of root or stem
- prepared slide of bacteria

Skills

Observing, Measuring, Calculating

Procedure  

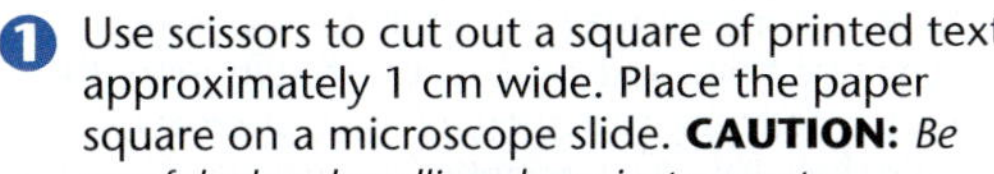

1. Use scissors to cut out a square of printed text approximately 1 cm wide. Place the paper square on a microscope slide. **CAUTION:** *Be careful when handling sharp instruments.*
2. Use a dropper pipette to place a drop of water on the paper square. Add a coverslip. Place the slide on the stage of a compound microscope. Use the stage clips to hold the slide in place.
3. Use the low-power objective to bring the letters on the paper square into focus. Slowly move the slide in different directions along the stage. Record how the image changes. **CAUTION:** *Handle the microscope carefully.*
4. Observe a prepared slide of crossed fibers through the low-power objective. Use the fine adjustment to focus up and down through the area where the fibers cross. Record the order of the fibers, from top to bottom.
5. Observe a transparent ruler through the low-power objective. Use the ruler to measure in millimeters the diameter of your field of view as precisely as you can. Record this distance and the magnification of the low-power objective.
6. Calculate and record the diameter of the field of view through the other objectives. For example, if a 4× objective has a field of 2 mm (2000 micrometers), then a 10× objective will have a field of (4 ÷ 10) × 2 mm = 0.8 mm (800 micrometers).
7. Examine a prepared slide of a plant stem or root at low and high powers. The small round shapes you see are cells. Use the field diameters you calculated in step 6 to estimate and record the size of a typical plant cell. For example, if 4 cells fit across an 800-micrometer field, then each cell is 200 micrometers long.
8. Repeat step 7 with a prepared slide of bacteria.

Analyze and Conclude

1. **Applying Concepts** What are the advantages of using the high-power objective? What are the disadvantages?
2. **Inferring** Some plant diseases are caused by bacteria. Could a bacterium injure a plant by surrounding a plant cell and consuming it? By entering a plant cell? Explain your answer.
3. **Drawing Conclusions** In what ways did the microscope alter the image in step 3? How did moving the slide affect the image?
4. **Drawing Conclusions** In what order were the fibers arranged on the slide you observed in step 4?

Go Further

Measuring With your teacher's permission, use the microscope to observe one of your hairs and estimate its width.

Analyze and Conclude

1. Advantages include the greater magnification of the image. Disadvantages include the relative darkness of the image when viewed with a high-power lens and that the size of the field of vision decreases as magnification increases.

2. Students should infer that a bacterium could injure plants by entering plant cells but not by consuming them, because observation showed that bacteria are much smaller than plant cells.

3. The microscope magnified the printed text. As students moved the slide, they should have observed the image moving in the opposite direction. For instance, if the slide is moved to the left, the image moves to the right.

4. Students should be able to distinguish the order of the fibers.

Exploration

Objective Students will be able to draw conclusions about the kinds of information that a compound microscope can provide. L2

Skills Focus **Observing, Measuring, Calculating**

Time 45 minutes

Alternative Materials Students may use inexpensive stage micrometers, which are available from science supply houses.

Teaching Tips

- At low power, most compound light microscopes have a field of view with a diameter of about 1.4 millimeters.
- Explain to students that the millimeter is usually too large a unit for microscopic calculations. Normally, biologists use the micrometer (μm); 1 μm = 1/1000 mm.
- Legal notices in a newspaper are an ideal size for this activity.

Procedure

5. Make sure students are using the low-power objective for this step. Explain how to estimate the diameter of the field of view. Have students place the ruler on the microscope stage and focus on the lines that divide the ruler into millimeters. Then, have them move the ruler so that one of these lines is at the left edge of the field of view. Students should add the number of whole millimeters—usually one—to the estimated fraction of a millimeter left over at the right.

Expected Outcomes Students will become familiar with the low-power and high-power objectives of a compound microscope and learn how the image moves as they move a slide.

Go Further

Encourage students to observe a hair under the microscope, and discuss how to estimate its width. Generally, students should compare the width of the magnified hair with the diameter of the field of view they've already calculated. For example, if the hair takes up about a third of the field of view and the diameter of that field is 375 micrometers, then the width of the hair is 125 micrometers.

Chapter 1 Study Guide

Study Tip

Divide the class into pairs, and have each pair make a list of review questions that incorporates all the Key Concepts and Vocabulary terms from the four sections. Ask that they answer the questions on separate sheets of paper. Then, have pairs of students exchange lists of questions. Once students have had time to answer the questions, have the same pairs exchange answer keys.

Thinking Visually

1. Hypotheses
2. Observations
3. Field studies

Chapter 1 Assessment

Reviewing Content

1. c	5. a	9. d
2. a	6. b	10. a
3. b	7. b	
4. c	8. d	

Understanding Concepts

11. The goal of science is to investigate and understand the natural world, to explain events in the natural world, and to use those explanations to make useful predictions.

12. An observation uses senses to gather information; an inference is a logical interpretation based on prior knowledge and experience.

13. Hypotheses help scientists by suggesting testable explanations for a set of observations. Hypotheses are starting points for discovering new information.

14. A hypothesis may arise from prior knowledge; logical inferences; or informed, creative imagination.

15. Scientists should test only one variable at a time so that only one observable factor affects the observed results of the experiment.

Chapter 1 Study Guide

1–1 What Is Science?

Key Concept 

- The goal of science is to investigate and understand the natural world, to explain events in the natural world, and to use those explanations to make useful predictions.

Vocabulary

science, p. 3 • observation, p. 4 • data, p. 4
inference, p. 4 • hypothesis, p. 5

1–2 How Scientists Work

Key Concepts 

- Whenever possible, a hypothesis should be tested by an experiment in which only one variable is changed at a time. All other variables should be kept unchanged, or controlled.
- In science, the word *theory* applies to a well-tested explanation that unifies a broad range of observations.

Vocabulary

spontaneous generation, p. 8
controlled experiment, p. 9
manipulated variable, p. 9
responding variable, p. 9 • theory, p. 13

1–3 Studying Life

Key Concepts

- Living things share characteristics including cellular organization, reproduction, a universal genetic code, growth and development, use of materials and energy, response to their environment, maintaining an internal stability, and, as a group, change over time.
- Some of the levels at which life can be studied include molecules, cells, organisms, populations of a single kind of organism, communities of populations living in the same area, and the biosphere. At all these levels, smaller living systems are found within larger systems.

Vocabulary

biology, p. 15 • cell, p. 16
homeostasis, p. 16
sexual reproduction, p. 17
asexual reproduction, p. 17
metabolism, p. 17
stimulus, p. 17

1–4 Tools and Procedures

Key Concepts 

- Most scientists use the metric system when collecting data and performing experiments.
- Light microscopes produce magnified images by focusing visible light rays. Electron microscopes produce magnified images by focusing beams of electrons.

Vocabulary

metric system, p. 24
microscope, p. 25
compound light microscope, p. 26
electron microscope, p. 26
cell culture, p. 27
cell fractionation, p. 27

Thinking Visually

Make a concept map that shows some ways scientists think and work. You can start with the partial concept map shown below or create your own. Recalling how scientists investigated spontaneous generation may help you identify important ideas to include.

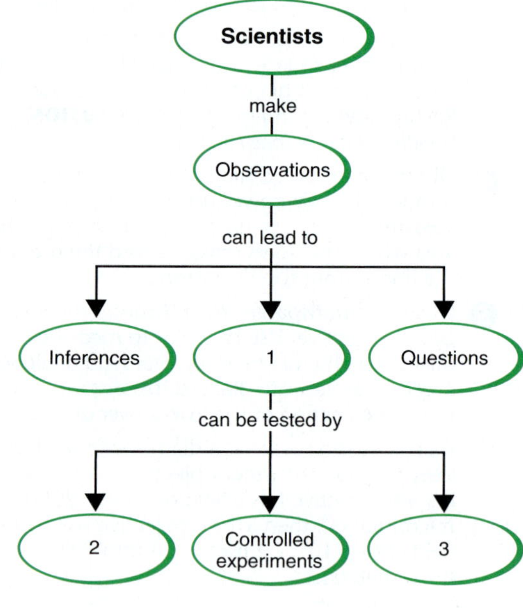

CHAPTER RESOURCES

Print:

- ***Teaching Resources,*** Chapter Vocabulary Review, Graphic Organizer, Chapter 1 Tests: Levels A and B

Technology:

- ***iText,*** Chapter 1 Assessment
- ***Computer Test Bank,*** Chapter 1 Test

Chapter 1 Assessment

Reviewing Content

Choose the letter that best answers the question or completes the statement.

1. Which of the following statements about the image shown below is NOT an observation?
   a. The insect has three legs on the left side.
   b. The insect has a pattern on its back.
   c. The insect's pattern shows that it is poisonous.
   d. The insect is green, white, and black.

2. The statement "the worm is 2 cm long" is a(an)
   a. quantitative observation.
   b. qualitative observation.
   c. inference.
   d. hypothesis.
3. An inference is
   a. the same as an observation.
   b. a logical interpretation of an observation.
   c. a statement involving numbers.
   d. a way to avoid bias.
4. To be useful in science, a hypothesis must be
   a. measurable. c. testable.
   b. observable. d. correct.
5. The term *spontaneous generation* means that
   a. living things can arise from nonliving matter.
   b. living things arise from other living things.
   c. a maggot is part of the life cycle of a fly.
   d. living things evolve over time.
6. Which of the following statements about a controlled experiment is true?
   a. All the variables must be kept the same.
   b. Only one variable is tested at a time.
   c. Scientists always use controlled experiments.
   d. Controlled experiments cannot be performed on living things.
7. A scientific theory is
   a. another word for hypothesis.
   b. a well-tested explanation that unifies a broad range of observations.
   c. the same as the conclusion of an experiment.
   d. the first step in a controlled experiment.

Interactive textbook with assessment at PHSchool.com 

8. The process in which cells from two different parents unite to produce the first cell of a new organism is called
   a. homeostasis.
   b. development.
   c. asexual reproduction.
   d. sexual reproduction.
9. The process by which organisms keep their internal conditions relatively stable is called
   a. metabolism. c. evolution.
   b. a genome. d. homeostasis.
10. An instrument that produces images by focusing light rays is called a(an)
    a. light microscope.
    b. transmission electron microscope.
    c. scanning electron microscope.
    d. electronic balance.

Understanding Concepts

11. What is the goal of science?
12. How does an observation about an object differ from an inference about that object?
13. How does a hypothesis help scientists understand the natural world?
14. Describe three possible ways in which a hypothesis may arise.
15. Why is it advantageous for scientists to test only one variable at a time during an experiment?
16. Distinguish between a variable and a control.
17. What steps are involved in making a valid conclusion?
18. What equipment did Redi use in his experiment? Why was the gauze important?
19. What question was Spallanzani's experiment designed to answer?
20. What must happen for a hypothesis to become a theory?
21. What is differentiation?
22. How can a graph of data be more informative than a table of the same data?
23. What is a cell culture? How can a cell culture be useful to biologists?

HOMEWORK GUIDE

Section:	Questions:
Section 1–1	1–4, 11–14, 25
Section 1–2	5–7, 15–20, 27, 30, 31
Section 1–3	8, 9, 21
Section 1–4	10, 22–24, 26, 28, 29, 31, 32

Interactive Textbook

The iText provides an interactive version of the Student Edition and a self-test.

(Continued from page 30)

16. A variable is a factor in an experiment that can change. A control is a factor in an experiment that is kept unchanged.
17. Asking a question, forming a hypothesis, setting up a controlled experiment, and recording and analyzing results
18. Redi used jars, meat, and gauze. The gauze was important because he used it to cover some jars; the gauze was his manipulated variable.
19. Whether microorganisms would grow in gravy that was boiled and then left in covered containers
20. It must be well supported by observation and experimentation.
21. Example: During its life cycle, a fly goes through these stages: egg → larva → pupa → adult fly.
22. A graph can make a pattern easier to recognize and understand.
23. A cell culture is a group of cells produced when a single cell is placed in a nutrient solution and allowed to reproduce. Scientists can use cell cultures to test cell responses under controlled conditions, to study interactions between cells, and to select specific cells for future study.

Chapter 1 Assessment

Critical Thinking

24. Check to be sure that students' measurements are in millimeters.

25. Because science is a process rather than unchanging knowledge

26. The magnification is greater with an electron microscope, but an electron microscope cannot be used to study organisms while they are alive. A light microscope produces magnified images by focusing a readily available source—visible light.

27. The strengths of the biogenesis theory include the fact that it is supported by numerous experiments and accounts for all known observations. At this time, there are no known weaknesses.

28. Student answers should reflect the idea that the number of organisms depends upon the lapsed time. Graph 1: As the time changed, the number of organisms increased. Graph 2: There was an increase in the number of individuals, then a decline. Graph 3: There were spikes in the population, followed by declines. The second spike was the most noticeable. Graph 4: The number of organisms remained constant.

29. Students' possible answers include: Graph 1 could be a chemical reaction in which product accumulates. Graph 2 could be an enzyme reaction in which heat is increased, affecting the rate of product formation, and then showing where the enzyme is deactivated by the diminishing heat and rate.

30. Check to be sure the experiment has one manipulated variable and a control. Sample experiment: Find two young animals of the same kind whose weight is approximately the same. Feed each animal a different food, and weigh the animals at intervals.

31. The other key variables may be responsible for the observed outcome of the experiment.

32. (1) Breakage; (2) Electric shock; (3) Sharp object; (4) Heat-resistant gloves.

Focus on the BIG Idea

Check students' writing for an understanding of a scientific attitude.

Chapter 1 Assessment

Critical Thinking

24. **Measuring** Use a ruler to find the precise length and width of this book in millimeters.

25. **Evaluating** Why is it misleading to describe science as a collection of facts?

26. **Comparing and Contrasting** What are some advantages and disadvantages of light microscopes and electron microscopes?

27. **Evaluating** Analyze and critique the theory of biogenesis. What are the strengths of the theory? Does it have any weaknesses?

28. **Analyzing Data** The following graphs show the sizes of four different populations over a period of time. Write a sentence summarizing what each graph shows.

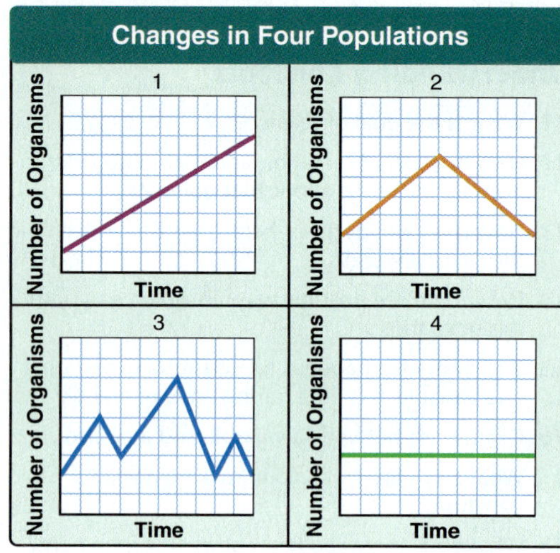

29. **Comparing and Contrasting** Graphs of completely different events can have the same appearance. Select one of the graphs from question 28 and explain how the shape of the graph could apply to a different set of events.

30. **Designing Experiments** Suggest an experiment that would show whether one type of food was better than another at helping an animal to grow faster.

31. **Controlling Variables** Explain why you cannot draw a conclusion about the effect of one variable in an investigation when the other key variables are not controlled.

32. **Interpreting Graphics** Each of the following safety symbols might appear in a laboratory activity in this book. Describe what each symbol stands for. (*Hint:* Refer to Appendix B.)

1 
2 
3 
4 

Science as a Way of Knowing Use the information in Section 1–2 to explain how having a scientific attitude might help you in everyday activities, for example, in trying to learn a new skill. Describe your ideas in your journal.

Writing in Science

Suppose you have a pet cat and want to determine which type of cat food it prefers. Write an explanation of how you might use scientific thinking, including making observations and inferences, to determine this. (*Hint:* To prepare to write, list the steps you might take, and then arrange them in order beginning with the first step.)

Performance-Based Assessment

Planning an Experiment Many people add fertilizers to house or garden plants. Make a hypothesis about whether you think these fertilizers really help plants grow. Next, design an experiment to test your hypothesis. Include in your plan what variable you will test and what variables you will control. Then, listen to other students' plans. Which plans would properly test their hypotheses?

For: An interactive self-test
Visit: PHSchool.com
Web Code: cba-1010

Writing in Science

Students' explanations will vary. All students, though, should define or describe how to make scientific observations and make inferences from those observations. A typical use of scientific thinking in determining which food a cat prefers will involve designing an experiment and drawing a conclusion. These steps should be included in this process: asking a question, forming a hypothesis, setting up a controlled experiment, recording and analyzing results, and drawing a conclusion. In the design of an experiment, students should identify a manipulated variable, a responding variable, and controlled variables.

Performance-Based Assessment

Student answers should include a testable hypothesis and a description of a controlled experiment in which the variable to be tested and the variables to be controlled are listed.

Standards Practice

Success Tracker™
Online at PHSchool.com

Test-Taking Tip Before taking a standardized test, it helps to become familiar with the format of the test, including the different question types. One helpful method is to complete practice tests, such as this one.

Questions 1–2

A researcher investigated two groups of fruit flies. Population A was kept in a 0.5-L container. Population B was kept in a 1-L container.

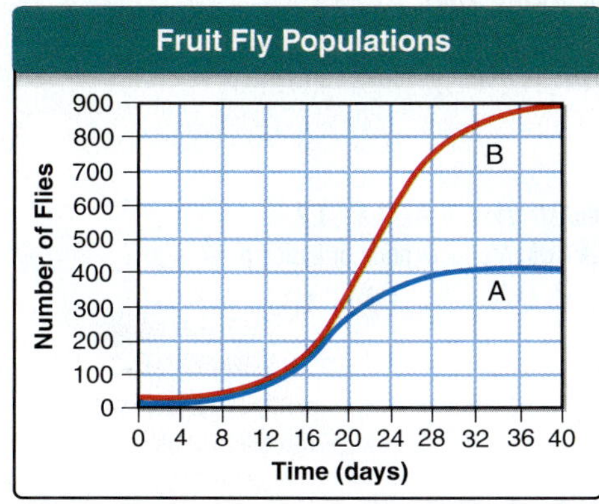

1. The manipulated variable was the **6IIE 7.c**
   A number of flies.
   B time in days.
   C difference in time per group.
   D size of the containers.

2. Which of the following is a logical inference based on the contents of the graph? **7IIE 7.c**
   A The flies in Group B were healthier than those in Group A.
   B A fly population with more available space will grow larger than a population with less space.
   C If Group B were observed for 40 more days, the size of the population would double.
   D In 40 more days, the sizes of both populations would decrease at the same rate.

Directions: Choose the letter that best answers the question or completes the statement.

3. Unlike sexual reproduction, asexual reproduction involves **7 2.a**
   A spontaneous generation.
   B two cells.
   C two parents.
   D one parent.

4. One meter is equal to
   A 1000 millimeters.
   B 1 millimeter.
   C 10 kilometers.
   D 1 milliliter.

Questions 5–6

Once a month, a pet owner recorded the mass of her puppy in a table. When the puppy was 3 months old, she started to feed it a "special puppy food" she saw advertised on TV.

Change in a Puppy's Mass Over Time

Age (months)	Mass at Start of Month (kg)	Change in Mass per Month (kg)
2	5	—
3	8	+3
4	13	+5

5. According to the table, which statement is true?
   A The puppy's mass increased at the same rate for each month shown.
   B The puppy's increase in mass during month 4 was greater than 4 kg.
   C The puppy added more mass during month 2 than during month 3.
   D The puppy added more mass during month 3 than during month 2.

6. All of the following statements about the pet owner's study are true EXCEPT
   A The owner made quantitative observations.
   B The owner used the metric system.
   C The owner recorded data.
   D The owner conducted a controlled experiment.

Standards Practice

1. D **2.** B **3.** D **4.** A **5.** B **6.** D

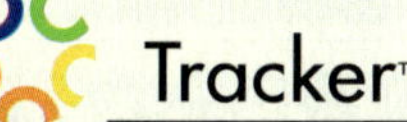

Success Tracker™
Online at PHSchool.com

Have students check their understanding of the chapter by logging onto Success Tracker.

Go Online PHSchool.com

Your students can independently test their knowledge of the chapter and print out their test results for your files.

Chapter Planner 2 The Chemistry of Life

Section and Section Objectives	Time	STANDARDS NCLB	STANDARDS Biology	Activities and Labs
2–1 The Nature of Matter, pp. 35–39 **2.1.1** ***Identify*** the three subatomic particles found in atoms. **2.1.2** ***Explain*** how all of the isotopes of an element are similar and how they are different. **2.1.3** ***Explain*** what chemical compounds are. **2.1.4** ***Describe*** the two main types of chemical bonds.	1 period (1/2 block)			**SE:** ***Inquiry Activity,*** Do large and small molecules behave exactly alike?, p. 34 L2 **TE:** ***Build Science Skills,*** p. 35 L2 **TE:** ***Build Science Skills,*** p. 36 L1 L2 **SE:** ***Careers in Biology,*** Forensic Scientist, p. 37 L2
2–2 Properties of Water, pp. 40–43 **2.2.1** ***Explain*** why water molecules are polar. **2.2.2** ***Differentiate*** between solutions and suspensions. **2.2.3** ***Explain*** what acidic solutions and basic solutions are.	1 period (1/2 block)			**TE:** ***Demonstration,*** p. 41 L1 L2 **SE:** ***Quick Lab,*** Are foods acidic or basic?, p. 42 L2 **PLM:** Are foods acidic or basic? L1 L2
2–3 Carbon Compounds, pp. 44–48 **2.3.1** ***Describe*** the functions of each group of organic compounds.	1 period (1/2 block)	8 6.b, 8 6.c	BI 1.h, BI 4.e, *BI 4.f	**TE:** ***Build Science Skills,*** p. 45 L2 **LMA:** Chapter 2 Lab L2 L3 **LMB:** Chapter 2 Lab L1 L2
2–4 Chemical Reactions and Enzymes, pp. 49–53 **2.4.1** ***Explain*** how chemical reactions affect chemical bonds in compounds. **2.4.2** ***Describe*** how energy changes affect how easily a chemical reaction will occur. **2.4.3** ***Explain*** why enzymes are important to living things.	1 period (1/2 block)		BI 1.b	**TE:** ***Demonstration,*** p. 49 L1 L2 **SE:** ***Analyzing Data,*** How does pH affect an enzyme?, p. 51 L2 L3 **TE:** ***Build Science Skills,*** p. 52 L1 L2, p. 53 L1 L2 **SE:** ***Design an Experiment,*** Investigating the Effect of Temperature on Enzyme Activity, pp. 54–55 L2 L3 **PLM:** Investigating the Effect of Temperature on Enzyme Activity L1 L2 L3
Chapter Assessment, pp. 56–59	1 period (1/2 block)			

ACTIVITY PLANNER

SE: ***Inquiry Activity,*** p. 34; 10 min.; tofu, soy sauce, butter, soap, cornstarch, sugar, teaspoon, 6 test tubes with stoppers, water

TE: ***Build Science Skills,*** p. 35; 15 min.; model of an atom, toothpicks, gumdrops

TE: ***Build Science Skills,*** p. 36; 10 min.; marbles of 2 different colors

TE: ***Demonstration,*** p. 41; 10 min.; flask, 25 g sugar, masking tape, stirring rod, metric ruler

SE: ***Quick Lab,*** p. 42; 15 min.; pH paper, solid foods and fruit juices, paper towel, scalpel, dropper pipette, plastic gloves

TE: ***Build Science Skills,*** p. 45; 20 min.; Lugol's solution, dropper, soda cracker, potato, white bread, oatmeal, granulated sugar, test tubes

TE: ***Demonstration,*** p. 49; 10 min.; baking soda, vinegar, 3 beakers

TE: ***Build Science Skills,*** p. 52; 15 min.; toothpicks, clock or watch with second hand

TE: ***Build Science Skills,*** p. 53; 10 min.; padlock, key

SE: ***Design an Experiment,*** pp. 54–55; 45 min.; liver, petri dish, dropper pipette, 1% H_2O_2, graduated cylinder, beakers, filter paper, forceps, glass-marker, ice- and warm-water baths, thermometers, watch

PLANNING KEY

Ability Levels
for students performing . . .
below grade level L1
at grade level L2
above grade level L3

Print Components

SE	Student Edition	LA	Lab Assessment
TE	Teacher's Edition	BTM	Biotechnology Manual
RSW	Reading & Study Workbook A	IDM	Issues and Decision Making
ARSW	Adapted Reading & Study Workbook B	LW	Lab Worksheets
TR	Teaching Resources	LMA	Laboratory Manual A
IF	Investigations in Forensics	LMB	Laboratory Manual B

Tech Components

CTB	Computer Test Bank
BD	BioDetectives DVD
TP	Transparencies Plus
PLM	Probeware Lab Manual
ABC	ABC DVD Library
LS	Lab Simulations
VL	Virtual Labs

Interactive textbook with assessment at PHSchool.com

Program Resources	Assessment	Media and Technology
TR: Lesson Plan 2–1, Section Summary, p. 47 L1, p. 59 L2, Worksheets, pp. 50–53 L1, pp. 61–62 L2 **RSW:** Section 2–1 L2 **ARSW:** Section 2–1 L1	**SE:** 2–1 Section Assessment, p. 39 **TR:** Section Review 2–1	**iText:** Section 2–1 **TP:** 2–1 Interest Grabber, Section Outline, An Element in the Periodic Table, Figure 2–2, Figure 2–3 **BD:** "History's Mystery: An Introduction to Forensic Science" **ABC:** 1 Atomic Structure, 2 Energy Levels and Ionic Bonding, 3 Covalent Bonding
TR: Lesson Plan 2–2, Section Summary, p. 47 L1, p. 59 L2, Worksheets, pp. 63–64 L2, Enrichment L2 L3 **RSW:** Section 2–2 L2	**SE:** 2–2 Section Assessment, p. 43 **TR:** Section Review 2–2	**iText:** Section 2–2 **TP:** 2–2 Interest Grabber, Section Outline, pH scale, Figure 2–9
TR: Lesson Plan 2–3, Section Summary, p. 48 L1, p. 60 L2, Worksheets, p. 54 L1, pp. 65–67 L2 **RSW:** Section 2–3 L2 **ARSW:** Section 2–3 L1	**SE:** 2–3 Section Assessment, p. 48 **TR:** Section Review 2–3	**iText:** Section 2–3 **TP:** 2–3 Interest Grabber, Section Outline, Concept Map, Figure 2–11, Figure 2–13, Figures 2–16 and 2–17 **Lab Simulations CD-ROM:** Properties of Biomolecules
TR: Lesson Plan 2–4, Section Summary, p. 49 L1, p. 60 L2, Worksheets, pp. 55–56 L1, pp. 68–69 L2 **LW:** Chapter 2 Design an Experiment L1 L2 L3 **RSW:** Section 2–4 L2 **ARSW:** Section 2–4 L1	**SE:** 2–4 Section Assessment, p. 53 **TR:** Section Review 2–4	**iText:** Section 2–4 **TP:** 2–4 Interest Grabber, Section Outline, Effect of Enzymes, Figure 2–19, Figure 2–21 **ABC:** 4 Enzymatic Reactions **VL:** Lab 1
	SE: Chapter 2 Assessment, pp. 56–59 **TR:** Chapter Vocabulary Review, Graphic Organizer, Chapter 2 Tests: Levels A and B **LA:** Laboratory Assessment 1	**iText:** Chapter 2 Assessment **CTB:** Chapter 2 Test **Go Online** Students can do research, share data, and test their knowledge online.

TIME SAVER

PRESSED FOR TIME?

To Preview the Chapter
- Introduce students to Key Concepts and Vocabulary terms in each section.
- Assign the Reading Strategies for each section.

To Cover the Chapter Quickly
- Have students read all of Section 2–1; Figures 2–6, 2–9, and 2–10 in Section 2–2; all of Section 2–3; and Chemical Reactions, Energy in Reactions, and Enzymes in Section 2–4.
- Assign 2–1 Section Review and 2–3 Section Review, as well as questions 1–3 and 5–9 in Chapter 2 Assessment and questions 1–10 in Chapter 2 Standards Practice.

To Review the Chapter
- Assign Sections 2–1, 2–3, and 2–4 in the Reading and Study Workbook or the Adapted Reading and Study Workbook.
- Assign Section Reviews for 2–1, 2–3, and 2–4 and the Chapter Vocabulary Review for Chapter 2 in the Teaching Resources.

CHAPTER 2

ENGAGE/EXPLORE

Inquiry Activity

Objective Students will be able to draw the conclusion that large molecules are less soluble in water than smaller related molecules. L2

Skill Focus **Observing, Drawing Conclusions**

Materials tofu, soy sauce, butter, soap, cornstarch, sugar, teaspoon, 6 test tubes with stoppers, water

Time 10 minutes

Advance Prep You can obtain each of the substances used in the activity at a grocery store.

Safety Caution students to make sure that the stopper is secure in the test tube before they shake it.

Strategies

- Explain that it is not important to add an exact amount of each material to the water, though students should not add too much. They should add about 1 teaspoon of each substance.
- Point out that the soy protein in tofu is the same protein that is broken down into amino acids to make soy sauce.

Expected Outcomes Students should observe that soy sauce, soap, and sugar dissolve in water, whereas tofu, butter, and starch do not.

Think About It

1. Soy sauce, soap, and sugar
2. The large molecules are less soluble than the smaller molecules.

Assess Prior Knowledge

To assess students' knowledge of basic chemistry, write this chemical equation on the board:

$C_6H_{12}O_6 + 6O_2 \rightarrow CO_2 + H_2O$

Ask students to write everything they know about this equation, including the compounds involved and how many atoms of each element are in each molecule. Also, ask students to balance the equation. *(Students may know that this is the summary equation for cellular respiration, in which glucose reacts with oxygen to produce carbon dioxide and water. Students should balance the equation as follows: $C_6H_{12}O_6 + 6O_2 \rightarrow 6CO_2 + 6H_2O$)*

CHAPTER 2

The Chemistry of Life

The beautiful feathers of this great egret are made up of protein. Proteins are one of the main groups of carbon compounds found in living things.

Inquiry Activity

Do large and small molecules behave exactly alike?

Procedure   

1. Label six test tubes as follows: tofu, soy sauce, butter, soap, starch, and sugar. Place a tiny amount of each sample in the appropriate test tube.
2. Half-fill each test tube with water. Stopper the test tubes. Shake each test tube for 2 minutes. Record your observations of each test tube.

Think About It

1. **Observing** Which substances dissolved easily in water?
2. **Drawing Conclusions** Tofu, starch, and butter consist mostly of large molecules (protein, starch, and fat, respectively). Soy sauce, sugar, and soap contain smaller molecules that are related to the large molecules. Are the larger molecules more or less soluble than the smaller molecules?

FACTS AND FIGURES

Biochemistry—the chemistry of life

Chemistry is the study of the composition and properties of substances, as well as the changes that substances can undergo. One major branch of chemistry is called organic chemistry, which is the study of organic compounds, or compounds that contain carbon. Inorganic chemistry is the rest of chemistry, or the study of all compounds that don't contain carbon, except for the oxides of carbon and the carbonates. Biochemistry is the study of the chemicals of living things and the changes that those chemicals undergo; that is, it is the chemistry of life, the focus of this chapter. Biochemistry is primarily concerned with organic chemistry and the structure and reactions of carbohydrates, lipids, nucleic acids, and proteins. It is also concerned with some inorganic compounds such as water and carbon dioxide.

2–1 The Nature of Matter

Life depends on chemistry. When you eat food or inhale oxygen, your body uses these materials in chemical reactions that keep you alive. Just as buildings are made from bricks, steel, glass, and wood, living things are made from chemical compounds. If the first task of an architect is to understand building materials, then the first job of a biologist is to understand the chemistry of life.

Guide for Reading

Key Concepts

- What three subatomic particles make up atoms?
- How are all of the isotopes of an element similar?
- What are the two main types of chemical bonds?

Vocabulary

atom
nucleus
electron
element
isotope
compound
ionic bond
ion
covalent bond
molecule
van der Waals forces

Reading Strategy: Using Prior Knowledge Before you read, write down what you already know about atoms, elements, and compounds. As you read, note the main new concepts you learn.

Atoms

The study of chemistry begins with the basic unit of matter, the **atom.** The Greek word *atomos,* which means "unable to be cut," was first used to refer to matter by the Greek philosopher Democritus nearly 2500 years ago. Democritus asked a simple question: If you take an object like a stick of chalk and break it in half, are both halves still chalk? The answer, of course, is yes. But what happens if you go on? Suppose you break it in half again and again and again. Can you continue to divide without limit, or does there come a point at which you cannot divide the fragment of chalk without changing it into something else? Democritus thought that there had to be a limit. He called the smallest fragment the atom, a name scientists still use today.

Atoms are incredibly small. Placed side by side, 100 million atoms would make a row only about 1 centimeter long—about the width of your little finger! Despite its extremely small size, an atom contains subatomic particles that are even smaller. **Figure 2–1** shows the subatomic particles in a helium atom. **The subatomic particles that make up atoms are protons, neutrons, and electrons.** Protons and neutrons have about the same mass. However, protons are positively charged particles (+) and neutrons carry no charge. Their name is a reminder that they are neutral particles. Strong forces bind protons and neutrons together to form the **nucleus,** which is at the center of the atom.

The **electron** is a negatively charged particle (–) with 1/1840 the mass of a proton. Electrons are in constant motion in the space surrounding the nucleus. They are attracted to the positively charged nucleus but remain outside the nucleus because of the energy of their motion. Because atoms have equal numbers of electrons and protons, and because these subatomic particles have equal but opposite charges, atoms are neutral.

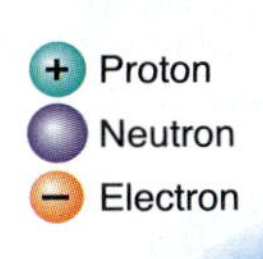

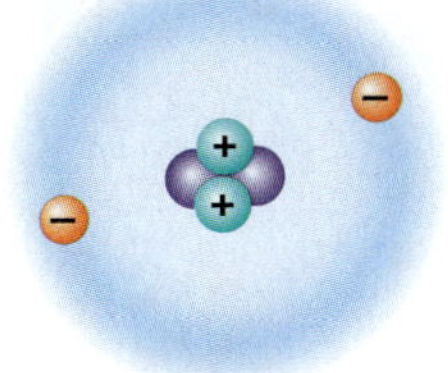

Figure 2–1 **Helium atoms contain protons, neutrons, and electrons.** The positively charged protons and uncharged neutrons are bound together in the dense nucleus, while the negatively charged electrons move in the space around the nucleus.

SECTION RESOURCES

Print:

- ***Teaching Resources,*** Lesson Plan 2–1, Adapted Section Summary 2–1, Adapted Worksheets 2–1, Section Summary 2–1, Worksheets 2–1, Section Review 2–1
- ***Reading and Study Workbook A,*** Section 2–1
- ***Adapted Reading and Study Workbook B,*** Section 2–1

Technology:

- ***BioDetectives DVD,*** "History's Mystery: An Introduction to Forensic Science"
- ***iText,*** Section 2–1
- ***Animated Biological Concepts DVD,*** 1 Atomic Structure, 2 Energy Levels and Ionic Bonding, 3 Covalent Bonding
- ***Transparencies Plus,*** Section 2–1

Section 2–1

1 FOCUS

Objectives

2.1.1 ***Identify*** the three subatomic particles found in atoms.
2.1.2 ***Explain*** how all of the isotopes of an element are similar and how they are different.
2.1.3 ***Explain*** what chemical compounds are.
2.1.4 ***Describe*** the two main types of chemical bonds.

Guide for Reading

Vocabulary Preview

Before students read the section, ask them to find each Vocabulary term and preview its meaning.

Reading Strategy

Encourage students to refer back regularly to their initial thoughts about atoms, elements, and compounds, editing their sentences as they revise their thinking in light of the section's discussion.

2 INSTRUCT

Atoms

Build Science Skills

Using Models Display a model of an atom, and have students identify the nucleus, protons, neutrons, and electrons. Then, have students build their own models of atoms, using toothpicks and gumdrops. Assign each student one or more of the elements mentioned in this section—helium, hydrogen, oxygen, carbon, sodium, and chlorine—and elements that will be discussed in future sections, such as nitrogen and calcium. Stress that all models have limitations. In the Figure 2–1 drawing, for example, electrons are shown as equal in size to the more massive protons and neutrons, and the constant motion of the electrons cannot be shown. L2

2–1 (continued)

Elements and Isotopes

Make Connections

Chemistry Display a wall-sized periodic table of elements and review with students the information it contains. Focus first on the names and symbols. Explain that new elements are assigned three-letter symbols until they are officially named. Ask: **How are the elements arranged in the table?** *(In order by increasing atomic number)* Remind students that the atomic number equals the number of protons in an atom. Ask: **What else does the atomic number equal?** *(The number of electrons in the atom)* Use the table to discuss the average atomic masses and the concept of a weighted average after students have learned about isotopes. L2

Build Science Skills

Using Models Help students grasp the concept of isotopes by using marbles of two different colors. Have dark-colored marbles represent protons and light-colored marbles represent neutrons. Place six of each color of marble in a student's hand, and explain that this represents the nucleus of a carbon-12 atom. Add a light-colored marble to the hand, and ask: **What do the marbles now represent?** *(The nucleus of a carbon-13 atom)* **How many electrons does this isotope of carbon contain?** *(The isotope has six electrons.)* Add another dark-colored marble to the hand, and ask: **Is the nucleus the marbles now represent a nucleus of a carbon isotope?** *(No. Carbon isotopes always have six protons.)* **Which element has seven protons?** *(Nitrogen)* L1 L2

Elements and Isotopes

A chemical **element** is a pure substance that consists entirely of one type of atom. More than 100 elements are known, but only about two dozen are commonly found in living organisms. Elements are represented by a one- or two-letter symbol. C, for example, stands for carbon, H for hydrogen, and Na for sodium. The number of protons in an atom of an element is the element's atomic number. Carbon's atomic number is 6, meaning that each atom of carbon has six protons and, consequently, six electrons. See Appendix G, The Periodic Table, which shows the elements.

Isotopes Atoms of an element can have different numbers of neutrons. For example, some atoms of carbon have six neutrons, some have seven, and a few have eight. Atoms of the same element that differ in the number of neutrons they contain are known as **isotopes.** The sum of the protons and neutrons in the nucleus of an atom is called its mass number. Isotopes are identified by their mass numbers. **Figure 2–2** shows the subatomic composition of carbon-12, carbon-13, and carbon-14 atoms. The weighted average of the masses of an element's isotopes is called its atomic mass. "Weighted" means that the abundance of each isotope in nature is considered when the average is calculated. **Because they have the same number of electrons, all isotopes of an element have the same chemical properties.**

Radioactive Isotopes Some isotopes are radioactive, meaning that their nuclei are unstable and break down at a constant rate over time. The radiation these isotopes give off can be dangerous, but radioactive isotopes have a number of important scientific and practical uses.

Geologists can determine the ages of rocks and fossils by analyzing the isotopes found in them. Radiation from certain isotopes can be used to treat cancer and to kill bacteria that cause food to spoil. Radioactive isotopes can also be used as labels or "tracers" to follow the movements of substances within organisms.

▼ **Figure 2–2** **Because they have the same number of electrons, these isotopes of carbon have the same chemical properties.** The difference among the isotopes is the number of neutrons in their nuclei.

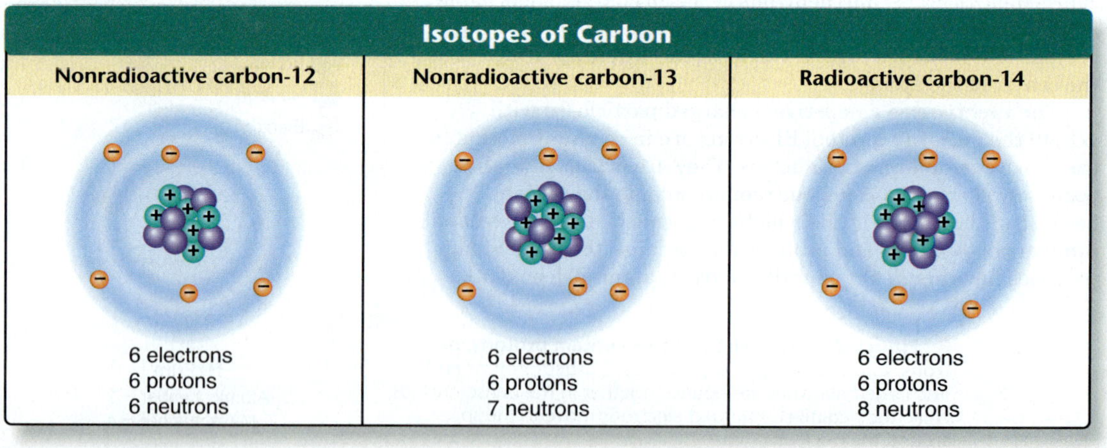

Isotopes of Carbon

Nonradioactive carbon-12	Nonradioactive carbon-13	Radioactive carbon-14
6 electrons 6 protons 6 neutrons	6 electrons 6 protons 7 neutrons	6 electrons 6 protons 8 neutrons

ESL — SUPPORT FOR ENGLISH LANGUAGE LEARNERS

Comprehension: Link to Visual

Beginning Use Figure 2–1 (page 35) to help students understand the structure of the atom. Review the terms *atom, proton, neutron,* and *electron* by pointing out the appropriate parts of the figure. Use the figure to differentiate between the similar-sounding terms *neutron* and *nucleus.* Add these terms to a word wall with other Vocabulary terms from the chapter. L1

Intermediate Pair ESL students with English-proficient students to construct a three-column table on subatomic particles. They can use both the text on page 35 and the information in Figure 2–1. The column heads should be *Particle, Charge,* and *Location.* The left column should list the subatomic particle (proton, neutron, electron), the middle column should list the charge (positive, negative, or none), and the right column should list the location (inside nucleus or outside nucleus). L2

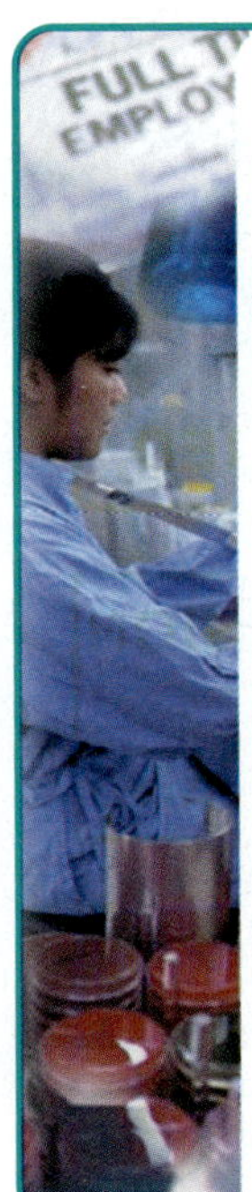

Careers in Biology

Forensic Scientist

Job Description: work as a forensic scientist for local, state, or federal investigative agencies in order to conduct scientific forensic examinations in criminal investigations

Education: a bachelor's degree in science—biology, physics, chemistry, metallurgy; some states require several years of forensic laboratory experience

Skills: analytical, logical, computer literate, detail oriented, able to take meticulous notes and to prepare evidence for presentation in court as well as to testify as an expert witness

Highlights: have the opportunity to use logic and science to solve unique or unusual problems in criminal investigations and to work collaboratively with other scientists

Quick View Video

Discovery School Video To find out more about forensic science, view track 1 "History's Mystery: An Introduction to Forensic Science" on the *BioDetectives* DVD.

Go Online PHSchool.com

For: Career links
Visit: PHSchool.com
Web Code: cbb-1021

Chemical Compounds

In nature, most elements are found combined with other elements in compounds. A chemical **compound** is a substance formed by the chemical combination of two or more elements in definite proportions. Scientists show the composition of compounds by a kind of shorthand known as a chemical formula. Water, which contains two atoms of hydrogen for each atom of oxygen, has the chemical formula H_2O. The formula for table salt, NaCl, indicates that the elements from which table salt forms—sodium and chlorine—combine in a 1 : 1 ratio.

The physical and chemical properties of a compound are usually very different from those of the elements from which it is formed. For example, hydrogen and oxygen, which are gases at room temperature, can combine explosively and form liquid water. Sodium is a silver-colored metal that is soft enough to cut with a knife. It reacts explosively with cold water. Chlorine is very reactive, too. It is a poisonous, greenish gas that was used to kill many soldiers in World War I. Sodium and chlorine combine to form sodium chloride (NaCl), or table salt. Sodium chloride is a white solid that dissolves easily in water. As you know, sodium chloride is not poisonous. In fact, it is essential for the survival of most living things.

CHECKPOINT *What information is contained in a chemical formula?*

BIO INSIGHTS — HISTORY OF SCIENCE

Same element, different atoms

In the early nineteenth century, British chemist John Dalton expounded a number of postulates about matter, including that all atoms of a given element are identical. His work had tremendous influence. About a century later, though, scientists working on radioactive decay detected scores of atoms that seemed to refute Dalton's postulate. English chemist Frederick Soddy provided a solution. In working with neon atoms, he found some atoms with a mass number of 20 and others with a mass number of 22. He suggested that atoms with both mass numbers can be considered neon because they have the same number of protons, even though they have different numbers of neutrons in their nuclei. Because both types of atoms could occupy the same place on the periodic table, he called them isotopes, from the Greek words for "same" and "place."

Careers in Biology

When a criminal investigation is needed, forensic scientists—also called criminalists—examine, compare, and analyze various types of physical evidence, including blood and other body fluids, hair and fibers, DNA and fingerprints.

An entry-level job as a forensic scientist usually requires a bachelor's degree in forensic science or some other science. L2

Resources Encourage interested students to contact a local university to see if it has a degree program in forensic science and what the program entails. Students might also contact a local police department and ask to talk to a forensic scientist or criminalist.

Go Online PHSchool.com

You can have students write a more extensive job description as well as list the educational requirements for a career in this field.

Quick View Video

Discovery School DVD Encourage students to view track 1 "History's Mystery: An Introduction to Forensic Science" on the *BioDetectives* DVD.

Chemical Compounds

Address Misconceptions

Many students may think that the smallest unit of every compound is a molecule. Chemists use the term *molecule* to describe the smallest unit of compounds whose atoms are joined by covalent bonds. You may want to note that atoms of some elements can join with other atoms of the same element and form molecules. For ionic compounds, the formula represents the lowest whole-number ratio of ions in the compound. L2

Answer to . . .

CHECKPOINT *The types of elements that are in the compound and the ratio in which atoms of those elements combine*

2–1 (continued)

Chemical Bonds

Build Science Skills

Using Models Arrange two circles of eight chairs each. The circles should be next to each other, about 1 meter apart. Then, invite nine students to take seats in one circle and seven students to take seats in the other. One student invited to sit in a circle will be left without a chair. Encourage that student to walk around the circle of eight chairs, looking for a place to sit. Then, ask: **How can this student's problem be resolved?** *(The student could sit in the empty seat in the other circle of chairs.)* **Assume the student is an electron. If the student takes a seat in the other circle, what kind of bond is being modeled?** *(An ionic bond, because the electron is transferred)* L1 L2

Use Visuals

Figure 2–3 Explain that an element's chemical properties are determined by the number and location of the electrons in its atoms. Ask: **Why does the transfer of an electron occur between a sodium atom and a chlorine atom?** *(The sodium atom, which has only one electron in its outermost level, easily loses that electron. The chlorine atom, which has seven electrons in its outermost level, easily gains an electron.)* Explain that the ions are more stable than the neutral atoms because their outermost levels are filled with electrons. Ask: **What is an ionic bond?** *(The attraction between two oppositely charged ions)* Students may notice that the name for the ion formed from a chlorine atom has an *-ide* ending. This is true for all monatomic negative ions. L2

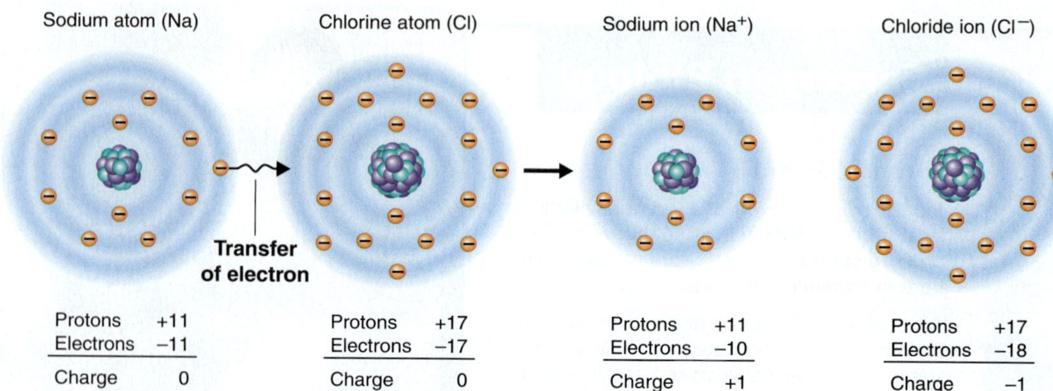

▲ **Figure 2–3** **The chemical bond in which electrons are transferred from one atom to another is called an ionic bond.** The compound sodium chloride forms when sodium loses its valence electron to chlorine.

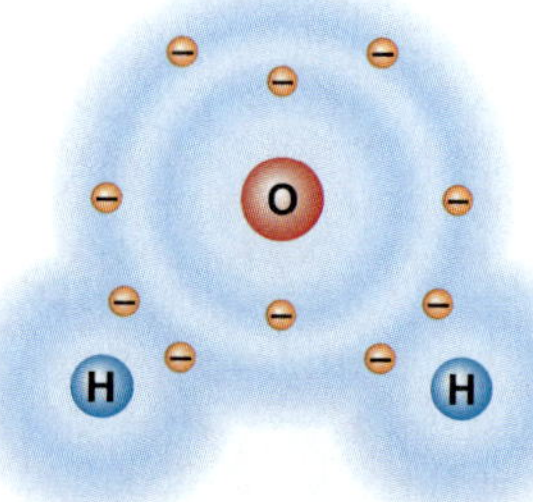

▲ **Figure 2–4** **The chemical bond in which electrons are shared between atoms is called a covalent bond.** In a water molecule, each hydrogen atom shares two electrons with the oxygen atom.

Chemical Bonds

The atoms in compounds are held together by chemical bonds. Much of chemistry is devoted to understanding how and when chemical bonds form. Bond formation involves the electrons that surround each atomic nucleus. The electrons that are available to form bonds are called valence electrons. **The main types of chemical bonds are ionic bonds and covalent bonds.**

Ionic Bonds An **ionic bond** is formed when one or more electrons are transferred from one atom to another. Recall that atoms are electrically neutral because they have equal numbers of protons and electrons. An atom that loses electrons has a positive charge. An atom that gains electrons has a negative charge. These positively and negatively charged atoms are known as **ions.**

Figure 2–3 shows how ionic bonds form between sodium and chlorine in table salt. A sodium atom easily loses its one valence electron and becomes a sodium ion (Na^+). A chlorine atom easily gains an electron and becomes a chloride ion (Cl^-). In a salt crystal, there are trillions of sodium and chloride ions. These oppositely charged ions have a strong attraction. The attraction between oppositely charged ions is an ionic bond.

Covalent Bonds Sometimes electrons are shared by atoms instead of being transferred. What does it mean to "share" electrons? It means that the moving electrons actually travel in the orbitals of both atoms. A **covalent bond** forms when electrons are shared between atoms. When the atoms share two electrons, the bond is called a single covalent bond. Sometimes the atoms share four electrons and form a double bond. In a few cases, atoms can share six electrons and form a triple bond.

The structure that results when atoms are joined together by covalent bonds is called a molecule. The **molecule** is the smallest unit of most compounds. The diagram of a water molecule in **Figure 2–4** shows that each hydrogen atom forms a single covalent bond with the oxygen atom.

TEACHER TO TEACHER

When I introduce chemical bonding, I remind the students that bonding, in general, means holding together. I use the following analogies: a shoe sole is bonded to the upper part of a shoe, a book cover is bonded to the pages within it, and paint is bonded to a surface. For covalent bonding, I use analogies such as the use of the prefix *co-* meaning together or jointly, as in soccer *co-captains* or *co-valedictorians*. For ionic bonding, I find that an analogy can also be used. Just as the opposite (positive and negative) poles of a magnet attract and exhibit holding power, so do oppositely charged ions: The positive sodium ion and the negative chloride ion attract and hold each other together.

—Dale Faughn
Biology Teacher
Caldwell County High School
Princeton, KY

Van der Waals Forces Because of their structures, atoms of different elements do not all have the same ability to attract electrons. Some atoms have a stronger attraction for electrons than do other atoms. Therefore, when the atoms in a covalent bond share electrons, the sharing is not always equal. Even when the sharing is equal, the rapid movement of electrons can create regions on a molecule that have a tiny positive or negative charge.

When molecules are close together, a slight attraction can develop between the oppositely charged regions of nearby molecules. Chemists call such intermolecular forces of attraction **van der Waals forces,** after the scientist who discovered them. Although van der Waals forces are not as strong as ionic bonds or covalent bonds, they can hold molecules together, especially when the molecules are large.

People who keep geckos as pets have already seen van der Waals forces in action. These remarkable little lizards can climb up vertical surfaces, even smooth glass walls, and then hang on by a single toe despite the pull of gravity. How do they do it? No, they do not have some sort of glue on their feet and they don't have suction cups.

A gecko foot like the one shown in **Figure 2–5** is covered by as many as half a million tiny hairlike projections. Each projection is further divided into hundreds of tiny, flat-surfaced fibers. This design allows the gecko's foot to come in contact with an extremely large area of the wall at the molecular level. Van der Waals forces form between molecules on the surface of the gecko's foot and molecules on the surface of the wall. The combined strength of all the van der Waals forces allows the gecko to balance the pull of gravity. When the gecko needs to move its foot, it peels the foot off at an angle and reattaches it at another location on the wall.

▼ **Figure 2–5** Van der Waals forces help geckos to grip smooth, vertical surfaces. **Applying Concepts** *Which product(s) might be developed based on van der Waals forces? Explain.*

2–1 Section Assessment

1. **Key Concept** Describe the structure of an atom.
2. **Key Concept** Why do all isotopes of an element have the same chemical properties? In what way do isotopes of an element differ?
3. **Key Concept** What is a covalent bond? An ionic bond?
4. What is a compound? How are compounds related to molecules?
5. How do van der Waals forces hold molecules together?
6. **Critical Thinking Comparing and Contrasting** How are ionic bonds and van der Waals forces similar? How are they different?

Writing in Science

Writing an Article
Write an article for your school newspaper on forensic science as a career. Assume that you have already interviewed a forensic scientist who works for a law enforcement agency. The article should be about 500 words long. *Hint:* Consider the interests of your readers.

Use Visuals

Figure 2–5 Ask students: **Are van der Waals forces stronger than ionic or covalent bonds?** *(No, they are much weaker.)* **How can such weak forces keep a gecko attached to a smooth vertical surface despite the gecko's weight?** *(The combined strength of all the van der Waals forces that form between molecules on the gecko's hairlike projections and the surface of the wall balance the pull of gravity.)* L2

3 ASSESS

Evaluate Understanding

Call on students at random to define each of the section's Vocabulary terms. Then, ask students to explain the difference between the chemical bond in a water molecule and the chemical bond in table salt.

Reteach

Have students write answers to the three Key Concept questions listed on the first page of the section.

Writing in Science

A good response will include several paragraphs, with an engaging "hook" about a crime scene that sets the stage for a description of what a forensic scientist does. Students should briefly describe some technical details about a career in forensic science as well as list the educational requirements needed to pursue such a career.

If your class subscribes to the iText, use it to review the Key Concepts in Section 2–1.

2–1 Section Assessment

1. Atoms have a nucleus made up of protons and neutrons. Electrons are in constant motion in the space around the nucleus.
2. They have the same number of electrons. They differ in number of neutrons.
3. A covalent bond forms when electrons are shared between atoms. An ionic bond forms when electrons are transferred.
4. A compound is a substance formed by the chemical combination of two or more elements in definite proportions. A molecule is the smallest unit of most compounds.
5. When the sharing of electrons is unequal, a molecule has regions that are charged. An attraction can occur between oppositely charged regions of nearby molecules.
6. In both cases, particles are held together by attractions between opposite charges, but the attractions are stronger between the ions than they are between the molecules.

Answer to . . .

Figure 2–5 *Answers may vary. Students should describe a product with tiny projections that provide a large surface area at the molecular level in order to utilize van der Waals forces to counterbalance the pull of gravity.*

Section 2–2

1 FOCUS

Objectives

2.2.1 ***Explain*** why water molecules are polar.

2.2.2 ***Differentiate*** between solutions and suspensions.

2.2.3 ***Explain*** what acidic solutions and basic solutions are.

Guide for Reading

Vocabulary Preview

Challenge students to divide the Vocabulary terms into three groups of related words. *(Cohesion, adhesion; mixture, solution, solute, solvent, suspension; pH scale, acid, base, buffer)*

Reading Strategy

Figure 2–7 shows that hydrogen bonds form between polar water molecules. Figure 2–9 shows that an ionic compound can dissolve in water because its ions are attracted to the polar water molecules, which surround and separate the ions.

2 INSTRUCT

The Water Molecule

Use Visuals

Figure 2–7 Point out that water is the most abundant compound in most living things, making an understanding of the chemical makeup of water extremely important for understanding how living things function. Then, ask: **What kind of bonds join the atoms in a water molecule?** *(Covalent bonds)* **Are the hydrogen atoms bonded to each other?** *(No, each is bonded to the oxygen atom.)* **Why is the hydrogen end of the molecule positive and the oxygen end negative?** *(In a water molecule, the electrons are shared unequally. At any moment, there is a greater probability of finding the shared electrons near the oxygen atom than near the hydrogen atoms.)* L1 L2

2–2 Properties of Water

Guide for Reading

Key Concepts
- Why are water molecules polar?
- What are acidic solutions? What are basic solutions?

Vocabulary
cohesion
adhesion
mixture
solution
solute
solvent
suspension
pH scale
acid
base
buffer

Reading Strategy: Using Visuals Before you read, preview **Figure 2–7** and **Figure 2–9.** As you read, note how these two figures are related.

After several days in space, one of the first astronauts to travel to the moon looked back longingly at Earth and marveled at its distant beauty. If there are other beings who have seen Earth, he said, they must surely call it "the blue planet." The astronaut was referring to the blue appearance of the water in the oceans, which cover three fourths of Earth's surface. Water is also the single most abundant compound in most living things.

Water is one of the few compounds that is a liquid at the temperatures found over much of Earth's surface. Unlike most substances, water expands as it freezes. Thus, ice is less dense than liquid water, which explains why ice floats on the surface of lakes and rivers. If the ice sank to the bottom, the situation would be disastrous for fish and plant life in regions with cold winters, to say nothing of the sport of ice skating!

The Water Molecule

Like all molecules, a water molecule (H_2O) is neutral. The positive charges on its 10 protons balance out the negative charges on its 10 electrons. However, there is more to the story.

Polarity With 8 protons in its nucleus, an oxygen atom has a much stronger attraction for electrons than does the hydrogen atom with a single proton in its nucleus. Thus, at any moment, there is a greater probability of finding the shared electrons near the oxygen atom than near the hydrogen atom. Because the water molecule has a bent shape, as shown in **Figure 2–6,** the oxygen atom is on one end of the molecule and the hydrogen atoms are on the other. As a result, the oxygen end of the molecule has a slight negative charge and the hydrogen end of the molecule has a slight positive charge.

A molecule in which the charges are unevenly distributed is called a polar molecule because the molecule is like a magnet with poles. **A water molecule is polar because there is an uneven distribution of electrons between the oxygen and hydrogen atoms.** The negative pole is near the oxygen atom and the positive pole is between the hydrogen atoms.

Figure 2–6 **The unequal sharing of electrons causes the water molecule to be polar.** The hydrogen end of the molecule is slightly positive, and the oxygen end is slightly negative.

TIME SAVER

SECTION RESOURCES

Print:
- ***Teaching Resources,*** Lesson Plan 2–2, Adapted Section Summary 2–2, Section Summary 2–2, Worksheets 2–2, Section Review 2–2, Enrichment
- ***Reading and Study Workbook A,*** Section 2–2
- ***Probeware Lab Manual,*** Are foods acidic or basic?

Technology:
- ***iText,*** Section 2–2
- ***Transparencies Plus,*** Section 2–2

Hydrogen Bonds Because of their partial positive and negative charges, polar molecules such as water can attract each other, as shown in **Figure 2–7.** The charges on a polar molecule are written in parentheses, (–) or (+), to show that they are weaker than the charges on ions such as Na^+ and Cl^-. The attraction between the hydrogen atom on one water molecule and the oxygen atom on another water molecule is an example of a hydrogen bond. Hydrogen bonds are not as strong as covalent or ionic bonds, but water's ability to form multiple hydrogen bonds is responsible for many of its special properties.

A single water molecule may be involved in as many as four hydrogen bonds at the same time. The ability of water to form multiple hydrogen bonds is responsible for many of water's properties. **Cohesion** is an attraction between molecules of the same substance. Because of hydrogen bonding, water is extremely cohesive. Water's cohesion causes molecules on the surface of water to be drawn inward, which is why drops of water form beads on a smooth surface. Cohesion also explains why some insects and spiders can walk on a pond's surface, as shown in **Figure 2–8.**

Adhesion is an attraction between molecules of different substances. Have you ever been told to read the volume in a graduated cylinder at eye level? The surface of the water in the graduated cylinder dips slightly in the center because the adhesion between water molecules and glass molecules is stronger than the cohesion between water molecules. Adhesion between water and glass also causes water to rise in a narrow tube against the force of gravity. This effect is called capillary action. Capillary action is one of the forces that draw water out of the roots of a plant and up into its stems and leaves. Cohesion holds the column of water together as it rises.

CHECKPOINT *How are cohesion and adhesion similar? Different?*

Solutions and Suspensions

Water is not always pure—it is often found as part of a mixture. A **mixture** is a material composed of two or more elements or compounds that are physically mixed together but not chemically combined. Salt and pepper stirred together constitute a mixture. So do sugar and sand. Earth's atmosphere is a mixture of gases. Living things are in part composed of mixtures involving water. Two types of mixtures that can be made with water are solutions and suspensions.

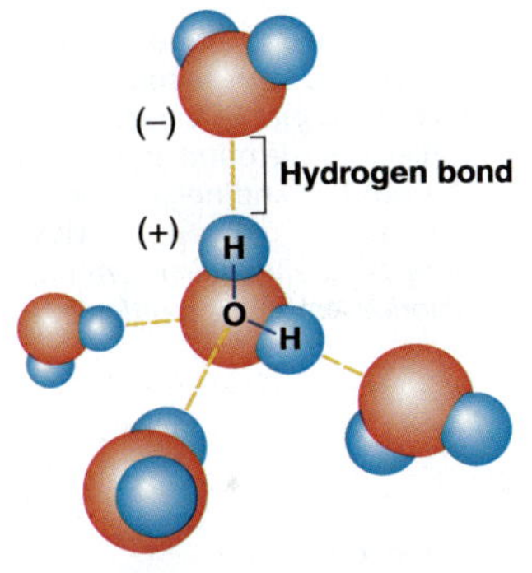

▲ **Figure 2–7** The illustration shows the hydrogen bonds that form between water molecules. **Applying Concepts** *Why are water molecules attracted to one another?*

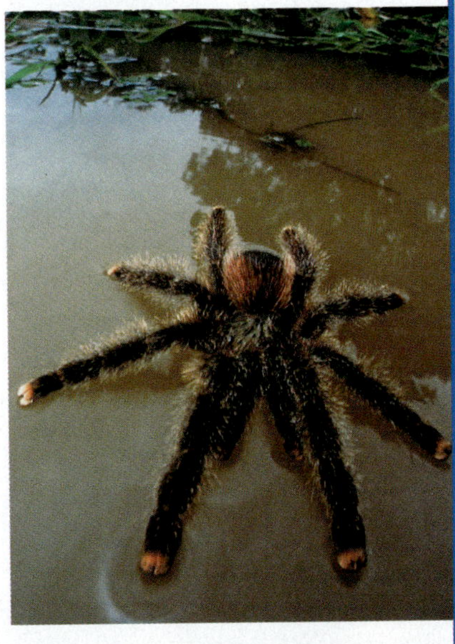

▶ **Figure 2–8** Cohesion is responsible for enabling this tarantula to rest on the water's surface. The strong attraction between water molecules produces a force sometimes called "surface tension," which can support very light objects, including this spider. **Observing** *How does the tarantula's physical structure help it to stay afloat?*

Download a worksheet on properties of water for students to complete, and find additional teacher support from NSTA SciLinks.

Solutions and Suspensions

Demonstration

Show students that when a solution is formed, the solute seems to disappear and yet takes up space. First, pour 225 mL of water into a 250-mL flask. Mark the level of the water with masking tape, and make sure students note this level. Then, stir in 25 g of sugar, which will dissolve almost immediately. Ask: **Is there any evidence that the sugar dissolved into the water?** *(Most students will note that the solution is transparent.)* Have students check to see if the level of the liquid is at the same height as before, as marked by the tape. Use a metric ruler to show that the liquid's level is about 1 cm higher than before, indicating that the sugar is present in the solution. L1 L2

Answers to . . .

CHECKPOINT *Cohesion and adhesion are similar because they are attractions between molecules, but cohesion occurs between molecules of the same substance and adhesion occurs between molecules of different substances.*

Figure 2–7 *Water molecules are polar, meaning they have regions with partial positive and negative charges. This polarity causes the attraction between water molecules.*

Figure 2–8 *Because of its multiple legs, a tarantula's mass is distributed over a large area on the surface of the water, which means that the pull of gravity is limited at any one location on the surface.*

UNIVERSAL ACCESS

Inclusion/Special Needs

Direct students' attention to the summary chemical equation on page 42, and call on volunteers to explain what it means that the reaction can occur in either direction. Make sure students understand what a hydrogen ion and a hydroxide ion are. Review the definition of *ion* in Section 2–1. Once students fully understand the definition of H^+ ions and OH^- ions, draw their attention to the definitions of *acid* and *base* on page 43. L1

English Language Learners

Explain that *cohesion* and *adhesion* are both derived from Latin verbs meaning "to stick." A subtle difference between the terms can be found in their prefixes. The prefix *co-* means "common," and the prefix *ad-* means "toward." Point out that *cohesion* means "an attraction," or "sticking," between molecules that have properties "in common." *Adhesion* means "attraction," or "sticking," from one substance "toward" another. L1 L2

2–2 (continued)

Acids, Bases, and pH

Quick Lab

BIIE 1.a

Objective Students will be able to conclude whether foods are acidic or basic. L2

Skill Focus Analyzing Data, Evaluating

Materials pH paper, solid foods and fruit juices, paper towel, scalpel, dropper pipette, plastic gloves

Time 15 minutes

Advance Prep Obtain a variety of foods for students to test, including orange juice, lemon juice, tomato juice, egg white, meat, fish, fruits, and vegetables. For the test to work, the samples must be moist. If you are using probeware in this activity, use the instructions in the *Probeware Lab Manual.*

Safety Demonstrate safe cutting techniques, such as holding the sample behind the cutting edge when using the scalpel. Make sure students wash their hands with soap and warm water before leaving the lab.

Strategies

- Ask students to write down their predictions.
- Make sure each student constructs a data table to record the pH of each sample. This simple table needs only two columns, headed Sample and pH.
- Review how pH paper acts as an indicator: a base turns red litmus paper blue; an acid turns blue litmus paper red.
- Either supply a pipette for each liquid or have students use one pipette and clean it between samples.

Expected Outcomes Students should discover that most foods are acidic.

Analyze and Conclude

1. Most of the samples were acidic.
2. Students were correct if they predicted that most foods are acidic.

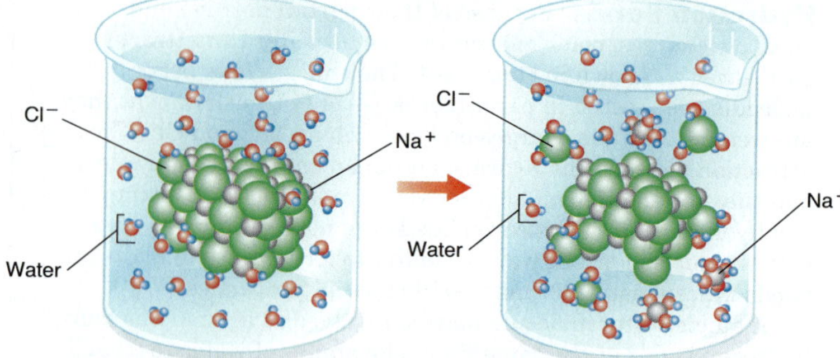

Figure 2–9 When an ionic compound such as sodium chloride is placed in water, water molecules surround and separate the positive and negative ions. **Interpreting Graphics** *What happens to the sodium ions and chloride ions in the solution?*

BIIE 1.a

Quick Lab

Are foods acidic or basic?

Materials pH paper, samples of food, paper towel, scalpel, dropper pipette

Procedure   

1. **Predicting** Predict whether most foods are acidic or basic.
2. 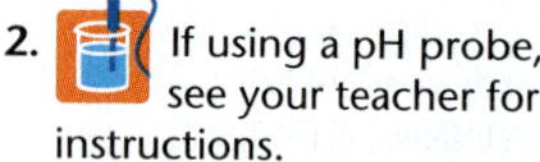 If using a pH probe, see your teacher for instructions.
3. Tear off a 2-inch piece of pH paper for each sample you will test. Place these pieces on a paper towel.
4. Construct a data table in which you will record the name and pH of each food sample.
5. Use a scalpel to cut a piece off each solid. **CAUTION:** *Be careful not to cut yourself. Do not eat the food.* Touch the cut surface of each sample to a square of pH paper. Use a dropper pipette to place a drop of any liquid sample on a square of pH paper. Record the pH of each sample in your data table.

Analyze and Conclude

1. **Analyzing Data** Were most of the samples acidic or basic?
2. **Evaluating** Was your prediction correct?

Solutions If a crystal of table salt is placed in a glass of warm water, sodium and chloride ions on the surface of the crystal are attracted to the polar water molecules. Ions break away from the crystal and are surrounded by water molecules, as illustrated in **Figure 2–9.** The ions gradually become dispersed in the water, forming a type of mixture called a solution. All the components of a **solution** are evenly distributed throughout the solution. In a saltwater solution, table salt is the **solute**—the substance that is dissolved. Water is the **solvent**—the substance in which the solute dissolves. Water's polarity gives it the ability to dissolve both ionic compounds and other polar molecules, such as sugar. Without exaggeration, water is the greatest solvent on Earth.

Suspensions Some materials do not dissolve when placed in water but separate into pieces so small that they do not settle out. The movement of water molecules keeps the small particles suspended. Such mixtures of water and nondissolved material are known as **suspensions.** Some of the most important biological fluids are both solutions and suspensions. The blood that circulates through your body is mostly water, which contains many dissolved compounds. However, blood also contains cells and other undissolved particles that remain in suspension as the blood moves through the body.

Acids, Bases, and pH

A water molecule can react to form ions. This reaction can be summarized by a chemical equation in which double arrows are used to show that the reaction can occur in either direction.

$$H_2O \rightleftharpoons H^+ + OH^-$$

$$\text{water} \rightleftharpoons \text{hydrogen ion} + \text{hydroxide ion}$$

How often does this happen? In pure water, about 1 water molecule in 550 million reacts and forms ions. Because the number of positive hydrogen ions produced is equal to the number of negative hydroxide ions produced, water is neutral.

BIO INSIGHTS

HISTORY OF SCIENCE

pH—a simpler way of expression

In 1909, the Danish chemist Søren Sørensen introduced the expression *pH*, or *p*otential of *H*ydrogen. A pH value represents the concentration of hydrogen ions in solution, an important factor in many chemical reactions. Before Sørensen's suggestion, chemists had to deal with negative logarithms of the concentration of the ions, such as a concentration of 1.0×10^{-4} moles/liter. Today, that would be expressed as a pH of 4, which is about the pH of wine. Pure water has a pH of 7, which means that the concentration of H^+ ions equals the concentration of OH^- ions. That is, there is about one ten-millionth of a mole of H^+ ions per liter of water and the same number of OH^- ions. If an acid is added to the water, the H^+ ions outnumber the OH^- ions, and the pH of the solution decreases. The opposite occurs if a base is added to the water.

The pH scale Chemists devised a measurement system called the **pH scale** to indicate the concentration of H^+ ions in solution. As **Figure 2–10** shows, the pH scale ranges from 0 to 14. At a pH of 7, the concentration of H^+ ions and OH^- ions is equal. Pure water has a pH of 7. Solutions with a pH below 7 are called acidic because they have more H^+ ions than OH^- ions. The lower the pH, the greater the acidity. Solutions with a pH above 7 are called basic because they have more OH^- ions than H^+ ions. The higher the pH, the more basic the solution. Each step on the pH scale represents a factor of 10. For example, a liter of a solution with a pH of 4 has 10 times as many H^+ ions as a liter of a solution with a pH of 5.

Acids Where do all those extra H^+ ions in a low-pH solution come from? They come from acids. An **acid** is any compound that forms H^+ ions in solution. **Acidic solutions contain higher concentrations of H^+ ions than pure water and have pH values below 7.** Strong acids tend to have pH values that range from 1 to 3. The hydrochloric acid produced by the stomach to help digest food is a strong acid.

Bases A **base** is a compound that produces hydroxide ions (OH^- ions) in solution. **Basic, or alkaline, solutions contain lower concentrations of H^+ ions than pure water and have pH values above 7.** Strong bases, such as lye, tend to have pH values ranging from 11 to 14.

Buffers The pH of the fluids within most cells in the human body must generally be kept between 6.5 and 7.5. If the pH is lower or higher, it will affect the chemical reactions that take place within the cells. Thus, controlling pH is important for maintaining homeostasis. One of the ways that the body controls pH is through dissolved compounds called buffers. **Buffers** are weak acids or bases that can react with strong acids or bases to prevent sharp, sudden changes in pH.

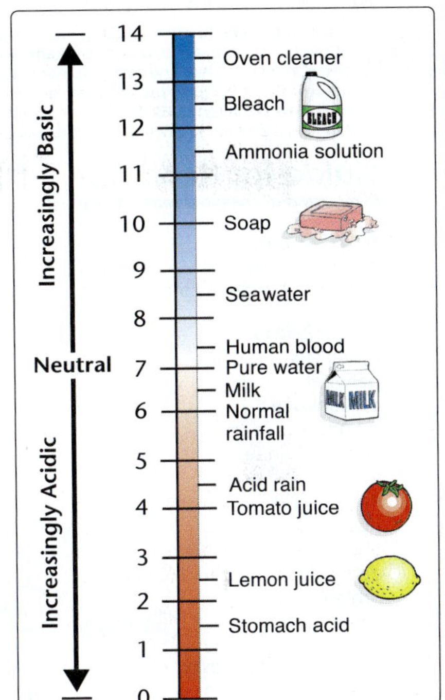

▲ **Figure 2–10** **The concentration of H^+ ions determines whether solutions are acidic or basic.** The most acidic material on this pH scale is stomach acid. The most basic material on this scale is oven cleaner.

2–2 Section Assessment

1. **Key Concept** Use the structure of a water molecule to explain why it is polar.
2. **Key Concept** Compare acidic and basic solutions in terms of their H^+ ion and OH^- ion concentrations.
3. What is the difference between a solution and a suspension?
4. What does pH measure?
5. **Critical Thinking** **Predicting** The strong acid hydrogen fluoride (HF) can be dissolved in pure water. Will the pH of the solution be greater or less than 7?

Thinking Visually

Creating a Concept Map
Draw a concept map on the properties of water. Include the following terms in your concept map: hydrogen bonds, polarity, cohesion, adhesion, capillary action, and solvent.

2–2 Section Assessment

1. The hydrogen atoms form covalent bonds with the oxygen atom. Because of oxygen's greater attraction for electrons, there is an unequal distribution of electrons. The oxygen end of the bent water molecule is negative; the hydrogen end is positive.
2. Per volume, there are more H^+ ions than OH^- ions in an acidic solution and more OH^- ions than H^+ ions in a basic solution.
3. In a solution, all components are evenly distributed. In a suspension, undissolved particles are suspended in the mixture and can settle out over time.
4. The pH scale measures the concentration of H^+ ions in a solution.
5. The pH will be less than 7.0.

Address Misconceptions

Students might mistakenly conclude that all water has a pH of 7. Explain that only pure water has a neutral pH. Normal rainwater, for example, can have a pH as low as 5.6, making it slightly acidic. As rain falls, it reacts with CO_2 in the atmosphere and forms carbonic acid, which lowers the pH of the rain. Acid rain has an even lower pH due to reactions between water and oxides of nitrogen and sulfur, which are pollutants found in air. Ask volunteers to collect rain or melt snow and use pH paper to check on the acidity of local precipitation. L2 L3

3 ASSESS

Evaluate Understanding

Ask students to write a paragraph that explains how the concentration of hydrogen ions determines the acid-base properties of a solution. Students should discuss how water reacts and forms ions, the difference between acids and bases, and the significance of the pH scale.

Reteach

Use Figure 2–9 to review the section's Key Concepts, including the polarity of water molecules, how this polarity gives water the ability to interact with other particles, how sodium and chloride ions become evenly dispersed in water to form a solution, and why some solutions are neutral, some are acidic, and others are basic.

Thinking Visually

Students' concept maps may vary. All should mention that water is polar, that because of hydrogen bonding water is extremely cohesive, that adhesion causes the capillary action of water in a narrow tube, and that water is the greatest solvent on Earth.

If your class subscribes to the iText, use it to review the Key Concepts in Section 2–2.

Answer to . . .

Figure 2–9 *They become evenly dispersed in the water.*

Section 2–3

 8 6.b, 8 6.c, BI 1.h, BI 4.e, *BI 4.f

1 FOCUS

Objective

2.3.1 ***Describe*** the functions of each group of organic compounds.

Guide for Reading

Vocabulary Preview

As students read, have them make a concept map using the section's Vocabulary terms, excluding the words *monomer* and *polymer.* In the initial oval, they should write *Four Groups of Organic Compounds in Living Things.* Then, students should add Vocabulary terms to their concept map as they read the section.

Reading Strategy

Explain that the boldface sentences are the key ideas. In writing their summaries, students should use key words from the key ideas, as well as any highlighted, boldface Vocabulary terms.

2 INSTRUCT

The Chemistry of Carbon

Make Connections

Chemistry Remind students that a stable carbon atom would have eight electrons in its outermost level. Then, ask: **How many electrons would a carbon atom have to gain to fill its outermost level?** *(Four)* Point out that such a transfer is unlikely. Instead, carbon completes its outermost level by sharing electrons and forming four covalent bonds. The atoms that carbon most often forms bonds with, besides other carbon atoms, are hydrogen, oxygen, and nitrogen. Have students look for these elements in the compounds discussed in this section. (Finding a definition of organic chemistry that does not require exceptions is difficult. The definition given in the text excludes methane and compounds derived from methane, but it includes the vast majority of organic compounds.) L2

2–3 Carbon Compounds

8 6.b. Students know that living organisms are made of molecules consisting largely of carbon, hydrogen, nitrogen, oxygen, phosphorus, and sulfur. **8 6.c.** Students know that living organisms have many different kinds of molecules, including small ones, such as water and salt, and very large ones, such as carbohydrates, fats, proteins, and DNA. **BI 1.h.** Students know most macromolecules (polysaccharides, nucleic acids, proteins, lipids) in cells and organisms are synthesized from a small collection of simple precursors. **BI 4.e.** Students know proteins can differ from one another in the number and sequence of amino acids. ***BI 4.f.** Students know why proteins having different amino acid sequences typically have different shapes and chemical properties.

Guide for Reading

Key Concept

- What are the functions of each group of organic compounds?

Vocabulary

monomer
polymer
carbohydrate
monosaccharide
polysaccharide
lipid
nucleic acid
nucleotide
ribonucleic acid (RNA)
deoxyribonucleic acid (DNA)
protein
amino acid

(a) 8 6.b

Reading Strategy: Summarizing As you read, find the key ideas. Write down a few key words from each main idea. Then, use the key words in your summary. Reread your summary, keeping only the most important ideas.

Until the early 1800s, many chemists thought that compounds created by organisms—organic compounds—were distinctly different from compounds in nonliving things. In 1828, a German chemist was able to synthesize the organic compound urea from a mineral called ammonium cyanate. Chemists soon realized that the principles governing the chemistry of nonliving things could be applied to living things. Scientists still use the term *organic chemistry,* but now it describes something a little different. Today, organic chemistry is the study of all compounds that contain bonds between carbon atoms.

The Chemistry of Carbon

CA (a) Is carbon so interesting that a whole branch of chemistry should be set aside just to study carbon compounds? It is indeed, for two reasons. First, carbon atoms have four valence electrons. Each electron can join with an electron from another atom to form a strong covalent bond. Carbon can bond with many elements, including hydrogen, oxygen, phosphorus, sulfur, and nitrogen. In fact, living organisms are made up of molecules that consist of carbon and these other elements.

Even more important, a carbon atom can bond to other carbon atoms, which gives carbon the ability to form chains that are almost unlimited in length. These carbon-carbon bonds can be single, double, or triple covalent bonds. Chains of carbon atoms can even close upon themselves to form rings, as shown in **Figure 2–11.** Carbon has the ability to form millions of different large and complex structures. No other element even comes close to matching carbon's versatility.

▼ **Figure 2–11** Carbon can form single, double, or triple bonds with other carbon atoms. Each line between atoms in a molecular drawing represents one covalent bond. **Observing** *How many covalent bonds are there between the carbon atoms in acetylene?*

Methane

Acetylene

Butadiene

Benzene

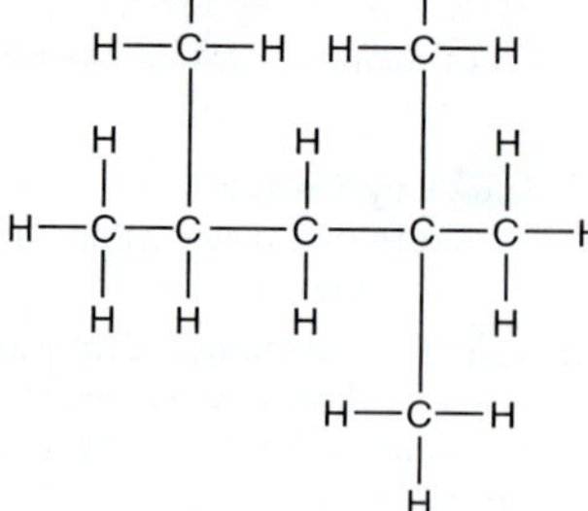

Isooctane

SECTION RESOURCES

Print:

- ***Laboratory Manual A,*** Chapter 2 Lab
- ***Laboratory Manual B,*** Chapter 2 Lab
- ***Teaching Resources,*** Lesson Plan 2–3, Adapted Section Summary 2–3, Adapted Worksheets 2–3, Section Summary 2–3, Worksheets 2–3, Section Review 2–3
- ***Reading and Study Workbook A,*** Section 2–3
- ***Adapted Reading and Study Workbook B,*** Section 2–3

Technology:

- ***iText,*** Section 2–3
- ***Transparencies Plus,*** Section 2–3
- ***Lab Simulations CD-ROM,*** Properties of Biomolecules

Macromolecules

Many of the molecules in living cells are so large that they are known as macromolecules, which means "giant molecules." Macromolecules are made from thousands or even hundreds of thousands of smaller molecules.

Macromolecules are formed by a process known as polymerization (pah-lih-mur-ih-ZAY-shun), in which large compounds are built by joining smaller ones together. The smaller units, or **monomers,** join together to form **polymers.** The monomers in a polymer may be identical, like the links on a metal watch band; or the monomers may be different, like the beads in a multicolored necklace. **Figure 2–12** illustrates the formation of a polymer from more than one type of monomer.

CA

a

It would be difficult to study the millions of organic compounds if they were not classified into groups. **Four groups of organic compounds found in living things are carbohydrates, lipids, nucleic acids, and proteins.** Sometimes these organic compounds are referred to as biomolecules. As you read about these molecules, compare their structures and functions.

CHECKPOINT *What is polymerization?*

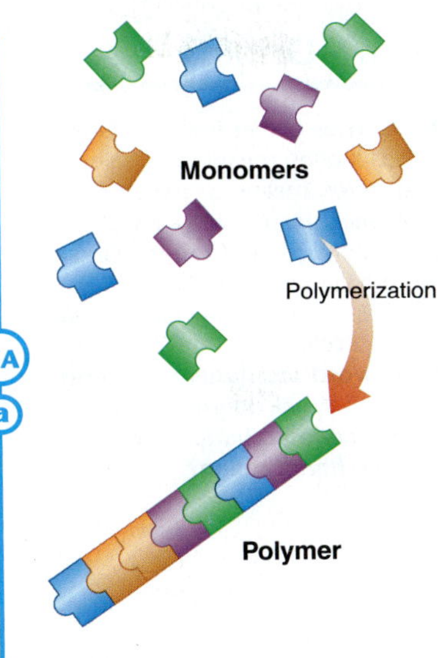

▲ **Figure 2–12** When small molecules called monomers join together, they form polymers, or large molecules. **Using Analogies** *How are monomers similar to links in a chain?*

Carbohydrates

Carbohydrates are compounds made up of carbon, hydrogen, and oxygen atoms, usually in a ratio of 1 : 2 : 1. **Living things use carbohydrates as their main source of energy. Plants and some animals also use carbohydrates for structural purposes.** The breakdown of sugars, such as glucose, supplies immediate energy for all cell activities. Living things store extra sugar as complex carbohydrates known as starches. As shown in **Figure 2–13**, the monomers in starch polymers are sugar molecules.

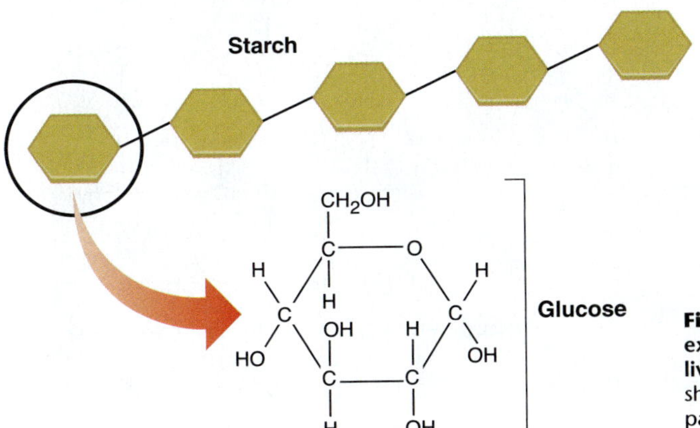

Figure 2–13 **Starches and sugars are examples of carbohydrates that are used by living things as a source of energy.** The chef shown here is drying pasta, which is made principally of starch. Starches form when sugars join together in a long chain.

Macromolecules

Use Visuals

Figure 2–12 After you introduce the four types of macromolecules, have students revisit Figure 2–12. Ask: **Which type of macromolecule could this drawing represent?** *(Students might say that the monomers represent different amino acids or nucleotides or sugars.)* Explain that plant starch, glycogen, and cellulose contain only glucose monomers. The drawing cannot represent a lipid because lipids are not polymers. L2

Build Science Skills

Using Tables and Graphs Have students make a compare/contrast table entitled "Four Groups of Organic Compounds." Column heads should read *Group Name, Chemical Composition, Examples,* and *Function in Living Things.* As students read the rest of the section, they should use the table to organize the information they learn about the groups of macromolecules. L1 L2

Carbohydrates

Build Science Skills

Observing Divide the class in pairs, and give each pair Lugol's solution, a dropper, test tubes, soda crackers, and several other foods, including a potato section, white bread, oatmeal, and granulated sugar. Explain that Lugol's solution is an indicator of starch—if the solution turns dark blue or black, starch is present. Then, have pairs test the foods for the presence of starch. For example, they should place pieces of soda crackers in a test tube, add 5 drops of Lugol's solution, and observe whether it darkens. Students should observe that all the foods listed contain starch except granulated sugar. L2

UNIVERSAL ACCESS

Less Proficient Readers

Have students make a concept map of the four groups of organic molecules found in living things—carbohydrates, lipids, nucleic acids, and proteins. For each group, they should attach bubbles for structure, functions, and examples. L1 L2

English Language Learners

Model how to divide Vocabulary words into parts—prefix, root word, and suffix. Explain that learning the parts of words will help them analyze the meanings of long and difficult terms, such as *deoxyribonucleic acid.* L1

Advanced Learners

Ask students to use a high-school or college chemistry text to research how chemists communicate information about compounds, including use of molecular formulas and various structural formulas. Have students collaborate on a presentation to the class about formulas. L3

Answers to . . .

CHECKPOINT *The process in which monomers are joined together to form larger molecules called polymers*

Figure 2–11 *Three*

Figure 2–12 *Like links in a chain, monomers are either identical or closely related units that connect together to form a larger structure.*

2–3 (continued)

Word Origins

The term *monosaccharide* means "single sugar"; the term *polysaccharide* means "many sugars." L2

Build Science Skills

Applying Concepts Display photos of various foods that contain high amounts of carbohydrates, including milk, potatoes, and fruits. Explain that milk contains the carbohydrates lactose and galactose, fruits contain fructose, and potatoes contain starch. Ask: **What is the source of these carbohydrates?** *(Energy from sunlight)* **What function do these carbohydrates serve in living things?** *(They store energy.)* L1 L2

Lipids

Use Visuals

Figure 2–14 After students study the structural formula of a lipid, ask: **What are the components of a lipid?** *(Glycerol and fatty acids)* **Would you describe the lipid shown in the structural formula as saturated, unsaturated, or polyunsaturated?** *(It is unsaturated because there is a single double bond in each fatty acid chain. Fatty acids with only one double bond are called monounsaturated.)* Then, direct students' attention to the photo, and ask: **Which is more likely to be polyunsaturated, a solid fat or a liquid oil?** *(Oils usually contain more unsaturated fatty acids.)* L2

Use Community Resources

Invite a dietician to address the class about why some fats are an important part of a healthy diet and why foods with a high fat content should be avoided. Ask the speaker to explain which fats are harmful and which aren't and which common foods have a high content of harmful fats. Make sure students ask about saturated, unsaturated, and polyunsaturated fats in foods. L2

Word Origins

Monomer comes from the Greek words *monos*, meaning "single," and *meros*, meaning "part." *Monomer* means "single part." The prefix *poly-* comes from the Greek word *polus*, meaning "many," so *polymer* means "many parts." **The word *saccharide* comes from the Latin word *saccharum*, meaning "sugar." What do you think the terms *monosaccharide* and *polysaccharide* mean?**

Single sugar molecules are also called **monosaccharides** (mahn-oh-SAK-uh-rydz). Besides glucose, monosaccharides include galactose, which is a component of milk, and fructose, which is found in many fruits.

The large macromolecules formed from monosaccharides are known as **polysaccharides.** Many animals store excess sugar in a polysaccharide called glycogen, or animal starch. When the level of glucose in your blood runs low, glycogen is released from your liver. The glycogen stored in your muscles supplies the energy for muscle contraction and, thus, for movement.

Plants use a slightly different polysaccharide, called plant starch, to store excess sugar. Plants also make another important polysaccharide called cellulose. Tough, flexible cellulose fibers give plants much of their strength and rigidity. Cellulose is the major component of both wood and paper, so you are actually looking at cellulose as you read these words!

Lipids

Lipids are a large and varied group of biological molecules that are generally not soluble in water. **Lipids** are made mostly from carbon and hydrogen atoms. The common categories of lipids are fats, oils, and waxes. **Lipids can be used to store energy. Some lipids are important parts of biological membranes and waterproof coverings.** Steroids are lipids as well. Many steroids serve as chemical messengers.

Many lipids are formed when a glycerol molecule combines with compounds called fatty acids, as shown in **Figure 2–14.** If each carbon atom in a lipid's fatty acid chains is joined to another carbon atom by a single bond, the lipid is said to be saturated. The term *saturated* is used because the fatty acids contain the maximum possible number of hydrogen atoms.

Figure 2–14 Lipids are used to store energy. Lipid molecules are made up of fatty acids and glycerol. Liquid lipids, such as olive oil, contain mainly unsaturated fatty acids.

Lipid

Glycerol

Fatty acids

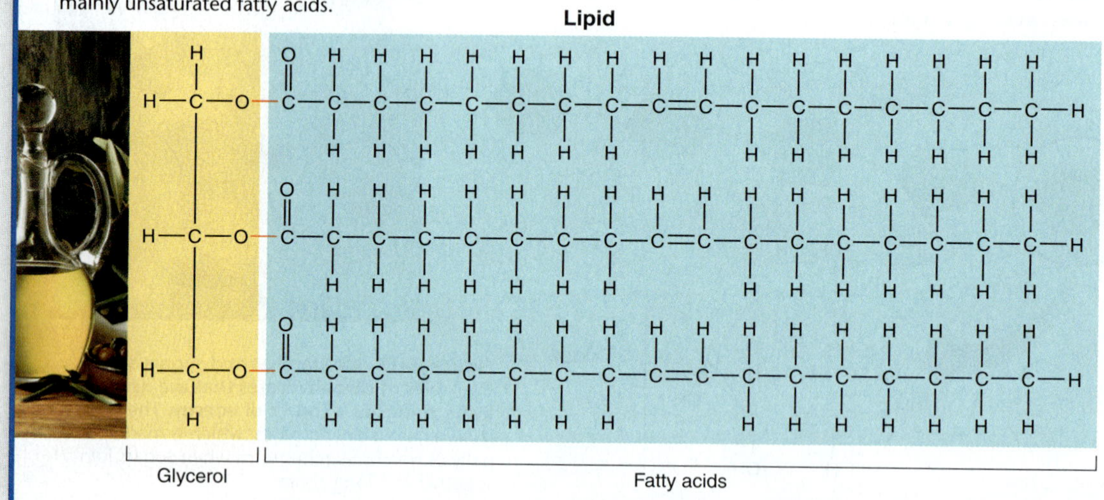

BIO INSIGHTS — FACTS AND FIGURES

Mono-, di-, and polysaccharides

The names of carbohydrates usually end in the suffix *-ose.* This includes glucose, which is the most common monosaccharide. Its formula is $C_6H_{12}O_6$, which conforms to the general formula of all carbohydrates: $C_x(H_2O)_x$. This general formula shows the derivation of *carbohydrate,* which means "carbon hydrate." Glucose is formed when a carbon compound, carbon dioxide, reacts with water. Monosaccharides, such as glucose, are important nutrients for cells, as evidenced by the central role glucose has in cellular respiration. Fructose and galactose are other monosaccharides. When a covalent bond links two monosaccharides, the result is called a disaccharide. An example is lactose, a sugar in milk. Polysaccharides, which include glycogen, starch, and cellulose—the most abundant organic chemical on Earth—can contain thousands of monosaccharides linked together.

If there is at least one carbon-carbon double bond in a fatty acid, the fatty acid is said to be unsaturated. Lipids whose fatty acids contain more than one double bond are said to be polyunsaturated. If the terms *saturated* and *polyunsaturated* seem familiar, you have probably seen them on food package labels. Lipids such as olive oil, which contains unsaturated fatty acids, tend to be liquid at room temperature. Cooking oils, such as corn oil, sesame oil, canola oil, and peanut oil, contain polyunsaturated lipids.

Nucleic Acids

Nucleic acids are macromolecules containing hydrogen, oxygen, nitrogen, carbon, and phosphorus. Nucleic acids are polymers assembled from individual monomers known as nucleotides. **Nucleotides** consist of three parts: a 5-carbon sugar, a phosphate group, and a nitrogenous base, as shown in **Figure 2–15.** Individual nucleotides can be joined by covalent bonds to form a polynucleotide, or nucleic acid.

Nucleic acids store and transmit hereditary, or genetic, information. There are two kinds of nucleic acids: **ribonucleic acid (RNA)** and **deoxyribonucleic acid (DNA).** As their names indicate, RNA contains the sugar ribose and DNA contains the sugar deoxyribose.

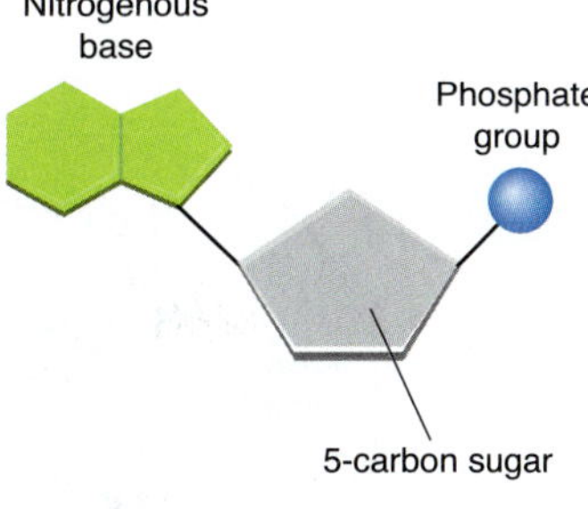

▲ **Figure 2–15 Nucleic acids store and transmit genetic information.** The monomers that make up a nucleic acid are nucleotides. Each nucleotide has a 5-carbon sugar, a phosphate group, and a nitrogenous base.

CHECKPOINT *What are the three parts of a nucleotide?*

Proteins

Proteins are macromolecules that contain nitrogen as well as carbon, hydrogen, and oxygen. Proteins are polymers of molecules called **amino acids.** Amino acids are compounds with an amino group ($-NH_2$) on one end and a carboxyl group ($-COOH$) on the other end.

Figure 2–16 shows one reason why proteins are among the most diverse macromolecules. More than 20 different amino acids are found in nature. All amino acids are identical in the regions where they may be joined together by covalent bonds. This uniformity allows any amino acid to be joined to any other amino acid—by bonding an amino group to a carboxyl group.

▶ **Figure 2–16** Amino acids are the monomers of proteins. All amino acids have an amino group at one end and a carboxyl group at the other end. What distinguishes one amino acid from another is the R-group section of the molecule. **Comparing and Contrasting** *How are proteins and carbohydrates similar? How are they different?*

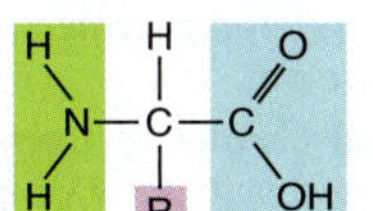
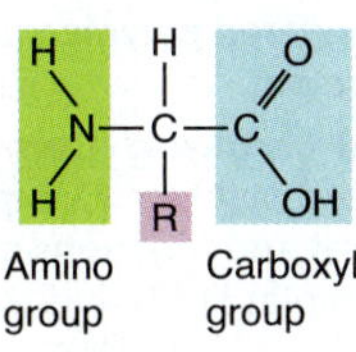
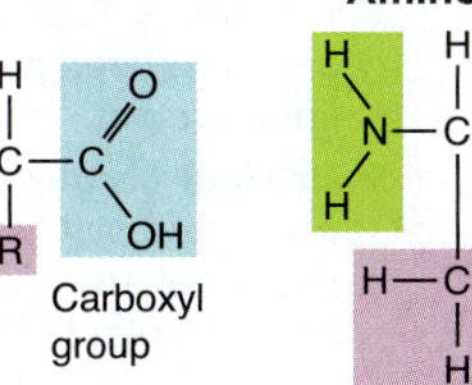
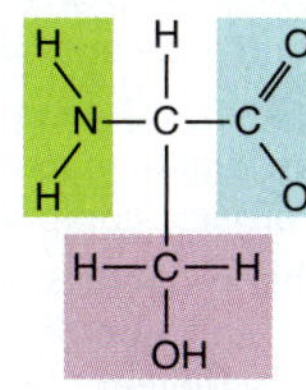

Nucleic Acids

Build Science Skills

Using Analogies To help students understand nucleic acids, ask: **What are the three basic parts of a nucleotide?** *(A 5-carbon sugar, a phosphate group, and a nitrogenous base)* Explain that each nucleotide in DNA contains one of four nitrogenous bases—adenine, guanine, cytosine, and thymine. The sequence of the nucleotides in a DNA molecule determines the information that it contains. Point out that the English alphabet contains only 26 letters, but different combinations of letters make virtually limitless numbers of words. Likewise, different combinations of the four nucleotides make endless numbers of different DNA molecules. L2

Proteins

Use Visuals

Figure 2–16 Ask students: **Which parts of an amino acid are the same in every amino acid?** *(The amino group, $-NH_2$, and the carboxyl group, $-COOH$)* Make sure students understand what composes the R group in alanine and serine. Ask: **In what ways are R groups different?** *(Some are acidic, some are basic, some are polar, and some are nonpolar.)* Stress that the joining of one amino acid to another, amino group to carboxyl group, creates a product that still has an amino group on one end and a carboxyl group on the other. L2

BIO INSIGHTS — FACTS AND FIGURES

Proteins serve many functions

The word *protein* is derived from a Greek word meaning "first or primary," and this class of molecules was so named because proteins are of "prime importance" in living things. They are so important because they have so many functions. As enzymes, they catalyze biological chemical reactions. Other proteins provide structural support, such as the protein collagen in bones and muscles. Proteins are important parts of cell membranes, where they play a role in reaction cycles such as the citric acid cycle. Proteins such as insulin function as hormones, regulating body metabolism. Actin and myosin are the proteins responsible for muscle contraction. The antibodies that protect against foreign invaders are proteins. Some proteins function as nutrient-storage molecules. Proteins are even used as toxins by some microorganisms.

Answers to . . .

CHECKPOINT *A 5-carbon sugar, a phosphate group, and a nitrogenous base*

Figure 2–16 *Carbohydrates and proteins are both polymers. The monomers in carbohydrates are monosaccharides. The monomers in proteins are amino acids.*

2–3 (continued)

Make Connections

Health Science Have students list foods that contain high amounts of protein, such as meats, fish, dairy products, and beans. Ask: **Why is it important to have an adequate amount of protein for a healthy diet?** *(Proteins perform numerous functions.)* **How can one group of compounds have so many different functions?** *(The diversity of amino acids and four levels of organization account for proteins with properties suited to a myriad of biological tasks.)* L2

3 ASSESS

Evaluate Understanding

Ask students to use their understanding of monomers, polymers, and polymerization to write an explanation of how polysaccharides, nucleic acids, and proteins are formed. They should use monosaccharides, nucleotides, and amino acids to explain polymerization.

Reteach

Ask a volunteer to explain what macromolecules are. Ask another student to list the four main groups of organic compounds found in living things. Then, call on students to explain the functions of each group of organic compounds.

Focus on the BIG Idea

Each level in a system is made up of smaller parts and is part of a larger system. For example, a nucleotide is made up of a sugar, a phosphate group, and a nitrogenous base. A nucleotide is part of a nucleic acid molecule. The nucleic acid molecule is larger and more complex than the nucleotide, which is larger and more complex than its components.

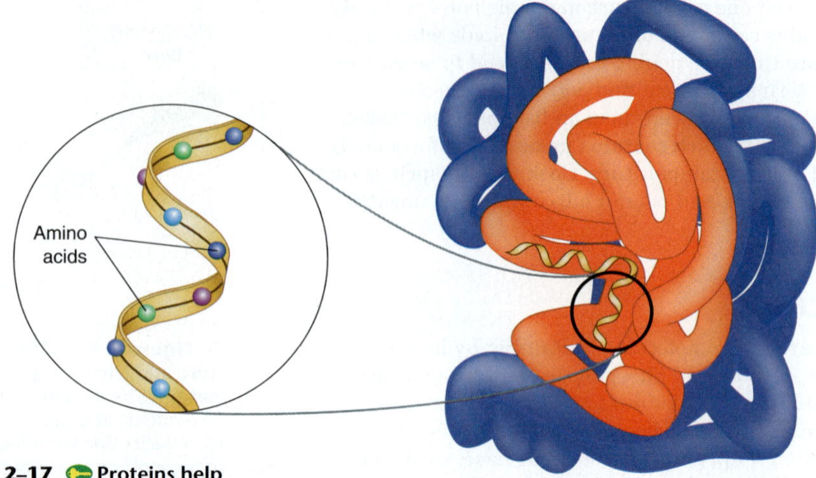

▲ **Figure 2–17 Proteins help to carry out chemical reactions, transport small molecules in and out of cells, and fight diseases.** Proteins are made up of chains of amino acids folded into complex structures.

The portion of each amino acid that is different is a side chain called an R-group. Some R-groups are acidic and some are basic. Some are polar and some are nonpolar. Some contain carbon rings. The instructions for arranging amino acids into many different proteins are stored in DNA. Each protein has a specific role. **Some proteins control the rate of reactions and regulate cell processes. Some are used to form bones and muscles. Others transport substances into or out of cells or help to fight disease.**

Proteins can have up to four levels of organization. The first level is the sequence of amino acids in a protein chain. Second, the amino acids within a chain can be twisted or folded. Third, the chain itself is folded. If a protein has more than one chain, each chain has a specific arrangement in space as shown by the red and blue structures in **Figure 2–17.** Van der Waals forces and hydrogen bonds help maintain a protein's shape. In the next section, you will learn why a protein's shape is so important.

2–3 Section Assessment

1. **Key Concept** Name four groups of organic compounds found in living things.
2. **Key Concept** Describe at least one function of each group of organic compounds.
3. What properties of carbon explain carbon's ability to form many different macromolecules?
4. **Critical Thinking Applying Concepts** Explain why proteins are considered polymers but lipids are not.
5. **Critical Thinking Comparing and Contrasting** Compare the structures and functions of the biomolecules lipids and starches.

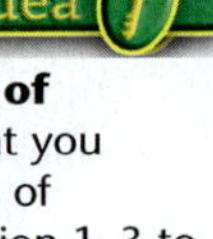

Focus on the BIG Idea

Science as a Way of Knowing Use what you learned about levels of organization in Section 1–3 to discuss the levels of organization in macromolecules. Begin your discussion with the smallest structure.

2–3 Section Assessment

1. Carbohydrates, lipids, nucleic acids, and proteins
2. A typical response might mention that living things use carbohydrates as their main source of energy, fats can be used to store energy, nucleic acids transmit hereditary information, and proteins form tissues.
3. Each carbon atom can form four covalent bonds, and carbon atoms can bond with other carbon atoms.
4. Proteins are made up of amino acid monomers joined in long chains. Although fatty acid chains may be mistaken for monomers, only three fatty acids can attach to a glycerol molecule.
5. Lipids are made mostly from carbon and hydrogen atoms; starch is a carbohydrate made up of carbon, hydrogen, and oxygen atoms. Both can be used to store energy.

2–4 Chemical Reactions and Enzymes

BI 1.b. Students know enzymes are proteins that catalyze biochemical reactions without altering the reaction equilibrium and the activities of enzymes depend on the temperature, ionic conditions, and the pH of the surroundings.

Living things, as you have seen, are made up of chemical compounds—some simple and some complex. But chemistry isn't just what life is made of—chemistry is also what life does. Everything that happens in an organism—its growth, its interaction with the environment, its reproduction, and even its movement—is based on chemical reactions.

Guide for Reading

Key Concepts
- What happens to chemical bonds during chemical reactions?
- How do energy changes affect whether a chemical reaction will occur?
- Why are enzymes important to living things?

Vocabulary
chemical reaction
reactant
product
activation energy
catalyst
enzyme
substrate

Reading Strategy: Building Vocabulary After you read, write a phrase or sentence in your own words to define or describe each highlighted, boldface term.

Chemical Reactions

A **chemical reaction** is a process that changes, or transforms, one set of chemicals into another. An important scientific principle is that mass and energy are conserved during chemical transformations. This is also true for chemical reactions that occur in living organisms. Some chemical reactions occur slowly, such as the combination of iron and oxygen to form an iron oxide called rust, shown in **Figure 2–18.** Other reactions occur quickly. The elements or compounds that enter into a chemical reaction are known as **reactants.** The elements or compounds produced by a chemical reaction are known as **products.** **Chemical reactions always involve changes in the chemical bonds that join atoms in compounds.**

One example of an important chemical reaction that occurs in your body involves carbon dioxide. Your cells constantly produce carbon dioxide as a normal part of their activity. This carbon dioxide is carried to your lungs through the bloodstream, and then is eliminated as you exhale. However, carbon dioxide is not very soluble in water. The bloodstream could not possibly dissolve enough carbon dioxide to carry it away from your tissues were it not for a chemical reaction. As it enters the blood, carbon dioxide reacts with water to produce a highly soluble compound called carbonic acid, H_2CO_3.

$$CO_2 + H_2O \longrightarrow H_2CO_3$$

The reaction shown above enables the bloodstream to carry carbon dioxide to the lungs. In the lungs, the reaction is reversed.

$$H_2CO_3 \longrightarrow CO_2 + H_2O$$

This reverse reaction produces carbon dioxide gas, which is released as you exhale.

▶ **Figure 2–18** **Chemical reactions always involve changes in chemical bonds.** The iron in these chain links gradually combined with oxygen to produce a compound known as rust.

SECTION RESOURCES

Print:
- ***Teaching Resources,*** Lesson Plan 2–4, Adapted Section Summary 2–4, Adapted Worksheets 2–4, Section Summary 2–4, Worksheets 2–4, Section Review 2–4
- ***Reading and Study Workbook A,*** Section 2–4
- ***Adapted Reading and Study Workbook B,*** Section 2–4
- ***Probeware Lab Manual,*** Investigating the Effect of Temperature on Enzyme Activity
- ***Lab Worksheets,*** Chapter 2 Design an Experiment

Technology:
- ***iText,*** Section 2–4
- ***Animated Biological Concepts DVD,*** 4 Enzymatic Reactions
- ***Transparencies Plus,*** Section 2–4
- ***Virtual Labs CD-ROM,*** Catalase Action in Living Tissue

Section 2–4

BI 1.b

1 FOCUS

Objectives

2.4.1 ***Explain*** how chemical reactions affect chemical bonds in compounds.

2.4.2 ***Describe*** how energy changes affect how easily a chemical reaction will occur.

2.4.3 ***Explain*** why enzymes are important to living things.

Guide for Reading

Vocabulary Preview

Before students read the section, call on volunteers to pronounce each word in the Vocabulary list. Correct any mispronunciations.

Reading Strategy

Students should focus their attention on the section's Vocabulary terms, not the words in the boldface Key Concepts. Before writing a definition using their own words, students might use the glossary at the back of their books. Explain that often words are defined in context within a section. The glossary sometimes provides a more general definition.

2 INSTRUCT

Chemical Reactions

Demonstration

To show students what a chemical reaction looks like, use baking soda and vinegar. In separate beakers, mix 5 mL of baking soda with 120 mL of water and 5 mL of vinegar with 120 mL of water. Have students observe that nothing extraordinary happens when these substances are mixed. Then, in a third beaker, mix 5 mL of baking soda with 5 mL of vinegar. Students should observe that this third mixture produces foaming and fizzling, indicating that a gas is produced in a chemical reaction. L1 L2

2–4 (continued)

Energy in Reactions

Use Visuals

Figure 2–19 Have students compare the graphs representing the two types of chemical reactions. Then, ask: **How would you compare the energy of the products and reactants in the two types of reactions?** *(In an energy-absorbing reaction, the products have more energy than the reactants. In an energy-releasing reaction, the products have less energy than the reactants.)* **Which type of reaction is more likely to be spontaneous?** *(An energy-releasing reaction)* L2

For: Enzyme Action activity
Visit: PHSchool.com
Web Code: cbe-1024
Students can interact with the art online.

Demonstration

Help students understand that enzymes lower the activation energy needed to get a reaction going by using the analogy of a book on the edge of a table. Show students that the book will not fall off the table without a push, which is the activation energy in this case. Then, place some kind of wedge under one side of the book, in such a way that the book is slanted off the edge of the table. Now, the push, or activation energy, needed to make the book fall is much less. Likewise, an enzyme lowers the activation energy needed to begin a chemical reaction. L1 L2

For: Enzyme Action activity
Visit: PHSchool.com
Web Code: cbp-1024

▼ **Figure 2–19** **Chemical reactions that release energy often occur spontaneously. Chemical reactions that absorb energy will occur only with a source of energy.** The peak of each graph represents the energy needed for the reaction to go forward. The difference between this required energy and the energy of the reactants is the activation energy.

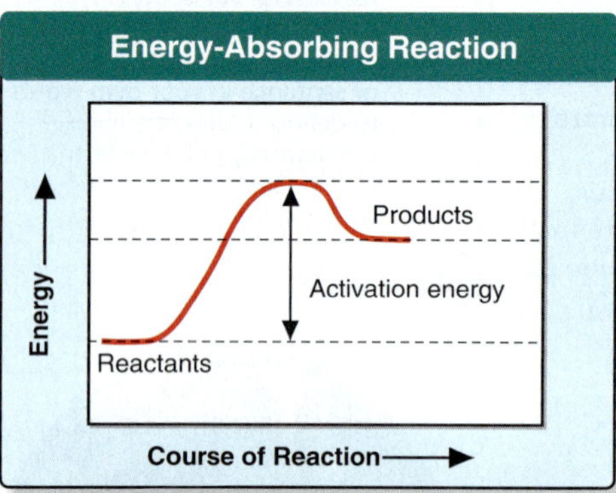

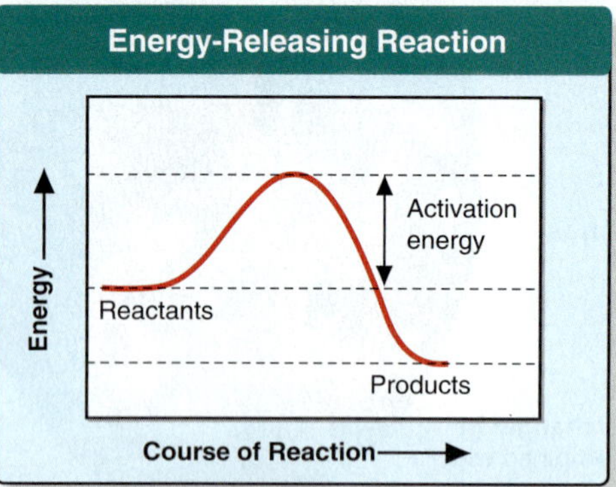

Energy in Reactions

Energy is released or absorbed whenever chemical bonds form or are broken. Because chemical reactions involve breaking and forming bonds, they involve changes in energy.

Energy Changes Some chemical reactions release energy, and other reactions absorb energy. Energy changes are one of the most important factors in determining whether a chemical reaction will occur. **Chemical reactions that release energy often occur spontaneously. Chemical reactions that absorb energy will not occur without a source of energy.** An example of an energy-releasing reaction is hydrogen gas burning, or reacting, with oxygen to produce water vapor.

$$2H_2 + O_2 \longrightarrow 2H_2O$$

The energy is released in the form of heat, and sometimes—when hydrogen gas explodes—light and sound.

The reverse reaction, in which water is changed into hydrogen and oxygen gas, absorbs so much energy that it generally doesn't occur by itself. In fact, the only practical way to reverse the reaction is to pass an electrical current through water to decompose water into hydrogen gas and oxygen gas. Thus, in one direction the reaction produces energy, and in the other direction the reaction requires energy.

In order to stay alive, organisms need to carry out reactions that require energy. Because matter and energy are conserved in chemical reactions, every organism must have a source of energy to carry out chemical reactions. Plants get that energy by trapping and storing the energy from sunlight in energy-rich compounds. Animals get their energy when they consume plants or other animals. Humans release the energy needed to grow tall, to breathe, to think, and even to dream through the chemical reactions that occur when humans metabolize, or break down, digested food.

Activation Energy Even chemical reactions that release energy do not always occur spontaneously. That's a good thing because if they did, the pages of this book might burst into flames. The cellulose in paper burns in the presence of oxygen and releases heat and light. However, the cellulose will burn only if you light it with a match, which supplies enough energy to get the reaction started. Chemists call the energy that is needed to get a reaction started the **activation energy.** As **Figure 2–19** shows, activation energy is a factor in whether the overall chemical reaction releases energy or absorbs energy.

CHECKPOINT *What is activation energy?*

UNIVERSAL ACCESS

Less Proficient Readers
Direct students' attention to the cycle diagram in Figure 2–21 on page 52. Go step-by-step around the diagram, calling on volunteers to explain what is being depicted in each step. As students mention Vocabulary terms, such as *enzyme* and *substrate*, have other students read the definitions in the text. After this oral lesson, ask students to make their own cycle diagrams of enzyme action, using their own words to describe what is illustrated in the figure. L1 L2

Advanced Learners
Students will learn about the enzyme amylase in Chapter 38 when they study the digestive system. Ask students who need an extra challenge to anticipate this study by researching the enzyme in saliva at this time and then presenting information about the action of this chemical to the class. Encourage students to use visual aids in their presentation. Students might want to prepare a demonstration of saliva's effect on a soda cracker. L3

Analyzing Data

How Does pH Affect an Enzyme?

Catalase is an enzyme that helps decompose the toxic hydrogen peroxide that is produced during normal cell activities. The products of this reaction are water and oxygen gas. The pressure of the oxygen gas in a closed container increases as oxygen is produced. Any increase in the rate of the reaction will cause an increase in the pressure of the oxygen.

The purple line on the graph represents the normal rate of the reaction in a water solution of hydrogen peroxide and catalase. The red line represents the rate of reaction when an acid is added to the solution. The blue line represents the rate of reaction when a base is added to the solution.

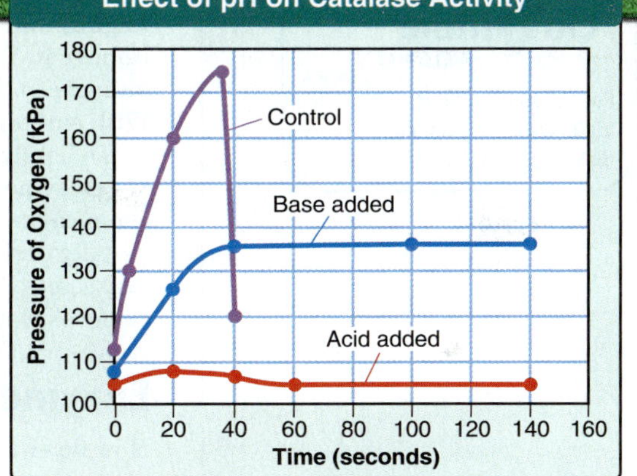

1. **Applying Concepts** What variable is plotted on the *x*-axis? What variable is plotted on the *y*-axis?
2. **Interpreting Graphics** How did the rate of reaction change over time in the control reaction?
3. **Inferring** Suggest an explanation for the change in the control reaction at about 40 seconds.
4. **Drawing Conclusions** What effect do acids and bases have on the enzyme catalase?
5. **Drawing Conclusions** Would it be valid to conclude that if a base were added, the rate of the reaction would slow down? Explain.
6. **Going Further** Predict what would happen if vinegar were added to a water solution of hydrogen peroxide and catalase.

Enzymes

Some chemical reactions that make life possible are too slow or have activation energies that are too high to make them practical for living tissue. These chemical reactions are made possible by a process that would make any chemist proud—cells make catalysts. A **catalyst** is a substance that speeds up the rate of a chemical reaction. Catalysts work by lowering a reaction's activation energy.

Enzymes are proteins that act as biological catalysts. **Enzymes speed up chemical reactions that take place in cells.** Like other catalysts, enzymes act by lowering the activation energies, as illustrated by the graph in **Figure 2–20.** Lowering the activation energy has a dramatic effect on how quickly the reaction is completed. How big an effect does it have? Consider the reaction in which carbon dioxide combines with water to produce carbonic acid.

$$CO_2 + H_2O \longrightarrow H_2CO_3$$

BI 1.b, 6IIE 7.c, 8IIE 9.c

▼ **Figure 2–20** **Enzymes speed up chemical reactions that take place in cells.** Notice how the addition of an enzyme lowers the activation energy in this reaction. This action speeds up the reaction.

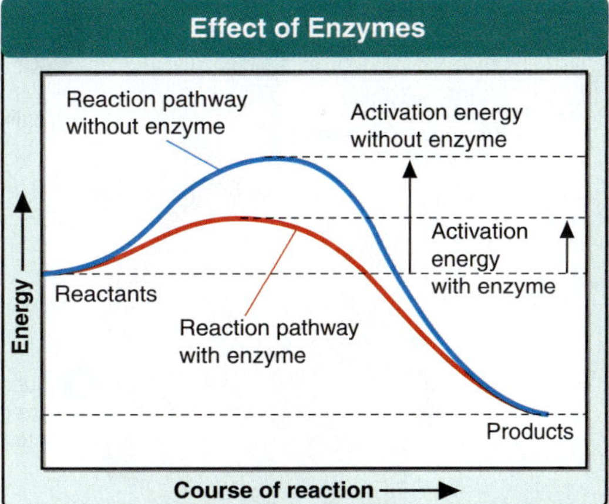

Analyzing Data

BI 1.b, 6IIE 7.c, 8IIE 9.c

Write the equation for the reaction on the chalkboard:

$2H_2O_2 \rightarrow O_2 + 2H_2O$

Explain that the pressure of oxygen gas is a measure of the amount of oxygen produced. The slope of the graphs is an indication of the rates of the reactions. L2 L3

Answers

1. Time is plotted on the *x*-axis and pressure of oxygen on the *y*-axis.
2. The rate was very rapid at first and then dropped off dramatically after about 40 seconds.
3. Students may suggest that the hydrogen peroxide was used up or that the reaction is reversible.
4. A base inhibits the enzyme so that it is less effective. An acid may deactivate the enzyme so that the reaction cannot take place.
5. It would be valid to draw that conclusion, because the blue line shows that the pressure of oxygen evened out when the base was added. That effect suggests that the rate of reaction slowed down, because any increase in the rate would cause an increase in the pressure of the oxygen.
6. Because vinegar is an acid, it would inhibit and possibly destroy the catalyst.

Enzymes

Use Visuals

Figure 2–20 Have students study the graph and explain its subject as well as what its axes represent. Then, ask: **What does the graph show would be the effect if enzymes were not available within a cell?** *(Without enzymes, reactions would need more activation energy to get started.)* **Would a reaction take a longer or shorter time with an enzyme?** *(A shorter time)* Explain that an enzyme may accelerate a reaction by a factor of 10^{10}, making it 10 billion times faster. L2

TEACHER TO TEACHER

To help students understand the action of enzymes, I have them do a lab in which they investigate bromelin, an enzyme in pineapple that breaks down certain proteins. Students mix liquid gelatin and fresh pineapple in one test tube, liquid gelatin and canned pineapple in a second, liquid gelatin and meat tenderizer in a third, and plain liquid gelatin in a fourth. After refrigerating the mixtures overnight, they let all four test tubes sit out at room temperature for 20 minutes and then assess each for how much the liquids have jelled.

—*LouEllen Parker Brademan*
Science Teacher
Potomac Senior High School
Dumfries, VA

Answer to . . .

CHECKPOINT *Activation energy is the energy that is needed to get a reaction started.*

2–4 (continued)

Download a worksheet on enzymes for students to complete, and find additional teacher support from NSTA SciLinks.

Build Science Skills

Using Models Have students model the action of enzymes by carrying out the "chemical reaction" of breaking toothpicks in half. Divide the class into groups, each with an increasing number of students. Group 1 should have two students, group 2 should have three students, and so on. Give each group 200 toothpicks, and ask one member to be a timer. The other student or students in each group represent enzyme molecules, and the toothpicks represent substrate molecules in a chemical reaction. Then, at your signal, all groups should begin breaking their toothpicks in half. The timer for each group should record the time it takes for the group to break all the toothpicks. Compare the times of each group. Students will find that the more "enzyme molecules" available, the faster the reaction is completed. L1 L2

Enzyme Action

Use Visuals

Figure 2–21 Ask students: **What are the substrates in this reaction?** *(Glucose and ATP)* **What are the products?** *(ADP and glucose-6-phosphate)* **How does the presence of an enzyme affect this reaction?** *(The enzyme speeds up the reaction.)* **What do the three arrows at the top left indicate?** *(Two arrows indicate that both products are released. The third arrow indicates that the enzyme is free to find new substrate molecules and start a new reaction cycle.)* L1

For: Links on enzymes
Visit: www.SciLinks.org
Web Code: cbn-1024

Left to itself, this reaction is so slow that carbon dioxide might build up in the body faster than the bloodstream could remove it. Your bloodstream contains an enzyme called carbonic anhydrase that speeds up the reaction by a factor of 10 million. With carbonic anhydrase on the job, the reaction takes place immediately and carbon dioxide is removed from the blood quickly.

Enzymes are very specific, generally catalyzing only one chemical reaction. For this reason, part of an enzyme's name is usually derived from the reaction it catalyzes. Carbonic anhydrase gets its name because it catalyzes the reaction that removes water from carbonic acid.

Enzyme Action

How do enzymes do their jobs? For a chemical reaction to take place, the reactants must collide with enough energy so that existing bonds will be broken and new bonds will be formed. If the reactants do not have enough energy, they will be unchanged after the collision.

The Enzyme-Substrate Complex Enzymes provide a site where reactants can be brought together to react. Such a site reduces the energy needed for reaction. The reactants of enzyme-catalyzed reactions are known as **substrates.**

▼ **Figure 2–21** The enzyme hexokinase converts the substrates glucose and ATP into glucose-6-phosphate and ADP. **Predicting** ***What happens to the hexokinase after the products are released?***

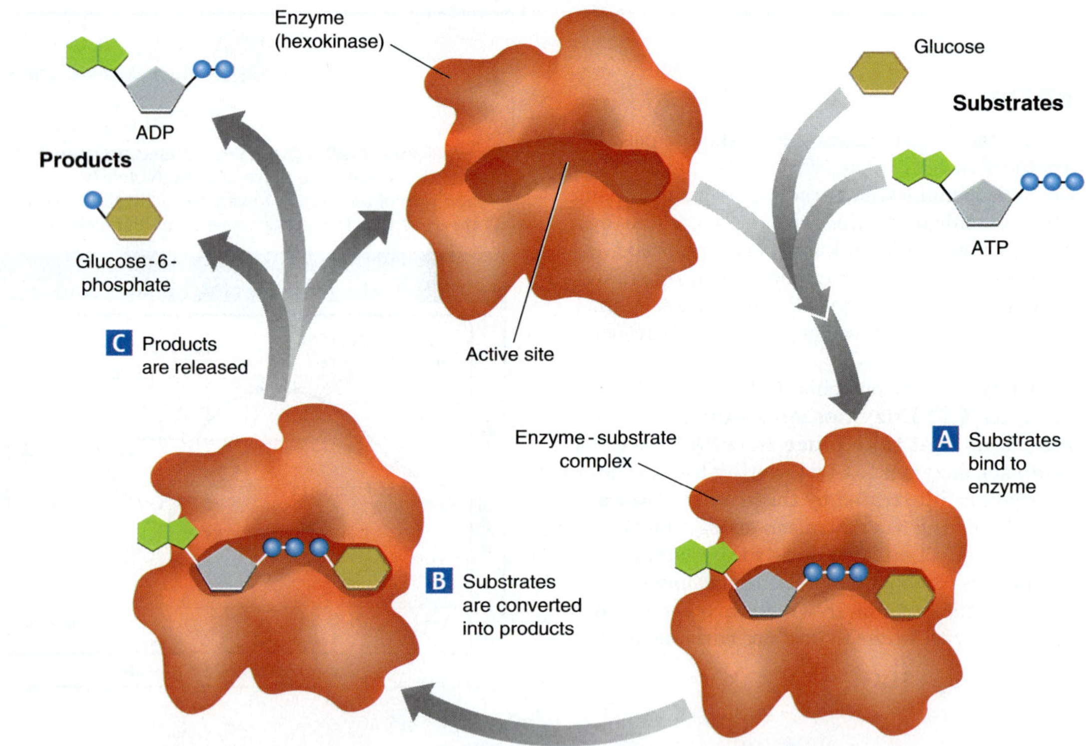

FACTS AND FIGURES

Just the right temperature
Each enzyme works best—that is, its reaction rate is fastest—at an optimal temperature. Enzymes in the human body generally function best near body temperature, or 35–40°C. Below an enzyme's optimal temperature, the reaction is slower. But, if the temperature rises above the optimal temperature, the reaction speed drops sharply because the high temperature disrupts the chemical bonds in the enzyme, which changes its shape; that is, the enzyme undergoes denaturation and is no longer functional. This is what occurs when the body has a high fever. Because denaturation is not reversible, a temperature higher than 44°C usually causes death. Enzymes in other organisms have different optimal temperatures. The bacteria in the hot springs of Yellowstone National Park, for instance, contain enzymes with optimal temperatures as high as 100°C.

Figure 2–21 provides an example of an enzyme-catalyzed reaction. The enzyme is hexokinase. The substrates are glucose and ATP. During the reaction, a phosphate group is transferred from ATP to the glucose molecule. Recall that each protein has a specific, complex shape. The substrates bind to a site on the enzyme called the active site. The active site and the substrates have complementary shapes. The fit is so precise that the active site and substrates are often compared to a lock and key.

Figure 2–22 shows a substrate fitting into an active site on an enzyme. The enzyme and substrate are bound together by intermolecular forces and form an enzyme-substrate complex. They remain bound together until the reaction is done. Once the reaction is over, the products of the reaction are released and the enzyme is free to start the process again.

Regulation of Enzyme Activity Because they are catalysts for reactions, enzymes can be affected by any variable that influences a chemical reaction. Enzymes, including those that help digest food, work best at certain pH values. Many enzymes are affected by changes in temperature. Not surprisingly, those enzymes produced by human cells generally work best at temperatures close to 37°C, the normal temperature of the human body.

Cells can regulate the activities of enzymes in a variety of ways. Most cells contain proteins that help to turn key enzymes "on" or "off" at critical stages in the life of the cell. Enzymes play essential roles in regulating chemical pathways, making materials that cells need, releasing energy, and transferring information.

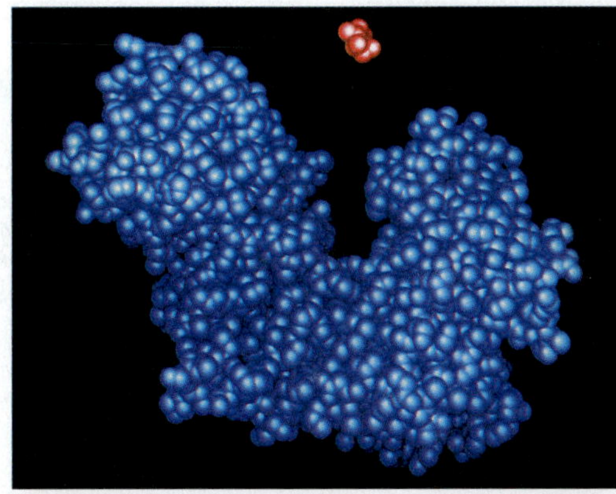

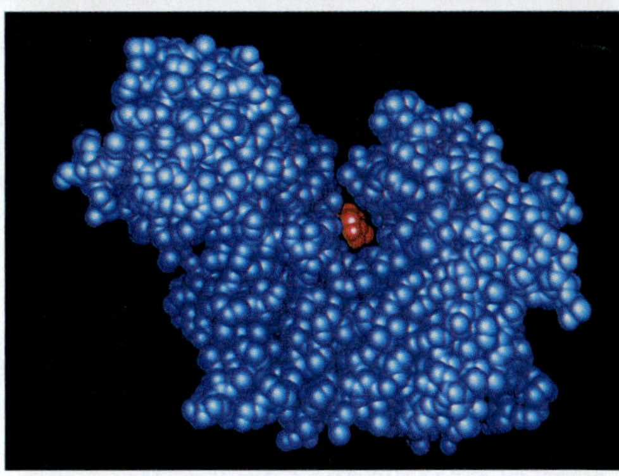

▲ **Figure 2–22** This space-filling model shows how a substrate binds to an active site on an enzyme. **Interpreting Graphics** *What happens after the substrate binds to the enzyme?*

2–4 Section Assessment

1. **Key Concept** What happens to chemical bonds during chemical reactions?
2. **Key Concept** Describe the role of energy in chemical reactions.
3. **Key Concept** What are enzymes, and how are they important to living things?
4. Describe how enzymes work, including the role of the enzyme-substrate complex.
5. **Critical Thinking Applying Concepts** A change in pH can change the shape of a protein. How might a change in pH affect the function of an enzyme such as hexokinase? (*Hint:* Think about the analogy of the lock and key.)

Sharpen Your Skills

Modeling

Make a model that demonstrates how an active site and a substrate are like a lock and a key. Give a brief talk in which you refer to your model as you explain how enzymes work.

Build Science Skills

Using Analogies As students watch, open a large padlock with its key. Ask: **In a chemical reaction, which of these is like the enzyme and which is like the substrate?** *(The padlock is like the enzyme and the key is like the substrate.)* **Which place on this padlock is like an active site?** *(The keyhole)* Direct students' attention to Figure 2–22. Ask: **How is inserting a key into a lock different from the formation of an enzyme-substrate complex?** *(The enzyme changes its shape when it binds to the substrate.)* L1 L2

3 ASSESS

Evaluate Understanding

Direct students' attention to Figure 2–21, and ask them to write as full a description as possible of the chemical reaction that is illustrated. They should mention the substrates and the products, the enzyme involved, how the enzyme lowers the activation energy, and the formation of the enzyme-substrate complex.

Reteach

Call on student volunteers to explain what a chemical reaction is, the energy changes involved in reactions, and how enzymes affect the rate of biochemical reactions.

Sharpen Your Skills

Provide students with a variety of materials, including modeling compound, fabric, sponges, construction paper, and papier-mâché. Labels on the model should include *enzyme, active site,* and *substrate.* Paragraphs should explain how the model demonstrates the enzyme function.

2–4 Section Assessment

1. Bonds are broken in reactants and new bonds are formed in products.
2. Some chemical reactions release energy, and other chemical reactions absorb energy. Energy changes determine how easily a chemical reaction will occur.
3. Enzymes are biological catalysts. Living cells use enzymes to speed up virtually every important chemical reaction that takes place in cells.
4. Substrates, the reactants of an enzyme-catalyzed reaction, attach to the enzyme at an active site and form an enzyme-substrate complex. Once the complex is formed, the enzyme helps convert substrate into product.
5. A change in pH could change the shape of hexokinase. This change would diminish or possibly eliminate the ability of glucose and ATP to bind to the active site on the enzyme.

If your class subscribes to the iText, use it to review the Key Concepts in Section 2–4.

Answers to . . .

Figure 2–21 *It is free to form a new enzyme-substrate complex.*

Figure 2–22 *The substrate reacts and forms one or more products.*

Design an Experiment

BI 1.b, 6IIE 7.c, 8IIE 9.c, BIIE 1.a, BIIE 1.b, BIIE 1.c

Objective Students will be able to design an experiment to investigate how temperature affects the rate of an enzyme-catalyzed reaction.

L2 L3

Skills Focus **Formulating Hypotheses, Predicting**

Time 45 minutes

Advance Prep

- If you are using probeware in this activity, use the instructions in the *Probeware Lab Manual.*
- Improvise controlled-temperature baths using a plastic dishpan filled with either ice water or warm water. A student volunteer can be stationed to check the temperature of the water with a thermometer, adding hot or cold water periodically to maintain a desired temperature.
- Liver puree, which you can prepare by mixing cut-up pieces of raw liver with a little distilled water in a blender, is often very concentrated in catalase. Before the lab, check the enzyme's activity by running through the procedure. Dilute the puree with distilled water, as necessary, to manipulate the time needed to float the disks into the measurable range. Refrigerate until ready to use.

Safety Caution students to be careful with the hydrogen peroxide, especially when they are pouring 25 mL of hydrogen peroxide solution into the 50-mL beaker. Make sure students wash their hands with soap and warm water before leaving the lab.

Pre-Lab Discussion Have students review the discussion of catalysts in Section 2–4 and read the procedure for this lab. Then, ask: **How are enzymes essential for living things?** *(Living things use enzymes to speed up virtually every important chemical reaction that takes place in cells.)* **The action of what enzyme is investigated in this lab?** *(The enzyme catalase)* **When you design your experiment, what will the manipulated variable be?** *(Temperature)* **What will the data be that you'll collect for your data table?** *(How many seconds it takes the filter-paper disk to float to the top of the liquid at various temperatures of the liver puree)*

Design an Experiment

BI 1.b, 6IIE 7.c, 8IIE 9.c, BIIE 1.a, BIIE 1.b, BIIE 1.c

Investigating the Effect of Temperature on Enzyme Activity

Almost all chemical reactions that occur in living organisms are catalyzed by enzymes. Many factors in a cell's environment affect the action of an enzyme. In this investigation, you will design an experiment to determine the effect of temperature on an enzyme-catalyzed reaction.

Problem How does temperature affect the rate of an enzyme-catalyzed reaction?

Materials

- raw liver
- petri dish
- dropper pipette
- 1% hydrogen peroxide solution
- liver puree
- 25-mL graduated cylinder
- five 50-mL beakers
- filter-paper disks
- forceps
- glass-marking pencil
- ice bath
- 3 thermometers
- warm water bath
- clock or watch with second hand
- paper towel

Skills Formulating Hypotheses, Predicting

Design Your Experiment

Part A: Observe the Catalase Reaction

1. Put on your apron, gloves, and safety goggles. Use forceps to place a small piece of raw liver in an open petri dish. Use a dropper pipette to put a drop of hydrogen peroxide solution on the liver. **CAUTION:** *Hydrogen peroxide can be irritating to skin and eyes. If you spill any on yourself or your clothes, wash it off immediately and tell your teacher.* Observe what happens. Liver contains the enzyme catalase, which breaks down hydrogen peroxide (H_2O_2) to water (H_2O) and oxygen gas (O_2). When hydrogen peroxide, which is formed in cells, is broken down by catalase, bubbles of oxygen gas are released.
2. With your teacher's guidance, select the proper equipment and technology to measure catalase activity—either a filter-paper disk or an oxygen probe. If using an oxygen probe, see your teacher for instructions.
3. To measure the activity of catalase, use a graduated cylinder to place 25 mL of hydrogen peroxide solution in a 50-mL beaker.
4. Use forceps to dip a filter-paper disk in liver puree. Place the filter-paper disk on a paper towel for 4 seconds to remove any excess liquid.
5. Use the forceps to place the filter-paper disk at the bottom of the beaker of hydrogen peroxide solution. Observe the filter-paper disk and record the number of seconds it takes to float to the top of the liquid.

Design Your Experiment

1. Demonstrate how to use a dropper pipette to put a drop of hydrogen peroxide solution on the piece of liver. When students perform this action, they should observe bubbles of oxygen appear in the hydrogen peroxide solution.

4. Demonstrate how to dip the filter-paper disk in the liver puree and then place it on a paper towel.

6., 7. Ask students to write down their hypothesis, prediction, and experimental design. Check these to make sure students are on the right track before they proceed.

9. Make sure each student or group has constructed a good data table in which to record the necessary data.

10. Graphs should show a rise until about 40°C and then show a sharp decline.

Expected Outcomes Students should discover that temperature has an effect on enzyme activity. Their data should show that catalase is most active near 40°C.

Part B: Design an Experiment

6 **Formulating Hypotheses** Use your observations and knowledge to develop a hypothesis. Develop a hypothesis about how temperature will affect the rate at which catalase breaks down hydrogen peroxide. Record your hypothesis.

7 **Designing Experiments** Design an experiment to test your hypothesis. Your experimental plan should include a prediction of the result based on your hypothesis, and any appropriate controls and replications (repetitions). Be sure to identify all manipulated, responding, and controlled variables in your experimental plan. Include any necessary safety precautions and safety equipment in your plan.

8 As you plan your investigative procedures, refer to the Lab Tips box on this page for information on demonstrating safe practices, making wise choices in the use of materials, and selecting equipment and technology.

9 Construct a data table in which to record the results of your experiment. Perform your experiment only after you have obtained your teacher's approval of your plan.

10 Make a graph of the results of your experiment. Plot temperature on the *x*-axis and the variable by which you measured catalase activity on the *y*-axis. With your teacher's guidance, select the proper equipment and technology to use—either graph paper or a graphing calculator.

Analyze and Conclude

1. **Inferring** How does the time required for a catalase-soaked filter-paper disk to float reflect the amount of catalase activity in the solution?
2. **Inferring** How did temperature affect catalase activity? Was your prediction confirmed?
3. **Drawing Conclusions** Many mammals, including cattle and pigs, have body temperatures close to 37°C. Does your graph indicate that catalase is most active close to that temperature? How might mammals benefit from that relationship?
4. **Evaluating** Identify and discuss possible sources of error in your procedure.
5. **SAFETY** Explain how you demonstrated safe practices when using hydrogen peroxide.

Lab Tips

Demonstrate Safe Practices

Consider what safety precautions you will need to take. Review the Science Safety Rules and Safety Symbols on pages 1066–1068. In your experimental plan, include any needed safety precautions. For example, if you will be using an irritating chemical, you should wear an apron, goggles, and plastic gloves. Review your plan with your teacher and get it approved before beginning your experiment.

Make Wise Choices in the Use of Materials

Consider how you will use materials wisely. For example, how can you use a reusable container rather than a disposable one? For materials that cannot be reused in the lab, consider whether they can be recycled. If a material cannot be recycled, determine whether any precautions for disposal must be taken to prevent soil or water contamination. Make sure your teacher has approved your material-use plan before beginning your experiment.

Select Equipment and Technology

Consider what equipment and technology you might need to use. If Probeware can be used to collect data, consider whether doing so will improve precision.

Evaluate Your Experimental Design

Follow scientific procedures, including those described in Appendix A. Identify and define the manipulated, responding, and controlled variables. Identify and discuss possible sources of error. Write needed operational definitions.

Go Further

Designing Experiments Catalase is also found in potatoes. Design an experiment using potato puree instead of liver puree to determine the temperature at which potato catalase is most active.

Analyze and Conclude

1. Catalase catalyzes a reaction that releases oxygen gas. Bubbles of oxygen form around the filter-paper disk, lifting it to the surface of the liquid. The more active the enzyme, the more quickly the bubbles are produced.

2. Students should observe that increasing the temperature increases the activity of catalase up to about 40–45°C.

3. Graphs should show that catalase is most active around 37°C. Mammals benefit from this, since the reactions occur inside the body.

4. Possible sources of error: variations in the amount of catalase in the liver and in the strength of hydrogen peroxide

5. Students should explain that they wore aprons, plastic gloves, and safety goggles when working with the hydrogen peroxide.

Go Further

Most students' experiments will be similar to the experimental design in this lab, with a substitution of potato puree for liver puree. Students should include a prediction and appropriate controls and replications.

Chapter 2 Study Guide

Study Tip

Divide the class into four groups, and have the members of each group collaborate in writing study questions tied to one of the four sections in the chapter. The questions should cover all the Key Concepts and Vocabulary terms in the section. Each group should also produce an answer key. Then, provide each student with a list of the questions developed by all four groups. Students should answer the questions, and then check their answers against the answer keys.

Thinking Visually

Tables may vary, though all should include information from Section 2–3 about each of the four groups of biomolecules. A typical table might have these column heads: *Group, Structure, Properties, Functions,* and *Examples.* Students should complete their tables with as much information as possible from pages 45–48.

Chapter 2 Assessment

Reviewing Content

1. c **5.** b **8.** c
2. d **6.** d **9.** a
3. b **7.** c **10.** d
4. b

Understanding Concepts

11. Elements are composed of atoms. Compounds are composed of atoms of two or more elements combined in definite proportions.

12. Radioactive isotopes are isotopes whose nuclei are unstable and break down at a constant rate over time. Radioactive isotopes are used in determining the ages of rocks, treating cancer, killing bacteria in food, and following the movements of substances within organisms.

13. Atoms in a compound are held together by a chemical bond.

14. Two electrons are shared in a single covalent bond, four in a double bond, and six in a triple bond.

Chapter 2 Study Guide

2–1 The Nature of Matter

Key Concepts

- The subatomic particles that make up atoms are protons, neutrons, and electrons.
- Because they have the same number of electrons, all isotopes of an element have the same chemical properties.
- The main types of chemical bonds are covalent bonds and ionic bonds.

Vocabulary

atom, p. 35 • nucleus, p. 35 • electron, p. 35
element, p. 36 • isotope, p. 36
compound, p. 37 • ionic bond, p. 38
ion, p. 38 • covalent bond, p. 38
molecule, p. 38 • van der Waals forces, p. 39

2–2 Properties of Water

Key Concepts

- A water molecule is polar because there is an uneven distribution of electrons between the oxygen and hydrogen atoms.
- Acidic solutions contain higher concentrations of H^+ ions than pure water and have pH values below 7.
- Basic, or alkaline, solutions contain lower concentrations of H^+ ions than pure water and have pH values above 7.

Vocabulary

cohesion, p. 41 • adhesion, p. 41 • mixture, p. 41
solution, p. 42 • solute, p. 42 • solvent, p. 42
suspension, p. 42 • pH scale, p. 43 • acid, p. 43
base, p. 43 • buffer, p. 43

2–3 Carbon Compounds

8 6.b, 8 6.c, BI 1.h, BI 4.e, *BI 4.f

Key Concepts

- Four groups of organic compounds found in living things are carbohydrates, lipids, nucleic acids, and proteins.
- Living things use carbohydrates as their main source of energy. Plants and some animals also use carbohydrates for structural purposes.
- Lipids can be used to store energy. Some lipids are important parts of biological membranes and waterproof coverings.
- Nucleic acids store and transmit hereditary, or genetic, information.
- Some proteins control the rate of reactions and regulate cell processes. Some proteins build tissues such as bone and muscle. Others transport materials or help to fight disease.

Vocabulary

monomer, p. 45 • polymer, p. 45
carbohydrate, p. 45 • monosaccharide, p. 46
polysaccharide, p. 46 • lipid, p. 46
nucleic acid, p. 47 • nucleotide, p. 47
ribonucleic acid (RNA), p. 47
deoxyribonucleic acid (DNA), p. 47
protein, p. 47 • amino acid, p. 47

2–4 Chemical Reactions and Enzymes

Key Concepts BI 1.b

- Chemical reactions always involve changes in the chemical bonds that join atoms in compounds.
- Chemical reactions that release energy often occur spontaneously. Chemical reactions that absorb energy will not occur without a source of energy.
- Enzymes speed up chemical reactions that take place in cells.

Vocabulary

chemical reaction, p. 49 • reactant, p. 49
product, p. 49 • activation energy, p. 50
catalyst, p. 51 • enzyme, p. 51 • substrate, p. 52

Thinking Visually

Create a table in which you compare the structures and functions of the following biomolecules: carbohydrates, lipids, proteins, and nucleic acids.

TIME SAVER — CHAPTER RESOURCES

Print:

- ***Teaching Resources,*** Chapter Vocabulary Review, Graphic Organizer, Chapter 2 Tests: Levels A and B
- ***Laboratory Assessment,*** Laboratory Assessment 1

Technology:

- ***Computer Test Bank,*** Chapter 2 Test
- ***iText,*** Chapter 2 Assessment

Chapter 2 Assessment

Reviewing Content

Choose the letter that best answers the question or completes the statement.

1. The positively charged particle in an atom is the
   a. neutron. c. proton.
   b. ion. d. electron.
2. Two or more different atoms are combined in definite proportions in any
   a. symbol. c. element.
   b. isotope. d. compound.
3. A covalent bond is formed by the
   a. transfer of electrons. c. gaining of electrons.
   b. sharing of electrons. d. losing of electrons.
4. When you shake sugar and sand together in a test tube, you cause them to form a
   a. compound. c. solution.
   b. mixture. d. suspension.
5. A compound that produces hydrogen ions in solution is a(an)
   a. salt. c. base.
   b. acid. d. polymer.
6. In polymerization, complex molecules are formed by the joining together of
   a. macromolecules. c. polymers.
   b. carbohydrates. d. monomers.
7. Which formula represents an amino acid?

a.
```
      H   H   H   OH  H   H
      |   |   |   |   |   |
  H—C—C—C—C—C—C=O
      |   |   |   |   |
      OH  OH  OH  H   OH
```

b.
```
        H                         H
        |                         |
    H—C—OH                   H—C—OH
        |                         |
        C———O                     C———O
   H  /  H   \   H          H  /  H   \   OH
    |/        \  |            |/        \  |
    C          C              C           C
    |\ OH   H  / \           / \ OH   H  /|
  HO  \ |   | /   \         /   \ |   | / H
       C———C        O            C———C
       |   |                     |   |
       H   OH                    H   OH
```

c.
```
      H   H   O
      |   |   ||
  H—N—C—C—OH
          |
      H—C—H
          |
          H
```

d.
```
      H   H   OH  OH  H   H
      |   |   |   |   |   |
  H—C—C—C—C—C—C=O
      |   |   |   |   |
      OH  OH  H   H   OH
```

Interactive textbook with assessment at PHSchool.com 

8. Proteins are polymers formed from
   a. lipids.
   b. carbohydrates.
   c. amino acids.
   d. nucleic acids.
9. An enzyme speeds up a reaction by
   a. lowering the activation energy.
   b. raising the activation energy.
   c. releasing energy.
   d. absorbing energy.
10. In a chemical reaction, a reactant binds to an enzyme at a region known as the
    a. catalyst.
    b. product.
    c. substrate.
    d. active site.

Understanding Concepts

11. Explain the relationship among atoms, elements, and compounds.
12. What is a radioactive isotope? Describe two scientific uses of radioactive isotopes.
13. How are atoms in a compound held together?
14. Distinguish among single, double, and triple covalent bonds.
15. Explain the properties of cohesion and adhesion. Give an example of each property.
16. What is the relationship among solutions, solutes, and solvents?
17. How are acids and bases different? How do their pH values differ?
18. Explain the relationship between monomers and polymers, using polysaccharides as an example.
19. Identify three major roles of proteins.
20. Describe the parts of a nucleotide.
21. Name the two basic kinds of nucleic acids. What sugar does each contain?
22. What is a chemical reaction?
23. Describe the two types of energy changes that can occur in a chemical reaction.
24. What relationship exists between an enzyme and a catalyst?
25. Describe some factors that may influence enzyme activity.

TIME SAVER — HOMEWORK GUIDE

Section:	Questions:
Section 2–1	1–3, 11–14, 32, 36
Section 2–2	4, 5, 15–17, 26, 34
Section 2–3	6–8, 18–21, 29–31
Section 2–4	9, 10, 22–25, 27, 28, 33, 35

Interactive Textbook

If your class subscribes to the iText, your students can go online to access an interactive version of the Student Edition and a self-test.

(Continued from page 56)

15. Cohesion is an attraction between molecules of the same substance. An example is drops of water forming beads on a smooth surface. Adhesion is an attraction between molecules of different substances. An example is capillary action.

16. A solution is a mixture in which one substance is dissolved in another. The solute is the substance that is dissolved. The solvent is the substance in which the solute is dissolved.

17. An acid is any compound that produces H^+ ions in solution; acidic solutions have pH values below 7. A base is a compound that produces hydroxide ions (OH^-) in solution; basic solutions have pH values above 7.

18. Polymers are large macromolecules made up of smaller molecules called monomers. For example, monomers called monosaccharides are joined together to form polymers called polysaccharides.

19. Proteins control the rate of chemical reactions, regulate cell processes, form tissues, transport substances, and help fight disease.

20. Nucleotides consist of a 5-carbon sugar, a phosphate group, and a nitrogenous base.

21. The two basic kinds are ribonucleic acid (RNA), which contains the sugar ribose, and deoxyribonucleic acid (DNA), which contains the sugar deoxyribose.

22. A chemical reaction is a process that changes one set of chemicals into another set of chemicals.

23. Some chemical reactions release energy, and others absorb energy.

24. An enzyme is a biological catalyst.

25. Factors that can influence enzyme activity include pH, temperature, and proteins in cells that help turn key enzymes "on" and "off" at critical stages.

Critical Thinking

26. Adding a base to the solution would increase its pH, because a base produces hydroxide ions in solution and basic solutions have pH values above 7.

27. To carry out all life processes, living things need the energy released in the chemical reactions involved in digesting food.

28. The total product was doubled when the temperature of the reaction increased from 25°C to 35°C, and it decreased to almost zero when the temperature was increased to 45°C. Enzymes work best at certain temperatures. Students should hypothesize that the enzyme involved in this reaction works best at about 35°C, and a much higher temperature inhibits the enzyme's function.

29. Students might suggest trying to dissolve the solid in water. Lipids are generally not water soluble. They also might suggest warming the solid to see if it would soften, which solid lipids tend to do when heated.

30. The mixture could be separated by adding water. The sodium chloride would dissolve in the water, whereas the silica would not. The salt could be retrieved by filtering the mixture and evaporating the filtrate.

31. The name indicates that carbohydrates contain carbon and the elements in water, oxygen and hydrogen.

32. The diagram should show that hydrogen and chlorine form a covalent bond. Students can use the chlorine atom in Figure 2–3 as a starting point and pair up one of the seven electrons in its outer level with hydrogen's single electron.

33. If the temperature or pH were changed, the shape of the enzyme hexokinase could change. It might lose its ability to bind with the substrates, glucose and ATP, and an enzyme-substrate complex would not form. As a result, the enzyme would not speed up the reaction.

34. Students should infer that magnesium hydroxide is a base. The base reacts with the acid in the stomach, and forms a product that is not acidic.

35. The fit of an enzyme and a substrate at the enzyme's active site is so precise that the substrate is like a key and the enzyme is like a lock. Like a key in a lock, only a substrate of a certain shape can fit into the active site of the enzyme. What occurs when a key is inserted into a lock is a physical process, unlike what occurs at an active site, which is a chemical process.

36. Answers will vary. A typical response might describe examples of a forensic scientist using knowledge about blood, human tissues, or animal life cycles to solve criminal cases.

Focus on the BIG Idea 

All responses should reflect an understanding of how scientists design an experiment using this procedure: stating the problem, forming a hypothesis, setting up a controlled experiment, recording and analyzing results, and drawing a conclusion. A typical experiment might involve observing differences in several plants' growth, with the pH of the soil being the manipulated variable.

Chapter 2 Assessment

Critical Thinking

26. Predicting Suppose you wanted to increase the pH of a solution. What could you add to the solution to increase the pH? Explain your prediction.

27. Inferring Why is it important that energy-releasing reactions take place in living organisms?

28. Interpreting Graphics The bar graph shows the total amount of product from a chemical reaction performed at three different temperatures. The same enzyme was involved in each case. Describe the results of each reaction. How can you explain these results?

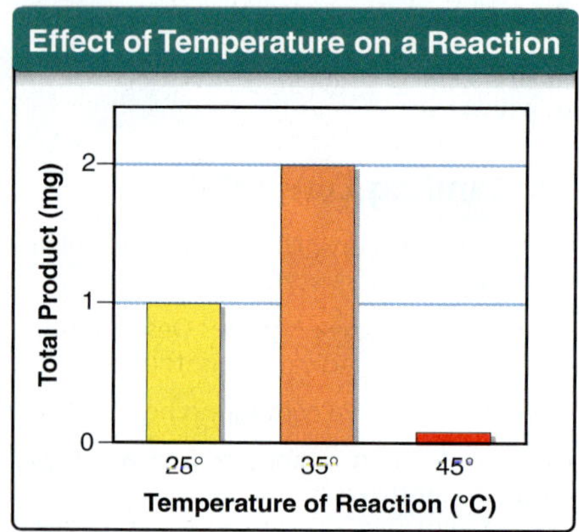

29. Designing Experiments Suggest one or two simple experiments to determine whether a solid white substance is a lipid or a carbohydrate. What evidence would you need to support each hypothesis?

30. Problem Solving Silica is a hard, glassy material that does not dissolve in water. Suppose sodium chloride is accidentally mixed with silica. Describe a way to remove the sodium chloride.

31. Inferring Explain what the name "carbohydrate" might indicate about the chemical composition of sugars.

32. Using Models Make a diagram like the one in **Figure 2–4** to show how chlorine and hydrogen form from the compound hydrogen chloride, HCl.

33. Predicting Changing the temperature or pH can change an enzyme's shape. Describe how changing the temperature or pH might affect the function of the enzyme in **Figure 2–21.**

34. Predicting As part of the digestive process, the human stomach produces hydrochloric acid, HCl. Sometimes excess acid causes discomfort. In such a case, a person might take an antacid such as magnesium hydroxide, $Mg(OH)_2$. Explain how this substance can reduce the amount of acid in the stomach.

35. Using Analogies Explain why a lock and key are used to describe the way an enzyme works. Describe any ways in which the analogy is not perfect.

36. Applying Concepts Using two or three examples, describe how a forensic scientist might use the knowledge of biology in his or her daily work.

Science as a Way of Knowing Refer back to Chapter 1 to review the way scientists work. Then, describe an experiment that would test the effects of pH on a plant species.

Writing in Science

Write a paragraph that includes the following: (a) a brief explanation of a polymer, (b) a description of the four major classes of organic compounds found in living things, and (c) a description of how these organic compounds are used by the human body. (*Hint*: Review each of the Key Concepts in Section 2–3.)

Performance-Based Assessment

Creative Writing At a yearly convention, individual atoms describe their recent experiences. Assume you are an oxygen atom that began the year in an O_2 molecule, and then spent time in a water molecule, in a hydroxide ion, and in carbonic acid. Write a speech describing the chemical reactions you experienced and the other molecules you met along the way.

For: An interactive self-test
Visit: PHSchool.com
Web Code: cba-1020

Standards Practice

Test-Taking Tip As you briefly scan the questions, mark those that may require pure guesswork on your part and save them for last. (Do not write in this book.) Use whatever time you have left for those questions to eliminate as many answers as possible through reasoning.

Questions 1–3 Each of the lettered choices below refers to the following numbered statements. Select the best lettered choice. A choice may be used once, more than once, or not at all.

A Cohesion
B Adhesion
C Catalysts
D Reactants

1. An attraction between different substances
2. Lower a chemical reaction's activation energy
3. The elements or compounds that enter into a chemical reaction

Directions: Choose the letter that best answers the question or completes the statement.

4. Which one of the following is NOT an organic molecule found in living organisms? **8 6.b**
   A protein
   B nucleic acid
   C carbohydrate
   D sodium chloride

5. Which combination of particle and charge is correct?
   A proton: positively charged
   B electron: positively charged
   C neutron: negatively charged
   D proton: negatively charged

6. In which of the following ways do isotopes of the same element differ?
   A in number of neutrons only
   B in number of protons only
   C in numbers of neutrons and protons
   D in number of protons and in mass

7. Which of the following molecules is made up of glycerol and fatty acids? **BI 1.h**
   A sugars
   B starches
   C lipids
   D nucleic acids

8. Nucleotides consist of a phosphate group, a nitrogenous base, and a **BI 1.h**
   A fatty acid.
   B starch.
   C lipid.
   D 5-carbon sugar.

Questions 9–10 Study the graph to answer the questions that follow.

The enzyme catalase speeds up the chemical reaction that changes hydrogen peroxide into oxygen and water. The amount of oxygen given off is an indication of the rate of the reaction.

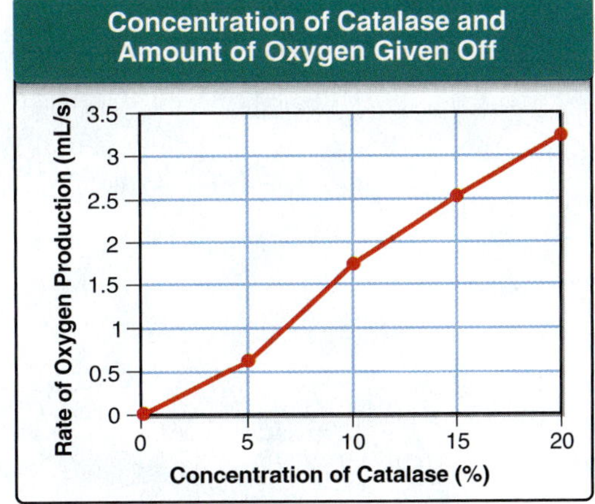

9. Based on the graph, what can you conclude about the relationship between enzyme concentration and reaction rate? **BI 1.b**
   A Reaction rate decreases with increasing enzyme concentration.
   B Reaction rate increases with decreasing enzyme concentration.
   C Reaction rate increases with increasing enzyme concentration.
   D The variables are indirectly proportional.

10. Which concentration of catalase will produce the fastest reaction rate? **BI 1.b**
    A 0%
    B 5%
    C 15%
    D 20%

Standards Practice

1. B	5. A	9. C
2. C	6. A	10. D
3. D	7. C	
4. D	8. D	

Success Tracker™
Online at PHSchool.com

Have students check their understanding of the chapter by logging onto Success Tracker.

Writing in Science

Students' paragraphs may vary. All students, though, should explain that a polymer is a macromolecule made up of monomers joined together. Students should also briefly describe the four groups of organic compounds found in living things: carbohydrates, lipids, nucleic acids, and proteins. For each of these groups, students should describe the composition and list important functions in the human body.

Performance-Based Assessment

A good speech will be both imaginative and scientifically accurate. Students should describe these events: being a part of an O_2 molecule, being in a polar water molecule with two hydrogen atoms, experiencing the decomposition of a water molecule into a hydrogen ion and a hydroxide ion, and being in the blood when carbon dioxide and water react and produce carbonic acid. Students should demonstrate knowledge of chemical compounds, chemical bonds, solutions, and chemical reactions.

Your students can independently test their knowledge of the chapter and print out their test results for your files.

UNIT 2

Dear Colleague,

Even those of us who love animals feel uncomfortable watching wild animals fight for food and resources. Why? Because they offer an unusual reminder that humans don't always have to be at the top of the food chain.

As modern Americans, of course, we are rarely reminded that food chains and other ecological processes even exist. Few of us grow our own vegetables. Fewer still think about where our chicken, beef, or veal dinners come from. And VERY few of us give a second thought to where our wastes go when we flush the toilet. Many of us are so isolated from the day-to-day workings of the biosphere that we forget them altogether. The only time we think about food chains, nutrient cycles, or rainfall is during food shortages, droughts, or floods. In other words, we ignore our planet's life-support systems unless or until they malfunction.

That level of ecological illiteracy is a pity. It's a shame that more people don't realize just how fascinating ecology really is. Imagine a carbon atom from your breath, wafted out to sea, absorbed by phytoplankton, settled into sediments, driven beneath the crust, belched out of a volcano, and becoming part of the global atmospheric greenhouse that has stabilized Earth's temperatures since life began. Imagine populations of insects and plants—predators and prey, parasites and hosts—growing and reproducing, passing through cycles of increase and decrease, rarely going extinct, yet never taking over the planet either.

These days, ecological illiteracy can be dangerous, too, because humans have become the most powerful force for change in the world. We transport more materials and use more energy than any other multicellular species. Our actions have even

Competition for resources is one of the underlying themes of ecology.

Chapters

Focus on the BIG Ideas

- Interdependence in Nature
- Matter and Energy

All forms of life on Earth are connected together into a biosphere, which literally means "living planet." Within the biosphere, organisms are linked to one another and to the land, water, and air around them by relationships that enable energy to flow and matter to cycle. Human life and the economies of human societies also require matter and energy, so human life depends directly on the economy of nature.

Go Online PHSchool.com
For: Latest discoveries
Visit: PHSchool.com
Web Code: cbe-2000

begun to affect the workings of vital systems, such as the ozone layer and the global greenhouse. This is not a healthy state of affairs. But there is an alternative. If enough people understand ecological principles well enough to work with them, the result can be profoundly positive.

On a national level, the Clean Air and the Clean Water acts fundamentally improved American air and water quality. Levels of lead in rivers and streams, for example, have fallen dramatically.

On a local level, the town I live in has wisely set aside nearly half its land area (much of it wetland) for conservation. It was no coincidence that when a multiyear drought forced mandatory water rationing in surrounding communities, our wells did not run dry.

On a personal level, I am delighted with a food chain currently in action near my son's bedroom. To my great satisfaction, platoons of beneficial insects—ladybugs, lacewings, predatory mites, and a beetle named *Cryptolaemus*—are munching their way through armies of aphids, spider mites, and mealybugs that had been devouring my "pet" plants. The Web sites of beneficial insect dealers supplied information on niche requirements for each predator, so I could select the correct species for my conditions of temperature and humidity. Those "good bugs" cost little more than the pesticides that I would have needed to do the same job. I can rest easy, knowing that I have protected my plants from herbivores without exposing my son to pesticides. Now, that's a food chain I can live with!

I hope these examples help inspire you to teach this unit vigorously. If enough of us teach our students that human society is part of the biosphere, that biological diversity is a treasure, that clean air and water and soil are invaluable resources, that old-growth forests are different from tree farms, and that all life is connected, our students and their descendants will enjoy a happier and healthier future.

Sincerely,

Joe Levine

Students can research ecology on the site developed by authors Ken Miller and Joe Levine.

Chapter Planner 3 The Biosphere

Section and Section Objectives	Time	STANDARDS NCLB	STANDARDS Biology	Activities and Labs
3–1 What Is Ecology?, pp. 63–65 **3.1.1** ***Identify*** the levels of organization that ecologists study. **3.1.2** ***Describe*** the methods used to study ecology.	1 period (1/2 block)			**SE:** ***Inquiry Activity,*** How do organisms affect one another's survival?, p. 62 L1 L2 **SE:** ***Technology & Society,*** Exploring Ecology From Space, p. 66 L2 L3
3–2 Energy Flow, pp. 67–73 **3.2.1** ***Identify*** the source of energy for life processes. **3.2.2** ***Trace*** the flow of energy through living systems. **3.2.3** ***Evaluate*** the efficiency of energy transfer among organisms in an ecosystem.	2 periods (1 block)	6 5.b, BI 6.d, BI 6.e, BI 6.f		**TE:** ***Build Science Skills,*** p. 67 L1 L2 **SE:** ***Quick Lab,*** How is a food chain organized?, p. 70 L1 L2 **TE:** ***Build Science Skills,*** p. 71 L2
3–3 Cycles of Matter, pp. 74–80 **3.3.1** ***Describe*** how matter cycles among the living and nonliving parts of an ecosystem. **3.3.2** ***Explain*** why nutrients are important in living systems. **3.3.3** ***Describe*** how the availability of nutrients affects the productivity of ecosystems.	2 periods (1 block)	BI 6.d		**TE:** ***Make Connections,*** p. 76 L2 L3 **TE:** ***Build Science Skills,*** p. 78 L1 L2 **SE:** ***Analyzing Data,*** Farming in the Rye, p. 79 L2 **SE:** ***Real-World Lab,*** Identifying a Limiting Nutrient, p. 81 L2 **LMA:** Chapter 3 Lab L2 L3 **LMB:** Chapter 3 Lab L1 L2 **BTM:** Issue 4 L2 L3
Chapter Assessment, pp. 82–85	1 period (1/2 block)			

ACTIVITY PLANNER

SE: *Inquiry Activity,* p. 62; 10 min.

TE: *Build Science Skills,* p. 67; 20 min.; heavy wrapping or butcher paper, meter stick, balance, various classroom objects

SE: *Quick Lab,* p. 70; 15 min.; 2 wide-mouth jars, 2 pieces of flexible screening, 2 rubber bands, 2 bean seedlings in small pots or paper cups, pea aphids, ladybird beetles (or crickets and praying mantises)

TE: *Build Science Skills,* p. 71; 25 min.; at least 25 pictures of producers and different-level consumers, masking tape, colored yarn

TE: *Make Connections,* p. 76; 15 min.; one empty vitamin container for each pair of students

TE: *Build Science Skills,* p. 78; 15 min.; variety of materials for making models of chemical formulas

SE: *Real-World Lab,* p. 81; 15 min. for setup; dropper pipette, algae culture, 2 test tubes with stoppers, test-tube rack, 50-mL graduated cylinder, pond water, glass-marking pencil, 10% trisodium phosphate solution

PLANNING KEY

Ability Levels

for students performing . . .

below grade level L1

at grade level L2

above grade level L3

Print Components

SE	Student Edition	LA	Lab Assessment
TE	Teacher's Edition	BTM	Biotechnology Manual
RSW	Reading & Study Workbook A	IDM	Issues and Decision Making
ARSW	Adapted Reading & Study Workbook B	LW	Lab Worksheets
TR	Teaching Resources	LMA	Laboratory Manual A
IF	Investigations in Forensics	LMB	Laboratory Manual B

Tech Components

CTB	Computer Test Bank
BD	BioDetectives DVD
TP	Transparencies Plus
PLM	Probeware Lab Manual
ABC	ABC DVD Library
LS	Lab Simulations
VL	Virtual Labs

Interactive textbook with assessment at PHSchool.com

Program Resources	Assessment	Media and Technology
TR: Lesson Plan 3–1, Section Summary, p. 4 L1, p. 15 L2, Worksheets, p. 7 L1, pp. 17–18 L2 **RSW:** Section 3–1 L2 **ARSW:** Section 3–1 L1	**SE:** 3–1 Section Assessment, p. 65 **TR:** Section Review 3–1	**iText:** Section 3–1 **TP:** 3–1 Interest Grabber, Section Outline, Compare/Contrast Table, Figure 3–2
TR: Lesson Plan 3–2, Section Summary, p. 4 L1, p. 15 L2, Worksheets, pp. 8–10 L1, pp. 19–21 L2 **RSW:** Section 3–2 L2 **ARSW:** Section 3–2 L1	**SE:** 3–2 Section Assessment, p. 73 **TR:** Section Review 3–2	**iText:** Section 3–2 **TP:** 3–2 Interest Grabber, Section Outline, Ecological Pyramids, Figure 3–8
TR: Lesson Plan 3–3, Section Summary, p. 6 L1, p. 16 L2, Worksheets, pp. 11–13 L1, pp. 22–23 L2, Enrichment L3 **LW:** Chapter 3 Exploration L1 L2 L3 **RSW:** Section 3–3 L2 **ARSW:** Section 3–3 L1	**SE:** 3–3 Section Assessment, p. 80 **TR:** Section Review 3–3	**iText:** Section 3–3 **TP:** 3–3 Interest Grabber, Section Outline, The Water Cycle, Figure 3–13, Figure 3–14 **BD:** *Pfiesteria:* A Killer in the Water
	SE: Chapter 3 Assessment, pp. 82–85 **TR:** Chapter Vocabulary Review, Graphic Organizer, Chapter 3 Test	**iText:** Chapter 3 Assessment **CTB:** Chapter 3 Test

Go Online
Students can do research, share data, and test their knowledge online.

TIME SAVER PRESSED FOR TIME?

To Preview the Chapter

- Have students read the Key Concepts in Sections 3–1 and 3–2.
- Assign the Reading Strategy for Section 3–3.

To Cover the Chapter Quickly

- Have students study Figure 3–2 and read Levels of Organization in Section 3–1, read pages 67–70 in Section 3–2, and read all of Section 3–3.
- Assign question 1 in 3–1 Section Assessment, questions 1 and 2 in 3–2 Section Assessment, question 1 in 3–3 Section Assessment, and questions 11–16, 18, and 21 in Chapter 3 Assessment. Assign questions 1–7 in Chapter 3 Standards Practice

To Review the Chapter

- Assign Sections 3–2 and 3–3 in the Reading and Study Workbook or the Adapted Reading and Study Workbook.
- Assign the Chapter Vocabulary Review for Chapter 3 in Teaching Resources.

CHAPTER 3

ENGAGE/EXPLORE

Inquiry Activity

Objective Students will be able to identify relationships among various types of organisms they have observed in their immediate environment. L1 L2

Skills Focus Classifying, Predicting, Asking Questions

Time 10 minutes

Strategies

- Emphasize to students that they should list specific types of organisms, not broad categories such as "trees" or "birds."
- If students have difficulty identifying different kinds of relationships, let them brainstorm ideas in a class discussion.

Expected Outcome Students should be able to identify at least five different types of common organisms and at least two different types of relationships among them, such as: feeding relationships; using plants for nesting sites, shelter, and hiding places; and creating favorable conditions for other organisms (for example, earthworms aerating soil).

Think About It

1. Students should identify most plants and several first- and second-order consumers as providing energy and nutrients to other organisms.
2. All other organisms would die, since they are dependent on plants either directly (as first-order consumers) or indirectly (as higher-order consumers, scavengers, or decomposers).
3. Accept all reasonable answers. Sample answer: Changes are difficult to predict because there are so many variables.

Brain Teaser

Challenge students' thinking by asking: **How do animals benefit plants?** *(Possible responses include: Some animals disperse plant seeds. Others help in pollination. Decomposers break down animal wastes and the remains of dead organisms into simpler substances that provide nutrients for plants. Some plants are nurtured and protected by humans.)*

CHAPTER 3

The Biosphere

A tawny owl prepares to seize a mouse. The mouse is carrying a berry in its mouth as it runs along a fallen, moss-covered tree trunk. The owl, the mouse, the tree trunk, and the moss are all members of this forest ecosystem.

Inquiry Activity

How do organisms affect one another's survival?

Procedure

1. Make a list of all the types of organisms, including plants, humans, insects, and so on, that you have seen near your home or school.
2. Make a diagram that shows how the organisms on your list interact with one another.

Think About It

1. **Classifying** Which organisms on your list provide energy or nutrients to the others?
2. **Predicting** What would you expect to happen if all the plants on your diagram died? Explain your answer.
3. **Asking Questions** Why is it difficult to make accurate predictions about changes in communities of organisms?

FACTS AND FIGURES

Earth's biosphere

In Earth's biosphere, populations of organisms interact not only with one another but also with the three major divisions of the abiotic environment: the lithosphere (the soil and rock of Earth's crust), the atmosphere (the gases surrounding Earth), and the hydrosphere (all of Earth's water, whether gaseous, liquid, or frozen, fresh or saline). Earth's biosphere is a closed system. Nothing leaves or enters—except energy from the sun, the ultimate source of all life on Earth. Much more solar energy reaches Earth each day than is needed to support Earth's producers. Most of the "extra" energy is absorbed or reflected by Earth's surface and atmosphere. In fact, only about .06 percent of the solar energy that reaches Earth's producers is converted to chemical energy through the process of photosynthesis. That amount, however, is sufficient to produce about 170 billion tons of organic matter every year!

3–1 What Is Ecology?

"Floods hit Texas!" "Wildfires char three states!" "Drought withers Florida!" Such news often flashes across television screens, newspapers, and the Internet. We are fascinated and frightened by these natural events, but there are other stories, as well. Some tell of projects to restore wetlands in southern Florida and along the Mississippi River for the purpose of controlling floods and droughts. Others report on improvements in air and water quality as a result of changes in the gasoline that we put in our cars. Like all organisms, we interact with our environment. To understand these interactions better and to learn how to control them, we turn to the science called ecology.

Guide for Reading

Key Concepts
- What different levels of organization do ecologists study?
- What methods are used to study ecology?

Vocabulary
ecology
biosphere
species
population
community
ecosystem
biome

Reading Strategy: Asking Questions Before you read, rewrite the headings in this section as *how, what,* or *why* questions about ecology. Then, as you read, write brief answers to your questions.

Interactions and Interdependence

Ecology (ee-KAHL-uh-jee) is the scientific study of interactions among organisms and between organisms and their environment, or surroundings. The word *ecology* was coined in 1866 by the German biologist Ernst Haeckel. Haeckel based this term on the Greek word *oikos,* meaning house, which is also the root of the word *economy.* Haeckel saw the living world as a household with an economy in which each organism plays a role.

Nature's "houses" come in many sizes—from single cells to the entire planet. The largest of these houses is called the biosphere. The **biosphere** contains the combined portions of the planet in which all of life exists, including land, water, and air, or atmosphere. It extends from about 8 kilometers above Earth's surface to as far as 11 kilometers below the surface of the ocean.

Interactions within the biosphere produce a web of interdependence between organisms and the environment in which they live. Whether it occurs on top of a glacier, in a forest like the one in **Figure 3–1,** or deep within an ocean trench, the interdependence of life on Earth contributes to an ever-changing, or dynamic, biosphere.

▶ **Figure 3–1** Organisms and their environment are interdependent. This giant land snail could not survive without plants and algae to eat, and the plants and algae could not grow unless bacteria and other organisms helped recycle nutrients in the water and soil. **Classifying** *List the organisms that you see in the photograph. Then, list the nonliving parts of the environment with which the organisms interact.*

Section 3–1

1 FOCUS

Objectives

3.1.1 ***Identify*** the levels of organization that ecologists study.
3.1.2 ***Describe*** the methods used to study ecology.

Guide for Reading

Reading Strategy

Before students begin their outlines, point out that one major topic below each heading is identified by bold type preceded by the key symbol. Encourage students to rephrase the Key Concepts in their own words. Also point out the highlighted, boldface Vocabulary terms and their definitions.

2 INSTRUCT

Interactions and Interdependence

Make Connections

Earth Science Call on a volunteer to read the definition of *ecology* aloud. Ask: **What nonliving things in their environment do organisms interact with?** *(Sunlight, air, water, soil, rocks)* **In what ways are these nonliving things essential to organisms?** *(Accept all reasonable descriptions of how abiotic factors meet organisms' needs.)* L2

Build Science Skills

Applying Concepts Point out that no organism exists in isolation but that all types of organisms on Earth depend on one another for their survival. Ask: **What evidence do you see that people in our society today are aware of the interdependence of living things?** *(Laws have been enacted to reduce air, water, and land pollution and to protect endangered species. People are encouraged to conserve natural resources through recycling and in other ways.)* L1 L2

Answer to . . .

Figure 3–1 *The snail, ferns, mosses, and other plants are organisms. They interact with the rocks, water, air, and light.*

TIME SAVER — SECTION RESOURCES

Print:
- ***Teaching Resources,*** Lesson Plan 3–1, Adapted Section Summary 3–1, Adapted Worksheets 3–1, Section Summary 3–1, Worksheets 3–1, Section Review 3–1
- ***Reading and Study Workbook A,*** Section 3–1
- ***Adapted Reading and Study Workbook B,*** Section 3–1

Technology:
- ***iText,*** Section 3–1
- ***Transparencies Plus,*** Section 3–1

3–1 (continued)

Levels of Organization

Use Visuals

Figure 3–2 As the class looks at the figure, call on students at random to define the term that identifies each level of organization: *population, community, ecosystem, biome,* and *biosphere.* Then, ask: **Can a group of rabbits and a group of field mice make up the same population in an ecosystem?** *(No, because individuals that make up a population must be of the same species)* **Could a biome in Brazil near the equator be the same as a biome in northern Canada? Explain.** *(No, because those two biomes would have different climates and different dominant communities)* L2

Build Science Skills

Applying Concepts To reinforce levels of organization, have students make posters or bulletin-board displays similar to the illustration in Figure 3–2, but with different examples of the six levels of organization. Students can draw the illustrations themselves or use pictures they have cut or photocopied from magazines and books. Have students work in small groups, and encourage each group to focus on a different biome. Have students scan Section 4–3 to identify major biomes. L2

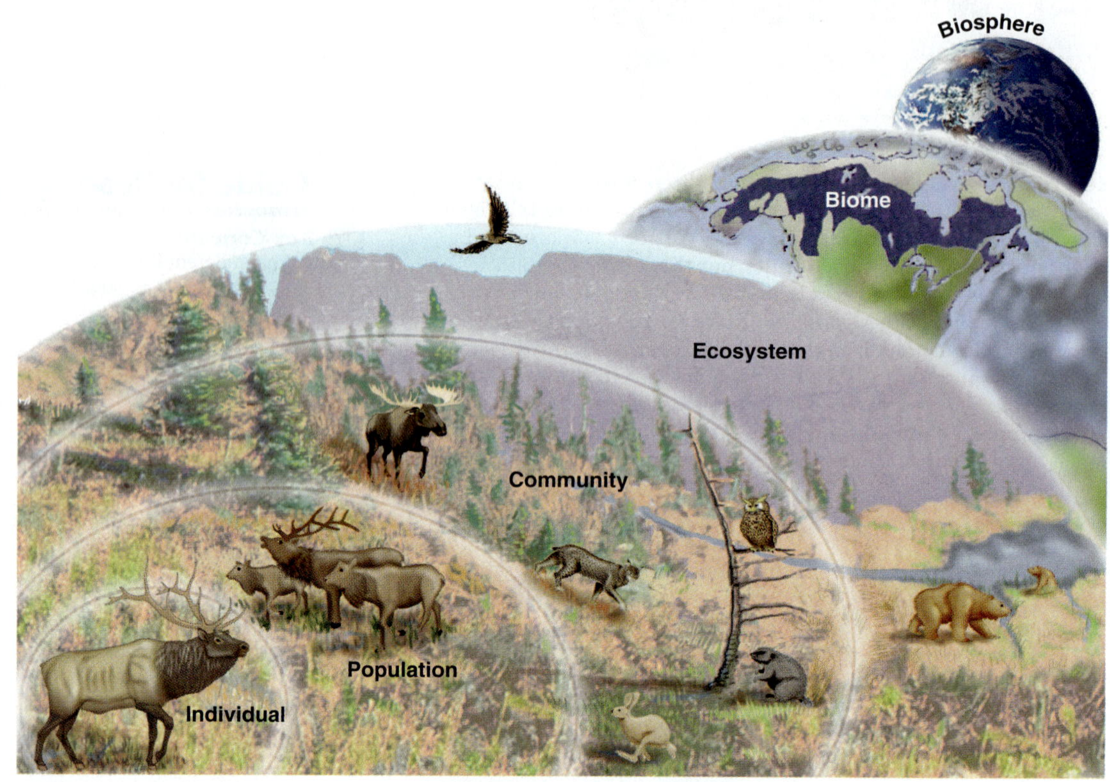

▲ **Figure 3–2** **The study of ecology ranges from the study of an individual organism to populations, communities, ecosystems, biomes—and, finally, to the entire biosphere.** The information that ecologists gain at each level contributes to our understanding of natural systems.

Levels of Organization

To understand relationships within the biosphere, ecologists ask questions about events and organisms that range in complexity from a single individual to the entire biosphere. The many levels of organization that ecologists study are shown in **Figure 3–2.**

Some ecologists study interactions between a particular kind of organism and its surroundings. Such studies focus on the species level. A **species** is a group of organisms so similar to one another that they can breed and produce fertile offspring. Other ecologists study **populations,** or groups of individuals that belong to the same species and live in the same area. Still other ecologists study **communities,** or assemblages of different populations that live together in a defined area.

Ecologists may study a particular ecosystem. An **ecosystem** is a collection of all the organisms that live in a particular place, together with their nonliving, or physical, environment. Larger systems called biomes are also studied by teams of ecologists. A **biome** is a group of ecosystems that have the same climate and similar dominant communities. The highest level of organization that ecologists study is the entire biosphere itself.

 *What is an ecosystem?*

ESL SUPPORT FOR ENGLISH LANGUAGE LEARNERS

Vocabulary: Word Analysis

Beginning Draw a circle labeled *Earth* on the board. Shade the outer portion of the circle and an area surrounding the circle, and label the shaded circle *biosphere.* Write *biosphere* on the board, and draw boxes around the prefix *bio-* and the base word *sphere.* Point out that *bio-* means "life" and *sphere* means "ball or circle." Have students write *biosphere* on their paper and define the term using short phrases, single words, or pictures. L1

Intermediate Extend the beginning-level activity by having the students list other words that use the prefix *bio-*. Possible answers include *biology,* the study of life, and *biography,* a book about someone's life. L2

Ecological Methods

Ecologists use a wide range of tools and techniques to study the living world. Some, like the scientists in **Figure 3–3**, use binoculars and field guides to assess changes in plant and wildlife communities. Others use studies of DNA to identify bacteria in the mud of coastal marshes. Still others use radio tags to track migrating wildlife or use data gathered by satellites.

Regardless of the tools they use, scientists conduct modern ecological research using three basic approaches: observing, experimenting, and modeling. All of these approaches rely on the application of scientific methods to guide ecological inquiry.

Observing Observing is often the first step in asking ecological questions. Some observations are simple: What species live here? How many individuals of each species are there? Other observations are more complex and may form the first step in designing experiments and models.

Experimenting Experiments can be used to test hypotheses. An ecologist may set up an artificial environment in a laboratory to imitate and manipulate conditions that organisms would encounter in the natural world. Other experiments are conducted within natural ecosystems.

Modeling Many ecological phenomena occur over long periods of time or on such large spatial scales that they are difficult to study. Ecologists make models to gain insight into complex phenomena such as the effects of global warming on ecosystems. Many ecological models consist of mathematical formulas based on data collected through observation and experimentation. The predictions made by ecological models are often tested by further observations and experiments.

▲ **Figure 3–3** **The three fundamental approaches to ecological research involve observing, experimenting, and modeling.** These ecologists are studying a rain forest ecosystem in Sri Lanka. They are using field observations to collect data on vines and other plants.

3–1 Section Assessment

1. **Key Concept** List the six different levels of organization that ecologists study, in order from smallest to largest.
2. **Key Concept** Describe the three basic methods of ecological research.
3. Identify two ways in which you interact every day with each of the three parts of the biosphere—land, water, and air.
4. **Critical Thinking Applying Concepts** Suppose you wanted to know if the water in a certain stream is safe to drink. Which ecological method(s) would you choose, and why?
5. **Critical Thinking Applying Concepts** Give an example of an ecological phenomenon that could be studied by modeling. Explain why modeling would be useful.

Thinking Visually

Creating a Table
Refer to **Figure 3–2**, which shows the various levels of organization that ecologists study. In a table, provide examples of the ecological levels where you live—individuals, populations, communities, and ecosystems—that could be studied by ecologists. *Hint:* You may wish to use library resources or the Internet.

Ecological Methods

Build Science Skills

Classifying Divide the class into groups of three, and have each group list one specific example of each ecological method, with all three examples relating to the same type of ecosystem. Then, let groups exchange lists and identify the ecological method that each example represents. L1 L2

3 ASSESS

Evaluate Understanding

Using the diagrams they drew for the Inquiry Activity on page 62, have students write a paragraph describing how the organisms shown in the diagram depend on one another and on nonliving things in their environment.

Reteach

Call on one student to name an individual organism, a second student to identify the population to which the organism belongs, a third student to describe the community of which the population is a part, and a fourth student to describe the community's ecosystem. Repeat this procedure until every student has had at least one turn.

Thinking Visually

The information in students' tables may vary, because students may choose to include any of the populations common in the ecosystems in the area where they live. Each table should include columns for individuals, populations, communities, and ecosystems. Library resources or the Internet could provide students with specific examples of populations that live in the types of ecosystems in their area.

3–1 Section Assessment

1. Individual, population, community, ecosystem, biome, biosphere
2. Observing involves using the senses to gather information. Experimenting involves testing hypotheses in a laboratory or natural ecosystem. Modeling involves making representations of ecological phenomena.
3. Student answers should give examples of interactions with land, water, and air.
4. Most students will choose experimenting, which would involve testing a hypothesis about whether the water is safe to drink. Some students might choose modeling, which would involve using a model to investigate whether pollutants or organisms could enter the water.
5. Answers may vary. A typical response might suggest using a mathematical model to study the effects of global warming on an ecosystem.

Interactive Textbook

If your class subscribes to the iText, use it to review the Key Concepts in Section 3–1.

Answer to . . .

CHECKPOINT *A collection of all the organisms that live in a particular place, together with their nonliving, or physical, environment*

TECHNOLOGY & SOCIETY

After students have read this feature, you might want to discuss one or more of the following:

- From their previous learning, students may know how the destruction of forests affects the global carbon-oxygen cycle and water cycle. Have them share this information in a class discussion. Then, ask: **Why is it important for ecologists to be aware of forest destruction? How do you think they would use this information?**
- Discuss the role of phytoplankton in the carbon-oxygen cycle. (You may want to have students preview Energy From the Sun on page 68.)

Research and Decide

Have students write a report on what they found in their research on satellite use in ecological studies. Ask students to expand on the discussion in this feature about such use by ecologists and then propose ways governments might use the data collected. For example, a local government might study satellite images over time to find out about wetlands in order to make sure development doesn't destroy important natural areas.

Students can research the use of satellites in ecology on the site developed by authors Ken Miller and Joe Levine.

TECHNOLOGY & SOCIETY

Exploring Ecology From Space

Modern research in global ecology would not be possible if all its tools were earthbound. Studies on a planetary scale require enormous data-gathering networks. Through a process called remote sensing, satellites extend the range of information that ecologists can collect within the biosphere.

Remote-sensing satellites are fitted with optical sensors that can scan several bands of the electromagnetic spectrum and convert those bands into electrical signals. The signals are run through a computer and converted into digital values, which are used to construct an image.

Remote sensing provides detailed images of essentially every square meter of Earth's surface. How else could scientists view all the world's lakes and oceans to see where concentrations of algae are the highest? Or view areas of destroyed forests in places like the Amazon Basin or northern Russia?

Global Change

The false-color image below was assembled from data gathered by NASA's Sea-viewing Wide Field-of-view Sensor (SeaWiFS) Project. The project's goal is to study factors that affect global change and to assess the oceans' role in the global carbon cycle, as well as other chemical cycles. The different ocean colors indicate varying concentrations of microscopic algae. Blue represents the least amount of algae, and red represents the highest amount. On land, the dark green areas have the most vegetation, and gold land areas have the least.

Rain Forest Destruction

Satellite images that show the presence or absence of vegetation are useful in studying the effects of human activity on natural ecosystems. The two images above, taken 26 years apart, show the same tract of land in a Brazilian rain forest. Red areas show undisturbed forest, and whitish areas show places where trees have been cut and cleared. Note the "fishbone" pattern of vegetation clearing. This pattern occurs because cutting of forests typically begins along existing roads and rivers and then spreads out as new roads and paths are cut.

Data in images such as these, especially when taken over time, help ecologists estimate the rate at which rain forests are being cut down. These data are also valuable in discussing the effects of development with local governments.

Research and Decide

Use library or Internet resources to learn more about the use of satellites in ecological studies. Decide how ecologists and local governments might use the data in their discussion.

For: Links from the authors
Visit: PHSchool.com
Web Code: cbe-2031

FACTS AND FIGURES

Terra in space

Launched in 1999, the school-bus-sized Terra—the "flagship" spacecraft in NASA's Earth Orbiting System—has been described as "a sort of Hubble Space Telescope aimed at Earth." The amount of data that Terra collects each day—about 100,000 encyclopedia volumes' worth—roughly equals the amount of data collected by the Hubble telescope in one year.

Terra circles 705 kilometers above Earth's surface in a polar orbit that carries it past the equator at 10:30 AM each day, when cloud cover over Earth's landmasses is minimal. The satellite's five instruments monitor Earth's radiation balance, sea surface temperatures, levels of greenhouse gases and changes in land cover use, ice sheet volume, and atmospheric chemistry. Data from Terra also may have practical applications, such as managing crops and coastal fisheries and assessing natural hazards such as volcanic activity, earthquakes, floods, and fires.

3–2 Energy Flow

6 5.b. Students know matter is transferred over time from one organism to others in the food web and between organisms and the physical environment. **BI 6.d.** Students know how water, carbon, and nitrogen cycle between abiotic resources and organic matter in the ecosystem and how oxygen cycles through photosynthesis and respiration. **BI 6.e.** Students know how a vital part of an ecosystem is the stability of its producers and decomposers. **BI 6.f.** Students know at each link in a food web some energy is stored in newly made structures but much energy is dissipated into the environment as heat. This dissipation may be represented in an energy pyramid.

At the core of every organism's interaction with the environment is its need for energy to power life's processes. Consider, for example, the energy that ants use to carry objects many times their size or the energy that birds use to migrate thousands of miles. Think about the energy that you need to get out of bed in the morning! The flow of energy through an ecosystem is one of the most important factors that determines the system's capacity to sustain life.

Guide for Reading

Key Concepts
- Where does the energy for life processes come from?
- How does energy flow through living systems?
- How efficient is the transfer of energy among organisms in an ecosystem?

Vocabulary
autotroph • producer
photosynthesis
chemosynthesis • heterotroph
consumer • herbivore
carnivore • omnivore
detritivore • decomposer
food chain • food web
trophic level
ecological pyramid • biomass

Reading Strategy: Building Vocabulary As you read, make notes about the meaning of each term in the list above and how it relates to energy flow in the biosphere. Then, draw a concept map to show the relationships among these terms.

Producers

Without a constant input of energy, living systems cannot function. **Sunlight is the main energy source for life on Earth.** Of all the sun's energy that reaches Earth's surface, only a small amount—less than 1 percent—is used by living things. This seemingly small amount is enough to produce as much as 3.5 kilograms of living tissue per square meter a year in some tropical forests.

In a few ecosystems, some organisms obtain energy from a source other than sunlight. **Some types of organisms rely on the energy stored in inorganic chemical compounds.** For instance, mineral water that flows underground or boils out of hot springs and undersea vents is loaded with chemical energy.

Only plants, some algae, and certain bacteria can capture energy from sunlight or chemicals and use that energy to produce food. These organisms are called **autotrophs.** Autotrophs use energy from the environment to fuel the assembly of simple inorganic compounds into complex organic molecules. These organic molecules combine and recombine to produce living tissue. Because they make their own food, autotrophs, like the kelp in **Figure 3–4**, are also called **producers.** Both types of producers—those that capture energy from sunlight and those that capture chemical energy—are essential to the flow of energy through the biosphere.

CA a

(a) BI 6.e

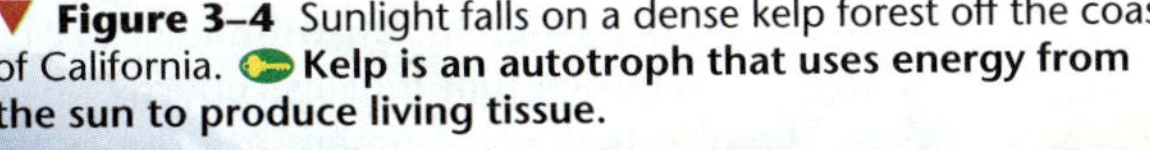

▼ **Figure 3–4** Sunlight falls on a dense kelp forest off the coast of California. **Kelp is an autotroph that uses energy from the sun to produce living tissue.**

SECTION RESOURCES

Print:
- ***Teaching Resources,*** Lesson Plan 3–2, Adapted Section Summary 3–2, Adapted Worksheets 3–2, Section Summary 3–2, Worksheets 3–2, Section Review 3–2
- ***Reading and Study Workbook A,*** Section 3–2
- ***Adapted Reading and Study Workbook B,*** Section 3–2

Technology:
- ***iText,*** Section 3–2
- ***Transparencies Plus,*** Section 3–2

Section 3–2

6 5.b, BI 6.d, BI 6.e, BI 6.f

1 FOCUS

Objectives

3.2.1 ***Identify*** the source of energy for life processes.
3.2.2 ***Trace*** the flow of energy through living systems.
3.2.3 ***Evaluate*** the efficiency of energy transfer among organisms in an ecosystem.

Guide for Reading

Vocabulary Preview

To help students understand related terms in this section, write the following sets of words and word parts on the board.
Set 1: *photo-, chemo-, synthesis*
Set 2: *herb-, carn-, omni-, detritus, -vore*
Have students look up the meaning of all words and parts in a dictionary and list them. As students read the section and make notes about the terms, they can check the text's definitions against this list.

Reading Strategy

Students' concept maps could be titled "Energy Flow" and begin with autotrophs, or producers, which make food through photosynthesis or chemosynthesis. Then, students should add the various types of heterotrophs to their concept maps and show how the various types of organisms are interrelated, using the terms *food chain, food web, trophic level,* and *ecological pyramid.*

2 INSTRUCT

Producers

Building Science Skills

Measuring Have groups of students cut out one-square-meter pieces of heavy wrapping or butcher paper. Next, let each group use a balance and various common objects in the classroom to measure out 3.5 kg of mass, and then place the objects on the paper square. Encourage the groups to examine one another's piles of objects. Emphasize that each pile represents the amount of living tissue produced per square meter each year in a tropical forest. L1 L2

3–2 (continued)

Make Connections

Chemistry On the board, write the chemical equation for photosynthesis:

$$6CO_2 + 6H_2O \xrightarrow[\text{energy}]{\text{light}} C_6H_{12}O_6 + 6O_2$$

Ask: **Which element does each letter in the formulas stand for?** *(C for carbon; O, oxygen; H, hydrogen)* Explain that the equation can be read as "Six molecules of carbon dioxide and six molecules of water combine in the presence of light energy to yield one molecule of glucose and six molecules of oxygen." Ask: **Why are the numbers needed in the equation?** *(Without numbers, the equation wouldn't be balanced.)* If students are not familiar with this concept, write the equation on the board, and then cross out the balanced pairs—6 carbon atoms (6C) on the left and 6 carbon atoms (C_6) on the right; 18 oxygen atoms ($6O_2$ + 6O) on the left and 18 (O_6 + $6O_2$) on the right; 12 hydrogen atoms ($6H_2$) on the left and 12 (H_{12}) on the right. L2

Consumers

Build Science Skills

Classifying Divide the class into small groups, and provide each group with photocopies of a wide variety of organisms, including plants, multicellular algae, invertebrates, and vertebrates. Then, have each group sort its organisms into two piles—producers and consumers—and then sort the consumers into piles representing the four subcategories of herbivores, carnivores, omnivores, and decomposers. L1 L2

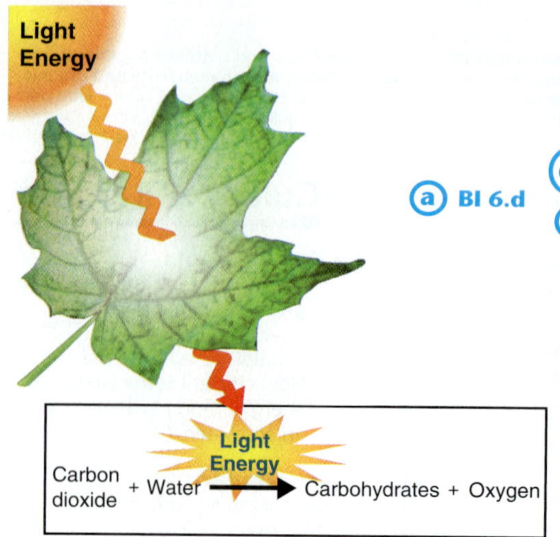

PHOTOSYNTHESIS IN PLANTS

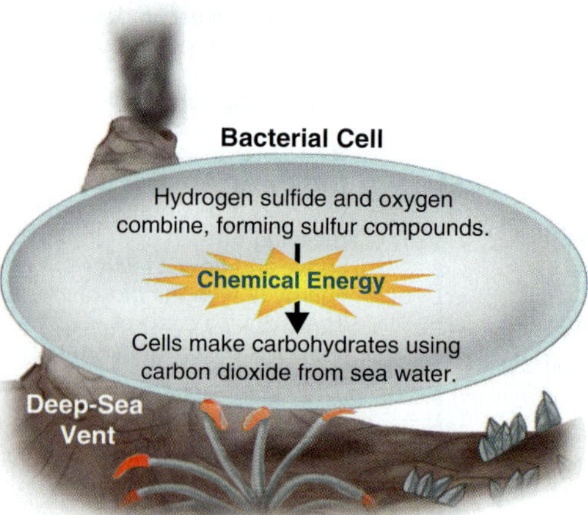

CHEMOSYNTHESIS IN SULFUR BACTERIA

Figure 3–5 **Sunlight is the main energy source for life on Earth. Some types of organisms rely on the energy stored in inorganic chemical compounds.** Plants use the energy from sunlight to carry out the process of photosynthesis. Other autotrophs, such as sulfur bacteria, use the energy stored in chemical bonds for chemosynthesis. In both cases, energy-rich carbohydrates are produced.

(a) BI 6.d

Energy From the Sun The best-known autotrophs are those that harness solar energy through a process known as photosynthesis. During **photosynthesis,** these autotrophs use light energy to power chemical reactions that convert carbon dioxide and water into oxygen and energy-rich carbohydrates such as sugars and starches. This process, shown in **Figure 3–5** (top), is responsible for adding oxygen to—and removing carbon dioxide from—Earth's atmosphere. In fact, were it not for photosynthetic autotrophs, the air would not contain enough oxygen for you to breathe!

On land, plants are the main autotrophs. In freshwater ecosystems and in the sunlit upper layers of the ocean, algae are the main autotrophs. Photosynthetic bacteria, the most common of which are the cyanobacteria (sy-an-oh-bak-TEER-ee-uh), are important in certain wet ecosystems such as tidal flats and salt marshes.

Life Without Light Although plants are the most visible and best-known autotrophs, some autotrophs can produce food in the absence of light. Such autotrophs rely on energy within the chemical bonds of inorganic molecules such as hydrogen sulfide. When organisms use chemical energy to produce carbohydrates, the process is called **chemosynthesis** (kee-moh-SIN-thuh-sis), as shown in **Figure 3–5** (bottom). This process is performed by several types of bacteria. Surprisingly, these bacteria represent a large proportion of living autotrophs. Some chemosynthetic bacteria live in very remote places on Earth, such as volcanic vents on the deep-ocean floor and hot springs in Yellowstone Park. Others live in more common places, such as tidal marshes along the coast.

CHECKPOINT *What is the difference between photosynthesis and chemosynthesis?*

Consumers

(b) BI 6.e

Many organisms—including animals, fungi, and many bacteria—cannot harness energy directly from the physical environment as autotrophs do. The only way these organisms can acquire energy is from other organisms. Organisms that rely on other organisms for their energy and food supply are called **heterotrophs** (HET-ur-oh-trohfs). Heterotrophs are also called **consumers.**

UNIVERSAL ACCESS

Inclusion/Special Needs
To engage students' interest in feeding relationships and ecological pyramids, ask students about feeding relationships with which they may have some familiarity. For example, most students will know that birds in their neighborhood feed on either seeds and berries or small animals such as worms and insects. Elicit from students ideas about relative numbers at different trophic levels, energy transfer, and biomass comparisons. L1

Advanced Learners
Point out to interested students this sentence on page 68 about chemosynthetic bacteria: "Surprisingly, these bacteria represent a large proportion of living autotrophs." Challenge students to find out about such bacteria, including those that live in hot springs and those that live in the deep ocean around vents. Have students prepare reports about what they find and present them to the class when students study bacteria in Chapter 19. L3

There are many different types of heterotrophs. **Herbivores** obtain energy by eating only plants. Some herbivores are cows, caterpillars, and deer. **Carnivores,** including snakes, dogs, and owls, eat animals. Humans, bears, crows, and other **omnivores** eat both plants and animals. **Detritivores,** (dee-TRYT-uh-vawrz), such as mites, earthworms, snails, and crabs, feed on plant and animal remains and other dead matter, collectively called detritus. Another important group of heterotrophs, called **decomposers,** breaks down organic matter. Bacteria and fungi, such as the one in **Figure 3–6,** are decomposers. CA a

▲ **Figure 3–6** This fungus, growing on the forest floor, is a decomposer that obtains nutrients by breaking down dead and decaying plants and animals. It is called a coral fungus because of its color and shape. **Classifying** *Is the fungus a producer or a consumer?*

ⓐ BI 6.e
ⓑ 6 5.b

Feeding Relationships

What happens to the energy in an ecosystem when one organism eats another? That energy moves along a one-way path. **Energy flows through an ecosystem in one direction, from the sun or inorganic compounds to autotrophs (producers) and then to various heterotrophs (consumers).** The relationships between producers and consumers connect organisms into feeding networks based on who eats whom.

Food Chains The energy stored by producers can be passed through an ecosystem along a **food chain,** a series of steps in which organisms transfer energy by eating and being eaten. For example, in a prairie ecosystem, a food chain might consist of a producer, such as grass, that is fed upon by a herbivore, such as a grazing antelope. The herbivore is in turn fed upon by a carnivore, such as a coyote. In this situation, the carnivore is only two steps removed from the producer. CA b

In some marine food chains, such as the one in **Figure 3–7,** the producers are microscopic algae that are eaten by very small organisms called zooplankton (zoh-oh-PLANK-tun). The zooplankton, in turn, are eaten by small fish, such as herring. The herring are eaten by squid, which are ultimately eaten by large fish, such as sharks. In this food chain, the top carnivore is four steps removed from the producer.

▼ **Figure 3–7** **Food chains show the one-way flow of energy in an ecosystem.** In this marine food chain, energy is passed from the producers (algae) to four different groups of consumers.

Feeding Relationships

Use Visuals

Figure 3–7 After students have studied the figure, ask: **Among the organisms shown, which are autotrophs and which are heterotrophs?** *(The algae are autotrophs; the others are heterotrophs.)* **Among the heterotrophs, which are herbivores and which are carnivores?** *(The zooplankton are herbivores; the other heterotrophs are carnivores.)* **What kind of heterotrophs might enter this food chain when the shark dies and falls to the ocean floor?** *(Detritivores and decomposers)* L1 L2

Build Science Skills

Applying Concepts Show students some acorns, sunflower seeds, or other common type of seed, and ask: **Where did these seeds come from?** *(A plant)* **What kind of animal might eat these seeds?** *(Depending on the type of seeds used, a squirrel, chickadee, mouse, or chipmunk might eat them.)* **What kind of animal might eat the animal that ate the seeds?** *(A larger carnivore such as a fox, hawk, or coyote)* **What is the feeding relationship that you just described called?** *(A food chain)* **What happens to energy in the food chain?** *(Energy is transferred from the organism being eaten to the organism doing the eating. Some energy from lower trophic levels is lost as heat.)* **What was the original source of energy in the food chain?** *(The sun)* L2

BIO INSIGHTS — FACTS AND FIGURES

Energy moves up the chain

In nature, simple "straight line" food chains are rare, primarily because few species eat or are eaten by only one other species. Nevertheless, a food chain is a useful model for studying the transfer of energy and materials in an ecosystem.

All food chains on land begin with producers that use light energy to synthesize organic compounds. Primary consumers are herbivores that feed directly on the producers. Above the primary consumers are secondary consumers, then tertiary consumers, and, in some food chains, quaternary consumers. Not many food chains extend beyond four consumer levels. Decomposers (also known as saprotrophs), detritivores, and parasites—organisms that live in or on other organisms and obtain energy from them—can occupy any level of a food chain.

Answers to . . .

CHECKPOINT *Photosynthesis uses light energy. Chemosynthesis uses the energy stored in chemical bonds.*

Figure 3–6 *A consumer*

3–2 (continued)

Quick Lab

Objective Students will be able to describe the organization of a simple food chain. L1 L2

Skill Focus **Classifying**

Materials 2 wide-mouth jars, 2 pieces of flexible screening, 2 rubber bands, 2 bean seedlings in small pots or paper cups, pea aphids, ladybird beetles

Time 15 minutes for initial setup, 5 minutes per day for one week to observe and record

Advance Prep

- About two weeks before students do this activity, plant bean seeds in pots or paper cups. Each group will need two seedlings. Plant extras in case some plants do not thrive.
- Aphids and ladybird beetles may be collected outdoors or ordered from a biological supply house. Ladybird beetles also may be available at garden centers as natural pest-controls. If the organisms are collected outdoors, make sure they are returned to their original locations at the conclusion of the activity.
- Because it may be difficult to obtain pea aphids and ladybird beetles, you may want to use crickets and praying mantises instead.

Safety Caution students to handle organisms without harming them. Make sure they wash their hands with soap and warm water before leaving the lab.

Strategies

- Make the aphids and ladybird beetles available to students in a central distribution center.
- You may want to let students examine the aphids with magnifiers before they place them in the jars.

Expected Outcome See Analyze and Conclude number 1 below.

Analyze and Conclude

1. In the jar without ladybird beetles, the uncontrolled aphids harmed (or perhaps killed) the seedling. In the jar with ladybird beetles, the seedling was less damaged and survived longer. The ladybird beetles helped protect the seedling by eating some of the aphids that were feeding on it.
2. The seedlings are producers; the aphids and ladybird beetles are consumers.

Quick Lab

How is a food chain organized?

Materials 2 wide-mouth jars, 2 pieces of flexible screening, 2 rubber bands, 2 bean seedlings in small pots or paper cups, pea aphids, ladybird beetles

Procedure

1. Place a potted bean seedling in each of the two jars.
2. Add 20 aphids to one jar and cover the jar with screening to prevent the aphids from escaping. Use a rubber band to attach the screening to the jar.
3. Add 20 aphids and 4 ladybird beetles to the second jar. Cover the second jar as you did the first one.
4. **Formulating Hypotheses** Record your hypothesis about how the presence of the ladybird beetles will affect the survival of the aphids and the bean seedling. Also, record your prediction of what will happen to the organisms in each jar during the next week.
5. Place both jars in a sunny location. Observe the jars each day for one week and record your observations each day. Water the seedlings as needed.

Analyze and Conclude

1. **Observing** What happened to the aphids and the seedling in the jar without the ladybird beetles? In the jar with the ladybird beetles? How can you explain this difference?
2. **Classifying** Identify each organism in the jars as a producer or a consumer.

CA a 6 5.b

Food Webs In most ecosystems, feeding relationships are more complex than can be shown in a food chain. Consider, for example, the relationships in a salt marsh. Although some producers—including marsh grass and other salt-tolerant plants—are eaten by water birds, grasshoppers, and other herbivores, most producers complete their life cycles, then die and decompose. Decomposers convert the dead plant matter to detritus, which is eaten by detritivores, such as sandhoppers. The detritivores are in turn eaten by smelt and other small fish. Some of those consumers will also eat detritus directly. Add mice, larger fish, and hawks to the scenario, and feeding relationships can get very confusing!

When the feeding relationships among the various organisms in an ecosystem form a network of complex interactions, ecologists describe these relationships as a **food web.** A food web links all the food chains in an ecosystem together. The food web in **Figure 3–8,** for example, shows the feeding relationships in a salt-marsh community.

Trophic Levels Each step in a food chain or food web is called a **trophic** (TRAHF-ik) **level.** Producers make up the first trophic level. Consumers make up the second, third, or higher trophic levels. Each consumer depends on the trophic level below it for energy.

CHECKPOINT *What is a food web?*

Word Origins

Trophic originates from the Greek word *trophe,* which means "food or nourishment." **What do you think are the original meanings of the words *heterotroph* and *autotroph*?**

FACTS AND FIGURES

Two types of food webs

There are two basic types of food webs: grazing food webs and detrital food webs. A grazing food web begins with photosynthesizing plants, algae, or phytoplankton. A detrital food web begins with decomposers and detritivores. It is the detrital type of food web that enables nutrients to be recycled in ecosystems.

Decomposers and detritivores obtain energy by breaking down organic wastes and the remains of dead organisms. This process releases simple inorganic molecules such as mineral salts, carbon, nitrogen, phosphorous, and potassium, making these nutrients available for reuse by producers and, eventually, all other organisms in the ecosystem. Without decomposers and detritivores, such essential elements would remain in animal wastes and dead organisms.

FIGURE 3–8 FOOD WEB IN A SALT MARSH

This illustration of a food web shows some of the feeding relationships in a salt marsh. **Interpreting Graphics** *What does the marsh hawk feed on?*

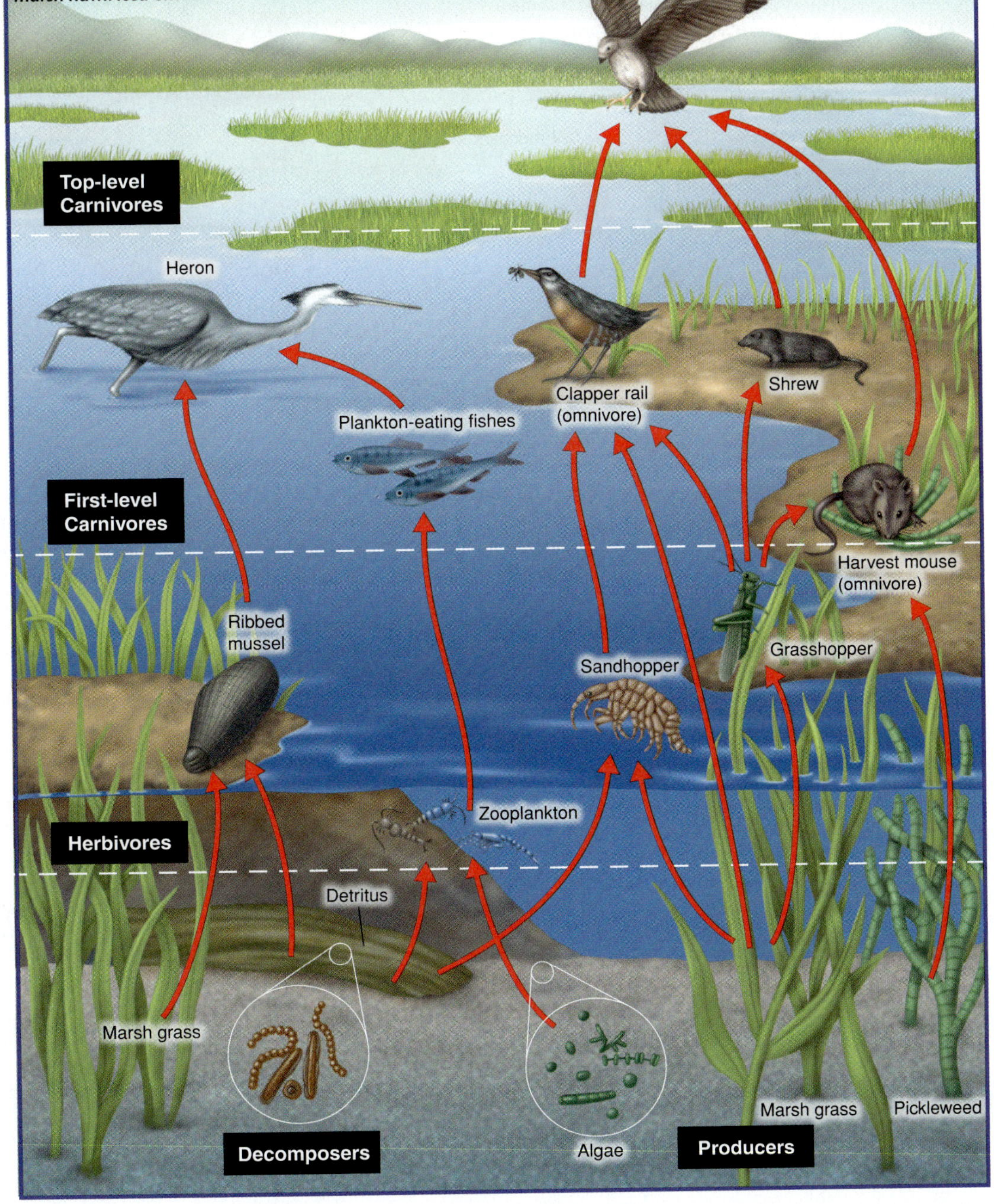

Top-level Carnivores
Marsh hawk
Heron
Clapper rail (omnivore)
Shrew
Plankton-eating fishes
First-level Carnivores
Harvest mouse (omnivore)
Ribbed mussel
Sandhopper
Grasshopper
Herbivores
Zooplankton
Detritus
Marsh grass
Decomposers
Algae
Producers
Marsh grass
Pickleweed

Use Visuals

Figure 3–8 To help students deal with the complexity of the food web, call on different students in turn to name the organisms in one food chain, beginning with a producer and working upward to the final consumer. For example, students might identify a food web including algae, zooplankton, plankton-eating fishes, and heron. L1 L2

Build Science Skills

Making Models Obtain at least 25 pictures of organisms—producers and different-level consumers—that could be found in an ecosystem other than the one shown in Figure 3–8. Tape the pictures in random order on the classroom walls, desktops, and other surfaces. Give each student a small ball of colored yarn and several small pieces of masking tape. Then, let four or five students at a time connect pictures with yarn to show different food chains. Students may crisscross the room with the yarn so the food web becomes quite complex. When every student has had a turn, let the class examine the results. Ask: **What is the name for this pattern of feeding relationships?** *(A food web)* **How is a food web different from a food chain?** *(A food web contains many overlapping food chains, so it is much more complex than a single food chain.)* L2

Word Origins

Hetero- means "other, different," and *auto-* means "self." Thus, *heterotroph* refers to an organism that feeds on other organisms, and *autotroph* refers to one that produces its own food.

TEACHER TO TEACHER

I have students make a food-web poster for a particular ecosystem or biome. The food web must contain at least five food chains consisting of a producer, a primary consumer, and a secondary consumer. Each consumer must be labeled as an herbivore, carnivore, omnivore, or decomposer. At least one predator-prey relationship must be shown. Five abiotic factors also must be included and labeled.

The posters may be drawn free-hand, or students may cut and paste pictures from magazines or computer printouts. I usually have students explain their posters to the class in oral presentations.

—LouEllen Parker Brademan
Teacher
Potomac Senior High School
Dumfries, Virginia

Answers to . . .

CHECKPOINT *A food web is the network of feeding relationships in an ecosystem.*

Figure 3–8 *Birds and small mammals*

3–2 (continued)

Ecological Pyramids

Make Connections

Mathematics Draw students' attention to the energy pyramid in Figure 3–9. Explain that the amount of energy available in food is measured in calories. One calorie is the amount of energy needed to raise the temperature of 1 gram of water 1°C. Scientists usually refer to the energy content of food in units of kilocalories. One kilocalorie equals 1000 calories. A kilocalorie is also expressed as a Calorie, with a capital C. Then, pose the following problem: **Suppose that the base of this energy pyramid consists of plants that contain 450,000 Calories of food energy. If all the plants were eaten by mice and insects, how much food energy would be available to those first-level consumers?** *(45,000 Calories)* **If all the mice and insects were eaten by snakes, how much food energy would be available to the snakes?** *(4500 Calories)* **If all the snakes were eaten by a hawk, how much food energy would be available to the hawk?** *(450 Calories)* **How much food energy would the hawk use for its body processes and lose as heat?** *(405 Calories—90 percent of 450)* **How much food energy would be stored in the hawk's body?** *(45 Calories)* L2

Build Science Skills

Applying Concepts Point out the exception described in the text of a numbers pyramid. Ask: **What would be the shape of a numbers pyramid for the forest?** *(The pyramid's base, representing the trees, would be much smaller than the second section, representing the insects that feed on the trees.)* L1 L2

Download a worksheet on energy pyramids for students to complete, and find additional teacher support from NSTA SciLinks.

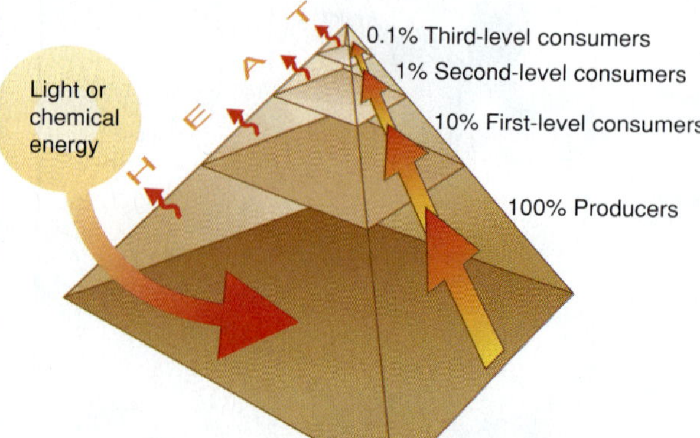

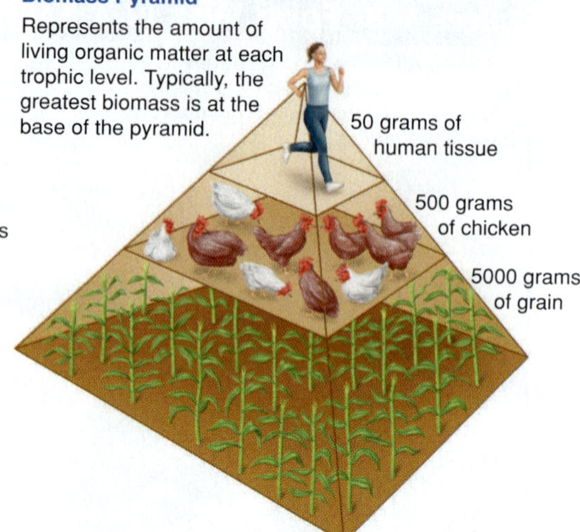

Ecological Pyramids

The amount of energy or matter in an ecosystem can be represented by an ecological pyramid. An **ecological pyramid** is a diagram that shows the relative amounts of energy or matter contained within each trophic level in a food chain or food web. Ecologists recognize three different types of ecological pyramids: energy pyramids, biomass pyramids, and pyramids of numbers. **Figure 3–9** shows an example of each type.

Energy Pyramid Theoretically, there is no limit to the number of trophic levels that a food chain can support. But there is one hitch. Only part of the energy that is stored in one trophic level is passed on to the next level. This is because organisms use much of the energy that they consume for life processes, such as respiration, movement, and reproduction. Some of the remaining energy is released into the environment as heat. **Only about 10 percent of the energy available within one trophic level is transferred to organisms at the next trophic level.** For instance, one tenth of the solar energy captured by grasses ends up stored in the tissues of cows and other grazers. Only one tenth of that energy—10 percent of 10 percent, or 1 percent total—is transferred to the humans that eat the cows. Thus, the more levels that exist between a producer and a top-level consumer in an ecosystem, the less energy that remains from the original amount.

For: Links on energy pyramids
Visit: www.SciLinks.org
Web Code: cbn-2032

Biomass Pyramid The total amount of living tissue within a given trophic level is called **biomass.** Biomass is usually expressed in terms of grams of organic matter per unit area. A biomass pyramid represents the amount of potential food available for each trophic level in an ecosystem.

BIOLOGY UPDATE

The rule of 10

The textbook's discussion of energy pyramids states that only about 10 percent of the energy available at each trophic level in a food chain is transferred to organisms at the next higher trophic level. This "rule of 10," which was based on early studies of aquatic ecosystems, is useful as a general approximation. However, it does not apply uniformly to all food chains.

More recent studies have demonstrated that energy efficiency varies between trophic levels in a food chain and between different food chains. In fact, these recent studies have yielded approximations of energy efficiency ranging from a low of 0.05 percent to a high of 20 percent.

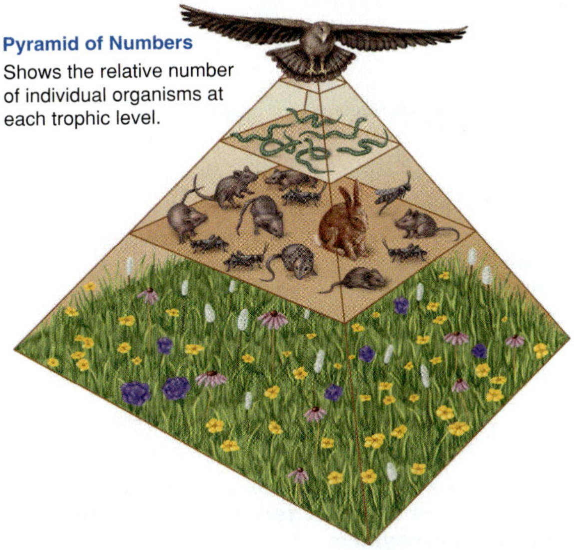

Pyramid of Numbers
Shows the relative number of individual organisms at each trophic level.

Figure 3–9 Ecological pyramids show the decreasing amounts of energy, living tissue, or number of organisms at successive feeding levels. The pyramid is divided into sections that represent each trophic level. **Because each trophic level harvests only about one tenth of the energy from the level below, it can support only about one tenth the amount of living tissue.**

Pyramid of Numbers Ecological pyramids can also be based on the numbers of individual organisms at each trophic level. For some ecosystems, such as the meadow shown in **Figure 3–9** above, the shape of the pyramid of numbers is the same as that of the energy and biomass pyramids. This, however, is not always the case. In most forests, for example, there are fewer producers than there are consumers. A single tree has a large amount of energy and biomass, but it is only one organism. Many insects live in the tree, but they have less energy and biomass. Thus, a pyramid of numbers for a forest ecosystem would not resemble a typical pyramid at all!

BI 6.f

3–2 Section Assessment

1. **Key Concept** What are the two main forms of energy that power living systems?
2. **Key Concept** Briefly describe the flow of energy among organisms in an ecosystem.
3. **Key Concept** What proportion of energy is transferred from one trophic level to the next in an ecosystem?
4. Explain the relationships in this food chain: omnivore, herbivore, and autotroph.
5. **Critical Thinking Calculating** Draw an energy pyramid for a five-step food chain. If 100 percent of the energy is available at the first trophic level, what percentage of the total energy is available at the highest trophic level?

Focus on the BIG Idea

Interdependence in Nature Refer to **Figure 3–8**, which shows a food web in a salt marsh. Choose one of the food chains within this web. Then, write a paragraph describing the feeding relationships among the organisms in the food chain. *Hint:* Use the terms *producers, consumers,* and *decomposers* in your description.

3–2 Section Assessment

1. Solar energy is harnessed by autotrophs that conduct photosynthesis. Chemical energy—the energy within the chemical bonds of inorganic molecules—is harnessed by autotrophs that conduct chemosynthesis.
2. Students should describe a one-way flow of energy from autotrophs (producers) to consumers—first herbivores, and then carnivores and/or omnivores.
3. In general, about 10 percent
4. The autotroph is the producer, and it is eaten by the herbivore. The herbivore is then eaten by the omnivore.
5. Students' pyramids should show 100 percent of the energy available at the first (producer) level, 10 percent at the second level, 1 percent at the third level, 0.1 percent at the fourth level, and 0.01 percent at the fifth level.

3 ASSESS

Evaluate Understanding

Have each student draw and label a food web for a specific ecosystem of his or her choice. Tell students that the web should contain at least four food chains and that each food chain should consist of at least three organisms.

Reteach

Display a list of organisms that would be found in a specific ecosystem. Call on students in turn to identify each organism as a producer or a consumer. Write *P* or *C* next to each organism's name. Then, have students further classify each consumer as an herbivore, a carnivore, or an omnivore; write *H, C,* or *O* next to each name. As a final step, have students in turn link together any three organisms—a producer, an herbivore, and a carnivore—in a food chain.

Focus on the BIG Idea

Students may choose to describe any of the several food chains shown in Figure 3–8. A typical choice might begin with marsh grass as the producer. The marsh grass is eaten by the grasshopper, which is eaten by the harvest mouse, which is eaten by the marsh hawk. All three animals should be identified as consumers. Students might suggest that any or all of these organisms eventually die and are consumed by decomposers.

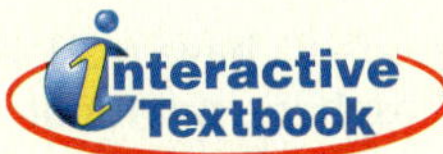

If your class subscribes to the iText, use it to review the Key Concepts in Section 3–2.

Section 3–3

 **BI 6.d**

1 FOCUS

Objectives

3.3.1 ***Describe*** how matter cycles among the living and nonliving parts of an ecosystem.

3.3.2 ***Explain*** why nutrients are important in living systems.

3.3.3 ***Describe*** how the availability of nutrients affects the productivity of ecosystems.

Guide for Reading

Vocabulary Preview

Figure 3–11, page 75, introduces seven terms. Two of the terms, *evaporation* and *transpiration,* are explicitly defined in the text. The meanings of the remaining five terms—*condensation, precipitation, runoff, seepage,* and *uptake*—can be inferred from their context. As students read about the water cycle on page 75, have them look for sentences that relate to the terms and copy them on a sheet of paper. Finally, using the sentences they copied as a basis, students can extrapolate a "formal" definition for each term. Have students share their definitions in a class discussion.

Reading Strategy

Have students make their own simplified cycle diagrams of the water cycle, carbon cycle, nitrogen cycle, and phosphorus cycle.

2 INSTRUCT

Recycling in the Biosphere

Build Science Skills

Inferring After students have read Recycling in the Biosphere, point out the sentence that begins *You are soon swallowed by a dung beetle . . .* Ask: **How can a molecule that's swallowed by a dung beetle "combine into"—or become part of—the body tissue of a tree shrew and then an owl?** *(The tree shrew takes in the molecule when it eats the dung beetle, and then an owl takes in the molecule when it eats the tree shrew.)* L2

3–3 Cycles of Matter

BI 6.d. Students know how water, carbon, and nitrogen cycle between abiotic resources and organic matter in the ecosystem and how oxygen cycles through photosynthesis and respiration.

Guide for Reading

Key Concepts
- How does matter move among the living and nonliving parts of an ecosystem?
- How are nutrients important in living systems?

Vocabulary
biogeochemical cycle
evaporation
transpiration
nutrient
nitrogen fixation
denitrification
primary productivity
limiting nutrient
algal bloom

Reading Strategy: Using Visuals Before you read, preview the cycles shown in **Figures 3–11, 3–13, 3–14,** and **3–15.** Notice how each diagram is similar to or different from the others. As you read, take notes on how each chemical moves through the biosphere.

Energy is crucial to an ecosystem. But all organisms need more than energy to survive. They also need water, minerals, and other life-sustaining compounds. In most organisms, more than 95 percent of the body is made up of just four elements: oxygen, carbon, hydrogen, and nitrogen. Although these four elements are common on Earth, organisms cannot use them unless the elements are in a chemical form that cells can take up.

Recycling in the Biosphere

Energy and matter move through the biosphere very differently. **Unlike the one-way flow of energy, matter is recycled within and between ecosystems.** Elements, chemical compounds, and other forms of matter are passed from one organism to another and from one part of the biosphere to another through **biogeochemical cycles.** As the long word suggests, biogeochemical cycles connect *bio*logical, *geo*logical, and *chemi*cal aspects of the biosphere.

Matter can cycle through the biosphere because biological systems do not use up matter, they transform it. The matter is assembled into living tissue or passed out of the body as waste products. Imagine, for a moment, that you are a carbon atom in a molecule of carbon dioxide floating in the air of a wetland like the one in **Figure 3–10.** The leaf of a blueberry bush absorbs you during photosynthesis. You become part of a carbohydrate molecule and are used to make fruit. The fruit is eaten by a caribou, and within a few hours, you are passed out of the animal's body. You are soon swallowed by a dung beetle, then combined into the body tissue of a hungry shrew, which is then eaten by an owl. Finally, you are released into the atmosphere once again when the owl exhales. Then, the cycle starts again.

Simply put, biogeochemical cycles pass the same molecules around again and again within the biosphere. Just think—with every breath you take, you inhale hundreds of thousands of oxygen atoms that might have been inhaled by dinosaurs millions of years ago!

Figure 3–10 Matter moves through an ecosystem in biogeochemical cycles. In this Alaskan wetland, matter is recycled through the air, the shrubs, the pond, and the caribou—as it is used, transformed, moved, and reused.

TIME SAVER — SECTION RESOURCES

Print:
- ***Laboratory Manual A,*** Chapter 3 Lab
- ***Laboratory Manual B,*** Chapter 3 Lab
- ***Teaching Resources,*** Lesson Plan 3–3, Adapted Section Summary 3–3, Adapted Worksheets 3–3, Section Summary 3–3, Worksheets 3–3, Section Review 3–3, Enrichment
- ***Reading and Study Workbook A,*** Section 3–3
- ***Adapted Reading and Study Workbook B,*** Section 3–3
- ***Biotechnology Manual,*** Issue 4
- ***Lab Worksheets,*** Chapter 3 Exploration

Technology:
- ***BioDetectives DVD,*** *Pfiesteria:* A Killer in the Water
- ***iText,*** Section 3–3
- ***Transparencies Plus,*** Section 3–3

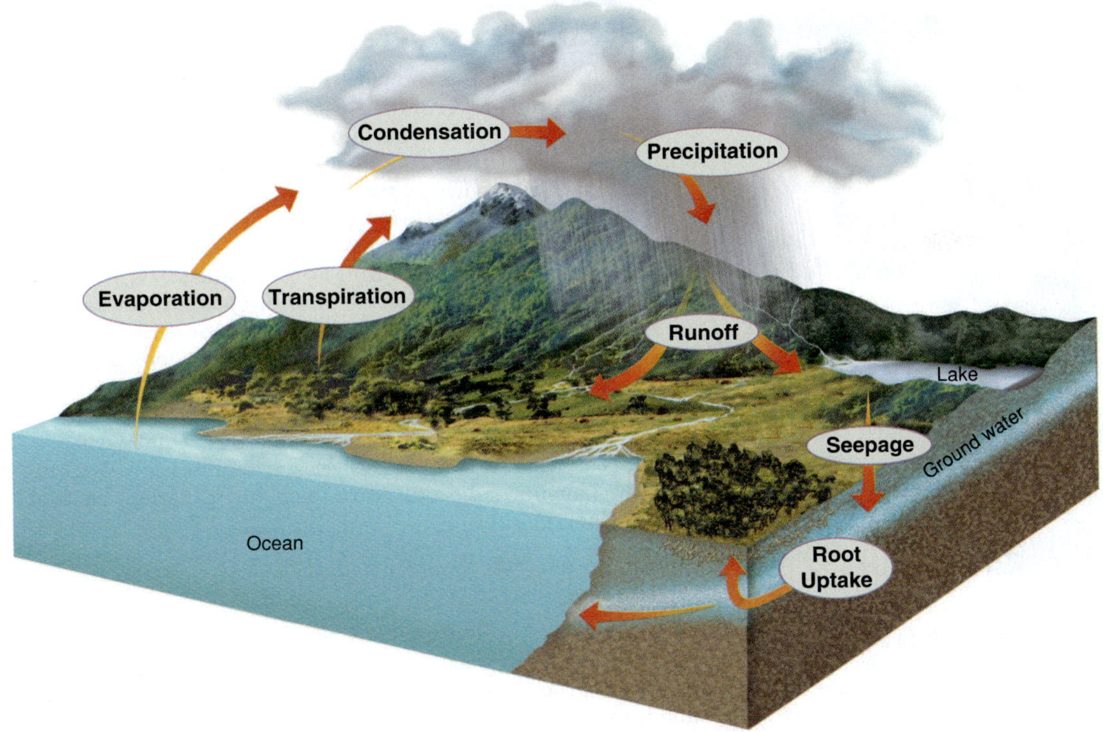

The Water Cycle

All living things require water to survive. Where does all this water come from? It moves between the ocean, atmosphere, and land. As **Figure 3–11** shows, water molecules enter the atmosphere as water vapor, a gas, when they evaporate from the ocean or other bodies of water. The process by which water changes from liquid form to an atmospheric gas is called **evaporation** (ee-vap-uh-RAY-shun). Water can also enter the atmosphere by evaporating from the leaves of plants in the process of **transpiration** (tran-spuh-RAY-shun).

During the day, the sun heats the atmosphere. As the warm, moist air rises, it cools. Eventually, the water vapor condenses into tiny droplets that form clouds. When the droplets become large enough, the water returns to Earth's surface in the form of precipitation—rain, snow, sleet, or hail.

On land, much of the precipitation runs along the surface of the ground until it enters a river or stream that carries the runoff back to an ocean or lake. Rain also seeps into the soil, some of it deeply enough to become ground water. Water in the soil enters plants through the roots, and the water cycle begins anew.

CHECKPOINT *How are evaporation and transpiration related?*

▲ **Figure 3–11** This diagram shows the main processes involved in the water cycle. Scientists estimate that it can take a single water molecule as long as 4000 years to complete one cycle. **Interpreting Graphics** *What happens to the water that evaporates from oceans and lakes?*

Go Online active art
For: Water Cycle activity
Visit: PHSchool.com
Web Code: cbp-2033

a BI 6.d

Go Online active art
For: Water Cycle activity
Visit: PHSchool.com
Web Code: cbe-2033
Students can examine how water moves through the water cycle.

The Water Cycle

Use Visuals

Figure 3–11 After students have studied the diagram and read the caption, have them recall what they learned about water in Chapter 2. Remind them that water is the single most abundant compound in most living things. Then, ask: **What are two ways that water can enter the atmosphere?** *(Evaporation and transpiration)* **What process moves water through the cycle from the air to the ground?** *(Precipitation)* **What are two routes by which water might make its way to the ocean?** *(Through runoff and through seepage into ground water and eventual flow into the ocean)* L1 L2

Build Science Skills

Comparing and Contrasting Emphasize that transpiration by plants releases water vapor, a gas, into the air, not liquid water. Ask: **What process in humans and other mammals also releases water vapor into the air?** *(Respiration)* **How are transpiration in plants and respiration in mammals different?** *(Sample answer: Mammals have specialized organs that are involved in respiration—the lungs, diaphragm, bronchial tubes, and so forth—but plants do not have "breathing" organs.)* L2

UNIVERSAL ACCESS

Less Proficient Readers
Some students might be unfamiliar with the terms used in Figure 3–11. Call on students at random to read aloud each sentence or set of sentences in the text that describes one of the processes in the water cycle. For example, the first two sentences in the second paragraph on page 75 describe condensation. After the text explanation for each process is read aloud, have students find that step in the cycle in Figure 3–11 and describe it in their own words. L1 L2

Advanced Learners
Encourage students who need an extra challenge to investigate further one of the biogeochemical cycles discussed in this section. You might assign one student to do further research on each of the four cycles discussed. Students can find more information on these cycles in higher-level biology texts as well as in earth science texts. Have students prepare a presentation to the class, complete with visual aids. L3

Answers to . . .

CHECKPOINT *Evaporation is part of the process of transpiration.*

Figure 3–11 *The water vapor rises into the atmosphere and then cools and condenses to form clouds.*

3–3 (continued)

Nutrient Cycles

Make Connections

Health Science For each pair of students, provide an empty vitamin container with its nutrition label intact. Try to provide a mix of vitamins for adults, for young children, and for infants. You may want to ask students in advance to bring in containers from home. Ask: **What types of information are given on the nutrition label?** *(The serving size, the total number of servings in the container, the specific nutrients in the pills or drops, the amount of each nutrient in one serving, and the percentage of daily value each amount represents.)* **What do you think a "daily value" is?** *(How much of a nutrient a person should take in each day)* **What does "percentage of daily value" mean?** *(How much of the daily value is in one serving of the vitamin)* Ask students if they recognize the names of any of the nutrients listed on the label and whether they know the nutrients' common dietary sources and their functions in maintaining good health. Depending on the extent of students' knowledge, you may want to suggest that they research this information and share their findings in posters or brief oral presentations. L2 L3

Download a worksheet on cycles of matter for students to complete, and find additional teacher support from NSTA SciLinks.

▲ **Figure 3–12** **Like all living organisms, the owl monkey needs nutrients to grow and carry out essential life functions.** This monkey, which is found in Central and South America, obtains most of its nutrients by eating plants.

Nutrient Cycles

The food you eat provides energy and chemicals that keep you alive. All the chemical substances that an organism needs to sustain life are its **nutrients.** Think of them as the body's chemical "building blocks." Primary producers, such as plants, usually obtain nutrients in simple inorganic forms from their environment. Consumers, such as the monkey in **Figure 3–12,** obtain nutrients by eating other organisms. **Every living organism needs nutrients to build tissues and carry out essential life functions. Like water, nutrients are passed between organisms and the environment through biogeochemical cycles.**

The carbon cycle, nitrogen cycle, and phosphorus cycle are especially important. Note also that oxygen participates in all these cycles by combining with these elements and cycling with them during various parts of their journey.

CHECKPOINT *What is a nutrient?*

The Carbon Cycle Carbon plays many roles. Carbon is a key ingredient of living tissue. In the form of calcium carbonate ($CaCO_3$), carbon is an important component of animal skeletons and is found in several kinds of rocks. Carbon and oxygen form carbon dioxide gas (CO_2), an important component of the atmosphere. Carbon dioxide is taken in by plants during photosynthesis and is given off by both plants and animals during respiration. Four main types of processes move carbon through its cycle:

- Biological processes, such as photosynthesis, respiration, and decomposition, take up and release carbon and oxygen.
- Geochemical processes, such as erosion and volcanic activity, release carbon dioxide to the atmosphere and oceans.
- Mixed biogeochemical processes, such as the burial and decomposition of dead organisms and their conversion under pressure into coal and petroleum (fossil fuels), store carbon underground.
- Human activities, such as mining, cutting and burning forests, and burning fossil fuels, release carbon dioxide into the atmosphere.

ⓐ BI 6.d

Scientists identified these processes decades ago, but they are still actively investigating them. For example, how much carbon moves through each part of the cycle? How do other parts of the carbon cycle respond to changes in atmospheric carbon dioxide? How much carbon dioxide can the ocean absorb? Later in this unit, you will learn why answers to these questions are so important.

Go Online NSTA SciLinks

For: Links on cycles of matter
Visit: www.SciLinks.org
Web Code: cbn-2033

BIO INSIGHTS — FACTS AND FIGURES

The rain in Spain, and elsewhere

Huge quantities of water cycle between Earth's surface and atmosphere. Hydrologists estimate that about 390,000 cubic kilometers of water evaporate from Earth's surface and enter the atmosphere each year.

Considering all forms of precipitation, about 77 percent falls on oceans and about 23 percent on land. However, this same proportion does not hold true for water that evaporates from Earth's surface: 84 percent of the water in the atmosphere comes from oceans and only 16 percent from land. The reason for the difference in proportions is simple: about a third of the precipitation that falls on land runs off into streams and rivers and is carried to oceans.

Figure 3–13 shows how these processes move carbon through the biosphere. In the atmosphere, carbon is present as carbon dioxide gas. Carbon dioxide is released into the atmosphere by volcanic activity, by respiration, by human activities such as the burning of fossil fuels and vegetation, and by the decomposition of organic matter. Plants take in carbon dioxide and use the carbon to build carbohydrates during photosynthesis. The carbohydrates are passed along food webs to animals and other consumers. In the ocean, carbon is also found, along with calcium and oxygen, in calcium carbonate, which is formed by many marine organisms. Calcium carbonate can also be formed chemically in certain marine environments. This chalky, carbon-based compound accumulates in marine sediments and in the bones and shells of organisms. Eventually these compounds break down and the carbon returns to the atmosphere.

ⓐ BI 6.d

▼ **Figure 3–13** Carbon is found in several large reservoirs in the biosphere. In the atmosphere, it is found as carbon dioxide gas; in the oceans as dissolved carbon dioxide; on land in organisms, rocks, and soil; and underground as coal, petroleum, and calcium carbonate rock. **Interpreting Graphics** *What are the main sources of carbon dioxide in the ocean?*

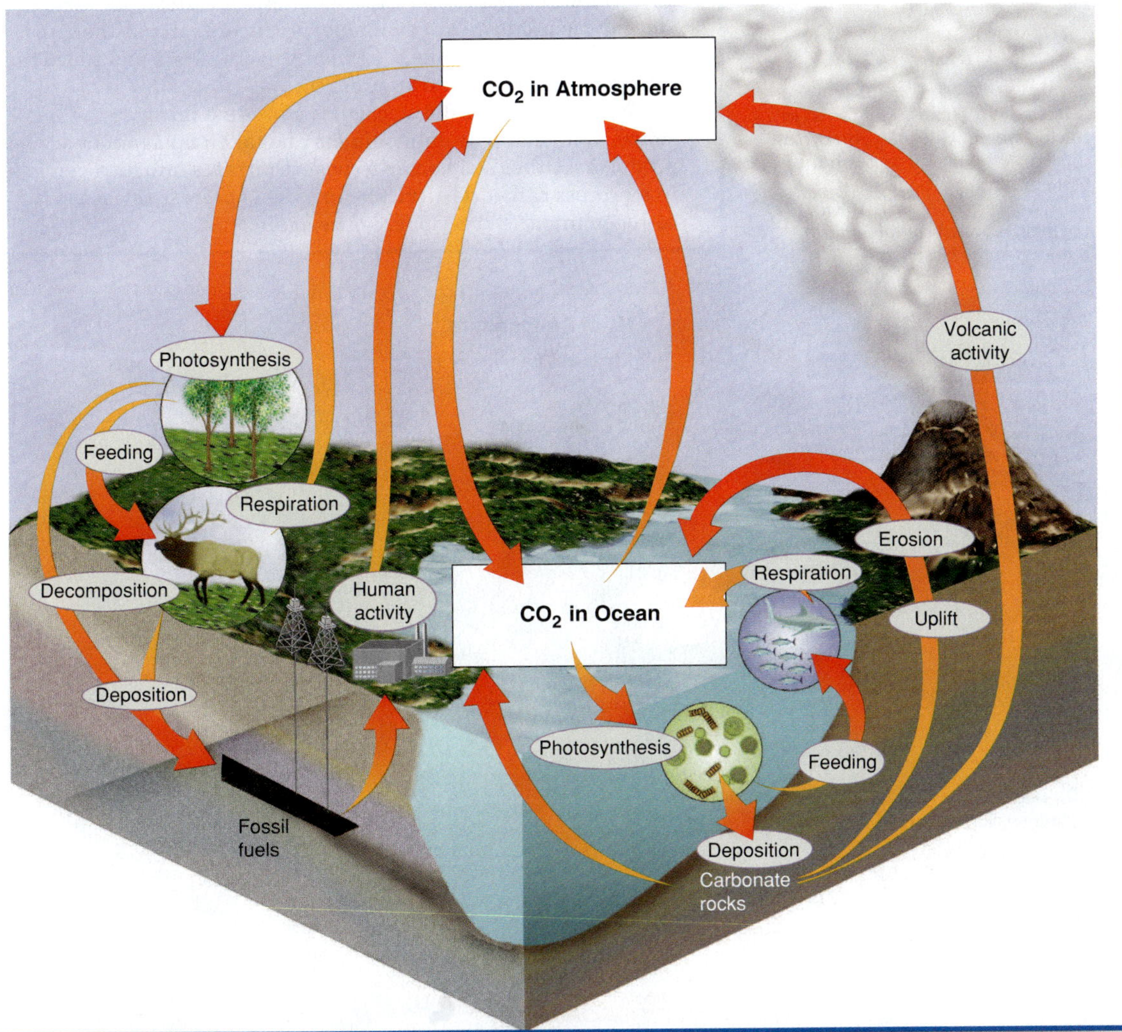

Use Visuals

Figure 3–13 Call on different students in turn to "translate" the diagram's pictures, labels, and arrows into complete, descriptive sentences. For example, the circled picture of trees, the arrows, and the *Photosynthesis* label on the left side of the diagram can be expressed as, "During photosynthesis, plants take in carbon dioxide from the atmosphere and release oxygen." The circled picture of the elk with two arrows can be translated as, "During respiration, animals take in oxygen given off by plants and release carbon dioxide into the atmosphere," and, "When animals die and decompose, carbon is released into the soil." Continue until all the processes in both pathways have been described this way. L2

FACTS AND FIGURES

The carbon pool

Scientists estimate the biosphere's total carbon pool to be approximately 49,000 metric gigatons. (1 metric gigaton equals 10^9 metric tons.) Of that total, 71 percent is contained in Earth's oceans, mainly in the form of carbonate and bicarbonate ions. Fossil carbon comprises 22 percent of the total pool. An additional 3 percent is contained in dead organic matter and phytoplankton, and another 3 percent is held in terrestrial ecosystems. The remaining 1 percent is held in the atmosphere, circulated, and used in photosynthesis.

The carbon that is contained in organic molecules—such as the wood in trees—may not be recycled back to the abiotic environment for several hundred years or even longer. Carbon compounds found in coal that formed from ancient trees, for example, are the products of photosynthesis that occurred millions of years ago.

Answers to . . .

CHECKPOINT *Any chemical substance that an organism needs to sustain life*

Figure 3–13 *Respiration by ocean animals, precipitation containing dissolved carbon dioxide, erosion of carbonate rocks formed from the skeletons of ocean organisms such as corals*

3–3 (continued)

Make Connections

Chemistry Write the chemical formulas for atmospheric nitrogen (N_2), ammonia (NH_3), the nitrate ion (NO_3^-), and the nitrite ion (NO_2^-) on the board. Ask students: **Which element is symbolized by each letter in these formulas?** *(N is the symbol for nitrogen; H for hydrogen; and O for oxygen.)* **What do the small numbers mean?** *(The small numbers tell how many atoms of the element are in one molecule or ion of the substance.)* **What atoms make up one molecule of atmospheric nitrogen?** *(Two atoms of nitrogen)* **One molecule of ammonia?** *(One atom of nitrogen and three atoms of hydrogen)* **The nitrate ion?** *(One atom of nitrogen and three atoms of oxygen)* **The nitrite ion?** *(One atom of nitrogen and two atoms of oxygen)* L1 L2

Build Science Skills

Using Models To reinforce students' understanding of the nitrogen cycle, have them make models of the four chemical formulas of the different forms of nitrogen. Provide a variety of materials, and let each student choose the type of model to make. For example, two-dimensional models could be made with circles cut from colored construction paper and glued to a larger sheet. Three-dimensional models could be made with clay balls of different colors held together with toothpicks. Students can use their models as they study the nitrogen cycle in Figure 3–14.

Use Visuals

Figure 3–14 The "translation" procedure described for use with Figure 3–13 would also work well with this diagram. For example, the part of the diagram that illustrates nitrogen fixation by bacteria could be described in the following way: "In nitrogen fixation, bacteria in the soil and on plant roots change atmospheric nitrogen into ammonia." L2

The Nitrogen Cycle All organisms require nitrogen to make amino acids, which in turn are used to build proteins. Many different forms of nitrogen occur naturally in the biosphere. Nitrogen gas (N_2) makes up 78 percent of Earth's atmosphere. Nitrogen-containing substances such as ammonia (NH_3), nitrate ions (NO_3^-), and nitrite ions (NO_2^-) are found in the wastes produced by many organisms and in dead and decaying organic matter. Nitrogen also exists in several forms in the ocean and other large water bodies. Human activity adds nitrogen to the biosphere in the form of nitrate—a major component of plant fertilizers.

CA a

Figure 3–14 shows how the different forms of nitrogen cycle through the biosphere. Although nitrogen gas is the most abundant form of nitrogen on Earth, only certain types of bacteria can use this form directly. Such bacteria, which live in the soil and on the roots of plants called legumes, convert nitrogen gas into ammonia in a process known as **nitrogen fixation.** Other bacteria in the soil convert ammonia into nitrates and nitrites. Once these products are available, producers can use them to make proteins. Consumers then eat the producers and reuse the nitrogen to make their own proteins.

When organisms die, decomposers return nitrogen to the soil as ammonia. The ammonia may be taken up again by producers. Other soil bacteria convert nitrates into nitrogen gas in a process called **denitrification.** This process releases nitrogen into the atmosphere once again.

▼ **Figure 3–14** The atmosphere is the main reservoir of nitrogen in the biosphere. Nitrogen also cycles through the soil and through the tissues of living organisms. **Interpreting Graphics** ***What are the main nitrogen-containing nutrients in the biosphere?***

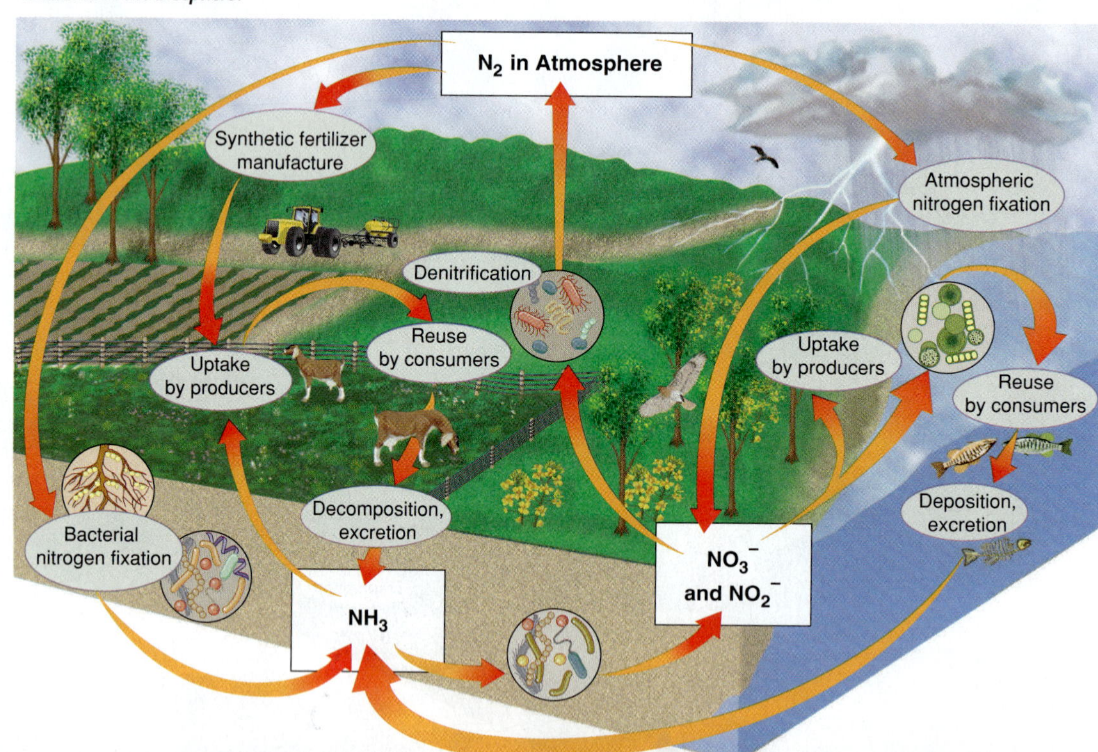

FACTS AND FIGURES

The scarcity of nitrogen
Although about 80 percent of the air surrounding Earth is nitrogen gas (N_2), usable forms of the element are scarce in ecosystems. The reason for this is that the two atoms in atmospheric nitrogen are held together by triple covalent bonds that only lightning, volcanic action, and certain bacteria can break. In addition, the ammonia, nitrite, and nitrate formed by nitrifying bacteria are very susceptible to leaching and runoff, which carry away nitrogen dissolved in the water.

Nitrifying bacteria use nitrogenase, an enzyme, to break the covalent bonds in N_2 molecules. Nitrogenase functions only when it is isolated from oxygen. On land, nitrogen-fixing bacteria accomplish this by living inside oxygen-excluding nodules or layers of insulating slime on plant roots. In aquatic ecosystems, cyanobacteria—the primary nitrogen-fixers—have specialized cells called heterocysts that exclude oxygen.

Analyzing Data

Farming in the Rye

6IIE 7.c, BIIE 1.I

Sometimes, farmers grow crops of rye and other grasses and then plow them under the soil to decay. This practice helps to increase crop yields of other plants. Farmers may also plow under legumes such as peas, vetch, and lentils. Legumes are plants that have colonies of nitrogen-fixing bacteria living in nodules on the plant roots.

In an effort to determine which practice produces the best crop yields, scientists performed an experiment in Georgia. They grew corn on land that had previously received one of five treatments. Three fields had previously been planted with three different legumes. A fourth field had been planted with rye. The fifth field was left bare before the corn was planted. None of the fields received fertilizer while the corn was growing. The table shows how much corn was produced per hectare of land (kg/ha) in each field. One hectare is equivalent to 10,000 square meters.

Corn Production

Previous Crop	Average Yield of Corn (kg/ha)
Monantha vetch	2876
Hairy vetch	2870
Austrian peas	3159
Rye	1922
None	1959

1. **Using Tables and Graphs** Use the data in the table to create a bar graph.
2. **Comparing and Contrasting** Compare the effect of growing legumes to that of growing grass on the yield of corn. How do the yields differ from the yield on the field that had received no prior treatment?
3. **Using Tables and Graphs** Which treatment produced the best yield of corn? The worst yield?
4. **Applying Concepts** Based on your knowledge of the nitrogen cycle, how can you explain these results?

The Phosphorus Cycle Phosphorus is essential to living organisms because it forms part of important life-sustaining molecules such as DNA and RNA. Although phosphorus is of great biological importance, it is not very common in the biosphere. Unlike carbon, oxygen, and nitrogen, phosphorus does not enter the atmosphere. Instead, phosphorus remains mostly on land in rock and soil minerals, and in ocean sediments. There, phosphorus exists in the form of inorganic phosphate. As the rocks and sediments gradually wear down, phosphate is released. On land, some of the phosphate washes into rivers and streams, where it dissolves. The phosphate eventually makes its way to the oceans, where it is used by marine organisms.

As **Figure 3–15** shows, some phosphate stays on land and cycles between organisms and the soil. When plants absorb phosphate from the soil or from water, the plants bind the phosphate into organic compounds. Organic phosphate moves through the food web, from producers to consumers, and to the rest of the ecosystem.

CA (a) (a) BI 6.d

CHECKPOINT *Where is most of the phosphorus stored in the biosphere?*

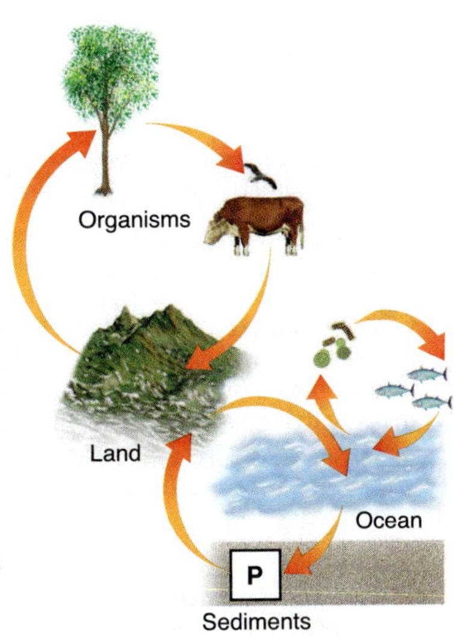

▶ **Figure 3–15** Phosphorus in the biosphere cycles among the land, ocean sediments, and living organisms. **Interpreting Graphics** *How is phosphorus important to living organisms?*

Analyzing Data

6IIE 7.c, BIIE 1.I

Help students understand the experiment procedure by asking: **Why was the fifth field left bare?** *(It was the control in the experiment. If the corn in the fifth field grew as well as or better than the corn in any of the other fields, the researchers would know that the previous year's plantings in those other fields did not increase corn productivity.)* L2

Answers

1. Students could plot plant names on the vertical axis and yields on the horizontal axis; use different increments for the yield axis; and/or arrange the crops in sequence from highest to lowest yield or from lowest to highest.

2. Growing legumes the previous year significantly increased the crop yields. Growing rye did not increase yields. In fact, the bare field's yield was slightly higher than the field planted with rye.

3. The legumes—particularly the Austrian peas—produced the highest yields. Rye produced the lowest yield.

4. The corn plants benefited greatly when the soil was enriched with nitrogen fixed by legumes the previous year.

Build Science Skills

Comparing and Contrasting

Point out the terms *inorganic* and *organic* in the description of the phosphorus cycle. Encourage students to consult science dictionaries and chemistry textbooks to determine the difference between organic and inorganic compounds and report their findings to the rest of the class.

L2 L3

BIO INSIGHTS — FACTS AND FIGURES

What makes a compound organic?

Organic compounds are often defined simply as compounds that contain carbon. However, not all carbon-containing compounds are considered organic. Carbon dioxide and hydrocarbons such as methane and propane are prime examples of carbon compounds that are not organic. A more precise definition of an organic compound is: a compound that contains carbon and is constructed in living cells.

A carbon atom has four electrons in its outer shell—but the shell is capable of holding eight electrons. For this reason, a carbon atom can form covalent bonds with as many as four atoms of other elements. Carbon atoms are usually joined together in a ring or chain that forms a stable "backbone" for building molecules. Such structures are not present in simple inorganic compounds such as carbon dioxide.

Answers to . . .

CHECKPOINT *In rock and soil minerals and in ocean sediments*

Figure 3–14 *Ammonia, nitrate, and nitrite*

Figure 3–15 *Phosphorus forms part of life-sustaining molecules such as RNA and DNA.*

3–3 (continued)

Nutrient Limitation

Build Science Skills

Making Judgments Call attention to the paragraph about farmers' use of fertilizers. Ask: **How might the use of fertilizers harm ecosystems nearby?** *(Runoff from the fields could carry fertilizers to bodies of water and cause algal blooms there.)* Have students discuss the pros and cons of fertilizer use. Then, let two teams debate the issue. L2 L3

3 ASSESS

Evaluate Understanding

Make one photocopy of Figure 3–11 (the water cycle), Figure 3–13 (the carbon cycle), and Figure 3–14 (the nitrogen cycle). Cover the diagrams' labels with white tape, and then use these "masters" to make a set of copies for students to add labels.

Reteach

Have each student write a brief description of each cycle discussed in the section referring to Figures 3–11, 3–13, 3–14, and 3–15. Let students share their work in a class discussion and correct any errors or omissions in one another's descriptions.

Thinking Visually

Students' flowcharts may vary. Each flowchart, though, should mention and describe the processes included in Figure 3–13. A good flowchart might incorporate the flow of energy, and carbon, through a food chain.

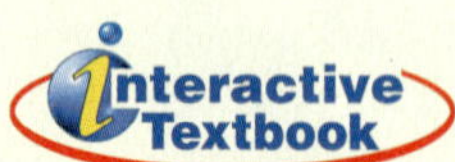

If your class subscribes to the iText, use it to review the Key Concepts in Section 3–3.

Answer to . . .

Figure 3–16 *Bacteria in a lake consume dead algae and deplete oxygen in the lake just as excess food in a fish tank is consumed by bacteria that deplete oxygen in the water.*

▲ **Figure 3–16** When an aquatic ecosystem receives a large input of a limiting nutrient, the result is often an increase in the number of producers. Here, an extensive algal bloom covers the shoreline of Tule Lake in California. **Using Analogies** *How is this situation similar to the one that occurs in a fish tank in which the fish have been overfed?*

Nutrient Limitation

Ecologists are often interested in the **primary productivity** of an ecosystem, which is the rate at which organic matter is created by producers. One factor that controls the primary productivity of an ecosystem is the amount of available nutrients. If a nutrient is in short supply, it will limit an organism's growth. When an ecosystem is limited by a single nutrient that is scarce or cycles very slowly, this substance is called a **limiting nutrient.**

Because they are well aware of this phenomenon, farmers apply fertilizers to their crops to boost their productivity. Fertilizers usually contain three important nutrients—nitrogen, phosphorus, and potassium. These nutrients help plants grow larger and more quickly than they would in unfertilized soil.

The open oceans of the world can be considered nutrient-poor environments compared to the land. Seawater contains at most only 0.00005 percent nitrogen, or 1/10,000 of the amount typically found in soil. In the ocean and other saltwater environments, nitrogen is often the limiting nutrient. In some areas of the ocean, however, silica or even iron can be the limiting nutrient. In streams, lakes, and freshwater environments, phosphorus is typically the limiting nutrient.

When an aquatic ecosystem receives a large input of a limiting nutrient—for example, runoff from heavily fertilized fields—the result is often an immediate increase in the amount of algae and other producers. This result is called an **algal bloom.** Why do algal blooms occur? There are more nutrients available, so the producers can grow and reproduce more quickly. If there are not enough consumers to eat the excess algae, conditions can become so favorable for growth that algae cover the surface of the water. Algal blooms, like the one shown in **Figure 3–16,** can sometimes disrupt the equilibrium of an ecosystem.

3–3 Section Assessment

1. **Key Concept** How does the way that matter flows through an ecosystem differ from the way that energy flows?
2. **Key Concept** Why do living organisms need nutrients?
3. Describe the path of nitrogen through its biogeochemical cycle.
4. Explain how a nutrient can be a limiting factor in an ecosystem.
5. **Critical Thinking Predicting** Based on your knowledge of the carbon cycle, what do you think might happen if vast areas of forests are cleared?
6. **Critical Thinking Applying Concepts** Summarize the role of algal blooms in disrupting the equilibrium in an aquatic ecosystem.

Thinking Visually

Making a Flowchart
Use a flowchart to trace the flow of energy in the carbon cycle. *Hint*: You may wish to refer to **Figure 3–13,** especially to the labels Photosynthesis, Feeding, Respiration, and Decomposition. Also, you may want to refer to **Figure 3–7** in Section 3–2 for a description of energy flow in an ecosystem.

3–3 Section Assessment

1. Unlike the one-way flow of energy, matter is recycled within and between ecosystems.
2. To build tissues and carry out life functions.
3. Students should summarize the steps in the nitrogen cycle as shown in Figure 3–14. A good response should describe the different forms of nitrogen as well as explain bacterial nitrogen fixation and denitrification.
4. If a nutrient is in short supply, it will limit an organism's growth.
5. If vast areas of forest were cleared, less carbon dioxide would be removed from the atmosphere by plants.
6. When an aquatic ecosystem receives a large input of a limiting nutrient, the result is often an algal bloom. Algal blooms can sometimes disrupt the equilibrium of an ecosystem by producing more algae than consumers can eat.

Real-World Lab

7IIE 7.c, 8IIE 9.b

Identifying a Limiting Nutrient

Limiting nutrients control the growth of organisms in many ecosystems. Excess nutrients can promote the growth of weeds, disease-causing bacteria, and other undesirable organisms. In this investigation, you will determine whether phosphate is a limiting nutrient for the growth of algae.

Problem

Does the supply of phosphate limit the growth of algae?

Materials

- dropper pipette
- algae culture
- 2 test tubes with stoppers
- test-tube rack
- 50-mL graduated cylinder
- pond water
- glass-marking pencil
- 10% trisodium phosphate solution

Skills

Formulating Hypotheses, Predicting

Procedure

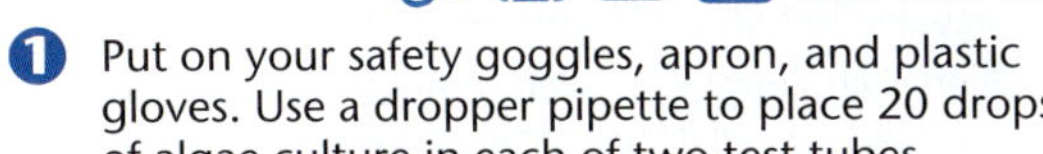

1. Put on your safety goggles, apron, and plastic gloves. Use a dropper pipette to place 20 drops of algae culture in each of two test tubes.
2. Use a 50-mL graduated cylinder to add 19 mL of pond water to each test tube.
3. Use the glass-marking pencil to label one test tube "control" and the other test tube "phosphate." Use a dropper pipette to add 2 drops of trisodium phosphate to the "phosphate" test tube. **CAUTION:** *Trisodium phosphate can injure your skin. Do not get it on your skin or touch your face after handling it.*
4. Stopper both test tubes and place them in a sunny place. Wash your hands.
5. **Formulating Hypotheses** Record your hypothesis of how phosphate will affect the growth of the algae if it is a limiting nutrient. Also, record your prediction of how the two test tubes will appear after 7 days.
6. Observe the two test tubes each day for the next week. Record your observations each day, including a labeled sketch of each test tube.

Analyze and Conclude

1. **Observing** How did the added phosphate affect the growth of the algae?
2. **Drawing Conclusions** Do your results indicate that phosphate is a limiting nutrient for algae?
3. **Evaluating and Revising** Do your results support your hypothesis? If not, how would you revise your hypothesis?
4. **Predicting** Some detergents are labeled as environmentally safe because they contain little or no phosphate. What differences might you expect to find between a lake that contains high levels of phosphate detergents and one that contains low levels of phosphate detergents?

Go Further

Designing Experiments Select another nutrient and design an experiment to determine whether it is a limiting nutrient for the growth of algae. With your teacher's permission, conduct the experiment and share your findings with the class.

Quick View Video

Discovery School Video To find out more about how scientists investigate algal blooms, view track 2 *"Pfiesteria: A Killer in the Water"* on the *BioDetectives* DVD.

Analyze and Conclude

1. The phosphate greatly increased the growth of algae.
2. Yes
3. Answers will vary depending on students' hypotheses.
4. Water that contains high levels of phosphate detergents would have algal blooms.

Discovery School DVD Encourage students to view track 2 "*Pfiesteria:* A Killer in the Water" on the *BioDetectives* DVD.

Real-World Lab

7IIE 7.c, 8IIE 9.b

Objective Students will be able to determine that the supply of phosphate is a limiting factor in the growth of algae. L2

Skills Focus Formulating Hypotheses, Predicting

Time 15 minutes for initial setup; follow-up of 5 minutes each day for 7 days to observe and record

Advance Prep

- Obtain a culture of *Chlorella.* Within four days, this alga will show more visible growth with phosphate than would other algae species such as *Spirogyra* or *Chlamydomonas.*
- **CAUTION:** Wear goggles, plastic gloves, and a lab apron while preparing the trisodium phosphate solution. In a beaker, completely dissolve 10 g of trisodium phosphate in about 80 mL of distilled or deionized water (*not* tap water). Transfer the solution to a 100-mL graduated cylinder and add enough water to bring the total to 100 mL.

Safety Read the MSDS on trisodium phosphate. Make sure that students wear plastic gloves, goggles, and lab aprons when handling the trisodium phosphate solution. Properly dispose of chemicals. Make sure students wash their hands with soap and warm water before leaving the lab.

Pre-Lab Discussion
Ask students to describe what a limiting nutrient is in their own words.

Teaching Tips

- Dispense the trisodium phosphate solution to students in small dropper bottles.
- Tell students to label the pair of test tubes with their initials so they can readily identify them.

Procedure
5. Sample hypothesis: The added phosphate will cause the algae in that test tube to grow more rapidly than the algae in the test tube without added phosphate. Sample prediction: The test tube with added phosphate will have more algae in it than the other test tube.

Expected Outcome The liquid in the test tube with added phosphate should be significantly cloudier and greener than the liquid in the test tube without added phosphate.

Chapter 3 Study Guide

Study Tip

For each section of the chapter, have students read the Key Concepts that are listed. Then, have them review the chapter text for any concepts that they do not fully understand. Next, students can define each Vocabulary term in their own words and check their definitions against the text's definitions. Tell students that when they check the text, they should read all the related text, not just the sentence that defines the highlighted, boldface Vocabulary term.

Thinking Visually

1. Autotroph or Producer
2. Consumer or Carnivore
3. Decomposer

Chapter 3 Assessment

Reviewing Content

1. c	5. c	9. d
2. b	6. c	10. d
3. c	7. a	
4. b	8. d	

Understanding Concepts

11. The scientific study of interactions among organisms and between organisms and their environment
12. Individual organism, population, community, ecosystem, biome, biosphere
13. Scientists use models to gain insight into ecological changes that are too complex or too long-range to study directly.
14. Sunlight is the ultimate source of energy in most ecosystems.
15. The process in which producers use chemical energy to produce carbohydrates
16. Autotrophs, such as plants, make their own food using the energy in sunlight or chemical bonds. Heterotrophs, such as animals, must rely on other organisms for energy and food.
17. A heterotroph that breaks down organic matter; bacteria, fungi
18. Autotrophs (producers)

Chapter 3 Study Guide

3–1 What Is Ecology?

Key Concepts

- To understand the various relationships within the biosphere, ecologists ask questions about events and organisms that range in complexity from a single individual to a population, community, ecosystem, or biome, or to the entire biosphere.
- Scientists conduct modern ecological research according to three basic approaches: observing, experimenting, and modeling. All of these approaches rely on the application of scientific methods to guide ecological inquiry.

Vocabulary

ecology, p. 63
biosphere, p. 63
species, p. 64
population, p. 64
community, p. 64
ecosystem, p. 64
biome, p. 64

3–2 Energy Flow

6 5.b, BI 6.d, BI 6.e, BI 6.f

Key Concepts

- Sunlight is the main energy source for life on Earth. In a few ecosystems, some organisms rely on the energy stored in inorganic chemical compounds.
- Energy flows through an ecosystem in one direction, from the sun or inorganic compounds to autotrophs (producers) and then to various heterotrophs (consumers).
- Only about 10 percent of the energy available within one trophic level is transferred to organisms at the next trophic level.

Vocabulary

autotroph, p. 67
producer, p. 67
photosynthesis, p. 68
chemosynthesis, p. 68
heterotroph, p. 68
consumer, p. 68
herbivore, p. 69
carnivore, p. 69
omnivore, p. 69
detritivore, p. 69
decomposer, p. 69
food chain, p. 69
food web, p. 70
trophic level, p. 70
ecological pyramid, p. 72
biomass, p. 72

3–3 Cycles of Matter

BI 6.d

Key Concepts

- Unlike the one-way flow of energy, matter is recycled within and between ecosystems.
- Every living organism needs nutrients to grow and carry out essential life functions. Like water, nutrients are passed between organisms and the environment through biogeochemical cycles.

Vocabulary

biogeochemical cycle, p. 74
evaporation, p. 75
transpiration, p. 75
nutrient, p. 76
nitrogen fixation, p. 78
denitrification, p. 78
primary productivity, p. 80
limiting nutrient, p. 80
algal bloom, p. 80

Thinking Visually

Using information from this chapter, complete the following flowchart:

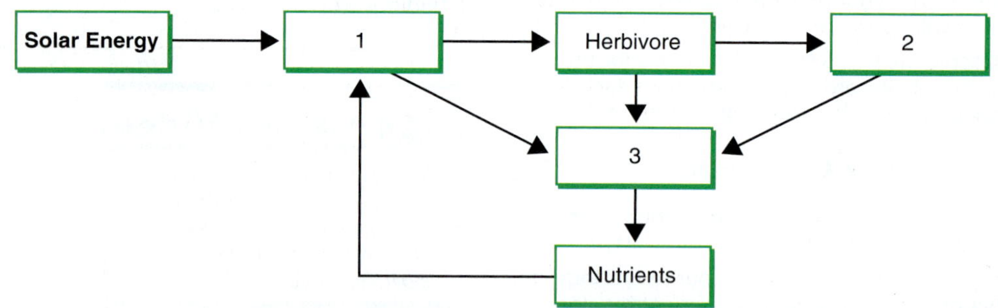

CHAPTER RESOURCES

TIME SAVER

Print:

- ***Teaching Resources,*** Chapter Vocabulary Review, Graphic Organizer, Chapter 3 Tests: Levels A and B

Technology:

- ***Computer Test Bank,*** Chapter 3 Test
- ***iText,*** Chapter 3 Assessment

Real-World Lab

7IIE 7.c, 8IIE 9.b

Identifying a Limiting Nutrient

Limiting nutrients control the growth of organisms in many ecosystems. Excess nutrients can promote the growth of weeds, disease-causing bacteria, and other undesirable organisms. In this investigation, you will determine whether phosphate is a limiting nutrient for the growth of algae.

Problem

Does the supply of phosphate limit the growth of algae?

Materials

- dropper pipette
- algae culture
- 2 test tubes with stoppers
- test-tube rack
- 50-mL graduated cylinder
- pond water
- glass-marking pencil
- 10% trisodium phosphate solution

Skills

Formulating Hypotheses, Predicting

Procedure

1. Put on your safety goggles, apron, and plastic gloves. Use a dropper pipette to place 20 drops of algae culture in each of two test tubes.
2. Use a 50-mL graduated cylinder to add 19 mL of pond water to each test tube.
3. Use the glass-marking pencil to label one test tube "control" and the other test tube "phosphate." Use a dropper pipette to add 2 drops of trisodium phosphate to the "phosphate" test tube. **CAUTION:** *Trisodium phosphate can injure your skin. Do not get it on your skin or touch your face after handling it.*
4. Stopper both test tubes and place them in a sunny place. Wash your hands.
5. **Formulating Hypotheses** Record your hypothesis of how phosphate will affect the growth of the algae if it is a limiting nutrient. Also, record your prediction of how the two test tubes will appear after 7 days.
6. Observe the two test tubes each day for the next week. Record your observations each day, including a labeled sketch of each test tube.

Analyze and Conclude

1. **Observing** How did the added phosphate affect the growth of the algae?
2. **Drawing Conclusions** Do your results indicate that phosphate is a limiting nutrient for algae?
3. **Evaluating and Revising** Do your results support your hypothesis? If not, how would you revise your hypothesis?
4. **Predicting** Some detergents are labeled as environmentally safe because they contain little or no phosphate. What differences might you expect to find between a lake that contains high levels of phosphate detergents and one that contains low levels of phosphate detergents?

Go Further

Designing Experiments Select another nutrient and design an experiment to determine whether it is a limiting nutrient for the growth of algae. With your teacher's permission, conduct the experiment and share your findings with the class.

Quick View Video

Discovery School Video To find out more about how scientists investigate algal blooms, view track 2 "*Pfiesteria:* A Killer in the Water" on the *BioDetectives* DVD.

Analyze and Conclude

1. The phosphate greatly increased the growth of algae.
2. Yes
3. Answers will vary depending on students' hypotheses.
4. Water that contains high levels of phosphate detergents would have algal blooms.

Discovery School DVD Encourage students to view track 2 "*Pfiesteria:* A Killer in the Water" on the *BioDetectives* DVD.

Real-World Lab

7IIE 7.c, 8IIE 9.b

Objective Students will be able to determine that the supply of phosphate is a limiting factor in the growth of algae. L2

Skills Focus Formulating Hypotheses, Predicting

Time 15 minutes for initial setup; follow-up of 5 minutes each day for 7 days to observe and record

Advance Prep

- Obtain a culture of *Chlorella.* Within four days, this alga will show more visible growth with phosphate than would other algae species such as *Spirogyra* or *Chlamydomonas.*
- **CAUTION:** Wear goggles, plastic gloves, and a lab apron while preparing the trisodium phosphate solution. In a beaker, completely dissolve 10 g of trisodium phosphate in about 80 mL of distilled or deionized water (*not* tap water). Transfer the solution to a 100-mL graduated cylinder and add enough water to bring the total to 100 mL.

Safety Read the MSDS on trisodium phosphate. Make sure that students wear plastic gloves, goggles, and lab aprons when handling the trisodium phosphate solution. Properly dispose of chemicals. Make sure students wash their hands with soap and warm water before leaving the lab.

Pre-Lab Discussion
Ask students to describe what a limiting nutrient is in their own words.

Teaching Tips

- Dispense the trisodium phosphate solution to students in small dropper bottles.
- Tell students to label the pair of test tubes with their initials so they can readily identify them.

Procedure
5. Sample hypothesis: The added phosphate will cause the algae in that test tube to grow more rapidly than the algae in the test tube without added phosphate. Sample prediction: The test tube with added phosphate will have more algae in it than the other test tube.

Expected Outcome The liquid in the test tube with added phosphate should be significantly cloudier and greener than the liquid in the test tube without added phosphate.

Chapter 3 Study Guide

Study Tip

For each section of the chapter, have students read the Key Concepts that are listed. Then, have them review the chapter text for any concepts that they do not fully understand. Next, students can define each Vocabulary term in their own words and check their definitions against the text's definitions. Tell students that when they check the text, they should read all the related text, not just the sentence that defines the highlighted, boldface Vocabulary term.

Thinking Visually

1. Autotroph or Producer
2. Consumer or Carnivore
3. Decomposer

Chapter 3 Assessment

Reviewing Content

1. c	5. c	9. d
2. b	6. c	10. d
3. c	7. a	
4. b	8. d	

Understanding Concepts

11. The scientific study of interactions among organisms and between organisms and their environment

12. Individual organism, population, community, ecosystem, biome, biosphere

13. Scientists use models to gain insight into ecological changes that are too complex or too long-range to study directly.

14. Sunlight is the ultimate source of energy in most ecosystems.

15. The process in which producers use chemical energy to produce carbohydrates

16. Autotrophs, such as plants, make their own food using the energy in sunlight or chemical bonds. Heterotrophs, such as animals, must rely on other organisms for energy and food.

17. A heterotroph that breaks down organic matter; bacteria, fungi

18. Autotrophs (producers)

Chapter 3 Study Guide

3–1 What Is Ecology?

Key Concepts

- To understand the various relationships within the biosphere, ecologists ask questions about events and organisms that range in complexity from a single individual to a population, community, ecosystem, or biome, or to the entire biosphere.
- Scientists conduct modern ecological research according to three basic approaches: observing, experimenting, and modeling. All of these approaches rely on the application of scientific methods to guide ecological inquiry.

Vocabulary

ecology, p. 63
biosphere, p. 63
species, p. 64
population, p. 64
community, p. 64
ecosystem, p. 64
biome, p. 64

3–2 Energy Flow

Key Concepts

6 5.b, BI 6.d, BI 6.e, BI 6.f

- Sunlight is the main energy source for life on Earth. In a few ecosystems, some organisms rely on the energy stored in inorganic chemical compounds.
- Energy flows through an ecosystem in one direction, from the sun or inorganic compounds to autotrophs (producers) and then to various heterotrophs (consumers).
- Only about 10 percent of the energy available within one trophic level is transferred to organisms at the next trophic level.

Vocabulary

autotroph, p. 67
producer, p. 67
photosynthesis, p. 68
chemosynthesis, p. 68
heterotroph, p. 68
consumer, p. 68
herbivore, p. 69
carnivore, p. 69
omnivore, p. 69
detritivore, p. 69
decomposer, p. 69
food chain, p. 69
food web, p. 70
trophic level, p. 70
ecological pyramid, p. 72
biomass, p. 72

3–3 Cycles of Matter

Key Concepts

BI 6.d

- Unlike the one-way flow of energy, matter is recycled within and between ecosystems.
- Every living organism needs nutrients to grow and carry out essential life functions. Like water, nutrients are passed between organisms and the environment through biogeochemical cycles.

Vocabulary

biogeochemical cycle, p. 74
evaporation, p. 75
transpiration, p. 75
nutrient, p. 76
nitrogen fixation, p. 78
denitrification, p. 78
primary productivity, p. 80
limiting nutrient, p. 80
algal bloom, p. 80

Thinking Visually

Using information from this chapter, complete the following flowchart:

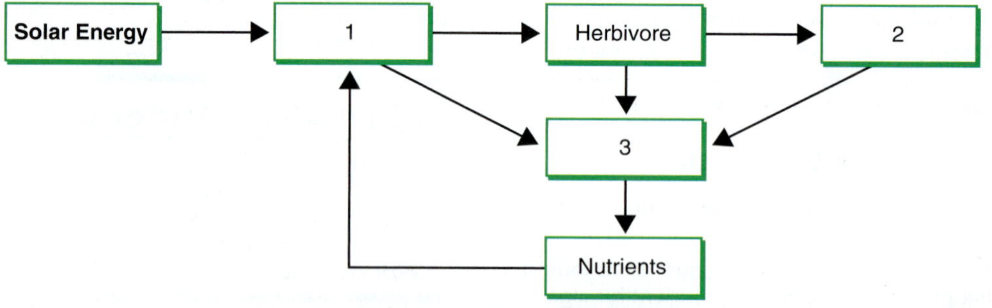

CHAPTER RESOURCES

Print:

- ***Teaching Resources,*** Chapter Vocabulary Review, Graphic Organizer, Chapter 3 Tests: Levels A and B

Technology:

- ***Computer Test Bank,*** Chapter 3 Test
- ***iText,*** Chapter 3 Assessment

Chapter 3 Assessment

Reviewing Content

Choose the letter that best answers the question or completes the statement.

1. All of life on Earth exists in a region known as
   a. an ecosystem.
   b. a biome.
   c. the biosphere.
   d. ecology.
2. Groups of different species that live together in a defined area make up a(an)
   a. population.
   b. community.
   c. ecosystem.
   d. biosphere.
3. Autotrophs are organisms that
   a. rely on other organisms for their energy and food supply.
   b. consume plant and animal remains and other dead matter.
   c. use energy they take in from the environment to convert inorganic molecules into complex organic molecules.
   d. obtain energy by eating only plants.
4. The series of steps in which a large fish eats a small fish that has eaten algae is a
   a. food web.
   b. food chain.
   c. pyramid of numbers.
   d. biomass pyramid.
5. Which of the following organisms is a decomposer?

a.

b.

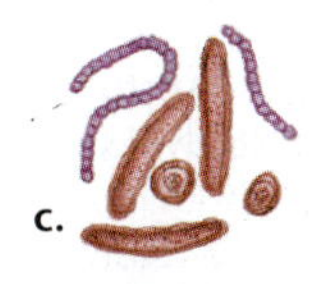

c.

d.

6. The total mass of living tissue at each trophic level can be shown in a(an)
   a. energy pyramid.
   b. pyramid of numbers.
   c. biomass pyramid.
   d. biogeochemical cycle.
7. Nutrients move through an ecosystem in
   a. biogeochemical cycles.
   b. water cycles.
   c. energy pyramids.
   d. ecological pyramids.

Interactive textbook with assessment at PHSchool.com

8. In the nitrogen cycle, bacteria that live on the roots of plants
   a. break down nitrogen compounds into nitrogen gas.
   b. denitrify nitrogen compounds.
   c. change nitrogen gas into plant proteins.
   d. change nitrogen gas into ammonia.
9. Which biogeochemical cycle does NOT involve a stage where the chemical enters the atmosphere?
   a. water cycle
   b. carbon cycle
   c. nitrogen cycle
   d. phosphorus cycle
10. When an ecosystem is limited by a single nutrient that either is scarce or cycles very slowly, this substance is called a(an)
    a. nitrogen compound.
    b. organic phosphate.
    c. biogeochemical cycle.
    d. limiting nutrient.

Understanding Concepts

11. What is the definition of ecology?
12. Name the different levels of organization within the biosphere, from smallest to largest.
13. How do scientists use modeling to study ecological changes?
14. How is sunlight important to most ecosystems?
15. What is chemosynthesis?
16. Distinguish between autotrophs and heterotrophs. Give an example of each.
17. What is a decomposer? Provide an example.
18. Which group of organisms is always found at the base of a food chain or food web?
19. What is an ecological pyramid? Describe the three different types of ecological pyramids.
20. Why is the transfer of energy and matter in a food chain only about 10 percent efficient?
21. What is a biogeochemical cycle?
22. List two ways in which water enters the atmosphere in the water cycle.
23. Explain the process of nitrogen fixation.
24. What are some of the similarities between the carbon cycle and the nitrogen cycle?
25. What is meant by "nutrient limitation"?

TIME SAVER — HOMEWORK GUIDE

Section:	Questions:
Section 3–1	1, 2, 11–13
Section 3–2	3–6, 14–20, 27, 30, 32
Section 3–3	7–10, 21–26, 28, 29, 31

If your class subscribes to the iText, your students can go online to access an interactive version of the Student Edition and a self-test.

(Continued from page 82)

19. An ecological pyramid is a diagram that shows the relative amounts of energy or matter contained within each trophic level of a food chain or food web. An energy pyramid shows the amount of energy available from one trophic level to the next. A biomass pyramid shows the total amount of living organic matter at each trophic level. A numbers pyramid shows the relative number of individual organisms at each trophic level.

20. Organisms use most of the energy they consume for life processes, and some is released into the environment as heat.

21. A repeating series of processes that passes the same molecules around again and again within the biosphere

22. Evaporation, transpiration

23. Bacteria that live in the soil and on plant roots called legumes convert nitrogen gas into ammonia.

24. In both cycles, the atmosphere is a major reservoir. Both cycles involve plants as transformers of the nutrients.

25. If a nutrient is in short supply, the ecosystem's growth will be limited.

Chapter 3 Assessment

Critical Thinking

26. The fertilizer was carried into the stream with runoff and promoted the growth of algae. The algae depleted oxygen in the water. Without oxygen, the fishes died.

27. Accept all food chains that begin with a producer and end with the student.

28. Students' answers should be logical and should provide some insights into the importance of water conservation.

29. As the rainfall amount increases, plant productivity also increases. Other factors that affect plant growth are the amount of sunlight, the types and amounts of nutrients in the soil, and the number of herbivores eating the plants.

30. Earthworm: detritivore; bear: omnivore; cow: herbivore; snail: detritivore; owl: carnivore; human: omnivore

31. Students' flowcharts may vary, depending on the organisms included in the food chain. A typical marine food chain might be similar to that shown in Figure 3–7, which begins with algae and ends with a shark. Students should also show that when the top-level carnivore in the chain dies, decomposers break down the dead organic matter and continue the biogeochemical cycle of nitrogen.

32. Several different food chains are possible. Make sure students identify a producer at the first level, an herbivore at the second level, and a carnivore at the third level.

Focus on the BIG Idea

Biogeochemical cycles pass molecules of essential nutrients among Earth's atmosphere, land, oceans and other bodies of water, and living organisms. In these cycles, complex substances are broken down into simple materials, transformed into forms that living organisms can use, and again assembled into complex substances such as proteins and carbohydrates.

Chapter 3 Assessment

Critical Thinking

26. Formulating Hypotheses Ecologists discovered that trout were dying in a stream that ran through some farmland where nitrogen fertilizer was used on the crops. How might you explain what happened?

27. Using Models Describe a food chain of which you are a member.

28. Problem Solving Water is a vital commodity. What are several ways in which you see water being wasted in your community? Can you offer some suggestions that will help limit the amount of water wasted? Can water consumption be reduced without a change in lifestyle?

29. Analyzing Data The graph below shows the effect of annual rainfall on the rate of primary productivity in an ecosystem. What happens to productivity as rainfall increases? What factors other than water might affect primary productivity?

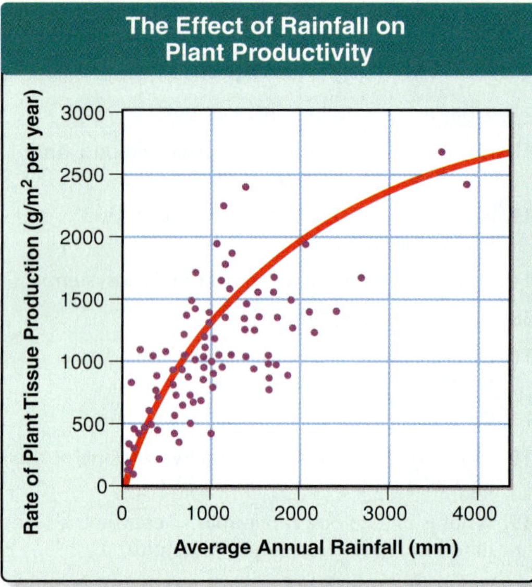

30. Classifying Classify each of the following as a herbivore, a carnivore, an omnivore, or a detritivore: earthworm, bear, cow, snail, owl, human.

31. Applying Concepts Using a flowchart, trace the flow of energy in a simple marine food chain. Then, show where nitrogen is cycled through the chain when the top-level carnivore dies and is decomposed.

32. Using Models Create flowcharts that show four different food chains in the food web shown below.

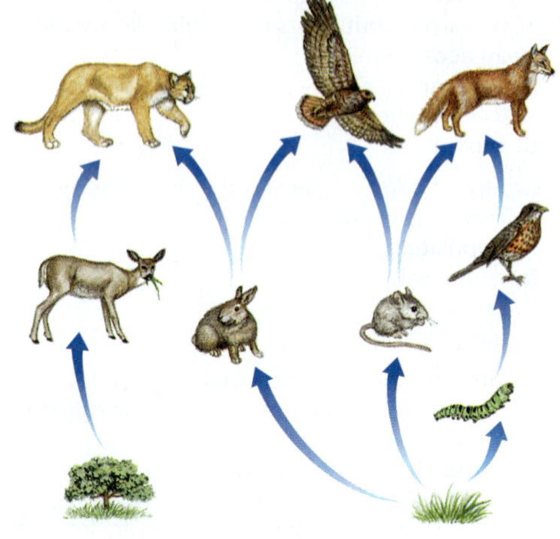

Focus on the BIG Idea

Matter and Energy Describe how biogeochemical cycles provide organisms with the raw materials necessary to synthesize complex organic compounds. Refer back to Chapter 2 for help in answering this question.

Writing in Science

Write a grammatically correct paragraph that (1) names and defines the levels of organization that an ecologist studies; (2) identifies the level that you would study if you were an ecologist; (3) describes the method you would use to study this level; and (4) gives a reason for your choice of a method.

Performance-Based Assessment

Make a Poster With a piece of string, mark off an area of about 4 m^2 in the schoolyard or in your own backyard. Create a poster that shows a food web of the organisms that you identify in the ecosystem you have sectioned off. Present your poster to the class.

For: An interactive self-test
Visit: PHSchool.com
Web Code: cba-2030

Writing in Science

Answers may vary. All students should name and define the levels of organization, including individual, population, community, ecosystem, biome, and biosphere. Students might choose any of the levels to study. Once that choice is made, students should describe how observing, experimenting, or modeling would be used in studying that level. The reason given for choice of method should be logical and supported in a way that suggests an understanding of that method.

Performance-Based Assessment

Make sure each food web begins with producers and includes several consumers.

Standards Practice

Online at PHSchool.com

Test-Taking Tip As you briefly scan the questions, identify those that may require pure guesswork on your part and save them for last. Then, use your time on those questions to reason through them and eliminate incorrect choices. Note: Do not write in this book.

Directions: Choose the letter that best answers the question or completes the statement.

1. A group of individuals belonging to a single species that lives together in a defined area is termed a(an)
   A population.
   B ecosystem.
   C community.
   D biome.

2. Which of the following is NOT characteristic of matter in the biosphere? **6 5.b**
   A Matter is recycled in the biosphere.
   B Biogeochemical cycles transform and reuse molecules.
   C The total amount of matter decreases over time.
   D Water and nutrients pass between organisms and the environment.

3. Which is a source of energy for Earth's living things?
   A sunlight
   B chemical energy
   C both A and B
   D none of the above

4. Which of the following is NOT a consumer?
   A autotroph
   B carnivore
   C omnivore
   D detritivore

5. Human activities, such as the burning of fossil fuels, cycle carbon through the carbon cycle. Which other processes also participate in the carbon cycle? **BI 6.d**
   A biological processes, such as photosynthesis
   B geochemical processes, such as the release of gas from volcanoes
   C mixed biogeochemical processes, such as the formation of fossil fuels
   D all of the above

Questions 6–7

The diagrams below represent the amount of biomass and the numbers of organisms in an ecosystem.

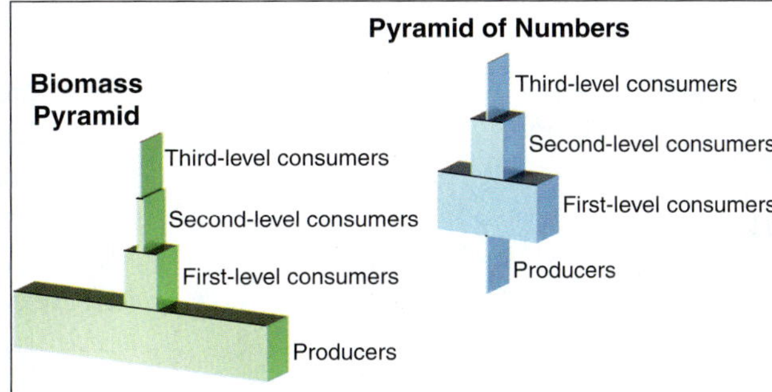

6. What is true about the pyramid of numbers? **BI 6.f**
   A First-level consumers compose the greatest number of individuals.
   B There are more third-level consumers than second-level consumers.
   C There are more producers than first-level consumers.
   D none of the above

7. What can you conclude based on the two pyramids? **BI 6.f**
   A The producers are probably small, like single-celled algae in a body of water.
   B The producers are probably large, like trees in a forest.
   C No reasonable conclusion can be drawn from the information given.
   D none of the above

Standards Practice

1. A 2. C 3. C 4. A 5. D 6. C 7. B

Success Tracker™

Online at PHSchool.com

Have students check their understanding of the chapter by logging onto Success Tracker.

Go Online PHSchool.com

Your students can independently test their knowledge of the chapter and print out their test results for your files.

Chapter Planner 4 Ecosystems and Communities

Section and Section Objectives	Time	STANDARDS NCLB	STANDARDS Biology	Activities and Labs
4–1 The Role of Climate, pp. 87–89 **4.1.1** ***Identify*** the causes of climate. **4.1.2** ***Explain*** how Earth's temperature range is maintained. **4.1.3** ***Identify*** Earth's three main climate zones.	1 period (1/2 block)			**SE:** ***Inquiry Activity,*** What relationships exist in an ecosystem?, p. 86 L2 **TE:** ***Build Science Skills,*** p. 88 L1 L2 **BTM:** Concept 8 L2 L3
4–2 What Shapes an Ecosystem?, pp. 90–97 **4.2.1** ***Explain*** how biotic and abiotic factors influence an ecosystem. **4.2.2** ***Identify*** the interactions that occur within communities. **4.2.3** ***Describe*** how ecosystems recover from a disturbance.	2 periods (1 block)	6 5.c, 6 5.e		**SE:** ***Quick Lab,*** How do abiotic factors affect different plant species?, p. 91 L2 **TE:** ***Demonstrations,*** pp. 92 L1 L2, 94 L2 **SE:** ***Careers in Biology,*** Forestry Technician, p. 95 L1 L2 **SE:** ***Build Science Skills,*** p. 96 L2 L3 **SE:** ***Exploration,*** Observing Succession, p. 113 L2 L3 **LMA:** Chapter 4 Lab L2 L3 **LMB:** Chapter 4 Lab L1 L2
4–3 Biomes, pp. 98–105 **4.3.1** ***Explain*** what microclimates are. **4.3.2** ***Identify*** the characteristics of major land biomes.	2 periods (1 block)	6 5.e		**TE:** ***Build Science Skills,*** p. 103 L2 L3 **IF:** Investigation 2 L1 L2 L3
4–4 Aquatic Ecosystems, pp. 106–112 **4.4.1** ***Identify*** the factors that govern aquatic ecosystems. **4.4.2** ***Identify*** the two types of freshwater ecosystems. **4.4.3** ***Describe*** the characteristics of the marine zones.	2 periods (1 block)	6 5.e		**TE:** ***Demonstration,*** p. 107 L2 **TE:** ***Build Science Skills,*** p. 110 L2 L3 **SE:** ***Analyzing Data,*** Ecosystem Productivity, p. 111 L2 L3
Chapter Assessment, pp. 114–117	1 period (1/2 block)			

ACTIVITY PLANNER

SE: *Inquiry Activity,* p. 86; 15 min.; small ecosystem

TE: *Build Science Skills,* p. 88; 5 min.; paper plate, pencil

SE: *Quick Lab,* p. 91; 15 min.; observation and recording each day for 2 weeks; rye (or wheat) and rice seeds, sand, potting soil, paper cups

TE: *Demonstration,* p. 92; 20 min.; string, uncolored and colored toothpicks

TE: *Demonstration,* p. 94; 15 min. for setup; dishpan, gravel, soil, shallow dish, water, grass seed, mixed birdseed

TE: *Build Science Skills,* p. 96; 15 min.; photos of succession

TE: *Build Science Skills,* p. 103; 15 min.; photographs of animals characteristic of each major land biome

TE: *Demonstration,* p. 107; 20 min.; aquarium, freshwater plants and animals, water, rocks, mud, sand, soil

TE: *Build Science Skills,* p. 110; 15 min.; variety of ocean organisms

SE: *Design an Experiment,* p. 113; 10 min. for setup, 20 min. every 2 days for 2 weeks; 1000-mL beaker, soil, grass clippings, dried leaves, 600-mL aged water, 4 coverslips, 4 glass slides, 4 dropper pipettes, microscope, guide for identifying microorganisms

PLANNING KEY

Ability Levels

for students performing . . .

below grade level L1

at grade level L2

above grade level L3

Print Components

SE	Student Edition	LA	Lab Assessment
TE	Teacher's Edition	BTM	Biotechnology Manual
RSW	Reading & Study Workbook A	IDM	Issues and Decision Making
ARSW	Adapted Reading & Study Workbook B	LW	Lab Worksheets
TR	Teaching Resources	LMA	Laboratory Manual A
IF	Investigations in Forensics	LMB	Laboratory Manual B

Tech Components

CTB	Computer Test Bank
BD	BioDetectives DVD
TP	Transparencies Plus
PLM	Probeware Lab Manual
ABC	ABC DVD Library
LS	Lab Simulations
VL	Virtual Labs

Interactive textbook with assessment at PHSchool.com

Program Resources	Assessment	Media and Technology
TR: Lesson Plan 4–1, Section Summary, p. 46 L1, p. 58 L2, Worksheets, p. 49 L1, pp. 60–61 L2 **RSW:** Section 4–1 L2 **ARSW:** Section 4–1 L1	**SE:** 4–1 Section Assessment, p. 89 **TR:** Section Review 4–1	**iText:** Section 4–1 **TP:** 4–1 Interest Grabber, Section Outline, Greenhouse Effect, Figure 4–1 and Figure 4–2 **VL:** The Effect of Temperature on Dissolved Oxygen
TR: Lesson Plan 4–2, Section Summary, p. 46 L1, p. 58 L2, Worksheets, pp. 50–53 L1, pp. 62–63 L2, Enrichment L2 L3 **LW:** Chapter 4 Exploration L1 L2 L3 **RSW:** Section 4–2 L2 **ARSW:** Section 4–2 L1	**SE:** 4–2 Section Assessment, p. 97 **TR:** Section Review 4–2	**iText:** Section 4–2 **TP:** 4–2 Interest Grabber, Section Outline, Abiotic and Biotic Factors, Figure 4–5
TR: Lesson Plan 4–3, Section Summary, p. 47 L1, p. 58 L2, Worksheets, pp. 54–55 L1, pp. 64–67 L2 **RSW:** Section 4–3 L2 **ARSW:** Section 4–3 L1 **IDM:** Issues and Decisions 46 L2 L3	**SE:** 4–3 Section Assessment, p. 105 **TR:** Section Review 4–3	**iText:** Section 4–3 **TP:** 4–3 Interest Grabber, Section Outline, Compare/Contrast Table, Figure 4–11
TR: Lesson Plan 4–4, Section Summary, p. 48 L1, p. 59 L2, Worksheets, p. 56 L1, pp. 68–70 L2 **RSW:** Section 4–4 L2 **ARSW:** Section 4–4 L1	**SE:** 4–4 Section Assessment, p. 112 **TR:** Section Review 4–4	**iText:** Section 4–4 **TP:** 4–4 Interest Grabber, Section Outline, Freshwater Pond Ecosystem, Figure 4–17
	SE: Chapter 4 Assessment, pp. 114–117 **TR:** Chapter Vocabulary Review, Graphic Organizer, Chapter 4 Test	**iText:** Chapter 4 Assessment **CTB:** Chapter 4 Test **Go Online** Students can do research, share data, and test their knowledge online.

PRESSED FOR TIME?

To Preview the Chapter

- Have students read What Is Climate? on page 87, Biotic and Abiotic Factors on page 90, The Major Biomes on page 99, and the two introductory paragraphs on page 106.

To Cover the Chapter Quickly

- Have students do the Reading Strategy for Section 4–1, page 87; read pages 90–93 of Section 4–2; review the land biome descriptions on pages 100–104; and read all of Section 4–4.

To Review the Chapter

- Assign Sections 4–1 through 4–4 in the Reading and Study Workbook or the Adapted Reading and Study Workbook.
- Assign the Chapter Vocabulary Review for Chapter 4 in Teaching Resources.

CHAPTER 4

ENGAGE/EXPLORE

Inquiry Activity

 6 5.c

Objective Students will be able to identify relationships among different organisms and between organisms and nonliving factors in a model ecosystem. L2

Skill Focus Classifying, Predicting

Materials terrarium, aquarium, or other small ecosystem

Time 15 minutes

Advance Prep If you do not already have a suitable small ecosystem in your classroom, prepare one before students do this activity. Set up the ecosystem sufficiently ahead of time so you are sure that it is fairly stable and the organisms are surviving well.

Strategy Provide times throughout the class period for pairs or small groups of students to take turns observing the ecosystem.

Expected Outcome Students should be able to identify some relationships between different organisms and between organisms and nonliving parts of the ecosystem.

Think About It

1. Answers will vary depending on the type of ecosystem and the kinds of organisms in it. Students should note any feeding relationships, competition, or nurturing behavior they observe. They also should identify organisms' interactions with air, water, sunlight, nutrients in the soil, and other nonliving factors.
2. Predictions will vary but should indicate differences due to the producers no longer adding energy to the ecosystem.

Assess Prior Knowledge

Determine whether students already understand the difference between climate and weather by asking them to define each term in their own words. Suggest that students note their definitions and compare them with those given in the text when they read Section 1.

CHAPTER 4

Ecosystems and Communities

In the Namib Desert, a Peringuey's sidewinder adder moves across the loose sand.

Inquiry Activity

 6 5.c

What relationships exist in an ecosystem?

Procedure

1. Observe a terrarium, aquarium, or other small ecosystem that your teacher provides.
2. Use your observations to construct a diagram (similar to a concept map) showing all the relationships that exist among the parts of the ecosystem.
3. Indicate on your diagram which relationships involve nonliving parts of the ecosystem.

Think About It

1. **Classifying** What types of relationships did you find among the organisms? What types of relationships did you find between the organisms and the nonliving parts of their environment?
2. **Predicting** How might your diagram change if the ecosystem were in the dark for a week?

HISTORY OF SCIENCE

Exploring the world
Prevailing winds and ocean currents played a vital role in world explorations of the fifteenth through eighteenth centuries. In some cases, sailors followed prevailing winds and currents to reach their desired location. In many cases, however, explorers encountered new lands by chance when they were carried off their intended course by unexpected winds or currents. Some voyagers met with difficulty or disaster when their ships entered the equatorial area of calm winds known as the doldrums or when they had to sail against prevailing winds and currents.

4–1 The Role of Climate

If you live in Michigan, you know you cannot grow banana trees in your backyard. Bananas are tropical plants that need plenty of water and heat. They won't survive in freezing temperatures. It may not be as obvious that cranberries won't grow in the Rio Grande Valley of Texas. Cranberries need plenty of water and a cold rest period. They cannot tolerate the months of very hot weather that often occur in the Rio Grande Valley.

Bananas and cranberries, like other plants and animals, vary in their adaptations to temperature, rainfall, and other environmental conditions. Species also vary in their tolerances for conditions outside their normal ranges. That's why climate is important in shaping ecosystems—and why understanding climate is important in ecology.

Guide for Reading

Key Concepts

- How does the greenhouse effect maintain the biosphere's temperature range?
- What are Earth's three main climate zones?

Vocabulary

weather • climate
greenhouse effect • polar zone
temperate zone • tropical zone

Reading Strategy: Outlining Before you read, use the headings in this section to make an outline about climate. As you read, fill in the subtopics and smaller topics. Then, add phrases or a sentence after each subtopic to provide key information.

What Is Climate?

In the atmosphere, temperature, precipitation, and other environmental factors combine to produce weather and climate. **Weather** is the day-to-day condition of Earth's atmosphere at a particular time and place. The weather where you live may be clear and sunny one day but cloudy and cold the next. **Climate,** on the other hand, refers to the average, year-after-year conditions of temperature and precipitation in a particular region.

Climate is caused by the interplay of many factors, including the trapping of heat by the atmosphere, the latitude, the transport of heat by winds and ocean currents, and the amount of precipitation that results. The shape and elevation of landmasses also contribute to global climate patterns.

The energy of incoming sunlight drives Earth's weather and helps determine climate. As you might expect, solar energy has an important effect on the temperature of the atmosphere. At the same time, the presence of certain gases in the atmosphere also has an effect on its temperature.

The Greenhouse Effect

Temperatures on Earth remain within a range suitable for life because the biosphere has a natural insulating blanket—the atmosphere. **Carbon dioxide, methane, water vapor, and a few other atmospheric gases trap heat energy and maintain Earth's temperature range.** These gases function like the glass windows of a greenhouse. Just as the glass keeps the greenhouse plants warm, these gases trap the heat energy of sunlight inside Earth's atmosphere. The natural situation in which heat is retained by this layer of greenhouse gases is called the **greenhouse effect,** shown in **Figure 4–1.**

▼ **Figure 4–1** **Carbon dioxide, water vapor, and several other gases in the atmosphere allow solar radiation to enter the biosphere but slow down the loss of heat to space.** These greenhouse gases cause the greenhouse effect, which helps maintain Earth's temperature range.

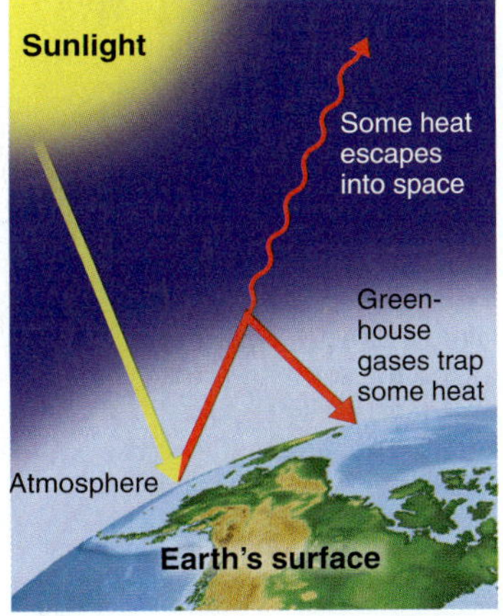

SECTION RESOURCES

Print:

- ***Teaching Resources,*** Lesson Plan 4–1, Adapted Section Summary 4–1, Adapted Worksheets 4–1, Section Summary 4–1, Worksheets 4–1, Section Review 4–1
- ***Reading and Study Workbook A,*** Section 4–1
- ***Adapted Reading and Study Workbook B,*** Section 4–1
- ***Biotechnology Manual,*** Concept 8

Technology:

- ***iText,*** Section 4–1
- ***Transparencies Plus,*** Section 4–1
- ***Virtual Labs CD-ROM,*** The Effect of Temperature on Dissolved Oxygen

Section 4–1

1 FOCUS

Objectives

4.1.1 ***Identify*** the causes of climate.
4.1.2 ***Explain*** how Earth's temperature range is maintained.
4.1.3 ***Identify*** Earth's three main climate zones.

Guide for Reading

Vocabulary Preview

Review the term *latitude* by asking students to describe what the term refers to. (*The distance north and south of the equator*) Display a large world map or globe, and have a volunteer point out the latitude lines on it.

Reading Strategy

Pair students who are not strong readers with proficient readers who can help them select main ideas, subtopics, and relevant details for the outline.

2 INSTRUCT

What Is Climate?

Use Community Resources

Encourage students to interview older family members and friends to find out what the climate was like in their area 25, 50, or more years ago. Instruct students to take notes during the interview. In class, let students compare notes to see whether the people they interviewed agree about climate changes in their lifetimes. L1 L2

The Greenhouse Effect

Make Connections

Physics Ask: **In what forms does Earth receive solar energy?** (*As light and other forms of radiation*) **Besides radiation, how is heat transferred?** (*By conduction [transfer from molecule to molecule within or between objects] and by convection [transfer in currents of a fluid, such as air]*) **What causes the greenhouse effect?** (*Earth's atmosphere traps much of the energy from the sun, raising the temperature of the atmosphere.*) L1 L2

Download a worksheet on climate and the greenhouse effect for students to complete, and find additional teacher support from NSTA SciLinks.

The Effect of Latitude on Climate

Use Visuals

Figure 4–2 After students have studied the figure and read the caption, ask: **Why does solar radiation strike different parts of Earth at an angle that varies throughout the year?** *(Earth is a sphere that is tilted on its axis.)* **What are the names given to the latitude lines of 23.5°N and 23.5°S?** *(The Tropic of Cancer and the Tropic of Capricorn, respectively)* **What climate zone is between the Tropic of Cancer and the Tropic of Capricorn?** *(The tropical zone)* **Which climate zone contains the United States?** *(The northern temperate zone)* **Why does the climate of a region in a temperate zone have a relatively wide range of temperatures, depending on the season?** *(The temperate zones are more affected by the changing angle of the sun over the course of a year.)* L1 L2

Heat Transport in the Biosphere

Build Science Skills

Using Models To reinforce students' understanding of how Earth's rotation affects currents and winds, give each pair of students a paper plate. Have one student hold a finger on the center of the plate while slowly turning the plate with the other hand. The second student should put the point of a pencil near the center of the plate and draw a line straight to the plate's edge. Students will see that the line drawn on the plate is not straight but curved, due to the plate's rotation. Explain that Earth's rotation has the same effect on winds and currents. L1 L2

For: Links on climate and the greenhouse effect
Visit: www.SciLinks.org
Web Code: cbn-2041

Greenhouse gases allow solar energy to penetrate the atmosphere in the form of sunlight. Much of the sunlight that hits the surface of our planet is converted into heat energy and then radiated back into the atmosphere. However, those same gases do not allow heat energy to pass out of the atmosphere as readily as light energy enters it. Instead, the gases trap heat inside Earth's atmosphere. If these gases were not present in the atmosphere, Earth would be 30 degrees Celsius cooler than it is today.

The Effect of Latitude on Climate

Because Earth is a sphere that is tilted on its axis, solar radiation strikes different parts of Earth's surface at an angle that varies throughout the year. At the equator, the sun is almost directly overhead at noon all year. At the North and South poles, however, the sun is much lower in the sky for months at a time. Look at **Figure 4–2**, and you will see that differences in the angle of sunlight directed at different latitudes result in the delivery of more heat to the equator than to the poles. The difference in heat distribution with latitude has important effects on Earth's climate zones.

As a result of differences in latitude and thus the angle of heating, Earth has three main climate zones: polar, temperate, and tropical. The **polar zones** are cold areas where the sun's rays strike Earth at a very low angle. These zones are located in the areas around the North and South poles, between 66.5° and 90° North and South latitudes. The **temperate zones** sit between the polar zones and the tropics. Because temperate zones are more affected by the changing angle of the sun over the course of a year, the climate in these zones ranges from hot to cold, depending on the season. The **tropical zone,** or tropics, is near the equator, between 23.5° North and 23.5° South latitudes. The tropics thus receive direct or nearly direct sunlight year-round, making the climate almost always warm. **Figure 4–2** shows Earth's main climate zones.

CHECKPOINT *What effect does latitude have on climate?*

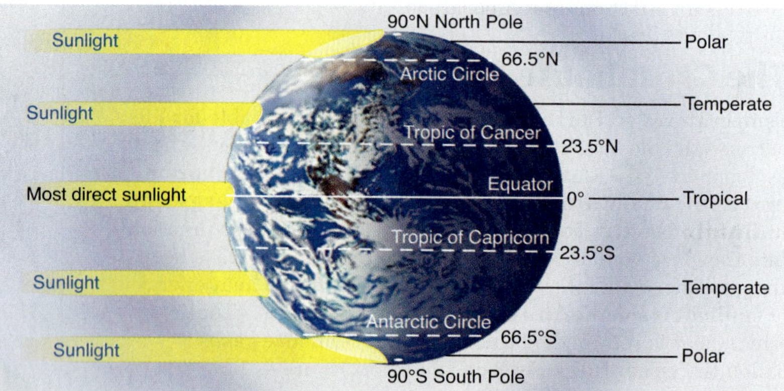

Figure 4–2 **Earth has three main climate zones.** These climate zones are caused by the unequal heating of Earth's surface. Near the equator, energy from the sun strikes Earth almost directly. Near the poles, the sun's rays strike Earth's surface at a lower angle. The same amount of solar energy is spread out over a larger area, heating the surface less than at the equator.

UNIVERSAL ACCESS

Inclusion/Special Needs
To help students who have difficulty grasping the information in the subsection Heat Transport in the Biosphere, read aloud the sentence about why winds form—warm air tends to rise and cool air tends to sink. This concept is common sense for most students, and once they understand that this phenomenon causes winds and ocean currents, they will be better able to understand how heat moves throughout the oceans and the atmosphere. L1

Advanced Learners
Point out to students who need an extra challenge that the word *tropics* derives from a Latin word for "solstice." Challenge these students to determine the connection between the solstices and the tropics of Cancer and Capricorn. Have them make a presentation of their findings to the class, complete with visual aids. L3

Heat Transport in the Biosphere

The unequal heating of Earth's surface drives winds and ocean currents, which transport heat throughout the biosphere. Winds form because warm air tends to rise and cool air tends to sink. Consequently, air that is heated near the equator rises. At the same time, cooler air over the poles sinks toward the ground. The upward movement of warm air and the downward movement of cool air create air currents, or winds, that move heat throughout the atmosphere, from regions of sinking air to regions of rising air. The prevailing winds, shown in **Figure 4–3**, bring warm or cold air to a region, affecting its climate.

Similar patterns of heating and cooling occur in Earth's oceans. Cold water near the poles sinks and then flows parallel to the ocean bottom, eventually rising again in warmer regions through a process called upwelling. Meanwhile, surface water is moved by winds. In both cases, the water flow creates ocean currents. Like air currents, ocean currents transport heat energy within the biosphere. Surface ocean currents warm or cool the air above them, thus affecting the weather and climate of nearby landmasses.

Continents and other landmasses can also affect winds and ocean currents. Landmasses can interfere with the movement of air masses. For example, a mountain range causes a moist air mass to rise. As this happens, the air mass cools and moisture condenses, forming clouds that bring precipitation to the mountains. Once the air mass reaches the far side of the mountains, it has lost much of its moisture. The result is a rain shadow—an area with a dry climate—on the far side of the mountains.

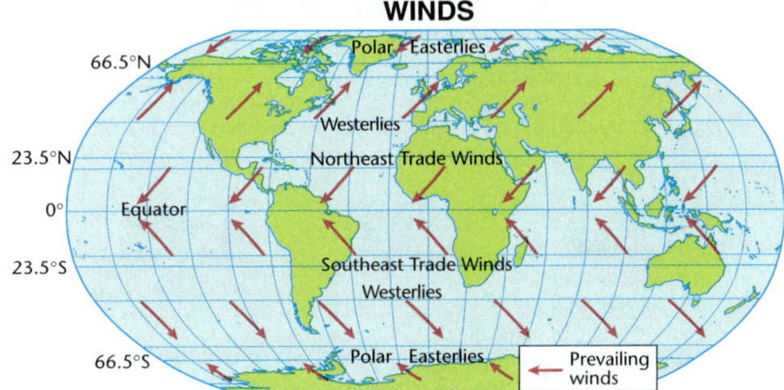

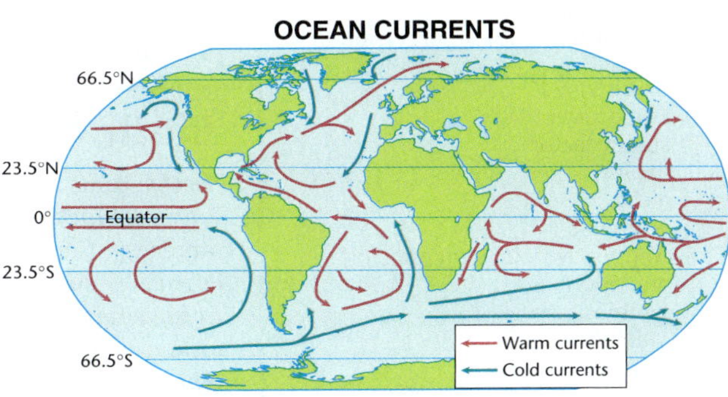

▲ **Figure 4–3** Earth's winds (top) and ocean currents (bottom) interact to help produce Earth's climates. The curved paths of some currents and winds are the result of Earth's rotation. **Interpreting Graphics** *In what direction do cold currents in Earth's oceans generally move?*

4–1 Section Assessment

1. **Key Concept** What is the greenhouse effect?
2. **Key Concept** Describe Earth's three main climate zones.
3. What are the main factors that determine Earth's climate?
4. Describe two ways in which heat is transported in the biosphere.
5. **Critical Thinking Applying Concepts** A biologist recorded the bird species in her region. Then, she spotted a bird that was not supposed to live in the region. How might variations relate to this occurrence?

Sharpen Your Skills

Modeling

Earth rotates daily on its axis and is tilted at an angle of 23.5° in relation to the sun. Using a flashlight to represent the sun and a globe to represent Earth, demonstrate different levels of light in Earth's three climate zones.

3 ASSESS

Evaluate Understanding

Call on students at random to identify the major climate factors discussed in this section and explain how each factor helps determine climate.

Reteach

Start a simple diagram of the greenhouse effect by drawing a curving section of Earth's surface on the board. Then, have different students in turn add features and labels to the drawing to explain the greenhouse effect step by step.

Sharpen Your Skills

Demonstrate how to hold the globe in a way that models the angle that Earth tilts on its axis, 23.5°. Have students note that if the North Pole is tilted away from the light, then the setup models the positions of sun and Earth during winter in the United States. If the North Pole is tilted toward the sun, then the setup models the positions during summer in the United States. Make sure students find these latitudes on the globe: 66.5° North and South, 90° North and South, 23.5° North and South, and the equator. Have students work in pairs or small groups.

Interactive Textbook

If your class subscribes to the iText, use it to review the Key Concepts in Section 4–1.

4–1 Section Assessment

1. Gases trap heat inside Earth's atmosphere.
2. Tropical zone: near equator; receives direct or nearly direct sunlight year-round, climate is almost always warm. Polar zones: near North and South poles; receive the sun's rays at a low angle, climate is cold. Temperate zones: between the other two zones; receive sunlight at changing angles during the year, climate ranges from hot to cold.
3. Trapping of heat by the atmosphere, latitude, transport of heat by winds and ocean currents, amount of precipitation
4. Winds and ocean currents
5. Animal species show variations in their tolerances for different climatic conditions. The bird was probably just a bit beyond its usual range. Because the species varies in its tolerance, it could survive beyond its range.

Answers to . . .

CHECKPOINT *Regions at higher latitudes receive less heat energy per unit area than do regions near the equator. As a result, the temperate and polar zones have cooler climates than the tropical zone.*

Figure 4–3 *Cold currents generally move in curving paths toward the equator.*

Section 4–2

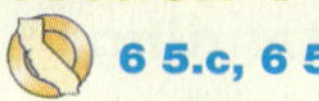

1 FOCUS

Objectives

4.2.1 ***Explain*** how biotic and abiotic factors influence an ecosystem.

4.2.2 ***Identify*** the interactions that occur within communities.

4.2.3 ***Describe*** how ecosystems recover from a disturbance.

Guide for Reading

Vocabulary Preview

The text provides pronunciations for most of the new Vocabulary terms in this section. Encourage students to use a dictionary to look up the phonetic spellings of the words for which pronunciations are not given, convert those spellings to the system used in this text, and include the phonetic spellings when they list the highlighted, boldface terms.

Reading Strategy

Students often confuse the terms *symbiosis, mutualism,* and *commensalism.* To help them understand and remember the distinctions, have them look up the derivations of the words in a dictionary and note the derivations when they list the highlighted, boldface terms.

2 INSTRUCT

Biotic and Abiotic Factors

Build Science Skills

Applying Concepts Point out to students that in any ecosystem, removing biotic elements can dramatically affect the ecosystem's abiotic conditions. For example, the trees in a forest hold topsoil with their roots, shade the soil, contribute organic matter to the soil in the form of dead leaves, and return water to the atmosphere through evaporation and transpiration. Removing trees from the forest ecosystem reduces these benefits. Ask students to suggest other examples of removing biotic elements from an ecosystem. L2 L3

4–2 What Shapes an Ecosystem?

6 5.c. Students know populations or organisms can be categorized by the functions they serve in an ecosystem.
6 5.e. Students know the number and types of organisms an ecosystem can support depend on the resources available and on abiotic factors, such as quantities of light and water, a range of temperatures, and soil composition.

Guide for Reading

Key Concepts

- How do biotic and abiotic factors influence an ecosystem?
- What interactions occur within communities?
- What is ecological succession?

Vocabulary

biotic factor
abiotic factor
habitat
niche
resource
competitive exclusion principle
predation
symbiosis
mutualism
commensalism
parasitism
ecological succession
primary succession
pioneer species
secondary succession

Reading Strategy: Building Vocabulary Before you read, preview new vocabulary terms by skimming the section and making a list of the highlighted, boldface terms. Leave space to make notes as you read.

If you ask an ecologist where a particular organism lives, that person might say the organism lives on a Caribbean coral reef, or in an Amazon rain forest, or in a desert in the American Southwest. Those answers provide a kind of ecological address not unlike a street address in a city or town. An ecological address, however, tells you more than where an organism lives. It tells you about the climate the organism experiences and what neighbors it is likely to have. But what shapes the ecosystem in which an organism lives?

Biotic and Abiotic Factors

CA a

Ecosystems are influenced by a combination of biological and physical factors. The biological influences on organisms within an ecosystem are called **biotic factors.** These include the entire living cast of characters with which an organism might interact, including birds, trees, mushrooms, and bacteria—in other words, the ecological community. Biotic factors that influence a bullfrog, for example, might include the tiny plants and algae it eats as a tadpole, the herons that eat the adult frog, and other species that compete with the bullfrog for food or space.

Physical, or nonliving, factors that shape ecosystems are called **abiotic** (ay-by-AHT-ik) **factors.** For example, the climate of an area includes abiotic factors such as temperature, precipitation, and humidity. Other abiotic factors are wind, nutrient availability, soil type, and sunlight. For example, the bullfrog in **Figure 4–4** is affected by abiotic factors such as the availability of water and the temperature of the air. **Together, biotic and abiotic factors determine the survival and growth of an organism and the productivity of the ecosystem in which the organism lives.** The area where an organism lives is called its **habitat.** A habitat includes both biotic and abiotic factors.

CHECKPOINT *Give an example of an abiotic factor.*

Figure 4–4 **Like all ecosystems, this pond is shaped by a combination of biotic and abiotic factors.** The bullfrog, plants, and other organisms in the pond are biotic factors. The water, the air, and the rock on which the bullfrog sits are abiotic factors.

SECTION RESOURCES

Print:

- ***Laboratory Manual A,*** Chapter 4 Lab
- ***Laboratory Manual B,*** Chapter 4 Lab
- ***Teaching Resources,*** Lesson Plan 4–2, Adapted Section Summary 4–2, Adapted Worksheets 4–2, Section Summary 4–2, Worksheets 4–2, Section Review 4–2, Enrichment
- ***Reading and Study Workbook A,*** Section 4–2
- ***Adapted Reading and Study Workbook B,*** Section 4–2
- ***Lab Worksheets,*** Chapter 4 Exploration

Technology:

- ***iText,*** Section 4–2
- ***Transparencies Plus,*** Section 4–2

Quick Lab

How do abiotic factors affect different plant species?

Materials presoaked rye and rice seeds, sand, potting soil, 4 paper cups

Procedure   

1. Use a pencil to punch three holes in the bottom of each cup. Fill 2 cups with equal amounts of sand and 2 cups with the same amount of potting soil.
2. Plant 5 rice seeds in one sand-filled cup and 5 rice seeds in one soil-filled cup. Plant 5 rye seeds in each of the other 2 cups. Label each cup with the type of seeds and soil it contains.
3. Place all the cups in a warm, sunny location. Each day for 2 weeks, water the cups equally and record your observations of any plant growth. **CAUTION:** *Wash your hands well with soap and warm water after handling plants or soil.*

Analyze and Conclude

1. **Analyzing Data** In which medium did the rice grow best—sand or soil? Which was the better medium for the growth of rye?
2. **Inferring** Soil retains more water than sand, providing a moister environment. What can you infer from your observations about the kind of environment that favors the growth of rice? The growth of rye?
3. **Drawing Conclusions** Which would compete more successfully in a dry environment—rye or rice? In a moist environment?

 6 5.e

The Niche

If an organism's habitat is its address, its niche is its occupation. A **niche** (NITCH) is the full range of physical and biological conditions in which an organism lives and the way in which the organism uses those conditions. For instance, part of the description of an organism's niche includes its place in the food web. Another part of the description might include the range of temperatures that the organism needs to survive. The combination of biotic and abiotic factors in an ecosystem often determines the number of different niches in that ecosystem.

A niche includes the type of food the organism eats, how it obtains this food, and which other species use the organism as food. For example, a mature bullfrog catches insects, worms, spiders, small fish, or even mice. Predators such as herons, raccoons, and snakes prey on bullfrogs.

The physical conditions that the bullfrog requires to survive are part of its niche. Bullfrogs spend their lives in or near the water of ponds, lakes, and slow-moving streams. A bullfrog's body temperature varies with that of the surrounding water and air. As winter approaches, bullfrogs burrow into the mud of pond or stream bottoms to hibernate.

The bullfrog's niche also includes when and how it reproduces. Female bullfrogs lay their eggs in water during the warmer months of the year. The young frogs, called tadpoles, live in the water until their legs and lungs develop.

UNIVERSAL ACCESS

Less Proficient Readers

Some students learn best when material is organized. Help these students better understand succession in a marine ecosystem by having them create a flowchart of the process discussed on pages 96 and 97. You could have students work in small groups to make these graphic organizers. When groups finish, display the flowcharts so that groups can compare their approaches. L1 L2

Advanced Learners

Encourage students who need an extra challenge to research the various types of defenses that have evolved in prey species as protection against predators. Such defenses include camouflage, mechanical defenses such as quills and thorns, chemical defenses such as toxins, warning coloration, and mimicry. Have students share their findings with the class in oral reports, posters, or displays. L3

Quick Lab

 6 5.e

Objective Students will be able to describe how abiotic factors affect growth in different species of plants. L2

Skill Focus Drawing Conclusions

Time 15 minutes for setup; brief observation and recording each day for 2 weeks

Advance Prep Soak the rice and rye seeds in water overnight.

Strategies

- Have students place the cups in trays or other shallow containers to hold any water, sand, and soil that may leak from the holes.
- Emphasize that except for the type of soil and type of seeds in each cup, all variables must be kept the same for all four cups.

Alternative Materials If rye is not available, you may use wheat seeds instead.

Expected Outcome Rice seeds will not grow well in the sand-filled cup because the water drains out and leaves the sand too dry. Rye seeds should grow well in soil or sand.

Analyze and Conclude

1. Both types of seeds will be more successful in soil. However, the effect on rice will be more pronounced.
2. Rice requires a moister environment than rye does. Rye can tolerate dry conditions better than rice can but also benefits from an ample supply of water.
3. Dry environment: rye; moist environment: rice

The Niche

Address Misconceptions

Students sometimes misunderstand what a niche is, believing it to be a part of an ecosystem. Use simple analogies to clarify the meaning of the term. For example, each player on a baseball team has a specific niche—a different role to play. L1 L2

Answer to . . .

The example should be any nonliving factor, such as air, water, soil, or rocks.

4–2 (continued)

Community Interactions

Demonstration

Mark off a 3-meter-square area with masking tape or string. Scatter 25 uncolored toothpicks (or other small objects) and 25 colored toothpicks over the area. Explain that the toothpicks represent two different species of insects. Choose two students to represent different species of lizards that eat both types of insects. At a signal from you, the two lizards start catching insects of both types. Signal the lizards to stop after 5–10 seconds, and ask them to count their insects. Rescatter the toothpicks and repeat the activity, but this time have one lizard eat only uncolored insects and the other lizard eat only colored insects. Compare the insect counts from the two different methods. Ask the "lizards": **Was it easier to catch insects when you were competing with each other or when you each had a different food?** *(When each had a different food)* Also ask the other students to describe competitive behaviors they observed.

Build Science Skills

Problem Solving Emphasize that any given ecosystem has only a certain amount of space, food, water, and other life essentials. Ask: **If one organism is involved in direct competition for life essentials, what are the possible outcomes for that organism?** *(The organism may win the struggle and survive, or it may lose the struggle and die.)* **Is there any other alternative for organisms that are in competition with other organisms?** *(If the competition is between different yet similar species, the organisms may change in ways that will decrease competition. In this way, both species may survive.)*

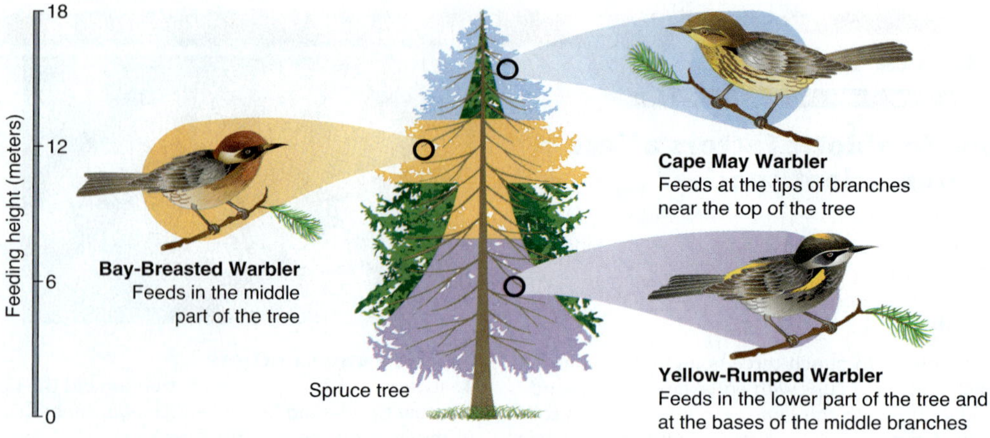

▲ **Figure 4–5** Each of these warbler species has a different niche in its spruce tree habitat. By feeding in different areas of the tree, the birds avoid competing with one another for food. **Inferring** ***What would happen if two of the warbler species attempted to occupy the same niche?***

As you will see, no two species can share the same niche in the same habitat. However, different species can occupy niches that are very similar. For instance, the three species of North American warblers shown in **Figure 4–5** live in the same spruce trees but feed at different elevations and in different parts of those trees. The species are similar, yet each warbler has a different niche within the forest.

What is a niche?

Community Interactions

When organisms live together in ecological communities, they interact constantly. These interactions help shape the ecosystem in which they live. **Community interactions, such as competition, predation, and various forms of symbiosis, can powerfully affect an ecosystem.**

Competition Competition occurs when organisms of the same or different species attempt to use an ecological resource in the same place at the same time. The term **resource** refers to any necessity of life, such as water, nutrients, light, food, or space. In a forest, for example, broad-leaved trees such as oak or hickory may compete for sunlight by growing tall, spreading out their leaves, and blocking the sunlight from shorter trees. Similarly, two species of lizards in a desert might compete by attempting to eat the same type of insect.

Direct competition in nature often results in a winner and a loser—with the losing organism failing to survive. A fundamental rule in ecology, the **competitive exclusion principle,** states that no two species can occupy the same niche in the same habitat at the same time. Look again at the distribution of the warblers in **Figure 4–5.** Can you see how this distribution avoids direct competition among the different warbler species?

HISTORY OF SCIENCE

The competitive exclusion principle
The competitive exclusion principle was first postulated by Russian ecologist G. F. Gause in 1934. In laboratory experiments, Gause studied the effect of interspecific competition on two closely related species of protists. When he cultured the two species separately, both populations grew rapidly and then leveled off at the culture's carrying capacity. When he cultured the two species together, however, one species apparently had a competitive edge in obtaining food, and the other species was driven to extinction in the culture. Gause concluded that two species so similar that they compete for the same limited resources cannot coexist in the same place. His conclusion was later confirmed by further studies.

Predation An interaction in which one organism captures and feeds on another organism is called **predation** (pree-DAY-shun). The organism that does the killing and eating is called the predator (PRED-uh-tur), and the food organism is the prey. Cheetahs are active predators with claws and sharp teeth. Their powerful legs enable them to run after prey. Other predators, such as anglerfishes, are more passive. An anglerfish has a fleshy appendage that resembles a fishing lure, which it uses to draw unsuspecting prey close to its mouth.

Symbiosis Any relationship in which two species live closely together is called **symbiosis** (sim-by-OH-sis), which means "living together." Biologists recognize three main classes of symbiotic relationships in nature: mutualism, commensalism, and parasitism. Examples of these three symbiotic relationships are shown in **Figure 4–6.**

Mutualism In **mutualism** (MYOO-choo-ul-iz-um), both species benefit from the relationship. Many flowers, for example, depend on certain species of insects to pollinate them. The flowers provide the insects with food in the form of nectar, pollen, or other substances, and the insects help the flowers reproduce.

Commensalism In **commensalism** (kuh-MEN-sul-iz-um), one member of the association benefits and the other is neither helped nor harmed. Small marine animals called barnacles, for example, often attach themselves to a whale's skin. The barnacles perform no known service to the whale, nor do they harm it. Yet, the barnacles benefit from the constant movement of water past the swimming whale, because the water carries food particles to them.

Parasitism In **parasitism** (PAR-uh-sit-iz-um), one organism lives on or inside another organism and harms it. The parasite obtains all or part of its nutritional needs from the other organism, called the host. Generally, parasites weaken but do not kill their host, which is usually larger than the parasite. Tapeworms, for example, are parasites that live in the intestines of mammals. Fleas, ticks, and lice live on the bodies of mammals, feeding on the blood and skin of the host.

Mutualism The ant cares for the aphids and protects them from predators. The aphids produce a sweet liquid that the ant drinks.

Commensalism The orchid benefits from its perch in the tree as it absorbs water and minerals from rainwater and runoff, but the tree is not affected.

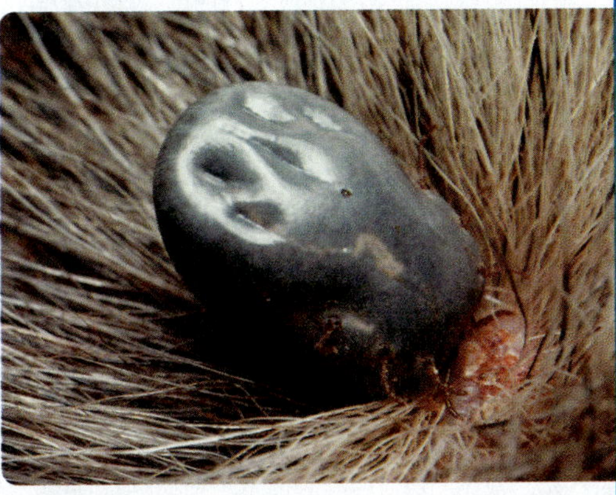

Parasitism A tick feeds on the blood of its host and may also carry disease-causing microorganisms.

Figure 4–6 Three examples of symbiosis are shown: mutualism, commensalism, and parasitism. **Predicting** ***What would happen to the aphids if the ant died?***

Build Science Skills

Problem Solving Explain that under normal conditions, prey populations seldom become extinct as a result of predation. Tell students to imagine an ecosystem in which a predator species has killed off an entire prey species. Ask: **What would the possible consequences be for the predators?** *(They would run out of food and die, they would have to change their eating habits and find other prey, or they would have to move to another area where that prey species still survives.)* L2

Build Science Skills

Applying Concepts Have each student list examples of symbiotic relationships that he or she knows from previous learning or has researched. In a class discussion, ask volunteers to describe examples without identifying the type of symbiosis each example represents. After each description, challenge other students to identify the relationship as mutualism, commensalism, or parasitism. L2 L3

BACKGROUND

Predation and diversity

In nature, predator species rarely kill and eat all their prey species, which would reduce community diversity. In fact, studies have shown that predation can actually help maintain diversity. One example of this process involves the gray wolf, a top predator in its ecosystem. Where wolves were hunted to extinction, such as in many parts of North America, populations of deer and other herbivores increased dramatically. As these populations overgrazed the vegetation, many plant species that could not tolerate such grazing pressure disappeared from the ecosystem. In turn, many insects and small animals that depended on the plants for food also disappeared. The elimination of wolves thus produced an ecosystem with considerably less species diversity.

Answers to . . .

CHECKPOINT *The full range of physical and biological conditions in which an organism lives and the way in which the organism uses those conditions*

Figure 4–5 *Most likely, one warbler species would be more successful in that niche, and the other species would not survive.*

Figure 4–6 *Without the ants, the aphids could be eaten by predators.*

4–2 (continued)

Ecological Succession

Demonstration

The following activity models stages of succession described on this page. Elicit student volunteers to help you create the model. Put a 2.5-cm layer of gravel in the bottom of a dishpan, and cover with a 10-cm layer of soil. Make a pond by sinking a shallow dish into the soil so its top is even with the soil surface. Put a 1-cm layer of soil in the bottom of the pond. Slowly pour water into the dishpan until the pond is completely full and the soil around it is wet. Sprinkle a handful of grass seeds over the entire dishpan. Leave the dishpan near a sunny window. Every 3 to 4 days, sprinkle grass seeds over the dishpan again. Lightly water the soil to keep it damp, but do not refill the pond or clean it out. Over time, the pond will become shallower and will eventually fill in with growing grass. When this has occurred, sprinkle a handful of mixed birdseed over the dishpan once a week for two weeks. The birdseed plants, which will be larger than the grass plants, represent the gradual invasion of shrubs and trees and the succession from a meadow to a forest. L1 L2

Build Science Skills

Problem Solving Ask: **What types of human activities can disturb an ecosystem and cause succession?** *(Examples include logging, strip mining, draining a marsh, clearing woodland to grow crops or graze livestock, removing a beaver dam, and the like.)* L2

Ecological Succession

On the time scale of a human life, some ecosystems may seem stable. The appearance of stability is often misleading, because ecosystems and communities are always changing. Sometimes, an ecosystem changes in response to an abrupt disturbance, such as a severe storm. At other times, change occurs as a more gradual response to natural fluctuations in the environment. **Ecosystems are constantly changing in response to natural and human disturbances. As an ecosystem changes, older inhabitants gradually die out and new organisms move in, causing further changes in the community.** This series of predictable changes that occurs in a community over time is called **ecological succession.** Sometimes succession results from slow changes in the physical environment. A sudden natural disturbance from human activities, such as clearing a forest, may also be a cause of succession.

Primary Succession On land, succession that occurs on surfaces where no soil exists is called **primary succession.** For example, primary succession occurs on the surfaces formed as volcanic eruptions build new islands or cover the land with lava rock or volcanic ash. Primary succession also occurs on bare rock exposed when glaciers melt.

In **Figure 4–7,** you can follow the stages of primary succession after a volcanic eruption. When primary succession begins, there is no soil, just ash and rock. The first species to populate the area are called **pioneer species.** The pioneer species on volcanic rocks are often lichens (LY-kunz). A lichen is made up of a fungus and an alga and can grow on bare rock. As lichens grow, they help break up the rocks. When they die, the lichens add organic material to help form soil in which plants can grow.

CHECKPOINT *What are pioneer species?*

▼ **Figure 4–7** Primary succession occurs on newly exposed surfaces, such as this newly deposited volcanic rock and ash. (1) A volcanic eruption destroys the previous ecosystem. (2) The first organisms to appear are lichens. (3) Mosses soon appear, and grasses take root in the thin layer of soil. (4) Eventually, tree seedlings and shrubs sprout among the plant community. **Predicting** *What types of animals would you expect to appear at each stage, and why?*

BIOLOGY UPDATE

Succession and chance

Many ecologists once believed that succession was an orderly and predictable process. Today, they realize that random, unpredictable events may influence which species succeed and which die off after a disturbance. For example, random variables such as the season of year the disturbance occurs, the wind direction and rainfall immediately after the disturbance, and which organisms are in an active stage of their breeding cycle can change the succession of a community after a fire, volcanic eruption, or other major disturbance. Ecologists have also found that climax communities are often not as stable as they were once thought to be. In studying coral reefs and tropical rain forests, for example, researchers find shifting patchworks of early, middle, and late successionary communities.

Secondary Succession Components of an ecosystem can be changed by natural events, such as fires, or by human activities, such as farming. These changes may affect the ecosystem in predictable or unpredictable ways. When the disturbance is over, community interactions tend to restore the ecosystem to its original condition through **secondary succession.** For example, secondary succession occurs after wildfires burn woodlands and when land cleared for farming is abandoned. **Figure 4–8** shows trees regrowing after a wildfire. In fact, fires set by lightning occur in many ecosystems, and some plants are so adapted to periodic fires that their seeds won't sprout unless exposed to fire!

Ecologists used to think that succession in a given area always proceeded through predictable stages to produce the same stable "climax community." Old-growth forests in the Pacific Northwest, for example, were considered climax communities. But natural disasters, climate change, and human activity such as introduction of nonnative species profoundly affect these communities today. Healthy ecosystems usually recover from natural disturbances because of the way components of the system interact. Ecosystems may or may not recover from long-term, human-caused disturbances.

▲ **Figure 4–8** Ten years after wildfires burned regions of Yellowstone National Park, small evergreen trees have begun to regenerate the forest. **Predicting** *How do you think this region will look 20 years after the fires?*

Careers in Biology

Forestry Technician

Job Description: work outdoors to help maintain, protect, and develop forests (by planting trees, fighting insects and diseases that attack trees, and controlling soil erosion)

Education: two- or four-year college degree in forestry, wildlife, or conservation; summer work in parks, state and national forests; and private industry provides on-the-job training

Skills: knowledge of the outdoors and basic safety precautions; communication skills for working with the public; keen observational skills; physical fitness for jobs that require walking long distances through forests

Highlights: help to manage and conserve forest biomes by analyzing data, planting trees, and managing fires when necessary; contribute to people's enjoyment of outdoor recreation

For: Career links
Visit: PHSchool.com
Web Code: cbb-2042

TEACHER TO TEACHER

To help students understand ecological succession, have them interview an older family member or neighbor who has lived in their neighborhood for a long time. Ask the person to describe how the neighborhood has changed over time. Make sure that students ask the following questions. (1) Have areas that were formerly grassy been paved or developed? (2) Have any farms, parks, or lots returned to their wild state? Ask students to write a summary of their interview and then share it with the class.

—Deidre Galvin
Biology Teacher
Ridgewood High School
Ridgewood, NJ

Use Community Resources

Invite students to cite examples of natural or human disturbances they have seen in their area. Emphasize that the disturbance need not be a large-scale event, such as cutting down all the trees in an area of woodland, but could be on a small scale—for example, homeowners removing thorny bushes from a narrow strip of land between their houses. Ask students to describe any changes they observed after the disturbance or, if the disturbance is very recent, to predict changes they think will occur over time. Take the class to a disturbed site, if feasible, or ask students to visit a site on their own periodically to observe changes that occur during the school year. L2 L3

Careers in Biology

Encourage students to use library resources to find out how to get started in a forestry career. Suggest that they present their findings in posters that include information such as the geographic locations where forestry professionals work, specific courses that are necessary, areas of research, and issues in the industry. L1 L2

Resources Society of American Foresters; International Union of Forestry Research Organizations; U.S. Department of Agriculture Forest Service

You can have students write a more extensive job description as well as list the educational requirements for a career in this field.

Answers to . . .

CHECKPOINT *The first species to populate an area at the beginning of the process of primary succession*

Figure 4–7 *Stage 2: insects and spiders are carried in by the wind; stage 3: rodents that feed on these arthropods and new grasses; stage 4: larger mammals and birds that feed on rodents*

Figure 4–8 *Answers may vary. Most students will suggest that succession will have proceeded in specific and predictable stages and the community in 20 years might be mature and stable.*

4–2 (continued)

Use Visuals

Figure 4–9 After students have studied the figure and read the caption, ask: **How is the situation shown in this illustration an example of ecological succession?** *(Ecological succession is the series of predictable changes that occurs in a community over time. In this situation, the predictable changes that occur are the different stages in the consumption of the dead whale.)* **What is the cause of succession in this situation?** *(The death and sinking of the whale causes the succession.)* **Is the succession in a marine ecosystem more like primary or secondary succession on land?** *(Students may compare it favorably to either kind of succession on land. Like primary succession, succession in a marine ecosystem begins with an event, a cause. It's also like secondary succession in that certain ocean organisms are adapted to the "disturbance" of a sinking dead whale, just as land organisms are adapted to the disturbance of fire.)* L2

Build Science Skills

Interpreting Graphics Collect, or ask students to find, several sets of photographs that show areas soon after a disturbance and at intervals as succession occurs. Good subjects for such photos include areas affected by a volcanic eruption or forest fire, such as the areas mentioned in the student text. Photos of succession after the eruption of Mount St. Helens are also widely available. Display each set of photos in random order, and have students identify the correct order. For each set, also ask: **How were you able to determine the correct order?** *(Sample answer: by the types and sizes of the plants growing in the area)* L2 L3

Figure 4–9 Ecosystems are constantly changing in response to disturbances. In natural environments, succession occurs in stages. A dead whale that falls to the ocean floor is soon covered with scavengers. After a time, only bare bones are left. The bones contain oil that supports several types of deep-sea bacteria. In the next stage of succession, the bacteria provide energy and nutrients for a different community of organisms that live on the bones and in the surrounding sediments.

Succession in a Marine Ecosystem Succession can occur in any ecosystem—even in the permanently dark, deep ocean. In 1987, scientists found an unusual community of organisms living on the remains of a dead whale in the deep waters off the coast of southern California. At first, ecologists did not know what to make of this extraordinary community. After several experiments and hours of observation, the ecologists found that the community represented a stage in succession amid an otherwise stable and well-documented deep-sea ecosystem. Since that discovery, several more whale carcasses have been found in other ocean basins with similar organisms surrounding them. **Figure 4–9** illustrates three stages in the succession of a whale-fall community.

1 The disturbance that causes this kind of succession begins when a large whale, such as a blue or fin whale, dies and sinks to the normally barren ocean floor. The whale carcass attracts a host of scavengers and decomposers, including amphipods (inset), hagfishes, and sharks, that feast on the decaying meat.

2 Within a year, most of the whale's tissues have been eaten. The carcass then supports only a much smaller number of fishes, crabs, marine snails (inset), and other marine animals. The decomposition of the whale's body, however, enriches the surrounding sediments with nutrients, forming an oasis of sediment dwellers, including many different species of marine worms.

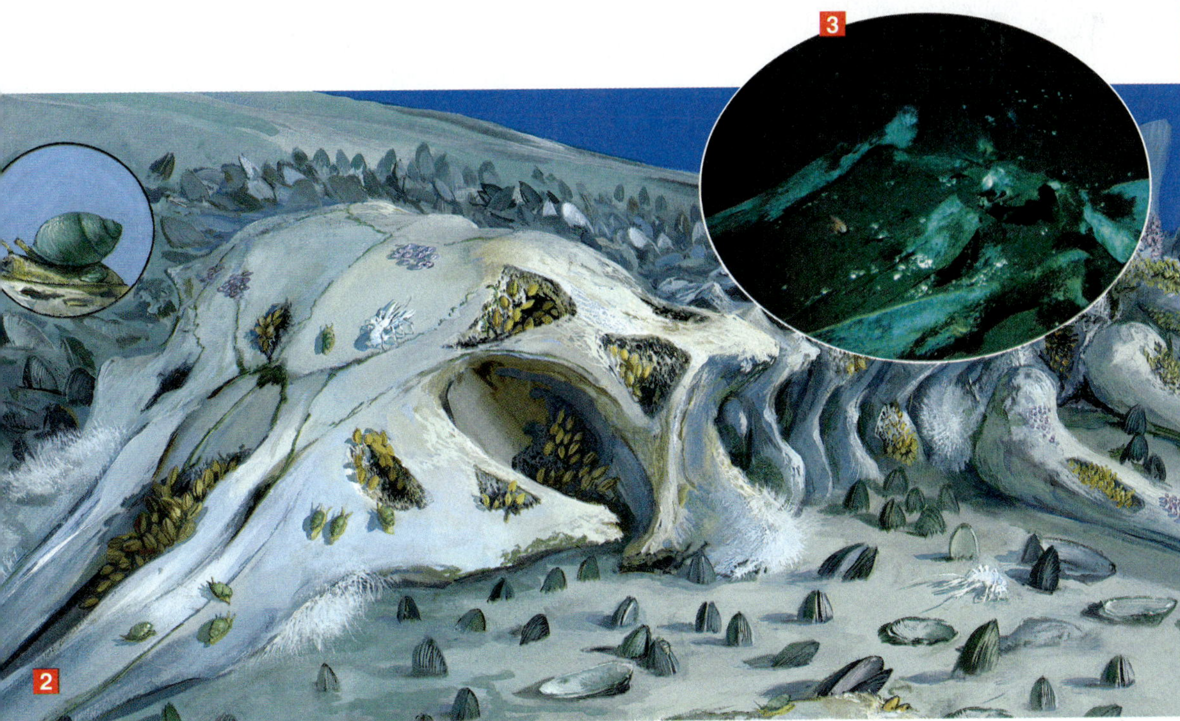

3 When only the whale's skeleton remains, a third community moves in. Heterotrophic bacteria begin to decompose oils inside the whale bones. In doing so, they release chemical compounds that serve as energy sources for other bacteria that are chemosynthetic autotrophs. The chemosynthetic bacteria, in turn, support a diverse community of mussels, limpets, snails, worms, crabs, clams, and other organisms that live on the bones and within the nearby sediments.

4–2 Section Assessment

1. **Key Concept** What is the difference between a biotic factor and an abiotic factor?
2. **Key Concept** Name three types of community interactions that can affect an ecosystem.
3. **Key Concept** What is the difference between primary succession and secondary succession?
4. How is an organism's niche determined?
5. **Critical Thinking Comparing and Contrasting** How are the three types of symbiotic relationships different? Similar?
6. **Critical Thinking Applying Concepts** Summarize the role of organisms, including microorganisms, in maintaining the equilibrium of a marine ecosystem while a dead whale decays on the ocean floor.

Writing in Science

Creative Writing

Use the information from this section to write a short story about an ecosystem that is disturbed and undergoes succession. *Hint:* Include a flowchart with your story to show the main stages of change.

3 ASSESS

Evaluate Understanding

Have each student select an example of succession—either one described in the student text or one of his or her own choice—and write a brief description of the sequence of changes that the ecosystem could undergo. As an alternative, students could draw sketches to show the changes.

Reteach

Using photographs of ecosystems that you have selected from other chapters in this textbook or from other sources, have students list the biotic and abiotic factors in each ecosystem.

Writing in Science

Let students use any ecosystem and any kind of disturbance of their choice. In general, students' stories should include information about a change in the biotic or abiotic factors in a stable ecosystem, resulting in succession. Students should chronicle the gradual changes that return the ecosystem to a climax community. If students have a hard time getting started, suggest that they begin by making a flowchart of steps in succession for a particular ecosystem and then use the flowchart as an outline for the story.

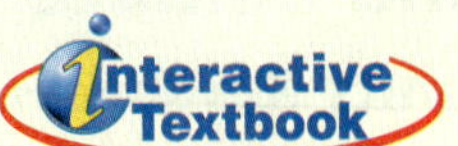

If your class subscribes to the iText, use it to review the Key Concepts in Section 4–2.

4–2 Section Assessment

1. A biotic factor is a living organism. An abiotic factor is nonliving.
2. Competition, predation, and symbiosis
3. Primary succession occurs on surfaces where no soil exists. Secondary succession occurs when a disturbance of some kind changes an existing community without removing the soil.
4. An organism's niche is determined by the physical and biological conditions in its environment and how it uses those conditions.
5. In mutualism, both species benefit. In commensalism, only one species benefits; the other is neither helped nor harmed. In parasitism, one species benefits; the other is harmed. In all three, two species live closely together.
6. Students should describe how scavengers and decomposers eat the decaying meat, how the decomposition of the whale's body forms an oasis for sediment dwellers, and how bacteria decompose the oils inside the whale's bones.

Section 4–3

1 FOCUS

Objectives

4.3.1 ***Explain*** what microclimates are.

4.3.2 ***Identify*** the characteristics of major land biomes.

Guide for Reading

Vocabulary Preview

Have students recall the definition of *climate* they learned earlier. Write *microclimate* on the board, and draw a box around the prefix *micro-*. Ask a volunteer to find the meaning of the prefix in a dictionary. *Micro-* means "small"; thus the term *microclimate* literally means "small climate"—a climate that exists over a small area.

Reading Strategy

Encourage students to create a table for recording the characteristics of each biome. Suggest that they include the following columns: *Name of Biome, Temperature, Precipitation, Soil Type, Dominant Plants, Dominant Animals,* and a final column labeled *Other Characteristics* in which to record any information that does not fit in the previous columns.

2 INSTRUCT

Biomes and Climate

Use Community Resources

Take students on a tour of the school grounds or immediate neighborhood to look for microclimates. Examples might include a south-facing embankment along a roadway; the sunny south side and shaded north side of a building; and the shaded, damp environment beneath a group of trees. Encourage students to check each microclimate periodically and note any changes—for example, spring flowers blooming along a building's south side. L2 L3

4–3 Biomes

6 5.e. Students know the number and types of organisms an ecosystem can support depend on the resources available and on abiotic factors, such as quantities of light and water, a range of temperatures, and soil composition. **BI 6.a.** Students know biodiversity is the sum total of different kinds of organisms and is affected by alterations of habitats.

Guide for Reading

Key Concept
- What are the unique characteristics of the world's major biomes?

Vocabulary
biome • tolerance
microclimate • canopy
understory • deciduous
coniferous • humus
taiga • permafrost

Reading Strategy: Using Visuals Before you read, preview **Figure 4–11.** Write down the names of the different biomes. As you read, examine the photographs and list the main characteristics of each biome. (a) 6 5.e

Ecologists group Earth's diverse environments into biomes. A **biome** is a complex of terrestrial communities that covers a large area and is characterized by certain soil and climate conditions and particular assemblages of plants and animals.

Can all kinds of organisms live in every biome? No. Species vary in their adaptations to different conditions. An adaptation is an inherited characteristic that increases an organism's ability to survive and reproduce.

The leaves of the saguaro cactus, for example, are reduced to spines to minimize water loss, and its stems store water during dry spells. Its shallow, wide-spreading roots absorb water rapidly. Desert rodents, such as kangaroo rats, have adaptations in their kidneys that help conserve water, and they extract water from food. Many rain forest plants, such as certain anthuriums, have long, thin leaves whose pointed tips help shed excess water. Some rain forest animals, such as certain tree frogs, spend their life in trees—their tadpoles grow in water pockets in leaf bases of plants such as bromeliads.

(CA) (a) These sorts of variations in plants and animals help different species survive under different conditions in different biomes. Plants and animals also exhibit variations in **tolerance,** or ability to survive and reproduce under conditions that differ from their optimal conditions. Plants and animals of the Arizona desert, for example, can tolerate temperatures that range from blisteringly hot to below freezing. Some rain forest plants and animals, by comparison, die quickly if the temperature drops below freezing or rises above 34°C for long. Either too much or too little of any environmental factor can make it difficult for an organism to survive. A saguaro would rot and die in a rain forest as surely as an anthurium or rain forest tree frog would shrivel and die in the desert!

▼ **Figure 4–10** Climate diagrams show the average temperature and precipitation at a given location during each month of the year. In this graph, and the others to follow, temperature is plotted as a red line. Precipitation is shown as vertical purple bars. **Interpreting Graphics** *What is the approximate average temperature and precipitation in New Orleans during the month of July?*

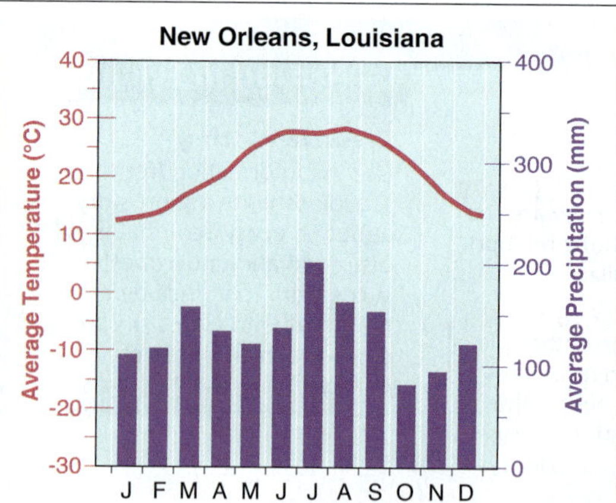

Biomes and Climate

Because each species is adapted to certain conditions, the climate of a region is an important factor in determining which organisms can survive there. Even within a biome, precise conditions of temperature and precipitation can vary over small distances. The climate in a small area that differs from the climate around it is called a **microclimate.** For example, certain streets in San Francisco are often blanketed in fog while the sun shines brightly just a few blocks away. Two main components of climate—temperature and precipitation—can be summarized in a graph called a climate diagram, as shown in **Figure 4–10.**

SECTION RESOURCES

Print:
- ***Teaching Resources,*** Lesson Plan 4–3, Adapted Section Summary 4–3, Adapted Worksheets 4–3, Section Summary 4–3, Worksheets 4–3, Section Review 4–3
- ***Reading and Study Workbook A,*** Section 4–3
- ***Adapted Reading and Study Workbook B,*** Section 4–3
- ***Issues and Decision Making,*** Issues and Decisions 46
- ***Investigations in Forensics,*** Investigation 2

Technology:
- ***iText,*** Section 4–3
- ***Transparencies Plus,*** Section 4–3

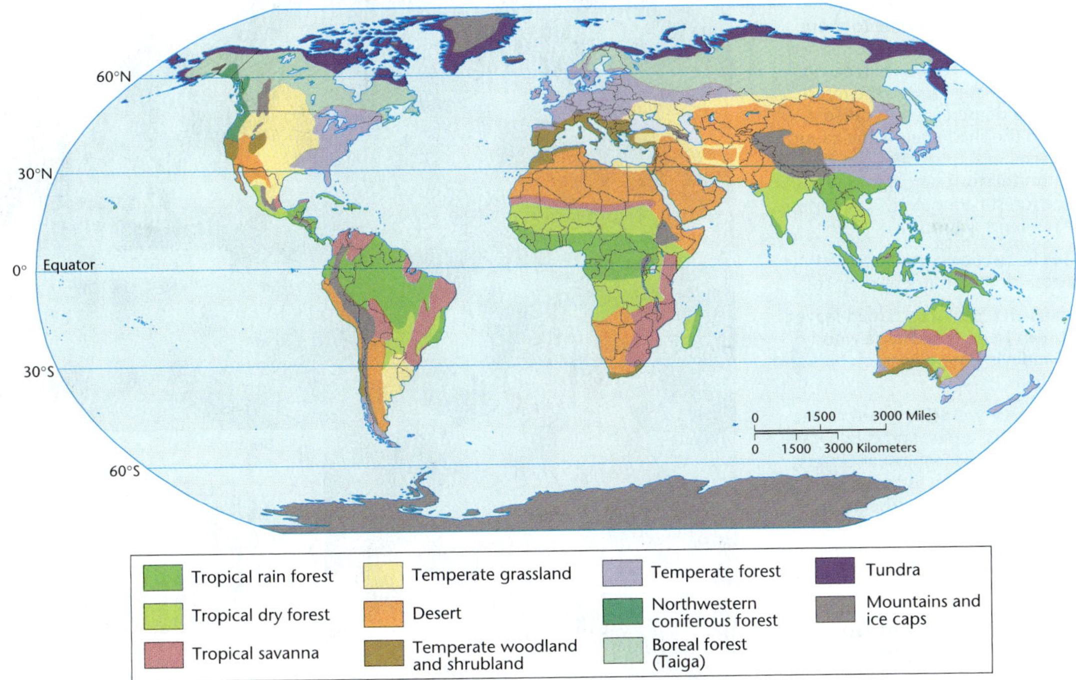

▲ **Figure 4–11** This map shows the locations of the world's major biomes. Other parts of Earth's surface are classified as mountains or ice caps. **Each biome has a characteristic climate and community of organisms.** These characteristics are shown on the pages that follow.

The Major Biomes

Ecologists recognize at least ten different biomes. **The world's major biomes include tropical rain forest, tropical dry forest, tropical savanna, desert, temperate grassland, temperate woodland and shrubland, temperate forest, northwestern coniferous forest, boreal forest, and tundra. Each of these biomes is defined by a unique set of abiotic factors—particularly climate—and a characteristic assemblage of plants and animals.** The distribution of major biomes is shown in **Figure 4–11**, and some of their most important characteristics are summarized over the next five pages.

There is often ecological variation within a biome. Sometimes, this variation is due to changes in microclimate caused by differences in exposure or elevation above sea level. Other times, variation may be related to geological factors such as local soil conditions or the presence of rock outcroppings. Note also that although boundaries between biomes on this map appear to be sharp, there are often transitional areas in which one biome's plants and animals become less common, whereas organisms of the adjacent biome become more common. These variations in distribution often can be related to the ranges of tolerances of plants and animals for different environmental factors. As you look at **Figure 4–11** and the following pages, see if you can relate the characteristics and locations of biomes to the patterns of global winds and ocean currents in **Figure 4–3.**

(a) 6 5.e

For: Earth's Biomes activity
Visit: PHSchool.com
Web Code: cbp-2043

Build Science Skills

Interpreting Tables and Graphs To ensure that students understand the format of a climate diagram, ask questions about Figure 4–10, such as the following: **In which month does New Orleans have the least precipitation?** *(October)* **The most precipitation?** *(July)* **What general trend do you see in the average monthly temperatures throughout the year?** *(Temperatures are lowest in winter, rise through the spring, are highest in summer, and decline through the fall and early winter.)* L2

The Major Biomes

Use Visuals

Figure 4–11 Direct students' attention to the map and ask: **Which biomes are found in the United States, not including Alaska and Hawaii?** *(Temperate grassland, desert, temperate woodland and shrubland, northwestern coniferous forest and temperate forest)* **Which biomes are found in Alaska?** *(Temperate forest, boreal forest, and tundra)* L1 L2

Build Science Skills

Inferring Direct students to look back at Figure 4–2 on page 88 and compare it with Figure 4–11 on this page. Ask: **Why do you think scientists classify land biomes into 10 categories when there are only three major climate zones on Earth?** *(Conditions vary somewhat within each climate zone, so several biomes may occur in some climate zones.)* L2

For: Earth's Biomes activity
Visit: PHSchool.com
Web Code: cbe-2043
Students compare and contrast the temperatures and rainfall levels of the different biomes.

ESL SUPPORT FOR ENGLISH LANGUAGE LEARNERS

Comprehension: Prior Knowledge

Beginning Have the students locate their native country on the biome map in Figure 4–11. Ask the students to use the key to identify the biome of their native country and the biome of their current home in the United States. Point out the names of the biomes in the figure's key, and read the names out loud to model correct pronunciation. L1

Intermediate Pair ESL students with English proficient students to prepare two lists. One list should contain words or phrases that describe the biome, climate, and common organisms of their native country. The other list should contain words or phrases that describe the biome, climate, and common organisms of their current home in the United States. Have the students add examples to their list by using pictures from newspapers and magazines. L2

Answer to . . .

Figure 4–10 *During the month of July in New Orleans, the average temperature is 25°C and the average precipitation is 200 mm.*

4–3 (continued)

Build Science Skills

Comparing and Contrasting Guide students through the wealth of information on pages 100–104 by having them focus on a single factor at a time across all the biomes. For example, first have students compare the biomes' temperature ranges and sequence them from lowest to highest. *(Tundra, boreal forest, temperate forest, northwestern coniferous forest, temperate grassland, temperate woodland and shrubland, desert, tropical savanna, tropical rain forest, tropical dry forest)* Then, have students compare the biomes' precipitation and sequence those amounts from lowest to highest. *(Desert and tundra, boreal forest, temperate woodland and shrubland, temperate grassland, temperate forest, tropical savanna, tropical dry forest, northwestern coniferous forest, tropical rain forest)* Next, have students compare the types of plants that are dominant in each biome and, finally, the dominant animals. Discuss any biome features or organisms that are unfamiliar to students. Encourage students to share any personal experiences they have had with different land biomes. L1

Address Misconceptions

Some students may have the misconception that all areas in tropical regions receive a great amount of rainfall all the time. Explain that it is true that many areas have abundant rainfall because of frequent thunderstorms caused by local heating of the air. Currents in the atmosphere, however, are extremely complex, and in some regions wind patterns result in much less precipitation than is found in regions with tropical rain forests. The result is that the tropics contain dry forests, savannas, and even deserts. L1 L2

Tropical Rain Forest

Tropical rain forests are home to more species than all other biomes combined. The leafy tops of tall trees—extending from 50 to 80 meters above the forest floor—form a dense covering called a **canopy.** In the shade below the canopy, a second layer of shorter trees and vines forms an **understory.** Organic matter that falls to the forest floor quickly decomposes, and the nutrients are recycled.

- **Abiotic factors:** hot and wet year-round; thin, nutrient-poor soils
- **Dominant plants:** broad-leaved evergreen trees; ferns; large woody vines and climbing plants; orchids and bromeliads
- **Dominant wildlife:** herbivores such as sloths, tapirs, and capybaras; predators such as jaguars; anteaters; monkeys; birds such as toucans, parrots, and parakeets; insects such as butterflies, ants, and beetles; piranhas and other freshwater fishes; reptiles such as caymans, boa constrictors, and anacondas
- **Geographic distribution:** parts of South and Central America, Southeast Asia, parts of Africa, southern India, and northeastern Australia

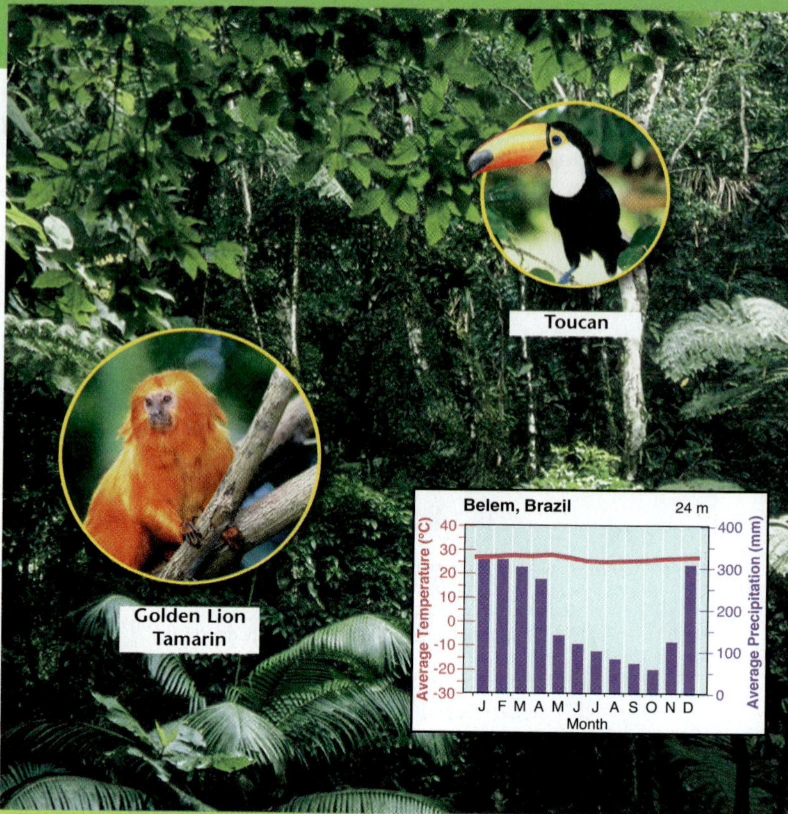

Tropical Dry Forest

Tropical dry forests grow in places where rainfall is highly seasonal rather than year-round. During the dry season, nearly all the trees drop their leaves to conserve water. A tree that sheds its leaves during a particular season each year is called **deciduous.**

- **Abiotic factors:** generally warm year-round; alternating wet and dry seasons; rich soils subject to erosion
- **Dominant plants:** tall, deciduous trees that form a dense canopy during the wet season; drought-tolerant orchids and bromeliads; aloes and other succulents
- **Dominant wildlife:** tigers; monkeys; herbivores such as elephants, Indian rhinoceroses, hog deer; birds such as great pied hornbills, pied harriers, and spot-billed pelicans; insects such as termites; reptiles such as snakes and monitor lizards
- **Geographic distribution:** parts of Africa, South and Central America, Mexico, India, Australia, and tropical islands

BACKGROUND

What's soil got to do with it? Soil is a mixture of rock, mineral ions, and organic matter. Each land biome tends to have a characteristic soil type. The top layer of soil in tropical rain forest biomes is acidic, with light-colored humus. The subsoil consists of iron and aluminum compounds mixed with clay. The soil in desert biomes is dry, brown to reddish brown with variable accumulations of clay, calcium carbonate, and soluble salts. A humus-mineral mixture exists in a thin layer of topsoil.

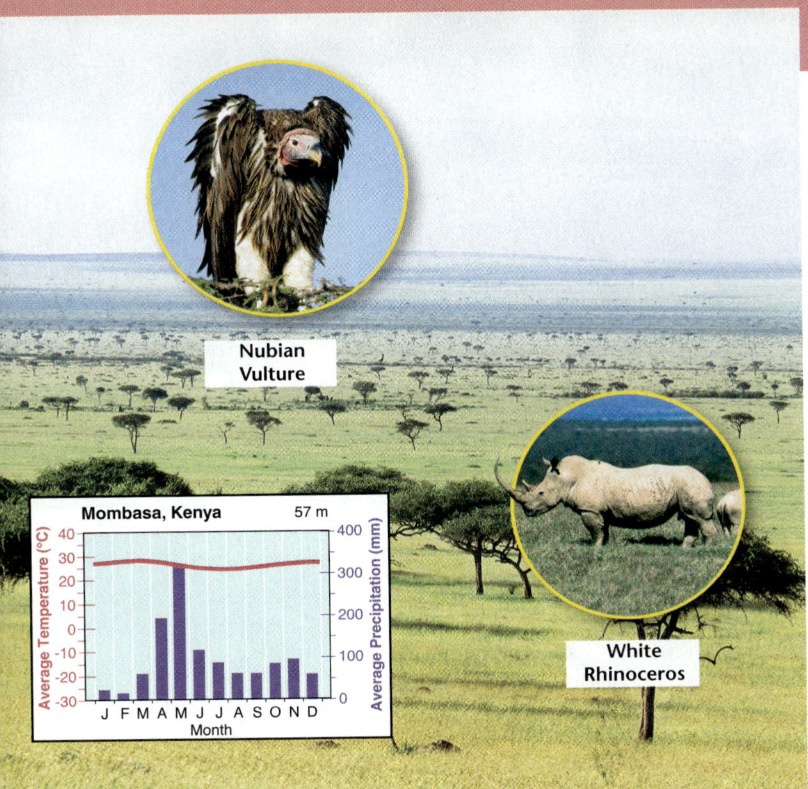

Tropical Savanna

Receiving more seasonal rainfall than deserts but less than tropical dry forests, tropical savannas, or grasslands, are characterized by a cover of grasses. Savannas are spotted with isolated trees and small groves of trees and shrubs. Compact soils, fairly frequent fires, and the action of large animals such as rhinoceroses prevent some savanna areas from turning into dry forest.

◀ **Abiotic factors:** warm temperatures; seasonal rainfall; compact soil; frequent fires set by lightning

◀ **Dominant plants:** tall, perennial grasses; sometimes drought-tolerant and fire-resistant trees or shrubs

◀ **Dominant wildlife:** predators such as lions, leopards, cheetahs, hyenas, and jackals; aardvarks; herbivores such as elephants, giraffes, antelopes, and zebras; baboons; birds such as eagles, ostriches, weaver birds, and storks; insects such as termites

◀ **Geographic distribution:** large parts of eastern Africa, southern Brazil, and northern Australia

Yuma, Arizona
60 m
Average Temperature (°C)
Average Precipitation (mm)
J F M A M J J A S O N D
Month

Golden Eagle

Desert Hairy Scorpion

Desert

All deserts are dry—in fact, a desert biome is defined as having annual precipitation of less than 25 centimeters. Beyond that, deserts vary greatly, depending on elevation and latitude. Many undergo extreme temperature changes during the course of a day, alternating between hot and cold. The organisms in this biome can tolerate the extreme conditions.

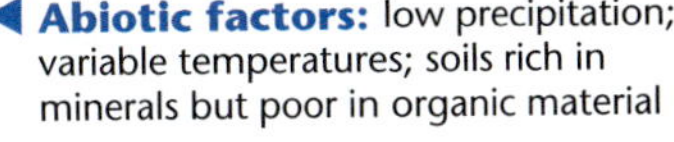

◀ **Abiotic factors:** low precipitation; variable temperatures; soils rich in minerals but poor in organic material

◀ **Dominant plants:** cacti and other succulents; creosote bush and other plants with short growth cycles

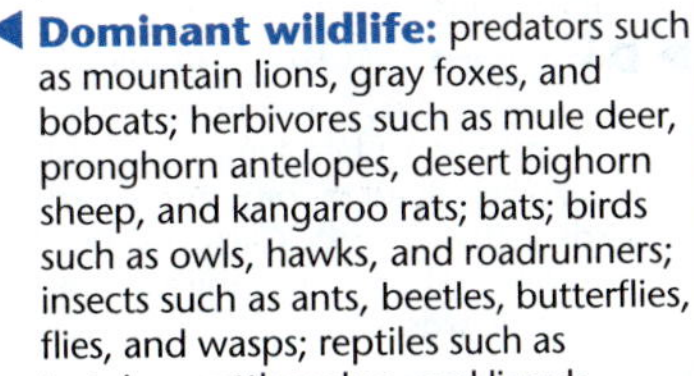

◀ **Dominant wildlife:** predators such as mountain lions, gray foxes, and bobcats; herbivores such as mule deer, pronghorn antelopes, desert bighorn sheep, and kangaroo rats; bats; birds such as owls, hawks, and roadrunners; insects such as ants, beetles, butterflies, flies, and wasps; reptiles such as tortoises, rattlesnakes, and lizards

◀ **Geographic distribution:** Africa, Asia, the Middle East, United States, Mexico, South America, and Australia

FACTS AND FIGURES

Convergent evolution

Plants and animals that appear to be quite similar often are found in similar environments but in widely separated parts of the world. For example, a member of the cactus family that grows in deserts of the southwestern United States is similar in appearance to a member of the spurge family that grows in the deserts of southwestern Africa. It would seem that these plants have evolved from a common ancestor, but this is not the case. The two species evolved from plants that are not related. This phenomenon of similar yet unrelated species occurring in different parts of the world is known as convergent evolution.

Build Science Skills

Communicating Divide the class into 10 groups, and assign a different biome to each group. Tell students that each group is to serve as the "class experts" on its assigned biome. Let each group's members divide responsibilities among themselves however they wish. For example, one student could handle abiotic factors, another student the dominant plants, and a third student the dominant animals. Encourage groups to do research to gain additional information about the biomes. Provide an opportunity for each group to present its biome to the class, share additional information they have gathered, and answer other students' questions. L2

Address Misconceptions

Most students—in fact, most people in general—think that all deserts are hot as well as dry. Emphasize that it is the amount of precipitation, not the temperature range, that distinguishes the desert from other biomes. Encourage students to find out about cold deserts, including the high-altitude deserts of Mongolia and China and the Great Basin in the western United States. L2 L3

4–3 (continued)

Build Science Skills

Comparing and Contrasting Have students refer back to the biome map in Figure 4–11 on page 99. Ask: **Which biome makes up the largest portion of the continental United States?** *(Temperate grassland)* Then, direct students to review the climate diagrams and text descriptions of the temperate grassland biome on this page and the tropical savanna biome on page 101. Ask: **What is the major similarity between these two biomes?** *(The dominant plants are grasses.)* **What are the major differences in the two biomes' climate?** *(The savanna gets more rainfall and has a greater range between the highest and lowest amounts. Savanna temperatures are higher but less variable than temperate grassland temperatures.)* L2

Make Connections

Earth Science Ask students: **What is the difference in the soils of temperate grassland and temperate woodland and shrubland?** *(Temperate grassland has fertile soils, whereas temperate woodland and shrubland has nutrient-poor soils.)* Have students compare the climate diagrams for the two biomes. Explain that soil is a combination of mineral and organic matter, and climate is perhaps the most influential factor in soil formation. Temperature and precipitation determine the kind of weathering, which determines the characteristics of the minerals that make up the soil. In addition, climate also is the main factor in the growth of vegetation and the abundance of microorganisms in the soil, both of which affect the soil's characteristics. Point out that just as the soils help determine the kind of vegetation found in a biome, the vegetation in turn contributes to how rich the soils are, since it's primarily the vegetation of an area that contributes the organic material in a rich soil. L2

Temperate Grassland

Characterized by a rich mix of grasses and underlaid by some of the world's most fertile soils, temperate grasslands—such as plains and prairies—once covered vast areas of the midwestern and central United States. Since the development of the steel plow, however, most have been converted to agricultural fields. Periodic fires and heavy grazing by large herbivores maintain the characteristic plant community.

- **Abiotic factors:** warm to hot summers; cold winters; moderate, seasonal precipitation; fertile soils; occasional fires
- **Dominant plants:** lush, perennial grasses and herbs; most are resistant to drought, fire, and cold
- **Dominant wildlife:** predators such as coyotes and badgers—historically included wolves and grizzly bears; herbivores such as mule deer, pronghorn antelopes, rabbits, prairie dogs, and introduced cattle—historically included bison; birds such as hawks, owls, bobwhites, prairie chickens, mountain plovers; reptiles such as snakes; insects such as ants and grasshoppers
- **Geographic distribution:** central Asia, North America, Australia, central Europe, and upland plateaus of South America

Black-Tailed Prairie Dog

Prairie Chicken

Dallas, Texas 400 m
Average Temperature (°C)
Average Precipitation (mm)
J F M A M J J A S O N D
Month

Temperate Woodland and Shrubland

This biome is characterized by a semiarid climate and a mix of shrub communities and open woodlands. In the open woodlands, large areas of grasses and wildflowers such as poppies are interspersed with oak trees. Communities that are dominated by shrubs are also known as chaparral. The growth of dense, low plants that contain flammable oils makes fires a constant threat.

- **Abiotic factors:** hot, dry summers; cool, moist winters; thin, nutrient-poor soils; periodic fires
- **Dominant plants:** woody evergreen shrubs with small, leathery leaves; fragrant, oily herbs that grow during winter and die in summer
- **Dominant wildlife:** predators such as coyotes, foxes, bobcats, and mountain lions; herbivores such as blacktailed deer, rabbits, and squirrels; birds such as hawks, California quails, warblers and other songbirds; reptiles such as lizards and snakes; butterflies
- **Geographic distribution:** western coasts of North and South America, areas around the Mediterranean Sea, South Africa, and Australia

BACKGROUND

More on soil The topsoil of temperate grassland biomes tends to be dark, alkaline, and rich in humus. This topsoil layer extends downward for more than a meter. Because topsoil formed on grasslands is often very fertile, most of the world's crops are grown on grassland soils. The subsoil consists of clay and calcium compounds. Soil in the boreal forest biomes is often quite acidic.

Temperate Forest

Temperate forests contain a mixture of deciduous and coniferous (koh-NIF-ur-us) trees. **Coniferous** trees, or conifers, produce seed-bearing cones, and most have leaves shaped like needles. These forests have cold winters that halt plant growth for several months. In autumn, the deciduous trees shed their leaves. In the spring, small plants burst out of the ground and flower. Soils of temperate forests are often rich in **humus** (HYOO-mus), a material formed from decaying leaves and other organic matter that makes soil fertile.

- **Abiotic factors:** cold to moderate winters; warm summers; year-round precipitation; fertile soils
- **Dominant plants:** broadleaf deciduous trees; some conifers; flowering shrubs; herbs; a ground layer of mosses and ferns
- **Dominant wildlife:** Deer; black bears; bobcats; nut and acorn feeders such as squirrels; omnivores such as raccoons and skunks; numerous songbirds; turkeys
- **Geographic distribution:** eastern United States; southeastern Canada; most of Europe; and parts of Japan, China, and Australia

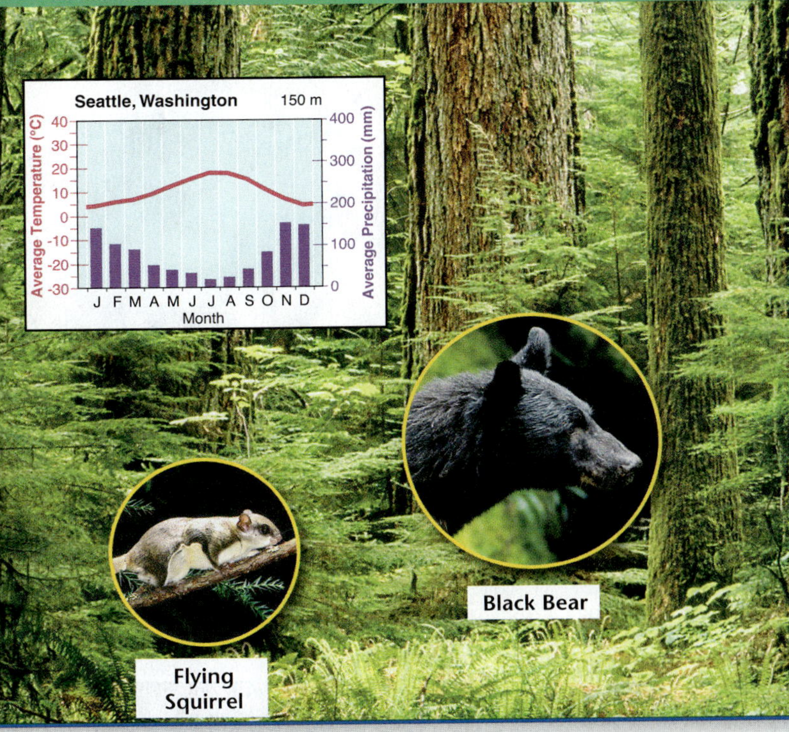

Northwestern Coniferous Forest

Mild, moist air from the Pacific Ocean provides abundant rainfall to this biome. The forest is made up of a variety of conifers, ranging from giant redwoods along the coast of northern California to spruce, fir, and hemlock farther north. Moss often covers tree trunks and the forest floor. Flowering trees and shrubs such as dogwood and rhododendron are also abundant. Because of its lush vegetation, the northwestern coniferous forest is sometimes called a "temperate rain forest."

- **Abiotic factors:** mild temperatures; abundant precipitation during fall, winter, and spring; relatively cool, dry summer; rocky, acidic soils
- **Dominant plants:** Douglas fir, Sitka spruce, western hemlock, redwood
- **Dominant wildlife:** bears; large herbivores such as elk and deer; beavers; predators such as owls, bobcats, and members of the weasel family
- **Geographic distribution:** Pacific coast of northwestern United States and Canada, from northern California to Alaska

Build Science Skills

Applying Concepts Point out that the temperate forest biome in northeastern regions of North America and Asia is noted for its striking colored fall foliage. If students do not live in an area that experiences this seasonal change, urge them to collect photographs of fall foliage. Also suggest that they obtain booklets and other tourist guides that describe the best times and locations for foliage viewing at different latitudes within the biome.  L2

Build Science Skills

Classifying Collect photographs of various types of animals that are characteristic of each major land biome. Number the photographs, and display them in random order. Working individually or in pairs, students should try to determine the biome(s) in which each animal might live. In a follow-up class discussion, let students compare their choices and explain their reasoning. L2 L3

FACTS AND FIGURES

Layers of plant growth

In a temperate forest, there may be up to five layers of plant growth. The tallest trees make up the canopy layer; often this layer consists of only one or two dominant species. Under the canopy is a layer of shorter trees called the understory. Below the understory is a shrub layer made up of short, branching, woody plants. An herb layer consisting of grasses, ferns, and annual wildflowers grows close to the ground. Finally, there is the ground layer, which consists of mosses, fungi, and leaf litter.

4–3 (continued)

Build Science Skills

Drawing Conclusions Focus students' attention on the climate diagram for the tundra biome. Ask: **In terms of precipitation throughout the year, which other biome does the tundra most resemble?** *(The desert biome)* Have students look back at the biome map on page 99. Ask: **Why does the tundra biome have the lowest temperatures of all the biomes?** *(The tundra is the farthest north of all biomes, so it receives the sun's rays at the lowest angles and for the shortest periods of time.)*

Other Land Areas

Make Connections

Earth Science Display a large world map that shows Earth's major mountain ranges. Have students locate the color-coded mountain areas on the biome map in Figure 4–11, page 99, and then find those areas on the large map and list the names of the mountain ranges. Separate groups could investigate each range's characteristics—the heights of its tallest peaks, the temperature ranges and dominant organisms at various elevations, and other data. Encourage students to also search out interesting facts about the ranges, such as the 1998 discovery of mummified children on high Andean peaks or tales of the elusive Yeti ("abominable snowman") high in the Himalayas. Let groups share their findings in oral reports, illustrated displays, or three-dimensional models. L2 L3

Boreal Forest

Along the northern edge of the temperate zone are dense evergreen forests of coniferous trees. These biomes are called boreal forests, or **taiga** (TY-guh). Winters are bitterly cold, but summers are mild and long enough to allow the ground to thaw. The word *boreal* comes from the Greek word for "north," reflecting the fact that boreal forests occur mostly in the Northern Hemisphere.

- **Abiotic factors:** long, cold winters; short, mild summers; moderate precipitation; high humidity; acidic, nutrient-poor soils
- **Dominant plants:** needleleaf coniferous trees such as spruce and fir; some broadleaf deciduous trees; small, berry-bearing shrubs
- **Dominant wildlife:** predators such as lynxes and timber wolves and members of the weasel family; small herbivorous mammals; moose and other large herbivores; beavers; songbirds and migratory birds
- **Geographic distribution:** North America, Asia, and northern Europe

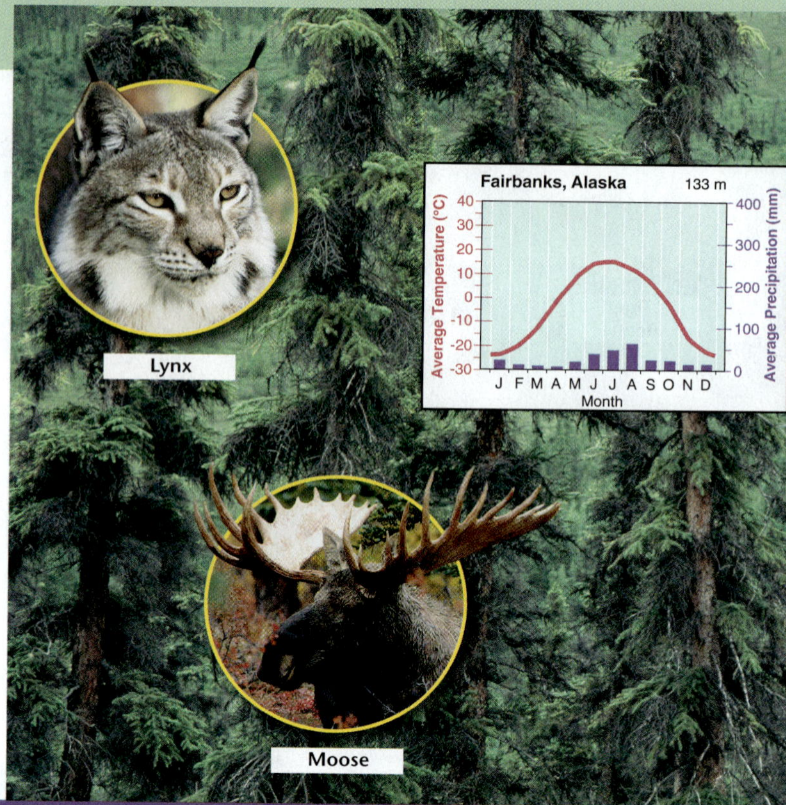

Tundra

The tundra is characterized by **permafrost,** a layer of permanently frozen subsoil. During the short, cool summer, the ground thaws to a depth of a few centimeters and becomes soggy and wet. In winter, the topsoil freezes again. This cycle of thawing and freezing, which rips and crushes plant roots, is one reason that tundra plants are small and stunted. Cold temperatures, high winds, the short growing season, and humus-poor soils also limit plant height.

- **Abiotic factors:** strong winds; low precipitation; short and soggy summers; long, cold, and dark winters; poorly developed soils; permafrost
- **Dominant plants:** ground-hugging plants such as mosses, lichens, sedges, and short grasses
- **Dominant wildlife:** a few resident birds and mammals that can withstand the harsh conditions; migratory waterfowl, shore birds, musk ox, Arctic foxes, and caribou; lemmings and other small rodents
- **Geographic distribution:** northern North America, Asia, and Europe

FACTS AND FIGURES

Oases in the tundra

As an example of the tundra's extreme dryness: In the Arctic regions north of mainland Canada, less than 15 cm of precipitation falls annually—about the same amount as falls in the desert regions of Arizona. Such dryness, coupled with intense cold, makes the tundra a barren place. Yet, like the oases in deserts, there are areas where living things can survive and even thrive. Some of these areas are sheltered valleys that are protected from bitterly cold winds. Other areas are meadows with an abundant water supply that can support large numbers of animals.

Other Land Areas

Some areas of land on Earth do not fall neatly into the major biome categories described on the previous pages. These areas include mountain ranges and polar ice caps.

Mountain Ranges Mountain ranges can be found on all continents. On mountains like the one in **Figure 4–12,** the abiotic and biotic conditions vary with elevation. As you move up from base to summit, temperatures become colder and precipitation increases. Therefore, the types of plants and animals also change. If you were to climb the Rocky Mountains in Colorado, for example, you would begin in a grassland. Then, you would pass through an open woodland of pines. Next, you would hike through a forest of spruce and other conifers. Near the summit, you would reach open areas of wildflowers and stunted vegetation resembling tundra. In the Canadian Rockies, ice fields occur at the peaks of some ranges.

Polar Ice Caps The icy polar regions that border the tundra are cold year-round. Outside of the ice and snow, plants and algae are few but do include mosses and lichens. In the north polar region, the Arctic Ocean is covered with sea ice, and a thick ice cap covers most of Greenland. Polar bears, seals, insects, and mites are the dominant animals. In the south polar region, the continent of Antarctica is covered by a layer of ice that is nearly 5 kilometers thick in some places. There, the dominant wildlife includes penguins and marine mammals.

▲ **Figure 4–12** Washington's Mount Rainier towers above the tree line. **Applying Concepts** *Based on what you have seen in the previous pages, which biome lies at the base of this mountain?*

For: Links on biomes
Visit: www.SciLinks.org
Web Code: cbn-2043

4–3 Section Assessment

1. **Key Concept** List the major biomes, and give one characteristic feature of each.
2. How are biomes classified?
3. What are the two types of tropical forest? How do they differ?
4. How might a mountain range affect the types of plants and animals found in an area?
5. **Critical Thinking Inferring** What characteristics would you expect tundra animals to have?
6. **Critical Thinking Comparing and Contrasting** Choose two very different biomes. From each biome, select a plant and an animal that are dominant. Compare how these plants' adaptations are suited to their biomes. Compare how these animals' adaptations are suited to their biomes.

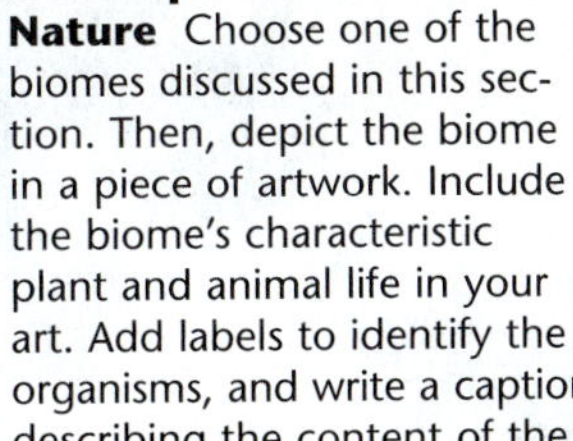

Interdependence in Nature Choose one of the biomes discussed in this section. Then, depict the biome in a piece of artwork. Include the biome's characteristic plant and animal life in your art. Add labels to identify the organisms, and write a caption describing the content of the artwork.

4–3 Section Assessment

1. Students should list the major biomes along with one characteristic of each.
2. By their climate, which is determined by precipitation and temperature, and by the community of organisms that live there
3. Tropical rain forests have higher temperatures and more rainfall annually than do tropical dry forests.
4. Animals and plants found in mountain ranges must be adapted to the generally cooler, wetter conditions that are found there.
5. Sample answer: Tundra animals need to be well insulated with thick coats of fur/hair or layers of feathers.
6. Answers may vary. Students might select any plants and animals mentioned in the profiles of the 10 biomes. In their comparisons, they should discuss specific adaptations of the organisms.

3 ASSESS

Evaluate Understanding

Briefly describe characteristics of various biomes, and call on students at random to identify each one. For example, if you say, "High temperatures that do not vary much throughout the year," students should identify the biome as a tropical rain forest or a tropical savanna. Base your descriptions on the information presented on pages 100–104 of the student text.

Reteach

Make overhead transparencies of the climate diagrams for each of the land biomes. Project the diagrams in any order. For each diagram, call on one student to summarize the diagram's information about temperature and precipitation *(for example, "High temperatures and heavy rainfall year-round")*, and call on a second student to identify the biome.

Focus on the BIG Idea

This activity can be completed individually or in small groups. Provide students with a variety of materials to choose from, including basic art supplies, modeling clay, pasta shapes, pipe cleaners, fabric, and construction paper. You might also encourage students to bring materials from home, or you might coordinate this activity with an art class at your school. Encourage students to be creative but accurate in depicting the biomes.

Download a worksheet on biomes for students to complete, and find additional teacher support from NSTA SciLinks.

If your class subscribes to the iText, use it to review the Key Concepts in Section 4–3.

Answer to . . .

Figure 4–12 *Boreal forest*

Section 4–4

 6 5.e

1 FOCUS

Objectives

4.4.1 ***Identify*** the factors that govern aquatic ecosystems.
4.4.2 ***Identify*** the two types of freshwater ecosystems.
4.4.3 ***Describe*** the characteristics of the marine zones.

Guide for Reading

Vocabulary Preview

Point out the words *photic* and *aphotic* in the Vocabulary list on this page. Explain that *phot-* in these words means the same thing as the prefix *photo-* in words such as *photograph.* Ask: **What does the prefix *photo-* mean?** *("Light")* **What does the prefix *a-* in the word *aphotic* mean?** *("Not" or "without")* **What do you think the terms *photic* and *aphotic* mean?** *("With light" and "without light")* Tell students to check their predictions when they encounter these words in the text.

Reading Strategy

As with the biomes in Section 4–3, have students set up a table for recording the similarities and differences they find as they read about aquatic ecosystems. Suggest that they divide the "Marine Ecosystems" section of the table into two subsections so they can keep separate notes on the photic and aphotic zones.

2 INSTRUCT

Freshwater Ecosystems

Use Community Sources

Have students consult road maps to find the locations and names of any freshwater ecosystems—lakes, ponds, rivers, or streams—in their area. If possible, arrange a trip to one of these locations so students can observe its characteristics and the types of organisms living there. L2

4–4 Aquatic Ecosystems

6 5.e. Students know the number and types of organisms an ecosystem can support depend on the resources available and on abiotic factors, such as quantities of light and water, a range of temperatures, and soil composition.

Guide for Reading

Key Concepts
- What are the main factors that govern aquatic ecosystems?
- What are the two types of freshwater ecosystems?
- What are the characteristics of the different marine zones?

Vocabulary
plankton • phytoplankton
zooplankton • wetland
estuary • detritus • salt marsh
mangrove swamp
photic zone • aphotic zone
zonation • coastal ocean
kelp forest • coral reef
benthos

ⓐ 6 5.e

Reading Strategy: Making Comparisons As you read, write down statements about similarities and differences among the different types of aquatic ecosystems.

Nearly three-fourths of Earth's surface is covered with water, so it is not surprising that many organisms make their homes in aquatic habitats. Oceans, streams, lakes, and marshes—indeed, nearly any body of water—contain a wide variety of communities. These aquatic communities are governed by biotic and abiotic factors, including light, nutrient availability, and oxygen.

CA ⓐ

Aquatic ecosystems are determined primarily by the depth, flow, temperature, and chemistry of the overlying water. In contrast to land biomes, which are grouped geographically, aquatic ecosystems are often grouped according to the abiotic factors that affect them. One such factor is the depth of water, or distance from shore. The depth of water, in turn, determines the amount of light that organisms receive. Water chemistry refers primarily to the amount of dissolved chemicals—especially salts, nutrients, and oxygen—on which life depends. For example, communities of organisms found in shallow water close to shore can be very different from the communities that occur away from shore in deep water. One abiotic factor that is important both to biomes and aquatic ecosystems is latitude. Aquatic ecosystems in polar, temperate, and tropical oceans all have distinctive characteristics.

▼ **Figure 4–13** The Menominee River in Michigan is a flowing-water ecosystem. **Like all aquatic ecosystems, this river's communities are determined by the depth, flow, and chemistry of the water.**

Freshwater Ecosystems

It may surprise you to know that only 3 percent of the surface water on Earth is fresh water. **Freshwater ecosystems can be divided into two main types: flowing-water ecosystems and standing-water ecosystems.**

Flowing-Water Ecosystems Rivers, streams, creeks, and brooks are all freshwater ecosystems that flow over the land. Organisms that live there are well adapted to the rate of flow. Some insect larvae have hooks that allow them to take hold of aquatic plants. Certain catfish have suckers that anchor them to rocks. Trout and many other fishes have streamlined bodies that help them move with or against the current.

Flowing-water ecosystems like the river in **Figure 4–13** originate in mountains or hills, often springing from an underground water source. Near the source, the turbulent water has plenty of dissolved oxygen but little plant life. As the water flows downhill, sediments build up and enable plants to establish themselves. Farther downstream, the water may meander more slowly through flat areas, where turtles, beavers, or river otters make their homes.

SECTION RESOURCES

Print:
- ***Teaching Resources,*** Lesson Plan 4–4, Adapted Section Summary 4–4, Adapted Worksheets 4–4, Section Summary 4–4, Worksheets 4–4, Section Review 4–4
- ***Reading and Study Workbook A,*** Section 4–4
- ***Adapted Reading and Study Workbook B,*** Section 4–4

Technology:
- ***iText,*** Section 4–4
- ***Transparencies Plus,*** Section 4–4

Standing-Water Ecosystems Lakes and ponds are the most common standing-water ecosystems. In addition to the net flow of water in and out of these systems, there is usually water circulating within them. This circulation helps to distribute heat, oxygen, and nutrients throughout the ecosystem.

The relatively still waters of lakes and ponds provide habitats for many organisms, such as plankton, that would be quickly washed away in flowing water. **Plankton** is a general term for the tiny, free-floating organisms that live in both freshwater and saltwater environments. See **Figure 4–14** for examples. Unicellular algae, or **phytoplankton** (fyt-oh-PLANK-tun), are supported by nutrients in the water and form the base of many aquatic food webs. Planktonic animals, or **zooplankton** (zoh-oh-PLANK-tun), feed on the phytoplankton.

CHECKPOINT *What are phytoplankton?*

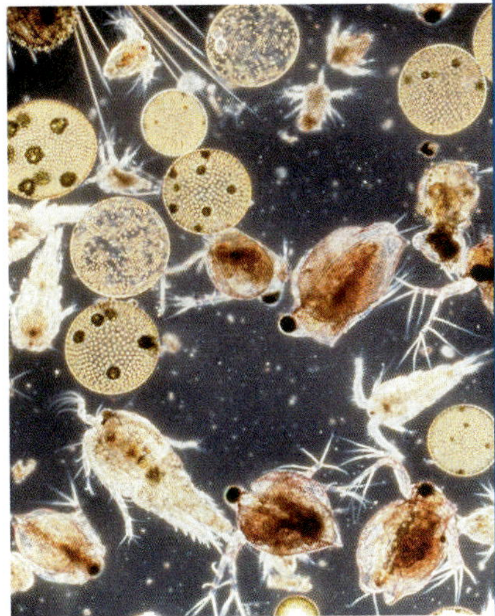

▲ **Figure 4–14** Both freshwater and saltwater ecosystems often include plankton. This photograph shows phytoplankton, zooplankton, and larger animals called water fleas. **Predicting** *What might happen to an aquatic food web if phytoplankton were removed from the ecosystem?*

Freshwater Wetlands A **wetland** is an ecosystem in which water either covers the soil or is present at or near the surface of the soil for at least part of the year. The water in wetlands may be flowing or standing and fresh, salty, or brackish, which is a mixture of fresh and salt water. Many wetlands are very productive ecosystems that serve as breeding grounds for insects, fishes and other aquatic animals, amphibians, and migratory birds.

The three main types of freshwater wetlands are bogs, marshes, and swamps. Bogs, which are wetlands that are often dominated by sphagnum moss, typically form in depressions where water collects. The water in sphagnum bogs is often very acidic. Marshes are shallow wetlands along rivers. They may be underwater for all or part of the year. Marshes often contain cattails, rushes, and other tall, grasslike plants. Water flows slowly through swamps, which often look like flooded forests. The presence of trees and shrubs is what distinguishes a swamp from a marsh.

Some wetlands, such as the swamp shown in **Figure 4–15**, are wet year-round. Other kinds of wetlands, however, may not always be covered in standing water. Such areas may be classified as wetlands because they have certain kinds of soils and are wet enough to support a specific community of water-loving plants and animals.

▼ **Figure 4–15** **Freshwater ecosystems can be divided into two main types: flowing-water ecosystems and standing-water ecosystems.** Although this swamp along the Loxahatchee River in Florida appears stagnant, water actually flows through it slowly. The swamp is home to turtles, otters, alligators, and herons that live among the baldcypress trees.

Build Science Skills

Comparing and Contrasting
As suggested for biomes, guide students through the information in this section by having them focus on one factor at a time—temperature range, light, oxygen and nutrient availability, and characteristic organisms—across all the aquatic ecosystems. Discuss any unfamiliar organisms, and provide field guides so students can do further research. Also, encourage students to share any personal experiences they have had with different aquatic biomes. L2

Demonstration

Collect several different types of freshwater plants and animals to set up a classroom aquarium. Also collect some abiotic elements—water, rocks, mud, sand, and the like—so the organisms will have as natural an environment as possible. Make sure you or students return all organisms to their original location at the end of this unit. L1 L2

Use Community Resources

Emphasize that a particular area of land is classified as a wetland not by whether it has water on it at any particular time of the year but by its soil type and the plants found there. In fact, many freshwater wetlands are dry for a good part of the year, so people may not even recognize them as wetlands. If a wetland exists near the school, take the class to observe it. Caution students to be very careful walking in the area, as many wetland plants are fragile and the soil, if damp, can be easily compacted. Do not allow students to collect any plants, animals, or abiotic materials.

L2 L3

UNIVERSAL ACCESS

Less Proficient Readers
Few students will have observed any marine ecosystems beyond the intertidal zone. To help students comprehend the text description of marine zones, provide a wide variety of visual resources—photographic books, nature magazines, videotapes, and CD-ROMs—so students can see what the different zones and their organisms look like. L1 L2

Advanced Learners
Students who need an additional challenge might enjoy researching and reading about Sylvia Earle, a marine biologist who earned international recognition for her pioneering studies of hydrothermal vents and the unique organisms found there. Encourage students to share their findings in posters, oral reports, mock radio shows, or skits. L3

Answers to . . .

CHECKPOINT *Unicellular algae*

Figure 4–14 *The consumers would die off because there would be no more producers to sustain them.*

4–4 (continued)

Estuaries

Word Origins

A detritivore is an organism that eats detritus. L2

Build Science Skills

Comparing and Contrasting Have students describe similarities and differences between the types of organisms found in freshwater ecosystems and those found in estuaries. Then, ask: **Do the same species of aquatic organisms live in both ecosystems?** *(No)* **Why not?** *(Estuaries are saltwater ecosystems. Species usually are adapted to live in either a saltwater environment or a freshwater environment, not both.)*

 L2

Marine Ecosystems

Build Science Skills

Predicting Draw a horizontal line on the chalkboard to represent the surface of the ocean. Then, draw a diagonal line slanting downward, and mark it to indicate ocean depths of 50 meters, 100 meters, 200 meters, 1000 meters, 2000 meters, and 10,000 meters. Invite students to relate what they already know about marine organisms. Then, ask: **What factors do you think determine the types of organisms that live at different depths in the ocean?** *(Most students will realize that available light is a major factor. Accept all responses without comment at this time.)* L2

Word Origins

Detritus is a Latin word meaning "worn away." In ecology, detritus refers to particles that have worn away from decaying organic material. **If the Latin word *vorare* means "to devour," what is a *detritivore?***

Estuaries

Estuaries (ES-tyoo-ehr-eez) are wetlands formed where rivers meet the sea. Estuaries thus contain a mixture of fresh water and salt water, and are affected by the rise and fall of ocean tides. Many are shallow, so sufficient sunlight reaches the bottom to power photosynthesis. Primary producers include plants, algae, and both photosynthetic and chemosynthetic bacteria. Estuary food webs differ from those of more familiar ecosystems because most primary production is not consumed by herbivores. Instead, much of that organic material enters the food web as detritus. **Detritus** is made up of tiny pieces of organic material that provide food for organisms at the base of the estuary's food web. Organisms that feed on detritus include clams, worms, and sponges.

Estuaries support an astonishing amount of biomass, although they usually contain fewer species than freshwater or marine ecosystems. Estuaries serve as spawning and nursery grounds for commercially important fishes and for shellfish such as shrimps and crabs. Many young animals feed and grow in estuaries, then head out to sea to mature, and return to reproduce. Many waterfowl use estuaries for nesting, feeding, and resting during migrations.

Salt marshes are temperate-zone estuaries dominated by salt-tolerant grasses above the low-tide line, and by seagrasses under water. Salt marshes like the one shown in **Figure 4–16** (left) are (or were once) found along great stretches of eastern North America from southern Maine to Georgia. One of the largest systems of connected salt marshes in America surrounds the Chesapeake Bay estuary in Maryland.

Mangrove swamps, shown in **Figure 4–16** (right), are coastal wetlands that are widespread across tropical regions, including southern Florida and Hawaii. Here, the dominant plants are several species of salt-tolerant trees, collectively called mangroves. Seagrasses are also common below the low-tide line. Like salt marshes, mangrove swamps are valuable nurseries for fish and shellfish. The largest mangrove area in the continental United States is within Florida's Everglades National Park.

Figure 4–16 Salt marshes occur in estuaries along seacoasts in the temperate zone. Salt-tolerant grasses are the dominant plants in this salt marsh (left) along the coast of Mount Desert Island in Maine. Mangrove swamps (right) occur in bays and estuaries along tropical coasts. The stiltlike roots of mangrove trees trap sediment that accumulates as mud behind the trees. This allows other plants to take root and helps to build the mangrove forest out from the shoreline. **Predicting** *Would you expect to find mangrove swamps or salt marshes on a coast exposed to large ocean waves? Explain.*

FACTS AND FIGURES

Bottoms up!

A problem that occurs in aquatic ecosystems is that nutrients tend to sink below the photic zone so organisms cannot use them. In lakes, strong winds usually mix the water. In oceans, deep nutrient-rich water rises to the photic zone in a process called upwelling. In upwelling, winds carry surface water away from land. Bottom water with valuable nutrients is pulled up into the photic zone to replace the surface water that has been moved out to sea. These nutrients support vigorous and rapid growth of phytoplankton, which provide the basis for marine food webs. Upwelling is common along the coastal margins of continents, where winds carry surface currents toward the open ocean.

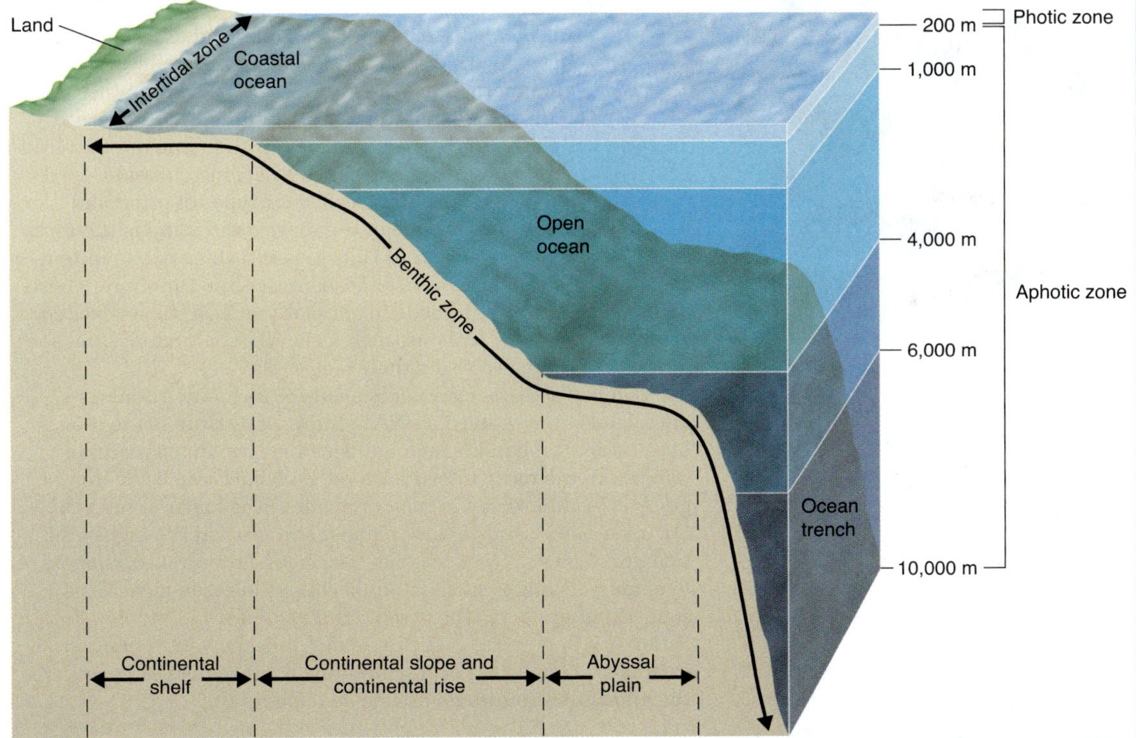

▲ **Figure 4–17** **The ocean can be divided into zones based on light penetration and into zones based on depth and the distance from shore.** Each zone contains a characteristic assemblage of organisms.

Marine Ecosystems

Unless you are an avid diver or snorkeler, it takes some imagination to picture what life is like in the vast, three-dimensional ocean. Sunlight penetrates only a relatively short distance through the surface of the water. Photosynthesis is limited to this well-lit upper layer known as the **photic** (FOH-tik) **zone.** Only in this relatively thin surface layer—typically down to a depth of about 200 meters—can algae and other producers grow. Below the photic zone is the **aphotic** (ay-FOH-tik) **zone,** which is permanently dark. Chemosynthetic autotrophs are the only producers that can survive in the aphotic zone.

CA a

There are several different classification systems that scientists use to describe marine ecosystems. **In addition to the division between the photic and aphotic zones, marine biologists divide the ocean into zones based on the depth and distance from shore: the intertidal zone, the coastal ocean, and the open ocean.** Each of these zones supports distinct ecological communities. The benthic zone covers the ocean floor and is, therefore, not exclusive to any of the other marine zones. **Figure 4–17** shows a generalized diagram of the marine zones.

a 6 5.e

CHECKPOINT *What factor is absent in the aphotic zone?*

For: Links on aquatic ecosystems
Visit: www.SciLinks.org
Web Code: cbn-2044

Build Science Skills

Problem Solving Explain that three main factors determine the types of marine organisms that live at different depths: available sunlight, water temperature, and water pressure. Ask: **At what depth do you think sunlight is most abundant?** *(Near the surface)* **How does this factor affect where organisms live?** *(Organisms that conduct photosynthesis live near the surface, as do many animals that depend on those organisms for food.)* **At what depth would you expect water temperatures to be the warmest? Why?** *(Near the surface, because sunlight warms the water there)* **How do you think water pressure changes with ocean depth?** *(Pressure increases as depth increases.)* **How would this factor affect where organisms live?** *(Most organisms cannot withstand great pressure on their bodies, so they must live near the surface.)* L2

Use Visuals

Figure 4–17 Have students locate the intertidal zone, coastal ocean, open ocean, and benthic zone on the figure and identify the characteristic organisms pictured for each of the four zones. Ask: **What are the abiotic characteristics of each zone?** *(Intertidal zone: extreme changes in conditions from being submerged in seawater to being exposed to air, sunlight, and heat; subject to waves and currents. Coastal ocean: receives sunlight. Open ocean: surface receives sunlight; deep ocean has high pressure, frigid temperatures, and total darkness. Benthic zone: includes ocean floor, various ocean depths, and deep-sea vents.)* L1 L2

Go Online NSTA SCILINKS

Download a worksheet on aquatic ecosystems for students to complete, and find additional teacher support from NSTA SciLinks.

Answers to . . .

CHECKPOINT *Sunlight*

Figure 4–16 *No, because large ocean waves would make it impossible for the roots of salt marsh grasses or mangrove trees to remain anchored.*

4–4 (continued)

Build Science Skills

Classifying To reinforce students' understanding of which organisms live in which zone, provide a variety of once-living ocean organisms for students to examine. Possibilities include dried sea stars and sea urchins; seashells; crab and lobster shells; dried kelp and other seaweed; pieces of coral; and dried, pickled, or fresh squid or octopus. Challenge students to sort the objects into groups based on the zones in which the living organisms are found. L1 L2

Build Science Skills

Using Analogies Direct students to consider what they learned about mountains when they studied biomes in the previous section. Then, ask: **How is the benthic zone like an upside-down mountain?** *(Sample answer: As you go up a mountain, temperatures become colder and precipitation increases, producing different conditions at different elevations. Similarly, as you go farther down in the ocean and the water depth increases, pressure also increases, available sunlight decreases, and temperatures become colder, producing different zones along the ocean floor.)* L2

▲ **Figure 4–18** **The main divisions in the ocean based on depth and distance from shore are the intertidal zone, the coastal ocean, and the open ocean.** Along the coast of Vancouver Island in Canada, low tide reveals sea stars, seaweed, and other organisms adapted to life in the intertidal zone.

Intertidal Zone Organisms that live in the intertidal zone are exposed to regular and extreme changes in their surroundings. Once or twice a day, they are submerged in seawater. The remainder of the time, they are exposed to air, sunlight, and temperature changes. Often, organisms in this zone are battered by waves and sometimes by strong currents.

There are many different types of intertidal communities. One of the most interesting is the rocky intertidal, shown in **Figure 4–18,** which exists in temperate regions where exposed rocks line the shore. There, barnacles and seaweed permanently attach themselves to the rocks. Other organisms, such as snails, sea urchins, and sea stars, cling to the rocks by their feet or suckers.

Competition among organisms in the rocky intertidal zone often leads to zonation (zoh-NAY-shun). **Zonation** is the prominent horizontal banding of organisms that live in a particular habitat. In the rocky intertidal zone, each band can be distinguished by differences in color or shape of the major organisms. For example, a band of black algae might grow at the highest high-tide line, followed by encrusting barnacles. Lower down, clusters of blue mussels might stick out amid clumps of green algae. This zonation is similar to the pattern that you might observe as you climb up a mountain. In the intertidal zone, however, zonation exists on a smaller vertical scale—just a few meters compared to the kilometers you would ascend on a mountain.

Coastal Ocean The **coastal ocean** extends from the low-tide mark to the outer edge of the continental shelf, the relatively shallow border that surrounds the continents. The continental shelf is often shallow enough to fall mostly or entirely within the photic zone, so photosynthesis can usually occur throughout its depth. As a result, the coastal ocean is often rich in plankton and many other organisms.

One of the most productive coastal ocean communities is the kelp forest. **Kelp forests** are named for their dominant organism: a giant brown alga that can grow at extraordinary rates—as much as 50 centimeters a day. Huge forests of this seaweed are found in cold-temperate seas around the world, including those along the coasts of California and the Pacific Northwest. Kelp forests, like the one shown in **Figure 4–19,** support a complex food web that includes snails, sea urchins, sea otters, a variety of fishes, seals, and whales.

CHECKPOINT *What is the coastal ocean?*

◀ **Figure 4–19** Kelp forests are ecosystems that occur in coastal oceans. The long strands of kelp create a habitat that shelters a variety of organisms. This kelp forest off the coast of California is part of a larger zone of kelp forests found along the western coast of North America from Alaska to Mexico. **Comparing and Contrasting** *How is a kelp forest like a forest on land?*

BACKGROUND

The ocean floor

The benthic zone, or ocean floor, extends from the high-tide mark to the deepest part of the ocean. Life in this zone consists of sessile and motile organisms. These organisms are distributed from near the shore to the depths of the ocean, and they play an important role in the ocean's food chain. Plants found in the benthic zone can live only in the photic zone, or area where sunlight can penetrate (30 to 200 meters below the ocean's surface). The portion of the benthic zone that is between 2000 meters and 6000 meters deep is known as the abyssal zone. The floor of the abyssal zone is covered with mud and organic debris. For the most part, food is in short supply. However, there are fishes (rattails), echinoderms, mollusks, and burrowing worms. In areas around hydrothermal vents (volcanic hot springs), clumps of bacteria growing on rocks use the hydrogen sulfide as an energy source. Living on these bacteria are filter-feeding animals such as giant clams and giant tube worms (up to 3.7 meters long).

Coral Reefs In the warm, shallow water of tropical coastal oceans are coral reefs, among the most diverse and productive environments on Earth. **Coral reefs** are named for the coral animals whose hard, calcium carbonate skeletons make up their primary structure. As you can see in **Figure 4–20**, an extraordinary diversity of organisms flourishes in these spectacular habitats.

Coral animals are tiny relatives of jellyfish that live together in vast numbers. Most coral animals are the size of your fingernail, or even smaller. Each one looks like a small sack with a mouth surrounded by tentacles. These animals use their tentacles to capture and eat microscopic creatures that float by. Coral animals cannot grow in cold water or water that is low in salt.

The types of corals that build reefs grow with the help of algae that live symbiotically within their tissues. These algae carry out photosynthesis using the coral animals' wastes as nutrients. In turn, the algae provide their coral hosts with certain essential carbon compounds. Because their algae require strong sunlight, most reef-building corals thrive only in brightly lit areas within 40 meters of the surface.

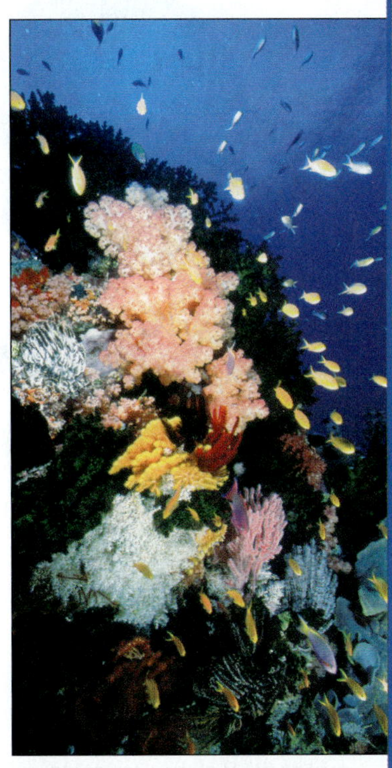

▶ **Figure 4–20** This coral reef off the island of New Britain in the Pacific Ocean supports a dazzling variety of corals and fishes. Reefs are most abundant around islands and along the eastern coasts of continents. In the United States, only the coasts of southern Florida and Hawaii have coral reefs. **Applying Concepts** *In what types of community interactions are coral animals involved?*

Analyzing Data

6IIE 7.c, 7IIE 7.c

Ecosystem Productivity

The data table on the right compares the primary productivity of some of the world's ecosystems. Use the data table to answer the following questions:

1. **Using Tables and Graphs** Construct a bar graph to display the data. Use different colors to distinguish aquatic and land ecosystems.
2. **Using Tables and Graphs** According to your graph, which ecosystem is most productive? Use what you know to explain that fact.
3. **Inferring** Although the open ocean is among the least productive ecosystems, it contributes greatly to the overall productivity of the biosphere. How can this situation be explained?
4. **Applying Concepts** What are two abiotic factors that might account for the differences in productivity among the land ecosystems in the table? (*Hint:* Review the relevant biomes on pages 100–104.)

Productivity of Aquatic and Land Ecosystems

Ecosystem	Average Primary Productivity (grams of organic matter produced per square meter per year)
Aquatic Ecosystems:	
Coral reef	2500
Estuary	1800
Lake	500
Open ocean	125
Land Ecosystems:	
Tropical rain forest	2200
Temperate forest	1250
Tropical savanna	900
Tundra	90

Analyzing Data

6IIE 7.c, 7IIE 7.c

Before students graph the data, have them review the characteristics of the listed types of ecosystems. L2 L3

1. Students should choose a scale for the axis of the graph representing average primary productivity that is large enough to enable them to graph the data accurately.
2. Coral reef ecosystems are the most productive. Students may infer that reefs are so productive because they are near the top of the photic zone.
3. The area of the open ocean far exceeds the area occupied by all the other ecosystems put together.
4. Latitude and precipitation are both factors that affect the productivity of the land ecosystems in the table. Ecosystems that are drier (tropical savanna) or closer to the polar zones (tundra) are less productive.

Answers to . . .

CHECKPOINT *The part of the ocean that extends from the low-tide mark to the outer edge of the continental shelf*

Figure 4–19 *Students' comparisons should include the idea that the producers in a kelp forest ecosystem—giant kelp—have a function similar to the producers in a forest on land.*

Figure 4–20 *Coral animals are involved in predation both as predators and as prey. They are also involved in a mutualistic symbiotic relationship with algae. Students might also infer that corals are involved in competition and are affected by parasitism and disease.*

4–4 (continued)

Use Visuals

Figure 4–21 Focus students' attention on the photo of the octopus, and ask: **Since this animal lives mainly on the ocean floor, can it be classified as a benthos organism?** *(Yes, but not exclusively so. Some octopi live in the depths of oceans, but others live in shallow coastal waters.)* Point out that marine animals can adapt to different environments, just as land animals can. L1 L2

3 ASSESS

Evaluate Understanding

As you did with biomes in the previous section, describe various aquatic ecosystems and ocean zones, and call on students at random to identify each one. Limit your descriptions to the information contained in this section.

Reteach

Have students work cooperatively to construct a bulletin board display showing the different kinds of aquatic ecosystems and ocean zones discussed in this section, using pictures they have drawn themselves or photocopied. Have students label the names of the aquatic ecosystems and ocean zones, their major characteristics, and the types of organisms found in each.

Writing in Science

Answers may vary. Students might select any plants and animals from three of the aquatic ecosystems discussed in this section. In their comparisons, they should describe how specific adaptations of the organisms help them live in their environments.

If your class subscribes to the iText, use it to review the Key Concepts in Section 4–4.

▲ **Figure 4–21** In the open ocean, the swordfish (top) can sometimes be seen swimming near the surface, yet these fish can also dive to more than 600 meters to prey on fishes of the deep ocean. Some types of octopus (bottom) live in the depths of the open ocean, although other types live in shallow coastal waters.

Open Ocean The open ocean, often referred to as the oceanic zone, begins at the edge of the continental shelf and extends outward. It is the largest marine zone, covering more than 90 percent of the surface area of the world's oceans. The open ocean ranges from about 500 meters deep along continental slopes to more than 11,000 meters at the deepest ocean trench. Organisms in the deep ocean are exposed to high pressure, frigid temperatures, and total darkness.

Typically, the open ocean has very low levels of nutrients and supports only the smallest producers. Productivity is generally low. Still, because of the enormous area, most of the photosynthetic activity on Earth occurs in the part of the open ocean within the photic zone. Fishes of all shapes and sizes dominate the open ocean. The swordfish and the octopus in **Figure 4–21** are just two examples of the organisms found in this zone. Marine mammals such as dolphins and whales also live there but must stay close to the surface to breathe.

Benthic Zone The ocean floor contains organisms that live attached to or near the bottom, such as sea stars, anemones, and marine worms. Scientists refer to these organisms as the **benthos.** That is why the ocean floor is called the benthic zone. This zone extends horizontally along the ocean floor from the coastal ocean through the open ocean.

Benthic ecosystems often depend on food from organisms that grow in the photic zone, particularly the producers. Animals that are attached to the bottom or do not move around much, such as clams and sea cucumbers, feed on pieces of dead organic material, or detritus, that drift down from the surface waters. Near deep-sea vents, where superheated water boils out of cracks on the ocean floor, dwell chemosynthetic primary producers that support life without light and photosynthesis.

4–4 Section Assessment

1. **Key Concept** List three characteristics that determine the structure of aquatic ecosystems.
2. **Key Concept** Compare standing-water ecosystems to flowing-water ecosystems. How are they alike? How are they different?
3. **Key Concept** List six distinct ecological zones that can be found in the ocean. Give two abiotic factors for each zone.
4. Define the terms *wetland* and *estuary*. Give at least one example of a freshwater wetland and of an estuary.
5. **Critical Thinking Predicting** How might the damming of a river affect an estuary at the river's mouth?

Writing in Science

Comparing and Contrasting
Choose three different aquatic ecosystems. From each of these ecosystems, select a plant and an animal and describe how the organisms are adapted to their environments. Show comparisons. *Hint*: Create a table to organize your ideas.

4–4 Section Assessment

1. Any three of these four: depth, flow, temperature, and chemistry of overlying water
2. Alike: freshwater ecosystems; water contains oxygen and nutrients. Different: Water in a flowing-water ecosystem moves rapidly near the source and slows near the mouth. Water in a standing-water ecosystem has little net flow but circulates within the system.
3. Photic zone, aphotic zone, intertidal zone, coastal ocean, open ocean, benthic zone; and the abiotic factors for each.
4. A wetland is an ecosystem in which water either covers the soil or is present at or near the surface of the soil for some of the year. An estuary is a wetland where a river meets the sea. Check students' examples.
5. Without fresh water from the river, the brackish estuary water would become saltier, changing the kinds of organisms that could survive in that ecosystem.

Exploration

6IIE 7.c, BIIE 1.a, BIIE 1.i

Observing Succession

The most obvious examples of succession involve large organisms, such as plants and animals. In this investigation, you will determine whether succession also occurs in a community of microorganisms.

Problem What changes occur in a microscopic community over time?

Materials

- 1000-mL beaker or large jar
- soil
- grass clippings
- dried leaves
- 600 mL aged water
- 4 coverslips
- 4 glass slides
- 4 dropper pipettes
- microscope
- reference book or chart for identifying common microorganisms

Skills Using Tables and Graphs, Analyzing Data

Procedure 

1. Place enough soil in the 1000-mL beaker to cover the bottom. Fill the beaker with a loosely packed mixture of grass clippings and dried leaves, and add the aged water.
2. Set the beaker aside in a cool place where it can remain undisturbed for 24 hours.
3. After 24 hours, check the water for signs of life. A strong odor or cloudy water is evidence of bacterial growth; fuzzy growths or threads indicate the presence of mold; and a green tint is due to algae. Record your observations.
4. Use a dropper pipette to transfer a drop of water from the beaker to a microscope slide. Add a coverslip.
5. Examine the slide under the low-power objective of the microscope to locate any microorganisms. Then, switch to high power. Use a reference book or chart to identify the organisms. Record the date and your observations, including labeled drawings, the number of each type of organism in your field of view, and the magnification.
6. Repeat steps 4 and 5 with water samples from several different areas of the beaker.
7. Repeat steps 3 through 6 every day for 2 weeks. Note any changes in the number or types of organisms in the beaker.
8. Wash your hands thoroughly with soap and warm water before leaving the lab.

Analyze and Conclude

1. **Using Tables and Graphs** Make a graph of the population of each type of organism. Plot time on the *x*-axis and number of organisms per field of view on the *y*-axis. With your teacher's guidance, select the equipment and technology to use—either graph paper or a graphing calculator.
2. **Observing** How did the number and variety of organisms in the beaker change over the 2-week period?
3. **Analyzing Data** What kinds of organisms appeared first in the microscopic water community? Which appeared last? How can you explain these changes?
4. **Drawing Conclusions** Do your observations support the idea that succession occurs in communities of microorganisms? Explain your answer.

Go Further

Analyzing Data With your teacher's approval, set up a simple community of only a few known species of microorganisms. Observe the community for two weeks, and try to explain any evidence of succession that you observe.

Exploration

6IIE 7.c, BIIE 1.a, BIIE 1.i

Objective Students will be able to identify changes that occur in a microscopic community as it undergoes succession L2 L3

Skills Focus Using Tables and Graphs, Analyzing Data

Time 10 minutes for setup, 20 minutes every 2 or 3 days for 2 weeks for observation and recording

Advance Prep For each group, fill a 600-mL beaker with tap water. Leave the beakers undisturbed for 48 hours so any gases harmful to microscopic organisms can evaporate.

Alternative Materials To shorten the time required to complete the activity, prepare several hay infusions 5 to 10 days apart, and let students observe samples of all the infusions on the same day.

Pre-Lab Discussion Ask students to recall the meaning of the term *succession.* Have them read the introductory paragraph, the problem, and the complete procedure.

Teaching Tips

- During the first week, show students how to stain a specimen with methylene blue to make bacteria more visible. (Read MSDS on methylene blue.)
- After the first week, offer students methyl cellulose or cotton fibers to slow down motile protists for observation. (Read MSDS on cellulose.)

Expected Outcome In general, no odor or organisms will become evident until day 4. By day 7, *Volvox, Spirogyra,* and *Paramecium* may be visible. By day 14, numerous fast-moving protists may appear. Between days 14 and 21, small numbers of nematodes, *Paramecium,* and *Spirostomum* and many small ciliates will probably be seen.

Analyze and Conclude

1. Graphs will vary depending on the numbers and types of organisms that appear over the two-week observation period.
2. Typically, bacteria are most numerous at first, followed by heterotrophic protists, microscopic animals, and algae.
3. Successional sequences will vary. Bacteria often appear first, followed by small protists and eventually larger predatory protists. The bacteria decompose the organic material present in the culture and support the populations of protists that prey on them. Larger protists and occasionally small animals appear later; these organisms may include some that prey on the protists.
4. Yes. The changes in types and numbers of microscopic organisms observed during the two-week period are evidence of succession.

Go Further

A community containing *Paramecium,* yeast as food, and the predatory protist *Didinium* can undergo succession within 2 to 6 weeks.

Chapter 4 Study Guide

Study Tip

This chapter presents a large number of Vocabulary terms—both the terms that are highlighted, boldface, and defined in the sections and other terms that may be unfamiliar to students. Have students prepare vocabulary flashcards, each card with a term written on one side and its definition written on the other side. Let students use these flashcards to quiz each other in pairs or small groups.

Thinking Visually

Student concept maps should indicate that community interactions affect ecosystems, which are made up of biotic and abiotic factors, and that abiotic factors include light, oxygen, and nutrients.

Chapter 4 Assessment

Reviewing Content

1. b
2. b
3. b
4. d
5. a
6. b
7. d
8. a
9. b
10. a

Understanding Concepts

11. Climate: year-after-year conditions of temperature and precipitation within a particular region. Weather: day-to-day condition of Earth's atmosphere at a particular time and place.

12. Temperature, precipitation, humidity, wind, nutrient availability, soil type, and sunlight

13. An organism's habitat is *where* it lives. Its niche is *how* it lives, or its occupation. A niche is the full range of physical and biological conditions in which an organism lives and the way in which the organism uses those conditions.

14. According to the competitive exclusion principle, no two species can occupy the same niche in the same habitat at the same time

15. Primary succession

Chapter 4 Study Guide

4–1 The Role of Climate

Key Concepts

- Carbon dioxide, methane, water vapor, and a few other atmospheric gases trap heat energy and maintain Earth's temperature range.
- As a result of differences in latitude and thus the angle of heating, Earth has three main climate zones: polar, temperate, and tropical.

Vocabulary

weather, p. 87
climate, p. 87
greenhouse effect, p. 87
polar zone, p. 88
temperate zone, p. 88
tropical zone, p. 88

4–2 What Shapes an Ecosystem?

Key Concepts 

- Together, biotic and abiotic factors determine the survival and growth of an organism and the productivity of the ecosystem in which the organism lives.
- Community interactions, such as competition, predation, and various forms of symbiosis, can powerfully affect an ecosystem.
- Ecosystems are constantly changing in response to natural and human disturbances. As an ecosystem changes, older inhabitants gradually die out and new organisms move in, causing further changes in the community.

Vocabulary

biotic factor, p. 90
abiotic factor, p. 90
habitat, p. 90
niche, p. 91
resource, p. 92
competitive exclusion principle, p. 92
predation, p. 93
symbiosis, p. 93
mutualism, p. 93
commensalism, p. 93
parasitism, p. 93
ecological succession, p. 94
primary succession, p. 94
pioneer species, p. 94
secondary succession, p. 95

4–3 Biomes

Key Concept 

- The world's major biomes include tropical rain forest, tropical dry forest, tropical savanna, temperate grassland, desert, temperate woodland and shrubland, temperate forest, northwestern coniferous forest, boreal forest, and tundra. Each of these biomes is defined by a unique set of abiotic factors—particularly climate—and has a characteristic ecological community.

Vocabulary

biome, p. 98 • tolerance, p. 98
microclimate, p. 98 • canopy, p. 100
understory, p. 100 • deciduous, p. 100
coniferous, p. 103 • humus, p. 103
taiga, p. 104 • permafrost, p. 104

4–4 Aquatic Ecosystems

Key Concepts 

- Aquatic ecosystems are determined primarily by the depth, flow, temperature, and chemistry of the overlying water.
- Freshwater ecosystems can be divided into two main types: flowing-water ecosystems and standing-water ecosystems.
- In addition to the division between the photic and aphotic zones, marine biologists also divide the ocean into zones based on the depth and distance from shore: the intertidal zone, the coastal ocean, and the open ocean.

Vocabulary

plankton, p. 107 • phytoplankton, p. 107
zooplankton, p. 107 • wetland, p. 107
estuary, p. 108 • detritus, p. 108
salt marsh, p. 108 • mangrove swamp, p. 108
photic zone, p. 109 • aphotic zone, p. 109
zonation, p. 110 • coastal ocean, p. 110
kelp forest, p. 110 • coral reef, p. 111
benthos, p. 112

Thinking Visually

Using information from this chapter, create a concept map that includes the following terms: *abiotic factors, biotic factors, community interactions, predation, competition, symbiosis, nutrients, ecosystems, light, oxygen.*

TIME SAVER — CHAPTER RESOURCES

Print:

- ***Teaching Resources,*** Chapter Vocabulary Review, Graphic Organizer, Chapter 4 Tests: Levels A and B

Technology:

- ***Computer Test Bank,*** Chapter 4 Test
- ***iText,*** Chapter 4 Assessment

Chapter 4 Assessment

Reviewing Content

Choose the letter that best answers the question or completes the statement.

1. The average, year-after-year conditions of temperature and precipitation within a particular region are its
   a. weather. c. greenhouse effect.
   b. climate. d. biotic factors.
2. The greenhouse effect causes an increase in
   a. carbon dioxide.
   b. temperature.
   c. oxygen.
   d. water.
3. All the biotic and abiotic factors in a pond form a(an)
   a. biosphere.
   b. ecosystem.
   c. community.
   d. niche.
4. A relationship in which one organism is helped and another organism is neither helped nor hurt is called
   a. mutualism.
   b. parasitism.
   c. competition.
   d. commensalism.
5. A form of symbiosis in which both organisms benefit is called
   a. mutualism.
   b. parasitism.
   c. commensalism.
   d. predation.
6. A type of symbiosis in which one organism benefits and the other is harmed is called
   a. mutualism.
   b. parasitism.
   c. commensalism.
   d. succession.
7. Natural disturbances, such as fires or hurricanes, can result in
   a. commensalism. c. parasitism.
   b. competition. d. succession.
8. In a tropical rain forest, the dense covering formed by the leafy tops of tall trees is called the
   a. canopy. c. niche.
   b. taiga. d. understory.
9. Organisms that live near or on the ocean floor are called
   a. parasites. c. plankton.
   b. benthos. d. mangroves.

Interactive textbook with assessment at PHSchool.com 

10. In the diagram of the ocean below, the feature labeled **A** is the
    a. open ocean. c. trench.
    b. coastal ocean. d. estuary.

Understanding Concepts

11. Distinguish between weather and climate.
12. Describe the major abiotic factors that produce Earth's main climate zones.
13. What is the difference between an organism's habitat and its niche?
14. What is the competitive exclusion principle?
15. What type of succession occurs after lava from a volcanic eruption covers an area?
16. Describe two major causes of ecological succession.
17. What is a biome?
18. What are two abiotic factors that cause deciduous trees to shed their leaves?
19. Describe the dominant vegetation found in a North American temperate forest.
20. Why are plants generally few and far between in a desert?
21. What is the meaning of the term *plankton*? Name the two types of plankton.
22. What are three types of freshwater wetlands?
23. How does the photic zone differ from the aphotic zone?
24. How are salt marshes and mangrove swamps alike? How are they different?
25. What are coral reefs? Explain.

TIME SAVER — HOMEWORK GUIDE

Section:	Questions:
Section 4–1	1, 2, 11, 12
Section 4–2	3–7, 13–16, 30, 33
Section 4–3	8, 17–20, 26, 27, 29, 31
Section 4–4	9, 10, 21–25, 28, 32

If your class subscribes to the iText, your students can go online to access an interactive version of the Student Edition and a self-test.

(Continued from page 114)

16. Sometimes succession results from slow changes in the physical environment, and sometimes it results from an abrupt disturbance, such as a severe storm or human activities.

17. A complex of terrestrial communities covering a large geographic area that is characterized by its soil, climate, and a certain combination of plants and animals

18. Low precipitation, such as in a tropical forest, and low temperatures, such as in a temperate forest

19. Broadleaf deciduous trees, some conifers, flowering shrubs, herbs, a ground layer of mosses and ferns

20. Lack of precipitation; annual precipitation is less than 25 centimeters.

21. Plankton are tiny, free-floating algae and animals that live in both freshwater and saltwater environments. Examples: unicellular algae called phytoplankton and planktonic animals called zooplankton

22. Bogs are formed in depressions that fill with water that is often very acidic. Sphagnum moss frequently grows in bogs. Marshes are shallow wetlands along rivers. Cattails and rushes often grow in marshes, which may be flooded for all or part of the year. Swamps are flooded forests through which water flows slowly.

23. The photic zone is the thin surface layer of the ocean that light can penetrate so that photosynthesis can occur. The aphotic zone is the permanently dark zone immediately below the photic zone.

24. Both salt marshes and mangrove swamps are coastal ecosystems that are influenced by tides. Salt marshes are flat, muddy areas that often surround estuaries and bays. Mangrove swamps occur only in warm climates.

25. Coral reefs are large structures made up of the calcium carbonate skeletons of coral animals that live in the warm, shallow waters of tropical oceans.

Chapter 4 Assessment

Critical Thinking

26. Check students' diagrams. They should appear similar to the diagrams on pages 102 through 104. The biome that is most likely to occur in Lillehammer is the boreal forest biome.

27. During the short, cool summers in the tundra, the ground thaws to a depth of a few centimeters and becomes soggy and wet.

28. The aphotic zone is permanently dark. Animals would need to be able to manufacture and obtain food without photosynthesis.

29. Because trees lose water through their leaves, dropping their leaves during an especially dry summer would enable the trees to conserve water and thus tolerate the drought.

30. This situation represents an example of secondary succession. In 5 years, the sun-loving plants may predominate, although seedlings of new trees may have begun to grow. In 50 years, the trees will have matured, reestablishing the forest ecosystem.

31. Students may discuss the adaptations of any animal that lives in the two biomes. A typical response might suggest one adaptation of the coyote that allows it to live in both biomes is the ability to tolerate periods of low precipitation. Another adaptation is the ability to range great distances for prey. Other adaptations could include the animal's color, its quickness, its heavy coat in winter, and its good senses of sight and smell.

32. Students' answers should demonstrate an understanding of the positive and negative effects of salt marsh development. Students' answers should also give reasons as to why they do or do not support the proposal.

33. No two species can occupy the same niche in the same habitat. Individuals within a single species living in the same niche would compete for the same resources.

Focus on the BIG Idea

Students' answers should demonstrate an understanding of biotic and abiotic factors in your area.

Chapter 4 Assessment

Critical Thinking

26. Using Tables and Graphs Using graph paper, construct a climate diagram for Lillehammer. Base your diagram on the ones for the biomes in this chapter. Use the completed diagram to identify the biome that is most likely to occur in Lillehammer.

Climate Data for Lillehammer, Norway

Month	Average Temperature (°C)	Precipitation (mm)
Jan.	-8.1	38.1
Feb.	-6.2	27.9
Mar.	-3.9	30.5
Apr.	3.3	35.6
May	8.9	45.7
June	13.9	63.5
July	16.4	81.3
Aug.	14.2	88.9
Sept.	9.5	58.4
Oct.	3.9	63.5
Nov.	-3.8	50.8
Dec.	-6.1	48.3

27. Applying Concepts Although the amount of precipitation is low, most parts of the tundra are very wet during the summer. What characteristics would explain this apparent contradiction?

28. Formulating Hypotheses The deep ocean is within the aphotic zone and is also very cold. Suggest some of the unique characteristics that might enable animals to live in the deep ocean.

29. Inferring Certain deciduous trees grow in tropical dry forests and lose water through their leaves every day. During summers with adequate rain, the leaves remain on the trees. During the cold, dry season, the trees drop their leaves. Suppose there is an especially dry summer. How might the adaptation of dropping leaves enable a tree to tolerate the drought?

30. Predicting A windstorm in a forest blows down the large trees in one part of the forest. Soon, sun-loving plants sprout in the new clearing. What type of succession is this? What might this area look like in 5 years? In 50 years?

31. Inferring Consider these two biomes: (1) the temperate grassland and (2) the temperate woodland and shrubland. Animals such as coyotes are known to live in both biomes. Describe two adaptations that might enable an animal to tolerate these two different biomes. Discuss the coyote or an animal of your choice.

32. Making Judgments A developer has proposed filling in a salt marsh to create a coastal resort. What positive and negative effects might this proposal have on wildlife and local residents? Would you support the proposal? Why or why not?

33. Inferring Competition for resources in an area is usually more intense within a single species than between two different species. Can you explain this observation? (*Hint*: Consider how niches help organisms of different species avoid competition.)

Interdependence in Nature Write a description of your niche in the environment. Include details about your ecosystem, including the biotic and abiotic factors around you. Be sure to describe your feeding habits as well as any interactions you have with members of other species.

Writing in Science

Select one of the ten major biomes. Write an overview of the characteristics of that biome. Explain how the abiotic factors and the dominant plants and wildlife are interrelated. Support your explanation with specific examples. (*Hint:* Review the descriptions of the biomes on pages 100–104.)

Performance-Based Assessment

Creating a Web Site A travel agent has asked you to develop a Web site on a biome of your choice. The goal of the site is to encourage tourism to the biome. Present accurate scientific information and images depicting the biome. Create a storyboard for this site, including the home page and two hot links.

Go Online
PHSchool.com
For: An interactive self-test
Visit: PHSchool.com
Web Code: cba-2040

Writing in Science

Answers may vary. Students might select any of the 10 biomes profiled in Section 4–3. For the biome selected, they should provide details about abiotic factors, dominant plants, and dominant animals, as well as various other characteristics. Students should explain and provide examples of how the plants and animals cited are adapted to the characteristics of the biome.

Performance-Based Assessment

Students' storyboards will vary but should include a general overview of the chosen biome, its abiotic and biotic factors, and examples of the dominant plants and wildlife that live there.

Standards Practice

Test-Taking Tip When you are asked to analyze a graph showing experimental data, first look at the shape of the curve. Identify the variables, and try to determine how they are related. Then, read and answer the questions about the graph.

Directions: Choose the letter that best answers the question or completes the statement.

1. Generally, which has the greatest effect on determining the climate of a region? **BI 6.b**
   A longitude
   B dominant plant species
   C distance from the equator
   D month of the year
2. Which is NOT an abiotic factor in an ecosystem? **6 5.e**
   A amount of plants
   B light
   C temperature
   D rainfall
3. What defines a species' niche?
   A abiotic factors
   B biotic factors
   C food web
   D all of the above
4. The disappearance of a population in a given niche as a result of direct competition with another species for a resource is called **BI 6.a**
   A competitive exclusion.
   B predation.
   C parasitism.
   D commensalism.
5. In which marine zone are you likely to find algae growing?
   A intertidal zone
   B photic zone
   C aphotic zone
   D both A and B
6. The water in an estuary is
   A salt water only.
   B poor in nutrients.
   C fresh water only.
   D a mixture of fresh water and salt water.
7. The attachment of barnacles to a whale's skin is an example of **6 5.c**
   A competition.
   B predation.
   C mutualism.
   D commensalism.

Questions 8–9
From 1960 to 1995, scientists recorded the concentration of carbon dioxide in the atmosphere and the average temperature at a remote site in Hawaii. Their data are shown in the graph.

Changes in Atmospheric Carbon Dioxide and Temperature

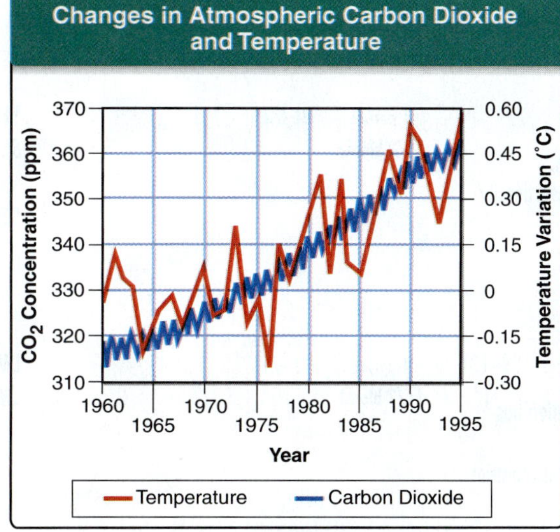

8. Based on the graph, which of the following is most likely?
   A Carbon dioxide levels and overall temperature will increase.
   B Carbon dioxide levels will soon decline.
   C Warm temperatures are increasing the carbon dioxide concentration.
   D The variables are indirectly proportional.
9. Which of the following would most likely cause an increase in atmospheric carbon dioxide?
   A increased biomass
   B a faster rate of photosynthesis
   C melting of the polar ice caps
   D increased burning of fossil fuels

Standards Practice

1. C	**4.** A	**7.** D
2. A	**5.** D	**8.** A
3. D	**6.** D	**9.** D

Online at PHSchool.com

Have students check their understanding of the chapter by logging onto Success Tracker.

Your students can independently test their knowledge of the chapter and print out their test results for your files.

Chapter Planner 5 Populations

Section and Section Objectives	Time	STANDARDS NCLB	STANDARDS Biology	Activities and Labs
5–1 How Populations Grow, pp. 119–123 **5.1.1** ***List*** the characteristics used to describe a population. **5.1.2** ***Identify*** factors that affect population size. **5.1.3** ***Differentiate*** between exponential and logistic growth.	1 period (1/2 block)	BI 6.b, BI 6.c		**SE:** ***Inquiry Activity,*** How do populations grow?, p. 118 L2 **TE:** ***Build Science Skills,*** p. 122 L1 L2 **SE:** ***Analyzing Data,*** Population Trends, p. 123 L2
5–2 Limits to Growth, pp. 124–127 **5.2.1** ***Identify*** factors that limit population growth. **5.2.2** ***Differentiate*** between density-dependent and density-independent limiting factors.	1 period (1/2 block)	BI 6.c		**SE:** ***Quick Lab,*** How does competition affect growth?, p. 125 L2 **SE:** ***Issues in Biology,*** Does the Gray Wolf Population Need Protection?, p. 128 L2 **SE:** ***Exploration,*** Investigating the Growth of a Population of Bacteria, p. 133 L2 L3
5–3 Human Population Growth, pp. 129–132 **5.3.1** ***Describe*** how the size of the human population has changed over time. **5.3.2** ***Explain*** why population growth rates differ in countries throughout the world.	1 period (1/2 block)	BI 6.c		**LMA:** Chapter 5 Lab L2 L3 **LMB:** Chapter 5 Lab L1 L2
Chapter Assessment, pp. 134–137	1 period (1/2 block)			

ACTIVITY PLANNER

SE: *Inquiry Activity*, p. 118; 15 min.; graph paper

TE: *Build Science Skills*, p. 122; 15 min.; box of 100 paper clips for each group

SE: *Quick Lab*, p. 125; 15 min. for setup; bean seeds, 2 paper cups, potting soil

SE: *Exploration*, p. 133; 5 min. for setup, 10–20 min./day for 5 days, 30 min. on day 6; 2 lima beans, 2 dropper pipettes, 100-mL beaker, coverslips, microscope slides, 10-mL graduated cylinder, 100-mL graduated cylinder, methylene blue stain, microscope, test tube rack, 4 test tubes, aluminum foil

PLANNING KEY

Ability Levels
for students performing . . .
below grade level L1
at grade level L2
above grade level L3

Print Components

SE	Student Edition	LA	Lab Assessment
TE	Teacher's Edition	BTM	Biotechnology Manual
RSW	Reading & Study Workbook A	IDM	Issues and Decision Making
ARSW	Adapted Reading & Study Workbook B	LW	Lab Worksheets
TR	Teaching Resources	LMA	Laboratory Manual A
IF	Investigations in Forensics	LMB	Laboratory Manual B

Tech Components

CTB	Computer Test Bank
BD	BioDetectives DVD
TP	Transparencies Plus
PLM	Probeware Lab Manual
ABC	ABC DVD Library
LS	Lab Simulations
VL	Virtual Labs

Interactive textbook with assessment at PHSchool.com

Program Resources	Assessment	Media and Technology
TR: Lesson Plan 5–1, Section Summary, p. 93 L1, p. 103 L2, Worksheets, pp. 96–97 L1, pp. 105–107 L2 **RSW:** Section 5–1 L2 **ARSW:** Section 5–1 L1	**SE:** 5–1 Section Assessment, p. 123 **TR:** Section Review 5–1	**iText:** Section 5–1 **TP:** 5–1 Interest Grabber, Section Outline, Concept Map, Figure 5–4
TR: Lesson Plan 5–2, Section Summary, p. 94 L1, p. 103 L2, Worksheets, pp. 98–99 L1, pp. 108–109 L2, Enrichment L2 L3 **RSW:** Section 5–2 L2 **ARSW:** Section 5–2 L1 **IDM:** Issues and Decisions 48 L2 L3	**SE:** 5–2 Section Assessment, p. 127 **TE:** Section Review 5–2	**iText:** Section 5–2 **TP:** 5–2 Interest Grabber, Section Outline, A Density-Dependent Limiting Factor, Figure 5–7
TR: Lesson Plan 5–3, Section Summary, p. 95 L1, p. 104 L2, Worksheets, pp. 100–101 L1, pp. 110–111 L2 **LW:** Chapter 5 Exploration L1 L2 L3 **RSW:** Section 5–3 L2 **ARSW:** Section 5–3 L1 **IDM:** Issues and Decisions 47 L2 L3	**SE:** 5–3 Section Assessment, p. 132 **TE:** Section Review 5–3	**iText:** Section 5–3 **TP:** 5–3 Interest Grabber, Section Outline, Human Population Growth, Figure 5–13
	SE: Chapter 5 Assessment, pp. 134–137 **TR:** Chapter Vocabulary Review, Graphic Organizer, Chapter 5 Test	**iText:** Chapter 5 Assessment **CTB:** Chapter 5 Test

Go Online
Students can do research, share data, and test their knowledge online.

PRESSED FOR TIME?

To Preview the Chapter
- Have students do the Reading Strategies for Sections 5–1, 5–2, and 5–3. Make sure students save their work for completion as they read the chapter.

To Cover the Chapter Quickly
- Have students read Section 5–1, exclusive of Analyzing Data on page 123; read all of Section 5–2; and review Figures 5–10 and 5–13 and their captions.
- Assign questions 1 through 3 in 5–1 Section Assessment, questions 1 and 2 in 5–2 Section Assessment, questions 1 and 2 in 5–3 Section Assessment, and questions 1–13 in the Standards Practice.

To Review the Chapter
- Assign Sections 5–1 and 5–2 in the Reading and Study Workbook or the Adapted Reading and Study Workbook.
- Assign the Chapter Vocabulary Review for Chapter 5 in Teaching Resources.

CHAPTER 5

ENGAGE/EXPLORE

Inquiry Activity

 6IIE 7.c, BIIE 1.a, BIIE 1.d

Objectives Students will be able to calculate the size of a population over time, given its rate of reproduction, and construct a graph based on the calculations. L2

Skills Focus **Using Tables and Graphs, Formulating Hypotheses**

Materials graph paper

Time 15 minutes

Strategies

- You may want to allow students to use calculators.
- Watch for common errors in calculations. In particular, students may forget that in each generation, only half of the population will be female.

Expected Outcome 6 offspring in one year, 18 in two years, 54 in three years, 162 in four years, 486 in five years

Think About It

1. The graph's shape is a curve that rises at an increasing rate.
2. In 10 years: about 120,000 rabbits; 20 years: about 7 billion rabbits
3. Natural predators, disease, and limited supplies of food and water limit rabbit populations. In addition, not all offspring survive to maturity, and some adults do not reproduce.

Brain Teaser

Tell students to think about the plant populations in the park. Ask students: **Once the original pair of rabbits started reproducing, what would happen to the plant populations, and why?** *(They would start decreasing, because the rabbits would eat them.)* **If the rabbits started to die off because there weren't enough plants to eat, what would happen to the plant populations, and why?** *(The plant populations would start to increase, because there would be fewer rabbits to eat them.)*

CHAPTER 5

Populations

This trio of sea otters is part of the population that lives near Monterey, California. Sea otters often rest by wrapping themselves in kelp to keep from drifting away.

Inquiry Activity

 6IIE 7.c, BIIE 1.a, BIIE 1.d

How do populations grow?

Procedure

1. Assume that a pair of rabbits produces 6 offspring, and that half the offspring are male and half are female. Assume that no offspring die. If each pair of rabbits breeds only once, how many offspring would be produced each year for 5 years?
2. Construct a graph of your data. Plot time on the *x*-axis and population on the *y*-axis.

Think About It

1. **Using Tables and Graphs** Describe the shape of your graph.
2. **Using Tables and Graphs** Use your graph to predict the population of rabbits in 10 years and in 20 years.
3. **Formulating Hypotheses** How can you explain the fact that Earth is not covered by rabbits?

FACTS AND FIGURES

Biotic potential of a species

The size that a population would reach if all offspring were to survive and produce young is called the biotic potential of a species. In order for this to happen, conditions would have to be ideal; there has to be enough food and living space to support the population, and there have to be no factors present that limit population growth. For instance, two elephants, under ideal conditions, would produce about 20 million descendents after 750 years, as shown in Figure 5–3. Such ideal conditions are also assumed in the projection of the growth of the rabbit population in the Inquiry Activity. These are both examples of exponential growth. In actuality, no population ever reaches its biotic potential. The factors that prevent this ideal growth are called limiting factors, or environmental resistance. Limiting factors are the focus of Section 5–2.

5–1 How Populations Grow

BI 6.b. Students know how to analyze changes in an ecosystem resulting from changes in climate, human activity, introduction of nonnative species, or changes in population size. **BI 6.c.** Students know how fluctuations in population size in an ecosystem are determined by the relative rates of birth, immigration, emigration, and death.

Sea otters are important members of the kelp forest community of America's Pacific Northwest coast. This "forest" is made up of algae called giant kelp, with stalks up to 30 meters long, and smaller types of kelp. The kelp forest provides a habitat as well as a food source for a variety of animals. Sea otters need a lot of energy to stay warm in cold water, so they eat large quantities of their favorite food: sea urchins. Sea urchins, in turn, feed on kelp.

The relationships along this food chain set the stage for a classic tale of population growth and decline. A century ago, otters were nearly eliminated by hunting. Sea urchin populations increased greatly, and kelp forests nearly disappeared. Why? Because the kelp was eaten down to the bare rock by hordes of sea urchins! The future of the kelp forests looked grim. Then, sea otters were declared an endangered species and were protected from hunting. With hunters out of the picture, otter populations recovered. Sea urchin numbers dropped dramatically. Kelp grew back. But now, some otter populations are shrinking again because otters are being eaten by killer whales. To better understand why populations such as these change as they do, we turn to the study of population biology.

Guide for Reading

Key Concepts
- What characteristics are used to describe a population?
- What factors affect population size?
- What are exponential growth and logistic growth?

Vocabulary
population density
immigration
emigration
exponential growth
logistic growth
carrying capacity

Reading Strategy: Asking Questions Before you read, rewrite the headings in the section as *how, why,* or *what* questions about populations. As you read, write down the answers to your questions.

Characteristics of Populations

Several terms can be used to describe a population in nature. **Three important characteristics of a population are its geographic distribution, density, and growth rate.** A fourth characteristic, the population's age structure, will be discussed later in this chapter. Geographic distribution, or range, is a term that describes the area inhabited by a population. The range can vary in size from a few cubic centimeters occupied by bacteria in a rotting apple to the millions of square kilometers occupied by migrating whales in the Pacific Ocean.

CA a

a **BI 6.c**

Population density is the number of individuals per unit area. This number can vary tremendously depending on the species and its ecosystem. The population of saguaro cactus in the desert plant community shown in **Figure 5–1,** for example, has a low density, whereas other plants in that community have a relatively high density.

▶ **Figure 5–1** The tall saguaro cactuses in this Arizona desert have a low population density compared to the smaller desert plants. **Density is one of the main characteristics that describe a natural population. Other characteristics of populations are their geographic distribution and growth rate.**

SECTION RESOURCES

Print:
- ***Teaching Resources,*** Lesson Plan 5–1, Adapted Section Summary 5–1, Adapted Worksheets 5–1, Section Summary 5–1, Worksheets 5–1, Section Review 5–1
- ***Reading and Study Workbook A,*** Section 5–1
- ***Adapted Reading and Study Workbook B,*** Section 5–1

Technology:
- ***iText,*** Section 5–1
- ***Transparencies Plus,*** Section 5–1

Section 5–1

BI 6.b, BI 6.c

1 FOCUS

Objectives

5.1.1 ***List*** the characteristics used to describe a population.
5.1.2 ***Identify*** factors that affect population size.
5.1.3 ***Differentiate*** between exponential and logistic growth.

Guide for Reading

Vocabulary Preview

To prepare students for the term *population density,* ask: **How many people are in this classroom?** *(Make sure students include you in the count.)* **What is the room's area?** *(Let students measure the room and calculate its area in square meters.)* **How many people are there in the room per square meter?** *(Have students divide the number of people by the room's area.)* Then, explain that the number of people per square meter is the density of the population in the room.

Reading Strategy

Suggest that students write their questions and the answers in outline format, with enough detail and explanation of terms that the outline can be used later as a study tool.

2 INSTRUCT

Characteristics of Populations

Make Connections

Mathematics Give students the equation for calculating population density:

$$\text{Population density} = \frac{\text{Number of individuals}}{\text{Unit area}}$$

Then, pose the following math problem for them to solve: **Suppose there are 150 bullfrogs living in a pond that covers an area of 3 square kilometers. What is the density of the bullfrog population?** *(50 bullfrogs per square kilometer)* Challenge students to make up similar problems for the rest of the class. L2

5–1 (continued)

Population Growth

Word Origins

Emigration means "out-migration." L1 L2

Build Science Skills

Applying Concepts Explain that populations can experience negative growth as well as positive growth. Then, pose the following problem: **Suppose that the total penguin population in Figure 5–2 was 1200 at the beginning of the year and 1600 at the end of the year. What was the population's growth?** *(An increase of 400 penguins)* **Suppose 250 penguin chicks died during the year. What was the population's growth?** *(A net increase of 150 penguins)* **Suppose that 200 adult penguins also died during the year. What was the population's growth?** *(A net decrease—negative growth—of 50 penguins)* L2

Download a worksheet on populations for students to complete, and find additional teacher support from NSTA SciLinks.

Word Origins

Immigration is formed from the Latin prefix *in-*, meaning "in," and *migrare*, meaning "to move from one place to another." **If the Latin prefix *e-* means "out," then what does *emigration* mean?**

Population Growth

Natural populations may stay the same size from year to year. But a population can grow rapidly, as sea otter populations did when they were first protected from hunting. Populations can also decrease in size, as otter populations are doing now because of predation by killer whales. But just how do interacting factors such as these influence population growth?

Three factors can affect population size: the number of births, the number of deaths, and the number of individuals that enter or leave the population. Simply put, a population will increase or decrease in size depending on how many individuals are added to it or removed from it.

Generally, populations grow if more individuals are born than die in any period of time. For some organisms, such as the penguins in **Figure 5–2,** being born may actually mean hatching. Plants can add new individuals as seeds sprout and begin to grow.

CA a

A population can grow when its birthrate is greater than its death rate. If the birthrate equals the death rate, the population stays more or less the same size. If the death rate is greater than the birthrate, the population shrinks. Sea otter populations grew when hunting stopped, because their death rate dropped. Those same otter populations are shrinking now because killer whales have raised the death rate of otters again.

Immigration (im-uh-GRAY-shun), the movement of individuals into an area, is another factor that can cause a population to grow. **Emigration** (em-uh-GRAY-shun), the movement of individuals out of an area, can cause a population to decrease in size. Wildlife biologists studying changes in populations of animals such as grizzly bears and wolves must consider immigration and emigration. For example, emigration can occur when young animals approaching maturity leave the area where they were born, find mates, and establish new territories. A shortage of food in one area may also lead to emigration. On the other hand, populations can increase by immigration as animals in search of mates or food arrive from outside.

▼ **Figure 5–2** This king penguin population has grown in size due to the recent births of chicks, recognizable by their downy brown feathers. **Population size is affected by the number of births, the number of deaths, and the number of individuals that enter or leave the population.**

UNIVERSAL ACCESS

Inclusion/Special Needs

Ask students to think about the carrying capacity of typical homes. Discuss how many people a two-bedroom apartment or a two-story home can comfortably house and the maximum number such a dwelling could house if absolutely necessary. Then, discuss how people are added or subtracted from homes—through birth, death, leaving, or arriving. Relate these everyday concepts to the biology concepts introduced in Section 5–1. L1

Less Proficient Readers

For students who have difficulty grasping the difference between exponential growth and logistic growth, draw the shapes of the graph lines of each on the board. Emphasize that each shape represents growth of a population over time. Point to the line for exponential growth, explain that at first growth occurs slowly, and then point out the sentence in the text on page 121 where students can read that. Continue this method with the parts of each line. L1 L2

Exponential Growth

If a population has abundant space and food, and is protected from predators and disease, then organisms in that population will multiply and the population size will increase. Let's conduct an imaginary investigation to understand how growth under ideal conditions might occur. Suppose you put a single bacterium in a petri dish. Supply it with enough nutrients and incubate the culture with the right amount of heat, moisture, and light. How will the population change over time?

Bacteria reproduce by splitting in half. If the bacteria have a doubling time of 20 minutes, then within 20 minutes the first bacterium will divide to produce 2 bacteria. Twenty minutes later, the 2 bacteria will divide to produce 4. After another 20 minutes, there will be 8 bacteria. In another hour, there will be 64 bacteria; and in just one more hour, there will be 512. And in just one day, this colony of bacteria will grow to an astounding size of 4,720,000,000,000,000,000,000. What would happen if this growth pattern continued for several days without slowing down? Bacteria would cover the planet!

Figure 5–3 shows a graph with the size of the bacterial population plotted against time. As you can see, the pattern of growth is a J-shaped curve. The J-shaped curve indicates that the population is undergoing exponential (eks-poh-NEN-shul) growth. **Exponential growth** occurs when the individuals in a population reproduce at a constant rate. At first, the number of individuals in an exponentially growing population increases slowly. Over time, however, the population becomes larger and larger until it approaches an infinitely large size. **Under ideal conditions with unlimited resources, a population will grow exponentially.**

With a doubling time of 20 minutes, some bacteria have the fastest rates of reproduction among living things. Populations of other species grow more slowly. For example, a female elephant can produce an infant only every 2 to 4 years, and then the offspring take about 10 years to mature. But as you can see in **Figure 5–3,** in the unlikely event that all the offspring of a single pair of elephants survived and reproduced for 750 years, there would be nearly 20 million elephants!

 *What is exponential growth?*

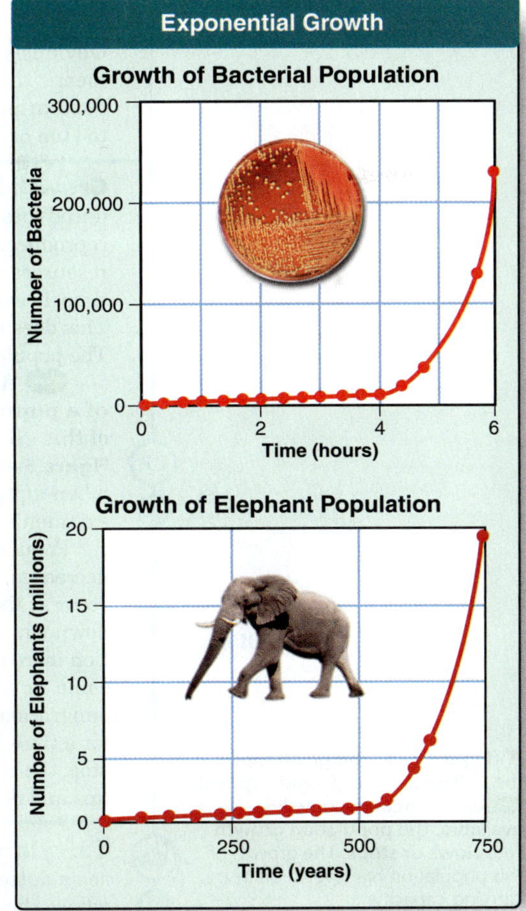

▲ **Figure 5–3**  **In the presence of unlimited resources and in the absence of predation and disease, a population will grow exponentially.** Both hypothetical graphs show the characteristic J-shape of exponential population growth.

(a) BI 6.b

For: Links on populations
Visit: www.SciLinks.org
Web Code: cbn-2051

Exponential Growth

Use Visuals

Figure 5–3 Have students study the two graphs; then, ask: **How are these graphs alike?** *(Both plot time on the horizontal axis and number of organisms on the vertical axis, and the curve on both graphs is J-shaped.)* **Besides showing different types of organisms, how do the graphs differ?** *(The size of the population is given in hundreds of thousands for bacteria and in millions for elephants. The elapsed time is in hours for bacteria and in hundreds of years for the elephants.)* **What do these differences indicate?** *(Bacteria reproduce very rapidly in a short period of time, but elephants reproduce much more slowly over a long period of time.)* **What is another major difference between the reproduction of bacteria and that of elephants?** *(Bacteria reproduce asexually; every bacterium is capable of producing two bacteria. Elephants reproduce sexually; two parents—a male and a female—are needed to produce one offspring.)* L2

Build Science Skills

Interpreting Graphics Have students compare the shape of the lines in the two graphs of Figure 5–3, and elicit from a volunteer that the shapes are identical. Ask: **If they are identical, does that mean the rates of reproduction for bacteria and for elephants are also identical?** *(No, because the rate is much faster for bacteria)* **Does the shape indicate that the rate of reproduction increases over time for both species?** *(No, because exponential growth occurs when individuals in a population reproduce at a constant rate)* **Why, then, does the shape of each line become gradually steeper and then shoot up dramatically?** *(Although individuals reproduce at a constant rate, the number of individuals accumulates over time. A doubling of a larger population yields greater numbers in a unit of time than a doubling of a smaller population in the same unit of time.)* L2 L3

Answer to . . .

CHECKPOINT *Growth that occurs when a population reproduces at a constant rate*

TEACHER TO TEACHER

Try the following activity when making the connection between population growth and spending money: Tell students a rich relative has left you $5 billion in cash. This money has been stacked in your basement in large piles of one-dollar denominations. You need to spend some of the money and have it removed so you can remodel part of the basement. Friends work eight hours each day, seven days a week, removing the bills at a rate of one dollar per second.

1. How long will it take to remove one billion dollars? *(Over 95 years).* 2. Explain how this money problem relates to population growth. *(The rate of money removed occurs at a constant rate because of certain factors. Population growth can occur at a constant rate as well.)*

—*Bob Culler*
Biology Teacher
Avon Lake High School
Avon Lake, Ohio

Logistic Growth

Use Visuals

Figure 5–4 Ask: **How frequently did the yeast population double?** *(Every 7 to 10 hours)* **How long did it take the yeast population to reach its carrying capacity?** *(About 32 hours)* **Based on the number of cells produced in 50 hours, would you say that yeast populations increase quickly or slowly?** *(Quickly, but not as rapidly as bacteria)* L1 L2

Build Science Skills

Using Models To help students understand the difference between exponential and logistic growth, divide the class into small groups. Give each group a box of 100 paper clips. Tell students that the clips represent amoebas, unicellular organisms that reproduce simply by splitting in half. Have students lay out paper clips in a branching dichotomous "tree" to represent exponential growth through six generations. (*The results will be: Generation 1: 1 amoeba; Generation 2: 2 amoebas; Generation 3: 4 amoebas; Generation 4: 8 amoebas; Generation 5: 16 amoebas; and Generation 6: 32 amoebas.*)

Next, have each group model logistic growth by repeating the procedure, but this time also removing clips to represent deaths, as follows: Generation 1: 1 amoeba; Generation 2: 2 amoebas; Generation 3: 4 amoebas, remove 1; Generation 4: 6 amoebas, remove 2; Generation 5: 8 amoebas, remove 3; and Generation 6: 10 amoebas. Have students compare the number of organisms in the last generation of both models.

Logistic Growth

Obviously, neither bacteria nor elephants cover the planet. This means that exponential growth does not continue in natural populations for very long. What might cause population growth to stop or to slow down?

Growth Slows Down Suppose that a few animals are introduced into a new environment. At first, as the animals begin to reproduce, the population increases slowly. Then, because resources are unlimited, the population grows exponentially. In time, however, the rate of population growth begins to slow down. This does not mean that the size of the population has dropped. The population is still growing, but at a much slower rate. **As resources become less available, the growth of a population slows or stops.** The general, S-shaped curve of this growth pattern, called logistic growth, is shown in **Figure 5–4** in a yeast population. **Logistic growth** occurs when a population's growth slows or stops following a period of exponential growth. How might this happen?

CA a

Population growth may slow down when the birthrate decreases, when the death rate increases, or when both events occur at the same rate. Similarly, population growth may slow down when the rate of immigration decreases, the rate of emigration increases, or both. When the birthrate and death rate are the same, or when the rate of immigration is equal to the rate of emigration, then population growth will slow down or even stop for a time. Note that even when the population growth is said to stop, the population is still rising and falling somewhat, but the ups and downs average out around a certain population size.

(a) BI 6.c
(b) BI 6.b

Carrying Capacity If you look again at **Figure 5–4**, you will see a dotted, horizontal line through the region of the graph where the growth of the yeast population has leveled off. The point at which that line intersects the *y*-axis tells you the size of the population when the average growth rate reaches zero. That number, in turn, represents the largest number of individuals—in this case, yeast cells—that a given environment can support. Ecologists call this number the **carrying capacity** of the environment for a particular species.

If you examine natural populations of familiar plant and animal species, you will find that many of them follow a logistic growth curve. In the natural world there are many factors that can slow the growth of a population. The factors that limit population growth are discussed in the next section.

▼ **Figure 5–4** This graph shows the S-shaped curve of logistic growth. **As resources become less available, the population growth rate slows or stops.** The growth of this population has leveled off at its carrying capacity.

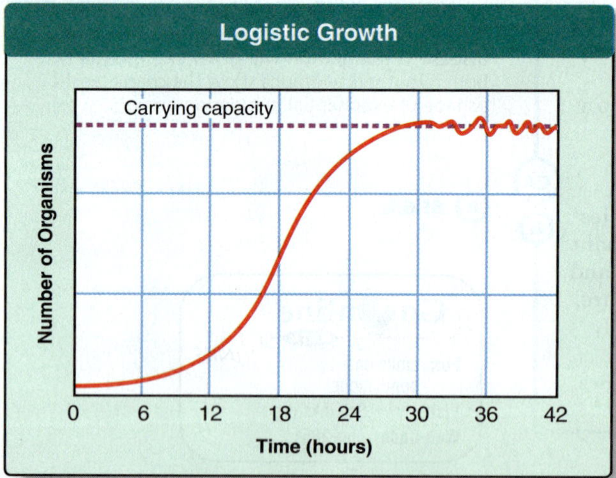

FACTS AND FIGURES

Close to carrying capacity

If the population density of a species is higher than the environment's carrying capacity, many individuals of the species may die. There are, however, several advantages to having a high population density that does not exceed the carrying capacity. One such advantage is that in sexually reproducing organisms, there is a greater opportunity for genetic diversity. Such diversity increases the chances of the population's adapting to environmental changes; this in turn increases its chances for survival. When population density becomes too low, the survival of the species is endangered. Scientists estimate that a minimum of 500 individuals is necessary to guarantee long-term survival in nature. A species with a very low population density may become extinct.

Analyzing Data

BI 6.b, 6IIE 7.c

Population Trends

Do fruit flies and rabbits show similar trends in population growth?

1. **Using Tables and Graphs** Make a graph using the data in each data table. One graph will show the growth rate of a fruit fly population. The other graph will show the growth rate of a population of rabbits.
2. **Using Tables and Graphs** What type of growth pattern is exhibited by the fruit fly population? Is it the same type of growth as in the rabbit population? Explain.
3. **Drawing Conclusions** Does either graph indicate that there is a carrying capacity for the population? If so, when does the population reach its carrying capacity? What is the maximum number of individuals that can be supported at that time?
4. **Predicting** Animals such as foxes and cats often prey on rabbits. Based on the growth curve of the rabbit population, what might happen if a group of predators move into the rabbits' habitat during the tenth generation and begin eating the rabbits?

Fruit Fly Population Growth

Days	Number of Fruit Flies
5	10
10	50
15	100
20	200
25	300
30	310
35	320
40	320

Rabbit Population Growth

Generations	Number of Rabbits
1	100
2	105
25	1000
37	1600
55	2400
72	3350
86	8000
100	13,150

5–1 Section Assessment

1. **Key Concept** List three characteristics that are used to describe a population.
2. **Key Concept** What factors can change a population's size?
3. **Key Concept** What is the difference between exponential growth and logistic growth?
4. What is meant by population density?
5. Define carrying capacity.
6. **Critical Thinking Inferring** What factors might cause the carrying capacity of a population to change?

Thinking Visually

Using Graphic Organizers
Draw a concept map that shows how populations grow. Include the following terms: *exponential growth, logistic growth, birthrate, death rate, immigration, emigration.* Add any other terms that you think are useful to complete the map.

5–1 Section Assessment

1. Geographic distribution, density, growth rate
2. Births, deaths, immigration, emigration
3. Exponential growth occurs when the population grows at a constant rate. Exponential growth occurs only under ideal conditions (ample space and food; protection from predators and disease). Logistic growth occurs when a population's growth rate slows or stops following a period of exponential growth.
4. The number of individuals per unit area
5. The largest number of individuals that a given environment can support
6. Accept all reasonable answers. Sample answer: A natural disaster such as a forest fire, flood, or hurricane might reduce the amount of resources available to a population.

Analyzing Data

BI 6.b, 6IIE 7.c

Before students create their graphs, help them decide on appropriate intervals for the *x*- and *y*-axes. L2

Answers

1. Check students' graphs to make sure they have plotted data correctly.
2. The fruit fly population exhibits logistic growth, while the rabbit population exhibits exponential growth. Limiting factors must have affected the growth of the fruit fly population but not the growth of the rabbit population.
3. The graph of the fruit fly population seems to reach its carrying capacity at 35 days, when 320 individuals can be supported.
4. With predators added, the rabbit population would exhibit logistic growth, not exponential growth, and the population's growth would slow, stop, or decrease in later generations.

3 ASSESS

Evaluate Understanding

Have students explain why the graph curves for exponential growth and logistic growth are different shapes and also identify some factors that cause population growth to slow or stop.

Reteach

Have each student draw two simplified graphs—one for exponential growth and the other for logistic growth—with each graph including only the correct shape of the curve and two axes labeled *Number* and *Time.* Have students compare their graphs with those in their textbook and make any necessary corrections in the shapes of the curves.

Thinking Visually

Students' concept maps will vary but should show logical connections between terms.

If your class subscribes to the iText, use it to review the Key Concepts in Section 5–1.

Section 5–2

BI 6.c

1 FOCUS

Objectives

5.2.1 ***Identify*** factors that limit population growth.

5.2.2 ***Differentiate*** between density-dependent and density-independent limiting factors.

Guide for Reading

Vocabulary Preview

To prepare students for the new Vocabulary terms *density-dependent* and *density-independent,* ask them to recall the definition of *population density* that they learned in Section 5–1. *(The number of individuals per unit of area)*

Reading Strategy

Suggest that students record their predictions in writing, leaving space below each one to note whether the prediction was correct or incorrect. In the case of incorrect predictions, have students correctly note how those limiting factors affect a population's growth.

2 INSTRUCT

Limiting Factors

Use Visuals

Figure 5–5 For each of the limiting factors shown in the diagram, have students suggest examples that are already familiar to them—for example, weeds and crop plants competing for light, space, and nutrients in a vegetable garden; the predator-prey relationship of a toad eating a moth; and so on. As students cite examples, have a volunteer list them on a large sheet of paper. Save the list for use again later in Evaluate Understanding, page 127.

L1 L2

5–2 Limits to Growth

BI 6.c. Students know how fluctuations in population size in an ecosystem are determined by the relative rates of birth, immigration, emigration, and death.

Guide for Reading

Key Concept

- What factors limit population growth?

Vocabulary

limiting factor
density-dependent limiting factor
predator-prey relationship
density-independent limiting factor

Reading Strategy: Predicting Before you read, preview the diagram below. Predict how each factor might limit the growth of a population. As you read, note whether your predictions were correct.

Now that you know a few things about population growth, think again about the sea otter example in the beginning of the previous section. When a sea otter population declines, something has changed the relationship between the birthrate and the death rate, or between the rates of immigration and emigration. For instance, in part of the sea otter's range, the death rate of sea otters is increasing because killer whales are eating the otters. Predation by killer whales creates a situation that reduces the growth of the sea otter population.

Limiting Factors

Recall from Chapter 3 that the primary productivity of an ecosystem can be reduced when there is an insufficient supply of a particular nutrient. Ecologists call such substances limiting nutrients. A limiting nutrient is an example of a more general ecological concept: a limiting factor. In the context of populations, a **limiting factor** is a factor that causes population growth to decrease. Some of the limiting factors that can affect a population are shown in **Figure 5–5.**

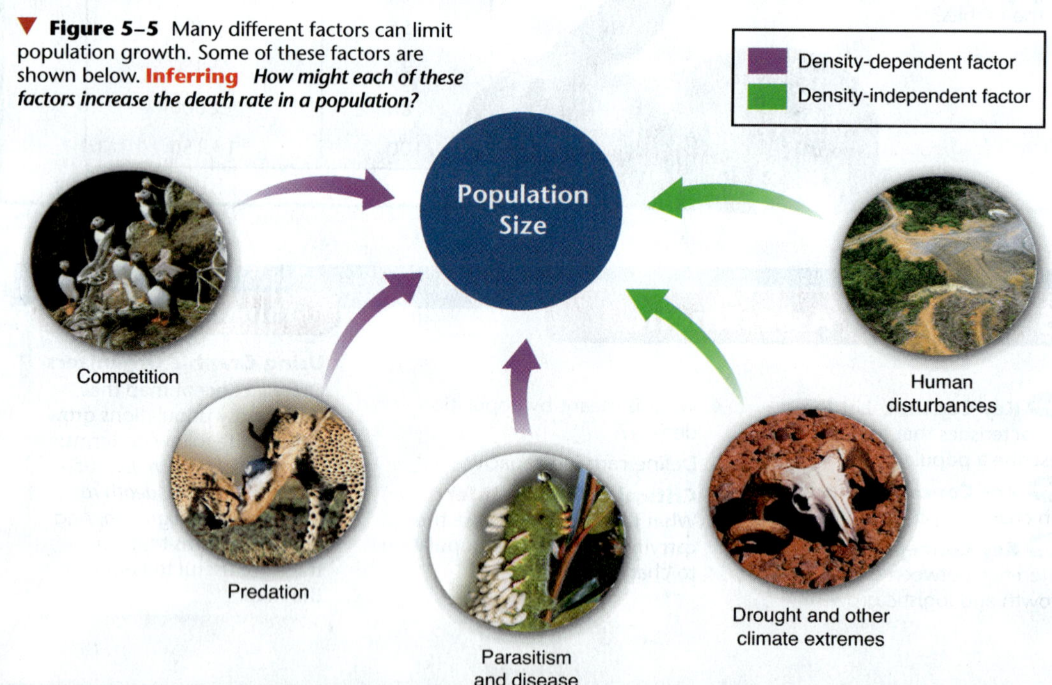

▼ **Figure 5–5** Many different factors can limit population growth. Some of these factors are shown below. **Inferring** ***How might each of these factors increase the death rate in a population?***

SECTION RESOURCES

TIME SAVER

Print:

- ***Teaching Resources,*** Lesson Plan 5–2, Adapted Section Summary 5–2, Adapted Worksheets 5–2, Section Summary 5–2, Worksheets 5–2, Section Review 5–2, Enrichment
- ***Reading and Study Workbook A,*** Section 5–2
- ***Adapted Reading and Study Workbook B,*** Section 5–2
- ***Issues and Decision Making,*** Issues and Decisions 48

Technology:

- ***iText,*** Section 5–2
- ***Transparencies Plus,*** Section 5–2

▶ **Figure 5–6** The panda is one of the most critically endangered species in the world today. Populations are declining, in large part because pandas depend on bamboo for food, which grows only in certain forests because of habitat destruction. **Inferring** *How might the panda population be saved?*

A resource base that is limited can also affect the long-term survival of a species. As shown in **Figure 5–6**, pandas depend on bamboo for food. Bamboo grows in certain kinds of temperate forests in China. Since the time that these forests have been cleared for timber and farmland, panda populations have fallen dramatically and have become isolated in small pockets of remaining forest.

Density-Dependent Factors

A limiting factor that depends on population size is called a **density-dependent limiting factor.** Density-dependent factors become limiting only when the population density—the number of organisms per unit area—reaches a certain level. These factors operate most strongly when a population is large and dense. They do not affect small, scattered populations as greatly. **Density-dependent limiting factors include competition, predation, parasitism, and disease.**

Competition

When populations become crowded, organisms compete with one another for food, water, space, sunlight, and other essentials. For example, puffins must compete for limited nesting sites. Competition among members of the same species is a density-dependent limiting factor. The more individuals living in an area, the sooner they use up the available resources. Likewise, the fewer the number of individuals, the more resources are available to them and the less they must compete with one another.

CA a

Competition can also occur between members of different species. This type of competition is a major force behind evolutionary change. When two species compete for the same resources, both species are under pressure to change in ways that decrease their competition. Over time, the species may evolve to occupy separate niches. That is because, as you may recall, no two species can occupy the same niche in the same place at the same time.

CHECKPOINT *What is a density-dependent limiting factor?* a BI 6.c

BI 6.b

Quick Lab

How does competition affect growth?

Materials bean seeds, 2 paper cups, potting soil

Procedure

1. Label two paper cups 3 and 15. Use a pencil to make several holes in the bottom of each paper cup. Fill each paper cup two-thirds full with potting soil. Plant 3 bean seeds in cup 3, and plant 15 bean seeds in cup 15.
2. Water both cups so that the soil is moist but not wet. Put them in a location that receives bright indirect light. Water the cups equally as needed.
3. Count the seedlings every other day for 2 weeks. **CAUTION:** *Wash your hands with soap and warm water before leaving the lab.*

Analyze and Conclude

Observing What differences did you observe between the two cups?

Density-Dependent Factors

Quick Lab

BI 6.b

Objective Students will be able to determine that crowding is a limiting factor in plant growth. L2

Skill Focus Observing

Materials bean seeds, 2 paper cups, potting soil

Time 15 minutes for initial setup, followed by observation and recording for 2 weeks

Strategy Remind students that the only variable that should be different between the two cups is the number of seeds planted. Ask: **What variables should you keep the same in both cups?** *(The depth at which the seeds are planted, the amount of water the cups are given, the amount of sunlight the cups receive, temperature)*

Expected Outcome The uncrowded seedlings will thrive. The crowded seedlings will show limited growth, and some may die.

Analyze and Conclude The seedlings in cup 15 will be smaller and less robust than those in cup 3, and some may die.

Answers to . . .

CHECKPOINT *A factor that limits population growth only when the population's density reaches a certain level*

Figure 5–5 *Each of the factors that limit population growth could cause deaths of individuals. Accept all reasonable responses.*

Figure 5–6 *The panda population might be saved if the habitat on which they depend—bamboo in certain forests—is prevented from being destroyed or is restored in areas that had been cleared.*

UNIVERSAL ACCESS

Less Proficient Readers
Have students make a compare/contrast table of the limiting factors discussed in the section. Column heads might include *Factor, Definition,* and *Example.* In the factor column, students should use subheads to divide the limiting factors into density-dependent and density-independent factors. L1 L2

English Language Learners
Have students pronounce the word *dependent*, and then discuss common usages of the word. Explain that the prefix *in-* means "not," and thus the word *independent* means "not dependent." This section introduces factors that do and do not depend upon the density of a population. L1

Advanced Learners
Encourage interested students to further research the relationship between predator and prey on Isle Royale, as mentioned on page 126. These populations of wolves and moose have been studied extensively, and students should readily find relevant resources. Have them report their research to the class. L3

5–2 (continued)

Use Visuals

Figure 5–7 Make sure students understand that two separate sets of data are plotted on the graph: the blue line represents the numbers of wolves labeled on the graph's left vertical axis, and the red line represents the numbers of moose labeled on the right vertical axis. L1

Make Connections

Mathematics Present the following math problems: In order to survive, a 50-kilogram wolf needs to eat about 2700 kilograms of moose per year. The average mass of a moose is about 385 kilograms; males have more mass, females less. Ask: **How many "average" moose does a wolf need to eat each year?** *(About 7)* **If there are 8 wolves in a pack, how many moose does the pack need to eat each year?** *(About 56)* L2 L3

For: Population Dynamics activity
Visit: PHSchool.com
Web Code: cbe-2059
Students can interact with the art online.

Density-Independent Factors

Build Science Skills

Applying Concepts Ask: **Does the graph in Figure 5–7 show a crash in either population?** *(Yes; the wolf population from 1980 to 1982 and the moose population from 1995 to 1996)* Read the caption and then ask: **What combination of density-dependent and density-independent factors may have caused the crash in the wolf population?** *(Decline in the moose population; unusually deep winter snows could have made it difficult for the wolves to hunt; parasites or disease could have weakened or killed the wolves.)* L2

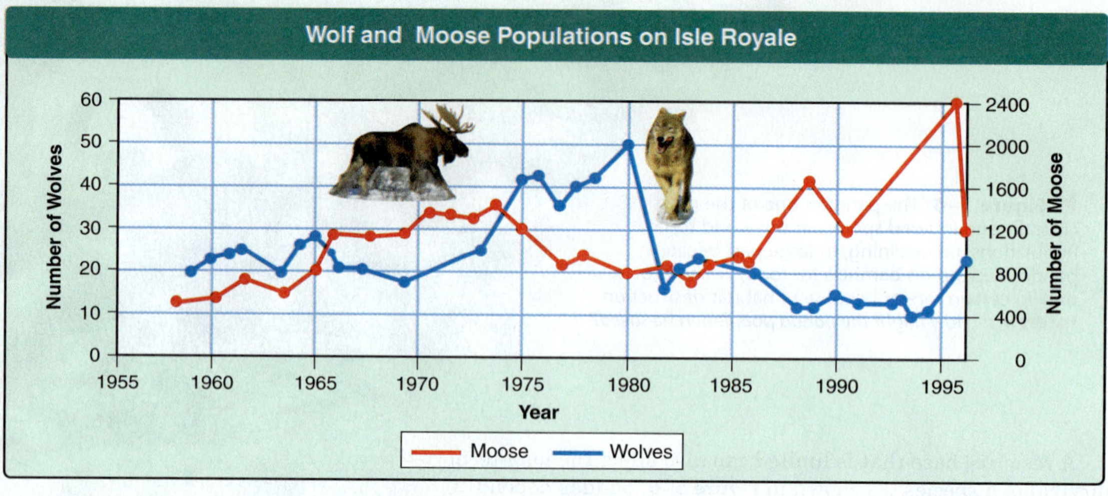

▲ **Figure 5–7** The relationship between moose and wolves on Isle Royale illustrates how predation can affect population growth. In this example, the moose population was also affected by changes in food supply, and the wolf population was also affected by disease. **Interpreting Graphics** ***How are the increases and decreases in the moose population related to the changes in the wolf population?***

ⓐ BI 6.c

Predation Populations in nature are often controlled by predation. The regulation of a population by predation takes place within a **predator-prey relationship,** one of the best-known mechanisms of population control. The relationships between sea otters and sea urchins and between sea otters and killer whales are examples of predator-prey interactions that affect population growth.

CA ⓐ A well-documented example of a predator-prey relationship is the interaction between wolves and moose on Isle Royale, an island in Lake Superior. The graph in **Figure 5–7** shows how periodic increases in the moose population—the prey—on Isle Royale are quickly followed by increases in the wolf population—the predators. As the wolves prey on the moose, the moose population falls. The decline in the moose population is followed, sooner or later, by a decline in the wolf population because there is less for the wolves to feed upon. A decline in the wolf population means that the moose have fewer enemies, so the moose population rises again. This cycle of predator and prey populations can be repeated indefinitely.

Parasitism and Disease Parasites can also limit the growth of a population. Parasitic organisms range in size from microscopic, disease-causing bacteria to tapeworms 30 centimeters or more in length. These organisms are similar to predators in many ways. Like predators, parasites take nourishment at the expense of their hosts, often weakening them and causing disease or death. The wasp cocoons in **Figure 5–8**, for example, can weaken or kill many caterpillars.

◀ **Figure 5–8** This larval sphinx moth has been attacked by a parasitic wasp. The wasp inserted its eggs beneath the moth's skin. After hatching, the wasp larvae fed on their host internally until they appeared as white cocoons on its back. **Predicting** ***How might the wasp larvae affect the sphinx moth population?***

126

TEACHER TO TEACHER

Use a short video clip of a forest fire, such as the National Park Service's video of fires in Yellowstone Park. Then, read one or two actual news articles that describe the fire and its effects.

Divide the class into groups of three or four, and assign each group the task of developing a management plan to study the ecological damage caused by the fire and to help reestablish plant and animal populations in the burned area. Students should research the following information: the types of populations living in the area before and after the fire; the initial and current size of each population; resources now available to the populations and resources no longer available; and possible steps to help reintroduce populations. Give each group an opportunity to explain its plan to the class.

—*Brenda Waldon*
Biology Teacher
Clayton County Public Schools
Morrow, Georgia

Density-Independent Factors

Density-independent limiting factors affect all populations in similar ways, regardless of the population size. **Unusual weather, natural disasters, seasonal cycles, and certain human activities—such as damming rivers and clear-cutting forests—are all examples of density-independent limiting factors.** In response to such factors, many species show a characteristic crash in population size. After the crash, the population may soon build up again, or it may stay low for some time.

For some species, storms or hurricanes can nearly extinguish a population. For example, thrips, aphids, and other insects that feed on plant buds and leaves might be washed out by a heavy rainstorm. Extremes of cold or hot weather also can take their toll on a population, regardless of the population's density. A severe winter frost, for example, can kill giant saguaro cactuses in the Arizona desert. In some areas, periodic droughts can affect entire populations of vegetation, as shown in **Figure 5–9.** Such events can, in turn, affect the populations of consumers within the food web.

Environments are always changing, and most populations can adapt to a certain amount of change. Populations often grow and shrink in response to such changes. Major upsets in an ecosystem, however, can lead to long-term declines in certain populations. Human activities have caused some of these major upsets, as you will soon read.

▶ **Figure 5–9** A drought can result in the abrupt decrease of a population, regardless of its size. **Droughts and other natural disasters are density-independent limiting factors.**

5–2 Section Assessment

1. **Key Concept** List three density-dependent factors and three density-independent factors that can limit the growth of a population.
2. What is the relationship between competition and population size?
3. If an entire lynx population disappears, what is likely to happen to the hare population on which it preys?
4. Identify how a limited resource can affect the size of a population. Give an example that illustrates this situation.
5. **Critical Thinking Applying Concepts** Give an example of a density-independent limiting factor that has affected a human population. Describe how this factor changed the human population.

Focus on the BIG Idea

Interdependence in Nature Study the factors that limit population growth as shown in **Figure 5–5.** Classify each factor as either biotic or abiotic. Refer to the information on biotic and abiotic factors in Section 4–2.

5–2 Section Assessment

1. Density-dependent: competition, predation, parasitism and disease; density-independent: unusual weather, natural disasters, seasonal cycles, human activities
2. When populations become larger and more crowded, organisms must compete with one another for food, water, space, sunlight, and other essential resources.
3. The hare population would probably undergo explosive growth.
4. Accept all reasonable responses. Students might mention any of the density-independent factors as limiting a resource. A limited resource limits the size of a population.
5. Accept all reasonable responses. Sample answer: A prolonged drought, with its associated crop loss, could cause deaths, financial hardship, and emigration to other countries.

3 ASSESS

Evaluate Understanding

Display the list of examples that the class created at the beginning of this section (Use Visuals, page 124). Call on students at random to identify each example as density-dependent or density-independent.

Reteach

Have students work in groups of three, with each student responsible for writing a brief description of how one of the three density-dependent limiting factors discussed in the text can limit a population's growth. Let the group members share their descriptions and offer corrections and improvements.

Focus on the BIG Idea 

Density-dependent limiting factors, such as competition, predation, parasitism, and disease, can be classified as biotic factors. Density-independent limiting factors, such as drought and other climate extremes as well as human disturbance to ecosystems, can be classified as abiotic factors. Some students may argue that human disturbance should be considered a biotic factor for the reason that humans are organisms interacting with other organisms. At the same time, however, human disturbances such as building roads, filling wetlands, or clearing forests cause large-scale changes in the physical environment that should be considered abiotic factors.

If your class subscribes to the iText, use it to review the Key Concepts in Section 5–2.

Answers to . . .

Figure 5–7 *As the moose population increased, the wolf population increased. Decreases in the moose population were followed by decreases in the wolf population.*

Figure 5–8 *Predation by wasp larvae would reduce the growth rate of the sphinx moth population.*

BIIE 1.m

Encourage students to research current nature publications to gather more detailed information on both sides of this issue. If students live in an area where ranchers or farmers suffer losses due to wolf predation, suggest that they interview affected people and research local newspaper articles to learn more.

You may wish to let students work in several small groups, with some groups representing ranchers and others representing conservationists and other stakeholders. Give the groups time to discuss their points of view and their reasoning. Then, hold a mock meeting in which each side presents its view to the "government official." (You may want to role-play the official yourself.)

Research and Decide

1. Students' lists will vary and may include researched information as well as information included in this feature.
2. Accept opinions on both sides of the issue so long as students defend their choices with reasonable explanations.

Students can research gray wolf protection on the site developed by authors Ken Miller and Joe Levine.

BIIE 1.m

Does the Gray Wolf Population Need Protection?

Wolves were once widely distributed around the world, occupying almost every habitat except tropical jungles. Today, however, wolves occupy only a fraction of their former range. In 1973, the Endangered Species Act was passed by the U.S. Congress to protect declining populations of gray wolves from becoming extinct. At the time, there were only about 400 wolves in the lower 48 states. By 2002, the population had swelled to an estimated 4000 individuals scattered mostly throughout the Rocky Mountains and Great Lakes areas.

Classifying the status of animals is a judgment call. In some cases, the judgment is easy. For instance, the California condor population now includes only a few remaining members and is clearly in great danger. With other species, such as the gray wolf, the situation is much more complex. How should the gray wolf be classified—and therefore managed—in the United States?

The Viewpoints

Keep the Endangered Classification

People who want to keep the gray wolf's status as an endangered species say that most of its former habitat in the 48 contiguous states is unsuitable because of human encroachment. Proponents of this view cite the fact that only after gray wolves were given protection under the Endangered Species Act did the wolf population in the United States begin to increase. There is concern that persecution by people and loss of habitat will confine gray wolves to more remote areas, or reduce their habitat even further, unless federal protection continues.

Reclassify the Wolf and Remove Federal Protection

Opponents of the endangered species classification counter that in states like Minnesota, the gray wolf population is growing at a rate of 4 to 5 percent each year. These people are confident that, because the populations are increasing at a healthy rate, the wolves no longer need federal protection. Ranchers are concerned that, at the current growth rate, wolves will encroach on their livestock. Many feel strongly that landowners should have the right to protect themselves from potential losses. The protection of wolves currently costs the U.S. government over $200,000 per year. If the wolves could be legally hunted and trapped, the money that would be saved could be used to help protect other, more endangered species.

Research and Decide

1. **Analyzing the Viewpoints** To make an informed decision, learn more about this issue by consulting library or Internet resources. List the pros and cons of each option as they relate to both humans and wolves. Consider the different perspectives of landowners, conservationists, and other interested groups.
2. **Forming Your Opinion** Decide whether the federal government should change the status of the gray wolf. Write a persuasive statement to support your decision.

For: Links from the authors
Visit: PHSchool.com
Web Code: cbe-2052

BACKGROUND

The gray wolf profiled

The gray wolf is a subspecies of *Canis lupus* and a member of the dog family, Canidae. Adult gray wolves are 1.5–1.8 meters long and stand 66–81 centimeters at the shoulder. Adult males average 31.8–45.4 kilograms; adult females average 24.9–38.6 kilograms. Wolves have long legs, and their bodies are suited for traveling great distances. Wolves prey on everything from large ungulates, such as moose and elk, to small rodents, such as field mice. Although wolves were once common in what is now the United States, populations of gray wolves are now found only in Alaska, Upper Michigan, Wisconsin, Minnesota, Wyoming, Montana, Idaho, and Washington State. Their decline was a result of loss of habitat, loss of prey, and hunting by humans. Bounties on wolves were once common. Wolf recovery in the United States is primarily the result of the Endangered Species Act.

5–3 Human Population Growth

BI 6.c. Students know how fluctuations in population size in an ecosystem are determined by the relative rates of birth, immigration, emigration, and death.

How quickly is the world's human population growing? In the United States and other developed countries, the current growth rate is very low. In some developing countries, the human population is growing at a rate of nearly 3 people per second. Because of this bustling growth rate, the human population is well on its way to reaching 9 billion within your lifetime.

Guide for Reading

Key Concepts
- How has the size of the human population changed over time?
- Why do population growth rates differ in countries throughout the world?

Vocabulary
demography
demographic transition
age-structure diagram

Reading Strategy: Asking Questions Before you read, preview the graphs in **Figures 5–10**, **5–12**, and **5–13.** Make a list of questions about the graphs. As you read, write down the answers to your questions.

Historical Overview

Like the populations of many other living organisms, the size of the human population tends to increase with time. For most of human existence, the population grew slowly. Life was harsh, and limiting factors kept population sizes low. Food was scarce. Incurable diseases were rampant. Until fairly recently, only half the children in the world survived to adulthood. Because death rates were so high, families had many children, just to make sure that some would survive.

About 500 years ago, the human population began growing more rapidly. Agriculture and industry made life easier and safer. The world's food supply became more reliable, and essential goods could be shipped around the globe. Improved sanitation, medicine, and healthcare dramatically reduced the death rate and increased longevity. At the same time, birthrates in most places remained high. With these advances, the human population experienced exponential growth, as shown in **Figure 5–10.**

▼ **Figure 5–10** **The size of the human population has increased over time.** After a long, slow start, the worldwide population grew exponentially following improvements in medicine, sanitation, agriculture, energy use, and technology.

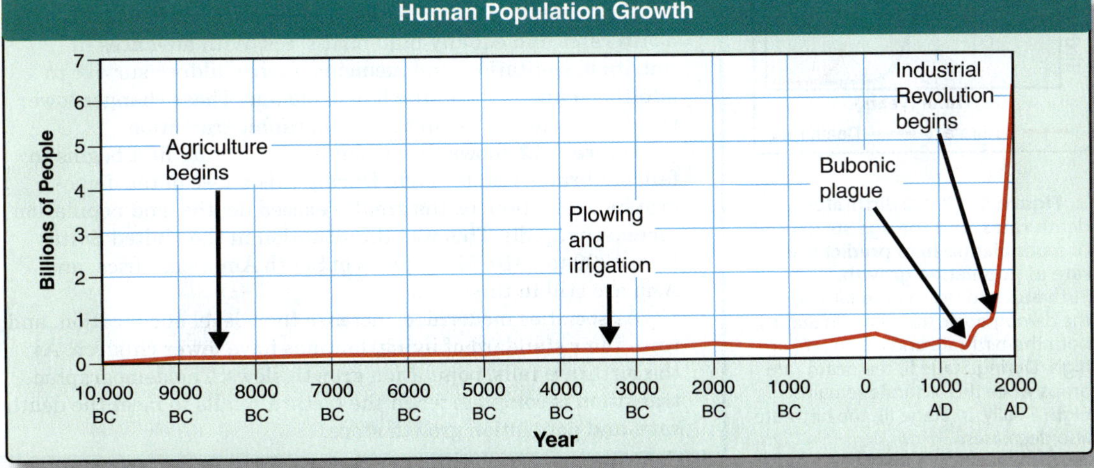

SECTION RESOURCES

Print:
- ***Laboratory Manual A,*** Chapter 5 Lab
- ***Laboratory Manual B,*** Chapter 5 Lab
- ***Teaching Resources,*** Lesson Plan 5–3, Adapted Section Summary 5–3, Adapted Worksheets 5–3, Section Summary 5–3, Worksheets 5–3, Section Review 5–3
- ***Reading and Study Workbook A,*** Section 5–3
- ***Adapted Reading and Study Workbook B,*** Section 5–3
- ***Issues and Decision Making,*** Issues and Decisions 47
- ***Lab Worksheets,*** Chapter 5 Exploration

Technology:
- ***iText,*** Section 5–3
- ***Transparencies Plus,*** Section 5–3

Section 5–3

BI 6.c

1 FOCUS

Objectives

5.3.1 ***Describe*** how the size of the human population has changed over time.

5.3.2 ***Explain*** why population growth rates differ from country to country.

Guide for Reading

Vocabulary Preview

Students would benefit from scanning the section's text to identify any unfamiliar words and terms—not only the highlighted, boldface Vocabulary terms but also others such as *essential goods* and *sanitation.* Have students record the terms and their dictionary definitions for use as a reference as they read the section.

Reading Strategy

To help students get started, let the entire class brainstorm ideas for each of the graphs. Review the purpose of the line graph (to show change over time) and a bar graph (to show comparisons).

2 INSTRUCT

Historical Overview

Build Science Skills

Predicting Ask: **If you extended the graph in Figure 5–10 thousands of years into the future, what do you think the curve would look like, and why?** *(Although a few students may say that the steep rise would continue, most will realize that at some point, Earth's carrying capacity for the human population would be reached, and population growth would slow and remain steady or might even drop—forming the S-shaped curve typical of logistic growth.)* L2 L3

5–3 (continued)

Patterns of Population Growth

Use Community Resources

Encourage small groups of students to research the demographics of their own city or town over a certain period of time. Statistics on births, deaths, total population, and other demographic data may be available from town/city hall, a library, county or state officials, or even real estate agencies. Suggest that the groups make graphs to share their findings. L2

Use Visuals

Figure 5–11 Make sure students understand what the photographs represent by asking them to identify the "positive change" shown and explain how the change has affected population growth. For example, the photograph showing a healthcare worker giving an injection of vaccine to an infant represents medical advances that have significantly reduced death rates. However, modernization must begin, as it has in many nations, before birthrates start to fall. L2

Figure 5–11 Medical advances can lead to a dramatic drop in a population's death rate. Dr. Leila Denmark (near right), who practiced medicine for 73 years, helped to invent the whooping cough vaccine in 1936. A healthcare worker in Rwanda (far right) vaccinates an infant, thereby helping to prevent certain diseases in that child. **Applying Concepts** ***Which other advances can reduce a population's death rate?***

Patterns of Population Growth

The human population cannot keep growing exponentially forever, because Earth and its resources are limited. The question is, when and how will our population growth slow? Two centuries ago, English economist Thomas Malthus observed that human populations were growing rapidly. Malthus predicted that such growth would not continue indefinitely. Instead, according to Malthus, war, famine, and disease would limit human population growth.

(a) BI 6.c

CA (a)

Today, scientists have identified a variety of other social and economic factors that can affect human populations. The scientific study of human populations is called **demography** (duh-MAH-gruh-fee). Demography examines the characteristics of human populations and attempts to explain how those populations will change over time. **Birthrates, death rates, and the age structure of a population help predict why some countries have high growth rates while other countries grow more slowly.**

The Demographic Transition Over the past century, population growth in the United States, Japan, and much of Europe has slowed dramatically. Demographers have developed a hypothesis to explain this shift. According to this hypothesis, these countries have completed the **demographic transition,** a dramatic change in birth and death rates.

Throughout most of history, human societies have had high death rates and equally high birthrates. With advances in nutrition, sanitation, and medicine, more children survive to adulthood and more adults live to old age. These changes lower the death rate and begin the demographic transition.

Figure 5–12 shows that when the death rate first begins to fall, birthrates remain high. During this phase of the demographic transition, births greatly exceed deaths, and population increases rapidly. This was the situation in the United States from 1790 to 1910. Many parts of South America, Africa, and Asia are still in this phase.

As societies modernize, increase their level of education, and raise their standard of living, families have fewer children. As the birthrate falls, population growth slows. The demographic transition is complete when the birthrate falls to meet the death rate, and population growth stops.

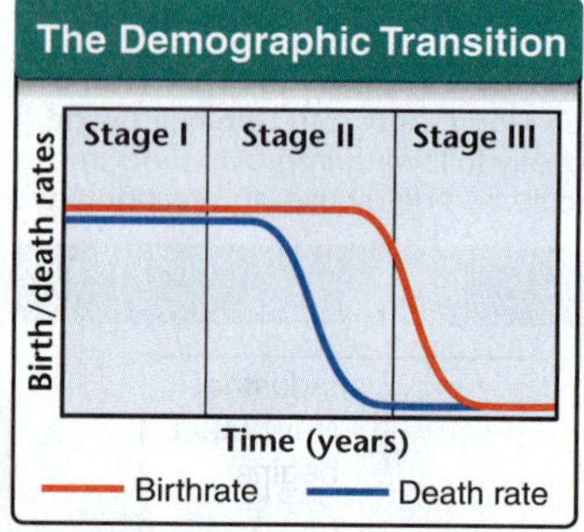

▲ **Figure 5–12** **Birthrates, death rates, and the age structure of a population help predict the rate of population growth.** Birthrates and death rates fall during the demographic transition. In Stage I, both the birthrate and death rate are high. During Stage II, the death rate drops while the birthrate remains high. Finally, in Stage III, the birthrate also decreases.

ESL SUPPORT FOR ENGLISH LANGUAGE LEARNERS

Vocabulary: Word Analysis

Beginning On the board, show the word *demography* broken into its component parts: *demo-*, meaning people, and *graphy*, meaning written or recorded. Then, write the complete word followed by the definition given in the text. Read aloud what you have written to model correct pronunciation. Have the students write the word and definition in their notebooks or science glossaries. Add the word *demography* to a word wall with other Vocabulary terms from the chapter. L1

Intermediate Extend the Beginning activity by writing the word *democracy* on the board. Pronounce the word, and use it in a sentence that defines the word. Point out the use of the prefix *demo-*, meaning people. Have the students infer the meaning of the word part *cracy* (government). L2

So far, the demographic transition has been completed in only a few countries. Despite the trend in the United States, Europe, and Japan, the worldwide human population is still growing exponentially. Most people live in countries that have not yet completed the demographic transition. Much of the population growth today is contributed by only 10 countries, with India and China in the lead, where birthrates remain high.

Age Structure Population growth depends, in part, on how many people of different ages make up a given population. Demographers can predict future growth using models called **age-structure diagrams,** or population profiles. Age-structure diagrams show the population of a country broken down by gender and age group. Each bar in the age-structure diagram represents individuals within a 5-year group. Percentages of males are to the left of the center line and females to the right in each group.

Consider **Figure 5–13,** which compares the age structure of the U.S. population with that of Rwanda, a country in east-central Africa. In the United States, there are nearly equal numbers of people in each age group. This age structure predicts a slow but steady growth rate for the near future. In Rwanda, on the other hand, there are many more young children than teenagers, and many more teenagers than adults. This age structure predicts a population that will double in about 30 years.

CHECKPOINT *What are age-structure diagrams?*

▼ **Figure 5–13** These graphs show the age structure of the U.S. population and the Rwandan population. **Analyzing Data** ***How do the United States and Rwanda differ in the percentages of 10- to 14-year-olds in the population?***

Age-Structure Diagrams

U.S. POPULATION — Males | Females; Age (years): 80+, 75–79, 70–74, 65–69, 60–64, 55–59, 50–54, 45–49, 40–44, 35–39, 30–34, 25–29, 20–24, 15–19, 10–14, 5–9, 0–4; Percentage of Population: 8 7 6 5 4 3 2 1 0 1 2 3 4 5 6 7 8

RWANDAN POPULATION — Males | Females; Age (years): 80+, 75–79, 70–74, 65–69, 60–64, 55–59, 50–54, 45–49, 40–44, 35–39, 30–34, 25–29, 20–24, 15–19, 10–14, 5–9, 0–4; Percentage of Population: 8 7 6 5 4 3 2 1 0 1 2 3 4 5 6 7 8

FACTS AND FIGURES

Controlling human population

Two examples illustrate the complexities of controlling human population growth in developing nations. In India, government-sponsored population-control programs have not done well, due largely to family resistance. In desperation, the government enacted a law subjecting some men to compulsory sterilization. Public outrage was so great that the law was rescinded. India's population continues to grow.

China has instituted the most extensive family-planning program in the world. Couples who pledge to have only one child are given benefits, including better housing and salary bonuses. Couples who break this pledge lose the benefits. There have also been credible reports of women being forced to undergo abortions. These policies have curtailed explosive growth. Growth remains rapid, though, primarily because of the many women entering their reproductive years.

Build Science Skills

Interpreting Graphics Focus students' attention on the right-hand graph in Figure 5–13 and ask: **What overall pattern do you see in the structure of Rwanda's population?** *(Moving from old to young, every five-year group is larger than the older group above.)* **Why would this pattern predict a large population increase in the future?** *(Each five-year group of younger Rwandans has a greater number of females than the group just above. As a result, there will be more and more women bearing children in the future than there are today.)* **If you compare the top halves of the two graphs, what can you tell about Rwanda's population?** *(Death rates of older people are higher in Rwanda than in the United States. People in Rwanda do not live as long as people in the United States. In the United States, women tend to live longer than men; in Rwanda, men tend to live longer than women.)* L1 L2

Answers to . . .

CHECKPOINT *Models that graph the numbers of people in different age groups in a population*

Figure 5–11 *A population's death rate can be reduced by improved prenatal care, improved sanitation, and an increase in education.*

Figure 5–13 *In the United States, 10- to 14-year-olds make up about 6.5 percent of the population, and in Rwanda they make up about 14 percent of the population. The difference is about 7.5 percent—about 3.5 percentage points for males and 4 percentage points for females.*

5–3 (continued)

Future Population Growth

Build Science Skills

Making Judgments Ask: **What two opposing points of view about future population growth are expressed in the last paragraph?** *(One view is stated in the sentence that begins "Most ecologists suggest . . ." The other view is stated in the last sentence.)* Let students meet to brainstorm ideas about both viewpoints. Have two teams debate the viewpoints for the class. L1 L2

3 ASSESS

Evaluate Understanding

Have students write a paragraph on why the human population grew very slowly for many thousands of years and why the growth increased dramatically about 500 years ago.

Reteach

If students need help with assessment questions, have them reread the related text material and work in small groups to quiz one another and offer corrections.

Writing in Science

A typical response will note that the projected world population in 2050 will be over three times what it was in 1950. Students might write that the average annual growth rate was 1.47 percent in 1950 but is projected to be only 0.43 percent in 2050. Thus, though the world population will continue to grow through 2050, the rate of growth will diminish.

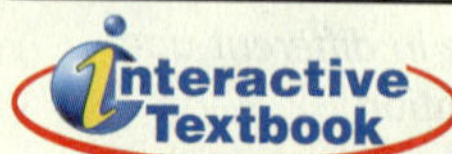

If your class subscribes to the iText, use it to review the Key Concepts in Section 5-3.

Answer to . . .

Figure 5–14 *Answers may vary. If the growth rate between 2040 and 2050 stays the same, the world population will be about 9.5 billion in 2060. If the growth rate falls—the trend shown on the table—the world population will be less than 9.5 billion.*

World Population: 1950–2050

Year	Average Annual Growth Rate (%)	Population
1950	1.47	2,555,360,972
1960	1.33	3,039,669,330
1962*	2.19	3,136,556,092
1963*	2.19	3,206,072,286
1970	2.07	3,708,067,105
1980	1.69	4,454,607,332
1990	1.58	5,275,407,789
2000	1.23	6,078,684,329
2010	1.06	6,812,009,338
2020	0.87	7,515,218,898
2030	0.68	8,127,277,506
2040	0.54	8,646,671,023
2050	0.43	9,078,850,714

*Highest growth rate during 100-year period

▲ **Figure 5–14** This table, based on actual and projected data from the U.S. Census Bureau, International Database, shows data on world population. **Predicting** ***Based on the projected trend between 2040 and 2050, what might the world population be in 2060?***

Future Population Growth

To predict how the world's human population will grow, demographers must consider many factors, including the age structure of each country and the prevalence of life-threatening diseases, such as AIDS, malaria, and cholera. The table in **Figure 5–14** shows statistics for world population growth from 1950 to 2000 with projected figures through the year 2050. Current projections suggest that by 2050, the world population may reach more than 9 billion people.

Will the human population grow at its current rate, or will it level out to a logistic growth curve and become stable? By 2050 the growth rate may level off or even decrease. This may happen if countries that are currently growing rapidly move toward the demographic transition. The figures in the table show that the growth rate in 2050 is projected to be 0.43 percent. This rate is a decrease from the peak growth rate of 2.19 percent, reached in the early 1960s.

A lower growth rate means that the human population will be growing more slowly over the next 50 years. But, because the growth rate is still larger than zero, our population will continue to grow. Most ecologists suggest that if this growth does not slow down even more, there could be serious damage to the environment as well as to the global economy. On the other hand, many economists assert that science, technology, and changes in society will control those negative impacts on the environment and economy.

ⓐ BI 6.c

5–3 Section Assessment

1. **Key Concept** Describe the general trend of human population growth that has occurred over time.
2. **Key Concept** What factors explain why populations in different countries grow at different rates?
3. What is demography?
4. Describe the demographic transition and explain how it might affect a country's population growth rate.
5. **Critical Thinking** **Evaluating** Why do you think age-structure diagrams can help predict future population trends?

Writing in Science

Explanatory Writing
Write a paragraph on the trends in the growth of world population from 1950 to 2050. Be sure to distinguish between population growth and population growth rate. *Hint:* Refer to **Figure 5–14** to help with your explanation.

5–3 Section Assessment

1. For tens of thousands of years, the human population grew very slowly. Then, about 500 years ago, the population started to grow exponentially and increased dramatically.
2. Birthrates, death rates, and the age structure of a population
3. The scientific study of human populations
4. When the demographic transition begins, the birthrate and the death rate are high. Then, the death rate drops while the birthrate remains high. Finally, the birthrate also drops. After the demographic transition, a population's growth rate would be very low, and growth could even stop.
5. Age-structure diagrams include data on younger individuals in age groups that will contribute to population growth as members of those groups mature.

7IIE 7.c, BIIE 1.e, BIIE 1.i

Investigating the Growth of a Population of Bacteria

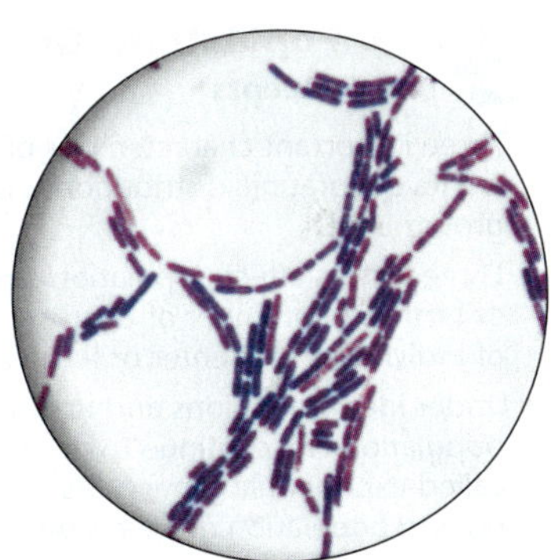

Bacteria are convenient for laboratory studies of populations because large numbers of bacteria live in a very small space and bacteria reproduce rapidly. In this investigation, you will examine the growth of a bacterial culture.

Problem What happens to a population that depends on limited resources?

Materials

- 2 lima beans
- 2 dropper pipettes
- 100-mL beaker
- coverslips
- microscope slides
- 10-mL graduated cylinder
- 100-mL graduated cylinder
- methylene blue stain
- microscope
- test-tube rack
- 4 test tubes
- aluminum foil

Skills Calculating, Using Tables and Graphs

Procedure

1. Before you begin, review the rules for sterile procedure with your teacher.
2. Wash your hands. Put on your plastic gloves. Then, to start a bacterial culture, put 2 lima beans into a 100-mL beaker. Add 50 mL of water. Allow this mixture to sit for 48 hours.
3. Construct a data table with four columns and five blank rows. At the top of the table, label the columns "Day," "Bacteria Observed," "Dilution Factor," and "Bacteria Present."
4. After 48 hours, use a dropper pipette to place a drop of the culture on a microscope slide. Add a coverslip. Place a drop of methylene blue stain on the slide next to the coverslip. Lightly touch a paper towel on the opposite side of the coverslip to draw the stain under the coverslip.
5. Use the high-power objective of a microscope to locate some bacteria. If you can count the bacteria in your field of view, go to step 7. If there are too many bacteria to count, go to step 6.
6. Use a dropper pipette to put 1 mL of the culture into a 10-mL graduated cylinder. Add 9 mL of water to the graduated cylinder. Empty the graduated cylinder into a test tube. This procedure dilutes the culture by a factor of 10. Examine the diluted sample under the microscope as in step 5. If there are still too many bacteria to count, dilute the sample again in the same way. Stop diluting when you can count the bacteria. Each time you dilute, multiply the dilution by 10.
7. Record the number of bacteria and the dilution factor in your data table. If you did not dilute, the dilution factor is 1. To determine the number of bacteria present, multiply the number of bacteria you observed by the dilution factor.
8. Cover the beaker with aluminum foil and set it aside overnight. Wash your hands thoroughly with soap and warm water when you are finished.
9. **Predicting** Record a prediction of how the population of bacteria will change.
10. Repeat steps 5 through 8 every day for 5 days.

Analyze and Conclude

1. **Using Tables and Graphs** Make a graph of the data from your data table. When did the population grow most quickly? Most slowly?
2. **Drawing Conclusions** How can you explain the changes in population growth?
3. **Inferring** What caused the changes in the population growth rate?

Go Further

Designing Experiments Design an experiment to investigate how a change in the food supply affects the growth of a bacterial population. With your teacher's approval, carry out your experiment.

Exploration

7IIE 7.c, BIIE 1.e, BIIE 1.i

Objective Students will be able to infer how limited resources affect a bacteria population. L2 L3

Skills Focus Calculating, Using Tables and Graphs

Time 5 minutes for initial setup, then 10–20 minutes each day for five days, 30 minutes on sixth day

Safety Read the safety information in the MSDS for methylene blue before doing the lab.

Pre-Lab Discussion Remind students that they saw a graph showing the growth of a bacteria population early in this chapter. Ask: **Did the graph's curve indicate exponential growth or logistic growth?** *(Exponential growth)* If students cannot recall the term, let them look back at page 121. Then, have students read the procedure, and address any questions they have.

Teaching Tips

- If students have limited experience using a microscope, show them the correct technique. Also demonstrate how to prepare the slide, add the stain, and use the dropper pipette.
- As students conduct their counts in steps 3–5, circulate among them to help with any processes that cause difficulty.

Procedure

3. You may want to draw a sample data table on the board or an overhead transparency for students to copy.
5. Point out the photograph of bacteria on this page, which will give students an idea of what to look for.
9. Remind students to record their predictions. Most students will probably predict that the bacteria population will increase.

Expected Outcome During the first few days, the bacteria count will increase. However, at some point near the end of the observation period, bacteria will start to die off as toxic wastes accumulate and the food supply becomes exhausted.

Analyze and Conclude

1. In a typical logistic pattern, the bacteria population will grow quickly at first and then will slow, stop, or decrease.
2. As the population grew, it consumed the food supply and produced toxic wastes that reduced growth.
3. The accumulation of toxic wastes and consumption of the food supply reduced population growth. Organisms that prey on bacteria also may have begun to infiltrate the culture.

Go Further

Check students' plans to make sure that their experiments will not cause rampant overgrowth of bacteria or development of mold.

Chapter 5 Study Guide

Study Tip

Have students work in pairs to review the Key Concepts and the Vocabulary for each section. Students might first quiz each other on the Key Concepts, with one student reading the text statement but omitting the key terms, and the other student supplying the terms. For the first Key Concept in Section 5–1, for example, the first student would say, "The main characteristics of a population are . . .," and the second student would identify the characteristics. A similar approach can be used to review Vocabulary.

Thinking Visually

1. Density-dependent factors
2. Density-independent factors
3. Competition
4. Unusual weather or seasonal cycles

Chapter 5 Assessment

Reviewing Content

1. c
2. c
3. b
4. b
5. b
6. a
7. b
8. a
9. d
10. a

Understanding Concepts

11. The movement of individuals into an area occupied by an existing population is called immigration. Emigration occurs when individuals move out of a population.

12. The graphs should show the characteristic J-shape of exponential population growth as illustrated in Figure 5–3 on page 121.

13. Logistic growth occurs when a population's growth rate slows or stops following a period of exponential growth. Population growth may slow down when the birthrate decreases or the death rate increases, or when both events occur at the same rate. Population growth may also slow down when the rate of immigration decreases, the rate of emigration increases, or both.

14. Carrying capacity represents the largest number of individuals that a given environment can support. Examples will vary.

Chapter 5 Study Guide

5–1 How Populations Grow

Key Concepts BI 6.b, BI 6.c

- Three important characteristics of a population are its geographic distribution, density, and growth rate.
- Three factors affect population size: the number of births, the number of deaths, and the number of individuals that enter or leave the population.
- Under ideal conditions and unlimited resources, a population will continue to grow in a pattern called exponential growth. As resources are used up and population growth slows or stops, the population exhibits logistic growth.

Vocabulary

population density, p. 119
immigration, p. 120
emigration, p. 120
exponential growth, p. 121
logistic growth, p. 122
carrying capacity, p. 122

5–2 Limits to Growth

Key Concepts  BI 6.c

- Density-dependent limiting factors include competition, predation, parasitism, and disease.
- Unusual weather, natural disasters, seasonal cycles, and certain human activities—such as damming rivers and clear-cutting forests—are all examples of density-independent limiting factors.

Vocabulary

limiting factor, p. 124
density-dependent limiting factor, p. 125
predator-prey relationship, p. 126
density-independent limiting factor, p. 127

5–3 Human Population Growth

Key Concepts  BI 6.c

- Like the populations of many other living organisms, the size of the human population tends to increase with time.
- The characteristics of populations, and the social and economic factors that affect them, explain why some countries have high population growth rates while populations of other countries grow slowly or not at all.

Vocabulary

demography, p. 130
demographic transition, p. 130
age-structure diagram, p. 131

Thinking Visually

Using information from this chapter, complete the following concept map:

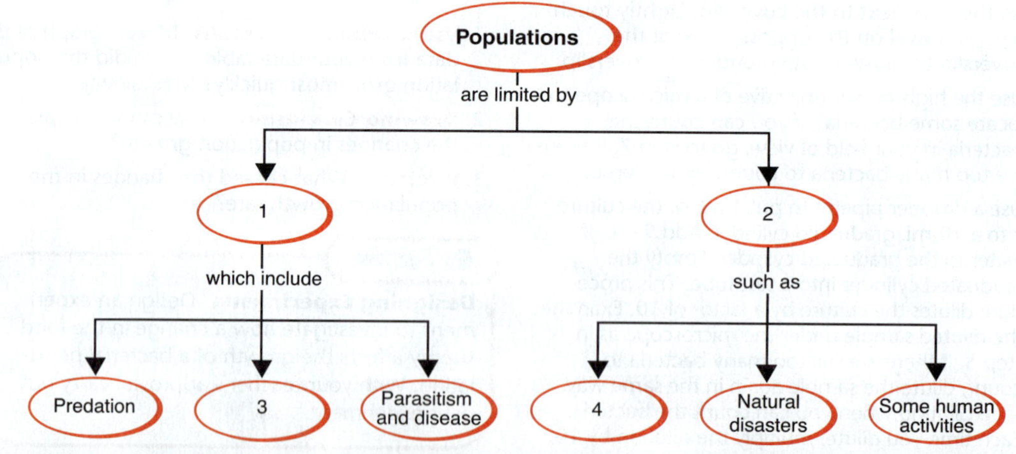

SECTION RESOURCES

Print:

- ***Teaching Resources,*** Chapter Vocabulary Review, Graphic Organizer, Chapter 5 Tests: Levels A and B

Technology:

- ***Computer Test Bank,*** Chapter 5 Test
- ***iText,*** Chapter 5 Assessment

Chapter 5 Assessment

Interactive textbook with assessment at PHSchool.com 

Reviewing Content

Choose the letter that best answers the question or completes the statement.

1. The number of individuals of a single species per unit area is known as
   a. carrying capacity. c. population density.
   b. logistic growth. d. population growth rate.
2. The movement of individuals into an area is called
   a. demography. c. immigration.
   b. carrying capacity. d. emigration.
3. The range or area occupied by a population is its
   a. growth rate.
   b. geographic distribution.
   c. age structure.
   d. population density.
4. The graph below represents

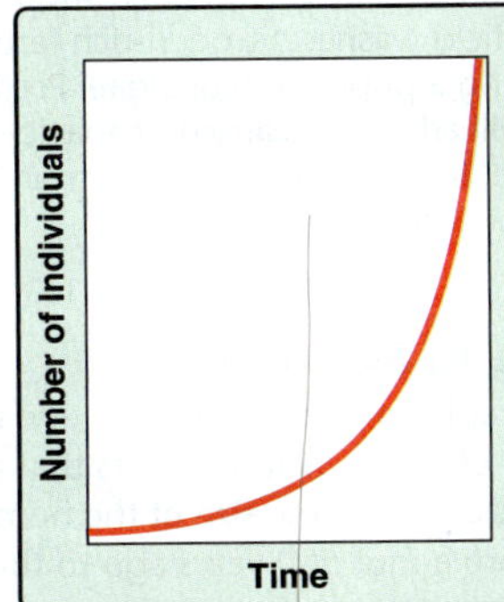

   a. carrying capacity.
   b. exponential growth.
   c. logistic growth.
   d. limiting factors.
5. The maximum number of organisms of a particular species that can be supported by an environment is called
   a. logistic growth.
   b. carrying capacity.
   c. exponential growth.
   d. population density.
6. If a population grows larger than the carrying capacity of its environment, the
   a. death rate may rise.
   b. birthrate may rise.
   c. death rate may fall.
   d. immigration rate may increase.
7. Density-independent limiting factors include
   a. predation. c. competition.
   b. hurricanes. d. parasitism.
8. A limiting factor that depends on population size is called a
   a. density-dependent limiting factor.
   b. density-independent limiting factor.
   c. predator-prey relationship.
   d. parasitic relationship.
9. The scientific study of human populations is called
   a. immigration.
   b. emigration.
   c. demographic transition.
   d. demography.
10. The demographic transition is complete when
   a. population growth stops.
   b. the birthrate is greater than the death rate.
   c. the death rate begins to fall.
   d. the death rate is greater than the birthrate.

Understanding Concepts

11. Distinguish between immigration and emigration.
12. Sketch the exponential growth curve of a hypothetical population.
13. Describe the conditions under which logistic growth occurs.
14. What is carrying capacity? Give an example.
15. How might the introduction of a limiting nutrient in a pond affect the carrying capacity of that pond?
16. Describe the long-term effects of competition on populations of two different species competing for the same resources.
17. Describe how a predator-prey relationship can be a mechanism of population control.
18. How do parasites serve as a density-dependent limiting factor?
19. Explain how density-independent limiting factors can affect populations.
20. How can you account for the fact that the human population has grown more rapidly during the past 500 years than throughout its previous history?
21. What is the significance of the demographic transition in studies of the human population?
22. How does the age structure of a population affect its growth rate?
23. Explain how a limited resource can affect the survival of a species. Give a specific example.

TIME SAVER HOMEWORK GUIDE

Section:	Questions:
Section 5–1	1–6, 11–14, 28
Section 5–2	7, 8, 15–19, 23–25, 29–31
Section 5–3	9, 10, 20–22, 26, 27, 32

Interactive Textbook

Your students can go online to access an interactive version of the Student Edition and a self-test.

(Continued from page 134)

15. The addition of a limiting nutrient to a pond would most likely cause an increase in the carrying capacity of those species directly dependent on that nutrient.

16. When two species compete for the same resources, both species are under pressure to change in ways that decrease their competition. Over time, the species may evolve to occupy separate niches.

17. The rise in the population of the prey would normally be followed by a rise in the predator population. As the population of predators rises, the population of prey declines. Since there is less prey available, the population of predators also declines. This cycle repeats itself and functions as a means of population control.

18. Parasites take nourishment from their hosts, often weakening them and causing disease or death.

19. Density-independent factors have similar effects on all individuals in a population regardless of the population's density. Examples include the effects of a prolonged drought, a killing frost, or a flood.

20. Human population began growing more rapidly 500 years ago due to favorable growth conditions. Agriculture and industry made life easier. The world's food supply became more reliable. Improved sanitation, medicine, and healthcare dramatically reduced the death rate. Simultaneously, the birthrate remained high.

21. Demographic transition is a prediction of population changes based on an analysis of changes in birthrate and death rate.

22. Populations with nearly equal numbers of people in each age group will have a slow but steady growth rate for the near future. Populations with many more young children than teenagers, and many more teenagers than adults, will grow at a fast rate.

23. A limited resource can affect the survival of a species if that species depends on the resource as part of its habitat. Most students will describe destruction of panda habitat.

Chapter 5 Assessment

Critical Thinking

24. Since the communicable virus is more likely to spread when people are crowded together, it is density-dependent.

25. In most cases, it will have a greater effect on the population of a small ecosystem. A small population will be more susceptible to serious damage from a density-independent limiting factor such as a flood or storm.

26. Because there are relatively small numbers of individuals in younger age groups, the population of Sweden is likely to stay about the same or even decline over the next 50 years.

27. The growth curve of a small town made up mostly of senior citizens would show a decline in population. A growth curve of a small town made up of newly married couples would show an increase in population.

28. The carrying capacity of a population is affected by limiting factors such as competition, predation, parasitism, disease, climate, drought, and human disturbances. Likewise, the carrying capacity of a city's roads depends on such limiting factors as the number and width of roads, the number of intersections, and the number of vehicles traveling on the road.

29. If there is a sudden increase in food for the prey, the population of predators would probably increase as well. An increase in food for prey would allow for a greater number of prey. More predators would then be supported.

30. In parasitic and predator-prey relationships, one member of the relationship benefits, while the other is harmed or killed.

31. The population of fish would most likely decrease due to a decrease in the size of the ecosystem. The decreased size would provide a smaller amount of resources.

32. A demographer would ask questions such as: "Have changes in society, such as access to healthcare and medicines, lowered the death rate?" and "Does the birthrate remain high, or are there signs that the birthrate is falling?"

Chapter 5 Assessment

Critical Thinking

24. **Applying Concepts** Why might a contagious virus that causes a fatal disease be considered a density-dependent limiting factor?

25. **Inferring** Would a density-independent limiting factor have more of an effect on population size in a large ecosystem or in a small ecosystem? Explain.

26. **Predicting** Study the age-structure diagram for Sweden below. Then, predict how Sweden's rate of population growth is likely to change over the next 50 years.

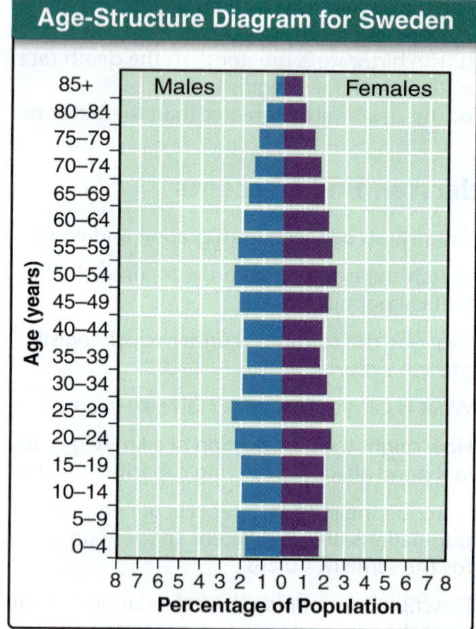

27. **Comparing and Contrasting** Describe the most likely population growth curve you would expect to see in a small town made up mainly of senior citizens. Compare this growth curve to that of a small town made up of newly married couples in their twenties.

28. **Using Analogies** How is the carrying capacity of a city's roads similar to the carrying capacity of an ecosystem?

29. **Predicting** What will happen to a population of predators if there is a sudden increase in food for the prey? Explain.

30. **Comparing and Contrasting** How is the relationship between parasites and their hosts similar to a predator-prey relationship?

31. **Applying Concepts** If the water level of a river drops, how might that affect a fish population living in that river?

32. **Asking Questions** What questions would a demographer need to answer in order to determine whether a country is approaching the demographic transition?

Focus on the BIG Idea

Science, Technology, and Society Nitrogen is a limiting factor in aquatic ecosystems. Suppose that runoff from a field washes nitrogen-rich fertilizer into a pond containing a population of algae. Predict how the fertilizer will affect the carrying capacity of the pond for algae. Refer to the information on limiting nutrients in Section 3–3.

Writing in Science

Write a paragraph on populations. Include the characteristics of a population, factors that affect its size, and the changes in the size of the human population from about 500 years ago to the present. Give a projection on how large the world population might be in the year 2050 and on how the growth rate in 2050 might compare to that in 2000. (*Hint:* Outline your ideas before you begin to write.)

Performance-Based Assessment

Multimedia Presentation Create a visual presentation that describes how limiting factors regulate population growth. Be sure to distinguish between density-dependent limiting factors and density-independent limiting factors.

For: An interactive self-test
Visit: PHSchool.com
Web Code: cba-2050

Focus on the BIG Idea

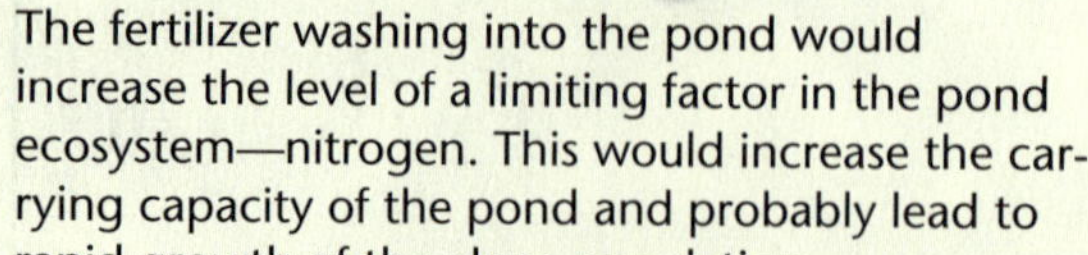

The fertilizer washing into the pond would increase the level of a limiting factor in the pond ecosystem—nitrogen. This would increase the carrying capacity of the pond and probably lead to rapid growth of the algae population.

Writing in Science

Students' paragraphs will vary. All should include mention of population density; carrying capacity; types of growth; and limiting factors, both density-dependent and density-independent. Students should also describe changes in the human population, drawing upon the text and figures in Section 5–3 for support for their descriptions. Using data in Figure 5–14, students should note that the projected population in 2050 is 9,078,850,714 and that the growth rate in 2050 is projected to be 0.43 percent annually, compared with an average annual growth rate of 1.23 percent in 2000.

Standards Practice

Online at PHSchool.com

Test-Taking Tip To answer questions that have different combinations of Roman numerals as answer choices, you must evaluate each Roman numeral separately in relation to the question. Then, look to see which answer choice corresponds to the numerals you have selected.

Directions: Choose the letter that best answers the question or completes the statement.

1. The total change in a population's size over time is BIIE 6.c
   A immigration.
   B emigration.
   C birthrate and death rate.
   D population growth rate.
2. Which factors increase the size of a population? BIIE 6.c
   A emigration
   B birthrate
   C carrying capacity
   D death rate
3. Which of the following is NOT an example of a density-dependent limiting factor?
   A natural disasters
   B predators
   C parasites
   D competitors
4. A hurricane nearly wipes out a population of insects. This is an example of a
   A demographic transition.
   B density-dependent limiting factor.
   C density-independent limiting factor.
   D predation.
5. Which of the following are necessary to complete the demographic transition?
   A the birthrate increases
   B the death rate decreases
   C the birthrate decreases
   D both B and C
6. In the presence of unlimited resources and in the absence of disease and predation, what will probably happen to a bacterial population?
   A logistic growth
   B exponential growth
   C endangerment
   D extinction

Questions 7–9 Use the graph below to answer the following questions.

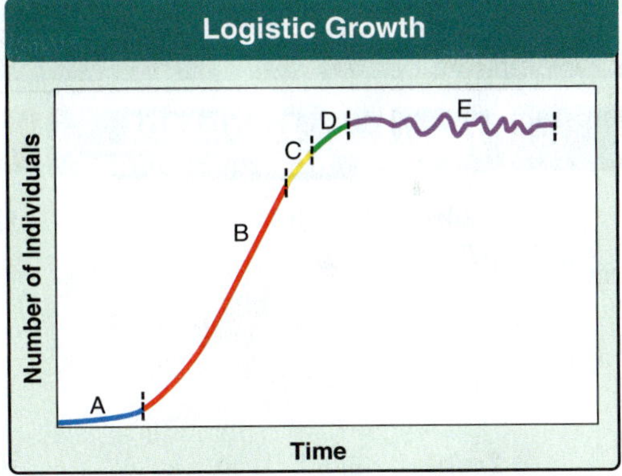

7. What is true of the time interval marked E in the graph?
   A Carrying capacity has been reached.
   B Birthrate is greater than the death rate.
   C Population is growing.
   D The population is declining.
8. Which time interval(s) in the graph shows exponential growth?
   A D and E
   B A and B
   C C and D
   D E only
9. Which time interval(s) in the graph depicts the effects of limiting factors on population?
   A A only
   B A and B
   C C, D, and E
   D C and D

Questions 10–13 Each of the lettered choices below refers to the following numbered statements. Select the best lettered choice. A choice may be used once, more than once, or not at all.

A Limiting factor
B Carrying capacity
C Exponential growth
D Population density

10. Birthrate = death rate BIIE 6.c
11. Slows the growth of a population BIIE 6.c
12. Number of individuals per unit area
13. Population grows at a constant rate

Standards Practice

1. D	5. D	9. C	13. C
2. B	6. B	10. B	
3. A	7. A	11. A	
4. C	8. C	12. D	

Online at PHSchool.com

Have students check their understanding of the chapter by logging onto Success Tracker.

Performance-Based Assessment

Visuals will vary but should include density-independent factors, such as fire, seasonal cycles, and natural disasters, and density-dependent factors, such as competition, predation, parasitism, and disease.

Your students can independently test their knowledge of the chapter and print out their test results for your files.

Chapter Planner 6 Humans in the Biosphere

Section and Section Objectives	Time	STANDARDS NCLB	STANDARDS Biology	Activities and Labs
6–1 A Changing Landscape, pp. 139–143 **6.1.1** ***Describe*** human activities that can affect the biosphere.	1 period (1/2 block)	BI 6.b		**SE:** ***Inquiry Activity,*** What happens to household trash?, p. 138 L1 L2
6–2 Renewable and Nonrenewable Resources, pp. 144–149 **6.2.1** ***Explain*** how environmental resources are classified. **6.2.2** ***Identify*** the characteristics of sustainable development. **6.2.3** ***Describe*** how human activities affect land, air, and water resources.	2 periods (1 block)	BI 6.b		**TE:** ***Demonstration,*** p. 148 L1 L2 **TE:** ***Build Science Skills,*** p. 148 L2 L3 **LMA:** Chapter 6 Lab L2 L3
6–3 Biodiversity, pp. 150–156 **6.3.1** ***Define*** biodiversity and explain its value. **6.3.2** ***Identify*** current threats to biodiversity. **6.3.3** ***Describe*** the goal of conservation biology.	2 periods (1 block)	BI 6.a, BI 6.b	*BI 6.g	**TE:** ***Build Science Skills,*** p. 151 L2 **SE:** ***Quick Lab,*** How does biological magnification occur?, p. 153 L1 L2 **SE:** ***Biology and History,*** Success in Conservation, pp. 154–155 L2 **TE:** ***Build Science Skills,*** p. 155 L1 L2
6–4 Charting a Course for the Future, pp. 157–160 **6.4.1** ***Describe*** two types of global change that are of concern to biologists.	1 period (1/2 block)	BI 6.b		**SE:** ***Analyzing Data,*** Banning CFCs, p. 158 L2 L3 **SE:** ***Design an Experiment,*** Observing the Effects of Acid Rain, p. 161 L2 **LMB:** Chapter 6 Lab L1 L2 **PLM:** Observing the Effects of Acid Rain L1 L2 L3
Chapter Assessment, pp. 162–165	1 period (1/2 block)			

ACTIVITY PLANNER

SE: *Inquiry Activity*, p. 138; 20 min.; bag containing dry trash

TE: *Demonstration*, p. 148; 15 min.; large freezer bag filled with car exhaust

TE: *Build Science Skills*, p. 148; 15 min.; samples of rainwater, sample of tapwater, litmus paper

TE: *Build Science Skills*, p. 151; 5 min.; object made of ivory

SE: *Quick Lab*, p. 153; 15 min.; paper cups (3 small, 1 medium, and 1 large), 1 L-beaker, sand, 12 beads, masking tape

TE: *Build Science Skills*, p. 155; 20 min.; large sheets of paper

SE: *Design an Experiment*, p. 161; 45 min. to design and set up experiment, 5 min./day for observation and recording; diluted sulfuric acid, filter paper, glass-marking pencil, 2 petri dishes, 100-mL graduated cylinder, 100 seeds (mustard or radish), pH paper, 2 100-mL beakers, hand lens

PLANNING KEY

Ability Levels
for students performing . . .
below grade level L1
at grade level L2
above grade level L3

Print Components

SE	Student Edition
TE	Teacher's Edition
RSW	Reading & Study Workbook A
ARSW	Adapted Reading & Study Workbook B
TR	Teaching Resources
IF	Investigations in Forensics
LA	Lab Assessment
BTM	Biotechnology Manual
IDM	Issues and Decision Making
LW	Lab Worksheets
LMA	Laboratory Manual A
LMB	Laboratory Manual B

Tech Components

CTB	Computer Test Bank
BD	BioDetectives DVD
TP	Transparencies Plus
PLM	Probeware Lab Manual
ABC	ABC DVD Library
LS	Lab Simulations
VL	Virtual Labs

Interactive textbook with assessment at PHSchool.com

Program Resources	Assessment	Media and Technology
TR: Lesson Plan 6–1, Section Summary, p. 134 L1, p. 142 L2, Worksheets, pp. 144–145 L2 **RSW:** Section 6–1 L2 **IDM:** Issues and Decisions 29 L2 L3	**SE:** 6–1 Section Assessment, p. 143 **TR:** Section Review 6–1	**iText:** Section 6–1 **TP:** 6–1 Interest Grabber, Section Outline, Concept Map
TR: Lesson Plan 6–2, Section Summary, p. 134 L1, p. 142 L2, Worksheets, p. 137 L1, pp. 146–148 L2, Enrichment L3 **RSW:** Section 6–2 L2 **ARSW:** Section 6–2 L1 **IDM:** Issues and Decisions 21, 23, 27, 31 L2 L3	**SE:** 6–2 Section Assessment, p. 149 **TR:** Section Review 6–2	**iText:** Section 6–2 **TP:** 6–2 Interest Grabber, Section Outline, Growth of Fish Catch, Figure 6–12
TR: Lesson Plan 6–3, Section Summary, p. 135 L1, p. 143 L2, Worksheets, pp. 138–139 L1, pp. 149–151 L2 **RSW:** Section 6–3 L2 **ARSW:** Section 6–3 L1 **IDM:** Issues and Decisions 22, 25, 26, 30, 32, 34, 36 L2 L3	**SE:** 6–3 Section Assessment, p. 156 **TR:** Section Review 6–3	**iText:** Section 6–3 **TP:** 6–3 Interest Grabber, Section Outline, Species Diversity, Figure 6–16
TR: Lesson Plan 6–4, Section Summary, p. 136 L1, p. 143 L2, Worksheets, p. 140 L1, pp. 152–153 L2 **LW:** Chapter 6 Exploration L1 L2 L3 **RSW:** Section 6–4 L2 **ARSW:** Section 6–4 L1 **IDM:** Issues and Decisions 1, 3, 50 L2 L3	**SE:** 6–4 Section Assessment, p. 160 **TR:** Section Review 6–4	**iText:** Section 6–4 **TP:** 6–4 Interest Grabber, Section Outline, Sustainable Agriculture, Figure 6–22
	SE: Chapter 6 Assessment, pp. 162–165 **TR:** Chapter Vocabulary Review, Graphic Organizer, Chapter 6 Test **LA:** Laboratory Assessment 2	**iText:** Chapter 6 Assessment **CTB:** Chapter 6 Test

Go Online
Students can do research, share data, and test their knowledge online.

PRESSED FOR TIME?

To Preview the Chapter
- Have students preview the major headings (in blue) and subheadings (green) in all three sections, and then review the following figures and answer any caption questions: Figures 6–8, 6–13, 6–19, and 6–20.

To Cover the Chapter Quickly
- Have students read pages 140–143 in Section 6–1, pages 144–145 in Section 6–2, pages 150–153 in Section 6–3, and all of Section 6–4.
- Assign question 1 in 6–1 Section Assessment, questions 1 and 2 in 6–2 Section Assessment, questions 1 and 2 in 6–3 Section Assessment, and question 1 in 6–4 Section Assessment. Assign questions 1–10 in Chapter 6 Standards Practice.

To Review the Chapter
- Assign Sections 6–1 through 6–4 in the Reading and Study Workbook or the Adapted Reading and Study Workbook.
- Assign the Chapter Vocabulary Review for Chapter 6 in Teaching Resources.

CHAPTER 6

ENGAGE/EXPLORE

Inquiry Activity

Objective Students will be able to suggest ways to reduce the amount of household trash produced. L1 L2

Skill Focus Analyzing Data, Predicting, Evaluating

Materials bag of dry trash

Time 20 minutes

Advance Prep For each group, prepare a large plastic garbage bag containing about 2 kg of dry trash, apportioned as follows: 0.94 kg paper and cardboard; 0.34 kg leaves and yard clippings; 0.15 kg glass; 0.18 kg metal; 0.22 kg plastic; and 0.17 kg wood. Make sure all glass, metal, and wood items are in the form of safe, unbroken items and all containers are empty and clean.

Safety Have students wear safety goggles, aprons, and plastic gloves.

Expected Outcome Students will sort the items and offer reasonable explanations for their choices.

Think About It

1. About half the material is paper and paper products. Yard waste is about 17 percent, and metal, glass, and plastic each account for about 10 percent. This is a typical household mixture, although the proportions may vary.
2. Answers may vary. Students might suggest their trash is buried, burned, or recycled. Trash can affect living things by poisoning them, harming them, or ruining habitats.
3. Students might suggest recycling, reducing their use of some materials, and reusing some items.

Brain Teaser

Challenge each student group to choose one item from the trash they sorted and list as many ways as they can think of for reusing the item. Encourage students to be creative in devising possible uses. Have groups share their ideas with the class.

CHAPTER 6

Humans in the Biosphere

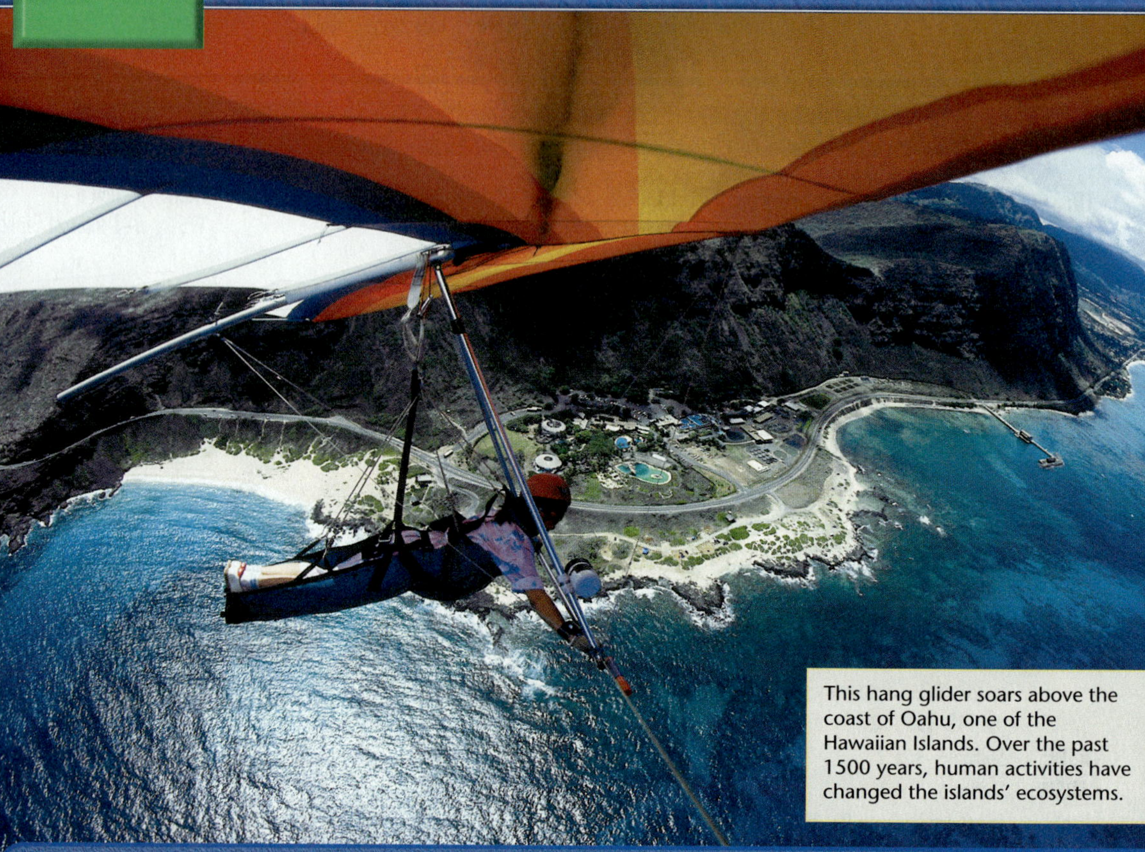

This hang glider soars above the coast of Oahu, one of the Hawaiian Islands. Over the past 1500 years, human activities have changed the islands' ecosystems.

Inquiry Activity

What happens to household trash?

Procedure   

1. Examine the contents of a bag containing roughly the amount of dry trash produced per person each day in the United States.
2. Sort the trash into items that can be reused, items that can be recycled, items that can be composted, and items that must be discarded because they cannot be recycled or composted.

Think About It

1. **Analyzing Data** Which materials make up most of the trash? Does this reflect the amount and types of trash you produce?
2. **Predicting** What do you think happens to the trash you produce? Think of at least three ways in which trash can have an impact on living things.
3. **Evaluating** List three ways you can reduce the amount of trash you produce.

FACTS AND FIGURES

Ecologists study islands

The study of the biology of islands, such as the Hawaiian Islands shown in the photo above, is one of many subspecialties of biology. Such a study is often called island biogeography. In this context, an *island* doesn't necessarily designate an ocean island. Rather, an island is any habitat surrounded by an environment that is unsuitable for the species that live within the island environment. Thus, islands include ocean islands, lake islands, mountain peaks, and even fragments of forests surrounded by suburbs. Such islands, because of their isolation and limited size, provide great places to study factors that affect the biodiversity of environments. The Hawaiian Islands—the most isolated archipelago in the world—have also been fertile ground for another branch of biology, historical biogeography, the study of the evolutionary history of groups of organisms.

6–1 A Changing Landscape

BI 6.b. Students know how to analyze changes in an ecosystem resulting from changes in climate, human activity, introduction of nonnative species, or changes in population size.

About 1600 years ago, people from Polynesia began settling in the islands of Hawaii. These island people were accustomed to limited living space, so they farmed and fished with limited resources in mind. To cut down a coconut palm, a person had to plant two palm trees in its place. Fishing for certain species was prohibited during the season in which the fishes reproduce. The first Hawaiians maintained the ecosystem in such a way that it continued to provide fresh water, fertile soil, and the other resources they needed to survive. Their society was self-sufficient.

Even though they respected the land, these early settlers changed Hawaii's ecology. They cleared forests for farmland and introduced nonnative crop plants, along with animals such as pigs and rats. Eventually, as a result of the Polynesian settlers' activities, many native plants and animals became extinct.

Beginning in the late 1700s, new settlers began to arrive in Hawaii. These new settlers, who eventually included Americans, Europeans, and Asians, continued the process of change begun by the Polynesians. For example, farmers cleared vast areas to grow sugar cane, pineapples, and other crops, and they used large amounts of water for agriculture.

Hawaii today is very different from the islands the Polynesians settled. Many native species, such as the bird in **Figure 6–1**, are becoming scarce. Although the islands boast some of the wettest spots on Earth, agricultural practices have seriously depleted drinking water in places. Because of overfishing, some fish species that were once common are now rare. And Hawaiians today, unlike their Polynesian predecessors, must import some necessities, including part of their food, that were once provided by local ecosystems.

Guide for Reading

Key Concept

- What types of human activities can affect the biosphere?

Vocabulary

agriculture
monoculture
green revolution

Reading Strategy: Finding Main Ideas As you read, make a list of facts that support the statement "The spreading influence of humans can and does affect the biosphere."

Earth as an Island

The history of humans in Hawaii offers an important lesson for the twenty-first century. In a sense, Earth, too, is an island. All of the organisms—including humans—that live on Earth share a limited resource base and depend on it for their long-term survival. We all rely on the natural ecological processes that sustain these resources.

To protect these resources, we need to understand how humans interact with the biosphere. You have learned about energy flow, chemical cycling, climate, and population-limiting factors. You must also understand how scientific models can be used to make predictions about complex systems. Studies of islands like Hawaii are important to people who don't live on an island—or don't think they do.

▼ **Figure 6–1** The iiwi, or Hawaiian honeycreeper, is one of the most beautiful birds in Hawaii. Like many native species in Hawaii, the iiwi is becoming scarce. Disease, habitat loss, and predation by introduced animals have taken their toll on the species. **Inferring** *Based on the photograph, what can you infer about the iiwi's niche?*

SECTION RESOURCES

Print:

- ***Teaching Resources,*** Lesson Plan 6–1, Adapted Section Summary 6–1, Section Summary 6–1, Worksheets 6–1, Section Review 6–1
- ***Reading and Study Workbook A,*** Section 6–1
- ***Issues and Decision Making,*** Issues and Decisions 29

Technology:

- ***iText,*** Section 6–1
- ***Transparencies Plus,*** Section 6–1

Section 6–1

BI 6.b

1 FOCUS

Objective

6.1.1 ***Describe*** human activities that can affect the biosphere.

Guide for Reading

Vocabulary Preview

Suggest that students use Word Origins on page 141 and a dictionary to derive the literal meaning of the Vocabulary term *monoculture.*

Reading Strategy

To help students focus on main ideas that support the statement, have them divide a sheet of paper into two columns. In the first column, they can write the types of human activities identified in this section as affecting the biosphere. In the second column, they can write sentences or phrases found in the text that explain how those activities affect the biosphere.

2 INSTRUCT

Earth as an Island

Build Science Skills

Predicting Have students recall the definition of *carrying capacity,* introduced in Chapter 5. *(Carrying capacity is the largest number of individuals that an environment can support.)* Then, explain that many biologists feel that in the not-too-distant future, the human population may reach or exceed the carrying capacity of Earth. Ask: **What do you think would be the consequences of exceeding Earth's carrying capacity for the human population?** *(Students will probably mention overcrowding; shortages of food, water, and fuel; malnutrition; increased disease; and the like.)* L1 L2

Answer to . . .

Figure 6–1 *Based on the unusual shape of its beak, the bird seems to depend on nectar that is deep within flowers.*

6–1 (continued)

Human Activities

Build Science Skills

Applying Concepts Point out that although many of the factors affecting the global environment are not under our control, each person can make a difference in the quality of the environment. Encourage students to list environmental problems and then brainstorm actions that they and their families can take to help resolve those problems. Students' suggestions might include conserving resources by recycling and by reducing total consumption, educating others about the issues, and voting on legislation. L1 L2

Hunting and Gathering

Build Science Skills

Inferring Ask: **What are some of the disadvantages of relying on hunting and gathering to obtain all the food you need?** *(Sample answers: You may have to move your home to follow animals that are used for food. Without being cared for by humans, plants may die from drought.)* L2

▲ **Figure 6–2** People of the Paleolithic, or Stone Age, relied on hunting and gathering for their existence. This cave painting from Northern Spain shows ancient hunters slaying a herd of deer with bows and arrows.  **Hunting and gathering are among the many human activities that have changed the biosphere.**

ⓐ BI 6.b

▼ **Figure 6–3** Like his Stone Age predecessors, this modern subsistence hunter from the Asmat tribe in New Guinea uses bows and spears. Other subsistence hunters may use modern tools like guns or motorized vehicles. **Predicting** ***What effects might subsistence hunters have on the environment in which they live?***

Human Activities

Like all organisms, we humans participate in food webs and chemical cycles. We depend on these ecological life-support systems to provide breathable air, drinkable water, and fertile soil that supports farming. In addition, ecosystem processes provide us with "services" such as storage and recycling of nutrients. Ecologists refer to these necessities as "ecosystem goods and services" because they have real value to us as individuals and societies. If we do not get these goods and services from the environment, we will need to spend money to produce them.

CA ⓐ Since we depend on ecosystem goods and services, we must be aware that human activities can change local and global environments. According to a recent study, global human activities use as much energy, and transport almost as much material, as all Earth's other multicellular species combined. We have become the most important source of environmental change on the planet. **Among human activities that affect the biosphere are hunting and gathering, agriculture, industry, and urban development.** We do not yet fully understand how human activities affect ecosystems. Happily, ecological research can help us understand and manage our impact on the environment.

Hunting and Gathering

For most of human history, our ancestors obtained food by hunting and gathering. They hunted birds and mammals and fished in rivers and oceans. They gathered wild seeds, fruits, and nuts. Even these prehistoric hunters and gatherers changed their environments. For example, some scientists hypothesize that the first humans to arrive in North America about 12,000 years ago caused a major mass extinction of animals. Woolly mammoths, giant ground sloths, and saber-toothed cats all became extinct. In addition, species that once lived in North America—cheetahs, zebras, and yaks, for example—disappeared from the continent.

Today groups of people in scattered parts of the world, from the Arctic to Central Africa, still follow the hunter-gatherer way of life to some degree. These people, such as the hunter shown in **Figure 6–3**, make relatively few demands on the environment. However, most of them use some form of technology, such as guns, snowmobiles, or manufactured tools.

✔ CHECKPOINT ***What are ecosystem goods and services?***

UNIVERSAL ACCESS

Inclusion/Special Needs

Engage students' interest in the section by reading aloud the sentences on page 141 that explain why the spread of agriculture was so important in human history. Then, elicit students' experiences with farms and farming. Some may have relatives who have farmed; others may have driven through farming country while on vacations. Direct their comments to an analysis of how agriculture benefits society as well as how it changes ecosystems. L1

Advanced Learners

Encourage students who need a challenge to investigate how urban growth has changed their community over the last 100 years. They can likely find descriptions and maps of the area with the help of a local librarian. Have these students make a presentation to the class about the native species of plants and animals that dominated the environment a century ago, complete with visual aids that would help the class understand the changes. L3

Agriculture

During thousands of years of searching for food, early hunter-gatherers learned how plants grew and ripened. They also discovered which ones were useful for food and medicines. By the end of the last ice age—about 11,000 years ago—humans began the practice of farming, or **agriculture.** Soon, people in different regions of the world were growing wheat, rice, and potatoes. The development of agriculture also included raising animals, such as sheep, goats, cows, pigs, and horses.

The spread of agriculture was among the most important developments in human history. Why? Because agriculture provides human societies with a fundamental need: a dependable supply of food that can be produced in large quantity and stored for later use. With a stable and predictable food supply, humans began to gather in larger settlements rather than travel in search of food. Stable communities, including towns and cities, enabled the development of the elements of civilization, such as government, laws, and writing.

From Traditional to Modern Agriculture Farming continued to develop for thousands of years. Farmers gradually acquired machinery, such as plows and the seed drill shown in **Figure 6–4,** to help with cultivation. World exploration led to an exchange of crops around the globe. For example, Europeans began to grow crops native to North and South America, such as potatoes and squash. Americans and Europeans cultivated rice, which is native to Asia.

In the 1800s and 1900s, advances in science and technology set the stage for a remarkable change in agriculture. Large-scale irrigation in dry areas such as the western United States allowed deserts to become breadbaskets. Machinery for plowing, planting, and harvesting helped farmers increase their yields tremendously. Agricultural scientists developed new varieties of crops that produce higher yields. These new crops were often grown using a practice called **monoculture,** in which large fields are planted with a single variety year after year. Chemical fertilizers boosted plant growth and pesticides controlled crop-damaging insects.

Word Origins

Agriculture is a combination of the Latin words *ager,* meaning "a field," and *cultura,* meaning "care." *Agriculture* is the science and art of farming, which includes the cultivation of field soils, production of crops, and the raising of livestock. **If the prefix *agro-* has the same meaning as *agri-*, what do you think the definition of the noun *agrochemical* is?**

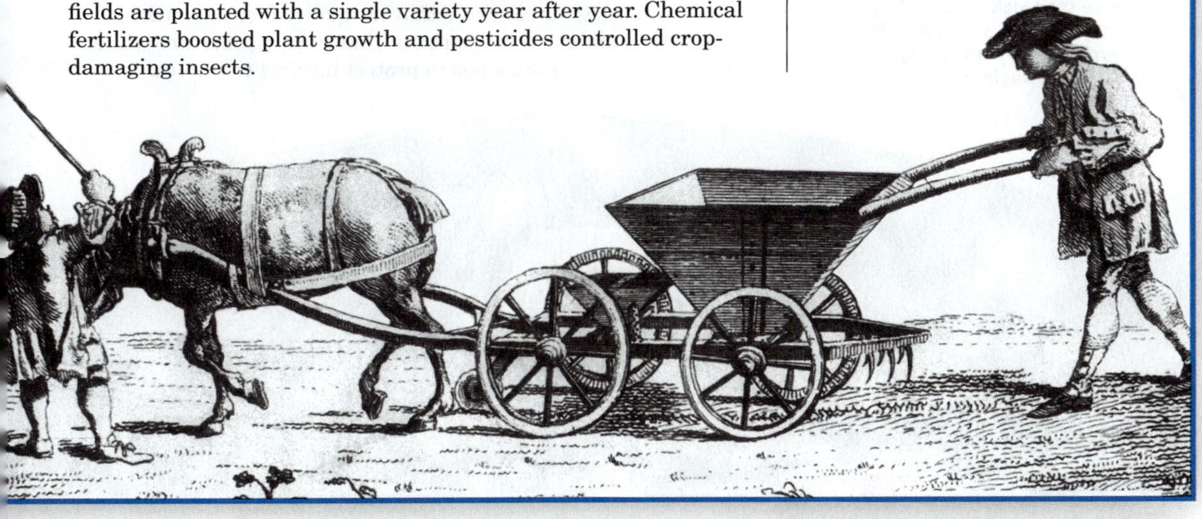

▼ **Figure 6–4** By the 1700s, most Europeans relied on simple tools and animal-drawn plows and vehicles to work the land. This illustration shows a farmer guiding a four-wheeled seed drill as his horse pulls it across a field. The seed drill was invented to help farmers plant seeds in straight lines. **Inferring** *Why is planting seeds in straight lines an advantage?*

Agriculture

Word Origins

An agrochemical is a chemical that is used to improve the growth and health of crops or livestock. L1 L2

Use Community Resources

Encourage students who are interested in careers in agriculture to research farming practices in your area. Sources of information include 4-H clubs, state and county agricultural agencies, and agricultural organizations listed in the *Encyclopedia of Associations,* including its separate volumes *Regional, State and Local Organizations* for different regions. Let students present their findings to the class in oral reports, posters, or bulletin board displays. L2 L3

Build Science Skills

Applying Concepts Role-playing is an effective learning tool, particularly for students who learn best through the spoken word. Have students work in five teams. Divide the four paragraphs on this page and the description of the green revolution on the next page among the five teams. Have each team create a skit in which they role-play farmers describing the agricultural practices of their assigned era. L2

Answers to . . .

CHECKPOINT *Ecological life-support systems that provide breathable air, drinkable water, and fertile soil that supports farming*

Figure 6–3 *Subsistence hunting may reduce the animal populations on which subsistence hunters depend for food.*

Figure 6–4 *Planting seeds in straight lines uses the space of the field more efficiently and ensures that each plant has room to grow.*

6–1 (continued)

Download a worksheet on sustainable agriculture for students to complete, and find additional teacher support from NSTA SciLinks.

Build Science Skills

Making Judgments Draw students' attention to Figure 6–5 and its caption. Then, ask: **What are the advantages of using agricultural machines such as tractors and harvesting combines?** *(Vast acreages can be plowed, sown, and harvested in less time and with fewer people, enabling farmers to produce large crops.)* **What are the disadvantages of such machines?** *(Accept a variety of responses, including their initial cost, costs of repairs and maintenance, increased energy resources they use, the exhaust gases they release into the air, and their noise.)* L2

Using Community Resources

Encourage students to interview farm owners and managers who represent different viewpoints and approaches, including both those farmers who employ green revolution practices, such as using chemical fertilizers and pesticides, and those who rely on organic practices with low environmental impact. Students could then stage a debate for the rest of the class. L2 L3

For: Links on sustainable agriculture
Visit: www.SciLinks.org
Web Code: cbn-2061

The Green Revolution By the middle of the twentieth century, despite agricultural advances, there were food shortages in many parts of the world. Governments and scientists began a major effort to increase food production in those countries. Plant breeders developed highly productive "miracle strains" of wheat and rice. Modern agricultural techniques were introduced, such as monoculture and the use of chemical fertilizers. This effort came to be called the **green revolution,** because it greatly increased the world's food supply.

The benefits of the green revolution have been enormous. In 20 years, Mexican farmers increased their wheat production 10 times. India and China, countries with the world's largest populations, produced enough food to feed their own people for the first time in years. Over the last 50 years, the green revolution has helped world food production double. Even though hunger is still a major problem in parts of the world, the green revolution has provided many people with better nutrition.

Challenges for the Future While increasing world food supplies, modern agriculture has created ecological challenges. For example, large-scale monoculture can lead to problems with insect pests and diseases. To a corn-eating insect, enormous fields of corn look like huge dinner tables, filled with tasty treats! When an insect population is surrounded by food, the population can grow rapidly. When populations of insect pests increase, farmers may increase their use of pesticides. Unfortunately, chemical pesticides can damage beneficial insects, contaminate water supplies, and accumulate in the environment.

A second challenge is finding enough water for irrigation. Less than a quarter of American farmland relies heavily on irrigation, but that land produces a major portion of our harvest. Several states in the West and Midwest, for example, depend heavily on an underground water deposit called the Ogallala aquifer for their water needs. However, evidence indicates that the Ogallala may run dry within 20 to 40 years.

Most ecologists conclude that humanity faces a challenge. We need to maintain the benefits of modern agriculture while developing new approaches to protect natural resources.

▼ **Figure 6–5** This farmer is using a tractor to cultivate a field of soybeans. Modern agricultural machinery such as this has helped increase crop yields. **Applying Concepts** *What is the name for the practice of planting large fields with a single crop?*

HISTORY OF SCIENCE

The green revolutionary

The central figure in the development of the farming practices known as the green revolution is the American plant biologist Norman Borlaug. He was born on a farm near Cresco, Iowa, in 1914 and graduated in forestry from the University of Minnesota in 1937. He received a doctorate from the same school in plant pathology. In 1944, he became director of a program in Mexico that focused on scientific research in plant breeding. In the years that followed at the International Maize and Wheat Center near Mexico City, he was tremendously successful in developing high-yielding, disease-resistant wheat. By the 1960s, his new strains of wheat were producing great harvests in famine-wracked areas of India and Pakistan. In 1970, Norman Borlaug was awarded the Nobel Peace Prize for this work.

Industrial Growth and Urban Development

Human society and its impact on the biosphere were transformed by the Industrial Revolution, which added machines and factories to civilization during the 1800s. That revolution led to the combination of industrial productivity and scientific know-how that provides us with most of the conveniences of modern life, from the homes we live in and the clothes we wear to the electronic devices we use in work and play. Mass-produced farm machinery makes efficient, large-scale agriculture possible. Automobiles give us mobility. Of course, to produce and power these machines, we need energy. We obtain most of this energy from fossil fuels—coal, oil, and natural gas.

For many years, cities and industries discarded wastes from manufacturing, energy production, and other sources into the air, water, and soil. Meanwhile, as urban centers became crowded, many people moved from the cities to the suburbs. The result of this movement was the growth of suburbs and the spread of suburban communities across the American landscape, as shown in **Figure 6–6.** Industrial development and the growth of cities and suburbs are closely tied to the high standard of living that so many people enjoy.

Many ecologists, however, are concerned about the effects of human activity on both local and global environments. Certain kinds of industrial processes pollute air, water, and soil. Dense human communities produce wastes that must be disposed of. Suburban growth consumes farmland and natural habitats, and can place additional stress on plant and animal populations and on the biosphere's life-support systems. Can we learn to control these harmful effects of human activity while preserving—or even improving—our standard of living? This is the enormous challenge that you and your children will face.

Figure 6–6 In the United States today, most people live and work either in cities or in the suburbs that surround them. **Problem Solving** ***List some ways that problems associated with the growth of cities and suburbs can be prevented.***

6–1 Section Assessment

1. **Key Concept** List three types of human activities that can affect the biosphere. For each activity, give one environmental cost and one benefit.
2. Identify three of Earth's resources on which humans and other organisms depend for the long-term survival of their species.
3. What did agriculture provide that changed the course of human history?
4. Identify two ways in which the Industrial Revolution has affected living things.
5. **Critical Thinking** **Predicting** How might improved agricultural practices in a developing nation affect that nation's human population?

You & Your Community

Mapping Community Growth
Are there signs of growth in your community, or in some other community you know? Map out some of the residential areas, shopping malls, and industrial parks in the community. Then, write a brief paragraph telling how this growth might impact local ecosystems.

Industrial Growth and Urban Development

Build Science Skills

Comparing and Contrasting Prompt students' thinking about what their world might be like in the future by discussing the changes they have already witnessed in their lifetime—for example, conversion of agricultural land to housing, shopping centers, or office buildings; highway construction; rehabilitation of vacant land or old buildings in cities. L2

3 ASSESS

Evaluate Understanding

Have each student write a brief paragraph identifying one type of human activity that has changed the biosphere and describing an example of that activity's effect.

Reteach

Write the headings Hunting and Gathering, Agriculture, and Industry and Urban Development on the board. Ask students to find examples in the text for each category describing how human activities have changed the biosphere.

You & Your Community

Before students write their paragraphs, lead a discussion about new developments in and near the students' community. Then, encourage students to think about what the area was like before these developments were built, in order to evaluate the impact such growth has had on local ecosystems.

Interactive Textbook

If your class subscribes to the iText, use it to review the Key Concepts in Section 6–1.

6–1 Section Assessment

1. Sample answers: Agriculture: cost—uses large amount of water; benefit—increased food production. Industry: cost—toxic wastes; benefit—large-scale production of products. Urban development: cost—destruction of habitat; benefit—housing and jobs for large numbers of people.
2. Breathable air, drinkable water, and fertile soil
3. A dependable supply of food that can be produced in large quantity and stored for later use.
4. Answers may vary. A typical response might mention pollution and urban growth that consumes natural habitats.
5. Sample answer: With a reliable food supply, children are more likely to survive to adulthood, so families might elect to have fewer children.

Answers to . . .

Figure 6–5 *Monoculture*

Figure 6–6 *Accept all reasonable responses. Some students may suggest that development in suburbs should be more compact, to preserve farmland and open space, and linked to public transit to reduce traffic congestion and the need to build more highways.*

Section 6–2

1 FOCUS

Objectives

6.2.1 ***Explain*** how environmental resources are classified.

6.2.2 ***Identify*** the characteristics of sustainable development.

6.2.3 ***Describe*** how human activities affect land, air, and water resources.

Guide for Reading

Vocabulary Preview

Help students understand the terms *aquaculture, deforestation,* and *desertification* by writing the words on the board, using lines or boxes to indicate the word parts (roots, prefixes, and suffixes). Then, have students use a dictionary to find the meaning of each word part.

Reading Strategy

Have students divide a sheet of paper into two columns. They can list the section's Vocabulary terms in one column and the definitions in the other column. This chart should assist students when they draw the concept map for the terms.

2 INSTRUCT

Classifying Resources

Build Science Skills

Applying Concepts Role-playing the villagers described in the first paragraph of the section could benefit many students. Divide the class into groups of three to discuss the tragedy of the commons, with one student representing the viewpoint of a villager who wants to keep grazing cattle on the commons, another student representing a villager who wants to have all the cattle removed from the commons, and the third student representing a town official who is trying to find a compromise between the two people. After students have discussed the issue, ask for volunteers to role-play a meeting in which the villagers and the official find a solution. L2

6–2 Renewable and Nonrenewable Resources

BI 6.b. Students know how to analyze changes in an ecosystem resulting from changes in climate, human activity, introduction of nonnative species, or changes in population size.

Guide for Reading

Key Concepts
- How are environmental resources classified?
- What effects do human activities have on natural resources?

Vocabulary

renewable resource
nonrenewable resource
sustainable development
soil erosion • desertification
deforestation • aquaculture
smog • pollutant • acid rain

Reading Strategy: Building Vocabulary

As you read, make notes about the meaning of each new term in the list above. Then, draw a concept map to show the relationships among the terms in this section.

A few hundred years ago, inhabitants of English villages could graze their cattle on shared pasture land called commons. Since grazing was free of charge, villagers often put as many cattle as possible on those commons. Occasionally there were more cattle on the commons than the land could support. Even as the land became overused, people kept putting more animals on it. After all, those who didn't use that free land would sacrifice their own profit while others would continue to benefit. Overgrazing on village commons sometimes caused the pastures to deteriorate so badly that they could no longer support cattle.

Today, environmentalists often talk about the *tragedy of the commons.* This phrase expresses the idea that any resource, such as water in the ground or fish in the sea, that is free and accessible to everyone, may eventually be destroyed. Why? Because if no one is responsible for protecting a resource, and if no one benefits from preserving it, people will use it up. If humans do not preserve the goods and services of an ecosystem, these resources may suffer the same fate as the common grazing lands in English villages.

Classifying Resources

Environmental goods and services may be classified as either renewable or nonrenewable. A tree is an example of a renewable resource, because a new tree can grow in place of an old tree that dies or is cut down. **Renewable resources** can regenerate if they are alive or can be replenished by biochemical cycles if they are nonliving. However, a renewable resource is not necessarily unlimited. Fresh water, for example, is a renewable resource that can easily become limited by drought or overuse.

▼ **Figure 6–7** **Natural resources can be classified as renewable or nonrenewable.** The grass growing in these pastures is a renewable resource—as long as the number of sheep grazing there is limited.

A **nonrenewable resource** is one that cannot be replenished by natural processes. The fossil fuels coal, oil, and natural gas are nonrenewable resources. Fossil fuels formed over hundreds of millions of years from deeply buried organic materials. When these fuels are depleted, they are gone forever.

The classification of a resource as renewable or nonrenewable depends on its context. Although a single tree is renewable, a population of trees in a forest ecosystem—on which a community of organisms depends—may not be renewable, because that ecosystem may change forever once those trees are gone.

CHECKPOINT *What is the "tragedy of the commons"?*

SECTION RESOURCES

Print:
- ***Laboratory Manual A,*** Chapter 6 Test
- ***Teaching Resources,*** Lesson Plan 6–2, Adapted Section Summary 6–2, Adapted Worksheets 6–2, Section Summary 6–2, Worksheets 6–2, Section Review 6–2, Enrichment
- ***Reading and Study Workbook A,*** Section 6–2
- ***Adapted Reading and Study Workbook B,*** Section 6–2
- ***Issues and Decision Making,*** Issues and Decisions 21, 23, 27, 31

Technology:
- ***iText,*** Section 6–2
- ***Transparencies Plus,*** Section 6–2

Sustainable Development

How can we provide for our needs while maintaining ecosystem goods and services that are renewable? The concept of sustainable development is one answer to this major question. **Sustainable development** is a way of using natural resources without depleting them and of providing for human needs without causing long-term environmental harm.

Human activities can affect the quality and supply of renewable resources such as land, forests, fisheries, air, and fresh water. Ecological research can help us understand how human activities affect the functioning of ecosystems. To work well, sustainable development must take into account both the functioning of ecosystems and the ways that human economic systems operate. Sustainable strategies must enable people to live comfortably and improve their situation. The use of insects to control insect pests, as shown in **Figure 6–8,** is one such strategy. In finding sustainable-development strategies, ecological research can have a practical, positive impact on the environment we create for ourselves and future generations.

CA a

▲ **Figure 6–8** This ladybug is eating an insect pest—a black aphid. New strategies for pest control that employ beneficial insects may help farmers reduce the use of pesticides. **Inferring** *How does biological pest control contribute to sustainable development?*

a BI 6.b

▼ **Figure 6–9 Human activities affect the supply and the quality of renewable resources.** In dry regions, human activities, such as farming practices that fail to protect the soil, can contribute to desertification.

Land Resources

Land is a resource that provides space for human communities and raw materials for industry. Land also includes the soils in which crops are grown. If managed properly, soil is a renewable resource. Soil, however, can be permanently damaged if it is mismanaged.

Food crops grow best in fertile soil, which is a mixture of sand, clay, rock particles, and humus (material from decayed organisms). Most of the humus that makes soil fertile is in the uppermost layer of the soil, called topsoil. Good topsoil absorbs and retains moisture yet allows excess water to drain. It is rich in nutrients but low in salts. Such soil is produced by long-term interactions between the soil and plants growing in it. Much agricultural land in the American Midwest, for example, was once covered by prairie ecosystems that produced and maintained a meter or more of very fertile topsoil. Deep roots of long-lived grasses held soil in place against rain and wind.

Plowing the land removes the roots that hold the soil in place. This increases the rate of **soil erosion**—the wearing away of surface soil by water and wind. A typical field on the High Plains of the Midwest loses roughly 47 metric tons of topsoil per hectare every year! In certain parts of the world with dry climates, a combination of farming, overgrazing, and drought has turned once productive areas into deserts, as shown in **Figure 6–9.** This process is called **desertification.** There are, however, a variety of sustainable-development practices that can guard against these problems. One practice is contour plowing, in which fields are plowed across the slope of the land to reduce erosion. Other strategies include leaving the stems and roots of the previous year's crop in place to help hold the soil and planting a field with rye rather than leaving it unprotected from erosion.

Sustainable Development

Use Community Resources

Encourage students to visit local nurseries, greenhouses, and garden centers to see if they sell natural "pest controllers" such as ladybugs and praying mantises. Also suggest that students ask about plants (nasturtiums, for example) that are used to repel insect pests in gardens. L2

Land Resources

Make Connections

Environmental Science Explain that when land is overgrazed by livestock, the grasses die and are replaced by scrub, weeds, and toxic plants that do not provide good pasture. The death of grasses with wide-branching roots increases runoff of precipitation, causing soil erosion. Overgrazing also ruins wildlife habitats. For example, livestock trample the fertile areas that border streams, killing plants, causing erosion of the stream banks, and making the water too muddy to support aquatic life. Encourage students to interview local ranchers and farmers or do library research to find out how damage from grazing can be minimized. (Methods include moving herds at intervals, which allows grass in the grazed area to regrow. Controlled burning destroys scrub brush and toxic plants without harming grass, whose roots sprout anew.) L2

SUPPORT FOR ENGLISH LANGUAGE LEARNERS

Comprehension: Prior Knowledge

Beginning Pronounce and define *sustainable* and *development* separately. Write each word on the board; then separate the suffixes *-able* and *-ment* from the roots *sustain* and *develop,* and define the roots and suffixes. Use concrete examples to clarify the concept of sustainable development. Then, ask students for examples from their own experience and cultures. For example: How do farmers keep soil fertile? What must be done to replace trees that are cut down? L1

Intermediate Expand on the Beginning activity by asking students to bring in photos that show specific examples that violate the principle of sustainable development. For each photo, ask students to write sentences describing things that people can do to remedy the situation. L2

Answers to . . .

CHECKPOINT *The "tragedy of the commons" is the idea that any resource that is free and accessible to everyone may eventually be destroyed.*

Figure 6–8 *Biological pest control does not cause pollution that can enter the food chain and harm other organisms.*

Forest Resources

Build Science Skills

Applying Concepts Have students review the diagram of the phosphorus cycle in Chapter 3. Explain that one consequence of the loss of forests is disruption of the phosphorus cycle. Normally, the rate of phosphorus loss from an undisturbed ecosystem is low. The removal of trees, however, causes a great deal of rainwater and snowmelt to wash over the soil as runoff. Large amounts of nutrients are washed away in this runoff. L1 L2

Build Science Skills

Predicting Encourage students to share any experiences with national forests and parks. Explain that these areas are one of the ways in which the federal government has sought to preserve and protect our forests and the wildlife living there. Explain that trees in national forests are available for logging on a regulated basis, but that national parks are protected from all commercial exploitation of their resources. Ask: **Do you think that these forests would remain as they are if the area were not set apart as a national forest or park? Why or why not?** *(Probably not, because the forests would probably be more extensively logged or destroyed to make room for industry, mining, housing, farming, or other uses.)* L1 L2

Forest Resources

Earth's forests are an important resource for the products they provide and for the ecological functions they perform. People use the wood from forests to make products ranging from homes to paper. In many parts of the world, wood is still burned as fuel for cooking and heating. But living forests also provide a number of important ecological services. Forests have been called "lungs of the Earth" because they remove carbon dioxide and produce oxygen. Forests also store nutrients, provide habitats and food for organisms, moderate climate, limit soil erosion, and protect freshwater supplies.

Whether a forest can be considered a renewable resource depends partly on the type of forest. For example, the temperate forests of the northeastern United States can be considered renewable. Most of these forests have been logged at least once in the past and have grown back naturally. However, today's forests differ somewhat in species composition from the forests they replaced.

Other forests, such as those in Alaska and the Pacific Northwest, are called old-growth forests because they have never before been cut. Worldwide, about half of the area originally covered by forests and woodlands has been cleared. Because it takes many centuries to produce old-growth forests, they are in effect nonrenewable resources. Old-growth forests often contain a rich variety of species. When logging occurs in these forests, the species they contain may be lost.

▼ **Figure 6–10** Planting new trees is one way to counteract the effects of deforestation. **Applying Concepts** *What are two ways in which reforestation might affect the biosphere?*

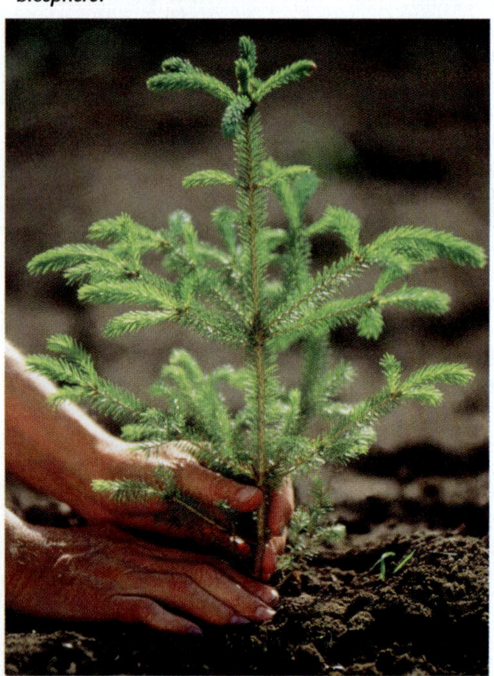

Deforestation Loss of forests, or **deforestation,** has several effects. Deforestation can lead to severe erosion as soil is exposed to heavy rains. Erosion can wash away nutrients in the topsoil. Grazing or plowing after deforestation can cause permanent changes to local soils and microclimates that in turn prevent the regrowth of trees.

Forest Management There are a variety of sustainable-development strategies for forest management. In some forests, mature trees can be harvested selectively to promote the growth of younger trees and preserve the forest ecosystem. In areas where forests have already been cut, foresters today often plant, manage, harvest, and replant tree farms, as shown in **Figure 6–10.** Tree farms can now be planted and harvested efficiently, making them fully renewable resources. Tree geneticists are also breeding new, faster-growing tree varieties that produce high-quality wood.

What is deforestation?

FACTS AND FIGURES

Trading forests for food

During the past 200 years, forest land in the United States has been reduced by approximately 20 percent. This amounts to an area of woodland about equal to the size of Texas. Forest land worldwide has been reduced by 20 percent in just the past 30 years. Many of these forests were cleared to grow crops for food—a need that no doubt continues to increase rapidly in developing nations.

A prime example of deforestation in a developing country is Madagascar, the island country off the southeast coast of Africa. Its forest is one of the most threatened in the world. Hundreds of hectares of forest disappear each year, mainly owing to slash-and-burn methods of clearing land to make way for the country's largest cash crop, maize. One result of this extensive deforestation is a sharp decline in the island's biodiversity.

Fishery Resources

Fishes and other animals that live in water are a valuable source of food for humanity. For example, consider the food provided by the Chesapeake Bay and its watershed, which includes the saltwater bay itself and the freshwater rivers and streams that flow into it. This complex ecosystem supplies people with fishes such as striped bass and American shad, and shellfishes such as crabs and oysters. The recent history of fisheries, or fishing grounds, is an example of the tragedy of the commons. Fortunately, it also shows how ecological research can help people begin to correct an environmental problem.

Overfishing Overfishing, or harvesting fish faster than they can be replaced by reproduction, greatly reduced the amount of fish in parts of the world's oceans. Between 1950 and 1990, the world fish catch grew from 19 million tons to more than 90 million tons. The fish that were caught helped feed the world's people. But as the catch increased, the populations of some fish species began to shrink. By the early 1990s, populations of cod and haddock had dropped so low that researchers feared these fishes might disappear from the sea.

The declining fish populations are an example of the tragedy of the commons. People from several countries were taking advantage of a resource—fisheries—but no one took responsibility for maintaining that resource. Until fairly recently, fisheries seemed to be a renewable resource, one that could be harvested indefinitely. But overfishing threatened to destroy what was once a renewable resource.

Sustainable Development Is there a way to manage fisheries sustainably? That's where ecological research has entered the picture. Fishery ecologists gathered data on the size of fish populations and their growth rate. The U.S. National Marine Fisheries Service used these data to create guidelines for United States commercial fishing. The guidelines specified how many fish, and of what size, could be caught in various parts of the oceans. The regulations are helping fish populations recover, as shown in **Figure 6–11.** The regulations caused loss of jobs in the short term, but are designed to protect the fishing industry for the future.

Aquaculture The raising of aquatic animals for human consumption, which is called **aquaculture,** is also helping to sustain fish resources. If not properly managed, aquaculture can pollute water and damage aquatic ecosystems. However, environment-friendly aquaculture techniques are being developed.

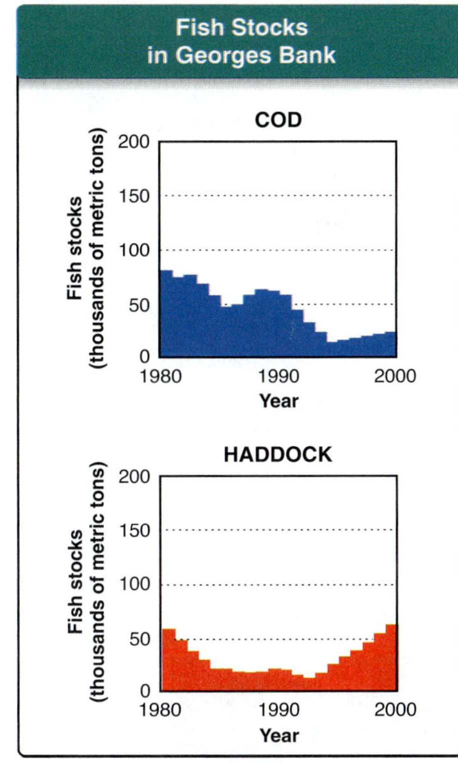

▲ **Figure 6–11** These graphs show how two fish populations—cod and haddock—have fluctuated in Georges Bank, a fishery off the New England coast. The fish populations began to rise after regulations restricted commercial fishing. **Interpreting Graphics** *Describe the history of the cod population in Georges Bank between 1980 and 2000.*

For: Fishery Resources activity
Visit: PHSchool.com
Web Code: cbp-2062

Fishery Resources

Build Science Skills

Applying Concepts Have interested students work as a group to learn about the fishing industry in the United States. Encourage students to find out about the history of the fishing industry as well as the various types of fishes that are caught and sold in different parts of the United States today. Have students present their findings to the class in the form of an oral report. L2 L3

Use Community Resources

Designate several pairs of students to interview the owners or managers of fish stores and the managers of fish and seafood departments in local supermarkets. Encourage students to gather the following information: Which types of fish being sold in the store are caught in the wild, and which are raised on fish farms? Is there a price difference between wild and farmed fish? Which wild fish are abundant? Which are harder for the store to obtain? After the interviews, let the student pairs meet as a group to share their findings and prepare an oral report to share with the class. L2 L3

For: Fishery Resources activity
Visit: PHSchool.com
Web Code: cbe-2069
Students experiment with various fish populations online.

Answers to . . .

The loss of forests

Figure 6–10 *Sample answer: Reforestation would prevent further soil erosion and help reduce atmospheric carbon dioxide.*

Figure 6–11 *In 1980, there were about 80,000 metric tons of cod fish stocks in Georges Bank. That total dropped until the late 1980s, when stocks rebounded for a few years. Then, in the early 1990s stocks fell precipitously. In the mid-1990s, stocks began to rise again, though by 2000 the total was still much below what it was in 1980.*

BIO INSIGHTS — FACTS AND FIGURES

Fisheries around the world

The meaning of the term *fishery* is confusing to many people. An area where fishes are caught, or harvested, is known as a fishery. Both the areas where commercial fishing occurs and the fishing industries themselves are known as fisheries. Here are some facts and figures about world fisheries.

- The world commercial catch for the year 2000 was almost 95 million metric tons, of which about 86 million metric tons came from the oceans.
- World aquaculture production for the year 2000 was almost 36 million metric tons.
- First on the list of commercial catches in 2000 was the grouping of herrings, sardines, and anchovies, with about 25 million metric tons.
- In 2000, the leading fishing countries were, in order of total production, China, Peru, Japan, India, the United States, Indonesia, Chile, and Russia.
- Pacific Ocean fisheries account for about half of the world's fish catch.

6–2 (continued)

Air Resources

Demonstration

Tie a 4-liter heavy-duty freezer-type bag over the end of the cold tailpipe of your car and start the engine. Turn the car off after 10 seconds or so, seal the bag tightly closed, and bring it to class. Let students use hand lenses to examine the emission particles in the bag. Point out that this bag of pollution is from only one car that ran for only 10 seconds. Ask students to imagine the amount of particles that would be released by hundreds or even thousands of vehicles during a morning commute. L1 L2

Build Science Skills

Analyzing Data Have students collect samples of rainwater from various outdoor locations, test each sample's pH level with litmus paper, and compare the pH level with that of a sample of tapwater. Explain that all rainwater is slightly acidic (pH 6–7) due to naturally occurring carbon dioxide in the air. However, a sample with a pH of less than 5.5 qualifies as acid rain. L2 L3

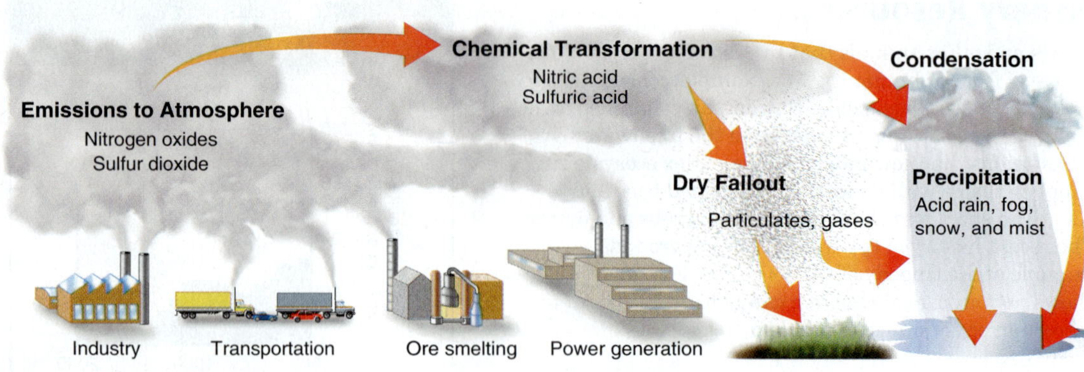

Figure 6–12 Acid rain results from the chemical transformation of nitrogen and sulfur products that come from human activities. The face of the statue (below) shows damage from acid rain. **Interpreting Graphics** *What pathways do the chemicals in atmospheric emissions take on their way to becoming acid rain?*

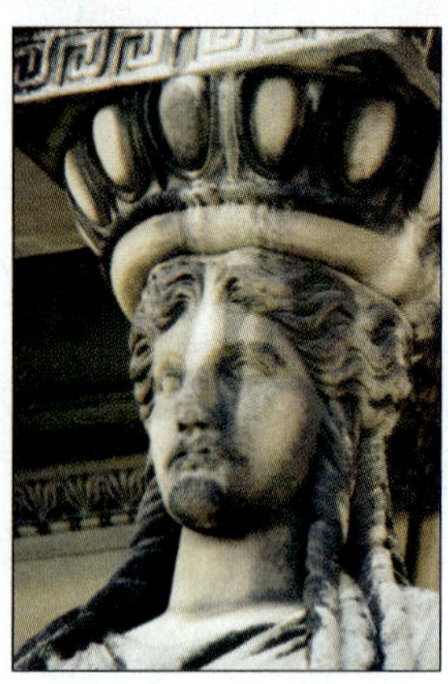

Air Resources

Air is a common resource that we use every time we breathe. The condition of the air affects people's health. The preservation of air quality remains a challenge for modern society.

If you live in a large city, you have probably seen **smog,** a mixture of chemicals that occurs as a gray-brown haze in the atmosphere. Smog is primarily due to automobile exhausts and industrial emissions. Because it threatens the health of people with asthma and other respiratory conditions, smog is considered a pollutant. A **pollutant** is a harmful material that can enter the biosphere through the land, air, or water.

The burning of fossil fuels can release pollutants that cause smog and other problems in the atmosphere. Potentially toxic chemicals, like nitrates, sulfates, and particulates (pahr-TIK-yoo-lits), are especially troublesome in large concentrations. Particulates are microscopic particles of ash and dust that can enter the nose, mouth, and lungs, causing health problems over the long term. Today, most industries use technology to control emissions from factory smokestacks. Strict automobile emission standards and clean-air regulations have improved air quality in many American cities, but air pollution is an ongoing problem in other parts of the world.

Many combustion processes, such as the burning of fossil fuels, release nitrogen and sulfur compounds into the atmosphere. When these compounds combine with water vapor in the air, they form drops of nitric and sulfuric acids. These strong acids can drift for many kilometers before they fall as **acid rain.** Acid rain can kill plants by damaging their leaves and changing the chemistry of soils and standing-water ecosystems. Acid rain may also dissolve and release toxic elements, such as mercury, from the soil, freeing those elements to enter other portions of the biosphere. **Figure 6–12** shows the processes that lead to the formation of acid rain.

CHECKPOINT *What is a pollutant?*

FACTS AND FIGURES

The Clean Water Act

Pressure by concerned voters resulted in the passage by Congress of the Water Pollution Control Act of 1972. This act and its amendments, now called the Clean Water Act, empower the federal government to set minimum water quality standards for rivers and streams. The act prohibits the discharge of any pollutant into a waterway unless a permit is first obtained from the state. The act gives the Environmental Protection Agency (EPA) the power to impose deadlines and levy fines on industries and municipalities that fail to comply with the law. For a long time, the EPA focused mainly on so-called point sources of pollution, including sewage plants and industrial facilities. In the 1980s, the agency began directing more of its attention to nonpoint sources of water pollution, including runoff from fertilized farmland and urban areas.

Freshwater Resources

Americans use billions of liters of fresh water daily for everything from drinking and washing to watering crops and making steel. Although water is a renewable resource, the total supply of fresh water is limited. For this reason, protecting water supplies from pollution and managing society's ever-growing demand for water are major priorities.

Pollution threatens water supplies in several ways. Improperly discarded chemicals can enter streams and rivers. Wastes discarded on land can seep through soil and enter underground water supplies that we tap with wells. Domestic sewage, which is the wastewater from sinks and toilets, contains nitrogen and phosphorous compounds that can encourage the growth of algae and bacteria in aquatic habitats. Sewage can also contain microorganisms that can spread disease among humans and animals. In this country, most cities and towns now treat their sewage in order to make it safer.

One way of ensuring the sustainable use of water resources is to protect the natural systems involved in the water cycle. For example, wetlands such as the one shown in **Figure 6–13** can help to purify the water passing through them. As water flows slowly through a swamp, densely growing plants filter certain pollutants out of the water. Similarly, forests and other vegetation help to purify the water that seeps into the ground or runs off into rivers and lakes.

As demand for water grows rapidly in many parts of the United States, water conservation is becoming an increasingly important aspect of sustainable development. There are many strategies for conserving water—in homes, industry, and agriculture. More than three-quarters of all water consumed in this country is used in agriculture, so conservation in this area can save large amounts of water. For example, drip irrigation delivers water directly to plant roots. This reduces the amount of water lost through evaporation.

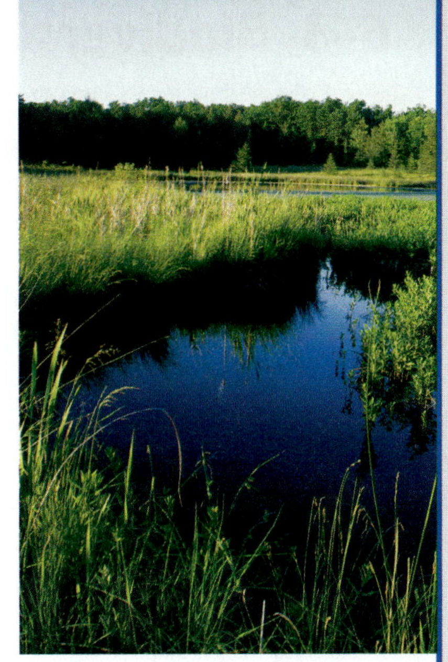

▲ **Figure 6–13** Wetlands provide a valuable ecosystem service by filtering certain pollutants from the water. **Applying Concepts** *How does this filtering process happen?*

6–2 Section Assessment

1. **Key Concept** What is the difference between a renewable and a nonrenewable resource?
2. **Key Concept** List two human activities that affect land resources, and explain the changes that can result. Do the same for air and water resources.
3. How does the decline in world fisheries represent a "tragedy of the commons"?
4. Identify two ways in which environmental resources are important to human health.
5. **Critical Thinking Applying Concepts** Describe sustainable development strategies to manage forests as a renewable resource.

Writing in Science

Cause-Effect Paragraph

Write a paragraph explaining the effect of fishing restrictions on fish populations. Your paragraph should explain why the regulations were needed as well as the effect of the regulations.

Freshwater Resources

Use Community Resources

Ask a member of your local health board to visit the class and tell students about problems with water pollution that have been encountered in your immediate area, the state, or the region. Make sure the guest also discusses whether and how any pollution problems are being resolved. L1 L2

3 ASSESS

Evaluate Understanding

Call on students at random to name harmful human activities discussed in the section and identify each activity's effects on the biosphere.

Reteach

Name different natural resources, and ask students to identify each as renewable or nonrenewable. Then, have students describe ways they can help to conserve resources.

If your class subscribes to the iText, use it to review the Key Concepts in Section 6–2.

Writing in Science

In explaining why regulations were needed, students should describe overfishing. A typical response will also explain that fishing restrictions may protect fish populations and cause their numbers to increase, using evidence from the graphs in Figure 6–11.

6–2 Section Assessment

1. A renewable resource can regenerate and is therefore replaceable. A nonrenewable resource cannot be replenished by natural processes.
2. Answers may vary. Students should draw from the examples discussed in the section as they explain changes that can result from six human activities that affect land, air, and water resources.
3. People from several countries were taking advantage of fisheries, but no one took responsibility for maintaining that resource.
4. Students may mention land, air, or water resources. A typical response might mention the air we breathe as well as the role that wetlands play in filtering pollutants from water.
5. Answers may vary. A typical response might mention selectively harvesting mature trees from forests and planting and harvesting trees from tree farms.

Answers to . . .

CHECKPOINT *A harmful material that can enter the biosphere through the land, air, or water*

Figure 6–12 *The gases combine with water vapor to form drops of nitric acid and sulfuric acid, which can drift long distances before they fall as acid rain.*

Figure 6–13 *As water flows slowly through a wetland, densely growing plants filter out certain pollutants.*

Section 6–3

 BI 6.a, BI 6.b, *BI 6.g

1 FOCUS

Objectives

6.3.1 ***Define*** biodiversity and explain its value.

6.3.2 ***Identify*** current threats to biodiversity.

6.3.3 ***Describe*** the goal of conservation biology.

Guide for Reading

Vocabulary Preview

Write the following terms on the board, and underline the parts as shown here: *habitat fragmentation, invasive species,* and *biological magnification*. Have students find the definition of each underlined part in a dictionary. Then, ask them to tell what they think the entire Vocabulary term means. Encourage students to write down their predicted definitions and make any necessary corrections when they encounter the terms in the text.

Reading Strategy

Encourage students to vary their questions so they don't simply keep repeating "What is . . ." for most headings. For example, the heading on page 153 could be rewritten as "Why are introduced species a threat to biodiversity?"

2 INSTRUCT

The Value of Biodiversity

Build Science Skills

Classifying Have each student find out about one specific example of how biodiversity is valuable to society. Tell students that the example should relate to agriculture, medicine, recreation, industry, or general health. After students have completed their research, let them meet in groups that are organized according to those fields and share their findings. Suggest that each group prepare a poster to summarize the information. L2

6–3 Biodiversity

BI 6.a. Students know biodiversity is the sum total of different kinds of organisms and is affected by alterations of habitats. **BI 6.b.** Students know how to analyze changes in an ecosystem resulting from changes in climate, human activity, introduction of nonnative species, or changes in population size. ***BI 6.g.** Students know how to distinguish between the accommodation of an individual organism to its environment and the gradual adaptation of a lineage of organisms through genetic change.

Guide for Reading

Key Concepts
- Why is biodiversity important?
- What are the current threats to biodiversity?
- What is the goal of conservation biology?

Vocabulary
biodiversity
ecosystem diversity
species diversity
genetic diversity
extinction
endangered species
habitat fragmentation
biological magnification
invasive species
conservation

Reading Strategy: Asking Questions Before you read, rewrite the headings in the section as *how, why,* or *what* questions about biodiversity. As you read, write brief answers to your questions.

Those of us who love nature find much to admire in the many forms of life that surround us. We marvel at the soaring flight of an eagle, the majestic movements of a whale, and the colors of spring wildflowers. "Variety," the saying goes, "is the spice of life." But variety in the biosphere gives us more than just interesting things to look at. Human society takes part in local and global food webs and energy cycles, and depends on both the physical and biological life-support systems of our planet. For that reason, our well-being is closely tied to the well-being of a great variety of other organisms—including many that are neither majestic nor beautiful to our eyes.

The Value of Biodiversity

Another word for variety is diversity. Therefore, biological diversity, or **biodiversity,** is the sum total of the genetically based variety of all organisms in the biosphere. **Ecosystem diversity** includes the variety of habitats, communities, and ecological processes in the living world. **Species diversity** refers to the number of different species in the biosphere. So far, biologists have identified and named about 1.5 million species and estimate that millions more may be discovered in the future. **Genetic diversity** refers to the sum total of all the different forms of genetic information carried by all organisms living on Earth today. Within each species, genetic diversity refers to the total of all different forms of genes present in that species. You will read about genetic information later in the book.

CA a — a BI 6.a

Biodiversity is one of Earth's greatest natural resources. Species of many kinds have provided us with foods, industrial products, and medicines—including painkillers, antibiotics, heart drugs, antidepressants, and anticancer drugs. For example, the rosy periwinkle plant in **Figure 6–14** is the source of substances used to treat certain cancers. The biodiversity represented by wild plants and animals is a kind of "library" of genetic information upon which humans can draw for future use. For example, most crop plants have wild relatives with useful traits such as resistance to disease or pests. When biodiversity is lost, potential sources of material with significant value to the biosphere and to humankind may be lost with it.

Figure 6–14 **Biodiversity is one of Earth's greatest natural resources. Species of many kinds have provided us with foods, industrial products, and medicines.** The rosy periwinkle is a pink-petaled flowering plant native only to Madagascar. Drugs derived from this plant, such as vincristine, are used to treat certain cancers, including leukemia.

SECTION RESOURCES

Print:
- ***Teaching Resources,*** Lesson Plan 6–3, Adapted Section Summary 6–3, Adapted Worksheets 6–3, Section Summary 6–3, Worksheets 6–3, Section Review 6–3
- ***Reading and Study Workbook A,*** Section 6–3
- ***Adapted Reading and Study Workbook B,*** Section 6–3
- ***Issues and Decision Making,*** Issues and Decisions 22, 25, 26, 30, 32, 34, 36

Technology:
- ***iText,*** Section 6–3
- ***Transparencies Plus,*** Section 6–3

Threats to Biodiversity

Human activity can reduce biodiversity by altering habitats, hunting species to extinction, introducing toxic compounds into food webs, and introducing foreign species to new environments. As human activities alter ecosystems, this may lead to the extinction of species. **Extinction** occurs when a species disappears from all or part of its range. A species whose population size is declining in a way that places it in danger of extinction is called an **endangered species.** As the population of an endangered species declines, the species loses genetic diversity—an effect that can make it even more vulnerable to extinction.

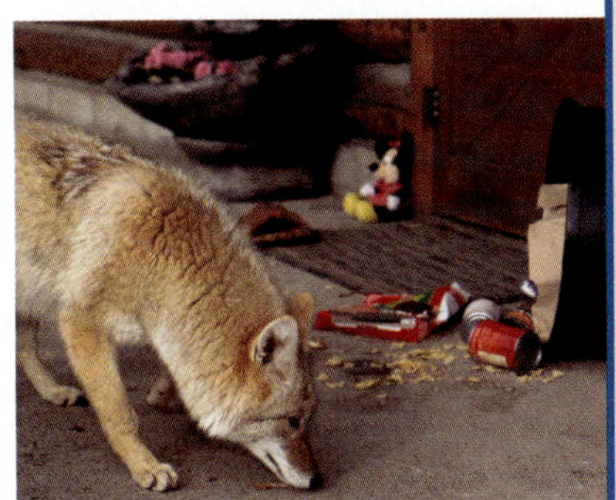

▲ **Figure 6–15** **Human activity can reduce biodiversity by altering habitats.** Normally this coyote would be hunting for small prey, but due to a changing habitat, it has learned to make an easy meal from garbage cans.

Habitat Alteration

When land is developed, natural habitats may be destroyed. Habitats supply organisms' needs, and they are a limited resource. The animals who live in these habitats, such as the coyote in **Figure 6–15**, must learn new behaviors in order to survive in these new environments. Species' long-term survival depends on the preservation of this limited resource.

CA a — a BI 6.b

As habitats disappear, the species that live in those habitats vanish. In addition, development often splits ecosystems into pieces, a process called **habitat fragmentation.** As a result, remaining pieces of habitat become biological "islands." We usually think of islands as bits of land surrounded by water. But a biological island can be any patch of habitat surrounded by a different habitat. New York's Central Park is an island of trees and grass in a sea of concrete. In suburbs, patches of forest can be surrounded by farms, houses, and shopping malls. Habitat islands are very different from large, continuous ecosystems. The smaller the "island," the fewer species can live there, the smaller their populations can be, and the more vulnerable they are to further disturbance or climate change.

CHECKPOINT *What is habitat fragmentation?*

Demand for Wildlife Products

Throughout history, humans have pushed some animal species to extinction by hunting them for food or other products. In the 1800s, hunting caused the extinction of species such as the Carolina parakeet and the passenger pigeon.

Today, in the United States, endangered species are protected from hunting. Hunting, however, still threatens rare animals in parts of Africa, South America, and Southeast Asia. Some species are hunted for meat, fur, or hides. Others are hunted because people think that their body parts such as horns have medicinal properties. The Convention on International Trade in Endangered Species, CITES, bans international trade in products derived from a list of endangered species. Unfortunately, it is difficult to enforce laws in remote wilderness areas.

For: Links on biodiversity
Visit: www.SciLinks.org
Web Code: cbn-2063

Threats to Biodiversity

Build Science Skills

Classifying Explain that endangered species are those considered to be in immediate danger of extinction. Ask: **What is extinction?** *(The dying out of an entire species so it no longer exists on Earth)* **Once a species becomes extinct, will it ever reappear?** *(No)* L1 L2

Habitat Alteration

Build Science Skills

Applying Concepts Ask students to name and estimate the size of all the parks or natural areas in their community, and make a list on the board. Add the areas of the parks together, and circle the sum. Then, ask: **What difference would it make for the species that live in these parks if, instead of many parks, there were just one park equal to the size of all added together?** *(Most students would suggest that species would be better protected in the larger area.)* Emphasize that species face more threats in fragmented habitats. L2

Demand for Wildlife Products

Build Science Skills

Predicting Show students an item made of ivory or a picture of such an item. This might be a billiard ball, a figurine, or jewelry. Explain that ivory comes mostly from elephant tusks. Ask: **What do you predict will happen to elephant populations in Africa if the demand for ivory remains high?** *(Students might suggest that elephants will become endangered or extinct.)* L1 L2

UNIVERSAL ACCESS

Inclusion/Special Needs

Diversity in American society is much discussed and praised. As students begin to study the concepts introduced in this section, talk about the value of diversity among the people of the United States, with an emphasis on the idea that various races, cultures, orientations, and faiths bring a richness to American life that is missing in many other countries around the world. Then, use this analogy to explain how biodiversity brings a richness to the living world. L1

Advanced Learners

Encourage students who need an extra challenge to make an enlarged version of the Biology and History timeline from pages 154–155 on the wall of the classroom. Then, have students research other conservation milestones and add them to the timeline. Students can draw their own pictures or photocopy ones from books and magazines and then write a paragraph explaining the significance of each person or event. L3

Download a worksheet on biodiversity for students to complete, and find additional teacher support from NSTA SciLinks.

Answer to . . .

CHECKPOINT *The splitting of ecosystems into small, isolated "islands"*

6–3 (continued)

Pollution

Use Visuals

Figure 6–16 After students have studied the figure and read the caption, have them turn back to Section 3–2 and look again at the illustrations of ecological pyramids in Figure 3–9. Then, ask: **What kind of ecological pyramid does the drawing on the left in Figure 6–16 represent?** *(It shows a pyramid of numbers.)* **What does a pyramid of numbers demonstrate about organisms in an ecosystem?** *(There are fewer organisms at each trophic level as you move up the pyramid.)* Then, direct students' attention to the arrow showing magnification of DDT concentration. Ask: **How is this illustration of DDT concentration opposite the pyramid of numbers to its left?** *(It's like an upside-down pyramid; the numbers are greater at each level as you move up.)* Point out that these pyramids are opposite because the same amount of DDT in organisms at the bottom of the pyramid of numbers is distributed in many fewer organisms at the top of the pyramid. L2

Make Connections

Chemistry Explain that DDT (dichlorodiphenyltrichloroethane) was first synthesized in the late 1930s. It was used in World War II to kill lice and ticks that carry typhus, and it was later used effectively to kill mosquitoes that carry malaria. Explain that DDT works to kill insects by wedging open the sodium channel in insect nerve cells. The result of opening that channel is that nerve impulses become continuous, and the insects die of exhaustion. The problem with DDT is that it is chemically very stable—that is, it doesn't degrade or break down easily. Because it is so stable, it persists in the environment and moves through food chains. L3

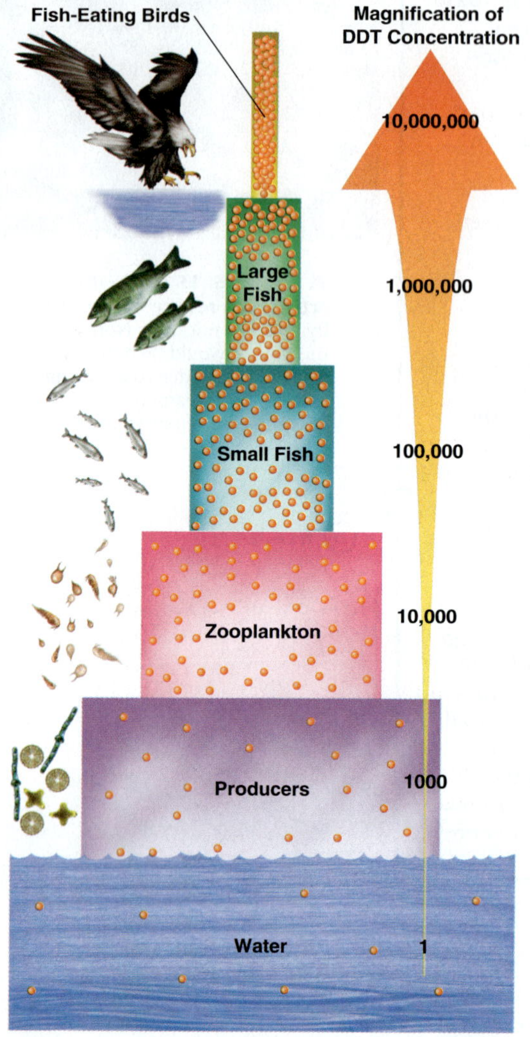

▲ **Figure 6–16** In the process of biological magnification, the concentration of a pollutant such as DDT—represented here by orange dots—is multiplied as it passes up the food chain from producers to consumers. By the time it reaches the top-level consumers, shown here as fish-eating birds, the amount of DDT in biological tissues can be magnified nearly 10 million times. **Calculating** *By what number is the concentration of DDT multiplied at each successive trophic level?*

Pollution

Many forms of pollution can threaten biodiversity, but one of the most serious problems occurs when toxic compounds accumulate in the tissues of organisms. The history of DDT, one of the first widely used pesticides, explains the situation well. At first, DDT seemed to be a perfect pesticide. It is cheap, remains active for a long time, kills many different insects, and can control agricultural pests and disease-carrying mosquitoes.

When DDT was sprayed, it drained into rivers and streams at low concentrations that seemed harmless. But DDT has two properties that make it hazardous. First, DDT is nonbiodegradable, which means that it is not broken down by metabolic processes in bacteria, plants, or animals. Second, when DDT is picked up by organisms, they do not eliminate it from their bodies. When aquatic plants pick up DDT from water, the pesticide is stored in their tissues. When herbivores eat those plants, they too store DDT. Because an herbivore eats many plants during its life, the DDT can become concentrated to levels ten times higher than levels found in the plants! When carnivores eat herbivores, the toxic substance is concentrated further, as shown in **Figure 6–16.** In this process, called **biological magnification,** concentrations of a harmful substance increase in organisms at higher trophic levels in a food chain or food web. Biological magnification affects the entire food web, although top-level carnivores are at highest risk.

In 1962, biologist Rachel Carson wrote a book called *Silent Spring* that alerted people to the dangers of biological magnification. The widespread spraying of DDT over many years had threatened populations of many animals—especially fish-eating birds like the osprey, brown pelican, and bald eagle—with extinction. One effect of DDT was to make eggs of these birds so fragile that the eggs could not survive intact. By the early 1970s, DDT was banned in the United States and in most other industrialized countries. In the years since, scientists have noted a marked recovery in the populations of birds that had been affected. Bald eagles, for example, can once again be seen around rivers, lakes, and estuaries in the lower 48 states.

CHECKPOINT *What is biological magnification?*

HISTORY OF SCIENCE

Tragedy in Minamata

A tragic example of biological magnification involved mercury, a byproduct in the manufacture of batteries. In humans, mercury affects the central nervous system, causing paralysis, mental illness, and even death. Some years ago, factories located around Minamata Bay in Japan discharged mercury into the sea in a supposedly safe insoluble form. Microorganisms in the bay changed the mercury's form, making it soluble in seawater. The dissolved mercury was ingested by phytoplankton and passed up the food chain. It reached dangerously high concentrations in fishes such as tuna and swordfish. Because the Japanese diet typically includes a great deal of fish, people in the Minamata area ingested large quantities of mercury, and many became terribly ill and died. Mothers gave birth to deformed and mentally retarded children. This tragedy is an example of why careful scientific studies are needed before disposing of waste products into the environment.

Quick Lab

BIIE 1.g

How does biological magnification occur?

Materials paper cups (3 small, 1 medium, and 1 large); 1-L beaker; sand; 12 beads; masking tape

Procedure  

1. Use a pencil to punch five holes in the bottom of each paper cup. Place tape over the outsides of the holes. The small cups represent grasshoppers, the medium-sized cup represents an insect-eating lizard, and the large cup represents a hawk.
2. Half-fill each small cup with sand and 4 beads. The sand represents food. The beads represent a chlorinated pesticide.
3. Hold each small cup over a beaker to catch the sand and remove the tape. The sand that flows out of the cup represents digested food. Record the number of beads in each cup.
4. To model the effects of biological magnification on the lizard, empty the contents of the three small cups into the medium-sized cup. Repeat step 3 with the medium-sized cup.
5. Empty your medium-sized cup and those of two classmates into a large cup to model a hawk eating the lizard. Repeat step 3 with the large cup.

Analyze and Conclude

1. **Inferring** Which animals accumulated the most pesticide?
2. **Predicting** Which level of the food chain is most affected by biological magnification?

Introduced Species

(a) BI 6.b

One of the most important threats to biodiversity today comes from an unexpected source: apparently harmless plants and animals that humans transport around the world either accidentally or intentionally. Introduced into new habitats, these organisms often become **invasive species** that reproduce rapidly. Invasive species increase their populations because their new habitat lacks the parasites and predators that control their population "back home."

Hundreds of invasive species, including the one in **Figure 6–17**, are already causing ecological problems in the United States. Zebra mussels, an aquatic pest, came on ships from Europe during the 1980s. They spread through the Great Lakes and several major rivers. These mussels reproduce and grow so quickly that they cause major ecological changes and are driving several native species close to extinction. There are also many examples on land. One European weed, the leafy spurge, now infests millions of hectares of grasslands across the Northern Great Plains, where it displaces native plants.

Figure 6–17 **Human activity can reduce biodiversity by introducing foreign species to new environments.** Native to South America, nutrias have become pests in coastal areas of the southeastern United States. These furry rodents eat water plants that protect fragile shorelines from erosion. This destroys the habitats of species native to those ecosystems.

BIO INSIGHTS — FACTS AND FIGURES

Costa Rica's megareserves

The Central American nation of Costa Rica has become a world leader in the effort to slow ecosystem destruction. In exchange for reductions in its international debt, the Costa Rican government has established eight megareserves—extensive regions that include one or more undisturbed areas surrounded by buffer zones that are used by people for economic gain.

The buffer zones provide a steady, lasting supply of forest products, water, and hydroelectric power and also support sustainable agriculture and ecotourism. Destructive practices that are incompatible with long-term ecosystem stability are prohibited in these zones. Costa Rica expects its megareserve system to maintain at least 80 percent of the country's native species. In addition, its thriving ecotourism industry is a significant source of income for the country.

Quick Lab

BIIE 1.g

Objective Students will be able to create a model of biological magnification. L1 L2

Skills Focus Inferring, Predicting

Materials paper cups (3 small, 1 medium, and 1 large); 1-L beaker; sand; 12 beads; masking tape

Time 15 minutes

Advance Preparation

- Use large beads that will not fall through the holes in the cups. Buttons or marbles can be substituted for the beads. Use waxed paper cups (plastic or foam cups will not puncture cleanly).

Strategies

- Before students begin, make sure they understand what each material represents.
- Have students set up a data table for recording results.

Expected Outcome Starting with 4 beads in each "grasshopper" cup, the "lizard" cup will contain 12 beads and the "hawk" cup 36 beads.

Analyze and Conclude

1. The hawks
2. The highest trophic level

Introduced Species

Build Science Skills

Applying Concepts Make a list of invasive species that compete with native species in the United States. Examples: starlings; zebra mussels in the Great Lakes; kudzu in Southeastern states; Asian long-horned beetles attacking New England maples; Eurasian milfoil choking lakes and ponds; phragmites and purple loosestrife crowding out native wetland plants; Mexican boll weevil attacking cotton crops; and cheatgrass crowding out native grasses in the West. Have students find out where each species originated, how it was transported to the United States, and what problems it causes. L2 L3

Answers to . . .

CHECKPOINT *The increasing concentration of a harmful substance in organisms at higher trophic levels in a food chain or food web*

Figure 6–16 *A factor of 10*

6–3 (continued)

Conserving Biodiversity

Use Community Resources

Find out if a nearby zoo, a university biology department, or a state agency has a captive breeding program. Invite a representative to address the class about this program. Make sure students have prepared questions in advance. If a speaker cannot come to the school, encourage volunteers to make an appointment with someone associated with such a program and conduct an interview. Ask that these students report back to the class about what they've learned. L2 L3

Biology and History

Call on fluent readers to read aloud the descriptive paragraphs on the timeline. Then, divide the class into eight groups, and assign a different timeline topic to each group. Challenge each group to prepare some sort of presentation—a debate, a role-play, or a taped radio show, for example—to dramatize the topic for the class.

Writing in Science

Encourage students to focus on endangered species found in their state or region. If students have difficulty identifying such species, let them choose threatened species instead. L2

Conserving Biodiversity

Most people would like to preserve Earth's biodiversity for future generations. In ecology, the term **conservation** is used to describe the wise management of natural resources, including the preservation of habitats and wildlife. The modern science of conservation biology seeks to protect biodiversity. To do so requires detailed information about ecological relationships—such as the way natural populations use their habitats—and integrates information from other scientific disciplines, such as genetics, geography, and natural resource management.

Strategies for Conservation Many conservation efforts are aimed at managing individual species to keep them from becoming extinct. Some zoos, for example, have established captive breeding programs, in which young animals are raised in protected surroundings until the population is stable, then are later returned to the wild. This strategy has succeeded with a few species, including the black-footed ferret.

Today, conservation efforts focus on protecting entire ecosystems as well as single species. Protecting an ecosystem will ensure that the natural habitats and the interactions of many different species are preserved at the same time. This effort is a much bigger challenge. Governments and conservation groups worldwide are working to set aside land, or expand existing areas, as parks and reserves.

Biology and History

Success in Conservation

Human activity can have a dramatic impact on the biosphere, to the point where other forms of life are threatened. Many efforts have been made to protect and preserve Earth's natural environments.

1854
Henry David Thoreau
Thoreau recommends the preservation of wildlife. In his book *Walden,* he cautions against seeking to dominate nature and suggests living in harmony with it.

1872
Yellowstone becomes the world's first national park.

1896
Harriet Hemenway
Hemenway and her cousin, Minna Hall, petition in Boston for legislation to prevent the extinction of birds due to unregulated hunting. By refusing to buy or wear plumed hats, the two cousins are among the first founders of the conservation movement.

1900
Lacey Act
Enacted by the U.S. Congress, the Lacey Act is the first major national conservation law. Transporting illegally killed animals across state borders becomes a federal crime.

1900

HISTORY OF SCIENCE

The Endangered Species Act
Originally passed in 1973 and updated in 1982, 1985, and 1988, the Endangered Species Act prohibits the sale or purchase of any product made from a species that has been listed by the U.S. government as endangered or threatened. In 2000, the U.S. Fish and Wildlife Service (FWS) listed 984 domestic species (388 animals and 596 plants) and 517 foreign species as endangered. These ranged from 65 domestic mammals to 2 domestic lichens. In addition, the FWS listed 276 domestic and 41 foreign species as threatened. For each species endangered or threatened, the act requires FWS to choose a suitable habitat and design a recovery plan. The effort to reestablish wolves in western regions is an example of such a plan. That effort is also an example of the great controversy some plans have engendered. Wolf protection is discussed in the Issues in Biology feature on page 128 in Chapter 5.

The United States has an extensive system of national parks, forests, and other protected areas. Marine sanctuaries are being designated to protect resources such as coral reefs and marine mammals. However, these areas may not be large enough, or contain the right resources, to protect biodiversity.

Protecting species and ecosystem diversity in many places around the world is an enormous challenge. As part of the effort to locate problem areas and set up a list of priorities, conservation biologists often identify biodiversity "hot spots," including those shown in **Figure 6–18** on the following page. Each hot spot is a place where significant numbers of habitats and species are in immediate danger of extinction as a result of human activity. The hot-spot strategy may help scientists and governments to focus their efforts where they are most needed.

Conservation Challenges Protecting resources for the future can require people to change the way they earn their living today. Regulations that restrict fishing, for example, can impose severe financial hardships on fishers for several years. That's why conservation regulations must be informed by solid research, and must try to maximize benefits while minimizing economic costs. But an ecological perspective tells us that if we do not take some difficult steps today, some resources may disappear. If that happens, many jobs that depend on ecosystem goods and services, such as fishing, will be lost permanently.

✓CHECKPOINT *Why is it important to preserve entire ecosystems?*

Writing in Science

Choose and research a specific endangered species and its habitat. Then, write a proposal that explains the problem and offers one or more possible conservation efforts for that species.

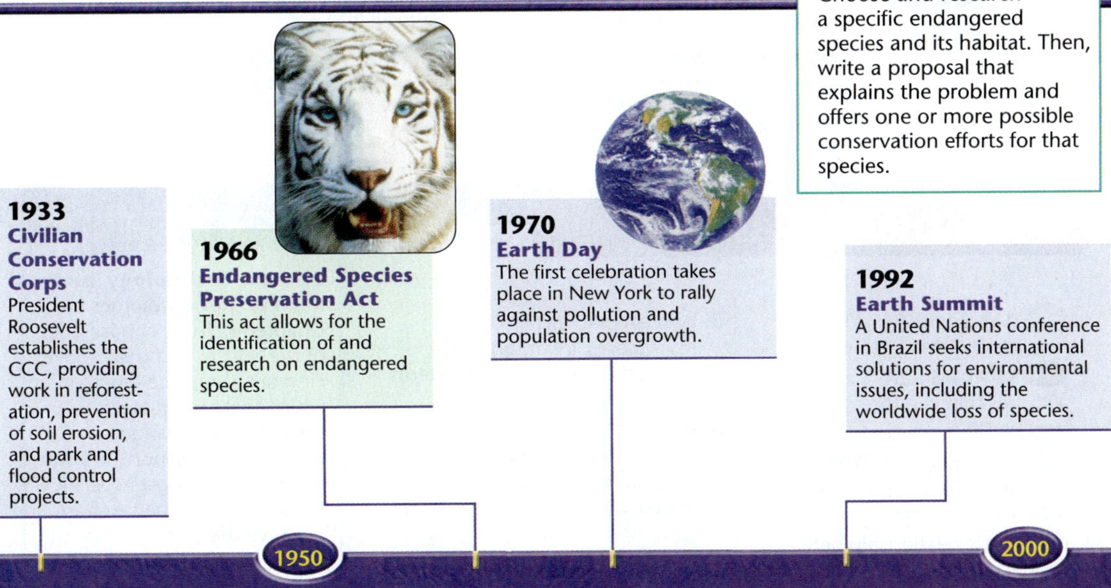

Use Community Resources

Contact local and state chapters of various conservation groups to see if they would provide speakers to visit the class. Ask each speaker to describe the group's efforts to preserve wildlife and ecosystems in your area. Also encourage the visitors to bring brochures, posters, and other materials to leave with students. If you are able to locate several such speakers, you might want to have them all visit at the same time for a Conservation Fair in the classroom.  L2

Build Science Skills

Applying Concepts Have students work in teams to create a mural entitled *Extinction Is Forever* to display in the classroom or a school hallway. Tell students that the goal of the display should be to dramatize the plight of endangered and threatened species and to motivate anyone viewing the display to become more concerned about protecting those species. L1 L2

FACTS AND FIGURES

Protecting ocean habitats
The National Marine Sanctuaries Act was part of the Marine Protection, Research, and Sanctuaries Act of 1972. That act established the National Marine Sanctuary Program, which is administered by the Sanctuaries and Reserves Division of the National Oceanic and Atmospheric Administration (NOAA). Since 1972, 12 national marine sanctuaries have been designated by the U.S. government. The smallest is an area of one-quarter square mile in Fagatele Bay in American Samoa. The largest is an area of over 5300 square miles in Monterey Bay, off the coast of California. Together, the 12 sanctuaries protect about 18,000 square miles of ocean habitats. Research is a major component of the program of each sanctuary. Regulations protect the habitats in these sanctuaries, and some activities are prohibited. Nevertheless, recreation, commercial fisheries, and shipping are allowed.

Answer to . . .

✓CHECKPOINT *Protecting an entire ecosystem will ensure that the natural habitats and the interactions of many different species are preserved at the same time.*

6–3 (continued)

Make Connections

Earth Science Let students take turns using a large world globe to find the "hot spots" that are highlighted on the map in Figure 6–18. If they present oral reports for the Connecting Concepts activity on this page, they could point out each biome's location on the globe. 

3 ASSESS

Evaluate Understanding

Call on students at random to identify one type of human activity that threatens biodiversity and to explain the effects of that activity.

Reteach

Have students prepare written or tape-recorded statements in which they discuss what it means to be a "citizen of Earth." For example, students might write a set of "eco-laws" that a good global citizen would follow or might create a bill of rights for all living things.

Focus on the BIG Idea

Students can use library or Internet sources. Consult with your school's or town's librarian to make sure adequate sources are available for students' research.

If your class subscribes to the iText, use it to review the Key Concepts in Section 6–3.

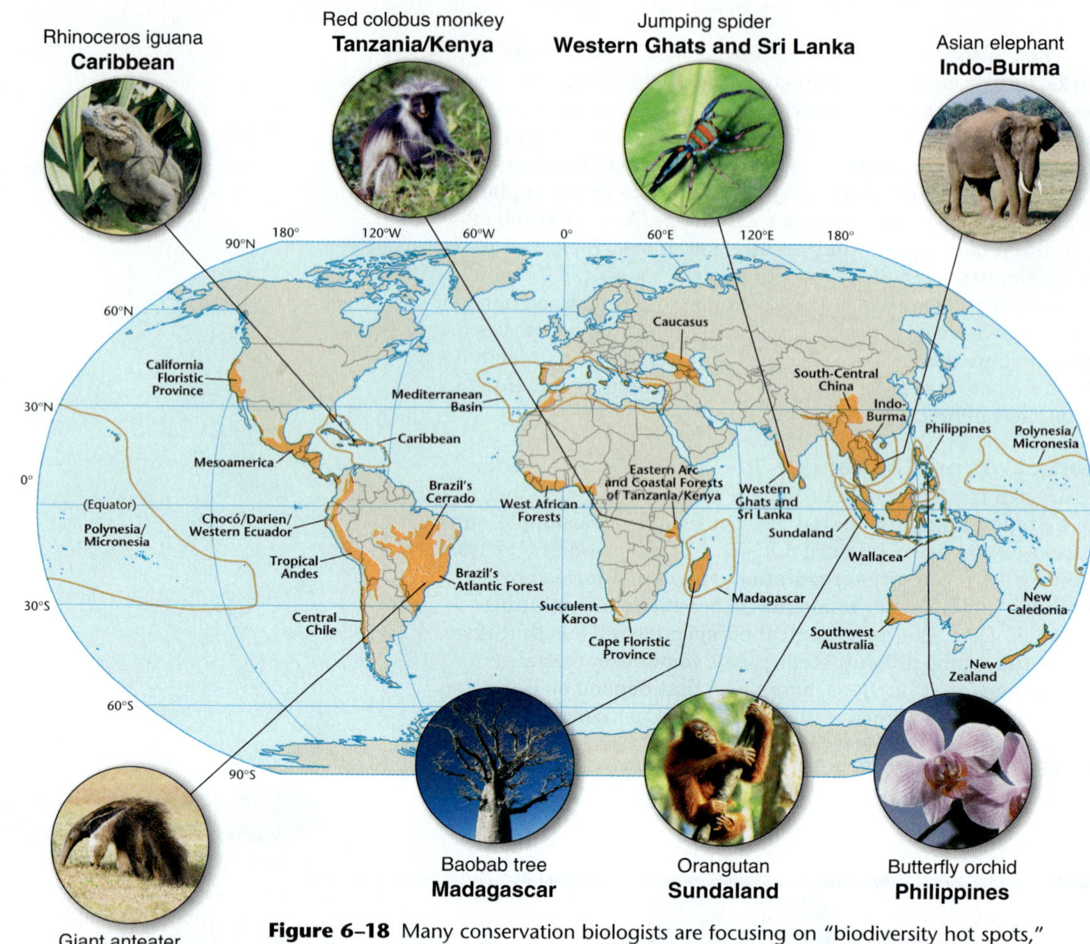

Figure 6–18 Many conservation biologists are focusing on "biodiversity hot spots," where the biodiversity of these unique ecosystems is threatened. The hot spots are shown in orange on the map. **By focusing on protecting specific ecosystems, biologists hope to preserve global biodiversity.**

6–3 Section Assessment

1. **Key Concept** Why is biodiversity worth preserving?
2. **Key Concept** List four activities that can threaten biodiversity.
3. **Key Concept** What is the current focus of conservation biologists worldwide?
4. Explain the relationship between habitat size and species diversity.
5. Why are habitats limited resources? How might their destruction affect the long-term survival of species?
6. **Critical Thinking Predicting** What problems could result if an endangered species were introduced into a nonnative habitat?

Focus on the BIG Idea

Science, Technology, and Society Review biomes in Chapter 4. Then, choose one of the hot spots shown above. Find out about the biome in which these unique ecosystems and endangered species occur. Report on your findings and suggest specific actions that can be taken to preserve the biome's biodiversity.

6–3 Section Assessment

1. Biodiversity is worth preserving because it is one of Earth's greatest natural resources and has provided us with foods, industrial products, and medicines.
2. Altering habitats, causing species extinction through hunting, polluting ecosystems, and introducing foreign species to new environments
3. Protecting entire ecosystems as well as single species
4. The smaller the habitat's size, the fewer the number of species that can live there.
5. Each habitat is unique; once destroyed or altered, a habitat may be gone forever. As habitats disappear, the species that depend on those habitats may not be able to survive.
6. An endangered species might become extinct if it is not suited to the new habitat. Conversely, an introduced species might reproduce rapidly and displace native species.

6–4 Charting a Course for the Future

BI 6.b. Students know how to analyze changes in an ecosystem resulting from changes in climate, human activity, introduction of nonnative species, or changes in population size.

For most of human history, environmental change was a local affair. For example, many animals in the Hawaiian Islands became extinct after humans arrived there. The effect of these extinctions on the biosphere at large was negligible. Since your parents and grandparents were born, however, global human population has grown from around 2.5 billion to more than 6.1 billion! Today, much of Earth's land surface has been altered by human activity.

In order to plan a sound environmental strategy for the twenty-first century, we need data provided by research. This research requires information from geology, chemistry, physics, and meteorology, as well as ecology.  **Researchers are gathering data to monitor and evaluate the effects of human activities on important systems in the biosphere. Two of these systems are the ozone layer high in the atmosphere and the global climate system.** Scientists' investigations of these two systems—and the actions taken as a result—show how research can have a positive impact on the global environment.

Guide for Reading

Key Concept
- What are two types of global change of concern to biologists?

Vocabulary
ozone layer
global warming

Reading Strategy: Summarizing As you read, find the key concept in the section. Write down a few words or phrases from the key concept, then use them in a summary of Section 6–4.

Ozone Depletion

Between 20 and 50 kilometers above Earth's surface, the atmosphere contains a relatively high concentration of ozone gas called the **ozone layer.** Molecules of ozone consist of three oxygen atoms. Although ozone at ground level is a pollutant, the naturally occurring ozone layer serves an important function. It absorbs a good deal of harmful ultraviolet, or UV, radiation from sunlight before it reaches Earth's surface. You may know that overexposure to UV radiation is the principal cause of sunburn. You may not know that exposure to UV can also cause cancer, damage eyes, and decrease organisms' resistance to disease. Intense UV radiation can also damage tissue in plant leaves and even phytoplankton in the oceans. Thus, by shielding the biosphere from UV light, the ozone layer serves as a global sunscreen.

Early Evidence Beginning in the 1970s, scientists found evidence from satellite data that the ozone layer was in trouble. The first problem sign was a gap, or "hole," in the ozone layer over Antarctica during winter. Since it was first discovered, the ozone hole has grown larger and lasted longer. A similar ozone hole also appeared over the Arctic. In 1974, a research team including Mario Molina of the Massachusetts Institute of Technology and F. Sherwood Rowland of the University of California at Irvine published data showing that gases called chlorofluorocarbons, or CFCs, could damage the ozone layer.

Figure 6–19 **Many biologists are concerned about the thinning of the ozone layer.** This image, taken by satellite in 2001, shows the thinning of the ozone layer in the Southern Hemisphere. The image is color-coded, with yellow being the area with the highest concentration of ozone and blue the lowest. The ozone hole is the bright blue area surrounding Antarctica.

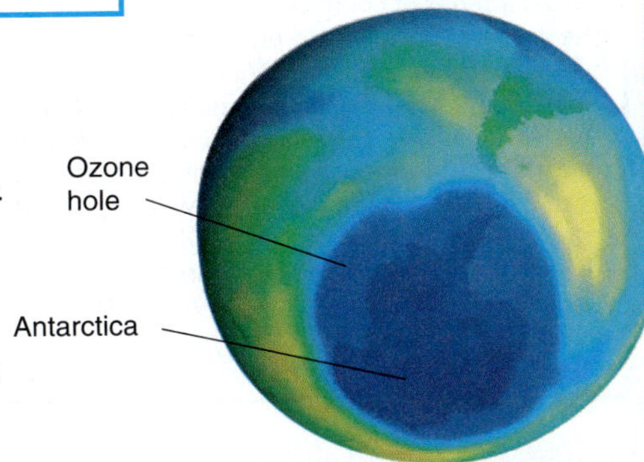

SECTION RESOURCES

Print:
- ***Laboratory Manual B,*** Chapter 6 Lab
- ***Teaching Resources,*** Lesson Plan 6–4, Adapted Section Summary 6–4, Adapted Worksheets 6–4, Section Summary 6–4, Worksheets 6–4, Section Review 6–4
- ***Reading and Study Workbook A,*** Section 6–4
- ***Adapted Reading and Study Workbook B,*** Section 6–4
- ***Issues and Decision Making,*** Issues and Decisions 1, 3, 50
- ***Lab Worksheets,*** Chapter 6 Exploration
- ***Probeware Lab Manual,*** Observing the Effects of Acid Rain

Technology:
- ***iText,*** Section 6–4
- ***Transparencies Plus,*** Section 6–4

Section 6–4

1 FOCUS

Objective

6.4.1 ***Describe*** two types of global change that are of concern to biologists.

Guide for Reading

Vocabulary Preview

Discuss with students the molecular structure of ozone (O_3), and make sure that they understand that its molecules are different from the diatomic oxygen molecules (O_2) in the atmosphere.

Review the greenhouse effect (Chapter 4). Ask: **What would happen to the temperature of the atmosphere if the proportion of greenhouse gases increased?** (*The atmosphere would become warmer—hence, the term* global warming.)

Reading Strategy

Students who are not fluent in written English would benefit from being paired with fluent readers who can help them identify main ideas and select relevant words and phrases.

2 INSTRUCT

Ozone Depletion

Making Connections

Earth Science Have students draw diagrams to scale that show the main layers of Earth's atmosphere, then shade the area occupied by the ozone layer. Ask: **Which layer contains most of the mass of the atmosphere?** (*The troposphere, which extends from 0 to 12 km above the surface*) **In which layer does the ozone layer occur?** (*The stratosphere, which extends from the top of the troposphere to about 50 km above the surface*) L1 L2

6–4 (continued)

Make Connections

Chemistry Explain that ozone (O_3) in the ozone layer naturally absorbs UV radiation, and such absorption results in an oxygen molecule (O_2) and an oxygen atom (O). Just as naturally, UV radiation adds energy to oxygen molecules, which causes them to combine with oxygen atoms to form ozone. The result of this cycle of destruction and formation is that the ozone layer tends to be relatively stable. CFCs also absorb UV radiation and also decompose into chemical products. Two of these products, chlorine and bromine atoms, react with ozone molecules, and oxygen molecules result from these reactions. The problem is that the oxygen molecules from those reactions do not as readily recombine with oxygen atoms to form ozone, and the natural cycle is broken. L3

Analyzing Data

 6IIE 7.e, 7IIE 7.c

Before students study the line graph in the feature, point out that the *y*-axis is labeled "Units of Ozone," which is more technically called the Dobson unit (DU). The Dobson unit, the basic unit used to measure ozone in the atmosphere, was named after G.M.B. Dobson, one of the first scientists to study ozone in the atmosphere. His Dobson spectrophotometer is an instrument that measures ozone in the atmosphere from the ground. The Dobson unit is defined as follows: 1 DU = 2.7×10^{16} ozone molecules per square centimeter.

Answers

1. The general trend from 1960 to the mid-1990s was a drop in the level of ozone in the atmosphere.
2. 1993
3. Between 1995 and 1999, the level of ozone in the atmosphere rose. This reversal of the previous trend may be the result of the reduction in production and use of CFCs, which was called for in the Montreal Protocol, signed in 1987.

Figure 6–20 Mario Molina (left), F. Sherwood Rowland, and Paul Crutzen shared the Nobel Prize in 1995 for their research on factors that can destroy ozone. **Applying Concepts** *What action did nations take to deal with the ozone hole?*

One Solution CFCs were once widely used as propellants in aerosol cans; as coolant in refrigerators, freezers, and air conditioners; and in the production of plastic foams. Because of the research of Molina, Rowland, and other scientists, the United States and many other nations began reducing the use of CFCs in 1987. Today, most uses of CFCs are banned.

Because CFC molecules can linger for as long as a century, their effects are not yet over. But the level of chlorine from CFCs in the atmosphere has already begun to fall, indicating that the CFC ban will have positive, long-term effects on the global environment. Current data predict that the ozone holes should shrink and disappear within 50 years.

CHECKPOINT *What is ozone depletion?*

Analyzing Data

Banning CFCs

 6IIE 7.e, 7IIE 7.c

A layer of ozone is normally present in Earth's upper atmosphere, or stratosphere. The ozone layer prevents much of the ultraviolet light emitted by the sun from reaching Earth's surface. In the 1970s, scientists noticed that ozone levels in the stratosphere were dropping. Evidence indicated that this was caused by the introduction of chlorofluorocarbons into the atmosphere.

In the lower atmosphere, CFCs are stable. However, when CFCs are carried into the stratosphere, UV rays bombard them and break them apart. This process causes a series of chemical reactions that break down the ozone molecules into ordinary oxygen, which offers no protection from UV light at all.

In 1987, forty-six nations signed an agreement called the Montreal Protocol, which called for an immediate reduction in production and use of CFCs. The following year, the United States passed a law to phase out the use of CFCs in aerosol cans by 2000. The members of the Montreal Protocol met again in 1990 and agreed to end the use of most CFCs by the year 2000. All of these resolutions have taken effect by now.

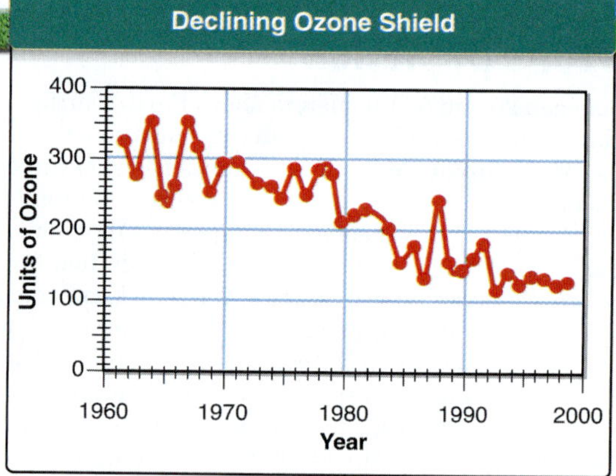

The graph shows ozone levels in the stratosphere from the 1960s to the late 1990s. Use the graph to answer the following questions.

1. **Using Tables and Graphs** Describe the general trend shown by the graph.
2. **Using Tables and Graphs** In what year did ozone drop to its lowest level?
3. **Applying Concepts** What happened between 1995 and 1999? Relate this to international actions regarding CFCs.

TEACHER TO TEACHER

I use the following activity to demonstrate the effects of ozone depletion. Ahead of time, I prepare a sufficient amount of yeast culture so each team can partially fill three or more petri dishes. The cultures can be started in large test tubes with baker's yeast in a sugar solution. I ask students to bring in sunscreen lotions of their choice, preferably several with different SPF ratings. Each team uses a microscope to get a rough population count of yeast in the starting culture. Students pour the culture into petri dishes and cover them. Then, they smear a different sunscreen on each cover. After exposing the dishes to direct sunlight or a sunlamp for a certain amount of time, students take a rough count of yeast in each dish and compare the counts with the starting counts.

—*Tamsen Meyer*
Biology Teacher
Boulder High School
Boulder, CO

Global Climate Change

All life on Earth depends on climate conditions such as temperature and rainfall. That's why many ecologists are concerned about strong evidence that climate is changing. Since the late nineteenth century, average atmospheric temperatures on Earth's surface have risen about 0.6 Celsius degrees. Data from sources such as the National Oceanic and Atmospheric Administration indicate that since about 1980, average temperatures have risen between 0.2 and 0.3 Celsius degrees. The 1990s were the warmest decade ever recorded, and 1998 was the warmest year since record-keeping began. The term used to describe this increase in the average temperature of the biosphere is **global warming.** One sign of global warming is melting polar ice, as shown in **Figure 6–21.**

Evidence of Global Warming The geological record shows that Earth's climate has changed repeatedly during its history. Therefore, researchers must determine whether the current warming trend is part of a larger, natural cycle of climate change, or whether it is caused by human activity. Research focuses on describing the warming trend, determining its cause, and predicting its effects on the biosphere.

The most widely accepted hypothesis is that current warming is related, at least in part, to human activities that are adding carbon dioxide and other greenhouse gases to the atmosphere. According to this hypothesis, the burning of fossil fuels, combined with the cutting and burning of forests worldwide, is adding carbon dioxide to the atmosphere faster than the carbon cycle removes it. Data show that concentrations of carbon dioxide in the atmosphere have been rising for 200 years. As a result, the atmosphere's natural greenhouse effect is intensified, causing the atmosphere to retain more heat.

Possible Effects of Global Warming How far might this warming go and what might its effects be? Researchers attempt to answer these questions with computer models based on data. Because these models are complex and involve assumptions, their predictions are open to debate. Nevertheless, most recent models suggest that average global surface temperatures will increase by 1 to 2 Celsius degrees by the year 2050.

What might this change mean? Sea levels may rise enough to flood some coastal areas. Flooding would affect coastal ecosystems as well as human communities. Some models suggest that parts of North America may experience more droughts during the summer growing season. Any long-term change in climate will affect ecosystems. New organisms may be able to live in places where they once could not. Other organisms may become threatened or extinct in areas where they once thrived.

Researchers are continuing to gather data and will use the data to refine current models. The new information should help provide society with ways of dealing with climate change.

For: Links on global warming
Visit: www.SciLinks.org
Web Code: cbn-2064

▼ **Figure 6–21** **Biologists are concerned about global warming.** This map of the Arctic is based on images taken by satellites in 1979 and 1999. Sea ice in the Arctic Ocean has receded so quickly that some scientists suggest that, within the next 50 years, the ice could disappear completely.

CA a BI 6.b

Global Climate Change

Use Visuals

Figure 6–21 Have students examine the map and read the caption. Then ask: **What do you think will happen if polar ice continues to melt?** *(Animals such as polar bears that live on the ice could be affected.)* L1 L2

Address Misconceptions

Students may think that an average climate change of only a degree or two would have little impact. Many researchers think that even slight global warming could cause storms to increase in strength and cause shifts in wind patterns that affect local temperatures and rainfall. Encourage students to find out about recent climatic events such as floods and droughts in the United States and elsewhere and the effects of those events on the human population. L2 L3

Download a worksheet on global warming for students to complete, and find additional teacher support from NSTA SciLinks.

UNIVERSAL ACCESS

Less Proficient Readers
Give students a better understanding of the location of the ozone layer by using an illustration of the atmosphere from a meteorology or earth science text. Most college-level textbooks that address the subject have a labeled illustration clearly showing this section of the stratosphere. L1 L2

English Language Learners
Explain to learners of English that the word *depletion* means a "loss of quantity." Thus, the heading *Ozone Depletion* simply means the loss of ozone. In this context, it means the loss of ozone molecules from a layer of the atmosphere that protects living things from the dangers of UV radiation. L1 L2

Advanced Learners
Encourage interested students to use library or Internet resources to find out what the current scientific thinking is about both ozone depletion and global climate change. Different students could collaborate on one or the other topic. Have them make a presentation of their findings. L3

Answers to . . .

CHECKPOINT *Thinning of the ozone layer resulting from release of chlorofluorocarbons into the atmosphere*

Figure 6–20 *Many nations reduced, and then banned, the use of CFCs.*

6–4 (continued)

The Value of a Healthy Biosphere

Build Science Skills

Problem Solving Tell students to imagine that they are conservation biologists, local developers, and town officials who are meeting to discuss the need to preserve natural areas in their community. Have students meet in small groups to outline the major points they would want to make. Let students role-play the meeting. L2

3 ASSESS

Evaluate Understanding

Have each student write two paragraphs: one explaining why it's important to stop releasing chlorofluorocarbons into the atmosphere, the other discussing the probable causes and possible long-term effects of global warming.

Reteach

Have small groups of students create an illustrated pamphlet designed to inform other students about one of the major topics in this section.

You & Your Community

Students should have no difficulty finding sources that express different opinions about global warming and the ozone hole. Make sure students note that more data are needed before scientists can make firm predictions about climate change.

If your class subscribes to the iText, use it to review the Key Concepts in Section 6–4.

Answer to . . .

Figure 6–22 *Most students will probably classify the ecological services as renewable resources, although some may argue that certain services are not renewable unless they are managed wisely.*

Ecosystem Services
Solar Energy
Production of oxygen
Storage and recycling of nutrients
Regulation of climate
Purification of water and air
Storage and distribution of fresh water
Food production
Nursery habitats for wildlife
Detoxification of human and industrial waste
Natural pest and disease control
Management of soil erosion and runoff

▲ **Figure 6–22** Human society depends on healthy, diverse, and productive ecosystems because of the environmental and economic benefits they provide. **Classifying** ***Should the ecosystem services in the chart be considered renewable or nonrenewable resources? Explain.***

The Value of a Healthy Biosphere

You might wonder why ecologists work so hard to study what seem to be small environmental changes. To understand, remember the concept of ecosystem goods and services. As shown in **Figure 6–22**, these range from water purification to waste recycling. Ecosystems provide many services besides these, however, such as the pollination of many crop plants by insects. Ecosystems are also a reservoir of organisms that might one day provide humans with new medicines and new varieties of crops. There is much that we don't understand about the systems that provide these services. Biologists are therefore concerned that human activities might affect them in unexpected ways.

Is there any way that people can help maintain the health of the biosphere without drastically changing their lifestyles? The answer is yes. People can make wise choices in the use and conservation of resources. For example, when people water gardens or take showers, they can avoid using more water than necessary. Like the Polynesians who settled Hawaii, people can plant trees to replace the ones they have cut down. Trash and other wastes can often be reused or recycled, and dangerous chemical wastes can be disposed in a way that does not harm ecosystems. Many communities now have facilities for recycling trash and methods of safely removing hazardous materials.

Studies of human impact on the environment are not about predicting disaster. You have seen how research led to actions that are replenishing fisheries in the North Atlantic and preserving the ozone layer. The biosphere is strong. Humans are very clever. Both humans and natural ecosystems can adapt to change of different kinds.

6–4 Section Assessment

1. **Key Concept** What are two major global changes affecting the biosphere today?
2. Why is the ozone layer important to living things?
3. How could a worldwide increase in temperature affect organisms?
4. What actions can people take in their daily lives to make wise choices in the use and conservation of resources?
5. **Thinking Critically** **Evaluating** Evaluate the impact of environmental research on the problem of ozone depletion. How did research identify the cause of the problem? To what action did this research lead?

You & Your Community

Comparing Media
Locate five print, radio, television, or Internet sources about global warming or the ozone hole. What attitudes and opinions are expressed in these sources? Compare them with the information in this section.

6–4 Section Assessment

1. Ozone depletion and global climate change
2. The ozone layer absorbs ultraviolet light from the sun that can harm organisms.
3. The effects of global warming include rising sea level, which could affect coastal ecosystems, and changes in climate that could affect the geographical distribution of species. Some species might be able to extend their ranges, while others might become extinct.
4. Recycling and energy conservation are wise choices in the use and conservation of resources.
5. Scientists first noticed a "hole" in the ozone layer over Antarctica through satellite data. A research team then discovered that CFCs could damage the ozone layer. This research led to the banning of CFCs.

Design an Experiment

 BI 6.b, 6IIE 7.e, 7IIE 7.c, 8IIE 9.c, BIIE 1.a, BIIE 1.j

Observing the Effects of Acid Rain

Acid rain is formed when the combustion of fossil fuels releases gases containing nitrogen and sulfur compounds into the atmosphere. It can damage crops, forests, soil, and buildings. In this investigation, you will design and perform an experiment to simulate and test the effect of acid rain on the germination of seeds.

Problem How does acid rain affect the germination of seeds?

Materials

- diluted sulfuric acid
- filter paper
- glass-marking pencil
- 2 petri dishes
- 100-mL graduated cylinder
- 100 seeds (mustard or radish)
- pH paper
- 2 100-mL beakers
- hand lens

Skills Designing Experiments, Controlling Variables

Design Your Experiment 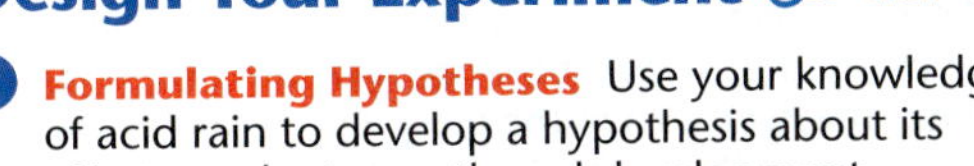

1. **Formulating Hypotheses** Use your knowledge of acid rain to develop a hypothesis about its effect on plant growth and development. Record your hypothesis.
2. **Predicting** Record a prediction about how acid rain will affect seed germination.
3. Design an experiment to test your prediction. It is not practical in the classroom to expose some plants to acid rain and others to rain without acid. You will need to choose a way to simulate acid rain.
4. As you plan your investigative procedures, refer to the Lab Tips box on page 55 for information on demonstrating safe practices, making wise choices in the use of materials, and selecting equipment and technology. With your teacher's guidance, select the equipment and technology to use to measure pH: either pH paper or a pH probe. If using a pH probe, see your teacher for instructions.
5. Check your experimental design to make sure you are testing only one variable and have included any necessary controls. Construct any data tables you will need to use for recording the results of your experiment. With your teacher's approval, carry out your experiment. **CAUTION:** *Wear goggles, an apron, and plastic gloves when handling diluted sulfuric acid.* Wash your hands thoroughly with soap and warm water before leaving the lab.

Analyze and Conclude

1. **Analyzing Data** What percentage of your control seeds germinated? What percentage of your acid-treated seeds germinated?
2. **Drawing Conclusions** What do your results imply about the short-term effects of acid rain?
3. **Predicting** Would you expect acid rain to injure plants after they have completed germination? Explain your answer.
4. **SAFETY** Explain how you demonstrated safe practices as you carried out this investigation.
5. **Asking Questions** What additional questions might you ask about the effects of acid rain on plants? (*Hint:* Think about seedlings that have already germinated.) Describe an experiment that might provide the answer.

Go Further

Problem Solving Conduct research and report to the class on the various methods used in industry to reduce the amounts of sulfur dioxide and nitrogen oxides being emitted into the atmosphere.

Analyze and Conclude

1. Actual counts and percentages will vary. Fewer acid-treated seeds will germinate than control seeds.
2. Acid rain inhibits seed germination.
3. Yes. If acid rain has a negative effect on seeds, it would probably injure young plants as well.
4. Students should explain that they wore plastic gloves, aprons, and safety goggles when working with diluted sulfuric acid.
5. Answers may vary. A typical question might be: How does acid rain affect the growth of plants? A typical design might use similar materials as in the experiment on this page, with a focus on observing plant growth and development over time when a plant is watered with an acidic solution.

Design an Experiment

 BI 6.b, 6IIE 7.e, 7IIE 7.c, 8IIE 9.c, BIIE 1.a, BIIE 1.j

Objective Students will be able to determine how acid rain affects seed germination. L2

Skills Focus Designing Experiments, Controlling Variables

Time 45 minutes to design and set up experiment; 5 minutes each day for observation and recording

Advance Prep To prepare the diluted sulfuric acid, dilute 10 mL of 0.1 N H_2SO_4 in water to a total of 1 L. **CAUTION:** *Always add acid to water, never water to acid.* Check the pH. Add additional 0.1 N sulfuric acid to bring the pH down to 3 or 4. If you are using probeware in this activity, use the instructions in the *Probeware Lab Manual.*

Safety Read the safety information on the MSDS for sulfuric acid before doing the lab. Wear goggles, lab apron, and plastic gloves when you prepare the diluted acid.

Pre-Lab Discussion Have students read the entire lab and ask any questions they may have about how they are to proceed. Review the difference between a testable hypothesis and a prediction.

Teaching Tips

- Have students work in groups of three or four.
- Circulate among the groups to check that they provide a safe and contained method of simulating acid rain, account for all variables that must be controlled, and plan data tables that will allow regular, detailed recording.

Expected Outcome The seeds exposed to acid rain will not germinate as well as those not exposed.

Go Further

Alert your school or town librarian to the topic of students' research so appropriate books can be set aside.

Chapter 6 Study Guide

6–1 A Changing Landscape

Key Concept 

- Among human activities that affect the biosphere are hunting and gathering, agriculture, industry, and urban development.

Vocabulary
agriculture, p. 141 • monoculture, p. 141
green revolution, p. 142

6–2 Renewable and Nonrenewable Resources

- Environmental goods and services may be classified as either renewable or nonrenewable.
- Human activities can affect the quality and supply of renewable resources such as land, forests, fisheries, air, and fresh water.

Vocabulary
renewable resource, p. 144
nonrenewable resource, p. 144
sustainable development, p. 145
soil erosion, p. 145 • desertification, p. 145
deforestation, p. 146 • aquaculture, p. 147
smog, p. 148 • pollutant, p. 148
acid rain, p. 148

6–3 Biodiversity

Key Concepts  

- Biodiversity is one of Earth's greatest natural resources. Many species have provided us with foods, industrial products, and medicines—including painkillers, antibiotics, heart drugs, antidepressants, and anticancer drugs.
- Human activity can reduce biodiversity by altering habitats, hunting species to extinction, introducing toxic compounds into food webs, and introducing foreign species to new environments.
- Today, conservation efforts focus on protecting entire ecosystems as well as single species. Protecting an ecosystem will ensure that the natural habitats and interactions of many different species are preserved at the same time.

Vocabulary
biodiversity, p. 150 • ecosystem diversity, p. 150
species diversity, p. 150 • genetic diversity, p. 150
extinction, p. 151 • endangered species, p. 151
habitat fragmentation, p. 151
biological magnification, p. 152
invasive species, p. 153 • conservation, p. 154

6–4 Charting a Course for the Future

Key Concept BI 6.b

- Researchers are gathering data to monitor and evaluate the effects of human activities on important systems in the biosphere. Two of these systems are the ozone layer high in the atmosphere and the global climate system.

Vocabulary
ozone layer, p. 157
global warming, p. 159

Thinking Visually

Using information from this chapter, complete the following concept map:

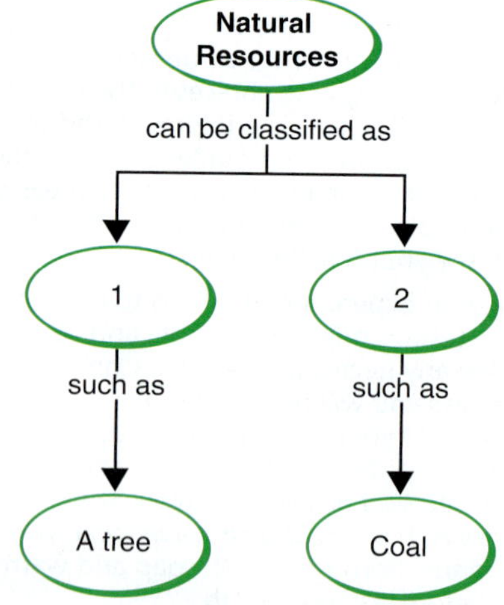

Chapter 6 Study Guide

Study Tip

Divide the class into four groups, and assign one section to each group. Tell students that each group will serve as the "class experts" on the assigned sections. Also, explain that they can divide the section's material among the group members in any way they wish. Encourage students to think of the kinds of questions other students might ask and to be prepared to answer them. Encourage groups to meet at least once to review their understanding of the sections.

Thinking Visually

1. Renewable
2. Nonrenewable

Chapter 6 Assessment

Reviewing Content

1. d	5. d	9. c
2. c	6. b	10. b
3. c	7. d	11. a
4. c	8. b	

Understanding Concepts

12. The greatest source of change in the biosphere is human activity.
13. The green revolution introduced farming strategies such as high-yield varieties of major food crops, which greatly increased agricultural production.
14. Answers may vary. A typical response might mention pollution and destruction of habitats.
15. Forests remove carbon dioxide from the atmosphere and produce oxygen.
16. Examples of environmental pollutants include sewage dumped into streams, oil spills at sea, pesticides that enter the food chain, and acidic gases from burning fossil fuels.

TIME SAVER — CHAPTER RESOURCES

Print:
- ***Teaching Resources,*** Chapter Vocabulary Review, Graphic Organizer, Chapter 6 Tests: Levels A and B
- ***Laboratory Assessment,*** Laboratory Assessment 2

Technology:
- ***Computer Test Bank,*** Chapter 6 Test
- ***iText,*** Chapter 6 Assessment

Chapter 6 Assessment

Reviewing Content

Choose the letter that best answers the question or completes the statement.

1. Which of the following human activities was NOT important in transforming the biosphere?
   a. agriculture
   b. industry
   c. urban development
   d. aquaculture

2. Civilizations could not develop without
   a. monoculture.
   b. hunter-gatherers.
   c. agriculture.
   d. crop exchange.

3. A resource that cannot be replenished by natural processes is called
   a. common.
   b. renewable.
   c. nonrenewable.
   d. conserved.

4. The conversion of a previously soil-rich area to a sandy desert is called
   a. habitat fragmentation.
   b. deforestation.
   c. desertification.
   d. acid rain.

5. The burning of fossil fuels may cause all of the following EXCEPT
   a. acid rain.
   b. global warming.
   c. smog.
   d. the ozone hole.

6. The sum total of the variety of organisms on Earth is referred to as
   a. ecosystem.
   b. biodiversity.
   c. forest.
   d. agriculture.

7. When land development divides a habitat into isolated "islands," the result is called
   a. deforestation.
   b. reforestation.
   c. magnification.
   d. fragmentation.

8. A species that enters an environment where it has not lived before is called a(an)
   a. endangered species.
   b. invasive species.
   c. threatened species.
   d. predator.

9. A species whose population size is declining so rapidly that it could soon become extinct is
   a. nonnative.
   b. fragmented.
   c. endangered.
   d. invasive.

10. The concept of using natural resources at a rate that does not deplete them is called
    a. conservation.
    b. sustainable development.
    c. reforestation.
    d. successful use.

Interactive textbook with assessment at PHSchool.com 

11. Examine the food web below and determine which of the following organisms would accumulate the highest levels of a chlorinated pesticide.

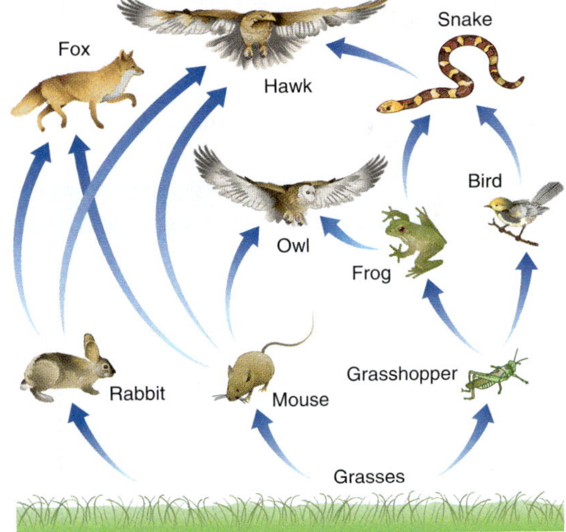

    a. hawk
    b. rabbit
    c. frog
    d. grasses

Understanding Concepts

12. What has been the greatest source of change in the biosphere?
13. What was the green revolution?
14. Identify two ways in which industrial development has affected ecosystems.
15. Why have forests been called the "lungs of the Earth"?
16. List three examples of an environmental pollutant.
17. Define biodiversity.
18. Give an example of biological magnification. How does it occur?
19. Describe the process by which chlorofluorocarbons deplete the ozone layer.
20. Speaking ecologically, what is conservation? What is the role of conservation biology?
21. Name four natural services that ecosystems provide for the biosphere.

If your class subscribes to the iText, your students can go online to access an interactive version of the Student Edition and a self-test.

(Continued from page 162)

17. Biodiversity is the sum total of the genetically based variety of organisms in the biosphere.

18. The increasing concentration of DDT released into the food chain from zooplankton to fish to eagles is an example of how biological magnification occurs.

19. CFCs are carried into the upper atmosphere, where UV radiation breaks them apart. A series of chemical reactions follows, breaking down ozone into ordinary oxygen.

20. In ecology, the term conservation is used to describe the wise management of natural resources, including preservation of habitats and wildlife. The modern science of conservation biology seeks to protect biodiversity.

21. Students should name any 4 of the 11 ecosystem services listed in Figure 6–22 on page 160.

HOMEWORK GUIDE

Section:	Questions:
Section 6–1	1, 2, 12–14, 25
Section 6–2	3–4, 10, 15, 16, 26, 28, 30, 31
Section 6–3	6–9, 11, 17, 18, 20, 22, 23, 27
Section 6–4	5, 19, 21, 24, 29

Chapter 6 Assessment

Critical Thinking

22. The loss of biodiversity may mean the loss of potential sources of material with significant value to humans. Students may suggest examples such as the loss of plants that can be used for medicines.

23. Species diversity refers to the number of species in the biosphere, and ecosystem diversity refers to the variety of different habitats, communities, and ecological processes in the living world.

24. **a.** The change in temperature, expressed in °C, is plotted on the *y*-axis. The unit 0.0 represents the global temperature in 1850. **b.** The world temperature change in 2000 was +0.7, or 0.7 degrees higher than in 1850. **c.** The data between 1970 and 2000 show an overall increase in temperature. **d.** The graph by itself does not predict the pattern of global warming in the future, because many different variables interact to produce temperature averages for a given year and can also modify climate trends in unpredictable ways.

25. Students may hypothesize that because the cotton crop was made up of plants that were all the same in their inability to resist disease, the new disease was able to sweep through and destroy the cotton crop.

26. Students' experiments should compare erosion of soil that is protected in various ways with erosion of unprotected soil.

27. To determine the concentration at each trophic level, multiply by 10. Thus, Ist level=40 ppm; 2nd level=400 ppm; 3rd level=4000 ppm; 4th level=40,000 ppm; 5th level=400,000 ppm.

28. Predictions may vary. A typical response might mention the sustainable-development strategies discussed in the text, including selectively harvesting mature trees, a greater reliance on tree farms, and the breeding of new, faster-growing tree varieties that produce high-quality wood.

29. Students' plans may vary. All guidelines should ensure that toxic or otherwise dangerous trash is either degraded before disposal or disposed in a manner that guarantees no harm will be done to the environment. Students should also describe ways to recycle paper, plastics, metals, and glass used in the classroom.

30. Acid rain might change the water chemistry of the lake, destroying life forms such as algae that can make lake water look cloudy.

31. Sulfur dioxide, which forms when sulfur-containing coal is burned, helps produce sulfuric acid, a component of acid rain. Low-sulfur coal produces less of the dioxide than high-sulfur coal, and thus less sulfuric acid and less acid rain.

Focus on the BIG Idea

The productivity of an ecosystem in which organisms live, and hence the potential variety of species (i.e., the level of biodiversity), depends on the ecosystem's abiotic and biotic factors. Most coastal waters are in the photic zone. As a result, they receive plenty of solar energy for the producers that support the food chain. In addition, runoff from rivers and streams may bring nutrients to coastal waters that also increase the productivity of coastal ecosystems. Finally, estuaries, the intertidal zone, and the coastal ocean provide varied habitats that encourage biodiversity.

Chapter 6 Assessment

Critical Thinking

22. **Predicting** How might the loss of biodiversity adversely affect humans?

23. **Comparing and Contrasting** Explain the difference between species diversity and ecosystem diversity.

24. **Using Tables and Graphs** Study the graph below that shows the change in global temperature from 1850 to 2000. Use the graph to answer the questions.

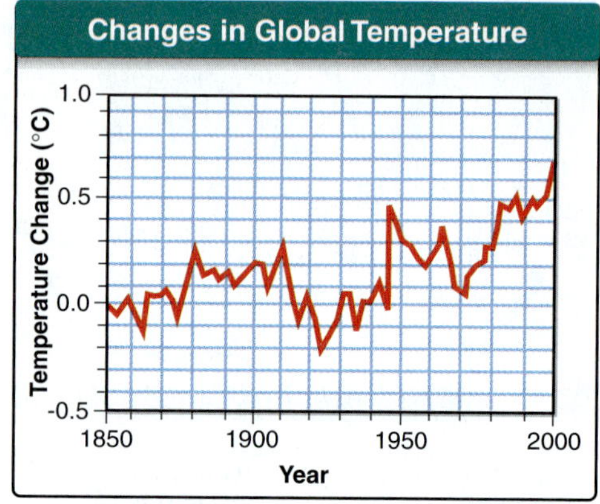

a. In your own words, explain what is plotted on the *y*-axis. What does the unit 0.0 represent?
b. How much did temperature change between 1850 and 2000?
c. Describe the trend in the data between 1970 and 2000.
d. Explain why this graph cannot predict global temperature change in the future.

25. **Formulating Hypotheses** A monoculture of cotton was planted in the 1980s in many southern states. A new disease invaded the cotton plants, almost completely destroying them. Explain how monoculture may have contributed to the effect of the disease.

26. **Designing Experiments** Can covering soil with mulch or compost near the bases of plants help to reduce soil erosion? Design an experiment to answer the question.

27. **Calculating** The concentration of a toxic chemical is magnified 10 times at each trophic level. What will be its concentration in organisms at the fifth trophic level if producers store the substance at concentrations of 40 parts per million?

28. **Predicting** Predict some ways in which scientific research might help the forest industry preserve forest ecosystems and maintain sustainable development and jobs.

29. **Applying Concepts** Devise guidelines that your biology class can use to dispose of the class's nonlab trash in a safe, "environment friendly" manner. Where possible, include recycling in your plan.

30. **Inferring** Lakes that are affected by acid rain often appear clear and blue. Why might this be so?

31. **Formulating Hypotheses** Different grades of coal contain different amounts of sulfur. Explain why burning low-sulfur coal can reduce acid rain.

Interdependence in Nature What environmental factors make high levels of biodiversity possible in most coastal waters? Refer to the discussion of abiotic and biotic factors in Chapter 4 if you need help answering this question.

Writing in Science

Write a paragraph explaining the value of wetlands to human societies. In your paragraph, include the concept of biodiversity as well as wetlands' role in maintaining water resources for human use. (*Hint*: To help think of ideas, create a cluster diagram or concept map with the word *wetlands* in the center. As you think of ideas, add them to the diagram. Then, group your ideas into related subtopics.)

Performance-Based Assessment

Designing an Educational Pamphlet You have been asked to design a pamphlet for fifth-graders about humans and the biosphere. The pamphlet must be scientifically accurate and contain illustrations. Create a thumbnail sketch of your pamphlet, including an outline of topics and images.

For: An interactive self-test
Visit: PHSchool.com
Web Code: cba-2060

Standards Practice

Test-Taking Tip When evaluating multiple-choice answers, be sure to read all of the answer choices, even if the first choice seems to be correct. By doing so, you can make sure that the answer you choose is the best one.

Directions: Choose the letter that best answers the question or completes the statement.

1. What is NOT true of a renewable resource?
   A It is unlimited.
   B It is replaceable by natural means.
   C It can regenerate quickly.
   D all of the above

2. Which of the following is NOT a renewable resource?
   A wind
   B sunlight
   C water
   D fossil fuels

3. Which of the following is NOT an effect of deforestation? **BI 6.b**
   A chemical change in soil
   B decreased productivity of the ecosystem
   C soil erosion
   D biological magnification

4. The sum total of the variety of organisms in the biosphere is called
   A biodiversity.
   B species diversity.
   C ecosystem diversity.
   D genetic diversity.

5. Which is NOT a characteristic of the sustainable development of natural resources? **BI 6.b**
   A instability
   B flexibility
   C appropriate technology
   D efficiency

6. Ozone is made up of
   A water.
   B hydrogen.
   C nitrogen.
   D oxygen.

7. Ozone depletion has been caused by **BI 6.b**
   A monoculture.
   B suburban sprawl.
   C aquaculture.
   D CFCs.

8. Concentrations of harmful substances increase in organisms at higher trophic levels in a food chain. This process is known as
   A aquaculture.
   B monoculture.
   C pesticide use.
   D biological magnification.

Questions 9–10 Use the information below to answer the questions that follow.

Fire ants first arrived in the United States in 1918, probably on a ship traveling from South America to Alabama. The maps show the geographic location of the U.S. fire ant population in 1953 and 1994.

1953

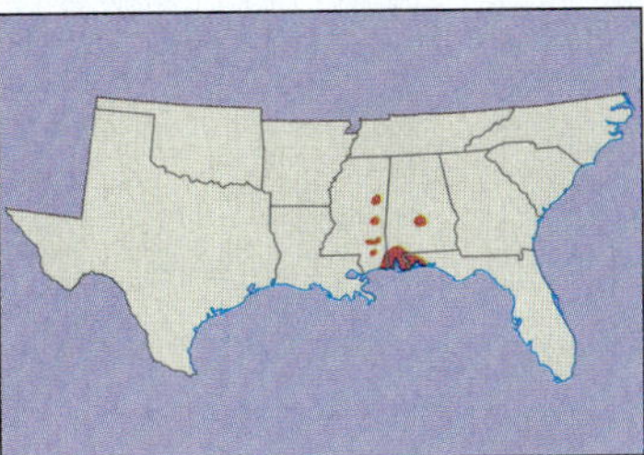

1994

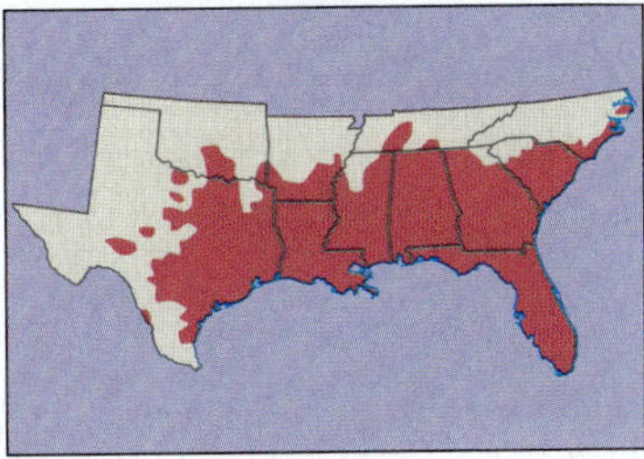

9. Which statement is true about fire ants in the United States? **BI 6.b**
   A They reproduce slowly.
   B They are a native species of the United States.
   C They are an invasive species.
   D Their numbers are declining.

10. By 2010, fire ants are likely to **BI 6.b**
   A occupy Florida only.
   B have reached their carrying capacity.
   C die out.
   D have spread to a larger area.

Standards Practice

1. A	5. A	9. C
2. D	6. D	10. D
3. D	7. D	
4. A	8. D	

Online at PHSchool.com

Have students check their understanding of the chapter by logging onto Success Tracker.

Writing in Science

Students' paragraphs may vary, though all should describe how wetlands provide a valuable ecosystem service by filtering certain pollutants from water. Students might also describe how pollution threatens water supplies and why wetlands are essential in maintaining a healthy environment, both for human uses and for other organisms.

Performance-Based Assessment

Student pamphlets should include highlights of the Key Concepts of the chapter: the effect of humans on the biosphere, renewable and nonrenewable resources, biodiversity, and sustainable use.

Your students can independently test their knowledge of the chapter and print out their test results for your files.

UNIT 3

Dear Colleague,

I can still remember the first time I looked through a microscope and saw a living cell. It was in Mr. Zong's ninth-grade biology class in my hometown in New Jersey. After carefully instructing us in the proper use of the microscope, our teacher placed a drop of water on every student's slide and told us to have a look.

I couldn't believe my eyes. Glistening creatures swam across the field of view. They twisted and turned, I thought, almost as if they were alive. I think I said that out loud, because I can remember Mr. Zong's deep, gentle laugh and a pat on my shoulder. "They *are* alive, Kenny! They're alive just like you and me."

Mr. Zong was famous among my classmates at Rahway High for his devotion to the "practicum" style of exam. Every other Friday, we walked into the classroom to be confronted by 30 "stations," one at the desk of every student. Each station had a specimen—a leaf, a butterfly, a seed, or a drop of water under a microscope. Taped to each desk was a question about that specimen.

We had 90 seconds to look at the specimen, read the question, and write down an answer. Then, we each moved on to the next station. No timeouts, no chances to go back. Forty-five minutes went by like a flash.

At first, I feared these semiweekly exams. After a while, however, I grew to love the challenge. In a way, I suppose, we sensed the passion in our teacher's insistence that the mysterious world of nature held stories—great stories. We students, he thought, could be expected to read, to learn, and then to tell those stories from the material of life itself.

All living things, including these ants, must use the energy they obtain from food in order to survive.

As fall turned toward winter, I remember my parents' surprise when I told them what I hoped to find under our Christmas tree that year—a microscope.

Only a few weeks later, I had transformed a tiny corner of the room I shared with my brother into a miniature laboratory. A tiny desk lamp glowed day and night, providing energy for nearly a dozen test-tube colonies of *Euglena*. At the end of the year, those cells would become a science project, the very first research I would ever do on my own.

I won second place that year in our school's science fair for my study of light's effect on the growth of *Euglena*. Although I have long since misplaced the ribbon my project was given, I hope I never lose the greater gift that came from a year of study in Paul Zong's classroom—a sense of amazement that returns every time I sit down at a microscope in my laboratory.

I hope that you and your students will find some of that amazement written into the pages of this unit. As a cell biologist, I especially hope to give students an appreciation of the roles that cells play in every aspect of life. In these four chapters, we have done our best to explain how cells live and grow, how they transform energy, and how they pass information along from one generation to the next.

I have been lucky enough to make biology my career, using the electron microscope as my primary research tool. Not all of your students can expect to do this, of course. But we can hope that with your guidance, each and every one of them will experience the same thrill I did when they focus their microscopes on living cells for the very first time.

Sincerely,

Ken Miller

Go Online PHSchool.com

Students can research cells on the site developed by authors Ken Miller and Joe Levine.

Chapter Planner 7 Cell Structure and Function

Section and Section Objectives	Time	STANDARDS NCLB	STANDARDS Biology	Activities and Labs
7–1 Life Is Cellular, pp. 169–173 **7.1.1** ***Explain*** what the cell theory is. **7.1.2** ***Describe*** how researchers explore the living cell. **7.1.3** ***Distinguish*** between eukaryotes and prokaryotes.	1 period (1/2 block)	BI 1.c	BIIE 1.k	**SE:** ***Inquiry Activity,*** What is a cell?, p. 168 L2 **SE:** ***Biology and History,*** The History of the Cell, pp. 170–171 L2 L3
7–2 Eukaryotic Cell Structure, pp. 174–181 **7.2.1** ***Describe*** the function of the cell nucleus. **7.2.2** ***Describe*** the functions of the major cell organelles. **7.2.3** ***Identify*** the main roles of the cytoskeleton.	2 periods (1 block)	7 1.c, 7 1.d, BI 1.c	BI 1.e, *BI 1.j	**TE:** ***Build Science Skills,*** p. 174, p. 175 L2 L3 **TE:** ***Build Science Skills,*** p. 178 L2 L3 **SE:** ***Quick Lab,*** How can you make a model of a cell?, p. 180 L2 L3
7–3 Cell Boundaries, pp. 182–189 **7.3.1** ***Identify*** the main functions of the cell membrane and the cell wall. **7.3.2** ***Describe*** what happens during diffusion. **7.3.3** ***Explain*** the processes of osmosis, facilitated diffusion, and active transport.	3 periods (1 1/2 blocks)	BI 1.a	*BI 1.j	**TE:** ***Build Science Skills,*** pp. 184 L1 L2, 189 L1 L2 **TE:** ***Demonstration,*** pp. 185 L1 L2, 186 L2 **SE:** ***Quick Lab,*** How can you model permeability in cells?, p. 187 L2 L3 **SE:** ***Analyzing Data,*** Crossing the Cell Membrane, p. 188 L2 L3 **SE:** ***Exploration,*** Investigating Cell Structures and Processes, pp. 194–195 L2 L3 **LMA:** Chapter 7 Lab L2 L3
7–4 The Diversity of Cellular Life, pp. 190–193 **7.4.1** ***Describe*** cell specialization. **7.4.2** ***Identify*** the organization levels in multicellular organisms.	1 period (1/2 block)	7 5.a		**SE:** ***Careers in Biology,*** Histotechnologist, p. 192 L2 **TE:** ***Build Science Skills,*** p. 192 L2 **LMB:** Chapter 7 Lab L1 L2
Chapter Assessment, pp. 196–199	1 period (1/2 block)			

ACTIVITY PLANNER

SE: *Inquiry Activity*, p. 168; 15 min.; microscopes, prepared slides of plant leaf or stem cross-section, nerve cell, bacteria, and paramecia

TE: *Build Science Skills*, p. 169; 15 min.; images of a variety of cells; p. 172; 15 min.; images produced by different kinds of microscopes; p. 175; 15 min.; prepared slides of animal cell and plant cell, microscope; p. 178; 20 min.; paramecium culture, yeast, Congo red, slide, coverslip, toothpick, microscope, dropper pipette

SE: *Quick Lab*, p. 180; 20 min.; variety of craft supplies, index cards

TE: *Build Science Skills*, p. 181; 5 min.; photo of a house being built; p. 184; 10 min.; 10 min. next day; 2 beakers, salt, teaspoon, food coloring, dropper

TE: *Demonstration*, p. 185; 5 min.; kitchen strainer, water, sugar, sand, small stones, marbles, paper clips; p. 186; 15 min.; paramecium culture, petri dish, microprojector, distilled water

SE: *Quick Lab*, p. 187; 20 min.; graduated cylinder, plastic sandwich bag, starch, twist tie, 500-mL beaker, iodine solution

TE: *Build Science Skills*, p. 189; 5 min.; board, books, tennis ball; p. 192; 10 min.; photographs, diagrams, or prepared slides of specialized cells

SE: *Exploration*, pp. 194–195; 90 min.; red onion, scalpel, 4 glass slides, dropper pipette, 4 coverslips, iodine solution, paper towel, microscope, prepared slide of human cheek cells, concentrated salt solution, distilled water, treated animal blood

PLANNING KEY

Ability Levels

for students performing . . .

below grade level L1

at grade level L2

above grade level L3

Print Components

SE	Student Edition	LA	Lab Assessment
TE	Teacher's Edition	BTM	Biotechnology Manual
RSW	Reading & Study Workbook A	IDM	Issues and Decision Making
ARSW	Adapted Reading & Study Workbook B	LW	Lab Worksheets
TR	Teaching Resources	LMA	Laboratory Manual A
IF	Investigations in Forensics	LMB	Laboratory Manual B

Tech Components

CTB	Computer Test Bank
BD	BioDetectives DVD
TP	Transparencies Plus
PLM	Probeware Lab Manual
ABC	ABC DVD Library
LS	Lab Simulations
VL	Virtual Labs

Interactive Textbook — Interactive textbook with assessment at PHSchool.com

Program Resources	Assessment	Media and Technology
TR: Lesson Plan 7–1, Section Summary, p. 5 L1, p. 17 L2, Worksheets, p. 8 L1, pp. 19–20 L2 **RSW:** Section 7–1 L2 **ARSW:** Section 7–1 L1	**SE:** 7–1 Section Assessment, p. 173 **TR:** Section Review 7–1	**iText:** Section 7–1 **TP:** 7–1 Interest Grabber, Section Outline, Prokaryotic and Eukaryotic Cells
TR: Lesson Plan 7–2, Section Summary, p. 5 L1, p. 17 L2, Worksheets, pp. 9–11 L1, pp. 21–25 L2 **RSW:** Section 7–2 L2 **ARSW:** Section 7–2 L1	**SE:** 7–2 Section Assessment, p. 181 **TR:** Section Review 7–2	**iText:** Section 7–2 **TP:** 7–2 Interest Grabber, Section Outline, Venn Diagrams, Figure 7–6, Figure 7–11
TR: Lesson Plan 7–3, Section Summary, p. 6 L1, p. 18 L2, Worksheets, pp. 12–14 L1, pp. 26–28 L2 **LW:** Chapter 7 Real-World Lab L1 L2 L3 **RSW:** Section 7–3 L2 **ARSW:** Section 7–3 L1	**SE:** 7–3 Section Assessment, p. 189 **TR:** Section Review 7–3	**iText:** Section 7–3 **TP:** 7–3 Interest Grabber, Section Outline, Facilitated Diffusion, Figure 7–12, Figure 7–15, Figure 7–19 **ABC:** 5 Diffusion and Osmosis, 6 Passive and Active Transport, 7 Endocytosis and Exocytosis **Lab Simulations CD-ROM:** Biomembranes I: Membrane Structure and Transport **VL:** Lab 3, Lab 4, Lab 5
TR: Lesson Plan 7–4, Section Summary, p. 7 L1, p. 18 L2, Worksheets, p. 15 L1, p. 29 L2, Enrichment L3 **RSW:** Section 7–4 L2 **ARSW:** Section 7–4 L1	**SE:** 7–4 Section Assessment, p. 193 **TR:** Section Review 7–4	**iText:** Section 7–4 **TP:** 7–4 Interest Grabber, Section Outline, Levels of Organization
	SE: Chapter 7 Assessment, pp. 196–199 **TR:** Chapter Vocabulary Review, Graphic Organizer, Chapter 7 Test	**iText:** Chapter 7 Assessment **CTB:** Chapter 7 Test

Go Online

Students can do research, share data, and test their knowledge online.

TIME SAVER

PRESSED FOR TIME?

To Preview the Chapter

- Introduce students to Key Concepts and Vocabulary terms in each section.
- Assign the Reading Strategies for each section.

To Cover the Chapter Quickly

- Have students read all of Section 7–1; the subsection Nucleus and Figures 7–6, 7–7, 7–8, 7–9, 7–10, and 7–11 in Section 7–2; the subsections Cell Membrane and Cell Walls and Figures 7–12, 7–14, 7–15, 7–16, 7–17, and 7–19 in Section 7–3; and all of Section 7–4.
- Assign Section Reviews for 7–1 through 7–4, as well as questions 1–10 in Chapter 7 Assessment and questions 1–9 in Chapter 7 Standards Practice.

To Review the Chapter

- Assign Sections 7–1 through 7–4 in the Reading and Study Workbook or the Adapted Reading and Study Workbook.
- Assign Section Reviews for 7–1 through 7–4 and the Chapter Vocabulary Review for Chapter 7 in the Teaching Resources.

CHAPTER 7

ENGAGE/EXPLORE

Inquiry Activity

Objectives Students will be able to
- form an operational definition of the term *cell*
- classify the cells they observe into two or more groups L2

Skills Focus **Forming Operational Definitions, Classifying**

Materials microscope, prepared slides of plant leaf or stem cross-section, nerve cell, bacteria, and paramecia

Time 15 minutes

Advance Prep If slides of some types of cells are unavailable, substitute slides of other types of cells or use photographs of different cell types. You may want to have students prepare fresh-mount slides of plant sections and microorganisms.

Strategy Set up the slides on microscopes around the room, and have students rotate through the stations to look at each slide.

Expected Outcomes Students should recognize that there are differences in structure and complexity among cells.

Think About It

1. Students should write a concise definition of *cell.* Sample definition: A cell is a structure within a living thing that has a definite boundary enclosing the material inside.
2. Typically, students might classify cells into plant cells and other cells, or into cells with and without nuclei.

Assess Prior Knowledge

Display a three-dimensional model of a cell, or use an overhead projector to display an enlarged photo of a eukaryotic cell. Then, challenge students to name any structures they think they recognize in the cell. Encourage debate about the names and the functions of various structures in the cell. Ask students: **Is this an animal cell or a plant cell?** *(Answers will depend on the displayed cell. Accept any reasonable explanation of why they classify it one way or another.)*

CHAPTER 7

Cell Structure and Function

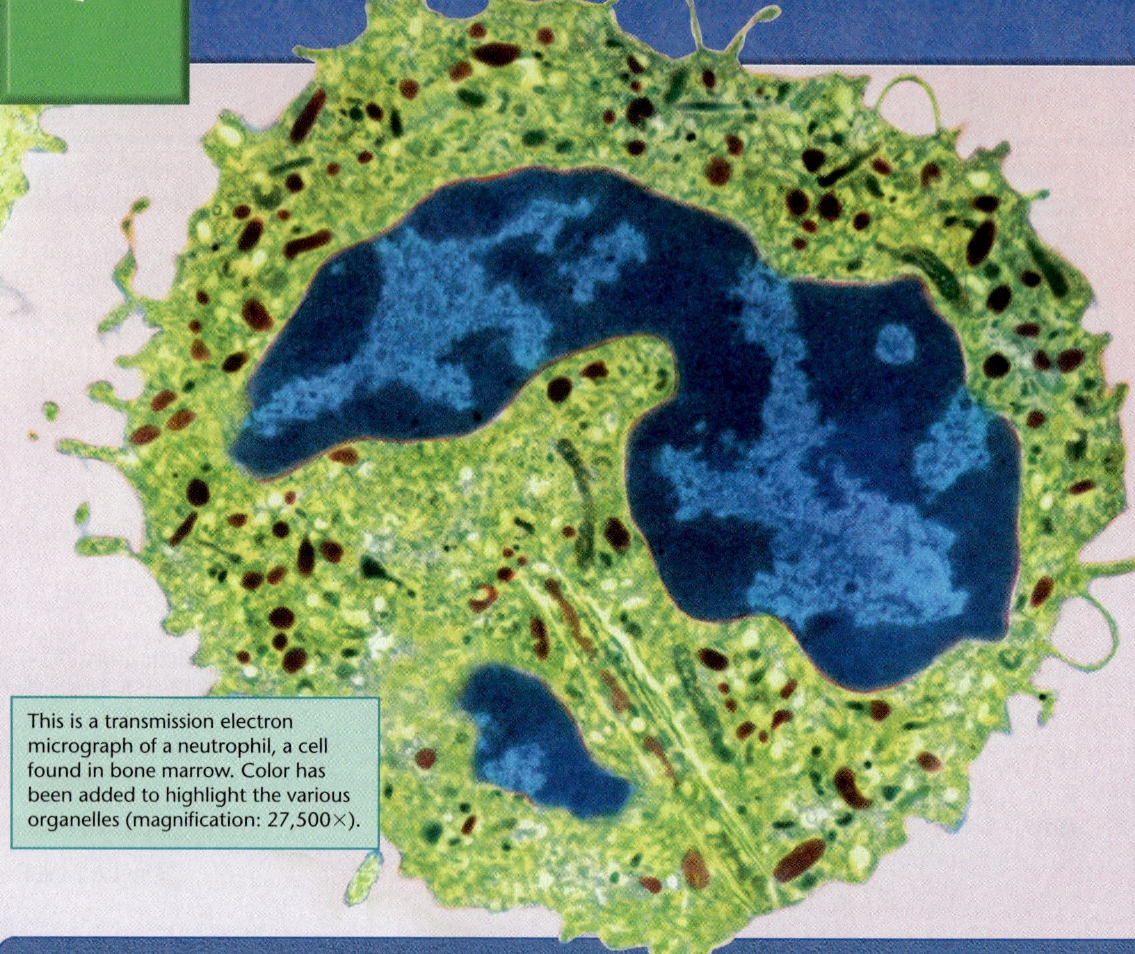

This is a transmission electron micrograph of a neutrophil, a cell found in bone marrow. Color has been added to highlight the various organelles (magnification: 27,500×).

Inquiry Activity

What is a cell?

Procedure

1. Look through a microscope at a slide of a plant leaf or stem cross section. **CAUTION:** *Handle the microscope and slide carefully to avoid breaking them.* Sketch one or more cells. Record a description of their features, such as shape and internal parts.
2. Repeat step 1 with slides of nerve cells, bacteria, and paramecia.
3. Compare the cells by listing the characteristics they have in common and some of the differences among them.

Think About It

1. **Forming Operational Definitions** Use your observations to write a definition of "cell."
2. **Classifying** Classify the cells you observed into two or more groups. Explain what characteristics you used to put each cell in a particular group.

HISTORY OF SCIENCE

Whatever happened to protoplasm?
At one time, practically everyone was taught that the fluid material of the cell was something called protoplasm, a colloid whose wonderful properties accounted for many of the unique abilities of the cell. The term actually means "first fluid," and it reflects the idea that the composition of a living cell is something so extraordinary that the common laws of chemistry cannot explain it. This is an idea whose time has passed. As biologists began to explore the composition of the cell with modern tools, it became increasingly clear that the properties of the cell could be explained in other ways. Instead of protoplasm, we now speak of cytoplasm, or "cell fluid," a term that encompasses all the complexity of the contents of the cell outside of the nucleus.

7–1 Life Is Cellular

BI 1.c. Students know how prokaryotic cells, eukaryotic cells (including those from plants and animals), and viruses differ in complexity and general structure. **BIIE 1.k.** Recognize the cumulative nature of scientific evidence.

Look closely at a part of a living thing, and what do you see? Hold a blade of grass up against the light, and you see tiny lines running the length of the blade. Examine the tip of your finger, and you see the ridges and valleys that make up fingerprints. Place an insect under a microscope, and you see the intricate structures of its wings and the spikes and bristles that protect its body. As interesting as these close-up views may be, however, they're only the beginning of the story. Look closer and deeper with a more powerful microscope, and you'll see that there is a common structure that makes up every living thing—the cell.

The Discovery of the Cell

"Seeing is believing," an old saying goes. It would be hard to find a better example of this than the discovery of the cell. Without the instruments to make them visible, cells remained out of sight and, therefore, out of mind for most of human history. All of this changed with a dramatic advance in technology—the invention of the microscope.

Early Microscopes It was not until the mid-1600s that scientists began to use microscopes to observe living things. In 1665, Englishman Robert Hooke used an early compound microscope to look at a thin slice of cork, a plant material. Under the microscope, cork seemed to be made of thousands of tiny, empty chambers. Hooke called these chambers "cells" because they reminded him of a monastery's tiny rooms, which were called cells. The term *cell* is used in biology to this day. Today we know that cells are not empty chambers, but contain living matter. One of Hooke's illustrations of cells is shown in **Figure 7–1**.

In Holland around the same time, Anton van Leeuwenhoek used a single-lens microscope to observe pond water and other things. To his amazement, the microscope revealed a fantastic world of tiny living organisms that seemed to be everywhere, even in the very water he and his neighbors drank.

Guide for Reading

Key Concepts
- What is the cell theory?
- What are the characteristics of prokaryotes and eukaryotes?

Vocabulary
cell
cell theory
nucleus
eukaryote
prokaryote

Reading Strategy: Finding Main Ideas
As you read, look for evidence to support the statement "The cell theory revolutionized how biologists thought about living things."

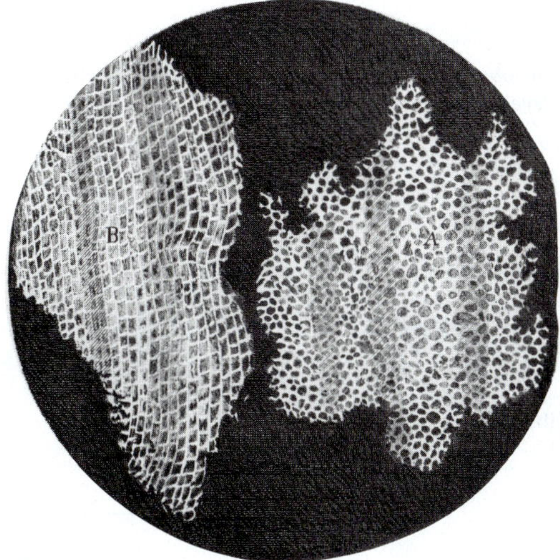

▶ **Figure 7–1** Using an early microscope, Hooke made this drawing of cork cells. In Hooke's drawings, the cells look like empty chambers because he was looking at dead plant matter. Today, we know that living cells are made up of many structures.

SECTION RESOURCES

Print:
- ***Teaching Resources,*** Lesson Plan 7–1, Adapted Section Summary 7–1, Adapted Worksheets 7–1, Section Summary 7–1, Worksheets 7–1, Section Review 7–1
- ***Reading and Study Workbook A,*** Section 7–1
- ***Adapted Reading and Study Workbook B,*** Section 7–1

Technology:
- ***iText,*** Section 7–1
- ***Transparencies Plus,*** Section 7–1

Section 7–1

BI 1.c, BIIE 1.k

1 FOCUS

Objectives

7.1.1 ***Explain*** what the cell theory is.
7.1.2 ***Describe*** how researchers explore the living cell.
7.1.3 ***Distinguish*** between eukaryotes and prokaryotes.

Guide for Reading

Vocabulary Preview

Have students write the Vocabulary terms, dividing each into its separate syllables as best they can. Remind students that each syllable usually has only one vowel sound. The correct syllabications are cell the•o•ry, nu•cle•us, pro•kar•y•ote, eu•kar•y•ote

Reading Strategy

Ask students to make an outline of the section, using the blue heads as their first level of the outline.

2 INSTRUCT

The Discovery of the Cell

Build Science Skills

Asking Questions Divide the class into small groups, and give each group a variety of drawings and photos of cells taken from numerous sources, such as college textbooks and Internet sites. These cells should include both unicellular organisms and cells from plants and animals. Have each group make drawings of the various cells, labeling any structure they recognize. Then, ask each group to brainstorm a list of questions about these cells that they expect will be answered as they read the chapter. L1 L2

Biology and History

BIIE 1.k

Discuss the contributions of each of the scientists leading up to the formulation of the cell theory. Be sure that students understand the importance of the individual accomplishments. It is also important that students understand the time span involved. Ask: **How did each observation influence the next scientist's work?** *(Answers will vary, but generally one clearly influenced the next. The microscope was essential to the discovery of the cell. Both van Leeuwenhoek and Hooke used early microscopes to observe cells and unicellular organisms. Schwann elaborated Schleiden's findings, and so on.)*

Writing in Science

Help students find appropriate books and Web sites as they investigate new discoveries about cells. Explain that the branch of biology that focuses on cells and their structures is called cytology, and the branch that is concerned with unicellular organisms is called microbiology. Encourage students to find out what scientist discovered each of the organelles they will learn about in Section 7–2 and when the discovery was made. L2 L3

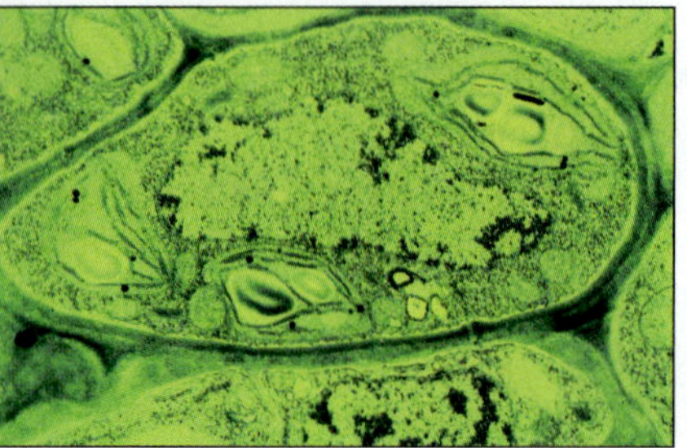

(magnification: 12,000×)

▲ **Figure 7–2** The cell theory states that cells are the basic units of all living things. This cell is from a plant leaf. Compare this micrograph with Hooke's drawing in **Figure 7–1.**

The Cell Theory Soon, numerous observations made it clear that **cells** were the basic units of life. In 1838, German botanist Matthias Schleiden concluded that all plants were made of cells like the one in **Figure 7–2.** The next year, German biologist Theodor Schwann stated that all animals were made of cells. In 1855, the German physician Rudolf Virchow concluded that new cells could be produced only from the division of existing cells. These discoveries, confirmed by other biologists, are summarized in the **cell theory,** a fundamental concept of biology. **The cell theory states:**

- **All living things are composed of cells.**
- **Cells are the basic units of structure and function in living things.**
- **New cells are produced from existing cells.**

Exploring the Cell

Following in the footsteps of Hooke, Virchow, and others, modern biologists still use microscopes to explore the cell. However, today's researchers use microscopes and techniques more powerful than the pioneers of biology could have imagined. Researchers can use fluorescent labels and light microscopy to follow molecules moving through the cell. Confocal light microscopy, which scans cells with a laser beam, makes it possible to build three-dimensional images of cells and their parts. High-resolution video technology makes it easy to produce movies of cells as they grow, divide, and develop.

BIIE 1.k

Biology and History

The History of the Cell

The observations and conclusions of many scientists helped to develop the current understanding of the cell.

1665
Robert Hooke
Hooke publishes his book *Micrographia,* which contains his drawings of sections of cork as seen through one of the first microscopes.

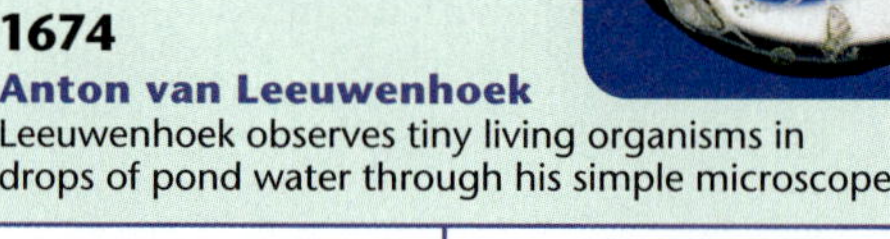

1674
Anton van Leeuwenhoek
Leeuwenhoek observes tiny living organisms in drops of pond water through his simple microscope.

1600 — 1700 — 1800

UNIVERSAL ACCESS

Less Proficient Readers
Focus students' attention on the cell theory by calling on students to read aloud the bulleted sentences on page 170. For each statement read aloud, call on other students to rephrase the concept in their own words and then explain the concept's significance. L1 L2

English Language Learners
Help students add to their personal science glossaries with Vocabulary words from this and subsequent sections of this chapter. For each word, encourage students to record definitions, note pronunciations, and perhaps add translations using their first languages. L2

Advanced Learners
Review the Writing Activity on page 171. Determine which discovery each student will research and present to the class. Emphasize that they must find more information than is given in the textbook. Encourage advanced students to pursue the more complicated discoveries. L2 L3

These new technologies make it possible for researchers to study the structure and movement of living cells in great detail. Unfortunately, light itself limits the detail, or resolution, of images that can be made with the light microscope. Like all forms of radiation, light waves are diffracted, or scattered, as they pass through matter, making it impossible to visualize tiny structures such as proteins and viruses with light microscopy.

Electron Microscopes By contrast, electron microscopes are capable of revealing details as much as 1000 times smaller than those visible in light microscopes because the wavelengths of electrons are much shorter than those of light. Transmission electron microscopes (TEMs) make it possible to explore cell structures and large protein molecules. Because beams of electrons can only pass through thin samples, cells and tissues must be cut first into ultrathin slices before they can be examined under a microscope.

With scanning electron microscopes (SEMs), a pencil-like beam of electrons is scanned over the surface of a specimen. For SEM images, specimens do not have to be cut into thin slices to be visualized. The scanning electron microscope produces stunning three-dimensional images of cells. Because electrons are easily scattered by molecules in the air, samples examined in both types of electron microscopes must be placed in a vacuum in order to be studied. As a result, researchers chemically preserve their samples first and then carefully remove all of the water before placing them in the microscope. This means that electron microscopy can be used to visualize only nonliving, preserved cells and tissues.

For: Links on cell theory
Visit: www.SciLinks.org
Web Code: cbn-3071

Writing in Science

Use the library or the Internet to research a new discovery relating to the cell or its structures. Be sure to include the scientist(s) responsible for the discovery. Then, present your findings in the form of an oral report.

1839
Theodor Schwann
Schwann concludes that all animals are made up of cells.

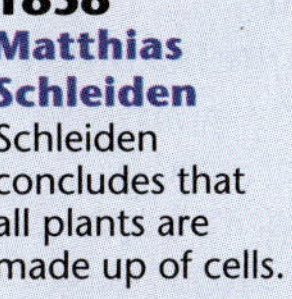

1838
Matthias Schleiden
Schleiden concludes that all plants are made up of cells.

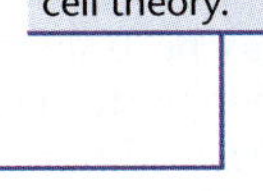

1855
Rudolph Virchow
Virchow proposes that all cells come from existing cells, completing the cell theory.

1970
Lynn Margulis
Margulis proposes the idea that certain organelles, tiny structures within some cells, were once free-living cells themselves.

1800 1900 2000

BIO INSIGHTS **HISTORY OF SCIENCE**

Hooke's observations

Robert Hooke (1635–1703) was the son of an English minister and a graduate of Oxford University. He did important work in mechanics and physics, and he became one of the most prominent microscopists of his time. The cork he observed through a compound microscope he had built was taken from the bark of an oak tree. Rectangular and boxlike cork cells are produced in woody plants as the woody stem increases its girth. Cork cells are dead at maturity, and thus Hooke was not looking at living cells when he gave them a name. Hooke never fully understood the significance of his findings, and it was some 150 years before the term *cell* took on its current meaning.

Go Online NSTA SCI LINKS

Download a worksheet on cell theory for students to complete, and find additional teacher support from NSTA SciLinks.

Exploring the Cell

Address Misconceptions

Many students have the misconception that a common egg, such as a chicken egg, is one cell. Some students might believe that the egg yolk is the nucleus and the egg white is the cytoplasm, while others may think that the yolk is the complete cell. Explain that an unfertilized egg does have only one cell, but that cell consists of a small, whitish disk at the top of the yolk. This disk can be seen if the yolk is carefully separated from the rest of the egg. When an egg is fertilized, that cell begins to divide and multiply. The yolk serves as nourishment for the developing embryo. L1

Make Connections

Mathematics Explain to students that cells are so small that the basic metric unit of length, the meter, has no usefulness in measuring cells. Ask: **What is one thousandth of a meter called?** *(1 millimeter)* Explain that 1 micrometer (μm) is one thousandth of 1 millimeter. Ask: **How long is 1 micrometer in terms of meters?** *(1 μm = 1/1000 · 1/1000 m = 1/1,000,000 m)* Thus, a micrometer is one millionth of a meter. Scientists use a unit called the nanometer (nm) to measure cell structures. A nanometer is 1/1000 of a micrometer. L2

7–1 (continued)

Use Visuals

Figure 7–3 After students have studied the photos in the figure and read the caption, have them turn back to Section 1–4 and review the text and figures that describe the different kinds of microscopes. Ask volunteers to read aloud the descriptions of the SEM and the TEM. Then, ask: **What advantage do the scanning probe microscopes have over the SEM and the TEM?** *(With scanning probe microscopes, scientists can study parts of living organisms. With the SEM and the TEM, only nonliving samples can be studied.)* L2

Build Science Skills

Classifying Photocopy images produced by the various kinds of microscopes. Find these images in college-level textbooks, especially those that focus on cell biology and molecular biology. Then, divide the class into small groups and give each group a set of these images. Each set should include at least one image associated with a light microscope, a TEM, an SEM, and a scanning probe microscope. Challenge the groups to classify the images according to which microscope was responsible for each. When groups have finished their classifications, have a member of each group present its conclusions to the class. Invite any objections to a group's classification, and emphasize the differences among the different types of microscopes. L2

FIGURE 7–3 VARIETY OF MICROGRAPHS

Different types of microscopes produce a variety of images of cells and cell parts.

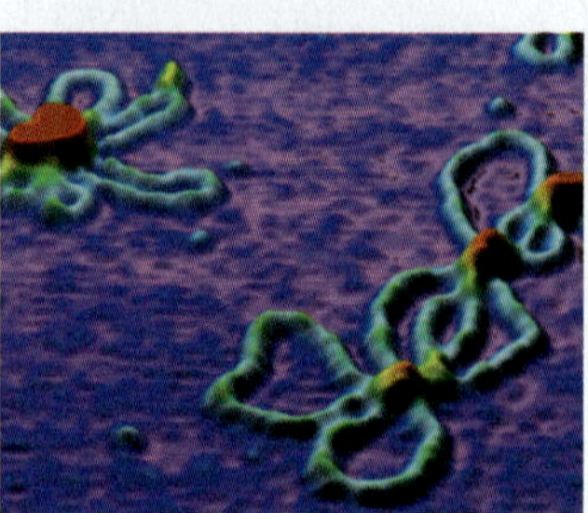

Scanning Probe Micrograph
A scanning probe microscope scans a tiny probe just above the surface of a sample and produces an image by recording the position of the probe. These powerful instruments can even visualize single molecules, such as DNA, on carefully prepared surfaces. (magnification: 320,000X)

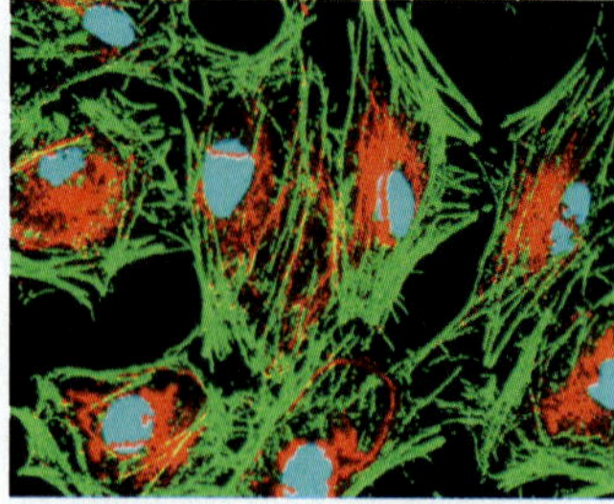

Confocal Light Micrograph
Confocal light microscopes construct images by scanning cells with a computer-controlled laser beam. In this fluorescent confocal light micrograph of HeLa cells, researchers attached fluorescent labels to the different molecules. By doing this, researchers can follow molecules as they move through a living cell. (magnification: 500X)

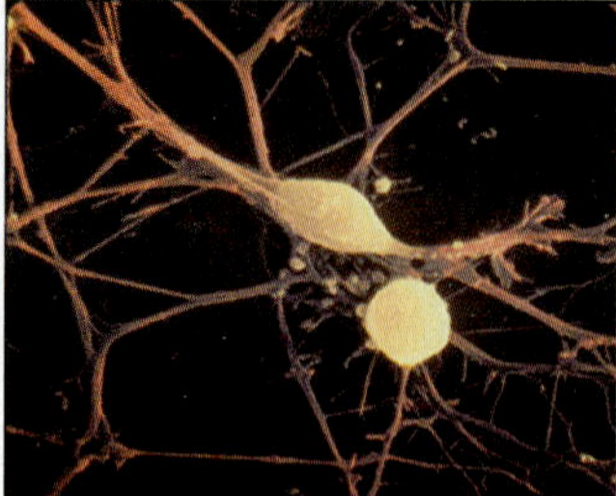

Scanning Electron Micrograph
Scanning electron microscopes produce three-dimensional images of the surfaces of cells, such as these neurons, and tissues. (magnification: 8900X)

Scanning Probe Microscopes In the 1990s, researchers perfected a new class of microscopes that produce images by tracing the surfaces of samples with a fine probe. These scanning probe microscopes have revolutionized the study of surfaces and made it possible to observe single atoms. Unlike electron microscopes, scanning probe microscopes can operate in ordinary air and can even show samples in solution. Researchers have already used scanning probe microscopes to image DNA and protein molecules as well as a number of important biological structures.

Prokaryotes and Eukaryotes

Cells come in a great variety of shapes and an amazing range of sizes. Although typical cells range from 5 to 50 micrometers in diameter, the tiniest mycoplasma bacteria are only 0.2 micrometers across, so small that they are difficult to see under even the best light microscopes. In contrast, the giant amoeba *Chaos chaos* may be 1000 micrometers in diameter, large enough to be seen with the unaided eye as a tiny speck in pond water. Despite their differences, all cells have two characteristics in common. They are surrounded by a barrier called a cell membrane; and, at some point in their lives, they contain the molecule that carries biological information—DNA.

FACTS AND FIGURES

Scanning probe microscopy
Scanning probe microscopes include a number of instruments that use a sharp point called a probe to scan a sample. These include the scanning tunneling microscope (STM) and the atomic force microscope (AFM). With the STM, the probe does not quite touch the sample. An electric current between the probe and the surface of the specimen is utilized to track the topography of a surface. The problem with an STM is that the sample must be a good conductor, and that limits the kinds of samples that can be studied. This problem was overcome with the development of the AFM, which utilizes a probe that gently touches the sample surface. The probe of an AFM is similar to the stylus (needle) on a turntable that plays LP records—that is, an AFM is like a record player. Like a stylus on a record, the probe slides over the surface of the sample and sends data about that surface back to a processor. The force is so slight that the probe usually causes no damage to the sample.

Cells fall into two broad categories, depending on whether they contain a nucleus. The **nucleus** (plural: nuclei) is a large membrane-enclosed structure that contains the cell's genetic material in the form of DNA. The nucleus controls many of the cell's activities. **Eukaryotes** (yoo-KAR-ee-ohts) are cells that contain nuclei. **Prokaryotes** (pro-KAR-ee-ohts) are cells that do not contain nuclei. Both words derive from the Greek words *karyon,* meaning "kernel," or nucleus, and *eu,* meaning "true," or *pro,* meaning "before." These words reflect the idea that prokaryotic cells evolved before nuclei developed.

Prokaryotes Prokaryotic cells are generally smaller and simpler than eukaryotic cells, although there are many exceptions to this rule. **Prokaryotic cells have genetic material that is not contained in a nucleus.** Some prokaryotes contain internal membranes, but prokaryotes are generally less complicated than eukaryotes. Despite their simplicity, prokaryotes carry out every activity associated with living things. They grow, reproduce, respond to the environment, and some can even move by gliding along surfaces or swimming through liquids. The organisms we call bacteria are prokaryotes.

CA

a

Eukaryotes Eukaryotic cells are generally larger and more complex than prokaryotic cells. As you can see in **Figure 7–4,** eukaryotic cells generally contain dozens of structures and internal membranes, and many are highly specialized. **Eukaryotic cells contain a nucleus in which their genetic material is separated from the rest of the cell.** Eukaryotes display great variety. Some eukaryotes live solitary lives as unicellular organisms. Others form large, multicellular organisms. Plants, animals, fungi, and protists are eukaryotes.

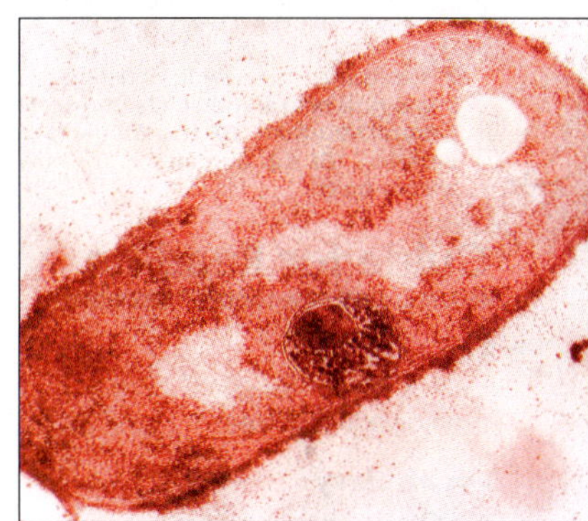

(magnification: 18,300×)

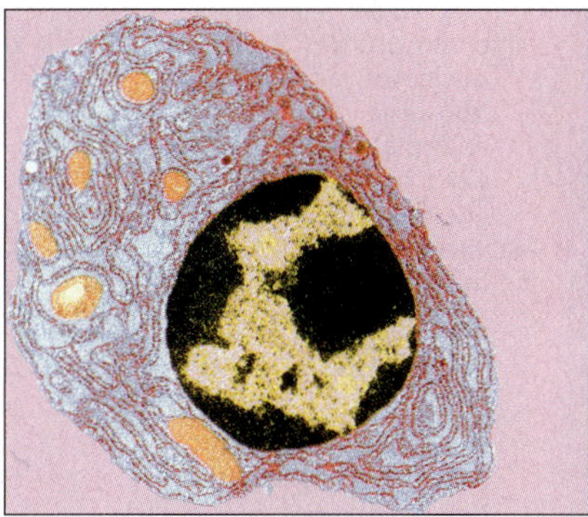

(magnification: 350×)

Figure 7–4 **The cells of eukaryotes have a nucleus, but the cells of prokaryotes do not.** Notice how many more structures are located in the eukaryotic cell (bottom) as compared with the prokaryotic cell (top).

7–1 Section Assessment

1. **Key Concept** What three statements make up the cell theory?
2. **Key Concept** What are the differences between prokaryotic cells and eukaryotic cells?
3. Compare the processes used to produce a TEM and an SEM.
4. What structures do all cells have?
5. **Critical Thinking** **Inferring** How did the invention of the microscope help the development of the cell theory?

Thinking Visually

Constructing a Chart
Make a three-column chart comparing prokaryotes with eukaryotes. In the first column, list the traits found in all cells. In the second column, list the features of prokaryotes. In the third column, list the features of eukaryotes.

7–1 Section Assessment

1. All living things are composed of cells. Cells are the basic units of structure and function in living things. New cells are produced only from existing cells.
2. Prokaryotic cells are generally smaller and simpler than eukaryotic cells. Eukaryotic cells contain a nucleus; prokaryotic cells do not. Eukaryotic cells generally contain dozens of structures and internal membranes.
3. A TEM is produced by passing electrons through an extremely thin sample. An SEM is produced by scanning a pencil-like beam of electrons over the surface of an object.
4. A cell membrane and DNA
5. The microscope was essential in that development because it allowed biologists to observe cells in living things.

Prokaryotes and Eukaryotes

Use Visuals

Figure 7–4 Ask students: **What is the main difference between prokaryotic cells and eukaryotic cells?** *(Eukaryotic cells contain a nucleus; prokaryotic cells do not.)* **Do bacterial cells contain a nucleus?** *(No. All bacteria are prokaryotes.)* **What else do eukaryotic cells contain that prokaryotic cells don't?** *(Eukaryotic cells generally contain dozens of structures and internal membranes.)* L1 L2

3 ASSESS

Evaluate Understanding

Call on students at random to describe how scientists use microscopes and other techniques to explore the living cell. Then, ask volunteers to explain the difference between prokaryotes and eukaryotes.

Reteach

Reinforce students' understanding of the three ideas that make up the cell theory by having them write statements that apply those ideas to specific living things.

Thinking Visually

Students' charts will vary, but they should include most of the information contained in the subsection Prokaryotes and Eukaryotes. Encourage students to add to their charts as they continue reading the chapter.

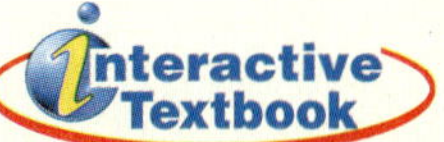

If your class subscribes to the iText, use it to review the Key Concepts in Section 7–1.

Section 7-2

 7 1.c, 7 1.d, BI 1.c, BI 1.e, *BI 1.j

1 FOCUS

Objectives

7.2.1 ***Describe*** the function of the cell nucleus.

7.2.2 ***Describe*** the functions of the major cell organelles.

7.2.3 ***Identify*** the main roles of the cytoskeleton.

Guide for Reading

Vocabulary Preview

Pronounce each Vocabulary word and have students repeat the pronunciation as a class. Pay special attention to words that are difficult for English language learners.

Reading Strategy

To help students begin their understanding of the differences between plant cells and animal cells, have them preview Figure 7–6 and answer the caption question.

2 INSTRUCT

Comparing the Cell to a Factory

Build Science Skills

Using Models Divide the class into small groups, and have groups make a labeled, two-dimensional drawing of a typical cell. First, have groups meet before reading the section to discuss what the inside of a cell might contain. Then, ask groups to meet again after learning about the structures of a cell to make the labeled drawing. L2

7–2 Eukaryotic Cell Structure

7 1.c. Students know the nucleus is the repository for genetic information in plant and animal cells. BI 1.c. Students know how prokaryotic cells, eukaryotic cells (including those from plants and animals), and viruses differ in complexity and general structure. BI 1.e. Students know the role of the endoplasmic reticulum and Golgi apparatus in the secretion of proteins. *BI 1.j. Students know how eukaryotic cells are given shape and internal organization by a cytoskeleton or cell wall or both.

Guide for Reading

Key Concept
- What are the functions of the major cell structures?

Vocabulary
organelle
cytoplasm
nuclear envelope
chromatin
chromosome
nucleolus
ribosome
endoplasmic reticulum
Golgi apparatus
lysosome
vacuole
mitochondrion
chloroplast
cytoskeleton
centriole

Reading Strategy: Building Vocabulary Before you read, preview the vocabulary by skimming the section and making a list of the highlighted boldface terms. Leave space to make notes as you read.

At first glance, a factory is a puzzling place. A bewildering variety of machines buzz and clatter, people move quickly in different directions, and the sheer diversity of so much activity can be confusing. However, if you take your time and watch carefully, before long you will begin to identify patterns. What might at first have seemed like chaos suddenly begins to make sense.

Comparing the Cell to a Factory

CA a

In some respects, the eukaryotic cell is like a factory. The first time you look at a microscope image of a cell, such as the one in **Figure 7–5**, the cell seems impossibly complex. Look closely at a eukaryotic cell, however, and patterns begin to emerge. To see those patterns more clearly, we'll look at some structures that are common to eukaryotic cells, shown in **Figure 7–6**. Because many of these structures act as if they are specialized organs, these structures are known as **organelles**, literally "little organs."

Cell biologists divide the eukaryotic cell into two major parts: the nucleus and the cytoplasm. The **cytoplasm** is the portion of the cell outside the nucleus. As you will see, the nucleus and cytoplasm work together in the business of life.

a BI 1.c

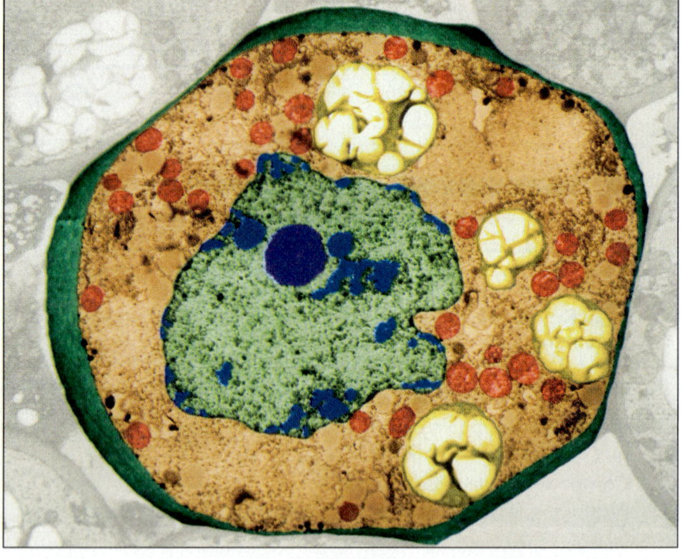

(magnification: 1500×)

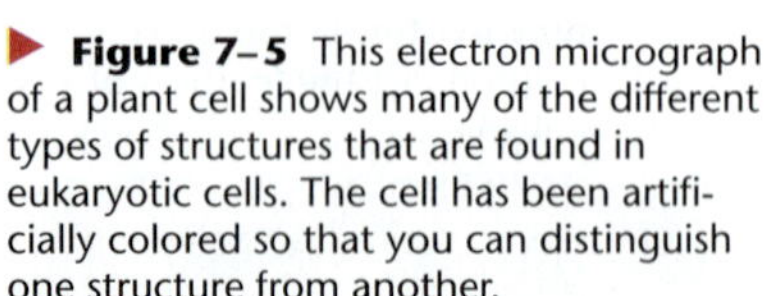

Figure 7–5 This electron micrograph of a plant cell shows many of the different types of structures that are found in eukaryotic cells. The cell has been artificially colored so that you can distinguish one structure from another.

SECTION RESOURCES

TIME SAVER

Print:
- ***Teaching Resources,*** Lesson Plan 7–2, Adapted Section Summary 7–2, Adapted Worksheets 7–2, Section Summary 7–2, Worksheets 7–2, Section Review 7–2
- ***Reading and Study Workbook A,*** Section 7–2
- ***Adapted Reading and Study Workbook B,*** Section 7–2

Technology:
- ***iText,*** Section 7–2
- ***Transparencies Plus,*** Section 7–2

Plant and Animal Cells

Figure 7–6 Both plant and animal cells contain a variety of organelles. Some structures are specific to either plant cells or animal cells only. **Interpreting Graphics** *What structures do plant cells have that animal cells do not?*

For: Cell Structure activity
Visit: PHSchool.com
Web Code: cbp-3072

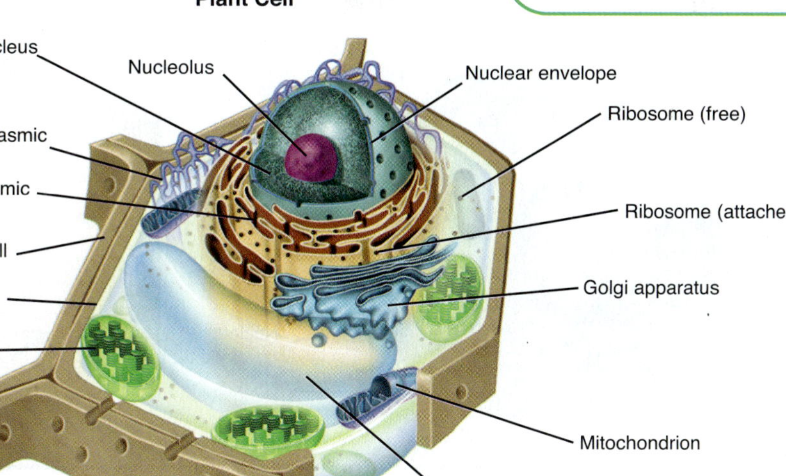

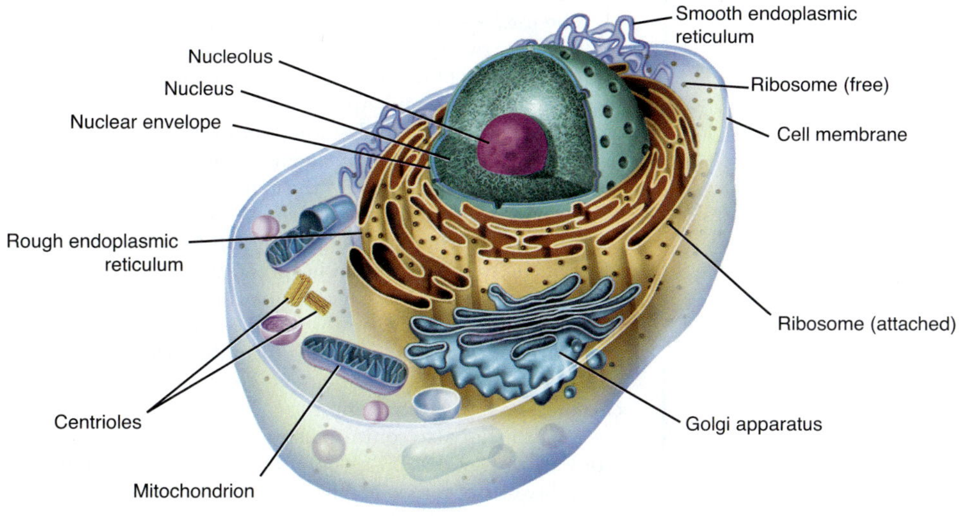

For: Cell Structure activity
Visit: PHSchool.com
Web Code: cbe-3072
Students can learn more about the structures of the cell online.

Build Science Skills

Predicting Ask students what specific functions a unicellular organism would need to carry out in order to live. Then, divide the class into small groups, and ask each group to make a table of predictions about what structures would likely be found inside a unicellular organism. The table should have two columns: *Necessary Function* and *Structure Needed to Carry Out Function.* L2

Use Visuals

Figure 7–6 Encourage students to make copies of these labeled illustrations in their notebooks. As they learn about the various structures that make up a cell, they can add definitions and descriptions of functions for each of the labels. Point out that when they have completed this task, they will have made the best possible tool for review. L1 L2

Build Science Skills

Comparing and Contrasting
Set up microscope stations at several locations around the room, and provide prepared slides of an animal cell and a plant cell at each location. Have students make labeled drawings of each and write a paragraph comparing and contrasting the two types of cells. L2 L3

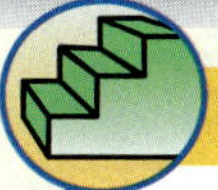

Universal Access

Less Proficient Readers
To reinforce students' understanding of cell structures, draw an animal cell on the board. Include and label the nucleus, the cell membrane, and the cytoplasm. Have students make a copy of the drawing on a sheet of paper. Then, as each organelle is studied and discussed, add labeled structures to the cell on the board, and have students add these structures to their own drawings.
 L1  L2

English Language Learners
When students read about the cytoskeleton on page 181, explain that *cyto-* means "cell," and thus *cytoskeleton* can be thought of as the "skeleton of the cell." Explain that this is an analogy, since the cytoskeleton is not like an animal skeleton. Also, explain that a filament is a threadlike material and a *tubule* is a "very slender tube." Thus, the cytoskeleton can be thought of as composed of threads and slender tubes. L1

Answer to . . .

Figure 7–6 *Plant cells have a cell wall and chloroplasts. Many plant cells also have a large, central vacuole.*

7–2 (continued)

Nucleus

Use Visuals

Figure 7–7 Ask students: **What is the nucleolus?** *(It is a small, dense region of the nucleus where the assembly of ribosomes begins.)* **Where is the DNA that a nucleus contains?** *(The DNA is part of the chromatin, which is spread throughout the nucleus most of the time.)* **Why is DNA important?** *(It holds coded instructions for making proteins and other important molecules.)* Point out that the genetic information is the coded instructions for making molecules. L1 L2

Build Science Skills

Inferring Remind students that prokaryotes do not contain a nucleus. Then, ask: **If the nucleus controls most cell processes in eukaryotes, how can prokaryotes live without a nucleus?** *(Some students might suggest that the lives of prokaryotes aren't as complex as those of eukaryotes. Others might correctly infer that the most important part of a nucleus is the DNA it contains, and prokaryotes have DNA without having a nucleus.)*

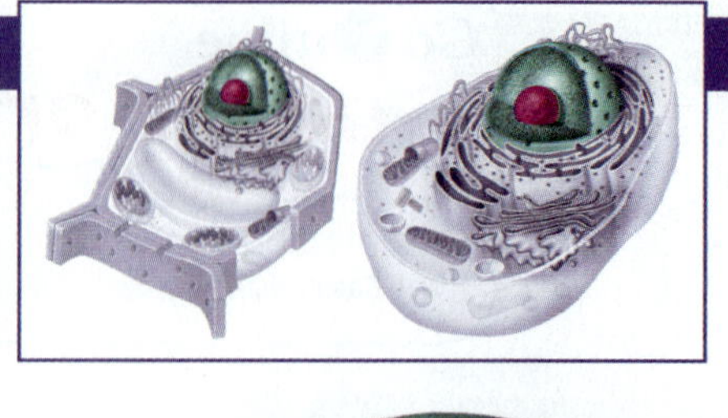

FIGURE 7–7 THE NUCLEUS

The nucleus controls most cell processes and contains the hereditary information of DNA. The DNA combines with protein to form chromatin, which is found throughout the nucleus. The small, dense region in the nucleus is the nucleolus.

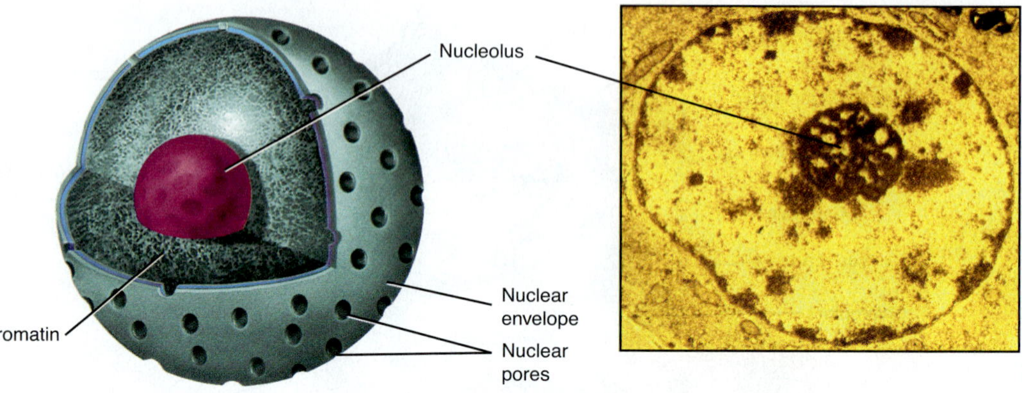

Nucleus

In the same way that the main office controls a large factory, the nucleus is the control center of the cell. **The nucleus contains nearly all the cell's DNA and with it the coded instructions for making proteins and other important molecules.** The structure of the nucleus is shown in **Figure 7–7.**

The nucleus is surrounded by a **nuclear envelope** composed of two membranes. The nuclear envelope is dotted with thousands of nuclear pores, which allow material to move into and out of the nucleus. Like messages, instructions, and blueprints moving in and out of a main office, a steady stream of proteins, RNA, and other molecules move through the nuclear pores to and from the rest of the cell.

CA a

The granular material you can see in the nucleus is called **chromatin.** Chromatin consists of DNA bound to protein. Most of the time, chromatin is spread throughout the nucleus. When a cell divides, however, chromatin condenses to form **chromosomes** (KROH-muh-sohms). These distinct, threadlike structures contain the genetic information that is passed from one generation of cells to the next. You will learn more about chromosomes in later chapters.

Most nuclei also contain a small, dense region known as the **nucleolus** (noo-KLEE-uh-lus). The nucleolus is where the assembly of ribosomes begins.

CHECKPOINT *What kind of information is contained in chromosomes?*

HISTORY OF SCIENCE

The nucleus controls the cell

During the 1930s and 1940s, researchers performed a series of experiments that demonstrated the link between a cell's nucleus and the physical characteristics of the cell. Two species of *Acetabularia* algae were used in the experiments. This marine alga, though 5 cm long, consists of a single cell. Each cell includes a holdfast at the bottom, a stalk, and a cuplike cap at the top, and the cell's nucleus is in the holdfast. The two species that were used had different-shaped caps. Researchers cut the cap off one cell, removed the nucleus from its holdfast, and transplanted a nucleus from a cell of the second species into the holdfast of the first cell. The cell regenerated a new cap, and researchers cut off that one. Eventually, the cap that grew was the shape of the cap from the second species, from which the transplanted nucleus came, and not the shape of the first cap.

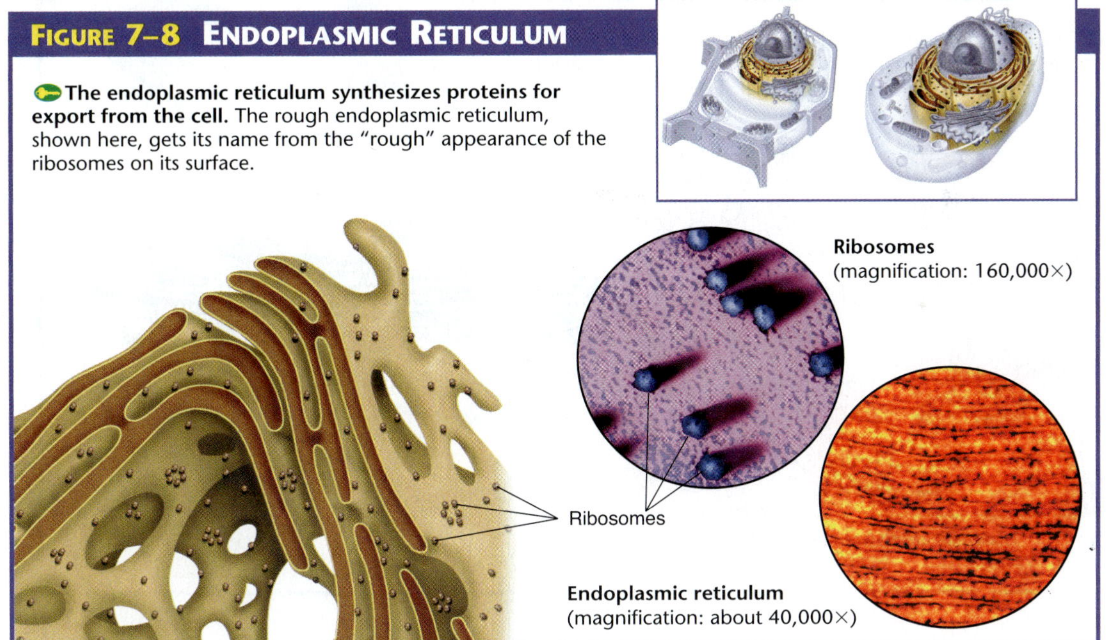

FIGURE 7–8 ENDOPLASMIC RETICULUM

The endoplasmic reticulum synthesizes proteins for export from the cell. The rough endoplasmic reticulum, shown here, gets its name from the "rough" appearance of the ribosomes on its surface.

Ribosomes

One of the most important jobs carried out in the cellular "factory" is making proteins. **Proteins are assembled on ribosomes. Ribosomes** are small particles of RNA and protein found throughout the cytoplasm. They produce proteins by following coded instructions that come from the nucleus. Each ribosome, in its own way, is like a small machine in a factory, turning out proteins on orders that come from its "boss"—the cell nucleus. Cells that are active in protein synthesis are often packed with ribosomes.

Endoplasmic Reticulum

Eukaryotic cells also contain an internal membrane system known as the **endoplasmic reticulum** (en-doh-PLAZ-mik rih-TIK-yuh-lum), or ER. **The endoplasmic reticulum is the site where lipid components of the cell membrane are assembled, along with proteins and other materials that are exported from the cell.**

The portion of the ER involved in the synthesis of proteins is called rough endoplasmic reticulum, or rough ER. It is given this name because of the ribosomes found on its surface. Newly made proteins leave these ribosomes and are inserted into the rough ER, where they may be chemically modified.

Ribosomes

Build Science Skills

Using Analogies Read aloud the sentence in the text that compares a ribosome to a machine. Use this comparison to discuss how a eukaryotic cell is like a factory. Then, encourage students who need an extra challenge to work together in writing a short play based on the analogy of the cell as a factory. Explain that a good play needs some conflict or danger. The "factory" might be under economic threat or some environmental threat. Advise students to include the functions of as many parts of the factory—cell organelles—as possible. Once the play has been written, encourage the "playwrights" to recruit class members to act out the drama. L3

Endoplasmic Reticulum

Use Visuals

Figure 7–8 Ask students: **What are ribosomes composed of?** *(RNA and protein)* **Where are ribosomes produced?** *(In the nucleolus)* **What do ribosomes produce?** *(Proteins)* **What happens to these proteins after they're produced by ribosomes?** *(Membrane proteins are inserted directly into the ER membrane. Many of the proteins produced on the rough ER are released or secreted from the cell.)* **If this were an illustration of smooth ER, how would it be different?** *(The ER would not have ribosomes on its surface.)* **What is the function of smooth ER?** *(The smooth ER contains enzymes that help synthesize lipids, such as steroids. Smooth ER also helps to detoxify and process chemicals.)* L1 L2

BIO INSIGHTS — HISTORY OF SCIENCE

Learning from sea urchin nuclei

The German cytologist Theodor Boveri (1862–1915) performed an experiment before the invention of microdissection that demonstrated the importance of the nucleus. By vigorous shaking, Boveri removed the nuclei from the eggs of sea urchins of the genus *Sphaerechinus.* He then fertilized the eggs (which had no nuclei) with sperm from sea urchins of the genus *Echinus.* In a practical sense, fertilization resulted in the substitution of one nucleus for another. The larvae that developed had only the traits of *Echinus*, even though the sperm contributed little more than a tiny bit of nucleus to the developing organism.

Answer to . . .

CHECKPOINT *Chromosomes contain the genetic information that is passed from one generation to the next.*

7–2 (continued)

Golgi Apparatus

Build Science Skills

Comparing and Contrasting Students often confuse the Golgi apparatus with the endoplasmic reticulum, because both are usually represented as folded membranes within the cytoplasm. Have students compare the illustrations in Figure 7–8 with those in Figure 7–9. Then, call on students at random to explain the differences in functions between ER and the Golgi apparatus. L2

Lysosomes

Build Science Skills

Observing Divide the class into small groups, and give each group access to a paramecium culture and a yeast suspension, as well as to a microscope slide, coverslip, toothpick, dropper pipette, and microscope. (Prepare the yeast suspension by adding a pinch of Congo red indicator to a thick mixture of yeast and water. Then, bring it to a gentle boil for 5 minutes. Cool before using. Transfer some paramecium culture from the stock culture at least a day ahead of time, and then limit the food supply to the transferred culture.) Have each group prepare a slide of live paramecia using the dropper pipette. Students should focus the slide under the low-power objective of the microscope. They should then obtain a small sample of the yeast solution. The indicator in the solution is red above pH 5 and blue below pH 3. The next step is to use a toothpick to transfer a small drop of yeast suspension to the edge of the slide and observe the paramecia under the microscope for 5 minutes. (*Students should observe that the paramecia sweep the yeast through their oral grooves and form vacuoles to enclose it. The vacuoles become blue at first and eventually red, as lysosomes fuse with the vacuole and release acids that digest the yeast.*)

FIGURE 7–9 GOLGI APPARATUS

The Golgi apparatus modifies, sorts, and packages proteins. Notice the stacklike membranes that make up the Golgi apparatus in this transmission electron micrograph.

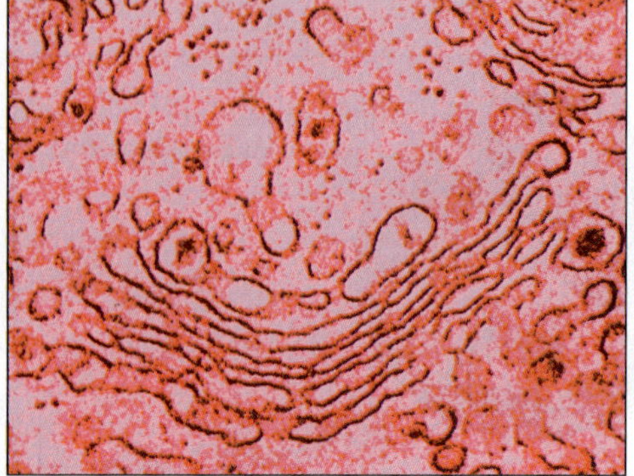

(magnification: about 45,700×)

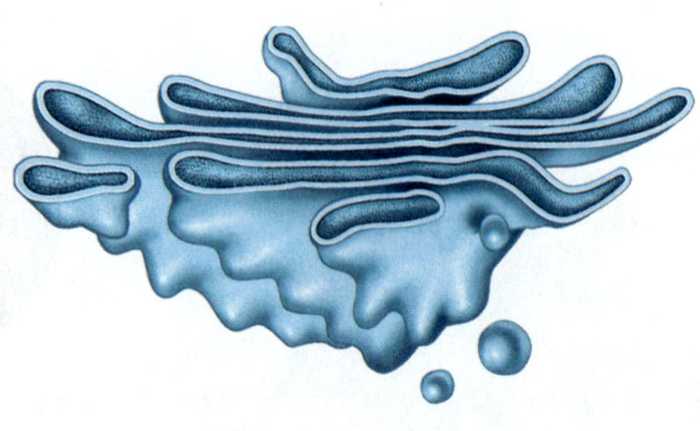

Proteins that are released, or exported, from the cell are synthesized on the rough ER, as are many membrane proteins. Rough ER is abundant in cells that produce large amounts of protein for export. Other cellular proteins are made on "free" ribosomes, which are not attached to membranes.

The other portion of the ER is known as smooth endoplasmic reticulum (smooth ER) because ribosomes are not found on its surface. In many cells, the smooth ER contains collections of enzymes that perform specialized tasks, including the synthesis of membrane lipids and the detoxification of drugs. Liver cells, which play a key role in detoxifying drugs, often contain large amounts of smooth ER.

Golgi Apparatus

Proteins produced in the rough ER move next into an organelle called the **Golgi apparatus,** discovered by the Italian scientist Camillo Golgi. As you can see in **Figure 7–9,** Golgi appears as a stack of closely apposed membranes. **The function of the Golgi apparatus is to modify, sort, and package proteins and other materials from the endoplasmic reticulum for storage in the cell or secretion outside the cell.** The Golgi apparatus is somewhat like a customization shop, where the finishing touches are put on proteins before they are ready to leave the "factory." From the Golgi apparatus, proteins are then "shipped" to their final destinations throughout the cell or outside of the cell.

FACTS AND FIGURES

Important products of the Golgi apparatus One of the most important cell components packaged and distributed by the Golgi apparatus is material for the membranes of the cell and its organelles. Lysosomes, which are essentially membranous bags filled with enzymes, are products of the Golgi apparatuses. These enzymes would destroy the cell if they were not surrounded by membrane. An example of how lysosomes function in cells can be seen in the way paramecia digest their food. Upon contact with a food organism or some other particle, the paramecium envelops the food in a vacuole. Lysosomes then fuse with the vacuole and release acids. The acids quickly digest the contents of the vacuole.

Lysosomes

Even the neatest, cleanest factory needs a cleanup crew, and that's what lysosomes (LY-suh-sohmz) are. **Lysosomes** are small organelles filled with enzymes. One function of lysosomes is the digestion, or breakdown, of lipids, carbohydrates, and proteins into small molecules that can be used by the rest of the cell.

Lysosomes are also involved in breaking down organelles that have outlived their usefulness. Lysosomes perform the vital function of removing "junk" that might otherwise accumulate and clutter up the cell. A number of serious human diseases, including Tay-Sachs disease, can be traced to lysosomes that fail to function properly.

CHECKPOINT *What is the role of lysosomes?*

Vacuoles

Every factory needs a place to store things, and cells contain places for storage as well. Some kinds of cells contain saclike structures called **vacuoles** (VAK-yoo-ohlz) that store materials such as water, salts, proteins, and carbohydrates. In many plant cells there is a single, large central vacuole filled with liquid. The pressure of the central vacuole in these cells makes it possible for plants to support heavy structures such as leaves and flowers.

Vacuoles are also found in some unicellular organisms and in some animals. The paramecium in **Figure 7–10** contains a vacuole called a contractile vacuole. By contracting rhythmically, this specialized vacuole pumps excess water out of the cell. The control of water content within the cell is just one example of an important process known as homeostasis. Homeostasis is the maintenance of a controlled internal environment.

Mitochondria and Chloroplasts

All living things require a source of energy. Factories are hooked up to the local power company, but what about cells? Most cells get energy in one of two ways—from food molecules or from the sun.

CA a **Mitochondria** Nearly all eukaryotic cells, including plants, contain **mitochondria** (myt-oh-KAHN-dree-uh; singular: mitochondrion).  **Mitochondria are organelles that convert the chemical energy stored in food into compounds that are more convenient for the cell to use.** Mitochondria are enclosed by two membranes—an outer membrane and an inner membrane. The inner membrane is folded up inside the organelle.

One of the most interesting aspects of mitochondria is the way in which they are inherited. In humans, all or nearly all of our mitochondria come from the cytoplasm of the ovum, or egg cell. This means that when your relatives are discussing which side of the family should take credit for your best characteristics, you can tell them that you got your mitchondria from Mom!

a 7 1.d

Figure 7–10 Vacuoles have a variety of functions. In the *Coleus* plant cell (top), the large blue structure is the central vacuole that stores salts, proteins, and carbohydrates. The paramecium (bottom) contains contractile vacuoles that fill with water and then pump the water out of the cell. **Applying Concepts** *How do vacuoles help support plant structures?*

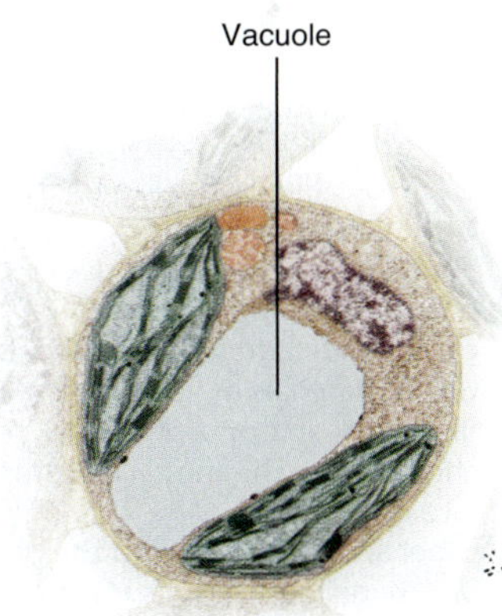

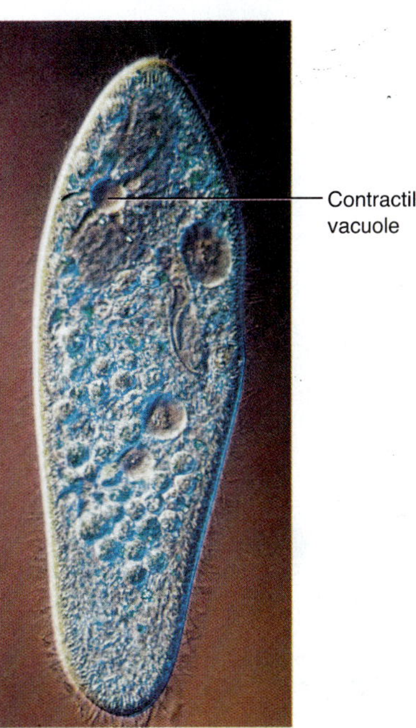

Vacuoles

Use Visuals

Figure 7–10 After students have studied the figure and read the caption, explain that the *Coleus* cell is from a multicellular, leafy plant, whereas the paramecium is a microscopic unicellular organism that is part of the kingdom Protista, which students will learn about in Chapter 20. Then, ask: **How is the function of a vacuole in a plant cell different from that in a unicellular organism?** *(A vacuole in a plant cell stores materials such as water, salts, proteins, and carbohydrates. It also helps support plant structures. A vacuole in a unicellular organism is specialized to pump water out of the cell.)* L1 L2

Mitochondria and Chloroplasts

Build Science Skills

Using Analogies Explain to students that mitochondria have long been called the "powerhouses" of cells. Ask: **What is a "powerhouse"?** *(A powerhouse is another name for a power plant, which produces electricity for cities and regions.)* **How is a mitochondrion like a powerhouse?** *(Powerhouses convert one source of energy to another more useful form. For example, energy from coal, oil, or gas is often converted to electricity, a more useful form for homes and industry. A mitochondrion also converts energy to a more useful form. It uses energy from food to make high-energy compounds that the cell can use in growth, development, and movement.)* L2

TEACHER TO TEACHER

When I introduce the structure of the cell, I try to analogize the cell with the students' city. Taking this analogy a step further, I organize a cooperative learning activity in which I ask teams of students to "create" an imaginary city that correlates cell structures with city components. Teams should include most of the organelles in their city. For example, they might use a mitochondrion as the local power plant or microtubules as major thoroughfares.

For this activity, each team will need a large sheet of paper or poster board for drawing the city, as well as colored pencils or similar materials. If possible, have teams display their work and explain their "creations" to the class.

—*Jorge E. Sanchez*
Biology Teacher
Green Valley High School
Henderson, NV

Answers to . . .

CHECKPOINT *Lysosomes break down lipids, carbohydrates, and proteins. They also break down organelles that have outlived their usefulness in the cell.*

Figure 7–10 *The pressure exerted by the liquid in the vacuole makes it possible for plants to support heavy structures.*

Quick Lab

BIIE 1.e, BIIE 1.g

Objective Students will make models of cell organelles and a large class model of a cell. L2 L3

Skill Focus Inferring, Calculating, Comparing and Contrasting, Evaluating

Materials craft supplies, index cards

Time 20 minutes

Advance Prep Collect a variety of craft supplies, including scissors, construction paper, cardboard tubes, plastic bags, yarn, glue, and beads.

Safety Caution students about the use of pins and about standing on chairs as they hang up their models. Supervise them as they do so.

Strategies

- You may want students to build a model of a different kind of cell. A model of a plant cell is suggested because plant cells have a great variety of structures and organelles.
- Make sure at least one group is working on these major structures: cell wall, cell membrane, nucleus, microtubules, microfilaments, ribosomes, smooth ER, rough ER, Golgi apparatus, lysosomes, vacuoles, mitochondria, and chloroplasts.

Expected Outcomes Students will make models of plant-cell structures and arrange them to form a complete cell.

Analyze and Conclude

1. Students' answers should reflect an understanding of the functions of plant cell organelles.
2. Scales will vary depending on the size of the cell model. A typical scale, assuming that the classroom is 5 m across, would be 5/0.00005 (50 micrometers = 0.00005 meters), or 100,000 : 1.
3. The model should be similar in shape and structure to a real cell part. The model is different in that it is much larger, is made of different materials, and does not function.
4. Students should explain how their model would be an improvement on their previous model.

Quick Lab

How can you make a model of a cell?

Materials variety of craft supplies, index cards

Procedure 

1. Your class is going to make a model of a plant cell using the whole classroom. Work with a partner or in a small group to decide what cell part or organelle you would like to model. (Use **Figure 7–6** as a starting point. It will give you an idea of the relative sizes of various cell parts and their possible positions. **Figures 7–7** through **7–10** can provide additional information.)
2. Using materials of your choice, make a three-dimensional model of the cell part or organelle you chose. Make the model as complete and as accurate as you can.
3. Label an index card with the name of your cell part or organelle and list its main features and functions. Attach the card to your model.
4. Attach your model to an appropriate place in the room. If possible, attach your model to another related cell part or organelle.

Analyze and Conclude

1. **Inferring** What are the functions of the different organelles in plant cells?
2. **Calculating** Assume that a typical plant cell is 50 micrometers wide. Calculate the scale of your classroom cell model. (*Hint:* Divide the width of the classroom by the width of a cell, making sure to use the same units.)
3. **Comparing and Contrasting** How is your model cell part or organelle similar to the real cell part or organelle? How is it different?
4. **Evaluating** Based on your work with this model, describe how you could make a better model. Specify what new information the improved model would demonstrate.

BIIE 1.e, BIIE 1.g

CA a 7 1.d

Chloroplasts Plants and some other organisms contain **chloroplasts.** **Chloroplasts are organelles that capture the energy from sunlight and convert it into chemical energy in a process called photosynthesis.** Chloroplasts are the biological equivalents of solar power plants. Like mitochondria, chloroplasts are surrounded by two membranes. Inside the organelle are large stacks of other membranes, which contain the green pigment chlorophyll. Interestingly, chloroplasts and mitochondria contain their own genetic information in the form of small DNA molecules. This has led to the idea that they may have descended from independent microorganisms. This idea, called the endosymbiotic theory, will be discussed in Chapter 17.

Cytoskeleton

A supporting structure and a transportation system complete our picture of the cell as a factory. As you know, a factory building is supported by steel or cement beams and by columns that support its walls and roof. Eukaryotic cells are given their shape and internal organization by a supporting structure known as the **cytoskeleton.**

Go Online PHSchool.com
For: Cell structure activity
Visit: PHSchool.com
Web Code: cbd-3072

FACTS AND FIGURES

The origin of eukaryotes?

The idea that chloroplasts and mitochondria originated in symbiotic relationships with prokaryotic cells is called the endosymbiont hypothesis. According to this hypothesis, the ancestors of eukaryotic cells were smaller species of prokaryotes living within larger species of prokaryotes. Chloroplasts possibly originated when cyanobacteria became established in larger prokaryotes either as parasites or as prey that were not digested. Mitochondria were once possibly anaerobic heterotrophs that found "safe harbor" inside larger prokaryotes as the world became increasingly aerobic. As the host and symbionts over time became more and more interdependent, the organisms merged to become a single organism.

The cytoskeleton is a network of protein filaments that helps the cell to maintain its shape. The cytoskeleton is also involved in movement. Microfilaments and microtubules are two of the principal protein filaments that make up the cytoskeleton.

Microfilaments Microfilaments are threadlike structures made of a protein called actin. They form extensive networks in some cells and produce a tough, flexible framework that supports the cell. Microfilaments also help cells move. Microfilament assembly and disassembly is responsible for the cytoplasmic movements that allow cells, such as amoebas, to crawl along surfaces.

Microtubules Microtubules are hollow structures made up of proteins known as tubulins. In many cells, they play critical roles in maintaining cell shape. Microtubules are also important in cell division, where they form a structure known as the mitotic spindle, which helps to separate chromosomes. In animal cells, structures known as centrioles are also formed from tubulin. **Centrioles** are located near the nucleus and help to organize cell division. Centrioles are not found in plant cells.

Microtubules also help to build projections from the cell surface, which are known as cilia (singular: cilium) and flagella (singular: flagellum), that enable cells to swim rapidly through liquids. As you can see in **Figure 7–11,** the microtubules are arranged in a "9 + 2" pattern. Small cross-bridges between the microtubules in these organelles use chemical energy to generate force, allowing cells to produce controlled movements using the cytoskeleton.

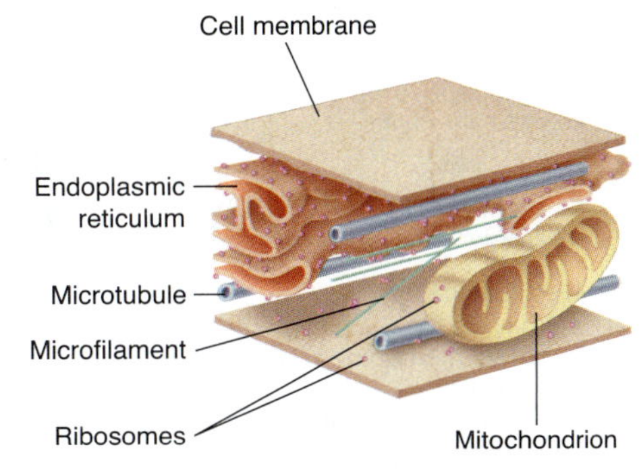

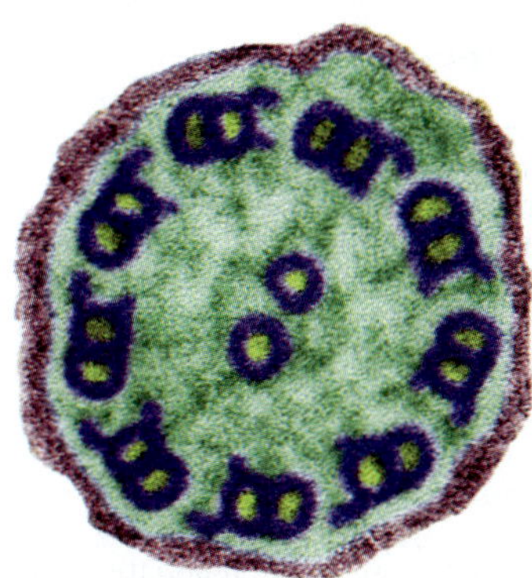

▲ **Figure 7–11 The cytoskeleton is a network of protein filaments that helps the cell to maintain its shape and is involved in many forms of cell movement.** The micrograph shows a cross section of an epithelial cell cilia. You can see the nine pairs of microtubules surrounding the two single microtubules, hence the "9 + 2" pattern.

7–2 Section Assessment

1. **Key Concept** Describe the functions of the endoplasmic reticulum, Golgi apparatus, chloroplast, and mitochondrion.
2. Describe the role of the nucleus in the cell.
3. What are two functions of the cytoskeleton?
4. How is a cell like a factory?
5. **Critical Thinking Inferring** You examine an unknown cell under the microscope and discover that the cell contains chloroplasts. What type of organism could you infer that the cell came from?

Thinking Visually

Creating Artwork
Create a work of art—such as a painting or sculpture—depicting a cross section of a plant cell or an animal cell. Include all the different organelles described in this section that would be found in that type of cell. Label each organelle in your artwork.

7–2 Section Assessment

1. Rough ER makes membranes and secretory proteins. Smooth ER makes lipids and helps in detoxification. The Golgi apparatus modifies, sorts, and packages proteins and other materials from the ER for storage or secretion. Chloroplasts capture the energy of sunlight and convert it into chemical energy. Mitochondria convert stored chemical energy into compounds that the cell can use.
2. It is the control center of the cell.
3. It helps the cell maintain its shape and also is involved in movement.
4. Answers may vary. A typical response will compare ribosomes to factory machines and the cytoskeleton to a supporting structure. Students should also compare other organelles to various parts of a factory.
5. Students should infer that the organism would either be a plant or some other organism that carries out photosynthesis.

Go Online PHSchool.com

Your students can extend their knowledge of cell structure through this online experience.

Cytoskeleton

Build Science Skills

Using Analogies Show students a photo of a house that's being built, with only the foundation laid and the basic frame constructed. Builders call this initial stage "framing" the house. Ask: **How is this house frame like a cell's cytoskeleton?** *(Just as a cytoskeleton is a network of protein filaments that helps a cell maintain its shape, the frame of a house is a network of boards and timbers that forms the shape of the house.)* L1 L2

3 ASSESS

Evaluate Understanding

Have students make a Venn diagram to show organelles that are found only in prokaryotic cells, those that are found only in eukaryotic cells, and those that are found in both types of cells.

Reteach

Ask students to make a compare/contrast table that lists all the parts of a typical cell. Column heads might include *Name, Structure,* and *Function.*

Thinking Visually

Encourage students to be creative yet accurate in their painting or sculpture. Provide them with a variety of materials to choose from, including paints, paintbrushes, plastic bags, balloons, various pasta shapes, pipe cleaners, gelatin, and pieces of fabric and construction paper. Also, have students bring materials from home.

If your class subscribes to the iText, use it to review the Key Concepts in Section 7–2.

Section 7–3

BI 1.a, *BI 1.j

1 FOCUS

Objectives

7.3.1 ***Identify*** the main functions of the cell membrane and the cell wall.

7.3.2 ***Describe*** what happens during diffusion.

7.3.3 ***Explain*** the processes of osmosis, facilitated diffusion, and active transport.

Guide for Reading

Vocabulary Preview

Suggest that students preview the meaning of the Vocabulary terms in the section by skimming the text to find the highlighted boldface words and their meanings.

Reading Strategy

Before students read, have them skim the section to identify and make a list of the main ideas. Then, as they read the section they should write down supporting details for each main idea.

2 INSTRUCT

Cell Membrane

Use Visuals

Figure 7–12 Ask students: **What does it mean that a cell membrane has a "lipid bilayer"?** *(A cell membrane is composed of two layers of lipid molecules.)* **What do the blue molecules represent in the illustration of the cell membrane?** *(They represent carbohydrate chains attached to the outside of the protein molecules embedded in the lipid bilayer.)* Explain that these carbohydrate molecules are particularly important in cell recognition. Nearly all cells have special carbohydrate molecules on their surfaces—cell markers—that are unique. L1 L2

7–3 Cell Boundaries

BI 1.a. Students know cells are enclosed within semipermeable membranes that regulate their interaction with their surroundings. ***BI 1.j.** Students know how eukaryotic cells are given shape and internal organization by a cytoskeleton or cell wall or both.

Guide for Reading

Key Concepts
- What are the main functions of the cell membrane and the cell wall?
- What happens during diffusion?
- What is osmosis?

Vocabulary
cell membrane • cell wall
lipid bilayer • concentration
diffusion • equilibrium
osmosis • isotonic
hypertonic • hypotonic
facilitated diffusion
active transport • endocytosis
phagocytosis • pinocytosis
exocytosis

Reading Strategy: Summarizing As you read, make a list of the ways in which substances can move through the cell membrane. Write one sentence describing each process.

When you first study a country, you may begin by examining a map of the country's borders. Before you can learn anything about a nation, it's important to understand where it begins and where it ends. The same principle applies to cells. Among the most important parts of a cell are its borders, which separate the cell from its surroundings. All cells are surrounded by a thin, flexible barrier known as the **cell membrane.** The cell membrane is sometimes called the plasma membrane because many cells in the body are in direct contact with the fluid portion of the blood—the plasma. Many cells also produce a strong supporting layer around the membrane known as a **cell wall.**

Cell Membrane

The cell membrane regulates what enters and leaves the cell and also provides protection and support. The composition of nearly all cell membranes is a double-layered sheet called a **lipid bilayer.** As you can see in **Figure 7–12,** there are two layers of lipids, hence the name bilayer. The lipid bilayer gives cell membranes a flexible structure that forms a strong barrier between the cell and its surroundings.

CA a

In addition to lipids, most cell membranes contain protein molecules that are embedded in the lipid bilayer. Carbohydrate molecules are attached to many of these proteins. In fact, there are so many kinds of molecules in cell membranes that scientists describe their understanding of the membrane as the "fluid mosaic model" of membrane structure. As you will see, some of the proteins form channels and pumps that help to move material across the cell membrane. Many of the carbohydrates act like chemical identification cards, allowing individual cells to identify one another.

a BI 1.a

Figure 7–12 **The cell membrane regulates what enters and leaves the cell.** This cell membrane is made up of a lipid bilayer in which proteins are embedded.

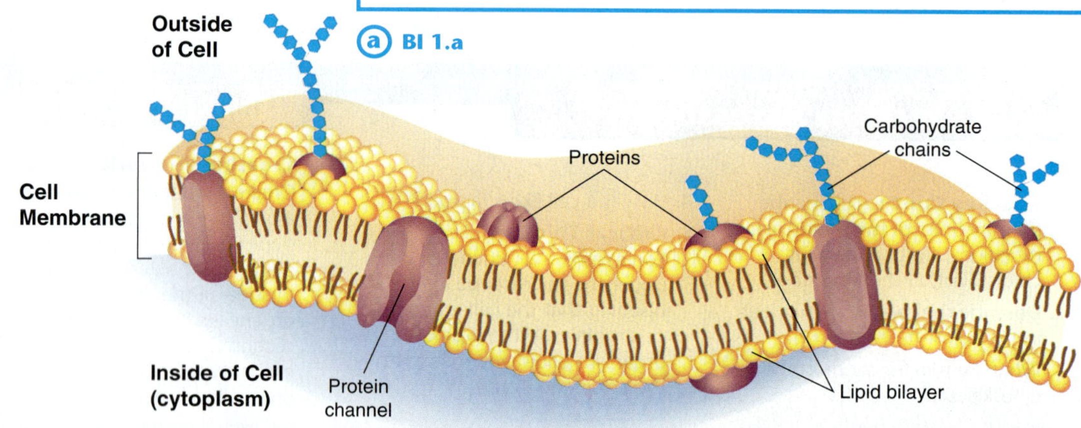

SECTION RESOURCES

Print:
- ***Laboratory Manual A,*** Chapter 7 Lab
- ***Teaching Resources,*** Lesson Plan 7–3, Adapted Section Summary 7–3, Adapted Worksheets 7–3, Section Summary 7–3, Worksheets 7–3, Section Review 7–3
- ***Reading and Study Workbook A,*** Section 7–3
- ***Adapted Reading and Study Workbook B,*** Section 7–3
- ***Lab Worksheets,*** Chapter 7 Real-World Lab

Technology:
- ***iText,*** Section 7–3
- ***Animated Biological Concepts DVD,*** 5 Diffusion and Osmosis, 6 Passive and Active Transport, 7 Endocytosis and Exocytosis
- ***Transparencies Plus,*** Section 7–3
- ***Lab Simulations CD-ROM,*** Biomembranes 1: Membrane Structure and Transport
- ***Virtual Labs,*** Lab 3, Lab 4, Lab 5

Cell Walls

Cell walls are present in many organisms, including plants, algae, fungi, and many prokaryotes. Cell walls lie outside the cell membrane. Most cell walls are porous enough to allow water, oxygen, carbon dioxide, and certain other substances to pass through easily. **The main function of the cell wall is to provide support and protection for the cell.**

Most cell walls are made from fibers of carbohydrate and protein. These substances are produced within the cell and then released at the surface of the cell membrane where they are assembled to form the wall. Plant cell walls are composed mostly of cellulose, a tough carbohydrate fiber. Cellulose is the principal component of both wood and paper, so every time you pick up a sheet of paper, you are holding the stuff of cell walls in your hand.

For: Links on cell membranes
Visit: www.SciLinks.org
Web Code: cbn-3073

Diffusion Through Cell Boundaries

Every living cell exists in a liquid environment that it needs to survive. It may not always seem that way; yet even in the dust and heat of a desert like the one in **Figure 7–13,** the cells of cactus plants, scorpions, and vultures are bathed in liquid. One of the most important functions of the cell membrane is to regulate the movement of dissolved molecules from the liquid on one side of the membrane to the liquid on the other side.

Measuring Concentration The cytoplasm of a cell contains a solution of many different substances in water. Recall that a solution is a mixture of two or more substances. The substances dissolved in the solution are called solutes. The **concentration** of a solution is the mass of solute in a given volume of solution, or mass/volume. For example, if you dissolved 12 grams of salt in 3 liters of water, the concentration of the solution would be 12 g/3 L, or 4 g/L (grams per liter). If you had 12 grams of salt in 6 liters of water, the concentration would be 12 g/6 L, or 2 g/L. The first solution is twice as concentrated as the second solution.

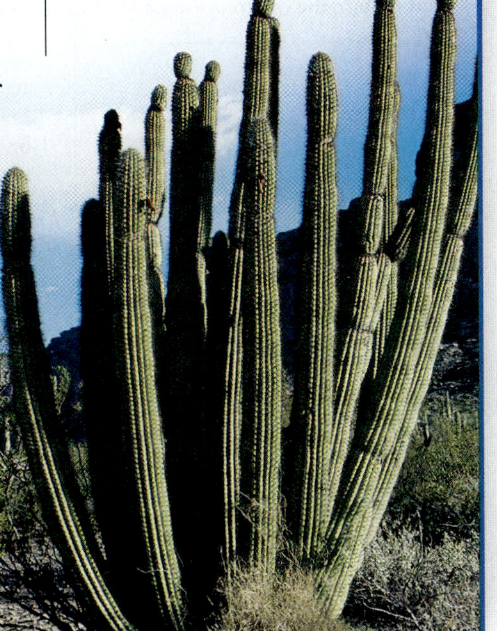

▼ **Figure 7–13** The cells of living things are bathed in liquid even in dry environments. When it rains, these cactus plants store the water in their stems. **Applying Concepts** *Which cell structure could serve as a storage location for water?*

Download a worksheet on cell membranes for students to complete, and find additional teacher support from NSTA SciLinks.

Cell Walls

Address Misconceptions

Some students may have the misconception that a cell wall takes the place of a cell membrane. Emphasize that all cells have a cell membrane. Some cells have the added characteristic of having a cell wall outside the cell membrane. Some students may also have the misconception that a cell wall is impenetrable, like the wall of a building. Read aloud the sentence in their text that explains that cell walls are porous. Point out that if cell walls weren't porous, nothing could pass into or out of plant cells, for instance. L1

Diffusion Through Cell Boundaries

Make Connections

Mathematics Reinforce students' understanding of concentration by building on the example in the text. Ask: **If you dissolved 12 grams of salt in 3 liters of water, what is the concentration of salt in the solution?** *(4 g/L)* **Suppose you added 12 more grams of salt to the solution. What would be the resulting concentration?** *(24 g/3 L = 8 g/L)* **What if you then added another 3 liters of water to that solution. What would be the resulting concentration?** *(24 g/6 L = 4 g/L)* **Which solution of the ones discussed would be called the most concentrated?** *(The solution in which the concentration is 8 g/L)* Point out that in each case the solute has a relatively small volume compared to the volume of the solvent. Yet, small differences in solute can have a great effect in living things. L2 L3

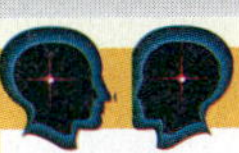

TEACHER TO TEACHER

To help students remember the structures and functions of an animal cell, give each pair of students an acetate sheet and a marking pen. Assign each student pair a different cell structure, and ask them to draw the cell structure in a specific place on their acetate sheet. As you discuss the parts of the cell, place all the sheets on an overhead projector. Then, draw a cell membrane surrounding all the cell structures on the top acetate sheet. Have students identify each structure and tell what its function is, including the cell membrane.

—*Beverly Cea*
Biology Teacher
Grimsley High School
Greensboro, NC

Answer to . . .

Figure 7–13 *Vacuoles*

For: Diffusion activity
Visit: PHSchool.com
Web Code: cbe-3073
Students explore the process of diffusion online.

Build Science Skills

Using Models Have students act out the process of diffusion. To begin, group class members at the classroom door. Then, tell them to spread out through the classroom in such a way that no two students are closer to each other than to any other students. Discuss how molecules randomly spread out through a liquid or a gas. L1 L2

Build Science Skills

Observing Students can observe the action of diffusion through this simple activity. Divide the class into small groups, and give each group two beakers, salt, a teaspoon, and food coloring, as well as access to water. Have groups follow this procedure. Fill one beaker about one-third full of water, and then add about a half teaspoon of salt and a few drops of food coloring. Fill the second beaker about half full of water. Then, pour the contents of the first beaker into the second beaker, and observe what happens. *(Students should observe that the colored saltwater will sink to the bottom of the beaker.)* Let the second beaker stand overnight, and observe any changes that have occurred. *(The next day, students should observe that the liquid in the beaker will be uniformly colored throughout.)* Ask students: **What process occurred that changed the mixture overnight?** *(Diffusion)*

Diffusion

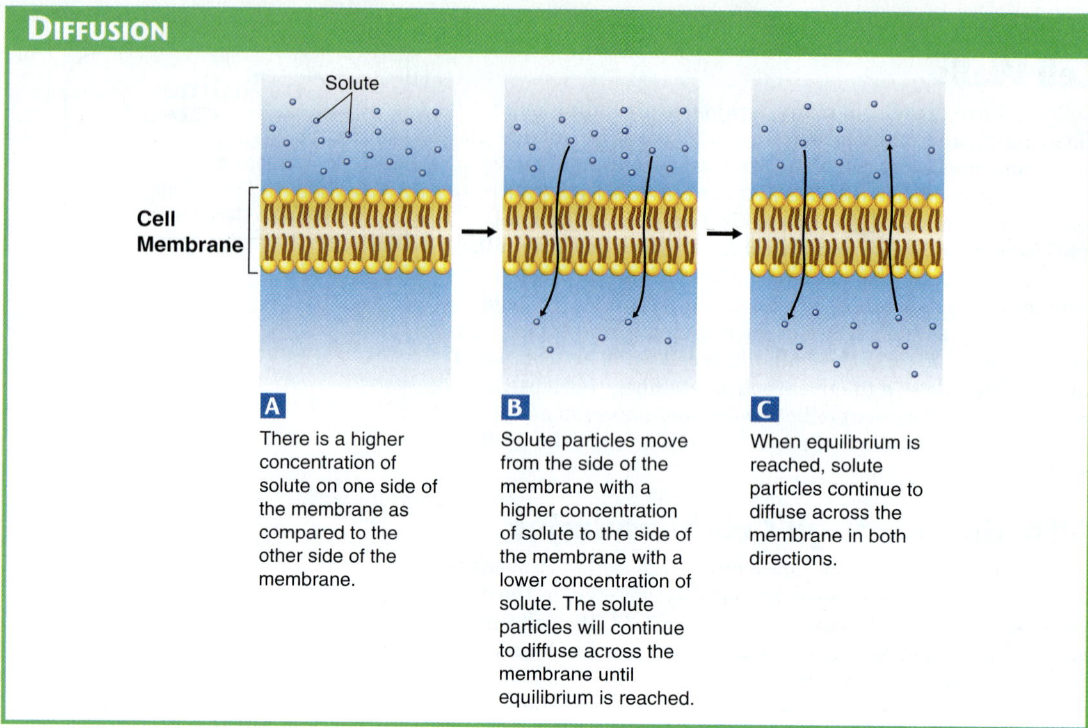

▲ **Figure 7–14** Diffusion is the process by which molecules of a substance move from areas of higher concentration to areas of lower concentration. **Diffusion does not require the cell to use energy.**

For: Diffusion activity
Visit: PHSchool.com
Web Code: cbp-3073

Diffusion In a solution, particles move constantly. They collide with one another and tend to spread out randomly. As a result, the particles tend to move from an area where they are more concentrated to an area where they are less concentrated, a process known as **diffusion** (dih-FYOO-zhun). When the concentration of the solute is the same throughout a system, the system has reached **equilibrium.**

What do diffusion and equilibrium have to do with cell membranes? Suppose a substance is present in unequal concentrations on either side of a cell membrane, as shown in **Figure 7–14.** If the substance can cross the cell membrane, its particles will tend to move toward the area where it is less concentrated until equilibrium is reached. At that point, the concentration of the substance on both sides of the cell membrane will be the same. **Because diffusion depends upon random particle movements, substances diffuse across membranes without requiring the cell to use energy.** Even when equilibrium is reached, particles of a solution will continue to move across the membrane in both directions. However, because almost equal numbers of particles move in each direction, there is no further change in concentration.

CHECKPOINT *What conditions are present when equilibrium is reached in a solution?*

UNIVERSAL ACCESS

Inclusion/Special Needs

To help students understand the difference between facilitated diffusion and active transport, use the analogy of going through a fence at an open gate or going through a turnstile. Walking through an open gate is like facilitated diffusion—it takes no energy to pass through that "carrier protein" in the fence. Moving through a turnstile is like active transport—a person has to use energy to move through that "molecular pump." L1

Advanced Learners

Point out that the human digestive system is unable to digest cellulose, and thus cellulose passes through the digestive tract without being broken down. Explain that cellulose is nevertheless an important part of a healthy diet. Cellulose in the diet is called fiber, and consuming enough fiber may help prevent some forms of cancer. Encourage students who need a challenge to find out how cellulose aids in digestion and helps prevent disease. L3

Osmosis

Although many substances can diffuse across biological membranes, some are too large or too strongly charged to cross the lipid bilayer. If a substance is able to diffuse across a membrane, the membrane is said to be permeable to it. A membrane is impermeable to substances that cannot pass across it. Most biological membranes are selectively permeable, meaning that some substances can pass across them and others cannot. Selectively permeable membranes are also called semipermeable membranes.

Water passes quite easily across most membranes, even though many solute molecules cannot. An important process known as **osmosis** is the result. **Osmosis is the diffusion of water through a selectively permeable membrane.**

CA a

How Osmosis Works Look at the beaker on the left in **Figure 7–15.** There are more sugar molecules on the left side of the membrane than on the right side. That means that the concentration of water is lower on the left than it is on the right. The membrane is permeable to water but not to sugar. This means that water can cross the membrane in both directions, but sugar cannot. As a result, there is a net movement of water from the area of high concentration to the area of low concentration.

Water will tend to move across the membrane until equilibrium is reached. At that point, the concentrations of water and sugar will be the same on both sides of the membrane. When this happens, the two solutions will be **isotonic,** which means "same strength." When the experiment began, the more concentrated sugar solution was **hypertonic,** which means "above strength," as compared to the dilute sugar solution. The dilute sugar solution was **hypotonic,** or "below strength."

Word Origins

Hypotonic comes from the Greek word *hupo,* meaning "under," and the New Latin word *tonicus,* meaning "tension" or "strength." So a hypotonic solution is less strong, or less concentrated, than another solution of the same type. **If *derma* means "skin," how would you describe a hypodermic injection?**

BI 1.a

For: Osmosis activity
Visit: PHSchool.com
Web Code: cbp-3075

Figure 7–15 **Osmosis is the diffusion of water through a selectively permeable membrane.** In the first beaker, water is more concentrated on the right side of the membrane. As a result, the water diffuses (as shown in the second beaker) to the area of lower concentration.

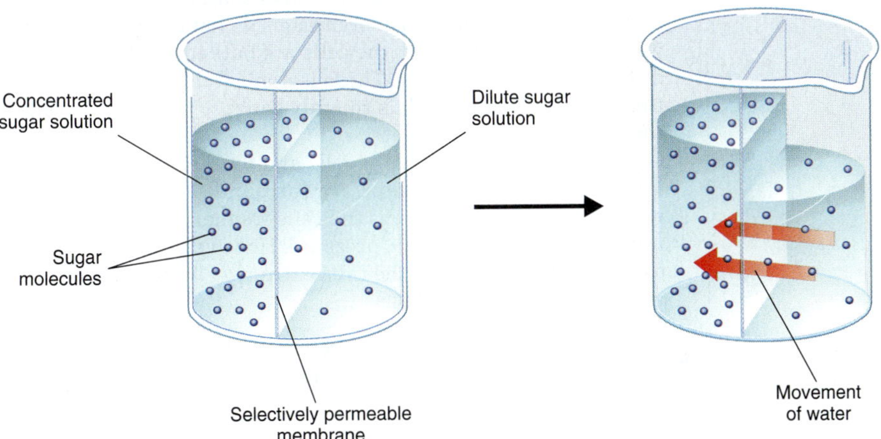

SCIENCE UPDATE

Water finds its way

Osmosis is easy to observe in cells, yet it was long a mystery as to how water can cross membranes so quickly. Water is a polar molecule, and as such it is not lipid soluble and should not be expected to cross a lipid bilayer. Many puzzled physical chemists suggested that biochemists should look for some kind of channels in the membrane. In the late twentieth century, such channels were in fact discovered. These channels, which are membrane-spanning proteins, are named aquaporins. They have been found in scores of cells, and some scientists think that they might be present in nearly all cells. Their discovery is so recent that a detailed analysis of how they work may be years away.

Osmosis

Word Origins

A hypodermic injection is one that is administered under the skin. L2

Demonstration

Demonstrate the concept of selective permeability by using a kitchen strainer. As students observe, pour different sorts of materials through the strainer, making sure to choose some materials that will go through the strainer and some that will not. Materials might include water, sugar, sand, small stones, marbles, and paper clips. Students will observe that the strainer is selectively permeable. L1 L2

Use Visuals

Figure 7–15 Have students study the figure and read the caption. Then, ask: **In the beaker on the left, which solution is hypertonic and which is hypotonic?** *(The solution on the left side of the membrane is hypertonic, and the solution on the right side is hypotonic.)* **In this model, to which material is the membrane permeable, water or sugar?** *(Water)* Emphasize that the membrane allows one material—water—to pass through it, while blocking the other material—sugar. This makes the membrane selectively permeable. Finally, ask students to draw a third beaker that would model a situation in which the two solutions on either side of the membrane are isotonic. *(Students should make a drawing in which the same number of sugar molecules are evenly distributed on both sides of the membrane.)* L2

For: Osmosis activity
Visit: PHSchool.com
Web Code: cbe-3075
Students interact with the art of osmosis online.

Answer to . . .

CHECKPOINT *Equilibrium is reached when the concentration of the solute is the same throughout the solution.*

7–3 (continued)

Build Science Skills

Applying Concepts Ask students to consider this real-life circumstance. A homeowner contracts a lawn company to add fertilizer to the lawn in order to make the grass grow better. This process is normally done by spraying a mixture of fertilizer and water onto the lawn. Ask: **What would happen if too much fertilizer and too little water were sprayed onto the lawn?** *(Students may know that the grass would appear to be burned.)* **Can you suggest what happened to the cells of the grass?** *(They lost water because of the concentrated solution of fertilizer around them.)* **In that case, was the fertilizer-water mixture hypotonic or hypertonic compared to the grass cells?** *(The mixture was hypertonic compared to the grass cells.)*

Demonstration

Place a small number of paramecia in a petri dish on a microprojector. Have students observe the paramecia as you discuss contractile vacuoles, which some unicellular organisms have to pump water out of the cell. Flood the environment of the paramecia with distilled water. As students continue to observe, point out the action of the contractile vacuoles. Ask: **What was added to the dish?** *(Pure water)* **How do you know?** *(The action of the contractile vacuoles increased.)* **What will eventually happen to the paramecia?** *(They will explode.)* **Why?** *(The vacuoles cannot keep up with the inward movement of water because of osmosis.)* **What would happen if a small amount of salt water were added?** *(Vacuole action would probably return to normal.)* L2

The Effects of Osmosis on Cells

Solution	Animal Cell	Plant Cell
Isotonic: The concentration of solutes is the same inside and outside the cell.	Water in; Water out	Water in; Water out; Vacuole; Cell wall; Cell membrane
Hypertonic: Solution has a higher solute concentration than the cell.	Water out	Water out
Hypotonic: Solution has a lower solute concentration than the cell.	Water in	Water in

▲ **Figure 7–16** Cells placed in an isotonic solution neither gain nor lose water. In a hypertonic solution, animal cells shrink, and plant cell vacuoles collapse. In a hypotonic solution, animal cells swell and burst. The vacuoles of plant cells swell, pushing the cell contents out against the cell wall. **Predicting** ***What would happen to the animal cell in the isotonic solution if it were placed in pure water?***

Osmotic Pressure For organisms to survive, they must have a way to balance the intake and loss of water. Osmosis exerts a pressure known as osmotic pressure on the hypertonic side of a selectively permeable membrane. Osmotic pressure can cause serious problems for a cell. Because the cell is filled with salts, sugars, proteins, and other molecules, it will almost always be hypertonic to fresh water. This means that osmotic pressure should produce a net movement of water into a typical cell that is surrounded by fresh water. If that happens, the volume of a cell will increase until the cell becomes swollen. Eventually, the cell may burst like an overinflated balloon.

Fortunately, cells in large organisms are not in danger of bursting. Most cells in such organisms do not come in contact with fresh water. Instead, the cells are bathed in fluids, such as blood, that are isotonic. These isotonic fluids have concentrations of dissolved materials roughly equal to those in the cells themselves.

Other cells, such as plant cells and bacteria, which do come into contact with fresh water, are surrounded by tough cell walls. The cell walls prevent the cells from expanding, even under tremendous osmotic pressure. However, the increased osmotic pressure makes the cells extremely vulnerable to injuries to their cell walls.

CHECKPOINT *What structures protect plant and bacterial cells from potential damage resulting from osmotic pressure?*

FACTS AND FIGURES

Penicillin works by osmosis

Penicillin, one of the most important antibiotic drugs in the history of medicine, depends on osmosis for its killing action. Penicillin inhibits an enzyme with which many bacteria produce chemical cross-links in their cell walls. This leads to the formation of a weakened cell wall that cannot stand the stress of osmotic pressure. Gradually, the cell wall becomes weaker and weaker until it breaks, and the bacterium bursts under the inrush of water caused by osmosis.

Facilitated Diffusion

A few molecules, such as the sugar glucose, seem to pass through the cell membrane much more quickly than they should. One might think that these molecules are too large or too strongly charged to cross the membrane, and yet they diffuse across quite easily.

How does this happen? Cell membranes have protein channels that act as carriers, making it easy for certain molecules to cross. Red blood cells, for example, have membrane proteins with carrier channels that allow glucose to pass through them. Only glucose can pass through this protein carrier, and it can move through in either direction. This is sometimes known as carrier-facilitated diffusion. These cell membrane channels are also said to facilitate, or help, the diffusion of glucose across the membrane. The process, shown in **Figure 7–17**, is known as **facilitated** (fuh-SIL-uh-tayt-ud) **diffusion.** Hundreds of different protein channels have been found that allow particular substances to cross different membranes.

Although facilitated diffusion is fast and specific, it is still diffusion. Therefore, a net movement of molecules across a cell membrane will occur only if there is a higher concentration of the particular molecules on one side than on the other side. This movement does not require the use of the cell's energy.

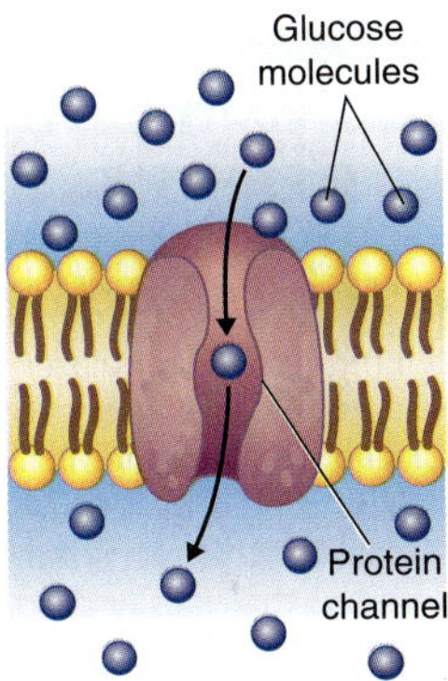

▲ **Figure 7–17** During facilitated diffusion, molecules, such as glucose, that cannot diffuse across the cell membrane's lipid bilayer on their own move through protein channels instead. **Applying Concepts** *Does facilitated diffusion require the cell to use energy?*

BIIE 1.d, BIIE 1.g

Quick Lab

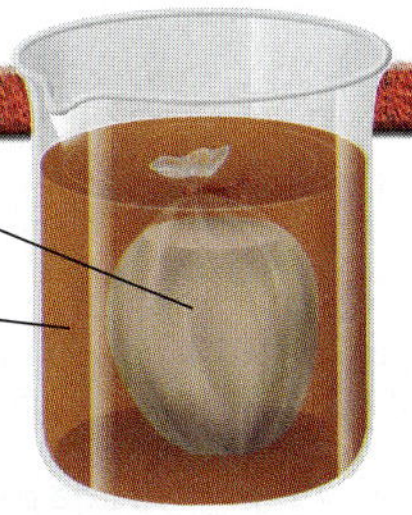

How can you model permeability in cells?

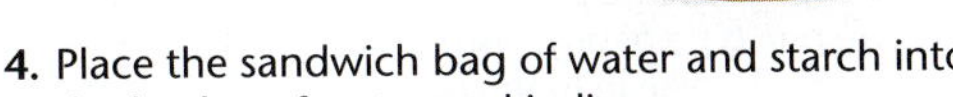

Materials graduated cylinder, plastic sandwich bag, starch, twist tie, 500-mL beaker, iodine solution

Procedure 

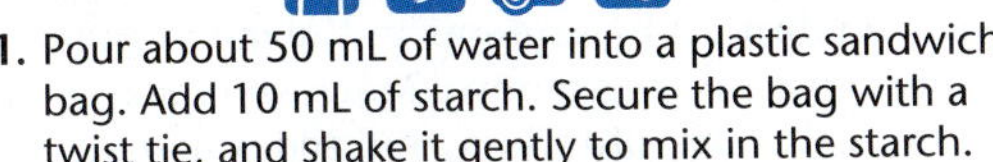

1. Pour about 50 mL of water into a plastic sandwich bag. Add 10 mL of starch. Secure the bag with a twist tie, and shake it gently to mix in the starch.
2. Put on your goggles, plastic gloves, and apron.
3. Pour 250 mL of water into a 500-mL beaker. **CAUTION:** *Handle the beaker carefully.* Add 15 drops of iodine. **CAUTION:** *Iodine is corrosive and irritating to the skin and can stain skin and clothing. Be careful not to spill it on yourself.*
4. Place the sandwich bag of water and starch into the beaker of water and iodine.
5. After 20 minutes, look at the sandwich bag in the beaker. Observe and record any changes that occurred.

Analyze and Conclude

1. **Using Models** What cell structure does the sandwich bag represent?
2. **Observing** What did you see inside the sandwich bag? Outside the sandwich bag?
3. **Inferring** Iodine turns blue-black in the presence of starch. What process do you think occurred that caused the results you observed? Explain.

FACTS AND FIGURES

Rate of facilitated diffusion

Facilitated diffusion depends on a difference in concentration. In simple diffusion, that is the only factor that affects rate. In facilitated diffusion, the rate also depends on the number of specific carrier protein molecules in the membrane, because the diffusing molecules can move across the membrane only through those proteins. An example is the diffusion of glucose into cells, as described on this page. Such diffusion occurs most of the time as facilitated diffusion. No matter how much the cell "needs" the glucose—no matter how great the difference is in concentration inside and outside the cell—the rate at which the glucose can diffuse into the cell has a limit because of the limited number of glucose carrier protein molecules in the lipid bilayer.

Facilitated Diffusion

Quick Lab

BIIE 1.d, BIIE 1.g

Objective Students will be able to make and investigate a model of permeability in cells. L2 L3

Skills Focus **Using Models, Observing, Inferring**

Time 20 minutes

Advance Prep To save time and reduce possible spills, you may want to prepare the starch mixture and iodine solution yourself in advance.

Safety Read the MSDS on iodine. If you prepare the iodine solution yourself, be sure to wear goggles, plastic gloves, and an apron.

Strategy It will take up to 20 minutes for the iodine to pass through the bag and react with the starch, so you may want to set up this lab at the beginning of the class and return to it at the end.

Expected Outcome Students should observe that the water inside the sandwich bag turned blue-black. The water outside the sandwich bag did not change.

Analyze and Conclude

1. The sandwich bag represents the cell membrane.
2. The water inside the sandwich bag turned blue-black. The water outside the sandwich bag did not change.
3. Diffusion occurred. The iodine molecules diffused through the sandwich bag and reacted with the starch inside. The starch molecules were too big to pass through the bag, and so there was no reaction outside the bag.

Answers to . . .

✓CHECKPOINT *Cell walls prevent the cells from expanding, even under tremendous osmotic pressure.*

Figure 7–16 *The volume of the cell would increase until it became swollen. Eventually, it could burst like an over-inflated balloon.*

Figure 7–17 *No*

Analyzing Data

BI 1.a

As students examine the bar graph of the different molecules, point out that some molecules move through the lipid bilayer by simple diffusion and others move through by facilitated diffusion. In most cases, for example, water moves through selectively permeable membranes by diffusion, whereas glucose moves through by facilitated diffusion. L2 L3

Answers

1. Students may predict that water will diffuse most quickly because it is the smallest and glucose will diffuse most slowly because it is the largest.
2. Students' hypotheses may include: The smaller a molecule is, the faster it diffuses.
3. Students' experiments should be designed to test their hypotheses and control variables.

Active Transport

Use Visuals

Figure 7–18 After students have studied the image and read the caption, ask: **Why is phagocytosis an example of active transport and not facilitated diffusion?** *(Phagocytosis requires the input of energy, because the organism uses energy to surround and engulf a large particle.)* L1 L2

Build Science Skills

Using Analogies Set up a ramp using a board propped up on one end by a stack of books. Then, as students observe, roll a ball down the ramp and push it back up again. Ask: **Which is like facilitated diffusion and which is like active transport, rolling the ball down the ramp or pushing it up? Explain.** *(Rolling the ball down is like facilitated diffusion, because neither requires addition of energy. Pushing the ball back up is like active transport, because it requires addition of energy.)* L1 L2

Analyzing Data

Crossing the Cell Membrane

The cell membrane regulates what enters and leaves the cell and also provides protection and support. The core of nearly all cell membranes is a double-layered sheet called a lipid bilayer. Most materials entering the cell pass across this membrane by diffusion. The graph shows the sizes of several molecules that can diffuse across a lipid bilayer.

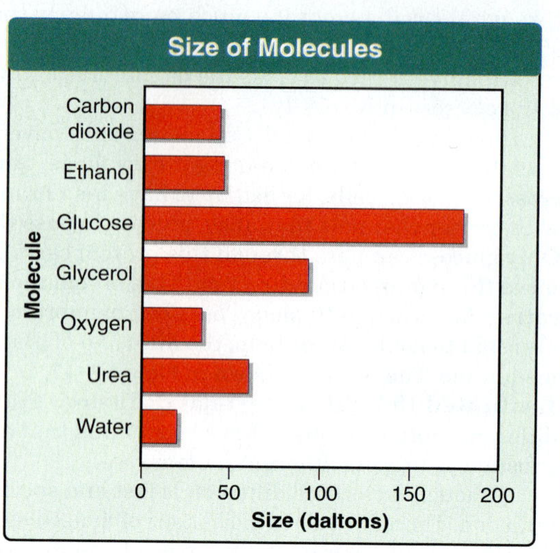

1. **Predicting** Which substances do you think will diffuse across the lipid bilayer most quickly? Most slowly? Explain your answers.
2. **Formulating Hypotheses** Formulate a hypothesis about the relationship between molecule size and rate of diffusion.
3. **Designing Experiments** Design an experiment to test your hypothesis.

BI 1.a

Figure 7–18 Phagocytosis is one form of active transport. During phagocytosis, extensions of cytoplasm surround and engulf large particles. Amoebas are one type of organism that uses this process to take in food and other materials.

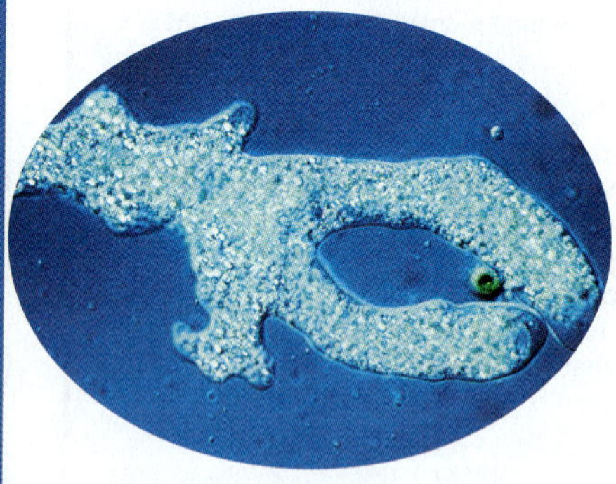

Active Transport

As powerful as diffusion is, cells sometimes must move materials in the opposite direction—against a concentration difference. This is accomplished by a process known as **active transport.** As its name implies, active transport requires energy. The active transport of small molecules or ions across a cell membrane is generally carried out by transport proteins or "pumps" that are found in the membrane itself. Larger molecules and clumps of material can also be actively transported across the cell membrane by processes known as endocytosis and exocytosis. The transport of these larger materials sometimes involves changes in the shape of the cell membrane.

Molecular Transport Small molecules and ions are carried across membranes by proteins in the membrane that act like energy-requiring pumps. Many cells use such proteins to move calcium, potassium, and sodium ions across cell membranes. Changes in protein shape, as shown in **Figure 7–19**, seem to play an important role in the pumping process. A considerable portion of the energy used by cells in their daily activities is devoted to providing the energy to keep this form of active transport working. The use of energy in these systems enables cells to concentrate substances in a particular location, even when the forces of diffusion might tend to move these substances in the opposite direction.

FACTS AND FIGURES

Protein molecules and active transport

One of the most important examples of active transport is known as the sodium potassium pump, in which sodium ions are maintained at a lower concentration inside the cell and potassium ions are maintained at a higher concentration inside the cell. The active transport by protein molecules of these ions is central to the production of electrical impulses by nerve cells. At one time, scientists thought that the protein molecules actually rotated as they transported substances through the cell membrane, picking up their parcels on the outside and dumping them on the inside. Now, scientists think that the transported molecules are somehow squeezed through the transport proteins, as the proteins change their configuration to accommodate their riders.

Endocytosis and Exocytosis Larger molecules and even solid clumps of material may be transported by movements of the cell membrane. One of these movements is called endocytosis (en-doh-sy-TOH-sis). **Endocytosis** is the process of taking material into the cell by means of infoldings, or pockets, of the cell membrane. The pocket that results breaks loose from the outer portion of the cell membrane and forms a vacuole within the cytoplasm. Large molecules, clumps of food, and even whole cells can be taken up in this way. Two examples of endocytosis are phagocytosis (fag-oh-sy-TOH-sis) and pinocytosis (py-nuh-sy-TOH-sis).

Phagocytosis means "cell eating." In **phagocytosis,** extensions of cytoplasm surround a particle and package it within a food vacuole. The cell then engulfs it. Amoebas use this method of taking in food. Engulfing material in this way requires a considerable amount of energy and, therefore, is correctly considered a form of active transport.

In a process similar to endocytosis, many cells take up liquid from the surrounding environment. Tiny pockets form along the cell membrane, fill with liquid, and pinch off to form vacuoles within the cell. This process is known as **pinocytosis.**

Many cells also release large amounts of material from the cell, a process known as exocytosis (ek-soh-sy-TOH-sis). During **exocytosis,** the membrane of the vacuole surrounding the material fuses with the cell membrane, forcing the contents out of the cell. The removal of water by means of a contractile vacuole is one example of this kind of active transport.

For: Active Transport activity
Visit: PHSchool.com
Web Code: cbp-3076

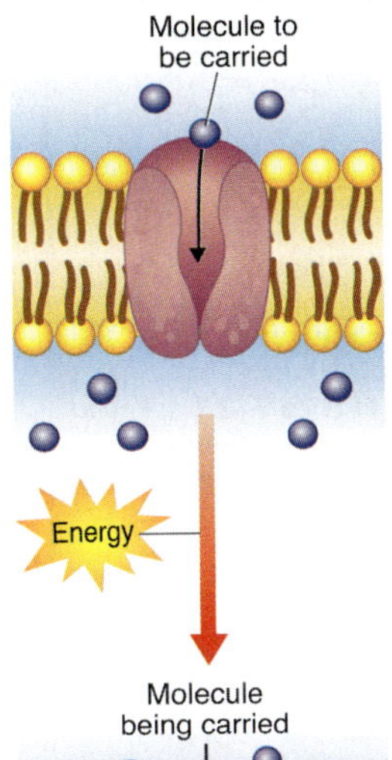

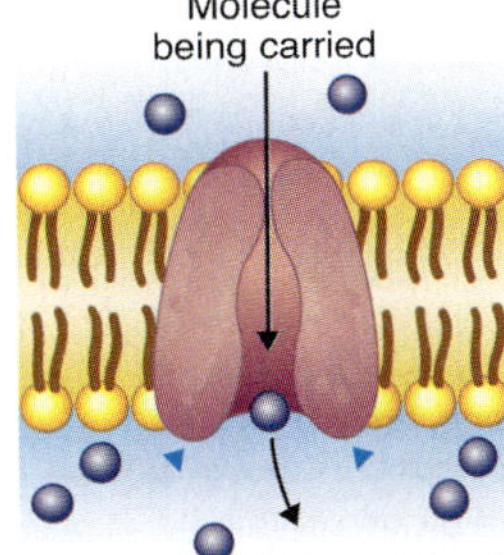

Figure 7–19 Active transport of particles against a concentration difference requires transport proteins and energy. **Interpreting Graphics** *What is happening in the illustration?*

7–3 Section Assessment

1. **Key Concept** Describe the functions of the cell membrane and cell wall.
2. **Key Concept** What happens during diffusion?
3. **Key Concept** Describe how water moves during osmosis.
4. What is the basic structure of a cell membrane?
5. What is the difference between phagocytosis and pinocytosis?
6. **Critical Thinking Comparing and Contrasting** What is the main way that active transport differs from diffusion?

Focus on the BIG Idea

Homeostasis
What is the relationship between active transport and homeostasis? Give one example of active transport in an organism, and explain how the organism uses energy to maintain homeostasis.

7–3 Section Assessment

1. The cell membrane regulates what enters and leaves the cell and also provides protection and support. The cell wall provides support and protection for the cell.
2. Particles tend to move from an area where they are more concentrated to an area where they are less concentrated.
3. Osmosis is the diffusion of water through a selectively permeable membrane.
4. The basic structure is a double-layered sheet called a lipid bilayer, in which proteins are embedded.
5. In phagocytosis, extensions of cytoplasm surround a particle and package it within a food vacuole. In pinocytosis, tiny pockets form along the cell membrane, fill with liquid, and pinch off to form vacuoles within the cell.
6. Active transport requires the input of energy, but diffusion does not require additional energy.

For: Active Transport activity
Visit: PHSchool.com
Web Code: cbe-3076
Students interact with the art of active transport online.

3 ASSESS

Evaluate Understanding

Make up a list of fictitious substances. Have students describe the method of transport a cell would use to move each substance through the cell membrane and why. Students need not be accurate; what you are looking for is correct reasoning.

Reteach

Have students write definitions of diffusion, osmosis, facilitated diffusion, and active transport. Then, discuss ways in which they are similar and ways in which they are different.

Focus on the BIG Idea 

Students should state the definition of both active transport and homeostasis, which they learned about in Section 1–3. Examples may vary. Students might suggest that any material taken into a cell by active transport that is necessary for normal cell activities helps maintain homeostasis, and active transport is a process that uses energy.

Interactive Textbook

If your class subscribes to the iText, use it to review the Key Concepts in Section 7–3.

Answer to . . .

Figure 7–19 *A molecule is moving across the cell membrane from an area of low concentration to an area of high concentration with the help of a transport protein and the use of energy.*

Section 7-4

 7 5.a

1 FOCUS

Objectives

7.4.1 ***Describe*** cell specialization.
7.4.2 ***Identify*** the organization levels in multicellular organisms.

Guide for Reading

Vocabulary Preview

On the chalkboard, make a concept map entitled Cell Specialization, using the section's Vocabulary terms. The map should show this hierarchy: cell, tissue, organ, organ system.

Reading Strategy

Have the students rewrite the section's blue headings as questions. Then, have them answer those questions as they read the section.

2 INSTRUCT

Unicellular Organisms

Use Visuals

Figure 7–20 Have students read the caption and study the unicellular organisms. Explain that the yeast cells are a form of fungi, which students will study in Chapter 21. *Volvox aureus* is a plantlike protist, which students will read about in Chapter 20. The disease caused by the bacterium shown is called leptospirosis, which is mostly a disease of wild animals but can affect humans as well. Then, ask: **Which of these organisms are prokaryotic, and which are eukaryotic?** *(The yeast cells and the* Volvox aureus *are eukaryotic. The bacterium* Leptospira interrogans *is prokaryotic).* Emphasize that not all unicellular organisms are bacteria or prokaryotic. L1 L2

7–4 The Diversity of Cellular Life

7 5.a. Students know plants and animals have levels of organization for structure and function, including cells, tissues, organs, organ systems, and the whole organism.

Guide for Reading

 **Key Concepts**

- What is cell specialization?
- What are the four levels of organization in multicellular organisms?

Vocabulary
cell specialization
tissue
organ
organ system

Reading Strategy: Using Visuals Before you read, preview **Figure 7–22.** As you read, note the different levels of organization in the body.

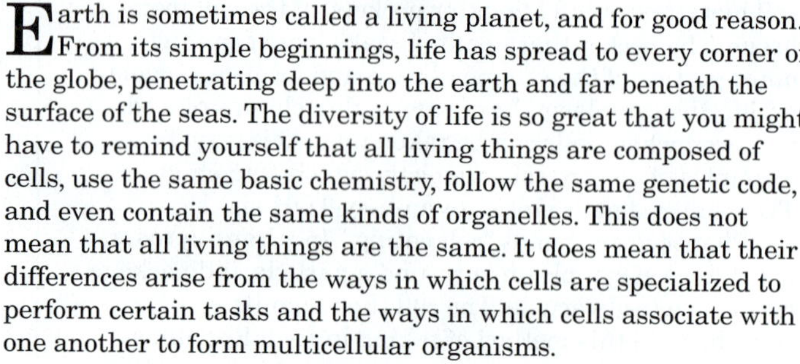

Earth is sometimes called a living planet, and for good reason. From its simple beginnings, life has spread to every corner of the globe, penetrating deep into the earth and far beneath the surface of the seas. The diversity of life is so great that you might have to remind yourself that all living things are composed of cells, use the same basic chemistry, follow the same genetic code, and even contain the same kinds of organelles. This does not mean that all living things are the same. It does mean that their differences arise from the ways in which cells are specialized to perform certain tasks and the ways in which cells associate with one another to form multicellular organisms.

Unicellular Organisms

Cells are the basic living units of all organisms, but sometimes a single cell is a little more than that. Sometimes, a cell *is* the organism. A single-celled organism is also called a unicellular organism. Unicellular organisms do everything that you would expect a living thing to do. They grow, respond to the environment, transform energy, and reproduce. In terms of their numbers, unicellular organisms dominate life on Earth. Some examples of unicellular organisms are shown in **Figure 7–20.**

Multicellular Organisms

Organisms that are made up of many cells are called multicellular. There is a great variety among multicellular organisms. However, all multicellular organisms depend on communication and cooperation among specialized cells. **Cells throughout an organism can develop in different ways to perform different tasks.** This process is called **cell specialization.** Some examples of specialized cells are shown in **Figure 7–21.**

Figure 7–20 Yeasts, which are often used in bread making, are unicellular fungi. The *Volvox aureus* cells shown are actually individual alga cells that live together in a colony. The unicellular spiral-shaped bacterium *Leptospira interrogans* causes a serious disease in humans.

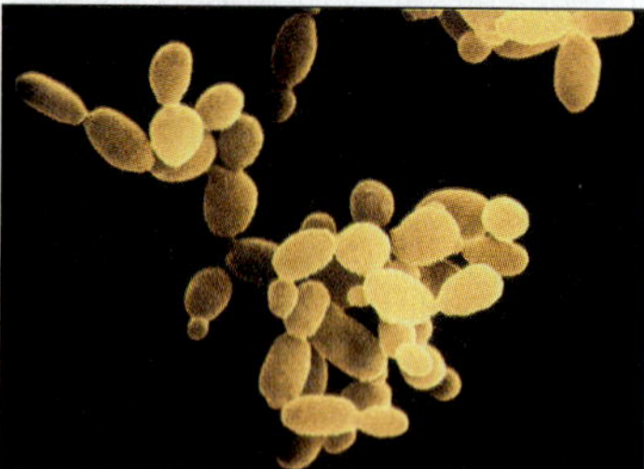

Yeast (magnification: 3400×)

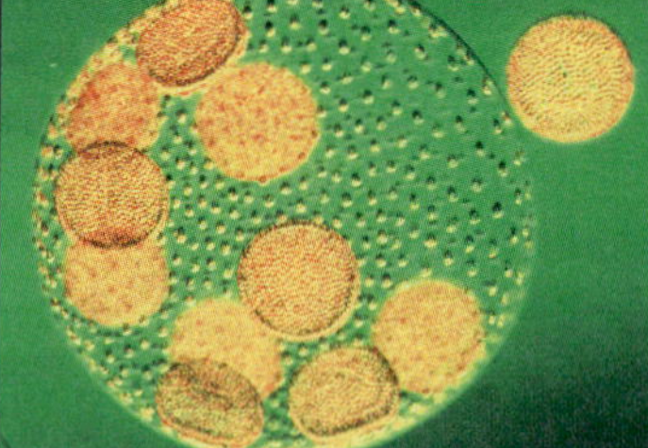

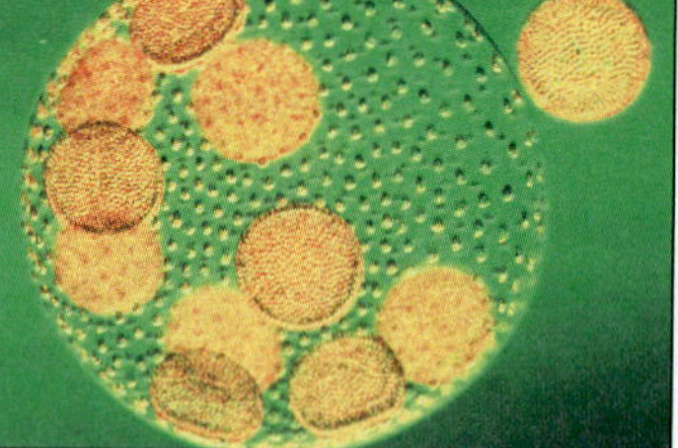

Volvox aureus (magnification: 250×)

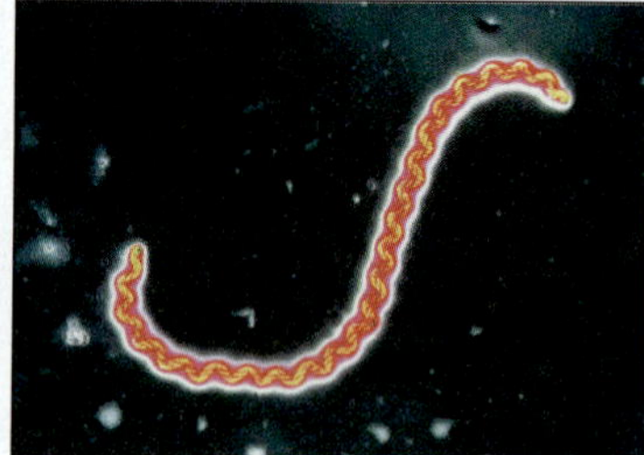

Leptospira interrogans (magnification: 27,000×)

SECTION RESOURCES

Print:

- ***Laboratory Manual B,*** Chapter 7 Lab
- ***Teaching Resources,*** Lesson Plan 7–4, Adapted Section Summary 7–4, Adapted Worksheets 7–4, Section Summary 7–4, Worksheets 7–4, Section Review 7–4, Enrichment
- ***Reading and Study Workbook A,*** Section 7–4
- ***Adapted Reading and Study Workbook B,*** Section 7–4

Technology:

- ***iText,*** Section 7–4
- ***Transparencies Plus,*** Section 7–4

Figure 7–21 Cell Specialization

Cells in multicellular organisms are specialized to perform particular functions within the organism. Red blood cells transport oxygen throughout the body. Pancreatic cells produce compounds such as insulin that the body needs. Muscle cells contract and relax to move parts of the body. Guard cells control the opening and closing of stomata on the undersides of leaves.

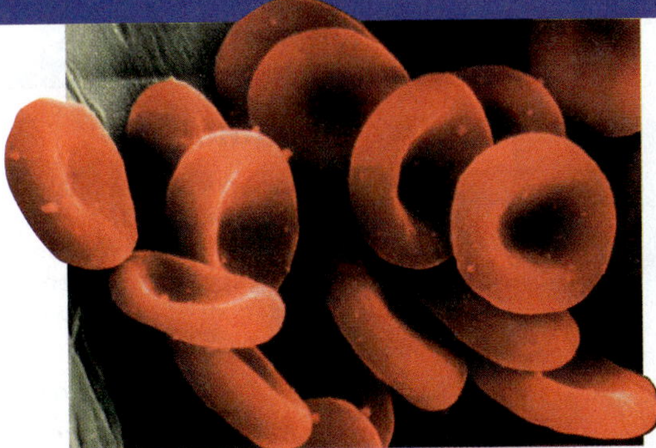

Red Blood Cells (magnification: 13,000×)

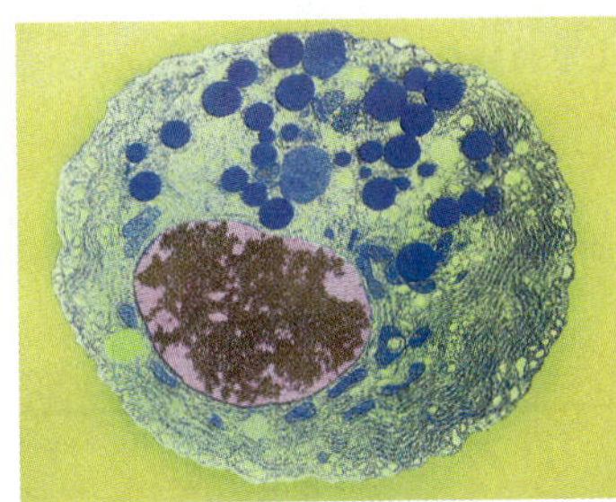

Pancreatic Cell (magnification: 4000×)

Muscle Cell (magnification: 350×)

Stomata (magnification: 510×)

Specialized Animal Cells Animal cells are specialized in many ways. Red blood cells are specialized to transport oxygen. Red blood cells contain a protein that binds to oxygen in the lungs and transports the oxygen throughout the body where it is released. Cells specialized to produce proteins, for example, are found in the pancreas. The pancreas is a gland that produces enzymes that make it possible to digest food. As you might expect, pancreatic cells are packed with ribosomes and rough ER, which are where proteins are produced. Pancreatic cells also possess large amounts of other organelles needed for protein export, including a well-developed Golgi apparatus and clusters of storage vacuoles loaded with enzymes.

The human ability to move is result of the specialized structures of muscle cells. These cells generate force by using a dramatically overdeveloped cytoskeleton. Skeletal muscle cells are packed with fibers arranged in a tight, regular pattern. Those fibers are actin microfilaments and a cytoskeletal protein called myosin. When they contract, muscle cells use chemical energy to pull these fibers past each other, generating force. Whether your muscles are large or small, your muscle cells themselves are "bulked up" with these specialized cytoskeletal proteins to a degree that makes them the body's undisputed heavy-lifting champions.

ESL Support for English Language Learners

Comprehension: Modified Cloze

Beginning Distribute a modified paragraph about levels of organization, but substitute blanks for some strategic words. For example, "There are four levels of organization in many-celled organisms. Cells that work together form _____. Tissues that work together form _____. Organs that work together form _____." Give students a list of the correct answers, and have them fill in each blank with one of the words. Post these terms on a word wall with other Vocabulary terms from the chapter. L1

Intermediate Have the students complete the beginning-level cloze activity, but add several sentences and terms. When students have completed the exercise, they can work in pairs to correct each other's answers. The students in each pair can also extend the activity by writing two examples of types of cells, tissues, organs, and organ systems. L2

Multicellular Organisms

Use Visuals

Figure 7–21 Discuss with students how each of the cells shown is specialized, carrying out only one or a few particular functions within the organism. Have students contrast these cells with those shown in Figure 7–20. Emphasize that the cells of unicellular organisms must carry out all the essential functions of life, whereas the cells of multicellular organisms are specialists. L1 L2

Build Science Skills

Using Analogies Introduce students to an analogy between the way cells evolved toward greater specialization and the way society evolved toward greater specialization during the Industrial Revolution. Just as cells became specialized to perform particular functions, people left their generalized lives in rural areas to take jobs in urban industries that produced particular goods or fulfilled particular functions. Challenge students to develop this analogy, either in a class discussion or in individual essays. L2 L3

7–4 (continued)

Careers in Biology

This is one of the many careers that are little known to the public but are essential to the functioning of a good health facility. L2

- Have students find out what kind of technology is being used by histotechnologists at a local hospital, clinic, or university. Students can gather information by interviewing a local histotechnician or administrator.

Resources Have interested students contact a local college or university to see if it has a certified histotechnology program. They might also gather information about this career by contacting the National Society for Histotechnology.

You can have students write a more extensive job description as well as list the educational requirements for a career in this field.

Levels of Organization

Build Science Skills

Applying Concepts Show students photographs, diagrams, or slides of various specialized cells. Discuss their specialization and what makes them uniquely suited to their function. For example, you might show human red blood cells. Then, ask: **How would you describe the shape of these cells?** *(They all have a disklike shape.)* **What important function do red blood cells have?** *(Students may know that red blood cells carry oxygen.)* Contrast these cells with cells from epithelial tissue. Elicit from students the idea that epithelial cells are closely packed and regular in appearance, a structure that suits their function of protection. L2

Careers in Biology

Histotechnologist

Job Description: work in a hospital laboratory, research institution, industrial laboratory, or government agency to prepare slides of body tissues for microscopic examination using special dyes and more advanced techniques, such as electron microscopy

Education: a bachelor's degree from a certified histotechnology program or a bachelor's degree with emphasis in biology and chemistry and one year's experience under a board-certified pathologist to become eligible for national certification exam, leading to a histotechnologist (HTL) certification

Skills: background in biology, anatomy, pathology, and/or chemistry; manual dexterity; attention to detail; good organizational skills; strong writing skills; computer literacy

For: Career links
Visit: PHSchool.com
Web Code: cbb-3074

Specialized Plant Cells A plant basking in the sunlight may seem quiet and passive, but it is actually interacting with the environment at every moment. It rapidly exchanges carbon dioxide, oxygen, water vapor, and other gases through tiny openings called stomata on the undersides of leaves. Highly specialized cells, known as guard cells, regulate this exchange. Guard cells monitor the plant's internal conditions, changing their shape according to those conditions. For example, when the plant can benefit from gas exchange, the stomata open. The stomata close tightly when the plant's internal conditions change.

Levels of Organization

Biologists have identified levels of organization that make it easier to describe the cells within a multicellular organism. **The levels of organization in a multicellular organism are individual cells, tissues, organs, and organ systems.** These levels of organization are shown in **Figure 7–22.**

Tissues In multicellular organisms, cells are the first level of organization. Similar cells are grouped into units called tissues. A **tissue** is a group of similar cells that perform a particular function. The collection of cells that produce digestive enzymes in the pancreas makes up one kind of tissue. Most animals have four main types of tissue: muscle, epithelial, nervous, and connective tissue. You will read about these tissues in later chapters.

TEACHER TO TEACHER

When teaching cell structure, I ask small groups of students to research the structure and function of a specific organelle, using a variety of sources, including college texts and relevant Internet sites. The members of each group work together to prepare a report to the class, complete with a detailed model of the organelle they researched. I have groups present their reports in the form of a justification of the importance of their organelles to their "parent organization," Cell Industries, with the understanding that they might be "downsized" if they don't make their case convincingly. Groups must cite the source of any information they present. The models students make are creative, and they are a strong learning reinforcement tool.

—*Tamsen K. Meyer*
Biology Teacher
Boulder High School
Boulder, CO

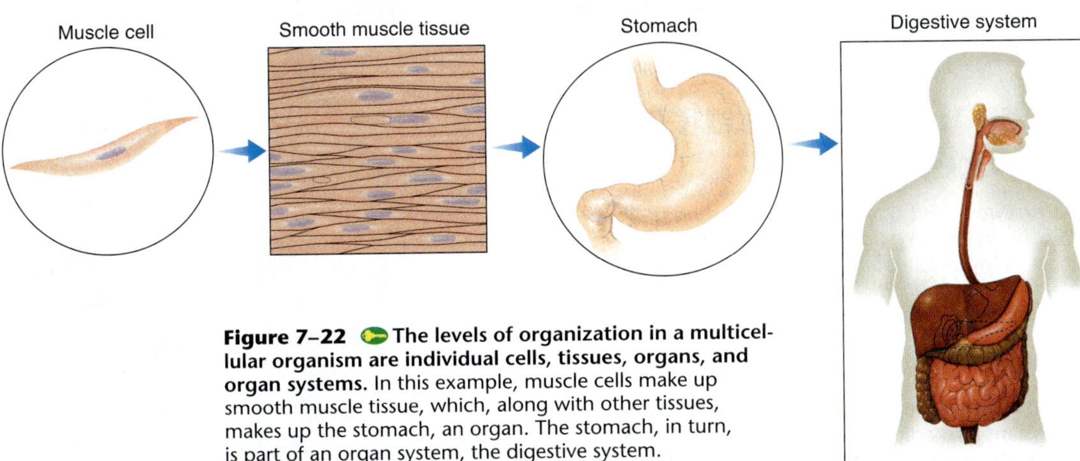

Figure 7–22 **The levels of organization in a multicellular organism are individual cells, tissues, organs, and organ systems.** In this example, muscle cells make up smooth muscle tissue, which, along with other tissues, makes up the stomach, an organ. The stomach, in turn, is part of an organ system, the digestive system.

Build Science Skills

Classifying To reinforce the concept of levels of organization, play a game of Name That Cell, Tissue, Organ, or System. Give students as many examples as you can in random order. Ask them to identify whether the example is a cell, a tissue, an organ, or an organ system. L2

Organs Many tasks within the body are too complicated to be carried out by just one type of tissue. In these cases, many groups of tissues work together as an **organ.** For example, each muscle in your body is an individual organ. Within a muscle, however, there is much more than muscle tissue. There are nervous tissues and connective tissues. Each type of tissue performs an essential task to help the organ function.

Organ Systems In most cases, an organ completes a series of specialized tasks. A group of organs that work together to perform a specific function is called an **organ system.**

The organization of the body's cells into tissues, organs, and organ systems creates a division of labor among those cells that makes multicellular life possible. Specialized cells such as nerve and muscle cells are able to function precisely because other cells are specialized to obtain the food and oxygen needed by those cells. This overall specialization and interdependence is one of the remarkable attributes of living things. Appreciating this characteristic is an important step in understanding the nature of living things.

7–4 Section Assessment

1. **Key Concept** In what kinds of organisms is cell specialization a characteristic?
2. **Key Concept** List the levels of biological organization in multicellular organisms from most simple to most complex.
3. How are unicellular organisms similar to multicellular organisms?
4. **Critical Thinking Predicting** Using what you know about the ways muscle moves, predict which organelles would be most common in muscle cells.

Writing in Science

Using Analogies
Use an organized area in your life—such as school, sports, or extracurricular activities—to construct an analogy to explain how the levels of organization in that chosen area can be compared with those of living organisms.

3 ASSESS

Evaluate Understanding

Ask students to explain the levels of organization involved in touch. (*A typical response might mention individual nerve cells, or receptors; brain tissue; the brain; the nervous system.*)

Reteach

Direct students' attention to Figure 7–21 on page 191. Ask them which level of organization is represented by the cells shown. (*Individual cells*) Then, for each kind of specialized cell, discuss the tissue, organ, and organ system of which that cell is a part.

Writing in Science

Make sure that each student's analogy appropriately relates an area of the student's life to the levels of organization in living things.

If your class subscribes to the iText, use it to review the Key Concepts in Section 7–4.

7–4 Section Assessment

1. Multicellular organisms have cell specialization.
2. Individual cells, tissues, organs, and organ systems
3. Both unicellular and multicellular organisms grow, respond to the environment, transform energy, and reproduce.
4. Muscle cells have a large number of mitochondria, because mitochondria release energy from stored food molecules and muscle cells need great amounts of energy to do the tasks they do.

Exploration

 **BIIE 1.d**

Objective Students will be able to draw conclusions about how the differences in structure between plant and animal cells affect the ways they respond to hypertonic and hypotonic solutions. L2 L3

Skills Focus **Observing, Comparing and Contrasting, Drawing Conclusions**

Time 90 minutes (45 minutes for each part)

Advance Prep Order prepared slides of human cheek cells and sterile heparinized sheep blood well in advance. Prepare the concentrated salt solution by dissolving 25 grams of sodium chloride (NaCl) in enough warm water to make a total of 100 milliliters of solution. Obtain or prepare a solution of "photographer's hypo," or 158 grams of sodium thiosulfate ($Na_2S_2O_3$) per liter of water. This solution will remove iodine stains from clothes and hands safely and quickly. Practice the procedure for staining the piece of onion on the slide so you can demonstrate the process to students.

Alternative Materials Other prepared slides of animal cells can be used instead of human cheek cells, as long as the cells' nuclei are clearly visible under the microscope.

Safety

- Read the safety information in the MSDS for iodine before doing the lab. If students should spill any of the iodine solution, instruct them to quickly wash it off with plenty of water. Do not allow students to use chipped glass slides.
- Use sterile animal blood from a biological supply company.
- Students should be very careful when handling animal blood. Be sure that students wear goggles, disposable plastic gloves, and lab aprons. Make sure to properly dispose of the gloves.

Prelab Discussion Have students read through the lab. Answer any questions they have about materials and procedure. Then, ask: **Why is the iodine solution used to stain the piece of onion?** *(The iodine will make some of the cell structures more visible under the microscope.)* **What is osmosis?** *(Osmosis is the diffusion of water through a selectively permeable membrane.)* **How do differences in the concentration of molecules of a substance affect diffusion across a cell membrane?** *(Diffusion across a cell membrane occurs as molecules of a substance move from areas of high concentration to areas of lower concentration.)*

Teaching Tips

- Review the proper use of a microscope before students perform this lab.
- If microscopes include a mirror rather than a built-in light source, make sure students do not use sunlight as a light source, because doing so could damage their eyes.

Procedure

Part A

2. Demonstrate how to peel a thin layer from the inner surface of a piece of red onion.

4. Demonstrate how to hold a piece of paper towel near the opposite edge of a coverslip in order to draw the iodine under it.

Part B

10. Demonstrate how to prepare a wet-mount slide using animal blood.

13. Make sure students rinse out the dropper pipette with distilled water.

Exploration

 **BIIE 1.d**

Investigating Cell Structures and Processes

A cell's structures affect how it responds to changes in its environment. In this investigation, you will observe the differences between plant and animal cells. You will then determine how plant and animal cells are affected by hypertonic and hypotonic solutions and relate those effects to the cells' structures.

Problem **How do the differences in structure between plant and animal cells influence how they are affected by hypertonic and hypotonic solutions?**

Materials

- forceps
- piece of red onion
- scalpel
- 4 glass slides
- dropper pipette
- 4 coverslips
- iodine solution
- paper towel
- microscope
- prepared slide of human cheek cells
- concentrated salt solution
- distilled water
- treated animal blood

Skills Observing, Comparing and Contrasting, Drawing Conclusions

Procedure     

Part A: Plant and Animal Cell Structures

1. Put on safety goggles and a lab apron. Using forceps, peel a thin layer from the inner surface of a piece of a red onion, as shown in the photograph.
2. Use a scalpel to cut a small piece out of the layer you removed. **CAUTION:** *The scalpel is very sharp. Handle it carefully, and make sure to cut away from yourself.*
3. Place the piece of onion in the center of a glass slide. Add a drop of distilled water to the piece of onion, and cover it with a coverslip.
4. Put on your plastic gloves. Use a dropper pipette to place a drop of iodine solution at one end of the coverslip. **CAUTION:** *Iodine can stain skin and clothing. Be careful not to spill it on yourself.* Hold a piece of paper towel near the opposite edge of the coverslip, as shown in the diagram on page 195. This will draw the iodine under the coverslip, where it will stain the onion cells.
5. Examine your slide under the low-power objective of the microscope. **CAUTION:** *Microscopes and slides are fragile. Handle them carefully.* Sketch one cell, and label any structures you recognize.
6. Carefully switch to high power, and observe the cell again. Try to identify other cell structures, and add them to your sketch with appropriate labels.
7. Repeat steps 5 and 6 using a prepared slide of human cheek cells.

Part B: Effects of Hypertonic and Hypotonic Solutions

8. Repeat steps 1 to 3 to prepare another onion cell wet mount. Using the same method as in step 4, add a drop of concentrated salt solution to the slide, and use a paper towel to draw it under the coverslip.

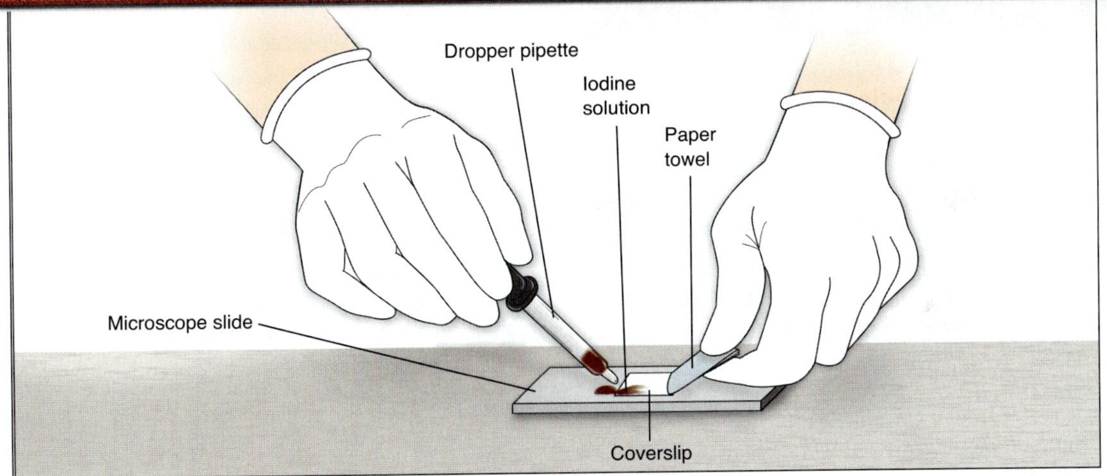

9. Observe the onion cells under the microscope under both low power and high power. Record your observations.
10. Prepare a wet-mount slide using treated animal blood. **CAUTION:** *Use only blood samples provided by your teacher.* Do not add water as you did with the onion cells.
11. Observe the blood cells under the microscope under both low power and high power. Sketch one cell, and label any structures you recognize.
12. Using the same method as in step 4, add a drop of concentrated salt solution to the slide, and use a paper towel to draw it under the coverslip.
13. Observe the blood cells under the microscope under both low power and high power. Record your observations. Rinse out the dropper pipette with distilled water.
14. Prepare another wet-mount slide of blood cells. This time, add a drop of distilled water to the slide and draw it under the coverslip.
15. Observe the blood cells under the microscope under both low power and high power. Record your observations.
16. Remove the plastic gloves and discard them according to your teacher's instructions. Wash your hands thoroughly with warm water and soap.

Analyze and Conclude

1. **Applying Concepts** Describe the shapes of the onion cells and the cheek cells you observed in Part A. What structures did you see in the onion cells? The cheek cells? Describe the functions of each of the structures you saw.
2. **Comparing and Contrasting** How are plant and animal cells similar in structure? How are they different?
3. **Drawing Conclusions** Explain your observations in step 9 of Part B in terms of osmosis and permeability.
4. **Drawing Conclusions** Explain your observations in steps 13 and 15 in terms of osmosis and permeability.
5. **Applying Concepts** What part of the cell is involved in the processes you observed in steps 9, 13, and 15? Explain your answer.
6. **Comparing and Contrasting** Why didn't the onion cells burst when they are in distilled water as in step 3? Relate your answer to the differences between plant and animal cells.

Go Further

Designing Experiments Design one or more experiments to test the effects of hypotonic and hypertonic solutions on other cells. Write a hypothesis for each experiment and control all variables. Get your teacher's permission before carrying out your experiments.

Analyze and Conclude

1. Onion cells are generally rectangular, with some variation in size and shape. Cheek cells are flat and roughly circular. The onion cells have rigid cell walls and distinct nuclei, both of which stain with iodine. Students may be able to see vacuoles in the centers of onion cells and dark spots (other organelles) outside the nucleus. The cheek cells do not have cell walls. Students should be able to see cell membranes as well as the nucleus within each cell. They may also see other dark spots (other organelles). Cell walls protect the cell and provide support. The nucleus directs cell activities and is where genetic material is stored. Vacuoles store water and other materials. Cell membranes regulate what enters and leaves the cell.

2. Plant and animal cells both have cell membranes and nuclei. Plant cells have cell walls, whereas animal cells do not.

3. The concentration of water was greater inside the cells than in the salt solution, so osmotic pressure moved water out of the cells. The cytoplasm of the cells then shrank away from the cell walls.

4. In step 13, the cells shrank. Because the concentration of water was greater inside the cells than in the salt solution outside the cells, water diffused out of the cells. In step 15, the cells expanded, and some may have burst. Because the concentration of water was greater in the distilled water than inside the cells, water diffused into the cells.

5. The cell membrane was involved. Water moves in and out of the cell by osmosis through the cell membrane.

6. The cell walls of the onion cells are strong enough to keep the cells from bursting. Animal cells do not have cell walls, so they may burst.

Expected Outcomes

- In Part A, students should observe and draw the cell membranes and nuclei of the plant and animal cells and the cell wall of the plant cell.
- In Part B, students should observe that the plant and animal cells shrink in the concentrated salt solution, while only the animal cells expand in the distilled water.

Go Further

A typical experiment will be similar to the steps in Part B of this lab. You may want to suggest that students design their experiments with protists or bacteria in mind.

Chapter 7 Study Guide

Study Tip

Divide the class into small groups, and have each group generate a list of questions about the Vocabulary terms and the Key Concepts for each of the four sections. When groups have completed their lists, have groups exchange lists of questions. Each group should end up with a list of questions for each section from four different groups. Ask the students in each group to collaborate in answering the questions they received from other groups.

Thinking Visually

Typically, a student's concept map will label the first level Movement Into and Out of a Cell. The next level should include Diffusion and Active Transport. A line from Diffusion should connect to Osmosis and Facilitated Diffusion. Lines from Active Transport should connect to Endocytosis and Exocytosis. Lines from Endocytosis should connect to Phagocytosis and Pinocytosis.

Chapter 7 Assessment

Reviewing Content

1. d	**5.** c	**9.** d
2. b	**6.** a	**10.** a
3. b	**7.** d	
4. b	**8.** c	

Understanding Concepts

11. Robert Hooke observed cork slices and named cells. Matthias Schleiden concluded that all plants are made of cells. Theodor Schwann concluded that all animals are made of cells. Rudolf Virchow concluded that all cells come from preexisting cells.

12. Both prokaryotic and eukaryotic cells have two characteristics in common: they are surrounded by a cell membrane, and they contain DNA. Prokaryotes are generally smaller and simpler, and they lack a nucleus. Eukaryotic cells generally contain dozens of structures and internal membranes, including a nucleus that contains their genetic material.

Chapter 7 Study Guide

7–1 Life Is Cellular

Key Concepts  BI 1.c, BIIE 1.k

- The cell theory states that all living things are composed of cells, cells are the basic units of structure and function in living things, and new cells are produced from existing cells.
- Prokaryotic cells have genetic material that is not contained in a nucleus. Eukaryotic cells contain a nucleus in which their genetic material is separated from the rest of the cell.

Vocabulary
cell, p. 170 • cell theory, p. 170
nucleus, p. 173 • eukaryote, p. 173
prokaryote, p. 173

7–2 Eukaryotic Cell Structure

Key Concepts 7 1.c, BI 1.c, BI 1.e, *BI 1.j

- The nucleus contains nearly all the cell's DNA and the coded instructions for making proteins and other important molecules.
- Proteins are assembled on ribosomes.
- One type of endoplasmic reticulum makes membranes and secretory proteins. The other type of ER makes lipids and helps to detoxify, or remove harmful substances.
- The Golgi apparatus modifies, sorts, and packages proteins and other materials from the endoplasmic reticulum for storage or secretion outside the cell.
- Mitochondria convert the chemical energy stored in food into compounds that are more convenient for the cell to use.
- Chloroplasts capture the energy from sunlight and convert it into chemical energy.
- The cytoskeleton is a network of protein filaments that helps the cell to maintain its shape. The cytoskeleton is also involved in movement of materials within and outside the cell.

Vocabulary
organelle, p. 174 • cytoplasm, p. 174
nuclear envelope, p. 176
chromatin, p. 176 • chromosome, p. 176
nucleolus, p. 176 • ribosome, p. 177
endoplasmic reticulum, p. 177
Golgi apparatus, p. 178
lysosome, p. 179 • vacuole, p. 179
mitochondrion, p. 179 • chloroplast, p. 180
cytoskeleton, p. 181 • centriole, p. 181

7–3 Cell Boundaries

Key Concepts  BI 1.a, *BI 1.j

- All cells have a cell membrane. The cell membrane regulates what enters and leaves the cell and also provides protection and support. Some cells also have cell walls. Cell walls provide additional support and protection.
- Diffusion causes many substances to move across a cell membrane but does not require the cell to use energy.
- Osmosis is the diffusion of water through a selectively permeable membrane.

Vocabulary
cell membrane, p. 182 • cell wall, p. 182
lipid bilayer, p. 182 • concentration, p. 183
diffusion, p. 184 • equilibrium, p. 184
osmosis, p. 185 • isotonic, p. 185
hypertonic, p. 185 • hypotonic, p. 185
facilitated diffusion, p. 187
active transport, p. 188
endocytosis, p. 189 • phagocytosis, p. 189
pinocytosis, p. 189 • exocytosis, p. 189

7–4 The Diversity of Cellular Life

Key Concepts 7 5.a

- Cells in multicellular organisms develop in different ways to perform particular functions within the organism.
- The levels of organization in a multicellular organism are individual cells, tissues, organs, and organ systems.

Vocabulary
cell specialization, p. 190
tissue, p. 192
organ, p. 193
organ system, p. 193

Thinking Visually

Use the information in this chapter to create a concept map about the ways substances can move into and out of cells. Use the following terms in your concept map: *diffusion, osmosis, facilitated diffusion, active transport, phagocytosis, endocytosis, pinocytosis, exocytosis.*

TIME SAVER — CHAPTER RESOURCES

Print:

- ***Teaching Resources,*** Chapter Vocabulary Review, Graphic Organizer, Chapter 7 Tests: Levels A and B

Technology:

- ***Computer Test Bank,*** Chapter 7 Test
- ***iText,*** Chapter 7 Assessment

Chapter 7 Assessment

Reviewing Content

Choose the letter that best answers the question or completes the statement.

1. In many cells, the structure that controls the cell's activities is the
   a. cell membrane.
   b. organelle.
   c. nucleolus.
   d. nucleus.
2. Despite differences in size and shape, all cells have cytoplasm and a
   a. cell wall.
   b. cell membrane.
   c. mitochondrion.
   d. nucleus.
3. If a cell of an organism contains a nucleus, the organism is a(an)
   a. plant.
   b. eukaryote.
   c. animal.
   d. prokaryote.
4. Distinct threadlike structures containing genetic information are called
   a. ribosomes.
   b. chromosomes.
   c. nuclei.
   d. mitochondria.
5. Which organelle converts the chemical energy in food into a form that cells can use?
   a. nucleolus
   b. chromosome
   c. mitochondrion
   d. chloroplast
6. Cell membranes are constructed mainly of
   a. lipid bilayers.
   b. protein pumps.
   c. carbohydrate gates.
   d. free-moving proteins.
7. The movement of water molecules across a selectively permeable membrane is known as
   a. exocytosis.
   b. phagocytosis.
   c. endocytosis.
   d. osmosis.
8. A substance that moves across a cell membrane without using the cell's energy tends to move
   a. away from the area of equilibrium.
   b. away from the area where it is less concentrated.
   c. away from the area where it is more concentrated.
   d. toward the area where it is more concentrated.
9. Which cell helps in gas exchange in plants?

a. 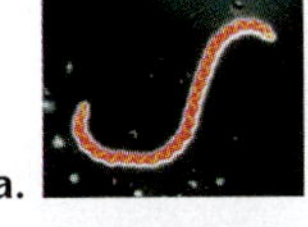

c. 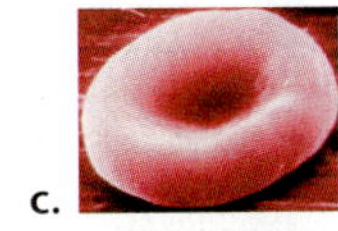

b. 

d. 

Interactive textbook with assessment at PHSchool.com 

10. A tissue is composed of a group of
    a. similar cells.
    b. related organelles.
    c. organ systems.
    d. related organs.

Understanding Concepts

11. Make a table to summarize the contributions made to the cell theory by Robert Hooke, Matthias Schleiden, Theodor Schwann, and Rudolf Virchow.
12. How are prokaryotic and eukaryotic cells alike? How do they differ?
13. Draw a cell nucleus. Label and give the function of the following structures: chromatin, nucleolus, and nuclear envelope.
14. What is the function of a ribosome?
15. What process takes place in the rough endoplasmic reticulum?
16. Describe the role of the Golgi apparatus.
17. Other than the nucleus, which two organelles contain their own DNA?
18. Name and describe the two types of structures that make up the cytoskeleton.
19. Briefly describe the structure of a cell membrane. How does the cell membrane affect the contents of a cell?
20. What is meant by the concentration of a solution? Give a specific example of concentration involving volume and mass.
21. Describe the process of diffusion. Name and describe the condition that exists when the diffusion of a particular substance is complete.
22. What is the relationship between osmosis and diffusion? By definition, what's the only substance that carries out osmosis?
23. Using the example of a cell in a sugar solution, explain what is meant by an isotonic solution.
24. Name and describe the cell structure that helps prevent damage to certain cells when they are subjected to high osmotic pressure.
25. Use an example to describe the relationship among cells, tissues, organs, and organ systems.

TIME SAVER

HOMEWORK GUIDE

Section:	Questions:
Section 7–1	1–3, 11, 12
Section 7–2	4, 5, 13–18, 29, 32
Section 7–3	6–8, 19–24, 26–28, 30, 33, 34
Section 7–4	9, 10, 25, 31

interactive Textbook

If your class subscribes to the iText, your students can go online to access an interactive version of the Student Edition and a self-test.

(Continued from page 196)

13. chromatin—granular material within nucleus consists of DNA bound to protein; nucleolus—small dense region where the assembly of ribosomes begins; nuclear envelope—a double membrane layer containing many pores that allow materials to move into and out of the nucleus.

14. Ribosomes produce proteins.

15. Rough ER makes membranes and secretory proteins.

16. The Golgi apparatus contains enzymes that attach carbohydrates and lipids to proteins.

17. Mitochondria and chloroplasts contain their own DNA.

18. Students should describe microfilaments and microtubules. Microfilaments are threadlike structures made of the protein actin. They produce a tough framework that supports the cell. Microtubules are hollow structures made of tubulin protein. They maintain cell shape.

19. The core of the cell membrane is made up of a lipid bilayer. Protein molecules run through this layer. The proteins form channels and pumps that enable materials to move across the cell membrane.

20. The concentration of a solution is the mass of solute in a given volume of solution, or mass/volume. For example, if you dissolved 12 grams of salt in 3 liters of water, the concentration of the solution would be 12 g / 3 L, or 4 grams per liter.

21. In diffusion, particles tend to move from an area where they are more concentrated to an area where they are less concentrated. When diffusion is complete, the system has reached equilibrium.

22. Osmosis is the diffusion of water through a selectively permeable membrane. Only water can move by osmosis.

23. An isotonic solution would have the same concentration of solute on both sides of a membrane. The result of placing cells in an isotonic sugar solution would be that the cells would neither shrink nor swell.

Chapter 7 Assessment

24. Cell walls prevent damage by preventing cells from expanding.

25. One possible answer: Muscle cells make up smooth muscle tissue, which is part of the stomach, an organ. The stomach is part of the digestive system.

Critical Thinking

26. The diffusing salt particles (that is, the sodium ions and chloride ions that make up salt) and water molecules will eventually reach equilibrium without a change in the fluid on either side.

27. Solution A is more concentrated because there are 3 grams of salt per liter compared to the 2 grams per liter in Solution B.

28. The blood cells would swell and probably burst.

29. Because muscle cells are responsible for movement, they require more energy than skin cells. Therefore, skin cells contain fewer mitochondria.

30. Most students will develop an experiment in which the rate of diffusion of food coloring is observed by dropping equal amounts of food coloring into each beaker. Make sure that students identify the control (water at room temperature).

31. Ribosomes are responsible for making proteins. Because enzymes are proteins, the ribosomes would be present in the pancreas.

32. Students should demonstrate an understanding of the functions of different parts of the cell.

33. In diffusion, particles tend to move from an area where they are more concentrated to an area where they are less concentrated. As waste chemicals build up in a cell, they become more concentrated inside the cell than outside. As a result, diffusion occurs from inside to outside, and the level of waste chemicals within the cell drops.

34. Answers may vary. Students should define both diffusion and active transport, and they should emphasize that active transport requires energy, whereas diffusion does not. A typical response might mention the excretion of wastes as an example of diffusion and the phagocytosis of large particles to ingest food as an example of active transport.

Chapter 7 Assessment

Critical Thinking

26. **Predicting** The beaker in the diagram has a selectively permeable membrane separating two solutions. Assume that the water molecules and salt can pass freely through the membrane. When equilibrium is reached, will the fluid levels be the same as they are now? Explain your answer.

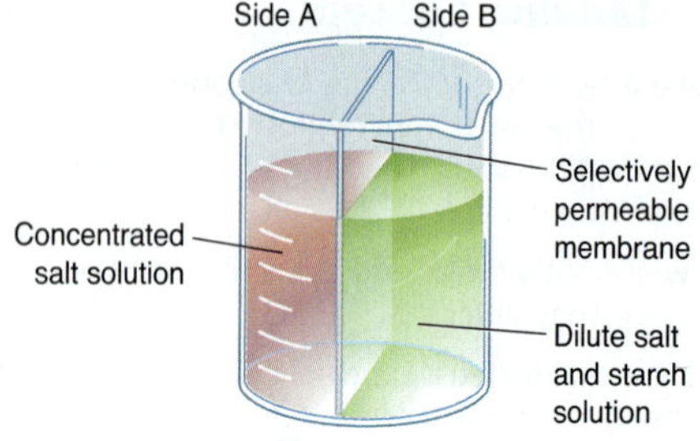

27. **Calculating** Which salt solution is more concentrated, solution A, which contains 18 g of salt in 6 L of water, or solution B, which contains 24 g of salt in 12 L of water? Explain.

28. **Predicting** What would happen to a sample of your red blood cells if they were placed into a hypotonic solution? Explain your prediction.

29. **Inferring** Would you expect skin cells to contain more or fewer mitochondria than muscle cells? Explain your answer.

30. **Designing Experiments** You are given vegetable coloring and three beakers. The first beaker contains water at room temperature, the second beaker contains ice water, and the third beaker contains hot water. Design an experiment to determine the effects of temperature on the rate of diffusion. Be sure to state your hypothesis and to include a control.

31. **Inferring** The pancreas, an organ present in certain animals, produces enzymes used elsewhere in the animals' digestive systems. Which type of cell structure(s) might produce those enzymes? Explain your answer.

32. **Using Analogies** Compare a cell to a factory, as in the chapter, or to something else, such as a school. (For example, a cell has a nucleus, and a school has a principal.) Use that analogy to describe the function of different parts of the cell.

33. **Applying Concepts** As waste chemicals build up in a cell, homeostasis is threatened. State how diffusion helps cells maintain homeostasis.

34. **Comparing and Contrasting** Diffusion and active transport are processes that are important to the maintenance of homeostasis in organisms. Compare the two processes, including examples that describe how they are important to living organisms.

Cellular Basis of Life In Chapter 2, you learned about four categories of carbon compounds called the "molecules of life." Explain where some of those compounds are found in a typical cell.

Writing in Science

Different beverages have different concentrations of solutes. Some beverages have low solute concentrations and can be a source of water for body cells. Other beverages have high solute concentrations and can actually dehydrate your body cells. Should companies that market these high-solute beverages say that these drinks quench your thirst?

Performance-Based Assessment

Prepare to Debate One day, unicellular organisms got tired of being referred to as simple organisms by the multicellular organisms. They felt that they should be recognized as complex individuals and challenged the multicellular organisms to a debate. As a unicellular organism, what arguments would you use to defend your position?

For: An interactive self-test
Visit: PHSchool.com
Web Code: cba-3070

Focus on the BIG Idea

Carbohydrates are found in the mitochondria, where they are converted into high-energy compounds. Lipids are found in the cell membrane, made up of the lipid bilayer. Proteins are found in ribosomes, where they are manufactured. Nucleic acids are found in the cells' chromosomes, where genetic information is stored.

Writing in Science

Answers may vary. Most students might suggest that companies that market such high-solute beverages should not say that the drinks quench a person's thirst. All responses should provide a logical reason for a position. Students might suggest that a high-solute beverage that dehydrates body cells would actually increase the sensation of thirst rather than quench it.

Standards Practice

Test-Taking Tip When you answer a question based on experimental data, read the description of the experiment carefully to determine the steps followed. Then, try to see if there are any trends in the data. For example, "if x increases, what happens to y?"

Directions: Choose the letter that best answers the question or completes the statement.

1. Animals cells have all of the following EXCEPT **BI 1.c**
   - **A** mitochondria.
   - **B** chloroplasts.
   - **C** a nucleus.
   - **D** a cell membrane.
2. The nucleus includes all of the following structures EXCEPT **7 1.c**
   - **A** cytoplasm.
   - **B** nuclear envelope.
   - **C** DNA.
   - **D** nucleolus.
3. Which statement best describes the expected result when a typical cell is placed into fresh water?
   - **A** Active transport of water into the cell would begin.
   - **B** There would be a net movement of water out of the cell.
   - **C** There would be a net movement of water into the cell.
   - **D** Protein synthesis would begin.
4. Which cell structures are sometimes found attached to the endoplasmic reticulum? **BI 1.e**
   - **A** chloroplasts
   - **B** mitochondria
   - **C** vacuoles
   - **D** ribosomes
5. Which process always involves the movement of materials from inside the cell to outside the cell?
   - **A** phagocytosis
   - **B** endocytosis
   - **C** diffusion
   - **D** exocytosis
6. Which of the following is an example of active transport?
   - **A** facilitated diffusion
   - **B** osmosis
   - **C** diffusion
   - **D** endocytosis

Questions 7–9

In an experiment, plant cells were placed in sucrose solutions of varying concentrations. The rate at which the plant cells absorbed sucrose from the solution was then measured for the different concentrations. The results are summarized in the graph below.

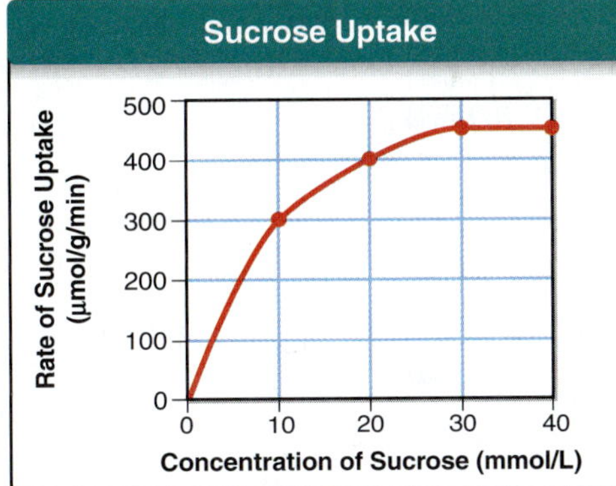

7. In this experiment, there was a positive sucrose uptake. Sucrose probably entered the cells by means of
   - **A** endocytosis.
   - **B** osmosis.
   - **C** active transport.
   - **D** phagocytosis.
8. The graph shows that as the concentration of sucrose increases from 10 to 30 mmol/L, the plant cells
   - **A** take in sucrose more slowly.
   - **B** take in sucrose more quickly.
   - **C** fail to take in more sucrose.
   - **D** secrete sucrose more slowly.
9. Which statement is best supported by information in the graph?
   - **A** The rate of sucrose uptake increases at a constant rate from 0 to 30 mmol/L.
   - **B** The rate of sucrose uptake decreases at a varying rate from 0 to 30 mmol/L.
   - **C** The rate of sucrose uptake is less at 25 mmol/L than at 5 mmol/L.
   - **D** The rate of sucrose uptake is constant between 30 and 40 mmol/L.

Standards Practice

1. B **2.** A **3.** C **4.** D **5.** D **6.** D **7.** C **8.** B **9.** D

Success Tracker™
Online at PHSchool.com

Have students check their understanding of the chapter by logging onto Success Tracker.

Performance-Based Assessment

Student answers should be scientifically accurate. Students' answers should demonstrate an understanding of the complex life processes that go on inside a cell.

Your students can independently test their knowledge of the chapter and print out their test results for your files.

Chapter Planner 8 Photosynthesis

Section and Section Objectives	Time	STANDARDS NCLB	STANDARDS Biology	Activities and Labs
8–1 Energy and Life, pp. 201–203 **8.1.1** ***Explain*** where plants get the energy they need to produce food. **8.1.2** ***Describe*** the role of ATP in cellular activities.	1 period (1/2 block)			**SE:** ***Inquiry Activity,*** How do organisms capture and use energy?, p. 200 L2
8–2 Photosynthesis: An Overview, pp. 204–207 **8.2.1** ***Explain*** what the experiments of van Helmont, Priestley, and Ingenhousz reveal about how plants grow. **8.2.2** ***State*** the overall equation for photosynthesis. **8.2.3** ***Describe*** the role of light and chlorophyll in photosynthesis.	1 period (1/2 block)	7 1.d	BIIE 1.k	**SE:** ***Biology and History,*** Understanding Photosynthesis, pp. 204–205 L2 L3 **SE:** ***Quick Lab,*** What waste material is produced during photosynthesis?, p. 206 L2 L3 **LMA:** Chapter 8 Lab L2 L3 **LMB:** Chapter 8 Lab L1 L2
8–3 The Reactions of Photosynthesis, pp. 208–214 **8.3.1** ***Describe*** the structure and function of a chloroplast. **8.3.2** ***Describe*** what happens in the light-dependent reactions. **8.3.3** ***Explain*** what the Calvin cycle is. **8.3.4** ***Identify*** factors that affect the rate at which photosynthesis occurs.	2 periods (1 block)	BI 1.f	*BI 1.i	**TE:** ***Demonstration,*** p. 210 L1 L2 **SE:** ***Analyzing Data,*** Rates of Photosynthesis, p. 213 L2 **SE:** ***Design an Experiment,*** Investigating Photosynthesis, p. 215 L2 L3 **BTM:** Lab 17 L2 L3, Issue 4 L2 L3
Chapter Assessment, pp. 216–219	1 period (1/2 block)			

ACTIVITY PLANNER

SE: *Inquiry Activity,* p. 200; 10 min.; 2 test tubes, aluminum foil, *Euglena* in water

SE: *Quick Lab,* p. 206; 30 min.; large clear plastic cup, sodium bicarbonate solution, elodea plant, large test tube

TE: *Demonstration,* p. 210; 10 min.; 2 potted green-leafed plants

SE: *Design an Experiment,* p. 215; 60 min.; scissors, black construction paper, potted plant, tape, cellophane (blue, red, and green), 5 large test tubes, glass-marking pencil, forceps, 400-mL beaker, 5 petri dishes, iodine solution, paper towels

PLANNING KEY

Ability Levels

for students performing . . .

below grade level L1

at grade level L2

above grade level L3

Print Components

SE	Student Edition	**LA**	Lab Assessment
TE	Teacher's Edition	**BTM**	Biotechnology Manual
RSW	Reading & Study Workbook A	**IDM**	Issues and Decision Making
ARSW	Adapted Reading & Study Workbook B	**LW**	Lab Worksheets
TR	Teaching Resources	**LMA**	Laboratory Manual A
IF	Investigations in Forensics	**LMB**	Laboratory Manual B

Tech Components

CTB	Computer Test Bank
BD	BioDetectives DVD
TP	Transparencies Plus
PLM	Probeware Lab Manual
ABC	ABC DVD Library
LS	Lab Simulations
VL	Virtual Labs

Interactive Textbook — Interactive textbook with assessment at PHSchool.com

Program Resources	Assessment	Media and Technology
TR: Lesson Plan 8–1, Section Summary, p. 52 L1, p. 61 L2, Worksheets, p. 54 L1, pp. 63–64 L2 **RSW:** Section 8–1 L2 **ARSW:** Section 8–1 L1	**SE:** 8–1 Section Assessment, p. 203 **TR:** Section Review 8–1	**iText:** Section 8–1 **TP:** 8–1 Interest Grabber, Section Outline, ATP, Figure 8–3 **ABC:** 8 ATP Formation
TR: Lesson Plan 8–2, Section Summary, p. 52 L1, p. 61 L2, Worksheets, pp. 65–66 L2, Enrichment L2 L3 **RSW:** Section 8–2 L2	**SE:** 8–2 Section Assessment, p. 207 **TR:** Section Review 8–2	**iText:** Section 8–2 **TP:** 8–2 Interest Grabber, Section Outline, Photosynthesis: Reactants and Products, Figure 8–5 **ABC:** 9 Photosynthesis **Lab Simulations CD-ROM:** Photosynthesis **VL:** Lab 6, Lab 7
TR: Lesson Plan 8–3, Section Summary, p. 53 L1, p. 63 L2, Worksheets, pp. 55–59 L1, pp. 67–69 L2 **LW:** Chapter 8 Design an Experiment L1 L2 L3 **RSW:** Section 8–3 L2 **ARSW:** Section 8–3 L1	**SE:** 8–3 Section Assessment, p. 214 **TR:** Section Review 8–3	**iText:** Section 8–3 **TP:** 8–3 Interest Grabber, Section Outline, Concept Map, Figure 8–7, Figure 8–10, Figure 8–11 **ABC:** 10 Light-Dependent Reactions, 11 Calvin Cycle **Lab Simulations CD-ROM:** Photosynthesis **VL:** Lab 7
	SE: Chapter 8 Assessment, pp. 216–219 **TR:** Chapter Vocabulary Review, Graphic Organizer, Chapter 8 Test	**iText:** Chapter 8 Assessment **CTB:** Chapter 8 Test

Go Online
Students can do research, share data, and test their knowledge online.

PRESSED FOR TIME?

To Preview the Chapter

- Introduce students to Key Concepts and Vocabulary terms in each section.
- Assign the Reading Strategies for each section.

To Cover the Chapter Quickly

- Have students read all of Section 8–1, read The Photosynthesis Equation and Figure 8–4 in Section 8–2, and Figures 8–7, 8–10, and 8–11 in Section 8–3.
- Assign the 8–1 Section Assessment and questions 1–14 in Chapter 8 Assessment and questions 1–9 in Chapter 8 Standards Practice.

To Review the Chapter

- Assign the Section Reviews for 8–1 through 8–3 in the Reading and Study Workbook or Adapted Reading and Study Workbook.
- Assign Section Reviews for 8–1 through 8–3 and the Chapter Vocabulary Review for Chapter 8 in the Teaching Resources.

CHAPTER 8

ENGAGE/EXPLORE

Inquiry Activity

Objective Students will be able to infer that photosynthetic organisms obtain energy from sunlight. L2

Skills Focus Observing, Inferring

Materials 2 test tubes, aluminum foil, *Euglena* in water

Time 10 minutes

Advance Prep Pour a culture containing *Euglena* into all the test tubes. Cover the test tubes completely with foil. Tear a small hole in the foil on the sides of half the test tubes. Set up the test tubes a day in advance so that the organisms will distribute accordingly.

Safety Remind students to handle the glass test tubes carefully.

Strategies
- Make sure that the test tubes are in bright light.
- Show students a test tube with a *Euglena* culture so that they know what to look for.

Expected Outcome Students should observe that the *Euglena* congregate near the hole in the foil where they can get light.

Think About It
1. In the completely covered test tube, the *Euglena* are evenly distributed. In the test tube with the hole in the foil, the *Euglena* should all be near the hole. The *Euglena* are drawn to the hole because of the light.
2. Light is the source of energy for the *Euglena*.

Assess Prior Knowledge

Challenge students to recall their observations of patterns of plant growth in parks and backyards. Ask: **Why don't bushes or other trees usually grow underneath large trees?** *(There's not enough sunlight for such plants to grow.)* **Why do plants need sunlight to grow?** *(Plants need sunlight to make food.)* Then, ask students to describe their understanding about how this food-making process occurs.

CHAPTER 8

Photosynthesis

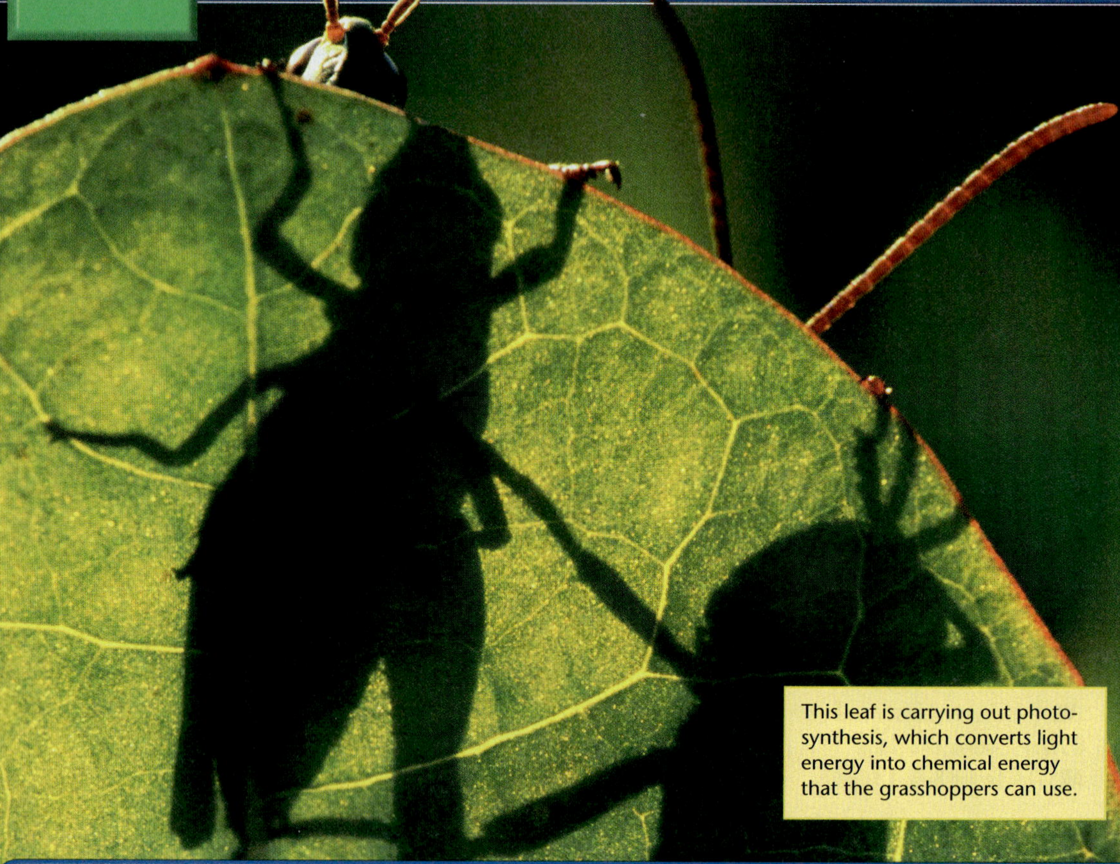

This leaf is carrying out photosynthesis, which converts light energy into chemical energy that the grasshoppers can use.

Inquiry Activity

How do organisms capture and use energy?

Procedure  

1. Obtain two test tubes wrapped in foil. Note the hole in the foil surrounding one test tube.
2. **Predicting** The test tubes contain *Euglena,* photosynthetic microorganisms that have chloroplasts and can move. Record your prediction of where in each test tube you will find *Euglena.*
3. Without shaking or disturbing the contents of the test tubes, carefully remove the foil. Record where *Euglena* are located in each test tube.

Think About It
1. **Observing** What pattern did you observe in the distribution of the *Euglena*? Why do you think they behave this way?
2. **Inferring** What is the source of energy that powers the *Euglena*'s swimming?

FACTS AND FIGURES

Photosynthesis drives carbon cycle
Photosynthesis is an integral part of one of the important biogeochemical cycles, the carbon cycle. Essentially, the carbon cycle consists of the complementary processes of photosynthesis and cellular respiration. Autotrophs, such as plants, produce carbohydrates using the carbon in carbon dioxide. Both autotrophs and heterotrophs, such as grasshoppers that eat plants, use those carbohydrates in cellular respiration, a product of which is carbon dioxide. In this way, carbon continually circulates through Earth's ecosystems. There is no corresponding cycle of energy, though. The energy captured from sunlight by photosynthetic organisms is used and released in the cellular respiration of living things. This energy is ultimately dissipated as heat. The energy used by living things must be continually replenished through photosynthesis.

8–1 Energy and Life

Energy is the ability to do work. Nearly every activity in modern society depends on one kind of energy or another. When a car runs out of fuel—more precisely, out of the chemical energy in gasoline—it comes to a sputtering halt. Without electrical energy, lights, appliances, and computers stop working.

Living things depend on energy, too. Sometimes, the need for energy is easy to see. It is obvious that energy is needed to play soccer or other sports. However, there are times when that need is less obvious. For example, when you are sleeping, your cells are busy using energy to build new proteins and amino acids. Clearly, without the ability to obtain and use energy, life would cease to exist.

Guide for Reading

Key Concepts

- Where do plants get the energy they need to produce food?
- What is the role of ATP in cellular activities?

Vocabulary

autotroph
heterotroph
adenosine triphosphate (ATP)

Reading Strategy: Asking Questions Before you read, study the diagram in **Figure 8–3.** Make a list of questions that you have about the diagram. As you read, write down the answers to your questions.

Autotrophs and Heterotrophs

Where does the energy that living things need come from? The simple answer is that it comes from food. Originally, though, the energy in most food comes from the sun. **Plants and some other types of organisms are able to use light energy from the sun to produce food.** Organisms such as plants, which make their own food, are called **autotrophs** (AW-toh-trohfs).

Other organisms, such as animals, cannot use the sun's energy directly. These organisms, known as **heterotrophs** (HET-uh-roh-trohfs), obtain energy from the foods they consume. Impalas, for example, eat grasses, which are autotrophs. Other heterotrophs, such as the leopard shown in **Figure 8–1,** obtain the energy stored in autotrophs indirectly by feeding on animals that eat autotrophs. Still other heterotrophs—mushrooms, for example—obtain food by decomposing other organisms. To live, all organisms, including plants, must release the energy in sugars and other compounds.

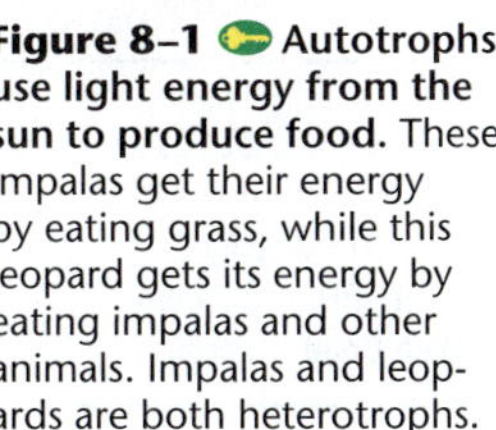

Figure 8–1 **Autotrophs use light energy from the sun to produce food.** These impalas get their energy by eating grass, while this leopard gets its energy by eating impalas and other animals. Impalas and leopards are both heterotrophs.

Section Resources

Print:

- ***Teaching Resources,*** Lesson Plan 8–1, Adapted Section Summary 8–1, Adapted Worksheets 8–1, Section Summary 8–1, Worksheets 8–1, Section Review 8–1
- ***Reading and Study Workbook A,*** Section 8–1
- ***Adapted Reading and Study Workbook B,*** Section 8–1

Technology:

- ***iText,*** Section 8–1
- ***Animated Biological Concepts DVD,*** 8 ATP Formation
- ***Transparencies Plus,*** Section 8–1

Section 8–1

1 FOCUS

Objectives

8.1.1 ***Explain*** where plants get the energy they need to produce food.

8.1.2 ***Describe*** the role of ATP in cellular activities.

Guide for Reading

Vocabulary Preview

Explain that the term *autotroph* comes from the Greek words *autos*, meaning "self," and *trophe*, meaning "food." Therefore, an autotroph is an organism that makes food for itself. Ask: **If *heteros* means "other," what does *heterotroph* mean?** *(A heterotroph is an organism that gets food from others.)*

Reading Strategy

Have students write a question for each head and subhead. For example, they might ask, "What are autotrophs and heterotrophs?" As students read the section, encourage them to write the answer to each question. Students can use their questions and answers as a study guide.

2 INSTRUCT

Autotrophs and Heterotrophs

Build Science Skills

Classifying Divide the class into small groups and have each group brainstorm a list of types of living things. Then, ask the groups to classify each type of living thing according to whether it is an autotroph or a heterotroph. After the groups have made their classifications, ask whether they found it difficult to classify any type of organism. Some students may know that certain bacteria—chemoautotrophs—are classified as autotrophs but do not obtain energy from the sun. L2

8–1 (continued)

Chemical Energy and ATP

Address Misconceptions

Some students may have difficulty with the concept that natural processes occur automatically when materials and conditions are right. Ask: **Do cells "think" about the life processes they carry out?** *(Some students might suggest that the nucleus is the "brain" of the cell, so maybe the nucleus directs cell processes in the same way a human brain directs body movements.)* Point out that cells have no thoughts. Although we often speak of how a cell "uses" energy or of how a cell can "add" a phosphate group, these words should not suggest that cells decide when or how to act. L1 L2

Use Visuals

Figure 8–2 Ask: **What does an ATP molecule consist of?** *(Adenine, ribose, and three phosphate groups)* **What do the lines between these parts of the molecule represent?** *(Chemical bonds)* **What would be the result if the third phosphate group were removed?** *(The remaining molecule would be ADP, and removing the third phosphate group would release energy.)* L2

Make Connections

Chemistry Use a large spring to help students understand the release of energy that occurs when the third phosphate group of ATP is removed. Explain that the "tail" of three phosphate groups is unstable and that the bonds that hold the phosphate groups together have high potential energy. In a sense, they are like a compressed spring. The chemical change that occurs when a phosphate group is removed and new products are formed is like letting that spring go. Energy is released as the spring relaxes—that is, as the spring changes from an unstable condition to a more stable condition. L2

Your students can extend their knowledge of ATP through this online experience.

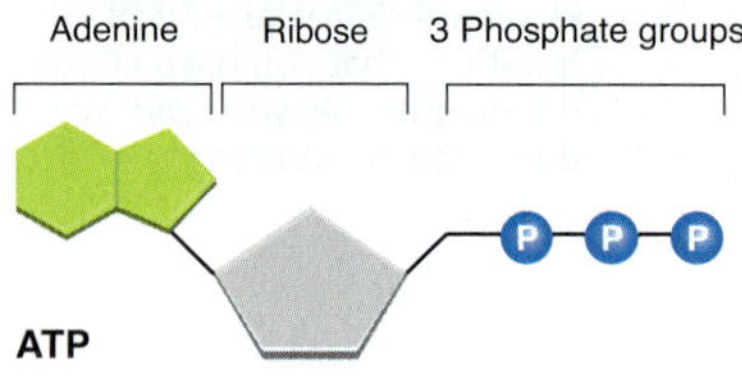

▲ **Figure 8–2 ATP is used by all types of cells as their basic energy source.** The energy needed by the cells of this soccer player comes from ATP.

For: ATP activity
Visit: PHSchool.com
Web Code: cbd-3081

Chemical Energy and ATP

Energy comes in many forms, including light, heat, and electricity. Energy can be stored in chemical compounds, too. For example, when you light a candle, the wax melts, soaks into the wick, and is burned, releasing energy in the form of light and heat. As the candle burns, high-energy chemical bonds between carbon and hydrogen atoms in the wax are broken. The high-energy bonds are replaced by low-energy bonds between these atoms and oxygen. The energy of a candle flame is released from electrons. When the electrons in those bonds are shifted from higher energy levels to lower energy levels, the extra energy is released as heat and light.

Living things use chemical fuels as well. One of the principal chemical compounds that cells use to store and release energy is **adenosine triphosphate** (uh-DEN-uh-seen try-FAHS-fayt), abbreviated **ATP.** As **Figure 8–2** shows, ATP consists of adenine, a 5-carbon sugar called ribose, and three phosphate groups. Those three phosphate groups are the key to ATP's ability to store and release energy.

Storing Energy Adenosine diphosphate (ADP) is a compound that looks almost like ATP, except that it has two phosphate groups instead of three. This difference is the key to the way in which living things store energy. When a cell has energy available, it can store small amounts of it by adding a phosphate group to ADP molecules, producing ATP, as shown in **Figure 8–3.** In a way, ATP is like a fully charged battery, ready to power the machinery of the cell.

Releasing Energy How is the energy that is stored in ATP released? Simply by breaking the chemical bond between the second and third phosphates, energy is released. Because a cell can subtract that third phosphate group, it can release energy as needed. ATP has enough energy to power a variety of cellular activities, including active transport across cell membranes, protein synthesis, and muscle contraction. **The characteristics of ATP make it exceptionally useful as the basic energy source of all cells.**

CHECKPOINT *What is the difference between ATP and ADP?*

Using Biochemical Energy

One way cells use the energy provided by ATP is to carry out active transport. Many cell membranes contain a sodium-potassium pump, a membrane protein that pumps sodium ions (Na^+) out of the cell and potassium ions (K^+) into it. ATP provides the energy that keeps this pump working, maintaining a carefully regulated balance of ions on both sides of the cell membrane. ATP produces movement, too, providing the energy for motor proteins that move organelles throughout the cell.

ESL SUPPORT FOR ENGLISH LANGUAGE LEARNERS

Comprehension: Prior Knowledge

Beginning To help students understand the concept of energy, show photos of people doing strenuous activities, e.g., running, loading moving vans. As you show each photo, briefly describe how energy is being used, for example, "Legs need energy to move." Pair beginning students with English-proficient students, and have the pairs identify other activities that require energy. Have the pairs explain aloud how energy is used in their examples. L1

Intermediate Write the following sentence on the board and read it aloud: "Cells need energy to do work." Call on volunteers to explain what energy means. Explain how the concept of energy relates to cells. Then, have students use what they learned in Chapter 7 to write lists of some cellular activities that require energy. Ask individual students to explain how these processes use energy. L2

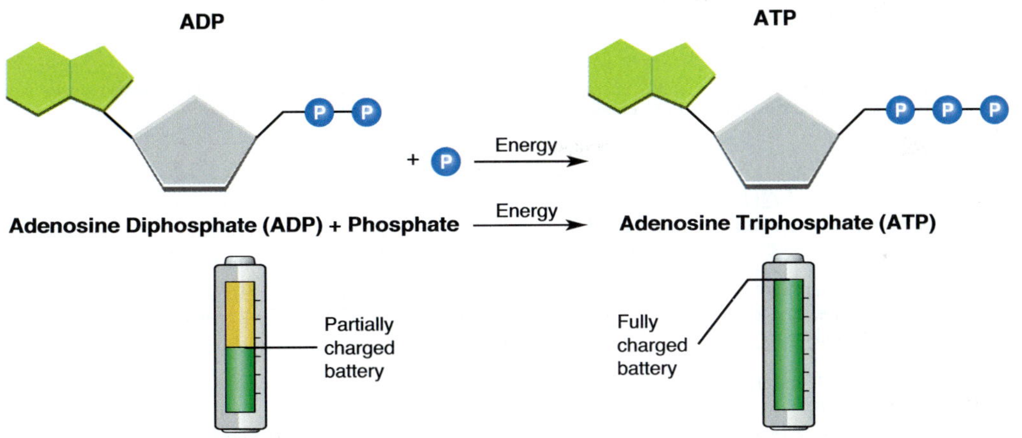

Energy from ATP powers other important events in the cell, including the synthesis of proteins and nucleic acids and responses to chemical signals at the cell surface. The energy from ATP can even be used to produce light. In fact, the blink of a firefly on a summer night comes from an enzyme powered by ATP!

ATP is such a useful source of energy that you might think the cells would be packed with ATP to get them through the day, but this is not the case. In fact, most cells have only a small amount of ATP, enough to last them for a few seconds of activity. Why? Even though ATP is a great molecule for transferring energy, it is not a good one for storing large amounts of energy over the long term. A single molecule of the sugar glucose stores more than 90 times the chemical energy of a molecule of ATP. Therefore, it is more efficient for cells to keep only a small supply of ATP on hand. Cells can regenerate ATP from ADP as needed by using the energy in foods like glucose. As you will see, that's exactly what they do.

▲ **Figure 8–3** ATP can be compared to a fully charged battery because both contain stored energy, whereas ADP resembles a partially charged battery. **Predicting** ***What happens when a phosphate group is removed from ATP?***

8–1 Section Assessment

1. **Key Concept** What is the ultimate source of energy for plants?
2. **Key Concept** What is ATP and what is its role in the cell?
3. Describe one cellular activity that uses the energy released by ATP.
4. How do autotrophs obtain energy? How do heterotrophs obtain energy?
5. **Critical Thinking Comparing and Contrasting** With respect to energy, how are ATP and glucose similar? How are they different?

Focus on the BIG Idea

Interdependence in Nature Recall that energy flows and that nutrients cycle through the biosphere. How does the process of photosynthesis impact the flow of energy and the cycling of nutrients? You may wish to refer to Chapter 3 to help you answer this question.

8–1 Section Assessment

1. The sun
2. ATP stands for adenosine triphosphate, which is one of the principal chemical compounds that living things use to store energy and release it for cell work to be done.
3. A typical answer might mention active transport, movements within the cell, synthesis of proteins and nucleic acids, or responses to chemical signals.
4. Autotrophs obtain energy by making their own food. Heterotrophs obtain energy from the foods they consume.
5. Similar: Both store chemical energy for a cell. Different: A single molecule of glucose stores more than 90 times the chemical energy of an ATP molecule.

Using Biochemical Energy

Build Science Skills

Using Analogies Some students may have difficulty understanding why cells keep only a small supply of ATP on hand. To clarify, display numerous coins and a number of paper bills of varying denominations. Explain that molecules of ATP are like the coins—coins are very useful, but too many of them fill a pocket fast. The paper money is like glucose—the bills represent much more value than an equal mass of coins. L1

3 ASSESS

Evaluate Understanding

Call on students at random to explain the difference between autotrophs and heterotrophs. Then, ask other students to explain the difference between ATP and ADP, describe how cells store and release energy, and explain why cells contain only a small amount of ATP.

Reteach

Have pairs of students work together to make a sequence of labeled illustrations that show how energy is stored and released through the addition and removal of a phosphate group.

Focus on the BIG Idea

Producers are essential to the flow of energy through the biosphere, since they help begin that flow. Photosynthesis is also important in the carbon cycle. Plants and other photosynthetic organisms take in carbon dioxide and use the carbon to build carbohydrates.

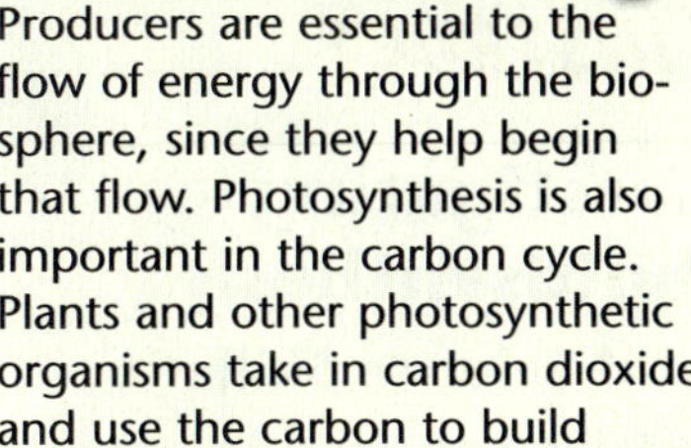

If your class subscribes to the iText, use it to review the Key Concepts in Section 8–1.

Answers to . . .

CHECKPOINT *ATP has three phosphate groups; ADP has two.*

Figure 8–3 *ADP is formed, and stored energy is released.*

Section 8–2

7 1.d, BIIE 1.k

1 FOCUS

Objectives

8.2.1 ***Explain*** what the experiments of van Helmont, Priestley, and Ingenhousz reveal about how plants grow.

8.2.2 ***State*** the overall equation for photosynthesis.

8.2.3 ***Describe*** the role of light and chlorophyll in photosynthesis.

Guide for Reading

Vocabulary Preview

Have students write the Vocabulary words, dividing each into its separate syllables as best they can. Remind students that each syllable usually has only one vowel sound. The correct syllabications are pho•to•syn•the•sis, pig•ment, chlo•ro•phyll.

Reading Strategy

Students' summaries should describe the findings of van Helmont, Priestley, and Ingenhousz and explain that plants use the energy of sunlight to convert water and carbon dioxide into oxygen and high-energy sugars. They should also describe the role of light and chlorophyll in photosynthesis.

2 INSTRUCT

Investigating Photosynthesis

Build Science Skills

Applying Concepts To help students grasp the basic problem faced by researchers centuries ago, on the board draw a large tree with leaves and roots. Point to the roots and ask: **What could trees obtain from underground that could help them grow?** *(Minerals, water)* Point to the leaves and ask: **What could trees obtain from the air that could help them grow?** *(Students might suggest oxygen or other gases. Some may mention light.)* Ask for their opinions about answers to the questions in the text about where a tall tree gets its mass. L1 L2

8–2 Photosynthesis: An Overview

7 1.d. Students know that mitochondria liberate energy for the work that cells do and that chloroplasts capture sunlight energy for photosynthesis. **BIIE 1.k.** Recognize the cumulative nature of scientific evidence.

Guide for Reading

Key Concepts

- What did the experiments of van Helmont, Priestley, and Ingenhousz reveal about how plants grow?
- What is the overall equation for photosynthesis?
- What is the role of light and chlorophyll in photosynthesis?

Vocabulary

photosynthesis
pigment
chlorophyll

Reading Strategy: Summarizing As you read, find the key ideas under each blue head. Write down a few key words from each key idea. Then, use the key words in your summary.

BIIE 1.k

a 7 1.d

The key cellular process identified with energy production is photosynthesis. In the process of **photosynthesis,** plants use the energy of sunlight to convert water and carbon dioxide into high-energy carbohydrates—sugars and starches—and oxygen, a waste product. The investigations of many scientists have contributed to the current understanding of the process of photosynthesis.

Investigating Photosynthesis

Research into photosynthesis began centuries ago with a simple question: When a tiny seedling grows into a tall tree with a mass of several tons, where does the tree's increase in mass come from? From the soil? From the water? From the air?

Van Helmont's Experiment In the 1600s, the Belgian physician Jan van Helmont devised an experiment to find out if plants grew by taking material out of the soil. Van Helmont determined the mass of a pot of dry soil and a small seedling. Then, he planted the seedling in the pot of soil. He watered it regularly. At the end of five years, the seedling, which by then had grown into a small tree, had gained about 75 kg.

Biology and History

Understanding Photosynthesis

Many scientists have contributed to understanding how plants carry out photosynthesis. Early research focused on the overall process. Later researchers investigated the detailed chemical pathways.

1643
Jan van Helmont
After careful measurements of a plant's water intake and mass increase, van Helmont concludes that trees gain most of their mass from water.

1771
Joseph Priestley
Using a bell jar, a candle, and a plant, Priestley finds that the plant releases oxygen.

1779
Jan Ingenhousz
Ingenhousz finds that aquatic plants produce oxygen bubbles in the light but not in the dark. He concludes that plants need sunlight to produce oxygen.

1600 1700 1800

SECTION RESOURCES

Print:

- ***Laboratory Manual A,*** Chapter 8 Lab
- ***Laboratory Manual B,*** Chapter 8 Lab
- ***Teaching Resources,*** Lesson Plan 8–2, Adapted Section Summary 8–2, Section Summary 8–2, Worksheets 8–2, Section Review 8–2, Enrichment
- ***Reading and Study Workbook A,*** Section 8–2

Technology:

- ***iText,*** Section 8–2
- ***Animated Biological Concepts DVD,*** 9 Photosynthesis
- ***Transparencies Plus,*** Section 8–2
- ***Lab Simulations CD-ROM,*** Photosynthesis
- ***Virtual Labs,*** Lab 6, Lab 7

The mass of the soil, however, was almost unchanged. He concluded that most of the gain in mass had come from water, because that was the only thing that he had added.

Van Helmont's experiment accounts for the "hydrate," or water, portion of the carbohydrate produced by photosynthesis. But where does the carbon of the "carbo-" portion come from? Although van Helmont did not realize it, carbon dioxide in the air made a major contribution to the mass of his tree. The carbon in carbon dioxide is used to make sugars and other carbohydrates in photosynthesis. Van Helmont had only part of the story, but he had made a major contribution to science.

Priestley's Experiment More than 100 years after van Helmont's experiment, the English minister Joseph Priestley performed an experiment that would give another insight into the process of photosynthesis. Priestley took a candle, placed a glass jar over it, and watched as the flame gradually died out. Something in the air, Priestley reasoned, was necessary to keep a candle flame burning. When that substance was used up, the candle went out. That substance was oxygen.

Priestley then found that if he placed a live sprig of mint under the jar and allowed a few days to pass, the candle could be relighted and would remain lighted for a while. The mint plant had produced the substance required for burning. In other words, it released oxygen.

CHECKPOINT *What did Priestley discover about photosynthesis?*

Word Origins

Photosynthesis comes from the Greek words *photo,* meaning "light," and *synthesis,* meaning "putting together." Therefore, *photosynthesis* means "using light to put something together," specifically, carbohydrates. *Chemo* means "having to do with chemicals or chemical reactions." **What do you think *chemosynthesis* means?**

Writing in Science

Use the Internet or library resources to research the experiments conducted by one of these scientists. Then, write a summary describing how the scientist contributed to the modern understanding of photosynthesis.

1845
Julius Robert Mayer
Mayer proposes that plants convert light energy into chemical energy.

1948
Melvin Calvin
Calvin traces the chemical path that carbon follows to form glucose. These reactions are also known as the Calvin cycle.

1992
Rudolph Marcus
Marcus wins the Nobel Prize in chemistry for describing the process by which electrons are transferred from one molecule to another in the electron transport chain.

2000

UNIVERSAL ACCESS

Less Proficient Readers
Focus students' attention on pages 204–206. Help them analyze the discoveries of the three scientists and develop a table to show what each one learned. Direct them to the word equation on page 206, and ask which part of the process each scientist discovered. L1 L2

English Language Learners
Have students compare the two equations on page 206. Relate each formula to its written name. Students who have studied the periodic table can use element symbols (such as C for carbon) to recognize each name. Help students restate the photosynthesis equation as a sentence. L1

Advanced Learners
With students, review the Writing Activity on this page. Have each student research a scientist and write a feature story on him or her. Stress that students must find more information than is given in the textbook. Emphasize that their stories should be written for the average citizen. L3

Word Origins

Chemosynthesis means "using chemical reactions to put something together." L2

Biology and History

 **BIIE 1.k**

Invite student volunteers to read aloud to the class the annotations on the timeline. Encourage students to add to the timeline by suggesting historical events that took place near in time to one of the discoveries mentioned. For each contribution to the understanding of photosynthesis mentioned in the timeline, challenge students to suggest how that discovery might have provided the basis for the next.

Writing in Science

Encourage students to look for descriptions of these experiments in books about photosynthesis, books about the history of biology, and college-level textbooks, as well as at Internet sites that specialize in biology. Provide several examples of news articles about medical and other scientific breakthroughs from a large daily newspaper. L2 L3

Build Science Skills

Designing an Experiment Divide the class into small groups and challenge them to design an experiment similar to the experiment that Joseph Priestley did in the 1700s. They should keep this concept in mind: Plant photosynthesis produces oxygen that animals need to breathe, while animal and plant respiration produces carbon dioxide that plants need in photosynthesis. Ask students to list the materials they would need and to write a step-by-step procedure. L2

Answer to . . .

CHECKPOINT *Priestley discovered that a plant releases a substance that keeps a candle burning. This substance, oxygen, is released during photosynthesis.*

8–2 (continued)

The Photosynthesis Equation

Quick Lab

Objective Students will be able to conclude that oxygen is produced by plants during photosynthesis.

Skills Focus **Observing, Inferring**

Materials large clear plastic cup, sodium bicarbonate solution, elodea plant, large test tube

Time 10 minutes for setup, 5 minutes for observations

Advance Prep Prepare the sodium bicarbonate solution by mixing 5 g of sodium bicarbonate into each liter of water. Obtain the elodea plants. If they are not available, any small water plants will do.

Safety If students break a test tube, warn them not to handle the glass.

Strategies

• It will take up to 30 minutes for oxygen to appear, so you may want to set up this lab at the beginning of the class and return to it at the end.

• To show that the gas is oxygen, you may want to demonstrate the glowing splint test. CAUTION: *Wear goggles and heat-resistant gloves during this demonstration.* Remove one of the test tubes, keeping it upside down. Remove the elodea and let the water drain out. Light a splint, blow it out, and then turn the tube sideways next to the splint. The splint will glow brighter and possibly reignite.

• Students may need to repeat step 3 several times to make sure no air is trapped.

Expected Outcome Students should observe a gas forming on the elodea leaves and conclude that it is oxygen.

Analyze and Conclude

1. Students should see bubbles of gas. An answer of "oxygen" is an inference, not an observation.

2. Photosynthesis produces sugars and oxygen. Because sugars are not gases, the gas must be oxygen. Oxygen is a waste product because it is released into the environment.

3. The chloroplast

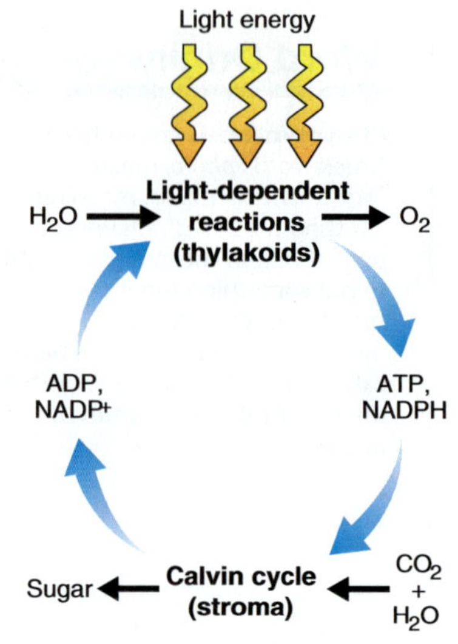

▲ **Figure 8–4** Photosynthesis is a series of reactions that uses light energy from the sun to convert water and carbon dioxide into sugars and oxygen.

Jan Ingenhousz Later, the Dutch scientist Jan Ingenhousz showed that the effect observed by Priestley occurred only when the plant was exposed to light. The results of both Priestley's and Ingenhousz's experiments showed that light is necessary for plants to produce oxygen. **The experiments performed by van Helmont, Priestley, and Ingenhousz led to work by other scientists who finally discovered that in the presence of light, plants transform carbon dioxide and water into carbohydrates, and they also release oxygen.**

The Photosynthesis Equation

Because photosynthesis usually produces 6-carbon sugars ($C_6H_{12}O_6$) as the final product, the overall equation for photosynthesis can be shown as follows:

$$6CO_2 + 6H_2O \xrightarrow{\text{light}} C_6H_{12}O_6 + 6O_2$$

$$\text{carbon dioxide} + \text{water} \xrightarrow{\text{light}} \text{sugars} + \text{oxygen}$$

Photosynthesis uses the energy of sunlight to convert water and carbon dioxide into high-energy sugars and oxygen. Plants then use the sugars to produce complex carbohydrates such as starches. Plants obtain carbon dioxide from the air or water in which they grow. The process of photosynthesis is shown in **Figure 8–4.**

Quick Lab

What waste material is produced during photosynthesis?

Materials large clear plastic cup, sodium bicarbonate solution, elodea plant, large test tube

Procedure

1. Fill a large clear plastic cup about half full with sodium bicarbonate solution. The sodium bicarbonate solution is a source of carbon dioxide.
2. Place an elodea plant in a large test tube with the cut stem at the bottom. Fill the tube with sodium bicarbonate solution. **CAUTION:** *Handle the test tube carefully.*
3. Hold your thumb over the mouth of the tube. Turn the tube over, and lower it to the bottom of the cup. Make sure there is no air trapped in the tube.
4. Place the cup in bright light.
5. After at least 20 minutes, look closely at the elodea leaves. Record your observations.

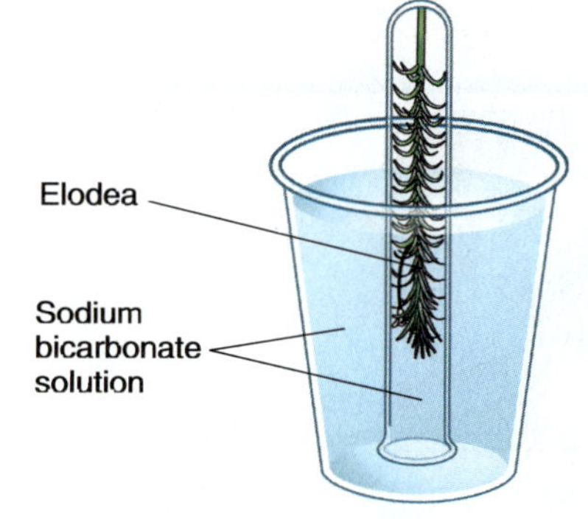

Analyze and Conclude

1. **Observing** What did you observe on the elodea leaves?
2. **Inferring** What substance accumulated in the leaves? Should that substance be considered a waste product? Explain.
3. **Applying Concepts** What plant organelle carries out photosynthesis and produces the gas?

HISTORY OF SCIENCE

Priestley's experiment "purifies" air Joseph Priestley (1733–1804), a British Unitarian minister, never formally studied science. His interest in science began when he met Benjamin Franklin in London in 1766. For one of his many experiments, Priestley devised an apparatus that consisted of enclosed containers of air sealed at the bottom by a trough of water. He discovered that a burning candle in one of the closed containers caused the air to become "impure," eventually putting out the flame. He also found that a mouse placed inside the container of "impure" air died. He expected the same to happen to a sprig of spearmint. Much to his surprise, instead of dying, the plant flourished. Furthermore, he discovered that the plant "purified" the air, since after leaving the plant in the space for several weeks, a candle would burn or a mouse could live in the same enclosed space.

Light and Pigments

Although the equation tells you that water and carbon dioxide are required for photosynthesis, it does not tell you how plants use these low-energy raw materials to produce high-energy sugars. To answer that question, you have to know how plants capture the energy of sunlight. **In addition to water and carbon dioxide, photosynthesis requires light and chlorophyll, a molecule in chloroplasts.**

Energy from the sun travels to Earth in the form of light. Sunlight, which your eyes perceive as "white" light, is actually a mixture of different wavelengths of light. Many of these wavelengths are visible to your eyes and make up what is known as the visible spectrum. Your eyes see the different wavelengths of the visible spectrum as different colors.

CA

a

Plants gather the sun's energy with light-absorbing molecules called **pigments.** The plants' principal pigment is **chlorophyll** (KLAWR-uh-fil). There are two main types of chlorophyll: chlorophyll *a* and chlorophyll *b*.

As **Figure 8–5** shows, chlorophyll absorbs light very well in the blue-violet and red regions of the visible spectrum. However, chlorophyll does not absorb light well in the green region of the spectrum. Green light is reflected by leaves, which is why plants look green. Plants also contain red and orange pigments such as carotene that absorb light in other regions of the spectrum.

Because light is a form of energy, any compound that absorbs light also absorbs the energy from that light. When chlorophyll absorbs light, much of the energy is transferred directly to electrons in the chlorophyll molecule, raising the energy levels of these electrons. These high-energy electrons make photosynthesis work.

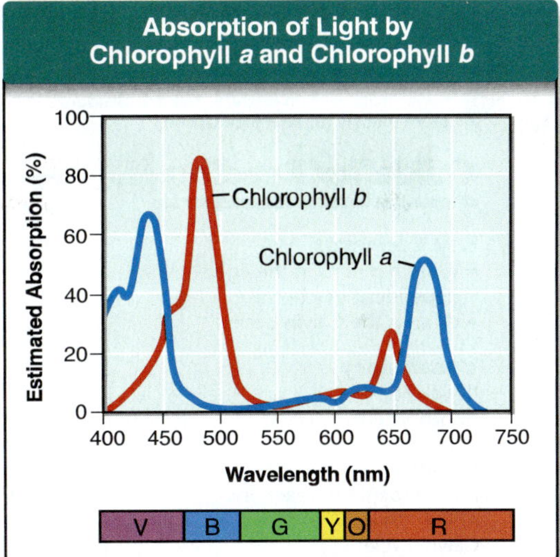

▲ **Figure 8–5 Photosynthesis requires light and chlorophyll.** In the graph above, notice how chlorophyll *a* absorbs light mostly in the blue-violet and red regions of the visible spectrum, whereas chlorophyll *b* absorbs light in the blue and red regions of the visible spectrum.

8–2 Section Assessment

1. **Key Concept** What did van Helmont, Priestley, and Ingenhousz discover about plants?
2. **Key Concept** Describe the process of photosynthesis, including the reactants and products.
3. **Key Concept** Why are light and chlorophyll needed for photosynthesis?
4. Describe the relationship between chlorophyll and the color of plants.
5. **Critical Thinking Predicting** How well would a plant grow under pure yellow light? Explain your answer.

Writing in Science

Descriptive Writing

Write a summary paragraph describing either van Helmont's, Priestley's, or Ingenhousz's experiments with plants and light. *Hint:* Use the first boldface key sentence on page 206 to give you an idea for the topic sentence.

8–2 Section Assessment

1. Van Helmont discovered that water was involved in increasing the mass of a plant. Priestley discovered that a plant produces the substance in air required for burning. Ingenhousz discovered that light is necessary for plants to produce oxygen.
2. Photosynthesis uses the energy of sunlight to convert water and carbon dioxide into oxygen and high-energy sugars.
3. Light provides the energy needed to produce high-energy sugars. Chlorophyll absorbs light, and the energy of that absorbed light makes photosynthesis work.
4. Plants are green because green light is reflected by the chlorophyll in leaves.
5. The plant would not grow well because chlorophyll does not absorb much light in the yellow region of visible light.

Light and Pigments

Build Science Skills

Using Tables and Graphs After students have examined the graph in Figure 8–5, ask: **How does the color spectrum at the bottom relate to the graph itself?** *(Each of the colors of the visible spectrum has a characteristic range of wavelengths, as designated on the horizontal axis of the graph.)* **In what region of the spectrum does chlorophyll *b* absorb light best?** *(In the blue region)* Challenge students to convert the data in the graph into a data table that shows, for example, the estimated absorption of chlorophyll *a* and chlorophyll *b* at 550 nm. L2

3 ASSESS

Evaluate Understanding

Have students write a paragraph, using their own words, that explains how plants produce high-energy sugars through the process of photosynthesis. Call on students at random to read their paragraphs.

Reteach

Ask students to make a labeled drawing based on Figure 8–4 but with more realistic objects, including a leafy tree, the sun, and clouds in the sky (visually representing the atmosphere). Ask that they use arrows and symbols in their drawing to show the same equation for photosynthesis that Figure 8–4 does.

Writing in Science

Students should write a paragraph summarizing the experiments of one of the three scientists discussed in the section. A good paragraph should have a topic sentence derived from the first boldface sentence on page 206, details about the experiments performed, and a concluding sentence that explains the significance of the scientist's work.

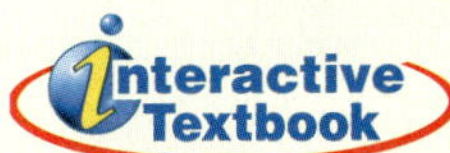

If your class subscribes to the iText, use it to review the Key Concepts in Section 8–2.

Section 8-3

BI 1.f, *BI 1.i

1 FOCUS

Objectives

8.3.1 ***Describe*** the structure and function of a chloroplast.

8.3.2 ***Describe*** what happens in the light-dependent reactions.

8.3.3 ***Explain*** what the Calvin cycle is.

8.3.4 ***Identify*** factors that affect the rate at which photosynthesis occurs.

Guide for Reading

Preview Vocabulary

Before reading, have students find each Vocabulary word in the section and preview its meaning.

Reading Strategy

Suggest that students write a summary of the information in Figures 8–7, 8–10, and 8–11. Have them revise their summaries after reading the section.

2 INSTRUCT

Inside a Chloroplast

Use Visuals

Figure 8–6 Have student volunteers read the annotations for the parts of a chloroplast. Then, with students' help, make a Venn diagram on the board that shows the relationships among a granum, thylakoids, and photosystems. The diagram should show a thylakoid within a granum and photosystems within the thylakoid. Then, ask: **Within the chloroplast, where do the light-dependent reactions occur, and where does the Calvin cycle occur?** *(The light-dependent reactions occur within the thylakoid membranes, and the Calvin cycle occurs in the stroma.)* Have students locate these places on the figure. L1 L2

8–3 The Reactions of Photosynthesis

BI 1.f. Students know usable energy is captured from sunlight by chloroplasts and is stored through the synthesis of sugar from carbon dioxide. ***BI 1.i.** Students know how chemiosmotic gradients in the mitochondria and chloroplasts store energy for ATP production.

Guide for Reading

Key Concepts

- What happens in the light-dependent reactions?
- What is the Calvin cycle?

Vocabulary

thylakoid
photosystem
stroma
NADP+
light-dependent reactions
ATP synthase
Calvin cycle

Reading Strategy: Using Visuals Before you read, preview **Figures 8–7, 8–10,** and **8–11.** As you read, notice where in the chloroplast each stage of photosynthesis takes place.

The requirements of photosynthesis were discovered in the 1800s. It was not until the second half of the 1900s, however, that biologists understood the complex reactions that make this important cellular process possible.

Inside a Chloroplast

In plants and other photosynthetic eukaryotes, photosynthesis takes place inside chloroplasts. The chloroplasts, shown in **Figure 8–6,** contain saclike photosynthetic membranes called **thylakoids** (THY-luh-koydz). Thylakoids are arranged in stacks known as grana (singular: granum). Proteins in the thylakoid membrane organize chlorophyll and other pigments into clusters known as **photosystems.** These photosystems are the light-collecting units of the chloroplast.

Scientists describe the reactions of photosystems in two parts: the light-dependent reactions and the light-independent reactions, or Calvin cycle. The relationship between these two sets of reactions is shown in **Figure 8–7.** The light-dependent reactions take place within the thylakoid membranes. The Calvin cycle takes place in the **stroma,** the region outside the thylakoid membranes.

Figure 8–6 In plants, photosynthesis takes place inside chloroplasts. **Observing** *What are thylakoids?*

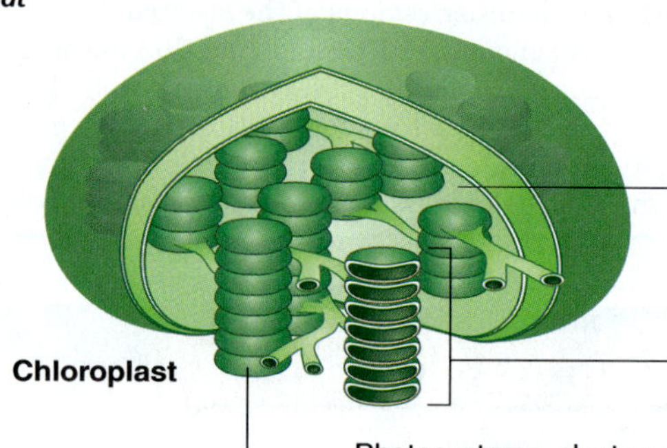

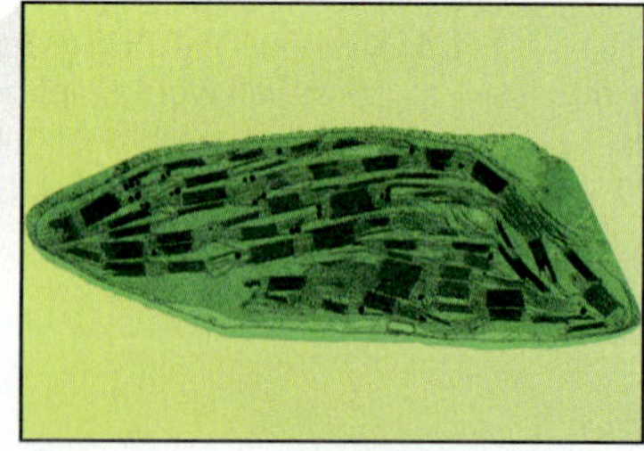

SECTION RESOURCES

Print:

- ***Teaching Resources,*** Lesson Plan 8–3, Adapted Section Summary 8–3, Adapted Worksheets 8–3, Section Summary 8–3, Worksheets 8–3, Section Review 8–3
- ***Reading and Study Workbook A,*** Section 8–3
- ***Adapted Reading and Study Workbook B,*** Section 8–3
- ***Biotechnology Manual,*** Lab 17, Issue 4
- ***Lab Worksheets,*** Chapter 8 Design an Experiment

Technology:

- ***iText,*** Section 8–3
- ***Animated Biological Concepts DVD,*** 10 Light-Dependent Reactions, 11 Calvin Cycle
- ***Transparencies Plus,*** Section 8–3
- ***Lab Simulations CD-ROM,*** Photosynthesis
- ***Virtual Labs,*** Lab 7

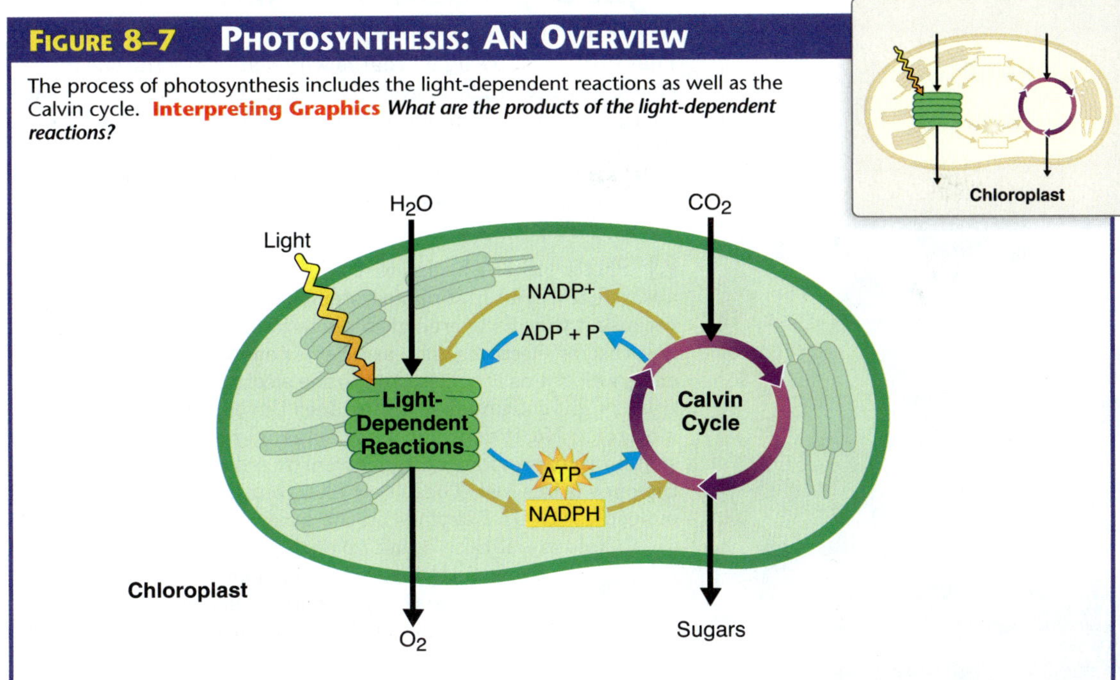

FIGURE 8–7 PHOTOSYNTHESIS: AN OVERVIEW

The process of photosynthesis includes the light-dependent reactions as well as the Calvin cycle. **Interpreting Graphics** *What are the products of the light-dependent reactions?*

Electron Carriers

When sunlight excites electrons in chlorophyll, the electrons gain a great deal of energy. These high-energy electrons require a special carrier. Think of a high-energy electron as being similar to a red-hot coal from a fireplace or campfire. If you wanted to move the coal from one place to another, you wouldn't pick it up in your hands. You would use a pan or bucket—a carrier—to transport it. Cells treat high-energy electrons in the same way. Instead of a pan or bucket, they use electron carriers to transport high-energy electrons from chlorophyll to other molecules, as shown in **Figure 8–8.** A carrier molecule is a compound that can accept a pair of high-energy electrons and transfer them along with most of their energy to another molecule. This process is called electron transport, and the electron carriers themselves are known as the electron transport chain.

One of these carrier molecules is a compound known as **$NADP^+$** (nicotinamide adenine dinucleotide phosphate). The name is complicated, but the job that $NADP^+$ has is simple. $NADP^+$ accepts and holds 2 high-energy electrons along with a hydrogen ion (H^+). This converts the $NADP^+$ into NADPH. The conversion of $NADP^+$ into NADPH is one way in which some of the energy of sunlight can be trapped in chemical form.

The NADPH can then carry high-energy electrons produced by light absorption in chlorophyll to chemical reactions elsewhere in the cell. These high-energy electrons are used to help build a variety of molecules the cell needs, including carbohydrates like glucose.

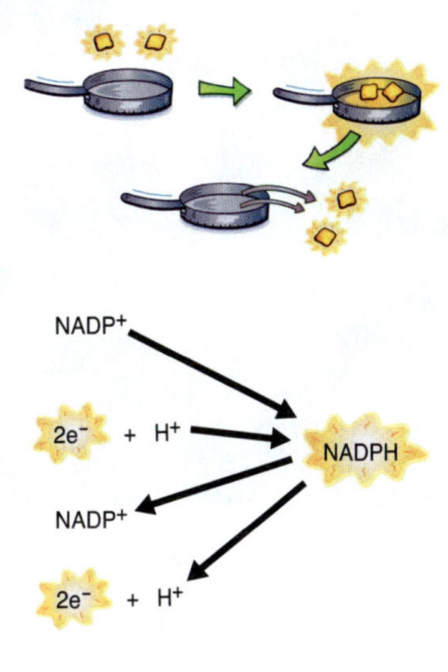

▲ **Figure 8–8** Like a pan being used to carry hot coals, electron carriers such as $NADP^+$ transport electrons. **Interpreting Graphics** *What eventually happens to those electrons?*

Electron Carriers

Use Visuals

Figure 8–7 After students have studied the figure and read the caption, have them answer the following questions on a sheet of paper: **What materials come into the chloroplast that are used in the light-dependent reactions?** *(Light and H_2O)* **What material comes into the chloroplast that is used in the Calvin cycle?** *(CO_2)* **What material moves out of the chloroplast from the light-dependent reactions?** *(O_2)* **What materials move out of the chloroplast from the Calvin cycle?** *(Sugars)* **What materials move from the light-dependent reactions to the Calvin cycle?** *(ATP and NADPH)* **What materials move from the Calvin cycle back to the light-dependent reactions?** *($NADP^+$ and ADP + P)* L1 L2

Make Connections

Chemistry Remind students that an ion is an atom, or group of atoms, that has a positive or negative charge because it has lost or gained electrons. Ask: **If an ion has more protons than electrons, is its charge positive or negative?** *(Positive)* Point out that $NADP^+$ is a positive ion, which explains why it can accept a negative electron. Then, ask: **What does a hydrogen atom consist of?** *(One proton and one electron)* **If a hydrogen atom loses its electron, what is the result?** *(A hydrogen ion, or H^+)* L2

UNIVERSAL ACCESS

Less Proficient Readers

To reinforce understanding of the Calvin cycle and the electron transport chain, divide the class into pairs, matching less proficient readers with students who have shown a grasp of the details of photosynthesis. Ask the paired students to quiz each other on the details of both the light-dependent reactions and the Calvin cycle, using Figure 8–10 and Figure 8–11 as their primary resources. L1 L2

Advanced Learners

The investigation of the light-independent reactions by Melvin Calvin in the late 1940s is a fascinating example of biochemical discovery. Encourage advanced learners to find out about Calvin's work through library research and to prepare a presentation to the class. Ask students to make drawings or provide other visual aids to help show how Calvin used carbon-14 to identify the sequence of reactions involved in the process. L3

Answers to . . .

Figure 8–6 *Thylakoids are saclike photosynthetic membranes contained in chloroplasts.*

Figure 8–7 *The products of the light-dependent reaction are O_2, ATP, and NADPH.*

Figure 8–8 *The electrons are carried to chemical reactions elsewhere in the cell, where they are used to help build a variety of molecules that the cell needs, including carbohydrates.*

8–3 (continued)

Light-Dependent Reactions

Make Connections

Physics Ask: **Does light radiate in waves or particles?** *(Some students may say waves, others particles.)* Explain that light has both the properties of waves and the properties of a stream of particles. A particle of light is called a photon, and some photons have more energy than others. The amount of energy in a photon depends on the wavelength; the shorter the wavelength, the more energy a photon has. Explain that when a photon of a certain amount of energy strikes a molecule of chlorophyll, the energy of that photon is transferred to an electron in that chlorophyll molecule. L2 L3

Demonstration

To reinforce the concept that light-dependent reactions require the presence of light, show students two healthy potted green-leafed plants of the same species and about the same size. Ask: **If one of these plants did not get any light for a week, what do you predict would happen?** *(Most students will predict that the plant will suffer from lack of light.)* Then, place one plant in a sunny spot in the room and the other in a dark place. Water each plant the same amount every other day. After a week, students should observe that the plant that received sunlight remained healthy, while the plant that spent the week in the dark became pale and straggly.

Light-Dependent Reactions

As you might expect from their name, the **light-dependent reactions** require light. That is why plants like the one in **Figure 8–9** need light to grow. The light-dependent reactions use energy from light to produce ATP and NADPH. **The light-dependent reactions produce oxygen gas and convert ADP and $NADP^+$ into the energy carriers ATP and NADPH.** Look at **Figure 8–10** to see what happens at each step of the process.

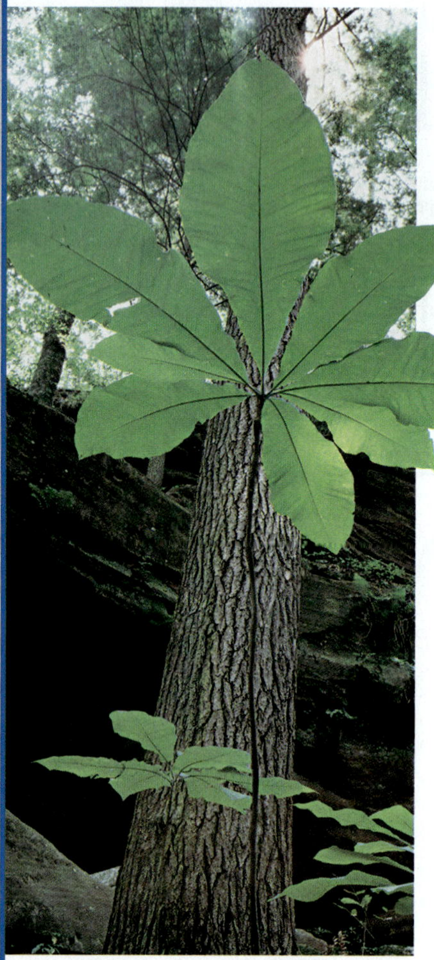

▲ **Figure 8–9** Like all plants, this seedling needs light to grow. **Applying Concepts** *What stage of photosynthesis requires light?*

A Photosynthesis begins when pigments in photosystem II absorb light. That first photosystem is called photosystem II because it was discovered after photosystem I. The light energy is absorbed by electrons, increasing their energy level. These high-energy electrons are passed on to the electron transport chain.

As light continues to shine, does the chlorophyll run out of electrons? No, it does not. The thylakoid membrane contains a system that provides new electrons to chlorophyll to replace the ones it has lost. These new electrons come from water molecules (H_2O). Enzymes on the inner surface of the thylakoid membrane break up each water molecule into 2 electrons, 2 H^+ ions, and 1 oxygen atom. The 2 electrons replace the high-energy electrons that chlorophyll has lost to the electron transport chain. As plants remove electrons from water, oxygen is left behind and is released into the air. This reaction is the source of nearly all of the oxygen in Earth's atmosphere, and it is another way in which photosynthesis makes our lives possible. The hydrogen ions left behind when water is broken apart are released inside the thylakoid membrane.

B High-energy electrons move through the electron transport chain from photosystem II to photosystem I. Energy from the electrons is used by the molecules in the electron transport chain to transport H^+ ions from the stroma into the inner thylakoid space.

C Pigments in photosystem I use energy from light to reenergize the electrons. $NADP^+$ then picks up these high-energy electrons, along with H^+ ions, at the outer surface of the thylakoid membrane, plus an H^+ ion, and becomes NADPH.

D As electrons are passed from chlorophyll to $NADP^+$, more hydrogen ions are pumped across the membrane. After a while, the inside of the membrane fills up with positively charged hydrogen ions. This makes the outside of the thylakoid membrane negatively charged and the inside positively charged. The difference in charges across the membrane provides the energy to make ATP. This is why the H^+ ions are so important.

E H^+ ions cannot cross the membrane directly. However, the cell membrane contains a protein called **ATP synthase** (SIN-thays) that spans the membrane and allows H^+ ions to pass through it. As H^+ ions pass through ATP synthase, the protein rotates like a turbine being spun by water in a hydroelectric power plant.

TEACHER TO TEACHER

When I introduce photosynthesis to students, I first present information about the physical properties of light, especially how light can be thought of as either waves or photons. This information both sparks the interest of students and helps them understand how the light-dependent reactions work. Then, I move on to the biochemistry of photosynthesis. Students often get bored with the specifics of the chemical reactions. Turning their attention to an illustration of chloroplast structure can help renew interest in the biochemistry. Using paper chromatography to identify the different pigments in plants also helps students understand photosynthesis.

—*Greg McCurdy*
Biology Teacher
Salem High School
Salem, IN

Light-Dependent Reactions

Figure 8–10 **The light-dependent reactions use energy from sunlight to produce ATP, NADPH, and oxygen.** The light-dependent reactions take place within the thylakoid membranes of chloroplasts.

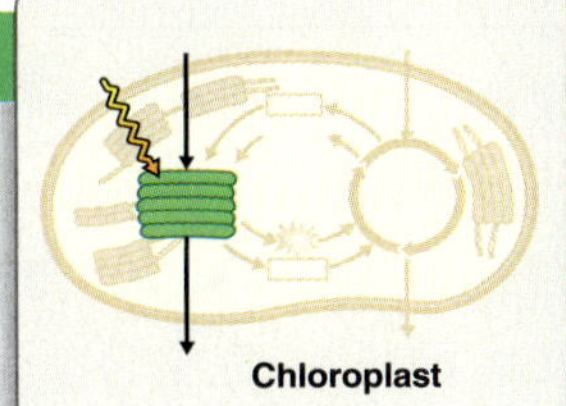

A Photosystem II
Light absorbed by photosystem II is used to break up water molecules into energized electrons, hydrogen ions (H^+), and oxygen.

D Hydrogen Ion Movement
The inside of the thylakoid membrane fills up with positively charged hydrogen ions. This action makes the outside of the thylakoid membrane negatively charged and the inside positively charged.

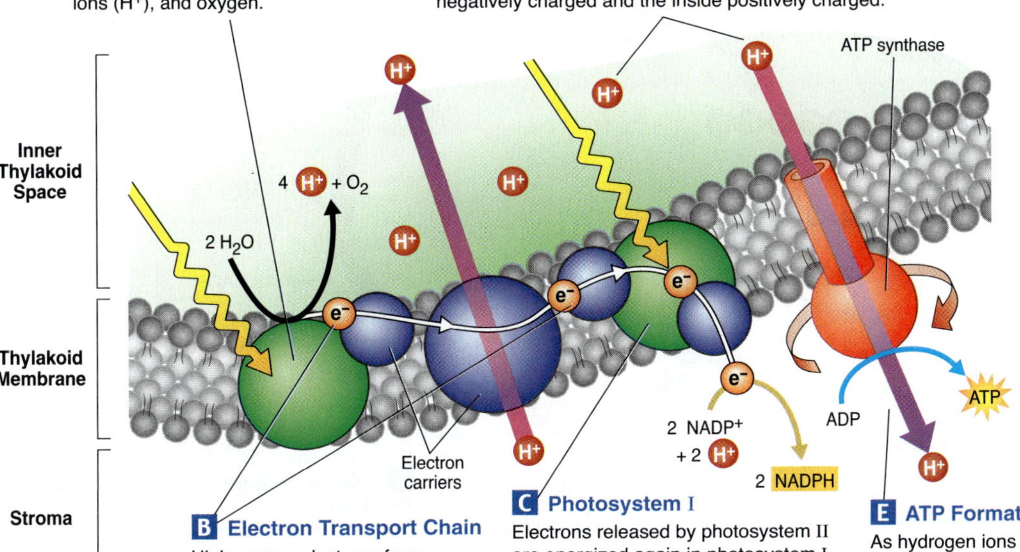

B Electron Transport Chain
High-energy electrons from photosystem II move through the electron transport chain to photosystem I.

C Photosystem I
Electrons released by photosystem II are energized again in photosystem I. Enzymes in the membrane use the electrons to form NADPH. NADPH is used to make sugar in the Calvin cycle.

E ATP Formation
As hydrogen ions pass through ATP synthase, their energy is used to convert ADP into ATP.

For: Photosynthesis activity
Visit: PHSchool.com
Web Code: cbp-3083

As it rotates, ATP synthase binds ADP and a phosphate group together to produce ATP. Because of this system, light-dependent electron transport produces not only high-energy electrons but ATP as well.

As we have seen, the light-dependent reactions use water, ADP, and $NADP^+$, and they produce oxygen and two high-energy compounds: ATP and NADPH. What good are these compounds? As we will see, they have an important role to play in the cell: They provide the energy to build energy-containing sugars from low-energy compounds.

CHECKPOINT ***What is the role of photosystem II? How does that role compare with the role of photosystem I?***

Go Online **active art**

For: Photosynthesis activity
Visit: PHSchool.com
Web Code: cbe-3083
Students identify the products and reactants of photosynthesis.

Make Connections

Earth Science Explain that Earth's atmosphere is about 21 percent oxygen. Point out that the atmosphere that surrounded Earth billions of years ago contained little oxygen. Then, about 3.3 billion years ago, photosynthetic organisms appeared on Earth. The atmosphere changed in composition over time, until it reached its present composition about 500 million years ago. Ask: **What process do you think increased the percentage of oxygen in the atmosphere over time?** *(Earth's photosynthetic organisms, including plants, added oxygen to the air as they carried out photosynthesis.)* **What is the source of the oxygen released into the atmosphere by photosynthetic organisms?** *(Oxygen released into the atmosphere is produced during the light-dependent reactions as water molecules are broken up.)* **L2**

TEACHER TO TEACHER

To illustrate the importance of light to the process of photosynthesis, describe what happens to sun-loving lawn plants such as grasses when a board, cloth, or some other object is left on the lawn for a number of days. Tell students that the lack of light causes photosynthesis to slow down. After a longer period of sun deprivation, the plants begin to die, the chlorophyll begins to break down, and a yellow color can be observed.

You also can describe what happens to a farm crop such as corn when it is planted in a field that borders a forest. Explain how the rows of corn next to the woodland will become pale green and stunted because the forest will block some of the corn's sunlight.

—Dale Faughn
Biology Teacher
Caldwell County High School
Princeton, KY

Answers to . . .

CHECKPOINT *In photosystem II, the energy from light is absorbed by chlorophyll and transferred to electrons, and then these high-energy electrons are passed on to the electron transport chain. In photosystem I, pigments use energy from light to reenergize the electrons.*

Figure 8–9 *The light-dependent reactions of photosynthesis require light.*

8–3 (continued)

The Calvin Cycle

Use Visuals

Figure 8–11 Have students study the figure and read the caption. Then, ask: **Where does the Calvin cycle take place?** *(It takes place in the stroma, outside the grana.)* **What enters the Calvin cycle from the atmosphere?** *(Six CO_2 molecules)* Ask a volunteer to describe where on the figure those molecules enter the cycle. Then, ask another volunteer to point out where in the cycle ATP and NADPH become involved. Ask: **Where do the ATP and NADPH come from?** *(Both ATP and NADPH come from the light-dependent reactions.)* Emphasize that the Calvin cycle uses the energy of those high-energy molecules from the light-dependent reactions to keep the cycle going. Ask: **What is the product of this cycle?** *(Two 3-carbon molecules)* Have a volunteer describe where in the cycle the two 3-carbon molecules are yielded. Ask: **What happens next to the 3-carbon molecules?** *(They are used to form one 6-carbon sugar.)* Ask: **How is the cycle completed?** *(The cycle is complete when the remaining 3-carbon molecules are converted back into 5-carbon molecules, which are ready to combine with new carbon dioxide molecules to begin the cycle again.)* L2

Download a worksheet on the Calvin cycle for students to complete, and find additional teacher support from NSTA SciLinks.

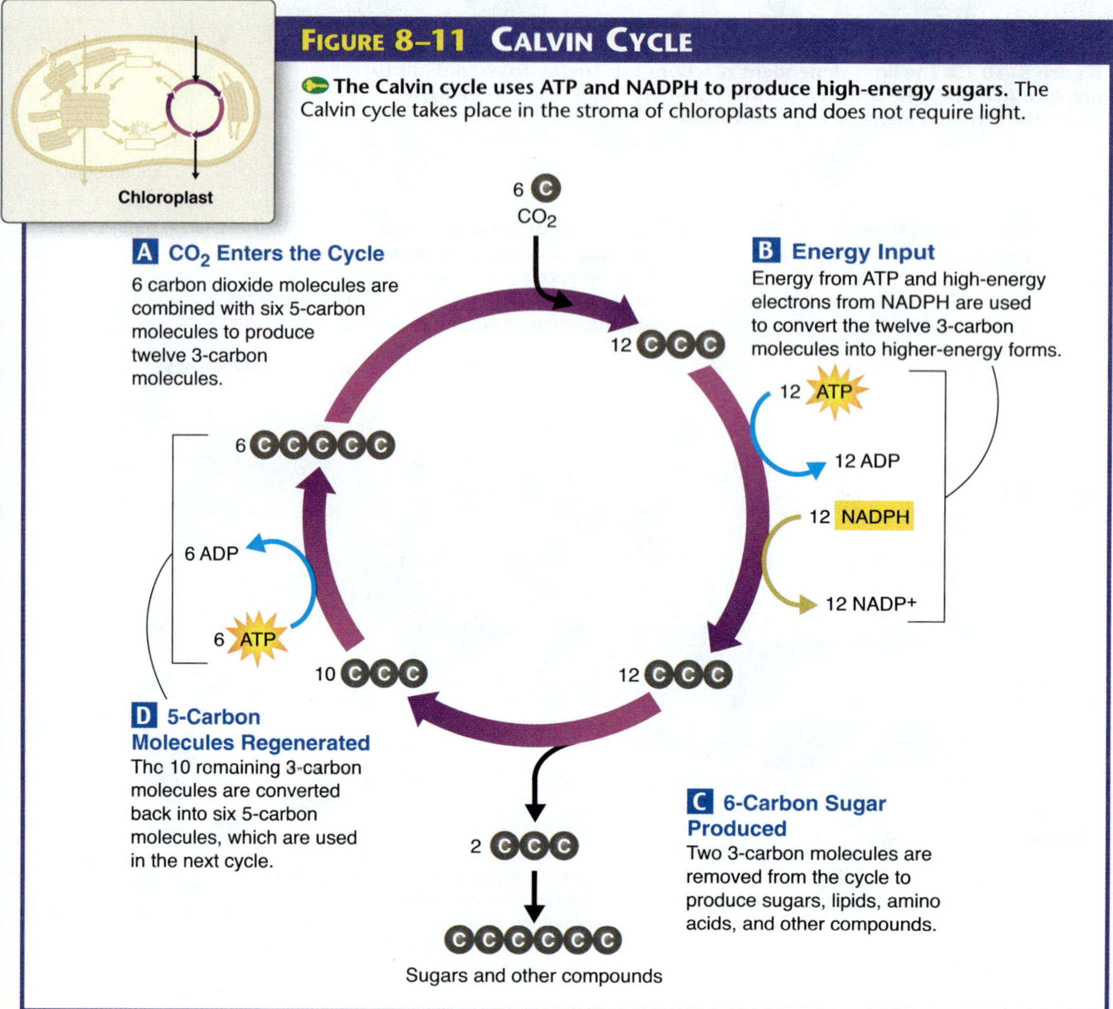

FIGURE 8–11 CALVIN CYCLE

The Calvin cycle uses ATP and NADPH to produce high-energy sugars. The Calvin cycle takes place in the stroma of chloroplasts and does not require light.

For: Links on Calvin cycle
Visit: www.SciLinks.org
Web Code: cbn-3082

ⓐ BI 1.f

The Calvin Cycle

CA ⓐ The ATP and NADPH formed by the light-dependent reactions contain an abundance of chemical energy, but they are not stable enough to store that energy for more than a few minutes. During the **Calvin cycle,** plants use the energy that ATP and NADPH contain to build high-energy compounds that can be stored for a long time. **The Calvin cycle uses ATP and NADPH from the light-dependent reactions to produce high-energy sugars.** The Calvin cycle is named after the American scientist Melvin Calvin, who worked out the details of this remarkable cycle. Because the Calvin cycle does not require light, these reactions are also called the light-independent reactions. Follow **Figure 8–11** to see how the Calvin cycle works.

BIO INSIGHTS — HISTORY OF SCIENCE

Same stages, different names

In the early 1900s, British plant physiologist F. F. Blackman concluded that photosynthesis occurs in two stages, a stage that depends on light followed by a stage that can take place in darkness. The terms *light reactions* and *dark reactions* have been commonly used for the two stages since that time. Yet, the term *dark reactions* implies that those reactions can occur only in darkness, which is not the case. It's just that the dark reactions don't depend on sunlight to occur. To avoid this ambiguity, the authors of many modern textbooks have labeled the two stages the *light-dependent reactions* and the *light-independent reactions.* The authors of this textbook have gone a step further toward clarity by labeling the light-independent reactions the *Calvin cycle,* the name of the series of reactions that make up the light-independent reactions in most photosynthetic organisms.

A Six carbon dioxide molecules enter the cycle from the atmosphere. The carbon dioxide molecules combine with six 5-carbon molecules. The result is twelve 3-carbon molecules.

B The twelve 3-carbon molecules are then converted into higher-energy forms. The energy for this conversion comes from ATP and high-energy electrons from NADPH.

C Two of the twelve 3-carbon molecules are removed from the cycle. The plant cell uses these molecules to produce sugars, lipids, amino acids, and other compounds needed for plant metabolism and growth.

D The remaining ten 3-carbon molecules are converted back into six 5-carbon molecules. These molecules combine with six new carbon dioxide molecules to begin the next cycle.

The Calvin cycle uses six molecules of carbon dioxide to produce a single 6-carbon sugar molecule. As photosynthesis proceeds, the Calvin cycle works steadily removing carbon dioxide from the atmosphere and turning out energy-rich sugars. The plant uses the sugars to meet its energy needs and to build more complex macromolecules such as cellulose that it needs for growth and development. When other organisms eat plants, they can also use the energy stored in carbohydrates.

ⓐ BI 1.f

CHECKPOINT *What are the main products of the Calvin cycle?*

6IIE 7.c, BIIE 1.d

Analyzing Data

Rates of Photosynthesis

The rate at which a plant carries out photosynthesis depends in part on its environment. Plants that grow in the shade, for example, carry out photosynthesis at low levels of light. Plants that grow in the sun, such as desert plants, typically carry out photosynthesis at much higher levels of light.

The graph compares the rates of photosynthesis between plants that grow in the shade and plants that grow in the sun. It shows how the rate of photosynthesis changes with the number of micromoles of photons per square meter per second (μmol photons/m²/s), a standard unit of light intensity.

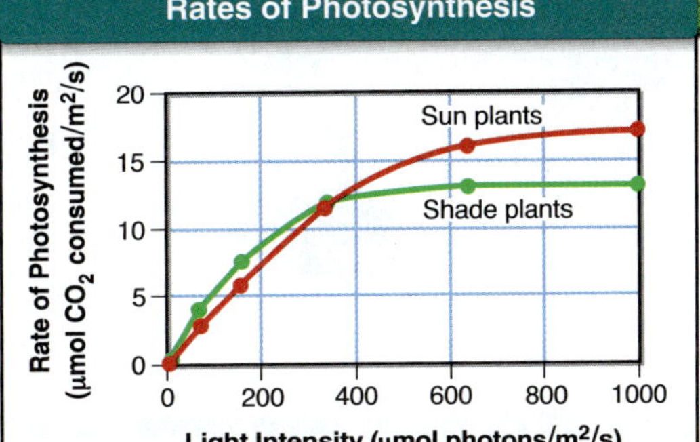

1. **Using Tables and Graphs** When light intensity is below 200 μmol photons/m²/s, do sun plants or shade plants have a higher rate of photosynthesis?
2. **Drawing Conclusions** Does the relationship in question 1 change when light intensity increases above 400 μmol photons/m²/s? Explain your answer.
3. **Inferring** The average light intensity in the Sonoran Desert is about 400 μmol photons/m²/s. According to the graph, what would be the approximate rate of photosynthesis for sun plants that grow in this environment?
4. **Going Further** Suppose you transplant a sun plant to a shaded forest floor that receives about 100 μmol photons/m²/s. Do you think this plant will grow and thrive? Why or why not? How does the graph help you answer this question?

BIO INSIGHTS — HISTORY OF SCIENCE

Calvin's investigation

In the late 1940s, University of California biochemist Melvin Calvin worked out the details of the sequence of reactions that now bears his name. For this investigation, Calvin exposed cells of *Chlorella,* a unicellular green alga, to carbon dioxide that contained the radioactive isotope carbon-14. After a short time, he dropped the algae into boiling alcohol, killing the cells and stopping the reactions at that point. He then identified the compounds in the dead cells that contained carbon-14, reasoning that these compounds were involved in the process of photosynthesis. By varying the time between exposure and killing the cells, Calvin was able to work out the steps in the light-independent reactions, or the Calvin cycle. For this work, Calvin received the 1961 Nobel Prize in Chemistry.

Go Online NSTA SciLinks

For: Links on photosynthesis
Visit: www.SciLinks.org
Web Code: cbn-3083

Go Online NSTA SciLinks

Download a worksheet on photosynthesis for students to complete, and find additional teacher support from NSTA SciLinks.

Build Science Skills

Comparing and Contrasting

Have students compare what happens in the light-dependent reactions of photosynthesis with what happens in the Calvin cycle. This could be done by each student in written form or orally in class discussion. Students should particularly compare the reactants and products of each series of reactions. L2

Analyzing Data

6IIE 7.c, BIIE 1.d

Have student volunteers explain what is measured on the vertical axis and the horizontal axis of this graph. Tell students that understanding the unit of measure for the rate of photosynthesis is not as important as recognizing that the rate increases in units of 5 along the vertical axis. L2

Answers

1. Shade plants
2. Yes; above 400 μmol photons/m²/s, sun plants have a higher rate of photosynthesis than shade plants.
3. 13 μmol CO_2 consumed/m²/s
4. The graph shows that a sun plant's rate of photosynthesis would decrease dramatically from its normal rate if transplanted to a shaded forest, from 13 μmol CO_2 consumed/m²/s at 400 μmol photons/m²/s to only about 4 μmol CO_2 consumed/m²/s at 100 μmol photons/m²/s.

Answer to . . .

CHECKPOINT *The main products of the Calvin cycle are high-energy sugars.*

8–3 (continued)

Factors Affecting Photosynthesis

Use Community Resources

Have students brainstorm a list of questions to ask a staff member at a local arboretum or conservatory about factors that limit or enhance plant growth. Ask a student volunteer to contact the person to set up an appointment for an interview. Have that student and one or two others use the list of questions as a basis for the interview. Then, have the interviewers make an oral report to the class. L2 L3

3 ASSESS

Evaluate Understanding

Call on students at random to define or explain each of the section's Vocabulary words. Encourage other students to add to any definition or explanation given by one of their classmates.

Reteach

Ask student volunteers to orally describe parts of Figures 8–10 and 8–11, in the sequence in which the light-dependent reactions and the Calvin cycle occur.

Thinking Visually

In their flowcharts, students should illustrate as many steps as they can find in the section, including events in both stages of photosynthesis. Some students may have 20 or more steps. After students have completed the task, post the flowcharts around the room and invite volunteers to present their work to the class.

If your class subscribes to the iText, use it to review the Key Concepts in Section 8–3.

Answer to . . .

Figure 8–12 *They both have a waxy coating on their leaves that reduces water loss.*

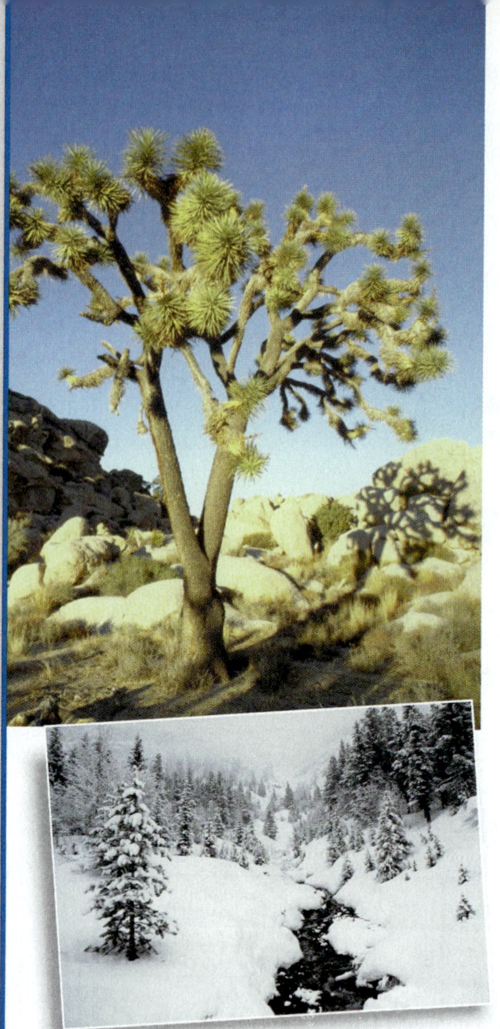

The two sets of photosynthetic reactions work together—the light-dependent reactions trap the energy of sunlight in chemical form, and the light-independent reactions use that chemical energy to produce stable, high-energy sugars from carbon dioxide and water. And, in the process, we animals get an atmosphere filled with oxygen. Not a bad deal at all.

Factors Affecting Photosynthesis

Many factors affect the rate at which photosynthesis occurs. Because water is one of the raw materials of photosynthesis, a shortage of water can slow or even stop photosynthesis. Plants that live in dry conditions, such as desert plants and conifers, have a waxy coating on their leaves that reduces water loss.

Temperature is also a factor. Photosynthesis depends on enzymes that function best between 0°C and 35°C. Temperatures above or below this range may damage the enzymes, slowing down the rate of photosynthesis. At very low temperatures, photosynthesis may stop entirely.

The intensity of light also affects the rate at which photosynthesis occurs. As you might expect, increasing light intensity increases the rate of photosynthesis. After the light intensity reaches a certain level, however, the plant reaches its maximum rate of photosynthesis. The level at which light intensity no longer affects photosynthesis varies from plant type to plant type. The conifers shown in **Figure 8–12** can carry out photosynthesis only on warm, sunny days.

Figure 8–12 Both temperature and the availability of water can affect rates of photosynthesis. Desert plants such as this Joshua tree (above) are adapted to survive with little water. During the cold winter months these conifers (below) may only occasionally carry out photosynthesis. **Comparing and Contrasting** ***What do both plants shown have that helps them conserve water?***

8–3 Section Assessment

1. **Key Concept** Summarize the light-dependent reactions.
2. **Key Concept** What reactions make up the Calvin cycle?
3. How is light energy converted into chemical energy during photosynthesis?
4. What is the function of NADPH?
5. **Critical Thinking Applying Concepts** Why are the light-dependent reactions important to the Calvin cycle?

Thinking Visually

Making a Flowchart

Construct a flowchart that illustrates the steps of photosynthesis. Begin with the energy of sunlight and end with the production of sugars. Include as much detail as possible in the numerous steps.

8–3 Section Assessment

1. The light-dependent reactions produce oxygen gas and convert ADP and $NADP^+$ into the energy carriers ATP and NADPH.
2. The Calvin cycle uses ATP and NADPH from the light-dependent reactions to produce high-energy sugars.
3. Light energy is converted into chemical energy by the pigments in the chloroplast.
4. The main function of NADPH is to carry high-energy electrons produced by light absorption in chlorophyll to chemical reactions elsewhere in the cell.
5. The light-dependent reactions provide the Calvin cycle with ATP and NADPH. The Calvin cycle uses the energy in ATP and NADPH to produce high-energy sugars.

Design an Experiment

BIIE 1.d

Investigating Photosynthesis

If only part of a leaf receives light, does the whole leaf perform photosynthesis? What if a leaf receives only light of one color? You are going to design an experiment to test the effects of colored light on photosynthesis.

Problem How do different colors of light affect starch synthesis during photosynthesis?

Materials

- scissors
- black construction paper
- potted plant
- tape
- blue, red, and green cellophane
- 5 large test tubes
- glass-marking pencil
- forceps
- 400-mL beaker
- 5 petri dishes
- iodine solution
- paper towels

Skills Predicting, Formulating Hypotheses

Design Your Experiment

1. **Predicting** As a result of photosynthesis, new starch molecules are synthesized and accumulate in leaves. Record your prediction of how keeping part of a leaf in darkness will affect starch synthesis.
2. Cut two pieces of black construction paper large enough to cover half of one leaf of the plant.
3. Sandwich half of the leaf between the pieces of black paper and tape the paper in place.
4. **Formulating Hypotheses** Develop a hypothesis that predicts how the color of light will affect photosynthesis. Record your hypothesis.
5. Design an experiment to test your hypothesis. Refer to the Lab Tips box on page 55. Have your teacher check your plan. Set up your experiment using whole leaves from the same plant as in step 3.
6. Leave your plant in a sunlit area for 2 days.
7. Cut off one leaf that was not treated as well as each of the experimental leaves, including the half-covered leaf. Roll up each leaf and put it in a large test tube. Label each tube and petri dish with the treatment the leaf received.
8. Put on your goggles and lab apron. Before you test the leaves for starch, the chlorophyll must be removed from the leaves. Your teacher will add alcohol to your test tubes and heat them in hot water. **CAUTION:** *Alcohol is toxic and flammable, and its fumes are irritating.* When the color has disappeared from each leaf, use forceps to swirl each leaf in a beaker of water. Place it in a labeled petri dish.
9. Put on your plastic gloves. Cover each leaf with iodine solution. Iodine solution stains starch blue or black. **CAUTION:** *Iodine is corrosive and irritating to the skin and can stain clothes and skin. Be careful not to spill it.*
10. After 1 minute, use forceps to gently swirl each leaf in the beaker of water and lay the leaf flat on a paper towel.
11. Observe each leaf and record your observations. Wash your hands before leaving the lab.

Analyze and Conclude

1. **Observing** Was your prediction about starch synthesis in the part of the first leaf covered in black paper correct? Explain your answer.
2. **Observing** What effect did each color of light have on starch synthesis in the leaves? Was your hypothesis correct?
3. **Communicating Results** Use your knowledge of chlorophyll to explain your results.

Go Further

Designing Experiments Where is starch found in the multicolored leaves of a coleus plant? Use your observations to propose a hypothesis. With your teacher's approval, perform an experiment to test your hypothesis. Explain your results.

Analyze and Conclude

1. The uncovered leaf and the leaves covered with red and blue cellophane contain starch, while the leaves covered with black paper or green cellophane contain little or no starch. Black paper or green cellophane prevents the right color of light from reaching the chlorophyll, preventing photosynthesis and thus starch synthesis.
2. The blue and red cellophane did not affect starch synthesis. The green cellophane reduced the amount of starch produced by the leaf. Students should explain why their hypothesis was or was not correct.
3. Chlorophyll absorbs red and blue light, but not green light. The leaves covered by red and blue cellophane received the energy they needed for photosynthesis to occur and produced starch. The leaf covered by green cellophane received little light energy that the chlorophyll could use, and thus produced little starch.

Design an Experiment

BIIE 1.d

Objective Students will be able to relate the effectiveness of different colors of light in photosynthesis to the absorption spectrum of chlorophyll. L2 L3

Skills Focus Predicting, Formulating Hypotheses

Time 30 minutes on each of two days

Advance Prep Use geraniums (or other uniformly green-leafed plants) with plenty of leaves so that covering and removing leaves will not harm the plants. Keep the plants in darkness for about two days before the activity begins to remove any starch stored in the leaves. Construct a hot-water bath by placing students' test tubes in a large beaker of water on a hot plate.

Safety Read the safety information in the MSDS for alcohol and iodine before doing the lab. Heat the sample tubes in a hot-water bath in a fume hood or other well-ventilated area. Wear safety goggles and heat-resistant gloves when handling the hot-water bath. Spilled iodine can be removed from skin and clothing with a solution of 12.5 g/L of sodium thiosulfate ($Na_2S_2O_3$—photographer's "hypo").

Teaching Tips

- In step 5, the cellophane should not cover the leaves so tightly that gas exchange is blocked.
- To save time, you can dispense with test tubes and heat all leaves that are treated identically as a batch in one beaker of alcohol.

Expected Outcome Leaves that are not covered or are covered by red or blue cellophane contain starch. Leaves that are covered by black paper or green cellophane contain little or no starch.

Go Further

Most students' experiments will involve testing different locations on a coleus leaf for the presence of starch. Students should find that the green leaf parts contain starch, while the white leaf parts do not, because only the green parts contain chlorophyll.

Chapter 8 Study Guide

Study Tip

Divide the class into pairs and have students quiz each other about the Vocabulary words and Key Concepts.

Thinking Visually

1. Light
2. Light-dependent reactions
3. NADPH
4. Carbon dioxide
5. Sugars

Chapter 8 Assessment

Reviewing Content

1. b	5. c	9. b
2. b	6. a	10. a
3. b	7. d	
4. d	8. a	

Understanding Concepts

11. Autotrophs are able to obtain energy by making their own food. Heterotrophs obtain their energy by consuming food.

12. An ATP molecule consists of a nitrogen-containing compound called adenine, a sugar called ribose, and three phosphate groups.

13. ATP resembles a fully charged battery because it can yield energy when the third phosphate group is removed, also forming ADP. ADP is like a partially charged battery that can be recharged when energy is added to link a third phosphate group, reforming ATP.

14. A single molecule of glucose stores more than 90 times the energy stored by ATP. However, ATP, which transfers energy quickly, is used by the cell as an immediate source of energy.

15. Priestley discovered that plants produce a substance needed to burn candles, now known to be oxygen. Ingenhousz found that plants produce oxygen only when exposed to light.

16. Carbon dioxide + water → sugars + oxygen

17. Plant pigments absorb energy from light and transfer it to electrons involved in photosynthesis.

Chapter 8 Study Guide

8–1 Energy and Life

 **Key Concepts**

- Plants and some other types of organisms are able to use light energy from the sun to produce food.
- The characteristics of ATP make it exceptionally useful as the basic energy source of all cells.

Vocabulary
autotroph, p. 201
heterotroph, p. 201
adenosine triphosphate (ATP), p. 202

8–2 Photosynthesis: An Overview

 **Key Concepts**  7 1.d, BIIE 1.k

- The experiments performed by van Helmont, Priestley, and Ingenhousz led to work by other scientists who finally discovered that in the presence of light, plants transform carbon dioxide and water into carbohydrates, and they also release oxygen.
- Photosynthesis uses the energy of sunlight to convert water and carbon dioxide into high-energy sugars and oxygen.
- In addition to water and carbon dioxide, photosynthesis requires light and chlorophyll, a molecule found in chloroplasts.

Vocabulary
photosynthesis, p. 204
pigment, p. 207
chlorophyll, p. 207

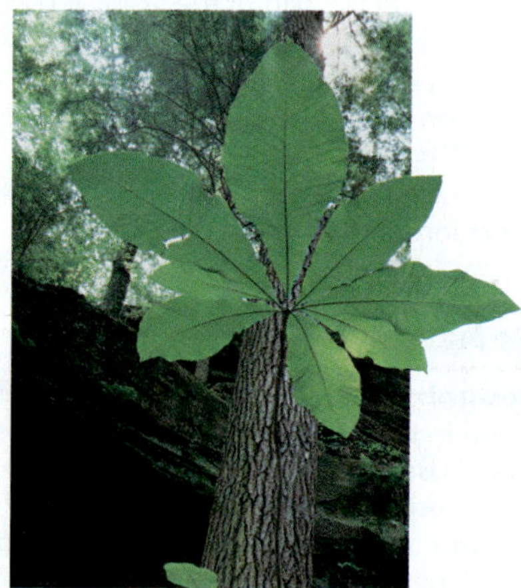

8–3 The Reactions of Photosynthesis

 **Key Concepts**  BI 1.f, *BI 1.i

- The process of photosynthesis includes the light-dependent reactions as well as the Calvin cycle.
- The light-dependent reactions produce oxygen gas and convert ADP and NADP+ into ATP and NADPH. The light-dependent reactions occur in the thylakoid.
- The Calvin cycle uses ATP and NADPH from the light-dependent reactions to produce high-energy sugars. The Calvin cycle is also known as the light-independent reactions.

Vocabulary
thylakoid, p. 208
photosystem, p. 208
stroma, p. 208
NADP+, p. 209
light-dependent reactions, p. 210
ATP synthase, p. 210
Calvin cycle, p. 212

Thinking Visually

Using the information in this chapter, complete the following flowchart about photosynthesis:

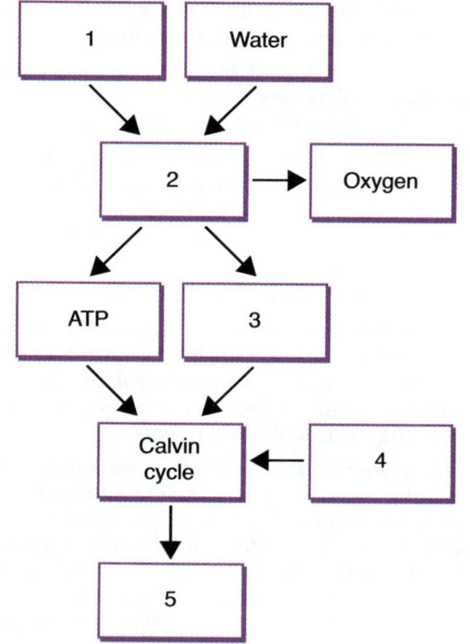

TIME SAVER — CHAPTER RESOURCES

Print:
- ***Teaching Resources,*** Chapter Vocabulary Review, Graphic Organizer, Chapter 8 Tests: Levels A and B

Technology:
- ***Computer Test Bank,*** Chapter 8 Test
- ***iText,*** Chapter 8 Assessment

Chapter 8 Assessment

Reviewing Content

Choose the letter that best answers the question or completes the statement.

1. Which of the following are autotrophs?
   a. impalas
   b. plants
   c. leopards
   d. mushrooms
2. One of the principal chemical compounds that living things use to store energy is
   a. DNA.
   b. ATP.
   c. H_2O.
   d. CO_2.
3. Which scientist concluded that most of a growing plant's mass comes from water?
   a. Priestley
   b. van Helmont
   c. Ingenhousz
   d. Calvin
4. In addition to light and chlorophyll, photosynthesis requires
   a. water and oxygen.
   b. water and sugars.
   c. oxygen and carbon dioxide.
   d. water and carbon dioxide.
5. The leaves of a plant appear green because chlorophyll
   a. reflects blue light.
   b. absorbs blue light.
   c. reflects green light.
   d. absorbs green light.
6. The products of photosynthesis are
   a. sugars and oxygen.
   b. sugars and carbon dioxide.
   c. water and carbon dioxide.
   d. hydrogen and oxygen.
7. Which organelle contains chlorophyll?

a. 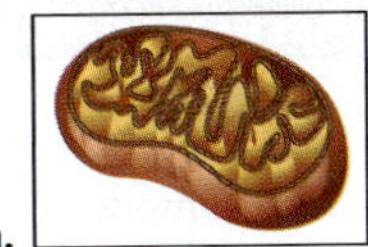

c. 

b. 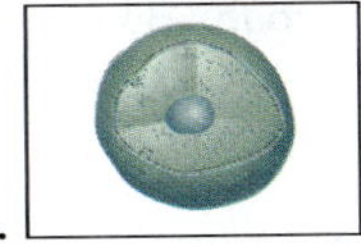

d. 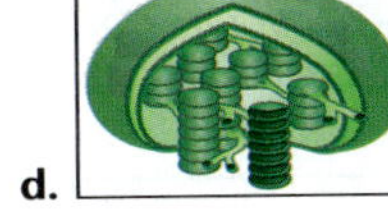

8. The first process in the light-dependent reactions of photosynthesis is
   a. light absorption.
   b. electron transport.
   c. oxygen production.
   d. ATP formation.

Interactive textbook with assessment at PHSchool.com 

9. Which substance from the light-dependent reactions of photosynthesis is a source of energy for the Calvin cycle?
   a. ADP
   b. NADPH
   c. H_2O
   d. pyruvic acid
10. The light-independent reactions of photosynthesis are also known as the
    a. Calvin cycle.
    b. Priestley cycle.
    c. Ingenhousz cycle.
    d. van Helmont cycle.

Understanding Concepts

11. How do heterotrophs and autotrophs differ in the way they obtain energy?
12. Describe the three parts of an ATP molecule.
13. Use the analogy of a battery to explain how energy is stored in and released from ATP.
14. Compare the amounts of energy stored by ATP and glucose. Which compound is used by the cell as an immediate source of energy?
15. How were Priestley's and Ingenhousz's discoveries about photosynthesis related?
16. Write the basic equation for photosynthesis using the names of the starting and final substances of the process.
17. What role do plant pigments play in the process of photosynthesis?
18. Identify the structures labeled A, B, C, and D. In which structure(s) do the light-dependent reactions occur? In which structure(s) does the Calvin cycle take place?

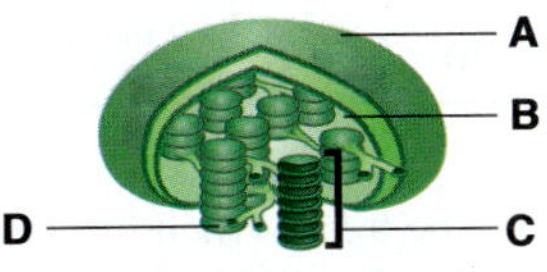

19. Explain the role of $NADP^+$ as an energy carrier in photosynthesis.
20. What is the role of ATP synthase? How does it work?
21. Summarize what happens during the Calvin cycle.
22. How do the events in the Calvin cycle depend on the light-dependent reactions?
23. Describe three factors that affect the rate at which photosynthesis occurs.

If your class subscribes to the iText, your students can go online to access an interactive version of the Student Edition and a self-test.

(Continued from page 216)

18. A: chloroplast; B: stroma; C: granum; D: thylakoid. The light-dependent reactions take place in the thylakoids. The Calvin cycle takes place in the stroma.
19. $NADP^+$ carries energy by holding two electrons and a hydrogen ion. It carries the stored energy to other reactions that help build sugar molecules.
20. ATP synthase is a protein found in the thylakoid membrane that allows H^+ ions to pass through it. As H^+ ions pass through this protein, it rotates and binds ADP and a phosphate group together to produce ATP.
21. During the Calvin cycle, plants use the energy that ATP and NADPH contain to build high-energy compounds that can be stored for a long time. The Calvin cycle uses six molecules of carbon dioxide to produce a single 6-carbon sugar molecule.
22. The Calvin cycle uses the ATP and NADPH produced during the light-dependent reactions to produce high-energy sugars.
23. Factors that affect the rate of photosynthesis include the temperature, the amount of available water, and the intensity of light.

HOMEWORK GUIDE

Section:	Questions:
Section 8–1	1, 2, 11–14
Section 8–2	3–6, 15–17, 24, 27, 28, 30
Section 8–3	7–10, 18–23, 25, 26, 29

Chapter 8 Assessment

Critical Thinking

24. The chlorophyll may be broken down by the cooling temperatures or the changing light, so the green color disappears. The leaf then shows the color of its remaining pigment(s).

25. Some students may build on the analogy of the battery from the chapter. Others may develop a new analogy. For example, ADP is like a ball at the bottom of the hill. Moving the ball to the top of the hill is like adding a phosphate group and making ATP. The ball now has the energy to roll downhill and move other objects in its path. ATP has energy to help change molecules.

26. No step of the Calvin cycle depends directly on light. Instead, it uses energy stored in the molecules ATP and NADPH.

27. Students' answers may include: Start with two samples of the same amount and type of pond algae in water. Put one sample in the dark and the other in a location that receives daylight, keeping the temperatures the same. After two weeks, compare the two samples to determine the amount and health of the algae.

28. a. The graph shows a curve that descends from left to right. The farther the light is from the plant, the fewer bubbles are produced.
b. 10 cm. **c.** The closer the plant is to the light, the more oxygen is produced. This occurs because more light energy is reaching the algae cells and thus is available for photosynthesis.

29. At first, photosynthesis would take place during daylight, but it would stop when the water was used up. If no more water was added, the plant might die.

30. Because the Indian pipe plant has no chlorophyll or other pigment involved in photosynthesis, it probably cannot make its own food. Therefore, it must obtain food from other sources the way a heterotroph does. Perhaps it absorbs partly decayed food in the soil.

Chapter 8 Assessment

Critical Thinking

24. Formulating Hypotheses Some plant leaves contain yellow and red pigments as well as chlorophyll. In the fall, those leaves may become red or yellow. Suggest an explanation for those color changes.

25. Using Analogies Develop an analogy to explain ATP and energy transfer to a classmate who does not understand the concept.

26. Interpreting Graphics The Calvin cycle is sometimes described as the light-independent reactions. Study **Figure 8–11** on page 212 and give evidence to support the idea that the Calvin cycle does not depend on light.

27. Designing Experiments Design an experiment that uses pond water and algae to demonstrate the importance of light energy to pond life. Be sure to identify the variables you will control and the variable you will change.

28. Using Tables and Graphs A water plant placed in a bright light gives off bubbles of oxygen. In the laboratory, you notice that if the light is placed at different distances from the plant, the rate at which the plant produces bubbles changes. Your data are shown in the following table.

Oxygen Production

Distance From Light (cm)	Bubbles Produced per Minute
10	39
20	22
30	8
40	5

a. On graph paper, plot the data on a line graph. Describe the trend. When the light was farther from the plant, did the number of bubbles produced increase or decrease? Explain.

b. At what distance is gas production at its highest?

c. What relationship exists between the distance from the plant to the light and the number of bubbles produced? Explain your answer.

29. Predicting Suppose you water a potted plant and place it by a window in an airtight jar. Predict when photosynthesis might occur over the next few days. Would you expect the pattern to change if the plant were left there for several weeks? Explain.

30. Inferring Examine the photograph of the Indian pipe plant shown below. What can you conclude about the ability of the Indian pipe plant to make its own food? Explain your answer.

Matter and Energy Recall what you learned about the flow of energy through an ecosystem. Explain how photosynthesis relates to that flow.

Writing in Science

Imagine that you are an oxygen atom and two of your friends are hydrogen atoms. Together, you make up a water molecule. Describe the events and changes that happen to you and your friends as you journey through the light-dependent reactions and Calvin cycle of photosynthesis. Include illustrations with your description.

Performance-Based Assessment

Making Models Construct a two- or three-dimensional model of an ATP molecule. Label the various parts of the molecule. Use the model to explain how ATP is broken down into ADP and AMP. (AMP contains one phosphate group.) How does your model change?

Go Online
PHSchool.com
For: An interactive self-test
Visit: PHSchool.com
Web Code: cba-3080

In autotrophs, the process of photosynthesis captures energy from sunlight and uses it to produce high-energy sugars. This energy passes from one organism to another in an ecosystem as organisms eat and are eaten.

Writing in Science

Stories and illustrations will vary. Students should recognize that both the oxygen atom and the hydrogen atoms enter a chloroplast together as a molecule of water: H_2O. The oxygen atom will split from the hydrogen atoms in the first stage of photosynthesis and leave the plant as oxygen gas. The hydrogen atoms will become involved in the formation of NADPH, the production of ATP, and the production of high-energy sugars in the Calvin cycle.

Standards Practice

Test-Taking Tip

When a paragraph and some related questions accompany a diagram, read the paragraph and all of the labels carefully. For example, in questions 7–9, the paragraph tells you that the drops of pigment were placed at the bottom of the strip. This information helps you interpret the events represented by the diagram.

Directions: Choose the letter that best answers the question or completes the statement.

1. The principal pigment in plants that captures sunlight energy is **7 1.d**
   - **A** chlorophyll.
   - **B** oxygen.
   - **C** ADP.
   - **D** ATP.
2. Which of the following is NOT produced in the light-dependent reactions of photosynthesis?
   - **A** NADPH
   - **B** sugars
   - **C** hydrogen ions
   - **D** ATP
3. Which equation best summarizes the process of photosynthesis? **BI 1.f**
   - **A** water + carbon dioxide $\xrightarrow{\text{light}}$ sugars + oxygen
   - **B** sugars + oxygen $\xrightarrow{\text{light}}$ water + carbon
   - **C** water + oxygen $\xrightarrow{\text{light}}$ sugars + carbon dioxide
   - **D** oxygen + carbon dioxide $\xrightarrow{\text{light}}$ sugars + oxygen
4. The color of light that is LEAST useful to a plant during photosynthesis is
   - **A** red.
   - **B** blue.
   - **C** green.
   - **D** orange.
5. The first step in photosynthesis is the
   - **A** synthesis of water.
   - **B** production of oxygen.
   - **C** formation of ATP.
   - **D** absorption of light energy.
6. In a typical plant, all of the following factors are necessary for photosynthesis EXCEPT
   - **A** chlorophyll.
   - **B** light.
   - **C** oxygen.
   - **D** carbon dioxide.

Questions 7–9

Several drops of concentrated pigment were extracted from spinach leaves. These drops were placed at the bottom of a strip of highly absorbent paper. After the extract dried, the paper was suspended in a test tube containing alcohol so that only the tip of the paper was in the alcohol. As the alcohol was absorbed and moved up the paper, the various pigments contained in the extract separated as shown in the diagram below.

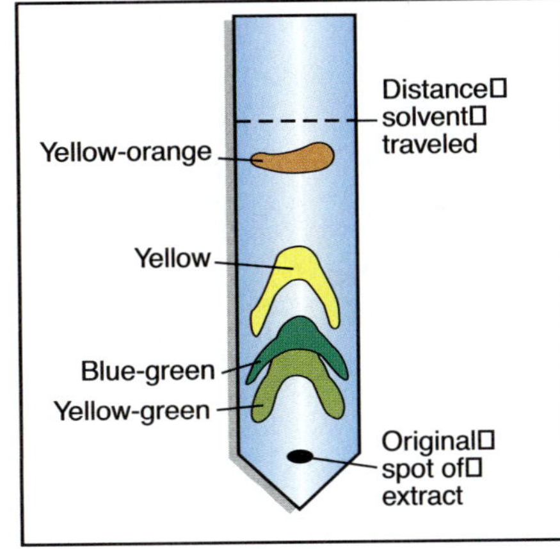

7. Which pigment traveled the shortest distance?
   - **A** yellow-orange
   - **B** yellow
   - **C** blue-green
   - **D** yellow-green
8. A valid conclusion that can be drawn from this information is that spinach leaves
   - **A** use only chlorophyll during photosynthesis.
   - **B** contain several pigments.
   - **C** contain more orange pigment than yellow pigment.
   - **D** are yellow-orange rather than green.
9. In which organelles would most of these pigments be found?
   - **A** vacuoles
   - **B** centrioles
   - **C** mitochondria
   - **D** chloroplasts

Standards Practice

1. A **4.** C **7.** D
2. B **5.** D **8.** B
3. A **6.** C **9.** D

Online at PHSchool.com

Have students check their understanding of the chapter by logging onto Success Tracker.

Performance-Based Assessment

Students may use modeling compound, toothpicks, pipe cleaners, or similar materials to construct a three-dimensional model of ATP, or they may simply use pencil and paper to make a two-dimensional model. The model of ATP should be similar to the depictions of ATP shown in Figure 8–2 and Figure 8–3. When ATP is broken down into ADP, the ADP compound has only two phosphate groups rather than the three of ATP. Students' models of ADP should be similar to that shown in Figure 8–3. Students should infer that AMP is an abbreviation for adenosine monophosphate. A model of AMP, then, should show only one phosphate group.

Your students can independently test their knowledge of the chapter and print their test results for your files.

Chapter Planner 9 Cellular Respiration

Section and Section Objectives	Time	STANDARDS NCLB	STANDARDS Biology	Activities and Labs
9–1 Chemical Pathways, pp. 221–225 ***9.1.1*** ***Explain*** what cellular respiration is. ***9.1.2*** ***Describe*** what happens during the process of glycolysis. ***9.1.3*** ***Name*** the two main types of fermentation.	2 periods (1 block)		BI 1.g	**SE:** ***Inquiry Activity,*** How do living things release energy?, p. 220 L2 **TE:** ***Build Science Skills,*** p. 224 L1 L2 **SE:** ***Problem Solving,*** A Family Recipe, p. 224 L2 L3 **SE:** ***Real-World Lab,*** Investigating Fermentation by Making Kimchi, pp. 234–235 L2 L3 **BTM:** Lab 1 **PLM:** Investigating Fermentation by Making Kimchi L1 L2 L3
9–2 The Krebs Cycle and Electron Transport, pp. 226–232 ***9.2.1*** ***Describe*** what happens during the Krebs cycle. ***9.2.2*** ***Explain*** how high-energy electrons are used by the electron transport chain. ***9.2.3*** ***Identify*** three pathways the body uses to release energy during exercise. ***9.2.4*** ***Compare*** photosynthesis and cellular respiration.	3 periods (1–1/2 blocks)	7 1.d	*BI 1.i	**TE:** ***Demonstration,*** p. 226 L2 **SE:** ***Quick Lab,*** How does exercise affect disposal of wastes from cellular respiration?, p. 231 L2 **SE:** ***Issues in Biology,*** Should Creatine Supplements Be Banned?, p. 233 L2 **LMA:** Chapter 9 Lab L2 L3 **LMB:** Chapter 9 Lab L1 L2 **PLM:** How does exercise affect disposal of wastes from cellular respiration? L1 L2 L3
Chapter Assessment, pp. 236–239	1 period (1/2 block)			

ACTIVITY PLANNER

SE: ***Inquiry Activity,*** p. 220; 15 min.; an electrical device such as a pencil sharpener, a chemically fueled device such as a candle, a live or preserved animal, a small plant in an opaque container

TE: ***Build Science Skills,*** p. 224; 5 min.; piece of leavened bread, piece of unleavened bread

TE: ***Demonstration,*** p. 226; 10 min.; clear glass beaker, bromthymol blue solution, a drinking straw

SE: ***Quick Lab,*** p. 231; 15 min.; 2 small test tubes, glass-marking pencil, 10-mL graduated cylinder, bromthymol blue solution, 2 straws, clock or watch with second hand

SE: ***Real-World Lab,*** pp. 234–235; 40 min., weekly follow-up; 2 resealable plastic sandwich bags, chopped Chinese cabbage, noniodized salt, 2.5-mL (1/2 teaspoon) measuring spoon, pH-indicator paper, thermometer

PLANNING KEY

Ability Levels
for students performing . . .
below grade level L1
at grade level L2
above grade level L3

Print Components

SE	Student Edition	**LA**	Lab Assessment
TE	Teacher's Edition	**BTM**	Biotechnology Manual
RSW	Reading & Study Workbook A	**IDM**	Issues and Decision Making
ARSW	Adapted Reading & Study Workbook B	**LW**	Lab Worksheets
TR	Teaching Resources	**LMA**	Laboratory Manual A
IF	Investigations in Forensics	**LMB**	Laboratory Manual B

Tech Components

CTB	Computer Test Bank
BD	BioDetectives DVD
TP	Transparencies Plus
PLM	Probeware Lab Manual
ABC	ABC DVD Library
LS	Lab Simulations
VL	Virtual Labs

Interactive textbook with assessment at PHSchool.com

Program Resources	Assessment	Media and Technology
TR: Lesson Plan 9–1, Section Summary, p. 90 L1, p. 99 L2, Worksheets, pp. 92–94 L1, pp. 101–103 L2, Enrichment L2 L3 **LW:** Chapter 9 Real-World Lab L1 L2 L3 **RSW:** Section 9–1 L2 **ARSW:** Section 9–1 L1	**SE:** 9–1 Section Assessment, p. 225 **TR:** Section Review 9–1	**iText:** Section 9–1 **TP:** 9–1, Interest Grabber, Section Outline, Chemical Pathways, Figure 9–2, Figure 9–3, Figure 9–4 **ABC:** 13 Glycolysis **Lab Simulations CD-ROM:** Cell Respiration
TR: Lesson Plan 9–2, Section Summary, p. 91 L1, p. 99 L2, Worksheets, pp. 95–97 L1, pp. 104–107 L2 **RSW:** Section 9–2 L2 **ARSW:** Section 9–2 L1	**SE:** 9–2 Section Assessment, p. 232 **TR:** Section Review 9–2	**iText:** Section 9–2 **TP:** 9–2 Interest Grabber, Section Outline, Flowchart, Figure 9–6, Figure 9–7 **ABC:** 12 Aerobic Respiration, 14 Krebs Cycle, 15 Electron Transport Chain **Lab Simulations CD-ROM:** Cell Respiration **VL:** Lab 8
	SE: Chapter 9 Assessment, pp. 236–239 **TR:** Chapter Vocabulary Review, Graphic Organizer, Chapter 9 Test	**iText:** Chapter 9 Assessment **CTB:** Chapter 9 Test **Go Online** Students can do research, share data, and test their knowledge online.

PRESSED FOR TIME?

To Preview the Chapter
- Introduce students to Key Concepts and Vocabulary terms in each section.
- Assign the Reading Strategies for each section.

To Cover the Chapter Quickly
- Have students read all of Section 9–1, Figures 9–6 and 9–7, and Comparing Photosynthesis and Cellular Respiration in Section 9–2.
- Assign the Section Reviews for 9–1 and 9–2, questions 1–10 in Chapter 9 Assessment, and questions 1–9 in Chapter 9 Standards Practice.

To Review the Chapter
- Assign the Section Reviews for 9–1 and 9–2 in the Reading and Study Workbook or Adapted Reading and Study Workbook.
- Assign Section Reviews for 9–1 and 9–2 and the Chapter Vocabulary Review for Chapter 9 in the Teaching Resources.

CHAPTER 9

ENGAGE/EXPLORE

Inquiry Activity

Objective Students will be able to formulate hypotheses for how organisms release energy from food. L2

Skills Focus Using Tables and Graphs, Formulating Hypotheses

Materials an electrical device such as a pencil sharpener, a chemically fueled device such as a candle, a live or preserved animal, a small plant in an opaque container

Time 15 minutes

Advance Prep Decide in advance which items will be provided to each group or student. To stimulate discussion, provide different examples of each type of item to different groups or students.

Safety If you provide some kind of flame-producing device, do not permit matches or other fire hazards to be present in the room.

Strategies

- Display a blank table with labeled columns on the board or with an overhead projector.
- Present items in order of difficulty, such as: electrical device, chemically fueled device, animal specimen, plant.

Expected Outcomes Students will identify the energy sources of various living and nonliving things. They will also identify the energy-releasing mechanisms of nonliving things and speculate about how living things release energy.

Think About It

1. Students will find it easier to describe how nonliving things use energy because the energy sources those things use are familiar to students.
2. Responses will vary depending on students' prior knowledge. Typical answers might include food, carbohydrates, and glucose.
3. A typical hypothesis might suggest that living things release energy from food through a chemical process within cells.

CHAPTER 9

Cellular Respiration

Athletes get the energy they need from the breakdown of glucose during cellular respiration.

Inquiry Activity

How do living things release energy?

Procedure

1. Draw a table with 5 rows and 4 columns. Label the columns from left to right: Item, Activities, Energy Source, and How Energy Is Released.
2. Fill in each row of your table for every item your teacher provides. List yourself as the last item and complete that row.

Think About It

1. **Using Tables and Graphs** Was it easier to describe how living things use energy or how nonliving things use energy?
2. **Using Tables and Graphs** What is the most common energy source for living things?
3. **Formulating Hypotheses** How do you think living things release the energy they need?

FACTS AND FIGURES

Respiration—converting ADP into ATP
Organisms pay a price in energy for the cellular work they do, including movement, molecular synthesis, active transport, and so on. Most of the energy used is gained through the conversion of ATP molecules into ADP molecules. To keep everything going, cells must convert the ADP molecules back into ATP molecules, and they do this mostly through the process of cellular respiration. For example, a working muscle cell converts ADP into ATP at a rate of about 10 million molecules per second. To accomplish this conversion, cells use the chemical energy stored in food.

9–1 Chemical Pathways

BI 1.g. Students know the role of the mitochondria in making stored chemical-bond energy available to cells by completing the breakdown of glucose to carbon dioxide.

When you are hungry, how do you feel? If you are like most people, your stomach may seem empty, you might feel a little dizzy, and above all, you feel weak. The sensations produced by hunger may vary, but the bottom line is always the same. Our bodies have a way of telling us when we need food.

Food provides living things with the chemical building blocks they need to grow and reproduce. Food serves as a source of raw materials for the cells of the body. Most of all, food serves as a source of energy.

Chemical Energy and Food

How much energy is actually present in food? Quite a lot, although it varies with the type of food, since our cells can use all sorts of molecules as food, including fats, sugars, and proteins. One gram of the sugar glucose ($C_6H_{12}O_6$), when burned in the presence of oxygen, releases 3811 calories of heat energy. A **calorie** is the amount of energy needed to raise the temperature of 1 gram of water 1 degree Celsius. The Calorie (capital "C") that is used on food labels is a kilocalorie, or 1000 calories. Cells, of course, don't "burn" glucose. Instead, they gradually release the energy from glucose and other food compounds.

This process begins with a pathway called **glycolysis** (gly-KAHL-ih-sis). Glycolysis releases only a small amount of energy. If oxygen is present, glycolysis leads to two other pathways that release a great deal of energy. If oxygen is not present, however, glycolysis is followed by a different pathway.

Guide for Reading

Key Concepts
- What is cellular respiration?
- What happens during the process of glycolysis?
- What are the two main types of fermentation?

Vocabulary
calorie
glycolysis
cellular respiration
NAD^+
fermentation
anaerobic

Reading Strategy: Asking Questions Before you read this section, rewrite the headings as *how, why,* or *what* questions about releasing energy. Then, as you read, write brief answers to your questions.

Figure 9–1 Living things get the energy they need from food. Both plant and animal cells carry out the final stages of cellular respiration in the mitochondria.

Animal
Plant
Animal Cells (magnification: 2500×)
Plant Cells (magnification: 500×)
Outer membrane
Intermembrane space
Inner membrane
Matrix
Mitochondrion
Mitochondrion (magnification: about 10,000×)

TIME SAVER

SECTION RESOURCES

Print:
- ***Teaching Resources,*** Lesson Plan 9–1, Adapted Section Summary 9–1, Adapted Worksheets 9–1, Section Summary 9–1, Worksheets 9–1, Section Review 9–1, Enrichment
- ***Reading and Study Workbook A,*** Section 9–1
- ***Adapted Reading and Study Workbook B,*** Section 9–1
- ***Biotechnology Manual,*** Lab 1
- ***Probeware Lab Manual,*** Investigating Fermentation by Making Kimchi
- ***Lab Worksheets,*** Chapter 9 Real-World Lab

Technology:
- ***iText,*** Section 9–1
- ***Animated Biological Concepts DVD,*** 13 Glycolysis
- ***Transparencies Plus,*** Section 9–1
- ***Lab Simulations CD-ROM,*** Cell Respiration

Section 9–1

 **BI 1.g**

1 FOCUS

Objectives

9.1.1 ***Explain*** what cellular respiration is.
9.1.2 ***Describe*** what happens during the process of glycolysis.
9.1.3 ***Name*** the two main types of fermentation.

Guide for Reading

Vocabulary Preview

Call on volunteers to pronounce the section's Vocabulary words. Correct any mispronunciations, and then have all students pronounce each word together.

Reading Strategy

Students should write a question for each head and subhead. For example, they might write, "How are chemical energy and food related?" Encourage students to write an answer to each question as they read the section.

2 INSTRUCT

Chemical Energy and Food

Use Visuals

Figure 9–1 Ask: **Would it be correct to say that only animal cells contain mitochondria?** *(No; both plant and animal cells contain mitochondria.)* Help students recall from Chapter 7 that all eukaryotic cells contain mitochondria, including plant and algal cells. Ask: **How is this cell organelle separated from the cytoplasm of the cell?** *(By an outer membrane)* **How would you describe the inner mitochondrial membrane?** *(It is convoluted, with many turns and folds.)* **What is the space between the inner and outer membranes called?** *(Intermembrane space)* L1 L2

9–1 (continued)

Overview of Cellular Respiration

Build Science Skills

Applying Concepts To reinforce where important reactions take place within cells, draw a large cell on the board. Within the cell, draw a nucleus, a chloroplast, and a mitochondrion. Then, ask students to point to and identify where in the cell photosynthesis occurs *(chloroplast)*, glycolysis occurs *(cytoplasm)*, and cellular respiration occurs *(mitochondrion)*. L1 L2

Use Visuals

Figure 9–2 Have students study the figure. Then, ask: **Where does the glucose used in respiration come from?** *(Cells obtain glucose mainly by breaking down carbohydrates such as starch.)* **How do you know that this series of reactions occurs in the presence of oxygen?** *(If there were no oxygen present, then fermentation would occur, not cellular respiration.)* **What does glycolysis supply to the Krebs cycle and to the electron transport chain?** *(It supplies pyruvic acid to the Krebs cycle and high-energy electrons via NADH to the electron transport chain.)* **What stages of cellular respiration occur in mitochondria?** *(The Krebs cycle and the electron transport chain)* L1 L2

For: Cellular Respiration activity
Visit: PHSchool.com
Web Code: cbe-3091
Students interact with the process of cellular respiration.

CELLULAR RESPIRATION: AN OVERVIEW

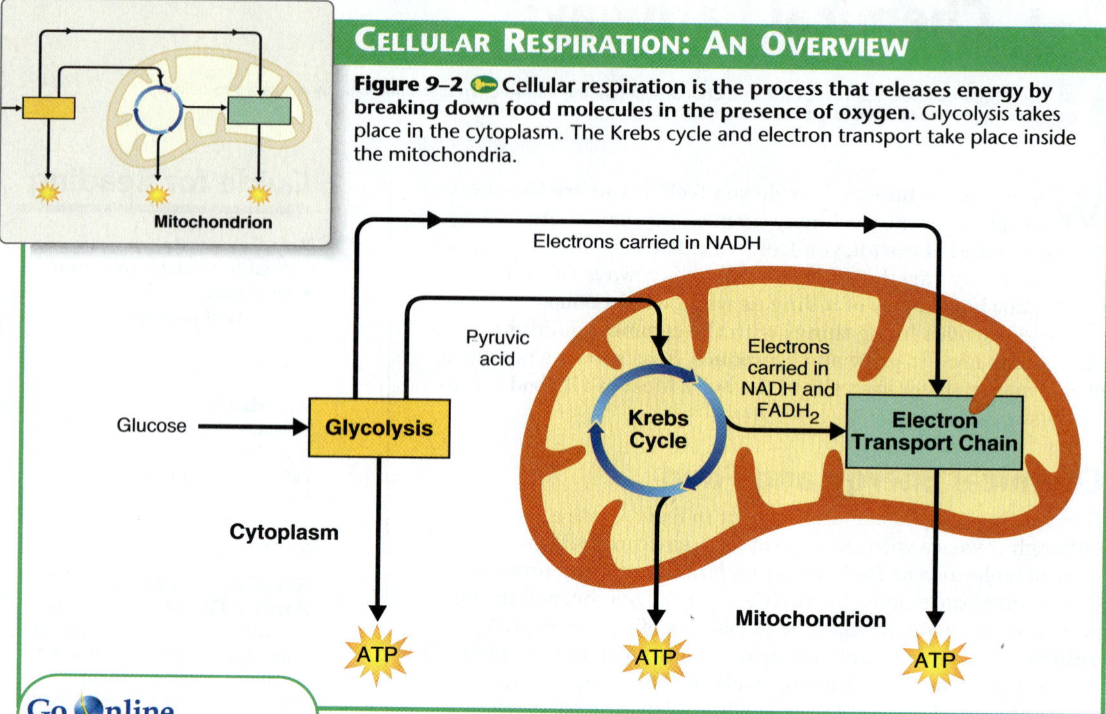

Figure 9–2 **Cellular respiration is the process that releases energy by breaking down food molecules in the presence of oxygen.** Glycolysis takes place in the cytoplasm. The Krebs cycle and electron transport take place inside the mitochondria.

Go Online active art
For: Cellular Respiration activity
Visit: PHSchool.com
Web Code: cbp-3091

Overview of Cellular Respiration

In the presence of oxygen, glycolysis is followed by the Krebs cycle and the electron transport chain. Glycolysis, the Krebs cycle, and the electron transport chain make up a process called **cellular respiration.** **Cellular respiration is the process that releases energy by breaking down glucose and other food molecules in the presence of oxygen.** The equation for cellular respiration is:

$$6O_2 + C_6H_{12}O_6 \longrightarrow 6CO_2 + 6H_2O + \text{Energy}$$

$$\text{oxygen} + \text{glucose} \longrightarrow \text{carbon dioxide} + \text{water} + \text{energy}$$

As you can see, cellular respiration requires oxygen, a food molecule such as glucose, and gives off carbon dioxide, water, and energy. Do not be misled, however, by the simplicity of this equation. If cellular respiration took place in just one step, all of the energy from glucose would be released at once, and most of it would be lost in the form of light and heat. Clearly, a living cell has to control that energy. It can't simply start a fire—it has to release the explosive chemical energy in food molecules a little bit at a time. The cell needs to find a way to trap those little bits of energy by using them to make ATP.

The three main stages of cellular respiration are shown in **Figure 9–2.** Each of the three stages captures some of the chemical energy available in food molecules and uses it to produce ATP.

ESL SUPPORT FOR ENGLISH LANGUAGE LEARNERS

Comprehension: Ask Questions

Beginning Write the chemical equation for cellular respiration on the board. Place labels under each of the molecules in the reaction, as shown on page 222. Read the equation aloud, pointing to the chemical symbols and the corresponding words as you do so. Explain the equation. Then, ask the students questions that can be answered orally or by pointing at the correct answer. For example, "What is one product of cellular respiration?" When students answer correctly, reinforce their comprehension by repeating the word they said or, if they pointed, saying the word aloud yourself. L1

Intermediate After students complete the beginning-level activity, ask questions that cannot be answered directly from the information on the board, for example, "What part of the equation represents the food you ate (will eat) at lunch today?" L2

Glycolysis

The first set of reactions in cellular respiration is glycolysis. **Glycolysis is the process in which one molecule of glucose is broken in half, producing two molecules of pyruvic acid, a 3-carbon compound.** The process of glycolysis is shown in **Figure 9–3.**

ATP Production Even though glycolysis is an energy-releasing process, the cell needs to put in a little energy to get things going. At the pathway's beginning, 2 molecules of ATP are used up. In a way, those 2 ATP molecules are like an investment that pays back interest. In order to earn interest from a bank, first you have to put money into an account. Although the cell puts 2 ATP molecules into its "account" to get glycolysis going, when glycolysis is complete, 4 ATP molecules have been produced. This gives the cell a net gain of 2 ATP molecules.

NADH Production One of the reactions of glycolysis removes 4 high-energy electrons and passes them to an electron carrier called **NAD^+,** or nicotinamide adenine dinucleotide. Like $NADP^+$ in photosynthesis, each NAD^+ accepts a pair of high-energy electrons. This molecule, known as NADH, holds the electrons until they can be transferred to other molecules. By doing this, NAD^+ helps to pass energy from glucose to other pathways in the cell.

Although the energy yield from glycolysis is small, the process is so fast that cells can produce thousands of ATP molecules in just a few milliseconds. Besides speed, another advantage is that glycolysis itself does not require oxygen. This means that glycolysis can supply chemical energy to cells when oxygen is not available.

However, when a cell generates large amounts of ATP from glycolysis, it runs into a problem. In just a few seconds, all of the cell's available NAD^+ molecules are filled up with electrons. Without NAD^+, the cell cannot keep glycolysis going, and ATP production stops.

CHECKPOINT *What does glycolysis break down?*

Word Origins

Glycolysis comes from the Greek word *glukus,* meaning "sweet," and the Latin word *lysis,* which indicates a process of loosening or decomposing. Thus, *glycolysis* means "breaking glucose." **If *hydro* means "water," what do you think the term *hydrolysis* means?**

▼ **Figure 9–3** Glycolysis is the first stage in cellular respiration. **During glycolysis, glucose is broken down into 2 molecules of pyruvic acid.**

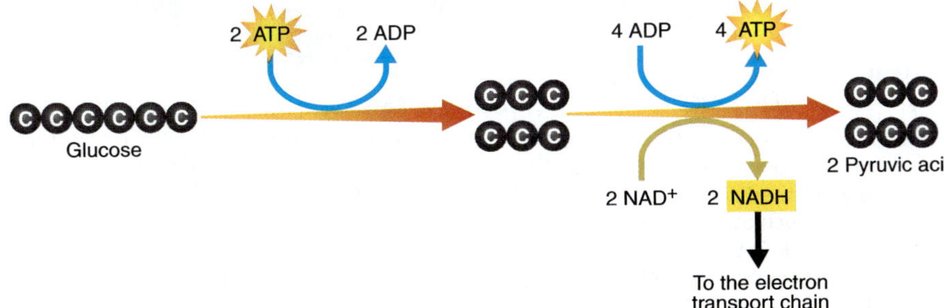

TEACHER TO TEACHER

When I introduce cellular respiration to students, I take a novel approach that sounds "off the wall," but it works. We first look at the overall equation for cellular respiration. I have the students take note of the products, and then we work backward. With this approach, I find that my students come away with a greater understanding of the total process and also have greater retention of the basic concepts. I also do a fermentation lab with my students using a variety of juices, including orange, grape, prune, apple, pineapple, and even diet cola. In addition, we make breads using different sugars and compare the weights of the resulting doughs. (CO_2 is a heavy gas.)

—*Greg McCurdy*
Biology Teacher
Salem High School
Salem, IN

Glycolysis

Word Origins

Hydrolysis means "breaking down water." L2

Build Science Skills

Using Analogies Some students may not be familiar with interest-bearing bank savings accounts. To clarify the analogy used in the text, show students a bank statement of a savings account. Point out that a person has to deposit money into the account in order to earn interest, just as a cell must put 2 ATPs into the "account" to earn the interest of additional ATPs. L2 L3

Use Visuals

Figure 9–3 Have students study the process of glycolysis. Remind students that the cell must expend energy to get the process going. Ask: **Where in the figure does it show that the cell is using energy to start glycolysis?** *(During the breakdown of glucose, 2 molecules of ATP change to 2 molecules of ADP.)* Have a volunteer point out where in the process 2 NAD^+ molecules accept electrons. Then, ask: **NAD^+ is an electron carrier in this process. What is an electron carrier?** *(An electron carrier is a compound that can accept a pair of high-energy electrons and transfer them along with most of their energy to another molecule.)* **Glycolysis is an energy-releasing process. Where in this figure does it show energy being released?** *(On the right side of the figure, 4 ATP molecules are produced from 4 ADP molecules using the energy released from the breakdown of the glucose molecule.)* L1

Download a worksheet on cellular respiration for students to complete, and find additional teacher support from NSTA SciLinks.

Answer to . . .

CHECKPOINT *Glycolysis breaks down a molecule of glucose into 2 molecules of pyruvic acid.*

9–1 (continued)

Fermentation

Build Science Skills

Comparing and Contrasting Display to students a piece of leavened bread and a piece of unleavened bread. Ask: **What is the difference between the two breads?** *(The unleavened bread is thinner than the leavened bread and has no holes, while the leavened bread is thicker than the unleavened bread and has little holes in it.)* Explain that *leaven* means "to raise," and so *unleavened* bread is bread that didn't rise when baked. Ask: **What was added to the leavened bread that made it rise?** *(Yeast)* **What process did the yeast carry out that caused the bread to rise?** *(Alcoholic fermentation)* L1 L2

Problem Solving

BIIE 1.j

Bread recipes are often precise about ingredients, though where and how to allow the dough to rise is often left up to the cook. Students may focus on the amount of yeast or flour, or they may want to focus on the conditions of the place where the dough is left to rise. This activity might be more appropriate for small groups than for individual students. L2 L3

Defining the Problem A typical definition of the problem: How can the production of bubbles of carbon dioxide be increased during the making of bread?

Organizing Information Students should know that temperature affects the action of enzymes and that temperature affects the processes of living things such as yeast. They should also understand that the amount of food available for a living thing to use will affect the outcome. Students should write a prediction for each factor listed.

Creating a Solution A typical experiment might identify temperature as the manipulated variable.

Presenting Your Plan Encourage students to include as many details as possible on their posters. Allow time for students or groups to present their experiments to the class.

Fermentation

When oxygen is not present, glycolysis is followed by a different pathway. The combined process of this pathway and glycolysis is called fermentation. **Fermentation** releases energy from food molecules by producing ATP in the absence of oxygen.

During fermentation, cells convert NADH to NAD^+ by passing high-energy electrons back to pyruvic acid. This action converts NADH back into the electron carrier NAD^+, allowing glycolysis to continue producing a steady supply of ATP. Because fermentation does not require oxygen, it is said to be **anaerobic.** The term *anaerobic* means "not in air." **The two main types of fermentation are alcoholic fermentation and lactic acid fermentation.**

Alcoholic Fermentation Yeasts and a few other microorganisms use alcoholic fermentation, forming ethyl alcohol and carbon dioxide as wastes. The equation for alcoholic fermentation after glycolysis is:

$$\text{pyruvic acid} + \text{NADH} \longrightarrow \text{alcohol} + CO_2 + NAD^+$$

Alcoholic fermentation produces carbon dioxide as well as alcohol. Alcoholic fermentation causes bread dough to rise. When yeast in the dough runs out of oxygen, it begins to ferment, giving off bubbles of carbon dioxide that form the air spaces you see in a slice of bread. The small amount of alcohol produced in the dough evaporates when the bread is baked.

Problem Solving

BIIE 1.j

A Family Recipe

You have opened a bakery, selling bread made according to your family's favorite recipe. Unfortunately, most of your customers find your bread too heavy. You need to make your bread more appealing to your customers. Before bread is baked, yeast cells in the dough ferment some of the carbohydrate in the flour, producing bubbles of carbon dioxide. These bubbles cause the dough to rise and give bread its light, spongy structure. How can you make your bread lighter?

Defining the Problem In your own words, write down what problem you are trying to solve.

Organizing Information The process of fermentation is a series of chemical reactions catalyzed by enzymes. Review what you've learned about such reactions. Make a list of factors, such as temperature and the amounts of yeast and flour in the dough, that might affect the process of fermentation. Predict how each factor will affect the rate of fermentation.

Creating a Solution Write a detailed description of an experiment that could determine if changing the process of fermentation would make the bread lighter. Identify each of your variables. What controls and experimental treatments will you use?

Presenting Your Plan Make a poster showing the procedures in your proposed experiment and explain it to your classmates.

FACTS AND FIGURES

Yeast leavens bread through fermentation

Yeast and other organisms that can carry out both fermentation and cellular respiration, including many kinds of bacteria, are called facultative anaerobes. Human muscle cells also behave as facultative anaerobes. What happens to the end product of glycolysis—pyruvic acid—depends on whether oxygen is present. If there is no oxygen, then fermentation begins.

Baker's yeast, *Saccharomyces cerevisiae,* is the most common organism used to leaven bread. Sourdough bread is leavened by lactobacilli and other lactic-acid bacteria found in flour and milk. Chemicals can also be used to leaven bread. Yeast multiplies best between temperatures of about 27°C and 43°C. It is dormant below 10°C, and it dies at temperatures above 49°C.

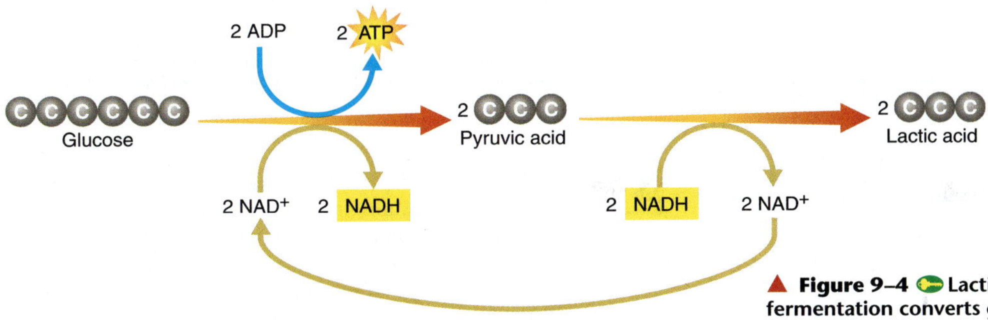

▲ **Figure 9–4 Lactic acid fermentation converts glucose into lactic acid.** The first part of the equation is glycolysis. The second part shows the conversion of pyruvic acid to lactic acid.

Lactic Acid Fermentation In many cells, the pyruvic acid that accumulates as a result of glycolysis can be converted to lactic acid. Because this type of fermentation produces lactic acid, it is called lactic acid fermentation. This process regenerates NAD^+ so that glycolysis can continue, as shown in **Figure 9–4.** The equation for lactic acid fermentation after glycolysis is:

$$\text{pyruvic acid} + \text{NADH} \longrightarrow \text{lactic acid} + \text{NAD}^+$$

Lactic acid is produced in your muscles during rapid exercise when the body cannot supply enough oxygen to the tissues. Without enough oxygen, the body is not able to produce all of the ATP that is required. When you exercise vigorously by running, swimming, or riding a bicycle as fast as you can, the large muscles of your arms and legs quickly run out of oxygen. Your muscle cells rapidly begin to produce ATP by lactic acid fermentation. The buildup of lactic acid causes a painful, burning sensation. This is why muscles may feel sore after only a few seconds of intense activity.

Unicellular organisms also produce lactic acid as a waste product during fermentation. For example, prokaryotes are used in the production of a wide variety of foods and beverages, such as cheese, yogurt, buttermilk, and sour cream. Pickles, sauerkraut, and kimchi are also produced using lactic acid fermentation.

9–1 Section Assessment

1. **Key Concept** Describe the process of cellular respiration.
2. **Key Concept** What are the products of glycolysis?
3. **Key Concept** Name the two main types of fermentation.
4. What is a calorie? A Calorie?
5. How is the function of NAD^+ similar to that of $NADP^+$?
6. **Critical Thinking Comparing and Contrasting** How are lactic acid fermentation and alcoholic fermentation similar? How are they different?

Focus on the BIG Idea

Matter and Energy
Write the conversion of ADP to ATP as a chemical equation. What are the reactants and the product? You may wish to refer back to Chapter 2 to review chemical equations.

9–1 Section Assessment

1. Cellular respiration is the process that releases energy by breaking down molecules in food in the presence of oxygen.
2. Glycolysis produces 2 molecules of pyruvic acid, 2 molecules of ATP, and 2 molecules of NADH.
3. Alcoholic fermentation and lactic acid fermentation
4. A calorie is the amount of energy required to raise the temperature of 1 gram of water 1 degree Celsius. A Calorie is 1000 calories.
5. Both are electron carriers.
6. Similar: Both provide energy to cells in the absence of oxygen. Different: Alcoholic fermentation produces alcohol, carbon dioxide, and NAD^+, while lactic acid fermentation produces lactic acid and NAD^+.

Use Visuals

Figure 9–4 Have students study the process shown in the figure. Point out that the process of glucose breaking down and giving off energy in the figure is similar to the process shown in Figure 9–3. Then, ask: **What is missing from this series of reactions that makes the process anaerobic?** *(There is no oxygen in the process.)* Point out that this pathway shows how an electron carrier behaves cyclically. In lactic acid fermentation, 2 NADH molecules become 2 NAD^+ molecules, resupplying the cell with the electron carriers needed in glycolysis. L2

3 ASSESS

Evaluate Understanding

Call on students at random to explain what occurs during glycolysis. Then, ask students to write the equations for alcoholic fermentation and lactic acid fermentation.

Reteach

Have students make three simple flowcharts, using words in each box that explain the processes of glycolysis, alcoholic fermentation, and lactic acid fermentation. Tell students that they can use Figures 9–3 and 9–4 for reference.

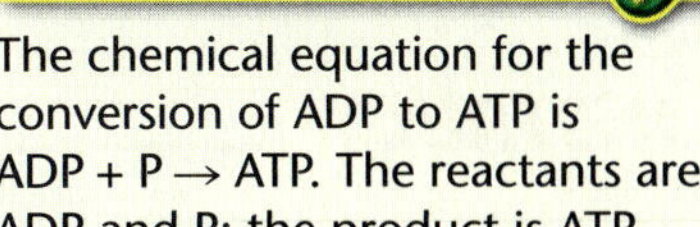

The chemical equation for the conversion of ADP to ATP is ADP + P $\rightarrow$ ATP. The reactants are ADP and P; the product is ATP.

If your class subscribes to the iText, use it to review the Key Concepts in Section 9–1.

Section 9–2

7 1.d, *BI 1.i

1 FOCUS

Objectives

9.2.1 ***Describe*** what happens during the Krebs cycle.

9.2.2 ***Explain*** how high-energy electrons are used by the electron transport chain.

9.2.3 ***Identify*** three pathways the body uses to release energy during exercise.

9.2.4 ***Compare*** photosynthesis and cellular respiration.

Guide for Reading

Vocabulary Preview

Explain that a prefix is a letter or group of letters placed at the beginning of a word to change its meaning. Remind students that *anaerobic* means "not in air." Explain that the prefix *an* means "not." Then, have a volunteer explain what the Vocabulary word *aerobic* means. (*"in air"*)

Reading Strategy

Before students read the section, have them examine Figures 9–6 and 9–7 and make a list of questions about what they see. Then, as they study the text, they can write answers to their questions.

2 INSTRUCT

The Krebs Cycle

Demonstration

To demonstrate production of carbon dioxide in the Krebs cycle, set up a beaker containing bromthymol blue solution. As students watch, blow slowly through a straw into the solution. Wait until it changes color, and then explain that bromthymol blue changes to yellow in the presence of carbon dioxide. Ask: **Where did the carbon dioxide in my breath come from?** *(It comes from reactions in the Krebs cycle, when one carbon atom from pyruvic acid becomes part of a molecule of carbon dioxide.)* L2

9–2 The Krebs Cycle and Electron Transport

7 1.d. Students know that mitochondria liberate energy for the work that cells do and that chloroplasts capture sunlight energy for photosynthesis. ***BI 1.i.** Students know how chemiosmotic gradients in the mitochondria and chloroplasts store energy for ATP production.

Guide for Reading

Key Concepts
- What happens during the Krebs cycle?
- How are high-energy electrons used by the electron transport chain?

Vocabulary
aerobic
Krebs cycle
electron transport chain

Reading Strategy: Using Visuals Before you read, review **Figure 9–2** on page 222. Then, preview **Figures 9–6** and **9–7.** As you read, notice where the Krebs cycle and electron transport take place.

At the end of glycolysis, about 90 percent of the chemical energy that was available in glucose is still unused, locked in the high-energy electrons of pyruvic acid. To extract the rest of that energy, the cell turns to one of the world's most powerful electron acceptors—oxygen. Oxygen is required for the final steps of cellular respiration. Because the pathways of cellular respiration require oxygen, they are said to be **aerobic.**

As you know, the word *respiration* is often used as a synonym for breathing. This is why we have used the term *cellular respiration* to refer to energy-releasing pathways within the cell. The double meaning of respiration points out a crucial connection between cells and organisms: The energy-releasing pathways within cells require oxygen, and that is the reason we need to breathe, to respire.

▲ **Figure 9–5** Hans Krebs won the Nobel Prize in 1953 for his discovery of the citric acid cycle, or Krebs cycle.

The Krebs Cycle

In the presence of oxygen, pyruvic acid produced in glycolysis passes to the second stage of cellular respiration, the **Krebs cycle.** The Krebs cycle is named after Hans Krebs, the British biochemist who demonstrated its existence in 1937. **During the Krebs cycle, pyruvic acid is broken down into carbon dioxide in a series of energy-extracting reactions.** Because citric acid is the first compound formed in this series of reactions, the Krebs cycle is also known as the citric acid cycle.

A The Krebs cycle begins when pyruvic acid produced by glycolysis enters the mitochondrion. One carbon atom from pyruvic acid becomes part of a molecule of carbon dioxide, which is eventually released into the air. The other two carbon atoms from pyruvic acid are joined to a compound called coenzyme A to form acetyl-CoA. (The acetyl part of acetyl-CoA is made up of 2 carbon atoms, 1 oxygen atom, and 3 hydrogen atoms.) Acetyl-CoA then adds the 2-carbon acetyl group to a 4-carbon molecule, producing a 6-carbon molecule called citric acid.

B As the cycle continues, citric acid is broken down into a 4-carbon molecule, more carbon dioxide is released, and electrons are transferred to energy carriers. Follow the reactions in **Figure 9–6,** and you will see how this happens. First, look at the 6 carbon atoms in citric acid. One is removed, and then another, releasing 2 molecules of carbon dioxide and leaving a 4-carbon molecule. This 4-carbon molecule is then ready to accept another 2-carbon acetyl group, which starts the cycle all over again.

Next, look for ATP. For each turn of the cycle, a molecule similar to ADP is converted to a molecule that is similar to ATP. Finally, look at the electron carriers, NAD^+ and FAD.

TIME SAVER

SECTION RESOURCES

Print:
- ***Teaching Resources,*** Lesson Plan 9–2, Adapted Section Summary 9–2, Adapted Worksheets 9–2, Section Summary 9–2, Worksheets 9–2, Section Review 9–2
- ***Reading and Study Workbook A,*** Section 9–2
- ***Adapted Reading and Study Workbook B,*** Section 9–2
- ***Laboratory Manual A,*** Chapter 9 Lab
- ***Laboratory Manual B,*** Chapter 9 Lab
- ***Probeware Lab Manual,*** How does exercise affect disposal of wastes from cellular respiration?

Technology:
- ***iText,*** Section 9–2
- ***Animated Biological Concepts DVD,*** 12 Aerobic Respiration, 14 Krebs Cycle, 15 Electron Transport Chain
- ***Transparencies Plus,*** Section 9–2
- ***Lab Simulations CD-ROM,*** Cell Respiration
- ***Virtual Labs,*** Cell Respiration

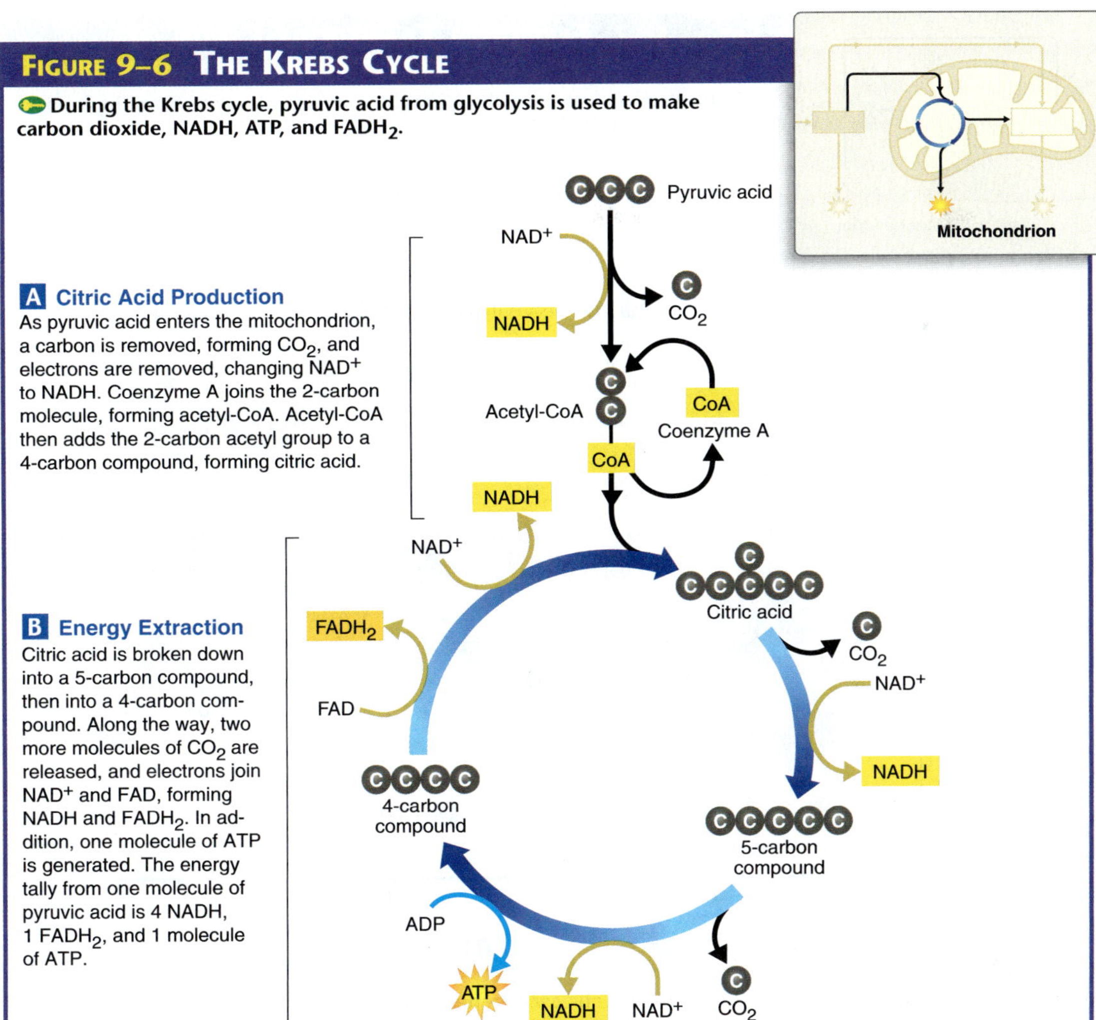

At five places in the cycle, a pair of high-energy electrons is accepted by electron carriers, changing NAD^+ to NADH and FAD to $FADH_2$. FAD (flavine adenine dinucleotide) and $FADH_2$ are molecules similar to NAD^+ and NADH, respectively.

What happens to each of these Krebs cycle products? First, the carbon dioxide released is the source of all the carbon dioxide in your breath. Every time you exhale, you expel the carbon dioxide produced by the Krebs cycle. Next, the ATP produced directly in the Krebs cycle can be used for cellular activities. However, what does the cell do with all those high-energy electrons in carriers like NADH? In the presence of oxygen, those high-energy electrons can be used to generate huge amounts of ATP.

CA a

a 7 1.d

 CHECKPOINT *Why is the Krebs cycle also known as the citric acid cycle?*

Use Visuals

Figure 9–6 Have students study the cycle of reactions, and then, ask: **Where does this cycle take place in the cell?** *(The Krebs cycle takes place in the mitochondrial matrix.)* Point out that the pyruvic acid produced in glycolysis moves from the cytoplasm through two membranes, the outer and inner membranes of a mitochondrion. Ask a volunteer to indicate the three places in the cycle where carbon dioxide is produced. Ask: **How many ATP molecules are generated for every one turn of the Krebs cycle?** *(One)* You may want to explain that the molecule GTP—guanosine triphosphate—is actually produced first. But the cell quickly uses GTP to produce ATP from ADP, and thus ATP is often considered a product of the Krebs cycle. Ask: **Where is most of the chemical energy in pyruvic acid transferred to as a result of the cycle?** *(Most of the energy is transferred to the electron carriers, NAD^+ and FAD^+, producing 4 NADHs and 1 $FADH_2$.)*  L2

Make Connections

Environmental Science Emphasize that the carbon dioxide produced in the Krebs cycle moves out of organisms as waste through exhalation and other processes. This gas becomes part of the atmosphere and becomes available for intake by plants for use in photosynthesis. Encourage students who need challenges to prepare a presentation to the class about the carbon cycle, which is the cycle of carbon through Earth's environment. L2

UNIVERSAL ACCESS

Inclusion/Special Needs

To help students understand electron transport, review the names and abbreviations of the electron carriers by writing them on the board and pronouncing their names: nicotinamide adenine dinucleotide (NAD^+) and flavine adenine dinucleotide (FAD). Emphasize that these ions accept high-energy electrons to form NADH and $FADH_2$. Make sure students recognize by the abbreviations when the carriers are carrying high-energy electrons. L1

Advanced Learners

On page 229, students learn about the charge difference that builds up on either side of the inner membrane. This is called a transmembrane electrochemical potential. Ask students who need a challenge to make a presentation to the class about how this electrochemical potential is similar to the potential difference between two terminals in an electric circuit. L3

Answer to . . .

CHECKPOINT *The Krebs cycle is also known as the citric acid cycle because citric acid is the first compound formed in this series of reactions.*

9–2 (continued)

Electron Transport

Use Visuals

Figure 9–7 After students have studied the figure, ask: **Where does the third stage of respiration take place?** *(Within the inner mitochondrial membrane)* **Where is the intermembrane space?** *(Between the outer membrane and the inner membrane)* Emphasize that the NADH and $FADH_2$ molecules are a product of the Krebs cycle. Then, ask: **What happens that causes NADH to change to NAD^+ and $FADH_2$ to change to FAD?** *(The electron carriers give up their high-energy electrons to the carrier proteins on the electron transport chain.)* **What happens to those electrons?** *(They are passed from one carrier protein to the next.)* **Where does the energy come from that moves hydrogen ions into the intermembrane space?** *(The energy comes from the electrons moving down the electron transport chain.)* **How is the difference in charge on either side of the membrane used to produce ATP molecules?** *(The charge differences cause H^+ ions to pass through ATP synthase in the membrane, and the energy released during the passing converts ADP molecules into ATP molecules.)* L2

Download a worksheet on the Krebs cycle for students to complete, and find additional teacher support from NSTA SciLinks.

Make Connections

Chemistry Remind students that a positive ion has fewer electrons than protons. Since a hydrogen atom contains only one electron and one proton, a positive hydrogen ion is simply one proton. Positive ions are attracted to negative ions, or ions with more electrons than protons. That attraction is the basis of ionic bonds. L1 L2

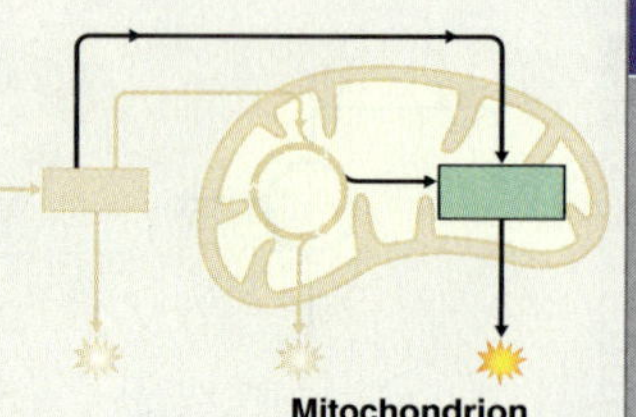

FIGURE 9–7 ELECTRON TRANSPORT CHAIN

The electron transport chain uses high-energy electrons from the Krebs cycle to convert ADP into ATP.

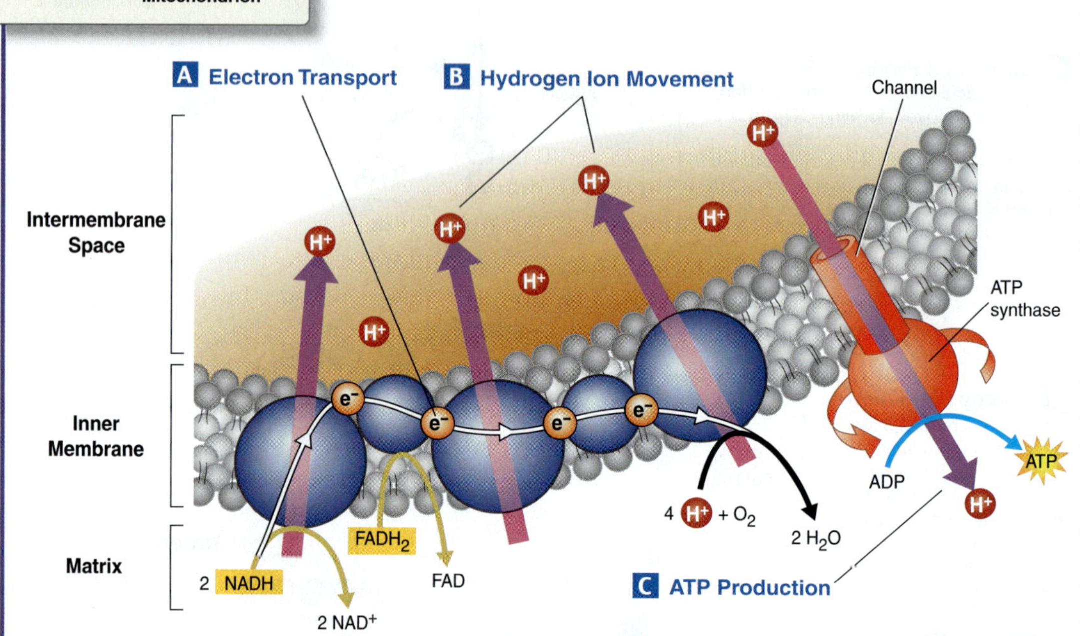

For: Links on the Krebs cycle
Visit: www.SciLinks.org
Web Code: cbn-3092

Electron Transport

The Krebs cycle generates high-energy electrons that are passed to NADH and $FADH_2$. The electrons are then passed from those carriers to the **electron transport chain.** **The electron transport chain uses the high-energy electrons from the Krebs cycle to convert ADP into ATP.** Look at **Figure 9–7** to see how this happens.

A High-energy electrons from NADH and $FADH_2$ are passed along the electron transport chain. In eukaryotes, the electron transport chain is composed of a series of carrier proteins located in the inner membrane of the mitochondrion. In prokaryotes, the same chain is in the cell membrane. High-energy electrons are passed from one carrier protein to the next. At the end of the electron transport chain is an enzyme that combines these electrons with hydrogen ions and oxygen to form water. Oxygen serves as the final electron acceptor of the electron transport chain. Thus, oxygen is essential for getting rid of low-energy electrons and hydrogen ions, the wastes of cellular respiration.

HISTORY OF SCIENCE

Hans Krebs discovers a cycle

Hans Krebs (1900–1981) grew up in Germany the son of a Jewish physician. In 1933, he was forced to leave Germany because of the Nazi persecution of the Jewish people. Krebs spent the rest of his life in Great Britain, where he taught and did research at universities. In 1937, he worked out the details of a cycle of chemical reactions in the breakdown of sugar in living organisms, a cycle in which citric acid is formed. He did most of his research about this cycle on pigeon tissues. His work was initially met with disbelief—the prestigious journal *Nature* rejected his paper on the findings. His discovery of what came to be called the Krebs cycle is of great importance in understanding cell metabolism. For his work, Krebs shared the 1953 Nobel Prize in Medicine and Physiology.

B Every time 2 high-energy electrons transport down the electron transport chain, their energy is used to transport hydrogen ions (H^+) across the membrane. During electron transport, H^+ ions build up in the intermembrane space, making it positively charged. The other side of the membrane, from which those H^+ ions have been taken, is now negatively charged.

C How does the cell use the charge differences that build up as a result of electron transport? The inner membranes of the mitochondria contain protein spheres called ATP synthases. As H^+ ions escape through channels into these proteins, the ATP synthases spin. Each time it rotates, the enzyme grabs a low-energy ADP and attaches a phosphate, forming high-energy ATP.

The beauty of this system is the way in which it couples the movement of high-energy electrons with the production of ATP. Every time a pair of high-energy electrons moves down the electron transport chain, the energy is used to move H^+ ions across the membrane. These ions then rush back across the membrane, producing enough force to spin the ATP synthase and generate enormous amounts of ATP. On average, each pair of high-energy electrons that moves down the electron transport chain provides enough energy to produce three molecules of ATP from ADP.

CHECKPOINT *What is the role of ATP synthase in cellular respiration?*

▼ **Figure 9–8** The complete breakdown of glucose through cellular respiration, including glycolysis, results in the production of 36 molecules of ATP. **Interpreting Graphics** ***How many molecules of ATP are produced during glycolysis?***

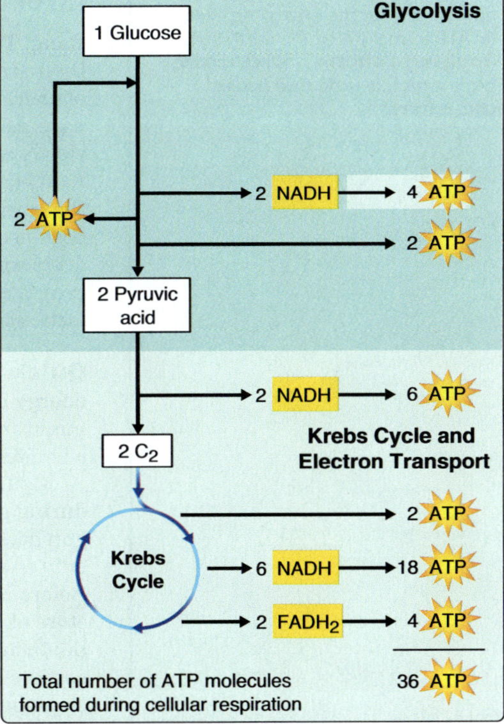

The Totals

Although glycolysis produces just 2 ATP molecules per molecule of glucose, in the presence of oxygen, everything changes. As **Figure 9–8** shows, the Krebs cycle and electron transport enable the cell to produce roughly 36 ATP molecules per glucose molecule, 18 times as much as can be generated in the absence of oxygen.

Our diets contain much more than just glucose, of course, but that's no problem for the cell. Complex carbohydrates are broken down to simple sugars like glucose. Lipids and proteins can be broken down into molecules that enter the Krebs cycle or glycolysis at one of several places. Like a furnace that can burn oil, gas, or wood, the cell can generate chemical energy in the form of ATP from just about any source.

How efficient is cellular respiration? The 36 ATP molecules represent about 38 percent of the total energy of glucose. That might not seem like much, but it means that the cell is actually more efficient at using food than the engine of a typical automobile is at burning gasoline. What happens to the remaining 62 percent? It is released as heat, which is one of the reasons your body feels warmer after vigorous exercise.

The Totals

Use Visuals

Figure 9–8 Students may ask why 4 ATPs in glycolysis are shown in a pale green box. The reason is that the 2 NADH molecules are transported to the electron transport chain, where they are used to make ATP. So, those 4 ATPs are counted under the total for the Krebs cycle and electron transport, not glycolysis. Students may also ask why each NADH from glycolysis produces only 2 ATPs, while each NADH from the Krebs cycle and electron transport produce 3 ATPs. The reason is that energy must be used to import the NADHs from glycolysis from the cytoplasm into the mitochondrion. **L2** **L3**

Build Science Skills

Calculating Explain to students that 1 mole of glucose (about 180 g) contains about 686 kilocalories of energy. A mole is the SI unit of the amount of a substance. Remind students that 1 kilocalorie = 1000 calories. Then, ask: **How much energy does respiration yield from 1 mole of glucose?** *(686 kilocalories × 0.38 = 261 kilocalories)* **How much energy is lost to heat?** *(686 kilocalories × 0.62 = 425 kilocalories; or 686 kilocalories – 261 kilocalories = 425 kilocalories)* **L2** **L3**

BIO INSIGHTS — FACTS AND FIGURES

Releasing energy in a series of steps
The final product of the electron transport chain is water, or H_2O. If hydrogen and oxygen gas were allowed to combine directly, there would be a great release of wasted energy. Instead, the cell uses a chain of carrier molecules, mostly proteins, embedded in the inner mitochondrial membrane to release the energy of electrons in a series of steps. At each step, the electrons lose a little bit of their energy. The flow of electrons along the chain begins, for example, when an NADH molecule passes two electrons and two protons to the first carrier protein. The two protons pass into the intermembrane space, making it positively charged. As the process continues, the electrons lose their energy and protons are pumped from the matrix out through the membrane. ATP is made when the H^+ ions are "pushed" back through the membrane, a process called chemiosmosis.

Answers to . . .

CHECKPOINT *ATP synthase uses energy from H^+ ions to convert ADP into ATP.*

Figure 9–8 *Glycolysis produces 2 ATP molecules per glucose molecule.*

9–2 (continued)

Energy and Exercise

Make Connections

Health Science Encourage student volunteers to research the differences between aerobic exercise and anaerobic exercise and the benefits of each. Have the students prepare a presentation to the class. L2 L3

Build Science Skills

Predicting After students have read the section Energy and Exercise, give them a list of sports and activities, including weight lifting, playing soccer, dancing, taking a long walk, cutting the grass, running a sprint, and running a marathon. For each activity, ask students to predict how much the muscles doing that activity would use lactic acid fermentation or cellular respiration as a source of energy. L2

Use Community Resources

Invite an aerobics exercise instructor to address the class and explain his or her understanding of the benefits of aerobic and anaerobic exercise. A day before the presentation, encourage students to brainstorm a list of questions to ask the instructor.

▲ **Figure 9–9** During a race, runners rely on the energy supplied by ATP to make it to the finish line. **Applying Concepts** *When runners begin a race, how do their bodies obtain energy?*

Energy and Exercise

Bang! The starter's pistol goes off, and the runners push off their starting blocks and sprint down the track. The initial burst of energy soon fades, and the runners settle down to a steady pace. After the runners hit the finish line, they walk around slowly and breathe deeply to catch their breath.

Let's look at what happens at each stage of the race in terms of the pathways the body uses to release energy. To obtain energy, the body uses ATP already in muscles and new ATP made by lactic acid fermentation and cellular respiration. At the beginning of a race, the body uses all three ATP sources, but stored ATP and lactic acid fermentation can only supply energy for a limited time.

Quick Energy What happens when your body needs lots of energy in a hurry? In response to sudden danger, quick actions might make the difference between life and death. To an athlete, a sudden burst of speed might win a race.

Cells normally contain small amounts of ATP produced during glycolysis and cellular respiration. When the starting gun goes off in a footrace, the muscles of the runners contain only enough of this ATP for a few seconds of intense activity. Before most of the runners have passed the 50-meter mark, that store of ATP is nearly gone. At this point, their muscle cells are producing most of their ATP by lactic acid fermentation. These sources can usually supply enough ATP to last about 90 seconds. In a 200- or 300-meter sprint, such as in **Figure 9–9,** this may be just enough to reach the finish line.

FACTS AND FIGURES

Aerobic and anaerobic training

During strenuous exercise, usually both aerobic and anaerobic pathways are at work in supplying muscles with ATP, though the percentage of each varies by the sport. For example, the quick and all-out action of lifting a heavy weight is 100 percent anaerobic. Running a marathon, by contrast, is about 99 percent aerobic. Playing soccer or basketball is about 20 percent anaerobic and 80 percent aerobic. Athletes can improve ATP production through training. Anaerobic training, including sprints and similar bursts of energy, can increase the level of glycogen in the muscles and increase tolerance of lactic acid. Aerobic training, including long runs, can increase the size and number of mitochondria in muscles and increase the delivery of oxygen to muscles by improving the heart and lungs. Thus, both types of training are beneficial.

Fermentation produces lactic acid as a byproduct. When the race is over, the only way to get rid of lactic acid is in a chemical pathway that requires extra oxygen. For that reason, you can think of a quick sprint building up an oxygen debt that a runner has to repay after the race with plenty of heavy breathing.

Long-Term Energy What happens if a race is longer? How does your body generate the ATP it needs to run 2 kilometers or more, or to play in a soccer game that lasts more than an hour? For exercise longer than about 90 seconds, cellular respiration is the only way to generate a continuing supply of ATP. Cellular respiration releases energy more slowly than fermentation, which is why even well-conditioned athletes have to pace themselves during a long race or over the course of a game. Your body stores energy in muscle and other tissues in the form of the carbohydrate glycogen. These stores of glycogen are usually enough to last for 15 or 20 minutes of activity. After that, your body begins to break down other stored molecules, including fats, for energy. This is one reason why aerobic forms of exercise such as running, dancing, and swimming are so beneficial for weight control.

CHECKPOINT *Why do runners breathe heavily after a race?*

Quick Lab

BIIE 1.a, BIIE 1.c

How does exercise affect disposal of wastes from cellular respiration?

Materials 2 small test tubes, glass-marking pencil, 10-mL graduated cylinder, bromthymol blue solution, 2 straws, clock or watch with second hand

Procedure   

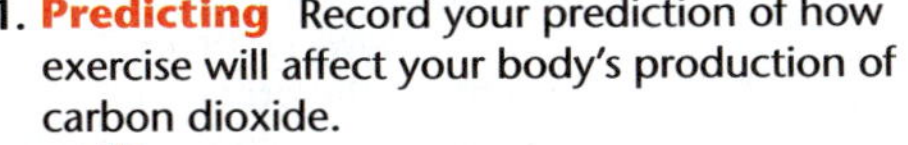

1. **Predicting** Record your prediction of how exercise will affect your body's production of carbon dioxide.
2. 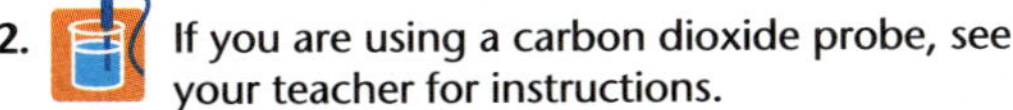 If you are using a carbon dioxide probe, see your teacher for instructions.
3. Label two test tubes A and B. Put 10 mL of water and a few drops of bromthymol blue solution in each test tube. Carbon dioxide causes bromthymol blue to turn yellow or green.
4. Your partner will time you during this step. When your partner says "go," slowly blow air through a straw into the bottom of test tube A. **CAUTION:** *Do not inhale through the straw.*

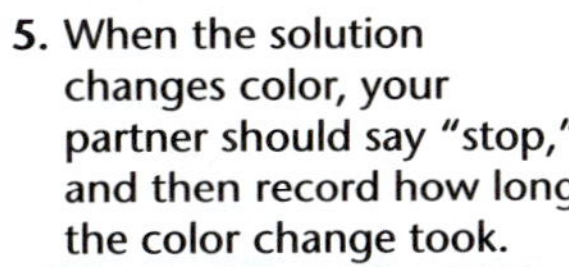

5. When the solution changes color, your partner should say "stop," and then record how long the color change took.
6. Jog in place for 1 minute. **CAUTION:** *Do not do this if you have a medical condition that interferes with exercise. If you feel faint or dizzy, stop immediately and sit down.*
7. Repeat steps 4 and 5 using test tube B.
8. Trade roles with your partner. Repeat steps 3 through 7.

Analyze and Conclude

1. **Analyzing Data** How did exercise affect the time for the solution to change color? Did these results support your prediction?
2. **Inferring** What process in your body produces carbon dioxide? How does exercise affect this process?
3. **SAFETY** What safety procedures did you follow? Why were these procedures important?

Quick Lab

BIIE 1.a, BIIE 1.c

Objective Students should conclude that exercise increases the body's production of carbon dioxide. L2

Skills Focus Analyzing Data, Inferring

Time 15 minutes

Advance Prep If you are using Probeware, use the instructions in the *Probeware Lab Manual.*

Safety Read the safety information on the MSDS for bromthymol blue before doing the lab. Warn students not to inhale or swallow the bromthymol blue solution. Make sure students wash their hands with soap and warm water before leaving the lab.

Strategies

- Demonstrate how to slowly blow air through a straw into a test tube that contains water and bromthymol blue solution.
- If students have difficulty understanding the significance of their results, have them think about which process in their own cells produces carbon dioxide and how that process is important to their survival. Then, have them think about how the rate of that process changes during exercise.

Expected Outcome Students should observe that the bromthymol blue solution changes color more rapidly after exercise than before exercise.

Analyze and Conclude

1. Exercise caused the time for the solution to change color to decrease. Whether the results supported a student's prediction will depend on that prediction.
2. Cellular respiration produces carbon dioxide. Exercise increases the rate of cellular respiration.
3. Answers should include: wearing a lab apron and goggles, and not inhaling through the straw.

BIO INSIGHTS — FACTS AND FIGURES

Using alternative fuels in cellular respiration Glucose is a common fuel for cells. Starch is broken down into glucose by the digestive system. Humans and many other animals store glycogen in their liver and muscle cells, and glycogen also can be changed into glucose. But, glucose is not the only fuel. For example, proteins and fats can also be used. Proteins are broken down into their constituent amino acids, and then modified amino acids are fed into the Krebs cycle with the help of enzymes. Fats, whether taken in with food or stored in the body, provide excellent fuel for respiration. The fatty acids of fats are broken down and carried into the mitochondrial matrix by special transport proteins, and then they enter the Krebs cycle in fragments as acetyl-CoA. Fats yield much more energy than glucose. A gram of fat produces more than double the ATP that a gram of carbohydrate does.

Answers to . . .

CHECKPOINT *They need extra oxygen to get rid of lactic acid that has built up in their muscles.*

Figure 9–9 *Their bodies obtain energy from ATP already in muscles and new ATP made by lactic acid fermentation and cellular respiration.*

9–2 (continued)

Comparing Photosynthesis and Cellular Respiration

Build Science Skills

Using Analogies Draw a hill on the board, and write *glucose* at the top of the hill. Then, tell students that photosynthesis might be considered an "uphill" process, whereas cellular respiration could be considered a "downhill" process. L2

3 ASSESS

Evaluate Understanding

Call on students at random to describe the steps in the process of cellular respiration, one at a time.

Reteach

Have students reexamine Figures 9–6 and 9–7. Ask each student to write a description of those figures using as many details as possible.

Thinking Visually

Students should use Figure 9–6 to find the main events in the Krebs cycle, including citric acid production and energy extraction. They should use Figure 9–7 to find the main events in the electron transport chain, including electron transport, hydrogen ion movement, and ATP production. Students should show that the Krebs cycle occurs inside the mitochondrion and the electron transport chain occurs within the inner mitochondrial membrane.

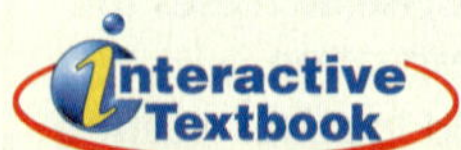

If your class subscribes to the iText, use it to review the Key Concepts in Section 9–2.

Answer to . . .

Figure 9–10 *The reactants in the equation for photosynthesis are the products in the equation for cellular respiration, and the products in the equation for photosynthesis are the reactants in the equation for cellular respiration.*

Comparing Photosynthesis and Cellular Respiration

	Photosynthesis	Cellular Respiration
Function	Energy capture	Energy release
Location	Chloroplasts	Mitochondria
Reactants	CO_2 and H_2O	$C_6H_{12}O_6$ and O_2
Products	$C_6H_{12}O_6$ and O_2	CO_2 and H_2O
Equation	$6CO_2 + 6H_2O \rightarrow C_6H_{12}O_6 + 6O_2$ (Energy)	$6O_2 + C_6H_{12}O_6 \rightarrow 6CO_2 + 6H_2O$ (Energy)

Figure 9–10 Photosynthesis and cellular respiration can be thought of as opposite processes. **Comparing and Contrasting** *Exactly how is the equation for photosynthesis different from the equation for cellular respiration?*

Comparing Photosynthesis and Cellular Respiration

(a) 7 1.d CA

The energy flows in photosynthesis and cellular respiration take place in opposite directions. Earlier in this chapter, the chemical energy in carbohydrates was compared to money in a savings account. Photosynthesis is the process that "deposits" energy. Cellular respiration is the process that "withdraws" energy. As you might expect, the equations for photosynthesis and cellular respiration, shown in **Figure 9–10,** are the reverse of each other.

On a global level, photosynthesis and cellular respiration are also opposites. Photosynthesis removes carbon dioxide from the atmosphere, and cellular respiration puts it back. Photosynthesis releases oxygen into the atmosphere, and cellular respiration uses that oxygen to release energy from food. The release of energy by cellular respiration takes place in all eukaryotes and some prokaryotes. Energy capture by photosynthesis, however, occurs only in plants, algae, and some bacteria.

9–2 Section Assessment

1. **Key Concept** What happens to pyruvic acid during the Krebs cycle?
2. **Key Concept** How does the electron transport chain use the high-energy electrons from the Krebs cycle?
3. Why is cellular respiration considered to be much more efficient than glycolysis alone?
4. How many molecules of ATP are produced in the entire breakdown of glucose?
5. **Critical Thinking Comparing and Contrasting** Compare the energy flow in photosynthesis to the energy flow in cellular respiration.
6. **Critical Thinking Using Analogies** How is the chemical energy in glucose similar to money in a savings account?

Thinking Visually

Organizing Information
Using **Figure 9–6** and **Figure 9–7** as guides, prepare a poster showing the main events of the process of cellular respiration. For each event, show the reactant and products and where in the mitochondrion the event occurs. Use your poster to explain cellular respiration to a classmate.

9–2 Section Assessment

1. Pyruvic acid is broken down into carbon dioxide in a series of energy-extracting reactions.
2. The electron transport chain uses the high-energy electrons from the Krebs cycle to convert ADP into ATP.
3. Cellular respiration enables the cell to produce 34 more ATP molecules per glucose molecule in addition to the 2 ATP molecules obtained from glycolysis.
4. 36
5. The energy flows in photosynthesis and cellular respiration take place in opposite directions. Photosynthesis is the process that "deposits" energy, while cellular respiration is the process that "withdraws" energy.
6. The energy in glucose is "saved" and can be "withdrawn" when the body needs it.

BIIE 1.m

Should Creatine Supplements Be Banned?

Many athletes now use a dietary supplement called creatine to enhance their performance. Creatine may improve athletic performance, but critics point to potentially serious side effects as a reason to control its use.

Although muscle cells contain only enough ATP for a few seconds of intense activity, most have a reserve nearly twice as large in the form of a molecule called creatine phosphate. When the muscle goes to work and starts to use up its available ATP, phosphates are transferred from creatine phosphate directly to ADP, regenerating ATP in a matter of milliseconds. The more creatine phosphate a muscle contains, the longer it can sustain intense activity. Hoping to increase their capacity for strong, short-term muscle contractions, many athletes have added creatine to their diets. Should athletes be allowed to use creatine supplements?

The Viewpoints

Creatine Supplements Should Be Allowed

Creatine is a natural substance found in human cells and in foods such as meat. Taken in recommended doses, creatine helps build muscle strength and performance, which can mean the difference between winning and losing. When athletes have followed instructions on container labels, no serious side effects have been reported. The risks are small and the rewards of winning are large enough to justify its use.

Creatine Supplements Should Be Banned

Like any natural substance, creatine can be abused. Creatine is known to cause water loss, putting the athletes who use it at risk for dehydration, muscle injury, diarrhea, kidney failure, and perhaps even death. Because creatine is considered a dietary supplement and not a drug, the Food and Drug Administration (FDA) has never determined its safety. Until a truly safe dose has been determined by careful scientific studies, athletes should not be allowed to use creatine.

Research and Decide

1. **Analyzing the Viewpoints** To make an informed decision, learn more about this issue by consulting library or Internet resources. Then, list the key arguments expressed by the proponents and critics of using creatine as a dietary supplement. What is known? What is not known? What are the benefits? What are the risks?
2. **Forming Your Opinion** Should athletes be allowed to take creatine to enhance performance? Weigh the pro and con arguments. Research to find out if some professional sports have banned the use of creatine by athletes. What were the reasons for this decision? Do some arguments outweigh others? Which arguments? Explain your answer.
3. **Writing an Editorial** Write an editorial for a sports magazine that takes a stand on creatine. Your editorial should persuade your readers that your opinion is justified.

For: Links from the authors
Visit: PHSchool.com
Web Code: cbe-3093

BACKGROUND

The creatine connection

Muscle cells have two backup systems when oxygen is in short supply. One is lactic acid fermentation, but before that begins, a muscle uses up its supply of a compound called creatine phosphate. That molecule can transfer its phosphate to ADP in the reaction: creatine phosphate + ADP → ATP + creatine. A good diet usually supplies an adequate amount of creatine. Meat and fish contain large quantities. In muscle cells, creatine is changed into creatine phosphate. Creatine supplements add to the amount already supplied in a good diet. Some research has shown that taking a recommended dose of creatine supplement can increase the level of creatine phosphate in muscles 10–20 percent, which can increase energy levels in muscles 2.5–10 percent. Research is incomplete about the health risks of taking the supplement.

BIIE 1.m

After students have read the feature, divide the class into small groups, and allow time for discussion. Then, have each group prepare questions for an interview with one of the following: the coach of one of the high-school teams, a physician associated with high-school teams, a high-school athlete, a salesperson at a health food store that sells creatine supplements, and a professor in the health or physical education department of a local college or university.

Work with each group to decide whom students want to talk to and how to go about setting up the interview. Encourage students to write several questions they want to ask, and anticipate asking follow-up questions.

After completing the interview, group members should collaborate in preparing a report to the class. Encourage students to research additional information to include in their report. Once all groups have given their reports, lead a class discussion of what students learned from the various sources.

Research and Decide

1. Students should list the key arguments discussed in the feature, including increasing strength and performance and the possibility of damage to health.

2. Some students may argue for taking the supplements, some may argue against, while others may be ambivalent. No matter which position a student takes, he or she should back up the opinion with facts and logic.

3. Students' editorials should concisely state their opinions, with good arguments for their positions.

Students can research creatine supplements on the site developed by authors Ken Miller and Joe Levine.

Real-World Lab

 BIIE 1.a, BIIE 1.b

Objective Students will be able to draw a conclusion about how fermentation affects pH. L2 L3

Skills Focus Predicting, Measuring, Drawing Conclusions

Time 40 minutes the first day; 10 minutes a day on one day in each of the following 4 weeks

Advance Prep Most of the materials are available at a local supermarket. Chinese cabbage is also sold at Asian food stores. Chop the cabbage in advance. If you are using probeware in this activity, use the instructions in the *Probeware Lab Manual.*

Alternative Materials Regular cabbage can be used if Chinese cabbage is unavailable.

Safety Acetic acid and other compounds produced during fermentation may irritate students' eyes. Using larger lab groups and fewer bags of fermenting cabbage will reduce the quantities of these compounds.

Pre-Lab Discussion Have students read the entire procedure, and answer any questions they have about the lab. Then, ask: **What is the purpose of this lab?** (*To measure the chemical changes of fermentation*) **What types of fermentation occur in making kimchi, and what are the products of those processes?** (*Both lactic acid and alcoholic fermentation occur. The products are lactic acid, carbon dioxide, and alcohol.*)

Teaching Tips

- Discuss with students how to construct the graph of their results.
- Demonstrate how to unseal the bags and expel any air.
- Show students how to use pH indicator paper to measure the pH of the liquid.

Procedure

1. Some students may correctly hypothesize that production of lactic acid will reduce the pH of the kimchi.

Expected Outcome The pH of the kimchi will gradually drop as *Lactobacillus* produces lactic acid and carbon dioxide.

Real-World Lab

 BIIE 1.a, BIIE 1.b

Investigating Fermentation by Making Kimchi

In this investigation, you will make a popular Korean side dish known as kimchi. Kimchi is made by allowing microorganisms to ferment Chinese cabbage. The main microorganism involved is a bacterium called Lactobacillus. *This bacterium mainly carries out lactic acid fermentation. Some species of* Lactobacillus *and other microorganisms on the cabbage carry out alcoholic fermentation. All of these microorganisms occur naturally on the surface of the Chinese cabbage. As these microorganisms ferment the Chinese cabbage, you will measure the chemical changes that occur during this process. You will use your knowledge of fermentation to explain the observations that you make.*

Problem
How does fermentation affect pH?

Materials

- 2 resealable plastic sandwich bags
- chopped Chinese cabbage
- noniodized salt
- 2.5-mL (1/2 teaspoon) measuring spoon
- pH-indicator paper
- thermometer

Skills
Predicting, Measuring, Drawing Conclusions

Procedure  

1. **Formulating Hypotheses** Recall that pH is a measure of how acidic or basic a solution is. Bases have pH levels between 7 and 14, and acids have pH levels between 0 and 7. Formulate a hypothesis that explains how fermentation leads to changes in pH. Record your hypothesis and your prediction of how the pH of the kimchi will change over time as it ferments.
2. Put one resealable plastic bag inside the other. Half-fill the inner bag with chopped cabbage. Add 2.5 mL of salt. Seal both bags and turn them upside down several times to mix the ingredients.
3. Unseal the bags and press down on them to expel any air. Then, reseal the bags. Label the plastic bags containing the kimchi with your name and place them in a cool area where they will remain undisturbed. Copy the data table shown. Measure and record the air temperature in your copy of the data table. Wash your hands at the end of each lab period.
4. Each day, observe the kimchi in the bags. Record your observations of any changes in the appearance of the kimchi or the bags in your data table. When a small amount of liquid appears in the bottom of the inner bag, open the bags. **CAUTION:** *Do not eat the kimchi.*

Data Table

Day	pH	Temperature	Observations
1			
8			
15			
22			
29			

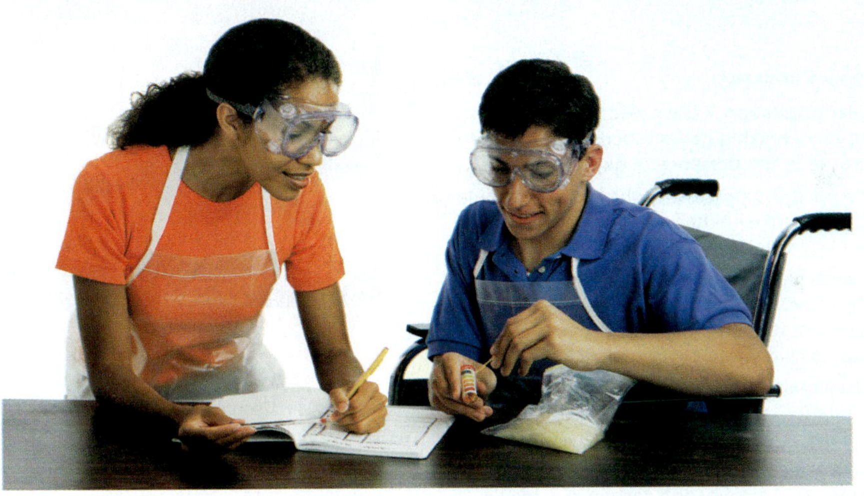

5 With your teacher's guidance, select the equipment and technology needed to measure pH—either pH-indicator paper or a pH probe. If you are using a pH probe, see your teacher for instructions.

6 Use pH-indicator paper to measure the pH of the liquid. Record the pH in your data table.

7 Press out any gas in the bags and reseal them. Return the bags to the cool area and leave them undisturbed for a week.

8 One week after you first measured the pH, repeat steps 6 and 7. Then, move the bags containing the kimchi to a refrigerator. Record the temperature of the refrigerator in your data table. Continue to observe the kimchi and record its pH every week for 4 weeks.

Analyze and Conclude

1. **Using Tables and Graphs** Use your data table to construct a graph showing the relationship between pH and time. With your teacher's guidance, select the appropriate equipment and technology—either graph paper or a graphing calculator. Describe how the pH of the kimchi changed over time.
2. **Inferring** What substance do you think was responsible for the change in pH? What process could have produced this substance?
3. **Evaluating and Revising** Was your prediction correct? What changes would you make in your hypothesis as a result of your observations?
4. **Inferring** Did you see any evidence that a gas was produced or consumed in the bags? If so, what was this gas? What process was responsible for this change? Explain the reasons for your answers.

Go Further

Designing Experiments Yogurt is made from milk using microorganisms that carry out lactic acid fermentation. Do research using scientific literature to form a hypothesis to determine how a factor, such as temperature or sugar concentration, affects the fermentation of yogurt. Your description should state your hypothesis, identify all variables, and explain how the outcome of the experiment could support or contradict your hypothesis.

For: Data Sharing
Visit: PHSchool.com
Web Code: cbd-3094

Share Your Data Online Enter your pH values in the data-sharing table online. Then, look at the data entered by other students. Based on the available data, how do you think a change in pH over time is related to fermentation? Why might your results differ from those of other students?

Go Further

A typical experiment might involve investigating how temperature affects fermentation by measuring changes in pH over time in two or more batches, each kept at a different temperature.

Students should see how fermentation affects pH, but their results will depend on their own data and the data on the site.

Analyze and Conclude

1. Students' graphs should have pH on the *y*-axis and time on the *x*-axis. The pH should decline from about 7 on Day 1 to about 4 on Day 29.
2. Lactic acid caused the change in pH. It was produced by the *Lactobacillus* during lactic acid fermentation. Production of carbon dioxide also helped to acidify the mixture.
3. Students predicted correctly if they predicted that the pH of the kimchi would decline. Students should revise their hypothesis if it was incorrect.
4. Students should have observed an accumulation of gas in the bags, evidence that gas was produced. They should infer that the gas was carbon dioxide, and they should also infer that the process responsible for gas production was alcoholic fermentation, because the sealed bags eliminated the possibility of oxygen being involved in the process.

Study Tip

Have students make Vocabulary flashcards by writing a Vocabulary word on one side of a card and its definition on the other side.

Thinking Visually

1. glucose
2. glucose and oxygen
3. glycolysis, several others
4. glycolysis, Krebs cycle, electron transport
5. either carbon dioxide and alcohol or lactic acid
6. carbon dioxide, water
7. 2
8. 36

Chapter 9 Assessment

Reviewing Content

1. c	4. c	7. c	10. b
2. b	5. b	8. b	
3. b	6. b	9. a	

Understanding Concepts

11. A calorie is the amount of energy needed to raise the temperature of 1 gram of water 1 degree Celsius. Cells break down high-calorie molecules in a series of steps, releasing the stored energy a small amount at a time.

12. During glycolysis, glucose is broken down into two molecules of pyruvic acid. The other products are ATP molecules and high-energy electrons that are picked up by NAD^+.

13. After glycolysis, if oxygen is available, a cell might carry out the rest of cellular respiration. If oxygen is not available, some cells carry out the rest of fermentation.

14. $6O_2 + C_6H_{12}O_6 \rightarrow 6CO_2 + 6H_2O$ + energy; oxygen + glucose $\rightarrow$ carbon dioxide + water + energy

15. Student diagrams should be similar to Figure 9–2.

16. NAD^+ picks up high-energy electrons produced during glycolysis, forming NADH. The large number of high-energy electrons quickly fill all of the cell's available NAD^+ molecules. Without NAD^+, the cell cannot keep glycolysis going, and ATP production stops.

Chapter 9 Study Guide

9–1 Chemical Pathways

Key Concepts BI 1.g

- Cellular respiration is the process that releases energy by breaking down glucose and other food molecules in the presence of oxygen.
- Glycolysis is the process in which one molecule of glucose is broken in half, producing two molecules of pyruvic acid, a 3-carbon compound.
- Glycolysis captures two pairs of high-energy electrons with the carrier NAD^+. Because glycolysis does not require oxygen, it supplies chemical energy to cells when oxygen is not available.
- The two main types of fermentation are alcoholic fermentation and lactic acid fermentation.
- In the absence of oxygen, yeast and a few other microorganisms use alcoholic fermentation, forming ethyl alcohol and carbon dioxide as wastes.
- Animals cannot perform alcoholic fermentation, but some cells, such as human muscle cells, can convert glucose into lactic acid. This is called lactic acid fermentation.

Vocabulary

calorie, p. 221
glycolysis, p. 221
cellular respiration, p. 222
NAD^+, p. 223
fermentation, p. 224
anaerobic, p. 224

9–2 The Krebs Cycle and Electron Transport

Key Concepts 7 1.d, *BI 1.i

- During the Krebs cycle, pyruvic acid is broken down into carbon dioxide in a series of energy-extracting reactions.
- The electron transport chain uses the high-energy electrons from the Krebs cycle to convert ADP into ATP.
- The products of photosynthesis are similar to the reactants of cellular respiration. The products of cellular respiration are the reactants of photosynthesis.

Vocabulary

aerobic, p. 226
Krebs cycle, p. 226
electron transport chain, p. 228

Thinking Visually

Using the information in this chapter, complete the following compare-and-contrast table about fermentation and cellular respiration:

Comparing Fermentation and Cellular Respiration

Characteristic	Fermentation	Cellular Respiration
Starting reactants	1	2
Pathways involved	3	4
End products	5	6
Number of ATP molecules produced	7	8

CHAPTER RESOURCES

TIME SAVER

Print:

- ***Teaching Resources,*** Chapter Vocabulary Review, Graphic Organizer, Chapter 9 Tests: Levels A and B

Technology:

- ***Computer Test Bank,*** Chapter 9 Test
- ***iText,*** Chapter 9 Assessment

Chapter 9 Assessment

Reviewing Content

Choose the letter that best answers the question or completes the statement.

1. In cells, the energy available in food is used to make an energy-rich compound called
   a. water. c. ATP.
   b. glucose. d. ADP.
2. The first step in releasing the energy of glucose in the cell is known as
   a. alcoholic fermentation.
   b. glycolysis.
   c. the Krebs cycle.
   d. electron transport.
3. The process that releases energy from food in the presence of oxygen is
   a. synthesis.
   b. cellular respiration.
   c. ATP synthase.
   d. photosynthesis.
4. Which organisms perform cellular respiration?

a.  b.  c.  d. 

   a. only c c. all of the above
   b. only a and c d. only a and b
5. The net gain of energy from glycolysis is
   a. 4 ATP molecules.
   b. 2 ATP molecules.
   c. 8 ADP molecules.
   d. 3 pyruvic acid molecules.
6. Because fermentation takes place in the absence of oxygen, it is said to be
   a. aerobic.
   b. anaerobic.
   c. cyclic.
   d. essential to oxygen production.
7. The Krebs cycle takes place within the
   a. chloroplast.
   b. nucleus.
   c. mitochondrion.
   d. cytoplasm.
8. The electron transport chain uses the high-energy electrons from the Krebs cycle to
   a. produce glucose.
   b. convert ADP to ATP.
   c. produce acetyl-CoA.
   d. produce GTP.

Interactive textbook with assessment at PHSchool.com 

9. A total of 36 molecules of ATP are produced from 1 molecule of glucose as a result of
   a. cellular respiration.
   b. glycolysis.
   c. alcoholic fermentation.
   d. lactic acid fermentation.
10. During heavy exercise, the buildup of lactic acid in muscle cells results in
    a. alcoholic fermentation.
    b. oxygen debt.
    c. the Calvin cycle.
    d. the Krebs cycle.

Understanding Concepts

11. What is a calorie? How do cells use a high-calorie molecule such as glucose?
12. How is glucose changed during glycolysis? What products are produced as a result of glycolysis?
13. What are the two pathways that might follow glycolysis? What factor can determine which of those pathways a cell might follow?
14. Use formulas to write a chemical equation for cellular respiration. Label the formulas with the names of the compounds.
15. Draw and label a mitochondrion surrounded by cytoplasm. Indicate where glycolysis, the Krebs cycle, and the electron transport chain occur.
16. How is NAD^+ involved in the products of glycolysis? What happens to a cell's NAD^+ when large numbers of high-energy electrons are produced in a short time?
17. Which two compounds react during fermentation? Which of these compounds passes high-energy electrons to the other?
18. Write equations to show how lactic acid fermentation compares with alcoholic fermentation. Which reactant(s) do they have in common?
19. How are fermentation and cellular respiration similar? What is the main difference between their starting compounds?
20. Summarize what happens during the Krebs cycle. What happens to the high-energy electrons generated during the Krebs cycle?
21. How is ATP synthase involved in making energy available to the cell?
22. When runners race for about 20 minutes, how do their bodies obtain energy?

If your class subscribes to the iText, your students can go online to access an interactive version of the Student Edition and a self-test.

(Continued from page 236)

17. Pyruvic acid and NADH react together as NADH passes high-energy electrons to pyruvic acid.

18. Lactic acid fermentation:
glucose → lactic acid
Alcoholic fermentation:
glucose → alcohol + CO_2
Both have glucose as the reactant.

19. Fermentation and cellular respiration are both processes that break down glucose and release the energy stored in the molecule. Both start with the process of glycolysis, which produces pyruvic acid. Cellular respiration requires oxygen as a reactant. Fermentation occurs without oxygen.

20. During the Krebs cycle, pyruvic acid is broken down into carbon dioxide in a series of reactions that give off energy. The high-energy electrons that are produced are picked up by a series of electron carriers, and the energy is used to convert ADP into ATP.

21. ATP synthase is a large protein through which hydrogen ions (H^+) pass, converting ADP into high-energy ATP.

22. At the beginning of a race, runners' energy comes from ATP that is present in their muscles and that is produced by lactic acid fermentation. When runners race for about 20 minutes, their bodies use cellular respiration to use stored carbohydrates to make ATP.

HOMEWORK GUIDE

Section:	Questions:
Section 9–1:	1–6, 11–19, 25, 27, 29
Section 9–2:	7–10, 20–24, 26, 28, 30

Chapter 9 Assessment

Critical Thinking

23. **Interpreting Graphics** Complete the following concept map showing the flow of energy in photosynthesis and cellular respiration.

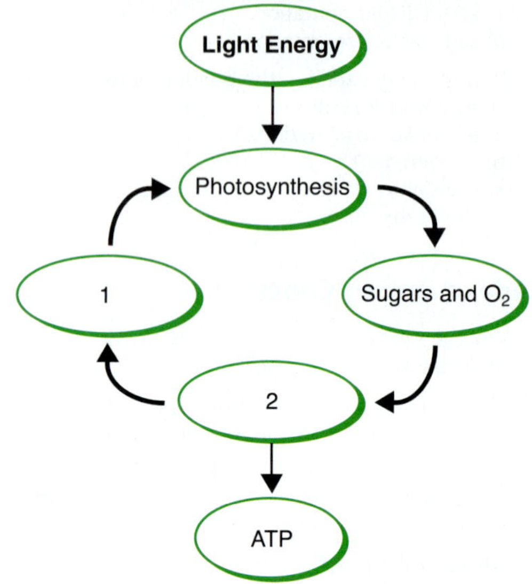

24. **Comparing and Contrasting** Where is the electron transport chain found in a eukaryotic cell? In a prokaryotic cell?

25. **Inferring** Certain types of bacteria thrive in conditions that lack oxygen. What does that fact indicate about the way they obtain energy?

26. **Predicting** In certain cases, regular exercise causes an increase in the number of mitochondria in muscle cells. How might that situation improve an individual's ability to perform energy-requiring activities?

27. **Formulating Hypotheses** Yeast cells can carry out both fermentation and cellular respiration, depending on whether oxygen is present. In which case would you expect yeast cells to grow more rapidly? Explain.

28. **Designing Experiments** Would individuals who carry out regular aerobic exercise suffer less muscle discomfort during intense exercise than other individuals? Outline an experiment that could answer this question.

29. **Inferring** To function properly, heart muscle cells require a steady supply of oxygen. After a heart attack, small amounts of lactic acid are present. What does this evidence suggest about the nature of a heart attack?

30. **Applying Concepts** Carbon monoxide (CO) molecules bring the electron transport chain in a mitochondrion to a stop by binding to an electron carrier. Use this information to explain why carbon monoxide gas kills organisms.

Focus on the BIG Idea

Matter and Energy In Chapter 3, you learned that certain substances are involved in chemical cycles. Draw a sketch that illustrates how cellular respiration fits into one of those cycles.

Writing in Science

Expand the analogy of deposits and withdrawals of money that was used in the chapter to write a short paragraph to explain cellular respiration. (*Hint:* You may wish to start out making a compare-and-contrast table that lists the similarities and differences between the two items.)

Performance-Based Assessment

Creating Diagrams Make one or more diagrams with labels or captions to show how two athletes get energy when the first athlete runs for 30 seconds and the second athlete runs for 20 minutes. How are the processes similar? How are they different? Be sure to show whether the energy is produced by an aerobic process or by an anaerobic process.

Chapter 9 Assessment

Critical Thinking

23. 1. CO_2 and H_2O
    2. cellular respiration

24. In a eukaryotic cell, the electron transport chain is found in the inner membrane of the mitochondrion. In a prokaryotic cell, the electron transport chain is in the cell membrane.

25. Bacteria that live without oxygen probably obtain energy through fermentation, because that process releases energy without involving oxygen.

26. An increased number of mitochondria in muscle cells would enable an individual to obtain energy from cellular respiration at a faster rate, so the individual might perform energy-requiring activities more quickly than others or for a longer period.

27. Yeast cells would probably grow more rapidly when they perform cellular respiration, because 18 times more ATP can be generated in the presence of oxygen than in anaerobic conditions.

28. Sample answer: Start with two groups of healthy volunteers who do not exercise regularly. Test their initial responses during intense activity, using the same definition of muscle discomfort for all. Monitor one group as they exercise regularly for a specific period, and then test both groups again to see whether the groups differ.

29. Lactic acid is produced by muscles when the supply of oxygen is insufficient, so the presence of lactic acid indicates that the heart did not receive the oxygen it needed.

30. An organism cannot continue to live without a constant supply of energy, which is provided by the Krebs cycle and the electron transport chain. Any event that cuts off that energy supply will cause the death of the organism.

Focus on the BIG Idea

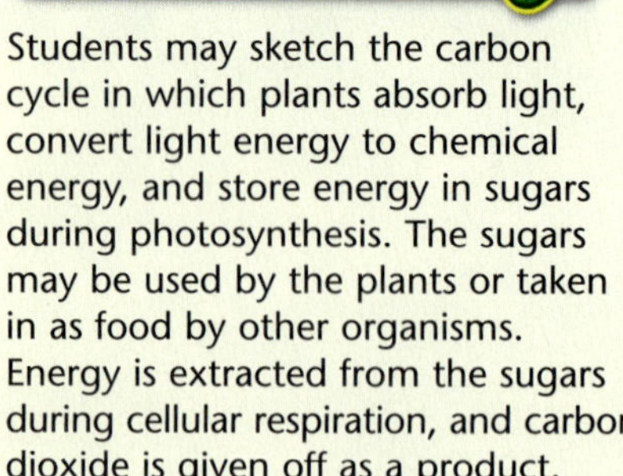

Students may sketch the carbon cycle in which plants absorb light, convert light energy to chemical energy, and store energy in sugars during photosynthesis. The sugars may be used by the plants or taken in as food by other organisms. Energy is extracted from the sugars during cellular respiration, and carbon dioxide is given off as a product.

Writing in Science

Students' paragraphs should expand the analogy by making a comparison in detail between cellular respiration and a savings account in a bank. After comparing the use of 2 ATPs in glycolysis to the initial bank deposit and the net gain of 2 ATPs to the first return of interest, students might compare the pyruvic acid and NADH from glycolysis for use in the next two stages of cellular respiration as the buildup of funds in a bank account that returns more interest. The total yield in ATPs from cellular respiration might be compared to the total interest gained after money is left in the bank for a year.

Standards Practice

Online at PHSchool.com

Test-Taking Tip When you are asked to analyze a graph showing experimental data, first look at the shape of the curve. Identify the variables and try to determine how they are related. Then, read and answer the questions that relate to the graph.

Directions: Choose the letter that best answers the question or completes the statement.

1. What raw materials are needed for cellular respiration?
   - **A** glucose and carbon dioxide
   - **B** glucose and oxygen
   - **C** carbon dioxide and oxygen
   - **D** oxygen and lactic acid
2. What happens during the Krebs cycle?
   - **A** Hydrogen ions and oxygen form water.
   - **B** The cell releases a small amount of energy through fermentation.
   - **C** Hydrogen ions build up on one side of the mitochondrial membrane.
   - **D** Pyruvic acid is broken down into carbon dioxide in a series of reactions.
3. Which substance is needed to begin the process of glycolysis?
   - **A** ATP
   - **B** NADP
   - **C** NADH
   - **D** pyruvic acid
4. In eukaryotic cells, most of cellular respiration takes place in the
   - **A** nuclei.
   - **B** cytoplasm.
   - **C** mitochondria.
   - **D** cell walls.
5. What substance produced by alcoholic fermentation makes bread dough rise?
   - **A** oxygen
   - **B** lactic acid
   - **C** carbon dioxide
   - **D** water
6. The human body can use all of the following as energy sources EXCEPT
   - **A** ATP in muscles.
   - **B** glycolysis.
   - **C** lactic acid fermentation.
   - **D** alcoholic fermentation.
7. Which of the following best represents the waste products of cellular respiration?
   - **A** CO_2
   - **B** H_2O
   - **C** O_2
   - **D** CO_2 and H_2O

Questions 8–9 The graph below shows the rate of alcoholic fermentation for yeast at different temperatures.

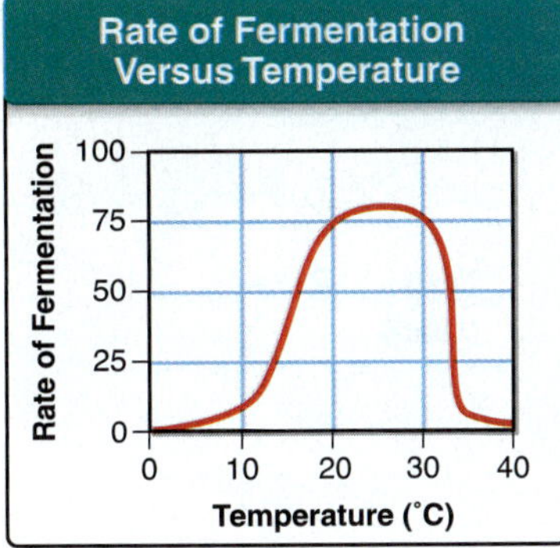

8. What is the relationship between the rate of fermentation and temperature?
   - **A** The rate of fermentation continually increases as temperature increases.
   - **B** The rate of fermentation continually decreases as temperature increases.
   - **C** The rate of fermentation increases with temperature, then it rapidly decreases.
   - **D** The rate of fermentation decreases with temperature, then it increases.
9. Which statement could explain the data shown in the graph?
   - **A** The molecules that regulate fermentation perform optimally at temperatures above 30°C.
   - **B** The yeast begins releasing carbon dioxide at 30°C.
   - **C** The yeast cannot survive at temperatures above 30°C.
   - **D** The molecules that regulate fermentation perform optimally below 10°C.

Standards Practice

1. B	**4.** C	**7.** D
2. D	**5.** C	**8.** C
3. A	**6.** D	**9.** C

Success Tracker™

Online at PHSchool.com

Have students check their understanding of the chapter by logging onto Success Tracker.

Performance-Based Assessment

Diagrams of the 30-second run should show that runners use the ATP that was already present in the muscles as well as that produced by lactic acid fermentation. Diagrams of the 20-minute run should show runners using carbohydrates to release energy through cellular respiration.

Go Online PHSchool.com

Your students can independently test their knowledge of the chapter and print out their test results for your files.

Chapter Planner 10 Cell Growth and Division

Section and Section Objectives	Time	STANDARDS NCLB	STANDARDS Biology	Activities and Labs
10–1 Cell Growth, pp. 241–243 **10.1.1** ***Explain*** the problems that growth causes for cells. **10.1.2** ***Describe*** how cell division solves the problems of cell growth.	1 period (1/2 block)			**SE:** ***Inquiry Activity,*** How do organisms grow?, p. 240 L2 **TE:** ***Build Science Skills,*** p. 241 L2 L3 **SE:** ***Quick Lab,*** What limits the sizes of cells?, p. 242 L2
10–2 Cell Division, pp. 244–249 **10.2.1** ***Name*** the main events of the cell cycle. **10.2.2** ***Describe*** what happens during the four phases of mitosis.	2 periods (1 block)	7 1.e		**TE:** ***Demonstration,*** p. 244 L1 L2 **TE:** ***Build Science Skills,*** p. 245, 246, 247 L2 **TE:** ***Build Science Skills,*** p. 247 L1 L2 **SE:** ***Analyzing Data,*** Life Spans of Human Cells, p. 249 L2 L3 **SE:** ***Exploration,*** Modeling the Phases of the Cell Cycle, pp. 254–255 L2 L3 **LMA:** Chapter 10 Lab L2 L3 **LMB:** Chapter 10 Lab L1 L2 **BTM:** Lab 3 L2 L3
10–3 Regulating the Cell Cycle, pp. 250–252 **10.3.1** ***Identify*** a factor that can stop cells from growing. **10.3.2** ***Describe*** how the cell cycle is regulated. **10.3.3** ***Explain*** how cancer cells are different from other cells.	1 period (1/2 block)			**SE:** ***Technology & Society,*** Stem Cells: Promises and Problems, p. 253 L2 **IF:** Investigation 3
Chapter Assessment, pp. 256–259	1 period (1/2 block)			

ACTIVITY PLANNER

SE: ***Inquiry Activity,*** p. 240; 15 min.; microscope, prepared slides of cells from large and small plants and similar tissues from large and small animals

SE: ***Build Science Skills,*** p. 241; 15 min.; 2 boxes of different sizes, metric ruler

SE: ***Quick Lab,*** p. 242; 15 min.; 2 peeled hard-boiled eggs, blue food coloring, 150-mL beaker, scalpel, spoon, paper towels, metric ruler

TE: ***Demonstration,*** p. 244; 5 min.; 2 pipe cleaners, pin

TE: ***Build Science Skills,*** p. 246; 15 min.; copies of pictures of each phase of mitosis

TE: ***Build Science Skills,*** p. 247; 20 min.; microscope, paramecium culture, slides, dropper pipette

TE: ***Build Science Skills,*** p. 247; 15 min.; pipe cleaners, string

SE: ***Exploration,*** pp. 254–255; 50 min.; microscope, prepared slides of onion root tips, scissors, tape or glue, craft materials such as beads, yarn, and pipe cleaners

PLANNING KEY

Ability Levels

for students performing . . .

below grade level L1

at grade level L2

above grade level L3

Print Components

SE	Student Edition
TE	Teacher's Edition
RSW	Reading & Study Workbook A
ARSW	Adapted Reading & Study Workbook B
TR	Teaching Resources
IF	Investigations in Forensics
LA	Lab Assessment
BTM	Biotechnology Manual
IDM	Issues and Decision Making
LW	Lab Worksheets
LMA	Laboratory Manual A
LMB	Laboratory Manual B

Tech Components

CTB	Computer Test Bank
BD	BioDetectives DVD
TP	Transparencies Plus
PLM	Probeware Lab Manual
ABC	ABC DVD Library
LS	Lab Simulations
VL	Virtual Labs

Interactive textbook with assessment at PHSchool.com

Program Resources	Assessment	Media and Technology
TR: Lesson Plan 10–1, Section Summary, p. 128 L1, p. 136 L2, Worksheets, p. 130 L1, p. 138 L2 **RSW:** Section 10–1 L2 **ARSW:** Section 10–1 L1	**SE:** 10–1 Section Assessment, p. 243 **TR:** Section Review 10–1	**iText:** Section 10–1 **TP:** 10–1 Interest Grabber, Section Outline, Ratio of Surface Area to Volume in Cells
TR: Lesson Plan 10–2, Section Summary, p. 128 L1, p. 136 L2, Worksheets, pp. 131–133 L1, pp. 139–141 L2, Enrichment L3 **LW:** Chapter 10 Exploration L1 L2 L3 **RSW:** Section 10–2 L2 **ARSW:** Section 10–2 L1	**SE:** 10–2 Section Assessment, p. 249 **TR:** Section Review 10–2	**iText:** Section 10–2 **TP:** 10–2 Interest Grabber, Section Outline, Concept Map, Figure 10–4, Figure 10–5 **ABC:** 16 Animal Cell Mitosis and Cytokinesis **Lab Simulations CD-ROM:** Mitosis **VL:** Lab 9, Lab 10
TR: Lesson Plan 10–3, Section Summary, p. 129 L1, p. 137 L2, Worksheets, p. 134 L1, p. 142 L2 **RSW:** Section 10–3 L2 **ARSW:** Section 10–3 L1	**SE:** 10–3 Section Assessment, p. 252 **TR:** Section Review 10–3	**iText:** Section 10–3 **TP:** 10–3 Interest Grabber, Section Outline, Control of Cell Division, Figure 10–8 **BD:** "Skin Cancer: Deadly Cells"
	SE: Chapter 10 Assessment, pp. 256–259 **TR:** Chapter Vocabulary Review, Graphic Organizer, Chapter 10 Test **LA:** Laboratory Assessment 3	**iText:** Chapter 10 Assessment **CTB:** Chapter 10 Test **Go Online** Students can do research, share data, and test their knowledge online.

PRESSED FOR TIME?

To Preview the Chapter
- Introduce students to Key Concepts and Vocabulary terms in each section.
- Assign the Reading Strategies for each section.

To Cover the Chapter Quickly
- Have students read the first page and Figure 10–2 of Section 10–1, The Cell Cycle and Figures 10–5 and 10–6 in Section 10–2, and Controls on Cell Division and Figure 10–8 in Section 10–3.
- Assign the Section Review 10–2, questions 1–10 in Chapter 10 Assessment, and Chapter 10 Standards Practice.

To Review the Chapter
- Assign Sections 10–1 through 10–3 in the Reading and Study Workbook or Adapted Reading and Study Workbook.
- Assign Section Reviews for 10–1 through 10–3 and the Chapter Vocabulary Review for Chapter 10 in the Teaching Resources.

CHAPTER 10

ENGAGE/EXPLORE

Inquiry Activity

Objective Students will be able to observe that the sizes of cells are about the same in small organisms as in large organisms. L2

Skills Focus **Observing, Comparing and Contrasting**

Materials microscope, prepared slides of cells from large and small plants and similar tissues from large and small animals

Time 15 minutes

Advance Prep Set up microscope stations at several locations around the classroom. Select prepared slides of corresponding tissues in large and small organisms, such as grass blades and tree leaves, as well as muscle tissue from a small and a large vertebrate.

Safety Caution students to handle prepared slides carefully.

Strategy Circulate among students to make sure they are focusing their microscopes correctly.

Expected Outcome Students should determine that growth in multicellular organisms is due mostly to an increase in cell number, not cell size.

Think About It

1. Students should observe that cells of small and large plants are about the same size and cells from small and large animals are about the same size.
2. A typical statement might suggest that there is a greater number of cells in large organisms than in small organisms, but the size of cells is about the same.

Assess Prior Knowledge

Ask students: **How would you describe the process by which a multicellular organism increases its size?** *(Accept all reasonable responses. Many students might suggest that the organism's cells grow larger.)* Point out that all the cells that students know about are quite small. Then, ask: **Why do cells stay small?** *(Some students might suggest that cells stay small because they are programmed to be small by their DNA. Larger cells face more problems in absorbing enough nutrients and ridding themselves of water effectively.)*

CHAPTER 10

Cell Growth and Division

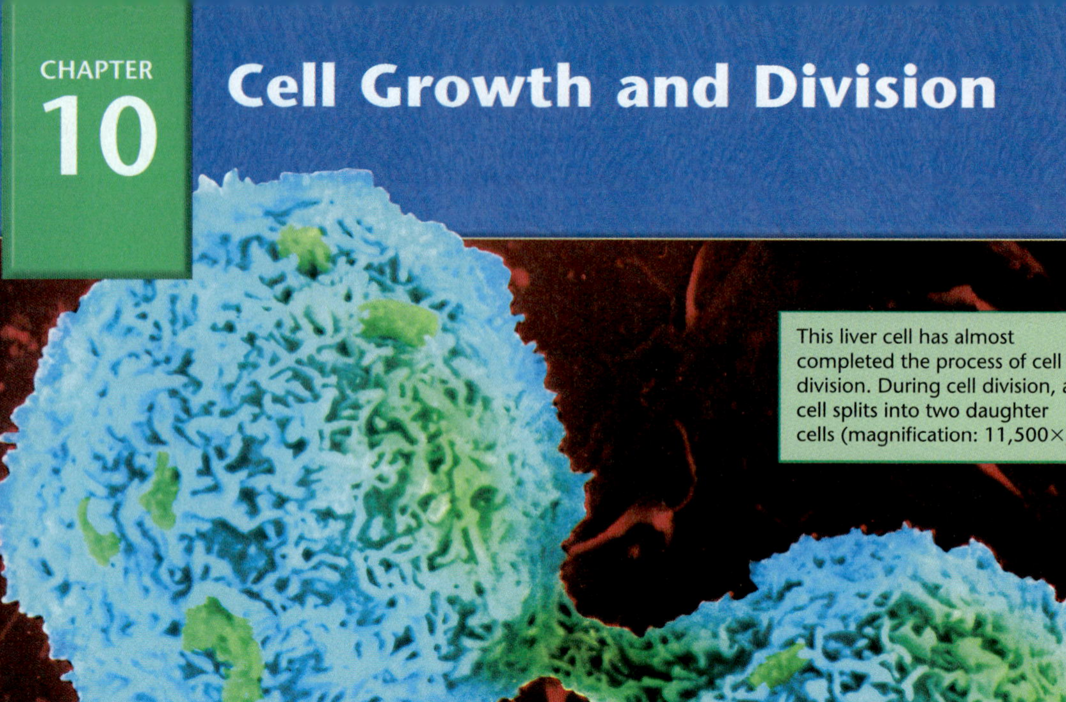

This liver cell has almost completed the process of cell division. During cell division, a cell splits into two daughter cells (magnification: 11,500×).

Inquiry Activity

How do organisms grow?

Procedure

1. Use a microscope to compare the sizes of similar cells in large and small plants. For example, you might compare the leaf cells of grass to the leaf cells of a tree. Be sure to use the same magnification when comparing the sizes of the cells.
2. Use a microscope to compare the sizes of cells in similar tissues from small and large animals, such as muscle tissue from a frog and from a human.

Think About It

1. **Observing** Are the cells of the small plant larger or smaller than those of the large plant? Are the cells of the small animal larger or smaller than those of the large animal?
2. **Comparing and Contrasting** Make a general statement that compares the number and size of cells in small organisms to those in larger organisms.

HISTORY OF SCIENCE

Human cells that keep dividing
To study cell division for medical and other purposes, biologists need human cells that continue to divide in culture in the laboratory. Yet, finding such cells proved difficult. In 1951, researchers at Johns Hopkins University tried to culture a line of cells that would continue to live and multiply. Every cell sample they tried died out in a few weeks, because normal mammalian cells will divide only 20–50 times in culture before they die. Finally, cells from one sample kept dividing week after week, and eventually, year after year. These were called HeLa cells after their original source, a young Baltimore woman named Henrietta Lacks. The sample had been taken from a malignant tumor in her body. Unfortunately, she died a few months later, but HeLa cells have been grown since that time in laboratories around the world.

10–1 Cell Growth

When a living thing grows, what happens to its cells? Does an animal get larger because each cell increases in size or because it produces more of them? In most cases, living things grow by producing more cells. On average, the cells of an adult animal are no larger than those of a young animal—there are just more of them.

Guide for Reading

Key Concept

- What problems does growth cause for cells?

Vocabulary

cell division

Reading Strategy: Asking Questions Before reading this section, rewrite each blue heading as a *what, where,* or *how* question. Then, as you read, fill in the answer to each question.

Limits to Cell Growth

There are two main reasons why cells divide rather than continuing to grow indefinitely. **The larger a cell becomes, the more demands the cell places on its DNA. In addition, the cell has more trouble moving enough nutrients and wastes across the cell membrane.**

DNA "Overload" As you may recall, the information that controls a cell's function is stored in a molecule known as DNA. In eukaryotic cells, DNA is found in the nucleus of the cell. When a cell is small, the information stored in that DNA is able to meet all of the cell's needs. But as a cell increases in size, it usually does not make extra copies of DNA. If a cell were to grow without limit, an "information crisis" would occur.

To help understand why a larger cell has a more difficult time functioning efficiently than a smaller cell, compare the cell to a growing town. Suppose a small town has a library with a few thousand books. If more people move into the town, the town will get larger. There will be more people borrowing books, and sometimes people may have to wait to borrow popular titles. Similarly, a larger cell would have to make greater demands on its available genetic "library." In time, the cell's DNA would no longer be able to serve the increasing needs of the growing cell.

Exchanging Materials There is another reason why the size of cells is limited. You may recall that food, oxygen, and water enter a cell through its cell membrane. Waste products leave in the same way. The rate at which this exchange takes place depends on the surface area of the cell, which is the total area of its cell membrane. However, the rate at which food and oxygen are used up and waste products are produced depends on the cell's volume. Understanding the relationship between a cell's volume and its surface area is the key to understanding why cells must divide as they grow.

▼ **Figure 10–1** Living things grow by producing more cells. Although the adult snail is larger than the young snail, the cells of both are the same size.

SECTION RESOURCES

Print:

- ***Teaching Resources,*** Lesson Plan 10–1, Adapted Section Summary 10–1, Adapted Worksheets 10–1, Section Summary 10–1, Worksheets 10–1, Section Review 10–1
- ***Reading and Study Workbook A,*** Section 10–1
- ***Adapted Reading and Study Workbook B,*** Section 10–1

Technology:

- ***iText,*** Section 10–1
- ***Transparencies Plus,*** Section 10–1

Section 10–1

1 FOCUS

Objectives

10.1.1 ***Explain*** the problems that growth causes for cells.

10.1.2 ***Describe*** how cell division solves the problems of cell growth.

Guide for Reading

Vocabulary Preview

Before students read the section, ask for volunteers to define *cell division.*

Reading Strategy

Have students preview Figure 10–2 and write an explanation of the implications the data in the table have for cell size and growth. Then, after they read the section, have them revise their explanation.

2 INSTRUCT

Limits to Cell Growth

Build Science Skills

Drawing Conclusions Divide the class into small groups, and give each group two cardboard boxes, one larger than the other. Ask each group to use a metric ruler to find the surface area of each box and then, the volume of each box. After students have collected data, ask them to compare the difference in surface area between the boxes and the difference in volume between the boxes. Challenge students to draw a conclusion about whether surface area or volume increases more rapidly as the size of a box increases. Students should discover that volume increases more rapidly than surface area. L2 L3

Your students can extend their knowledge of cell growth through this online experience.

Quick Lab

BIIE 1.g

Objective Students will be able to use a model to explain why a cell cannot continue to grow indefinitely. L2

Skills Focus Observing, Using Models

Materials 2 peeled hard-boiled eggs, blue food coloring, 150-mL beaker, scalpel, spoon, paper towels, metric ruler

Time 15 minutes

Safety Tell students not to eat the pieces of egg.

Advance Prep Boil eggs the day of the activity, two per group of students. Blue coloring works best, though other colors can be used. You may want to cut egg cubes ahead of time.

Strategy Food coloring will diffuse farther if the eggs are warm.

Expected Outcome Students should find that the food coloring diffuses almost to the center of the egg cube but just through the surface of the whole egg.

Analyze and Conclude

1. The coloring almost reaches the center of the egg cube but moves only a few millimeters into the whole egg.
2. Just as the food coloring entered the eggs, food must enter a living cell, and wastes must be removed. The food coloring diffused into more of the egg cube than the whole egg because the egg cube had a smaller ratio of surface area to volume than the whole egg. Similarly, a very large cell would not have a large enough surface area for substances to move easily into and out of the cell.

For: Links on cell growth
Visit: PHSchool.com
Web Code: cbd-3101

Ratio of Surface Area to Volume Imagine a cell that is shaped like a cube, like those in **Figure 10–2.** If this cell has a length of 1 cm, its surface area would be equal to length × width × number of sides, or 1 cm × 1 cm × 6 = 6 cm². The volume of the cell would be equal to length × width × height, or 1 cm × 1 cm × 1 cm = 1 cm³. To obtain the ratio of surface area to volume, divide the surface area by the volume. In this case, the ratio of surface area to volume would be 6 / 1, or 6 : 1.

If the length of the cell doubled, what would happen to the cell's surface area compared to its volume? The cell's surface area would be equal to 2 cm × 2 cm × 6 = 24 cm². The volume would be equal to 2 cm × 2 cm × 2 cm = 8 cm³. The cell's ratio of surface area to volume would be 24 / 8, or 3 : 1.

What if the length of the cell triples? The cell's surface area now would be 3 cm × 3 cm × 6 = 54 cm². The volume would be 3 cm × 3 cm × 3 cm = 27 cm³. The ratio of surface area to volume would be 54 / 27, or 2 : 1.

Note that the volume increases much more rapidly than the surface area, causing the ratio of surface area to volume to decrease. This decrease creates serious problems for the cell.

To use the town analogy again, suppose that the small town has a two-lane main street. As the town grows, more people will begin to use this street. The main street leading through town, however, has not increased in size. As a result, people will encounter more traffic as they enter and leave the town. A cell that continues to grow larger would experience similar problems.

BIIE 1.g

Quick Lab

What limits the sizes of cells?

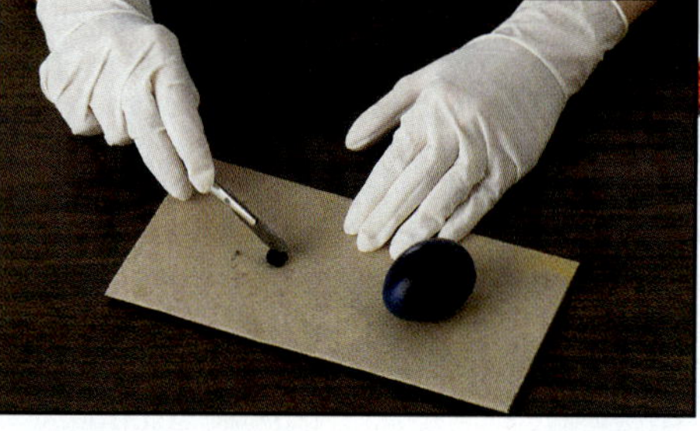

Materials 2 peeled hard-boiled eggs, blue food coloring, 150-mL beaker, scalpel, spoon, paper towels, metric ruler

Procedure    

1. Put on your plastic gloves and apron. Place 100 mL of water in a beaker. Add 10 drops of blue food coloring, and stir with a spoon. **CAUTION:** *Food coloring may stain hands and clothing.*
2. Use the scalpel to cut through the middle of 1 hard-boiled egg. **CAUTION:** *Be careful with the scalpel.* Remove the yolk. Cut an 8-mm cube from the thickest part of the egg white.
3. Place the egg cube and a peeled hard-boiled egg gently into the beaker of food coloring and water. Allow the eggs to sit in the beaker for 10 minutes.
4. After 10 minutes, use a spoon to carefully remove the egg cube and the whole egg from the beaker, and place them on a paper towel. Cut the egg cube in half. Clean the scalpel blade and cut the whole egg in half. Measure how far the blue color penetrated the egg cube and the whole egg.

Analyze and Conclude

1. **Observing** How close to the centers of the egg cube and the whole egg did the color reach?
2. **Using Models** Compare the whole egg and the egg cube to cells to explain why a cell cannot continue to grow indefinitely.

UNIVERSAL ACCESS

Inclusion/Special Needs

The concept of ratio of surface area to volume may be a difficult one for some students to grasp. To help these students, have them determine simple ratios, such as students in their class to students in the school. Then, have them use tape measures to make measurements of the classroom and a larger room in the school, such as the cafeteria. With your guidance, have them use their measurements to determine a ratio of surface area to volume for each room. L1

Advanced Learners

Encourage interested students to extend the Quick Lab on this page by determining ratio of surface area to volume for each object. First, they should measure the volume of water that each object displaces by using a graduated cylinder. They can then measure the surface area of each object by tightly wrapping aluminum foil around both the egg and the cube. They can then trace the pieces of foil onto graph paper and count the squares within each tracing. L3

Ratio of Surface Area to Volume in Cells			
Cell Size	 1 cm × 1 cm × 1 cm	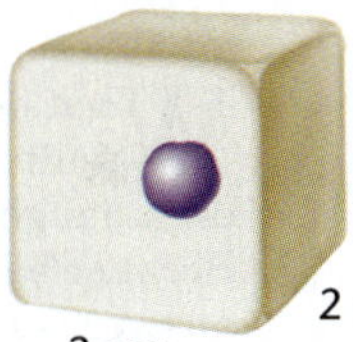 2 cm × 2 cm × 2 cm	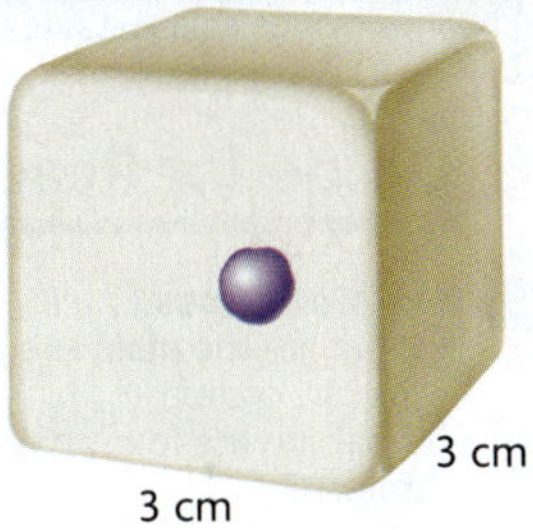 3 cm × 3 cm × 3 cm
Surface Area (length × width × 6)	1 cm × 1 cm × 6 = 6 cm^2	2 cm × 2 cm × 6 = 24 cm^2	3 cm × 3 cm × 6 = 54 cm^2
Volume (length × width × height)	1 cm × 1 cm × 1 cm = 1 cm^3	2 cm × 2 cm × 2 cm = 8 cm^3	3 cm × 3 cm × 3 cm = 27 cm^3
Ratio of Surface Area to Volume	6 / 1 = 6 : 1	24 / 8 = 3 : 1	54 / 27 = 2 : 1

▲ **Figure 10–2** As the length of a cell increases, its volume increases faster than its surface area. **The resulting decrease in the cell's ratio of surface area to volume makes it more difficult for the cell to move needed materials in and waste products out.**

If a cell got too large, it would be more difficult to get sufficient amounts of oxygen and nutrients in and waste products out. This is one reason why cells do not grow much larger even if the organism of which they are a part does.

Division of the Cell

Before it becomes too large, a growing cell divides forming two "daughter" cells. The process by which a cell divides into two new daughter cells is called **cell division.**

Before cell division occurs, the cell replicates, or copies, all of its DNA. This replication of DNA solves the problem of information storage because each daughter cell gets one complete set of genetic information. Thus, each daughter cell receives its own genetic "library." Cell division also solves the problem of increasing size by reducing cell volume. Each daughter cell has an increased ratio of surface area to volume. This allows efficient exchange of materials with the environment.

10–1 Section Assessment

1. **Key Concept** Give two reasons why cells divide.
2. How is a cell's DNA like the books in a library?
3. As a cell increases in size, which increases more rapidly, its surface area or its volume?
4. **Critical Thinking Calculating** Calculate the surface area, volume, and ratio of surface area to volume of an imaginary cubic cell measuring 4 cm on each side.

Focus on the BIG Idea

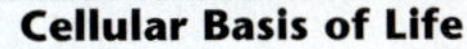

Cellular Basis of Life
Select two cell organelles and describe how their functions might be impaired if the cell were to become too large. A review of Chapter 7 may help you with this task.

10–1 Section Assessment

1. The larger a cell becomes, the more demands the cell places on its DNA and the more trouble the cell has moving enough nutrients and wastes across the cell membrane.
2. The information that controls a cell's function is stored in DNA, just as information needed by the public is stored in the books of a library. A cell's DNA, then, is a "genetic" library.
3. Its volume
4. The surface area is 96 cm^2, the volume is 64 cm^3, and the ratio of surface area to volume is 96/64 = 3 : 2.

Make Connections

Mathematics Some students may have limited experience with ratios. Explain that a ratio is a measure of the relative size of two quantities, expressed as a proportion or as a fraction. A ratio can be expressed as a fraction, such as *1/2*, or with a colon, such as *1 : 2*. Like a fraction, a ratio can be reduced to the lowest numbers, and thus 50 : 25 is reduced to 2 : 1. Ask: **What is the ratio of vowels to consonants in the alphabet?** *(5 : 21)* L1 L2

Division of the Cell

Use Visuals

Figure 10–2 Have students compare the largest cell and the smallest cell in the figure. Ask: **Which of the two cells has the greater volume?** *(The larger cell)* **Which of the two has the greater surface area?** *(The larger cell)* Point out that both volume and surface area increase with cell size. L2

3 ASSESS

Evaluate Understanding

Ask students to write a paragraph that explains why a cell in the human body never grows as large as a fist.

Reteach

Tell students that an imaginary cubic cell has doubled from a length of 3 mm to a length of 6 mm. Have them calculate the ratio of surface area to volume for each cell. *(The first cell has a ratio of 2 : 1; the larger cell has a ratio of 1 : 1.)*

Focus on the BIG Idea

Sample answer: The function of a mitochondrion might be impaired because it might not be able to get enough oxygen from outside the cell. Similarly, a chloroplast might not be able to get enough water from outside the cell.

If your class subscribes to the iText, use it to review the Key Concepts in Section 10–1.

Section 10-2

1 FOCUS

Objectives

10.2.1 ***Name*** the main events of the cell cycle.

10.2.2 ***Describe*** what happens during the four phases of mitosis.

Guide for Reading

Vocabulary Preview

Ask students at random to pronounce the Vocabulary words in the order in which they appear. Correct any mispronunciations.

Reading Strategy

Suggest that students write a summary of the information in Figure 10–5. Then, have them revise their summaries after reading the section.

2 INSTRUCT

Chromosomes

Address Misconceptions

Students may think that there is a chemical or structural difference between chromosomes and chromatids. Explain that there is really no difference between chromosomes and chromatids except that the chromatids are always double structures (DNA replicas) fastened together at their centromeres. Biologists avoid saying that an organism has "double" the number of "chromosomes," because each kind of organism has a specific number of chromosomes. A chromatid becomes a chromosome when the sister chromatids separate during anaphase. L1 L2

Demonstration

Reinforce students' understanding of chromatids and centromeres by using two pipe cleaners and a pin. Show students a pipe cleaner and explain that it represents a chromosome. As you explain the process of duplication of chromosomes during interphase, pick up another pipe cleaner of the same size and wind it around the first one. Then, push a pin through the contact joint of the two pipe cleaners and explain that the pin represents a centromere. L1 L2

10–2 Cell Division

7 1.e. Students know cells divide to increase their numbers through a process of mitosis, which results in two daughter cells with identical sets of chromosomes.

Guide for Reading

Key Concepts
- What are the main events of the cell cycle?
- What are the four phases of mitosis?

Vocabulary
mitosis
cytokinesis
chromatid
centromere
interphase
cell cycle
prophase
centriole
spindle
metaphase
anaphase
telophase

Reading Strategy: Outlining As you read this section, outline the major events of the cell cycle. Write a few sentences to describe the activity of chromosomes as they progress through each part of the cell cycle.

What do you think would happen if a cell were simply to split into two, without any advance preparation? Would each daughter cell have everything it needed to survive? Because each cell has only one set of genetic information, the answer is no. Every cell must first copy its genetic information before cell division begins. Each daughter cell then gets a complete copy of that information.

In most prokaryotes, the rest of the process of cell division is a simple matter of separating the contents of the cell into two parts. In eukaryotes, cell division is more complex and occurs in two main stages. The first stage, division of the cell nucleus, is called **mitosis** (my-TOH-sis). The second stage, division of the cytoplasm, is called **cytokinesis** (sy-toh-kih-NEE-sis).

CA a Many organisms, especially unicellular ones, reproduce by means of mitosis and cytokinesis. Reproduction by mitosis is classified as asexual, since the cells produced by mitosis are genetically identical to the parent cell. Mitosis is also the source of new cells when a multicellular organism grows and develops. In humans, for example, mitosis begins shortly after the egg is fertilized, producing the vast numbers of cells needed for the embryo to take form.

Chromosomes

In eukaryotic cells, the genetic information that is passed on from one generation of cells to the next is carried by chromosomes. Chromosomes are made up of DNA—which carries the cell's coded genetic information—and proteins. The cells of every organism have a specific number of chromosomes. The cells of fruit flies, for example, have 8 chromosomes; human cells have 46 chromosomes; and carrot cells have 18 chromosomes.

Chromosomes are not visible in most cells except during cell division. This is because the DNA and protein molecules that make up the chromosomes are spread throughout the nucleus. At the beginning of cell division, however, the chromosomes condense into compact, visible structures that can be seen through a light microscope.

Well before cell division, each chromosome is replicated, or copied. Because of this, each chromosome consists of two identical "sister" **chromatids** (KROH-muh-tidz), as shown in **Figure 10–3.** When the cell divides, the "sister" chromatids separate from each other. One chromatid goes to each of the two new cells.

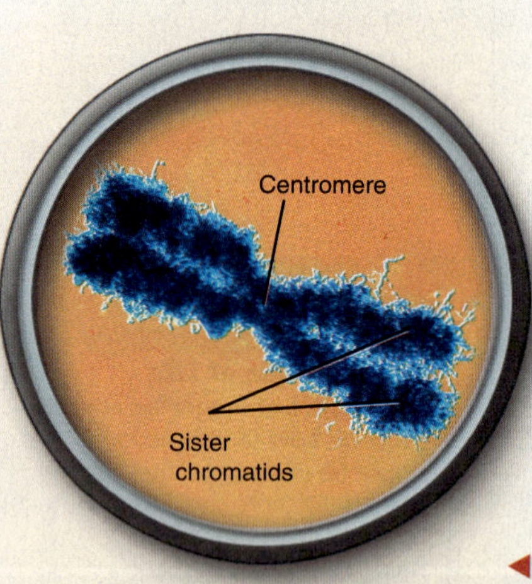

(magnification: 20,000×)

Figure 10–3 This is a human chromosome shown as it appears through an electron microscope. Each chromosome has two sister chromatids attached at the centromere. **Inferring** *Why is it important that the sister chromatids are identical?*

SECTION RESOURCES

Print:
- ***Laboratory Manual A,*** Chapter 10 Lab
- ***Laboratory Manual B,*** Chapter 10 Lab
- ***Teaching Resources,*** Lesson Plan 10–2, Adapted Section Summary 10–2, Adapted Worksheets 10–2, Section Summary 10–2, Worksheets 10–2, Section Review 10–2, Enrichment
- ***Reading and Study Workbook A,*** Section 10–2
- ***Adapted Reading and Study Workbook B,*** Section 10–2
- ***Biotechnology Manual,*** Lab 3
- ***Lab Worksheets,*** Chapter 10 Exploration

Technology:
- ***iText,*** Section 10–2
- ***Animated Biological Concepts DVD,*** 16 Animal Cell Mitosis and Cytokinesis
- ***Transparencies Plus,*** Section 10–2
- ***Lab Simulations CD-ROM,*** Mitosis
- ***Virtual Labs,*** Lab 9, Lab 10

Each pair of chromatids is attached at an area called the centromere (SEN-troh-meer). **Centromeres** are usually located near the middle of the chromatids, although some lie near the ends. A human body cell entering cell division contains 46 chromosomes, each of which consists of two chromatids.

The Cell Cycle

At one time, biologists described the life of a cell as one cell division after another separated by an "in-between" period of growth called **interphase.** We now appreciate that a great deal happens in the time between cell divisions, and use a concept known as the cell cycle to represent recurring events in the life of the cell. The **cell cycle** is the series of events that cells go through as they grow and divide. **During the cell cycle, a cell grows, prepares for division, and divides to form two daughter cells, each of which then begins the cycle again.** The cell cycle is shown in **Figure 10–4.**

The cell cycle consists of four phases. Mitosis and cytokinesis take place during the M phase. Chromosome replication, or synthesis, takes place during the S phase. When the cell copies the chromosomes, it makes a duplicate set of DNA. Between the M and S phases are G_1 and G_2. The *G* in the names of these phases stands for "gap," but the G_1 and G_2 are definitely not periods when nothing takes place. They are actually periods of intense growth and activity.

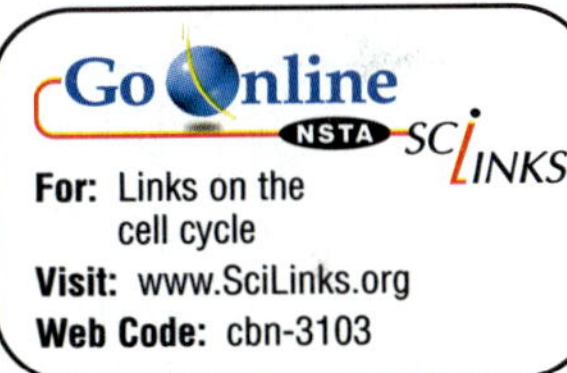

Events of the Cell Cycle

During the normal cell cycle, interphase can be quite long, whereas the process of cell division takes place quickly. Interphase is divided into three phases: G_1, S, and G_2.

The G_1 phase is a period of activity in which cells do most of their growing. During this phase, cells increase in size and synthesize new proteins and organelles.

G_1 is followed by the S phase, in which chromosomes are replicated and the synthesis of DNA molecules takes place. Key proteins associated with the chromosomes are also synthesized during the S phase. Usually, once a cell enters the S phase and begins the replication of its chromosomes, it completes the rest of the cell cycle.

When the DNA replication is completed, the cell enters the G_2 phase. G_2 is usually the shortest of the three phases of interphase. During the G_2 phase, many of the organelles and molecules required for cell division are produced. When the events of the G_2 phase are completed, the cell is ready to enter the M phase and begin the process of cell division.

▼ **Figure 10–4 During the cell cycle, the cell grows, replicates its DNA, and divides into two daughter cells.** DNA synthesis takes place during the S phase. Cell division takes place during the M phase. G_1 and G_2 are gap phases.

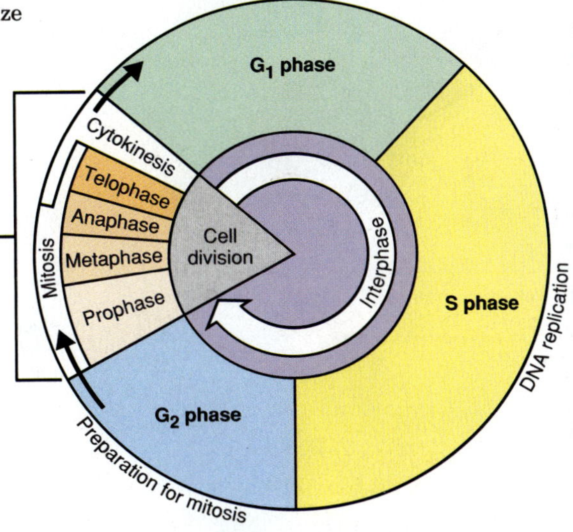

CHECKPOINT *What happens during the G_1 phase?*

The Cell Cycle

Use Visuals

Figure 10–4 After students have examined the figure, ask: **What are the four phases of the cell cycle?** *(G_1 phase, S phase, G_2 phase, and M phase)* **If you were to divide the cell cycle into two parts, what would they be?** *(Interphase and cell division)* Explain that this is called a cycle because the process is continuous through generations of cells, and one phase leads into the next. Then, ask: **For each individual cell, when does the cell cycle begin?** *(When the daughter cells form, at the end of the M phase, or after cytokinesis has occurred)* L2

Download a worksheet on the cell cycle for students to complete, and find additional teacher support from NSTA SciLinks.

Events of the Cell Cycle

Build Science Skills

Using Models Divide the class into eight groups, making sure each group contains a mix of students of varying abilities. Assign one group the G_1 phase, a second group the S phase, a third group the G_2 phase, four groups one of the four phases of mitosis, and the eighth group cytokinesis. Explain that together, the groups will make a wall-length cartoon strip that shows the events in the cell cycle. Give each group four frames—four large sheets of paper—for its part of the total cartoon sequence. Advise group members to work together to plan what should be shown in the four frames, which should contain cartoon figures that creatively tell the story of that part of the cell cycle. When all groups have completed their work, tape all cartoons in sequence across the side of the classroom. L2

Answers to . . .

CHECKPOINT *Cells increase in size and synthesize new proteins and organelles.*

Figure 10–3 *Each cell must receive the same genetic information.*

ESL SUPPORT FOR ENGLISH LANGUAGE LEARNERS

Comprehension: Link to Visual

Beginning Use Figure 10–4 (page 245) to help students understand the cell cycle. In the figure, point out the labels *cell growth, DNA replication, preparation for mitosis*, and *cell division*. Then, hand out a two-column graphic organizer titled "The Cell Cycle." The left column should be labeled *Phase*, and the rows of the left column should be blank. The right column should be labeled *Activity*. Each row of the right column should be filled in with a description of the activity associated with one phase of the cell cycle (for example, *cell growth*). Working with an English-proficient partner, the students can use the information in Figure 10–4 to complete the left column of the graphic organizer. L1

Intermediate Modify the activity for beginning students by requiring the students to fill in both columns of the graphic organizer using the information found in Figure 10–4. L2

10–2 (continued)

Download a worksheet on cell division for students to complete, and find additional teacher support from NSTA SciLinks.

Mitosis

Build Science Skills

Predicting Divide the class into small groups, and give each group a packet of pictures, each of which represents a phase of mitosis. To make each packet, copy photos or illustrations from a college textbook, eliminating any labels. Challenge each group to make a prediction about how mitosis proceeds by placing the pictures in the correct sequence. Then, have groups present their predictions to the class. L2

Use Visuals

Figure 10–5 Explain that this figure shows each event in the cell cycle in two ways, as a photomicrograph and as a labeled illustration. Ask: **When are the cell's chromosomes replicated during the cell cycle?** *(During the S phase of interphase)* **What function does the spindle serve during mitosis?** *(The spindle helps separate the chromosomes.)* Have students look back at Figure 10–4, and ask: **Does cytokinesis start when telophase ends?** *(No. The figure shows that cytokinesis ends after telophase, but it begins during mitosis.)* Explain that cytokinesis overlaps mitosis and usually begins during telophase. Finally, have students use the figure to make their own drawings of each phase of mitosis. L2

For: Links on cell division
Visit: www.SciLinks.org
Web Code: cbn-3102

CA a

a 7 1.e

Mitosis

Biologists divide the events of mitosis into four phases: prophase, metaphase, anaphase, and telophase. Depending on the type of cell, the four phases of mitosis may last anywhere from a few minutes to several days. As you read about each phase of mitosis, look at **Figure 10–5.**

Prophase The first and longest phase of mitosis, **prophase,** can take as much as 50 to 60 percent of the total time required to complete mitosis. During prophase, the chromosomes become visible. The **centrioles** (SEN-tree-ohlz), two tiny structures located in the cytoplasm near the nuclear envelope, separate and take up positions on opposite sides of the nucleus.

▼ **Figure 10–5** Most eukaryotic cells go through a regular cycle of interphase, mitosis, and cytokinesis. **Mitosis has four phases: prophase, metaphase, anaphase, and telophase.** The events shown here are typical of animal cells. The photographs shown are from a developing whitefish embryo (magnification: 625×).

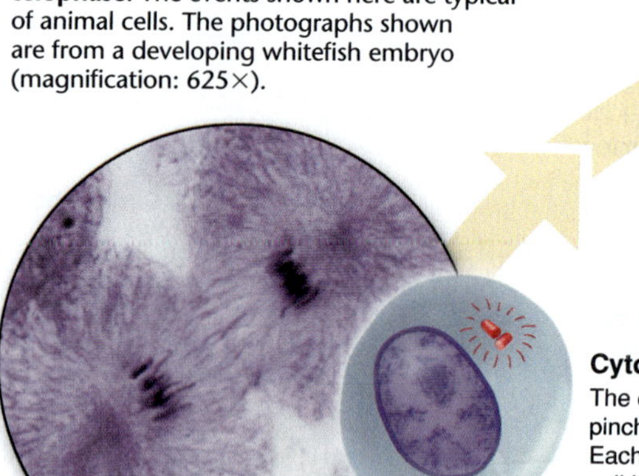

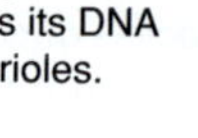

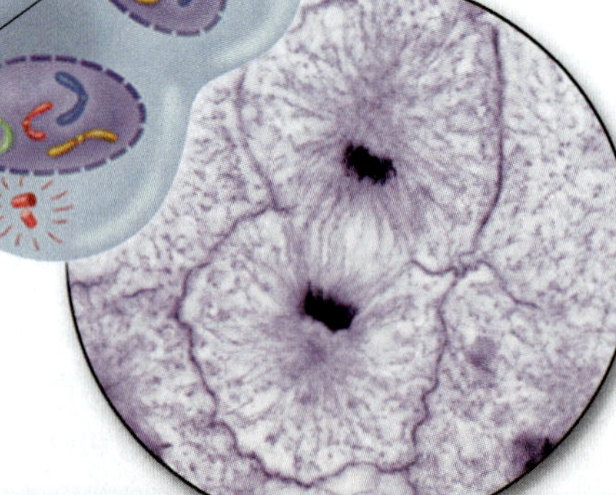

TEACHER TO TEACHER

Write the numbers 1 to 23 on two sets of index cards. Distribute the cards to students, and have them stand in a group. Tell them that they symbolize a human body cell and each card represents a chromosome. Then, have students illustrate replication of chromosomes during interphase by finding their matching number and holding the cards out in front so that each student is holding a card. To illustrate metaphase, have student pairs stand side by side in a line while holding each other's cards. Students should let go of their partner's card while still holding their own and walk to the opposite side of the room, illustrating anaphase. Now each of the two groups represents a new cell.

—*Michael Lopatka*
Biology Teacher
Edgewater High School
Orlando, FL

The centrioles lie in a region called the centrosome that helps to organize the **spindle,** a fanlike microtubule structure that helps separate the chromosomes. During prophase, the condensed chromosomes become attached to fibers in the spindle at a point near the centromere of each chromatid. Interestingly, plant cells do not have centrioles, but still organize their mitotic spindles from similar regions.

Near the end of prophase, the chromosomes coil more tightly. In addition, the nucleolus disappears, and the nuclear envelope breaks down.

CA a

a 7 1.e

CHECKPOINT *What is the function of the spindle?*

Spindle forming

Prophase
The chromatin condenses into chromosomes. The centrioles separate, and a spindle begins to form. The nuclear envelope breaks down.

Centromere

Chromosomes (paired chromatids)

Centriole

Metaphase
The chromosomes line up across the center of the cell. Each chromosome is connected to a spindle fiber at its centromere.

Spindle

Centriole

Anaphase
The sister chromatids separate into individual chromosomes and are moved apart.

Individual chromosomes

Build Science Skills

Observing Set up microscope stations around the room, and provide a paramecium culture. Ask each student to make a slide from the culture. Have students examine their slides, using low power, to find any paramecia that are pinched in the middle or that look like "double cells." When such an example is found, the student should switch to high power and make a sketch of the organism. Students should also write a short description of what they think is occurring. L2

Build Science Skills

Using Models Divide the class into small groups, and give each group pieces of pipe cleaner and string. Have each group form a cell with the string and use the pipe cleaners for chromosomes. Then, call on student volunteers to explain what occurs during prophase, metaphase, anaphase, and telophase. As a student explains each event, group members should manipulate their materials to model that phase of mitosis. Circulate among the groups to correct any misconceptions. L1 L2

Go Online
active art

Students can interact with the art of mitosis online.

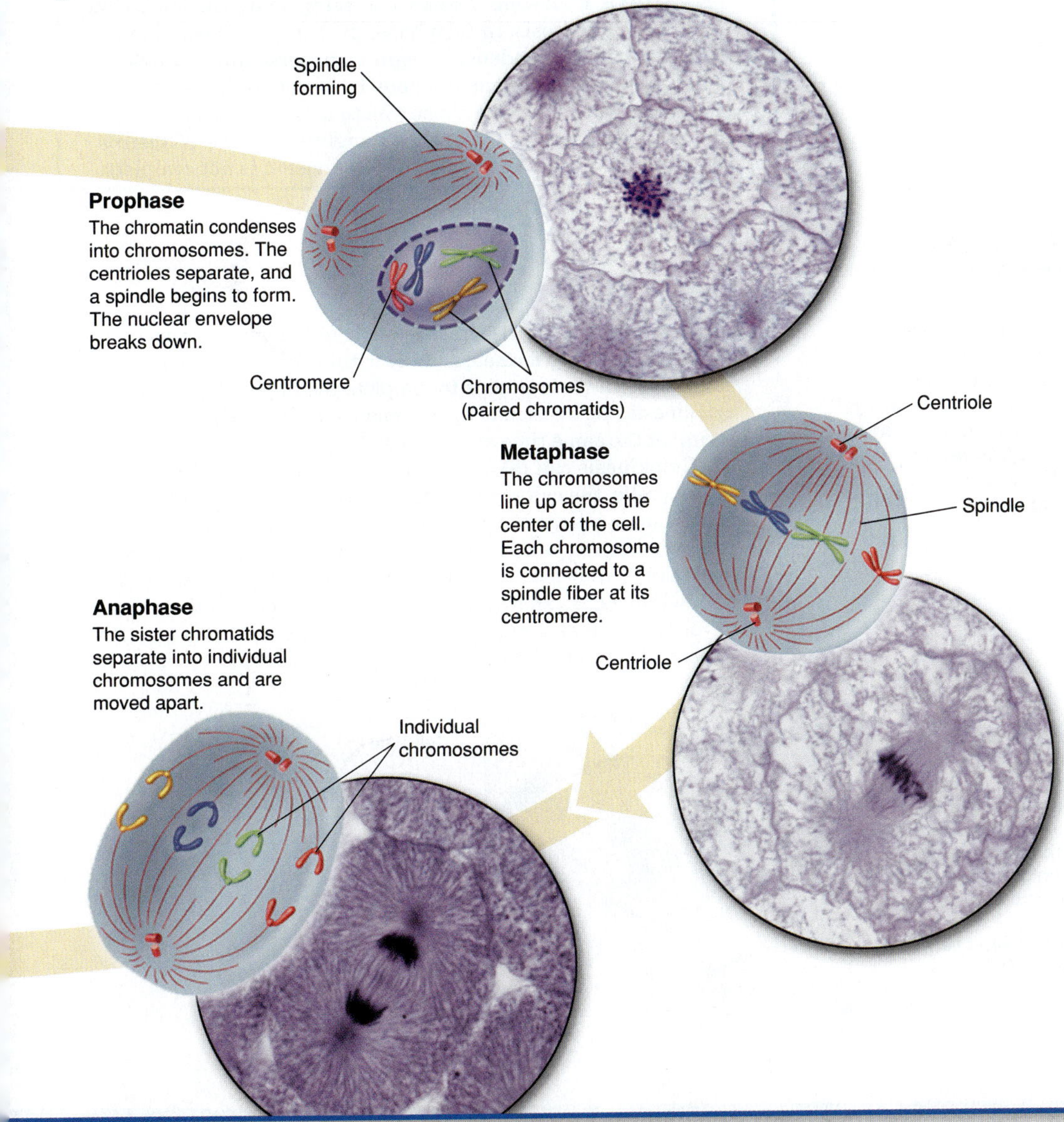

TEACHER TO TEACHER

To reinforce students' understanding of the processes of mitosis, I have them manipulate common materials as they mirror the sequence of phases. I supply them with a paper towel to represent the cell, gummy worms (which are bicolored) to represent chromosomes, and toothpicks to represent spindle fibers. They use plastic knives to cut the gummy worms, making sister chromatids. For mitosis, they organize a spindle with toothpicks on opposite sides of the towel (prophase), line up the chromosomes (metaphase), separate the chromosomes into two groups (anaphase), form the chromosomes into clusters (telophase), and split the paper towel in two (cytokinesis).

—Sheila Smith
Biology Teacher
Terry High School
Terry, MS

Answer to . . .

CHECKPOINT *The spindle helps separate the chromosomes.*

10–2 (continued)

Cytokinesis

Word Origins

The word *cytotoxic* means "related to something poisonous to a cell." L2

Analyzing Data

6IIE 7.c, 7IIE 7.c

Many students have the misconception that mitosis occurs regularly in all cells. The information in the data table will help address that mistaken notion. L2 L3

Answers

1. Most white blood cells are needed by the body only for a short time to fight infection, so they do not have to be long-lived.

2. Because cardiac muscle cells and neurons cannot divide, injuries to the heart or spinal cord cannot heal through the production of new heart or nerve cells. In contrast, because the cells of smooth muscle can divide, an injury to smooth muscle may be able to heal through cell division.

3. A typical hypothesis might suggest that cells lining the digestive system, where chemical and mechanical digestion occur, are more apt to be destroyed or damaged by these processes.

4. A typical prediction will correctly suggest that cancer cells (in a cell culture) are long-lived and division can occur a seemingly unlimited number of times.

Metaphase The second phase of mitosis, **metaphase,** often lasts only a few minutes. During metaphase, the chromosomes line up across the center of the cell. Microtubules connect the centromere of each chromosome to the two poles of the spindle.

Anaphase **Anaphase** is the third phase of mitosis. During anaphase, the centromeres that join the sister chromatids split, allowing the sister chromatids to separate and become individual chromosomes. The chromosomes continue to move until they have separated into two groups near the poles of the spindle. Anaphase ends when the chromosomes stop moving.

CA a 7 1.e

Telophase Following anaphase is **telophase,** the fourth and final phase of mitosis. In telophase, the chromosomes, which were distinct and condensed, begin to disperse into a tangle of dense material. A nuclear envelope re-forms around each cluster of chromosomes. The spindle begins to break apart, and a nucleolus becomes visible in each daughter nucleus. Mitosis is complete. However, the process of cell division is not complete.

CHECKPOINT *What happens during anaphase?*

Word Origins

Cytokinesis comes from the Greek words *kytos,* meaning "hollow vessel," and *kinesis,* meaning "motion." The prefix *cyto-* refers to cells, so *cytokinesis* means movement within the cell. **What do you think the term *cytotoxic* means?**

Cytokinesis

As a result of mitosis, two nuclei—each with a duplicate set of chromosomes—are formed, usually within the cytoplasm of a single cell. All that remains to complete the M phase of the cycle is cytokinesis, the division of the cytoplasm itself. Cytokinesis usually occurs at the same time as telophase.

Cytokinesis can take place in a number of ways. In most animal cells, the cell membrane is drawn inward until the cytoplasm is pinched into two nearly equal parts. Each part contains its own nucleus and cytoplasmic organelles. In plants, a structure known as the cell plate forms midway between the divided nuclei, as shown in **Figure 10–6.** The cell plate gradually develops into a separating membrane. A cell wall then begins to appear in the cell plate.

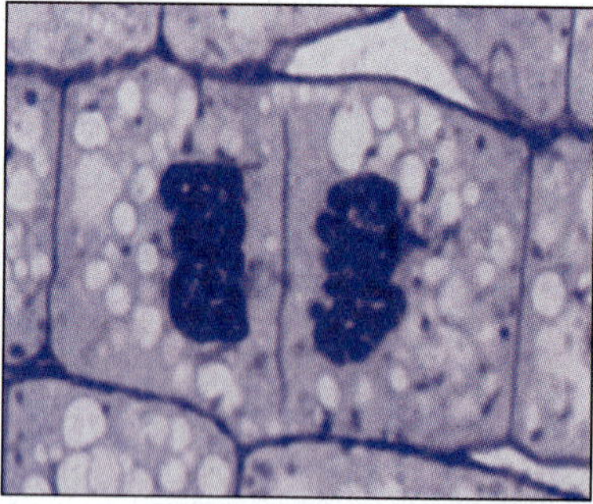

(magnification: 2200×)

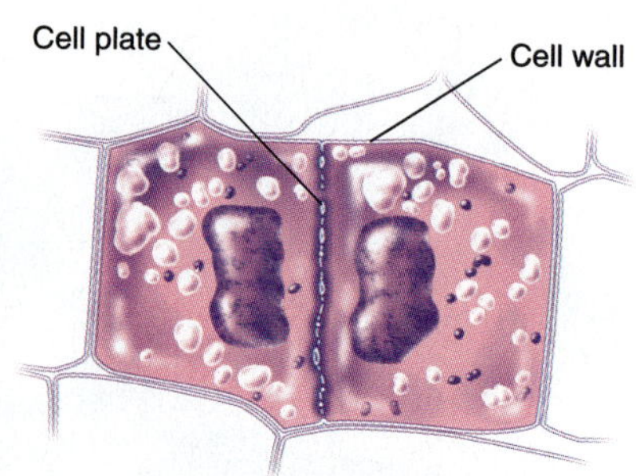

Figure 10–6 During cytokinesis in plant cells, the cytoplasm is divided by a cell plate. The thin line you can see between the two dark nuclei in this electron micrograph of onion cells dividing is the cell plate forming. **Interpreting Graphics** ***What structure forms between the divided nuclei?***

FACTS AND FIGURES

How long does a cell cycle take?
The time it takes for a cell to complete a cell cycle, called the generation time, varies widely among cells. The minimum time for a complete cell cycle is about 10 minutes. It takes about 2 hours for cells to divide in a newly forming sea urchin. In animal and plant cells that are actively growing, generation time is often between 8 and 10 hours. The generation time for a bean cell is 19 hours; the G_1 phase lasts about 5 hours, the S phase lasts about 7 hours, the G_2 phase lasts about 5 hours, and the M phase lasts about 2 hours. The generation time for some mouse cells is about 22 hours; for these cells, the G_1 phase lasts about 9 hours, the S phase lasts about 10 hours, the G_2 phase lasts about 2 hours, and the M phase lasts about 1 hour. Many mature cells, such as nerve and red blood cells, never divide; they are said to be in the G_0 phase, which is much like the G_1 phase.

Analyzing Data

Life Spans of Human Cells

Like all organisms, cells have a given life span from birth to death. In multicellular organisms, such as humans, the health of the organism depends on cells not exceeding their life span. This is especially true of cells that tend to divide rapidly. If these cells did not die on schedule, overcrowding of cells would occur, causing uncontrolled growth that would be life-threatening.

The data table shows the life spans of various human cells. It also contains information about the ability of the cells to multiply through cell division.

Life Spans of Various Human Cells

Cell Type	Life Span	Cell Division
Lining of esophagus	2–3 days	Can divide
Lining of small intestine	1–2 days	Can divide
Lining of large intestine	6 days	Can divide
Red blood cells	Less than 120 days	Cannot divide
White blood cells	10 hours to decades	Many do not divide
Smooth muscle	Long-lived	Can divide
Cardiac (heart) muscle	Long-lived	Cannot divide
Skeletal muscle	Long-lived	Cannot divide
Neuron (nerve cell)	Long-lived	Most do not divide

1. **Inferring** White blood cells help protect the body from infection and disease-producing organisms. How might their function relate to their life span?
2. **Comparing and Contrasting** Based on the data, how are the consequences of injuries to the heart and spinal cord similar to each other? How are they different from the consequences of injuries to smooth muscle?
3. **Formulating Hypotheses** Propose a hypothesis to account for the data related to the cell life spans of the lining of the esophagus, small intestine, and large intestine.
4. **Going Further** Cancer is a disease related to cell life span and cell division. If cancer cells were added to the data table, predict what would be written under the columns headed "Life Span" and "Cell Division." Explain the reasoning underlying your predictions.

6IIE 7.c, 7IIE 7.c

10–2 Section Assessment

1. **Key Concept** Name the main events of the cell cycle.
2. **Key Concept** Describe what happens during each of the four phases of mitosis.
3. Describe what happens during interphase.
4. What are chromosomes made of?
5. How do prokaryotic cells divide?
6. **Critical Thinking Comparing and Contrasting** How is cytokinesis in plant cells similar to cytokinesis in animal cells? How is it different?

Writing in Science

Creative Writing

Suppose you were small enough to hitch a ride on a chromosome located in a plant cell that goes through mitosis and cytokinesis. Describe what you would see happening during each phase of the process.

10–2 Section Assessment

1. A cell grows, prepares for division, and divides to form two daughter cells.
2. Students should describe what happens during prophase, metaphase, anaphase, and telophase, as in Figure 10–5.
3. Students should describe what happens during the G_1 phase, S phase, and G_2 phase.
4. DNA, which carries the cell's coded genetic information, and proteins
5. A prokaryotic cell first replicates its genetic information before cell division begins. In most prokaryotes, the rest of the process of cell division is a simple matter of separating the contents of the cell into two parts.
6. Cytokinesis is the division of the cytoplasm in both types of cells. The difference is that in plant cells a cell plate forms midway between the divided nuclei.

3 ASSESS

Evaluate Understanding

Ask students to look at the pie chart in Figure 10–4. Then, call on volunteers to describe the events in each phase of interphase and each phase of mitosis.

Reteach

Have students make a flowchart of the cell division, including what occurs in each of the four phases of mitosis as well as in cytokinesis.

Writing in Science

Answers may vary. An excellent response will be a well-written, engaging "travelogue" through the M phase of the cell cycle. Students should include important details from the subsections Mitosis and Cytokinesis in Section 10–2, including events presented in the cycle diagram in Figure 10–5.

If your class subscribes to the iText, use it to review the Key Concepts in Section 10–2.

Answers to . . .

CHECKPOINT *The centromeres that join the sister chromatids split, allowing the sister chromatids to separate. The chromosomes continue to move until they separate into two groups near the poles of the spindle.*

Figure 10–6 *A cell wall forms in the cell plate.*

Section 10–3

1 FOCUS

Objectives

10.3.1 ***Identify*** a factor that can stop cells from growing.
10.3.2 ***Describe*** how the cell cycle is regulated.
10.3.3 ***Explain*** how cancer cells are different from other cells.

Guide for Reading

Vocabulary Preview

Have students write the Vocabulary words, dividing each into its separate syllables as best they can. Remind students that each syllable usually has only one vowel sound. The correct syllabications are cy•clin and can•cer.

Reading Strategy

Before they read, have students skim the section to find the Key Concepts and copy each onto a note card. Then, as they read, they should make notes of supporting details.

2 INSTRUCT

Controls on Cell Division

Use Visuals

Figure 10–7 Ask: **What happened to the cells between the first petri dish and the second petri dish?** *(The cells divided until a thin layer of cells covered the bottom of the dish.)* Explain that researchers then removed cells from the center of the petri dish, as shown in the third dish. Ask: **What caused the difference shown between the third and fifth petri dishes?** *(The cells began dividing again until they filled the empty space.)* **Why didn't the cells keep dividing until they spilled over the edge of the petri dish?** *(When the cells came into contact with other cells, they responded by not growing.)* L1 L2

10–3 Regulating the Cell Cycle

Guide for Reading

Key Concepts
- How is the cell cycle regulated?
- How are cancer cells different from other cells?

Vocabulary
cyclin
cancer

Reading Strategy: Summarizing Summarizing helps you understand and remember what you read. Write a main-idea statement for each blue head. When you have finished the section, compare your statements with those in the study guide.

One of the most striking aspects of cell behavior in a multicellular organism is how carefully cell growth and cell division are controlled. Not all cells move through the cell cycle at the same rate. In the human body, most muscle cells and nerve cells do not divide at all once they have developed. In contrast, the cells of the skin and digestive tract, and cells in the bone marrow that make blood cells, grow and divide rapidly throughout life. Such cells may pass through a complete cycle every few hours. This process provides new cells to replace those that wear out or break down.

Controls on Cell Division

Scientists can observe the effects of controlled cell growth in the laboratory by placing some cells in a petri dish containing nutrient broth. The nutrient broth provides food for the cells. Most cells will grow until they form a thin layer covering the bottom of the dish, as shown in **Figure 10–7.** Then, the cells stop growing. When cells come into contact with other cells, they respond by not growing.

If cells are removed from the center of the dish, however, the cells bordering the open space will begin dividing until they have filled the empty space. These experiments show that the controls on cell growth and cell division can be turned on and off.

Something similar happens within the body. When an injury such as a cut in the skin or a break in a bone occurs, cells at the edges of the injury are stimulated to divide rapidly. This action produces new cells, starting the process of healing. When the healing process nears completion, the rate of cell division slows down, controls on growth are restored, and everything returns to normal.

▼ **Figure 10–7** Cells in a petri dish will continue to grow until they come into contact with other cells. **Applying Concepts** *What would happen if the cells continued to divide?*

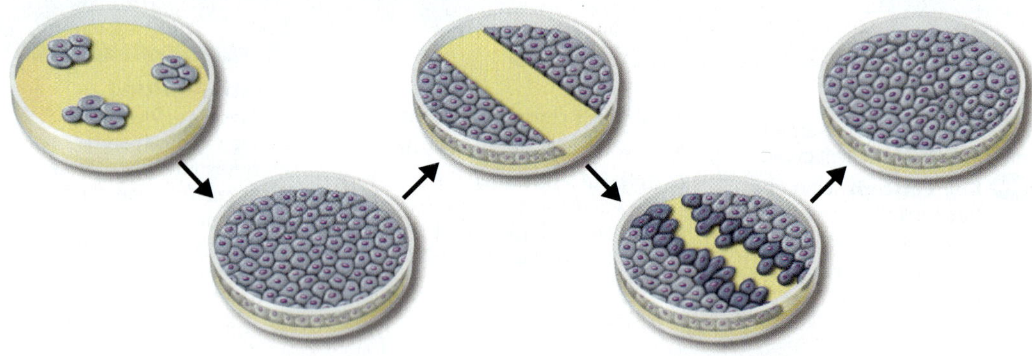

SECTION RESOURCES

Print:
- ***Teaching Resources,*** Lesson Plan 10–3, Adapted Section Summary 10–3, Adapted Worksheets 10–3, Section Summary 10–3, Worksheets 10–3, Section Review 10–3
- ***Reading and Study Workbook A,*** Section 10–3
- ***Adapted Reading and Study Workbook B,*** Section 10–3
- ***Investigations in Forensics,*** Investigation 3

Technology:
- ***iText,*** Section 10–3
- ***BioDetectives DVD,*** "Skin Cancer: Deadly Cells"
- ***Transparencies Plus,*** Section 10–3

Cell Cycle Regulators

For many years, biologists searched for a substance that might regulate the cell cycle—something that would "tell" cells when it was time to divide, duplicate their chromosomes, or enter another phase of the cycle. In the early 1980s, biologists found the substance.

Several scientists, including Tim Hunt of Great Britain and Mark Kirschner of the United States, discovered that cells in mitosis contained a protein that when injected into a nondividing cell, would cause a mitotic spindle to form. Such an experiment is shown in **Figure 10–8.** To their surprise, they discovered that the amount of this protein in the cell rose and fell in time with the cell cycle. They decided to call this protein **cyclin** because it seemed to regulate the cell cycle. Investigators have since discovered a family of closely related proteins, known as cyclins, that are involved in cell cycle regulation. **Cyclins regulate the timing of the cell cycle in eukaryotic cells.**

The discovery of cyclins was just the beginning. More recently, dozens of other proteins have been discovered that also help to regulate the cell cycle. There are two types of regulatory proteins: those that occur inside the cell and those that occur outside the cell.

Internal Regulators Proteins that respond to events inside the cell are called internal regulators. Internal regulators allow the cell cycle to proceed only when certain processes have happened inside the cell. For example, several regulatory proteins make sure that a cell does not enter mitosis until all its chromosomes have been replicated. Another regulatory protein prevents a cell from entering anaphase until all its chromosomes are attached to the mitotic spindle.

External Regulators Proteins that respond to events outside the cell are called external regulators. External regulators direct cells to speed up or slow down the cell cycle. Growth factors are among the most important external regulators. They stimulate the growth and division of cells. Growth regulators are especially important during embryonic development and wound healing. Molecules found on the surfaces of neighboring cells often have an opposite effect, causing cells to slow down or stop their cell cycles. These signals prevent excessive cell growth and keep the tissues of the body from disrupting one another.

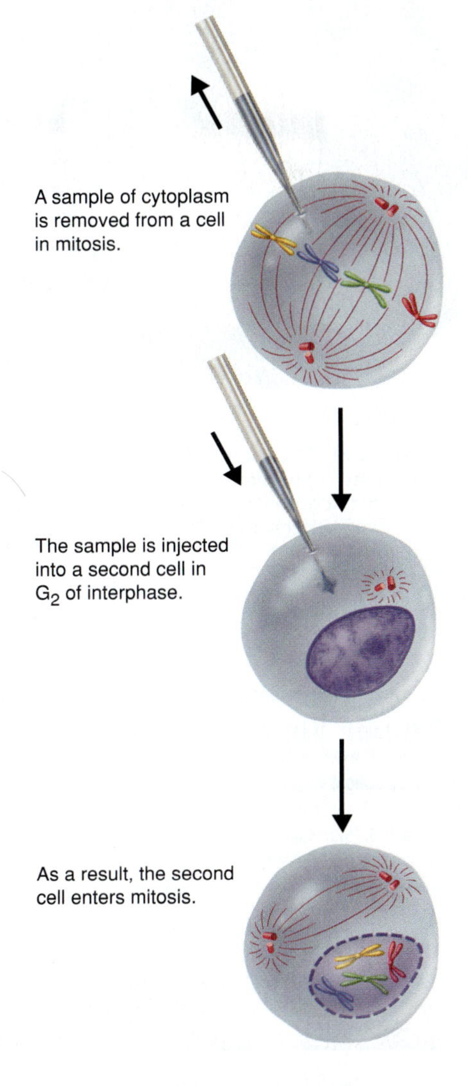

▲ **Figure 10–8 The timing of the cell cycle is regulated by cyclins.** When cytoplasm from a cell in mitosis is injected into another cell, the second cell enters mitosis. The reason for this effect is a protein called cyclin, which triggers cell division.

CHECKPOINT *What are cyclins?*

Cell Cycle Regulators

Use Visuals

Figure 10–8 Emphasize that this sequence shows an experiment carried out by scientists who were researching what regulates the cell cycle. Ask: **How can you tell that the first cell shown is in mitosis?** *(The illustration shows that a spindle has formed and the chromosomes are visible and lined up across the middle of the cell. The cell is therefore in metaphase.)* **How can you tell that the second cell shown is in interphase?** *(The illustration shows that the nuclear envelope is intact and no chromosomes are visible.)* **How can you tell that the third cell shown has begun mitosis?** *(The chromosomes are visible, and the spindle has begun to form. This is prophase.)* **What caused the second cell to enter mitosis?** *(The material injected into the second cell from the first cell caused the second cell to enter mitosis, which suggests that the sample contained cyclin.)* L2

Build Science Skills

Designing Experiments Divide the class into small groups, and ask each group to design an experiment to test the following hypothesis: Substance C regulates when a cell begins each phase of the cell cycle. Groups' experiments will vary. Each group, though, should designate Substance C as the variable in its experiment. A typical experiment will focus on either increasing or decreasing the amount of Substance C at various points in the cell cycle and then observing what effect this has on the cell. L2 L3

UNIVERSAL ACCESS

Less Proficient Readers
Have students who are having trouble understanding the function of cyclins make a flowchart of the steps in the experiment described on p. 251 and illustrated in Figure 10–8. Then, call on volunteers to help you make a flowchart of the experiment on the board. L1 L2

English Language Learners
Point out to learners of English that the word *cyclin* is similar and related to the word *cycle*, which derives from a Greek word for "circle" or "wheel." Have students look up the definition of *cycle* in a dictionary and then look up the meanings of such related words as *cyclic, cyclone, cylinder,* and *cyclist.* L1

Advanced Learners
Encourage students who need a challenge to further investigate the discoveries about gene defects in cancer cells, as mentioned on p. 252. Ask students to report their findings to the class. This could be the start of a larger project that anticipates students' further study of cancer in Chapter 40. L3

Answers to . . .

CHECKPOINT *Cyclins are proteins that regulate the timing of the cell cycle in eukaryotic cells.*

Figure 10–7 *The cells would form more layers but would probably begin to die off when space and nutrients ran short and wastes accumulated.*

10–3 (continued)

Uncontrolled Cell Growth

Quick View Video

Discovery School DVD Encourage students to view track 3 "Skin Cancer: Deadly Cells" on the *BioDetectives* DVD.

Use Community Resources

Invite a representative of a local cancer support group to address the class about the causes, symptoms, and treatments of various kinds of cancer. A day before the speaker makes the presentation, discuss with students the kinds of questions they might ask, and then have each student write two or three questions. L2

3 ASSESS

Evaluate Understanding

Call on students at random to explain what controls cell division, what regulates the cell cycle, and why cancer cells are different from normal cells in the body.

Reteach

Have students write a few paragraphs that could be used in a pamphlet given to the public. The purpose of the pamphlet is to explain the regulation of cell division and how cancer cells have lost the growth control that normal body cells have.

Sharpen Your Skills

The strategies of student-designed drugs will vary. The drugs should, however, function to interrupt the cell cycle and prevent cell division.

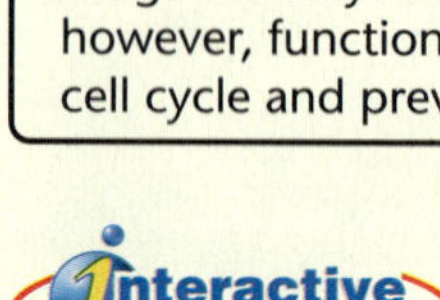

If your class subscribes to the iText, use it to review the Key Concepts in Section 10–3.

(magnification: 6900×)

▲ **Figure 10–9** **Cancer cells do not respond to the signals that regulate the growth of most cells.** Masses of cancer cells form tumors that can damage normal tissues. These cancer cells are from a tumor in the large intestine.

Quick View Video

Discovery School Video To find out more about how scientists study cancer, view track 3 "Skin Cancer: Deadly Cells" on the *BioDetectives* DVD.

Uncontrolled Cell Growth

Why is cell growth regulated so carefully? The principal reason may be that the consequences of uncontrolled cell growth in a multicellular organism are very severe. **Cancer,** a disorder in which some of the body's own cells lose the ability to control growth, is one such example. **Cancer cells do not respond to the signals that regulate the growth of most cells.** As a result, they divide uncontrollably and form masses of cells called tumors that can damage the surrounding tissues. Cancer cells may break loose from tumors and spread throughout the body, disrupting normal activities and causing serious medical problems or even death. **Figure 10–9** shows typical cancer cells.

What causes the loss of growth control that characterizes cancer? The various forms of cancer have many causes, including smoking tobacco, radiation exposure, and even viral infection. All cancers, however, have one thing in common: The control over the cell cycle has broken down. Some cancer cells will no longer respond to external growth regulators, while others fail to produce the internal regulators that ensure orderly growth.

An astonishing number of cancer cells have a defect in a gene called p53, which normally halts the cell cycle until all chromosomes have been properly replicated. Damaged or defective p53 genes cause the cells to lose the information needed to respond to signals that would normally control their growth.

Cancer is a serious disease. Understanding and combating cancer remains a major scientific challenge, but scientists at least know where to start. Cancer is a disease of the cell cycle, and conquering cancer will require a much deeper understanding of the processes that control cell division.

10–3 Section Assessment

1. **Key Concept** What chemicals regulate the cell cycle? How do they work?
2. **Key Concept** What happens when cells do not respond to the signals that normally regulate their growth?
3. How do cells respond to contact with other cells?
4. Why can cancer be considered a disease of the cell cycle?
5. **Critical Thinking Formulating Hypotheses** Write a hypothesis about what you think would happen if cyclin were injected into a cell that was in mitosis.

Sharpen Your Skills

Problem Solving

Imagine that you are developing a drug that will inhibit the growth of cancer cells. Use your knowledge of the cell cycle to describe how the drug would target and prevent the multiplication of cancer cells. Use the Internet to compare your anticancer drug with those currently in use.

10–3 Section Assessment

1. Cyclins regulate the timing of the cell cycle in eukaryotic cells. Cyclin may cause a mitotic spindle to form and trigger cell division.
2. Such cells, called cancer cells, divide uncontrollably and form masses of cells called tumors that can damage the surrounding tissues.
3. Normal cells respond by not growing.
4. The cell cycle is the series of events that cells go through as they grow and divide, and cancer is a disorder in which some of the body's cells lose the ability to control growth.
5. A typical hypothesis might suggest that cyclin would have no effect because the cell was already in mitosis.

Stem Cells: Promises and Problems

Where do the different cells and tissues in your body come from? Incredible as it seems, every cell was produced by mitosis from a small number of cells called stem cells. Stem cells are unspecialized cells that have the potential to differentiate—to become specialized in structure and function—into a wide variety of cell types. In early embryonic development, stem cells produce every tissue in the body. Evidence indicates that stem cells also are found in adults. Stem cells in the bone marrow, for example, produce more than a dozen types of blood cells, replacing those lost due to normal wear and tear.

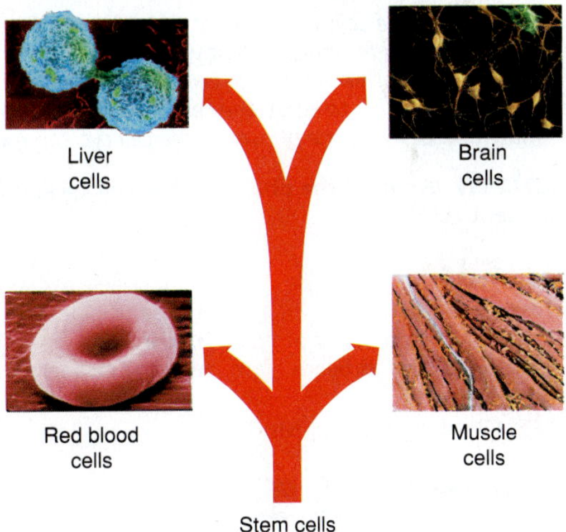

Stem Cells in Medicine

Although your body produces billions of new cells every day, it is not always able to produce the right kind of cell to replace those damaged by injury or disease. For example, the body is not able to produce new neurons to repair serious spinal cord injuries, such as those that cause paralysis. Because of this, at present, there is no way for doctors to restore movement and feeling to people who are paralyzed.

Stem cells may be the perfect solution to this problem. Recently, researchers have found that implants of stem cells can reverse the effects of brain injuries in mice. There is hope that the same will hold true for humans and that stem cells might be used to reverse brain and spinal cord injuries. It also may be possible to use stem cells to grow new liver tissue, to replace heart valves, and to reverse the effects of diabetes.

Sources of Stem Cells

Human embryonic stem cells were first isolated in 1998 by scientists in Wisconsin. In 2004, Korean scientists produced such cells by transferring adult cell nuclei into the cytoplasms of egg cells. However, since such cells are taken from human embryos, these techniques raise serious moral and ethical questions. Because of such issues, embryonic stem cell research is highly controversial.

Researchers have also found that nerve, muscle, and liver cells sometimes can be grown from adult stem cells isolated from the bone marrow and other tissues in the body. Experiments such as these, although still in the early stages of development, may usher in a new era of therapy in which replacement tissue is grown from a person's own stem cells.

Research and Decide

Use library or Internet resources to learn more about stem-cell research. Then, write a brief report on how this technology will impact the future of medicine.

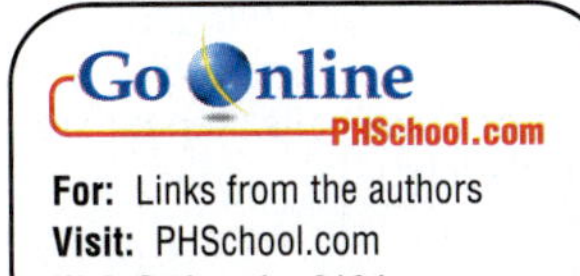

For: Links from the authors
Visit: PHSchool.com
Web Code: cbe-3104

FACTS AND FIGURES

Three kinds of stem cells

A human fertilized egg has the potential to form a whole organism, and therefore the egg and the cells that result from early cell division are called totipotent stem cells. About five days after fertilization, the cells develop into a blastocyst, with an outer layer of cells and an inner cell mass. The inner cells go on to form almost all the tissues of the human body, although they don't have the potential to form a whole organism. They are called pluripotent stem cells. These cells eventually specialize further to become stem cells that can give rise to specific kinds of cells. For example, a blood stem cell can give rise to both red and white blood cells, and a skin stem cell can give rise to different kinds of skin cells. These stem cells are called multipotent stem cells, and they are present in adults. For most stem-cell medical therapies, pluripotent stem cells are used.

TECHNOLOGY & SOCIETY

After students have read this feature, you might want to do one or more of the following:

- Lead a discussion about how cells become differentiated as an embryo grows.
- Ask students to hypothesize why adults don't have stem cells that can give rise to every kind of cell in the body.
- The use of stem cells has many applications in medicine. Diseases that might benefit from stem-cell therapy include heart disease, arthritis, Parkinson's disease, Alzheimer's disease, and diabetes. Stem cells might also be used in treating such conditions as stroke, burns, and spinal-cord injuries. Discuss with students how stem cells might be useful in treating each of these diseases and conditions.
- Although researchers are working on ways to derive stem cells from adult cells, the primary sources of stem cells are still embryos and fetal tissue. Lead a discussion about the moral and ethical objections to using such cells in research and therapy.

Research and Decide

Students should be able to find information relating to stem cells in library books on biology or in science or current events magazines. Their reports should expand on the information given in the feature on this page. Most students may be optimistic about the future of stem-cell research and its impact, though some may express moral concerns about the technology.

Students can research stem cells on the site developed by authors Ken Miller and Joe Levine.

Exploration

 6IIE 7.c, 6IIE 7.e, BIIE 1.g

Objective Students will be able to observe what the phases of the cell cycle look like in a typical plant cell.  

Skills Focus **Classifying, Using Models**

Time 50 minutes

Advance Prep Assemble a variety of materials for students to make their models, including index cards, beads, yarn, pipe cleaners, licorice, and gum drops.

Pre-Lab Discussion Have students read the procedure and ask any questions they have about materials or about what they are to do. Then, ask: **In the data table, why are the phases listed in that sequence?** *(That is the sequence in which those phases occur in the cell cycle.)* **Of the phases listed in the table, which do you predict will have the greatest number of cells once you have made your observations?** *(Many students will predict that interphase will have the greatest number, because it encompasses most of the cell cycle.)*

Teaching Tips

- Circulate among students as they work, asking such questions as: What do you think is going on in this phase? What phases are you seeing the most?
- You may want to calculate class averages and compare them to the results of individuals or groups to demonstrate the importance of sample size.

Procedure

1. Help students find the root tips on the slides.
2. Make sure that students are looking at the meristematic cells on the slides. Point out the darkly stained chromosomes.
6. Discuss with students how to choose 25 cells at random. They could choose 25 cells that are touching or randomly point to 25 cells. Make sure that they are careful not to choose a cell twice.

Expected Outcome Students will identify and make models of the phases of the cell cycle, and they will determine that most of the onion cells are in interphase.

Exploration

 6IIE 7.c, 6IIE 7.e, BIIE 1.g

Modeling the Phases of the Cell Cycle

In a growing root, the cells at the tip of the root are constantly dividing. Because each cell divides independently of the others, a root tip contains many cells at different phases of the cell cycle. This makes a root tip an excellent tissue in which to study the cell cycle. In this investigation, you will identify and describe the phases of the cell cycle in root tip cells.

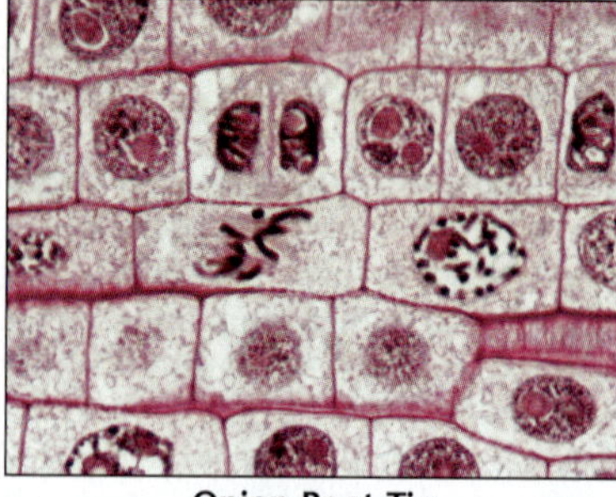
Onion Root Tip
(magnification: 700×)

Problem **What do the phases of the cell cycle look like in a typical plant cell?**

Materials

- microscope
- prepared slides of onion root tips
- craft materials such as beads, yarn, and pipe cleaners
- tape or glue
- scissors

Skills Classifying, Using Models

Procedure   

1. Obtain a prepared slide of an onion root tip. Hold the slide up to the light and find the pointed end of the root section. This is the root tip where cells were actively dividing.
2. Place the slide on the microscope stage with the root tip pointing away from you. Using the low-power objective, adjust the focus of the microscope until the root tip is clearly visible. Just above the root tip is a region that contains many new small cells. The larger cells of this region were in the process of dividing when the slide was made. These are the cells you will be observing.
3. Observe the boxlike cells that are arranged in rows. Scan across one row and down to the next row to compare the cells. The chromosomes of the cells have been stained to make them easily visible. Select one cell whose chromosomes are clearly visible. Switch to high power and sketch this cell.
4. Use the craft materials to make a model of the cell that you sketched, showing how its chromosomes are arranged.
5. Select at least four more cells whose internal appearances are different from the first cell you sketched. Switch to high power and sketch each of these cells. Repeat step 4 for each cell you sketch.
6. On a separate sheet of paper, make a copy of the data table shown. Choose 25 root tip cells at random and decide which phase of the cell cycle each is in. Record the number of cells in each phase in your copy of the data table. If you find that some cells appear to be between two phases, record those observations as well.
7. Look closely at your sketches and models. Arrange the models in order to represent the process of cell division.
8. Refer to **Figure 10–5** on pages 246 and 247 to determine whether you have ordered the phases of the cell cycle accurately. Correct the order of your models, if necessary. Label each of the models and sketches with the name of the phase it represents. Use the models to explain the process of cell division to another student.
9. Wash your hands with soap and warm water before you leave the lab.

Data Table

Phase	Number of Cells
Interphase	
Prophase	
Metaphase	
Anaphase	
Telophase	

Sample Data Table

Phase	Number of Cells
Interphase	19
Prophase	3
Metaphase	1
Anaphase	1
Telophase	1

Go Further

Students' models should show that cells repeatedly proceed through the four phases of mitosis but that cytokinesis never occurs.

Go Online PHSchool.com

Students should see data on the number of cells in the phases of the cell cycle, but their results will depend on their own data and the data on the site.

Analyze and Conclude

1. **Analyzing Data** Do your results indicate that there were more cells in some phases than in others? Identify the most common phase(s) and explain what these differences in numbers of cells might mean.
2. **Drawing Conclusions** What evidence did you observe that shows mitosis is a continuous process, not a series of separate events?
3. **Using Models** Describe what is happening in each phase of your cell models.
4. **Using Models** Propose an alternative model to illustrate the same concept.
5. **Applying Concepts** Cells in the root divide many times as the root grows longer and thicker. With each cell division, the chromosomes are divided between two daughter cells, yet the number of chromosomes in each cell does not change. What process ensures that the normal number of chromosomes is restored after each cell division? During which part of the cell cycle does this process occur?

Go Further

Making Models In muscle cells, mitosis is not always followed by cell division. Instead, repeated cycles of mitosis result in long, tubular cells with many nuclei. Make a model that shows mitosis in a muscle cell.

For: Data sharing
Visit: PHSchool.com
Web Code: cbd-3104

Share Your Data Online Enter your data on the number of cells in the phases of the cell cycle. Then, look at the data entered by other students. Based on the available data, were there more cells in some phases than in others? Why might your results differ from those of other students?

Analyze and Conclude

1. Most students will observe that more cells are in interphase than any other phase of mitosis, because interphase is the longest phase of the cell cycle.
2. Students should observe that many cells appear to be in intermediate phases rather than in a specific mitotic phase.
3. Students should describe what is happening to cells in the four phases of mitosis.
4. Student models should accurately illustrate mitosis.
5. The replication of chromosomes during the S phase of the cell cycle and the mitotic process of chromosome separation ensure that each daughter cell has the normal number of chromosomes after cell division.

Chapter 10 Study Guide

Study Tip

Divide the class into pairs, and have students quiz each other about the Vocabulary words and the chapter Key Concepts.

Thinking Visually

1. The cell grows and replicates its DNA and centrioles.
2. The chromosomes line up across the middle of the cell.
3. The sister chromatids separate into individual chromosomes and move apart.
4. The cell membrane pinches the cytoplasm in half.

Chapter 10 Assessment

Reviewing Content

1. d	5. c	9. a
2. c	6. a	10. a
3. b	7. b	
4. c	8. b	

Understanding Concepts

11. During cell division, a cell divides into two new daughter cells.

12. When a cell is small, the information stored in its DNA is able to meet all of the cell's needs. But if a cell were to grow without limit, an "information crisis" would occur.

13. Cell volume is the amount of material inside the cell. Surface area is the total area of the cell's membrane. Ratio of surface area to volume is the surface area divided by the volume.

14. A cell's ratio of surface area to volume decreases as it grows larger. This means that the area available for diffusion also decreases. Thus, if a cell grows too large, it is unable to take in all needed materials and expel all its wastes. These problems impose limits on the growth of a cell.

15. Well before cell division, each chromosome is replicated. At the beginning of cell division, each chromosome consists of two identical sister chromatids.

16. Together, interphase and cell division make up the cell cycle.

Chapter 10 Study Guide

10–1 Cell Growth

Key Concept

- The larger a cell becomes, the more demands the cell places on its DNA. In addition, the cell has more trouble moving enough nutrients and wastes across the cell membrane.

Vocabulary

cell division, p. 243

10–2 Cell Division

7 1.e

Key Concepts

- During the cell cycle, a cell grows, prepares for division, and divides to form two daughter cells, each of which then begins the cycle again.
- Biologists divide the events of mitosis into four phases: prophase, metaphase, anaphase, and telophase. Mitosis insures that each daughter cell has the same genetic information as the parent cell.
- During prophase in animal cells, the centrioles separate and take up positions on opposite sides of the nucleus. In addition, chromosomes condense and the spindle appears.
- During metaphase, the chromosomes line up across the center of the cell. Microtubules connect the chromosome to each pole of the spindle.
- During anaphase, the centromeres that join the sister chromatids split, and the sister chromatids separate and become individual chromosomes.
- In telophase, the chromosomes, which were distinct and condensed, uncoil and disperse as the nuclear envelope re-forms.
- Cytokinesis is the division of the cytoplasm.

Vocabulary

mitosis, p. 244
cytokinesis, p. 244
chromatid, p. 244
centromere, p. 245
interphase, p. 245
cell cycle, p. 245
prophase, p. 246
centriole, p. 246
spindle, p. 247
metaphase, p. 248
anaphase, p. 248
telophase, p. 248

10–3 Regulating the Cell Cycle

Key Concepts

- Cyclins regulate the timing of the cell cycle in eukaryotic cells.
- Cancer cells do not respond to the signals that regulate the growth of most cells.

Vocabulary

cyclin, p. 251
cancer, p. 252

Thinking Visually

Using the information in this chapter, complete the following cycle diagram of the cell cycle:

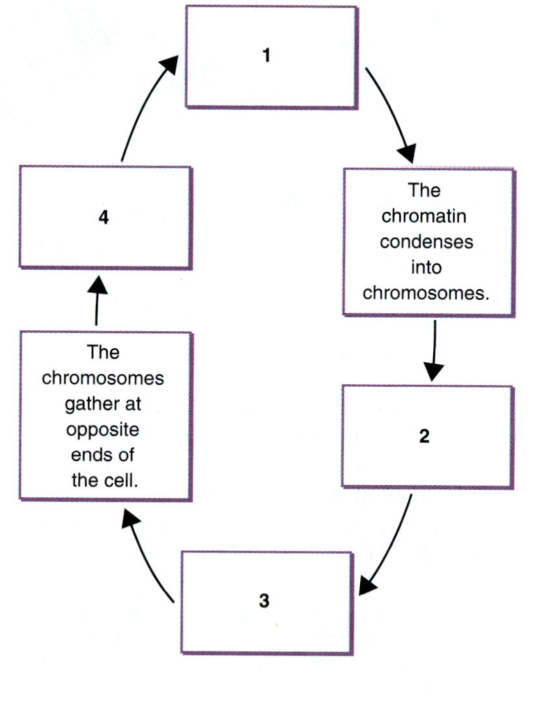

CHAPTER RESOURCES

Print:

- ***Teaching Resources,*** Chapter Vocabulary Review, Graphic Organizer, Chapter 10 Tests: Levels A and B
- ***Laboratory Assessment,*** Laboratory Assessment 3

Technology:

- ***Computer Test Bank,*** Chapter 10 Test
- ***iText,*** Chapter 10 Assessment

Chapter 10 Assessment

Reviewing Content

Choose the letter that best answers the question or completes the statement.

1. The rate at which materials enter and leave through the cell membrane depends on the cell's
   a. volume. c. mass.
   b. weight. d. surface area.

2. The process of cell division results in
   a. sister chromatids. c. two daughter cells.
   b. mitosis. d. unregulated growth.

3. Sister chromatids are attached to each other at an area called the
   a. centriole. c. spindle.
   b. centromere. d. chromosome.

4. If a cell has 12 chromosomes, how many chromosomes will each of its daughter cells have after mitosis?
   a. 4 c. 12
   b. 6 d. 24

5. At the beginning of cell division, a chromosome consists of two
   a. centromeres. c. chromatids.
   b. centrioles. d. spindles.

6. The phase of mitosis during which chromosomes become visible and the centrioles separate from one another is
   a. prophase. c. metaphase.
   b. anaphase. d. telophase.

7. Which of the illustrations below best represents metaphase of mitosis?

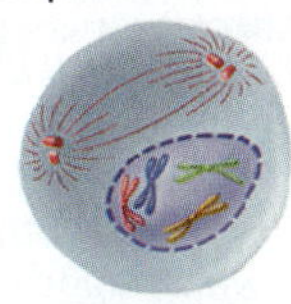
a.

c.

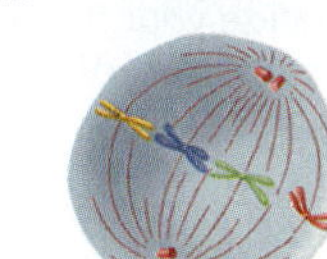
b.

d.

8. The timing of the cell cycle in eukaryotic cells is believed to be controlled by a group of closely related proteins known as
   a. chromatids.
   b. cyclins.
   c. centromeres.
   d. centrioles.

Interactive textbook with assessment at PHSchool.com 

9. In the cell cycle, external regulators direct cells to
   a. speed up or slow down the cell cycle.
   b. remain unchanged.
   c. proceed and then stop the cell cycle.
   d. grow uncontrollably.

10. Uncontrolled cell division occurs in
    a. cancer.
    b. mitosis.
    c. cytokinesis.
    d. cyclin.

Understanding Concepts

11. Summarize what happens during the process of cell division.
12. Explain how a cell's DNA can limit the cell's size.
13. Describe what is meant by each of the following terms: cell volume, cell surface area, ratio of surface area to volume.
14. How is a cell's potential growth affected by its ratio of surface area to volume?
15. Describe how a cell's chromosomes change as a cell prepares to divide.
16. What is the relationship between interphase and cell division?
17. Summarize what happens during interphase.
18. Explain how the following terms are related to one another: DNA, centromere, chromosome, chromatid.
19. List the following events in the correct sequence, and describe what happens during each event: anaphase, metaphase, prophase, and telophase.
20. How does the number of chromosomes in the two new cells compare with the number in the original cell at the end of cell division?
21. Summarize what happens during the cell cycle.
22. When some cells are removed from the center of a tissue culture, will new cells replace the cells that were removed? Explain.
23. Describe the role of cyclins in the cell cycle.
24. Why is it important that cell growth in a multicellular organism be regulated so carefully?
25. How do cancer cells differ from noncancerous cells? How are they similar?

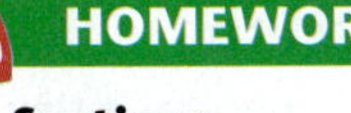

HOMEWORK GUIDE

Section:	Questions:
Section 10–1:	1, 2, 11–14, 26, 27
Section 10–2:	3–7, 15– 21, 28–33
Section 10–3:	8–10, 22–25

If your class subscribes to the iText, use it to review the Key Concepts in this chapter.

(Continued from page 256)

17. During interphase, a cell increases in size, synthesizes new proteins and organelles, replicates its chromosomes, and prepares for cell division by producing needed spindle proteins.

18. The genetic information that is passed on from one generation of cells to the next is carried by chromosomes, which are made up of DNA. Before cell division, chromosomes are replicated, so that each chromosome consists of two identical "sister" chromatids. Sister chromatids are attached at an area called the centromere.

19. Prophase: Chromatin condenses into chromosomes; centrioles separate; spindle begins to form; nuclear membrane breaks down. Metaphase: Chromosomes line up across middle of cell with spindle fibers connected to their centromeres. Anaphase: Sister chromatids separate and move apart. Telophase: Chromosomes gather at opposite ends of cell and lose distinct shape; new nuclear membranes form.

20. The number of chromosomes in each of the two cells equals the number in the original cell.

21. A cell grows, prepares for division, and divides to form two daughter cells, each of which then begins the cycle again.

22. Yes, new cells will replace the removed cells because of the process of cell division, which will continue until the new cells come in contact with other cells. When that occurs, cell division will stop.

23. Cyclins regulate the timing of the cell cycle in eukaryotic cells.

24. The consequences of uncontrolled cell growth are severe, as in cancer, for example.

25. Cancer cells do not respond to the signals that regulate the growth of most cells. As a result, they form masses of cells called tumors that can damage the surrounding tissues.

Chapter 10 Assessment

Critical Thinking

26. Students' models should demonstrate that as the size of a cube increases, its volume increases faster than its surface area. As a result, the ratio of surface area to volume decreases as the size of the cube increases.

27. Surface area = 5 mm × 5 mm × 6 = 150 mm^2. Volume = 5 mm × 5 mm × 5 mm = 125 mm^3.
Ratio of surface area to volume = 150/125 = 6 : 5.

28. A typical experiment might suggest comparing the rate of cell division over time in the same kind of plant cell at various temperatures.

29. a. The cell is in metaphase. It most resembles that of an animal because there is no evidence of a cell wall, as there would be in the cell of a plant. Also, this cell has centrioles at opposite ends of the spindle, and plant cells do not have centrioles.
b. The two strands carry the same genetic information, which is important because the cell needs this information to function.

30. The presence of many nuclei indicates that mitosis has occurred repeatedly without cytokinesis having occurred, because there is still only one cell.

31. Cell division is similar in animal and plant cells. In prophase, though, plant cells do not have centrioles, as animal cells do. Plant cells organize their mitotic spindles from regions known as centrosomes. Also, during cytokinesis in most animal cells, the cell membrane moves inward until the cytoplasm is pinched into two nearly equal parts. In plant cells, a cell plate forms midway between the divided nuclei and gradually develops into a separating membrane. A cell wall then appears in the cell plate.

32. Because nerve cells seldom undergo mitosis, the body is usually unable to repair damage to parts of the nervous system. Thus, complete recovery may not occur.

33. If the pattern were not constant, each type of organism could not stay the same, and there would be no species continuity.

Chapter 10 Assessment

Critical Thinking

26. Using Models Use paper, blocks, or another material to create three-dimensional models demonstrating how the ratio of surface area to volume changes as the size of a cube changes.

27. Calculating Calculate the surface area, volume, and ratio of surface area to volume of an imaginary cubic cell measuring 5 mm on each side.

28. Designing Experiments A classmate suggests that temperature might affect the rate of mitosis in plant cells. Design an experiment to test this hypothesis.

29. Interpreting Graphics The diagram below shows a phase of mitosis. Use the diagram to answer the questions.

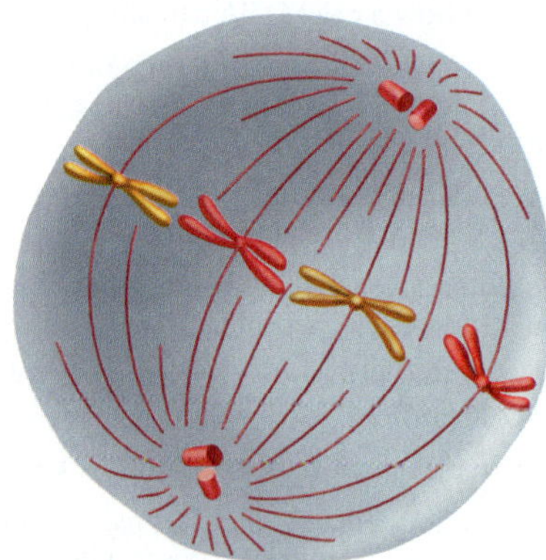

a. Identify the phase and indicate whether the cell most resembles that of a plant or an animal. Explain your answer.

b. The four chromosomes shown in the center of this cell each have two connected strands. Explain how the two strands on the same chromosome compare with regard to the genetic information they carry. In your answer, be sure to explain why this is important to the cell.

30. Formulating Hypotheses Some cells have several nuclei within the cytoplasm of a single cell. Considering the events in a typical cell cycle, which phase of the cell cycle is not operating when such cells form?

31. Comparing and Contrasting Describe the differences between cell division in an animal cell and cell division in a plant cell.

32. Applying Concepts The nerve cells in the human nervous system seldom undergo mitosis. Based on this information, explain why complete recovery from injuries to the nervous system may not occur.

33. Formulating Hypotheses Each type of eukaryotic organism has a characteristic number of chromosomes. Human cells, for example, generally have 46 chromosomes in their nuclei; fruit fly cells have 8 chromosomes. How might a particular type of organism be affected if this pattern were not repeated in each generation?

Focus on the BIG Idea

Science as a Way of Knowing Recall what you learned about the characteristics of life in Chapter 1. How is cell division related to one or more of those characteristics?

Writing in Science

In this chapter, you learned that cells can reproduce asexually by mitosis. In some cases, animals have the ability to reproduce asexually by a process called regeneration. If a planarian is cut into pieces, for example, it can regenerate an entire body from each piece. If large mammals were capable of regeneration, how do you think this would affect ecosystems?

Performance-Based Assessment

Demonstrate the Cell Cycle A flip-book consists of pages of sequential drawings that, when flipped, appear to move. Create a flip-book movie of the steps in the cell cycle. Be sure to show what happens to the chromosomes at each step. Exchange your flip-book with another student. Look at the other student's movie, and write a review of it.

For: An interactive self-test
Visit: PHSchool.com
Web Code: cba-3100

Focus on the BIG Idea

Students might mention that organisms are made of units called cells and that organisms grow and develop as their cells divide.

Writing in Science

Explain that a planarian is a flatworm, a tiny animal with a very simple body plan, which students will study in Chapter 27. Students' responses to the question may vary. A typical response may assert that if mammals were capable of regeneration, populations would tend to increase more rapidly than they would otherwise, and such population growth would have effects throughout a food web.

Standards Practice

Success Tracker™
Online at PHSchool.com

Test-Taking Tip If after reading all of the answer choices you are not sure which one is correct, eliminate the choices that you know are wrong. Then, select your answer from the remaining choices.

Directions: Choose the letter that best answers the question or completes the statement.

1. Which of the following is NOT related to a cell's ratio of surface area to volume?
   A cell size
   B rate of growth
   C number of nuclei
   D efficiency of cell's transport of oxygen
2. Which family of proteins regulates the timing of the cell cycle in eukaryotes?
   A chromatids
   B DNA and RNA
   C cyclins
   D chromosomes
3. Which of the following is NOT a phase of mitosis?
   A anaphase **7 1.e**
   B metaphase
   C telophase
   D interphase
4. Chromatids are attached to each other at the
   A nucleus.
   B centriole.
   C centromere.
   D cell plate.
5. In the cell cycle, the period between cell divisions is called
   A interphase.
   B prophase.
   C G_3 phase.
   D telophase.

Questions 6–9 Each of the lettered choices below may refer to the following numbered statements. Select the best lettered choice.

A Mitosis
B Cell cycle
C Cytokinesis
D Cancer

6. a process in which unregulated cell division occurs
7. a process of cytoplasmic division
8. series of events that cells go through as they divide and grow **7 1.e**
9. the division of the cell nucleus **7 1.e**

Questions 10–12

The spindle fibers of a dividing cell were labeled with a fluorescent dye. At the beginning of anaphase, a laser beam was used to stop the dye from glowing on one side of the cell, thereby marking the fibers, as shown in the second diagram. The laser did not inhibit the normal function of the fibers.

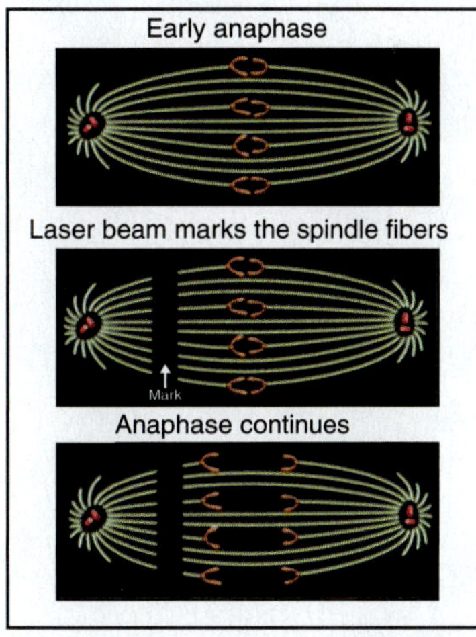

10. This experiment tests a hypothesis about **7IIE 7.c**
    A how chromosomes migrate during cell division.
    B how fluorescent dyes work in the cell.
    C the effect of lasers on cells.
    D the effect of lasers on fluorescent dye.
11. The diagram shows that the spindle fibers
    A shorten on the chromosome side of the mark.
    B lengthen on the chromosome side of the mark.
    C shorten on the centriole side of the mark.
    D lengthen on the centriole side of the mark.
12. A valid conclusion that can be drawn from this experiment is that **7IIE 7.c**
    A centrioles pull chromosomes toward the poles of the cell.
    B chromosomes do not migrate in the presence of dye.
    C chromosomes migrate only when treated with dye.
    D chromosomes travel along the fibers toward the poles of the cell.

Standards Practice

1. C	**5.** A	**9.** A
2. C	**6.** D	**10.** A
3. D	**7.** C	**11.** A
4. C	**8.** B	**12.** D

Success Tracker™
Online at PHSchool.com

Have students check their understanding of the chapter by logging onto Success Tracker.

Performance-Based Assessment

Students' flip-books should include several illustrations for each of the four phases of the cell cycle, including several pages for each phase of mitosis. Those pages illustrating mitosis should be similar to the illustrations in Figure 10–5. The flip-books should illustrate all the major events in the cell cycle on pages 246–247. Initiate a way that students can exchange flip-books at random, such as by drawing names out of a hat. Students should evaluate a flip-book by deciding how well the flip-book movie puts across the events of the cell cycle.

Your students can independently test their knowledge of the chapter and print out their test results for your files.

UNIT 4

Dear Colleague,

The year was 1963, and the news article was from Stockholm. My teacher reserved a small bulletin board right next to the blackboard for newspaper clippings that dealt with science, and this particular one caught my eye. It seemed that three people named Watson, Crick, and Wilkins had received the 1962 Nobel Prize in Physiology or Medicine for unraveling the structure of DNA.

A few days after the article appeared, our teacher took some time to tell us a little about DNA and about something called the "double helix" model. To tell the truth, I was a little confused. Our textbook barely mentioned DNA, and it was only our teacher's enthusiasm that made me remember this as something important.

As the years went by, I came to appreciate the clippings on that bulletin board more and more. Not everything worth knowing, it was clear, was in the textbook. One of the most exciting things about science, and biology in particular, is how quickly things can change.

In the 1970s, I had the good fortune to start my professional career in the same building in which Allan Maxam and Walter Gilbert first developed their technique for reading the sequence of DNA. Such techniques, Gilbert would later point out, might well revolutionize the study of genetics. Before long, it became clear that such talk was, if anything, an understatement.

In 1999, one of my colleagues returned from a conference and handed me a shiny computer disk. On that disk was the complete DNA sequence of the fruit fly *Drosophila melanogaster*. In just a few months of intensive work, a private laboratory had sequenced the genome of the most important of all organisms for the study of genetics. Only a bit more than a year later, the human genome followed.

Mendel's principles of heredity were based on his early experiments with pea plants.

This albino ring-tailed lemur inherited the recessive trait for albinism from its parents.

Today, you or I or any of your students can sit down at a computer and access the DNA sequences of each and every human chromosome. We can test for many genetic disorders, hope to cure at least a few of them, and routinely insert new genes into bacteria, plants, and laboratory animals.

In every respect, we are living not only in a new century, but also in a truly new world. Our students will spend most of their lives in what may eventually come to be know as the Biological Century. They'd better be prepared.

Where does that preparation start? Well, in many respects, it starts with us—a scientific community composed of researchers and teachers. We owe it to each of our students to teach them what science has learned. That's important work. However, we must also keep in mind that it's just as important to teach them *how* science learns. That's where the bulletin board in *your* classroom comes in.

In preparing this unit, Joe Levine and I had access to the complete DNA sequence of the human genome. That information enabled us to put more detail than ever before into our description of human genetics.

Try as we might, however, we cannot predict the future, and that's one of the many places where you come in. At best, this book should serve as a starting point for you and for your students. Where you go from this starting point is up to you. I hope, however, whether you use a newspaper clipping or a Web page, you'll find a way to convey to your students the same thing my biology teacher showed me. The future isn't in the book—it's up there on the board that changes every day.

Sincerely,

Ken Miller

Go Online PHSchool.com

Students can research genetics on the site developed by authors Ken Miller and Joe Levine.

Chapter Planner 11 Introduction to Genetics

Section and Section Objectives	Time	STANDARDS NCLB	STANDARDS Biology	Activities and Labs
11–1 The Work of Gregor Mendel, pp. 263–266 11.1.1 ***Describe*** how Mendel studied inheritance in peas. 11.1.2 ***Summarize*** Mendel's conclusion about inheritance. 11.1.3 ***Explain*** the principle of dominance. 11.1.4 ***Describe*** what happens during segregation.	1 period (1/2 block)	7 2.c, 7 2.d, BI 2.d	BI 3.b	**SE:** ***Inquiry Activity,*** Are traits inherited?, p. 262 L2 **TE:** ***Build Science Skills,*** p. 263 L1 L2 **TE:** ***Demonstration,*** p. 265 L2 **TE:** ***Build Science Skills,*** p. 266 L1 L2
11–2 Probability and Punnett Squares, pp. 267–269 11.2.1 ***Explain*** how geneticists use the principles of probability. 11.2.2 ***Describe*** how geneticists use Punnett squares.	1 period (1/2 block)	7 2.c, 7 2.c, BI 3.a	BI 2.g, BI 3.b	**TE:** ***Make Connections,*** p. 267 L1 L2 **SE:** ***Quick Lab,*** How are dimples inherited?, p. 268 L2 **TE:** ***Build Science Skills,*** p. 269 L2
11–3 Exploring Mendelian Genetics, pp. 270–274 11.3.1 ***Explain*** the principle of independent assortment. 11.3.2 ***Describe*** other inheritance patterns. 11.3.3 ***Explain*** how Mendel's principles apply to organisms.	1 period (1/2 block)	7 2.c, 7 2.d	BI 2.g, BI 3.b	**TE:** ***Build Science Skills,*** p. 270 L2, p. 274 L2 **SE:** ***Problem Solving,*** Producing True-Breeding Seeds, p. 271 L2 L3 **TE:** ***Demonstration,*** p. 273 L2 **LMA:** Chapter 11 Lab L2 L3 **LMB:** Chapter 11 Lab L1 L2
11–4 Meiosis, pp. 275–278 11.4.1 ***Contrast*** the chromosome number of body cells and gametes. 11.4.2 ***Summarize*** the events of meiosis. 11.4.3 ***Contrast*** meiosis and mitosis.	1 period (1/2 block)	BI 2.b, BI 2.d, BI 2.e	BI 2.a	**TE:** ***Demonstration,*** p. 277 L2 **TE:** ***Build Science Skills,*** p. 278 L2 **SE:** ***Exploration,*** Modeling Meiosis, p. 281 L2
11–5 Linkage and Gene Maps, pp. 279–280 11.5.1 ***Identify*** the structures that actually assort independently. 11.5.2 ***Explain*** how gene maps are produced.	1 period (1/2 block)		BI 3.b, *BI 3.d	**TE:** ***Build Science Skills,*** p. 279 L1 L2 **BTM:** Lab 2 L2 L3
Chapter Assessment, pp. 282–285	1 period (1/2 block)			

ACTIVITY PLANNER

SE: *Inquiry Activity,* p. 262; 10 min.

TE: *Build Science Skills,* p. 263; 15 min.; flowers, scissors, dissecting microscope, compound microscope, microscope slides, tweezers, coverslips

TE: *Demonstration,* p. 265; 10 min.; P and F_1 corn cobs for specific traits

TE: *Build Science Skills,* p. 266; 15 min. on two days; 10 days apart; F_2 corn seeds, potting soil, water, aluminum pans

TE: *Make Connections,* p. 267; 15 min.; bag, different-colored items

SE: *Quick Lab,* p. 268; 15 min.; page from phone book, calculator

TE: *Build Science Skills,* p. 269; 15 min.; coin, or bag with 2 or 3 beads

TE: *Build Science Skills,* p. 270; 10 min.; F_1 corn cobs for specific traits

TE: *Demonstration,* p. 273; 15 min. on two days; 2 weeks apart; wild-type fruit flies, fruit flies with vestigial wings, microscope, fruit fly growth medium, culture jars, ether, jar with mineral oil, paintbrush, index cards

TE: *Build Science Skills,* p. 274; 5 min. daily for 2 weeks; cuttings from coleus plant started in pots

TE: *Demonstration,* p. 277; 10 min.; pipe cleaners, beads, scissors, tape

TE: *Build Science Skills,* p. 278; 10 min.; red and yellow gloves, green and blue socks, white and black shoes

TE: *Build Science Skills,* p. 279; 10 min.; pipe cleaners, beads, scissors

SE: *Exploration,* p. 281; 45 min.; yarn, scissors, tape, index cards, marker

PLANNING KEY

Ability Levels
for students performing . . .
below grade level L1
at grade level L2
above grade level L3

Print Components
SE Student Edition
TE Teacher's Edition
RSW Reading & Study Workbook A
ARSW Adapted Reading & Study Workbook B
TR Teaching Resources
IF Investigations in Forensics
LA Lab Assessment
BTM Biotechnology Manual
IDM Issues and Decision Making
LW Lab Worksheets
LMA Laboratory Manual A
LMB Laboratory Manual B

Tech Components
CTB Computer Test Bank
BD BioDetectives DVD
TP Transparencies Plus
PLM Probeware Lab Manual
ABC ABC DVD Library
LS Lab Simulations
VL Virtual Labs

Interactive textbook with assessment at PHSchool.com

Program Resources	Assessment	Media and Technology
TR: Lesson Plan 11–1, Section Summary, p. 6 L1, p. 14 L2, Worksheets, p. 9 L1, pp. 16–17 L2 **RSW:** Section 11–1 L2 **ARSW:** Section 11–1 L1	**SE:** 11–1 Section Assessment, p. 266 **TR:** Section Review 11–1	**iText:** Section 11–1 **TP:** 11–1 Interest Grabber, Section Outline, Principles of Dominance, Figure 11–3 **ABC:** 19 Segregation of Chromosomes
TR: Lesson Plan 11–2, Section Summary, p. 7 L1, p. 14 L2, Worksheets, p. 10 L1, pp. 18–19 L2, Enrichment L2 L3 **RSW:** Section 11–2 L2 **ARSW:** Section 11–2 L1	**SE:** 11–2 Section Assessment, p. 269 **TR:** Section Review 11–2	**iText:** Section 11–2 **TP:** 11–2 Interest Grabber, Section Outline, *Tt* × *Tt* Cross
TR: Lesson Plan 11–3, Section Summary, p. 7 L1, p. 15 L2, Worksheets, p. 11 L1, pp. 20–22 L2 **RSW:** Section 11–3 L2 **ARSW:** Section 11–3 L1	**SE:** 11–3 Section Assessment, p. 274 **TR:** Section Review 11–3	**iText:** Section 11–3 **TP:** 11–3 Interest Grabber, Section Outline, Concept Map, Figure 11–10, Figure 11–11 **Lab Simulations CD-ROM:** Mendelian Inheritance
TR: Lesson Plan 11–4, Section Summary, p. 8 L1, p. 15 L2, Worksheets, p. 12 L1, pp. 23–25 L2 **LW:** Chapter 11 Exploration L1 L2 L3 **RSW:** Section 11–4 L2 **ARSW:** Section 11–4 L1	**SE:** 11–4 Section Assessment, p. 278 **TR:** Section Review 11–4	**iText:** Section 11–4 **TP:** 11–4 Interest Grabber, Section Outline, Crossing-Over, Figure 11–15, I, II **ABC:** 17 Meiosis Overview, 18 Animal Cell Meiosis, 22 Crossing-Over **Lab Simulations CD-ROM:** Meiosis
TR: Lesson Plan 11–5, Section Summary, p. 8 L1, p. 15 L2, Worksheets, p. 26 L2 **RSW:** Section 11–5 L2	**SE:** 11–5 Section Assessment, p. 280 **TR:** Section Review 11–5	**iText:** Section 11–5 **TP:** 11–5 Interest Grabber, Section Outline, Comparative Scale of a Gene Map, Figure 11–19
	SE: Chapter 11 Assessment, pp. 282–285 **TR:** Chapter Vocabulary Review, Graphic Organizer, Chapter 11 Test	**iText:** Chapter 11 Assessment **CTB:** Chapter 11 Test

Go Online
Students can do research, share data, and test their knowledge online.

PRESSED FOR TIME?

To Preview the Chapter
- Introduce students to Key Concepts and Vocabulary in each section.
- Encourage students to study all chapter figures and captions.

To Cover the Chapter Quickly
- Have students read all of Sections 11–1 and 11–2, Independent Assortment in Section 11–3, all of Section 11–4, and Gene Linkage in Section 11–5.
- Assign the Section Reviews 11–1, 11–2, and 11–4; questions 1–5, 7–9, 12, 13, 17–20, 22–26, 29 and 30 in Chapter 11 Assessment; and questions 1–13 in Chapter 11 Standards Practice.

To Review the Chapter
- Have students study Figure 11–15 and complete the flowchart in the Chapter 11 Study Guide.
- Assign Section Reviews 11–1 through 11–5 and Chapter Vocabulary Review in the Teaching Resources.

CHAPTER 11

ENGAGE/EXPLORE

Inquiry Activity

Objective Students will be able to infer whether traits are inherited. L2

Skill Focus Inferring

Time 10 minutes

Strategies

- Help students identify examples of widow's peak vs. straight hairline, attached earlobes vs. free earlobes, and gapped vs. ungapped front teeth.
- Ask students if these traits run in families. Follow by inquiring exactly what that means, soliciting the idea that "you get them from your parents."

Expected Outcomes Students will recognize two or more forms of a trait and infer that these traits are inherited from parents.

Think About It

1. Yes; parents
2. Genes are passed from generation to generation, but they are not all expressed in every generation. If students mention adoption as an explanation, remind them that the question asks only about biological relatives.

Brain Teaser

Challenge students to explain how two brown rabbits could have white offspring. *(Accept all reasonable responses. The parents are heterozygous for fur color. The white offspring inherited both recessive alleles, thereby showing the recessive coat color.)* Challenge students to predict the coat color of offspring produced in a cross between two white rabbits. *(All offspring will be white.)* Revisit this question at the end of the chapter. Invite student volunteers to explain whether or not they would change their prediction and why.

CHAPTER 11 Introduction to Genetics

The varied patterns of stripes on zebras are due to differences in genetic makeup. No two zebras have identical stripe patterns.

Inquiry Activity

Are traits inherited?

Procedure

1. Look at your classmates. Note how they vary in the shape of the front hairline, the space between the two upper front teeth, and the way in which the earlobes are attached.
2. Make a list of the different forms of these traits that you have observed in the class or among other people you know.

Think About It

1. **Inferring** Could these traits be inherited? From whom could they be inherited?
2. **Inferring** How is it possible that these traits could be found in a person and his or her biological grandparents but not in the biological parents?

HISTORY OF SCIENCE

Changing theories of inheritance

Greek philosophers were the first to hypothesize how traits are passed from parent to offspring. Their concept of pangenesis explained that body fluids were composed of a mixture of particles secreted from all organs of the body. New individuals formed from a blend of male and female fluids. The discovery of eggs and sperm in the seventeenth century led to the theory of preformation—sex cells contain preformed miniatures of the adult. This idea was disproved by Caspar Wolff's work with chicken embryos. So when Darwin was developing an explanation for the mechanism of evolution, he took the ancient Greek idea of pangenesis and expanded it to include the inheritance of acquired characters. He proposed that as parts of the body changed, so did the pangenes (particles) that they produced.

11–1 The Work of Gregor Mendel

7 2.c. Students know an inherited trait can be determined by one or more genes. **7 2.d.** Students know plant and animal cells contain many thousands of different genes and typically have two copies of every gene. The two copies (or alleles) of the gene may or may not be identical, and one may be dominant in determining the phenotype while the other is recessive. **BI 2.d.** Students know new combinations of alleles may be generated in a zygote through the fusion of male and female gametes (fertilization). **BI 3.b.** Students know the genetic basis for Mendel's laws of segregation and independent assortment.

What is an inheritance? To most people, it is money or property left to them by a relative who has passed away. That kind of inheritance is important, of course. There is another form of inheritance, however, that matters even more. This inheritance has been with you from the very first day you were alive—your genes.

Every living thing—plant or animal, microbe or human being—has a set of characteristics inherited from its parent or parents. Since the beginning of recorded history, people have wanted to understand how that inheritance is passed from generation to generation. More recently, however, scientists have begun to appreciate that heredity holds the key to understanding what makes each species unique. As a result, **genetics,** the scientific study of heredity, is now at the core of a revolution in understanding biology.

Gregor Mendel's Peas

The work of an Austrian monk named Gregor Mendel, shown in **Figure 11–1,** was particularly important to understanding biological inheritance. Gregor Mendel was born in 1822 in what is now the Czech Republic. After becoming a priest, Mendel spent several years studying science and mathematics at the University of Vienna. He spent the next 14 years working in the monastery and teaching at the high school. In addition to his teaching duties, Mendel was in charge of the monastery garden. In this ordinary garden, he was to do the work that changed biology forever.

Mendel carried out his work with ordinary garden peas. He knew that part of each flower produces pollen, which contains the plant's male reproductive cells, or sperm. Similarly, the female portion of the flower produces egg cells. During sexual reproduction, male and female reproductive cells join, a process known as **fertilization.** Fertilization produces a new cell, which develops into a tiny embryo encased within a seed. Pea flowers are normally self-pollinating, which means that sperm cells in pollen fertilize the egg cells in the same flower. The seeds that are produced by self-pollination inherit all of their characteristics from the single plant that bore them. In effect, they have a single parent.

When Mendel took charge of the monastery garden, he had several stocks of pea plants. These peas were **true-breeding,** meaning that if they were allowed to self-pollinate, they would produce offspring identical to themselves. One stock of seeds would produce only tall plants, another only short ones. One line produced only green seeds, another only yellow seeds. These true-breeding plants were the basis of Mendel's experiments.

Guide for Reading

Key Concepts
- What is the principle of dominance?
- What happens during segregation?

Vocabulary
genetics • fertilization
true-breeding • trait • hybrid
gene • allele • segregation
gamete

Reading Strategy: Finding Main Ideas As you read, find evidence to support the following statement: Mendel's ideas about genetics were the beginning of a new area of biology.

▲ **Figure 11–1** Gregor Mendel's experiments with pea plants laid the foundations of the science of genetics.

SECTION RESOURCES

TIME SAVER

Print:
- ***Teaching Resources,*** Lesson Plan 11–1, Adapted Section Summary 11–1, Adapted Worksheets 11–1, Section Summary 11–1, Worksheets 11–1, Section Review 11–1
- ***Reading and Study Workbook A,*** Section 11–1
- ***Adapted Reading and Study Workbook B,*** Section 11–1

Technology:
- ***iText,*** Section 11–1
- ***Animated Biological Concepts DVD,*** 19
- ***Transparencies Plus,*** Section 11–1

Section 11–1

7 2.c, 7 2.d, BI 2.d, BI 3.b

1 FOCUS

Objectives

11.1.1 ***Describe*** how Mendel studied inheritance in peas.
11.1.2 ***Summarize*** Mendel's conclusion about inheritance.
11.1.3 ***Explain*** the principle of dominance.
11.1.4 ***Describe*** what happens during segregation.

Guide for Reading

Vocabulary Preview

Help students become comfortable with the language of genetics by showing them how the Vocabulary words are related to one another. For example, a true-breeding individual is the opposite of a hybrid; an allele is one form of a gene, and genes specify particular traits. Construct a word web on the board to show these relationships.

Reading Strategy

Students should mention Mendel's research approach, as well as his results and interpretations, as support for the main idea.

2 INSTRUCT

Gregor Mendel's Peas

Build Science Skills

Observing Give students lilies, tulips, freesia, or other flowers with large stamens and pistils. Instruct them to cut off the stamens and pistils with small scissors and examine them under a dissecting microscope. If students carefully section the anther and the pistil, they may be able to observe pollen and egg cells on microscope slides with a compound microscope. Help them distinguish between pollen and sperm, and egg and ovule. Encourage students to draw labeled diagrams of their flowers. L1 L2

11–1 (continued)

Build Science Skills

Classifying Explain that much of Mendel's success came from his choice of experimental organism. Pea plants are useful for genetic study because they have many contrasting characters, they reproduce sexually, their crosses can be controlled, they have short life cycles, they produce a large number of offspring, and they are easy to handle in a laboratory. Invite students to apply these same criteria to other organisms, such as humans, fruit flies, bacteria, oak trees, dogs, and mice. For each organism, students should explain why it would or would not be useful for genetic study. *(Fruit flies, bacteria, and mice are most useful.)* L2

Genes and Dominance

Use Visuals

Figure 11–3 Review the results of Mendel's crosses. Make sure students can identify which traits are dominant and which are recessive. Ask: **Why was Mendel surprised when the offspring had the character of only one of the parents?** *(In Mendel's time, people thought that characters of the parents blended to form the offspring.)* Relate the terms *genes* and *alleles* to the results shown in the table. Make sure students are comfortable with the terminology. L1 L2

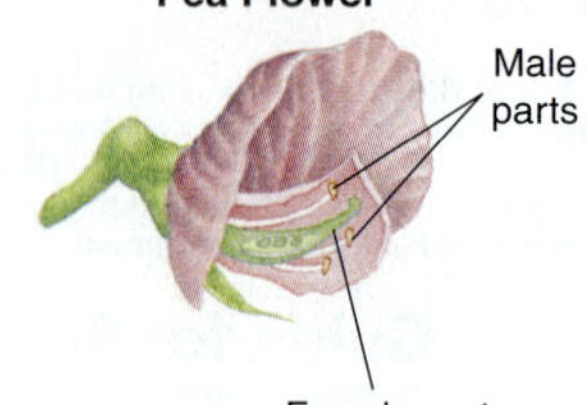

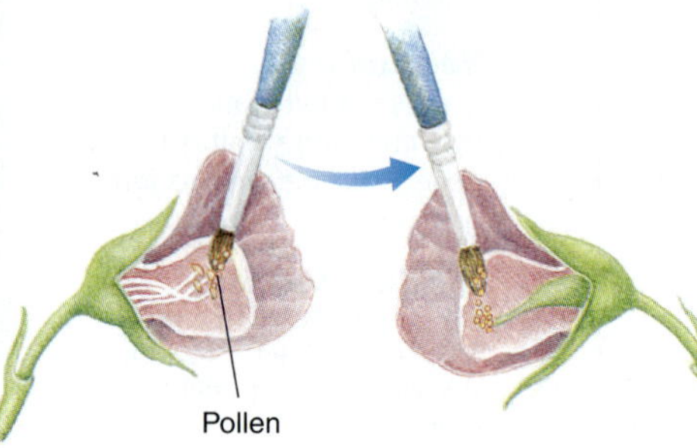

◀ **Figure 11–2** To cross-pollinate pea plants, Mendel cut off the male parts of one flower and then dusted it with pollen from another flower. **Applying Concepts** *How did this procedure prevent self-pollination?*

Mendel wanted to produce seeds by joining male and female reproductive cells from two different plants. To do this, he had to prevent self-pollination. He accomplished this by cutting away the pollen-bearing male parts as shown in **Figure 11–2** and then dusting pollen from another plant onto the flower. This process, which is known as cross-pollination, produced seeds that had two different plants as parents. This made it possible for Mendel to cross-breed plants with different characteristics and then to study the results.

CHECKPOINT *What is fertilization?*

Genes and Dominance

Mendel studied seven different pea plant traits. A **trait** is a specific characteristic, such as seed color or plant height, that varies from one individual to another. Each of the seven traits Mendel studied had two contrasting characters, for example, green seed color and yellow seed color. Mendel crossed plants with each of the seven contrasting characters and studied their offspring. We call each original pair of plants the P (parental) generation. The offspring are called the F_1, or "first filial," generation. *Filius* and *filia* are the Latin words for "son" and "daughter." The offspring of crosses between parents with different traits are called **hybrids.**

CA (a) (a) BI 2.d

▼ **Figure 11–3** When Mendel crossed plants with contrasting characters for the same trait, the resulting offspring had only one of the characters. **From these experiments, Mendel concluded that some alleles are dominant and others are recessive.**

Mendel's Seven F_1 Crosses on Pea Plants

	Seed Shape	Seed Color	Seed Coat Color	Pod Shape	Pod Color	Flower Position	Plant Height
P	Round X Wrinkled	Yellow X Green	Gray X White	Smooth X Constricted	Green X Yellow	Axial X Terminal	Tall X Short
F_1	Round	Yellow	Gray	Smooth	Green	Axial	Tall

ESL SUPPORT FOR ENGLISH LANGUAGE LEARNERS

Vocabulary: Prior Knowledge

Beginning Write the word *trait* on the board. Say *trait* and its definition aloud. Then, display photos of various kinds of organisms. For the first few photos, point to a trait and say the trait aloud in a simple sentence, such as "This bear has the trait of brown fur." Then, ask students to point to other traits exhibited by the organism. As they point, say the trait aloud. Finally, work with students to compose concept circles (cluster diagrams) of traits shown in additional photos. After the students understand the concept, call their attention to the pea-plant traits in Figure 11–3. L1

Intermediate Extend the activity for beginning students by having intermediate students work individually to write traits of organisms shown in photos in this book, such as the mammals on pages 831–832. L2

What were those F_1 hybrid plants like? Did the characters of the parent plants blend in the offspring? Not at all. To Mendel's surprise, all of the offspring had the character of only one of the parents, as shown in **Figure 11–3.** In each cross, the character of the other parent seemed to have disappeared.

From this set of experiments, Mendel drew two conclusions. Mendel's first conclusion was that biological inheritance is determined by factors that are passed from one generation to the next. Today, scientists call the chemical factors that determine traits **genes.** Each of the traits Mendel studied was controlled by one gene that occurred in two contrasting forms. These contrasting forms produced the different characters of each trait. For example, the gene for plant height occurs in one form that produces tall plants and in another form that produces short plants. The different forms of a gene are called **alleles** (uh-LEELZ).

CA ⓐ

ⓐ 7 2.c

Mendel's second conclusion is called the principle of dominance.  **The principle of dominance states that some alleles are dominant and others are recessive.** An organism with a dominant allele for a particular form of a trait will always exhibit that form of the trait. An organism with a recessive allele for a particular form of a trait will exhibit that form only when the dominant allele for the trait is not present. In Mendel's experiments, the allele for tall plants was dominant and the allele for short plants was recessive. The allele for yellow seeds was dominant, while the allele for green seeds was recessive.

CA ⓑ

ⓑ 7 2.d

Segregation

Mendel wanted the answer to another question: Had the recessive alleles disappeared, or were they still present in the F_1 plants? To answer this question, he allowed all seven kinds of F_1 hybrid plants to produce an F_2 (second filial) generation by self-pollination. In effect, he crossed the F_1 generation with itself to produce the F_2 offspring, as shown in **Figure 11–4.**

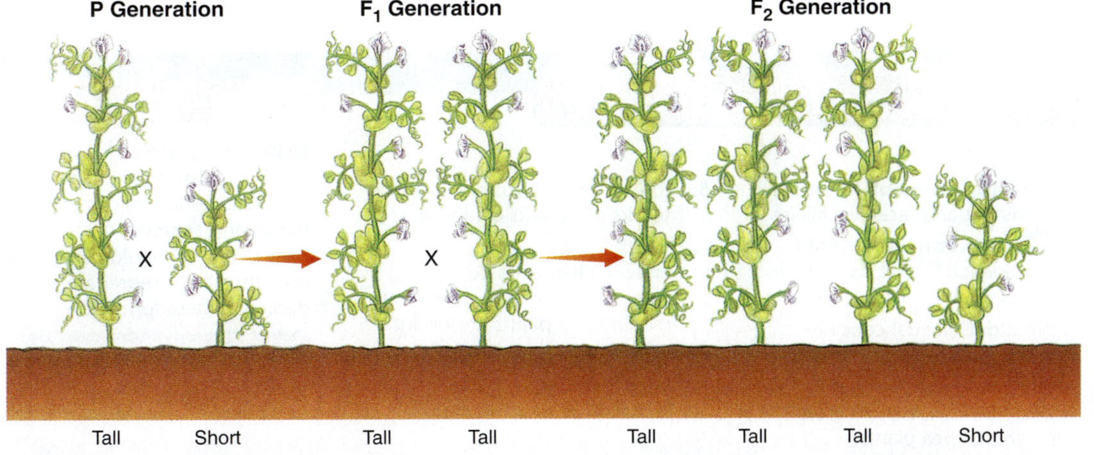

▼ **Figure 11–4** When Mendel allowed the F_1 plants to reproduce by self-pollination, the traits controlled by recessive alleles reappeared in about one fourth of the F_2 plants in each cross. **Calculating** *What proportion of the F_2 plants had a trait controlled by a dominant allele?*

Demonstration

Display the parental corn cobs and the F_1 corn cobs produced in a cross between purple *(PP)* corn and yellow *(pp)* corn, as well as those produced in a cross between starchy *(SS)* corn and sweet *(ss)* corn. Have students identify the traits associated with each allele for each cross and which allele is dominant and which is recessive. L2

Segregation

Use Visuals

Figure 11–4 Walk students through the crosses that Mendel set up as they are illustrated in the figure. Ask: **Did Mendel cross-pollinate F_1 plants to get F_2 plants?** *(No, he allowed them to self-pollinate.)* **Was the recessive allele for shortness lost in the F_1 generation?** *(No, it was masked by the dominant allele for tallness.)* **Are the F_1 plants true-breeding?** *(No, they did not produce offspring identical to themselves.)* Have student volunteers identify the gametes that each plant would produce in the P generation and in the F_1 generation. L2

Address Misconceptions

Some students might think it is impossible for two tall pea plants to produce short pea plants. For these students, review the cross as shown in Figure 11–4. Make sure they see that the tall pea plants came from a tall plant crossed to a short plant. Ask: **Why aren't any offspring short?** *(The allele for tallness is dominant and masks the allele for shortness.)* **Why do these plants have an allele for shortness?** *(One of their parents was short and could contribute only alleles for shortness to its offspring.)* L1 L2

HISTORY OF SCIENCE

Methods of Mendel's success

Mendel was the first scientist of his time to obtain successful results from inheritance studies because of the methods he employed. In fact, his methods continue to be used today. Mendel studied only one trait at a time. He also took the time to verify that the parent plants were true-breeding for the particular trait he was studying. Mendel used a quantitative approach to analyze his results. He counted the number of offspring from every cross and used statistical analysis to interpret his numbers. Most important, Mendel formulated hypotheses to explain his results, and he developed experimental tests to confirm them.

Answers to . . .

✓CHECKPOINT *The process during sexual reproduction when male and female cells join*

Figure 11–2 *The flower no longer had its own source of pollen.*

Figure 11–4 *Three-fourths*

11–1 (continued)

Build Science Skills

Calculating Instruct students to plant F_2 corn seeds produced in a cross between two plants heterozygous for green and white color *(Gg)*. When the seeds sprout, students should get a mixture of green plants and white plants. Ask: **Which allele is dominant?** *(Green)* **Which is recessive?** *(White)* **How do you know?** *(More green plants)* Have students calculate the ratio of green plants to white plants. Discuss how their results compare with Mendel's. *(The class should have a ratio close to 3 green : 1 white.)* L1 L2

3 ASSESS

Evaluate Understanding

Assign students a trait in pea plants. Have them set up a cross as Mendel did to show the F_1 and F_2 offspring. Students should identify the dominant and recessive alleles.

Reteach

Help students devise a flowchart that outlines Mendel's method for his breeding experiments in pea plants. Encourage students to include as many Vocabulary words as possible.

Thinking Visually

Students' diagrams should be similar to Figures 11–3 and 11–5. Segregation of alleles ensures that each gamete carries only a single copy of each gene.

If your class subscribes to the iText, use it to review the Key Concepts in Section 11–1.

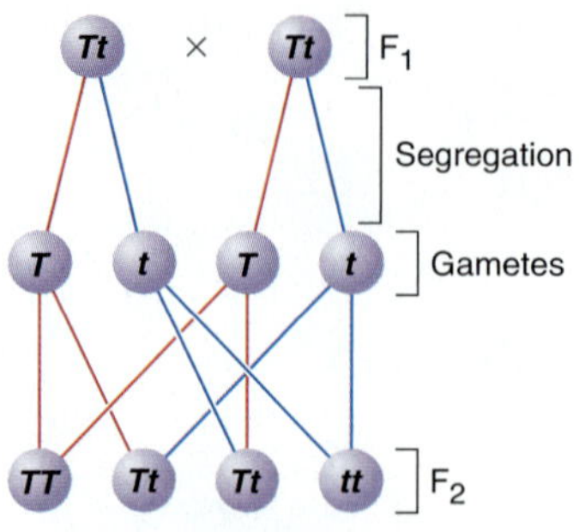

▲ **Figure 11–5** **During gamete formation, alleles segregate from each other so that each gamete carries only a single copy of each gene. Each F_1 plant produces two types of gametes—those with the allele for tallness and those with the allele for shortness.** The alleles are paired up again when gametes fuse during fertilization. The *TT* and *Tt* allele combinations produce tall pea plants; *tt* is the only allele combination that produces a short pea plant.

The F_1 Cross The results of the F_1 cross were remarkable. When Mendel compared the F_2 plants, he discovered that the traits controlled by the recessive alleles had reappeared! Roughly one fourth of the F_2 plants showed the trait controlled by the recessive allele. Why did the recessive alleles seem to disappear in the F_1 generation and then reappear in the F_2 generation? To answer this question, let's take a closer look at one of Mendel's crosses.

Explaining the F_1 Cross To begin with, Mendel assumed that a dominant allele had masked the corresponding recessive allele in the F_1 generation. However, the trait controlled by the recessive allele showed up in some of the F_2 plants. This reappearance indicated that at some point the allele for shortness had been separated from the allele for tallness. How did this separation, or **segregation,** of alleles occur? Mendel suggested that the alleles for tallness and shortness in the F_1 plants segregated from each other during the formation of the sex cells, or **gametes** (GAM-eetz). Did that suggestion make sense?

Let's assume, as perhaps Mendel did, that the F_1 plants inherited an allele for tallness from the tall parent and an allele for shortness from the short parent. Because the allele for tallness is dominant, all the F_1 plants are tall. **When each F_1 plant flowers and produces gametes, the two alleles segregate from each other so that each gamete carries only a single copy of each gene. Therefore, each F_1 plant produces two types of gametes—those with the allele for tallness and those with the allele for shortness.**

Look at **Figure 11–5** to see how alleles separated during gamete formation and then paired up again in the F_2 generation. A capital letter *T* represents a dominant allele. A lowercase letter *t* represents a recessive allele. The result of this process is an F_2 generation with new combinations of alleles.

11–1 Section Assessment

1. **Key Concept** What are dominant and recessive alleles?
2. **Key Concept** What is segregation? What happens to alleles during segregation?
3. What did Mendel conclude determines biological inheritance?
4. Describe how Mendel cross-pollinated pea plants.
5. Why did only about one fourth of Mendel's F_2 plants exhibit the recessive trait?
6. **Critical Thinking Applying Concepts** Why were true-breeding pea plants important for Mendel's experiments?

Thinking Visually

Using Diagrams
Use a diagram to explain Mendel's principles of dominance and segregation. Your diagram should show how the alleles segregate during gamete formation.

11–1 Section Assessment

1. Dominant: form of an allele whose trait always shows up if it is present; recessive: form of an allele whose trait shows up only when the dominant allele is not present
2. Separation of paired alleles; the alleles are separated during the formation of gametes, with the result that each gamete carries only a single allele from the original pair.
3. Factors that are passed from one generation to the next
4. Mendel cut away the male parts of one flower, then dusted it with pollen from another flower.
5. Only one-fourth of the possible gamete combinations did not have a dominant allele.
6. True-breeding pea plants have two identical alleles for a gene, so in a genetic cross each parent contributed only one form of a gene, making inheritance patterns more detectable.

11–2 Probability and Punnett Squares

7 2.c. Students know an inherited trait can be determined by one or more genes. **7 2.d.** Students know plant and animal cells contain many thousands of different genes and typically have two copies of every gene. The two copies (or alleles) of the gene may or may not be identical, and one may be dominant in determining the phenotype while the other is recessive. **BI 2.g.** Students know how to predict possible combinations of alleles in a zygote from the genetic makeup of the parents. **BI 3.a.** Students know how to predict the probable outcome of phenotypes in a genetic cross from the genotypes of the parents and mode of inheritance (autosomal or X-linked, dominant or recessive). **BI 3.b.** Students know the genetic basis for Mendel's laws of segregation and independent assortment.

Guide for Reading

Key Concepts

- How do geneticists use the principles of probability?
- How do geneticists use Punnett squares?

Vocabulary

probability
Punnett square
homozygous
heterozygous
phenotype
genotype

Reading Strategy: Building Vocabulary Before you read, preview the list of new vocabulary words. Predict the relationship between phenotype and genotype. As you read, check to see if your predictions were correct.

Whenever Mendel performed a cross with pea plants, he carefully categorized and counted the many offspring. Every time Mendel repeated a particular cross, he obtained similar results. For example, whenever Mendel crossed two plants that were hybrid for stem height (*Tt*), about three fourths of the resulting plants were tall and about one fourth were short. Mendel realized that the principles of probability could be used to explain the results of genetic crosses.

Genetics and Probability

The likelihood that a particular event will occur is called **probability.** As an example of probability, consider an ordinary event like the coin flip shown in **Figure 11–6.** There are two possible outcomes: The coin may land heads up or tails up. The chances, or probabilities, of either outcome are equal. Therefore, the probability that a single coin flip will come up heads is 1 chance in 2. This is 1/2, or 50 percent.

If you flip a coin three times in a row, what is the probability that it will land heads up every time? Because each coin flip is an independent event, the probability of each coin's landing heads up is 1/2. Therefore, the probability of flipping three heads in a row is:

$$\frac{1}{2} \times \frac{1}{2} \times \frac{1}{2} = \frac{1}{8}.$$

As you can see, you have 1 chance in 8 of flipping heads three times in a row. That the individual probabilities are multiplied together illustrates an important point—past outcomes do not affect future ones.

How is coin flipping relevant to genetics? The way in which alleles segregate is completely random, like a coin flip. **The principles of probability can be used to predict the outcomes of genetic crosses.**

CHECKPOINT *What is the probability that a tossed coin will come up tails twice in a row?*

Figure 11–6 The mathematical concept of probability allows you to calculate the likelihood that a particular event will occur. **Predicting** *What is the probability that the coin will land heads up?*

SECTION RESOURCES

Print:

- ***Teaching Resources,*** Lesson Plan 11–2, Adapted Section Summary 11–2, Adapted Worksheets 11–2, Section Summary 11–2, Worksheets 11–2, Section Review 11–2, Enrichment
- ***Reading and Study Workbook A,*** Section 11–2
- ***Adapted Reading and Study Workbook B,*** Section 11–2

Technology:

- ***iText,*** Section 11–2
- ***Transparencies Plus,*** Section 11–2

Section 11–2

7 2.c, 7 2.d, BI 2.g, BI 3.a, BI 3.b

1 FOCUS

Objectives

11.2.1 ***Explain*** how geneticists use the principles of probability.
11.2.2 ***Describe*** how geneticists use Punnett squares.

Guide for Reading

Vocabulary Preview

Ask: **What suffix do the words *homozygous* and *heterozygous* share?** (-zygous) Tell students that *-zygous* means "yoked" or "joined," and the prefix *homo-* means "same." Also explain that a homozygous organism has two identical alleles for a certain gene. Ask: **If *hetero-* means "other," what does *heterozygous* describe?** *(An organism with two different alleles for a gene)*

Reading Strategy

Encourage students to write down the main headings of the section before they begin reading. Tell them to leave room below each heading to record important ideas as they read.

2 INSTRUCT

Genetics and Probability

Make Connections

Mathematics Give pairs of students a paper bag that has 4 items that are identical except for color. The items should be the same shape and size. Ask: **What is the probability of picking a red item?** *(1/4 or 25 percent)* **Of picking a red item two times in a row?** *(1/4 × 1/4 = 1/16)* Then, instruct students to pick an item from the bag 20 times, then 50 times. Ask: **Did your results equal your calculated probabilities?** *(The more times students pick from the bag, the closer their actual results will be to the predicted probability.)* L1 L2

Answers to . . .

CHECKPOINT *1/4 or 25 percent*

Figure 11–6 *1/2 or 50 percent*

11–2 (continued)

Punnett Squares

Quick Lab

Objective Students will be able to conclude how dimples are inherited. L2

Skills Focus **Applying Concepts, Drawing Conclusions**

Materials copy of page from telephone book, calculator

Time 15 minutes

Advance Prep Photocopy several pages from a telephone book.

Strategies

- Demonstrate the use of a 4-digit number to represent the genotypes of the parents in a genetic cross.
- Show students how to set up and use Punnett squares, if necessary.

Expected Outcomes Students will determine the probability of having a child with dimples based on the genotypes of the parents. Calculated probabilities will vary depending on the genotypes of the parents.

Analyze and Conclude

1. Class averages will vary but will usually be close to 75 percent dimples, the result of a cross between two heterozygotes.
2. 100 percent because the allele for dimples (*D*) is a dominant allele.

Probability and Segregation

Address Misconceptions

Beginning genetics students often misinterpret probable genotypic and phenotypic ratios as actual numbers of offspring. Provide opportunities to calculate "actual" ratios using F_2 corn cobs or experimental data. Students should set up Punnett squares and compare the predicted ratios with the "actual" ratios. L1 L2

Quick Lab

How are dimples inherited?

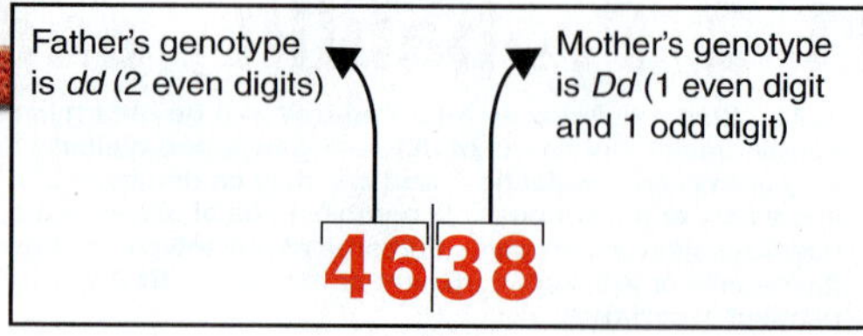

Materials copy of page from telephone book, calculator

Procedure

1. Write the last 4 digits of any telephone number. These 4 random digits represent the alleles of a gene that determines whether a person will have dimples. Odd digits represent the allele for the dominant trait of dimples. Even digits stand for the allele for the recessive trait of no dimples.
2. Use the first 2 digits to represent a certain father's genotype. Use the symbols *D* and *d* to write his genotype, as shown in the example.
3. Use the last 2 digits the same way to find the mother's genotype. Write her genotype.
4. Use **Figure 11–7** as an example to construct a Punnett square for the cross of these parents. Then, using the Punnett square, determine the probability that their child will have dimples.
5. Determine the class average of the percent of children with dimples.

Analyze and Conclude

1. **Applying Concepts** How does the class average compare with the result of a cross of two heterozygous parents?
2. **Drawing Conclusions** What percentage of the children will be expected to have dimples if one parent is homozygous for dimples *(DD)* and the other is heterozygous *(Dd)*?

CA a 7 2.c, 7 2.d

Punnett Squares

The gene combinations that might result from a genetic cross can be determined by drawing a diagram known as a **Punnett square.** The Punnett square in **Figure 11–7** shows one of Mendel's segregation experiments. The types of gametes produced by each F_1 parent are shown along the top and left sides of the square. The possible gene combinations for the F_2 offspring appear in the four boxes that make up the square. The letters in the Punnett square represent alleles. In this example, *T* represents the dominant allele for tallness and *t* represents the recessive allele for shortness. **Punnett squares can be used to predict and compare the genetic variations that will result from a cross.**

Organisms that have two identical alleles for a particular trait—*TT* or *tt* in this example—are said to be **homozygous** (hoh-moh-ZY-gus). Organisms that have two different alleles for the same trait are **heterozygous** (het-ur-oh-ZY-gus). Homozygous organisms are true-breeding for a particular trait. Heterozygous organisms are hybrid for a particular trait.

All of the tall plants have the same **phenotype,** or physical characteristics. They do not, however, have the same **genotype,** or genetic makeup. The genotype of one third of the tall plants is *TT,* while the genotype of two thirds of the tall plants is *Tt*. The plants in **Figure 11–8** have the same phenotype but different genotypes.

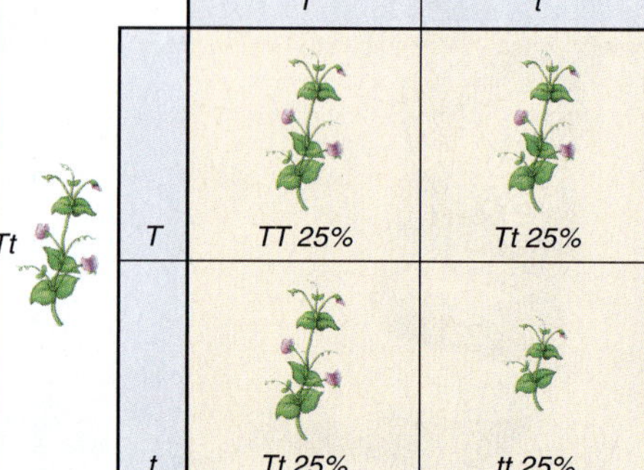

▲ **Figure 11–7** **The principles of probability can be used to predict the outcomes of genetic crosses.** This Punnett square shows the probability of each possible outcome of a cross between hybrid tall *(Tt)* pea plants.

UNIVERSAL ACCESS

Inclusion/Special Needs

Give students additional opportunities to practice calculating probabilities by making available a "probabilities kit." In this "kit," provide coins and a grab bag with colored beads, colored sticks, or any other manipulative that differs only in color. You might have these students pair up with advanced students to predict probabilities and observe the outcomes. L1

Less Proficient Readers

Challenge students to write an instructional manual for using Punnett squares. Students should include a labeled diagram of a Punnett square in their manual, as well as step-by-step directions on how to use one and why Punnett squares are useful tools for geneticists. L1 L2

Probability and Segregation

Look again at **Figure 11–7.** One fourth (1/4) of the F_2 plants have two alleles for tallness *(TT);* 2/4, or 1/2, of the F_2 plants have one allele for tallness and one allele for shortness *(Tt).* Because the allele for tallness is dominant over the allele for shortness, 3/4 of the F_2 plants should be tall. Overall, there are 3 tall plants for every 1 short plant in the F_2 generation. Thus, the ratio of tall plants to short plants is 3 : 1. This assumes, of course, that Mendel's model of segregation is correct.

Did the data from Mendel's experiments fit his model? Yes. The predicted ratio—3 dominant to 1 recessive—showed up consistently, indicating that Mendel's assumptions about segregation had been correct. For each of his seven crosses, about 3/4 of the plants showed the trait controlled by the dominant allele. About 1/4 showed the trait controlled by the recessive allele. Segregation did indeed occur according to Mendel's model.

CA
a

▲ **Figure 11–8** Although these plants have different genotypes (*TT* and *Tt*), they have the same phenotype (tall). **Predicting** ***If you crossed these two plants, would their offspring be tall or short?***

a **BI 3.a**

Probabilities Predict Averages

Probabilities predict the average outcome of a large number of events. However, probability cannot predict the precise outcome of an individual event. If you flip a coin twice, you are likely to get one head and one tail. However, you might also get two heads or two tails. To be more likely to get the expected 50 : 50 ratio, you would have to flip the coin many times.

The same is true of genetics. The larger the number of offspring, the closer the resulting numbers will get to expected values. If an F_1 generation contains just three or four offspring, it may not match Mendelian predicted ratios. When an F_1 generation contains hundreds or thousands of individuals, however, the ratios usually come very close to matching expectations.

11–2 Section Assessment

1. **Key Concept** How are the principles of probability used to predict the outcomes of genetic crosses?
2. **Key Concept** How are Punnett squares used?
3. What is probability?
4. Define the terms *genotype* and *phenotype.*
5. **Critical Thinking Problem Solving** An F_1 plant that is homozygous for shortness is crossed with a heterozygous F_1 plant. What is the probability that a seed from the cross will produce a tall plant? Use a Punnett square to explain your answer and to compare the probable genetic variations in the F_2 plants.

Thinking Visually

Drawing Punnett Squares
Imagine that you came upon a tall pea plant similar to those Mendel used in his experiments. How could you determine the plant's genotype with respect to height? Draw two Punnett squares to show your answer.

Probabilities Predict Averages

Build Science Skills

Designing Experiments Give students a coin or a bag with 2 or 3 beads that differ in color. Ask them to design an experiment to show that probabilities cannot predict the outcome of an individual event. L2

3 ASSESS

Evaluate Understanding

Assign students different traits in peas. Then, instruct them to set up a Punnett square to show the cross between two heterozygous pea plants for their trait. Students should give both the genotypic and phenotypic ratio of the offspring.

Reteach

Give student pairs a list of genetic crosses between parents of various genotypes. Instruct pairs to use Punnett squares to show the possible outcomes of the crosses.

Thinking Visually

The genotype of the tall pea plant is determined by allowing the plant to self-pollinate. If the plant is heterozygous, there is a 25 percent chance that an offspring will be short. If the plant is homozygous, then all offspring will be tall. Students should draw Punnett squares to show both possibilities.

Interactive Textbook

If your class subscribes to the iText, use it to review the Key Concepts in Section 11–2.

11–2 Section Assessment

1. The way in which the alleles segregate is random, and probability allows the calculation of the likelihood that a particular allele combination will occur in offspring.
2. To predict and compare the genetic variations that will result from a cross
3. The likelihood that a particular event will occur
4. Genotype: actual alleles present for a trait, or genetic makeup; phenotype: visible expression of the alleles, or physical characteristics
5. 50 percent; Punnett square:

	t	*t*
T	*Tt*	*Tt*
t	*tt*	*tt*

Answer to . . .

Figure 11–8 *All of the offspring would be tall.*

Section 11–3

7 2.c, 7 2.d, BI 2.g, BI 3.b

1 FOCUS

Objectives

11.3.1 ***Explain*** the principle of independent assortment.

11.3.2 ***Describe*** the inheritance patterns that exist aside from simple dominance.

11.3.3 ***Explain*** how Mendel's principles apply to all organisms.

Guide for Reading

Vocabulary Preview

Explain that the prefix *poly-* means "more than one." Ask: **What do you think a polygenic trait is?** *(A trait controlled by more than one gene)*

Reading Strategy

Before students read the section, suggest that they read the captions and study the art and diagrams in each figure.

2 INSTRUCT

Independent Assortment

Build Science Skills

Applying Concepts Give students F_1 corn cobs produced in a dihybrid cross between homozygous purple, starchy *(PPSS)* and yellow, sweet parents *(ppss)*. Ask: **Which traits are controlled by dominant alleles?** *(Purple and starchy)* Then, have students construct a Punnett square to show all the possible gametes and offspring from the cross. (*Punnett squares should look similar to the one in Figure 11–9. Possible gametes for the* ppss *parent are* ps. *Those for the* PPSS *parent are* PS. *All offspring will be heterozygous,* PpSs.*)* L2

11–3 Exploring Mendelian Genetics

7 2.c. Students know an inherited trait can be determined by one or more genes. **7 2.d.** Students know plant and animal cells contain many thousands of different genes and typically have two copies of every gene. The two copies (or alleles) of the gene may or may not be identical, and one may be dominant in determining the phenotype while the other is recessive. **BI 2.g.** Students know how to predict possible combinations of alleles in a zygote from the genetic makeup of the parents. **BI 3.b.** Students know the genetic basis for Mendel's laws of segregation and independent assortment.

Guide for Reading

Key Concepts
- What is the principle of independent assortment?
- What inheritance patterns exist aside from simple dominance?

Vocabulary
independent assortment
incomplete dominance
codominance
multiple alleles
polygenic traits

Reading Strategy: Finding Main Ideas Before you read, draw a line down the center of a sheet of paper. On the left side, write down the main topics of the section. On the right side, note supporting details and examples.

After showing that alleles segregate during the formation of gametes, Mendel wondered if they did so independently. In other words, does the segregation of one pair of alleles affect the segregation of another pair of alleles? For example, does the gene that determines whether a seed is round or wrinkled in shape have anything to do with the gene for seed color? Must a round seed also be yellow?

Independent Assortment

To answer these questions, Mendel performed an experiment to follow two different genes as they passed from one generation to the next. Mendel's experiment is known as a two-factor cross.

The Two-Factor Cross: F_1 First, Mendel crossed true-breeding plants that produced only round yellow peas (genotype *RRYY*) with plants that produced wrinkled green peas (genotype *rryy*). All of the F_1 offspring produced round yellow peas. This shows that the alleles for yellow and round peas are dominant over the alleles for green and wrinkled peas. A Punnett square for this cross, shown in **Figure 11–9,** shows that the genotype of each of these F_1 plants is *RrYy*.

This cross does not indicate whether genes assort, or segregate, independently. However, it provides the hybrid plants needed for the next cross—the cross of F_1 plants to produce the F_2 generation.

Figure 11–9 Mendel crossed plants that were homozygous dominant for round yellow peas with plants that were homozygous recessive for wrinkled green peas. All of the F_1 offspring were heterozygous dominant for round yellow peas. **Interpreting Graphics** *How is the genotype of the offspring different from that of the homozygous dominant parent?*

rryy / RRYY

	ry	ry	ry	ry
RY	RrYy	RrYy	RrYy	RrYy
RY	RrYy	RrYy	RrYy	RrYy
RY	RrYy	RrYy	RrYy	RrYy
RY	RrYy	RrYy	RrYy	RrYy

SECTION RESOURCES

TIME SAVER

Print:
- ***Laboratory Manual A,*** Chapter 11 Lab
- ***Laboratory Manual B,*** Chapter 11 Lab
- ***Teaching Resources,*** Lesson Plan 11–3, Adapted Section Summary 11–3, Adapted Worksheets 11–3, Section Summary 11–3, Worksheets 11–3, Section Review 11–3
- ***Reading and Study Workbook A,*** Section 11–3
- ***Adapted Reading and Study Workbook B,*** Section 11–3

Technology:
- ***iText,*** Section 11–3
- ***Transparencies Plus,*** Section 11–3
- ***Lab Simulations CD-ROM,*** Mendelian Inheritance

The Two-Factor Cross: F_2 Mendel knew that the F_1 plants had genotypes of *RrYy*. In other words, the F_1 plants were all heterozygous for both the seed shape and seed color genes. How would the alleles segregate when the F_1 plants were crossed to each other to produce an F_2 generation? Remember that each plant in the F_1 generation was formed by the fusion of a gamete carrying the dominant *RY* alleles with another gamete carrying the recessive *ry* alleles. Did this mean that the two dominant alleles would always stay together? Or would they "segregate independently," so that any combination of alleles was possible?

In Mendel's experiment, the F_2 plants produced 556 seeds. Mendel compared the variation in the seeds. He observed that 315 seeds were round and yellow and another 32 were wrinkled and green, the two parental phenotypes. However, 209 of the seeds had combinations of phenotypes—and therefore combinations of alleles—not found in either parent. This clearly meant that the alleles for seed shape segregated independently of those for seed color—a principle known as **independent assortment.** Put another way, genes that segregate independently—such as the genes for seed shape and seed color in pea plants—do not influence each other's inheritance. Mendel's experimental results were very close to the 9 : 3 : 3 : 1 ratio that the Punnett square shown in **Figure 11–10** predicts. Mendel had discovered the principle of independent assortment. **The principle of independent assortment states that genes for different traits can segregate independently during the formation of gametes. Independent assortment helps account for the many genetic variations observed in plants, animals, and other organisms.**

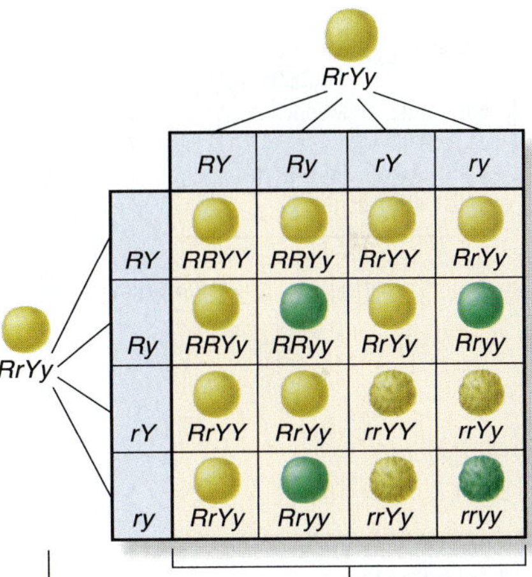

▲ **Figure 11–10** **When Mendel crossed plants that were heterozygous dominant for round yellow peas, he found that the alleles segregated independently to produce the F_2 generation.**

7 2.c, 7 2.d, **BI 2.c, BI 2.g**

Problem Solving

Producing True-Breeding Seeds

Suppose you work for a company that specializes in ornamental flowers. One spring, you find an ornamental plant with beautiful lavender flowers. Knowing that these plants are self-pollinating, you harvest seeds from it. You plant the seeds the following season. Of the 106 test plants, 31 have white flowers. Is there a way to develop seeds that produce only lavender flowers?

Defining the Problem Describe the problem that must be solved to make the lavender-flowered plants a commercial success.

Organizing Information The first lavender flower produced offspring with both lavender and white flowers when allowed to self-pollinate. Use your knowledge of Mendelian genetics, including Punnett squares, to draw conclusions about the nature of the allele for these lavender flowers.

Creating a Solution Write a description of how you would produce seeds guaranteed to produce 100 percent lavender plants. A single plant can produce as many as 1000 seeds.

Presenting Your Plan Prepare a step-by-step outline of your plan, including Punnett squares when appropriate. Present the procedure to your class.

Use Visuals

Figure 11–10 Have students give the phenotypic and genotypic ratios of the offspring for the cross shown in the figure. Ask: **What phenotypes would you observe if the alleles did not segregate independently?** *(Round, yellow seeds and wrinkled, green seeds)* L2

Problem Solving

7 2.c, 7 2.d, **BI 2.c, BI 2.g**

The 106 test plants were the result of the self-fertilization, or selfing, of the original lavender-flowering plant. Because the male and female gametes came from the same plant, they have the same genotype. You can compare this to the F_1 crosses set up by Mendel. L2 L3

Defining the Problem
Develop true-breeding, or homozygous, lavender-flowering plants.

Organizing Information
The allele for lavender flowers is dominant. The lavender-flowering plant is heterozygous. Students should show Punnett squares for a self-pollinating homozygous plant (would expect only one flower color) and a heterozygous plant (would expect two colors in a 3:1 ratio).

Creating a Solution
The best plans will suggest collecting seeds from many plants with lavender flowers and sowing them in separate plots, one plot for seeds produced by each plant. Some plants should produce offspring with only lavender flowers. Sow seeds from these plants to be absolutely sure the plants are true-breeding.

Presenting Your Plan
The best plans will include a step-by-step outline of the procedure to collect lavender-flowering plants that is genetically sound. The plan should include Punnett squares to support the genetic predictions of the crosses.

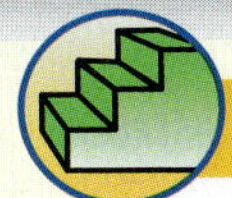

UNIVERSAL ACCESS

Inclusion/Special Needs
Have students develop a table in which they list the five different patterns of gene expression, along with descriptions and examples of each. Encourage students to include Punnett squares that illustrate each pattern of inheritance. L1 L2

English Language Learners
Make sure students can differentiate between Mendel's principles of segregation and independent assortment. Use diagrams like the one in Figure 11–5 to illustrate how alleles from different traits segregate independently. L1 L2

Advanced Learners
Enable students to set up genetic crosses with fruit flies. Have enough varieties available for students to observe independent assortment and different inheritance patterns. Tell them how to use test crosses. Invite them to share their findings with the class. L3

Answer to . . .

Figure 11–9 *The offspring are heterozygous.*

11–3 (continued)

A Summary of Mendel's Principles

Download a worksheet on Mendelian genetics for students to complete, and find additional teacher support from NSTA SciLinks.

Build Science Skills

Applying Concepts Challenge students to work in pairs to illustrate the summarized list of Mendel's principles. For reference, they can study figures in this chapter and in Chapter 12. L1 L2

Beyond Dominant and Recessive Alleles

Build Science Skills

Applying Concepts Explain that for alleles that show incomplete dominance, such as those in **Figure 11–11,** the alleles work together to produce a "dosage effect." For example, if a plant has one allele for red pigment and one allele for no pigment (which produces white flowers), then only half as much red pigment is produced, making the flowers pink. L2

Build Science Skills

Using Models Challenge students to devise a model that shows the difference between incomplete dominance and codominance. One way to do this is to use paper and crayons. In incomplete dominance, two colors are blended together to form a new color. In codominance, the two individual colors are still distinctly visible; they are not blended together. L1 L2

For: Punnett Square activity
Visit: PHSchool.com
Web Code: cbe-4112
Students can make their own Punnett squares.

For: Links on Mendelian genetics
Visit: www.SciLinks.org
Web Code: cbn-4113

a 7 2.c, 7 2.d

A Summary of Mendel's Principles

CA a

Mendel's principles form the basis of the modern science of genetics. These principles can be summarized as follows:

- The inheritance of biological characteristics is determined by individual units known as genes. Genes are passed from parents to their offspring.
- In cases in which two or more forms (alleles) of the gene for a single trait exist, some forms of the gene may be dominant and others may be recessive.
- In most sexually reproducing organisms, each adult has two copies of each gene—one from each parent. These genes are segregated from each other when gametes are formed.
- The alleles for different genes usually segregate independently of one another.

For: Punnett Square activity
Visit: PHSchool.com
Web Code: cbp-4112

Beyond Dominant and Recessive Alleles

Despite the importance of Mendel's work, there are important exceptions to most of his principles. For example, not all genes show simple patterns of dominant and recessive alleles. In most organisms, genetics is more complicated, because the majority of genes have more than two alleles. In addition, many important traits are controlled by more than one gene. **Some alleles are neither dominant nor recessive, and many traits are controlled by multiple alleles or multiple genes.**

Incomplete Dominance A cross between two four o'clock (Mirabilis) plants shows one of these complications. The F_1 generation produced by a cross between red-flowered *(RR)* and white-flowered *(WW)* plants consists of pink-colored flowers *(RW),* as shown in **Figure 11–11.** Which allele is dominant in this case? Neither one. Cases in which one allele is not completely dominant over another are called **incomplete dominance.** In incomplete dominance, the heterozygous phenotype is somewhere in between the two homozygous phenotypes.

Figure 11–11 **Some alleles are neither dominant nor recessive.** In four o'clock plants, for example, the alleles for red and white flowers show incomplete dominance. Heterozygous *(RW)* plants have pink flowers—a mix of red and white coloring.

Codominance A similar situation is **codominance,** in which both alleles contribute to the phenotype. For example, in certain varieties of chicken, the allele for black feathers is codominant with the allele for white feathers. Heterozygous chickens have a color described as "erminette," speckled with black and white feathers. Unlike the blending of red and white colors in heterozygous four o'clocks, black and white colors appear separately. Many human genes show codominance, too, including one for a protein that controls cholesterol levels in the blood. People with the heterozygous form of the gene produce two different forms of the protein, each with a different effect on cholesterol levels.

BIO INSIGHTS

HISTORY OF SCIENCE

Testing to identify F_1 genotypes

Mendel was very thorough in his methodology, so it really comes as no surprise that he devised a method to test his hypotheses in various ways. One method he used, which is used frequently by geneticists today, has come to be known as the testcross. A testcross is used to identify the genotype of F_1 hybrids. For this cross, F_1 hybrids are crossed back to the parent with the trait controlled by the recessive allele. When Mendel used a testcross for his F_1 offspring, he expected to observe approximately equal numbers of offspring with the traits controlled by the dominant and recessive alleles. That is what he observed. Today, a testcross is used to determine whether an individual with the phenotype controlled by the dominant allele is heterozygous or homozygous. If the individual is homozygous, none of the offspring will have the phenotype controlled by the recessive allele.

FIGURE 11–12 MULTIPLE ALLELES

Coat color in rabbits is determined by a single gene that has at least four different alleles. Different combinations of alleles result in the four colors you see here. **Interpreting Graphics** *What allele combinations can a chinchilla rabbit have?*

Full color: CC, Cc^{ch}, Cc^{h}, or Cc

Chinchilla: $c^{ch}c^{h}$, $c^{ch}c^{ch}$, or $c^{ch}c$

Himalayan: $c^{h}c$ or $c^{h}c^{h}$

Albino: cc

Key

C = full color; dominant to all other alleles

c^{ch} = chinchilla; partial defect in pigmentation; dominant to c^{h} and c alleles

c^{h} = Himalayan; color in certain parts of body; dominant to c allele

c = albino; no color; recessive to all other alleles

Multiple Alleles Many genes have more than two alleles and are therefore said to have **multiple alleles.** This does not mean that an individual can have more than two alleles. It only means that more than two possible alleles exist in a population. One of the best-known examples is coat color in rabbits. A rabbit's coat color is determined by a single gene that has at least four different alleles. The four known alleles display a pattern of simple dominance that can produce four possible coat colors, as shown in **Figure 11–12.** Many other genes have multiple alleles, including the human genes for blood type.

Polygenic Traits Many traits are produced by the interaction of several genes. Traits controlled by two or more genes are said to be **polygenic traits,** which means "having many genes." For example, at least three genes are involved in making the reddish-brown pigment in the eyes of fruit flies. Different combinations of alleles for these genes produce very different eye colors. Polygenic traits often show a wide range of phenotypes. For example, the wide range of skin color in humans comes about partly because more than four different genes probably control this trait.

What are multiple alleles?

For: Links on Punnett squares
Visit: www.SciLinks.org
Web Code: cbn-4112

TEACHER TO TEACHER

When I teach introductory genetics, I find that students often lose interest studying only the inheritance of traits in pea plants. To keep them more interested, I like to relate inheritance to their world and insert many examples of human traits. Some human traits that show simple dominance include cystic fibrosis (recessive), freckles (dominant), and widow's peak (dominant). Blood type is controlled by 3 alleles in which A (I^A) and B (I^B) are codominant, and both are dominant over O (ii). I devise genetics problems using these and other human traits for students to practice setting up Punnett squares and identifying genotypes and phenotypes.

—*James Boal*
Biology Teacher
Natrona County High School
Casper, WY

Address Misconceptions

Students might try to apply the ideas of simple dominance to other types of gene expression. Give students many different examples of incomplete dominance, codominance, multiple alleles, and polygenic traits. Collect pictures for students to compare the various phenotypes. L1 L2

Use Visuals

Figure 11–12 Explain that coat color in rabbits does show a pattern of simple dominance among four alleles. Have students study the genotypes of the rabbits in the figure. Challenge them to arrange the alleles for coat color in order from the most dominant to the least dominant. *($C > c^{ch} > c^{h} > c$)* Then, have students make up genetic crosses for coat color in rabbits and exchange them with partners. Partners should solve the problems using Punnett squares. L2

Download a worksheet on Punnett squares for students to complete, and find additional teacher support from NSTA SciLinks.

Applying Mendel's Principles

Demonstration

Set up crosses between wild-type fruit flies and fruit flies with vestigial wings. Allow students to observe the parents of the cross and the F_1 offspring. Ask: **Which trait is controlled by a dominant allele?** *(Normal wings)* Then, have student volunteers diagram a Punnett square on the board to predict the phenotypic ratio of the F_2 offspring. Count all the F_2 progeny from the cross and have students compare the actual phenotypic ratio with the predicted ratio. L2

Answers to . . .

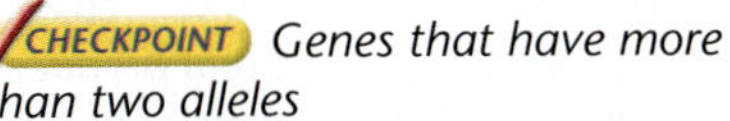

Genes that have more than two alleles

Figure 11–12 $c^{ch}c^{h}$, $c^{ch}c^{ch}$, or $c^{ch}c$

11–3 (continued)

Genetics and the Environment

Build Science Skills

Designing Experiments Give student groups two cuttings from the coleus plant that you started in potting soil about two weeks before. (The cuttings are genetically identical.) Challenge students to use these cuttings to design an experiment that shows how the environment affects phenotype. Students might grow one of the plants with less daylight, at warmer temperatures, or with added fertilizer. L2

3 ASSESS

Evaluate Understanding

Play a game in which you ask student teams to solve various problems in genetics—from identifying the pattern of inheritance, such as simple dominance, incomplete dominance, or multiple alleles, to predicting the outcome of dihybrid crosses.

Reteach

Students can make flashcards for each of the Vocabulary words. Student pairs can quiz each other on the meanings of the words.

Sharpen Your Skills

Students' problems should follow the rules of genetics and include correct and complete answers. Have pairs of students exchange and try to solve each other's problems.

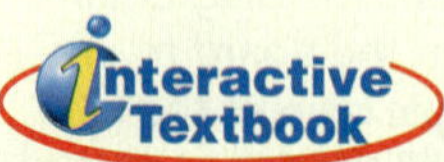

If your class subscribes to the iText, use it to review the Key Concepts in Section 11–3.

Answer to . . .

Figure 11–13 *They are small, easy to keep in the laboratory, and produce large numbers of offspring in a short time.*

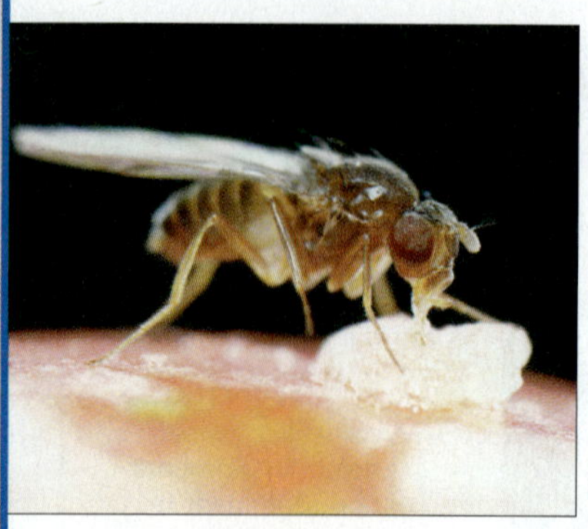

▲ **Figure 11–13** The common fruit fly is a popular organism for genetic research. **Inferring** *Why are fruit flies easier to use for genetic research than large animals, such as dogs?*

Applying Mendel's Principles

Mendel's principles don't apply only to plants. At the beginning of the 1900s, the American geneticist Thomas Hunt Morgan decided to look for a model organism to advance the study of genetics. He wanted an animal that was small, easy to keep in the laboratory, and able to produce large numbers of offspring in a short period of time. He decided to work on a tiny insect that kept showing up, uninvited, in his laboratory. The insect was the common fruit fly, *Drosophila melanogaster,* shown in **Figure 11–13.**

Morgan grew the flies in small milk bottles stoppered with cotton gauze. *Drosophila* was an ideal organism for genetics because it could produce plenty of offspring, and it did so quickly. A single pair of flies could produce as many as 100 offspring. Before long, Morgan and other biologists had tested every one of Mendel's principles and learned that they applied not just to pea plants but to other organisms as well.

Mendel's principles also apply to humans. The basic principles of Mendelian genetics can be used to study the inheritance of human traits and to calculate the probability of certain traits appearing in the next generation. You will learn more about human genetics in Chapter 14.

Genetics and the Environment

The characteristics of any organism, whether bacterium, fruit fly, or human being, are not determined solely by the genes it inherits. Rather, characteristics are determined by interaction between genes and the environment. For example, genes may affect a sunflower plant's height and the color of its flowers. However, these same characteristics are also influenced by climate, soil conditions, and the availability of water. Genes provide a plan for development, but how that plan unfolds also depends on the environment.

11–3 Section Assessment

1. **Key Concept** Explain what *independent assortment* means.
2. **Key Concept** Describe two inheritance patterns besides simple dominance.
3. What is the difference between incomplete dominance and codominance?
4. Why are fruit flies an ideal organism for genetic research?
5. **Critical Thinking Comparing and Contrasting** A geneticist studying coat color in animals crosses a male rabbit having the genotype *CC* with a female having genotype Cc^{ch}. The geneticist then crosses a cc^{ch} male with a Cc^{c} female. In which of the two crosses are the offspring more likely to show greater genetic variation? Use Punnett squares to explain your answer.

Sharpen Your Skills

Problem Solving

Construct a genetics problem to be given as an assignment to a classmate. The problem must test incomplete dominance, codominance, multiple alleles, or polygenic traits. Your problem must have an answer key that includes all of your work.

11–3 Section Assessment

1. During gamete formation, pairs of alleles for different traits segregate, or separate, independently of each other.
2. Answers include descriptions for any two: incomplete dominance, codominance, multiple alleles, or polygenic traits.
3. In incomplete dominance, two alleles combine their effects to produce a single in-between phenotype, such as pink flowers from red and white parents. In codominance, each allele is expressed separately, as when erminette chickens have both black and white feathers.
4. They are small, easy to keep in the laboratory, and produce large numbers of offspring in a short period of time.
5. The offspring in the second cross will show greater variation because 100 percent of the offspring from the first cross ($CC \times Cc^{ch}$) will be full color.

11–4 Meiosis

BI 2.a. Students know meiosis is an early step in sexual reproduction in which the pairs of chromosomes separate and segregate randomly during cell division to produce gametes containing one chromosome of each type. **BI 2.b.** Students know only certain cells in a multicellular organism undergo meiosis. **BI 2.d.** Students know new combinations of alleles may be generated in a zygote through the fusion of male and female gametes (fertilization). **BI 2.e.** Students know why approximately half of an individual's DNA sequence comes from each parent.

Gregor Mendel did not know where the genes he had discovered were located in the cell. Fortunately, his predictions of how genes should behave were so specific that it was not long before biologists were certain they had found them. Genes are located on chromosomes in the cell nucleus.

Mendel's principles of genetics require at least two things. First, each organism must inherit a single copy of every gene from each of its "parents." Second, when an organism produces its own gametes, those two sets of genes must be separated from each other so that each gamete contains just one set of genes. This means that when gametes are formed, there must be a process that separates the two sets of genes so that each gamete ends up with just one set. Although Mendel didn't know it, gametes are formed through exactly such a process. CA (a)

Chromosome Number

As an example of how this process works, let's consider the fruit fly, *Drosophila*. A body cell in an adult fruit fly has 8 chromosomes, as shown in **Figure 11–14.** Four of the chromosomes came from the fruit fly's male parent, and 4 came from its female parent. These two sets of chromosomes are **homologous** (hoh-MAHL-uh-guhs), meaning that each of the 4 chromosomes that came from the male parent has a corresponding chromosome from the female parent. CA (b)

A cell that contains both sets of homologous chromosomes is said to be **diploid,** which means "two sets." The number of chromosomes in a diploid cell is sometimes represented by the symbol 2N. Thus for *Drosophila,* the diploid number is 8, which can be written 2N = 8. Diploid cells contain two complete sets of chromosomes and two complete sets of genes. This agrees with Mendel's idea that the cells of an adult organism contain two copies of each gene.

By contrast, the gametes of sexually reproducing organisms, including fruit flies and peas, contain only a single set of chromosomes, and therefore only a single set of genes. Such cells are said to be **haploid,** which means "one set." For *Drosophila,* this can be written as N = 4, meaning that the haploid number is 4.

Phases of Meiosis

How are haploid (N) gamete cells produced from diploid (2N) cells? That's where **meiosis** (my-OH-sis) comes in. **Meiosis is a process of reduction division in which the number of chromosomes per cell is cut in half through the separation of homologous chromosomes in a diploid cell.**

Guide for Reading

Key Concepts
- What happens during the process of meiosis?
- How is meiosis different from mitosis?

Vocabulary
homologous
diploid
haploid
meiosis
tetrad
crossing-over

Reading Strategy: Using Visuals Before you read, preview **Figure 11–15.** As you read, note what happens at each stage of meiosis.

(a) BI 2.e

(b) BI 2.d

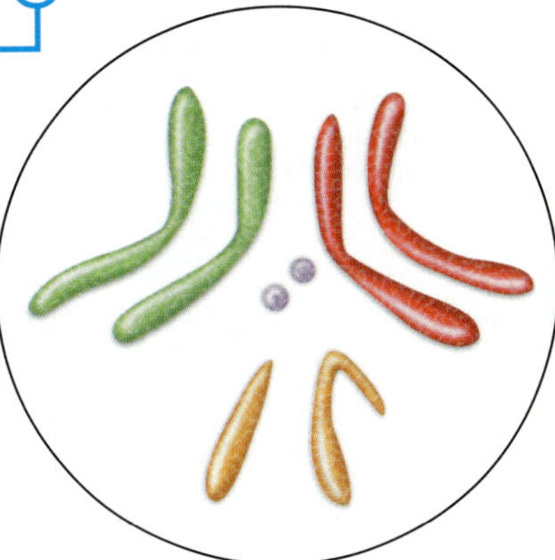

▶ **Figure 11–14** These chromosomes are from a fruit fly. Each of the fruit fly's body cells has 8 chromosomes.

SECTION RESOURCES

TIME SAVER

Print:
- ***Teaching Resources,*** Lesson Plan 11–4, Adapted Section Summary 11–4, Adapted Worksheets 11–4, Section Summary 11–4, Worksheets 11–4, Section Review 11–4
- ***Reading and Study Workbook A,*** Section 11–4
- ***Adapted Reading and Study Workbook B,*** Section 11–4
- ***Lab Worksheets,*** Chapter 11 Exploration

Technology:
- ***iText,*** Section 11–4
- ***Animated Biological Concepts DVD,*** 17, 18, 22
- ***Transparencies Plus,*** Section 11–4
- ***Lab Simulations CD-ROM,*** Meiosis

Section 11–4

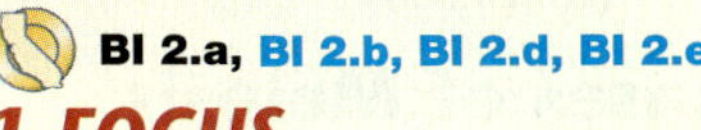

BI 2.a, **BI 2.b, BI 2.d, BI 2.e**

1 FOCUS

Objectives

11.4.1 ***Contrast*** the chromosome number of body cells and gametes.

11.4.2 ***Summarize*** the events of meiosis.

11.4.3 ***Contrast*** meiosis and mitosis.

Guide for Reading

Vocabulary Preview

Explain that the prefix *hapl-* comes from the Greek word *haplous,* which means "single." The word *haploid* refers to cells that have a single set of chromosomes. Ask: **If the prefix *diplo-* means "double," what does the word *diploid* refer to?** *(A cell with two sets of chromosomes)*

Reading Strategy

Before students read the section, encourage them to preview the Vocabulary words by finding the highlighted, boldface terms in the section and listing them. Tell students to leave space on their lists to make notes as they read.

2 INSTRUCT

Chromosome Number

Use Visuals

Figure 11–14 Point out that the homologous chromosomes in the illustration are the same color. Make sure students understand that one complete set of chromosomes—one green, one red, one yellow, and one purple—came from each parent. Ask: **What would happen if the gametes were 2N?** *(Offspring would have 4N chromosomes.)* L1 L2

11–4 (continued)

Phases of Meiosis

Use Visuals

Figure 11–15 Have volunteers use their own words to describe what is occurring during each step of meiosis. Ask: **Which cell is diploid?** *(The original cell)* **Which cell is haploid?** *(The daughter cells of meiosis I through the daughter cells of meiosis II)* Discuss the difference between the divisions in meiosis I and meiosis II. Make sure students understand that homologous chromosomes separate during meiosis I and the centromeres and sister chromatids separate during meiosis II. L2

Address Misconceptions

Some students might confuse mitosis and meiosis. The most difficult point to understand is that the daughter cells produced after meiosis I are already haploid; they contain only one set of chromosomes. Have students compare diagrams of mitosis and meiosis. Point out that DNA replication occurs in prophase I; however, the duplicate chromosomes (sister chromatids) do not separate until meiosis II. Also point out that the division in meiosis II is like that of mitosis—centromeres divide to separate the sister chromatids. Emphasize that meiosis occurs only in cells that form gametes; it does not occur in body cells. L2

For: Meiosis activity
Visit: PHSchool.com
Web Code: cbe-4114
Students interact with the art of meiosis online.

Meiosis

Figure 11–15 **During meiosis, the number of chromosomes per cell is cut in half through the separation of the homologous chromosomes.** The result of meiosis is 4 haploid cells that are genetically different from one another and from the original cell.

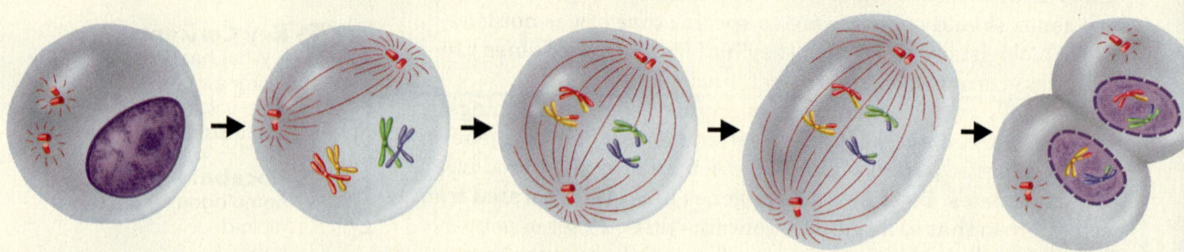

MEIOSIS I

Interphase I
Cells undergo a round of DNA replication, forming duplicate chromosomes.

Prophase I
Each chromosome pairs with its corresponding homologous chromosome to form a tetrad.

Metaphase I
Spindle fibers attach to the chromosomes.

Anaphase I
The fibers pull the homologous chromosomes toward opposite ends of the cell.

Telophase I and Cytokinesis
Nuclear membranes form. The cell separates into two cells.

For: Meiosis activity
Visit: PHSchool.com
Web Code: cbp-4114

For: Links on meiosis
Visit: www.SciLinks.org
Web Code: cbn-4114

Meiosis usually involves two distinct divisions, called meiosis I and meiosis II. By the end of meiosis II, the diploid cell that entered meiosis has become 4 haploid cells. **Figure 11–15** shows meiosis in an organism that has a diploid number of 4 (2N = 4).

Meiosis I Prior to meiosis I, each chromosome is replicated. The cells then begin to divide in a way that looks similar to mitosis. In mitosis, the 4 chromosomes line up individually in the center of the cell. The 2 chromatids that make up each chromosome then separate from each other.

In prophase of meiosis I, however, each chromosome pairs with its corresponding homologous chromosome to form a structure called a **tetrad.** There are 4 chromatids in a tetrad. This pairing of homologous chromosomes is the key to understanding meiosis.

As homologous chromosomes pair up and form tetrads in meiosis I, they exchange portions of their chromatids in a process called **crossing-over.** Crossing-over, shown in **Figure 11–16,** results in the exchange of alleles between homologous chromosomes and produces new combinations of alleles.

What happens next? The homologous chromosomes separate, and two new cells are formed. Although each cell now has 4 chromatids (as it would after mitosis), something is different.

UNIVERSAL ACCESS

Inclusion/Special Needs
Review the location of chromosomes in the cell. Diagram a pair of homologous chromosomes in a cell. Then, work backward to show how one chromosome came from the mother and one from the father. Point out the location of a gene. Show how it can have two alleles. L1

Less Proficient Readers
Have students develop a flowchart that shows the phases of meiosis. Students can refer to Figure 11–15 but should draw their own diagrams and use their own words to describe what is occurring during each step. L1 

Advanced Learners
Challenge students to write a story about a chromosome going through meiosis for the first time. Encourage students to use illustrations and to be creative, but they must give accurate information about the movement of chromosomes. L3

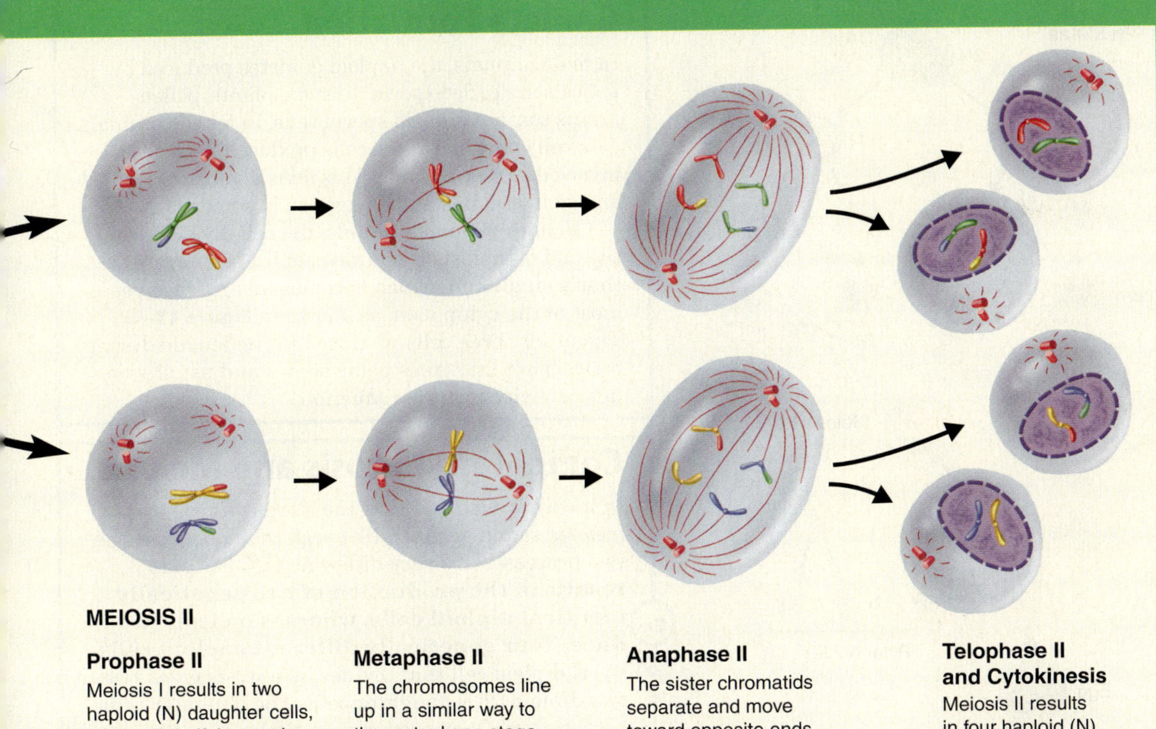

MEIOSIS II

Prophase II
Meiosis I results in two haploid (N) daughter cells, each with half the number of chromosomes as the original cell.

Metaphase II
The chromosomes line up in a similar way to the metaphase stage of mitosis.

Anaphase II
The sister chromatids separate and move toward opposite ends of the cell.

Telophase II and Cytokinesis
Meiosis II results in four haploid (N) daughter cells.

Because each pair of homologous chromosomes was separated, neither of the daughter cells has the two complete sets of chromosomes that it would have in a diploid cell. Those two sets have been shuffled and sorted almost like a deck of cards. The two cells produced by meiosis I have sets of chromosomes and alleles that are different from each other and from the diploid cell that entered meiosis I.

Meiosis II The two cells produced by meiosis I now enter a second meiotic division. Unlike the first division, neither cell goes through a round of chromosome replication before entering meiosis II. Each of the cell's chromosomes has 2 chromatids. During metaphase II of meiosis, chromosomes line up in the center of each cell. In anaphase II, the paired chromatids separate. In this example, each of the four daughter cells produced in meiosis II receives 2 chromatids. Those four daughter cells now contain the haploid number (N)—just 2 chromosomes each.

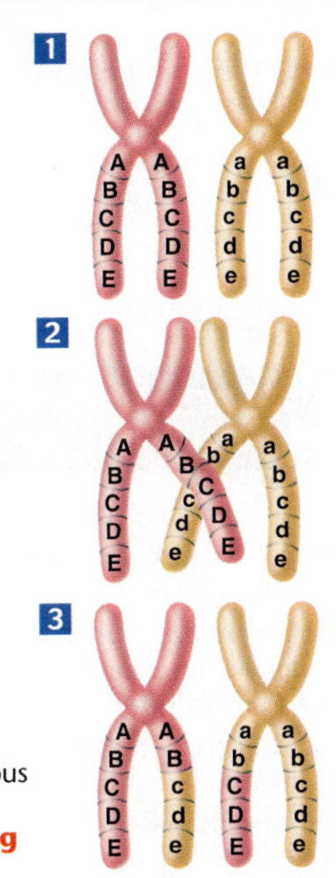

▶ **Figure 11–16** Crossing-over occurs during meiosis. (1) Homologous chromosomes form a tetrad. (2) Chromatids cross over one another. (3) The crossed sections of the chromatids are exchanged. **Interpreting Graphics** *How does crossing-over affect the alleles on a chromatid?*

TEACHER TO TEACHER

I find that mitosis and meiosis are difficult for students to understand, so I use an overhead projector and pipe cleaners to model both processes. I demonstrate that chromosomes occur in pairs and show how chromosomes are involved in genetic continuity and variety. After I finish, I have students actively participate in using the overhead projector and pipe cleaners to model the processes for their peers. This teaching strategy facilitates their understanding of these challenging topics.

—*Tracy Swedlund*
Biology Teacher
Medford Area Senior High
Medford, WI

Build Science Skills

Applying Concepts Challenge students to draw diagrams of meiosis that show how seed color and seed shape in Mendel's peas are traits whose genes assort independently. Make sure students realize that the genes for seed shape and seed color are on different chromosomes. Ask: **If the genes for seed shape and seed color had not assorted independently, what could you assume about the genes for these traits?** *(The genes for these traits are located on the same chromosome.)* L2 L3

Demonstration

Use pipe cleaners of different colors to show how a tetrad forms from two homologous chromosomes. Connect sister chromatids together by threading two pipe cleaners through a bead. Ask: **What structure does the bead represent?** *(Centromere)* Overlap the pipe cleaners to simulate crossing-over. Then, cut and tape the pipe cleaners to simulate the breaking and recombination of chromosomes to form the genetically different chromatids. Discuss the significance of crossing-over. Elicit from students that crossing-over increases genetic diversity. Ask: **Will crossing-over cause a different phenotype in the offspring of true-breeding parents?** *(No, the homologous chromosomes are homozygous for the particular trait because they have the same allele for the gene that encodes the trait. Crossing-over will cause portions of the chromosomes to be mixed, but if the alleles are identical, crossing-over is not detected.)* L2

Download a worksheet on meiosis for students to complete, and find additional teacher support from NSTA SciLinks.

Answer to . . .

Figure 11–16 *The alleles can be exchanged between chromatids of homologous chromosomes to produce new combinations of alleles.*

11–4 (continued)

Gamete Formation

Use Visuals

Figure 11–17 Use the illustrations to help students see the end results of meiosis. Emphasize that the cells are haploid after meiosis I. Ask: **In what cells does meiosis occur?** *(Only in cells of the reproductive organs that will form gametes)* L1 L2

Comparing Mitosis and Meiosis

Build Science Skills

Using Analogies Challenge students to contrast the results of mitosis and meiosis using three "pairs of alleles": a red glove and a yellow glove, a green sock and a blue sock, and a white shoe and a black shoe. *(After mitosis, all cells would have the same six items. After meiosis, a gamete could have any combination of glove, sock, and shoe, such as a red glove, blue sock, and black shoe.)* L2

3 ASSESS

Evaluate Understanding

Have students list the stages of meiosis in order and describe what occurs during each stage.

Reteach

Have students review Figure 11–15. Then, instruct them to diagram the movement of chromosomes as a cell goes through the stages of meiosis.

Focus on the BIG Idea 

Sexual reproduction, shuffling and separating of homologous chromosomes, and crossing-over events during meiosis produce gametes that are genetically different from each other and from the original cell. Fertilization with a gamete from a different parent further increases genetic variation.

If your class subscribes to the iText, use it to review the Key Concepts in Section 11–4.

In Males
2N
Meiosis I
N
N
Meiosis II
N
N
N
N
Sperm

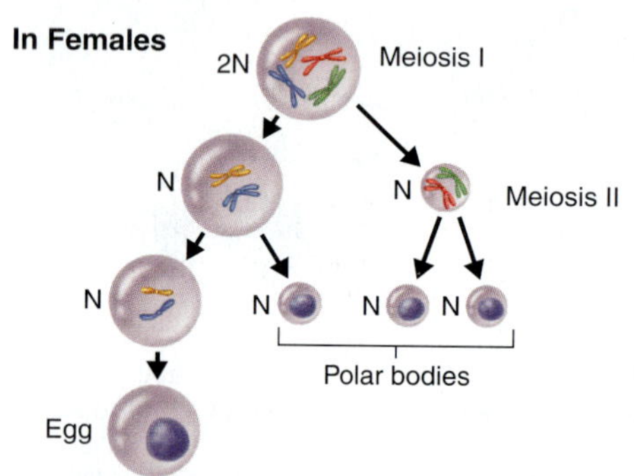

▲ **Figure 11–17** **Meiosis produces four genetically different haploid cells.** In males, meiosis results in four equal-sized gametes called sperm. In females, only one large egg cell results from meiosis. The other three cells, called polar bodies, usually are not involved in reproduction.

(a) BI 2.d

(b) BI 2.b

Gamete Formation

CA (a) In male animals, the haploid gametes produced by meiosis are called sperm. In some plants, pollen grains contain haploid sperm cells. In female animals, generally only one of the cells produced by meiosis is involved in reproduction. This female gamete is called an egg in animals and an egg cell in some plants.

In many female animals, the cell divisions at the end of meiosis I and meiosis II are uneven, so that a single cell, which becomes an egg, receives most of the cytoplasm, as shown in **Figure 11–17.** The other three cells produced in the female during meiosis are known as polar bodies and usually do not participate in reproduction.

Comparing Mitosis and Meiosis

CA (b) In a way, it's too bad that the words *mitosis* and *meiosis* sound so much like each other, because the two processes are very different. **Mitosis results in the production of two genetically identical diploid cells, whereas meiosis produces four genetically different haploid cells.**

A diploid cell that divides by mitosis gives rise to two diploid (2N) daughter cells. The daughter cells have sets of chromosomes and alleles that are identical to each other and to the original parent cell. Mitosis allows an organism's body to grow and replace cells. In asexual reproduction, a new organism is produced by mitosis of the cell or cells of the parent organism.

Meiosis, on the other hand, begins with a diploid cell but produces four haploid (N) cells. These cells are genetically different from the diploid cell and from one another. Meiosis is how sexually reproducing organisms produce gametes. In contrast, asexual reproduction involves only mitosis.

11–4 Section Assessment

1. **Key Concept** Describe the main results of meiosis.
2. **Key Concept** What are the principal differences between mitosis and meiosis?
3. What do the terms *diploid* and *haploid* mean?
4. What is crossing-over?
5. **Critical Thinking Applying Concepts** In human cells, 2N = 46. How many chromosomes would you expect to find in a sperm cell? In an egg cell? In a white blood cell? Explain.

Focus on the BIG Idea 

Information and Heredity
In asexual reproduction, mitosis occurs, but not meiosis. Which type of reproduction—sexual or asexual—results in offspring with greater genetic variation? Explain your answer.

11–4 Section Assessment

1. Four haploid cells genetically different from one another and from the original cell
2. Mitosis produces two genetically identical diploid cells; meiosis produces four genetically different haploid cells.
3. Diploid: two sets of chromosomes; haploid: one set of chromosomes
4. Homologous chromosomes pair up and form tetrads, which may exchange portions of their chromatids, resulting in the exchange of alleles between the homologous chromosomes.
5. Both sperm and egg cells have 23 chromosomes because they are gametes, which are haploid cells. A white blood cell has 46 chromosomes because it is a diploid body cell.

11–5 Linkage and Gene Maps

BI 3.b. Students know the genetic basis for Mendel's laws of segregation and independent assortment. ***BI 3.d.** Students know how to use data on frequency of recombination at meiosis to estimate genetic distances between loci and to interpret genetic maps of chromosomes.

If you thought carefully about Mendel's principle of independent assortment as you analyzed meiosis, one question might have been bothering you. It's easy to see how genes located on different chromosomes assort independently, but what about genes located on the same chromosome? Wouldn't they generally be inherited together?

Gene Linkage

The answer to these questions, as Thomas Hunt Morgan first realized in 1910, is yes. Morgan's research on fruit flies led him to the principle of linkage. After identifying more than 50 *Drosophila* genes, Morgan discovered that many of them appeared to be "linked" together in ways that, at first glance, seemed to violate the principle of independent assortment. For example, a fly with reddish-orange eyes and miniature wings, like the one shown in **Figure 11–18,** was used in a series of crosses. The results showed that the genes for those traits were almost always inherited together and only rarely became separated from each other.

Morgan and his associates observed so many genes that were inherited together that before long they could group all of the fly's genes into four linkage groups. The linkage groups assorted independently, but all of the genes in one group were inherited together. *Drosophila* has four linkage groups. It also has four pairs of chromosomes, which led to two remarkable conclusions. First, each chromosome is actually a group of linked genes. Second, Mendel's principle of independent assortment still holds true. **It is the chromosomes, however, that assort independently, not individual genes.**

How did Mendel manage to miss gene linkage? By luck, or by design, six of the seven genes he studied are on different chromosomes. The two genes that are found on the same chromosome are so far apart that they also assort independently.

Gene Maps

If two genes are found on the same chromosome, does this mean that they are linked forever? Not at all. Crossing-over during meiosis sometimes separates genes that had been on the same chromosome onto homologous chromosomes. Crossover events occasionally separate and exchange linked genes and produce new combinations of alleles. This is important because it helps to generate genetic diversity.

Guide for Reading

Key Concept
- What structures actually assort independently?

Vocabulary
gene map

Reading Strategy: Predicting Before you read, preview **Figure 11–19.** Predict how a diagram like this one can be used to determine how likely genes are to assort independently. As you read, note whether or not your prediction was correct.

▼ **Figure 11–18** The genes for this fruit fly's reddish-orange eyes and miniature wings are almost always inherited together. The reason for this is that the genes are close together on a single chromosome. **It is the chromosomes that assort independently, not individual genes.**

SECTION RESOURCES

Print:
- ***Teaching Resources,*** Lesson Plan 11–5, Adapted Section Summary 11–5, Section Summary 11–5, Worksheets 11–5, Section Review 11–5
- ***Reading and Study Workbook A,*** Section 11–5
- ***Adapted Reading and Study Workbook B,*** Section 11–5
- ***Biotechnology Manual,*** Lab 2

Technology:
- ***iText,*** Section 11–5
- ***Transparencies Plus,*** Section 11–5

Section 11–5

BI 3.b, *BI 3.d

1 FOCUS

Objectives

11.5.1 ***Identify*** the structures that actually assort independently.

11.5.2 ***Explain*** how gene maps are produced.

Guide for Reading

Vocabulary Preview

Have student volunteers describe what a map is. Elicit the fact that maps show the locations of places and things. Ask: **What do you think a gene map is?** *(It shows the locations of genes on a chromosome.)*

Reading Strategy

As students read, encourage them to write down the main ideas that lead them to determine whether or not their prediction was correct.

2 INSTRUCT

Gene Linkage

Build Science Skills

Using Models Students can construct a model of a chromosome with beads threaded on a pipe cleaner. The beads represent genes, and the pipe cleaner represents the chromosome. Challenge students to demonstrate why linked genes do not usually assort independently. Ask: **Could there be exceptions to this?** *(Yes, if crossing-over occurs.)* **How could crossing-over affect the linked genes of a fruit fly?** *(Alleles could be exchanged between a maternal chromatid and a paternal chromatid.)* L1 L2

Gene Maps

Use Visuals

Figure 11–19 As students study the gene map, ask: **Would you expect more crossing-over events to occur between star eye and speck wing or between star eye and black body? Explain.** *(Star eye and speck wing; because these genes are located farther apart, it is more likely that a crossing-over event will occur between*

(continued)

11–5 (continued)

them.) Explain that recombination rates are calculated by determining the percentage of recombinants produced in a cross. Recombinant offspring have a phenotype that is different from either parent. For example, in a cross between a homozygous male with a black body *(bb)* and vestigial wings *(vv)* and a heterozygous female *(BbVv)* with a brown body and normal wings, most of the F_2 offspring will look like either parent. However some of the offspring, about 20%, will have either a black body and normal wings or a brown body and vestigial wings.

3 ASSESS

Evaluate Understanding

Draw a hypothetical gene map on the board. Have students tell which genes would have high frequencies of crossing-over and which would not.

Reteach

Have students diagram a crossing-over event to show how genes that are located close together have a lower frequency of recombination than genes that are located far apart.

Writing in Science

Paragraphs should explain that if the genes are usually inherited together, they are located near each other on the same chromosome. If they were far apart, crossing-over events would make them appear to be located on different linkage groups.

If your class subscribes to the iText, use it to review the Key Concepts in Section 11–5.

Answer to . . .

Figure 11–19 *The "purple eye" gene is located at 54.5.*

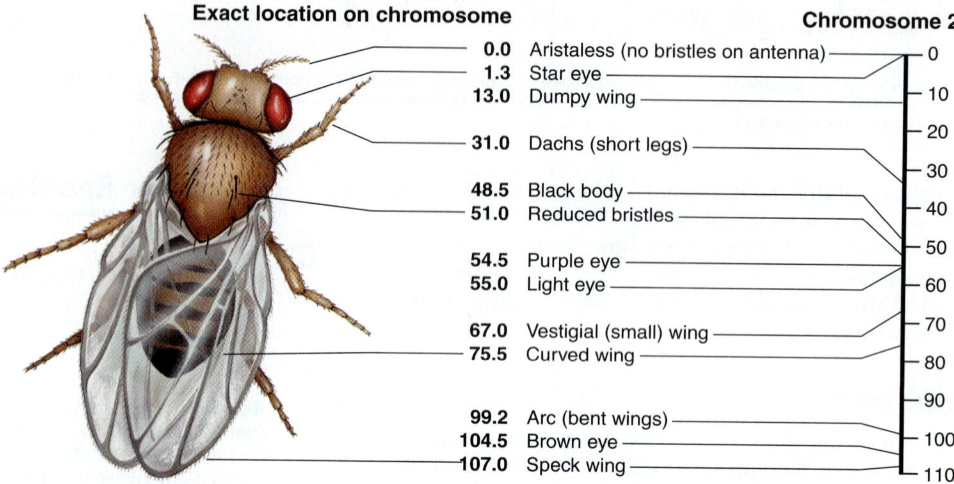

▲ **Figure 11–19** This gene map shows the location of a variety of genes on chromosome 2 of the fruit fly. The genes are named after the problems abnormal alleles cause, not the normal structure. **Interpreting Graphics** *Where on the chromosome is the "purple eye" gene located?*

In 1911, a Columbia University student was working part time in Morgan's lab. This student, Alfred Sturtevant, wondered if rates of crossing-over between genes in meiosis might be a clue to something important. Sturtevant reasoned that the farther apart two genes were, the more likely they were to be separated by a crossover in meiosis. That meant that he could use recombination frequencies to determine the distances between genes. Sturtevant gathered up several notebooks of lab data and took them back to his room. The next morning, he presented Morgan with a **gene map** showing the relative locations of each known gene on one of the *Drosophila* chromosomes, as shown in **Figure 11–19.** If two genes are close together, the recombination frequency between them should be low, since crossovers are rare. If they are far apart, recombination rates between them should be high. Sturtevant's method has been used to construct genetic maps, including maps of the human genome, ever since.

11–5 Section Assessment

1. **Key Concept** How does the principle of independent assortment apply to chromosomes?
2. What are gene maps, and how are they produced?
3. How does crossing-over make gene mapping possible?
4. **Critical Thinking Inferring** If two genes are on the same chromosome but usually assort independently, what does that tell you about how close together they are?

Writing in Science

Cause-Effect Paragraph
In your own words, explain why the alleles for reddish-orange eyes and miniature wings in *Drosophila* are usually inherited together. Include the idea of gene linkage. *Hint:* To organize your ideas, draw a cause-effect diagram that shows what happens to the two alleles during meiosis.

11–5 Section Assessment

1. It is the chromosomes that assort independently, not individual genes.
2. A gene map shows the relative locations of genes on a chromosome. The frequency of crossing-over between genes is used to produce a map of distances between genes.
3. The farther apart two genes are, the more likely they are to be separated during a crossover in meiosis. Therefore, the frequency of crossing-over is equal to the distance between two genes.
4. The two genes are located very far apart from each other.

Exploration

BI 2.a, BIIE 1.g

Modeling Meiosis

Meiosis results in 4 new cells, each containing half the number of chromosomes in the original cells. Using the procedures below, you will build a model to demonstrate the process of meiosis and explore how it can lead to genetic changes.

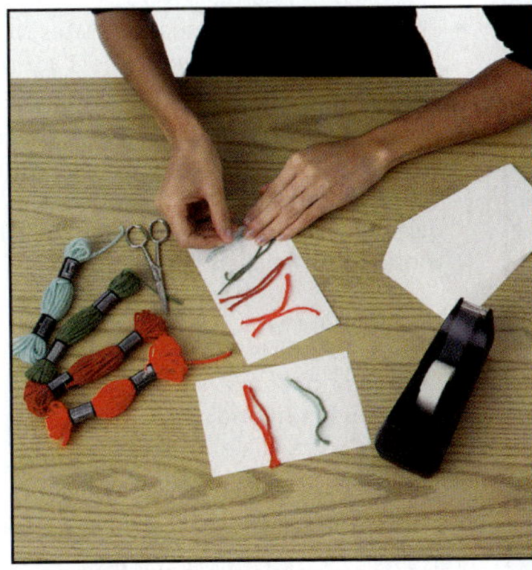

Problem

What happens to the chromosomes in cells during meiosis?

Materials

- 4 colors of yarn (2 shades of red and 2 shades of green)
- scissors
- transparent tape
- index cards
- felt-tip marker

Skills

Using Models, Communicating Results

Procedure

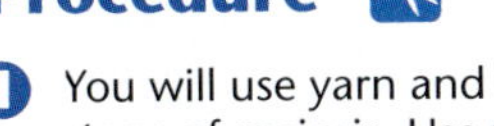

1. You will use yarn and index cards to model each stage of meiosis. Use two shades of red yarn to represent one homologous pair of chromosomes and two shades of green yarn to represent another pair. Use an index card to represent a cell.
2. Cut two pieces of yarn about 5 cm long from each color of yarn. Each piece of yarn will represent a chromatid.
3. Tape pieces of red and green yarn to an index card to show the appearance of two tetrads in a cell at the beginning of meiosis.
4. Tape pieces of yarn to additional index cards to model the numbers and positions of the chromosomes and cells at each stage of meiosis. Be sure to include an example of crossing-over at the correct stage. Use a felt-tip marker to label each card with the name of the stage it represents.
5. Arrange the finished cards to show the complete process of meiosis. Label the stages at which genetic segregation and crossing-over occur and chromosome number changes.
6. Use your cards to explain the process of meiosis to a classmate. Then, trade roles and have your classmate use his or her models to explain the process of meiosis to you.

Analyze and Conclude

1. **Using Models** What is the result of the first meiotic division (meiosis I)?
2. **Using Models** What is the result of the second meiotic division (meiosis II)?
3. **Drawing Conclusions** How does meiosis lead to increased genetic variation?
4. **Predicting** How would the gametes be affected if a pair of chromatids failed to separate in the second meiotic division?
5. **Using Models** What parts of the cell did the yarn represent?
6. **Evaluating** How well do you think this investigation modeled the process of meiosis? Explain your answer.

Go Further

Using Models Make a second set of models that shows the differences between the formation of sperm and the formation of eggs.

Analyze and Conclude

1. Two cells with a haploid number of duplicated chromosomes
2. Four cells, each with a haploid number of chromosomes
3. Meiosis leads to increased genetic variation through crossing-over and independent assortment. During crossing-over, alleles are exchanged between chromosome pairs, changing the original parental chromosomes. In independent assortment, the parental chromosomes are lined up and randomly distributed to the daughter cells.
4. One gamete would have an extra copy of a chromosome, and another gamete would not have any copies of that chromosome.
5. The yarn represented the chromosomes.
6. Students may say that the investigation modeled meiosis fairly well because all of the processes of meiosis could be shown, including segregation and crossing-over.

Exploration

BI 2.a, BIIE 1.g

Objective Students will be able to use models to show what happens to the chromosomes in cells during meiosis. L2

Skills Focus **Using Models, Communicating Results**

Time 45 minutes

Alternative Materials Yarn of any color may be used. However, use two shades of one color and two shades of another color.

Pre-Lab Discussion Discuss how gametes form. Ask: **Why is it important for gametes to have only half the number of chromosomes that body cells have?** *(When gametes combine, the zygote has the proper number of chromosomes.)*

Teaching Tips

- Refer students to Figure 11–15 as a guide for constructing their models.
- Students should use the lighter shade of yarn to represent the chromosomes that come from one parent and the darker shade to represent the chromosomes from the other parent. Sister chromatids should be the same shade.
- Circulate among students to make sure they understand what homologous chromosomes and chromatids are.

Procedure

5. Student models should look similar to the diagrams in Figure 11–15. Crossing-over occurs during prophase I. Segregation, or the separation of alleles, occurs during anaphase I. The chromosome number becomes haploid at the end of meiosis I.

Expected Outcomes Students will have constructed a usable model for meiosis.

Go Further

In sperm formation, all four daughter cells develop into sperm cells, whereas in egg formation, only one daughter cell develops into an egg. In most species, the polar bodies die.

Chapter 11 Study Guide

Study Tip

Give students various problems in genetics in which they must identify genotypes and phenotypes of parents and offspring, identify patterns of inheritance, or predict the outcomes of crosses with Punnett squares.

Thinking Visually

1. Each chromosome pairs with its corresponding homologous chromosome.
2. Spindle fibers pull homologous chromosomes toward opposite ends of the cell.
3. Sister chromatids separate and move toward opposite ends of the cell.

Chapter 11 Assessment

Reviewing Content

1. c	**5.** c	**9.** d
2. a	**6.** d	**10.** b
3. a	**7.** d	
4. c	**8.** d	

Understanding Concepts

11. (1) The inheritance of biological characteristics is determined by genes. (2) Where there are two or more forms (alleles) of the gene for a single trait, some forms of the gene may be dominant and others recessive. (3) In most sexually reproducing organisms, each adult has two copies of each gene, one from each parent. These genes are segregated when gametes form. (4) The alleles for different genes (actually, the chromosomes) usually segregate independently.

12. Probability is the likelihood that an event will occur. This principle can be used to predict the outcomes of genetic crosses.

Chapter 11 Study Guide

11–1 The Work of Gregor Mendel

Key Concepts 7 2.c, 7 2.d, BI 2.d, BI 3.b

- The principle of dominance states that some alleles are dominant and others are recessive.
- When each F_1 plant flowers, the two alleles segregate from each other so that each gamete carries only a single copy of each gene. Therefore, each F_1 plant produces two types of gametes—those with the allele for tallness and those with the allele for shortness.

Vocabulary
genetics, p. 263 • fertilization, p. 263
true-breeding, p. 263
trait, p. 264 • hybrid, p. 264
gene, p. 265 • allele, p. 265
segregation, p. 266 • gamete, p. 266

11–2 Probability and Punnett Squares

Key Concepts 7 2.c, 7 2.d, BI 2.g, BI 3.a, BI 3.b

- The principles of probability can be used to predict the outcomes of genetic crosses.
- Punnett squares can be used to predict and compare the genetic variations that will result from a cross.

Vocabulary
probability, p. 267 • Punnett square, p. 268
homozygous, p. 268 • heterozygous, p. 268
phenotype, p. 268 • genotype, p. 268

11–3 Exploring Mendelian Genetics

Key Concepts 7 2.c, 7 2.d, BI 2.g, BI 3.b

- The principle of independent assortment states that genes for different traits can segregate independently during the formation of gametes. Independent assortment helps account for the many genetic variations observed in plants, animals, and other organisms.
- Some alleles are neither dominant nor recessive, and many traits are controlled by multiple alleles or multiple genes.

Vocabulary
independent assortment, p. 271
incomplete dominance, p. 272
codominance, p. 272
multiple alleles, p. 273
polygenic traits, p. 273

11–4 Meiosis

Key Concepts BI 2.a, BI 2.b, BI 2.d, BI 2.e

- Meiosis is a process of reduction division in which the number of chromosomes per cell is cut in half through the separation of homologous chromosomes in a diploid cell.
- Mitosis results in the production of two genetically identical diploid cells, whereas meiosis produces four genetically different haploid cells.

Vocabulary
homologous, p. 275 • diploid, p. 275
haploid, p. 275 • meiosis, p. 276
tetrad, p. 276 • crossing-over, p. 277

11–5 Linkage and Gene Maps

Key Concept BI 3.b, *BI 3.d

- Chromosomes assort independently; individual genes do not.

Vocabulary
gene map, p. 280

Thinking Visually

Using the information in this chapter, complete the following flowchart about meiosis:

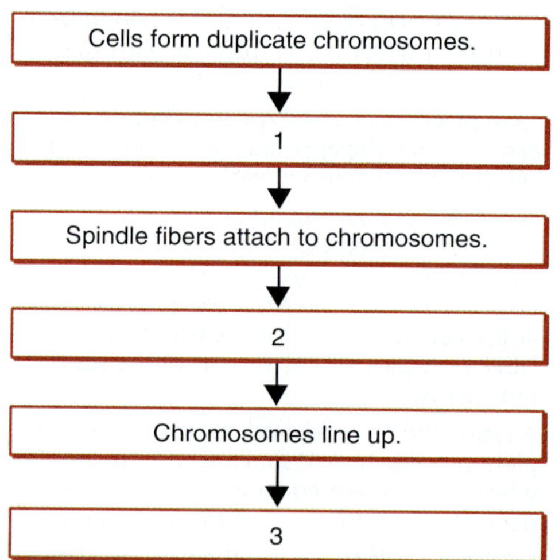

CHAPTER RESOURCES

Print:
- ***Teaching Resources,*** Chapter Vocabulary Review, Graphic Organizer, Chapter 11 Tests: Levels A and B

Technology:
- ***Computer Test Bank,*** Chapter 11 Test
- ***iText,*** Chapter 11 Assessment

Chapter 11 Assessment

Interactive textbook with assessment at PHSchool.com 

Reviewing Content

Choose the letter that best answers the question or completes the statement.

1. Different forms of a gene are called
   a. hybrids. c. alleles.
   b. dominant factors. d. recessive factors.
2. If a homozygous tall pea plant and a homozygous short pea plant are crossed,
   a. the recessive trait seems to disappear.
   b. the offspring are of medium height.
   c. no hybrids are produced.
   d. all the offspring are short.
3. A Punnett square is used to determine the
   a. probable outcome of a cross.
   b. actual outcome of a cross.
   c. result of mitosis.
   d. result of meiosis.
4. Organisms that have two identical alleles for a particular trait are said to be
   a. hybrid. c. homozygous.
   b. heterozygous. d. dominant.
5. The physical characteristics of an organism are its
   a. genetics. c. phenotype.
   b. heredity. d. genotype.
6. A situation in which a gene has more than two alleles is known as
   a. complete dominance.
   b. codominance.
   c. polygenic dominance.
   d. multiple alleles.
7. The illustration below represents what stage of meiosis?

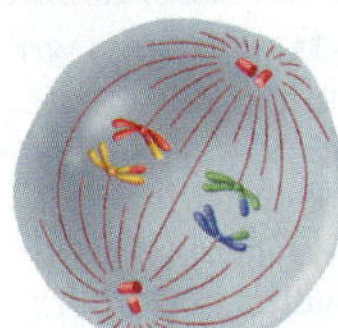

   a. prophase I c. telophase I
   b. anaphase II d. metaphase I
8. Unlike mitosis, meiosis in male mammals results in the formation of
   a. one haploid cell.
   b. three diploid polar bodies.
   c. four diploid gamete cells.
   d. four haploid gamete cells.
9. To maintain the chromosome number of an organism, the gametes must
   a. become diploid.
   b. become recessive.
   c. be produced by mitosis.
   d. be produced by meiosis.
10. A gene map shows
    a. the number of possible alleles for a gene.
    b. the relative locations of genes on a chromosome.
    c. where chromosomes are in a cell.
    d. how crossing-over occurs.

Understanding Concepts

11. List the four basic principles of genetics that Mendel discovered in his experiments. Briefly describe each of these principles.
12. What is probability? How does probability relate to genetics?
13. In pea plants, the allele for yellow seeds is dominant to the allele for green seeds. Predict the genotypic ratio of offspring produced by crossing two parents heterozygous for this trait. Draw a Punnett square to illustrate your prediction.
14. How do multiple alleles and polygenic traits differ?
15. Why can multiple alleles provide many different phenotypes for a trait?
16. Are an organism's characteristics determined only by its genes? Explain.
17. Suppose that for an organism, 2N = 8. How many chromosomes do the organism's gametes contain?
18. In rabbits, *B* is an allele for black coat and *b* is an allele for brown coat. Write the genotypes for a rabbit that is homozygous for black coat and another rabbit that is heterozygous for black coat.
19. Describe the process of meiosis.
20. Compare the phases of meiosis I with the phases of meiosis II in terms of the number and arrangement of the chromosomes.
21. Explain why it is chromosomes, not individual genes, that assort independently.

Interactive Textbook

If your class subscribes to the iText, your students can go online to access an interactive version of the Student Edition and a self-test.

(Continued from page 282)

13. 1 *YY* : 2 *Yy* : 1 *yy*

	Y	*y*
Y	*YY*	*Yy*
y	*Yy*	*yy*

14. A gene has multiple alleles if it has more than two alleles. Two or more genes control polygenic traits.

15. With two alleles for a trait, up to three phenotypes are possible. With three alleles, up to six phenotypes are possible.

16. No, genes provide a plan for development, but how the plan unfolds depends on the environment.

17. Four

18. Homozygous black coat: *BB*; heterozygous black coat: *Bb*

19. Meiosis is a process of reduction division in which the number of chromosomes per cell is cut in half through the separation of homologous chromosomes.

20. DNA replicates during interphase so that during meiosis I, all of the chromosomes are doubled and consist of duplicate chromosomes (sister chromatids). At anaphase I, the homologous chromosomes separate, with the sister chromatids still together, as two haploid daughter cells form. During meiosis II, the sister chromatids separate to produce four haploid daughter cells.

21. It is the chromosomes that are separated during gamete formation. The genes are linked to the chromosomes.

TIME SAVER — HOMEWORK GUIDE

Section:	Questions:
Section 11–1	1, 2
Section 11–2	3–5, 12, 13, 18, 22, 24–26, 29
Section 11–3	6, 11, 14–16, 30
Section 11–4	7–9, 17, 19, 20, 23
Section 11–5	10, 21, 27, 28

Chapter 11 Assessment

Critical Thinking

22. By crossing the white ram to a number of black ewes; if any offspring are black, then the white ram is heterozygous

23.

	Mitosis	Meiosis
Number of cells produced	2	4
Type of cell	body	gamete
Chromosome number	diploid (2N)	haploid (N)

24. Both parents are heterozygous.

25. The predicted outcome of the cross is 50% rough and 50% smooth. However, since the result of each fertilization (joining of egg and sperm) is independent of any previous fertilization, it is possible for all offspring to have smooth coats.

26. The original genotypes and the crosses could have been *Tt* x *tt* or *Tt* x *Tt*. The genotype *TT* could not have been present; if it were, all the offspring would be tall.

27. There would be less genetic variation in the F_2 generation between two closely linked genes because these genes will not be separated during the chromosomal movements of meiosis and the chances of crossing-over events separating the genes are slim.

28. Gene M

29. The allele for black color is dominant, and the allele for brown color is recessive. The black parent is homozygous, and the brown parent is heterozygous.

30. The color helps the ptarmigan hide from predators. In winter, its white coat color blends in with its snowy surroundings. In summer, its brown coat blends in with the bare ground and grass.

Focus on the BIG Idea 

Punnett squares could be used to raise questions for investigation, to predict the possible outcomes of a cross when writing the hypothesis, to analyze data, and to explain results.

Chapter 11 Assessment

Critical Thinking

22. Designing Experiments In sheep, the allele for white wool *(A)* is dominant over the allele for black wool *(a)*. How would you determine the genotype of a white ram, or male sheep?

23. Comparing and Contrasting Design and complete a table to compare and contrast meiosis and mitosis.

24. Applying Concepts In dogs, the allele for short hair is dominant over the allele for long hair. Two short-haired dogs are the parents of a litter of eight puppies. Six puppies have short hair, and two have long hair. What are the genotypes of the parents?

25. Applying Concepts In guinea pigs, the allele for a rough coat *(R)* is dominant over the allele for a smooth coat *(r)*. A heterozygous guinea pig *(Rr)* and a homozygous recessive guinea pig *(rr)* have a total of nine offspring. Explain how all nine offspring can have smooth coats.

26. Inferring Suppose Mendel crossed two pea plants and got both tall and short offspring. What could have been the genotypes of the two original plants? What genotype could not have been present?

27. Comparing and Contrasting Suppose a plant geneticist uses true-breeding plants to make a two-factor cross involving genes that are closely linked on a chromosome. How would the genetic variation in the F_2 generation probably differ from a cross in which two genes assort independently?

28. Calculating Three genes, stumpy (S), mottled (M), and pale (P) are found on the same chromosome in a newly-discovered species of fly. A preliminary gene map places gene S in the middle, with M and P on opposite sides. The frequency of genetic recombination between genes M and S is 5%, which means that a crossover occurs between these two genes in meiosis 5% of the time (one gamete in 20 has a crossover). The frequency between genes S and P is 8%. Which gene is closer to S—gene P or gene M?

29. Formulating Hypotheses Suppose you found out that a mating between a black animal and a brown animal produced all black offspring. Propose a hypothesis to explain the color of the offspring.

30. Interpreting Graphics Genes that control hair or feather color in some animals have different effects in the winter than in the summer. How might such a difference be beneficial to the ptarmigan shown below?

Information and Heredity How might a scientist use a Punnett square in designing and carrying out an experiment?

Writing in Science

Write an explanation of dominant and recessive alleles that would be appropriate to give to an eighth-grade science class. You can assume that the eighth-grade students already know the meanings of *gene* and *allele*. (*Hint:* Use examples to make your explanation clear.)

Performance-Based Assessment

Creating Storyboards You are a writer for a TV station. The producer asks you to write a series that takes the viewer on an imaginary voyage back in time. The show is designed to provide insight into the work of the person being interviewed and to give the viewers a feel for the events of that era. The first person you visit will be Gregor Mendel. Create storyboards that plan one scene for this program.

For: An interactive self-test
Visit: PHSchool.com
Web Code: cba-4110

Writing in Science

Student explanations should be clear and concise and include at least two different examples. They should explain that a gene has at least two alleles. Some alleles are dominant and others are recessive. An organism with a dominant allele will always exhibit that form of the trait. Recessive alleles are expressed only in the absence of dominant alleles.

Performance-Based Assessment

Storyboards will vary but should describe Mendel's work, including his experimental design and results, his principles, and how his principles are relevant to modern genetics.

Standards Practice

Test-Taking Tip For questions containing the word NOT, begin by jotting down items that do fit the characteristic in question. Then, compare your notes with the answer choices and eliminate those that correspond to your list. Finally, check to see that your answer is correct by confirming that it does not fit the characteristic in question.

Directions: Choose the letter that best answers the question or completes the statement.

1. What happens to the chromosome number during meiosis?
   A It doubles.
   B It stays the same.
   C It halves.
   D It becomes diploid.

2. Which ratio did Mendel find in his F_2 generation?
   A 3 : 1
   B 1 : 3 : 1
   C 1 : 2
   D 1 : 9

3. During which phase of meiosis is the chromosome number reduced?
   A anaphase I
   B metaphase I
   C telophase I
   D prophase II

4. Two pink-flowering plants are crossed. The offspring flower as follows: 25% red, 25% white, 50% pink. What pattern of inheritance does flower color in these flowers follow?
   A dominance
   B multiple alleles
   C incomplete dominance
   D recessiveness

5. Which of the following is used to construct a gene map? ***BI 3.d**
   A chromosome number
   B litter count
   C rate of meiosis
   D recombination rate

6. Alleles for the same trait are separated from each other during the process of **7 2.d**
   A mitosis.
   B meiosis I.
   C meiois II.
   D interphase.

Questions 7–8

Genes A, B, C, and D are located on the same chromosome. After calculating recombination frequencies, a student determines that these genes are separated by the following map units: C-D: 25 map units; A-B: 12 map units; B-D: 20 map units; and A-C: 17 map units.

7. How many map units apart are genes A and D? ***BI 3.d**
   A 5
   B 8
   C 10
   D 12.5

8. Which gene map best reflects the student's data? ***BI 3.d**

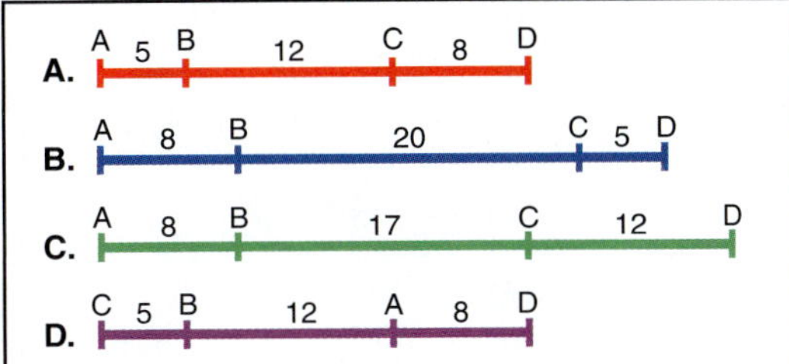

9. Which of the following is NOT one of Gregor Mendel's principles?
   A The alleles for different genes usually segregate independently.
   B Some forms of a gene may be dominant.
   C The inheritance of characteristics is determined by factors (genes).
   D Crossing-over occurs during meiosis.

Questions 10–13 Each of the lettered choices below refers to the following numbered statements. Select the best lettered choice. A choice may be used once, more than once, or not at all.

A Phenotype
B Hybrids
C Genotype
D Homozygous

10. Offspring of crosses between parents with different traits
11. Appearance due to genetic makeup
12. Having two identical alleles for a given gene
13. Physical characteristics

Standards Practice

1. C	**5.** D	**9.** D	**13.** C
2. A	**6.** B	**10.** B	
3. A	**7.** B	**11.** A	
4. C	**8.** D	**12.** D	

Success Tracker™
Online at PHSchool.com

Have students check their understanding of the chapter by logging onto Success Tracker.

Go Online PHSchool.com

Your students can independently test their knowledge of the chapter and print out their test results for your files.

Chapter Planner 12 DNA and RNA

Section and Section Objectives	Time	STANDARDS NCLB	STANDARDS Biology	Activities and Labs
12–1 DNA, pp. 287–294 *12.1.1* ***Summarize*** the relationship between genes and DNA. *12.1.2* ***Describe*** the overall structure of the DNA molecule.	2 periods (1 block)	7 2.e, BI 5.a	BIIE 1.k	**SE:** ***Inquiry Activity,*** How do codes work?, p. 286 L2 **TE:** ***Demonstration,*** p. 291 L1 L2 **SE:** ***Biology and History,*** Discovering the Role of DNA, pp. 292–293 L2 **TE:** ***Build Science Skills,*** p. 293 L1 L2 **LMA:** Chapter 12 Lab L2 L3 **LMB:** Chapter 12 Lab L1 L2 **BTM:** Labs 4, 5, 6 L2 L3
12–2 Chromosomes and DNA Replication, pp. 295–299 *12.2.1* ***Summarize*** the events of DNA replication. *12.2.2* ***Relate*** the DNA molecule to chromosome structure.	1 period (1/2 block)	7 2.e	BI 5.b	**TE:** ***Demonstration,*** p. 295 L2, p. 298 L1 L2 **SE:** ***Analyzing Data,*** Synthesis of New DNA Molecules, p. 296 L2 **TE:** ***Build Science Skills,*** p. 297 L1 L2 **SE:** ***Exploration,*** Modeling DNA Replication, p. 313 L2
12–3 RNA and Protein Synthesis, pp. 300–306 *12.3.1* ***Tell*** how RNA differs from DNA. *12.3.2* ***Name*** the three main types of RNA. *12.3.3* ***Describe*** transcription and the editing of RNA. *12.3.4* ***Identify*** the genetic code. *12.3.5* ***Summarize*** translation. *12.3.6* ***Explain*** the relationship between genes and proteins.	2 periods (1 block)	BI 5.a	BI 1.d, BI 4.a, BI 4.b	**TE:** ***Demonstration,*** p. 302 L1 L2 **TE:** ***Build Science Skills,*** p. 303 L2 **SE:** ***Quick Lab,*** How does a cell interpret DNA?, p. 303 L2
12–4 Mutations, pp. 307–308 *12.4.1* ***Contrast*** gene mutations and chromosomal mutations.	1 period (1/2 block)		BI 4.c	**TE:** ***Demonstration,*** p. 307 L1 L2
12–5 Gene Regulation, pp. 309–312 *12.5.1* ***Describe*** a typical gene. *12.5.2* ***Describe*** how *lac* genes are turned off and on. *12.5.3* ***Explain*** how most eukaryotic genes are controlled. *12.5.4* ***Relate*** gene regulation to development.	1 period (1/2 block)		BI 4.d	**BTM:** Lab 13 L2 L3
Chapter Assessment, pp. 314–317	1 period (1/2 block)			

ACTIVITY PLANNER

SE: *Inquiry Activity,* p. 286; 15 min.; 12 pop beads of four colors

TE: *Demonstration,* p. 291; 15 min.; paper clips, beads, safety pins

TE: *Build Science Skills,* p. 293; 20 min.; pipe cleaners, beads, foam balls

TE: *Demonstration,* p. 295; 10 min.; about 1 meter of string

TE: *Build Science Skills,* p. 297; 15 min.; yarn, beads, dowels, film canister

TE: *Demonstration,* p. 298; 10 min.; red and green yarn

TE: *Demonstration,* p. 302; 10 min.; string, marker, scissors, tape, yarn

TE: *Build Science Skills,* p. 303; 30 min.; diagram of a simple object, building set or colored blocks

TE: *Demonstration,* p. 307; 10 min.; different colors of modeling clay

SE: *Exploration,* p. 313; 45 min.; construction paper (tan, gray, green, yellow, red, and purple), metric ruler, scissors, transparent tape

PLANNING KEY

Ability Levels

for students performing . . .

below grade level **L1**

at grade level **L2**

above grade level **L3**

Print Components

SE	Student Edition	**LA**	Lab Assessment
TE	Teacher's Edition	**BTM**	Biotechnology Manual
RSW	Reading & Study Workbook A	**IDM**	Issues and Decision Making
ARSW	Adapted Reading & Study Workbook B	**LW**	Lab Worksheets
TR	Teaching Resources	**LMA**	Laboratory Manual A
IF	Investigations in Forensics	**LMB**	Laboratory Manual B

Tech Components

CTB	Computer Test Bank
BD	BioDetectives DVD
TP	Transparencies Plus
PLM	Probeware Lab Manual
ABC	ABC DVD Library
LS	Lab Simulations
VL	Virtual Labs

Interactive textbook with assessment at PHSchool.com

Program Resources	Assessment	Media and Technology
TR: Lesson Plan 12–1, Section Summary, p. 52 L1, p. 64 L2, Worksheets, pp. 55–56 L1, pp. 66–68 L2, Enrichment L3 **RSW:** Section 12–1 L2 **ARSW:** Section 12–1 L1	**SE:** 12–1 Section Assessment, p. 294 **TR:** Section Review 12–1	**iText:** Section 12–1 **TP:** 12–1 Interest Grabber, Section Outline, Percentage of Bases in Four Organisms, Figure 12–2, Figure 12–4, Figure 12–5, Figure 12–7 **ABC:** 20 Griffith's Experiment **Lab Simulations CD-ROM:** DNA Structure and Replication
TR: Lesson Plan 12–2, Section Summary, p. 52 L1, p. 64 L2, Worksheets, pp. 69–70 L2 **LW:** Chapter 12 Exploration L1 L2 L3 **RSW:** Section 12–2 L2	**SE:** 12–2 Section Assessment, p. 299 **TR:** Section Review 12–2	**iText:** Section 12–2 **TP:** 12–2 Interest Grabber, Section Outline, Prokaryotic Chromosome Structure, Figure 12–10, Figure 12–11 **ABC:** 21 DNA Replication **Lab Simulations CD-ROM:** DNA Structure and Replication
TR: Lesson Plan 12–3, Section Summary, p. 53 L1, p. 64 L2, Worksheets, pp. 58–60 L1, pp. 71–73 L2 **RSW:** Section 12–3 L2 **ARSW:** Section 12–3 L1	**SE:** 12–3 Section Assessment, p. 306 **TR:** Section Review 12–3	**iText:** Section 12–3 **TP:** 12–3 Interest Grabber, Section Outline, Concept Map, Figure 12–14, Figure 12–17, Figure 12–18 **ABC:** 25 DNA Transcription, 26 Protein Synthesis
TR: Lesson Plan 12–4, Section Summary, p. 54 L1, p. 65 L2, Worksheets, p. 61 L1, pp. 74–75 L2 **RSW:** Section 12–4 L2 **ARSW:** Section 12–4 L1	**SE:** 12–4 Section Assessment, p. 308 **TR:** Section Review 12–4	**iText:** Section 12–4 **TP:** 12–4 Interest Grabber; Section Outline; Gene Mutations: Substitution, Insertion, and Deletion; Figure 12–20 **ABC:** 27, 28, 29
TR: Lesson Plan 12–5, Section Summary, p. 54 L1, p. 65 L2, Worksheets, p. 62 L1, pp. 76–78 L2 **RSW:** Section 12–5 L2 **ARSW:** Section 12–5 L1	**SE:** 12–5 Section Assessment, p. 312 **TR:** Section Review 12–5	**iText:** Section 12–5 **TP:** 12–5 Interest Grabber, Section Outline, Typical Gene Structure
	SE: Chapter 12 Assessment, pp. 314–317; **TR:** Chapter Vocabulary Review, Graphic Organizer, Chapter 12 Test	**iText:** Chapter 12 Assessment **CTB:** Chapter 12 Test

Go Online

Students can do research, share data, and test their knowledge online.

TIME SAVER

PRESSED FOR TIME?

To Preview the Chapter

- Instruct students to find all of the Vocabulary terms in the chapter and write a definition for each.
- Have students look at the chapter figures and read the captions.

To Cover the Chapter Quickly

- Have students read The Structure of DNA in Section 12–1 and all of Sections 12–2 and 12–3.
- Assign the Section Reviews for 12–2 and 12–3.

To Review the Chapter

- Assign Sections 12–1 through 12–5 in the Reading and Study Workbook or the Adapted Reading and Study Workbook.
- Assign Section Reviews for 12–1 through 12–5 and the Chapter Vocabulary Review for Chapter 12 in the Teaching Resources.

CHAPTER 12

ENGAGE/EXPLORE

Inquiry Activity

Objective Students will be able to determine how codes work. L2

Skills Focus **Using Models, Calculating, Analyzing Data**

Materials 12 pop beads of four different colors

Time 15 minutes

Strategies

- Explain to students that each letter of the word should have its own combination of bead colors.
- Students should connect their pop beads to form a chain that represents the encoded word.

Expected Outcomes Students will devise a code in which two colors represent one letter.

Think About It

1. Each letter must be encoded by a sequence of at least two beads.
2. A two-bead code can represent 16 different letters. ($4 \times 4 = 16$)
3. Yes, a three-bead code could represent 64 different letters. ($4 \times 4 \times 4 = 64$)

Assess Prior Knowledge

To find out what students already know about DNA and RNA, ask: **What organelle is known as the "control center" of the cell?** *(Nucleus)* **What structures are found in the nucleus?** *(Chromosomes)* **What are located on chromosomes?** *(Genes)* **What are chromosomes composed of?** *(DNA wound around proteins)* **How do genes and chromosomes control the activity of a cell?** *(By producing proteins that regulate cellular functions or become part of the cell structure)*

CHAPTER 12

DNA and RNA

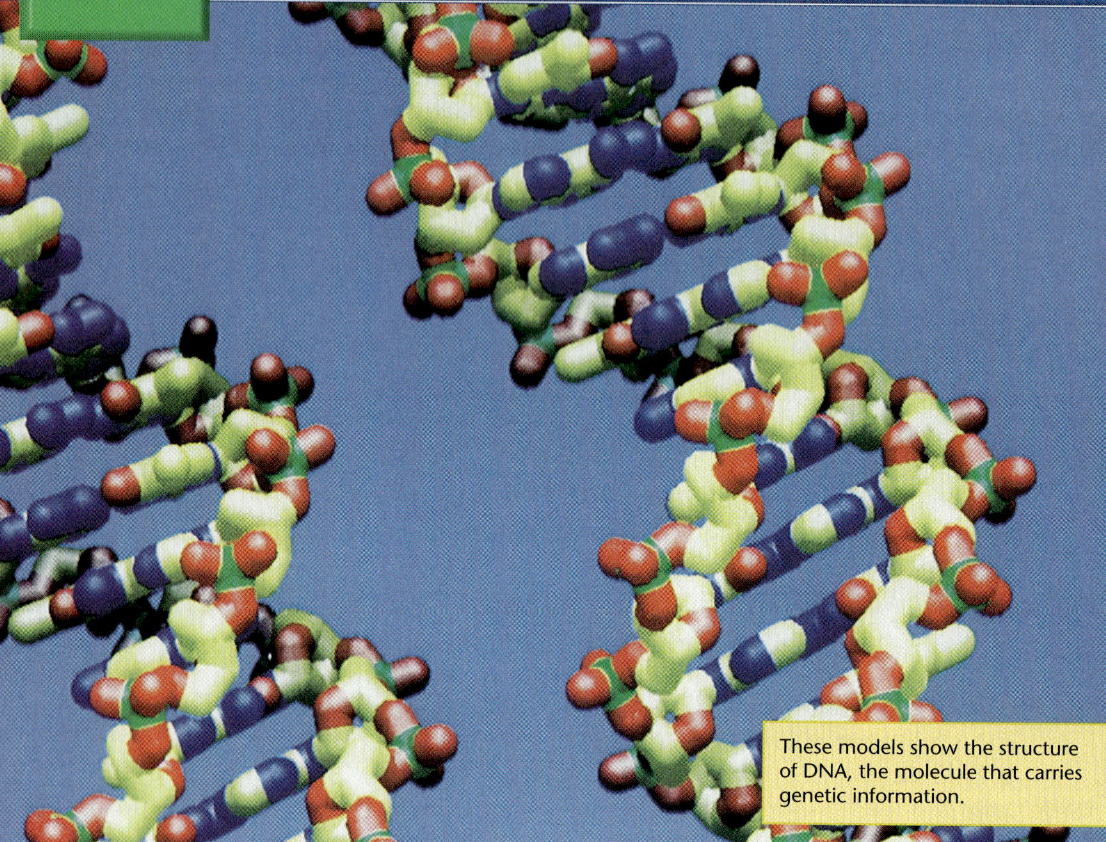

These models show the structure of DNA, the molecule that carries genetic information.

Inquiry Activity

How do codes work?

Procedure

1. Obtain 12 pop beads of four different colors.
2. Select a word that contains at least five different letters from the text on the next page. Use your beads to develop a code for your word.
3. Exchange your code and your coded bead chain with a classmate. Use the classmate's code to decipher his or her word.

Think About It

1. **Using Models** How were you able to encode five different letters using only four colors?
2. **Calculating** How many different letters could you encode by using two beads to stand for each letter used in your message?
3. **Analyzing Data** Could you encode the whole alphabet by using three beads for each letter?

HISTORY OF SCIENCE

The search for genes

After Mendel's work was rediscovered in the 1900s, two scientists, Walter Sutton and Thomas Hunt Morgan, showed that genes are the units of heredity and are located on chromosomes. In the 1940s, George Beadle and Edward Tatum showed that genes control the structure and function of an organism by directing the synthesis of enzymes, which were known to control chemical reactions in cells. Soon, scientists wanted to know the structure of genes. They already knew that chromosomes were made up of proteins and DNA. Most scientists then believed that genes were composed of proteins, because proteins were important to the chemical processes of the cell. They thought the chemical structure of DNA was too simple to contain all the information needed to direct cell processes.

12–1 DNA

7 2.e. Students know DNA (deoxyribonucleic acid) is the genetic material of living organisms and is located in the chromosomes of each cell. **BI 5.a.** Students know the general structures and functions of DNA, RNA, and protein. **BIIE 1.k.** Recognize the cumulative nature of scientific evidence.

How do genes work? What are they made of, and how do they determine the characteristics of organisms? Are genes single molecules, or are they longer structures made up of many molecules? In the middle of the 1900s, questions like these were on the minds of biologists everywhere.

To truly understand genetics, biologists first had to discover the chemical nature of the gene. If the structures that carry genetic information could be identified, it might be possible to understand how genes control the inherited characteristics of living things.

Guide for Reading

Key Concepts
- What did scientists discover about the relationship between genes and DNA?
- What is the overall structure of the DNA molecule?

Vocabulary
transformation
bacteriophage
nucleotide
base pairing

Reading Strategy: Summarizing As you read, find the key ideas for the text under each blue heading. Write down a few key words from each main idea. Then, use the key words in your summary. Revise your summary, keeping only the most important ideas.

Griffith and Transformation

Like many stories in science, the discovery of the molecular nature of the gene began with an investigator who was actually looking for something else. In 1928, British scientist Frederick Griffith was trying to figure out how bacteria make people sick. More specifically, Griffith wanted to learn how certain types of bacteria produce a serious lung disease known as pneumonia.

Griffith had isolated two slightly different strains, or types, of pneumonia bacteria from mice. Both strains grew very well in culture plates in his lab, but only one of the strains caused pneumonia. The disease-causing strain of bacteria grew into smooth colonies on culture plates, whereas the harmless strain produced colonies with rough edges. The differences in appearance made the two strains easy to distinguish.

◀ **Figure 12–1** White mice like these are commonly used in scientific experiments.

SECTION RESOURCES

Print:
- ***Laboratory Manual A,*** Chapter 12 Lab
- ***Laboratory Manual B,*** Chapter 12 Lab
- ***Teaching Resources,*** Lesson Plan 12–1, Adapted Section Summary 12–1, Adapted Worksheets 12–1, Section Summary 12–1, Worksheets 12–1, Section Review 12–1, Enrichment
- ***Reading and Study Workbook A,*** Section 12–1
- ***Adapted Reading and Study Workbook B,*** Section 12–1
- ***Biotechnology Manual,*** Labs 4, 5, 6

Technology:
- ***iText,*** Section 12–1
- ***Animated Biological Concepts DVD,*** 20
- ***Transparencies Plus,*** Section 12–1
- ***Lab Simulations CD-ROM,*** DNA Structure and Replication

Section 12–1

7 2.e, BI 5.a, BIIE 1.k

1 FOCUS

Objectives

12.1.1 ***Summarize*** the relationship between genes and DNA.
12.1.2 ***Describe*** the overall structure of the DNA molecule.

Guide for Reading

Vocabulary Preview

Read the Vocabulary terms aloud to the class. Then, invite students to write the words and divide them into syllables as best they can. The correct syllabications are trans•for•ma•tion, bac•te•ri•o•phage, nu•cle•o•tide, base pair•ing.

Reading Strategy

Before students read the section, have them write a question for each of the section heads. As they read for key ideas to summarize the section, they should also write the answers to their questions.

2 INSTRUCT

Griffith and Transformation

Build Science Skills

Asking Questions Engage students in a discussion about the scientific question that Griffith originally set out to answer. Explain that Griffith set out to learn whether or not a toxin produced by the bacteria was the cause of pneumonia. Brainstorm a list of scientific questions that Griffith might have asked when he designed his experiment. Write the questions on the board. Work together as a class to decide which questions could serve as the basis for scientific inquiry and which could not. L2

12–1 (continued)

Use Visuals

Figure 12–2 Review Griffith's transformation experiment. Ask: **What was Griffith trying to learn when he set up this experiment?** *(How bacteria caused pneumonia)* Encourage students to evaluate Griffith's experimental design and discuss the controls he used. Then, ask: **How did Griffith show that the disease-causing bacteria were killed by the heat?** *(He tried to grow them in a petri dish. If the bacteria grew, then he knew that he had not killed them.)* **What result was Griffith expecting when he injected the mixture of live harmless bacteria and heat-killed disease-causing bacteria?** *(He expected the mice to live.)* L2

Make Connections

Health Science Poll the class to find out who remembers getting immunizations for tetanus and diphtheria. Find out if anyone knows why he or she received the immunizations and how they work. Explain that for these diseases, the immunizations are actually toxoids, or inactivated toxins. These diseases are not caused by the bacteria themselves but by toxins that the bacteria produce. Ask: **Why do you think it's important to learn how bacteria cause disease?** *(To find a cure for the disease or a means to prevent it)* Explain that Griffith set up his experiment to show that a toxin produced by the bacteria causes pneumonia. It was later learned that pneumonia is caused instead by bacterial growth damaging healthy lung tissue. L2

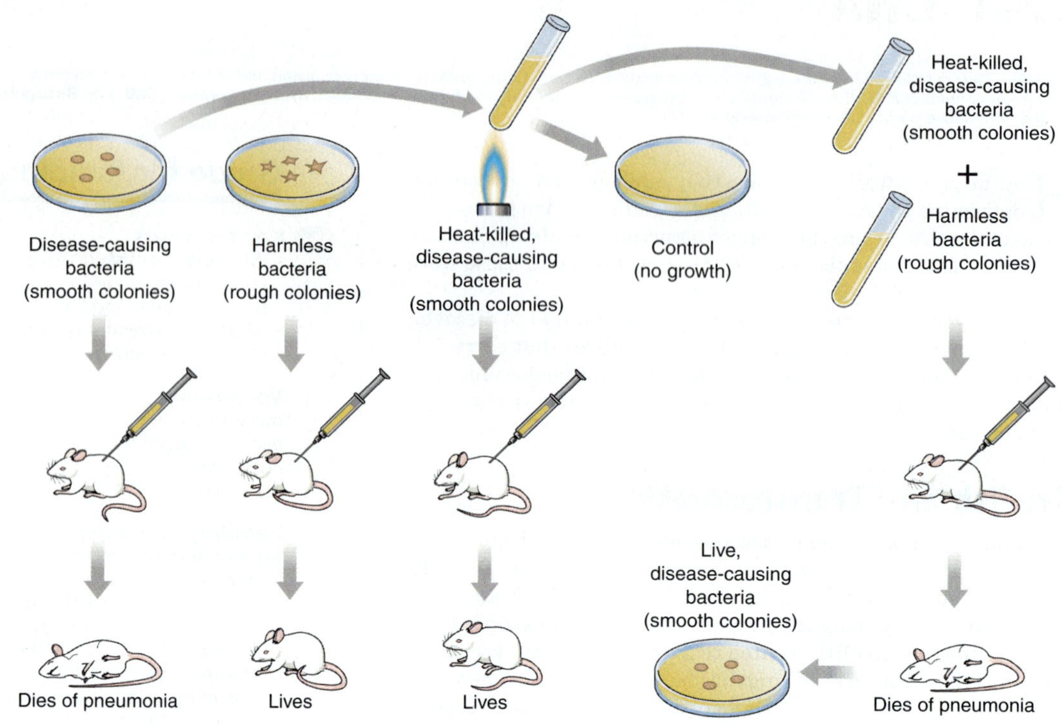

▲ **Figure 12–2** Griffith injected mice with four different samples of bacteria. When injected separately, neither heat-killed, disease-causing bacteria nor live, harmless bacteria killed the mice. The two types injected together, however, caused fatal pneumonia. From this experiment, biologists inferred that genetic information could be transferred from one bacterium to another. **Inferring** ***After heating the disease-causing bacteria, why did Griffith test whether material from the bacterial culture would produce new colonies in a petri dish?***

Griffith's Experiments When Griffith injected mice with the disease-causing strain of bacteria, the mice developed pneumonia and died. When mice were injected with the harmless strain, they didn't get sick at all. Griffith wondered if the disease-causing bacteria might produce a poison.

To find out, he took a culture of these cells, heated the bacteria to kill them, and injected the heat-killed bacteria into mice. The mice survived, suggesting that the cause of pneumonia was not a chemical poison released by the disease-causing bacteria. Griffith's experiments are shown in **Figure 12–2.**

Transformation Griffith's next experiment produced an amazing result. He mixed his heat-killed, disease-causing bacteria with live, harmless ones and injected the mixture into mice. By themselves, neither should have made the mice sick. But to Griffith's amazement, the mice developed pneumonia and many died. When he examined the lungs of the mice, he found them filled not with the harmless bacteria, but with the disease-causing bacteria. Somehow the heat-killed bacteria had passed their disease-causing ability to the harmless strain. Griffith called this process **transformation** because one strain of bacteria (the harmless strain) had apparently been changed permanently into another (the disease-causing strain).

UNIVERSAL ACCESS

Less Proficient Readers
Students can review the vocabulary of DNA structure by making a concept map that includes the terms *nucleotide, deoxyribose, phosphate group, nitrogenous base, purine, pyrimidine, adenine, guanine, cytosine,* and *thymine.* L1

English Language Learners
Have students assemble a glossary of terms for this chapter. They can include phonetic spellings of words and definitions in their own words. Use synonyms or mnemonics to help with meanings. Students can also use illustrations and phrases from their native languages. L1 L2

Advanced Learners
Students might enjoy reading *The Double Helix: A Personal Account of the Discovery of the Structure of DNA* by James Watson, and *Rosalind Franklin: The Dark Lady of DNA* by Brenda Maddox. Invite students to discuss the books and their characters. L2 L3

Griffith hypothesized that when the live, harmless bacteria and the heat-killed bacteria were mixed, some factor was transferred from the heat-killed cells into the live cells. That factor, he hypothesized, must contain information that could change harmless bacteria into disease-causing ones. Furthermore, since the ability to cause disease was inherited by the transformed bacteria's offspring, the transforming factor might be a gene.

Avery and DNA

In 1944, a group of scientists led by Canadian biologist Oswald Avery at the Rockefeller Institute in New York decided to repeat Griffith's work. They did so to determine which molecule in the heat-killed bacteria was most important for transformation. If transformation required just one particular molecule, that might well be the molecule of the gene.

Avery and his colleagues made an extract, or juice, from the heat-killed bacteria. They then carefully treated the extract with enzymes that destroyed proteins, lipids, carbohydrates, and other molecules, including the nucleic acid RNA. Transformation still occurred. Obviously, since these molecules had been destroyed, they were not responsible for the transformation.

Avery and the other scientists repeated the experiment, this time using enzymes that would break down DNA. When they destroyed the nucleic acid DNA in the extract, transformation did not occur. There was just one possible conclusion. DNA was the transforming factor. **Avery and other scientists discovered that the nucleic acid DNA stores and transmits the genetic information from one generation of an organism to the next.**

The Hershey-Chase Experiment

Scientists are a skeptical group. It usually takes several experiments to convince them of something as important as the chemical nature of the gene. The most important of these experiments was performed in 1952 by two American scientists, Alfred Hershey and Martha Chase. They collaborated in studying viruses, nonliving particles smaller than a cell that can infect living organisms.

Bacteriophages One kind of virus that infects bacteria is known as a **bacteriophage** (bak-TEER-ee-uh-fayj), which means "bacteria eater." **Figure 12–3** shows typical bacteriophages. Bacteriophages are composed of a DNA or RNA core and a protein coat. When a bacteriophage enters a bacterium, the virus attaches to the surface of the cell and injects its genetic information into it. The viral genes act to produce many new bacteriophages, and they gradually destroy the bacterium. When the cell splits open, hundreds of new viruses burst out.

CHECKPOINT *What is a bacteriophage?*

▼ **Figure 12–3** A bacteriophage is a type of virus that infects and kills bacteria. This image shows two T2 bacteriophages (purple) invading an *E. coli* cell (green). **Comparing and Contrasting** *How large are viruses compared with bacteria?*

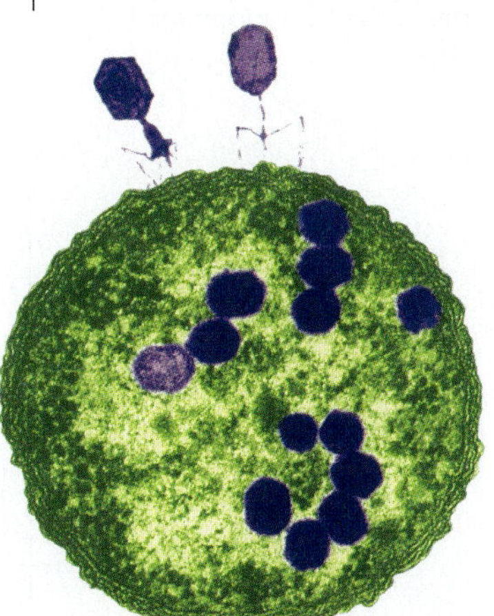

(magnification: 25,000×)

Avery and DNA

Build Science Skills

Designing Experiments Challenge students to diagram the experiments conducted by Avery and his group to repeat Griffith's work. Students should identify the variable in the experiment. *(The enzyme used to destroy a certain molecule)* Make sure students realize that Avery used only one enzyme at a time. Explain that for these experiments, they didn't need mice because they had developed a test for the presence of transformed bacterial cells that could be done in a test tube. Ask: **How did this experiment show that it was DNA and not any other molecule?** *(Transformation occurred every time, except when DNA was destroyed.)*

The Hershey-Chase Experiment

Demonstration

Diagram on the board the process by which a bacteriophage infects and replicates in bacteria. Show how the bacteriophage injects its DNA into a bacterium and how DNA incorporates itself into the bacterial DNA (which is usually circular). Explain that the bacterium is tricked into thinking that the viral DNA is its own and begins to make the bacteriophage's DNA and proteins. These parts assemble into new bacteriophages and burst out of the bacterial cell, killing it in the process. If possible, find electron micrographs of this process to show to students.

BIO INSIGHTS **HISTORY OF SCIENCE**

Scientists are a skeptical bunch

Today, Avery's results show without a doubt that DNA makes up genes. However, in 1944 the results were questionable. Then, inheritance in bacteria was just beginning to be studied. Scientists didn't know if bacteria had genes like those in more complex organisms. And even if DNA were the hereditary substance in bacteria, it might not be the hereditary substance in more complex organisms. DNA was still considered a very simple molecule. Scientists were more excited about Hershey and Chase's results with bacteriophages in 1952. By that time, genetic studies showed that bacteriophages had properties of heredity similar to those of more complex organisms. Also, experiments showed that DNA was more complex than originally thought.

Answers to . . .

CHECKPOINT *A virus that infects and kills bacteria*

Figure 12–2 *If the bacteria grew, then he knew that he had not killed them.*

Figure 12–3 *Viruses are smaller.*

12–1 (continued)

Use Visuals

Figure 12–4 Use the diagram to discuss Hershey and Chase's experimental design. Make sure students understand that the radioactive elements can be easily observed in the laboratory. Ask: **How were Hershey and Chase able to determine whether bacteriophages injected DNA or protein into bacteria?** *(By growing the bacteriophages in cultures containing either ^{32}P or ^{35}S so that the bacteriophage DNA—which contains phosphorus—or protein—which contains sulfur—would be labeled in a way that was easy to follow)* **What would you expect if a bacteriophage injected protein into a bacterial cell?** *(If the bacteriophage injected protein, the bacterial cell would contain ^{35}S. If it injected DNA, it would contain ^{32}P.)*

Make Connections

Chemistry Explain that radioactive elements are unstable isotopes of an element. Diagram an atom of hydrogen on the board with one proton in the nucleus and one electron. Add one neutron to the nucleus. Ask: **Now what element is this?** *(It's still hydrogen, but it is an isotope of hydrogen, deuterium.)* Add another neutron to the nucleus, and ask a volunteer to tell what element it is now. *(Another hydrogen isotope, tritium)* Point out that the three isotopes of hydrogen all have the same chemical properties—they each have one proton and one electron. However, they have very different physical properties because of their differences in mass. Ask: **What causes their mass to be different?** *(Neutrons)* **Do neutrons affect the chemical properties of an element?** *(No)* **Why not?** *(They are not charged particles; they do not repel or attract other particles.)* Explain that tritium is an unstable, radioactive isotope because its nucleus tends to break down and release small particles of energy. This release of energy is called radioactivity. L2 L3

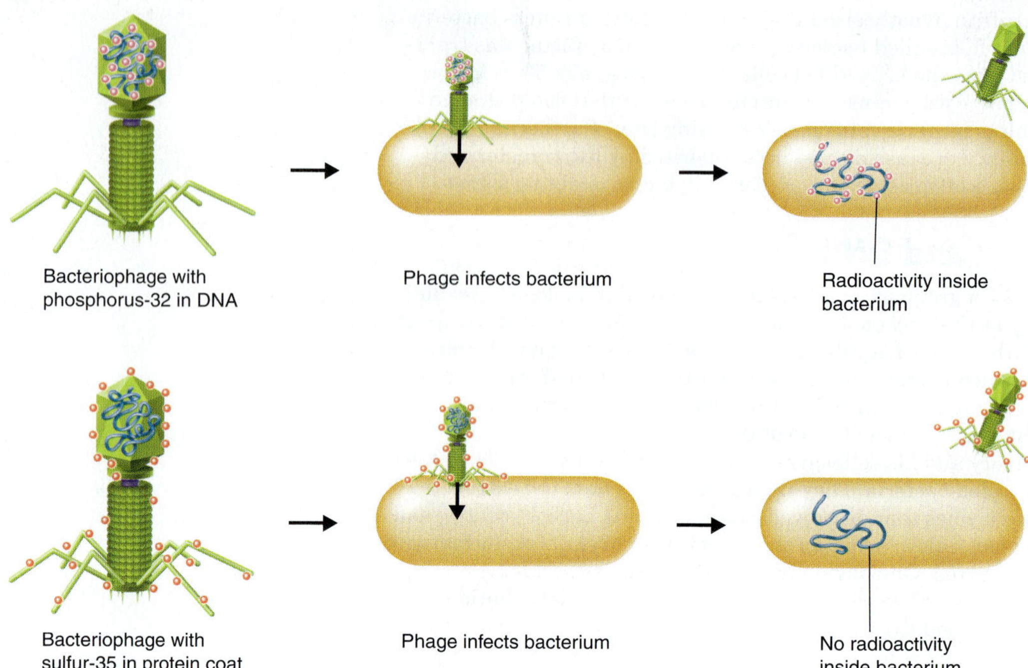

▲ **Figure 12–4** Alfred Hershey and Martha Chase used different radioactive markers to label the DNA and proteins of bacteriophages. The bacteriophages injected only DNA into the bacteria, not proteins. **From these results, Hershey and Chase concluded that the genetic material of the bacteriophage was DNA.**

Radioactive Markers Hershey and Chase reasoned that if they could determine which part of the virus—the protein coat or the DNA core—entered the infected cell, they would learn whether genes were made of protein or DNA. To do this, they grew viruses in cultures containing radioactive isotopes of phosphorus-32 (^{32}P) and sulfur-35 (^{35}S). This was a clever strategy because proteins contain almost no phosphorus and DNA contains no sulfur. The radioactive substances could be used as markers. If ^{35}S was found in the bacteria, it would mean that the viruses' protein had been injected into the bacteria. If ^{32}P was found in the bacteria, then it was the DNA that had been injected.

The Hershey-Chase experiment is shown in **Figure 12–4.** The two scientists mixed the marked viruses with bacteria. Then, they waited a few minutes for the viruses to inject their genetic material. Next, they separated the viruses from the bacteria and tested the bacteria for radioactivity. Nearly all the radioactivity in the bacteria was from phosphorus (^{32}P), the marker found in DNA. **Hershey and Chase concluded that the genetic material of the bacteriophage was DNA, not protein.**

CHECKPOINT *What part of the virus did the Hershey-Chase experiment show had entered the bacteria?*

FACTS AND FIGURES

Radioisotopes—a tool for biologists
Biologists commonly use radioisotopes—radioactive isotopes—to learn about cell processes, because they can be substituted into biochemical reactions without changing the chemistry of the reaction. Radioactive isotopes are unstable and break apart or "decay" into a stable form. Because of this decay, their presence can be detected. When they decay, two different kinds of particles are given off—alpha particles, which are 2 neutrons and 2 protons, and beta particles, which are high-speed electrons. In some cases, gamma rays are also given off. Gamma rays are electromagnetic waves of energy that act like X-rays. All forms of radiation, but especially gamma rays, can damage tissues.

The Components and Structure of DNA

You might think that knowing genes were made of DNA would have satisfied scientists, but that was not the case at all. Instead, they wondered how DNA, or any molecule for that matter, could do the three critical things that genes were known to do: First, genes had to carry information from one generation to the next; second, they had to put that information to work by determining the heritable characteristics of organisms; and third, genes had to be easily copied, because all of a cell's genetic information is replicated every time a cell divides. For DNA to do all of that, it would have to be a very special molecule indeed.

DNA is a long molecule made up of units called **nucleotides.** As **Figure 12–5** shows, each nucleotide is made up of three basic components: a 5-carbon sugar called deoxyribose, a phosphate group, and a nitrogenous (nitrogen-containing) base. There are four kinds of nitrogenous bases in DNA. Two of the nitrogenous bases, adenine (AD-uh-neen) and guanine (GWAH-neen), belong to a group of compounds known as purines. The remaining two bases, cytosine (SY-tuh-zeen) and thymine (THY-meen), are known as pyrimidines. Purines have two rings in their structures, whereas pyrimidines have one ring.

a 7 2.e, BI 5.a

The backbone of a DNA chain is formed by sugar and phosphate groups of each nucleotide. The nitrogenous bases stick out sideways from the chain. The nucleotides can be joined together in any order, meaning that any sequence of bases is possible.

If you don't see much in **Figure 12–5** that could explain the remarkable properties of the gene, don't be surprised. In the 1940s and early 1950s, the leading biologists in the world thought of DNA as little more than a string of nucleotides. They were baffled, too. The four different nucleotides, like the 26 letters of the alphabet, could be strung together in many different ways, so it was possible they could carry coded genetic information. However, so could many other molecules, at least in principle. Was there something more to the structure of DNA?

For: Links on DNA
Visit: www.SciLinks.org
Web Code: cbn-4121

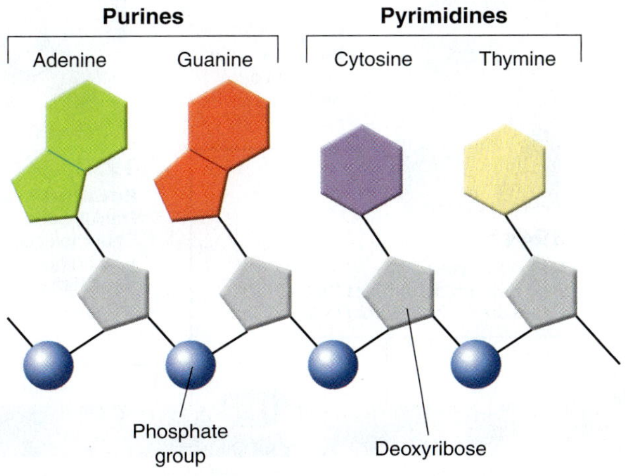

Figure 12–5 DNA is made up of nucleotides. Each nucleotide has three parts: a deoxyribose molecule, a phosphate group, and a nitrogenous base. There are four different bases in DNA: adenine, guanine, cytosine, and thymine. **Interpreting Graphics** *How are the nucleotides joined together to form the DNA chain?*

TEACHER TO TEACHER

Students often have difficulty understanding how a nucleic acid such as DNA is constructed, even after viewing models or laserdisc presentations. The idea "clicks," however, when they're allowed to construct a nucleic acid from the members of the class in an activity we do outside of the classroom. Students are assigned a specific nitrogenous base and must pair with their complementary base until the DNA molecule is replicated. I also use the activity to teach the different kinds of bonds in DNA and the workings of enzymes such as DNA polymerase. Students really get to understand DNA from this experience, and most of all, they have fun doing the project.

—Leon Lange
Biology Teacher
Fort Campbell High School
Fort Campbell, KY

The Components and Structure of DNA

Download a worksheet on DNA for students to complete, and find additional teacher support from NSTA SciLinks.

Build Science Skills

Predicting Challenge students to predict how DNA is able to carry out the three critical things that genes are known to do. Have them write their predictions in their lab manuals. When you complete the chapter, have students check their predictions to see if they are correct. Encourage students to share the facts or inferences on which they based their predictions. L2 L3

Demonstration

Demonstrate what a polymer is by linking together paper clips to make a chain. Explain that a polymer is a very large molecule made up of repeating units that are bonded together. The individual paper clips act as the repeating units of the polymer chain. You can make the polymer chain more complex by making the repeating unit more complex, for example, by adding beads or safety pins to the paper clips. Ask: **How many basic units does DNA have?** *(Three: deoxyribose, a phosphate group, and a nitrogenous base)* Explain that polymers can be very strong and flexible and have a variety of uses. For example, nylon is a polymer. L1 L2

Answers to . . .

 *The DNA*

Figure 12–5 *By the deoxyribose sugar and the phosphate group*

Biology and History

BIIE 1.k

Tell students that the DNA and RNA molecules were discovered not long after Mendel published his ideas about inheritance. Discuss how long it was before scientists made the connection between DNA and genes and why it took so long to establish the molecular basis of inheritance. Then, focus on the short period of time between Avery's work and Watson and Crick's proposal for the DNA molecule.

Writing in Science

Students' essays should describe the research activities of James Watson or Francis Crick since the early 1950s. They might write something similar to a timeline, or they might write a summary. Students should mention what the scientist they choose is doing now. L2

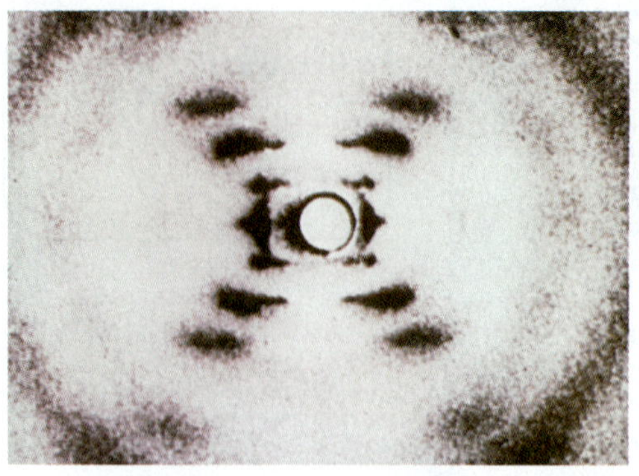

▲ **Figure 12–6** This X-ray diffraction photograph of DNA was taken by Rosalind Franklin in the early 1950s. The X-shaped pattern in the center indicates that the structure of DNA is helical.

Chargaff's Rules One of the puzzling facts about DNA was a curious relationship between its nucleotides. Years earlier, Erwin Chargaff, an American biochemist, had discovered that the percentages of guanine [G] and cytosine [C] bases are almost equal in any sample of DNA. The same thing is true for the other two nucleotides, adenine [A] and thymine [T]. The observation that [A] = [T] and [G] = [C] became known as Chargaff's rules. Despite the fact that DNA samples from organisms as different as bacteria and humans obeyed this rule, neither Chargaff nor anyone else had the faintest idea why.

X-Ray Evidence In the early 1950s, a British scientist named Rosalind Franklin began to study DNA. She used a technique called X-ray diffraction to get information about the structure of the DNA molecule. Franklin purified a large amount of DNA and then stretched the DNA fibers in a thin glass tube so that most of the strands were parallel. Then, she aimed a powerful X-ray beam at the concentrated DNA samples and recorded the scattering pattern of the X-rays on film. Franklin worked hard to make better and better patterns from DNA until the patterns became clear. The result of her work is the X-ray pattern shown in **Figure 12–6.**

BIIE 1.k

Biology and History

Discovering the Role of DNA

Genes and the laws of heredity were discovered before scientists identified the molecules that genes are made of. With the discovery of DNA, scientists have been able to explain how genes are replicated and how they function.

1928
Frederick Griffith
Griffith discovers that a factor in heat-killed, disease-causing bacteria can "transform" harmless bacteria into ones that can cause disease.

1944
Oswald Avery
Avery's team determines that genes are composed of DNA.

1951
Linus Pauling
Robert Corey
Pauling and Corey determine that the structure of a class of proteins is a helix.

1952
Rosalind Franklin
Franklin studies the DNA molecule using a technique called X-ray diffraction.

1925

HISTORY OF SCIENCE

Watson and Crick's discoveries
When Watson and Crick were ready to announce their double-helix model in 1953, they made drawings of DNA and sent their paper to *Nature* magazine. They ended their first paper by writing, "It has not escaped our notice that the specific pairing we have postulated immediately suggests a possible copying mechanism for the genetic material." Within a few weeks, Watson and Crick had written another paper describing the copying mechanism.

By itself, Franklin's X-ray pattern does not reveal the structure of DNA, but it does carry some very important clues. The X-shaped pattern in the photograph in **Figure 12–6** shows that the strands in DNA are twisted around each other like the coils of a spring, a shape known as a helix. The angle of the *X* suggests that there are two strands in the structure. Other clues suggest that the nitrogenous bases are near the center of the molecule.

CHECKPOINT ***What technique did Franklin use to study DNA?***

The Double Helix At the same time that Franklin was continuing her research, Francis Crick, a British physicist, and James Watson, an American biologist, were trying to understand the structure of DNA by building three-dimensional models of the molecule. Their models were made of cardboard and wire. They twisted and stretched the models in various ways, but their best efforts did nothing to explain DNA's properties.

Then, early in 1953, Watson was shown a copy of Franklin's remarkable X-ray pattern. The effect was immediate. In his book *The Double Helix,* Watson wrote: "The instant I saw the picture my mouth fell open and my pulse began to race." Using clues from Franklin's pattern, within weeks Watson and Crick had built a structural model that explained the puzzle of how DNA could carry information and how it could be copied. They published their results in a historic one-page paper in April of 1953. **Watson and Crick's model of DNA was a double helix, in which two strands were wound around each other.**

1953
James Watson
Francis Crick
Watson and Crick develop the double-helix model of the structure of DNA.

1960
Sydney Brenner
Brenner and other scientists show the existence of messenger RNA.

1977
Walter Gilbert
Gilbert, Allan Maxam, and Frederick Sanger develop methods to read the DNA sequence.

2000
Human Genome Project
The Human Genome Project—an attempt to sequence all human DNA—is essentially complete.

1950 1975 2000

Writing in Science

Do research in the library or on the Internet to find out what James Watson or Francis Crick has worked on since discovering the structure of DNA. Organize your findings about the scientist's work and write a short essay describing it.

Build Science Skills

Using Models Make available various materials for building models of the DNA molecule. You might provide pipe cleaners, an assortment of beads, and small foam balls. Encourage student groups to use the materials to build a model of the DNA molecule. They may use the illustration in Figure 12–7 on page 294 as a guide. Help students see that the structure is like a twisted ladder. Make sure they understand that this structure is called a helix. DNA is a double helix because it has two strands, like the two rails of a ladder.

Answer to . . .

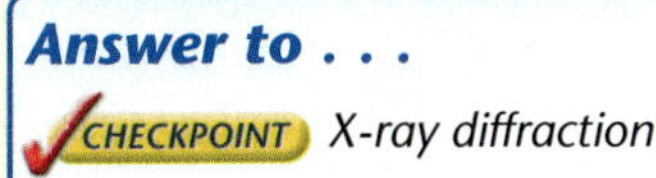

CHECKPOINT *X-ray diffraction*

12–1 (continued)

Use Visuals

Figure 12–7 As students study the diagram, point out that the dotted lines represent the hydrogen bonds that hold together the two DNA strands. Ask: **How does the arrangement of base pairs relate to Chargaff's rules?** *(Adenine and thymine are present in equal percentages because the two bases always pair together; guanine and cytosine are present in equal percentages because they always pair together.)* L2

3 ASSESS

Evaluate Understanding

Devise a question-and-answer game for the class in which teams of three or four students work together to answer questions about the discovery of DNA and its structure.

Reteach

Encourage students to draw their own diagram of the DNA molecule using Figure 12–7 as a guide. Students should label all parts of the molecule.

Focus on the BIG Idea

Students can choose the experiments of Griffith, Avery, or Hershey and Chase for their flowcharts. You might divide the class into thirds to ensure that each experiment is covered. Organizers should include the procedure and the conclusions of each experiment.

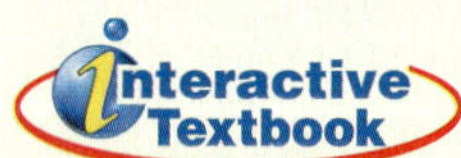

If your class subscribes to the iText, use it to review the Key Concepts in Section 12–1.

Figure 12–7 **DNA is a double helix in which two strands are wound around each other.** Each strand is made up of a chain of nucleotides. The two strands are held together by hydrogen bonds between adenine and thymine and between guanine and cytosine.

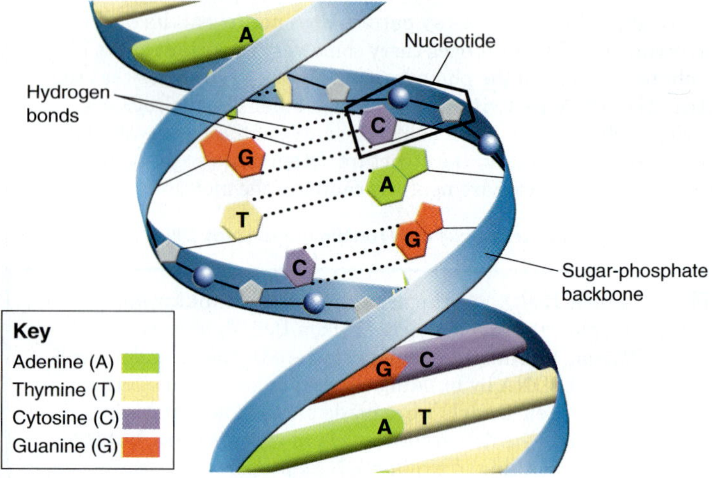

A double helix looks like a twisted ladder or a spiral staircase. When Watson and Crick evaluated their DNA model, they realized that the double helix accounted for many of the features in Franklin's X-ray pattern but did not explain what forces held the two strands together. They then discovered that hydrogen bonds could form between certain nitrogenous bases and provide just enough force to hold the two strands together. As **Figure 12–7** shows, hydrogen bonds can form only between certain base pairs—adenine and thymine, and guanine and cytosine. Once they saw this, they realized that this principle, called **base pairing,** explained Chargaff's rules. Now there was a reason that [A] = [T] and [G] = [C]. For every adenine in a double-stranded DNA molecule, there had to be exactly one thymine molecule; for each cytosine molecule, there was one guanine molecule.

12–1 Section Assessment

1. **Key Concept** List the conclusions Griffith, Avery, Hershey, and Chase drew from their experiments.
2. **Key Concept** Describe Watson and Crick's model of the DNA molecule.
3. What are the four kinds of bases found in DNA?
4. Did Watson and Crick's model account for the equal amounts of thymine and adenine in DNA? Explain.
5. **Critical Thinking Inferring** Why did Hershey and Chase grow viruses in cultures that contained both radioactive phosphorus and radioactive sulfur? What might have happened if they had used only one radioactive substance?

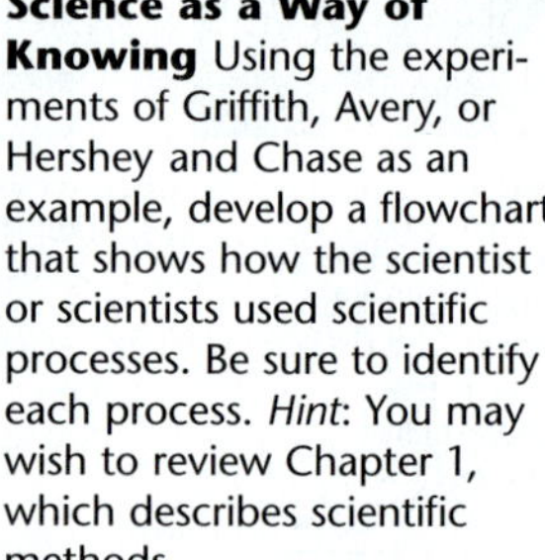

Focus on the BIG Idea

Science as a Way of Knowing Using the experiments of Griffith, Avery, or Hershey and Chase as an example, develop a flowchart that shows how the scientist or scientists used scientific processes. Be sure to identify each process. *Hint*: You may wish to review Chapter 1, which describes scientific methods.

12–1 Section Assessment

1. Griffith and Avery: genes were probably made of DNA; Hershey and Chase: genetic material of bacteriophage was DNA, not protein.
2. DNA is a double helix in which two strands are wound around each other.
3. Adenine, thymine, guanine, cytosine
4. Yes; hydrogen bonds can form only between certain base pairs—adenine with thymine and guanine with cytosine.
5. So that both the viral DNA and viral proteins would be marked; either they would not have been able to trace the location of the unmarked molecule in the bacterial cell, or the results would not have been conclusive.

12–2 Chromosomes and DNA Replication

7 2.e. Students know DNA (deoxyribonucleic acid) is the genetic material of living organisms and is located in the chromosomes of each cell. **BI 5.b.** Students know how to apply base-pairing rules to explain precise copying of DNA during semiconservative replication and transcription of information from DNA to mRNA.

DNA is present in such large amounts in many tissues that it's easy to extract and analyze. But where is DNA found in the cell? How is it organized? Where are the genes that Mendel first described a century and a half ago?

Guide for Reading

Key Concept
- What happens during DNA replication?

Vocabulary
chromatin
histone
replication
DNA polymerase

Reading Strategy: Asking Questions Before you read, study the diagram in **Figure 12–11.** Make a list of questions about the diagram. As you read, write down the answers to your questions.

DNA and Chromosomes

Prokaryotic cells lack nuclei and many of the organelles found in eukaryotes. Their DNA molecules are located in the cytoplasm. Most prokaryotes have a single circular DNA molecule that contains nearly all of the cell's genetic information. This large DNA molecule is usually referred to as the cell's chromosome, as shown in **Figure 12–8.**

Eukaryotic DNA is a bit more complicated. Many eukaryotes have as much as 1000 times the amount of DNA as prokaryotes. This DNA is not found free in the cytoplasm. Eukaryotic DNA is generally located in the cell nucleus in the form of a number of chromosomes. The number of chromosomes varies widely from one species to the next. For example, diploid human cells have 46 chromosomes, *Drosophila* cells have 8, and giant sequoia tree cells have 22.

7 2.e

DNA Length DNA molecules are surprisingly long. The chromosome of the prokaryote *E. coli,* which can live in the human colon (large intestine), contains 4,639,221 base pairs. The length of such a DNA molecule is roughly 1.6 mm, which doesn't sound like much until you think about the small size of a bacterium. To fit inside a typical bacterium, the DNA molecule must be folded into a space only one one-thousandth of its length.

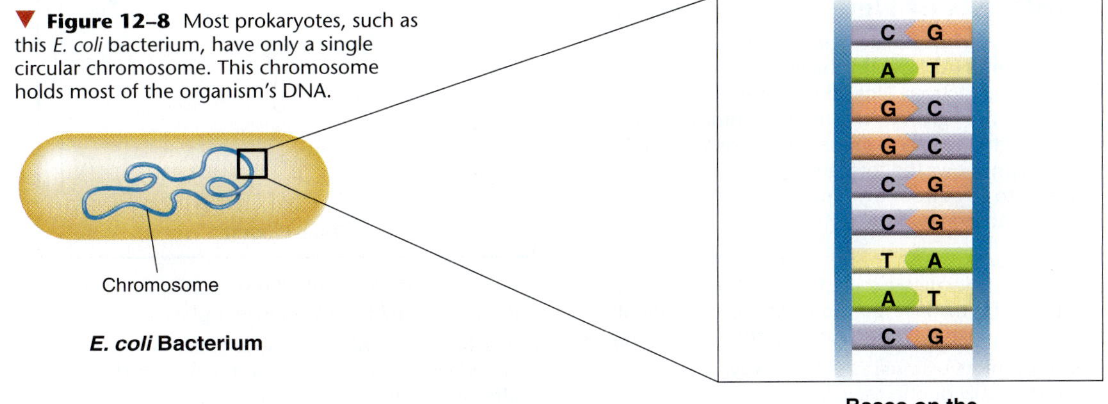

▼ **Figure 12–8** Most prokaryotes, such as this *E. coli* bacterium, have only a single circular chromosome. This chromosome holds most of the organism's DNA.

SECTION RESOURCES

Print:
- ***Teaching Resources,*** Lesson Plan 12–2, Adapted Section Summary 12–2, Section Summary 12–2, Worksheets 12–2, Section Review 12–2
- ***Reading and Study Workbook A,*** Section 12–2
- ***Lab Worksheets,*** Chapter 12 Exploration

Technology:
- ***iText,*** Section 12–1
- ***Animated Biological Concepts DVD,*** 21
- ***Transparencies Plus,*** Section 12–2
- ***Lab Simulations CD-ROM,*** DNA Structure and Replication

Section 12–2

7 2.e, BI 5.b

1 FOCUS

Objectives

12.2.1 ***Summarize*** the events of DNA replication.
12.2.2 ***Relate*** the DNA molecule to chromosome structure.

Guide for Reading

Vocabulary Preview

Explain that the suffix *-ase* is used to denote molecules that are enzymes, proteins that catalyze biochemical reactions. Challenge students to look carefully at the term *DNA polymerase.* Ask: **Based on the root of the word, what do you think DNA polymerase does?** *(It synthesizes the DNA molecule by adding individual nucleotides to the DNA polymer.)*

Reading Strategy

Encourage students to preview all diagrams in this section before reading. For Figure 12–11, have students list questions for the diagram and write answers to those questions as they read.

2 INSTRUCT

DNA and Chromosomes

Demonstration

To give students an idea of how large a DNA molecule is compared to the cell into which it is packed, show students a ball formed from a piece of string that is about 1 meter long. Then, draw a circle on the board that has a diameter of about 1 mm. If needed, review the metric equivalents so that students can see the relationship between micrometers (diameter of a bacterium) and millimeters (10^{-3} to 1) and millimeters to meters (also 10^{-3} to 1). Explain that the string represents the DNA molecule that must fit inside the circle drawn on the board. Encourage students to speculate about how the DNA molecule is able to fit into the cell and why it is so long. L2

12–2 (continued)

Build Science Skills

Using Models Give students a very long piece of yarn (30–50 cm), some beads, short wooden dowels, and a film canister. Challenge students to use the materials to help them fit the yarn inside the container, making sure that the yarn can be unwound fairly easily. Encourage students to make comparisons between their models and chromatin. L1 L2

Analyzing Data

Review the cell cycle with students. Remind them that interphase is the phase that occurs before mitosis, or cell division. After the cell has divided, its daughter cells are in interphase until they divide. Discuss the three phases of interphase: G_1, S, and G_2. Remind students that cell growth occurs during G_1, DNA replication occurs during S, and the cell prepares for mitosis in G_2. L2

Answers

1. (a) No radioactivity is incorporated. (b) Very large amounts of radioactivity are incorporated. (c) No additional radioactivity is incorporated.
2. No, DNA is synthesized at one point in the cell cycle about halfway between the two cell divisions. DNA synthesis lasts about an hour.
3. The chromosomes in the cell nucleus would contain the most radioactivity because thymine is part of the DNA molecule and chromosomes are composed of DNA.

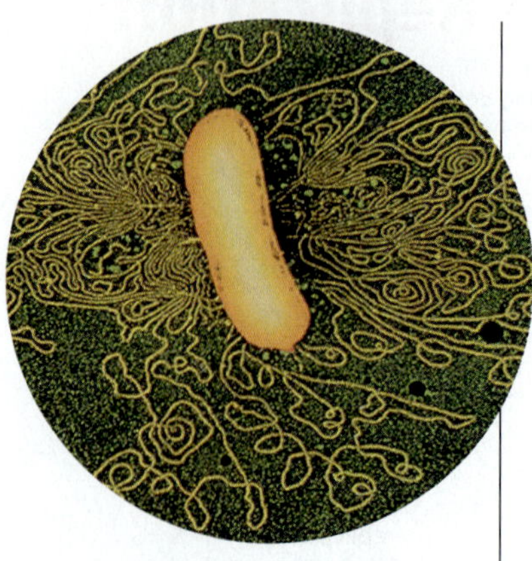

▲ **Figure 12–9** The DNA in a bacterium is about 1000 times as long as the bacterium itself. It must therefore be very tightly folded. **Using Analogies** *Compare DNA in a bacterium to a rope jammed into a backpack.*

To get a rough idea of what this means, think of a large school backpack. Then, imagine trying to pack a 300-meter length of rope into the backpack! **Figure 12–9,** which shows DNA spilling out from a ruptured bacterium, indicates how dramatically the DNA must be folded to fit within the cell.

Chromosome Structure The DNA in eukaryotic cells is packed even more tightly. A human cell contains almost 1000 times as many base pairs of DNA as a bacterium. The nucleus of a human cell contains more than 1 meter of DNA. How is so much DNA folded into tiny chromosomes? The answer can be found in the composition of eukaryotic chromosomes.

Eukaryotic chromosomes contain both DNA and protein, tightly packed together to form a substance called **chromatin.** Chromatin consists of DNA that is tightly coiled around proteins called **histones,** as shown in **Figure 12–10.** Together, the DNA and histone molecules form a beadlike structure called a nucleosome. Nucleosomes pack with one another to form a thick fiber, which is shortened by a system of loops and coils.

During most of the cell cycle, these fibers are dispersed in the nucleus so that individual chromosomes are not visible. During mitosis, however, the fibers of each individual chromosome are drawn together, forming the tightly packed chromosomes you can see through a light microscope in dividing cells. The tight packing of nucleosomes may help separate chromosomes during mitosis. There is also some evidence that changes in chromatin structure and histone-DNA binding are associated with changes in gene activity and expression.

Analyzing Data

Synthesis of New DNA Molecules

How can you investigate when and where cells synthesize DNA? Scientists have done this by briefly adding radioactively labeled thymine to the medium in which a cell grows. A cell that is synthesizing DNA will take the labeled thymine nucleotide into its DNA. The graph shows the total amount of radioactive label taken into DNA from thymine during an eight-hour period between two cell divisions.

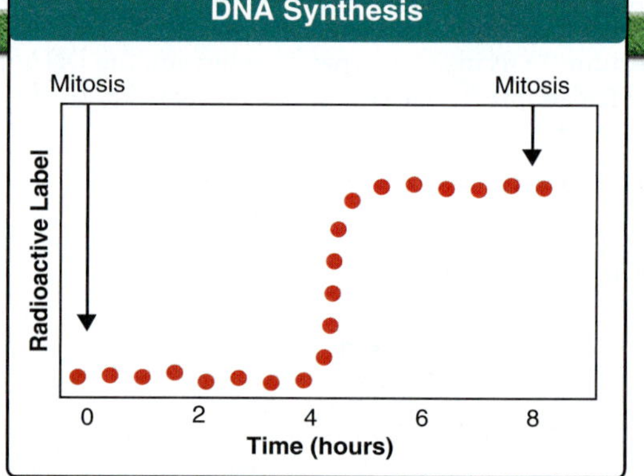

1. **Interpreting Graphics** Contrast the amounts of radioactivity incorporated during the following times: (a) the first four hours of the experiment, (b) the next two hours, and (c) the final two hours.
2. **Drawing Conclusions** Is DNA synthesized continually during the cell cycle (the period between cell divisions)? If not, during what phase is it synthesized? How long is that phase?
3. **Predicting** Which organelle or cell structure would you expect to contain the most radioactivity after this experiment? Explain.

UNIVERSAL ACCESS

Inclusion/Special Needs

Show students a picture of a bacterial cell and an animal cell. Talk about the location of DNA in each cell and where DNA replication occurs. Then, discuss situations in which the cell would need copies of its DNA molecule. Elicit from students that replication occurs when new cells are needed, either during healing and growth (mitosis) or during the production of sex cells (meiosis). L1

Less Proficient Readers

Encourage students to outline this section as they read it. Students should include at least two main points for each green head in the section. Students can also use illustrations in their outlines to help describe the main points. Check the outlines to make sure that students have included all Vocabulary terms and Key Concepts.  L2

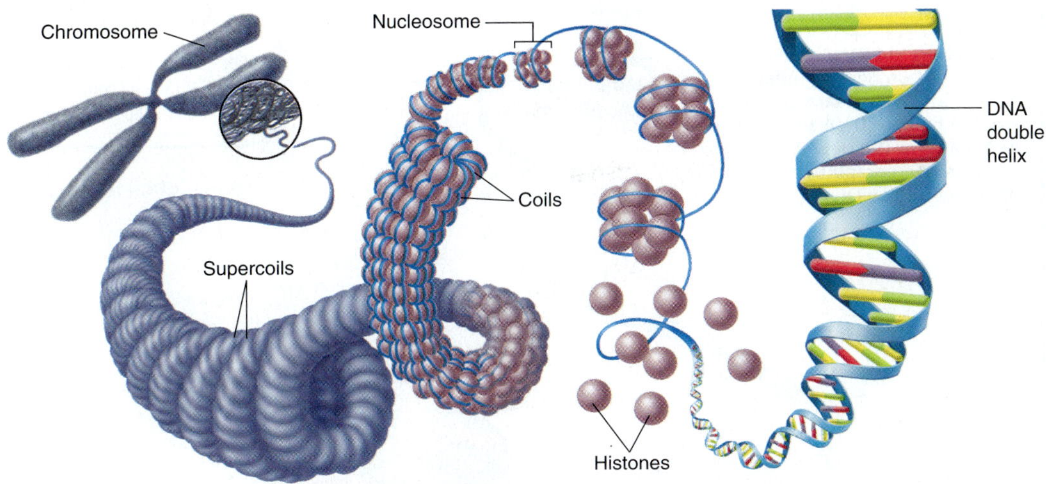

▲ **Figure 12–10** Eukaryotic chromosomes contain DNA wrapped around proteins called histones. The strands of nucleosomes are tightly coiled and supercoiled to form chromosomes. **Interpreting Graphics** *What is each DNA-histone complex called?*

What do nucleosomes do? Nucleosomes seem to be able to fold enormous lengths of DNA into the tiny space available in the cell nucleus. This is such an important function that the histone proteins themselves have changed very little during evolution—probably because mistakes in DNA folding could harm a cell's ability to reproduce.

CHECKPOINT *What is chromatin?*

DNA Replication

When Watson and Crick discovered the double helix structure of DNA, there was one more remarkable aspect that they recognized immediately. The structure explained how DNA could be copied, or replicated. Each strand of the DNA double helix has all the information needed to reconstruct the other half by the mechanism of base pairing. Because each strand can be used to make the other strand, the strands are said to be complementary. If you could separate the two strands, the rules of base pairing would allow you to reconstruct the base sequence of the other strand.

In most prokaryotes, DNA replication begins at a single point in the chromosome and proceeds, often in two directions, until the entire chromosome is replicated. In the larger eukaryotic chromosomes, DNA replication occurs at hundreds of places. Replication proceeds in both directions until each chromosome is completely copied. The sites where separation and replication occur are called replication forks.

For: Links on DNA replication
Visit: www.SciLinks.org
Web Code: cbn-4122

Use Visuals

Figure 12–10 Use Figure 12–10 to reinforce the structure of chromosomes. Ask: **What are chromosomes composed of?** *(Proteins and DNA)* Discuss the role of histones in compacting the DNA molecule. Ask: **What is a nucleosome?** *(A beadlike structure composed of DNA wrapped around a histone molecule)* **Why would it be advantageous to the cell to have its DNA molecules tightly condensed into nucleosomes during mitosis?** *(To prevent the chromatin from tangling and to make separation and division of the chromatin more efficient during mitosis)* Then, challenge students to infer why changes in chromatin structure are associated with gene expression. Help students realize that the DNA molecule must be unwound from the histone molecule so that the individual nucleotide bases can be exposed if the DNA molecule is to be copied or translated into protein. L1 L2

DNA Replication

Download a worksheet on DNA replication for students to complete, and find additional teacher support from NSTA SciLinks.

BIO INSIGHTS — FACTS AND FIGURES

Straight talk about nomenclature
Chromatin is a general term that describes a substance that is made up of DNA, histone and nonhistone proteins, and some RNA that is identified by its special staining properties. Chromosomes are composed of chromatin. Chromosomes have specific structures. Bacteria usually have a single circular chromosome. Multicellular plants and animals have rod-shaped chromosomes. A chromatid is found only in replicated chromosomes after DNA replication has occurred in the S phase of the cell cycle. Chromatids are the two highly visible chromosome replicas held together at their centromeres during prophase and metaphase of mitosis and meiosis.

Answers to . . .

CHECKPOINT *Chromatin is DNA and protein tightly packed together.*

Figure 12–9 *Both situations involve packing a very long, narrow material (the DNA or rope) into a compact space (the bacterium or backpack).*

Figure 12–10 *A nucleosome*

12–2 (continued)

Use Visuals

Figure 12–11 As students examine the diagram of DNA replication, have volunteers explain what a complementary strand of DNA is and what happens when the DNA molecule unzips. *(Hydrogen bonds break.)* Discuss how the strand being copied acts as a template for the new strand being synthesized. Ask: **Why is the new strand complementary to the original strand?** *(It is made up of a base sequence of purines and pyrimidines that match, or base pair, with the sequence of purines and pyrimidines of the original strand.)* Remind students of the tightly wound chromosome structure. Have students infer how chromosome structure might change during replication. *(The nucleosomes unwind.)* L2

Demonstration

Demonstrate that each new DNA molecule is composed of one original strand and one new strand. Use two strands of red yarn to represent the DNA molecule of a chromosome. As you separate the strands of yarn for replication, lay down a new strand of green yarn to represent the replicated strand of DNA. When replication is complete, the result will be two sets of yarn molecules composed of one red strand and one green strand. Explain that these two sets of yarn molecules are connected by centromeres (represent this with a paper clip) until they are separated during mitosis. L1 L2

For: DNA Replication activity
Visit: PHSchool.com
Web Code: cbe-4122
Students learn about DNA replication by producing complementary strands of DNA.

DNA Replication

Figure 12–11 During DNA replication, the DNA molecule produces two new complementary strands. Each strand of the double helix of DNA serves as a template for the new strand. The electron micrograph shows a double strand of human DNA.

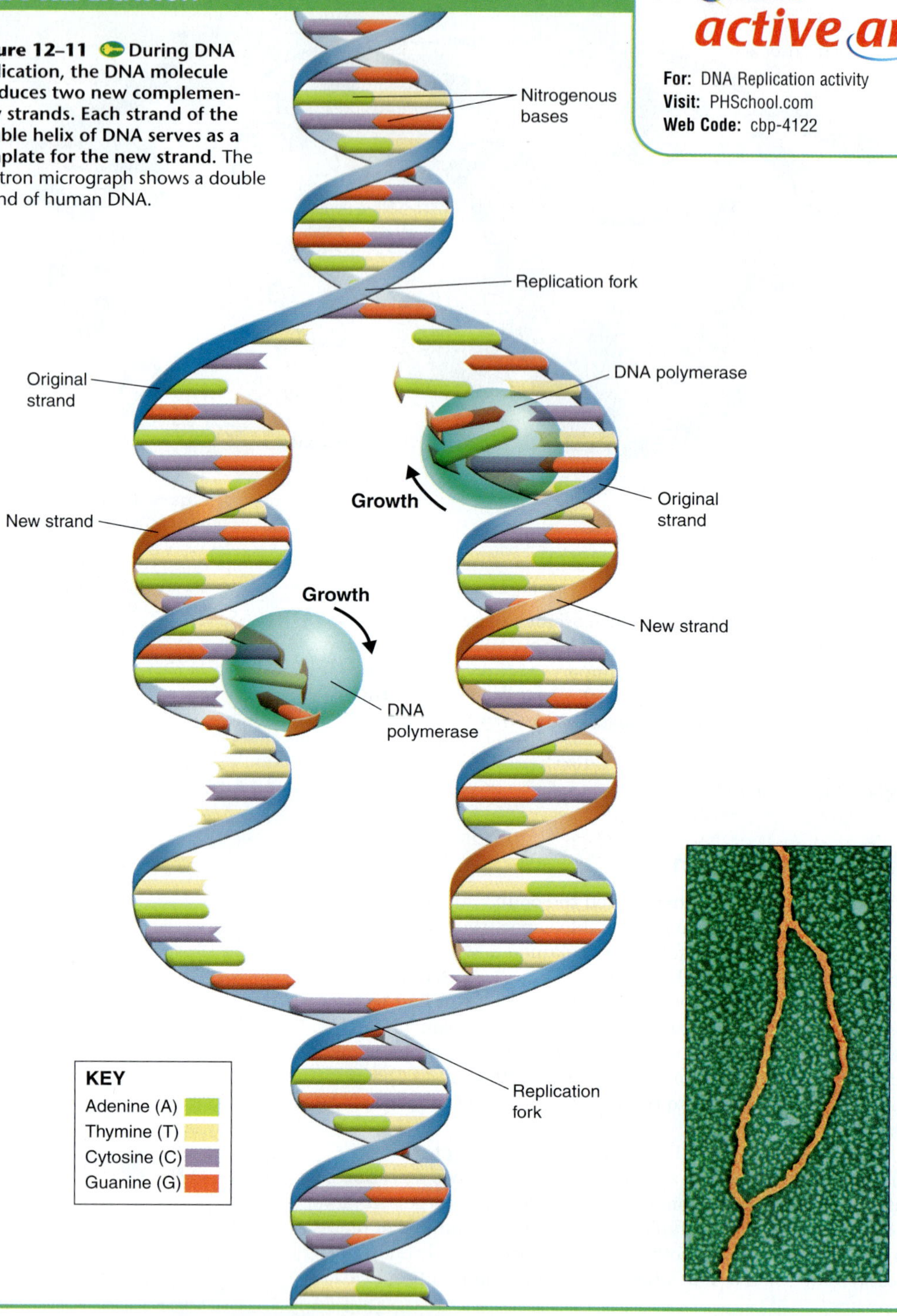

Nitrogenous bases
Replication fork
Original strand
DNA polymerase
Growth
Original strand
New strand
Growth
New strand
DNA polymerase
Replication fork

KEY	
Adenine (A)	green
Thymine (T)	yellow
Cytosine (C)	purple
Guanine (G)	red

Go Online active art

For: DNA Replication activity
Visit: PHSchool.com
Web Code: cbp-4122

FACTS AND FIGURES

Where other genes are located

All the genes in a cell are not located in the nucleus, although for many years scientists thought they were. However, researchers began to notice that some inherited traits—such as Leber disorder, a type of blindness—seem to follow an unusual inheritance pattern. Could the genes for such traits be located somewhere else in the cell? In the 1970s, researchers found that mitochondria and chloroplasts have their own genes that code for proteins.

In the 1980s, Douglas Wallace of Emory University first demonstrated that human mitochondrial DNA is inherited from the mother and later showed that most cases of Leber disorder are due to a mutation in mitochondrial DNA. Other mitochondrial genetic disorders have since been discovered.

Duplicating DNA Before a cell divides, it duplicates its DNA in a copying process called **replication.** This process ensures that each resulting cell will have a complete set of DNA molecules. **During DNA replication, the DNA molecule separates into two strands, and then produces two new complementary strands following the rules of base pairing. Each strand of the double helix of DNA serves as a template, or model, for the new strand.**

Figure 12–11 shows the process of DNA replication. The two strands of the double helix have separated, allowing two replication forks to form. As each new strand forms, new bases are added following the rules of base pairing. In other words, if the base on the old strand is adenine, thymine is added to the newly forming strand. Likewise, guanine is always paired to cytosine.

For example, a strand that has the bases TACGTT produces a strand with the complementary bases ATGCAA. The result is two DNA molecules identical to each other and to the original molecule. Note that each DNA molecule resulting from replication has one original strand and one new strand.

How Replication Occurs DNA replication is carried out by a series of enzymes. These enzymes "unzip" a molecule of DNA. The unzipping occurs when the hydrogen bonds between the base pairs are broken and the two strands of the molecule unwind. Each strand serves as a template for the attachment of complementary bases.

DNA replication involves a host of enzymes and regulatory molecules. You may recall that enzymes are highly specific. For this reason, they are often named for the reactions they catalyze. The principal enzyme involved in DNA replication is called **DNA polymerase** (PAHL-ih-mur-ayz) because it joins individual nucleotides to produce a DNA molecule, which is, of course, a polymer. DNA polymerase also "proofreads" each new DNA strand, helping to maximize the odds that each molecule is a perfect copy of the original DNA.

12–2 Section Assessment

1. **Key Concept** Explain how DNA is replicated.
2. Where and in what form is eukaryotic DNA found?
3. How are the long DNA molecules found in eukaryotes packed into short chromosomes?
4. How are histones related to nucleosomes?
5. What is the role of DNA polymerase in DNA replication?
6. **Critical Thinking Comparing and Contrasting** How is the structure of chromosomes in eukaryotes different from the structure of chromosomes in prokaryotes?

Thinking Visually

Creating a Venn Diagram
Make a Venn diagram that compares the process of DNA replication in prokaryotes and eukaryotes. Compare the location, steps, and end products of the process in each kind of cell. (For more on Venn diagrams, see Appendix A.)

12–2 Section Assessment

1. The DNA molecule separates into two strands, which serve as templates against which the new strands are made, following the rules of base pairing.
2. In the cell nucleus as chromosomes
3. DNA is tightly wound around histones, forming nucleosomes. Nucleosomes are tightly coiled and supercoiled to form chromosomes.
4. Nucleosomes are composed of DNA wound around histones.
5. Polymerizes individual nucleotides to produce DNA
6. Prokaryotes: single, circular DNA molecule; eukaryotes: many chromosomes composed of tightly coiled DNA and proteins called histones

Build Science Skills

Applying Concepts Divide the class into pairs. Instruct each student to write a base pair sequence for one strand of DNA. Partners should exchange their DNA sequences with each other and write the sequence of the complementary strand. Monitor students to be sure they understand the process. L1 L2

3 ASSESS

Evaluate Understanding

Ask students to describe the steps that occur in the process of DNA replication. Ask other students to explain how DNA is packaged to fit inside cells.

Reteach

Have students review Figure 12–10 and Figure 12–11. Encourage them to draw a diagram that combines the ideas described in each figure. Remind students to clearly label their diagrams.

Thinking Visually

In the Venn diagrams, students should describe prokaryotic DNA replication as beginning at a single point and occurring in the cytoplasm. Eukaryotic DNA replication begins in hundreds of places at once and occurs in the nucleus. DNA replication in both eukaryotes and prokaryotes proceeds in both directions, results in two identical strands of DNA, and so on. You might use the diagrams to emphasize that the process of DNA replication is very similar in the two types of cells.

If your class subscribes to the iText, use it to review the Key Concepts in Section 12–2.

Section 12-3

BI 1.d, BI 4.a, BI 4.b, BI 5.a

1 FOCUS

Objectives

12.3.1 ***Tell*** how RNA differs from DNA.

12.3.2 ***Name*** the three main types of RNA.

12.3.3 ***Describe*** transcription and the editing of RNA.

12.3.4 ***Identify*** the genetic code.

12.3.5 ***Summarize*** translation.

12.3.6 ***Explain*** the relationship between genes and proteins.

Guide for Reading

Vocabulary Preview

Ask: **What does it mean to transcribe something?** *(To write a copy of it)* Explain that in transcription, DNA is transcribed to produce a molecule of RNA. Ask: **What does it mean to translate something?** *(To express something in another language)* Explain that the message encoded by RNA is translated into a protein sequence during the process of translation.

Reading Strategy

Encourage students to preview all the figures in the section by carefully reading the captions and studying the diagrams. Remind students to refer to the diagrams while reading the section.

2 INSTRUCT

The Structure of RNA

Use Visuals

Figure 12–12 Have students compare and contrast the structures of the three RNA molecules. Make sure students are aware that rRNA also has nitrogenous bases; the scale of the illustration doesn't allow room for them. Ask: **What do all forms of RNA have in common?** *(Single-stranded chain of nucleotides composed of a ribose sugar, a phosphate group, and a nitrogenous base)* L1 L2

12–3 RNA and Protein Synthesis

BI 1.d. Students know the central dogma of molecular biology outlines the flow of information from transcription of ribonucleic acid (RNA) in the nucleus to translation of proteins on ribosomes in the cytoplasm. **BI 4.a.** Students know the general pathway by which ribosomes synthesize proteins, using tRNAs to translate genetic information in mRNA. **BI 4.b.** Students know how to apply the genetic coding rules to predict the sequence of amino acids from a sequence of codons in RNA. **BI 5.a.** Students know the general structures and functions of DNA, RNA, and protein.

Guide for Reading

Key Concepts
- What are the three main types of RNA?
- What is transcription?
- What is translation?

Vocabulary
gene
messenger RNA
ribosomal RNA
transfer RNA
transcription
RNA polymerase
promoter
intron
exon
codon
translation
anticodon

Reading Strategy: Using Visuals Before you read, preview **Figure 12–18.** As you read, notice what happens in each step of translation, or protein synthesis.

The double helix structure explains how DNA can be copied, but it does not explain how a gene works. In molecular terms, **genes** are coded DNA instructions that control the production of proteins within the cell. The first step in decoding these genetic messages is to copy part of the nucleotide sequence from DNA into RNA, or ribonucleic acid. These RNA molecules contain coded information for making proteins.

(a) BI 5.a

The Structure of RNA

CA (a)

RNA, like DNA, consists of a long chain of nucleotides. As you may recall, each nucleotide is made up of a 5-carbon sugar, a phosphate group, and a nitrogenous base. There are three main differences between RNA and DNA: The sugar in RNA is ribose instead of deoxyribose, RNA is generally single-stranded, and RNA contains uracil in place of thymine.

You can think of an RNA molecule as a disposable copy of a segment of DNA. In many cases, an RNA molecule is a working copy of a single gene. The ability to copy a single DNA sequence into RNA makes it possible for a single gene to produce hundreds or even thousands of RNA molecules.

Types of RNA

RNA molecules have many functions, but in the majority of cells most RNA molecules are involved in just one job—protein synthesis. The assembly of amino acids into proteins is controlled by RNA. **There are three main types of RNA: messenger RNA, ribosomal RNA, and transfer RNA.** The structures of these molecules are shown in **Figure 12–12.**

Figure 12–12 **The three main types of RNA are messenger RNA, ribosomal RNA, and transfer RNA.** Ribosomal RNA is combined with proteins to form ribosomes.

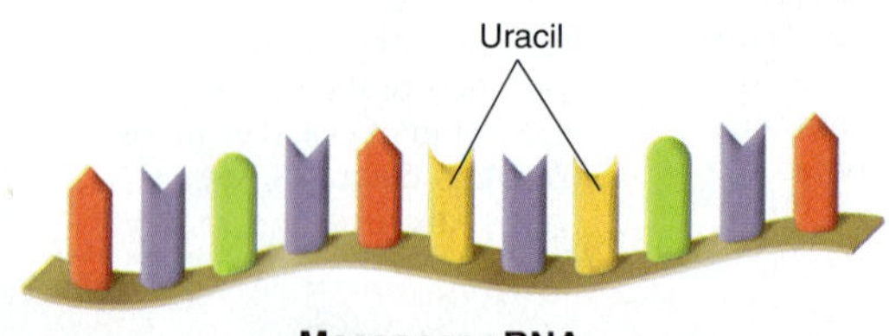

TIME SAVER

SECTION RESOURCES

Print:
- ***Teaching Resources,*** Lesson Plan 12–3, Adapted Section Summary 12–3, Adapted Worksheets 12–3, Section Summary 12–3, Worksheets 12–3, Section Review 12–3
- ***Reading and Study Workbook A,*** Section 12–3
- ***Adapted Reading and Study Workbook B,*** Section 12–3

Technology:
- ***iText,*** Section 12–3
- ***Animated Biological Concepts DVD,*** 25, 26
- ***Transparencies Plus,*** Section 12–3

Most genes contain instructions for assembling amino acids into proteins. The RNA molecules that carry copies of these instructions are known as **messenger RNA** (mRNA) because they serve as "messengers" from DNA to the rest of the cell.

Proteins are assembled on ribosomes, shown in **Figure 12–13.** Ribosomes are made up of several dozen proteins, as well as a form of RNA known as **ribosomal RNA** (rRNA).

During the construction of a protein, a third type of RNA molecule transfers each amino acid to the ribosome as it is specified by coded messages in mRNA. These RNA molecules are known as **transfer RNA** (tRNA).

CHECKPOINT *What are ribosomes made of?*

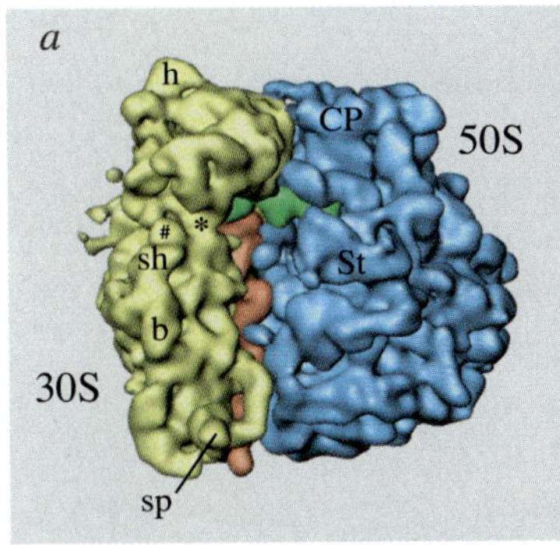

▲ **Figure 12–13** In this detailed model of a ribosome, the two subunits of the ribosome are shown in yellow and blue. The model was produced using cryo-electron microscopy. Data from more than 73,000 electron micrographs, taken at ultra-cold temperatures to preserve ribosome structure, were analyzed to produce the model.

Transcription

RNA molecules are produced by copying part of the nucleotide sequence of DNA into a complementary sequence in RNA, a process called **transcription.** Transcription requires an enzyme known as **RNA polymerase** that is similar to DNA polymerase. **During transcription, RNA polymerase binds to DNA and separates the DNA strands. RNA polymerase then uses one strand of DNA as a template from which nucleotides are assembled into a strand of RNA.** The process of transcription is shown in **Figure 12–14.**

How does RNA polymerase "know" where to start and stop making an RNA copy of DNA? The answer to this question begins with the observation that RNA polymerase doesn't bind to DNA just anywhere. The enzyme will bind only to regions of DNA known as **promoters,** which have specific base sequences. In effect, promoters are signals in DNA that indicate to the enzyme where to bind to make RNA. Similar signals in DNA cause transcription to stop when the new RNA molecule is completed.

▼ **Figure 12–14** **During transcription, RNA polymerase uses one strand of DNA as a template to assemble nucleotides into a strand of RNA.**

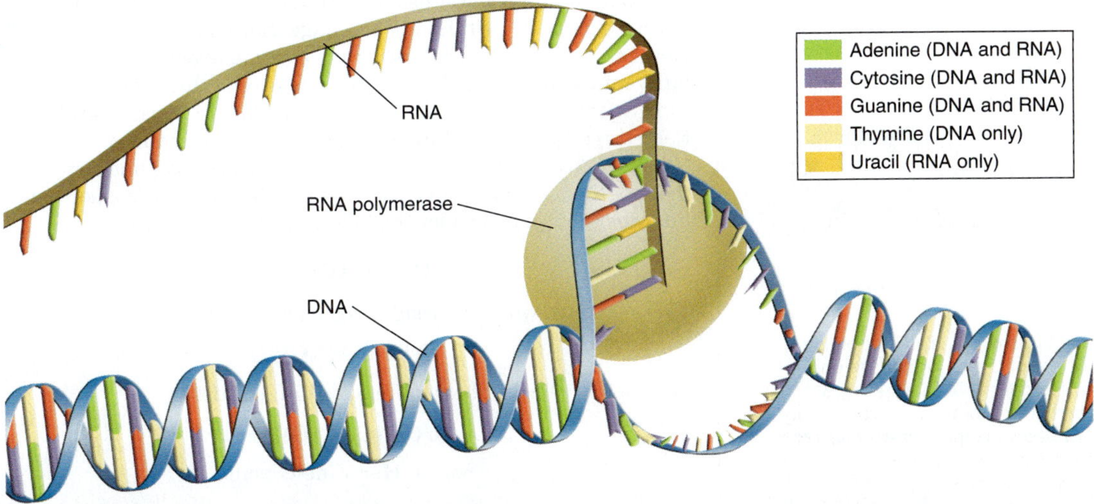

ESL SUPPORT FOR ENGLISH LANGUAGE LEARNERS

Vocabulary: Writing

Beginning Help students understand the functions of—and differences between—messenger RNA, ribosomal RNA, and transfer RNA. Point to each type of RNA in Figures 12–12 and 12–18. Then, pair beginning ESL students with English-proficient students. The pairs can collaborate to make a table that compares the three kinds of RNA (column heads: *Where Located* and *Function*). They can use the two illustrations. L1

Intermediate Have students draw a cell and label the locations of messenger RNA, transfer RNA, and ribosomal RNA. Then, ask students to write explanations of the functions of the three kinds of RNA. Model the process by writing the function of messenger RNA on the board. L2

Types of RNA

Build Science Skills

Predicting Explain that each type of RNA has a specific job in the process of making proteins. Have students examine the structures of each type of RNA molecule. Either provide diagrams of your own or have students look at the diagrams in Figure 12–12. From the structures of each type of RNA, challenge students to predict what function that RNA has in protein synthesis. Students should write their predictions and their reasons for making them. After studying transcription and translation, have students review their predictions.
 L2

Transcription

Use Visuals

Figure 12–14 As students study the diagram, ask: **Where is DNA located in the eukaryotic cell?** *(In the nucleus)* **Where does transcription take place?** *(In the nucleus)* **Where does protein synthesis take place?** *(In the cytoplasm)* Discuss the role of mRNA and its significance as a copy of DNA. Challenge students to consider why DNA stays inside the nucleus and produces expendable copies of RNA that leave the nucleus to direct protein synthesis. L2

Address Misconceptions

Some students might think that mRNA is transcribed from DNA and then processed into tRNA and/or rRNA. Review the roles and the structures of each form of RNA. Point out that rRNA and tRNA must bind to other proteins in the cytoplasm of the cell before they are activated. Emphasize that mRNA is transcribed only from genes that encode proteins. Ribosomal RNA and transfer RNA are transcribed from other genes that cannot be translated into proteins. L1 L2

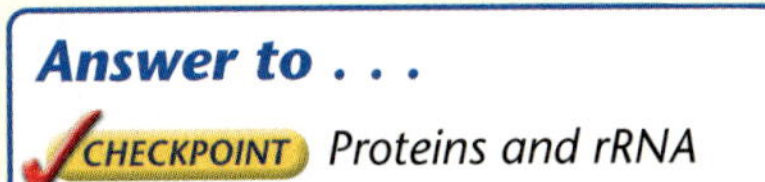

Answer to . . .

CHECKPOINT *Proteins and rRNA*

12–3 (continued)

RNA Editing

Demonstration

Show students what occurs during RNA editing by using a length of string to represent the pre-mRNA molecule. Color the string with markers to show which segments are introns and which are exons. Remind students that this process occurs in the nucleus before the mRNA moves into the cytoplasm. Demonstrate that the introns form loops so that the exons are situated next to each other. Cut the introns off with scissors and tape together the adjacent exons. Then, tape yarn to both ends of the string to represent the cap and the tail added to the mRNA sequence before it leaves the nucleus. L1 L2

The Genetic Code

Build Science Skills

Applying Concepts Give student pairs different sequences of DNA, and tell them that a mutation has occurred in the sequence that changed one of the nucleotide bases. Have students show two possible sites for this mutation, one that affects the protein product and one that does not. Ask students to explain how the genetic code can help prevent some DNA mutations from affecting an organism's phenotypes. Direct them to review Figure 12–17 as they try to formulate their explanation. *(A mutation can change a nucleotide base, but the resulting codon can specify the same amino acid as the original codon.)* L2 L3

Use Visuals

Figure 12–17 Encourage students to closely examine the genetic code in the diagram. Make sure students are reading the diagram correctly to decode a codon. Ask: **What amino acid is specified by CAU?** *(Histidine)* **What is the codon for tryptophan?** *(UGG)* **What are two possible codons for glutamine?** *(CAG, CAA)* **What amino acid is usually the first amino acid of a protein?** *(Methionine)* **How do you know?** *(AUG is the start codon.)* L1 L2

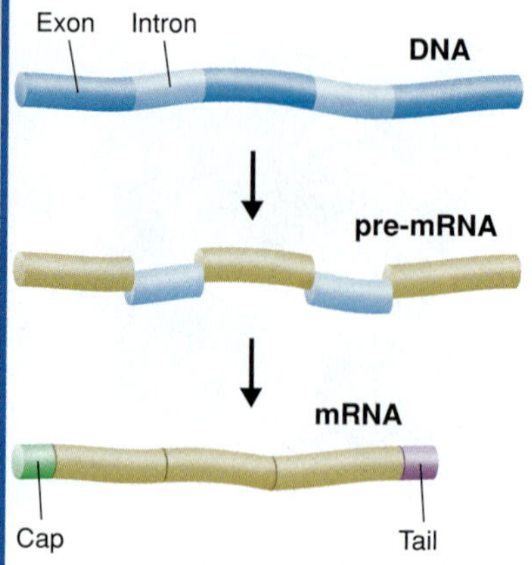

▲ **Figure 12–15** Many RNA molecules have sections, called introns, edited out of them before they become functional. The remaining pieces, called exons, are spliced together. Then, a cap and tail are added to form the final RNA molecule. **Predicting** *What do you think would happen if the introns were not removed from the pre-mRNA?*

RNA Editing

Like a writer's first draft, many RNA molecules require a bit of editing before they are ready to go into action. Remember that an RNA molecule is produced by copying DNA. Surprisingly, the DNA of eukaryotic genes contains sequences of nucleotides, called **introns,** that are not involved in coding for proteins. The DNA sequences that code for proteins are called **exons** because they are "expressed" in the synthesis of proteins. When RNA molecules are formed, both the introns and the exons are copied from the DNA. However, the introns are cut out of RNA molecules while they are still in the nucleus. The remaining exons are then spliced back together to form the final mRNA as shown in **Figure 12–15.**

Why do cells use energy to make a large RNA molecule and then throw parts of it away? That's a good question, and biologists still do not have a complete answer to it. Some RNA molecules may be cut and spliced in different ways in different tissues, making it possible for a single gene to produce several different forms of RNA. Introns and exons may also play a role in evolution. This would make it possible for very small changes in DNA sequences to have dramatic effects in gene expression.

✓CHECKPOINT *What are introns and exons?*

The Genetic Code

Proteins are made by joining amino acids into long chains called polypeptides. Each polypeptide contains a combination of any or all of the 20 different amino acids. The properties of proteins are determined by the order in which different amino acids are joined together to produce polypeptides. How, you might wonder, can a particular order of nitrogenous bases in DNA and RNA molecules be translated into a particular order of amino acids in a polypeptide?

The "language" of mRNA instructions is called the genetic code. As you know, RNA contains four different bases: A, U, C, and G. In effect, the code is written in a language that has only four "letters." How can a code with just four letters carry instructions for 20 different amino acids? The genetic code is read three letters at a time, so that each "word" of the coded message is three bases long. Each three-letter "word" in mRNA is known as a codon, as shown in **Figure 12–16.** A **codon** consists of three consecutive nucleotides that specify a single amino acid that is to be added to the polypeptide. For example, consider the following RNA sequence:

UCGCACGGU

This sequence would be read three bases at a time as:

UCG-CAC-GGU

The codons represent the different amino acids:

UCG-CAC-GGU

Serine-Histidine-Glycine

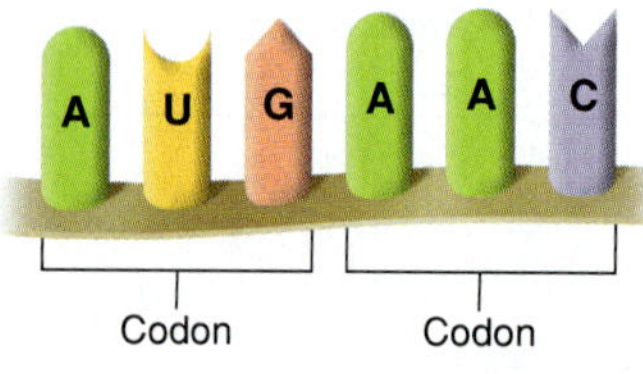

▲ **Figure 12–16** A codon is a group of three nucleotides on messenger RNA that specify a particular amino acid. **Observing** *What are the three-letter groups of the two codons shown here?*

FACTS AND FIGURES

RNA wobble

Cells do not produce 61 tRNA molecules—one for each codon. Most cells produce between 22 and 30 kinds of tRNA. The third nucleotide base in a codon is often called the wobble position, because the strength of the bond between the codon and the anticodon is weak. Because of this weakness, Chargaff's rules can be broken, and bases that would not normally pair up, do. This wobble effect is evident in the genetic code. In many cases, the first two bases are the most important in specifying an amino acid. It often does not matter what the third base is.

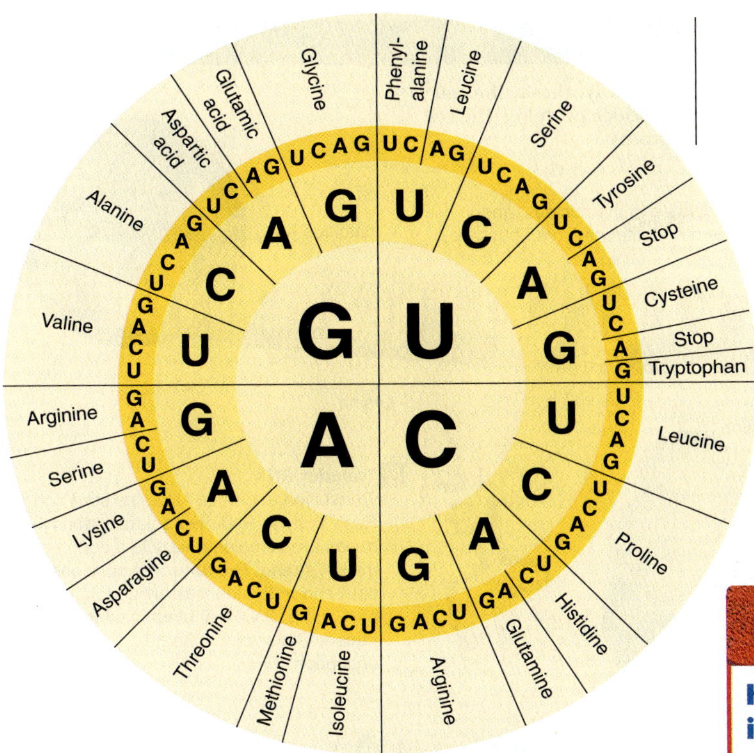

◀ **Figure 12–17** The genetic code shows the amino acid to which each of the 64 possible codons corresponds. To decode a codon, start at the middle of the circle and move outward. **Interpreting Graphics** *For what amino acid does the codon UGC code?*

Because there are four different bases, there are 64 possible three-base codons ($4 \times 4 \times 4 = 64$). **Figure 12–17** shows all 64 possible codons of the genetic code. As you can see, some amino acids can be specified by more than one codon. For example, six different codons specify the amino acid leucine, and six others specify arginine.

There is also one codon, AUG, that can either specify methionine or serve as the initiation, or "start," codon for protein synthesis. Notice also that there are three "stop" codons that do not code for any amino acid. Stop codons act like the period at the end of a sentence; they signify the end of a polypeptide, which consists of many amino acids.

Translation

The sequence of nucleotide bases in an mRNA molecule serves as instructions for the order in which amino acids should be joined together to produce a polypeptide. However, anyone who has tried to assemble a complex toy knows that instructions generally don't do the job themselves. They need something to read them and put them to use. In the cell, that "something" is a tiny factory called the ribosome.

Quick Lab

How does a cell interpret DNA?

Procedure  **BI 4.b**

1. A certain gene has the following sequence of nucleotides:
   GACAAGTCCACAATC
   Write this sequence on a sheet of paper.
2. From left to right, write the sequence of the mRNA molecule transcribed from this gene.
3. Look at **Figure 12–17.** Reading the mRNA codons from left to right, write the amino acid sequence of the polypeptide translated from the mRNA.
4. Repeat step 3, reading the codons from right to left.

Analyze and Conclude

1. **Applying Concepts** Why did steps 3 and 4 produce different polypeptides?
2. **Inferring** Do cells usually decode nucleotides in one direction only or in either direction?

Translation

Build Science Skills

Using Models Give small groups of students a diagram of a simple object to build using colored blocks or other building sets. Explain that the diagram must stay in one spot and the building materials and building site must be in a different spot. Instruct students to devise a method by which they can build the object accurately despite the distance between the building plan and site. L2

Quick Lab

 **BI 4.b**

Objective Students will be able to conclude how a cell interprets DNA. L2

Skills Focus **Applying Concepts, Inferring**

Time 15 minutes

Strategy Diagram a molecule of DNA on the board, or show students a three-dimensional model of one. Show students that ends of the DNA are different and that the molecule is directional. Discuss the importance of the directionalism of DNA and how it affects the sequence of amino acids making up proteins.

Expected Outcomes Students should conclude that translation in both directions yields two different amino acid sequences.

Analyze and Conclude

1. The mRNA sequence is not the same in both directions. Reading the sequence backward specifies a different amino acid sequence.
2. Cells usually decode nucleotides in only one direction.

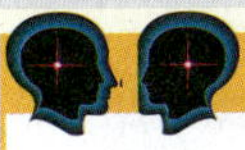

TEACHER TO TEACHER

To help my students better understand how DNA encodes proteins, I like to give them a worksheet on which they practice transcribing and translating DNA. More specifically, I instruct them to write the mRNA sequence of the DNA, then write the tRNA anticodon sequence that is complementary to the mRNA. However, instead of using amino acids, I substitute words so that students produce a sentence instead of a protein sequence. I like to make up sentences such as "I love biology." or "Biology is often fun." I also instruct students to write their own DNA molecules and have their lab partners decode them.

—*James Boal*
Biology Teacher
Natrona County High School
Casper, WY

Answers to . . .

✓CHECKPOINT *Introns: sequences of mRNA not involved in coding for proteins; exons: expressed sequences of mRNA*

Figure 12–15 *The protein would be made incorrectly.*

Figure 12–16 *AUG, AAC*

Figure 12–17 *Cysteine*

12–3 (continued)

Use Visuals

Figure 12–18 As students study the process of translation in the diagram, discuss the roles of mRNA, tRNA, and rRNA. Explain that ribosomes begin translation by binding to mRNA at an initiation site, which includes the start codon, AUG. Also point out that as soon as the initiation site is open on mRNA, another ribosome binds to it and begins translating another polypeptide. For example, B lymphocytes are infection-fighting white blood cells. When stimulated by invading germs, they begin a frenzy of cell division, forming huge numbers of plasma cells. These cells produce vast amounts of protein antibody, each cell secreting 2000 molecules per second throughout its short, four-day life span. Make sure students understand where translation occurs within a cell *(in the cytoplasm).* L2

Download a worksheet on protein synthesis for students to complete, and find additional teacher support from NSTA SciLinks.

Translation

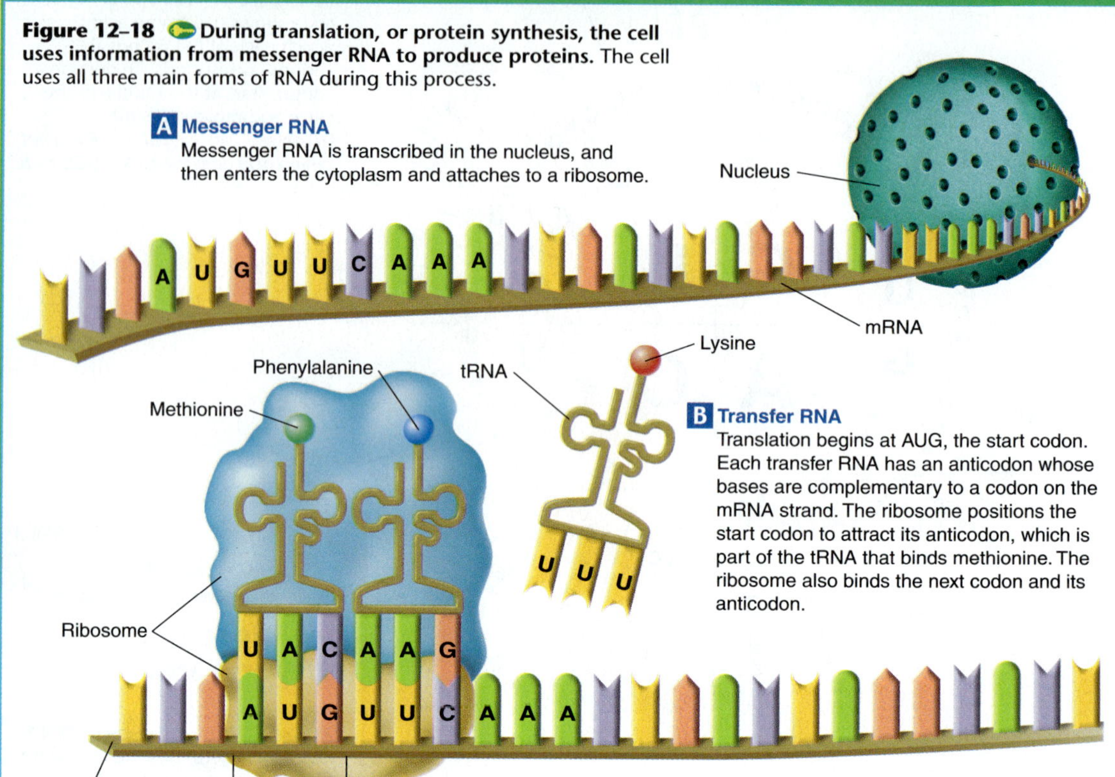

Figure 12–18 **During translation, or protein synthesis, the cell uses information from messenger RNA to produce proteins.** The cell uses all three main forms of RNA during this process.

A Messenger RNA
Messenger RNA is transcribed in the nucleus, and then enters the cytoplasm and attaches to a ribosome.

B Transfer RNA
Translation begins at AUG, the start codon. Each transfer RNA has an anticodon whose bases are complementary to a codon on the mRNA strand. The ribosome positions the start codon to attract its anticodon, which is part of the tRNA that binds methionine. The ribosome also binds the next codon and its anticodon.

For: Links on protein synthesis
Visit: www.SciLinks.org
Web Code: cbn-4123

The decoding of an mRNA message into a polypeptide chain (protein) is known as **translation.** Translation takes place on ribosomes. **During translation, the cell uses information from messenger RNA to produce proteins.** Refer to **Figure 12–18** as you read about translation.

A Before translation occurs, messenger RNA is transcribed from DNA in the nucleus and released into the cytoplasm.

B Translation begins when an mRNA molecule in the cytoplasm attaches to a ribosome. As each codon of the mRNA molecule moves through the ribosome, the proper amino acid is brought into the ribosome by tRNA. In the ribosome, the amino acid is transferred to the growing polypeptide chain.

Each tRNA molecule carries only one kind of amino acid. For example, some tRNA molecules carry methionine, others carry arginine, and still others carry serine. In addition to an amino acid, each tRNA molecule has three unpaired bases. These bases, called the **anticodon,** are complementary to one mRNA codon.

Facts and Figures

The importance of protein synthesis

The synthesis of proteins is a carefully orchestrated and controlled process that begins with a coded message on a DNA molecule. The cell goes to a lot of trouble to synthesize proteins correctly because proteins define what the cell looks like, how it functions, how it grows, and how it passes this information to its daughter cells. Some of the specific roles played by proteins include enzymatic action, transport, motion, protection, support, communication, and regulation.

C The Polypeptide "Assembly Line"
The ribosome joins the two amino acids—methionine and phenylalanine—and breaks the bond between methionine and its tRNA. The tRNA floats away from the ribosome, allowing the ribosome to bind another tRNA. The ribosome moves along the mRNA, binding new tRNA molecules and amino acids.

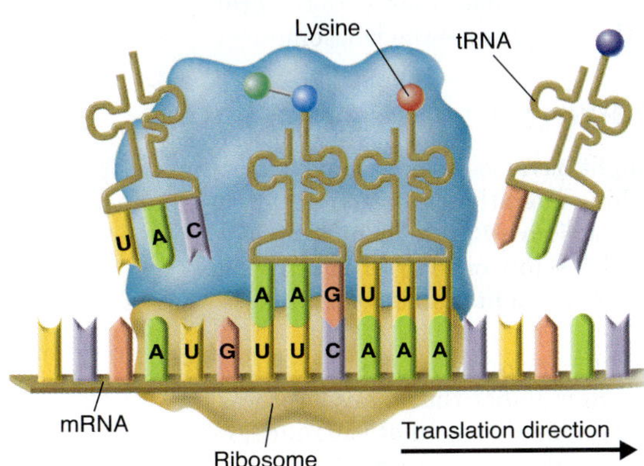

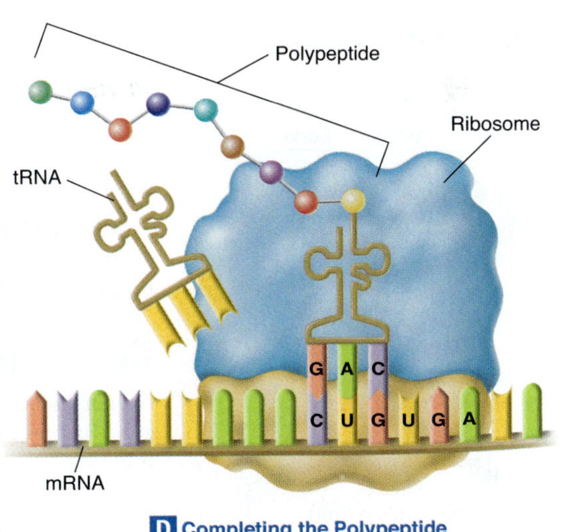

D Completing the Polypeptide
The process continues until the ribosome reaches one of the three stop codons. The result is a complete polypeptide.

Go Online
active art
For: Protein Synthesis activity
Visit: PHSchool.com
Web Code: cbp-4123

In the case of the tRNA molecule for methionine, the anticodon bases are UAC, which pair with the methionine codon, AUG. The ribosome has a second binding site for a tRNA molecule for the next codon. If that next codon is UUC, a tRNA molecule with an AAG anticodon would fit against the mRNA molecule held in the ribosome. That second tRNA molecule would bring the amino acid phenylalanine into the ribosome.

C Like an assembly line worker who attaches one part to another, the ribosome forms a peptide bond between the first and second amino acids, methionine and phenylalanine. At the same time, the ribosome breaks the bond that had held the first tRNA molecule to its amino acid and releases the tRNA molecule. The ribosome then moves to the third codon, where a tRNA molecule brings it the amino acid specified by the third codon.

D The polypeptide chain continues to grow until the ribosome reaches a stop codon on the mRNA molecule. When the ribosome reaches a stop codon, it releases the newly formed polypeptide and the mRNA molecule, completing the process of translation.

Build Science Skills

Asking Questions After studying translation, invite students to choose one component of the process to consider in depth. They might choose a ribosome, tRNA, mRNA, or a step in the process, such as ribosomal binding or elongation of the polypeptide chain. Then, have students write a question or a series of questions about their component of choice. Challenge students to refine their questions so they could potentially be answered by experimentation. L2

Go Online

For: Protein Synthesis activity
Visit: PHSchool.com
Web Code: cbe-4123
Students interact with the art of protein synthesis online.

12–3 (continued)

The Roles of RNA and DNA

Build Science Skills

Using Analogies Have students evaluate the analogy used in the text to compare the roles of RNA and DNA. Ask them how well the analogy describes the roles. Then, challenge small groups of students to develop another analogy to describe the roles of DNA and RNA. Lead the class in a discussion about the accuracy of each group's analogy. L2

Genes and Proteins

Address Misconceptions

Some students might have difficulty visualizing the connections between genes, DNA, and proteins. Take this opportunity to put Gregor Mendel's findings into the context of DNA and RNA. Make sure students understand that proteins cause the phenotypes observed by Mendel. Also, emphasize that a DNA sequence that codes for a protein is a gene. L1 L2

3 ASSESS

Evaluate Understanding

Invite student volunteers to give the steps in the processes of transcription and translation. Write the steps on the board in the form of a flowchart.

Reteach

Have students study the process of translation in Figure 12–18. Instruct them to describe the roles of mRNA, tRNA, and rRNA in the synthesis of proteins. Make sure students know where transcription and translation occur in the cell.

Writing in Science

Students' résumés should clearly describe the functions of each type of RNA.

If your class subscribes to the iText, use it to review the Key Concepts in Section 12–3.

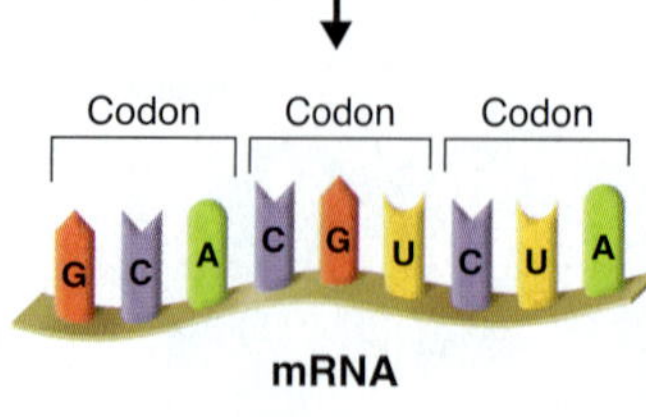

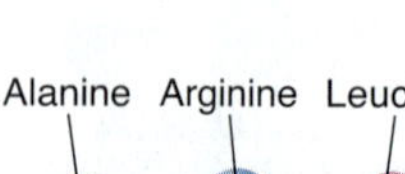

▲ **Figure 12–19** This diagram illustrates how information for specifying the traits of an organism is carried in DNA. The sequence of bases in DNA is used as a template for mRNA. The codons of mRNA specify the sequence of amino acids in a protein, and proteins play a key role in producing an organism's traits.

The Roles of RNA and DNA

You can compare the different roles played by DNA and RNA molecules in directing protein synthesis to the two types of plans used by builders. A master plan has all the information needed to construct a building. But builders never bring the valuable master plan to the building site, where it might be damaged or lost. Instead, they prepare inexpensive, disposable copies of the master plan called blueprints. The master plan is safely stored in an office, and the blueprints are taken to the job site. Similarly, the cell uses the vital DNA "master plan" to prepare RNA "blueprints." The DNA molecule remains within the safety of the nucleus, while RNA molecules go to the protein-building sites in the cytoplasm—the ribosomes.

Genes and Proteins

Gregor Mendel might have been surprised to learn that most genes contain nothing more than instructions for assembling proteins, as shown in **Figure 12–19.** He might have asked what proteins could possibly have to do with the color of a flower, the shape of a leaf, a human blood type, or the sex of a newborn baby.

The answer is that proteins have everything to do with these things. Remember that many proteins are enzymes, which catalyze and regulate chemical reactions. A gene that codes for an enzyme to produce pigment can control the color of a flower. Another gene produces an enzyme specialized for the production of red blood cell surface antigen. This molecule determines your blood type. Genes for certain proteins can regulate the rate and pattern of growth throughout an organism, controlling its size and shape. In short, proteins are microscopic tools, each specifically designed to build or operate a component of a living cell.

12–3 Section Assessment

1. **Key Concept** List the three main types of RNA.
2. **Key Concept** What happens during transcription?
3. **Key Concept** What happens during translation?
4. Describe the three main differences between RNA and DNA.
5. **Critical Thinking Applying Concepts** Using the genetic code, identify the amino acids that have the following messenger RNA strand codes: UGGCAGUGC.

Writing in Science

Creative Writing

An RNA molecule is looking for a job in a protein synthesis factory, and it asks you to write its résumé. This RNA molecule is not yet specialized and could, with some structural changes, function as either mRNA, tRNA, or rRNA. The résumé you create should reflect the qualifications needed for each type of RNA.

12–3 Section Assessment

1. Messenger RNA, transfer RNA, ribosomal RNA
2. RNA polymerase binds to DNA, separates the strands, and then uses one strand as a template to assemble RNA.
3. The cell uses information from messenger RNA to produce proteins.
4. The sugar in RNA is ribose instead of deoxyribose; RNA is generally single-stranded; RNA contains uracil in place of thymine.
5. Tryptophan-glutamine-cysteine

12–4 Mutations

BI 4.c. Students know how mutations in the DNA sequence of a gene may or may not affect the expression of the gene or the sequence of amino acids in the encoded protein.

Now and then cells make mistakes in copying their own DNA, inserting an incorrect base or even skipping a base as the new strand is put together. These mistakes are called **mutations,** from a Latin word meaning "to change."  **Mutations are changes in the genetic material.**

Guide for Reading

Key Concept
- What are mutations?

Vocabulary
mutation
point mutation
frameshift mutation
polyploidy

Reading Strategy: Using Visuals Before you read, preview **Figure 12–20** and **Figure 12–21.** As you read, notice the changes that occur in gene and chromosomal mutations.

Kinds of Mutations

Like the mistakes that people make in their daily lives, mutations come in many shapes and sizes. Mutations that produce changes in a single gene are known as gene mutations. Those that produce changes in whole chromosomes are known as chromosomal mutations.

Gene Mutations Gene mutations involving changes in one or a few nucleotides are known as **point mutations,** because they occur at a single point in the DNA sequence. Point mutations include substitutions, in which one base is changed to another, as well as insertions and deletions, in which a base is inserted or removed from the DNA sequence.

Substitutions usually affect no more than a single amino acid. The effects of insertions or deletions can be much more dramatic. Remember that the genetic code is read in three-base codons. If a nucleotide is added or deleted, the bases are still read in groups of three, but now those groupings are shifted for every codon that follows, as shown in **Figure 12–20.** Changes like these are called **frameshift mutations** because they shift the "reading frame" of the genetic message. By shifting the reading frame, frameshift mutations may change every amino acid that follows the point of the mutation. Frameshift mutations can alter a protein so much that it is unable to perform its normal functions.

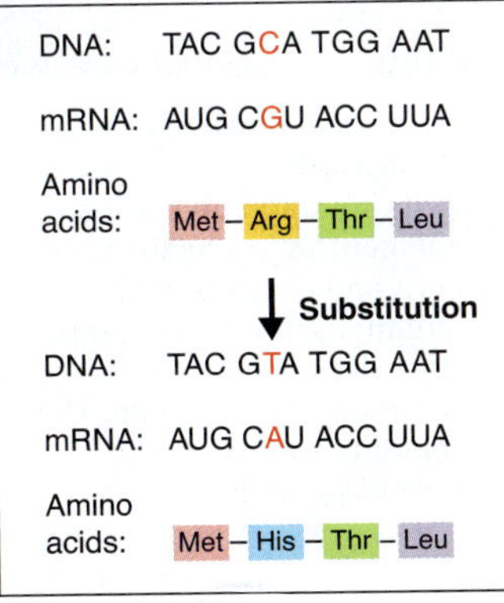

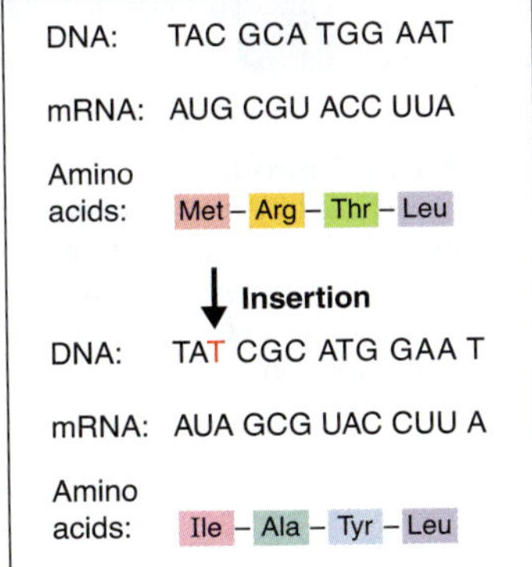

Figure 12–20 **Gene mutations result from changes in a single gene.** These diagrams illustrate the different types of mutations, or changes, in DNA. They also show how the mutations affect the amino acid sequences of the proteins for which they code. In a substitution (left), one base replaces another. In an insertion (center), an extra base is inserted into a base sequence. The loss of a single letter in a sentence (below) models the effects of the deletion of one base in a DNA sequence.

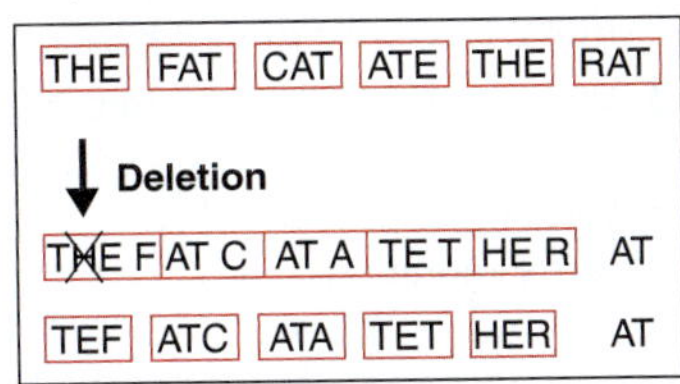

Section 12–4

 BI 4.c

1 FOCUS

Objective

12.4.1 ***Contrast*** gene mutations and chromosomal mutations.

Guide for Reading

Vocabulary Preview

Some students will already know what a mutation is. Ask: **What is a mutation?** *(A change in genetic material)* **What do you think a point mutation is?** *(A mutation that affects one nucleotide)*

Reading Strategy

Encourage students to preview Figures 12–20 and 12–21 and develop a table to note the changes that occur in gene and chromosomal mutations.

2 INSTRUCT

Kinds of Mutations

Build Science Skills

Comparing and Contrasting Encourage students to compare point mutations and frameshift mutations. First, have students write a DNA sequence and show how it is changed by a point mutation and a frameshift mutation. Then, have students compare the mRNA sequence and the protein sequence produced by both "mutated" DNA sequences. Discuss which type of mutation causes more damage and why. *(Frameshift; it changes all codons after the point of the mutation)* L2

Demonstration

Use a thin, clay log composed of different colors to represent different genes on a chromosome, like the one shown in Figure 12–21. Manipulate the clay to show how an inversion can occur. Point out that a translocation requires two different chromosomes. Tell students that these mutations often occur during crossing-over in meiosis. L1 L2

TIME SAVER — SECTION RESOURCES

Print:
- ***Teaching Resources,*** Lesson Plan 12–4, Adapted Section Summary 12–4, Adapted Worksheets 12–4, Section Summary 12–4, Worksheets 12–4, Section Review 12–4
- ***Reading and Study Workbook A,*** Section 12–4
- ***Adapted Reading and Study Workbook B,*** Section 12–4

Technology:
- ***iText,*** Section 12–4
- ***Animated Biological Concepts DVD,*** 27, 28, 29
- ***Transparencies Plus,*** Section 12–4

12–4 (continued)

Significance of Mutations

Build Science Skills

Classifying Have student groups generate five examples of gene mutations and five examples of chromosomal mutations. These examples should include DNA or gene sequences for both the normal and mutated sequences. Have groups exchange examples and then classify the mutations as being possibly harmful, harmless, or even helpful. *(Many inversions and translocations are harmless because all the genes are still present. Many nucleotide substitutions are harmless because of redundancy in the code. Some nucleotide substitutions are harmful. Few mutations are helpful.)* L2

3 ASSESS

Evaluate Understanding

Ask: **What kinds of mutations can occur in organisms?** *(Gene mutations—point and frameshift mutations; chromosomal mutations)* Have students describe the significance of these mutations.

Reteach

Have students review Figures 12–20 and 12–21 and describe the types of mutations. Make sure that students understand the difference between gene mutations and chromosomal mutations.

Writing in Science

Student paragraphs should define each category of mutation and clearly describe the different types of gene mutations and chromosomal mutations and their possible effects on an organism.

If your class subscribes to the iText, use it to review the Key Concepts in Section 12–4.

▼ **Figure 12–21** **Chromosomal mutations involve changes in whole chromosomes.** The illustration below shows four types of chromosomal mutations.

Original chromosome

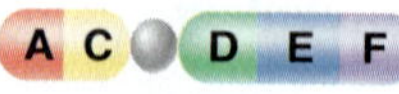

Deletion

A B B C D E F

Duplication

A E D C B F

Inversion

A B C J K L

G H I D E F

Translocation

Chromosomal Mutations Chromosomal mutations involve changes in the number or structure of chromosomes. Such mutations may change the locations of genes on chromosomes, and may even change the number of copies of some genes.

Figure 12–21 shows four types of chromosomal mutations: deletions, duplications, inversions, and translocations. Deletions involve the loss of all or part of a chromosome, while duplications produce extra copies of parts of a chromosome. Inversions reverse the direction of parts of chromosomes, and translocations occur when part of one chromosome breaks off and attaches to another.

Significance of Mutations

Many, if not most, mutations are neutral, meaning that they have little or no effect on the expression of genes or the function of the proteins for which they code. Mutations that cause dramatic changes in protein structure or gene activity are often harmful, producing defective proteins that disrupt normal biological activities. However, mutations are also the source of genetic variability in a species. Some of this variation may be highly beneficial.

Mutations are the causes of many genetic disorders, including sickle cell disease and cystic fibrosis, both discussed in Chapter 14. Harmful mutations are also associated with many types of cancer. In contrast, beneficial mutations may produce proteins with new or altered activities that can be useful in changing environments. One such mutation produces resistance to HIV, the virus that causes AIDS.

Plant and animal breeders often take advantage of such beneficial mutations. For example, when a complete set of chromosomes fails to separate during meiosis, the gametes that result may produce triploid (3N) or tetraploid (4N) organisms. The condition in which an organism has extra sets of chromosomes is called **polyploidy.** Polyploid plants are often larger and stronger than diploid plants. Important crop plants have been produced in this way, including bananas and many citrus fruits.

12–4 Section Assessment

1. **Key Concept** What is a mutation?
2. What is the significance of mutations to living things?
3. What are two kinds of frameshift mutations?
4. What are four types of chromosomal mutations?
5. **Critical Thinking Inferring** The effects of a mutation are not always visible. How might a biologist determine whether a mutation has occurred, and if so, what type of mutation it is?

Writing in Science

Compare/Contrast Paragraph

Write a paragraph comparing and contrasting gene mutations and chromosomal mutations. *Hint:* To organize your ideas, use a compare/contrast table. The column heads might be *Definition, Types,* and *Effects.*

12–4 Section Assessment

1. A change in genetic material.
2. Mutations can be harmful by producing defective proteins that disrupt normal biological activities. Mutations are also the source of genetic variability and can be beneficial.
3. Two kinds of frameshift mutations are insertions and deletions.
4. Four kinds of chromosomal mutations are deletions, duplications, inversions, and translocations.
5. A researcher could compare the DNA sequence of normal DNA to that of the mutated DNA. The base sequence should reveal the type of mutation.

12–5 Gene Regulation

BI 4.d. Students know specialization of cells in multicellular organisms is usually due to different patterns of gene expression rather than to differences of the genes themselves.

Only a fraction of the genes in a cell are expressed at any given time. An expressed gene is a gene that is transcribed into RNA. How does the cell determine which genes will be expressed and which will remain "silent"? A close look at the structure of a gene provides some important clues.

At first glance, the DNA sequence of a gene is nothing more than a confusing jumble of the four letters that represent the bases in DNA. However, if we take the time to analyze those letters, patterns emerge. Molecular biologists have found that certain DNA sequences serve as promoters, binding sites for RNA polymerase. Others serve as start and stop signals for transcription. In fact, cells are filled with DNA-binding proteins that attach to specific DNA sequences and help to regulate gene expression. A typical gene might look something like **Figure 12–22.**

As we've seen, there is a promoter just to one side of the gene. But what are the "regulatory sites" next to the promoter? These are places where other proteins, binding directly to the DNA sequences at those sites, can regulate transcription. The actions of these proteins help to determine whether a gene is turned on or turned off.

Guide for Reading

Key Concepts

- How are *lac* genes turned off and on?
- How are most eukaryotic genes controlled?

Vocabulary

operon
operator
differentiation
hox gene

Reading Strategy: Outlining Before you read, use the headings of the section to make an outline about gene regulation. As you read, fill in subtopics and smaller topics. Then, add phrases or a sentence after each subtopic to provide key information.

Gene Regulation: An Example

How does an organism "know" whether to turn a gene on or off? The common bacterium *E. coli* provides us with a perfect example of how gene expression can be regulated. The 4288 protein-encoding genes in this bacterium include a cluster of three genes that are turned on or off together. A group of genes that operate together is known as an **operon.** Because these genes must be expressed in order for the bacterium to be able to use the sugar lactose as a food, they are called the *lac* operon.

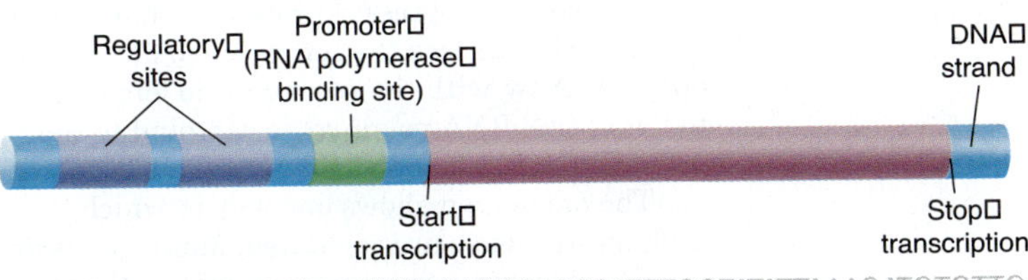

GAATTCTAATCTCCCTCTCAACCCTACAGTCACCCATTTGGTATATTAAAGATGTGTTG
TCTACTGTCTAGTATCCCTCAAGTAGTGTCAGGAATTAGTCATTTAAATAGTCTGCAAG
CCAGGAGTGGTGGCTCATGTCTGTAATTCCAGCACTGGAGAGGTAGAAGTGGGAG
GACTGCTTGAGCTCAAGAGTTTGATATTATCCTGGACAACATAGCAAGACCTCGTCT
CTACTTAAAAAAAAAAAAAATTAGCCAGGCATGTGATGTACACCTGTAGTCCCAGCTAC
TCAGGAGGCCGAAATGGGAGGATCCCTTGAGCTCAGGAGGTCAAGGCTGCAGTGA
GACATGATCTTGCCACTGCACTCCAGCCTGGACAGCAGAGTGAAACCTTGCCTCAC
GAAACAGAATACAAAAACAAACAAACAAAAAACTGCTCCGCAATGCGCTTCCTTGAT
GCTCTACCACATAGGTCTGGGTACTTT

◀ **Figure 12–22** A typical gene includes start and stop signals, with the nucleotides to be translated in between. The DNA sequence shown is only a very small part of an actual gene. **Interpreting Graphics** *What is the function of the promoter?*

Section Resources

Print:

- ***Teaching Resources,*** Lesson Plan 12–5, Adapted Section Summary 12–5, Adapted Worksheets 12–5, Section Summary 12–5, Worksheets 12–5, Section Review 12–5
- ***Reading and Study Workbook A,*** Section 12–5
- ***Adapted Reading and Study Workbook B,*** Section 12–5
- ***Biotechnology Manual,*** Lab 13

Technology:

- ***iText,*** Section 12–5
- ***Transparencies Plus,*** Section 12–5

Section 12–5

BI 4.d

1 FOCUS

Objectives

12.5.1 ***Describe*** a typical gene.
12.5.2 ***Describe*** how the *lac* genes are turned off and on.
12.5.3 ***Explain*** how most eukaryotic genes are controlled.
12.5.4 ***Relate*** gene regulation to development.

Guide for Reading

Vocabulary Preview

Have students write the terms *operon* and *operator,* noting their difference. As students read, they can write tips to help themselves distinguish the terms. (Example: Operon means genes act as one)

Reading Strategy

As students complete their outlines, encourage them to include sketches of the diagrams in the section. Students should label the sketches as they are labeled in the text.

2 INSTRUCT

Gene Regulation: An Example

Use Visuals

Figure 12–22 As students examine the structure of a typical gene in the diagram, have volunteers describe the function of each part. Ask: **What codon sequence would you expect to find in the mRNA at the place where transcription starts?** *(AUG, the start codon)* **At the place where transcription ends?** *(Any one of the three stop codons—UAA, UAG, or UGA)* **What kinds of molecules bind to the regulatory sites of genes?** *(DNA-binding proteins)* **What is the action of these proteins on genes?** *(They turn genes off or on.)* L2

Answer to . . .

Figure 12–22 *It's the RNA polymerase binding site.*

12–5 (continued)

Use Visuals

Figure 12–23 Reinforce the operation of the *lac* operon by diagramming the illustration on the board while students follow along in their textbooks. Ask: **When is the repressor protein bound to the operator?** *(When lactose is not present)* **Can transcription occur when the repressor is bound to the operator?** *(No)* **Why not?** *(The repressor protein blocks RNA polymerase from binding to the promoter.)* **How does the presence of lactose help start transcription of the *lac* genes?** *(Lactose binds to the repressor protein, causing it to release from the operator site, and RNA polymerase can bind to the promoter.)* You may wish to discuss what inactivates a *lac* operon once it has become active. The enzymes produced by the active *lac* operon eventually digest the lactose, including the molecules that had bound up the repressor protein. Once this happens, the repressors again bind the operator, and the operon closes down. L2

Build Science Skills

Inferring Help students realize how efficiently the cell is able to control its production of proteins involved in the utilization of lactose. Challenge students to make inferences about why the cell has evolved such an elaborate method of gene regulation. Have them consider why regulating the production of proteins that utilize lactose is advantageous to the cell. They can also consider why it is not advantageous to produce the *lac* proteins continuously. L2 L3

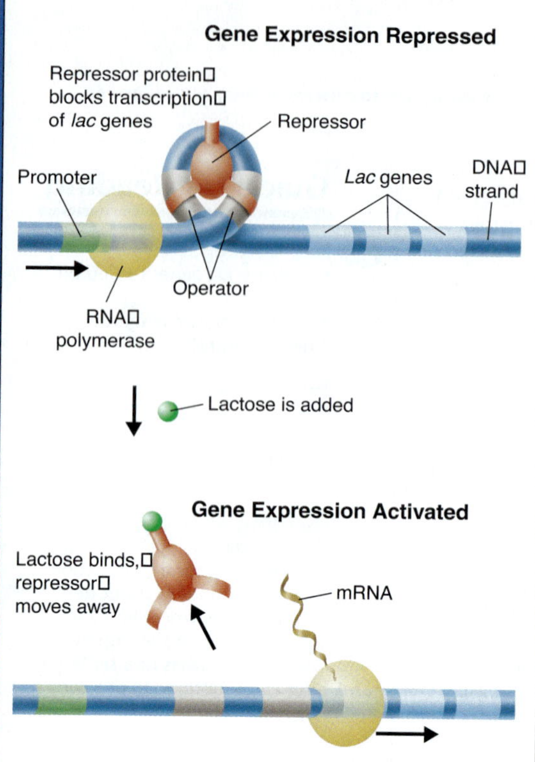

▲ **Figure 12–23** **The *lac* genes in *E. coli* are turned off by repressors and turned on by the presence of lactose.** When lactose is not present, the repressor binds to the operator region, preventing RNA polymerase from beginning transcription. Lactose causes the repressor to be released from the operator region.

Why must *E. coli* turn on the *lac* genes in order to use lactose for food? Lactose is a compound made up of two simple sugars, galactose and glucose. To use lactose for food, the bacterium must take lactose across its cell membrane and then break the bond between glucose and galactose. These tasks are performed by proteins coded for by the genes of the *lac* operon. This means, of course, that if the bacterium is grown in a medium where lactose is the only food source, it must transcribe the genes and produce these proteins. If grown on another food source, such as glucose, it would have no need for these proteins.

Remarkably, the bacterium almost seems to "know" when the products of these genes are needed. **The *lac* genes are turned off by repressors and turned on by the presence of lactose.** This process tells us a great deal about how genes are regulated.

On one side of the operon's three genes are two regulatory regions. In the promoter (P), RNA polymerase binds and then begins transcription. The other region is the **operator** (O). *E. coli* cells contain several copies of a DNA-binding protein known as the *lac* repressor, which can bind to the O region. As **Figure 12–23** shows, when the *lac* repressor binds to the O region, RNA polymerase is prevented from beginning the process of transcription. In effect, the binding of the repressor protein turns the operon "off" by preventing the transcription of its genes.

If the repressor protein is always present, how are the *lac* genes turned on in the presence of lactose? Besides its DNA binding site, the *lac* repressor protein has a binding site for lactose itself. When lactose is added to the medium in which *E. coli* is growing, sugar molecules diffuse into the cell and bind to the repressor proteins. This causes the repressor protein to change shape in a way that causes the repressor to fall off the operator. Now, with the repressor no longer bound to the O site, RNA polymerase can bind to the promoter and transcribe the genes of the operon.

The *lac* operon shows one way in which prokaryotic genes are regulated. Many genes are regulated by repressor proteins, while others use proteins that speed transcription. Sometimes regulation occurs at the level of protein synthesis. Regardless of the system, the result is the same: Cells turn their genes on and off as needed.

CHECKPOINT *What is the operator?*

UNIVERSAL ACCESS

Inclusion/Special Needs
Have students model the action of the repressor protein, lactose, and RNA polymerase on the *lac* operon. Students can use a pipe cleaner to represent the *lac* operon and beads connected to paper clips to represent the repressor protein, RNA polymerase, and lactose. They can use a marker to color-code the promoter, the operator, and the *lac* genes on the pipe cleaner, using Figure 12–23 as a guide. L1

Advanced Learners
Students can use library and Internet sources for additional research on topics from this section. Topics in prokaryotic gene expression *(E. coli)* include the *trp* operon and the regulation of the *lac* operon by the cAMP receptor protein. Topics in eukaryotic gene expression include control of development, formation of antibodies, and causes of cancer. Students can develop a poster presentation of their findings. L3

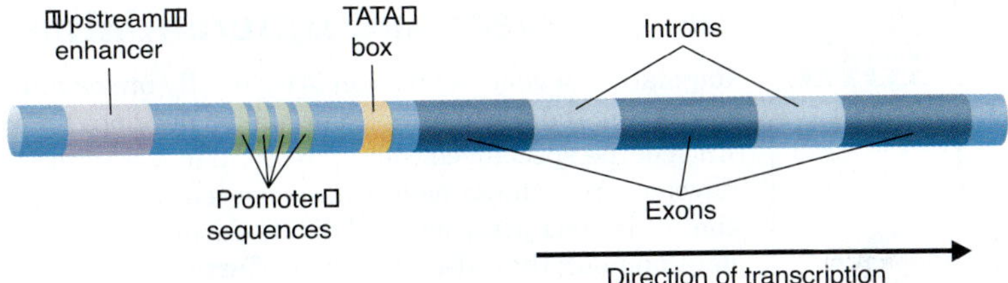

Figure 12–24 Many eukaryotic genes include a sequence called the TATA box that may help position RNA polymerase. **Eukaryotic genes have regulatory sequences that are more complex than prokaryotic genes.**

Eukaryotic Gene Regulation

The general principles of gene regulation in prokaryotes also apply to eukaryotic cells, although there are some important differences. Operons are generally not found in eukaryotes. **Most eukaryotic genes are controlled individually and have regulatory sequences that are much more complex than those of the *lac* operon.**

Figure 12–24 shows some of the features of a typical eukaryotic gene. One of the most interesting is a short region of DNA about 30 base pairs long, containing a sequence of TATATA or TATAAA, before the start of transcription. This region is found before so many eukaryotic genes that it even has a name: the "TATA box." The TATA box seems to help position RNA polymerase by marking a point just before the point at which transcription begins. Eukaryotic promoters are usually found just before the TATA box, and they consist of a series of short DNA sequences.

Genes are regulated in a variety of ways by enhancer sequences located before the point at which transcription begins. An enormous number of proteins can bind to different enhancer sequences, which is why eukaryotic gene regulation is so complex. Some of these DNA-binding proteins enhance transcription by opening up tightly packed chromatin. Others help to attract RNA polymerase. Still other proteins block access to genes, much like prokaryotic repressor proteins.

Why is gene regulation in eukaryotes more complex than in prokaryotes? Think for a moment about the way in which genes are expressed in a multicellular organism. The genes that code for liver enzymes, for example, are not expressed in nerve cells. Keratin, an important protein in skin cells, is not produced in blood cells. Cell specialization requires genetic specialization, but all of the cells in a multicellular organism carry the complete genetic code in their nucleus. Therefore, for proper overall function, only a tiny fraction of the available genes needs to be expressed in the appropriate cells of different tissues throughout the body. The complexity of gene regulation in eukaryotes makes this specificity possible.

Eukaryotic Gene Regulation

Build Science Skills

Forming Operational Definitions Challenge students to write an operational definition for a eukaryotic gene. In their definitions, students should include all the parts that make up a eukaryotic gene, including enhancer sequences, promoter sequences, the TATA box, introns, and exons. L2

Address Misconceptions

Many students might think that all genes are expressed in all cells of a eukaryotic organism. Help students understand that not every gene is expressed in every body cell. Explain that the pancreas secretes many digestive enzymes, such as amylase, which help break down starches. Expression of the amylase-coding gene in the pancreas enables it to perform one of its main functions—secreting this starch-digesting enzyme. However, the same gene in bone marrow cells and in most other body cells has never been activated, so those cells do not secrete amylase. The activated genes in bone marrow and other cells respond to different conditions, and each produces its own appropriate proteins. L1 L2

Answer to . . .

CHECKPOINT *The operator is a region to which a repressor can bind, preventing transcription of the genes.*

12–5 (continued)

Development and Differentiation

Build Science Skills

Formulating Hypotheses
Challenge students to devise a hypothesis that describes how a hox gene might be regulated. To help them get started, suggest that they review the way in which eukaryotic genes are regulated. Encourage students to diagram the method of regulation that they hypothesize. L2 L3

3 ASSESS

Evaluate Understanding

Instruct students to make a table in which they compare and contrast the regulation of gene expression in prokaryotes and eukaryotes.

Reteach

Have students sketch the regulation of the *lac* operon, using the diagram in Figure 12–23. Students should label their sketch with the parts of the operon and describe the functions of each part.

Writing in Science

In one possible analogy, students might compare the *lac* operon to a lamp, in which the promoter is the electricity, the operator is the lamp socket, the repressor is the lamp switch in the "off" position, and lactose is the lamp switch in the "on" position. Even if student analogies do not carry through all of the components of the *lac* operon, students will internalize the main concepts of the model in the process of creating the analogy.

If your class subscribes to the iText, use it to review the Key Concepts in Section 12–5.

Answer to . . .

Figure 12–25 *Rear section*

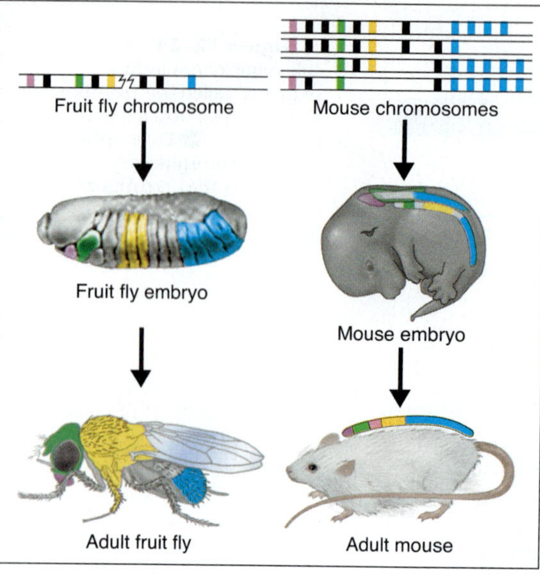

▲ **Figure 12–25** In fruit flies, a series of hox genes along a chromosome determines the basic structure of the fly's body. Mice have very similar genes on four different chromosomes. The color bars along the mouse's back show the approximate body area affected by genes of the corresponding colors. **Interpreting Graphics** *What section of the bodies of flies and mice is coded by the genes shown in blue?*

Development and Differentiation

Regulation of gene expression is especially important in shaping the way a complex organism develops. Each of the specialized cell types found in the adult develops from the same fertilized egg cell. This means that cells don't just grow and divide during embryonic development; they also undergo **differentiation,** meaning they become specialized in structure and function. The study of genes that control development and differentiation is one of the most exciting areas in biology today.

A series of genes, known as the **hox genes,** control the differentiation of cells and tissues in the embryo. A mutation in one of these "master control genes" can completely change the organs that develop in specific parts of the body. Mutations affecting the hox genes in the fruit fly, *Drosophila,* for example, can replace the fly's antennae with legs growing on its head!

In flies, the hox genes are located side-by-side in a single cluster, as shown in **Figure 12–25.** Remarkably, similar clusters exist in the DNA of other animals, including humans. The function of the hox genes in humans seems to be almost the same—to tell the cells of the body how they should differentiate as the body grows. Careful control of expression in these genes is essential for normal development.

The striking similarity of genes that control development has a simple scientific explanation: Common patterns of genetic control exist because all these genes have descended from the genes of common ancestors. One such gene, called Pax 6, controls eye growth in *Drosophila*. A similar gene was found to guide eye growth in mice and other mammals. When a copy of the mouse gene was inserted into the "knee" of a *Drosophila* embryo, the resulting fruit fly grew an eye on its leg! The fly gene and the mouse gene are similar enough to trade places and still function—even though they come from animals that have not shared a common ancestor in at least 600 million years.

12–5 Section Assessment

1. **Key Concept** How is the *lac* operon regulated?
2. **Key Concept** Describe how most eukaryotic genes are controlled.
3. What genes control cell differentiation during development?
4. What is a promoter?
5. **Critical Thinking Comparing and Contrasting** How is the way hox genes are expressed in mice similar to the way they are expressed in fruit flies? How is it different?

Writing in Science

Making an Analogy
Make an analogy to demonstrate the different components of the *lac* operon. Then, explain in a short paragraph—using your analogy—how the *lac* operon works.

12–5 Section Assessment

1. It is turned off by repressors and turned on by the presence of lactose.
2. Most are controlled individually and have regulatory sequences that are much more complex than those of the *lac* operon.
3. The hox genes
4. The region of mRNA where RNA polymerase binds and starts transcription
5. The genes themselves are very similar and have the same function. In fruit flies, the genes are located on one chromosome. In mice, the genes are spread among four chromosomes.

Exploration

BI 5.b, 6IIE 7.e, 8IIE 9.b, BIIE 1.g

Modeling DNA Replication

Living cells synthesize exact copies of DNA molecules that are passed on to each daughter cell during cell division. In this investigation, you will model DNA replication.

Problem How is DNA replicated?

Materials

- construction paper (tan, gray, green, yellow, red, and purple)
- metric ruler
- scissors
- transparent tape

Skills Using Models

Procedure

1. Cut out rectangles of construction paper in the sizes and colors indicated below:

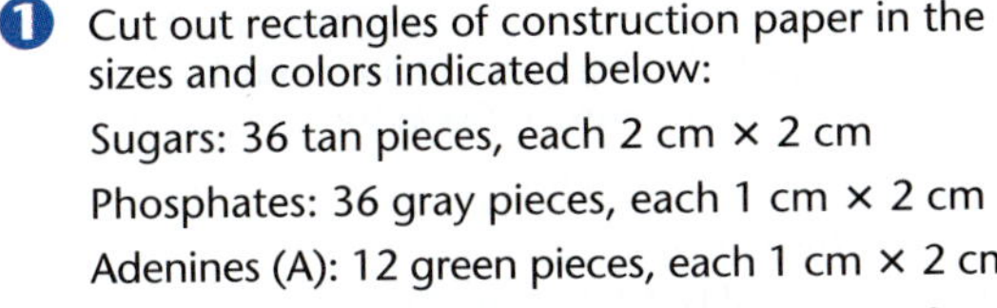

Sugars: 36 tan pieces, each 2 cm × 2 cm
Phosphates: 36 gray pieces, each 1 cm × 2 cm
Adenines (A): 12 green pieces, each 1 cm × 2 cm
Thymines (T): 12 yellow pieces, each 1 cm × 2 cm
Guanines (G): 6 red pieces, each 1 cm × 2 cm
Cytosines (C): 6 purple pieces, each 1 cm × 2 cm

2. To model a nucleotide, tape together a phosphate group, a sugar, and a guanine (G) molecule (see **Figure 12–5**).
3. Assemble eight additional nucleotide models with the following nitrogenous bases: 3 thymines (T); 3 adenines (A); 2 cytosines (C).
4. To model a single strand of DNA, tape the sugar of each nucleotide to the phosphate group of the next nucleotide in the following order: G T T A C A A T C.
5. Construct a strand of DNA that is complementary to the first strand. Tape the nucleotides of the second strand together as you did in step 4. Record the positions of the bases in both strands of your model.
6. Place the two strands side by side so that their complementary nucleotides face each other. Do not tape the two strands together. Write "original" on each strand.
7. Separate the two strands. Simulate the action of DNA polymerase by constructing a new complementary strand for each original strand.
8. Tape the bases of each new strand to the complementary bases of its matching strand.

Analyze and Conclude

1. **Comparing and Contrasting** Compare the new double-stranded DNA models with your original DNA model. Are their nucleotide sequences identical?
2. **Using Models** After a cell's DNA is replicated, the cell may divide in two. Each new cell receives one copy of the original cell's DNA. According to your model, how are the new strands and the original strands divided between the two new cells?
3. **Drawing Conclusions** What problems would you expect to occur if DNA was not copied accurately as it is replicated?
4. **Evaluating** Do you consider this procedure an adequate model of DNA replication? Explain your answer.
5. **Using Models** Describe an alternative way of modeling DNA replication.

Go Further

Using Models Cells use the information in DNA to make proteins. First, part of the nucleotide sequence of DNA is copied into a complementary sequence of RNA in the process of transcription. Then, during translation, the cell uses information in the RNA to make proteins. Modify your model or make a new model to show how transcription and translation occur.

Exploration

BI 5.b, 6IIE 7.e, 8IIE 9.b, BIIE 1.g

Objective Students will be able to use models to determine how DNA is replicated. L2

Skill Focus Using Models

Time 45 minutes

Pre-Lab Discussion Review how DNA is replicated. Invite volunteers to describe the steps in the process. Ask: **How does the structure of DNA make it easy to copy?** *(The weak hydrogen bonds holding the two strands are easily broken to separate the strands. The sequence of base pairs specifies the synthesis of a new strand because of Chargaff's base-pairing rules.)*

Teaching Tip Monitor students as they construct their models to make sure they understand how the DNA molecule is assembled.

Procedure

4. The color sequence of the DNA model should be red-yellow-yellow-green-purple-green-green-yellow-purple.
5. Color sequence should be purple-green-green-yellow-red-yellow-yellow-green-red.

Expected Outcomes Students should construct two strands of DNA that have a complementary sequence to the two original DNA strands.

Analyze and Conclude

1. Yes, the new DNA sequence should be identical to the original sequence.
2. Each cell receives a DNA molecule consisting of a new strand and an original strand.
3. Mutations would occur that might affect the functions of the proteins specified by the DNA sequence. These mutations could affect the life of the cell.
4. Students may say that the procedure modeled DNA replication fairly well because all the steps of DNA replication could be shown, including the structure of DNA, complementary nucleotides, and the action of DNA polymerase in forming a new strand of DNA.
5. Students' models should accurately represent DNA replication.

Go Further

Student models will vary but should show how transcription and translation occur.

Chapter 12 Study Guide

Study Tip

Have students make a glossary for the Vocabulary terms in which they use their own words for the definitions. Also, encourage students to use illustrations or mnemonics to help them remember meanings.

Thinking Visually

1. The mRNA enters the cytoplasm and attaches to a ribosome.
2. The tRNA anticodon matches with the mRNA codon in the ribosome. The ribosome assembles the amino acids brought by tRNA.

Chapter 12 Assessment

Reviewing Content

1. c	4. c	7. b	10. b
2. d	5. a	8. c	
3. b	6. d	9. b	

Understanding Concepts

11. Genes carry information from one generation to the next, determine heritable characteristics, and are replicated easily.

12. DNA is a long molecule made up of nucleotides. Each nucleotide has three parts: a 5-carbon sugar called deoxyribose, a phosphate group, and a nitrogenous base. The four nitrogenous bases are adenine and guanine, which are purines, and cytosine and thymine, which are pyrimidines.

13. The two strands of DNA are held together by hydrogen bonds between certain bases—A and T, and G and C—which explained Chargaff's rules.

14. Base pairing is the principle that hydrogen bonds form only between certain base pairs—A and T, and C and G. In DNA replication, base pairing ensures that the complementary strands produced are identical to the original strands.

15. A prokaryote has a single, circular DNA molecule that contains nearly all of the cell's genetic information.

16. DNA separates into two strands, then produces two new complementary strands following the rules of base pairing. Each new DNA molecule has one strand from the original molecule and one new strand.

Chapter 12 Study Guide

12–1 DNA

 **Key Concepts**  7 2.e, BI 5.a, BIIE 1.k

- Avery and other scientists discovered that DNA is the nucleic acid that stores and transmits the genetic information from one generation of an organism to the next.
- Hershey and Chase concluded that the genetic material of the bacteriophage was DNA.
- Watson and Crick's model of DNA was a double helix, in which two strands were wound around each other.

Vocabulary
transformation, p. 288 • bacteriophage, p. 289
nucleotide, p. 291 • base pairing, p. 294

12–2 Chromosomes and DNA Replication

 **Key Concept**  7 2.e, BI 5.b

- During DNA replication, the DNA molecule separates into two strands, and then produces two new complementary strands following the rules of base pairing. Each strand of the double helix of DNA serves as a template, or model, for the new strand.

Vocabulary
chromatin, p. 296 • histone, p. 296
replication, p. 299 • DNA polymerase, p. 299

12–3 RNA and Protein Synthesis

 **Key Concepts**  BI 1.d, BI 4.a, BI 4.b, BI 5.a

- There are three main types of RNA: messenger RNA, ribosomal RNA, and transfer RNA.
- During transcription, RNA polymerase binds to DNA and separates the DNA strands. RNA polymerase then uses one strand of DNA as a template from which nucleotides are assembled into a strand of RNA.
- During translation, the cell uses information from messenger RNA to produce proteins.

Vocabulary
gene, p. 300 • messenger RNA, p. 301
ribosomal RNA, p. 301
transfer RNA, p. 301 • transcription, p. 301
RNA polymerase, p. 301 • promoter, p. 301
intron, p. 302 • exon, p. 302 • codon, p. 302
translation, p. 304 • anticodon, p. 304

12–4 Mutations

  BI 4.c

- Mutations are changes in genetic material. Gene mutations result from changes in a single gene. Chromosomal mutations involve changes in whole chromosomes.

Vocabulary
mutation, p. 307 • point mutation, p. 307
frameshift mutation, p. 307 • polyploidy, p. 308

12–5 Gene Regulation

Key Concepts  BI 4.d

- The *lac* genes are turned off by repressors and turned on by the presence of lactose.
- Most eukaryotic genes are controlled individually and have regulatory sequences that are much more complex than those of the *lac* operon.

Vocabulary
operon, p. 309 • operator, p. 310
differentiation, p. 312 • hox gene, p. 312

Thinking Visually

Using the information in this chapter, complete the following flowchart about protein synthesis:

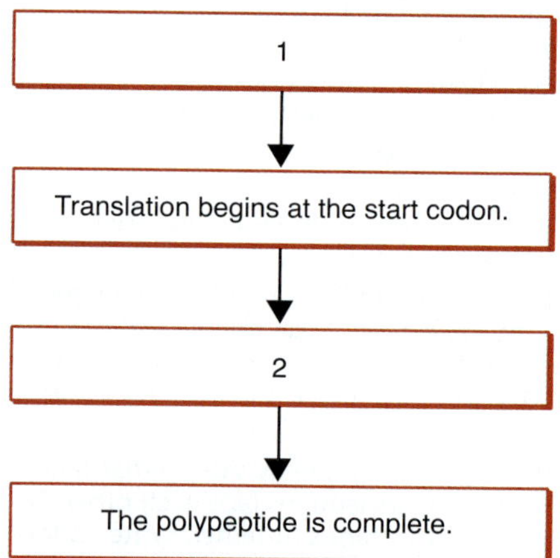

TIME SAVER — CHAPTER RESOURCES

Print:
- ***Teaching Resources,*** Chapter Vocabulary Review, Graphic Organizer, Chapter 12 Tests: Levels A and B

Technology:
- ***iText,*** Chapter 12 Assessment
- ***Computer Test Bank,*** Chapter 12 Test

Chapter 12 Assessment

Reviewing Content

Choose the letter that best answers the question or completes the statement.

1. The process by which one strain of bacteria is apparently changed into another strain is called
   a. transcription. c. transformation.
   b. translation. d. replication.

2. Bacteriophages are
   a. tiny bacteria. c. coils of RNA.
   b. enzymes. d. viruses.

3. A nucleotide does NOT contain
   a. a 5-carbon sugar.
   b. polymerase.
   c. a nitrogen base.
   d. a phosphate group.

4. In prokaryotes, DNA molecules are located in the
   a. nucleus. c. cytoplasm.
   b. ribosome. d. histone.

5. The diagram below shows the process of DNA

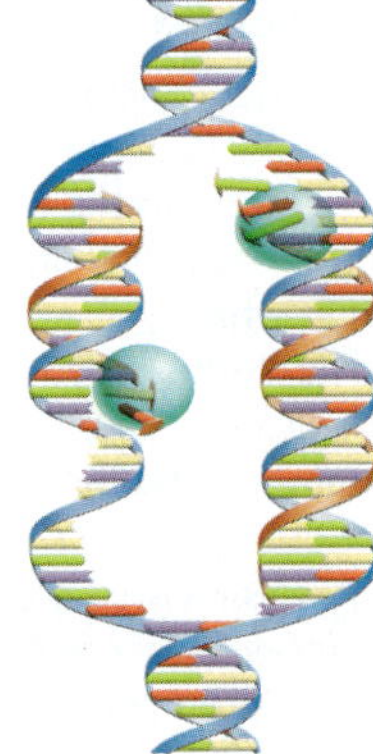

   a. replication. c. translation.
   b. transcription. d. transformation.

6. The main enzyme involved in linking individual nucleotides into DNA molecules is
   a. transfer RNA. c. RNA polymerase.
   b. ribose. d. DNA polymerase.

7. The process by which the genetic code of DNA is copied into a strand of RNA is called
   a. translation. c. transformation.
   b. transcription. d. replication.

8. In messenger RNA, each codon specifies a particular
   a. nucleotide. c. amino acid.
   b. purine. d. pyrimidine.

Interactive textbook with assessment at PHSchool.com

9. Changes in the DNA sequence that affect genetic information are known as
   a. replications. c. transformations.
   b. mutations. d. prokaryotes.

10. An expressed gene is one that
   a. functions as a promoter.
   b. is transcribed into RNA.
   c. codes for only one amino acid.
   d. is made of mRNA.

Understanding Concepts

11. As scientists tried to discover the nature of genes, what three critical gene functions had they identified?
12. Describe the components and structure of a DNA nucleotide.
13. Explain how Chargaff's rules helped Watson and Crick model DNA.
14. What is meant by the term *base pairing*? How is base pairing involved in DNA replication?
15. Describe the appearance of DNA in a typical prokaryotic cell.
16. Explain the process of replication. When a DNA molecule is replicated, how do the new molecules relate to the original molecule?
17. Describe the relationship between DNA, chromatin, histones, and nucleosomes.
18. What is the difference between exons and introns?
19. What is a codon?
20. What is an anticodon? How does it function?
21. If a code on a DNA molecule for a specific amino acid is CTA, what would be the messenger RNA codon? The transfer RNA anticodon?
22. Explain why controlling the proteins in an organism controls the organism's characteristics.
23. Name two major types of mutations. What do they have in common? How are they different? Give an example of each.
24. Describe how a TATA box helps position RNA polymerase in a eukaryotic cell.
25. Describe the role of an operon in a prokaryotic cell, and give an example of how an operon works.

TIME SAVER HOMEWORK GUIDE

Section:	Questions:
Section 12–1	1–3, 11–14, 26, 27, 32
Section 12–2	4–6, 15–17, 28
Section 12–3	7, 8, 18–22, 24, 29–31, 34
Section 12–4	9, 23, 33
Section 12–5	10, 25

Interactive Textbook

If your class subscribes to the iText, your students can go online to access an interactive version of the Student Edition and a self-test.

(Continued from page 314)

17. Nucleosomes are made up of DNA wrapped around histones. Chromatin is long chains of tightly coiled nucleosomes.

18. Pre-RNA contains introns that must be removed before RNA becomes active. The remaining RNA, the exons, or expressed sequences, are the actual genetic message that is used to assemble proteins.

19. A codon consists of three consecutive nucleotides that specify a single amino acid that is to be added to a polypeptide.

20. An anticodon consists of the three bases on the tRNA molecule that are complementary to an mRNA codon. Anticodons determine which tRNA binds to the codon on mRNA, and thus which amino acid is attached to the polypeptide chain.

21. GAU; CUA

22. Proteins are responsible for catalyzing and regulating chemical reactions, as well as regulating the rate and pattern of growth. These actions help determine an organism's characteristics.

23. Gene and chromosomal; both change the DNA sequence that affects genetic information. Gene mutations involve a change in one or several nucleotides in a single gene, whereas chromosomal mutations involve changes in the number or structure of whole chromosomes. Examples should reflect those given in Section 12–4.

24. The TATA box marks a point just before the point at which transcription begins.

25. An operon regulates gene expression. In the *lac* operon, the *lac* genes are turned off by a repressor that binds to the operator, blocking RNA polymerase from the promoter. When lactose is present, it binds to the repressor, causing it to release from the operator, allowing RNA polymerase to transcribe the *lac* genes.

Chapter 12 Assessment

Critical Thinking

26. Griffith heated a culture of the disease-causing strain, which killed the bacteria but did not destroy the DNA. When he mixed the heat-killed, disease-causing bacteria with the live, harmless bacteria, the DNA from the disease-causing bacteria was picked up by the live bacteria. The disease-causing DNA began replicating and was passed on to new bacteria cells. The new bacteria cells were disease-causing because of their DNA. These bacteria caused pneumonia in the mice.

27. Watson and Crick's model includes all the components of DNA arranged in such a way as to explain Chargaff's rules and X-ray evidence, and provide a mechanism for replication.

28. DNA replication is similar to photocopying because an exact duplicate is made. DNA replication is different because the strands are templates for the production of two DNA molecules. Each new molecule contains half the original molecule. In photocopying, the copy is an entirely new image and the original is preserved intact.

29. UGGCAGUG; AGCGUGCA

30. Additional amino acids would be added to the protein, and it would probably not function properly in the cell.

31. In genetics, transcription is the process by which a complementary strand of RNA is produced from DNA. It is similar to its meaning in ordinary language in that the order of DNA nucleotides is written out. In genetics, translation refers to the decoding of the RNA "message" into an amino acid sequence. In ordinary language, it refers to the similar process of converting one language into another.

32. Adenine and guanine are larger than cytosine and thymine. The equal distance between the backbones suggested that a small base must always be paired with a large base.

33. Chromosomal mutations that occur during meiosis affect the gametes and could appear in the offspring. Mitotic chromosomal mutations will affect only a few body cells.

Chapter 12 Assessment

Critical Thinking

26. Interpreting Graphics Look back at Griffith's experiment, shown in **Figure 12–2.** Describe the occasion in which the bacterial DNA withstood conditions that killed the bacteria. Describe what happened to the DNA from that point until the end of the experiment.

27. Using Models Evaluate Watson and Crick's model of the DNA molecule. How adequately does it represent the structure of DNA?

28. Using Analogies Is photocopying a document similar to DNA replication? Think of the original materials, the copying process, and the final products. Explain how the two processes are alike. Identify major differences.

29. Applying Concepts Suppose you start with two DNA strands: ACCGTCAC and TCGCACGT. Use the "rules" of base pairing to list the bases on messenger RNA strands transcribed from those DNA strands.

30. Predicting Examine the first intron in the diagram below. What difference would result in the protein produced by the messenger RNA if that intron were not removed but instead functioned as an exon?

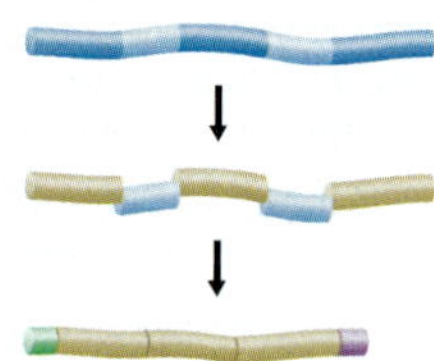

31. Using Analogies The word *transcribe* means "to write out," and the word *translate* means "to express in another language." Review the meanings of *transcription* and *translation* in genetics. How do the technical meanings of these words relate to meanings of the words in ordinary language?

32. Inferring Rosalind Franklin's X-ray patterns showed that the distance between the two phosphate-sugar "backbones" of a DNA molecule is the same throughout the length of the molecule. How did that information help Watson and Crick determine how the bases are paired?

33. Comparing and Contrasting How does the possible impact of a chromosomal mutation that occurs during meiosis differ from that of a similar event that occurs during mitosis of a body cell not involved in reproduction?

34. Predicting A researcher identifies the nucleotide sequence AAC in a long strand of RNA inside a nucleus. In the genetic code, AAC codes for the amino acid asparagine. When that RNA becomes involved in protein synthesis, will asparagine necessarily appear in the protein? Explain.

Focus on the BIG Idea

Information and Heredity Recall what you learned about mitosis in Chapter 10 and meiosis in Chapter 11. Describe what happens to a cell's DNA during each of these processes.

Writing in Science

Recall that Gregor Mendel concluded that factors, which we now call genes, determine the traits that are passed from one generation to the next. Imagine that you could send a letter backwards in time to Mendel. Write a letter to him in which you explain what a gene consists of in molecular terms. In your letter, you will need to explain, briefly, what DNA and proteins are. (*Hint:* Review Chapter 2 for the definition of protein.)

Performance-Based Assessment

Make a Model Make a three-dimensional model representing protein synthesis. Your "protein" should be a sequence of three different amino acids. Show the DNA molecule and the related RNA molecules that would be involved in producing your protein.

For: An interactive self-test
Visit: PHSchool.com
Web Code: cba-4120

34. No, asparagine will not necessarily appear in the protein. The sequence may be part of two adjacent codons that specify different amino acids, or it may be part of an intron.

Focus on the BIG Idea

During mitosis, the cell's DNA is replicated and each daughter cell receives a copy. Each new cell has the same amount of DNA as the original cell. During meiosis, the cell's DNA is also replicated. But two divisions result in four daughter cells that have half the chromosome number of the original cell.

Writing in Science

In their letters to Mendel, students should describe the structure of a typical eukaryotic gene and how these genes are part of DNA sequences that, along with DNA-binding proteins, form chromatin, the substance that forms chromosomes. Students should describe the genetic code and how it specifies proteins. They should also include a description of what proteins are and how they affect the characteristics of an organism.

Standards Practice

Online at PHSchool.com

Test-Taking Tip When asked to find the solution to a problem, such as the complementary sequence of DNA or RNA, first solve the problem on scratch paper. Then, compare your answer with the options provided.

Directions: Choose the letter that best answers the question or completes the statement.

1. During replication, which sequence of nucleotides would bond with the DNA sequence TATGA? **BI 5.b**
   A TATGA **C** ATACT
   B UAUGA **D** AUAGA
2. In which of the following ways does RNA differ from DNA? **BI 5.a**
   A RNA contains uracil and deoxyribose.
   B RNA contains ribose and thymine.
   C RNA contains uracil and ribose.
   D RNA contains adenine and ribose.
3. Which of the following nucleotide(s) bond(s) with adenine? **BI 5.b**
   A thymine only
   B uracil only
   C cytosine and guanine
   D thymine and uracil
4. The process of decoding mRNA into a polypeptide chain is known as **BI 1.d**
   A transformation.
   B transpiration.
   C translation.
   D transcription.
5. Which of the following does NOT describe the structure of DNA? **BI 5.a**
   A double helix
   B nucleotide polymer
   C sugar-phosphate backbone
   D contains adenine-uracil pairs
6. What did Hershey and Chase's work show?
   A Genes are probably made of DNA.
   B Genes are probably made of protein.
   C Genes are made of both DNA and protein.
   D Viruses contain DNA but not protein.
7. Anticodons are part of the structure of
   A DNA.
   B messenger RNA.
   C transfer RNA.
   D ribosomal RNA.

Questions 8–9

A scientist analyzed several DNA samples from exons to determine the relative proportions of purine and pyrimidine bases. Her data are summarized in the table below.

Percentages of Bases in Three Samples

Sample	G	C	A	T
A	35	35	15	15
B	40	10	40	10
C	25	25	25	25

8. Which sample(s) support(s) the base-pairing rules? **BI 5.b**
   A Sample A only **C** Sample C only
   B Sample B only **D** Samples A and C
9. If the scientist had analyzed mRNA rather than DNA, what percentage of uracil would you expect to find in Sample B? **BI 5.b**
   A 10 **C** 35
   B 25 **D** 40

Questions 10–12 Each of the lettered choices below refers to the following numbered statements. Select the best lettered choice.

A Mutation **C** Genetic code
B Double helix **D** Transcription

10. RNA molecules are produced by copying part of the nucleotide sequence of DNA into a complementary sequence in RNA **BI 1.d**
11. Structure of DNA **BI 5.a**
12. Heritable change in the DNA sequence that affects genetic information **BI 4.c**

Standards Practice

1. C	**5.** D	**9.** A
2. C	**6.** A	**10.** D
3. D	**7.** C	**11.** B
4. C	**8.** D	**12.** A

Success Tracker™

Online at PHSchool.com

Have students check their understanding of the chapter by logging onto Success Tracker.

Performance-Based Assessment

Check student models for structural accuracy of DNA, mRNA, and tRNA. Student models should reflect an understanding of the roles of DNA, RNA, and ribosomes in protein synthesis and the significance of codons and anticodons in the process.

Your students can independently test their knowledge of the chapter and print out their test results for your files.

Chapter Planner 13 Genetic Engineering

Section and Section Objectives	Time	STANDARDS NCLB	STANDARDS Biology	Activities and Labs
13–1 Changing the Living World, pp. 319–321 *13.1.1* ***Explain*** the purpose of selective breeding. *13.1.2* ***Describe*** two techniques used in selective breeding. *13.1.3* ***Tell*** why breeders try to induce mutations.	1 period (1/2 block)		BI 5.c	**SE:** ***Inquiry Activity,*** Can you improve plant breeding?, p. 318 L2 **SE:** ***Design an Experiment,*** Investigating the Effects of Radiation on Seeds, pp. 334–335 L2
13–2 Manipulating DNA, pp. 322–326 *13.2.1* ***Explain*** how scientists manipulate DNA.	1 period (1/2 block)		BI 5.c, *BI 5.d	**TE:** ***Demonstration,*** p. 324 L2 **SE:** ***Quick Lab,*** How can restriction enzymes be modeled?, p. 326 L2 **LMA:** Chapter 13 Lab L2 L3 **LMB:** Chapter 13 Lab L1 L2 **BTM:** Issue 1; Labs 8, 9, 12 L2 **IF:** Investigation 4 L1 L2 L3
13–3 Cell Transformation, pp. 327–329 *13.3.1* ***Summarize*** what happens during transformation. *13.3.2* ***Explain*** how you can tell if a transformation experiment has been successful.	1 period (1/2 block)		BI 5.c, *BI 5.e	**TE:** ***Build Science Skills,*** p. 329 L1 L2 **SE:** ***Issues in Biology,*** Do Genetically Modified Foods Need Stricter Controls?, p. 330 L2 **BTM:** Concepts 5, 7; Labs 14, 15 L2
13–4 Applications of Genetic Engineering, pp. 331–333 *13.4.1* ***Describe*** the usefulness of some transgenic organisms to humans. *13.4.2* ***Summarize*** the main steps in cloning.	1 period (1/2 block)			**BTM:** Lab 17; Issue 4 L2
Chapter Assessment, pp. 336–339	1 period (1/2 block)			

ACTIVITY PLANNER

SE: *Inquiry Activity,* p. 318; 10 min.; 5 apples of different varieties

TE: *Demonstration,* p. 324; 20 min. on two days; prepared kit for DNA restriction analysis and gel electrophoresis

SE: *Quick Lab,* p. 326; 20 min.; construction paper, scissors, transparent tape

TE: *Build Science Skills,* p. 329; 15 min.; pipe cleaners or pop beads of different colors

SE: *Design an Experiment,* pp. 334–335; 45 min.; irradiated seeds and nonirradiated seeds of the same species, petri dishes, paper towels, plant pots with commercial potting soil, glass-marking pencil

PLANNING KEY

Ability Levels
for students performing . . .
below grade level L1
at grade level L2
above grade level L3

Print Components

SE	Student Edition	**LA**	Lab Assessment
TE	Teacher's Edition	**BTM**	Biotechnology Manual
RSW	Reading & Study Workbook A	**IDM**	Issues and Decision Making
ARSW	Adapted Reading & Study Workbook B	**LW**	Lab Worksheets
TR	Teaching Resources	**LMA**	Laboratory Manual A
IF	Investigations in Forensics	**LMB**	Laboratory Manual B

Tech Components

CTB	Computer Test Bank
BD	BioDetectives DVD
TP	Transparencies Plus
PLM	Probeware Lab Manual
ABC	ABC DVD Library
LS	Lab Simulations
VL	Virtual Labs

Interactive textbook with assessment at PHSchool.com

Program Resources	Assessment	Media and Technology
TR: Lesson Plan 13–1, Section Summary, p. 103 L1, p. 111 L2, Worksheets, p. 106 L1, pp. 113–114 L2 **RSW:** Section 13–1 L2 **ARSW:** Section 13–1 L1 **LW:** Chapter 13 Design an Experiment L1 L2 L3	**SE:** 13–1 Section Assessment, p. 321 **TR:** Section Review 13–1	**iText:** Section 13–1 **TP:** 13–1 Interest Grabber, Section Outline, Concept Map
TR: Lesson Plan 13–2, Section Summary, p. 103 L1, p. 111 L2, Worksheets, pp. 107–108 L1, pp. 115–117 L2 **RSW:** Section 13–2 L2 **ARSW:** Section 13–2 L1 **IDM:** Issues and Decisions 24 L2 L3	**SE:** 13–2 Section Assessment, p. 326 **TR:** Section Review 13–2	**iText:** Section 13–2 **TP:** 13–2 Interest Grabber, Section Outline, Restriction Enzymes, Figure 13–6, Figure 13–7, Figure 13–8 **VL:** Lab 11
TR: Lesson Plan 13–3, Section Summary, p. 104 L1, p. 112 L2, Worksheets, p. 109 L1, pp. 118–119 L2 **RSW:** Section 13–3 L2 **ARSW:** Section 13–3 L1	**SE:** 13–3 Section Assessment, p. 329 **TR:** Section Review 13–3	**iText:** Section 13–3 **TP:** 13–3 Interest Grabber, Section Outline, Knockout Genes, Figure 13–9, Figure 13–10 **VL:** Lab 11
TR: Lesson Plan 13–4, Section Summary, p. 105 L1, p. 112 L2, Worksheets, pp. 120–121 L2, Enrichment L2 L3 **RSW:** Section 13–4 L2 **IDM:** Issues and Decisions 18 L2 L3	**SE:** 13–4 Section Assessment, p. 333 **TR:** Section Review 13–4	**iText:** Section 13–4 **TP:** 13–4 Interest Grabber, Section Outline, Flowchart, Figure 13–13 **ABC:** 30 Gene Transfer and Cloning
	SE: Chapter 13 Assessment, pp. 336–339 **TR:** Chapter Vocabulary Review, Graphic Organizer, Chapter 13 Test	**iText:** Chapter 13 Assessment **CTB:** Chapter 13 Test

Go Online
Students can do research, share data, and test their knowledge online.

PRESSED FOR TIME?

To Preview the Chapter
- Instruct students to read the Key Concepts and Vocabulary terms in each section.
- Have students examine all the figures in the chapter and read the captions.

To Cover the Chapter Quickly
- Have students read all of Sections 13–1, 13–2, and 13–3.
- Assign the Section Assessments for 13–1, 13–2, and 13–3.

To Review the Chapter
- Review the concept map in the Chapter 13 Study Guide.
- Assign Sections 13–1, 13–2, 13–3, and 13–4 in the Reading and Study Workbook or the Adapted Reading and Study Workbook.

CHAPTER 13

ENGAGE/EXPLORE

Inquiry Activity

Objective Students will be able to determine how to improve plant breeding. L2

Skill Focus **Formulating Hypotheses**

Materials 5 apples of different varieties

Time 10 minutes

Advance Prep Purchase five different varieties of apples at a grocery store or fruit market.

Strategy You might want students to use a cloth tape measure or string to determine the circumference of the apples at their widest point.

Expected Outcomes Students will identify the apple varieties that they consider to be best in color, shape, and size.

Think About It

1. Crossbreed the existing varieties until a hybrid with the desired traits is developed.

2. Isolate the genes that encode the desirable traits from the different apple varieties. These genes can be combined in one of the apple varieties to produce a new apple variety.

Brain Teaser

Challenge students to consider how a sheep that is 12 years old can have an identical twin that is only 4 years old. *(The 4-year-old sheep is a clone of the older sheep.)* To help students get started, first discuss with them what identical twins are. *(Two individuals that are genetically identical)* If students cannot solve the puzzle, write the puzzle on the board and revisit it periodically while studying this chapter.

CHAPTER 13

Genetic Engineering

Excessive inbreeding of cheetahs has resulted in a lack of genetic diversity and a higher rate of mortality.

Inquiry Activity

Can you improve plant breeding?

Procedure 

1. Examine 5 apples of different varieties. Record the color, shape, and size of each apple.
2. Record your choices of the varieties that you consider best in color, shape, and size.

Think About It

1. **Formulating Hypotheses** How could you produce an apple that has the best traits of all 5 varieties?
2. **Formulating Hypotheses** Most apple trees do not produce fruit until they are about 15 years old. How could you use your knowledge of DNA to produce a new variety of apple more quickly?

HISTORY OF SCIENCE

Giant steps in genetics
Watson and Crick discovered the structure of the DNA molecule in 1953. Researchers cracked the genetic code by the mid-1960s. In the early 1970s, researchers first developed the techniques for manipulating DNA, including the use of restriction enzymes and gel electrophoresis. In the late 1970s, researchers successfully engineered bacteria to produce insulin and interferon. In 1982, the first drug produced by recombinant bacteria—insulin—was approved for use in people. It was also in 1982 that researchers were successful in transferring genes between plant and animal species. In the early 1990s, researchers began inserting DNA into human patients to treat genetic diseases. By 2001, the human genome had been sequenced.

13–1 Changing the Living World

BI 5.c. Students know how genetic engineering (biotechnology) is used to produce novel biomedical and agricultural products.

Visit a dog show, and what do you see? You can compare dogs of every breed imaginable, distinguished from one another by an enormous range of characteristics that are the result of genetic variation. Striking contrasts are everywhere—the size of a tiny Chihuahua and that of a massive great Dane, the short coat of a Labrador retriever and the curly fur of a poodle, the long muzzle of the wolfhound and the pug nose of a bulldog. The differences among breeds of dogs are so great that someone who had never seen such animals before might think that many of these breeds are different species. They're not, of course, but where did such differences come from? What forces gave rise to the speed of a greyhound, the courage of a German shepherd, and the herding instincts of a border collie?

Guide for Reading

Key Concepts
- What is the purpose of selective breeding?
- Why might breeders try to induce mutations?

Vocabulary
selective breeding
hybridization
inbreeding

Reading Strategy: Outlining Before you read, write down the blue headings of the section. As you read, list the important information under each heading.

Selective Breeding

The answer, of course, is that *we* did it. Humans have kept and bred dogs for thousands of years, always looking to produce animals that might be better hunters, better retrievers, or better companions. By **selective breeding,** allowing only those animals with desired characteristics to produce the next generation, humans have produced many different breeds of dogs.

Humans use selective breeding, which takes advantage of naturally occurring genetic variation in plants, animals, and other organisms, to pass desired traits on to the next generation of organisms. Nearly all domestic animals—including horses, cats, and farm animals—and most crop plants have been produced by selective breeding. American botanist Luther Burbank (1849–1926) may have been the greatest selective plant breeder of all time. He developed the disease-resistant Burbank potato, which was later exported to Ireland to help fight potato blight and other diseases. During his lifetime, Burbank developed more than 800 varieties of plants.

Figure 13–1 **Humans use selective breeding to pass desired traits on to the next generation of organisms.** Luther Burbank used selective breeding to develop these Shasta daisies, a popular variety.

Hybridization

As one of his tools, Burbank used **hybridization,** crossing dissimilar individuals to bring together the best of both organisms. Hybrids, the individuals produced by such crosses, are often hardier than either of the parents. In many cases, Burbank's hybrid crosses combined the disease resistance of one plant with the food-producing capacity of another. The result was a new line of plants that had the characteristics farmers needed to increase food production. **Figure 13–1** shows hybrid daisies developed using Burbank's techniques.

SECTION RESOURCES

Print:
- ***Teaching Resources,*** Lesson Plan 13–1, Adapted Section Summary 13–1, Adapted Worksheets 13–1, Section Summary 13–1, Worksheets 13–1, Section Review 13–1
- ***Reading and Study Workbook A,*** Section 13–1
- ***Adapted Reading and Study Workbook B,*** Section 13–1
- ***Lab Worksheets,*** Chapter 13 Design an Experiment

Technology:
- ***iText,*** Section 13–1
- ***Transparencies Plus,*** Section 13–1

Section 13–1

 **BI 5.c**

1 FOCUS

Objectives

13.1.1 ***Explain*** the purpose of selective breeding.
13.1.2 ***Describe*** two techniques used in selective breeding.
13.1.3 ***Tell*** why breeders try to induce mutations.

Guide for Reading

Vocabulary Preview

Read aloud the Vocabulary terms for this section. Invite students to identify parts of the words that give clues about the words' meaning. For example, *hybrid-* gives a clue to the meaning of *hybridization,* and the prefix *in-* gives a clue to the meaning of the word *inbreeding.*

Reading Strategy

Instruct students to include the green subheadings from the section in their outlines. Remind students to include at least one piece of information for each green subhead. Also encourage them to add information to their outlines that is described in the figure captions, especially if the caption has a Key Concept.

2 INSTRUCT

Selective Breeding

Build Science Skills

Designing Experiments Challenge student pairs to develop a breeding plan to improve the traits of any domestic organism. Students should choose the organism and describe a way to improve the organism. In other words, students should choose a real problem or real characteristics. (*Some examples include purebred dogs that do not have hip dysplasia, roses resistant to fungal diseases, or oak trees resistant to gypsy moths.*) If students need help getting started, refer them to Mendel's breeding experiments with peas. Have students present their breeding plans to the class.

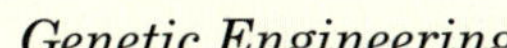

13–1 (continued)

Use Visuals

Figure 13–2 Have students look at the puppies in the photograph, and ask: **How can you tell that these puppies are inbred?** *(They all look identical.)* Discuss how the puppies might look instead if they were hybrids. Ask: **What differences might these puppies have if they were hybrids?** *(Differences in coloring, fur, shape and size of body; might look different from mother)* L1 L2

Increasing Variation

Address Misconceptions

Emphasize that sometimes creating mutants is a totally random process because of the action of the mutagens. The offspring that survive such mutagenic effects may have mutations that either are not detectable or are not useful to the researcher. Because of the laws of probability, researchers often must create thousands of mutants before they can isolate the particular one they are searching for. L2

Build Science Skills

Applying Concepts Explain that researchers also induce mutations to learn the function of a protein. By comparing the structure and function of the normal individual to those of the mutant, they can elucidate the protein's function. Challenge students to devise a plan to determine the function of a known protein. They should describe the expected phenotype of a mutant based on the protein's function. L2 L3

▶ **Figure 13–2** Inbreeding is required to maintain the characteristics of pedigreed dogs, such as these golden retrievers. However, inbreeding has also increased the breed's susceptibility to diseases and deformities. **Applying Concepts** *What other animals are likely to be inbred?*

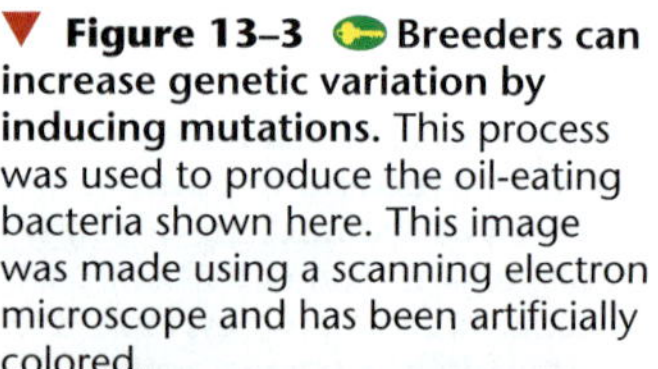

▼ **Figure 13–3** **Breeders can increase genetic variation by inducing mutations.** This process was used to produce the oil-eating bacteria shown here. This image was made using a scanning electron microscope and has been artificially colored.

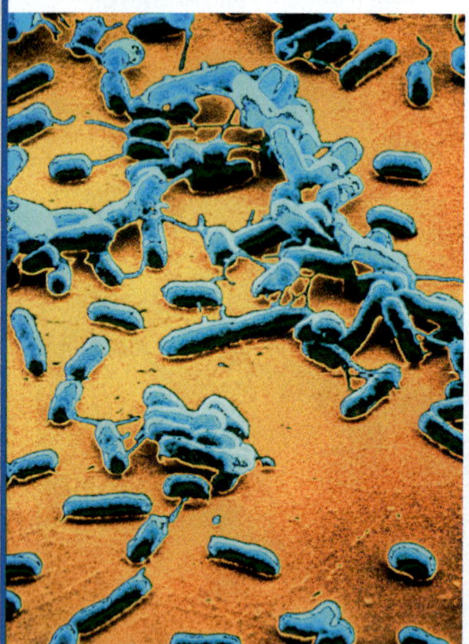

(magnification: 6200×)

Inbreeding To maintain the desired characteristics of a line of organisms, breeders often use a technique known as inbreeding. **Inbreeding** is the continued breeding of individuals with similar characteristics. The many breeds of dogs—from beagles to poodles—are maintained by inbreeding. Inbreeding helps to ensure that the characteristics that make each breed unique will be preserved. The golden retrievers shown in **Figure 13–2** are an example of inbred animals.

Although inbreeding is useful in retaining a certain set of characteristics, it does have its risks. Most of the members of a breed are genetically similar. Because of this, there is always a chance that a cross between two individuals will bring together two recessive alleles for a genetic defect. Serious problems in many breeds of dogs, including blindness and joint deformities in German shepherds and golden retrievers, have resulted from excessive inbreeding.

✓ CHECKPOINT *What is inbreeding?*

Increasing Variation

Selective breeding would be nearly impossible without the wide variation that is found in natural populations. This is one of the reasons biologists are interested in preserving the diversity of plants and animals in the wild. However, sometimes breeders want more variation than exists in nature. **Breeders can increase the genetic variation in a population by inducing mutations, which are the ultimate source of genetic variability.**

As you may recall, mutations are inheritable changes in DNA. Mutations occur spontaneously, but breeders can increase the mutation rate by using radiation and chemicals. Many mutations are harmful to the organism. With luck and perseverance, however, breeders can often produce a few mutants—individuals with mutations—with desirable characteristics that are not found in the original population.

ESL SUPPORT FOR ENGLISH LANGUAGE LEARNERS

Comprehension: Modified Cloze

Beginning Distribute a modified paragraph about selective breeding, but leave some strategic words blank. For example, "Crossing individuals with different traits is called _____. Breeding individuals with similar characteristics is called _____." Provide students with the missing terms, such as *inbreeding* and *hybridization*, and have students fill in each blank with one of these terms. Post these terms on a word wall with other Vocabulary terms from the chapter. L1

Intermediate Distribute the cloze paragraph described for beginning students, but add several more sentences and terms. Students can work in pairs to correct each other's answers. The students in each pair can also collaborate in writing about examples of the terms *selective breeding, hybridization,* and *inbreeding.* L2

Producing New Kinds of Bacteria This technique has been particularly useful with bacteria. Their small size enables millions of organisms to be treated with radiation or chemicals at the same time. This increases the chances of producing a useful mutant. Using this technique, scientists have been able to develop hundreds of useful bacterial strains. It has even been possible to produce bacteria that can digest oil, as shown in **Figure 13–3,** and that were once used to clean up oil spills. (Today, naturally occurring strains of oil-digesting bacteria are used to clean up oil spills.)

Producing New Kinds of Plants Drugs that prevent chromosomal separation during meiosis have been particularly useful in plant breeding. Sometimes these drugs produce cells that have double or triple the normal number of chromosomes. Plants grown from such cells are called polyploid because they have many sets of chromosomes. Polyploidy is usually fatal in animals. However, for reasons that are not clear, plants are much better at tolerating extra sets of chromosomes. Polyploidy may instantly produce new species of plants that are often larger and stronger than their diploid relatives. **Figure 13–4** shows some polyploid day lilies. Many important crop plants have been produced in this way, including bananas and many varieties of citrus fruits.

Word Origins

Polyploid comes from the Greek words *polus,* meaning "many," and *-ploos,* meaning "fold." So *polyploid* means "many-fold" or "many times." **How many sets of chromosomes do you think a triploid plant has?**

Figure 13–4 The day lilies at the right are examples of polyploid plants. New species of plants are produced when the chromosome number is doubled or tripled. **Applying Concepts** ***What are some other examples of polyploid plants?***

13–1 Section Assessment

1. **Key Concept** Give one example of selective breeding.
2. **Key Concept** Relate genetic variation and mutations to each other.
3. How might a breeder induce mutations?
4. What is polyploidy?
5. **Critical Thinking Comparing and Contrasting** You are a geneticist trying to develop a sunflower with red flowers and a short stem. As you compare the sunflowers you have, what genetic variations would you look for? What kinds of plants would you select for crossing?

Focus on the BIG Idea

Science, Technology, and Society Write a paragraph in which you suggest ways that plants could be genetically altered to improve the world's food supply. *Hint:* The first sentence in your paragraph should express the paragraph's main idea.

13–1 Section Assessment

1. Nearly all domestic animals, including horses, cats, and farm animals, and most crop plants have been produced by selective breeding.
2. Mutations are the ultimate source of genetic variation.
3. By using radiation and chemicals
4. The condition of having many sets of chromosomes
5. Plants with shorter stems and plants with more red pigment in their flowers

Word Origins

A triploid plant has three sets of chromosomes. L2

3 ASSESS

Evaluate Understanding

Describe some breeding situations, and invite students to classify each as an example of hybridization or inbreeding. Have students describe the effects of genetic variation on selective breeding.

Reteach

Have students make a concept map to show the relationships among selective breeding, hybridization, inbreeding, and increasing variation. Encourage students to write notes on the maps to clarify meanings of words and concepts.

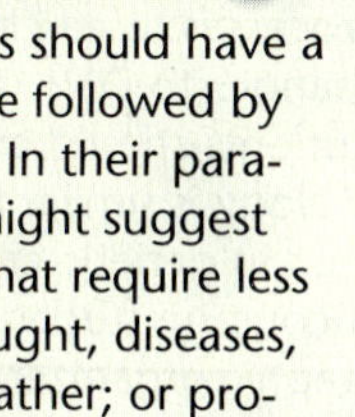

Focus on the BIG Idea

Student paragraphs should have a clear topic sentence followed by supporting details. In their paragraphs, students might suggest producing plants that require less fertilizer; resist drought, diseases, pests, and cold weather; or produce more nutritious or abundant fruit. Students should also suggest methods to produce these plants.

If your class subscribes to the iText, use it to review the Key Concepts in Section 13–1.

Answers to . . .

CHECKPOINT *Continued breeding of individuals with similar characteristics*

Figure 13–2 *Any domesticated animal*

Figure 13–4 *Bananas, citrus fruits*

Section 13–2

 BI 5.c, *BI 5.d

1 FOCUS

Objective

13.2.1 ***Explain*** how scientists manipulate DNA.

Guide for Reading

Vocabulary Preview

Explain that the word *recombinant* is an adjective that came from the word *recombine.* Discuss what recombinant DNA is (*new DNA molecules produced by inserting different DNA sequences, often from different organisms*).

Reading Strategy

As students read the section, encourage them to answer the questions or correct their predictions made while previewing the figures.

2 INSTRUCT

The Tools of Molecular Biology

Build Science Skills

Using Analogies Challenge student pairs to develop an analogy for the processes researchers use to make changes to DNA. In their analogies, students should explain how the analogy is similar to the techniques used in genetic engineering. Encourage students to develop a graphic organizer, poster, computer slide show, or videotape to present their analogy to the class. L2

Use Visuals

Figure 13–5 Explain that restriction enzymes are used as "scissors" to cut a DNA molecule. Emphasize that every restriction enzyme has a specific sequence of DNA that it recognizes and cuts. You might remind students about the specificity of other DNA-binding proteins, such as repressor proteins and polymerases. Also, point out that like *Eco*R I, many restriction enzymes leave sticky ends, but others leave blunt ends—a single-stranded "tail" is not left. Fragments with blunt ends will recombine indiscriminately with other blunt-ended fragments. L2

13–2 Manipulating DNA

BI 5.c. Students know how genetic engineering (biotechnology) is used to produce novel biomedical and agricultural products. ***BI 5.d.** Students know how basic DNA technology (restriction digestion by endonucleases, gel electrophoresis, ligation, and transformation) is used to construct recombinant DNA molecules.

Guide for Reading

Key Concept
- How do scientists make changes to DNA?

Vocabulary
genetic engineering
restriction enzyme
gel electrophoresis
recombinant DNA
polymerase chain reaction (PCR)

Reading Strategy: Previewing Graphics Before you read this section, examine the figures. Read the captions, and identify questions about or predict relationships among the techniques illustrated.

Until very recently, animal and plant breeders could not modify the genetic code of living things. They were limited by the need to work with the variation that already exists in nature. Even when they tried to add to that variation by introducing mutations, the changes they produced in the DNA were random and unpredictable. Imagine, however, that one day biologists were able to go right to the genetic code and rewrite an organism's DNA. Imagine that biologists could transfer genes at will from one organism to another, designing new living things to meet specific needs. That day, as you may know from scientific stories in the news, is already here.

How are changes made to DNA? **Scientists use their knowledge of the structure of DNA and its chemical properties to study and change DNA molecules. Different techniques are used to extract DNA from cells, to cut DNA into smaller pieces, to identify the sequence of bases in a DNA molecule, and to make unlimited copies of DNA.** Understanding how these techniques work will help you develop an appreciation for what is involved in genetic engineering.

The Tools of Molecular Biology

Suppose you had a computer game you wanted to change. Knowing that the characteristics of that game are determined by a coded computer program, how would you set about rewriting parts of the program? To make such changes, a software engineer would need a way to get the program out of the computer, read it, make changes in it, and then put the modified code back into the game. **Genetic engineering,** making changes in the DNA code of a living organism, works almost the same way.

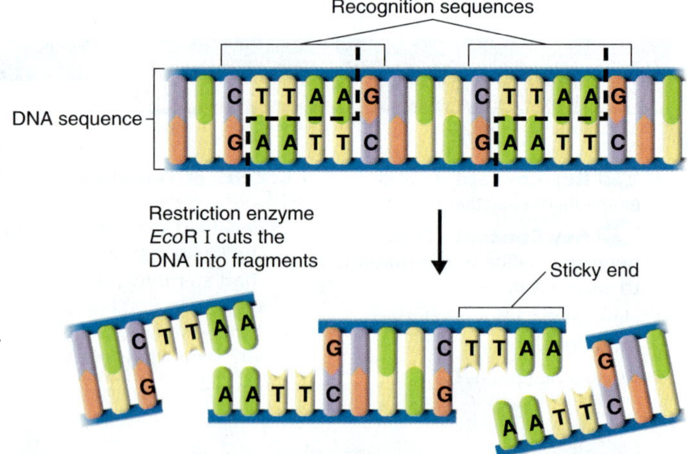

Figure 13–5 **Molecular biologists have developed different techniques that allow them to study and change DNA molecules.** Endonucleases—enzymes that cut DNA molecules into fragments—are one of their most important tools. The most useful endonucleases are restriction enzymes, which cut DNA at specific sequences. This drawing shows how restriction enzymes are used to edit DNA. The restriction enzyme *Eco*R I, for example, finds the sequence CTTAAG on DNA. Then, the enzyme cuts the molecule at each occurrence of CTTAAG. The cut ends are called sticky ends because they may "stick" to complementary base sequences by means of hydrogen bonds.

SECTION RESOURCES

Print:
- ***Laboratory Manual A,*** Chapter 13 Lab
- ***Laboratory Manual B,*** Chapter 13 Lab
- ***Teaching Resources,*** Lesson Plan 13–2, Adapted Section Summary 13–2, Adapted Worksheets 13–2, Section Summary 13–2, Worksheets 13–2, Section Review 13–2
- ***Reading and Study Workbook A,*** Section 13–2
- ***Adapted Reading and Study Workbook B,*** Section 13–2
- ***Issues and Decision Making,*** 24
- ***Biotechnology Manual,*** Issue 1; Labs 8, 9, 12
- ***Investigations in Forensics,*** Investigation 4

Technology:
- ***iText,*** Section 13–2
- ***Transparencies Plus,*** Section 13–2
- ***Virtual Labs,*** Lab 11

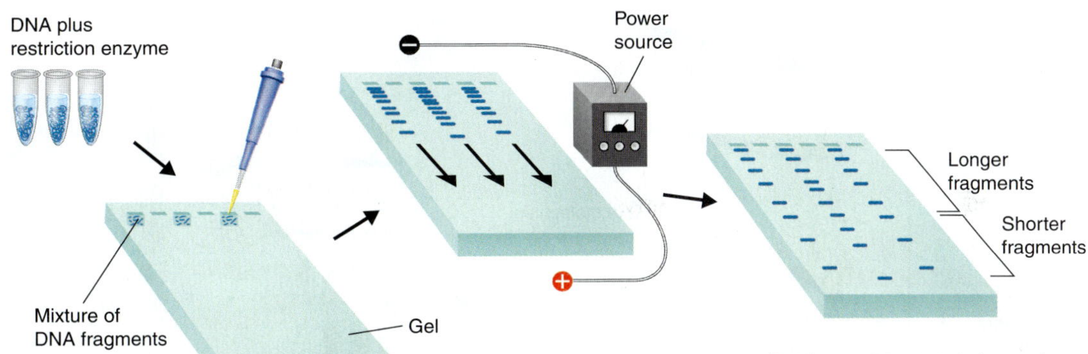

▲ **Figure 13–6** Gel electrophoresis is used to separate DNA fragments. First, restriction enzymes cut DNA into fragments. The DNA fragments are then poured into wells on a gel, which is similar to a thick piece of gelatin. An electric voltage moves the DNA fragments across the gel. Because longer fragments of DNA move through the gel more slowly, they do not migrate as far across the gel as shorter fragments of DNA. Based on size, the DNA fragments make a pattern of bands on the gel. These bands can then be compared with other samples of DNA. **Inferring** *What kinds of information might the bands from two different DNA sources provide?*

DNA Extraction How do biologists get DNA out of a cell? DNA can be extracted from most cells by a simple chemical procedure: The cells are opened and the DNA is separated from the other cell parts.

Cutting DNA DNA molecules from most organisms are much too large to be analyzed, so biologists cut them precisely into smaller fragments using restriction enzymes. Hundreds of **restriction enzymes** are known, and each one cuts DNA at a specific sequence of nucleotides. As shown in **Figure 13–5,** restriction enzymes are amazingly precise. Like a key that fits only one lock, a restriction enzyme will cut a DNA sequence only if it matches the sequence precisely.

Separating DNA How can DNA fragments be separated and analyzed? One way, a procedure known as gel electrophoresis (ee-lek-troh-fuh-REE-sis), is shown in **Figure 13–6.** In **gel electrophoresis,** a mixture of DNA fragments is placed at one end of a porous gel, and an electric voltage is applied to the gel. When the power is turned on, DNA molecules, which are negatively charged, move toward the positive end of the gel. The smaller the DNA fragment, the faster and farther it moves. Gel electrophoresis can be used to compare the genomes, or gene composition, of different organisms or different individuals. It can also be used to locate and identify one particular gene out of the tens of thousands of genes in an individual's genome.

Using the DNA Sequence

Once DNA is in a manageable form, its sequence can be read, studied, and even changed. Knowing the sequence of an organism's DNA allows researchers to study specific genes, to compare them with the genes of other organisms, and to try to discover the functions of different genes and gene combinations. The following are some techniques scientists use to read and change the sequence of DNA molecules.

Use Visuals

Figure 13–6 Walk students through the processes of preparing DNA for gel electrophoresis. Also use Figure 13–5 to make sure students understand the action of restriction enzymes. Then, discuss the steps in gel electrophoresis. Explain that the gel is a porous material that looks and feels like gelatin. A "comb" is used to form holes, called wells, when the gel is "poured." After the gel hardens, the comb is removed and the gel is "loaded." The different samples of DNA are micropipetted into the wells. Then, the voltage is applied. Ask: **Where are the shorter DNA fragments located on a completed gel?** *(At the end of the gel.)* **Why?** *(The shorter fragments move much faster through the porous gel.)* L2

Make Connections

Chemistry Explain that the DNA molecule has a negative charge because the phosphate group, PO_3, is negatively charged. Draw diagrams on the board to show that phosphorus has five electrons in its outermost level and the oxygen atoms have six electrons in the outermost level. Remind students that atoms with eight electrons are more stable, so the oxygen atoms bind to phosphorus. The deoxyribose sugars are bonded to the phosphate group by the oxygen atoms. However, one atom of oxygen in the phosphate group does not bind to any component of the DNA molecule. This is the atom that confers the negative charge. Also, explain that in the cell, DNA is always found bound to positively charged proteins (histones) or other cations. L2

UNIVERSAL ACCESS

Inclusion/Special Needs

Students can model many of the abstract ideas in this section using yarn to represent the DNA molecule. Work with students yourself or pair them with another student to describe the steps of the processes that are diagrammed in the section figures. Students can follow the explanation by manipulating the yarn in the same manner that the DNA is manipulated. L1

Less Proficient Readers

Have students devise a flowchart that shows the steps to prepare DNA for gel electrophoresis, as well as the protocol for setting up and running a gel. Encourage students to add diagrams to the flowchart and add detailed notes to help them understand the procedures. L1 L2

Answer to . . .

Figure 13–6 *Possible answers include differences in the DNA sequences of the two sources and the relative sizes of particular genes.*

13–2 (continued)

Using the DNA Sequence

Demonstration

Demonstrate DNA restriction analysis and gel electrophoresis for the class. Some biological supply companies have prepared kits that contain restriction enzymes, DNA, agarose gel materials, electrophoresis equipment, and all the other supplies and detailed instructions required for this procedure. You might wish to perform a restriction map analysis in which a DNA sequence is cut separately with two different restriction enzymes and then cut with a mixture of the two enzymes. These three different samples are run together on a gel along with a sample of uncut DNA and marker DNA with fragments of known lengths. From the bands on the gel, the order of the fragments in the DNA sequence can be determined. L2

For: Gel Electrophoresis activity
Visit: PHSchool.com
Web Code: cbe-4132
Students interact with the art online.

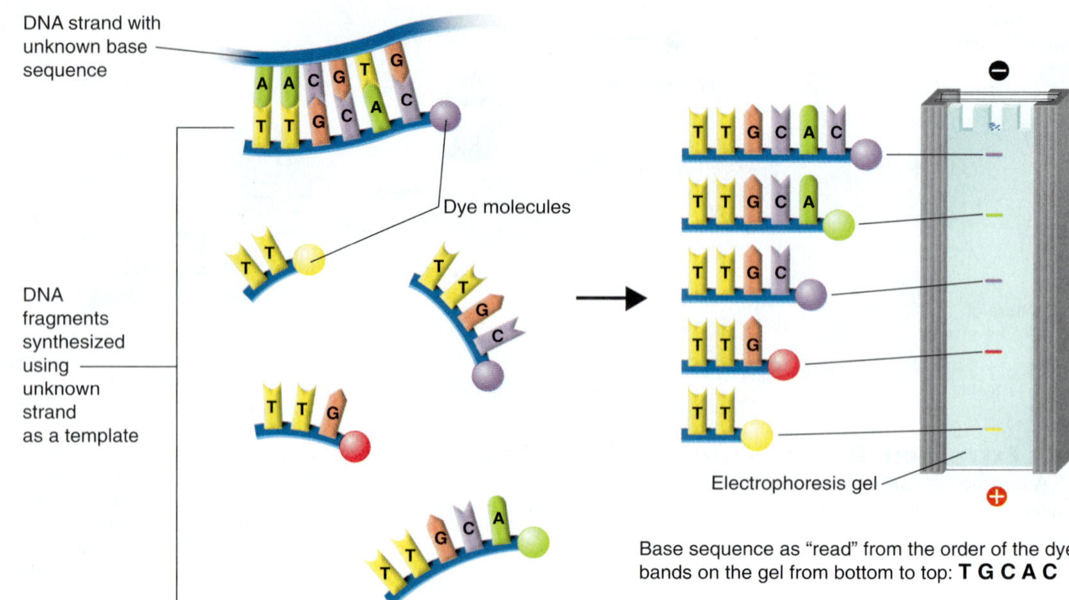

▲ **Figure 13–7** **Knowing the sequence of an organism's DNA allows researchers to study specific genes.** In DNA sequencing, a complementary DNA strand is made using a small proportion of fluorescently labeled nucleotides. Each time a labeled nucleotide is added, it stops the process of replication, producing a short color-coded DNA fragment. When the mixture of fragments is separated on a gel, the DNA sequence can be read directly from the gel.

For: Gel Electrophoresis activity
Visit: PHSchool.com
Web Code: cbp-4132

Reading the Sequence Researchers use a clever chemical trick to "read" DNA by determining the order of its bases. A single strand of DNA whose sequence of bases is not known is placed in a test tube. DNA polymerase, the enzyme that copies DNA, and the four nucleotide bases, A, T, G, and C, are added to the test tube. As the enzyme goes to work, it uses the unknown strand as a template to make one new DNA strand after another. The tricky part is that researchers also add a small number of bases that have a chemical dye attached.

Each time a dye-labeled base is added to a new DNA strand, the synthesis of that strand is terminated. When DNA synthesis is completed, the new DNA strands are different lengths, depending on how far synthesis had progressed when the dye-tagged base was added. Since each base is labeled with a different color, the result is a series of dye-tagged DNA fragments of different lengths. These fragments are then separated according to length, often by gel electrophoresis, as shown in **Figure 13–7.** The order of colored bands on the gel tells the exact sequence of bases in the DNA.

Cutting and Pasting DNA sequences can be changed in a number of ways. Short sequences can be assembled using laboratory machines known as DNA synthesizers. "Synthetic" sequences can then be joined to "natural" ones using enzymes that splice DNA together. The same enzymes make it possible to take a gene from one organism and attach it to the DNA of another organism. Such DNA molecules are sometimes called **recombinant DNA** because they are produced by combining DNA from different sources.

TEACHER TO TEACHER

To help students understand how restriction enzymes work, I like to give them a sentence, such as "My twin sister Sherry, older brother Larry, and I all went to the shopping mall to purchase a gift for our mother and new baby brother Harry." Then, I tell half the class to cut the sentence using a restriction enzyme that cuts between "rr." I instruct the other half to cut the sentence between "he." Next, I have both groups compare the sizes and numbers of fragments by arranging the fragments on a grid according to their lengths. Finally, I have them cut the same sentence using both enzymes and compare the grid pattern with the pattern produced when using the enzymes singly.

—*Mary Colvard*
Biology Teacher
Cobleskill-Richmondville High School
Cobleskill, NY

Making Copies In order to study genes, biologists often need to make many copies of a particular gene. Like a photocopy machine stuck on "print," a technique known as **polymerase chain reaction (PCR)** allows biologists to do exactly that. **Figure 13–8** shows how PCR works.

The idea behind PCR is surprisingly simple. At one end of a piece of DNA a biologist wants to copy, he or she adds a short piece of DNA that is complementary to a portion of the sequence. At the other end, the biologist adds another short piece of complementary DNA. These short pieces are known as "primers" because they provide a place for the DNA polymerase to start working.

The DNA is heated to separate its two strands, then cooled to allow the primers to bind to single-stranded DNA. DNA polymerase starts making copies of the region between the primers. Because the copies themselves can serve as templates to make still more copies, just a few dozen cycles of replication can produce millions of copies of the DNA between those primers.

Where did Kary Mullis, the American inventor of PCR, find a DNA polymerase enzyme that could stand repeated cycles of heating and cooling? Mullis found it in bacteria living in the hot springs of Yellowstone National Park—a perfect example of the importance of biodiversity to biotechnology.

CHECKPOINT *What is a polymerase chain reaction?*

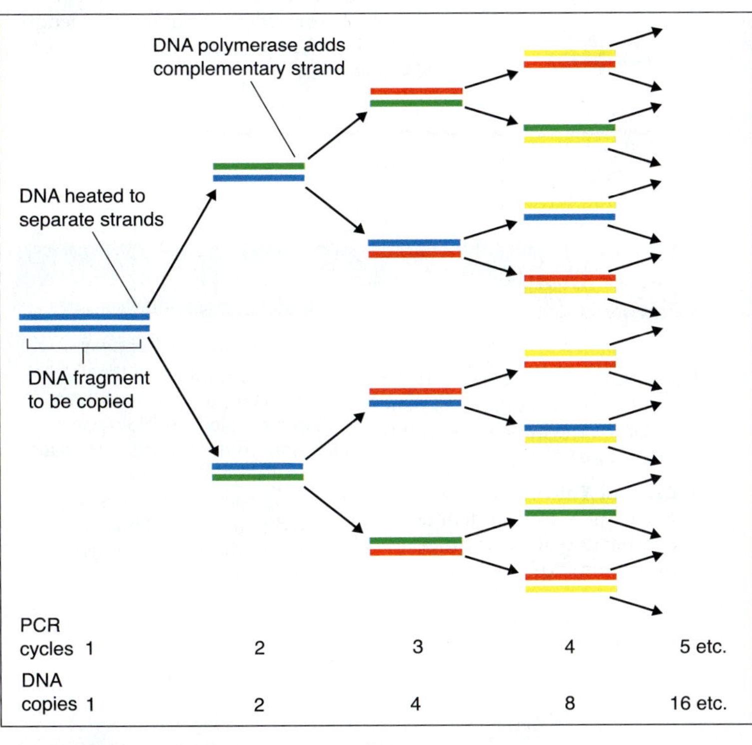

Figure 13–8 Polymerase chain reaction (PCR) is used to make multiple copies of genes. **Calculating** *How many copies of the DNA will there be after six cycles?*

For: Links on recombinant DNA
Visit: www.SciLinks.org
Web Code: cbn-4132

Go Online NSTA SCiLINKS

Download a worksheet on recombinant DNA for students to complete, and find additional teacher support from NSTA SciLinks.

Address Misconceptions

Students might not fully understand how so many different-sized bands can be produced in a sequencing gel. Diagram the process on the board, beginning with preparing the small, single-stranded piece of DNA that is to be sequenced. Make sure students realize that more than one piece of this DNA is in the test tube. Emphasize that all nucleotides required to form the complementary strand are in the test tube; however, only a small percentage of the nucleotides are marked with the chemical dye. Remind them of the laws of probability to explain why a complementary sequence of every length, from one nucleotide to the complete sequence, is produced in the reaction. Use a short nucleotide sequence of 5 bases to demonstrate this idea on the board. Correlate the length of the marked complementary strand with the band on a gel.

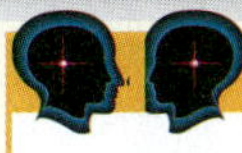

TEACHER TO TEACHER

Using a model of bacterial transformation is a great way to help students understand gene manipulation. When discussing transformation, I provide students with manipulatives. My favorite is garden hose cut into lengths to represent the original plasmid, along with short pieces of doweling covered with tape of different colors to represent the inserted genes. (Models made of colored paper or pop beads also work well.) Having students carry out changes using their model makes the idea of transformation concrete. Using the model to assess learning quickly points out any misconceptions that students may have.

—*Amelia Quillen*
Biology Teacher
Smyrna High School
Smyrna, DE

Answers to . . .

CHECKPOINT *A technique in which biologists can make many copies of a particular gene*

Figure 13–8 *32*

13–2 (continued)

Quick Lab

BIIE 1.g, *BI 5.d

Objective Students will model how restriction enzymes are used. L2

Skills Focus **Observing, Evaluating**

Materials construction paper, scissors, transparent tape

Time 20 minutes

Advance Prep To increase the chance of students finding a matching cut site, provide them with several 50-base sequences that include one or more cut sites.

Expected Outcomes Students will construct recombinant DNA models.

Analyze and Conclude

1. Answers will depend on students' sequences.

2. Students might think their model well represents the action of restriction enzymes. However, the number of fragments produced in the model is much smaller than produced in the actual process.

3 ASSESS

Evaluate Understanding

Have students describe what is occurring in each figure in the section.

Reteach

Have students develop a table about the procedures and uses of each technique for manipulating DNA.

Writing in Science

Student paragraphs should correctly describe, in order, the steps in the process of reading a DNA sequence, as they are described in this section.

If your class subscribes to the iText, use it to review the Key Concepts in Section 13–2.

Quick Lab

BIIE 1.g, *BI 5.d

How can restriction enzymes be modeled?

Materials construction paper, scissors, transparent tape

Procedure 

1. Write a 50-base double-stranded DNA sequence using the letters A, C, G, and T in random order. Include each of the base sequences shown below at least once in your 50 base-pair sequences.
2. Make three copies of your double-stranded sequence on three different-colored strips of paper.
3. Use the drawings below to see how the restriction enzyme *Eco*R I would cut your double-stranded sequence. Use scissors to cut one copy of the sequence as *Eco*R I would.

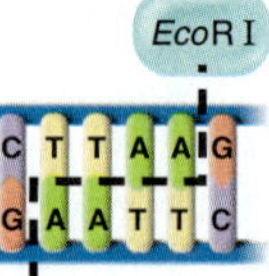

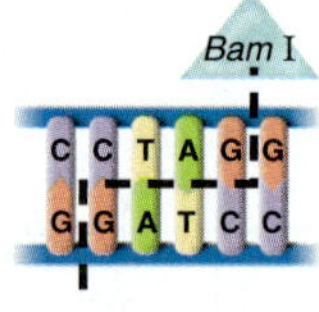

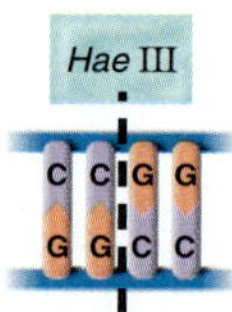

4. Use the procedure in step 3 to cut apart another copy of your sequence as the restriction enzyme *Bam* I would. Cut apart the third copy as the restriction enzyme *Hae* III would.
5. To model the building of recombinant DNA, tape the single-stranded end of one of your pieces of DNA sequences to a complementary, single-stranded end of one of a classmate's pieces. This will form a single, long DNA molecule.

Analyze and Conclude

1. **Observing** Which restriction enzyme produced the most pieces? The fewest pieces?
2. **Evaluating** Evaluate your model of restriction-enzyme function according to how well it represents the actual process. (*Hint:* Contrast the length of your model DNA sequence to the actual length of a DNA molecule.)

13–2 Section Assessment

1. **Key Concept** Describe the process scientists use to manipulate DNA.
2. Why might a scientist want to know the sequence of a DNA molecule?
3. How does gel electrophoresis work?
4. Which technique can be used to make multiple copies of a gene? What are the basic steps in this procedure?
5. **Critical Thinking** **Using Analogies** How is genetic engineering like computer programming?

Writing in Science

Explaining a Process

Write a paragraph that explains, in your own words, how molecular biologists determine the order of bases in a segment of a DNA molecule. *Hint:* Before you write, use a flowchart to organize the steps in the process.

13–2 Section Assessment

1. Biologists use various tools to extract, read, edit, and reinsert DNA into living organisms, including DNA extraction, restriction enzymes, gel electrophoresis, sequencing DNA, and PCR.
2. To study specific genes; compare them with the genes of other organisms; and discover the functions of different genes
3. A mixture of DNA fragments in a porous gel are separated by their sizes with electric voltage.
4. PCR; short pieces of complementary DNA are added to each end of a DNA sequence. DNA is heated, then cooled, and DNA polymerase makes copies of the sequence.
5. Both rely on a code that can be manipulated to change the function of the system.

13–3 Cell Transformation

BI 5.c. Students know how genetic engineering (biotechnology) is used to produce novel biomedical and agricultural products. ***BI 5.e.** Students know how exogenous DNA can be inserted into bacterial cells to alter their genetic makeup and support expression of new protein products.

It would do little good to modify a DNA molecule in the test tube if it were not possible to put that DNA back into a living cell and make it work. This sounds tricky, and it is, but you have already seen an example of how this can be done. Remember Griffith's experiments on bacterial transformation? **During transformation, a cell takes in DNA from outside the cell. This external DNA becomes a component of the cell's DNA.**

Today, biologists understand that Griffith's extract of heat-killed bacteria must have contained DNA fragments. When he mixed those fragments with live bacteria, a few of them actually took up the DNA molecules. This suggests that bacteria can be transformed simply by placing them in a solution containing DNA molecules—and indeed they can.

Guide for Reading

Key Concepts
- What happens during cell transformation?
- How can you tell if a transformation experiment has been successful?

Vocabulary
plasmid
genetic marker

Reading Strategy: Summarizing As you read, take notes on how each kind of cell can be transformed. After you read, go back to your notes and compare the different techniques.

Transforming Bacteria

Figure 13–9 shows how bacteria can be transformed using recombinant DNA. The foreign DNA is first joined to a small, circular DNA molecule known as a **plasmid.** Plasmids are found naturally in some bacteria and have been very useful for DNA transfer. Why? The plasmid DNA has two essential features. First, it has a DNA sequence that helps promote plasmid replication. If the plasmid containing the foreign DNA manages to get inside a bacterial cell, this sequence ensures that it will be replicated.

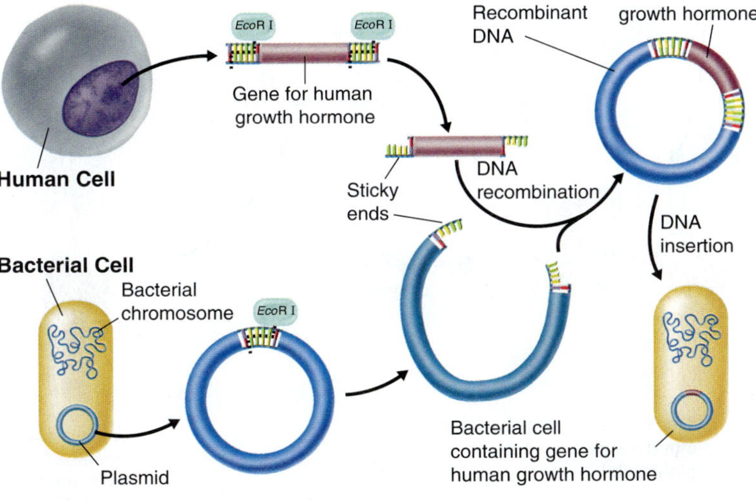

Figure 13–9 **During transformation, a cell incorporates DNA from outside the cell into its own DNA.** One way to use bacteria to produce human growth hormone is to insert a human gene into bacterial DNA. The new combination of genes is then returned to a bacterial cell. The bacterial cell containing the gene replicates over and over.

SECTION RESOURCES

Print:
- ***Teaching Resources,*** Lesson Plan 13–3, Adapted Section Summary 13–3, Adapted Worksheets 13–3, Section Summary 13–3, Worksheets 13–3, Section Review 13–3
- ***Reading and Study Workbook A,*** Section 13–3
- ***Adapted Reading and Study Workbook B,*** Section 13–3
- ***Biotechnology Manual,*** Concepts 5, 7; Labs 14, 15

Technology:
- ***iText,*** Section 13–3
- ***Transparencies Plus,*** Section 13–3
- ***Virtual Labs,*** Lab 12

Section 13–3

BI 5.c, *BI 5.e

1 FOCUS

Objectives

13.3.1 ***Summarize*** what happens during transformation.
13.3.2 ***Explain*** how you can tell if a transformation experiment has been successful.

Guide for Reading

Vocabulary Preview

Explain that the word *plasmid* is derived from the prefix *plasm-*, which refers to the cytoplasm in the cell, and the suffix *-id,* which means particle. Then, ask: **Where do you think a plasmid is located?** *(In the cytoplasm of a cell)* **What do you think a plasmid is?** If students can't answer this question, explain that it's a small, circular piece of DNA.

Reading Strategy

Encourage students to include in their notes sketches of the diagrams of the three kinds of transformation.

2 INSTRUCT

Transforming Bacteria

Use Visuals

Figure 13–9 Go through the procedure of producing recombinant DNA as it is outlined in the diagram. Make sure students know that a plasmid is a small, circular piece of DNA found in some bacteria. Bacteria will readily take up plasmids under the right conditions. Ask: **Why must both the plasmid and the human gene be cut with the same restriction enzyme?** *(So that both DNA sequences have sticky ends that are complementary to each other.)* **How do you think the human gene was isolated from the DNA in a human cell?** *(The gene was isolated by cutting the band of DNA out of a gel.)* L2

13–3 (continued)

Build Science Skills

Applying Concepts Challenge student pairs to brainstorm a list of reasons why researchers might transform bacteria in the course of their studies. Students should describe how bacterial transformation is useful in the experiment. Make a class list of these uses, and add to or subtract from the list as you continue with the chapter. L2

Transforming Plant Cells

Use Visuals

Figure 13–10 As students study the procedure diagrammed in the figure, point out that the transformed bacteria are mixed in a test tube with plant cells before the plant cells are placed out onto a petri dish. As with bacteria, genetic markers are used so that only transformed plant cells will grow on the petri dish. Individual plant colonies are removed from the petri dish and placed in a special growing medium where they will grow into a plant. Ask: **How do you think researchers inactivate the tumor-producing gene on the plasmid?** *(They remove part of the gene sequence—create a mutation—that inactivates the gene.)* L2

Second, the plasmid has a **genetic marker**—a gene that makes it possible to distinguish bacteria that carry the plasmid (and the foreign DNA) from those that don't. Genes for resistance to antibiotics, compounds that can kill bacteria, are commonly used as markers. A marker makes it possible for researchers to mix recombinant plasmids with a culture of bacteria, add enough DNA to transform one cell in a million, and still be able to "find" that cell. After transformation, the culture is treated with an antibiotic. Only those rare cells that have been transformed survive—because only they carry a resistance gene.

CHECKPOINT *What is a genetic marker?*

Transforming Plant Cells

Many plant cells can be transformed by using a process that takes advantage of a bacterium. In nature, this bacterium inserts a small DNA plasmid that produces tumors into a plant's cells. Researchers have discovered that they can inactivate the tumor-producing gene and insert a piece of foreign DNA into the plasmid. The recombinant plasmid can then be used to infect plant cells, as shown in **Figure 13–10.**

▼ **Figure 13–10** The bacterium *Agrobacterium tumefaciens* can be used to introduce foreign DNA into plant cells. **If the transformation is successful, the DNA will be integrated into one of the cell's chromosomes.**

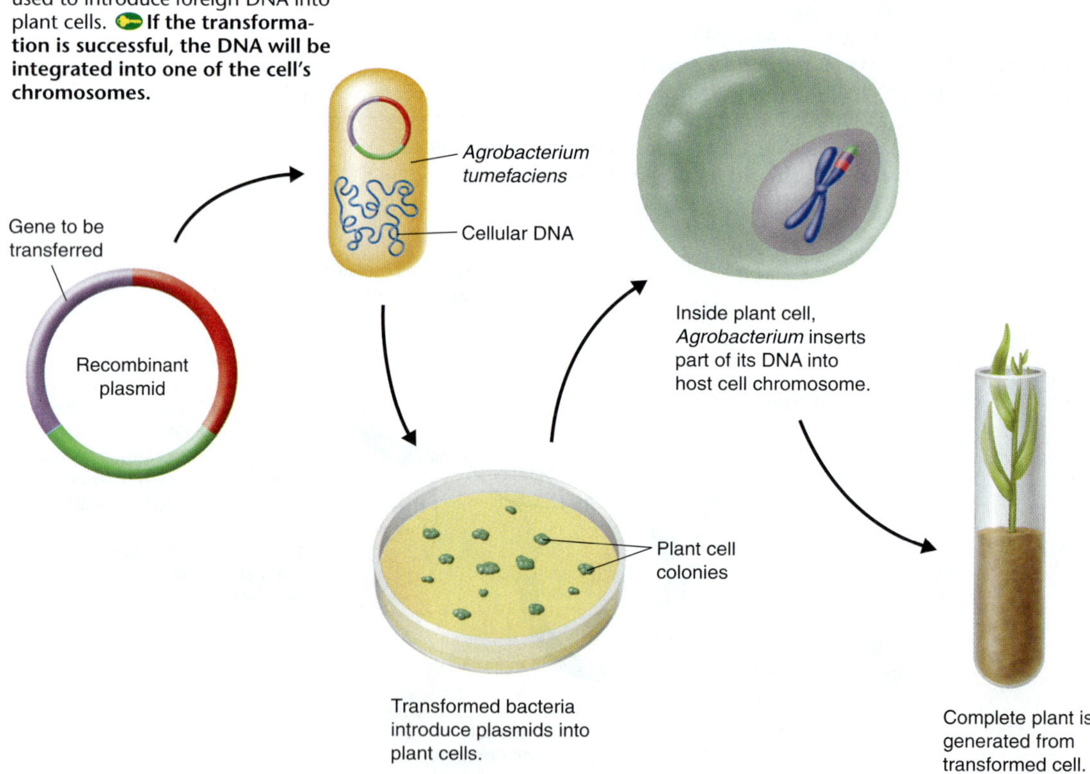

UNIVERSAL ACCESS

English Language Learners
Assess how well students understand transformation by giving them the opportunity to explain the three different processes in their own words. You might accomplish this by setting up small discussion groups. Students can use the figures in the section as visual aids in their explanations. Allow students to use their native languages to help them convey their understanding of the concepts. L1 L2

Advanced Learners
Interested students might want to learn more about how scientists use transformation. Encourage students to use library and Internet sources to research an example of how transformation is used. Possible topics include producing medicines, producing insect-resistant plants, or determining gene function. Students can prepare a poster or computer presentation about their findings. L3

When their cell walls are removed, plant cells in culture will sometimes take up DNA on their own. DNA can also be injected directly into some cells. Cells transformed by either procedure can be cultured to produce adult plants. **If transformation is successful, the recombinant DNA is integrated into one of the chromosomes of the cell.**

Transforming Animal Cells

Animal cells can be transformed in some of the same ways as plant cells. Many egg cells are large enough that DNA can be directly injected into the nucleus. Once inside the nucleus, enzymes normally responsible for DNA repair and recombination may help to insert the foreign DNA into the chromosomes of the injected cell. Like bacterial plasmids, the DNA molecules used for transformation of animal and plant cells contain marker genes that enable biologists to identify which cells have been transformed.

Recently, it has become possible to eliminate particular genes by careful design of the DNA molecules that are used for transformation. As **Figure 13–11** shows, DNA molecules can be constructed with two ends that will sometimes recombine with specific sequences in the host chromosome. Once they do, the host gene normally found between those two sequences may be lost or specifically replaced with a new gene. This kind of gene replacement has made it possible to pinpoint the specific functions of genes in many organisms, including mice.

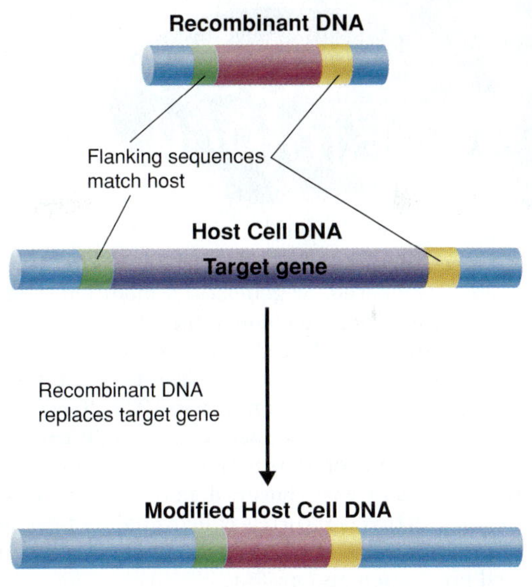

▲ **Figure 13–11** Recombinant DNA can replace a gene in an animal's genome. The ends of the recombinant DNA recombine with sequences in the host cell DNA. When the recombinant DNA is inserted into the target location, the host cell's original gene is lost or knocked out of its place. **Applying Concepts** *How might this technique be used to treat disorders caused by a single gene? What might be some risks?*

13–3 Section Assessment

1. **Key Concept** What is transformation?
2. **Key Concept** How can you tell if a transformation experiment has been successful?
3. How are genetic markers related to transformation?
4. What are two features that make plasmids useful for transforming cells?
5. **Critical Thinking Comparing and Contrasting** Compare the transformation of a bacterium cell with the transformation of a plant cell.

Writing in Science

Writing a Plan for an Experiment

Imagine that you are a genetic engineer. Determine what your next experiment will be. Then, write up the steps you will follow and what your intended result will be.

13–3 Section Assessment

1. A process in which a cell incorporates DNA from outside the cell into its own DNA
2. If transformation is successful, the DNA will be integrated into one of the cell's chromosomes.
3. A genetic marker makes it possible to distinguish a cell that has been transformed from those that have not.
4. They have DNA sequences that promote plasmid replication, and they have genetic markers.
5. Recombinant plasmids are simply taken up by bacterial cells. Plant cells do not naturally take up DNA. Recombinant plasmids are either directly injected into cells or carried into the cell by an infecting bacterium.

Transforming Animal Cells

Build Science Skills

Using Models Have students model the changes made to the DNA molecule when an animal cell is transformed. Students can use different-colored pipe cleaners or pop beads. While students demonstrate what happens to the chromosome, encourage them to narrate the process. L1 L2

3 ASSESS

Evaluate Understanding

Have students devise a table in which they compare and contrast the process of transformation in bacteria, plant cells, and animal cells. Make sure students describe how the processes are similar and how they are different.

Reteach

Have students review the procedures for transforming bacteria, plant cells, and animal cells by diagramming the procedure for each. For each step of the procedure, students should explain what is occurring. They can use the figures in the section as guides.

Writing in Science

Help students get started by suggesting that they first determine what their end product will be. Then, students can write the protocol. Students might choose the techniques described in this section, as well as in the previous section.

If your class subscribes to the iText, use it to review the Key Concepts in Section 13–3.

Answers to . . .

CHECKPOINT *A gene that makes it possible to distinguish bacteria that carry the plasmid and foreign DNA*

Figure 13–11 *The mutated gene causing the disorder can be replaced by the normal gene. It could disrupt the sequence of a normal gene, or too many copies could be inserted.*

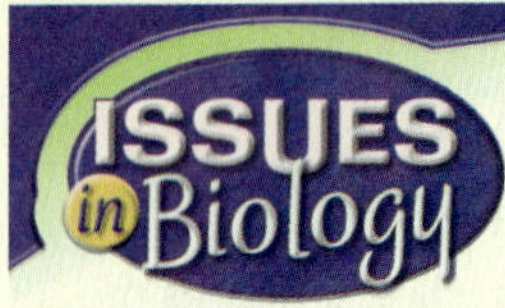

 **BI 5.c, BIIE 1.m**

After students have read the feature, invite them to learn more about this issue. First, encourage students to learn how genetically modified foods are produced. Then, have them research one specific example of a genetically modified food. They should learn what genes were added to the plant or animal and why the plant or animal was altered. They should learn what benefit or improvement researchers were trying to make. Finally, have students present their findings to the class. Encourage the class to debate the pros and cons of each example.

Research and Decide

1. Risks: could cause unexpected effects on people, such as allergic reactions; could kill beneficial insects; could cause antibiotic-resistant bacteria; could produce weeds that don't respond to herbicides. Benefits: provide essential vitamins; higher yields could help prevent famine in some parts of world; eliminate need for chemical pesticides; could be inexpensive sources of medicines, fuels, and plastics
2. Students should give sound reasons to support their opinions.

Students can research genetically modified foods on the site developed by authors Ken Miller and Joe Levine.

BI 5.c, BIIE 1.m

Do Genetically Modified Foods Need Stricter Controls?

Since they were first introduced in 1994, bioengineered, or genetically modified (GM), crops have become common in the American supermarket and diet. Most GM plants are engineered to produce pest-killing chemicals or to resist weed-killing chemicals. For example, in 1998, 20 percent of U.S. corn crops contained a gene for *Bt-toxin,* a natural insecticide that protects corn plants from the European corn borer, a major insect pest. *Bt*-corn, as this GM corn is called, enables farmers to produce more food on fewer acres, increasing food production and profits.

Many consumers, however, are concerned about the long-term impact of these crops. The European Union, for example, has effectively stopped the import of many GM food crops and required that others be prominently labeled as genetically modified. Should GM foods be more tightly controlled?

The Viewpoints

GM Foods Need Tighter Controls

Some people are concerned that GM foods might have unexpected effects on people. For example, one type of GM corn approved only for animal feed has appeared accidentally in tortillas. The corn contains a protein that could cause allergic reactions in people. The contaminated tortillas show that GM crops can get mixed in with crops that have not been genetically modified.

Genetically modified crops also could pose a hazard to the environment. Antibiotic-resistant genes used as markers could spread into the environment, resulting in antibiotic-resistant bacteria. Pollen from GM plants might transfer genes to wild plants, resulting in "super weeds" that are impossible to control with weed killers. Plants engineered to produce insecticides can kill beneficial insects as well as pests. The spread of these pesticide genes from crop plants into wild plants might harm beneficial insects, such as bees and butterflies.

GM Foods Do Not Need Tighter Controls

Recently developed GM food crops contain essential vitamins that are lacking in the diets of many people. For example, golden rice contains genes that greatly increase its content of beta-carotene, which the body uses to make vitamin A. The high productivity and nutritional benefits of GM crops are especially important in developing countries, where their use may prevent famine and ease suffering.

Because they increase production and reduce the need for chemical pesticides, GM crops can be beneficial to the environment. Someday, GM plants could be sources of medicines, fuels, and plastics. If GM products are more strictly controlled, companies might not research new applications.

Research and Decide

1. **Analyzing the Viewpoints** To make an informed decision, learn more about this issue by consulting library or Internet resources. Then, list the risks and benefits of GM plants.
2. **Forming Your Opinion** Are stricter regulations needed? Give reasons for your opinion.

For: Links from the authors
Visit: PHSchool.com
Web Code: cbe-4133

13–4 Applications of Genetic Engineering

BI 5.c. Students know how genetic engineering (biotechnology) is used to produce novel biomedical and agricultural products.

Genetic engineering makes it possible to transfer DNA sequences, including whole genes, from one organism to another. Does this mean that genes from organisms as different as animals and plants can be made to work in each other? American researcher Steven Howell and his associates provided the answer in 1986. They isolated the gene for luciferase, an enzyme that allows fireflies to glow, and inserted it into tobacco cells. When whole plants were grown from the recombinant cells and the gene was activated, the plants glowed in the dark, as you can see in **Figure 13–12.** The gene for luciferase, which comes from an animal, can specify a trait in a plant. This shows that the basic mechanisms of gene expression are shared by plants and animals.

Guide for Reading

Key Concept
- How are transgenic organisms useful to human beings?

Vocabulary
transgenic
clone

Reading Strategy: Monitoring Your Understanding Make a table with three columns. Before you read, write what you already know about cloning in the first column. Under the next heading, write down what you want to learn about cloning. After you read, write down what you learned about cloning in the last column.

Transgenic Organisms

The universal nature of genetic mechanisms makes it possible to construct organisms that are **transgenic,** meaning that they contain genes from other species. Using the basic techniques of genetic engineering, a gene from one organism can be inserted into cells from another organism. These transformed cells can then be used to grow new organisms. **Genetic engineering has spurred the growth of biotechnology, which is a new industry that is changing the way we interact with the living world.**

Transgenic Microorganisms

Because they reproduce rapidly and are easy to grow, transgenic bacteria now produce a host of important substances useful for health and industry. The human forms of proteins such as insulin, growth hormone, and clotting factor, which are used to treat serious human diseases and conditions, were once rare and expensive. Bacteria transformed with the genes for human proteins now produce these important compounds cheaply and in great abundance. People with insulin-dependent diabetes are now treated with pure human insulin produced by human genes inserted into bacteria. In the future, transgenic microorganisms may produce substances designed to fight cancer, as well as the raw materials for plastics and synthetic fibers.

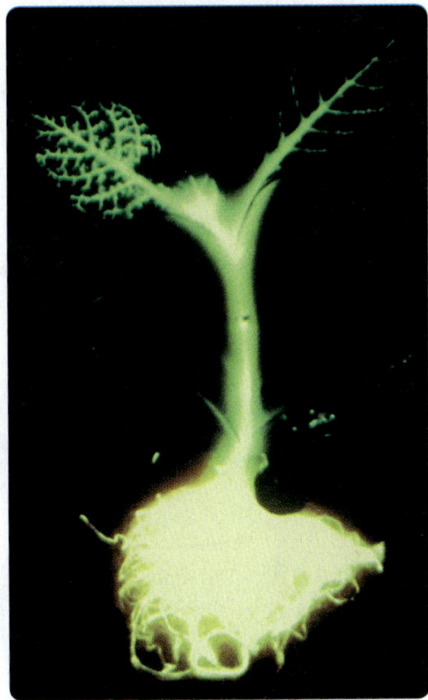

▶ **Figure 13–12** **Genetic engineering has changed the way we interact with living things.** This transgenic tobacco plant, which glows in the dark, was grown from a tobacco cell transformed with the firefly luciferase gene. The plant illustrates how DNA from one organism contains information that can specify traits in another organism.

SECTION RESOURCES

Print:
- ***Teaching Resources,*** Lesson Plan 13–4, Adapted Section Summary 13–4, Section Summary 13–4, Worksheets 13–4, Section Review 13–4, Enrichment
- ***Reading and Study Workbook A,*** Section 13–4
- ***Issues and Decision Making,*** Issues and Decisions 18
- ***Biotechnology Manual,*** Lab 17; Issue 4

Technology:
- ***iText,*** Section 13–4
- ***Transparencies Plus,*** Section 13–4

Section 13–4

BI 5.c

1 FOCUS

Objectives

13.4.1 ***Describe*** the usefulness of some transgenic organisms to humans.

13.4.2 ***Summarize*** the main steps in cloning.

Guide for Reading

Vocabulary Preview

Challenge students to infer the meaning of the word *transgenic* by first explaining that the prefix *trans-* means "across or beyond." Write students' inferences on the board, and review them as you study the section. After completing the section, compare the inferences with the actual meaning.

Reading Strategy

Encourage students to make a list of the events involved in cloning. You might also want students to add diagrams to their list of events.

2 INSTRUCT

Transgenic Organisms

Build Science Skills

Using Models Challenge students to create a model of a transgenic organism. Encourage them to be creative. Students may choose a bacterium, a plant, or an animal. If possible, try to get a mixture of organisms in the class. Students can use various materials to create a three-dimensional organism, or they can simply diagram the organism. In either case, students must describe what gene or genes were inserted into the organism, how the foreign gene or genes affect the phenotype of the organism, and how this new phenotype is beneficial. Have students present their models to the class. L2

13–4 (continued)

Download a worksheet on genetic engineering for students to complete, and find additional teacher support from NSTA SciLinks.

Address Misconceptions

Students might have the mistaken idea that performing genetic engineering techniques and transformations is easy. Emphasize that these procedures are complicated and often fail for no apparent reasons. For example, on average, scientists inject 50 mouse eggs with DNA before one egg survives to form a living, developing embryo. Encourage students to read articles about the experiments described in the section to learn the success rates of the procedures. L2

For: Links on genetic engineering
Visit: www.SciLinks.org
Web Code: cbn-4134

Transgenic Animals Transgenic animals have been used to study genes and to improve the food supply. Mice have been produced with human genes that make their immune systems act similarly to those of humans. This allows scientists to study the effects of diseases on the human immune system. Some transgenic livestock now have extra copies of growth hormone genes. Such animals grow faster and produce leaner meat than ordinary animals. Researchers are trying to produce transgenic chickens that will be resistant to the bacterial infections that can cause food poisoning.

In the future, transgenic animals might also provide us with an ample supply of our own proteins. Several labs have engineered transgenic sheep and pigs that produce human proteins in their milk, making it easy to collect and refine the proteins.

Transgenic Plants Transgenic plants are now an important part of our food supply. In the year 2000, 52 percent of the soybeans and 25 percent of the corn grown in the United States were transgenic, or genetically modified (GM). Many of these plants contain genes that produce a natural insecticide, so the crops do not have to be sprayed with synthetic pesticides. Other crop plants have genes that enable them to resist weed-killing chemicals. These genes allow crop plants to survive while weeds are still controlled.

▼ **Figure 13–13** In early 1997, Dolly made headlines as the first clone of an adult mammal. **Applying Concepts** *Why did Dolly not look like her foster mother?*

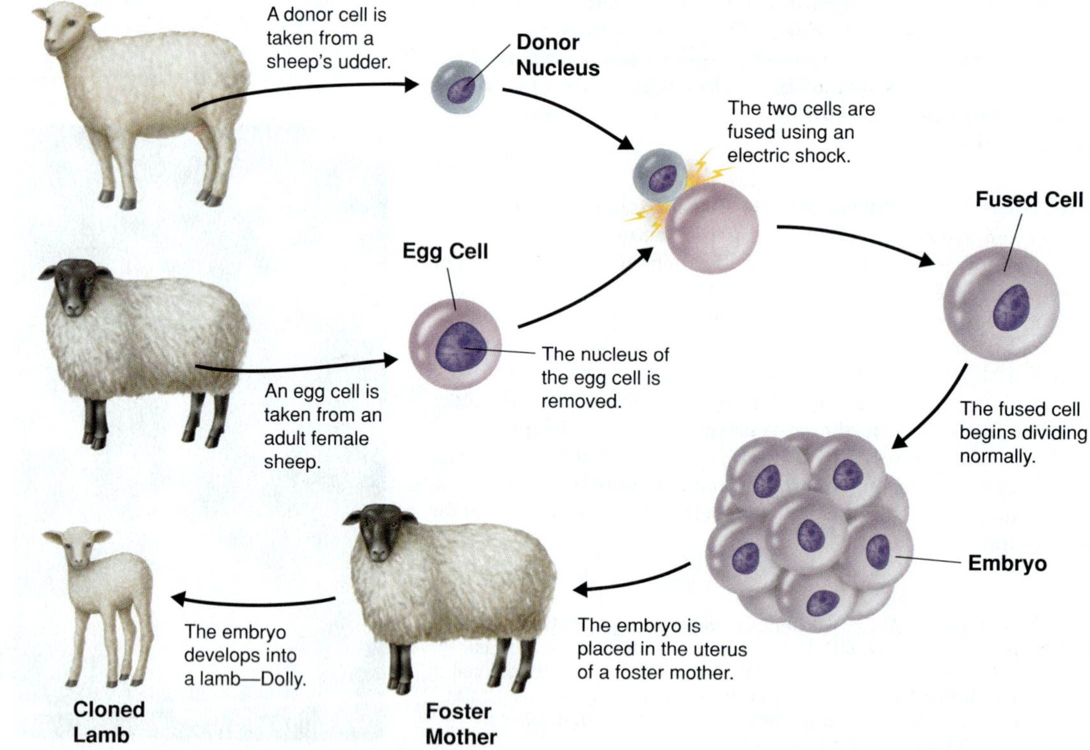

UNIVERSAL ACCESS

Inclusion/Special Needs

Have groups of students with mixed abilities choose one specific example of applied genetic engineering, such as producing a human protein to treat a disease. Then, groups should discuss how the transgenic organism was produced, beginning with the isolation of the desired gene and ending with how the phenotype of the transgenic organism is different. L1 L2

Less Proficient Readers

Make sure students have made the transition from manipulating DNA molecules to engineering new organisms. Have students make flowcharts that show the steps in developing a transgenic organism. Remind them that first the DNA fragment to be inserted into the organism must be constructed. Then, one of the transformation techniques described in Section 13–3 must be used. L1 L2

Transgenic plants may soon produce human antibodies that can be used to fight disease, plastics that can now be produced only from petroleum, and foods that are resistant to rot and spoilage. One of the most important new developments in GM foods is a rice plant that contains vitamin A, a nutrient that is essential for human health. Since rice is the major food for billions of the world's people, this rice may improve the diets and health of many people by supplying an important nutrient.

Cloning

A **clone** is a member of a population of genetically identical cells produced from a single cell. Cloned colonies of bacteria and other microorganisms are easy to grow, but this is not always true of multicellular organisms, especially animals. For many years, biologists wondered if it might be possible to clone a mammal—to use a single cell from an adult to grow an entirely new individual that is genetically identical to the organism from which the cell was taken. After years of research, many scientists had concluded that this was impossible.

In 1997, Scottish scientist Ian Wilmut stunned biologists by announcing that he had cloned a sheep. How did he do it? **Figure 13–13** shows the basic steps. In Wilmut's technique, the nucleus of an egg cell is removed. The cell is fused with a cell taken from another adult. The fused cell begins to divide and the embryo is then placed in the reproductive system of a foster mother, where it develops normally. The sheep, which Wilmut named Dolly, is shown in **Figure 13–14.** Cloned cows, pigs, mice, and other mammals have been produced by similar techniques. Researchers hope that cloning will enable them to make copies of transgenic animals and even help save endangered species. On the other hand, the technology is controversial for many reasons, including studies suggesting that cloned animals may suffer from a number of genetic defects and health problems.

The use of cloning technology on humans, while scientifically possible, raises serious ethical and moral issues that have caused many people to oppose such work. As techniques improve, these important issues will become even more pressing.

▲ **Figure 13–14** The adult sheep is Dolly, the first mammal cloned from an adult cell. The lamb is Dolly's first offspring, called Bonnie. The fact that Dolly was cloned did not affect her ability to produce a live offspring. **Inferring** *Why might it be important for cloned animals to be able to reproduce?*

13–4 Section Assessment

1. **Key Concept** List one practical application for each of the following: transgenic bacteria, transgenic animals, transgenic plants.
2. **Key Concept** What is a transgenic organism?
3. What basic steps were followed to produce Dolly?
4. **Critical Thinking Making Judgments** List reasons you would or would not be concerned about eating genetically modified food.

You & Your Community

Conducting a Survey
Survey at least ten people about their viewpoints on cloning animals. To help the people you survey understand the topic, prepare an illustrated explanation of the process of cloning.

13–4 Section Assessment

1. Sample answers: transgenic bacteria—to produce human proteins for medical use, produce materials for plastics; animals—study genes, improve food supply, provide human proteins; plants—improve food supply, produce human antibodies, produce plastics
2. An organism that contains genes from another species
3. The nucleus of an egg cell is removed and replaced with a nucleus taken from another adult. This egg is then placed in the reproductive system of a foster mother, where it develops normally.
4. Some may be concerned because the foods might harm humans, for example, by causing allergies. Others will not be concerned because they think the genetic modifications will not affect humans adversely.

Cloning

Use Visuals

Figure 13–13 Go through Ian Wilmut's procedure for producing a clone of a sheep. Discuss how this procedure is similar to and different from transformation. Point out that Dolly was not a transgenic animal because she did not have any DNA sequences from a different organism. Her DNA was exactly the same as the DNA from the donor sheep. Also, relate the cloning procedure to meiosis and fertilization, having volunteers point out which cells are diploid (*donor nucleus*) and which are haploid (*egg cell nucleus*). L1 L2

3 ASSESS

Evaluate Understanding

Have students draw diagrams to show how a transgenic organism is produced and how a clone is produced.

Reteach

Instruct students to make a table to describe the uses and the examples of transgenic microorganisms, animals, and plants.

You & Your Community

Results will depend on the viewpoints of the people interviewed. However, all results should include at least 10 different people and their viewpoints, either for or against cloning animals.

Interactive Textbook

If your class subscribes to the iText, use it to review the Key Concepts in Section 13–4.

Answers to . . .

Figure 13–13 *Dolly received all of her genetic material from the donor sheep, not from the foster mother.*

Figure 13–14 *To make it possible to pass on the desired trait to future generations*

Design an Experiment

7IIE 7.c, 8IIE 9.c, BIIE 1.a, BIIE 1.b

Objective Students will be able to investigate whether plants grown from irradiated seeds have more mutations. L2

Skill Focus Forming Operational Definitions

Time 45 minutes

Advance Prep Purchase irradiated seeds from a biological supply company, or arrange to have your seeds irradiated at a local university or medical clinic.

Safety
- If commercial potting soil is not used, students should wear plastic gloves. Dispose of the gloves properly.

Pre-Lab Discussion Review with the class how mutations can be induced in DNA. Remind students that radiation, or exposure to X-rays, damages the DNA molecule. Then, encourage students to brainstorm a list of mutations that they might observe in the plants grown from irradiated seeds. If no one mentions it, point out that lethality is one possibility. In other words, they might observe a lower germination rate in irradiated seeds. Finally, go over the procedure with students and answer any questions they have.

Teaching Tips
- Review each group's experimental design before students proceed with their experiment. Make sure their data table is organized properly to include the observations that they plan to record.
- Place the petri dishes in a warm, dark place while the seeds are germinating. After germination, move the petri dishes into direct light.

Expected Outcomes Students should observe that irradiated seeds have variable growth and development, whereas nonirradiated seeds grow and develop normally.

Design an Experiment

7IIE 7.c, 8IIE 9.c, BIIE 1.a, BIIE 1.b

Investigating the Effects of Radiation on Seeds

Mutations occur naturally in all organisms. However, an organism's mutation rate increases when it is exposed to certain chemicals or types of radiation. In this investigation, you will design an experiment to test the effects of X-ray exposure on seeds.

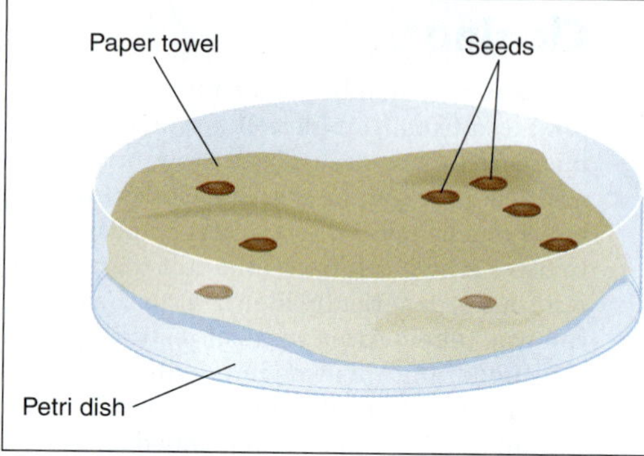

Problem
Do plants grown from irradiated seeds show evidence of increased mutation?

Materials
- irradiated seeds and nonirradiated seeds of the same species
- petri dishes
- paper towels
- plant pots with commercial potting soil
- glass-marking pencil

Skills
Forming Operational Definitions

Design Your Experiment

Part A: Plan the Experiment

1. **Designing Experiments** Working with two of your classmates, design an experiment to test the hypothesis that radiation increases the rate of mutation in seeds.
2. As you plan your investigative procedures, refer to the Lab Tips box on page 55 for information on demonstrating safe practices, making wise choices in the use of materials, and selecting equipment and technology.
3. Discuss your experimental plan with your group. Make certain that you have identified and controlled all important variables and included both irradiated and control seeds in your experimental plan.
4. You will not be able to observe mutations in DNA directly. What observations or measurements can you make that will provide evidence of the number of mutations that have occurred in a seed? With your group, plan what observations you will use to estimate the number of mutations that have occurred in a seed.
5. Design a data table in which to record your observations.
6. Show your experimental plan to your teacher. Once your teacher approves your plan, begin your experiment.

Part B: Carry Out Your Experiment

7. To grow the seeds, follow any instructions that are on the seed packages. If there are no instructions, line a petri dish with a paper towel for each experimental group of seeds. Place the seeds in the petri dishes, as shown in the diagram above. Cover the seeds with water. **CAUTION:** *Wash your hands well with warm water and plenty of soap after handling seeds, plants, or soil and before leaving the laboratory.*
8. Place the covers on the petri dishes to protect the seeds from mold and bacteria. Record everything you do to the seeds.
9. Use a glass-marking pencil to label each petri dish. Every petri dish that you use in this experiment should be identified by a different label that includes your name. Store the petri dishes in the location that your teacher designates.
10. Record your observations of each group of seed every day for 2 weeks. Add water to the petri dishes as necessary to keep the seeds moist.
11. After 2 weeks, count the seeds that failed to germinate. Carefully transfer the young plants from the petri dishes to pots of soil. Water each plant. Label each pot with your name and the kind of plants it contains.

12 Place the potted plants in sunlight or under a fluorescent lamp as your teacher directs. Water the plants regularly. Continue to observe the plants daily, according to your experimental plans, for the next 2 weeks. Record your observations each day.

Analyze and Conclude

1. **Comparing and Contrasting** What differences did you observe between the irradiated seeds and the nonirradiated seeds?
2. **Designing Experiments** How could you best determine whether a seed contains mutant DNA?
3. **Forming Operational Definitions** What kinds of observations did you decide to use as evidence of mutations? Explain why you think that these observations are reliable evidence.
4. **Analyzing Data** Did the irradiated seeds show evidence of more mutations than the nonirradiated seeds?
5. **Formulating Hypotheses** Mutations sometimes cause part of an otherwise healthy-looking leaf or other plant part to appear abnormal. Did you see abnormal-looking areas on any plants? Would you expect this kind of abnormality to be inherited? Explain.
6. **Evaluating** What explanations, other than mutation, can you think of for the differences you observed between the irradiated seeds and the nonirradiated seeds?
7. **SAFETY:** Explain how you demonstrated safe practices during this investigation.

Go Further

Communicating Valid Conclusions
Compare your data to those of other students in your class. Work with the rest of the students in your class to reach a conclusion about the effect of radiation on seeds. Your conclusion should be based on class data. Then, write a short report about your experiment that would be suitable to submit to a scientific journal. Your report should communicate your conclusion and explain why it is valid.

Analyze and Conclude

1. Observations will vary. Some irradiated seeds will grow into plants that look the same as those from nonirradiated seeds. Other irradiated seeds will produce plants with very different phenotypes, or they may not grow at all.
2. A seed that produces an abnormal plant probably has mutant DNA.
3. Students should show evidence of understanding that mutations often cause random, usually damaging, changes in growth and development.
4. Observations will vary, but irradiated seeds will probably produce plants with more mutations than nonirradiated seeds, if they grow at all.
5. Observations will vary, but this type of damage is common in irradiated plants. Localized damage is often a sign of a mutation in somatic (nongamete) cells. These mutations are not inherited because they do not affect the genes of the gametes.
6. Possible explanations include that the seeds contained mutant DNA before they were irradiated; the seeds were not produced by homozygous parents; or the seeds were subjected to different environmental conditions.
7. Students should say that they washed their hands well with soap and warm water after handling seeds, plants, and soil, and before leaving the lab.

Go Further

In their reports, students should begin with their scientific question, some background information about mutations, and a description of their expected results. Then, they should present the class data, analyze the data, and clearly describe their conclusions about the effect of radiation on seeds. They should give reasons and evidence to support their conclusions.

Chapter 13 Study Guide

Study Tip

Have students develop a crossword puzzle, word search, or other word puzzle that incorporates the Vocabulary terms and some of the Key Concepts. Students can exchange their puzzles and solve them.

Thinking Visually

1. Selective Breeding
2. Genetic Engineering
3. Hybridization

Chapter 13 Assessment

Reviewing Content

1. c	5. a	9. a
2. a	6. b	10. a
3. c	7. c	
4. a	8. c	

Understanding Concepts

11. Hybridization: cross dissimilar organisms; inbreeding: breed similar organisms; both involve selecting to breed organisms with the desired characteristics.

12. By inducing mutations with chemicals or radiation

13. The condition in which cells have many sets of chromosomes; it may instantly produce new plant species that are larger and stronger.

14. Both have codes that can be isolated and altered to change the characteristics of the game or the organism.

15. With restriction enzymes that recognize and cut specific nucleotide sequences of DNA

16. Gel electrophoresis enables scientists to separate and analyze DNA fragments, to compare genomes of different individuals and organisms, and to identify a specific gene.

17. A DNA molecule produced by combining DNA from other sources

Chapter 13 Study Guide

13–1 Changing the Living World

Key Concepts 

- Humans use selective breeding, which takes advantage of naturally occurring genetic variation in plants, animals, and other organisms, to pass desired traits on to the next generation of organisms.
- Breeders can increase the genetic variation in a population by inducing mutations, which are the ultimate source of genetic variability.

Vocabulary

selective breeding, p. 319
hybridization, p. 319
inbreeding, p. 320

13–2 Manipulating DNA

Key Concept 

- Scientists use their knowledge of the structure of DNA and its chemical properties to study and change DNA molecules. Different techniques are used to extract DNA from cells, to cut DNA into smaller pieces, to identify the sequence of bases in a DNA molecule, and to make unlimited copies of DNA.

Vocabulary

genetic engineering, p. 322
restriction enzyme, p. 323
gel electrophoresis, p. 323
recombinant DNA, p. 324
polymerase chain reaction (PCR), p. 325

13–3 Cell Transformation

 **Key Concepts** 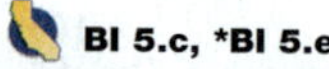

- During transformation, a cell takes in DNA from outside the cell. This external DNA becomes a component of the cell's DNA.
- If transformation is successful, the recombinant DNA is integrated into one of the chromosomes of the cell.

Vocabulary

plasmid, p. 327
genetic marker, p. 328

13–4 Applications of Genetic Engineering

Key Concept 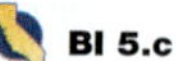

- Genetic engineering has spurred the growth of biotechnology, which is a new industry that is changing the way we interact with the living world.

Vocabulary

transgenic, p. 331
clone, p. 333

Thinking Visually

Using the information in this chapter, complete the following concept map:

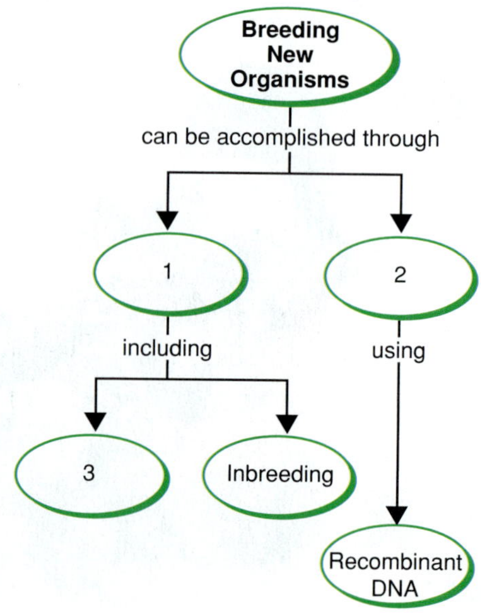

CHAPTER RESOURCES

Print:

- ***Teaching Resources,*** Chapter Vocabulary Review, Graphic Organizer, Chapter 13 Tests: Levels A and B

Technology:

- ***iText,*** Chapter 13 Assessment
- ***Computer Test Bank,*** Chapter 13 Test

Chapter 13 Assessment

Reviewing Content

Choose the letter that best answers the question or completes the statement.

1. A cross between dissimilar individuals to bring together their best characteristics is called
   a. genetic engineering. c. hybridization.
   b. inbreeding. d. sequencing.

2. Crossing individuals with similar characteristics so that those characteristics will appear in the offspring is called
   a. inbreeding. c. hybridization.
   b. electrophoresis. d. genetic engineering.

3. Varieties of purebred dogs are maintained by
   a. selective breeding. c. inbreeding.
   b. hybridization. d. genetic engineering.

4. Changing the DNA of an organism is called
   a. genetic engineering.
   b. hybridization.
   c. selective breeding.
   d. inbreeding.

5. DNA can be cut into shorter sequences by proteins known as
   a. restriction enzymes.
   b. plasmids.
   c. mutagens.
   d. clones.

6. What has been produced in the drawing below?

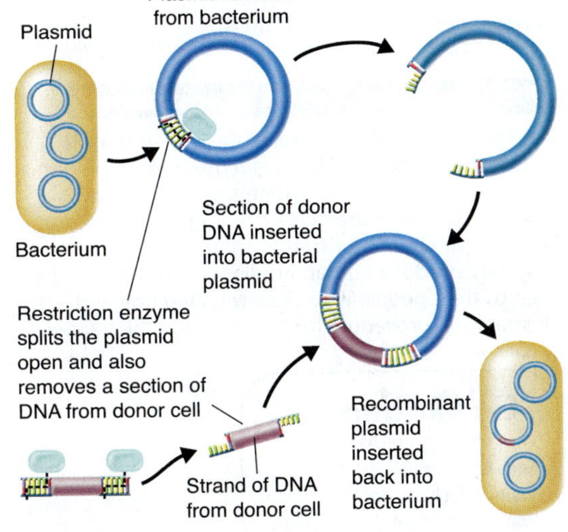

   a. a clone c. a genome
   b. recombinant DNA d. a species

Interactive textbook with assessment at PHSchool.com

7. When cell transformation is successful, the recombinant DNA
   a. undergoes mutation.
   b. is treated with antibiotics.
   c. becomes part of the transformed cell's genome.
   d. becomes a nucleus.

8. Bacteria often contain small circular molecules of DNA known as
   a. clones. c. plasmids.
   b. restriction enzymes. d. hybrids.

9. Organisms that contain genes from other organisms are called
   a. transgenic. c. donor organisms.
   b. mutagenic. d. cloned organisms.

10. A member of a population of genetically identical cells produced from a single cell is a
   a. clone. c. mutant.
   b. plasmid. d. sequence.

Understanding Concepts

11. Compare hybridization and inbreeding. Why are they considered forms of selective breeding?
12. How do breeders produce new genetic variations not found in nature?
13. What is polyploidy? When is this condition useful?
14. Explain why genetic engineering can be compared to reprogramming a computer game.
15. How are large DNA molecules cut up?
16. What role does gel electrophoresis play in the study of DNA?
17. What is recombinant DNA?
18. Describe what occurs during a polymerase chain reaction (PCR).
19. What happens during cell transformation? What are some types of cells that have been transformed?
20. Explain what genetic markers are, and describe how scientists use them.
21. What did the successful transfer of the luciferase gene from an animal to a plant indicate about the functioning of genes?
22. What is a transgenic organism? Explain how transgenic bacteria have been useful.
23. How did Ian Wilmut clone the sheep known as Dolly?
24. Explain how a transgenic plant differs from a hybrid plant.

HOMEWORK GUIDE

TIME SAVER

Section:	Questions:
Section 13–1	1–3, 11–13, 27
Section 13–2	4, 5, 14–18, 28
Section 13–3	6–8, 19, 20, 30
Section 13–4	9, 10, 21–26, 29, 31–34

If your class subscribes to the iText, your students can go online to access an interactive version of the Student Edition and a self-test.

(Continued from page 336)

18. A short piece of complementary DNA—a primer—is added to both ends of the DNA fragment to be copied. The DNA is heated to separate the two strands, and then cooled. DNA polymerase makes copies of the region between the two primer sequences. The copies also serve as templates to make more copies.

19. A cell takes in DNA from outside the cell, and the external DNA becomes a part of the cell's DNA. Bacteria and plant and animal cells are types of cells that have been transformed.

20. Genetic markers make it possible to distinguish bacteria that carry plasmids and foreign DNA from those that do not; genetic markers are inserted into plasmids so that scientists can identify transformed bacteria.

21. That the basic mechanisms for gene expression are shared by plants and animals

22. An organism that contains genes from other organisms; produce important substances for health and industry

23. Ian Wilmut removed the nucleus of an egg cell and replaced it with a nucleus taken from a cell from another adult. This egg was then placed in the reproductive system of a foster mother, where it developed normally.

24. A transgenic plant contains DNA from another organism via genetic engineering. A hybrid plant contains DNA only from both parents via fertilization.

Chapter 13 Assessment

Critical Thinking

25. They can be produced relatively inexpensively in large quantities; they are the actual human protein; and they are pure.

26. No, the change involves body (somatic) cells, not germ cells.

27. Answers should involve crossing the different varieties of roses and selecting the offspring with the desired traits for further crosses. For example: cross the pink and yellow roses until a thornless plant with sweet-smelling flowers is obtained. Cross this plant with purple roses until thornless plants with sweet-smelling purple flowers are obtained. Inbreed these plants until the traits breed true.

28. T-A-C-G-C-T-T-T-T-C-G-C-A-A-A-G-A-C-C-T-G-C-C-A-G-T-G-A-T-T

29. Breeding techniques require little technology and take much time. It is also difficult to achieve the desired combination of traits. Genetic engineering requires extensive training and expensive equipment. Specific combinations of traits can be made, and traits from organisms that cannot be crossed naturally can be combined.

30. DNA from one organism can be inserted into another, and the gene is successfully expressed to produce the same protein.

31. The blood proteins that people need could be produced by bacteria that have been transformed with the human gene that encodes the needed protein.

32. Sample answers: Transgenic microorganisms might produce substances designed to fight cancer, as well as the raw materials for plastics and synthetic fibers. Transgenic animals might provide humans with sources of human proteins. Transgenic plants might produce human antibodies that can be used to fight disease, foods that are resistant to spoilage, and foods that contain extra vitamins.

33. All DNA contains the same four nucleotides and is translated by the same mechanism and genetic code, so the DNA from a bacterium could be used to make a human protein.

Chapter 13 Assessment

Critical Thinking

25. Applying Concepts Describe one or more advantages of producing needed proteins such as insulin through genetic engineering.

26. Inferring If a human patient's bone marrow cells were removed, altered genetically, and reimplanted, would the change be passed on to the patient's children? Explain your answer.

27. Problem Solving Suppose a plant breeder has a thornless rose bush with scentless pink flowers, a thorny rose bush with sweet-smelling yellow flowers, and a thorny rose bush with scentless purple flowers. How might the plant breeder develop a purebred variety of thornless sweet-smelling purple roses?

28. Problem Solving The following fragments were obtained when a gene that consists of ten codons was cut by restriction enzymes. What is the sequence of bases in the gene? (*Hint:* Look for overlapping sections on the fragments.)

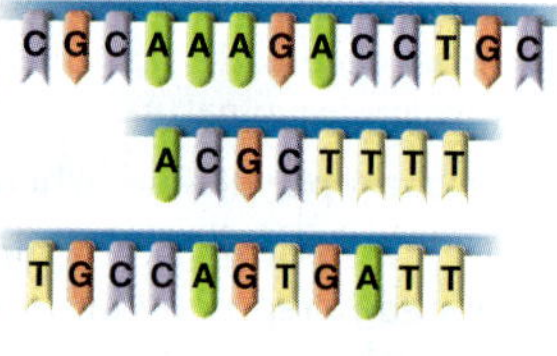

29. Comparing and Contrasting Compare the advantages and disadvantages of breeding techniques and genetic engineering.

30. Formulating Hypotheses Almost every organism has DNA that is made of the same four nucleotides and translated by the same genetic code. Explain why this fact is significant in cell transformation.

31. Inferring Some people need blood transfusions because their blood lacks important proteins, such as those needed for blood clotting. People who receive blood transfusions have some risk of being exposed to disease-causing viruses. How might genetic engineering eliminate this risk?

32. Predicting Predict three ways in which you think genetically engineered organisms will be used in the future.

33. Applying Concepts Bacteria and human beings are very different organisms. Why is it sometimes possible to combine their DNA and use a bacterium to make a human protein?

34. Applying Concepts Your friend proposes that using genetic engineering, biologists should be able to produce an organism with any combination of characteristics. For example, they could create an animal with the body of a frog and the wings of a bat. Do you think this is a reasonable proposal? Explain your answer.

Focus on the BIG Idea

Information and Heredity In Chapter 12, you learned how DNA and RNA molecules specify the traits of an organism. Use this knowledge to illustrate how, at the molecular level, the DNA and RNA of a transgenic tobacco plant produce the trait of glowing in the dark.

Writing in Science

Your local newspaper has published an editorial against the use of genetic engineering. The editorial states that genetic engineering is still too new to use, while traditional selective breeding can accomplish anything that genetic engineering can do. Write a letter to the newspaper either in support of the newspaper's position or against it.

Performance-Based Assessment

Design a Procedure Insulin is a protein that enables body cells to take in glucose from the blood. People with one type of diabetes do not produce enough insulin, so their cells cannot take in glucose. Devise a procedure for transforming bacterial cells so that they produce human insulin, which can then be used to treat people with diabetes. Describe and illustrate the procedure for transforming the bacteria.

For: An interactive self-test
Visit: PHSchool.com
Web Code: cba-4130

34. Students should disagree. Possible explanations include: too many genetic differences exist between frogs and bats; it is too difficult to control the expression of so many genes in such a specific location.

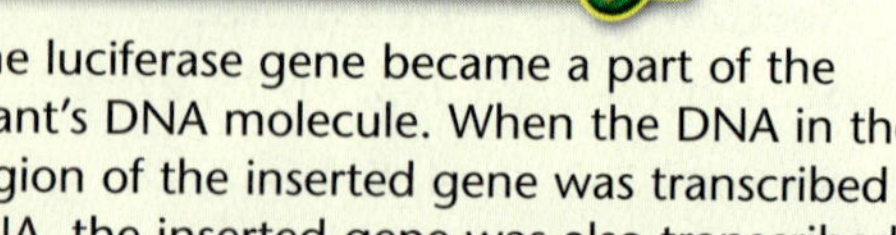

The luciferase gene became a part of the plant's DNA molecule. When the DNA in the region of the inserted gene was transcribed into RNA, the inserted gene was also transcribed. This mRNA sequence was translated by the ribosomes to produce the protein responsible for producing the trait of glowing in the dark.

Standards Practice

Online at PHSchool.com

Test-Taking Tip For questions containing the words NOT or EXCEPT, begin by eliminating each answer choice that *does* fit the characteristic in question. After eliminating all but one of the choices, check to see that your answer is correct by confirming that it does *not* fit the characteristic in question.

Directions: Choose the letter that best answers the question or completes the statement.

1. Which of the following can be used to produce organisms with desirable traits?
   A inbreeding
   B genetic engineering
   C inducing mutations
   D all of the above
2. Which of the following characteristics does NOT apply to a plasmid?
   A made of DNA
   B in bacterial cells
   C circular
   D accepts foreign DNA

Questions 3–4

A researcher chooses a plasmid with a gene that confers resistance to the antibiotic ampicillin. She isolates and tries to insert a human gene that codes for a protein into the plasmid. Next, she transforms bacteria using the plasmid. She then cultures the new bacteria on a nutrient medium containing ampicillin.

3. What can the researcher conclude about the bacteria that grow on the nutrient medium? ***BI 5.e**
   A They are resistant to ampicillin.
   B They contain recombinant DNA.
   C They contain a human gene.
   D all of the above
4. Which of the following would indicate that the bacteria contain the human gene? ***BI 5.e**
   A They produce the human protein encoded by the human gene.
   B They produce ampicillin.
   C both A and B
   D neither A nor B

Questions 5–8 Each of the lettered choices below refers to the following numbered statements. Select the best lettered choice. A choice may be used once, more than once, or not at all.

A Gel electrophoresis
B Plasmid
C Polymerase chain reaction
D Inbreeding

5. Used to insert new genes into plant cells **BI 5.c**
6. Makes many copies of a DNA sample
7. Continued breeding of individuals with similar characteristics
8. Separates DNA fragments

Questions 9–10

The graph below shows the number of accurate copies of DNA produced by polymerase chain reaction (PCR).

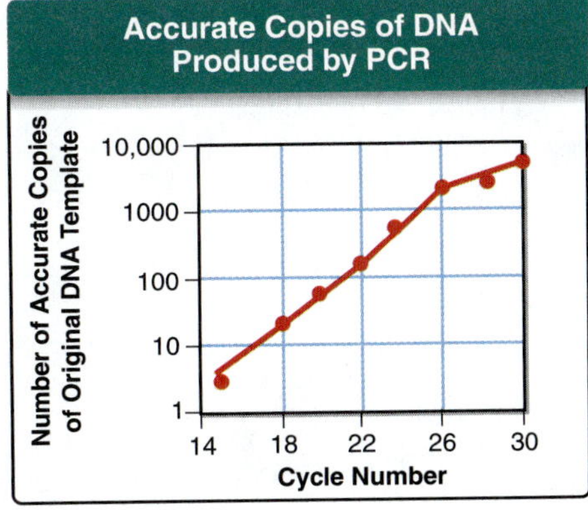

9. What can you conclude about cycles 18–26?
   A PCR produced accurate copies of template DNA at an exponential rate.
   B The amount of DNA produced by PCR doubled with each cycle of the reaction.
   C The DNA copies produced by PCR were not accurate copies of the original DNA template.
   D A and B only
10. Based on the graph, which of the following might have happened between cycles 26 and 28?
   A PCR stopped producing accurate copies of the template.
   B The rate of the reaction slowed down.
   C All the template DNA was used up.
   D A and C only

Standards Practice

1. D 2. B 3. A 4. A 5. B 6. C 7. D 8. A 9. A 10. B

Success Tracker™
Online at PHSchool.com

Have students check their understanding of the chapter by logging onto Success Tracker.

Writing in Science

Students should support their positions with examples of genetic engineering. They should demonstrate an understanding of both selective breeding and genetic engineering and the advantages and disadvantages of each.

Performance-Based Assessment

In their procedures, students should first describe the insertion of the human insulin into the bacterial plasmid by cutting both DNA molecules with the same restriction enzyme and mixing the fragments together. Then, they should describe transforming the plasmid into the bacterial cell as it is described in Section 13–3. Illustrations should look similar to Figure 13–9.

Your students can independently test their knowledge of the chapter and print out their test results for your files.

Chapter Planner 14 The Human Genome

Section and Section Objectives	Time	STANDARDS NCLB	STANDARDS Biology	Activities and Labs
14–1 Human Heredity, pp. 341–348 14.1.1 ***Identify*** the types of human chromosomes in a karyotype. 14.1.2 ***Explain*** how sex is determined. 14.1.3 ***Explain*** how pedigrees are used to study human traits. 14.1.4 ***Describe*** examples of the inheritance of human traits. 14.1.5 ***Explain*** how small changes in DNA cause genetic disorders.	2 periods (1 block)	7 2.c, 7 2.d, BI 2.e, BI 2.f, BI 3.a	BI 2.g, *BI 3.c	SE: ***Inquiry Activity,*** Can you predict chin shape?, p. 340 L2 SE: ***Problem Solving,*** Using a Pedigree, p. 343 L2 LMA: Chapter 14 Lab L2 L3 LMB: Chapter 14 Lab L1 L2 BTM: Lab 10; Issues 2, 3 L2 L3
14–2 Human Chromosomes, pp. 349–354 14.2.1 ***Identify*** characteristics of human chromosomes. 14.2.2 ***Describe*** some sex-linked disorders and explain why they are more common in males than in females. 14.2.3 ***Explain*** the process of X-chromosome inactivation. 14.2.4 ***Summarize*** nondisjunction and the problems it causes.	1 period (1/2 block)	BI 3.a, BI 7.b	BI 2.g	TE: ***Address Misconceptions,*** p. 350 L2 SE: ***Quick Lab,*** How is colorblindness transmitted?, p. 351 L2 TE: ***Build Science Skills,*** p. 352 L2 SE: ***Issues in Biology,*** Who Controls Your DNA?, p. 354 L2
14–3 Human Molecular Genetics, pp. 355–360 14.3.1 ***Summarize*** methods of human DNA analysis. 14.3.2 ***State*** the goal of the Human Genome Project. 14.3.3 ***Describe*** how researchers are attempting to cure genetic disorders.	1 period (1/2 block)			TE: ***Demonstration,*** p. 357 L2 SE: ***Careers in Biology,*** Geneticist, p. 359 L2 SE: ***Real-World Lab,*** Modeling DNA Probes, p. 361 L2 BTM: Labs 2, 11, 12; Concepts 2, 3, 4, 6 L2 L3
Chapter Assessment, pp. 362–365	1 period (1/2 block)			

ACTIVITY PLANNER

SE: *Inquiry Activity,* p. 340; 10 min.

TE: *Address Misconceptions,* p. 350; 10 min.; charts used to diagnose colorblindness

SE: *Quick Lab,* p. 351; 20 min.; 2 plastic cups, 3 white beans, black marker, red bean

TE: *Build Science Skills,* p. 352; 20 min.; prepared slides of female cells with Barr bodies and cells without Barr bodies

TE: *Demonstration,* p. 357; 15 min.; yarn, scissors

SE: *Real-World Lab,* p. 361; 45 min.; graph paper, scissors, colored pencil or marker

PLANNING KEY

Ability Levels
for students performing . . .
below grade level **L1**
at grade level **L2**
above grade level **L3**

Print Components

SE	Student Edition	LA	Lab Assessment
TE	Teacher's Edition	BTM	Biotechnology Manual
RSW	Reading & Study Workbook A	IDM	Issues and Decision Making
ARSW	Adapted Reading & Study Workbook B	LW	Lab Worksheets
TR	Teaching Resources	LMA	Laboratory Manual A
IF	Investigations in Forensics	LMB	Laboratory Manual B

Tech Components

CTB	Computer Test Bank
BD	BioDetectives DVD
TP	Transparencies Plus
PLM	Probeware Lab Manual
ABC	ABC DVD Library
LS	Lab Simulations
VL	Virtual Labs

Interactive textbook with assessment at PHSchool.com

Program Resources	Assessment	Media and Technology
TR: Lesson Plan 14–1, Section Summary, p. 144 L1, p. 152 L2, Worksheets, pp. 146–147 L1, pp. 154–156 L2 **RSW:** Section 14–1 L2 **ARSW:** Section 14–1 L1	**SE:** 14–1 Section Assessment, p. 348 **TR:** Section Review 14–1	**iText:** Section 14–1 **TP:** 14–1 Interest Grabber, Section Outline, Concept Map, Figure 14–3, Figure 14–4, Figure 14–8 **ABC:** 23 Human Sex Determination
TR: Lesson Plan 14–2, Section Summary, p. 145 L1, p. 152 L2, Worksheets, p. 148 L1, pp. 157–159 L2, Enrichment L2 L3 **RSW:** Section 14–2 L2 **ARSW:** Section 14–2 L1 **IDM:** Issues and Decisions 7 L2 L3	**SE:** 14–2 Section Assessment, p. 353 **TR:** Section Review 14–2	**iText:** Section 14–2 **TP:** 14–2 Interest Grabber, Section Outline, Nondisjunction, Figure 14–13 **BD:** "Coming Home: A Nation's Pledge" **ABC:** 24 Nondisjunction
TR: Lesson Plan 14–3, Section Summary, p. 145 L1, p. 153 L2, Worksheets, pp. 149–150 L1, pp. 160–162 L2 **LW:** Chapter 14 Real-World Lab L1 L2 L3 **RSW:** Section 14–3 L2 **ARSW:** Section 14–3 L1 **IDM:** Issues and Decisions 9, 10, 11, 12 L2 L3	**SE:** 14–3 Section Assessment, p. 360 **TR:** Section Review 14–3	**iText:** Section 14–3 **TP:** 14–3 Interest Grabber, Section Outline, Locating Genes, Figure 14–18, Figure 14–21 **ABC:** 30 Gene Transfer and Cloning
	SE: Chapter 14 Assessment, pp. 362–365 **TR:** Chapter Vocabulary Review, Graphic Organizer, Chapter 14 Test **LA:** Laboratory Assessment 4	**iText:** Chapter 14 Assessment **CTB:** Chapter 14 Test **Go Online** Students can do research, share data, and test their knowledge online.

PRESSED FOR TIME?

To Preview the Chapter
- Have students read the Key Concepts and Vocabulary terms in each section.
- Have students examine all the figures in the chapter and read their captions.

To Cover the Chapter Quickly
- Have students read Human Chromosomes and Human Traits in Section 14–1; Sex-Linked Genes, X-Chromosome Inactivation, and Chromosomal Disorders in Section 14–2; and all of Section 14–3.
- Assign the 14–3 Section Assessment and questions 1–7 in Chapter 14 Standards Practice.

To Review the Chapter
- Review the concept map in the Chapter 14 Study Guide.
- Assign Sections 14–1, 14–2, and 14–3 in the Reading and Study Workbook or the Adapted Reading and Study Workbook.

CHAPTER 14

ENGAGE/EXPLORE

Inquiry Activity

 6IIE 7.e, 8IIE 9.b, BIIE 1.c, BI 3.a

Objective Students will be able to predict chin shape with Punnett squares. L2

Skill Focus Predicting, Using Models

Time 10 minutes

Strategy Use photographs of famous people to demonstrate cleft and uncleft chins. Emphasize that cleft chin is used here as an illustrative example. In practice, the inheritance of traits such as cleft chin is a complex process affected by other factors in addition to Mendel's laws. Students should not assume that they can analyze their own or anyone's ancestry simply by examination of such traits.

Expected Outcomes Students will use Punnett squares to predict that the parents will have a 75 percent chance of having a child with a cleft chin.

Think About It

1. Punnett squares give the possible genotypic and phenotypic ratios of the offspring of a cross. No; the Punnett square suggests that the parents have a 3 in 4, or 75 percent, chance of their fourth child's having a cleft chin.
2. 75 percent; Each child is the result of an independent combination of chromosomes from each parent. The phenotype of one child does not affect the phenotype of the next.

Brain Teaser

List on the board the phenotypes of the following members of a family. The mother, father, one son, and the two daughters have normal vision. The other son is colorblind. The mother's mother, two sisters, and three brothers have normal vision, but the mother's father is colorblind. The father's mother, father, sister, and three brothers all have normal vision. Challenge students to determine how the allele for colorblindness is inherited. *(The mother has one X chromosome that carries the allele for colorblindness, which she inherited from her father.)* Continue working on the puzzle throughout the chapter until students are able to successfully solve it.

CHAPTER 14

The Human Genome

The children in this family have some traits that are similar to their mother's and some that are similar to their father's.

Inquiry Activity

 6IIE 7.e, 8IIE 9.b, BIIE 1.c, BI 3.a

Can you predict chin shape?

Procedure

1. Two parents with cleft chins, both heterozygous for cleft chin *(Cc)*, have three children with cleft chins. The parents are sure that their fourth child will not have a cleft chin. Draw a Punnett square to see if this is possible.
2. Determine the probability that the fourth child will have a cleft chin.

Think About It

1. **Using Models** What information does a Punnett square give? Does the Punnett square support the parents' prediction? Explain your answer.
2. **Predicting** If these parents have a fifth child, what are the chances that the child will have a cleft chin? Explain your answer.

14–1 Human Heredity

BI 2.e. Students know why approximately half of an individual's DNA sequence comes from each parent. **BI 2.f.** Students know the role of chromosomes in determining an individual's sex. **BI 2.g.** Students know how to predict possible combinations of alleles in a zygote from the genetic makeup of the parents. **BI 3.a.** Students know how to predict the probable outcome of phenotypes in a genetic cross from the genotypes of the parents and mode of inheritance (autosomal or X-linked, dominant or recessive). ***BI 3.c.** Students know how to predict the probable mode of inheritance from a pedigree diagram showing phenotypes.

Of all the living things that inhabit this remarkable world, there is one in particular that has always drawn our interest, one that has always made us wonder, one that will always fire our imagination. That creature is, of course, ourselves, *Homo sapiens.*

Scientists once knew much less about humans than about other organisms. Until very recently, human genetics lagged far behind the genetics of "model" organisms such as fruit flies and mice. That, however, has changed. Scientists are now on the verge of understanding human genetics at least as well as they understand that of some other organisms. From that understanding will come a new responsibility to use that information wisely.

Guide for Reading

Key Concepts

- How is sex determined?
- How do small changes in DNA cause genetic disorders?

Vocabulary

karyotype
sex chromosome
autosome
pedigree

Reading Strategy: Using Prior Knowledge Before you read, write down what you already know about the inheritance of traits. As you read, compare the information in the text to your notes.

Human Chromosomes

What makes us human? Biologists can begin to answer that question by taking a look under the microscope to see what is inside a human cell. To analyze chromosomes, cell biologists photograph cells in mitosis, when the chromosomes are fully condensed and easy to see. The biologists then cut out the chromosomes from the photographs and group them together in pairs. A picture of chromosomes arranged in this way is known as a **karyotype** (KAR-ee-uh-typ).

CA a 

The chromosomes shown in **Figure 14–1** are from a typical human body cell. The number of chromosomes—46—helps identify this karyotype as human. This karyotype is the result of a haploid sperm, carrying just 23 chromosomes, fertilizing a haploid egg, also with 23 chromosomes. The diploid zygote, or fertilized egg, contained the full complement of 46 chromosomes.

Two of those 46 chromosomes are known as **sex chromosomes,** because they determine an individual's sex. Females have two copies of a large X chromosome. Males have one X and one small Y chromosome. To distinguish them from the sex chromosomes, the remaining 44 chromosomes are known as autosomal chromosomes, or **autosomes.** To quickly summarize the total number of chromosomes present in a human cell, both autosomes and sex chromosomes, biologists write 46,XX for females and 46,XY for males.

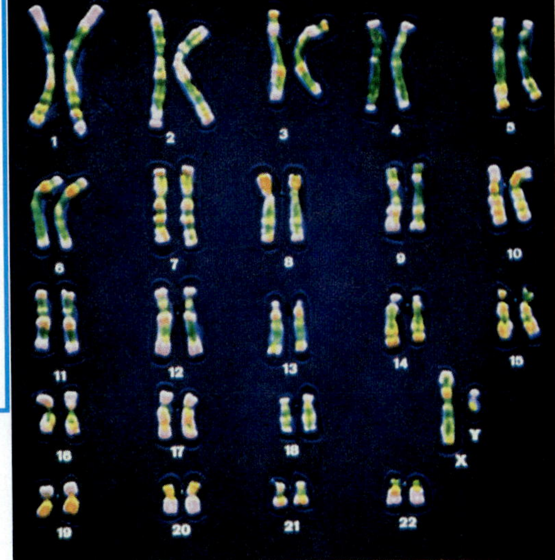

▶ **Figure 14–1** These human chromosomes have been cut out of a photograph and arranged to form a karyotype. **Interpreting Graphics** *Analyze this karyotype and identify the person's sex.*

SECTION RESOURCES

Print:

- ***Laboratory Manual A,*** Chapter 14 Lab
- ***Laboratory Manual B,*** Chapter 14 Lab
- ***Teaching Resources,*** Lesson Plan 14–1, Adapted Section Summary 14–1, Adapted Worksheets 14–1, Section Summary 14–1, Worksheets 14–1, Section Review 14–1
- ***Reading and Study Workbook A,*** Section 14–1
- ***Adapted Reading and Study Workbook B,*** Section 14–1
- ***Biotechnology Manual,*** Lab 10; Issues 2, 3

Technology:

- ***iText,*** Section 14–1
- ***Animated Biological Concepts DVD,*** 23
- ***Transparencies Plus,*** Section 14–1

Section 14–1

7 2.c, 7 2.d, BI 2.e, BI 2.f, BI 2.g, BI 3.a, *BI 3.c

1 FOCUS

Objectives

14.1.1 ***Identify*** the types of human chromosomes in a karyotype.
14.1.2 ***Explain*** how sex is determined.
14.1.3 ***Explain*** how pedigrees are used to study human traits.
14.1.4 ***Describe*** examples of the inheritance of human traits.
14.1.5 ***Explain*** how small changes in DNA cause genetic disorders.

Guide for Reading

Vocabulary Preview

Explain that the word *autosome* is the opposite of the term *sex chromosome.* Challenge students to infer the meaning of the word *autosome. (A chromosome that is not a sex chromosome)* Also find out what students think the sex chromosomes are and correct any misconceptions they have.

Reading Strategy

As students read this section, encourage them to write at least one main idea from each subsection under a blue heading. Remind students to include information given in figure captions.

2 INSTRUCT

Human Chromosomes

Use Visuals

Figure 14–1 Point out that the chromosomes are arranged by size. Encourage students to make inferences about why this is so. *(For organizational purposes, making it easier to see abnormalities)* Explain that the human chromosomes were originally assigned numbers based on their sizes and positions in a karyotype.

Answer to . . .

Figure 14–1 *The person is male.*

14–1 (continued)

Build Science Skills

Using Models Give student pairs of pipe-cleaner chromosomes to represent the sex chromosomes. Students should use the pipe cleaners to model the movement of the sex chromosomes during meiosis. Make sure students can explain why egg cells carry only an X chromosome but sperm cells can carry either an X chromosome or a Y chromosome.

Human Traits

Use Visuals

Figure 14–3 Copy the pedigree from Figure 14–3 onto the board. Have student volunteers identify the symbols used in the chart—circles, squares, and vertical and horizontal lines. Ask: **What does a shaded circle or square indicate?** *(That person expresses the trait.)* Emphasize that pedigree charts are based on observable traits—phenotypes—and only one trait is studied on each chart. Also explain that pedigree charts are most often used by geneticists when tracking the inheritance of genetic disorders, such as hemophilia or colorblindness. They are used to help parents understand the probability of having a child with a genetic disorder. L1 L2

For: Pedigree activity
Visit: PHSchool.com
Web Code: cbe-4141
Students can interact with the art of a pedigree online.

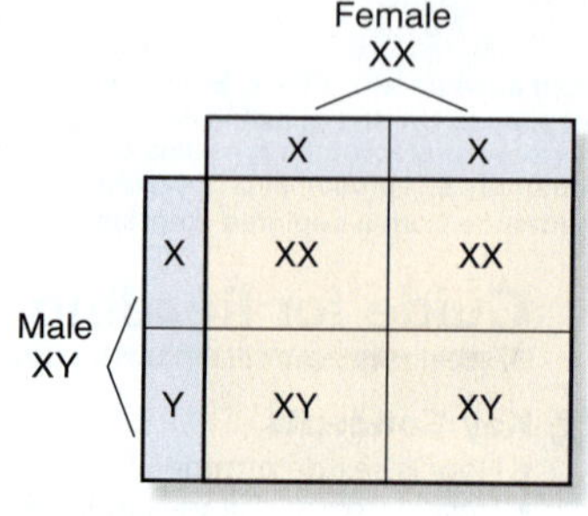

▲ **Figure 14–2** **In humans, egg cells contain a single X chromosome. Sperm cells contain either one X chromosome or one Y chromosome.** In a population, approximately half of the zygotes are XX (female) and half are XY (male).

For: Pedigree activity
Visit: PHSchool.com
Web Code: cbp-4141

CA a As you can see in **Figure 14–2,** males and females are born in a roughly 50 : 50 ratio because of the way in which sex chromosomes segregate during meiosis. **All human egg cells carry a single X chromosome (23,X). However, half of all sperm cells carry an X chromosome (23,X) and half carry a Y chromosome (23,Y). This ensures that just about half of the zygotes will be 46,XX and half will be 46,XY.**

 *What is a karyotype?*  BI 2.f

Human Traits

Human genes are inherited according to the same principles that Gregor Mendel discovered in his work with garden peas. However, in order to apply Mendelian genetics to humans, biologists must identify an inherited trait controlled by a single gene. First, they must establish that the trait is actually inherited and not the result of environmental influences. Then, they have to study how the trait is passed from one generation to the next.

Pedigree Charts A **pedigree** chart, which shows the relationships within a family, can be used to help with this task. The pedigree in **Figure 14–3** shows how an interesting human trait, a white lock of hair just above the forehead, is transmitted through three generations of a family. The allele for the white forelock trait is dominant. At the top of the chart is a grandfather who had the white forelock trait. Two of his three children inherited the trait, although one child did not. Three grandchildren have the trait, and two do not.

Genetic counselors analyze pedigree charts to infer the genotypes of family members. For example, since the white forelock trait is dominant, all the family members that lack the trait must have homozygous recessive alleles. Since one of the grandfather's children lacks the white forelock trait, the grandfather must be heterozygous for the trait.

▼ **Figure 14–3** This drawing shows what the symbols in a pedigree represent. **Interpreting Graphics** *What are the genotypes of both parents on the left in the second row? How do you know?*

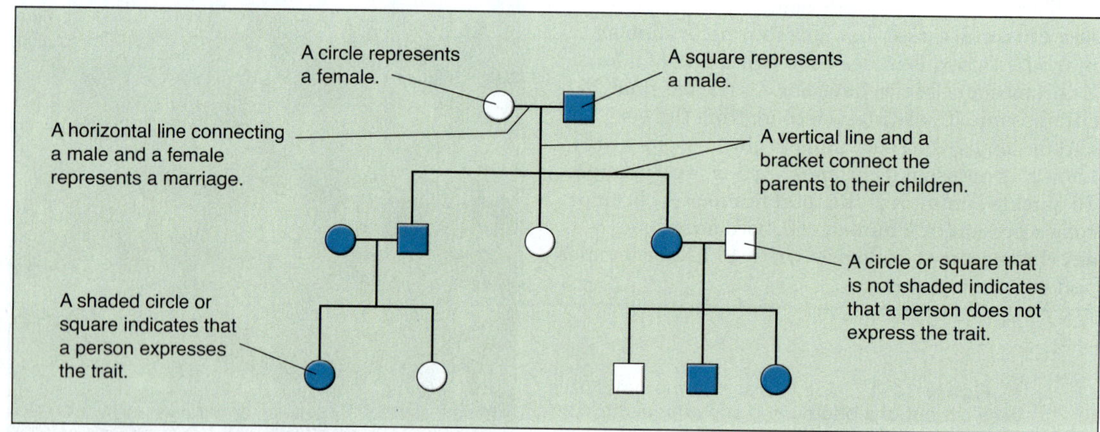

SUPPORT FOR ENGLISH LANGUAGE LEARNERS

Vocabulary: Link to Visual

Beginning Clarify what *pedigree* means by discussing Figure 14–3. Explain each label in Figure 14–3. Then, distribute a description of how a trait—for example, widow's peak, which is autosomal dominant—appears in three generations of a fictional family. (To modify the information, draw faces that show—or do not show—this trait.) Have students construct and label pedigrees using this information. They should use the labels "Shows the trait" and "Does not show the trait" for each person. L1

Intermediate To supplement the Beginning activity, pairs of intermediate students can work together to write sentences. The sentences should use the words *genotype* and *phenotype* to describe three people in the pedigree. L2

Genes and the Environment Unfortunately for folks who would like to settle burning issues, like which side of the family is responsible for your good looks, some of the most obvious human traits are almost impossible to associate with single genes. There are two reasons for this. First, things you might think of as single traits, such as the shape of your eyes or ears, are actually polygenic, meaning they are controlled by many genes. Second, many of your personal traits are only partly governed by genetics. Remember that the phenotype of an organism is only partly determined by its genotype. Many traits are strongly influenced by environmental, or nongenetic, factors, including nutrition and exercise. For example, even though a person's maximum possible height is largely determined by genetic factors, nutritional improvements in the United States and Europe have increased the average height of these populations about 10 centimeters over their average height in the 1800s.

Although it is important to consider the influence of the environment on the expression of some genes, it must be understood that environmental effects on gene expression are not inherited; genes are. Genes may be denied a proper environment in which to reach full expression in one generation. However, these same genes can, in a proper environment, achieve full potential in a later generation.

(a) 7 2.c

Problem Solving

*BI 3.c

Using a Pedigree

Imagine that you are a genetic counselor. The pedigree shown illustrates the inheritance of albinism, a condition in which a person's skin, hair, and eyes lack normal coloring, in three generations of a family. A couple from the family have come to you for advice about how the trait is inherited. Your task is to determine whether the allele for albinism is dominant or recessive.

Defining the Problem Define the problem that must be solved.

Organizing Information Copy the pedigree and the key onto a piece of paper. Label each person on the pedigree with his or her phenotype: normal-pigmented skin or albino.

Creating a Solution Write down how you would analyze the pattern in the inheritance of the albinism trait. Describe how you will use your analysis to infer the genotype of as many individuals as possible.

Presenting Your Plan Prepare a step-by-step outline of your plan. Present the plan to your class as if you were explaining the process to the couple involved.

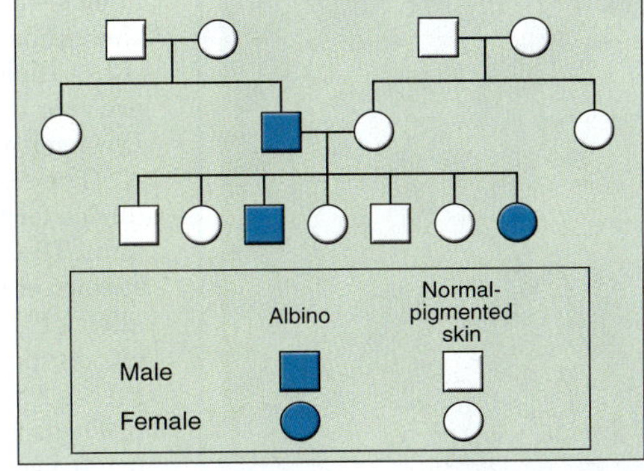

FACTS AND FIGURES

Multiple genes, multiple phenotypes
Polygenic traits include height, skin color, and eye color. None of the genes for a polygenic trait are dominant. Each gene has an active allele and an inactive allele. Active alleles have an additive effect on the phenotype. Inactive alleles do not affect the phenotype. Because of these additive effects, a continuous range of phenotypes is possible. Environmental conditions also affect the phenotype of polygenic traits. For example, height and weight are affected by nutrition, disease, and exercise.

Problem Solving

***BI 3.c**

About 1 in 17,000 people have albinism. It is caused by a recessive allele that disrupts the normal production of melanin. People with albinism sometimes have underpigmented hair and skin. More commonly, they have impaired vision. L2

Defining the Problem Is the allele for albinism dominant or recessive?

Organizing Information Students should copy the pedigree onto their own papers and label each individual as normal-pigmented or albino.

Creating a Solution To analyze the pattern in the inheritance of the albinism trait, students should assume that the allele for the trait is dominant and then observe the phenotypes in the pedigree to see if they match that pattern of inheritance. Then, they should do the same for the recessive inheritance pattern. Students can use Punnett squares to help them make inferences about genotypes and phenotypes. By assigning the known genotypes to individuals first, students can work backward and make assumptions about the genotypes of some individuals. For normal-pigmented individuals that are heterozygous, they will not be able to assign definitive genotypes. Students should conclude that the allele for albinism is recessive.

Presenting Your Plan Students should explain why they think the allele for the trait is recessive. Plans should include phenotypes of first- and third-generation individuals as part of their explanations. Students might present a pedigree to show how the phenotypes of the family would be different if the allele for the trait were dominant. They might also present a Punnett square to show the probability of the couple's having another albino child.

Answers to . . .

CHECKPOINT *A picture of chromosomes arranged in pairs*

Figure 14–3 *Both are heterozygous because they have a child with the recessive phenotype.*

14–1 (continued)

Human Genes

Build Science Skills

Applying Concepts Give students genetics practice problems that involve the blood group genes. Ask: **What blood types would you expect the children to have if their parents are type A and type B with genotypes of I^Ai and I^Bi?** *(1 AB: 1 A: 1B: 1 O)* **If this couple has Rh^+ blood, could they have a child with Rh^- blood? Explain.** *(Yes; if both parents are heterozygous; Rh^+/Rh^-.)* **Could a child with type A blood have parents that have type O and type B blood?** *(No, this couple can only have children with type O and type B blood.)* Encourage students to make up their own problems and trade them with other students to solve. L1 L2

Make Connections

Health Science Explain the importance of transfusing the correct blood group into an individual. On the board, diagram a blood cell with "A" antigens on the outside of the cell. Do the same for a blood cell with "B" antigens and an O blood cell with no antigens. Explain that if type A or type B blood were given to a type O person, the immune system would recognize the blood cells as foreign because of the A or B antigens on the cells' surfaces. The immune system would produce antibodies against these blood cells and destroy them. Then, challenge students to infer why people with type AB blood are called universal acceptors, while people with type O blood are called universal donors. Ask: **What blood type do you think blood centers want the most?** *(Type O, because it has no antigens and it can be given to any blood type without causing an antibody reaction.)* L2 L3

▶ **Figure 14–4** This table shows the relationship between genotype and phenotype for the ABO blood group. It also shows which blood types can safely be transfused into people with other blood types. **Applying Concepts** *How can there be four different phenotypes, even though there are six different genotypes?*

Blood Groups

Phenotype (Blood Type)	Genotype	Antigen on Red Blood Cell	Safe Transfusions	
			To	From
A	I^AI^A or I^Ai	A	A, AB	A, O
B	I^BI^B or I^Bi	B	B, AB	B, O
AB	I^AI^B	A and B	AB	A, B, AB, O
O	ii	none	A, B, AB, O	O

Human Genes

The human genome—our complete set of genetic information—includes tens of thousands of genes. The DNA sequences on these genes carry information for specifying many characteristics, from the color of your eyes to the detailed structures of proteins within your cells. The exploration of the human genome has been a major scientific undertaking. In 2003, the DNA sequence of the human genome was published.

Studying the genetics of our species has not been easy. Until recently, the identification of a human gene took years of scientific work. Humans have long generation times and a complex life cycle, and they produce, at least compared with peas and fruit flies, very few offspring. Still, in a few cases, biologists were able to identify genes that directly control a single human trait. Some of the very first human genes to be identified were those that control blood type.

▼ **Figure 14–5** This medical worker is drawing blood from a patient. The blood will be tested to see what type of blood it is. **Applying Concepts** *Why is blood typing so important during a blood transfusion?*

(a) 7 2.d

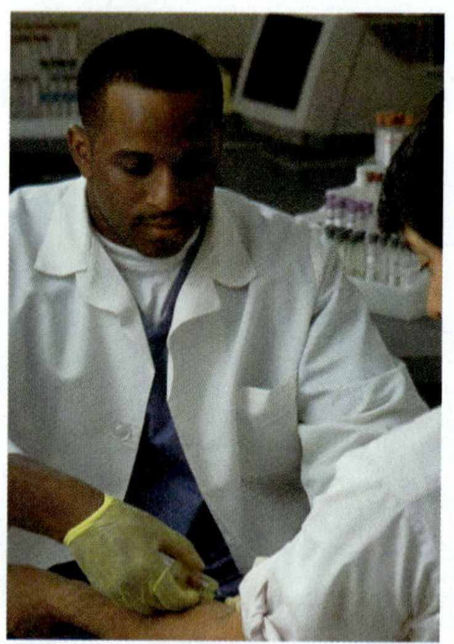

CA (a)

Blood Group Genes Human blood comes in a variety of genetically determined blood groups. Knowing a person's blood group is critical because using the wrong type of blood for a transfusion during a medical procedure can be fatal. A number of genes are responsible for human blood groups, but the best known are the ABO blood groups and the Rh blood groups.

The Rh blood group is determined by a single gene with two alleles—positive and negative. *Rh* stands for "rhesus monkey," the animal in which this factor was discovered. The positive (Rh^+) allele is dominant, so persons who are Rh^+/Rh^+ or Rh^+/Rh^- are said to be Rh-positive. Individuals with two Rh^- alleles are Rh-negative.

The ABO blood group is more complicated. There are three alleles for this gene, I^A, I^B, and i. Alleles I^A and I^B are codominant. These alleles produce molecules known as antigens on the surface of red blood cells. As **Figure 14–4** shows, individuals with alleles I^A and I^B produce both A and B antigens, making them blood type AB. The i allele is recessive. Individuals with alleles I^AI^A or I^Ai produce only the A antigen, making them blood type A. Those with I^BI^B or I^Bi alleles are type B. Those who are homozygous for the i allele (ii) produce no antigen and are said to have blood type O.

TEACHER TO TEACHER

I usually have students choose a human genetic mutation or disorder and research it. I encourage them to use the Internet, printed materials, or interviews. I ask them to learn about the genetics behind the condition, including the condition's pattern of inheritance and its frequency of occurrence in the population. Students must also learn about the specifics of the condition, such as its phenotype, any cures, treatments, or life-altering measures—diet, medications, exercise—to survive the condition. After students complete their research, I invite them to share their knowledge with the class in short presentations. This process seems to make the terminology and the genetics more understandable to students.

—Myron E. Blosser
Biology Teacher
Harrisonburg High School
Harrisonburg, VA

When a medical worker refers to blood groups, he or she usually mentions both groups at the same time. For example, if a patient has AB-negative blood, it means the individual has I^A and I^B alleles from the ABO gene and two Rh^- alleles from the Rh gene.

Recessive Alleles Many human genes have become known through the study of genetic disorders. **Figure 14–6** lists some common genetic disorders. In most cases, the presence of a normal, functioning gene is revealed only when an abnormal or nonfunctioning allele affects the phenotype.

One of the first genetic disorders to be understood this way was phenylketonuria (fen-ul-ket-oh-NOOR-ee-uh), or PKU. People with PKU lack the enzyme that is needed to break down phenylalanine. Phenylalanine is an amino acid found in milk and many other foods. If a newborn has PKU, phenylalanine may build up in the tissues during the child's first years of life and cause severe mental retardation. Fortunately, newborns can be tested for PKU and then placed on a low-phenylalanine diet that prevents most of the effects of PKU. PKU is caused by an autosomal recessive allele carried on chromosome 12.

Many other disorders are also caused by autosomal recessive alleles. One is Tay-Sachs disease, which is caused by an allele found mostly in Jewish families of central and eastern European ancestry. Tay-Sachs disease results in nervous system breakdown and death in the first few years of life. Although there is no treatment for Tay-Sachs disease, there is a test for the allele. By taking this test, prospective parents can learn whether they are at risk of having a child with the disorder.

▼ **Figure 14–6** This table shows the major symptoms of some well-known genetic disorders. **Interpreting Graphics** *Which disorder causes galactose to accumulate in the tissues?*

Some Autosomal Disorders in Humans

Type of Disorder	Disorder	Major Symptoms
Disorders caused by recessive alleles	Albinism	Lack of pigment in skin, hair, and eyes
	Cystic fibrosis	Excess mucus in lungs, digestive tract, liver; increased susceptibility to infections
	Galactosemia	Accumulation of galactose (a sugar) in tissues; mental retardation; eye and liver damage
	Phenylketonuria (PKU)	Accumulation of phenylalanine in tissues; lack of normal skin pigment; mental retardation
	Tay-Sachs disease	Lipid accumulation in brain cells; mental deficiency; blindness; death in early childhood
Disorders caused by dominant alleles	Achondroplasia	Dwarfism (one form)
	Huntington disease	Mental deterioration and uncontrollable movements; symptoms usually appear in middle age
	Hypercholesterolemia	Excess cholesterol in blood; heart disease
Disorders caused by codominant alleles	Sickle cell disease	Misshapen, or sickled, red blood cells; damage to many tissues

Build Science Skills

Designing Experiments Challenge students to outline an experimental plan that uses genetic engineering techniques to cure phenylketonuria. Encourage students to review the techniques in genetic engineering that they learned about in Chapter 13 and to apply those techniques to treating a human genetic disorder. Have students point out the steps in their plan that will be especially difficult to carry out. L2

Address Misconceptions

Many students might be under the impression that all genetic disorders are caused by recessive alleles. When describing various disorders, be sure to point out ones that are caused by dominant or codominant alleles. Explain that when a disorder is inherited as a recessive trait, body cells can produce enough of the normal protein with only one normal copy of the gene. However when a disorder is caused by a dominant allele, the protein product produced by the altered gene either inactivates the normal protein or not enough normal protein is being produced. L2

FACTS AND FIGURES

Achondroplasia

Achondroplasia is a type of dwarfism in which the affected person never reaches a height greater than 4 feet 4 inches tall. When long bones develop in an affected child, cartilage forms in such a way that the arms and legs end up being disproportionately short. About 1 in every 10,000 individuals is affected by achondroplasia.

Answers to . . .

Figure 14–4 *Because the allele for no antigens, i, is recessive to I^A and I^B, it is hidden by the I^A and I^B genes.*

Figure 14–5 *Using the wrong type of blood for a transfusion could be fatal.*

Figure 14–6 *Galactosemia*

14–1 (continued)

Building Science Skills

Posing Questions Make sure students realize that the genetic disorders they are learning about were not always known to be inheritable. Doctors were the first to try to treat and characterize these disorders, and it was through their observations that they identified these disorders as inheritable. Challenge students to imagine that they are doctors who have identified a disorder that has not been identified before. Instruct them to develop a list of questions that will help them determine whether the disorder is due to an inherited gene, an environmental factor such as poor nutrition, or infection by bacteria or viruses. L2

Download a worksheet on pedigrees for students to complete, and find additional teacher support from NSTA SciLinks.

From Gene to Molecule

Use Visuals

Figure 14–8 Walk through the illustration to make sure students understand the biochemistry of the disease. Review membrane-bound proteins and their functions, if necessary. Ask: **Why do the airways of people with cystic fibrosis become clogged with thick mucus?** *(The cells in the airways are unable to transport chloride ions.)* **Why can't the cells transport chloride ions?** *(The protein required to transport chloride ions does not function properly because of its abnormal structure.)* Discuss the type of mutation that has occurred in the most common allele of CF. Ask: **Why isn't this mutation a frame-shift mutation?** *(Exactly one codon has been deleted, so the reading frame has not been affected. The entire protein sequence is translated correctly, except for the missing phenylalanine.)* L1 L2

For: Links on pedigrees
Visit: www.SciLinks.org
Web Code: cbn-4141

ⓐ BI 3.a

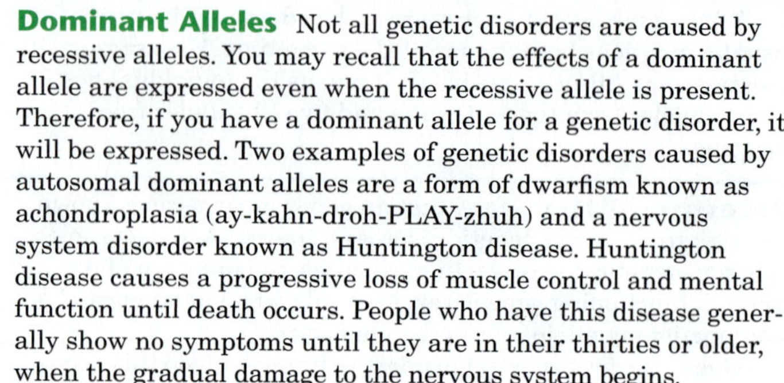

Dominant Alleles Not all genetic disorders are caused by recessive alleles. You may recall that the effects of a dominant allele are expressed even when the recessive allele is present. Therefore, if you have a dominant allele for a genetic disorder, it will be expressed. Two examples of genetic disorders caused by autosomal dominant alleles are a form of dwarfism known as achondroplasia (ay-kahn-droh-PLAY-zhuh) and a nervous system disorder known as Huntington disease. Huntington disease causes a progressive loss of muscle control and mental function until death occurs. People who have this disease generally show no symptoms until they are in their thirties or older, when the gradual damage to the nervous system begins.

Codominant Alleles Sickle cell disease, a serious disorder found in about 1 out of 500 African Americans, is caused by a codominant allele. As you will read, the reason for the high incidence of sickle cell in the United States is a story that links genetics, human history, and molecular biology.

CHECKPOINT *What type of allele causes Huntington disease?*

From Gene to Molecule

How do the actual DNA sequences in genes affect phenotype so profoundly? What is the link between the DNA bases in the allele for a genetic disorder and the disorder itself? For many genetic disorders, scientists are still working to find the answer. But for two disorders, the connection is understood very well indeed. **In both cystic fibrosis and sickle cell disease, a small change in the DNA of a single gene affects the structure of a protein, causing a serious genetic disorder.**

Cystic Fibrosis Cystic fibrosis, or CF, is a common genetic disease. Cystic fibrosis is most common among people whose ancestors came from Northern Europe. The disease is caused by a recessive allele on chromosome 7. Children with cystic fibrosis have serious digestive problems. In addition, they produce a thick, heavy mucus that clogs their lungs and breathing passageways.

Cystic fibrosis involves a very small genetic change. **Figure 14–8** illustrates how information carried in a chromosome's DNA specifies the trait of cystic fibrosis. Most cases of cystic fibrosis are caused by the deletion of 3 bases in the middle of a sequence for a protein. This protein normally allows chloride ions (Cl^-) to pass across biological membranes. The deletion of these 3 bases removes just one amino acid from this large protein, causing it to fold improperly. Because of this, the cells do not transport the protein to the cell membrane, and the misfolded protein is destroyed. Unable to transport chloride ions, tissues throughout the body malfunction. People with one normal copy of the allele are unaffected, because they can produce enough of the chloride channel protein to allow their tissues to function properly.

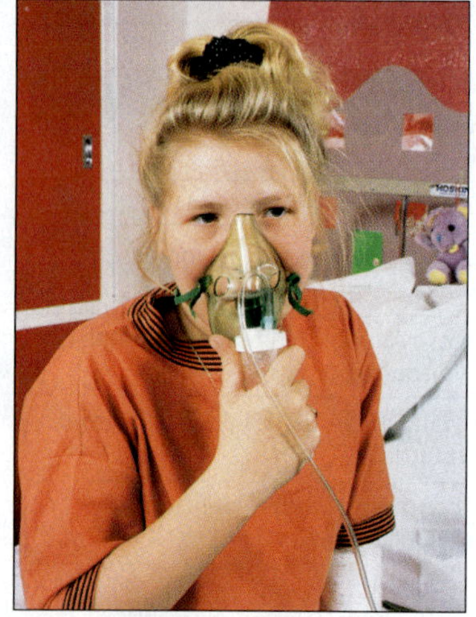

▲ **Figure 14–7** This girl is inhaling a fine mist through a nebulizer. The medication in the mist thins the mucus in the lungs, making breathing easier. **Inferring** *Why is it important for people with CF to thin the mucus in their lungs?*

BIO INSIGHTS — FACTS AND FIGURES

Founder effect and Huntington disease
One of the highest known frequencies of Huntington disease is found in the Afrikaner population of South Africa. Researchers have discovered that the affected persons are descendants of a settler from the Netherlands who arrived there in the 1700s.

This phenomenon of one or a few individuals with a genetic abnormality causing the establishment of a new population is known as the founder effect. The founder effect is most likely to occur in remote areas where the total population is relatively small. (The founder effect is discussed on page 400.)

▼ **Figure 14–8** **Cystic fibrosis is usually caused by the deletion of three bases in the DNA of a single gene.** As a result, the body does not produce normal CFTR, a protein needed to transport chloride ions. Cystic fibrosis causes serious digestive and respiratory problems.

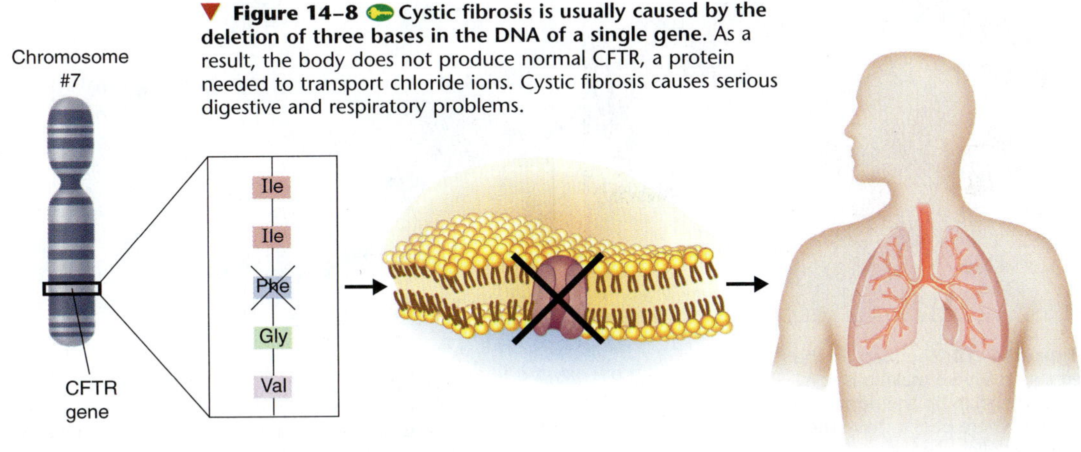

A The most common allele that causes cystic fibrosis is missing 3 DNA bases. As a result, the amino acid phenylalanine is missing from the CFTR protein.

B Normal CFTR is a chloride ion channel in cell membranes. Abnormal CFTR cannot be transported to the cell membrane.

C The cells in the person's airways are unable to transport chloride ions. As a result, the airways become clogged with a thick mucus.

Sickle Cell Disease Sickle cell disease is a common genetic disorder found in African Americans. Sickle cell disease is characterized by the bent and twisted shape of the red blood cells, like those shown in **Figure 14–9.** These sickle-shaped red blood cells are more rigid than normal cells and tend to get stuck in the capillaries, the narrowest blood vessels in the body. As a result, blood stops moving through these vessels, damaging cells, tissues, and organs. Sickle cell disease produces physical weakness and damage to the brain, heart, and spleen. In some cases, it may be fatal.

Hemoglobin is the protein in red blood cells that carries oxygen. The normal allele for the gene differs little from the sickle cell allele—just one DNA base is changed. This change substitutes the amino acid valine for glutamic acid. As a result, the abnormal hemoglobin is somewhat less soluble than normal hemoglobin. Any decrease in blood oxygen levels causes many of the hemoglobin molecules to come out of solution and stick together. The stuck-together molecules form long chains and fibers that produce the characteristic shape of sickled cells.

Why do so many African Americans carry the sickle cell allele? Most African Americans can trace their ancestry to west central Africa. Malaria, a serious parasitic disease that infects red blood cells, is common in this region of Africa. People who are heterozygous for the sickle cell allele are generally healthy. In addition, they have the benefit of being resistant to malaria. The relationship between the incidence of malaria and the presence of the sickle cell allele is shown in **Figure 14–10** on the next page.

▼ **Figure 14–9** These red blood cells contain the abnormal hemoglobin characteristic of sickle cell disease. **Observing** ***How is this cell different from a normal red blood cell?***

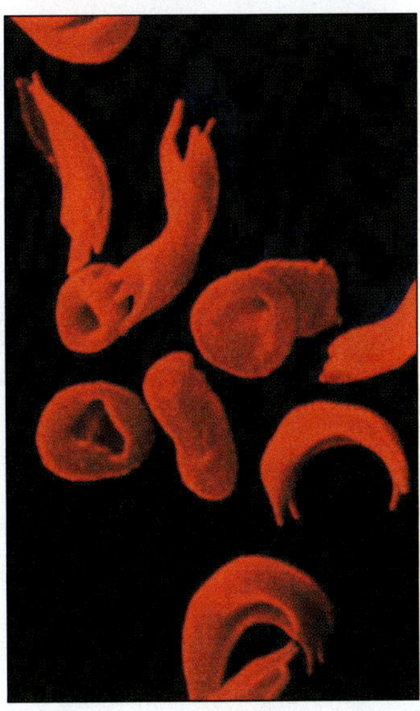

(magnification: 1800×)

Use Visuals

Figure 14–9 Have students compare and contrast the shapes of the normal red blood cells and the sickle-shaped red blood cells. Discuss how the shape of the sickle cells affects their movement through capillaries. Ask: **Why don't the heterozygous individuals suffer from sickle cell disease?** *(They have normal-shaped red blood cells moving through their bodies.)* L1 L2

Build Science Skills

Forming Hypotheses The allele for sickle cell disease is a positive adaptation to malaria for people living in areas where malaria is a problem. Challenge students to form a hypothesis that explains how this allele became so common among the ancestors of African Americans who lived in west central Africa, where malaria was prevalent. *(Hypotheses should explain that after the mutated allele appeared in the population, those individuals who inherited a copy of that allele were more likely to survive malaria and pass the allele on to their children. Individuals without the allele and individuals with both alleles were more likely to die; either from malaria or from sickle cell disease. In this case, "nature" was selecting for the heterozygote.)* L2

BIO INSIGHTS — FACTS AND FIGURES

Fetal hemoglobin and sickle cell disease
Hemoglobin F is the form of hemoglobin found only in developing fetuses. This form of hemoglobin is different from the adult form of hemoglobin and is not affected by the sickle cell mutation.

Unfortunately, production of hemoglobin F is stopped a few months after the birth of a baby. Some scientists think that hemoglobin F could provide a key to better medical treatment for sickle cell patients.

Answers to . . .

CHECKPOINT *An autosomal dominant allele*

Figure 14–7 *Thinning the mucus makes it easier for people with CF to breathe.*

Figure 14–9 *The sickle cells have elongated, sickle shapes.*

14–1 (continued)

Build Science Skills

Using Models Challenge student pairs to create a model that shows why an allele is dominant or recessive. Their model may be a diagram, a short skit with props, or three-dimensional structures. The models should show how the role of the gene's protein product and the action of the normal protein versus the mutant protein determine whether the mutant allele is dominant or recessive. L2

3 ASSESS

Evaluate Understanding

Quiz students about the pattern of inheritance of the human genetic traits described in the section. Give them sample genetic problems that they can solve with Punnett squares to predict probabilities of couples' having children with specific genotypes or phenotypes.

Reteach

Review the karyotype in Figure 14–1. Make sure students know the difference between autosomes and sex chromosomes and can identify them on the karyotype.

Thinking Visually

If students have a difficult time finding a family to use for their pedigree, you might allow them to fabricate one. Students should use the standard pedigree symbols used in this section in their pedigrees and include a key.

If your class subscribes to the iText, use it to review the Key Concepts in Section 14–1.

Answer to . . .

Figure 14–10 *In many locations, the area where malaria is common is the same as the area where people have the sickle cell allele.*

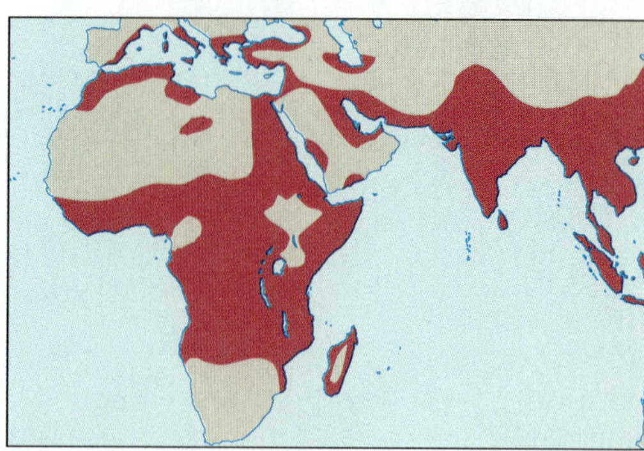

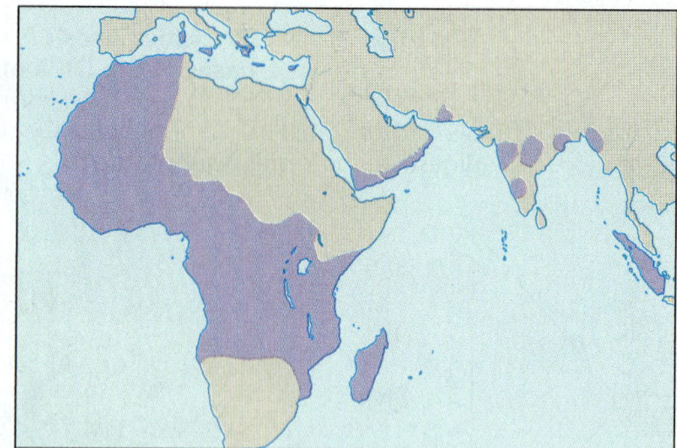

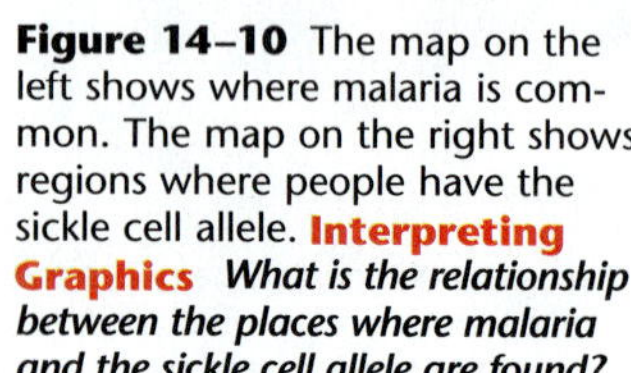

Figure 14–10 The map on the left shows where malaria is common. The map on the right shows regions where people have the sickle cell allele. **Interpreting Graphics** ***What is the relationship between the places where malaria and the sickle cell allele are found?***

Low oxygen levels cause some red blood cells to become sickle shaped. When the body destroys the sickled cells, it also destroys the parasite that causes malaria. Therefore, in parts of the world such as west central Africa, where malaria is a major threat to health, the sickle cell allele is actually beneficial in heterozygous persons.

Dominant or Recessive? What makes an allele dominant, recessive, or codominant? CF and sickle cell disease show biologists that it all depends on the nature of a gene's protein product and its role in the cell. In the case of CF, just one copy of the normal allele can supply cells with enough chloride channel proteins to function. Therefore, the trait has only two phenotypes: the normal phenotype or the cystic fibrosis phenotype. Because of this, the normal allele is considered dominant over the recessive CF allele.

The allele for normal hemoglobin was once also considered dominant over the sickle cell allele, but biologists now know that this situation is more complex. In contrast to cystic fibrosis, there are three phenotypes associated with the sickle cell gene. An individual with both normal and sickle cell alleles has a different phenotype—resistance to malaria—from someone with only normal alleles. Therefore, the sickle cell alleles are thought to be codominant because both alleles contribute to the phenotype.

14–1 Section Assessment

1. **Key Concept** What are sex chromosomes? What determines whether a person is male or female?
2. **Key Concept** Using an example, explain how a small change in a person's DNA can cause a genetic disorder.
3. How does studying genetic disorders such as PKU help biologists understand normal alleles?
4. **Critical Thinking Predicting** If a woman with type O blood and a man with type AB blood have children, what are the children's possible genotypes?

Thinking Visually

Drawing a Pedigree
Choose a family and a trait, such as facial dimples, that you can trace through three generations. Find out who in the family has had the trait and who has not. Then, draw a pedigree to represent the family history of the trait.

14–1 Section Assessment

1. X and Y chromosomes; Females have two X chromosomes; males have one X and one Y chromosome.
2. In cystic fibrosis, for example, the deletion of three DNA bases alters the structure of a protein and prevents its normal function. This damages tissues throughout the body.
3. A specific genetic disorder produced by an abnormal or nonfunctioning allele gives researchers clues about the normal functionings of the gene, as when PKU was shown to result from a missing enzyme.
4. $I^{A}i$ and $I^{B}i$

14–2 Human Chromosomes

BI 2.g. Students know how to predict possible combinations of alleles in a zygote from the genetic makeup of the parents. **BI 3.a.** Students know how to predict the probable outcome of phenotypes in a genetic cross from the genotypes of the parents and mode of inheritance (autosomal or X-linked, dominant or recessive). **BI 7.b.** Students know why alleles that are lethal in a homozygous individual may be carried in a heterozygote and thus maintained in a gene pool.

A human diploid cell contains more than 6 billion base pairs of DNA. All of this DNA is neatly packed into the 46 chromosomes present in every diploid human cell. In its own way, each of these chromosomes is like a library containing hundreds or even thousands of books. Although biologists are many decades away from mastering the contents of those books, biology is now in the early stages of learning just how many books there are and what they deal with.

You may be surprised to learn that genes make up only a small part of chromosomes. In fact, only about 2 percent of the DNA in your chromosomes functions as genes—that is, is transcribed into RNA. Genes are scattered among long segments of DNA that do not code for RNA. The average human gene consists of about 3000 base pairs, while the largest gene in the human genome has more than 2 million base pairs!

Human Genes and Chromosomes

Chromosomes 21 and 22 are the smallest human autosomes. Chromosome 22 contains approximately 43 million DNA base pairs. Chromosome 21 contains roughly 32 million base pairs. These chromosomes were the first two human chromosomes whose sequences were determined. Their structural features seem to be representative of other human chromosomes.

Chromosome 22 contains as many as 545 different genes, some of which are very important for health. Genetic disorders on chromosome 22 include an allele that causes a form of leukemia and another associated with neurofibromatosis, a tumor-causing disease of the nervous system. However, chromosome 22 also contains long stretches of repetitive DNA that do not code for proteins. These long stretches of repetitive DNA are unstable sites where rearrangements can occur.

The structure of chromosome 21 is similar. It contains about 225 genes, including one associated with amyotrophic lateral sclerosis (ALS), also known as Lou Gehrig's disease. Chromosome 21 also has many regions with no genes at all.

As exploration of the larger human chromosomes continues, molecular biologists may gradually learn more about how the arrangements of genes on chromosomes affect gene expression and development.

As you may recall, genes located close together on the same chromosome are linked, meaning that they tend to be inherited together. This is true for human genes. You also read earlier that linked genes may be separated by crossing-over during meiosis; this applies to human chromosomes as well.

Guide for Reading

Key Concepts
- Why are sex-linked disorders more common in males than in females?
- What is nondisjunction, and what problems does it cause?

Vocabulary
sex-linked gene
nondisjunction

Reading Strategy: Outlining Before you read, use the headings of the section to make an outline about human chromosomes. As you read, write a sentence under each head to provide key information.

▲ **Figure 14–11** Lou Gehrig died at age 37 of ALS. ALS causes a progressive loss of muscle control due to the destruction of nerves in the brain and spinal cord.

SECTION RESOURCES

Print:
- ***Teaching Resources,*** Lesson Plan 14–2, Adapted Section Summary 14–2, Adapted Worksheets 14–2, Section Summary 14–2, Worksheets 14–2, Section Review 14–2, Enrichment
- ***Reading and Study Workbook A,*** Section 14–2
- ***Adapted Reading and Study Workbook B,*** Section 14–2
- ***Issues and Decision Making,*** Issues and Decisions 7

Technology:
- ***BioDetectives DVD,*** "Coming Home: A Nation's Pledge"
- ***iText,*** Section 14–2
- ***Animated Biological Concepts DVD,*** 24
- ***Transparencies Plus,*** Section 14–2

Section 14–2

1 FOCUS

Objectives

14.2.1 ***Identify*** characteristics of human chromosomes.
14.2.2 ***Describe*** some sex-linked disorders and explain why they are more common in males than in females.
14.2.3 ***Explain*** the process of X-chromosome inactivation.
14.2.4 ***Summarize*** nondisjunction and the problems it causes.

Guide for Reading

Vocabulary Preview

Write the word *nondisjunction* on the board. Challenge students to identify the prefixes in the word. Ask: **What does *junction* mean?** *(Joining together)* Add the suffix *dis-*, and ask: **What does *disjunction* mean?** *(The act of separating)* Finally, challenge students to infer the meaning of *nondisjunction. (The act of not separating)*

Reading Strategy

Encourage students to add the green subheadings to their outlines and write a sentence under each. Remind students to include information in their outlines that is presented in figure captions.

2 INSTRUCT

Human Genes and Chromosomes

Build Science Skills

Calculating Have students reexamine the human karyotype on page 341. Ask: **Which chromosomes are the largest?** *(1 and 2)* **The smallest?** *(18 through 22)* **Considering the chromosome sizes, how many bases might chromosome 1 have if chromosome 22 has about 43 million bases?** *(About three times as many, or 129 million)* L1 L2

14–2 (continued)

Sex-Linked Genes

Use Visuals

Figure 14–13 Discuss the symbols used in the Punnett square and relate them to pedigree. Ask: **Why is the box for one son shaded?** *(He expresses the trait for colorblindness.)* **Would you expect the colorblind son to have sons who are colorblind?** *(No, the son can pass only the Y chromosome to his sons.)* **What is the probability that the daughter who is a carrier will have a colorblind child if she marries a man with normal vision?** *(25%)* L2

Build Science Skills

Using Models Challenge student pairs to design a pedigree that traces the inheritance of colorblindness in a family over several generations. Students can invent the family and the affected individuals. Then, students should write three questions about their pedigree and the inheritance of colorblindness. Have groups exchange pedigrees and answer the questions. L2

Address Misconceptions

Students might think that colorblind people see the world only in black and white. Show students charts used to diagnose colorblindness. Explain that a colorblind person either cannot see the object in the pattern or might see a different object. Help students realize that people who are red-green colorblind do see objects as blue or yellow or shades of red; they cannot see objects as green. L2

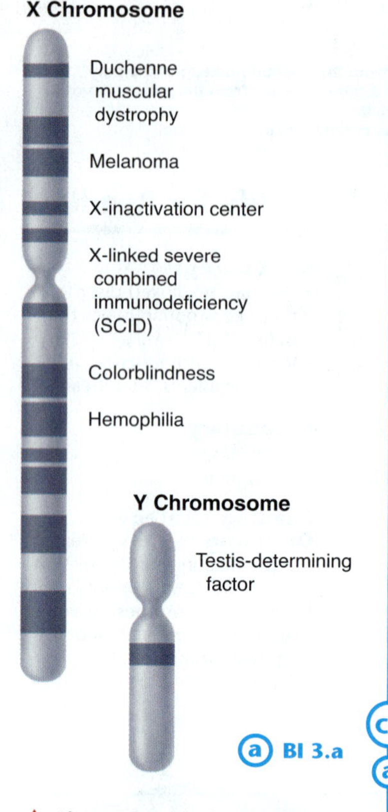

ⓐ BI 3.a

▲ **Figure 14–12** Genes on X and Y chromosomes, such as those shown in the diagrams, are called sex-linked genes. **Interpreting Graphics** *Which chromosome carries more genes?*

Sex-Linked Genes

Is there a special pattern of inheritance for genes located on the X chromosome or the Y chromosome? The answer is yes. Because these chromosomes determine sex, genes located on them are said to be **sex-linked genes.** Many sex-linked genes are found on the X chromosome, as shown in **Figure 14–12.** More than 100 sex-linked genetic disorders have now been mapped to the X chromosome. The human Y chromosome is much smaller than the X chromosome and appears to contain only a few genes.

Colorblindness Three human genes associated with color vision are located on the X chromosome. In males, a defective version of any one of these genes produces colorblindness, an inability to distinguish certain colors. The most common form of this disorder, red-green colorblindness, is found in about 1 in 10 males in the United States. Among females, however, colorblindness is rare—only about 1 female in 100 has colorblindness. Why the difference?

Males have just one X chromosome. Thus, all X-linked alleles are expressed in males, even if they are recessive. In order for a recessive allele, such as the one for colorblindness, to be expressed in females, there must be two copies of the allele, one on each of the two X chromosomes. This means that the recessive phenotype of a sex-linked genetic disorder tends to be much more common among males than among females. In addition, because men pass their X chromosomes along to their daughters, sex-linked genes move from fathers to their daughters and may then show up in the sons of those daughters, as shown in **Figure 14–13.**

CA ⓐ

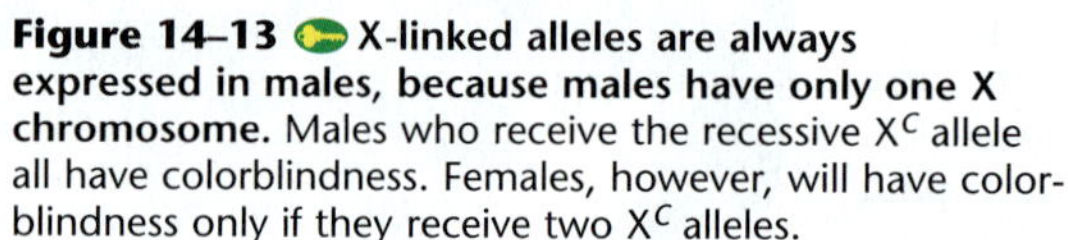

Figure 14–13 **X-linked alleles are always expressed in males, because males have only one X chromosome.** Males who receive the recessive X^c allele all have colorblindness. Females, however, will have colorblindness only if they receive two X^c alleles.

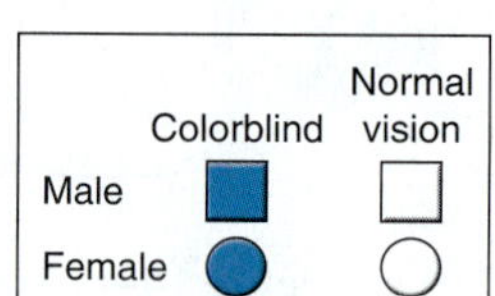

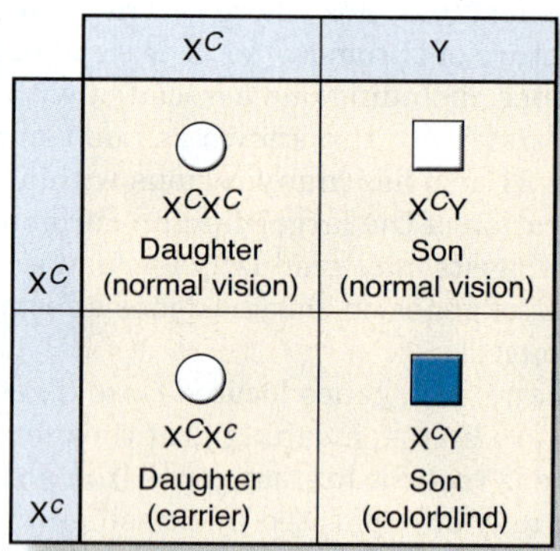

UNIVERSAL ACCESS

Inclusion/Special Needs

Have students draw diagrams to show how chromosomal disorders can occur. Make sure students realize that nondisjunction occurs during the formation of the egg cell or sperm cell. You might also have students draw Punnett squares to show the possible genotypes produced in a cross between a normal sex cell and a cell in which nondisjunction has occurred. L1

Less Proficient Readers

For each blue heading in the section, have students write a sentence that describes the main idea of that subsection. Encourage students to write the sentences in their own words, after reading the subsection and thinking about what it is about. You might also encourage students to illustrate their main ideas, if they wish.  

Quick Lab

 BI 2.g, 8IIE 9.b, BIIE 1.g

How is colorblindness transmitted?

Materials 2 plastic cups, 3 white beans, black marker, red bean

Procedure

1. On a sheet of paper, draw a data table with the column headings "Trial," "Colors," "Sex of Individual," and "Number of X-Linked Alleles." Draw 10 rows under the headings and fill in the numbers 1 through 10 under "Trial." Use the marker to label one cup "father" and the other "mother."
2. The white beans represent X chromosomes. Use the marker to mark a dot on 1 white bean to represent the X-linked allele for colorblindness. Place this bean, plus 1 unmarked white bean, into the cup labeled "mother."
3. Mark a black dot on 1 more white bean. Place this bean, plus 1 red bean, into the cup labeled "father." The red bean represents a Y chromosome.
4. Close your eyes and pick one bean from each cup to represent how each parent contributes a sex chromosome to a fertilized egg.
5. In your data table, record the color of each bean and the sex of an individual who would carry this pair of sex chromosomes. Also record how many X-linked alleles the individual has. Put the beans back in the cups they came from.
6. Determine whether the individual would have colorblindness.
7. Repeat steps 4 to 6 for a total of 10 pairs of beans.

Analyze and Conclude

1. **Drawing Conclusions** How do the sex chromosomes keep the numbers of males and females roughly equal?
2. **Calculating** Share your data with your classmates. Calculate the class totals for each table column. How many females were colorblind? How many males? How would you explain these results?
3. **Using Models** Evaluate the adequacy of your model. How accurately does it represent the transmission of colorblindness in a population?

Hemophilia Hemophilia is another example of a sex-linked disorder. Two important genes carried on the X chromosome help control blood clotting. A recessive allele in either of these two genes may produce a disorder called hemophilia (hee-moh-FIL-ee-uh). In hemophilia, a protein necessary for normal blood clotting is missing. About 1 in 10,000 males is born with a form of hemophilia. People with hemophilia can bleed to death from minor cuts and may suffer internal bleeding from bumps or bruises. Fortunately, hemophilia can be treated by injections of normal clotting proteins, which are now produced using recombinant DNA.

Duchenne Muscular Dystrophy Duchenne muscular dystrophy (DIS-truh-fee) is a sex-linked disorder that results in the progressive weakening and loss of skeletal muscle. In the United States, one out of every 3000 males is born with this condition. Duchenne muscular dystrophy is caused by a defective version of the gene that codes for a muscle protein. Researchers in many laboratories are trying to find a way to treat or cure this disorder, possibly by inserting a normal allele into the muscle cells of Duchenne muscular dystrophy patients.

CHECKPOINT *What causes Duchenne muscular dystrophy?*

FACTS AND FIGURES

Hemophilia and royalty
The frequency of hemophilia was much higher among the royal families of nineteenth-century Europe than among the general population. This was probably due to the fact that these families often intermarried. Queen Victoria of England was a carrier of the disease, as were two of her daughters. At one time, it was calculated that of Victoria's 69 descendants, 18 were either affected males or female carriers, though none of these individuals were British.

Quick Lab

 BI 2.g, 8IIE 9.b, BIIE 1.g

Objective Students will be able to model how colorblindness is transmitted.

Skill Focus **Using Models, Calculating, Drawing Conclusions**

Materials 2 plastic cups, 3 white beans, black marker, red bean

Time 20 minutes

Strategies

- After students read the procedure, ask: **Is either parent colorblind?** *(Yes, the father)* **Is the mother heterozygous or homozygous for colorblindness?** *(Heterozygous)* **Is she a carrier?** *(Yes, she has one allele for colorblindness.)*
- Remind students to keep their eyes closed while picking the beans so that they choose randomly.

Expected Outcomes Students will conclude that colorblindness occurs more frequently in males because they have only one copy of the X chromosome.

Analyze and Conclude

1. There is a 50 : 50 chance that a child will receive an X or Y chromosome from the father.
2. About 50% of the females will be colorblind and about 50% of the males will be colorblind. The mother is heterozygous, so her sons have a 50% chance of inheriting the X chromosome that carries the allele for colorblindness. The father is colorblind, so the daughters have a 50% chance of inheriting X chromosomes from both parents that carry the allele for colorblindness.
3. The model was accurate in representing the randomness of chromosome movement during meiosis and gametes joining during fertilization. It also accurately models the independence of each fertilization event. However, in a real population, the ratio of colorblind to noncolorblind people will be much lower, because the allele for colorblindness is not present in 50% of the people.

Answers to . . .

CHECKPOINT *A defective gene that codes for a muscle protein*

Figure 14–12 *The X chromosome*

14–2 (continued)

X-Chromosome Inactivation

Build Science Skills

Observing Set up microscope stations with slides of animal body cells that have Barr bodies. Encourage students to draw their observations, labeling the cell cytoplasm, nucleus, nucleoplasm, chromosomes, and Barr bodies. Then, give students two unknown slides and challenge them to identify which slide came from a female. L2

Chromosomal Disorders

Use Visuals

Figure 14–15 Ask: **What phase of meiosis is illustrated by the first cell?** *(Metaphase I)* If necessary, review meiosis so that students remember that in meiosis I, homologous chromosomes separate to produce a haploid cell and that in meiosis II, chromosome copies (or sister chromatids) separate. Ask: **What types of gametes are produced when nondisjunction occurs?** *(Some gametes that have two copies of the chromosome and other gametes with no copies of it)* L1 L2

▲ **Figure 14–14** This cat's fur color is controlled by a gene on the X chromosome. **Drawing Conclusions** *Is the cat shown a male or a female?*

▼ **Figure 14–15** **Nondisjunction causes gametes to have abnormal numbers of chromosomes.** The result of nondisjunction may be a chromosome disorder such as Down syndrome.

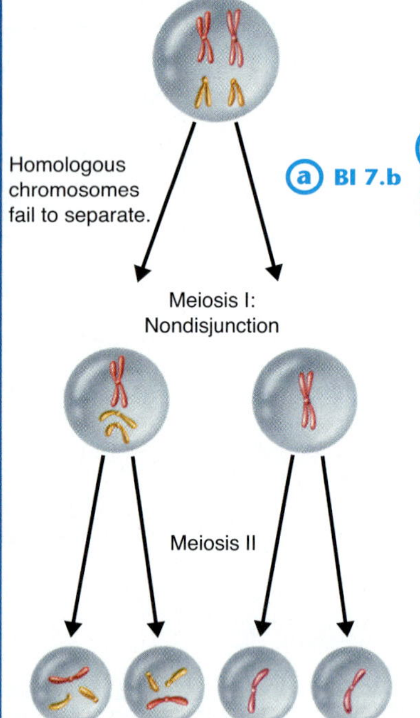

X-Chromosome Inactivation

Females have two X chromosomes, but males have only one. If just one X chromosome is enough for cells in males, how does the cell "adjust" to the extra X chromosome in female cells? The answer was discovered by the British geneticist Mary Lyon. In female cells, one X chromosome is randomly switched off. That turned-off chromosome forms a dense region in the nucleus known as a Barr body. Barr bodies are generally not found in males because their single X chromosome is still active.

The same process happens in other mammals. In cats, for example, a gene that controls the color of coat spots is located on the X chromosome. One X chromosome may have an allele for orange spots and the other may have an allele for black spots. In cells in some parts of the body, one X chromosome is switched off. In other parts of the body, the other X chromosome is switched off. As a result, the cat's fur will have a mixture of orange and black spots, as shown in **Figure 14–14.** Male cats, which have just one X chromosome, can have spots of only one color. By the way, this is one way to tell the sex of a cat. If the cat's fur has three colors—white with orange and black spots, for example—you can almost be certain that it is female.

Chromosomal Disorders

Most of the time, the mechanisms that separate human chromosomes in meiosis work very well, but every now and then something goes wrong. The most common error in meiosis occurs when homologous chromosomes fail to separate. This is known as **nondisjunction,** which means "not coming apart." Nondisjunction is illustrated in **Figure 14–15.** **If nondisjunction occurs, abnormal numbers of chromosomes may find their way into gametes, and a disorder of chromosome numbers may result.**

CA a

Down Syndrome If two copies of an autosomal chromosome fail to separate during meiosis, an individual may be born with three copies of a chromosome. This is known as a trisomy, meaning "three bodies." The most common form of trisomy involves three copies of chromosome 21 and is called Down syndrome. **Figure 14–16** shows a karyotype of a person with Down syndrome. In the United States, approximately 1 baby in 800 is born with Down syndrome. Down syndrome produces mild to severe mental retardation. It is also characterized by an increased susceptibility to many diseases and a higher frequency of some birth defects.

Why should an extra copy of one chromosome cause so much trouble? That is still not clear, and it is one of the reasons scientists have worked so hard to learn the DNA sequence for chromosome 21. Now that researchers know all of the genes on the chromosome, they can begin experiments to find the exact genes that cause problems when present in three copies.

HISTORY OF SCIENCE

Barr bodies

Barr bodies were named for Murray Barr, who first observed them in the nerve cells of female cats in 1949. It was not until the early 1960s that Mary Lyon proposed that one X chromosome is randomly inactivated. In body cells, she observed that one X chromosome replicated later than the other. The late-replicating X chromosome is inactivated when the embryo implants in the uterine wall. All body cells have the same activated and inactivated X chromosomes as the embryonic cell from which they were derived.

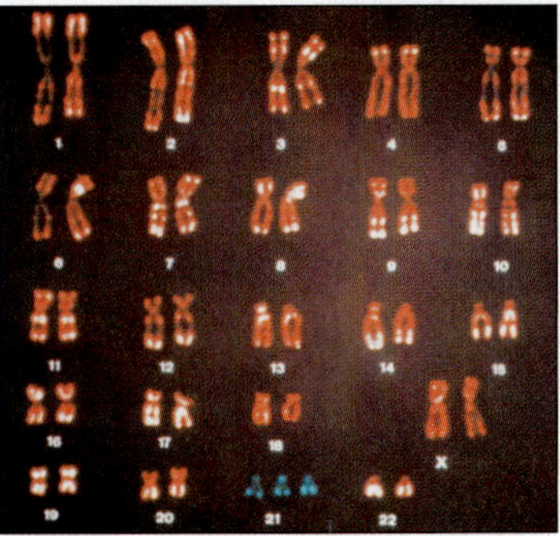

Figure 14–16 The karyotype on the right is from a person with Down syndrome. Down syndrome causes mental retardation and various physical problems. People with Down syndrome can, however, lead active, happy lives. **Observing** *Analyze this karyotype. What characteristic enables you to identify it as belonging to a person with Down syndrome? Is that person male or female?*

Sex Chromosome Disorders Disorders also occur among the sex chromosomes. Two of these abnormalities are Turner's syndrome and Klinefelter's syndrome.

In females, nondisjunction can lead to Turner's syndrome. A female with Turner's syndrome usually inherits only one X chromosome (karyotype 45,X). Women with Turner's syndrome are sterile, which means that they are unable to reproduce. Their sex organs do not develop at puberty.

In males, nondisjunction causes Klinefelter's syndrome (karyotype 47,XXY). The extra X chromosome interferes with meiosis and usually prevents these individuals from reproducing. Cases of Klinefelter's syndrome have been found in which individuals were XXXY or XXXXY. There have been no reported instances of babies being born without an X chromosome, indicating that the X chromosome contains genes that are vital for the survival and development of an embryo.

These sex chromosome abnormalities point out the essential role of the Y chromosome in male sex determination in humans. The human Y chromosome contains a sex-determining region that is necessary to produce male sexual development, and it can do this even if several X chromosomes are present. However, if this region of the Y chromosome is absent, the embryo develops as a female.

14–2 Section Assessment

1. **Key Concept** Why are sex-linked disorders more common in males than in females?
2. **Key Concept** How does nondisjunction cause chromosome number disorders?
3. List at least two examples of human sex-linked disorders.
4. Describe two sex chromosome disorders.
5. **Critical Thinking** **Comparing and Contrasting** Distinguish between sex-linked disorders and sex chromosome disorders.

Writing in Science

Explaining a Process
Write a paragraph explaining the process of nondisjunction. *Hint:* To organize your writing, refer to **Figure 14–15** and use this diagram to create a flowchart that shows the steps in the process.

Build Science Skills

Drawing Conclusions From patients with sex chromosomes disorders, physicians and geneticists have been able to infer the functions of the X and Y chromosomes to sex determination. Ask: **Why do geneticists believe that the X chromosome contains genes that are vital for survival?** *(Babies without an X chromosome have never been born.)* **Why is the Y chromosome thought to cause male sexual development?** *(In the absence of a Y chromosome, the embryo develops as a female.)* L1 L2

3 ASSESS

Evaluate Understanding

Have students construct a concept map that summarizes the concepts described in this section. Students should include the Vocabulary terms and Key Concepts in the map.

Reteach

Have students use Punnett squares to model how sex-linked traits are transmitted from parents to offspring. Challenge students to show how a dominant sex-linked allele has a different pattern of inheritance from a recessive sex-linked allele.

Writing in Science

Paragraphs should describe in a step-by-step process the failure of one pair of homologous chromosomes to separate during anaphase I or the failure of one pair of chromatids to separate during anaphase II.

If your class subscribes to the iText, use it to review the Key Concepts in Section 14–2.

14–2 Section Assessment

1. Males have just one X chromosome. Thus, all X-linked alleles are expressed in males, even if they are recessive.
2. Chromosomes fail to separate, causing gametes to have abnormal numbers of chromosomes.
3. Answers include colorblindness, hemophilia, and Duchenne muscular dystrophy.
4. A female with Turner's syndrome has only one X chromosome and is sterile. A male with Klinefelter's syndrome has one or more extra X chromosomes and is usually sterile.
5. Sex-linked disorders are caused by alleles of genes usually carried on the X chromosome. Sex chromosome disorders are caused by nondisjunction, or sex chromosomes failing to separate correctly during meiosis.

Answers to . . .

Figure 14–14 *The cat is female.*

Figure 14–16 *Since it has three copies of chromosome 21, it is the karyotype of a person with Down syndrome; the two X chromosomes indicate a female.*

 **BIIE 1.m**

Encourage one group of students to learn what companies or agencies are interested in knowing about an individual's DNA. Students should find out what the motives of these agencies and companies are. Have another group of students learn about medical records and who has access to that information. A third group of students can research how DNA information has allegedly been used to discriminate against individuals. Have each group present its findings to the class. Then, have a class discussion about the pros and cons of keeping DNA information private.

Research and Decide

1. Accept all reasonable answers. Justified: Employers use DNA information as a record of employees' identity, as in the case of the military. Withhold: Individuals are concerned that DNA information could be used against them, causing them to lose promotions or even their jobs.
2. Students will have different opinions, but all opinions should include reasonable explanations.
3. Some students might think the insurance company has a right to test for cystic fibrosis so that it can decide not to insure a family carrying the allele to prevent a profit loss. Others might think the insurance company does not have the right to test for the cystic fibrosis allele, because DNA information is private and should not be used to discriminate against an individual.

Students can research the right to control DNA information on the site developed by authors Ken Miller and Joe Levine.

Who Controls Your DNA?

 **BIIE 1.m**

The U.S. Department of Defense requires that soldiers submit DNA samples for a database that could be used to identify soldiers' remains. Two Marines, Corporal John C. Mayfield and Corporal Joseph Vlacovsky, refused. At their court martial, the two Marines argued that DNA samples could be examined for genes related to disease or even behavior and, therefore, the database was an invasion of privacy. As a result of the concerns raised by this case, the U.S. Department of Defense has changed its policies. It now destroys DNA samples upon request when an individual leaves military service. Do people have a right to control their own DNA samples?

The Viewpoints

DNA Information Is Not Private

As the court recognized, the U.S. Department of Defense had good reasons for requiring that DNA samples be taken and stored. Furthermore, DNA sequences are no more private and personal than fingerprints or photographs, which are taken by private and government agencies all the time. An employer has a right to take and keep such information. Individuals should have no reason to fear the abuse of such databases.

DNA Infomation Is Private and Personal

The use of DNA for personal identification by the military may be justified. An individual's genetic information, however, is a private matter. A recent study at Harvard and Stanford universities turned up more than 200 cases of discrimination because of genes individuals carried or were suspected of carrying. Employers with DNA information might use it to discriminate against workers who carry genes they suspect might cause medical or behavioral problems. Individuals must have the right to control their own DNA and to withhold samples from such databases.

Research and Decide

1. **Analyzing the Viewpoints** Learn more about this issue by consulting library or Internet resources. Then decide whether there are any circumstances in which an employer might be justified in demanding DNA samples from its employees. Why might an employee wish to withhold such samples?
2. **Forming Your Opinion** Should the control of DNA databases be a matter of law, or should it be a matter to be negotiated between people, their employers, and insurance companies?
3. **Persuasive Speaking** Suppose you were a doctor working as a consultant to a health insurance company. The insurance company is trying to decide whether to test adults for cystic fibrosis alleles before agreeing to insure their families. What advice would you give to the company about this?

For: Links from the authors
Visit: PHSchool.com
Web Code: cbe-4142

14–3 Human Molecular Genetics

Watson and Crick took the first step in making genetics a molecular science when they discovered the double-helical structure of DNA in 1953. Today, the transformation they started is complete. The exploration of human genes is now a major scientific undertaking. Biologists can now read, analyze, and even change the molecular code of genes.

Guide for Reading

Key Concepts
- What is the goal of the Human Genome Project?
- What is gene therapy?

Vocabulary
DNA fingerprinting

Reading Strategy: Finding Main Ideas As you read, find evidence to support the following statement: The influence of human molecular genetics on society is growing rapidly.

Human DNA Analysis

The roughly 6 billion base pairs you carry in your DNA are a bit like an encyclopedia with thousands of volumes. In principle, biologists would like to know everything the volumes contain, but as a practical matter there isn't enough time to read all of them. Nonetheless, if you've used an encyclopedia you've already learned one of the ways to handle huge amounts of information—you find a way to look up only what you need. In an encyclopedia, you can use an index or an alphabetical list of articles. As you might suspect, biologists search the volumes of the human genome using sequences of DNA bases.

Testing for Alleles If two prospective parents suspect they might be carrying recessive alleles for a genetic disorder such as cystic fibrosis (CF) or Tay-Sachs disease, how could they find out for sure? Because the Tay-Sachs and CF alleles have slightly different DNA sequences from their normal counterparts, a variety of genetic tests have been developed that can spot those differences. Sometimes these genetic tests use labeled DNA probes. These are specific DNA base sequences that detect the complementary base sequences found in disease-causing alleles. Other tests search for changes in restriction enzyme cutting sites. Tests also detect differences between the lengths of normal and abnormal alleles.

Genetic tests are now available for hundreds of disorders, making it possible to determine whether prospective parents risk passing such alleles to their children. In an increasing number of such cases, DNA testing can pinpoint the exact genetic basis of a disorder, making it possible to develop more effective treatment for individuals affected by genetic disease.

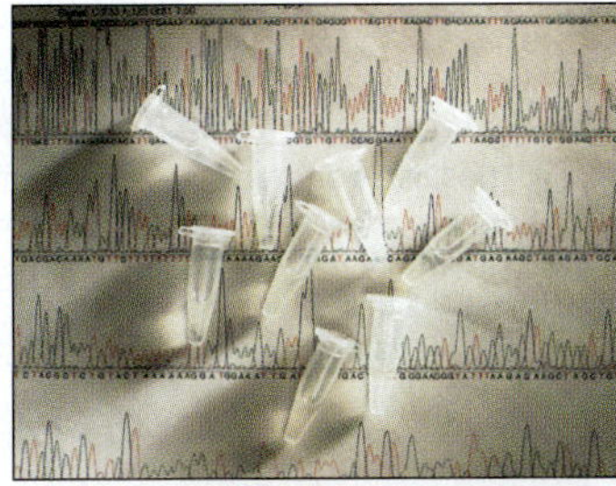

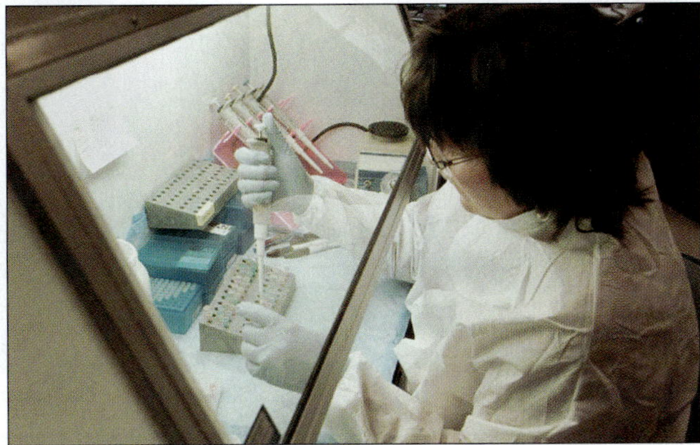

▶ **Figure 14–17** This laboratory worker is preparing a report on DNA evidence. The inset shows vials of DNA lying on a printout of a DNA analysis chart.

SECTION RESOURCES

Print:
- ***Teaching Resources,*** Lesson Plan 14–3, Adapted Section Summary 14–3, Adapted Worksheets 14–3, Section Summary 14–3, Worksheets 14–3, Section Review 14–3
- ***Reading and Study Workbook A,*** Section 14–3
- ***Adapted Reading and Study Workbook B,*** Section 14–3
- ***Issues and Decision Making,*** Issues and Decisions 9, 10, 11, 12
- ***Biotechnology Manual,*** Labs 2, 11, 12; Concepts 2, 3, 4, 6
- ***Lab Worksheets,*** Chapter 14 Real-World Lab

Technology:
- ***iText,*** Section 14–3
- ***Animated Biological Concepts DVD,*** 30
- ***Transparencies Plus,*** Section 14–3

Section 14–3

1 FOCUS

Objectives

14.3.1 ***Summarize*** methods of human DNA analysis.
14.3.2 ***State*** the goal of the Human Genome Project.
14.3.3 ***Describe*** how researchers are attempting to cure genetic disorders.

Guide for Reading

Vocabulary Preview

Invite student volunteers to describe what a fingerprint is and what it is used for. Then, challenge them to make inferences about what DNA fingerprinting is. List the inferences on the board, and narrow them down to two or three. Revisit this list throughout the section, if necessary, until the class correctly defines the term.

Reading Strategy

Instruct students to write the statement from the text onto a sheet of paper. As they read, students should list under the statement the evidence that supports it.

2 INSTRUCT

Human DNA Analysis

Build Science Skills

Designing Experiments Challenge students to write the steps in a protocol in which they test for the allele of a gene that causes a genetic disorder using restriction enzymes and gel electrophoresis. Students who need an extra challenge can list the steps to testing for alleles using a labeled DNA probe. Encourage students to use what they learned in Chapter 13. They might also wish to use the Internet to find additional resources. 

14–3 (continued)

Use Visuals

Figure 14–18 Go over the steps in the procedure used in DNA fingerprinting. Have volunteers describe what occurs in each step. Make sure all students understand which DNA sequences are being targeted and how restriction enzymes are used to find similarities and differences between DNA samples. Ask: **Why is DNA fingerprinting more accurate if the samples are cut with more than one restriction enzyme?** *(There is a greater chance of finding differences in the sequences, which translates to restriction fragments of varying sizes.)* L1 L2

Use Community Resources

Invite a forensics expert to the class to describe how DNA evidence is used in criminal cases. Suggest that the expert describe how DNA evidence is collected at the crime scene and how it is manipulated in the laboratory. Before the expert visits the class, have students brainstorm for questions to ask the expert. Encourage students to ask their questions during the expert's presentation. L2

FIGURE 14–18 DNA FINGERPRINTING

DNA fingerprinting can be used to determine whether blood, sperm, or other material left at a crime scene matches DNA from a suspect. **Interpreting Graphics** *In the DNA fingerprint below, does the DNA fingerprint from the evidence (E) match suspect 1 (S1) or suspect 2 (S2)?*

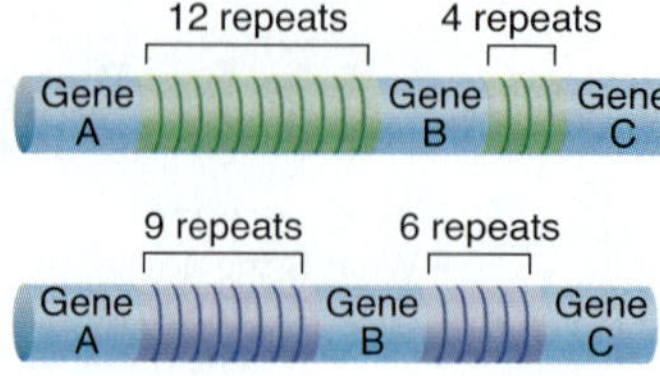

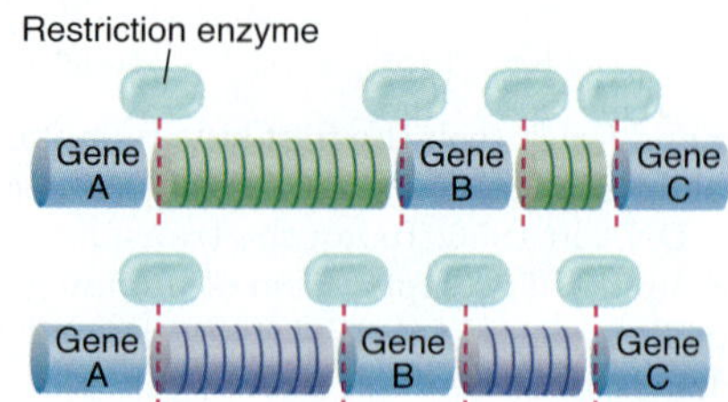

A Chromosomes contain large amounts of DNA called repeats that do not code for proteins. This DNA varies from person to person. Here, one sample has 12 repeats between genes A and B, while the second sample has 9 repeats.

B Restriction enzymes are used to cut the DNA into fragments containing genes and repeats. Note that the repeat fragments from these two samples are of different lengths.

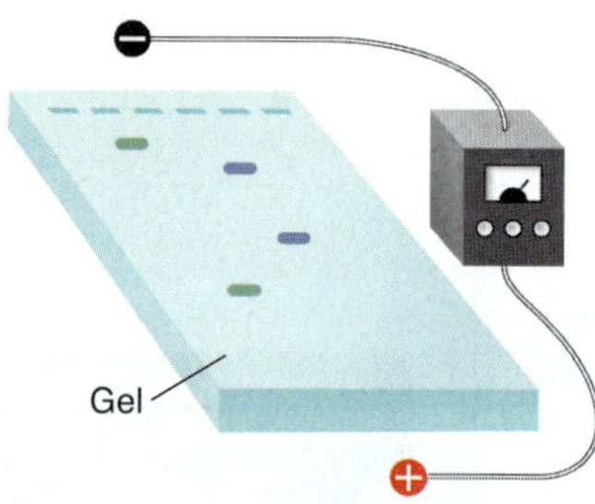

C The DNA fragments are separated according to size using gel electrophoresis. The fragments containing repeats are then labeled using radioactive probes. This produces a series of bands—the DNA fingerprint.

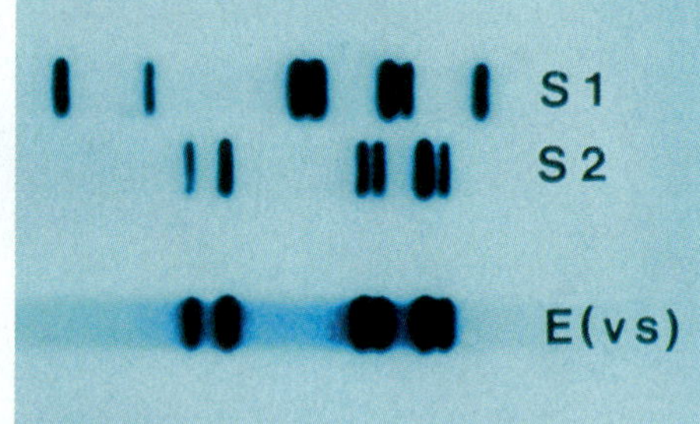

DNA fingerprint

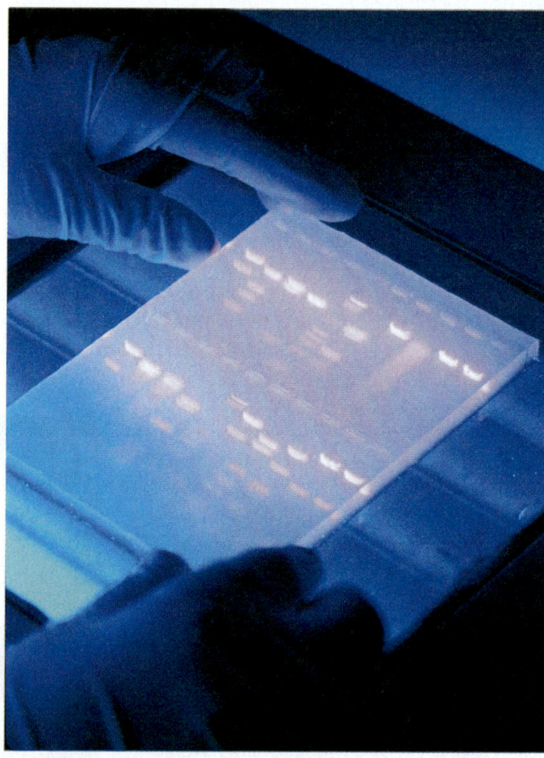

Gel electrophoresis

UNIVERSAL ACCESS

English Language Learners

To help students have a clearer understanding of what the Human Genome Project signifies, introduce the word *genome* to them. Explain that a genome is the genetic content of a cell. Remind students that all of the cells in the human body have the same genetic content, or genome. If they don't understand why, review mitosis and its role in growth and development. L1 L2

Advanced Learners

Some students might wish to learn about the actual human DNA sample that was sequenced. Have them find out if this DNA came from only one person or if it was a mixture from many people. Also have them find out how scientists plan to handle the fact that every human individual has a different DNA sequence. Encourage students to present their findings to the class. L3

DNA Fingerprinting The great complexity of the human genome ensures that no individual is exactly like any other genetically—except, of course, for identical twins. Molecular biology has used this biological fact to add a powerful new tool called **DNA fingerprinting** to the identification of individuals. Unlike other forms of testing, DNA fingerprinting does not analyze the cell's most important genes, which are largely identical among most people. Rather, DNA fingerprinting analyzes sections of DNA that have little or no known function but vary widely from one individual to another.

Figure 14–18 shows how DNA fingerprinting works. A small sample of human DNA is cut with a restriction enzyme. The resulting fragments are separated by size using gel electrophoresis. Fragments containing these highly variable regions are then detected with a DNA probe, revealing a series of DNA bands of various sizes. If enough combinations of restriction enzymes and probes are used, a pattern of bands is produced that can be distinguished statistically from the pattern of any other individual in the world. DNA samples can be obtained from blood, sperm, and even hair strands with tissue at the base.

DNA fingerprinting has been used in the United States since the late 1980s. The reliability of DNA evidence has helped convict criminals as well as overturn many convictions. The precision that molecular biology brings to the justice system is good news not only for those who are victims of crime but also for those who have been wrongly convicted.

The Human Genome Project

Advances in DNA sequencing technologies at the close of the twentieth century made it possible, for the first time, to sequence entire genomes. At first, biologists worked on relatively small genomes, such as those of viruses and bacteria. The DNA sequence of the common bacterium *Escherichia coli,* which was determined in 1996, contains "only" 4,639,221 base pairs, making it just about as long as this textbook if it were printed on paper in a readable typeface. The genomes of even the simplest eukaryotic organisms are much larger, and the human genome, which contains over 6 billion base pairs, is nearly 1400 times as large.

Despite the problem of size, in 1990, scientists in the United States and other countries began the Human Genome Project. **The Human Genome Project is an ongoing effort to analyze the human DNA sequence.** Along the way, investigators completed the genomes of several other organisms, including yeast—a unicellular eukaryote—and *Drosophila melanogaster,* the fruit fly. In June 2000, scientists announced that a working copy of the human genome was essentially complete.

▲ **Figure 14–19 The Human Genome Project is an ongoing effort to analyze the human DNA sequence.** Dr. Francis Collins and Dr. Craig Venter, who headed the public and private portions of the project, jointly announced the completion of a working draft of the human genome sequence.

The Human Genome Project

Demonstration

Demonstrate to students how sequencing the human genome was much like putting together a puzzle or solving a word puzzle. Copy on the board the X chromosome and its genes from Figure 14–12 on page 350. Make up short sequences of DNA on the board and assign them to various places on the X chromosome. Explain that these sequences are the "markers" sequenced by government scientists. Then, demonstrate the "shotgun" sequencing method by cutting up into very short pieces a length of yarn that represents the X chromosome. Choose four or five of these short yarn pieces, and give each a DNA sequence. Write the sequences on the board. Set it up so that students can determine where the DNA segments from the yarn fragments are located on the X chromosome based on the marker sequences. L2

HISTORY OF SCIENCE

The beginning of the genomic race

The Human Genome Project officially began in 1990 with two ultimate goals: identify and map every gene to its chromosome and determine the entire DNA sequence for the human genome. Research centers, universities, and private companies in the United States and around the world began work on this multibillion-dollar project, which was first estimated to take 20 years to complete. The first step of the project was completed in 1993, when a group in France completed a rough map of genetic markers for the entire genome. These markers were used to help researchers map the locations of various DNA fragments.

Answer to . . .

Figure 14–18 *It matches suspect 2.*

14–3 (continued)

Address Misconceptions

Students may think that scientists now know everything there is to know about the human genome. Point out that researchers have uncovered the "big picture," but they still need to learn many details. Ask: **About how many bases are present in a small human chromosome, such as chromosome 22?** *(About 43 million base pairs, as noted on page 349)* **What does that number indicate about the total number of bases in all the chromosomes?** *(There are probably well over 1 billion bases.)* **What are some questions about the human genome that researchers still need to investigate?** *(Samples: Which bases form genes that code for major traits? Which genes play a major role in human health?)* L2

Careers in Biology

- High school students interested in genetics should take courses in biology, chemistry, and physics, as well as English and math. College students should choose majors such as biochemistry, biology, or chemistry.
- Encourage students interested in studying genetics to find out about research going on in the social sciences, such as anthropology, history, and psychology. L2

Resources

Students can contact a university genetics department, the Genetics Society of America, the American Board of Genetic Counseling, or the genetics department of a local hospital.

You can have students write a more extensive job description as well as list the educational requirements for a career in this field.

Rapid Sequencing How did they do it? Scientists first determined the sequence of bases in widely separated regions of DNA. These regions were then used as markers, not unlike the mile markers along a road thousands of miles long. The markers made it possible to locate and return to specific locations in the genome.

Scientists then used a technique known as "shotgun sequencing." This method involved cutting DNA into random fragments and then determining the sequence of bases in each fragment. Computers found areas of overlap between the fragments and put the fragments together by linking the overlapping areas. The computers then aligned the fragments relative to the known markers on each chromosome. The entire process is something like putting a jigsaw puzzle together, but instead of matching shapes, the scientists match identical base sequences.

Searching for Genes Only a small part of a human DNA molecule is made up of genes. In fact, one of the genome's scientific surprises was how few genes it seems to contain—possibly as few as 25,000. Since the genome of the fruit fly *Drosophila* contains approximately 14,000 genes and that of a tiny worm roughly 20,000, many researchers had expected to find far more in our own DNA. The final number, however, is far from certain.

Molecular biologists continue to search for genes, which they can locate in several ways. In one method, they find genes by finding DNA sequences that are known to be promoters, which are binding sites for RNA polymerase. Promoters indicate the start of a gene. Shortly behind the promoter, there should be an open reading frame. An open reading frame is a sequence of DNA bases that will produce an mRNA sequence, which then specifies a series of amino acids. Recall that for most genes, the mRNA coding regions, or exons, are interrupted by introns, which are noncoding regions. Therefore, investigators have to find the introns as well as the exons in order to follow the gene through its complete length, as shown in **Figure 14–20.**

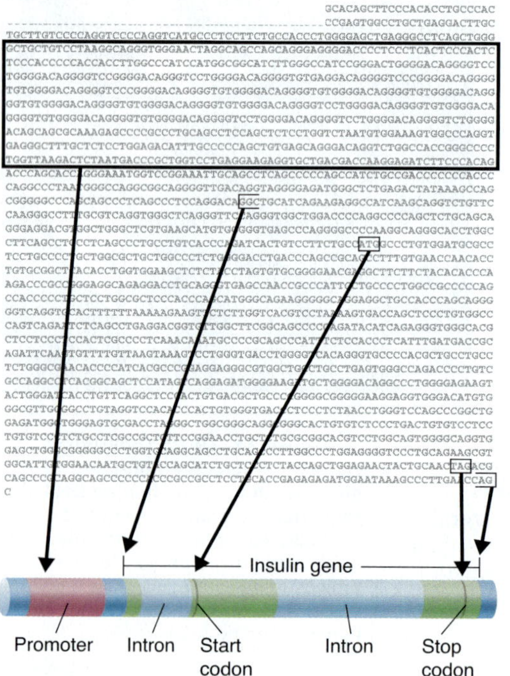

▼ **Figure 14–20** Researchers exploring the human genome can use DNA sequences to locate many genes. Promoters are sequences in which RNA polymerase can bind to DNA. A typical gene, such as the gene for insulin shown below, has other DNA sequences that may serve as signals for RNA polymerase to start and stop transcription. **Interpreting Graphics** ***In which direction would RNA polymerase move in transcribing the insulin gene?***

Research groups around the world are analyzing the huge amount of information in the DNA sequence, looking for genes that may provide useful clues to some of the basic properties of life. In addition to its scientific significance, understanding the structure and control of key genes may have commercial value. Biotechnology companies are rushing to find genetic information that may be useful in developing new drugs and treatments for diseases.

A Breakthrough for Everyone One of the remarkable things about genome research is the open availability of nearly all its data. From its very beginning, data from publicly supported research on the human genome have been posted on the Internet on a daily basis. You can read the latest genome data there and, if you wish, analyze it. The Web site for this textbook links to the Human Genome Project.

TEACHER TO TEACHER

After completing the unit on genetics, I have students work cooperatively searching the Internet and scientific journals for the current research on one of these topics: the Human Genome Project, genetic engineering, DNA fingerprinting, genetic screening, gene therapy, genetic counseling, or specific ethical issues in genetics. Then I have each group create a presentation to their classmates by means of a pamphlet, a multimedia presentation, or a role-playing activity. This strategy successfully helps students develop an awareness of the latest innovations in genetics.

—*Tracy Swedlund*
Biology Teacher
Medford Area Senior High
Medford, WI

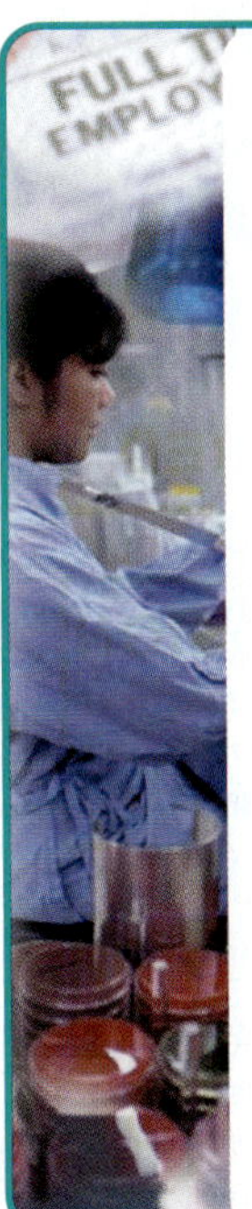

Careers in Biology

Geneticist

Job Description: work in the laboratories of universities or large companies doing molecular-level research, or work in a clinic collecting family histories and counseling people who have a genetic disorder or who may carry a genetic disorder

Education: a master's degree or doctorate in genetics or related field; some medical research positions require a medical degree, as well

Skills: good verbal and written communication skills, analytical, detail-oriented, caring, organized, curious, and able to meet deadlines

Highlights: You have the opportunity to discover new genes or patterns of heredity that can help treat or cure genetic disorders or to make sure that these types of discoveries are put into practice to improve public health.

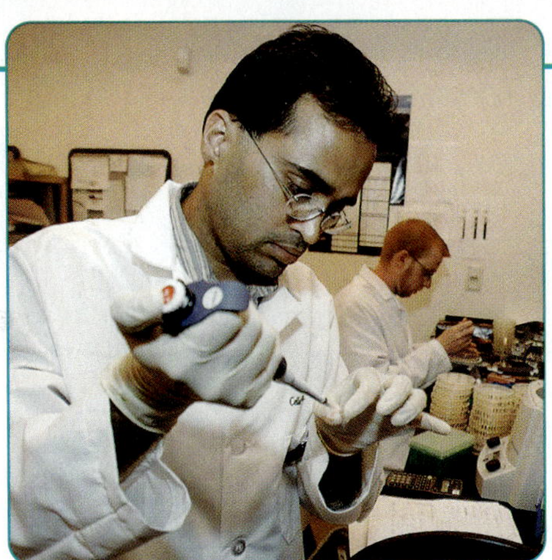

For: Career links
Visit: PHSchool.com
Web Code: cbb-4143

Gene Therapy

The Human Genome Project will have an impact on society as well as on scientific thought. For example, information about the human genome might be used to cure genetic disorders by gene therapy. Gene therapy is the process of changing the gene that causes a genetic disorder. **In gene therapy, an absent or faulty gene is replaced by a normal, working gene.** This way, the body can make the correct protein or enzyme it needs, which eliminates the cause of the disorder.

The first authorized attempt to cure a human genetic disorder by gene transfer occurred in 1990. Then, in 1999, a young French girl was apparently cured of an inherited immune disorder when cells from her bone marrow were removed, modified in the laboratory, and then placed back in her body. However, scientists do not yet know how long the beneficial effects of this treatment will last.

Figure 14–21 on the next page shows one of the ways in which researchers have attempted to practice gene therapy. Viruses are often used because of their ability to enter a cell's DNA. The virus particles are modified so that they cannot cause disease. Then, a DNA fragment containing a replacement gene is spliced to viral DNA. The patient is then infected with the modified virus particles, which should carry the gene into cells to correct genetic defects.

For: More information on the Human Genome Project
Visit: PHSchool.com
Web Code: cbe-4143

Gene Therapy

Use Visuals

Figure 14–21 Help students understand the procedure of gene therapy. Encourage them to compare it to animal cell transformation. Ask: **What is used to carry the DNA into the cell instead of a plasmid?** *(A virus)* **Why doesn't the virus cause disease in an individual?** *(The viral DNA has been modified to prevent the virus from causing disease.)* Remind students about the control of gene expression in eukaryotes. Ask: **Would all body cells produce hemoglobin?** *(No, only cells in which hemoglobin is produced would express the hemoglobin gene.)* **Why do researchers inject the hemoglobin gene into bone marrow cells and not into muscle cells or skin cells?** *(Muscle and skin cells do not produce hemoglobin; the hemoglobin gene is not expressed in these cells. It is expressed only in bone marrow cells, where red blood cells are produced.)* L2

BIO INSIGHTS — HISTORY OF SCIENCE

Transforming human cells

The first federally approved transfer of cells with foreign genes into a human occurred in May 1989, at the Clinical Center of the National Institutes of Health in Bethesda, Maryland.

Cancer-fighting cells into which a foreign gene had been inserted were infused into the bloodstream of a cancer patient who had volunteered for the experiment. The primary purpose of the manipulation was to make the cells easily identifiable so that doctors could track them in the patient's body. The patient was not expected to benefit directly.

The cells, tumor-infiltrating lymphocytes, had been taken from the patient's cancerous tissue and treated in the laboratory to increase their numbers and, thus, their ability to attack the cancer tissue.

You can have students visit the Web site of the Human Genome Project for additional information.

Answer to . . .

Figure 14–20 *It moves from the promoter to the stop signal (in the diagram, from left to right).*

14–3 (continued)

Ethical Issues in Human Genetics

Build Science Skills

Making Judgments Have groups work together to devise a set of guidelines for the use of the human genome. Make sure students understand the consequences of the guidelines they develop. L2 L3

3 ASSESS

Evaluate Understanding

Challenge students to choose a topic in genetics and briefly describe its implications for society. Challenge them to explain how an understanding of science will help them make informed decisions.

Reteach

Have students design a flowchart to show the steps in gene therapy. They should also include the steps required to engineer the virus that carries the human gene. Students can use Figure 14–21 as a guide.

Focus on the BIG Idea

Students will have different opinions, but their opinions should be fully developed and supported by specific examples.

If your class subscribes to the iText, use it to review the Key Concepts in Section 14–3.

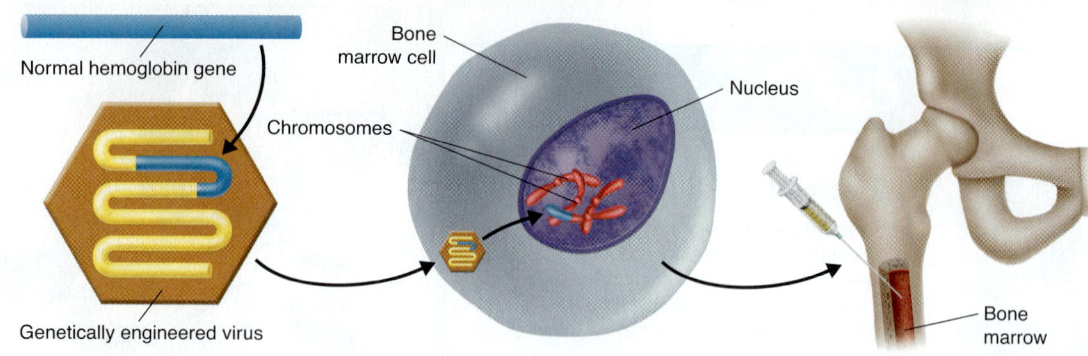

▲ **Figure 14–21 Gene therapy is the process of changing the genes that cause a genetic disorder.** This drawing shows how a virus might be used to deliver the gene for normal hemoglobin into a person's bone marrow.

Unfortunately, gene therapy experiments have not always been successful. Attempts to treat cystic fibrosis by spraying genetically engineered viruses into the breathing passages have not produced a lasting cure. For all the promise it holds, in most cases gene therapy remains a high-risk, experimental procedure.

Ethical Issues in Human Genetics

It would be marvelous to be able to cure hemophilia or other genetic diseases. But if human cells can be manipulated to cure disease, should biologists try to engineer taller people or change their eye color, hair texture, sex, blood group, or appearance? What will happen to the human species if we gain the opportunity to design our bodies? What will be the consequences if biologists develop the ability to clone human beings by making identical copies of their cells? These are questions with which society must come to grips.

The goal of biology is to gain a better understanding of the nature of life. As our knowledge increases, however, so does our ability to manipulate the genetics of living things, including ourselves. In a democratic nation, all citizens—not just scientists—are responsible for ensuring that the tools science has given us are used wisely. This means that you should be prepared to help develop a thoughtful and ethical consensus of what should and should not be done with the human genome. To do anything less would be to lose control of two of our most precious gifts: our intellect and our humanity.

14–3 Section Assessment

1. **Key Concept** What is the Human Genome Project?
2. **Key Concept** Describe how gene therapy works.
3. Name two common uses for DNA testing.
4. Describe how molecular biologists identify genes in sequences of DNA.
5. **Critical Thinking Making Judgments** Evaluate the potential impact of the Human Genome Project on both scientific thought and society. How has it improved our understanding of human genetics? How might it be used to benefit humankind? What potential ethical problems might it create?

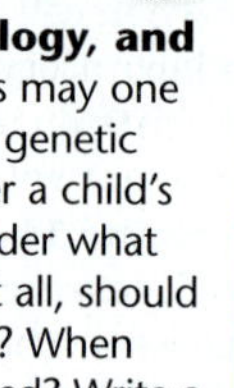

Focus on the BIG Idea

Science, Technology, and Society Biologists may one day be able to use genetic engineering to alter a child's inherited traits. Under what circumstances, if at all, should this ability be used? When should it not be used? Write a persuasive paragraph expressing your opinion. *Hint:* Use specific examples of traits to support your ideas.

14–3 Section Assessment

1. An ongoing effort to analyze the human DNA sequence
2. An absent or faulty gene is replaced by a normal, working gene.
3. To detect alleles for a genetic disorder and to identify individuals
4. By looking for promoters, which are binding sites for RNA polymerase; an open reading frame; and introns as well as exons
5. Possible answer: Learn causes of genetic disorders and how the inheritance and expression of human traits is controlled. Helpful in curing diseases, but could cause discrimination and the manipulation of human traits for profit

Real-World Lab

 6IIE 7.e, BIIE 1.d, BIIE 1.g

Modeling DNA Probes

A DNA probe is a short, single-stranded DNA molecule bound to a detectable tag such as a fluorescent dye. Because the probe is single stranded, it can bind to other DNA that has a complementary sequence. To find a specific DNA sequence, scientists mix a probe with an unknown DNA sample. The probe will only bind to a DNA sample that has a complementary sequence, showing where the desired sequence is. In this lab, you will model how scientists use DNA probes.

Problem

How do DNA probes help to identify individuals?

Materials

- graph paper
- scissors
- colored pencil or marker

Skills

Using Models, Classifying

Procedure 

Individual 1	ATCTCGAGACTGATAGGCTCTAAGCTCGAG
Individual 2	ATTGGCCACTCGAGACGTTGGCCAAGTCCG
Individual 3	ATGACCATGGCCAGGCTCGAGCTGATGACG
Individual 4	ATATGGCCATTGCTCGAGTGGCCAGATCCG
Individual 5	ACTCGAGGTCCCTCGAGTGTAGGCTCATCG

1. DNA sequences from five individuals are shown. Copy each individual's number and DNA sequence onto graph paper, putting one letter from the DNA sequence into each square. Skip five lines between each sequence and the next one.
2. Copy the following sequence for a six-base DNA probe onto graph paper, as you did the DNA sequences in step 1: T C C G A G
3. Fill in the square that follows the probe sequence with a colored pencil or marker to represent the fluorescent dye bound to the probe.
4. Cut out the strip of graph paper that represents the probe and its attached fluorescent dye.
5. Move the probe along each individual's DNA sequence. As you do so, look for parts of the DNA sequences that are complementary to the probe's sequence.
6. Circle the part of any individual's DNA sequence that is complementary to the sequence of the DNA probe.
7. Record the numbers of the individuals who were identified by the DNA probe.
8. Choose one of the five individuals, and construct a new DNA probe that will identify only that individual. Write out the DNA sequence of this new probe as you did in step 2. Your new probe does not have to be six bases long.
9. Cut out your new probe and exchange it for one written by a classmate.
10. Repeat steps 5 and 6 with the probe you received to identify the individual that your classmate selected.

Analyze and Conclude

1. **Observing** What DNA sequence is complementary to the sequence of the probe shown in step 2?
2. **Classifying** Which individual(s) was (were) identified by the DNA probe given in step 2?
3. **Using Models** Is it possible for the same DNA probe to identify more than one individual? Explain your answer.
4. **Drawing Conclusions** Would DNA probes with longer or shorter sequences be more likely to identify only one individual? Explain your answer.

Go Further

Using Models Restriction enzymes cut DNA at specific base sequences. Make a model of a DNA probe and a restriction enzyme. Use your models to show how DNA probes and restriction enzymes could be used together to create DNA fingerprints for the five individuals shown.

Analyze and Conclude

1. A G G C T C
2. Individuals 1, 3, and 5
3. Yes, if the complementary sequence occurs in more than one individual's DNA, then the probe will bind to the DNA of all those individuals.
4. Longer, because the longer the probe sequence is, the less often the complementary sequence is likely to occur

Real-World Lab

 6IIE 7.e, BIIE 1.d, BIIE 1.g

Objective Students will be able to use models to determine how DNA probes help to identify individuals.  L2

Skills Focus Using Models, Classifying

Time 45 minutes

Pre-Lab Discussion After students read the procedure, review what a complementary sequence is. Write several DNA sequences on the board, and have student volunteers give the complementary sequence of each.

Teaching Tips

- Use quarter-inch graph paper so that students have room to write.
- Have students write the complementary sequence under the DNA sequence of the probe.
- Suggest that students circle or highlight the complementary sequences in the individuals' DNA with the colored pencil or marker.
- Remind students to read the DNA sequence from left to right.

Procedure

7. Individuals 1, 3, and 5

10. Answers depend on the probe sequence written by students.

Expected Outcomes Students should observe that the DNA probe identified individuals 1, 3, and 5.

Go Further

Students should specify the DNA sequence that is cut by their restriction enzymes. They should cut the DNA samples from the individuals with the restriction enzymes (using scissors), and then order the fragments by size. Only the fragments with the complementary sequence to the probe will be highlighted. Individuals will show different bands that are highlighted.

Chapter 14 Study Guide

Study Tip

Write each Vocabulary term on a separate card, as well as a question for each Key Concept. Place the cards into a hat or a bowl. Have students draw a card and either give the definition of the word or answer the question. Continue until all the cards have been used.

Thinking Visually

1. Autosomes

2.–5. Tay-Sachs disease, achondroplasia, Huntington disease, sickle cell disease (or any other disorder listed in Figure 14–6 on page 345)

6.–7. Colorblindness, Duchenne muscular dystrophy

Chapter 14 Assessment

Reviewing Content

1. b	**5.** d	**9.** a
2. a	**6.** a	**10.** a
3. c	**7.** d	
4. b	**8.** c	

Understanding Concepts

11. Biologists photograph cells in mitosis, cut out the chromosomes from the photographs, and group them together in pairs. They then check whether any chromosomes are missing or have extra copies.

12. The sex chromosomes, X and Y, determine an individual's sex; the remaining chromosomes are autosomal.

13. A pedigree shows how a genetic trait has been passed from one generation to the next. This information can be used to infer the genotypes of family members and predict the likelihood that a child will have the disorder.

14. Mothers 1 and 6 are carriers. Person 3 can pass his affected X chromosome only to his daughters; his sons inherit his Y chromosome and an X chromosome from their mother.

15. No, the I^A and I^B alleles are codominant. When both alleles are present in an individual, that person has blood type AB.

Chapter 14 Study Guide

14–1 Human Heredity

BI 2.e, BI 2.f, BI 2.g, BI 3.a, *BI 3.c

Key Concepts

- All human egg cells carry a single X chromosome (23,X). However, half of all sperm cells carry an X chromosome (23,X) and half carry a Y chromosome (23,Y). This ensures that just about half of the zygotes will be 46,XX (female), and half will be 46,XY (male).
- In both cystic fibrosis and sickle cell disease, a small change in the DNA of a single gene affects the structure of a protein, causing a serious genetic disorder.

Vocabulary
karyotype, p. 341
sex chromosome, p. 341
autosome, p. 341
pedigree, p. 342

14–2 Human Chromosomes

BI 2.g, BI 3.a, BI 7.b

Key Concepts

- Males have just one X chromosome. Thus, all X-linked alleles are expressed in males, even if they are recessive.
- If nondisjunction occurs, abnormal numbers of chromosomes may find their way into gametes, and a disorder of chromosome numbers may result.

Vocabulary
sex-linked gene, p. 350
nondisjunction, p. 352

14–3 Human Molecular Genetics

Key Concepts

- The Human Genome Project is an ongoing effort to analyze the human DNA sequence.
- In gene therapy, an absent or faulty gene is replaced by a normal, working gene.

Vocabulary
DNA fingerprinting, p. 357

Thinking Visually

Using the information in this chapter, complete the following concept map about chromosome disorders:

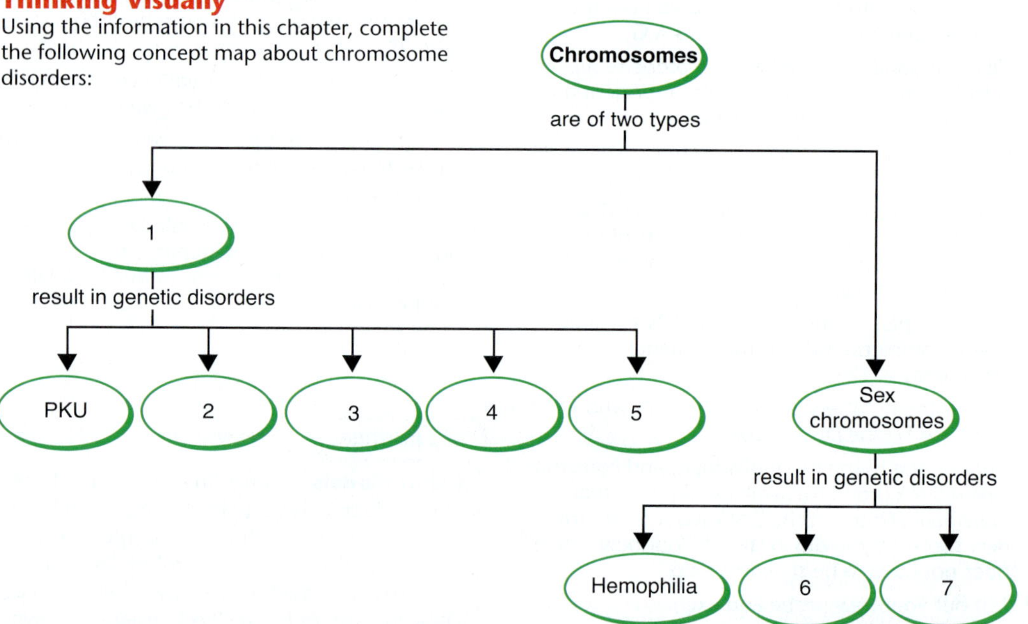

CHAPTER RESOURCES

Print:

- ***Teaching Resources,*** Chapter Vocabulary Review, Graphic Organizer, Chapter 14 Tests: Levels A and B
- ***Laboratory Assessment,*** Laboratory Assessment 4

Technology:

- ***Computer Test Bank,*** Chapter 14 Test
- ***iText,*** Chapter 14 Assessment

Chapter 14 Assessment

Reviewing Content

Choose the letter that best answers the question or completes the statement.

1. A normal human diploid zygote contains
 a. 23 chromosomes. c. 44 chromosomes.
 b. 46 chromosomes. d. XXY chromosomes.
2. A chart that traces the inheritance of a trait in a family is called a(an)
 a. pedigree. c. genome.
 b. karyotype. d. autosome.
3. Traits that are caused by the interaction of many genes are said to be
 a. polyploid. c. polygenic.
 b. linked. d. autosomal.
4. An example of a trait that is determined by multiple alleles is
 a. Huntington disease. c. Down syndrome.
 b. ABO blood groups. d. hemophilia.
5. Most sex-linked genes are found on the
 a. Y chromosome. c. YY chromosomes.
 b. O chromosome. d. X chromosome.
6. Hemophilia is a genetic disorder that is
 a. sex-linked.
 b. sex-influenced.
 c. fairly common.
 d. more common in women than men.
7. Which parental pair could produce females with colorblindness?
 a. homozygous normal-vision mother, father with colorblindness
 b. mother with colorblindness, normal-vision father
 c. heterozygous normal-vision mother, normal-vision father
 d. heterozygous normal-vision mother, father with colorblindness
8. A common genetic disorder characterized by bent and twisted red blood cells is
 a. cystic fibrosis.
 b. hemophilia.
 c. sickle cell disease.
 d. muscular dystrophy.
9. Which of the following techniques takes advantage of repeated DNA sequences that do not code for proteins?
 a. DNA fingerprinting
 b. DNA sequencing
 c. genetic engineering
 d. rapid sequencing

Interactive textbook with assessment at PHSchool.com 

10. The process of attempting to cure genetic disorders by placing copies of healthy genes into cells that lack them is known as
 a. gene therapy.
 b. DNA fingerprinting.
 c. rapid sequencing.
 d. the Human Genome Project.

Understanding Concepts

11. Describe how a karyotype is prepared and analyzed.
12. What is the difference between autosomes and sex chromosomes?
13. How can a family pedigree be helpful in determining the probability of having a child with a genetic disorder?
14. In the pedigree below, the shaded symbols indicate people who have hemophilia. Which mothers certainly are carriers? Why did the sons of person 3 not inherit the trait?

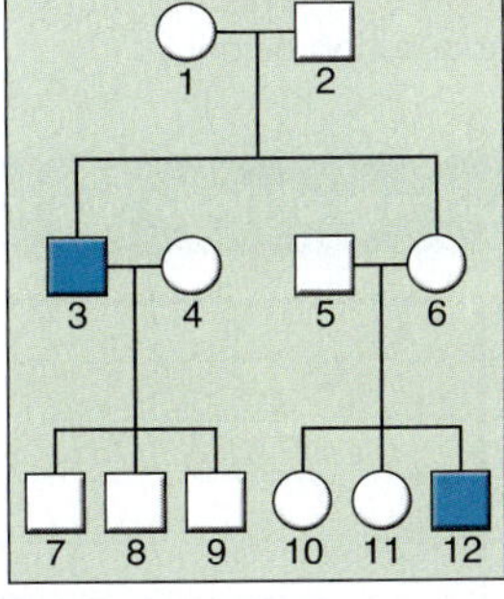

15. Is it possible for a person with blood type alleles I^A and I^B to have blood type A? Explain your answer.
16. Explain the significance of the Rh factor in blood groups.
17. What is Tay-Sachs disease?
18. What determines whether an allele is dominant, recessive, or codominant?
19. What is a chromosomal disorder? Name one chromosomal disorder that can result from nondisjunction.
20. Describe the process of DNA fingerprinting.
21. Describe what is meant by the term *rapid sequencing.*
22. How does an open reading frame help molecular biologists search for genes?

HOMEWORK GUIDE

Section:	Questions:
Section 14–1	1–4, 11–18, 23, 24, 27
Section 14–2	5–8, 19, 25, 26, 28, 29
Section 14–3	9, 10, 20–22

Interactive Textbook

If your class subscribes to the iText, your students can go online to access an interactive version of the Student Edition and a self-test.

(Continued from page 362)

16. Giving a person a transfusion of blood with the wrong Rh factor could be fatal.

17. Tay-Sachs disease is an autosomal recessive genetic disease that causes nervous system breakdown and death.

18. The nature of the gene's protein product and its role in the cell; for example, if one copy of the normal allele can supply cells with enough protein to function, then the normal allele is dominant. If both alleles contribute to the phenotype, they are codominant.

19. A chromosomal disorder occurs when abnormal numbers of chromosomes find their way into the gametes. Chromosomal disorders resulting from nondisjunction include Down syndrome, Turner's syndrome, and Klinefelter's syndrome.

20. A small sample of DNA is cut with restriction enzymes. The fragments are separated by size using electrophoresis. Fragments containing highly variable regions of DNA are detected with a DNA probe.

21. It is a sequencing technique in which widely separated regions of DNA on each chromosome are first sequenced. Then, the sequence of bases on randomly generated fragments of DNA are determined. Computers then find overlapping regions between the fragments and put the fragments together by linking overlapping areas. Computers then align the fragments relative to the known markers to assemble the final sequence.

22. An open reading frame helps biologists find a gene's promoter as well as its introns.

Chapter 14 Study Guide

Critical Thinking

23. Neither parent has the disease because the Tay-Sachs allele is recessive. They have a 1 : 4 chance of having a child with Tay-Sachs disease and a 1 : 2 chance of having a healthy child who will carry the Tay-Sachs allele.

24. One hypothesis is that sickled red blood cells lack a substance *P. falciparum* needs to live. Another is that when the body destroys the sickled red blood cell, it also destroys *P. falciparum.*

25. There is a 50 percent chance that either a son or a daughter will have the disorder.

26. 0.1%; 0.2%; 1.0%; 8.0%; The incidence of Down syndrome increases with the age of the mother.

27. No, cystic fibrosis is caused by a gene mutation. Karyotypes can only detect abnormalities in chromosome number.

28. Possible genotypes of the parents of a male child with colorblindness are X^CX^c and X^CY, X^CX^c and X^cY, X^cX^c and X^CY, or X^cX^c and X^cY. Students may point out that the father's genotype does not affect his son's colorblindness, since he does not pass on an X chromosome to his son.

29. Turner's syndrome; only one X chromosome is present, and there is no Y chromosome.

Focus on the BIG Idea

All three disorders are caused by the nondisjunction of chromosomes during meiosis. Nondisjunction can occur when the homologous chromosomes fail to separate during anaphase I.

Writing in Science

Students should explain in their paragraphs that hemophilia is a recessive disorder linked to the X chromosome. It is more common in men because men have just one X chromosome, so the allele for hemophilia is always expressed if it is present. People with hemophilia lack a protein required for normal blood clotting and can bleed to death from minor cuts.

Chapter 14 Assessment

Critical Thinking

23. Predicting Two prospective parents learn that they each carry one allele for Tay-Sachs disease. Why does neither of them suffer from Tay-Sachs disease? If they decide to have children, what are the chances a pregnancy will produce a baby with Tay-Sachs disease? What are the chances that one of their healthy children will carry the Tay-Sachs allele?

24. Formulating Hypotheses *Plasmodium falciparum,* a protist, causes a fatal form of malaria. Propose a testable hypothesis to explain why *P. falciparum* can live in red blood cells that contain normal hemoglobin but not in red blood cells that contain the sickle cell allele.

25. Predicting A man with colorblindness marries a woman who is a carrier of the disorder. Determine the probability that any son will have the disorder. Determine the probability that any daughter will have the disorder.

26. Using Tables and Graphs Study the graph and answer the question below.

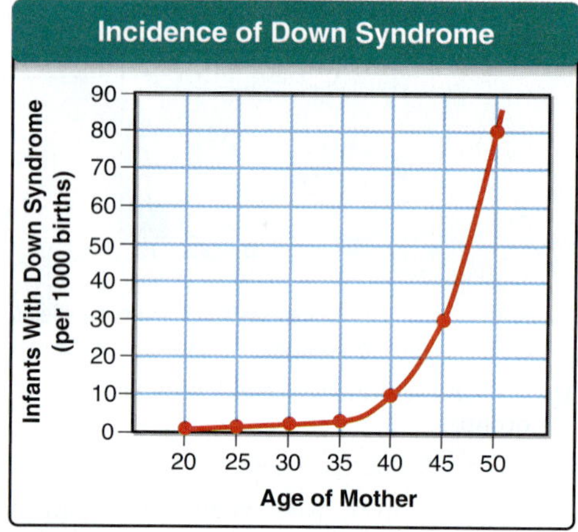

What percent of children born to women under age 30 has Down syndrome? Age 35? Age 40? Age 50? What can you infer about how the age of the mother is related to the incidence of Down syndrome?

27. Inferring Can a genetic counselor use a karyotype to identify a carrier of cystic fibrosis? Explain.

28. Predicting What are the possible genotypes of the parents of a male child with colorblindness?

29. Interpreting Graphics Analyze the human karyotype below. Identify the chromosomal disorder that it shows.

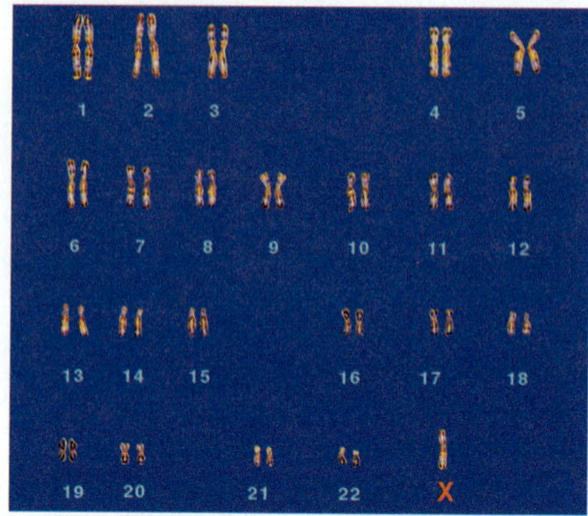

Information and Heredity Explain the relationship between meiosis and Down syndrome, Turner's syndrome, and Klinefelter's syndrome. You may wish to refer to Chapter 11.

Writing in Science

Write a paragraph explaining, in your own words, how hemophilia is inherited. Your paragraph should include both a description of the disease and an explanation of why the disease is found almost exclusively in men. (*Hint:* Begin your paragraph with a topic sentence that expresses the main idea.)

Performance-Based Assessment

Interviewing a Geneticist Your career ambition is to be a science reporter. You are sent by your school newspaper to interview a geneticist who works with human genetic disorders. Prepare a script of the questions you would like answered.

For: An interactive self-test
Visit: PHSchool.com
Web Code: cba-4140

Performance-Based Assessment

Some questions that students might wish to pose include the following: What are the most commonly occurring genetic disorders? How are they inherited? What effects do they have on the body? Can they be detected by genetic screening methods? Can they be treated? If so, how?

Your students can independently test their knowledge of the chapter and print out their test results for your files.

Standards Practice

Test-Taking Tip When interpreting a pedigree, first read through all the generations given. Then, go back and assign (either mentally or on scratch paper) a possible genotype to each person represented in the pedigree. Use Punnett squares to test your assigned genotypes to ensure that they could produce each successive generation's phenotypes.

Directions: Choose the letter that best answers the question or completes the statement.

1. Which of the following can be observed in a person's karyotype?
   A colorblindness
   B trisomy 21
   C hemophilia
   D Huntington disease

2. Which of the following conditions is caused by a sex-linked gene? **BI 3.a**
   A Klinefelter's syndrome
   B Down syndrome
   C muscular dystrophy
   D cystic fibrosis

3. A child has colorblindness. Which genotype-phenotype combination is NOT possible in the child's parents? **BI 3.a**
   A The father does not carry the allele and does not have colorblindness.
   B The mother carries one allele but does not have colorblindness.
   C The father carries one allele but does not have colorblindness.
   D The father carries one allele and has colorblindness.

4. A woman is homozygous for A-negative blood type. A man has AB-negative blood type. What is the probability that the couple's child will be type B-negative? **BI 3.a**
   A 0%
   B 25%
   C 50%
   D 75%

Questions 5–7

A student traced a widow's peak hairline in her family. Based on her interviews and observations, she drew the following pedigree:

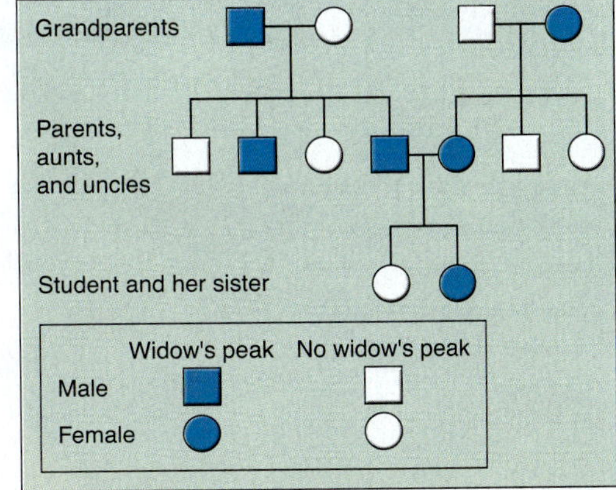

5. Which pattern(s) of inheritance are consistent with the pedigree? **BI 3.a**
   A sex-linked
   B complete dominance
   C codominance
   D incomplete dominance

6. What are the probable genotypes of the student's parents? **7 2.d**
   A mother—*Ww*; father—*ww*
   B mother—*ww*; father—*ww*
   C mother—*WW*; father—*Ww*
   D mother—*Ww*; father—*Ww*

7. The student does not have a widow's peak hairline, but her sister does. What are the girls' probable genotypes? **7 2.d**
   A student—*Ww*; her sister—*ww*
   B student—*WW*; her sister—*Ww*
   C student—*ww*; her sister—*Ww*
   D student—*ww*; her sister—*ww*

Standards Practice

1. B
2. A
3. C
4. A
5. B
6. D
7. C

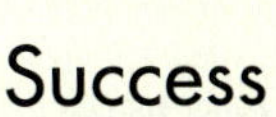

Online at PHSchool.com

Have students check their understanding of the chapter by logging onto Success Tracker.

UNIT 5

Dear Colleague,

Galápagos finches and tortoises ranked high among the inspirations for Darwin's theory of evolution by natural selection—described by leading scientists as the "single most important scientific idea that anyone has ever had." During the century and a half since Darwin's day, as new branches of science have appeared and matured, scientists have gathered evidence beyond Darwin's wildest dreams. Any of that evidence—from biochemistry, molecular genetics, geology, and physics—could have either confirmed or negated Darwin's work. Astonishingly, all those new data have not only supported and reinforced Darwin's insight but have strengthened and expanded it so that evolutionary theory now informs every aspect of biological thought, from global ecology to human genome studies. Evolutionary change is now as well documented as anything we have ever learned in science.

"But why," you might ask, "is evolutionary theory really *that* important to teach, and to teach properly?" There are many answers, but here are a few points most relevant to high-school biology.

Science attempts to describe events in the natural world based on phenomena that we can observe, measure, and replicate. It tries to explain the past in terms of events and processes we can observe today.

UNIT 5 Evolution

Sally lightfoot crabs are commonly found on the shoreline of the Galápagos Islands. The crabs are born black to blend in with the lava. As they mature, they get brighter and redder.

Chapters

Focus on the BIG Ideas

- Evolution
- Science as a Way of Knowing

Humans have always wondered about the organisms that share our planet. In some ways they are so different, yet in other ways they have so much in common. The first scientific explanation for the unity and diversity of life was offered by Darwin's theory of evolution by natural selection. Scientists are still unraveling the details of the evolutionary puzzle. Yet, evolutionary theory stands as one of the most important, and most central, contributions to our scientific understanding of life on Earth.

Go Online PHSchool.com
For: Latest discoveries
Visit: PHSchool.com
Web Code: cbe-5000

Science also attempts to make useful predictions about future events in the same way. That's what science is all about, and that is *all* that science is about. Evolutionary biology uses Darwinian theory to produce scientific explanations and predictions about certain kinds of events in the living world around us.

How, for example, do bacteria become resistant to antibiotics? They evolve under pressure from natural selection. In fact, one physician wrote that humanity would be in a lot better shape with regard to bacteria and antibiotics "if doctors had been taught in medical schools as much about Darwin as they learned about Pasteur." What is the best scientific explanation for the heartbreaking reality that we have not yet been able to develop either a vaccine or a cure for AIDS? The fact is, the human immunodeficiency virus is evolving even faster than bacteria.

But more than simply providing *descriptions* of these phenomena, evolutionary theory enables us to make valuable *predictions* about how living systems will respond to human activity. Evolutionary theory is now informing new treatments for AIDS, new approaches to the production and use of antibiotics, and new strategies for using insecticides against agricultural pests. These and other applications, which hold great promise for humanity, explain why having an understanding of evolution is vital to making informed judgments about many issues in the modern world.

The goal of this unit is to help students understand the evolutionary worldview. As scientists and teachers, we believe very strongly that the purpose of education is to promote understanding, not to compel belief. That applies to evolution, too, which, if properly taught, should *never* threaten the beliefs of students. As biologists, we genuinely feel, as Darwin wrote, there is ". . . grandeur in this view of life." We hope you agree.

Sincerely,

Joe Levine

Students can research evolution on the site developed by authors Ken Miller and Joe Levine.

Chapter Planner 15 Darwin's Theory of Evolution

Section and Section Objectives	Time	STANDARDS NCLB	STANDARDS Biology	Activities and Labs
15–1 The Puzzle of Life's Diversity, pp. 369–372 15.1.1 ***Describe*** the pattern Darwin observed among organisms of the Galápagos Islands.	1 period (1/2 block)	BIIE 1.f		SE: ***Inquiry Activity,*** Do lima beans show variation?, p. 368 L1 L2
15–2 Ideas That Shaped Darwin's Thinking, pp. 373–377 15.2.1 ***State*** how Hutton and Lyell described geological change. 15.2.2 ***Identify*** how Lamarck thought species evolve. 15.2.3 ***Describe*** Malthus's theory of population growth.	2 periods (1 block)	7 3.b	BIIE 1.n	SE: ***Biology and History,*** Origins of Evolutionary Thought, pp. 374–375 L2 L3 TE: ***Demonstration,*** p. 377 L2
15–3 Darwin Presents His Case, pp. 378–386 15.3.1 ***List*** events leading to Darwin's publication of *On the Origin of Species*. 15.3.2 ***Describe*** how natural variation is used in artificial selection. 15.3.3 ***Explain*** how natural selection is related to species' fitness. 15.3.4 ***Identify*** evidence Darwin used to present his case for evolution. 15.3.5 ***State*** Darwin's theory of evolution by natural selection.	3 periods (1 1/2 blocks)	7 3.a, 7 3.b, 7 3.c, BI 7.a, BI 7.d, BI 8.a, BI 8.b		SE: ***Quick Lab,*** New vegetables from old?, p. 379 L2 TE: ***Build Science Skills,*** p. 382 L2 TE: ***Demonstration,*** p. 382 L1 SE: ***Exploration,*** Modeling Adaptation, p. 387 L2 LMA: Chapter 15 Lab L2 L3 LMB: Chapter 15 Lab L1 L2
Chapter Assessment, pp. 388–391	1 period (1/2 block)			

ACTIVITY PLANNER

SE: *Inquiry Activity,* p. 368; 15 min.; 10 lima beans, ruler, calculator, graph paper

TE: *Demonstration,* p. 377; 10 min.; green pepper

SE: *Quick Lab,* p. 379; 20 min.; various *Brassica* vegetables

TE: *Build Science Skills,* p. 382; 5 min.; tree-of-life taxonomic chart

TE: *Demonstration,* p. 382; 15 min.; several beakers, water, several small objects such as leaves and shells, sand and soil mixture

SE: *Exploration,* p. 387; 45 min.; coin

PLANNING KEY

Ability Levels
for students performing . . .
below grade level L1
at grade level L2
above grade level L3

Print Components

SE	Student Edition	**LA**	Lab Assessment
TE	Teacher's Edition	**BTM**	Biotechnology Manual
RSW	Reading & Study Workbook A	**IDM**	Issues and Decision Making
ARSW	Adapted Reading & Study Workbook B	**LW**	Lab Worksheets
TR	Teaching Resources	**LMA**	Laboratory Manual A
IF	Investigations in Forensics	**LMB**	Laboratory Manual B

Tech Components

CTB	Computer Test Bank
BD	BioDetectives DVD
TP	Transparencies Plus
PLM	Probeware Lab Manual
ABC	ABC DVD Library
LS	Lab Simulations
VL	Virtual Labs

Interactive textbook with assessment at PHSchool.com

Program Resources	Assessment	Media and Technology
TR: Lesson Plan 15–1, Section Summary, p. 12 L1, p. 20 L2, Worksheets, p. 15 L1, pp. 22–23 L2, Enrichment L2 L3 **RSW:** Section 15–1 L2 **ARSW:** Section 15–1 L1	**SE:** 15–1 Section Assessment, p. 372 **TR:** Section Review 15–1	**iText:** Section 15–1 **TP:** 15–1 Interest Grabber, Section Outline, Giant Tortoises of the Galápagos Islands, Figure 15–1
TR: Lesson Plan 15–2, Section Summary, p. 12 L1, p. 20 L2, Worksheets, pp. 24–25 L2 **RSW:** Section 15–2 L2	**SE:** 15–2 Section Assessment, p. 377 **TR:** Section Review 15–2	**iText:** Section 15–2 **TP:** 15–2 Interest Grabber, Section Outline, Movement of Earth's Crust, Figure 15–7
TR: Lesson Plan 15–3, Section Summary, p. 13 L1, p. 21 L2, Worksheets, pp. 16–18 L1, pp. 26–28 L2 **LW:** Chapter 15 Exploration L1 L2 L3 **RSW:** Section 15–3 L2 **ARSW:** Section 15–3 L1	**SE:** 15–3 Section Assessment, p. 386 **TR:** Section Review 15–3	**iText:** Section 15–3 **TP:** 15–3 Interest Grabber, Section Outline, Concept Map, Figure 15–14, Figure 15–15
	SE: Chapter 15 Assessment, pp. 388–391 **TR:** Chapter Vocabulary Review, Graphic Organizer, Chapter 15 Test	**iText:** Chapter 15 Assessment **CTB:** Chapter 15 Test

Go Online
Students can do research, share data, and test their knowledge online.

TIME SAVER

PRESSED FOR TIME?

To Preview the Chapter
- Introduce students to Key Concepts and Vocabulary terms in each section.
- Assign the Reading Strategies for each section.

To Review the Chapter
- Assign the Section Review 15–1 through 15–3 in the Reading and Study Workbook or the Adapted Reading and Study Workbook.
- Assign the Section Review for 15–1 through 15–3 and the Chapter Vocabulary Review for Chapter 15 in the Teaching Resources.

To Cover the Chapter Quickly
- Have students read all of Section 15–1, the Biology and History timeline in Section 15–2, and all of Section 15–3.
- Assign Section Review 15–1; Section Review 15–3; questions 1–34 in Chapter 15 Assessment; and questions 1–10 in Chapter 15 Standards Practice.

CHAPTER 15

ENGAGE/EXPLORE

Inquiry Activity

 **BIIE 1.a, BIIE 1.e, BIIE 1.k**

Objectives Students will be able to:
- analyze differences in length of a sample of lima beans
- predict how the data are affected by sample size L1 L2

Skills Focus **Analyzing Data, Predicting**

Materials 10 lima beans, ruler, calculator, graph paper

Time 15 minutes

Strategy Students can write their measurements in pencil directly on each lima bean.

Expected Outcome Students should find slight differences in length of the lima beans in their sample.

Think About It

1. Most lima beans are close to the average length.
2. Students should predict that a graph of data from the entire class would have the same general shape but a smoother curve.

Brain Teaser

Show students pictures of several different species of familiar animals in which the feet or other means of locomotion are visible. Ask: **What different ways do these animals use to move about?** *(Students should state the means of locomotion, for example, a robin flies or a rabbit hops.)* **What traits does each animal have that help it move about as it does?** *(Students should identify the traits. For example, robins have wings for flying and rabbits have large hind legs for hopping.)* Conclude by telling students that observing these different traits was helpful to Darwin in developing his theory of evolution.

CHAPTER 15 Darwin's Theory of Evolution

If you look closely at the top of what appears to be a leaf in the center of this photograph, you can see a head. This walking-leaf insect is a superb example of camouflage.

Inquiry Activity

 BIIE 1.a, BIIE 1.e, BIIE 1.k

Do lima beans show variation?

Procedure 

1. Count out 10 lima beans and measure the length of each in millimeters. Record your results in a data table.
2. Combine your data with the data of two other classmates. Place all the data on one graph. Plot the length on the *x*-axis and the number of beans of each length on the *y*-axis.

Think About It

1. **Analyzing Data** Calculate the average length of the beans. Are most lima beans close to the average length?
2. **Predicting** How do you think a graph of data from the entire class would be different from your graph of data?

HISTORY OF SCIENCE

How Darwin became a naturalist

Charles Darwin came from a family of doctors, and he almost became one, too. Both his father and grandfather were doctors, and they urged him to follow in their footsteps. Charles started out in medical school but soon found that he did not like it. He then went to theological school to study to become a minister. Darwin had always been interested in nature, so he also took courses in biology and geology. These courses were the extent of his formal training as a naturalist when he accepted a job on the *Beagle*. Darwin was not the most qualified applicant, but he was hired anyway because the captain, Robert Fitz Roy, thought Darwin would make a good companion for the five-year voyage.

15–1 The Puzzle of Life's Diversity

7 3.b. Students know the reasoning used by Charles Darwin in reaching his conclusion that natural selection is the mechanism of evolution.

Nature presents scientists with a puzzle. Humans share the Earth with millions of other kinds of organisms of every imaginable shape, size, and habitat. This variety of living things is called biological diversity. How did all these different organisms arise? How are they related? These questions make up the puzzle of life's diversity.

What scientific explanation can account for the diversity of life? The answer is a collection of scientific facts, observations, and hypotheses known as evolutionary theory. **Evolution,** or change over time, is the process by which modern organisms have descended from ancient organisms. A scientific **theory** is a well-supported testable explanation of phenomena that have occurred in the natural world.

CA ⓐ

ⓐ BIIE 1.f

Voyage of the *Beagle*

The individual who contributed more to our understanding of evolution than anyone was Charles Darwin. Darwin was born in England on February 12, 1809—the same day as Abraham Lincoln. Shortly after completing his college studies, Darwin joined the crew of the H.M.S. *Beagle*. In 1831, he set sail from England for a voyage around the world. His route is shown in **Figure 15–1.** Although no one knew it at the time, this was to be one of the most important voyages in the history of science.

 **During his travels, Darwin made numerous observations and collected evidence that led him to propose a revolutionary hypothesis about the way life changes over time.** That hypothesis, now supported by a huge body of evidence, has become the theory of evolution.

Guide for Reading

 **Key Concepts**

- What was Charles Darwin's contribution to science?
- What pattern did Darwin observe among organisms of the Galápagos Islands?

Vocabulary
evolution
theory
fossil

Reading Strategy: Using Visuals Before you read, examine **Figure 15–1.** Find the British Isles, where Darwin's journey began, and then trace his route. Write a statement describing his travels.

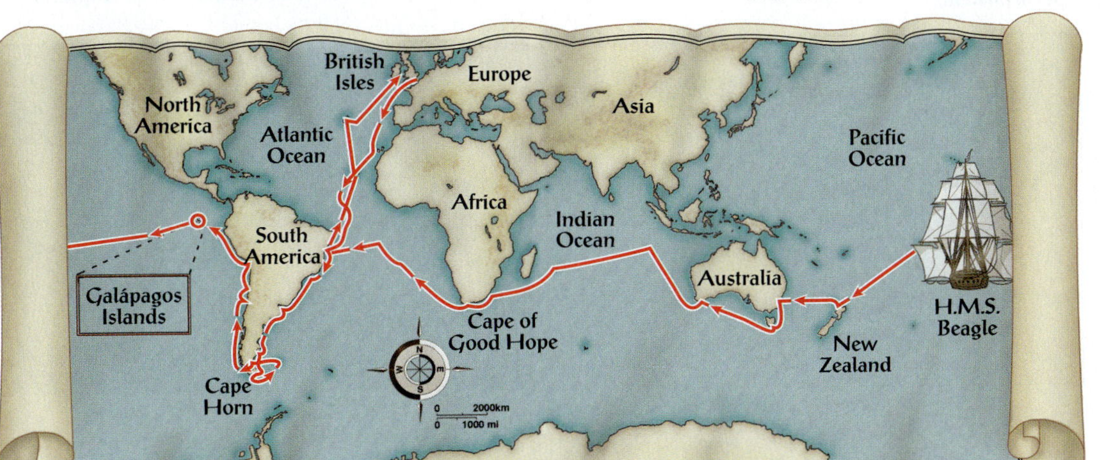

▼ **Figure 15–1** On a five-year voyage on the *Beagle*, Charles Darwin visited several continents and many remote islands. **Darwin's observations led to a revolutionary theory about the way life changes over time.**

Section 15–1

BIIE 1.f

1 FOCUS

Objectives

15.1.1 ***Describe*** the pattern Darwin observed among organisms of the Galápagos Islands.

Guide for Reading

Vocabulary Preview

Challenge students to predict how the three Vocabulary terms are related. Then, after they read the section, have them check to see if they were correct.

Reading Strategy

As students read, have them identify questions Darwin asked during his journey. Such questions include: Why were there no rabbits in Australia and no kangaroos in England? Why had some species disappeared, and how were they related to living species? Had animals living on different Galápagos Islands once been members of the same species?

2 INSTRUCT

Address Misconceptions

Students may hold the misconception that because evolution is called a theory, it is no more likely to be true than any other explanation for biological diversity. Point out that in science a theory is a well-tested concept that is supported by evidence. Explain that scientists do not dispute the fact that evolution has occurred, because so much evidence supports it. L1 L2

Voyage of the *Beagle*

Use Visuals

Figure 15–1 Have students use the figure to trace Darwin's voyage as they read about it in the chapter. 

TIME SAVER — SECTION RESOURCES

Print:

- ***Teaching Resources,*** Lesson Plan 15–1, Adapted Section Summary 15–1, Adapted Worksheets 15–1, Section Summary 15–1, Worksheets 15–1, Section Review 15–1, Enrichment
- ***Reading and Study Workbook A,*** Section 15–1
- ***Adapted Reading and Study Workbook B,*** Section 15–1

Technology:

- ***iText,*** Section 15–1
- ***Transparencies Plus,*** Section 15–1

15–1 (continued)

Darwin's Observations

Use Community Resources

Invite the director of a local zoo or a zoologist from a nearby university or college to speak to the class about similarities and differences between Australian and North American animals that fill similar niches on the two continents. Relate the speaker's presentation to Darwin's observations, as described in the text.

L1 L2

Make Connections

Earth Science Explain to students that climate on the Galápagos Islands varies with elevation. Ask: **Why do you think the islands are drier at lower elevations and wetter at higher elevations?** *(At higher elevations, the air is cooler and cannot hold as much moisture, which causes clouds and precipitation.)* L2

Wherever the ship anchored, Darwin went ashore to collect plant and animal specimens that he added to an ever-growing collection. At sea, he studied his specimens, read the latest scientific books, and filled many notebooks with his observations and thoughts. Darwin was well educated and had a strong interest in natural history. His curiosity and analytical nature were ultimately the keys to his success as a scientist. During his travels, Darwin came to view every new finding as a piece in an extraordinary puzzle: a scientific explanation for the diversity of life on this planet.

Darwin's Observations

Darwin knew a great deal about the plants and animals of his native country. But he saw far more diversity during his travels. For example, during a single day in a Brazilian forest, Darwin collected 68 different beetle species—despite the fact that he was not even searching for beetles! He began to realize that an enormous number of species inhabit the Earth.

Patterns of Diversity Darwin was intrigued by the fact that so many plants and animals seemed remarkably well suited to whatever environment they inhabited. He was impressed by the many ways in which organisms survived and produced offspring. He wondered if there was some process that led to such a variety of ways of reproducing.

Darwin was also puzzled by where different species lived—and did not live. He visited Argentina and Australia, for example, which had similar grassland ecosystems. Yet, those grasslands were inhabited by very different animals. Also, neither Argentina nor Australia was home to the sorts of animals that lived in European grasslands. For Darwin, these patterns posed challenging questions. Why were there no rabbits in Australia, despite the presence of habitats that seemed perfect for them? Similarly, why were there no kangaroos in England?

Figure 15–2 Many of the fossils that Darwin discovered resembled living organisms but were not identical to them. The glyptodon, an extinct animal known only from fossil remains, is an ancient relative of the armadillo of South America. **Comparing and Contrasting** *What are some similarities and differences between these two types of animals?*

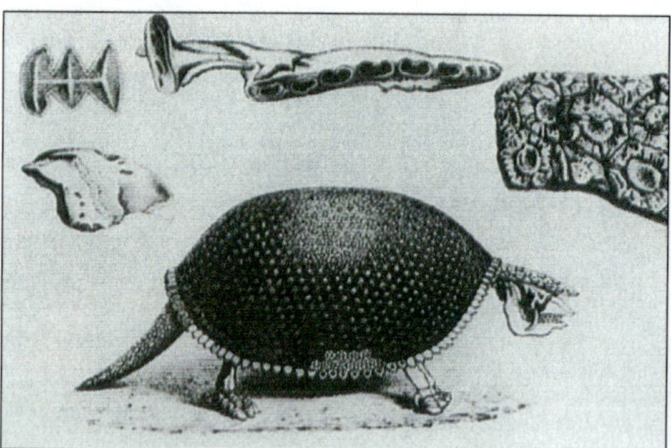

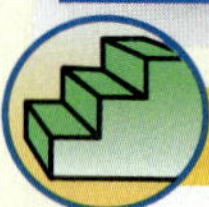

UNIVERSAL ACCESS

Inclusion/Special Needs

Tell at-risk students that the most important thing Darwin learned from his voyage was that organisms vary through time and space. Provide visual examples of each type of variation by showing students pictures of extinct organisms and their living relatives and pictures of related organisms that differ geographically. In each case, point out the similarities as well as the differences in the organisms being compared. L1

Advanced Learners

Have students obtain a copy of Darwin's book *On the Origin of Species* and find passages in which Darwin describes his observations of plants and animals on the Galápagos Islands. Urge students to put a few of Darwin's observations in their own words and share them with the class in a written or an oral report. If possible, students should illustrate their reports with copies of Darwin's original drawings. L3

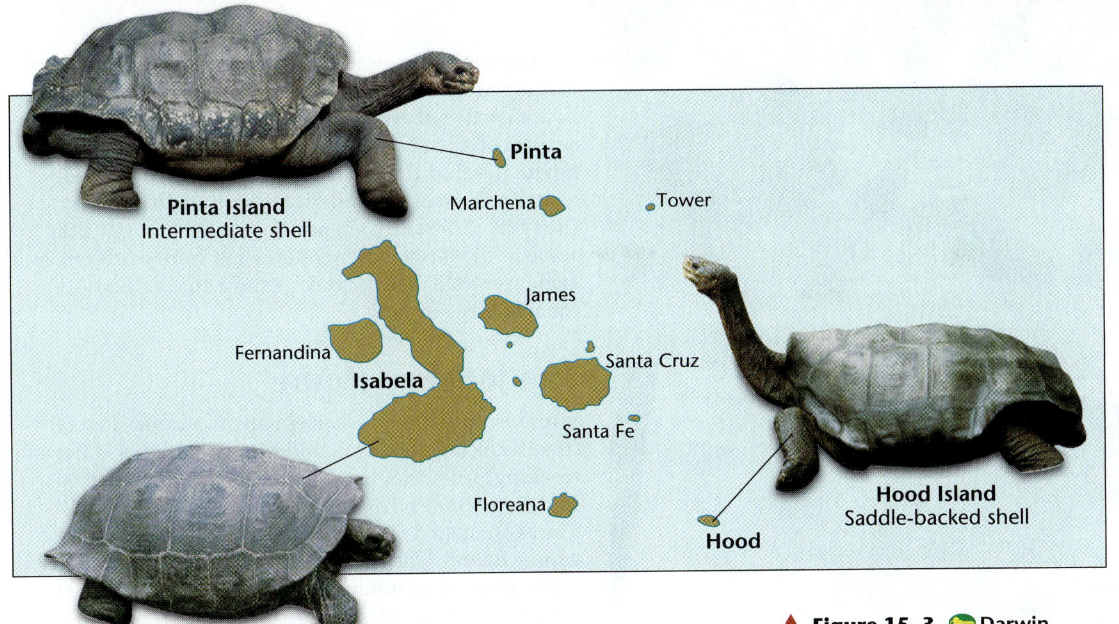

Living Organisms and Fossils Darwin soon realized that living animals represented just part of the puzzle posed by the natural world. In many places during his voyage, Darwin collected the preserved remains of ancient organisms, called **fossils.** Some of those fossils resembled organisms that were still alive, as shown in **Figure 15–2.** Others looked completely unlike any creature he had ever seen. As Darwin studied fossils, new questions arose. Why had so many of these species disappeared? How were they related to living species?

The Galápagos Islands Of all the *Beagle*'s ports of call, the one that influenced Darwin the most was a group of small islands located 1000 km west of South America. These are the Galápagos Islands. Darwin noted that although they were close together, the islands had very different climates. The smallest, lowest islands were hot, dry, and nearly barren. Hood Island, for example, had sparse vegetation. The higher islands had greater rainfall and a different assortment of plants and animals. Isabela Island had rich vegetation.

Darwin was fascinated in particular by the land tortoises and marine iguanas in the Galápagos. He learned that the giant tortoises varied in predictable ways from one island to another, as shown in **Figure 15–3.** The shape of a tortoise's shell could be used to identify which island a particular tortoise inhabited. Darwin later admitted in his notes that he "did not for some time pay sufficient attention to this statement."

CHECKPOINT *How did the fossils Darwin observed compare with the living organisms he studied?*

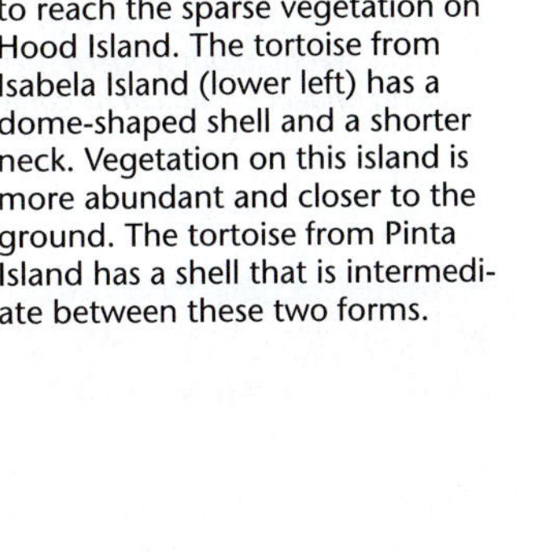

▲ **Figure 15–3** **Darwin observed that the characteristics of many animals and plants varied noticeably among the different Galápagos Islands.** Among the tortoises, the shape of the shell corresponds to different habitats. The Hood Island tortoise (right) has a long neck and a shell that is curved and open around the neck and legs, allowing the tortoise to reach the sparse vegetation on Hood Island. The tortoise from Isabela Island (lower left) has a dome-shaped shell and a shorter neck. Vegetation on this island is more abundant and closer to the ground. The tortoise from Pinta Island has a shell that is intermediate between these two forms.

For: Links on evolution
Visit: www.SciLinks.org
Web Code: cbn-5151

Build Science Skills

Inferring Help students appreciate why the Galápagos Islands were such an important influence on Darwin. Discuss why islands make good places for studying evolution. Point out how different some of the Galápagos are from one another in climate and other environmental features, despite their close proximity. If possible, show students pictures taken on different islands that illustrate these differences. Ask: **What traits do you think an animal might need to survive on a hot, dry, rocky island?** *(Students might describe traits that help conserve water, provide protection from the sun, or make use of scarce food resources.)* **What traits might an animal need to survive on an island with a lot of rainfall and vegetation?** *(Students might describe traits that help the animal move around in trees or tolerate dim, damp conditions.)* Conclude by pointing out that the sharply contrasting environments on the Galápagos Islands and the different animals found on them helped Darwin surmise how evolution could occur. L1 L2

Download a worksheet on evolution for students to complete, and find additional teacher support from NSTA SciLinks.

FACTS AND FIGURES

Galápagos Islands

The Galápagos Islands lie almost 1000 km off the coast of South America. They have a total land area of about 8000 square km, or about three quarters the land area of the Hawaiian Islands. The Galápagos were formed by volcanoes that rise out of the ocean at different elevations, from barely above sea level to 1500 m above the sea. About 15,000 people live on the islands, which are best known for their unusual animals, including the giant tortoises for which the islands were named. The largest species weigh more than 230 kg. The Galápagos also have an unusual history. They were once known as the Enchanted Isles, and pirates buried their treasure there. Ships also abandoned mutineers on the islands. During World War II, the United States established a military base on the Galápagos to guard the Panama Canal.

Answers to . . .

CHECKPOINT *Some fossils resembled organisms that were still alive, while others looked completely unlike any organism Darwin had ever seen.*

Figure 15–2 *Both animals have a type of shell that covers their bodies. The armadillo's covering consists of overlapping plates, whereas the glyptodon's covering consists of one entire piece.*

15–1 (continued)

The Journey Home

Build Science Skills

Inferring Challenge students to make inferences about what a particular species of animal needs to survive. Point out that not only do the physical characteristics of an organism help it to survive, but also its behaviors and relationship with its environment. Have each student choose a particular organism and explain how its characteristics help it survive in its particular environment.

3 ASSESS

Evaluate Understanding

Call on students at random to explain in their own words what the Vocabulary terms mean.

Reteach

Work with students to develop a list of examples of the biological diversity that Darwin observed.

Focus on the BIG Idea

Students should note that biotic factors are those that are living, such as predators and vegetation, and abiotic factors are those that are not living, such as climate and topography. Students' examples will vary. One possible example is that sparse vegetation (biotic factor) led to the evolution of long-necked tortoises.

If your class subscribes to the iText, use it to review the Key Concepts in Section 15–1.

Answer to . . .

Figure 15–4 *They can learn how the earlier investigators formed their ideas based on the evidence they had. They might also interpret the evidence in new ways.*

▲ **Figure 15–4** Darwin's notebooks and some of the finch specimens he collected have been preserved for today's scientists to study. **Inferring** *What might modern scientists learn from examining evidence collected by earlier investigators?*

Darwin also saw several types of small, ordinary-looking brown birds hopping around, looking for seeds. As an eager naturalist, he collected many specimens, several of which are shown in **Figure 15–4.** However, he did not find them particularly unusual or important. As Darwin examined the birds, he noted that they had differently shaped beaks. He thought that some of the birds were wrens, some were warblers, and some were blackbirds. But he came to no other conclusions—at first.

The Journey Home

While heading home, Darwin spent a great deal of time thinking about his findings. Examining different mockingbirds from the Galápagos, Darwin noticed that individual birds collected from the island of Floreana looked different from those collected on James Island. They also looked different from individuals collected on other islands. Darwin also remembered that the tortoises differed from island to island. Although Darwin did not immediately understand the reason for these patterns of diversity, he had stumbled across an important finding. **Darwin observed that the characteristics of many animals and plants varied noticeably among the different islands of the Galápagos.** After returning to England, Darwin began to wonder if animals living on different islands had once been members of the same species. According to this hypothesis, these separate species would have evolved from an original South American ancestor species after becoming isolated from one another. Was this possible? If so, it would turn people's view of the natural world upside down.

15–1 Section Assessment

1. **Key Concept** What did Darwin's travels reveal to him about the number and variety of living species?
2. **Key Concept** How did tortoises and birds differ among the islands of the Galápagos?
3. What is evolution? Why is evolution referred to as a theory?
4. What is a fossil?
5. **Critical Thinking Inferring** Darwin found fossils of many organisms that were different from any living species. How would this finding have affected his understanding of life's diversity?

Focus on the BIG Idea

Interdependence in Nature In Chapter 5, you learned that both biotic and abiotic factors affect ecosystems. Distinguish between these two factors, give some examples of each, and explain how they might have affected the tortoises that Darwin observed on the Galápagos Islands.

15–1 Section Assessment

1. Darwin's travels showed him that the diversity of living species was far greater than he had previously known.
2. Each Galápagos island had its own type of tortoises and birds that were clearly different from the tortoises and birds on other islands.
3. Evolution, or change over time, is the process by which modern organisms have descended from ancient ones. Evolution is referred to as a theory because it is a well-supported explanation of phenomena that have occurred in the natural world.
4. A fossil is the preserved remains of an ancient organism.
5. It would have greatly increased his estimates of biological diversity.

15–2 Ideas That Shaped Darwin's Thinking

7 3.b. Students know the reasoning used by Charles Darwin in reaching his conclusion that natural selection is the mechanism of evolution. **BIIE 1.n.** Know that when an observation does not agree with an accepted scientific theory, the observation is sometimes mistaken or fraudulent (e.g. the Piltdown Man fossil or unidentified flying objects) and that the theory is sometimes wrong (e.g. the Ptolemaic model of the movement of the Sun, Moon, and planets).

If Darwin had lived a century earlier, he might have done little more than think about the questions raised during his travels. But Darwin's voyage came during one of the most exciting periods in the history of Western science. Explorers were traversing the globe, and great thinkers were beginning to challenge established views about the natural world. Darwin was powerfully influenced by the work of these scientists, especially those who were studying the history of Earth. In turn, he himself greatly changed the thinking of many scientists and nonscientists. Some people, however, found Darwin's ideas too shocking to accept. To understand how radical Darwin's thoughts appeared, you must understand a few things about the world in which he lived.

Most Europeans in Darwin's day believed that the Earth and all its forms of life had been created only a few thousand years ago. Since that original creation, they concluded, neither the planet nor its living species had changed. A robin, for example, has always looked and behaved as robins had in the past. Rocks and major geological features were thought to have been produced suddenly by catastrophic events that humans rarely, if ever, witnessed.

By the time Darwin set sail, numerous discoveries had turned up important pieces of evidence. A rich fossil record, including the example in **Figure 15–5**, was challenging that traditional view of life. In light of such evidence, some scientists even adjusted their beliefs to include not one but several periods of creation. Each of these periods, they contended, was preceded by a catastrophic event that killed off many forms of life. At first, Darwin may have accepted these beliefs. But he began to realize that much of what he had observed did not fit neatly into this view of unchanging life. Slowly, after studying many scientific theories of his time, Darwin began to change his thinking dramatically.

(a) 7 3.b

Guide for Reading

Key Concepts

- How did Hutton and Lyell describe geological change?
- According to Lamarck, how did species evolve?
- What was Malthus's theory of population growth?

Reading Strategy: Finding Main Ideas

As you read about the individuals who influenced Darwin's thinking, write a sentence briefly describing what Darwin learned from each one.

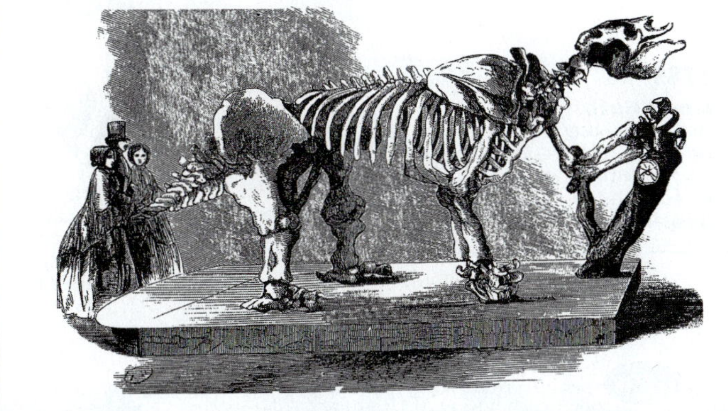

Figure 15–5 This engraving, made around 1850, shows the fossil remains of a giant sloth from South America. During the 1800s, explorers were finding the remains of numerous animal types that had no living representatives. **Inferring** *What did such fossil evidence indicate about life in the past?*

Section 15–2

7 3.b, **BIIE 1.n**

1 FOCUS

Objectives

15.2.1 ***State*** how Hutton and Lyell described geological change.

15.2.2 ***Identify*** how Lamarck thought species evolve.

15.2.3 ***Describe*** Malthus's theory of population growth.

Guide for Reading

Reading Strategy

Students should list Hutton, Lyell, Lamarck, and Malthus. Before students read the section, have them look at the figures, read the captions, and write down each Key Concept they find in the captions. As they read the section, they should match each Key Concept they listed with a related Key Concept in the text.

2 INSTRUCT

Address Misconceptions

With the rapid pace of technological change today, students may not appreciate how revolutionary the idea of evolution was in Darwin's time. Point out that, from ancient times, most people believed that all living things were created by a divine being at the same time and that, once created, living things remained unchanged. L1 L2

SECTION RESOURCES

Print:

- ***Teaching Resources,*** Lesson Plan 15–2, Adapted Section Summary 15–2, Section Summary 15–2, Worksheets 15–2, Section Review 15–2
- ***Reading and Study Workbook A,*** Section 15–2

Technology:

- ***iText,*** Section 15–2
- ***Transparencies Plus,*** Section 15–2

Answer to . . .

Figure 15–5 *That some organisms from the past had no modern representatives, and that some organisms may have become extinct*

15–2 (continued)

An Ancient, Changing Earth

Use Visuals

Figure 15–6 Call students' attention to the figure, and have them read the caption. Ask: **How did Hutton's and Lyell's proposals about Earth support Darwin's ideas about the changes he had observed in living things?** *(Hutton and Lyell proposed that Earth had changed. This helped support Darwin's idea that living things change. Hutton and Lyell also proposed that Earth was millions of years old. This provided the long time span Darwin thought was needed for changes in living things to occur.)* L1 L2

Biology and History

 BIIE 1.k

Point out to students that most of the dates in the timeline refer to the dates of publications that influenced Darwin. After students read the timeline, suggest that they refer back to it as they read about each of the scientists in the text. Doing so will help students appreciate the role each scientist played in the development of Darwin's theory.

Writing in Science

Students might write about how similar Darwin's and Wallace's theories are. They also might write about how different the backgrounds and careers of the two men were. Wallace came from a large family with little money and only went to grammar school, whereas Darwin came from a small, well-to-do family and graduated from college. Darwin became one of the most famous scientists of all time for his theory of evolution by natural selection, whereas Wallace is not very well known by the general public today. However, Wallace is considered the founder of biogeography, the study of the distribution of living things.

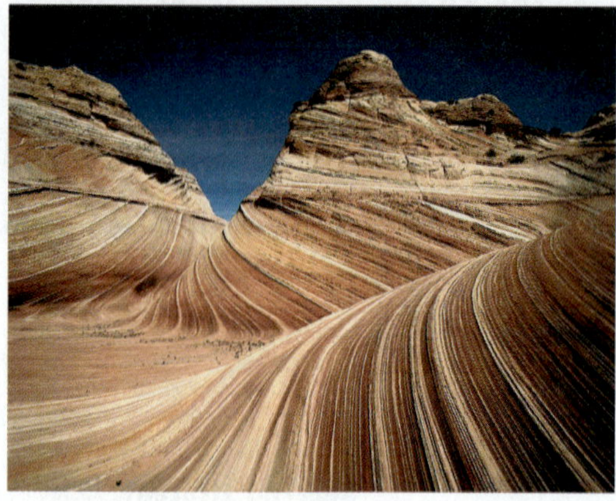

▲ **Figure 15–6** These huge rocks, which are composed of sandstone, show distinct layers that were laid down over millions of years. **Hutton and Lyell cited geological features such as these rocks as evidence that Earth is many millions of years old.**

An Ancient, Changing Earth

During the eighteenth and nineteenth centuries, scientists examined Earth in great detail. They gathered information suggesting that Earth was very old and had changed slowly over time. Two scientists who formed important theories based on this evidence were James Hutton and Charles Lyell. **Hutton and Lyell helped scientists recognize that Earth is many millions of years old, and the processes that changed Earth in the past are the same processes that operate in the present.**

Hutton and Geological Change In 1795, the geologist James Hutton published a detailed hypothesis about the geological forces that have shaped Earth. Hutton proposed that layers of rock, such as those shown in **Figure 15–6,** form very slowly. Also, some rocks are moved up by forces beneath Earth's surface. Others are buried, and still others are pushed up from the sea floor to form mountain ranges. The resulting rocks, mountains, and valleys are then shaped by a variety of natural forces—including rain, wind, heat, and cold temperatures. Most of these geological processes operate extremely slowly, often over millions of years. Hutton, therefore, proposed that Earth had to be much more than a few thousand years old.

 BIIE 1.k

Biology and History

Origins of Evolutionary Thought

The groundwork for the modern theory of evolution was laid during the 1700s and 1800s. Charles Darwin developed the central idea of evolution by natural selection, but others before and during his time also built essential parts of the theory.

1785
James Hutton
Hutton proposes that Earth is shaped by geological forces that took place over extremely long periods of time. He estimates Earth to be millions—not thousands—of years old.

1798
Thomas Malthus
In his *Essay on the Principle of Population,* Malthus predicts that the human population will grow faster than the space and food supplies needed to sustain it.

1809
Jean-Baptiste Lamarck
Lamarck publishes his hypotheses of the inheritance of acquired traits. The ideas are flawed, but he is one of the first to propose a mechanism explaining how organisms change over time.

HISTORY OF SCIENCE

In Darwin's shadow
Alfred Russel Wallace was born in 1823 in Wales. He received only six years of formal education but was very well read. His first job, as a surveyor, gave him practical experience in the natural world and furthered his love of nature. Wallace began his career as a naturalist in 1848, when he went on an expedition to the Amazon River basin. There, he spent four years traveling, collecting, mapping, and writing. He later went to Malaysia, where he spent eight years involved in the same pursuits. His evolutionary theory, which is strikingly similar to Darwin's, was developed during this time. Because Wallace was a vocal proponent of unpopular social and religious views, he never held a permanent academic position. Part-time jobs and a small inheritance allowed him to spend much of his time writing. By the time he died in 1913, he had over 700 publications and two honorary doctorate degrees.

Lyell's *Principles of Geology* Just before the *Beagle* set sail, Darwin had been given the first volume of geologist Charles Lyell's book *Principles of Geology*. Lyell stressed that scientists must explain past events in terms of processes that they can actually observe, since processes that shaped the Earth millions of years earlier continue in the present. Volcanoes release hot lava and gases now, just as they did on an ancient Earth. Erosion continues to carve out canyons, just as it did in the past.

Lyell's work explained how awesome geological features could be built up or torn down over long periods of time. Lyell helped Darwin appreciate the significance of geological phenomena that he had observed. Darwin had witnessed a spectacular volcanic eruption. Darwin wrote about an earthquake that had lifted a stretch of rocky shoreline—with mussels and other animals attached to it—more than 3 meters above its previous position. He noted that fossils of marine animals were displaced many feet above sea level. Darwin then understood how geological processes could have raised these rocks from the sea floor to a mountaintop.

This understanding of geology influenced Darwin in two ways. First, Darwin asked himself: If the Earth could change over time, might life change as well? Second, he realized that it would have taken many, many years for life to change in the way he suggested. This would have been possible only if the Earth were extremely old.

CHECKPOINT *What are some ways the Earth has changed over time?*

Go Online NSTA SCILINKS
For: Links on Darwin
Visit: www.SciLinks.org
Web Code: cbn-5152

Writing in Science

Use the library or the Internet to find out more about Darwin and Wallace. Write a dialogue between these two men, where the conversation shows the similarities in their careers and theories.

1831
Charles Darwin
Darwin sets sail on the H.M.S. *Beagle*, a voyage that will provide him with vast amounts of evidence leading to his theory of evolution.

1833
Charles Lyell
In the second and final volume of *Principles of Geology*, Lyell explains that processes occurring now have shaped Earth's geological features over long periods of time.

1850

1858
Alfred Wallace
Wallace writes to Darwin, speculating on evolution by natural selection, based on his studies of the distribution of plants and animals.

1859
Darwin publishes *On the Origin of Species*.

1900

Make Connections

Earth Science Help students appreciate how slowly geological forces such as erosion occur. Ask: **How did the Grand Canyon form?** *(Through the erosion of rock layers by the Colorado River)* Tell students that the Colorado River is currently eroding Earth's surface at a rate of about 0.3 m per millennium, which is actually a rather rapid rate of erosion. Point out that the Grand Canyon is as deep as 1800 m in some places. Urge students to develop a real-world example for 1800 m, such as the distance from school to a particular location. Ask: **Using the current rate of erosion, about how long did it take the Colorado River to erode the Grand Canyon to its current depth?** *(About six million years)* L2

Use Community Resources

Have students visit a local road bed, ravine, rock outcrop, or other site where sedimentary layers have been exposed to view by construction activities or by natural processes, such as erosion or faults. Challenge students to predict how long it took for the sediments in each layer to be deposited and turned into rock. If possible, arrange to have a geologist from a local college, university, or state department of natural resources meet with your class at the site to explain how the exposed layers were formed and how long it took them to form. L2

Download a worksheet on Darwin for students to complete, and find additional teacher support from NSTA SciLinks.

UNIVERSAL ACCESS

Less Proficient Readers

Work with less proficient readers to make a concept map that simplifies and clarifies the main points in the section. The concept map should show the major contributions to Darwin's thought by Hutton, Lyell, Lamarck, and Malthus. Place the concept map on the chalkboard and leave it until students have finished studying the section, or have students copy the concept map into their class notebooks. L1 L2

Advanced Learners

Challenge students to research Count de Buffon, the eighteenth-century French naturalist who influenced Darwin with his voluminous writings about the natural history of organisms. Encourage students to locate some of Buffon's original writings and skim through them to find passages that might have influenced Darwin's ideas about evolution. Ask students to share their findings with the class. L3

Answer to . . .

CHECKPOINT *Geological features on Earth have been built up and torn down over long periods of time through processes such as volcanic activity, earthquakes, and erosion.*

15–2 (continued)

Lamarck's Evolution Hypotheses

Address Misconceptions

The way evolution is often discussed may lead students to hold the misconception that scientists today still view evolution as a Lamarckian process. Give students the following example, which is typical of what they might read in a textbook: "The bird evolved a larger beak." This sounds as though an individual bird has intentionally changed its biological traits. Ask: **What would be a more accurate way of stating this?** *(Over many generations, larger beaks evolved in certain bird species.)* L2

Build Science Skills

Designing Experiments Challenge students to design an experiment to test Lamarck's hypothesis of the inheritance of acquired traits. Students' experimental designs should include a specific hypothesis, procedure, and possible outcomes. Ask: **What species would you use, and what variable would you test?** *(Answers will vary depending on students' experimental designs.)* Have students explain how the different possible outcomes of their experiment would or would not support Lamarck's hypothesis. L2 L3

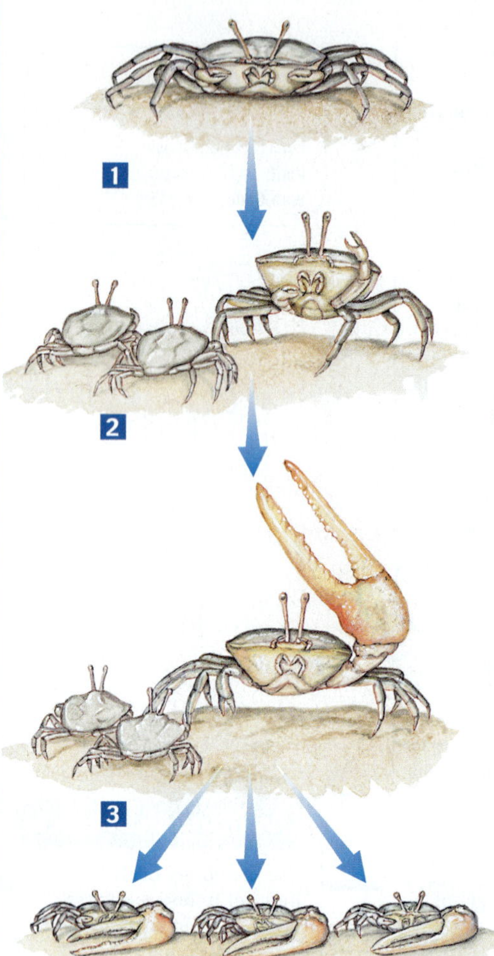

▲ **Figure 15–7** **Lamarck proposed that the selective use or disuse of an organ led to a change in that organ that was then passed on to offspring.** This proposed mechanism is shown here applied to fiddler crabs. (1) The male crab uses its small front claw to attract mates and ward off predators. (2) Because the front claw has been used repeatedly, it becomes larger. (3) The acquired characteristic, a larger claw, is then passed on to the crab's offspring. Lamarck's explanation, proposed in 1809, was found to be incorrect.

Lamarck's Evolution Hypotheses

The French naturalist Jean-Baptiste Lamarck was among the first scientists to recognize that living things have changed over time—and that all species were descended from other species. He also realized that organisms were somehow adapted to their environments. In 1809, the year that Darwin was born, Lamarck published his hypotheses. **Lamarck proposed that by selective use or disuse of organs, organisms acquired or lost certain traits during their lifetime. These traits could then be passed on to their offspring. Over time, this process led to change in a species.**

Tendency Toward Perfection Lamarck proposed that all organisms have an innate tendency toward complexity and perfection. As a result, they are continually changing and acquiring features that help them live more successfully in their environments. In Lamarck's view, for instance, the ancestors of birds acquired an urge to fly. Over many generations, birds kept trying to fly, and their wings increased in size and became more suited to flying.

Use and Disuse Because of this tendency toward perfection, Lamarck proposed that organisms could alter the size or shape of particular organs by using their bodies in new ways. For example, by trying to use their front limbs for flying, birds could eventually transform those limbs into wings. Conversely, if a winged animal did not use its wings—an example of disuse—the wings would decrease in size over generations and finally disappear.

Inheritance of Acquired Traits Like many biologists of his time, Lamarck thought that acquired characteristics could be inherited. For example, if during its lifetime an animal somehow altered a body structure, leading to longer legs or fluffier feathers, it would pass that change on to its offspring. By this reasoning, if you spent much of your life lifting weights to build muscles, your children would inherit big muscles, too.

Evaluating Lamarck's Hypotheses Lamarck's hypotheses of evolution, illustrated in **Figure 15–7,** are incorrect in several ways. Lamarck, like Darwin, did not know how traits are inherited. He did not know that an organism's behavior has no effect on its heritable characteristics. However, Lamarck was one of the first to develop a scientific hypothesis of evolution and to realize that organisms are adapted to their environments. He paved the way for the work of later biologists.

HISTORY OF SCIENCE

Lamarck's successes and failures

French naturalist Jean-Baptiste Lamarck worked as a soldier and a bank clerk before becoming a botanist. He spent many years collecting and studying plants, and he wrote numerous books and articles on his research. Lamarck was also a museum curator and one of the originators of the modern concept of the museum collection. In addition, he coined the terms *invertebrate* and *biology*. In 1801, Lamarck's carefully researched book *System of Invertebrate Animals* presented a revision of the Linnaean classification of invertebrates that is still accepted by most scientists today. Unfortunately, some of Lamarck's other publications were based more on fancy than fact, including his 1809 *Zoological Philosophy*. Lamarck became a scientific outcast primarily because he supported the idea of evolution, and he died a poor, lonely man.

Population Growth

Another important influence on Darwin came from the English economist Thomas Malthus. In 1798, Malthus published a book in which he noted that babies were being born faster than people were dying. **Malthus reasoned that if the human population continued to grow unchecked, sooner or later there would be insufficient living space and food for everyone.** The only forces he observed that worked against this growth were war, famine, and disease. Conditions in certain parts of nineteenth-century England, illustrated in **Figure 15–8,** reinforced Malthus's somewhat pessimistic view of the human condition.

When Darwin read Malthus's work, he realized that this reasoning applied even more strongly to plants and animals than it did to humans. Why? Because humans produce far fewer offspring than most other species do. A mature maple tree can produce thousands of seeds in a single summer, and one oyster can produce millions of eggs each year. If all the offspring of almost any species survived for several generations, they would overrun the world.

Obviously, this has not happened, because continents are not covered with maple trees, and oceans are not filled with oysters. The overwhelming majority of a species' offspring die. Further, only a few of those offspring that survive succeed in reproducing. What causes the death of so many individuals? What factor or factors determine which ones survive and reproduce, and which do not? Answers to these questions became central to Darwin's explanation of evolutionary change.

CA a

a 7 3.b

▶ **Figure 15–8** **Malthus reasoned that if the human population continued to grow unchecked, sooner or later there would be insufficient food and living space for everyone.** He supported his theory with the evidence he observed in the streets of London.

15–2 Section Assessment

1. **Key Concept** What two ideas from geology were important to Darwin's thinking?
2. **Key Concept** According to Lamarck, how did organisms acquire traits?
3. **Key Concept** According to Malthus, what factors limited population growth?
4. How did Lyell's *Principles of Geology* influence Darwin?
5. **Critical Thinking Evaluating** Imagine that you are Thomas Malthus. Write an article describing your ideas. Explain the impact of a growing population on society and the environment.

Focus on the BIG Idea

Science as a Way of Knowing Describe the idea and observations proposed by Lamarck regarding his theory of evolution. Include in your description what Lamarck observed and the conclusions he made based on his observations. In addition, include the scientific evidence that eventually proved Lamarck's theory incorrect.

15–2 Section Assessment

1. Earth is very old, and the same processes that shaped Earth millions of years ago continue in the present.
2. Lamarck thought that organisms acquired traits by using their bodies in new ways.
3. War, famine, and disease
4. It suggested Earth was very old and continued to change, allowing time for living things to change and for evolution to occur.
5. Students' articles will vary. However, students should include that if human population growth continues to grow unchecked, eventually resources will become scarce.

Population Growth

Demonstration

Help students appreciate the tremendous reproductive potential of organisms. Have each student or small group count all the seeds in a green pepper that has been cut in half. Then, ask: **How many seeds would there be in one generation if all the seeds in your pepper grew into plants that each produced the same number of seeds?** *(There would be x^2 seeds, where x is the number of seeds in the original pepper.)* Challenge students to calculate how many seeds there would be in two generations. *(There would be $(x^2)^2$, or x^4 seeds.)* Conclude by saying that, if pepper plants actually reproduced at their potential rate, there would be billions of offspring in just a few generations. L2

3 ASSESS

Evaluate Understanding

Read each of the Key Concepts in the section, leaving the names *Hutton, Lyell, Lamarck,* or *Malthus* blank. Call on students at random to fill in the correct name.

Reteach

Using the chalkboard or an overhead transparency, work with students to create a concept map summarizing the contributions of other scientists to Darwin's ideas about evolution.

Focus on the BIG Idea

Students' responses should incorporate the boldface Key Concept on page 376 as well as the fiddler crab example illustrated in Figure 15–7. Because Lamarck did not know how traits were inherited or that behavior had no effect on inherited characteristics, his theory was eventually proven incorrect.

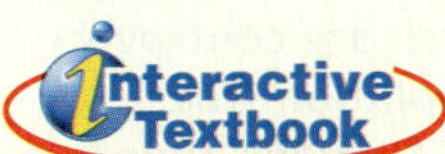

If your class subscribes to the iText, use it to review the Key Concepts in Section 15–2.

Section 15-3

7 3.a, 7 3.b, 7 3.c, BI 7.a, BI 7.d, BI 8.a, BI 8.b

1 FOCUS

Objectives

15.3.1 ***List*** events leading to Darwin's publication of *On the Origin of Species.*

15.3.2 ***Describe*** how natural variation is used in artificial selection.

15.3.3 ***Explain*** how natural selection is related to species' fitness.

15.3.4 ***Identify*** evidence Darwin used to present his case for evolution.

15.3.5 ***State*** Darwin's theory of evolution by natural selection.

Guide for Reading

Vocabulary Preview

Have students think of examples of each of the concepts in the Vocabulary list. As they read the section, they should check to see if their examples are suitable.

Reading Strategy

Suggest that students write the headings and subheadings in outline form and fill in details under each topic as they read the section.

2 INSTRUCT

Publication of *On the Origin of Species*

Build Science Skills

Making Judgments Whether Darwin delayed publishing his work because of possible criticism by fellow scientists or the general public, his reluctance to publish is a good example of how science is influenced by its social context. Help students appreciate this by challenging them to think of similar examples from today. Ask: **What current areas of scientific research are controversial, much as evolution was controversial in Darwin's time?** *(Possible answers include cloning, genetic engineering, and research involving animals or human fetal tissue.)* L2

15–3 Darwin Presents His Case

7 3.a. Students know both genetic variation and environmental factors are causes of evolution and diversity of organisms. **BI 7.a.** Students know why natural selection acts on the phenotype rather than the genotype of an organism. **BI 7.d.** Students know variation within a species increases the likelihood that at least some members of a species will survive under changed environmental conditions. **BI 8.a.** Students know how natural selection determines the differential survival of groups of organisms. **BI 8.b.** Students know a great diversity of species increases the chance that at least some organisms survive major changes in the environment.

Guide for Reading

Key Concepts

- How is natural variation used in artificial selection?
- How is natural selection related to a species' fitness?
- What evidence of evolution did Darwin present?

Vocabulary

artificial selection
struggle for existence
fitness
adaptation
survival of the fittest
natural selection
descent with modification
common descent
homologous structure
vestigial organ

Reading Strategy: Building Vocabulary As you read, write a phrase or sentence in your own words to define each highlighted, boldface term.

When Darwin returned to England in 1836, he brought back specimens from around the world. Subsequent findings about these specimens soon had the scientific community abuzz. Darwin learned that his Galápagos mockingbirds actually belonged to three separate species found nowhere else in the world! Even more surprising, the brown birds that Darwin had thought to be wrens, warblers, and blackbirds were all finches. They, too, were found nowhere else. The same was true of the Galápagos tortoises, the marine iguanas, and many plants that Darwin had collected on the islands. Each island species looked a great deal like a similar species on the South American mainland. Yet, the island species were clearly different from the mainland species and from one another.

Publication of *On the Origin of Species*

Darwin began filling notebooks with his ideas about species diversity and the process that would later be called evolution. However, he did not rush out to publish his thoughts. Recall that Darwin's ideas challenged fundamental scientific beliefs of his day. Darwin was not only stunned by his discoveries, he was disturbed by them. Years later, he wrote, "It was evident that such facts as these . . . could be explained on the supposition that species gradually became modified, and the subject haunted me." Although he discussed his work with friends, he shelved his manuscript for years and told his wife to publish it in case he died.

In 1858, Darwin received a short essay from Alfred Russel Wallace, a fellow naturalist who had been doing field work in Malaysia. That essay summarized the thoughts on evolutionary change that Darwin had been mulling over for almost 25 years! Suddenly, Darwin had an incentive to publish his own work. At a scientific meeting later that year, Wallace's essay was presented together with some of Darwin's work.

◀ **Figure 15–9** Each zebra inherits genes that give it a distinctive pattern of stripes. Those visibly different patterns are an example of natural variation in a species. **Formulating Hypotheses** *What might be some genetic variations that are not visible?*

SECTION RESOURCES

Print:

- ***Laboratory Manual A,*** Chapter 15 Lab
- ***Laboratory Manual B,*** Chapter 15 Lab
- ***Teaching Resources,*** Lesson Plan 15–3, Adapted Section Summary 15–3, Adapted Worksheets 15–3, Section Summary 15–3, Worksheets 15–3, Section Review 15–3
- ***Reading and Study Workbook A,*** Section 15–3
- ***Adapted Reading and Study Workbook B,*** Section 15–3
- ***Lab Worksheets,*** Chapter 15 Exploration

Technology:

- ***iText,*** Section 15–3
- ***Transparencies Plus,*** Section 15–3

Eighteen months later, in 1859, Darwin published the results of his work, *On the Origin of Species.* In his book, he proposed a mechanism for evolution that he called natural selection. He then presented evidence that evolution has been taking place for millions of years—and continues in all living things. Darwin's work caused a sensation. Many people considered his arguments to be brilliant, while others strongly opposed his message. But what did Darwin actually say?

CA a

CHECKPOINT *What event motivated Darwin to publish his ideas?*

Inherited Variation and Artificial Selection

One of Darwin's most important insights was that members of each species vary from one another in important ways. Observations during his travels and conversations with plant and animal breeders convinced him that variation existed both in nature and on farms. For example, some plants in a species bear larger fruit than others. Some cows give more milk than others. From breeders, Darwin learned that some of this was heritable variation—differences that are passed from parents to offspring. Darwin had no idea of how heredity worked. Today, we know that heritable variation in organisms is caused by variations in their genes. We also know that genetic variation is found in wild species as well as in domesticated plants and animals.

CA b

Darwin argued that this variation mattered. This was a revolutionary idea, because in Darwin's day, variations were thought to be unimportant, minor defects. But Darwin noted that plant and animal breeders used heritable variation—what we now call genetic variation—to improve crops and livestock. They would select for breeding only the largest hogs, the fastest horses, or the cows that produced the most milk. Darwin termed this process **artificial selection.** **In artificial selection, nature provided the variation, and humans selected those variations that they found useful.** Artificial selection has produced many diverse domestic animals and crop plants, including the plants shown in **Figure 15–10**, by selectively breeding for different traits.

CA c

Quick Lab

New vegetables from old?

Materials various *Brassica* (cabbage family) vegetables

Procedure

Examine each of the vegetables and compare them. Determine which organ of the ancestral plant breeders may have chosen to produce each vegetable.

Analyze and Conclude

Formulating Hypotheses

Choose one of the vegetables. Explain how breeders might have produced that variety from the ancestral plant, shown below.

a 7 3.b

b 7 3.a, BI 7.a, BI 8.b

c 7 3.a

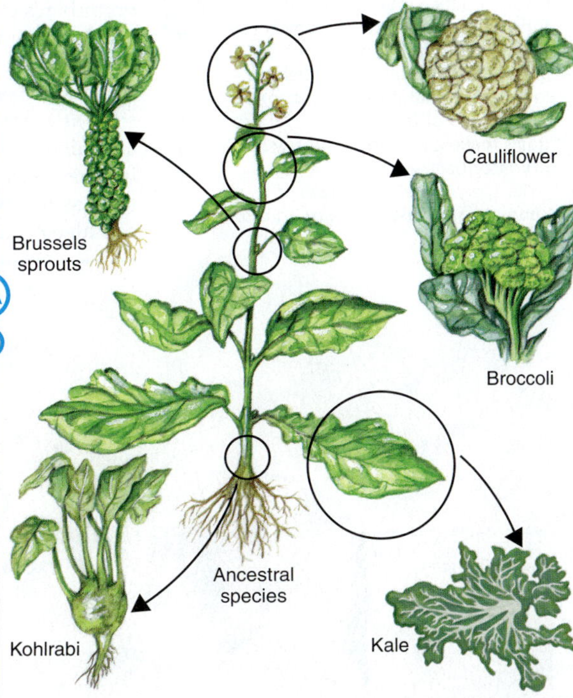

Figure 15–10 **In artificial selection, humans select from among the naturally occurring genetic variations in a species.** From a single ancestral plant, breeders selecting for enlarged flower buds, leaf buds, leaves, or stems have produced all these plants.

Inherited Variation and Artificial Selection

Quick Lab

Objective Students will be able to formulate hypotheses to explain how agricultural scientists use selective breeding to develop new vegetables. L2

Skill Focus Formulating Hypotheses

Materials various *Brassica* vegetables

Time 20 minutes

Advance Prep Obtain a variety of fresh *Brassica* vegetables, such as broccoli, Brussels sprouts, cauliflower, cabbage, and rutabaga.

Strategies

- Urge students to recall the smell and taste of cooked *Brassica* vegetables, noting their similar cabbagelike characteristics, in addition to making observations of the uncooked specimens.
- After students have completed the procedure, challenge them to recall what selective breeding is. (If necessary, prompt them to review Section 13–1.) Then, encourage them to observe the ancestral species in Figure 15–10.

Expected Outcome Students should identify the organ that was developed in each plant, such as flowers in cauliflower and leaves in kale.

Analyze and Conclude Students should hypothesize that plants in the ancestral species must have shown great variation, for example, some probably had larger leaves or flowers. Breeders would have selected plants with similar traits and crossed them to produce new vegetables. Students may also suggest that chemicals were used for generating polyploids, thereby developing new variants to work with.

ESL SUPPORT FOR ENGLISH LANGUAGE LEARNERS

Comprehension: Key Concepts

Beginning Write the Key Concept sentence about artificial selection on the board, and read it aloud. Draw boxes around the following words: *artificial selection, nature, variation, organisms, humans,* and *selected.* Form groups that include beginners and—if possible—more advanced students who speak the beginners' native languages. Students in the groups should work together to ensure that all comprehend the meaning of the boxed words and the Key Concept. Ask each group questions to check comprehension. L1

Intermediate To help students comprehend the Key Concept, give them English words and phrases that mean the same as some of the more difficult words in the statement, for example, *selected/chose, organisms/living things, variations/differences.* L2

Answers to . . .

CHECKPOINT *Darwin received Wallace's essay.*

Figure 15–9 *Answers may include: differences in speed of the animal, physical strength, resistance to disease, vision, hearing, and so on.*

15–3 (continued)

Evolution by Natural Selection

Download a worksheet on natural selection for students to complete, and find additional teacher support from NSTA SciLinks.

Use Community Resources

Arrange for students to visit a local zoo, wildlife preserve, or museum of natural history. Challenge small groups of students to identify adaptive traits in 10 different animal species. Tell students to consider behavioral as well as biological traits. After the visit, urge groups to share their lists of adaptive traits. In the case of traits for which the adaptive significance is not obvious, ask: **Why do you think the trait is adaptive?** *(Answers will vary depending on the species and trait identified. For example, students might say that an orangutan's long arms are adaptive because they help the animal swing through trees in its arboreal habitat.)* L1 L2

Address Misconceptions

The phrase "struggle for existence" may lead to the misconception that the struggle is a physical contest in which bigger or stronger individuals always win. Challenge students to think of situations in which smaller, weaker individuals might be winners, for example, because small size helps them hide from predators, locate food, or find safe resting places. Stress that fitness involves passing inherited traits to the next generation.

For: Links on natural selection
Visit: www.SciLinks.org
Web Code: cbn-5153

ⓐ BI 7.d, BI 8.a

ⓑ 7 3.b, BI 7.d, BI 8.a, BI 8.b

ⓒ 7 3.a, BI 7.d, BI 8.a

Evolution by Natural Selection

CA ⓐ Darwin's next insight was to compare processes in nature to artificial selection. By doing so, he developed a scientific hypothesis to explain how evolution occurs. This is where Darwin made his greatest contribution—and his strongest break with the past.

The Struggle for Existence Darwin was convinced that a process like artificial selection worked in nature. But how? He recalled Malthus's work on population growth. Darwin realized that high birth rates and a shortage of life's basic needs would eventually force organisms into a competition for resources. CA ⓑ The **struggle for existence** means that members of each species compete regularly to obtain food, living space, and other necessities of life. In this struggle, the predators that are faster or have a particular way of ensnaring other organisms can catch more prey. Those prey that are faster, better camouflaged, or better protected, such as the porcupine shown in **Figure 15–11**, can avoid being caught. This struggle for existence was central to Darwin's theory of evolution.

Survival of the Fittest A key factor in the struggle for existence, Darwin observed, was how well suited an organism is to its environment. Darwin called the ability of an individual to survive and reproduce in its specific environment **fitness.** Darwin proposed that fitness is the result of adaptations. An **adaptation** is any inherited characteristic that increases an CA ⓒ organism's chance of survival. Successful adaptations, Darwin concluded, enable organisms to become better suited to their environment and thus better able to survive and reproduce. Adaptations can be anatomical, or structural, characteristics, such as a porcupine's sharp quills. Adaptations also include an organism's physiological processes, or functions, such as the way in which a plant performs photosynthesis. More complex features, such as behavior in which some animals live and hunt in groups, can also be adaptations.

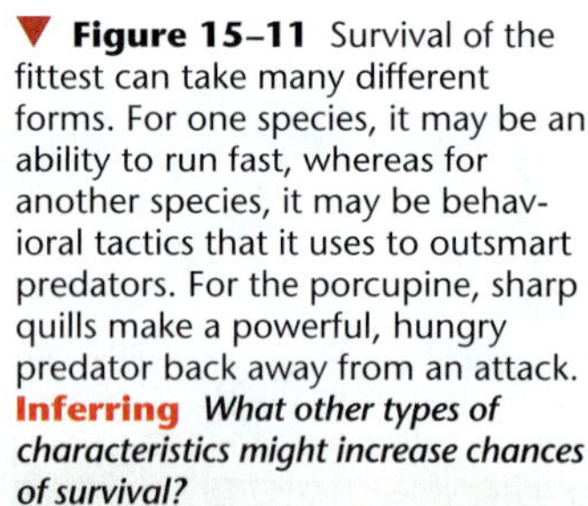

▼ **Figure 15–11** Survival of the fittest can take many different forms. For one species, it may be an ability to run fast, whereas for another species, it may be behavioral tactics that it uses to outsmart predators. For the porcupine, sharp quills make a powerful, hungry predator back away from an attack. **Inferring** *What other types of characteristics might increase chances of survival?*

TEACHER TO TEACHER

I like to take my class to the gym and play "survival of the fittest." Several exercises are set up to test for different abilities, such as jumping, crawling, hearing soft sounds, and seeing color distinctions. The "winners" are likely to have adaptations for their specialty areas. For example, students who excel in crawling through tight openings are likely to be smaller than average. This activity highlights individual uniqueness and is a great springboard for discussing adaptations that contribute to fitness.

—Dick Jordan
Biology Teacher
Timberline High School
Boise, ID

◀ **Figure 15–12** Each of these baby tanagers has its own set of inherited traits that affect its survival. A stronger bird may take food from a weaker sibling. A faster bird may escape predators more easily. Only those birds that survive and reproduce have the chance to pass their traits to the next generation. **Over time, natural selection results in changes in the inherited characteristics of a population.**

The concept of fitness, Darwin argued, was central to the process of evolution by natural selection. Generation after generation, individuals compete to survive and produce offspring. The baby birds in **Figure 15–12,** for example, compete for food and space while in the nest. Because each individual differs from other members of its species, each has unique advantages and disadvantages. Individuals with characteristics that are not well suited to their environment—that is, with low levels of fitness—either die or leave few offspring. Individuals that are better suited to their environment—that is, with adaptations that enable fitness—survive and reproduce most successfully. Darwin called this process **survival of the fittest.**

CA (a)

Because of its similarities to artificial selection, Darwin referred to the survival of the fittest as **natural selection.** In both artificial selection and natural selection, only certain individuals of a population produce new individuals. However, in natural selection, the traits being selected—and therefore increasing over time—contribute to an organism's fitness in its environment. Natural selection also takes place without human control or direction. **Over time, natural selection results in changes in the inherited characteristics of a population. These changes increase a species' fitness in its environment.** Natural selection cannot be seen directly; it can only be observed as changes in a population over many successive generations.

CA (b)

(a) 7 3.b, BI 7.d, BI 8.a

(b) BI 7.d, BI 8.a, BI 8.b

CHECKPOINT What did Darwin mean when he described certain organisms as "more fit" than others?

Descent With Modification Darwin proposed that over long periods, natural selection produces organisms that have different structures, establish different niches, or occupy different habitats. As a result, species today look different from their ancestors. Each living species has descended, with changes, from other species over time. He referred to this principle as **descent with modification.**

Build Science Skills

Applying Concepts Divide the class into small groups. Instruct each group to brainstorm ways Earth might change over the next 1000 years. Have each group select an organism living today and explain how populations descended from that organism might evolve to adapt to the changes. The groups should describe or sketch specific adaptations in their organism. Invite each group to share its ideas with the class. L2 L3

Address Misconceptions

Students may hold the misconception that if a trait is favored by natural selection, it must be adaptive in every respect. Provide an example to make the point that some adaptive traits have drawbacks as well as benefits. Show students a picture of (or have them imagine) a deer with large antlers. Tell students that the antlers help the deer to compete for a mate and, therefore, to reproduce. However, a deer uses energy to produce the antlers and they may get in the way when the deer tries to run through thick woods or feed in dense brush. The reproductive advantage of antlers outweighs these risks to survival. L1

TEACHER TO TEACHER

I like to use a make-believe scenario to illustrate natural selection. I have students pretend that a small group of humans is rocketed at "warp speed" to Planet X, without any books, weapons, or technology. Planet X has no ozone layer to protect its surface from cancer-causing ultraviolet radiation, but native plants and animals have evolved to live safely there. Below the surface, the planet has a network of underground tunnels, just a meter high, that are inhabited by carnivorous predators. I challenge students to describe how descendants of the group of humans would look and act after evolving for 100,000 years on Planet X.

—*Dennis Glasgow*
Biology Teacher
Little Rock School District
Little Rock, AR

Answers to . . .

CHECKPOINT He meant organisms that are better suited to survive in their environment and pass their traits on to the next generation.

Figure 15–11 *Possible answers include characteristics that help the organism evade predators, such as a chameleon's ability to change color, or help the organism obtain resources, such as a giraffe's long neck.*

15–3 (continued)

Build Science Skills

Applying Concepts Find a tree of life that includes major taxonomic categories, including the kingdoms, phyla, and classes. Explain that the classification is based on similarities in traits among living organisms. The classification also shows how different kinds of organisms are related to one another as shown by the "tree of life." Have students look closely at one of the lineages in the chart, such as the lineage that leads to the species *Homo sapiens*. Check their interpretation of the chart as a record of evolution by asking: **To which family do humans belong?** *(The hominid family)* **Which other families are most closely related to the hominids?** *(The pongids, or great apes, and the hylobatids, or lesser apes)* **What type of animal was the common ancestor of humans and apes?** *(A hominoid)* L2

Evidence of Evolution

Demonstration

Half fill some beakers with water. Place a small leaf, shell, or other object in the bottom of each beaker. As students observe, gradually add a couple of handfuls of a mixture of sand and soil to each beaker. Do not stir or shake the beakers. Have students observe the beakers again at the end of class and once a day for the next two days. Then, ask: **What happened to the leaves, shells, and other objects?** *(They became covered with deposits of sediment.)* Point out that this is also what happens to organisms when they die and fall into ponds or lakes. Explain how the pressure of water and additional deposits eventually turns the sediments into rock. Ask: **What might eventually happen to organic remains that are covered over with sediments?** *(They turn into fossils.)* L1

Descent with modification also implies that all living organisms are related to one another. Look back in time, and you will find common ancestors shared by tigers, panthers, and cheetahs. Look farther back, and you will find ancestors that these felines share with horses, dogs, and bats. Farther back still are the common ancestors of mammals, birds, alligators, and fishes. If we look far enough back, the logic concludes, we could find the common ancestors of all living things. This is the principle known as **common descent.** According to this principle, all species—living and extinct—were derived from common ancestors. Therefore, a single "tree of life" links all living things.

Evidence of Evolution

With this unified, dynamic theory of life, Darwin could finally explain many of the observations he had made during his travels aboard the *Beagle.* **Darwin argued that living things have been evolving on Earth for millions of years. Evidence for this process could be found in the fossil record, the geographical distribution of living species, homologous structures of living organisms, and similarities in early development, or embryology.**

CA a

The Fossil Record By Darwin's time, scientists knew that fossils were the remains of ancient life and that different layers of rock had been formed at different times during Earth's history. Darwin saw fossils as a record of the history of life on Earth. Darwin, like Lyell, proposed that Earth was many millions—rather than thousands—of years old. During this long time, Darwin proposed, countless species had come into being, lived for a time, and then vanished. By comparing fossils from older rock layers with fossils from younger layers, scientists could document the fact that life on Earth has changed over time as shown in **Figure 15–13.**

▼ **Figure 15–13 Darwin argued that the fossil record provided evidence that living things have been evolving for millions of years.** Often, the fossil record includes a variety of different extinct organisms that are related to one another and to living species. The four fossil organisms shown here are cephalopods, a group that includes squid, octopi, and the chambered nautilus. The fossil record contains more than 7500 species of cephalopods, which vary, as these fossils show, from species with short, straight shells, to species with longer, coiled shells. Darwin and his colleagues noticed that the sizes, shapes, and varieties of related organisms preserved in the fossil record changed over time.

HISTORY OF SCIENCE

Monkeys old and new

Until a few decades ago, scientists had long believed that Old and New World monkeys diverged from a common prosimian ancestor at least 50 million years ago. According to this view, the two primate groups became separated as Africa and South America drifted apart, but they evolved many of the same traits because of their similar tropical arboreal habitats. This interpretation was challenged in the 1970s by Richard Hoffstetter, an anthropologist, who hypothesized that Old and New World monkeys evolved from a common monkey ancestor much more recently. According to Hoffstetter, small numbers of monkeys accidentally rafted on fallen trees across the Atlantic Ocean from Africa to South America, after the two continents had already drifted apart. Later, genetic evidence was found to support Hoffstetter's hypothesis, which is accepted by most experts today.

Since Darwin's time, the number of known fossil forms has grown enormously. Researchers have discovered many hundreds of transitional fossils that document various intermediate stages in the evolution of modern species from organisms that are now extinct. Gaps remain, of course, in the fossil records of many species, although a lot of them shrink each year as new fossils are discovered. These gaps do not indicate weakness in the theory of evolution itself. Rather, they point out uncertainties in our understanding of exactly how some species evolved.

CA a

Geographic Distribution of Living Species

a 7 3.c

Geographic Distribution of Living Species Remember that many parts of the biological puzzle that Darwin saw on his *Beagle* voyage involved living organisms. After Darwin discovered that those little brown birds he collected in the Galápagos were all finches, he began to wonder how they came to be similar, yet distinctly different from one another. Each species was slightly different from every other species. They were also slightly different from the most similar species on the mainland of South America. Could the island birds have changed over time, as populations in different places adapted to different local environments? Darwin struggled with this question for a long time. He finally decided that all these birds could have descended with modification from a common mainland ancestor.

There were other parts to the living puzzle as well. Recall that Darwin found entirely different species of animals on the continents of South America and Australia. Yet, when he looked at similar environments on those continents, he sometimes saw different animals that had similar anatomies and behaviors. Darwin's theory of descent with modification made scientific sense of this part of the puzzle as well. Species now living on different continents, as shown in **Figure 15–14,** had each descended from different ancestors. However, because some animals on each continent were living under similar ecological conditions, they were exposed to similar pressures of natural selection. Because of these similar selection pressures, different animals ended up evolving certain striking features in common.

CHECKPOINT *How can two species that look very different from each other be more closely related than two other species that look similar to each other?*

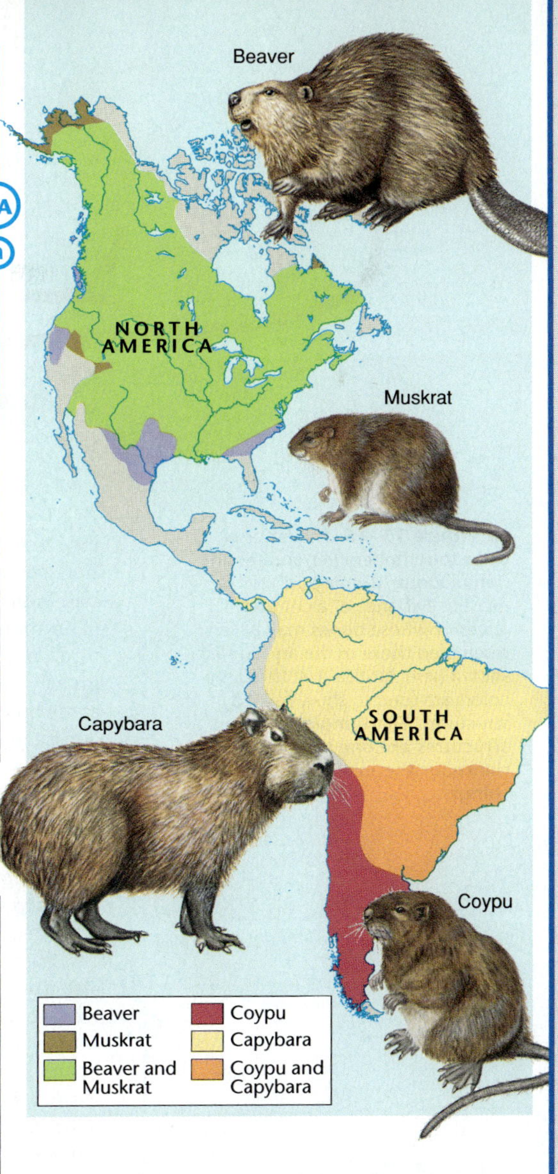

▲ **Figure 15–14** The existence of similar but unrelated species was a puzzle to Darwin. Later, he realized that similar animals in different locations were the product of different lines of evolutionary descent. Here, the beaver and the capybara are similar species that inhabit similar environments of North America and South America. The South American coypu also shares many characteristics with the North American muskrat. **Interpreting Graphics** *Which animal has a larger geographical range, the coypu or the muskrat?*

Build Science Skills

Using Analogies Explain to students that the evolution of shared traits in unrelated species because of similar environments is called convergent evolution. Give students a chance to see how convergent evolution works by using an analogy similar to one that Darwin himself suggested. Have small groups of students brainstorm several ways to solve the same problem, such as improving traffic flow in the school or decreasing crowding in the classrooms. Tell students to be creative as they brainstorm ideas. After several minutes, have the groups share their ideas and identify those that are similar. Ask: **What do the different groups represent in terms of convergent evolution?** *(Unrelated species)* **What do the similar ideas represent?** *(Similar adaptations)* **What does the common problem that the groups worked on represent?** *(Similarities in the environments of the unrelated species)* L2

BIO INSIGHTS

FACTS AND FIGURES

Comparing DNA
Instead of comparing homologous structures or embryos, a more direct way of determining evolutionary relationships among species is to compare the sequence of the four nitrogenous bases—adenine, guanine, cytosine, and thymine—in the DNA of all living things on Earth. The exact sequence of nitrogenous bases is unique to each species, but it is more similar in closely related species than in species that are not as closely related. Scientists can use this information, along with knowledge of mutation rates, to estimate how long it has been since two species shared a common ancestor. Since the 1990s, scientists have also been able to sequence the DNA of fossils to determine how extinct organisms were related to one another and to their living descendants.

Answers to . . .

CHECKPOINT *Regardless of their appearance, two species are closely related when they share a common ancestry. If one of those species experienced natural selection in a particular kind of environment, such as a desert, it may look similar to some unrelated desert species from a different location.*

Figure 15–14 *Muskrat*

15–3 (continued)

Build Science Skills

Applying Concepts Help students understand homologous structures by contrasting them with analogous structures. Tell students that homologous structures are similar because they were inherited from a common ancestor, whereas analogous structures are similar because they evolved to fulfill the same function in unrelated species. Challenge students to apply the concepts by asking: **Are bat wings and butterfly wings homologous or analogous structures?** *(Analogous)* L1 L2

Use Visuals

Figure 15–15 Call students' attention to the figure. Ask: **What similarities in the limbs suggest that they developed from the same basic structure?** *(The number and placement of the bones)* **How is the form of each limb adapted for a specific type of movement?** *(Students might say, for example, that the thin, light bones of a bird's wing help it to fly and the thick, strong bones of an alligator's leg help it maneuver in the water.)* L1 L2

Build Science Skills

Classifying Challenge students to use the information in the text to create a graphic organizer to classify the following animals according to their similarities and differences: snakes, lizards, robins, hawks, bats, and whales. *(Students' graphics should show that snakes are most closely related to lizards, robins to hawks, and bats to whales. Graphic organizers also should show that robins and hawks are more closely related to snakes and lizards than they are to bats and whales.)* Urge students to share their work with the class. Then, ask: **Would you expect the vestigial limb bones of a snake to be more like the bones of a bird's wing or a rabbit's leg?** *(A bird's wing)* L2

Word Origins

Homomorphic structures are different structures that have the same, or similar, shapes. L2

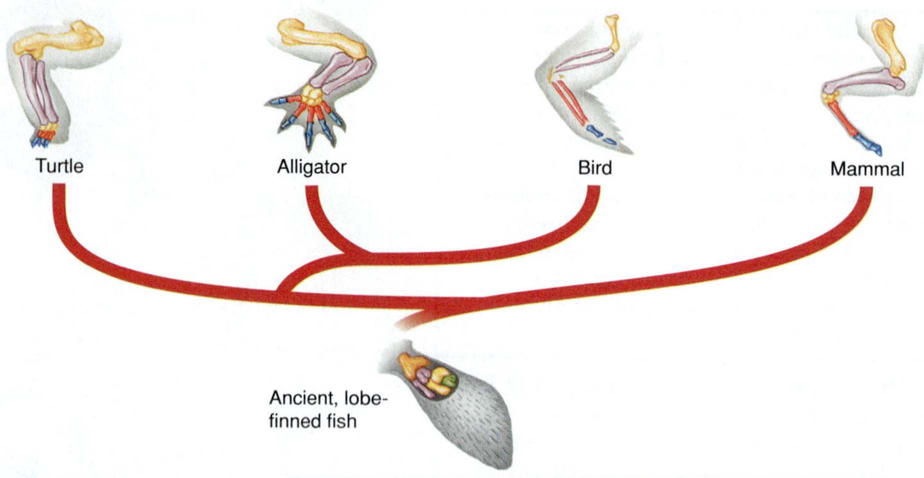

▲ **Figure 15–15** The limbs of these four modern vertebrates are homologous structures. They provide evidence of a common ancestor whose bones may have resembled those of the ancient fish shown here. Notice that the same colors are used to show related structures. **Homologous structures are one type of evidence for the evolution of living things.**

CA a

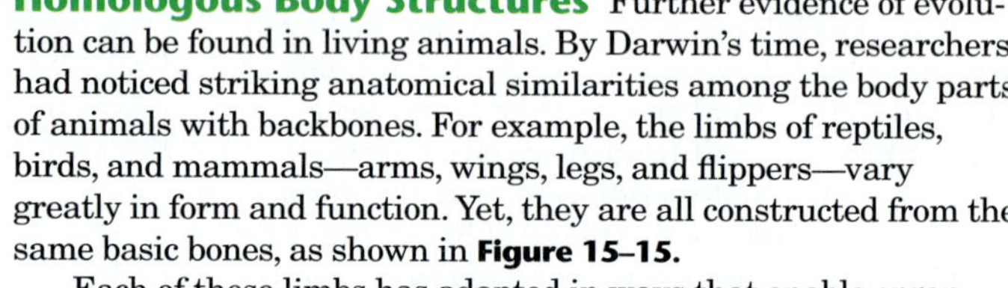

Homologous Body Structures Further evidence of evolution can be found in living animals. By Darwin's time, researchers had noticed striking anatomical similarities among the body parts of animals with backbones. For example, the limbs of reptiles, birds, and mammals—arms, wings, legs, and flippers—vary greatly in form and function. Yet, they are all constructed from the same basic bones, as shown in **Figure 15–15.**

Each of these limbs has adapted in ways that enable organisms to survive in different environments. Despite these different functions, however, these limb bones all develop from the same clumps of cells in embryos. Structures that have different mature forms but develop from the same embryonic tissues are called **homologous** (hoh-MAHL-uh-guhs) **structures.** Homologous structures provide strong evidence that all four-limbed vertebrates have descended, with modifications, from common ancestors.

There is still more information to be gathered from homologous structures. If we compare the front limbs, we can see that all bird wings are more similar to one another than any of them are to bat wings. Other bones in bird skeletons most closely resemble the homologous bones of certain reptiles—including crocodiles and extinct reptiles such as dinosaurs. The bones that support the wings of bats, by contrast, are more similar to the front limbs of humans, whales, and other mammals than they are to those of birds. These similarities and differences help biologists group animals according to how recently they last shared a common ancestor.

Not all homologous structures serve important functions. The organs of many animals are so reduced in size that they are just vestiges, or traces, of homologous organs in other species. These **vestigial organs** may resemble miniature legs, tails, or other structures. The legs of the skinks shown in **Figure 15–16** are an example of vestigial organs. Why would an organism possess organs with little or no function? One possibility is that the presence of a vestigial organ may not affect an organism's ability to survive and reproduce. In that case, natural selection would not cause the elimination of that organ.

Word Origins

Homologous, from the Greek words *homos,* meaning "same," and *legein,* meaning "say," describes similar body structures that come from a common ancestor. **If the word *morphe* means "shape," what are homomorphic structures?**

FACTS AND FIGURES

Clues to evolution

Many species of animals have vestigial organs. An example is the human appendix, an extension of the cecum at the beginning of the large intestine. Some plant-eating mammals such as koalas also have cecal extensions, which they require for digestion. Humans also have a set of miniature tailbones at the base of the spine, even though humans do not have tails. In addition, in humans the muscles that move the ears are vestigial. Vestigial organs often persist in a species indefinitely because they are unaffected by natural selection. Natural selection increases the frequency of useful traits and decreases the frequency of harmful traits, but it does not change the frequency of traits that have little or no effect on an organism's ability to survive and reproduce.

Homologies also appear in other aspects of plant and animal anatomy and physiology. Certain groups of plants and algae, for example, share homologous variations in stem, leaf, root, and flower structures, and in the way they carry out photosynthesis. Mammals share many homologies that distinguish them from other vertebrates. Dolphins may look something like fishes, but homologies show that they are mammals. For example, like other mammals, they have lungs rather than gills and obtain oxygen from air rather than water.

Similarities in Embryology The early stages, or embryos, of many animals with backbones are very similar. This does not mean that a human embryo is ever identical to a fish or a bird embryo. However, as you can see in **Figure 15–17,** many embryos look especially similar during early stages of development. What do these similarities mean?

There have, in the past, been incorrect explanations for these similarities. Also, the biologist Ernst Haeckel fudged some of his drawings to make the earliest stages of some embryos seem more similar than they actually are! Errors aside, however, it is clear that the same groups of embryonic cells develop in the same order and in similar patterns to produce the tissues and organs of all vertebrates. These common cells and tissues, growing in similar ways, produce the homologous structures discussed earlier.

ⓐ 7 3.c

Figure 15–16 These three animals are skinks, a type of lizard. In some species of skinks, legs have become vestigial. They are so reduced that they no longer function in walking. In humans, the appendix is an example of a vestigial organ because it carries out no function in digestion. **Inferring** ***How might vestigial organs provide clues to an animal's evolutionary history?***

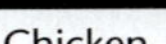

CHECKPOINT *What are homologous structures?*

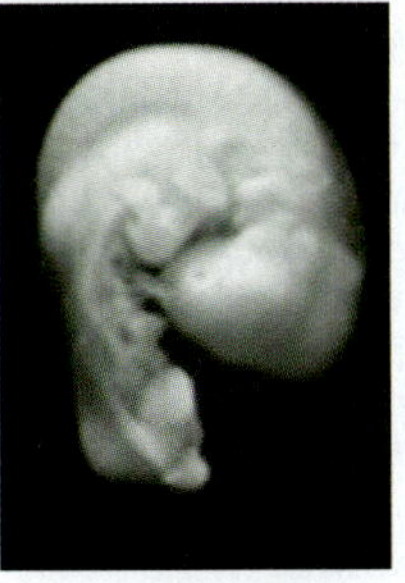

Chicken

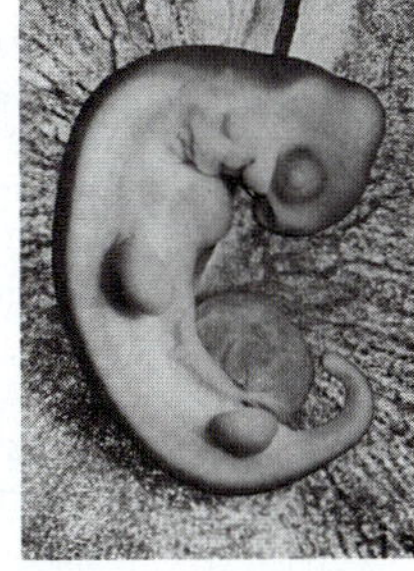

Turtle

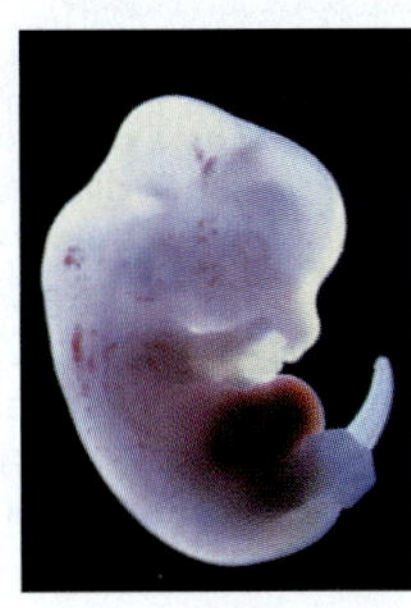

Rat

Figure 15–17 In their early stages of development, chickens, turtles, and rats look similar, providing evidence that they shared a common ancestry. **Inferring** ***How could a study of these embryos help show the relationships among animals with backbones?***

Build Science Skills

Inferring Tell students that similarities and differences in the DNA of different species are used to reconstruct evolutionary relationships. Ask: **Why do DNA comparisons provide the most direct evidence of evolutionary relationships?** *(Because DNA is passed directly from common ancestors to their descendants and controls the development of other traits)* L2

Use Visuals

Figure 15–17 Find a picture of a human embryo, and show it to students. Call their attention to the embryos in the figure. Ask: **In what ways is the human embryo similar and in what ways is it different?** *(There will be slight differences, but overall the human embryo should be very similar to the embryos in the figure.)* **What do the similarities suggest?** *(That humans are related to these other animals with backbones)*

If your class subscribes to the iText, use it to review the Key Concepts in Section 15–3.

BIO INSIGHTS — FACTS AND FIGURES

Comparative embryology explained

The explanation for embryonic similarities in organisms that are very different as adults lies with the timing of gene action. All of an organism's genes are not active at the same time. In addition, those that are active during early development are less subject to change than those that are active later. This is because mutations occurring early in development have such far-reaching effects that they tend to be lethal. Therefore, they are not passed on to successive generations. Mutations occurring later in development, on the other hand, tend to have more limited effects, so they are less likely to be lethal and more likely to be passed on. Thus, genes controlling later development are more subject to evolutionary change, explaining why humans and chickens are so different at later stages despite their similarity as embryos.

Answers to . . .

CHECKPOINT *Homologous structures are structures that have different mature forms but develop from the same embryonic tissue.*

Figure 15–16 *A specific vestigial organ suggests that an organism's ancestor once used that organ.*

Figure 15–17 *Embryos of less closely related species would likely look different earlier in their development, while embryos of more closely related species probably look similar for longer periods.*

15–3 (continued)

Summary of Darwin's Theory

Build Science Skills

Applying Concepts Darwin's "struggle for existence" refers to competition but may be confused with predation. Explain the difference between the two. Describe several cases of each, and have students identify which are examples of Darwin's concept. L1 L2

Strengths and Weaknesses of Evolutionary Theory

Make Connections

Health Science Describe antibiotic resistance in bacteria. Ask students to use Darwin's theory of natural selection to explain how it comes about. L2

3 ASSESS

Evaluate Understanding

Ask students to make a table listing similarities and differences between artificial and natural selection and to give examples of each.

Reteach

Write the following concepts on the board, and review their meaning: *fitness, adaptation, natural selection, struggle for existence, survival of the fittest,* and *descent with modification.* Then, have students write a paragraph in which they correctly use each concept.

Writing in Science

Students' newspaper articles should explain how heritable traits that help organisms survive and reproduce tend to be passed on to successive generations and increase in frequency in populations.

Answer to . . .

Figure 15–18 *Based on Darwin's theory, you could observe how these species are adapted to survive and reproduce in their environments.*

▲ **Figure 15–18** Darwin's *On the Origin of Species* presented a revolutionary view of the living world. Many scientists agree with Darwin's statement that "There is a grandeur in this view of life, . . . that . . . from so simple a beginning, endless forms so beautiful and wonderful have been and are being evolved." **Applying Concepts** ***New species are continually being discovered. How could you use Darwin's theory to learn more about these new species?***

Summary of Darwin's Theory

CA a

Darwin's theory of evolution can be summarized as follows:

- Individual organisms differ, and some of this variation is heritable.
- Organisms produce more offspring than can survive, and many that do survive do not reproduce.
- Because more organisms are produced than can survive, they compete for limited resources.
- Each unique organism has different advantages and disadvantages in the struggle for existence. Individuals best suited to their environment survive and reproduce most successfully. These organisms pass their heritable traits to their offspring. Other individuals die or leave fewer offspring. This process of natural selection causes species to change over time.
- Species alive today are descended with modification from ancestral species that lived in the distant past. This process, by which diverse species evolved from common ancestors, unites all organisms on Earth into a single tree of life.

Strengths and Weaknesses of Evolutionary Theory

Scientific advances in many fields of biology, along with geology and physics, have confirmed and expanded most of Darwin's hypotheses. Today, evolutionary theory offers vital insights to all biological and biomedical sciences—from infectious-disease research to ecology. In fact, evolution is often called the "grand unifying theory of the life sciences."

Like any scientific theory, evolutionary theory continues to change as new data are gathered and new ways of thinking arise. As you will see shortly, researchers still debate such important questions as precisely how new species arise and why species become extinct. There is also uncertainty about how life began.

15–3 Section Assessment

1. **Key Concept** How is artificial selection dependent on variation in nature?
2. **Key Concept** The theory of evolution by natural selection explains, in scientific terms, how living things evolve over time. What is being selected in this process?
3. **Key Concept** What types of evidence did Darwin use to support his theory of change over time?
4. **Critical Thinking Evaluating** Use scientific evidence to evaluate Darwin's theory of evolution by natural selection.

Writing in Science

Newspaper Article

Write a newspaper article about the meeting in which Darwin's and Wallace's hypotheses of evolution were first presented. Explain the theory of evolution by natural selection for an audience who knows nothing about the subject.

15–3 Section Assessment

1. Nature provides the variation, and humans select the variations that are useful.
2. The traits that help an organism survive in a particular environment
3. The fossil record, geographic distribution of species, homologous structures, and similarities in embryology
4. Scientific advances in many fields of biology, along with geology and physics, have confirmed most of Darwin's hypotheses. Specific examples of evidence supporting Darwin's theory include similarities in embryology and homologous structures.

Exploration

BIIE 1.d, BIIE 1.e, BIIE 1.g

Modeling Adaptation

In this game, three families land on an alien planet. At home, the Hunter family survived by hunting in the cold north. The Seeder family farmed the temperate zone. The Fisher family lived on a tropical island. In this investigation, you will model how well each family survives in a new environment.

Problem How do organisms survive in new habitats?

Material

- coin

Skills Using Models, Using Tables and Graphs, Calculating

Procedure

1. Work in groups of three, with each member playing a Hunter, Seeder, or Fisher.
2. Flip a coin. Record the result as 1 for heads, 0 for tails. Toss the coin three more times to produce a series of four 1s and 0s. This 4-digit number is the code for your new habitat.
3. If the first digit in your code is 1, you live in a hot area. If it is 0, the climate is cold. If the second digit is 1, the climate is wet. If it is 0, it's dry. If the third digit is 1, you have a dry cave to live in. If it is 0, you sleep under the stars. If the last digit is 1, there is enough food. If it is 0, food is scarce. Record a description of your habitat.
4. Find your family in the table below. Then, record each number in your row that falls under a heading that describes your habitat (hot or cold and so forth). Record the total of these 4 numbers. This total represents the energy you have accumulated from your food.
5. Subtract 8 from your total to model the energy you must use to survive. If you don't have enough energy to do this, you're out of the game. The player with the most energy wins. Record the score and habitat of each family.
6. **Predicting** Record a prediction of what would happen if you reversed each player's habitat code by changing all the 1s to 0s and the 0s to 1s.
7. Reverse your habitat code as described in step 6. Play a second round with these conditions.

Analyze and Conclude

1. **Comparing and Contrasting** In which habitat were you most successful? Was it similar to your home environment?
2. **Using Models** The numbers in the table are different for each family. How did this fact help you model the survival of different organisms?
3. **Drawing Conclusions** Is one habitat best for all players? Explain in terms of adaptation.

Go Further

Applying Concepts Revise the game to reflect the different conditions of summer and winter. Then, demonstrate your game to the class.

Energy Points for Survival

	Temperature		Water		Shelter		Food	
	Cold	Hot	Dry	Wet	None	Cave	Scarce	Plenty
Hunter	8	-2	0	4	-6	7	-5	8
Seeder	0	3	2	2	-1	2	-2	6
Fisher	-5	8	-2	5	0	1	-1	4

Exploration

BIIE 1.d, BIIE 1.e, BIIE 1.g

Objective Students will be able to use a model to determine how adaptations affect survival of organisms in new habitats. L2

Skills Focus Using Models, Using Tables and Graphs, Calculating

Time 45 minutes

Advance Prep Before assigning the lab, you may want to play a round of the game by yourself to get a feel for how it works.

Teaching Tips
Have students read the entire procedure. Then, ask:
- **Why do the Hunters score the most points in a cold habitat?** *(Because they are adapted to a cold environment)*
- **Why do the Fishers score the least points in a cold habitat?** *(Because they are adapted to a hot habitat)*

Procedure
6. Have groups share their results by recording their scores and habitats on the board or a transparency.

Analyze and Conclude

1. Answers will vary by family. Each family will be most successful in a habitat that is similar to its home environment.
2. The different numbers in the table for each family reflect differences in their adaptations. In nature, different organisms have different adaptations that help them to survive in their environments.
3. No, because the players have different adaptations that are suited for some environments but not others.

Go Further

For summer, students might give the Fisher family more energy points, because they have adaptations for heat. For winter, students might give the Hunter family more energy points, because they have adaptations for cold. For both seasons, students might give the Seeder family fewer energy points, because they lack adaptations for heat or cold.

Chapter 15 Study Guide

Study Tip

Suggest that students review their answers to the Key Concept questions in the section assessments. Divide the class into pairs and have students quiz each other on definitions of the Vocabulary words.

Thinking Visually

Check students' tables. See pages 382–385.

Chapter 15 Assessment

Reviewing Content

1. c 2. a 3. a 4. a 5. d 6. b 7. a 8. a 9. c 10. b

Understanding Concepts

11. Evolution, or change over time, is the process by which modern organisms have descended from ancient organisms. An example is a population of predators in which the fastest animals passed on their traits to new generations.

12. Darwin observed fossils, some of which resembled living organisms and others that were unlike any organisms he knew; that organisms everywhere seemed remarkably well suited to their environments; and that similar organisms, such as tortoises, were different on each island.

13. Darwin's visit to the Galápagos Islands convinced him that new species might arise from existing species over time.

14. Hutton proposed that Earth had to be millions—not thousands—of years old. Lyell argued that the same forces change Earth in the present as in the past, so scientists should explain Earth's history in terms of processes that are observable in the present.

15. Lamarck said that structures that are used develop and are passed on to offspring, whereas structures that are not used are not passed on.

16. Natural variation provides the raw material for natural selection, which, in turn, leads to evolution.

17. Artificial selection is the process by which humans select certain naturally occurring variations to use in breeding new plants and animals.

(continued)

Chapter 15 Study Guide

15–1 The Puzzle of Life's Diversity

Key Concepts 7 3.b

- During his travels, Charles Darwin made numerous observations and collected evidence that led him to propose a revolutionary hypothesis about the way life changes over time.
- Darwin observed that the characteristics of many animals and plants varied noticeably among the different islands of the Galápagos.

Vocabulary
evolution, p. 369
theory, p. 369
fossil, p. 371

15–2 Ideas That Shaped Darwin's Thinking

Key Concepts  7 3.b, BIIE 1.n

- Hutton and Lyell helped scientists realize that Earth is many millions of years old, and the processes that changed Earth in the past are the same processes that operate in the present.
- Lamarck proposed that by selective use or disuse of organs, organisms acquired or lost certain traits during their lifetime. These traits could then be passed on to their offspring. Over time, this process led to change in a species.
- Malthus reasoned that if the human population continued to grow unchecked, sooner or later there would be insufficient living space and food for everyone.

15–3 Darwin Presents His Case

Key Concepts 7 3.a, BI 7.a, BI 7.d, BI 8.a, BI 8.b

- In artificial selection, nature provides the variation among different organisms, and humans select those variations that they find useful.
- Over time, natural selection results in changes in the inherited characteristics of a population. These changes increase a species' fitness in its environment.
- Darwin argued that living things have been evolving on Earth for millions of years. Evidence for this process could be found in the fossil record, the geographical distribution of living species, homologous structures of living organisms, and similarities in early development, or embryology.

Vocabulary
artificial selection, p. 379
struggle for existence, p. 380
fitness, p. 380
adaptation, p. 380
survival of the fittest, p. 381
natural selection, p. 381
descent with modification, p. 381
common descent, p. 382
homologous structure, p. 384
vestigial organ, p. 384

Thinking Visually

Use the information in this chapter to complete the table below.

Evidence of Evolution

Type of Evidence	Example	What Evidence Reveals
The fossil record	1	2
Geographic distribution of living species	3	4
Homologous body structures	5	6
Similarities in embryological development	7	8

CHAPTER RESOURCES

TIME SAVER

Print:
- ***Teaching Resources,*** Chapter Vocabulary Review, Graphic Organizer, Chapter 15 Tests: Levels A and B

Technology:
- ***Computer Test Bank,*** Chapter 15 Test
- ***iText,*** Chapter 15 Assessment

Chapter 15 Assessment

Reviewing Content

Choose the letter that best answers the question or completes the statement.

1. Who observed variations in the characteristics of animals and plants on the different islands of the Galápagos?
   a. James Hutton
   b. Charles Lyell
   c. Charles Darwin
   d. Thomas Malthus
2. In addition to observing living organisms, Darwin studied the preserved remains of ancient organisms, called
   a. fossils.
   b. adaptations.
   c. homologous structures.
   d. vestigial organs.
3. Which of the following ideas proposed by Lamarck was later found to be incorrect?
   a. Acquired characteristics can be inherited.
   b. All species were descended from other species.
   c. Living things change over time.
   d. Organisms are adapted to their environments.
4. Differences among individuals of a species are referred to as
   a. natural variation.
   b. fitness.
   c. natural selection.
   d. adaptation.
5. Which would an animal breeder use to produce cows that give more milk?
   a. overproduction
   b. genetic isolation
   c. acquired characteristics
   d. artificial selection
6. An inherited characteristic that increases an organism's ability to survive and reproduce in its specific environment is called a(an)
   a. vestigial organ.
   b. adaptation.
   c. speciation.
   d. radiation.
7. The concept that each living species has descended, with changes, from other species over time is referred to as
   a. descent with modification.
   b. artificial selection.
   c. theory of acquired characteristics.
   d. natural selection.
8. Fitness is a result of
   a. adaptations.
   b. homologies.
   c. common descent.
   d. variation.
9. Structures that have different mature forms but develop from the same embryonic tissue are
   a. vestigial organs.
   b. adaptations.
   c. homologous structures.
   d. fossils.

Interactive textbook with assessment at PHSchool.com 

10. The economist who reasoned that if the human population continued to grow unchecked, eventually there would not be enough resources was
    a. Lamarck.
    b. Darwin.
    c. Malthus.
    d. Lyell.

Understanding Concepts

11. Explain what is meant by the term *evolution*, and give an example.
12. Describe three of Darwin's observations about animals in South America and on the Galápagos Islands.
13. How did the visit to the Galápagos Islands affect Darwin's thoughts on evolution?
14. How did Hutton's and Lyell's views of Earth differ from that of most people of their time?
15. Explain Lamarck's principle of use and disuse.
16. How does natural variation affect evolution?
17. What is artifical selection? How did this concept influence Darwin's thinking?
18. Distinguish between fitness and adaptation. Give an example of each.
19. How is the process of survival of the fittest related to a population's environment?
20. How does Darwin's principle of descent with modification explain the characterisitics of today's species?
21. What does fossil evidence show about evolution?
22. What evidence of evolution can be found in the geographic distribution of living animals? Give an example.
23. What is a vestigial organ? Give an example.
24. How do scientists use similarities in embryology as evidence for evolution?
25. Summarize the main ideas in Darwin's theory.

TIME SAVER — HOMEWORK GUIDE

Section:	Questions:
Section 15–1	1, 2, 11–13
Section 15–2	3, 14, 15
Section 15–3	4–10, 16–25, 26–34

Interactive Textbook

If your class subscribes to the iText, your students can go online to access an interactive version of the Student Edition and a self-test.

(Continued from page 388)

Darwin thought that a similar process in nature could explain how organisms change over time.

18. Fitness, the ability of an individual to survive and reproduce in its specific environment, occurs through ongoing adaptation. An example is an animal that survives through camouflage. An adaptation is any inherited characteristic that increases an organism's chance of survival. Examples include a porcupine's quills and a lion's teeth and claws.

19. In the survival of the fittest, individuals that are best suited to their environment survive and reproduce most successfully.

20. Descent with modification explains why organisms living today may be different from their ancestors, for example, by having different structures.

21. Fossils that formed in different layers of rock provide evidence of the way species changed over time.

22. Evidence of evolution in living animals includes the existence of unrelated organisms from different locations that share traits because they evolved from similar environments. An example is the beaver in North America and the capybara in South America.

23. A vestigial organ is an organ, such as the human appendix, that is reduced in size and no longer has a function.

24. Similarities in embryology of different species have been used as evidence that the species evolved from a common ancestor.

25. Variations occur within populations, and some of the variations are favorable. More offspring are produced than can survive, and individuals with favorable variations are more likely to survive. Because of this, changes accumulate in populations over long periods of time.

Chapter 15 Assessment

Critical Thinking

26. Natural selection leads to organisms being better adapted to their environments and explains the diversity of organisms Darwin observed on the Galápagos Islands, which have varied environments.

27. Giraffes with slightly longer necks could reach plant materials that those with shorter necks could not reach and, therefore, would have a better chance of surviving and passing on their genes. Over many generations of natural selection, the long necks of modern giraffes evolved.

28. The few mosquitoes that were resistant to DDT survived and reproduced, whereas those that were not resistant were killed by the insecticide. The succeeding populations of mosquitoes were more resistant to DDT.

29. Their survival might depend on how well the turkey could avoid predators and whether there was an adequate food supply.

30. Most endangered species are endangered because human actions have changed or destroyed their habitats. Protecting endangered species—for example, by preserving their habitats or providing them with nesting sites—may restore the natural conditions.

31. On Hood Island where vegetation is sparse, tortoises with a shell that is curved and open around the neck and legs could use their legs and long neck to obtain food more easily; thus they had a better chance to survive and pass their genes to the next generation. Vegetation on Isabela Island is abundant and close to the ground, so tortoises with domed shells and short necks were able to find food, survive, and reproduce.

32. It might protect the eggs and young birds from predators and accidents, helping to ensure that they survive to adulthood and reproduce.

33. A whale could have vestigial hip and leg bones, because the ancestral vertebrate had hips and legs.

34. It indicates that animals with backbones share a common ancestor.

Chapter 15 Assessment

Critical Thinking

26. Inferring How does the process of natural selection account for the diversity of organisms that Darwin observed on the Galápagos Islands?

27. Applying Concepts Explain how natural selection might have produced the modern giraffe from short-necked ancestors.

28. Formulating Hypotheses DDT is an insecticide that was first used in the 1940s to kill mosquitoes and stop the spread of malaria. At first, it was very effective. However, over a period of years, people began to notice that it was becoming less and less effective. A possible explanation for this was that the insects were becoming resistant to the DDT. Explain how the resistance may have evolved.

29. Predicting Although wild turkeys can fly, domesticated turkeys cannot. Suppose that a population of domesticated turkeys escaped from a farm into a new environment. Give examples of environmental conditions that might determine whether that population would survive over time.

30. Making Judgments Is protecting an endangered species upsetting the process of natural selection? Explain your answer.

31. Applying Concepts Charles Darwin discovered that different types of tortoises lived on the different Galápagos Islands. Two of those types are shown below. Darwin learned that each type of tortoise had adaptations that enabled it to feed on the vegetation that was characteristic of its particular island. Use **Figure 15–3** and what you learned about Darwin's theory to explain how the different types of tortoises may have evolved.

Hood Island Tortoise

Isabela Island Tortoise

32. Inferring Many species of birds build nests in which they lay eggs and raise the newly hatched birds. How might nest-building behavior be an adaptation that helps ensure reproductive fitness?

33. Applying Concepts A whale flipper and a human arm are considered homologous. Do you think a whale might have vestigial hip and leg bones? Explain.

34. Inferring In all animals with backbones, oxygen is carried in blood by a molecule called hemoglobin. What might this physiological similarity indicate about the evolutionary history of animals with backbones?

Information and Heredity Refer back to Chapter 11 to refresh what you learned about Mendel. If Mendel and Darwin had met, how might Mendel have helped Darwin develop his theory? Include parts of Mendel's theory in your answer.

Writing in Science

Write a paragraph in which you explain Darwin's concept of the struggle for existence. The paragraph should include specific examples to clarify the meaning of the concept. (*Hints:* Think of a few examples that illustrate the concept, and then choose the best two to write about. When you write your paragraph, begin it with a sentence that expresses the main idea.)

Performance-Based Assessment

Alternative Scenarios Select an adaptation of a plant or an animal. Write a scenario explaining how the trait might have evolved according to Lamarck, and then write a second scenario using Darwin's ideas. Present your essay, and challenge classmates to identify the theory on which each scenario is based.

For: An interactive self-test
Visit: PHSchool.com
Web Code: cba-5150

Focus on the BIG Idea

Darwin did not understand how traits were passed from parents to offspring. Mendel explained that traits were determined by "factors" that were inherited from the parents.

Writing in Science

Make sure students use examples of intraspecific, and not interspecific, struggles. Examples might include the overpopulation of deer in an eastern woodland, leading to starvation for many of the animals.

Standards Practice

Success Tracker™
Online at PHSchool.com

Test-Taking Tip If you have trouble answering a question, make a mark beside it and go on. (Do not write in this book.) You may find information in later questions that will allow you to eliminate some answer choices in your unanswered question.

Directions: Choose the letter that best answers the question or completes the statement.

1. Which scientist formulated the theory of evolution through natural selection?
A Charles Darwin
B James Hutton
C Charles Lyell
D Gregor Mendel

2. The ability of an individual organism to survive and reproduce in its natural environment is called
A natural selection.
B evolution.
C adaptation.
D fitness.

3. The French scientist Jean-Baptiste Lamarck proposed which of the following theories?
I. All organisms have a common ancestor.
II. Species change over time.
III. A single organism can acquire traits over its lifetime that are then passed to its offspring.
A I only
B II only
C I and II only
D II and III only

4. Which of the following is an important concept in Darwin's theory of evolution by natural selection?
A struggle for existence
B survival of the fittest
C descent with modification
D all of the above

5. Which of the following does NOT provide sufficient evidence that living things have been evolving for millions of years?
A fossil record
B natural variation within a species
C geographical distribution of living things
D homologous structures of living organisms

6. A farmer's use of the best livestock for breeding is an example of
A natural selection.
B artificial selection.
C fitness.
D common descent.

7. Lyell's *Principles of Geology* influenced Darwin because it explained how **7 3.c**
A organisms change over time.
B adaptations occur.
C the surface of the Earth changes over time.
D the Galápagos Islands were formed.

8. A bird's wings are homologous to a(an) **7 3.c**
A fish's tailfin.
B alligator's claws.
C dog's front legs.
D mosquito's wings.

Questions 9–10
The birds shown below are two species of the 13 species of finches Darwin found on the Galápagos Islands.

Woodpecker finch

Large ground finch

9. What process produced the two different types of beaks shown?
A artificial selection
B natural selection
C geographical distribution
D inheritance of acquired traits

10. The large ground finch obtains food by cracking seeds. Its short, strong beak is an example of
A the struggle for existence.
B the tendency toward perfection.
C the inheritance of acquired traits.
D an adaptation.

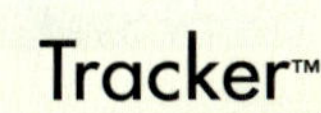

Standards Practice

1. A	**5.** B	**8.** C
2. D	**6.** B	**9.** B
3. D	**7.** C	**10.** D
4. D		

Success Tracker™
Online at PHSchool.com

Have students check their understanding of the chapter by logging onto Success Tracker.

Performance-Based Assessment

Students' first scenarios should explain that the adaptive trait was acquired through use and then inherited by future generations. Their second scenarios should explain that the adaptive trait was present in the population and it increased in the population over time because it enhanced the survival or reproduction of individuals with the trait.

Go Online PHSchool.com

Your students can independently test their knowledge of the chapter and print out their test results for your files.

Chapter Planner 16 Evolution of Populations

Section and Section Objectives	Time	STANDARDS NCLB	STANDARDS Biology	Activities and Labs
16–1 Genes and Variation, pp. 393–396 **16.1.1** ***Explain*** what a gene pool is. **16.1.2** ***Identify*** the main sources of inheritable variation in a population. **16.1.3** ***State*** what determines how a phenotype is expressed.	1 period (1/2 block)	7 3.a, BI 7.c, BI 7.d		**SE:** ***Inquiry Activity,*** Does sexual reproduction change genotype ratios?, p. 392 L2 **TE:** ***Build Science Skills,*** p. 396 L1 L2 **SE:** ***Exploration,*** Investigating Genetic Diversity in Bacteria, p. 411 L2 **LMA:** Chapter 16 Lab L2 L3
16–2 Evolution as Genetic Change, pp. 397–402 **16.2.1** ***Explain*** how natural selection affects single-gene and polygenic traits. **16.2.2** ***Describe*** genetic drift. **16.2.3** ***List*** the five conditions needed to maintain genetic equilibrium.	2 periods (1 block)	BI 7.a	*BI 7.e, *BI 7.f, BI 8.c	**TE:** ***Build Science Skills,*** p. 400 L2 **SE:** ***Quick Lab,*** Can the environment affect survival?, p. 398 L1 L2 **SE:** ***Issues in Biology,*** Should the Use of Antibiotics Be Restricted?, p. 403 L2 **LMB:** Chapter 16 Lab L1 L2
16–3 The Process of Speciation, pp. 404–410 **16.3.1** ***Identify*** the condition necessary for a new species to evolve. **16.3.2** ***Describe*** the process of speciation in the Galápagos finches.	1 period (1/2 block)	BI 8.a, BI 8.b, BIIE 1.f	BI 8.d	**SE:** ***Analyzing Data,*** How Are These Fish Related?, p. 408 L2 L3
Chapter Assessment, pp. 412–415	1 period (1/2 block)			

ACTIVITY PLANNER

SE: *Inquiry Activity*, p. 392; 10 min.; 33 red beads, 67 black beads, large paper cup

TE: *Build Science Skills*, p. 396; 15 min.; tape measure

TE: *Build Science Skills*, p. 400; 15 min.; 10 beans each of 5 different types (per group)

SE: *Quick Lab*, p. 398; 20 min.; scissors, construction paper (several colors), transparent tape, 15-cm ruler, watch with a second hand

SE: *Exploration*, p. 411; 15 min. one day, 30 min. the next day; liquid bacterial culture, sterile swabs, sterile agar plate, glass-marking pencil, antibiotic paper disks, forceps, transparent tape, 70% alcohol, metric ruler, dilute bleach solution and plastic container for cleanup and disposal

PLANNING KEY

Ability Levels

for students performing . . .

below grade level L1

at grade level L2

above grade level L3

Print Components

SE	Student Edition	LA	Lab Assessment
TE	Teacher's Edition	BTM	Biotechnology Manual
RSW	Reading & Study Workbook A	IDM	Issues and Decision Making
ARSW	Adapted Reading & Study Workbook B	LW	Lab Worksheets
TR	Teaching Resources	LMA	Laboratory Manual A
IF	Investigations in Forensics	LMB	Laboratory Manual B

Tech Components

CTB	Computer Test Bank
BD	BioDetectives DVD
TP	Transparencies Plus
PLM	Probeware Lab Manual
ABC	ABC DVD Library
LS	Lab Simulations
VL	Virtual Labs

Interactive textbook with assessment at PHSchool.com

Program Resources	Assessment	Media and Technology
TR: Lesson Plan 16–1, Section Summary, p. 50 L1, p. 62 L2, Worksheets, pp. 53–54 L1, pp. 64–66 L2 **LW:** Chapter 16 Exploration L1 L2 L3 **RSW:** Section 16–1 L2 **ARSW:** Section 16–1 L1	**SE:** 16–1 Section Assessment, p. 396 **TR:** Section Review 16–1	**iText:** Section 16–1 **TP:** 16–1 Interest Grabber, Section Outline, Generic Bell Curve for a Polygenic Trait, Figure 16–2, Figure 16–3 **VL:** Lab 13
TR: Lesson Plan 16–2, Section Summary, p. 51 L1, p. 62 L2, Worksheets, pp. 55–58 L1, pp. 67–68 L2 **RSW:** Section 16–2 L2 **ARSW:** Section 16–2 L1	**SE:** 16–2 Section Assessment, p. 402 **TR:** Section Review 16–2	**iText:** Section 16–2 **TP:** 16–2 Interest Grabber, Section Outline, Genetic Drift, Figure 16–6, Figure 16–7, Figure 16–8 **VL:** Lab 14, Lab 15
TR: Lesson Plan 16–3, Section Summary, p. 52 L1, pp. 63 L2, Worksheets, pp. 59–60 L1, pp. 69–70 L2, Enrichment L2 L3 **RSW:** Section 16–3 L2 **ARSW:** Section 16–3 L1 **IDM:** Issues and Decisions 16 L2 L3	**SE:** 16–3 Section Assessment, p. 410 **TR:** Section Review 16–3	**iText:** Section 16–3 **TP:** 16–3 Interest Grabber, Section Outline, Concept Map **BD:** "The Galápagos Islands: A Glimpse Into the Past"
	SE: Chapter 16 Assessment, pp. 412–415 **TR:** Chapter Vocabulary Review, Graphic Organizer, Chapter 16 Test	**iText:** Chapter 16 Assessment **CTB:** Chapter 16 Test

Go Online

Students can do research, share data, and test their knowledge online.

TIME SAVER

PRESSED FOR TIME?

To Preview the Chapter

- Have students read the headings and boldface sentences in each section.
- Have students study the figures and read the captions.

To Cover the Chapter Quickly

- Have students read all of Section 16–1, the introduction and Natural Selection on Single-Gene Traits in Section 16–2, and the introduction and Speciation of Darwin's Finches in Section 16–3.
- Assign Section Assessment 16–1 and question 1 in Section Assessment 16–2; questions 1–3, 9–15, 24, and 30–32 in Chapter 16 Assessment; and questions 1–10 in Chapter 16 Standards Practice.

To Review the Chapter

- Assign Sections 16–1 through 16–3 in the Reading and Study Workbook or the Adapted Reading and Study Workbook.
- Assign the Section Reviews for 16–1 through 16–3 and the Chapter Vocabulary Review for Chapter 16 in the Teaching Resources.

CHAPTER 16

ENGAGE/EXPLORE

Inquiry Activity

 BIIE 1.j

Objective Students will be able to calculate genotype ratios in a model population and compare them with Mendelian ratios. L2

Skills Focus **Calculating, Comparing and Contrasting, Predicting**

Materials 33 red beads, 67 black beads, large paper cup

Time 10 minutes

Strategy Provide a data table on the board where students can pool their results.

Expected Outcome Genotype ratios calculated from the individual samples will vary, but the ratios calculated from the pooled data for the class should be very close to 4:4:1.

Think About It

1. For the pooled data, there should be an approximate ratio of four homozygous black offspring to four heterozygous offspring to one homozygous red offspring.
2. No, because a 1:2:1 ratio would be expected only if there were equal numbers of red and black beads.
3. The genotype ratios would change only slightly because you are selecting from the same pool of alleles.

Assess Prior Knowledge

Introduce inheritable traits by explaining that they are traits controlled by genes. Then, ask: **In what ways are you like your parents?** *(Students might mention physical traits such as hair color and behavioral traits such as sense of humor.)* **Which traits do you think you inherited?** *(Students are likely to know that most physical traits are largely inherited but may not realize that many behavioral traits, including personality and IQ, are also at least partly inherited.)* Explain that in this chapter students will learn how inheritable traits evolve in populations.

CHAPTER 16

Evolution of Populations

This group of ladybug beetles illustrates a population with a number of inherited traits. Darwin recognized such variation as the raw material for evolution.

Inquiry Activity

 BIIE 1.j

Does sexual reproduction change genotype ratios?

Procedure

1. Put 33 red and 67 black beads in a large paper cup to represent two alleles of a certain gene in a population.
2. To model the genotype of an offspring, remove two beads. Record the genotype. Return the beads.
3. Repeat step 2 for a total of 10 offspring. Add your data to the class total.

Think About It

1. **Calculating** What was the genotype ratio of the offspring?
2. **Comparing and Contrasting** Was the genotype ratio the same as the 1 : 2 : 1 genotype ratio for a cross between two heterozygotes ($Aa \times Aa$)? Explain.
3. **Predicting** If you repeated this activity over and over, would you expect the genotype ratios to change? Explain.

16–1 Genes and Variation

7 3.a. Students know both genetic variation and environmental factors are causes of evolution and diversity of organisms. BI 7.c. Students know new mutations are constantly being generated in a gene pool. BI 7.d. Students know variation within a species increases the likelihood that at least some members of a species will survive under changed environmental conditions.

As Darwin developed his theory of evolution, he worked under a serious handicap. He didn't know how heredity worked! Although Mendel's work on inheritance in peas was published during Darwin's lifetime, its importance wasn't recognized for decades. This lack of knowledge left two big gaps in Darwin's thinking. First, he had no idea how heritable traits pass from one generation to the next. Second, although variation in heritable traits was central to Darwin's theory, he had no idea how that variation appeared.

Evolutionary biologists connected Mendel's work to Darwin's during the 1930s. By then, biologists understood that genes control heritable traits. They soon realized that changes in genes produce heritable variation on which natural selection can operate. Genes became the focus of new hypotheses and experiments aimed at understanding evolutionary change. Another revolution in evolutionary thought began with Watson and Crick's studies on DNA. Their model of the DNA molecule helped evolutionary biologists because it demonstrated the molecular nature of mutation and genetic variation.

Today, molecular techniques are used to test hypotheses about how heritable variation appears and how natural selection operates on that variation. As you will learn in this chapter, fitness, adaptation, species, and evolutionary change are now defined in genetic terms. We understand how evolution works better than Darwin ever could, beginning with heritable variation.

CA a

Guide for Reading

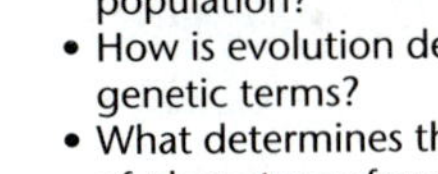

Key Concepts
- What are the main sources of heritable variation in a population?
- How is evolution defined in genetic terms?
- What determines the numbers of phenotypes for a given trait?

Vocabulary
gene pool
relative frequency
single-gene trait
polygenic trait

Reading Strategy: Building Vocabulary Before you read, make a list of the vocabulary terms above. As you read, take notes about the meaning of each term.

a 7 3.a

How Common Is Genetic Variation?

We now know that many genes have at least two forms, or alleles. Animals such as horses, dogs, and mice often have several alleles for traits such as body size or coat color. Plants, such as peas, often have several alleles for flower color. All organisms have additional genetic variation that is "invisible" because it involves small differences in biochemical processes. In addition, an individual organism is heterozygous for many genes. An insect may be heterozygous for as many as 15 percent of its genes. Individual fishes, reptiles, and mammals are typically heterozygous for between 4 and 8 percent of their genes.

▼ **Figure 16–1 There are two main sources of genetic variation: mutations and the gene shuffling that results from sexual reproduction.** Each of these babies has inherited a collection of traits. Some, such as hair color, are visible, while others, such as the ability to resist certain diseases, are not.

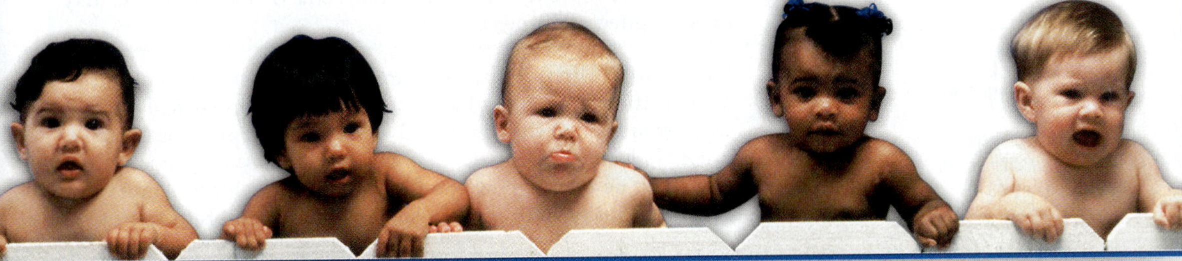

Section 16–1

7 3.a, BI 7.c, BI 7.d

1 FOCUS

Objectives

16.1.1 ***Explain*** what a gene pool is.
16.1.2 ***Identify*** the main sources of inheritable variation in a population.
16.1.3 ***State*** what determines how a phenotype is expressed.

Guide for Reading

Vocabulary Preview

Help students understand the Vocabulary terms by reviewing the terms *gene (segment of DNA that codes for a particular protein)* and *allele (one of a number of different forms of the same gene for a specific trait).*

Reading Strategy

Suggest that students preview the section by studying the figures and reading the captions. Advise them to look for Key Concepts in the captions.

2 INSTRUCT

How Common Is Genetic Variation?

Build Science Skills

Applying Concepts Help students appreciate how much genetic variation there can be with just one gene. Remind them that the gene for ABO blood type has three major alleles. Ask: **How many ABO genotypes are possible?** *(Six genotypes: AA, AB, AO, BB, BO, OO)* **How many genotypes would be possible with four alleles?** *(Ten genotypes)* Challenge students to continue counting the number of possible genotypes for increasing numbers of alleles. Then, point out that there may be thousands of variable genes. L2

TIME SAVER SECTION RESOURCES

Print:
- ***Laboratory Manual A,*** Chapter 16 Lab
- ***Teaching Resources,*** Lesson Plan 16–1, Adapted Section Summary 16–1, Adapted Worksheets 16–1, Section Summary 16–1, Worksheets 16–1, Section Review 16–1
- ***Reading and Study Workbook A,*** Section 16–1
- ***Adapted Reading and Study Workbook B,*** Section 16–1
- ***Lab Worksheets,*** Chapter 16 Exploration

Technology:
- ***iText,*** Section 16–1
- ***Transparencies Plus,*** Section 16–1
- ***Virtual Labs,*** Lab 13

16–1 (continued)

Variation and Gene Pools

Use Visuals

Figure 16–2 Explain that the gene pool modeled in the drawing is a simplification of reality. In a real gene pool, each person has alleles for thousands of different genetic traits, not just one. Help students understand the concept of relative allele frequency by asking: **If the relative frequency of the B allele decreased in the gene pool, what would happen to the relative frequency of the other allele?** *(It would increase in frequency, because the total of the two frequencies must remain 100 percent.)*

Sources of Genetic Variation

Address Misconceptions

Perhaps because mutations are often the subjects of science fiction, many people have misconceptions about them. One misconception is that most mutations have drastic effects on the organism, for example, by causing major physical deformities. Point out that most mutations involve only minor changes in the DNA and that many mutations do not lead to visible changes in the phenotype. Add that most people carry hundreds of mutations that have little or no effect on their fitness. Avoid giving students the impression that most mutations are harmless, however. Explain that some minor changes in DNA can have drastic effects on the organism. For example, the allele that codes for sickle cell hemoglobin differs by just one codon from the allele that codes for normal hemoglobin, yet a person with two sickle cell alleles suffers from a life-threatening disease that affects virtually every organ of the body. L1

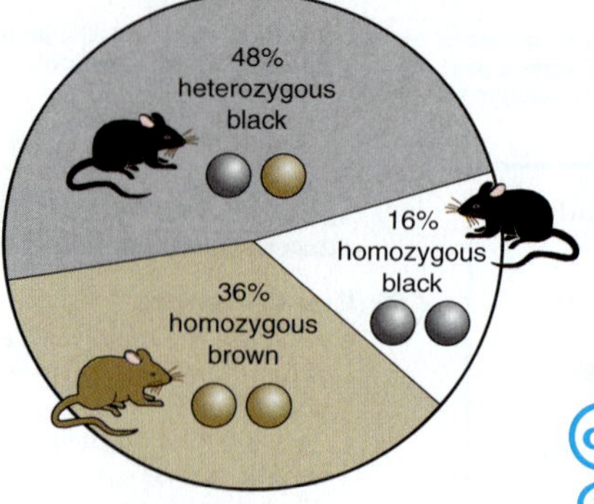

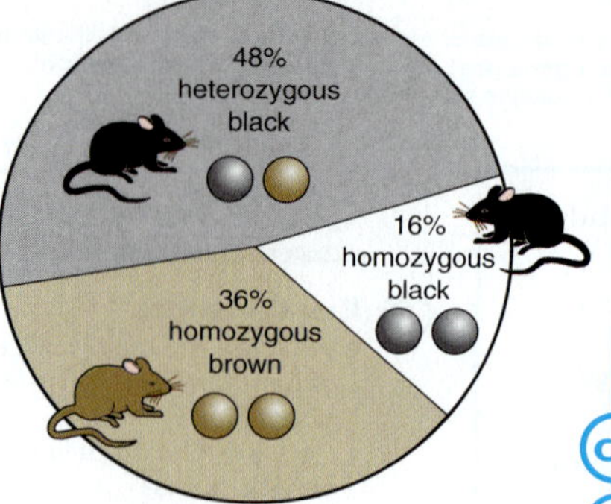

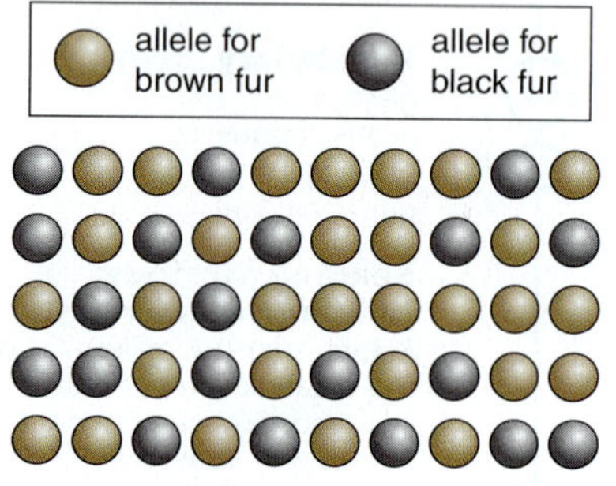

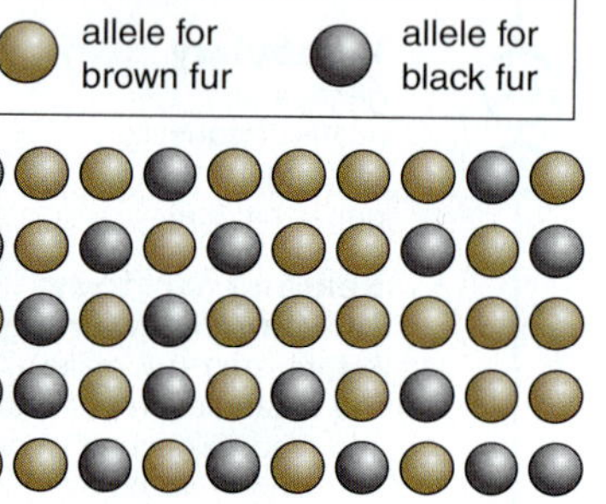

▲ **Figure 16–2** When scientists determine whether a population is evolving, they may look at the sum of the population's alleles, or its gene pool. This diagram shows the gene pool for fur color in a population of mice. **Calculating** *Here, in a total of 50 alleles, 20 alleles are B (black), and 30 are b (brown). How many of each allele would be present in a total of 100 alleles?*

Variation and Gene Pools

Genetic variation is studied in populations. A population is a group of individuals of the same species that interbreed. Because members of a population interbreed, they share a common group of genes called a gene pool. A **gene pool** consists of all genes, including all the different alleles, that are present in a population.

The **relative frequency** of an allele is the number of times that the allele occurs in a gene pool, compared with the number of times other alleles for the same gene occur. Relative frequency is often expressed as a percentage. For example, in the mouse population in **Figure 16–2,** the relative frequency of the dominant *B* allele (black fur) is 40 percent, and the relative frequency of the recessive *b* allele (brown fur) is 60 percent. The relative frequency of an allele has nothing to do with whether the allele is dominant or recessive. In this particular mouse population, the recessive allele occurs more frequently than the dominant allele.

Gene pools are important to evolutionary theory, because evolution involves changes in populations over time. **In genetic terms, evolution is any change in the relative frequency of alleles in a population.** For example, if the relative frequency of the *B* allele in the mouse population changed over time to 30 percent, the population is evolving.

CHECKPOINT *What is a gene pool?*

Sources of Genetic Variation

Biologists can now explain how variation is produced. **The two main sources of genetic variation are mutations and the genetic shuffling that results from sexual reproduction.**

Mutations A mutation is any change in a sequence of DNA. Mutations can occur because of mistakes in the replication of DNA or as a result of radiation or chemicals in the environment. Mutations do not always affect an organism's phenotype. For example, a DNA codon altered from GGA to GGU will still code for the same amino acid, glycine. That mutation has no effect on phenotype. Many mutations do produce changes in phenotype, however. Some can affect an organism's fitness, or its ability to survive and reproduce in its environment. Other mutations may have no effect on fitness.

Gene Shuffling Mutations are not the only source of heritable variation. You do not look exactly like your biological parents, even though they provided you with all your genes. You probably look even less like any brothers or sisters you may have. Yet, no matter how you feel about your relatives, mutant genes are not primarily what makes them so different from you.

Most heritable differences are due to gene shuffling that occurs during the production of gametes. Recall that each chromosome of a homologous pair moves independently during meiosis. As a result, the 23 pairs of chromosomes found in humans can produce 8.4 million different combinations of genes!

Another process, crossing-over, also occurs during meiosis. Crossing-over further increases the number of different genotypes that can appear in offspring. Recall that a genotype is an organism's genetic makeup. When alleles are recombined during sexual reproduction, they can produce dramatically different phenotypes. Thus, sexual reproduction is a major source of variation within many populations.

Sexual reproduction can produce many different phenotypes, but it does not change the relative frequency of alleles in a population. To understand why, compare a population's gene pool to a deck of playing cards. Each card represents an allele found in the population. The exchange of genes during gene shuffling is similar to shuffling a deck of cards. Shuffling leads to different types of hands, but it can never change the relative numbers of aces, kings, or queens in the deck. The probability of drawing an ace off the top of the deck will always be 4 in 52, or one thirteenth (4/52 = 1/13). No matter how many times you shuffle the deck, this probability will remain the same. Similarly, sexual reproduction produces many different combinations of genes, but in itself it does not alter the relative frequencies of each type of allele in a population.

CHECKPOINT *What are the sources of heritable variation?*

Word Origins

Gene comes from the Greek word *gignesthai,* meaning "to be born," and refers to factors that produce an organism. The prefix *poly-* comes from the Greek word *polys,* meaning "many," so *polygenic* means "having many genes." The prefix *mono-* means "one." **What do you think the term *monogenic* means?**

Single-Gene and Polygenic Traits

Heritable variation can be expressed in a variety of ways. **The number of phenotypes produced for a given trait depends on how many genes control the trait.** Among humans, a widow's peak—a downward dip in the center of the hairline—is a **single-gene trait.** It is controlled by a single gene that has two alleles. The allele for a widow's peak is dominant over the allele for a hairline with no peak. As a result, variation in this gene leads to only two distinct phenotypes, as shown in **Figure 16–3.**

As you can see, the frequency of phenotypes caused by this single gene is represented on the bar graph. This graph shows that the presence of a widow's peak may be less common in a population than the absence of a widow's peak, even though the allele for a widow's peak is the dominant form. In real populations, phenotypic ratios are determined by the frequency of alleles in the population as well as by whether the alleles are in the dominant or recessive form. Allele frequencies may not match Mendelian ratios.

Figure 16–3 In humans, a single gene with two alleles controls whether a person has a widow's peak (left) or does not have a widow's peak (right). As a result, only two phenotypes are possible. **The number of phenotypes a given trait has is determined by how many genes control the trait.**

Single-Gene Trait

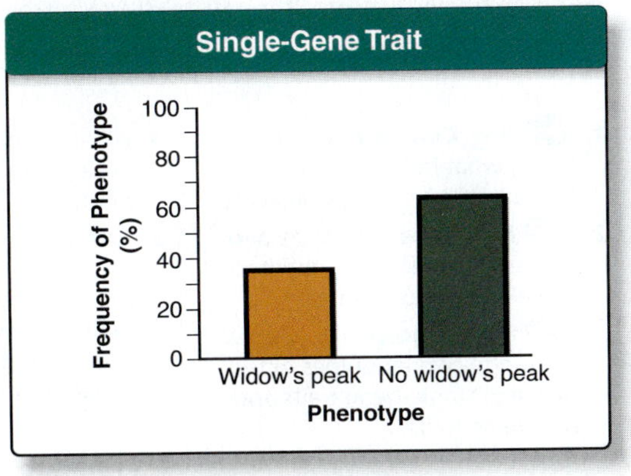

Build Science Skills

Calculating To reinforce the point that reshuffling genes does not change allele frequencies, describe genotype proportions in two hypothetical populations: population 1 (50% *AA,* 50% *aa*) and population 2 (25% *AA,* 50% *Aa,* 25% *aa*). Then, ask: **What are the frequencies of *A* and *a* in the two populations?** (A = a = *50%*) L1 L2

Word Origins

Monogenic means having a single gene. L2

Single-Gene and Polygenic Traits

Demonstration

Find students with and without widow's peaks to demonstrate this trait. Then, explain that there are a number of other single-gene traits that are easy to see and that are either present or absent in individuals because of dominance. Invite students to demonstrate each of the following single-gene traits (or their absence) to the class: tongue rolling (the ability to fold up the sides of the tongue into a pea-shooter shape) and attached ear lobes (ear lobes with no notch or indentation where they are attached to the side of the face). Challenge students to count the number of phenotypes in the class for each of the traits and then draw a graph for each trait like the graph in Figure 16–3 for widow's peak. L1

UNIVERSAL ACCESS

Inclusion/Special Needs

Students may benefit from a review of meiosis. Refer them to the diagram of meiosis in Chapter 11. Point out that gene shuffling refers to the crossover event that occurs during the first stage of meiosis. Discuss how crossing-over exchanges alleles between chromosomes so that the chromosomes that are passed on to the offspring are different from chromosomes that were inherited from the parents. L1

Advanced Learners

Have interested students learn about the lives and works of scientists who synthesized Darwin's theory of evolution and Mendel's work on inheritance. They include Julian Huxley, Theodosius Dobzhansky, Ronald Fisher, J.B.S. Haldane, Sewall Wright, and Sergei Chetverikov. Ask students to report to the class on the contributions made by the scientist they researched. L3

Answers to . . .

CHECKPOINT *A gene pool consists of all genes, including all the different alleles, that are present in a population.*

CHECKPOINT *Mutations and the genetic shuffling that results from sexual reproduction*

Figure 16–2 *40* B *and 60* b

16–1 (continued)

Build Science Skills

Using Tables and Graphs Measure and record the height of each student in class, and have students use the data to create a bar graph showing the distribution of students by height. After the graph is completed, ask: **How does the bar graph for the class compare with a normal distribution?** *(Like a normal distribution, the bar graph for the class should have more individuals at or near the average height and increasingly fewer students at shorter and taller heights.)*

3 ASSESS

Evaluate Understanding

Ask students to explain whether fur color in the mice shown in Figure 16–2 is a single-gene or polygenic trait. *(It's a single-gene trait because it is produced by one gene, which has two alleles.)*

Reteach

Have students draw two graphs, one to show the frequency of phenotypes for a hypothetical single-gene trait and the other to show the frequency of phenotypes for a hypothetical polygenic trait. Review why the two graphs differ as they do.

Focus on the BIG Idea

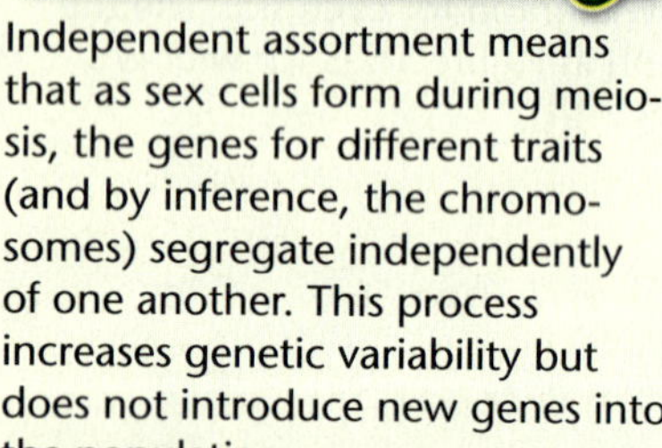

Independent assortment means that as sex cells form during meiosis, the genes for different traits (and by inference, the chromosomes) segregate independently of one another. This process increases genetic variability but does not introduce new genes into the population.

If your class subscribes to the iText, use it to review the Key Concepts in Section 16–1.

Answer to . . .

Figure 16–4 *It indicates that the height of most people is at or near the average, with a small number of individuals at either extreme.*

Figure 16–4 The graph below shows the distribution of phenotypes that would be expected for a trait if many genes contributed to the trait. The photograph shows the actual distribution of heights of a group of young men. **Using Tables and Graphs** *What does the shape of the graph indicate about height in humans?*

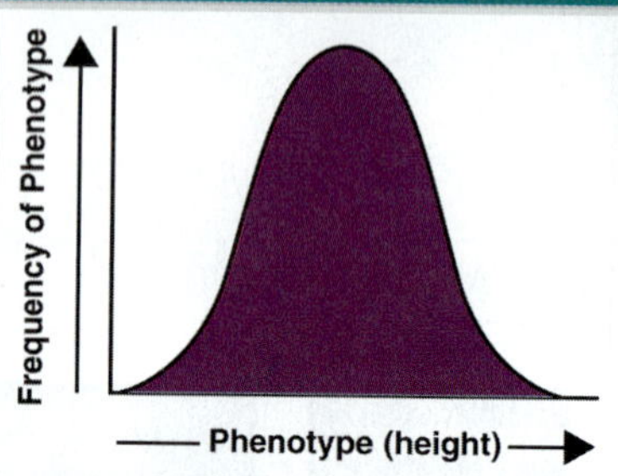

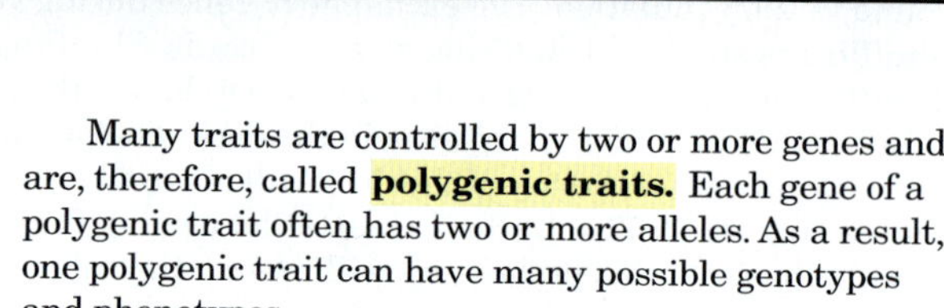

Many traits are controlled by two or more genes and are, therefore, called **polygenic traits.** Each gene of a polygenic trait often has two or more alleles. As a result, one polygenic trait can have many possible genotypes and phenotypes.

Height in humans is one example of a polygenic trait. You can sample phenotypic variation in this trait by measuring the height of all the students in your class. You can then calculate the average height of this group. Many students will be just a little taller or shorter than average. Some of your classmates, however, will be very tall or very short. If you graph the number of individuals of each height, you may get a graph similar to the one in **Figure 16–4.** The symmetrical bell-like shape of this curve is typical of polygenic traits. A bell-shaped curve is also called a normal distribution.

16–1 Section Assessment

1. **Key Concept** In genetic terms, what indicates that evolution is occurring in a population?
2. **Key Concept** What two processes can lead to inherited variation in populations?
3. **Key Concept** How does the range of phenotypes differ between single-gene traits and polygenic traits?
4. What is a gene pool? How are allele frequencies related to gene pools?
5. **Critical Thinking Evaluating** Evaluate the significance of mutations to the process of biological evolution. (*Hint*: How does mutation affect genetic variation?)

Focus on the BIG Idea

Information and Heredity
How does the process known as independent assortment relate to the genetic variation that results from sexual reproduction? *Hint:* Refer to Chapter 11.

16–1 Section Assessment

1. Evolution is occurring when there is a change in the relative frequency of alleles in a population.
2. Mutations and the genetic shuffling that results from sexual reproduction
3. Single-gene traits have only two distinct phenotypes. Polygenic traits can have many possible phenotypes.
4. A gene pool is the combined genetic information of all members of a particular population. Allele frequencies are the number of times certain alleles occur in a particular gene pool compared with other alleles.
5. Mutations increase genetic variation, which is needed for natural selection to bring about evolutionary change.

16–2 Evolution as Genetic Change

BI 7.a. Students know why natural selection acts on the phenotype rather than the genotype of an organism. ***BI 7.e.** Students know the conditions for Hardy-Weinberg equilibrium in a population and why these conditions are not likely to appear in nature. ***BI 7.f.** Students know how to solve the Hardy-Weinberg equation to predict the frequency of genotypes in a population, given the frequency of phenotypes. **BI 8.c.** Students know the effects of genetic drift on the diversity of organisms in a population.

A genetic view of evolution offers a new way to look at key evolutionary concepts. Each time an organism reproduces, it passes copies of its genes to its offspring. We can therefore view evolutionary fitness as an organism's success in passing genes to the next generation. In the same way, we can view an evolutionary adaptation as any genetically controlled physiological, anatomical, or behavioral trait that increases an individual's ability to pass along its genes.

Natural selection never acts directly on genes. Why? Because it is an entire organism—not a single gene—that either survives and reproduces or dies without reproducing. Natural selection, therefore, can only affect which individuals survive and reproduce and which do not. If an individual dies without reproducing, the individual does not contribute its alleles to the population's gene pool. If an individual produces many offspring, its alleles stay in the gene pool and may increase in frequency.

Now recall that evolution is any change over time in the relative frequencies of alleles in a population. This reminds us that it is populations, not individual organisms, that can evolve over time. Let us see how this can happen in different situations.

Guide for Reading

Key Concepts

- How does natural selection affect single-gene and polygenic traits?
- What is genetic drift?
- What is the Hardy-Weinberg principle?

Vocabulary

directional selection
stabilizing selection
disruptive selection
genetic drift
founder effect
Hardy-Weinberg principle
genetic equilibrium

Reading Strategy: Outlining Before you read, use the headings to make an outline. As you read, add a sentence after each heading to provide key information.

Natural Selection on Single-Gene Traits

BI 7.a

Natural selection on single-gene traits can lead to changes in allele frequencies and thus to evolution. Imagine that a hypothetical population of lizards, shown in **Figure 16–5**, is normally brown, but experiences mutations that produce red and black forms. What happens to those new alleles? If red lizards are more visible to predators, they might be less likely to survive and reproduce, and the allele for red coloring might not become common.

▼ **Figure 16–5** **Natural selection on single-gene traits can lead to changes in allele frequencies and thus to evolution.** Organisms of one color, for example, may produce fewer offspring than organisms of other colors.

Effect of Color Mutations on Lizard Survival

Initial Population	Generation 10	Generation 20	Generation 30
80%	80%	70%	40%
10%	0%	0%	0%
10%	20%	30%	60%

SECTION RESOURCES

Print:

- ***Laboratory Manual B,*** Chapter 16 Lab
- ***Teaching Resources,*** Lesson Plan 16–2, Adapted Section Summary 16–2, Adapted Worksheets 16–2, Section Summary 16–2, Worksheets 16–2, Section Review 16–2
- ***Reading and Study Workbook A,*** Section 16–2
- ***Adapted Reading and Study Workbook B,*** Section 16–2

Technology:

- ***iText,*** Section 16–2
- ***Transparencies Plus,*** Section 16–2
- ***Virtual Labs,*** Lab 14, Lab 15

Section 16–2

BI 7.a, *BI 7.e, *BI 7.f, BI 8.c

1 FOCUS

Objectives

16.2.1 ***Explain*** how natural selection affects single-gene and polygenic traits.
16.2.2 ***Describe*** genetic drift.
16.2.3 ***List*** the five conditions needed to maintain genetic equilibrium.

Guide for Reading

Vocabulary Preview

Challenge students to predict what the Vocabulary terms *directional selection, stabilizing selection*, and *disruptive selection* refer to. They should check to see if their predictions were correct after they read the section.

Reading Strategy

When completing their outlines, students should pay special attention to the highlighted, boldface terms and the boldface sentences.

2 INSTRUCT

Natural Selection on Single-Gene Traits

Use Visuals

Figure 16–5 Ask: How does color affect the fitness of the lizards? *(Both red and brown lizards are less fit than black lizards.)* **What do you predict the lizard population will look like by generation 50? Explain.** *(Students are likely to say that the lizard population will have more black lizards, fewer brown lizards, and no red lizards by generation 50. They should describe the environmental conditions that would support their prediction.)*

16–2 (continued)

Quick Lab

Objective Students will be able to analyze data and infer that the environment affects survival. L1 L2

Skills Focus Analyzing Data, Inferring

Materials scissors, construction paper (several colors), transparent tape, 15-cm ruler, watch with a second hand

Time 20 minutes

Advance Prep Select surfaces that will not be harmed by tape. Provide students with construction paper in some colors that blend with and other colors that contrast with the selected surfaces.

Strategy Relate the lab to natural selection.

Expected Outcome Students will find that butterflies in contrasting colors are easier to see.

Analyze and Conclude

1. Butterflies in colors that contrast with the surfaces are the easiest to see. These butterflies would be the most easily caught by a predator.
2. After many generations, the population will be made up only of butterflies in colors that are difficult to see.

Natural Selection on Polygenic Traits

Build Science Skills

Inferring Explain that polygenic traits are often susceptible to environmental influences. In fact, a shift in the environment can lead to a corresponding shift in the phenotypes of a polygenic trait, which can mimic directional selection. Give students an example. Explain that during the 1900s, average height in the United States increased because of environmental factors. Ask: **What environmental factors do you think led to this shift in phenotype?** *(The increase in average height has been attributed largely to changes in diet and health care that maximized growth potential.)* L2

Quick Lab

Can the environment affect survival?

Materials scissors, construction paper (several colors), transparent tape, 15-cm ruler, watch with a second hand

Procedure 

1. Choose three different-colored sheets of construction paper. Cut out a butterfly shape from each sheet, 5 × 10 cm in size. **CAUTION:** *Be careful with scissors.*
2. Tape your butterflies to different-colored surfaces. Then, return to your seat.
3. Record how many shapes of each color you can count from your desk in 5 seconds.
4. Exchange your observations with your classmates to determine the class total for each color.

Analyze and Conclude

1. **Analyzing Data** According to your class data, which colors of butterfly are easiest to see? Which color of butterfly would be most easily caught by a predator?
2. **Inferring** What will happen to the butterfly population after many generations if predators consume most of the easy-to-see butterflies?

Black lizards, on the other hand, might absorb more sunlight and warm up faster on cold days. If high body temperature allows them to move faster to feed and to avoid predators, they might produce more offspring than brown forms. The allele for black color might then increase in relative frequency. If a color change has no effect on fitness, the allele that produces it would not be under pressure from natural selection.

Natural Selection on Polygenic Traits

When traits are controlled by more than one gene, the effects of natural selection are more complex. As you learned earlier, the action of multiple alleles on traits such as height produces a range of phenotypes that often fit a bell curve. The fitness of individuals close to one another on the curve will not be very different. But fitness can vary a great deal from one end of such a curve to the other. And where fitness varies, natural selection can act. **Natural selection can affect the distributions of phenotypes in any of three ways: directional selection, stabilizing selection, or disruptive selection.**

CA a

Directional Selection When individuals at one end of the curve have higher fitness than individuals in the middle or at the other end, **directional selection** takes place. The range of phenotypes shifts as some individuals fail to survive and reproduce while others succeed. To understand this, consider how limited resources, such as food, can affect the long-term survival of individuals and the evolution of populations.

Among seed-eating birds such as Darwin's finches, for example, birds with bigger, thicker beaks can feed more easily on larger, harder, thicker-shelled seeds. Suppose a food shortage causes the supply of small and medium-sized seeds to run low, leaving only larger seeds. Birds whose beaks enable them to open those larger seeds will have better access to food. Birds with the big-beak adaptation would therefore have higher fitness than small-beaked birds. The average beak size of the population would probably increase, as shown in **Figure 16–6.**

a BI 7.a

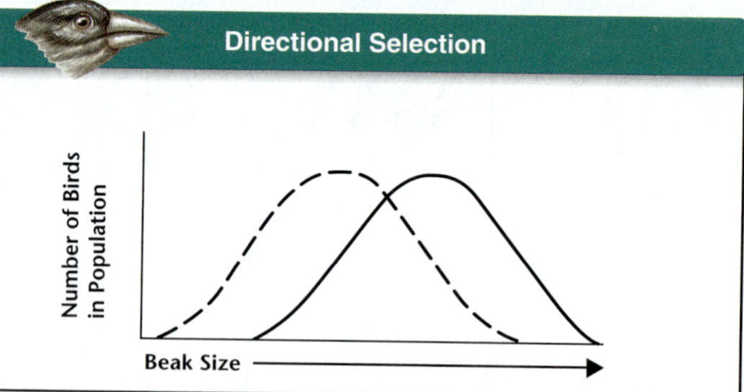

Figure 16–6 Directional selection occurs when individuals at one end of the curve have higher fitness than individuals in the middle or at the other end. In this example, a population of seed-eating birds experiences directional selection when a food shortage causes the supply of small seeds to run low. The dotted line shows the original distribution of beak sizes. The solid line shows how the distribution of beak sizes would change as a result of selection.

ESL SUPPORT FOR ENGLISH LANGUAGE LEARNERS

Comprehension: Ask Questions

Beginning To help students understand the relationship between genetics and natural selection, distribute a rewritten, modified version of the first three paragraphs on page 397 that includes the most important information. Ask students questions that can be answered directly from the rewritten text. For example: When an organism reproduces, what does it pass to its offspring? How do genes affect an organism's adaptations? L1

Intermediate Have students read the modified text that you prepared for beginning students and then read the actual text in the book. Students can work in groups to write questions about the text. Provide answers both orally and in writing. L2

Stabilizing Selection When individuals near the center of the curve have higher fitness than individuals at either end of the curve, **stabilizing selection** takes place. This situation keeps the center of the curve at its current position, but it narrows the overall graph.

As shown in **Figure 16–7**, the mass of human infants at birth is under the influence of stabilizing selection. Human babies born much smaller than average are likely to be less healthy and thus less likely to survive. Babies that are much larger than average are likely to have difficulty being born. The fitness of these larger or smaller individuals is, therefore, lower than that of more average-sized individuals.

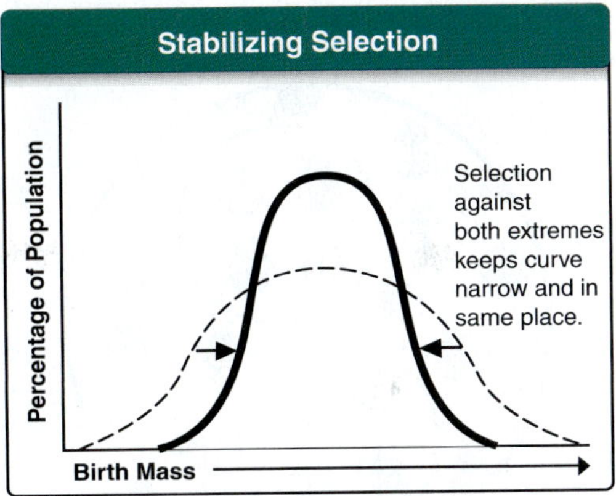

▲ **Figure 16–7** In this example of stabilizing selection, human babies born at an average mass are more likely to survive than babies born either much smaller or much larger than average.

Disruptive Selection When individuals at the upper and lower ends of the curve have higher fitness than individuals near the middle, **disruptive selection** takes place. In such situations, selection acts most strongly against individuals of an intermediate type. If the pressure of natural selection is strong enough and lasts long enough, this situation can cause the single curve to split into two. In other words, selection creates two distinct phenotypes.

CA a

For example, suppose a population of birds lives in an area where medium-sized seeds become less common and large and small seeds become more common. Birds with unusually small or large beaks would have higher fitness. As shown in **Figure 16–8**, the population might split into two subgroups: one that eats small seeds and one that eats large seeds.

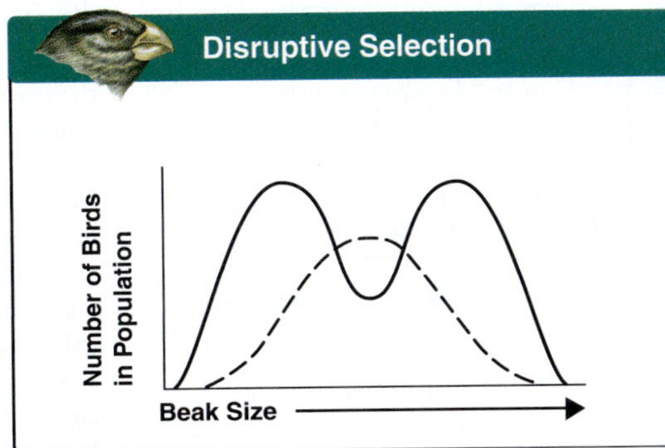

▲ **Figure 16–8** In this example of disruptive selection, average-sized seeds become less common, and larger and smaller seeds become more common. As a result, the bird population splits into two subgroups specializing in eating different-sized seeds.

Genetic Drift

a BI 7.a

In small populations, an allele can become more or less common simply by chance, rather than because it has positive or negative effects on fitness. The smaller a population is, the greater the chance that it will experience this kind of random change in allele frequency. This kind of random change in allele frequency is called **genetic drift.** How does genetic drift take place? **In small populations, individuals that carry a particular allele may leave more descendants than other individuals, just by chance. Over time, a series of chance occurrences of this type can cause an allele to become common in a population.**

Demonstration

Show students illustrations of monarch and viceroy butterflies. Challenge them to detect any visible differences between the two species. Explain that monarch butterflies are avoided by bird predators because they taste bitter and that viceroy butterflies are avoided by bird predators because they resemble the bitter-tasting monarch butterflies, a situation called mimicry that has evolved through natural selection.

Use Visuals

Figure 16–7 Ask: **If the fitness of phenotypes at both ends of the curve were to decrease even more, how would it affect the shape of the curve?** *(The curve would become narrower.)* **If medical advances could prevent problems for high birth weight babies but not for low birth weight babies, how might the curve change then?** *(There might be a shift in the curve toward higher birth weights or at least a broadening of the curve at the high end.)* L1 L2

Genetic Drift

Build Science Skills

Using Models Divide the class into groups, and provide each group with a bowl containing 10 beans each of 5 different types, such as pinto, kidney, navy, white, and lima beans. Challenge groups to brainstorm for a way to use the beans to model genetic drift. *(One way is by randomly selecting only some of the beans from the bowl to represent alleles in the next generation.)* Ask: **How would you show with your model that genetic change had occurred?** *(By calculating the relative frequencies of the different types of beans in the next generation to show that their frequencies had changed)* L2

16–2 (continued)

Make Connections

Environmental Science State that the founder effect may be especially likely to occur when natural disasters take place. Challenge students to think of ways in which natural disasters might result in a small number of individuals from a population becoming and remaining isolated from the rest of the group. *(As one example, students might describe how a forest fire isolates a few rodents in a small remnant of forest.)* L1 L2

For: Genetic Drift activity
Visit: PHSchool.com
Web Code: cbe-5169

Students explore the concept of genetic drift online.

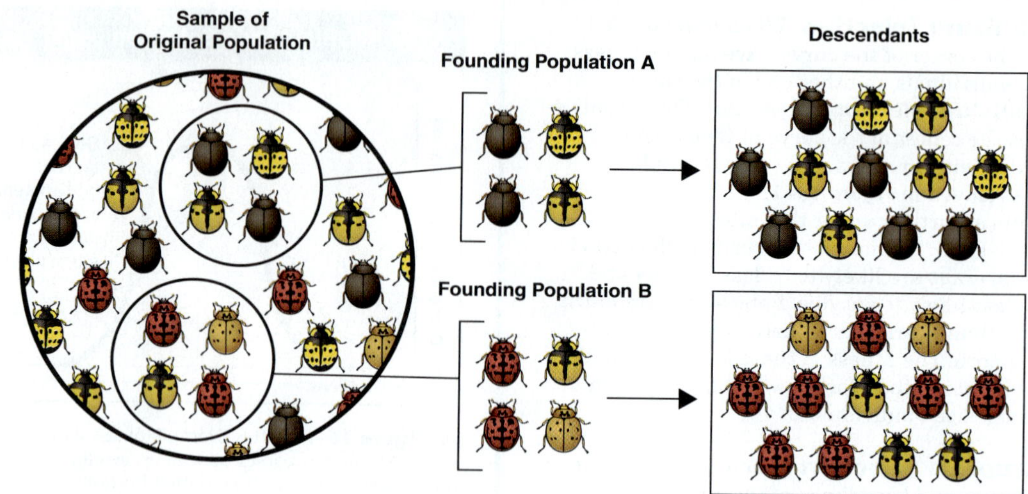

For: Genetic Drift activity
Visit: PHSchool.com
Web Code: cbp-5162

Figure 16–9 **In small populations, individuals that carry a particular allele may have more descendants than other individuals. Over time, a series of chance occurrences of this type can cause an allele to become more common in a population.** This model demonstrates how two small groups from a large, diverse population could produce new populations that differ from the original group.

Genetic drift may occur when a small group of individuals colonizes a new habitat. These individuals may carry alleles in different relative frequencies than did the larger population from which they came. If so, the population that they found will be genetically different from the parent population. Here, however, the cause is not natural selection but simply chance—specifically, the chance that particular alleles were in one or more of the founding individuals, as shown in **Figure 16–9.** A situation in which allele frequencies change as a result of the migration of a small subgroup of a population is known as the **founder effect.** One example of the founder effect is the evolution of several hundred species of fruit flies found on different Hawaiian Islands. All of those species descended from the same original mainland population. Those species in different habitats on different islands now have allele frequencies that are different from those of the original species.

Hardy-Weinberg and Genetic Equilibrium

To clarify how evolutionary change operates, scientists often find it helpful to determine what happens when *no* change takes place. So biologists ask: Are there any conditions under which evolution will not occur? Is there any way to recognize when that is the case? The answers to those questions are provided by the Hardy-Weinberg principle, named after two researchers who independently proposed it in 1908.

The **Hardy-Weinberg principle** states that allele frequencies in a population will remain constant unless one or more factors cause those frequencies to change. The situation in which allele frequencies remain constant is called **genetic equilibrium.** If the allele frequencies do not change, the population will not evolve.

FACTS AND FIGURES

***Mutiny on the* Bounty**

A good example of founder effect in human populations is the population of Pitcairn Island in the South Pacific. The island's population today has limited genetic variability because it was founded by only a handful of people in the late 1700s. The founders consisted of nine mutineers from the HMS *Bounty*, all of whom were English, along with a small number of Tahitian men and Tahitian women. A few years after the population was founded, the number of people declined even more because of a disagreement between the English and Tahitian men. When Pitcairn Island was discovered by American whalers in 1808, the population consisted of just one Englishman, several Tahitian women, and some children. Because the population was geographically isolated, few new genes entered the gene pool over subsequent years, and genetic variation remained limited.

Under what conditions does the Hardy-Weinberg principle hold? **Five conditions are required to maintain genetic equilibrium from generation to generation: (1) There must be random mating: (2) the population must be very large; and (3) there can be no movement into or out of the population, (4) no mutations, and (5) no natural selection.**

In some populations and in rare situations, these five conditions may be met or nearly met for long periods of time. If, however, the conditions are not met, the genetic equilibrium will be disrupted, and the population will evolve.

Solving Problems Using Hardy-Weinberg

It turns out that the Hardy-Weinberg principle is based on an equation that allows us to check its predictions. That equation can also be used to calculate and predict the frequency of certain genotypes.

Imagine that you are a geneticist studying a trait controlled by two alleles, *A* and *a*. You know that these alleles follow rules of simple dominance. You survey a population for the trait, and discover that 4% of the population exhibits the phenotype produced by the homozygous recessive genotype *aa*. Fully 96% of the population is *AA* or *Aa* and exhibits the dominant phenotype.

The Hardy-Weinberg equations represent the frequency of the dominant *A* allele as *p* and the frequency of the recessive *a* allele as *q*. The sum of the frequencies must always equal the entire population (100%). In mathematical form, this can be written as the equation:

$$r + q = 1$$

Recall from Chapter 11, that any cross that involves these alleles can produce three possible genotypes: *AA*, *Aa*, and *aa*.

Now, when eggs and sperm are produced in members of this population, those gametes will carry these alleles in the same relative frequencies at which those alleles occur in the population. Thus, the relative frequency of eggs and sperm that carry the *A* allele will be equal to *p*, and the relative frequency of eggs and sperm that carry the *a* allele will be equal to *q*. The three types of zygotes produced by these eggs and sperm will have the same relative numbers as the individuals in the Punnett square.

▲ **Figure 16–10** **One of the five conditions that are needed to maintain genetic equilibrium from one generation to the next is large population size.** The allele frequencies of large populations, such as this group of birds, are less likely to be changed through the process of genetic drift.

Hardy-Weinberg and Genetic Equilibrium

Make Connections

Mathematics Explain that in addition to allele frequencies remaining constant when a population is in genetic equilibrium, genotype proportions also remain constant and can be calculated from the allele frequencies. If p is the frequency of allele *A* for a trait and q is the frequency of allele *a* for the same trait, then genotype proportions are given by $(p + q)^2 = p^2$ (*AA*) + 2pq (*Aa*) + q^2 (*aa*). Ask: **If a population is in genetic equilibrium and the value of p is 0.3, what proportion of the population has each genotype?** *(The proportion of* AA *individuals is p^2, or 0.09; the proportion of* Aa *individuals is 2pq, or 0.42; and the proportion of* aa *individuals is q^2, or 0.49.)* Point out that the genotype proportions must add up to 1.00. L2 L3

Solving Problems Using Hardy-Weinberg

Build Science Skills

Inferring Explain that selection for heterozygotes can also lead to equilibrium in allele frequencies, and give the following example. State that, in some African populations where malaria is prevalent, heterozygotes for sickle cell hemoglobin have the highest fitness, because they are somewhat resistant to malaria and largely unaffected by sickle cell anemia. Homozygotes for sickle cell hemoglobin have the lowest fitness, because they have sickle cell anemia. Normal homozygotes have somewhat reduced fitness, because they have no resistance to malaria. As a result, the allele for sickle cell hemoglobin persists in these populations. Ask: **What do you think would happen to the sickle cell allele in these populations if malaria were eradicated?** *(The allele would be selected against and become less common.)* L2

TEACHER TO TEACHER

Using a series of overhead transparencies, I explain the Hardy-Weinberg principle to the entire class. Then, I distribute a problem sheet to the students and have them work in pairs. One student is the tutor, and the other is the learner. While students are teaching one another, I circulate through the classroom, providing help where needed. After each pair of students has solved three problems, I have the students reverse roles with their partners. I find that students understand the Hardy-Weinberg principle much more quickly and thoroughly when they are able to explain it to one another. At the end of this activity, I have each pair write a new problem on an overhead transparency. I then use these new problems as a warm-up activity for genetics.

—Marion LaFemina
Biology Teacher
Ridgewood High School
Ridgewood, NJ

16–2 (continued)

3 ASSESS

Evaluate Understanding

Ask students to write a paragraph summarizing the different types of natural selection on polygenic traits.

Reteach

Using the board or a transparency, work with students to make a concept map showing the conditions required for genetic equilibrium.

Sharpen Your Skills

One way students can model selection is to use the different-sized squares to represent individual phenotypes in a population. They can increase the number of either small or large squares to model directional selection, of medium-sized squares to model stabilizing selection, and of both small and large squares to model disruptive selection.

If your class subscribes to the iText, use it to review the Key Concepts in Section 16–2.

Those numbers can be expressed by the following equation:

$$p^2 + 2pq + q^2 = 1$$

p^2 = frequency of *AA* homozygotes

$2pq$ = the frequency of *Aa* heterozygotes

q^2 = the frequency of *aa* homozygotes

1 = the sum of frequencies of all genotypes (100%)

In a particular generation, we find that $p = 0.8$, and $q = 0.2$. How can you figure out the relative frequencies of *AA, Aa,* and *aa* individuals?

1. First, write the following equation:

   $p^2 + 2pq + q^2 = 1$ (or $A^2 + 2Aa + a^2 = 1$)

2. Fill in the values.

   $(0.8)^2 + 2(0.8 \times 0.2) + (0.2)^2 = 1$

3. Calculate.

   $(0.8 \times 0.8) + 2(0.16) + (0.2 \times 0.2) = 1$

   $0.64 + 0.32 + 0.04 = 1.00$

4. Convert the fractions to percentages.

   $0.64 \times 100 = 64\%$, so 64% is the frequency of homozygous dominant individuals (*AA*).

   $0.32 \times 100 = 32\%$, so 32% is the frequency of heterozygous recessive individuals (*Aa*).

   $0.04 \times 100 = 4\%$, so 4% is the frequency of homozygous recessive individuals (*aa*).

As long as the Hardy-Weinberg equilibrium conditions hold, neither the frequency of the genotypes nor the frequencies of the alleles (p and q) will change from generation to generation.

16–2 Section Assessment

1. **Key Concept** Describe how natural selection can affect traits controlled by single genes.
2. **Key Concept** Describe three patterns of natural selection on polygenic traits. Which one leads to two distinct phenotypes?
3. **Key Concept** How does genetic drift lead to a change in a population's gene pool?
4. **Key Concept** What is the Hardy-Weinberg principle?
5. **Critical Thinking Calculating** You are studying a population of 100 people and discover that 36 of these people are *ss* for a genetic condition. Use the Hardy-Weinberg equation to figure out the frequencies of the *S* and *s* alleles. What are the frequencies of the *SS, Ss,* and *ss* genotypes?

Sharpen Your Skills

Using Models

Demonstrate natural selection on polygenic traits by cutting a sheet of paper into squares of five different sizes to represent sizes in a population. Use the squares to model directional, stabilizing, and disruptive selection.

16–2 Section Assessment

1. It can lead to changes in allele frequencies and the evolution of traits.
2. Directional selection favors one extreme; stabilizing selection favors the middle of the range; disruptive selection favors both extremes and leads to two phenotypes.
3. Genetic drift causes random changes in allele frequencies in small populations.
4. Allele frequencies in a population remain constant unless one or more factors cause the frequencies to change.
5. SS = 12.96%; Ss = 46.08%; ss = 40.96%

BIIE 1.m

Should the Use of Antibiotics Be Restricted?

Natural selection is everywhere. One dramatic example of evolution in action poses a serious threat to public health. Many kinds of disease-causing bacteria are evolving resistance to antibiotics—drugs intended to kill them or interfere with their growth.

Antibiotics are one of medicine's greatest weapons against bacterial diseases. When antibiotics were discovered, they were called "magic bullets" and "wonder drugs" because they were so effective. They have made diseases like pneumonia much less of a threat than they were about sixty years ago. However, people may be overusing antibiotics. Doctors sometimes prescribe them for diseases for which they are not effective. Commercial feed for chickens and other farm animals is laced with antibiotics to prevent infection.

This wide use has caused many bacteria—including *Mycobacterium tuberculosis,* which causes tuberculosis—to evolve resistance to antibiotics. This resistance is a prime example of the evolution of a genetically controlled physiological trait. Resistance evolved because bacterial populations contained a few individuals with genes that enabled them to destroy, inactivate, or eliminate antibiotics. Descendants of those physiologically similar individuals survived and reproduced, and became today's resistant strains. Once-powerful antibiotics are now useless against resistant bacteria. Given this risk, should government agencies restrict the use of antibiotics?

The Viewpoints

Antibiotic Use Should Be Restricted

The danger of an incurable bacterial epidemic is so high that action must be taken on a national level as soon as possible. Doctors overuse antibiotics in humans because patients demand them. The livestock industry likes using antibiotics in animal feeds and will not change their practice unless forced to do so.

Antibiotic Use Should Not Be Restricted

Researchers are coming up with new drugs all the time. These drugs can be reserved for human use only. Doctors need to be able to prescribe antibiotics as they choose, and our food supply depends on the use of antibiotics in agriculture. The medical profession and the livestock industry need the freedom to find solutions that work best for them.

Research and Decide

1. **Analyzing the Viewpoints** To make an informed decision, learn more about this issue by consulting library and Internet resources. Then, list the advantages and disadvantages of restricting the use of antibiotics.
2. **Forming Your Opinion** Should antibiotics be restricted? Are there some situations in which such regulations would be more appropriate than others?

For: Links from the authors
Visit: PHSchool.com
Web Code: cbe-5162

BIIE 1.m

Suggest that students investigate the role patients play in the development of resistance by demanding antibiotics and then failing to take them correctly. Also, have students investigate bacterial resistance to other agents because of the widespread use of antibacterial products, ranging from disinfectant sprays to hand gels, soaps, and lotions.

Research and Decide

1. Advantages of restricting the use of antibiotics include a reduced risk of bacteria becoming resistant to antibiotics and less danger of an incurable bacterial epidemic. Disadvantages include the likelihood of more deaths and suffering from infectious diseases and a possible reduction in the food supply because of more infections in farm animals.
2. Some students might say that antibiotics should be restricted to human use or to people who have serious infectious diseases.

Students can research antibiotic resistance on the site developed by authors Ken Miller and Joe Levine.

Section 16-3

BI 8.a, BI 8.b, **BI 8.d,** BIIE 1.f

1 FOCUS

Objectives

16.3.1 ***Identify*** the condition necessary for a new species to evolve.

16.3.2 ***Describe*** the process of speciation in the Galápagos finches.

Guide for Reading

Vocabulary Preview

Introduce students to the Vocabulary terms by explaining that speciation, or the formation of new species, comes about because of one or more types of reproductive isolation: behavioral, geographic, or temporal isolation.

Reading Strategy

Suggest that students make two graphic organizers as they read to summarize the information in the two parts of the section. For example, they might make a concept map to show the types of isolating mechanisms that lead to speciation and a flowchart to show how speciation of Darwin's finches occurred.

2 INSTRUCT

Isolating Mechanisms

Address Misconceptions

Students may think that being able to mate more widely rather than just within a species would be an evolutionary advantage, not a disadvantage. Explain that attempting to mate with a member of another species almost always results in reproductive failure and therefore wastes time and energy that might have been spent mating effectively with a conspecific. Also, even if mating does take place and offspring are produced, they are likely to be less well adapted to the niche of either of the parent species and, thus, selected against. L1 L2

16–3 The Process of Speciation

BI 8.a. Students know how natural selection determines the differential survival of groups of organisms. **BI 8.b.** Students know a great diversity of species increases the chance that at least some organisms survive major changes in the environment. **BI 8.d. Students know reproductive or geographic isolation affects speciation.** **BIIE 1.f.** Distinguish between hypothesis and theory as scientific terms.

Guide for Reading

Key Concepts
- What factors are involved in the formation of new species?
- Describe the process of speciation in the Galápagos finches.

Vocabulary
speciation
reproductive isolation
behavioral isolation
geographic isolation
temporal isolation

Reading Strategy: Using Visuals Before you read, preview **Figure 16–16.** As you read about speciation of Darwin's finches, notice what happens at each step in the diagram.

(a) BI 8.b

(b) BI 8.a

Factors such as natural selection and chance events can change the relative frequencies of alleles in a population. But how do these changes lead to the formation of new species, or **speciation**?

CA (a) Recall that biologists define a species as a group of organisms that breed with one another and produce fertile offspring. This means that individuals in the same species share a common gene pool. Because a population of individuals has a shared gene pool, a genetic change that occurs in one individual can spread through the population as that individual and its offspring reproduce. If a genetic change increases fitness, that allele will eventually be found in many individuals of that population.

Isolating Mechanisms

Given this genetic definition of species, what must happen for a species to evolve into two new species? The gene pools of two populations must become separated for them to become new species. **As new species evolve, populations become reproductively isolated from each other.** When the members of two populations cannot interbreed and produce fertile offspring, **reproductive isolation** has occurred. CA (b) At that point, the populations have separate gene pools. They respond to natural selection or genetic drift as separate units. Reproductive isolation can develop in a variety of ways, including behavioral isolation, geographic isolation, and temporal isolation.

Behavioral Isolation One type of isolating mechanism, **behavioral isolation,** occurs when two populations are capable of interbreeding but have differences in courtship rituals or other reproductive strategies that involve behavior. For example, the eastern and western meadowlarks shown in **Figure 16–11** are very similar birds whose habitats overlap in the center of the United States. Members of the two species will not mate with each other, however, partly because they use different songs to attract mates. Eastern meadowlarks will not respond to western meadowlark songs, and vice versa.

Figure 16–11 The eastern meadowlark (left) and western meadowlark (right) have overlapping ranges. They do not interbreed, however, because they have different mating songs. **Applying Concepts** *What type of reproductive isolation does this situation illustrate?*

TIME SAVER — SECTION RESOURCES

Print:
- ***Teaching Resources,*** Lesson Plan 16–3, Adapted Section Summary 16–3, Adapted Worksheets 16–3, Section Summary 16–3, Worksheets 16–3, Section Review 16–3, Enrichment
- ***Reading and Study Workbook A,*** Section 16–3
- ***Adapted Reading and Study Workbook B,*** Section 16–3
- ***Issues and Decision Making,*** Issues and Decisions 16

Technology:
- ***iText,*** Section 16–3
- ***Transparencies Plus,*** Section 16–3
- ***BioDetectives DVD,*** "The Galápagos Islands: A Glimpse Into the Past"

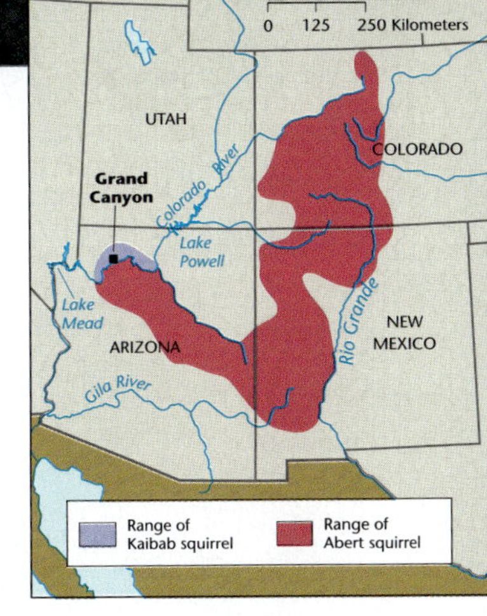

Figure 16–12  **When two populations of a species become reproductively isolated, new species can develop.** The Kaibab squirrel evolved from the Abert squirrel. The Kaibab squirrels were isolated from the main population by the Colorado River.

Geographic Isolation With **geographic isolation,** two populations are separated by geographic barriers such as rivers, mountains, or bodies of water. The Abert squirrel in **Figure 16–12,** for example, lives in the Southwest. About 10,000 years ago, the Colorado River split the species into two separate populations. Two separate gene pools formed. Genetic changes that appeared in one group were not passed to the other. Natural selection worked separately on each group and led to the formation of a distinct subspecies, the Kaibab squirrel. The Abert and Kaibab squirrels have very similar anatomical and physiological characteristics, indicating that they are closely related. However, the Kaibab squirrel differs from the Abert squirrel in significant ways, such as fur coloring.

Geographic barriers do not guarantee the formation of new species, however. Separate lakes may be linked for a time during a flood, or a land bridge may temporarily form between islands, enabling separated populations to mix. If two formerly separated populations can still interbreed, they remain a single species. Also, any potential geographic barrier may separate certain types of organisms but not others. A large river will keep squirrels and other small rodents apart, but it does not necessarily isolate bird populations.

Temporal Isolation A third isolating mechanism is **temporal isolation,** in which two or more species reproduce at different times. For example, three similar species of orchid all live in the same rain forest. Each species releases pollen only on a single day. Because the three species release pollen on different days, they cannot pollinate one another.

(a) BI 8.a

 *How can temporal isolation lead to speciation?*

Build Science Skills

Applying Concepts Divide the class into several groups, and challenge each group to brainstorm for a scenario in which a small population of a species becomes geographically isolated from the remainder of the species long enough to evolve into a separate species. Urge groups to consider both natural events and human activities when they brainstorm for ways that geographic isolation could come about. Have each group elect a spokesperson to describe their scenario to the class. In each case, ask: **Why did the geographically isolated population evolve into a different species?** *(Answers will vary depending on scenarios. Students might say, for example, that the isolated population was genetically different to begin with because of founder effect and that it became even more different through time due to different selective pressures.)* 

Use Visuals

Figure 16–12 Have students use the key to locate the range of each type of squirrel. Point out how the Colorado River effectively isolates the two types of squirrels geographically, despite the closeness of their ranges. L1 L2

Build Science Skills

Inferring Have students infer the reproductive characteristics of species most likely to be affected by temporal isolation. Ask: **What must be true about the reproductive behavior of species that are isolated by temporal isolation?** *(Their reproductive behavior must be limited to a certain time of day or a certain season.)* 

UNIVERSAL ACCESS

Inclusion/Special Needs
Create a flowchart showing in a simple way the steps that occurred in the speciation of Darwin's finches. Include the following steps: founders arriving; founders remaining geographically isolated; directional selection occurring in different environments; reproductive isolation developing; and interspecific competition leading to improved adaptation to the species' niches. L1

Advanced Learners
Invite students who need extra challenges to research the process of speciation in Hawaiian birds called honeycreepers. Like Darwin's finches, honeycreepers underwent adaptive radiation after colonizing islands with vacant niches. Ask students to share their findings with the class and to point out similarities and differences between the Hawaiian and Galápagos cases. L3

Answers to . . .

 *If two populations reproduce at different times, they are unlikely to reproduce with each other. Eventually they may become separate species.*

Figure 16–11 *Behavioral isolation*

16–3 (continued)

Testing Natural Selection in Nature

Use Visuals

Figure 16–13 Point out that the woodpecker finch uses its beak to hold a cactus spine, which it pokes into holes in trees in order to spear insects. Ask: **What tool does its beak resemble?** *(Students might say pliers or needle-nosed pliers.)* **If another species of fruit-eating finch was discovered, what type of beak do you think it would have?** *(Students are likely to infer that it would have a beak like the vegetarian tree finch, which also eats fruit.)* L2

Build Science Skills

Applying Concepts Point out that the Grants used the scientific method in their research on the Galápagos Islands. Challenge students to recall the steps typically involved in the scientific method. Assign a student to record the steps on the board. *(Ask a question, gather information and form hypothesis, experiment, record and analyze data, draw conclusion)* Then, have students describe each step of the scientific method as it applies to the Grants' research. *(For example, the Grants' problem was to demonstrate natural selection in action. Their hypotheses were that there was enough inheritable variation in beak size and shape to provide raw material for natural selection and that variation in beak size and shape produced differences in fitness.)* L1 L2

Download a worksheet on speciation for students to complete, and find additional teacher support from NSTA SciLinks.

Galápagos Islands Finches

Shape of Head and Beak						
Common Name of Finch Species	Vegetarian tree finch	Large insectivorous tree finch	Woodpecker finch	Cactus ground finch	Sharp-beaked ground finch	Large ground finch
Main Food	Fruits	Insects	Insects	Cacti	Seeds	Seeds
Feeding Adaptation	Parrotlike beak	Grasping beak	Uses cactus spines	Large crushing beak	Pointed crushing beak	Large crushing beak
Habitat	Trees	Trees	Trees	Ground	Ground	Ground

▲ **Figure 16–13** Detailed genetic studies have shown that these finches evolved from a species with a more-or-less general-purpose beak. **Formulating Hypotheses** ***Suggest how one of these beaks could have resulted from natural selection.***

Testing Natural Selection in Nature

Now that you know the basic mechanisms of evolutionary change, you might wonder if these processes can be observed in nature. The answer is yes. In fact, some of the most important studies showing natural selection in action involve descendants of the finches that Darwin observed in the Galápagos Islands.

Those finch species looked so different from one another that when Darwin first saw them, he did not realize they were all finches. He thought they were blackbirds, warblers, and other kinds of birds. The species he examined differed greatly in the sizes and shapes of their beaks and in their feeding habits, as shown in **Figure 16–13.** Some species fed on small seeds, while others ate large seeds with thick shells. One species used cactus spines to pry insects from dead wood. One species, not shown here, even pecked at the tails of large sea birds and drank their blood!

Once Darwin discovered that these birds were all finches, he hypothesized that they had descended from a common ancestor. Over time, he proposed, natural selection shaped the beaks of different bird populations as they adapted to eat different foods.

That was a reasonable hypothesis. But was there any way to test it? No one thought so, until the work of Peter and Rosemary Grant from Princeton University proved otherwise. For more than twenty years, the Grants, shown in **Figure 16–14,** have been collaborating to band and measure finches on the Galápagos Islands. They realized that Darwin's hypothesis relied on two testable assumptions. First, in order for beak size and shape to evolve, there must be enough heritable variation in those traits to provide raw material for natural selection. Second, differences in beak size and shape must produce differences in fitness that cause natural selection to occur.

For: Links on speciation
Visit: www.SciLinks.org
Web Code: cbn-5163

BIO INSIGHTS — FACTS AND FIGURES

Fruit fly speciation

The North American fruit fly *Rhagoletis pomonella* appears to be in the process of speciation. Before the 1800s, *R. pomonella* infested only hawthorn trees. Then, when apple trees were introduced to North America, the fruit fly began infesting them as well. Today, the species exists in separate populations on each type of fruit tree. The different populations do not interbreed and have some genetic differences. Although they are still one species, they appear to be on their way to becoming separate species.

The Grants tested these hypotheses on the medium ground finch on Daphne Major, one of the Galápagos Islands. This island is large enough to support good-sized finch populations, yet small enough to enable the Grants to catch and identify nearly every bird belonging to the species under study.

Variation The Grants first identified and measured as many individual birds as possible on the island. They recorded which birds were still living and which had died, which had succeeded in breeding and which had not. For each individual, they also recorded anatomical characteristics such as wing length, leg length, beak length, beak depth, beak color, feather colors, and total mass. Many of these characteristics appeared in bell-shaped distributions typical of polygenic traits. These data indicate that there is great variation of heritable traits among the Galápagos finches.

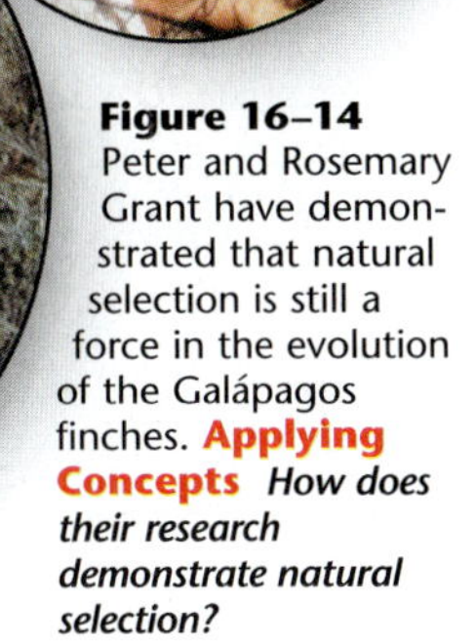

Figure 16–14 Peter and Rosemary Grant have demonstrated that natural selection is still a force in the evolution of the Galápagos finches. **Applying Concepts** *How does their research demonstrate natural selection?*

Natural Selection Other researchers who had visited the Galápagos did not see the different finches competing or eating different foods. During the rainy season, when these researchers visited, there is plenty of food. Under these conditions, finches often eat the most available type of food. During dry-season drought, however, some foods become scarce, and others disappear altogether. At that time, differences in beak size can mean the difference between life and death. To survive, birds become feeding specialists. Each species selects the type of food its beak handles best. Birds with big, heavy beaks, for example, select big, thick seeds that no other species can crack open.

CA
a

a BI 8.b

The Grants' most interesting discovery was that individual birds with different-sized beaks had different chances of survival during a drought. When food for the finches was scarce, individuals with the largest beaks were more likely to survive, as shown in **Figure 16–15.** Beak size also plays a role in mating behavior, because big-beaked birds tend to mate with other big-beaked birds. The Grants observed that average beak size in that finch population increased dramatically over time. This change in beak size is an example of directional selection operating on an anatomical trait.

By documenting natural selection in the wild, the Grants provided evidence of the process of evolution: The next generation of finches had larger beaks than did the generation before selection had occurred. An important result of this work was their finding that natural selection takes place frequently—and sometimes very rapidly. Changes in the food supply on the Galápagos caused measurable fluctuations in the finch populations over a period of only decades. This is markedly different from the slow, gradual evolution that Darwin envisioned.

▼ **Figure 16–15** This graph shows the survival rate of one species of ground-feeding finches, the medium ground finch, *Geospiza fortis.* **Using Tables and Graphs** *What trend does this graph show?*

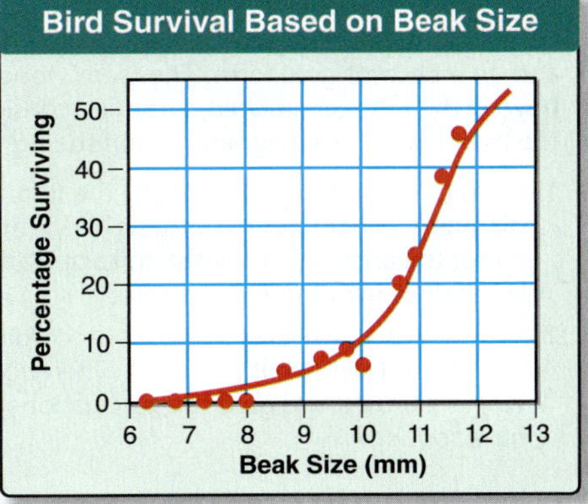

CHECKPOINT *What type of natural selection did the Grants observe in the Galápagos?*

Build Science Skills

Inferring Challenge students to assume the role of an evolutionary biologist. First, have them choose a population that they will study. Then, ask them to list the kinds of observations they would need to make to determine if the population were undergoing natural selection. *(You would need to observe evidence of inheritable variation in the population and evidence that different phenotypes vary in fitness.)* Ask: **What might you observe if speciation were occurring?** *(You might observe that various populations of the species had become separated so they no longer shared the same gene pool. You also might observe genetic differences between the populations.)* L2 L3

Use Visuals

Figure 16–15 Challenge students to predict how the graph would be different if birds with medium-sized beaks were more likely to survive. *(It would resemble a normal curve.)* Ask: **What type of natural selection would this represent?** *(Stabilizing selection)* L1 L2

Answers to . . .

CHECKPOINT *Directional selection*

Figure 16–13 *Sample answer: For the large ground finch, natural selection favored birds with large, heavy beaks that could crush tough seeds.*

Figure 16–14 *Their research shows that birds with larger beaks have a better chance of surviving during a drought and that average beak size has increased dramatically over time as a result.*

Figure 16–15 *The larger a bird's beak, the greater its chances of survival.*

BIO INSIGHTS — FACTS AND FIGURES

Birds and flies in Hawaii

In the process of adaptive radiation on the Galápagos Islands, one species of finches gave rise to many species of finches. Similarly, five million years of adaptive radiation in Hawaiian birds known as honeycreepers resulted in a wide array of beak shapes and as many as 43 species. However, human actions have resulted in the extinction of most of these species.

Diverging physical traits do not cause all speciation. In Hawaii, a variety of courtship songs has separated the native *Drosophila* fruit fly into more than 500 species! Some Hawaiian *Drosophila* sound more like cicadas than flies. Others make a cricketlike noise. Still others make a sound like that of a North American fruit fly, but they create the sound by vibrating their abdomen instead of their wings.

16–3 (continued)

Speciation in Darwin's Finches

Quick View Video

Discovery School DVD Encourage students to view track 5 "The Galápagos Islands: A Glimpse Into the Past" on the *BioDetectives* DVD.

Build Science Skills

Applying Concepts Challenge students to apply the concept of founder effect to the example of Darwin's finches. Ask: **How did the first finches to arrive on the Galápagos compare genetically with finches on the mainland?** *(They had only a tiny fraction of the total genetic variability of the mainland finches and, through chance, may not have been genetically representative of mainland finches.)* L2

Analyzing Data

Explain to students that the arrows in the diagrams imply evolutionary relationships. For example, in hypothesis A, both B and G are presumed to have evolved from A.

Answers

1. Hypothesis A suggests that Lake 1 and Lake 2 brown fishes are unrelated, and the gold fishes from the two lakes are unrelated. This differs from hypothesis B, which suggests that Lake 1 gold fishes evolved from Lake 2 gold fishes and that Lake 2 brown fishes evolved from Lake 1 brown fishes.
2. In hypothesis A, the brown (B) and gold (G) fish populations each evolved independently. In hypothesis B, the brown (B) fish populations in both lakes evolved from fish type A in Lake 1, and the gold (G) fish populations in both lakes evolved from fish type A in Lake 2.
3. This evidence supports hypothesis A.
4. Scientists would need to ask whether fishes from the two lakes can interbreed and produce fertile offspring. If not, then they are members of different species.

Quick View Video

Discovery School Video To find out more about ongoing research on the Galápagos, view track 5 "The Galápagos Islands: A Glimpse Into the Past" on the *BioDetectives* DVD.

Speciation in Darwin's Finches

The Grants' work demonstrates that finch beak size can be changed by natural selection. If we combine this information with other evolutionary concepts you have learned in this chapter, we can show how natural selection can lead to speciation. We can devise a hypothetical scenario for the evolution of all Galápagos finches from a single group of founding birds.  **Speciation in the Galápagos finches occurred by founding of a new population, geographic isolation, changes in the new population's gene pool, reproductive isolation, and ecological competition.**

Founders Arrive Many years ago, a few finches from the South American mainland—species A—flew or were blown to one of the Galápagos Islands, as shown in **Figure 16–16.** Finches are small birds that do not usually fly far over open water. These birds may have gotten lost, or they may have been blown off course by a storm. Once they arrived on one of the islands, they managed to survive and reproduce.

Geographic Isolation Later on, some birds from species A crossed to another island in the Galápagos group. Because these birds do not usually fly over open water, they rarely move from island to island. Thus, finch populations on the two islands were essentially isolated from each other and no longer shared a common gene pool.

CHECKPOINT *How did finches arrive in the Galápagos Islands?*

Analyzing Data

How Are These Fish Related?

A research team studied two lakes in an area that sometimes experiences flooding. Each lake contained two types of similar fish: a dull brown form and an iridescent gold form. The team wondered how all the fish were related, and they considered the two hypotheses diagrammed on the right.

Hypothesis A

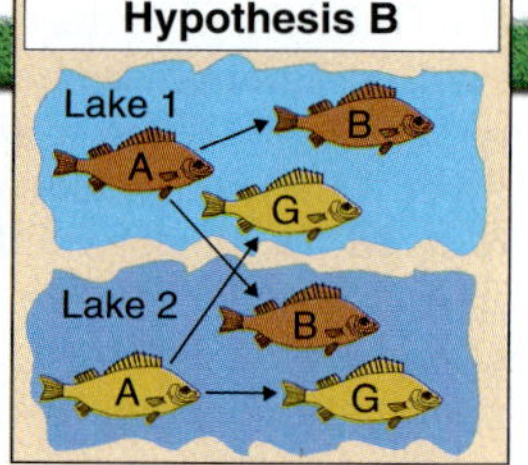

A = Possible ancestor
B = Contemporary brown form
G = Contemporary gold form
→ Shows possible line of descent

1. **Interpreting Graphics** Study the two diagrams. What does hypothesis A indicate about the ancestry of the fish in Lake 1 and Lake 2? What does hypothesis B indicate?
2. **Comparing and Contrasting** According to the two hypotheses, what is the key difference in the way the brown and gold fish populations might have formed?
3. **Drawing Conclusions** A DNA analysis showed that the brown and gold fish from Lake 1 are the most closely related. Which hypothesis does this evidence support?
4. **Asking Questions** To help determine whether the brown and gold fish are members of separate species, what question might scientists ask?

BIO INSIGHTS — FACTS AND FIGURES

Not just finches

Among birds on the Galápagos Islands, Darwin's finches are better known than the mockingbirds, but it was the four species of mockingbirds that first drew Darwin's attention to the diversity of species on the islands. Darwin discovered that three of the mockingbird species were each confined to a single island, and it surprised him to learn that the islands were all similar and within sight of one another. Like Darwin's finches, the mockingbird species had evolved differences primarily in the size and shape of their beaks that reflected the different food sources they relied upon.

Figure 16–16 **Speciation in the Galápagos finches occurred by founding of new populations, geographic isolation, gene pool changes, reproductive isolation, and ecological competition.** Small groups of finches moved from one island to another, became reproductively isolated, and evolved into new species.

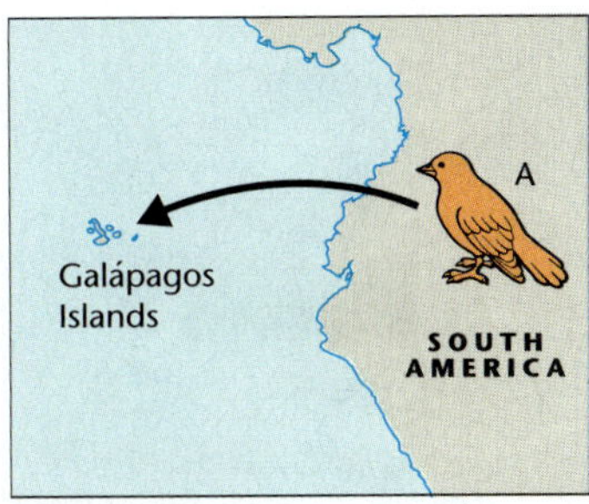

Founders Arrive
A few finches travel from South America to one of the islands. There, they survive and reproduce.

Geographic Isolation
Some birds from species A cross to a second island. The two populations no longer share a gene pool.

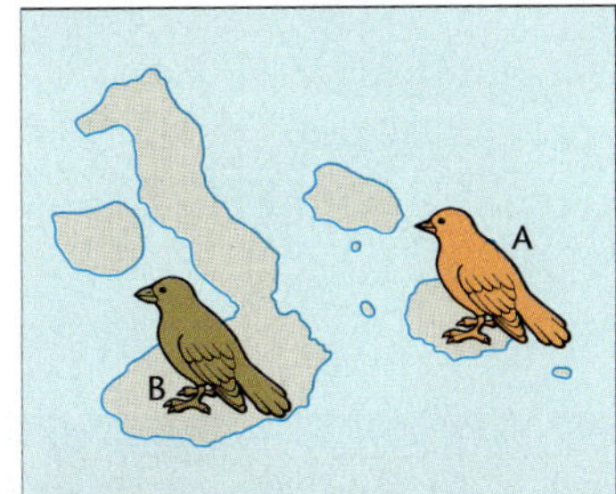

Changes in the Gene Pool
Seed sizes on the second island favor birds with larger beaks. The population on the second island evolves into a population, B, with larger beaks. Eventually, populations A and B evolve into separate species.

Changes in the Gene Pool Over time, populations on each island became adapted to their local environments. The plants growing on the first island may have produced small thin-shelled seeds, whereas the plants on the second island may have produced larger thick-shelled seeds. On the second island, directional selection would favor individuals with larger, heavier beaks. These birds could crack open and eat the large seeds more easily. Thus, birds with large beaks would be better able to survive on the second island. Over time, natural selection would have caused that population to evolve larger beaks, forming a separate population, B.

Reproductive Isolation Now, imagine that a few birds from the second island cross back to the first island. Will the population-A birds breed with the population-B birds? Probably not. These finches choose their mates carefully. As part of their courtship behavior, they inspect a potential partner's beak very closely. Finches prefer to mate with birds that have the same-sized beak as they do. In other words, big-beaked birds prefer to mate with other big-beaked birds, and smaller-beaked birds prefer to mate with other smaller-beaked birds. Because the birds on the two islands have different-sized beaks, it is likely that they would not choose to mate with each other. Thus, differences in beak size, combined with mating behavior, could lead to reproductive isolation. The gene pools of the two bird populations remain isolated from each other—even when individuals live together in the same place. The two populations have now become separate species.

Ecological Competition As these two new species live together in the same environment (the first island), they compete with each other for available seeds. During the dry season, individuals that are most different from each other have the highest fitness. The more specialized birds have less competition for certain kinds of seeds and other foods, and the competition among individual finches is also reduced. Over time, species evolve in a way that increases the differences between them. The species-B birds on the first island may evolve into a new species, C.

Continued Evolution This process of isolation on different islands, genetic change, and reproductive isolation probably repeated itself time and time again across the entire Galápagos island chain. Over many generations, it produced the 13 different finch species found there today. Use the steps in this illustration to explain how other Darwin finches, such as the vegetarian tree finch that feeds on fruit, might have evolved.

Make Connections

Environmental Science Introduce students to the concept of adaptive radiation, which is the evolution of many diversely adapted species from a common ancestor. Explain that Darwin's finches could not have evolved into so many different species if the niche resources they found had already been put to use by other birds. Point out that the Galápagos are volcanic islands that at one time had many available niche resources for land birds. Ask: **Besides the formation of islands by volcanoes, how might an area come to support so many niches established by invading species through adaptive radiation?** *(One possible answer is the occurrence of a natural disaster, such as a forest fire or flood, that destroys habitats. As the original habitats gradually return, the species reestablish niches.)* L2

Build Science Skills

Inferring Point out the role of ecological competition in the speciation of Darwin's finches. Ask: **How does competition increase the differences between species?** *(Individuals that are more specialized and less like the other species have less competition and higher fitness. This leads to an increase in the differences between the species.)* L2

Use Visuals

Figure 16–16 Challenge students to create new captions for the sequence of drawings to explain how another species of Darwin's finches, such as the vegetarian tree finch, might have evolved. Ask volunteers to share their captions with the class. L2

CHECKPOINT *They flew, or were blown, from South America.*

16–3 (continued)

Studying Evolution Since Darwin

Build Science Skills

Applying Concepts Challenge students to explain in two or three sentences the process of speciation, using concepts of Mendelian inheritance. Ask volunteers to share their statements with the class. L2

3 ASSESS

Evaluate Understanding

Call on students at random to name and give examples of each of the ways reproductive isolation comes about.

Reteach

Have students write on a note card a brief summary of each step in the speciation of Darwin's finches. Then, have students shuffle the cards and try to put them back in the correct order.

Writing in Science

Assess students' paragraphs on the basis of their completeness, accuracy, and organization. The paragraphs should begin with a topic sentence, such as the Grants' hypothesis, followed by sentences providing details related to the topic sentence. Paragraphs should also include the conclusions the Grants reached based on their research.

If your class subscribes to the iText, use it to review the Key Concepts in Section 16–3.

▲ **Figure 16–17** Paleontologists study fossils to find clues about previous life-forms.

Studying Evolution Since Darwin

It is useful to review and critique the strengths and weaknesses of evolutionary theory. Darwin made bold assumptions about heritable variation, the age of Earth, and relationships among organisms. New data from genetics, physics, and biochemistry could have proved him wrong on many counts. They didn't. Scientific evidence supports the theory that living species descended with modification from common ancestors that lived in the ancient past.

Limitations of Research The Grants' research clearly shows the effects of directional selection in nature. The Grants' data also show how competition and climate change affect natural selection. The work does have limitations. For example, while the Grants observed changes in the size of the finches' beaks, they did not observe the formation of a new species. Scientists predict that as new fossils are found, they will continue to expand our understanding of how species evolved.

(a) BIIE 1.f

CA (a)

Unanswered Questions The studies of the Grants fit into an enormous body of scientific work supporting the theory of evolution. Millions of fossils show that life has existed on Earth for more than 3 billion years and that organisms have changed dramatically over this time. These fossils form just a part of the evidence supporting the conclusion that life has evolved. Remember that a scientific theory is defined as a well-tested explanation that accounts for a broad range of observations. Evolutionary theory fits this definition. To be sure, many new discoveries have led to new hypotheses that refine and expand Darwin's original ideas. No scientist suggests that all evolutionary processes are fully understood. Many unanswered questions remain.

Why is understanding evolution important? Because evolution continues today, driving changes in the living world such as drug resistance in bacteria and viruses, and pesticide resistance in insects. Evolutionary theory helps us understand and respond to these changes in ways that improve human life.

16–3 Section Assessment

1. **Key Concept** How is reproductive isolation related to the formation of new species?
2. **Key Concept** What type of isolating mechanism was important in the formation of Galápagos finch species?
3. Explain how behavior can play a role in the evolution of species.
4. What recent research findings support Darwin's theory of evolution?
5. **Critical Thinking Inferring** Suppose that a drought on an island eliminates all but plants that produce large, tough seeds. All the finches on the island have very small beaks. How might this environmental change impact the survival of this finch population?

Writing in Science

Summarizing
Write a paragraph that summarizes the Grants' research with Galápagos finches. Your summary should include the main points of the research. *Hint:* The first sentence in your summary might state the Grants' hypothesis.

16–3 Section Assessment

1. For new species to evolve, populations must be reproductively isolated from each other.
2. Geographic isolation
3. Behavioral isolation can occur when two populations that could otherwise interbreed do not because of differences in behavior. This can lead to the evolution of different species.
4. Peter and Rosemary Grant have provided evidence of the process of evolution through their studies of changes of beak size and shape in Galápagos finches.
5. Only those finches that can find another food source or those with beaks large enough to crack the seeds will survive.

Exploration

 BI 7.d, BI 8.b, **BI 8.d**, 6IIE 7.e, 8IIE 9.b, BIIE 1.c

Investigating Genetic Diversity in Bacteria

Genetic diversity can make a population of organisms more adaptable. Some bacteria are able to survive in the presence of antibiotics that kill other bacteria. In this investigation, you will test a population of bacteria for the presence of antibiotic-resistant bacteria.

Problem **How common are antibiotic-resistant bacteria?**

Materials

- liquid bacterial culture
- sterile swabs
- sterile agar plate
- glass-marking pencil
- antibiotic paper disks
- forceps
- transparent tape
- 70% alcohol
- metric ruler

Skills Observing, Analyzing Data

Procedure

   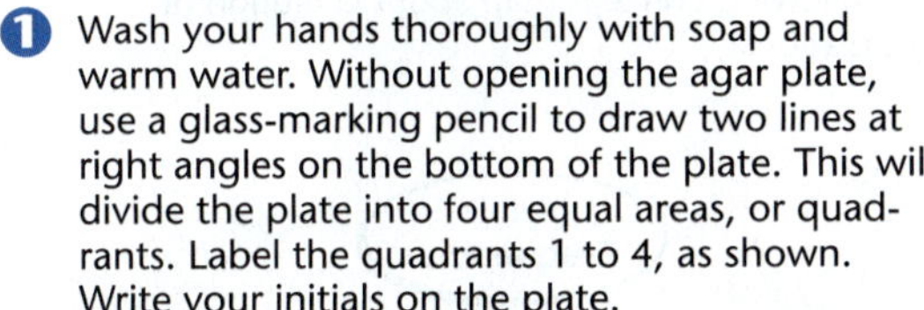

1. Wash your hands thoroughly with soap and warm water. Without opening the agar plate, use a glass-marking pencil to draw two lines at right angles on the bottom of the plate. This will divide the plate into four equal areas, or quadrants. Label the quadrants 1 to 4, as shown. Write your initials on the plate.
2. Wearing plastic gloves, dip a sterile swab in the bacterial culture. Remove the cover of the agar plate and rub the swab gently over the entire surface of the agar. Immediately replace the cover. Follow your teacher's directions for disposing of the swab.
3. Remove the cover of the agar plate again. Use clean forceps to place an antibiotic disk on the agar in the center of each quadrant. Replace the cover; then tape the plate closed.
4. Place the plate upside down in the area designated by your teacher.
5. Return the forceps to your teacher for disinfection. Wipe your work surface with 70% alcohol and a paper towel. Wash your hands well with soap and warm water before leaving the lab.
6. After 24 hours, observe the growth of bacteria around each antibiotic disk. Record your observations. **CAUTION:** *Do not open the plate.*
7. Use the metric ruler to measure the diameter of the zone of reduced bacterial growth, called the zone of inhibition, around each antibiotic disk. Record the diameter of each zone of inhibition.
8. Carefully observe the zones of inhibition. Do you see any evidence of bacterial growth there? Record your observations. Give the used plate to your teacher for safe disposal. Wipe your work surface with 70% alcohol and a paper towel. Wash your hands well with soap and warm water before leaving the lab.

Analyze and Conclude

1. **Observing** How did the antibiotic disks affect the growth of the bacteria?
2. **Classifying** What type of selection (directional, stabilizing, or disruptive) occurred in this experiment? Explain your answer.
3. **Drawing Conclusions** Did your data support the idea that antibiotic-resistant bacteria are common? Explain your answer.
4. **Evaluating** How do you know your data and conclusion are valid? (*Hint*: Compare your data and conclusion with those of other students.)

Go Further

Applying Concepts Investigate genetic diversity further by using your school library and the Internet to research the use of wild relatives of food crops to increase genetic variation in plants.

Exploration

 BI 7.d, BI 8.b, **BI 8.d**, 6IIE 7.e, 8IIE 9.b, BIIE 1.c

Objective Students will be able to observe how antibiotics affect bacteria cultures. L2

Skills Focus Observing, Analyzing Data

Time 15 minutes one day; 30 minutes the next day

Advance Prep
- Provide a liquid culture of noninfectious bacteria, such as *E. coli* obtained from a biological supply house. Do not use *Serratia marcescens* or *Bacillus subtilis*.
- Students with weakened immunity, immunosuppressive or cancer therapy, or alcohol or drug abuse should not participate in the lab. School administrators and parents or guardians should be notified of the lab and its risks to these students.

Safety
- Stress the need to handle the bacteria with great care.
- Make sure that students wear disposable plastic gloves when handling the bacterial culture. Dispose of the gloves properly.
- Supervise the disposal of used swabs and plates in a plastic container filled with dilute bleach.
- After steps 5 and 8, wipe down all surfaces with dilute bleach and have students thoroughly wash their hands with soap and warm water.
- Read the safety information on the MSDS for alcohol prior to doing the lab.

Teaching Tip **Ask: How do you predict the antibiotic disks will affect the bacteria?** (*Students might predict that the disks will prevent the bacteria from growing around them.*)

Expected Outcome Students are likely to observe limited bacterial growth around the antibiotic disks.

Go Further

Improvement of food crops through plant breeding requires genetic variation in traits, such as resistance to disease, that must be sought in the wild relatives of the food crops.

Procedure

4. Provide students with a warm, dark place to put their disks.

Analyze and Conclude

1. The antibiotic disks reduced the growth of the bacteria nearby.
2. Directional selection occurred in this experiment because the genes of the bacteria that were susceptible to the antibiotic have been lost.
3. Answers will depend on the data. In general, some bacterial growth will be observed around most or all of the antibiotic disks. This suggests that antibiotic-resistant bacteria are common enough that the swab deposited some in each zone of inhibition.
4. Students are likely to say their data and conclusions are valid because other students obtained the same or similar results.

Chapter 16 Study Guide

Study Tip

Have pairs of students quiz each other on the Vocabulary terms. Suggest that students review the answers to the Key Concept questions in the Section Assessments.

Thinking Visually

1. Genetic drift
2. Single-gene traits
3. Stabilizing selection
4. Disruptive selection

Chapter 16 Assessment

Reviewing Content

1. a 2. a 3. b 4. b 5. c 6. b 7. b 8. c 9. c 10. b

Understanding Concepts

11. The relative frequency of an allele is the number of times that the allele occurs in a gene pool compared with the number of times other alleles occur. For example, there are two alleles for the gene that controls fur color in mice. If one of the alleles is present in half the members of the population, its frequency is 50 percent.

12. In sexual reproduction, alleles can recombine to produce different genotypes, resulting in different phenotypes and hence variation within a population.

13. The number of phenotypes produced for a given trait depends on how many genes control the trait.

14. A single-gene trait is a trait controlled by one gene.

15. A polygenic trait is controlled by two or more genes, and each gene often has two or more alleles. As a result, there can be many possible phenotypes, represented by a bell curve.

Chapter 16 Study Guide

16–1 Genes and Variation

Key Concepts 

- In genetic terms, evolution is any change in the relative frequency of alleles in a population.
- Biologists have discovered that there are two main sources of genetic variation: mutations and the genetic shuffling that results from sexual reproduction.
- The number of phenotypes produced for a given trait depends on how many genes control the trait.

Vocabulary

gene pool, p. 394
relative frequency, p. 394
single-gene trait, p. 395
polygenic trait, p. 396

16–2 Evolution as Genetic Change

Key Concepts BI 7.a, BI 7.e, BI 7.f, BI 8.c

- Natural selection on single-gene traits can lead to changes in allele frequencies and thus to evolution.
- Natural selection can affect the distributions of phenotypes in any of three ways: directional selection, stabilizing selection, or disruptive selection.
- In small populations, individuals that carry a particular allele may leave more descendants than other individuals, just by chance. Over time, a series of chance occurrences of this type can cause an allele to become common in a population.
- The Hardy-Weinberg principle states that allele frequencies in a large, randomly mating population will remain constant if immigration, emigration, and mutation do not take place and if natural selection does not place selective pressure on the population.

Vocabulary

directional selection, p. 398
stabilizing selection, p. 399
disruptive selection, p. 399
genetic drift, p. 399
founder effect, p. 400
Hardy-Weinberg principle, p. 400
genetic equilibrium, p. 400

16–3 The Process of Speciation

Key Concepts BI 8.a, BI 8.b, BI 8.d, BIIE 1.f

- As new species evolve, populations become reproductively isolated from each other.
- Speciation in the Galápagos finches occurred by founding of a new population, geographic isolation, changes in the new population's gene pool, reproductive isolation, and ecological competition.

Vocabulary

speciation, p. 404
reproductive isolation, p. 404
behavioral isolation, p. 404
geographic isolation, p. 405
temporal isolation, p. 405

Thinking Visually

Using the information in this chapter, complete the following concept map about evolution of populations:

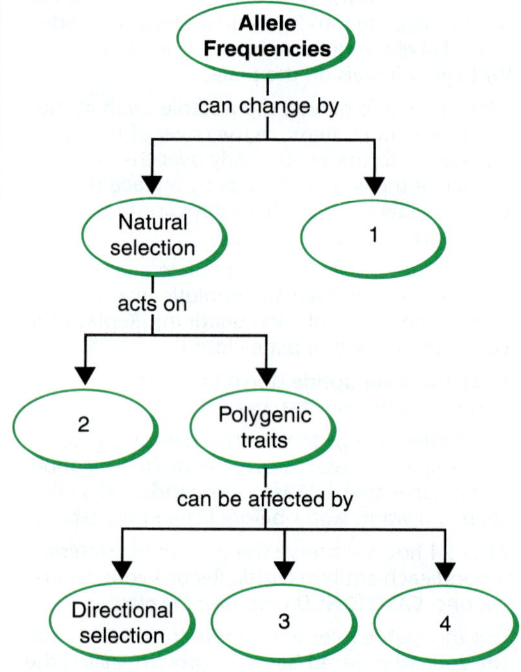

TIME SAVER

CHAPTER RESOURCES

Print:

- ***Teaching Resources,*** Chapter Vocabulary Review, Graphic Organizer, Chapter 16 Tests: Levels A and B

Technology:

- ***iText,*** Chapter 16 Assessment
- ***Computer Test Bank,*** Chapter 16 Test

Reviewing Content

Choose the letter that best answers the question or completes the statement.

1. The combined genetic information of all members of a particular population forms a
   a. gene pool. c. phenotype.
   b. niche. d. population.
2. The success of an organism in surviving and reproducing is a measure of its
   a. fitness. c. speciation.
   b. polygenic traits. d. gene pool.
3. Traits that are controlled by more than one gene, such as human height, are known as
   a. single-gene traits. c. recessive traits.
   b. polygenic traits. d. dominant traits.
4. The type of selection in which individuals of average size have greater fitness than small or large individuals is called
   a. disruptive selection.
   b. stabilizing selection.
   c. directional selection.
   d. genetic drift.
5. The type of selection in which individuals at one end of a curve have the highest fitness is called
   a. stabilizing selection.
   b. disruptive selection.
   c. directional selection.
   d. the founder effect.
6. If coat color in a rabbit population is a polygenic trait, which process might have produced the graph below?

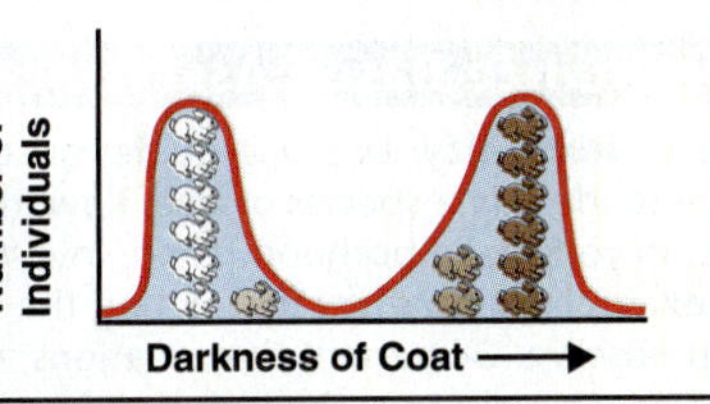

   a. stabilizing selection
   b. disruptive selection
   c. directional selection
   d. genetic equilibrium
7. A random change in a small population's allele frequency is known as
   a. a gene pool.
   b. genetic drift.
   c. variation.
   d. fitness.

Interactive textbook with assessment at PHSchool.com 

8. A change in allele frequency that results from the migration of a small subgroup of a population is called
   a. natural selection.
   b. the Hardy-Weinberg principle.
   c. the founder effect.
   d. genetic equilibrium.
9. A group of individuals of the same species that interbreed make up a
   a. species. c. population.
   b. gene pool. d. genetic drift.
10. The evolution of Darwin's finches is an example of
   a. equilibrium. c. stabilizing selection.
   b. speciation. d. artificial selection.

Understanding Concepts

11. Explain what the term *relative frequency* means. Include an example in your answer.
12. Explain why sexual reproduction is a source of genetic variation.
13. Explain what determines the number of phenotypes for a given trait.
14. What is meant by the term *single-gene trait*?
15. Why are certain polygenic traits represented by a bell curve?
16. Define evolution in genetic terms.
17. How are speciation and reproductive isolation related?
18. How do stabilizing selection and disruptive selection differ?
19. What is genetic drift? In what kinds of situations is it likely to occur?
20. What is genetic equilibrium? What conditions are required to maintain genetic equilibrium?
21. Explain how isolation of groups can be involved in speciation.
22. What two testable assumptions were the basis for Darwin's hypothesis about the evolution of the Galápagos finches?
23. What evidence did the work of Rosemary and Peter Grant provide that strengthened Darwin's hypothesis about finch evolution in the Galápagos Islands?
24. Explain how the Galápagos finches may have evolved.

TIME SAVER — HOMEWORK GUIDE

Section:	Questions:
Section 16–1	1–3, 11–15
Section 16–2	4–8, 16, 18–20
Section 16–3	9, 10, 17, 21–29, 30–32

If your class subscribes to the iText, your students can go online for an interactive version of the Student Edition and a self-test.

(Continued from page 412)

16. Evolution can be defined as a change in the relative frequency of alleles in the gene pool of a population.

17. Speciation occurs only when populations are reproductively isolated. Reproductively isolated populations have different gene pools and eventually form new species.

18. In stabilizing selection, individuals near the center of the curve have higher fitness than individuals at either end. In disruptive selection, individuals at both ends of the curve have higher fitness than individuals near the center.

19. Genetic drift is the random change in allele frequencies in a population. It is most likely to occur in small populations or when a small group of organisms colonizes a new habitat.

20. Genetic equilibrium occurs when the allele frequencies in a population remain constant. Five conditions are required to maintain genetic equilibrium: random mating, extremely large population size, no movement into or out of the population, no mutations, and no natural selection.

21. When two populations of a species become isolated, each group can evolve independently until they become separate species.

22. The assumptions were that there had to be enough inheritable variation to provide raw material for natural selection, and the variation, such as differences in beak size, must produce differences in fitness.

23. The Grants showed that beak size changed as a result of changes in food supply. This showed that the various Galápagos finches could have evolved from a common ancestor.

24. Students' answers should be consistent with the material on pages 408–409.

Chapter 16 Assessment

Critical Thinking

25. The shortest length of beak is 6 mm. About 2 percent of these birds have a beak this length.

26. Species A: 9.5 mm; Species B: 14.5 mm; Species C: 22 mm

27. The range is from 15.5 mm to 22 mm.

28. Species A probably eats small seeds. Species B can probably eat seeds larger than those eaten by species A. Species C can probably eat seeds that are larger than those eaten by either species A or species B.

29. The limited genetic variation in the isolated individuals might make them less able to adapt to changing conditions, and this would threaten their survival. However, by chance, they could possess genetic traits that made them especially well suited to the new environment, and this would enhance their survival.

30. The Grants tested this hypothesis by measuring the survival of birds with different sizes of beaks. Their data supported Darwin's hypothesis by showing that fitness varied with beak size.

31. It might lead to the death of the individual organism. It also might threaten the long-term survival of a species unless the species evolved the ability to use other food sources.

32. One hypothesis may be that the other violets are the result of variation arising from genetic recombination between two plant species.

Focus on the BIG Idea

Ecology involves the study of interactions among populations of organisms and their environment. Changes in these interactions that occur over time result in evolution.

Chapter 16 Assessment

Critical Thinking

The graph below shows data on the lengths of the beaks of three species of Darwin's finches. The percentage of individuals in each category of beak length is given. Use this information to answer questions 25–28.

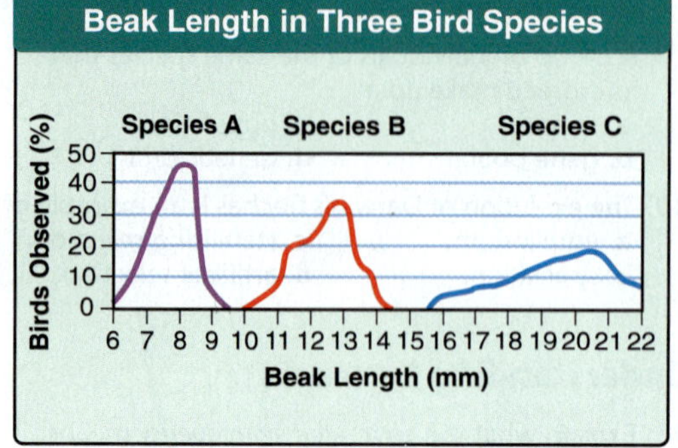

25. **Interpreting Graphics** What is the shortest beak length observed in species A? About what percentage of the birds of species A have this beak length?

26. **Interpreting Graphics** What are the longest beak lengths of each of the three species?

27. **Interpreting Graphics** What is the range of beak lengths for the birds of species C?

28. **Inferring** Based on these data, what can you infer about the sizes of the seeds eaten by each of these species of birds?

29. **Applying Concepts** Suppose a rock slide isolates a very small number of animals from the rest of their population. How might this reproductive isolation impact the long-term survival of the new, smaller population? (*Hint*: Think of the role that genetic variation might play, both positively and negatively.)

30. **Evaluating** Darwin hypothesized that natural selection shaped the beaks of different finch populations on the Galápagos Islands. Describe how the Grants tested this hypothesis. Did their data support or refute Darwin's hypothesis? Explain.

31. **Inferring** How might a limited resource, such as food, affect the survival of an individual organism? How might a severe limitation affect the long-term survival of a species?

32. **Formulating Hypotheses** A botanist identifies two distinct species of violets growing in a field. Also in the field are several other types of violets that, although somewhat similar to the two known species, appear to be new species. Develop a hypothesis explaining how the new species may have originated.

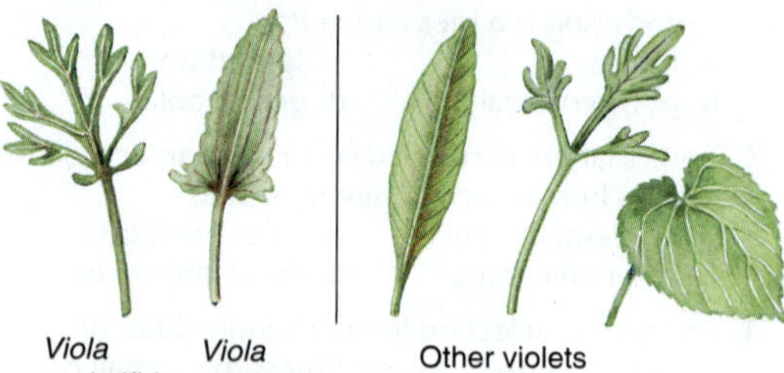

Focus on the BIG Idea

Evolution Sometimes biologists say, "Evolution is ecology over time." Use what you learned in Unit 2 to explain that statement.

Writing in Science

Write a summary of the ways in which natural selection operates on polygenic traits. (*Hint*: Use the graphs in **Figures 16–6, 16–7,** and **16–8** to help identify the main ideas.)

Performance-Based Assessment

In Your Community Use field guides or scientific literature to identify a species of tree, flowering plant, or insect in your neighborhood. Then, investigate several examples of that species, noting the variations that you observe. Document the variations, using descriptive notes along with photographs or drawings. Describe how the variations may have contributed to the evolution of the species.

For: An interactive self-test
Visit: PHSchool.com
Web Code: cba-5160

Writing in Science

Students' summaries should clearly and correctly explain, and also distinguish among, the three types of polygenic selection represented in the figures: stabilizing, disruptive, and directional selection.

Performance-Based Assessment

Variations might include differences in size, shape, color, and form. In their responses, students should demonstrate an understanding of the factors that influence evolution.

Your students can independently test their knowledge of the chapter and print out their test results for your files.

Standards Practice

Online at PHSchool.com

Test-Taking Tip If you have trouble answering a question, make a mark beside it and go on. (Do not write in this book.) You may find information in later questions that will allow you to eliminate some answer choices in your unanswered question.

Directions: Choose the letter that best answers the question or completes the statement.

1. Which of the following conditions is likely to result in speciation?
   A random mating
   B small population size
   C no migrations into or out of the population
   D absence of natural selection
2. Which of the following is a source of genetic variation?
   I. Mutations
   II. Polygenic traits
   III. Genetic shuffling that results from sexual reproduction
   A I only
   B I and III only
   C II and III only
   D I, II, and III
3. In a population of lizards, the smallest and largest lizards are more easily preyed upon than middle-sized lizards. What kind of natural selection is most likely to occur in this situation?
   A genetic drift
   B sexual selection
   C stabilizing selection
   D directional selection
4. When two species reproduce at different times, the situation is called
   A temporal isolation.
   B speciation.
   C temporal selection.
   D geographic isolation.
5. A situation in which a population's allele frequencies remain relatively constant is called
   A genetic equilibrium.
   B a gene pool.
   C fitness.
   D genetic variation.

Questions 6–8 Each of the lettered choices below refers to the following numbered statements. Select the best lettered choice. A choice may be used once, more than once, or not at all.

A Fitness
B Single-gene trait
C Polygenic trait
D Gene pool

6. The combined genetic information of all members of a particular population
7. Survival and reproduction of individuals best suited to their environment
8. Characteristic of the traits that Mendel tracked in pea plants

Questions 9–10

The graphs show the changes in crab color at one beach.

Graph A (1950)

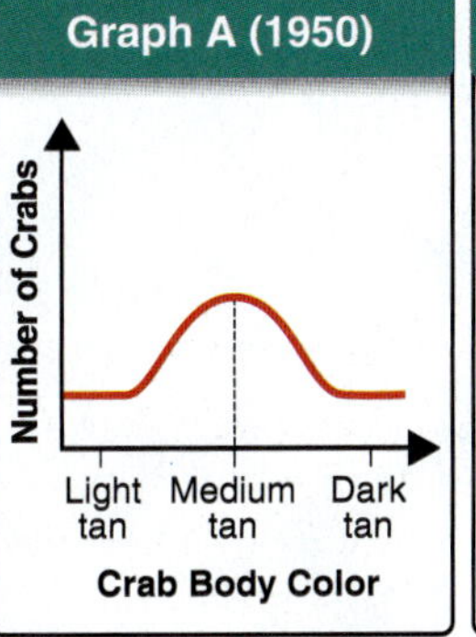

Graph B (1990)

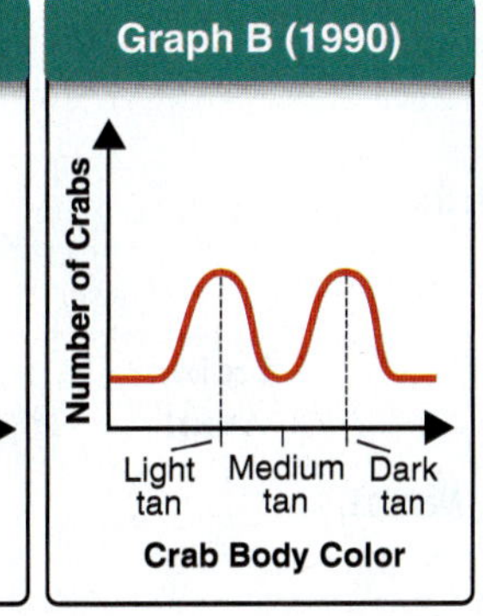

9. What process occurred over the 40-year period?
   A artificial selection
   B sexual selection
   C stabilizing selection
   D disruptive selection
10. Which of the following is most likely to have caused the change in distribution?
    A A new predator prefers dark-tan crabs.
    B A new predator prefers light-tan crabs.
    C A new beach color makes medium-tan crabs the least visible to predators.
    D A new beach color makes medium-tan crabs the most visible to predators.

Standards Practice

1. B	5. A	9. D
2. B	6. D	10. D
3. C	7. A	
4. A	8. B	

Success Tracker™

Online at PHSchool.com

Have students check their understanding of the chapter by logging onto Success Tracker.

Chapter Planner 17 The History of Life

Section and Section Objectives	Time	STANDARDS NCLB	STANDARDS Biology	Activities and Labs
17–1 The Fossil Record, pp. 417–422 **17.1.1** ***Describe*** the fossil record. **17.1.2** ***State*** the information that relative dating and radioactive dating provide about fossils. **17.1.3** ***Identify*** the divisions of the geologic time scale.	2 periods (1 block)	BI 8.e, BIIE 1.i		SE: ***Inquiry Activity,*** How can you date a rock?, p. 416 L2 TE: ***Demonstration,*** p. 417 L1 L2 TE: ***Build Science Skills,*** p. 418 L1 L2 TE: ***Build Science Skills,*** p. 419 L1 L2 SE: ***Quick Lab,*** What is a half-life?, p. 420 L1 L2 LMB: Chapter 17 Lab L1 L2
17–2 Earth's Early History, pp. 423–428 **17.2.1** ***Describe*** how conditions on early Earth were different from conditions today. **17.2.2** ***Explain*** what Miller and Urey's experiments showed. **17.2.3** ***State*** the hypotheses that have been proposed for how life first arose on Earth. **17.2.4** ***Identify*** some of the main evolutionary steps in the early evolution of life.	2 periods (1 block)			TE: ***Demonstration,*** p. 424 L1 L2 LMA: Chapter 17 Lab L2 L3
17–3 Evolution of Multicellular Life, pp. 429–434 **17.3.1** ***Describe*** the key forms of life in the Paleozoic, Mesozoic, and Cenozoic eras.	2 periods (1 block)	BI 8.e		SE: ***Careers in Biology,*** Fossil Preparer, p. 433 L2
17–4 Patterns of Evolution, pp. 435–440 **17.4.1** ***Identify*** important patterns of macroevolution.	1 period (1/2 block)	7 3.c, BI 8.e		SE: ***Analyzing Data,*** Changing Number of Marine Families, p. 438 L2 SE: ***Exploration,*** Modeling Coevolution, p. 441 L2
Chapter Assessment, pp. 442–445	1 period (1/2 block)			

ACTIVITY PLANNER

SE: *Inquiry Activity,* p. 416; 10 min.; piece of shale, hand lens, transparent metric ruler

TE: *Demonstration,* p. 417; 5 min.; fossils or casts of fossils

TE: *Build Science Skills,* p. 418; 15 min.; plaster of Paris, water, flat-bottomed container, organic specimen such as a shell or leaf

TE: *Build Science Skills,* p. 419; 20 min.; slabs of clay or sheets of colored paper or other suitable materials

SE: *Quick Lab,* p. 420; 15 min.; 100 1-cm squares of paper, plastic or paper cup

TE: *Demonstration,* p. 424; 5 min.; box of wooden matches

SE: *Exploration,* p. 441; 45 min.; long forceps, spoon, dried peas, 3 25-mL graduated cylinders, 3 100-mL beakers, watch or clock with second hand

PLANNING KEY

Ability Levels
for students performing . . .

below grade level **L1**
at grade level **L2**
above grade level **L3**

Print Components

SE	Student Edition
TE	Teacher's Edition
RSW	Reading & Study Workbook A
ARSW	Adapted Reading & Study Workbook B
TR	Teaching Resources
IF	Investigations in Forensics
LA	Lab Assessment
BTM	Biotechnology Manual
IDM	Issues and Decision Making
LW	Lab Worksheets
LMA	Laboratory Manual A
LMB	Laboratory Manual B

Tech Components

CTB	Computer Test Bank
BD	BioDetectives DVD
TP	Transparencies Plus
PLM	Probeware Lab Manual
ABC	ABC DVD Library
LS	Lab Simulations
VL	Virtual Labs

Interactive Textbook — Interactive textbook with assessment at PHSchool.com

Program Resources	Assessment	Media and Technology
TR: Lesson Plan 17–1, Section Summary, p. 93 L1, p. 103 L2, Worksheets, pp. 96–97 L1, pp. 105–107 L2, Enrichment L2 L3 **RSW:** Section 17–1 L2; **ARSW:** Section 17–1 L1 **IDM:** Issues and Decisions 14 L2 L3	**SE:** 17–1 Section Assessment, p. 422 **TR:** Section Review 17–1	**iText:** Section 17–1 **TP:** 17–1 Interest Grabber, Section Outline, Compare/Contrast Table, Figure 17–2, Figure 17–5 **BD:** "Mummies: Ties to the Past"
TR: Lesson Plan 17–2, Section Summary, p. 93 L1, p. 103 L2, Worksheets, p. 98 L1, pp. 108–110 L2 **RSW:** Section 17–2 L2 **ARSW:** Section 17–2 L1	**SE:** 17–2 Section Assessment, p. 428 **TR:** Section Review 17–2	**iText:** Section 17–2 **TP:** 17–2 Interest Grabber, Section Outline, Flowchart, Figure 17–8, Figure 17–12
TR: Lesson Plan 17–3, Section Summary, p. 94 L1, p. 104 L2, Worksheets, p. 99 L1, pp. 111–113 L2 **RSW:** Section 17–3 L2 **ARSW:** Section 17–3 L1	**SE:** 17–3 Section Assessment, p. 434 **TR:** Section Review 17–3	**iText:** Section 17–3 **TP:** 17–3 Interest Grabber, Section Outline, Geologic Time Scale With Key Events
TR: Lesson Plan 17–4, Section Summary, p. 95 L1, p. 104 L2, Worksheets, pp. 100–101 L1, pp. 114–115 L2 **LW:** Chapter 17 Exploration L1 L2 L3 **RSW:** Section 17–4 L2 **ARSW:** Section 17–4 L1 **IDM:** Issues and Decisions 13 L2 L3	**SE:** 17–4 Section Assessment, p. 440 **TR:** Section Review 17–4	**iText:** Section 17–4 **TP:** 17–4 Interest Grabber, Section Outline, Concept Map
	SE: Chapter 17 Assessment, pp. 442–445 **TR:** Chapter Vocabulary Review, Graphic Organizer, Chapter 17 Test	**iText:** Chapter 17 Assessment **CTB:** Chapter 17 Test

Go Online
Students can do research, share data, and test their knowledge online.

TIME SAVER — PRESSED FOR TIME?

To Preview the Chapter

- Introduce students to the Vocabulary terms and Key Concepts in each section.
- Assign the Reading Strategies for each section.

To Cover the Chapter Quickly

- Have students read Fossils and Ancient Life and Geologic Time Scale in Section 17–1, the boldface sentences in Sections 17–2 and 17–3, and the introduction in Section 17–4.
- Assign questions 1 and 3 in Section Assessments 17–1 through 17–3; questions 1, 14, and 18 in Chapter 17 Assessment; and questions 1–8 in Chapter 17 Standards Practice.

To Review the Chapter

- Assign Sections 17–1 through 17–4 in the Reading and Study Workbook or the Adapted Reading and Study Workbook.
- Assign the Section Reviews for 17–1 through 17–4 and the Chapter Vocabulary Review for Chapter 17 in the Teaching Resources.

CHAPTER 17

ENGAGE/EXPLORE

Inquiry Activity

 BIIE 1.i

Objective Students will be able to infer how long it took for a sample of shale to form. L2

Skills Focus Inferring, Calculating

Materials piece of shale, hand lens, transparent metric ruler

Time 10 minutes

Advance Prep Shale billets from the Green River formation in Colorado, Wyoming, and Utah can be obtained from mineralogy suppliers and scientific supply houses.

Strategies

- Offer students dissecting probes or toothpicks for counting layers.
- Explain that the shale samples are from an ancient lake floor and that each pair of light and dark layers formed during a single year when sediment washed into the lake in summers and winters, respectively.

Expected Outcomes Sample: 35 dark layers in 5 mm = 7 dark layers (years) per mm. 600 m = 600,000 mm. 600,000 mm × 7 years/mm = 4,200,000 years that the lake existed.

Think About It

1. Students should multiply the average number of layers per millimeter from step 3 by the thickness of their specimen.
2. Students should multiply the average number of layers per millimeter by 600,000 mm.

Discrepant Event

Engage students' interest in evolutionary change by describing living fossils, which are members of species that have remained virtually unchanged for tens of millions of years. Examples include sea stars, crocodiles, turtles, opossums, ants, and dragonflies. Ask: **What are some other examples of living fossils?** *(Sharks and cockroaches are well-known examples.)* Explain that living fossils are rare, because most species have undergone observable evolutionary change since they first appeared on Earth, as students will learn in this chapter.

CHAPTER 17

The History of Life

About 25 million years ago, this scorpion was caught in sticky tree resin, which later hardened into amber. Fossils like this one provide evidence that enables scientists to build up a picture of Earth's history.

Inquiry Activity

 BIIE 1.i

How can you date a rock?

Procedure

1. Examine a piece of shale with a hand lens. This rock formed from the sediment deposited at the bottom of an ancient lake. As the shale formed, one dark layer and one light layer were deposited each year.
2. Place a transparent metric ruler next to the shale sample. Count and record the number of dark layers in a 5-mm section of the shale.
3. Divide your result in step 2 by 5 to determine the average number of layers per millimeter.

Think About It

1. **Inferring** How many years did it take for your specimen to form?
2. **Calculating** Suppose your specimen came from a deposit of shale that is 600 meters thick. How long did it take for the complete deposit to form?

17–1 The Fossil Record

BI 8.e. Students know how to analyze fossil evidence with regard to biological diversity, episodic speciation, and mass extinction. **BIIE 1.i.** Analyze the locations, sequences, or time intervals that are characteristic of natural phenomena (e.g., relative ages of rocks, locations of planets over time, and succession of species in an ecosystem).

The history of life on Earth is filled with mystery, life-and-death struggles, and bizarre plants and animals as amazing as any mythological creatures. Studying life's history is one of the most fascinating and challenging parts of biology, and researchers go about it in several ways. One technique is to read the pieces of the story that are "written" in ancient rocks, in the petrified sap of ancient trees, in peat bogs and tar pits, and in polar glaciers. You may recall that these traces and preserved remains of ancient life are called fossils.

Guide for Reading

Key Concepts

- What is the fossil record?
- What information do relative dating and radioactive dating provide about fossils?
- What are the main divisions of the geologic time scale?

Vocabulary

paleontologist • fossil record
extinct • relative dating
index fossil • half-life
radioactive dating
geologic time scale • era
period

Reading Strategy: Finding Main Ideas Before you read, write down this idea: Scientists use the fossil record to learn about the history of life on Earth. As you read, make a list of the kinds of evidence that support this main idea.

Fossils and Ancient Life

Paleontologists (pay-lee-un-TAHL-uh-jists) are scientists who study fossils. They collect fossils such as the one shown in **Figure 17–1.** From these fossils, they infer what past life-forms were like—the structure of the organisms, what they ate, what ate them, and the environment in which they lived. Paleontologists also classify fossil organisms. They group similar organisms together and arrange them in the order in which they lived—from oldest to most recent. Together, all this information about past life is called the **fossil record.**  **The fossil record provides evidence about the history of life on Earth. It also shows how different groups of organisms, including species, have changed over time.**

The fossil record reveals a remarkable fact: Fossils occur in a particular order. Certain fossils appear only in older rocks, and other fossils appear only in more recent rocks. In other words, the fossil record shows that life on Earth has changed over time. In fact, more than 99 percent of all species that have ever lived on Earth have become **extinct,** which means the species died out. Meanwhile, over billions of years, ancient unicellular organisms have given rise to the modern bacteria, protists, fungi, plants, and animals that you will study in later units.

▶ **Figure 17–1** This remarkably complete dinosaur fossil reveals many characteristics of the original animal. **Observing** *What anatomical similarities can you observe between this fossil and any organism alive today?*

SECTION RESOURCES

Print:

- ***Laboratory Manual B,*** Chapter 17 Lab
- ***Teaching Resources,*** Lesson Plan 17–1, Adapted Section Summary 17–1, Adapted Worksheets 17–1, Section Summary 17–1, Worksheets 17–1, Section Review 17–1, Enrichment
- ***Reading and Study Workbook A,*** Section 17–1
- ***Adapted Reading and Study Workbook B,*** Section 17–1
- ***Issues and Decision Making,*** Issues and Decisions 14

Technology:

- ***BioDetectives DVD,*** "Mummies: Ties to the Past"
- ***iText,*** Section 17–1
- ***Transparencies Plus,*** Section 17–1

Section 17–1

BI 8.e, BIIE 1.i

1 FOCUS

Objectives

17.1.1 ***Describe*** the fossil record.
17.1.2 ***State*** the information that relative dating and radioactive dating provide about fossils.
17.1.3 ***Identify*** the divisions of the geologic time scale.

Guide for Reading

Vocabulary Preview

Ask: **What is a fossil?** *(Traces and preserved remains of ancient life)* Point out that traces are footprints, droppings, or any other type of evidence an organism might leave behind.

Reading Strategy

The kinds of evidence that students might list include the fossils themselves, as well as the types of environments and time periods in which the organisms lived.

2 INSTRUCT

Fossils and Ancient Life

Demonstration

Display fossils or casts of fossils for students to inspect. If possible, pass fossils around the room for students to examine. Ask: **Do any of these fossils resemble organisms that still exist today?** *(Answers will depend on the fossils.)* **Can you guess how these organisms might have lived, based on their fossils?** *(Students might say, for example, that an organism might have lived in water because it resembles a living aquatic organism.)* Explain that, in this section, students will learn how fossils form and what they reveal about the history of life on Earth. L1 L2

Answer to . . .

Figure 17–1 *Students might note similarities between the fossil's jaws and teeth and those of alligators and other reptiles alive today.*

17–1 (continued)

How Fossils Form

Build Science Skills

Using Models Help students appreciate how fossils form by giving them an opportunity to make a model fossil of a shell, leaf, fern frond, nut, or other small organic specimen. First, have students pour a plaster of Paris mixture into a small, flat-bottomed container. When the plaster just begins to harden, students should press the specimen into its surface. After the plaster hardens, they should carefully remove the specimen. Explain that the resulting imprint models a type of fossil called a mold. Add that fossils also form when minerals replace organic materials in a decaying specimen. This process, called petrification, creates a stony duplicate of the original specimen. L1 L2

Interpreting Fossil Evidence

Make Connections

Chemistry Point out that scientists now use molecular clocks to help interpret the fossil record and date important evolutionary events. Explain that molecular clocks are based on the assumption that mutations occur at a known rate over time, like the ticking of a clock. Thus, the DNA of an organism diverges more and more from the DNA of its ancestors—the greater the differences between the DNA of living related species, the longer the time since the species shared a common ancestor. L2

For: Fossil Formation activity
Visit: PHSchool.com
Web Code: cbe-5171
Students explore how fossils are formed.

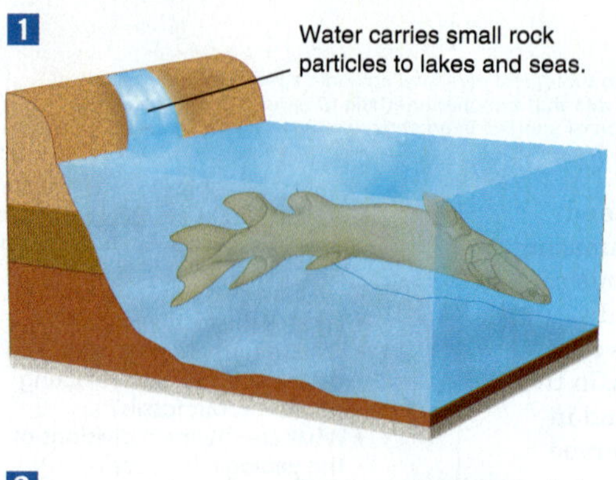

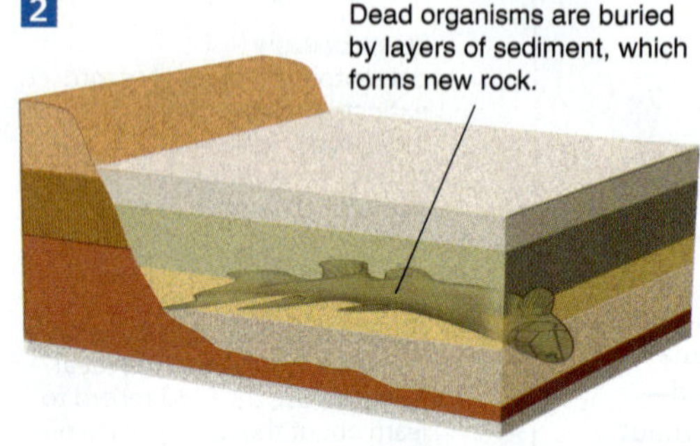

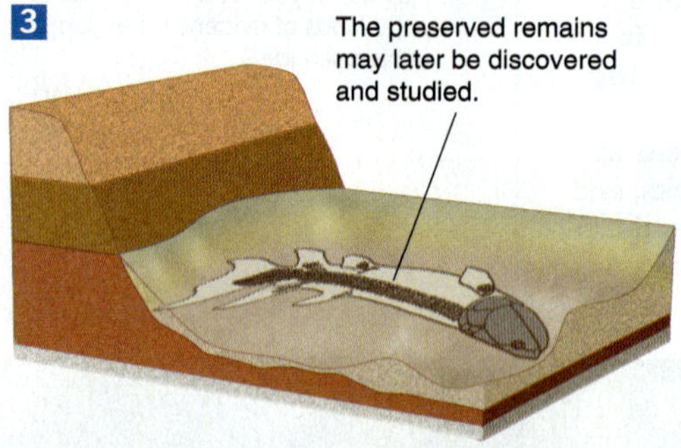

▲ **Figure 17–2** **The fossil record provides evidence about the history of life on Earth.** Most fossils are formed in sedimentary rock.

For: Fossil Formation activity
Visit: PHSchool.com
Web Code: cbp-5171

How Fossils Form

A fossil can be as large and complete as an entire, perfectly preserved animal, or as small and incomplete as a tiny fragment of a jawbone or leaf. There are fossil eggs, fossil footprints, and even fossilized animal droppings. For a fossil to form, either the remains of the organism or some trace of its presence must be preserved. The formation of any fossil depends on a precise combination of conditions. Because of this, the fossil record provides incomplete information about the history of life. For every organism that leaves a fossil, many more die without leaving a trace.

Most fossils form in sedimentary rock, as shown in **Figure 17–2.** Sedimentary rock is formed when exposure to rain, heat, wind, and cold breaks down existing rock into small particles of sand, silt, and clay. These particles are carried by streams and rivers into lakes or seas, where they eventually settle to the bottom. As layers of sediment build up over time, dead organisms may also sink to the bottom and become buried. If conditions are right, the remains may be kept intact and free from decay. The weight of layers of sediment gradually compresses the lower layers and, along with chemical activity, turns them into rock.

The quality of fossil preservation varies. In some cases, the small particles of rock surrounding the remains of an organism preserve an imprint of its soft parts. In other cases, the hard parts are preserved when wood, shells, or bones are saturated or replaced with long-lasting mineral compounds. Occasionally, organisms are buried quickly in fine-grained clay or volcanic ash before they begin to decay, so they are perfectly preserved.

CHECKPOINT *Why is the fossil record described as an incomplete record of life's history?*

Interpreting Fossil Evidence

CA a The natural forces that form sedimentary rock can also reveal fossils that have been hidden in layers of rock for millions of years. Forces inside Earth lift rocks up into mountain ranges, where wind, rain, and running water erode the rock. Bit by bit, water and wind wear away the upper, younger layers, exposing the older fossil-bearing layers beneath.

When a fossil is exposed, a fortunate (and observant) paleontologist may happen along at just the right time and remove the fossil for study.

Paleontologists occasionally unearth the remains of an entire organism. More often, though, they must reconstruct an extinct species from a few fossil bits—remains of bone, a shell, leaves, or pollen. When paleontologists study a fossil, they look for anatomical similarities—and differences—between the fossil and living organisms. Also, a fossil's age is extremely important. Paleontologists determine the age of fossils using two techniques: relative dating and radioactive dating.

Relative Dating About two centuries ago, geologists noted that rock layers containing certain fossils consistently appeared in the same vertical order no matter where they were found. Also, a particular species of trilobite—a common fossil and an extinct relative of horseshoe crabs—might be found in one rock layer but be absent from layers above or below it. How might such a pattern be useful?

In **relative dating,** the age of a fossil is determined by comparing its placement with that of fossils in other layers of rock, as shown in **Figure 17–3.** Recall that sedimentary rock is formed from the gradual deposition of layers of sand, rock, and other types of sediment. The rock layers form in order by age—the oldest layers on the bottom, with more recent layers on top, closer to Earth's surface.

Scientists also use **index fossils** to compare the relative ages of fossils. To be used as an index fossil, a species must be easily recognized and must have existed for a short period but have had a wide geographic range. As a result, it will be found in only a few layers of rock, but these specific layers will be found in different geographic locations. **Relative dating allows paleontologists to estimate a fossil's age compared with that of other fossils.** However, it provides no information about its absolute age, or age in years.

CA

a

Word Origins

The word part *paleo-* means "ancient" or "early," and *-zoic* means "life." The word part *meso-* means "middle." The word part *ceno-* means "recent." **Use this information to explain the meanings of *paleozoic, mesozoic,* and *cenozoic.***

a BIIE 1.i

▼ **Figure 17–3 In relative dating, a paleontologist estimates a fossil's age in comparison with that of other fossils.** Each of these fossils is an index fossil. It enables scientists to date the rock layer in which it is found. Scientists can also use index fossils to date rocks from different locations.

Word Origins

The Paleozoic Era is the era of ancient life, the Mesozoic Era is the era of middle life, and the Cenozoic Era is the era of recent life. L2

Build Science Skills

Using Models Divide the class into small groups, and have each group design and build a model showing how the fossils contained in one sequence of rock layers can be used to determine the relative ages of fossils in another sequence of rock layers. To represent the rock layers, students can use slabs of clay, stacks of paper of different colors, or other suitable materials. They should label the layers with pictures of fossils they have sketched, photocopied from books, or printed from the Internet. Give each group a chance to present its model to the class and explain how relative dating can be used to date one sequence of fossils based on the other. L1 L2

Use Visuals

Figure 17–3 Have students read the figure caption. Then, ask: **What assumption do paleontologists make when they use relative dating to estimate the ages of fossils?** *(They assume that fossils found in the upper layers of sedimentary rock are younger than fossils found in the lower layers of rock.)* **What might happen to invalidate this assumption?** *(Anything that disturbs rock layers so that older layers end up on top of younger layers, including movement of rock layers at a fault or human activities such as mining)* L2

UNIVERSAL ACCESS

Inclusion/Special Needs

Help students make a scale model of the geologic time scale, using a long roll of paper and a scale of 1 cm : 5 million years. Ask volunteers to label the eras, periods, and years. Then, challenge students to read the text and find the major "ages" that occurred during each era, such as the Age of Reptiles in the Mesozoic and the Age of Mammals in the Cenozoic. Have students add these to the timeline. L1

Advanced Learners

Challenge interested students to research the use of molecular clocks to date evolutionary events. For example, have them investigate how data from molecular clocks suggest that mammals began evolving long before dinosaurs disappeared, a conclusion not apparent from the fossil record alone. Urge students to share what they learn with the class in a brief oral report or computer presentation. L3

Answer to . . .

CHECKPOINT *Many organisms die without leaving fossils because fossil formation requires a precise combination of conditions.*

17–1 (continued)

Quick Lab

 6IIE 7.c, BIIE 1.a, BIIE 1.e

Objective Students will be able to analyze data and calculate the "half-life" of a model radioactive element. 

Skills Focus **Analyzing Data, Calculating**

Materials 100 1-cm squares of paper, plastic or paper cup

Time 15 minutes

Advance Prep Students can make their own paper squares in advance.

Strategy Explain to students that, on average, about half the remaining squares will be removed each time step 4 is repeated. Ask: **Why does this model radioactive decay?** *(Because half the radioactive element decays during each half-life)*

Expected Outcome Students will need to spill and remove paper squares about four or five times to reduce the number of squares to five or fewer.

Analyze and Conclude

1. In most cases, about half the squares will be removed in one spill and about three-fourths of the squares will be removed in two spills.
2. One year

Quick View Video

Discovery School DVD Encourage students to view track 6 "Mummies: Ties to the Past" on the *BioDetectives* DVD.

Use Visuals

Figure 17–4 Ask: **Why does the curve fall steeply and then start to level out?** *(Because it is decreasing by half of an ever smaller amount)* **What fraction of potassium-40 will be present after five half-lives?** *(1/32)* Some students may have a better appreciation for the rate of decay if they convert the fractions into percentages. L1 L2

Quick Lab

What is a half-life?

Materials 100 1-cm squares of paper, plastic or paper cup

Procedure 

1. Construct a data table or spreadsheet with 2 columns and 5 blank rows. Label the columns "Spill Number" and "Number of Squares Returned."
2. Place an *X* on each square of paper, and put all the squares in the cup.
3. Mix up the squares in the cup. Then, spill them out and separate all squares that overlap.
4. Remove the squares that have an *X* showing. Record the number of squares remaining and return them to the cup.
5. Repeat steps 3 and 4 until there are 5 or fewer squares remaining. Make a graph of your results with the number of spills on the *x*-axis and the number of squares remaining on the *y*-axis.

Analyze and Conclude

1. **Analyzing Data** How many spills were required to remove half of the squares? To remove three fourths?
2. **Calculating** If each spill represents one year, what is the half-life of the squares?

Quick View Video

Discovery School Video To find out about radioactive dating, view track 6 "Mummies: Ties to the Past" on the *BioDetectives* DVD.

Radioactive Dating Scientists use radioactive decay to assign absolute ages to rocks. Some elements found in rocks are radioactive. Radioactive elements decay, or break down, into nonradioactive elements at a steady rate, which is measured in a unit called a half-life. A **half-life** is the length of time required for half of the radioactive atoms in a sample to decay. As shown in **Figure 17–4**, after one half-life, half of the original radioactive atoms in a sample have decayed. Of those remaining atoms, half again are decayed after another half-life.

CA a **Radioactive dating** is the use of half-lives to determine the age of a sample. **In radioactive dating, scientists calculate the age of a sample based on the amount of remaining radioactive isotopes it contains.** Different radioactive elements have different half-lives and therefore provide natural clocks that "tick" at different rates. Carbon-14, for example, has a half-life of about 5730 years. Carbon-14 is taken up by living things while they are alive. After an organism dies, the carbon-14 in its body begins to decay to form nitrogen-14, which escapes into the air. Carbon-12, the most common isotope of carbon, is not radioactive and does not decay. By comparing the amounts of carbon-14 and carbon-12 in a fossil, researchers can determine when the organism lived. The more carbon-12 there is in a sample compared to carbon-14, the older the sample is.

Because carbon-14 has a relatively short half-life, it is useful only for dating fossils younger than about 60,000 years. To date older rocks, researchers use elements with longer half-lives. Potassium-40, for example, decays to the inert gas argon-40 and has a half-life of 1.26 billion years.

CHECKPOINT *What is a half-life?* 

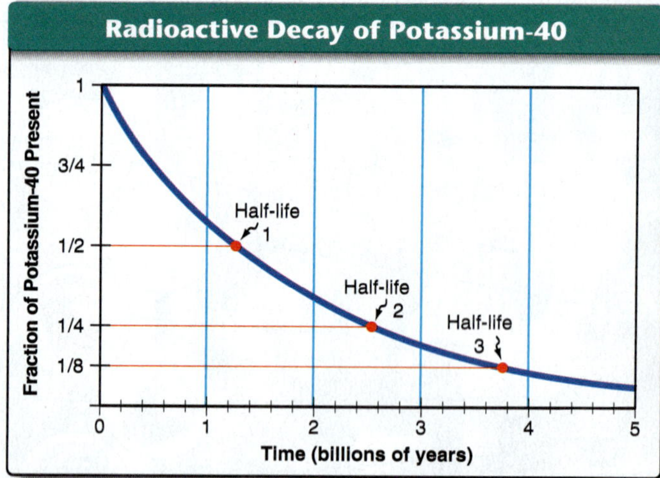

▲ **Figure 17–4** **Radioactive dating involves measuring the amounts of radioactive isotopes in a sample to determine its actual age.** Such measurements enable scientists to determine the absolute age of rocks and the fossils they contain.

BIO INSIGHTS — HISTORY OF SCIENCE

Pliny's footprints and Noah's ravens

The first dinosaur footprints ever discovered in the United States were found by a 12-year-old boy. In 1802, while plowing a field on his family's farm in western Massachusetts, Pliny Moody turned up a flat stone with footprints on it that resembled bird footprints but were much too large to have been made by any living bird. When news of Pliny's discovery spread, crowds came to view the prints. People thought that the prints must have been made by giant ravens released by Noah from the Ark. Prompted by Pliny's discovery, Edward Hitchcock, who was president of Amherst College in Massachusetts, began a 30-year search for more prints. He eventually discovered tracks of about 50 different types of dinosaurs. Believing the tracks to have been made by large, ostrichlike birds, Hitchcock called the prints ornithichites, which means "stony bird tracks."

Geologic Time Scale

Paleontologists use divisions of the **geologic time scale** to represent evolutionary time. **Figure 17–5** shows the most recent version of the geologic time scale. Scientists first developed the geologic time scale by studying rock layers and index fossils worldwide. With this information, they placed Earth's rocks in order according to relative age. As geologists studied the fossil record, they found major changes in the fossil animals and plants at specific layers in the rock. These times were used to mark where one segment of geologic time ends and the next begins—long before anyone knew how long these various segments actually were.

Years later, radioactive dating techniques were used to assign specific ages to the various rock layers. Not surprisingly, the divisions of the geologic time scale did not turn out to be of standard lengths, such as 100 million years. Instead, geologic divisions vary in duration by many millions of years. Scientists use several levels of divisions for the geologic time scale. Geologic time begins with Precambrian (pree-KAM-bree-un) Time. Although few multicellular fossils exist from this time, the Precambrian actually covers about 88 percent of Earth's history, as shown in **Figure 17–6** on the next page. **After Precambrian Time, the basic divisions of the geologic time scale are eras and periods.**

Eras Geologists divide the time between the Precambrian and the present into three **eras.** They are the Paleozoic Era, the Mesozoic Era, and the Cenozoic Era. The Paleozoic (pay-lee-oh-ZOH-ik) began about 544 million years ago and lasted for almost 300 million years. Many vertebrates and invertebrates—animals with and without backbones—lived during the Paleozoic.

The Mesozoic (mez-uh-ZOH-ik) began about 245 million years ago and lasted about 180 million years. Some people call the Mesozoic the Age of Dinosaurs, yet dinosaurs were only one of many kinds of organisms that lived during this era. Mammals began to evolve during the Mesozoic.

Earth's most recent era is the Cenozoic (sen-uh-ZOH-ik). It began about 65 million years ago and continues to the present. The Cenozoic is sometimes called the Age of Mammals because mammals became common during this time.

Geologic Time Scale

Era	Period	Time (millions of years ago)
Cenozoic	Quaternary	1.8 – present
	Tertiary	65 – 1.8
Mesozoic	Cretaceous	145 – 65
	Jurassic	208 – 145
	Triassic	245 – 208
Paleozoic	Permian	290 – 245
	Carboniferous	360 – 290
	Devonian	410 – 360
	Silurian	440 – 410
	Ordovician	505 – 440
	Cambrian	544 – 505
Precambrian Time	Vendian	650 – 544

▲ **Figure 17–5** **The basic units of the geologic time scale after Precambrian Time are eras and periods.** Each era is divided into periods.

a **BI 8.e**

For: Links on the fossil record
Visit: www.SciLinks.org
Web Code: cbn-5171

Geologic Time Scale

Use Visuals

Figure 17–5 Make sure students understand the table by asking: **What is the name of the earliest era in geologic time?** *(Precambrian Time)* **What are the periods of the Paleozoic Era, from oldest to youngest?** *(Cambrian, Ordovician, Silurian, Devonian, Carboniferous, and Permian)* **When did the Cretaceous Period end?** *(65 million years ago)* **Which era and period do we live in?** *(Cenozoic Era and Quaternary Period)* L1 L2

Download a worksheet on the fossil record for students to complete, and find additional teacher support from NSTA SciLinks.

TEACHER TO TEACHER

To help students remember the geological time scale, I divide the class into four groups, assigning a geological era to each group. Then, I have each group make a poster of their era, showing the periods within the era and a drawing of at least two types of organisms that appeared in the period. I display the posters in the classroom and refer to them as we discuss the evolution of multicellular life.

—*Janice Lagatol*
Biology Teacher
Fort Lee High School
Fort Lee, NJ

Answer to . . .

CHECKPOINT *The length of time required for half of the radioactive atoms in a sample to decay*

17–1 (continued)

Build Science Skills

Using Analogies Point out that Figure 17–6 uses a particular time analogy—a 12-hour period—to show Earth's history. Students may also encounter analogies based on a 24-hour day, a month, or a year. For example, if you compare Earth's age to a 24-hour day and Earth was formed at 12:01 AM, then the oldest known fossils appeared at about 6 AM, the oldest nucleated cells between 4 and 5 PM, the oldest complex organisms between 8 and 9 PM, the oldest plants between 9 and 10 PM, and the oldest mammals at about 11 PM. Ask: **How do the various time analogies compare?** *(The actual times representing particular events will vary, but the proportions remain the same.)* L2

3 ASSESS

Evaluate Understanding

Have students make a Venn diagram to compare and contrast relative and absolute dating.

Reteach

Make a copy of the geologic time scale in Figure 17–5 with several of the eras and periods left blank. Have students work in pairs to fill in the missing terms.

Thinking Visually

Students' timelines should be based on Figure 17–5 and the information found on pages 421 and 422 of the text.

If your class subscribes to the iText, use it to review the Key Concepts in Section 17–1.

Answer to . . .

Figure 17–6 *The first prokaryotes appeared at about 2:00 PM; the first land plants at 11:00 PM; the first humans about 12:00 AM.*

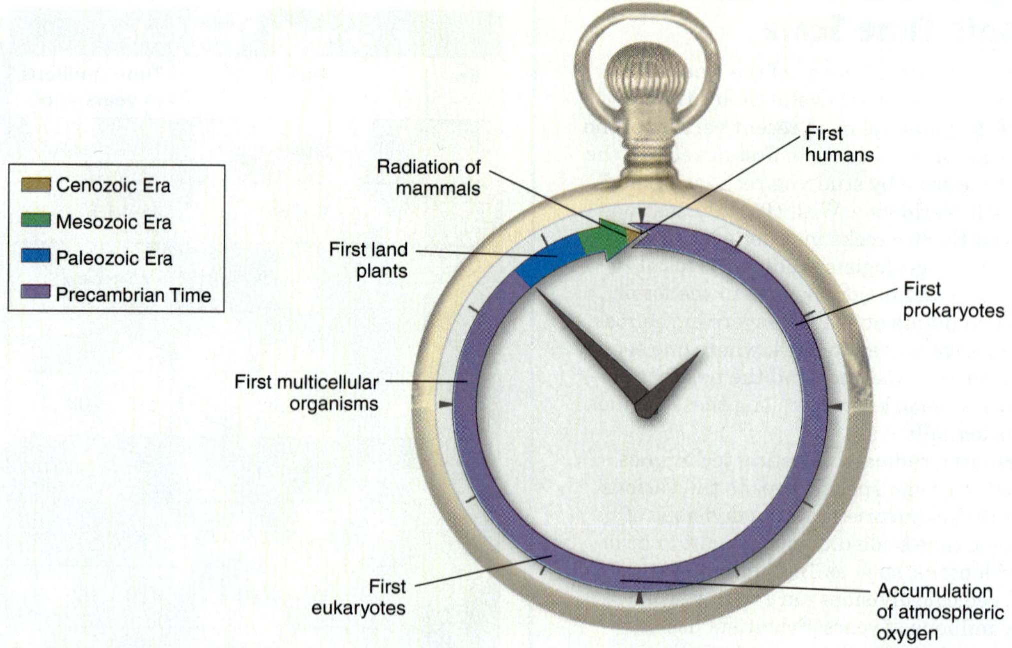

▲ **Figure 17–6** Earth's history is often compared to a familiar measurement, such as the twelve hours between noon and midnight. In such a comparison, notice that Precambrian Time lasts from noon until after 10:30 PM. **Interpreting Graphics** ***Using this model, about what time did life appear? The first plants? The first humans?***

Periods Eras are subdivided into **periods,** which range in length from tens of millions of years to less than two million years. The Mesozoic Era, for example, includes three periods: the Triassic Period, the Jurassic Period, and the Cretaceous Period. Many periods are named for places around the world where geologists first described the rocks and fossils of that period. The name Cambrian, for example, refers to Cambria, the old Roman name for Wales. Jurassic refers to the Jura Mountains in France. The Carboniferous ("carbon-bearing") Period, on the other hand, is named for the large coal deposits that formed during that period.

CA a

17–1 Section Assessment

1. **Key Concept** What can be learned from the fossil record?
2. **Key Concept** Which type of dating provides an absolute age for a given fossil? Describe how this is done.
3. **Key Concept** How are eras and periods related?
4. How do fossils form?
5. What geologic era is known as the Age of Mammals? When did this era begin?
6. **Critical Thinking Drawing Conclusions** Many more fossils have been found since Darwin's day, allowing several gaps in the fossil record to be filled. How might this information make relative dating more accurate?

Thinking Visually

Constructing a Timeline
Create a timeline that shows the four main divisions in the geologic time scale and the key events that occurred during those divisions. Then, as you read Section 17–3, add more events to your timeline.

17–1 Section Assessment

1. The fossil record provides evidence about the history of life on Earth and how different groups of organisms changed over time.
2. Radioactive dating provides an absolute age for a given fossil. Scientists calculate the age of a sample based on the amount of remaining radioactive isotopes it contains.
3. Periods are subdivisions of the eras of the geologic time scale.
4. Most fossils form when dead organisms are covered with layers of sediment.
5. The Cenozoic Era; 65 million years ago
6. More fossils might make relative dating more accurate because the method depends on comparison of fossils.

17–2 Earth's Early History

Guide for Reading

 **Key Concepts**
- What substances made up Earth's early atmosphere?
- What did Miller and Urey's experiments show?
- What occurred when oxygen was added to Earth's atmosphere?
- What hypothesis explains the origin of eukaryotic cells?

Vocabulary
proteinoid microsphere
microfossil
endosymbiotic theory

Reading Strategy: Making Comparisons Before you read, write three sentences about Earth as it is today. As you read, write three sentences that describe how Earth was very different in the past.

If life comes only from life, then how did life on Earth first begin? This section presents the current scientific view of events on the early Earth. These hypotheses, however, are based on a relatively small amount of evidence. The gaps and uncertainties make it likely that scientific ideas about the origin of life will change.

Formation of Earth

Geologic evidence shows that Earth, which is about 4.6 billion years old, was not "born" in a single event. Instead, pieces of cosmic debris were probably attracted to one another over the course of about 100 million years. While the planet was young, it was struck by one or more objects, possibly as large as the planet Mars. This collision produced enough heat to melt the entire globe.

Once Earth melted, its elements rearranged themselves according to density. The most dense elements formed the planet's core. There, radioactive decay generated enough heat to convert Earth's interior into molten rock. Moderately dense elements floated to the surface, much as fat floats to the top of hot chicken soup. These elements ultimately cooled to form a solid crust. The least dense elements—including hydrogen and nitrogen—formed the first atmosphere.

This infant planet was very different from today's Earth. **Figure 17–7** shows how it might have looked. The sky was probably not blue but pinkish-orange. **Earth's early atmosphere probably contained hydrogen cyanide, carbon dioxide, carbon monoxide, nitrogen, hydrogen sulfide, and water.** Had you been there, a few deep breaths would have killed you!

▼ **Figure 17–7** The early Earth was much hotter than it is now, and there was little or no oxygen in the atmosphere. **Earth's early atmosphere was probably made up of hydrogen cyanide, carbon dioxide, carbon monoxide, nitrogen, hydrogen sulfide, and water.**

SECTION RESOURCES

Print:
- ***Laboratory Manual A,*** Chapter 17 Lab
- ***Teaching Resources,*** Lesson Plan 17–2, Adapted Section Summary 17–2, Adapted Worksheets 17–2, Section Summary 17–2, Worksheets 17–2, Section Review 17–2
- ***Reading and Study Workbook A,*** Section 17–2
- ***Adapted Reading and Study Workbook B,*** Section 17–2

Technology:
- ***iText,*** Section 17–2
- ***Transparencies Plus,*** Section 17–2

Section 17–2

1 FOCUS

Objectives

17.2.1 ***Describe*** how conditions on early Earth were different from conditions today.
17.2.2 ***Explain*** what Miller and Urey's experiments showed.
17.2.3 ***State*** the hypotheses that have been proposed for how life first arose on Earth.
17.2.4 ***Identify*** some of the main evolutionary steps in the early evolution of life.

Guide for Reading

Vocabulary Preview

Break down some Vocabulary terms into their components so their meanings are easier to decipher. Explain that *-oid* means "resembling" and that *micro-* means "tiny." Ask: **What is a proteinoid microsphere?** *(A tiny sphere resembling a protein)* **What is a microfossil?** *(A tiny fossil)*

Reading Strategy

Students may find it beneficial to summarize information in a graphic organizer.

2 INSTRUCT

Formation of Earth

Use Visuals

Figure 17–7 Show students a recent photograph of Earth taken from a satellite in space. Have them compare the recent photograph with the drawing of early Earth shown in the figure. Ask: **What features can you see on Earth's surface in the photograph and in the drawing?** *(Features in the photograph include white clouds, blue oceans, and green and brown landmasses. Features in the drawing include erupting volcanoes, meteors, and lightning.)* Then, ask: **What are the basic requirements for human life that are found on Earth today?** *(Water, oxygen, and plants and animals for nutrients)* **Which basic requirements were present on early Earth?** *(Water, energy, and gases other than oxygen.)* L2

17–2 (continued)

The First Organic Molecules

Demonstration

Demonstrate the importance of energy as a prerequisite for chemical reactions. Have students observe as you light a match by running it across its striker. Challenge students to identify the factors involved in lighting the match. *(Energy and a chemical reaction)* Relate the demonstration to the work done by Miller and Urey. Explain that for amino acids to form, energy was required for chemical reactions. Ask: **Where did this energy come from on early Earth?** *(Lightning)* L1 L2

Build Science Skills

Inferring Explain that several years after Miller and Urey's experiment, a meteorite crashed to Earth in Australia. It was carefully split open and analyzed. Inside were found the same amino acids that had been produced in Miller and Urey's apparatus. Ask: **Why did this support Miller and Urey's experimental results?** *(Because the amino acids in the meteorite were most likely not produced by living organisms)* L2 L3

Use Visuals

Figure 17–8 Ask: **Why did Miller and Urey use a mixture of nitrogen, hydrogen, methane, and ammonia in their apparatus?** *(Because this mixture of gases resembles Earth's early atmosphere)* **Why was it necessary to perform their experiment in a sterilized, closed system?** *(To prevent oxygen from entering, because Earth's early atmosphere had no oxygen, and to prevent contamination by modern bacteria or fungi)* **Why did they boil water to produce water vapor?** *(Because water vapor was present in the early atmosphere)* **What was the purpose of the electric sparks?** *(To simulate lightning and provide energy for the chemical reactions)* **Does the Miller-Urey experiment show what actually happened on early Earth?** *(No, it is only a model showing how organic molecules could have been produced from inorganic components.)*
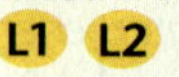

Geologists infer that about 4 billion years ago, Earth cooled enough to allow the first solid rocks to form on its surface. For millions of years afterward, violent volcanic activity shook Earth's crust. Comets and asteroids bombarded its surface. Oceans did not exist because the surface was extremely hot.

About 3.8 billion years ago, Earth's surface cooled enough for water to remain a liquid. Thunderstorms drenched the planet, and oceans covered much of the surface. Those primitive oceans were brown because they contained lots of dissolved iron. The earliest sedimentary rocks, which were deposited in water, have been dated to this period. This was the Earth on which life appeared.

CHECKPOINT *Why did the early Earth not have oceans?*

The First Organic Molecules

For several reasons, atoms do not assemble themselves into complex organic molecules or living cells on Earth today. For one thing, the oxygen in the atmosphere is very reactive and would destroy many kinds of organic molecules not protected within cells. In addition, as soon as organic molecules appeared, something—bacteria or some other life form—would probably eat them! But the early Earth was a very different place. Could organic molecules have evolved under those conditions?

In the 1950s, American chemists Stanley Miller and Harold Urey tried to answer that question by simulating conditions on the early Earth in a laboratory setting. They filled a flask with hydrogen, methane, ammonia, and water to represent the atmosphere. They made certain that no microorganisms could contaminate the results. Then, as shown in **Figure 17–8,** they passed electric sparks through the mixture to simulate lightning.

The results were spectacular. Over a few days, several amino acids—the building blocks of proteins—began to accumulate. **Miller and Urey's experiments suggested how mixtures of the organic compounds necessary for life could have arisen from simpler compounds present on a primitive Earth.** Scientists now know that Miller and Urey's original simulations of Earth's early atmosphere were not accurate. However, similar experiments based on more current knowledge of Earth's early atmosphere have also produced organic compounds. In fact, one of Miller's experiments in 1995 produced cytosine and uracil, two of the bases found in RNA.

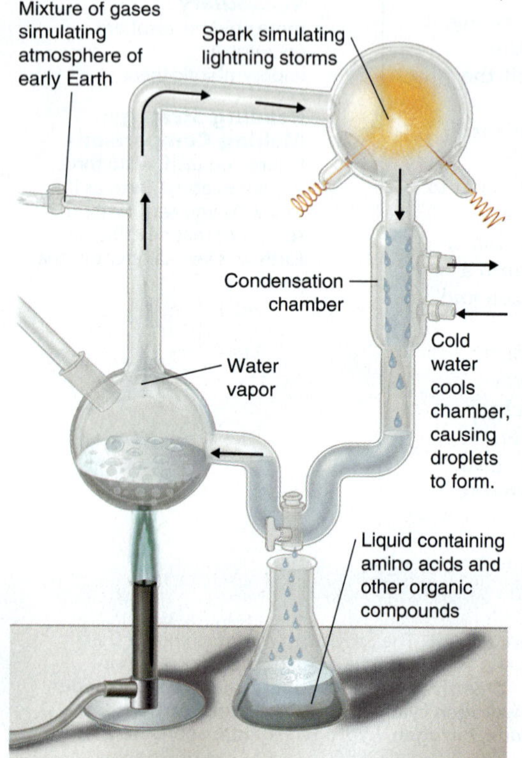

▲ **Figure 17–8** Miller and Urey produced amino acids, which are needed to make proteins, by passing sparks through a mixture of hydrogen, methane, ammonia, and water. **This and other experiments suggested how simple compounds found on the early Earth could have combined to form the organic compounds needed for life.**

The Puzzle of Life's Origins

A stew of organic molecules is a long way from a living cell, and the leap from nonlife to life is the greatest gap in scientific hypotheses of Earth's early history. Geological evidence suggests that about 200 to 300 million years after Earth cooled enough to carry liquid water, cells similar to modern bacteria were common. How might these cells have originated?

Formation of Microspheres Under certain conditions, large organic molecules can form tiny bubbles called **proteinoid microspheres,** as shown in **Figure 17–9.** Microspheres are not cells, but they have some characteristics of living systems. Like cells, they have selectively permeable membranes through which water molecules can pass. Microspheres also have a simple means of storing and releasing energy. Several hypotheses suggest that structures similar to proteinoid microspheres might have acquired more and more characteristics of living cells.

Evolution of RNA and DNA Another unanswered question in the evolution of cells is the origin of DNA and RNA. Remember that all cells are controlled by information stored in DNA, which is transcribed into RNA and then translated into proteins. How could this complex biochemical machinery have evolved?

Science cannot yet solve this puzzle, although molecular biologists have made surprising discoveries in this area. Under the right conditions, some RNA sequences can help DNA replicate. Other RNA sequences process messenger RNA after transcription. Still others catalyze chemical reactions. Some RNA molecules can even grow and duplicate themselves—suggesting that RNA might have existed before DNA. A series of experiments that simulated conditions of the early Earth have suggested that small sequences of RNA could have formed and replicated on their own. From this relatively simple RNA-based form of life, several steps could have led to the system of DNA-directed protein synthesis that exists now. This hypothesis is shown in **Figure 17–10.** Future experiments are aimed at refining and retesting this hypothesis.

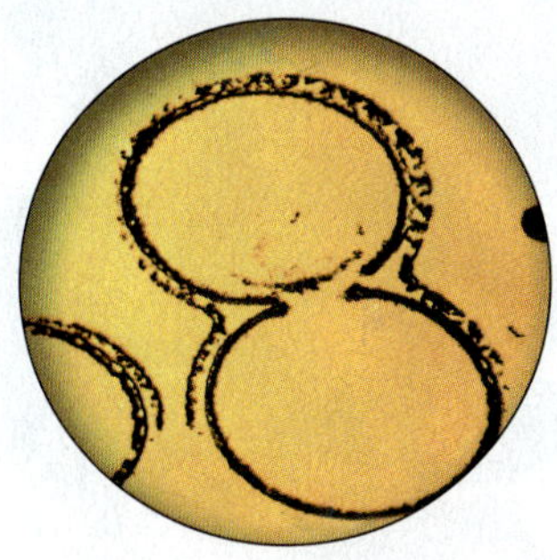

(magnification: about 10,000×)

▲ **Figure 17–9** Large organic molecules can sometimes form tiny proteinoid microspheres like the ones shown here. **Comparing and Contrasting** *How are proteinoid microspheres similar to cells? How are they different?*

▼ **Figure 17–10** One hypothesis about the origin of life, illustrated here, suggests that RNA could have evolved before DNA. Scientists have not yet demonstrated the later stages of this process in a laboratory setting. **Interpreting Graphics** *How might RNA have stored genetic information?*

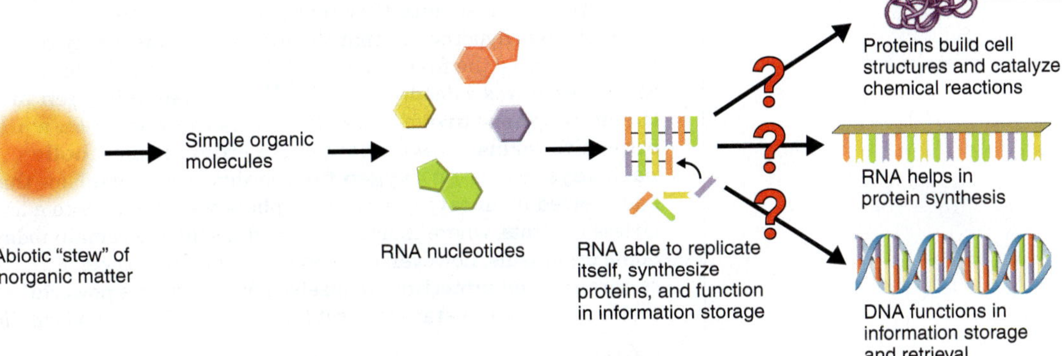

The Puzzle of Life's Origins

Build Science Skills

Inferring Help students understand the importance of proteinoid microspheres. Remind students that cells are the basic functional units of most living things and that cells cannot exist without semipermeable cell membranes. Ask: **Why do cells need membranes?** *(To control which substances move into and out of the cells)* Conclude by saying that the development of membranes in proteinoid microspheres was a crucial step in the evolution of living cells. L1 L2

Use Visuals

Figure 17–10 Help students relate the visual to the information in the text. Ask: **What data support the hypothesis that is modeled in the figure?** *(RNA molecules can help DNA replicate. They can also process messenger RNA, catalyze chemical reactions, grow and duplicate themselves, and form and replicate on their own under simulated conditions of early Earth.)* L1 L2

UNIVERSAL ACCESS

Less Proficient Readers
Some students may have a better understanding of the material on the evolution of RNA and DNA if they first review the structure of the two molecules, how they replicate, and how proteins are synthesized. Advise the students to review these parts of Chapter 12 at this time. L1

English Language Learners
Suggest that English language learners focus on the diagrams in this section. Guide them in interpreting Figures 17–8, 17–10, and 17–12, and relate the figures to the main topics of the section. Give students adequate time to ask questions about the figures. L1

Advanced Learners
Challenge students who need extra work to develop a television program for young children that explains the origin of life on Earth. Have students write a script for the program and then videotape a presentation using the script. Show students' videotapes to the class. L3

Answers to . . .

CHECKPOINT *Because the surface was extremely hot*

Figure 17–9 *Like cells, proteinoid microspheres have a selectively permeable membrane and a simple means of storing and releasing energy. Unlike cells, they do not have DNA or RNA.*

Figure 17–10 *RNA may have acted much like the present DNA molecules—groups of nucleotides may have served as codes for genetic information.*

17–2 (continued)

Free Oxygen

Build Science Skills

Using Tables and Graphs Tell students that Earth's early atmosphere was about 92% carbon dioxide, 5% nitrogen, 0% oxygen, and 3% other gases, whereas Earth's present-day atmosphere is about 78% nitrogen, 21% oxygen, and 1% other gases, including carbon dioxide. Have students display the data in a table and in a bar or line graph. Then, ask: **Where did the oxygen come from?** *(It was produced by photosynthesis.)* L2

Address Misconceptions

Some students might think that the first organisms must have been able to make their own food. Emphasize that the first known fossils do not represent autotrophs, organisms that can make their own food, but instead heterotrophs, organisms that depend on organic compounds for energy. Explain that autotrophs, such as photosynthetic bacteria, are chemically more complex organisms than the simplest heterotrophs. Therefore, it is unlikely that autotrophs evolved first. L1 L2

Build Science Skills

Inferring Ask: **If photosynthetic organisms had not evolved, what do you think life would be like on Earth today?** *(Students should describe ways Earth would be different without oxygen in the oceans and atmosphere. Oxygen-based life would not have evolved, and organisms that did not depend on oxygen would no doubt have evolved further than they did.)* L2

▲ **Figure 17–11** **Ancient photosynthetic organisms produced a rise in oxygen in Earth's atmosphere.** These rocklike formations, called stromatolites, were made by cyanobacteria, which were probably among the earliest organisms to evolve on Earth.

Free Oxygen

Microscopic fossils, or **microfossils,** of unicellular prokaryotic organisms that resemble modern bacteria have been found in rocks more than 3.5 billion years old, as shown in **Figure 17–11.** Those first life-forms must have evolved in the absence of oxygen, because Earth's first atmosphere contained very little of that highly reactive gas.

Over time, as indicated by fossil evidence, photosynthetic bacteria became common in the shallow seas of the Precambrian. By 2.2 billion years ago at the latest, these organisms were steadily churning out oxygen, an end product of photosynthesis. One of the first things oxygen did was to combine with iron in the oceans. In other words, it caused the oceans to rust! When iron oxide was formed, it fell from the sea water to the ocean floor. There, it formed great bands of iron that are the source of most of the iron ore mined today. Without iron, the oceans changed color from brown to blue-green.

Next, oxygen gas started accumulating in the atmosphere. As atmospheric oxygen concentrations rose, concentrations of methane and hydrogen sulfide began to decrease, the ozone layer began to form, and the skies turned their present shade of blue. Over the course of several hundred million years, oxygen concentrations rose until they reached today's levels.

Biologists hypothesize that the increase in this highly reactive gas created the first global "pollution" crisis. To the first cells, oxygen was a deadly poison!  **The rise of oxygen in the atmosphere drove some life-forms to extinction, while other life-forms evolved new, more efficient metabolic pathways that used oxygen for respiration.** Organisms that had evolved in an oxygen-free atmosphere were forced into a few airless habitats, where their anaerobic descendants remain today. Some organisms, however, evolved ways of using oxygen for respiration and protecting themselves from oxygen's powerful reactive abilities. The stage was set for the evolution of modern life.

CHECKPOINT *What process added oxygen to Earth's atmosphere?*

FACTS AND FIGURES

Polymers on the rocks

After small organic molecules formed on prebiotic Earth, the second major chemical step before life appeared was most likely polymerization, or the formation of organic polymers from monomers. Polymers are synthesized by dehydration reactions. In living cells, specific enzymes catalyze these reactions. However, polymerization also occurs in laboratory situations without enzymes, for example, when dilute solutions of organic monomers are dripped onto hot sand, clay, or rock. The heat vaporizes the water in the solutions and concentrates the monomers on the underlying substance. Some of the monomers then spontaneously bond together in chains, forming polymers. In a similar way on early Earth, rain or waves may have splashed dilute solutions of organic monomers onto fresh lava or other hot rocks and then rinsed proteinoids and other polymers into the sea.

Origin of Eukaryotic Cells

Several important events in the history of life have been revealed through molecular studies of cells and their organelles. One of these events is the origin of eukaryotic cells, which are cells that have nuclei. About 2 billion years ago, prokaryotic cells—cells without nuclei—began evolving internal cell membranes. The result was the ancestor of all eukaryotic cells.

The Endosymbiotic Theory Then, something radical seems to have happened. Other prokaryotic organisms entered this ancestral eukaryote. These organisms did not infect their host, as parasites would have done, and the host did not digest them, as it would have digested prey. Instead, the smaller prokaryotes began living inside the larger cell, as shown in **Figure 17–12.** Over time, a symbiotic, or interdependent, relationship evolved. According to the **endosymbiotic theory,** eukaryotic cells formed from a symbiosis among several different prokaryotic organisms. One group of prokaryotes had the ability to use oxygen to generate energy-rich molecules of ATP. These evolved into the mitochondria that are now in the cells of all multicellular organisms. Other prokaryotes that carried out photosynthesis evolved into the chloroplasts of plants and algae. **The endosymbiotic theory proposes that eukaryotic cells arose from living communities formed by prokaryotic organisms.**

This hypothesis was proposed more than a century ago, when microscopists saw that the membranes of mitochondria and chloroplasts resembled the plasma membranes of free-living prokaryotes. Yet, the endosymbiotic theory did not receive much support until the 1960s, when it was championed by Lynn Margulis of Boston University.

For: Links on eukaryotic cells
Visit: www.SciLinks.org
Web Code: cbn-5172

▼ **Figure 17–12** **The endosymbiotic theory proposes that eukaryotic cells arose from living communities formed by prokaryotic organisms.** Ancient prokaryotes may have entered primitive eukaryotic cells and remained there as organelles.

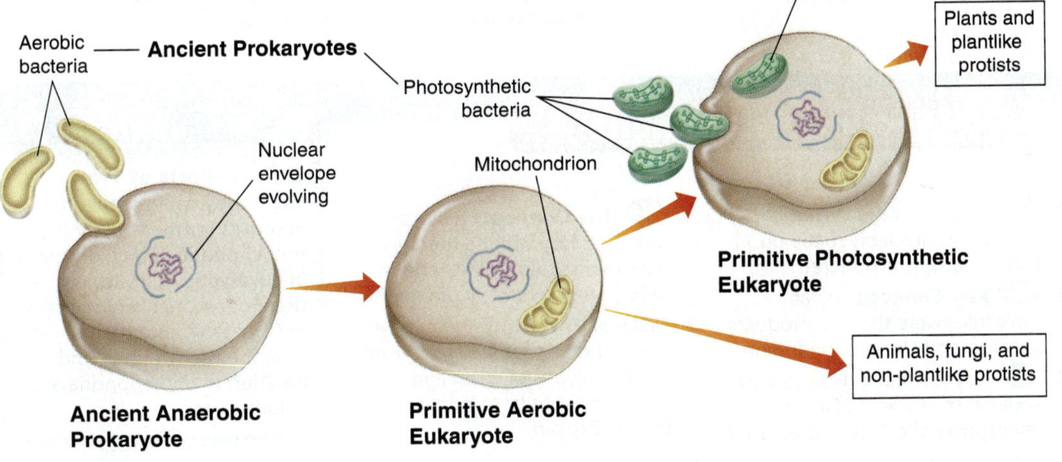

Origin of Eukaryotic Cells

Download a worksheet on eukaryotic cells for students to complete, and find additional teacher support from NSTA SciLinks.

Use Visuals

Figure 17–12 Have students trace the path of the arrows through the figure. Check their understanding of the processes being modeled by asking: **According to the endosymbiotic theory, which organelles did aerobic bacteria become in primitive eukaryotes?** *(Mitochondria)* **Which organelles did photosynthetic bacteria become in primitive photosynthetic eukaryotes?** *(Chloroplasts)* **What did primitive aerobic eukaryotes give rise to?** *(Primitive photosynthetic eukaryotes and animals, fungi, and non-plantlike protists)* **What did primitive photosynthetic eukaryotes give rise to?** *(Plants and plantlike protists)* L1 L2

Answer to . . .

CHECKPOINT *Photosynthesis added oxygen to Earth's atmosphere.*

17–2 (continued)

Sexual Reproduction and Multicellularity

Build Science Skills

Drawing Conclusions Ask: How do you think the evolution of life-forms on Earth might have been different if sexual reproduction had not evolved? *(There would have been less genetic variation, so evolution by natural selection would have proceeded more slowly.)* L2 L3

3 ASSESS

Evaluate Understanding

Have students write a concise paragraph describing the role of photosynthetic bacteria in the evolution of early life on Earth.

Reteach

Work with students to make a simple timeline of Earth's early history that includes the following events: formation of Earth, first organic molecules, first prokaryotic cells, formation of free oxygen, first eukaryotic cells, first cells to reproduce sexually, and first multicellular organisms.

Focus on the BIG Idea

Students should note that both mitochondria and chloroplasts are cell organelles that are enclosed by an outer and inner membrane. They also should say that chloroplasts use energy from sunlight to make energy-rich food molecules and that mitochondria use energy from food to make high-energy compounds needed for cellular activities.

If your class subscribes to the iText, use it to review the Key Concepts in Section 17–2.

Answer to . . .

Figure 17–13 *Impressions in the fossil radiate out from a central point.*

▲ **Figure 17–13** This ancient jellyfish, an early multicellular animal from Precambrian Time, did not have bones or other hard parts, but it left behind a fossil that allowed biologists to infer its overall shape. **Observing** *What evidence shows that this organism had body parts arranged around a central point?*

The Evidence Lynn Margulis and her supporters built their argument on several pieces of evidence: First, mitochondria and chloroplasts contain DNA similar to bacterial DNA. Second, mitochondria and chloroplasts have ribosomes whose size and structure closely resemble those of bacteria. Third, like bacteria, mitochondria and chloroplasts reproduce by binary fission when the cells containing them divide by mitosis. Thus, mitochondria and chloroplasts have many of the features of free-living bacteria. These similarities provide strong evidence of a common ancestry between free-living bacteria and the organelles of living eukaryotic cells.

Sexual Reproduction and Multicellularity

Some time after eukaryotic cells arose, those cells began to reproduce sexually. This development enabled evolution to take place at far greater speeds than ever before. How did sexual reproduction speed up the evolutionary process?

Most prokaryotes reproduce asexually. Often, they simply duplicate their genetic material and divide into two new cells. Although this process is efficient, it yields daughter cells that are exact duplicates of the parent cell. This type of reproduction restricts genetic variation to mutations in DNA. Sexual reproduction, on the other hand, shuffles and reshuffles genes in each generation, much like a person shuffling a deck of cards. The offspring of sexually reproducing organisms, therefore, never resemble their parents exactly. By increasing the number of gene combinations, sexual reproduction increases the probability that favorable combinations will be produced. Favorable gene combinations greatly increase the chances of evolutionary change in a species due to natural selection.

A few hundred million years after the evolution of sexual reproduction, evolving life forms crossed another great threshold: the development of multicellular organisms from unicellular organisms. These first multicellular organisms, such as the one shown in **Figure 17–13,** experienced a great increase in diversity. The evolution of life was well on its way.

17–2 Section Assessment

1. **Key Concept** What substances probably made up Earth's early atmosphere?
2. **Key Concept** What molecules were the end products in Miller and Urey's experiments?
3. **Key Concept** How did the addition of oxygen to Earth's atmosphere affect life of that time?
4. **Key Concept** According to the endosymbiotic theory, how might chloroplasts and mitochondria have originated?
5. **Critical Thinking** **Predicting** You just read that life arose from nonlife billions of years ago. Could life arise from nonlife today? Explain.

Focus on the BIG Idea 

Cellular Basis of Life

The endosymbiotic theory accounts for the evolution of mitochondria and chloroplasts in eukaryotic cells. Review the description of eukaryotic cells in Chapter 7, and then describe the structure and function of mitochondria and chloroplasts.

17–2 Section Assessment

1. Hydrogen cyanide, carbon dioxide, carbon monoxide, nitrogen, hydrogen sulfide, and water
2. Amino acids, which are the building blocks of proteins
3. Oxygen drove some life-forms to extinction; others became restricted to oxygen-free habitats; still others evolved ways of using oxygen for respiration.
4. Ancient aerobic and photosynthetic bacteria may have been engulfed by primitive eukaryotes and evolved into mitochondria and chloroplasts.
5. Probably not. The same conditions no longer exist on Earth. The oxygen in the atmosphere would likely react with and destroy any new kinds of organic molecules or they would be consumed by bacteria and molds.

17–3 Evolution of Multicellular Life

7 3.c. Students know how independent lines of evidence from geology, fossils, and comparative anatomy provide the bases for the theory of evolution. **BI 8.e.** Students know how to analyze fossil evidence with regard to biological diversity, episodic speciation, and mass extinction.

Although the fossil record has missing pieces, paleontologists have assembled good evolutionary histories for many groups of organisms. Furthermore, the fossil record indicates that major changes occurred in Earth's climate, geography, and life-forms. In this section, you will get an overview of how multicellular life evolved from its earliest forms to its present-day diversity.

Guide for Reading

Key Concept
- What were the characteristic forms of life in the Paleozoic, Mesozoic, and Cenozoic eras?

Vocabulary
mass extinction

Reading Strategy: Using Graphic Organizers As you read, make a table of the three geologic eras described in the section. Include information about the typical organisms and main evolutionary events of each era.

Precambrian Time

Recall that almost 90 percent of Earth's history occurred during the Precambrian. During this time, simple anaerobic forms of life appeared and were followed by photosynthetic forms, which added oxygen to the atmosphere. Aerobic forms of life evolved, and eukaryotes appeared. Some of those organisms gave rise to multicellular forms that continued to increase in complexity. Few fossils exist from this time because the animals were all soft-bodied. Life existed only in the sea.

Paleozoic Era

Rich fossil evidence shows that early in the Paleozoic Era, there was a diversity of marine life. Scientists once thought that those different forms of life evolved rapidly at the beginning of the Paleozoic, but increasing evidence from Precambrian fossils and DNA studies suggests that life began to diversify much earlier. Regardless of when these forms evolved, fossil evidence shows that life was highly diverse by the first part of the Paleozoic Era, the Cambrian Period. An artist's portrayal of Cambrian life, which included many kinds of invertebrate animals, is shown in **Figure 17–14.**

CA a BI 8.e

Figure 17–14 **The fossil record shows evidence of many types of marine life early in the Paleozoic Era.** These and other unfamiliar organisms dwelt in the sea during the Cambrian Period, a time when animals with hard parts evolved.

SECTION RESOURCES

Print:
- ***Teaching Resources,*** Lesson Plan 17–3, Adapted Section Summary 17–3, Adapted Worksheets 17–3, Section Summary 17–3, Worksheets 17–3, Section Review 17–3
- ***Reading and Study Workbook A,*** Section 17–3
- ***Adapted Reading and Study Workbook B,*** Section 17–3

Technology:
- ***iText,*** Section 17–3
- ***Transparencies Plus,*** Section 17–3

Section 17–3

BI 8.e

1 FOCUS

Objective

17.3.1 ***Describe*** the key forms of life in the Paleozoic, Mesozoic, and Cenozoic eras.

Guide for Reading

Vocabulary Preview

Read the names of the periods aloud and encourage students to repeat them after you. Knowing how to pronounce the words correctly will help students remember them.

Reading Strategy

Depending on the amount of detail you expect students to learn, you might want to suggest that they make a separate row in their table for each period.

2 INSTRUCT

Precambrian Time

Demonstration

The information in the text on Precambrian Time provides a concise summary of the detailed material in Section 17–2. Students may benefit from a review of the material. Work with the class to create a simple flowchart on the chalkboard or an overhead transparency. Call on students to identify the correct sequence of events for the flowchart. L1

Paleozoic Era

Use Visuals

Figure 17–14 Call students' attention to the figure. Ask: **Why are only aquatic organisms represented for the Cambrian Period?** *(There were no terrestrial life-forms at that time.)*

L1 L2

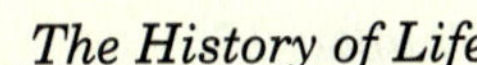

17–3 (continued)

Build Science Skills

Inferring Point out that the first organisms with shells and outer skeletons evolved during the Cambrian Period. Then, ask: **Why would having hard parts such as shells be an advantage to organisms?** *(The hard body parts would help protect the organisms from predators.)* L2

Make Connections

Environmental Science Help students appreciate why the evolution of the first land-dwelling organisms, which occurred during the Ordovician Period, was an important evolutionary event. Point out how the earliest terrestrial organisms would have had virtually no competitors for the diversity of potential niches available on land. L1 L2

Build Science Skills

Drawing Conclusions Ask: **How did life on Earth differ before and after the Permian extinction?** *(Most marine life and many land vertebrates—particularly large ones—were lost. Small reptiles and land plants were less affected.)* L2

Cambrian Period Paleontologists call the diversification of life during the early Cambrian Period the "Cambrian Explosion." For the first time, many organisms had hard parts, including shells and outer skeletons. During the Cambrian Period, the first known representatives of most animal phyla evolved. Invertebrates—such as jellyfishes, worms, and sponges—drifted through the water, crawled along the sandy bottom, or attached themselves to the ocean floors. Brachiopods, which were small animals with two shells, were especially common. They resembled—but were unrelated to—modern clams. Trilobites were also common. Trilobites were arthropods, which are invertebrates with segmented bodies, jointed limbs, and an external skeleton.

a BI 8.e

CHECKPOINT *What is the "Cambrian Explosion"?*

▲ **Figure 17–15** During the Ordovician Period, aquatic arthropods like this eurypterid evolved. Eurypterids had segmented bodies and lived in water. Some of them grew to a length of almost 13 meters. Eurypterids are now extinct. **Comparing and Contrasting** *Which of today's animals do eurypterids resemble?*

Ordovician and Silurian Periods During the Ordovician (awr-duh-VISH-un) and Silurian (sih-LOOR-ee-un) periods, the ancestors of the modern octopi and squid appeared, as did aquatic arthropods like the one in **Figure 17–15.** Some arthropods became the first animals to live on land. Among the first vertebrates (animals with backbones) to appear were jawless fishes, which had suckerlike mouths. The first land plants evolved from aquatic ancestors. These simple plants grew low to the ground in damp areas.

Devonian Period By the Devonian (dih-VOH-nee-un) Period, some plants, such as ferns, had adapted to drier areas, allowing them to invade more habitats. Insects, which are arthropods, appeared on land. In the seas, both invertebrates and vertebrates thrived. Even though the invertebrates were far more numerous, the Devonian is often called the Age of Fishes because many groups of fishes were present in the oceans. Most fishes of this time had jaws, bony skeletons, and scales on their bodies. Sharks appeared in the late Devonian.

During the Devonian, vertebrates began to invade the land. The first fishes to develop the ability to crawl awkwardly on leglike fins were still fully aquatic animals. Some of these early four-legged vertebrates evolved into the first amphibians. An amphibian (am-FIB-ee-un) is an animal that lives part of its life on land and part of its life in water.

Carboniferous and Permian Periods Throughout the rest of the Paleozoic Era, life expanded over Earth's continents. Other groups of vertebrates, such as reptiles, evolved from certain amphibians. Reptiles are animals that have scaly skin and lay eggs with tough, leathery shells. Winged insects evolved into many forms, including huge dragonflies and cockroaches. Giant ferns and other plants formed vast swampy forests, shown in **Figure 17–16.** The remains of those ancient plants formed thick deposits of sediment that changed into coal over millions of years, giving the Carboniferous its name.

ESL SUPPORT FOR ENGLISH LANGUAGE LEARNERS

Vocabulary: Writing

Beginning On the board, make a box labeled *Paleozoic Era.* Write several words or simple phrases describing the life-forms of Precambrian time in the box. To clarify the descriptions, call students' attention to the organisms in Figure 17–14. Then, have the students draw two boxes, one labeled *Mesozoic Era* and one labeled *Cenozoic Era.* Have pairs of students work together to draw a picture or write a word or phrase describing the dominant life-forms of that era. L1

Intermediate Extend the beginning-level activity by writing a complete sentence on the board to describe the life-forms present in the Paleozoic Era. Then, ask students to fill in their labeled boxes using complete sentences. If an ESL student needs assistance, pair him or her with a student who is proficient in English. L2

At the end of the Paleozoic, many organisms died out. This was a **mass extinction,** in which many types of living things became extinct at the same time. **The mass extinction at the end of the Paleozoic affected both plants and animals on land and in the seas. As much as 95 percent of the complex life in the oceans disappeared.** For example, trilobites, which had existed since early in the Paleozoic, suddenly became extinct. Many amphibians also became extinct. Not all organisms disappeared, however. The mass extinction did not affect many fishes. Numerous reptiles also survived.

▲ **Figure 17–16** Ancient forests like this one from the Carboniferous Period were characterized by a huge variety of life-forms. **At the end of the Paleozoic Era, many types of animals and plants became extinct.**

CA

ⓐ BI 8.e

Mesozoic Era

The Mesozoic Era lasted approximately 180 million years. **Events during the Mesozoic include the increasing dominance of dinosaurs. The Mesozoic is marked by the appearance of flowering plants.**

Triassic Period Those organisms that survived the Permian mass extinction became the main forms of life early in the Triassic (try-AS-ik) Period. Important organisms in this new ecosystem were fishes, insects, reptiles, and cone-bearing plants like the one in **Figure 17–17.** Reptiles were so successful during the Mesozoic Era that this time is often called the Age of Reptiles.

About 225 million years ago, the first dinosaurs appeared. One of the earliest dinosaurs, *Coelophysis,* was a meat-eater that had light, hollow bones and ran swiftly on its hind legs. Mammals also first appeared during the late Triassic Period, probably evolving from mammal-like reptiles. Mammals of the Triassic were very small, about the size of a mouse or shrew.

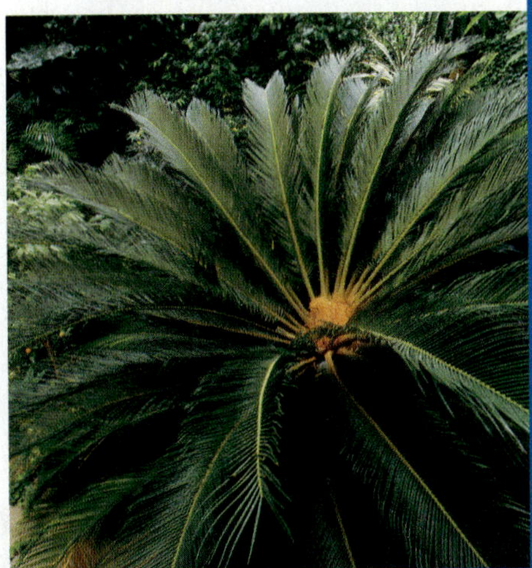

▼ **Figure 17–17** Among the seed plants of the Triassic Period were cone-bearing plants called cycads, which left this modern descendant. **Applying Concepts** *What other organisms were important in the Triassic Period?*

Mesozoic Era

Make Connections

Earth Science Show students maps of the location of Earth's landmasses at various times during the Mesozoic Era. Include a map showing Earth at around 225 million years ago, when all the major landmasses were joined together in the supercontinent of Pangaea, and also around 180 million years ago, when Pangaea had split apart to form Laurasia and Gondwanaland. Have students compare these maps with the present-day locations of the continents. Ask: **Why would the drifting of continents have affected climate?** *(Because climate is determined by the distance north and south of the equator and by the position of large bodies of water)* **How might various kinds of organisms have been affected by those climate changes?** *(Changes in climate might have led to the extinction of some species, while favoring others. Also, the separation of landmasses might have led to geographic isolation and the emergence of new and different species on the different landmasses.)* L2 L3

Answers to . . .

CHECKPOINT *The diversification of life during the early Cambrian Period*

Figure 17–15 *Possible answers include a crab, a scorpion, and a lobster.*

Figure 17–17 *Fishes, insects, and reptiles*

17–3 (continued)

Address Misconceptions

Some students might think that dinosaurs were not very successful in evolutionary terms because, with the possible exception of the ancestors of modern birds, dinosaurs became extinct at the end of the Cretaceous Period. Point out that dinosaurs "ruled" Earth for a total period of about 150 million years. Put this time span in perspective by comparing it with the length of time that the human family, the hominids, has been in existence, which is less than 10 million years. L2

Use Visuals

Figure 17–18 Call on students to describe the environment that is depicted in the figure. *(They may say it is hot and wet or tropical.)* Explain that, during the Mesozoic, many places on Earth, including much of North America, had this type of environment. Remind students that dinosaurs were reptiles and probably could not internally regulate their body temperature. Ask: **What would happen to dinosaurs if they were in North America today?** *(It might be difficult for them to survive because of the cold and other differences in environment.)* L1 L2

▲ **Figure 17–18** **During the Mesozoic Era, dinosaurs were dominant.** *Dicraeosaurus* (foreground) was a plant-eater that grew to about 20 meters in length.

Jurassic Period During the Jurassic (joo-RAS-ik) Period, dinosaurs became the dominant animals on land. Dinosaurs "ruled" Earth for about 150 million years, but different types lived at different times. At 20 meters long, *Dicraeosaurus*, shown in **Figure 17–18**, was one of the larger dinosaurs of the Jurassic Period.

One of the first birds, called *Archaeopteryx*, appeared during this time. Many paleontologists now think that birds are close relatives of dinosaurs. Since the 1990s, scientists working in China have found evidence for this hypothesis in other fossils that have the skulls and teeth of dinosaurs but the body structure and feathers of birds.

Cretaceous Period Reptiles were still the dominant vertebrates throughout the Cretaceous (krih-TAY-shus) Period. Dinosaurs such as the meat-eating *Tyrannosaurus rex* dominated land ecosystems, while flying reptiles and birds soared in the sky. Flying reptiles, however, became extinct during the Cretaceous. In the seas, turtles, crocodiles, and extinct reptiles such as plesiosaurs swam among fishes and marine invertebrates.

The Cretaceous also brought new forms of life, including leafy trees, shrubs, and small flowering plants like those you see today. Unlike the conifers, flowering plants produce seeds enclosed in a fruit, which protects the seed and aids in dispersing it to new locations.

At the close of the Cretaceous, another mass extinction occurred. More than half of all plant and animal groups were wiped out, including all of the dinosaurs.

When did flowering plants evolve?

FACTS AND FIGURES

How sweet it is

Fruits and seeds were a major evolutionary advance in the reproduction of plants. However, if animals eat unripe fruits, the immature seeds in them are not capable of sprouting and growing. As a result, natural selection led to plants that have ways to discourage animals from eating their unripe fruits. Many unripe fruits are green and contain bitter-tasting chemical compounds. The green color of the unripe fruits makes them more difficult to see among a plant's leaves, and the bitter taste helps discourage animals from eating them. As the seeds mature, the bitter-tasting chemical compounds break down, and the fruits become laden with sugars. While this process occurs, the fruits also change color from green to red, orange, purple, or whatever color indicates ripeness in that species. These colors are more easily seen by animals against the background of green leaves, and the fruits' sweet taste reinforces the eating response.

▶ **Figure 17–19** **During the Cenozoic Era, mammals evolved adaptations that allowed them to live on land, in water, and even in the air.** Two of the traits that contributed to the success of mammals were a covering of hair that provided insulation against the cold and the protection of the young before and after birth.

Cenozoic Era

During the Mesozoic, early mammals competed with dinosaurs for food and places to live. The extinction of dinosaurs at the end of the Mesozoic, however, created a different world. **During the Cenozoic, mammals evolved adaptations that allowed them to live in various environments—on land, in water, and even in the air.** One land mammal from the early Cenozoic is shown in **Figure 17–19.** Paleontologists often call the Cenozoic the Age of Mammals.

Tertiary Period During the Tertiary Period, Earth's climates were generally warm and mild. In the oceans, marine mammals such as whales and dolphins evolved. On land, flowering plants and insects flourished. Grasses evolved, providing a food source that encouraged the evolution of grazing mammals, the ancestors of today's cattle, deer, sheep, and other grass-eating mammals. Some mammals became very large, as did some birds.

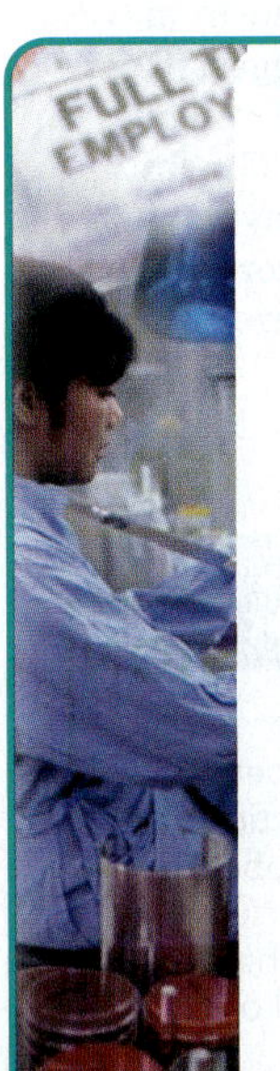

Careers in Biology

Fossil Preparer

Job Description: work for private industries, museums, or universities to expose fossils covered by rock or soil or to construct missing fossil parts

Education: a college degree in biology or geology, knowledge about the fossils being worked on

Skills: be knowledgeable about many areas of science, ability to use fine tools under a microscope, self-motivated, patient, ability to handle very fragile specimens for long periods

Highlights: work with fossils; collaborate with many types of people—from amateur fossil collectors to professional paleontologists

For: Career links
Visit: PHSchool.com
Web Code: cbb-5173

Cenozoic Era

Build Science Skills

Drawing Conclusions Point out that the first mammals probably evolved during the Triassic Period but that mammals did not flourish until the Cenozoic Era. Ask: **Why did mammals not become successful for more than 100 million years after they first evolved?** *(During the Mesozoic, early mammals had to compete with many kinds of reptiles, including dinosaurs, for food and places to live. When dinosaurs went extinct at the end of the Mesozoic, many resources became available for mammals to utilize.)* L2

Careers in Biology

- Sculpting is a good skill to have for this career because fossil preparers occasionally must fabricate missing fossil parts.
- Some fossil preparers spend months working in a field camp at a paleontological dig. They may also spend time in the field collecting fossils. L2

Resources Students can contact a university paleontology department, the Paleontological Association, the Paleontological Research Institute, or the personnel department of a natural history museum.

You can have students write a more extensive job description as well as list the educational requirements for a career in this field.

Answer to . . .

 *During the Cretaceous Period*

17–3 (continued)

Make Connections

Environmental Science Provide students with background information on the ice ages. Explain that over the past two million years, there were four major ice ages, each lasting at least 100,000 years or longer and between which were long periods of warmer climate. During the peak of the most recent ice age, which ended about 20,000 years ago, ice covered much of North America, reaching as far south as the present-day lower midwestern states. Scientists think the ice ages were caused by variations in the position of the Earth relative to the sun, changes in the sun's energy output due to sunspots, and continental movement. L2

3 ASSESS

Evaluate Understanding

Read each of the Key Concepts in the section, leaving the name of the era or period blank. Call on students at random to fill in the blanks.

Reteach

Have pairs of students make and quiz each other with flashcards that each have an important evolutionary event on one side and the correct era and period on the other side.

Writing in Science

If students have a hard time developing ideas for their stories, suggest that they brainstorm in small groups. Stories should include information from the text as well as additional reliable sources.

If your class subscribes to the iText, use it to review the Key Concepts in Section 17–3.

Answer to . . .

Figure 17–20 *Organisms that could not migrate to a warmer climate or adapt to the change in climate would have gone extinct.*

▶ **Figure 17–20** During the Quaternary Period, Earth's climate cooled, producing a series of ice ages. Among the characteristic animals of the time were these huge mammoths. **Inferring** ***How might the change to a colder climate have affected different types of organisms?***

Quaternary Period Mammals that had evolved during the Tertiary Period eventually faced a changing environment during the Quaternary Period. During this time, Earth's climate cooled, causing a series of ice ages. Repeatedly, thick continental glaciers advanced and retreated over parts of Europe and North America. So much of Earth's water was frozen in continental glaciers that the level of the oceans fell by more than 100 meters. Then, about 20,000 years ago, Earth's climate began to warm. Over the course of thousands of years, the continental glaciers melted. This caused sea levels to rise again.

In the oceans, algae, coral, mollusks, fishes, and mammals thrived. Insects and birds shared the skies. On land, mammals—such as bats, cats, dogs, cattle, and the mammoths shown in **Figure 17–20**—became common. The fossil record suggests that the early ancestors of our species appeared about 4.5 million years ago but that they did not look entirely human. The first fossils assigned to our own species, *Homo sapiens,* may have appeared as early as 200,000 years ago in Africa. According to one hypothesis, members of our species began a series of migrations from Africa that ultimately colonized the world.

17–3 Section Assessment

1. **Key Concept** Where did life exist during the early Paleozoic Era?
2. **Key Concept** What evolutionary milestone involving animals occurred during the Devonian Period?
3. **Key Concept** What are two key events from the Mesozoic Era?
4. **Critical Thinking Inferring** If you were a paleontologist investigating fossils from the Cenozoic Era, what fossils might you find?

Writing in Science

Creative Writing
Choose one of the periods described in this section. Then, write a story about life during that time. Include information about the life-forms, weather, and other characteristics.

17–3 Section Assessment

1. Early life existed in the sea.
2. During the Devonian Period, animals began to invade the land.
3. Events include the first appearance of dinosaurs and the appearance of seed plants, including cone-bearing and flowering types.
4. You might find fossils of flowering plants, insects, birds, and mammals, including humans.

17–4 Patterns of Evolution

7 3.c. Students know how independent lines of evidence from geology, fossils, and comparative anatomy provide the bases for the theory of evolution. **BI 8.e.** Students know how to analyze fossil evidence with regard to biological diversity, episodic speciation, and mass extinction.

Biologists often use the term **macroevolution** to refer to large-scale evolutionary patterns and processes that occur over long periods of time.  **Six important topics in macroevolution are extinction, adaptive radiation, convergent evolution, coevolution, punctuated equilibrium, and changes in developmental genes.**

Guide for Reading

Key Concept
- What are six important patterns of macroevolution?

Vocabulary
macroevolution
adaptive radiation
convergent evolution
coevolution
punctuated equilibrium

Reading Strategy: Summarizing
List the six patterns of macroevolution described in this section. As you read, write a statement describing each pattern.

Extinction

More than 99 percent of all species that have ever lived are now extinct. Usually, extinctions happen for the reasons that Darwin proposed. Species compete for resources, and environments change. Some species adapt and survive. Others gradually become extinct in ways that are often caused by natural selection.

Several times in Earth's history, however, mass extinctions wiped out entire ecosystems. Food webs collapsed, and this disrupted energy flow through the biosphere. During these events, some biologists propose, many species became extinct because their environment was collapsing around them, rather than because they were unable to compete. Under these environmental pressures, extinction is not necessarily related to ordinary natural selection.

Until recently, most researchers looked for a single, major cause for each mass extinction. For example, one hypothesis suggests that at the end of the Cretaceous Period, the impact of a huge asteroid, as shown in **Figure 17–21**, wiped out the dinosaurs and many other organisms. Scientific evidence confirms that an asteroid did strike Earth at that time. The impact threw huge amounts of dust and water vapor into the atmosphere and probably caused global climate change. It is reasonable to assume that this kind of event played a role in the end of the dinosaurs.

Many paleontologists, however, think that most mass extinctions were caused by several factors. During several mass extinctions, many large volcanoes were erupting, continents were moving, and sea levels were changing. Researchers have not yet determined the precise causes of mass extinctions.

What effects have mass extinctions had on the history of life? Each disappearance of so many species left habitats open and provided ecological opportunities for those organisms that survived. The result was often a burst of evolution that produced many new species. The extinction of the dinosaurs, for example, cleared the way for the evolution of modern mammals and birds.

▼ **Figure 17–21** **Mass extinctions are one pattern of macroevolution.** A huge asteroid hitting Earth may have caused the extinction of the dinosaurs at the end of the Cretaceous Period. This illustration shows an artist's conception of that event.

SECTION RESOURCES

Print:
- ***Teaching Resources,*** Lesson Plan 17–4, Adapted Section Summary 17–4, Adapted Worksheets 17–4, Section Summary 17–4, Worksheets 17–4, Section Review 17–4
- ***Reading and Study Workbook A,*** Section 17–4
- ***Adapted Reading and Study Workbook B,*** Section 17–4
- ***Issues and Decision Making,*** Issues and Decisions 13
- ***Lab Worksheets,*** Chapter 17 Exploration

Technology:
- ***iText,*** Section 17–4
- ***Transparencies Plus,*** Section 17–4

Section 17–4

1 FOCUS

Objective

17.4.1 ***Identify*** important patterns of macroevolution.

Guide for Reading

Vocabulary Preview

Explain that *co-* means "together" and that *macro-* means "large scale." Then, ask: **What do you think the terms *macroevolution* and *coevolution* mean?** *(Macroevolution means large-scale evolution, and coevolution means the evolution of two species in response to each other.)*

Reading Strategy

Suggest that students add to their summary an example of each type of macroevolutionary pattern, such as the mass extinction of dinosaurs that occurred during the Cretaceous Period or the adaptive radiation of mammals during the Cenozoic Era.

2 INSTRUCT

Extinction

Make Connections

Environmental Science Help put mass extinctions in perspective and relate them to environmental changes with which students are more familiar. Have students research the number of extinctions of plant and animal species that have occurred in the past 100 years. Students should also find out the names of several particular species that have gone extinct and the reason for their extinction. Have students share what they learn with the class. Then, ask: **Do you think extinctions are occurring at a faster rate today than they were in 1900?** *(Because most extinctions today are due to human activities, destroying habitats, they are occurring more rapidly now than they were in 1900.)* L2

Section 17–4

Adaptive Radiation

Build Science Skills

Applying Concepts Review the evolution of Darwin's finches, which is the example of adaptive radiation mentioned in the text. Remind students that a single species of finch from mainland South America traveled to the Galápagos Islands and evolved into multiple species that used different food resources. Ask: **If mass extinction was not responsible for the adaptive radiation of Darwin's finches, what was?** *(The ancestral finch was one of the first land birds ever to reach the islands. Therefore, many niche resources were available.)* L2

Use Visuals

Figure 17–22 Point out that the common ancestor at the bottom of the diagram is the oldest species and that present-day species are at the top of the diagram. Explain that each branching as you travel up the "tree" represents a point where speciation has occurred and the two resulting groups have gone on to evolve separately. The more recently the branching occurred, the less different the two lines of evolution are.

Convergent Evolution

Use Visuals

Figure 17–23 Review the shared traits shown by the shark, penguin, and dolphin, and explain how the traits provide examples of convergent evolution. Ask students to note differences as well as analogous structures, such as the fishlike shape of the bodies.

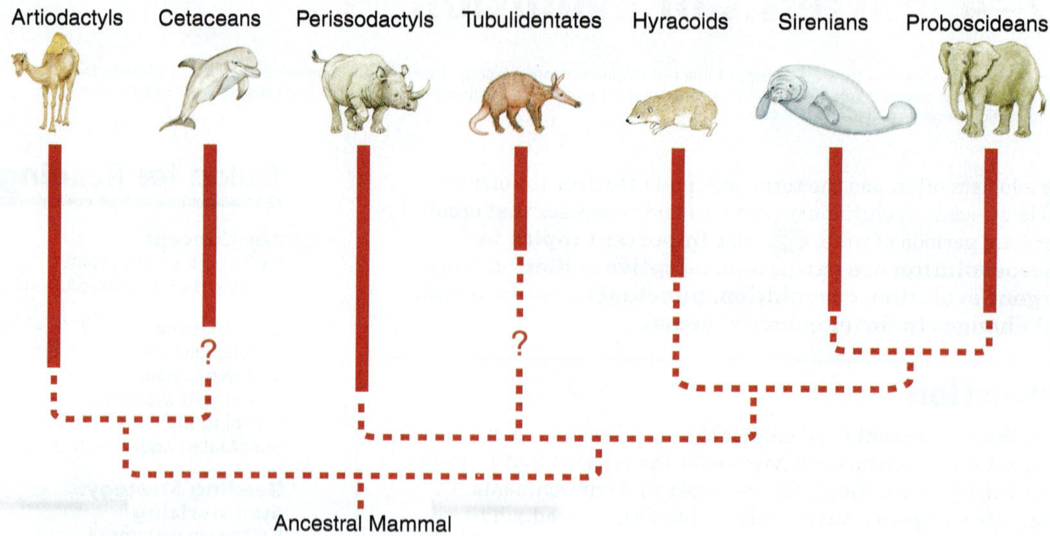

▲ **Figure 17–22** This diagram shows part of the adaptive radiation of mammals, emphasizing current hypotheses about how a group of ancestral mammals diversified over millions of years into several related living orders. Note that the dotted lines and question marks in this diagram indicate a combination of gaps in the fossil record and uncertainties about the timing of evolutionary branching. **Interpreting Graphics** ***According to this diagram, which mammal group is the most closely related to elephants?***

Adaptive Radiation

CA a

Often, studies of fossils or of living organisms show that a single species or a small group of species has evolved, through natural selection and other processes, into diverse forms that live in different ways. This process is known as **adaptive radiation.** In the adaptive radiation of Darwin's finches, more than a dozen species evolved from a single species.

Adaptive radiations can also occur on a much larger scale. Dinosaurs, for example, were the products of a spectacular adaptive radiation among ancient reptiles. The first dinosaurs and the earliest mammals evolved at about the same time. Dinosaurs and other ancient reptiles, however, underwent an adaptive radiation first and "ruled" Earth for about 150 million years. During that time, mammals remained small and relatively scarce. But the disappearance of the dinosaurs cleared the way for the great adaptive radiation of mammals. This radiation, part of which is shown in **Figure 17–22,** produced the great diversity of mammals of the Cenozoic.

Convergent Evolution

Adaptive radiations can have an interesting evolutionary "side effect." They can produce unrelated organisms that look remarkably similar to one another. How does that happen? Sometimes, groups of different organisms, such as mammals and dinosaurs, undergo adaptive radiation in different places or at different times but in ecologically similar environments. These organisms start out with different "raw material" for natural selection to work on, but they face similar environmental demands, such as moving through air, moving through water, or eating similar foods.

Figure 17–23 Each of these animals has a streamlined body and various appendages that enable it to move rapidly through water. Yet, the shark (above) is a fish, the penguin (center) is a bird, and the dolphin (bottom) is a mammal. **Applying Concepts** *How did these different animals come to resemble one another?*

CA a

In these situations, natural selection may mold different body structures, such as arms and legs, into modified forms, such as wings or flippers. The wings or flippers function in the same way and look very similar. This process, by which unrelated organisms come to resemble one another, is called **convergent evolution.** Convergent evolution has occurred time and time again in both animals and plants.

Consider swimming animals, for example. An animal can move through the water rapidly with the least amount of energy if its body is streamlined and if it has body parts that can be used like paddles. That is why convergent evolution involving fishes, two different groups of aquatic mammals, and swimming birds has resulted in sharks, dolphins, seals, and penguins whose streamlined bodies and swimming appendages look a lot alike, as shown in **Figure 17–23.** Structures such as a dolphin's flukes and a fish's tail fin, which look and function similarly but are made up of parts that do not share a common evolutionary history, are called analogous structures. There are a surprising number of animals (including one of Darwin's finches) that have evolved adaptations analogous to those of woodpeckers for feeding on insects living beneath the bark of trees and in rotted wood.

a 7 3.c

CHECKPOINT *How do biologists explain the similar shapes of sharks and dolphins?*

Coevolution

Sometimes organisms that are closely connected to one another by ecological interactions evolve together. Many flowering plants, for example, can reproduce only if the shape, color, and odor of their flowers attract a specific type of pollinator. Not surprisingly, these kinds of relationships can change over time. An evolutionary change in one organism may also be followed by a corresponding change in another organism. The process by which two species evolve in response to changes in each other over time is called **coevolution.**

Coevolution

Build Science Skills

Applying Concepts Point out that to coevolve, species must interact in some way over a long period of time. For example, flowering plants and the bees that pollinate them have mutualistic relationships, whereas plants and some plant-eating insects have parasitic relationships. Ask: **What other pairs of species do you think might have coevolutionary relationships?** *(Students should name pairs of species that interact in a symbiotic, predator-prey, or other type of long-term relationship. One example is humans and their intestinal bacteria, which have a mutualistic relationship.)* L2 L3

UNIVERSAL ACCESS

English Language Learners
Have students write the terms *Adaptive Radiation* and *Convergent Evolution* at the top of a sheet of paper. Then, as they read about the processes in the section, encourage them to list terms and phrases that are associated with each process. Have students find drawings or photographs to illustrate the points listed. Then, tell them to prepare a visual summary of the two processes, using the terms, phrases, and illustrations. L1 L2

Advanced Learners
Have students who need extra challenges learn more about hox genes and their possible role in major evolutionary transformations. Students should use credible Internet sources to find out about the most recent research in this new field. Encourage them to share what they learn in an oral report to the class. Suggest that they illustrate their talk with diagrams or pictures from the research. L3

Answers to . . .

CHECKPOINT *The similar shapes of sharks and dolphins resulted from convergent evolution: natural selection in a water environment resulted in streamlined bodies with parts that work like paddles.*

Figure 17–22 *Sirenians*

Figure 17–23 *By the process of convergent evolution*

17–4 (continued)

Analyzing Data

BIIE 1.k

Help students appreciate the significance of the data in the graph. Point out that marine organisms are of special interest because they evolved long before land organisms and, therefore, have a much longer evolutionary history to study. L2

Answers

1. Overall, there is an increase in the number of marine families.
2. The number of marine families decreased by about 200 families at the end of the Paleozoic Era. The number decreased by about 100 families at the end of the Mesozoic.
3. The mass extinction at the end of the Mesozoic may have involved a large asteroid colliding with Earth and causing changes in climate. Other extinctions, including the one at the end of the Paleozoic, may be due to climate changes related to cooling and drying periods, volcanic activity, continental drift, and other factors.
4. Sample answer: Global warming or pollution of ocean water might lead to a decline in the number of marine families in the next 1000 years. In the next 10,000,000 years, there might be an increase in marine families due to natural selection. Natural selection may cause the development of modified body structures that may help organisms survive in a hostile environment. Eventually, those surviving marine families would produce offspring that would evolve into new species and, in turn, new families.

◀ **Figure 17–24** This orchid has an unusually long spur containing a supply of nectar within its tip. The hawk moth has an equally long feeding tube that enables it to feed on the nectar. The flower spur and the feeding tube are an example of coevolution. **Inferring** *How might natural selection bring about the evolution of this orchid and the moth?*

The pattern of coevolution involving flowers and insects is so common that biologists in the field often discover additional examples. When Charles Darwin saw an orchid like the one in **Figure 17–24,** he closely examined the long structure called a spur. Inside the tip of that 40-centimeter spur is a supply of nectar, which serves as food for many insects. Darwin predicted the discovery of a pollinating insect with a 40-centimeter structure that could reach the orchid's nectar. About fifty years later, researchers discovered a moth that matched Darwin's prediction.

Consider another example, the relationships between plants and plant-eating insects. Insects have been feeding on flowering plants since both groups emerged during the Mesozoic. Over time, a number of plants have evolved poisonous compounds that prevent insects from feeding on them. In fact, some of the most powerful poisons known in nature are plant compounds that have evolved in response to insect attacks. But once plants began to produce poisons, natural selection in herbivorous insects began to favor any variants that could alter, inactivate, or eliminate those poisons. In a few cases, coevolutionary relationships can be traced back over millions of years.

CHECKPOINT *What happens during coevolution?*

BIIE 1.k

Analyzing Data

Changing Number of Marine Families

Using fossil evidence, scientists make inferences about the kinds and number of organisms that lived at different times in the past. Further, they classify those organisms in ways that facilitate comparisons between past and present types. The graph on the right gives an estimate of the number of ocean-dwelling families over time. In biology, a family consists of several groups of related species.

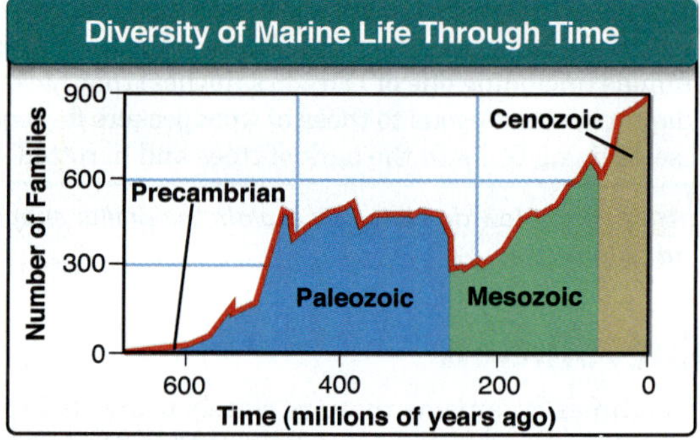

1. **Using Tables and Graphs** What overall trend does this graph show?
2. **Calculating** What was the change in the number of marine families at the end of the Paleozoic Era? At the end of the Mesozoic?
3. **Inferring** What kind of event(s) might explain the changes at the end of the Paleozoic and Mesozoic eras?
4. **Predicting** What factors might cause this graph to change in the next 1000 years? The next 10,000,000 years? Explain.

BIO INSIGHTS — FACTS AND FIGURES

The birds and the bees

An unusual example of coevolution occurs among certain orchids. These plants are pollinated by species of insects in which the males emerge in the spring before the females. The orchid flowers have evolved shapes and odors that mimic the stimuli presented by the female insects. The males fly around searching for females. They happen upon the insect-mimicking orchid flowers and try to mate with one after another. In the process, they pollinate the orchids. Some other kinds of plants and their pollinators are so highly adapted to each other that only one species of insect is able to pollinate a given plant. In Hawaii, *Brighamia* flowers can be pollinated only by nectar-feeding birds known as Hawaiian honeycreepers. Because the birds have declined greatly in number, the plants as well as the birds are facing extinction.

Punctuated Equilibrium

How quickly does evolution operate? Does it always occur at the same speed? These are questions on which some modern biologists would disagree with Darwin. Recall that Darwin was enormously impressed by the way Hutton and Lyell discussed the slow and steady nature of geologic change. Darwin, in turn, felt that biological change also needed to be slow and steady, an idea known as gradualism. In many cases, the fossil record confirms that populations of organisms did, indeed, change gradually over time.

But there is also evidence that this pattern does not always hold. Some species, such as horseshoe crabs, have changed little from the time they first appeared in the fossil record. In other words, much of the time these species are in a state of equilibrium, which means they do not change very much. Every now and then, however, something happens to upset the equilibrium. At several points in the fossil record, changes in animals and plants occurred over relatively short periods of time. Some biologists suggest that most new species are produced by periods of rapid change. (Remember that "short" and "rapid" are relative to the geologic time scale. Short periods of time for geologists can be hundreds of thousands—even millions—of years!)

Rapid evolution after long periods of equilibrium can occur for several reasons. It may occur when a small population becomes isolated from the main part of the population. This small population can then evolve more rapidly than the larger one because genetic changes can spread more quickly among fewer individuals. Or it may occur when a small group of organisms migrates to a new environment. That's what happened with the Galápagos finches, for example. Organisms evolve rapidly to fill available niches. In addition, mass extinctions can open many ecological niches and provide new opportunities to those organisms that survive. Thus, it is not surprising that some groups of organisms have evolved rapidly following mass extinctions.

Scientists use the term **punctuated equilibrium** to describe this pattern of long, stable periods interrupted by brief periods of more rapid change. The concept of punctuated equilibrium, illustrated in **Figure 17–25**, has generated much debate and is still somewhat controversial among biologists today. It is clear, however, that evolution has often proceeded at different rates for different organisms at different times during the long history of life on Earth.

▲ **Figure 17–25** Biologists have considered two different explanations for the rate of evolution, as illustrated in these diagrams. Gradualism involves a slow, steady change in a particular line of descent. Punctuated equilibrium involves stable periods interrupted by rapid changes involving many different lines of descent. **Interpreting Graphics** ***How do the diagrams illustrate these explanations?***

Punctuated Equilibrium

Build Science Skills

Inferring Challenge students to infer how the fossil record would differ if evolution is modeled by punctuated equilibrium instead of by gradualism. *(Students should infer that the fossil record would show only minor changes in fossils for long time periods and then sudden, major changes if evolution is modeled by punctuated equilibrium, whereas the fossil record would show continuous minor changes if evolution is modeled by gradualism.)* Point out that both patterns have been found in different organisms, suggesting that both models may apply in different cases. L2

Answers to . . .

CHECKPOINT *Over time, two species evolve in response to changes in each other.*

Figure 17–24 *The original flowers may have had moderately long spurs that only a few moths could feed on. These moths survived and reproduced more successfully than others and also helped fertilize flowers with longer spurs. Over time, the flower spurs and the moth's feeding tubes both became longer.*

Figure 17–25 *The broad, branching effect shows the slow, steady change of gradualism. The thin branching lines representing punctuated equilibrium show stable periods, interrupted by rapid changes involving many lines of descent.*

17–4 (continued)

Developmental Genes and Body Plans

Use Visuals

Figure 17–26 Ask: **How could hox genes produce the modern insects shown at the bottom of the figure from the ancestral insect shown at the top?** *(By turning other genes off or on, hox genes could transform the ancestral insect's many winglike structures into the one or two pairs of large wings seen in modern insects.)* L2

3 ASSESS

Evaluate Understanding

Have students write a paragraph explaining mass extinction and adaptive radiation and how the two are related.

Reteach

Divide the class into pairs, and have each pair create a Venn diagram showing the similarities and differences between gradualism and punctuated equilibrium. Encourage pairs to exchange and compare Venn diagrams.

Thinking Visually

Students' tables should have rows for each of the six patterns of macroevolution and columns for explanations and examples of the patterns. Students should fill in each row of the table with appropriate information. For example, they might explain that adaptive radiation is the evolution of several different forms from a single species and give the example of Darwin's finches. Tables should also have a title, such as "Patterns of Macroevolution."

If your class subscribes to the iText, use it to review the Key Concepts in Section 17–4.

Ancient Insect

Two Types of Modern Insects

▲ **Figure 17–26** Some ancient insects, such as the mayfly nymph (top), had winglike structures on many body segments. Modern insects have only four wings or two wings. **Changes in the expression of developmental genes may explain how these differences evolved.**

Developmental Genes and Body Plans

Biologists have long suspected that changes in the genes for growth and differentiation during embryological development could produce transformations in body shape and size. Until recently, however, researchers had only limited ability to affect gene activity in embryos. Therefore, they couldn't develop many of those hunches into testable scientific hypotheses. Molecular tools have changed all that. We can now perform experiments with gene expression by turning genes on or off and examining the results. These studies shed new light on how genetic change can produce major evolutionary transformations.

CA a For example, as you saw in Chapter 12, "master control genes," called hox genes, guide development of major body structures in animals. Some determine which parts of an embryo become front and rear, or top and bottom. Others control the size and shape of arms, legs, or wings. Homologous control genes serve similar functions in animals as different as insects and humans—even though those animals haven't shared a common ancestor in at least 700 million years!

Small changes in the activity of control genes can affect many other genes to produce large changes in adult animals. If one gene, called "wingless," is turned on in an insect body segment, that segment grows no wings. This is interesting because some ancient insects, shown in **Figure 17–26,** had winglike structures on all body segments. Yet modern insects have wings on only one or two segments. Changes in the activation of this gene could have enabled many-winged ancestors of modern insects to evolve into four-winged and two-winged forms.

Small changes in the timing of cell differentiation and gene expression can make the difference between long legs and short ones, between long, slender fingers or short, stubby toes. In fact, recent studies suggest that differences in gene expression may cause many of the differences between chimpanzee brains and human brains. Small wonder that this new field is one of the hottest areas in all of evolutionary biology!

 7 3.c

17–4 Section Assessment

1. **Key Concept** What is macroevolution? Describe two patterns of macroevolution.
2. What role have mass extinctions played in the history of life?
3. What is convergent evolution? Describe an example.
4. How might hox genes contribute to variation?
5. **Critical Thinking Comparing and Contrasting** Compare and contrast the hypotheses of gradualism and punctuated equilibrium.

Thinking Visually

Making a Table
Create a table that lists each of the six patterns of macroevolution, explains each pattern, and gives one example for each. Add a title to your table.

17–4 Section Assessment

1. Macroevolution is large-scale evolutionary change over long time periods. Students should describe any two patterns.
2. Mass extinctions periodically wiped out huge numbers of species and made way for the rapid evolution of new species.
3. The process by which unrelated organisms, such as dolphins and sharks, come to resemble one another
4. Hox genes regulate timing of genetic control in the embryo. Even small changes in timing can cause variation in traits.
5. Gradualism: evolutionary change is slow and steady. Punctuated equilibrium: evolutionary change occurs in spurts of rapid change after long periods of little change.

Exploration

 BIIE 1.d, BIIE 1.g

Modeling Coevolution

Flowering plants and the animals that pollinate their flowers include many examples of coevolving species. In this investigation, you will model how these plants and animals evolve in response to one another.

Problem How do flowering plants and their pollinators coevolve?

Materials

- long forceps
- spoon
- dried peas
- 3 25-mL graduated cylinders
- 3 100-mL beakers
- watch or clock with second hand

Skills Using Models, Inferring

Procedure 

1. Work in groups of three. Each group member represents a different bird species. To represent the birds' beaks, one group member will use forceps, the second group member will use a spoon, and the third will use two fingertips.
2. On a separate sheet of paper, make a copy of the data table shown. The beakers represent short, open flowers and the graduated cylinders represent long, narrow flowers. The dried peas represent the flowers' nectar, which is the birds' food. Fill the beakers and the graduated cylinders halfway with dried peas. **CAUTION:** *Handle the beakers and graduated cylinders carefully. If one breaks, tell your teacher immediately.*
3. For 1 minute, use the method you chose in step 1 to remove the peas. Remove them one at a time from your beaker. Do not move or tip the beaker as you do this.
4. Record the number of peas you removed in your data table.
5. To produce seeds, a flower must be pollinated by a member of its own species. Assume that 1 flower was pollinated for every 5 peas removed. Record the number of pollinations for each bird.
6. Repeat steps 3 through 5, using the graduated cylinders instead of the beakers.
7. **Calculating** Exchange data with your classmates and record the class averages for each bird species in your data table.

Data Table

Beak Type	Individual Data		Class Average	
	Peas	Pollinations	Peas	Pollinations
Forceps				
Spoon				
Fingers				

Analyze and Conclude

1. **Analyzing Data** Which bird species obtained the most nectar from the beakers? From the graduated cylinders?
2. **Analyzing Data** From which type of flower was each bird most successful in obtaining food?
3. **Inferring** What is the benefit to a plant of short, open flowers?
4. **Inferring** What is the benefit to a bird of a long, narrow beak?
5. **Drawing Conclusions** Which type of bird is the best pollinator for long, narrow flowers?
6. **Evaluating and Revising** How does this model represent coevolution? How could you improve this model?

Go Further

Using Models Construct an alternative model of coevolution between flowering plants and birds that feed on their nectar. Then, compare your model to the one you used in this lab. Analyze the strengths and weaknesses of each model.

Analyze and Conclude

1. Spoon beaks obtained the most nectar from the beakers. Forceps beaks obtained the most nectar from the graduated cylinders.
2. Spoon beaks and finger beaks were most successful with short, open flowers. Forceps beaks were most successful with long, narrow flowers.
3. Short, open flowers allow a plant to be pollinated by more types of birds.
4. A long, narrow beak allows a bird to feed from long, narrow flowers that other birds cannot feed from.
5. The bird with the long, narrow beak is the best pollinator for long, narrow flowers.
6. The model represents coevolution because it shows how traits in a species evolve in response to changes in another species. A better model would show how the birds and flowers change in response to one another through time.

Exploration

 **BIIE 1.d, BIIE 1.g**

Objectives Students will be able to
- model coevolution;
- infer how plants and animals evolve in response to one another. L2

Skills Focus Using Models, Inferring

Time 45 minutes

Advance Prep You can obtain dried peas from a supermarket or bulk foods store. Other small dried legumes, such as pinto beans, could be used instead.

Safety Advise students who are using their fingers for beaks not to force their hands into the beakers or cylinders because they could break.

Teaching Tip Have students read the entire procedure. Then, ask: **What type of relationship exists between the birds and the flowering plants in the model?** *(A mutualistic relationship)* **How does each type of organism benefit from the relationship?** *(The birds benefit by obtaining nectar for food. The plants benefit by being pollinated so they can reproduce.)*

Procedure

5. To obtain the number of pollinations for each bird, students should divide the number of peas removed by that bird by five.

7. Make a data table on the chalkboard for students to use in compiling data for the class. Check that all the students have correctly calculated the class average for each bird species.

Expected Outcome Students should be able to remove the most peas from the beaker with the spoon and from the graduated cylinder with the forceps.

Go Further

One possible alternative model is to use water for nectar and droppers, straws, spoons, or other such items for beaks. This model would be closer to reality, because nectar, like water, is a liquid.

Chapter 17 Study Guide

Study Tip

Suggest that students review the Key Concept questions in the section assessments. Also suggest that they make flashcards for the Vocabulary terms and use them to quiz a partner.

Thinking Visually

Students' flowcharts should show competition or environmental change leading to natural selection against a species due to problems in survival or reproduction and, ultimately, to extinction of the species.

Chapter 17 Assessment

Reviewing Content

1. b	**5.** d	**9.** c
2. d	**6.** d	**10.** a
3. a	**7.** a	
4. a	**8.** b	

Understanding Concepts

11. The age of a fossil is estimated by comparing its placement in rock layers with the placement of fossils in other rock layers.

12. Radioactive elements decay at a steady rate, measured in units called half-lives. Radioactive dating uses half-lives to determine the age of a sample. Scientists can calculate the age of fossil-bearing rocks based on the amount of remaining radioactive isotopes they contain.

13. The geologic time scale represents evolutionary time. It was developed by scientists who studied rock layers and index fossils worldwide.

14. When Earth was young, a collision with a very large object produced enough heat to melt Earth. Elements then rearranged themselves by density. The least dense elements, including hydrogen and nitrogen, formed the first atmosphere. About 3.8 billion years ago, Earth cooled enough for water to remain a liquid. Thunderstorms drenched the planet, eventually forming the oceans.

15. Miller and Urey first demonstrated how organic matter might have formed in Earth's primitive atmosphere. By re-creating the early atmosphere (ammonia, water, hydrogen, and methane) and passing a spark (lightning) through the mixture, they demonstrated that organic matter, such as amino acids, could have arisen from simpler compounds.

Chapter 17 Study Guide

17–1 The Fossil Record

BI 8.e, BIIE 1.i

Key Concepts

- The fossil record provides evidence about the history of life on Earth. It also shows how different groups of organisms, including species, have changed over time.
- Relative dating allows paleontologists to estimate a fossil's age compared with that of other fossils.
- In radioactive dating, scientists calculate the age of a sample based on the amount of remaining radioactive isotopes it contains.
- After Precambrian Time, the basic divisions of the geologic time scale are eras and periods.

Vocabulary

paleontologist, p. 417
fossil record, p. 417
extinct, p. 417
relative dating, p. 419
index fossil, p. 419
half-life, p. 420
radioactive dating, p. 420
geologic time scale, p. 421
era, p. 421
period, p. 422

17–2 Earth's Early History

Key Concepts

- Earth's early atmosphere probably contained hydrogen cyanide, carbon dioxide, carbon monoxide, nitrogen, hydrogen sulfide, and water.
- Miller and Urey's experiments suggested how mixtures of the organic compounds necessary for life could have arisen from simpler compounds present on a primitive Earth.
- The rise of oxygen in the atmosphere drove some life-forms to extinction, while other life-forms evolved new, more efficient metabolic pathways that used oxygen for respiration.
- The endosymbiotic theory proposes that eukaryotic cells arose from living communities formed by prokaryotic organisms.

Vocabulary

proteinoid microsphere, p. 425
microfossil, p. 426
endosymbiotic theory, p. 427

17–3 Evolution of Multicellular Life

Key Concepts

7 3.c, BI 8.e

- Rich fossil evidence shows that early in the Paleozoic Era, there was a diversity of marine life.
- During the Devonian, vertebrates began to invade the land.
- The mass extinction at the end of the Paleozoic affected both plants and animals on land and in the seas. As much as 95 percent of the complex life in the oceans disappeared.
- Events during the Mesozoic include the increasing dominance of dinosaurs. The Mesozoic is marked by the appearance of flowering plants.
- During the Cenozoic, mammals evolved adaptations that allowed them to live in various environments—on land, in water, and even in the air.

Vocabulary

mass extinction, p. 431

17–4 Patterns of Evolution

Key Concept

7 3.c, BI 8.e

- Six important topics in macroevolution are extinctions, adaptive radiation, convergent evolution, coevolution, punctuated equilibrium, and changes in developmental genes.

Vocabulary

macroevolution, p. 435
adaptive radiation, p. 436
convergent evolution, p. 437
coevolution, p. 437
punctuated equilibrium, p. 439

Thinking Visually

Use information from the chapter to create a flowchart that illustrates how natural selection can lead to the extinction of a species.

CHAPTER RESOURCES

Print:

- ***Teaching Resources,*** Chapter Vocabulary Review, Graphic Organizer, Chapter 17 Tests: Levels A and B

Technology:

- ***Computer Test Bank,*** Chapter 17 Test
- ***iText,*** Chapter 17 Assessment

Chapter 17 Assessment

Interactive textbook with assessment at PHSchool.com 

Reviewing Content

Choose the letter that best answers the question or completes the statement.

1. Scientists who specialize in the study of fossils are called
   a. biologists. c. zoologists.
   b. paleontologists. d. anthropologists.
2. Sedimentary rocks form when layers of small particles are compressed
   a. in the atmosphere. c. in mountains.
   b. in a snow field. d. under water.
3. Radioactive dating of rock samples
   a. is a method of absolute dating.
   b. is a method of relative dating.
   c. forms a geologic column.
   d. forms a geologic time scale.
4. Half-life is the length of time required for half the atoms in a radioactive sample to
   a. decay. c. expand.
   b. double. d. be created.
5. Earth's first atmosphere contained little or no
   a. hydrogen cyanide. c. nitrogen.
   b. hydrogen sulfide. d. oxygen.
6. In Miller and Urey's experiments with the origin of life-forms, electric sparks were passed through a mixture of gases to
   a. simulate temperature.
   b. simulate sunlight.
   c. sterilize the gases.
   d. simulate lightning.
7. Outlines of ancient cells that are preserved well enough to identify them as prokaryotes are
   a. microfossils. c. autotrophs.
   b. heterotrophs. d. phototrophic.
8. Which event occurred at the end of the Paleozoic Era?
   a. coevolution c. punctuated equilibrium
   b. mass extinction d. convergent evolution
9. The process that produces a similar appearance among unrelated groups of organisms is
   a. adaptive radiation. c. convergent evolution.
   b. coevolution. d. mass evolution.
10. As a group, the large-scale evolutionary changes that take place over long periods of time are called
    a. macroevolution. c. convergent evolution.
    b. coevolution. d. geologic time.

Understanding Concepts

11. How does relative dating enable paleontologists to estimate a fossil's age?
12. Explain how radioactivity is used to date rocks.
13. What is the geologic time scale? How was it developed?
14. Discuss what scientists hypothesize about Earth's early atmosphere and the way oceans formed.
15. Use the diagram below to explain the significance of Miller and Urey's experiment.

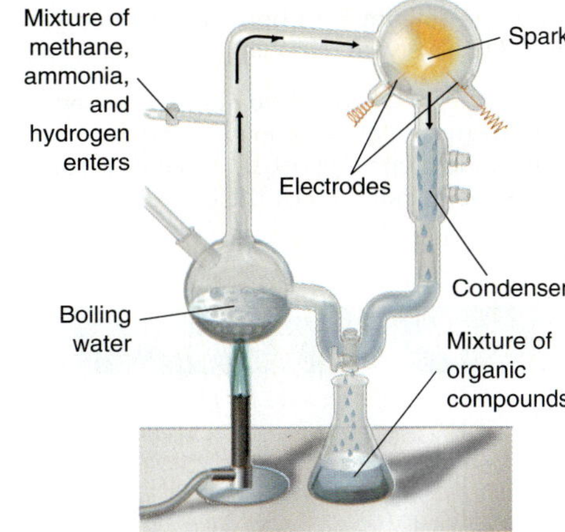

16. How are proteinoid microspheres like living cells?
17. How did the addition of oxygen to Earth's atmosphere affect the evolution of life?
18. Describe the endosymbiotic theory.
19. Describe life as it existed in Precambrian Time.
20. During what era did marine life become diverse?
21. What significant mammalian adaptations led to their success during the Cenozoic Era?
22. What events led to the diversification of mammals?
23. Explain the process of adaptive radiation. Give an example.
24. Explain the pattern known as punctuated equilibrium.
25. Use an example to explain the concept of coevolution.
26. How can hox genes provide evidence of evolution?

TIME SAVER — HOMEWORK GUIDE

Section:	Questions:
Section 17–1	1–4, 11–13, 30, 32, 34
Section 17–2	5–7, 14–18, 27, 28, 31
Section 17–3	8, 19–22, 29
Section 17–4	9, 10, 23–26, 33

Interactive Textbook

If your class subscribes to the iText, your students can go online to access an interactive version of the Student Edition and a self-test.

(Continued from page 442)

16. Proteinoid microspheres, like cells, have a selectively permeable membrane across which water molecules can travel and have a simple means of storing and releasing energy.

17. Some organisms began to evolve more efficient metabolic pathways that used oxygen for respiration; others became restricted to oxygen-free habitats.

18. The endosymbiotic theory states that the first eukaryotic cells were formed from symbiosis among different prokaryotic cells. One type with the ability to use oxygen to generate ATP evolved into mitochondria. Another type that carried out photosynthesis evolved into chloroplasts. Both types were engulfed by other cells.

19. The first organisms were anaerobic, heterotrophic bacteria. Photosynthetic bacteria followed, adding oxygen to the atmosphere. Some bacteria adapted to the presence of oxygen, using it in cell respiration. The next to appear were eukaryotes, which gave rise to multicellular organisms.

20. The Paleozoic Era

21. Mammalian adaptations included hair that provided insulation against the cold and the protection of young before and after birth.

22. Disappearance of the dinosaurs enabled the smaller, relatively scarce mammals to flourish and diversify.

23. In adaptive radiation, species evolve into several different forms that live in different ways; examples: dinosaurs, mammals.

24. Punctuated equilibrium is a pattern in which long periods of little or no evolutionary change are interrupted by brief periods of rapid change.

25. Students can use any example from the text to convey the concept of two species evolving in response to changes in each other over time.

26. Homologous hox genes established body plans in organisms that had not shared common ancestors for millions of years.

Chapter 17 Assessment

Critical Thinking

27. Condensing water vapor represents rain. Rain carried many chemicals from the atmosphere into the primitive sea. The sea was also the site of the first steps in chemical evolution.

28. When prokaryotes engulfed other bacteria that evolved into mitochondria and chloroplasts, they gained energy in two new ways: by using oxygen to form energy-rich ATP and by using light to carry out photosynthesis.

29. Geological changes such as volcanic eruptions and meteorite collisions can send enormous ash and dust clouds into Earth's atmosphere, quickly changing the climate and the conditions that support life. Those changes can bring on local and mass extinctions of Earth's producers, followed quickly by the loss of consumers.

30. After one half-life, half of the original radioactive atoms in a sample have decayed. It would take four half-lives for the sample to contain 1/16 of the amount of carbon-14. One half-life is 5730 years, so four half-lives are 22,920 years. Therefore, the age of the fossil would be about 22,920 years.

31. At 2.5 billion years ago, photosynthetic organisms appeared. They added oxygen to the atmosphere.

32. Some organisms never became fossils because they did not live near water and their remains never became part of sedimentary rock. Other organisms may not have had hard body parts that could be preserved.

33. Both processes occur because organisms cannot successfully adapt to changing environmental conditions. In mass extinctions, major environmental changes cause severe selective pressure against many or most species. In other extinctions, environmental changes are smaller or more gradual, generally lead to less severe selective pressure, and affect fewer species.

34. Possible questions might include: In which rock stratum was the fossil found? What other types of organisms lived at that time? The fossil might provide evidence of a species change in locomotion or body size.

Chapter 17 Assessment

Critical Thinking

27. Using Models What part of Miller and Urey's apparatus represents rain? What important part would rain play in chemical evolution?

28. Applying Concepts In what way might the cells that took in the ancestors of mitochondria and chloroplasts have benefited from the relationship?

29. Inferring Geologic changes often accompany mass extinctions of life-forms. Why do you think this is true?

30. Problem Solving The half-life of carbon-14 is 5730 years. What is the age of a fossil containing 1/16 the amount of carbon-14 of living organisms? Explain your reasoning.

31. Applying Concepts The graph shows an approximation of the amount of oxygen in the atmosphere since life began. What event occurred at the point indicated by the arrow?

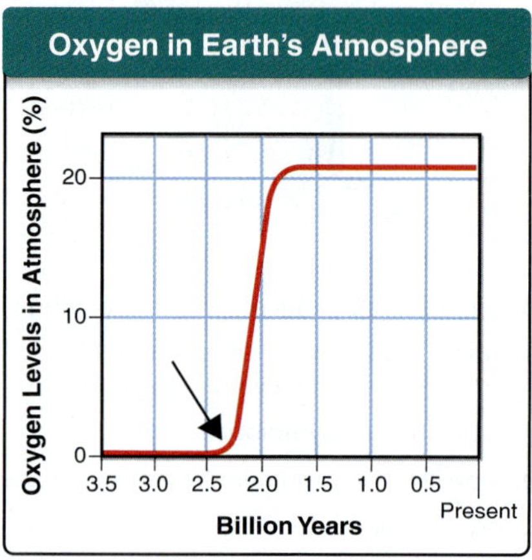

32. Applying Concepts Evolutionary biologists say that there is good reason for gaps in the fossil record. Can you explain why some extinct animals and plants were never fossilized?

33. Comparing and Contrasting Compare mass extinction to the extinction of species through the more typical processes of natural selection. Be sure to say how the processes are similar as well as different.

34. Asking Questions Suppose you are part of a scientific expedition searching for fossils. Someone brings you a fossilized bone that resembles one of the leg bones of a modern frog. What are some questions you would need to have answered in order to determine the age of the fossil? In what ways might the fossil provide evidence of change in species?

Focus on the BIG Idea

Matter and Energy Recall what you learned about chemistry in Chapter 2. When Earth's atmosphere first began to form, it did not contain oxygen (O_2), and hydrogen (H_2) was the most abundant element in the solar system. However, there is very little H_2 in the atmosphere today, and the element makes up less than 1 percent of Earth's mass. What might have happened to the H_2?

Writing in Science

When you compare two items, you explain how they are similar and different. Write a paragraph comparing conditions on early Earth (about 3.8 billion years ago) with those on modern Earth. (*Hint:* When you write a comparison, it isn't sufficient to summarize the characteristics of both items separately. Instead, you need to say specifically how the items are like each other and how they differ from each other.)

Performance-Based Assessment

Prepare a Booklet Suppose you could observe the formation and early history of Earth. Write your experiences in the form of a booklet four to six pages long to be read by middle-school students. Include a table of contents, color illustrations, and an activity at the end to evaluate students' understanding of the concept. The activity could be a puzzle, a completion activity, or another similar activity.

For: An interactive self-test
Visit: PHSchool.com
Web Code: cba-5170

Focus on the BIG Idea

The hydrogen reacted with other elements and became part of compounds, especially water and organic compounds. Some students may also say that hydrogen, the lightest element, could have escaped Earth's gravity and become spread out in space.

Writing in Science

Students' paragraphs should compare the physical conditions on Earth, including presence or absence of oceans, geological activity, and atmospheric content. They should also compare the types of life-forms.

Standards Practice

Success Tracker™ Online at PHSchool.com

Test-Taking Tip If you find particular questions difficult, put a light mark beside them and keep working. As you answer later questions, you may find information that helps you find the answers you still need. (Do not write in this book.)

Directions: Choose the letter that best answers the question or completes the statement.

1. Which of the following is characteristic of an index fossil? BI 8.e
   I. Distinctive species
   II. Lived in a wide geographic range
   III. Lived for a long period of time
   A I only
   B II only
   C I and II only
   D II and III only

2. In which geologic era do you live?
   A Cenozoic
   B Mesozoic
   C Cambrian
   D Precambrian

3. The endosymbiotic theory includes all of the following EXCEPT
   A Photosynthetic prokaryotes evolved into chloroplasts.
   B Aerobic prokaryotes evolved into mitochondria.
   C Eukaryotic cells arose from the merging of different prokaryotic organisms.
   D All organelles evolved from specialized enfoldings of the plasma membrane.

4. Which of the following is evidence for the endosymbiotic theory?
   I. Mitochondria and chloroplasts contain DNA similar to bacterial DNA.
   II. Mitochondria and chloroplasts contain ribosomes that differ from bacterial ribosomes.
   III. Mitochondria and chloroplasts reproduce by binary fission.
   A I only
   B II only
   C I and III only
   D II and III only

5. Potassium-40 is useful for dating very old fossils because BI 8.e
   A it has a very long half-life.
   B it has a very short half-life.
   C most organisms contain more potassium than carbon.
   D it does not undergo radioactive decay.

6. The Cambrian Period is also called the
   A Age of Humans.
   B Age of Fishes.
   C Age of Dinosaurs.
   D Age of Invertebrates.

Questions 7 and 8

The graph shows the radioactive decay of an isotope. Use the information in the graph to answer the questions that follow.

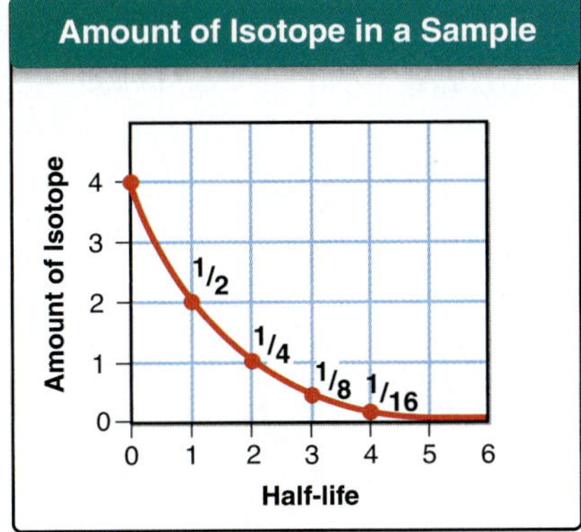

7. The half-life of thorium-230 is 75,000 years. How long will it take for 7/8 of the original amount of thorium-230 in a sample to decay?
   A 75,000 years
   B 225,000 years
   C 25,000 years
   D 70,000 years

8. The half-life of potassium-40 is about 1300 million years. After four half-lives have passed, how much of the original sample will be left?
   A $\frac{1}{16}$
   B $\frac{1}{16} \times$ 1300 million grams
   C $\frac{1}{4}$
   D $\frac{1}{4} \times$ 1300 million grams

Standards Practice

1. C 5. A
2. A 6. D
3. D 7. B
4. C 8. A

Success Tracker™ Online at PHSchool.com

Have students check their understanding of the chapter by logging onto Success Tracker.

Performance-Based Assessment

Students' booklets will vary, but they should contain information about the geologic time scale, Earth's early atmosphere, how early Earth was formed, and the appearance of eukaryotes and other early forms of life.

Go Online PHSchool.com

Your students can independently test their knowledge of the chapter and print out their test results for your files.

Chapter Planner 18 Classification

Section and Section Objectives	Time	STANDARDS NCLB	STANDARDS Biology	Activities and Labs
18–1 Finding Order in Diversity, pp. 447–450 **18.1.1** ***Explain*** how living things are organized for study. **18.1.2** ***Describe*** binomial nomenclature. **18.1.3** ***Explain*** Linnaeus's system of classification.	1 period (1/2 block)			**SE:** ***Inquiry Activity,*** How can you classify fruits?, p. 446 L2 **TE:** ***Demonstration,*** p. 449 L1 L2 **TE:** ***Build Science Skills,*** p. 450 L2 **IF:** Investigation 5 L1 L2 L3
18–2 Modern Evolutionary Classification, pp. 451–455 **18.2.1** ***Explain*** how evolutionary relationships are important in classification. **18.2.2** ***Identify*** the principle behind cladistic analysis. **18.2.3** ***Explain*** how we can compare very dissimilar organisms.	1 period (1/2 block)		*BI 8.f, *BI 8.g	**TE:** ***Demonstration,*** p. 451 L1 L2 **SE:** ***Quick Lab,*** How is a cladogram constructed?, p. 453 L2 L3 **TE:** ***Demonstration,*** p. 454 L2 **SE:** ***Technology and Society,*** The Search for New Species in Tropical Forests, p. 456 L2
18–3 Kingdoms and Domains, pp. 457–461 **18.3.1** ***Name*** the six kingdoms of life as they are now identified. **18.3.2** ***Describe*** the three-domain system of classification.	1 period (1/2 block)			**TE:** ***Demonstration,*** p. 460 L1 L2 **SE:** ***Real-World Lab,*** Classifying Organisms Using Dichotomous Keys, pp. 462–463 L2 **LMA:** Chapter 18 Lab L2 L3 **LMB:** Chapter 18 Lab L1 L2
Chapter Assessment, pp. 464–467	1 period (1/2 block)			

ACTIVITY PLANNER

SE: ***Inquiry Activity,*** p. 446; 15 min.; 5 different fruits, knife

TE: ***Demonstration,*** p. 449; 5 min.; pictures of domestic dog, wolf, fox, and mountain lion

TE: ***Build Science Skills,*** p. 450; 10 min.; hair clip, bobby pin, safety pin, straight pin, screw, nail, paper clip, and staple

TE: ***Demonstration,*** p. 451; 5 min.; pictures of plants, animals, and protists

SE: ***Quick Lab,*** p. 453; 15 min.; no materials needed

TE: ***Demonstration,*** p. 454; 5 min.; cytochrome-c family tree

TE: ***Demonstration,*** p. 460; 10 min.; microprojector, slides of amoebas and paramecia

TE: ***Real-World Lab,*** pp. 462–463; 45 min.; group of common items such as nuts and bolts or coins

PLANNING KEY

Ability Levels
for students performing . . .
below grade level L1
at grade level L2
above grade level L3

Print Components

SE	Student Edition	LA	Lab Assessment
TE	Teacher's Edition	BTM	Biotechnology Manual
RSW	Reading & Study Workbook A	IDM	Issues and Decision Making
ARSW	Adapted Reading & Study Workbook B	LW	Lab Worksheets
TR	Teaching Resources	LMA	Laboratory Manual A
IF	Investigations in Forensics	LMB	Laboratory Manual B

Tech Components

CTB	Computer Test Bank
BD	BioDetectives DVD
TP	Transparencies Plus
PLM	Probeware Lab Manual
ABC	ABC DVD Library
LS	Lab Simulations
VL	Virtual Labs

Interactive textbook with assessment at PHSchool.com

Program Resources	Assessment	Media and Technology
TR: Lesson Plan 18–1, Section Summary, p. 138 L1, p. 147 L2, Worksheets, p. 141 L1, pp. 149–150 L2, Enrichment L2 L3 **RSW:** Section 18–1 L2 **ARSW:** Section 18–1 L1	**SE:** 18–1 Section Assessment, p. 450 **TR:** Section Review 18–1	**iText:** Section 18–1 **TP:** 18–1 Interest Grabber, Section Outline, Flowchart, Figure 18–5
TR: Lesson Plan 18–2, Section Summary, p. 139 L1, p. 147 L2, Worksheets, pp. 142–143 L1, pp. 151–152 L2 **RSW:** Section 18–2 L2 **ARSW:** Section 18–2 L1	**SE:** 18–2 Section Assessment, p. 455 **TR:** Section Review 18–2	**iText:** Section 18–2 **TP:** 18–2 Interest Grabber, Section Outline, Traditional Classification Versus Cladogram
TR: Lesson Plan 18–3, Section Summary, p. 140 L1, p. 148 L2, Worksheets, pp. 144–145 L1, pp. 153–155 L2 **LW:** Chapter 18 Real-World Lab L1 L2 L3 **RSW:** Section 18–3 L2 **ARSW:** Section 18–3 L1	**SE:** 18–3 Section Assessment, p. 461 **TR:** Section Review 18–3	**iText:** Section 18–3 **TP:** 18–3 Interest Grabber, Section Outline, Concept Map, Figure 18–12, Figure 18–13
	SE: Chapter 18 Assessment, pp. 464–467 **TR:** Chapter Vocabulary Review, Graphic Organizer, Chapter 18 Test **LA:** Laboratory Assessment 5	**iText:** Chapter 18 Assessment **CTB:** Chapter 18 Test

Go Online
Students can do research, share data, and test their knowledge online.

PRESSED FOR TIME?

To Preview the Chapter
- Have students read the boldface sentences in each section.
- Introduce students to the Vocabulary terms in each section.

To Cover the Chapter Quickly
- Have students read Assigning Scientific Names and Linnaeus's System of Classification in Section 18–1, Evolutionary Classification in Section 18–2, and all of Section 18–3.
- Assign questions 2 and 3 in 18–1 Section Assessment, question 1 in 18–2 Section Assessment, and all of 18–3 Section Assessment; questions 2, 5, 8–10, 13, 14, 21–30, and 32 in Chapter 18 Assessment; and questions 1–8 in the Chapter 18 Standards Practice.

To Review the Chapter
- Assign Sections 18–1 through 18–3 in the Reading and Study Workbook or the Adapted Reading and Study Workbook.
- Assign the Section Reviews for 18–1 through 18–3 and the Chapter Vocabulary Review for Chapter 18 in the Teaching Resources.

CHAPTER 18

ENGAGE/EXPLORE

Inquiry Activity

Objective Students will be able to conclude which of five fruits are most closely related based on observable characteristics. L2

Skills Focus **Observing, Classifying**

Materials 5 different fruits, knife

Time 15 minutes

Advance Prep Choose some fruits that are similar, such as apples and pears or oranges and grapefruits, and also some fruits that are dissimilar, such as peaches and bananas or lemons and kiwis.

Safety Remind students to be careful using knives. Make sure students wash their hands with soap and hot water before leaving the lab.

Strategy If students are having difficulty thinking of four different characteristics, mention some they may not have thought of, such as scent, firmness, and thickness of skin.

Expected Outcome Students will be able to classify a sample of fruits based on how similar the fruits are in observable characteristics.

Think About It

1. Students are likely to have selected such readily observable characteristics as size, shape, color, and presence or absence of seeds.
2. Students should conclude that the most closely related fruits are those sharing the greatest number of characteristics.

Assess Prior Knowledge

Find out if students are familiar with Linnaeus's binomial classification system. Ask: **What is the scientific name for the human species?** *(Homo sapiens)* **What do you think are the common names for *Felis catus* and *Canis familiaris*?** *(Cat, dog)* **In each case, what does the first of the two names refer to?** *(The genus)* **What do the two names together refer to?** *(The species)* **Which group, *genus* or *species*, is more inclusive?** *(Genus)* Point out that, in this chapter, students will learn more about how organisms are classified.

CHAPTER 18

Classification

Each person might divide these shells into different categories. Scientists often group and name, or classify, organisms using certain guidelines. This makes it easier to discuss the types and characteristics of living things.

Inquiry Activity

How can you classify fruits?

Procedure  

1. Obtain five different fruits. Use a paring knife to cut each fruit open and examine its structure. **CAUTION:** *Use caution with sharp instruments. Do not eat any of the fruit.*
2. Construct a table with five rows and four columns. Label each row with the name of a different fruit.
3. Observe each fruit and choose four characteristics by which you can tell the fruits apart. Label the columns in your table with these four characteristics.
4. Record a description of each fruit in your table.

Think About It

1. **Observing** What characteristics did you use to describe the fruits?
2. **Classifying** Based on your table, which fruits are most closely related? Explain.

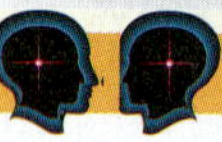

TEACHER TO TEACHER

Near the beginning of the chapter on classification, I do a demonstration using characteristics of students' shoes to develop a dichotomous key. Each student takes off his or her left shoe and puts it on the floor in the front of the room. As a group, we identify characteristics that vary in the sample of shoes, such as white/nonwhite and tennis/nontennis, and develop a dichotomous key that identifies all the shoes and their owners. If possible, I have the principal or another teacher come into the classroom at this point and return some of the shoes to their owners by following the key. I usually let the rest of the students retrieve their own shoes once they see that the dichotomous key really works. The demonstration is fun for students and makes the concept of dichotomous key easier to understand.

—Bob Demmink
Biology Teacher
East Kentwood High School
Kentwood, MI

18–1 Finding Order in Diversity

For more than 3.5 billion years, life on Earth has been constantly changing. Natural selection and other processes have led to a staggering diversity of organisms. A tropical rain forest, for example, may support thousands of species per acre. Recall that a species is a population of organisms that share similar characteristics and can breed with one another and produce fertile offspring. Biologists have identified and named about 1.5 million species so far. They estimate that anywhere between 2 and 100 million additional species have yet to be discovered.

Why Classify?

To study this great diversity of organisms, biologists must give each organism a name. Biologists must also attempt to organize living things into groups that have biological meaning. **To study the diversity of life, biologists use a classification system to name organisms and group them in a logical manner.**

In the discipline known as **taxonomy,** scientists classify organisms and assign each organism a universally accepted name. One example appears in **Figure 18–1.** By using a scientific name, biologists can be certain that everyone is discussing the same organism. When taxonomists classify organisms, they organize them into groups that have biological significance. When you hear the word "bird," for example, you immediately form a mental picture of the organism being discussed—a flying animal that has feathers. But science often requires smaller categories as well as larger, more general categories. In a good system of classification, organisms placed into a particular group are more similar to one another than they are to organisms in other groups.

You use classification systems also, for example, when you refer to "teachers" or "mechanics," or more specifically, "biology teachers" or "auto mechanics." Such a process, like scientific classification, uses accepted names and common criteria to group things.

Figure 18–1 Depending on where you live, you might recognize this as a mountain lion, a puma, a cougar, or a panther—all of which are common names for the same animal. The scientific name for this animal is *Felis concolor.* **To avoid the confusion caused by regional names, biologists use a classification system to group organisms in a logical manner and to assign names.**

Guide for Reading

Key Concepts
- How are living things organized for study?
- What is binomial nomenclature?
- What is Linnaeus's system of classification?

Vocabulary
taxonomy
binomial nomenclature
genus
taxon
family
order
class
phylum
kingdom

Reading Strategy: Building Vocabulary
As you read about the seven categories established by Linnaeus, list those categories in order, starting with the smallest group. Then, create a memory aid to help you remember them.

SECTION RESOURCES

Print:
- ***Teaching Resources,*** Lesson Plan 18–1, Adapted Section Summary 18–1, Adapted Worksheets 18–1, Section Summary 18–1, Worksheets 18–1, Section Review 18–1
- ***Reading and Study Workbook A,*** Section 18–1
- ***Adapted Reading and Study Workbook B,*** Section 18–1
- ***Investigations in Forensics,*** Investigation 5

Technology:
- ***iText,*** Section 18–1
- ***Transparencies Plus,*** Section 18–1

Section 18–1

1 FOCUS

Objectives

18.1.1 ***Explain*** how living things are organized for study.
18.1.2 ***Describe*** binomial nomenclature.
18.1.3 ***Explain*** Linnaeus's system of classification.

Guide for Reading

Vocabulary Preview

Explain how the Vocabulary terms are related. State that in biology the term *taxonomy* refers to the classification of organisms and that *binomial nomenclature* refers to the system of assigning names developed by Linnaeus. In Linnaeus's system, organisms are classified into a hierarchy of categories. Ask: **Which of the Vocabulary terms refer to categories in Linnaeus's system?** *(Genus, family, order, class, phylum, and kingdom)*

Reading Strategy

One example of a memory aid to help students remember the seven taxonomic categories is: *Sam gave Fred one copper padlock key.*

2 INSTRUCT

Why Classify?

Demonstration

Introduce students to dichotomous classification with a quick demonstration. First, have all the students stand up. Then, as you read aloud each of the following physical characteristics, have students without the characteristic sit down: over 5 feet tall, brown eyes, female, left-handed. By the time you have named all the characteristics, all or nearly all of the students are likely to be sitting down. Point out that with each characteristic you named, the remaining group became narrower. Conclude that grouping organisms based on comparing characteristics makes it easier to study the diversity of life. L1

18–1 (continued)

Assigning Scientific Names

Build Science Skills

Applying Concepts Challenge students to brainstorm other examples of species with more than one common name. *(Possible examples include the woodchuck, which is also called ground hog, and the yellow poplar tree, which is also called tulip tree.)* L2

Use Community Resources

Display several field guides for your region. Explain how field guides are used to help identify the species of a plant or animal based on physical characteristics similar to the ones that were used in early efforts at naming. For example, a field guide to trees identifies holly trees based on such characteristics as whether the leaf edges are scalloped and whether they are hairy on their undersides. Encourage interested students to borrow the field guides and use them to identify flora or fauna in the community. Give students a chance to share their observations with the class. L2

Download a worksheet on classification for students to complete, and find additional teacher support from NSTA SciLinks.

Word Origins

A biped has two feet. L2

▲ **Figure 18–2** The problem of naming organisms efficiently continues to challenge biologists as they discover new species. This barking deer was recently discovered near the border of Laos and Vietnam. Its scientific name, which is based on Latin, is *Muntiacus muntjak.* **In binomial nomenclature, each animal is assigned a two-part scientific name.**

For: Links on classification
Visit: www.SciLinks.org
Web Code: cbn-5181

Word Origins

Binomial **and** ***nomenclature*** are built from some familiar roots. *Bi-* is Latin for "two." *Nomen-* is Latin for "name." So *binomial nomenclature* means a two-name system of assigning names. **If *pedis* is Latin for "of the foot," how many feet does a *biped* have?**

Assigning Scientific Names

By the eighteenth century, European scientists recognized that referring to organisms by common names was confusing. Common names vary among languages and even among regions within a single country. The animal you saw in **Figure 18–1,** for example, can be called a cougar, a puma, a panther, or a mountain lion. Furthermore, different species sometimes share a single common name. In the United Kingdom, the word *buzzard* refers to a hawk, whereas in many parts of the United States, *buzzard* refers to a vulture. To eliminate such confusion, scientists agreed to use a single name for each species. Because eighteenth-century scientists understood Latin and Greek, they used those languages for scientific names. This practice is still followed today in naming newly discovered species, such as the barking deer in **Figure 18–2.**

Early Efforts at Naming Organisms The first attempts at standard scientific names often described the physical characteristics of a species in great detail. As a result, these names could be twenty words long! For example, the English translation of the scientific name of a particular tree might be "Oak with deeply divided leaves that have no hairs on their undersides and no teeth around their edges." This system of naming had another major drawback. It was difficult to standardize the names of organisms because different scientists described different characteristics.

Binomial Nomenclature A major step was taken by Carolus Linnaeus, shown in **Figure 18–3,** a Swedish botanist who lived during the eighteenth century. He developed a two-word naming system called **binomial nomenclature** (by-NOH-mee-ul NOH-mun-klay-chur). This system is still in use today. **In binomial nomenclature, each species is assigned a two-part scientific name.** The scientific name is always written in italics. The first word is capitalized, and the second word is lowercased.

For example, the grizzly bear shown in **Figure 18–4** is called *Ursus arctos.* The first part of the scientific name—in this case, *Ursus*—is the genus to which the organism belongs. A **genus** (JEE-nus; plural: genera, JEN-ur-uh) is a group of closely related species. The genus *Ursus* contains five other kinds of bears, including *Ursus maritimus,* the polar bear.

The second part of a scientific name—in this case, *arctos* or *maritimus*—is unique to each species within the genus. Often, this part of the name is a Latinized description of some important trait of the organism or an indication of where the organism lives. The Latin word *maritimus,* referring to the sea, comes from the fact that polar bears often live on pack ice that floats in the sea.

CHECKPOINT *Do* **Ursus arctos** *and* **Ursus maritimus** *belong to the same species? To the same genus?*

ESL SUPPORT FOR ENGLISH LANGUAGE LEARNERS

Comprehension: Prior Knowledge

Beginning To introduce binomial nomenclature, hand out a graphic organizer with four columns. The far left column should be labeled *Organism,* and each cell in the left column should have a picture of a common organism. The next column should be labeled *Scientific Name,* and the cells should be filled with the scientific names of the organisms in the left column. The next two columns should be completed by ESL students paired with English-proficient students. The pairs should fill in the English names of the organisms and the names of the organisms in the ESL students' native languages. L1

Intermediate Ask students to list, in English, several organisms with which they are familiar. The students should work with English-proficient students to research and write the scientific names of these organisms. L2

Linnaeus's System of Classification

Linnaeus's classification system is hierarchical; that is, it consists of levels. **Linnaeus's hierarchical system of classification includes seven levels. They are—from smallest to largest—species, genus, family, order, class, phylum, and kingdom.** In taxonomic nomenclature, or naming system, each of those levels is called a **taxon** (plural: taxa), or taxonomic category.

The two smallest categories, genus and species, were discussed in the example of the bears. The giant panda, shown in **Figure 18–4,** resembles the grizzly bear and the polar bear. However, it differs enough from them and other species in the genus *Ursus* that it is placed in its own genus, *Ailuropoda*.

Genera that share many characteristics, such as *Ursus* and *Ailuropoda,* are grouped in a larger category, the **family**—in this case, Ursidae. These bears, together with six other families of animals, such as dogs (Canidae) and cats (Felidae), are grouped together in the order Carnivora. An **order** is a broad taxonomic category composed of similar families. The next larger category, the **class,** is composed of similar orders. For example, order Carnivora is placed in the class Mammalia, which includes animals that are warm-blooded, have body hair, and produce milk for their young.

Several different classes make up a **phylum** (FY-lum; plural: phyla). A phylum includes many different organisms that nevertheless share important characteristics. The class Mammalia is grouped with birds (class Aves), reptiles (class Reptilia), amphibians (class Amphibia), and all classes of fishes into the phylum Chordata. All these organisms share important features of their body plan and internal functions. Finally, all animals are placed in the kingdom Animalia. The **kingdom** is the largest and most inclusive of Linnaeus's taxonomic categories. Linnaeus named two kingdoms, Animalia and Plantae. You can see the seven taxonomic levels in **Figure 18–5** on the next page.

▲ **Figure 18–3** Carolus Linnaeus (1707–1778) brought order to the process of naming species and classifying them into groups. **Evaluating** ***Why do biologists consider Linnaeus's system an improvement over earlier systems?***

Figure 18–4 The grizzly bear, *Ursus arctos,* and the polar bear, *Ursus maritimus,* are classified as different species in the same genus, *Ursus.* The giant panda is placed in a separate genus. **Inferring** ***What do the scientific names of the polar and grizzly bears tell you about their similarity to each other?***

Linnaeus's System of Classification

Address Misconceptions

Students might think that different breeds of dogs, cats, and other domesticated animals are different species. Explain that the term *breed* refers to a domesticated variety of an organism that is a subgroup of a species. For example, dogs of different breeds, no matter how dissimilar they look, all belong to the species *Canis familiaris.* Because they are members of the same species, they can mate and produce fertile offspring. L1 L2

Demonstration

Demonstrate how Linnaeus's system of classification consists of organisms that are increasingly similar as you go from the level of kingdom to the level of species. Show students pictures of a domestic dog, wolf, fox, and mountain lion. Ask: **What are some ways these animals are similar, and what are some ways they are different?** *(Accept all reasonable responses.)* Then, explain that the mountain lion, fox, wolf, and dog are classified together at the level of order (Carnivora); the fox, wolf, and dog, at the level of family (Canidae); and the wolf and dog, together at the level of genus (*Canis*). L1 L2

BIO INSIGHTS — FACTS AND FIGURES

Why pandas are carnivores

Most people are familiar with the bamboo-eating habits of the giant panda. In fact, pandas depend so much on bamboo in their diet that they have evolved a sixth front "toe" to help them grasp and eat their favorite food. If pandas are herbivores, why are they classified in the order *Carnivora*, as shown in Figure 18–5? The answer lies in their evolutionary past. Like other bears, their most recent ancestor was a carnivorous bearlike animal. All of today's bears, however, have evolved into omnivores, meaning they will eat almost anything, including fruit, seeds, honey, insects, fish, and meat. Pandas have evolved to depend on a narrower omnivorous diet than most other bears, depending as they do almost exclusively on bamboo. However, they may feed on gardens, crops, and even chickens if their usual food supply is threatened.

Answers to . . .

CHECKPOINT *They do not belong to the same species, but they do belong to the same genus.*

Figure 18–3 *Because it provides a brief and unique name for each species*

Figure 18–4 *The shared genus name* Ursus *indicates that the two species are in the same genus and thus are closely related.*

18–1 (continued)

Build Science Skills

Classifying Have the class work in groups to develop a system, similar to the Linnaean system, to classify a collection that includes a hair clip, bobby pin, safety pin, straight pin, screw, nail, paper clip, and staple. *(All are fasteners, and subsets might be classified on the basis of other shared characteristics. For example, hair clips and bobby pins are fasteners of hair, screws and nails are fasteners of wood, and paper clips and staples are fasteners of paper. Other characteristics that might be used include sharpness, shape, or color.)* Have groups share their systems. Then, ask: **How is the classification affected by the characteristics selected?** *(Different objects are grouped together if different characteristics are selected.)* L2

3 ASSESS

Evaluate Understanding

Have students write a paragraph explaining why it is important to classify the diversity of living things.

Reteach

Call on students to name the categories of the Linnaean classification system in order from smallest to largest. Write each term on the board. Have students brainstorm examples of each category, such as Chordata for phylum and Mammalia for class.

Writing in Science

Possible paragraphs might describe how students use the raters' classification system to choose movies or an alphabetical classification system to find names in a phone book. Encourage students to think of classification systems they use that are obviously hierarchical like the Linnaean system, such as the Library of Congress classification system they use to find a nonfiction book in the library.

If your class subscribes to the iText, use it to review the Key Concepts in Section 18–1.

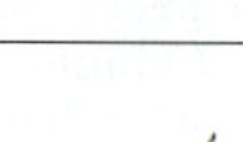

Figure 18–5 Linnaeus's hierarchical system of classification uses seven taxonomic categories. This illustration shows how a grizzly bear, *Ursus arctos,* is grouped within each taxonomic category. Only some representative species are illustrated for each category above the species level.

18–1 Section Assessment

1. **Key Concept** How are living things organized for study?
2. **Key Concept** Describe the system for naming species that Linnaeus developed.
3. **Key Concept** What are the seven taxonomic categories of Linnaeus's classification system? Rank these taxa in hierarchical order, beginning with the largest level and ending with the smallest.
4. Why do scientists avoid using common names when discussing organisms?
5. What is binomial nomenclature?
6. **Critical Thinking Applying Concepts** Look at **Figure 18–5** above. Are foxes more closely related to sea stars or to snakes? Explain.

Writing in Science

Explanatory Paragraph
Think of a classification system that you use in everyday life, and then write a paragraph explaining how the classification system organizes objects or other things. *Hint:* Before you write, make a diagram that shows the organization of the classification system.

18–1 Section Assessment

1. Biologists use a classification system to name organisms with a universally accepted name. They also group organisms in a logical manner. Organisms placed into a particular group are more similar to one another than they are to organisms in other groups.
2. Each species is assigned a two-part scientific name.
3. Kingdom, phylum, class, order, family, genus, species
4. Because common names vary among languages and even among regions within a single country
5. A two-word naming system
6. They are more closely related to snakes, because they are in the same phylum.

18–2 Modern Evolutionary Classification

***BI 8.f. Students know how to use comparative embryology, DNA or protein sequence comparisons, and other independent sources of data to create a branching diagram (cladogram) that shows probable evolutionary relationships. *BI 8.g. Students know how several independent molecular clocks, calibrated against each other and combined with evidence from the fossil record, can help to estimate how long ago various groups or organisms diverged evolutionarily from one another.**

In a sense, organisms determine who belongs to their species by choosing with whom they will mate! Taxonomic groups above the level of species are "invented" by researchers who decide how to distinguish between one genus, family, or phylum, and another. Linnaeus and other taxonomists have always tried to group organisms according to biologically important characteristics. Like any taxonomic system, however, Linnaeus's system had limitations and problems.

Which Similarities Are Most Important?

Linnaeus grouped species into larger taxa, such as genus and family, mainly according to visible similarities and differences. But which similarities and differences are most important? If you lived in Linneaus's time, for example, how would you have classified dolphins? Would you have called them fishes because they live in water and have finlike limbs? Or would you call them mammals because they breathe air and feed their young with milk? How about the animals shown in **Figure 18–6**? Adult barnacles and limpets live attached to rocks and have similarly shaped shells with holes in the center. Crabs, on the other hand, have body shapes unlike those of barnacles or limpets. Based on these features, would you place limpets and barnacles together, and crabs in a different group?

Guide for Reading

Key Concepts
- How are evolutionary relationships important in classification?
- How can DNA and RNA help scientists determine evolutionary relationships?

Vocabulary
phylogeny
evolutionary classification
derived character
cladogram
molecular clock

Reading Strategy: Predicting Before you read, preview **Figure 18–7.** Predict how the field of taxonomy has changed since Linnaeus's time. As you read, note whether or not your prediction was correct.

Figure 18–6 Classifying species based on easily observed adult traits can pose problems. Observe the crab (top left), barnacles (bottom left), and limpet (right). Which seem most alike? **Asking Questions** *What additional information might you gather to help inform your decision?*

SECTION RESOURCES

Print:
- ***Teaching Resources,*** Lesson Plan 18–2, Adapted Section Summary 18–2, Adapted Worksheets 18–2, Section Summary 18–2, Worksheets 18–2, Section Review 18–2
- ***Reading and Study Workbook A,*** Section 18–2
- ***Adapted Reading and Study Workbook B,*** Section 18–2

Technology:
- ***iText,*** Section 18–2
- ***Transparencies Plus,*** Section 18–2

Section 18–2

***BI 8.f, *BI 8.g**

1 FOCUS

Objectives

18.2.1 ***Explain*** how evolutionary relationships are important in classification.
18.2.2 ***Identify*** the principle behind cladistic analysis.
18.2.3 ***Explain*** how we can compare very dissimilar organisms.

Guide for Reading

Vocabulary Preview

Explain how some of the Vocabulary terms are related. Point out that the term *cladogram* refers to a type of evolutionary classification. Ask: **What do you think the term *evolutionary classification* refers to?** *(A type of classification based on the evolutionary history of organisms)*

Reading Strategy

In comparing the traditional classification and the cladogram in Figure 18–7, students might point out that the cladogram includes references to different stages of an organism's life.

2 INSTRUCT

Which Similarities Are Most Important?

Demonstration

Show students pictures of a variety of plants and animals. In each case, ask them to identify the kingdom to which the organism belongs. Point out that plants and animals are the only two kingdoms in Linnaeus's system. Then, show students pictures of unicellular protists, such as paramecia, and challenge them to identify the kingdom to which they belong. *(Students may or may not be able to identify the kingdom of paramecia as Protista.)* L1 L2

Answer to . . .

Figure 18–6 *You might gather information on embryology or on environmental adaptations in the three species to see if any of them are more similar in these ways.*

18–2 (continued)

Evolutionary Classification

Build Science Skills

Using Models Tell students that some scientists used to think that monkeys of the New and Old Worlds had diverged from a monkeylike common ancestor fairly recently. Other scientists think that New and Old World monkeys diverged from a more generalized common ancestor much longer ago and later evolved similar characteristics because of similar environments. Challenge students to represent each of these theories with an evolutionary family tree, or phylogenetic tree. *(A phylogenetic tree for the first theory would show a recent branching. A tree for the second theory would show a much less recent branching, followed by parallel evolution in the two groups.)* L2 L3

Use Visuals

Figure 18–7 Call students' attention to the figure. Ask: **In the early classification on the left, which traits are used to classify barnacles and limpets together?** *(A conical shell and absence of appendages)* **In the cladogram on the right, which traits are used to classify crabs and barnacles together?** *(A segmented body and an external skeleton that is shed during growth)* Call on students to explain why different traits are used in the two systems of evolutionary classification. Correct any misconceptions. L2

For: Cladogram activity
Visit: PHSchool.com
Web Code: cbe-5189
Students get additional practice with cladograms.

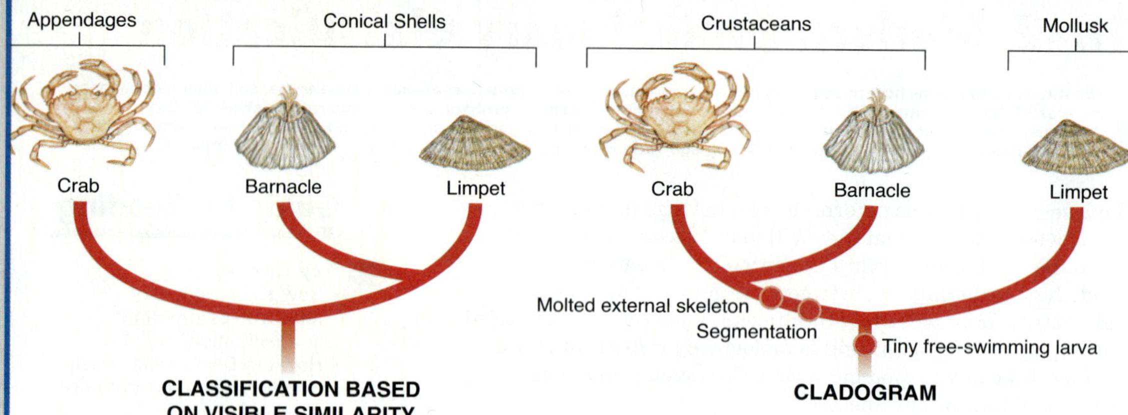

Figure 18–7 Early systems of classification grouped organisms together based on visible similarities. That approach might result in classifying limpets and barnacles together (left). **Biologists now group organisms into categories that represent lines of evolutionary descent, or phylogeny, not just physical similarities.** Crabs and barnacles are now grouped together (right) because they share several characteristics that indicate that they are more closely related to each other than either is to limpets. These characteristics include segmented bodies, jointed limbs, and an external skeleton that is shed during growth.

For: Cladogram activity
Visit: PHSchool.com
Web Code: cbp-5182

Evolutionary Classification

Darwin's ideas about descent with modification have given rise to the study of **phylogeny,** or evolutionary relationships among organisms. **Biologists now group organisms into categories that represent lines of evolutionary descent, or phylogeny, not just physical similarities.** The strategy of grouping organisms together based on their evolutionary history is called **evolutionary classification.**

Species within a genus are more closely related to one another than to species in another genus. According to evolutionary classification, that is because all members of a genus share a recent common ancestor. Similarly, all genera in a family share a common ancestor. This ancestor is further in the past than the ancestor of any genus in the family but more recent than the ancestor of the entire order. The higher the level of the taxon, the further back in time is the common ancestor of all the organisms in the taxon.

Organisms that appear very similar may not share a recent common ancestor. Natural selection, operating on species in similar ecological environments, has often caused convergent evolution. For example, superficial similarities once led barnacles and limpets to be grouped together, as shown on the left in **Figure 18–7.**

However, barnacles and limpets are different in important ways. For example, their free-swimming larvae, or immature forms, are unlike one another. Certain adult characteristics are different too. Adult barnacles have jointed limbs and a body divided into segments. Barnacles periodically shed, or molt, their external skeleton. These characteristics make barnacles more similar to crabs than to limpets. Limpets, in turn, have an internal anatomy that is closer to that of snails, which are mollusks. And like mollusks, limpets do not shed their shells. Because of such characteristics, taxonomists infer that barnacles are more closely related to crabs than to mollusks. In other words, barnacles and crabs share an evolutionary ancestor that is more recent than the ancestor that barnacles share with limpets. Thus, both barnacles and crabs are classified as crustaceans, and limpets are mollusks.

UNIVERSAL ACCESS

Less Proficient Readers

Help students understand evolutionary classification systems by showing them a family tree with at least three generations. Point out that both the family tree and the phylogenetic trees in their text show relationships among descendants of a common ancestor. Say that species with a recent common ancestor are like siblings in a family, and species with a remote common ancestor are like distant cousins. L1 L2

Advanced Learners

Have interested students research similarities in the DNA of humans and a number of other different organisms. They should include organisms that are closely related to humans, such as other species of primates, as well as those that are only distantly related to humans, such as sharks or other species of fish. Suggest to students that they present their findings in a table and share it with the rest of the class. L3

Classification Using Cladograms

To refine the process of evolutionary classification, many biologists now prefer a method called cladistic analysis. Cladistic analysis identifies and considers only those characteristics of organisms that are evolutionary innovations—new characteristics that arise as lineages evolve over time. Characteristics that appear in recent parts of a lineage but not in its older members are called **derived characters.**

Derived characters can be used to construct a **cladogram,** a diagram that shows the evolutionary relationships among a group of organisms. You can see an example of a cladogram on the right-hand side of **Figure 18–7.** Notice how derived characters, such as "free-swimming larva" and "segmentation," appear at certain locations along the branches of the cladogram. These locations are the points at which these characteristics first arose. You can see that crabs and barnacles share some derived characters that barnacles and limpets do not. One such shared derived character is a segmented body. Another is a molted external skeleton. Thus, this cladogram groups crabs and barnacles together as crustaceans and separates them from limpets, which are classified as a type of mollusk.

Cladograms are useful tools that help scientists understand how one lineage branched from another in the course of evolution. Just as a family tree shows the relationships among different lineages within a family, a cladogram represents a type of evolutionary tree, showing evolutionary relationships among a group of organisms.

CHECKPOINT *What is a cladogram?*

 BI 8.f

Quick Lab

How is a cladogram constructed?

Procedure

1. Identify the organism in the table that is least closely related to the others.
2. Use the information in the table to construct a cladogram of these animals.

Derived Characters in Organisms

Organism	Derived Character		
	Backbone	Legs	Hair
Earthworm	Absent	Absent	Absent
Trout	Present	Absent	Absent
Lizard	Present	Present	Absent
Human	Present	Present	Present

Analyze and Conclude

1. **Using Tables and Graphs** What trait separates the least closely related organism from the other animals?
2. **Classifying** List the animals in your cladogram in order of distance from the least closely related organism.
3. **Drawing Conclusions** Does your cladogram indicate that lizards and humans share a more recent common ancestor than either does with an earthworm? Explain.
4. **Inferring** Where would you insert a frog if you added it to the cladogram? Explain your answer.

BIO INSIGHTS **FACTS AND FIGURES**

Homologous vs. analogous
When classifying organisms, taxonomists are careful to distinguish between homologous structures and analogous structures. Homologous structures have a similar structure and development pattern. However, the function of homologous structures may be different. The wing of a bird and the human arm are homologous structures due to their similar structure pattern of development. Analogous structures appear similar and perform similar functions; however, their structure and developmental patterns are quite different. The wing of a bird and the wing of a butterfly are analogous structures.

Classification Using Cladograms

Quick Lab

 **BI 8.f**

Objective Students will be able to construct a cladogram to classify a group of animals. L2 L3

Skills Focus Using Tables and Graphs, Classifying, Drawing Conclusions, Inferring

Time 15 minutes

Strategies

- Advise students to start with the organism that lacks at least one characteristic that all the other organisms share.
- Check that students have correctly identified the earthworm as the organism that lacks all three listed traits.
- Refer students to Figure 18–7 for ideas about how to construct a cladogram.

Expected Outcome Students should draw a cladogram that shows backbones evolved first, followed by legs, and then by hair.

Analyze and Conclude

1. Lack of a backbone
2. Trout, lizard, and human
3. Yes; lizards and humans shared an ancestor that had legs and a backbone and that evolved after the earthworm's lineage branched off on another evolutionary pathway.
4. A frog would occupy a branch between the trout and the lizard, because it has the derived character of legs. Another derived character, such as dry skin, would then have to be added for the lizard.

Answer to . . .

CHECKPOINT *A cladogram is a diagram that shows evolutionary relationships among organisms based on shared derived characters.*

18–2 (continued)

Similarities in RNA and DNA

Make Connections

Chemistry Explain that the most precise method of comparing the DNA of two species is DNA sequencing, in which the researcher first prepares comparable DNA segments from two species and then determines the extent to which nucleotide sequences are the same in the two segments. (See Chapter 13, Section 2.) Another method, called DNA–DNA hybridization, measures the extent of hydrogen bonding between single strands of DNA from different species. The more hydrogen bonding that occurs, the greater the similarity between the DNA strands of the two species. L2 L3

Demonstration

Obtain and display a copy of a cytochrome-c family tree, which is a phylogenetic tree based solely on mutations in the protein cytochrome-c. (Alternatively, you might want to ask students to research and locate a cytochrome-c tree.) Explain that cytochrome-c, a protein that plays a role in cellular respiration, was chosen for study because it is present in most organisms. Point out how closely the phylogenetic tree based on this single important protein resembles traditional phylogenetic trees based on other kinds of evidence. L2

▲ **Figure 18–8** **Similarities at the DNA level in the genes of organisms can be used to help determine classification.** Traditionally, African vultures (top) and American vultures (center) were classified together in the falcon family. But DNA analysis has revealed that American vultures are actually more closely related to storks (bottom).

Similarities in DNA and RNA

All of the classification methods discussed so far are based primarily on physical similarities and differences. But even organisms with very different anatomies have common traits. For example, all organisms use DNA and RNA to pass on information and to control growth and development. Hidden in the genetic code of all organisms are remarkably similar genes. Because DNA and RNA are so similar across all forms of life, these molecules provide an excellent way of comparing organisms at their most basic level—their genes.

The genes of many organisms show important similarities at the molecular level. Similarities in DNA can be used to help determine classification and evolutionary relationships. Now that scientists can sequence, or "read," the information coded in DNA, they can compare the DNA of different organisms to trace the history of genes over millions of years.

Similar Genes Even the genes of diverse organisms such as humans and yeasts show many surprising similarities. For example, humans have a gene that codes for myosin, a protein found in our muscles. Researchers have found a gene in yeast that codes for a myosin protein. As it turns out, myosin in yeast helps enable internal cell parts to move. Myosin is just one example of similarities at the molecular level—an indicator that humans and yeasts share a common ancestry.

DNA Evidence DNA evidence can also help show the evolutionary relationships of species and how species have changed. The more similar the DNA sequences of two species, the more recently they shared a common ancestor, and the more closely they are related in evolutionary terms. And the more two species have diverged from each other, or changed in comparison to each other during evolution, the less similar their DNA will be.

Consider the birds in **Figure 18–8.** The bird in the top photograph looks a lot like the bird in the middle photograph. Both birds have traditionally been classified together as "vultures." One group of birds inhabits Africa and Asia, and the other, the Americas. But American vultures have a peculiar behavior: When they get overheated, they urinate on their legs, and evaporative cooling removes some body heat. The only other birds known to behave this way are storks, which look quite different and have always been put in a separate family. Does this similarity in behavior indicate a close evolutionary relationship?

Scientists analyzed the DNA of these three birds. The analysis showed that the DNA sequences of the American vulture and the stork were more similar than those of the American vulture and the African vulture. This similarity in DNA sequences indicates that the American vulture and the stork share a more recent common ancestor than do the American vulture and the African vulture. Therefore, the American vulture is more closely related to storks than to other vultures.

Molecular Clocks

Comparisons of DNA can also be used to mark the passage of evolutionary time. A model known as a **molecular clock** uses DNA comparisons to estimate the length of time that two species have been evolving independently. To understand molecular clocks, think about a pendulum clock. It marks time with a periodically swinging pendulum. A molecular clock also relies on a repeating process to mark time—mutation.

Simple mutations occur all the time, causing slight changes in the structure of DNA, as shown in **Figure 18–9.** Some mutations have a major positive or negative effect on an organism's phenotype. These mutations are under powerful pressure from natural selection. Other mutations have no effects on phenotype. These neutral mutations accumulate in the DNA of different species at about the same rate. A comparison of such DNA sequences in two species can reveal how dissimilar the genes are. The degree of dissimilarity is, in turn, an indication of how long ago the two species shared a common ancestor.

The use of molecular clocks is not simple, however, because there is not just one molecular clock in a genome. Instead, there are many, each of which "ticks" at a different rate. This is because some genes accumulate mutations faster than others. These different clocks allow researchers to time different kinds of evolutionary events. Think of a conventional clock. If you want to time a brief event, you pay attention to the second hand. To time an event that lasts longer, you use the minute hand or the hour hand. In the same way, researchers would use a different molecular clock to compare modern bird species than they would to estimate the age of the common ancestor of yeasts and humans.

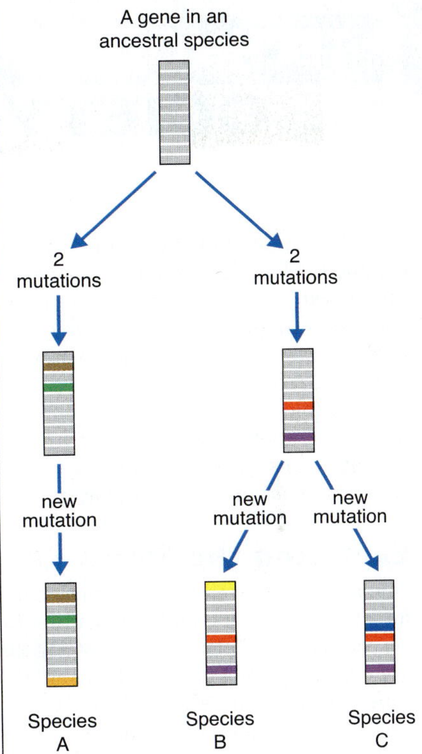

▲ **Figure 18–9** By comparing the DNA sequences of two or more species, biologists estimate how long the species have been separated. **Analyzing Data** ***What evidence indicates that species C is more closely related to species B than to species A?***

18–2 Section Assessment

1. **Key Concept** How is information about evolutionary, or phylogenetic, relationships useful in classification?
2. **Key Concept** How are genes used to help scientists classify organisms?
3. What is the principle behind cladistic analysis?
4. What gene indicates that yeasts and humans share a common ancestor?
5. Describe the relationship between evolutionary time and the similarity of genes in two species.
6. **Critical Thinking Inferring** Would a barnacle's DNA be more similar to the DNA of a crab or that of a limpet? Explain.

Thinking Visually

Constructing a Chart
Draw a cladogram of a manufactured item, such as an automobile or a household item, that has changed over the years. Label derived characters that appeared as new models arose. For example, automobiles came to have electronic fuel injection and antilock brakes.

18–2 Section Assessment

1. Organisms are placed in various taxonomic groups based on evolutionary descent.
2. Scientists compare the DNA of different organisms to establish similarities between them and reconstruct possible evolutionary relationships.
3. Cladistic analysis traces the process of evolution in a group of organisms by focusing on unique features that appear in some organisms but not in others.
4. A gene that codes for the protein myosin
5. The longer it has been since two species descended from a common ancestor, the more different their genes are likely to be.
6. It would be more similar to the DNA of a crab, because barnacles and crabs have a closer evolutionary relationship.

Molecular Clocks

Use Visuals

Figure 18–9 Have students examine the figure. Then, ask: **Why do biologists study mutations in genes that do not code for essential proteins?** *(Those mutations occur in different species at about the same rate, and they can be used as a basis for comparison.)* L1 L2

3 ASSESS

Evaluate Understanding

Have students make a Venn diagram to show similarities and differences between traditional classification diagrams and cladograms.

Reteach

Call on students to explain in their own words what molecular clocks are, how they are used, and why some molecular clocks "tick" at different rates. Correct any errors or misunderstandings.

Thinking Visually

Students should draw a cladogram based on several derived characteristics of a type of manufactured item. Instead of the automobile, they might choose the television, video game, or camera. Their diagrams should show the order in which innovations were developed in the item they chose. For example, a cladogram for the television might show that this item first acquired colored pictures, then solid-state circuitry, and then remote controls.

If your class subscribes to the iText, use it to review the Key Concepts in Section 18–2.

Answer to . . .

Figure 18–9 *The DNA molecules in species B and C show two common mutations that do not appear in the DNA in species A.*

After students have read this feature, you might want to discuss one or more of the following:

- The reasons that newly discovered species are likely to live in remote, hard-to-reach places
- Why tropical forests have so many different species compared with other types of ecosystems
- How advances in technology, such as portable computers, wireless communication devices, and the Internet, have made research in remote locations easier and more efficient
- The ways that technological advances, such as electron microscopy and DNA analysis, are used to determine whether a particular organism represents a newly discovered species

Research and Decide

Students should describe and sketch ideas for inventions that would help them search for new species high up in the tree canopy of a forest or in some other hard-to-reach place, such as a sheer rock wall, a deep cave, or the ocean floor. For example, students might describe and sketch a system of harnesses and platforms, similar to those used by window washers, to search for new species on sheer rock walls, or they might describe a pressurized compartment, like a bathysphere, to search for new species on the ocean floor.

Students can research the search for new species on the site developed by authors Ken Miller and Joe Levine.

The Search for New Species in Tropical Forests

So far, scientists have identified about 1.5 million species. Yet, millions more have never been discovered. Researchers continue to find new species—not just tiny organisms, but also fish, birds, and mammals. Because new species are likely to live in hard-to-reach places, scientists call on technology to help in the search, including scuba gear, helicopters, and ultralight airplanes. Remote cameras and e-mail let scientists follow the work of others continents away.

Exploring the Forest Canopy

One place to search for new species is in tropical forests, which are teeming with life. Researchers especially want better ways to study the canopy—the upper layers of the forest. Scientists have used ropes to climb the tall trees, but it is hard to stay up long or collect specimens. Then, French researchers invented an unusual "raft" suspended from a hot-air balloon that floats over the tops of the trees. Scientists on the raft could work together for longer periods of time, collecting many more species.

One canopy explorer, biologist Margaret Lowman, worked with a structural engineer to design and build a canopy walkway as her "green laboratory." The walkway looks like a huge treehouse 75 feet above the forest floor, with platforms on which researchers can work. Another new and dramatic route into the canopy is a huge construction crane like those used in building skyscrapers. Scientists on the arm of the crane get a close-up look at trees. Today there is a worldwide network of forest sites.

New Species or Not?

When researchers spot an unfamiliar organism, they may use simple observation to classify it. How many petals are on the flower? How many toes are on the animal? If the organism does not match known categories, the species may be new. Unusual antlers, for instance, were a major clue in identifying a new deer species in Vietnam.

External appearances can fool you, however. X-rays and electron microscopes may reveal differences that set one species apart from another. The most exciting advances have come with studies of DNA. By analyzing DNA, scientists can demonstrate how two organisms are—or are not—related.

Research and Decide

Use library or Internet resources to learn more about the search for new species. Then, describe and sketch your own ideas for an invention that would help scientists search in a forest canopy or other location that is hard to reach.

For: Links from the authors
Visit: PHSchool.com
Web Code: cbe-5182

18–3 Kingdoms and Domains

As in all areas of science, systems of classification adapt to new discoveries. Ideas and models change as new information arises. Some explanations have been discarded altogether, whereas others, such as Darwin's theory of evolution by natural selection, have been upheld and refined through years of research. So, it should not be surprising that early attempts at drawing life's universal tree were based on some misguided assumptions. Some of the earliest trees of life were dominated by humans. These models represented vertebrates as the most important and abundant animals. They also implied that "higher" animals evolved from "lower" animals that were identical to modern forms. Biologists now know these notions are incorrect.

Guide for Reading

Key Concepts
- What are the six kingdoms of life as they are now identified?
- What is the three-domain system of classification?

Vocabulary
domain
Bacteria
Eubacteria
Archaea
Archaebacteria
Eukarya
Protista
Fungi
Plantae
Animalia

Reading Strategy: Classifying As you read, write the names of the six kingdoms recognized by biologists. Label each group as either prokaryotes or eukaryotes.

The Tree of Life Evolves

The scientific view of life was simpler in Linnaeus's time. The only known differences among living things were the fundamental traits that separated animals from plants. Animals were mobile organisms that used food for energy. Plants were green, photosynthetic organisms that used energy from the sun.

Five Kingdoms As biologists learned more about the natural world, they realized that Linnaeus's two kingdoms, Animalia and Plantae, did not adequately represent the full diversity of life. First, microorganisms, such as the protist and bacterium in **Figure 18–10,** were recognized as being significantly different from plants and animals. Scientists soon agreed that microorganisms merited their own kingdom, which was named Protista. Then, the mushrooms, yeasts, and molds were placed in their own kingdom, Fungi. Later still, scientists realized that bacteria lack the nuclei, mitochondria, and chloroplasts found in other forms of life. Therefore, they were placed in another new kingdom, Monera. This process produced five kingdoms—Monera, Protista, Fungi, Plantae, and Animalia.

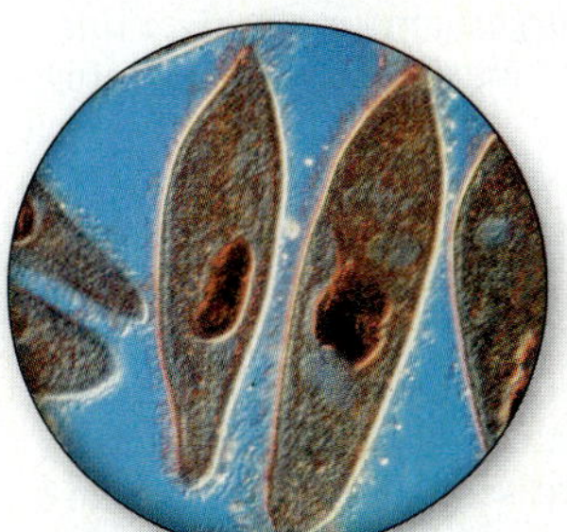

Paramecium caudatum
(magnification: about 1000×)

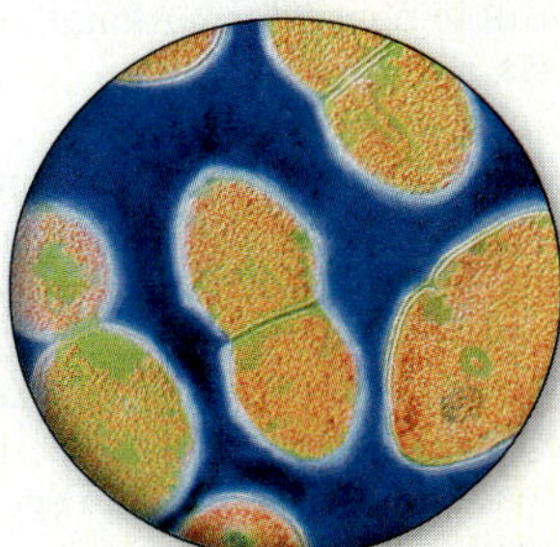

Streptococcus faecalis
(magnification: 26,000×)

Figure 18–10 The paramecium (left) is a unicellular organism that is eukaryotic, or has a nucleus. *Streptococcus faecalis* (right) is a bacterium that evolved long before eukaryotic cells. Bacteria are prokaryotes—they do not have nuclei. The classification of these two organisms has changed greatly over the years. **Classifying** ***List reasons that these two organisms should be classified in separate kingdoms.***

Section 18–3

1 FOCUS

Objectives

18.3.1 ***Name*** the six kingdoms of life as they are now identified.

18.3.2 ***Describe*** the three-domain system of classification.

Guide for Reading

Vocabulary Preview

Introduce students to the Vocabulary terms by explaining that the term *domain,* like the term *kingdom,* refers to a very broad grouping of related organisms. Add that all of the other Vocabulary terms are the names of specific kingdoms or domains.

Reading Strategy

Students should label the Archaebacteria and Eubacteria as prokaryotes, and they should label the Protists, Plantae, Fungi, and Animalia as eukaryotes.

2 INSTRUCT

The Tree of Life Evolves

Build Science Skills

Inferring Remind students that all the kingdoms in the six-kingdom system are eukaryotes except for the two bacterial kingdoms. Ask: **As the only prokaryotic kingdoms, how do Eubacteria and Archaebacteria differ from the other four kingdoms?** *(They lack nuclei, mitochondria, and chloroplasts, and they reproduce by binary fission.)* L2

SECTION RESOURCES

Print:
- ***Laboratory Manual A,*** Chapter 18 Lab
- ***Laboratory Manual B,*** Chapter 18 Lab
- ***Teaching Resources,*** Lesson Plan 18–3, Adapted Section Summary 18–3, Adapted Worksheets 18–3, Section Summary 18–3, Worksheets 18–3, Section Review 18–3
- ***Reading and Study Workbook A,*** Section 18–3
- ***Adapted Reading and Study Workbook B,*** Section 18–3
- ***Lab Worksheets,*** Chapter 18 Real-World Lab

Technology:
- ***iText,*** Section 18–3
- ***Transparencies Plus,*** Section 18–3

Answer to . . .

Figure 18–10 *The differences between paramecia and bacteria are significant:* Paramecia *(and other eukaryotes) contain nuclei, mitochondria, and other membrane-bound organelles. Bacteria (and other prokaryotes) do not contain these structures. The DNA of bacteria forms one circular chromosome.*

18–3 (continued)

The Three-Domain System

Address Misconceptions

Students may not understand why bacteria are put into two separate domains while all other living things are put into just one domain. Stress that organisms are grouped into domains according to how long they have been evolving independently. Remind students that bacteria have been evolving for 3.5 billion years, as compared with 2.0 billion years or less for eukaryotic organisms. L2

Use Visuals

Figure 18–11 Call students' attention to the diagram. Ask: **Which two kingdoms were introduced first?** *(Plantae and Animalia)* **Why do you think the other kingdoms were introduced later?** *(In the case of Protista, Monera, Eubacteria, and Archaebacteria, because they are mostly unicellular organisms and, therefore, difficult to observe; in the case of Fungi, because they are similar to plants)* L1 L2

Download a worksheet on domains of life for students to complete, and find additional teacher support from NSTA SciLinks.

Changing Number of Kingdoms

First Introduced	Names of Kingdoms						
1700s	Plantae						Animalia
Late 1800s	Protista			Plantae			Animalia
1950s	Monera		Protista	Fungi	Plantae		Animalia
1990s	Eubacteria	Archaebacteria	Protista	Fungi	Plantae		Animalia

▲ **Figure 18–11** This diagram shows some of the ways organisms have been classified into kingdoms over the years. **The six-kingdom system includes the following kingdoms: Eubacteria, Archaebacteria, Protista, Fungi, Plantae, and Animalia.**

Six Kingdoms In recent years, as evidence about microorganisms continued to accumulate, biologists came to recognize that the Monera were composed of two distinct groups. Some biologists consider the differences between these two groups to be as great as those between animals and plants. As a result, the Monera have been separated into two kingdoms, Eubacteria and Archaebacteria, bringing the total number of kingdoms to six. **The six-kingdom system of classification includes the kingdoms Eubacteria, Archaebacteria, Protista, Fungi, Plantae, and Animalia.** This system of classification is shown in the bottom row of **Figure 18–11.**

The Three-Domain System

Some of the most recent evolutionary trees have been produced using comparative studies of a small subunit of ribosomal RNA that occurs in all living things. Using a molecular clock model, scientists have grouped modern organisms according to how long they have been evolving independently.

Molecular analyses have given rise to a new taxonomic category that is now recognized by many scientists. The **domain** is a more inclusive category than any other—larger than a kingdom. **The three domains are the domain Eukarya, which is composed of protists, fungi, plants, and animals; the domain Bacteria, which corresponds to the kingdom Eubacteria; and the domain Archaea, which corresponds to the kingdom Archaebacteria.** As scientists continue to accumulate new information about organisms in the domains Bacteria and Archaea, these domains may be subdivided into additional kingdoms.

Clearly, modern classification is a rapidly changing science, and we must pick a convention to classify life's diversity for the purposes of this book. In this book, we recognize the three domains and also refer frequently to the six kingdoms. The relationship between the three domains and the six kingdoms is shown in **Figure 18–12.** It also summarizes the key characteristics of each kingdom. You can see that some groups share one or more traits with other groups.

What are the three domains?

For: Link on domains of life
Visit: www.SciLinks.org
Web Code: cbn-5183

UNIVERSAL ACCESS

Inclusion/Special Needs

Help students become more familiar with the Eukarya domain. Have them use field guides, encyclopedias, textbooks, or other sources to find examples of different organisms in each kingdom of Eukarya. Suggest that they sketch or copy photographs of several species in each kingdom and use the images to create a poster illustrating the diversity of this domain. L1

Advanced Learners

Encourage interested students to research the proposed nine-kingdom system of classification, in which protists are divided into three kingdoms. Students should determine what criteria are used for dividing protists into kingdoms and why the criteria were selected. They also should try to assess how widely accepted the nine-kingdom system is. L3

Domain Bacteria

The members of the domain **Bacteria** are unicellular and prokaryotic. Their cells have thick, rigid cell walls that surround a cell membrane. The cell walls contain a substance known as peptidoglycan. The domain Bacteria corresponds to the kingdom **Eubacteria.** These bacteria are ecologically diverse, ranging from free-living soil organisms to deadly parasites. Some photosynthesize, while others do not. Some need oxygen to survive, while others are killed by oxygen.

Domain Archaea

Also unicellular and prokaryotic, members of the domain **Archaea** live in some of the most extreme environments you can imagine—volcanic hot springs, brine pools, and black organic mud totally devoid of oxygen. Indeed, many of these bacteria can survive only in the absence of oxygen. Their cell walls lack peptidoglycan, and their cell membranes contain unusual lipids that are not found in any other organism. The domain Archaea corresponds to the kingdom **Archaebacteria.**

CHECKPOINT ***What characteristics distinguish members of the domain Bacteria from members of the domain Archaea?***

▼ **Figure 18–12**  **Organisms are grouped in three domains. There is a simple relationship between the three domains and the six kingdoms.** This table summarizes key evidence used in classifying organisms into these major taxonomic groups.

Classification of Living Things

DOMAIN	Bacteria	Archaea	Eukarya			
KINGDOM	Eubacteria	Archaebacteria	Protista	Fungi	Plantae	Animalia
CELL TYPE	Prokaryote	Prokaryote	Eukaryote	Eukaryote	Eukaryote	Eukaryote
CELL STRUCTURES	Cell walls with peptidoglycan	Cell walls without peptidoglycan	Cell walls of cellulose in some; some have chloroplasts	Cell walls of chitin	Cell walls of cellulose; chloroplasts	No cell walls or chloroplasts
NUMBER OF CELLS	Unicellular	Unicellular	Most unicellular; some colonial; some multicellular	Most multicellular; some unicellular	Multicellular	Multicellular
MODE OF NUTRITION	Autotroph or heterotroph	Autotroph or heterotroph	Autotroph or heterotroph	Heterotroph	Autotroph	Heterotroph
EXAMPLES	*Streptococcus, Escherichia coli*	Methanogens, halophiles	*Amoeba, Paramecium,* slime molds, giant kelp	Mushrooms, yeasts	Mosses, ferns, flowering plants	Sponges, worms, insects, fishes, mammals

Domain Bacteria

Build Science Skills

Classifying Have students assume that they are biologists and that they have just discovered an unclassified species. The organism makes its own food, has no nucleus, and has peptidoglycan in its cell walls. Ask: **In which domain should you classify this species?** *(Bacteria)* **In which kingdom does it belong?** *(Eubacteria)* L2

Domain Archaea

Build Science Skills

Inferring Point out that Archaea are the most ancient organisms on Earth and they exist in extreme environments. Ask: **What explains the ability of Archaea to live in extreme environments?** *(The early Earth had extreme environments, and this was when Archaea first evolved.)* L2 L3

Use Visuals

Figure 18–12 Check students' comprehension of the table. Ask: **How many cells do Archaea have?** *(Archaea are unicellular.)* **What makes Fungi different from Protists?** *(Fungi have cell walls of chitin.)* **What sets Animalia apart from all other kingdoms of organisms?** *(Animals do not have cell walls or chloroplasts.)* **Which kingdom contains some species that share characteristics with Plantae? Explain.** *(Protista; some species of Protista are multicellular autotrophs, have cell walls composed of cellulose, and have chloroplasts.)* L1 L2

Answers to . . .

CHECKPOINT *Eukarya, Bacteria, and Archaea*

CHECKPOINT *Members of domain Archaea live in extreme environments, whereas members of domain Bacteria are ecologically diverse. Also, the cell walls of Bacteria contain peptidoglycan, while those of Archaea do not.*

18–3 (continued)

Domain Eukarya

Demonstration

Use a microprojector to show students examples of unicellular protists, including amoebas and paramecia. Have students identify some of the characteristics—such as nuclei, cell walls, and chloroplasts—that are used to classify the organisms as protists. Suggest that students sketch the organisms and label the important structures. L1 L2

Make Connections

Health Science Students are likely to recognize the role of foods from plants and animals in a healthy diet, but they may not realize the important role played by fungi. Obtain from a supermarket and bring to class a variety of different types of fresh and canned mushrooms and a package of dried yeast. Ask students to name some of the foods they eat containing mushrooms. *(Students might name pizza, salad, and pasta.)* Then, following package instructions, use warm water to activate the yeast. Explain that the bubbles generated by the living yeast organisms cause bread and other baked goods to have a light, fluffy texture. Ask: **How often do you eat foods containing yeast?** *(Most students are likely to say that they eat bread or other yeast-containing foods virtually every day.)* L1 L2

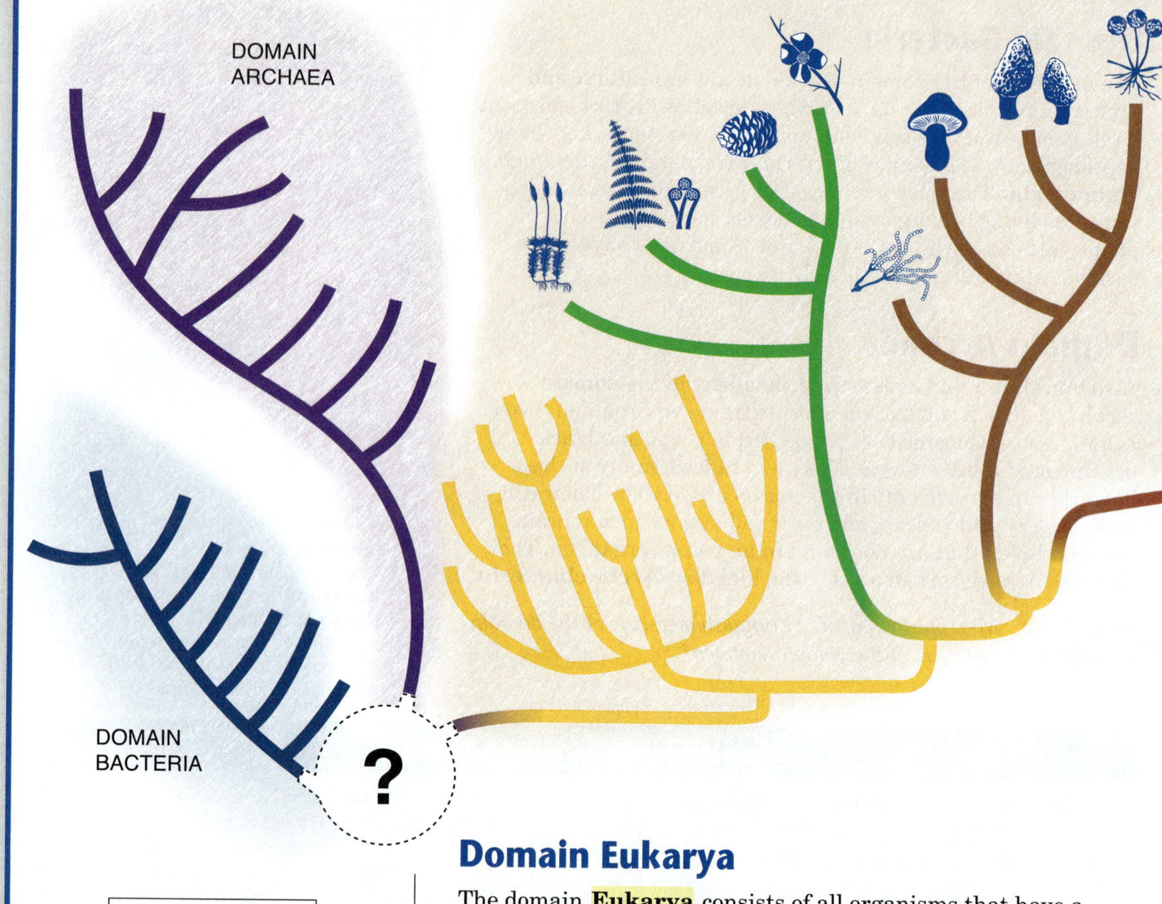

Kingdoms

- Eubacteria
- Archaebacteria
- Protista
- Plantae
- Fungi
- Animalia

Domain Eukarya

The domain **Eukarya** consists of all organisms that have a nucleus. It is organized into the four remaining kingdoms of the six-kingdom system: Protista, Fungi, Plantae, and Animalia, as shown in **Figure 18–13.**

Protista The kingdom **Protista** is composed of eukaryotic organisms that cannot be classified as animals, plants, or fungi. Of the six kingdoms, Protista is the least satisfying classification, because its members display the greatest variety. Most protists are unicellular organisms, but some, such as the multicellular algae, are not. Some protists are photosynthetic, while others are heterotrophic. Some share characteristics with plants, others with fungi, and still others with animals.

Fungi Members of the kingdom **Fungi** are heterotrophs. Most feed on dead or decaying organic matter. Unlike other heterotrophs, these fungi secrete digestive enzymes into their food source. They then absorb the smaller food molecules into their bodies. The most recognizable fungi, including mushrooms, are multicellular. Some fungi, such as yeasts, are unicellular.

FACTS AND FIGURES

By any other name

The term *algae* is the plural form of the Latin word *alga*, which means seaweed. However, according to some, not all algae are seaweeds, and not all seaweeds are algae. The term *algae* is currently used to refer to a range of organisms: yellow-green algae, golden-brown algae, brown algae, red algae, and green algae. The classification of these organisms at the kingdom level is still in question and is likely to change as evidence accumulates.

▲ **Figure 18–13** The domains Bacteria and Archaea include the same organisms that are in the kingdoms Eubacteria and Archaebacteria. The domain Eukarya includes the protists, fungi, plants, and animals. Biologists continue to investigate how these three large groups originated. **Interpreting Graphics** *Which domain includes organisms from more than one kingdom?*

Plantae Members of the kingdom **Plantae** are multicellular organisms that are photosynthetic autotrophs. In other words, they carry out photosynthesis. Plants are nonmotile—they cannot move from place to place. They also have cell walls that contain cellulose. The plant kingdom includes cone-bearing and flowering plants as well as mosses and ferns. Although older classification systems regard multicellular algae as plants, in this book we group algae with the protists.

Animalia Members of the kingdom **Animalia** are multicellular and heterotrophic. The cells of animals do not have cell walls. Most animals can move about, at least for some part of their life cycle. As you will see in later chapters, there is incredible diversity within the animal kingdom, and many species of animals exist in nearly every part of the planet.

18–3 Section Assessment

1. **Key Concept** What are the six kingdoms of life as they are now identified?
2. **Key Concept** What are the three domains of life?
3. Why was the kingdom Monera divided into two separate kingdoms?
4. Why might kingdom Protista be thought of as the "odds and ends" kingdom?
5. How are members of the kingdom Fungi different from members of the kingdom Plantae? How are members of the two kingdoms similar?
6. **Critical Thinking Classifying** Which kingdoms include only prokaryotes? Which kingdoms include only heterotrophs?

Focus on the BIG Idea

Unity and Diversity
Review what you learned in Chapter 7 about how the cells of various organisms differ. Then, write a riddle (What kingdom am I?) describing the characteristics of members of a particular kingdom. Exchange your riddle with a classmate, and see if you can guess the kingdom being described.

18–3 Section Assessment

1. The six kingdoms are Archaebacteria, Eubacteria, Protista, Plantae, Fungi, and Animalia.
2. The three domains are Archaea, Bacteria, and Eukarya.
3. Monera was divided into two kingdoms because scientists have come to recognize profound differences among two broad groups of Monera.
4. Members of the kingdom Protista display the greatest variety, sharing characteristics with plants, fungi, or animals; protists cannot be classified in any other group.
5. Fungi are heterotrophic; Plantae are autotrophic. Both are nonmotile.
6. Eubacteria and Archaebacteria include only prokaryotes. Fungi and Animalia contain only heterotrophs.

Use Visuals

Figure 18–13 Ask students to identify by color each of the kingdoms of Eukarya in the diagram. *(The red segment is Animalia; the brown segment is Fungi; the green segment is Plantae; and the yellow segment is Protista.)* L1

3 ASSESS

Evaluate Understanding

Call on students at random to name the kingdoms in the six-kingdom classification system. Call on other students to name examples of organisms in each kingdom.

Reteach

Write the name of each of the three domains on the chalkboard. Then, have students brainstorm characteristics of organisms in each domain. List the characteristics on the board under the name of the corresponding domain.

Focus on the BIG Idea 

Students' riddles should include several of the characteristics listed in Figure 18–12 on page 459.

If your class subscribes to the iText, use it to review the Key Concepts in Section 18–3.

Answer to . . .

Figure 18–13 *Domain Eukarya*

Real-World Lab

7IIE 7.c

Objective Students will be able to make and use a dichotomous key to classify a group of items. L2

Skills Focus **Observing, Classifying, Forming Operational Definitions**

Time 45 minutes

Advance Prep

- For Part B, obtain graphite pencils (with and without erasers) and ballpoint and felt-tip pens. Other groups of items may include: different types of nuts and bolts or a group of coins.

Teaching Tips

- Explain that the term *dichotomous* means "having two forms." Add that a dichotomous key uses two forms of each of several characteristics to identify a species.
- Ask: **What characteristics are used in the dichotomous key for leaves?** *(Whether a leaf is simple or compound, how the leaflets are arranged, leaflet shapes, how the leaf veins are arranged, the shape of the leaf, and the appearance of the leaf edge)*
- Ask: **How many choices does the key give for each characteristic?** *(Two)*
- Ask: **Could you give the same set of choices to identify leaves of species other than the ones shown in the book?** *(Yes, if they belong to the genera named in the key)*

Procedure

1.–3. Make sure students take time to familiarize themselves with the two forms of each characteristic so they will be less likely to make a mistake in the identification process.

5. Characteristics students select will vary depending on the group of items. For example, if writing implements are used, they might select the characteristic ink/inkless. Each characteristic they select should vary in at least one of the items.

6. Make sure that all of the characteristics students select are dichotomous. For example, color is not a dichotomous characteristic, but black or nonblack is a dichotomous characteristic.

Real-World Lab

7IIE 7.c

Classifying Organisms Using Dichotomous Keys

One tool used to identify unfamiliar organisms is a dichotomous key. A dichotomous key is a series of paired statements that describe physical characteristics of different organisms. In this activity, you will use a dichotomous key to identify tree leaves.

Problem

How are dichotomous keys used and made?

Materials

- 6–8 writing implements or other group of common items

Skills

Observing, Classifying, Forming Operational Definitions

Procedure

Part A: Using a Dichotomous Key

1. To use the dichotomous key for leaves, begin by reading paired statements 1a and 1b. Notice that the statements are opposites.
2. Carefully observe the leaf labeled I on the next page. Decide which statement, 1a or 1b, applies to this leaf. Then, follow the direction at the end of the statement. In other words, because the leaf is a simple leaf, go to statement 4.
3. Continue reading the paired statements and following the direction at the end of the applicable statement until you determine the identity of leaf I.
4. Repeat steps 2 and 3 for leaves II through VII.

Part B: Constructing a Dichotomous Key

5. Examine the group of items your teacher gives you. List some characteristics you could use to classify these items into groups.
6. Using the dichotomous key from Part A as a model, construct a dichotomous key for your group of items. You may wish to use some of the characteristics you listed in step 5 to construct your key. Make sure that each of the paired statements in your key are opposites.
7. Once your dichotomous key is complete, test it with each item and revise your key, if necessary.
8. Exchange keys and items with a classmate. Use your classmate's key to identify his or her items. Then, suggest ways to improve that key.

Dichotomous Key for Leaves

1. Compound or simple leaf
   1a) Compound leaf (leaf divided into leaflets) ....go to step 2
   1b) Simple leaf (leaf not divided into leaflets) ....go to step 4
2. Arrangement of leaflets
   2a) Palmate arrangement of leaflets (leaflets all attached at one central point) ....*Aesculus* (buckeye)
   2b) Pinnate arrangement of leaflets (leaflets attached at several points) ....go to step 3
3. Leaflet shape
   3a) Leaflets taper to pointed tips ....*Carya* (pecan)
   3b) Oval leaflets with rounded tips ....*Robinia* (locust)
4. Arrangement of leaf veins
   4a) Veins branch out from one central point ....go to step 5
   4b) Veins branch off main vein in the middle of the leaf ....go to step 6
5. Overall shape of leaf
   5a) Leaf is heart shaped..........*Cercis* (redbud)
   5b) Leaf is star shaped ....*Liquidambar* (sweet gum)
6. Appearance of leaf edge
   6a) Leaf has toothed (jagged) edge ....*Betula* (birch)
   6b) Leaf has untoothed (smooth) edge ....*Magnolia* (magnolia)

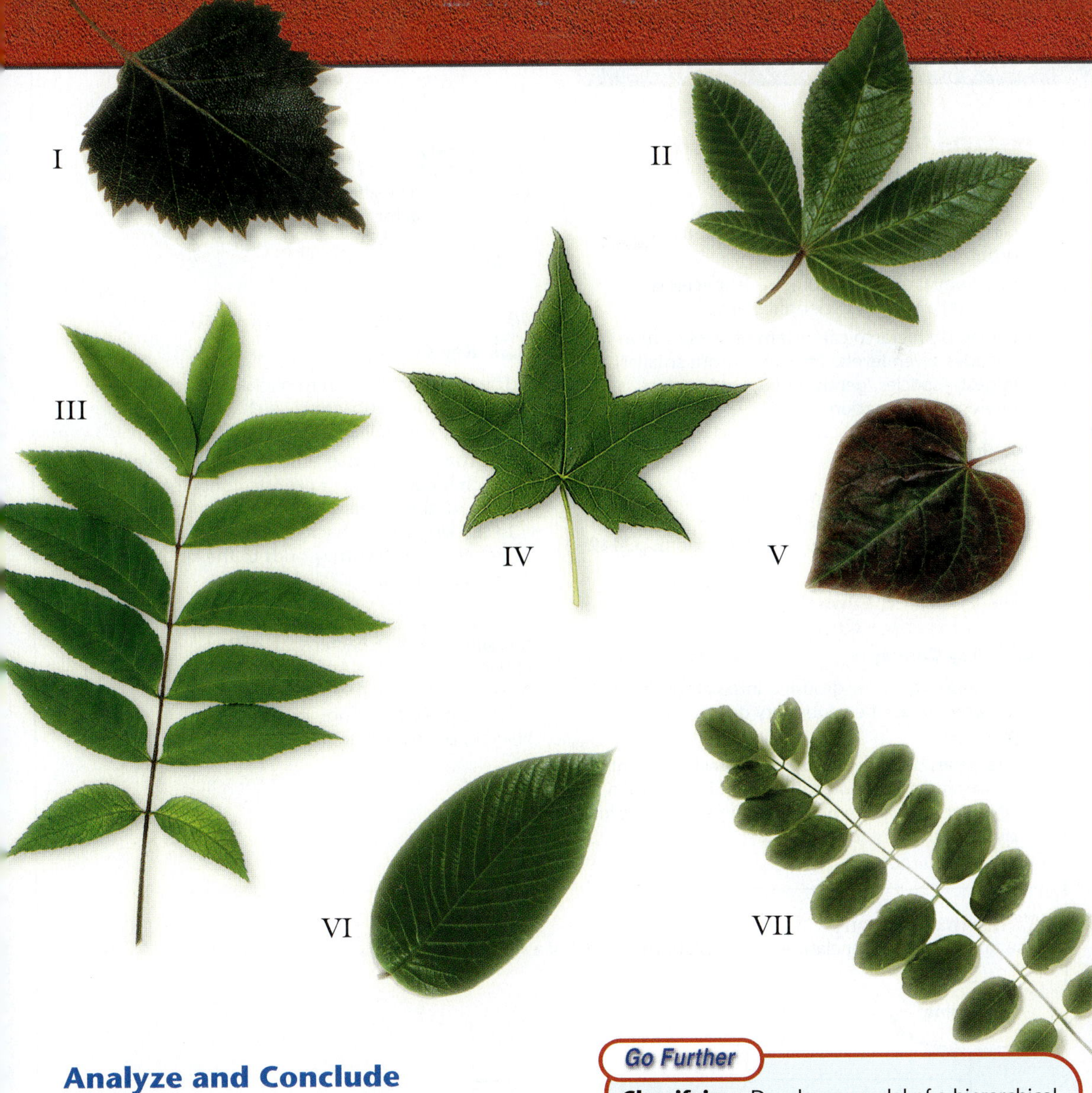

Analyze and Conclude

1. **Classifying** In Part A, identify leaves I through VII.
2. **Applying Concepts** In Part B, how did you choose the characteristics for your key? How did you decide on the key's order?
3. **Evaluating and Revising** Based on your classmate's feedback, does the key you developed in Part B need to be revised? If so, how?
4. **Inferring** Why is it important that the paired statements in a dichotomous key be opposites?

Go Further

Classifying Develop a model of a hierarchical classification system for a group of small objects, such as nuts, bolts, and screws. Your classification should be based on observable similarities and differences. Invent your own taxonomic nomenclature for the levels of your classification system. Then, develop a dichotomous key that someone can use to identify the items in your classification system. Use the dichotomous key in this lab as a model.

Expected Outcomes In Part A, students should correctly classify the leaves using the dichotomous key. In Part B, they should develop a dichotomous key to correctly classify another group of items.

Additional Activity

Collect 3 or 4 leaves from different trees in your neighborhood. Then, use a field guide to trees in your area to determine the identity of each tree. Which characteristics of the leaves were useful in determining their identity? In addition to leaves, does the field guide use other characteristics of the trees to help identify them? If so, which ones? (**Answer:** *Students may indicate that the descriptions and drawings of the basic leaf types and tree shapes helped to determine the identity of each tree. Field guides may also provide information about types of fruits and flowers as well as habitats.*)

Go Further

Examples of groups of objects students might use include eating utensils, postage stamps, and model vehicles. They should select only observable characteristics, such as color or shape, and make all the choices dichotomous; for example, black or silver, car or truck, and round or square. Have pairs of students exchange completed keys to check that the keys work correctly to classify the selected objects.

Analyze and Conclude

1. I: *Betula* (birch); II: *Aesculus* (buckeye); III: *Carya* (pecan); IV: *Liquidambar* (sweetgum); V: *Cercis* (redbud); VI: *Magnolia* (magnolia); VII: *Robinia* (locust)

2. Characteristics chosen will depend on the writing implements or groups of items provided.

3. Students' answers will depend on which characteristics they chose for their classifications.

4. Paired statements must be opposites because each statement leads to either another step or identification of the species.

Chapter 18 Study Guide

Study Tip

Suggest that students review the chapter by studying the figures and their captions.

Thinking Visually

1. Classes

2.–6. Archaebacteria, Protista, Plantae, Fungi, Animalia (in any order)

Chapter 18 Assessment

Reviewing Content

1. b	5. a	9. b
2. d	6. d	10. c
3. c	7. d	
4. a	8. c	

Understanding Concepts

11. Biologists assign each organism a universally accepted name to provide consistency and avoid confusion.

12. Evolutionary relationships are used as well as structural similarities of the organisms.

13. Binomial nomenclature is useful to all scientists because each name is unique, a combination of the genus name and a term that is different for each species in the genus. Each scientific name is assigned to only one species, so different species are not confused.

14. The seven taxonomic groups are species, genus, family, order, class, phylum, and kingdom.

15. The goal of evolutionary classification is to group organisms based on their evolutionary history instead of grouping only according to physical similarities.

16. A derived character is a characteristic that appears in recent parts of a lineage but not in its older members; a molted exoskeleton in crustaceans is an example; this trait was not present in early crustacean ancestors.

17. A cladogram is an attempt to trace the process of evolution in a group of organisms by focusing on unique shared derived features that appear in some organisms but not in others.

Chapter 18 Study Guide

18–1 Finding Order in Diversity

Key Concepts

- To study the diversity of life, biologists use a classification system to name organisms and group them in a logical manner.
- In binomial nomenclature, each species is assigned a two-part scientific name.
- Linnaeus's hierarchical system of classification includes seven levels. They are—from smallest to largest—species, genus, family, order, class, phylum, and kingdom.

Vocabulary

taxonomy, p. 447
binomial nomenclature, p. 448 • genus, p. 448
taxon, p. 449 • family, p. 449 • order, p. 449
class, p. 449 • phylum, p. 449 • kingdom, p. 449

18–2 Modern Evolutionary Classification

 **Key Concepts** 

*BI 8.f, *BI 8.g

- Organisms are now grouped into categories that represent lines of evolutionary descent, or phylogeny.
- The genes of many organisms show important similarities at the molecular level. Similarities in DNA can be used to help determine classification and evolutionary relationships.

Vocabulary

phylogeny, p. 452
evolutionary classification, p. 452
derived character, p. 453
cladogram, p. 453
molecular clock, p. 455

18–3 Kingdoms and Domains

Key Concepts

- The six-kingdom system of classification includes the kingdoms Eubacteria, Archaebacteria, Protista, Fungi, Plantae, and Animalia.
- The three domains are the domain Eukarya, which is composed of protists, fungi, plants, and animals; the domain Bacteria, which corresponds to the kingdom Eubacteria; and the domain Archaea, which corresponds to the kingdom Archaebacteria.

Vocabulary

domain, p. 458 • Bacteria, p. 459
Eubacteria, p. 459 • Archaea, p. 459
Archaebacteria, p. 459 • Eukarya, p. 460
Protista, p. 460 • Fungi, p. 460
Plantae, p. 461 • Animalia, p. 461

Thinking Visually

Use taxonomic nomenclature to complete the model of a hierarchical classification system below.

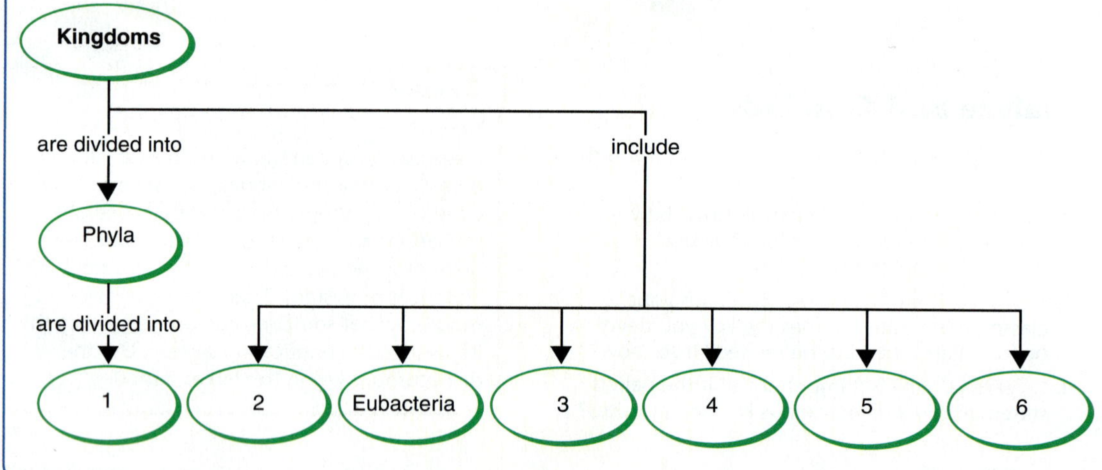

CHAPTER RESOURCES

TIME SAVER

Print:

- ***Teaching Resources,*** Chapter Vocabulary Review, Graphic Organizer, Chapter 18 Tests: Levels A and B
- ***Laboratory Assessment,*** Laboratory Assessment 5

Technology:

- ***Computer Test Bank,*** Chapter 18 Test
- ***iText,*** Chapter 18 Assessment

Chapter 18 Assessment

Reviewing Content

Choose the letter that best answers the question or completes the statement.

1. The science that specializes in the classification of organisms is
   a. anatomy.
   b. taxonomy.
   c. botany.
   d. paleontology.
2. Solely from its name, you know that *Rhizopus nigricans* must be
   a. a plant.
   b. an animal.
   c. in the genus *nigricans.*
   d. in the genus *Rhizopus.*
3. A useful classification system does NOT
   a. show relationships.
   b. reveal evolutionary trends.
   c. use different scientific names for the same organism.
   d. change the taxon of an organism based on new data.
4. In classifying organisms, orders are grouped together into
   a. classes.
   b. phyla.
   c. families.
   d. genera.
5. The largest and most inclusive of Linnaeus's taxonomic categories is the
   a. kingdom.
   b. order.
   c. phylum.
   d. species.
6. Which of the following shows the evolutionary relationships among a group of organisms?
   a. taxon
   b. domain
   c. binomial nomenclature
   d. cladogram
7. A unique trait that is used to construct a cladogram is called a
   a. taxon.
   b. molecular clock.
   c. domain.
   d. derived character.
8. The three domains are
   a. Animalia, Plantae, Archaebacteria.
   b. Plantae, Fungi, Eubacteria.
   c. Bacteria, Archaea, Eukarya.
   d. Protista, Bacteria, Animalia.
9. A kingdom that includes only heterotrophs is
   a. Protista.
   b. Fungi.
   c. Plantae.
   d. Eubacteria.

Interactive textbook with assessment at PHSchool.com 

10. Which organism belongs in the kingdom Animalia?

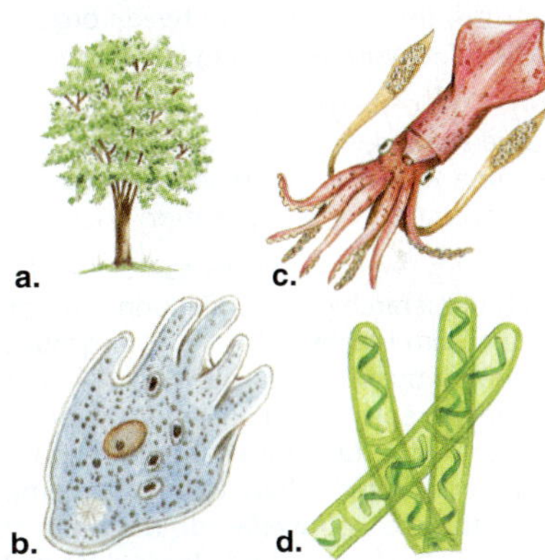

Understanding Concepts

11. Why do biologists assign each organism a universally accepted name?
12. What criteria are used to classify an organism?
13. What features of binomial nomenclature make it useful for scientists of all nations?
14. Sequence Linnaeus's seven taxonomic categories from smallest to largest.
15. Explain the goal of evolutionary classification.
16. What is a derived character? Give an example of a derived character.
17. How is a cladogram used in classification?
18. How do biologists use DNA and RNA to help classify organisms?
19. What is phylogeny?
20. Describe how a molecular clock is used to estimate the length of time that two related species have been evolving independently.
21. How do domains and kingdoms differ?
22. What characteristics are used to place an organism in the domain Bacteria?
23. Which domain consists of prokaryotes whose cell walls lack peptidoglycan?
24. Describe the four kingdoms that comprise the domain Eukarya.
25. What characteristic(s) differentiate the kingdom Animalia from the kingdom Plantae?

HOMEWORK GUIDE

Section:	Questions:
Section 18–1	1–5, 11–14, 26, 28
Section 18–2	6, 7, 15–20, 27, 31, 32
Section 18–3	8–10, 21–25, 29, 30

If your class subscribes to the iText, your students can go online to access an interactive version of the Student Edition and a self-test.

(Continued from page 464)

18. Biologists choose segments of DNA and RNA that are similar in all or many organisms, and compare the sequences within those molecules. The more similar the DNA or RNA between species, the more closely related the species are assumed to be. Such comparisons can provide information that supports or refutes inferences based on visible structural characteristics.
19. Phylogeny is the study of evolutionary relationships among organisms.
20. A molecular clock relies on a repeating process, a mutation, to estimate the length of time that two species have been evolving independently. A comparison of DNA sequences in two species indicates how alike or dissimilar the genes are. The degree of dissimilarity is, in turn, an indication of how long ago the species shared a common ancestor.
21. A domain is more inclusive and larger than a kingdom.
22. Members of domain Bacteria are all unicellular and prokaryotic. Cell walls contain peptidoglycan.
23. They are placed in the kingdom Archaea.
24. The four kingdoms making up the domain Eukarya are Protists, Fungi, Plantae, and Animalia.
25. Unlike members of the Plantae kingdom, members of the Animalia kingdom are heterotrophic, do not have cell walls, and are motile.

Chapter 18 Assessment

Critical Thinking

26. Taxonomic classification emphasizes both. Similarities place organisms together in large groups, and differences separate organisms into smaller groups.

27. Students' answers should indicate that the internal structures would have to be examined for similarities and that the organisms would have to be examined for genetic similarities and differences.

28. A is labeled *All Animals,* B is labeled *Animals With Backbones,* C is labeled *Mammals,* and D is labeled *Insects.*

29. This organism would be placed in the kingdom Protista because it is unicellular, contains a nuclear membrane, and has chloroplasts.

30. Organism A belongs in the kingdom Plantae. Organism B belongs in the kingdom Archaebacteria. Organism C belongs in the kingdom Protista.

31. If the DNA of beetles A and B is more similar than that of beetle C to either, you could conclude that beetles A and B are more closely related to each other than to beetle C.

32. The two groups of organisms are closely related, although not as closely as species within a genus.

Focus on the BIG Idea 

Gene mutations would probably be more useful because chromosomal mutations may cause abnormalities that can be harmful. Gene mutations are more likely to be neutral and thus suitable for use as molecular clocks.

Writing in Science

Students should explain that similarities in the DNA of two different organisms suggest that the organisms recently shared a common ancestor and that the more recently they shared a common ancestor, the more closely related they are. Students might use the example of African and American vultures and storks that is described on page 454.

Chapter 18 Assessment

Critical Thinking

26. **Applying Concepts** Does taxonomic classification place emphasis on the similarities between organisms, the differences between organisms, or both? Explain your reasoning.

27. **Applying Concepts** Both snakes and worms are tube-shaped, with no legs. How could you determine whether the similarity in shape means that they share a recent common ancestor?

28. **Classifying** Venn diagrams can be used to make models of hierarchical classification schemes. A Venn diagram is shown below. Four groups are represented by circular regions—A, B, C, and D. Each region represents a collection of organisms or members of a taxonomic level. Regions that overlap, or intersect, share common members. Regions that do not overlap do not have members in common. Use the following terms to label the regions shown in the diagram: All Animals, Animals That Have Backbones, Insects, Mammals.

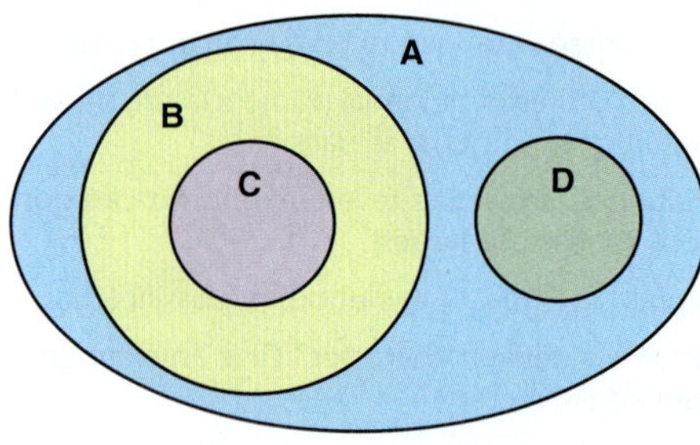

29. **Classifying** Suppose you discovered a new unicellular organism. This organism has a nucleus, mitochondria, and a giant chloroplast. In which kingdom would you place this organism? What are your reasons?

30. **Classifying** Study the descriptions of the following organisms and place them in the correct kingdom.

    Organism A: Multicellular, photosynthetic autotrophs, with cell walls that contain cellulose

    Organism B: Their cell walls lack peptidoglycan, and their cell membranes contain certain lipids that are not found in any other organisms. Many live in some of the most extreme environments and can survive only in the absence of oxygen.

    Organism C: Unicellular, eukaryotic organisms that have chloroplasts

31. **Applying Concepts** You are a biologist who is searching for new species in the Amazon jungle. You find two new species of beetles, beetle A and beetle B, that resemble each other closely but have somewhat different markings on their wings. In addition, both beetle A and beetle B resemble a species of beetle, beetle C, that has already been identified. How could you use DNA similarities and differences to determine whether beetle A and beetle B are more closely related to each other than to beetle C?

32. **Applying Concepts** Two groups of organisms are in different genera, but they are included in the same family. What does this information tell you about the phylogenetic relationship of the two groups?

Focus on the BIG Idea

Information and Heredity Refer back to Chapter 12 to help you answer the following question: Which type of mutations would be more useful to scientists as molecular clocks—gene mutations or chromosomal mutations? Explain.

Writing in Science

Write a short explanation of the way in which taxonomists use similarities and differences in DNA to help classify organisms and infer evolutionary relationships. (*Hint*: Use a specific example to help clarify your explanation.)

Performance-Based Assessment

Illustrate Storyboards It has been estimated that there are more unknown species in the tropical rain forests than there are known species in the world. Scientists are concerned that these rain forests might be destroyed before the species in them can be classified. Illustrate storyboards for a television news program explaining this issue to the general public. Show your storyboards to the class.

For: An interactive self-test
Visit: PHSchool.com
Web Code: cba-5180

Performance-Based Assessment

Some students may present ethical reasons that organisms in rain forests should be protected. Other students may focus on the potential benefits to humans of learning about and classifying organisms. Students also may mention economic benefits, medicines, or new sources of food.

Your students can independently test their knowledge of the chapter and print out their test results for your files.

Standards Practice

Success  Tracker™
Online at PHSchool.com

Test-Taking Tip When you open your test booklet, reassure yourself that the question format is similar to the ones that you have seen in these practice tests. Notice that the directions and the number of choices are similar to those with which you have experience.

Directions: Choose the letter that best answers the question or completes the statement.

1. Which of the following is NOT a characteristic of Linnaeus's system for naming organisms?
   A two-part name
   B multi-part name describing several traits
   C name that identifies the organism's genus
   D name that includes the organism's species identifier

2. What is true about using similarities to classify different species?
   A Only similar species, such as two species of rabbits, can be meaningfully compared.
   B Genetic similarities are no indication of the relationship between two species.
   C Even dissimilar species can be compared at the level of certain genes.
   D Species are not compared for the purpose of classification.

3. In the six-kingdom system of classifying living things, the kingdom(s) that contain(s) microscopic organisms is(are)
   A Eubacteria
   B Archaebacteria
   C Protista
   D all of the above

4. If species A and B have very similar genes and proteins, what is probably true? ***BI 8.f**
   A Species A and B shared a relatively recent common ancestor.
   B Species A evolved independently of species B for a long period.
   C Species A and species B are the same species.
   D Species A is older than species B.

5. The length of time that two taxa have been evolving separately can be estimated using a model called a ***BI 8.g**
   A phylogenetic tree.
   B cladogram.
   C molecular clock.
   D six-kingdom system.

6. The taxon called Eukarya is a(an)
   A order.
   B class.
   C species.
   D domain.

7. Bacteria are classified into
   A three kingdoms.
   B three domains.
   C three species.
   D two domains.

8. The figure below shows the presumed relationships between three insect taxa.

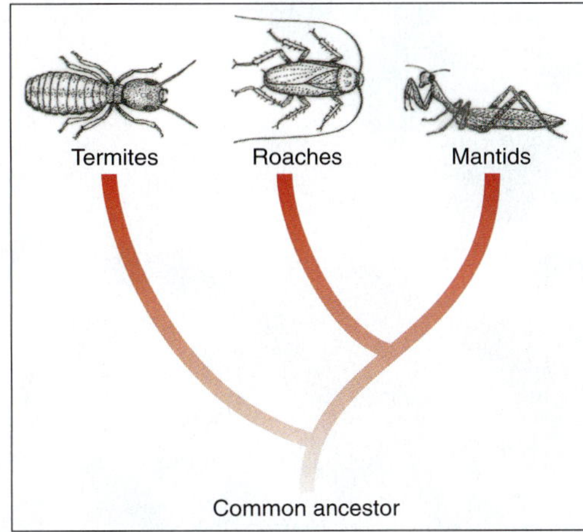

What is true about these three groups of insects?

I. Roaches and mantids share a more recent common ancestor than do roaches and termites.
II. Roaches and mantids share a more recent common ancestor than do mantids and termites.
III. Termites, roaches, and mantids share a common ancestor.

A I only
B II only
C I and III only
D I, II, and III

Standards Practice

1. B	**4.** A	**7.** D
2. C	**5.** C	**8.** D
3. D	**6.** D	

Success  Tracker™
Online at PHSchool.com

Have students check their understanding of the chapter by logging onto Success Tracker.

UNIT 6

Scarlet hood mushrooms growing on a forest floor

Dear Colleague,

To be perfectly honest, this unit is one of my favorite parts of this textbook. You might not expect this, since most of my teaching and research deals with the material in Units 3 and 4, but it's true nonetheless. Some of this comes from the challenges presented by the study of these organisms. Students don't always appreciate the importance of living things such as protists and bacteria, and it's a special challenge to open their eyes to these remarkable forms of life.

I think this is important for a number of reasons. Every time I take a walk through the woods near my house, I'm struck by the obvious ways in which decomposers such as fungi and slime molds shape the living world. Students take it for granted that dead things "rot." But why should they? Most living things, humans included, simply can't break down cork, cellulose, and other complex substances found in the forest. If this were true of all organisms, after a few years, the floors of the forests around the world would be littered with leaves and twigs and the undecayed bodies of insects.

As I point out in Chapter 21, fungi are different. They produce enzymes that can break down just about anything, even the chitinous exoskeletons of insects, and it's a good thing, too. Fungi's biochemical magic returns nutrients and organic matter to the soil, making it possible for new organisms to thrive in the recycled environment.

This is just one way in which these organisms shape the world around us. Even more amazing are the protists, whose various members exemplify nearly every conceivable way of making a living on this little planet. Molecular studies of these organisms have confirmed the suspicions of many biologists—this single

All multicellular fungi, including these mushrooms, are made up of thin filaments called hyphae.

phylum contains organisms whose differences from one another are so great that the protists themselves could easily be split into several phyla of their own. At least a few taxonomists have done exactly that, although we decided to spare you and your students these complications, at least for now.

Knowing that bacteria and viruses cause any number of serious diseases, I'm sure your students will understand many of the reasons for studying them. On a global scale, however, there is good evidence that we are just beginning to learn the extent to which bacteria dominate life on Earth.

Drilling samples, taken hundreds of meters below the surface of Earth, have now confirmed something that bacteriologists have long suspected. Great numbers of bacteria live deep beneath the surface, thriving in darkness, often under some of the most extreme conditions imaginable. A few biologists have suggested that the abundance of underground bacteria is so great that their mass might dwarf all life found on Earth's surface.

The jury is still out as to whether such remarkable estimates are correct. One thing, however, is certain. There is no corner of this planet that does not harbor microbial life.

We humans tend to think of ourselves as the dominant forms of life on planet Earth, and, in some respects, that is true. The organisms discussed in this unit, however, may have a better claim. They were here before us, they outnumber us, and our lives depend upon their presence in ways almost too numerous to count.

As teachers, one of the greatest gifts we can give our students is to extend their vision beyond the obvious. I can think of no better way to do exactly that than to spend some time investigating these extraordinary organisms.

Sincerely,

Ken Miller

Go Online PHSchool.com

Students can research microorganisms and fungi on the site developed by authors Ken Miller and Joe Levine.

Chapter Planner 19 Bacteria and Viruses

Section and Section Objectives	Time	STANDARDS NCLB	STANDARDS Biology	Activities and Labs
19–1 Bacteria, pp. 471–477 *19.1.1* ***Explain*** how the two groups of prokaryotes differ. *19.1.2* ***Describe*** the factors that are used to identify prokaryotes. *19.1.3* ***Explain*** why bacteria are vital to maintaining the living world.	2 periods (1 block)	BI 10.d		**SE:** ***Inquiry Activity,*** Where are bacteria found?, p. 470 L2 L3 **TE:** ***Build Science Skills,*** p. 472 L2, p. 473 L2 L3 **TE:** ***Demonstration,*** p. 473 L1 L2, p. 475 L1 L2 **TE:** ***Build Science Skills,*** p. 477 L1 L2 **SE:** ***Exploration,*** Identifying Limits to the Growth of Bacteria, p. 491 L2 L3 **LMB:** Chapter 19 Lab L1 L2
19–2 Viruses, pp. 478–483 *19.2.1* ***Describe*** the structure of a virus. *19.2.2* ***Explain*** how viruses cause infection.	1 period (1/2 block)	BI 1.c, BI 10.d		**TE:** ***Build Science Skills,*** p. 479 L2 **TE:** ***Build Science Skills,*** p. 480 L2 **SE:** ***Quick Lab,*** How do viruses differ in structure?, p. 482 L1 L2
19–3 Diseases Caused by Bacteria and Viruses, pp. 485–490 *19.3.1* ***Explain*** how bacteria cause disease. *19.3.2* ***Describe*** how bacterial growth can be controlled. *19.3.3* ***Explain*** how viruses cause disease.	1 period (1/2 block)	BI 10.c, BI 10.d		**SE:** ***Issues in Biology,*** Should Mass Vaccinations Be Required?, p. 484 L2 L3 **SE:** ***Biology and History,*** The History of Vaccines, p. 486 **TE:** ***Build Science Skills,*** p. 488 L2 **SE:** ***Careers in Biology,*** p. 489 L2 **LMA:** Chapter 19 Lab L2 L3 **BTM:** Lab 16 L2 L3 **IF:** Investigation 6 L2 L3
Chapter Assessment, pp. 492–495	1 period (1/2 block)			

ACTIVITY PLANNER

SE: ***Inquiry Activity,*** p. 470; 15 min. each for 2 days; 2 sterile agar plates, 2 plate covers, glass-marking pencil, transparent tape

TE: ***Build Science Skills,*** p. 472; 20 min.; variety of craft materials

TE: ***Demonstration,*** p. 473; 10 min.; marbles, beads, spheres of modeling clay or malted milk balls; unsharpened pencils, pieces of chalk, or short dowels; spring, pipe cleaners

TE: ***Build Science Skills,*** p. 473; 20 min.; prepared slides of various species of bacteria, microscope

TE: ***Demonstration,*** p. 475; 15 min. each for 2 days; soil, freezer, 2 petri dishes of agar, plastic container, incubator

TE: ***Build Science Skills,*** p. 477; 20 min.; plain yogurt, bowl, dropper pipette, microscope slide, coverslip, methylene blue, microscope

TE: ***Build Science Skills,*** p. 479; 10 min.; sunflower seeds (or other easily shelled seeds including pumpkin seeds or pistachio nuts)

TE: ***Build Science Skills,*** p. 480; 10 min.; electron micrograph of a virus particle attaching to a cell membrane

SE: ***Quick Lab,*** p. 482; 20 min.; metric ruler, scissors, tape, craft materials such as colored paper, foam balls, pipe cleaners, yarn, sandpaper

TE: ***Build Science Skills,*** p. 488; 15 min.; advertisements and packages of cold remedies

SE: ***Exploration,*** p. 491; 15 min. each for 2 days, 45 min. for day 3; 3 sterile agar plates, hand lens, bacterial culture, sterile cotton swabs, glass-marking pencil, transparent tape

PLANNING KEY

Ability Levels
for students performing . . .
below grade level L1
at grade level L2
above grade level L3

Print Components

SE	Student Edition	LA	Lab Assessment
TE	Teacher's Edition	BTM	Biotechnology Manual
RSW	Reading & Study Workbook A	IDM	Issues and Decision Making
ARSW	Adapted Reading & Study Workbook B	LW	Lab Worksheets
TR	Teaching Resources	LMA	Laboratory Manual A
IF	Investigations in Forensics	LMB	Laboratory Manual B

Tech Components

CTB	Computer Test Bank
BD	BioDetectives DVD
TP	Transparencies Plus
PLM	Probeware Lab Manual
ABC	ABC DVD Library
LS	Lab Simulations
VL	Virtual Labs

Interactive textbook with assessment at PHSchool.com

Program Resources	Assessment	Media and Technology
TR: Lesson Plan 19–1, Section Summary, p. 4 L1, p. 14 L2, Worksheets, pp. 7–8 L1, pp. 16–19 L2 **LW:** Chapter 19 Exploration L1 L2 L3 **RSW:** Section 19–1 L2 **ARSW:** Section 19–1 L1	**SE:** 19–1 Section Assessment, p. 477 **TR:** Section Review 19–1	**iText:** Section 19–1 **TP:** 19–1 Interest Grabber, Section Outline, Concept Map, The Structure of a Eubacterium
TR: Lesson Plan 19–2, Section Summary, p. 5 L1, p. 14 L2, Worksheets, pp. 9–11 L1, pp. 20–22 L2 **RSW:** Section 19–2 L2 **ARSW:** Section 19–2 L1	**SE:** 19–2 Section Assessment, p. 483 **TR:** Section Review 19–2	**iText:** Section 19–2 **TP:** 19–2 Interest Grabber, Section Outline, Figure 19–9, Figure 19–10, Figure 19–11 **BD:** "Influenza: Tracking a Virus" **ABC:** 31 Lytic and Lysogenic Cycles
TR: Lesson Plan 19–3, Section Summary, p. 5 L1, p. 15 L2, Worksheets, p. 12 L1, pp. 23–24 L2 **RSW:** Section 19–3 L2 **ARSW:** Section 19–3 L1	**SE:** 19–3 Section Assessment, p. 490 **TR:** Section Review 19–3	**iText:** Section 19–3 **TP:** 19–3 Interest Grabber, Section Outline, Common Diseases Caused by Bacteria, Common Diseases Caused by Viruses
	SE: Chapter 19 Assessment, pp. 492–495 **TR:** Chapter Vocabulary Review, Graphic Organizer, Chapter 19 Test	**iText:** Chapter 19 Assessment **CTB:** Chapter 19 Test **Go Online** Students can do research, share data, and test their knowledge online.

PRESSED FOR TIME?

To Preview the Chapter

- Introduce students to Key Concepts and Vocabulary terms in each section.
- Assign the Reading Strategies for each section.

To Cover the Chapter Quickly

- Have students read Classifying Prokaryotes, Identifying Prokaryotes, and Importance of Bacteria in Section 19–1; What Is a Virus? and Viruses and Living Cells in Section 19–2; and Bacterial Disease in Humans, Controlling Bacteria, and Viral Diseases in Humans in Section 19–3.
- Assign the Section Reviews 19–1, 19–2, and 19–3; questions 1–6, 8, 10–12, 20, 24, 26, 29, and 30 in Chapter 19 Assessment; and questions 1–11 in Chapter 19 Standards Practice.

To Review the Chapter

- Assign Sections 19–1 through 19–3 in the Reading and Study Workbook or the Adapted Reading and Study Workbook.
- Assign Section Reviews for 19–1 through 19–3 and the Chapter Vocabulary Review for Chapter 19 in the Teaching Resources.

CHAPTER 19

ENGAGE/EXPLORE

Inquiry Activity

Objective Students will be able to draw a conclusion that there are bacteria in the air.

Skills Focus **Observing, Drawing Conclusions, Asking Questions**

Materials 2 sterile agar plates, 2 plate covers, glass-marking pencil, transparent tape

Time 15 minutes each for 2 days

Safety Make sure that students wash their hands with soap and warm water after handling the plates. Use a disinfectant, such as diluted bleach, to wipe down all surfaces where bacteria might have been deposited. Inform parents that students will be doing a lab involving bacteria. Parents of students with compromised immune systems may wish them not to participate in the lab. Provide a container in which students can safely dispose of used plates. For safe disposal, soak the plates overnight in undiluted chlorine bleach, 70% isopropyl alcohol, or another disinfectant. Read the safety information in the MSDS for chlorine bleach and isopropyl alcohol prior to doing the lab. It may be possible to place the used plates in biohazard bags and dispose of them through a local hospital.

Strategies

- Emphasize to students the importance of not touching the exposed plates. Plastic gloves must be worn to emphasize this safety precaution.
- Show students how to tape the plates closed.
- Sealing the plates with parafilm can help prevent agar from drying out.

Expected Outcomes On the exposed plate, there will typically be 12 colonies after 24 hours and 16 colonies after 48 hours.

Think About It

1. The exposed plate
2. Students should conclude that bacterial spores and dust-borne bacteria landed on the agar when the plate was exposed.
3. Students' questions should focus on their particular results.

CHAPTER 19

Bacteria and Viruses

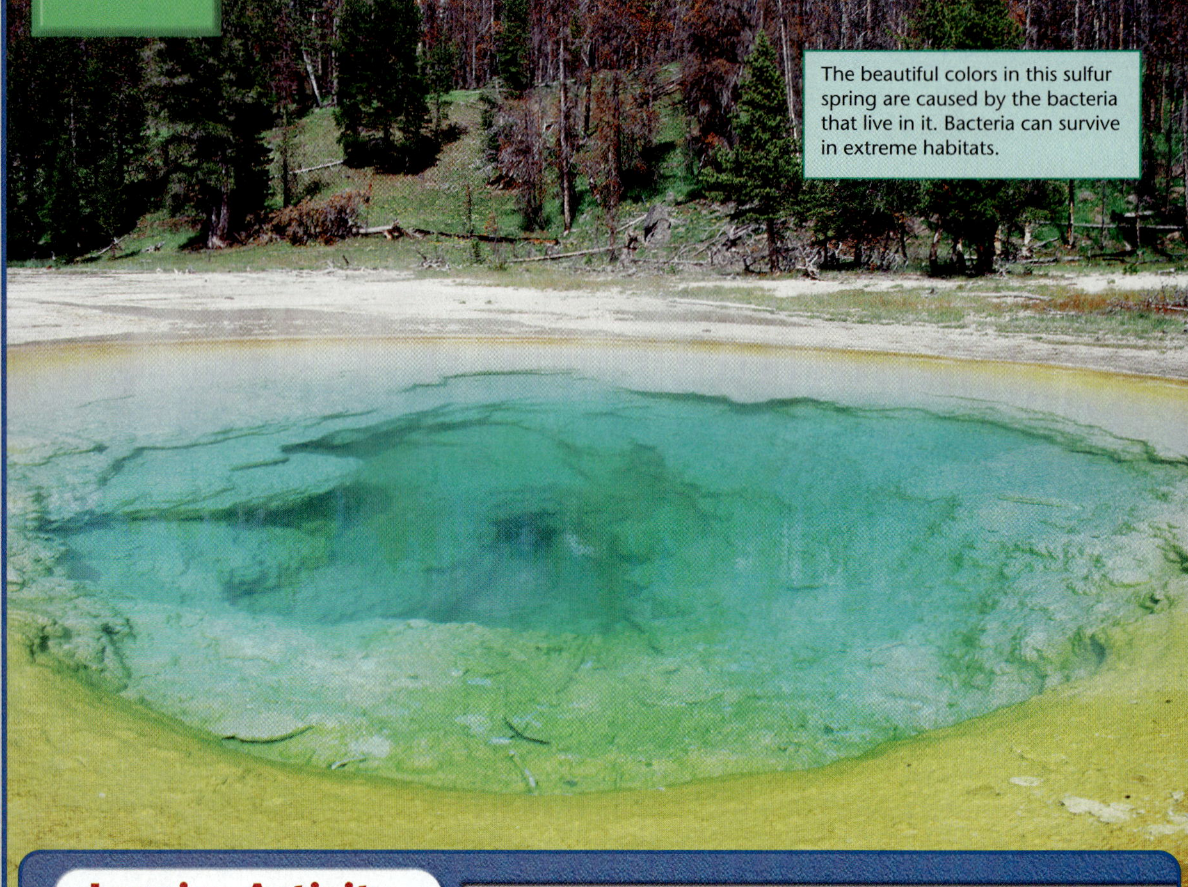

The beautiful colors in this sulfur spring are caused by the bacteria that live in it. Bacteria can survive in extreme habitats.

Inquiry Activity

Where are bacteria found?

Procedure   

1. Label 2 sterile agar plates "control" and "exposed."
2. Tape closed the cover of the control plate. Remove the cover of the exposed plate. Leave both plates on the table for 5 minutes. Do not touch or breathe on the agar.
3. After 5 minutes, tape closed the lid of the exposed plate. Store both plates upside down in a warm place.
4. After 2 days, record the number of bacterial colonies on each plate. **CAUTION:** *Do not open the plates. Give them to your teacher for disposal.*

Think About It

1. **Observing** Which plate had more colonies?
2. **Drawing Conclusions** Where did the bacteria on your plates come from? Explain your answer.
3. **Asking Questions** Write three questions you could investigate using your observations and results.

Assess Prior Knowledge

Display a variety of photographs of bacteria and viruses taken from old microbiology and biology texts and science journals. You could use a microprojector or videocamera to show slides of the major shapes of bacteria and several shapes of viruses. Tell students that some of these photos are of bacteria and some are of viruses. Then, have small groups of students classify a pile of photos into two groups—bacteria and viruses. After all groups have finished their classifications, have them present their results to the class. Invite students from other groups to challenge the classification of various photos. Then, after students have read about bacteria and viruses, ask that groups reconsider their classifications.

19–1 Bacteria

BI 10.d. Students know there are important differences between bacteria and viruses with respect to their requirements for growth and replication, the body's primary defenses against bacterial and viral infections, and effective treatments of these infections.

Imagine living all your life as a member of the only family on your street. Then, one morning, you open the front door and discover houses all around you. You see neighbors tending their gardens and children walking to school. Where did all the people come from? What if the answer turned out to be that they had always been there—you just hadn't seen them? In fact, they had lived on your street for years and years before your house was even built. How would your view of the world change? What would it be like to go, almost overnight, from thinking that you and your family were the only folks on the block to just one family in a crowded community? A bit of a shock!

Humans once had just such a shock. Suddenly, the street was very crowded! Thanks to Robert Hooke and Anton van Leeuwenhoek, the invention of the microscope opened our eyes to the hidden, living world around us.

Microscopic life covers nearly every square centimeter of Earth. There are microorganisms of many different sizes and shapes, even in a single drop of pond water. The smallest and most common microorganisms are **prokaryotes**—unicellular organisms that lack a nucleus. For many years, most prokaryotes were called "bacteria." The word *bacteria* is so familiar that we will use it as a common term to describe prokaryotes.

Prokaryotes typically range in size from 1 to 5 micrometers, making them much smaller than most eukaryotic cells, which generally range from 10 to 100 micrometers in diameter. There are exceptions to this, of course. One example is *Epulopiscium fisheloni,* a gigantic prokaryote, shown in **Figure 19–1**, that is about 500 micrometers long.

Guide for Reading

Key Concepts

- How do the two groups of prokaryotes differ?
- What factors are used to identify prokaryotes?
- What is the importance of bacteria?

Vocabulary

prokaryote • bacillus
coccus • spirillum
chemoheterotroph
photoheterotroph
photoautotroph
chemoautotroph
obligate aerobe
obligate anaerobe
facultative anaerobe
binary fission
conjugation • endospore
nitrogen fixation

Reading Strategy: Finding Main Ideas Before you read this section, write down the major headings of the section. Then, as you read the section, list the important information under each heading.

Classifying Prokaryotes

Until fairly recently, all prokaryotes were placed in a single kingdom—Monera. More recently, however, biologists have begun to appreciate that prokaryotes can be divided into two very different groups: the eubacteria (yoo-bak-TEER-ee-uh) and the archaebacteria (ahr-kee-bak-TEER-ee-uh). Each group is now considered to be a separate kingdom. Some biologists think that the split between these two groups is so ancient and so fundamental that they should be called domains, a level of classification even higher than kingdom.

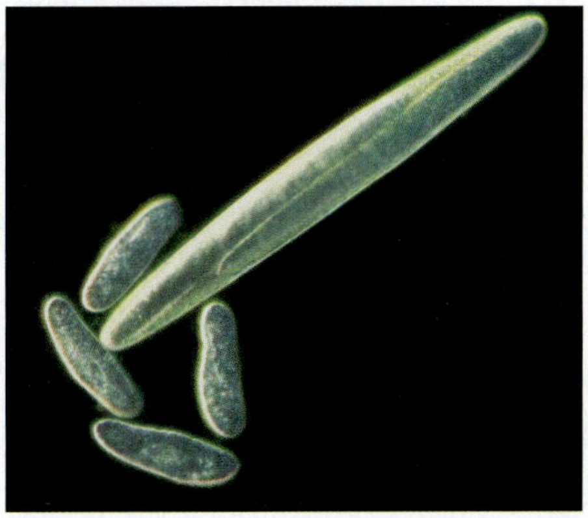

(magnification: 100×)

▶ **Figure 19–1** The large cell in this photograph is *Epulopiscium fisheloni,* one of the largest prokaryotes. Notice its size in relation to the neighboring cells, which are eukaryotic paramecia.

Section 19–1

BI 10.d

1 FOCUS

Objectives

19.1.1 ***Explain*** how the two groups of prokaryotes differ.

19.1.2 ***Describe*** the factors that are used to identify prokaryotes.

19.1.3 ***Explain*** why bacteria are vital to maintaining the living world.

Guide for Reading

Vocabulary Preview

Call on students at random to pronounce the Vocabulary terms in the order in which they appear. Correct any mispronunciations.

Reading Strategy

Have students make an outline of the section, using the blue headings as the first level of the outline and the green side headings as the second level. Explain that they should add third and fourth levels to their outlines by finding details in the section that support each of the headings.

2 INSTRUCT

Classifying Prokaryotes

Make Connections

Mathematics Point out that 1 micrometer equals 1/1,000,000 meter, or 1/10,000 centimeter. A typical prokaryote ranges in size from 1 to 5 micrometers. Then, ask students: **How many prokaryotic cells could be lined up across a coin that is 1 centimeter in diameter?** *(2000 to 10,000 cells)* L2

SECTION RESOURCES

TIME SAVER

Print:

- ***Laboratory Manual B,*** Chapter 19 Lab
- ***Teaching Resources,*** Lesson Plan 19–1, Adapted Section Summary 19–1, Adapted Worksheets 19–1, Section Summary 19–1, Worksheets 19–1, Section Review 19–1
- ***Reading and Study Workbook A,*** Section 19–1
- ***Adapted Reading and Study Workbook B,*** Section 19–1
- ***Lab Worksheets,*** Chapter 19 Exploration

Technology:

- ***iText,*** Section 19–1
- ***Transparencies Plus,*** Section 19–1

19–1 (continued)

Use Visuals

Figure 19–2 To reinforce for students the difference between prokaryotic cells and eukaryotic cells, have them make a labeled drawing of each kind of cell. For the typical prokaryotic cell, they can use the illustration in Figure 19–2 as a model. For the typical eukaryotic cell, have them turn back to Figure 7–6 on page 175 and use the animal cell as a model. L1 L2

Build Science Skills

Using Models Have students gather a variety of craft materials from school and home to make models of bacteria. These materials might include yarn, sandpaper, textured fabrics, and pipe cleaners. As a resource for this model, students may use any of the photos or illustrations of bacteria in this chapter or in another textbook or one of the drawings they made in observing bacteria with a microscope. L2

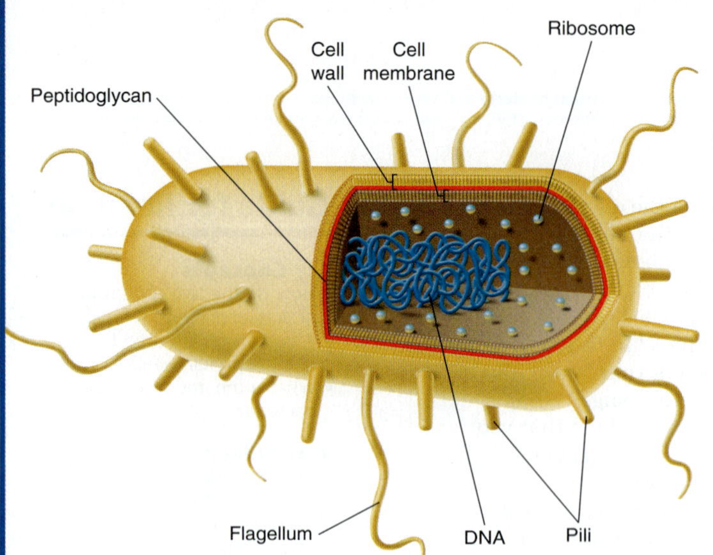

(magnification: 32,300×)

Figure 19–2 A bacterium such as *E. coli* has the basic structure typical of most prokaryotes: cell wall, cell membrane, and cytoplasm. Some prokaryotes have flagella that they use for movement. The pili are involved in cell-to-cell contact. **The cell walls of eubacteria contain peptidoglycan.**

Eubacteria The larger of the two kingdoms of prokaryotes is the eubacteria. Eubacteria include a wide range of organisms with different lifestyles. The variety is so great, in fact, that biologists do not agree on exactly how many phyla are needed to classify this group. Eubacteria live almost everywhere. They live in fresh water, salt water, on land, and on and within the human body. **Figure 19–2** shows a diagram of *Escherichia coli,* a typical eubacterium that lives in human intestines.

Eubacteria are usually surrounded by a cell wall that protects the cell from injury and determines its shape. The cell walls of eubacteria contain peptidoglycan, a carbohydrate. Inside the cell wall is a cell membrane that surrounds the cytoplasm. Some eubacteria have a second membrane, outside the cell membrane, that makes them especially resistant to damage.

Archaebacteria Under a microscope, archaebacteria look very similar to eubacteria. They are equally small, lack nuclei, have cell walls, but chemically archaebacteria are quite different. **Archaebacteria lack the peptidoglycan of eubacteria and also have different membrane lipids. Also, the DNA sequences of key archaebacterial genes are more like those of eukaryotes than those of eubacteria.** Based on this and other data, scientists reason that archaebacteria may be the ancestors of eukaryotes.

Many archaebacteria live in extremely harsh environments. One group of archaebacteria is the methanogens, prokaryotes that produce methane gas. Methanogens live in oxygen-free environments, such as thick mud and the digestive tracts of animals. Other archaebacteria live in extremely salty environments, such as Utah's Great Salt Lake, or in hot springs where temperatures approach the boiling point of water.

CHECKPOINT *Where do archaebacteria live?*

UNIVERSAL ACCESS

Inclusion/Special Needs
Explain to students who have trouble understanding distinctions among prokaryotes that the section divides these organisms in several ways, and each way of division doesn't necessarily have anything to do with the other ways. For instance, cocci bacteria can be aerobic or anaerobic. L1

Less Proficient Readers
To help students understand the text following the green heading Releasing Energy on page 474, have them turn back to Chapter 9 to review the processes of fermentation and cellular respiration. L1 L2

English Language Learners
For learners of English, read aloud the definitions in the text for *obligate* and *facultative*. Then, review the pronunciations of all the new terms in the subsection Metabolic Diversity. Encourage students to add these terms to their personal science glossaries. L1 L2

Identifying Prokaryotes

Because prokaryotes are so small, it may seem difficult to tell one type of prokaryote from another. **Prokaryotes are identified by characteristics such as shape, the chemical nature of their cell walls, the way they move, and the way they obtain energy.**

Shapes Look at the different shapes of the prokaryotes shown in **Figure 19–3.** Rod-shaped prokaryotes are called **bacilli** (buh-SIL-eye; singular: bacillus). Spherical prokaryotes are called **cocci** (KAHK-sy; singular: coccus). Spiral and corkscrew-shaped prokaryotes are called **spirilla** (spy-RIL-uh; singular: spirillum).

Cell Walls Two different types of cell walls are found in eubacteria. A method called Gram staining is used to tell them apart. The Gram stain consists of two dyes—one violet (the primary stain) and the other red (the counterstain). The violet stain, applied first, stains peptidoglycan cell walls. This is followed by an alcohol treatment that tends to wash out the stain. Gram-positive bacteria have thick peptidoglycan walls that retain the dark color of the violet stain even after the alcohol wash. Gram-negative bacteria have much thinner walls inside an outer lipid layer. Alcohol dissolves the lipid and removes the dye from the walls of these bacteria. The counterstain then makes these bacteria appear pink or light red.

Movement You can also identify prokaryotes by whether they move and how they move. Some prokaryotes do not move at all. Others are propelled by flagella, whiplike structures used for movement. Other prokaryotes lash, snake, or spiral forward. Still others glide slowly along a layer of slimelike material they secrete.

Metabolic Diversity

No characteristic of prokaryotes illustrates their diversity better than the ways in which they obtain energy. Depending on their source of energy and whether or not they use oxygen for cellular respiration, prokaryotes can be divided into two main groups. Most prokaryotes are heterotrophs, meaning that they get their energy by consuming organic molecules made by other organisms. Other prokaryotes are autotrophs and make their own food from inorganic molecules.

Heterotrophs Most heterotrophic prokaryotes must take in organic molecules for both energy and a supply of carbon. These prokaryotes are called **chemoheterotrophs** (kee-moh-HET-ur-oh-trohfs). Most animals, including humans, are chemoheterotrophs. A smaller group of heterotrophic prokaryotes are called **photoheterotrophs** (foh-toh-HET-ur-oh-trohfs). These organisms are photosynthetic, using sunlight for energy, but they also need to take in organic compounds as a carbon source.

Figure 19–3 **Prokaryotes can be identified by their shapes.** Prokaryotes usually have one of three basic shapes: rods (bacilli), spheres (cocci), or spirals (spirilla).

Bacilli
(magnification: 3738×)

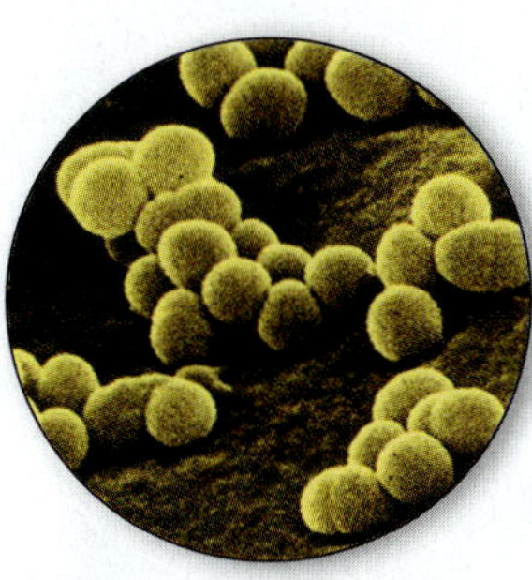

Cocci
(magnification: 30,000×)

Spirilla
(magnification: about 7000×)

BIO INSIGHTS — FACTS AND FIGURES

Prokaryotes in a cow's gut
The kingdom Archaebacteria includes exotic prokaryotes that live in such extreme environments as deep ocean vents and hot sulfur springs. Archaebacteria also include common prokaryotes that live in the digestive tracts of all animals, especially in the rumina of cows and other grazing beasts. These prokaryotes, called methanogens, use hydrogen and carbon to produce methane (CH_4), and most of the methane in the atmosphere is the result of this process. In the atmosphere, the methane reacts with oxygen to produce CO_2. If it were not for methanogens, Earth would be a much different place. Carbon would pile up in huge deposits in the ground, and oxygen would make up a much greater percentage of the atmosphere.

Identifying Prokaryotes

Demonstration

Collect some common items that can be used to model the three basic shapes of bacteria as you discuss the shapes with students. For example, you can represent cocci with marbles, beads, spheres of modeling clay, or malted milk balls. You can represent bacilli with unsharpened pencils, pieces of chalk, or short dowels. You can represent spirilla with springs or pipe cleaners that have been shaped into spirals by wrapping them around a pencil. L1 L2

Build Science Skills

Observing Set up at least one learning station with a microscope and a number of prepared slides showing various species of bacteria, each labeled with the species name. Provide opportunities for students to use the station during class periods. To guide students as they make their observations, prepare a study sheet containing the following instructions to use with each slide:

- What is the scientific name of this bacterium?
- What magnification did you use to see the bacterium clearly?
- How would you classify this bacterium according to cell shape?

Metabolic Diversity

Build Science Skills

Applying Concepts After students have read about chemoautotrophs, ask: **Suppose you leave a jar of mayonnaise on the counter with the top off for a day, make a sandwich with the mayonnaise, and get sick. With what you know about chemoautotrophs, what do you think caused your illness?** *(Chemoautotrophic bacteria began eating the mayonnaise, multiplied, and released toxins. The toxins in the mayonnaise caused the illness.)* L2

Answer to . . .

CHECKPOINT *Many archaebacteria live in harsh environments, including thick mud, animal digestive tracts, salt lakes, and hot springs.*

19–1 (continued)

Use Visuals

Figure 19–4 Ask students: **What kind of prokaryotes might you find near an ocean vent?** *(Chemoautotrophs)* **How do chemoautotrophs obtain the energy they need to carry out life processes?** *(They get energy from chemical reactions involving ammonia, hydrogen sulfide, nitrites, sulfur, or iron.)* **From what chemical do chemoautotrophs obtain energy near ocean vents?** *(From hydrogen sulfide gas that flows from the vents)* 

Build Science Skills

Forming Operational Definitions Help students differentiate among the different groups of prokaryotes by reviewing the word parts that make up the terms used to describe these organisms. On the board, write the following:

- *auto* = "self"
- *chemo* = "chemical"
- *photo* = "light"
- *hetero* = "other"
- *troph* = "nourishment"

Then, have students write definitions for the terms using these equivalencies.

- *autotroph,* an organism that gets "nourishment from itself"
- *photoautotroph,* an organism that gets "nourishment from itself using light"
- *chemoautotroph,* an organism that gets "nourishment from itself using chemicals"
- *heterotroph,* an organism that gets "nourishment from others"
- *photoheterotroph,* an organism that gets "nourishment from others and from using light" L1 L2

▲ **Figure 19–4** Ocean vents, such as this one, are often home to a variety of organisms, including tube worms and other exotic organisms. **Applying Concepts** *Would photoautotrophs survive in this environment? Why or why not?*

Autotrophs Other groups of prokaryotes are autotrophs. Some autotrophs, the **photoautotrophs** (foh-toh-AW-toh-trohfs), use light energy to convert carbon dioxide and water to carbon compounds and oxygen in a process similar to that used by green plants. As you might expect, these organisms are found where light is plentiful, such as near the surfaces of lakes, streams, and oceans. One group, the cyanobacteria (sy-uh-noh-bak-TEER-ee-uh), contains a bluish pigment and chlorophyll *a*, the key pigment in photosynthesis. Cyanobacteria are found throughout the world—in fresh water, salt water, and even on land. In fact, cyanobacteria are often the very first species to recolonize the site of a natural disaster such as a volcanic eruption.

Other prokaryotes can perform chemosynthesis and are called **chemoautotrophs** (kee-moh-AW-toh-trohfs). Like photoautotrophs, chemoautotrophs make organic carbon molecules from carbon dioxide. Unlike photoautotrophs, however, they do not require light as a source of energy. Instead, they use energy directly from chemical reactions involving ammonia, hydrogen sulfide, nitrites, sulfur, or iron. Some chemoautotrophs live deep in the darkness of the ocean. They obtain energy from hydrogen sulfide gas that flows from hydrothermal vents on the ocean floor, such as the one shown in **Figure 19–4.**

✓CHECKPOINT *What are the two groups of autotrophs found in prokaryotes?*

Releasing Energy Like all organisms, bacteria need a constant supply of energy. This energy is released by the processes of cellular respiration or fermentation or both. Organisms that require a constant supply of oxygen in order to live are called **obligate aerobes.** (*Obligate* means that the organisms are obliged, or required, by their life processes to live only in that particular way.) *Mycobacterium tuberculosis,* the bacterium that causes tuberculosis, is an obligate aerobe.

Some bacteria, however, do not require oxygen and, in fact, may be killed by it! These bacteria are called **obligate anaerobes,** and they must live in the absence of oxygen. *Clostridium botulinum* is an obligate anaerobe found in soil. Because of its ability to grow without oxygen, it can grow in canned food that has not been properly sterilized.

A third group of bacteria can survive with or without oxygen and are known as **facultative anaerobes.** (*Facultative* means that the organisms are able to function in different ways, depending on their environment.) Facultative anaerobes do not require oxygen, but neither are they killed by its presence. Their ability to switch between the processes of cellular respiration and fermentation means that facultative anaerobes are able to live just about anywhere. *E. coli* is a facultative anaerobe that lives anaerobically in the large intestine and aerobically in sewage or contaminated water.

FACTS AND FIGURES

Anaerobes get energy

There are four main ways that anaerobes obtain energy. In fermentation, which is performed by many bacteria as well as by fungi such as yeasts, an energy-rich molecule such as glucose is split, releasing energy. In nitrate reduction, which occurs in a number of bacteria that are facultative anaerobes, the oxygen in the nitrate ion is used to oxidize an organic compound and so obtain energy. In carbonate reduction, which is carried out by methanogens, the oxygen in carbon dioxide or carbonate is used to oxidize hydrogen produced by other microorganisms and so obtain energy. In sulfate reduction, the oxygen in the sulfate ion is used to oxidize organic matter or hydrogen and so obtain energy. One of the products of this reaction under acidic conditions is hydrogen sulfide (H_2S), a foul-smelling gas that is poisonous to most living things.

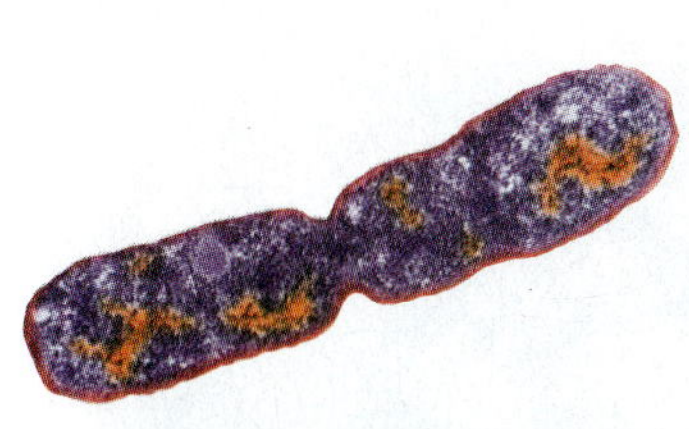

Binary Fission
(magnification: 26,500×)

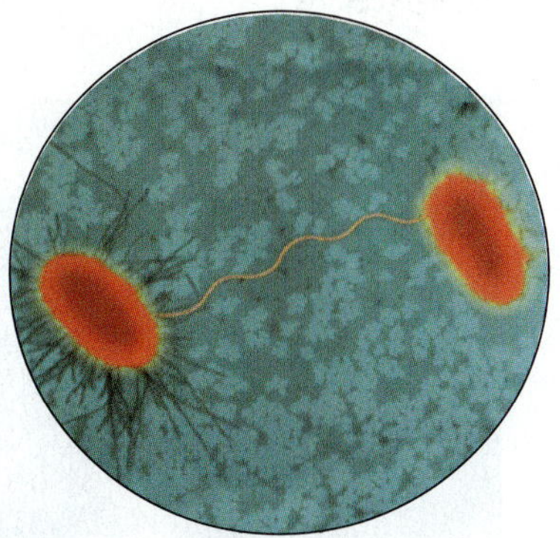

Conjugation
(magnification: 7000×)

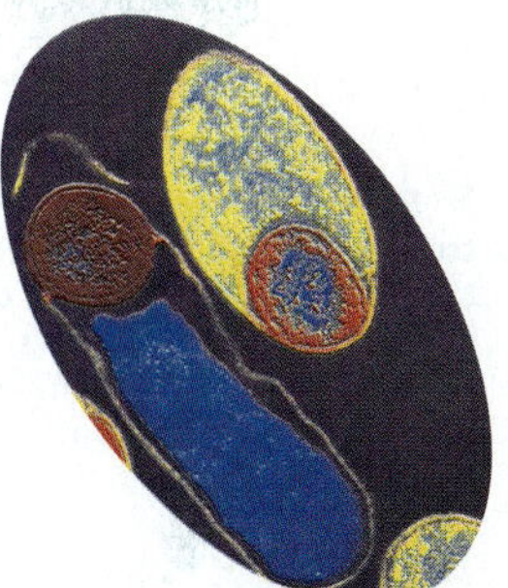

Spore Formation
(magnification: 7800×)

Figure 19–5 Most prokaryotes reproduce by binary fission, producing two identical "daughter" cells. Some prokaryotes take part in conjugation, in which genetic information is transferred from one cell to another by way of a hollow bridge. Other prokaryotes produce endospores, which allow them to withstand harsh conditions. **Comparing and Contrasting** *Compare the process of conjugation to binary fission.*

Growth and Reproduction

When conditions are favorable, bacteria can grow and divide at astonishing rates. Some divide as often as every 20 minutes! If unlimited space and food were available to a single bacterium and if all of its offspring divided every 20 minutes, in just 48 hours they would reach a mass approximately 4000 times the mass of Earth! Fortunately, this does not happen. In nature, growth is held in check by the availability of food and the production of waste products.

Binary Fission When a bacterium has grown so that it has nearly doubled in size, it replicates its DNA and divides in half, producing two identical "daughter" cells. This type of reproduction is known as **binary fission.** Because binary fission does not involve the exchange or recombination of genetic information, it is an asexual form of reproduction.

Conjugation Many bacteria are also able to exchange genetic information by a process called conjugation. During **conjugation,** a hollow bridge forms between two bacterial cells, and genes move from one cell to the other. This transfer of genetic information increases genetic diversity in populations of bacteria.

Spore Formation When growth conditions become unfavorable, many bacteria form structures called spores. One type of spore, called an **endospore,** is formed when a bacterium produces a thick internal wall that encloses its DNA and a portion of its cytoplasm. Spores can remain dormant for months or even years while waiting for more favorable growth conditions. The ability to form spores makes it possible for some bacteria to survive harsh conditions that might otherwise kill them. The bacterium *Bacillus anthracis,* which causes the disease anthrax, is one such bacterium. The ability to form these endospores has led some groups to develop anthrax as a biological warfare agent.

Growth and Reproduction

Use Visuals

Figure 19–5 Focus students' attention on the photo of conjugation, and have a student read aloud the text explanation of the process. Then, ask: **Since two bacterial cells are involved in conjugation, should this be considered a form of sexual reproduction?** *(No. Although genes move from one cell to the other, no daughter cells are produced.)* L1 L2

Demonstration

To show that bacteria can survive through such harsh conditions as freezing temperatures, place a small amount of soil into a plastic container. Cover the container and place it in a freezer overnight. The next day, sprinkle some soil onto a petri dish of agar. On another dish of agar, sprinkle some of the soil from the container that was in the freezer overnight. Cover the dishes and place them in an incubator overnight. The next day, have students observe both dishes for evidence of bacterial colonies growing on the agar.

Answers to . . .

CHECKPOINT *Photoautotrophs and chemoautotrophs*

Figure 19–4 *No, because sunlight does not reach deep into the ocean*

Figure 19–5 *In conjugation, genetic information is transferred from one cell to another by way of a hollow bridge. In binary fission, a cell replicates its DNA and divides in half, producing two daughter cells.*

19–1 (continued)

Importance of Bacteria

Use Community Resources

Encourage interested students to schedule a visit to a local wastewater treatment plant to find out how bacteria are utilized in purifying wastewater. Have students who visit the treatment plant gather information and any pamphlets about the process used and then make a report to the class. L2 L3

Use Visuals

Figure 19–7 Point out that the relationship between the soybean plant and the *Rhizobium* bacteria is an example of mutualism, a symbiotic relationship in which both organisms benefit. Ask students: **What process in the plant provides food for the bacteria?** *(Photosynthesis)* Then, have students take a deep breath, and emphasize that most of what they take into their lungs is nitrogen. Ask: **Can you use any of this nitrogen?** *(Some students may know that none of the nitrogen is used.)* Remind students that nitrogen is an essential element in protein and that we need proteins to survive. Ask: **How do humans and other animals get the nitrogen needed to make proteins?** *(They eat plants or animals that have eaten plants, which get nitrogen from such nitrogen-fixing bacteria as* Rhizobium *that can use nitrogen from the air.)* Tell students that soybeans are a good food source of protein, and now they know why. L2

Download a worksheet on bacteria for students to complete, and find additional teacher support from NSTA SciLinks.

▶ **Figure 19–6** **Bacteria help to break down the nutrients in this tree, allowing other organisms to use the nutrients.** In this way, bacteria help maintain equilibrium in the environment.

Importance of Bacteria

You probably remember the principal actors in the last film you saw. You might even recall some of the supporting actors. Have you ever thought that there would be no film at all without the hundreds of workers who are never seen on screen? Bacteria are just like those unseen workers. **Bacteria are vital to maintaining the living world. Some are producers that capture energy by photosynthesis. Others are decomposers that break down the nutrients in dead matter and the atmosphere. Still other bacteria have human uses.**

Decomposers Every living thing depends directly or indirectly on a supply of raw materials. If these materials were lost when an organism died, life could not continue. Before long, plants would drain the soil of minerals and die, and animals that depend on plants for food would starve. As decomposers, bacteria help the ecosystem recycle nutrients, therefore maintaining equilibrium in the environment. When a tree dies, such as the one in **Figure 19–6,** armies of bacteria attack and digest the dead tissue, breaking it down into simpler materials, which are released into the soil. Other organisms, including insects and fungi, also play important roles in breaking down dead matter.

Bacteria also help in sewage treatment. Sewage contains human waste, discarded food, and chemical waste. Bacteria break down complex compounds in the sewage into simpler ones. This process produces purified water, nitrogen and carbon dioxide gases, and leftover products that can be used as fertilizers.

Nitrogen Fixers Plants and animals depend on bacteria for nitrogen. You may recall that plants need nitrogen to make amino acids, the building blocks of proteins. Nitrogen gas (N_2) makes up approximately 80 percent of Earth's atmosphere.

For: Links on bacteria
Visit: www.SciLinks.org
Web Code: cbn-6191

BIO INSIGHTS — FACTS AND FIGURES

Earth's cycles depend on bacteria

Earth's environment depends on a cycling of substances through the world ecosystem. These substances include water, carbon, nitrogen, sulfur, phosphorus, sodium, potassium, and other materials. Their cycles are sometimes called biogeochemical cycles, because they involve both biological and geologic parts of the ecosystem. Bacteria play essential roles in all of these cycles. For instance, the cyanobacteria are a primary component of the carbon cycle, for through their photosynthesis they contribute much of the oxygen to the atmosphere that is used in cellular respiration. The nitrogen-fixing bacteria, such as *Rhizobium,* are central to the nitrogen cycle. The many bacteria that decompose dead organisms contribute to all of the cycles.

However, plants cannot use nitrogen gas directly. Nitrogen must first be changed chemically to ammonia (NH_3) or other nitrogen compounds. Expensive synthetic fertilizers contain these nitrogen compounds, but certain bacteria in the soil produce them naturally. The process of converting nitrogen gas into a form plants can use is known as **nitrogen fixation.** Nitrogen fixation allows nitrogen atoms to continually cycle through the biosphere.

Many plants have symbiotic relationships with nitrogen-fixing bacteria. For example, soybeans and other legumes host the bacterium *Rhizobium. Rhizobium* grows in nodules, or knobs, on the roots of the soybean plant, as shown in **Figure 19–7.** The plant provides a source of nutrients for *Rhizobium*, which converts nitrogen in the air into ammonia, helping the plant. Thus, soybeans have their own fertilizer factories in their roots!

▲ **Figure 19–7** The knoblike structures on the roots of this soybean plant are called nodules. Within these nodules are populations of the nitrogen-fixing bacteria *Rhizobium*. **Applying Concepts** *What is the name of the relationship between* **Rhizobium** *and soybean plants?*

Human Uses of Bacteria Many of the remarkable properties of bacteria provide us with products we depend on every day. For example, bacteria are used in the production of a wide variety of foods and beverages. Bacteria can also be used in industry. One type of bacteria can digest petroleum, making it very helpful in cleaning up small oil spills. Some bacteria remove waste products and poisons from water. Others can even help to mine minerals from the ground. Still others are used to synthesize drugs and chemicals through the techniques of genetic engineering.

Our intestines are inhabited by large numbers of bacteria, including *E. coli*. The term *coli* was derived from the fact that these bacteria were discovered in the human colon, or large intestine. In the intestines, the bacteria are provided with a warm and safe home, plenty of food, and free transportation. These bacteria also make a number of vitamins that the body cannot produce by itself. So both we and the bacteria benefit from this symbiotic relationship.

Biologists continue to discover new uses for bacteria. For example, biotechnology companies have begun to realize that bacteria adapted to extreme environments may be a rich source of heat-stable enzymes. These enzymes can be used in medicine, food production, and industrial chemistry.

19–1 Section Assessment

1. **Key Concept** Describe the characteristics of the two kingdoms of prokaryotes.
2. **Key Concept** What factors can be used to identify prokaryotes?
3. **Key Concept** Give one example of how bacteria maintain equilibrium in the environment.
4. Identify the parts of a prokaryote.
5. What are some ways that prokaryotes obtain energy?
6. **Critical Thinking Inferring** Why might an infection by Gram-negative bacteria be more difficult to treat than a Gram-positive bacterial infection?

Thinking Visually

Making a Venn Diagram
Create a Venn diagram that illustrates the similarities and differences between eubacteria and archaebacteria. *Hint*: Before you start, you may want to list the similarities and differences.

Build Science Skills

Observing Tell students that you are preparing a microscope slide to examine fresh yogurt under the microscope. As you prepare the slide, involve them by asking questions about the process. Add water to a tiny amount of plain yogurt to make a thin, cloudy mixture. The sample has to be thinned for light to pass through and for individual particles to be more visible. Place a drop of the yogurt mixture on a microscope slide. Stain the sample with a drop of methylene blue. Put on a coverslip. Then, have students observe the slide under high magnification. Ask students: **What do you see?** (*Blue ovals or cylinders*) Explain that the cylinders are *Lactobacillus* bacteria. Ask: **Why might there be bacteria in yogurt?** *(Students might suggest that the yogurt is spoiled or that the bacteria are used to make yogurt.)* Explain that *Lactobacillus* is used to make milk into yogurt. L1 L2

3 ASSESS

Evaluate Understanding

Call on students to explain the differences between eubacteria and archaebacteria.

Reteach

Direct students' attention to the labeled illustration of a eubacterium in Figure 19–2, and review the basic structure and function of prokaryotes.

Thinking Visually

Students' Venn diagrams should show that both eubacteria and archaebacteria are prokaryotic, have cell walls, and contain DNA. The diagrams should also show that archaebacteria lack peptidoglycan, have different membrane lipids, and have different DNA sequences in key genes.

19–1 Section Assessment

1. Archaebacteria lack peptidoglycan, and their membrane lipids are quite different. Also, the DNA of key archaebacterial genes are like those of eukaryotes.
2. They are identified by their shapes, the chemical natures of their cell walls, the ways they move, and the ways they obtain energy.
3. Bacteria are vital to maintaining the living world. Some are producers, others are decomposers, and others have human uses.
4. Cell wall, cell membrane, cytoplasm, DNA, ribosomes, pili, and flagella
5. Some consume organic molecules made by other organisms, whereas others make their own food from inorganic molecules.
6. Gram-positive bacteria have only one cell membrane, whereas gram-negative bacteria have a second, outer, layer of lipid and carbohydrates. Therefore, gram-negative bacteria might be more difficult to kill.

Interactive Textbook

If your class subscribes to the iText, use it to review the Key Concepts in Section 19–1.

Answer to . . .

Figure 19–7 *Mutualism*

Section 19–2

 BI 1.c, BI 10.d

1 FOCUS

Objectives

19.2.1 ***Describe*** the structure of a virus.

19.2.2 ***Explain*** how viruses cause infection.

Guide for Reading

Vocabulary Preview

Have students preview the Vocabulary words by skimming the section for the highlighted, boldface terms and recording the definition of each.

Reading Strategy

Before students read, have them preview the different viral structures shown in Figure 19–9 and make a list of questions about the structures and functions of viruses. Students should look for answers to their questions as they read the section.

2 INSTRUCT

What Is a Virus?

Use Visuals

Figure 19–8 Before students have read the introduction to the section or the caption to the figure, have them look at the photo of the infected tobacco leaf. Then, describe the puzzle that faced scientists who were trying to determine the cause of tobacco mosaic disease. Review the experiments that led to the discovery of viruses. Have students analyze for themselves the results of each experiment and suggest to them further experiments that could be performed. Then, have students read the text. By looking into the problem for themselves, students will gain a much better understanding of the way viruses were discovered. L2

19–2 Viruses

BI 1.c. Students know how prokaryotic cells, eukaryotic cells (including those from plants and animals), and viruses differ in complexity and general structure. **BI 10.d.** Students know there are important differences between bacteria and viruses with respect to their requirements for growth and replication, the body's primary defenses against bacterial and viral infections, and effective treatments of these infections.

Guide for Reading

Key Concepts
- What is the structure of a virus?
- How do viruses cause infection?

Vocabulary
virus
capsid
bacteriophage
lytic infection
lysogenic infection
prophage
retrovirus

Reading Strategy: Using Visuals As you read about viral replication in this section, trace each step in **Figure 19–10.** Then, list the steps, and write a few sentences to describe each step.

 BI 10.d

 BI 1.c

Imagine that you have been presented with a great puzzle. Farmers have begun to lose a valuable crop to a plant disease. The disease produces large pale spots on the leaves of plants similar to those shown in **Figure 19–8.** The diseased leaves look like mosaics of yellow and green. As the disease progresses, the leaves turn completely yellow, wither, and fall off, killing the plant.

To determine what is causing the disease, you take leaves from a diseased plant and extract a juice. You place a few drops of the juice on the leaves of healthy plants. A few days later, the mosaic pattern appears where you put the drops. Could the source of the disease be in the juice?

You use a light microscope to look for a germ that might cause the disease, but none can be seen. Even when the tiniest of cells are filtered out of the juice, it still causes the disease. You hypothesize that the juice must contain disease-causing agents so small that they are not visible under the microscope. Although you cannot see the disease-causing particles, you're sure they are there. You give them the name *virus*, from the Latin word for "poison."

If you think you could have carried out this investigation, congratulations! You're walking in the footsteps of a 28-year-old Russian biologist, Dmitri Ivanovski. In 1892, Ivanovski identified the cause of tobacco mosaic disease as juice extracted from infected plants. In 1897, Dutch scientist Martinus Beijerinck suggested that tiny particles in the juice caused the disease, and he named these particles viruses.

What Is a Virus?

In 1935, the American biochemist Wendell Stanley obtained crystals of tobacco mosaic virus. Living organisms do not crystallize, so Stanley inferred that viruses were not alive. **Viruses** are particles of nucleic acid, protein, and in some cases, lipids.

CA a Viruses can reproduce only by infecting living cells. Viruses differ widely in terms of size and structure, as you can see in **Figure 19–9.** As different as they are, all viruses have one thing in common: They enter living cells and, once inside, use the machinery of the infected cell to produce more viruses.

CA b Most viruses are so small they can be seen only with the aid of a powerful electron microscope. **A typical virus is composed of a core of DNA or RNA surrounded by a protein coat.** The simplest viruses contain only a few genes, whereas the most complex may have more than a hundred genes.

▼ **Figure 19–8** Tobacco mosaic virus causes the leaves of tobacco plants to develop a pattern of spots called a mosaic.

SECTION RESOURCES

Print:
- ***Teaching Resources,*** Lesson Plan 19–2, Adapted Section Summary 19–2, Adapted Worksheets 19–2, Section Summary 19–2, Worksheets 19–2, Section Review 19–2
- ***Reading and Study Workbook A,*** Section 19–2
- ***Adapted Reading and Study Workbook B,*** Section 19–2

Technology:
- ***iText,*** Section 19–2
- ***BioDetectives DVD,*** "Influenza: Tracking a Virus"
- ***Animated Biological Concepts DVD,*** 31 Lytic and Lysogenic Cycles
- ***Transparencies Plus,*** Section 19–2

Figure 19–9 Virus Structures

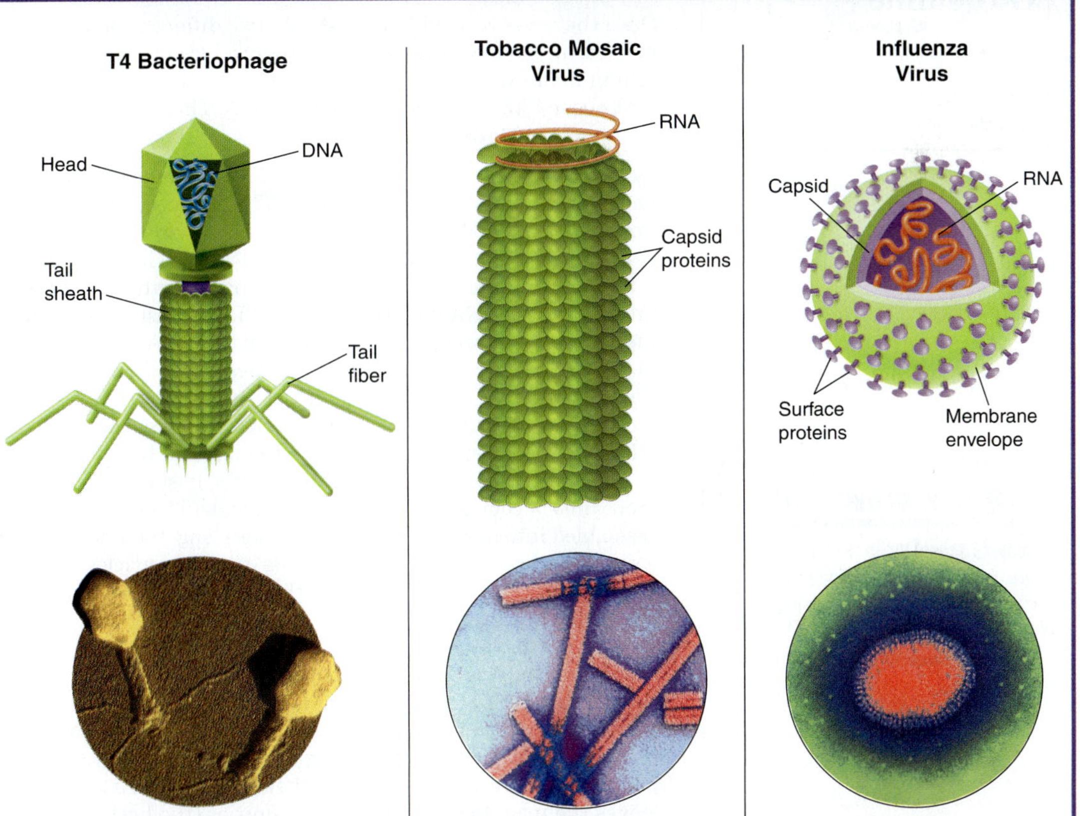

T4 Bacteriophage (magnification: 82,000×)

Tobacco Mosaic Virus (magnification: 200,000×)

Influenza Virus (magnification: 1,000,000×)

A virus's protein coat is called its **capsid.** The capsid includes proteins that enable a virus to enter a host cell. The capsid proteins of a typical virus bind to receptors on the surface of a cell and "trick" the cell into allowing it inside. Once inside, the viral genes are expressed. The cell transcribes and translates the viral genetic information into viral capsid proteins. Sometimes that genetic program causes the host cell to make copies of the virus, and in the process the host cell is destroyed.

Because viruses must bind precisely to proteins on the cell surface and then use a host's genetic system, most viruses are highly specific to the cells they infect. Plant viruses infect plant cells; most animal viruses infect only certain related species of animals; and bacterial viruses infect only certain types of bacteria. Viruses that infect bacteria are called **bacteriophages.**

CA a

▲ **Figure 19–9** Viruses come in a wide variety of sizes and shapes.  **A typical virus is composed of a core of either DNA or RNA, which is surrounded by a protein coat, or capsid.**

a BI 1.c

CHECKPOINT *What happens when a cell transcribes a viral gene?*

Use Visuals

Figure 19–9 Ask students: **From these three examples, can you describe the typical shape of a virus?** *(No. The shapes are so different that there is no typical shape.)* **What parts do all three kinds of viruses have in common?** *(A capsid and a core of nucleic acid, either DNA or RNA)* Point out that each of the three examples in the figure infects different kinds of organisms—bacteria, plants, and animals. Explain that viruses are often classified according to the type of organism they infect. L2

Build Science Skills

Using Models Give each student an unshelled sunflower seed. (Other easily shelled seeds will also work well, including peanuts, pumpkin seeds, and pistachio nuts.) Then, ask: **In what ways is the structure of a virus like the structure of a sunflower seed?** *(Students should recognize that both sunflower seeds and viruses consist of a protective outer shell that encases vital contents.)* **What does the shell of the sunflower seed represent in a virus?** *(The capsid)* **How are the functions of a sunflower seed's shell and a virus's capsid similar?** *(Both protect the contents.)* **What does the kernel of the sunflower seed represent?** *(The virus's core of DNA or RNA)* **What is the function of the virus's core?** *(To put the genetic program of the virus into effect)* L2

ESL Support for English Language Learners

Vocabulary: Link to Visual

Beginning Use Figure 19–9 to help clarify the meaning of the Vocabulary words *virus*, *capsid*, and *bacteriophage*. Write each of these words on the board, and model the pronunciation of each term. While the students have Figure 19–9 in front of them, give a short definition of each term and point to the appropriate part of the figure. Write the definitions on the board. Post these terms on a word wall with other Vocabulary terms from the chapter. L1

Intermediate To extend the beginning-level activity, pair ESL students with English-proficient students to write three sentences, one using each of the following terms: *virus*, *capsid*, and *bacteriophage*. The student pairs can use the text on pages 478 and 479 and the information in Figure 19–9 to write their sentences. Ask one student in each pair to read the sentences aloud. L2

Answer to . . .

CHECKPOINT *The cell transcribes and translates the viral genetic information into viral capsid proteins. Sometimes that genetic program may simply cause the cell to make copies of the virus, and in the process the host cell is destroyed.*

19–2 (continued)

Download a worksheet on the lytic cycle for students to complete, and find additional teacher support from NSTA SciLinks.

Viral Infection

Build Science Skills

Predicting Before students read about viral infection, show them an electron micrograph that shows a virus particle attaching to a cell membrane. Give a simple description of what the image shows, and then ask students what they think will happen to the virus and the cell. Have students consider this question by making a prediction about what events will occur next and how the virus will ultimately affect the cell. 

Build Science Skills

Using Analogies Ask a volunteer to read aloud the paragraph that uses the analogy of an outlaw to explain the function of a lytic virus. Then, after students have reread the description of a lysogenic infection, ask: **If a lytic infection is like an outlaw taking over a town in the Old West, what is a lysogenic infection like?** *(Responses will vary. Students might suggest that a lysogenic infection is like a relative or family friend who moves into a family's home and stays there for a long time, using everything in the home and borrowing money as well.)* L1 L2

For: Links on the lytic cycle
Visit: www.SciLinks.org
Web Code: cbn-6192

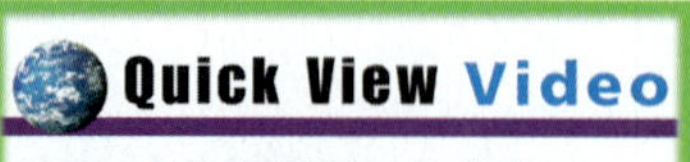

Discovery School Video To find out more about the transmission of a virus, view track 10 "Influenza: Tracking a Virus" on the *BioDetectives* DVD.

Viral Infection

Once the virus is inside the host cell, two different processes may occur. Some viruses replicate themselves immediately, killing the host cell. Other viruses replicate themselves in a way that doesn't kill the host cell immediately. These two processes are shown in **Figure 19–10.**

Lytic Infection Bacteriophage T4 is an example of a bacteriophage that causes a lytic infection. **In a lytic infection, a virus enters a cell, makes copies of itself, and causes the cell to burst.** Bacteriophage T4 has a DNA core inside an intricate protein capsid that is activated by contact with a host cell. It then injects its DNA directly into the cell. The host cell cannot tell the difference between its own DNA and the DNA of the virus. Consequently, the cell begins to make messenger RNA from the genes of the virus. This viral mRNA is translated into viral proteins that act like a molecular wrecking crew, chopping up the cell DNA, a process that shuts down the infected host cell.

The virus then uses the materials of the host cell to make thousands of copies of its own DNA molecule. The viral DNA gets assembled into new virus particles. Before long, the infected cell lyses, or bursts, and releases hundreds of virus particles that may go on to infect other cells. Because the host cell is lysed and destroyed, this process is called a **lytic infection.**

In its own way, a lytic virus is similar to an outlaw in the American Old West. First, the outlaw eliminates the town's existing authority (host cell DNA). Then, the outlaw demands to be outfitted with new weapons, horses, and riding equipment by terrorizing the local people (using the host cell to make viral proteins and viral DNA). Finally, the outlaw forms a gang that leaves the town to attack new communities (the host cell bursts, releasing hundreds of virus particles).

Lysogenic Infection Other viruses, including the bacteriophage lambda, cause **lysogenic infections** in which a host cell makes copies of the virus indefinitely. **In a lysogenic infection, a virus integrates its DNA into the DNA of the host cell, and the viral genetic information replicates along with the host cell's DNA.** Unlike lytic viruses, lysogenic viruses do not lyse the host cell right away. Instead, a lysogenic virus remains inactive for a period of time.

The viral DNA that is embedded in the host's DNA is called a **prophage.** The prophage may remain part of the DNA of the host cell for many generations before becoming active. A virus may not stay in the prophage form indefinitely. Eventually, any one of a number of factors may activate the DNA of a prophage, which will then remove itself from the host cell DNA and direct the synthesis of new virus particles.

The steps of lytic and lysogenic infections may be different from those of other viruses when they attack eukaryotic cells. Most animal viruses, however, show patterns of infection similar to either the lytic or lysogenic patterns of infection of bacteria.

Quick View Video

Discovery School DVD Encourage students to view track 10 "Influenza: Tracking a Virus" on the *BioDetectives* DVD.

FACTS AND FIGURES

Viruses get in

Although bacteriophages typically inject their DNA into the host cell, not all viruses invade a host cell in this manner. Many animal viruses, such as the Semliki virus, enter the host through endocytosis—the binding of the virus to the cell membrane, inducing the cell to take in the virus. Once inside the host cell, the virus sheds its protein coat and either undergoes replication or becomes part of the host's DNA. Interestingly, a few animal viruses, such as those responsible for rabies, AIDS, and influenza, leave the host cell through budding, which can be thought of as the opposite of endocytosis.

Lytic and Lysogenic Infections

Figure 19–10 Bacteriophages may infect cells in two ways: lytic infection and lysogenic infection.

Bacteriophage injects DNA into bacterium.

Bacteriophage DNA forms a circle.

Lytic Infection

Bacteriophage takes over bacterium's metabolism, causing synthesis of new bacteriophage proteins and nucleic acids.

Bacteriophage proteins and nucleic acids assemble into complete bacteriophage particles.

Bacteriophage enzyme lyses the bacterium's cell wall, releasing new bacteriophage particles that can attack other cells.

Lysogenic Infection

Prophage

Bacteriophage DNA inserts itself into bacterial chromosome.

Bacteriophage DNA (prophage) may replicate with bacterium for many generations.

Bacteriophage DNA (prophage) can exit the bacterial chromosome. Bacteriophage enters lytic cycle.

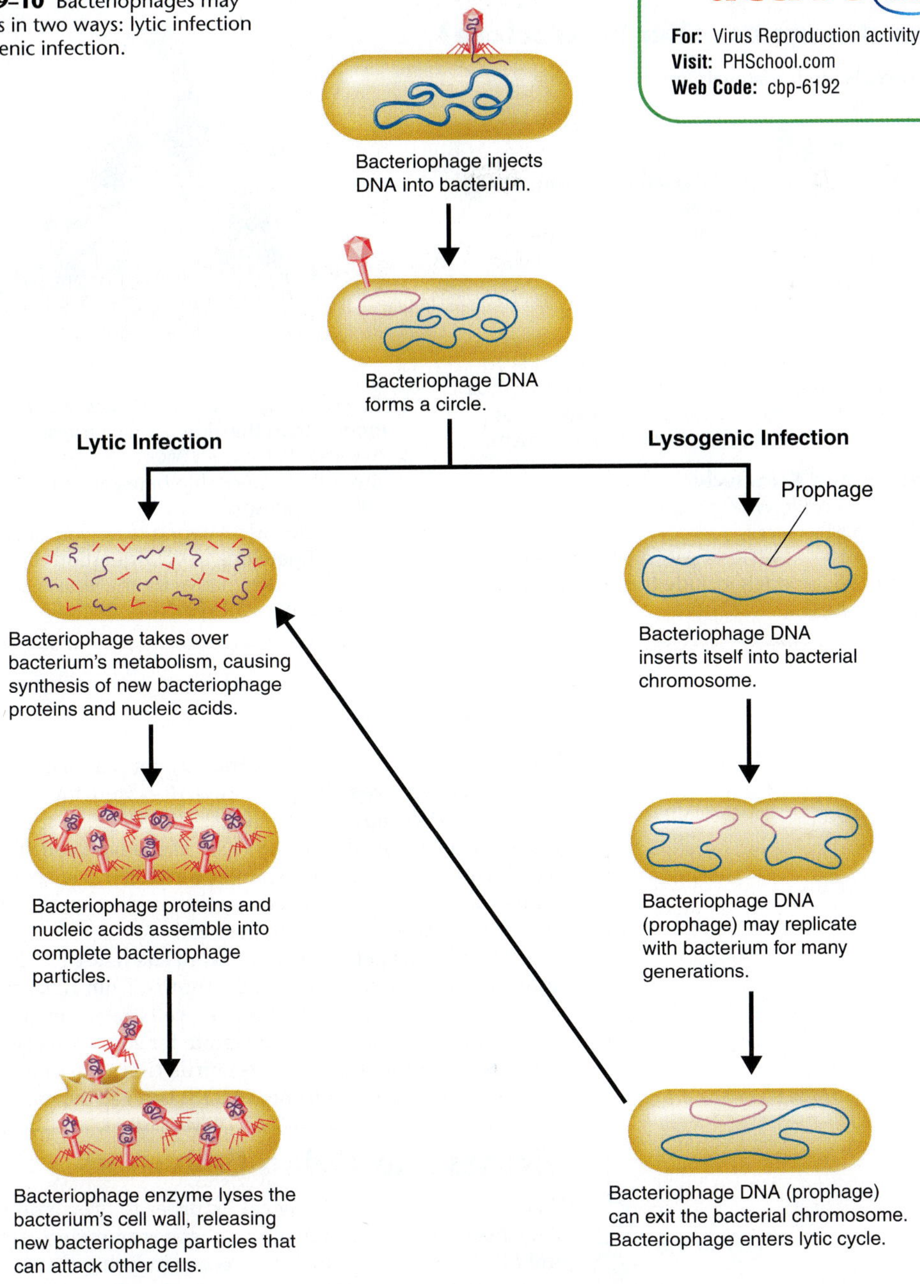

Go Online
active art
For: Virus Reproduction activity
Visit: PHSchool.com
Web Code: cbp-6192

Use Visuals

Figure 19–10 Ask students: **In the lysogenic cycle, what happens to the virus DNA?** *(It inserts itself into the bacterial chromosome.)* **What is the viral DNA called while it is embedded in the bacterial DNA?** *(A prophage)* Explain that the bacterium can replicate for many generations with the prophage embedded in its DNA, giving rise to many host cells that contain a prophage. When conditions change, the virus can switch from the lysogenic cycle to the lytic cycle. Explain that it is usually some kind of environmental change that causes the switch, such as a chemical change or radiation. As you describe this process to students, have them trace the path with a finger. Move the finger through the lysogenic cycle to the bottom, where a switch in cycles can occur. Make sure that students understand that a switch in cycles may not occur. The virus can move through the lysogenic cycle for many generations of the bacteria. L2

Address Misconceptions

Point out to students that in the description of each type of infection (both lytic and lysogenic), the virus is described as making copies of itself. In a lytic infection, though, the virus uses the materials of the host cell to make copies of itself. In a lysogenic infection, the virus uses the DNA of the host cell to make copies of itself. Explain that, for this reason, biologists often talk about viral "replication" or "multiplication" rather than "reproduction."

For: Virus Reproduction activity
Visit: PHSchool.com
Web Code: cbe-6192
Students explore the two methods viruses use to multiply.

19–2 (continued)

Retroviruses

Quick Lab

BIIE 1.g

Objective Students will make models of two different viruses and conclude that viruses differ in structure.

Skills Focus **Using Models, Drawing Conclusions, Calculating**

Materials metric ruler, scissors, tape, craft materials

Time 20 minutes

Strategy Make sure that students accurately follow steps 3 and 4.

Expected Outcomes Students will learn that viruses differ in structure.

Analyze and Conclude

1. A capsid and a core of either DNA or RNA

2. A model of a T4 bacteriophage should include a head, a tail sheath, and a tail fiber. A model of an influenza virus should include surface proteins and a membrane envelope.

3. Students should measure the image of the virus they modeled in Figure 19–9 and divide this length by the magnification, to determine the actual size of the virus. For example, the image of the T4 bacteriophage is 3 cm long; 3 cm = 3×10^{-2} m;
3×10^{-2} m/82,000 =
0.37×10^{-6} m = 370 nm.

4. Students' questions may vary. Typical questions might include: How does a virus particle get into a cell? How does a virus inject its core of viral genetic material into the cell's DNA?

5. Students' models should directly relate to one of the questions they listed in question 4.

Build Science Skills

Using Analogies Point out that retroviruses, such as the virus that causes AIDS, can remain dormant for various lengths of time. Explain that this is like a plant seed that can remain dormant until conditions are right for growth. Some seeds, for example, have thick coats that don't allow the embryo inside the seed to grow. This seed coat might be broken by abrasion, fire, or the action of soil microorganisms. L2

Quick Lab

BIIE 1.g

How do viruses differ in structure?

Materials craft materials, metric ruler, scissors, tape

Procedure 

1. Make models of two of the viruses shown in **Figure 19–9** on page 479.
2. Label the parts of each of your virus models.
3. Measure and record the length of each of your virus models in centimeters. Convert the length of each model into nanometers: 1 cm = 10 million nm.
4. Calculate the length of each virus you modeled. Divide the length of each model by the length of the actual virus to determine how many times larger each model is than the virus it represents.

Analyze and Conclude

1. **Using Models** What parts of your models are found in all viruses?
2. **Drawing Conclusions** What parts do one or both of your models include that are found in only some viruses?
3. **Calculating** How many times larger are your models than the viruses they represent?
4. **Asking Questions** Write two or more questions about the relationship between viruses and single-celled organisms.
5. **Using Models** Suggest ways you can use models to investigate one of your questions in question 4. Suggest an alternative for the virus model you made in this activity.

Retroviruses

Some viruses contain RNA as their genetic information and are called **retroviruses.** When retroviruses infect a cell, they produce a DNA copy of their RNA. This DNA, much like a prophage, is inserted into the DNA of the host cell. There the retroviruses may remain dormant for varying lengths of time before becoming active, directing the production of new viruses, and causing the death of the host cell.

Retroviruses get their name from the fact that their genetic information is copied backward—that is, from RNA to DNA instead of from DNA to RNA. (The prefix *retro-* means "backward.") Retroviruses are responsible for some types of cancer in animals, including humans. The virus that causes acquired immune deficiency syndrome (AIDS) is a retrovirus.

Viruses and Living Cells

Viruses must infect a living cell in order to grow and reproduce. They also take advantage of the host's respiration, nutrition, and all the other functions that occur in living things. Therefore, viruses can be considered to be parasites. A parasite depends entirely upon another living organism for its existence, harming that organism in the process.

FACTS AND FIGURES

Classifying viruses

Because viruses are unique, they are not part of any kingdom, and they are not identified as species. Classification of viruses depends on the chemical and physical properties of the virus. The major division focuses on their genetic material; thus, there are DNA viruses and RNA viruses. Viruses are then further divided by the shapes of their protein coats and their sizes. This scheme results in a major group called the picornaviruses, which are small RNA viruses with a polyhedral shape. Both poliovirus and the rhinoviruses (which cause the common cold) are subgroups of the picornaviruses. Another way of grouping viruses is by the type of host a virus infects. Thus, animal viruses infect animals, plant viruses infect plants, and bacterial viruses—or bacteriophages—infect bacteria.

Viruses and Cells		
Characteristic	**Virus**	**Cell**
Structure	DNA or RNA core, capsid	Cell membrane, cytoplasm; eukaryotes also contain nucleus and organelles
Reproduction	only within a host cell	independent cell division either asexually or sexually
Genetic Code	DNA or RNA	DNA
Growth and Development	no	yes; in multicellular organisms, cells increase in number and differentiate
Obtain and Use Energy	no	yes
Response to Environment	no	yes
Change Over Time	yes	yes

▲ **Figure 19–11** The differences between viruses and cells are listed in this chart. **Applying Concepts** ***Based on this information, would you classify viruses as living or nonliving? Explain.***

Are viruses alive? If we require that living things be made up of cells and be able to live independently, then viruses are not alive. Yet, viruses have many of the characteristics of living things. After infecting living cells, viruses can reproduce, regulate gene expression, and even evolve. Some of the main differences between cells and viruses are summarized in **Figure 19–11.** Viruses are at the borderline of living and nonliving things.

Although viruses are smaller and simpler than the smallest cells, it is not likely that they could have been the first living things. Because viruses are completely dependent upon living things, it seems more likely that viruses developed after living cells. In fact, the first viruses may have evolved from the genetic material of living cells. Once established, however, viruses have continued to evolve, along with the cells they infect, over billions of years.

19–2 Section Assessment

1. **Key Concept** What are the parts of a virus?
2. **Key Concept** Describe the two ways that viruses cause infection.
3. What is the difference between a bacteriophage and a prophage?
4. What is a retrovirus?
5. **Critical Thinking** **Making Judgments** Do you think viruses should be considered a form of life? Describe the reasons for your opinion.

Focus on the BIG Idea

Structure and Function
Viruses and cells are similar yet different. Compare the structure of a virus to the structure of a eukaryotic cell. Organize your information in a table. You may wish to refer to Chapter 7, which discusses the structures of cells in detail.

19–2 Section Assessment

1. A typical virus is composed of a core of either DNA or RNA surrounded by a protein coat, which is called a capsid.
2. In a lytic infection, a virus enters a cell, makes copies of itself, and causes the cell to burst. In a lysogenic infection, a virus embeds its DNA into the DNA of the host cell and replicates.
3. A bacteriophage is a virus that infects bacteria. A prophage is the lysogenic viral DNA that is embedded in the host's DNA.
4. A retrovirus is a virus that contains RNA.
5. Most students will assert that viruses should not be considered a form of life because they do not exhibit all the characteristics of life.

Viruses and Living Cells

Use Visuals

Figure 19–11 Point out that the characteristics listed in the table are similar to the list of characteristics of living things students studied in Section 1–3. Help students recall that the first characteristic from that list is "Living things are made up of units called cells." Ask: **How do the column heads of this table answer the question of whether a virus fulfills that characteristic?** *(Since a distinction is made between Virus and Cell in the column heads, viruses obviously aren't made up of units called cells.)*

3 ASSESS

Evaluate Understanding

Have students make two flowcharts to show two examples of the way viruses infect cells.

Reteach

Have students compare the illustrations of virus structures in Figure 19–9 with the illustration of bacterium structure in Figure 19–2. Place emphasis on what viruses don't have.

Focus on the BIG Idea

Students' tables might be similar to the one in Figure 19–11, though the column head for the first column might be Structure. Students might list a variety of cell structures in that first column, including cell membrane, cytoplasm, nucleus, and the several cell organelles. In completing this table, students might write a *no* in the virus column and a *yes* in the cell column for all of the structures, except in a row for genetic material.

If your class subscribes to the iText, use it to review the Key Concepts in Section 19–2.

Answer to . . .

Figure 19–11 *Most students will state that viruses are nonliving. However, accept all responses that are adequately supported.*

 **BIIE 1.m, BI 10.c**

The issue of whether to require smallpox vaccinations for military personnel and civilians in the United States became quite important following the terrorist attacks of September 11, 2001. In late 2002, President Bush ordered smallpox vaccinations for military personnel. Before students read this feature, find out or have student volunteers find out what today's government policies about vaccinations for smallpox and other diseases are. After students read the feature, encourage them to use library and Internet resources to learn more about this issue. Also, encourage students to contact local health officials about the risks and benefits of various vaccinations. After students have answered the Research and Decide questions, organize role-playing with students who have opinions on both sides of the issue.

Research and Decide

1. The risks of nationwide vaccination include deaths and illnesses. Students should find out how great the risk is for certain vaccinations. The benefits include prevention of a devastating epidemic as well as possible cost savings.
2. Answers may vary. A typical response might discuss the risks involved in vaccination, the risks involved in not having the population vaccinated, and the costs involved to administer vaccines or to store the amount of vaccine that might be needed in the case of a terrorist attack that uses a pathogen as a weapon.
3. Whichever position a student takes, the opinion should be supported by logical arguments.

Students can research vaccinations on the site developed by authors Ken Miller and Joe Levine.

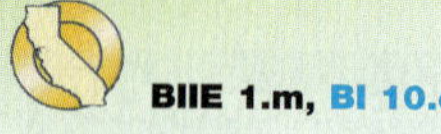 **BIIE 1.m, BI 10.c**

Should Mass Vaccinations Be Required?

Smallpox is a deadly disease for which there is no treatment. Smallpox had been brought under control by a worldwide vaccination program. It appeared that vaccination had eradicated every trace of smallpox in nature. As a result, the routine vaccination of children against smallpox was ended in the United States in 1971. No new smallpox cases have been reported anywhere since 1978. Only two laboratories, one in Atlanta, Georgia, and the other in Russia, are known to have samples of the virus.

Today there is concern that certain infectious diseases, such as smallpox, will be used as a biological weapon. This has led authorities in the United States and other countries to order the production of new stocks of certain vaccines. Preparing millions of doses of a vaccine as a precaution against attack certainly seems like a good idea. But it also raises an important social and scientific question—should a nation require its citizens to be vaccinated against a particular disease, or should we wait until there is evidence of an outbreak of a disease in a given area?

The Viewpoints

Require Vaccinations

Human history shows just how deadly certain infectious diseases can be. Therefore, it makes sense to preempt an outbreak by requiring vaccinations as soon as enough doses of the vaccine are available. The benefits of immunity would outweigh any possible adverse reactions to the vaccine. In addition, it is cheaper to vaccinate everyone, rather than to treat infectious diseases on an individual basis.

Hold the Vaccine in Reserve

As serious as the threat from certain infectious diseases may be, we should keep in mind the rule of medicine that is taught to all doctors: First, do no harm. We already know, unfortunately, that administering vaccines to an entire population will indeed do harm. For example, U. S. health statistics

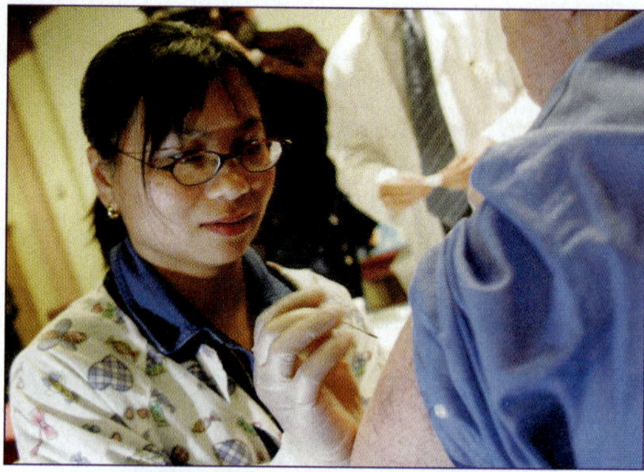

show that for every 1 million infants vaccinated for smallpox, as many as 5 may have died from reactions to the vaccine. The exact number of deaths that will result from a nationwide vaccination program is not certain, but any number of deaths is too many when the risk of infection is only hypothetical.

Research and Decide

1. **Analyzing the Viewpoints** To make an informed decision, learn more about this issue by consulting library or Internet resources. Then, list both the risks and benefits of nationwide vaccination.
2. **Forming Your Opinion** How do you balance the risks and benefits of vaccination now against the risks and benefits of stockpiling the vaccine? What factors should you consider?
3. **Role-Playing** You are a researcher for the Centers for Disease Control in Atlanta. You have been offered the chance to be inoculated with a vaccine such as smallpox. Would you get the vaccination? Explain your answer and support it with facts from your research.

For: Links from the authors
Visit: PHSchool.com
Web Code: cbe-6194

HISTORY OF SCIENCE

An end to smallpox
In 1980, the World Health Organization announced that the smallpox virus had been eradicated. This virus was the cause of many terrible epidemics throughout human history, and as recently as 1967 it caused 2 million deaths worldwide. The introduction of the virus into the Americas by Europeans caused epidemics among Native Americans because they had no immunity. In Europe and Asia, people had long recognized that someone who had contracted the less severe form of smallpox was forever immunized to the more severe form. In the late 1700s, English physician Edward Jenner noticed that milkmaids who contracted cowpox also gained immunity from smallpox. From that observation and subsequent experimentation, Jenner developed the first vaccine, a term he named from the Latin word for cow, *vacca,* because it was made from the cowpox virus.

19–3 Diseases Caused by Bacteria and Viruses

BI 10.c. Students know how vaccinations protect an individual from infectious diseases. **BI 10.d.** Students know there are important differences between bacteria and viruses with respect to their requirements for growth and replication, the body's primary defenses against bacterial and viral infections, and effective treatments of these infections.

Have you ever heard a teacher say that when a few people misbehave, they ruin it for everybody? In a way, that saying could be applied to bacteria and viruses. Bacteria and viruses are everywhere in nature, but only a few cause disease. However, these **pathogens,** or disease-causing agents, get all the attention.

Disease can be considered a conflict between the pathogen and the host. All viruses reproduce by infecting living cells, and disease results when the infection causes harm to the host. All bacteria require nutrients and energy; however, disease results when bacteria interfere with the host's ability to obtain enough of those elements to function properly.

Guide for Reading

Key Concepts
- How do bacteria cause disease?
- How can bacterial growth be controlled?
- How do viruses cause disease?

Vocabulary
pathogen
vaccine
antibiotic
viroid
prion

Reading Strategy: Outlining Before you read, use the headings of this section to make an outline about disease. As you read, fill in subtopics. Then, add phrases or a sentence after each to provide key information.

Bacterial Disease in Humans

Many bacteria live on and within our bodies, and some bacteria even help us to perform essential functions, such as digesting our food. The growth of pathogenic bacteria, on the other hand, disrupts the body's equilibrium by interfering with its normal activities and producing disease.

The French chemist Louis Pasteur, shown in **Figure 19–12,** was the first person to show convincingly that bacteria cause disease. Pasteur helped to establish what has become known as the germ theory of disease when he showed that bacteria were responsible for a number of human and animal diseases.

Bacteria produce disease in one of two general ways. Some bacteria damage the cells and tissues of the infected organism directly by breaking down the cells for food. Other bacteria release toxins (poisons) that travel throughout the body interfering with the normal activity of the host.

▲ **Figure 19–12** By testing multiple hypotheses, Louis Pasteur was able to show that bacteria cause disease.

Using Cells for Food The bacterium *Mycobacterium tuberculosis*, which causes tuberculosis, is inhaled into the lungs, where it destroys the lung tissue. The bacterium also may enter a blood vessel and travel to new sites in the body where it destroys more tissue.

Releasing Toxins Bacterial toxins can travel throughout the body. For example, the *Streptococcus* bacterium that causes strep throat can release toxins into the bloodstream. These toxins can cause scarlet fever. A red rash appears on the skin of someone infected with scarlet fever. Diphtheria, another disease caused by the *Corynebacterium diphtheriae* bacterium, infects the tissues of the throat. *C. diphtheriae* releases toxins into the bloodstream, where they destroy tissues. Diphtheria can lead to breathing problems, heart failure, paralysis, and death.

TIME SAVER — SECTION RESOURCES

Print:
- ***Laboratory Manual A,*** Chapter 19 Lab
- ***Teaching Resources,*** Lesson Plan 19–3, Adapted Section Summary 19–3, Adapted Worksheets 19–3, Section Summary 19–3, Worksheets 19–3, Section Review 19–3
- ***Reading and Study Workbook A,*** Section 19–3
- ***Adapted Reading and Study Workbook B,*** Section 19–3
- ***Biotechnology Manual,*** Lab 16
- ***Investigations in Forensics,*** Investigation 6

Technology:
- ***iText,*** Section 19–3
- ***Transparencies Plus,*** Section 19–3

Section 19–3

1 FOCUS

Objectives

19.3.1 ***Explain*** how bacteria cause disease.
19.3.2 ***Describe*** how bacterial growth can be controlled.
19.3.3 ***Explain*** how viruses cause disease.

Guide for Reading

Vocabulary Preview

Have students write the Vocabulary words, dividing each into its separate syllables as best they can. Remind students that each syllable usually has only one vowel sound. The correct syllabications are path•o•gen, vac•cine, an•ti•bi•ot•ic, vir•oid, pri•on.

Reading Strategy

Before they read, have students rewrite the blue headings as questions about bacteria and viruses. Then, as they read the section, they should write brief answers to those questions using the main ideas from the text.

2 INSTRUCT

Bacterial Disease in Humans

Use Visuals

Figure 19–12 Ask a student volunteer to recall for the class the experiment Louis Pasteur carried out that disproved the theory of spontaneous generation. If no student can recall this experiment, have the class turn back to Section 1–2 and review the details of his work. Explain that this experiment was one of many that Pasteur carried out with microorganisms.

19–3 (continued)

Word Origins

A carcinogen is a substance that causes cancer. L2

Build Science Skills

Applying Concepts Ask students: **What are antibiotics?** *(Antibiotics are compounds that block the growth and reproduction of bacteria.)* Explain that, although antibiotics have proved amazingly effective in combating bacterial diseases, many bacteria have become increasingly resistant to most antibiotics, worrying medical authorities. Ask: **What is the process among living things that results in the appearance of such resistant bacteria?** *(Natural selection)* Call on students at random to describe the process of natural selection that results in antibiotic resistance. Then, have students reread the description of antibiotic resistance on page 403 in Chapter 16. L2

Biology and History

 **BIIE 1.k**

Help place these discoveries in historical context by asking when events from other fields occurred during the period covered by this timeline. For instance, in 1815, Napoleon Bonaparte was defeated at the battle of Waterloo; in 1865, President Abraham Lincoln was assassinated at Ford's Theater; in 1901, legendary trumpeter Louis Armstrong was born in New Orleans; in 1937, Pablo Picasso painted the mural *Guernica*; and in 1969, Neil Armstrong set foot on the moon. Then, discuss how each of the discoveries on the timeline affected society as a whole.

Writing in Science

Students might find information about these scientists and their discoveries in books about the history of medicine. They also might look for books that contain short biographies of noted scientists.

Word Origins

Pathogen comes from the Greek words *pathos*, meaning "suffering," and *-genes*, meaning "born" or "produced." So a pathogen is something that produces suffering. **The Greek word *karkinos* means "cancer." What do you think a carcinogen is?**

Preventing Bacterial Disease Some of the diseases caused by pathogenic bacteria include Lyme disease, tetanus, strep throat, and tooth decay. Many bacterial diseases can be prevented by stimulating the body's immune system with vaccines. A **vaccine** is a preparation of weakened or killed pathogens. When injected into the body, a vaccine sometimes prompts the body to produce immunity to the disease. Immunity is the body's ability to destroy new pathogens. You will learn more about immunity in Chapter 40.

If a bacterial infection does occur, a number of drugs can be used to attack and destroy the invading bacteria. These drugs include antibiotics, such as penicillin and tetracycline. **Antibiotics** are compounds that block the growth and reproduction of bacteria. They can be used to cure many bacterial diseases. One of the major reasons for the dramatic increase in human life expectancy during the past two centuries is an increased understanding of how to prevent and cure bacterial infections. The history of the use of vaccines is illustrated in the Biology and History timeline below.

(a) BI 10.c

(b) BI 10.d

Controlling Bacteria

Although most bacteria are harmless, and many are beneficial, the risks of bacterial infection are great enough to warrant efforts to control bacterial growth. **There are various methods used to control bacterial growth, including sterilization, disinfectants, and food processing.**

 BIIE 1.k

Biology and History

The History of Vaccines

Early discoveries with vaccination allowed new braches of science and medicine to develop. These new fields, such as bacteriology and immunology, would help in the crusade against diseases caused by bacteria and viruses.

1769
Edward Jenner
Jenner performs the first inoculation against smallpox by infecting a boy with cowpox.

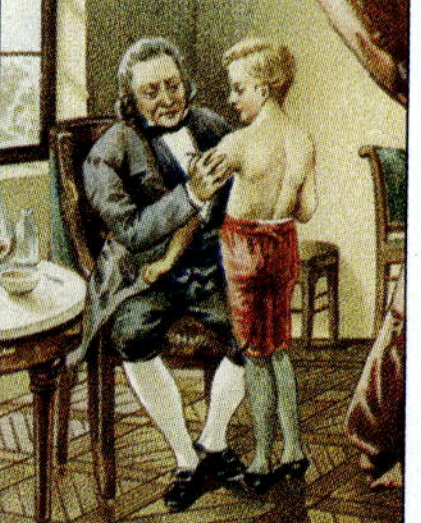

1880
Louis Pasteur develops germ theory of disease.

1881
Louis Pasteur
Pasteur develops the first effective vaccine against anthrax, a bacterial disease that affects both animals and humans.

1750 1850 1900

UNIVERSAL ACCESS

Less Proficient Readers
Engage students' interest in the difference in the uses of vaccinations and antibiotics by leading a discussion about students' experiences with each. Most students will know that they began receiving vaccinations as babies. Use this to emphasize that vaccines are used to prevent disease by activating the immune response. Students' experiences with antibiotics can also be useful as a way of distinguishing between bacteria and viruses. L1

Advanced Learners
Ask students who need an extra challenge to research one of the bacterial or viral diseases listed in Figure 19–13 or Figure 19–15. Ask them to prepare a report on the disease, including detailed information on the specific pathogen involved as well as the symptoms, transmission, treatment, and prevention of the disease. Ask these students to prepare a brief presentation to the class, with visual aids that could include photos, drawings, and graphic organizers. L3

Sterilization by Heat One method used to control the growth of potentially dangerous bacteria is sterilization. Sterilization destroys all bacteria by subjecting them to great heat. Most bacteria cannot survive high temperatures for a long time, so most can be killed by exposure to high heat.

Disinfectants Another method of controlling bacteria is by using disinfectants—chemical solutions that kill pathogenic bacteria. Disinfectants are used in the home to clean bathrooms, kitchens, and other rooms where bacteria may flourish.

Today, some manufacturers of soaps, cleansers, and even kitchen utensils have added antibacterial chemicals to their products. If you wash your hands properly, ordinary soaps do a good job of removing bacteria. Overuse of antibacterial compounds increases the likelihood that common bacteria will eventually evolve to become resistant to them—and therefore much more dangerous and difficult to kill.

Food Storage and Processing As you read earlier, bacteria can cause food to spoil. One method of stopping food from spoiling is storing it in a refrigerator. Food that is stored at a low temperature will stay fresh longer because the bacteria will take much longer to multiply. In addition, boiling, frying, or steaming can sterilize many kinds of food. Each of these cooking techniques raises the temperature of the food to a point where the bacteria are killed.

CHECKPOINT *Why might scientists recommend the use of regular soap over antibacterial soap?*

Writing in Science

Use the Internet or a library to find out more about one of the people in this timeline. Write a summary of the person's discovery as it might appear in a newspaper story of the time.

Spitting is DANGEROUS and ILLEGAL! TUBERCULOSIS is transmitted in this way and kills more people than any other disease.
Baltimore and Ohio Railroad Co.

1923
Albert Calmette
Camille Guérin
Calmette and Guérin develop a vaccine against tuberculosis.

1928
Alexander Fleming
Fleming discovers penicillin accidentally when an experiment with bacteria is contaminated by mold. He finds that penicillin is nontoxic but inhibits the growth of many types of disease-causing bacteria.

1952
Jonas Salk
Salk develops a polio vaccine using killed viruses.

1957
Albert Sabin
Sabin develops a polio vaccine based on live, weakened viruses.

1900 1950 2000

Controlling Bacteria

Build Science Skills

Designing Experiments Challenge groups of students to design an experiment to test the hypothesis that washing hands with antibacterial soap reduces the number of bacteria on the hands. A typical experiment will suggest dragging a washed and an unwashed finger across agar in separate petri dishes and then comparing bacterial growth on the agar.

L2 L3

TEACHER TO TEACHER

When the class is ready to discuss antibiotic resistance, I try to tie in the topics of genetics and natural selection, which the class has already discussed. For instance, I review Frederick Griffith's experiment dealing with transformation of DNA, as well as the concept of natural selection. This review helps lead into a discussion of how some bacteria have become resistant to antibiotics and makes the topic more understandable. (If your class has not yet covered DNA transformation and natural selection, you may wish to give a brief overview of the topics to the class.)

—*Leon Lange*
Biology Teacher
Fort Campbell High School
Fort Campbell, KY

Answer to . . .

CHECKPOINT *Because overuse of antibacterial soap increases the chance of bacteria becoming resistant*

19–3 (continued)

Viral Disease in Humans

Build Science Skills

Making Judgments Prepare a display of advertisements and packages of cold remedies. Ask students: **What is the purpose of these products?** *(To relieve cold symptoms)* **How do they relieve cold symptoms?** *(Lower fever, relieve aches and pains, reduce congestion, stop cough, and so on)* **Is this a sign that you are cured?** *(No. Point out that these medications merely provide relief from symptoms. A cure would have to disable the virus that causes the cold.)* L2

Use Visuals

Figure 19–13 After students have studied the information in the table, explain that droplets of saliva or mucus can be spread through the air by sneezing and coughing—and also by laughing and talking. Usually, these droplets spread less than 1 meter before dissipating. Point out that this kind of transmission is different from transfer by contact, by bodily fluids, or by insects. Ask: **Which of the viral diseases listed are spread by droplet inhalation?** *(Common cold, influenza, smallpox, and chickenpox)* **How is AIDS spread?** *(By contact with contaminated blood or bodily fluids; by pregnant women to babies during delivery or breast-feeding)* Emphasize that AIDS is not spread by droplet inhalation, casual contact, or insects. Then, discuss specific ways that AIDS is spread. L1 L2

Viral Disease in Humans

Like bacteria, viruses produce disease by disrupting the body's normal equilibrium. In many viral infections, viruses attack and destroy certain cells in the body, causing the symptoms of the disease. Poliovirus infects and kills cells of the nervous system, producing paralysis. Other viruses cause infected cells to change their patterns of growth and development.

CA (a) BI 10.d

Unlike bacterial diseases, viral diseases cannot be treated with antibiotics. The best way to protect against most viral diseases lies in prevention, often by the use of vaccines. Most vaccines provide protection only if they are used before an infection begins. Once a viral disease has been contracted, it may be too late to control the infection. However, sometimes the symptoms of the infection can be treated with over-the-counter medicines. **Figure 19–13** lists some common diseases caused by both viruses and bacteria.

▼ **Figure 19–13 Some common bacterial and viral diseases are shown in the table below.** Bacterial diseases are shown in the blue rows, while viral diseases are shown in the white rows.

Bacterial and Viral Diseases

Disease	Effect on Body	Transmission
Lyme disease	"Bull's-eye" rash at site of tick bite, fever, fatigue, headache	Bite from an infected tick
Tetanus	Lockjaw, stiffness in neck and abdomen, difficulty swallowing, fever, elevated blood pressure, severe muscles spasms	Bacteria enters the body through a break in the skin
Tuberculosis	Fatigue, weight loss, fever, night sweats, chills, appetite loss	Bacterial particles are inhaled
Bacterial meningitis	High fever, headache, stiff neck, nausea, fatigue	Bacteria are spread in respiratory droplets caused by coughing and sneezing; close or prolonged contact with someone infected with meningitis
Strep throat	Fever, sore throat, headache, fatigue, nausea	Direct contact with mucus from an infected person or direct contact with infected wounds or breaks in the skin
Common cold	Sneezing, sore throat, fever, headache, muscle aches	Contact with contaminated objects; droplet inhalation
Influenza	Body aches, fever, sore throat, headache, dry cough, fatigue, nasal congestion	Flu viruses spread in respiratory droplets caused by coughing and sneezing
AIDS	Helper T cells, which are needed for normal immune system function, are destroyed	Contact with contaminated blood or bodily fluids; pregnant women to babies during delivery or during breastfeeding
Chicken pox	Skin rash of blisterlike lesions	Virus particles are spread in respiratory droplets caused by coughing and sneezing; highly contagious
Hepatitis B	Jaundice, fatigue, abdominal pain, nausea, vomiting, joint pain	Contact with contaminated blood or bodily fluids
West Nile	Fever, headache, body ache	Bite from an infected mosquito

FACTS AND FIGURES

Extremely poisonous exotoxins

Bacterial toxins are usually divided into two groups: exotoxins and endotoxins. Exotoxins are produced and released as part of the normal metabolism of certain bacteria. Endotoxins are typically lipopolysaccharides that were originally part of the cell wall and that are released by the lysis of the bacterium. In general, exotoxins are much more potent than endotoxins. Diseases caused by exotoxins include botulism, cholera, diphtheria, gas gangrene, food poisoning, scarlet fever, tetanus, and toxic shock syndrome.

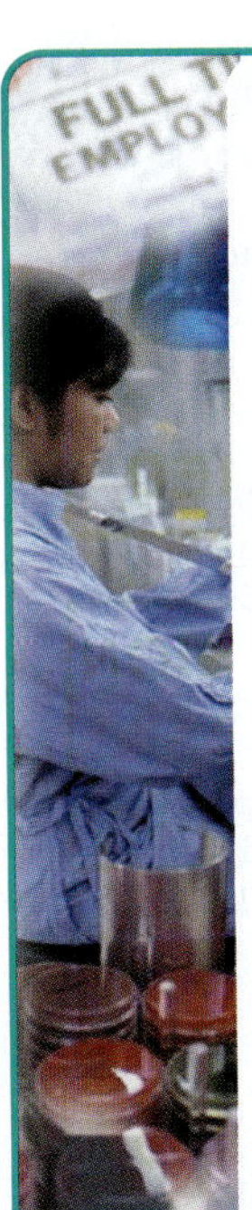

Careers in Biology

Epidemiologist

Job Description: work for a university, health department, research or health organization, or medical corporation to identify and track diseases and develop programs that prevent or control the spread of disease

Education: master's or doctoral degree in epidemiology, including course work in statistics, demography, research design, and public health

Skills: good communication skills, strong computer skills, knowledge of health and medical conditions

Highlights: You get to ask lots of questions and travel. You can work on infectious diseases such as tuberculosis. Some epidemiologists work on specific issues such as tobacco addiction.

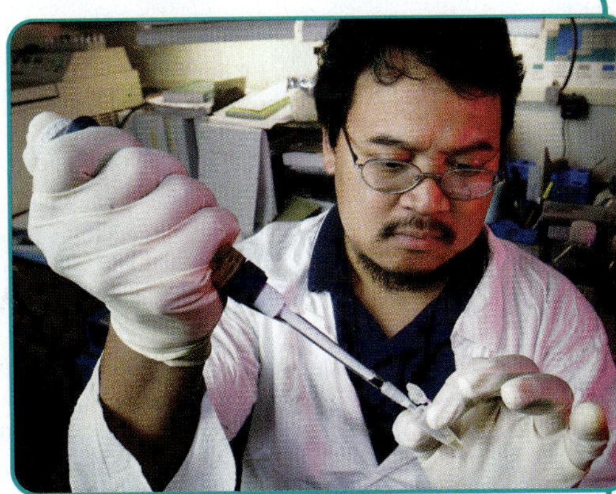

For: Career links
Visit: PHSchool.com
Web Code: cbb-6195

Viral Disease in Animals

Viruses produce serious animal diseases as well. An epidemic of foot-and-mouth (or hoof-and-mouth) disease, caused by a virus that infects cattle, sheep, and pigs, swept through parts of Europe in the late 1990s. Thousands of cattle were destroyed in efforts to control the disease. American authorities took special precautions to guard against the spread of the foot-and-mouth virus to North America.

Viral Disease in Plants

Many viruses, including tobacco mosaic virus, infect plants. These viruses pose a serious threat to many agricultural crops. Farmers in many countries, including the United States, struggle to control them. Like other viruses, plant viruses contain a core of nucleic acid and a protein coat.

Unlike animal viruses, most plant viruses have a difficult time entering the cells they infect. This is partly because plant cells are surrounded by tough cell walls that viruses alone cannot break through. As a result, most plant viruses are adapted to take advantage of breaks in the cell wall caused by even minor damage to plant tissues. Viruses can enter through tears in leaf tissue, breaks in stems or roots, or simply through microscopic cell wall damage caused by human or animal contact with the plant.

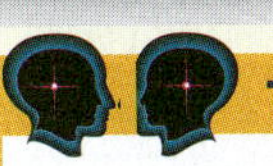

TEACHER TO TEACHER

When I teach students about bacteria and viruses, I try to give students as many examples that relate to real-life experiences as possible. With such examples, the material becomes more interesting for students and keeps their attention on the subject at hand. For example, we spend a good amount of time on the causes, symptoms, and spread of bacterial and viral diseases. I encourage students to relate their own experiences with such diseases, as well as those of family members. I also try to provide as many graphic organizers, diagrams, and charts as possible in order to help students organize what they are learning. Finally, I design experiences in which students can actively participate.

—*Brenda Waldon*
Biology Teacher
Clayton County Public Schools
Morrow, GA

Careers in Biology

- Epidemiology focuses on where, when, and how often diseases occur; on how diseases are transmitted; and on how diseases can be controlled.
- Epidemiologists collect and analyze data that are relevant in describing the occurrence of a disease under study and its probable cause.
- When investigating a disease epidemic, an epidemiologist may collect information about the gender, age, occupation, socioeconomic status, personal habits, and history of immunization of those who have contracted the disease. L2

Resources All states and many large cities employ epidemiologists in their public health departments.

You can have students write a more extensive job description as well as list the educational requirements for a career in this field.

Viral Disease in Animals

Use Community Resources

Ask a local farmer or agricultural agent to address the class about bacterial and viral diseases that affect farm animals in your area. Ask the speaker to talk about specific diseases and their symptoms, treatments, and preventive measures. One topic students might focus on is whether farmers in your area use preventive doses of antibiotics to prevent bacterial diseases. L2 L3

Viral Disease in Plants

Build Science Skills

Posing Questions After students have read about viral disease in plants, have them turn back to Figure 19–8 on page 478 and reconsider the disease caused by the tobacco mosaic virus (TMV). Explain that tobacco mosaic is a common plant disease that has been extensively studied. Then, ask each student to write two questions that could be investigated about this virus. Examples might be: How is the virus spread? How can the disease be prevented? Collect the questions, and ask interested students to find the answers to some of them. L2 L3

19–3 (continued)

Viroids and Prions

Build Science Skills

Comparing and Contrasting Ask students to make a table that they can use to compare viruses, viroids, and prions. Column heads might include Particle, Structure, and Method of Infection. After they have created their own tables, call on students at random to help you create a similar table on the board. Advise students to revise their own tables at the end of the discussion. L1 L2

3 ASSESS

Evaluate Understanding

Ask students to write a paragraph explaining why antibiotics are used to treat bacterial diseases but not viral diseases. In their paragraphs, students should demonstrate an understanding of the differences between the two microorganisms as well as an understanding of what antibiotics are.

Reteach

Have pairs of students work together to make a public-health pamphlet that focuses on the prevention and treatment of bacterial and viral diseases.

Writing in Science

A typical story might focus on the carrying of disease-causing bacteria by the travelers from Earth and the lack of immunity to those bacteria by the residents of another planet. The result would be an epidemic of bacterial diseases. Accept all logical explanations relating to protection from disease.

Interactive Textbook

If your class subscribes to the iText, use it to review the Key Concepts in Section 19–3.

Answer to . . .

Figure 19–14 *Like viruses, prions can cause diseases. Unlike viruses, prions do not contain DNA or RNA—only protein.*

▲ **Figure 19–14** Prions may cause several infectious diseases, including mad cow disease. This cow was killed by mad cow disease. **Comparing and Contrasting** *How are prions similar to viruses? How are they different?*

Once inside the plant, many viruses spread rapidly, causing severe tissue damage, mottled leaves, and wilting, and sometimes killing the infected plant. Plant viruses infect many valuable fruit trees, including apples and peaches, and have caused serious losses in the potato crop.

Viroids and Prions

Scientists have discovered two other viruslike particles that also cause disease: viroids and prions. Viroids cause disease in plants. Prions cause disease in animals.

Viroids Many plants, including potatoes, tomatoes, apples, and citrus fruits, can be infected by viroids. **Viroids** are single-stranded RNA molecules that have no surrounding capsids. It is believed that viroids enter an infected cell and direct the synthesis of new viroids. The viroids then disrupt the metabolism of the plant cell and stunt the growth of the entire plant.

Prions In 1972, American Stanley Prusiner became interested in scrapie, an infectious disease in sheep for which the exact cause was unknown. Although he first suspected a virus, experiments suggested the disease might actually be caused by tiny particles found in the brains of infected sheep. Unlike viruses, these particles contained no DNA or RNA, only protein. Prusiner called these particles **prions,** short for "protein infectious particles." Although prions were first discovered in sheep, many animals, including humans, can become infected with prions.

There is some evidence that prions cause disease by forming protein clumps. These clumps induce normal protein molecules to become prions. Eventually, there are so many prions in the nerve tissue that cells become damaged. There is strong evidence that mad cow disease may be caused by prions.

19–3 Section Assessment

1. **Key Concept** What are the two ways that bacteria cause disease?
2. **Key Concept** Describe the three methods of preventing bacterial growth in food.
3. **Key Concept** Describe how viruses cause disease.
4. What are viroids?
5. **Critical Thinking Applying Concepts** You think you might have a bacterial infection. Would you ask for a vaccination against the bacteria? Why or why not?
6. **Critical Thinking Applying Concepts** How might epidemiologists collaborate with scientists who study viruses as they investigate viral diseases?

Writing in Science

Creative Writing
In *War of the Worlds,* Earth is invaded by aliens. No weapons can kill the invaders. Earth is saved when the invaders die from diseases they contract. Write a summary of a story about people from Earth voyaging to another planet. Include information on how the people from Earth might protect themselves from possible new diseases.

19–3 Section Assessment

1. Some damage cells and tissues directly by breaking down the host's cells for food. Others release toxins that interfere with the host's normal activity.
2. Students should describe sterilization, disinfectants, and food storage and processing.
3. Viruses cause disease by disrupting the body's normal equilibrium.
4. Single-stranded RNA molecules that have no surrounding capsids
5. It would probably not be a good idea because vaccinations prevent infection rather than attacking and destroying bacteria.
6. Epidemiologists are primarily concerned with tracking and preventing the spread of diseases. They might collaborate with virologists to find out the characteristics of specific viruses, including how they spread and how they infect a host.

Exploration

BIIE 9.b, BIIE 1.b, BIIE 1.d, BI 10.d

Identifying Limits to the Growth of Bacteria

In this investigation, you will determine whether an environmental factor such as temperature can control the growth and reproduction of bacteria.

Problem Does temperature limit the growth and reproduction of bacteria?

Materials

- glass-marking pencil
- 3 sterile agar plates
- sterile cotton swabs
- bacterial culture
- transparent tape
- hand lens

Skills Analyzing Data, Drawing Conclusions

Procedure

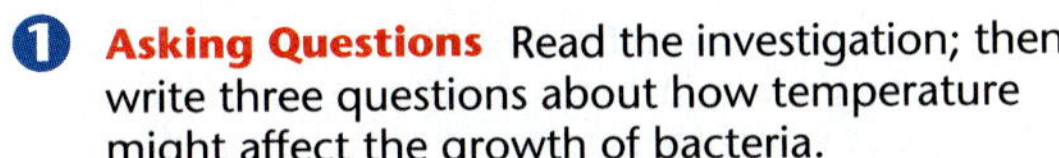

1. **Asking Questions** Read the investigation; then, write three questions about how temperature might affect the growth of bacteria.
2. **Predicting** Predict how temperature will affect the growth rate of bacterial colonies.
3. Put on your plastic gloves. Use a glass-marking pencil to label the edges of the agar plates "3°C," "20°C," and "37°C." Also, write your name on each plate.
4. Dip a sterile swab in the bacterial culture and wipe it back and forth in a zigzag pattern over the entire surface of the agar on one plate. Cover the plate and seal it with transparent tape. **CAUTION:** *Do not open the plates once they have been exposed to the air.*
5. Repeat step 4 with each plate, using a new sterile swab for each plate.
6. Place the plate labeled "3°C" in a refrigerator. Leave the plate labeled "20°C" in a place designated by your teacher. Place the plate labeled "37°C" in an incubator. Be sure to store each plate upside down.
7. Make a copy of the data table. After 24 hours, examine each plate with a hand lens. Bacterial colonies look like small white or colored dots on the agar surface. In your data table, record the number of bacterial colonies on each agar plate. Return each plate to its location.
8. After a second period of 24 hours, record in your data table the number of bacterial colonies on each agar plate. Return your agar plates to your teacher for safe disposal.
9. Make a graph of the results in your data table. Plot time on the *x*-axis and number of bacterial colonies on the *y*-axis. Use a different symbol to represent data from each day. After you have plotted all your data on your graph, draw a straight line or smooth curve as close as possible to all the points that represent observations after 24 hours. Draw a second curve or line through the points that represent observations after 48 hours.

Data Table

Temperature	Number of Colonies	
	24 hours	48 hours
3°C		
20°C		
37°C		

Analyze and Conclude

1. **Analyzing Data** At what temperature were the most bacterial colonies visible after 24 hours? At what temperature were the fewest bacterial colonies visible after 24 hours?
2. **Analyzing Data** Did the same plate have the most bacteria after 48 hours? The fewest?
3. **Analyzing Data** Describe the effect of temperature on the growth of bacteria.
4. **Evaluating** Do you consider your data reliable? Explain. Did the results of your experiment confirm your prediction?

Go Further

Formulating Hypotheses Propose a hypothesis about the effects of another variable on the growth of bacteria. Design an experiment that could test your hypothesis.

Analyze and Conclude

1. Students should observe that the most colonies were visible at 37°C and the fewest at 3°C after 24 hours.
2. The same plate has the most bacteria after 48 hours, though differences may be smaller than after 24 hours.
3. Higher temperatures promoted the growth of bacteria. Raising the temperature more might reduce growth, not enhance it.
4. Answers will depend on students' predictions. Most students' predictions were probably confirmed.

Exploration

BIIE 9.b, BIIE 1.b, BIIE 1.d, BI 10.d

Objective Students will be able to draw the conclusion that temperature limits the growth and reproduction of bacteria.

Skills Focus Analyzing Data, Evaluating, Drawing Conclusions

Time 15 min. on day 1, 15 min. on day 2, and 45 min. on day 3

Advance Prep Provide a diluted liquid culture of noninfectious bacteria, such as *E. coli* obtained from a biological supply house. Do not use *Serratia marcescens* or *Bacillus subtilis*. Check the dilution by culturing in advance, and then refrigerate the diluted culture. Check all of the plates to make sure there is no bacterial or mold growth. You will need to use a 37°C incubator.

Safety Don't allow students to touch the agar. Make sure students wash their hands with soap and warm water after handling. Use a disinfectant to wipe down all surfaces. Inform parents that students will be doing a lab involving bacteria, especially parents of students with compromised immune systems. Provide a container in which students can dispose of used plates. For safe disposal, soak the plates overnight in undiluted chlorine bleach, 70% isopropyl alcohol, or another disinfectant. Read the safety information in the MSDS for chlorine bleach and isopropyl alcohol prior to use. Place plates in a biohazard bag and dispose of them through a local hospital.

Expected Outcome Students should find that bacteria grow more at 37°C than at 3°C. They should therefore draw the conclusion that a low temperature does limit the growth and reproduction of bacteria.

Go Further

One hypothesis is that higher or lower pH will affect the growth of bacteria. Other hypotheses might focus on how osmotic conditions, such as salt solutions or sugary syrups, affect bacterial growth.

Chapter 19 Study Guide

Study Tip

Divide the class into small groups, and have students quiz one another about the Vocabulary terms and the Key Concepts.

Thinking Visually

1. Archaebacteria
2. Bacilli
3. Cocci
4. Spirilla

Chapter 19 Assessment

Reviewing Content

1. a	5. a	9. b
2. a	6. d	10. c
3. b	7. d	
4. b	8. c	

Understanding Concepts

11. Prokaryotes are the smallest and most common microorganisms. They are unicellular and lack a nucleus.

12. The three most common shapes of prokaryotes are the rod-shaped bacilli, spherical-shaped cocci, and corkscrew-shaped spirilli.

13. Gram-positive bacteria with a single cell wall layer absorb only the violet primary stain. Gram-negative bacteria have a thin layer of peptidoglycan. This layer absorbs the red stain so that the bacteria appear red.

14. Some prokaryotes move by flagella, some spiral forward, and some glide along on a slimelike material they secrete.

15. Both photoautotrophs and chemoautotrophs make their own food. Photoautotrophs obtain energy from photosynthesis and thus depend upon light. Chemoautotrophs obtain energy from chemical reactions involving ammonia, hydrogen sulfide, nitrates, sulfur, or iron.

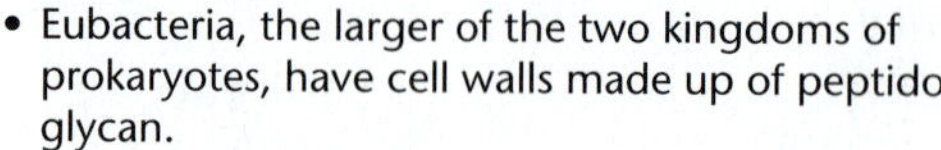

Chapter 19 Study Guide

19–1 Bacteria

Key Concepts  BI 10.d

- Eubacteria, the larger of the two kingdoms of prokaryotes, have cell walls made up of peptidoglycan.
- Archaebacteria do not contain peptidoglycan. The DNA sequences of key archaebacterial genes are more like those of eukaryotes than those of eubacteria.
- Prokaryotes are identified by their shapes, the chemical natures of their cell walls, the ways they move, and the way they obtain energy.
- Some bacteria are producers that capture energy by photosynthesis. Others break down the nutrients in dead matter and the atmosphere. Still other bacteria have human uses.

Vocabulary

prokaryote, p. 471 • bacillus, p. 473
coccus, p. 473 • spirillum, p. 473
chemoheterotroph, p. 473
photoheterotroph, p. 474
photoautotroph, p. 474
chemoautotroph, p. 474
obligate aerobe, p. 474
obligate anaerobe, p. 474
facultative anaerobe, p. 474
binary fission, p. 475
conjugation, p. 475
endospore, p. 475
nitrogen fixation, p. 477

19–2 Viruses

Key Concepts  BI 1.c, BI 10.d

- A typical virus is composed of a core of DNA or RNA surrounded by a protein coat.
- In a lytic infection, a virus enters a cell, makes copies of itself, and causes the cell to burst.
- In a lysogenic infection, a virus integrates its DNA into the DNA of the host cell, and the viral genetic information replicates along with the host cell's DNA.

Vocabulary

virus, p. 478 • capsid, p. 479
bacteriophage, p. 479
lytic infection, p. 480
lysogenic infection, p. 480
prophage, p. 480
retrovirus, p. 482

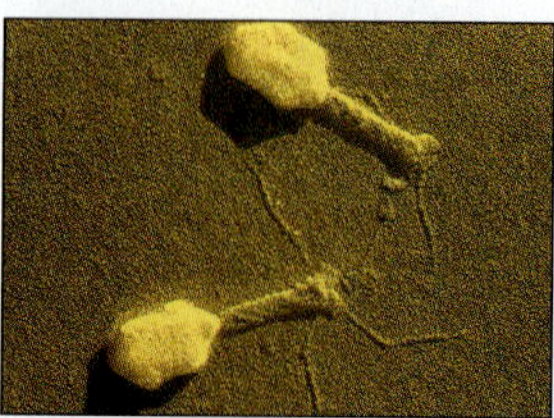

19–3 Diseases Caused by Bacteria and Viruses

Key Concepts   BI 10.c, BI 10.d

- Bacteria produce disease in one of two general ways. Some bacteria damage the cells and tissues of the infected organism directly by breaking down the cells for food. Other bacteria release toxins (poisons) that travel throughout the body interfering with the normal activity of the host.
- There are various methods used to control bacterial growth, including sterilization, disinfectants, and food processing.
- Viruses produce disease by disrupting the body's normal equilibrium.

Vocabulary

pathogen, p. 485
vaccine, p. 486
antibiotic, p. 486
viroid, p. 490
prion, p. 490

Thinking Visually

Complete this concept map about prokaryotes:

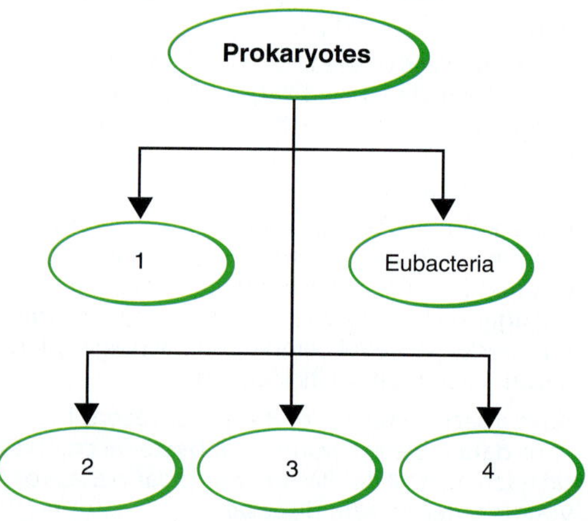

CHAPTER RESOURCES

Print:

- ***Teaching Resources,*** Chapter Vocabulary Review, Graphic Organizer, Chapter 19 Tests: Levels A and B

Technology:

- ***Computer Test Bank,*** Chapter 19 Test
- ***iText,*** Chapter 19 Assessment

Chapter 19 Assessment

Interactive textbook with assessment at PHSchool.com

Reviewing Content

Choose the letter that best answers the question or completes the statement.

1. Prokaryotes are unlike all other organisms in that their cells
   a. lack nuclei.
   b. have organelles.
   c. have cell walls.
   d. lack nucleic acids.
2. Archaebacteria that live in oxygen-free environments include
   a. methanogens.
   b. retroviruses.
   c. bacteriophages.
   d. protists.
3. Which micrograph shows bacillus bacteria?

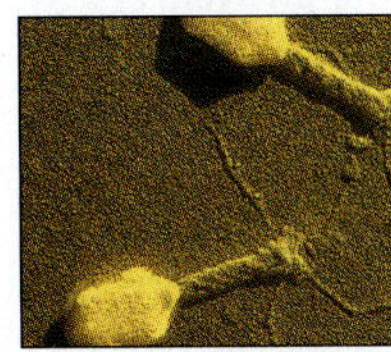
a.

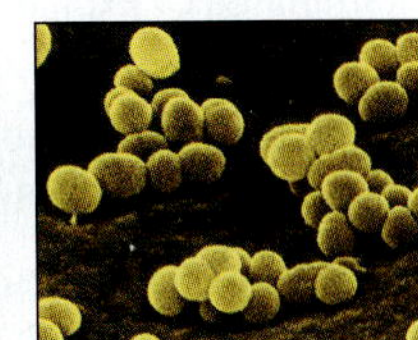
c.

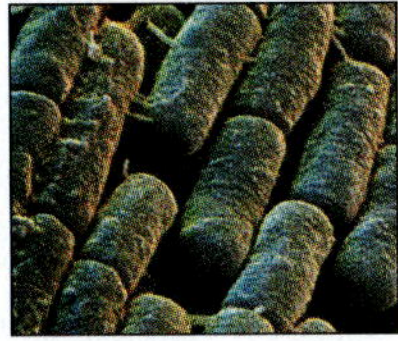
b.

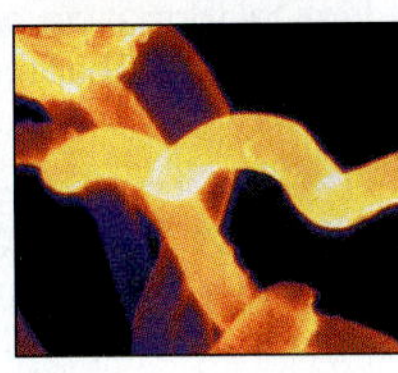
d.

4. Bacteria that contain chlorophyll *a* belong in the group
   a. archaebacteria.
   b. cyanobacteria.
   c. chemoautotrophs.
   d. pathogens.
5. Bacteria reproduce asexually by
   a. binary fission.
   b. spores.
   c. conjugation.
   d. fixation.
6. The process of converting nitrogen into a form plants can use is known as nitrogen
   a. conjugation.
   b. sterilization.
   c. decomposition.
   d. fixation.
7. Particles made up of nucleic acids, proteins, and in some cases, lipids that can reproduce only by infecting living cells are known as
   a. bacteria.
   b. capsids.
   c. prophages.
   d. viruses.
8. The outer protein coat of a virus is a
   a. core of DNA.
   b. core of RNA.
   c. capsid.
   d. membrane envelope.
9. One group of viruses that contain RNA as their genetic information is
   a. oncogenic viruses.
   b. retroviruses.
   c. capsids.
   d. prophages.
10. Disease-causing organisms are known as
   a. cocci.
   b. bacilli.
   c. pathogens.
   d. archaebacteria.

Understanding Concepts

11. What are two distinguishing characteristics of prokaryotes?
12. Describe the three main cell shapes of prokaryotes.
13. How do scientists distinguish between Gram-positive and Gram-negative bacteria?
14. Describe two methods by which prokaryotes move.
15. How are photoautotrophs similar to chemoautotrophs? How are they different?
16. State one way in which photoheterotrophs are similar to chemoheterotrophs.
17. Distinguish between an obligate aerobe and an obligate anaerobe.
18. Facultative anaerobes can survive with or without oxygen. How is this advantageous to them?
19. What is the role of certain bacteria in changing atmospheric nitrogen into a form usable by plants?
20. What one characteristic do all viruses have in common?
21. How is the capsid protein important to the functioning of a virus?
22. Describe the sequence of events that occur during a lytic infection.
23. Describe what happens to the host cell of a lysogenic virus.
24. What is the best way to protect humans against most viral diseases?
25. How are viruses highly specific to the cells they infect?

HOMEWORK GUIDE

Section:	Questions:
Section 19–1	1–6, 11–19, 26–29, 33–35
Section 19–2	7–9, 20–23, 25, 32
Section 19–3	10, 24, 30, 31

Interactive Textbook

If your class subscribes to the iText, your students can go online to access an interactive version of the Student Edition and a self-test.

(Continued from page 492)

16. They are similar in that both require organic compounds in order to stay alive.

17. Obligate aerobes require oxygen to survive. Obligate anaerobes are killed by oxygen.

18. Because facultative anaerobes are able to switch between cellular respiration and fermentation for their energy demands, they are able to live anywhere.

19. Plants can't use nitrogen gas directly. Certain bacteria that have symbiotic relationships with plants carry out nitrogen fixation, which is the process of converting nitrogen gas into a form plants can use.

20. One thing all viruses have in common is that they enter living cells and, once inside, use the machinery of the infected cell to multiply.

21. The capsid protein of a virus is important because it binds to the surface of a cell and tricks the cell into allowing it inside. Once inside, the viral genes take over.

22. In a lytic infection, a virus enters a cell, makes copies of itself, and causes the cell to burst.

23. In a lysogenic infection, a virus integrates its DNA into the DNA of the host cell, and the viral genetic information replicates along with the host cell's DNA.

24. The best way to protect against most viral diseases is prevention. Once a viral disease has been contracted, it might be too late to control the disease.

25. Viruses are highly specific to the cells they infect because they must bind precisely to proteins on the cell surface in order to penetrate the cytoplasm.

Chapter 19 Assessment

Critical Thinking

26. Because other organisms depend on bacteria for converting nitrogen gas into nitrogen compounds, these organisms might die if bacteria lost their ability to fix nitrogen.

27. Viruses can replicate only within living things. As a result, bacteriophages can grow on cultures of bacteria but not on synthetic media.

28. Not brushing your teeth leaves particles on teeth that bacteria can use for food. This encourages bacterial growth.

29. The organism probably belongs to Eubacteria because it is unicellular, has a cell wall containing peptidoglycan, and lacks a nucleus.

30. Antibiotics B and C were the least effective. The growth of the bacteria was not retarded at all.

31. Antibiotics A and D would be good treatments because both retarded the growth of the bacteria.

32. Viruses, prokaryotes, and eukaryotes all have nucleic acids and proteins. Prokaryotes and eukaryotes have cell membranes, and eukaryotes have organelles.

33. Binary fission produces two cells from one, whereas endospore formation and conjugation do not increase the number of cells. In addition, conjugation results in genetic recombination.

34. Two labeled agar plates are needed. Touch one plate with a finger. Leave both plates uncovered for 20 minutes. Then, cover the plates, and store them in a protected area of the classroom. Use a hand lens to count the bacteria colonies after 24 and 48 hours.

35. Students should infer that if the agar plates are not sterile at the beginning of the lab, the results of the lab may be suspect. The reason is that the bacterial colonies that grow on the plates may not be the result of wiping the swab across the plate. For instance, the bacterial colonies that develop might not be of the same species as the bacteria in the bacterial culture and might grow at different rates under the same conditions.

Focus on the BIG Idea 

Bacteria break down carbon compounds, so they can be used to make all four types of organic compounds.

Chapter 19 Assessment

Critical Thinking

26. Predicting Suppose that bacteria lost the ability to fix nitrogen. How would this affect other organisms?

27. Applying Concepts Bacteria can be grown in the laboratory on synthetic media. Can bacteriophages be grown on cultures of bacteria? Can bacteriophages be grown on synthetic media? Explain your answers.

28. Problem Solving Bacteria that live on teeth produce an acid that causes decay. Why do people who do not brush their teeth regularly tend to have more cavities than those who do?

29. Classifying A scientist finds a new organism but is unsure to which kingdom it belongs. The organism is unicellular, has a cell wall containing peptidoglycan, has a circular DNA molecule and ribosomes, but it lacks a nucleus. Based on those characteristics, to which kingdom does it belong?

Questions 30–31

An experiment was conducted to determine the effectiveness of different antibiotics against a certain strain of bacteria. Four disks, each soaked in a different antibiotic, were placed in a petri dish where the bacteria were growing. The results are summarized below.

Effects of Antibiotics

Antibiotic	Observation After One Week
A	Growth retarded for 6 mm diameter
B	Growth not retarded
C	Growth not retarded
D	Growth retarded for 2 mm diameter

30. Analyzing Data Which antibiotics were the least effective at retarding the growth of the bacteria? Explain your answer using data from the experiment.

31. Inferring Which antibiotics might be most effective treatments for an infection caused by this strain of bacteria? Explain your answer using data from the experiment.

32. Comparing and Contrasting Make a chart that compares the structure and function of viruses with prokaryotes and eukaryotes.

33. Comparing and Contrasting Explain how the outcome of binary fission differs from that of both endospore formation and conjugation.

34. Designing Experiments Design an experiment to test the hypothesis that contact of an agar plate with a finger results in more bacterial growth than the exposure of the plate to classroom air.

35. Evaluating In science, sources of error are factors or conditions that cause recorded data to be inaccurate. Review the lab procedures on page 491. Is the following a possible source of error for that investigation: "At the beginning of the lab, the agar plates may not be sterile (may be contaminated)." Explain your answer.

Focus on the BIG Idea

Interdependence in Nature Many prokaryotes are decomposers, helping to recycle materials, including organic molecules. How are chemical reactions involved in the formation of organic molecules? You may wish to review Chapter 2.

Writing in Science

You are writing a science article entitled "Viruses in the Biosphere" for the local newspaper. Explain the role viruses play in the environment. Describe the harm they cause.

Performance-Based Assessment

Demonstrating a Lytic Infection A flip-book consists of pages of sequential drawings that, when flipped, appear to move. Create a flip-book movie of the steps in a lytic infection. Be sure to show what happens to the bacteriophage at each step. Exchange your flip-book with another student. Look at the other student's movie, and write a review of it.

For: An interactive self-test
Visit: PHSchool.com
Web Code: cba-6190

Writing in Science

Helpful aspects that student essays might mention: Viruses can be used in the production of vaccines that could eradicate specific diseases such as measles and polio; genetic engineers can correct genetic defects by using viruses to carry desirable genes from one cell to another. Harmful aspects: Viruses are pathogens and resistant to antibiotics. Viral diseases that affect humans include the common cold, measles, chickenpox, mumps, AIDS, and polio. Viral diseases that affect animals include distemper, rabies, and pneumonia. Viral diseases that affect plants may discolor leaves, stunt growth, or even kill the plant.

Standards Practice

Online at PHSchool.com

Test-Taking Tip For questions containing the word NOT, begin by jotting down items that do fit the characteristic in question. Then, compare your notes with the answer choices and eliminate those that correspond to your list. Finally, check to see that your answer is correct by confirming that it does not fit the characteristic in question.

Questions 1–4 Each of the lettered choices below refers to the following numbered statements. Select the best lettered choice. A choice may be used once, more than once, or not at all.

A Cocci
B Conjugation
C Binary fission
D Bacteriophage

1. Type of parasite that attacks certain prokaryotes

2. Process of transferring genetic information

3. Spherical prokaryotes

4. Process of asexual reproduction

Choose the letter that best answers the question or completes the statement.

5. Which of the following is NOT used to identify specific prokaryotes?
A size
B shape
C movement
D energy source

6. Which method is NOT used to protect food against microorganisms?
A salting
B freezing
C sterilization
D vaccination

7. Which illness is caused by a bacterium?
A AIDS
B polio
C diphtheria
D common cold

8. Which process is used for the exchange of genetic information between two bacterial cells?
A lytic cycle
B lysogenic cycle
C conjugation
D binary fission

9. All bacteria are classified as
A eukaryotes.
B protists.
C archaea.
D prokaryotes.

Questions 10–11 Use the graph below to answer the questions.

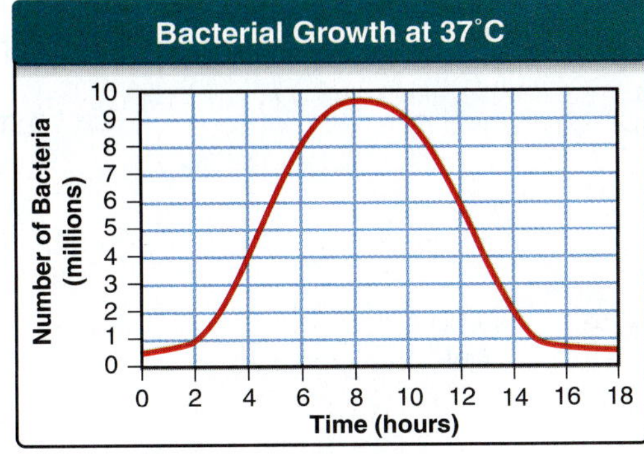

10. At which point in the graph does the number of living bacteria increase at the greatest rate? **BI 10.d**
A Between hours 2 and 4
B Between hours 4 and 6
C Between hours 6 and 8
D Between hours 10 and 12

11. Which is the most likely reason for the decrease in bacteria shown? **BI 10.d**
A The temperature of the bacterial culture was too high after 8 hours.
B The bacteria stopped reproducing after 8 hours.
C More nutrients were added to the culture at regular intervals.
D Waste products from the bacteria accumulated in the nutrient solution.

Standards Practice

1. D
2. B
3. A
4. C
5. A
6. D
7. C
8. C
9. D
10. B
11. D

Online at PHSchool.com

Have students check their understanding of the chapter by logging onto Success Tracker.

Performance-Based Assessment

Students' flip-books should reflect the steps involved in the lytic infection as shown in Figure 19–10. Once students have completed their flip-books, divide the class into pairs and have students in each pair write a review of the other student's flip-book. Advise students to focus their critiques on whether a flip-book accurately reflects what occurs in a lytic infection.

Your students can independently test their knowledge of the chapter and print out their test results for your files.

Chapter Planner 20 Protists

Section and Section Objectives	Time	STANDARDS NCLB	STANDARDS Biology	Activities and Labs
20–1 The Kingdom Protista, pp. 497–498 **20.1.1** ***Explain*** what a protist is.	1 period (1/2 block)			SE: ***Inquiry Activity,*** What are protists?, p. 496 L2 TE: ***Build Science Skills,*** p. 497 L2 L3 TE: ***Build Science Skills,*** p. 498 L2
20–2 Animal-like Protists: Protozoans, pp. 499–505 **20.2.1** ***Describe*** the major phyla of animal-like protists. **20.2.2** ***Explain*** how animal-like protists harm other living things.	2 periods (1 block)			TE: ***Build Science Skills,*** pp. 500 L2 L3, 501 L2 SE: ***Quick Lab,*** What are the functions of a paramecium's gullet and food vacuoles?, p. 504 L2 L3 TE: ***Demonstration,*** p. 505 L2 SE: ***Design an Experiment,*** Investigating Contractile Vacuoles, p. 521 L2 L3 LMB: Chapter 20 Lab L1 L2
20–3 Plantlike Protists: Unicellular Algae, pp. 506–509 **20.3.1** ***Describe*** the function of chlorophyll and accessory pigments in algae. **20.3.2** ***Describe*** the major phyla of unicellular algae. **20.3.3** ***Summarize*** the ecological roles of unicellular algae.	2 periods (1 block)			TE: ***Demonstration,*** p. 506 L2 TE: ***Build Science Skills,*** p. 507 L2 L3 TE: ***Build Science Skills,*** p. 507 L2 L3 SE: ***Analyzing Data,*** Fertilizers and Algae, p. 508 L2
20–4 Plantlike Protists: Red, Brown, and Green Algae, pp. 510–515 **20.4.1** ***Describe*** the major phyla of multicellular algae. **20.4.2** ***Explain*** how multicellular algae reproduce. **20.4.3** ***Identify*** some human uses of algae.	2 periods (1 block)	7 2.a		TE: ***Build Science Skills,*** p. 511 L2 TE: ***Build Science Skills,*** p. 512 L2 L3
20–5 Funguslike Protists, pp. 516–520 **20.5.1** ***Compare and Contrast*** funguslike protists and fungi. **20.5.2** ***Describe*** slime molds and water molds. **20.5.3** ***Summarize*** the ecological roles of funguslike protists.	1 period (1/2 block)	7 2.a		TE: ***Demonstration,*** p. 517 L1 L2 TE: ***Demonstration,*** p. 518 L1 L2 LMA: Chapter 20 Lab L2 L3
Chapter Assessment, pp. 522–525	1 period (1/2 block)			

ACTIVITY PLANNER

SE: *Inquiry Activity*, p. 496; 20 min.; mixed protist culture, microscope slide, methyl cellulose, coverslip, microscope

TE: *Build Science Skills*, p. 497; 20 min.; pond water, jars, microscope slides, coverslips, microscope

TE: *Build Science Skills*, p. 498; 10 min.; photographs/slides of protists, microprojector

TE: *Build Science Skills*, p. 500; 10 min.; grass, glass jar with lid, bottled water, dropper pipette, microscope slide, coverslip, microscope

TE: *Build Science Skills*, p. 501; 15 min.; slide of paramecium, microscope

SE: *Quick Lab*, p. 504; 20 min.; paramecium culture, 2 dropper pipettes, microscope, microscope slide, coverslip, *Chlorella* culture, toothpick, carmine dye

TE: *Demonstration*, p. 506; 20 min.; termite, microscope slide, coverslip, microscope, distilled water

TE: *Demonstration*, p. 506; 15 min.; filter paper; denatured ethyl alchohol; 3 beakers; scissors; green, brown, and red algae

TE: *Build Science Skills*, p. 506; 15 min.; slide of euglena, microscope

TE: *Build Science Skills*, p. 507; 20 min.; jar, coverslip, slide, microscope

TE: *Build Science Skills*, p. 511; 20 min.; sea lettuce, fern, mushroom, moss, flowering plant

TE: *Build Science Skills*, p. 512; 20 min.; living cultures of green algae, microscope slides, coverslips, dropper pipette, microscope

TE: *Demonstration*, p. 517; 15 min.; dead leaf or piece of bark, dry oatmeal flakes, petri dish with cover

TE: *Demonstration*, p. 518; 10 min.; dead fish, water, jar with lid

SE: *Design an Experiment*, p. 521; 90 minutes; *Paramecium caudatum* cultures, dropper pipette, slides, coverslips, microscope, cotton ball, forceps, clock

PLANNING KEY

Ability Levels

for students performing . . .

below grade level L1

at grade level L2

above grade level L3

Print Components

SE	Student Edition	LA	Lab Assessment
TE	Teacher's Edition	BTM	Biotechnology Manual
RSW	Reading & Study Workbook A	IDM	Issues and Decision Making
ARSW	Adapted Reading & Study Workbook B	LW	Lab Worksheets
TR	Teaching Resources	LMA	Laboratory Manual A
IF	Investigations in Forensics	LMB	Laboratory Manual B

Tech Components

CTB	Computer Test Bank
BD	BioDetectives DVD
TP	Transparencies Plus
PLM	Probeware Lab Manual
ABC	ABC DVD Library
LS	Lab Simulations
VL	Virtual Labs

Interactive textbook with assessment at PHSchool.com

Program Resources	Assessment	Media and Technology
TR: Lesson Plan 20–1, Section Summary, p. 48 L1, p. 58 L2, Worksheets, pp. 60–61 L2 **RSW:** Section 20–1 L2	**SE:** 20–1 Section Assessment, p. 498 **TR:** Section Review 20–1	**iText:** Section 20–1 **TP:** 20–1 Interest Grabber, Section Outline, Concept Map
TR: Lesson Plan 20–2, Section Summary, p. 48 L1, p. 58 L2, Worksheets, pp. 51–52 L1, pp. 62–64 L2 **RSW:** Section 20–2 L2 **ARSW:** Section 20–2 L1 **LW:** Chapter 20 Design an Experiment L1 L2 L3	**SE:** 20–2 Section Assessment, p. 505 **TR:** Section Review 20–2	**iText:** Section 20–2 **TP:** 20–2 Interest Grabber, Section Outline, Conjugation, Figure 20–4, Figure 20–5, Figure 20–7
TR: Lesson Plan 20–3, Section Summary, p. 49 L1, p. 58 L2, Worksheets, pp. 53–54 L1, pp. 65–67 L2, Enrichment L2 L3 **RSW:** Section 20–3 L2 **ARSW:** Section 20–3 L1	**SE:** 20–3 Section Assessment, p. 509 **TR:** Section Review 20–3	**iText:** Section 20–3 **TP:** 20–3 Interest Grabber, Section Outline, Euglena
TR: Lesson Plan 20–4, Section Summary, p. 49 L1, p. 59 L2, Worksheets, p. 55 L1, pp. 68–70 L2 **RSW:** Section 20–4 L2 **ARSW:** Section 20–4 L1	**SE:** 20–4 Section Assessment, p. 515 **TR:** Section Review 20–4	**iText:** Section 20–4 **TP:** 20–4 Interest Grabber, Section Outline, *Ulva* Life Cycle, Figure 20–17
TR: Lesson Plan 20–5, Section Summary, p. 50 L1, p. 59 L2, Worksheets, p. 56 L1, pp. 71–72 L2 **RSW:** Section 20–5 L2 **ARSW:** Section 20–5 L1	**SE:** 20–5 Section Assessment, p. 520 **TR:** Section Review 20–5	**iText:** Section 20–5 **TP:** 20–5 Interest Grabber, Section Outline, The Life Cycle of a Water Mold, Figure 20–22, Figure 20–23
	SE: Chapter 20 Assessment, pp. 522–525 **TR:** Chapter Vocabulary Review, Graphic Organizer, Chapter 20 Test	**iText:** Chapter 20 Assessment **CTB:** Chapter 20 Test

Go Online
Students can do research, share data, and test their knowledge online.

PRESSED FOR TIME?

To Preview the Chapter

- Introduce students to Key Concepts and Vocabulary terms in each section.
- Assign the Reading Strategies for each section.

To Cover the Chapter Quickly

- Have students read all of Section 20–1; Zooflagellates, Sarcodines, Ciliates, and Sporozoans in Section 20–2; Euglenophytes, Dinoflagellates, Chrysophytes, and Diatoms in Section 20–3; Red Algae, Brown Algae, and Green Algae in Section 20–4; and Slime Molds and Water Molds in Section 20–5.
- Assign the 20–1 Section Review and questions 1–11 in Chapter 20 Assessment and Chapter 20 Standards Practice.

To Review the Chapter

- Assign Sections 20–1 through 20–5 in the Reading and Study Workbook or the Adapted Reading and Study Workbook.
- Assign Section Reviews for 20–1 through 20–5 and the Chapter Vocabulary Review for Chapter 20 in the Teaching Resources.

CHAPTER 20

ENGAGE/EXPLORE

Inquiry Activity

Objective Students will be able to form an operational definition of what a protist is.

Skill Focus **Forming Operational Definitions, Classifying**

Materials mixed protist culture, microscope slide, methyl cellulose, coverslip, microscope

Time 20 minutes

Advance Prep Prepare a mixed culture that contains various protists for students to observe, including amoebas, paramecia, euglenas, and multicellular algae.

Safety Caution students to wash their hands after concluding the activity.

Strategy Remind students that they have learned about structures within cells, and that they should call upon that knowledge in drawing and labeling what they observe in these microorganisms.

Expected Outcomes Students should observe a variety of microorganisms and be able to get a sense of what a protist is.

Think About It

1. Bacteria may be present but will not be visible at the magnification used to see most protists. Protists observed will be visibly eukaryotic (nucleated). Some students may assume incorrectly that motile organisms are animals and green, nonmotile organisms are plants.

2. A typical definition might suggest that protists are unicellular eukaryotes.

Brain Teaser

Have students compare the photo on this chapter-opening page with those in Figure 20–1 on page 497. As students observe the photographs, ask: **What similarities are there among the four types of organisms shown in these photographs?** *(Students may mention that three of the four appear to be unicellular. Many will say that these organisms share few, if any, similarities.)* Reinforce students' feeling that these organisms make up a diverse group. Develop the idea that this kingdom is a catchall in which membership is determined mainly by exclusion from the other kingdoms.

CHAPTER 20 Protists

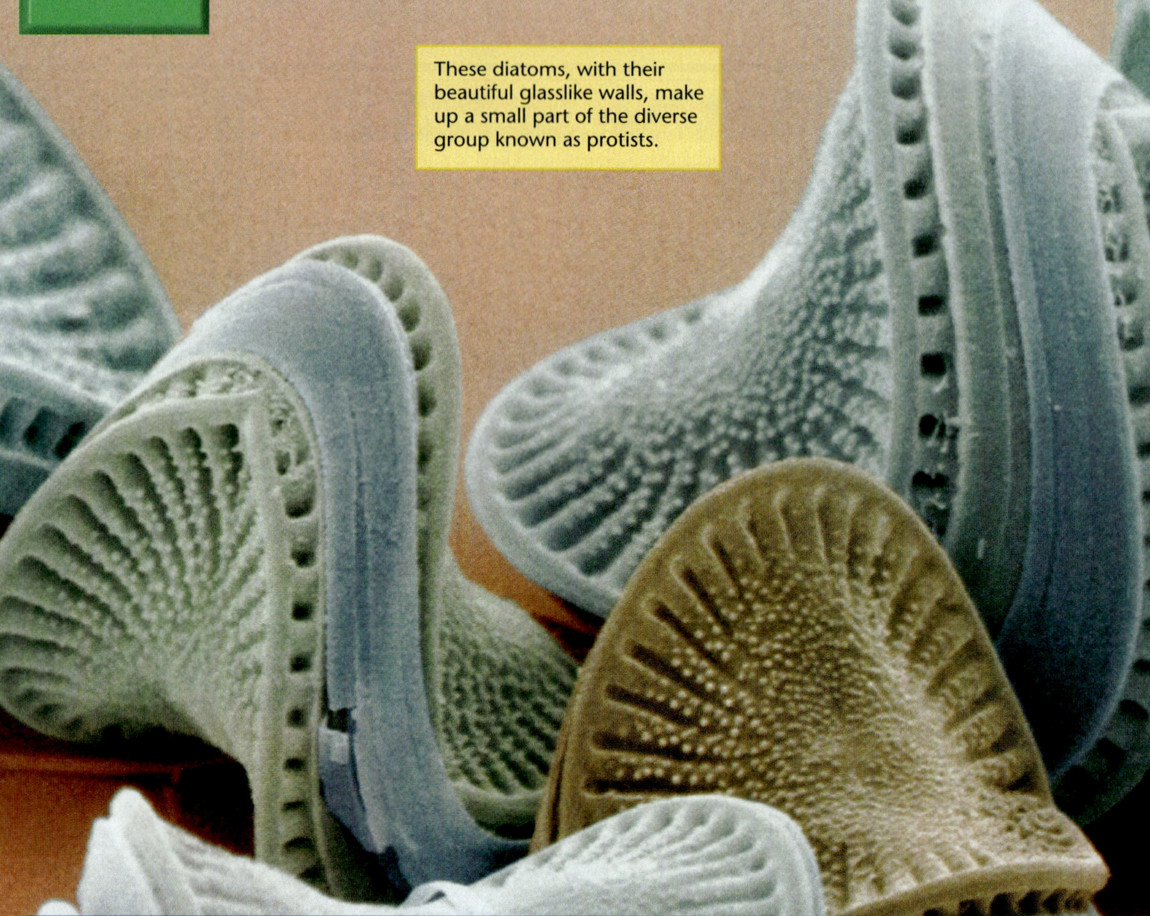

These diatoms, with their beautiful glasslike walls, make up a small part of the diverse group known as protists.

Inquiry Activity

What are protists?

Procedure

1. Place a drop of water containing a variety of microorganisms on a microscope slide. Add a drop of methyl cellulose and a coverslip. Observe the slide under the microscope at low and high magnifications.
2. Record your observations. Draw and label each type of organism.
3. Draw a chart listing each type of organism that you observed and its characteristics.

Think About It

1. **Classifying** Are any of these organisms bacteria, animals, or plants? Explain your answer.
2. **Forming Operational Definitions** The organisms you observed are members of a group called protists. Write a definition of *protist*.

HISTORY OF SCIENCE

A new kingdom
In the nineteenth century, microscopes were refined to the point where biologists began to describe many different kinds of unicellular organisms. Some scientists, including the German naturalist Ernst Haeckel (1834–1919), proposed that a new kingdom needed to be created to include all these organisms that were not really plants or animals. But not until the 1960s, with the advent of more powerful biochemical microscopic technology, did most biologists recognize the gross inadequacy of the two-kingdom, animal/plant system. By the 1970s, the term *protist*, which means "first organism," came to be used for unicellular, nucleated organisms and their derivatives. Some biologists have used another term, *protoctist*, to encompass the same organisms because *protist* has too often been used as a synonym for *protozoan.*

20–1 The Kingdom Protista

On a dark, quiet night you sit at the stern of a tiny sailboat as it glides through the calm waters of a coastal inlet. Suddenly, the boat's wake sparkles with its own light. As the stern cuts through the water, glimmering points of light leave a ghostly trail into the darkness. What's responsible for this eerie display? You've just had a close encounter with one group of some of the most remarkable organisms in the world—the protists.

What Is a Protist?

The kingdom Protista is a diverse group that may include more than 200,000 species. Biologists have argued for years over the best way to classify protists, and the issue may never be settled. In fact, protists are defined less by what they are and more by what they are not: A **protist** is any organism that is not a plant, an animal, a fungus, or a prokaryote. **Protists are eukaryotes that are not members of the kingdoms Plantae, Animalia, or Fungi.** Recall that a eukaryote has a nucleus and other membrane-bound organelles. Although most protists are unicellular, quite a few are not, as you can see in **Figure 20–1.** A few protists actually consist of hundreds or even thousands of cells but are still considered protists because they are so similar to other protists that are truly unicellular.

CHECKPOINT *What is the classification of an organism that is not a plant, an animal, a fungus, or a prokaryote?*

Guide for Reading

Key Concept
- What are protists?

Vocabulary
protist

Reading Strategy: Summarizing As you read, find the main ideas for each blue heading. Write down a few key words from each main idea. Then, use the key words in your summary. Reread and revise your summary, keeping only the most important ideas.

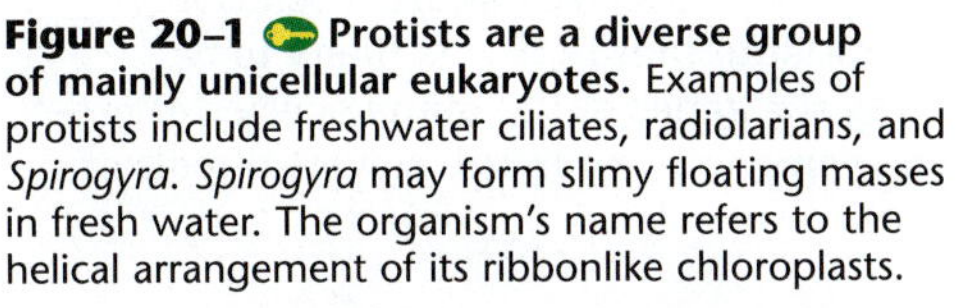

Figure 20–1 Protists are a diverse group of mainly unicellular eukaryotes. Examples of protists include freshwater ciliates, radiolarians, and *Spirogyra*. *Spirogyra* may form slimy floating masses in fresh water. The organism's name refers to the helical arrangement of its ribbonlike chloroplasts.

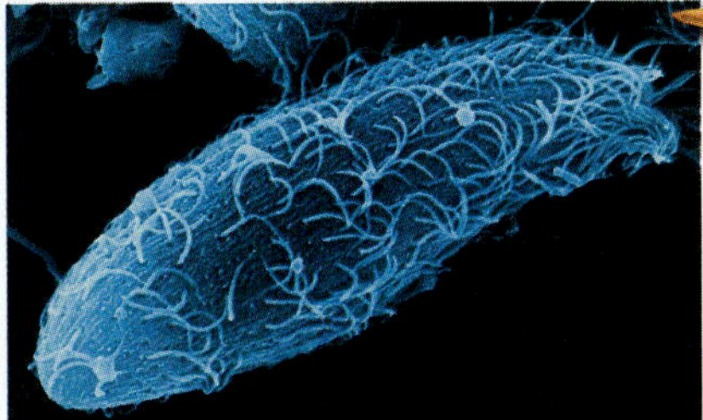

Euplotes (a freshwater ciliate) (magnification: about 140×)

Radiolarian (magnification: 3400×)

Spirogyra (magnification: 400×)

SECTION RESOURCES

Print:
- ***Teaching Resources,*** Lesson Plan 20–1, Adapted Section Summary 20–1, Adapted Worksheets 20–1, Section Summary 20–1, Worksheets 20–1, Section Review 20–1
- ***Reading and Study Workbook A,*** Section 20–1

Technology:
- ***iText,*** Section 20–1
- ***Transparencies Plus,*** Section 20–1

Section 20–1

1 FOCUS

Objective

20.1.1 ***Explain*** what a protist is.

Guide for Reading

Vocabulary Preview

Before students read the section, call on volunteers to propose a definition for the word *protist.*

Reading Strategy

Ask students to find evidence in the section for this statement: The kingdom Protista is a catchall grouping for organisms that don't fit into other kingdoms.

2 INSTRUCT

What Is a Protist?

Build Science Skills

Observing Collect samples of pond water in several jars. In each jar, include some mud from the pond's bottom. Have students make slides of samples from the water and observe the slides through a microscope. Ask students to make drawings of at least two of the organisms and to pay special attention to how they move. L2 L3

Evolution of Protists

Make Connections

Earth Science Explain that nearly 1.5 billion years ago, when the first protists appeared, the world was much different than it is today. Point out that the ocean covered much of Earth. Explain that Earth itself formed about 4.6 billion years ago, so eukaryotic organisms appeared about 3 billion years after the planet formed and more than a billion years after the first prokaryotes. L2

Answer to . . .

CHECKPOINT *A protist*

20–1 (continued)

Classification of Protists

Build Science Skills

Classifying Display photographs of protists. Include some images of animal-like, plantlike, and funguslike protists. Use a microprojector to show slides of various organisms, such as an amoeba, a euglena, and a paramecium. Have students brainstorm for lists of similarities and differences that exist among the protists they observe. Ask students to create a classification system. L2

Download a worksheet on protists for students to complete, and find additional teacher support from NSTA SciLinks.

3 ASSESS

Evaluate Understanding

Call on students to explain the classification of protists based on nutrition. Students should describe animal-like protists, plantlike protists, and funguslike protists.

Reteach

Have students look at the organisms shown in Figure 20–1 and explain why none of the three could be classified as a fungus or an animal.

Writing in Science

Students' newspaper stories should explain that early in Earth's history, different kinds of prokaryotic cells, including photosynthetic prokaryotes, probably began to live inside larger cells. This relationship began as a parasitic one, but over time the different cells came to be mutually dependent.

If your class subscribes to the iText, use it to review the Key Concepts in Section 20–1.

Answer to . . .

Figure 20–2 *Chloroplast*

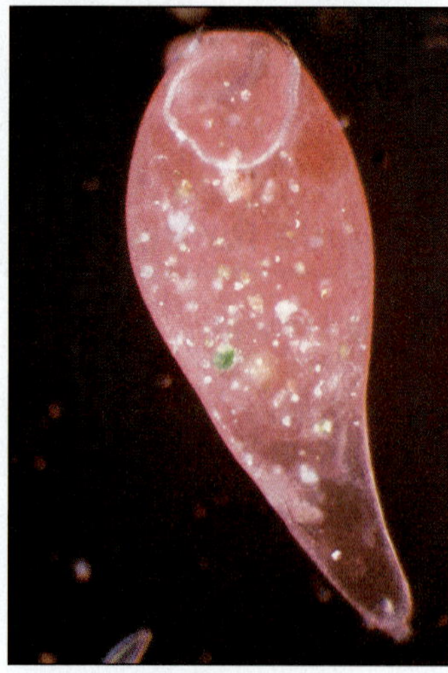

Stentor (magnification: 350×)

▲ **Figure 20–2** According to one hypothesis, some organelles in eukaryotic cells were once symbiotic prokaryotes that lived inside other cells. For example, the mitochondria found in this *Stentor* may be descended from early prokaryotes. **Applying Concepts** ***What other organelle may originally have been symbiotic cells?***

For: Links on protists
Visit: www.SciLinks.org
Web Code: cbn-6201

Evolution of Protists

Protists are members of a kingdom whose formal name, *Protista,* comes from Greek words meaning "the very first." The name is appropriate. The first eukaryotic organisms on Earth, which appeared nearly 1.5 billion years ago, were protists.

Where did the first protists come from? Biologist Lynn Margulis has hypothesized that the first eukaryotes evolved from a symbiosis of several cells. Mitochondria and chloroplasts found in eukaryotic cells may be descended from aerobic and photosynthetic prokaryotes that began to live inside larger cells. **Figure 20–2** shows a representative protist.

Classification of Protists

Protists are so diverse that many biologists suggest that they should be broken up into several kingdoms. This idea is supported by recent studies of protist DNA indicating that different groups of protists evolved independently from archaebacteria. Unfortunately, at present, biologists don't agree on how to classify the protists. Therefore, we will take the traditional approach of considering the protists as a single kingdom.

One way to classify protists is according to the way they obtain nutrition. Thus, many protists that are heterotrophs are called animal-like protists. Those that produce their own food by photosynthesis are called plantlike protists. Finally, those that obtain their food by external digestion—either as decomposers or parasites—are called funguslike protists. This is the way in which we will organize our investigation of the protists.

It is important to understand that these categories are an artificial way to organize a very diverse group of organisms. Categories based on the way protists obtain food do not reflect the evolutionary history of these organisms. For example, all animal-like protists did not necessarily share a relatively recent ancestor. The protistan family tree is likely to be redrawn many times as the genes of the many species of protists are analyzed and compared using the powerful tools of molecular biology.

20–1 Section Assessment

1. **Key Concept** What is a protist?
2. Describe Margulis's theory about the evolution of protists.
3. Are most protists unicellular or multicellular?
4. What are the three methods that protists use to obtain food?
5. Identify the characteristics of organisms belonging to the kingdom Protista.
6. **Critical Thinking Using Analogies** In what way is the kingdom Protista similar to a group of people who do not belong to a political party?

Writing in Science

Creative Writing
Write and illustrate a brief newspaper story explaining the hypothesis that eukaryotic cells evolved from a symbiosis of several prokaryotes with larger cells. *Hint:* Begin with a draft and then revise that draft, looking at organization and word choice.

20–1 Section Assessment

1. A protist is a eukaryote that is not a member of the kingdoms Plantae, Animalia, or Fungi.
2. The first eukaryotic cells may have evolved from a symbiosis of several prokaryotes with larger cells.
3. Most are unicellular.
4. Animal-like protists ingest or absorb food; plantlike protists produce food by photosynthesis; and funguslike protists obtain their food by external digestion either as decomposers or as parasites.
5. Protists are eukaryotic organisms, and most are unicellular.
6. Like people who do not belong to a political party, protists are defined less by what they are and more by what they are not.

20–2 Animal-like Protists: Protozoans

At one time, animal-like protists were called protozoa, which means "first animals," and were classified separately from more plantlike protists. Like animals, these organisms are heterotrophs. The four phyla of animal-like protists are distinguished from one another by their means of movement. As you will read, zooflagellates swim with flagella, sarcodines move by extensions of their cytoplasm, ciliates move by means of cilia, and sporozoans do not move on their own at all.

Guide for Reading

Key Concepts
- What are the distinguishing features of the major phyla of animal-like protists?
- How do animal-like protists harm other living things?

Vocabulary
pseudopod
amoeboid movement
food vacuole • cilium
trichocyst • macronucleus
micronucleus • gullet
anal pore • contractile vacuole
conjugation

Reading Strategy: Building Vocabulary
Before you read, preview new vocabulary by skimming the section and making a list of the highlighted, boldface terms. Leave space to make notes as you read.

Zooflagellates

Many protists easily move through their aquatic environments propelled by flagella. Flagella are long, whiplike projections that allow a cell to move. **Animal-like protists that swim using flagella are classified in the phylum Zoomastigina and are often referred to as zooflagellates.** Most zooflagellates (zoh-oh-FLAJ-uh-lits) have either one or two flagella, although a few species have many flagella. Two representative zooflagellates are shown in **Figure 20–3.**

Zooflagellates are generally able to absorb food through their cell membranes. Many live in lakes and streams, where they absorb nutrients from decaying organic material. Others live within the bodies of other organisms, taking advantage of the food that the larger organism provides.

Most zooflagellates reproduce asexually by mitosis and cytokinesis. Mitosis followed by cytokinesis results in two cells that are genetically identical. Some zooflagellates, however, have a sexual life cycle as well. During sexual reproduction, gamete cells are produced by meiosis. When gametes from two organisms fuse, an organism with a new combination of genetic information is formed.

Figure 20–3 **Zooflagellates are animal-like protists that swim using flagella.** Most zooflagellates live as solitary cells. Some form colonies of cells.

Trichomonas vaginalis (magnification: 11,500×)

Leishmania donovani (magnification: 4800×)

SECTION RESOURCES

Print:
- ***Laboratory Manual B,*** Chapter 20 Lab
- ***Teaching Resources,*** Lesson Plan 20–2, Adapted Section Summary 20–2, Adapted Worksheets 20–2, Section Summary 20–2, Worksheets 20–2, Section Review 20–2
- ***Reading and Study Workbook A,*** Section 20–2
- ***Adapted Reading and Study Workbook B,*** Section 20–2
- ***Lab Worksheets,*** Chapter 20 Design an Experiment

Technology:
- ***iText,*** Section 20–2
- ***Transparencies Plus,*** Section 20–2

Section 20–2

1 FOCUS

Objectives

20.2.1 ***Describe*** the major phyla of animal-like protists.

20.2.2 ***Explain*** how animal-like protists harm other living things.

Guide for Reading

Vocabulary Preview

Have students write the Vocabulary terms, dividing each into its separate syllables as best they can. Remind students that each syllable usually has only one vowel sound. The correct syllabications are pseu•do•pod, a•moe•boid move•ment, food vac•u•ole, cil•i•um, trich•o•cyst, mac•ro•nu•cle•us, mi•cro•nu•cle•us, gul•let, a•nal pore, con•trac•tile vac•u•ole, con•ju•ga•tion.

Reading Strategy

Before students read, ask them to skim the section to find the boldface Key Concepts. Have them copy each of the concepts onto a notecard. Then, as they read they should note details and examples that support each Key Concept.

2 INSTRUCT

Zooflagellates

Make Connections

Health Science Explain that the zooflagellates include several parasitic protists that cause human diseases, such as the pathogens that cause African sleeping sickness and giardiasis. The zooflagellate *Trichomonas vaginalis* causes a common sexually transmitted disease that afflicts women, called vaginitis. Encourage interested students to find out how this disease is spread, what the symptoms are, and how it can be treated. L2 L3

20–2 (continued)

Sarcodines

Word Origins

The word *pseudonym* means "false name." L2

Use Visuals

Figure 20–4 Ask students: **Which animal-like protist phylum includes** ***Amoeba proteus?*** *(Sarcodina)* **Why do you think an amoeba is often described as "shape-shifting"?** *(It has no permanent shape. It changes its shape as it pushes out projections called pseudopods.)* **What is the function of the food vacuole?** *(It temporarily stores and digests food.)* L1 L2

Build Science Skills

Observing Have each student gather a handful of grass from a field near the school. The grass should then be dried on a flat tray for at least one day. After the grass is dried, have students place the grass in a clean glass jar, add bottled water until the jar is about three-quarters full, and seal it tightly with a lid. After three days, students should open the jar in a well-ventilated area and gently stir the contents. Have students then use a dropper pipette to make slides from the water in the jar and observe the slides under a microscope. Typically, students will observe several different types of protists, such as paramecia and amoebas. Ask students to make drawings and try to identify the organisms they see. L2 L3

Word Origins

Pseudopod comes from the Greek words *pseudes,* meaning "false," and *-pous,* meaning "foot." So *pseudopod* means "false foot." The suffix *-onym* comes from the Greek word *onama,* meaning "name." **What do you think the word** ***pseudonym*** **means?**

Sarcodines

Members of the phylum Sarcodina, or sarcodines, move via temporary cytoplasmic projections known as **pseudopods** (SOO-doh-pahdz). **Sarcodines are animal-like protists that use pseudopods for feeding and movement.** The best-known sarcodines are the amoebas, shown in **Figure 20–4.** Amoebas are flexible, active cells with thick pseudopods that extend out of the central mass of the cell. The cytoplasm of the cell streams into the pseudopod, and the rest of the cell follows. This type of locomotion is known as **amoeboid movement.**

Amoebas can capture and digest particles of food and even other cells. They do this by surrounding their meal, then taking it inside themselves to form a food vacuole. A **food vacuole** is a small cavity in the cytoplasm that temporarily stores food. Once inside the cell, the material is digested rapidly and the nutrients are passed along to the rest of the cell. Undigestible waste material remains inside the vacuole until its contents are eliminated by releasing them outside the cell. Amoebas reproduce by mitosis and cytokinesis.

Foraminiferans, another member of Sarcodina, are abundant in the warmer regions of the oceans. Foraminiferans secrete shells of calcium carbonate ($CaCO_3$). As they die, the calcium carbonate from their shells accumulates on the bottom of the ocean. In some regions, thick deposits of foraminiferan shells have formed on the ocean floor. The white chalk cliffs of Dover, England, are huge deposits of foraminiferan skeletons that were raised above sea level by geological processes.

Heliozoans comprise another group of sarcodines. The name *heliozoa* means "sun animal." Thin spikes of cytoplasm, supported by microtubules, project from their silica (SiO_2) shells, making heliozoans look like the sun's rays.

▼ **Figure 20–4** **Sarcodines use pseudopods for feeding and movement.** The amoeba, a common sarcodine, moves by first extending a pseudopod away from its body. The organism's cytoplasm then streams into the pseudopod. Amoebas also use pseudopods to surround and ingest prey.

Amoeba proteus (magnification: 330×)

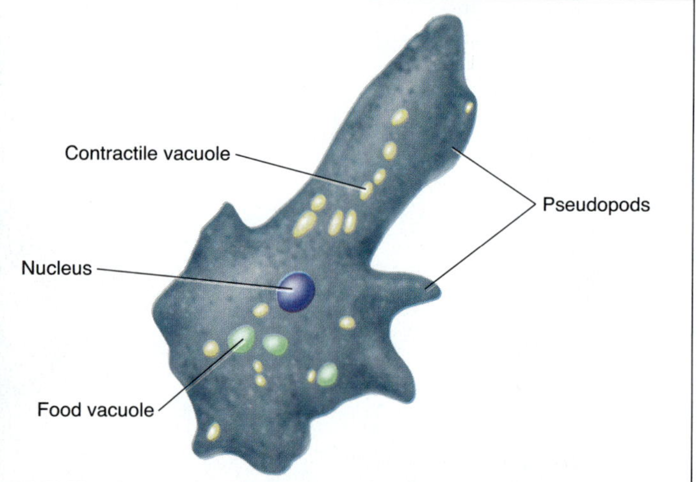

UNIVERSAL ACCESS

Less Proficient Readers

To reinforce the anatomies of two important animal-like protists, have students make their own labeled drawings of *Amoeba proteus* and a paramecium, using Figures 20–4 and 20–5 for reference. Then, call on students at random to describe the function of each of the labeled structures in both drawings. L1 L2

English Language Learners

Help English language learners pronounce the term *sporozoite,* which is introduced on page 502. Explain that the word is derived from a Greek word meaning "seed." Point out that knowledge of derivation can aid in understanding, but derivation can sometimes be misleading. For instance, a *sporozoite* is a unicellular stage of the sporozoan life cycle. A seed, by contrast, is a multicellular structure with clearly organized and specialized tissues. L1 L2

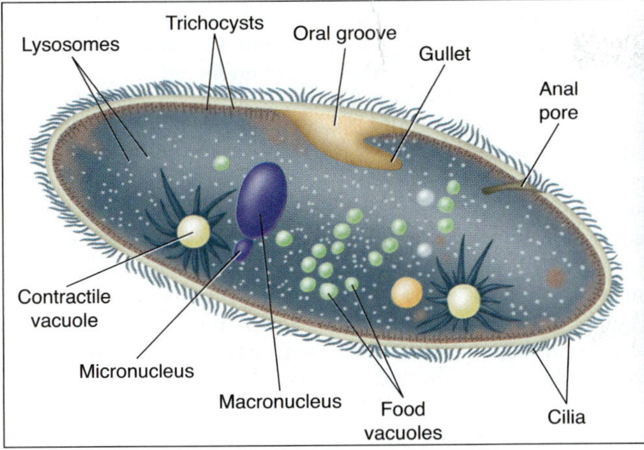

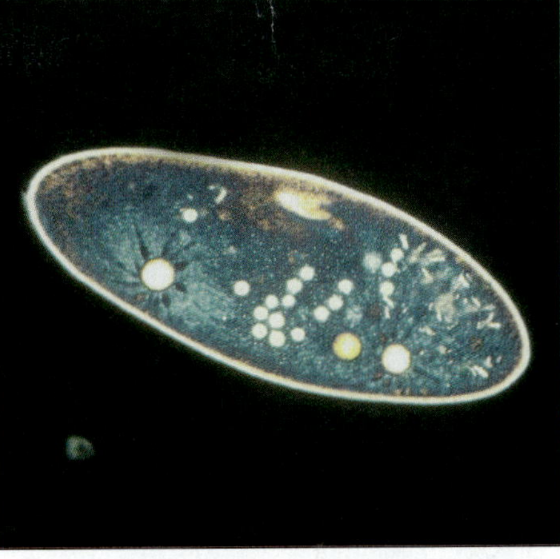

Paramecium caudatum (magnification: 2500×)

Ciliates

The phylum Ciliophora is named for **cilia** (singular: cilium), short hairlike projections similar to flagella. **Members of the phylum Ciliophora, known as ciliates, use cilia for feeding and movement.** The internal structure of cilia and flagella are identical. The beating of cilia, like the pull of hundreds of oars in an ancient ship, propels a cell rapidly through water.

Ciliates are found in both fresh and salt water. In fact, a lake or stream near your home might contain many different ciliates. Most ciliates are free living, which means that they do not exist as parasites or symbionts.

CHECKPOINT *What are cilia, and how do ciliates use them?*

Internal Anatomy Some of the best-known ciliates belong to the genus *Paramecium.* A paramecium can be as long as 350 micrometers. Its cilia, which are organized into evenly spaced rows and bundles, beat in a regular, efficient pattern. The cell membrane of a paramecium is highly structured and has trichocysts just below its surface. **Trichocysts** (TRY-koh-sists) are very small, bottle-shaped structures used for defense. When a paramecium is confronted by danger, such as a predator, the trichocysts release stiff projections that protect the cell.

A paramecium's internal anatomy is shown in **Figure 20–5.** Like most ciliates, a paramecium possesses two types of nuclei: a macronucleus and one or more smaller micronuclei. Why does a ciliate need two types of nuclei? The **macronucleus** is a "working library" of genetic information—a site for keeping multiple copies of most of the genes that the cell needs in its day-to-day existence. The **micronucleus,** by contrast, contains a "reserve copy" of all of the cell's genes.

▲ **Figure 20–5** **Ciliates use hairlike projections called cilia for feeding and movement.** Ciliates, including this paramecium, are covered with cilia that propel them through the water. Cilia also line the organism's gullet and move its food—usually bacteria—to the organism's interior. There, the food particles are engulfed, forming food vacuoles. The contractile vacuoles collect and remove excess water, thereby helping to achieve homeostasis, a stable internal environment.

For: Amoeba and Paramecium activity
Visit: PHSchool.com
Web Code: cbp-6202

Ciliates

Use Visuals

Figure 20–5 Ask students: **Which animal-like protist phylum includes paramecia?** *(Ciliophora)* **What structures do paramecia use for movement?** *(Cilia)* **What are some other structures in a paramecium cell?** *(An oral groove, a gullet, an anal pore, a contractile vacuole, a micronucleus, a macronucleus, and food vacuoles)* L1 L2

Build Science Skills

Observing Provide students with a prepared slide of a paramecium. Have them use a microscope to observe the slide and make a labeled drawing of what they see. L2

For: Amoeba and Paramecium activity
Visit: PHSchool.com
Web Code: cbe-6209
Students learn about two types of protozoans—the amoeba and the paramecium.

FACTS AND FIGURES

No difference

Students may wonder what the real difference is between a cilium and a flagellum. Some might suspect that there must be a subtle difference in internal structure about which their textbook or teacher is not telling them. The truth is that there is no difference—a cilium and a flagellum are the same organelle. The difference in terminology is derived from the days of the light microscope, when biologists thought that the many fine hairs surrounding some cells might well turn out to be different from the few long whips that move other cells. With the advent of the electron microscope, however, it became clear that the structure and biochemistry of both organelles are identical, at least in protists. There is a real difference, however, between the flagella of prokaryotes and those of protists.

Answer to . . .

CHECKPOINT *Cilia are short hairlike projections that ciliates use for feeding and movement.*

20–2 (continued)

Use Visuals

Figure 20–6 After students have studied the figure, ask: **What is conjugation?** *(Conjugation is the process that allows paramecia to exchange genetic material with other individuals in times of stress.)* **What is the advantage of conjugation for a paramecium species?** *(Conjugation provides new combinations of genes, which help create and maintain genetic diversity. Biologists believe that genetic diversity provides a better chance for species to survive unfavorable changes in their environments.)* L1 L2

Sporozoans

Build Science Skills

Comparing and Contrasting Have students make a compare/contrast table that organizes the information they have learned about the four phyla of animallike protists. Column heads for this table should include Phylum, Means of Movement, Feeding, Other Characteristics, and Examples. After students have individually worked on their tables, divide the class into small groups and have students in each group compare tables, trade information, and collaborate on a group table. L2

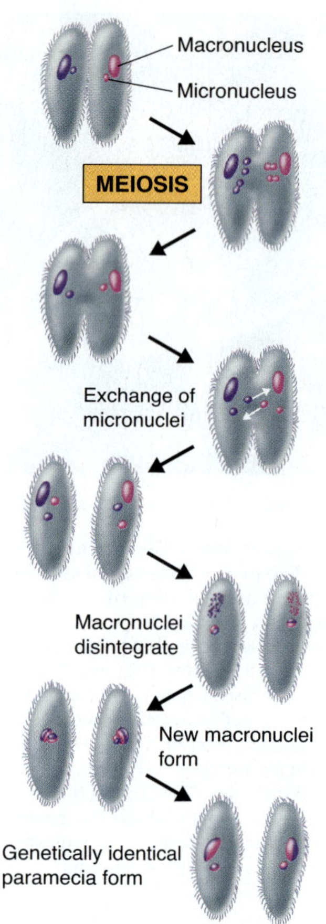

▲ **Figure 20–6** During conjugation, two paramecia attach themselves to each other and exchange genetic information. The process is not reproduction because no new individuals are formed. Conjugation is a sexual process, however, and it results in an increase in genetic diversity. **Interpreting Graphics** *What structures do paramecia exchange during conjugation?*

Many ciliates obtain food by using cilia to sweep food particles into the **gullet,** an indentation in one side of the organism. The particles are trapped in the gullet and forced into food vacuoles that form at its base. The food vacuoles pinch off into the cytoplasm and eventually fuse with lysosomes, which contain digestive enzymes. The material in the food vacuoles is digested, and the organism obtains nourishment. Waste materials are emptied into the environment when the food vacuole fuses with a region of the cell membrane called the **anal pore.**

In fresh water, water may move into the paramecium by osmosis. This excess water is collected in vacuoles. These vacuoles empty into canals that are arranged in a star-shaped pattern around contractile vacuoles. **Contractile vacuoles** are cavities in the cytoplasm that are specialized to collect water. When a contractile vacuole is full, it contracts abruptly, pumping water out of the organism. The expelling of excess water via the contractile vacuole is one of the ways the paramecium maintains homeostasis.

Conjugation Under most conditions, ciliates reproduce asexually by mitosis and cytokinesis. When placed under stress, paramecia may engage in a process known as **conjugation** that allows them to exchange genetic material with other individuals. The process of conjugation is shown in **Figure 20–6.**

Conjugation begins when two paramecia attach themselves to each other. Meiosis of their diploid micronuclei produces four haploid micronuclei, three of which disintegrate. The remaining micronucleus in each cell divides mitotically, forming a pair of identical micronuclei. The two cells then exchange one micronucleus from each pair. The macronuclei disintegrate, and each cell forms a new macronucleus from its micronucleus. The two paramecia that leave conjugation are genetically identical to each other, but both have been changed by the exchange of genetic information.

Conjugation is not a form of reproduction, because no new individuals are formed. It is, however, a sexual process—because it uses meiosis to produce new combinations of genetic information. In a large population, conjugation helps to produce and maintain genetic diversity.

Sporozoans

While many animal-like protists are free living, some are parasites.  **Members of the phylum Sporozoa do not move on their own and are parasitic.** Sporozoans are parasites of a wide variety of organisms, including worms, fish, birds, and humans. Many sporozoans have complex life cycles that involve more than one host. Sporozoans reproduce by sporozoites. Under the right conditions, a sporozoite can attach itself to a host cell, penetrate it, and then live within it as a parasite.

How do sporozoans reproduce?

BIO INSIGHTS

FACTS AND FIGURES

Why conjugation?

Conjugation is an interesting aspect of ciliate reproduction, but many students find it confusing. During the process, the two cells exchange part of their micronuclear "libraries" and form new combinations of genetic information. Once these new combinations are formed, the cell destroys its old macronucleus and makes a new one from the new set of information. Each cell leaves the conjugation event with a genetic makeup that is different from the one with which it entered. The macronuclei seem to contain the genes that must function on a daily basis to keep the cell alive. For the sake of efficiency, those genes have been copied hundreds of times. The existence of two kinds of nuclei seems to help the cell to express the genes required all the time. It also allows the cell to keep a repository of genetic information that may be passed on to future generations.

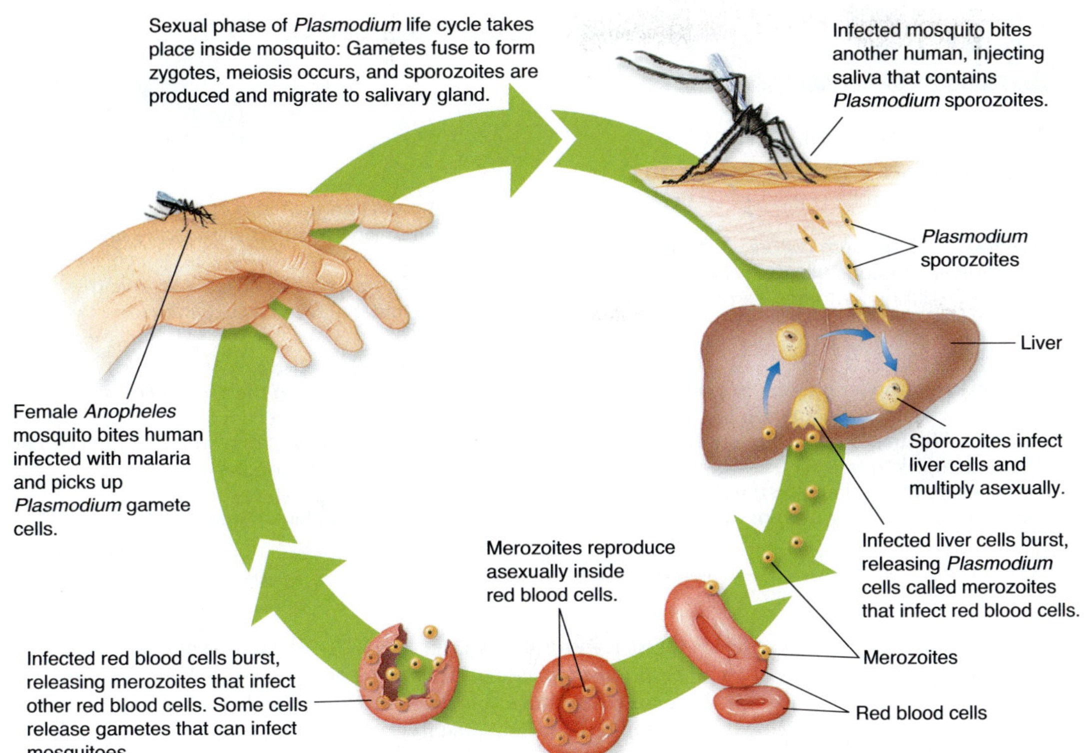

Animal-like Protists and Disease

Unfortunately for humans and for other organisms, many protists are disease-causing parasites. **Some animal-like protists cause serious diseases, including malaria and African sleeping sickness.**

Malaria Malaria is one of the world's most serious infectious diseases. As many as 2 million people still die from malaria every year. The sporozoan *Plasmodium,* which causes malaria, is carried by the female *Anopheles* mosquito.

The cycle of malarial infection is shown in **Figure 20–7.** When an infected mosquito bites a human, the mosquito's saliva, which contains sporozoites, enters the human's bloodstream. Once inside the blood, *Plasmodium* infects liver cells and then red blood cells, where it multiplies rapidly. When the red blood cells burst, the release of the parasites into the bloodstream produces severe chills and fever, symptoms of malaria.

Although drugs such as chloroquinine are effective against some forms of the disease, many strains of *Plasmodium* are resistant to these drugs. Scientists have developed a number of vaccines against malaria, but to date most are only partially effective. For the immediate future, the best means of controlling malaria involve controlling the mosquitoes that carry it.

Figure 20–7 **Animal-like protists can cause serious diseases, including malaria.** The bite of an *Anopheles* mosquito can transmit *Plasmodium* sporozoites. Once in the human body, *Plasmodium* first infects liver cells and then red blood cells.

Animal-like Protists and Disease

Make Connections

Health Science Ask students: **Where is malaria most common?** *(Some students may know that malaria is common in tropical and subtropical regions of the world, including Africa, Southeast Asia, and Central and South America.)* Explain that the classic treatment of malaria was with quinine, a medicine derived from the bark of the cinchona tree. Stronger synthetic forms of that drug are used today. Eradicating the mosquito carriers and their breeding areas is an important preventive measure against malaria. 

Use Community Resources

Invite a health professional to give a brief talk about this disease that still affects so many people around the world. There are many forms of malaria, so it makes an interesting discussion topic. L2

BIO INSIGHTS

FACTS AND FIGURES

The nighttime is the right time

The symptoms of malaria include chills and fever. These symptoms are associated with the rupture of red blood cells and the release into the bloodstream of huge numbers of merozoites. Not all red blood cells become infected with merozoites. Yet, if only 1 percent of the red blood cells contain the protist cells, there would be about 100 trillion parasite cells in the circulatory system at the same time. The rupture of blood cells in a person occurs simultaneously and at regular intervals—always a multiple of 24 hours. Between periods of rupture, the infected person feels normal. Why is there such perfect timing of these periods of rupture? Some scientists think that the parasite has evolved this adaptation to ensure that the gametes released are mature at night, which is when mosquitoes are more likely to be feeding. Thus, there is a greater likelihood that the sporozoans will be transmitted to new hosts.

Answers to . . .

CHECKPOINT *Sporozoans reproduce by means of sporozoites that live within host cells as parasites.*

Figure 20–6 *Two paramecia exchange one micronucleus from a pair of identical micronuclei in each.*

Quick Lab

Objective Students will be able to formulate a hypothesis about how paramecia feed.

Skills Focus **Observing, Inferring, Formulating Hypotheses**

Materials *Paramecium* culture, 2 dropper pipettes, microscope, microscope slide, coverslip, *Chlorella* culture, toothpick, carmine dye

Time 20 minutes

Advance Prep Order cultures of *Paramecium* and *Chlorella*, as well as carmine dye, from a biological supply house.

Safety Make sure that students wash their hands with warm soap and water before they leave the lab.

Strategies

- Demonstrate the use of a toothpick in transferring granules of carmine dye to the drops on the slide.
- You may choose to have students observe the organisms through the microscope before adding carmine red.

Expected Outcomes Students should observe that the paramecia feed on the *Chlorella* cells by trapping the cells in the gullet and then moving the cells into the cytoplasm in food vacuoles.

Analyze and Conclude

1. Students should observe that the *Chlorella* cells and the carmine dye accumulate inside the paramecia.
2. Students should infer from their observations that the paramecia trapped the *Chlorella* cells and dye granules in the gullet and then forced the particles into food vacuoles.
3. Students should hypothesize that the paramecia took in the *Chlorella* cells and the dye granules by endocytosis.

Quick Lab

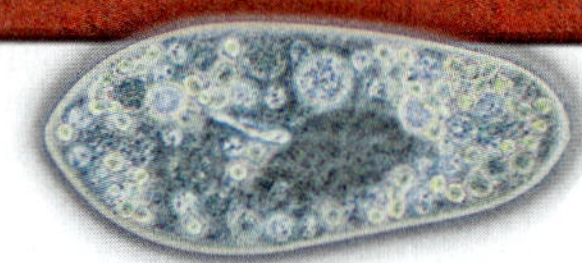

What are the functions of a paramecium's gullet and food vacuoles?

Materials paramecium culture, 2 dropper pipettes, microscope, microscope slide, coverslip, *Chlorella* (green alga) culture, toothpick, carmine dye

Procedure 

1. Use separate dropper pipettes to place a drop of paramecium culture and a drop of *Chlorella* culture next to each other on a microscope slide.
2. Use a toothpick to transfer a few granules of carmine dye to the drops on the slide. Add a coverslip so that the two drops mix.
3. Place the slide on the stage of a microscope. Use the low-power objective to locate several paramecia.
4. Use the high-power objective to observe the contents and behavior of the paramecia.

Analyze and Conclude

1. **Observing** Where did the *Chlorella* cells and carmine dye granules accumulate?
2. **Inferring** How do you think this accumulation of cells and dye granules occurs?
3. **Formulating Hypotheses** What process in the paramecia do you think resulted in this change?

Other Protistan Diseases Zooflagellates of the genus *Trypanosoma* cause African sleeping sickness. The trypanosomes that cause this disease are spread from person to person by the bite of the tsetse fly. Trypanosomes destroy blood cells and infect other tissues in the body. Symptoms of infection include fever, chills, and rashes. Trypanosomes also infect nerve cells. Severe damage to the nervous system causes some individuals to lose consciousness, lapsing into a deep and sometimes fatal sleep from which the disease gets its name. The control of the tsetse fly and the protist pathogens that it spreads is a major goal of health workers in Africa.

In certain regions of the world, many people are infected with species of *Entamoeba.*The parasitic protist *Entamoeba* causes a disease known as amebic dysentery. The parasitic amoebas that cause this disease live in the intestines, where they absorb food from the host. They also attack the wall of the intestine itself, destroying parts of it in the process and causing severe bleeding. These amoebas are passed out of the body in feces. In places where sanitation is poor, the amoebas may then find their way into supplies of food and water. In some areas of the world, amebic dysentery is a major health problem, weakening the human population and contributing to the spread of other diseases.

Amebic dysentery is common in areas with poor sanitation, but even crystal-clear streams may be contaminated with the flagellated pathogen *Giardia*. *Giardia* produces tough, microscopic cysts that can be killed only by boiling water thoroughly or by adding iodine to the water. Infection by *Giardia* can cause severe diarrhea and digestive system problems.

What is one method for controlling amebic dysentery?

FACTS AND FIGURES

Trypanosomes in disguise

African sleeping sickness is one of the worst infectious diseases known, and it has had a devastating effect across central Africa. About 45,000 new cases of the disease are diagnosed each year, and without treatment it is almost always fatal. There is no good treatment for the disease because the protist that causes it, *Trypanosoma,* has a remarkable ability to thwart the human immune system. Normally, when a pathogen invades the body, the immune system makes antibodies that can destroy the invader and end the infection. When trypanosomes infect a person, the immune system produces antibodies that destroy almost all of the invading cells. But about 1 percent of the trypanosomes react through changes in the proteins on the surfaces of their cells, and the antibodies made to destroy trypanosomes no longer recognize the cells as enemies.

(magnification: 10×)

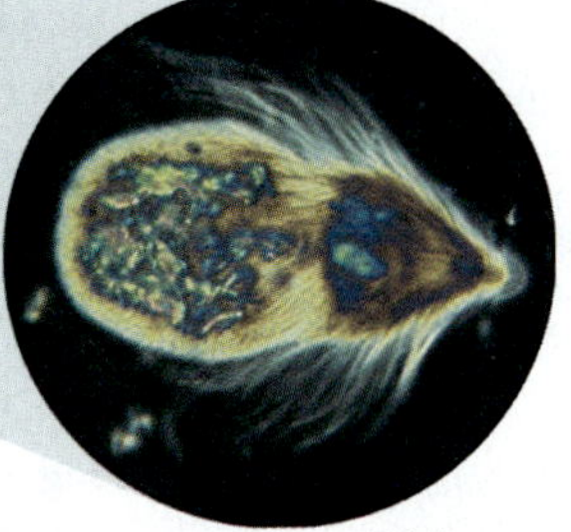

(magnification: about 250×)

Trichonympha

Figure 20–8 *Trichonympha* (below), a wood-digesting protist, lives in the digestive systems of insects such as a termite (left). Digestive enzymes produced by the protist break down the particles of wood, which you can see inside the protist's body. **Predicting** ***What would happen to a termite if its* Trichonympha *colony died?***

Ecology of Animal-like Protists

Many animal-like protists play essential roles in the living world. Some live symbiotically within other organisms. Others recycle nutrients by breaking down dead organic matter. Many animal-like protists live in seas and lakes, where they are eaten by tiny animals, which in turn serve as food for larger animals.

Some animal-like protists are beneficial to other organisms. *Trichonympha,* shown in **Figure 20–8,** is a zooflagellate that lives within the digestive systems of termites. This protist makes it possible for the termites to eat wood. Termites do not have enzymes to break down the cellulose in wood. (Incidentally, neither do humans, so it does us little good to nibble on a piece of wood.) How, then, does a termite digest cellulose? In a sense, it doesn't. *Trichonympha* does.

Trichonympha and other organisms in the termite's gut manufacture cellulase. Cellulase is an enzyme that breaks the chemical bonds in cellulose and makes it possible for termites to digest wood. Thus, with the help of their protist partners, termites can munch away, busily digesting all the wood they can eat.

20–2 Section Assessment

1. **Key Concept** What are the four major phyla of animal-like protists? How do members of each of these groups move?
2. **Key Concept** What animal-like protists cause disease?
3. How does a macronucleus differ in function from a micronucleus?
4. Describe the role of animal-like protists in the environment.
5. **Critical Thinking Comparing and Contrasting** Compare animal-like protists that have flagella to those that have cilia.
6. **Critical Thinking Making Judgments** Summarize how *Plasmodium* can cause a major disruption in the equilibrium of a human population.

Focus on the BIG Idea

Information and Heredity
Compare asexual and sexual processes in paramecia. Include the terms *mitosis* and *meiosis* in your answer. You may wish to refer back to Chapters 10 and 11 to review mitosis and meiosis.

20–2 Section Assessment

1. Zooflagellates swim with flagella; sarcodines move by extensions of their cytoplasm; ciliates move by means of cilia; and sporozoans do not move at all.
2. *Plasmodium* causes malaria; *Trypanosoma* causes African sleeping sickness; *Entamoeba* causes amebic dysentery; and *Giardia* can cause diarrhea and digestive problems.
3. A macronucleus contains multiple copies of most of the genes that the cell needs; a micronucleus contains a copy of all the genes.
4. Some live symbiotically. Others recycle nutrients by breaking down dead matter. Many live in seas and lakes, where they are eaten.
5. Zooflagellates have flagella; some live within other organisms. Ciliates have cilia; most are free living.
6. Students should describe the effects of the disease malaria, caused by *Plasmodium.*

Ecology of Animal-like Protists

Demonstration

Trichonympha lives in the gut of the termite. It is relatively easy to make a squash slide of a termite. Pull the head off the termite, bringing the intestinal tract with it. Squash the digestive tract in a drop of distilled water, and look for the movement of the protists. Once you have located the protists, either project them on a screen or allow students to look into the microscope. L2

3 ASSESS

Evaluate Understanding

Ask students to write a paragraph that compares an amoeba to a paramecium. In this comparison, students should emphasize differences in the way the two protists move and feed.

Reteach

Have students make a concept map about animal-like protists. Ask that this concept map include information about the four phyla of animal-like protists, the means of movement of members of each phyla, and examples of each phylum.

Focus on the BIG Idea

Students should define the terms *mitosis* and *meiosis*. Then, they should explain that under most conditions, paramecia reproduce by mitosis and cytokinesis. Under certain conditions, paramecia engage in conjugation, which is not a form of reproduction but is a sexual process because it uses meiosis.

Interactive Textbook

If your class subscribes to the iText, use it to review the Key Concepts in Section 20–2.

Answers to . . .

CHECKPOINT *Improve sanitation*

Figure 20–8 *The termite would also die because of its inability to break down cellulose for food.*

Section 20–3

1 FOCUS

Objectives

20.3.1 ***Describe*** the function of chlorophyll and accessory pigments in algae.

20.3.2 ***Describe*** the major phyla of unicellular algae.

20.3.3 ***Summarize*** the ecological roles of unicellular algae.

Guide for Reading

Vocabulary Preview

Have students preview the Vocabulary terms by skimming the section for the highlighted, boldface terms and writing down their definitions.

Reading Strategy

Point out that in several of the sections, the phrases or sentences students should write after each heading would be the Key Concepts, which are in boldface type.

2 INSTRUCT

Chlorophyll and Accessory Pigments

Demonstration

Before class, under a vent hood, use a water bath to boil some samples of green, brown, and red algae in separate beakers of alcohol to dissolve their pigments. Take three disks of filter paper large enough to cover the tops of the beakers, and in each, cut two parallel slits 0.5 cm apart. Bend each paper strip so that it extends into the liquid and acts as a wick. Within a class period, the streaks of the different pigments can be seen. Have students observe and compare the pigments on the filter paper. Then, ask: **What pigment(s) seem to be present in every type of alga?** *(Chlorophylls)* **Why aren't all algae green?** *(The other pigments—the accessory pigments—mask the color of the chlorophyll.)* **Why do algae have pigments other than chlorophyll?** *(The accessory pigments are capable of absorbing wavelengths of light that chlorophyll cannot, making photosynthesis more efficient.)* L2

20–3 Plantlike Protists: Unicellular Algae

Guide for Reading

Key Concepts

- What is the function of chlorophyll and accessory pigments in algae?
- What are the distinguishing features of the major phyla of unicellular algae?

Vocabulary

accessory pigment
eyespot
pellicle
phytoplankton

Reading Strategy: Summarizing As you read, make a list of the types of unicellular algae. Write a sentence about each type.

Many protists contain the green pigment chlorophyll and carry out photosynthesis. Many of these organisms are highly motile, or able to move about freely. Despite this, the fact that they perform photosynthesis is so important that we group these protists in a separate category, the plantlike protists. Plantlike protists are commonly called "algae."

Some scientists place those algae that are more closely related to plants in the kingdom Plantae. In this textbook, we will consider all forms of algae, including those most closely related to plants, to be protists. There are seven major phyla of algae classified according to a variety of cellular characteristics. The first four phyla, which contain unicellular organisms, are discussed in this section. These four phyla are the euglenophytes, the chrysophytes, the diatoms, and the dinoflagellates. The last three phyla include many multicellular organisms and will be discussed in the next section.

Chlorophyll and Accessory Pigments

One of the key traits used to classify algae is the type of photosynthetic pigments they contain. As you will remember, light is necessary for photosynthesis, and it is chlorophyll and the accessory pigments that trap the energy of sunlight.

Life in deep water poses a major difficulty for algae—a shortage of light. As sunlight passes through water, much of the light's energy is absorbed by the water. In particular, seawater absorbs large amounts of the red and violet wavelengths. Thus, light becomes dimmer and bluer, in deeper water. Because chlorophyll *a* is most efficient at capturing red and violet light, the dim blue light that penetrates into deep water contains very little light energy that chlorophyll *a* can use.

In adapting to conditions of limited light, various groups of algae have evolved different forms of chlorophyll. Each form of chlorophyll—chlorophyll *a*, chlorophyll *b*, and chlorophyll *c*—absorbs different wavelengths of light. The result of this evolution is that algae can use more of the energy of sunlight than just the red and violet wavelengths.

Many algae also have compounds called **accessory pigments** that absorb light at different wavelengths than chlorophyll. Accessory pigments pass the energy they absorb to the algae's photosynthetic machinery. **Chlorophyll and accessory pigments allow algae to harvest and use the energy from sunlight.** Because accessory pigments reflect different wavelengths of light than chlorophyll, they give algae a wide range of colors.

▼ **Figure 20–9 Chlorophyll and other pigments allow algae to collect and use energy from sunlight.** These green algae of the species *Acetabularia calyculus* live on the roots of mangrove trees in Florida.

SECTION RESOURCES

Print:

- ***Teaching Resources,*** Lesson Plan 20–3, Adapted Section Summary 20–3, Adapted Worksheets 20–3, Section Summary 20–3, Worksheets 20–3, Section Review 20–3, Enrichment
- ***Reading and Study Workbook A,*** Section 20–3
- ***Adapted Reading and Study Workbook B,*** Section 20–3

Technology:

- ***iText,*** Section 20–3
- ***Transparencies Plus,*** Section 20–3

Euglenophytes

Members of the phylum Euglenophyta (yoo-GLEE-nuh-fyt-uh), or euglenophytes, are closely related to the animal-like flagellates. **Euglenophytes are plantlike protists that have two flagella but no cell wall.** Although euglenophytes have chloroplasts, in most other ways they are like zooflagellates.

The phylum takes its name from the genus *Euglena*. Euglenas are found in ponds and lakes throughout the world. A typical euglena, such as the one shown in **Figure 20–10,** is about 50 micrometers in length. Euglenas are excellent swimmers. Two flagella emerge from a gullet at one end of the cell, and the longer of these two flagella spins in a pattern that pulls the organism rapidly through the water. Near the gullet end of the cell is a cluster of reddish pigment known as the **eyespot,** which helps the organism find sunlight to power photosynthesis. If sunlight is not available, euglenas can also live as heterotrophs, absorbing the nutrients available in decayed organic material. Euglenas store carbohydrates in small storage bodies.

Euglenas do not have cell walls, but they do have an intricate cell membrane called a **pellicle.** The pellicle is folded into ribbonlike ridges, each ridge supported by microtubules. The pellicle is tough and flexible, letting euglenas crawl through mud when there is not enough water for them to swim. Euglenas reproduce asexually by binary fission.

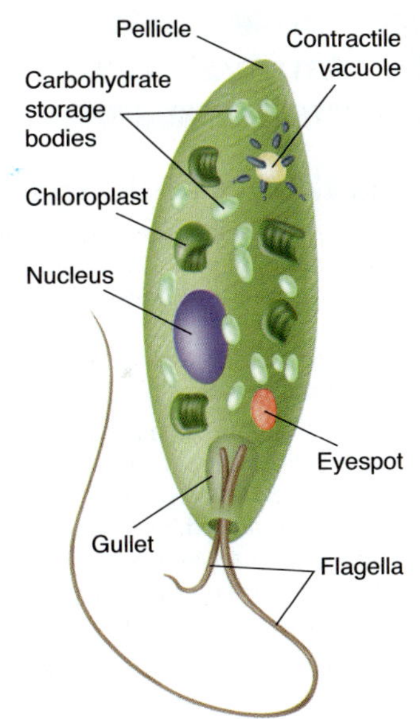

▲ **Figure 20–10 Euglenophytes are plantlike protists that have two flagella but no cell wall.** The green structures inside the euglena shown are chloroplasts, which allow the organism to carry on photosynthesis. Like paramecia, euglenas expel excess water through a contractile vacuole.

Chrysophytes

The phylum Chrysophyta (KRIS-oh-fyt-uh) includes the yellow-green algae and the golden-brown algae. The chloroplasts of these organisms contain bright yellow pigments that give the phylum its name. Chrysophyta means "golden plants." **Members of the phylum Chrysophyta are a diverse group of plantlike protists that have gold-colored chloroplasts.**

The cell walls of some chrysophytes contain the carbohydrate pectin rather than cellulose, and others contain both pectin and cellulose. Chrysophytes generally store food in the form of oil rather than starch. They reproduce both asexually and sexually. Most are solitary, but some form threadlike colonies.

Diatoms

Members of the phylum Bacillariophyta (buh-sil-LAHR-ee-oh-fyt-uh), or diatoms, are among the most abundant and beautiful organisms on Earth. **Diatoms produce thin, delicate cell walls rich in silicon (Si)—the main component of glass.** These walls are shaped like the two sides of a petri dish or flat pillbox, with one side fitted snugly into the other. The cell walls have fine lines and patterns that almost seem to be etched into their glasslike brilliance, as shown in **Figure 20–11.**

▼ **Figure 20–11 Tiny jewellike diatoms such as this centric diatom have cell walls rich in silicon.**

(magnification: 2200×)

CHECKPOINT *How are diatoms and glass alike?*

Section 20-3

Euglenophytes

Build Science Skills

Observing Provide students with a prepared slide of a euglena. Ask them to use a microscope to observe the slide and make a labeled drawing of what they see. Point out that students should use the labeled drawing in Figure 20–10 to help them find the structures of a euglena. L2 L3

Chrysophytes

Make Connections

Chemistry Ask students: **What is unusual about the way chrysophytes store food?** *(They generally store food in the form of oils rather than starch.)* **How do the energy-storing abilities of oils compare to those of starch?** *(Oils, which are lipids, can store more than twice as much energy per gram as starches, which are carbohydrates.)* L2

Diatoms

Build Science Skills

Observing Ask students how they think they could collect diatoms to observe. Suggest that they look for brownish-yellow, crusty coatings on rocks, twigs, or shells in shallow ocean, lake, or pond water. Have students follow these steps to collect and observe diatoms:

1. Place a coated rock, twig, or shell and some of the water in a jar.
2. In the lab, drain off most of the water, and then float a clean glass coverslip in the remaining water. If left for 1–2 days, diatoms will attach to the coverslip.
3. Scrape the coverslip with a scalpel, spread the material on a slide, and observe with a microscope.

Have students make drawings and try to identify the diatoms they observe. L2 L3

ESL SUPPORT FOR ENGLISH LANGUAGE LEARNERS

Vocabulary: Science Glossary

Beginning Write the following Vocabulary terms on the board: *eyespot* and *pellicle*. Say each term aloud, and have students repeat it after you. Help students identify these structures in Figure 20–10. Then, distribute unlabeled copies of Figure 20–10. Have students write the two terms as labels. Finally, students can write definitions of each term in their science glossary and paste their labeled copies of the illustration next to the definition. L1

Intermediate Students should complete the beginning-level activity. Working with an English-proficient student, they can extend the activity by writing two complete sentences, one using each of the Vocabulary terms. Then, to give students an opportunity to practice pronunciation, ask for individuals to volunteer to read their sentences aloud. L2

Answers to . . .

CHECKPOINT *The cell walls of diatoms are rich in silicon, which is the main component of glass.*

20–3 (continued)

Dinoflagellates

Use Visuals

Figure 20–12 Have students examine the figure and read the caption. Then, ask: **Which protist phylum includes the dinoflagellates?** *(Pyrrophyta)* **What is a luminescent organism?** *(An organism that produces light)* **Which group of animallike protists are dinoflagellates most like? Explain why.** *(They are most like the zooflagellates, because both groups of protists use flagella for movement.)* L1 L2

Ecology of Unicellular Algae

Analyzing Data

 8IIE 9.c

Fertilizer in runoff from agricultural fields as well as from lawns in suburban areas can cause algal blooms in lakes and other bodies of water. The experiment described in this Analyzing Data is typical of those investigating such pollution problems. L2

Answers

1. The responding variable in the students' experiment is the amount of undiluted liquid plant fertilizer added to a container of pond water.
2. The container to which no fertilizer was added serves as the control.
3. The algae grew the most in the container in which 2 mL of fertilizer were added.
4. Students should draw the conclusion that fertilizers increase the growth of algae.

Analyzing Data

Fertilizers and Algae

The growth of algae in bodies of water is affected by the addition of plant fertilizers—a pollutant. A group of students collected three large, clear containers of pond water. They used a turbidity meter to measure the cloudiness of the water. The cloudiness, or turbidity, is a rough indicator of the amount of algae present.

The students did not add anything to the first container. To the second container, they added 1 mL of undiluted liquid plant fertilizer. To the third container, they added 2 mL of fertilizer. They then left the containers in a window for 1 week and measured the turbidity again on the eighth day. Their data are summarized in the table.

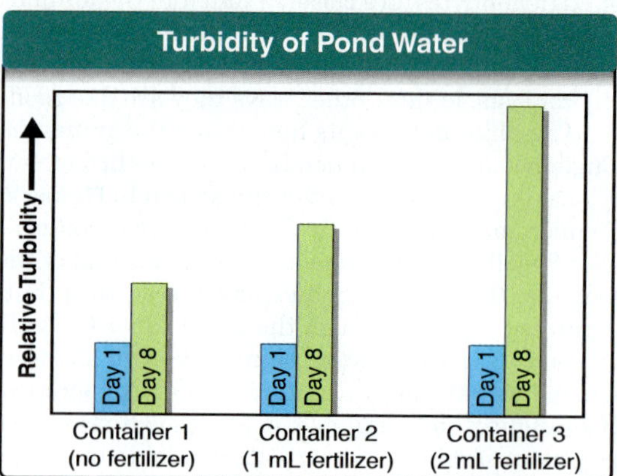

1. **Controlling Variables** What is the responding variable in the students' experiment?
2. **Designing Experiments** What is the role of the first container of water, to which no fertilizer was added?
3. **Using Tables and Graphs** In which container did the algae grow the most?
4. **Drawing Conclusions** What can you conclude about the effect of fertilizers on the growth of algae?

 8IIE 9.c

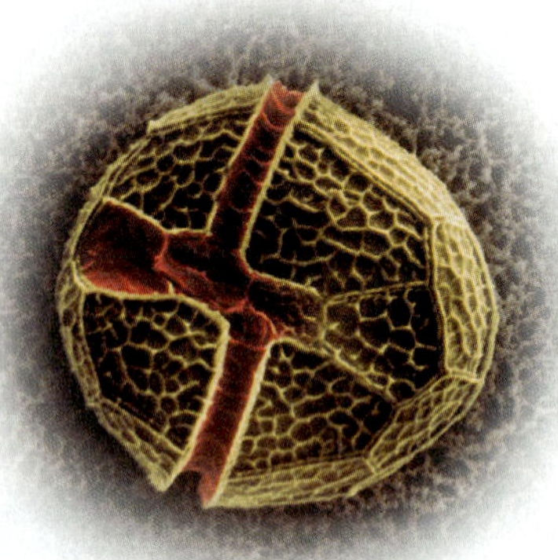

(magnification: 1280×)

▲ **Figure 20–12 Some dinoflagellates are photosynthetic, whereas others are heterotrophs.** The paired flagella of a dinoflagellate lie in grooves around its circumference, shown here in red. The flagella propel the organism, spinning, through the water.

Dinoflagellates

Dinoflagellates are members of the phylum Pyrrophyta (PIR-oh-fyt-uh). **About half of the dinoflagellates are photosynthetic; the other half live as heterotrophs.** Dinoflagellates generally have two flagella, and these often wrap around the organism in grooves between two thick plates of cellulose that protect the cell, as shown in **Figure 20–12.** Most dinoflagellates reproduce asexually by binary fission.

Many dinoflagellate species are luminescent, and when agitated by sudden movement in the water, give off light. Some areas of the ocean are so filled with dinoflagellates that the movement of a boat's hull will cause the dark water to shimmer with a ghostly blue light. This luminescent property gives the phylum its name, *Pyrrophyta*, which means "fire plants."

Ecology of Unicellular Algae

Plantlike protists are common in both fresh and salt water, and thus are an important part of freshwater and marine ecosystems. A few species of algae, however, can cause serious problems.

Plantlike protists play a major ecological role on Earth. They are important organisms whose position at the base of the food chain makes much of the diversity of aquatic life possible. They make up a considerable part of the phytoplankton.

FACTS AND FIGURES

The base of the ocean's food web

Oceans cover about three fourths of Earth. In the deep ocean, relatively few species live far below a few meters. But much life can be found at and near the ocean's surface in a collection of floating organisms known as plankton. In fact, most of Earth's biomass can be found drifting with ocean currents. The zooplankton include various protozoa, larvae and eggs, and tiny invertebrates. The phytoplankton, the photosynthesizing portion of the plankton, consists of plantlike algae, including dinoflagellates, diatoms, and many other forms. These producers capture the energy of sunlight and, in so doing, provide the basis of the food web in the marine ecosystem. The zooplankton depend on the phytoplankton for food, and the other organisms in the sea gain their sustenance from the zooplankton.

Phytoplankton (fyt-oh-PLANK-tun) constitute the population of small, photosynthetic organisms found near the surface of the ocean. About half of the photosynthesis that occurs on Earth is carried out by phytoplankton, which provide a direct source of nourishment for organisms as diverse as shrimp and whales. Even such land animals as humans get nourishment indirectly from phytoplankton. When you eat tuna fish, you are eating fish that fed on smaller fish that fed on still smaller animals that fed on plantlike protists.

Algal Blooms Many protists grow rapidly in regions where sewage is discharged. These protists play a vital role in recycling sewage and other waste materials. When the amount of waste is excessive, however, populations of euglenophytes and other algae may grow into enormous masses known as blooms. These algal blooms deplete the water of nutrients, and the cells die in great numbers. The decomposition of these dead algae can rob water of its oxygen, choking its resident fish and invertebrate life. As a result, these microorganisms disrupt the equilibrium of the aquatic ecosystem.

Great blooms of the dinoflagellates *Gonyaulax* and *Karenia* have occurred in recent years on the east coast of the United States, although scientists are not sure of the reason. These blooms, such as the one shown in **Figure 20–13,** are known as "red tides." These species produce a potentially dangerous toxin. Filter-feeding shellfish such as clams can trap *Gonyaulax* and *Karenia* for food and become filled with the toxin. Eating shellfish from water infected with red tide can cause serious illness, paralysis, and even death in humans and fish.

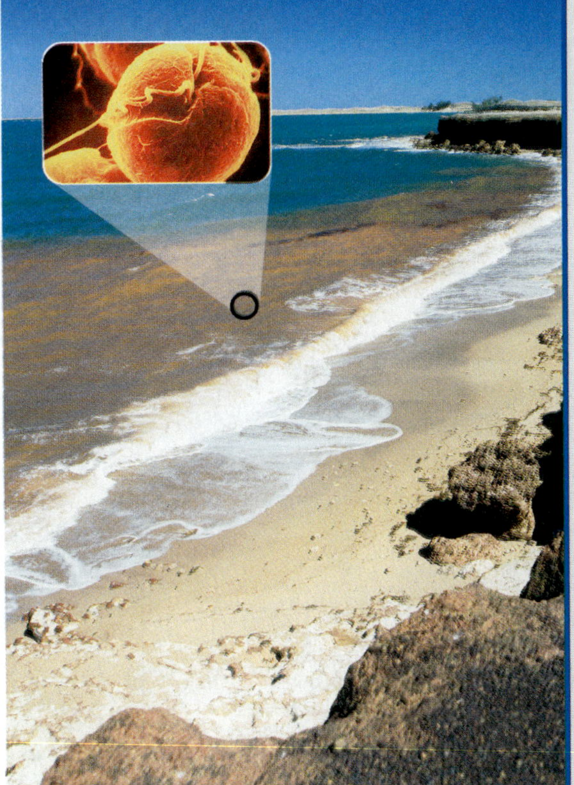

Figure 20–13 Blooms of the dinoflagellate *Karenia brevis* (inset) can produce red tides. *Karenia* contains a toxin that becomes concentrated in the tissue of filter feeders such as clams and oysters. **Inferring** *How can red tides be harmful to humans?*

20–3 Section Assessment

1. **Key Concept** What do chlorophyll and accessory pigments do in algae?
2. **Key Concept** What are the four phyla of unicellular plantlike protists?
3. How do most unicellular algae get food? How does this differ from the way most animal-like protists get food?
4. What is the role of unicellular algae in the environment?
5. **Critical Thinking Problem Solving** Identify two ways to reduce the problem of algal blooms in fresh water.
6. **Critical Thinking Problem Solving** Summarize the role of a red tide in disrupting an ecosystem.

Writing in Science

Write a News Broadcast
Use the library or the Internet to investigate the number of algal blooms off the California coast in the last five years. Be sure to note the causes, the types of protists identified, and the effects on wildlife and people. Present your findings to the class as an unbiased investigative report.

20–3 Section Assessment

1. They allow algae to harvest and use the energy from sunlight.
2. Euglenophyta, Pyrrophyta, Chrysophyta, Bacillariophyta
3. Most unicellular algae use the energy of sunlight to produce food. Animal-like protists get food by absorbing, capturing, or trapping it.
4. They are at the base of aquatic food chains, and they make up a considerable part of the phytoplankton. Unicellular algae also form symbiotic relationships with other organisms.
5. Sample answer: Eliminate sewage discharge and reduce the amount of plant fertilizers.
6. The dinoflagellates that cause a red tide produce a potentially dangerous toxin. Filter-feeding shellfish become filled with the toxin, and fish that eat those shellfish can become seriously ill.

Use Visuals

Figure 20–13 After students have studied the photo and read the caption, ask: **What are red tides?** *(Red tides are great blooms of the dinoflagellates* Gonyaulax *and* Karenia.*)* **How might people who live in the area of a red tide be harmed?** *(Filter-feeding shellfish trap the dinoflagellates for food and become filled with the toxin. When people eat the shellfish, they can become seriously ill.)* L2

3 ASSESS

Evaluate Understanding

Call on students to name the phylum, describe the characteristics, and give examples for each of the groups of plantlike protists discussed: the euglenophytes, the dinoflagellates, the chrysophytes, and the diatoms.

Reteach

Have students compare the labeled illustration of a euglena in Figure 20–10 with that of a paramecium in Figure 20–5. Help students see the similarities and differences between these two organisms.

Writing in Science

Encourage students to visit the science news sections of newspaper Web sites and organizations like the National Marine Fisheries Service. California's Monterey area is a good example of an area affected by algal blooms. All students should include where the blooms occurred and the species as well as its effect on other marine wildlife, such as shellfish. Students' broadcasts should include acknowledgment of any sources.

If your class subscribes to the iText, use it to review the Key Concepts in Section 20–3.

Answer to . . .

Figure 20–13 *Toxins from the algae that produce red tides can get into clams and cause illness, paralysis, and death in humans who eat the clams.*

Section 20–4

 7 2.a

1 FOCUS

Objectives

20.4.1 ***Describe*** the major phyla of multicellular algae.

20.4.2 ***Explain*** how multicellular algae reproduce.

20.4.3 ***Identify*** some human uses of algae.

Guide for Reading

Vocabulary Preview

Pronounce each of the Vocabulary words out loud, and ask students to pronounce the terms back in unison.

Reading Strategy

Explain that an outline should include several levels of entries, with each of the entries providing support for the level above. To make an outline of this section, students should use the blue headings as their first level of entries. The green headings, such as those under Green Algae, should form the second level of entries. Third and fourth levels should include supporting details, concepts, and examples.

2 INSTRUCT

Red Algae

Make Connections

Physics Some students may not know that the color of an object depends on which colors of the visible spectrum of light are absorbed and which are reflected. Point to a pair of blue pants and ask students: **Are these pants blue because they absorb blue light or reflect blue light?** *(The pants are blue because they reflect blue light.)* Point out that the pants not only reflect blue light but also absorb the other colors in the visible light spectrum. Explain that the different pigments in the different kinds of algae absorb some colors and reflect others. The pigments in red algae, for example, reflect red light and absorb other colors. L1 L2

20–4 Plantlike Protists: Red, Brown, and Green Algae

 7 2.a. Students know the differences between the life cycles and reproduction methods of sexual and asexual organisms.

Guide for Reading

Key Concepts

- What are the distinguishing features of the major phyla of multicellular algae?
- How do multicellular algae reproduce?

Vocabulary

phycobilin
filament
alternation of generations
gametophyte
spore
sporophyte

Reading Strategy: Outlining Before you read, use the blue and the green headings to make an outline about multicellular algae. As you read, add phrases or a sentence after each heading to provide key information.

Have you ever taken a walk along a rocky beach at low tide? As the water recedes, in many places it reveals a damp forest of green and brown "plants" clinging to the rocks. These seaweeds have the size, color, and appearance of plants, but they are not plants. They are actually algae. Unlike the algae in the previous section, most of these algae are multicellular, like plants. They also have reproductive cycles that are sometimes very similar to those of plants. Many of them have cell walls and photosynthetic pigments that are identical to those of plants. Many of these algae also possess highly specialized tissues.

The three phyla of algae that are largely multicellular are commonly known as red algae, brown algae, and green algae. The most important differences among these phyla involve their photosynthetic pigments.

Red Algae

Red algae are members of the phylum Rhodophyta (roh-duh-FYT-uh), meaning "red plants." **Red algae are able to live at great depths due to their efficiency in harvesting light energy. Red algae contain chlorophyll *a* and reddish accessory pigments called phycobilins.** **Phycobilins** (fy-koh-BIL-inz) are especially good at absorbing blue light, enabling red algae to live deeper in the ocean than many other photosynthetic algae. Many red algae are actually green, purple, or reddish black, depending upon the other pigments they contain. Red algae are an important group of marine algae that can be found in waters from the polar regions to the tropics. The highly efficient light-harvesting pigments in these algae enable them to grow anywhere from the ocean's surface to depths of up to 260 meters.

Most species of red algae are multicellular, and all species have complex life cycles. Red algae lack flagella and centrioles. Red algae also play an important role in the formation of coral reefs, as shown in **Figure 20–14.** These microorganisms help to maintain the equilibrium of the coral ecosystem, providing nutrients from photosynthesis that nourish coral animals. Coralline red algae provide much of the calcium carbonate that helps to stabilize the growing coral reef.

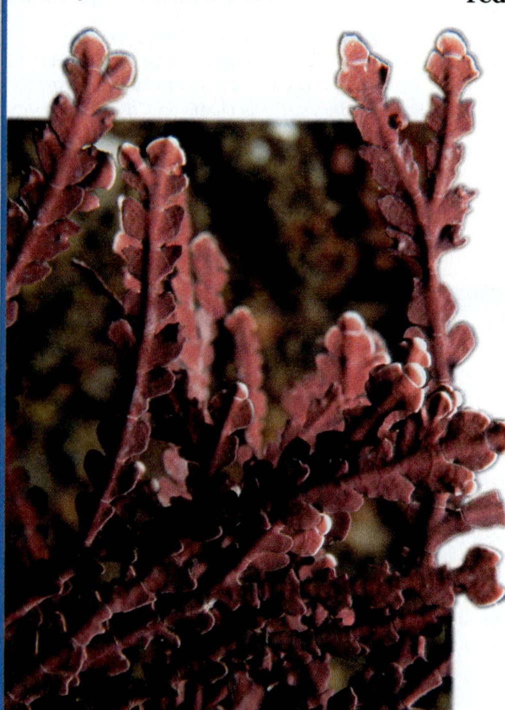

Figure 20–14 **Red algae contain chlorophyll *a* and reddish pigments called phycobilins.** Coralline algae, a type of red alga, collect calcium carbonate in their cell walls, giving them a tough, stony texture.

SECTION RESOURCES

Print:

- ***Teaching Resources,*** Lesson Plan 20–4, Adapted Section Summary 20–4, Adapted Worksheets 20–4, Section Summary 20–4, Worksheets 20–4, Section Review 20–4
- ***Reading and Study Workbook A,*** Section 20–4
- ***Adapted Reading and Study Workbook B,*** Section 20–4

Technology:

- ***iText,*** Section 20–4
- ***Transparencies Plus,*** Section 20–4

Brown Algae

Brown algae belong to the phylum Phaeophyta (fay-uh-FYT-uh), meaning "dusky plants." **Brown algae contain chlorophyll *a* and *c*, as well as a brown accessory pigment, fucoxanthin.** The combination of fucoxanthin (fyoo-koh-ZAN-thin) and chlorophyll *c* gives most of these algae a dark, yellow-brown color. Brown algae are the largest and most complex of the algae. All brown algae are multicellular and most are marine, commonly found in cool, shallow coastal waters of temperate or arctic areas.

The largest known alga is giant kelp, a brown alga that can grow to more than 60 meters in length. Another brown alga called *Sargassum* forms huge floating mats many kilometers long in an area of the Atlantic Ocean near Bermuda known as the Sargasso Sea. Bunches of *Sargassum* often drift on currents to beaches in the Caribbean and southern United States.

One of the most common brown alga is *Fucus*, or rockweed, found along the rocky coast of the eastern United States. Each *Fucus* alga has a holdfast, a structure that attaches the alga to the bottom. The body of the alga consists of flattened stemlike structures called stipes, leaflike structures called blades, and gas-filled swellings called bladders, which float and keep the alga upright in the water. **Figure 20–15** shows the structures of a brown alga.

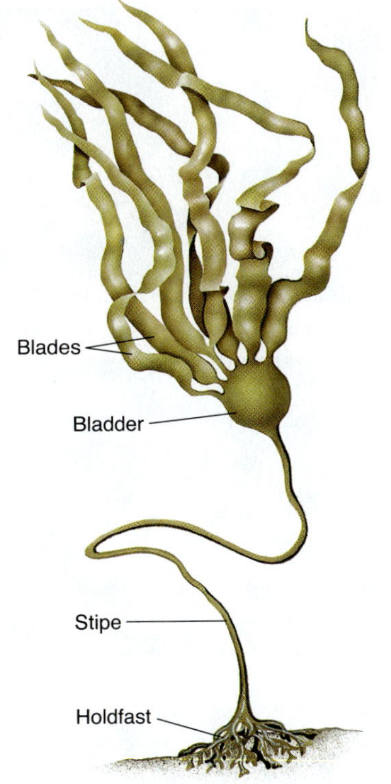

▲ **Figure 20–15** **Brown algae contain chlorophyll *a* and *c*, plus fucoxanthin, a brown pigment.**

CHECKPOINT *What does a holdfast do?*

Green Algae

Green algae are members of the phylum Chlorophyta (klawr-uh-FYT-uh), which means "green plants" in Greek. **Green algae share many characteristics with plants, including their photosynthetic pigments and cell wall composition.** Green algae have cellulose in their cell walls, contain chlorophyll *a* and *b*, and store food in the form of starch, just like land plants. One stage in the life cycle of mosses—small land plants you will learn about in the next unit—looks remarkably like a tangled mass of green algae strands. All these characteristics lead scientists to hypothesize that the ancestors of modern land plants looked a lot like certain species of living green algae. Unfortunately, algae rarely form fossils, so there is no single specific fossil that scientists can call an ancestor of both living algae and mosses. However, scientists think that mosses and green algae shared such a common algalike ancestor millions of years ago.

Green algae are found in fresh and salt water, and even in moist areas on land. Many species live most of their lives as single cells. Others form colonies, groups of similar cells that are joined together but show few specialized structures. A few green algae are multicellular and have well-developed specialized structures.

For: Links on algae
Visit: www.SciLinks.org
Web Code: cbn-6204

Brown Algae

Demonstration

Display a large map of North America or the Western Hemisphere for students to see. Point out the area of ocean called the Sargasso Sea, which is southeast of Bermuda. Explain that some brown algae, such as kelp, have a holdfast that attaches the seaweed to rocks or other surfaces. The *Sargassum* in the Sargasso Sea, by contrast, has no holdfast. Instead, this form of brown algae has gas-filled bladders—floats—at the base of the seaweed's blades that keep the algae afloat in the Sargasso Sea. Explain that some students may have seen this brown alga on the Florida shores of the Gulf of Mexico. After tropical storms, large quantities of *Sargassum* are washed up along the beaches there. L2

Green Algae

Build Science Skills

Classifying Before students read about green algae, divide the class into small groups and give each group several samples to observe, including a sample of "sea lettuce" or another kind of multicellular green alga, a fern, a mushroom, a flowering plant, and some kind of moss. Ask students to examine these organisms and speculate about the environment to which each organism is adapted. Have each group consider which of the samples could be considered a plant and which could not be. Then, have several groups present their findings to the class. Challenge groups to give reasons why they classified some organisms as plants but not others. L2

Download a worksheet on algae for students to complete, and find additional teacher support from NSTA SciLinks.

UNIVERSAL ACCESS

Inclusion/Special Needs
Emphasize that although the organisms discussed in this section have characteristics in common with plants, they are not plants. Remind students again of the definition of protists—eukaryotes that are not members of other kingdoms. L1

Less Proficient Readers
Ask students to make a concept map to organize information in the section about multicellular algae. The concept map should include the phylum names, the common names, and examples of members of each phylum. L1 L2

English Language Learners
Make sure students understand *alternation of generations.* After discussing the meaning of *generation* in this context, explain that *alternation* derives from a Latin word that means "by turns"—shifting from one thing to another and back again. The verb *alternate* is a related word. L2

Answer to . . .

CHECKPOINT *A holdfast is a structure that attaches the alga to the bottom.*

20–4 (continued)

Build Science Skills

Comparing and Contrasting Provide students with access to living cultures of different forms of green algae, such as *Chlamydomonas, Spirogyra,* and *Ulva,* and have them make slides from these cultures. (To make a slide from the *Chlamydomonas* culture, they can use a dropper pipette to place one drop of the culture on a slide and cover with a coverslip. To make a slide from the *Spirogyra* culture, they can separate a strand into a 2-centimeter segment using a dissecting needle, add a drop of water, and cover with a coverslip. To make a slide from the *Ulva* culture, they can separate a small piece of the alga from the sample, add a drop of water, and cover with a coverslip.) Ask students to observe the slides under a microscope and make labeled drawings of what they see. After students have concluded their observations, have them compare the different kinds of green algae in a class discussion. L2 L3

Reproduction in Green Algae

Address Misconceptions

The idea of alternation of generations may confuse some students. They might conclude that every other generation of an organism is radically different from the previous generation. Point out that this use of the term *generation* has a different meaning from what it might have in another context, such as the generations in a person's family. Synonyms for *generation* in this context include *phase* and *stage.* L1 L2

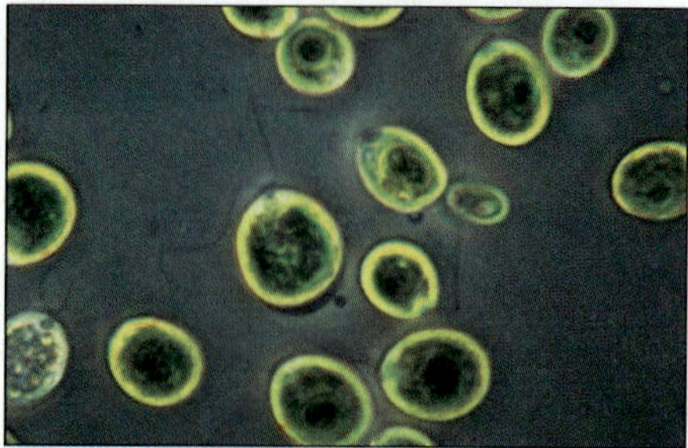

Chlamydomonas (magnification: 1000×)

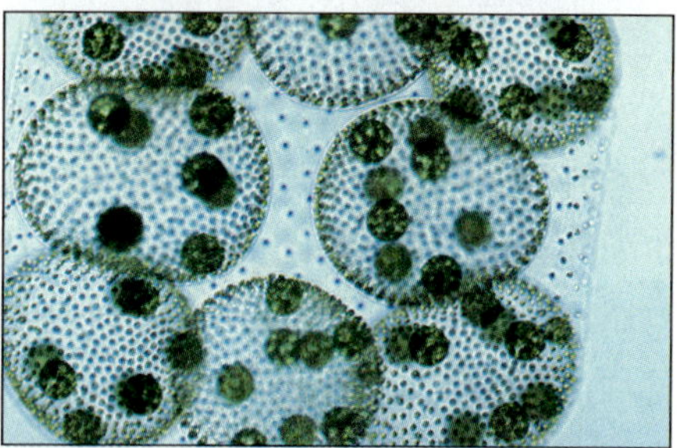

Volvox (magnification: 450×)

Ulva

Figure 20–16 Green algae have the same photosynthetic pigments and cell wall compositions as green plants. *Chlamydomonas* is a unicellular green alga that lives in ponds. Delicate spherical colonies of the green alga *Volvox* live in fresh water. New colonies can develop within existing colonies and are released when an older colony ruptures. *Ulva* is a multicellular green alga that lives along seacoasts.

Unicellular Green Algae *Chlamydomonas* (kluh-mid-uh-MOHN-uz), a typical single-celled green alga, grows in ponds, ditches, and wet soil. *Chlamydomonas* is a small egg-shaped cell with two flagella and a single large, cup-shaped chloroplast. Within the base of the chloroplast is a region that synthesizes and stores starch. *Chlamydomonas* lacks the large vacuoles found in the cells of land plants. Instead, it has two small contractile vacuoles. *Chlamydomonas* and two other green algae are shown in **Figure 20–16.**

Colonial Green Algae Several species of green algae live in multicellular colonies. The freshwater alga *Spirogyra,* shown in **Figure 20–1,** forms long threadlike colonies called **filaments,** in which the cells are stacked almost like aluminum cans placed end to end. *Volvox* colonies are more elaborate, consisting of as few as 500 to as many as 50,000 cells arranged to form hollow spheres. The cells in a *Volvox* colony are connected to one another by strands of cytoplasm, enabling them to coordinate movement. When the colony moves, cells on one side of the colony "pull" with their flagella, and the cells on the other side of the colony have to "push." Although most cells in a *Volvox* colony are identical, a few gamete-producing cells are specialized for reproduction. Because it shows some cell specialization, *Volvox* straddles the fence between colonial and multicellular life.

Multicellular Green Algae *Ulva,* or "sea lettuce," is a bright-green marine alga that is commonly found along rocky seacoasts. *Ulva* is a true multicellular organism, containing several specialized cell types. Although the body of *Ulva* is only two cells thick, it is tough enough to survive the pounding of waves on the shores where it lives. A group of cells at its base forms holdfasts that attach *Ulva* to the rocks.

Reproduction in Green Algae

The life cycles of many algae include both a diploid and a haploid generation. Recall from Chapter 11 that diploid cells have two sets of chromosomes, whereas haploid cells have a single set. Many algae switch back and forth between haploid and diploid stages during their life cycles, in a process known as **alternation of generations.** Many species also shift back and forth between sexual and asexual forms of reproduction.

Reproduction in *Chlamydomonas* The unicellular *Chlamydomonas* spends most of its life in the haploid stage. As long as its living conditions are suitable, this haploid cell reproduces asexually, producing cells called zoospores by mitosis. Reproduction by mitosis is asexual. The two haploid daughter cells produced by mitosis are genetically identical to the single haploid cell that entered mitosis.

FACTS AND FIGURES

Ancestors of land plants

It is generally believed that the chlorophytes, or green algae, are the group from which land plants evolved. Among the algae, only the chlorophytes have cellulose in their cell walls, contain chlorophylls *a* and *b,* and store their food in the form of starch, all of which are also characteristics of land plants. Because algae ordinarily do not form fossils, we do not have direct evidence of an evolutionary relationship. But one stage in the life cycle of mosses looks remarkably like a tangle of green algal filaments. Perhaps both mosses and the modern multicellular green algae descended from a common algalike ancestor.

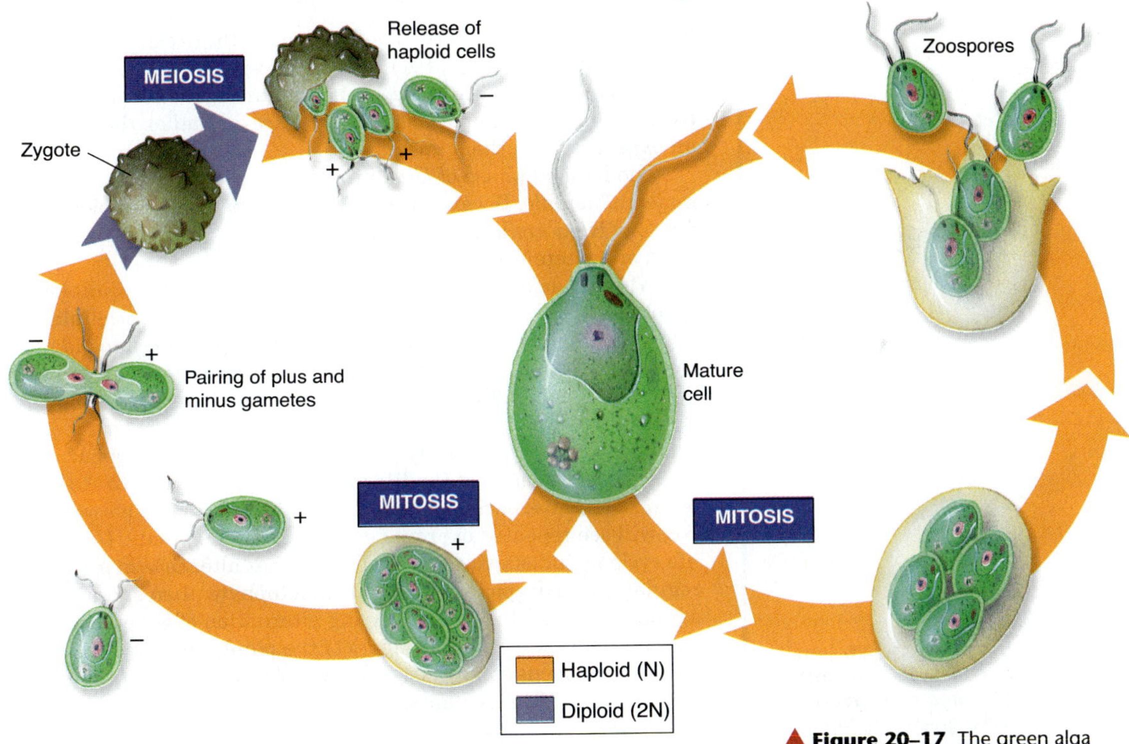

▲ **Figure 20–17** The green alga *Chlamydomonas* reproduces asexually by producing zoospores and sexually by producing zygotes, which release haploid gametes. **Interpreting Graphics** ***Which form of reproduction includes a diploid organism that can survive adverse conditions?***

If conditions become unfavorable, *Chlamydomonas* can also reproduce sexually. The life cycle of *Chlamydomonas* is shown in **Figure 20–17.** The haploid cells continue to undergo mitosis, but instead of releasing zoospores, the cells release gametes. The gametes, which look identical, are of two opposite mating types, + (plus) and − (minus). During sexual reproduction, the gametes gather in large groups. Then + and − gametes form pairs that soon move away from the group. The paired gametes join flagella and spin around in the water. Both members of the pair then shed their cell walls and fuse, forming a diploid zygote.

The zygote sinks to the bottom of the pond and grows a thick protective wall. Within this protective wall, *Chlamydomonas* can survive freezing or drying conditions that otherwise would kill it. When conditions once again become favorable, the zygote begins to grow. It divides by meiosis to produce four flagellated haploid cells. These haploid cells can swim away, mature, and reproduce asexually. Thus, during its life cycle, *Chlamydomonas* alternates between a haploid stage, in which it spends most of its life, and a brief diploid stage, represented by the zygote cell.

 ***What two types of gametes does*** **Chlamydomonas** ***produce?***

CA a

a 7 2.a

Use Visuals

Figure 20–17 To understand the life cycle of *Chlamydomonas*, students may need to review what they have learned about reproduction. Ask students: **What is the difference between asexual and sexual reproduction?** *(Asexual reproduction involves the division of a single parent cell. Sexual reproduction involves the joining of two parent cells, or gametes.)* **What is the difference between cells with a diploid number of chromosomes and cells with a haploid number?** *(Diploid cells have the full complement of chromosomes for a particular species; haploid cells have half the complement.)* **What is meant by alternation of generations?** *(Shifting back and forth between haploid and diploid stages during the life cycle)* **In the life cycle of *Chlamydomonas*, which generation, the haploid or the diploid, produces zoospores?** *(Haploid)* **When *Chlamydomonas* does produce zoospores, is it reproducing sexually or asexually?** *(Asexually)* **What does the organism release when it is reproducing sexually?** *(Plus and minus gametes)* L2

BIO INSIGHTS — FACTS AND FIGURES

Alternating phases

The basic plan of alternation of generations is a life cycle in which diploid (2N) and haploid (N) phases alternate. Use of the term *generation* can be confusing, since these are phases in one complete life cycle of an organism rather than the production of offspring. The following are generalizations that apply to an alternation of generations in any organism, from algae to vascular plants:

- Any cell of the sporophyte generation is usually diploid (2N).
- Any cell of the gametophyte generation is usually haploid (N).
- The change from sporophyte to gametophyte occurs as the result of meiosis.
- The change from gametophyte to sporophyte occurs as a result of fertilization, or the fusion of gametes.

Answers to . . .

CHECKPOINT Chlamydomonas *produces two gametes of opposite mating types, + (plus) and − (minus).*

Figure 20–17 *Sexual reproduction*

20–4 (continued)

Use Visuals

Figure 20–18 Ask students: **What is the term for the pattern by which *Ulva* reproduces?** *(Alternation of generations)* **Which generation, or phase, produces haploid spores?** *(The sporophyte generation)* **What cellular process is involved in producing these spores?** *(Meiosis)* **Which generation produces gametes?** *(The gametophyte generation)* **Does this generation undergo meiosis to produce gametes?** *(No. It is already haploid, which is how most fungi spend their life cycles.)* **What does the fusion of the gametes produce?** *(A zygote)* **What does the zygote grow to become?** *(The sporophyte generation)* L2

Reproduction in *Ulva* The life cycle of the green alga *Ulva* involves an alternation of generations in which both the diploid and haploid phases are large, multicellular organisms. In fact, the haploid and diploid phases of *Ulva* are so similar that only an expert can tell them apart!

The haploid phase of *Ulva* produces two forms of gametes—male and female. Because they produce gametes, the haploid forms of *Ulva* are known as **gametophytes** (guh-MEET-uh-fyts), or gamete-producing plants.

CA ⓐ 7 2.a

When male and female gametes fuse, they produce a diploid zygote cell, which then grows into a large, diploid multicellular *Ulva*. The diploid *Ulva* undergoes meiosis to produce haploid reproductive cells called **spores.** Each of these spores is able to grow into a new individual without fusing with another cell. Because the diploid *Ulva* produces spores, it is known as a **sporophyte** (SPOH-ruh-fyt), or spore-producing organism.

Take a close look at the life cycle of *Ulva* in **Figure 20–18,** because the alternation of generations it displays is a pattern you will see repeated over and over again in the plants. *Ulva*'s life cycle includes two separate phases that alternate in a regular pattern: sporophyte, then gametophyte, then sporophyte again. Complex life cycles involving alternation of generations are characteristic of the members of the plant kingdom. This is one of the reasons some biologists favor classifying multicellular algae such as *Ulva* as plants.

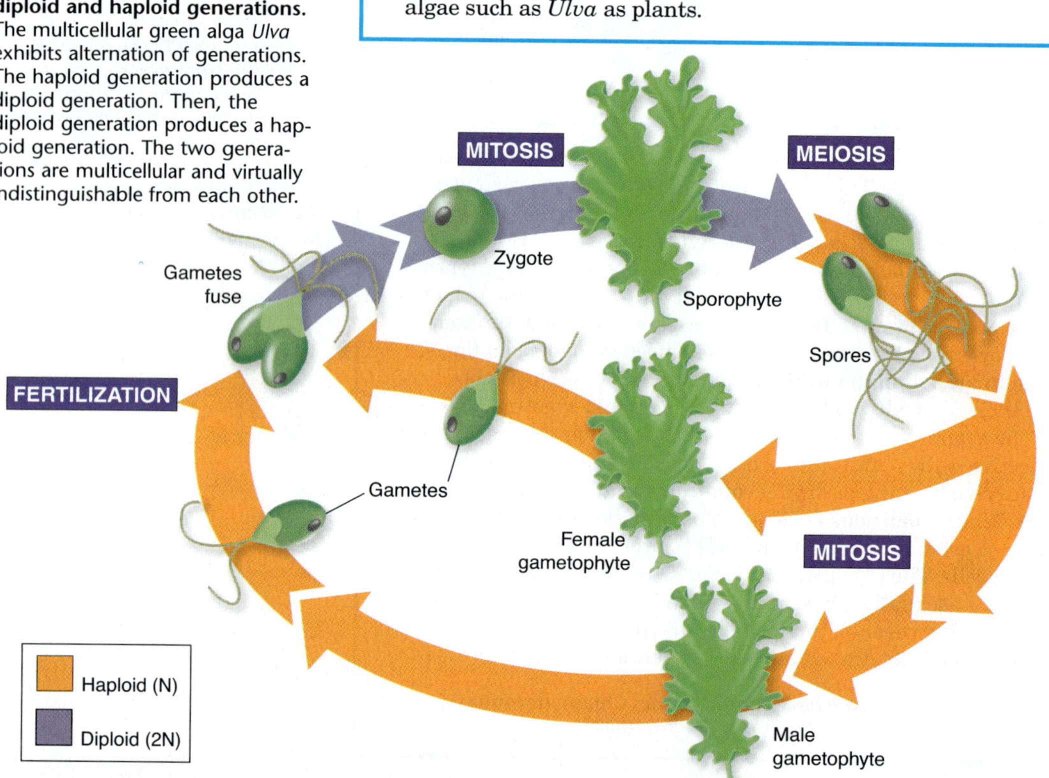

▼ **Figure 20–18** **The life cycles of most algae include both diploid and haploid generations.** The multicellular green alga *Ulva* exhibits alternation of generations. The haploid generation produces a diploid generation. Then, the diploid generation produces a haploid generation. The two generations are multicellular and virtually indistinguishable from each other.

FACTS AND FIGURES

An evolutionary link

The characteristics of the green alga *Ulva*—often called sea lettuce—demonstrate an evolutionary link between simpler green algae and more complex land plants. Although only two cells thick, *Ulva* is truly multicellular, forming such specialized structures as holdfasts. *Ulva* exhibits isomorphic alternation of generations, in which sporophytes and gametophytes are similar in shape and size.

Ecology of Algae

Algae are a major food source for life in the oceans. Algae have even been called the "grasses" of the seas, because they make up much of the base of the food chain upon which sea animals "graze." The enormous brown kelp forests off the coasts of North America are home to many animal species.

Algae produce much of Earth's oxygen through photosynthesis. Scientists calculate that about half of all the photosynthesis that occurs on Earth is performed by algae. This fact alone makes algae one of the most important groups of organisms on the entire planet.

Over the years, people have learned to use algae—and the chemicals produced by algae—in many different ways. Many species of algae are rich in vitamin C and iron. Chemicals in algae are used to treat stomach ulcers, high blood pressure, arthritis, and other health problems.

Have you ever eaten algae? Almost certainly, your answer should be yes. In Japan, the red alga *Porphyra* is grown on special marine farms. Dried *Porphyra*—called *nori* in Japanese—is dark green and paper-thin. Nori is used to wrap portions of rice, fish, and vegetables to make sushi, as shown in **Figure 20–19.** You say you've never had sushi? Well, you've probably eaten ice cream, salad dressing, pudding, or a candy bar. Other products from algae are used in pancake syrups and eggnog.

Industry has even more uses for algae. Chemicals from algae are used to make plastics, waxes, transistors, deodorants, paints, lubricants, and even artificial wood. Algae even have an important use in scientific laboratories. The compound agar, derived from certain seaweeds, thickens the nutrient mixtures scientists use to grow bacteria and other microorganisms.

▲ **Figure 20–19** People have found many different uses for algae. The red alga *Porphyra* is used as a wrapper in Japanese sushi rolls. Ice cream often contains algin, a thickener made from brown algae. **Predicting** ***How would your life be different without products made from algae?***

20–4 Section Assessment

1. **Key Concept** Describe the main features of the major phyla of multicellular algae.
2. **Key Concept** What is alternation of generations?
3. How are multicellular algae important at a global level?
4. Why can red algae live in deeper water than green algae?
5. **Critical Thinking Comparing and Contrasting** Choose a green alga and illustrate its life cycle. Identify which parts are haploid and which are diploid. Show where meiosis and mitosis occur. Illustrate which part of the life cycle involves sexual reproduction and which involves asexual reproduction.

Thinking Visually

Organizing Information
Make a poster illustrating three types of multicellular algae. Your poster should have detailed drawings or photographs of each group. Each illustration should show the correct classification and list two written characteristics of each group.

Ecology of Algae

Use Community Resources

Some seaweeds, or multicellular algae, are edible and part of the cuisine of Japan and other countries. Have students look for seaweed foods at a specialty market and report to the class about the products they found. Also encourage students interested in cooking to make an appointment to interview a chef at a local Japanese restaurant about how seaweed is used in Japanese recipes. You might ask these students to prepare a seaweed dish for the class. L2 L3

3 ASSESS

Evaluate Understanding

Ask students to make a table that contains information about the three phyla of multicellular plantlike protists. This table should include the phylum names, the common names, characteristics, and examples of each.

Reteach

Ask students to make their own drawings of the life cycle of the multicellular green alga *Ulva,* using Figure 20–18 as a model. Then, call on students to define the terms *alternation of generations, gametophyte,* and *sporophyte.*

Thinking Visually

A student's poster should show several drawings or photographs of multicellular algae, including at least one example each of red algae, brown algae, and green algae. Each illustration should be clearly labeled with the alga's phylum as well as the alga's scientific name.

20–4 Section Assessment

1. Students should describe the main features of algae in the phyla Rhodophyta, Phaeophyta, and Chlorophyta.
2. A process in which algae switch back and forth between haploid and diploid during their life cycles
3. Multicellular algae provide food and generate oxygen and are an important part of the food chain along coastal waters and in the Sargasso Sea.
4. Red algae contain the reddish accessory pigments known as phycobilins, which are especially good at absorbing blue light, which penetrates deeper, enabling red algae to live deeper in the ocean than other algae.
5. Students may choose any of the examples of green algae discussed in the section. A typical response will illustrate either *Chlamydomonas* or *Ulva* and use Figure 20–17 or 20–18 for reference.

If your class subscribes to the iText, use it to review the Key Concepts in Section 20–4.

Answer to . . .

Figure 20–19 *Many products might be different, including ice cream, salad dressing, and pudding.*

Section 20–5

7 2.a

1 FOCUS

Objectives

20.5.1 ***Compare and Contrast*** funguslike protists and fungi.

20.5.2 ***Describe*** slime molds and water molds.

20.5.3 ***Summarize*** the ecological roles of funguslike protists.

Guide for Reading

Vocabulary Preview

Call on students at random to pronounce the Vocabulary words in the order in which they appear. Correct any mispronunciations.

Reading Strategy

Before students read, have them rewrite the blue headings in the section as *how, why,* or *what* questions about funguslike protists. Then, as they read, they can write down answers to the heading questions.

2 INSTRUCT

Slime Molds

Address Misconceptions

Because of the terminology involved in the two groups of slime molds, students may infer that cellular slime molds are the rule and acellular slime molds the exception. Explain that the majority of slime mold species are acellular and form plasmodia. L2

20–5 Funguslike Protists

7 2.a. Students know the differences between the life cycles and reproduction methods of sexual and asexual organisms.

Guide for Reading

Key Concepts

- What are the similarities and differences between funguslike protists and fungi?
- What are the defining characteristics of the slime molds and water molds?

Vocabulary

cellular slime mold
acellular slime mold
fruiting body
plasmodium
hypha
zoosporangium
antheridium
oogonium

Reading Strategy: Predicting Before you read, preview the life cycles in **Figure 20–22** and **Figure 20–23.** Predict how these life cycles are similar and how they are different.

If you look closely at the debris-laden floor of a forest after several days of rain, you may see patches of what looks like brightly colored mold. Funguslike protists, such as in **Figure 20–20** and **Figure 20–21,** grow in damp, nutrient-rich environments and absorb food through their cell membranes, much like fungi. These organisms have sometimes been classified as fungi, even though their cellular structure more closely resembles that of the protists. **Like fungi, the funguslike protists are heterotrophs that absorb nutrients from dead or decaying organic matter. But unlike most true fungi, funguslike protists have centrioles. They also lack the chitin cell walls of true fungi.** The funguslike protists include the cellular slime molds, the acellular slime molds, and the water molds.

Slime Molds

Slime molds are found in places that are damp and rich in organic matter, such as the floor of a forest or a backyard compost pile. **Slime molds are funguslike protists that play key roles in recycling organic material.** At one stage of their life cycle, slime molds look just like amoebas. At other stages, they form moldlike clumps that produce spores, almost like fungi.

Two broad groups of slime molds are recognized. The individual cells of **cellular slime molds** remain distinct—separated by cell membranes—during every phase of the mold's life cycle. Slime molds that pass through a stage in which their cells fuse to form large cells with many nuclei are called **acellular slime molds.**

▼ **Figure 20–20** **Funguslike protists absorb nutrients from dead organic matter.** Slime molds like this red raspberry slime mold are often found in the damp, shaded environments preferred by many fungi.

Cellular Slime Molds Cellular slime molds belong to the phylum Acrasiomycota (ak-ruh-see-oh-my-KOH-tuh). They spend most of their lives as free-living cells that are not easily distinguishable from soil amoebas. In nutrient-rich soils, these amoeboid cells reproduce rapidly. When their food supply is exhausted, they go through a reproductive process to produce spores that can survive adverse conditions. First, they send out chemical signals that attract other cells of the same species. Within a few days, thousands of cells aggregate into a large sluglike colony that begins to function like a single organism. The colony migrates for several centimeters, then stops and produces a **fruiting body,** a slender reproductive structure that produces spores. Eventually, the spores are scattered from the fruiting body. Each spore gives rise to a single amoeba-like cell that starts the cycle all over again, as shown in **Figure 20–22.**

7 2.a

SECTION RESOURCES

Print:

- ***Laboratory Manual A,*** Chapter 20 Lab
- ***Teaching Resources,*** Lesson Plan 20–5, Adapted Section Summary 20–5, Adapted Worksheets 20–5, Section Summary 20–5, Worksheets 20–5, Section Review 20–5
- ***Reading and Study Workbook A,*** Section 20–5
- ***Adapted Reading and Study Workbook B,*** Section 20–5

Technology:

- ***iText,*** Section 20–5
- ***Transparencies Plus,*** Section 20–5

◀ **Figure 20–21** **Slime molds help recycle organic matter.** The bright yellow acellular slime mold shown here, *Fuligo septica*, is often found growing in gardens on damp, rich soil.

In many ways, these remarkable organisms challenge our understanding of what it means to be multicellular. During much of their life cycle, cellular slime molds are unicellular organisms that look and behave like animal-like protists. When they aggregate, however, they act very much like multicellular organisms. Slime molds have been especially interesting to biologists who study how cells send chemical signals and regulate development. They have kept biologists busy for decades, but their secrets are still not fully understood.

CA a — a 7 2.a

CHECKPOINT ***Why is it difficult to classify cellular slime molds as unicellular or multicellular?***

▼ **Figure 20–22** Cellular slime molds reproduce asexually and sexually. **Interpreting Graphics** ***Is most of the cellular slime mold life cycle haploid or diploid?***

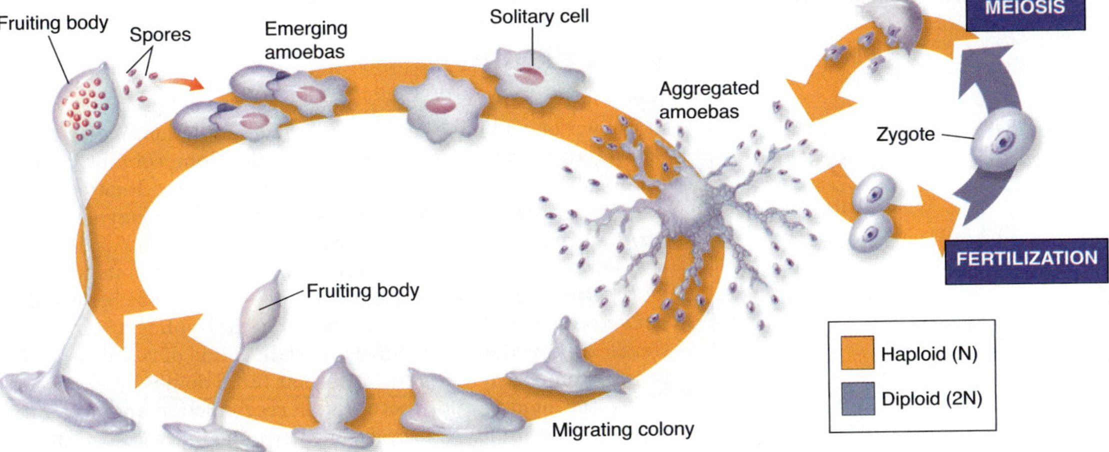

Use Visuals

Figure 20–22 Have students study the life cycle of cellular slime molds, and ask: **What are slime molds?** *(Funguslike protists that play key roles in recycling organic material)* **How are cellular slime molds different from acellular slime molds?** *(The individual cells of cellular slime molds remain distinct, while the cells of acellular slime molds fuse to form large cells with many nuclei.)* **How do the individual cells of cellular slime molds reproduce?** *(They reproduce by cell division.)* Emphasize that most of the life cycle is haploid. L2

Demonstration

The spores of slime molds are abundant in airborne dusts. To demonstrate, place a dead leaf or piece of bark on a few dry oatmeal flakes in a petri dish. Sprinkle some water over the flakes, and cover the dish. If you put the dish aside for a few days, an acellular slime mold called plasmodium will likely grow on the oatmeal flakes. Have students observe the funguslike protist and make drawings. L1 L2

UNIVERSAL ACCESS

English Language Learners

Focus students' attention on the terms *cellular* and *acellular*. Point out that the prefix *a-* means "not." Thus, an acellular slime mold is a slime mold that is "not cellular." Point out that this organism does actually consist of cells. The distinction—and the derivation of the term—is that in acellular slime molds the amoeba-like cells fuse together to produce structures with many nuclei. Such a structure is not "cellular" in the common meaning of that term. L1 L2

Advanced Learners

Encourage students who need an extra challenge to research the Great Potato Famine in nineteenth-century Ireland. Have them find out how the potato blight was diagnosed at the time, whether there were any attempts to attack the pest, and what is done today to prevent or treat attacks by *P. infestans*. Also, have them investigate the ramifications of the human crisis that the potato blight caused. Ask students to report what they learned to the class. L3

Answers to . . .

CHECKPOINT *During most of their life cycle, cellular slime molds are unicellular organisms that look and behave like animal-like protists. When they aggregate, however, they act very much like a multicellular organism.*

Figure 20–22 *Haploid*

20–5 (continued)

Use Visuals

Figure 20–23 Ask students: **What forms when cells of acellular slime molds aggregate?** *(A plasmodium forms.)* **What contains the many nuclei within the plasmodium?** *(A single cell membrane)* Explain that when environmental conditions change, a plasmodium will break up and produce fruiting bodies, which are reproductive structures. Ask: **What are produced within the fruiting bodies?** *(Spores)* **Are the spores haploid or diploid?** *(Haploid)* L2

Water Molds

Demonstration

Several days before students read about water molds, ask a local pet store to provide you with a dead tropical fish. Put the dead fish in a jar of water, place a top on the jar, and set it aside for a few days. Have students observe the fuzzy water mold that grows on the dead fish. Explain that the "fuzziness" is actually a mass of hyphae, which students will learn more about when they study fungi. Ask students: **What is the food source for this water mold?** *(The decaying body of the dead fish)* Point out that the water mold is providing a necessary environmental service in recycling this dead organic matter. L1 L2

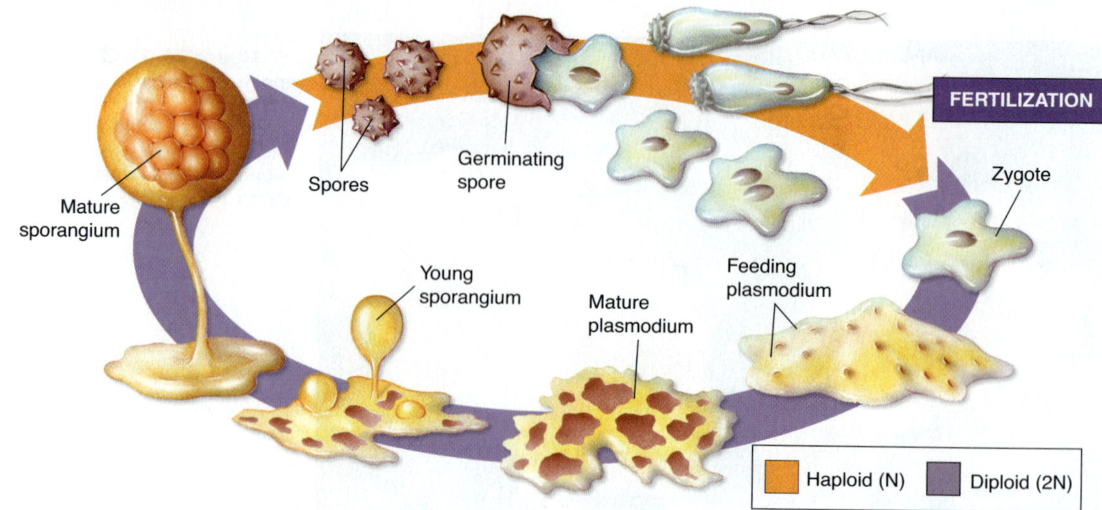

Figure 20–23 The plasmodium of an acellular slime mold is the collection of many amoeba-like organisms contained in a single cell membrane. The plasmodium will eventually produce sporangia, which in turn will undergo meiosis and produce haploid spores. **Interpreting Graphics** *What stage of the life cycle is shown in the photograph?*

Acellular Slime Molds Acellular slime molds belong to the phylum Myxomycota (myk-suh-my-KOH-tuh). Like cellular slime molds, acellular slime molds begin their life cycles as amoeba-like cells. However, when they aggregate, their cells fuse to produce structures with many nuclei.

These structures are known as **plasmodia** (singular: plasmodium). The large plasmodium of an acellular slime mold, such as the one shown in **Figure 20–23,** is actually a single structure with many nuclei. A plasmodium may grow as large as several meters in diameter!

Eventually, small fruiting bodies, or sporangia, spring up from the plasmodium. The sporangia produce haploid spores by meiosis. These spores scatter to the ground where they germinate into amoeba-like or flagellated cells. The flagellated cells then fuse in a sexual union to produce diploid zygotes that repeat the cycle.

Water Molds

a 7 2.a

If you have seen white fuzz growing on the surface of a dead fish in the water, you have seen a water mold in action. Water molds, or oomycetes, are members of the phylum Oomycota (oh-oh-my-KOH-tuh). **Oomycetes thrive on dead or decaying organic matter in water and some are plant parasites on land.** Oomycetes are commonly known as water molds, but they are not true fungi. Water molds produce thin filaments known as **hyphae** (singular: hypha). These hyphae do not have walls between their cells; as a result, water mold hyphae are multinucleate. Also, water molds have cell walls made of cellulose and produce motile spores, two traits that fungi do not have.

Water molds display both sexual reproduction and asexual reproduction in their life cycle, as shown in **Figure 20–24.** In asexual reproduction, portions of the hyphae develop into **zoosporangia** (singular: zoosporangium), which are spore cases.

FACTS AND FIGURES

The attack of the giant amoeba
An acellular slime mold begins its life as an amoeba-like cell. When the cells aggregate to form a plasmodium, it becomes more like a giant amoeba. Plasmodia are usually white, but they may also be colorless, orange, yellow, violet, blue, or black. In a favorable environment, a plasmodium may increase to 25 times its original size in just one week, and it can grow to become 45 centimeters in length. A plasmodium tends to creep in one direction at a rate of 2.5 centimeters per hour. If the environment suddenly becomes unfavorable—if, for example, the food supply suddenly diminishes—a plasmodium will usually change into many separate, small sporangia, each of which contains thousands of spores. In some species, the plasmodium forms a single spore-bearing body.

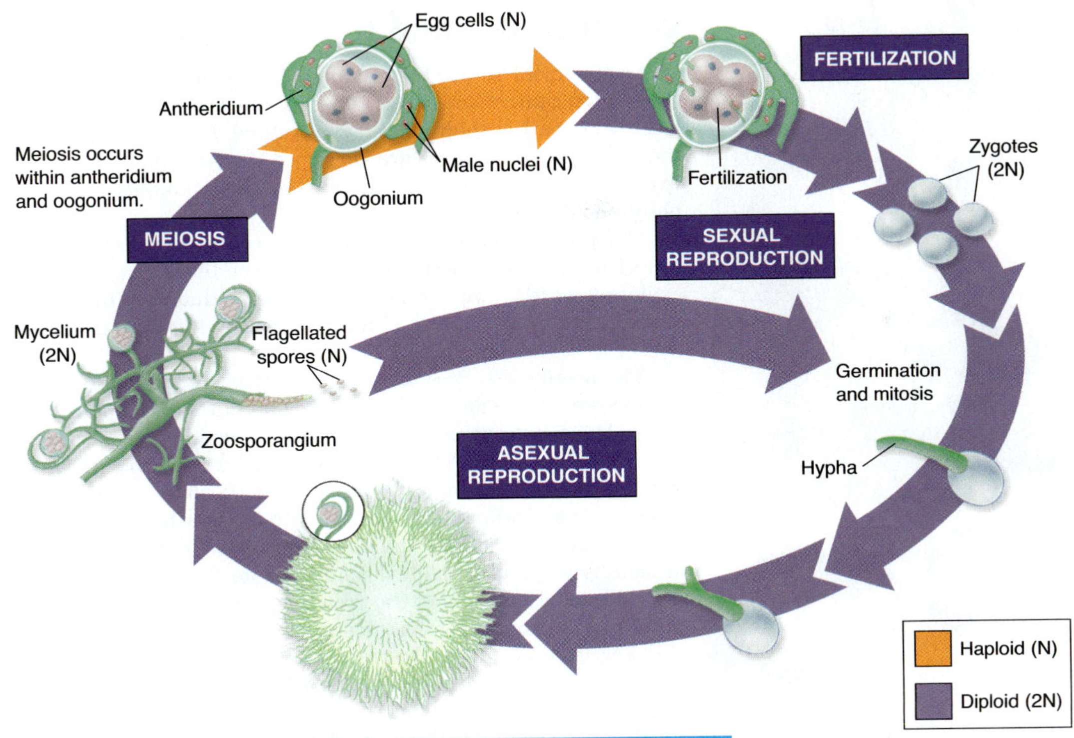

Each zoosporangium produces flagellated spores that swim away in search of food. When they find food, the spores develop into hyphae, which then grow into new organisms.

Sexual reproduction takes place in specialized structures that are formed by the hyphae. One structure, the **antheridium** (an-thur-ID-ee-um), produces male nuclei. The other structure, the **oogonium** (oh-oh-GOH-nee-um), produces female nuclei. Fertilization, or sexual fusion, occurs within the oogonium, and the spores that form develop into new organisms.

CA

a

CHECKPOINT *Where does sexual reproduction in water molds take place?*

▲ **Figure 20–24 Water molds live on decaying organic matter in water.** Water molds reproduce both asexually and sexually. During asexual reproduction, flagellated spores are produced by the diploid (2N) mycelium. These spores grow into new mycelia. During sexual reproduction, a male nucleus fuses with a female nucleus.

a 7 2.a

Ecology of Funguslike Protists

Slime molds and water molds are important as recyclers of organic material. In other words, they help things rot. A walk through woods or grassland shows that the ground is not littered with the bodies of dead animals and plants. After these organisms die, their tissues are broken down by slime molds, water molds, and other decomposers. The dark, rich topsoil that provides plants with nutrients results from this decomposition.

Some funguslike protists can harm living things. In addition to their beneficial function as decomposers, land-dwelling water molds cause a number of important plant diseases. These diseases include mildews and blights of grapes and tomatoes.

For: Links on funguslike protists
Visit: PHSchool.com
Web Code: cbe-6205

Use Visuals

Figure 20–24 Ask students: **What is the cellular process that produces male and female nuclei in water molds?** *(Meiosis)* **Where are these nuclei produced?** *(The male nuclei are produced in the antheridium, and the female nuclei are produced in the oogonium.)* **Are the spores produced by the mycelia haploid or diploid?** *(Diploid)* Explain that a mycelium is a mass of hyphae, as shown in the bottom left of the figure. Ask: **How are oomycetes different from true fungi?** *(Oomycetes have cell walls made of cellulose and produce motile spores, whereas fungi have chitin cell walls and do not have motile stages.)* L2

Ecology of Funguslike Protists

Make Connections

Environmental Science Focus students' attention on the role that funguslike protists play in the environment. Ask: **What do funguslike protists feed on?** *(Dead or decaying organic matter)* **What are organisms called that feed on dead material?** *(Decomposers)* **How is the role played by decomposers like that of the recyclers who collect the glass and paper you put in recycle bins?** *(Like the recyclers of glass and paper, the decomposers use the material accumulated in dead organisms for new purposes instead of letting that material go to waste.)* L1 L2

Your students can extend their knowledge of funguslike protists through this online experience.

TEACHER TO TEACHER

As a review of the many different organisms included in the kingdom Protista, I use a game with a format like Bingo. The game uses a card or grid with either the written name or a picture of each organism being reviewed. I develop several different cards and copy them onto card stock. Plastic pieces cut from colored transparencies can be used as game pieces. In this game, the teacher draws a description of an organism from a container and reads it to the class. The students match the description with the name or picture of the organism, and in doing so, try to get Bingo. The degree of difficulty depends on the descriptions you write for the protists.

—*Lynne M. McElhaney*
Special Services Teacher
Leflore High School
Mobile, AL

Answers to . . .

CHECKPOINT *Sexual reproduction takes place within the oogonium.*

Figure 20–23 *The photograph shows a mature sporangium.*

20–5 (continued)

Water Molds and the Potato Famine

Use Visuals

Figure 20–25 Ask students: **In some history books, the Great Potato Famine is blamed on a fungus. Is that true?** *(No, it was not caused by a fungus, but by an oomycete, or water mold.)* **When spores of *P. infestans* reached a potato during that period in Ireland, how did the spore change, and what caused that change?** *(The spores developed into hyphae, which grew into new organisms, because that's what occurs when spores find food.)* L2

3 ASSESS

Evaluate Understanding

Call on students at random to compare and contrast cellular slime molds with acellular slime molds. Students should mention that both types are funguslike heterotrophs, and they should distinguish between the "slug" of the cellular slime mold and the plasmodium of the acellular slime mold.

Reteach

Use Figure 20–23 to reteach the basics of funguslike protists. Make sure students understand the formation of fruiting bodies and the production of haploid spores. This knowledge will set the stage for the next chapter, which focuses on fungi.

Thinking Visually

The steps in the students' flowcharts should reflect an understanding of the life cycles illustrated in Figure 20–22 for cellular slime molds and Figure 20–23 for acellular slime molds.

If your class subscribes to the iText, use it to review the Key Concepts in Section 20–5.

Answer to . . .

Figure 20–25 *Many Irish people migrated to the United States, where they changed the ethnic and social character of many American cities.*

Figure 20–25 *Phytophthora infestans* is an oomycete that attacks potatoes (bottom right). In the summer of 1846, *P. infestans* destroyed nearly the entire potato crop of Ireland within weeks, leading to the Great Potato Famine. **Applying Concepts** ***How did the famine affect the United States?***

Water Molds and the Potato Famine

One water mold helped to permanently change the character of the United States. Roughly 40 million Americans can trace at least some part of their ancestry to Ireland. If you are one of those people, the chances are very good that your life and the lives of your ancestors were changed by the combination of a plant and a protist.

The plant was the potato. Potatoes are native to South America, where they were cultivated by the Incas. Spanish explorers were so impressed with this plant that they introduced it to Europe. By the 1840s, potatoes had become the major food crop of Ireland.

The protist was *Phytophthora infestans*, an oomycete that produces airborne spores that destroy all parts of the potato plant. The oomycete can disrupt an ecosystem and cause disease in a potato crop. Potatoes that are infected with *P. infestans* may appear normal at harvest time. Within a few weeks, however, the protist makes its way into the potato, reducing it to a spongy sac of spores and dust. The summer of 1845 was unusually wet and cool, ideal conditions for the growth of *P. infestans*. By the end of the growing season, the potato blight caused by this pathogen had destroyed as much as 60 percent of the Irish potato crop. The photographs in **Figure 20–25** show the effects of *P. infestans* on a potato. The art shows a woman digging for potatoes in a field.

Because the poorest farmers depended upon potatoes for their food, the effects were tragic. In 1846, nearly the entire potato crop was lost, leading to mass starvation. Between 1845 and 1851, at least 1 million Irish people died of starvation or disease. During this same period, more than 1 million people emigrated from Ireland to the United States and other countries. The Great Potato Famine, as this tragic event was known, changed the ethnic and social character of many American cities, the new home of so many Irish immigrants.

20–5 Section Assessment

1. **Key Concept** How are funguslike protists and fungi similar? How are they different?
2. **Key Concept** Compare acellular slime molds, cellular slime molds, and water molds.
3. What is the role of slime molds in the environment?
4. How can water molds affect other living things?
5. **Critical Thinking Comparing and Contrasting** How is the sluglike mass of cellular slime molds similar to the plasmodium of acellular slime molds? How do they differ?

Thinking Visually

Constructing a Flowchart
Draw two flowcharts—one showing the steps from unicellular existence through multicellular existence and reproduction in cellular slime molds and one showing those steps in acellular slime molds.

20–5 Section Assessment

1. Like fungi, funguslike protists are heterotrophs that absorb nutrients from dead or decaying organic matter. Unlike most true fungi, funguslike protists have centrioles and lack the chitin cell walls of true fungi.
2. The individual cells of cellular slime molds remain distinct throughout the life cycle. Acellular slime molds pass through a stage in which their cells fuse to form large cells with many nuclei. Water molds have a diploid life cycle. The only haploid stage is the gamete.
3. They recycle organic material.
4. Water molds can cause plant diseases, such as potato blight.
5. Both the cellular slime mold mass and the plasmodium function like a single organism, and both produce a fruiting body. They differ in that the cells of a plasmodium fuse, while cells in a slime mold mass preserve their separate cellular identities.

Design an Experiment

BIIE 1.a, BIIE 1.d, BIIE 1.j

Investigating Contractile Vacuoles

Most freshwater protists have contractile vacuoles. The function of these organelles is to regulate the concentration of water in the cytoplasm, thereby maintaining homeostasis within the organism. In this investigation, you will observe how this structure works under various conditions.

Problem How do the salt concentration and temperature of the environment affect the action of contractile vacuoles?

Materials

- 3 *Paramecium caudatum* cultures at room temperature, 25°C (fresh water, 0.5% salt solution, 1.0% salt solution)
- *Paramecium caudatum* culture at 2°C in fresh water
- dropper pipette
- 4 microscope slides
- coverslips
- microscope
- cotton ball
- forceps
- clock with second hand

Skills Designing Experiments, Observing

Design Your Experiment

1. Use a dropper pipette to put one drop of *Paramecium caudatum* culture in fresh water at 25°C on a microscope slide.
2. Use forceps to pull apart a cotton ball and put a few threads in the drop of water. Cover the drop with a coverslip.
3. Use the low-power objective to locate and focus on one paramecium. If necessary, increase the magnification to observe the alternating contractions of the two contractile vacuoles.
4. Record how long a contractile vacuole takes to contract and refill.
5. **Formulating Hypotheses** Formulate a hypothesis about how salt concentration and temperature will affect the rate of expansion and contraction of a contractile vacuole.
6. **Designing Experiments** Design an experiment to test your hypothesis. As you plan your procedures, refer to the Lab Tips box on page 55 for ways to demonstrate safe practices, make wise choices in the use of materials, and select equipment and technology.
7. Construct a data table to record your observations. With your teacher's approval, carry out your experiment.

Analyze and Conclude

1. **Observing** How did an increase in the concentration of salt in its environment affect the paramecium's contractile vacuoles?
2. **Inferring** What can you infer from this result about the rate at which water enters the paramecium in salt solutions? Explain your answer.
3. **Inferring** What can you infer about the relationship between the contractile vacuole and homeostasis?
4. **Observing** How did temperature affect the contractile vacuoles?
5. **Drawing Conclusions** What can you conclude about the paramecium's use of energy from the effect of temperature on the contractile vacuole?

Go Further

Designing Experiments Does temperature affect paramecia in other ways? Design an experiment to investigate the effects of temperature on movement or feeding. With your teacher's approval, carry out your experiment.

Analyze and Conclude

1. Increasing the salt concentration slowed down the contractions of the contractile vacuoles.
2. The higher the salt concentration outside the organism, the less water that diffuses into the paramecium, because water will diffuse from an area of high concentration to an area of low concentration.
3. Contractile vacuoles help maintain homeostasis by regulating the concentration of water in the cytoplasm.
4. Students should observe that the action of the contractile vacuoles slowed down at a lower temperature.
5. The greater activity of the contractile vacuoles at higher temperatures implies that the paramecium uses energy in contracting its contractile vacuoles.

Design an Experiment

BIIE 1.a, BIIE 1.d, BIIE 1.j

Objective Students will conclude that salt concentration and temperature affect the action of contractile vacuoles.

Skills Focus Designing Experiments, Observing

Time 90 minutes

Advance Prep
- Order cultures of *Paramecium* from a biological supply house; one culture is usually adequate for a class of 24.
- To prepare a 0.5% salt solution, add 0.5 gram of table salt to 99.5 milliliters of water and mix well.
- Prepare a 1.0% salt solution by adding 1 gram of table salt to 99 milliliters of water.

Teaching Tips Notice that as water evaporates from the slide, the coverslip presses down on the paramecium, making the contraction of the contractile vacuoles easier to see.

Design Your Experiment

1. Demonstrate how to use a dropper pipette to put one drop of culture on a slide.
2. Demonstrate how to pull apart the cotton ball, and put a few threads in the drop of water.
5. Make sure that students record a hypothesis that predicts for both salt concentration and temperature.
6. Check each experimental design to make sure that it tests the students' hypotheses and is feasible.

Expected Outcomes Students should observe that higher salt concentrations and lower temperatures reduce the rate at which the contractile vacuole contracts.

Go Further

A typical experiment might investigate whether paramecia feed more or less at a higher temperature. Such an experiment might involve observing paramecia feeding on *Chlorella* or yeast at two temperatures. Students should clearly designate the variable they are testing.

Chapter 20 Study Guide

Study Tip

Divide the class into small groups, and have students quiz one another about the Vocabulary terms and the Key Concepts.

Thinking Visually

In their tables, students should include information about animal-like protists, unicellular plantlike protists, multicellular plantlike protists, and funguslike protists. Students should indicate that animal-like protists and funguslike protists are heterotrophic, while plantlike protists are autotrophic. Movement varies among protists. Three of the four groups of animal-like protists are motile, as are most of the unicellular plantlike protists.

Chapter 20 Assessment

Reviewing Content

1. c
2. c
3. c
4. b
5. d
6. c
7. a
8. d
9. b
10. d

Understanding Concepts

11. Possible answer: Yes, the terms are useful because many protists have characteristics similar to those of plants, animals, or fungi.

12. In fresh water, the water may move into a protozoan by osmosis. The excess water is collected by contractile vacuoles.

13. Ciliates use short, hairlike projections called cilia to move. The cilia beat, propelling the ciliate through water. Sarcodines use pseudopods for movement. These pseudopods extend out of the central mass of the cell. Cytoplasm streams into the pseudopod, and the rest of the cell follows.

Chapter 20 Study Guide

20–1 The Kingdom Protista

Key Concept

- Protists are eukaryotes that are not members of the kingdoms Plantae, Animalia, or Fungi.

Vocabulary

protist, p. 497

20–2 Animal-like Protists: Protozoans

Key Concepts

- Animal-like protists that swim using flagella are classified in the phylum Zoomastigina and are often referred to as zooflagellates.
- Sarcodines are animal-like protists that use pseudopods for feeding and movement.
- Members of the phylum Ciliophora, known as ciliates, use cilia for feeding and movement.
- Members of the phylum Sporozoa do not move on their own and are parasitic.
- Some animal-like protists cause serious diseases, including malaria and African sleeping sickness.

Vocabulary

pseudopod, p. 500
amoeboid movement, p. 500
food vacuole, p. 500 • cilium, p. 501
trichocyst, p. 501 • macronucleus, p. 501
micronucleus, p. 501 • gullet, p. 502
anal pore, p. 502 • contractile vacuole, p. 502
conjugation, p. 502

20–3 Plantlike Protists: Unicellular Algae

Key Concepts

- Chlorophyll and accessory pigments allow algae to harvest and use the energy from sunlight.
- Euglenophytes are plantlike protists that have two flagella but no cell wall.
- Members of the phylum Chrysophyta are a diverse group of plantlike protists that have gold-colored chloroplasts.
- Diatoms produce thin, delicate cell walls rich in silicon (Si)—the main ingredient in glass.
- About half of dinoflagellates are photosynthetic; the other half live as heterotrophs.

Vocabulary

accessory pigment, p. 506 • eyespot, p. 507
pellicle, p. 507 • phytoplankton, p. 509

20–4 Plantlike Protists: Red, Brown, and Green Algae

Key Concepts 7 2.a

- Red algae are able to live at great depths due to their efficiency in harvesting light energy. Red algae contain chlorophyll *a* and reddish accessory pigments called phycobilins.
- Brown algae contain chlorophyll *a* and *c*, as well as a brown accessory pigment, fucoxanthin.
- Green algae share many characteristics with plants, including their photosynthetic pigments and cell wall composition.
- The life cycles of most algae include both a diploid and a haploid generation.

Vocabulary

phycobilin, p. 510
filament, p. 512
alternation of generations, p. 512
gametophyte, p. 514
spore, p. 514
sporophyte, p. 514

20–5 Funguslike Protists

Key Concepts 7 2.a

- Funguslike protists lack chlorophyll and absorb nutrients from dead or decaying organic matter. But unlike most true fungi, funguslike protists have centrioles. They also lack the chitin cell walls of true fungi.
- Slime molds are funguslike protists that play key roles in recycling organic material.
- Oomycetes thrive on dead or decaying organic matter in water and are plant parasites on land.

Vocabulary

cellular slime mold, p. 516
acellular slime mold, p. 516
fruiting body, p. 516
plasmodium, p. 518
hypha, p. 518
zoosporangium, p. 518
antheridium, p. 519
oogonium, p. 519

Thinking Visually

Make a table that compares the means of feeding and movement of the four main groups of protists.

TIME SAVER — CHAPTER RESOURCES

Print:

- ***Teaching Resources,*** Chapter Vocabulary Review, Graphic Organizer, Chapter 20 Tests: Levels A and B

Technology:

- ***Computer Test Bank,*** Chapter 20 Test
- ***iText,*** Chapter 20 Assessment

Chapter 20 Assessment

Reviewing Content

Choose the letter that best answers the question or completes the statement.

1. Which of the following descriptions applies to most protists?
   a. unicellular prokaryotes
   b. multicellular prokaryotes
   c. unicellular eukaryotes
   d. multicellular eukaryotes
2. Which of the following is NOT true of amoebas?
   a. They reproduce by binary fission.
   b. They move by pseudopodia.
   c. They have a definite shape.
   d. They form temporary food vacuoles.
3. For defense, a paramecium uses small, bottle-shaped structures known as
   a. cilia.
   b. pseudopodia.
   c. trichocysts.
   d. micronuclei.
4. Which of the diagrams below shows the process of conjugation?

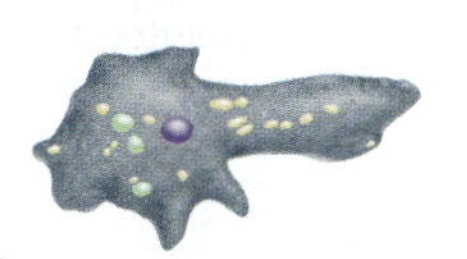
a.

c.

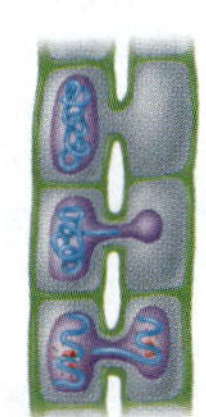
b.

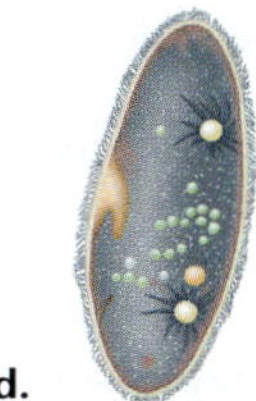
d.

5. The wide range of colors in algae depends upon the presence of
   a. chlorophyll *a* and *b*.
   b. chlorophyll *a* and *c*.
   c. chlorophyll *a* and *d*.
   d. accessory pigments.
6. The population of small, photosynthetic organisms found near the surface of the ocean is called
   a. euglenophytes.
   b. chrysophytes.
   c. phytoplankton.
   d. dinoflagellates.

Interactive textbook with assessment at PHSchool.com 

7. What characteristics do green algae share with plants?
   a. photosynthetic pigments and cell wall composition
   b. photosynthetic and accessory pigment composition
   c. accessory pigments and cell wall composition
   d. accessory pigments and cell membrane composition
8. Alternation of generations is defined as the switching back and forth between the production of
   a. cells by mitosis and meiosis.
   b. asexual and sexual reproductive cells.
   c. gametophytes and sporophytes.
   d. diploid and haploid cells.
9. Slime molds are found primarily in
   a. oceans.
   b. rotting wood or compost piles.
   c. fast-moving streams.
   d. deserts.
10. The thin filaments produced by water molds are known as
    a. oogonia.
    b. antheridia.
    c. zoosporangia.
    d. hyphae.

Understanding Concepts

11. Are the categories animal-like, plantlike, or funguslike useful in classifying protists? Explain your answer.
12. All freshwater protozoans have contractile vacuoles to get rid of excess water. Describe the process responsible for this excess water.
13. Compare the structures used for movement in the ciliates and sarcodines.
14. Describe the process of conjugation. Is conjugation a form of reproduction? Explain your answer.
15. What characteristics distinguish algae from other protists?
16. Describe the two methods euglenophytes can use to obtain energy.
17. Explain why plantlike protists are so important to aquatic food chains.
18. List the three phyla of multicellular plantlike protists. Give an example of an organism in each phylum.
19. Describe the process of alternation of generations. Explain its significance.

TIME SAVER HOMEWORK GUIDE

Section:	Questions:
Section 20–1	1, 11, 26
Section 20–2	2–4, 12–14, 20, 22, 28
Section 20–3	5, 6, 15–17, 21, 27
Section 20–4	7, 8, 18, 19
Section 20–5	9, 10, 23–25

Students can use the iText to access an interactive version of the Student Edition and a self-test.

(Continued from page 522)

14. Conjugation allows ciliates to exchange genetic material. Two paramecia join together. After meiosis of their diploid micronuclei, each organism is left with four haploid micronuclei. Three of the nuclei disintegrate, leaving one nucleus in each organism to divide by mitosis, forming a pair of identical nuclei. The two paramecia then exchange one nucleus from their pairs. Conjugation is not a form of reproduction, because no new offspring are formed. The two paramecia are genetically changed from their former state, but they are identical to each other.

15. Algae contain the green pigment chlorophyll and carry out photosynthesis, unlike other protists.

16. Euglenophytes obtain energy by photosynthesis. If sunlight is not available, euglenophytes can obtain energy by absorbing nutrients available in decayed organic material.

17. Their position at the bottom of the food chain allows much of the diversity of aquatic life. Phytoplankton provide a source of energy for organisms as diverse as shrimp and whales.

18. Phyla of plantlike protists are (1) Rhodophyta or red algae; example: *Chondros crispus;* (2) Phaeophyta or brown algae; example: *Sargassum*; and (3) Chlorophyta or green algae; example: *Volvox*.

19. Many algae switch back and forth between haploid and diploid stages during their life cycles, enabling them to survive unfavorable conditions. Under adverse conditions, a single-celled organism will produce haploid gametes by mitosis. These gametes, which are of two opposing mating types, bind to each other, shed their cell walls, and fuse to from a diploid zygote. The zygote can form a protective wall, enabling it to survive freezing or drying conditions. When conditions are favorable, the zygote begins to grow.

Chapter 20 Assessment

Critical Thinking

20. The antibiotic kills wood-digesting symbiotic bacteria that live inside the cytoplasm of the protists. Because the termites can no longer digest wood, they will die of starvation.

21. Water pollution involving an excess of nutrients might cause a bloom of dinoflagellates which results in a red tide.

22. Sexual reproduction allows for an exchange of genes. New combinations of genes can enable species to adapt to changes in the environment.

23. Answers will vary, depending on the group of protists selected. A typical response might describe the effect that an oomycete had on Ireland and the ethnic and social character of many American cities.

24. Protist A belongs to the phylum Sarcodina; protist B belongs to the phylum Euglenophyta; protist C belongs to the phylum Myxomycota.

25. Slime molds produce sporangia when subjected to environmental stress for two reasons: greater mobility and increased genetic diversity. Greater spore mobility increases the organism's chances of finding another source of food. Greater diversity helps the slime mold adapt to changes in environmental conditions.

26. Protists that belong to the phylum Euglenophyta have characteristics of animallike protists in the ways they move and ingest food. However, they also have characteristics of plantlike protists in that they contain chloroplasts and they produce starch. These organisms cannot be classified as either animals or plants.

27. If the radiation slows the growth of phytoplankton or kills it, the amount of oxygen in the air might decrease and the amount of carbon dioxide might increase. If the radiation speeds up the growth of phytoplankton, the amount of oxygen in the air might increase and the amount of carbon dioxide decrease.

28. If red blood cells are infected with *Plasmodium* cells and are present in blood, they could be passed along by a transfusion. Once inside the recipient, the infected red blood cells could burst, releasing *Plasmodium* cells, which would then infect other red blood cells.

Chapter 20 Assessment

Critical Thinking

20. Formulating Hypotheses A scientist observes that termites that are fed a certain antibiotic die of starvation after a few days. The scientist also notices that the antibiotic affects certain protists that live inside the termite's gut in a peculiar way. Although the protists continue to thrive, they lose a certain kind of structure in their cytoplasm. Develop a hypothesis to explain these observations.

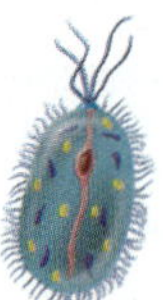

Protist before exposure to antibiotic

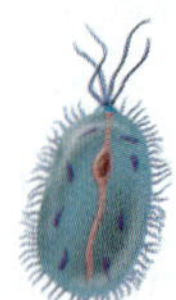

Protist after exposure to antibiotic

21. Applying Concepts How might water pollution result in a red tide?

22. Inferring During its lifetime, a paramecium can reproduce asexually about 700 times. However, it can reproduce many more times if it conjugates as well. How could the capability for sexual reproduction affect the evolution of paramecia?

23. Making Judgments Summarize the role of a selected group of protists in disrupting the equilibrium in an ecosystem and in a human population. Explain how the role of these organisms could contradict the statement that "small organisms are not important in life and in history." Provide specific examples in your answer.

24. Classifying Your teacher asks you to observe and classify into the correct phylum the following protists:

Protist A: Organism has no cell wall, lacks chlorophyll, and moves using pseudopodia.

Protist B: Organism has no cell wall, contains chlorophyll, and has two flagella.

Protist C: Cells appear amoeba-like and appear to fuse to produce structures with many nuclei, lack chlorophyll, and have sporangia that produce spores that germinate into flagellated cells.

25. Inferring Slime molds produce sporangia and spores only when food is scarce. Why do you think this is so? What advantages do slime molds gain from this?

26. Applying Concepts At one time, living things were classified as animals if they moved or ingested food, and as plants if they did not move or ingest food. What difficulties would arise in trying to classify the protists according to these criteria?

27. Predicting Growing "holes" in Earth's ozone layer may increase the amount of radiation that reaches the surface of the ocean. If this radiation were to affect the growth of phytoplankton, what long-term consequences might this have on Earth's atmosphere?

28. Inferring Examine the life cycle of *Plasmodium* illustrated in **Figure 20–7.** Based on the illustration, do you think malaria could be transmitted by a blood transfusion?

Focus on the BIG Idea

Matter and Energy What are the reactants and products of photosynthesis? Where might algae get the raw materials they need to carry out photosynthesis? You may wish to refer back to Chapter 8 for help answering this question.

Writing in Science

Write one or two paragraphs about the four groups of protists described in this chapter. In your description, list the distinguishing characteristics of the organisms in each of the groups and identify at least one organism from each group. (*Hint:* Use a concept map to organize your ideas.)

Performance-Based Assessment

Making Models Select a representative protist from each of the four animal-like protist groups. Make a model of each organism. Describe the characteristics that place it in that group.

For: An interactive self-test
Visit: PHSchool.com
Web Code: cba-6200

Focus on the BIG Idea

The reactants of photosynthesis are carbon dioxide and water. The products are sugars and oxygen. Algae would get water from the water they live in and carbon dioxide from the water it is dissolved in.

Writing in Science

Students' paragraphs may vary, though all responses should differentiate among animal-like protists, unicellular plantlike protists, multicellular plantlike protists, and funguslike protists. In their descriptions, students should include the distinguishing features of the major phyla of each of the four groups of protists. Examples of organisms from each group may be any of the organisms described in the chapter.

Standards Practice

Online at PHSchool.com

Test-Taking Tip As you briefly scan the questions, mark those that may be pure guesswork on your part and save them for last. (Do not write in this book.) Use your time on those questions that you can reason through and for which you can eliminate answers.

Directions: Choose the letter that best answers the question or completes the statement.

1. Which of the following is NOT a characteristic of protists?
   - **A** cell wall containing peptidoglycan
   - **B** membrane-bound nucleus
   - **C** flagella
   - **D** cilia
2. In amoebas, what structure helps the organism move and feed?
   - **A** flagellum
   - **B** cilia
   - **C** food vacuole
   - **D** pseudopod
3. Which of the following is true of the process of conjugation in protists?
   - **A** It occurs only in photosynthetic protists.
   - **B** It results in the trading of some genetic material with another organism.
   - **C** It produces offspring that are genetically identical to the parent.
   - **D** Four new individuals are formed from each single organism.
4. Which of the following is NOT a characteristic of funguslike protists such as slime molds?
   - **A** eukaryotic
   - **B** lack cell walls of chitin
   - **C** multicellular at some time in life cycle
   - **D** photosynthetic
5. Which of the following is characteristic of some types of algae?
   - **A** alternation of generations
   - **B** multicellularity
   - **C** parasitism
   - **D** both A and B

Questions 6–9 Select the best lettered choice for each of the following numbered statements.

- **A** Contractile vacuole
- **B** Anal pore
- **C** Gullet
- **D** Food vacuole

6. Contains food particles in organism's body
7. Indentation leading to organism's mouth
8. Collects and gets rid of excess water
9. Site where waste is released to the environment

Questions 10–11 Use the graph below to answer the following questions.

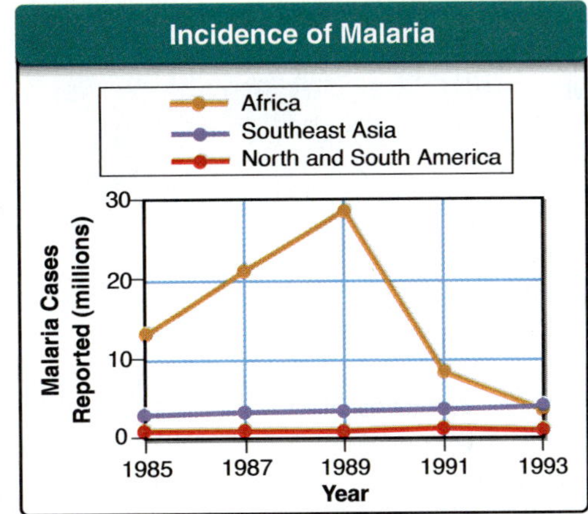

10. It is estimated that there are at least 10 actual cases of malaria for every one reported and shown in the graph. Based on this estimate, how many millions of cases of malaria were there in Africa in 1991?
    - **A** 9
    - **B** 5
    - **C** 50
    - **D** 90
11. Based on the data in the graph, the incidence of malaria is
    - **A** declining in Africa.
    - **B** increasing in Southeast Asia.
    - **C** both A and B
    - **D** none of the above

Standards Practice

1. A	**5.** D	**9.** B
2. D	**6.** D	**10.** D
3. B	**7.** C	**11.** C
4. D	**8.** A	

Success Tracker™

Online at PHSchool.com

Have students check their understanding of the chapter by logging onto Success Tracker.

Performance-Based Assessment

Students should make models of any of the animal-like protists described in Section 20–2. Typically, students will make a model of *Trichomonas,* an amoeba, and a paramecium. You might want to provide illustrations from college biology books for an example of a sporozoan; *Plasmodium* would be a good choice. Provide craft materials for students to use in making their models, including some kind of commercial gelatin for cytoplasm. You might have students label their models with toothpick-and-paper flags. Students should describe each of the organisms they model, especially the means of movement of each organism.

PHSchool.com

Your students can independently test their knowledge of the chapter and print out their test results for your files.

Chapter 21 Planner — Fungi

Section and Section Objectives	Time	STANDARDS NCLB	STANDARDS Biology	Activities and Labs
21–1 The Kingdom Fungi, pp. 527–529 **21.1.1** ***Identify*** the defining characteristics of fungi. **21.1.2** ***Describe*** the main structures of a fungus. **21.1.3** ***Explain*** how fungi reproduce.	1 period (1/2 block)	7 2.a		**SE:** ***Inquiry Activity,*** What are mushrooms made of?, p. 526 L2 **TE:** ***Build Science Skills,*** p. 527 L2 **TE:** ***Build Science Skills,*** p. 529 L2
21–2 Classification of Fungi, pp. 530–536 **21.2.1** ***Identify*** the characteristics of the four main groups of fungi.	2 periods (1 block)	7 2.a		**TE:** ***Build Science Skills,*** p. 530 L2 L3 **SE:** ***Quick Lab,*** What is the structure of bread mold?, p. 531 L2 L3 **TE:** ***Build Science Skills,*** p. 533 L2 L3, p. 535 L2 **TE:** ***Demonstration,*** p. 535 L2 L3 **LMA:** Chapter 21 Lab L2 L3 **LMB:** Chapter 21 Lab L1 L2
21–3 Ecology of Fungi, pp. 537–542 **21.3.1** ***Explain*** what the ecological role of fungi is. **21.3.2** ***Describe*** problems that parasitic fungi cause. **21.3.3** ***Describe*** the kinds of mutualistic relationships that fungi form with other organisms.	2 periods (1 block)	BI 6.e		**TE:** ***Build Science Skills,*** p. 540 L2 L3 **SE:** ***Problem Solving,*** Repotting Orchids, p. 541 L2 L3 **SE:** ***Real-World Lab,*** Examining Seeds for Fungi, p. 543 L2 L3
Chapter Assessment, pp. 544–547	1 period (1/2 block)			

ACTIVITY PLANNER

SE: *Inquiry Activity*, p. 526; 10 min.; mushroom

TE: *Build Science Skills*, p. 527; 5 min.; ball of yarn

TE: *Build Science Skills*, p. 529; 15 min.; mature mushroom cap, paper, microscope slides, microscope

TE: *Build Science Skills*, p. 530; 10 min. for setup, 15 min. 2–3 days later; various foods, plastic container, dampened paper towel

SE: *Quick Lab*, p. 531; 15 min.; transparent tape, moldy bread, microscope slide, microscope

TE: *Build Science Skills*, p. 533; 45 min.; package of dry yeast, beaker, molasses, aluminum foil, dropper pipette, microscope, microscope slide, coverslip, methylene blue

TE: *Demonstration*, p. 535; 15 min.; samples of wild basidiomycetes, field guides

TE: *Build Science Skills*, p. 535; 20 min.; modeling compound, paper, paints, paint brushes

TE: *Build Science Skills*, p. 540; 10 min.; photos of lichens

SE: *Real-World Lab*, p. 543; 45 min.; seeds stored in cold and dry conditions, seeds stored in warm and moist conditions, forceps, microscope slide, coverslip, microscope, aniline blue stain, dropper pipette, paper towels

PLANNING KEY

Ability Levels

for students performing . . .

below grade level **L1**

at grade level **L2**

above grade level **L3**

Print Components

SE	Student Edition	**LA**	Lab Assessment
TE	Teacher's Edition	**BTM**	Biotechnology Manual
RSW	Reading & Study Workbook A	**IDM**	Issues and Decision Making
ARSW	Adapted Reading & Study Workbook B	**LW**	Lab Worksheets
TR	Teaching Resources	**LMA**	Laboratory Manual A
IF	Investigations in Forensics	**LMB**	Laboratory Manual B

Tech Components

CTB	Computer Test Bank
BD	BioDetectives DVD
TP	Transparencies Plus
PLM	Probeware Lab Manual
ABC	ABC DVD Library
LS	Lab Simulations
VL	Virtual Labs

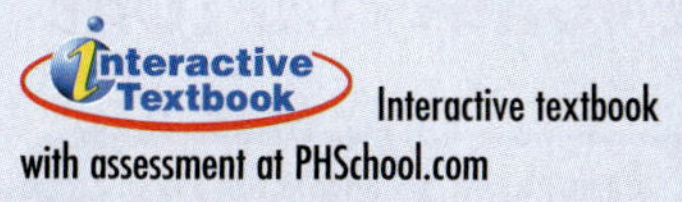

Interactive textbook with assessment at PHSchool.com

Program Resources	Assessment	Media and Technology
TR: Lesson Plan 21–1, Section Summary, p. 96 L1, p. 105 L2, Worksheets, pp. 99–100 L1, pp. 107–109 L2 **RSW:** Section 21–1 L2 **ARSW:** Section 21–1 L1	**SE:** 21–1 Section Assessment, p. 529 **TR:** Section Review 21–1	**iText:** Section 21–1 **TP:** 21–1 Interest Grabber, Section Outline, Hyphae Structure, Figure 21–2
TR: Lesson Plan 21–2, Section Summary, p. 97 L1, p. 105 L2, Worksheets, pp. 101–102 L1, pp. 110–113 L2, Enrichment L2 L3 **RSW:** Section 21–2 L2 **ARSW:** Section 21–2 L1 **IDM:** Issues and Decisions 20 L2 L3	**SE:** 21–2 Section Assessment, p. 536 **TR:** Section Review 21–2	**iText:** Section 21–2 **TP:** 21–2 Interest Grabber, Section Outline, Concept Map, Figure 21–5, Figure 21–7, Figure 21–8
TR: Lesson Plan 21–3, Section Summary, p. 98 L1, p. 106 L2, Worksheets, p. 103 L1, pp. 114–115 L2 **LW:** Chapter 21 Real-World Lab L1 L2 L3 **RSW:** Section 21–3 L2 **ARSW:** Section 21–3 L1	**SE:** 21–3 Section Assessment, p. 542 **TR:** Section Review 21–3	**iText:** Section 21–3 **TP:** 21–3 Interest Grabber, Section Outline, Lichen Structure
	SE: Chapter 21 Assessment, pp. 544–547 **TR:** Chapter Vocabulary Review, Graphic Organizer, Chapter 21 Test **LA:** Laboratory Assessment 6	**iText:** Chapter 21 Assessment **CTB:** Chapter 21 Test

Go Online

Students can do research, share data, and test their knowledge online.

PRESSED FOR TIME?

To Preview the Chapter

- Introduce students to Key Concepts and Vocabulary terms in each section.
- Assign the Reading Strategies for each section.

To Cover the Chapter Quickly

- Have students read all of Section 21–1; the introductory paragraph and Figures 21–5, 21–7, and 21–8 of Section 21–2; and all of Section 21–3.
- Assign the 21–1 Section Review and 21–3 Section Review, as well as questions 1–10 in Chapter 21 Assessment and questions 1–11 in Chapter 21 Standards Practice.

To Review the Chapter

- Assign Sections 21–1 through 21–3 in the Reading and Study Workbook or the Adapted Reading and Study Workbook.
- Assign Section Reviews for 21–1 through 21–3 and the Chapter Vocabulary Review for Chapter 21 in the Teaching Resources.

CHAPTER 21

ENGAGE/EXPLORE

Inquiry Activity

Objective Students will be able to distinguish a mushroom from a plant and describe the structure of a mushroom.

Skill Focus **Comparing and Contrasting, Observing**

Materials mushroom

Time 10 minutes

Advance Prep Buy common mushrooms from a grocery store.

Safety Use only store-bought edible mushrooms, but do not allow students to eat the mushrooms. Make certain students do not have allergies to mushrooms.

Strategy Ask students whether they think mushrooms should be classified as plants, as they once were.

Expected Outcomes
Students will observe that mushrooms are different from plants and are composed of compressed filaments, called hyphae.

Think About It

1. Students should observe that mushrooms are composed of threadlike parts, or hyphae.
2. They are similar in that both have a stalk or a stem. They are different in that plants have green leaves, stems, roots, flowers, fruits, and seeds, none of which mushrooms have. Mushrooms, in contrast, have a cap with gills.

Assess Prior Knowledge

Ask students: **What are all the different kinds of fungi you can think of?** *(Many students will mention molds, yeasts, morels, and mushrooms sold in groceries. Some might also mention rusts, mildew, and lichens.)* **How do you think fungi reproduce?** *(Accept all reasonable responses. Some students might correctly suggest that fungi reproduce through the broadcast of spores.)*

CHAPTER 21

Fungi

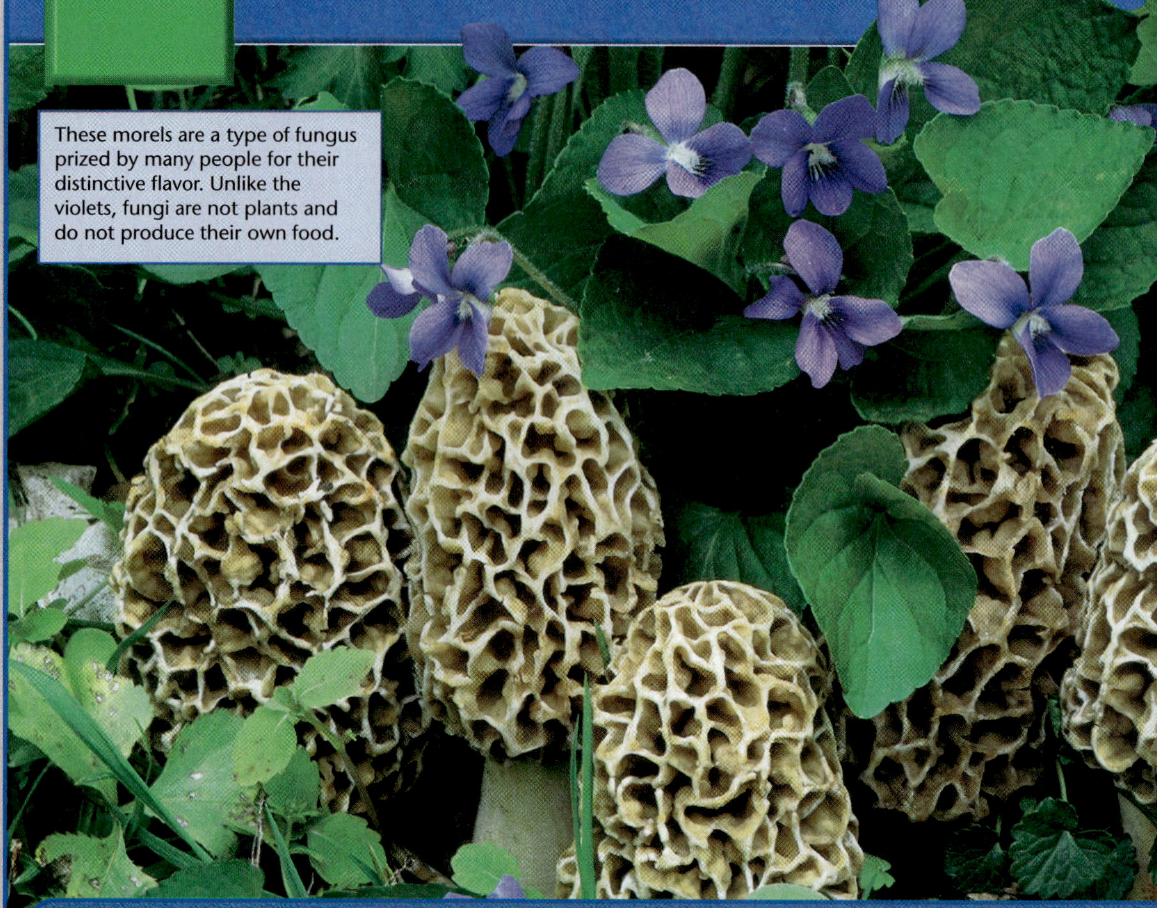

These morels are a type of fungus prized by many people for their distinctive flavor. Unlike the violets, fungi are not plants and do not produce their own food.

Inquiry Activity

What are mushrooms made of?

Procedure 

1. Examine a mushroom without damaging it. Record your observations, and include a sketch.
2. Carefully separate the stalk and cap of the mushroom. Try to break the stalk across and lengthwise.
3. Crumble a piece of the stalk. Describe the shape of the parts that make up the stalk.
4. Break the cap in two, and examine the thin sheets on the underside of the cap. Record your observations.

Think About It

1. **Observing** Was the stalk made up of parts with specific shapes? If so, what are the shapes of those parts?
2. **Comparing and Contrasting** Compare a mushroom to a plant. How are they similar? Different?

FACTS AND FIGURES

The oldest and biggest
The kingdom Fungi is known in some sources as the kingdom Mycota, from the Greek word *mykes,* which means "fungus." The branch of botany that focuses on fungi is mycology, and biologists who specialize in the study of fungi are called mycologists. Fungi include a wide variety of organisms, from unicellular yeasts to perhaps the largest multicellular organisms on Earth. In the 1990s, researchers in Michigan discovered an example of the fungus *Armillaria bulbosa* that spread through more than 15 hectares of forest soil—the size of more than 33 football fields. Biologists estimated that it was over 1500 years old. Researchers also documented an individual of *Armillaria ostoyae* in Washington State that was even larger.

21–1 The Kingdom Fungi

In spring, if you know where to look, you can find one of the most prized of all foods—the common morel—growing wild in woodlands throughout the United States. Its ridged cap is often camouflaged by dead leaves that collect in abandoned orchards or underneath old oaks or tulip poplars. Some morels grow alone, but others grow in groups. They appear suddenly, often overnight, and live for only a few days. What are these mysterious organisms? How do they grow so quickly?

Guide for Reading

Key Concepts
- What are the defining characteristics of fungi?
- What is the internal structure of a fungus?
- How do fungi reproduce?

Vocabulary
chitin
hypha
mycelium
fruiting body
sporangium
sporangiophore

Reading Strategy: Asking Questions Before you read, preview **Figures 21–1** and **21–2.** Make a list of questions you have about the structure of fungi. As you read, look for answers to your questions.

What Are Fungi?

Like mushrooms and molds, morels are fungi. The way in which many fungi grow from the ground once led scientists to classify them as nonphotosynthetic plants. But they aren't plants at all. In fact, fungi are very different from plants.

Fungi are eukaryotic heterotrophs that have cell walls. The cell walls of fungi are made up of **chitin,** a complex carbohydrate that is also found in the external skeletons of insects. Recall that heterotrophs depend on other organisms for food. Unlike animals, fungi do not ingest their food. Instead, they digest food outside of their bodies and then absorb it. Many fungi feed by absorbing nutrients from decaying matter in the soil. Others live as parasites, absorbing nutrients from the bodies of their hosts.

Structure and Function of Fungi

Except for yeasts, all fungi are multicellular. Multicellular fungi are composed of thin filaments called **hyphae** (HY-fee; singular: hypha). Each hypha is only one cell thick. In some fungi, cross walls divide the hyphae into cells containing one or two nuclei, as shown in **Figure 21–1.** In the cross walls, there are tiny openings through which the cytoplasm and nuclei can move. Other hyphae lack cross walls and contain many nuclei.

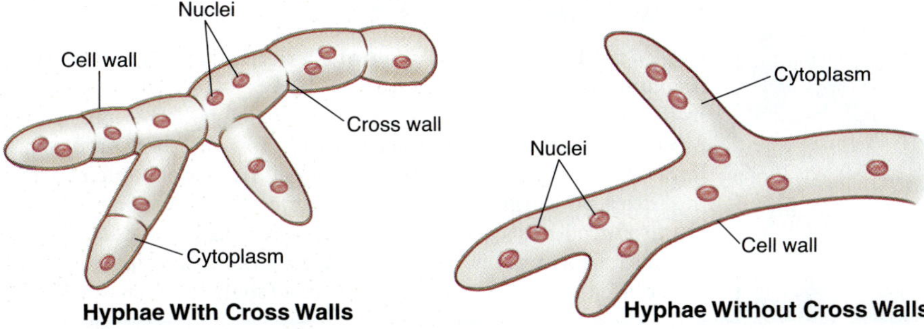

▼ **Figure 21–1 Fungi are eukaryotes that have cell walls made of chitin.** Most fungi are made up of filaments called hyphae. In some fungi, the hyphae are divided by cross walls. In other fungi, the hyphae lack cross walls and contain many nuclei.

SECTION RESOURCES

Print:
- ***Teaching Resources,*** Lesson Plan 21–1, Adapted Section Summary 21–1, Adapted Worksheets 21–1, Section Summary 21–1, Worksheets 21–1, Section Review 21–1
- ***Reading and Study Workbook A,*** Section 21–1
- ***Adapted Reading and Study Workbook B,*** Section 21–1

Technology:
- ***iText,*** Section 21–1
- ***Transparencies Plus,*** Section 21–1

Section 21–1

7 2.a

1 FOCUS

Objectives

21.1.1 ***Identify*** the defining characteristics of fungi.
21.1.2 ***Describe*** the main structures of a fungus.
21.1.3 ***Explain*** how fungi reproduce.

Guide for Reading

Vocabulary Preview

Ask volunteers to pronounce each Vocabulary word. Correct any mispronunciations. Survey students for their ideas of what the words mean.

Reading Strategy

Have students copy the Key Concepts into their notebooks. As they read the section, have students write supporting details for each Key Concept.

2 INSTRUCT

What Are Fungi?

Build Science Skills

Comparing and Contrasting Have students make a compare/contrast table that compares characteristics of bacteria, protists, fungi, plants, and animals. Column headings should include *Prokaryotes/Eukaryotes, Autotrophs/Heterotrophs,* and *Method of Obtaining Nutrition.* To complete this table, students can draw on the knowledge gained from previous chapters in this unit, as well as on their common knowledge about plants and animals. L2

Structure and Function of Fungi

Build Science Skills

Using Analogies Explain that a filament is a thin, flexible, threadlike object. Then, show students a ball of yarn. Point out that the yarn when wrapped in a ball feels like a large, solid object. As students watch, unravel part of the ball. Explain that fungal hyphae are like the yarn—they can aggregate into a large object or they can be thin threads underground. L2

21–1 (continued)

Use Visuals

Figure 21–2 Point out that fungi have a great variety of shapes and sizes, and the fungus illustrated here is only a representative that is helpful as an introduction to fungus structure. Ask: **What is the function of the mushroom you see aboveground?** *(The mushroom, or fruiting body, is the reproductive structure of the fungus.)* **What are both the mushroom and the mycelium made of?** *(Tiny filaments called hyphae)* **What are the cell walls of these hyphae made of?** *(Chitin, a complex carbohydrate)* L1 L2

Build Science Skills

Inferring Have students recall that in Chapter 10 they learned about cell size and ratio of surface area to volume. Ask: **As cell volume increases, what happens to the ratio of surface area to volume?** *(It decreases.)* **Why is such a decrease a disadvantage to a cell?** *(With a smaller ratio, it becomes more difficult for a cell to bring materials into the cell and send waste materials out.)* **With this concept in mind, how does the structure of the mycelium correlate with its function for the organism?** *(The structure of the mycelium provides a large ratio of surface area to volume for the organism's cells. This large ratio correlates with the structure's function, which is absorbing nutrients from the soil or from the decaying matter in the soil or from the body of the host.)* L2 L3

Reproduction in Fungi

Build Science Skills

Designing Experiments Ask students to investigate what causes an organism to reproduce either sexually or asexually. Students should discover that in some organisms, asexual reproduction occurs when conditions are stable and favorable to growth. Sexual reproduction, by contrast, occurs when environmental conditions are changing. Once students have researched the topic, have them collaborate in designing an experiment that tests what conditions would cause a fungus to reproduce sexually. L3

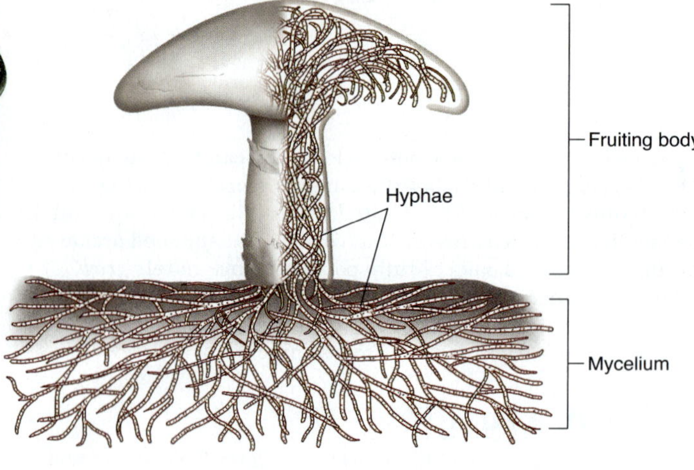

Figure 21–2 The body of a mushroom is part of a mycelium formed from many tangled hyphae. The major portion of the mycelium grows below ground. The visible portion of the mycelium is the reproductive structure, or fruiting body, of the mushroom.

Fungus Structure **Figure 21–2** shows the structure of a multicellular fungus. **The bodies of multicellular fungi are composed of many hyphae tangled together into a thick mass called a mycelium.** The **mycelium** (my-SEE-lee-um; plural: mycelia) is well suited to absorb food because it permits a large surface area to come in contact with the food source through which it grows.

What you recognize as a mushroom is actually the fruiting body of a fungus. A **fruiting body** is a reproductive structure growing from the mycelium in the soil beneath it. Clusters of mushrooms are often part of the same mycelium, which means that they are part of the same organism.

Fairy Rings Some mycelia can live for many years. As time goes by, soil nutrients near the center of the mycelium become depleted. As a result, new mushrooms sprout only at the edges of the mycelium, producing a ring like the one in **Figure 21–3.** People once thought fairies dancing in circles during warm nights produced these rings, so they were called "fairy rings." Over many years, fairy rings can become enormous—from 10 to 30 meters in diameter.

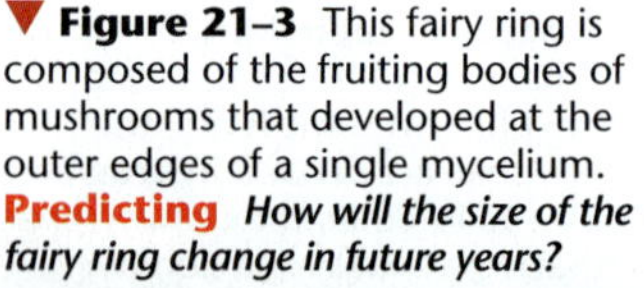

▼ **Figure 21–3** This fairy ring is composed of the fruiting bodies of mushrooms that developed at the outer edges of a single mycelium. **Predicting** *How will the size of the fairy ring change in future years?*

Reproduction in Fungi

Most fungi reproduce both asexually and sexually. Asexual reproduction takes place when cells or hyphae break off from a fungus and begin to grow on their own. Some fungi also produce spores, which can scatter and grow into new organisms. Recall that a spore is a reproductive cell that is capable of growing into a new organism by mitosis alone. In some fungi, spores are produced in structures called **sporangia** (spoh-RAN-jee-uh; singular: sporangium). Sporangia are found at the tips of specialized hyphae called **sporangiophores** (spoh-RAN-jee-oh-fawrz).

CA a

a 7 2.a

ESL SUPPORT FOR ENGLISH LANGUAGE LEARNERS

Vocabulary: Link to Visual

Beginning Use Figure 21–2 to help students visualize the Vocabulary terms *fruiting body, hyphae,* and *mycelium.* After students have examined the figure, provide an unlabeled copy of the figure and a list of the three Vocabulary terms. Ask the students to label the diagram. Check the students' work, and pronounce each term for the students. Have the students repeat the Vocabulary terms to practice pronunciation. L1

Intermediate Students should do the activity described for beginning students. Then, to extend the activity, have the students provide a brief definition of each term in either oral or written form. Students who need assistance in preparing definitions should be paired with a student who is proficient in English. L2

Sexual reproduction in fungi usually involves two different mating types. Because gametes of both mating types are about the same size, they are not called male and female. Rather, one mating type is called "+" (plus) and the other "–" (minus). When hyphae of opposite mating types meet, they start the process of sexual reproduction by fusing, bringing plus and minus nuclei together in the same cell. After a period of growth and development, these nuclei form a diploid zygote nucleus. In most fungi, the diploid zygote then enters meiosis, completing the sexual phase of its life cycle by producing haploid spores. Like the spores produced asexually, these spores are also capable of growing, by repeated rounds of mitosis, into new organisms.

CA a

a 7 2.a

How Fungi Spread

Fungal spores are found in almost every environment. This is why molds seem to spring up in any location that has the right combination of moisture and food. Many fungi produce dry, almost weightless spores, as shown in **Figure 21–4.** These spores scatter easily in the wind. On a clear day, a few liters of fresh air may contain hundreds of spores from many species of fungi.

If these spores are to germinate, they must land in a favorable environment. There must be the proper combination of temperature, moisture, and food so that the spores can grow. Even under the best of circumstances, the probability that a spore will produce a mature organism can be less than one in a billion.

Other fungi are specialized to lure animals, which disperse fungal spores over long distances. Stinkhorns smell like rotting meat, which attracts flies. When they land on the stinkhorn, the flies ingest the sticky, smelly fluid on the surface of the fungus. The spore-containing fluid will pass unharmed out of the flies' digestive systems, depositing spores over many kilometers.

▲ **Figure 21–4** **Most fungi reproduce both sexually and asexually.** One form of asexual reproduction is spore formation. Here, an earthstar puffball *(Geastrum saccatum)* that has been struck by a raindrop expels a cloud of spores.

21–1 Section Assessment

1. **Key Concept** Identify the characteristics all fungi have in common.
2. **Key Concept** Describe the structure of the body of a typical fungus.
3. **Key Concept** Briefly describe asexual and sexual reproduction in fungi.
4. By what means are fungal spores spread to new locations?
5. **Critical Thinking** **Applying Concepts** Tissue from several mushrooms gathered near the base of a tree were tested and found to be genetically identical. How might you explain this?

Writing in Science

Writing a Proposal

A house may become uninhabitable because of the presence of mold spores. Research how to detect and identify mold allergens in the home. Assume you are a contractor. Write a proposal for how you will assess this problem in preparation for a cleanup. *Hint:* Write a draft of your proposal.

How Fungi Spread

Build Science Skills

Observing Shake or scrape spores from the underside of a mature mushroom cap onto a sheet of paper. Invite students to observe the spores with the naked eye, and then, transfer some of the spores to slides. Have each student observe spores under a microscope. Ask: **How would you describe these spores?** *(The spores are tiny, dry structures. The shape varies with the variety of mushroom.)* L2

3 ASSESS

Evaluate Understanding

Have volunteers explain different parts of Figure 21–2. Ask about the structures of a typical fungus, its asexual and sexual reproductive parts, and how its spores are spread.

Reteach

Have students draw and label a typical fungus, as in Figure 21–2. Students may add other drawings to their page as they learn about the main groups of fungi in the next section.

Writing in Science

Advise students to look for library books or Internet sites that address allergies to molds. Students should find that identifying molds involves collecting samples and examining spores under a microscope. Eliminating molds from buildings involves washing thoroughly with antiseptic detergents. Students may also discover that heating and cooling systems would have to be disassembled and washed to eliminate mold spores.

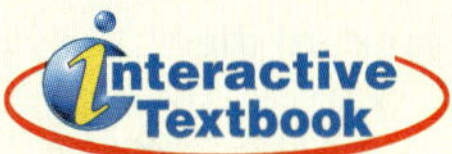

If your class subscribes to the iText, use it to review the Key Concepts in Section 21–1.

21–1 Section Assessment

1. Fungi are eukaryotic heterotrophs that have cell walls. Fungi do not ingest food; they digest food outside their cells and absorb it.
2. The bodies of multicellular fungi are composed of many hyphae tangled together into a thick mass called a mycelium. The visible portion of the mycelium is the reproductive structure, or fruiting body.
3. Asexual reproduction takes place when cells or hyphae break off from a fungus and begin to grow on their own. Some fungi also produce asexual spores. Sexual reproduction in fungi usually involves two different mating types, which mate to form zygote nuclei.
4. Some spores are scattered by the wind and some, by animals.
5. The genetically identical mushrooms were part of the same mycelium, which means they were part of the same organism.

Answer to . . .

Figure 21–3 *The fairy ring will become larger as the mycelium grows.*

Section 21–2

 7 2.a

1 FOCUS

Objective

21.2.1 ***Identify*** the characteristics of the four main groups of fungi.

Guide for Reading

Vocabulary Preview

Help students remember the meanings of the second and third Vocabulary words by explaining that *rhizoid* is derived from a Greek word meaning "root" and *stolon* is derived from a Latin word meaning "branch."

Reading Strategy

Students' main topics should be the four groups of fungi. For each, students should note details about structure and function and list examples.

2 INSTRUCT

The Common Molds

Build Science Skills

Observing Divide the class into small groups, and give each group a different food sample in an open plastic container with a dampened paper towel lining the bottom. Foods might include bread (without preservatives), fruit, vegetables, or potato chips. Have students dampen the food with water and expose it to the air for the rest of the day. Then, place all samples in a warm, dark place for two or three days. Have students observe and make drawings of any mold that grows on their samples. Ask students to compare their observations. L2 L3

Download a worksheet on fungi for students to complete, and find additional support from NSTA SciLinks.

21–2 Classification of Fungi

7 2.a. Students know the differences between the life cycles and reproduction methods of sexual and asexual organisms.

Guide for Reading

 **Key Concept**

- What are the characteristics of the four main phyla of fungi?

Vocabulary

zygospore
rhizoid
stolon
gametangium
conidium
ascus
ascospore
budding
basidium
basidiospore

Reading Strategy: Finding Main Ideas Before you read, skim the section to identify the four main groups of fungi. Write the name of each group on a notecard. As you read, make note of the characteristics of each group.

The kingdom Fungi has over 100,000 species. Fungi are classified according to their structure and method of reproduction. The methods by which fungi reproduce are unlike those of any other kingdom. The four main groups of fungi are the common molds (Zygomycota), the sac fungi (Ascomycota), the club fungi (Basidiomycota), and the imperfect fungi (Deuteromycota).

The Common Molds

The familiar molds that grow on meat, cheese, and bread are members of the phylum Zygomycota, also called zygomycetes. **Zygomycetes have life cycles that include a zygospore.** A **zygospore** (ZY-goh-spawr) is a resting spore that contains zygotes formed during the sexual phase of the mold's life cycle. The hyphae of zygomycetes generally lack cross walls, although the cells of their reproductive structures do have cross walls.

Structure and Function of Bread Mold Black bread mold, *Rhizopus stolonifer,* is a familiar zygomycete. Expose preservative-free bread to dust, and you can grow the mold. Keep the bread warm and moist in a covered jar, and in a few days dark fuzz will appear. With a hand lens, you can see delicate hyphae on moldy bread. There are two different kinds of hyphae. The rootlike hyphae that penetrate the bread's surface are **rhizoids** (RY-zoydz). Rhizoids anchor the fungus to the bread, release digestive enzymes, and absorb digested organic material. The stemlike hyphae that run along the surface of the bread are **stolons.** The hyphae that push up into the air are the sporangiophores, which form sporangia at their tips. A single sporangium may contain up to 40,000 spores.

CHECKPOINT *What is a zygospore?*

 7 2.a

Life Cycle of Molds The life cycle of black bread mold is shown in **Figure 21–5.** Its sexual phase begins when hyphae from different mating types fuse to produce gamete-forming structures known as **gametangia** (gam-uh-TAN-jee-uh; singular: gametangium). Haploid (N) gametes produced in the gametangia fuse with gametes of the opposite mating type to form diploid (2N) zygotes. These zygotes develop into thick-walled zygospores, which may remain dormant for months. When conditions become favorable, the zygospore germinates, then undergoes meiosis, and new haploid spores are released. The significance of this sexual process—zygote formation followed by meiosis—is that it produces new combinations of genetic information that may help the organism meet changing environmental conditions.

For: Links on fungi
Visit: www.SciLinks.org
Web Code: cbn-6211

SECTION RESOURCES

Print:

- ***Laboratory Manual A,*** Chapter 21 Lab
- ***Laboratory Manual B,*** Chapter 21 Lab
- ***Teaching Resources,*** Lesson Plan 21–2, Adapted Section Summary 21–2, Adapted Worksheets 21–2, Section Summary 21–2, Worksheets 21–2, Section Review 21–2, Enrichment
- ***Reading and Study Workbook A,*** Section 21–2
- ***Adapted Reading and Study Workbook B,*** Section 21–2
- ***Issues and Decision Making,*** Issues and Decisions 20

Technology:

- ***iText,*** Section 21–2
- ***Transparencies Plus,*** Section 21–2

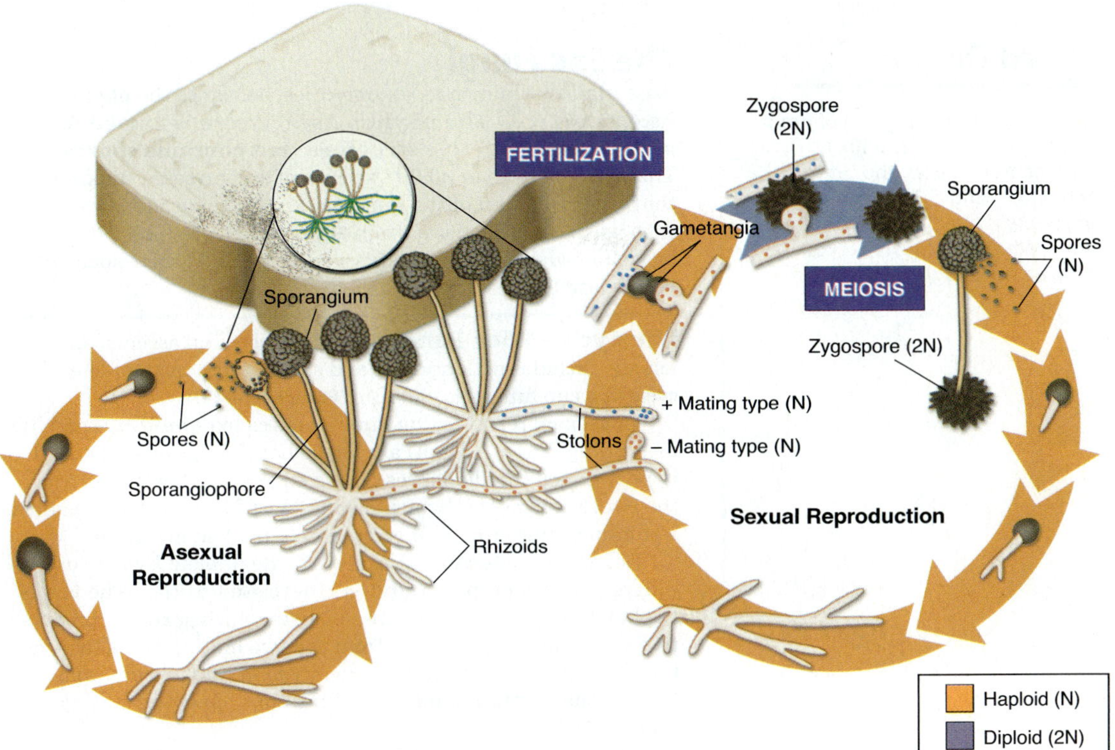

▲ **Figure 21–5** **Zygomycetes have life cycles that include a zygospore.** During sexual reproduction in the bread mold *Rhizopus stolonifer,* hyphae from two different mating types form gametangia. The gametangia fuse, and zygotes form within a zygospore. The zygospore develops a thick wall and can remain dormant for long periods. The zygospore eventually germinates, and a sporangium emerges. The sporangium reproduces asexually by releasing haploid spores produced by meiosis.

Quick Lab

 **BIIE 1.d**

What is the structure of bread mold?

Materials transparent tape, moldy bread, microscope slide, microscope

Procedure  

1. Touch the sticky side of a 2-cm piece of transparent tape to the black "fuzzy" area of a bread mold.
2. Gently stick the tape to a glass slide. Observe the slide under the compound microscope. Make a sketch of your observations.
3. Return all slides to your teacher for proper disposal. Wash your hands before leaving the laboratory.

Analyze and Conclude

1. **Observing** Describe the structures you observed in the bread mold.
2. **Formulating Hypotheses** What do you think the function of the round structures is? Why might it be advantageous for a single mass of bread mold to produce so many of the round structures?
3. **Inferring** How can your observations help explain the ability of molds to appear on foods even in very clean kitchens?

UNIVERSAL ACCESS

Less Proficient Readers

Focus students' attention on Figure 21–8, and call on students at random to explain what is occurring at each step in the diagram. If a student has trouble with an explanation, read aloud the sentences from the text that would provide insight into that step. Then, ask the student again to explain what is occurring at that place on the diagram. Continue this questioning process around the diagram more than once, emphasizing its cyclic character. L1 L2

Advanced Learners

Encourage students who need a challenge to research and prepare a report on the discovery of the "wonder drug," penicillin. Direct students to books about famous scientists to read about Alexander Fleming, who won a Nobel Prize for his work. Make sure students focus on the initial experiment that showed how a culture of *Penicillium notatum* killed bacteria. 

Quick Lab

 **BIIE 1.d**

Objective Students will be able to observe the major structures of a mold and hypothesize why bread mold produces so many sporangia. 

Skill Focus **Formulating Hypotheses, Observing, Inferring**

Materials transparent tape, moldy bread, microscope slide, microscope

Time 15 minutes

Advance Prep Prepare moldy bread by moistening slices of bread and placing them in a warm, dark place several days in advance of the activity.

Safety Students who have allergies to molds should avoid any exposure to the bread mold. Make sure students wash their hands with soap and warm water before leaving the lab.

Strategies

- Suggest that students look at the slide near the edge of the tape, where it may be easier for them to see the hyphae and spores.
- If students are unable to identify the sporangia, encourage them to review the subsection Structure and Function of Bread Molds and Figure 21–5.

Expected Outcomes Students should observe hyphae and reproductive structures in bread mold.

Analyze and Conclude

1. The tangled filaments are hyphae, including rhizoids, stolons, and sporangiophores. The round structures are sporangia.
2. Sporangia produce and release spores. The production of such a large number of sporangia increases the number of spores released, thus increasing the chances of the mold's reproduction.
3. Molds produce large numbers of very tiny spores that are easily spread by wind and animals. Keeping all spores out of a kitchen is impossible.

Answer to . . .

CHECKPOINT *A zygospore is a resting spore that contains zygotes formed during the sexual phase of the mold's life cycle.*

21–2 (continued)

The Sac Fungi

Word Origins

A mycologist studies fungi. L2

Address Misconceptions

Make sure students understand that ascomycetes produce two different kinds of spores. Which kind they produce depends on the environmental conditions. Ask: **Which kind of spores do sac fungi produce in asexual reproduction?** *(Conidia)* **Which kind of spores do they produce in sexual reproduction?** *(Ascospores)* Point out that bread yeasts, which are ascomycetes, reproduce asexually by budding, not by the production of conidia. Yet, when yeasts reproduce sexually, they produce ascospores. L2

Use Visuals

Figure 21–7 Have students study the life cycle. Then, ask: **Are the conidia produced in asexual reproduction haploid or diploid?** *(Haploid)* **Which type of reproduction involves development of a fruiting body?** *(Sexual reproduction)* **What cellular process results in haploid ascospores?** *(Meiosis)* **After mitosis occurs, how many ascospores are there per ascus?** *(Eight)* L2

Word Origins

The name of each phylum of fungi ends in *-mycota.* This suffix is derived from *mukes,* the Greek word for "fungi." The term *mycelium* is also derived from this root. **What organisms do you think a mycologist studies?**

a 7 2.a

The Sac Fungi

Sac fungi, also known as ascomycetes, belong to the phylum Ascomycota. **The phylum Ascomycota is named for the ascus, a reproductive structure that contains spores.** There are more than 30,000 species of ascomycetes, making it the largest phylum of the kingdom Fungi. Some ascomycetes, such as the cup fungi shown in **Figure 21–6**, are large enough to be visible when they grow above the ground. Others, such as yeasts, are microscopic.

Life Cycle of Sac Fungi The life cycle of an ascomycete usually includes both asexual and sexual reproduction. The life cycle of a cup fungus is shown in **Figure 21–7.**

In asexual reproduction, tiny spores called **conidia** (koh-NID-ee-uh; singular: conidium) are formed at the tips of specialized hyphae called conidiophores. These spores get their name from the Greek word *konis,* which means "dust." If a conidium lands in a suitable environment, it grows into a haploid mycelium.

Sexual reproduction occurs when the haploid hyphae of two different mating types (+ and –) grow close together. The N + N hyphae then produce a fruiting body in which sexual reproduction continues. Gametangia from the two mating types fuse, but the haploid (N) nuclei do not fuse. Instead, this fusion produces hyphae that contain haploid nuclei from each of the mating types (N + N).

The **ascus** (plural: asci) forms within the fruiting body. Within the ascus, two nuclei of different mating types fuse to form a diploid zygote (2N). The zygote soon divides by meiosis, producing four haploid cells. In most ascomycetes, meiosis is followed by a cycle of mitosis, so that eight cells known as **ascospores** are produced. In a favorable environment, an ascospore can germinate and grow into a haploid mycelium.

CHECKPOINT *Where are ascospores formed? Are they haploid or diploid?*

▼ **Figure 21–6** These cup fungi are members of the phylum Ascomycota. In cup fungi, asci lie on the interior surface of the cup. At maturity, the spore-filled asci burst, releasing the spores into the air. **Applying Concepts** *What type of spores are formed by the cup fungi?*

BIO INSIGHTS **FACTS AND FIGURES**

The sport of mushroom hunting

In springtime across the northern United States, scores of intrepid souls tramp over fields and through woods hunting for a highly prized "mushroom." Actually, they are searching for morels, which are ascomycetes, rather than basidiomycetes, the true mushrooms. Morels, most commonly *Morchella esculenta,* are small and tan and have a wrinkled, conelike top, as shown in this chapter's opening photograph. Each of the cup-shaped depressions on the morel's surface contains thousands of asci. Some morels produce mycorrhizae. Mushroom hunters find morels growing in a wide range of habitats, though they are often found in orchards. Another ascomycete found in southern Europe is even more prized—the delicious black truffle, *Tuber melanosporum.*

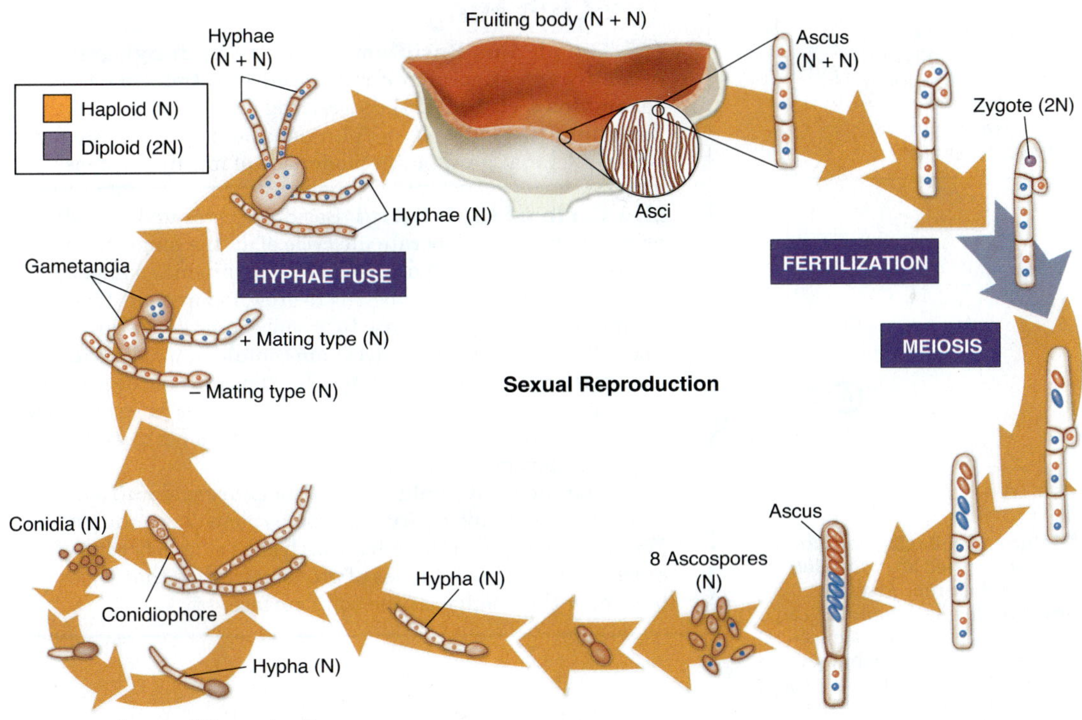

▲ **Figure 21–7** The life cycle of ascomycetes includes both asexual and sexual reproduction. During asexual reproduction, spores called conidia are formed at the tips of specialized hyphae called conidiophores. During sexual reproduction, hyphae of two mating types fuse to form hyphae with two haploid nuclei (N + N). The N + N hyphae then form a fruiting body, which eventually releases ascospores. **Ascomycetes are named for the ascus, the reproductive structure that contains ascospores.**

Yeasts Yeasts are unicellular fungi. The yeasts used by humans for baking and brewing are classified as ascomycetes because they form asci with ascospores during the sexual phase of their life cycle.

You might think of yeast as a lifeless, dry powder that is used to make bread. Actually, the dry granules contain ascospores, which become active in a moist environment. To see this for yourself, add a spoonful of dry yeast to half a cup of warm water that contains some sugar. In about 20 minutes, when you examine a drop of this mixture under a microscope, you will be able to see cell division in the rapidly growing yeast cells. The process of asexual reproduction you are observing is called **budding.**

The common yeasts used for baking and brewing are members of the genus *Saccharomyces,* which means "sugar fungi." These yeasts are grown in a rich nutrient mixture containing very little oxygen. Prior to baking, the nutrient mixture is a mound of thick dough. Lacking oxygen, the yeasts within the mixture use the process of alcoholic fermentation to obtain energy. The byproducts of alcoholic fermentation are carbon dioxide and alcohol. The carbon dioxide gas makes beverages bubble and bread rise (by producing bubbles within the dough). The alcohol in bread dough evaporates during baking. In brewing, alcohol remains in the resulting alcoholic beverages.

Build Science Skills

Observing Allow students to carry out the activity described in paragraph 2. Divide the class into small groups, and provide each group with a package of dry yeast, beaker, molasses, aluminum foil, dropper pipette, microscope, microscope slide, coverslip, and methylene blue. Have students mix 5 mL of molasses and 500 mL of warm water in the beaker and then stir in half the package of dry yeast. They should cover the top of the beaker and place it in a warm spot for 20–30 minutes. Then, students should make slides of the yeast cells that have grown in the beaker and observe them under a microscope at low and high power. Adding a drop of methylene blue under the coverslip will ensure that the cells can be clearly observed. Have students make drawings of the yeast cells and share their observations in a class discussion. L2 L3

Build Science Skills

Designing Experiments Explain to students that bromthymol blue solution turns green then yellow in the presence of carbon dioxide, which is one of the byproducts of alcoholic fermentation. Then, divide the class into small groups, and ask each group to design an experiment that investigates at what temperature yeast is most active. A typical experiment will involve adding bromthymol blue solution to a yeast-molasses mixture at various temperatures and observing how fast the color changes. L2

BIO INSIGHTS — FACTS AND FIGURES

Yeast on the shower curtain!
Yeasts are unicellular ascomycetes that reproduce both asexually and sexually. When yeasts reproduce asexually, it is mostly by budding. A parent cell forms a bud on its outer surface that eventually breaks off. Yeasts also reproduce by fission. Sexual reproduction occurs when two haploid yeasts fuse to form a diploid zygote. The zygote then undergoes meiosis, which results in haploid spores. These haploid spores remain for some period within the diploid cell wall—the ascospores and ascus of these ascomycetes. Yeasts are found widely in nature, mostly in liquid or moist environments. Yeasts are often seen as a white powder on leaves and fruits. One yeast, *Rhodotorula,* is seen in the home as a pink coating on shower curtains. *Saccharomyces* is used not only in baking and brewing but also often in research, because it is so easily cultured.

Answers to . . .

CHECKPOINT *Ascospores are formed in the asci. They are haploid.*

Figure 21–6 *Cup fungi form conidia (asexually) and ascospores (sexually).*

Download a worksheet on asexual reproduction for students to complete, and find additional support from NSTA SciLInks.

The Club Fungi

Use Visuals

Figure 21–8 After students have studied the figure, ask: **What occurs that produces a secondary mycelium?** *(Mycelia of different mating types fuse.)* Explain that each cell of the secondary mycelium has both plus (+) and minus (-) nuclei. **What is a button?** *(A thick bulge of growing hyphae at the soil's surface)* The common mushrooms found in the produce section at the grocery are buttons of the basidiomycete *Agaricus bisporus*. Ask: **What happens in the basidia?** *(The plus and minus nuclei fuse in fertilization, forming diploid zygotes.)* **What cellular process results in haploid basidiospores?** *(Meiosis)* Point out that the basidiospores are forcibly discharged from the gills, as shown in one of the bottom illustrations. **What force distributes these basidiospores far from the mushroom cap?** *(The wind)* L1 L2

Address Misconceptions

Show students a photo of a mushroom growing in the wild, and ask: **Is there a difference between this mushroom and a toadstool?** *(Some students may suggest that a toadstool is a kind of poisonous mushroom.)* Explain that folklore in some places makes distinctions between mushrooms and toadstools; however, mycologists make no such distinctions. A toadstool is a folk term—not a scientific term—for some kinds of mushrooms. L2

For: Links on asexual reproduction
Visit: www.SciLinks.org
Web Code: cbn-6212

The Club Fungi

The phylum Basidiomycota, or club fungi, gets its name from a specialized reproductive structure that resembles a club. The spore-bearing structure is called the **basidium** (buh-SID-ee-um; plural: basidia). Basidia are found on the gills that grow on the underside of mushroom caps.

CA a ⓐ 7 2.a

Life Cycle of Club Fungi Basidiomycetes undergo what is probably the most elaborate life cycle of all the fungi. As shown in **Figure 21–8,** a basidiospore germinates to produce a haploid primary mycelium, which begins to grow. Before long, the mycelia of different mating types fuse to produce a secondary mycelium. The cells of the secondary mycelium contain haploid nuclei of each mating type. Secondary mycelia may grow in the soil for years, reaching an enormous size. A few mycelia have been found to be hundreds of meters across, making them perhaps the largest organisms in the world.

When the right combination of moisture and nutrients occurs, spore-producing fruiting bodies push above the ground. You would recognize these fruiting bodies as mushrooms. Each mushroom begins as a mass of growing hyphae that forms a button, or thick bulge, at the soil's surface.

▼ **Figure 21–8 The club fungi are named after the club shape of their reproductive structure, the basidium.** The cap of a basidiomycete such as a mushroom is composed of tightly packed hyphae. The lower side of the cap is composed of gills—thin blades of tissue lined with basidia that produce basidiospores.

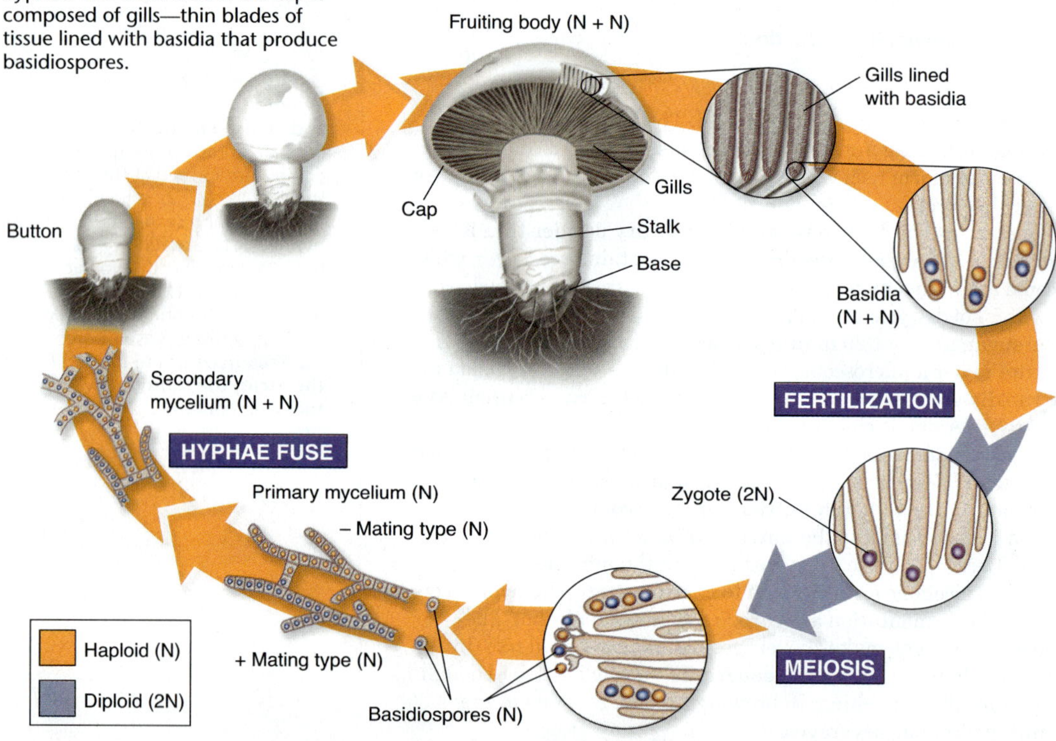

BIO INSIGHTS — FACTS AND FIGURES

Cultivated mushrooms

The common "white button" mushrooms sold in grocery stores are the buttons of *Agaricus bisporus*. This mushroom was probably first cultivated in and around Paris, France, in the mid-1600s. In the United States, one of the main centers for commercial cultivation of white buttons is Kennett Square, a small town in southeastern Pennsylvania. Large-scale mushroom growing is generally done in long, windowless warehouses, or "mushroom houses." The mushrooms are cultivated on compost made from straw and manure, first pasteurized to destroy harmful microorganisms. The compost is seeded with compact mycelium and watered regularly. The temperature is kept cool (9–13°C) to cut down on disease and insect attacks. For taste reasons, mushrooms are harvested as immature buttons, before spores are produced in great numbers.

Figure 21–9 Diversity of Club Fungi

Orange Jelly

Pigskin Poison Puffball

Fly Agaric

Star Stinkhorn Fungi

Shelf Fungus

Bird's Nest Fungus

▲ The club fungi are a very diverse group. These fungi are all decomposers, but other kinds of club fungi are parasites of plants and animals. At least two of these fungi, the pigskin poison puffball and the fly agaric, are poisonous. **Inferring** *Can you tell by looking at a fungus whether or not it is poisonous?*

Fruiting bodies expand with astonishing speed, sometimes producing fully developed mushrooms overnight. This remarkable growth rate is caused by cell enlargement, not cell division. The cells of the hyphae enlarge by rapidly taking in water.

When the mushroom cap opens, it exposes hundreds of tiny gills on its underside. Each gill is lined with basidia. The two nuclei in each basidium fuse to form a diploid (2N) zygote cell, which then undergoes meiosis, forming clusters of haploid **basidiospores.** The basidiospores form at the edge of each basidium and, within a few hours, are ready to be scattered. Mushrooms are truly amazing reproductive structures—a single mushroom can produce billions of spores, and giant puffballs can produce trillions.

CA a 7 2.a

Diversity of Club Fungi In addition to mushrooms, basidiomycetes include shelf fungi, which grow near the surfaces of dead or decaying trees. The visible bracketlike structure that forms is a reproductive structure, and it, too, is a prolific producer of spores. Puffballs, earthstars, jelly fungi, and plant parasites known as rusts are other examples of basidiomycetes. **Figure 21–9** shows some examples of basidiomycetes.

CHECKPOINT *On which part of a mushroom would you find basidia?*

Demonstration

Collect samples of basidiomycetes from local wild areas and bring them to class. (To collect a sample, use a self-sealing plastic sandwich bag. Turn it inside out, place it over a hand like a glove, pick the fungus, and invert the bag over the sample. You can use a plastic fork or similar tool to pry up the sample. If collecting proves impractical, obtain samples from a biological supply house or use photographs.) Display your collection for students to examine. Challenge students to identify the fruiting body, the hyphae, and the mycelium of each sample. Provide field guides, and encourage students to identify the different samples displayed. L2 L3

Build Science Skills

Using Models Provide modeling compound, and challenge students to make a simple model of a basidiomycete. For an example of what to make, students can use illustrations in their textbook, photos in other books, or samples collected by teacher or students. Have students also make labels for the parts they include in their model. When the modeling compound dries, encourage students to use paints to simulate the colors of real basidiomycetes. L2

Teacher to Teacher

To help students understand how fungal spores spread, I have them make "mushroom prints." Give each student a mature mushroom and have them remove the stalk from the cap with a knife. Place the cap on a piece of white paper, with the gills down. Place a glass, cup, or bowl over the cap to make sure it is undisturbed, and leave it overnight. When the cover and mushroom are removed, there will be a radiating pattern on the paper, caused by basidiospores falling to the paper from the gills. Students can transfer some of the basidiospores onto a slide and examine them with a microscope. They can preserve their print by lightly spraying it with an artist's fixative or varnish.

—*Audra Williams*
Biology Teacher
Sprayberry High School
Marietta, GA

Answers to . . .

CHECKPOINT *Basidia are found on the gills in the caps of mushrooms.*

Figure 21–9 *You cannot tell by looking, because many species of poisonous mushrooms look very similar to edible mushrooms.*

21–2 (continued)

The Imperfect Fungi

Use Visuals

Figure 21–10 Ask students: **What is this blue-green deuteromycete growing on?** *(An orange)* Have students relate experiences with this same phenomenon at home, and point out that they may have observed an important and famous fungus in their own homes without realizing it. Ask: **What is the antibiotic penicillin used to kill?** *(Harmful bacteria)* Review with students what they learned in Chapter 19 about bacteria and antibiotics. L1 L2

3 ASSESS

Evaluate Understanding

Have students write a paragraph that compares and contrasts the life cycles of a sac fungus and a club fungus.

Reteach

Ask students to make a compare/contrast table entitled The Four Main Groups of Fungi. Column heads could include *Name, Phylum Name, Characteristic Structures, Life Cycle,* and *Examples*. Students should include as many important details about each of the four main groups as possible.

You & Your Community

Encourage students to talk to the produce manager at a local supermarket. Students might also talk with the chefs of local restaurants, including Asian restaurants. Suggest that they investigate foods using portobello mushrooms (*Agaricus bisporus*), oyster mushrooms (*Pleurotus ostratus*), shiitake mushrooms (*Lentinus edodes*), or enoki mushrooms (*Flammulina velutipes*). Blue cheese is made using a *Penicillium* mold. *Aspergillus* fungi are used to produce soy sauce, as well as the Japanese food called *miso.*

If your class subscribes to the iText, use it to review the Key Concepts in Section 21–2.

Figure 21–10 **The phylum Deuteromycota is made up of fungi that cannot be classified in any other phylum.** Under the microscope, the brushlike clusters of many small, spherical conidia characterize *Penicillium notatum.* This organism was the first of the *Penicillium* fungi used to produce the antibiotic penicillin.

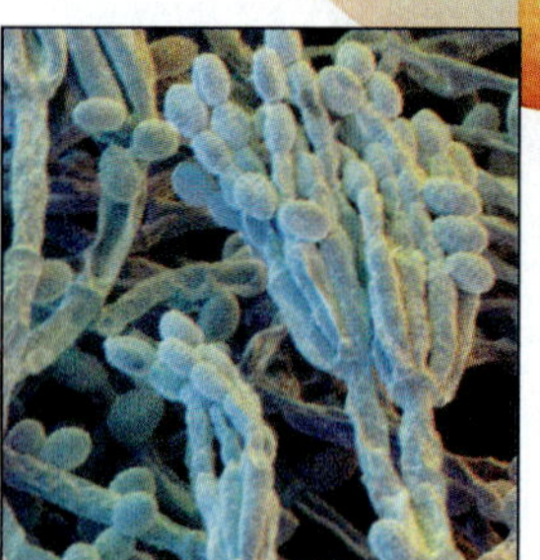

(magnification: 930×)

Edible and Inedible Mushrooms Many types of fungi have long been considered delicacies, and several different species of mushrooms are cultivated for food. You may have already tasted sliced mushrooms on pizza, feasted on delicious sautéed portobello mushrooms, or eaten shiitake mushrooms. When properly cooked and prepared, domestic mushrooms are tasty and nutritious.

Wild mushrooms are a different story: Although some are edible, many are poisonous. Because many species of poisonous mushrooms look almost identical to edible mushrooms, you should never pick or eat any mushrooms found in the wild. Instead, mushroom gathering should be left to experts who can positively identify each mushroom they collect. The result of eating a poisonous mushroom can be severe illness, or even death.

The Imperfect Fungi

Fungi are usually classified by the sexual phase of their life cycle. So, what do biologists do when they discover a fungus that does not seem to have a sexual phase? Until a sexual phase is discovered, scientists place it in the phylum called Deuteromycota, or imperfect fungi. The term *imperfect*, by the way, doesn't mean that there's anything wrong with these organisms. It simply means that *our* understanding of their life cycles may not be perfect. **The Deuteromycota are fungi that cannot be placed in other phyla because researchers have never been able to observe a sexual phase in their life cycles.** A majority of the imperfect fungi closely resemble ascomycetes. Others are similar to basidiomycetes, and a few resemble the zygomycetes.

One of the best-known genera of the imperfect fungi is *Penicillium*. The species *Penicillium notatum*, shown in **Figure 21–10**, is a mold that frequently grows on fruit and is the source of the antibiotic penicillin. Like the ascomycetes, *Penicillium* reproduces asexually by means of conidia, leading many biologists to conclude that *Penicillium* evolved from an ascomycete that lost the sexual phase of its life cycle.

21–2 Section Assessment

1. **Key Concept** List the four phyla of fungi, and identify the main characteristics of the members of each phylum.
2. How do conidia form? What is their function?
3. Which fungal phylum contains the largest number of species?
4. **Critical Thinking Comparing and Contrasting** Compare the structure and function of an ascus and a basidium.
5. **Critical Thinking Comparing and Contrasting** Compare asexual and sexual reproduction in bread mold. At what stage does meiosis occur?

You & Your Community

Exploring Your Community

Visit a local supermarket to find out how fungi are used in the cuisines of different cultures. Select a particular fungus, research recipes in which it is used, and try one of the recipes. You may also want to find the scientific name of the fungus you have selected.

21–2 Section Assessment

1. Zygomycota have life cycles that include a zygospore. Ascomycota have asci that contain spores. Basidiomycota have a reproductive structure that resembles a club. Deuteromycota do not have an observed sexual phase.
2. In asexual reproduction of some ascomycetes, tiny spores called conidia are formed at the tip of specialized hyphae.
3. Phylum Ascomycota
4. The ascus, a sac that contains spores, forms within the fruiting body of an ascomycete. Within the ascus, two nuclei fuse to form a diploid zygote. The spore-bearing structure of a basidiomycete, called the basidium, is found on the gills of mushrooms. A basidiospore germinates to produce a haploid primary mycelium.
5. Students should describe both sexual and asexual reproduction, as discussed on page 530 and in Figure 21–5. Meiosis occurs when conditions become favorable and the zygospore germinates.

21–3 Ecology of Fungi

BI 6.e. Students know a vital part of an ecosystem is the stability of its producers and decomposers.

Guide for Reading

Key Concepts
- What is the main role of fungi in natural ecosystems?
- What problems do parasitic fungi cause?
- What kinds of symbiotic relationships do fungi form with other organisms?

Vocabulary
saprobe
lichen
mycorrhiza

Reading Strategy: Using Prior Knowledge Before you read this section, write down all the different ways that you think fungi interact in the environment. As you read, add to or revise your list as necessary.

Fungi have been around since life first moved onto land. In fact, the oldest known fossils of fungi, shown in **Figure 21–11**, were formed about 460 million years ago. At that time, the largest land plants were small organisms similar to mosses. Paleontologists think that fungi helped early plants to obtain nutrients from the ground. Their early appearance suggests that fungi may have been essential to plants' successful colonization of the land, one of the key events in the history of life.

Over time, fungi have become an important part of virtually all ecosystems, adapting to conditions in every corner of Earth. Because most fungi live their lives out of our sight, people often overlook them. But without fungi, the world would be a very different place.

All Fungi Are Heterotrophs

As heterotrophs, fungi cannot manufacture their own food. Instead, they must rely on other organisms for their energy. Unlike animals, fungi cannot move to capture food, but their mycelia can grow very rapidly into the tissues and cells of plants and other organisms. Many fungi are **saprobes,** organisms that obtain food from decaying organic matter. Others are parasites, which harm other organisms while living directly on or within them. Still other fungi are symbionts that live in close and mutually beneficial association with other species.

Although most fungi feed on decaying matter, a few feed by capturing live animals. *Pleurotus ostreatus* is a carnivorous fungus that lives on the sides of trees. As roundworms crawl into the fungus to feed, they are exposed to a fungal chemical that makes them become sluggish. As the worms slow to a stop, fungal hyphae penetrate their bodies, trapping them in place and then digesting them.

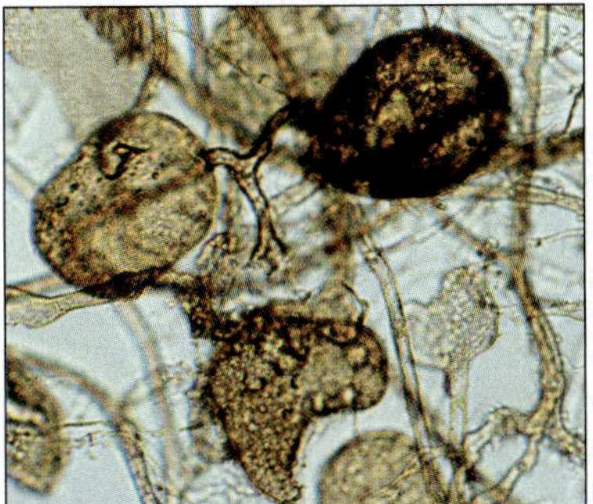

(magnification: 280×)

(magnification: 560×)

Figure 21–11 These microscopic images show fossils of the earliest known fungi, zygomycetes that lived about 460 million years ago. An overview of fossilized hyphae with spores is shown on the left. The close-up of hyphae growing out of a spore is shown on the right. **Observing** *Can you identify structures similar to those of modern molds?*

SECTION RESOURCES

Print:
- ***Teaching Resources,*** Lesson Plan 21–3, Adapted Section Summary 21–3, Adapted Worksheets 21–3, Section Summary 21–3, Worksheets 21–3, Section Review 21–3
- ***Reading and Study Workbook A,*** Section 21–3
- ***Adapted Reading and Study Workbook B,*** Section 21–3
- ***Lab Worksheets,*** Chapter 21 Real-World Lab

Technology:
- ***iText,*** Section 21–3
- ***Transparencies Plus,*** Section 21–3

Section 21–3

BI 6.e

1 FOCUS

Objectives

21.3.1 ***Explain*** what the ecological role of fungi is.
21.3.2 ***Describe*** problems that parasitic fungi cause.
21.3.3 ***Describe*** the kinds of mutualistic relationships that fungi form with other organisms.

Guide for Reading

Vocabulary Preview
Have students write the Vocabulary words, dividing each into its separate syllables as best they can. Remind students that each syllable usually has only one vowel sound. The correct syllabications are sap•robe, li•chen, my•cor•rhi•za.

Reading Strategy
Have students rewrite each of the section's blue headings in the form of a question and then find details within each subsection to answer their questions.

2 INSTRUCT

All Fungi Are Heterotrophs

Build Science Skills

Formulating Hypotheses Point out the statement on page 537 that fungi may have been essential to plants' successful colonization of the land. Also review the definitions of the three kinds of fungi: saprobes, parasites, and mutualists. Then, ask each student to write a hypothesis about how fungi helped in plants' colonization of the land. Their hypotheses should be in the form of a brief statement. Tell students that they will learn whether their hypotheses are correct later in the section. L2 L3

Answer to . . .

Figure 21–11 *Modern molds have hyphae and spores, just as the fossil fungi had.*

21–3 (continued)

Fungi as Decomposers

Make Connections

Earth Science To help students understand how fungi aid in soil formation, explain that soil is a combination of mineral and organic matter, water, and air. Soil forms through the weathering, or breaking down, of rock at the surface of the earth. Although rock and mineral fragments form the major part of soil, it also contains a significant amount of organic matter, called humus. Display a pile of sand and a mound of potting soil, and have students examine and compare both materials. Then, ask: **Which of these materials will best support plant life, and why?** *(Students should know that the potting soil will best support plant life. Some may know that it does so because it contains humus.)* Explain that geologists don't classify a material as soil unless it contains humus. The humus is the result of decomposers, including bacteria and fungi. L1 L2

Fungi as Parasites

Build Science Skills

Posing Questions Divide the class into small groups, and ask each group to brainstorm for a list of questions about parasitic fungi. Typical questions might include: How do parasitic fungi harm plants? Are any human diseases caused by parasitic fungi serious or fatal? How can human diseases caused by parasitic fungi be prevented? Are pets susceptible to fungal diseases? Once groups have made their lists, discuss as a class which questions would be most productive to investigate. Then, encourage interested students to find the answers to some of the questions. L2

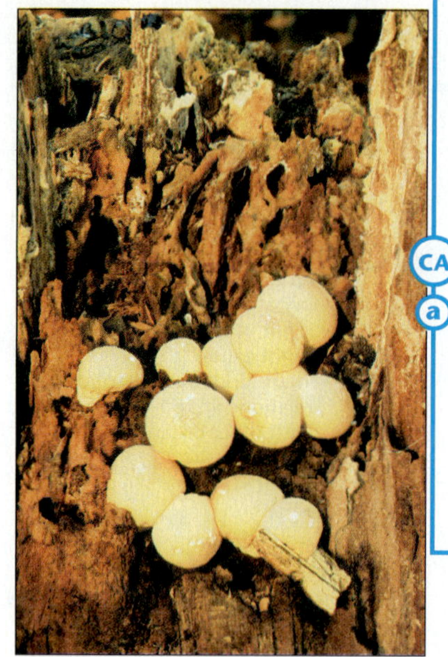

▲ **Figure 21–12** **Many fungi are decomposers that recycle nutrients by breaking down the bodies of other organisms.** The mycelia of these mushrooms have released enzymes that are breaking down the wood tissues of the decaying tree stump.

Fungi as Decomposers

Fungi play an essential role in maintaining equilibrium in nearly every ecosystem, where they recycle nutrients by breaking down the bodies and wastes of other organisms. Like the fungi in **Figure 21–12,** many fungi feed by releasing digestive enzymes that break down leaves, fruit, and other organic material into simple molecules. These molecules then diffuse into the fungus. The mycelia of fungi produce digestive enzymes that speed the breakdown of wastes and dead organisms. In so doing, they promote the recycling of nutrients and essential chemicals, helping to maintain ecosystem equilibrium.

CA a

Imagine a world without decomposers. Without decay, the energy-rich compounds that organisms accumulate during their lifetimes would be lost forever. Many organisms, especially plants, remove important trace elements and nutrients from the soil. If these materials were not returned, the soil would quickly be depleted, and Earth would become lifeless and barren.

Fungi as Parasites

As useful as many fungi are, others can infect both animals and plants, disrupting their internal equilibrium and causing disease. **Parasitic fungi cause serious plant and animal diseases. A few cause diseases in humans.**

Plant Diseases Fungi cause diseases such as corn smut, which destroys the corn kernels, as shown in **Figure 21–13.** Mildews, which infect a wide variety of fruits, are also fungi. Fungal diseases are responsible for the loss of approximately 15 percent of the crops grown in temperate regions of the world. In tropical areas, where high humidity favors fungal growth, the loss of crops is sometimes as high as 50 percent. Fungi are in direct competition with humans for food. Unfortunately for us, sometimes fungi win that competition.

One fungal disease—wheat rust—affects one of the most important crops grown in North America. Rusts are caused by a type of basidiomycete that needs two different plants to complete its life cycle. Spores produced by rust in barberry plants are carried by the wind into wheat fields. There, the spores germinate and infect wheat plants. The patches of rust produce a second type of spore that infects other wheat plants, allowing the disease to spread through the field like wildfire.

Later in the growing season, a new variety of spore is produced by the rust. These tough black spores easily survive through the winter. In spring, they go through a sexual phase and produce spores that infect barberry plants. Once on the barberry leaves, the rust produces the spores that infect wheat plants, and the cycle continues. Fortunately, once agricultural scientists understood the life cycle of the rust, they were able to slow its spread by destroying barberry plants.

CHECKPOINT *What are two examples of plant diseases caused by fungi?*

UNIVERSAL ACCESS

Less Proficient Readers

Help students understand the importance of recycling nutrients by having them recall what they learned about organic molecules in Chapter 2. Elicit from volunteers that there are four groups of compounds in living things—carbohydrates, lipids, proteins, and nuclei acids. Remind students that carbohydrates and lipids are energy-rich compounds that decomposers help recycle, and those compounds would be lost to living things without decomposers. L1

Advanced Learners

Encourage interested students to further investigate the problem of wheat rust. Explain that the fungus that causes the disease is *Puccinia graminis*, which is often known as black stem rust of wheat. Ask students to prepare a presentation about wheat rust, including an illustration of the organism's life cycle. Students will discover that the wheat-rust problem persists despite development of rust-resistant strains of wheat. 

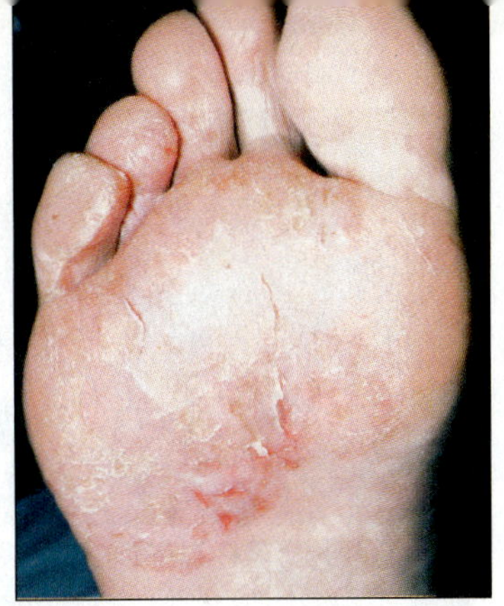

Figure 21–13 Parasitic fungi cause serious diseases in plants and animals. Corn smut (left) grows on a corn plant, harming it. The fungus releases millions of spores that survive in the soil during the winter and begin their life cycle again in the spring. Wheat rust (center) is a basidiomycete that infects both wheat and barberry plants. Athlete's foot (right) infects the outer layers of human skin.

Human Diseases Fungal parasites can also infect humans. One deuteromycete can infect the areas between the toes, causing the infection known as athlete's foot. The fungus forms a mycelium directly within the outer layers of the skin. This produces a red, inflamed sore from which the spores can easily spread from person to person. When the same fungus infects other areas, such as the skin of the scalp, it produces a red scaling sore known as ringworm, which is not a worm at all.

The microorganism *Candida albicans,* a yeast, can disrupt the equilibrium within the human body, causing fungal disease. *Candida,* which grows in moist regions of the body, is usually kept in check by competition from bacteria that grow in the body and by the body's immune system. This normal balance can be upset by many factors, including the use of antibiotics, which kill bacteria, or by damage to the immune system. When this happens, *Candida* may produce thrush, a painful mouth infection. Yeast infections of the female reproductive tract usually are due to overgrowth of *Candida*.

Other Animal Diseases As problematic as human fungal diseases can be, few fungal diseases are as deadly as the infection by one fungus from the genus *Cordyceps*. This fungus infects grasshoppers in rain forests in Costa Rica. Microscopic spores become lodged in the grasshopper, where they germinate and produce enzymes that slowly penetrate the insect's tough external skeleton. The spores multiply in the insect's body, digesting all its cells and tissues until the insect dies. To complete the process of digestion, hyphae develop, cloaking the decaying exoskeleton in a web of fungal material. Reproductive structures, which will produce more spores that will spread the infection, then emerge from the grasshopper's remains, as shown in **Figure 21–14.**

▲ **Figure 21–14** This grasshopper is the victim of *Cordyceps,* a fungus. Once the fungus's tiny spore enters the insect's body, it multiplies rapidly and digests body tissues. The structures growing out of the grasshopper's body are the fungus's fruiting bodies. **Comparing and Contrasting** ***Some pathogens rely on their host to spread them to other potential hosts. How does this fungus spread?***

Use Visuals

Figure 21–13 After students have examined the photos and read the caption, ask: **What is a parasite?** *(An organism that lives within or on another organism and harms that organism by feeding on it)* Have students recall that parasitism is one of the three symbiotic relationships they learned about in Chapter 4. Point out that parasites generally weaken but do not kill their hosts. Ask: **What hosts are shown in this figure?** *(Corn, wheat, and human)* **Does athlete's foot kill the host?** *(No)* Explain that corn smut and wheat rust also don't kill their hosts, though they do enough damage to their hosts that the plants become worthless to the farmer who grows them. L2

Make Connections

Health Science After students have read about the fungal parasite that causes athlete's foot, ask: **In what kind of location are you most likely to "catch" this disease?** *(Many students will know that athlete's foot is spread in locker rooms.)* Point out that the disease is spread from person to person by spores. Ask: **What is it about locker rooms that enhances the spread of these fungal spores?** *(Locker rooms are warm and damp and people walk around barefoot, especially from the shower to lockers. Spores in a sore on one person's foot can easily spread to other people's feet.)* L1 L2

BIO INSIGHTS

FACTS AND FIGURES

The fungus among us

Fungal infections in humans are called mycoses. Fungi that cause superficial skin, or cutaneous, infections are known as dermatophytes. These pathogens are generally classified as deuteromycetes, and they include members of the fungi genera *Trichophyton, Epidermophyton,* and *Microsporum.* The medical names of cutaneous mycoses look like genus and species names, but they really identify the infected part of the body. For example, the common "athlete's foot" is known as tinea pedis. *Tinea* means "worm," and *pedis* means "foot." Other cutaneous mycoses are tinea capitis (ringworm of the scalp), tinea cruris (ringworm of the groin, or "jock itch"), and tinea unguium (ringworm of the nails). Usually, these cutaneous infections occur when there are cuts and other breaks in the skin that become infected with fungal spores.

Answers to . . .

CHECKPOINT *Corn smut, wheat rust*

Figure 21–14 *The spores of* Cordyceps *are spread by fruiting bodies that grow out of the grasshopper's body.*

21–3 (continued)

Symbiotic Relationships

Make Connections

Earth Science Explain that lichens are able to break down rocks through both mechanical and chemical weathering. Mechanical weathering includes processes that break rock into smaller pieces. Chemical weathering actually changes the chemical makeup of rocks. The fungus part of a lichen sends its hyphae into cracks in a rock, eventually wedging the rock apart. This is mechanical weathering. More important, the fungus produces acids that seep into rock and break it apart. This is chemical weathering. In addition to these weathering processes, lichens that grow on bare rock trap soil particles. As soil builds up, plants are able to grow. Thus, lichens are often the most important part of the so-called pioneer community on bare rock. 

Use Visuals

Figure 21–16 Call students' attention to the lichen's layers. Then, ask: **Which of the organisms in this mutualistic association provides a protective upper layer?** *(The fungus)* **How would you describe the photosynthetic component of a lichen?** *(The algal or cyanobacterial cells are scattered among strands of fungal hyphae in the second layer of the lichen.)* **What attaches the lichen to a rock or tree?** *(Small projections)* Explain that these lichen anchors are fungal hyphae called rhizines. L1 L2

Build Science Skills

Observing Provide students with photos of different species of lichens. Explain that lichens are found on trees and rocks, as well as on the sides of buildings, gravestones, and other rocklike structures. Encourage students to find one or two examples of lichens near their homes. For each example, they should make a drawing and write a description. L2 L3

Figure 21–15 Lichens grow in one of three forms. Crustose lichens (top) are flat; foliose lichens (middle) resemble leaves; and fruticose lichens (bottom) grow upright. **Inferring** *How do lichens assist in soil formation?*

Symbiotic Relationships

Fungi often grow in close association with members of other species in symbiotic relationships. Although fungi are parasites in many of these relationships, that is not always the case. **Some fungi form symbiotic relationships in which both partners benefit. Two such mutualistic associations, lichens and mycorrhizae, are essential to many ecosystems.** Lichens are shown in **Figure 21–15.**

Lichens **Lichens** (LY-kunz) are not single organisms. Rather, they are symbiotic associations between a fungus and a photosynthetic organism. The fungi in lichens are usually ascomycetes, although a few are basidiomycetes. The photosynthetic organism is either a green alga or a cyanobacterium, or both. **Figure 21–16** shows the structure of a lichen.

Lichens are extremely resistant to drought and cold. Therefore, they can grow in places where few other organisms can survive—on dry, bare rock in deserts and on the tops of mountains. Lichens are able to survive in these harsh environments because of the relationship between the two partner organisms. The algae or cyanobacteria carry out photosynthesis, providing the fungus with a source of energy. The fungus, in turn, provides the algae or bacteria with water and minerals that it collects and protects the delicate green cells from intense sunlight.

Lichens are often the first organisms to enter barren environments, gradually breaking down the rocks on which they grow. In this way, lichens help in the early stages of soil formation. Lichens are also remarkably sensitive to air pollution, and they are among the first organisms to be affected when air quality deteriorates.

CHECKPOINT *What two groups of organisms grow together in lichens?*

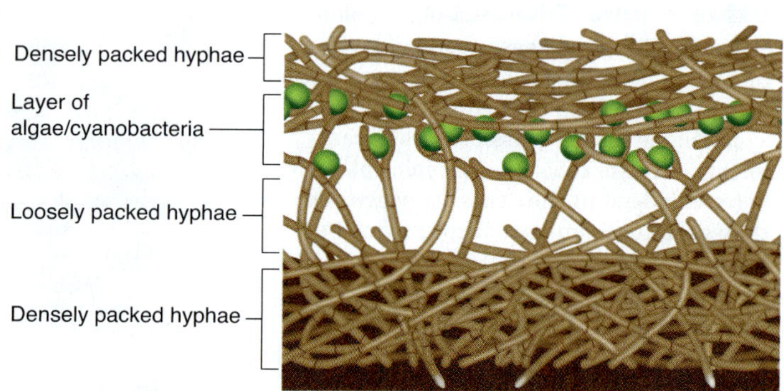

▲ **Figure 21–16 Lichens are a mutualistic relationship between a fungus and an alga or a cyanobacterium, or both.** The protective upper surface of a lichen is composed of fungal hyphae. Below this is the layer of cyanobacteria or algae with loosely woven hyphae. The third layer consists of loosely packed hyphae. The bottom layer is a protective surface covered by small projections that attach the lichen to a rock or tree.

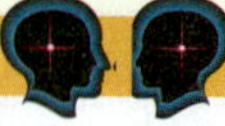

TEACHER TO TEACHER

A day before discussing lichens in class, I show students a sample of tree bark with a lichen growing on it. Each student is asked to describe what he or she sees and make a few notes about the physical appearance of the lichen. (It is typically gray and lifeless in appearance.) After each student has had a chance to observe the bark, I spray the lichen with water, place the bark in a large plastic bag, and put it under a plant light. In a day or two, the lichen will develop a green color. I use this to emphasize that a photosynthetic organism is part of the lichen.

—*Debbie Richards*
Biology Teacher
Bryan High School
Bryan, TX

Problem Solving

BIIE 1.d

Repotting Orchids

You are working in a greenhouse that has just begun to grow orchids. The plants arrive in small pots from a nursery. When they outgrow the pots, your supervisor asks you to place them in larger pots with fresh soil, just as you have done with other plants. However, every time you follow the greenhouse procedure for repotting, which includes carefully washing off the "old" soil and placing the roots into a sterilized soil mix, the plants soon wither and die.

Defining the Problem In your own words, what is the problem the greenhouse faces?

Organizing Information What problems could sterile, microbe-free soil present to a plant? Are there microorganisms in soil that might be essential to orchids? Might the loss of such organisms cause problems for the plants? What kinds of problems?

Creating a Solution Describe an experiment that you could use to find out if the use of sterile soil is causing the problems with repotting. Be sure to devise controls that might determine whether the mechanical stress of repotting, rather than the soil mixture, is causing the problems.

Presenting Your Plan Make a poster showing the steps and procedures in your proposed experiment, and explain it to the class.

Mycorrhizae Fungi also form mutualistic relationships with plants. Almost half of the tissues of trees are hidden beneath the ground in masses of tangled roots. These roots are woven into a partnership with an even larger web of fungal mycelia. These associations of plant roots and fungi are **mycorrhizae** (my-koh-RY-zee; singular: mycorrhiza).

Scientists have known about this partnership for years, but recent research shows that it is more common and more important than was previously thought. Researchers now estimate that 80 percent of all plant species form mycorrhizae with fungi.

How do plants and fungi benefit from each other? The tiny hyphae of the fungi aid plants in absorbing water and minerals. They do this by producing a network that covers the roots of the plants and increases the effective surface area of the root system. This allows the roots to absorb more water and minerals from the soil. In addition, the fungi release enzymes that free nutrients in the soil. The plants, in turn, provide the fungi with the products of photosynthesis.

The presence of mycorrhizae is essential for the growth of many plants. The seeds of some plants, such as orchids, cannot germinate in the absence of mycorrhizal fungi. Many trees are unable to survive without fungal symbionts. Mycorrhizal associations have even been cited as an adaptation that was critical in the evolution of land plants from more-aquatic ancestors.

FACTS AND FIGURES

Fungus roots

The term *mycorrhizae* means "fungus roots," and the name aptly describes the association that develops between plant roots and fungi. The hyphae of some fungi form a sheath around the root, and hyphae also penetrate a short way into the root, growing between the root cells. These are called ectomycorrhizae. Other fungi have hyphae that penetrate root cells, through which materials are exchanged. These are called endomycorrhizae. Many plants have difficulty absorbing such elements as phosphorus from the soil, and the hyphae provide these elements to the plant. In return, the plant provides the fungus with sugars and amino acids. About half of all basidiomycetes that form mushrooms live in mycorrhizae with trees such as oaks and pines. The mushrooms that pop up at the base of these trees are evidence of the "fungus roots" underground.

Problem Solving

BIIE 1.d

Explain that the problem described is a common one experienced by greenhouse workers. Although many plants can be repotted into fresh, sterile soil, those that depend on mycorrhizae cannot. The fungi that form mycorrhizae with orchids are zygomycetes that live in soil. L2 L3

Defining the Problem Students' definitions of the problem will differ, though all should mention that repotting plants in a sterilized soil mix causes the plants to die.

Organizing Information Students should suggest that sterilized soil would not contain the fungi for the mycorrhizal relationships with orchids that the plants need to absorb necessary minerals.

Creating a Solution A typical experiment might retain some of the old soil attached to the roots when repotting a plant. To determine whether mechanical stress is part of the problem, students might suggest adding fungicide to soil instead of replacing it.

Presenting Your Plan Students' plans should show the steps necessary to carry out the proposed experiment. Each plan should designate a control, a variable, and a means to collect the data needed to evaluate the results.

Use Community Resources

Invite a manager of a local greenhouse to speak to the class about repotting plants and whether and why sterilized soil is ever used. Have students write questions ahead of time both about mycorrhizal associations and about fungal diseases that affect greenhouse plants. L2

Answers to . . .

CHECKPOINT *A lichen is a symbiotic association between a fungus and an alga or a cyanobacterium.*

Figure 21–15 *They gradually break down the rocks on which they grow.*

21–3 (continued)

Use Visuals

Figure 21–17 Ask students: **In the bottom photograph, what did the seedlings on the left, grown without mycorrhizae, have less of in comparison with the seedlings on the right?** *(They had less water and nutrients, which fungal symbionts aid plants in absorbing in mycorrhizae.)* **If the plants on the right benefited from a mycorrhizal association, how did the fungi in that association benefit?** *(The fungi were provided with the products of photosynthesis by the plants.)* L2

3 ASSESS

Evaluate Understanding

Call on students at random to compare and contrast the relationship between the fungus that causes corn smut and a corn plant and the relationship between a mycorrhizal fungus and a Douglas fir. Students should contrast a parasitic relationship with a symbiotic relationship.

Reteach

Have students make a chart listing the beneficial roles and the harmful roles of fungi in the environment.

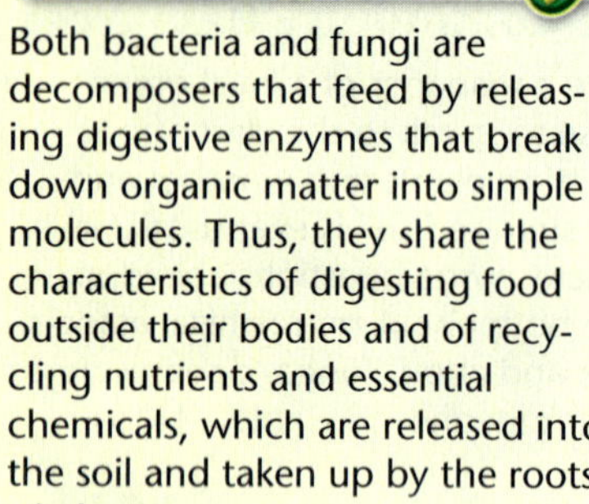

Both bacteria and fungi are decomposers that feed by releasing digestive enzymes that break down organic matter into simple molecules. Thus, they share the characteristics of digesting food outside their bodies and of recycling nutrients and essential chemicals, which are released into the soil and taken up by the roots of plants.

If your class subscribes to the iText, use it to review the Key Concepts in Section 21–3.

Answer to . . .

Figure 21–17 *Mutualism*

Figure 21–17 Plants and fungi often form associations called mycorrhizae (top photograph). The fungi in the mycorrhizae allow the host plant to absorb more water and nutrients. In the bottom photograph, the lemon seedlings on the left were grown without mycorrhizae. Those on the right, of the same age, were grown with mycorrhizae. **Applying Concepts** *What type of symbiotic relationship is illustrated by mycorrhizae?*

Mycorrhizal relationships are often very specialized. For example, the Douglas fir forests of the Pacific Northwest are dependent on the presence of a particular species of white truffle. In Europe, black truffles are found growing with oak and beech trees. The fly agaric grows mostly with birch and pine trees. **Figure 21–17** shows how mycorrhizae affect the growth of young lemon trees.

Why is this networking relationship so important? The partnership between plant and fungus does not end with a single plant. The roots of each plant are plugged into mycorrhizal networks that connect many plants. What's more astounding is that these networks appear to connect plants of different species.

A recent experiment showed that carbon atoms from one tree often end up in another nearby tree. In an experiment using carbon isotopes to track the movement of carbon, ecologist Suzanne Simard found that mycorrhizal fungi transferred carbon from paper birch trees growing in the sun to Douglas fir trees growing in the shade. As a result, the sun-starved fir trees thrived, basically by being "fed" carbon from the birches.

Simard's findings suggest that plants are far from being isolated individuals, as was previously thought. Instead, plants—and their associated fungi—may be evolving as part of an ecological partnership.

21–3 Section Assessment

1. **Key Concept** What is the major role of fungi in an ecosystem?
2. **Key Concept** Explain the roles of fungi in causing disease in humans and in other living things.
3. **Key Concept** Describe two mutualistic relationships that fungi form with other organisms.
4. Describe the life cycle of wheat rust.
5. **Critical Thinking Applying Concepts** What might happen to a garden if it were sprayed with a long-acting fungicide?
6. **Critical Thinking Applying Concepts** Summarize the role of fungi in disrupting the equilibrium in an ecosystem. Give one specific example.

Structure and Function
Both bacteria and fungi are decomposers. What characteristics do these two groups share that allow them to function in this ecological role? Use the information in Chapter 19 to help answer this question.

21–3 Section Assessment

1. To recycle nutrient material by breaking down organic matter
2. Parasitic fungi cause serious plant and animal diseases, including those in humans.
3. A lichen is a symbiotic association between a fungus and an alga or a cyanobacterium. Mycorrhizae are mutualistic relationships between plant roots and fungi.
4. Spores produced by the rust in barberry plants are carried by wind into wheat fields, where they infect wheat plants and produce a second type of spore that infects other wheat plants. Another type of spore survives through the winter and produces yet another spore that infects barberry plants.
5. The garden plants would not flourish, because the mycorrhizae between plants and fungi benefit both plants and fungi.
6. Answers will vary. Most students will focus on plant or animal diseases caused by fungi.

Real-World Lab

BIIE 1.d

Examining Seeds for Fungi

The fungi that you are probably most familiar with are mushrooms and the molds that attack stored foods. In this investigation, you will examine how storage conditions affect the growth of fungi on seeds.

Problem

What storage conditions best protect seeds from fungi?

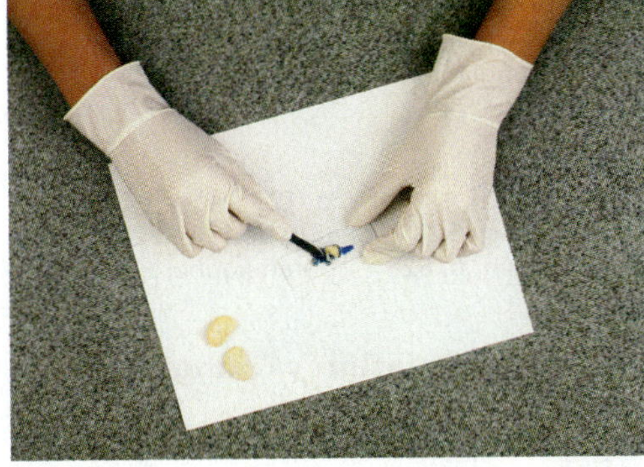

Materials

- seeds stored in cold, dry conditions
- seeds stored in warm, moist conditions
- forceps
- microscope slide
- coverslip
- microscope
- aniline blue stain
- dropper pipette
- paper towels

Skill

Formulating Hypotheses

Procedure

1. **Formulating Hypotheses** Develop a hypothesis about the effect of temperature and moisture on the growth of a seed-destroying fungus. Predict whether you will find more hyphae in seeds stored in cold, dry conditions or in seeds stored in warm, moist conditions.
2. Put on your plastic gloves. Use a dropper pipette to place a drop of aniline blue stain on a microscope slide. **CAUTION:** *Avoid getting the stain on your hands or clothing.*
3. Use forceps to carefully remove the outer seed coat from a seed stored in cool, dry conditions. Place the seed in the drop of aniline blue stain.
4. Use the flat side of the forceps to gently mash and flatten the seed in the drop of stain. Place a coverslip on top of the mashed seed. Leave the seed in the stain for 1 minute.
5. Use a dropper pipette to place a drop of water on the slide, touching one edge of the coverslip.
6. Touch a paper towel to the edge of the coverslip opposite the drop of water to draw the water under the coverslip. Repeat steps 4 and 5 until you have removed the drop of stain.
7. Use the high-power objective of the microscope to examine the stained seed. Any hyphae that are present will be stained blue. Record your observations as notes and sketches.
8. Repeat steps 2 through 7 with a seed stored in warm, moist conditions.

Analyze and Conclude

1. **Observing** Which seeds had more hyphae?
2. **Analyzing Data** What conditions favor the growth of fungi? What conditions are better for storing seeds?
3. **Drawing Conclusions** Did your observations support your hypothesis? Are the environmental requirements of this fungus typical of most fungi?
4. **Inferring** Aniline blue stains the cell walls of fungi more easily than plant cell walls. What substance in fungi do you think aniline blue binds to? Explain your answer.
5. **SAFETY** Explain how you demonstrated safe practices as you carried out this investigation.

Go Further

Designing Experiments Plan an experiment to compare the growth of plants from both healthy and fungus-infected seeds. Define your controlled and manipulated variables. Obtain your teacher's permission before carrying out your experiment.

Analyze and Conclude

1. Seeds stored in warm, moist conditions have more hyphae.

2. Warm, moist conditions favor the growth of fungi, and thus, cool, dry conditions are better for storing seeds.

3. Answer will depend on a student's hypothesis. Observations should support the hypothesis that fungal growth is greater in seeds stored in warm, moist conditions. This is typical of the environmental requirements of most fungi.

4. Aniline blue stain binds to chitin, which is common in fungal cells but lacking in plant cell walls.

5. Students should say that they wore plastic gloves, goggles, and aprons when working with aniline blue and handled it carefully to avoid getting the stain on their hands or clothing.

Real-World Lab

BIIE 1.d

Objectives Students will be able to:
- formulate and test a hypothesis about the effects of temperature and moisture on a fungus;
- draw a conclusion about what storage conditions best protect seeds from fungi. L2 L3

Skill Focus Formulating Hypotheses

Time 45 minutes

Advance Prep At least ten days in advance, put one batch of dry seeds—such as corn, wheat, or beans—in a sealed, airtight container in a refrigerator. Put a second batch in a dark, warm, moist place. Don't use seeds that are stained pink, which indicates treatment with a fungicide. The day before the activity, soak the seeds in 1 M sodium hydroxide (40 g/L NaOH) overnight to soften them. Wear safety goggles and rubber gloves when working with the liquid. The next day, drain the seeds and rinse them with several changes of tap water until the water is neutral pH.

Safety Make sure all students wear plastic gloves and safety goggles. Read the MSDS on NaOH.

Procedure

1. Ask students what their hypotheses and predictions are. If a prediction does not follow from a hypothesis, ask the student to explain how he or she arrived at the prediction.

3. Demonstrate how to remove the outer seed coat from a seed.

6. Demonstrate how to touch a paper towel to the edge of a coverslip to draw water under the coverslip.

Expected Outcome Students should conclude that fungal infestation is more severe in seeds stored in warm, moist conditions than in cool, dry conditions.

Go Further

Have students develop a detailed plan for how to go about carrying out such an experiment. Then, provide a sunny space in the classroom for the plants to grow. Make sure students collect growth data every two days or so for several weeks.

Chapter 21 Study Guide

Study Tip

Divide the class into small groups, and ask each group to write a list of review questions that address all the Vocabulary words and Key Concepts. Then, have groups exchange lists and answer one another's questions.

Thinking Visually

1. Life cycle includes zygospore; have rhizoids and stolons; reproduce both sexually and asexually
2. Hyphae form a gametangium
3. Cup fungi, some yeasts
4. Conidia on conidiophores
5. Hyphae form a gametangium
6. Mycelia form a secondary mycelium
7. No observed sexual phase of life cycle
8. Unknown

Chapter 21 Assessment

Reviewing Content

1. a
2. b
3. c
4. a
5. b
6. c
7. c
8. d
9. d
10. c

Understanding Concepts

11. The cells of fungi are similar to the exoskeletons of insects in that both contain chitin.

12. Hyphae are tiny filaments that are only one cell thick, whereas a mycelium is a thick mass composed of many hyphae tangled together.

13. Spores are produced in sporangia, which are found at the tops of specialized hyphae called sporangiophores. Spores can grow into new organisms.

14. Many fungi produce dry, almost weightless spores, which scatter easily in the wind. Other fungi are specialized to lure animals, which disperse fungal spores.

15. Spores must land in a favorable environment. There must be a proper combination of temperature, moisture, and food.

16. Fungi are classified according to their structure and method of reproduction.

Chapter 21 Study Guide

21–1 The Kingdom Fungi

Key Concepts

- Fungi are eukaryotic heterotrophs that have cell walls made of chitin.
- The bodies of multicellular fungi are composed of many hyphae tangled together into a thick mass called a mycelium.
- Most fungi reproduce both asexually and sexually.

Vocabulary

chitin, p. 527 • hypha, p. 527
mycelium, p. 528 • fruiting body, p. 528
sporangium, p. 528 • sporangiophore, p. 528

21–2 Classification of Fungi

Key Concepts 

- Zygomycetes have life cycles that include a zygospore.
- The phylum Ascomycota is named for the ascus, a reproductive structure that contains spores.
- The phylum Basidiomycota, or club fungi, gets its name from the basidium, a specialized reproductive structure that resembles a club.
- Deuteromycota are fungi that cannot be placed in other phyla because researchers have never been able to observe a sexual phase in their life cycles.

Vocabulary

zygospore, p. 530 • rhizoid, p. 530
stolon, p. 530 • gametangium, p. 530
conidium, p. 532 • ascus, p. 532
ascospore, p. 532 • budding, p. 533
basidium, p. 534 • basidiospore, p. 535

21–3 Ecology of Fungi

Key Concepts 

- Fungi play an essential role in maintaining equilibrium in nearly every ecosystem, where they recycle nutrients by breaking down the bodies and wastes of other organisms.
- Parasitic fungi cause serious plant and animal diseases. A few fungi cause diseases in humans.
- Some fungi form symbiotic relationships in which both partners benefit. Two such mutualistic associations, lichens and mycorrhizae, are essential to many ecosystems.

Vocabulary

saprobe, p. 537
lichen, p. 540
mycorrhiza, p. 541

Thinking Visually

Use the information in Section 21–2 to complete the following compare-and-contrast table about the different phyla of Fungi.

Four Phyla of Fungi

Phylum	Examples	Characteristics	Reproduction	
			Asexual	Sexual
Zygomycota (common molds)	*Rhizopus stolonifer* (black bread mold)	1	Spores in sporangiophores	2
Ascomycota (sac fungi)	3	Long stage in which cells have two nuclei; yeasts are unicellular	4	5
Basidiomycota (club fungi)	Mushrooms, puffballs, earthstars, shelf fungi, jelly fungi, rusts	Extremely variable; long stage in which cells have two nuclei	None or conidia on conidiophores	6
Deuteromycota (imperfect fungi)	*Penicillium,* ringworm, and athlete's foot fungus	7	Conidia on conidiophores	8

TIME SAVER

CHAPTER RESOURCES

Print:

- ***Teaching Resources,*** Chapter Vocabulary Review, Graphic Organizer, Chapter 21 Tests: Levels A and B
- ***Laboratory Assessment,*** Laboratory Assessment 6

Technology:

- ***Computer Test Bank,*** Chapter 21 Test
- ***iText,*** Chapter 21 Assessment

Chapter 21 Assessment

Interactive textbook with assessment at PHSchool.com 

Reviewing Content

Choose the letter that best answers the question or completes the statement.

1. Which of the following is NOT a characteristic of the kingdom Fungi?
   a. All are unicellular. **c.** All are eukaryotic.
   b. All have cell walls. **d.** All are heterotrophs.
2. The body of a typical fungus consists of a tangled mass of filaments called a(an)
   a. basidium. **c.** hypha.
   b. mycelium. **d.** antheridium.
3. When hyphae of opposite mating types of fungi meet, each hypha forms a
   a. sporangium. **c.** gametangium.
   b. zygospore. **d.** zoospore.
4. In the diagram of bread mold shown below, X is pointing to what structure?

   a. stolon **c.** basidium
   b. rhizoid **d.** ascus
5. The asexual spores of ascomycetes are called
   a. zygospores. **c.** ascospores.
   b. conidia. **d.** zoospores.
6. In baking, yeast cells bud and carry out the process of
   a. lactic acid fermentation.
   b. aerobic respiration.
   c. alcoholic fermentation.
   d. digestion.
7. A mushroom that you see above the ground is actually a
   a. basidiospore. **c.** fruiting body.
   b. gametangium. **d.** basidium.
8. Sexual reproduction has never been observed in
   a. zygomycetes. **c.** basidiomycetes.
   b. ascomycetes. **d.** deuteromycetes.
9. Organisms that obtain food from decaying organic matter are called
   a. mutualists.
   b. autotrophs.
   c. parasites.
   d. saprobes.
10. A symbiotic association between a fungus and an alga or a cyanobacterium is a
   a. mycorrhiza.
   b. fruiting body.
   c. lichen.
   d. mushroom.

Understanding Concepts

11. How are the cell walls of fungi similar to the exoskeletons of insects?
12. Distinguish between the terms *hyphae* and *mycelium.*
13. How does a sporangiophore function in the reproduction of fungi?
14. Describe one way in which fungi are adapted to disperse spores.
15. What conditions are necessary for fungal spores to germinate?
16. Explain the basis for the classification of fungi.
17. Describe the reproductive cycle of bread mold.
18. Compare the structure and function of rhizoids and stolons.
19. Yeasts are unicellular fungi. In which phylum are most yeasts classified? What is the basis of this classification?
20. Why is it dangerous to eat wild mushrooms?
21. Why do many biologists think that *Penicillium* evolved from an ascomycete?
22. Distinguish between a saprobe and a parasite. Give an example of each.
23. How does the method by which fungi obtain nutrients help in recycling nutrients and essential chemicals?
24. Describe two symbiotic relationships involving fungi and members of another kingdom.
25. What is the evolutionary significance of mycorrhizae?

TIME SAVER — HOMEWORK GUIDE

Section:	Questions:
Section 21–1	1–3, 11–15, 26, 27, 29, 32, 33
Section 21–2	4–8, 16–21, 28, 30, 35
Section 21–3	9, 10, 22–25, 31, 34

Interactive Textbook

If your class subscribes to the iText, your students can go online to access an interactive version of the Student Edition and a self-test.

(Continued from page 544)

17. Two hyphae from different mating types come together, forming gametangia. Haploid gametes produced in the gametangia fuse with gametes of the opposite mating type to form diploid nuclei. A thick wall develops around the nuclei, producing a zygospore that may remain dormant for months. When conditions become favorable, the zygospore germinates, undergoes meiosis, and develops into a new individual.

18. Rhizoids: rootlike hyphae that penetrate surfaces, anchor fungi, release digestive enzymes, and absorb digested matter; stolons: stemlike hyphae that run along surfaces and are used in reproduction

19. Most yeasts are classified in the phylum Ascomycota because they form asci with ascospores during the sexual phase of their life cycle.

20. Many species of poisonous mushrooms look like edible mushrooms.

21. Like ascomycetes, *Penicillium* reproduces asexually via conidia.

22. A saprobe, such as a mushroom, obtains food from decaying organic matter. A parasite, such as wheat rust, harms other organisms while living directly on or within them.

23. The mycelia of fungi produce digestive enzymes that speed the breakdown of dead organisms, thereby helping to recycle nutrients and essential chemicals.

24. A lichen is a symbiotic association between a fungus and an alga or a cyanobacterium. The alga or cyanobacterium provides the fungus with a source of energy; the fungus provides the alga or cyanobacterium with water and minerals. Mycorrhizae are mutualistic relationships between plant roots and fungi. The fungi aid plants in absorbing water and minerals; the plants provide the fungi with the products of photosynthesis.

25. Mycorrhizal associations may have been critical in the evolution of land plants from aquatic ancestors.

Chapter 21 Assessment

Critical Thinking

26. **Classifying** Fungi can reproduce both sexually and asexually. Identify which of the following structures can be involved in a process of asexual reproduction: hyphae, fruiting bodies, sporangia, gametangia, zygospores, conidia, ascospores, basidiospores, yeast buds.

27. **Comparing and Contrasting** Both humans and fungi are heterotrophs. Compare the way fungi obtain food with the way humans do.

28. **Classifying** Suppose someone gave you an unknown fungus to classify. What criteria would you use to determine the phylum to which the fungus belongs?

29. **Applying Concepts** Why are fungi a more serious problem to agriculture in tropical regions of the world than they are in temperate regions?

30. **Formulating Hypotheses** The antibiotic penicillin is a natural secretion of a certain kind of fungus—a green mold called *Penicillium.* Penicillin kills bacteria. Why might a mold species have evolved a way of killing bacteria?

31. **Interpreting Graphics** The graph below illustrates the growth rates of three species of trees—two individuals of each. One tree of each species grew with mycorrhizae, and one grew without mycorrhizae. For each species, how does the growth of the two plants compare? Make a generalization about the growth rate of plants with mycorrhizae.

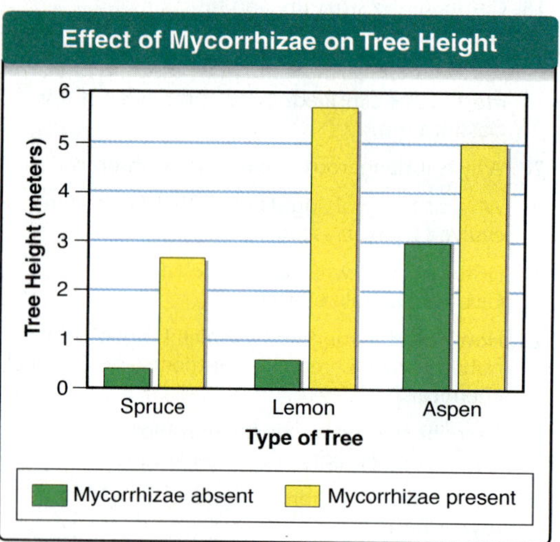

32. **Inferring** Most fungi have evolved the ability to produce spores through both sexual and asexual reproduction. How is this an advantage to fungi?

33. **Inferring** Suppose mushrooms appeared repeatedly in only one small part of your yard. What would this indicate about the soil in that area?

34. **Predicting** Heavily polluted fresh water contains few fungi. How might this affect life in a lake?

35. **Comparing and Contrasting** Compare sexual and asexual reproduction in ascomycetes. Explain the role of meiosis and mitosis in the life cycle.

Structure and Function How do fungal cells differ from the cells of plants or animals? Draw a diagram or make a chart that compares the cells of multicellular organisms in these three kingdoms: Animalia, Plantae, and Fungi. Use the information in Chapters 7 and 18 to help in answering this question.

Writing in Science

Write a paragraph explaining how fungi either maintain or disrupt the equilibrium of an ecosystem. Use examples from each of the groups of fungi described in this chapter. (*Hint:* To organize your ideas, develop a table before you begin writing your paragraph.)

Performance-Based Assessment

In Your Community Use a field guide to find and identify fungi growing near your home. Sketch what you find, but do not touch or collect them. Note the environment in which each fungus is growing. What do you think is their source of nutrition? Share your findings with your class.

For: An interactive self-test
Visit: PHSchool.com
Web Code: cba-6210

Critical Thinking

26. All of the structures listed are used in sexual reproduction except conidia and yeast buds.

27. Fungi obtain food by absorbing nutrients from decaying matter in the soil or by absorbing nutrients from the bodies of their hosts. Humans obtain food by ingesting plants and animals.

28. The division to which an unknown fungus belongs can be determined by examining its structures for sexual production. Common molds produce zygospores. Club fungi have basidia, and sac fungi have asci. Imperfect fungi do not have known structures for sexual reproduction.

29. Tropical regions are warmer and have more moisture, which are conditions that favor fungal growth.

30. Answers may vary. A typical answer might suggest that bacteria and fungi compete for the same food source, and as a result fungi evolved a mechanism for killing bacteria.

31. The trees with mycorrhizae grew taller. Plants with mycorrhizae have a faster rate of growth than those without mycorrhizae.

32. With both methods of reproduction, fungi increase their chance of reproducing in different environmental conditions. Asexual reproduction is adaptive to more constant, favorable conditions, whereas sexual reproduction is adaptive to those that are harsh and unstable.

33. Students might suggest that the soil in the area where the mushrooms grow must contain a lot of nutrients. Some students may mention the possibility that the mushrooms are evidence of mycorrhizae in that area.

34. A principal role of fungi in the environment is to decompose dead organisms and recycle nutrients. If a lake contains few fungi, little decomposition and recycling will occur, and the water will become a less hospitable place for other organisms to survive.

35. During asexual reproduction of ascomycetes, spores called conidia are formed at the tips of specialized hyphae called conidiophores. If a conidium lands in a suitable environment, it grows into a haploid mycelium. During sexual reproduction, haploid hyphae of two different mating types grow close together. The N + N hyphae then produce a fruiting body. The ascus forms within the fruiting body. Within the ascus, two nuclei of different mating types fuse to form a diploid zygote, which soon divides by meiosis, producing four haploid cells. In most ascomycetes, meiosis is followed by a cycle of mitosis, so that ascospores are produced. In a favorable environment, an ascospore can germinate and grow into a haploid mycelium.

Focus on the BIG Idea 

Animal cells have no cell walls or chloroplasts. Plant cells have chloroplasts and cell walls of cellulose. Fungal cells have cell walls of chitin and do not have chloroplasts.

Standards Practice

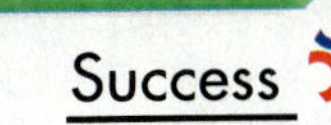

Success Tracker™ Online at PHSchool.com

Test-Taking Tip Before you begin answering questions, determine the total number of questions on the test and how much time, on average, you have to answer each question. Try to allocate your time accordingly.

Directions: Choose the letter that best answers the question or completes the statement.

1. Which of the following organisms is NOT a fungus?
   - **A** mushroom
   - **B** morel
   - **C** water mold
   - **D** bread mold
2. Which of the following is characteristic of some types of fungi?
   - **A** decomposition
   - **B** parasitism
   - **C** mutualism
   - **D** all of the above
3. Which of the following is a club fungus?
   - **A** mushroom
   - **B** yeast
   - **C** bread mold
   - **D** *Penicillium*
4. Which of the following is the rootlike structure of a mold?
   - **A** gametangium
   - **B** zygospore
   - **C** rhizoid
   - **D** stolon

Questions 5–8 Each of the lettered choices below refers to the following numbered statements. Select the best lettered choice. A choice may be used once, more than once, or not at all.

- **A** Mycorrhiza
- **B** *Penicillium*
- **C** Mycelium
- **D** Chitin

5. Cell wall carbohydrate
6. Tangled mass of hyphae
7. Fungal source of antibiotic
8. Association of plant roots and fungi

Questions 9–11

Ripe grapes are covered with a grayish film called "bloom," which contains yeasts and sometimes other microorganisms. A group of students prepared three test tubes of fresh, mashed grapes. They heated two of the test tubes to the boiling point, and then cooled them. They inoculated one of these test tubes with live yeast. They incubated all three test tubes at 30°C for 48 hours and then examined the test tubes for signs of fermentation—the presence of bubbles and alcohol. Their data are summarized in the table below.

Evidence of Fermentation

Test-Tube Contents	Alcohol Odor (yes or no)	Bubbles (yes or no)
Unheated grape mash	yes	yes
Boiled grape mash	no	no
Boiled grape mash inoculated with yeast	yes	yes

9. What is the independent variable in the students' investigation? **8IIE 9.c**
   - **A** presence of live yeast or other microorganisms
   - **B** light
   - **C** bubbles
   - **D** odor of alcohol
10. What is the dependent variable in the students' investigation? **8IIE 9.c**
    - **A** boiling
    - **B** odor of alcohol
    - **C** presence of bubbles
    - **D** both B and C
11. What can you conclude, based on the students' results? **7IIE 7.c**
    - **A** Uninoculated, boiled grape mash does not seem to ferment over a 48-hour period.
    - **B** Boiled grape mash that contains live yeast undergoes fermentation.
    - **C** Grape mash does not ferment unless live yeast is added.
    - **D** both A and B

Standards Practice

1. C 2. D 3. A 4. C 5. D 6. C 7. B 8. A 9. A 10. D 11. D

Success Tracker™ Online at PHSchool.com

Have students check their understanding of the chapter by logging onto Success Tracker.

Writing in Science

Paragraphs may vary. A typical response will mention fungi as decomposers, fungi as parasites, and fungi in mutualistic associations. As students provide examples of fungi that either maintain or disrupt an ecosystem, they should mention organisms from each of the four main groups of fungi discussed in Section 21–2, including the common molds, the sac fungi, the club fungi, and the imperfect fungi.

Performance-Based Assessment

Students can use field guides for fungi or mushroom hunters' guides. If there is a limited supply of field guides, divide the class into pairs or small groups. Before students attempt to find fungi, lead a brainstorming session with the class about where there are nearby wild areas, especially city, state, or national parks. The fungi students find will depend on the season and the area they search. For each example found, students should attempt an identification and note details of the environment in their field notebooks.

Go Online PHSchool.com

Your students can independently test their knowledge of the chapter and print out their test results for your files.

UNIT 7

Dear Colleague,

Each spring, I teach a large freshman course in general biology at my university. At the beginning of the class, students ask all sorts of questions about what I intend to cover during the semester, and, every now and then, one of them asks whether or not I intend to teach any botany. When I say "yes," they aren't always pleased. They've got an image of plant science as dull, pointless, and old-fashioned. But they are wrong.

As I do my best to explain, plant biology today is one of the most exciting and interesting areas of biology. Think of it this way: Imagine that you had to find a way to survive with your feet permanently anchored in cement. You couldn't move, couldn't hide, couldn't seek food, couldn't even walk to water. Doesn't sound like much of a life, does it? Let's suppose, however, that you managed not only to survive under such conditions but to prosper. Let's suppose that you and your descendants became the dominant form of life on land, transforming the landscape and making life possible for thousands of other organisms. Would you find this remarkable? Would you wonder how you managed to pull it off? I'll bet you would.

Well, that's exactly what plants have done. They stand there for all to see, surrounded by potential predators, and they prevail. They inhabit a landscape where water and nutrients are often hidden from view, and yet they find them. They have no way to search for mates; nonetheless, they manage to bring their reproductive cells together, often over great distances. Plants are, in many ways, the ultimate survivors, the ultimate winners in the battle for control of life on land.

UNIT 7 Plants

The vibrant colors of these autumn leaves are a result of various plant pigments.

I don't know how your students will approach the study of plants, but we have done our best to make sure that they'll understand just how remarkable these organisms really are. In New England, plants mark the coming of spring and the passage of summer; they celebrate autumn with colors so vibrant that they draw tourists from across the country to enjoy the spectacle. In the great American Midwest, plants produce a harvest that sustains our nation's growing population and millions of others around the world. Plants shape the landscape of the desert, cover the freshwater marshes of the Everglades, and produce forests that are homes to an endless variety of wildlife.

When the first complete DNA sequence for a plant (*Arabadopsis*) was determined in the year 2000, many people were surprised that it contained nearly 25,500 genes, almost double that of the fruit fly, *Drosophila*. They shouldn't have been surprised. Plants may not be able to move, but in their own way, they have figured out ways to do many things better than animals. Far from being "simple" organisms, plants survive and succeed because they are complex and sophisticated. Perhaps the best way to think of this is to tell students that plants have evolved a survival strategy so different from that of animals that organisms like us have a hard time even noticing it.

The next time students are in doubt about whether plants are anything more than passive spectators in the game of life, ask them what an animal is *really* doing when it eats an apple. The answer, as we try to make clear in Chapter 24, is that an act of deception is going on. The plant is "bribing" the unsuspecting creature into spreading its seeds over great distances. The apple, of course, still tastes great, and the animal never knows it's been taken advantage of. Now, that's clever!

Sincerely,

Ken Miller

Go Online PHSchool.com

Students can research plants on the site developed by authors Ken Miller and Joe Levine.

Chapter Planner 22 Plant Diversity

Section and Section Objectives	Time	STANDARDS NCLB	STANDARDS Biology	Activities and Labs
22–1 Introduction to Plants, pp. 551–555 22.1.1 ***Explain*** what a plant is. 22.1.2 ***Describe*** what plants need to survive. 22.1.3 ***Describe*** how the first plants evolved.	2 periods (1 block)	7 2.a		SE: ***Inquiry Activity,*** Are all plants the same?, p. 550 L2 TE: ***Build Science Skills,*** p. 552 L1 L2 SE: ***Problem Solving,*** "Plantastic" Voyage, p. 553 L2 TE: ***Make Connections,*** p. 554 L2 L3
22–2 Bryophytes, pp. 556–559 22.2.1 ***Describe*** the adaptations of bryophytes. 22.2.2 ***Identify*** the three groups of bryophytes. 22.2.3 ***Explain*** how bryophytes reproduce.	1 period (1/2 block)	7 2.a		TE: ***Build Science Skills,*** p. 556 L2 TE: ***Make Connections,*** p. 557 L2 L3 TE: ***Demonstration,*** p. 558 L2 TE: ***Build Science Skills,*** p. 559 L2 L3 LMA: Chapter 22 Lab L2 L3 LMB: Chapter 22 Lab L1 L2
22–3 Seedless Vascular Plants, pp. 560–563 22.3.1 ***Explain*** how vascular tissue is important to ferns and their relatives. 22.3.2 ***Describe*** the three phyla of spore-bearing plants. 22.3.3 ***Identify*** the stages in the life cycle of ferns.	1 period (1/2 block)	7 2.a		TE: ***Build Science Skills,*** p. 561 L2 TE: ***Demonstration,*** p. 561 L2 TE: ***Build Science Skills,*** p. 562 L2 SE: ***Exploration,*** Comparing Adaptations of Mosses and Ferns, p. 573 L2
22–4 Seed Plants, pp. 564–568 22.4.1 ***Describe*** the reproductive adaptations of seed plants. 22.4.2 ***Describe*** the evolution of seed plants. 22.4.3 ***Identify*** the four groups of gymnosperms.	2 periods (1 block)			SE: ***Quick Lab,*** How do seeds differ from spores?, p. 565 L2
22–5 Angiosperms—Flowering Plants, pp. 569–572 22.5.1 ***Identify*** the characteristics of angiosperms. 22.5.2 ***Explain*** what monocots and dicots are. 22.5.3 ***Describe*** the three different life spans of angiosperms.	1 period (1/2 block)			TE: ***Build Science Skills,*** p. 569 L2 SE: ***Careers in Biology,*** Botanical Illustrator, p. 571 L2
Chapter Assessment, pp. 574–577	1 period (1/2 block)			

ACTIVITY PLANNER

SE: *Inquiry Activity,* p. 550; 15 min.; hand lens, metric ruler, specimens of mosses, mature ferns with sori, flowering plants with flowers

TE: *Build Science Skills,* p. 552; 15 min.; potting soil, small pot, seeds; p. 556; 15 min.; samples of bryophytes; p. 559; 20 min.; peat moss, soil, beakers; p. 561; 15 min.; fern frond, metric ruler, scissors, microscope slides, microscope; p. 562; 20 min.; 2-L soda bottle, scissors, peat moss, fern spores; p. 569; 15 min.; ripe apple, knife, scalpel

TE: *Make Connections,* p. 554; 15 min.; fossil specimens of mosses and ferns; p. 557; 15 min.; potting soil, moss plants, small pots

TE: *Demonstration,* p. 558; 15 min.; moss plant; p. 561; 15 min.; specimens of mosses and club mosses

SE: *Quick Lab,* p. 565; 20 min.; fern frond with sori, microscope, scalpel, slide, coverslip, dropper pipette, sunflower seeds in the shell, brown paper bag, hand lens

SE: *Exploration,* p. 573; 45 min.; fern plant, moss plants, hand lens, forceps, microscope slide, dropper pipette, coverslip, microscopes

PLANNING KEY

Ability Levels
for students performing . . .
below grade level L1
at grade level L2
above grade level L3

Print Components
SE Student Edition
TE Teacher's Edition
RSW Reading & Study Workbook A
ARSW Adapted Reading & Study Workbook B
TR Teaching Resources
IF Investigations in Forensics
LA Lab Assessment
BTM Biotechnology Manual
IDM Issues and Decision Making
LW Lab Worksheets
LMA Laboratory Manual A
LMB Laboratory Manual B

Tech Components
CTB Computer Test Bank
BD BioDetectives DVD
TP Transparencies Plus
PLM Probeware Lab Manual
ABC ABC DVD Library
LS Lab Simulations
VL Virtual Labs

Interactive Textbook — Interactive textbook with assessment at PHSchool.com

Program Resources	Assessment	Media and Technology
TR: Lesson Plan 22–1, Section Summary, p. 6 L1, p. 16 L2, Worksheets, pp. 9–10 L1, pp. 18–20 L2 **RSW:** Section 22–1 L2 **ARSW:** Section 22–1 L1	**SE:** 22–1 Section Assessment, p. 555 **TR:** Section Review 22–1	**iText:** Section 22–1 **TP:** 22–1 Interest Grabber, Section Outline, Generalized Plant Life Cycle, Figure 22–6, Figure 22–7
TR: Lesson Plan 22–2, Section Summary, p. 6 L1, p. 16 L2, Worksheets, p. 11 L1, pp. 21–23 L2 **RSW:** Section 22–2 L2 **ARSW:** Section 22–2 L1	**SE:** 22–2 Section Assessment, p. 559 **TR:** Section Review 22–2	**iText:** Section 22–2 **TP:** 22–2 Interest Grabber, Section Outline, The Structure of a Moss, Figure 22–11
TR: Lesson Plan 22–3, Section Summary, p. 7 L1, p. 16 L2, Worksheets, p. 12 L1, pp. 24–26 L2 **LW:** Chapter 22 Exploration L1 L2 L3 **RSW:** Section 22–3 L2 **ARSW:** Section 22–3 L1	**SE:** 22–3 Section Assessment, p. 563 **TR:** Section Review 22–3	**iText:** Section 22–3 **TP:** 22–3 Interest Grabber, Section Outline, Compare/Contrast Table, Figure 22–17
TR: Lesson Plan 22–4, Section Summary, p. 7 L1, p. 17 L2, Worksheets, p. 13 L1, pp. 27–30 L2 **RSW:** Section 22–4 L2 **ARSW:** Section 22–4 L1	**SE:** 22–4 Section Assessment, p. 568 **TR:** Section Review 22–4	**iText:** Section 22–4 **TP:** 22–4 Interest Grabber, Section Outline, Compare/Contrast Table, Figure 22–19
TR: Lesson Plan 22–5, Section Summary, p. 8 L1, p. 17 L2, Worksheets, p. 14 L1, pp. 31–32 L2, Enrichment L3 **RSW:** Section 22–5 L2 **ARSW:** Section 22–5 L1	**SE:** 22–5 Section Assessment, p. 572 **TR:** Section Review 22–5	**iText:** Section 22–5 **TP:** 22–5 Interest Grabber, Section Outline, Concept Map, Figure 22–25
	SE: Chapter 22 Assessment, pp. 574–577 **TR:** Chapter Vocabulary Review, Graphic Organizer, Chapter 22 Test	**iText:** Chapter 22 Assessment **CTB:** Chapter 22 Test

Go Online Students can do research, share data, and test their knowledge online.

TIME SAVER — PRESSED FOR TIME?

To Preview the Chapter
- Introduce students to Key Concepts and Vocabulary terms in each section.
- Assign the Reading Strategies for each section.

To Cover the Chapter Quickly
- Have students read all of Section 22–1; Life Cycle of Bryophytes in Section 22–2; Evolution of Vascular Tissue and Life Cycle of Ferns in Section 22–3; Reproduction Free From Water in Section 22–4; and Flowers and Fruits in Section 22–5.
- Assign the 22–1 Section Review, questions 1–10 in Chapter 22 Assessment, and Chapter 22 Standards Practice.

To Review the Chapter
- Assign Sections 22–1 through 22–5 in the Reading and Study Workbook or the Adapted Reading and Study Workbook.
- Assign Section Reviews for 22–1 through 22–5 and the Chapter Vocabulary Review for Chapter 22 in the Teaching Resources.

CHAPTER 22

ENGAGE/EXPLORE

Inquiry Activity

Objective Students will be able to compare and contrast the structures of three different plants. L2

Skill Focus **Comparing and Contrasting, Inferring, Classifying**

Materials hand lens, metric ruler, plants such as mosses, mature ferns with sori, and flowering plants with flowers

Time 15 minutes

Advance Prep Obtain moss plants in damp, shady areas or through a biological supply house. Obtain mature ferns and potted plants from a garden store or florist.

Strategy You could divide the class into small groups and provide each group with a set of specimens.

Expected Outcomes Students will observe similarities among the plants, as well as differences.

Think About It

1. Answers will vary, depending on the plants. All the plants will contain chlorophyll. The plants will differ in the structure of their leaves, stems, and roots (or the analogous structures in bryophytes and ferns) and in their reproductive structures.
2. Students should be able to infer the functions of roots, stems, leaves, and reproductive structures.
3. Accept all reasonable answers. Students should justify their classifications based on specific aspects of plant structure that they observed.

Assess Prior Knowledge

Have students brainstorm for a list of plants that are common to their area. Then, ask them whether they know any logical way to classify the plants they have named into a few large groups, or phyla. Typically, students will divide plants into needle-leaved and broad-leaved plants. Some students might also place mosses and ferns in separate phyla.

CHAPTER 22

Plant Diversity

A great diversity of plants can be found in the Hoh Rain Forest of Olympic National Park in Washington.

Inquiry Activity

Are all plants the same?

Procedure 

1. Obtain three plants, a metric ruler, and a hand lens.
2. Construct a table for recording your data.
3. Identify the major parts of each plant. Measure the heights of the plants and the sizes of their parts.
4. Use the hand lens to examine the plants. Record your observations.

Think About It

1. **Comparing and Contrasting** How are the three plants alike? How do they differ?
2. **Inferring** What are the functions of the major parts of each plant?
3. **Classifying** Use your observations to classify the three plants into two groups. Explain your reasons for classifying them in these groups.

FACTS AND FIGURES

The success of flowering plants

Angiosperms have enjoyed remarkable success. The pea family (Leguminosae) alone has around 16,000 to 19,000 living species. This single family of angiosperms outnumbers all the surviving ferns, which number about 11,000 species. That is adaptive radiation in a big way!

22–1 Introduction to Plants

What color is life? That's a silly question, of course, because living things can be just about any color. But consider it in a different way. Imagine yourself in a place on Earth where the sounds and scents of life are all around you. The place is so abundant with life that when you stand on the ground, living things blot out the sun. Now, what color do you see? If you have imagined a thick forest or a teeming jungle, then one color will fill the landscape of your mind—green—the color of plants.

Plants dominate the landscape. Where plants are plentiful, other organisms, such as animals, fungi, and microorganisms, take hold and thrive. Plants provide the base for food chains on land. They also provide shade, shelter, and oxygen for animals of every size and kind. The oldest fossil evidence of plants dates from about 470 million years ago. Since then, plants have colonized and transformed nearly every corner of Earth.

Guide for Reading

Key Concepts

- What is a plant?
- What do plants need to survive?
- How did the first plants evolve?

Vocabulary

sporophyte
gametophyte

Reading Strategy: Using Prior Knowledge Before you read the chapter, make a list of the different groups of plants that you know. As you read, revise your list to include new information about plant groups.

What Is a Plant?

Plants are members of the kingdom Plantae. **Plants are multicellular eukaryotes that have cell walls made of cellulose. They develop from multicellular embryos and carry out photosynthesis using the green pigments chlorophyll *a* and *b*.** Plants include trees, shrubs, and grasses, as well as other organisms, such as mosses and ferns. Most plants, including the one in **Figure 22–1,** are autotrophs, although a few are parasites or saprobes that live on decaying materials.

Plants are so different from animals that sometimes there is a tendency to think of them as not being alive. With few exceptions, plants do not gather food nor do they move about or struggle directly with their predators. Plants can neither run away from danger nor strike blows against an adversary. But as different as they are from animals, plants are everywhere. How have they managed to be so successful?

That question has many answers. In the next few chapters, we will explore some of them. For now, it might help to think of plants as a well-known botanist once described them—as "stationary animals that eat sunlight"!

Figure 22–1 **All plants are multicellular eukaryotes that have cell walls made of cellulose.** Their leaves appear green because of the photosynthetic pigments chlorophyll *a* and *b*, which are located in chloroplasts.

SECTION RESOURCES

Print:

- ***Teaching Resources,*** Lesson Plan 22–1, Adapted Section Summary 22–1, Adapted Worksheets 22–1, Section Summary 22–1, Worksheets 22–1, Section Review 22–1
- ***Reading and Study Workbook A,*** Section 22–1
- ***Adapted Reading and Study Workbook B,*** Section 22–1

Technology:

- ***iText,*** Section 22–1
- ***Transparencies Plus,*** Section 22–1

Section 22–1

 7 2.a

1 FOCUS

Objectives

22.1.1 ***Explain*** what a plant is.
22.1.2 ***Describe*** what plants need to survive.
22.1.3 ***Describe*** how the first plants evolved.

Guide for Reading

Vocabulary Preview

Explain to students that the suffix *-phyte* means "plant." Thus, *sporophyte* means "spore plant," and *gametophyte* means "gamete plant."

Reading Strategy

Before students read, ask them to skim the section to find the three boldface Key Concepts. Have them copy each onto a notecard. Then, as they read, they should make notes of supporting details.

2 INSTRUCT

What Is a Plant?

Build Science Skills

Observing Take students on a guided tour of the exterior of your school building. Look for the many places that terrestrial plants can grow. You might begin by looking in some of the obvious locations first, such as the lawn or garden of the school. Then, look in some of the less obvious places—in pavement cracks, on the shady sides of the building or walls, on rocks, on trees, or near a source of standing water. Examine each plant and have the students note the following:

- Does it have leaves?
- Does the leaf have veins?
- Where is the plant growing?
- What is the approximate size of the plant?
- Is the plant mosslike, or does it have a green or woody stem? L1 L2

22–1 (continued)

The Plant Life Cycle

Use Visuals

Figure 22–2 Ask students: **Which generation of a plant is diploid and which is haploid?** *(The sporophyte generation is diploid, and the gametophyte generation is haploid.)* **Which generation produces gametes?** *(The gametophyte)* **What does the sporophyte produce?** *(Spores)* **What process produces spores?** *(Meiosis)* **When does mitosis occur in this life cycle?** *(It occurs after meiosis in the gametophyte plant and after fertilization in the growth of the sporophyte.)* L2

For: Alternation of Generation activity
Visit: PHSchool.com
Web Code: cbe-7222
Students can interact with the art online.

What Plants Need to Survive

Build Science Skills

Applying Concepts Perhaps the best way to help students understand what plants need to survive is to allow them to grow their own seedlings. Provide potting soil, small containers, and seeds. Any seeds will do, but those that germinate quickly are more fun—small flowers, beans, corn, and so on. Put these in a warm, light area and allow students brief opportunities to observe and care for them every day. You can make this as basic or elaborate as you wish. Challenge students to experiment with the presence and absence of specific plant requirements to observe their effects on growth. The seedlings can be used in subsequent chapters to study plant structure, although some students may want to take them home. L1 L2

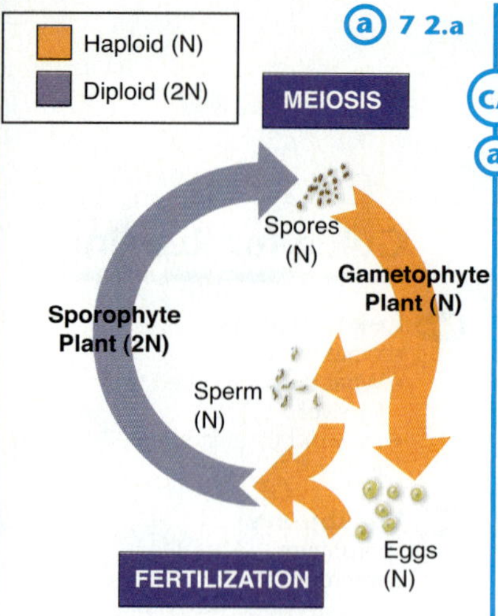

▲ **Figure 22–2** All plants have a life cycle with alternation of generations, in which the haploid gametophyte phase alternates with the diploid sporophyte phase.

For: Alternation of Generation activity
Visit: PHSchool.com
Web Code: cbp-7222

▼ **Figure 22–3** **All plants need sunlight, water, minerals, oxygen, carbon dioxide, and a way to move water and nutrients to all their cells.** Adaptations allow them to live in even the driest locations, such as this desert.

a 7 2.a

The Plant Life Cycle

CA a

Plant life cycles have two alternating phases, a diploid (2N) phase and a haploid (N) phase, known as alternation of generations. During the two phases of the life cycle, shown in **Figure 22–2,** mitosis and meiosis alternate to produce the two types of reproductive cells—gametes and spores. The diploid (2N) phase is known as the **sporophyte,** or spore-producing plant. The haploid (N) phase is known as the **gametophyte,** or gamete-producing plant. Plant spores are haploid (N) reproductive cells formed in the sporophyte plant by meiosis that can grow into new individuals. The new individual is the gametophyte. A gamete is a reproductive cell that is produced by mitosis and fuses during fertilization with another gamete to produce a new individual, the diploid sporophyte.

The earliest plants, mosses and ferns, require water to reproduce. Seed plants, which appeared more recently, have reproductive cycles that can be carried out without water. Many plants also have forms of vegetative, or asexual, reproduction.

What Plants Need to Survive

Surviving as stationary organisms on land is a difficult task, but plants have developed a number of adaptations that enable them to succeed. **The lives of plants center on the need for sunlight, water and minerals, gas exchange, and the transport of water and nutrients throughout the plant body.**

Sunlight Plants use the energy from sunlight to carry out photosynthesis. As a result, every plant displays adaptations shaped by the need to gather sunlight. Photosynthetic organs such as leaves are typically broad and flat and are arranged on the stem so as to maximize light absorption.

Water and Minerals All cells require a constant supply of water. For this reason, plants must obtain and deliver water to all their cells—even those that grow aboveground in the dry air. Water is one of the raw materials of photosynthesis, so it is used up quickly when the sun is shining. Sunny conditions can cause living tissues to dry out. Thus, plants have developed structures that limit water loss. As they absorb water, plants also absorb minerals. Minerals are nutrients in the soil that are needed for plant growth.

Gas Exchange Plants require oxygen to support cellular respiration as well as carbon dioxide to carry out photosynthesis. They must exchange these gases with the atmosphere without losing excessive amounts of water through evaporation.

Movement of Water and Nutrients Plants take up water and minerals through their roots but make food in their leaves. Most plants have specialized tissues that carry water and nutrients upward from the soil and distribute the products of photosynthesis throughout the plant body. Simpler types of plants carry out these functions by diffusion.

UNIVERSAL ACCESS

Inclusion/Special Needs

Build on students' hands-on experiences of using pipe cleaner chromosomes to model the haploid and diploid cells in the plant life cycle. Students can use two pairs of chromosome pipe cleaners, each pair a different color to model the alternation of generations in plants. Have them draw and label their own life cycle diagram and actually move the pipe cleaner chromosome pairs through it. L1

Less Proficient Readers

Encourage students to look carefully at Figure 22–2 as they read about the plant life cycle. Instruct them to construct a Venn diagram to compare and contrast the gametophyte and the sporophyte phases. Students should use information from Figure 22–2 and the text to complete the Venn diagrams. Ask students to explain how the illustration in the figure helped them understand the plant life cycle. L1 L2

Problem Solving

 BIIE 1.d

"Plantastic" Voyage

You are part of a team that is planning a space mission that will send astronauts into space for two years. As part of their food, the astronauts will be growing yam plants, *Dioscorea composita*. Your job is to develop a plan to help plants grow on the spacecraft.

Defining the Problem In your own words, state the problem at hand.

Organizing Information Research the types of conditions these plants would need. What requirements would the plants have for moisture? Soil conditions? Light intensity? Day length?

Creating a Solution Make a detailed scale drawing of a container for growing 10 of these plants. (*Dioscorea* plants are vines; assume that each is 10 cm long and 0.5 cm wide.) Determine what material(s) you will use for your container. As you devise your plan, be sure to keep a journal in which you record your team's ideas, drawings, data, and other information.

Presenting Your Plan Prepare a multimedia presentation for your classmates as if they were the managers of the space mission. Describe how your team solved the problem, the sources of information you used, the design itself, and what you learned during the project.

Early Plants

For most of Earth's history, plants did not exist. Life was concentrated in oceans, lakes, and streams. Algae and photosynthetic prokaryotes added the oxygen to our planet's atmosphere and provided food for animals and microorganisms.

When plants appeared, much of the existing life on Earth changed. As these new photosynthetic organisms colonized the land, they changed the environment in ways that made it possible for other organisms to develop. New ecosystems emerged, and organic matter began to form soil. How did plants adapt to the conditions of life on land? How plants evolved structures that acquire, transport, and conserve water is the key to answering this question.

Origins in the Water You may recall from Chapter 20 that green algae, shown in **Figure 22–4,** are photosynthetic, plantlike protists. Many of these algae are multicellular. **The first plants evolved from an organism much like the multicellular green algae living today.** Multicellular green algae have the size, color, and appearance of plants. But the resemblance of many green algae to plants is more than superficial. They have reproductive cycles that are similar to those of plants. In addition, green algae have cell walls and photosynthetic pigments that are identical to those of plants.

CHECKPOINT *What was the greatest "challenge" to plants as they began to live on land?*

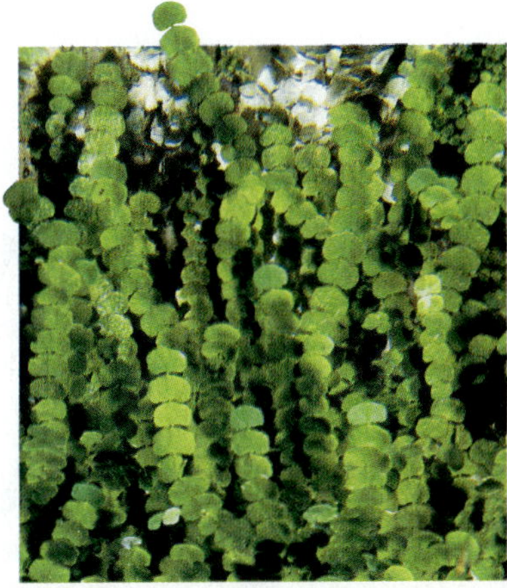

▲ **Figure 22–4** **The first plants evolved from an organism much like the modern multicellular green algae.** The alga *Halimeda* is found in Honduras in Central America. It has many cellular features in common with plants.

BIO INSIGHTS — FACTS AND FIGURES

Arriving on land first

When students think of life first emerging from the sea, they invariably envision an amphibian-like creature skulking around the shore. In truth, much smaller animals—such as insects—were the first to colonize dry land. But plants arrived on land before any animal species. Without plants, land animals would have had to remain close to the water or would have had nothing to eat. Some biologists believe that plants did not make the transition to land by themselves. Their theory is that plants coevolved with fungi, developing the very first mycorrhizae. The term *mycorrhiza* (plural: mycorrhizae) refers to the symbiotic relationship between certain fungi and the root cells of some vascular plants, such as orchids. This plant–fungi partnership allowed necessary minerals to be extracted from sterile, inorganic soils.

Problem Solving

 **BIIE 1.d**

A yam is a plant, similar to a sweet potato, in which the branch roots swell and provide storage for large quantities of carbohydrates. The yam plant is thought to have originated in or near India, and these food-storage roots are a staple in some tropical regions of the world. L2

Defining the Problem The problem is to grow yams successfully under artificial conditions aboard a spacecraft.

Organizing Information To determine the optimal conditions a yam plant needs, students might use the reference section of their public library or contact an expert, either at a garden store or the botany department of a local university.

Creating a Solution Teams should make detailed drawings of the proposed container. For 10 plants, the bottom of this container needs to be at least 50 square centimeters. Students might suggest using a container with a solid bottom with tops and sides that have openings, so that gas exchange is adequate.

Presenting Your Plan Budget class time for each team to make its multimedia presentation. All plans should take into account what plants need to survive, including light, water, gas exchange, and nutrients.

Early Plants

Use Visuals

Figure 22–4 As students study the algae in the photograph, ask: **How are green algae like plants?** *(Green algae and plants have chlorophyll, store carbohydrates, and have cell walls made of cellulose. Larger green algae are similar in color and size to some plants and may have alternating generations.)* L2

Answer to . . .

CHECKPOINT *Acquiring, transporting, and conserving water*

22–1 (continued)

Make Connections

Earth Science Display specimens, pictures, or slides of early plant fossils, including mosses and ferns. Review with students the process by which fossils form. For example, these are the steps that occur in the formation of a mold fossil: (1) a plant is buried in sediment; (2) the sediment hardens into rock; (3) the organic material of the plant decays, leaving an empty space in the rock. After reviewing fossil formation, discuss how geologists and paleontologists determine the age of fossils. Explain relative age to students, including the law of superposition. Also explain the basics of radioactive dating, in which the decay of radioactive elements is used to date certain rock formations. L2 L3

Use Visuals

Figure 22–6 After students have studied the cladogram, ask: **What are the four main groups of plants?** *(Mosses and their relatives, ferns and their relatives, cone-bearing plants [gymnosperms], and flowering plants [angiosperms])* **What do mosses and their relatives lack that all other plants have?** *(Vascular tissue)* **Which groups of plants don't have seeds?** *(Mosses and their relatives and ferns and their relatives)* **How do the seeds of flowering plants differ from the seeds of cone-bearing plants?** *(Flowering plants have seeds enclosed in fruit.)* L2

▲ **Figure 22–5** One of the earliest fossil vascular plants was *Cooksonia,* which looked similar to mosses living today. *Cooksonia* had simple branched stalks that bore reproductive structures at their tips. The figure above shows an artist's drawing of *Cooksonia* and a photograph of the fossil. **Inferring** ***Which structures of this early plant might have carried out photosynthesis? Obtained water and minerals?***

The First Plants Plants share many characteristics with the green algae described in Chapter 20, including their photosynthetic pigments and the composition of their cell walls. DNA sequences confirm that plants are closely related to certain groups of green algae, further suggesting that the ancestors of the first plants were indeed algae. The oldest known fossils of plants, nearly 450 million years old, show that the earliest plants were similar to today's mosses. As shown in **Figure 22–5,** they had a simple structure and grew close to the damp ground. The fossils also suggest that the first true plants were still dependent on water to complete their life cycles. Over time, the demands of life on land favored the evolution of plants more resistant to the drying rays of the sun, more capable of conserving water, and more capable of reproducing without water.

From these plant pioneers, several major groups of plants evolved. One group developed into the mosses and their relatives. Another lineage gave rise to all the other plants on Earth today—ferns, cone-bearing plants, and flowering plants. All of these groups of plants are now successful in living on dry land, but they have evolved very different adaptations for a wide range of terrestrial environments.

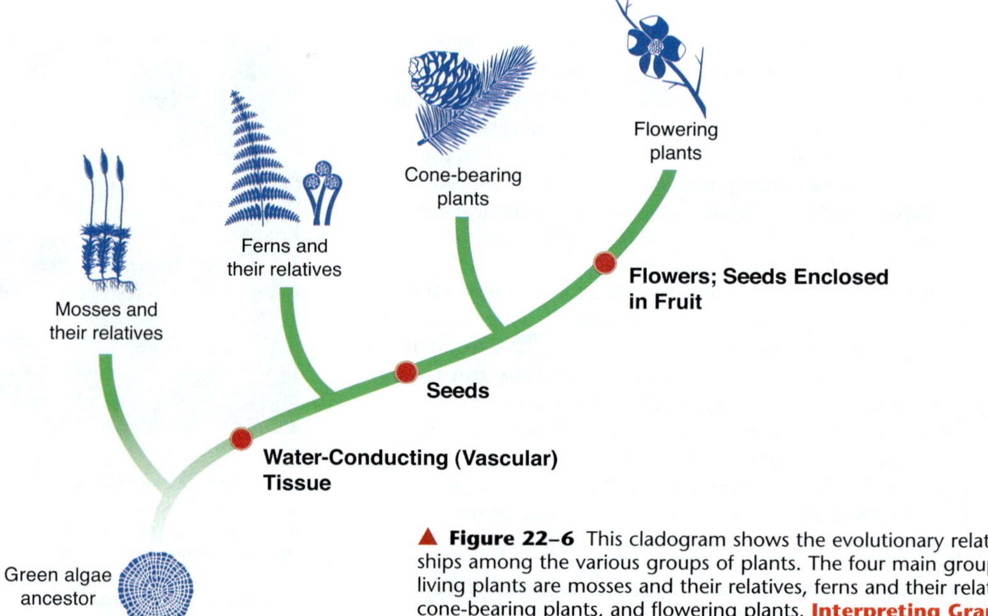

▲ **Figure 22–6** This cladogram shows the evolutionary relationships among the various groups of plants. The four main groups of living plants are mosses and their relatives, ferns and their relatives, cone-bearing plants, and flowering plants. **Interpreting Graphics** ***Which two groups of plants contain seeds?***

TEACHER TO TEACHER

Before beginning the chapter on plants, give each student a bottle cap (or have students bring them to class). If you have a wooded area near your school, have each student find a plant that can be grown in a bottle cap. Limiting the size of the plant to a bottle cap will force students to look beyond the obvious common plants that they normally observe. If there is not a wooded area available, ask students to bring plants to class from areas near their homes. Place the caps in a large plastic container. All the caps from one lab group should fit in one container. During the course of the unit, students should be able to identify their plant species, as well as any reproductive structures that appear.

—*Kathey A. Roberts*
Biology Teacher
Lakeside High School
Hot Springs, AR

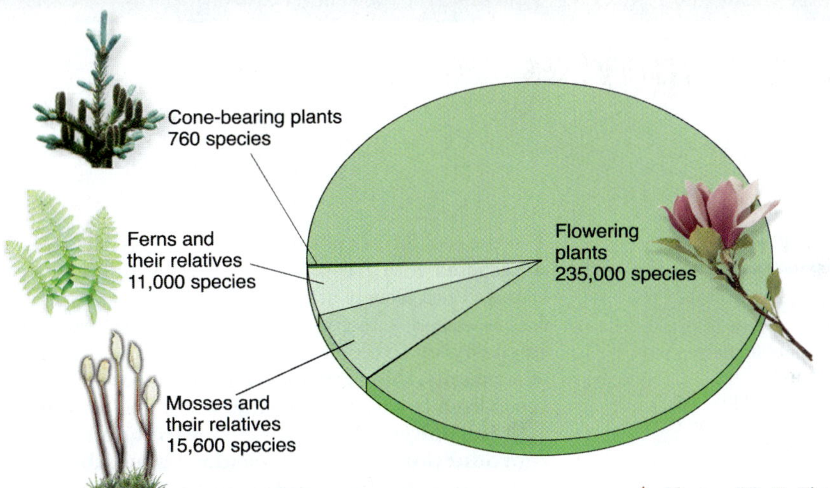

▲ **Figure 22–7** The great majority of plants alive today are angiosperms, which are also known as flowering plants. **Interpreting Graphics** *What is the second largest group of plants?*

Overview of the Plant Kingdom

Botanists divide the plant kingdom into four groups based on three important features: water-conducting tissues, seeds, and flowers. The relationship of these groups is shown in **Figure 22–6.** There are, of course, many other features by which plants are classified, including reproductive structures and body plan.

Today, plant scientists can classify plants more precisely by comparing the DNA sequences of various species. Since 1994, a team of biologists from twelve nations has begun to change our view of plant relationships. Their project, Deep Green, has provided strong evidence that the first plants evolved from green algae living in fresh water, not in the sea as had been thought.

In the rest of this chapter, we will explore how important plant traits evolved over the course of millions of years. In particular, we will examine the success of the flowering plants. As shown in **Figure 22–7,** flowering plants consist of 235,000 species—almost 90 percent of all living species of plants.

For: Links on classifying plants
Visit: www.SciLinks.org
Web Code: cbn-7221

22–1 Section Assessment

1. **Key Concept** Identify the characteristics of the plant kingdom.
2. **Key Concept** To live successfully on land, what substances must plants obtain from their environment?
3. **Key Concept** From which group of protists did the first plants evolve? How are plants similar to these protists?
4. **Critical Thinking Comparing and Contrasting** Compare the gametophyte and sporophyte stages of the plant life cycle. Which is haploid? Which is diploid?
5. **Critical Thinking Comparing and Contrasting** Compare the roles of mitosis and meiosis in a plant life cycle. Which of these processes is related to sexual reproduction? To asexual reproduction?

Focus on the BIG Idea

Structure and Function

How do the cells of plants differ from those of animals? How are they different from those of fungi? You may wish to use labeled diagrams or a compare-and-contrast table to present your results. Refer to Chapters 7 and 21 for help in answering these questions.

22–1 Section Assessment

1. Multicellular eukaryotes; cell walls made of cellulose; develop from multicellular embryos; the green pigments, chlorophyll *a* and *b*, carry out photosynthesis
2. Sunlight, water and minerals, and oxygen and carbon dioxide
3. Multicellular green algae; similar in size, color, appearance, reproductive cycles, cell walls, and photosynthetic pigments
4. Gametophyte: haploid, produces eggs and sperm by mitosis, formed from spores; Sporophyte: diploid, produces spores by meiosis, formed during fertilization with fusion of egg and sperm
5. Mitosis: sexual reproduction; occurs in the haploid gametophytes to produce the haploid gametes. Meiosis: asexual reproduction; produces haploid spores in the sporophyte, which grow into the gametophyte.

Overview of the Plant Kingdom

Use Visuals

Figure 22–7 Ask students: **What are the three most important features of plants that botanists use to classify them into four groups?** *(Water-conducting tissue, seeds, and flowers)* **From what kind of organism did all plants evolve?** *(Freshwater green algae)* L2

Download a worksheet on classifying plants for students to complete, and find additional teacher support from NSTA SciLinks.

3 ASSESS

Evaluate Understanding

Call on students at random to list the main groups of the plant kingdom, explain which plant characteristics were important in the evolution of the different groups, and describe the generalized plant life cycle.

Reteach

Have students list the characteristics that define a living thing as a plant. Then, review the characteristics that divide plants into major groups.

Focus on the BIG Idea

Plant cells contain cell walls made of cellulose, large vacuoles, and chloroplasts. Animal cells do not have cell walls or chloroplasts. The cells of fungi have no chloroplasts and have cell walls made of chitin rather than cellulose.

Interactive Textbook

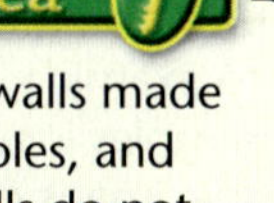

If your class subscribes to the iText, use it to review the Key Concepts in Section 22–1.

Answers to . . .

Figure 22–5 *The green, stemlike structures; the rootlike structures*

Figure 22–6 *Cone-bearing plants and flowering plants*

Figure 22–7 *Mosses and their relatives*

Section 22–2

1 FOCUS

Objectives

22.2.1 ***Describe*** the adaptations of bryophytes.

22.2.2 ***Identify*** the three groups of bryophytes.

22.2.3 ***Explain*** how bryophytes reproduce.

Guide for Reading

Vocabulary Preview

Call on students at random to pronounce the Vocabulary words in the order in which they appear. Correct any mispronunciations.

Reading Strategy

Ask students to write a paragraph that explains the life cycle of a moss, using the information in Figure 22–11. After they have read the section, have them revise their paragraphs.

2 INSTRUCT

Groups of Bryophytes

Build Science Skills

Observing Display samples of bryophytes—including mosses, liverworts, and hornworts—for students to examine. If you are unable to find samples locally, living or preserved specimens can be ordered from a biological supply house. Ask students to observe and record the color, size, and appearance of the bryophytes. Encourage them to diagram the parts of each plant and label the parts using the pictures in this book and other reference books as guides. L2

22–2 Bryophytes

Guide for Reading

Key Concepts

- What adaptations of bryophytes enable them to live on land?
- What are the three groups of bryophytes?
- How do bryophytes reproduce?

Vocabulary

bryophyte
rhizoid
gemma
protonema
antheridium
archegonium

Reading Strategy: Using Visuals

Before you read, preview **Figure 22–11,** which shows the life cycle of a moss. In your own words, describe the basic process of reproduction shown. As you read the section, add information that you learn about reproduction in bryophytes.

In the cool forests of the northern woods, the moist ground is carpeted with green. When you walk, this soft carpet feels spongy. Look closely and you will see the structure of this carpet—mosses. Mosses and their relatives are generally called **bryophytes** (BRY-oh-fyts), or nonvascular plants. Unlike all other plants, these organisms do not have vascular tissues, or specialized tissues that conduct water and nutrients. **Bryophytes have life cycles that depend on water for reproduction. Lacking vascular tissue, these plants can draw up water by osmosis only a few centimeters above the ground.** This method of development keeps them relatively small. During at least one stage of their life cycle, bryophytes produce sperm that must swim through water to reach the eggs of other individuals. Therefore, they must live in places where there is rainfall or dew for at least part of the year.

Groups of Bryophytes

The most recognizable feature of bryophytes is that they are low-growing plants that can be found in moist, shaded areas. Wherever water is in regular supply—in habitats from the polar regions to the tropics—these plants thrive. **Bryophytes include mosses, liverworts, and hornworts.** Today, most botanists classify these groups of plants in three separate phyla.

Mosses The most common bryophytes are mosses, which are members of the phylum Bryophyta (bry-oh-FYT-uh). Mosses grow most abundantly in areas with water—in swamps and bogs, near streams, and in rain forests. Bryophytes are well adapted to life in wet habitats and nutrient-poor soils. Many mosses can tolerate low temperatures, allowing them to grow in harsh environments where other plants cannot. In fact, mosses are the most abundant plants in the polar regions.

Mosses vary in appearance from miniature evergreen trees to small, filamentous plants that together form a threadlike carpet of green, as shown in **Figure 22–8.** The moss plants that you might have observed on a walk through the woods are actually clumps of gametophytes growing close together. Each moss plant has a thin, upright shoot that looks like a stem with tiny leaves. These are not true stems or leaves, however, because they do not contain vascular tissue. When mosses reproduce, they produce thin stalks, each containing a capsule. This is the sporophyte stage, as shown in **Figure 22–9.**

Figure 22–8 Mosses grow best in moist environments, such as on the rocks by this waterfall. **Like all bryophytes, mosses have life cycles that depend on water for reproduction.**

SECTION RESOURCES

Print:

- ***Laboratory Manual A,*** Chapter 22 Lab
- ***Laboratory Manual B,*** Chapter 22 Lab
- ***Teaching Resources,*** Lesson Plan 22–2, Adapted Section Summary 22–2, Adapted Worksheets 22–2, Section Summary 22–2, Worksheets 22–2, Section Review 22–2
- ***Reading and Study Workbook A,*** Section 22–2
- ***Adapted Reading and Study Workbook B,*** Section 22–2

Technology:

- ***iText,*** Section 22–2
- ***Transparencies Plus,*** Section 22–2

Because the "leaves" of mosses are only one cell thick, these plants lose water quickly if the surrounding air is dry. The lack of vascular tissues also means that mosses do not have true roots. Instead, they have **rhizoids,** which are long, thin cells that anchor them in the ground and absorb water and minerals from the surrounding soil. Water moves from cell to cell through the rhizoids and into the rest of the plant.

Liverworts If you have come across odd little plants that look almost like flat leaves attached to the ground, you have probably seen a liverwort, shown in **Figure 22–10.** These plants belong to the phylum Hepaticophyta (hih-PAT-ik-oh-fy-tuh) and get their name from the fact that some species resemble the shape of a liver. In their method of development, the liverwort gametophytes form broad and thin structures that draw up moisture directly from the surface of the soil. When the plants mature, the gametophytes produce structures that look like tiny green umbrellas. These "umbrellas" carry the structures that produce eggs and sperm.

Some liverworts can also reproduce asexually by means of gemmae. **Gemmae** (JEM-ee; singular: gemma) are small multicellular reproductive structures. In some species of liverworts, gemmae are produced in cuplike structures called gemma cups. When washed out of the gemma cup, the gemmae can divide by mitosis to produce a new individual.

Hornworts Hornworts are members of the phylum Anthocerophyta (an-tho-SEHR-oh-fy-tuh). Like the liverworts, hornworts are generally found only in soil that is damp nearly year-round. Their gametophytes look very much like those of liverworts. The hornwort sporophyte, however, looks like a tiny green horn.

CHECKPOINT *How do bryophytes reproduce asexually?*

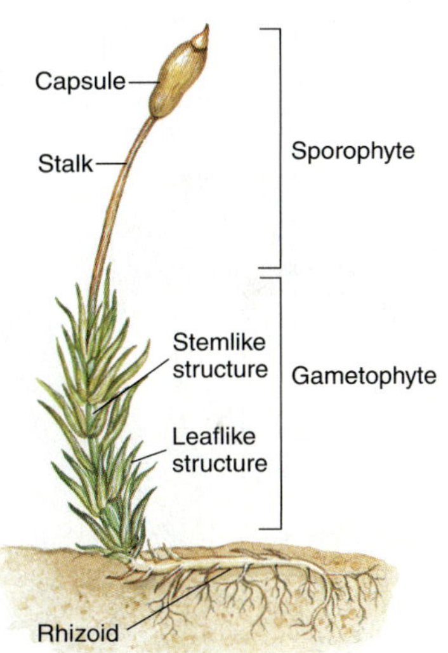

▲ **Figure 22–9** This illustration shows the structure of a typical moss plant. The green photosynthetic portion is the gametophyte. The brown structure on the tip of the gametophyte is the sporophyte. **Applying Concepts** *Which stage of the moss plant provides nutrients for the other stage?*

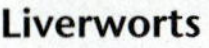

Liverworts

Hornworts

◄ **Figure 22–10** **Bryophytes include liverworts and hornworts.** The liverworts produce gametes in structures that look like little green umbrellas. The tiny cuplike structures on the liverworts are gemma cups. The hornworts have sporophytes that look like tiny green horns.

Make Connections

Environmental Science Help students understand the importance of bryophytes in the environment. Explain that they provide protected locations for seeds to germinate. Bryophytes also capture and recycle nutrients that the rain washes from the canopy layer, and they help prevent soil erosion. Mosses especially help keep moisture in the soil because of their ability to hold water. Students can observe this by comparing how long soil stays moist when covered with moss and without any covering. They can use two equal-sized flower pots filled with potting soil and moistened with equal amounts of water. They should determine how long it takes for the soil to dry out when it is covered with moss and when it is uncovered. Ask: **In what ways do mosses help the other plants in the environment?** *(By providing places for seeds to sprout and by keeping moisture in the soil)* L2 L3

Use Visuals

Figure 22–10 As students study the photos of liverworts and hornworts, discuss the characteristics of each and ask if any students can remember seeing these plants in the area. Then, ask students who need an extra challenge to investigate hornworts and liverworts and make a presentation to the class. Help them find visual aids that would enhance their presentation, such as pictures or slides that could be used in a microprojector. Ask that as part of their investigation, they find out where in the local area students can observe these bryophytes, such as in a park or woodland. L2

UNIVERSAL ACCESS

English Language Learners

Break apart the word *bryophyte* for students. The prefix *bryo-* means "moss." Remind them that the suffix *-phyte* means "plant." Then, write the words *liverwort* and *hornwort* on the board. Explain that the suffix *-wort* is an Old English word that also means "plant." Use Figure 22–10 to point out how the shapes of the plants help define their names. Have students add these words to their science glossaries. L2

Advanced Learners

Explain that bryophytes are adapted to life on land because their specialized structures, antheridia and archegonia, protect the gametes. Developing zygotes are also protected within the archegonia. Explain that because of this adaptation, botanists often refer to terrestrial plants as embryophytes. Ask: **What are these specialized structures protecting the gametes and zygotes from?** *(Drying out)* L3

Answers to . . .

CHECKPOINT *Liverworts, for example, reproduce asexually by producing gemmae, small multicellular reproductive structures. Gemmae can divide by mitosis to produce a new individual.*

Figure 22–9 *The gametophyte*

22–2 (continued)

Life Cycle of Bryophytes

Use Visuals

Figure 22–11 Have students examine the life cycle and read the caption. Then, ask: **Which generation of moss is the form of the plant with which you are most familiar?** *(Gametophyte)* **Is the gametophyte haploid or diploid?** *(Haploid)* **Where does the sporophyte develop?** *(It develops within the gametophyte.)* **Is the sporophyte haploid or diploid?** *(Diploid)* **What does the sporophyte produce?** *(Spores)* **When a spore germinates, what does it produce?** *(Protonema)* L1 L2

Demonstration

Take students outside the school building, and take along a moss plant that includes a mature sporophyte. As students observe, compress the capsule—the sporangium—of the sporophyte between your fingers, which will release the spores contained within. Ask students: **In what sort of environment do you suppose these spores must land for them to germinate?** *(They must land in a moist environment.)* **If one of these spores does germinate, what will it first grow into?** *(A protonema)* **What will the protonema become?** *(A gametophyte)* L2

Your students can extend their knowledge of bryophytes through this online experience.

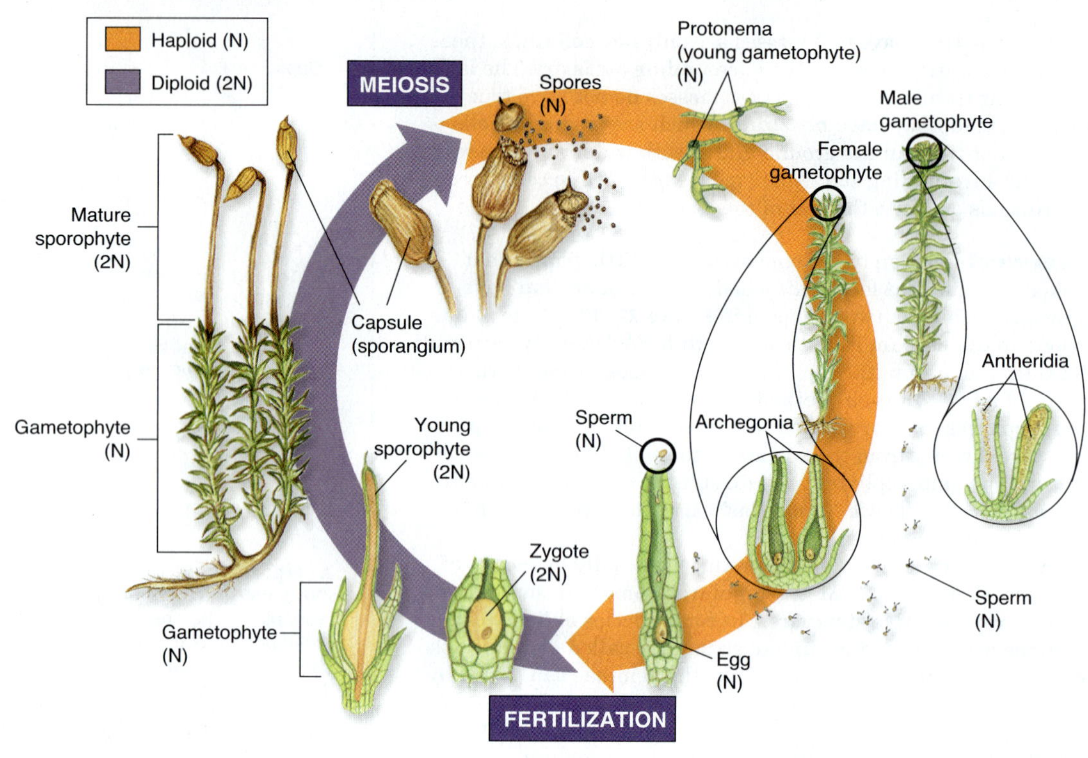

▲ **Figure 22–11** **In bryophytes, the gametophyte is the dominant, recognizable stage of the life cycle and is the form that carries out photosynthesis.** Sporophytes, which produce haploid spores, grow at the top of the gametophyte plant. When the spores are ripe, they are shed from the capsule like pepper from a shaker. In some species, gametes (sperm and eggs) are produced on separate male and female gametophyte plants.

For: Bryophyte activity
Visit: PHSchool.com
Web Code: cbd-7222

Life Cycle of Bryophytes

Like all plants, bryophytes display a method of reproduction and development involving alternation of generations. **In bryophytes, the gametophyte is the dominant, recognizable stage of the life cycle and is the stage that carries out most of the plant's photosynthesis.** The sporophyte is dependent on the gametophyte for supplying water and nutrients.

Dependence on Water For fertilization to occur, the sperm of a bryophyte must swim to an egg. Because of this dependence on water for reproduction, bryophytes must live in habitats where water is available at least part of the year.

Life Cycle of a Moss The life cycle of a moss, shown in **Figure 22–11,** helps illustrate how bryophytes reproduce and develop. When a moss spore lands in a moist place, it germinates and grows into a mass of tangled green filaments called a **protonema** (proh-toh-NEE-muh). As the protonema grows, it forms rhizoids that grow into the ground and shoots that grow into the air. These shoots grow into the familiar green moss plants, which are the gametophyte stage of its life cycle.

CHECKPOINT *What is a protonema?*

FACTS AND FIGURES

Mosses in surprising places

As the text emphasizes, mosses need abundant water to grow and reproduce. Yet, many mosses are found in areas with seasonal droughts. Even more surprising, some mosses live in tundras and other frigid climates, where liquid water may be unavailable for months at a time. Mosses survive such habitats by entering a state similar to suspended animation. Their tissues virtually dehydrate when water is not available, and they neither grow nor reproduce. But, though they may not prosper without water, mosses have adapted to periods without it, and that has let them live in some surprising places.

Gametes are formed in reproductive structures at the tips of the gametophytes. Sperm with whiplike tails are produced in **antheridia** (an-thur-ID-ee-uh; singular: antheridium), and egg cells are produced in **archegonia** (ahr-kuh-GOH-nee-uh; singular: archegonium). Some species produce both sperm and eggs on the same plant, whereas other species produce sperm and eggs on separate plants. Once sperm are released and reach egg cells, fertilization produces a diploid zygote. This zygote is the beginning of the sporophyte stage of the life cycle. It grows directly out of the body of the gametophyte and actually depends on it for water and nutrients. The mature sporophyte is a long stalk ending in a capsule that looks like a saltshaker. Inside the capsule, haploid spores are produced by meiosis. When the capsule ripens, it opens and haploid spores are scattered to the wind to start the cycle again.

a 7 2.a

Human Use of Mosses

Sphagnum (SFAG-num) mosses are a group of mosses that thrive in the acidic water of bogs. Dried sphagnum moss absorbs many times its own weight in water and thus acts as a sort of natural sponge. In certain environments the dead remains of sphagnum accumulate to form thick deposits of peat. Peat can be cut from the ground, as shown in **Figure 22–12,** and then burned as a fuel.

Peat moss is also used in gardening. Gardeners add peat moss to the soil because it improves the soil's ability to retain water. Peat moss also has a low pH, so when added to the soil it increases the soil's acidity. Some plants, such as azaleas, grow well only if they are planted in acidic soil.

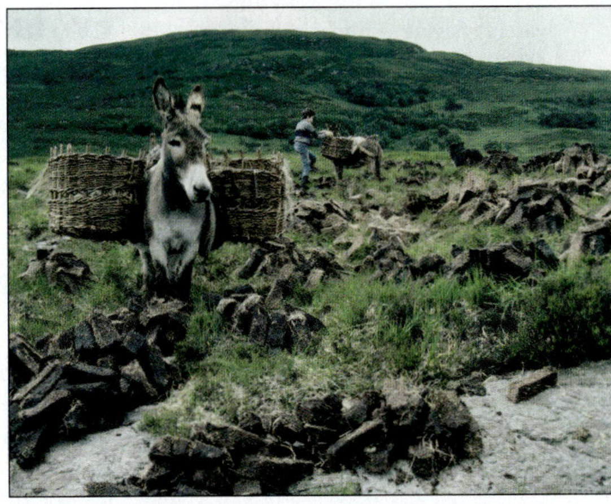

▼ **Figure 22–12** The compacted remains of sphagnum moss may eventually form thick deposits of peat. When it is cut and dried, it can be burned to produce heat. Peat has been used as a form of fuel in Ireland for many centuries. **Inferring** *What can you infer about the climate of an area where sphagnum moss grows abundantly in peat bogs?*

22–2 Section Assessment

1. **Key Concept** How is water essential in the life cycle of a bryophyte?
2. **Key Concept** List the three groups of bryophytes. In what type of habitat do they live?
3. **Key Concept** What is the relationship between the gametophyte and the sporophyte in mosses and other bryophytes?
4. What is an archegonium? An antheridium? How are these structures important in the life cycle of a moss?
5. **Critical Thinking Inferring** What characteristic of bryophytes is responsible for their small size? Explain.

Writing in Science

Descriptive Writing
You are writing a pocket field guide about plants and are working on the bryophytes chapter. Develop several paragraphs to help your readers distinguish among the mosses, hornworts, and liverworts. *Hint:* Do additional library or Internet research to find examples of bryophytes in your locality.

22–2 Section Assessment

1. Bryophytes produce sperm that must swim through water to reach the eggs of others.
2. Mosses, liverworts, and hornworts; in moist, shaded areas
3. The gametophyte is the dominant, recognizable stage and is the form that carries out most of the plant's photosynthesis. The sporophyte depends on the gametophyte for water and nutrients.
4. An archegonium is the reproductive structure that produces egg cells; an antheridium is the reproductive structure that produces sperm. These gametes fuse to form a diploid zygote, the beginning of the sporophyte stage.
5. Bryophytes are limited in size because they lack vascular tissue and therefore can draw only a few centimeters of water up from the ground by osmosis.

Human Use of Mosses

Build Science Skills

Designing Experiments Ask students why they think people use peat moss for growing plants. Then, provide groups of students with peat moss (*Sphagnum* spp.), soil, beakers, and water. Challenge each group to design an experiment that will demonstrate a characteristic of peat moss that would be useful to a gardener. *(Most students will design an experiment to show the superior water-absorbing ability of peat moss when compared with soil.)* L2 L3

3 ASSESS

Evaluate Understanding

Call on students at random to describe the life cycle of a moss. Make sure students know that in bryophytes, the gametophyte is the dominant stage of the life cycle.

Reteach

Point out the differences in structure among the three kinds of bryophytes shown in Figures 22–9 and 22–10. Ask students to point to the gametophyte and the sporophyte in each.

Writing in Science

Student paragraphs should highlight the differences among mosses, hornworts, and liverworts, focusing on visual differences that will aid in identification. With the examples of local bryophytes, students should give clear and concise examples of representative plants from each bryophyte group.

iNteractive Textbook

If your class subscribes to the iText, use it to review the Key Concepts in Section 22–2.

Answers to . . .

CHECKPOINT *The young gametophyte that develops into a moss plant*

Figure 22–12 *The climate is probably wet.*

Section 22-3

 7 2.a

1 FOCUS

Objectives

22.3.1 ***Explain*** how vascular tissue is important to ferns and their relatives.

22.3.2 ***Describe*** the three phyla of spore-bearing plants.

22.3.3 ***Identify*** the stages in the life cycle of ferns.

Guide for Reading

Vocabulary Preview

Have students write the Vocabulary words, dividing each into its separate syllables as best they can. Remind students that each syllable usually has only one vowel sound. The correct syllabications are vas•cu•lar tis•sue, tra•che•id, xy•lem, phlo•em, lig•nin, root, leaf, vein, stem, rhi•zome, frond, spor•an•gi•um, so•rus.

Reading Strategy

Have students preview the life cycle of a typical fern, shown in Figure 22–17. Ask them to write a paragraph describing the life cycle. Then, have them make any necessary revisions to their paragraphs after reading the section.

2 INSTRUCT

Evolution of Vascular Tissue: A Transport System

Use Visuals

Figure 22–13 Ask students: **What cells are shown in the bottom photo?** *(Tracheids)* **Tracheids are key cells in what plant tissue?** *(Xylem)* **What is the function of xylem?** *(To carry water upward from roots to every part of a plant)* **What is the other kind of vascular tissue in plants?** *(Phloem)* **Why were tracheids one of the great evolutionary innovations of the plant kingdom?** *(Because tracheids allow water to move efficiently through the plant body, even against gravity, plants can grow upright and tall.)* L2

22–3 Seedless Vascular Plants

Guide for Reading

 **Key Concepts**

- How is vascular tissue important to ferns and their relatives?
- What are the characteristics of the three phyla of seedless vascular plants?
- What are the stages in the life cycle of ferns?

Vocabulary

vascular tissue • tracheid xylem • phloem • lignin root • leaf • vein • stem rhizome • frond sporangium • sorus

Reading Strategy: Building Vocabulary Before you read, preview new vocabulary by skimming the section and making a list of the highlighted, boldface terms. Leave space to make notes about each term as you read.

Bryophytes have only one way to transport water—from cell to cell by osmosis. This fact limits their height to just a few centimeters; for millions of years, plants grew no larger. About 420 million years ago, something remarkable happened. The small, mosslike plants on land were suddenly joined by some plants more than a meter tall and others as large as small trees. Fossil evidence shows that these new plants were the first to have a transport system with **vascular tissue,** which is specialized to conduct water and nutrients throughout the plant.

Evolution of Vascular Tissue: A Transport System

The first vascular plants had a new type of cell that was specialized to conduct water. **Tracheids** (TRAY-kee-idz), shown in **Figure 22–13,** were one of the great evolutionary innovations of the plant kingdom. They are the key cells in **xylem** (ZY-lum), a transport subsystem that carries water upward from the roots to every part of a plant. Tracheids are hollow cells with thick cell walls that resist pressure. They are connected end to end like a series of drinking straws. Tracheids allow water to move through a plant more efficiently than by diffusion alone.

Vascular plants have a second transport subsystem composed of vascular tissue called phloem. **Phloem** (FLOH-um) transports solutions of nutrients and carbohydrates produced by photosynthesis. Like xylem, the main cells of phloem are long and specialized to move fluids throughout the plant body. **Both forms of vascular tissue—xylem and phloem—can move fluids through the plant body, even against the force of gravity.** Together, xylem and phloem form an integrated transport system that moves water, nutrients, and other dissolved materials from one end of the plant to the other. In many plants, the combination of the thick walls of xylem and **lignin,** a substance that makes cell walls rigid, enables vascular plants to grow upright and reach great heights.

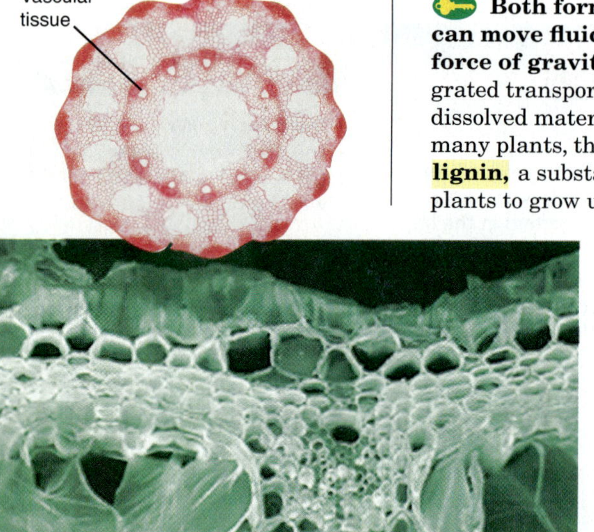

◀ **Figure 22–13** **Vascular tissue conducts water and nutrients throughout the plant body.** It also provides support for the leaves and other organs of the plant. The two types of vascular tissue are xylem, which conducts water, and phloem, which conducts solutions of nutrients. The cross section (top) shows the vascular tissue of the horsetail stem. The bottom photo shows a much-magnified view of tracheids from the xylem of the horsetail.

SECTION RESOURCES

Print:

- ***Teaching Resources,*** Lesson Plan 22–3, Adapted Section Summary 22–3, Adapted Worksheets 22–3, Section Summary 22–3, Worksheets 22–3, Section Review 22–3
- ***Reading and Study Workbook A,*** Section 22–3
- ***Adapted Reading and Study Workbook B,*** Section 22–3
- ***Lab Worksheets,*** Chapter 22 Exploration

Technology:

- ***iText,*** Section 22–3
- ***Transparencies Plus,*** Section 22–3

Ferns and Their Relatives

Seedless vascular plants include club mosses, horsetails, and ferns. The most numerous phylum of these is the ferns. Like other vascular plants, ferns and their relatives have true roots, leaves, and stems. **Roots** are underground organs that absorb water and minerals. Water-conducting tissues are located in the center of the root. **Leaves** are photosynthetic organs that contain one or more bundles of vascular tissue. This vascular tissue is gathered into **veins** made of xylem and phloem. **Stems** are supporting structures that connect roots and leaves, carrying water and nutrients between them.

Club Mosses What was once a large and ancient group of land plants—phylum Lycophyta (LY-koh-fy-tuh)—exists now as a much smaller group that includes the club mosses. Once, ancient club mosses grew into huge trees—up to 35 meters tall—and some produced Earth's first forests. The fossilized remains of these forests exist today as huge beds of coal.

Today, club mosses are small plants that live in moist woodlands. Members of the genus *Lycopodium,* the common club mosses shown in **Figure 22–14,** look like miniature pine trees. For this reason they are also called "ground pines."

Horsetails The only living genus of Arthrophyta (AHR-throh-fy-tuh) is *Equisetum,* which is a plant that usually grows about a meter tall. Like the club mosses, *Equisetum* has true leaves, stems, and roots. Its nonphotosynthetic, scalelike leaves are arranged in distinctive whorls at joints along the stem. *Equisetum* is called horsetail, or scouring rush, because its stems look similar to horses' tails and contain crystals of abrasive silica. During colonial times, horsetails were commonly used to scour pots and pans.

CHECKPOINT *What substance makes the stems of* Equisetum *abrasive?*

Figure 22–14 Club mosses and horsetails are seedless vascular plants. The club moss *Lycopodium* (left) looks like a tiny pine tree growing on the forest floor. The only living genus of Arthrophyta is *Equisetum*, or horsetail (above).

ESL SUPPORT FOR ENGLISH LANGUAGE LEARNERS

Comprehension: Key Concepts

Beginning Write the Key Concept statement (page 560) on the board, and read it aloud. To convey the idea that vascular tissue can move fluids through the plant body, show students photos of pipes and relate vascular tissue to the function of water pipes. Then, draw a Venn diagram on the board that contrasts the functions of xylem and phloem. Label the left circle *Xylem* and the right circle *Phloem*. In the area where the two circles overlap, write "transport fluids," and say these words aloud. Under *Xylem,* write and say "transports water." Under *Phloem,* write and say "transports food made in photosynthesis." L1

Intermediate Extend the Beginning activity by having students write sentences using five additional terms in the list on page 560. Model the process by writing a sample sentence on the board. L2

Ferns and Their Relatives

Build Science Skills

Observing Most students probably have never closely examined a fern frond. Give each student a frond from a fern plant. Also provide metric rulers, scissors, slides, and microscopes. Ask students to write the best description of the frond that they can, including such characteristics as size, color, structure, and so on. Make sure they look for sporangia on the undersides of the fronds. Have students make diagrams of what they see, both with the unaided eye and with the microscope under low power. Once everyone has completed the activity, have volunteers present their findings. L2

Demonstration

Use specimens of mosses and club mosses or pictures of them to demonstrate the differences between bryophytes and seedless vascular plants. Ask students: **What is the dominant form of mosses?** *(The gametophyte)* **What is the dominant form of club mosses?** *(The sporophyte)* Using your specimens or photographs, point out that the moss sporophyte is unbranched and that the club moss sporophyte is branched. Ask: **What is an advantage to having a branched sporophyte?** *(Students can infer that branching increases the number of sporangia that an individual plant can produce.)* Also point out the true roots, stems, and leaves of the club moss. Ask: **What anchors moss to the ground?** *(A rhizome)* Remind students that mosses do not have true roots, stems, or leaves. L2

Download a worksheet on seedless vascular plants for students to complete, and find additional teacher support from NSTA SciLinks.

Answer to . . .

Silica

22–3 (continued)

Life Cycle of Ferns

Build Science Skills

Using Models Students can model the environment in which ferns grow in a homemade terrarium. Have students follow these steps:

- Obtain an empty 2-liter soda bottle that is made of colorless plastic and has an opaque plastic base.
- Remove the base from the bottom of the bottle. Fill the base with peat moss to within 2 centimeters of the top and moisten thoroughly with water.
- Cut the transparent portion of the bottle in half horizontally. Discard the top portion containing the cap. The bottom half will become the dome of the terrarium.
- Collect fern spores from a frond of an actively growing fern plant. Sprinkle the spores over the moistened peat moss.
- Cover the terrarium with the dome. In about three weeks, prothallia, the fern gametophytes, should be visible.

Keep the terrarium out of direct sunlight. Monitor it periodically to correct for improper water balance. There should always be some moisture clinging to the dome of the terrarium. If the terrarium is completely fogged and the contents are not visible, the top should be removed for a few minutes. If the dome appears to be dry, water the peat moss using a spray bottle and replace the dome immediately. As the ferns grow, make sure students identify the gametophyte and sporophyte generations. Encourage them to draw their observations and label the parts of the fern. L2

▲ **Figure 22–15** Ferns are easily recognized because of their delicate leaves, which are called fronds. Fronds grow from a rhizome, which grows horizontally through the soil. **Applying Concepts** *Is the plant shown a sporophyte or a gametophyte?*

a 7 2.a

Ferns Ferns, members of phylum Pterophyta (TEHR-oh-fy-tuh), probably evolved about 350 million years ago, when great club moss forests covered ancient Earth. Ferns have survived during Earth's long history in numbers greater than any other group of spore-bearing vascular plants. More than 11,000 species of ferns are living today.

Ferns have true vascular tissues, strong roots, creeping or underground stems called **rhizomes,** and large leaves called **fronds,** shown in **Figure 22–15.** Ferns can thrive in areas with little light. They are most abundant in wet, or at least seasonally wet, habitats around the world. They are often found living in the shadows of forest trees, where direct sunlight hardly penetrates the forest's leafy umbrella. Ferns are found in great numbers in the rain forests of the Pacific Northwest. In tropical forests, some species grow as large as small trees.

Life Cycle of Ferns

CA a

The large plants we recognize as ferns are actually diploid sporophytes. **Ferns and other vascular plants have a life cycle in which the diploid sporophyte is the dominant stage.** Fern sporophytes develop haploid spores on the underside of their fronds in tiny containers called **sporangia** (spoh-RAN-jee-uh; singular: sporangium). Sporangia are grouped into clusters called **sori** (SOH-ry; singular: sorus), shown in **Figure 22–16.** The life cycle and method of development of a typical fern are shown in **Figure 22–17.**

When the spores germinate, they develop into haploid gametophytes. The small gametophyte first grows a set of rootlike rhizoids. It then flattens into a thin, heart-shaped, green structure that is the mature gametophyte. Although it is tiny, the gametophyte grows independently of the sporophyte.

The antheridia and archegonia are found on the underside of the gametophyte. As in bryophytes, fertilization requires at least a thin film of water, allowing the sperm to swim to the eggs. The diploid zygote produced by fertilization immediately begins to develop into a new sporophyte plant. As the sporophyte grows, the gametophyte withers away. Fern sporophytes often live for many years. In some species, the fronds produced in the spring die in the fall, but the rhizomes live through the winter and produce new leaves again the following spring.

▶ **Figure 22–16** Many clusters of sporangia form on the underside of fern leaves—each cluster is called a sorus. In each sporangium, cells undergo meiosis to produce spores. **Inferring** *Are these spores haploid or diploid?*

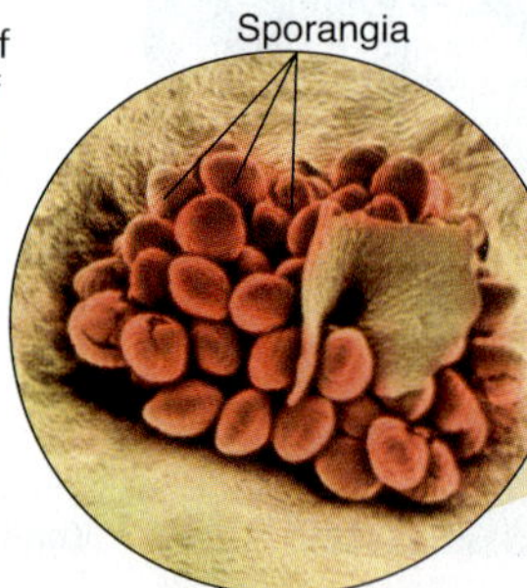

TEACHER TO TEACHER

To introduce students to the great diversity of plants, I give each team of students a set of 10 related plants and have them devise a classification system for that set. For example, one team might be given 10 different gymnosperms. Students classify the plants according to length of needle, number of needles in a whorl, or any other characteristic they consider significant. Other teams are given 10 angiosperms, 10 ferns, or 10 bryophytes, and each team devises a system based on a significant characteristic of their choosing. After 20 minutes, I have the teams present their systems to the class. This activity dramatically demonstrates the diversity of plants.

—*John E. Gonzales*
Biology Teacher
Temescal Canyon High School
Lake Elsinore, CA

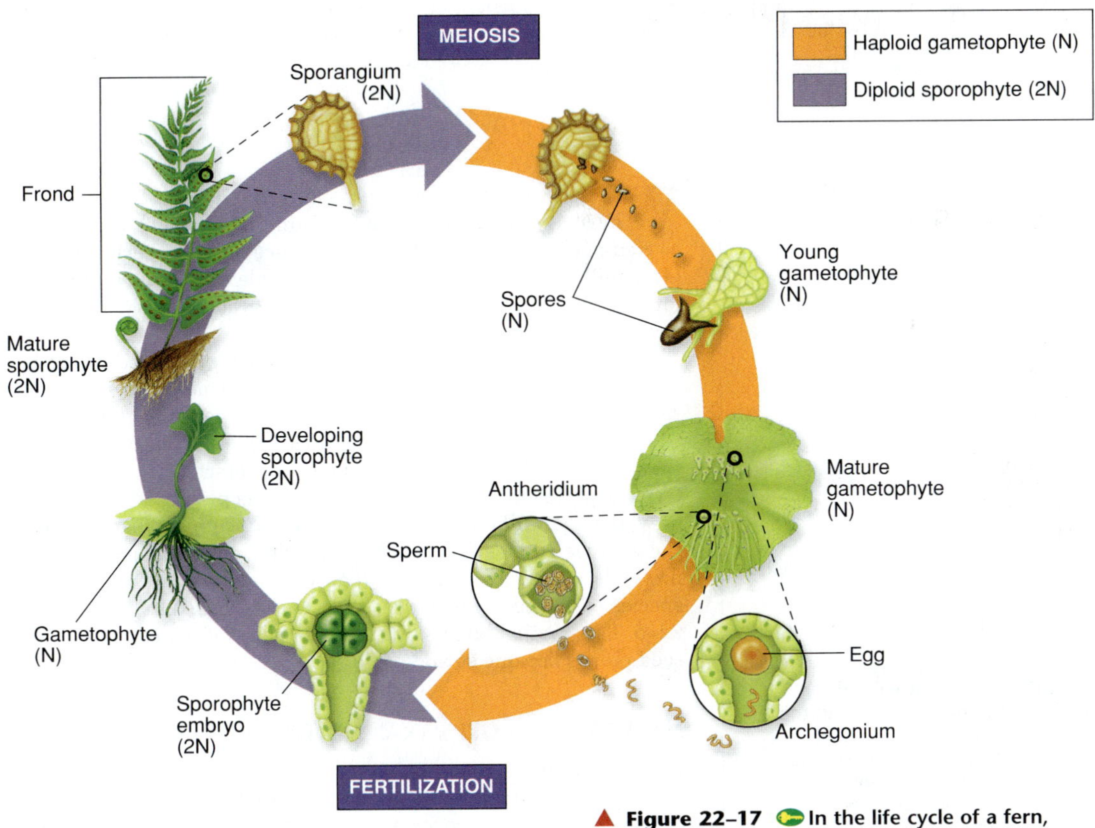

▲ **Figure 22–17** **In the life cycle of a fern, the dominant and recognizable stage is the diploid sporophyte.** The tiny, heart-shaped gametophyte grows close to the ground and relies on dampness for the sperm it produces to fertilize an egg. The young sporophyte grows from the gametophyte.

22–3 Section Assessment

1. **Key Concept** What are the two types of vascular tissue? Describe the function of each.
2. **Key Concept** What are the three phyla of seedless vascular plants? Give an example of each.
3. **Key Concept** What is the dominant stage of the fern life cycle? What is the relationship of the fern gametophyte and sporophyte?
4. **Critical Thinking Inferring** The size of plants increased dramatically with the evolution of vascular tissue. How might these two events be related?
5. **Critical Thinking Applying Concepts** Explain why xylem and phloem together can be considered to be a transport system.

Thinking Visually

Making a Visual Essay
Find out more about club mosses, horsetails, and ferns. Research information such as description, method of development, ecology, and scientific name. Use this information along with photographs or drawings of these plants to create a two-page photo essay about seedless vascular plants.

22–3 Section Assessment

1. Xylem carries water from the roots to the rest of the plant. Phloem transports solutions of nutrients and the products of photosynthesis.
2. Lycophyta: club mosses; Arthrophyta: horsetails; and Pterophyta: ferns
3. The diploid sporophyte; the gametophyte grows independently of the sporophyte. The young sporophyte grows from the gametophyte.
4. Plants without vascular tissue can draw up water by osmosis only a few centimeters above the ground. Vascular tissue moves fluids efficiently throughout a plant, even against gravity. The rigidity of vascular tissue also helps support a tall plant.
5. Xylem moves water from roots to leaves, and phloem moves nutrients from leaves to roots. Together they move materials throughout a plant, forming a transport system.

Use Visuals

Figure 22–17 Have students examine the life cycle and read the caption. Then, ask: **Which generation in the life cycle of the fern is the large, leafy plant we all know?** *(The sporophyte)* **How is the gametophyte produced?** *(The sporophyte produces spores. A spore grows into a gametophyte.)* **What does the gametophyte produce?** *(Sperm and eggs, or gametes)* **Is the gametophyte diploid or haploid?** *(Haploid)* **Is the sporophyte diploid or haploid?** *(Diploid)* L2

3 ASSESS

Evaluate Understanding

Ask students to make a flowchart that describes the steps in the life cycle of a fern using information from the text and from Figure 22–17.

Reteach

Ask students to write a paragraph that explains what vascular tissue is and why it was important in the evolution of ferns and their relatives.

Thinking Visually

Students could use a camera to take their own photos of club mosses, horsetails, and ferns. A good place to take pictures is a local botanical garden. Students might also copy photographs from botany textbooks or library books about plants. As an alternative, students could make drawings of these plants from the photos they find. For each illustration in the photo essay, students should include the common name of the plant, the scientific name, where the photo was taken or obtained, method of development, and an ecological description.

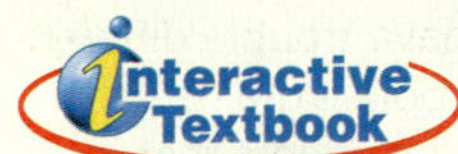

If your class subscribes to the iText, use it to review the Key Concepts in Section 22–3.

Answers to . . .

Figure 22–15 *Sporophyte*

Figure 22–16 *Haploid*

Section 22–4

1 FOCUS

Objectives

22.4.1 ***Describe*** the reproductive adaptations of seed plants.
22.4.2 ***Describe*** the evolution of seed plants.
22.4.3 ***Identify*** the four groups of gymnosperms.

Guide for Reading

Vocabulary Preview

Pronounce each term in the list of Vocabulary words, and ask that students repeat the correct pronunciation back to you in unison.

Reading Strategy

Before students read, ask them to draw a line down the center of a piece of paper. Then, as they read, they should write the main topics of the section on the left side of the line and supporting details on the right side of the line.

2 INSTRUCT

Reproduction Free From Water

Build Science Skills

Designing Experiments Ask students how long they think a seed for a common garden plant could be kept out of soil and still grow if planted in proper conditions. Then, have pairs of students work together to design an experiment that would test the survivability of a certain kind of seed kept away from soil under a variety of conditions. L2 L3

Address Misconceptions

Many students have trouble differentiating between pollen grains and gametes. Remind students that a gamete is a cell that must fuse with another gamete to form a new individual. Point out that pollen grains, therefore, are not gametes; they are spores, because they grow by mitosis into a new individual—the gametophyte. L1 L2

22–4 Seed Plants

Guide for Reading

Key Concepts

- What adaptations allow seed plants to reproduce without standing water?
- What are the four groups of gymnosperms?

Vocabulary

gymnosperm
angiosperm
cone
flower
pollen grain
pollination
seed
embryo
seed coat

Reading Strategy: Building Vocabulary As you read, make notes about the meaning of each term listed above. After you have read the section, draw a concept map to show the relationship among these terms.

Whether they are acorns, pine nuts, dandelion seeds, or kernels of corn, seeds can be found everywhere. Seeds are so common, in fact, that their importance may be overlooked. Over millions of years, plants with a single trait—the ability to form seeds—became the most dominant group of photosynthetic organisms on land.

Seed plants are divided into two groups: gymnosperms and angiosperms. **Gymnosperms** (JIM-noh-spurmz) bear their seeds directly on the surfaces of cones, whereas **angiosperms** (AN-jee-oh-spurmz), which are also called flowering plants, bear their seeds within a layer of tissue that protects the seed. Gymnosperms include the conifers, such as pines and spruces, as well as palmlike plants called cycads, ancient ginkgoes, and the very weird gnetophytes. Angiosperms include grasses, flowering trees and shrubs, and all wildflowers and cultivated species of flowers. The angiosperms are discussed in Section 22–5. This section begins by exploring some of the reasons that seed plants became so successful.

Reproduction Free From Water

Like all plants, seed plants have a life cycle that alternates between a gametophyte stage and a sporophyte stage. Unlike mosses and ferns, however, seed plants do not require water for fertilization of gametes. Because of this method of development, seed plants can live just about anywhere—from moist habitats that are often dominated by seedless plants, to dry and cold habitats where most seedless plants cannot survive. **Adaptations that allow seed plants to reproduce without water include flowers or cones, the transfer of sperm by pollination, and the protection of embryos in seeds.**

Cones and Flowers The gametophytes of seed plants grow and mature within sporophyte structures called **cones,** which are the seed-bearing structures of gymnosperms, and **flowers,** which are the seed-bearing structures of angiosperms. The cones of a common gymnosperm are shown in **Figure 22–18.** The gametophyte generations of seed plants live inside these reproductive structures.

Figure 22–18 **Adaptations that allow seed plants to reproduce without water include reproduction in flowers or cones, the transfer of sperm by pollination, and the protection of embryos in seeds.** Gymnosperms, such as this spruce tree, bear their seeds on the scales of cones.

TIME SAVER

SECTION RESOURCES

Print:

- ***Teaching Resources,*** Lesson Plan 22–4, Adapted Section Summary 22–4, Adapted Worksheets 22–4, Section Summary 22–4, Worksheets 22–4, Section Review 22–4
- ***Reading and Study Workbook A,*** Section 22–4
- ***Adapted Reading and Study Workbook B,*** Section 22–4

Technology:

- ***iText,*** Section 22–4
- ***Transparencies Plus,*** Section 22–4

Pollen In seed plants, the entire male gametophyte is contained in a tiny structure called a **pollen grain.** Sperm produced by this gametophyte do not swim through water to fertilize the eggs. Instead, the pollen grain is carried to the female reproductive structure by wind, insects, or small animals. The transfer of pollen from the male reproductive structure to the female reproductive structure is called **pollination.**

Seeds A **seed** is an embryo of a plant that is encased in a protective covering and surrounded by a food supply. An **embryo** is an organism in its early stage of development. A plant embryo is diploid and is the early developmental stage of the sporophyte plant. The seed's food supply provides nutrients to the embryo as it grows. The **seed coat** surrounds and protects the embryo and keeps the contents of the seed from drying out. Seeds may also have special tissues or structures that aid in their dispersal to other habitats. Some seed coats are textured so that they stick to the fur or feathers of animals. Other seeds are contained in fleshy tissues that are eaten and dispersed by animals.

After fertilization, the zygote contained within a seed grows into a tiny plant—the embryo. The embryo often stops growing while it is still small and contained within the seed. The embryo can remain in this condition for weeks, months, or even years. When the embryo begins to grow again, it uses nutrients from the stored food supply. Seeds can survive long periods of bitter cold, extreme heat, or drought—beginning to grow only when conditions are once again right.

✓CHECKPOINT *What is a pollen grain?*

Seed coat
Embryo
Stored food supply
A
Seed
Wing
B

▲ **Figure 22–19** (A) This longitudinal section shows the internal structure of the seed of a pine tree. (B) The pine tree seed, found on the scale of a cone, is winged. **Predicting** *How might the food stored in the seed affect the reproductive success of the pine tree?*

Quick Lab

How do seeds differ from spores?

Materials Fern frond with sori, microscope, scalpel, microscope slide, coverslip, dropper pipette, sunflower seeds in shells, brown paper bag, hand lens

Procedure   

1. Use a scalpel to scrape sporangia from the underside of a fern frond onto a microscope slide. Add a drop of water and a coverslip and examine the slide under low power. Sketch a few spores. **CAUTION:** *Use care with the scalpel.*
2. **CAUTION:** *Do not perform steps 2 and 3 if you are allergic to sunflower seeds. Do not eat the sunflower seeds.* Open a sunflower seed. With a hand lens, examine the nutlike kernel of the seed and sketch the embryo.
3. Rub the seed on brown paper and hold the paper up to the light. A bright spot indicates lipids. Wash your hands.

Analyze and Conclude

1. **Observing** What evidence do you have that nutrients are stored in sunflower seeds?
2. **Predicting** A spore and a seed are deposited in an area where the soil is poor in nutrients. Which is more likely to survive in a nutrient-poor environment? Explain.
3. **Formulating Hypotheses** Consider two populations of ferns and seed plants. How might their reproductive strategies, or methods of reproduction, have an impact on their survival? Over time, how might these events affect the overall diversity of plants?

UNIVERSAL ACCESS

Inclusion/Special Needs
Review pollination in conifers. Show a picture of a pollen cone. Explain that the pollen grains contain the male gametophyte and each scale of the cone contains the female gametophyte. Review how seeds form after fertilization, and diagram both pollination and fertilization. Then, give students a mature cone to examine. Help them find the seed at the end of each scale. L1

English Language Learners
Give special attention to pronouncing the names of the four groups of gymnosperms. Point out that the initial letter in *cycad* and *conifer* is the same but stands for different sounds because of the vowel that follows each. Make sure students understand that the *g* in *gnetophyte* is silent. L1 L2

Quick Lab

Objective Students will be able to observe how seeds differ from spores. L2

Skills Focus Observing, Predicting, Formulating Hypotheses

Materials fern frond with sori, microscope, scalpel, microscope slide, coverslip, dropper pipette, sunflower seeds in shells, brown paper bag, hand lens

Time 20 minutes

Advance Prep Obtain mature fern fronds from a garden store or florist. Obtain a bag of sunflower seeds in shells.

Safety Make sure students are careful with the scalpel. **CAUTION:** If students are allergic to sunflower seeds, excuse them from this activity.

Strategies
- Demonstrate how to scrape the sori from the underside of the frond onto a microscope slide.
- Demonstrate how to separate the cotyledons of the sunflower seed.

Expected Outcomes Students should observe that seeds contain an embryo plant and stored food while spores do not, and they should infer that fern spores are able to travel great distances through the air.

Analyze and Conclude
1. The brown spot on the paper bag where the seed was rubbed indicates the presence of lipid.
2. The seed; a seed can store nutrients that allow the young plant to survive in poor soil until it is able to support itself by photosynthesis.
3. Ferns depend on water for fertilization. Seed plants do not require water during fertilization. Instead, transfer of the male to the female gamete in seed plants occurs via wind or animals. Seed plants can survive in a broader range of habitats than ferns. Fern spores do not contain stored food, whereas seeds of seed plants have an embryo surrounded by endosperm. The seed is largely responsible for the success and proliferation of seed plants.

Answers to . . .

✓CHECKPOINT *The structure that contains the male gametophyte*

Figure 22–19 *The stored food supply provides nutrients for the seed in the early stages of its growth.*

22–4 (continued)

Evolution of Seed Plants

Use Visuals

Figure 22–20 Ask students: **Do ferns today reproduce using seeds?** *(No, ferns are spore-bearing vascular plants.)* **Why did the evolution of seeds allow plants to live in places where mosses and ferns could not?** *(Seeds provide protection and a food supply for the embryo. With seeds, plants can reproduce free from water.)* L2

Gymnosperms—Cone Bearers

Build Science Skills

Forming Operational Definitions Before students read about gymnosperms, display photographs of a variety of gymnosperms taken from old botany books, nature magazines, or personal photographs. You might also show commercial slides of conifers and other gymnosperms on a slide projector. Then, divide the class into groups to brainstorm for a list of characteristics that they think all gymnosperms exhibit. L1 L2

Address Misconceptions

Some students might think that all gymnosperms have cones. Emphasize that the ginkgo, shown in Figure 22–22, doesn't have a cone but is classified as a gymnosperm. Point out that although this seed might look like a "berry," the outer surface is actually the seed coat. Contrast this with an angiosperm, in which the fruit is on the outside of the seed coat. Then, remind students that *gymnosperm* means "naked seed." Ask: **Why is a ginkgo classified as a gymnosperm?** *(Its seed is not protected by a layer of tissue, or fruit.)* L1 L2

▲ **Figure 22–20** Seed ferns are part of the fossil record. They represent a link between ferns, which do not form seeds, and seed plants. This ancient plant had leaves that resemble the leaves of modern ferns. **Comparing and Contrasting** *If this plant were alive, what structures would distinguish it from a fern?*

Evolution of Seed Plants

The fossil record indicates that ancestors of seed plants evolved new adaptations that enabled them to survive in many places where most mosses and ferns could not—from frigid mountains to scorching deserts. The most important of these adaptations was the seed itself, which can survive dry conditions and extreme temperatures.

Mosses and ferns underwent major adaptive radiations during the Carboniferous and Devonian periods, 300 to 400 million years ago. During these periods, land environments were much wetter than they are today. Tree ferns and other seedless plants flourished and developed into forests that covered much of Earth. Over millions of years, however, continents became much drier, making it harder for seedless plants to survive and reproduce. Many moss and fern species became extinct, replaced by seed plants adapted to live in drier conditions. Similarities in DNA sequences from modern plants provide evidence that today's seed plants are all descended from common ancestors.

Fossils of seed-bearing plants exist from almost 360 million years ago. As shown in **Figure 22–20,** some of these early seed plants outwardly resembled ferns. Seed fern fossils document several evolutionary stages in the development of the seed.

The early seed plants reached every landmass on Earth. Together with now-extinct seed ferns and other seedless vascular plants, seed plants formed dense forests and swamps that spread over much of what is now the eastern United States. Their remains now exist in the form of coal deposits.

Gymnosperms—Cone Bearers

The most ancient surviving seed plants are the gymnosperms. **Gymnosperms include gnetophytes, cycads, ginkgoes, and conifers.** These plants all reproduce with seeds that are exposed—gymnosperm means "naked seed."

Gnetophytes About 70 present-day species of the phylum Gnetophyta (NEE-toh-fy-tuh) are known, placed in just three genera. The reproductive scales of these plants are clustered into cones. *Welwitschia,* an inhabitant of the Namibian desert in southwestern Africa, is one of the most remarkable gnetophytes. It has only two huge leathery leaves, shown in **Figure 22–21,** which grow continuously and spread across the ground.

▼ **Figure 22–21** The *Welwitschia* plant (below), a type of gnetophyte, is an odd desert plant that produces only two leaves during its entire life. Cones are produced at the bases of the two leaves. **Classifying** *In what phylum is this plant classified?*

Figure 22–22 **Cycads, ginkgoes, and conifers are gymnosperms.** Some cycads (top left) produce seeds in reproductive structures that look like giant pine cones. The bristlecone pine (top right) is a conifer that can live for thousands of years. The ginkgo tree (bottom) is sometimes called a "living fossil" because it has changed little over millions of years.

Cycads Cycads, members of the phylum Cycadophyta (SY-kad-oh-fy-tuh), are beautiful palmlike plants that reproduce with large cones. Cycads first appeared in the fossil record during the Triassic Period, 225 million years ago. Huge forests of cycads thrived when dinosaurs roamed Earth. Today, only nine genera of cycads exist. Cycads can be found growing naturally in tropical and subtropical places such as Mexico, the West Indies, Florida, and parts of Asia, Africa, and Australia.

Ginkgoes Ginkgoes were common when dinosaurs were alive, but today the phylum Ginkgophyta (GING-koh-fy-tuh) contains only one species, *Ginkgo biloba.* The living *Ginkgo* species looks similar to its fossil ancestors, so it is truly a living fossil. In fact, *G. biloba,* shown in **Figure 22–22,** may be one of the oldest seed plant species alive today. Ginkgo trees were carefully cultivated in China, where they were often planted around temples. Ginkgoes are now often planted in urban settings in the United States, where their toughness and resistance to air pollution make them popular shade trees.

CHECKPOINT *How many different species of ginkgoes exist?*

Conifers By far the most common gymnosperms, with more than 500 known species, are the conifers. The phylum Coniferophyta (koh-nif-ur-oh-FYT-uh) includes pines, spruces, firs, cedars, sequoias, redwoods, junipers, and yews. Some conifers, such as the bristlecone pine tree, can live for more than 4000 years. Other species, such as giant redwoods, can grow to more than 100 meters in height.

Build Science Skills

Comparing and Contrasting Initiate a discussion of students' knowledge and experience with gymnosperms, including common shrubs such as taxus and junipers and common pine and spruce trees. Ask students to compare and contrast "evergreens" with leafy trees—angiosperms—such as maples and oaks. In this comparison, students should mention that both gymnosperms and angiosperms produce pollen and seeds. They should also mention that only gymnosperms have needles and pine cones and stay green throughout the year. L2

Build Science Skills

Observing Have student groups make a survey of gymnosperms in a specific area near the school. Ask groups to find a field guide in a library to help them identify specific trees and shrubs. Their product should be a table that lists observed gymnosperms, locations, descriptions of habitat, and characteristics.

BIO INSIGHTS **FACTS AND FIGURES**

In the pines

The conifers make up the largest phylum of gymnosperms, and the largest genus of conifers is *Pinus,* which includes 100 species of pine trees. Pines make up much of the coniferous forests, or taiga, of the Northern Hemisphere. Only one species of pine occurs naturally in the Southern Hemisphere. The pines also claim the oldest living organisms, the bristlecone pines. A bristlecone pine cut down in 1964 was estimated to be 4900 years old. The wood of the eastern white pine, *Pinus strobus,* has long been used in furniture making and flooring. It was valued so greatly for use in the masts of sailing ships that in colonial days large trees were marked for use by the English navy.

Answers to . . .

CHECKPOINT *Only one species,* Ginkgo biloba

Figure 22–20 *Its seeds*

Figure 22–21 *Gnetophyta*

Download a worksheet on seed plants for students to complete, and find additional teacher support from NSTA SciLinks.

3 ASSESS

Evaluate Understanding

Call on students at random to describe the features that allow seed plants to reproduce without water. Ask students to explain why this is significant in the evolution of plants.

Reteach

Direct students' attention to Figure 22–19 and ask them to point out the seed, the embryo, the stored food supply, and the seed coat. Then, ask students to explain how the evolution of seeds helped allow plants to reproduce free from water.

Sharpen Your Skills

Students should explain that seed plants can reproduce without water. As a result, seed plants can live just about anywhere. Seedless plants decreased in number as the climate became drier. Angiosperms flourished over gymnosperms because of their protected seeds.

If your class subscribes to the iText, use it to review the Key Concepts in Section 22–4.

Figure 22–23 These longleaf pines in North Carolina grow in an area that receives abundant rainfall. Yet water sinks quickly through the sandy soil, limiting the availability of water to tree roots. In this environment, the pines' water-conserving needles (inset) are an adaptation that contributes to the trees' survival. **Predicting** ***What might happen to a tree with large, flat leaves planted in this environment? Explain.***

For: Links on seed plants
Visit: www.SciLinks.org
Web Code: cbn-7224

Ecology of Conifers Today, conifers thrive in a wide variety of habitats in several biomes: on mountains, in sandy soil, and in cool, moist areas such as the temperate rain forest of the Pacific Northwest. Surprisingly, conifer leaves have specific adaptations to dry conditions. How did these adaptations develop? Scientists have hypothesized that more than 250 million years ago, when conifers evolved, climate conditions were dry and cool. In response to these conditions, most conifers developed leaves that are long and thin, like the pine needles in **Figure 22–23.** This shape reduces the surface area from which water can be lost by evaporation. Another water-conserving adaptation is the thick, waxy layer that covers conifer leaves. In addition, the openings of leaves that allow for gas exchange are located in cavities below the surface of the leaves, also reducing water loss.

Most conifers are "evergreens"—that is, they retain their leaves throughout the year. The needles of most conifer species remain on the plant for 2 to 14 years. Older needles are gradually replaced by new needles, so the trees never become bare. However, not all species are evergreen. Larches and bald-cypresses, for example, lose their needles every fall.

22–4 Section Assessment

1. **Key Concept** Identify the main characteristics of seed plants.
2. **Key Concept** What are the different groups of gymnosperms?
3. What major change in Earth's climate favored the evolution of seed plants?
4. **Critical Thinking Applying Concepts** Pollination is a process that occurs only in seed plants. What process in seedless plants is analogous to pollination?

Sharpen Your Skills

Comparing and Contrasting

Compare reproduction in nonseed plants and seed plants. Then, explain how the evolution of the seed was critical to the success of gymnosperms and angiosperms.

22–4 Section Assessment

1. The ability to reproduce without water, the formation of cones or flowers, the transfer of sperm by pollination, and the protection of embryos in seeds
2. Gnetophytes, cycads, ginkgoes, and conifers
3. Earth's climate became much drier.
4. In seedless plants, the swimming of the male gametes to the female gametes is analogous to pollination in seed plants.

Answer to . . .

Figure 22–23 *Large, flat leaves might lose water rapidly by evaporation, causing the tree to dry out.*

22–5 Angiosperms—Flowering Plants

Flowering plants, or angiosperms, are members of the phylum Anthophyta (AN-tho-fy-tuh). They first appeared during the Cretaceous Period, about 135 million years ago, making their origin the most recent of all plant phyla. Flowering plants originated on land and soon came to dominate Earth's plant life. The vast majority of living plant species have a method of reproduction and development involving flowers and fruits.

Guide for Reading

Key Concepts

- What are the characteristics of angiosperms?
- What are monocots and dicots?
- What are the three categories of plant life spans?

Vocabulary

fruit
monocot
dicot
cotyledon
annual
biennial
perennial

Reading Strategy: Finding Main Ideas Angiosperms are the most diverse group of plants. As you read, take notes on the ways by which their diversity can be organized.

Flowers and Fruits

Angiosperms develop unique reproductive organs known as flowers. In general, flowers are an evolutionary advantage to plants because they attract animals such as bees, moths, or hummingbirds, which then transport pollen from flower to flower. This means of pollination is much more efficient than the wind pollination of most gymnosperms.

Flowers contain ovaries, which surround and protect the seeds. The presence of an ovary gives angiosperms their name: Angiosperm means "enclosed seed." After pollination, the ovary develops into a fruit, which protects the seed and aids in its dispersal.

The unique angiosperm **fruit**—a wall of tissue surrounding the seed—is another reason for the success of these plants. When an animal eats a fruit, seeds from the core of the fruit generally enter the animal's digestive system. By the time these seeds leave the digestive system—ready to sprout—the animal may have traveled many kilometers. By using fruit to attract animals, flowering plants increase the ranges they inhabit, spreading seeds over hundreds of square kilometers.

Figure 22–24 Angiosperms develop unique reproductive structures known as flowers, which contain ovaries that surround and protect the seeds. Apple flowers (left) produce seeds inside ovaries, which mature into fruits (right).

SECTION RESOURCES

Print:

- ***Teaching Resources,*** Lesson Plan 22–5, Adapted Section Summary 22–5, Adapted Worksheets 22–5, Section Summary 22–5, Worksheets 22–5, Section Review 22–5, Enrichment
- ***Reading and Study Workbook A,*** Section 22–5
- ***Adapted Reading and Study Workbook B,*** Section 22–5

Technology:

- ***iText,*** Section 22–5
- ***Transparencies Plus,*** Section 22–5

Section 22–5

1 FOCUS

Objectives

22.5.1 ***Identify*** the characteristics of angiosperms.
22.5.2 ***Explain*** what monocots and dicots are.
22.5.3 ***Describe*** the three different life spans of angiosperms.

Guide for Reading

Vocabulary Preview

Before students read, have them write definitions of what they think each of the Vocabulary terms means. Then, have them skim the section to find the highlighted, boldface terms; read the definitions; and revise what they have written.

Reading Strategy

Before students read, ask them to preview the photographs of angiosperms shown in the section and make a list of questions they have about the diversity of flowering plants. Then, as they read, they can write down the answers to their questions.

2 INSTRUCT

Flowers and Fruits

Build Science Skills

Formulating Hypotheses Before students read about fruits, give each pair of students a ripe apple and a scalpel or paring knife. Ask students to write a description of the outside of the apple before cutting into it. Then, instruct them to cut the apple in half and closely examine the inside. (Caution students to be careful when handling the scalpel or knife.) Ask students to write descriptions of the inside of the apple and make drawings of the apple's core. Also, ask them to count whatever objects are inside the apple. As a final task, have students formulate a hypothesis about the role the apple plays in the life cycle of an apple tree. L2

22–5 (continued)

Diversity of Angiosperms

Build Science Skills

Forming Operational Definitions Before students read about angiosperms, display photographs of a variety of angiosperms taken from old botany books, nature magazines, or personal photographs. You might also show commercial slides of angiosperms on a slide projector. Make sure many of the photographs or slides show plants in bloom. Then, have students brainstorm for a list of characteristics that they think all angiosperms exhibit. L1 L2

Use Visuals

Figure 22–25 Ask students: **If the veins in the leaves of an unknown plant are parallel, what do you know about that plant?** *(It is a monocot.)* **What is a main characteristic of dicot seeds?** *(They have two cotyledons.)* **What is the difference in stem structure between monocots and dicots?** *(Monocots have vascular bundles scattered throughout the stem; dicots have vascular bundles arranged in a ring.)* L1 L2

Diversity of Angiosperms

The angiosperms are an incredibly diverse group. There are many different ways of categorizing them. These include monocots and dicots; woody and herbaceous plants; and annuals, biennials, and perennials. Keep in mind that the categories can overlap. An iris, for example, is a monocot plant that is also an herbaceous perennial. These categories simply provide a way of organizing the diversity of angiosperms.

Monocots and Dicots There are two classes within the angiosperms: the Monocotyledonae, or **monocots,** and the Dicotyledonae, or **dicots.** The general characteristics of both groups are shown in **Figure 22–25.** **Monocots and dicots are named for the number of seed leaves, or cotyledons, in the plant embryo. Monocots have one seed leaf, and dicots have two.** A **cotyledon** is the first leaf or the first pair of leaves produced by the embryo of a seed plant. Other differences include the distribution of vascular tissue in stems, roots, and leaves, and the number of petals per flower. Monocots include corn, wheat, lilies, orchids, and palms. Dicots include roses, clover, tomatoes, oaks, and daisies.

Figure 22–25 **Monocots and dicots are named for the number of seed leaves, or cotyledons, in the plant embryo.** The table compares the characteristics of monocots and dicots.

Characteristics of Monocots and Dicots

	Monocots	Dicots
Seeds	Single cotyledon 	Two cotyledons 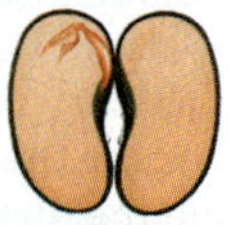
Leaves	Parallel veins 	Branched veins 
Flowers	Floral parts often in multiples of 3 	Floral parts often in multiples of 4 or 5 
Stems	Vascular bundles scattered throughout stem 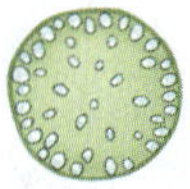	Vascular bundles arranged in a ring 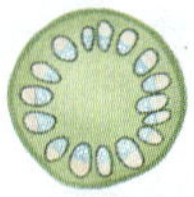
Roots	Fibrous roots 	Taproot 

UNIVERSAL ACCESS

Inclusion/Special Needs
Display a packet of annual flower seeds. Then, have students think of trees that they know of. Ask: **Why don't garden stores usually sell seeds for trees?** *(Many garden flowers are annuals. Trees are perennials and too slow-growing for most gardeners to start from seed.)* L1

Less Proficient Readers
Before students read Section 22–5, have them predict the meanings of *annual, biennial,* and *perennial.* They should write their predictions on a sheet of paper. After reading, have students check the accuracy of their predictions and correct them if necessary. L1

Advanced Learners
Explain that weed plants also fall into the categories of annuals, biennials, and perennials. Challenge students to develop a weed-control plan based on the life span of the weeds. Encourage them to develop alternatives to herbicides. Have students use additional resources. L3

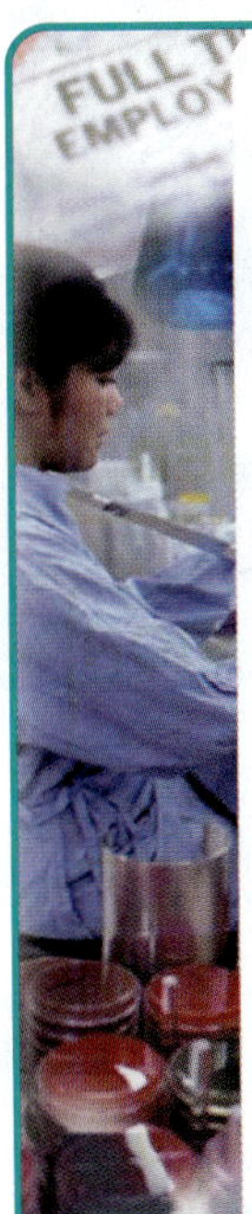

Careers in Biology

Botanical Illustrator

Job Description: work in a museum, outdoors, in a botanical garden, or at home to illustrate plants and organisms related to the plants

Education: two- or four-year college degree in an art school or other school noted for its art and design department

Skills: ability to observe nature; artistic talent; knowledge of biology; detail oriented; knowledge of the Internet, library, and museum research sources

Highlights: You provide illustrations that help people understand and appreciate biology. You have the pleasure of taking people of all ages on exciting visual adventures into the world of plants.

For: Career links
Visit: PHSchool.com
Web Code: cbb-7225

Careers in Biology

Botanical illustrators, also called botanical artists, combine artistic skills with detailed knowledge of botany. Those who follow this career path try to communicate their scientific knowledge and appreciation of plants and flowers in an artistically pleasing way. L2 L3

- Some botanical illustrators work for museums or similar institutions. Many also work at home as freelance commercial artists. Their skills are utilized by book publishers, magazines, and organizations that publish pamphlets and brochures.
- A botanical illustrator usually markets his or her work with an artist's portfolio, which is a collection of samples of the artist's best work.

Resources For additional information on this career, students can contact the American Society of Botanical Artists (ASBA), a nonprofit organization that promotes awareness of botanical art. To contact local botanical illustrators, you can call the art department of a local magazine, publishing company, or university and ask for a reference.

You can have students write a more extensive job description as well as list the educational requirements for a career in this field.

Woody and Herbaceous Plants The flowering plants can be subdivided into various groups according to the characteristics of their stems. One of the most important and noticeable stem characteristics is woodiness. Woody plants are made primarily of cells with thick cell walls that support the plant body. Woody plants include trees, shrubs, and vines. Shrubs are typically smaller than trees, and vines have stems that are long and flexible. Examples of woody vines are grapes and ivy. Examples of shrubs include blueberries, rhododendrons, and roses.

Plant stems that are smooth and nonwoody are characteristic of herbaceous plants. Herbaceous plants do not produce wood as they grow. Examples of herbaceous plants include dandelions, zinnias, petunias, and sunflowers.

CHECKPOINT *What is one example of a woody plant? One example of a herbaceous plant?*

Annuals, Biennials, and Perennials If you've ever planted a garden, you know that many flowering plants grow, flower, and die in a single year. Other types of plants continue to grow from year to year. The life span of plants is determined by a combination of genetic and environmental factors. Many long-lived plants continue growing despite yearly environmental fluctuations. However, harsh environmental conditions can shorten the life of other plants.
 **There are three categories of plant life spans: annual, biennial, and perennial.**

Word Origins

Annual comes from the Latin word *annus,* which means "year." The Latin prefix *bi-* means "two." **Based on the characteristics of perennials, what do you think the Latin prefix *per-* means?**

Word Origins

Students might infer from the description of perennials that the Latin word *per* means "through." Thus, a perennial lives "through the years." L2

BIO INSIGHTS — FACTS AND FIGURES

Evolution of angiosperms

The oldest angiosperm fossils are fossils of pollen grains found in southern England that date from the early Cretaceous Period. By the middle of that geologic period, flowering plants had spread and diversified and were very successful. Many reasons account for their success, including seeds protected inside ovaries. Some biologists also point to the relative quickness with which angiosperms set their seed and grow. During this same period, the giant dinosaurs that had ruled Earth during the Jurassic Period were disappearing. They were replaced by much smaller, low-feeding species. If a plant could not gain a foothold and grow quickly, it would be eaten by the smaller dinosaurs. In this respect, the slow-growing gymnosperms were at a disadvantage compared to the fast-growing angiosperms.

Answer to . . .

CHECKPOINT *Woody plants: trees, shrubs, and vines; herbaceous plants: dandelions, zinnias, petunias, and sunflowers*

22–5 (continued)

Use Community Resources

Invite a landscape architect or designer or a master gardener to the class to help students design a flower garden. Ask the designer to describe how to select plants for a garden, as well as the basics of garden design. Students can use gardening catalogues and gardening reference books to choose plants for their gardens. Stipulate that students use some annuals, some biennials, and some perennials in their plans. Students should submit a design plan for their garden that shows the placement of the plants in the garden and a description of each plant, including common name, scientific name, height, color, bloom time, and life span. L2 L3

3 ASSESS

Evaluate Understanding

Ask students to write a paragraph that explains why flowers and fruit aid in the reproduction of angiosperms.

Reteach

Have students study the table in Figure 22–25. Then, call on students to describe the differences between monocots and dicots.

Thinking Visually

Have students use reference sources such as encyclopedias, field guides, gardening magazines, or seed catalogues to research specific plants. Students' displays should show how the plants they selected have the characteristics of monocots or dicots listed in Figure 22–25.

If your class subscribes to the iText, use it to review the Key Concepts in Section 22–5.

Figure 22–26 **Categories of plant life spans include annuals, biennials, and perennials.** Zinnias (left) are annual plants, which germinate, grow to maturity, set seed, and die in one growing season. Biennials such as the evening primrose (middle) grow roots, stems, and leaves in their first year, then produce flowers and seeds in their second year. Perennials such as peonies (right) live through many years.

Some plants grow from seed to maturity, flower, produce seeds, and die all in the course of one growing season. Flowering plants that complete a life cycle within one growing season are called **annuals.** Annuals include many garden plants, such as marigolds, petunias, pansies, and the zinnias in **Figure 22–26.** Wheat and cucumbers are also annuals.

Angiosperms that complete their life cycle in two years are called **biennials** (by-EN-ee-ulz). In the first year, biennials germinate and grow roots, very short stems, and sometimes leaves. During their second year, biennials grow new stems and leaves and then produce flowers and seeds. Once the flowers produce seeds, the plant dies. Evening primrose, parsley, celery, and foxglove are biennials.

Flowering plants that live for more than two years are called **perennials.** Perennials usually live through many years. Some perennials, such as peonies, asparagus, and many grasses, have herbaceous stems that die each winter and are replaced in the spring. Most perennials, however, have woody stems. Palm trees, sagebrush, maple trees, and honeysuckle are examples of woody perennials.

22–5 Section Assessment

1. **Key Concept** What reproductive structures are unique to angiosperms? Briefly describe the function of each.
2. **Key Concept** What are monocots and dicots?
3. **Key Concept** How do annuals, biennials, and perennials differ?
4. Compare the growth forms of plants with woody stems and those with herbaceous stems.
5. **Critical Thinking Forming Hypotheses** Which are more likely to be dispersed by animals—the seeds of an angiosperm or the spores of a fern? Explain your reasoning.

Thinking Visually

Creating a Display
Prepare a display comparing two specific plants, one monocot and one dicot. On this display, show photographs or drawings of the plants and write a brief summary of the basic differences between these two types of angiosperms.

22–5 Section Assessment

1. Flowers and fruits; flowers attract pollinators; fruits protect the seed and aid in its dispersal.
2. Monocots have one seed leaf, or cotyledon, in the plant embryo; dicots have two.
3. Annuals complete a life cycle within one growing season. Biennials complete their life cycle in two years. Perennials live for more than two years, usually many years.
4. Plants with woody stems are trees, shrubs, or vines. Plants with herbaceous stems include flowers such as zinnias and petunias.
5. The seeds of angiosperms, because the seeds are enclosed in fruit, which animals eat

Exploration

 BIIE 1.d

Comparing Adaptations of Mosses and Ferns

As plants evolved from their aquatic ancestors, they adapted to increasingly drier environments. In this investigation, you will compare a moss and a fern to determine which plant is better adapted for life in a dry environment.

Problem Are ferns or mosses better adapted for life in a dry environment?

Materials

- fern plant
- clump of moss plants
- hand lens
- forceps
- scalpel
- microscope slide
- dropper pipette
- coverslip
- compound microscope

Skills Observing, Comparing and Contrasting

Procedure    

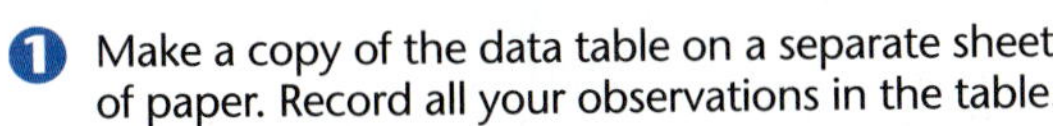

1. Make a copy of the data table on a separate sheet of paper. Record all your observations in the table.

Data Table

Characteristic	Fern	Moss
Appearance of surface		
Flexibility		
Presence or absence of veins		

2. Remove a single moss plant from the clump of plants. Examine the plant. Record whether its leaf surface is dull or shiny. Examine a fern frond. Record whether its surface is dull or shiny.
3. Gently bend the leafy moss plant and the fern frond back and forth. Record the flexibility (ability to bend) of the moss and the fern.
4. Use a forceps to gently transfer a single moss "leaf" to the center of a clean microscope slide. Use a dropper pipette to place a drop of water on top of it, and cover the drop with a coverslip.
5. Examine the slide under the low-power objective of your microscope. Note whether you find veins in the moss. Record your observations.
6. Use a scalpel to cut a thin slice of a fern frond. Using the slice of fern as your specimen, follow the procedure in steps 4 and 5.

Analyze and Conclude

1. **Inferring** Describe the surface of the moss leaf and the fern leaf. What substance did you find on the surface of the fern? How does this substance help ferns live on dry land?
2. **Comparing and Contrasting** Which plant was firmer—the fern or the moss? How can you explain this difference?
3. **Observing** Did you observe veins in the fern? In the moss?
4. **Formulating Hypotheses** Why do you think the fern is able to grow larger than the moss?
5. **Drawing Conclusions** Which plant has structural adaptations that make it better able to survive in a dry environment? Explain.

Go Further

Observing Use a microscope to examine prepared slides of cross sections of mosses and ferns. Where do you see vascular tissue? Explain how these variations in traits might impact the survival of moss and fern species.

Exploration

 **BIIE 1.d**

Objective Students will be able to draw the conclusion that ferns are better adapted than mosses for life in a dry environment. L2

Skills Focus Observing, Comparing and Contrasting

Time 45 minutes

Advance Prep Obtain fern plants from a garden store or florist. Ferns can also be found in damp, wooded areas. Obtain moss plants in damp, shady areas or through a biological supply house.

Teaching Tips

- Remind students to use only the low-power objective in examining their slides.
- Students usually take too large a sample for microscope observation and may attempt to fit a clump of moss under a coverslip, instead of a single moss plant.

Procedure

3. Bending the fronds back and forth is a way of seeing if the fern has supporting tissue to hold its fronds upright.

4. Demonstrate how to transfer a single moss plant to a slide, add a drop of water, and cover with a coverslip.

Expected Outcomes Students should observe a waxy cuticle and vascular tissue in the fern that help them draw the conclusion that ferns are better adapted than mosses for life in a dry environment.

Go Further

Mosses do not contain vascular tissue. Water can be transported only a short distance in moss "leaves" and in their rhizoids, the rootlike structures. Because of the absence of vascular tissue, mosses can easily dry out and cannot grow in areas that lack a good supply of moisture. Ferns have true vascular tissue. They can transport water greater distances within their vascular tissue and are more likely than mosses to survive extremes of temperature and moisture.

Analyze and Conclude

1. Students should observe that the moss plant was dull. The fern frond was shiny, especially on its upper surface, because of the waxy cuticle there. This layer of wax helps ferns live on dry land by preventing them from drying out.

2. The fern should be firmer. Students might correctly suggest that the fern is firmer because it has vascular tissue.

3. The fern has veins in its fronds; the moss does not have veins.

4. Students should hypothesize that the fern can grow larger because it contains vascular tissue that provides support and supplies water to the plant's top. The moss has no vascular tissue.

5. Both the waxy cuticle and the vascular tissue help prevent the fern from drying out, and the vascular tissue also provides support. Therefore, the fern is better adapted for life in a dry environment.

Chapter 22 Study Guide

Study Tip

Divide the class into small groups, and ask each group to make a list of questions that would cover all the Key Concepts in the chapter. Then, have groups exchange lists and answer the questions they receive from another group.

Thinking Visually

Students should construct a table with column headings similar to the following: *Plant Groups*, *Reproduction*, *Tissues*, *Typical Size*, and *Habitat*. Students should list characteristics of each plant group based on the information provided in this chapter.

Chapter 22 Assessment

Reviewing Content

1. b **2.** b **3.** d **4.** c **5.** d **6.** b **7.** a **8.** d **9.** c **10.** c

Understanding Concepts

11. The two alternating phases of a plant's life cycle: the gametophyte, or haploid phase, and the sporophyte, or diploid phase.

12. The fact that some green algae resemble small plants in color and shape. Green algae also have photosynthetic pigments, cell walls, and reproductive cycles that are similar to those in plants.

13. Botanists divide the plant kingdom into four groups based on water-conducting tissues, seeds, and flowers.

14. Because they lack vascular tissue, bryophytes draw up water by osmosis.

15. Bryophytes depend upon the presence of water to complete their life cycle, because the only way the sperm can reach the egg is to swim through standing water or dew.

16. In bryophytes, a protonema is the tangled mass of green filaments that forms the young gametophyte. It is haploid.

17. Tracheids are hollow cells with thick cell walls that make up xylem. The function of tracheids is to transport water through a plant.

Chapter 22 Study Guide

22–1 Introduction to Plants

Key Concepts

- Plants are multicellular eukaryotes that have cell walls made of cellulose. They develop from multicellular embryos and carry out photosynthesis using the green pigments chlorophyll *a* and *b*.
- The lives of plants revolve around the need for sunlight, water and minerals, gas exchange, and the movement of water and nutrients throughout the plant body.
- The first plants evolved from an organism much like the multicellular green algae living today.

Vocabulary

sporophyte, p. 552
gametophyte, p. 552

22–2 Bryophytes

Key Concepts

- Bryophytes have life cycles that depend on water for reproduction. Lacking vascular tissue, these plants can draw up water by osmosis only a few centimeters above the ground.
- Bryophytes include mosses, liverworts, and hornworts.
- In bryophytes, the gametophyte is the dominant, recognizable stage of the life cycle and is the stage that carries out most of the plant's photosynthesis.

Vocabulary

bryophyte, p. 556 • rhizoid, p. 557
gemma, p. 557
protonema, p. 558
antheridium, p. 559
archegonium, p. 559

22–3 Seedless Vascular Plants

Key Concepts

- Both forms of vascular tissue—xylem and phloem—can move fluids throughout the plant body, even against the force of gravity.
- Seedless vascular plants include club mosses, horsetails, and ferns.
- Ferns and other vascular plants have a life cycle in which the diploid sporophyte is the dominant stage.

Vocabulary

vascular tissue, p. 560 • tracheid, p. 560
xylem, p. 560 • phloem, p. 560
lignin, p. 560 • root, p. 561
leaf, p. 561 • vein, p. 561 • stem, p. 561
rhizome, p. 562 • frond, p. 562
sporangium, p. 562 • sorus, p. 562

22–4 Seed Plants

Key Concepts

- Adaptations that allow seed plants to reproduce in areas without water include flowers or cones, the transfer of sperm by pollination, and the protection of embryos in seeds.
- Gymnosperms include gnetophytes, cycads, ginkgoes, and conifers.

Vocabulary

gymnosperm, p. 564 • angiosperm, p. 564
cone, p. 564 • flower, p. 564
pollen grain, p. 565 • pollination, p. 565
seed, p. 565 • embryo, p. 565
seed coat, p. 565

22–5 Angiosperms—Flowering Plants

Key Concepts

- Angiosperms develop unique reproductive organs known as flowers. Flowers contain ovaries, which surround and protect the seeds.
- Monocots and dicots are named for the number of seed leaves, or cotyledons, in the plant embryo. Monocots have one seed leaf, and dicots have two.
- There are three categories of plant life spans: annual, biennial, and perennial.

Vocabulary

fruit, p. 569 • monocot, p. 570 • dicot, p. 570
cotyledon, p. 570 • annual, p. 572
biennial, p. 572 • perennial, p. 572

Thinking Visually

Using the information in this chapter, make a compare-and-contrast table comparing bryophytes, ferns, gymnosperms, and angiosperms. Compare these groups of plants in terms of reproduction (seeds or seedless), tissues (vascular or nonvascular), typical size, and type of habitat.

TIME SAVER

CHAPTER RESOURCES

Print:

- ***Teaching Resources,*** Chapter Vocabulary Review, Graphic Organizer, Chapter 22 Tests: Levels A and B

Technology:

- ***Computer Test Bank,*** Chapter 22 Test
- ***iText,*** Chapter 22 Assessment

Chapter 22 Assessment

Interactive textbook with assessment at PHSchool.com 

Reviewing Content

Choose the letter that best answers the question or completes the statement.

1. Which of the following is NOT a characteristic of plants?
   a. eukaryotic
   b. cell walls contain chitin
   c. multicellular
   d. contain chlorophyll
2. The first plants evolved from
   a. brown algae.
   b. green algae.
   c. red algae.
   d. golden algae.
3. The most recognizable stage of a moss is the
   a. sporophyte.
   b. protonema.
   c. archegonium.
   d. gametophyte.
4. The small, multicellular structures by which liverworts reproduce asexually are
   a. protonemas. c. gemmae.
   b. rhizoids. d. archegonia.
5. Water is carried upward from the roots to every part of a plant by
   a. cell walls. c. cuticle.
   b. phloem. d. xylem.
6. The leaves of ferns are called
   a. sori. c. rhizomes.
   b. fronds. d. spores.
7. To which group does this plant belong?

   a. bryophytes c. gymnosperms
   b. ferns d. angiosperms
8. The reproductive structures of cycads are called
   a. flowers.
   b. sporangia.
   c. sori.
   d. cones.
9. In angiosperms, the mature seed is surrounded by a
   a. cone.
   b. flower.
   c. fruit.
   d. cotyledon.
10. A plant that has a life cycle that lasts two years is a
   a. dicot.
   b. monocot.
   c. biennial.
   d. perennial.

Understanding Concepts

11. What is alternation of generations?
12. What evidence supports the theory that plants evolved from multicellular green algae?
13. Describe the three important features used by botanists to divide the plant kingdom into four groups.
14. By what process does water move through the body of a bryophyte?
15. During the life cycle of a moss, what environmental conditions are necessary for fertilization to occur?
16. What is a protonema? Is it haploid or diploid?
17. What are tracheids? What is their function in a vascular plant?
18. How was the ability to produce lignin significant to the evolution of plants?
19. Describe the dominant stage in the life cycle of a fern.
20. Compare the structure and function of rhizomes, rhizoids, and roots.
21. Describe the male gametophyte of a seed plant.
22. What adaptations allow conifers to live in dry habitats?
23. Which group of plants contains the most species?
24. How do fruits aid in the dispersal of angiosperms?
25. How does the pattern of veins differ in a monocot and a dicot leaf? Draw an example of each.

Interactive Textbook

If your class subscribes to the iText, your students can go online to access an interactive version of the Student Edition and a self-test.

(Continued from page 574)

18. The evolution of lignin made the cell walls of plants rigid. This enabled plants to grow upright and reach great heights.

19. The dominant stage in the life cycle of a fern is the diploid sporophyte, which when mature consists of roots, underground stems called rhizomes, and fronds, which are large leaves. On the undersides of the fronds grow small containers called sporangia, which grow in clusters called sori that release spores.

20. Rhizoids are long, thin cells that anchor bryophytes in the ground and absorb water and minerals. The water moves from cell to cell through the rhizoids to the rest of the plant. Rhizomes are creeping or underground stems that live through the winter and produce new leaves in spring. Roots are underground organs that absorb water and minerals from the soil.

21. In seed plants, the male gametophyte is contained in pollen grains.

22. Features of conifers that suggest they evolved to live in dry habitats include long, thin needles to reduce the surface area of their leaves; the leaves' waxy outer covering; and the placement of leaf openings in cavities in the surface of the leaves to reduce water loss by evaporation.

23. Angiosperms contain the most living species.

24. Fruits attract and are eaten by animals that spread the seeds enclosed in the fruits widely, increasing the ranges that the angiosperms inhabit.

25. Drawings should show that monocots have leaves with parallel veins. Dicots have leaves with branched veins.

TIME SAVER — HOMEWORK GUIDE

Section:	Questions:
Section 22–1	1, 2, 11–13, 26, 30
Section 22–2	3, 4, 7, 14–16, 28, 31
Section 22–3	5, 6, 17–20, 27, 33
Section 22–4	8, 21, 22
Section 22–5	9, 10, 23–25, 29, 32, 34

Chapter 22 Assessment

Critical Thinking

26. Student answers should be consistent with the information in the chapter.

27. Vascular tissue supports a tall plant and carries water and nutrients from the soil to its upper regions. Thus, ferns, which have vascular tissue, grow tall, whereas moss plants cannot grow tall, because they lack vascular tissue. Plants require a method to transport water and nutrients throughout the plant body in order to survive.

28. She needs to provide constant moisture for the mosses and liverworts and protection from too much sun.

29. Student answers should reflect the concept that angiosperms have protected seeds and many ways in which the seeds can be dispersed, which increase the chances of survival.

30. The rootlike structures, similar to rhizoids, might have been used for transport of water and minerals. The branched stalks have capsulelike structures on the ends that might have been used for reproduction.

31. *Cooksonia* resembles mosses living today. Both have simple structures and grow close to the ground. They have similar rootlike structures and reproductive structures. Mosses today have more complex leaflike structures absent in *Cooksonia.*

32. Essays should include the major characteristics of plants: multicellular eukaryotes with cell walls made of cellulose; multicellular embryos; photosynthetic pigments, chlorophyll *a* and *b*. Students should also describe the characteristics of bryophytes, seedless vascular plants, gymnosperms, and angiosperms that are used to classify these plant groups. Last, students should explain how similarities in DNA sequences are used to show which plant species are more closely related.

33. Concept maps should show *vascular tissue* as the main system with *xylem* and *phloem* branching off it as subsystems. *Tracheids* should branch off *xylem* as cells that carry water. Branching off *phloem* should be cells that transport dissolved nutrients.

34. The plant is a monocot, since monocots can have floral parts in multiples of three.

Chapter 22 Assessment

Critical Thinking

26. Comparing and Contrasting Select four major groups of plants, and describe their methods of reproduction and development. Include information about the size of the mature plants.

27. Comparing and Contrasting Moss plants are small. Ferns can grow as tall as a small tree. Explain why this is so. How does your answer illustrate a major characteristic of the plant kingdom?

28. Predicting A friend of yours lives in a desert area of New Mexico. She wants to grow a garden of mosses and liverworts. What environmental conditions would she need to provide in her garden for it to be successful?

29. Formulating Hypotheses Propose a hypothesis to explain why angiosperms have become the dominant type of plant on Earth.

30. Interpreting Graphics The plant below is called *Cooksonia.* Identify the structures that are shown in this drawing. Which structures might have been used for transport of water and minerals? Which structures might have been for reproduction?

31. Applying Concepts Identify fossil evidence of a change in a plant species. Using *Cooksonia* as your example, which present-day species resembles this organism? Explain how the modern plant compares to *Cooksonia.*

32. Classifying Recently, taxonomists have added several kingdoms to the classification system of living things. Mostly, these additions have come about as scientists try to organize different types of unicellular organisms. Write an essay explaining the classification system for the plant kingdom. Be sure to include (a) four groups of plants, (b) the important features used to organize these groups, and (c) the role of DNA in classification.

33. Comparing and Contrasting Develop a concept map illustrating systems and subsystems in plant vascular tissue.

34. Classifying Study the photograph of the orchid below. Is this plant a monocot or dicot? Explain your answer.

Focus on the BIG Idea

Evolution Use what you know about natural selection to explain how the first nonvascular land plants might have evolved into vascular plants. Refer to Chapter 15 for help in answering this question.

Writing in Science

Choose a particular group of seedless vascular plants and a particular group of seed plants. Then, write a paragraph that compares reproduction in the groups of plants that you have chosen. (*Hint:* Use the Key Concepts and the Study Guide to help you organize your ideas.)

Performance-Based Assessment

Making a Timeline Make a timeline to show the major milestones in the evolution of plants. Include a representative plant to show major evolutionary changes in the development of plants. Use the geologic time scale and other information in Chapter 17 for help in drawing your timeline.

For: An interactive self-test
Visit: PHSchool.com
Web Code: cba-7220

Focus on the BIG Idea

Accept all reasonable hypotheses. Answers should include the idea that vascular tissue evolved as a result of variations in plant structure due to mutations. The evolution of vascular tissue improved the transport of water and nutrients within the plant and the absorption of water and minerals from the soil. This development, along with the evolution of lignin, also allowed plants to grow taller. Thus, vascular plants were able to colonize drier habitats and compete for sunlight by raising leaves above surrounding plants.

Standards Practice

Success Tracker™
Online at PHSchool.com

Test-Taking Tip If you find particular questions difficult, put a light pencil mark beside them and keep working. (Do not write in this book.) As you answer later questions, you may find information that helps you answer the difficult questions.

Directions: Choose the letter that best answers the question or completes the statement.

1. Which of the following is a basic requirement of plants?
   A sunlight
   B carbon dioxide
   C water
   D all of the above
2. What stage is represented by cones?
   A sporophytes
   B gametophytes
   C pollen grains
   D spores
3. Which of the following is NOT a characteristic of dicots?
   A branched veins
   B taproot
   C parallel veins
   D vascular bundles in a ring
4. Which of the following is the structure associated with gymnosperms?
   A flower
   B cone
   C branched veins
   D covered seed

Questions 5–8 Each of the lettered choices below refers to the following numbered statements. Select the best lettered choice. A choice may be used once, more than once, or not at all.

A Gymnosperm
B Pollen grain
C Fruit
D Cotyledon

5. Male gametophyte
6. Cone-bearing plant
7. Seed leaf
8. Plant ovary

Questions 9–11

A group of students placed a sprig of a conifer in a beaker of water. They measured the amount of oxygen given off during a set period of time to determine the rate of photosynthesis. They changed the temperature of the beaker using an ice bucket and a hot plate. Their data are summarized in the graph below.

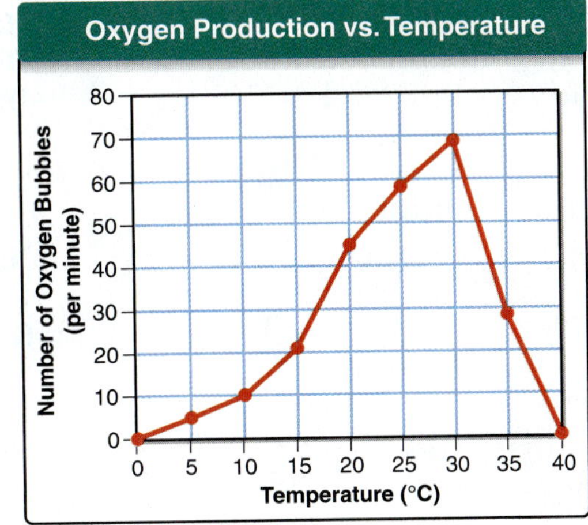

9. What is the independent variable in the students' investigation? **8IIE 9.c**
   A light intensity
   B temperature
   C plant growth
   D oxygen bubbles
10. Which variables should the students have held constant? **8IIE 9.c**
    I. Plant type
    II. Temperature
    III. Light intensity
    A I only
    B II only
    C I and III only
    D II and III only
11. What can you conclude based on the graph? **7IIE 7.c**
    A The higher the temperature, the more oxygen bubbles are released.
    B There is an optimum temperature for photosynthesis in this species of conifer.
    C All plants are most efficient at 30°C.
    D The lower the temperature, the more oxygen bubbles are released.

Standards Practice

1. D	5. B	9. B
2. B	6. A	10. C
3. C	7. D	11. B
4. B	8. C	

Success Tracker™
Online at PHSchool.com

Have students check their understanding of the chapter by logging onto Success Tracker.

Writing in Science

Student paragraphs should include comparisons between the location of spore production, how sperm reach eggs, what occurs during fertilization, and the seed compared to the young gametophyte of seedless plants.

Performance-Based Assessment

Student timelines should include a multicellular green alga, a moss, a fern, a gymnosperm such as a conifer, and an angiosperm such as a geranium. Major milestones include vascular tissue, seeds, and seeds enclosed in fruits.

Go Online
PHSchool.com

Your students can independently test their knowledge of the chapter and print out their test results for your files.

Chapter Planner 23 Roots, Stems, and Leaves

Section and Section Objectives	Time	STANDARDS NCLB	STANDARDS Biology	Activities and Labs
23–1 Specialized Tissues in Plants, pp. 579–583 **23.1.1** ***Describe*** the organs and tissues of vascular plants. **23.1.2** ***Identify*** the specialized cells of vascular tissue. **23.1.3** ***Contrast*** meristematic tissue with other plant tissues.	1 period (1/2 block)			**SE:** ***Inquiry Activity,*** What parts of plants do we eat?, p. 578 L2 **TE:** ***Build Science Skills,*** p. 579 L2 **TE:** ***Build Science Skills,*** p. 581 L2 L3 **TE:** ***Build Science Skills,*** p. 582 L2
23–2 Roots, pp. 584–588 **23.2.1** ***Describe*** the two main types of roots. **23.2.2** ***Identify*** the tissues and structures in a mature root. **23.2.3** ***Describe*** the different functions of roots.	1 period (1/2 block)			**TE:** ***Build Science Skills,*** p. 584 L1 L2, p. 585 L1 L2, p. 587 L2, p. 588 L1 L2 **TE:** ***Make Connections,*** p. 586 L2 **TE:** ***Demonstration,*** p. 586 L2 **SE:** ***Exploration,*** Identifying the Growth Zones in a Plant, p. 603 L2 **LMB:** Chapter 23 Lab L1 L2
23–3 Stems, pp. 589–594 **23.3.1** ***Describe*** the three main functions of stems. **23.3.2** ***Contrast*** monocot and dicot stems. **23.3.3** ***Explain*** how primary growth and secondary growth occur in stems.	1 period (1/2 block)			**TE:** ***Build Science Skills,*** p. 589 L2 **SE:** ***Analyzing Data,*** Reading a Tree's History, p. 592 L2 **TE:** ***Demonstration,*** p. 593 L2 **LMA:** Chapter 23 Lab L2 L3
23–4 Leaves, pp. 595–598 **23.4.1** ***Describe*** how the structure of a leaf enables it to carry out photosynthesis. **23.4.2** ***Describe*** how gas exchange takes place in a leaf.	1 period (1/2 block)	BI 1.f		**TE:** ***Build Science Skills,*** p. 595 L2 **TE:** ***Build Science Skills,*** p. 597 L2
23–5 Transport in Plants, pp. 599–602 **23.5.1** ***Explain*** how water is transported throughout a plant. **23.5.2** ***Describe*** how the products of photosynthesis are transported throughout a plant.	1 period (1/2 block)			**TE:** ***Demonstration,*** p. 599 L2 **TE:** ***Build Science Skills,*** p. 600 L1 L2 **SE:** ***Quick Lab,*** What is the role of leaves in transpiration?, p. 601 L2
Chapter Assessment, pp. 604–607	1 period (1/2 block)			

ACTIVITY PLANNER

SE: *Inquiry Activity,* p. 578; 15 min.; onion, potato, artichoke

TE: *Build Science Skills,* p. 579; 20 min.; plant, dissecting tools, dissecting microscope, petri dish

TE: *Build Science Skills,* p. 581; 20 min.; prepared slides, microscope

TE: *Build Science Skills,* p. 582; 20 min.; prepared slides, microscope

TE: *Build Science Skills,* p. 584; 15 min.; photos of plants with roots

TE: *Build Science Skills,* p. 585; 15 min.; microscope, prepared slides

TE: *Make Connections,* p. 586; 10 min.; soil samples, beaker

TE: *Demonstration,* p. 586; 5 min.; various fertilizer bags and cartons

TE: *Build Science Skills,* p. 587; 10 min.; building blocks or bricks

TE: *Build Science Skills,* p. 588; 5 min.; water, balloon, water dropper

TE: *Build Science Skills,* p. 589; 15 min.; stems, tools, microscope

TE: *Demonstration,* p. 593; 10 min.; bark samples from several trees

TE: *Build Science Skills,* p. 595; 15 min.; several plant leaves, dissecting microscope, dissecting tools, microscope, slides, coverslips, stain

TE: *Build Science Skills,* p. 597; 10 min.; 2 elongated balloons, water

TE: *Demonstration,* p. 599; 10 min.; colored water, glass tubes, pan

TE: *Build Science Skills,* p. 600; 5 min.; potted plant, clear plastic bag

SE: *Quick Lab,* p. 601; Day 1: 20 min.; Day 2: 10 min.; celery, plastic container, food coloring, petroleum jelly, cotton swab, scalpel, metric ruler

SE: *Exploration,* p. 603; 35 min. to set up; 150-mL beaker, metric ruler, paper towels, India ink, 4 large seeds, toothpick, petri dish

PLANNING KEY

Ability Levels

for students performing . . .

below grade level L1

at grade level L2

above grade level L3

Print Components

SE	Student Edition	LA	Lab Assessment
TE	Teacher's Edition	BTM	Biotechnology Manual
RSW	Reading & Study Workbook A	IDM	Issues and Decision Making
ARSW	Adapted Reading & Study Workbook B	LW	Lab Worksheets
TR	Teaching Resources	LMA	Laboratory Manual A
IF	Investigations in Forensics	LMB	Laboratory Manual B

Tech Components

CTB	Computer Test Bank
BD	BioDetectives DVD
TP	Transparencies Plus
PLM	Probeware Lab Manual
ABC	ABC DVD Library
LS	Lab Simulations
VL	Virtual Labs

Interactive Textbook: Interactive textbook with assessment at PHSchool.com

Program Resources	Assessment	Media and Technology
TR: Lesson Plan 23–1, Section Summary, p. 58 L1, p. 70 L2, Worksheets, pp. 61–62 L1, pp. 72–74 L2 **RSW:** Section 23–1 L2; **ARSW:** Section 23–1 L1	**SE:** 23–1 Section Assessment, p. 583 **TR:** Section Review 23–1	**iText:** Section 23–1 **TP:** 23–1 Interest Grabber, Section Outline, Concept Map, Figure 23–1
TR: Lesson Plan 23–2, Section Summary, p. 59 L1, p. 70 L2, Worksheets, p. 63 L1, pp. 75–76 L2 **LW:** Chapter 23 Exploration L1 L2 L3 **RSW:** Section 23–2 L2; **ARSW:** Section 23–2 L1	**SE:** 23–2 Section Assessment, p. 588 **TR:** Section Review 23–2	**iText:** Section 23–2 **TP:** 23–2 Interest Grabber, Section Outline, Essential Plant Nutrients, Figure 23–7, Figure 23–9 **Lab Simulations CD-ROM:** Plant Structure and Growth
TR: Lesson Plan 23–3, Section Summary, p. 59 L1, p. 70 L2, Worksheets, pp. 64–65 L1, pp. 77–79 L2 **RSW:** Section 23–3 L2; **ARSW:** Section 23–3 L1	**SE:** 23–3 Section Assessment, p. 594 **TR:** Section Review 23–3	**iText:** Section 23–3 **TP:** 23–3 Interest Grabber, Section Outline, Compare/Contrast Table, Figure 23–14, Figure 23–15 **Lab Simulations CD-ROM:** Plant Structure and Growth **VL:** Examining Plant Stem Structure
TR: Lesson Plan 23–4, Section Summary, p. 60 L1, p. 71 L2, Worksheets, pp. 66–67 L1, pp. 80–81 L2, Enrichment L2 L3 **RSW:** Section 23–4 L2; **ARSW:** Section 23–4 L1	**SE:** 23–4 Section Assessment, p. 598 **TR:** Section Review 23–4	**iText:** Section 23–4 **TP:** 23–4 Interest Grabber, Section Outline, Function of Guard Cells, Figure 23–18
TR: Lesson Plan 23–5, Section Summary, p. 60 L1, p. 71 L2, Worksheets, p. 68 L1, pp. 82–84 L2 **RSW:** Section 23–5 L2; **ARSW:** Section 23–5 L1	**SE:** 23–5 Section Assessment, p. 602 **TR:** Section Review 23–5	**iText:** Section 23–5 **TP:** 23–5 Interest Grabber, Section Outline, Transpiration, Figure 23–24 **ABC:** 32 Water Transport in Plants, 33 Sugar Movement in Plants
	SE: Chapter 23 Assessment, pp. 604–607 **TR:** Chapter Vocabulary Review, Graphic Organizer, Chapter 23 Test	**iText:** Chapter 23 Assessment **CTB:** Chapter 23 Test

Go Online
Students can do research, share data, and test their knowledge online.

PRESSED FOR TIME?

To Preview the Chapter
- Instruct students to find all of the Vocabulary terms in the chapter and write a definition for each.
- Have students look at the figures in the chapter and read the captions.

To Cover the Chapter Quickly
- Have students read all of Sections 23–1, 23–2, 23–3, 23–4, and 23–5. This entire chapter is required to understand structure and function in plants.
- Assign all Section Reviews and all questions in the Section Assessment.

To Review the Chapter
- Assign Sections 23–1 through 23–5 in the Reading and Study Workbook or the Adapted Reading and Study Workbook.
- Assign the Chapter Vocabulary Review for Chapter 23 in the Teaching Resources.

CHAPTER 23

ENGAGE/EXPLORE

Inquiry Activity

Objective Students will be able to infer what parts of plants they eat. L2

Skills Focus Classifying, Inferring

Materials onion, potato, artichoke

Time 15 minutes

Advance Prep Trim the stems off the artichoke to avoid having students confuse the leaf bud with the stem. You can substitute Brussels sprouts. Obtain onions that have visible roots.

Strategies

- Suggest that students label on their sketches the stems, roots, and leaves of each vegetable.
- Many students will assume incorrectly that onions and potatoes are roots because they grow underground.

Expected Outcomes Students will classify each vegetable as a root, stem, leaf, or other plant part based on their own knowledge of plants.

Think About It

1. Some students might correctly classify the onion as a small stem surrounded by leaves. The leaves are thin and flat, and are attached to the stem at the base. The stem is the part of the onion that joins the leaves to the roots.
2. Some students might correctly identify the potato as a stem. The "eyes" are buds that grow into branches.
3. Some students might correctly identify the artichoke as a floral bud surrounded by modified leaves. The leaves are green because they contain chloroplasts, indicating that they are active in photosynthesis.

Assess Prior Knowledge

Write the words *Roots, Stems,* and *Leaves* on the board. Encourage students to tell what they know about each plant structure. Record their responses under the appropriate heading. Throughout the chapter, correct and add to the information under each heading as students learn about that plant structure.

CHAPTER 23

Roots, Stems, and Leaves

Cacti leaves are modified into thin, sharp spines. The reduced-leaf surface area prevents excess water loss.

Inquiry Activity

What parts of plants do we eat?

Procedure 

1. Examine an onion, a potato, and an artichoke. Record your observations as notes and labeled sketches.
2. Use your observations to classify each vegetable as a root, stem, leaf, or other plant part.

Think About It

1. **Classifying** How did you classify the onion? Explain what characteristics you used to make this decision.
2. **Inferring** How did you classify the potato? How is its structure related to its function?
3. **Inferring** How did you classify the artichoke? What does its inner structure tell you about its function?

FACTS AND FIGURES

Soil and plants

Soil, climate, and plants interact in ways that affect the response of ecosystems to disturbance. Across the American Midwest, for example, deep, sandy soil was covered for many years by native grasses whose leaves and roots decayed to produce thick, humus-laden soil. That soil is superbly suited to production of crops that can be sustained for decades with proper management. In most tropical rain forests, on the other hand, heavy rainfall, high temperatures, and high humidity cause organic matter to break down so quickly that humus is restricted to a thin surface layer. When vegetation is removed for farming, humus quickly vanishes. The remaining soil is exhausted of nutrients, and compacts into clay so hard that it can break a plow. Such land turns to wasteland in about five years after clearing.

23–1 Specialized Tissues in Plants

Have you ever wondered if plants were really alive? Compared to animals, plants don't seem to do much. Yet, in one sense, plants have been more successful than animals. Individual plants outnumber animals and also make up far more of Earth's biomass. So, it's only fair to admit that plants must be doing something right. And so they are.

If you look deep inside a living plant, that first impression of inactivity vanishes. Instead, you will find a busy and complex organism packed with specialized systems and subsystems. Materials move throughout the plant, and growth and repair take place continuously. Plants may act at a pace that seems slow to us, but their cells work together in remarkably effective ways to ensure the plant's survival.

Guide for Reading

Key Concepts
- What are the three principal organs and tissues of seed plants?
- What are the three main tissue systems of plants?
- What specialized cells make up vascular tissue?
- How does meristematic tissue differ from other plant tissue?

Vocabulary
epidermal cell
vessel element
sieve tube element
companion cell
parenchyma
collenchyma
sclerenchyma
meristem
meristematic tissue
apical meristem
differentiation

Reading Strategy: Building Vocabulary
Before you read, preview new vocabulary by skimming the section and making a list of the highlighted, boldface terms. Leave space to make notes of definitions as you read.

Seed Plant Structure

The cells of a seed plant are organized into different tissues and organs. **Three of the principal organs of seed plants are roots, stems, and leaves.** These organs are linked together by systems and subsystems that run the length of the plant, performing functions such as transport of nutrients, protection, and coordinating plant activities.

Roots The root system of a plant absorbs water and dissolved nutrients. Roots anchor plants in the ground, holding soil in place and preventing erosion. Root systems also protect the plant from harmful soil bacteria and fungi, transport water and nutrients to the rest of the plant, and hold plants upright against forces such as wind and rain.

Stems A stem has a support system for the plant body, a transport system that carries nutrients, and a defense system that protects the plant against predators and disease. Stems can be as short as a few millimeters or as tall as 100 meters. Whatever its size, the support system of a stem must be strong enough to hold up its leaves and branches. Similarly, the stem's transport system must contain subsystems that can lift water from roots up to the leaves and carry the products of photosynthesis from the leaves back down to the roots.

Leaves Leaves are the plant's main photosynthetic systems. The broad, flat surfaces of many leaves help increase the amount of sunlight plants absorb. Leaves also expose a great deal of tissue to the dryness of the air and, therefore, must contain subsystems to protect against water loss. Adjustable pores in leaves help conserve water while letting oxygen and carbon dioxide enter and exit the leaf.

SECTION RESOURCES

Print:
- ***Teaching Resources,*** Lesson Plan 23–1, Adapted Section Summary 23–1, Adapted Worksheets 23–1, Section Summary 23–1, Worksheets 23–1, Section Review 23–1
- ***Reading and Study Workbook A,*** Section 23–1
- ***Adapted Reading and Study Workbook B,*** Section 23–1

Technology:
- ***iText,*** Section 23–1
- ***Transparencies Plus,*** Section 23–1

Section 23–1

1 FOCUS

Objectives

23.1.1 ***Describe*** the organs and tissues of vascular plants.
23.1.2 ***Identify*** the specialized cells of vascular tissue.
23.1.3 ***Contrast*** meristematic tissue with other plant tissues.

Guide for Reading

Vocabulary Preview

Read aloud the Vocabulary terms to students. Then, instruct students to copy the words from their textbook and divide them into syllables. (ep• i• der• mal cell, ves• sel el• e• ment, sieve tube el• e• ment, com• pan• ion cell, pa• ren• chy• ma, col• len• chy• ma, scle• ren• chy• ma, mer• i• stem, mer• i• ste mat• ic tis• sue, ap• i• cal mer• i• stem, dif• fer• en• ti• a• tion)

Reading Strategy

Encourage students to practice saying the Vocabulary terms aloud as they read the chapter. They should use the phonetic spellings to help them with correct pronunciation.

2 INSTRUCT

Seed Plant Structure

Build Science Skills

Observing Have students examine small, bare-root plants. Instruct them to locate and observe the three principal organs of the plant. Have them diagram the plant and label the leaves, stems, and roots. Then, have students examine the roots, stems, and leaves under a dissecting microscope. Encourage them to use dissecting tools to tease apart the plant tissue to observe the cells inside. Instruct students to record and illustrate their observations. L2

23–1 (continued)

Plant Tissue Systems

Use Visuals

Figure 23–1 Use the figure to help students understand the hierarchy of plant structure. Ask: **What are the three principal plant organs?** *(Leaves, stems, and roots)* **What three types of tissues are found in each organ?** *(Dermal, vascular, ground)* Have student volunteers identify the location of each type of tissue in each plant organ. Point out that each tissue has the same function in each organ. At this point, you might also explain that organs are made up of specialized tissues working together and tissues are made up of specialized cells working together. L2

Dermal Tissue

Build Science Skills

Using Analogies Have small groups of students work together to develop analogies for the four types of epidermal cells—cuticle, trichomes, root hair cells, and guard cells. Emphasize that analogies describe a similarity between two things that are otherwise not comparable. For example, dermal tissue might be compared to a coat of armor that protects the internal parts of the plant from injury. Invite a spokesperson from each group to share the group's analogies with the class. Discuss the analogies as a class to determine if they seem to fit the structure or function of the epidermal cells. L2 L3

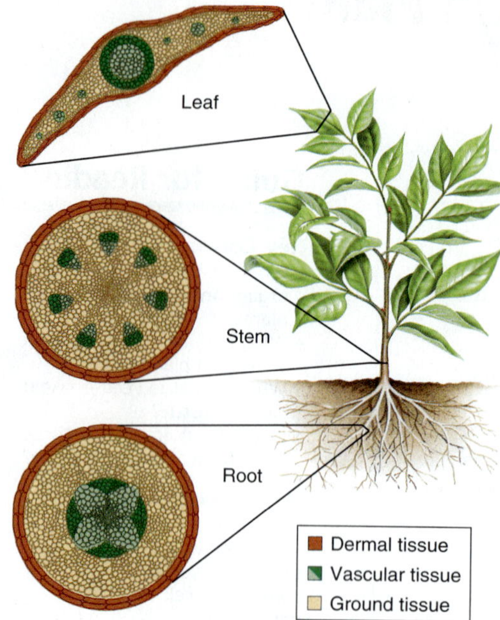

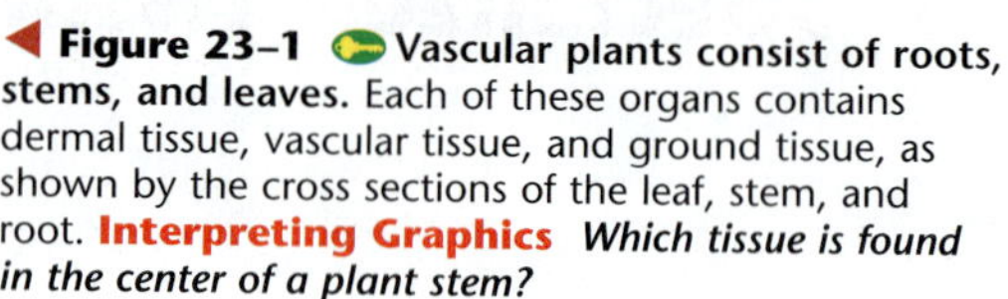

◀ **Figure 23–1** **Vascular plants consist of roots, stems, and leaves.** Each of these organs contains dermal tissue, vascular tissue, and ground tissue, as shown by the cross sections of the leaf, stem, and root. **Interpreting Graphics** *Which tissue is found in the center of a plant stem?*

Plant Tissue Systems

Within the roots, stems, and leaves of plants are specialized tissue systems. **Plants consist of three main tissue systems: dermal tissue, vascular tissue, and ground tissue.** Dermal tissue is like the "skin" of a plant in that it is the outmost layer of cells. Vascular tissue is like the plant's "bloodstream," transporting water and nutrients throughout the plant, and ground tissue is everything else. On this and the following page, you will see how the cells in these systems compare to one another.

Dermal Tissue

The outer covering of a plant consists of dermal tissue, which typically consists of a single layer of **epidermal cells,** shown in **Figure 23–2.** The outer surfaces of these are often covered with a thick waxy layer that protects against water loss and injury. The thick waxy coating of the epidermal cells is known as the cuticle. Some epidermal cells have tiny projections known as trichomes (TRY-kohmz), which help protect the leaf and also give it a fuzzy appearance. In roots, dermal tissue includes root hair cells that provide a large amount of surface area and aid in water absorption. On the underside of leaves, dermal tissue contains guard cells, which regulate water loss and gas exchange.

▼ **Figure 23–2** This scanning electron micrograph shows the specialized cells of the epidermis of a rosebud. The epidermis is covered with thin, unicellular trichomes as well as large, bulbous trichomes that secrete chemicals that protect the plant against insect attack (magnification: 150×). **Formulating Hypotheses** *Develop a hypothesis to explain how natural selection might have led to the development of plants with large trichomes.*

Vascular Tissue

Vascular tissue forms a transport system that moves water and nutrients throughout the plant. The principal subsystems in vascular tissue are xylem, a water-conducting tissue, and phloem, a food-conducting tissue. **Vascular tissue contains several types of specialized cells. Xylem consists of tracheids and vessel elements. Phloem consists of sieve tube elements and companion cells.** As you can see in **Figure 23–3,** both xylem and phloem are made up of networks of hollow connected cells that carry fluids throughout the plant.

UNIVERSAL ACCESS

Inclusion/Special Needs
Provide students with fresh leaves from a wide variety of plants. Have them compare and contrast the textures of the leaf surfaces. Then, challenge students to infer, based on their knowledge of dermal tissue, how these various textures help the plants survive. L2

Less Proficient Readers
Have students create a concept map in which they show the levels of organization in plants. Their concept maps should include the three plant organs, the three types of plant tissue, and the specialized cells of each plant tissue. L1 L2

English Language Learners
Make an audiotape of the Vocabulary words for this chapter. Also make copies of Figures 23–1, 23–3, 23–4, and 23–5, and label them with the words and their phonetic spellings. Show students how to use the audiotape and labeled diagrams to practice saying the words aloud. L1

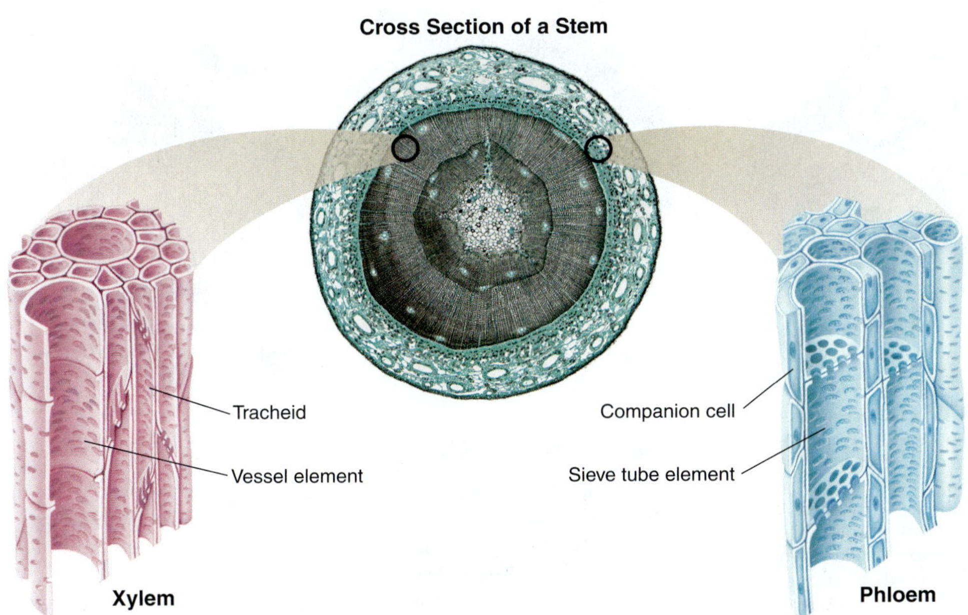

Xylem All seed plants have a type of xylem cell called a tracheid. Recall that tracheids are long, narrow cells with walls that are impermeable to water. These walls, however, are pierced by openings that connect neighboring cells to one another. When tracheids mature, they die, and their cytoplasm disintegrates.

Angiosperms have another kind of xylem cell that is called a **vessel element.** Vessel elements are much wider than tracheids. Like tracheids, they mature and die before they conduct water. Vessel elements are arranged end to end on top of one another like a stack of tin cans. The cell walls at both ends are lost when the cells die, transforming the stack of vessel elements into a continuous tube through which water can move freely.

Phloem The main phloem cells are **sieve tube elements.** These cells are arranged end to end, like vessel elements, to form sieve tubes. The end walls of sieve tube elements have many small holes in them. Materials can move through these holes from one adjacent cell to another. As sieve tube elements mature, they lose their nuclei and most of the other organelles in their cytoplasm. The remaining organelles hug the inside of the cell wall. The rest of the space is a pipeline through which sugars and other foods are carried in a watery stream.

Companion cells are phloem cells that surround sieve tube elements. Companion cells keep their nuclei and other organelles through their lifetime. Companion cells support the phloem cells and aid in the movement of substances in and out of the phloem.

CHECKPOINT *What are the three main tissue systems?*

▲ **Figure 23–3 Vascular tissue is made up of xylem and phloem.** Xylem tissue (left) conducts water from the roots to the rest of the plant. Phloem tissue (right) conducts a variety of materials, mostly carbohydrates, throughout a plant.

Vascular Tissue

Use Visuals

Figure 23–3 Have students compare and contrast the structure of xylem and phloem in the figure. Ask: **What cells make up xylem?** *(Tracheids and vessel elements)* **What cells make up phloem?** *(Companion cells and sieve tube elements)* Then, have students recall what xylem *(water)* and phloem *(food)* transport through the plant. Ask: **How does the structure of vessel elements differ from that of sieve tube elements?** *(Vessel elements lose the cell walls at both ends to form a continuous tube. Sieve tube elements have small holes on the ends through which materials can move.)* Discuss how the structure of the cells is related to their function. L2

Build Science Skills

Comparing and Contrasting Provide prepared microscope slides of xylem and phloem tissues for students to observe. If possible, provide samples from the roots, stems, and leaves of dicots and monocots. First, have students compare and contrast the structures of xylem and phloem. Encourage students to diagram the tissues and label the tracheids, vessel elements, companion cells, and sieve tube elements. Then, challenge them to compare the distribution of xylem and phloem in the different organs of monocots and dicots. L2 L3

TEACHER TO TEACHER

In order to focus student interest on the organs of seed plants, I bring to class examples of roots, stems, and leaves and have students sketch them and describe any unusual adaptations. I also set up microscopes with cross sections of roots, stems, and leaves as concrete examples to help students understand the structure of plant tissues. Then, I focus student attention on meristematic, dermal, vascular, and ground tissues and their cells. I challenge students to identify the different types of cells in each of the tissues and show how cell structure determines its function.

—*Lora L. Marschall*
Biology Teacher
Nathan Hale High School
Tulsa, OK

Answers to . . .

CHECKPOINT *Dermal tissue, vascular tissue, and ground tissue*

Figure 23–1 *Ground tissue*

Figure 23–2 *Plants with larger trichomes might have been better able to protect themselves against insects, which allowed them to survive and reproduce better than plants with smaller trichomes.*

23–1 (continued)

Ground Tissue

Build Science Skills

Observing Have students examine prepared microscope slides of parenchyma cells, collenchyma cells, and sclerenchyma cells. Instruct students to draw labeled diagrams of the cells they observe. Encourage them to label as many parts of the plant cell as they can, such as nucleus, cell wall, cytoplasm, chloroplast, nuclear membrane, and vacuole. L2

Plant Growth and Meristematic Tissue

Use Visuals

Figure 23–5 Have students find the location of the root and shoot apical meristems in the diagram. Ask: **How are both meristems similar?** *(Both contain new cells that have formed by mitosis.)* **How are they different?** *(They have a different structure.)* Discuss the structure of an undifferentiated cell and a differentiated cell. Make sure students understand what is occurring during differentiation. L1

Use Community Resources

Invite a horticulturist to the class to demonstrate how pinching and trimming plants affect their growth. Then, give student groups two plant shoots to experiment with. With the help of the horticulturist, they can pinch back one of the shoots and leave the other shoot alone. Have them compare the growth of the two shoots. L1 L2

Download a worksheet on plant anatomy for students to complete, and find additional teacher support from NSTA SciLinks.

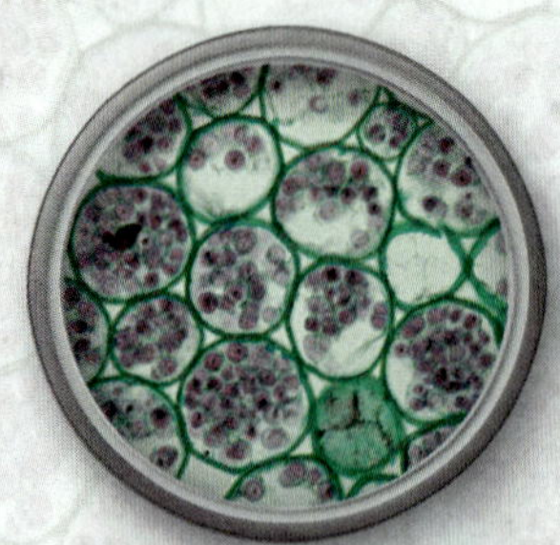

Parenchyma
(magnification: about 50×)

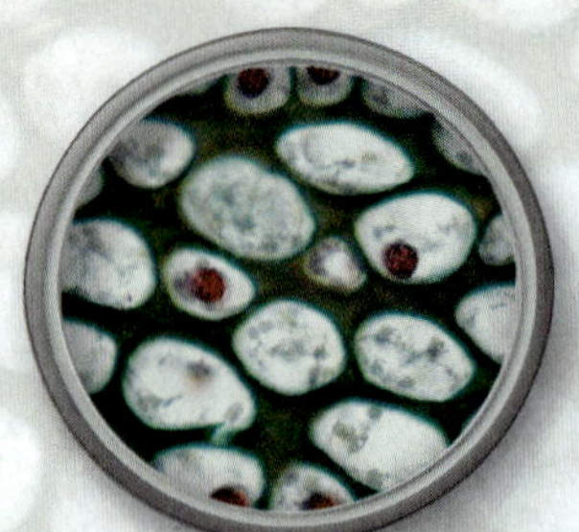

Collenchyma
(magnification: about 150×)

Sclerenchyma
(magnification: about 200×)

Figure 23–4 Ground tissue is made of cells whose cell walls have different thicknesses. Parenchyma cells function mainly in storage and photosynthesis. The root cells shown are filled with purple-staining starch grains. Collenchyma and sclerenchyma cells both function in support. **Predicting** *Where would you expect to find more sclerenchyma—in the leaves or the stem of a plant?*

For: Links on plant anatomy
Visit: www.SciLinks.org
Web Code: cbn-7231

Ground Tissue

The cells that lie between dermal and vascular tissues make up the ground tissues, shown in **Figure 23–4.** In most plants, ground tissue consists mainly of parenchyma. **Parenchyma** (puh-RENG-kih-muh) cells have thin cell walls and large central vacuoles surround by a thin layer of cytoplasm. In leaves, these cells are packed with chloroplasts and are the site of most of a plant's photosynthesis. Ground tissue may also contain two types of cells with thicker cell walls. **Collenchyma** (kuh-LENG-kih-muh) cells have strong, flexible cell walls that help support larger plants. Collenchyma cells make up the familiar "strings" of a stalk of celery. **Sclerenchyma** (sklih-RENG-kih-muh) cells have extremely thick, rigid cell walls that make ground tissue tough and strong.

✓CHECKPOINT *How do the cells of the three kinds of ground tissue compare with one another?*

Plant Growth and Meristematic Tissue

Most plants have a method of development that involves an open, or indeterminate, type of growth. Indeterminate growth means that they grow and produce new cells at the tips of their roots and stems for as long as they live. These cells are produced in **meristems** (MEHR-uh-stems), clusters of tissue that are responsible for continuing growth throughout a plant's lifetime. The new cells produced in **meristematic tissue** are undifferentiated—that is, they have not yet become specialized for specific functions, such as transport.

Near the end, or tip, of each growing stem and root is an apical meristem. An **apical meristem** is a group of undifferentiated cells that divide to produce increased length of stems and roots. **Figure 23–5** shows examples of root and shoot apical meristems. **Meristematic tissue is the only plant tissue that produces new cells by mitosis.**

FACTS AND FIGURES

Characteristics of specialized plant cells
Parenchyma cells are found in all the major parts of plants. Although these cells are usually spherical when first produced, their thin walls are easily flattened as they are packed against one another. The majority end up having a shape with 14 sides. The main function of parenchyma cells with chloroplasts is photosynthesis; those without chloroplasts store water or food.

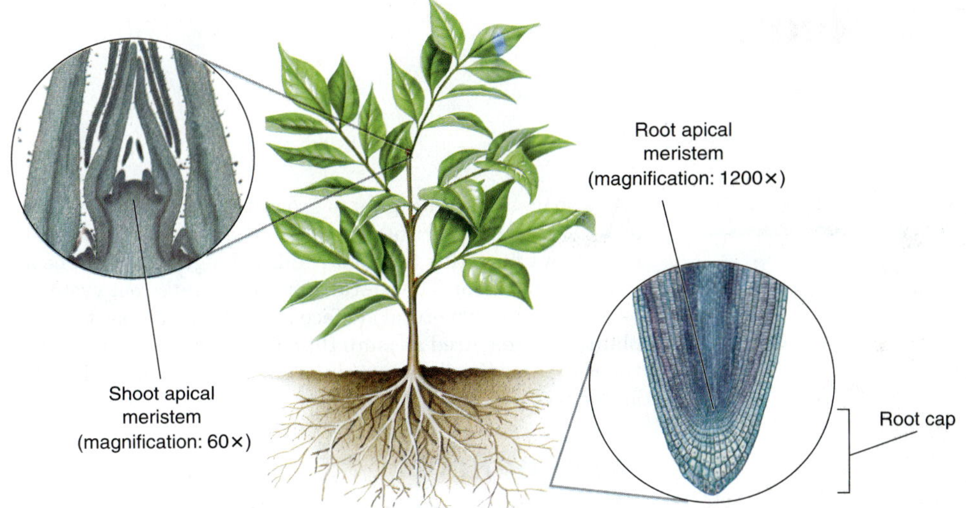

▲ **Figure 23–5 Meristematic tissue produces new cells by mitosis.** Apical meristems, which consist of many actively dividing cells, are located at the tips of shoots (left) and roots (right). The apical meristem of a root is surrounded by a root cap that protects the root as it grows through the soil.

At first, the cells that originate in meristems look very much alike: They divide rapidly and have thin cell walls. Gradually, these cells develop into mature cells with specialized structures and functions, a process called **differentiation.** As these cells differentiate, they produce each of the tissue systems of the plant, including dermal, ground, and vascular tissue.

The highly specialized cells found in flowers, which make up the reproductive systems of flowering plants, are also produced in meristems. Flower development begins when certain genes are turned on in a shoot apical meristem. The actions of these genes transform the apical meristem into a floral meristem, producing the modified leaves that become the flower's colorful petals, as well as the reproductive tissues of the flower. Many plants also grow in width as a result of meristematic tissue that lines the stems and roots of a plant. Later in the chapter, you will learn how this method of growth and development takes place.

23–1 Section Assessment

1. **Key Concept** What are the three main organs of seed plants? Describe the structure of each.
2. **Key Concept** List the three tissue systems of plants. Describe how each tissue is distributed in stems, tissues, and leaves.
3. **Key Concept** What two cell types make up xylem? Phloem?
4. **Key Concept** What is the function of meristematic tissue in a plant?
5. In a stem that needs to support heavy leaves, what type of ground tissue might you expect to find?
6. **Critical Thinking Comparing and Contrasting** Choose a group of cells making up vascular tissue in the root, the stem, and the leaf. Compare these cells, showing how they are alike and different.

Writing in Science

Comparing and Contrasting

You probably have some knowledge of the human circulatory system. Based on this knowledge, write a paragraph comparing and contrasting the vascular system of a plant to the human circulatory system. *Hint:* Show how the systems are alike and different.

3 ASSESS

Evaluate Understanding

Play a word-association game in which you name a type of plant cell and a student volunteer names the tissue from which it comes.

Reteach

Have students create a table in which they organize and describe the three types of plant tissue (dermal, vascular, and ground) and the types of cells that make them up. Students might also wish to include sketches of the cells in their tables.

Writing in Science

Student paragraphs should explain that both the vascular system of plants and the human circulatory system are systems of tubes that transport materials through the body of the organism. In the human circulatory system, fluids move by the pumping action of the heart.

If your class subscribes to the iText, use it to review the Key Concepts in Section 23–1.

23–1 Section Assessment

1. Roots: tissue to transport and anchor; stems: tissue for transport and to support leaves and branches; leaves: flat surfaces for light absorption
2. Dermal tissue: outermost layer of cells; vascular tissue: cells that transport water and nutrients throughout the plant; ground tissue: all other cells making up the plant
3. Tracheids and vessel elements; sieve tube elements and companion cells
4. Produces new cells by mitosis
5. Sclerenchyma cells; they have thicker and harder cell walls that make ground tissue stronger.
6. The structure of cells making up vascular tissue in roots, stems, and leaves is similar. However, the arrangement of the cells differs in each. Figure 23–1 shows this arrangement.

Answers to . . .

CHECKPOINT *Parenchyma cells have thin cell walls; collenchyma cells have strong, flexible cell walls; and sclerenchyma cells have thick, rigid cell walls.*

Figure 23–4 *Stem*

Section 23–2

1 FOCUS

Objectives

23.2.1 ***Describe*** the two main types of roots.

23.2.2 ***Identify*** the tissues and structures in a mature root.

23.2.3 ***Describe*** the different functions of roots.

Guide for Reading

Vocabulary Preview

As you read aloud the Vocabulary terms that refer to root structure, point out their location in Figure 23–7. Contrast the words *endodermis* and *epidermis.* Explain that the suffix *-dermis* means "skin." Challenge students to infer what the prefixes *endo-* *(inside)* and *epi-* *(upon)* mean based on the location of these structures in the root.

Reading Strategy

Encourage students to include diagrams of types of roots and root structures in their outlines. Also suggest that they include all Vocabulary terms and Key Concepts in their outlines.

2 INSTRUCT

Types of Roots

Build Science Skills

Classifying Give students 10 to 15 pictures of different plants with their root structures. Instruct students to classify the roots as being taproots or fibrous roots. Then, have students determine what other characteristics the members of each group share. Challenge students to write a general statement to describe the types of plants in each group. L1 L2

23–2 Roots

Guide for Reading

Key Concepts

- What are the two main types of roots?
- What are the main tissues in a mature root?
- What are the different functions of roots?

Vocabulary

taproot
fibrous root
root hair
cortex
endodermis
vascular cylinder
root cap
Casparian strip

Reading Strategy: Outlining Before you read, use the headings of the section to make an outline about plant roots. As you read, fill in phrases or a sentence after each heading to provide key information.

As soon as a seed begins to grow, it puts out its first root to draw water and nutrients from the soil. Other roots soon branch out from this first root, adding length and surface area to the root system. The overall size of a plant's root system can be astonishing: The total surface area of the root system of a rye plant was measured at more than 600 square meters—130 times greater than the combined surface areas of both the stems and leaves.

Types of Roots

The two main types of roots are taproots, which are found mainly in dicots, and fibrous roots, which are found mainly in monocots. In some plants, the primary root grows long and thick while the secondary roots remain small. This type of primary root is called a **taproot,** shown in **Figure 23–6.** Taproots of oak and hickory trees grow so long that they can reach water far below Earth's surface. Carrots, dandelions, beets, and radishes have short, thick taproots that store sugars or starches.

In other plants, such as grasses, **fibrous roots** branch to such an extent that no single root grows larger than the rest. The extensive fibrous root systems produced by many plants help prevent topsoil from being washed away by heavy rain.

CHECKPOINT *How do roots help prevent erosion?*

Figure 23–6 Plants have taproots, fibrous roots, or both. Taproots have a central primary root and generally grow deep into the soil. Fibrous roots are usually shallow and consist of many thin roots.

SECTION RESOURCES

Print:

- ***Laboratory Manual B,*** Chapter 23 Lab
- ***Teaching Resources,*** Lesson Plan 23–2, Adapted Section Summary 23–2, Adapted Worksheets 23–2, Section Summary 23–2, Worksheets 23–2, Section Review 23–2
- ***Reading and Study Workbook A,*** Section 23–2
- ***Adapted Reading and Study Workbook B,*** Section 23–2
- ***Lab Worksheets,*** Chapter 23 Exploration

Technology:

- ***iText,*** Section 23–2
- ***Transparencies Plus,*** Section 23–2
- ***Lab Simulations CD-ROM,*** Plant Structure and Growth

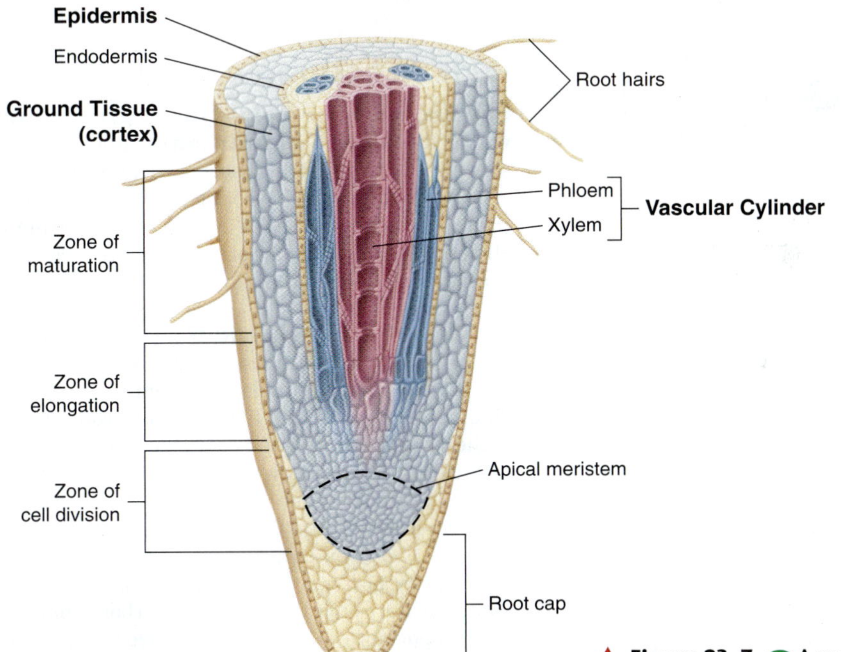

▲ **Figure 23–7** **A root consists of a central vascular cylinder surrounded by ground tissue and the epidermis.** Root hairs along the surface of the root aid in water absorption. Only the cells in the root tip divide. In the area just behind the root tip, the newly divided cells increase in length, pushing the root tip farther into the soil. The root cap, located just ahead of the root tip, protects the dividing cells as they are pushed forward. Dicot roots, such as the one shown in the cross section, have a central column of xylem cells arranged in a radiating pattern.

Root Structure and Growth

Roots contain cells from the three tissue systems—dermal, vascular, and ground tissue. **A mature root has an outside layer, the epidermis, and a central cylinder of vascular tissue. Between these two tissues lies a large area of ground tissue.** The root system plays a key role in water and mineral transport. Its cells and tissues, as shown in **Figure 23–7,** contain a number of subsystems that carry out these functions. The root's epidermal subsystem performs the dual functions of protection and absorption. Its surface is covered with tiny cellular projections called **root hairs.** These hairs penetrate the spaces between soil particles and produce a large surface area through which water can enter the plant. Just inside the epidermis is a spongy layer of ground tissue called the **cortex.** This layer extends to another layer of cells, the **endodermis.** The endodermis completely encloses the root's vascular subsystem in a region called the **vascular cylinder.**

Roots grow in length as their apical meristem produces new cells near the root tip. These fragile new cells are covered by a tough **root cap** that protects the root as it forces its way through the soil. As the root grows, the root cap secretes a slippery substance that lubricates the progress of the root through the soil. Cells at the very tip of the root cap are constantly being scraped away, and new root cap cells are continually added by the meristem. Most of the increase in root length occurs immediately behind the meristem, where cells are growing longer. At a later stage, these cells mature and take on specialized functions. The process by which unspecialized cells change to become specialized in structure and function is known as cell differentiation.

Root Structure and Growth

Use Visuals

Figure 23–7 Relate the three plant tissue systems to the diagram of the root in the figure. Make sure students can identify the location of dermal tissue, vascular tissue, and ground tissue. Help students identify the different cell types within each tissue. Ask: **Would you expect to observe chlorophyll in the parenchyma cells of a root?** *(No, roots do not receive sunlight and have no need for chlorophyll.)* Then, discuss where new growth originates from. Ask: **As roots grow, which portion of the root actually elongates?** *(The portion located just behind the apical meristem)* L2

Build Science Skills

Observing Set up microscope stations at which students can observe prepared slides of longitudinal segments and cross sections of plant roots. Include both monocot and dicot plant roots to give students the opportunity to compare and contrast their structures. Students should draw labeled diagrams of their observations. They can use Figure 23–7 to help them identify the root structures. L1 L2

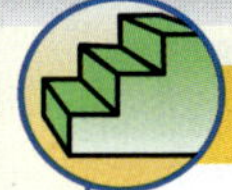

UNIVERSAL ACCESS

Less Proficient Readers
Review with students the processes of active transport and osmosis. Have students apply the diagrams describing active transport and osmosis from Chapter 7 to the movement of water and minerals in a root. Then, ask them to write definitions for osmosis and active transport as they relate to the movement of materials in a root. L1 L2

Advanced Learners
Challenge students to learn about the symbiotic relationship that some plants have with bacteria. These plants have nodules, or bumps, on their roots that contain these bacteria. The bacteria convert atmospheric nitrogen to a form of nitrogen that the plants can absorb. Students can report to the class what plants have nodules, the advantages of this symbiotic relationship, and how farmers use these plants. L3

Answer to . . .

CHECKPOINT *Extensive, branching fibrous roots hold soil in place.*

23–2 (continued)

Root Functions

Download a worksheet on root structures for students to complete, and find additional teacher support from NSTA SciLinks.

Make Connections

Earth Science Display samples of sand, silt, clay, and various soils that are combinations of each. Demonstrate how the pore size of sand enables water to quickly filter through it, while the small pore size of clay causes water to seep through it slowly. Explain that this pore size directly relates to the amount of nutrients held in a soil. Ask: **Why can't sandy soils hold as many nutrients as silt and clay soils?** *(Water washes the nutrients out of sandy soils more quickly and carries them away.)* **Why do you think clay soils are difficult for many plants to grow in?** *(They tend to be water-logged due to poor drainage.)* L2

Demonstration

Display different types of plant fertilizers to the class. Show students how to read the nutrient analysis information on the bag or carton, especially the Nitrogen-Phosphorus-Potassium number. Discuss when and why fertilizers are used for plants, as well as the dangers of overfertilizing and the potential for harming lakes and ponds from fertilizer runoff *(increased phosphates in the pond stimulate algae growth)*. L2

For: Links on root structures
Visit: www.SciLinks.org
Web Code: cbn-7232

Root Functions

Roots anchor a plant in the ground and absorb water and dissolved nutrients from the soil. How does a root go about the job of absorbing water and minerals from the soil? Although it might seem to, water does not just "soak" into the root from soil. It takes energy on the part of the plant to absorb water. Our explanation of this process begins with a description of soil and plant nutrients.

Uptake of Plant Nutrients An understanding of soil helps explain how plants function. Soil is a complex mixture of sand, silt, clay, air, and bits of decaying animal and plant tissue. Soil in different places and at different depths contains varying amounts of these ingredients. Sandy soil, for example, is made of large particles that retain few nutrients, whereas the finely textured silt and clay soils of the Midwest and southeastern United States are high in nutrients. The ingredients define the soil and determine, to a large extent, the kinds of plants that can grow in it.

To grow, flower, and produce seeds, plants require a variety of inorganic nutrients in addition to carbon dioxide and water. The most important of these nutrients are nitrogen, phosphorus, potassium, magnesium, and calcium. The functions of these essential nutrients within a plant are described in **Figure 23–8.** These nutrients are located in varying amounts in the soil and are drawn up by the roots of a plant. In addition to these essential nutrients, trace elements are required in small quantities to maintain proper plant growth. Trace elements include sulfur, iron, zinc, molybdenum, boron, copper, manganese, and chlorine. Large amounts of trace elements in the soil can be poisonous.

CHECKPOINT *What are essential nutrients and trace nutrients?*

▼ **Figure 23–8** Soil contains several nutrients that are essential for plant growth. Each nutrient plays a different role in plant functioning and development, and produces distinct effects when deficient in the soil. **Interpreting Graphics** ***If you notice that a plant is becoming paler and more yellow, what nutrient might need to be added?***

Essential Plant Nutrients

Nutrient	Role in Plant	Result of Deficiency
Nitrogen	Proper leaf growth and color; synthesis of amino acids, proteins, nucleic acids, and chlorophyll	Stunted plant growth; pale yellow leaves
Phosphorus	Synthesis of DNA; development of roots, stems, flowers, and seeds	Poor flowering; stunted growth
Potassium	Synthesis of proteins and carbohydrates; development of roots, stems, and flowers; resistance to cold and disease	Weak stems and stunted roots; edges of leaves turn brown
Magnesium	Synthesis of chlorophyll	Thin stems; mottled, pale leaves
Calcium	Cell growth and division; cell wall structure; cellular transport; enzyme action	Stunted growth; curled leaves

BIO INSIGHTS **FACTS AND FIGURES**

Roots and the underground
Many plants produce roots above ground as well as below. Corn plants, for example, form roots that emerge from the stems and grow toward the ground. Orchids frequently grow perched high on tree trunks and branches. They attach themselves to the tree with roots that secrete a kind of cement. Orchids actually grow on other plants. They gain no nourishment from their unintended hosts. They get nutrients from leaves that fall and decompose near their roots.

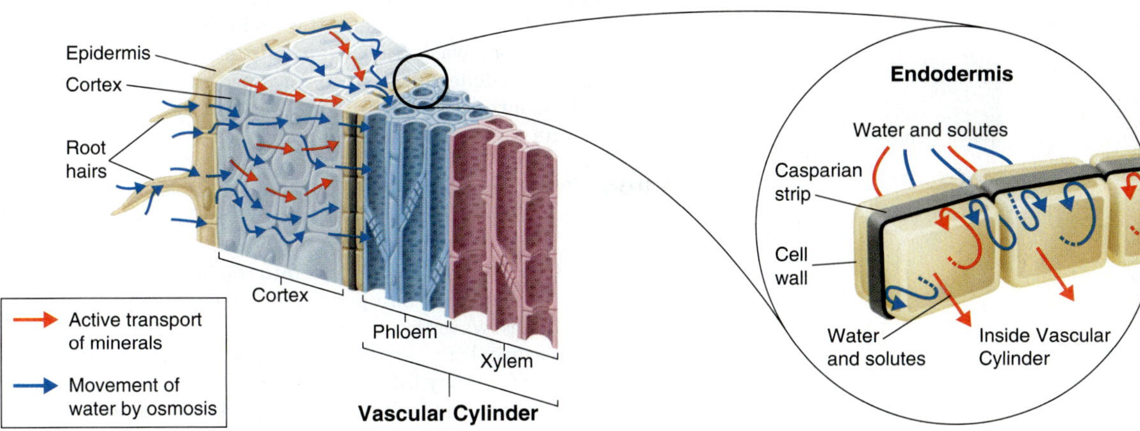

▲ **Figure 23–9** **Roots absorb water and dissolved nutrients from the soil.** Most water and minerals enter a plant through the tiny root hairs. Water moves into the cortex, through the cells of the endodermis, and into the vascular cylinder. Finally, water reaches the xylem, where it is transported throughout the plant. Cells in the endodermis are made waterproof by the Casparian strip. The Casparian strip is another example of how cells are specialized to perform a particular function—in this case, preventing the backflow of water out of the vascular cylinder into the root cortex.

Active Transport of Minerals The cell membranes of root hairs and other cells in the root epidermis contain active transport proteins. These proteins use ATP to pump mineral ions from the soil into the plant. The high concentration of mineral ions in the plant cells causes water molecules to move into the plant by osmosis, as shown in **Figure 23–9.**

You may recall that osmosis is the movement of water across a membrane toward an area where the concentration of dissolved material is higher. By using active transport to accumulate ions from the soil, cells of the root epidermis create conditions under which osmosis causes water to "follow" those ions and flow into the root. Note that the root does not actually pump water. But by pumping dissolved minerals into its own cells, the end result is almost the same—the water moves from the epidermis through the cortex into the vascular cylinder.

Movement Into the Vascular Cylinder Both osmosis and active transport cause water and minerals to move from the root epidermis into the cortex. From there, the water and dissolved minerals pass the inner boundary of the cortex and enter the endodermis. This process is shown in **Figure 23–9.**

The endodermis encloses the vascular cylinder and stretches up and down the entire length of the root, like a cylinder. It is composed of many individual cells, each shaped a bit like a brick. Each of these cells is surrounded on four sides by a waterproof strip called a **Casparian strip.** To imagine what the Casparian strip looks like, think of a brick with a thick rubber band stretched around it. The rubber bands stick together like mortar between the bricks. Imagine many of these bricks placed edge to edge to build a cylinder. When a root is viewed in cross section, the endodermis forms a circle.

Use Visuals

Figure 23–9 As students study how water and minerals move through the epidermis, through the cortex, and into the vascular cylinder, point out that water moves through the cortex cells, as well as around them in the spaces between. Make sure students understand that the Casparian strips only prevent water and nutrients from moving around the endodermal cells—not through them. Ask: **What stops dissolved minerals from moving back through the endodermal cells into the cortex?** *(These cells use active transport to force the nutrients into the vascular cylinder.)* **What stops water from diffusing backward through endodermal cells?** *(If water moved backward, it would be moving from an area of low water concentration to one of high water concentration.)* L2

Build Science Skills

Using Analogies Students can visualize the function of the Casparian strip by making a small wall with bricks or blocks. Ask: **Why could air blow through this wall?** *(There are spaces between the bricks.)* **How could the air be blocked?** *(By filling the spaces between the bricks with caulk or mortar)* Discuss how the caulk or mortar is analogous in function to the Casparian strip. *(Both block the in-between spaces so that air or water does not move through the "wall.")* L2

FACTS AND FIGURES

Nutrients and active transport

Active transport is required to move nutrients into roots, because nutrient ions are present in soil water in lower concentrations than they are in epidermal cells. In fact, these ions would tend to move out of root hairs by diffusion if active transport did not pull them inside. Active transport requires ATP and oxygen. Thus, roots need a constant supply of oxygen. Roots normally obtain oxygen from the air in soil spaces. But, if the soil spaces are filled with water, the roots of most land plants cannot obtain the oxygen they need. This is why overwatering houseplants can kill them. However, if the concentration of water in soil spaces is too low, water may even move out of root hairs and back into the soil. This is called root burn.

Answers to . . .

CHECKPOINT *Inorganic nutrients required by plants to grow, flower, and produce seeds*

Figure 23–8 *Nitrogen*

23–2 (continued)

Build Science Skills

Using Models Students can model the effect of the Casparian strip by filling a balloon with water and then filling a water dropper. Encourage students to describe which model is more similar to what occurs in roots *(the dropper)* and explain how the Casparian strip contributes to root pressure. L1 L2

3 ASSESS

Evaluate Understanding

Play a game in which students must draw a picture of the word they have on a card for the other students to guess. Make up word cards that include all Vocabulary terms from the section, as well as some of the Key Concepts. While drawing, students may not speak or give clues using body language.

Reteach

Have students make a chart with the headings Water Absorption and Nutrient Uptake. Under each heading, have them describe how each process occurs in the root. Then, have them list in order the root tissues that are involved in the process.

Thinking Visually

Encourage students to base their diagrams on either actual plants or photographs from gardening magazines and books or botany books. They should also describe how roots work, based on the information from this section.

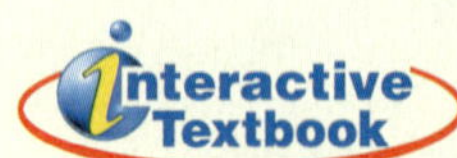

If your class subscribes to the iText, use it to review the Key Concepts in Section 23–2.

Answer to . . .

Figure 23–10 *Roots; this is where root pressure is created—by the movement of water into the root from the soil.*

Osmosis Recall that water moves into the vascular cylinder by osmosis. Because water and minerals cannot pass through the waxy Casparian strip, once they pass through the endodermis, they are trapped in the vascular cylinder. As a result, there is a one-way passage of materials into the vascular cylinder in plant roots.

Root Pressure Why do plants "need" a system that ensures the one-way movement of water and minerals? That system is how the plant generates enough pressure to move water out of the soil and up into the body of the plant. As minerals are pumped into the vascular cylinder, more and more water follows by osmosis, producing a strong pressure. If the pressure were not contained, roots would expand as they filled with water.

Instead, contained within the Casparian strip, the water has just one place to go—up. Root pressure, produced within the cylinder by active transport, forces water through the vascular cylinder and into the xylem. As more water moves from the cortex into the vascular cylinder, more water in the xylem is forced upward through the root into the stem. In **Figure 23–10**, you can see a demonstration of root pressure in a carrot root. Root pressure is the starting point for the movement of water through the vascular system of the entire plant. But it is just the beginning. Once you have learned about stems and leaves, you will see how water and other materials are transported within an entire plant.

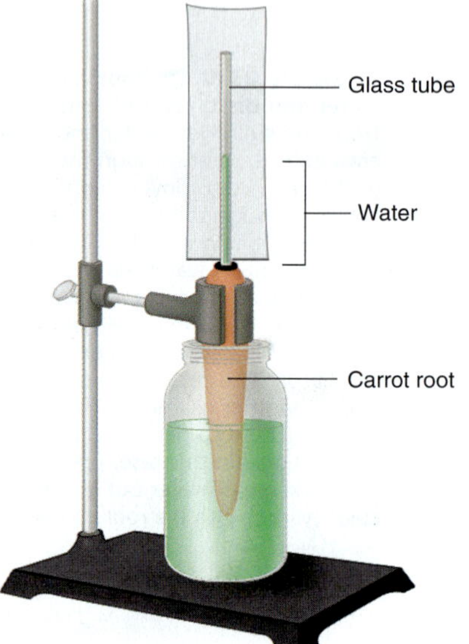

◀ **Figure 23–10** As a carrot root absorbs water, root pressure forces water upward into the glass tube, which takes the place of the stem and leaves of the carrot in this demonstration. **Applying Concepts** *Would you expect root pressure to be higher in the leaves or in the roots? Explain your answer.*

23–2 Section Assessment

1. **Key Concept** Compare a taproot and a fibrous root.
2. **Key Concept** How are tissues distributed in a plant root?
3. **Key Concept** Describe the two main functions of roots.
4. How is osmosis involved in the absorption of water and nutrients?
5. Analyze how a root is part of a plant's transport system. Which parts of a root may be thought of as a subsystem?
6. **Critical Thinking Inferring** Why is it important that the root endodermis permit only a one-way passage of materials?

Thinking Visually

Making a Diagram
Make two diagrams, one showing a root's structure and growth, the other showing how roots absorb water and nutrients. Label the diagrams and write brief descriptions of the processes shown in each.

23–2 Section Assessment

1. Taproots: central primary root, grow deep; fibrous roots: shallow, many thin roots
2. Roots have an outside layer of epidermal cells and a central cylinder of vascular tissue; between these lies ground tissue.
3. Anchor a plant in the ground and absorb water and dissolved nutrients from the soil
4. Active transport through the root epidermis results in a high concentration of mineral ions in the root cells that causes water molecules to move into the root by osmosis.
5. A root is the starting point for the movement of water through the vascular system. Subsystems: epidermis, cortex, endodermis, vascular cylinder
6. The one-way passage of materials creates the root pressure that moves water up into the stem and leaves.

23–3 Stems

What do a barrel cactus, a tree trunk, a dandelion stem, and a potato have in common? They are all types of stems. Stems vary in size, shape, and method of development. Some grow entirely underground; others reach high into the air. Stems also vary in structure and internal arrangement of cells.

Guide for Reading

Key Concepts
- What are the three main functions of stems?
- How do monocot and dicot stems differ?
- How do primary growth and secondary growth occur in stems?

Vocabulary
node • internode • bud
vascular bundle • pith
primary growth
secondary growth
vascular cambium
cork cambium • heartwood
sapwood • bark

Reading Strategy: Using Visuals Before you read, preview the art in **Figure 23–15.** As you read the section, refer to this art to learn about the structure of mature woody stems.

Stem Structure and Function

In general, stems have three important functions: They produce leaves, branches, and flowers; they hold leaves up to the sunlight; and they transport substances between roots and leaves. Stems make up an essential part of the water and mineral transport systems of the plant. The vascular tissue in stems conducts water, nutrients, and other compounds throughout the plant. Xylem and phloem, the major subsystems of the transport system, form continuous tubes from the roots through the stems to the leaves. These vascular tissues link all parts of the plant, allowing water and nutrients to be carried throughout the plant. In many plants, stems also function as storage systems and aid in the process of photosynthesis.

Like the rest of the plant, the stem is composed of three tissue systems: dermal, vascular, and ground tissue. Stems are surrounded by a layer of epidermal cells that have thick cell walls and a waxy protective coating.

In most plants, stems contain distinct **nodes,** where leaves are attached, and **internode** regions between the nodes, as shown in **Figure 23–11.** Small buds are found where leaves attach to the nodes. **Buds** contain undeveloped tissue that can produce new stems and leaves. In larger plants, stems develop woody tissue that helps support leaves and flowers.

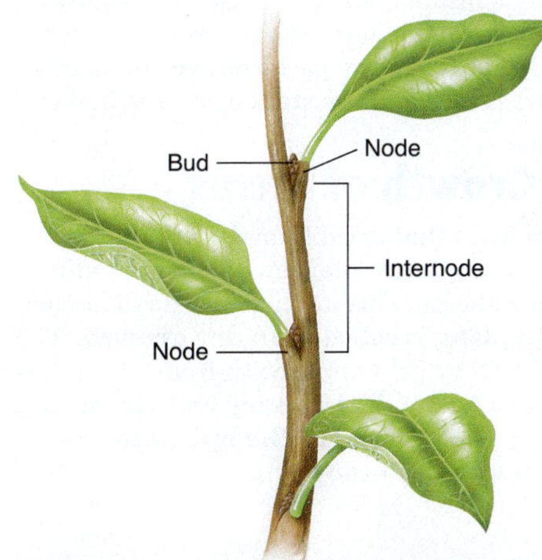

Figure 23–11 **Stems produce leaves and branches and hold leaves up to the sunlight, where they carry out photosynthesis.** Leaves are attached to a stem at structures called nodes. These nodes are separated by regions of the stem called internodes.

SECTION RESOURCES

Print:
- ***Laboratory Manual A,*** Chapter 23 Lab
- ***Teaching Resources,*** Lesson Plan 23–3, Adapted Section Summary 23–3, Adapted Worksheets 23–3, Section Summary 23–3, Worksheets 23–3, Section Review 23–3
- ***Reading and Study Workbook A,*** Section 23–3
- ***Adapted Reading and Study Workbook B,*** Section 23–3

Technology:
- ***iText,*** Section 23–3
- ***Transparencies Plus,*** Section 23–3
- ***Lab Simulations CD-ROM,*** Plant Structure and Growth
- ***Virtual Labs,*** Examining Plant Stem Structure

Section 23–3

1 FOCUS

Objectives

23.3.1 ***Describe*** the three main functions of stems.
23.3.2 ***Contrast*** monocot and dicot stems.
23.3.3 ***Explain*** how primary growth and secondary growth occur in stems.

Guide for Reading

Vocabulary Preview

List the Vocabulary terms on the board. Invite students to identify terms they already know and give definitions for them. Then, challenge students to infer the meanings of the remaining terms. Review the definitions throughout the section, and correct earlier definitions as needed.

Reading Strategy

As students preview the figure, encourage them to identify the Vocabulary terms used as labels in the diagram. Have students find their meanings as they read the section.

2 INSTRUCT

Stem Structure and Function

Build Science Skills

Observing Provide students with examples of various stems, such as woody tree branches, flower stems, ivy, sprouted tulip or daffodil bulbs, and sprouted potatoes. Challenge students to find the nodes, internodes, and buds on these stems. Suggest that they use dissecting tools to tease apart stem tissue and examine it under a dissecting microscope. Remind students to use sharp dissecting tools with care. Also encourage students to examine cross sections of stems. Students should draw labeled diagrams of their observations. Make sure they observe the differences between underground stems and more “traditional” stems. L2

23–3 (continued)

Monocot and Dicot Stems

Use Visuals

Figure 23–12 Use the stem cross sections in the figure to compare and contrast stem structure in monocots and dicots. Discuss characteristics of the stem structures that are different. Also discuss their similarities. Make sure students can correctly identify all parts of the stem, including the locations of the three types of plant tissue. L2

Primary Growth of Stems

Address Misconceptions

Some students might think that as plants grow, the stems get taller from the point where they attach to the roots. Help students understand where primary growth occurs by looking at trees on the school grounds. Point out that as a tree grows taller, the branches at the bottom do not get higher off the ground, they stay where they are. Apply this concept to other plants growing on the school grounds until it is clear that students understand. L1 L2

Build Science Skills

Designing Experiments Challenge students to design an experiment to determine if all plants have the same rate of primary growth. Students should decide how they will measure primary growth and determine what plants they will study. They should write a complete procedure and estimate the time it will take to complete the study. L2 L3

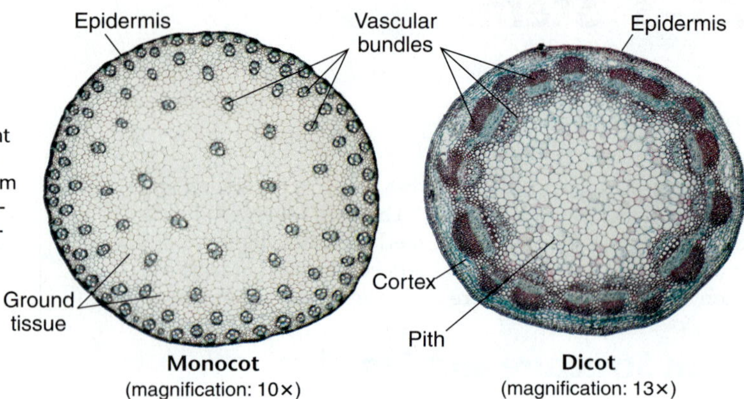

▶ **Figure 23–12** The arrangement of vascular bundles in the stem of a monocot differs from that in the stem of a dicot. **In a monocot, vascular bundles are scattered throughout the stem. In a dicot, vascular bundles are arranged in a ring.**

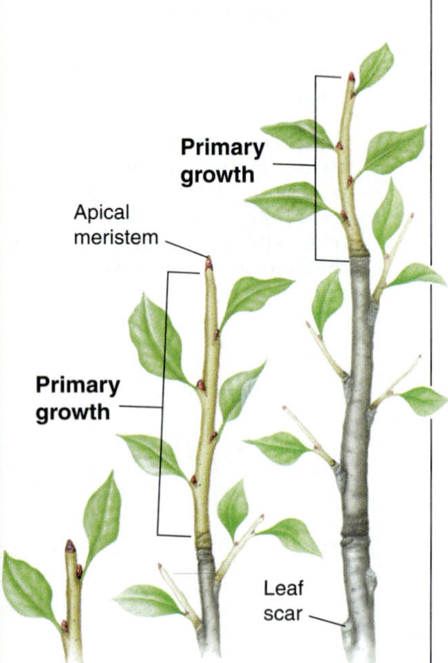

▲ **Figure 23–13** **All seed plants undergo primary growth, which is an increase in length.** Every year, apical meristems, shown in red, divide to produce new growth. The primary growth for one season consists of a stem and several leaves.

Monocot and Dicot Stems

The arrangement of tissues in a stem differs among seed plants. **In monocots, vascular bundles are scattered throughout the stem. In dicots and most gymnosperms, vascular bundles are arranged in a cylinder.** Recall that monocots and dicots are two types of flowering plants, or angiosperms. For a comparison of monocot and dicot stems, look at **Figure 23–12.**

Monocot Stems The cross section of a young monocot stem shows all three tissue systems clearly. The stem has a distinct epidermis, which encloses a series of **vascular bundles,** each of which contains xylem and phloem tissue. Phloem faces the outside of the stem, and xylem faces the center. In monocots, these bundles are scattered throughout the ground tissue. The ground tissue is fairly uniform, consisting mainly of parenchyma cells.

Dicot Stems Young dicot stems have vascular bundles, but they are generally arranged in an organized, ringlike pattern. The parenchyma cells inside the ring of vascular tissue are known as **pith,** while those outside form the cortex of the stem. In dicots, these relatively simple tissue patterns become more complex as the plant grows larger and the stem increases in diameter.

Primary Growth of Stems

Plants grow in ways that are distinctly different from other organisms. For their entire life, new cells are produced at the tips of roots and shoots. This method of growth, occurring only at the ends of a plant, is called **primary growth.** The increase in length produced by primary growth from year to year is shown in **Figure 23–13.** **Primary growth of stems is produced by cell divisions in the apical meristem. It takes place in all seed plants.**

ESL SUPPORT FOR ENGLISH LANGUAGE LEARNERS

Comprehension: Link to Visual

Beginning Use Figure 23–12 (page 590) to help students contrast monocots and dicots. On the board, write the boldface sentences found in the caption of Figure 23–12. Use the figure to clarify the meanings of the sentences. Review the Vocabulary terms *vascular bundle* and *pith* by pointing out these structures in the figure. Ask the students to draw and label their own cross sections of a monocot and a dicot. L1

Intermediate Have the students complete the beginning-level activity. Then, pair ESL students with students who are proficient in English to write several sentences summarizing the differences between monocots and dicots in their own words. Ask one member of each pair to read the sentences out loud. L2

Secondary Growth of Stems

If a plant is to grow larger year after year, its stems must increase in thickness as well as in length. They have more mass to support and more fluid to move through their vascular tissues. Yet, only meristematic tissue can produce new cells for growth. Some monocots, such as palm trees, produce thick stems from a meristem that becomes wider as the plant grows. However, most monocots, such as grasses, produce only fleshy growth and do not grow very tall. Many dicots grow extremely tall and also grow in width to support this extra weight. This growth occurs as a result of meristems other than the apical meristem.

The method of growth in which stems increase in width is called **secondary growth.** In **Figure 23–14** you can see the pattern of secondary growth in a dicot stem. **In conifers and dicots, secondary growth takes place in lateral meristematic tissues called the vascular cambium and cork cambium.** The type of lateral meristematic tissue called **vascular cambium** produces vascular tissues and increases the thickness of stems over time. **Cork cambium** produces the outer covering of stems. Another kind of cambium enables roots to grow thicker and branch. The addition of new tissue in these cambium layers increases the thickness of the stem.

Formation of the Vascular Cambium In a young dicot stem produced by primary growth, bundles of xylem and phloem are arranged in a ring. Once secondary growth begins, the vascular cambium appears as a thin layer situated between clusters of vascular tissue. This new meristematic tissue forms between the xylem and phloem of each vascular bundle. Divisions in the vascular cambium give rise to new layers of xylem and phloem. As a result, the stem becomes wider. The cambium continues to produce new layers of vascular tissue, causing the stem to become thicker and thicker.

CHECKPOINT *What tissue divides to produce secondary growth in dicots?*

▼ **Figure 23–14 Dicots produce secondary growth from meristematic tissue called vascular cambium.** This tissue forms between the xylem and phloem of the individual vascular bundles, as shown in A. Once the tissue forms, as shown in B, it divides to produce xylem cells toward the center of the stem and phloem cells toward the outside. These different tissues form the bark and wood of a mature stem, shown in C.

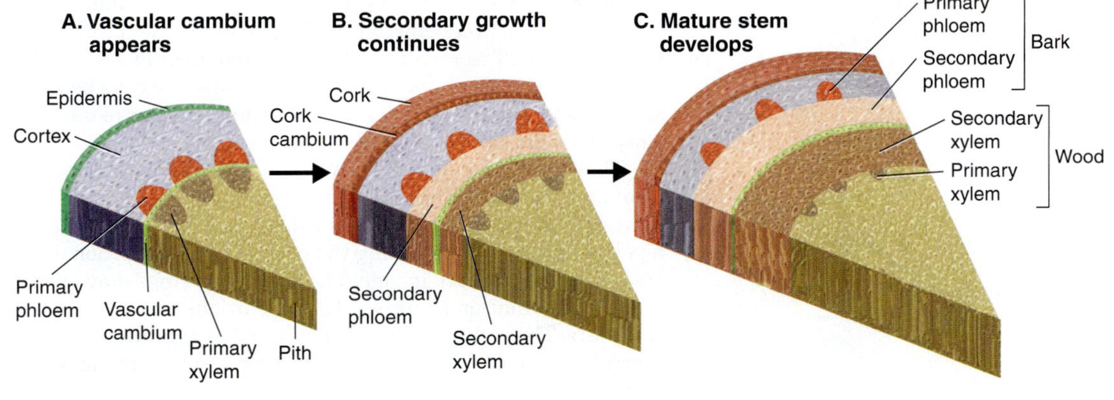

Secondary Growth of Stems

Use Visuals

Figure 23–14 Use the diagram to review the formation of vascular cambium and secondary growth. Ask: **Where does the vascular cambium appear when secondary growth begins?** *(Between the xylem and phloem of primary vascular tissue)* **What causes the stem to become wider?** *(Divisions of vascular cambium give rise to new layers of xylem and phloem, widening the stem)* **Where do new phloem cells form?** *(Toward the outside of the stem)* **Where do new xylem cells form?** *(Toward the center of the stem)* L1 L2

Use Science Skills

Inferring Challenge students to make an inference to explain why secondary growth does not commonly occur in monocots. To get students thinking, ask: **How does the structure of the monocot stem differ from that of the dicot stem?** *(In a monocot stem, the vascular bundles are scattered throughout. In dicots, they are arranged in a ring.)* Review the process of secondary growth in a dicot stem. Then, ask students to infer if that same process could occur in a monocot stem. *(No, there is no definite location for the lateral meristematic tissue to form.)* Discuss whether secondary growth is even necessary in monocots and why. *(Monocots are generally shorter plants and do not require the extra support of a wider stem.)* L2

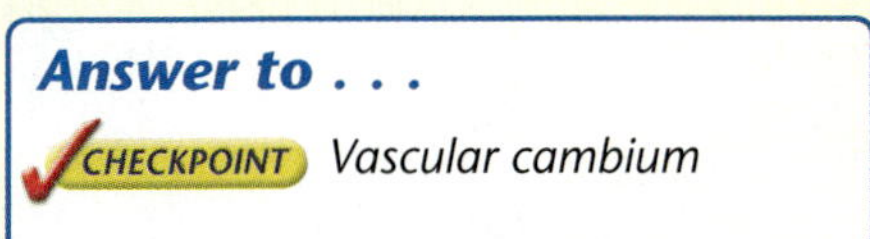

Answer to . . .

CHECKPOINT *Vascular cambium*

Analyzing Data

Thick growth rings indicate that the growing season had adequate moisture. Narrow growth rings form during dry years. L2

Answers

1. About 25 years old
2. Rainfall and temperature
3. The tree laid down more new wood on the side away from the fire than on the side of the fire.
4. Area D is heartwood. Area E is sapwood. Heartwood consists of older xylem that no longer conducts water. Sapwood contains active xylem that transports water and minerals.
5. Diagrams should show a cross section of the tree trunk with the youngest xylem cells next to the vascular cambium toward the center of the stem. The youngest phloem cells are next to the vascular cambium toward the outside of the stem. These tissues are produced by the vascular cambium. See Figure 23–15 for reference.

Analyzing Data

Reading a Tree's History

The field of dendrochronology (*dendron* means "tree"; *chronos* means "time") analyzes tree rings to determine information about a tree and the environment in which it grew. A tree's age, for example, can be measured by counting its growth rings—each produced by a year of growth. The specific environmental conditions can be inferred for each year of its growth by examining the relative width and color of each ring. Use the photograph below to answer each question.

1. **Interpreting Graphics** Approximately how old was this tree when it was cut down?
2. **Inferring** Areas A and B were both produced by four years of growth, yet they are different widths. What climatic conditions might account for this difference?
3. **Interpreting Graphics** The area at C is blackened from a fire that apparently affected only one side of the tree. Describe how the tree grew after this fire.
4. **Comparing and Contrasting** Areas D and E are two types of wood. Give their names, and explain how they differ.
5. **Applying Concepts** On a separate sheet of paper, draw a simple sketch of the tree, indicating where the xylem and phloem are located. Where are the youngest xylem cells located? The youngest phloem cells? What tissue produces both of these cells?

Formation of Wood Most of what we call "wood" is actually layers of xylem. These cells build up year after year, layer on layer. As woody stems grow thicker, the older xylem near the center of the stem no longer conducts water and instead becomes what is known as **heartwood.** Heartwood usually darkens with age because it accumulates impurities that cannot be removed. Heartwood is surrounded by **sapwood,** which is active in fluid transport and therefore usually lighter in color. Both heartwood and sapwood are shown in **Figure 23–15.**

In most of the temperate zone, tree growth is seasonal. When growth begins in the spring, the vascular cambium begins to grow rapidly, producing large, light-colored xylem cells with thin cell walls. The result is a light-colored layer of wood called early wood. As the growing season continues, the cells become smaller and have thicker cell walls, forming a layer of dark wood. This darker wood is called late wood.

This alternation of dark and light wood produces what we commonly call tree rings. Each ring is composed of a band of light wood and a band of dark wood. Thus, a ring corresponds to a year of growth. By counting the rings in a cross section of a tree, you can estimate its age. The size of the rings may even provide information about weather conditions, such as wet or dry years. Thick rings indicate that weather conditions were favorable for tree growth, whereas thin rings indicate less favorable conditions.

FACTS AND FIGURES

Dating archaeological sites with annual rings Some tropical trees produce a uniform wood without annual rings because the cambium makes xylem throughout the year. But most wood shows seasonal variations. For instance, the trees of the American Southwest grow for only a few months a year, when water is available, and thus show distinct rings. In that region, archaeologists have studied the rings of ancient wooden beams found in Native American pueblos. Through careful correlation, they have established an accurate chronology for the region going back to 59 BC. That is, they can now date a specific site by matching the rings of beams at that site with those of beams at other sites. In Europe, similar efforts have been made throughout the continent, using old trees and beams in German cathedrals and Roman ruins.

Formation of Bark On most trees, **bark** includes all of the tissues outside the vascular cambium, as shown in **Figure 23–15.** These tissues include phloem, the cork cambium, and cork. How does bark form? Picture a tree as new xylem is being laid down. It is expanding in width, or girth. Recall that the phloem tissue lies to the outside of this xylem. Phloem must grow to accommodate the larger size of the tree. As the vascular cambium increases in diameter, it forces the phloem tissue outward. This expansion causes the oldest tissues to split and fragment as they are stretched by the expanding stem. Were this expansion left unchecked, the outer covering of the stem might eventually split and break.

Another layer of growing tissue, the cork cambium, solves this potential problem. The cork cambium surrounds the cortex and produces a thick protective layer of cork. Cork consists of cells that have thick walls and usually contain fats, oils, or waxes. These waterproof substances help prevent the loss of water from the stem. The outermost cork cells are usually dead. As the stem increases in size, this dead bark often cracks and flakes off in strips or patches.

CHECKPOINT *What is heartwood?*

▼ **Figure 23–15** In a mature tree that has undergone several years of secondary growth, the vascular cambium lies between layers of xylem to the inside and layers of phloem to the outside. The youngest xylem, called sapwood, transports water and minerals. **Classifying** *Which layer contains meristematic cells?*

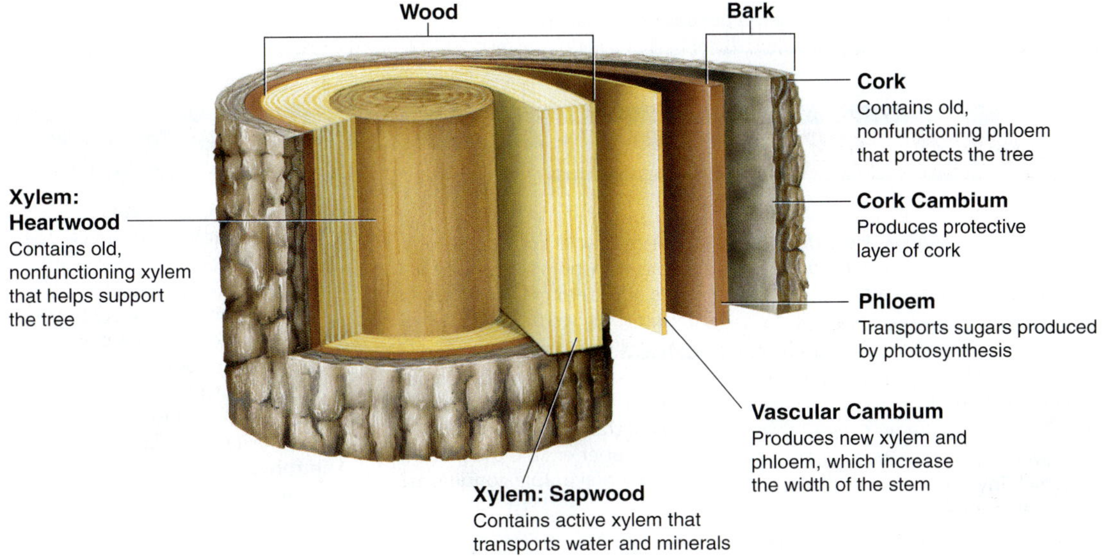

Using Science Skills

Formulating Hypotheses Explain to students that when European settlers were struggling to clear heavily wooded land in North America for farming, they often "girdled" large trees by removing a strip of bark all the way around the base of the tree. Ask students to form a hypothesis to explain why the practice of girdling would cause the tree to die. *(Girdling removes the phloem from the entire circumference of the tree, preventing the tree from transporting sugars to the roots. Without sugar, active transport cannot occur and the roots will not take up nutrients and water.)* L2 L3

Demonstration

Display samples of bark from several species of trees. Explain that because the appearance of bark differs among species of trees, bark appearance is used to identify trees. Encourage students to examine the bark. Ask: **What types of cells make up the bark?** *(Secondary phloem, cork, and cork cambium)* **Why does bark split?** *(As the stem increases in size, the dead bark often cracks and flakes off in strips or patches.)* Discuss reasons why different species exhibit different patterns of bark. L2

Answers to . . .

CHECKPOINT *Older xylem near the center of a woody stem that no longer conducts water*

Figure 23–15 *Vascular cambium*

23–3 (continued)

Use Visuals

Figure 23–16 Have students identify how each stem is adapted for storage and dormancy. Discuss how each of these stems helps the plant survive during periods of poor growing conditions. Ask: **When do plants use the food that was stored in the stems?** *(When the plant begins to grow after dormancy, until its new growth can make enough food)* L2

3 ASSESS

Evaluate Understanding

Have students write three review questions for the section. Invite students to take turns asking one question of the class. Continue until everyone has had a turn or until all unique questions have been answered.

Reteach

Have students use Figure 23–14 and Figure 23–15 to describe the structure of a mature stem and how secondary growth occurs in stems. Students can describe this process to you or to another student.

Writing in Science

Travelogues should trace the path of water and nutrients into a plant's roots from the soil and up into the stem. Travelogues should include a description of the plant's root structures, type of root system, and the process of absorbing materials from the soil and transporting them up through the plant's stem. You might consider having students continue their travelogues to include leaf structure and transpiration in the next section.

Interactive Textbook

If your class subscribes to the iText, use it to review the Key Concepts in Section 23–3.

FIGURE 23–16 STEMS ADAPTED FOR STORAGE AND DORMANCY

Many kinds of plants have modified stems that store food. Tubers, rhizomes, bulbs, and corms can remain dormant during cold or dry periods until favorable conditions for growth return.

Tuber
A tuber is a stem, usually growing underground, that stores food. In potato plants grown from cuttings (shown here), the tubers form at the end of underground stems. In potato plants grown from seed, tubers form at the tips of stems that grow along the ground surface.

Potato

Amaryllis

Bulb
A bulb is made up of a central stem surrounded by short, thick leaves. As in the amaryllis bulb shown here, the leaves wrap around and protect the stem and also store food. A bulb may remain dormant for a long time, yet still grow into a plant.

Corm
A corm looks similar to a bulb, but is a thickened stem that stores food. A corm has an outer covering that consists of layers of thin leaves. Plants such as the gladiolus (shown here) and the crocus form corms.

Gladiolus

Ginger

Rhizome
The stem of a ginger is a rhizome, which is a horizontal, underground stem. As shown in the ginger, new shoots can form from a rhizome, allowing plants to undergo periods of dormancy.

23–3 Section Assessment

1. **Key Concept** How do the functions of a stem relate to the roots and leaves of a plant?
2. **Key Concept** Describe how the arrangement of vascular bundles differs between monocot and dicot stems.
3. **Key Concept** Define primary and secondary growth. Which involves divisions of the apical meristem?
4. How do heartwood and sapwood differ?
5. Analyze how a stem is part of a plant's transport system. Which parts of a stem may be thought of as a subsystem?
6. **Critical Thinking Applying Concepts** Evaluate the significance of the structural adaptations of the white potato. How does a tuber enable the plant to survive unfavorable conditions?

Writing in Science

Descriptive Writing
Pretend that you are small enough to enter a plant through its root system. Describe what you would see as you traveled into a plant and through one of its stems. Include illustrations to enhance your description. *Hint:* Review the illustrations in this chapter for ideas.

23–3 Section Assessment

1. Stems transport substances between roots and leaves.
2. Monocots: scattered throughout stem; dicots: arranged in a cylinder
3. Primary growth occurs only at the ends of plants. Secondary growth is a pattern in which stems increase in width. Primary growth involves the apical meristem.
4. Heartwood contains old, nonfunctioning xylem. Sapwood contains active xylem.
5. The stem conducts water and nutrients; xylem and phloem form a subsystem.
6. The plant uses the food stored in the tuber for survival until favorable conditions return and the plant can make food again.

23–4 Leaves

BI 1.f. Students know usable energy is captured from sunlight by chloroplasts and is stored through the synthesis of sugar from carbon dioxide.

The leaves of a plant are its main organs of photosynthesis. In a sense, plant leaves are the world's most important manufacturers of food. Sugars, starches, and oils manufactured by plants in their leaves are sources of food for virtually all land animals.

Recall from Chapter 8 that photosynthesis uses carbon dioxide and water to produce sugars and oxygen. Leaves, therefore, must have a way of obtaining the materials needed for photosynthesis as well as distributing its end products. Much of the internal structure of leaves can be understood in terms of their functions in carrying out photosynthesis.

CA a

Guide for Reading

Key Concepts
- How does the structure of a leaf enable it to carry out photosynthesis?
- How does gas exchange take place in a leaf?

Vocabulary
blade
petiole
mesophyll
palisade mesophyll
spongy mesophyll
stoma
guard cell
transpiration

Reading Strategy: Monitoring Your Understanding Make a table with three columns, labeled K, W, and L. Before you read, write what you already know about leaves in the first column (K). Under the next heading, write down what you want to learn about leaves (W). After you read, write down what you learned about leaves in the last column (L).

Leaf Structure

a BI 1.f

The structure of a leaf is optimized for absorbing light and carrying out photosynthesis. As you can see in **Figure 23–17,** leaves may differ greatly in shape, yet share certain structural features. To collect sunlight, most leaves have thin, flattened sections called **blades.** The blade is attached to the stem by a thin stalk called a **petiole.** Like roots and stems, leaves have an outer covering of dermal tissue and inner regions of ground and vascular tissues. As shown in **Figure 23–18** on page 596, leaves are covered on the top and bottom by epidermis made of a layer of tough, irregularly shaped cells. The epidermis of many leaves is also covered by the cuticle. Together, the cuticle and epidermal cells form a waterproof barrier that protects tissues and limits the loss of water through evaporation.

The vascular tissues of leaves are connected directly to the vascular tissues of stems, making them part of the plant's transport system. In leaves, xylem and phloem tissues are gathered together into bundles that run from the stem into the petiole. Once they are in the leaf blade, the vascular bundles are surrounded by parenchyma and sclerenchyma cells.

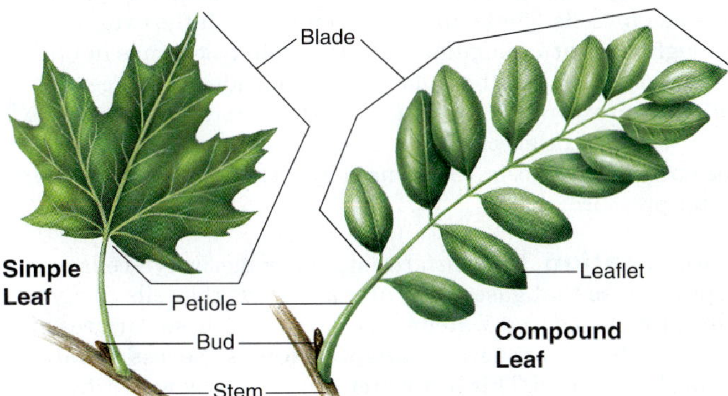

Figure 23–17 Most of a leaf consists of a blade attached to the stem by a petiole. The blade of a simple leaf (left) can be different shapes. In a compound leaf (right), the blade is divided into many separate leaflets.

SECTION RESOURCES

Print:
- ***Teaching Resources,*** Lesson Plan 23–4, Adapted Section Summary 23–4, Adapted Worksheets 23–4, Section Summary 23–4, Worksheets 23–4, Section Review 23–4, Enrichment
- ***Reading and Study Workbook A,*** Section 23–4
- ***Adapted Reading and Study Workbook B,*** Section 23–4

Technology:
- ***iText,*** Section 23–4
- ***Transparencies Plus,*** Section 23–4

Section 23–4

BI 1.f

1 FOCUS

Objectives

23.4.1 ***Describe*** how the structure of a leaf enables it to carry out photosynthesis.

23.4.2 ***Describe*** how gas exchange takes place in a leaf.

Guide for Reading

Vocabulary Preview

Explain that the prefix *meso-* means "middle," and the suffix *-phyll* means "leaf." Challenge students to infer what mesophyll is. *(Tissue that makes up the middle of a leaf)* Then, explain that a palisade is a tall wooden fence. Have students infer how palisade mesophyll might differ from spongy mesophyll. *(Palisade mesophyll has tall, column-shaped cells. Spongy mesophyll is loose, with many air spaces between cells.)*

Reading Strategy

As students read the section, encourage them to sketch diagrams of leaf structures in their table. Also encourage students to write the Vocabulary terms and their definitions in the table.

2 INSTRUCT

Leaf Structure

Build Science Skills

Observing Provide leaves from several species of plants for students to observe. Choose leaves that represent a wide range of shapes and sizes. Encourage students to examine the leaves under a dissecting microscope and draw labeled diagrams of their observations. Also have students use a light microscope to examine leaf cross sections, either those that they prepare themselves or prepared slides. L2

23–4 (continued)

Leaf Functions

Use Visuals

Figure 23–18 Review the structure of a leaf as diagrammed in the figure. If students diagrammed leaf structure from their observations of leaves, encourage them to compare their diagrams to the diagram in the figure. Discuss the function of each leaf part labeled in the diagram. For each part, have students describe how it works to help the leaf produce carbohydrates in the process of photosynthesis. L1 L2

Make Connections

Chemistry Review the process of photosynthesis. Write the equation for photosynthesis on the board: carbon dioxide + water (light) → sugar + oxygen. Discuss specific structures in the leaves that enable a plant to get the molecules it requires for photosynthesis. *(Xylem brings water to the mesophyll cells. Stomata enable carbon dioxide to diffuse into the leaf. The palisade mesophyll absorbs most of the light that enters the leaf.)* Then, discuss the importance of water to photosynthesis. Point out that carbon dioxide alone cannot enter the cell. It must be dissolved in water. When water moves through the cell membrane in the process of diffusion, it carries the dissolved carbon dioxide with it. L2 L3

Word Origins

Chlorophyll means "green leaf." L2

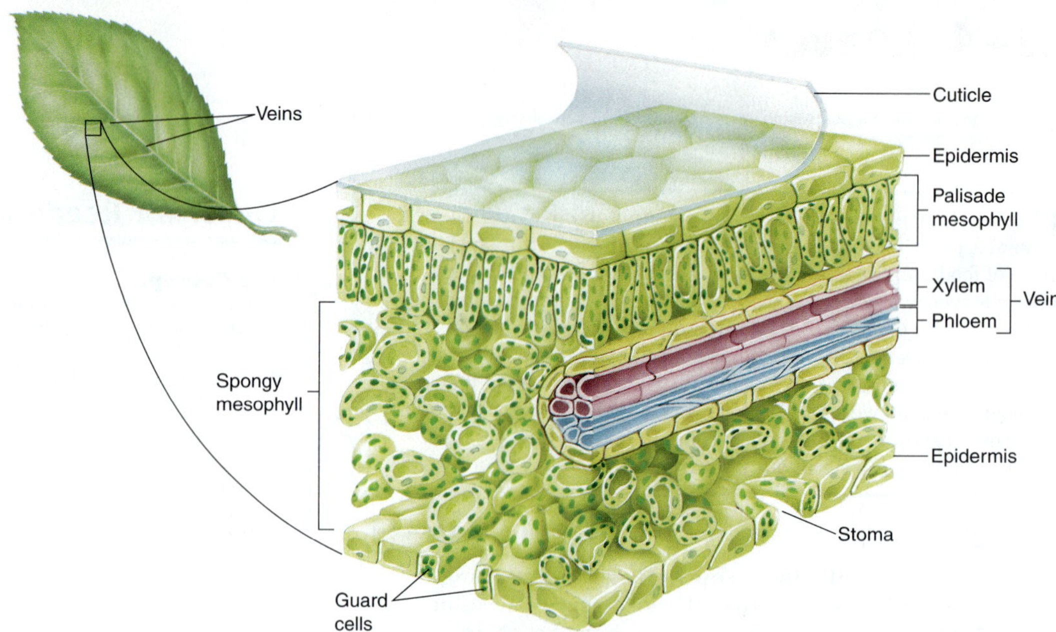

▲ **Figure 23–18** **Leaves absorb light and carry out most of the photosynthesis in a plant.** Some of the most important manufacturing sites on Earth are found in the leaves of plants. The cells in plant leaves are able to use light energy to make carbohydrates. **Comparing and Contrasting** *Compare the structure of the different kinds of cells in a leaf.*

Word Origins

Mesophyll comes from two Greek words: *meso,* meaning "middle," and *phyllon,* meaning "leaf." **If the Greek word *chloro* means "green," what does the term *chlorophyll* mean?**

Leaf Functions

A leaf can be considered a system specialized for photosynthesis. Subsystems of the leaf include tissues that bring gases, water, and nutrients to the cells that carry out photosynthesis.

Photosynthesis The bulk of most leaves consists of a specialized ground tissue known as **mesophyll,** shown in **Figure 23–18.** Photosynthesis in most plants occurs in the mesophyll. The carbohydrates produced move into phloem vessels of the transport system, which carry them to the rest of the plant.

A leaf has specialized cells that enable it to carry out photosynthesis. Under the epidermis is a layer of mesophyll cells called the **palisade mesophyll.** These closely packed cells absorb light that enters the leaf. Beneath the palisade layer is the **spongy mesophyll,** a loose tissue with many air spaces between its cells. These air spaces connect with the exterior through **stomata** (singular: stoma), porelike openings in the underside of the leaf that allow carbon dioxide and oxygen to diffuse into and out of the leaf. Each stoma consists of two **guard cells,** the specialized cells in the epidermis that control the opening and closing of stomata by responding to changes in water pressure.

Transpiration The surfaces of spongy mesophyll cells are kept moist so that gases can enter and leave the cells easily. This also means that water evaporates from these surfaces and is lost to the atmosphere. **Transpiration** is the loss of water through its leaves. This lost water is replaced by water drawn into the leaf through xylem vessels in the vascular tissue.

UNIVERSAL ACCESS

Inclusion/Special Needs
Give students a worksheet on which you have copied Figure 23–18 and drawn the outline for a two-column chart. Students should list in the chart all parts of the leaf that are labeled in Figure 23–18. You might wish to review with students the pronunciations of the words, especially Vocabulary words. Then, students should write the function of each leaf part. Provide help as needed. L1

Less Proficient Readers
Have students create a comic strip in which they show how photosynthesis occurs in the plant. They should describe how the raw materials required for photosynthesis get into the leaf and its cells and how the products move from the leaf cells to the rest of the plant. Help students plan their comic strip to mirror the step-by-step process of photosynthesis as it relates to leaf structure. L1 L2

Gas Exchange Leaves take in carbon dioxide and give off oxygen during photosynthesis. When plant cells use the food they make, the cells respire, taking in oxygen and giving off carbon dioxide (just as animals do). Plant leaves allow gas exchange between air spaces in the spongy mesophyll and the exterior by opening their stomata.

It might seem that stomata should be open all the time, allowing gas exchange to take place and photosynthesis to occur at top speed. However, this is not what happens! If stomata were kept open all the time, water loss due to transpiration would be so great that few plants would be able to take in enough water to survive. So, plants maintain a kind of balance. **Plants keep their stomata open just enough to allow photosynthesis to take place but not so much that they lose an excessive amount of water.**

Guard cells are epidermal cells found on the undersides of leaves. They are structurally specialized to control stomata and thus regulate the movement of gases, especially water vapor, into and out of leaf tissues. The stomata open and close in response to changes in water pressure within the guard cells, as shown in **Figure 23–19.** When water pressure within the guard cells is high, the thin outer walls of the cells are forced into a curved shape. This pulls the thick inner walls of the guard cells away from one another, opening the stoma. When water pressure within the guard cells decreases, the inner walls pull together and the stoma closes. Guard cells respond to conditions in the environment, such as wind and temperature, helping to maintain homeostasis within a leaf. Notice how the structure of guard cells, which is quite different from the structure of other epidermal cells, helps them to carry out this task.

In general, stomata are open during the daytime, when photosynthesis is active, and closed at night, when open stomata would only lead to water loss. However, stomata may be closed even in bright sunlight under hot, dry conditions in which water conservation is a matter of life and death.

CHECKPOINT *What factor regulates the opening and closing of stomata?*

Figure 23–19 Plants regulate the opening and closing of their stomata to balance water loss with rates of photosynthesis. A stoma opens or closes in response to the changes in pressure within the guard cells that surround the opening. When the guard cells are swollen with water (left), the stoma is open. When the guard cells lose water (right), the opening closes, limiting further water loss from the leaf.

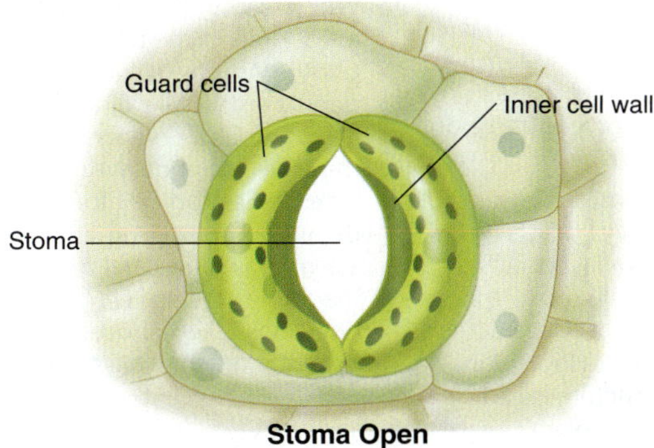

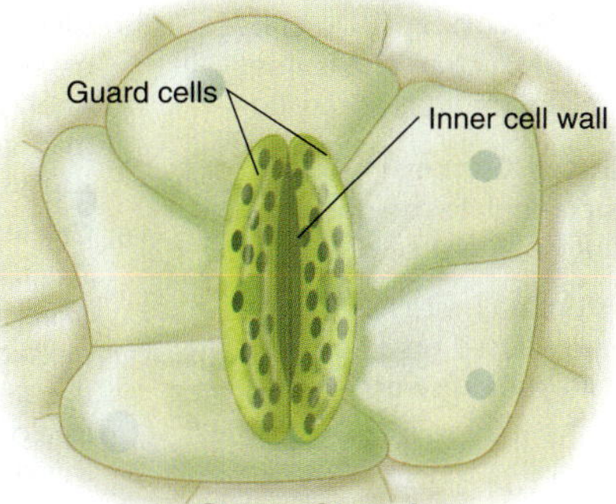

Build Science Skills

Using Models Give student pairs two elongated balloons and challenge them to use the balloons to model the action of stomata. Point out to the class how stomata are a plant adaptation that helps to protect plants in their environment. Have students draw diagrams showing how their balloon model is similar to the action of guard cells. They should describe the conditions under which the stomata are open and when they are closed. L2

Address Misconceptions

Some students might think that plants have no use for oxygen, because they focus only on the process of photosynthesis as a way for plants to manufacture carbohydrates. Make sure students realize that plants also use the carbohydrates they manufacture for growth, repair, and the active transport required to take up nutrients and water through roots. Identify for students the locations of plant cells that require oxygen and what the oxygen is used for. If needed, review the process of cellular respiration and plant cell structure. L1 L2

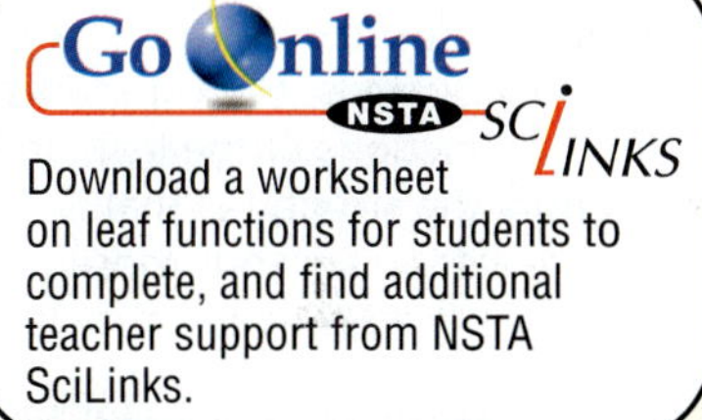

TEACHER TO TEACHER

I like to provide as many opportunities as possible for students to observe actual plant structures. In a simple strategy to examine stomata, I have students coat the underside of a leaf with clear fingernail polish. After the polish has dried, I instruct students to carefully peel it off and place it on a slide. I have them add a coverslip and examine it under a microscope.

To observe transpiration, I have students fill plastic tubing with colored water and place a bean stem with leaves into the tubing. The stem must fit tightly. I then have the students tape the apparatus to a white board and mark the water level. The students measure the change in water level due to transpiration by measuring every 10 minutes.

—John E. Gonzales
Biology Teacher
Temescal Canyon High School
Lake Elsinore, CA

Answer to . . .

CHECKPOINT *Changes in water pressure within guard cells*

23–4 (continued)

Use Visuals

Figure 23–20 Have students compare and contrast the leaf adaptations of the rock plant, cactus, and pine. Discuss how these plants are adapted to living in dry conditions. Ask: **How is the pine leaf adapted to reduce water loss?** *(Waxy epidermis and stomata sunken below surface of the leaf both act to keep water in the leaf.)* **How are the adaptations of the cactus leaf similar to those of the pine leaf?** *(Cactus leaves are very different from pine leaves; cactus leaves do not carry out photosynthesis. However, both are structured to reduce water loss.)* L2

3 ASSESS

Evaluate Understanding

Have students write a paragraph in which they describe how a leaf functions to produce energy for a plant. Students can include diagrams to help describe the process if they wish. Stipulate that students use all Vocabulary terms in their paragraphs.

Reteach

Have students construct a concept map that relates the structure of a leaf with its functions. Help students identify the functions of the leaf, and then identify the structures that enable the leaf to carry out those functions.

Focus on the BIG Idea

Photosynthesis takes place in the chloroplasts contained in a leaf's mesophyll cells. The light-dependent reactions occur in the thylakoid membranes. The light-independent reactions (or Calvin cycle) take place in the stroma. The leaf obtains water for photosynthesis through the xylem and carbon dioxide through the stomata in the leaf's lower surface.

If your class subscribes to the iText, use it to review the Key Concepts in Section 23–4.

FIGURE 23–20 ADAPTATIONS OF LEAVES

The plants shown here grow in different biomes. The leaves of these plants show variations and adaptations to the dry or low-nutrient conditions in which they live.

Pitcher plant
The leaf of a pitcher plant is modified to attract and then digest insects and other small prey. Such plants typically live in nutrient-poor soils and rely on insects as their source of nitrogen.

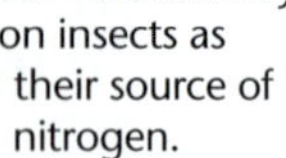

Cactus
Cactus leaves are actually nonphotosynthetic thorns that protect against herbivores. Most of the plant's photosynthesis is carried out in its stem.

Pine
The narrow leaves of a pine tree contain a waxy epidermis as well as stomata that are sunken below the surface of the leaf. This arrangement reduces water loss from the leaf.

Rock plant
The leaves of a rock plant are adapted for hot, dry conditions. They are round, with few stomata, and often have clear tissue that allows light to penetrate into the leaf.

23–4 Section Assessment

1. **Key Concept** Describe how the structure of a leaf is optimized for light absorption.
2. **Key Concept** What factors regulate the opening and closing of guard cells?
3. Are stomata more likely to be open or closed on a hot day? Explain your answer.
4. Describe the cell types found within a typical leaf.
5. Identify the parts of a leaf that make up its transport system. Analyze how some of these parts may be thought of as a transport subsystem.
6. **Critical Thinking Inferring** The leaves of desert plants often have two or more layers of palisade mesophyll, rather than the single layer that is characteristic of most leaves. How might this modified structure be advantageous to a desert plant?

Focus on the BIG Idea

Structure and Function
Where within the structure of a leaf does each stage of photosynthesis occur? How does the structure of a leaf allow it to obtain energy and materials for photosynthesis? Refer to Section 8–3 for details on photosynthesis. Then, draw and label a diagram that answers the questions asked above.

23–4 Section Assessment

1. Most leaves have thin, flattened sections, called blades, to collect sunlight.
2. Rate of photosynthesis and changes in water pressure within the guard cells
3. Closed; to prevent the loss of too much water from the plant
4. Leaves are covered on the top and bottom with tough, irregularly shaped epidermal cells. Xylem and phloem tissues are gathered together in bundles that are surrounded by parenchyma and sclerenchyma cells.
5. Veins and petiole; they contain vascular bundles composed of xylem and phloem that carry water and nutrients.
6. To help reduce the loss of water from the plant

23–5 Transport in Plants

The pressure created by water entering the tissues of a root can push water upward in a plant stem. This creates more than enough pressure to force water into the vascular system and out of the root. However, root pressure does not exert enough pressure to lift water up into trees, such as the topmost needles of a redwood tree 90 meters above the ground. To draw water to such great heights, plants take advantage of some of water's most interesting physical properties.

Guide for Reading

Key Concepts
- How is water transported throughout a plant?
- How are the products of photosynthesis transported throughout a plant?

Vocabulary
adhesion
capillary action
pressure-flow hypothesis

Reading Strategy: Making Comparisons This section describes how xylem and phloem function in transport. As you read, write down statements about similarities and differences between the functions of these two tissues.

Water Transport

Recall that xylem tissue forms a continuous set of tubes that stretch from roots through stems and out into the spongy mesophyll of leaves. This set of tubes forms a complex transport system within a plant. The transport is carried out by a subsystem of cells and tissues. Active transport and root pressure cause water to move from soil into plant roots. Root pressure alone, however, cannot account for the movement of water and dissolved materials throughout an entire plant. Obviously, other forces are at work. These include capillary action and transpiration. **The combination of root pressure, capillary action, and transpiration provides enough force to move water through the xylem tissue of even the tallest plant.** As you will learn, transpiration is the most powerful of these forces.

Capillary Action

Water molecules are attracted to one another by a force called cohesion. Recall from Chapter 2 that cohesion is the attraction of molecules of the same substance to each other. Because of cohesion, water molecules have a tendency to form hydrogen bonds with each other. Water molecules can also form hydrogen bonds with other substances.This results from a force called **adhesion,** which is attraction between unlike molecules. Place empty glass tubes of various widths into a dish of water, as shown in **Figure 23–21,** and you will see both forces at work. The tendency of water to rise in a thin tube is called **capillary action.** Water is attracted to the walls of the tube, and water molecules are attracted to one another. The thinner the tube, the higher the water will rise inside it.

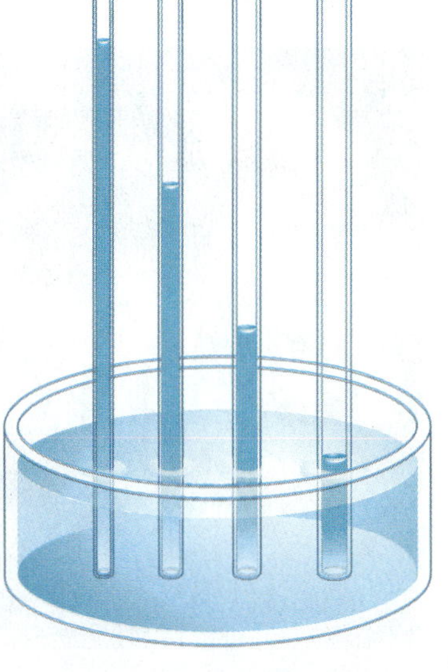

▶ **Figure 23–21** Capillary action—the result of water molecules' ability to stick to one another and to the walls of a tube—contributes to the movement of water up the cells of xylem tissue. As shown here, capillary action causes water to move much higher in a narrow tube than in a wide tube. **Applying Concepts** *Which force—adhesion or cohesion—causes the water to stick to the walls of the glass tube?*

SECTION RESOURCES

TIME SAVER

Print:
- ***Teaching Resources,*** Lesson Plan 23–5, Adapted Section Summary 23–5, Adapted Worksheets 23–5, Section Summary 23–5, Worksheets 23–5, Section Review 23–5
- ***Reading and Study Workbook A,*** Section 23–5
- ***Adapted Reading and Study Workbook B,*** Section 23–5

Technology:
- ***iText,*** Section 23–5
- ***Animated Biological Concepts DVD,*** 32 Water Transport in Plants, 33 Sugar Movement in Plants
- ***Transparencies Plus,*** Section 23–5

Section 23–5

1 FOCUS

Objectives

23.5.1 ***Explain*** how water is transported throughout a plant.
23.5.2 ***Describe*** how the products of photosynthesis are transported throughout a plant.

Guide for Reading

Vocabulary Preview

Have students study Figure 23–21 and read the caption to learn what is meant by capillary action. Then, have them do the same for Figure 23–24 to learn about pressure-flow hypothesis.

Reading Strategy

After students read the section, encourage them to use their notes about the similarities and differences of xylem and phloem to construct a graphic organizer, such as a table or a concept map.

2 INSTRUCT

Water Transport

Demonstration

Demonstrate capillary action by placing empty glass tubes of various sizes in a dish of colored water, as shown in Figure 23–21. As students observe the water moving, ask: **What causes the water to move up the tubes?** *(Water molecules are attracted to the walls of the tube and to one another.)* **Do you expect water to move highest up the thinnest tube or the thickest tube?** *(Thinnest tube)* **Why doesn't gravity pull the water down?** *(It does. However, the forces of adhesion and cohesion are greater and work together to pull the water molecules up inside the tube.)* L2

Answer to . . .

Figure 23–21 *Adhesion*

23–5 (continued)

Build Science Skills

Observing Students can easily observe transpiration by covering a potted plant with a plastic bag. The plant should have been watered normally and placed in a well-lighted area. After a few days, have students describe any changes. *(Moisture accumulated inside the bag.)* Discuss where the water came from. Make sure students understand that as each molecule of water evaporates, it pulls up the next molecule of water to take its place. L1 L2

Use Visuals

Figure 23–22 Use the figure to discuss the three forces that work to move water through a plant: root pressure, capillary action, and transpiration. Ask: **What is the importance of transpiration pull?** *(Without transpiration pull, water would never reach the tops of trees and other large plants, because the combination of root pressure and capillary action does not provide enough force to lift water high enough.)* **Where is capillary action working to move water?** *(Within the tracheids and vessel elements of xylem)* L1 L2

▶ **Figure 23–22 Root pressure, capillary action, and transpiration contribute to the movement of water within a plant.** Transpiration is the movement of water molecules out of leaves. The faster water evaporates from a plant, shown in A, the stronger the pull of water upward from the roots, shown in B.

▼ **Figure 23–23** In hot, dry conditions, transpiration can lead to water loss that is severe enough to cause wilting. High transpiration rates can cause a loss of osmotic pressure in a plant's cells. In leaves, this loss of pressure causes guard cells to close, thereby slowing down the rate of transpiration. **Inferring** *Why do hot, dry conditions cause transpiration rates to increase?*

What does capillary action have to do with water movement through xylem? Recall that there are two main types of xylem tissue in flowering plants: tracheids and vessel elements. Both tracheids and vessel elements form hollow connected tubes similar to a thin, glass capillary tube. Capillary action in the tubelike structures formed by both types of cells causes water to rise well above the level of the ground.

Transpiration For trees and other tall plants, the combination of root pressure and capillary action does not provide enough force to lift water to the topmost branches and leaves. The major force in water transport is provided by the evaporation of water from leaves during transpiration. When water is lost through transpiration, osmotic pressure moves water out of the vascular tissue of the leaf, as shown in **Figure 23–22.** Then, like a locomotive pulling a train with hundreds of cars, the movement of water out of the leaf "pulls" water upward through the vascular system all the way from the roots. This process is known as transpirational pull.

How important is transpirational pull? On a hot day, even a small tree may lose as much as 100 liters of water to transpiration. The hotter and drier the air, and the windier the day, the greater the amount of water lost. As a result of this water loss, the plant draws up even more water from the roots.

Controlling Transpiration The leaf's gas exchange subsystem helps to maintain homeostasis by keeping the water content of the leaf relatively constant. For example, when water is abundant, it flows into the leaf, raising water pressure in the guard cells, which then open the stomata. Excess water is then lost through the open stomata by transpiration. When water is scarce, the opposite occurs. Water pressure in the leaf falls, and the guard cells respond by closing the stomata. This reduces further water loss by limiting transpiration.

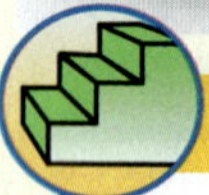

UNIVERSAL ACCESS

Inclusion/Special Needs
Have students describe how water moves through xylem, from the roots to the leaves. Encourage students to talk through the process in a "play-by-play" manner, like a sportscaster. A student could focus on one method—capillary action, transpiration, or root pressure—at a time. L1

English Language Learners
Students can diagram the movement of nutrients through phloem tissue in a fruit tree. Students should show seasonal movements, as well as the movement of sugars to the developing fruit. Students should label their diagrams and define all terms. L1 L2

Advanced Learners
Challenge students to learn about antidesiccant products, such as Wilt-Pruf®, used in horticulture. They should find out what these products are used for and how they work. Students can present their findings to the class with diagrams and plant specimens. L3

Quick Lab

What is the role of leaves in transpiration?

Materials 3 stalks of celery with leaves, plastic container, food coloring, petroleum jelly, cotton swab, scalpel, metric ruler

Procedure 

1. Cut 1 cm off the bottoms of the celery stalks. **CAUTION:** *Use the scalpel with care.*
2. Remove the leaves from one stalk. Use a cotton swab to apply petroleum jelly to both sides of all the leaves on another stalk. Place all three stalks into a plastic container containing about 200 mL of water and food coloring.
3. Place the plastic container in a sunny location. Observe the celery at the end of the class and the next day. Record your observations each day.

Analyze and Conclude

1. **Observing** In which stalk did the colored water rise the most? The least?
2. **Inferring** What effect did the petroleum jelly have on transpiration? What part of the leaf did the petroleum jelly affect?
3. **Drawing Conclusions** How are leaves involved in transpiration?

Transpiration and Wilting Osmotic pressure keeps a plant's leaves and stems rigid, or stiff. High transpiration rates can lead to wilting, shown in **Figure 23–23.** Wilting results from the loss of water—and therefore of the pressure in a plant's cells. Without this internal pressure to support them, the plant's cell walls bend inward, and the plant's leaves and stems wilt. When a leaf wilts, its stomata close. As a result, transpiration slows down significantly. Thus, wilting helps a plant to conserve water.

What happens when a plant wilts?

Nutrient Transport

You have learned how transpiration *pulls* water upward through a plant. But most plant nutrients, including sugars, minerals, and complex organic compounds, are *pushed* through phloem.

Functions of Phloem Many plants pump sugars into their fruits. This action often requires moving sugars out of leaves or roots into stems, and then through stems to the fruits. All of this movement takes place in the phloem. In cold climates, many plants pump food down into their roots for winter storage. This stored food must be moved back into the trunk and branches of the plant before growth begins again in the spring. Phloem carries out this seasonal movement of sugars within a plant.

FACTS AND FIGURES

The nutrient highway

The exact mechanism by which phloem transport occurs is not fully known. It is difficult to investigate, because phloem is extremely delicate. One technique for the study of phloem is the use of aphids. An aphid's mouthpart forms a long tube that it can insert into a plant so that the end of the tube enters a single sieve element. The contents of the element are under pressure. The fluid in the phloem goes into the mouthpart tube and through the aphid's gut with such force that the feeding aphids often have a drop of "honeydew" on their posterior ends. The fluid that comes from the phloem can be collected and analyzed. By using several aphids on different parts of the plant, a scientist can introduce substances into the phloem at certain points and study their speed and direction of flow.

Quick Lab

Objective Students will be able to observe the role of leaves in transpiration. L2

Skills Focus Inferring, Drawing Conclusions, Observing

Materials 3 stalks of celery with leaves, plastic container, food coloring, petroleum jelly, cotton swab, scalpel, metric ruler

Time Day 1: 20 minutes; Day 2: 10 minutes

Advance Prep Purchase celery, and separate the individual stalks. You can substitute one leafless stalk for one of the three leafy stalks listed in the materials.

Strategies

- Discuss the purpose of each celery stalk. Ask: **Which celery stalk is the control?** *(The leafy stalk without petroleum jelly)*
- Have students place the celery stalks on a paper towel or a cutting board to help keep the stalks from slipping.
- Students should cut the stalks to the same length.

Expected Outcomes The water will rise the most in the leafy stalk without petroleum jelly. It will rise the least in the stalk without leaves.

Analyze and Conclude

1. Leafy stalk not coated with petroleum jelly; stalk without leaves
2. The petroleum jelly reduces transpiration by plugging up the stomata.
3. Transpiration occurs through leaf stomata.

Nutrient Transport

Build Science Skills

Forming Operational Definitions Have student groups work together to define the "source" and the "sink" in the process of phloem transport. Definitions should be composed in the students' own words. If they wish, they may use diagrams in their definitions. L1 L2

Answers to . . .

CHECKPOINT *When water is lost from the plant's cells, the cell walls bend inward and the plant wilts.*

Figure 23–23 *More water evaporates into the air during hot, dry conditions.*

23–5 (continued)

Using Visuals

Figure 23–24 Use the diagram in the figure to make sure students understand the pressure-flow hypothesis. Ask: **Where is the pressure in the phloem the highest?** *(At the source, where nutrients enter and water follows, as it moves from areas of high concentration to low concentration)* **How does low pressure at the sink help move nutrients through the phloem?** *(Low pressure pulls the nutrients toward it, much like a straw or vacuum cleaner.)* L2

3 ASSESS

Evaluate Understanding

Randomly ask students to describe how capillary action and transpiration work to move water through xylem tissue. Base your questions on the diagrams in Figures 23–21 and 23–22. Do the same for Figure 23–24 and the pressure-flow hypothesis for the movement of nutrients through phloem tissue.

Reteach

Have students create a concept map to show the ways in which water and nutrients are transported through a plant. Students need to include the Vocabulary terms from the section, as well as the words *xylem* and *phloem*.

Sharpen Your Skills

Experimental designs can be similar to that of the Quick Lab on page 601. However, students should design experiments to test the effects of changes in temperature, humidity, and light on the rate of transpiration.

If your class subscribes to the iText, use it to review the Key Concepts in Section 23–5.

Answer to . . .

Figure 23–24 *Water from the nearby xylem follows the movement of nutrients by osmosis.*

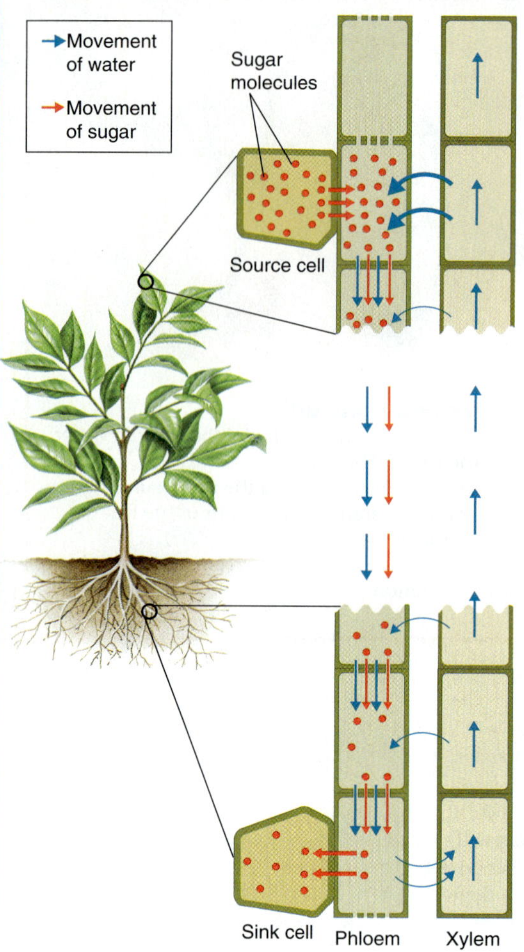

Figure 23–24 The diagram shows the movement of sugars and water throughout the phloem and xylem as explained by the pressure-flow hypothesis. Materials move from a source cell, where photosynthesis produces a high concentration of sugars, to a sink cell, where sugars are lower in concentration. **Interpreting Graphics** *What is the source of the water that forces nutrients through phloem tissue?*

Movement From Source to Sink A process of phloem transport moves sugars through a plant from a source to a sink. The source can be any cell in which sugars are produced by photosynthesis. The sink is a cell where the sugars are used or stored. How does phloem transport take place?

One idea put forward by many plant scientists is called the **pressure-flow hypothesis.** As you can see in **Figure 23–24,** sugars are pumped into the phloem at one point, called the source. For example, sugars produced by photosynthesis may move from a leaf. As concentrations of sugar increase in the phloem, water from the xylem moves in by osmosis. This movement causes an increase in pressure at that point, forcing nutrient-rich fluid to move through the phloem away from nutrient-producing regions and toward a region that uses these nutrients, called the sink.

Conversely, if part of a plant actively absorbs nutrients from the phloem, osmosis causes water to follow. This movement of water decreases pressure and causes a movement of fluid in the phloem toward the sink. **When nutrients are pumped into or removed from the phloem system, the change in concentration causes a movement of fluid in that same direction. As a result, phloem is able to move nutrients in either direction to meet the nutritional needs of the plant.**

23–5 Section Assessment

1. **Key Concept** What three processes work together to cause water to flow upward through a plant?
2. **Key Concept** How does the pressure-flow hypothesis explain the function of phloem?
3. Why is capillary action insufficient to move water through a plant?
4. **Critical Thinking Predicting** If a plant's stomata close on a hot, dry day, how could this affect the plant's rate of photosynthesis?

Sharpen Your Skills

Designing Experiments Devise an experiment to measure the rate of transpiration from a plant cutting. Describe results you would expect with changes in temperature, humidity, and light.

23–5 Section Assessment

1. The three processes are: root pressure, capillary action, and transpiration.
2. The change in concentration of nutrients in the phloem system causes a movement of nutrients in either direction.
3. It does not provide enough force to lift water to the topmost parts of large plants.
4. With their stomata closed, leaves would not be able to take in carbon dioxide, thus slowing the plant's rate of photosynthesis.

Exploration

7IIE 7.c

Identifying the Growth Zones in a Plant

Do roots grow at the tips or do existing root tissues grow longer? In this investigation, you will answer this question by examining root growth.

Problem In which part of a root does most growth occur?

Materials

- 150-mL beaker
- metric ruler
- paper towels
- India ink
- 4 large seeds
- toothpick
- petri dish

Skills Measuring, Analyzing Data

Procedure

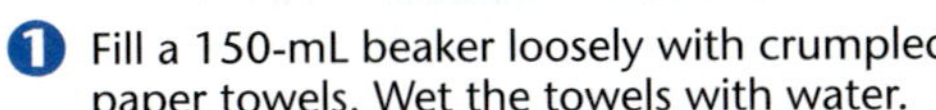

1. Fill a 150-mL beaker loosely with crumpled paper towels. Wet the towels with water.
2. Place 4 seeds between the towels and the sides of the beaker. Cover the beaker with a petri dish. Keep the paper towels damp.
3. On a separate sheet of paper, make a copy of the data table shown.
4. When the roots appear, gently place one seedling on a wet paper towel. Use a ruler to measure the length of the root. Record this length in your copy of the data table. Use another sprout if this one becomes damaged.
5. Pick up a very small drop of India ink on the tip of a toothpick. Use the toothpick to mark the root with small dots of ink 3, 10, 15, and 20 mm from the root tip. **CAUTION:** *India ink stains skin and clothing.*
6. Allow the ink dots to dry. Return the sprout to the beaker and replace the cover. Keep the paper towels in the beaker moist.
7. **Predicting** Record your prediction of which part of the root will grow the most over the next 3 days. Wash your hands before you leave the lab.
8. **Measuring** Measure precisely and record the length of the root and the positions of the dots in your data table each day for 3 days. Wash your hands.

Data Table

Days	Position of Mark (mm from root tip)				Root Length (mm)
	3	10	15	20	
1					
2					
3					

Analyze and Conclude

1. **Observing** Did most of the growth occur at the tip of the root (0–3 mm) or farther up?
2. **Analyzing Data** Which part of the root grew the most?
3. **Drawing Conclusions** Do your data support the idea that roots grow mostly at their tips or that growth farther up the root pushes the root tip through the soil?

Go Further

Designing Experiments Design a similar experiment to determine where most stem growth occurs. With your teacher's permission, perform your experiment.

Go Online PHSchool.com

For: Data sharing
Visit: PHSchool.com
Web Code: cbd-7235

Share Your Data Online Enter your data on the growth of the roots. Then, look at the data entered by other students. Based on the available data, which part of the root grew the most? Which grew the least? Why might your data differ from those of other students?

Analyze and Conclude

1. Most growth occurred at a region a few millimeters above the root cap.
2. In most cases, growth is concentrated in the area that was initially a few millimeters above the root cap.
3. Roots grow in length mainly in a region farther up the root tip.

Go Online PHSchool.com

Students should see most root growth occurring near the tip of the root, but their results will depend on their own data and the data on the site.

Exploration

7IIE 7.c

Objective Students will be able to analyze data to determine in which part of a root the most growth occurs. L2

Skills Focus Measuring, Analyzing Data

Time 35 minutes to set up; 10 minutes every day for 3 days to record measurements

Advance Prep Obtain seeds such as bean, corn, or pea.

Alternative Materials You can use a fine-tipped permanent marker instead of India ink.

Safety Caution students about India-ink stains. Students should wear lab aprons and gloves and wash their hands with soap and warm water before they leave the lab.

Teaching Tips

- Have students use forceps to handle the seeds.
- Instruct students to measure and mark all sprouts in their beakers in case one is damaged. They should have separate data tables for each.
- Water should not puddle at the bottom of the beakers. Have students use water droppers to remoisten the toweling.

Procedure

7. Some will predict that the root tip grows the most. Others might predict the part closest to the seed grows the most.

8. Typically, a root might grow to a length of 43 mm in 3 days, with 19 mm of the 23 mm increase occurring near the root tip.

Expected Outcome Nearly all root growth occurs at the tip of the root (within the region that was initially 3 mm from the tip).

Go Further

Students should set up their experiments in the way described in this laboratory, except they would measure stem length.

Chapter 23 Study Guide

Study Tip

Write each Vocabulary term on a separate card. Divide the class into two teams. Draw a vocabulary card, and have one member from each team draw diagrams or use pantomime to convey the meaning of the term to their team members. The first team to guess the term correctly wins a point. Continue until all the cards have been used.

Thinking Visually

Terms in the flowchart should be listed in the following order: *root epidermis, cortex, endodermis, xylem, spongy mesophyll, stomata.*

Chapter 23 Assessment

Reviewing Content

1. b **2.** a **3.** c **4.** c **5.** c **6.** a **7.** b **8.** c **9.** b **10.** d

Understanding Concepts

11. The two kinds of vascular tissue in plants are xylem and phloem. Xylem consists of tracheids and vessel elements, and phloem consists of sieve tube elements and companion cells.

12. Parenchyma cells function mainly in storage and photosynthesis. Collenchyma cells help support large plants, and sclerenchyma cells make tissue tough and strong.

13. A dicot root has a vascular cylinder at its center, surrounded by a cortex of ground tissue. A dicot stem has ground tissue in the center, surrounded by a ring of vascular tissue.

14. The cell membranes of root hairs contain active transport proteins, which pump mineral ions from the soil into the plant, a process that leads to the movement of water into the plant by osmosis. Root hairs absorb most of the water taken in by plants.

Chapter 23 Study Guide

23–1 Specialized Tissues in Plants

Key Concepts

- Three of the principal organs of seed plants are roots, stems, and leaves.
- Plants consist of three tissue systems: dermal tissue, vascular tissue, and ground tissue.
- Vascular tissue contains several different cell types. Xylem consists of tracheids and vessel elements, and phloem consists of sieve tube elements and companion cells.
- Meristematic tissue is the only plant tissue that produces new cells by mitosis.

Vocabulary

epidermal cell, p. 580 • vessel element, p. 581
sieve tube element, p. 581
companion cell, p. 581 • parenchyma, p. 582
collenchyma, p. 582 • sclerenchyma, p. 582
meristem, p. 582 • meristematic tissue, p. 582
apical meristem, p. 582 • differentiation, p. 583

23–2 Roots

Key Concepts

- The two main types of roots are taproots, found mainly in dicots, and fibrous roots, found mainly in monocots.
- A mature root has an outside layer of epidermal cells and a central cylinder of vascular tissue separated by a large area of ground tissue called the cortex.
- Roots anchor a plant in the ground and absorb water and dissolved nutrients from the soil.

Vocabulary

taproot, p. 584 • fibrous root, p. 584
root hair, p. 585 • cortex, p. 585
endodermis, p. 585 • vascular cylinder, p. 585
root cap, p. 585 • Casparian strip, p. 587

23–3 Stems

Key Concepts

- Stems have three important functions: They produce leaves, branches, and flowers; they hold leaves up in the sunlight; and they transport various substances between roots and leaves.
- In monocots, vascular bundles are scattered throughout the stem. In dicots and most gymnosperms, vascular bundles are arranged in a cylinder.
- In all seed plants, primary growth of stems is produced by cell divisions in the apical meristem.
- In conifers and dicots, secondary growth takes place in lateral meristematic tissues called the vascular cambium and cork cambium.

Vocabulary

node, p. 589 • internode, p. 589
bud, p. 589 • vascular bundle, p. 590
pith, p. 590 • primary growth, p. 590
secondary growth, p. 591
vascular cambium, p. 591 • cork cambium, p. 591
heartwood, p. 592 • sapwood, p. 592 • bark, p. 593

23–4 Leaves

Key Concepts

- The structure of a leaf is optimized for absorbing light and carrying out photosynthesis.
- Plants keep their stomata open just enough to allow photosynthesis to take place but not so much that they lose an excessive amount of water.

Vocabulary

blade, p. 595 • petiole, p. 595
mesophyll, p. 596 • palisade mesophyll, p. 596
spongy mesophyll, p. 596 • stoma, p. 596
guard cell, p. 596 • transpiration, p. 596

23–5 Transport in Plants

Key Concepts

- Root pressure, capillary action, and transpiration work together to move water through the xylem tissue of even the tallest plant.
- When nutrients are pumped into or removed from the phloem system, the change in concentration causes a movement of fluid in that same direction. As a result, phloem is able to move nutrients in either direction to meet the nutritional needs of the plant.

Vocabulary

adhesion, p. 599 • capillary action, p. 599
pressure-flow hypothesis, p. 602

Thinking Visually

Make a flowchart of the tissues through which water passes, from when it enters a plant at the root until it escapes from the plant through the leaves. Use the following terms in your flowchart: *spongy mesophyll, root epidermis, stomata, cortex, endodermis, xylem.*

TIME SAVER — CHAPTER RESOURCES

Print:
- ***Teaching Resources,*** Chapter Vocabulary Review, Graphic Organizer, Chapter 23 Tests: Levels A and B

Technology:
- ***Computer Test Bank,*** Chapter 23 Test
- ***iText,*** Chapter 23 Assessment

Chapter 23 Assessment

Interactive textbook with assessment at PHSchool.com 

Reviewing Content

Choose the letter that best answers the question or completes the statement.

1. The plant structure that is responsible for support of the plant body and for carrying nutrients between different parts of the plant is the
   a. root. c. leaf.
   b. stem. d. flower.
2. Which type of plant tissue would be found ONLY in the circled areas of the plant shown below?
   a. meristematic tissue c. dermal tissue
   b. vascular tissue d. ground tissue

3. Phloem functions primarily in
   a. transport of water.
   b. growth of the root.
   c. transport of products of photosynthesis.
   d. increasing stem diameter.
4. Tracheids and vessel elements make up
   a. phloem. c. xylem.
   b. trichomes. d. meristem.
5. The waterproof strip that surrounds cells of the endodermis is the
   a. vascular cambium. c. Casparian strip.
   b. vascular cylinder. d. cortex.
6. Increases in the thickness of stems over time result from the production of vascular tissue by the
   a. vascular cambium.
   b. cork cambium.
   c. apical meristem.
   d. ground tissue.
7. Within a leaf, there are many air spaces between the cells of the
   a. palisade layer. c. meristem.
   b. spongy mesophyll. d. cuticle.
8. Stomata open and close in response to pressure within
   a. root cells. c. guard cells.
   b. cell walls. d. xylem.
9. The tissue that conducts the products of photosynthesis through a plant's stem is
   a. xylem.
   b. phloem.
   c. mesophyll.
   d. ground tissue.
10. The rise of water in a tall plant depends on root pressure and
    a. osmosis.
    b. evaporation.
    c. capillary action.
    d. transpiration pull.

Understanding Concepts

11. What are the two different kinds of vascular tissue in plants? Briefly describe each kind.
12. Explain the functions of these cells: parenchyma, collenchyma, and sclerenchyma.
13. If your classmate gave you a cross section of a dicot, how would you know whether the section was from a root or a stem?
14. How are root hairs important to plants?
15. What is the function of the vascular cambium in the secondary growth of stems?
16. From what type of plant tissue does bark develop?
17. What are the three main functions of leaves?
18. What is the function of the epidermis and cuticle layers in a leaf? What is the function of the pore-like openings in these layers?
19. What properties of water are important in its movement up a plant?
20. What is the function of guard cells in regulating transpiration and wilting?
21. What are the functions of phloem?
22. What are source cells and sink cells? Explain.

HOMEWORK GUIDE

Section:	Questions:
Section 23–1	1–4, 11, 12
Section 23–2	5, 14, 25
Section 23–3	6, 13, 15, 16, 23, 28, 30
Section 23–4	7, 8, 17, 18, 20, 26, 27, 29
Section 23–5	9, 10, 19, 21, 22, 24, 31, 32

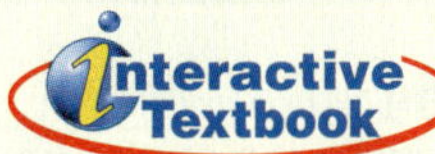

If your class subscribes to the iText, your students can go online to access an interactive version of the Student Edition and a self-test.

(Continued from page 604)

15. In the secondary growth of a stem, the vascular cambium produces vascular tissue and increases the thickness of stems over time.

16. Bark develops from the cork cambium.

17. The three main functions of leaves are photosynthesis, transpiration, and gas exchange.

18. The epidermis and cuticle layers of dermal tissue that form the outer covering of a plant prevent water loss. The function of porelike openings in these layers is to allow gas exchange between the plant and the environment.

19. The properties of water that are important in its movement up a plant are cohesion, or the attraction of water molecules to one another, and adhesion, or the attraction of water molecules to the walls of a tube. As a result of this combination of forces, water is able to rise in tubes by capillary action.

20. When the guard cells are filled with water, the pressure within them increases, and they swell. This causes the stomata to open and transpiration to occur. When the guard cells lose water, the stomata close, preventing water from leaving the leaf. This in turn prevents wilting due to excessive loss of water by the leaf.

21. The function of phloem is to pump food down from the leaves into the stems and roots for storage and back again from the roots to other parts of the plant when the food is needed.

22. Source cells are located where sugars are pumped into the phloem, and sink cells are located where there is a low concentration of sugars. The pressure-flow hypothesis explains how phloem moves sugars and water from source cells to sink cells.

Chapter 23 Assessment

Critical Thinking

23. The person training the miniature tree trims off the apical meristems at the tips of shoots and roots. This keeps the tree short. However, the person does not touch the vascular cambium in the stem, so the stem continues to increase in thickness.

24. Students might choose cells from any of the three types of plant tissue: dermal tissue, vascular tissue, or ground tissue. Students should describe how the structure of the cell types is specialized to move water and minerals through the plant.

25. Without the Casparian strip, water could flow out of the xylem and back into the cortex of the root. The Casparian strip seals and waterproofs the cells of the endodermis around their edges so that water can move through them in only one direction.

26. a. How the rates of water intake and transpiration vary with the time of day **b.** Between about 12:30 and 3:30 PM **c.** About 35 grams of water **d.** As transpiration increases or decreases, water intake also increases or decreases.

27. Cactus: spinelike leaves reduce water loss; pine: waxy epidermis and sunken stomata reduce water loss.

28. Students' experimental designs should include reasonable hypotheses and controls.

29. Students' definitions should reflect an understanding of how leaf structures catch light and take in carbon dioxide and water for photosynthesis, as well as how they move the products of photosynthesis to the rest of the plant.

30. Grasses have monocot stems, which grow only by primary growth at the apical meristems. Conifers grow by both primary growth at the apical meristems and secondary growth at the vascular cambium.

31. Sample answers: Like a skyscraper, a tree has structures that transport materials from its lowest level to its highest. Unlike a skyscraper, a tree is an organism that functions without human intervention.

32. In early spring, the daily rise and fall of temperature causes the sap to start flowing up from the maple trees' roots. During the summer and autumn, the flow would be in the opposite direction and the sap would not be as concentrated.

Chapter 23 Assessment

Critical Thinking

23. **Inferring** In Japan, the art of growing miniature trees is highly valued. By cutting the roots and tips of the branches, gardeners can keep the tree small. The trunk of the tree, however, continues to increase in diameter. How do you explain the ever-increasing growth of the diameter of the trunk?

24. **Comparing and Contrasting** Choose a group of cells in the root, in the stem, and in the leaf. Explain how these cells are specialized for transport of water and minerals.

25. **Predicting** How would the function of a plant root be affected if the endodermis cells did not have Casparian strips? Explain.

26. **Using Tables and Graphs** During transpiration, water evaporates from the leaves of plants into the air. Examine the graph that follows and answer the following questions.
    a. What does the graph show?
    b. During which span of time is the greatest amount of water lost through transpiration?
    c. About how many grams of water are lost every 2 hours when the transpiration curve is at its highest peak?
    d. What can you conclude about the relationship between transpiration and water intake?

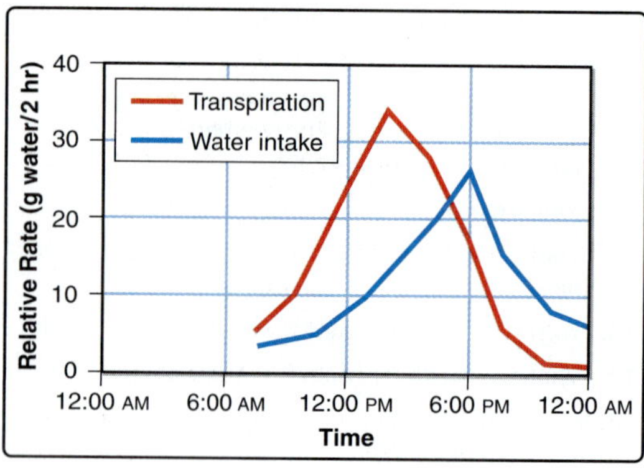

27. **Comparing and Contrasting** Choose a plant from a desert and a plant from a coniferous forest, and compare the ways in which their leaves are adapted to their biomes.

28. **Designing Experiments** What relationship would you expect between a plant's lifespan and its ability to undergo secondary growth? What data could you collect to test your hypothesis? Describe an experiment to collect the data.

29. **Forming Operational Definitions** Review the structure and functions of a leaf and use this information to write an operational definition that explains in your own words what a leaf is.

30. **Comparing and Contrasting** Identify and compare the methods of stem growth in grasses and conifers. Use the terms *primary growth* and *secondary growth* in your answer.

31. **Using Analogies** Someone has said, "A tree is like a skyscraper." In what ways would you agree or disagree with this statement? In your answer, refer to the processes responsible for the transport of water and nutrients in trees and other plants.

32. **Applying Concepts** Why are maple trees tapped for their sugar in the early spring rather than in the summer or autumn?

Structure and Function Recall from Chapter 22 four things that plants need to survive. Describe how roots, stems, and leaves each contribute to meeting at least two of those needs.

Writing in Science

Consider the vascular tissue in a root, a stem, and a leaf. Write a paragraph showing how the cells in this tissue are specialized for transport of water and minerals. (*Hint:* Create an outline to organize your ideas.)

Performance-Based Assessment

Making Models Make a three-dimensional model of one of the following: the layers in a plant leaf, the structure of a plant root, or the structure of a woody stem with secondary growth. Label the major structures in your model. On a separate sheet of paper, describe the function of each structure.

For: An interactive self-test
Visit: PHSchool.com
Web Code: cba-7230

Focus on the BIG Idea

Students' answers should discuss how roots, stems, and leaves contribute to meeting a plant's needs for two of the following: sunlight, water, gas exchange, and the movement of water and nutrients.

Writing in Science

Students should describe how the cell structures of tracheids, vessel elements, sieve tube elements, and companion cells are specialized for their functions. They should also describe how the location of vascular tissue within roots, stems, and leaves contributes to its function.

Standards Practice

Success Tracker™
Online at PHSchool.com

Test-Taking Tip When presented with questions that are related to data in a table, study each column and row of the table for the information you need to answer the questions.

Directions: Choose the letter that best answers the question or completes the statement.

1. Which of the following cell types is NOT found in a plant's vascular tissue?
   A tracheid
   B vessel element
   C guard cell
   D companion cell
2. Where in a plant does mitosis produce new cells?
   A meristematic tissue
   B shoots
   C roots
   D all of the above
3. Tree bark is made of which of the following tissues?
   A phloem
   B cork
   C cork cambium
   D all of the above
4. Which is NOT a factor in the movement of water through a plant's vascular tissues?
   A transpiration
   B capillary action
   C osmotic pressure
   D meristems
5. All of the following conduct fluids in a plant EXCEPT
   A heartwood.
   B sapwood.
   C vascular tissue.
   D phloem.
6. Where does most of the photosynthesis occur in a plant? **BI 1.f**
   A stomata
   B guard cells
   C bark
   D mesophyll tissue
7. Which of the following structures prevents the backflow of water into the root cortex?
   A palisade mesophyll
   B root cap
   C cambium
   D Casparian strip
8. Which of the following plants has a fibrous root system?
   A dandelion
   B potato
   C radish
   D grass

Questions 9–10

A student compared the average number of stomata on the top side and the underside of different plants. Her data are summarized in the table.

Average Number of Stomata (per square mm)

Plant	Top Surfaces of Leaves	Bottom Surfaces of Leaves
Pumpkin	29	275
Tomato	12	122
Bean	40	288

9. What generalization can be made based on the data?
   A All plants have more stomata on the top side of their leaves than on the bottom side.
   B Plants have fewer stomata on the top side of their leaves than on the bottom side.
   C Some plants have more stomata on the top side of their leaves than on the bottom side.
   D The number of stomata varies greatly from plant to plant.
10. Pumpkins, tomatoes, and beans all grow in direct sunlight. Assuming the plants receive plenty of water, stomata on the lower surface of their leaves
    A are always closed.
    B are usually clogged with dust.
    C are unlikely to close at night.
    D stay open during daylight hours.

Standards Practice

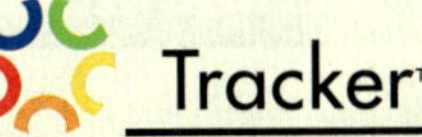

1. C
2. D
3. D
4. D
5. A
6. D
7. D
8. D
9. B
10. D

Success Tracker™
Online at PHSchool.com

Have students check their understanding of the chapter by logging onto Success Tracker.

Performance-Based Assessment

Students' models and descriptions should reflect an understanding of the structure and function of leaves, stems, or roots.

Go Online PHSchool.com

Your students can independently test their knowledge of the chapter and print out their test results for your files.

Chapter Planner 24 Reproduction of Seed Plants

Section and Section Objectives	Time	STANDARDS NCLB	STANDARDS Biology	Activities and Labs
24–1 Reproduction With Cones and Flowers, pp. 609–616 **24.1.1** ***Identify*** the reproductive structures of gymnosperms and angiosperms. **24.1.2** ***Explain*** how pollination and fertilization differ between angiosperms and gymnosperms.	2 periods (1 block)	7 2.a		**SE:** ***Inquiry Activity,*** How do seeds and fruits vary?, p. 608 L2 **TE:** ***Demonstrations,*** pp. 608 L1 L2, 610 L2 **TE:** ***Build Science Skills,*** pp. 610 L1 L2, 611 L1 L2 **SE:** ***Quick Lab,*** What is the structure of a flower?, p. 613 L2 **SE:** ***Technology and Society,*** Using Technology to Design Flowers, p. 617 L2 L3 **SE:** ***Design an Experiment,*** Investigating Pollination, p. 627 L2 **IF:** Investigation 7 L2 L3
24–2 Seed Development and Germination, pp. 618–621 **24.2.1** ***Describe*** the development of seeds and fruits. **24.2.2** ***Explain*** how seeds are dispersed. **24.2.3** ***List*** the factors that influence the dormancy and germination of seeds.	1 period (1/2 block)			**TE:** ***Demonstration,*** p. 618 L2 **SE:** ***Analyzing Data,*** Temperature and Seed Germination, p. 620 L2 **TE:** ***Demonstration,*** p. 621 L2 **LMA:** Chapter 24 Lab L2 L3 **LMB:** Chapter 24 Lab L1 L2
24–3 Plant Propagation and Agriculture, pp. 622–626 **24.3.1** ***Identify*** the forms of plant vegetative reproduction. **24.3.2** ***Describe*** plant propagation. **24.3.3** ***Identify*** the major food-supply crops for humans.	1 period (1/2 block)	7 2.a		**TE:** ***Demonstrations,*** pp. 622 L2, 623 L2 L3 **TE:** ***Build Science Skills,*** pp. 623 L1 L2, 624 L1 L2 **SE:** ***Biology and History,*** The Evolution of Agriculture, pp. 624–625 L2 L3
Chapter Assessment, pp. 628–631	1 period (1/2 block)			

ACTIVITY PLANNER

SE: *Inquiry Activity*, p. 608; 15 min.; hand lens, seeds, fruits, petri dish, scalpel

TE: *Demonstration*, p. 608; 5 min.; pine cone, apple, knife

TE: *Build Science Skills*, p. 610; 5 min.; small pine branch with pollen cones and seed cones

TE: *Demonstration*, p. 610; 10 min.; pollen cone, slide, coverslip

TE: *Build Science Skills*, p. 611; 5 min.; pine seed, knife, hand lens

SE: *Quick Lab*, p. 613; 20 min.; flower, forceps, scalpel, microscope slide, dropper pipette, coverslips, microscope

TE: *Demonstration*, p. 618; 5 min.; variety of fruits, knife

TE: *Demonstration*, p. 621; 5 min.; variety of monocot and dicot seeds, 2 paper towels, plate, plastic wrap

TE: *Demonstration*, p. 622; 5 min.; spider plant, crab grass, daffodil bulb

TE: *Build Science Skills*, p. 623; 5 min., 5 min.; raw sweet potato, 4 toothpicks, small container of water

TE: *Demonstration*, p. 623; 5 min.; tree-branch sections, knife, cloth tape

TE: *Build Science Skills*, p. 624; 5 min.; oranges with and without seeds, knife

SE: *Design an Experiment*, p. 627; 45 min.; flowering plants, hand lens, small paintbrush, forceps, pollen nutrient solution, pollen nutrient solution without calcium, conc. calcium chloride solution, dissecting probe, microscope slides, coverslips, dropper pipette, microscope

PLANNING KEY

Ability Levels

for students performing . . .

below grade level L1

at grade level L2

above grade level L3

Print Components

SE	Student Edition	LA	Lab Assessment
TE	Teacher's Edition	BTM	Biotechnology Manual
RSW	Reading & Study Workbook A	IDM	Issues and Decision Making
ARSW	Adapted Reading & Study Workbook B	LW	Lab Worksheets
TR	Teaching Resources	LMA	Laboratory Manual A
IF	Investigations in Forensics	LMB	Laboratory Manual B

Tech Components

CTB	Computer Test Bank
BD	BioDetectives DVD
TP	Transparencies Plus
PLM	Probeware Lab Manual
ABC	ABC DVD Library
LS	Lab Simulations
VL	Virtual Labs

Interactive textbook with assessment at PHSchool.com

Program Resources	Assessment	Media and Technology
TR: Lesson Plan 24–1, Section Summary, p. 108 L1, p. 117 L2, Worksheets, pp. 111–113 L1, pp. 119–123 L2 **LW:** Chapter 24 Design an Experiment L1 L2 L3 **RSW:** Section 24–1 L2 **ARSW:** Section 24–1 L1	**SE:** 24–1 Section Assessment, p. 616 **TR:** Section Review 24–1	**iText:** Section 24–1 **TP:** 24–1 Interest Grabber, Section Outline, Compare/Contrast Table, Figure 24–1, Figure 24–4, Figure 24–5, Figure 24–7 **ABC:** Angiosperm Reproduction
TR: Lesson Plan 24–2, Section Summary, p. 109 L1, p. 118 L2, Worksheets, pp. 114–115 L1, pp. 124–125 L2, Enrichment L3 **RSW:** Section 24–2 L2 **ARSW:** Section 24–2 L1	**SE:** 24–2 Section Assessment, p. 621 **TR:** Section Review 24–2	**iText:** Section 24–2 **TP:** 24–2 Interest Grabber, Section Outline, Concept Map
TR: Lesson Plan 24–3, Section Summary, p. 110 L1, p. 118 L2, Worksheets, pp. 126–127 L2 **RSW:** Section 24–3 L2	**SE:** 24–3 Section Assessment, p. 626 **TR:** Section Review 24–3	**iText:** Section 24–3 **TP:** 24–3 Interest Grabber, Section Outline, Compare/Contrast Table
	SE: Chapter 24 Assessment, pp. 628–631 **TR:** Chapter Vocabulary Review, Graphic Organizer, Chapter 24 Test	**iText:** Chapter 24 Assessment **CTB:** Chapter 24 Test

Students can do research, share data, and test their knowledge online.

PRESSED FOR TIME?

To Preview the Chapter

- Have students read the Key Concepts in each section.
- Introduce students to the Vocabulary terms in each section.

To Cover the Chapter Quickly

- Have students read Gymnosperms, Angiosperms, Pollination, and Fertilization in Section 24–1; all of Section 24–2; and the Biology and History timeline in Section 24–3.
- Assign Section Assessments 24–1 and 24–2; questions 1–10, 12–19, 22–30, 32, 33 in Chapter 24 Assessment; and questions 1–11 in Chapter 24 Standards Practice.

To Review the Chapter

- Assign Sections 24–1 and 24–2 in the Reading and Study Workbook or the Adapted Reading and Study Workbook.
- Assign the Section Reviews for 24–1 and 24–2 and the Chapter Vocabulary Review for Chapter 24 in the Teaching Resources.

CHAPTER 24

ENGAGE/EXPLORE

Inquiry Activity

 BIIE 1.d

Objective Students will be able to observe structures in seeds and predict which structures are involved in reproduction. L2

Skills Focus **Observing, Formulating Hypotheses, Predicting**

Materials hand lens, variety of seeds and fruits, petri dish, scalpel

Time 15 minutes

Advance Prep If you soak the seeds in water overnight before the lab, they will be easier to cut open.

Strategy Make sure students cut the seeds lengthwise, or they may not be able to see all the structures.

Expected Outcome Students should observe the embryo and other structures inside the seeds.

Think About It

1. All seeds have an embryo, seed coat, stored food, and one or two cotyledons.
2. The cotyledons and endosperm contain stored nutrients.
3. Depending on the type of seed, students might have observed burrs, "wings," or other structures that enable the seeds, or the fruits that contain the seeds, to attach to fur or clothing or to glide on the wind.

Demonstration

Display a pine cone and an apple. Cut the apple in half to expose the seeds and shake some of the seeds out of the pine cone. Then, ask: **What do the pine cone and apple have in common?** *(Both contain the plant's seeds.)* Explain that cone-bearing plants such as pine trees and fruit-bearing plants such as apple trees produce seeds in different ways. Add that students will learn more about the reproduction of both types of plants in this chapter. L1 L2

CHAPTER 24

Reproduction of Seed Plants

Red nodding thistle flowers show a dramatic change as they undergo fertilization and seed development. At maturity, the seeds—each attached to long, white threads—detach from the flowers and are dispersed by wind.

Inquiry Activity

 BIIE 1.d

How do seeds and fruits vary?

Procedure  

1. Use a hand lens to examine a variety of seeds and fruits. (*Hint:* Review the material on seeds in Section 22–4.) Record your observations.
2. Place each seed in a petri dish and use a scalpel to cut the seed lengthwise. **CAUTION:** *Use care with sharp instruments.* Use a hand lens to examine the inside of each seed. Draw and label the structures you observe. Label the embryo of each seed.

Think About It

1. **Observing** What types of structures did you observe in all the seeds?
2. **Formulating Hypotheses** A seed contains stored nutrients that nourish the new plant until it becomes autotrophic. Which part of the seed might contain these nutrients?
3. **Predicting** What structures did you observe that could help spread the offspring of a plant over a larger area? Explain your answer.

HISTORY OF SCIENCE

In 1879, a botany professor at Michigan Agricultural College (now Michigan State University) designed a long-term experiment to investigate the survivability of common weed seeds. Dr. W. J. Beal gathered 50 freshly grown seeds from each of 23 different types of plants, including common mallow and common mullein. He then prepared 20 sets of seeds by mixing each set in moist sand that filled a pint bottle. He buried those bottles in a row on a sandy knoll, with the tops left uncovered and the bottles slanting down so that they would not fill with water. Since then, one of Beal's bottles has been dug up every five or ten years to see if any of the seeds in it would germinate. Some of the seeds of three species in the bottle dug up in 1980—after 100 years—still germinated when placed in good growing conditions.

24–1 Reproduction With Cones and Flowers

7 2.a. Students know the difference between the life cycles and reproduction methods of sexual and asexual organisms.

Seed plants are well adapted to the demands of life on land, especially in how they reproduce. The gametes of seedless plants, such as ferns and mosses, need water for fertilization to be successful. Water allows gametes to move from plant to plant. The gametes of seed plants, however, can achieve fertilization even when the plants are not wet from rain or dew. So, they can reproduce nearly anywhere. The way in which seed plants reproduce has allowed them to survive the dry conditions on land.

Guide for Reading

Key Concepts

- What are the reproductive structures of gymnosperms and angiosperms?
- How does pollination differ between angiosperms and gymnosperms?

Vocabulary

pollen cone • seed cone
ovule • pollen tube
sepal • petal • stamen
filament • anther • carpel
ovary • style • stigma
embryo sac • endosperm
double fertilization

Reading Strategy: Making Comparisons

Before you read, preview **Figure 24–4** and **Figure 24–7.** As you read, compare the life cycles of gymnosperms and angiosperms.

Alternation of Generations

All plants have a life cycle in which a diploid sporophyte generation alternates with a haploid gametophyte generation. Gametophyte plants produce male and female gametes—sperm and eggs. When the gametes join, they form a zygote that begins the next sporophyte generation. In some plants, the two stages of the life cycle are distinct, independent plants. In most ferns, for instance, the gametophyte is a small, heart-shaped plant that grows close to the ground. The sporophyte is the familiar fern plant itself made up of graceful fronds.

Where are these two generations in seed plants? You may remember from Mendel's work on peas that such plants are diploid. Therefore, in seed plants, the familiar, recognizable form of the plant is the diploid sporophyte.

If the sporophyte is what we recognize as the plant, then where is the gametophyte? The answer may surprise you. As shown in **Figure 24–1,** the gametophytes of seed plants are actually hidden deep within tissues of the sporophyte plant. In gymnosperms they are found inside cones, and in angiosperms they are found inside flowers. Cones and flowers represent two different methods of reproduction.

7 2.a

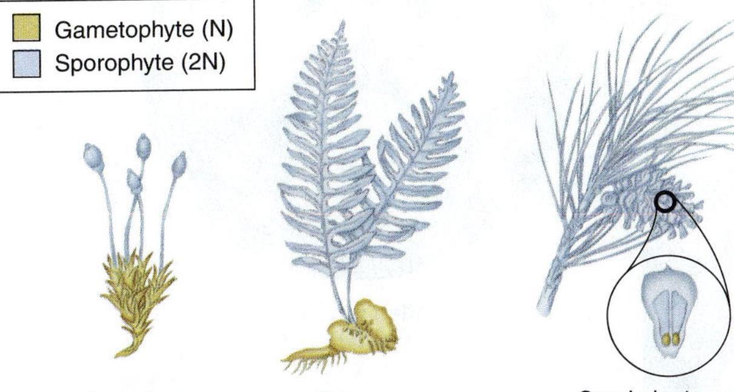

◀ **Figure 24–1** An important trend in plant evolution is the reduction of the gametophyte and the increasing size of the sporophyte. Bryophytes consist of a relatively large gametophyte and smaller sporophytes. Seedless vascular plants, such as ferns, have a small gametophyte and a larger sporophyte. Seed plants have an even smaller gametophyte that is contained within sporophyte tissues. **Interpreting Graphics** *How does the relative size of the haploid and diploid stages of plants differ between bryophytes and seed plants?*

SECTION RESOURCES

TIME SAVER

Print:

- ***Teaching Resources,*** Lesson Plan 24–1, Adapted Section Summary 24–1, Adapted Worksheets 24–1, Section Summary 24–1, Worksheets 24–1, Section Review 24–1
- ***Reading and Study Workbook A,*** Section 24–1
- ***Adapted Reading and Study Workbook B,*** Section 24–1
- ***Investigations in Forensics,*** Investigation 7
- ***Lab Worksheets,*** Chapter 24 Design an Experiment

Technology:

- ***iText,*** Section 24–1
- ***Animated Biological Concepts DVD,*** 34 Angiosperm Reproduction
- ***Transparencies Plus,*** Section 24–1

Section 24–1

7 2.a

1 FOCUS

Objectives

24.1.1 ***Identify*** the reproductive structures of gymnosperms and angiosperms.

24.1.2 ***Explain*** how pollination and fertilization differ between angiosperms and gymnosperms.

Guide for Reading

Vocabulary Preview

Ask students to predict which Vocabulary terms refer to the reproductive parts of gymnosperms, or cone-bearing plants, and which terms refer to the reproductive parts of angiosperms, or flowering plants. *(Pollen cone and seed cone are parts of gymnosperms. Sepal, petal, stamen, anther, carpel, ovary, style, and stigma are parts of angiosperms. Both types of plants have pollen tubes and ovules.)*

Reading Strategy

Suggest that students find each highlighted, boldface term in the text; read its definition; and then locate it in Figure 24–4 or Figure 24–7.

2 INSTRUCT

Alternation of Generations

Use Visuals

Figure 24–1 Have students compare and contrast the differences in the sizes of the diploid sporophyte and the haploid gametophyte in different plant groups. Review the life cycle for each plant group shown, if needed. Challenge students to make inferences about the evolutionary advantage of a reduced haploid gametophyte stage. Have them consider water requirements, complexity of structure, and size. L2

Answer to . . .

Figure 24–1 *Seed plants have a highly reduced haploid or gametophyte stage; the visible plant is nearly all diploid sporophyte.*

24–1 (continued)

Life Cycle of Gymnosperms

Build Science Skills

Observing Obtain a small pine branch that has both pollen cones and seed cones. Point out how the two types of cones are arranged on the branch so that pollen from a pollen cone is likely to fall on a seed cone. Call students' attention to the scales on a seed cone and how they are arranged. Remove some of the scales, and let students examine the base of the scales. *(Even if the seeds have been shed, an impression of the seeds still remains.)* Also, have students examine the scales of a seed cone that has been soaked in water. *(The scales are closed.)* Ask: **What is the function of the scales of a seed cone?** *(To produce and protect the seeds)* L1 L2

Demonstration

Dust some pollen grains from a cone on a microscope slide. Prepare a wet-mount slide and focus on low power. Use a microprojector or have students take turns observing the pollen. Suggest that students sketch what they see. Ask: **How is the structure of the pollen grain related to its function?** *(A pine pollen grain has two tiny wings on either side of its rounded center that aid in its dispersal by wind.)* L1 L2

▲ **Figure 24–2** **Reproduction in gymnosperms takes place in structures called cones.** In this pine tree, pollen cones, shown on the top, produce male gametophytes, which are pollen grains. Seed cones, such as the one shown on the bottom, produce female gametophytes that develop into a new embryo following fertilization.

Life Cycle of Gymnosperms

Pine trees and other gymnosperms are diploid sporophytes. As you will see, this sporophyte develops from a zygote that is contained within a seed. How and where is this seed produced? **Reproduction in gymnosperms takes place in cones, which are produced by a mature sporophyte plant.** Gymnosperms produce two types of cones: pollen cones and seed cones.

Pollen Cones and Seed Cones **Pollen cones,** shown in **Figure 24–2,** are also called male cones. Pollen cones produce the male gametophytes, which are called pollen grains. As tiny as it is, the pollen grain makes up the entire male gametophyte stage of the gymnosperm life cycle. One of the haploid nuclei in the pollen grain will divide later to produce two sperm nuclei.

The more familiar **seed cones,** which produce female gametophytes, are generally much larger than pollen cones. Near the base of each scale are two **ovules** in which the female gametophytes develop. Within the ovules, meiosis produces haploid cells that grow and divide to produce female gametophytes. These gametophytes may contain hundreds or thousands of cells. When mature, each gametophyte contains a few large egg cells, each ready for fertilization by sperm nuclei.

CA a

Pollination The gymnosperm life cycle typically takes two years to complete. The cycle begins in the spring as male cones release enormous numbers of pollen grains. The pollen is carried by the wind, as shown in **Figure 24–3.** Some of these pollen grains reach female cones. There, some pollen grains are caught in a sticky secretion on one of the scales of the female cone. This sticky material, known as a pollination drop, ensures that pollen grains stay on the female cone.

CHECKPOINT *What are pollen cones and seed cones?*

Figure 24–3 Pollen grains are male gametophytes. Pollen is carried by the wind until it reaches a female cone. **Inferring** *Male and female cones are distributed on a plant such that pollen usually lands on a different plant from where it started. Why might this strategy have evolved?*

Pollen Grains
(magnification: 750×)

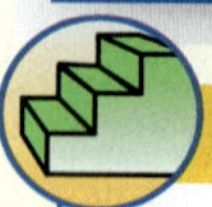

UNIVERSAL ACCESS

Less Proficient Readers
Because the double fertilization process is complicated, encourage students to carefully reread that subsection, and have each student draw a flowchart to illustrate the process. In their flowcharts, they should indicate which cells are haploid, diploid, and triploid. L2

English Language Learners
Invite students to diagram several very different types of flowers, such as orchids, magnolias, and daisies. Students should label each with the following: sepals, petals, stamen, anthers, ovary, style, and stigma. They may also include labels in their native languages. L1 L2

Advanced Learners
Encourage students to write a "biography" of any mature seed plant. Their biographies should incorporate all of the important events in the plant's life cycle, including formation as a seed, germination, transportation away from the parent plant, and growth to maturity. L3

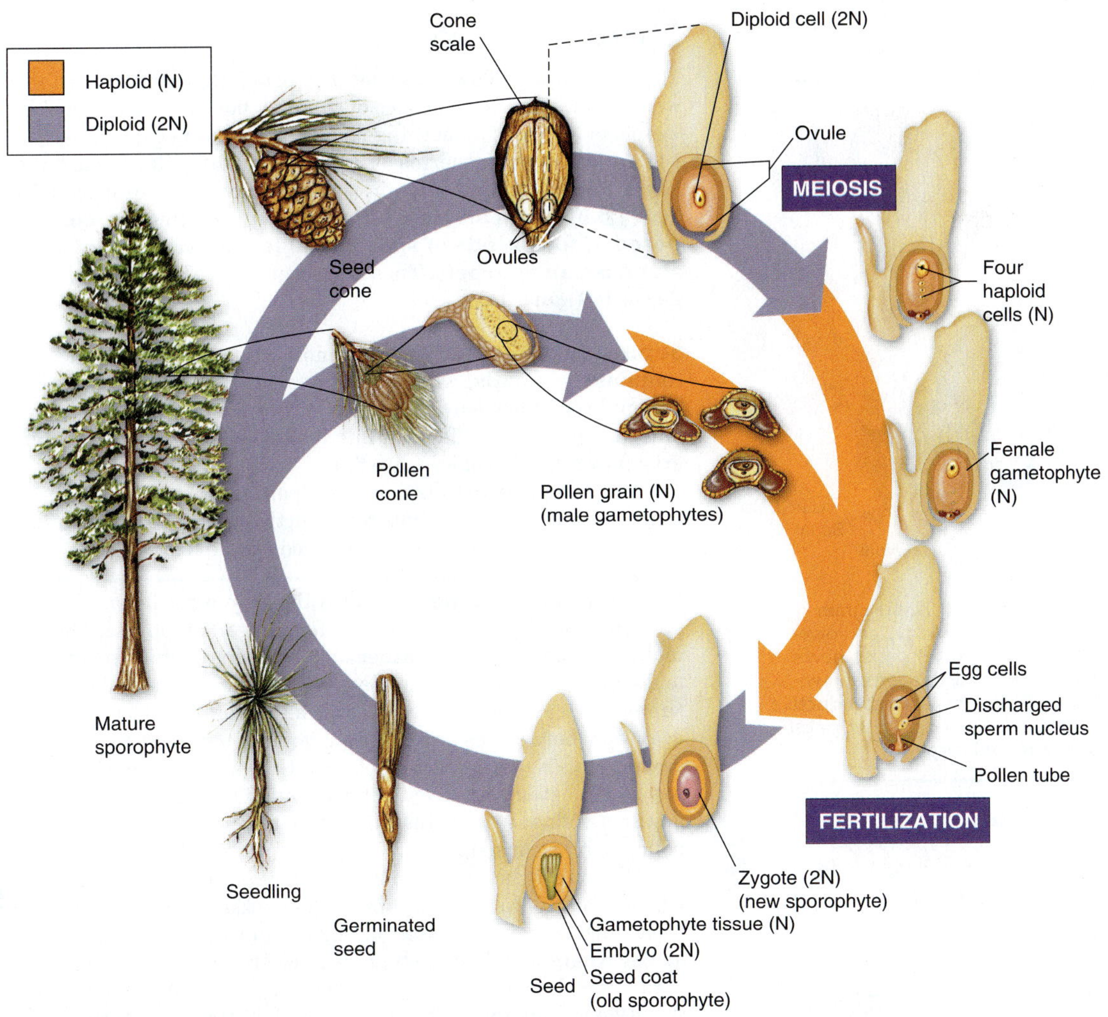

Fertilization and Development If a pollen grain lands near an ovule, the grain splits open and begins to grow a structure called a **pollen tube,** which contains two haploid sperm nuclei. Once the pollen tube reaches the female gametophyte, one sperm nucleus disintegrates, and the other fertilizes the egg contained within the female gametophyte. If sperm from another pollen tube reaches the female gametophyte, more than one egg cell may be fertilized, but just one embryo develops. As shown in **Figure 24–4,** fertilization produces a diploid zygote—the new sporophyte plant. This zygote grows into an embryo. During this time, it is encased within what will soon develop into a seed. The seed consists of three generations of the life cycle. The outer seed coat is part of the old sporophyte generation, the haploid cells surrounding the embryo are part of the female gametophyte, and the embryo is the new sporophyte plant.

CA a

▲ **Figure 24–4** This illustration shows the life cycle of a typical gymnosperm. A pine tree—the mature sporophyte—produces male and female cones. Male cones produce pollen, and female cones produce ovules located on cone scales. If an egg is fertilized by the sperm, it becomes a zygote that is nourished by the female cone. In time, the zygote develops into a new sporophyte plant. **Classifying** *Classify each of the following terms as to whether they belong to the haploid or diploid stage of the pine tree's life cycle: pollen tube, seed cone, embryo, ovule, seedling.*

a 7 2.a

Use Visuals

Figure 24–4 Make sure students understand the diagram. Point out all the steps where the next drawing in the sequence is an enlargement of the previous drawing. For example, explain how the single cone scale at the top of the diagram is just one of many cone scales on the seed cone in the previous drawing. Similarly, the drawing that shows the diploid cell in the cone scale is an enlargement of the previous drawing of the cone scale. Add that the same holds true for the male pollen cone and its pollen grains. Then, review the entire life cycle of a pine tree, and have students follow along in the diagram. As you identify the structures involved in each stage, students should locate them in the diagram. Check students' comprehension of the life cycle by asking: **Which parts of the plant are haploid?** *(The haploid cell in the ovule, the female gametophyte, and the male gametophytes in the pollen grains)* **Why is the zygote diploid?** *(Because fertilization has occurred)* L1 L2

Build Science Skills

Applying Concepts As students watch, cut a pine seed in half. Point out the three layers of the seed: the outer seed coat, the gametophyte, and the embryo. You may want to provide students with a hand lens to examine the three layers. Explain that the seed consists of three generations of the pine tree. Ask: **Which generation of the pine tree is represented by each layer of the seed?** *(The outer seed coat is part of the old sporophyte plant, the cells surrounding the embryo are part of the female gametophyte, and the embryo is the new sporophyte plant.)* L1 L2

BIO INSIGHTS BACKGROUND

In an attempt to simplify the terminology, pollen grains often are referred to as gametes. It is important, though, to be clear about exactly what is a gamete and what is a spore. Recall that a gamete is a cell that must fuse with another gamete to form a new organism. Pollen grains, therefore, are not gametes; they are spores because they grow by mitosis into a new organism—the gametophyte. In angiosperms, the true male gametes are the two sperm nuclei that appear in the pollen tube. The true female gametes are the egg cell and the polar nuclei that fuse with the sperm nuclei to form the embryo and endosperm, respectively.

Answers to . . .

CHECKPOINT *Pollen cones produce the male gametophytes. Seed cones produce the female gametophytes.*

Figure 24–3 *Because it increases genetic variation*

Figure 24–4 *Haploid stage: pollen tube; diploid stage: seed cone, embryo, ovule, seedling*

24–1 (continued)

Structure of Flowers

Build Science Skills

Classifying Display pictures of a wide variety of angiosperms. Include trees, shrubs, perennial and annual herbaceous plants, ground covers, grasses, and water plants. Give students a chance to view the pictures, and then have them brainstorm a list of characteristics that they think all angiosperms share. *(Students might identify green leaves, flowers, and fruits, among other possible shared characteristics.)* Then, ask: **How do angiosperms differ from gymnosperms?** *(Students might say that angiosperms have broad leaves instead of needles and that they produce flowers and fruits instead of cones.)* L2

Build Science Skills

Using Models Give students a chance to create a model of a flower using whatever materials they find around the classroom or at home. For example, they might use colored construction paper for sepals and petals; toothpicks for filaments; modeling clay for anthers, stigma, and ovary; cornmeal for pollen; a drinking straw for the style; and dry peas for ovules. Invite students to share their models with the class and identify the parts of each model. L1 L2

For: The Structure of a Flower activity
Visit: PHSchool.com
Web Code: cbe-7249
Students can interact with the art online.

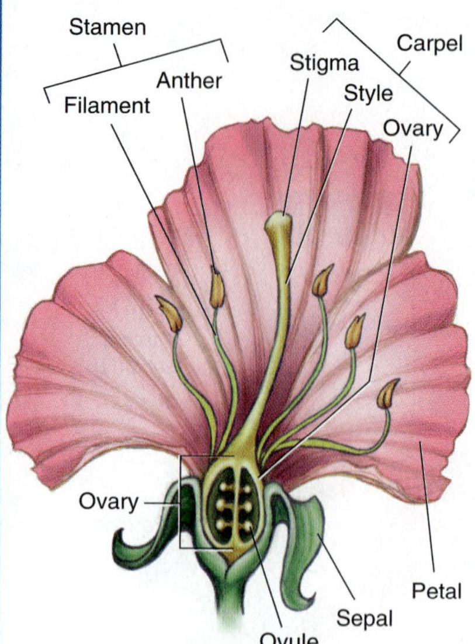

▲ **Figure 24–5** This diagram shows the parts of a typical flower. The flowers of some species, however, may not have all the parts shown here. **Flowers are reproductive organs that include sepals, petals, stamens, and carpels.**

For: The Structure of a Flower activity
Visit: PHSchool.com
Web Code: cbp-7241

Structure of Flowers

You may think of flowers as decorative objects that brighten the world. However, the presence of so many flowers in the world is visible evidence of something else—the stunning evolutionary success of the angiosperms, or flowering plants. Flowers are the key to understanding why angiosperms have been so successful. **Flowers are reproductive organs that are composed of four kinds of specialized leaves: sepals, petals, stamens, and carpels.** These structures are shown in the flower in **Figure 24–5.**

Sepals and Petals The outermost circle of floral parts contains the **sepals,** which in many plants are green and closely resemble ordinary leaves. Sepals enclose the bud before it opens, and they protect the flower while it is developing. **Petals,** which are often brightly colored, are found just inside the sepals. The petals attract insects and other pollinators to the flower. Because they do not produce reproductive cells, the sepals and petals of a flower are sometimes called sterile leaves.

CA a

Stamens and Carpels Within the ring of petals are the structures that produce male and female gametophytes. The male parts consist of an anther and a filament, which together make up the **stamen.** The **filament** is a long, thin stalk that supports an anther. At the tip of each filament is an **anther,** an oval sac where meiosis takes place, producing haploid male gametophytes—pollen grains. In most angiosperms, each flower has several stamens. If you rub your hand on the anthers of a flower, a yellow-orange dust may stick to your skin. This is pollen, which consists of thousands of individual pollen grains.

The innermost floral parts are **carpels,** also called pistils, which produce the female gametophytes. Each carpel has a broad base forming an **ovary,** which contains one or more ovules where female gametophytes are produced. The diameter of the carpel narrows into a stalk called the **style.** At the top of the style is a sticky portion known as the **stigma,** where pollen grains frequently land. Some flowers have several carpels fused together to form a single reproductive structure called a compound carpel.

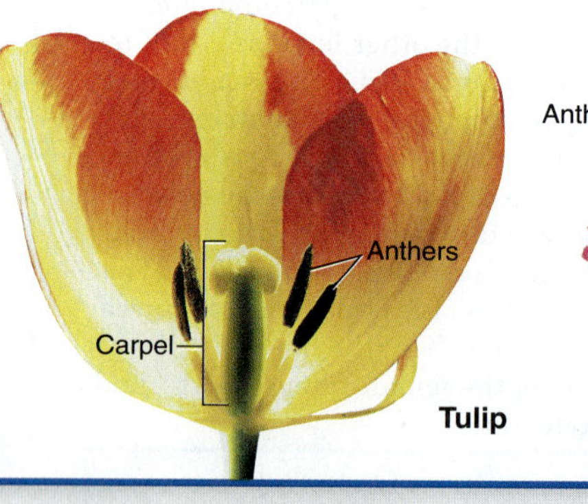

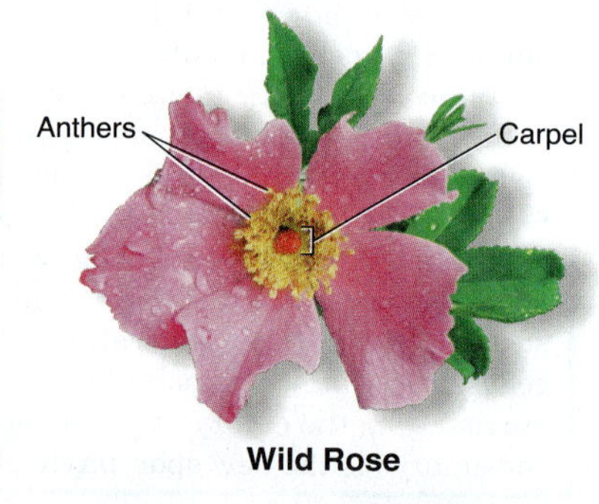

FACTS AND FIGURES

Flowery facts

In many flowers, both sepals and petals are brightly colored and help attract pollinators. In other plants, sepals are smaller and thicker than petals and green in color. In these plants, the sepals' function is to protect the more fragile flower bud from damage.

Some angiosperm plants have evolved unique ways to attract pollinators. For example, an African plant, *Anchomanes difformis*, does the botanical equivalent of burning incense. The flower has a foot-tall structure called a spadix. The plant's tissues generate heat and warm the spadix to about 40°C, so that it produces a sweet aroma that attracts the beetles that pollinate the flower. Most angiosperm flowers contain both pistils and stamens. However, some species—including date palms, willows, and poplars—produce unisexual flowers that have only stamens (staminate flowers) or pistils (pistillate flowers).

Quick Lab

What is the structure of a flower?

Materials flower, forceps, scalpel, microscope slide, dropper pipette, coverslips, microscope

Procedure 

1. Examine a flower carefully. Make a detailed drawing of the flower and label as many parts as you can. Note whether the anthers are above or below the stigma.
2. Remove an anther and place it on a slide. While holding the anther with forceps, use the scalpel to cut one or more thin slices across the anther. **CAUTION:** *Be careful with sharp tools.*
3. Lay the slices flat on the microscope slide and add a drop of water and a coverslip. Observe the slices with the microscope at low power. Make a labeled drawing of your observations.
4. Repeat steps 2 and 3 with the ovary.

Analyze and Conclude

1. **Observing** Are the anthers in this flower located above or below the stigma? How could this affect what happens to the pollen produced by the anthers? Explain your answer.
2. **Applying Concepts** What structures did you identify in the anther? What is the function of these structures?
3. **Applying Concepts** What structures did you identify in the ovary? What is the function of these structures?
4. **Drawing Conclusions** Which parts of the flower will become the seeds? The fruit?

Flowers vary greatly in shape, color, and size, as shown in **Figure 24–6.** A typical flower produces both male and female gametophytes. In some plants, however, male and female gametophytes are produced in separate flowers on the same individual. Corn, for example, has separate male and female flowers on the same plant. The tassel is a flower that produces male gametophytes, and the silk is the style of a flower that contains the female gametophyte. In other cases, many flowers grow together to form a composite structure that looks like a single flower, as shown in the sunflower.

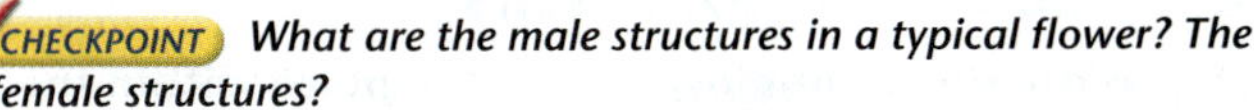

CHECKPOINT *What are the male structures in a typical flower? The female structures?*

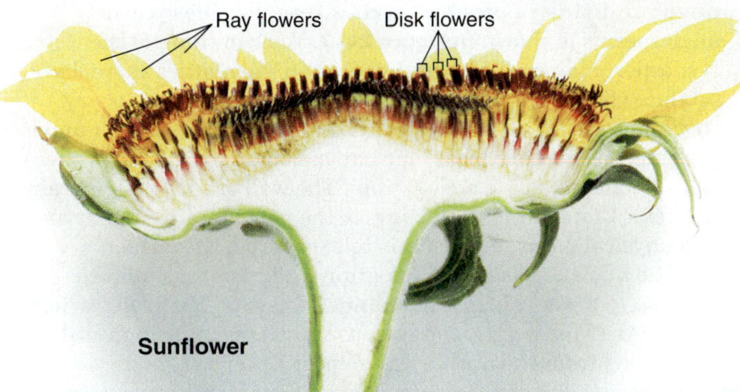

Figure 24–6 Flowers vary enormously in structure. The tulip has only a single carpel, whereas the wild rose has many carpels. Some flowerlike structures are actually clusters of many individual flowers. In the sunflower, disk flowers toward the inside of the cluster are reproductive, whereas ray flowers toward the outside are nonreproductive and form what look like petals. **Formulating Hypotheses** *How might it be an advantage for a plant to have many flowers together in a single structure?*

Quick Lab

Objective Students will be able to observe the structures of a flower and conclude which structures become seeds and which structures become the fruit. L2

Skills Focus Observing, Applying Concepts, Drawing Conclusions

Materials flower, forceps, scalpel, microscope slide, dropper pipette, coverslips, microscope

Time 20 minutes

Strategy Before students cut their flower, make sure they have noted whether the anthers are above or below the stigma.

Analyze and Conclude

1. Self-pollinated flowers typically have anthers higher than the stigma, and pollen falls directly from the anthers onto the stigma. Many cross-pollinated plants have taller stigmas that receive windblown or animal-borne pollen from other flowers.
2. Students may be able to observe mature or immature pollen in the anthers. The pollen grains form male gametophytes that can fertilize female gametophytes and form zygotes that will grow into new plants.
3. Students may be able to observe mature or immature ovules in the ovary. The ovules produce female gametophytes that can be fertilized by male gametophytes.
4. The ovules will become the seeds. Generally, the ovary becomes the fruit, although other parts of the flower may also contribute to fruit formation.

Answers to . . .

CHECKPOINT *The male structures are the stamen and anthers; the female structures are the carpels, ovary, style, and stigma.*

Figure 24–6 *Many flowers together in a single structure might attract more insects, which might improve the chances of pollination.*

24–1 (continued)

Life Cycle of Angiosperms

Use Visuals

Figure 24–7 Some students might be confused by the figure. Check their comprehension by asking: **Where does fertilization take place?** *(Inside the ovary)* **How do pollen grains reach the ovary?** *(By growing pollen tubes down through the style)* **After fertilization, how many sets of chromosomes are contained within the endosperm?** *(Three)* **How many sets of chromosomes does the embryo have?** *(Two)* **From which part of the plant does the seed coat develop?** *(The outer part of the ovule)* L1 L2

Address Misconceptions

Students may not fully recognize the alternation of generations in the angiosperm life cycle. Review the definitions of sporophyte and gametophyte. Then, superimpose the angiosperm life cycle on the general plant life cycle in Figure 22–2 on page 552. Make sure students can identify the gametophyte stage and the sporophyte stage in angiosperms. Emphasize the single mitotic divisions that the haploid cells of the male and female gametophytes undergo. Identify pollen as the spores of the sporophyte. L1 L2

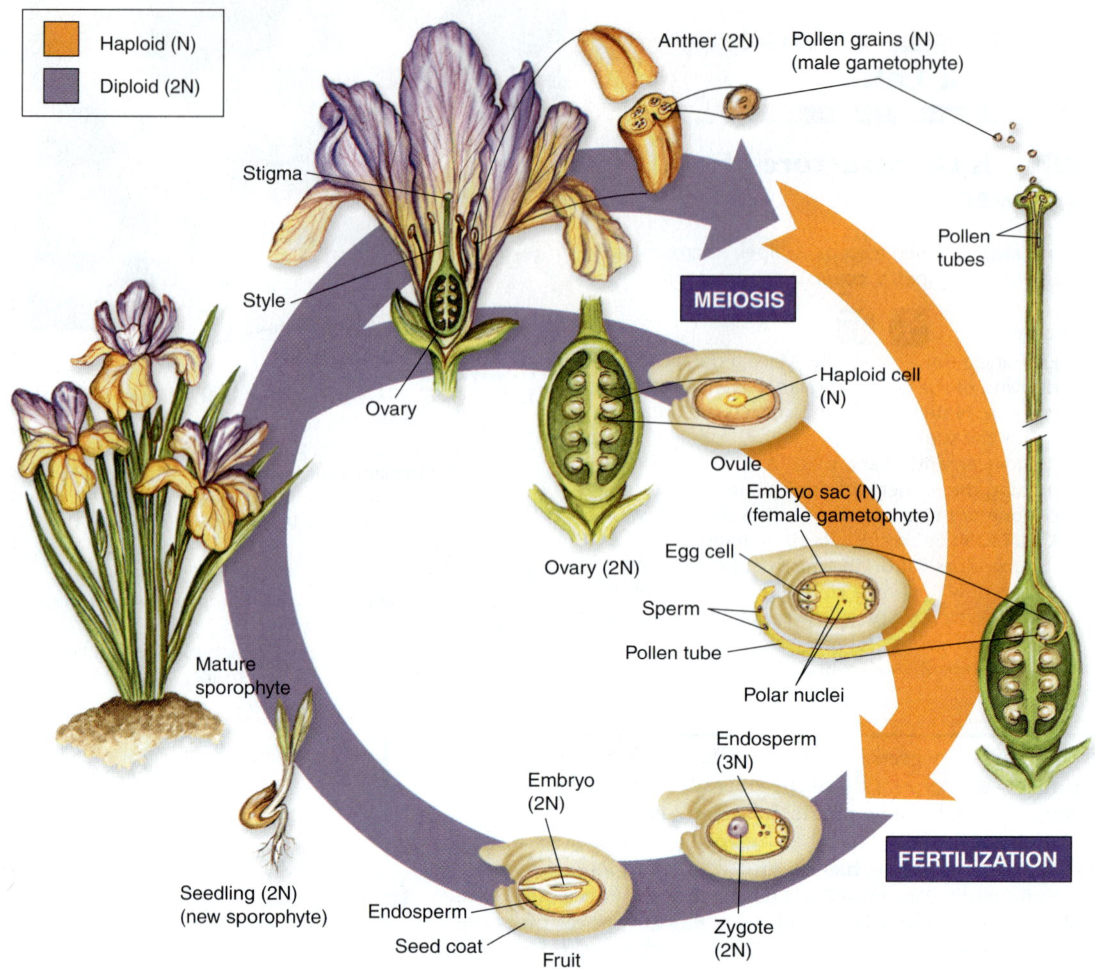

▲ **Figure 24–7** This illustration shows the life cycle of a typical angiosperm—an iris. The developing seeds of a flowering plant are protected and nourished inside the ovary, which is located at the base of the flower. **Reproduction in angiosperms takes place within the flower. After pollination, the seeds of angiosperms develop inside protective structures.**

Life Cycle of Angiosperms

Reproduction in angiosperms takes place within the flower. Following pollination and fertilization, the seeds develop inside protective structures. The life cycle of angiosperms is shown in **Figure 24–7.** You can think of the angiosperm life cycle as beginning when the mature sporophyte produces flowers. Each flower contains anthers and an ovary. Inside the anthers—the male part of the flower—each cell undergoes meiosis and produces four haploid spore cells. Each of these cells becomes a single pollen grain. The wall of each pollen grain thickens, protecting the contents of the pollen grain from dryness and physical damage when it is released from the anther.

The nucleus of each pollen grain undergoes one mitotic division to produce two haploid nuclei. The pollen grain, which is the entire male gametophyte, usually stops growing until it is released from the anther and deposited on a stigma.

CA a

FACTS AND FIGURES

All about angiosperms

There are at least 250,000 known species of angiosperms. Given their numbers, it is not surprising that they show great variability. For example, the length of time for completion of the angiosperm life cycle ranges from less than a month to as long as 150 years. Pollen tubes also show great variation. In corn, the pollen tube may be as long as 50 cm, but in most plants the pollen tube is much shorter. In addition, a pollen tube may complete its growth in less than 24 hours, but in some plants it takes over a year. The size of flowers varies greatly as well. The smallest flowers are those of the tiny duckweed *Wolffia columbiana.* Its flowers are only about 0.1 mm long. The largest flowers are those of the *Rafflesia* plant, which is indigenous to Indonesia. Its huge blooms can grow to 1 m in diameter and attain a mass of 9 kg.

The ovary of the flower contains the ovules, in which the female gametophyte develops. A single diploid cell goes through meiosis to produce four haploid cells, three of which disintegrate. The remaining cell undergoes mitosis to produce eight nuclei. These eight nuclei and the surrounding membrane are called the **embryo sac.** The embryo sac, contained within the ovule, is the female gametophyte of a flowering plant. One of the eight nuclei, near the base of the gametophyte, is the egg nucleus—the female gamete. If fertilization takes place, this cell will become the zygote that grows into a new sporophyte plant. Inside the ovary, the cells of the growing embryo begin to differentiate. That is, they begin to specialize, developing from a ball of cells into an embryonic sporophyte. The new sporophyte, or seedling, is shown in **Figure 24–7.**

CHECKPOINT *Where does the female gametophyte develop?*

Pollination

Once the gametophytes have developed inside the flower, pollination takes place. **Most gymnosperms and some angiosperms are wind pollinated, whereas most angiosperms are pollinated by animals.** These animals, mainly insects, birds, and bats, carry pollen from one flower to another. Because wind pollination is less efficient than animal pollination, wind-pollinated plants, such as the oak tree in **Figure 24–8,** rely on favorable weather and sheer numbers to get pollen from one plant to another. Animal-pollinated plants have a variety of adaptations, such as bright colors and sweet nectar, to attract animals. Animals have evolved body shapes that enable them to reach nectar deep within certain flowers.

Insect pollination is beneficial to insects and other animals because it provides a dependable source of food—pollen and nectar. Plants also benefit because the insects take the pollen directly from flower to flower. Insect pollination is more efficient than wind pollination, giving insect-pollinated plants a greater chance of reproductive success. Botanists suggest that insect pollination is the factor largely responsible for the displacement of gymnosperms by angiosperms during the past 100 million years.

(a) 7 2.a

Figure 24–8 **Most angiosperms are pollinated by animals, although some are pollinated by wind.** The shape of a flower often indicates how it is pollinated. The flowers of an oak tree (A) are typical of wind-pollinated flowers in that they are small, are not brightly colored, and produce vast amounts of pollen. To attract insects and other animals, many animal-pollinated flowers are large and brightly colored. The rose flower (B) is pollinated by a variety of insects, whereas the trumpet creeper flower (C) has a tube shape that is adapted specifically to the long beak of a hummingbird.

Pollination

Build Science Skills

Applying Concepts Have students imagine that they are botanists who have just discovered a new plant that has not yet been identified. They note that the plant has tiny green flowers that are difficult to see against the background of green leaves. Ask: **How do you think this plant is pollinated?** *(By the wind, because it does not have large colorful flowers to attract animal pollinators)* L2

Make Connections

Health Science Point out that many people are allergic to the pollen of flowers. Explain that allergies to pollen are actually reactions to proteins in the coat of the pollen grain and that people may be allergic to certain pollens but not to others because each type has a different protein coat. One of the most common pollen allergies is the allergic reaction known as "hay fever." You might want to take a poll of students to see how many have this type of allergy. Explain that hay fever is not an allergy to hay but to certain wind-pollinated plants. Ask: **Why might wind-pollinated plants create more problems for allergy sufferers than animal-pollinated plants?** *(Wind-pollinated plants usually produce more pollen because these plants release their pollen into the air in large amounts, and it is easily carried all over by wind.)* L2

Answer to . . .

CHECKPOINT *The female gametophyte develops in the ovules, which are contained in the ovary of the flower.*

24–1 (continued)

Fertilization in Angiosperms

Use Visuals

Figure 24–9 Have students identify the parts of the corn seed that are haploid *(none)*, diploid *(embryo)*, and triploid *(endosperm)*. Review the process of double fertilization. Discuss its adaptive advantage. L2

3 ASSESS

Evaluate Understanding

Trace Figure 24–5 and give students a copy without the labels. Then, have students label the parts of the flower shown in the diagram.

Reteach

Review the life cycle of gymnosperms and angiosperms as students follow the stages shown in Figure 24–4 and Figure 24–7.

Focus on the BIG Idea

Seed plants: Dominant stage—Diploid (2N); Zygote formation—Two sperm nuclei in a pollen tube reach a female gametopyhte. One sperm nucleus disintegrates and the other fertilizes the egg, forming a diploid zygote; Occurrence of meiosis—In gymnosperms, meiosis occurs in the pollen grains and in the ovules. In angiosperms, meiosis occurs in anthers and in ovules. *Chlamydomonas*: Dominant stage—Haploid (N); Zygote formation—Gametes gather in large groups, and then – and + gametes form pairs, which join flagella and shed their cell walls and fuse, forming a diploid zygote; Occurrence of meiosis—The thick-walled zygote divides and produces four flagellated haploid cells.

If your class subscribes to the iText, use it to review the Key Concepts in Section 24–1.

Answer to . . .

Figure 24–9 *As the seed develops, the food stored in the endosperm is absorbed by the cotyledon and then used by the growing embryo.*

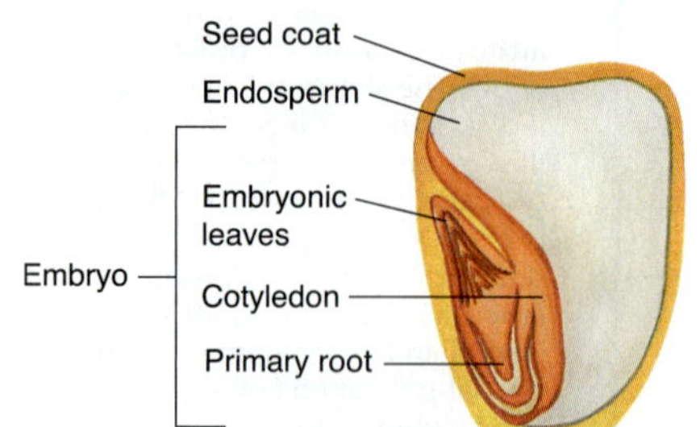

▲ **Figure 24–9** The endosperm of a corn seed develops through the process of double fertilization. After one sperm nucleus fertilizes the egg cell, the zygote forms. Then, the other sperm nucleus fuses with the two polar nuclei to form a triploid cell, which develops into the endosperm. **Predicting** ***What will happen to the endosperm when the seed begins to grow?***

Fertilization in Angiosperms

If a pollen grain lands on the stigma of an appropriate flower of the same species, it begins to grow a pollen tube. The generative nucleus within the pollen grain divides and forms two sperm nuclei. The pollen tube now contains a tube nucleus and two sperm nuclei. The pollen tube grows into the style. There, it eventually reaches the ovary and enters the ovule.

Inside the embryo sac, two distinct fertilizations take place. First, one of the sperm nuclei fuses with the egg nucleus to produce a diploid zygote. The zygote will grow into the new plant embryo. Second, the other sperm nucleus does something truly remarkable—it fuses with two polar nuclei in the embryo sac to form a triploid (3N) cell. This cell will grow into a food-rich tissue known as **endosperm,** which nourishes the seedling as it grows.

As shown in **Figure 24–9,** a seed of corn, a monocot, contains a rich supply of endosperm. In many dicots, including garden beans, the cotyledons absorb the endosperm as the seed develops. The cotyledons then serve as the stored food supply for the embryo when it begins to grow.

Because two fertilization events take place between the male and female gametophytes, this process is known as **double fertilization.** Double fertilization may be one of the reasons why the angiosperms have been so successful. Recall that in gymnosperms, the food reserve built up in seeds is produced before fertilization takes place. As a result, if an ovule is not fertilized, those resources are wasted. In angiosperms, if an ovule is not fertilized, the endosperm does not form, and food is not wasted by preparing for a nonexistent zygote.

24–1 Section Assessment

1. **Key Concept** What are the reproductive structures of gymnosperms?
2. **Key Concept** Describe the flower and how it is involved in reproduction.
3. **Key Concept** Are angiosperms typically wind pollinated or animal pollinated? How does this process occur?
4. What is endosperm? Where does it form in a flowering plant?
5. **Critical Thinking Inferring** Many flowers have bright patterns of coloration that directly surround the reproductive structures. How might this type of coloration be advantageous to the plant?

Focus on the BIG Idea

Information and Heredity
Review the life cycle of the green alga *Chlamydomonas* in Section 20–4. Make a compare-and-contrast table comparing alternation of generations in seed plants and *Chlamydomonas*. Include which stage (haploid or diploid) of each organism's life cycle is dominant and when meiosis occurs.

24–1 Section Assessment

1. The reproductive structures of gymnosperms are pollen cones, pollen grains, seed cones, ovules, and pollen tubes.
2. Flowers are reproductive organs that are composed of four kinds of specialized leaves: sepals, petals, stamens, and carpels. The stamens produce male gametophytes, and the carpels produce female gametophytes.
3. Angiosperms are typically pollinated by animals. Insects, birds, and bats carry pollen from one flower to another as they gather nectar.
4. A food-rich tissue that nourishes a seedling as it grows; inside the embryo sac
5. Bright patterns of coloration might attract insects and other animals to the reproductive structures of the flower and increase the chances of pollination.

Using Technology to Design Flowers

What's your favorite flower? Perhaps your answer was "the rose." Roses are the world's most popular ornamental flowers. They come in many colors. Chances are you've seen red, white, pink, or even yellow roses. But have you ever seen a blue rose? Probably not! Roses do not have the enzymes to produce blue pigments, so even the best efforts of plant breeders have not produced a blue rose.

What Makes a Flower?

Botanists have discovered that flower development is controlled by a series of genes. By manipulating these genes, scientists have produced plants that will flower earlier and much faster than normal.

Changing the color of a flower, however, has proved a little more difficult. Knowing that petunias often produce blue flowers, in 1991 Australian researchers isolated the gene for the enzyme that produces blue pigment. Then, they transferred this "blue gene" to a rose. To their disappointment, however, the new roses were just as red as ever. Apparently, flower color is a tricky and unpredictable business—particularly in roses—that involves complex interactions with other genes and pigments.

Violet Carnations?

When the Australian scientists turned from roses to carnations, they produced a carnation with unique violet flowers. Again, they inserted the gene from the blue petunias into a carnation plant. The result, shown in the photos, was a deep violet carnation unlike any ever seen in nature. In 1999, these genetically modified carnation plants were introduced for sale in Europe and the United States. A number of biotech companies are hoping to master the intricacies of color genetics in flowers. Someday, one of these companies may have what they've all been seeking—a blue rose.

Research and Decide

1. Use library or Internet resources to learn more about the relationship between genetics and new flower varieties. Then, choose a common food crop and find out how breeders have modified the plants to give the crop specific traits.
2. Suppose you are a plant geneticist and you want to create a new color of lily. Decide which flower color you would like to produce. Then, write down the scientific steps that you would take to produce the new flower color.

PHSchool.com

For: Links from the authors
Visit: PHSchool.com
Web Code: cbe-7241

After students have read this feature, you might want to discuss one or more of the following:

- Genetic engineering methods, such as the use of restriction enzymes and DNA insertion, that are used to isolate a gene from one plant or insert it into another plant
- Other traits of flowers, besides color, that breeders might try to modify, such as season of bloom, length of bloom period, size of flowers, number of petals, and number of flowers
- Examples of plants produced by breeders that have unusual characteristics, such as plants that have black or nearly black flowers (for example, columbine, hollyhock, viola, and sweet pea)
- Reasons why varieties of plants bred for certain traits, such as color, may not be as hardy as the standard varieties

Research and Decide

1. Students should choose any common food crop that has been genetically modified, such as tomatoes, potatoes, squash, or corn. They should describe how the plants have been modified to exhibit certain traits.
2. Students should select any color they would like to produce in a lily plant, such as yellow, pink, red, or orange. The steps they would take might include first isolating a gene from another plant that codes for the color of their choice and then inserting the gene into a lily plant.

PHSchool.com

Students can research genetically modified plants on the site developed by authors Ken Miller and Joe Levine.

Section 24–2

1 FOCUS

Objectives

24.2.1 ***Describe*** the development of seeds and fruits.

24.2.2 ***Explain*** how seeds are dispersed.

24.2.3 ***List*** the factors that influence the dormancy and germination of seeds.

Guide for Reading

Vocabulary Preview

Ask: **What are some examples of fruits?** *(Examples might include apples, oranges, bananas, and grapes.)* Explain that the common meaning of the term *fruit* is not the same as its scientific meaning. In biological terms, *fruit* means a ripened ovary that contains angiosperm seeds. Add that many foods not commonly thought of as fruits fit this definition, including tomatoes and cucumbers.

Reading Strategy

Suggest that students include the highlighted, boldface terms and sentences in their summaries.

2 INSTRUCT

Seed and Fruit Development

Demonstration

Display an apple, peach, tomato, bean pod, and acorn. Ask: **How are these specimens similar?** *(They are all fruits, although students may not realize that the tomato, bean, and acorn are fruits.)* Explain that each specimen is actually an enlarged and ripened ovary, which, by definition, is a fruit. Ask: **Which fruits have soft, fleshy outer walls?** *(Apple, peach, and tomato)* Point out that these fruits are classified as fleshy fruits, whereas the bean pod and acorn are classified as dry fruits. Cut the fruits in half and ask students to describe what they see inside. *(Mature, fertilized seeds)* L2

24–2 Seed Development and Germination

Guide for Reading

Key Concepts
- How do fruits form?
- How are seeds dispersed?
- What factors influence the dormancy and germination of seeds?

Vocabulary
dormancy
germination

Reading Strategy: Summarizing As you read, take notes on the development, dispersal, dormancy, and germination of seeds. Write a few sentences summarizing each of these processes.

The development of the seed, which provides protection and nutrition for the embryo, was a major factor in the success of plants on land. The angiosperm seed, encased within a fruit formed by the ovary wall, offers even more. As you will see, by helping a seed get into the best possible location to start its new life, angiosperm seeds were immediately favored by natural selection.

Seed and Fruit Development

Once fertilization is complete, nutrients flow into the flower tissue and support the development of the growing embryo within the seed. **As angiosperm seeds mature, the ovary walls thicken to form a fruit that encloses the developing seeds.** A fruit is a ripened ovary that contains angiosperm seeds. Examples of fruits are shown in **Figure 24–10.** Parts of the ovule toughen to form a seed coat, which is the outer layer that protects the delicate embryo and its tiny food supply. The ovary wall then thickens and may join with other parts of the flower stem. These structures together form a fruit that encloses the seeds.

The term *fruit,* biologically speaking, applies to any seed that is enclosed within its embryo wall. The term applies to the things we usually think of as fruits, such as apples, grapes, and strawberries. However, foods such as peas, corn, beans, rice, cucumbers, and tomatoes, which we commonly call vegetables, are also fruits. Whether it tastes sweet or not, if it contains a seed enclosed inside the ovary wall, it is a fruit.

The ovary wall surrounding a simple fruit may be fleshy, as it is in grapes and tomatoes, or tough, like the pod of a bean. In some fruits, such as peaches and cherries, the inner wall of the ovary is attached rigidly to the surface of the seed. In others, such as the maple, the dry fruit forms an aerodynamic shape that helps the seed whirl gracefully down when it is released from the parent plant.

CHECKPOINT *What is a fruit?*

Figure 24–10 **As seeds mature, the ovary walls thicken to form a fruit that encloses the developing seeds.** Like the flowers from which they develop, fruits vary in structure. They can contain one seed, as in the lychee nut, or several, as in the apple. Fruits also have different amounts of tissue, which often relates to the mode of seed dispersal.

TIME SAVER

SECTION RESOURCES

Print:
- ***Laboratory Manual A,*** Chapter 24 Lab
- ***Laboratory Manual B,*** Chapter 24 Lab
- ***Teaching Resources,*** Lesson Plan 24–2, Adapted Section Summary 24–2, Adapted Worksheets 24–2, Section Summary 24–2, Worksheets 24–2, Section Review 24–2, Enrichment
- ***Reading and Study Workbook A,*** Section 24–2
- ***Adapted Reading and Study Workbook B,*** Section 24–2

Technology:
- ***iText,*** Section 24–2
- ***Transparencies Plus,*** Section 24–2

Seed Dispersal

What are fruits for, and why have they been favored by natural selection? They are not there to nourish the seedling—the endosperm does that. Why should an entire phylum of plants have seeds that are wrapped in an additional layer of nutrient-packed tissue—tissue that is later discarded when the fruit is released from the plant? It seems pointless, but in evolutionary terms, it makes all the sense in the world.

Think of the blackberries that grow wild in the forests of North America. Each seed is enclosed in a sweet, juicy fruit, making it a tasty treat for all kinds of birds and mammals. What good does all that sweetness do the fruit? All it does is get the seed eaten! Well, believe it or not, that's exactly the point.

Dispersal by Animals The seeds of many plants, especially those with sweet, fleshy fruits, are eaten by animals, such as the cedar waxwing in **Figure 24–11.** The seeds are covered with tough coatings that protect them from digestive chemicals, enabling them to pass through an animal's digestive system unharmed. The seeds then sprout in the feces eliminated from the animal. **Seeds dispersed by animals are typically contained in fleshy, nutritious fruits.** These fruits provide nutrition for the animal and also help the plant disperse its seeds—often to areas where there is less competition with the parent plants.

Dispersal by Wind and Water Animals are not the only means by which plants can scatter their seeds. Seeds are also adapted for dispersal by wind and water. **Seeds dispersed by wind or water are typically lightweight, allowing them to be carried in the air or to float on the surface of the water.** The seeds of ash and maple trees are encased in winglike structures that spin and twirl as they are released, helping them glide considerable distances from their parent plants. Westerners are familiar with tumbleweed plants, shown in **Figure 24–12.** These plants break off at their roots and tumble along the dry plains, scattering their seeds as they are blown by the wind. An example of a seed that is dispersed by water is the coconut. This seed contains a liquid endosperm layer (the "milk" of the coconut). A coconut is buoyant enough to float in seawater within its protective coating for many weeks. Water dispersal is one reason for the success of this species in reaching remote islands.

▲ **Figure 24–11 Seeds that are dispersed by animals typically contain fleshy, sweet tissue.** A cedar waxwing feasts on mountain ash berries. Berries are enclosed in sugary tissue that is eaten by birds or other animals. Berries contain seeds that pass through the animal and are dispersed away from the parent plant.

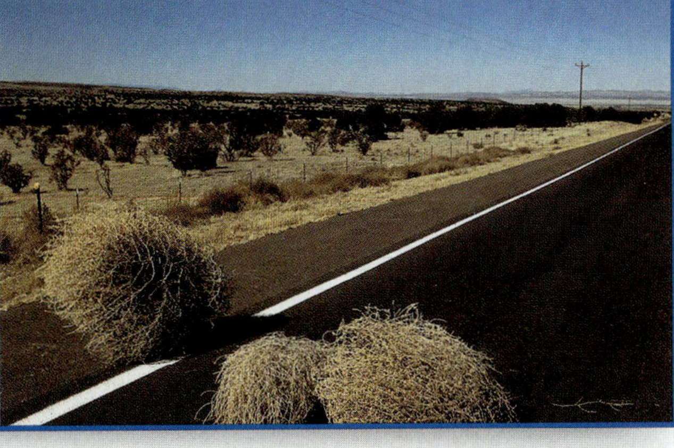

▶ **Figure 24–12 Wind-dispersed seeds are typically lightweight.** Tumbleweed plants, which live in a hot, dry, and windy environment, release small seeds as the plants are blown along open stretches of land. **Inferring** *How do the structural adaptations of tumbleweeds enable them to survive?*

Seed Dispersal

Build Science Skills

Inferring Explain that the seeds of some plants, such as clover, do not germinate well unless their seed coats have been scarified, or scratched. Mention that clover is eaten by grazing animals. You could ask: **How does scarification ensure that the clover seed will germinate, and how does the seed's trip through an animal's digestive system improve the conditions in which it begins to grow?** *(Scarification by enzymes and acid in the animal's digestive system weakens the tough seed coat, improving the chances of its taking up water and germinating. The animal's feces, which surround the seed, may improve the fertility of the nearby soil.)* L2

Build Science Skills

Designing Experiments Divide the class into groups, and have each group brainstorm a way of determining whether fruit-eating animals are attracted to the color of fruit or to its scent. Each group should formulate a hypothesis and design an experiment to test the hypothesis. Remind students to include a control in their experimental design. Give groups a chance to share their ideas. *(Students should hypothesize that animals are attracted either more by scent or more by color. For example, they might design an experiment to see if animals are attracted to fruit when they cannot see it because it is in a darkened room or when they cannot detect its scent because the fruit is wrapped in plastic.)* L2

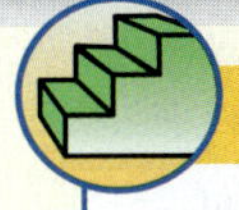

UNIVERSAL ACCESS

Inclusion/Special Needs

Give students a chance to differentiate between seeds that are dispersed by animals and those that are dispersed by wind. Provide a large selection of various fruits, such as berries, apples, maple seeds, and dandelion seeds. Challenge students to characterize each fruit and infer from those characteristics the process by which the seed is dispersed. L1 L2

Advanced Learners

Invite students to learn more about the relationships between animals and seed plants. Encourage them to find a specific example of an animal dispersing plant seeds. Challenge them to make inferences about what would happen to the plant if the animal became endangered or extinct. Students can display a poster in the classroom summarizng their findings. L3

Answers to . . .

CHECKPOINT *A fruit is a ripened ovary that contains angiosperm seeds.*

Figure 24–12 *Tumbleweed seeds are widely dispersed by wind, ensuring that at least a few seeds land in locations favorable for growth with less competition from the parent plants.*

24–2 (continued)

Seed Dormancy

Analyzing Data

7IIE 7.c

Help students put the data in an experimental context. Ask: **What variables do the data represent?** *(Climate of origin, temperature during dormancy, and whether or not germination occurred)* **What other variables do you think the plant biologists had to control?** *(Possible answers include the amount of water the seeds received and the temperature at which germination took place.)* L2

Answers

1. Chilling increases the percentage of seeds that germinate, especially for seeds from Ontario.
2. The increase in the percentage of seeds that germinate at lower temperatures might indicate an adaptation to lower temperatures.

Build Science Skills

Applying Concepts Explain that arctic lupines are plants whose seeds can remain dormant for thousands of years. Ask: **Why might this be an advantage for a plant living in an arctic environment?** *(For much of the year, the arctic is extremely cold and dark. Lupine seeds might have to wait many years until a suitable combination of soil, moisture, light, and temperature would allow for successful germination.)* L2

Analyzing Data

Temperature and Seed Germination

Arisaema dracontium—"green dragon"—is a plant that grows from the southern United States to Canada. The graph shows germination properties of *Arisaema* seeds gathered from Clinton, Ontario, and from Baton Rouge, Louisiana. Seeds from both locations were stored at two different temperatures: 3°C and 24°C. The graph indicates the rate of seed germination following storage at these different temperatures.

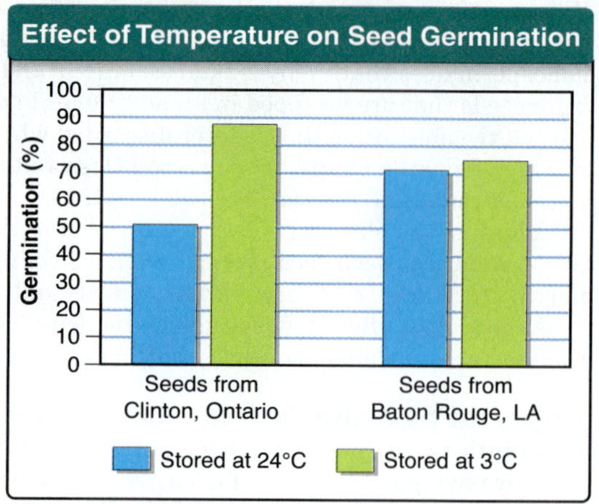

1. **Interpreting Graphics** What effect does chilling have on germination of seeds from Ontario? How does chilling affect the seeds from Louisiana?
2. **Formulating Hypotheses** Keeping in mind that annual temperatures are much lower in Ontario than in Louisiana, describe how the different rates of seed germination might be explained in terms of adaptation to the local climate.

7IIE 7.c

Seed Dormancy

Some seeds sprout so rapidly that they are practically instant plants. Bean seeds are a good example. With proper amounts of water and warmth, a newly planted mature bean seed rapidly develops into a bean plant. But many seeds will not grow when they first mature. Instead, these seeds enter a period of **dormancy,** during which the embryo is alive but not growing. The length of dormancy varies in different plant species. **Environmental factors such as temperature and moisture can cause a seed to end dormancy and germinate.**

Seed dormancy can be adaptive in several ways. It can allow for long-distance dispersal, as in a coconut that floats across the sea for weeks or even months until it washes ashore. It may also allow seeds to germinate under ideal growth conditions. The seeds of many temperate plants do not germinate during the summer or winter, since the extremes of temperature would make it impossible for seedlings to survive. Instead, most seeds germinate in the spring, when conditions are best for growth. The long period of cold temperatures during which the seeds are dormant is required before growth can begin.

Other environmental conditions can end seed dormancy. Some pine trees, for example, produce seeds in sealed cones. These seeds remain dormant until the high temperatures generated by forest fires cause the cones to open, as shown in **Figure 24–13.** This process activates the seeds, allowing the plants to reclaim the forest floor quickly after a fire.

▼ **Figure 24–13** **Environmental factors such as temperature and moisture can end dormancy.** The cones of this bishop pine open and release seeds only after being exposed to the heat of a forest fire. **Inferring** *How do the adaptations of this tree illustrate the results of natural selection?*

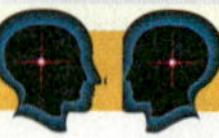

TEACHER TO TEACHER

How about a scavenger hunt? Have groups of three students bring in three examples each of fruits that they have found around the school. Make sure that students wear disposable plastic gloves and have been instructed how to properly collect specimens. (Students may not purchase their fruits.) Have each group sort the fruits according to their particular method of seed dispersal. Make a class chart showing all the different types of fruits and seed dispersal methods.

—*Kathey A. Roberts*
Biology Teacher
Lakeside High School
Hot Springs, AR

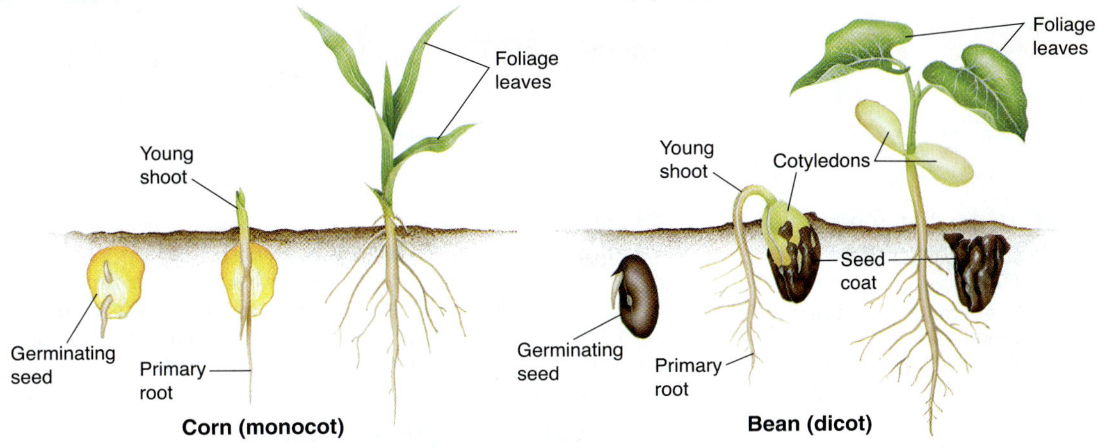

▲ **Figure 24–14** The corn seedling (left) is a monocot in which the shoot grows directly upward, protected by its sheath. The garden bean (right) is a dicot in which the cotyledons emerge aboveground. **Applying Concepts** *What roles do cotyledons play in the early growth of plants?*

Seed Germination

Seed **germination** is the early growth stage of the plant embryo. **Figure 24–14** shows germination in monocots and dicots. When seeds germinate, they absorb water. The absorbed water causes food-storing tissues to swell, cracking open the seed coat. Through the cracked seed coat, the young root emerges and begins to grow.

Recall that monocots have a single cotyledon, or seed leaf. In most monocots, the single cotyledon remains underground. The growing shoot emerges while protected by a sheath. In dicots, which have two cotyledons, germination takes place in one of two ways. In some species, the cotyledons emerge aboveground, protecting the stem and first foliage leaves. The cotyledons may then wither and drop off the plant or become photosynthetic, such as in the pumpkin. In other species, such as the garden pea, the cotyledons stay underground and provide a food source for the growing seedling. In this case, the young stem grows longer and forms an arch that protects the delicate shoot tip.

For: Links on seed structure and function
Visit: www.SciLinks.org
Web Code: cbn-7242

24–2 Section Assessment

1. **Key Concept** Describe what happens as fertilized angiosperm seeds mature.
2. **Key Concept** Compare the typical structure of seeds that are dispersed by animals to those dispersed by wind and water.
3. **Key Concept** Why is it adaptive for some seeds to remain dormant before they germinate?
4. **Critical Thinking Applying Concepts** The seeds of a bishop pine germinate only after they have undergone a forest fire. Evaluate the significance of this structural adaptation.
5. **Critical Thinking Applying Concepts** Describe which adaptations of a seed would enable it to germinate in a vacant lot where a building once stood.

Writing in Science

Writing a Book

Imagine that you are writing a children's book on seeds and that you are working on the chapter on dispersal. Write from one to three paragraphs on seed dispersal by wind. *Hint:* Try to include details that you would have found appealing when you were about 8 years old.

24–2 Section Assessment

1. Nutrients flow into the flower tissue and support the development of the embryo within the seed. Parts of the ovule toughen to form a seed coat, and the ovary wall thickens and joins with other flower parts to form a fruit that encloses and protects the seed.
2. Seeds dispersed by animals typically have a tough coat and are contained in fleshy fruits. Seeds dispersed by wind and water typically are lightweight and may be encased in winglike structures.
3. It allows for long-distance dispersal and for germination under ideal conditions.
4. It enables the species to recover after a fire and ensures that seedlings grow in a favorable environment.
5. Dispersal by wind and possibly animals

Seed Germination

Demonstration

Place a variety of seeds, including monocots such as corn and dicots such as beans, between two wet paper towels on a plate. Place plastic wrap over the plate, and put the plate in a warm place where it will not be disturbed. After a few days, remove the plastic and the top paper towel and point out the germinated seeds. Have students locate the root and shoot of each seed and determine whether it is a monocot or dicot. L2

Download a worksheet on seed structure and function for students to complete, and find additional teacher support from NSTA SciLinks.

3 ASSESS

Evaluate Understanding

Read the boldface sentences and the sentences defining the Vocabulary terms, in each case leaving blank the most significant term in the sentence. Call on students to fill in the blanks.

Reteach

Work with students to create flowcharts summarizing seed germination. Create one flowchart for monocots and another for dicots.

Writing in Science

Seed characteristics should be described in relation to their being dispersed by animals, wind, or water.

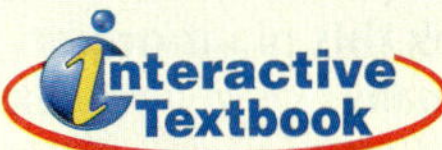

If your class subscribes to the iText, use it to review the Key Concepts in Section 24–2.

Answers to . . .

Figure 24–13 *Seeds that germinate only after a fire not only enable a species to recover but also allow seedlings to grow without competition from parent plants.*

Figure 24–14 *Cotyledons protect the young shoot as it emerges and provide food to the seedling.*

Section 24–3

 7 2.a

1 FOCUS

Objectives

24.3.1 ***Identify*** the forms of plant vegetative reproduction.
24.3.2 ***Describe*** plant propagation.
24.3.3 ***Identify*** the major food-supply crops for humans.

Guide for Reading

Vocabulary Preview

Point out that the word *vegetative* in the term *vegetative reproduction* means "growing" and not "having to do with vegetables," as students might assume. Explain that the term *vegetative reproduction* refers to any type of reproduction in plants that involves vegetative, or growing, tissues instead of reproductive tissues and seeds.

Reading Strategy

Students should list the following methods of growing food plants: seeds, cuttings, grafting, and budding.

2 INSTRUCT

Vegetative Reproduction

Demonstration

Bring to class several different plants or plant parts that grow by vegetative reproduction. You might include a spider plant, a clump of crab grass, and a daffodil bulb. As you display each plant or plant part in turn, ask: **How do you think this plant or part reproduces asexually?** *(A spider plant produces plantlets that can take root to form new plants. Crab grass produces horizontal stems or stolons that can put down roots to form new plants. A daffodil bulb produces roots and shoots when placed underground and given moisture.)* L2

24–3 Plant Propagation and Agriculture

7 2.a. Students know the differences between the life cycles and reproduction methods of sexual and asexual organisms.

Guide for Reading

 **Key Concepts**
- What forms of vegetative reproduction occur in plants?
- What is plant propagation?
- Which crops are the major food supply for humans?

Vocabulary
vegetative reproduction
stolon
grafting
budding

Reading Strategy: Using Prior Knowledge Before you read the section, make a list of methods that humans use to grow food plants such as fruit trees and grains. As you read, add new information to your list.

Seed plants have been essential to human life from the beginnings of our existence on this planet. The earliest humans gathered plants for food, shelter, and medicine. Over time, humans learned to collect and plant edible seeds, thus domesticating wild plants. The technology of growing crops and propagating desirable plant species is the basis of modern society.

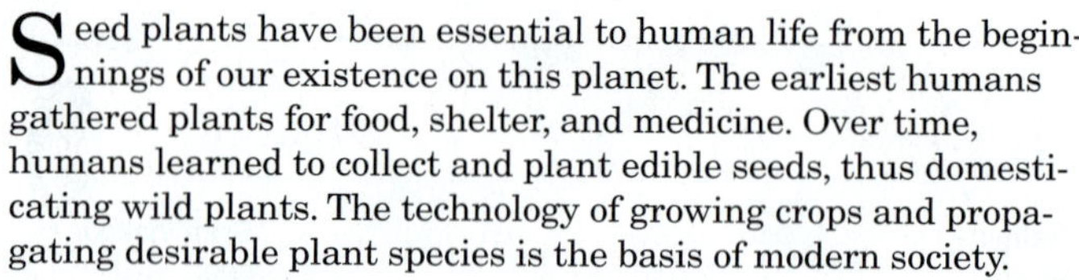

Vegetative Reproduction

Although the chapter so far has concentrated on patterns of sexual reproduction, this section deals with the many flowering plants that reproduce asexually by **vegetative reproduction.** Growing a new plant by mitosis alone, vegetative reproduction enables a single plant to produce many offspring genetically identical to itself. This process takes place naturally in many plants, and it is also used as a technique by horticulturalists who want to produce many copies of an individual plant.

Vegetative reproduction includes the production of new plants from horizontal stems, from plantlets, and from underground roots. Because vegetative reproduction does not involve pollination or seed formation, it can enable plants to reproduce very quickly. Several species of angiosperms, such as the spider plant shown in **Figure 24–15,** produce tiny plants, or plantlets, at the tips of elongated stems. If the parent plant is knocked over or if plantlets fall to the soil, they can take root and grow into new plants. New plants can also grow from the leaves of a parent plant if the leaves fall to the ground under conditions that allow them to root.

Another way in which plants reproduce vegetatively is by growing horizontal stems. Strawberry plants, shown in **Figure 24–16,** send out long trailing stems called **stolons** that produce roots when they touch the ground. Once the roots are well established, each stolon may be broken, forming a new plant that is truly independent of its parent. Bamboo plants grow long underground stems that can send up new shoots in several places. In fact, bamboo forests that cover huge areas are often the descendants of a single bamboo plant that reproduced asexually.

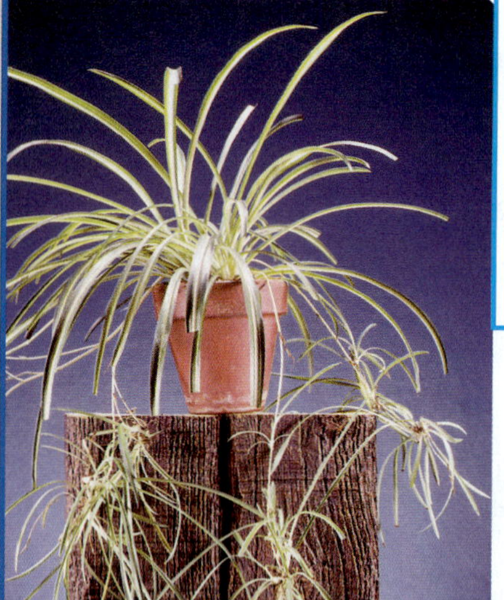

Figure 24–15 **The production of plantlets is a form of asexual reproduction.** The spider plant produces plantlets at the tips of elongated stems. When a plantlet reaches the soil, it can develop roots and grow into a new spider plant.

TIME SAVER — SECTION RESOURCES

Print:
- ***Teaching Resources,*** Lesson Plan 24–3, Adapted Section Summary 24–3, Section Summary 24–3, Worksheets 24–3, Section Review 24–3, Enrichment
- ***Reading and Study Workbook A,*** Section 24–3

Technology:
- ***iText,*** Section 24–3
- ***Transparencies Plus,*** Section 24–3

◀ **Figure 24–16** The strawberry plant reproduces vegetatively by producing thin, horizontal stems called stolons. Each node along the stolon produces roots that anchor the plant into the ground. **Applying Concepts** *Describe how asexual reproduction might allow a plant to become established rapidly in a new area.*

Plant Propagation

Sometimes the characteristics of a particular plant are so attractive or beneficial that horticulturists want to make many exact copies of the plant. But the growers also want to avoid the variation that would result if the plant reproduced sexually by seeds. In addition, new varieties of some plants, such as grapefruits and navel oranges, do not produce seeds. **In plant propagation, horticulturists use cuttings, grafting, or budding to make many identical copies of a plant or to produce offspring from seedless plants.**

Cuttings One of the simplest ways to reproduce plants vegetatively is by cuttings. A grower "cuts" from the plant a length of stem that includes a number of buds containing meristematic tissue. That stem is then partially buried in soil or in a special rooting mixture. Some common plants, such as coleus, root so easily that no other treatment is necessary. The cuttings of many woody plants, however, do not develop roots easily. To help cuttings of these plants form roots, growers use mixtures of plant hormones called rooting powders.

Grafting and Budding Grafting and budding are used to reproduce seedless plants and varieties of woody plants that do not produce strong root systems. In both of these techniques, new plants are grown on plants that have strong root systems. To do this, a piece of stem or a lateral bud is cut from the parent plant and attached to another plant. The cut piece is called the scion, and the plant to which it is attached is called the stock. When stems are used as scions, the process is called **grafting,** shown in **Figure 24–17.** When buds are used as scions, the process is called **budding.**

Grafting usually works best when plants are dormant because the wounds created can heal before new growth starts. In all cases, grafts are successful only if the vascular cambiums of scion and stock are firmly connected to each other.

CHECKPOINT *What are the different techniques used to propagate woody plants?*

▼ **Figure 24–17** **Plant propagation uses a variety of techniques to make identical copies of a single plant.** Here, a scion of a commercial orange tree is being grafted to a larger, established tree.

Build Science Skills

Observing Provide each student with a raw sweet potato. Show students how to insert four toothpicks into the sweet potato around the middle so that the bottom half of it can be suspended in a container of water. Have students keep the water level above the bottom of the sweet potato and observe it each day until it starts to grow roots and shoots. Ask: **What type of reproduction is represented by the growth of the sweet potato?** *(Vegetative reproduction)* L1 L2

Plant Propagation

Demonstration

Obtain two small sections of a tree branch and use them to demonstrate grafting. Using a sharp knife, make a deep notch in the end of one section (the stock) and cut the end of the other section (the scion) into a V-shaped point. (Use care when cutting with the sharp knife.) Insert the pointed end of the scion into the deeply notched end of the stock. Wrap the two pieces tightly together with cloth tape, making sure that the cambium layers are properly aligned. Explain that the stock and scion must be fastened tightly together, their secondary cambia touching, before grafts will grow together. Ask: **If the stock came from a red delicious apple tree and the scion came from a yellow delicious apple tree, what color fruit would the scion produce?** *(Yellow)* L2 L3

ESL SUPPORT FOR ENGLISH LANGUAGE LEARNERS

Comprehension: Prior Knowledge

Beginning On the board, write the key idea found on page 624: *Most of the people of the world depend on a few crop plants, such as wheat, rice, and corn, for the bulk of their food supply.* Read the sentence out loud. On the board, write a list of food crops commonly grown in your region of the U.S. Ask the students to name or draw a picture of the main food crops grown in their native country. L1

Intermediate Pair each ESL student with a student proficient in English. Have the students draw a T chart, one side labeled *food* and the other side labeled *crop plant.* The students should list pairs of terms such as *bread-wheat* and *tortilla-corn* in the T chart. Make sure each list includes foods from the United States and the ESL student's native country. Students can add visual examples to the T chart by using pictures from magazines or newspapers. L2

Answers to . . .

CHECKPOINT *Cuttings, grafting, and budding*

Figure 24–16 *It might put out stolons that take root to form new plants all around the original plant.*

24–3 (continued)

Build Science Skills

Inferring Bring two oranges to class, one with seeds and one without. Cut the oranges in half, and ask students to explain how they differ. Challenge students to explain how offspring could be produced from each type of orange. *(The orange with seeds can be grown from seed. The orange without seeds must be grown by grafting or budding.)* L1 L2

Agriculture

Use Community Resources

Ask a local farmer or the owner of a greenhouse in the community to visit the class and describe advances in agricultural or horticultural methods that are used in his or her type of business. Possible methods might include plant propagation techniques, the use of pesticides or herbicides, soil-conservation practices such as crop rotation or contour plowing, the use of irrigation, or the introduction of genetically engineered plants. Ask the speaker to address how the methods have increased production, led to the production of better plants, or otherwise improved the business. Encourage students to ask questions. L2 L3

Biology and History

Provide interested students with the challenge of continuing the timeline to the present. They should add more recent changes in agriculture, such as the invention of the iron plow and the development of genetically engineered food crops.

Writing in Science

Arrange to have students share their research so that they can compare the effect of climate and other factors on the type of crop that was important in each region. Students should give examples of ways in which the cultivation of crops in the region they selected affected the human population and its culture. L2 L3

▲ **Figure 24–18** **Most of the world's food supply comes from a few crop plants.** Rice, here being planted by hand, is a staple crop in China and many nations of Southeast Asia.

Agriculture

The importance of agriculture—the systematic cultivation of plants—should be obvious, even to those of us who live in urban areas and seldom visit a farm. Modern farming is the foundation on which human society is built. North America has some of the richest, most productive cropland in the world. As a result, farmers in the United States and Canada produce so much food that they are able to feed millions of people around the world as well as their own citizens.

Worldwide Patterns of Agriculture Many scholars now trace the beginnings of human civilization to the cultivation of crop plants. Evidence suggests that agriculture developed separately in many parts of the world about 10,000 to 12,000 years ago. Once people discovered how to grow plants for food, the planting and harvesting of crops tended to keep them in one place for much of the year, leading directly to the establishment of social institutions. Even today, agriculture, shown in **Figure 24–18**, is the principal occupation of more human beings than any other activity.

Thousands of different plants—nearly all of which are angiosperms—are raised for food in various parts of the world. **Most of the people of the world depend on a few crop plants, such as wheat, rice, and corn, for the bulk of their food supply.** The same crops are also used to feed livestock.

Biology and History

The Evolution of Agriculture

More than 10,000 years ago, humans began a gradual transition from hunter-gatherer societies to civilizations that were reliant on cultivated crops—many of which are still cultivated today.

8000 BC
Inhabitants of the Middle East begin to cultivate wheat. The change from gathering a crop in the wild to farming it eventually contributes to the rise of one of the earliest Middle Eastern civilizations.

7000 BC
Chilies and avocados are cultivated as important additions to the diets of Mesoamerican people. Chilies are used for flavoring foods, and avocados provide vitamins and oils.

5500 BC
Barley is cultivated in the Nile Valley of Egypt. About 2000 years later, farming settlements are united throughout the Nile Valley, and Egyptian culture flourishes.

8000 — 7000 — 6000

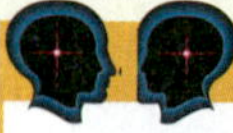

TEACHER TO TEACHER

To introduce students to the concept of vegetative reproduction, I ask them to bring small jars to class. I have the students fill the jars almost to the top with water. After carefully removing stems from either coleus plants or impatiens plants, I have the students place the stems in the water. I instruct students to write the date the cutting was inserted into the water on the jar, using a permanent marker. For the next two weeks, I have the students observe their cuttings every day, recording any changes they see. Hairlike roots should begin to appear in about one to two weeks. Then, I plant the rooted cuttings in soil so that students see how the plants continue to grow. This also gives me a new supply of plants that I can use for this activity next year.

—Janice Lagatol
Biology Teacher
Fort Lee High School
Fort Lee, NJ

You may not have thought of it this way, but the food we eat from most crop plants is taken from their seeds. In monocots, nearly all of this food is stored in the endosperm. Worldwide, most of humanity depends for food on the endosperm of only a few carefully cultivated species of grass. The pattern in the United States is similar. Roughly 80 percent of all U.S. cropland is used to grow just four crops: wheat, corn, soybeans, and hay. Of these crops, three—wheat, corn, and hay—are derived from grasses.

CHECKPOINT *What is agriculture?*

Changes in Agriculture The discovery and introduction of new plants has changed human history. Before they were discovered in the Americas, many important crops—including corn, peanuts, beans, and potatoes—were unknown in Europe. The introduction of these plants changed European agriculture rapidly. Within a century, many of these foods had become important parts of the European diet. We think of boiled potatoes, for example, as traditional staples of German and Irish cooking, but 400 years ago they were new items in the diets of Europeans.

The efficiency of agriculture has been improved through the selective breeding of crop plants and improvements in farming techniques. The corn grown by Native Americans, for example, was developed more than 8000 years ago from teosinte (tee-oh-SIN-tee), a wild grass found in Mexico.

Writing in Science

The domestication of all major crops had a huge impact on the growth of civilizations. Choose one of the crops discussed below and research how that crop contributed to the rise of civilization and culture in that region.

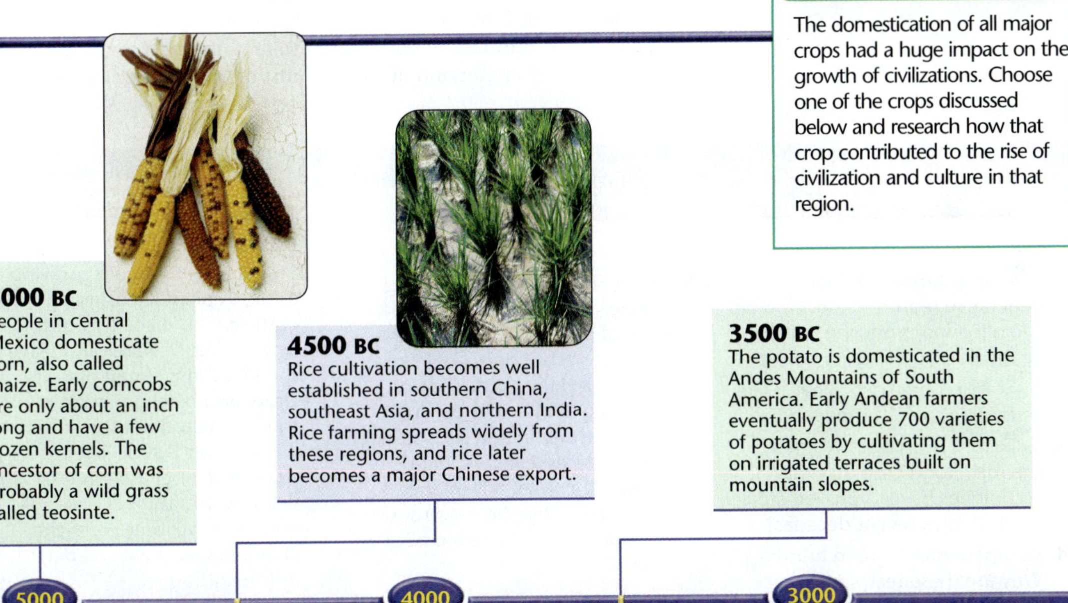

5000 BC
People in central Mexico domesticate corn, also called maize. Early corncobs are only about an inch long and have a few dozen kernels. The ancestor of corn was probably a wild grass called teosinte.

4500 BC
Rice cultivation becomes well established in southern China, southeast Asia, and northern India. Rice farming spreads widely from these regions, and rice later becomes a major Chinese export.

3500 BC
The potato is domesticated in the Andes Mountains of South America. Early Andean farmers eventually produce 700 varieties of potatoes by cultivating them on irrigated terraces built on mountain slopes.

BIO INSIGHTS — HISTORY OF SCIENCE

Grafting in history

There is evidence that the Chinese understood grafting as early as 1000 B.C. The Greek botanist Theophrastus, who is sometimes called the founder of botany, wrote about grafting and other forms of vegetative reproduction in the second century B.C. in his book *Causes of Plants*. The history of the navel orange provides an example of the benefits of careful grafting. Around 1820, a farmer near Bahia, Brazil, noticed that the fruit on one branch of one of his orange trees—probably a natural mutant—was superior to all his other fruit. Through grafting, he multiplied that form of the fruit. Some 50 years later, a missionary sent a dozen of the orange trees to Washington, D.C., and two of those were sent to a farm near Riverside, California. From those two trees sprang almost the entire navel orange industry the world over.

Make Connections

Health Science Have students compare the nutrient content of unbleached wheat flour, brown rice, and cornmeal. Students should display their findings in a compare/contrast table that lists the amount of nutrients contained in one serving of each of the three foods. Also, have students compare the nutrients in their table with recommended daily allowances. Ask: **Which major nutrient are these foods high in?** *(Carbohydrates)* **Which major nutrient are these foods low in?** *(Protein)* Point out how each food is also high in some vitamins and minerals but low in others. Explain that people in many countries often have little to eat besides one of these staple crops. Ask: **If you ate almost nothing except one of these foods, how healthy do you think you would be?** *(You probably would not be very healthy, because you would be deficient in protein and other important nutrients.)* L2 L3

Answer to . . .

CHECKPOINT *Agriculture is the systematic cultivation of plants.*

24–3 (continued)

Use Visuals

Figure 24–19 Check students' understanding of the graph. Ask: **What was the corn yield in the United States in 1974?** *(About 71 bushels per acre)* **In which year was the corn yield the highest?** *(1994)* **What do you think explains the ups and downs from year to year in the graph?** *(Variations in the weather from year to year)* L1 L2

3 ASSESS

Evaluate Understanding

Ask students to write a paragraph summarizing worldwide patterns of agriculture.

Reteach

Have pairs of students work together to create graphic organizers comparing and contrasting vegetative reproduction and plant propagation. Call on several pairs of students to share their graphic organizers with the class.

Sharpen Your Skills

The diagram for Day 1 should show the cutting—a stem with some leaves—in a beaker of water. By Day 8, roots should be growing from the stem in the water. Students should label both diagrams. Changes in the cutting that students might list include growth of roots and leaves.

If your class subscribes to the iText, use it to review the Key Concepts in Section 24–3.

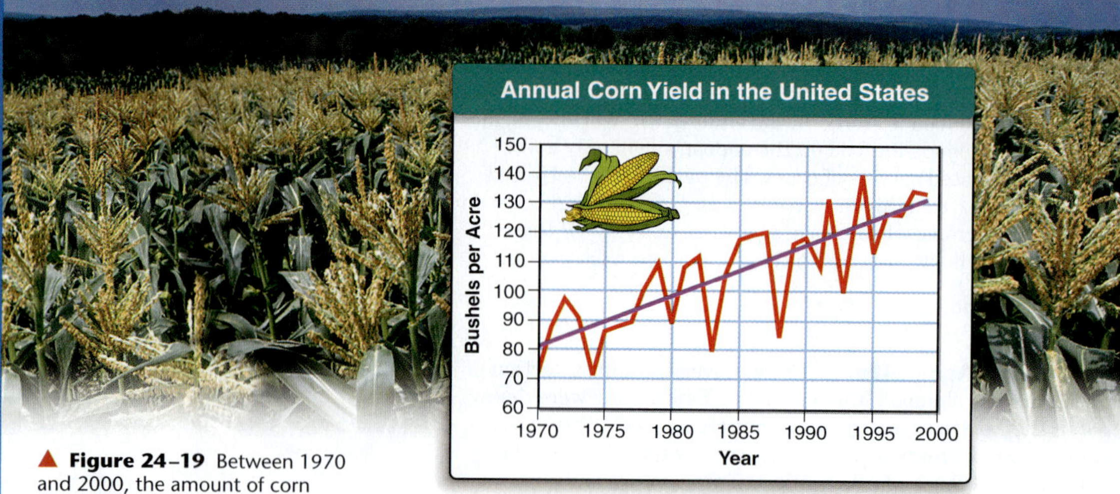

▲ **Figure 24–19** Between 1970 and 2000, the amount of corn grown per acre in the United States increased more than 60 percent. A field of corn, also called *Zea mays,* is shown in the photograph. **Interpreting Graphics** *Describe the trend shown in the graph for the years 1983 and 1988.*

Recall from Chapter 13 that selective breeding is a method for improving a species by allowing only organisms with certain traits to produce the next generation. In more recent times, other familiar crops have been the product of selective breeding. Sugar beets, the source of most refined sugar from the United States, were produced from the ordinary garden beet using selective breeding. Plants as different as cabbage, broccoli, and Brussels sprouts have been developed from a single species of wild mustard.

Improvements in farming techniques have contributed to dramatic improvements in crop yields, as shown in **Figure 24–19.** Some of the most important techniques have been the use of pesticides and fertilizers. These improvements have lowered the price of food and enabled farmers to feed many more people without any expansion of the amount of land under cultivation.

24–3 Section Assessment

1. **Key Concept** Define vegetative reproduction. How do the offspring produced compare to the parent plant?
2. **Key Concept** What is the purpose of plant propagation?
3. **Key Concept** What are the main food crops? What techniques have improved crop yields during recent decades?
4. Compare grafting and budding. Why are these techniques preferable to sexual propagation of woody plants?
5. **Critical Thinking Inferring** Dandelions employ an unusual form of reproduction that produces seeds but does not involve meiosis and the production of haploid gametes. The pollen produced within flowers is sterile and produces seeds without fertilization. What advantages might this system have over sexual reproduction of viable seeds?

Sharpen Your Skills

Predicting

Imagine that you are growing a *Coleus* plant by using a cutting. You place the cutting in a beaker of water and leave the plant in a sunny place. Draw and label a picture of the way you think the cutting will look on Day 1. Then, draw and label a picture of the way you think it will look on Day 8. Write a list of the changes you think will occur in the cutting.

24–3 Section Assessment

1. Vegetative reproduction is the production of new plants from horizontal stems, plantlets, or underground roots. The offspring are genetically identical to the parent plant.
2. To make identical copies of a plant or to produce offspring from seedless plants
3. The main crops are wheat, rice, and corn. Selective breeding, pesticides, and fertilizers have improved crop yields.
4. In grafting, a stem is attached. In budding, a bud is attached. Both involve growing a new plant by cutting a piece from a parent plant with desirable traits and attaching it to another plant that has a strong root system.
5. This system might have the advantages of not requiring other plants nearby in order for pollination and fertilization to occur and of producing new plants that are genetically identical to the parent plant.

Answer to . . .

Figure 24–19 *Both 1983 and 1988 showed a significant drop in the annual corn yield.*

Design an Experiment

BIIE 1.a

Investigating Pollen Tube Growth

In this investigation, you will design an experiment to test a hypothesis about the chemical signals that steer the growth of pollen tubes toward the ovary.

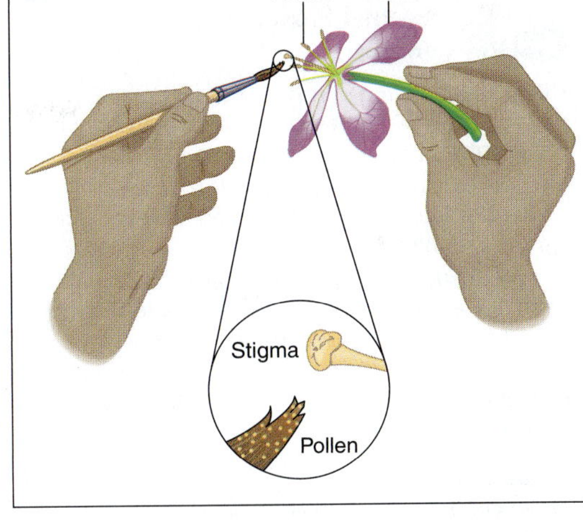

Problem

What controls the direction of pollen tube growth?

Materials

- flowering plants, such as beans or *Brassicas*
- hand lens
- small paintbrush
- forceps
- pollen nutrient solution
- pollen nutrient solution without calcium
- concentrated calcium chloride solution
- dissecting probe
- microscope slides
- coverslips
- dropper pipette

Skills

Designing Experiments, Controlling Variables

Design Your Experiment

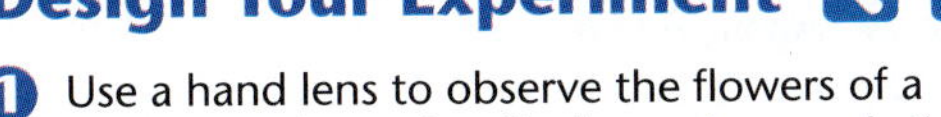

1. Use a hand lens to observe the flowers of a flowering plant. Identify the anthers and stigma of a flower.
2. Use a small paintbrush to transfer pollen from several flowers to the stigmas of other flowers.
3. Use forceps to transfer several anthers to a microscope slide. Add a drop of pollen nutrient solution. Gently tap the anthers with the tip of a dissecting probe to release pollen.
4. Discard the anthers and add a coverslip. Observe the pollen with the microscope at low power. Make a labeled drawing of your observations.
5. Your teacher will provide slides containing pollen that has been in pollen nutrient solution for several hours. Observe these slides with the microscope. Record your observations.
6. Pollen tubes have been found to grow toward calcium or pieces of ovaries. Design an experiment to test the hypothesis that calcium is the chemical signal that guides the growing pollen tube toward the ovary.
7. As you plan your investigative procedures, refer to the Lab Tips box on page 55 for information on demonstrating safe practices, making wise choices in the use of materials, and selecting equipment and technology.
8. In your plan, also be sure to define and control all important variables. If observing pollen tube growth in a flower directly is too difficult, you will need to choose some other method to test the hypothesis. Have your teacher check your plan before you begin your experiment.

Analyze and Conclude

1. **Applying Concepts** The pollen of most plants will not germinate in pure water. What function of the stigma and style did the pollen nutrient solution replace?
2. **Observing** Did the pollen tubes grow toward a source of calcium? Toward ovary tissue?
3. **Drawing Conclusions** In many experiments, pollen tubes grow toward either calcium or ovary tissue. From these results, could you conclude that calcium directs pollen tube growth toward the ovary in flowers? Explain.

Go Further

Formulating Hypotheses Use scientific literature to form a hypothesis on the effect of light on pollen tube growth.

Design an Experiment

BIIE 1.a

Objective Students will be able to design an experiment to determine what controls the direction of pollen tube growth. L2

Skills Focus **Designing Experiments, Controlling Variables**

Time 45 minutes

Advance Prep

- Prepare the pollen nutrient solution with 30% sucrose, 0.01% boric acid, and 0.02% calcium chloride.
- Prepare the pollen nutrient solution without calcium in the same way, but omit the calcium chloride.
- Prepare a 1% solution of calcium chloride for the concentrated calcium chloride solution.
- Prepare slides with several grains of pollen in a drop of nutrient solution, cover the slides with a coverslip, and let them stand for several hours before students use them in step 5 of the lab.

Teaching Strategies Have students read the entire procedure. Point out how the procedure models the pollination of flowers by insects. Then, ask: **What role does the paintbrush play?** *(The role of the insect pollinator)* **What role is played by the pollen nutrient solution on the slide?** *(The role of the stigma and style)*

Design Your Experiment

6. One experimental design is to begin as described in step 3, but using pollen nutrient solution without calcium. Then, add a coverslip. Place a drop of concentrated calcium chloride solution next to the coverslip so that it touches the solution under the coverslip. Let the slide stand for several hours, and then look at it under a microscope to see whether the pollen tubes have grown toward the calcium chloride solution. Other designs are also possible.

Analyze and Conclude

1. It replaced the nutrients provided by the stigma and style.

2. In general, pollen tubes grow toward calcium and toward ovary tissue.

3. The results would support but not prove the hypothesis. Proof would require demonstrating a biochemical mechanism by which calcium directs pollen tube growth.

Go Further

A possible hypothesis is that light is required for pollen tube growth and affects the rate and direction of growth.

Chapter 24 Study Guide

Study Tip

Have students rewrite the boldface sentences as questions and answer them. They should look up the answers to any questions they are unsure of.

Thinking Visually

1. Mature sporophyte; **2.** Pollen cone; **3.** Seed cone; **4.** Pollen grains; **5.** Female gametophyte; **6.** Zygote; **7.** Seed

Chapter 24 Assessment

Reviewing Content

1. a	**5.** b	**9.** c
2. a	**6.** a	**10.** d
3. a	**7.** d	**11.** c
4. a	**8.** a	

Understanding Concepts

12. A gametophyte plant produces male and female gametes (sperm and eggs). A sporophyte plant produces spores.

13. An ovule is a structure in which the female gametophyte develops. When a pollen grain reaches an ovule, the grain splits open and grows a pollen tube, which contains two haploid sperm nuclei. Once the pollen tube reaches the female gametophyte, one sperm nucleus disintegrates and the other fertilizes the egg within the female gametophyte.

14. Male pollen cones produce male gametophytes called pollen grains. Later, one of the nuclei in the pollen grain divides to produce two sperm nuclei.

15. Check students' diagrams against Figure 24–4 for accuracy.

16. The carpel, which produces the female gametophytes, is the innermost part of the flower. Each carpel has a broad base that contains an ovary. The diameter narrows into a stalk called the style. At the top of the style is the stigma.

17. Pollen may be transferred from plant to plant by wind, insects, birds, or bats.

Chapter 24 Study Guide

24–1 Reproduction With Cones and Flowers

 7 2.a

 **Key Concepts**

- Reproduction in gymnosperms takes place in cones, which are produced by a mature sporophyte plant.
- Flowers are reproductive organs that are composed of four kinds of specialized leaves: sepals, petals, stamens, and carpels.
- Reproduction in angiosperms takes place within the flower. Following pollination and fertilization, the seeds develop inside protective structures called fruits.
- Most gymnosperms are wind pollinated, whereas most flowering plants are pollinated by animals.

Vocabulary

pollen cone, p. 610 • seed cone, p. 610
ovule, p. 610 • pollen tube, p. 611
sepal, p. 612 • petal, p. 612
stamen, p. 612 • filament, p. 612
anther, p. 612 • carpel, p. 612
ovary, p. 612 • style, p. 612
stigma, p. 612 • embryo sac, p. 615
endosperm, p. 616 • double fertilization, p. 616

24–2 Seed Development and Germination

 **Key Concepts**

- As angiosperm seeds mature, the ovary walls thicken to form a fruit that encloses the developing seeds.
- Seeds dispersed by animals are typically contained in fleshy, nutritious fruits.
- Seeds dispersed by wind or water are typically lightweight, allowing them to be carried in the air or to float on the surface of the water.
- Environmental factors such as temperature and moisture can cause a seed to end dormancy and germinate.

Vocabulary

dormancy, p. 620
germination, p. 621

24–3 Plant Propagation and Agriculture

 7 2.a

Key Concepts

- Vegetative reproduction includes the production of new plants from horizontal stems, cuttings, leaves, plantlets, and underground roots.
- Horticulturists use plant propagation to make many identical copies of a plant or to produce offspring from seedless plants.
- Most of the people of the world depend on a few crop plants, such as wheat, rice, and corn, for the bulk of their food supply.

Vocabulary

vegetative reproduction, p. 622
stolon, p. 622 • grafting, p. 623
budding, p. 623

Thinking Visually

Use the following terms to complete the flowchart about reproduction in gymnosperms: *female gametophyte, seed, pollen cone, mature sporophyte, seed cone, zygote, pollen grains.*

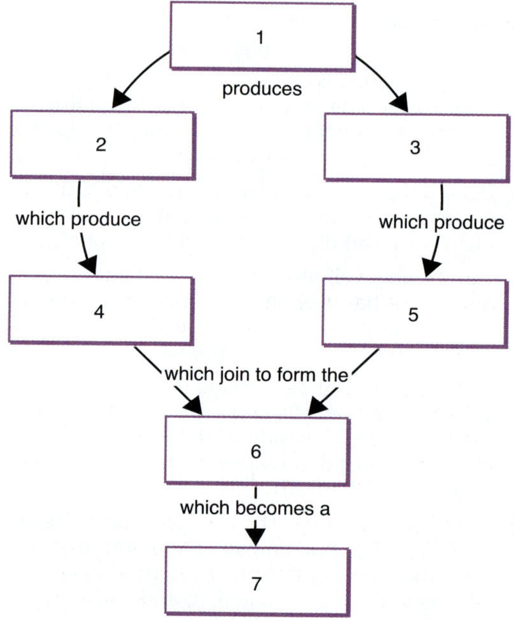

CHAPTER RESOURCES

Print:
- ***Teaching Resources,*** Chapter Vocabulary Review, Graphic Organizer, Chapter 24 Tests: Levels A and B

Technology:
- ***Computer Test Bank,*** Chapter 24 Test
- ***iText,*** Chapter 24 Assessment

Chapter 24 Assessment

Interactive textbook with assessment at PHSchool.com

Reviewing Content

Choose the letter that best answers the question or completes the statement.

1. Two structures specialized for sexual reproduction in seed plants are
   a. cones and flowers.
   b. cones and lateral buds.
   c. lateral and terminal buds.
   d. meristems and flowers.
2. Which of the following is NOT true of reproduction in a pine tree?
   a. The pollen tube contains two diploid sperm.
   b. One sperm fertilizes the egg.
   c. One sperm disintegrates.
   d. The zygote grows into an embryo.
3. In angiosperms, the structures that produce the male gametophyte are called the
   a. anthers.
   b. sepals.
   c. pollen tubes.
   d. stigmas.
4. The outermost circle of flower parts consists of several
   a. sepals. c. carpels.
   b. petals. d. corollas.
5. Pollination occurs when pollen lands on the
   a. style. c. filament.
   b. stigma. d. anther.
6. The thickened ovary wall of a plant may join with other parts of the flower stem to become the
   a. fruit. c. endosperm.
   b. seed. d. cotyledon.
7. The seed leaves of a flowering plant are known as
   a. endosperm. c. radicles.
   b. carpels. d. cotyledons.
8. In seed plants, the structure that encloses the male gametophyte and transports it to another plant is called a
   a. pollen grain. c. flower.
   b. seed. d. pollinator.
9. The period during which the embryo is alive but not growing is called
   a. fertilization. c. dormancy.
   b. vegetative growth. d. germination.
10. The process in which a single plant produces many offspring genetically identical to itself is called
    a. sexual reproduction.
    b. agriculture.
    c. dormancy.
    d. vegetative reproduction.
11. The illustration below shows the germination of a pea plant. The feature labeled A is a(an)
    a. anther. c. cotyledon.
    b. seed coat. d. root.

Understanding Concepts

12. What is a gametophyte plant? How is it different from a sporophyte plant?
13. What is an ovule? Describe what happens to an ovule of a pine cone if it is fertilized by the male gametophyte.
14. What role do male pine cones play in reproduction?
15. Draw and label a diagram showing the stages in the life cycle of a typical gymnosperm.
16. What is a carpel? Where is it located in a typical flower?
17. Describe at least two ways in which pollen is transferred from one plant to another.
18. Briefly describe each stage in the life cycle of an angiosperm, starting with germination of the seed.
19. What purposes are served by seed dormancy?
20. What is vegetative reproduction?
21. Describe three ways in which plants can be propagated artificially.
22. What is the function of endosperm?

HOMEWORK GUIDE

Section:	Questions:
Section 24–1	1–5, 7, 8, 12–18, 22–25, 30
Section 24–2	6, 9, 11, 19, 26–29, 32
Section 24–3	10, 20, 21, 31

If your class subscribes to the iText, your students can go online to access an interactive version of the Student Edition and a self-test.

(Continued from page 628)

18. Germination is followed by growth of the sporophyte. In anthers, cells undergo meiosis, reproducing haploid spore cells that develop into pollen grains. In ovules, cells undergo meiosis, producing eggs. Pollen grains are released from the anther and deposited on a stigma. After pollination and fertilization, eggs develop into zygotes, ovules develop into seeds, and ovaries develop into fruits. Seeds are disbursed, and the cycle repeats.

19. Seed dormancy can allow for long-distance dispersal, and it may allow seeds to germinate under ideal conditions.

20. Vegetative reproduction is asexual reproduction in which new plants are produced from horizontal stems, plantlets, or underground roots.

21. Plants can be propagated asexually by cuttings, grafting, and budding. In cuttings, a length of stem is cut and placed in a rooting mixture. In grafting and budding, a piece of a parent plant is attached to another plant.

22. Endosperm is the stored food supply in angiosperm seeds that nourishes the embryo plant.

Chapter 24 Assessment

Critical Thinking

23. It provides a sticky landing site for pollen grains. Without it, pollen grains would not stick to the cones and fertilization would not occur.

24. Fruit could not form on flowers that lack carpels because fruit develops from the ovary, which is part of the carpel.

25. If pollen grains of wind-pollinated flowers were sticky, they might stick to anything, not just the female flowers. To test their answers, students should suggest a controlled experiment.

26. One possible answer is that, in such harsh environments, a seed might have to wait many years before suitable conditions for germination and growth occur.

27. Students' experimental designs will vary. One possible answer is to choose seeds with large cotyledons and remove the cotyledons before planting. Leave the cotyledons on some seeds as a control.

28. In monocots, the single cotyledon remains within the seed. The growing shoot emerges while protected by a sheath. In some species of dicots, the cotyledons emerge above the ground and protect the first foliage leaves. In other species, the cotyledons remain below the ground, providing a food source for the developing seedling.

29. The seed needs water from the soil for germination. The root emerges first to obtain water and nutrients from the soil.

30. Pollen is produced inside the anthers, labeled C. The stigma is labeled A; it is where pollen grains land. Seeds develop in the ovary, labeled F. A sepal is labeled G and a petal is labeled H.

31. Grafting is the method of artificial propagation that fuses together pieces of two different plants, so it would be an appropriate method for producing an apple tree that will bear two different kinds of apples. Cuttings, however, generate clones of a plant but do not combine two different plants.

Chapter 24 Assessment

Critical Thinking

23. Inferring What is the function of the pollination drop (sticky substance) secreted by female pine cones? What would happen if it were not present?

24. Predicting Some plants form flowers that produce stamens but no carpels. Could fruit form on one of these flowers? Explain your answer.

25. Formulating Hypotheses Would you expect pollen grains of wind-pollinated flowers to be sticky? How would you test the accuracy of your answer?

26. Inferring The seeds of lupines, an arctic plant, can remain dormant for thousands of years. Why might this trait be important to a plant in an arctic environment?

27. Designing Experiments A friend suggests that seeds do not need cotyledons to grow. You argue that cotyledons are important to seeds. Design an experiment that shows the effect of removing cotyledons on seed growth.

28. Comparing and Contrasting How is seed germination similar in monocots and dicots? How is it different?

29. Inferring What does a plant need that makes it necessary for seed germination to start with the emergence of a root rather than a shoot?

30. Interpreting Graphics The diagram below shows the parts of a typical flower.

a. Inside which structure is pollen produced? What is the name of this structure?
b. What structure is represented by A? What is its function?
c. In which structure do seeds develop?
d. What are the names of structures G and H?

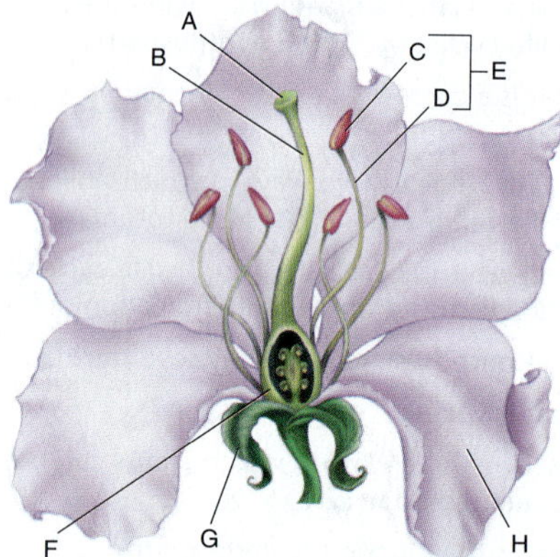

31. Applying Concepts Suppose that you want to produce an apple tree that will bear two different kinds of apples. Which method of artificial propagation would you choose? Why would the other method of artificial propagation not be suitable?

32. Applying Concepts Many ecologists have argued that the historic policy of preventing all wildfires in the western United States has affected the structures of western ecosystems. How might the example of seed dormancy in certain types of pines support their case?

Focus on the BIG Idea

Evolution Review the discussion of coevolution in Chapter 17, Section 17–4. Discuss how the coevolution of plants and the animals that pollinate them might have taken place. (*Hint*: What are several characteristics of plants that represent adaptations to animal pollinators? What characteristics of these animals are the result of coevolution with plants?)

Writing in Science

Write a paragraph that compares and contrasts the most important aspects of reproduction in gymnosperms and angiosperms. Then, explain why the flower is the key to the evolutionary success of the angiosperm. (*Hint:* Develop a concept map before you begin to write.)

Performance-Based Assessment

Create a Video Prepare a video presentation in which you demonstrate different types of vegetative reproduction. If possible, prepare the video over a long period so that you can show the growth of propagated plants. Include in your documentary a discussion of the advantages and disadvantages of vegetative reproduction.

For: An interactive self-test
Visit: PHSchool.com
Web Code: cba-7240

32. Certain species of pines require the heat of a fire for seed germination. If forest fires are prevented, these pines will not produce more seedlings and will eventually be crowded out by other plant species that do not require heat for germination.

Focus on the BIG Idea

Coevolution is the process by which two organisms evolve in response to changes in each other. A relationship exists between the evolution of angiosperms and the evolution of modern insects, mammals, and birds. Animals rely on the plants for food, and the plants rely on the animals for reproduction.

Standards Practice

Success Tracker™
Online at PHSchool.com

Test-Taking Tip When answering questions pertaining to experimental situations, read all of the questions first. Then, read the passage carefully and examine any accompanying data, looking for the specific information required to answer the questions.

Directions: Choose the letter that best answers the question or completes the statement.

1. Which of the following are NOT part of a flower?
   A sepals
   B petals
   C stamens
   D stems
2. Where in a flower are pollen grains produced?
   A sepals
   B carpels
   C anthers
   D ovary
3. Which part of a flower develops into a fruit?
   A pollen tube
   B sepals
   C anthers
   D ovary
4. Which flower structure includes all the others listed below?
   A style
   B carpel
   C stigma
   D ovary
5. Which is an example of vegetative reproduction?
   A grafting
   B budding
   C both A and B
   D none of the above
6. What is endosperm?
   A a 3N cell
   B food-rich tissue
   C tissue formed from the second stage of double fertilization
   D all of the above
7. The trumpet honeysuckle has long, red, narrow tubular flowers. What is its most likely means of pollination?
   A wind
   B water
   C bee
   D hummingbird
8. A scientist wants to artificially pollinate a flower. In what part of a typical flower would she find the pollen grains?
   A sepal
   B carpel
   C anther
   D ovary
9. All of the following are fruits EXCEPT
   A tomato.
   B corn.
   C beet.
   D cucumber.

Questions 10–11

A scientist measured the average time it took different fruits to fall 1 meter (m) from the parent tree. Assume that for every second a fruit falls, it is carried 1.5 m away from the parent tree.

Relationship Between Fruit Type and Dispersal Time

Type of Tree	Average Time (sec) for Seed to Fall 1 m
Norway maple	0.98
Silver maple	0.64
White ash	0.30
Shagbark hickory	0.16
Red oak	0.16

Norway maple
Silver maple
White ash
Shagbark hickory
Red oak

10. Which fruit was carried the farthest from the parent tree?
    A silver maple
    B Norway maple
    C white ash
    D red oak
11. According to these data, what benefit does a winged fruit have over an acorn?
    A It is lighter.
    B It is heavier.
    C It will travel farther.
    D none of the above

Standards Practice

1. D
2. C
3. D
4. B
5. C
6. D
7. D
8. C
9. C
10. B
11. C

Success Tracker™
Online at PHSchool.com

Have students check their understanding of the chapter by logging onto Success Tracker.

Writing in Science

Students should compare the reproductive organs (cones and flowers) of gymnosperms and angiosperms, as well as differences in pollination and seed dispersal. The flower is key to the evolutionary success of angiosperms because of its ability to attract pollinators, but more important is its development into a fruit that protects the seed and enhances its chances for dispersal.

Performance-Based Assessment

Students' videos should demonstrate an understanding of cuttings, grafting, and budding.

Your students can independently test their knowledge of the chapter and print out their test results for your files.

Chapter Planner 25 Plant Responses and Adaptations

Section and Section Objectives	Time	STANDARDS NCLB	STANDARDS Biology	Activities and Labs
25–1 Hormones and Plant Growth, pp. 633–638 **25.1.1** ***Describe*** patterns of plant growth. **25.1.2** ***Explain*** what plant hormones are. **25.1.3** ***Describe*** how auxins, cytokinins, gibberellins, and ethylene affect plant growth.	2 periods (1 block)			**SE:** ***Inquiry Activity,*** How are plants adapted to their environments?, p. 632 L2 **TE:** ***Demonstrations,*** pp. 633 L1 L2, 637 L2 **TE:** ***Build Science Skills,*** pp. 635 L1 L2, 635 L2, 636 L2 **SE:** ***Analyzing Data,*** Auxins and Plant Growth, p. 637 L2 **TE:** ***Make Connections,*** p. 638 L2 **LMA:** Chapter 25 Lab L2 L3 **BTM:** Concept 7 L2 L3
25–2 Plant Responses, pp. 639–642 **25.2.1** ***Explain*** what plant tropisms are. **25.2.2** ***Explain*** what photoperiodism is. **25.2.3** ***Describe*** how deciduous plants prepare for winter.	1 period (1/2 block)			**TE:** ***Demonstration,*** p. 640 L2 **SE:** ***Quick Lab,*** Can a plant find its way through a maze?, p. 640 L2 **TE:** ***Build Science Skills,*** p. 642 L1 L2 **LMB:** Chapter 25 Lab L1 L2
25–3 Plant Adaptations, pp. 643–646 **25.3.1** ***Summarize*** how plants are adapted to different environments. **25.3.2** ***Describe*** how plants obtain nutrients. **25.3.3** ***Explain*** how plants use chemical defenses.	1 period (1/2 block)			**TE:** ***Build Science Skills,*** pp. 643 L2, 644 L2 **SE:** ***Issues in Biology,*** Should Herbal Remedies Be Regulated?, p. 647 L2 **SE:** ***Real-World Lab,*** Using Hormones to Control Plant Development, pp. 648–649 L1 L2 L3
Chapter Assessment, pp. 650–653	1 period (1/2 block)			

ACTIVITY PLANNER

SE: *Inquiry Activity*, p. 632; 15 min.; desert and rain forest plants

TE: *Demonstration*, p.633; 10 min.; plant such as geranium

TE: *Build Science Skills*, p. 635; 10 min.; balloon, transparent tape

TE: *Build Science Skills*, p. 635; 5 min. for setup, 5 min. for observation; plant such as coleus in four-sided plastic pot

TE: *Build Science Skills*, p. 636; 15 min.; twigs with terminal and lateral buds

TE: *Demonstration*, p. 637; 20 min. for setup, 10 min. for observations; wheat seeds, potting soil, 2 small flats, gibberellic acid, ethyl alcohol, distilled water, spray bottle

TE: *Make Connections*, p. 638; 10 min.; artificially ripened fruit

TE: *Demonstration*, p. 640; 5 min.; *Mimosa pudica*

SE: *Quick Lab*, p. 640; 20 min. for setup, 5 min. for observation every 2 to 3 days for 2 weeks; scissors, masking tape, cardboard box, cardboard dividers, bean seeds, small flowerpots containing commercial potting soil

TE: *Build Science Skills*, p. 642; 10 min.; dormant tree branches

TE: *Build Science Skills*, p. 643; 15 min.; aquatic plants

TE: *Build Science Skills*, p. 644; 15 min.; various desert plants

SE: *Real-World Lab*, pp. 648–649; 45 min. for setup, 10 min. for observation several times over 3 weeks; coleus plants, dissecting pins, scalpels, metric rulers, rooting compound, commercial potting soil, paper cups, flat wooden toothpicks

PLANNING KEY

Ability Levels
for students performing . . .
below grade level L1
at grade level L2
above grade level L3

Print Components
SE Student Edition
TE Teacher's Edition
RSW Reading & Study Workbook A
ARSW Adapted Reading & Study Workbook B
TR Teaching Resources
IF Investigations in Forensics
LA Lab Assessment
BTM Biotechnology Manual
IDM Issues and Decision Making
LW Lab Worksheets
LMA Laboratory Manual A
LMB Laboratory Manual B

Tech Components
CTB Computer Test Bank
BD BioDetectives DVD
TP Transparencies Plus
PLM Probeware Lab Manual
ABC ABC DVD Library
LS Lab Simulations
VL Virtual Labs

Interactive textbook with assessment at PHSchool.com

Program Resources	Assessment	Media and Technology
TR: Lesson Plan 25–1, Section Summary, p. 149 L1, p. 159 L2, Worksheets, pp. 152–154 L1, pp. 161–163 L2 **LW:** Chapter 25 Real-World Lab L1 L2 L3 **RSW:** Section 25–1 L2 **ARSW:** Section 25–1 L1	**SE:** 25–1 Section Assessment, p. 638 **TR:** Section Review 25–1	**iText:** Section 25–1 **TP:** 25–1 Interest Grabber, Section Outline, Hormone Action in Plants, Figure 25–3, Figure 25–5
TR: Lesson Plan 25–2, Section Summary, p. 150 L1, p. 159 L2, Worksheets, pp. 155–156 L1, pp. 164–165 L2, Enrichment L2 L3 **RSW:** Section 25–2 L2 **ARSW:** Section 25–2 L1	**SE:** 25–2 Section Assessment, p. 642 **TR:** Section Review 25–2	**iText:** Section 25–2 **TP:** 25–2 Interest Grabber, Section Outline, Photoperiodism and Flowering
TR: Lesson Plan 25–3, Section Summary, p. 151 L1, p. 160 L2, Worksheets, p. 157 L1, pp. 166–167 L2 **RSW:** Section 25–3 L2 **ARSW:** Section 25–3 L1	**SE:** 25–3 Section Assessment, p. 646 **TR:** Section Review 25–3	**iText:** Section 25–3 **TP:** 25–3 Interest Grabber, Section Outline, Compare/Contrast Table
	SE: Chapter 25 Assessment, pp. 650–653 **TR:** Chapter Vocabulary Review, Graphic Organizer, Chapter 25 Test **LA:** Laboratory Assessment 7	**iText:** Chapter 25 Assessment **CTB:** Chapter 25 Test

Go Online
Students can do research, share data, and test their knowledge online.

PRESSED FOR TIME?

To Preview the Chapter
- Have students read the Key Concepts and Vocabulary terms in each section.
- Have students examine all the figures and read their captions.

To Cover the Chapter Quickly
- Have students read Patterns of Plant Growth and Plant Hormones in Section 25–1 and Tropisms in Section 25–2.
- Assign questions 1 and 2 in Section Assessment 25–1 and questions 1 and 5 in Section Assessment 25–2.

To Review the Chapter
- Assign Sections 25–1 through 25–3 in the Reading and Study Workbook or the Adapted Reading and Study Workbook.
- Assign the Section Review for Sections 25–1 through 25–3 and the Chapter Vocabulary Review for Chapter 25 in the Teaching Resources.

CHAPTER 25

ENGAGE/EXPLORE

Inquiry Activity

Objective Students will be able to identify characteristics that make plants adapted to their environments.

Skills Focus **Classifying, Formulating Hypotheses, Predicting**

Materials Two groups of plants: desert plants, such as cactus and crown-of-thorns, and rain forest plants, such as philodendron, fern, and African violet

Time 15 minutes

Safety Check for students with allergies to plants. Warn students to avoid cactus spines and not to crush the leaves of plants.

Strategy You can place the plants at stations around the classroom and have students observe the plants at each station.

Expected Outcome Students should observe that some desert plants have thick leaves and cuticles while others have a few small leaves or no leaves at all; spines or thorns; and thick, fleshy stems. Rain forest plants have large, broad leaves with thinner cuticles and may be vines with aerial roots. Both types of plants have chlorophyll, stems, roots, and some type of leaves.

Think About It

1. Variations of desert plants that students might identify include reduced surface area and leaf size; thick leaves and cuticles; spines or thorns; and thick, fleshy stems. Rain forest plants have larger, thinner leaves and thinner cuticles, and fewer of them have thorns or spines. Vines are also common rain forest plants.
2. The reduced leaf surface area and thick cuticle of desert plants help conserve water. The thick, green, fleshy stems of cactuses perform photosynthesis and store water. Tropical rain forest plants have large, broad leaves that capture the dim light available below the tree canopy and provide a large surface area for evaporation that helps to keep the plants cool. Climbing vines are also common in the rain forest, where they grow up around trees toward the brighter light high in the leaf canopy.
3. Student drawings and descriptions should include adaptations both to dry conditions (such as deep roots or thick cuticles) and to cold conditions (such as seeds, bulbs, or woody perennial stems that can survive through winter dormancy).

CHAPTER 25

Plant Responses and Adaptations

In what may be its last moments, an ant peers down into a pitcher plant's specialized leaf. The leaf is lined with slippery hairs and is filled with digestive enzymes that will extract nutrients from any unsuspecting prey.

Inquiry Activity

How are plants adapted to their environments?

Procedure  

1. Examine several desert plants and several rain forest plants. Note any differences between these two groups of plants. Record your observations.
2. List the characteristics that vary between desert plants and rain forest plants. List any characteristics that you observed in both types of plants.

Think About It

1. **Classifying** What variations did you identify that distinguish desert plants and rain forest plants?
2. **Formulating Hypotheses** How could these variations help desert and rain forest plants survive in their environments?
3. **Predicting** Draw a real or an imaginary plant that is adapted for warm, dry summers and rainy, cold winters. Write a paragraph describing the adaptations of your plant.

Assess Prior Knowledge

Ask students: **How does a plant "know" how to grow right side up?** *(Some students might know that stems grow against the force of gravity and roots grow with it.)* Invite students to share their observations of unusual plant growth. List their observations on the board. At the end of the chapter, challenge students to give an explanation for these unusual growth patterns.

25–1 Hormones and Plant Growth

Unlike most animals, plants do not have a rigidly set organization to their bodies. Cows have four legs, ants have six, and spiders have eight; but tomato plants do not have a predetermined number of leaves or branches. However, plants such as the baobab tree in **Figure 25–1** show distinct patterns of growth. As a result, you can easily tell the difference between a tomato plant and a corn plant, between an oak tree and a pine tree.

Patterns of Plant Growth

Although plant growth is not determined precisely, it still follows general patterns that differ among species. What controls these patterns of development? Biologists have discovered that plant cells send signals to one another that indicate when to divide and when not to divide, and when to develop into a new kind of cell.

There is another difference between growth in plants and animals. Once most animals reach adulthood, they stop growing. In contrast, even plants that are thousands of years old continue to grow new needles, add new wood, and produce cones or new flowers, almost as if parts of their bodies remained "forever young." As you have learned, the secrets of plant growth are found in meristems, regions of tissue that can produce cells that later develop into specialized tissues. Meristems are found at places where plants grow rapidly—the tips of growing stems and roots, and along the outer edges of woody tissues that produce new growth every year.

If meristems are the source of plant growth, how is that growth controlled and regulated? Plants grow in response to environmental factors such as light, moisture, temperature, and gravity. But how do roots "know" to grow down, and how do stems "know" to grow up toward light? How do the tissues of a plant determine the right time of year to produce flowers? How do plants ensure that their growth is evenly balanced—that the trunk of a tree grows large enough to support the weight of its leaves and branches? The answers to these questions involve the actions of chemicals that direct, control, and regulate plant growth.

Guide for Reading

 **Key Concepts**
- What are plant hormones?
- How do auxins, cytokinins, gibberellins, and ethylene affect plant growth?

Vocabulary
hormone
target cell
phototropism
auxin
gravitropism
lateral bud
apical dominance
herbicide
cytokinin
gibberellin
ethylene

Reading Strategy: Finding Main Ideas
Before you read, skim the section to identify the key ideas about plant hormones. Then, read the section carefully, making a list of supporting details for each main idea.

▶ **Figure 25–1** All plants follow a highly regulated pattern of growth that continues throughout the life of the plant. This pattern of growth leads to distinct shapes, such as the thick trunk and widely spaced branches of this baobab tree. **Applying Concepts** *In which plant tissue does growth occur?*

SECTION RESOURCES

Print:
- ***Laboratory Manual A,*** Chapter 25 Lab
- ***Teaching Resources,*** Lesson Plan 25–1, Adapted Section Summary 25–1, Adapted Worksheets 25–1, Section Summary 25–1, Worksheets 25–1, Section Review 25–1
- ***Reading and Study Workbook A,*** Section 25–1
- ***Adapted Reading and Study Workbook B,*** Section 25–1
- ***Lab Worksheets,*** Chapter 25 Real-World Lab
- ***Biotechnology Manual,*** Concept 7

Technology:
- ***iText,*** Section 25–1
- ***Transparencies Plus,*** Section 25–1

Section 25–1

1 FOCUS

Objectives

25.1.1 ***Describe*** patterns of plant growth.
25.1.2 ***Explain*** what plant hormones are.
25.1.3 ***Describe*** how auxins, cytokinins, gibberellins, and ethylene affect plant growth.

Guide for Reading

Vocabulary Preview

Call students' attention to the Vocabulary terms *phototropism* and *gravitropism.* Explain that the root word *tropism* is from a Greek word meaning "turning." Challenge students to infer the meaning of the two terms. (*Phototropism: turning due to light; gravitropism: turning due to gravity*)

Reading Strategy

Have students read the Key Concepts in the text to find the main ideas about plant hormones. Students can organize the main ideas and supporting details under the heads Auxins, Cytokinins, Gibberellins, and Ethylene.

2 INSTRUCT

Patterns of Plant Growth

Demonstration

Display a common houseplant, such as a geranium, that has had the soil removed from the roots. Also be sure the stem can be plainly seen. Ask: **How does growth occur in this plant?** (*Growth is the result of cell division and cell enlargement.*) **Where do these kinds of cell activities take place in this plant?** (*In the meristematic regions at the tips of the roots and stems*) Next, show a small woody twig and a tree branch. Ask: **In what other way does this kind of plant stem grow?** (*Some plants grow in thickness as well as in length.*) L1 L2

Answer to . . .

Figure 25–1 *In meristems*

25–1 (continued)

Plant Hormones

Use Visuals

Figure 25–2 Ask: **Where are hormone-producing cells in a plant?** (*In apical meristems, young leaves, roots, and growing flowers and fruits*) **What are target cells?** (*Cells that contain a hormone receptor and are affected by particular hormones*) **How do hormones affect target cells?** (*By changing their metabolism, affecting their growth rate, or activating the transcription of certain genes*) **In the figure, how do you think the hormones produced in the flower will affect the target cells in the flower bud?** (*They will probably affect their growth rate so that the flower opens and activate the transcription of certain genes so that the reproductive organs in the flower mature.*) L2

Download a worksheet on plant hormones for students to complete, and find additional teacher support from NSTA SciLinks.

Auxins

Build Science Skills

Designing Experiments Some students might enjoy trying to duplicate Charles and Francis Darwin's experiment with phototropism, described in the text and illustrated in Figure 25–3. Like the Darwins, they can use oat seedlings, which are fast growing. They can use aluminum foil for the opaque caps and bands on the oat shoots and clear plastic wrap for the clear caps. Have students share their results with the class. L2

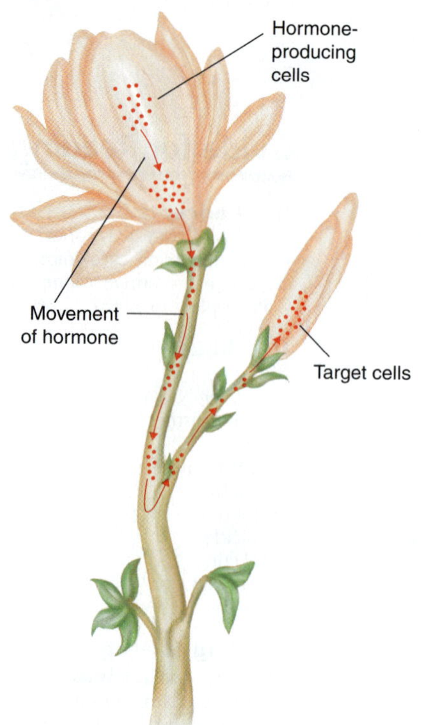

▲ **Figure 25–2** **Plant hormones are chemical substances that control patterns of development as well as plant responses to the environment.** Hormones are produced in apical meristems, in young leaves, in roots, and in growing flowers and fruits. From their place of origin, hormones move to other parts of the plant, where target cells respond in a way that is specific to the hormone.

For: Links on plant hormones
Visit: www.SciLinks.org
Web Code: cbn-7251

Plant Hormones

In plants, the division, growth, maturation, and development of cells are controlled by a group of chemicals called hormones. A **hormone** is a substance that is produced in one part of an organism and affects another part of the same individual. **Plant hormones are chemical substances that control a plant's patterns of growth and development, and the plant's responses to environmental conditions.**

The general mechanism of hormone action in plants is shown in **Figure 25–2.** As you can see, the hormone moves through the plant from the place where it is produced to the place where it triggers its response. The portion of an organism affected by a particular hormone is known as its **target cell** or target tissue. To respond to a hormone, the target cell must contain a hormone receptor—usually a protein—to which the hormone binds. If the appropriate receptor is present, the hormone can exert an influence on the target cell by changing its metabolism, affecting its growth rate, or activating the transcription of certain genes. Cells that do not contain receptors are generally unaffected by hormones.

Different kinds of cells may have different receptors for the same hormone. As a result, a single hormone may affect two different tissues in different ways. For example, a particular hormone may stimulate growth in stem tissues but inhibit growth in root tissues.

✓ CHECKPOINT *In which cells do hormones carry out their functions?*

Auxins

The experiment that led to the discovery of the first plant hormone was carried out by Charles Darwin. In 1880, Darwin and his son Francis published a book called *The Power of Movement in Plants.* In this book, they described an experiment in which oat seedlings demonstrated a response known as phototropism. **Phototropism** is the tendency of a plant to grow toward a source of light.

Figure 25–3 shows an experiment similar to the one carried out by the Darwins. Notice that the tip of one of the oat seedlings was covered with an opaque cap. This plant did not bend toward the light, even though the rest of the plant was uncovered. However, if an opaque shield was placed a few centimeters below the tip, the plant would bend toward the light as if the shield were not there. Clearly, something was taking place at the tip of the seedling.

UNIVERSAL ACCESS

Less Proficient Readers

After students have read the section, instruct them to review the definitions of the Vocabulary terms. Then, have them separate the words into groups based on their own methods of classification. From these word groups, students should devise a graphic organizer, such as a concept map, to show the relationships among the words. L1

Advanced Learners

The first cytokinin to be discovered was zeatin, which was isolated from corn kernels in 1964. Since then, three other cytokinins have been identified, including kinetin. Kinetin is the cytokinin that has been most used in research. Encourage students to learn more about cytokinins and their roles in plant growth and aging. Ask students to present their findings to the class in an oral report or poster display. L3

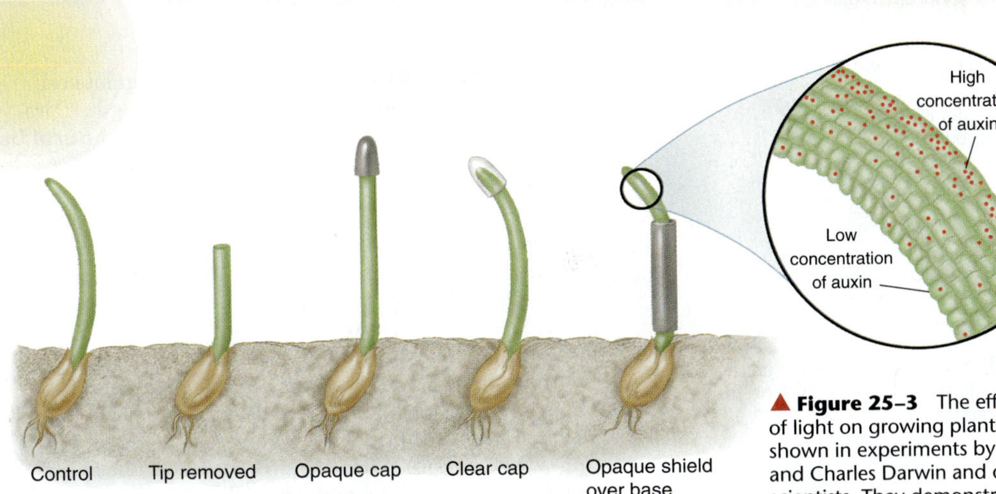

▲ **Figure 25–3** The effect of light on growing plants was shown in experiments by Francis and Charles Darwin and other scientists. They demonstrated that chemical substances are produced in the growing tip of a plant. **Auxins stimulate cell elongation.** A higher concentration of auxins accumulate in the shaded part of a stem and cause the plant to bend toward a light source.

Auxins and Phototropism The Darwins suspected that the tip of each seedling produced substances that regulated cell growth. Forty years later, these substances were identified and named **auxins.** **Auxins are produced in the apical meristem and are transported downward into the rest of the plant. They stimulate cell elongation.** When light hits one side of the stem, a higher concentration of auxins develops in the shaded part of the stem. This change in concentration stimulates cells on the dark side to elongate. As a result, the stem bends away from the shaded side and toward the light. Recent experiments have shown that auxins migrate toward the shaded side of the stem, possibly due to changes in membrane permeability in response to light.

Auxins and Gravitropism Auxins are also responsible for **gravitropism,** which is the response of a plant to the force of gravity. By mechanisms that are still not understood, auxins build up on the lower sides of roots and stems. In stems, auxins stimulate cell elongation, helping turn the trunk upright, as shown in **Figure 25–4.** In roots, however, the effects of auxins are exactly the opposite. There, auxins inhibit cell growth and elongation, causing the roots to grow downward.

Auxins are also involved in the way roots grow around objects in the soil. If a growing root is forced sideways by an obstacle such as a rock, auxins accumulate on the lower side of the root. Once again, high concentrations of auxins inhibit the elongation of root cells. The uninhibited cells on the top elongate more than the auxin-inhibited cells on the bottom of the root. As a result, the root grows downward.

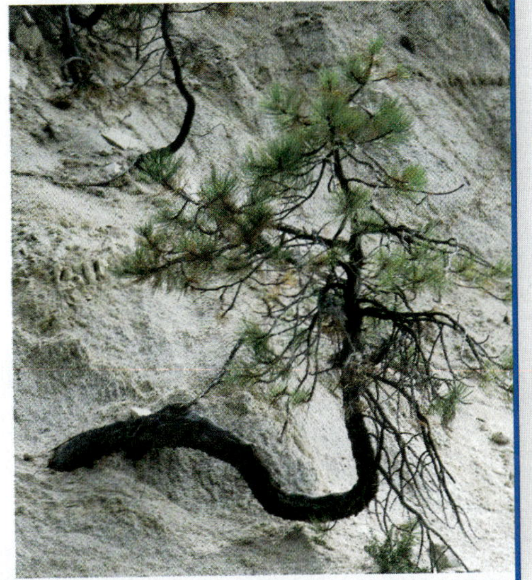

▶ **Figure 25–4** Auxins are responsible for the plant response called gravitropism. Auxins caused the tip of this tree stem to grow upright. **Comparing and Contrasting** *Compare how auxins affect the growth of stems and roots.*

Build Science Skills

Using Models Use a long balloon and transparent tape to model the elongation of one side of a stem versus the other side of the stem. To represent a stem growing straight, blow the balloon up partway and hold the end closed. Then, ask a volunteer to apply a long piece of transparent tape lengthwise to one side of the balloon. Point out that the tape represents an area of low auxin concentration. Ask: **What do you predict will happen as the stem continues to grow?** (*It will curve inward relative to the low auxin concentration.*) Blow up the balloon so that students can confirm their predictions. Ask: **Where is the concentration of auxins higher?** (*On the outside curve of the stem*) **What causes the stem to curve in this fashion?** (*High concentrations of auxin stimulate cells to elongate, so the cells on the outside of the curve are longer than the cells on the inside of the curve.*) L1 L2

Build Science Skills

Predicting Divide the class into small groups, and give each group a small, fast-growing potted plant, such as a coleus plant. The activity works best if the plant is in a four-sided plastic pot. Ask each group to write a prediction of how the plant will react if the pot is placed on its side. Once the predictions are made, ask each group to find a location in the classroom to turn the pot on its side. (If the plant is in a round pot, students can prop the pot with books or other objects.) After a day or two, students should observe that all the plant stems have turned upward. L2

HISTORY OF SCIENCE

Charles Darwin is hailed as one of the greatest scientists in history. It is less well known, however, that he had an inauspicious beginning to his career. He failed both at medical school and in an attempt to become a minister. It was at Cambridge University that Darwin found his calling, under the tutelage of the botanist John Stevens Henslow. Around school, Darwin became known as "the man who walks with Henslow" because he spent many days in the field learning about plants from the professor. Darwin never lost his interest in plants, and late in his life he made great strides in understanding what he called heliotropism.

Answers to . . .

CHECKPOINT *In target cells*

Figure 25–4 *Auxins cause stems to grow upward and roots to grow downward.*

25–1 (continued)

Build Science Skills

Applying Concepts Gather a few twigs with terminal buds and lateral buds that can be easily seen. Distribute the twigs for examination by small groups. Direct students' observations by asking: **Where will this stem grow in length?** (*It will lengthen at the tip.*) **What name is given to the region of rapidly dividing cells at the tip?** (*It is called the apical meristem.*) Point out that the meristematic cells are located in the bud. The bud itself is made up of newly formed, unopened leaves. If the bud is dormant, it will be covered by a ring of bud scales. Direct students to look for bud scales covering the bud. Explain that woody stems produce bud scales to protect the bud at the end of a growing season. The bud scales fall away in the spring when new growth begins. Ask: **When bud scales fall off, a set of rings called bud scale scars are left on the stem. Can bud scale scars be seen on your stem?** (*Answers will vary.*) **How can you determine the amount of growth that occurred during a year?** (*Because bud scale scars mark the location of former terminal buds, the distance between them indicates one year's growth.*) Next, call attention to the lateral buds on the side of the stem. Ask: **What do you think develops from the lateral buds?** (*New branches, leaves, and sometimes flowers develop from lateral buds.*) L2

Cytokinins

Use Visuals

Figure 25–5 Use the figure to reinforce the effects of auxins and cytokinins on plant growth. Ask: **What inhibits the growth of lateral buds?** (*Auxins produced in the apical meristem*) **What happens when the apical meristem is removed?** (*Cytokinins stimulate cell division, and lateral buds grow into branches.*) Then, make a chart on the board to compare and contrast the effects of auxins and cytokinins on plant growth. L1 L2

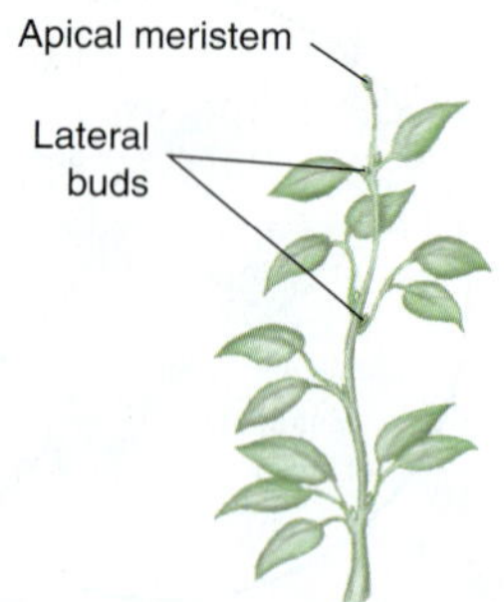

A Auxins produced in the apical meristem inhibit the growth of lateral buds.

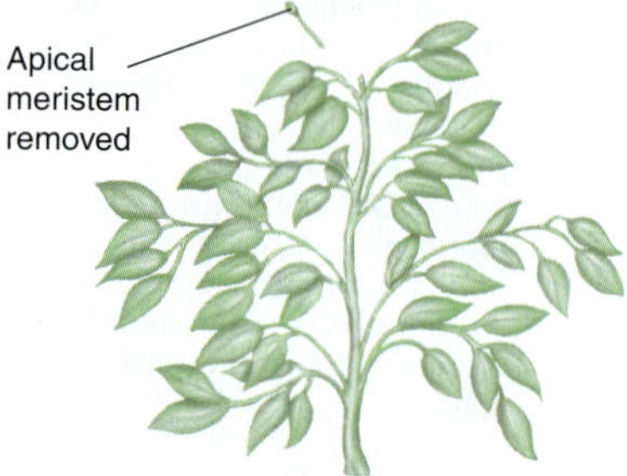

B Without the inhibiting effect of auxins from the apical meristem, lateral buds produce many branches.

▲ **Figure 25–5** Apical dominance, shown here, is controlled by the relative amounts of auxins and cytokinins. During normal growth (A), lateral buds are kept dormant because of the production of auxins in the apical meristem. If the apical meristem is removed (B), the concentration of auxins drops. **Applying Concepts** **How can a gardener use this knowledge of hormones to produce fuller, bushier plants?**

Auxins and Branching Auxins also regulate cell division in meristems. As a stem grows in length, it produces lateral buds, as shown in **Figure 25–5.** A **lateral bud** is a meristematic area on the side of a stem that gives rise to side branches. Most lateral buds do not start growing right away. The reason for this delay is that growth at the lateral buds is inhibited by auxins. Because auxins move out from the apical meristem, the closer a bud is to the stem's tip, the more it is inhibited. This phenomenon is called **apical dominance.**

Although not all gardeners have heard of auxins, most of them know how to overcome apical dominance. If you snip off the tip of a plant, the side branches begin to grow more quickly, resulting in a rounder, fuller plant. Why does this happen? When the tip is removed, the apical meristem—the source of the growth-inhibiting auxins—goes with it. Without the influence of auxins, meristems in the side branches grow more rapidly, changing the overall shape of the plant.

Auxinlike Weed Killers Chemists have produced many compounds that mimic the effects of auxins. Because high concentrations of auxins inhibit growth, many of these compounds are used as **herbicides,** which are compounds that are toxic to plants. Herbicides include a chemical known as 2,4-D (2,4-dichlorophenoxyacetic acid), which is used to kill weeds. A mixture containing 2,4-D was used as Agent Orange, a chemical defoliant sprayed during the Vietnam War.

What role do auxins play in apical dominance?

Cytokinins

Cytokinins are plant hormones that are produced in growing roots and in developing fruits and seeds. **In plants, cytokinins stimulate cell division and the growth of lateral buds, and cause dormant seeds to sprout.** Cytokinins also delay the aging of leaves and play important roles in the early stages of plant growth.

Cytokinins often produce effects opposite to those of auxins. For example, auxins stimulate cell elongation, whereas cytokinins inhibit elongation and cause cells to grow thicker. Auxins inhibit the growth of lateral buds, whereas cytokinins stimulate lateral bud growth. Recent experiments show that the rate of cell growth in most plants is determined by the ratio of the concentration of auxins to cytokinins. In growing plants, therefore, the relative concentrations of auxins, cytokinins, and other hormones determine how the plant grows.

FACTS AND FIGURES

Hanging tight
Growers of apples and citrus fruits used to lose considerable amounts of their crop when fruits fell from trees before harvest time. Now, orchards are often sprayed with synthetic auxins, such as 2,4-D, to induce fruits to remain on trees longer. The auxins apparently retard the formation of the abscission layer that forms between the fruit petiole and the stem.

Analyzing Data

BIIE 1.d

Auxins and Plant Growth

Auxins affect plant growth in a variety of ways. This graph shows the results of experiments in which carrot cells were grown in the presence of varying concentrations of auxins. The orange line on the graph shows the growth pattern of the carrot plants' roots. The green line shows the growth pattern of the carrot plants' stems.

1. **Using Tables and Graphs** At what auxin concentration are the stems stimulated to grow the most?
2. **Using Tables and Graphs** How is the growth of the roots affected by the auxin concentration at which stems grow the most?
3. **Drawing Conclusions** Use the data in the graph to describe the relationship between the concentration of auxins and the growth of carrot plant stems.
4. **Inferring** If you were a carrot farmer, what concentration of auxin should you apply to your fields to produce the largest-sized carrots?

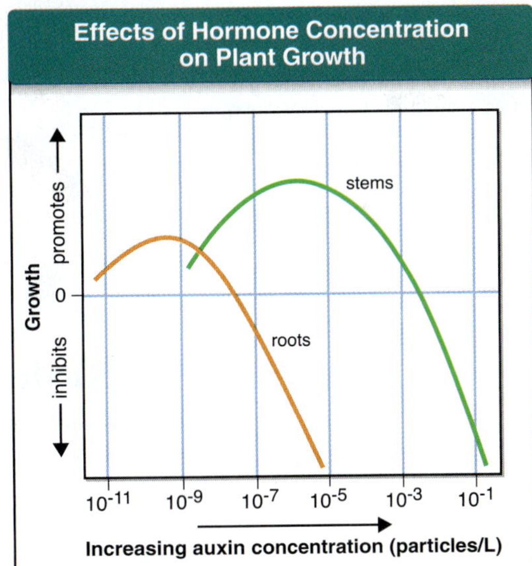

Analyzing Data

BIIE 1.d

The graph shows how carrot cells respond to varying concentrations of auxins. Review with students how data are shown on the graph: increasing auxin concentration is shown on the *x*-axis and plant growth is shown on the *y*-axis. The effects on stem and root cells are shown using green and orange lines, respectively. L2

Answers

1. Maximum stem growth occurs at about 10^{-6} particles/L.
2. That concentration inhibits the growth of roots.
3. Concentrations between approximately 10^{-9} and 10^{-3} particles/L promote stem growth. Concentrations above about 10^{-2} particles/L inhibit stem growth.
4. Because carrots are roots, a concentration of approximately 10^{-10} to 10^{-9} particles/L would produce the largest-sized carrots.

Gibberellins

For years, farmers in Japan knew of a disease that weakened rice plants by causing them to grow unusually tall. They called the disease the "foolish seedling" disease. In 1926, Japanese biologist Eiichi Kurosawa discovered that this extraordinary growth was caused by a fungus: *Gibberella fujikuroi.* His experiments showed that the fungus produced a growth-promoting substance that was named **gibberellin.**

Before long, other researchers had learned that plants themselves produce more than 60 similar compounds, all of which are now known as gibberellins. **Gibberellins produce dramatic increases in size, particularly in stems and fruit.** Their effects on a flower are shown in **Figure 25–6.** Gibberellins are also produced by seed tissue and are responsible for the rapid early growth of many plants.

CHECKPOINT *How were gibberellins discovered?*

▼ **Figure 25–6** **Gibberellins cause an increase in the overall size of plants and individual plant structures.** Their effect can be seen in the difference between an untreated geranium plant (left) and a geranium plant treated with gibberellin (right).

Gibberellins

Demonstration

To demonstrate the effect of gibberellins on plant growth, first plant wheat seeds in soil in two flats. After the seedlings grow to about 3 cm high, water one flat with a gibberellin solution and the other with plain water. (Gibberellic acid is available from biological supply companies. To use it, dissolve about 25 mg in a few milliliters of 70% ethyl alcohol, then mix with 1 liter of distilled water. Solutions of gibberellic acid may also be available at garden stores.) Students should see a marked difference in the growth of the treated and untreated seedlings. L2

TEACHER TO TEACHER

To illustrate the effects of ethylene on the ripening of fruit, I set up a simple experiment for students to participate in and observe. I bring to class several pears, apples, and bananas in different stages of ripeness—none, though, that are overly ripe. I ask students to predict which will ripen first: a combination of the fruits left out in the classroom exposed to light or a similar combination of fruits enclosed in a paper bag. I encourage students to formulate a hypothesis and identify the variables in the experiment. Then, we set up the experiment and observe the fruit each day. After a few days, students conclude that the fruit in the paper bag ripens first, because the bag holds the ethylene around the fruit more than the fruit left in the open.

—*Mary Colvard*
Biology Teacher
Cobleskill-Richmondville High School
Cobleskill, NY

Answers to . . .

CHECKPOINT *Auxins produced in the apical meristem inhibit the growth of lateral buds. The closer a bud is to a stem's tip, the more it is inhibited, a phenomenon called apical dominance.*

CHECKPOINT *Eiichi Kurosawa, a Japanese biologist, discovered that a fungus,* Gibberella fujikuroi, *caused rice plants to grow unusually tall.*

Figure 25–5 *The gardener would cut off the tip of the plant.*

25–1 (continued)

Ethylene

Make Connections

Health Science Show students a fruit from the supermarket that has the color of a ripe fruit but feels hard and unripened. Ask: **Does this fruit look good enough to eat?** (*Most students will probably say yes.*) Hand the fruit to a student, and ask: **Does this fruit feel good enough to eat?** (*Probably not*) Encourage students to share their experiences with fruit that looked good but didn't taste ripe. Challenge interested students to find out about the nutritional value of unripened fruits treated with synthetic ethylene compared with fruits that ripen naturally. 

3 ASSESS

Evaluate Understanding

Call on students at random to identify the four types of plant hormones and explain their roles in the control of plant growth.

Reteach

Have students make a table that lists and describes the effects of the four types of plant hormones.

Focus on the BIG Idea

Check students' flowcharts for accuracy. Flowcharts should list the steps described on pages 634–635 and illustrated in Figure 25–3.

If your class subscribes to the iText, use it to review the Key Concepts in Section 25–1.

Figure 25–7 **Ethylene is a plant hormone that causes fruits to ripen.** The tomatoes on the left were allowed to ripen naturally, whereas those in the middle were genetically altered to prevent transcription of the gene that produces ethylene. Only when ethylene gas was added did the tomatoes ripen, as you can see on the right.

Ethylene

When natural gas was used in city street lamps in the nineteenth century, people noticed that trees along the street suffered leaf loss and stunted growth. This effect was eventually traced to **ethylene,** one of the minor components of natural gas.

Today, scientists know that plants produce their own ethylene, and that it affects plants in a number of ways. **In response to auxins, fruit tissues release small amounts of the hormone ethylene. Ethylene then stimulates fruits to ripen.**

Commercial producers of fruit sometimes use this hormone to control the ripening process. Many crops, including lemons and tomatoes, shown in **Figure 25–7,** are picked before they ripen so that they can be handled without damage to the fruit. Just before they are delivered to market, the fruits are treated with synthetic ethylene to produce a ripe color quickly. This trick does not always produce a ripe flavor, which is one reason why naturally ripened fruits often taste much better.

25–1 Section Assessment

1. **Key Concept** What effects do hormones have within a growing plant?
2. **Key Concept** Identify the four main types of hormones. What parts of the plant does each hormone affect?
3. Compare the effects of auxins and cytokinins on plant growth.
4. **Critical Thinking Inferring** A person who trims trees for a living must know the effect of apical dominance on the shape of trees. Explain.
5. **Critical Thinking Interpreting Graphics** Using **Figure 25–3,** describe the experiment by Francis and Charles Darwin. Explain why the seedling at the far right is curved.

Focus on the BIG Idea

Science as a Way of Knowing Using the Darwins' experiment as an example, develop a flowchart that shows the scientific process. Be sure to identify each process. (*Hint:* You may wish to review Chapter 1, which describes the scientific method.)

25–1 Section Assessment

1. They control a plant's branching pattern, the rate at which its stems elongate, and its responses to environmental conditions.
2. Auxins: stems, roots, lateral buds; cytokinins: lateral buds, seeds, leaves; gibberellins: stems, fruits, flowers; ethylene: fruits
3. Auxins stimulate cell elongation; cytokinins inhibit elongation and cause cells to grow thicker. Auxins inhibit lateral bud growth; cytokinins stimulate lateral bud growth.
4. The person will know to remove the apical meristem to make the tree grow rounder and fuller or leave it to make the tree grow taller and narrower.
5. The seedling curved because there was more auxin on the shaded side of the stem.

25–2 Plant Responses

Like all living things, plants respond to changes in their environments. Some biologists call these responses "plant behavior," which is a useful way of thinking about them. Plants generally do not respond as quickly as animals do, but that does not make their responses any less effective. Some plant responses are so fast that even animals cannot keep up with them!

Guide for Reading

Key Concepts
- What are plant tropisms?
- What is photoperiodism?
- How do deciduous plants prepare for winter?

Vocabulary
tropism
thigmotropism
short-day plant
long-day plant
photoperiodism
phytochrome
dormancy
abscission layer

Reading Strategy: Using Visuals Before you read, preview **Figure 25–10.** From this figure, what can you conclude about the topic of photoperiodism?

Tropisms

Plants change their patterns and directions of growth in response to a multitude of cues. The responses of plants to external stimuli are called **tropisms,** from a Greek word that means "turning." **Plant tropisms include gravitropism, phototropism, and thigmotropism. Each of these responses demonstrates the ability of plants to respond effectively to external stimuli, such as gravity, light, and touch.**

Gravitropism and Phototropism You have already read about gravitropism, the response of a plant to gravity, and phototropism, the response of a plant to light. Both of these responses are controlled by the hormone auxin. Gravitropism causes the shoot of a germinating seed to grow out of the soil—against the force of gravity. It also causes the roots of a plant to grow with the force of gravity and into the soil.

Phototropism causes a plant to grow toward a light source. This response can be so quick that young seedlings reorient themselves in a matter of hours.

Thigmotropism The response of plants to touch is called **thigmotropism** (thig-MAH-troh-piz-um). A plant that is touched regularly, for example, may be stunted in its growth—sometimes quite dramatically. Another example of thigmotropism is the growth of vines and climbing plants. The stems of these plants do not grow straight up. Rather, the growing tip of each stem points sideways and twists in circles as the shoot grows. When the tip encounters an object, it quickly wraps around it. Some climbing plants have long, twisting leaf tips or petioles that wrap tightly around small objects. Other plants, such as the grapes in **Figure 25–8,** have extra growths called tendrils that emerge near the base of the leaf and wrap tightly around any object they encounter.

Figure 25–8 **Plant tropisms include gravitropism, phototropism, and thigmotropism.** One effect of thigmotropism is that plants curl and twist around objects, as shown by the stems of this grapevine.

SECTION RESOURCES

Print:
- ***Laboratory Manual B,*** Chapter 25 Lab
- ***Teaching Resources,*** Lesson Plan 25–2, Adapted Section Summary 25–2, Adapted Worksheets 25–2, Section Summary 25–2, Worksheets 25–2, Section Review 25–2, Enrichment
- ***Reading and Study Workbook A,*** Section 25–2
- ***Adapted Reading and Study Workbook B,*** Section 25–2

Technology:
- ***iText,*** Section 25–2
- ***Transparencies Plus,*** Section 25–2

Section 25–2

1 FOCUS

Objectives

25.2.1 ***Explain*** what plant tropisms are.
25.2.2 ***Explain*** what photoperiodism is.
25.2.3 ***Describe*** how deciduous plants prepare for winter.

Guide for Reading

Vocabulary Preview

Ask students to review the meaning of the term *phototropism* from Section 25–1. (*The tendency of a plant to grow toward a source of light*) Then, call students' attention to the Vocabulary term *photoperiodism* and challenge them to infer its meaning. Have students skim the text to find the term and verify their predictions.

Reading Strategy

As students read the section, have them use the blue heads and the green heads to create an outline. They should include relevant details under each heading.

2 INSTRUCT

Tropisms

Building Science Skills

Inferring Point out that in environments such as tropical rain forests where there is dense growth, there are many varieties of vining plants. Ask: **How are vines an adaptation to that kind of environment?** (*The tall tree canopy and subcanopy are so dense that little sunlight reaches the forest floor and new growth is inhibited. Vines have a unique adaptation to this situation—these slender plants grow on the trunks of the tall trees, soon emerging into the sunlight. This is done without the energy-costly investment regular plants must make to produce regular, tall tree trunks.*) L2 L3

25–2 (continued)

Rapid Responses

Demonstration

Obtain a *Mimosa pudica.* Ask a volunteer to touch the plant at the end of its leaves so that the other students can watch as the leaves fold closed. Challenge students to infer how this response is an adaptative advantage for this plant. (*The leaves are less prone to damage by insects and other animals when they are folded closed.*) Have a volunteer time how long it takes for the leaves to reopen. L2

Quick Lab

 **BIIE 1.d**

Objective Students will be able to observe the effects of phototropism on plants. L2

Skills Focus **Observing, Inferring**

Materials scissors, masking tape, cardboard box, cardboard dividers, 4 bean seeds, small flowerpot containing commercial potting soil

Time 20 minutes for setup; 5 minutes every 2 to 3 days for 2 weeks for observation

Advance Prep Collect copy-paper boxes from an office or copy center. Cut holes in the boxes before class.

Safety If you do not use commercial potting soil, make sure students wear plastic gloves and dispose of them properly.

Strategies

- After placing the boxes next to a light source and covering them, students should secure the covers with weights or easily removable tape to prevent the seedlings from pushing the box lids up and growing over the walls of the maze.
- Emphasize that the lids should be opened only briefly to water and observe the plants.

Expected Outcome The seedlings will grow around the barriers toward the source of light at the hole in the box.

Analyze and Conclude

1. Growth of the seedlings followed an increasing light gradient around the barriers, toward the light source.
2. The seedlings exhibited a phototropic response, growing toward the light source.

Figure 25–9 The mimosa plant responds to touch by folding in its leaves quickly. This response is produced by decreased osmotic pressure in cells near the base of each leaflet. **Inferring** *What adaptive value might rapid responses have for a plant?*

Rapid Responses

Some plant responses do not involve growth. In fact, they are so rapid that it would be a mistake to call them tropisms. **Figure 25–9** shows what happens if you touch a leaf of *Mimosa pudica,* appropriately called the "sensitive plant." Within only two or three seconds, its two leaflets fold together completely. The secret to this movement is changes in osmotic pressure. Recall that osmotic pressure is caused by the diffusion of water into cells. The leaves are held apart due to osmotic pressure where the two leaflets join. When the leaf is touched, cells near the center of the leaflet pump out ions and lose water due to osmosis. Pressure from cells on the underside of the leaf, which do not lose water, force the leaflets together.

The carnivorous Venus' flytrap also demonstrates rapid responses. When a fly triggers sensory cells on the inside of the flytrap's leaf, electrical signals are sent from cell to cell. A combination of changes in osmotic pressure and cell wall expansion causes the leaf to snap shut, trapping the insect inside.

Quick Lab

 **BIIE 1.d**

Can a plant find its way through a maze?

Materials scissors, masking tape, cardboard box, cardboard dividers, 4 bean seeds, small flowerpot containing soil

Procedure  

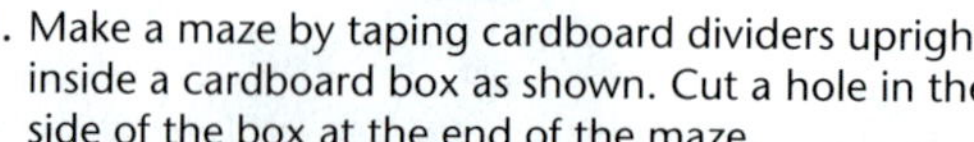

1. Make a maze by taping cardboard dividers upright inside a cardboard box as shown. Cut a hole in the side of the box at the end of the maze. **CAUTION:** *Use care when handling scissors.*
2. Plant 4 bean seeds in a small flowerpot of soil. Water the flowerpot.
3. Place the flowerpot in the box at the beginning of the maze. Close the box so that the only light in the box comes from the hole that you cut. **CAUTION:** *Wash your hands with soap and warm water after handling soil or plants.*
4. Over the next 2 weeks, open the box every 2 to 3 days to water the seeds and observe the seedlings. Record your observations each day.

Analyze and Conclude

1. **Observing** Summarize what happened to the seedlings.
2. **Inferring** What caused the plants to grow the way they did?

ESL SUPPORT FOR ENGLISH LANGUAGE LEARNERS

Comprehension: Key Concept

Beginning On the board, rewrite the boldface sentences on page 639 as three individual sentences, e.g., "Plant tropisms include gravitropism, a response to gravity." Explain each plant response. Then, write the following word pairs on the board: *gravitropism-gravity, phototropism-*_____, and *thigmotropism-*_____. Ask students to fill in the blanks using the information on the board. Read aloud each word pair. L1

Intermediate Pair each ESL student with a student who is proficient in English. Have the students write a short paragraph that restates the boldface sentences found on page 639. If the ESL student is comfortable reading the paragraph aloud, have him or her do so. If not, have the English-proficient student read the paragraph aloud. L2

Photoperiodism

"To every thing there is a season." Nowhere is this more evident than in the regular cycles of plant growth. Year after year, some plants flower in the spring, others in summer, and still others in the fall. Plants such as chrysanthemums and poinsettias flower when days are short and are therefore called **short-day plants.** Plants such as spinach and irises flower when days are long and are therefore known as **long-day plants.**

How do all these plants manage to time their flowering so precisely? In the early 1920s, scientists discovered that tobacco plants flower according to the number of hours of light and darkness they receive. Additional research showed that many other plants also respond to periods of light and darkness, a response called **photoperiodism.** This type of response is summarized in **Figure 25–10.** **Photoperiodism in plants is responsible for the timing of seasonal activities such as flowering and growth.**

It was later discovered that a plant pigment called **phytochrome** (FYT-oh-krohm) is responsible for photoperiodism. Phytochrome absorbs red light and activates a number of signaling pathways within plant cells. By mechanisms that are still not understood completely, plants respond to regular changes in these pathways. These changes determine the patterns of a variety of plant responses.

Effect of Photoperiod on Flowering

	Short-Day Plant	Long-Day Plant
Midnight / Noon — Long Day		
Midnight / Noon — Short Day		
Midnight / Noon — Interrupted Night		

▲ **Figure 25–10** **Photoperiodism controls the timing of flowering and seasonal growth.** Short-day plants flower only when exposed to an extended period of darkness every night—and thus a short period of light during the day. Long-day plants flower when exposed to a short period of darkness or to a long period of darkness interrupted by a brief period of light.

For: Photoperiodism activity
Visit: PHSchool.com
Web Code: cbp-7252

Winter Dormancy

Phytochrome also regulates the changes in activity that prepare many plants for dormancy as winter approaches. **Dormancy** is the period during which an organism's growth and activity decrease or stop.

The changes that prepare a plant for dormancy are important adaptations that protect plants over the cold winter months. **As cold weather approaches, deciduous plants turn off photosynthetic pathways, transport materials from leaves to roots, and seal leaves off from the rest of the plant.** In early autumn, the shorter days and lower temperatures gradually reduce the efficiency of photosynthesis. With these changing conditions, the plant gains very little by keeping its leaves alive. In fact, the thin, delicate leaves produced by most flowering plants would have little chance of surviving a tough winter, and their continued presence would be costly in terms of water loss.

CHECKPOINT ***What is dormancy? What changes do plants undergo as colder weather approaches?***

Photoperiodism

Use Community Resources

Invite a floriculturist or a manager of a greenhouse to speak to the class about photoperiodism and how plants are brought to bloom for specific seasons. For example, ask how poinsettias are grown so that they are in bloom for the winter. L2

For: Photoperiodism activity
Visit: PHSchool.com
Web Code: cbe-7252
Students learn how plants respond to daylight and darkness.

Winter Dormancy

Address Misconceptions

Point out that many plants in environments with seasonal dry periods go through a time of dormancy. The plants may lose their leaves and form drought-resistant buds, in a way similar to the way in which plants respond in winter dormancy. Many seeds also have dormancy periods and will not germinate immediately after they are released from the parent plant. Some seeds remain dormant until they have the right temperature and moisture conditions for growth. Other seeds require a period of low temperatures or intense heat, such as from a forest fire, before they will germinate. Challenge students to infer the adaptive advantages of these different types of dormancy. L1 L2

TEACHER TO TEACHER

Before introducing photoperiodism, arrange photos of typical flowering long-day plants that you have covered with black construction paper around your classroom. Next to each one, place a photo of the same long-day plant that is not flowering. Do not cover these photos with black construction paper. Darken the room for a short period of time. While in the dark, cover the photos of the plants that are not flowering and uncover the photos of the plants that are flowering. Turn on the light. Have students explain what they observed. Discuss what makes the plants flower. What effect does light/dark duration have on these plants? Finally, discuss how photoperiodism helps florists with orders for flowers for holidays at different seasons of the year.

—Bob Culler
Biology Teacher
Avon Lake High School
Avon Lake, OH

Answers to . . .

CHECKPOINT *Dormancy is the period during which an organism's growth and activity decrease or stop. Deciduous plants turn off photosynthetic pathways, transport materials from leaves to roots, and seal leaves off from the rest of the plant.*

Figure 25–9 *Rapid responses might help reduce damage to leaves or, in the case of carnivorous plants, help the plant to capture prey.*

25–2 (continued)

Build Science Skills

Observing Provide dormant tree branches for students to observe. (If dormant branches are not available, nondormant branches can be used.) Have students find an abscission layer. Ask: **What grew from this area?** (*A leaf*) Challenge students to find the small holes where the vascular bundles passed from the leaf into the branch. Ask: **Why is it important that the vascular system be sealed before the leaf drops off?** (*So that nutrients and water are not lost*) Have students locate a terminal bud. Ask: **How is this bud prepared to survive winter?** (*Thick, waxy scales form a protective layer around the new leaf buds, and ions and organic compounds are pumped into the vascular tissue to prevent the tree's sap from freezing.*)

3 ASSESS

Evaluate Understanding

Have students use the Vocabulary terms to create a concept map that summarizes the Key Concepts of the section.

Reteach

Ask students to create a table to compare and contrast the various plant responses discussed in the section.

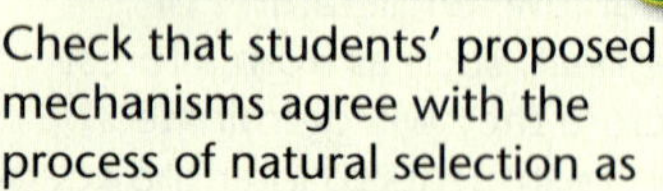

Check that students' proposed mechanisms agree with the process of natural selection as described in Chapter 15.

If your class subscribes to the iText, use it to review the Key Concepts in Section 25–2.

Figure 25–11 Deciduous plants undergo changes in preparation for winter dormancy. Photosynthetic pathways in leaves shut down (top). An abscission layer of cells forms at the petiole to seal the leaf off from the rest of the plant (bottom). Eventually, the leaf falls off.

Leaf Abscission In temperate regions, most flowering plants lose their leaves during the colder months. During the warm growing season, auxins are produced in leaves. At summer's end, the phytochrome in leaves absorbs less light as days shorten and nights become longer. Auxin production drops, but the production of ethylene increases. The change in the relative amounts of these two hormones starts a series of events that gradually shut down the leaf.

The chemical pathways for chlorophyll synthesis stop first. When light destroys the remaining green pigment, other pigments that have been present all along—including yellow and orange carotenoids—become visible for the first time. Production of new plant pigments—the reddish anthocyanins—begins in the autumn. The brilliant colors of autumn leaves are a direct result of these processes.

Behind the scenes, enzymes extract nutrients from the broken-down chlorophyll. These nutrients are then transported to other parts of the plant, where they are stored until spring. Every available carbohydrate is transported out of the leaf, and much of the leaf's water is extracted. Finally, an **abscission layer** of cells at the petiole seals the leaf off from the plant's vascular system. The location of the abscission layer is shown in **Figure 25–11.** Before long, the leaf falls to the ground, a sign that the tree is fully prepared for winter.

Overwintering of Meristems Hormones also produce important changes in apical meristems. Instead of continuing to produce leaves, meristems produce thick, waxy scales that form a protective layer around new leaf buds. Enclosed in its coat of scales, a terminal bud can survive the coldest winter days. At the onset of winter, xylem and phloem tissues pump themselves full of ions and organic compounds. These molecules act like antifreeze in a car, preventing the tree's sap from freezing, thus making it possible to survive the bitter cold.

25–2 Section Assessment

1. **Key Concept** Identify three types of plant tropisms that show how plants respond to external stimuli.
2. **Key Concept** Compare short-day and long-day plants. Which type of plant is likely to bloom in the summer?
3. **Key Concept** What changes occur in plants before winter? How do these changes help the plant to survive?
4. Describe the process of leaf abscission.
5. **Critical Thinking Designing Experiments** How could a garden-store owner determine what light conditions are needed for a particular flowering plant to bloom? Design a controlled experiment to find out.

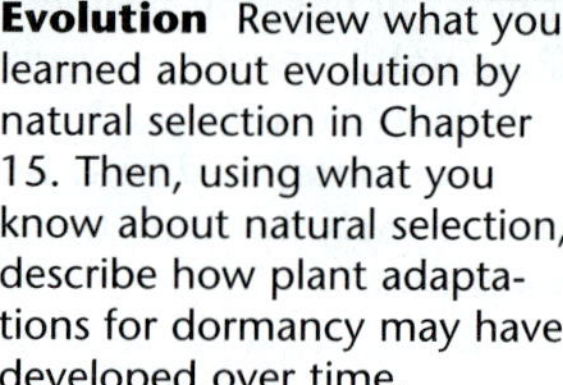

Evolution Review what you learned about evolution by natural selection in Chapter 15. Then, using what you know about natural selection, describe how plant adaptations for dormancy may have developed over time.

25–2 Section Assessment

1. Gravitropism: response to gravity; phototropism: response to light; thigmotropism: response to touch
2. Short-day plants flower when days are short. Long-day plants flower when days are long. Long-day plants bloom in the summer.
3. Lose leaves to reduce water loss; form scales to protect buds from cold; produce ions and organic compounds to act as an antifreeze
4. Auxin production drops and production of ethylene increases; chlorophyll synthesis stops; carbohydrates and water are transported out of leaf; abscission layer seals off vascular system; leaf falls
5. Students' experiments should involve exposing the plant to different amounts of light.

25–3 Plant Adaptations

Flowering plants grow in a variety of biomes—in deserts, savannas, and tundras—to name a few. They also grow in various aquatic ecosystems, such as ponds and streams. Angiosperms can survive in many different locations. How is this possible? Through natural selection they have evolved tolerances and structural and physiological adaptations to meet the conditions of each biome. In this section, we explore how plants have become adapted to various environments through evolutionary change.

Aquatic Plants

Aquatic plants are able to tolerate mud that is saturated with water and nearly devoid of oxygen. **To take in sufficient oxygen, many aquatic plants have tissues with large air-filled spaces through which oxygen can diffuse.** In waterlilies, shown in **Figure 25–12,** there are large open spaces in the long petioles that reach from the leaves down to the roots at the bottom. Oxygen diffuses from these open spaces into the roots.

Many other plants show similar adaptations. Several species of mangrove trees grow in shallow water along tropical seacoasts. Mangroves tolerate this environment by means of specialized air roots with air spaces in them, just like waterlily stems. These spaces conduct air down to the buried roots, allowing the root tissues to respire normally. Stately bald cypress trees thrive in freshwater swamps in the southern United States. These trees grow structures called knees, which protrude above the water. The knees bring oxygen-rich air down to the roots.

The reproductive adaptations of aquatic plants include seeds that float in water and delay germination for long periods. Many aquatic plants grow quickly after germination, extending the growing shoot above the water's surface.

Guide for Reading

Key Concepts
- How are plants adapted to different environments?
- How do plants obtain nutrients from sources other than photosynthesis?
- How do plants defend themselves from insects?

Vocabulary
xerophyte
epiphyte

Reading Strategy: Using Prior Knowledge Before you read, list the different environments in which plants grow. Next to each environment listed, describe adaptations you might expect to find in plants. As you read, compare your predictions with information about different plant adaptations.

▼ **Figure 25–12 Aquatic plants have air-filled spaces in their tissues that allow for the uptake and diffusion of oxygen.** These waterlilies transport oxygen from the air to their roots through large spaces in their petioles.

TIME SAVER — SECTION RESOURCES

Print:
- ***Teaching Resources,*** Lesson Plan 25–3, Adapted Section Summary 25–3, Adapted Worksheets 25–3, Section Summary 25–3, Worksheets 25–3, Section Review 25–3
- ***Reading and Study Workbook A,*** Section 25–3
- ***Adapted Reading and Study Workbook B,*** Section 25–3

Technology:
- ***iText,*** Section 25–3
- ***Transparencies Plus,*** Section 25–3

Section 25–3

1 FOCUS

Objectives

25.3.1 ***Summarize*** how plants are adapted to different environments.
25.3.2 ***Describe*** how plants obtain nutrients.
25.3.3 ***Explain*** how plants use chemical defenses.

Guide for Reading

Vocabulary Preview

Explain that the root word *phyte* comes from a Greek word meaning "plant." Have students skim the text to find out what kinds of plants xerophytes and epiphytes are.

Reading Strategy

To help students get started making their lists of different environments, have them look at the figures and read the captions in the section.

2 INSTRUCT

Aquatic Plants

Build Science Skills

Inferring Provide specimens of waterlily leaves, water hyacinth plants, and any other aquatic plants that you can obtain. Invite students to observe the plants and look for special adaptations that the plants have for aquatic environments. You might cut open the long petiole of a waterlily leaf for students to observe the large air spaces through which oxygen diffuses. Also point out the stomata on the upper surface of the waterlily leaf. Ask: **How are these stomata an adaptation to an aquatic environment?** (*They allow the plant to take in carbon dioxide directly from the air.*) **Why do you think there are no stomata on the bottom of the leaf?** (*They would be useless for exchanging gases because they are under the water level.*) Challenge students to make inferences about other adaptations they observe. L2

25–3 (continued)

Word Origins

Hydrophytes live in water. L2

Salt-Tolerant Plants

Make Connections

Environmental Science Tell students how soils in arid climates and poor-draining soils are susceptible to the accumulation of salts. Salts tend to accumulate in irrigated soils when evaporation occurs faster than drainage. When water evaporates, the minerals dissolved in it are left behind, building up as salts in the soil. In well-drained soils, the minerals are carried away. Since food crops cannot grow in salty soils, these soils become unproductive. Challenge students to consider solutions to this problem. Have the class evaluate the merits of each solution. *(Solutions include providing adequate drainage; converting mineral-laden water to fresh water; and developing salt-tolerant crops via selection, hybridization, and genetic engineering.)* L2 L3

Desert Plants

Build Science Skills

Inferring Display various cactuses, a crown-of-thorns plant, and any other desert plants that you can obtain. Invite students to observe the plants and look for special adaptations that the plants have for a desert environment. Point to a cactus and ask: **Where are the leaves on this plant?** *(The spines are modified leaves.)* **What function do the spines serve?** *(They provide defense against predators that might try to eat the plant.)* **Where do you think photosynthesis is carried out in this cactus?** *(In the green stem)* **What other function does the stem serve?** *(It stores water.)* Challenge students to make inferences about other adaptations they observe. L2

Word Origins

Xerophyte comes from the Greek words *xeros,* meaning "dry," and *phyton,* meaning "plant." **Where do you think hydrophytes live?**

Salt-Tolerant Plants

When plant roots take in dissolved minerals, a difference in the concentration of water molecules is created between the root cells and the surrounding soil. This concentration difference causes water to enter the root cells by osmosis. For plants that grow in salt water, such as mangroves, this means taking in much more salt than the plant can use. The roots of salt-tolerant plants are adapted to salt concentrations that would quickly destroy the root hairs on most plants. The leaves of these plants have specialized cells that pump salt out of the plant tissues and onto the leaf surfaces, where it is washed off by rain.

Desert Plants

Plants that live in the desert biome are called **xerophytes.** Xerophytes must tolerate a variety of extreme conditions, including strong winds, daytime heat, sandy soil, and infrequent rain. Rainwater sinks rapidly through desert soils instead of staying near the surface. The hot, dry air quickly removes moisture from any wet surface, making life difficult for plants. **Plant adaptations to a desert climate include extensive roots, reduced leaves, and thick stems that can store water.**

One familiar group of desert plants is the cactus (family Cactaceae), shown in **Figure 25–13.** Cactuses have root systems that either spread out for long distances just beneath the soil surface or that reach deep down into the soil. In addition, the roots have many hairs that quickly absorb water after a rainstorm, before the water sinks too deeply into the soil.

To reduce water loss due to transpiration, cactus leaves have been reduced to thin, sharp spines. Cactuses also have thick green stems that carry out photosynthesis and are adapted to store water. The stems of cactuses swell during rainy periods and shrivel during dry spells, when the plants are forced to use up their water reserves.

Figure 25–13 Desert plants have evolved different adaptations to survive desert conditions. For example, the shallow root systems of cactuses allow them to pick up surface water. The deep taproots of the mesquite tree and the sagebrush collect underground water. Spines, which are found on many desert plants, are actually reduced leaves that carry out little or no photosynthesis and, as a result, lose little water. Most of a plant's photosynthesis is carried out in its fleshy stem.

UNIVERSAL ACCESS

Less Proficient Readers
Some students might need to review osmosis. Have them turn back to Section 7–3. Review selectively permeable membranes and how the concentration of water molecules "powers" osmosis. Relate osmosis to salt-tolerant plants. L1

English Language Learners
Students can devote an entire page in their science glossaries to each plant group described in this section. For each plant group, students can diagram a representative plant with its adaptations labeled. Help students define terms that give them difficulties. L1 L2

Advanced Learners
Encourage students to choose one of the groups of plants described in this section and find out more about it. They could present their findings in an oral report or a poster. Students should focus on the adaptations of the plants that make them suited to their environments. L3

Seeds of many desert plants can remain dormant for years, germinating only when sufficient moisture guarantees them a chance for survival. Other desert plants have bulbs, tubers, or other specialized stems that can remain dormant for years. When rain does come, the plants mature, flower, and set seed in a matter of weeks or even days, before the water disappears.

CHECKPOINT *How are the roots and leaves of desert plants specialized for the environment in which they live?*

Nutritional Specialists

Some plants grow in environments that have low concentrations of nutrients in the soil. **Plants that have specialized features for obtaining nutrients include carnivorous plants and parasites.**

Carnivorous Plants Some plants live in bogs, wet and acidic environments where there is very little or no nitrogen present. Because conditions are too wet and too acidic, bacteria that cause decay cannot survive. Without these bacteria, neither plant nor animal material is broken down into the nutrients plants can use.

A number of plants that live in these habitats obtain nutrients using specialized leaves that trap and digest insects. Pitcher plants drown their prey in pitcher-shaped leaves that hold rainwater and digestive enzymes. Sundews trap insects on leaf hairs tipped with sticky secretions. The best known of the carnivorous plants is the Venus' flytrap, shown in **Figure 25–14.** This plant has leaf blades that are hinged at the middle. If an insect touches the trigger hairs on the leaf, the leaf folds up suddenly, trapping the animal inside. Over a period of several days, the leaf secretes enzymes that digest the insect and release nitrogen for the plant to use.

Parasites Some plants extract water and nutrients directly from a host plant. Like all parasites, these plants harm their host organisms and sometimes even pose a serious threat to other species. The dodder plant *Cuscuta* is a parasitic plant that has no chlorophyll and thus does not produce its own food. The plant grows directly into the vascular tissue of its host. There, it extracts nutrients and water. Mistletoe grows as a parasite on many plants, including conifers in the western United States.

Epiphytes

Epiphytes are plants that are not rooted in soil but instead grow directly on the bodies of other plants. Most epiphytes are found in the tropical rain forest biome, but they grow in other moist biomes as well. Epiphytes are not parasites. They gather their own moisture, generally from rainfall, and produce their own food. One of the most common epiphytes is Spanish moss. This plant is actually not a moss at all but a member of the bromeliad family. Over half the species of orchids are epiphytes.

Carnivorous Plant: Venus' flytrap

Parasite: Mistletoe

Figure 25–14 Plants that have specialized features for obtaining nutrients include carnivorous plants and parasites. Carnivorous plants, such as the Venus' flytrap, digest insects—and occasionally frogs—as a source of nutrients. Parasites grow into the tissues of their host plant and extract water and nutrients, causing harm to the host.

Nutritional Specialists

Build Science Skills

Predicting Scientists speculate that carnivorous plants evolved when plants in nitrogen-poor soil collected rainwater in depressions on their leaves. Insects landing in the water drowned and decomposed, providing the plants with needed nutrients. Thus, plants in nitrogen-poor environments with certain shaped leaves had a reproductive advantage. Eventually, the leaves became more specialized for capturing insects and other small animals. Have students predict how plants without specialized leaves will survive in nitrogen-poor environments. *(These plants either die or adapt to the environment in some way.)* Ask: **Would carnivorous plants have developed in nutrient-rich soils?** *(No, there would be no adaptive advantage for carnivorous plants in nutrient-rich soils.)* L2 L3

Epiphytes

Use Community Resources

Visit a local public conservatory or botanical garden so students can observe examples of epiphytes, including orchids and bromeliads. Some commercial greenhouses grow epiphytes and may be willing to offer a tour. Point out the aerial roots of these plants, and explain that they are modified with a spongy outer layer that absorbs moisture in the air. Ask: **In what type of environment do you think epiphytes naturally live?** (*In a humid environment such as a tropical rain forest*) Point out how bromeliads trap water in the spaces around the base of their leaves. Ask: **How do you think this helps bromeliads survive in their environment?** (*Because bromeliads do not have roots in the ground, this is a way for these plants to store water for times when there is less water available.*) L2

FACTS AND FIGURES

Plant carnivores

Carnivorous plants have adaptations in their lives that provide the plants with needed nutrients. The tentacle-covered leaves of the sundew are one of four kinds of insect-trapping mechanisms. Another is found in the Venus' flytrap. Its leaves are fashioned like a steel trap, with two halves of the blade hinged along a middle rib. Stiff projections along the leaf margins trap an insect when it touches trigger hairs on the leaf surface. Still another mechanism is found in bladderworts, which float in shallow water. These plants have stomach-shaped bladders at the base of their leaves. When an insect touches a trigger hair, a "trapdoor" springs open and water rushes into the bladder, taking the insect in with it. Finally, the leaves of pitcher plants are formed like vases. When an insect ventures to the bottom of the "vase," a pool of liquid and a slippery inner surface make it difficult for the insect to climb out.

Answer to . . .

CHECKPOINT *Desert plants have extensive root systems that spread out for long distances just beneath the surface or grow down deep into the soil. The roots have many root hairs to absorb water. To reduce water loss, the leaves are often reduced to spines.*

25–3 (continued)

Chemical Defenses

Make Connections

Health Science Point out that many common plants are poisonous to humans. Even some familiar food plants have poisonous parts. For example, the seeds of peaches, apricots, and cherries are poisonous, as are the leaves of potatoes and tomatoes. Emphasize to students that they should never put any part of a plant in their mouths unless they are sure that it is harmless. Explain that some poisonous plants, such as poison ivy, cause irritation to the skin. Encourage interested students to create a chart of local poisonous plants for a bulletin board. L2

3 ASSESS

Evaluate Understanding

Ask students to compare and contrast the adaptations that aquatic plants have with the adaptations that desert plants have.

Reteach

List the different environments discussed in the section. Then, randomly call on students to identify adaptations that plants have to live in that environment.

Thinking Visually

This activity can be completed individually or in small groups. Provide students with a variety of materials to choose from, including basic art supplies, paint, watercolors, charcoal, fabric, and construction paper. You might also allow students to bring materials from home to include in their artwork or coordinate this activity with an art class at your school. Students should depict a plant in its natural environment. Encourage students to be creative, yet accurate, in their artwork.

If your class subscribes to the iText, use it to review the Key Concepts in Section 25–3.

Figure 25–15 **Many plants produce chemical compounds that ward off potential predators.** *Digitalis* (left), which is also called foxglove, is poisonous when eaten. The monarch caterpillar (right) can eat milkweed—which is toxic to most animals—because it can store the toxic compounds in its body.

Chemical Defenses

Seed plants and insects have had such a long relationship that each has had plenty of time to adapt to the other. The beginnings of the relationship are obvious—plants represent an important source of food for insects, as shown in **Figure 25–15.** Plants, therefore, fall prey to a host of plant-eating insects. Because plants cannot run away, you might think that they are defenseless against insects that are armed with biting and sucking structures. But plants have their own defenses.

Many plants defend themselves against insect attack by manufacturing compounds that have powerful effects on animals. Some of these chemicals are poisons that can be lethal when eaten. Other chemicals act as insect hormones, disrupting normal growth and development and preventing insects from reproducing. These chemicals include those used in aspirin, codeine, and scores of other drugs that humans use as medicines.

As you may know, nicotine is a chemical that is found in tobacco plants. When a person smokes tobacco in the form of cigarettes, the nicotine in the tobacco affects the human nervous system. Biologists hypothesize that nicotine is a natural insecticide that disrupts the nervous system of many insects, protecting tobacco plants from potential predators.

25–3 Section Assessment

1. **Key Concept** Compare the variations and adaptations of aquatic plants and desert plants. Which plants have adaptations for obtaining sufficient oxygen?
2. **Key Concept** Describe how carnivorous plants and parasites obtain their nutrients.
3. **Key Concept** How do some plants defend themselves from insect predators?
4. How are salt-tolerant plants adapted to their environment?
5. **Critical Thinking** **Predicting** Suppose a temperate region underwent a drought. Predict which structural and physiological adaptations would enable some plants to survive. Give at least two examples.
6. **Critical Thinking** **Comparing and Contrasting** Choose two different biomes and then compare adaptations of two different groups of plants in those biomes.

Thinking Visually

Creating Artwork
Choose one of the plants discussed in this section. Then, create a piece of artwork that shows how the plant is adapted to live in its natural environment. Label the particular adaptation you are illustrating.

25–3 Section Assessment

1. Aquatic plants have adaptations to take in sufficient oxygen, whereas desert plants have adaptations to take in and conserve water.
2. Carnivorous plants obtain nutrients by trapping and digesting insects. Parasitic plants obtain nutrients from the tissues of other plants.
3. Some plants make compounds that are poisonous to animals or disrupt their growth and development.
4. Salt-tolerant plants are able to pump excess salt out of tissues.
5. Adaptations for getting water, such as deep root systems, and reducing water loss due to transpiration, such as spiny leaves or waxy cuticles
6. Student answers should reflect an understanding of the ways in which plants are adapted to live in different environments.

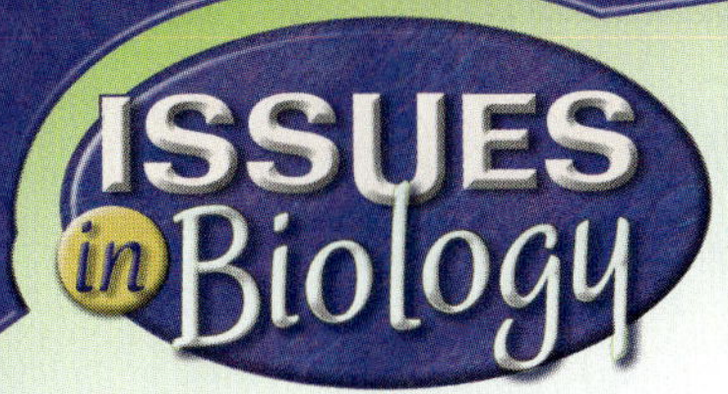

Should Herbal Remedies Be Regulated?

 BIIE 1.m

Natural herbal medicines and dietary supplements can be found in the medicine cabinets of millions of Americans. Annually, Americans spend about $2 billion on herbal remedies. These remedies include St. John's wort, for treatment of depression; *Echinacea,* for colds and flu; and *Ephedra,* for weight loss.

Because these preparations are made from plants and plant extracts, they are considered to be foods and food supplements, not drugs. As a result, the Food and Drug Administration (FDA) cannot require studies to determine the safety and effectiveness of herbal substances. Advocates for herbal products say that additional regulations are not needed. Critics worry that many of these products are as powerful and as dangerous as drugs.

SNEEZING? CHILLS? FLU?

Try Echinacea to **RELIEVE** your cold and flu symptoms!

Echinacea will boost your immune system to fight upper respiratory tract infections!

Warning: Do not use Echinacea if you are pregnant, intend to become pregnant, have an autoimmune disease, liver disease, or are allergic to daisies, chrysanthemums, or ragweed. Consult with your physician or pharmacist before beginning any self-medication.

The Viewpoints

Are Herbal Remedies Safe?

Natural herbal products have been used for thousands of years by people of every culture. *Ephedra,* for example, comes from the Chinese herb *ma huang* and has been used to treat asthma and nasal congestion for centuries. Remedies using *Echinacea* were developed long ago by Native Americans. Such substances should continue to be exempt from new FDA regulations and available without a prescription. Herbal substances present consumers with increased health benefits combined with low risks.

Are Herbal Remedies Dangerous?

Just because a product is "natural" does not mean that it is safe. Plants produce many substances that are more powerful and dangerous than synthetic drugs. *Ephedra,* sometimes used for weight loss, is itself a powerful stimulant that can cause hypertension, stroke, and perhaps death. St. John's wort interferes with the functions of many drugs, including medications for AIDS, epilepsy, and heart disease. As with other drugs, the FDA should regulate and test herbal substances for safety and effectiveness.

Research and Decide

1. **Analyzing the Viewpoints** To make an informed decision, learn more about this issue by consulting library or Internet sources. Write why some people prefer herbal remedies to drugs. Explain why some people think that herbal remedies should be better regulated.
2. **Forming Your Opinion** If an extract of an herb such as *Echinacea* produces effects as powerful as those of synthetic drugs, should it be regulated in the same way? What principles should shape government policies regarding these substances?
3. **Persuasive Writing** Write an e-mail to a friend who is thinking about taking *Echinacea.* Provide guidelines for evaluating labels and ads for *Echinacea* so that your friend can discuss this topic with an adult family member.

For: Links from the authors
Visit: PHSchool.com
Web Code: cbe-7253

 **BIIE 1.m**

Ask student volunteers to look through popular magazines to find advertisements for herbal remedies and dietary supplements. Other students can look for articles supporting or opposing the sale of herbal remedies. Have students bring the advertisements and articles, or copies of them, to class so other students may also read them. Challenge students to find any claims the manufacturers make about the products and any verification of the products' efficacy.

Research and Decide

1. Some people prefer herbal remedies because they believe these products are "natural" as opposed to synthetic. Others think that herbal remedies are potentially dangerous because they have not undergone rigorous testing.
2. Students' opinions may vary. Some students might believe that if the effects of an herbal extract are as powerful as those of synthetic drugs, the herbal substance should be regulated in the same way, because the misuse or abuse of the herbal substance could be harmful to people's health. Students might suggest that the principles that should shape public policy regarding herbal substances are freedom of choice versus public safety.
3. In their e-mails, students should provide guidelines for evaluating the safety and effectiveness of *Echinacea.* For example, they might advise the friend to look on the label for dosage information and possible drug interactions. They should not tell the friend whether or not to take the product, but give accurate information so that the friend can discuss the product with an adult family member.

Students can research herbal remedies on the site developed by authors Ken Miller and Joe Levine.

Real-World Lab

 **BIIE 1.b**

Objective Students will be able to identify the locations of meristems that can be forced to form roots on leaf and stem cuttings through the use of rooting hormone. L1 L2 L3

Skills Focus **Observing, Formulating Hypotheses, Comparing and Contrasting**

Time 45 minutes for setup; 10 minutes for observation several times over 3 weeks

Advance Prep Assemble materials ahead of time. Coleus plants are readily available either by purchase or on loan from a houseplant grower. They must routinely be cut back, so taking cuttings should not be a problem. To avoid confounding variables, all cuttings should come from the same cultivar. Rooting hormone and potting soil are available at most lawn and garden centers.

Safety
- Students should use caution with scalpels. Keep the potting soil moist and provide dust masks to any students who may be allergic to dust or mold.
- Make sure that students wear plastic gloves when applying rooting compound and if commercial potting soil is not used. Properly dispose of gloves.
- Make sure that students wash their hands with soap and warm water before leaving the lab.

Teaching Tips
- Rooting hormone belongs to a class of chemical messengers called auxins. Their general effect is to control cell size and shape, but they often act in concert with cytokinins to initiate cell proliferation and differentiation.
- Before students take their cuttings, you may need to remind them that each branch is a stem segment; they do not need to take "stem tip" cuttings from only the central stem of each plant.
- Compare and contrast the nervous system and the chemical system of hormones in animals and plants. Point out that animals have both, but plants must rely on only a chemical system. Thus, plants are dependent on hormones for sophisticated developmental control, as seen in the effects of auxins on both root and leaf development.

Expected Outcomes
- In Part A, all plants should develop roots. The greatest difference in root development should be seen in the week 1 plants. By 2 weeks, the natural proliferation of roots should begin to overshadow the "jump-start" effect of using rooting hormone. The tip cuttings in Part A that are treated at the tops should show apical dominance, while the untreated ones will show lateral dominance.
- In Part B, no roots should develop in the internodal segments. It is possible that treating only an internode will cause roots to develop from an adjacent node as the rooting hormone is transported to the node. Roots will develop from the vascular tissue on the undersides of leaves, but the veins must be nicked before treating in order to expose the terminal meristem inside the outer layer of cells. Students must make sure the leaves are firmly in contact with moist soil for this procedure to work.

Real-World Lab

 **BIIE 1.b**

Using Hormones to Control Plant Development

Plant hormones have many practical uses. Growers spray gibberellins on sugar cane and fruits to promote their growth. Orchid growers use cytokinins when they clone orchids. Auxins are used to keep potatoes from sprouting and apples from falling from trees before they are ripe. Auxins are also used to stimulate pineapples to flower and develop fruits. In this investigation, you will use auxins to identify the locations of meristems that can be forced to form roots on leaf and stem cuttings.

Problem How do auxins affect plant development?

Materials
- large coleus plants (total of at least 4 branches)
- dissecting pin
- scalpel
- metric ruler
- rooting compound (auxin powder)
- commercial potting soil
- 12 paper cups
- flat, wooden toothpick

Skills Observing, Formulating Hypotheses, Comparing and Contrasting

Procedure    

Part A: Observing the Effects of Auxins on Root and Leaf Development

1. Use a scalpel to cut a piece containing a stem tip from a coleus plant as shown. The stem-tip cutting should include a stem tip and 2 nodes that are at least 1 cm from the tip of the stem. Cut the stem tip 3 mm below these 2 nodes. Cut 3 more stem-tip cuttings. **CAUTION:** *Be careful with sharp instruments.*
2. Cut off the petioles growing from the bottom node of each stem-tip cutting. Make sure the cut is 3 mm from the stem. See the illustration.
3. Put on plastic gloves. Cut the top from each stem-tip cutting, 3 mm above the top node. Using a toothpick, apply only enough rooting compound to coat the cut surfaces on the tops of 2 stem-tip cuttings.
4. Cut 8 pieces from the lower stems of each plant as shown. As in step 1, each stem cutting should contain at least 2 nodes and be cut 3 mm below the lower node.
5. Dip the stem-tip cuttings and 6 of the lower stem cuttings into powdered rooting hormone (an auxin) so that the bottom nodes are covered with powder. Leave 2 stem cuttings untreated.
6. Use a dissecting pin to punch several small drainage holes in the bottoms of the paper cups. Fill each paper cup with potting soil. Push the bottom of each cutting into the potting soil in a paper cup so that the bottom nodes are buried. Keep the soil moist but not wet. Label the paper cups to indicate what type of cutting each cup contains.
7. After 1 week, carefully pull 1 treated and 1 untreated stem cutting from the potting soil. Gently wash the soil off the roots and observe the differences. Record your observations and discard the cuttings you removed. Repeat this procedure after 2 weeks.
8. Allow the stem-tip cuttings to grow for 3 weeks. Observe, measure with precision, and record any differences in leaf growth between the treated and untreated plants.

Stem-Tip Cutting

At least 1 cm
Nodes
Petioles
3 mm
Cut here
Step 1

Cut here
Cut here
3 mm
Step 2

Cut here
3 mm
Step 3

Stem Cutting

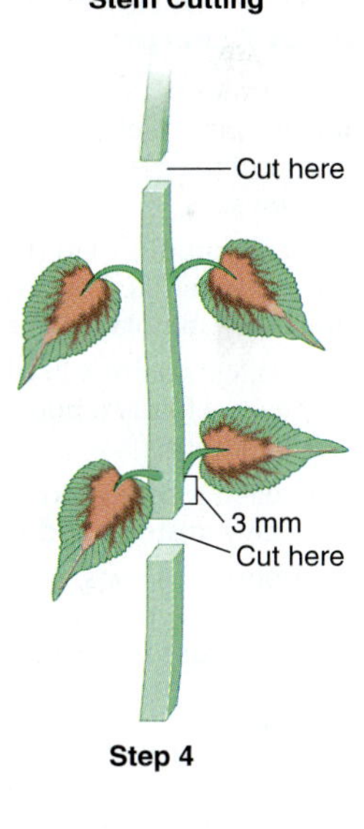

Part B: Using the Effects of Auxins

9. **Formulating Hypotheses** Because auxins stimulate meristems to produce new roots and other plant parts, auxins can be used to locate meristems. Record a hypothesis about whether there are meristems in stems between nodes and in the veins on the bottoms of leaves.

10. **Designing Experiments** Design an experiment to test your hypothesis. You may need to nick the leaf veins slightly with a scalpel to expose any meristems in the veins to the rooting compound and moist soil. With your teacher's approval, carry out your experiment.

Analyze and Conclude

1. **Comparing and Contrasting** What differences did you see between the roots of the auxin-treated and untreated cuttings after 1 week? How can you explain these differences?
2. **Comparing and Contrasting** Was there more difference between roots of treated cuttings and untreated cuttings after 1 week or 2 weeks? How can you explain this result?
3. **Inferring** In step 8, what differences did you observe between the leaves of the treated and untreated stem-tip cuttings? Explain your observations.
4. **Drawing Conclusions** Did the results of your experiment in step 10 show that there are meristem cells in the stem between nodes? In the veins on the underside of the leaves? Explain your conclusions.
5. **Evaluating** Do you consider your conclusions in step 4 to be valid? Explain your answer.

Go Further

Designing Experiments Examine a coleus plant and list questions about the effect of ethylene gas on the development of flowers and new leaves. Design an experiment to answer one of your questions. Use a bruised apple as a source of ethylene gas.

Analyze and Conclude

1. The treated plants have more roots than untreated ones. The effect of the rooting hormone initiating root development accounts for this.

2. There is relatively greater difference between treated and untreated plants in the first week. Rooting hormone is effective only to start the rooting process. After it is initiated, normal proliferation of roots controls development.

3. Treated plants should show signs of apical dominance, such as longer internodes and smaller leaves. Untreated plants should show a general uniformity of leaf size.

4. No roots should develop in the internodal regions. Meristematic tissue is scarce between nodes; it is present in leaf veins.

5. Students should explain that their conclusions are valid because they followed the procedure carefully.

Go Further

The first effects of ethylene gas should be withered flowers followed by leaves dying.

Chapter 25 Study Guide

Study Tip

Write each Vocabulary term on a separate card, as well as a question for each Key Concept. Place the cards into a box. Have each student draw a card and give the definition of the Vocabulary term or the answer to the Key Concept question. Continue until all cards have been selected.

Thinking Visually

1. Ethylene production increases.
2. Chlorophyll is destroyed.
3. An abscission layer forms.

Chapter 25 Assessment

Reviewing Content

1. a
2. a
3. d
4. c
5. b
6. d
7. b
8. b
9. b
10. a

Understanding Concepts

11. Auxins cause growth in plants by stimulating cell elongation. These substances are produced in the apical meristem, or growing tip, of a plant.

12. Auxins migrate to the side of a stem away from light. High concentrations of auxin on the shady side of a stem cause these cells to increase in length. Thus, the stem bends toward the light.

13. Apical dominance is the delay in growth at the lateral bud because auxins move out from the apical meristem. The closer the bud to the stem's tip, the more it is inhibited. Example: If you remove the tip of a stem, more side branches will grow, changing the shape of the plant.

14. The responses of plants to external stimuli are called tropisms. Stems show phototropism when they grow toward light and gravitropism when they grow against gravity. Roots show gravitropism when they grow with the force of gravity.

Chapter 25 Study Guide

25–1 Hormones and Plant Growth

Key Concepts

- Plant hormones are chemical substances that control a plant's patterns of growth and development, and the plant's responses to environmental conditions.
- Auxins are produced in the apical meristem and are transported downward into the rest of the plant. They stimulate cell elongation.
- In plants, cytokinins stimulate cell division and the growth of lateral buds, and cause dormant seeds to sprout.
- Gibberellins produce dramatic increases in size, particularly in stems and fruit.
- In response to auxins, fruit tissues release small amounts of the hormone ethylene. Ethylene then stimulates fruits to ripen.

Vocabulary

hormone, p. 634 • target cell, p. 634
phototropism, p. 634 • auxin, p. 635
gravitropism, p. 635 • lateral bud, p. 636
apical dominance, p. 636 • herbicide, p. 636
cytokinin, p. 636 • gibberellin, p. 637
ethylene, p. 638

25–2 Plant Responses

Key Concepts

- Plant tropisms include gravitropism, phototropism, and thigmotropism. Each of these responses demonstrates the ability of plants to respond effectively to external stimuli, such as gravity, light, and touch.
- Photoperiodism in plants is responsible for the timing of seasonal activities such as flowering and growth.
- As cold weather approaches, deciduous plants turn off photosynthetic pathways, transport materials from leaves to roots, and seal leaves off from the rest of the plant.

Vocabulary

tropism, p. 639
thigmotropism, p. 639
short-day plant, p. 641
long-day plant, p. 641
photoperiodism, p. 641
phytochrome, p. 641
dormancy, p. 641
abscission layer, p. 642

25–3 Plant Adaptations

Key Concepts

- To take in sufficient oxygen, many aquatic plants have tissues with large air-filled spaces through which oxygen can diffuse.
- Plant adaptations to a desert climate include extensive roots, reduced leaves, and thick stems that can store water.
- Plants that have specialized features for obtaining nutrients include carnivorous plants and parasites.
- Many plants defend themselves against insect attack by manufacturing compounds that have powerful effects on animals.

Vocabulary

xerophyte, p. 644
epiphyte, p. 645

Thinking Visually

Using the information in this chapter, complete the following flowchart about leaf abscission.

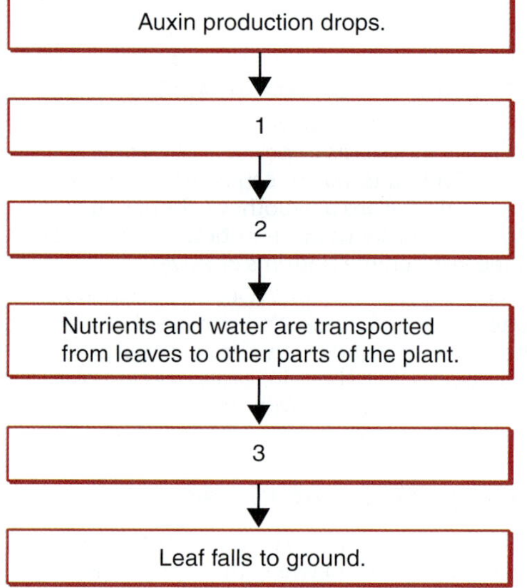

CHAPTER RESOURCES

Print:

- ***Teaching Resources,*** Chapter Vocabulary Review, Graphic Organizer, Chapter 25 Tests: Levels A and B
- ***Laboratory Assessment,*** Laboratory Assessment 7

Technology:

- ***Computer Test Bank,*** Chapter 25 Test
- ***iText,*** Chapter 25 Assessment

Chapter 25 Assessment

Reviewing Content

Choose the letter that best answers the question or completes the statement.

1. A substance produced in one part of a plant that affects another part is a(an)
   a. hormone.
   b. enzyme.
   c. auxin.
   d. phytochrome.
2. A high concentration of auxins can inhibit plant growth. Many of these compounds are used as
   a. herbicides.
   b. pesticides.
   c. fruit ripeners.
   d. growth stimulants.
3. In the illustration below, what phenomenon is responsible for the shape of the plant on the left?
   a. gravitropism
   b. dormancy
   c. phytochromes
   d. apical dominance

4. Substances that stimulate cell division and cause dormant seeds to sprout are
   a. gibberellins.
   b. auxins.
   c. cytokinins.
   d. phytochromes.
5. Japanese scientists found that the extraordinary growth of a certain rice plant was caused by
   a. auxin.
   b. gibberellin.
   c. cytokinin.
   d. ethylene.
6. The response of a plant to touch is
   a. gravitropism. **c.** photoperiodism.
   b. phototropism. **d.** thigmotropism.

Interactive textbook with assessment at PHSchool.com

7. Photoperiodism is the response of plants to
   a. water and dryness.
   b. light and darkness.
   c. gravity.
   d. nutrients.
8. The period during which an organism's growth and activity decreases or stops is called
   a. abscission.
   b. dormancy.
   c. thigmotropism.
   d. gravitropism.
9. Plants that have air-filled spaces in their tissues are likely to be
   a. desert plants.
   b. aquatic plants.
   c. epiphytes.
   d. parasites.
10. Plants that grow directly on the bodies of other plants but manufacture their own food are
    a. epiphytes.
    b. aquatic plants.
    c. carnivorous plants.
    d. parasites.

Understanding Concepts

11. What is the role of auxins in a plant? Where are these substances produced?
12. How do auxins cause a plant to grow toward a light source?
13. Explain and give an example of apical dominance.
14. What is a tropism? Give an example of a tropism that affects plant stems and one that affects roots.
15. What is photoperiodism?
16. Describe two different ways in which a plant may respond to changes in day length.
17. Many Arctic plants flower in the late spring when the days are very long. Are these plants more likely to be long-day plants or short-day plants? Explain.
18. What roles does phytochrome play in plants?
19. Describe what happens to deciduous plants during winter dormancy.
20. What are two adaptations found in many desert plants?

If your class subscribes to the iText, your students can go online to access an interactive version of the Student Edition and a self-test.

(Continued from page 650)

15. Photoperiodism is responsible for the timing of seasonal activities such as flowering and growth according to the length of day and night.

16. Many plants time their flowering by day length. Plants that flower in the late spring or early summer when days are longer are called long-day plants. Plants that flower in late summer, autumn, or winter when days are short are called short-day plants. Many plants also prepare for winter dormancy with changes (a shortening) in day length.

17. They are long-day plants because they flower when days are very long.

18. Phytochrome is a plant pigment responsible for photoperiodism. Phytochrome absorbs red light and activates a number of signaling pathways within plant cells. Plants respond to regular changes in these pathways. The changes determine the patterns of a variety of plant responses.

19. During winter dormancy, a plant's growth and activity decrease or stop. As cold weather approaches, deciduous trees turn off the pathways of photosynthesis, transport materials from leaves to the roots, and seal the leaf off from the rest of the plant.

20. Adaptations of desert plants include extensive shallow, fibrous root systems, or very deep-growing taproot systems; reduced leaves; and thick stems that can store water.

TIME SAVER

HOMEWORK GUIDE

Section:	Questions:
Section 25–1	1–5, 11–13, 24
Section 25–2	6–8, 14–19, 21–23, 25, 27
Section 25–3	9, 10, 20, 26, 28, 29

Chapter 25 Assessment

Critical Thinking

21. Flowers of a species need to open at the same time to ensure pollination.

22. The gravitropic response would cause the root to grow downward with the pull of gravity and the stem to grow upward against it.

23. (a) Even when a plant is placed in a horizontal or inverted position, the plant stem will grow upward due to negative gravitropism. (b) No, the presence of the overhead lights in the experimental setup added an additional variable—plant stems also show positive phototropism—so the upward growth of the stems cannot be simply attributed to negative gravitropism. (c) Possible answers include setting up the experiment so that the light is coming from the side.

24. Trees continue to grow taller because the top of each shoot has an apical meristem that contains cells that are actively dividing. Thus, tree branches continue to increase in length as long as the tree is alive.

25. Nights near the equator are too long to allow spinach to flower and grow properly.

26. Carnivorous plants grow in nitrogen-poor soil. They get their nitrogen from capturing and digesting animals.

27. Loss of leaves also prevents the loss of water through transpiration and the freezing of tissues.

28. Being able to climb allows the plants to grow high enough to expose their leaves to light without a sizable energy investment in producing a tall, strong trunk.

29. Student answers should reflect an understanding of the plant adaptations described in Section 25–3 that enable plants to survive in particular environments.

Chapter 25 Assessment

Critical Thinking

21. Inferring Why is it important that the flowers of a particular species open at about the same time?

22. Predicting What would happen if you accidentally planted a seed wrong side up?

23. Interpreting Graphics The growth responses of plants to external stimuli are called tropisms. The response is positive if the plant part grows toward the stimulus. The response is negative if the plant part grows away from the stimulus. Different parts of the same plant may respond differently to the same external stimulus. The experiment shown below tested the effect of gravitropism on plant growth. The conclusion drawn from the experiment was that the plant stems grow upward due to negative gravitropism.

a. What was the probable hypothesis for this experiment?

b. From the experimental setup shown, was the hypothesis successfully tested? Explain.

c. Indicate what kinds of changes you would make to improve this experimental design.

24. Applying Concepts The tallest humans stop growing eventually, yet a tall tree increases its height year after year. Why are plants able to continue to grow taller as long as they live?

25. Inferring Spinach is a long-day plant that grows best with a night length of 10 hours or less. Why is spinach not usually grown in regions near the equator?

26. Applying Concepts How is trapping and digesting insects an adaptation that contributes to the survival of the Venus' flytrap?

27. Problem Solving Many plants and trees exhibit a seasonal loss of leaves as a means of conserving nutrients. Can you think of another advantage that the loss of leaves would provide?

28. Inferring Why might climbing plants have a survival advantage over some nonclimbing plants in tropical rain forests and other densely grown areas?

29. Applying Concepts Choose an environment. Then, describe at least two structural and physiological adaptations that enable a plant to thrive in that environment.

Unity and Diversity Review the characteristics shared by members of the kingdom Plantae that you learned about in Chapter 18 and Chapter 22. Can you make a case for not including some parasitic plants in this kingdom?

Writing in Science

Sometimes people grow houseplants on a windowsill. Books on houseplants often advise giving the plants a one-quarter turn every other week. Write a paragraph explaining why turning the plant is a good idea. (*Hint:* Be sure to include an explanation of tropisms in your answer.)

Performance-Based Assessment

Bulletin Board Display Create a bulletin board display that shows the effects that auxins, cytokinins, gibberellins, and ethylene have on plant growth and development. You can use photos from gardening catalogs or magazines. Include information on how gardeners can use this knowledge to achieve desired effects.

For: An interactive self-test
Visit: PHSchool.com
Web Code: cba-7250

Focus on the BIG Idea

One of the defining characteristics of plants is that they produce their own food by photosynthesis. Because some parasitic plants do not do this, students may argue that they should not be considered to be plants.

Writing in Science

In their paragraphs, students should explain that window light comes from one direction only. A plant growing in a window will grow toward the light. Turning the plant will keep exposing a new part of the stem to light. The stem will continue to grow straight.

Performance-Based Assessment

Review for accuracy the information that students will use in their bulletin board displays. The illustrations and examples they cite should show an understanding of the role each hormone plays in plant development. For example, students can illustrate and explain how auxin and cytokinin levels control the shape of some plants.

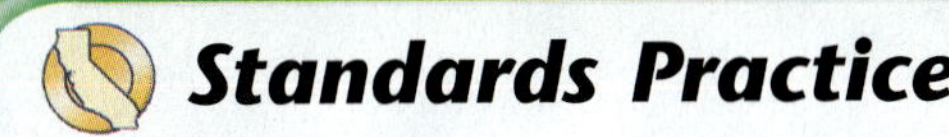

Test-Taking Tip Take the time to read each question completely, including all the answer choices. Consider each possible choice before determining which answer is correct.

Directions: Choose the letter that best answers the question or completes the statement.

1. Which of the following are caused by auxins?
   A apical dominance
   B cell elongation
   C phototropism
   D all of the above
2. Which of the following cause fruit to ripen?
   A auxins
   B cytokinins
   C ethylene
   D 2,4-D chemicals
3. Which is an example of thigmotropism?
   A leaf abscission
   B climbing vines
   C blooming
   D photoperiodism
4. All of the following are plant adaptations to a desert climate EXCEPT
   A thick stems.
   B small leaves.
   C deep root system.
   D salt tolerance.
5. What causes a short-day plant to flower?
   A continuous darkness for a certain length of time
   B phytochromes
   C at least 10 hours of continuous red light
   D both A and B

Questions 6–8 Each of the lettered choices below refers to the following numbered statements. Select the best lettered choice. A choice may be used once, more than once, or not at all.

A Lateral bud
B Apical dominance
C Gibberellin
D Dormancy

6. Meristematic area on the side of a stem that gives rise to side branches
7. Includes turning off photosynthesis and sealing the leaf off from the rest of the plant
8. Increases growth in plant stems and fruits

Questions 9–10 The results of an experiment are summarized in the art below. Use information from the art to answer the questions that follow.

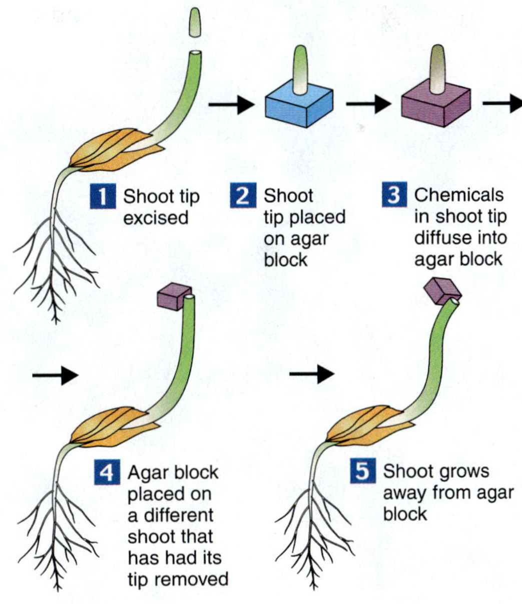

9. Which of the following can be concluded from the results of this experiment alone?
   A Hormones are produced in the growing tips of plants.
   B Plants grow toward the sun because of compounds produced in their stems.
   C Agar blocks contain a variety of plant compounds.
   D Compounds produced in shoot tips can cause stems to bend.
10. Based on your knowledge of plant hormones, which of the following best explains the results of this experiment?
   A Auxins produced in the shoot tip caused cell enlargement in the growing stem.
   B Cytokinins produced in the shoot tip caused cell enlargement in the growing stem.
   C Auxins produced in the shoot tip caused lateral bud growth.
   D Cytokinins caused the shoot tip to die.

Standards Practice

1. D 2. C 3. B 4. D 5. C 6. A 7. D 8. C 9. D 10. A

Online at PHSchool.com

Have students check their understanding of the chapter by logging onto Success Tracker.

Your students can independently test their knowledge of the chapter and print out their test results for your files.

UNIT 8

Dear Colleague,

There's no doubt about it. Those of us who live mostly indoors in urban areas usually see invertebrates as nuisances—if we even see them at all. There are cockroaches that ensure that life will persist on Earth, even if we humans eradicate one another. There are ants that, sooner or later, infest nearly any structure we build. There are Japanese beetles that devour our gardens. And there are mosquitoes that seem determined to devour us whenever we try to enjoy the outdoor life.

I moved to a woodsy place outside Boston last year and was immediately dazzled by—of all things—dragonflies! I had almost forgotten them, but here they were—red ones, blue ones, small ones, huge ones—darting about and settling on every plant in sight. So it seemed especially fitting to me that a dragonfly would grace the cover of this book!

But what really took me aback, once I settled in, were the odd and unusual (to me, anyway) hymenopterans. I was accustomed to run-of-the-mill honeybees, bumblebees, and yellow jackets. I was not prepared for some of their relatives and look-alikes that swarmed over our yard. Several were just hymenopteran species I hadn't seen before, and which I still haven't identified. Others were hymenopteran mimics; stingless, harmless insects that mimic the body forms and colors of their less palatable cousins. "Yes, Joe," they seemed to be buzzing, "all that evolution and natural history stuff you write about us in these books *is* real after all—and not just in tropical rain forests!"

UNIT 8 Invertebrates

Like most spiders, the female jumping spider protects her eggs until they hatch.

Chapters

Internal structures of a typical spider

Focus on the BIG Ideas

- Structure and Function
- Unity and Diversity

From sponges and corals to insects and sea stars, the countless species of animals without backbones offer an incredible variety of body plans whose structures serve the essential functions of life. Within each major group of animals, similarities and differences in structure reveal the unity that underlies this diversity.

Go Online PHSchool.com
For: Latest discoveries
Visit: PHSchool.com
Web Code: cbe-8000

Joe Levine

I can imagine, though, that—personal fascination with inverts aside—more than a few of you look at this unit with mixed feelings. How can you cover all this stuff? Should you even try? The answers depend on your own likes and dislikes (and local standards), but here's my take: Invertebrates have profound effects on our lives in scores of ways—depending, in large part, on where we live. To my mind, the best way to approach this material is to zero in on cases that you can make relevant to your particular collection of students.

If you live in Florida, focus on coral reefs—their otherworldly collection of creatures and their major ecological importance to southern Florida and to the tropics beyond. If you live in the South or Southwest, consider insects and arachnids that carry diseases of humans and livestock. Some of these "bugs" might become more important to our lives than we might like; global warming seems to be encouraging disease-carrying tropical mosquitoes to move north and settle on our side of the Rio Grande and along the Gulf Coast. Wherever you live, the story of plant-pollinator coevolution is as vibrant and important today as it has ever been; if we lose our pollinating bees (and several species are in trouble), many crops across the country could face a pollination crisis.

There is also the sobering reality that if we think about "success" on Earth in terms of total numbers of species and individuals, invertebrates win the prize hands down over the piddling few of us with backbones. Their phenomenal diversity of body forms and ways of making a living are endlessly fascinating—and instructive—to those of us with open minds. And if you need some comic relief, there is always Jonathan Swift's perceptive ditty:

So, naturalists observe, a flea
Hath smaller fleas that on him
  prey;
And those have smaller still to bite
  'em;
And so proceed *ad infinitum.*

Joe Levine

Students can research invertebrates on the site developed by authors Ken Miller and Joe Levine.

Chapter Planner 26 Sponges and Cnidarians

Section and Section Objectives	Time	STANDARDS NCLB	STANDARDS Biology	Activities and Labs
26–1 Introduction to the Animal Kingdom, pp. 657–663 **26.1.1** ***List*** the characteristics that all animals share. **26.1.2** ***Describe*** the essential functions that animals carry out. **26.1.3** ***Identify*** the important trends in animal evolution.	1 period (1/2 block)	7 5.a		**SE:** ***Inquiry Activity,*** What makes an animal an animal?, p. 656 L2 **TE:** ***Build Science Skills,*** p. 660 L3, p. 660 L2 L3, p. 661 L2 **SE:** ***Quick Lab,*** How can body symmetry affect movement?, p. 662 L2
26–2 Sponges, pp. 664–667 **26.2.1** ***Explain*** what a sponge is. **26.2.2** ***Describe*** how sponges carry out essential functions. **26.2.3** ***Describe*** the ecology of sponges.	1 period (1/2 block)	7 2.a		**TE:** ***Build Science Skills,*** p. 664 L2 **TE:** ***Demonstration,*** p. 666 L2
26–3 Cnidarians, pp. 669–675 **26.3.1** ***Explain*** what a cnidarian is. **26.3.2** ***Describe*** the two body plans that exist in the cnidarian life cycle. **26.3.3** ***Describe*** how cnidarians carry out essential functions. **26.3.4** ***Identify*** the three groups of cnidarians. **26.3.5** ***Describe*** the ecology of cnidarians.	1 period (1/2 block)	7 2.a		**SE:** ***Technology & Society,*** Using Nature to Produce Sunscreen, p. 668 L2 L3 **TE:** ***Demonstration,*** p. 670 L1 L2, p. 671 L1 L2 **SE:** ***Analyzing Data,*** Coral Vanishing Act, p. 674 L2 L3 **SE:** ***Exploration,*** Investigating the Responses of Hydras to External Stimuli, pp. 676–677 L2 L3 **LMA:** Chapter 26 Lab L2 L3 **LMB:** Chapter 26 Lab L1 L2
Chapter Assessment, pp. 678–681	1 period (1/2 block)			

ACTIVITY PLANNER

SE: *Inquiry Activity,* p. 656; 15 min.; specimens or photos of a variety of organisms, including animals, plants, protists, fungi, and bacteria

TE: *Build Science Skills,* p. 660; 20 min.; prepared slides of cells from the four types of animal tissues, microscope

TE: *Build Science Skills,* p. 660; 15 min.; prepared slides of animal cells and plant cells, microscope

TE: *Build Science Skills,* p. 661; 20 min.; 3 different-colored blocks of modeling compound, plastic knife

SE: *Quick Lab,* p. 662; 15 min.; modeling clay

TE: *Build Science Skills,* p. 664; 15 min.; natural sponge, hand lens, prepared slide of sponge, microscope

TE: *Demonstration,* p. 666; 5 min.; natural sponge, synthetic sponge, balance scale, water

TE: *Demonstration,* p. 670; 5 min.; clear plastic cup, colored plastic cup

TE: *Demonstration,* p. 671; 5 min.; oblong balloon, umbrella

SE: *Exploration,* pp. 676–677; 45 minutes, 10 minutes the following day; 6 test tubes with screw caps, test-tube rack, green hydras, brown hydras, aluminum foil, pond or spring water, glass-marking pencil, dropper pipette, transparent tape

PLANNING KEY

Ability Levels

for students performing . . .

below grade level L1

at grade level L2

above grade level L3

Print Components

SE	Student Edition	LA	Lab Assessment
TE	Teacher's Edition	BTM	Biotechnology Manual
RSW	Reading & Study Workbook A	IDM	Issues and Decision Making
ARSW	Adapted Reading & Study Workbook B	LW	Lab Worksheets
TR	Teaching Resources	LMA	Laboratory Manual A
IF	Investigations in Forensics	LMB	Laboratory Manual B

Tech Components

CTB	Computer Test Bank
BD	BioDetectives DVD
TP	Transparencies Plus
PLM	Probeware Lab Manual
ABC	ABC DVD Library
LS	Lab Simulations
VL	Virtual Labs

Interactive textbook with assessment at PHSchool.com

Program Resources	Assessment	Media and Technology
TR: Lesson Plan 26–1, Section Summary, p. 4 L1, p. 15 L2, Worksheets, pp. 7–8 L1, pp. 17–20 L2 **RSW:** Section 26–1 L2 **ARSW:** Section 26–1 L1	**SE:** 26–1 Section Assessment, p. 663 **TR:** Section Review 26–1	**iText:** Section 26–1 **TP:** 26–1 Interest Grabber, Section Outline, Concept Map, Figure 26–5
TR: Lesson Plan 26–2, Section Summary, p. 5 L1, p. 15 L2, Worksheets, pp. 9–10 L1, pp. 21–22 L2 **RSW:** Section 26–2 L2 **ARSW:** Section 26–2 L1	**SE:** 26–2 Section Assessment, p. 667 **TR:** Section Review 26–2	**iText:** Section 26–2 **TP:** 26–2 Interest Grabber, Section Outline, Sponge Life Cycle, Figure 26–8
TR: Lesson Plan 26–3, Section Summary, p. 6 L1, p. 16 L2, Worksheets, pp. 11–13 L1, pp. 23–25 L2, Enrichment L2 L3 **RSW:** Section 26–3 L2 **ARSW:** Section 26–3 L1 **LW:** Chapter 26 Exploration L1 L2 L3	**SE:** 26–3 Section Assessment, p. 675 **TR:** Section Review 26–3	**iText:** Section 26–3 **TP:** 26–3 Interest Grabber, Section Outline, Jellyfish Life Cycle, Figure 26–12
	SE: Chapter 26 Assessment, pp. 678–681 **TR:** Chapter Vocabulary Review, Graphic Organizer, Chapter 26 Test	**iText:** Chapter 26 Assessment **CTB:** Chapter 26 Test

Go Online
Students can do research, share data, and test their knowledge online.

PRESSED FOR TIME?

To Preview the Chapter
- Introduce students to Key Concepts and Vocabulary terms in each section.
- Assign the Reading Strategies for each section.

To Cover the Chapter Quickly
- Have students read all of Section 26–1, read What Is a Sponge? in Section 26–2, and read What Is a Cnidarian? and Groups of Cnidarians in Section 26–3.
- Assign the 26–1 Section Review and questions 1–10, 11–16, 24, 28, and 32 in Chapter 26 Assessment and questions 1–11 in Chapter 26 Standards Practice.

To Review the Chapter
- Assign the Sections 26–1 through 26–3 in the Reading and Study Workbook or the Adapted Reading and Study Workbook.
- Assign Section Reviews for 26–1 through 26–3 and the Chapter Vocabulary Review for Chapter 26 in the Teaching Resources.

CHAPTER 26

ENGAGE/EXPLORE

Inquiry Activity

Objective Students should form an operational definition of an animal. 

Skill Focus **Classifying, Forming Operational Definitions**

Materials specimens or photos of a variety of organisms, including animals, plants, protists, fungi, and bacteria

Time 15 minutes

Safety Avoid exposing students to noxious preservatives and to potential allergens such as animal hair or pollen. Make sure students wash their hands with soap and warm water before leaving the lab.

Strategies

- Include a plant that responds to touch, such as a Venus' flytrap.
- You may want to set up the specimens and photos at stations around the room and have students move from station to station.

Expected Outcomes Students should easily classify most of the organisms into categories, though they may have difficulty classifying sponges and motile protists.

Think About It

1. Students should give at least one reason for how they classified each organism.
2. Students might list such characteristics as multicellular structure, movement, response to stimuli, and lack of chlorophyll.

Assess Prior Knowledge

Remind students that the classification system used in this text includes six kingdoms. Ask a volunteer to list the kingdoms. *(Archaebacteria, Eubacteria, Protista, Fungi, Plantae, Animalia)* Then, ask: **What characteristics distinguish animals from organisms of the other kingdoms?** *(Animals are multicellular heterotrophs that have the ability to move.)* **Are there any animals that don't move during their lives?** *(Some students may know that sponges, for instance, are sessile animals.)* Have students speculate about what functions animals must carry out to survive.

CHAPTER 26

Sponges and Cnidarians

Tube sponges (pink objects) are the most common variety of sponge. Water is constantly filtered through the sponge's body and ejected through the large hole at the top. The golden yellow objects and red objects are crinoids (a type of echinoderm).

Inquiry Activity

What makes an animal an animal?

Procedure 

1. Observe the specimens or photographs of organisms provided by your teacher. Some of the organisms are animals, whereas others are not. Examine each organism carefully.
2. Make a list of each organism's characteristics.

Think About It

1. **Classifying** Classify the organisms into two groups: animals and nonanimals. Give your reasons for putting each organism into a particular group.
2. **Forming Operational Definitions** List at least three characteristics shared by each of the organisms you classified as animals. Describe how these characteristics separate them from the nonanimals.

FACTS AND FIGURES

Why so many kinds of animals?

Animals are tremendously diverse. Animals can be found in almost all habitats, though most animal phyla inhabit Earth's seas. There are about 35 animal phyla, encompassing more than 1.5 million recognized species. Although plants far outnumber animals if you count individuals, plant species aren't nearly as numerous as animal species, and the reasons for that have to do with how plants and animals live. Plants are generally nonmotile, and they obtain the energy they need to carry out cellular functions through photosynthesis. Animals, by contrast, obtain their energy by ingesting other organisms, and they generally must move about and expend energy to acquire the foods they need to live. The great variety of animal shapes and sizes is in large part a consequence of the adaptations made to the great variety of foods that animals eat—or to avoid being eaten.

26–1 Introduction to the Animal Kingdom

7 5.a. Students know plants and animals have levels of organization for structure and function, including cells, tissues, organs, organ systems, and the whole organism.

Of all the kingdoms of organisms, the animal kingdom is the most diverse in appearance. Some animals are so small that they live on or inside the bodies of other animals. Others are many meters long and live in the depths of the sea. They may walk, swim, crawl, burrow, or fly—or not move at all. As you will see, each major group, or phylum, has its own typical body plan.

What Is an Animal?

All members of the animal kingdom share certain characteristics. Animals are all heterotrophs, meaning that they obtain nutrients and energy by feeding on organic compounds from other organisms. Animals are multicellular, or composed of many cells. The cells that make up animal bodies are eukaryotic, meaning that they contain a nucleus and membrane-bound organelles. Unlike the cells of algae, fungi, and plants, animal cells do not have cell walls. **Animals, members of the kingdom Animalia, are multicellular, eukaryotic heterotrophs whose cells lack cell walls.**

The bodies of most animals contain tissues. Recall that a tissue is a group of cells that perform a similar function. Animals have epithelial, muscular, connective, and nervous tissues. Epithelial tissues cover body surfaces. The epithelial cells that line lung surfaces, for example, have thin, flat structures through which gases move in and out easily. The cells of muscle tissue contain proteins that enable the cells to contract, moving parts of animals' bodies. Connective tissue, such as bone and blood, support an animal's body and connect its parts. Cells embedded in bone tissue produce minerals that give strength and hardness to bone. Nervous tissue is composed of nerve cells, which have threadlike projections that act like telephone wires to carry information throughout the body.

CA a

Over 95 percent of all animal species are often grouped in a single, informal category: invertebrates. This group is defined in an odd way—by describing a characteristic that its members do *not* have. **Invertebrates** are animals that do not have a backbone, or vertebral column. They range in size from microscopic dust mites to the giant squid, which is more than 20 meters in length. They include groups as diverse as sea stars, worms, jellyfishes, and insects. The other 5 percent of animals, including fishes, amphibians, reptiles, birds, and mammals, are called **vertebrates,** because they have a backbone.

Guide for Reading

Key Concepts
- What characteristics do all animals share?
- What essential functions do animals carry out?
- What are the important trends in animal evolution?

Vocabulary
invertebrate • vertebrate
feedback inhibition
blastula • protostome
deuterostome • anus
endoderm • mesoderm
ectoderm • radial symmetry
bilateral symmetry
cephalization

Reading Strategy: Monitoring Your Understanding Before you read, write down what you already know about animals. After you have read this section, write down what you learned about animals.

a 7 5.a

Figure 26–1 The animal kingdom includes an incredible diversity of forms and lifestyles. **Despite their differences in appearance, both the collared lizard and the grasshopper are eukaryotic heterotrophs whose cells lack cell walls.**

Section 26–1

7 5.a

1 FOCUS

Objectives

26.1.1 ***List*** the characteristics that all animals share.
26.1.2 ***Describe*** the essential functions that animals carry out.
26.1.3 ***Identify*** the important trends in animal evolution.

Guide for Reading

Vocabulary Preview

Call on volunteers to pronounce each of the Vocabulary words aloud. Correct any mispronunciations, and note any words that English language learners have special trouble pronouncing.

Reading Strategy

Consider conducting a class brainstorming activity in which students together identify everything they know about animals. Write their answers on the board or chart paper that can be saved. At this point, accept all ideas uncritically. After students have read the section, have them check the characteristics they listed earlier, revising them or adding to them as necessary.

2 INSTRUCT

What Is an Animal?

Build Science Skills

Classifying Have the class brainstorm a list of animals they commonly see in their environment, including birds, insects, mammals, worms, fishes, and so on. Then, divide the class into groups, and have each group classify each animal as either a vertebrate or an invertebrate. Then, ask a member of one group to read aloud its classification. The list will likely favor vertebrates. Ask students to speculate why more vertebrates were mentioned when over 95 percent of all animal species are invertebrates. L1 L2

TIME SAVER — SECTION RESOURCES

Print:
- ***Teaching Resources,*** Lesson Plan 26–1, Adapted Section Summary 26–1, Adapted Worksheets 26–1, Section Summary 26–1, Worksheets 26–1, Section Review 26–1
- ***Reading and Study Workbook A,*** Section 26–1
- ***Adapted Reading and Study Workbook B,*** Section 26–1

Technology:
- ***iText,*** Section 26–1
- ***Transparencies Plus,*** Section 26–1

26–1 (continued)

What Animals Do to Survive

Build Science Skills

Comparing and Contrasting Divide the class into small groups, and ask each group to make a large compare/contrast table on poster board that shows how a variety of different animals carry out the essential physiological processes. Encourage students to add drawings to their tables where appropriate. Check to make sure no two groups are doing the same animals. Display the tables on the classroom wall when the groups have finished. You may want groups to leave space on their posters for the addition of other animals they learn about in this and subsequent chapters. L2

Build Science Skills

Applying Concepts Challenge students to create an animal that has never lived before. They can create a three-dimensional model, draw an illustration, or write a verbal description. Each new animal should meet the definition of *animal* learned in this section, and it must have specializations to enable it to carry out the seven essential animal functions. Tell students they can be as creative as they want in the form of their animals, as long as form meets function in the seven essential ways. L2 L3

What Animals Do to Survive

Animals carry out the following essential functions: feeding, respiration, circulation, excretion, response, movement, and reproduction. Over millions of years, animals have evolved in a variety of ways that enable them to do this. The study of the functions of organisms is called physiology. The structure, or anatomy, of an animal's body enables it to carry out physiological processes.

Many body functions help animals maintain homeostasis, or a relatively stable internal environment. Homeostasis is often maintained by internal feedback mechanisms called feedback loops. Most of these feedback loops involve **feedback inhibition,** in which the product or result of a process stops or limits the process. For example, when a dog becomes too hot, it pants. Panting releases heat, and the animal's body temperature decreases.

Feeding

Feeding Most animals cannot absorb food; instead, they ingest (or eat) it. Animals have evolved a variety of ways to feed. Herbivores eat plants; carnivores eat other animals; and omnivores feed on both plants and animals. Detritivores feed on decaying plant and animal material. Filter feeders are aquatic animals that strain tiny floating organisms from water.

Animals can also form symbiotic relationships, in which two species live in close association with each other. A parasite, for example, is a type of symbiont that lives within or on another organism, the host. The parasite feeds on the host, harming it.

Respiration

Respiration Whether they live in water or on land, all animals respire, which means that they take in oxygen and give off carbon dioxide. Because of their very simple, thin-walled bodies, some animals can rely on the diffusion of these substances through their skin. Most other animals, however, have evolved complex tissues and organ systems for respiration.

Circulation Many small aquatic animals, such as some aquatic worms, rely solely on diffusion to transport oxygen, nutrient molecules, and waste products among all their cells. Diffusion is sufficient because these animals are only a few cell layers thick. Larger animals, however, have some kind of circulatory system to move materials around within their bodies.

Circulation

Excretion

ESL **SUPPORT FOR ENGLISH LANGUAGE LEARNERS**

Vocabulary: Word Analysis

Beginning Contrast the meanings of *vertebrate* and *invertebrate.* Point out that the prefix *in-* sometimes means "not," and that words with this prefix may mean the opposite of the word without the prefix. Explore the meanings of *active/inactive* and *correct/incorrect.* You might look ahead to Chapter 28 and contrast the meanings of complete and incomplete metamorphosis. L1

Intermediate Analyze the terms *ectoderm, endoderm,* and *mesoderm* on page 661. Explain the meaning of the prefixes *endo-* ("inside"), meso- ("middle"), and *ecto-* ("outside"). Also explain that the word part *derm* derives from the Latin word for skin, which here can be interpreted as "tissue." Then, have students speak or write sentences using the three terms.

Excretion A primary waste product of cells is ammonia, a poisonous substance that contains nitrogen. A buildup of ammonia and other waste products would kill an animal. Most animals have an excretory system that either eliminates ammonia quickly or converts it into a less toxic substance that is removed from the body. By eliminating metabolic wastes, excretory systems help maintain homeostasis.

Response Animals respond to events in their environment using specialized cells called nerve cells. In most animals, nerve cells hook up together to form a nervous system. Some cells, called receptors, respond to sound, light, and other external stimuli. Other nerve cells process information and determine how the animal responds. The arrangement of nerve cells in the body changes dramatically from phylum to phylum.

Movement Some adult animals stay attached to a single spot. Most animals, however, are motile, meaning they can move. But both stick-in-the-muds and jet-setters usually have either muscles or musclelike tissues that generate force by becoming shorter. Muscle contraction enables motile animals to move around, usually by working in combination with a support structure called a skeleton. Muscles also help even sedentary animals feed and pump water and fluids through their bodies.

Reproduction Most animals reproduce sexually by producing haploid gametes. Sexual reproduction helps create and maintain genetic diversity in populations. It therefore helps improve species' abilities to evolve when the environment changes. Many invertebrates can also reproduce asexually. Asexual reproduction produces offspring that are genetically identical to the parent. It allows animals to increase their numbers rapidly.

CHECKPOINT *How do sexual and asexual reproduction differ?*

Figure 26–2 Animals carry out seven essential functions: feeding, respiration, circulation, excretion, response, movement, and reproduction. Some snakes feed by constricting, or squeezing, their prey. Humans respire by breathing oxygenated air into lungs. A rabbit's circulatory system pumps blood through closed vessels, which are visible in its ears. Crabs rid their bodies of metabolic wastes by excreting fluid. Like many insects, moths respond to stimuli that they detect from the environment using specialized sense organs such as antennae. Herons move using a system of muscles attached to a low-density skeleton. Animals reproduce either sexually or asexually; lions reproduce sexually and have only a few offspring per litter.

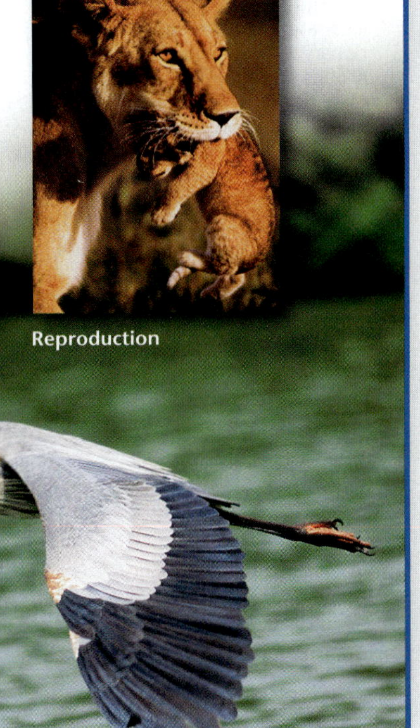

Reproduction

Response

Movement

Build Science Skills

Communicating Results Divide students into small groups, and have each group choose one of the seven essential functions and do an in-depth study of the way several animals carry out that function. These animals should be a diverse group of specific animals from various phyla. For example, a group might study how circulation is accomplished in a jellyfish, a worm, a spider, and a dog. Each group could prepare a brief presentation about each animal, to be delivered when the class is studying the phylum in which the animal is included. L2

Use Community Resources

Contact a local zoo for a speaker to address the class about how modern zoos try to create environments in which animals can carry out essential functions in the most natural ways possible. Have students prepare questions ahead of time related to the seven functions discussed in their text and dealing with animals from phyla they will learn about in the next several chapters. L1 L2

FACTS AND FIGURES

Taking advantage of good times

An animal that can reproduce asexually has the perfect response to good conditions—a rapid increase in population. For instance, the food supply in an area may suddenly become abundant or the living space for a species may suddenly expand. By reproducing asexually in great numbers, some animals can gain a competitive edge by taking advantage of the favorable environment. Methods of asexual reproduction include not only fission and budding but also fragmentation. Some organisms—including sponges as well as certain cnidarians, echinoderms, and annelids—exploit an ability to regrow lost parts (regeneration) and to produce new individuals from parts (fragmentation). A sea star, for example, can produce a new individual from a single arm.

Answer to . . .

CHECKPOINT *Sexual reproduction, which involves the joining of two haploid gametes, helps create and maintain genetic diversity in populations, while asexual reproduction produces offspring that are genetically identical to the parent.*

26–1 (continued)

Trends in Animal Evolution

Use Visuals

Figure 26–3 Emphasize that the diagram shows the evolutionary relationships of groups of organisms. It branches where characteristics, or traits, can distinguish between the different phyla. Then, ask: **Which group of animals is more closely related to annelids: flatworms or arthropods?** *(Arthropods)* **How should you interpret this cladogram in that it shows chordates farther away from mollusks than from echinoderms?** *(Chordates are more closely related to echinoderms than to mollusks.)* L1 L2

Build Science Skills

Applying Concepts To help students understand levels of organization, display an illustration of a human figure that shows internal structures, such as digestive organs, bones, muscles, and nerves. Explain that animals have four types of tissues: epithelial, connective, muscle, and nervous. Call on students to describe the tissues that make up the digestive system, the skeletal system, the nervous system, and so on. Then, have students use a microscope to observe prepared slides of cells from each of the four types of animal tissues. Ask students to write a description of each type of cell. L3

Build Science Skills

Comparing and Contrasting
Have students use a microscope to observe prepared slides of animal cells and plant cells, and ask them to compare the two types of cells. For example, have them compare animal skin cells and plant epidermal cells, such as epidermal cells of leaves. Have students make drawings and write descriptions of the differences in the two types of cells. L2 L3

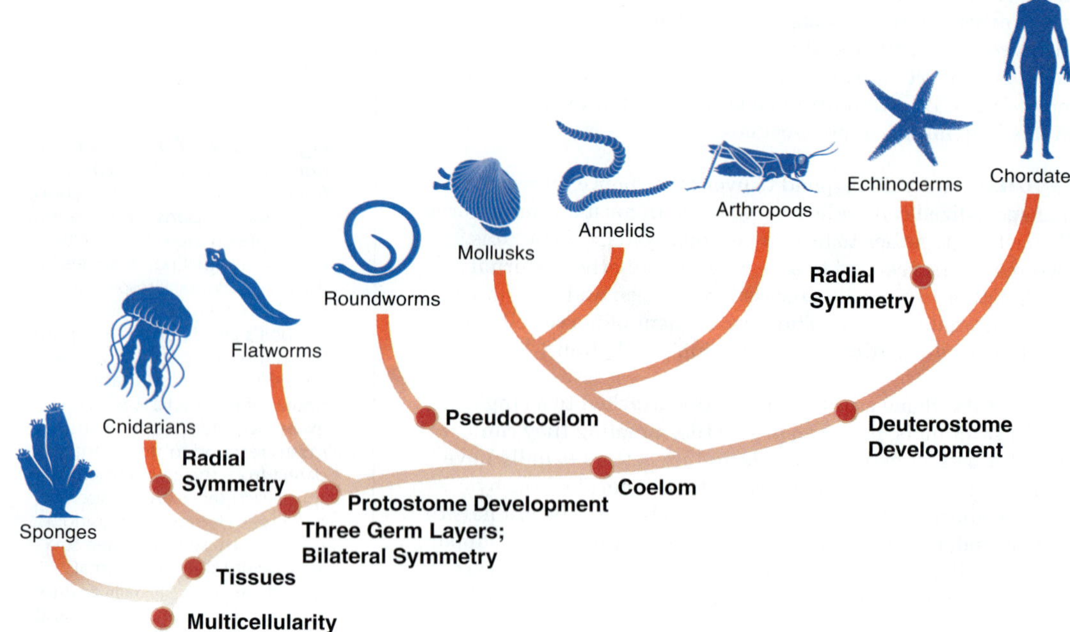

▲ **Figure 26–3** This diagram illustrates phylogenetic, or evolutionary, relationships among major groups of animals. Groups shown close together, such as echinoderms and chordates, are more closely related than groups that are shown farther apart, such as echinoderms and cnidarians. During the course of evolution that produced these different groups, important traits evolved. **Animals that are more complex typically have specialized cells, bilateral body symmetry, cephalization, and a body cavity.**

Trends in Animal Evolution

Your survey of the animal kingdom will begin with simple forms and move through more complicated ones. These different phyla are related to one another by a common evolutionary heritage. The diagram in **Figure 26–3** shows our most current understanding of phylogenetic relationships among groups of living animals. A comparison of the groups in the diagram shows important trends in animal evolution. **Complex animals tend to have high levels of cell specialization and internal body organization, bilateral body symmetry, a front end or head with sense organs, and a body cavity.** In addition, the embryos of complex animals develop in layers.

CA a

Cell Specialization and Levels of Organization As animals have evolved, by natural selection and other evolutionary processes, their cells have become specialized to carry out different functions, such as movement and response. Large animals need greater efficiency in body processes than do very small animals. Unicellular organisms, such as amoebas, move nutrients and waste products directly across their cell membranes. In multicellular organisms such as animals, however, each cell type has a structure and chemical composition that enable it to perform a specialized function. Groups of specialized cells form tissues. Tissues join together to form organs and organ systems—all of which work together to carry out a variety of complex functions.

BIO INSIGHTS — FACTS AND FIGURES

The basic types of tissues
A tissue is a group of specialized cells that have a common structure and a common function. Despite the great diversity of kinds of animals that have evolved, there are only four basic types of animal tissues: epithelial, connective, muscle, and nervous. Epithelial tissue, which consists of tightly packed cells, lines the cavities inside the body and covers the body's outside. A primary function of epithelial tissue is protection against injury, invaders, and fluid loss. Connective tissue connects and supports other tissues. It includes threadlike fibers, bone, cartilage, and blood. Muscle tissue consists of long cells that can contract. It is the most abundant kind of tissue in most animals, which makes sense for an organism that needs to move to survive. Nervous tissue includes cells that are specialized to sense stimuli and transmit signals from one place to another.

Early Development Animals that reproduce sexually begin life as a zygote, or fertilized egg. **Figure 26–4** shows patterns of embryology, or development of the embryo after fertilization. The zygote undergoes a series of divisions to form a **blastula** (BLAS-tyoo-luh), which is a hollow ball of cells. The blastula folds in on itself, forming a single opening called a blastopore. The process of blastopore formation changes a simple ball of cells—similar to an inflated balloon—into an elongated structure with a tube inside, as if you were holding the balloon and pushing your thumbs toward the center.

The blastopore leads into a central tube that runs the length of the developing embryo. This tube becomes the digestive tract and is formed in one of two ways. A **protostome** (PROH-tuh-stohm) is an animal whose mouth is formed from the blastopore. Most invertebrate animals are protostomes. A **deuterostome** (DOO-tur-uh-stohm) is an animal whose anus is formed from the blastopore. The **anus** is the opening through which wastes leave the digestive tract. The mouth is formed second, after the anus. Echinoderms and all vertebrates are deuterostomes. This similarity in embryology may indicate that vertebrates have a closer evolutionary relationship to echinoderms than to other invertebrates.

During early development, the cells of most animal embryos differentiate into three layers called germ layers. The cells of the **endoderm,** or innermost germ layer, develop into the linings of the digestive tract and much of the respiratory system. The cells of the **mesoderm,** or middle layer, give rise to muscles and much of the circulatory, reproductive, and excretory organ systems. The **ectoderm,** or outermost layer, gives rise to sense organs, nerves, and the outer layer of the skin.

CHECKPOINT *Which germ layer gives rise to the muscles?*

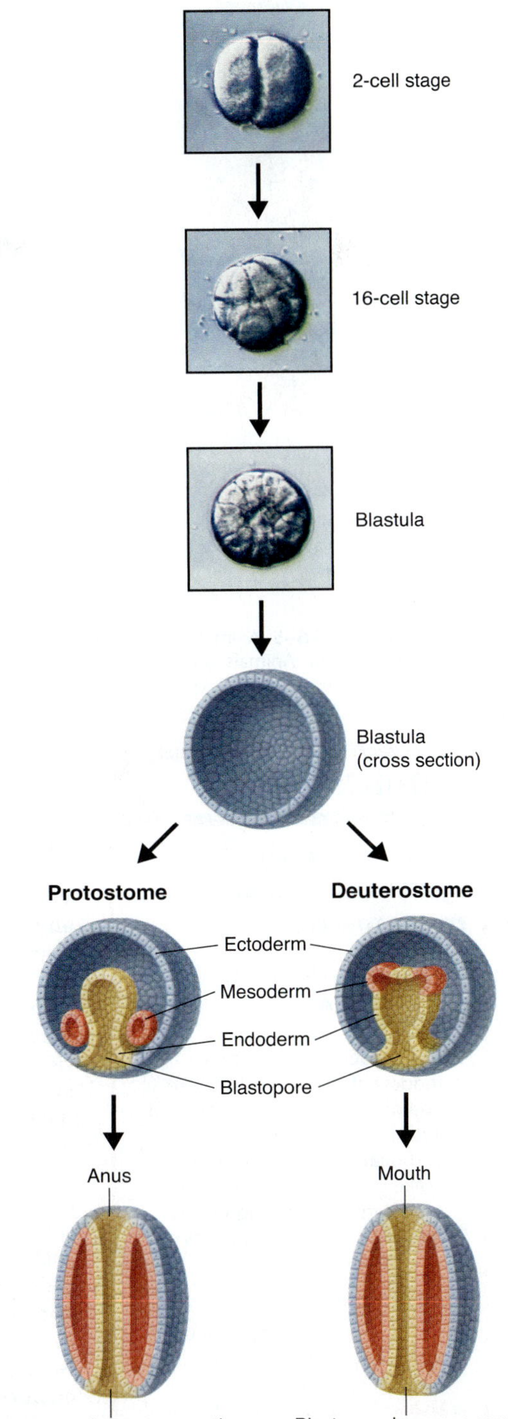

▶ **Figure 26–4** During the early development of animal embryos, cells divide to produce a hollow ball of cells called a blastula. An opening called a blastopore forms in this ball. In protostomes, the blastopore develops into the mouth. In deuterostomes, the blastopore forms an anus. **Interpreting Graphics** *Which cell layer lines the digestive tract in both protostomes and deuterostomes?*

Use Visuals

Figure 26–4 Ask: **What does the illustrated process show about the differences in patterns of embryology among kinds of animals?** *(In protostomes, the blastopore develops into a mouth; in deuterostomes, the blastopore develops into an anus.)* Call on volunteers to identify the three tissue layers by color and to explain what each layer gives rise to in the adult organism. *(Endoderm—lining of the digestive tract and much of the respiratory system; mesoderm—muscles and much of the circulatory, reproductive, and excretory organ systems; ectoderm—sense organs, nerves, and outer layer of the skin)* L2

Build Science Skills

Using Models Divide the class into pairs, and give each pair three colors of modeling compound. Challenge students to work with their partners to create a series of models showing the process of early animal development from zygote to protostome or deuterostome, including how cells differentiate into three germ layers. Students can use Figure 26–4 for reference. L2

BIO INSIGHTS — HISTORY OF SCIENCE

Following the path of stained cells

During early animal development, the cells of the blastula are rearranged to become an embryo called the gastrula, usually with three tissue layers. This process, called gastrulation, involves dramatic movements of cells from the surface of the blastula to interior locations. How do biologists know exactly what happens during this process? In the 1920s, German embryologist W. Vogt carried out classic studies of frog blastulas that showed where cells ended up. His method involved staining blastula cells with different colors of nontoxic dyes. After allowing the process to proceed for different intervals, he would slice open embryos to see where the stained cells had moved. Through this method, he charted "fate maps" for the various cells in the blastula and, thus, mapped out gastrulation. Today, similar studies are done using fluorescent substances.

Answers to . . .

CHECKPOINT *The mesoderm*

Figure 26–4 *The endoderm*

26–1 (continued)

Quick Lab

Objective Students will be able to relate bilateral symmetry to the ability to walk forward. L2

Skill Focus **Inferring, Using Models**

Materials modeling clay

Time 15 minutes

Advance Prep Provide each student with two paper towels—one for each model—to prevent staining their desks with the modeling compound.

Strategy After students have completed the activity, point out that bilateral symmetry is not superior to radial symmetry. The two kinds of symmetry adapt animals to different ways of life. See Facts and Figures below.

Expected Outcomes Students will find it much easier to devise a plausible model of a bilaterally symmetrical walking animal than a radially symmetrical one.

Analyze and Conclude

1. Bilateral symmetry
2. Paired legs make it easier to coordinate walking.

Build Science Skills

Applying Concepts To give students practice with the terms *ventral, dorsal, anterior,* and *posterior,* have them complete the following sentences: (1) The belly is on the [*ventral*] surface of a fish. (2) The back of a wasp is its [*dorsal*] surface. (3) The head is on the [*anterior*] end of a snail. (4) The tail is on the [*posterior*] end of a lizard. L1 L2

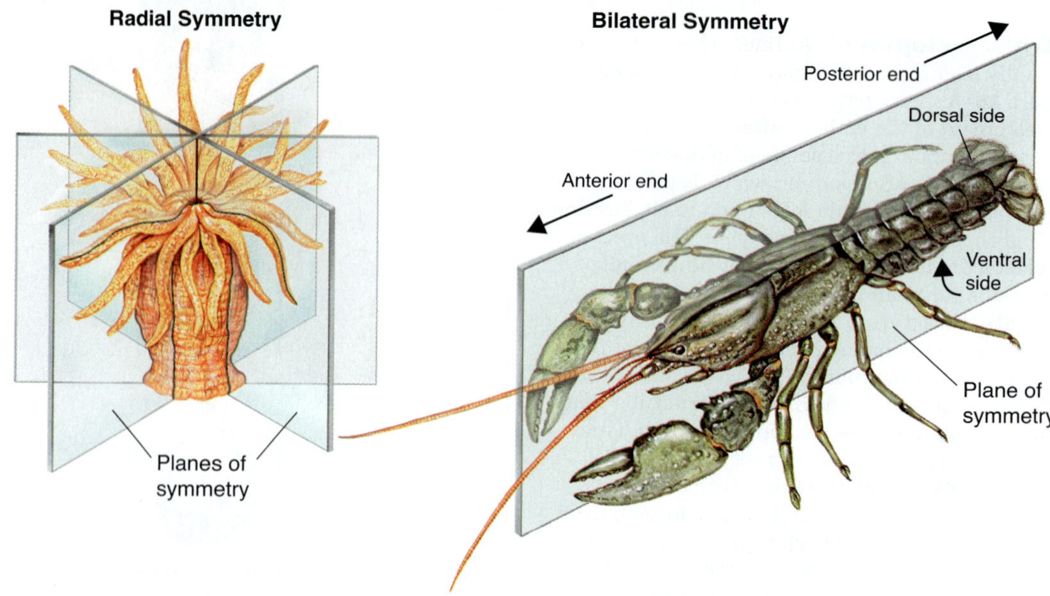

▲ **Figure 26–5** Animals with radial symmetry have body parts that extend from a central point. Animals with bilateral symmetry have distinct anterior and posterior ends and right and left sides. **Interpreting Graphics** *How many planes of symmetry does the crayfish, above right, have?*

Quick Lab

How can body symmetry affect movement?

Material modeling clay

Procedure 

1. Use modeling clay to make models of two animals. Make one model radially symmetrical and the other long, narrow, and bilaterally symmetrical.
2. Make grooves to divide each model into similar segments.
3. Add legs to some segments of your models.

Analyze and Conclude

1. **Inferring** Which type of body symmetry is more suited to walking forward?
2. **Using Models** How is bilateral symmetry an advantage to animals that walk or run?

Body Symmetry With the exception of sponges, every kind of animal exhibits some type of body symmetry in its anatomy, or body structure. Many simple animals, such as the sea anemone shown on the left in **Figure 26–5,** have body parts that repeat around the center of the body. These animals exhibit **radial symmetry,** similar to that of a bicycle wheel, in which any number of imaginary planes can be drawn through the center, each dividing the body into equal halves.

In animals with **bilateral symmetry,** such as the crayfish, only a single imaginary plane can divide the body into two equal halves. Animals with bilateral symmetry have left and right sides. They also usually have front and back ends and upper and lower sides. The anterior is the front end, and the posterior is the back end. The dorsal is the upper side, and the ventral is the lower side.

An anatomy with bilateral symmetry allows for segmentation, in which the body is constructed of many repeated and similar parts, or segments. Animals with bilateral symmetry, such as worms, insects, and vertebrates, typically have external body parts that repeat on either side of the body. The combination of bilateral symmetry and segmentation is found in two of the most successful animal groups—arthropods and vertebrates. Geneticists are learning how gene interactions during development control the growth and form of segments. Amazingly, the same controls are found in humans and insects!

✓CHECKPOINT *How do radial symmetry and bilateral symmetry differ?*

FACTS AND FIGURES

Variations on a theme

Most animals that have radial symmetry have a body like a cylinder, with a main axis around which the body parts are arranged. This main axis runs from the oral end—where the mouth is—to the aboral end—the end opposite the mouth. Any plane passing through that axis splits the animal into mirror images. For animals that are sessile, such as coral, or drifting, such as jellyfishes, this arrangement is adaptive because the animal can meet the environment equally in all directions. Radially symmetrical animals have variations on the theme. Sea anemones, for example, have biradial symmetry, since parts of the body are specialized and only two planes through the central axis will produce a mirror image. Many jellyfishes have quadriradial symmetry, and many sea stars have pentamerous radial symmetry.

Figure 26–6 Animals with cephalization have the brain and other sense organs toward the front of the body. This end of the body comes into contact with the environment first, allowing animals to respond effectively to stimuli. **Inferring** *How might cephalization help animals to move quickly?*

Cephalization Animals with bilateral symmetry usually exhibit the anatomical characteristic called cephalization (sef-uh-lih-ZAY-shun). **Cephalization** is the concentration of sense organs and nerve cells at the front end of the body. Animals with cephalization, such as the dragonfly in **Figure 26–6,** respond to the environment more quickly and in more complex ways than simpler animals can. Animals with bilateral symmetry usually move with the anterior end forward, so this end comes in contact with new parts of the environment first. As sense organs such as eyes have evolved, they have tended to gather at the anterior end, as have nerve cells that process information and "decide" what the animal should do. In general, the more complex animals become, the more pronounced their cephalization. The anterior end is often different enough from the rest of the body that it is called a head.

Body Cavity Formation Most animals have a body cavity, which is a fluid-filled space that lies between the digestive tract and the body wall. A body cavity is important because it provides a space in which internal organs can be suspended so that they are not pressed on by muscles or twisted out of shape by body movements. Body cavities also allow for specialized regions to develop, and they provide room for internal organs to grow and expand. In some animals, body cavities contain fluids that are involved in circulation, feeding, and excretion.

For: Links on classifying animals
Visit: www.SciLinks.org
Web Code: cbn-8261

26–1 Section Assessment

1. **Key Concept** What are the characteristics of members of the animal kingdom?
2. **Key Concept** Describe the seven essential functions performed by all animals.
3. **Key Concept** In what ways are complex animals different from simple animals?
4. How is the embryology of echinoderms similar to that of vertebrates? What might this similarity indicate about their evolutionary relationship?
5. How are body symmetry and cephalization related?
6. **Critical Thinking Applying Concepts** How is hunger an internal feedback mechanism for maintaining homeostasis?

Thinking Visually

Constructing a Chart
Make a two-column chart of the different functions that enable animals to survive and respond to the environment. In the first column, list each function. In the second column, include a drawing, photograph, or magazine clipping that illustrates an example of that function.

26–1 Section Assessment

1. An animal is a multicellular, eukaryotic heterotroph whose cells lack cell walls.
2. Students should describe feeding, respiration, circulation, excretion, response, movement, and reproduction.
3. Complex animals tend to have high levels of cell specialization and internal organization, bilateral symmetry, cephalization, and a body cavity.
4. Echinoderms and all vertebrates are deuterostomes. This similarity may indicate that vertebrates have a close evolutionary relationship to echinoderms.
5. Animals with bilateral symmetry usually exhibit cephalization.
6. An animal becomes hungry when it needs energy to maintain homeostasis. Hunger subsides when enough food has been taken in to maintain homeostasis.

3 ASSESS

Evaluate Understanding

List the seven essential functions of animals on the board. Then, call on individual students to explain what each function entails. After each student has spoken, invite the rest of the class to contribute additional details.

Reteach

Help students create two flowcharts that explain the processes involved in an animal's early development, as shown in Figure 26–4. One chart should show protostome development, and the other should show deuterostome development.

Download a worksheet on classifying animals for students to complete, and find additional teacher support from NSTA SciLinks.

Thinking Visually

Provide students with an assortment of nature magazines from which they can cut photographs. Students' charts should include the functions of feeding, respiration, circulation, excretion, response to the environment, movement, and reproduction.

If your class subscribes to the iText, use it to review the Key Concepts in Section 26–1.

Answers to . . .

CHECKPOINT *With radial symmetry, any number of imaginary planes can be drawn through the center, each dividing the body into equal halves. With bilateral symmetry, only a single imaginary plane can be drawn to divide the body into two equal halves.*

Figure 26–5 *One*

Figure 26–6 *The concentration of nerve cells and sense organs at the front end enables quick detection of stimuli and processing of the response.*

Section 26–2

7 2.a

1 FOCUS

Objectives

26.2.1 ***Explain*** what a sponge is.
26.2.2 ***Describe*** how sponges carry out essential functions.
26.2.3 ***Describe*** the ecology of sponges.

Guide for Reading

Vocabulary Preview

Have students write the Vocabulary terms, dividing each into its separate syllables as best they can. Remind students that each syllable usually has only one vowel sound. The correct syllabications are cho•a•no•cyte, os•cu•lum, spic•ule, arch•ae•o•cyte, in•ter•nal fer•til•i•za•tion, lar•va, gem•mule.

Reading Strategy

Before students read the section, have them draw a line down the center of a piece of paper. Explain that as they read through the section, they should write down the main topics of the section on the left side of the line. On the right side, they should make notes of supporting details and examples.

2 INSTRUCT

What Is a Sponge?

Build Science Skills

Observing Divide the class into small groups, and give each group a natural sponge and a hand lens. Explain that they will be observing the nonliving part of a sponge; the living material was removed during processing. Ask students to observe the sponge with the hand lens and make drawings of what they see. Then, have students use a microscope to observe prepared slides of sections of a sponge. Have them make drawings of what they observe. L2

26–2 Sponges

7 2.a. Students know the differences between the life cycles and reproduction methods of sexual and asexual organisms.

Guide for Reading

Key Concepts
- Why are sponges classified as animals?
- How do sponges carry out essential functions?

Vocabulary
choanocyte
osculum
spicule
archaeocyte
internal fertilization
larva
gemmule

Reading Strategy: Using Visuals Before you read, preview **Figure 26–8** and **Figure 26–9.** For each figure, write a brief statement that summarizes the content of the illustration. Once you have read the section, explain how each illustration reinforces or enhances the content of the section.

Sponges are the simplest and probably the most unusual animals. Living on Earth for at least 540 million years, sponges are also the most ancient animals. Today, most sponges live in the ocean, from the Arctic and Antarctic regions to the tropics, and from shallow water to depths of several hundred meters. To humans, however, they are probably best known in their dried form—the natural sponges used for bathing.

What Is a Sponge?

Sponges are placed in the phylum Porifera (poh-RIF-ur-uh), which means "pore-bearers." This name is appropriate because sponges have tiny openings, or pores, all over their bodies, as shown in **Figure 26–7.** Sponges are sessile, meaning that they live their entire adult life attached to a single spot.

Given these unusual features, why are sponges considered animals? **Sponges are classified as animals because they are multicellular, heterotrophic, have no cell walls, and contain a few specialized cells.** Because sponges are so different from other animals, some scientists think that they evolved independently from all other animals. Other evidence suggests that sponges share a common ancestor with other animals but that they separated from this ancestor long before the other groups did.

CHECKPOINT *Why is the phylum name Porifera appropriate for sponges?*

Form and Function in Sponges

Sponges have nothing resembling a mouth or gut, and they have no tissues or organ systems. Simple physiological processes are carried out by a few specialized cells.

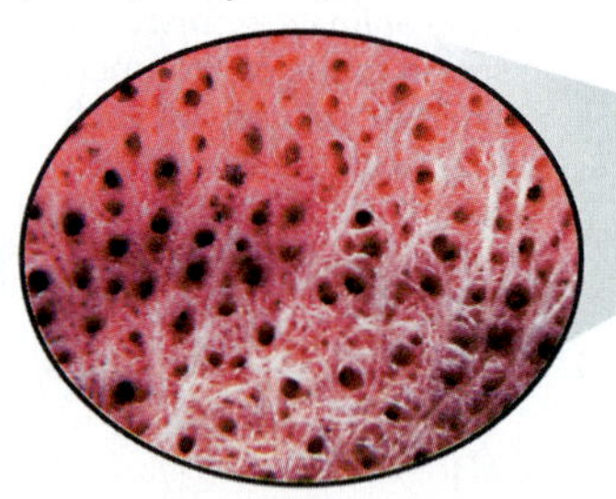

Figure 26–7 Sponges are animals because they are heterotrophic and have specialized cells. Sponges are probably the least typical of what we think of as animals. They grow in irregular shapes and live attached to the floor of oceans and freshwater bodies. Water enters the body of a sponge through small holes called pores (inset photo).

SECTION RESOURCES

Print:
- ***Teaching Resources,*** Lesson Plan 26–2, Adapted Section Summary 26–2, Adapted Worksheets 26–2, Section Summary 26–2, Worksheets 26–2, Section Review 26–2
- ***Reading and Study Workbook A,*** Section 26–2
- ***Adapted Reading and Study Workbook B,*** Section 26–2

Technology:
- ***iText,*** Section 26–2
- ***Presentation Assistant Plus,*** Section 26–2

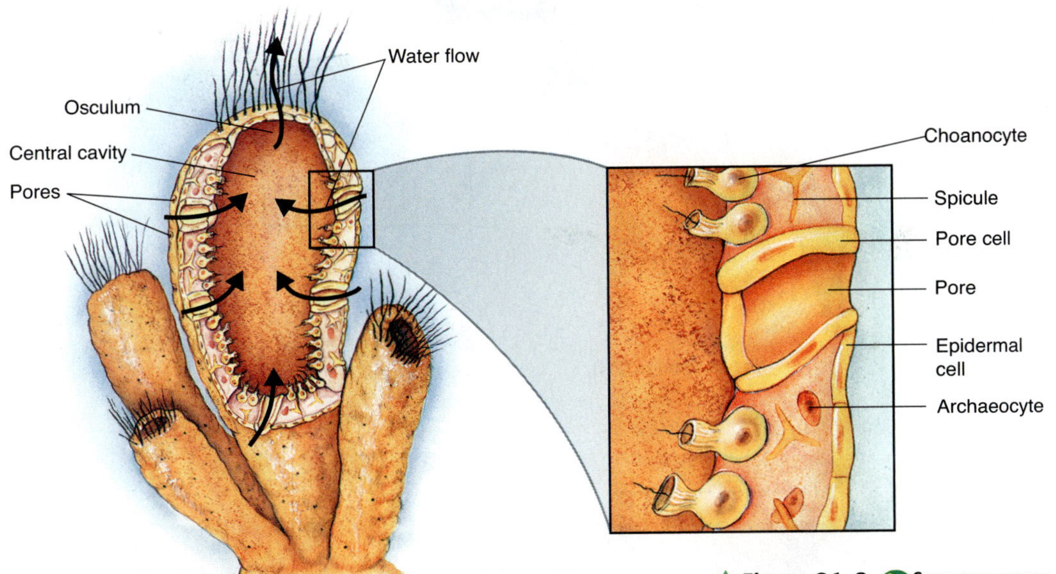

▲ **Figure 26–8** **Sponges carry out basic functions, such as feeding and circulation, by moving water through their bodies.** Choanocytes use flagella to move water through pores in the wall of the osculum. As water moves through the sponge, food particles are filtered from the water, and wastes are removed from the sponge.

Body Plan Sponges are asymmetrical; they have no front or back ends, and no left or right sides. A sponge can be thought of as a large, cylindrical water pump. The body of a sponge, shown in **Figure 26–8,** forms a wall around a large central cavity through which water is circulated continually. **Choanocytes** (koh-AN-uh-sytz) are specialized cells that use flagella to move a steady current of water through the sponge. This water enters through pores located in the body wall. Water then leaves through the **osculum** (AHS-kyoo-lum), a large hole at the top of the sponge. **The movement of water through the sponge provides a simple mechanism for feeding, respiration, circulation, and excretion.**

Sponges have a simple skeleton. In harder sponges, the skeleton is made of spiny spicules. A **spicule** is a spike-shaped structure made of chalklike calcium carbonate or glasslike silica. Spicules are made by **archaeocytes** (ARK-ee-uh-sytz), which are specialized cells that move around within the walls of the sponge. Softer sponges have an internal skeleton made of spongin, a network of flexible protein fibers. These are the sponges that are harvested and used as natural bath sponges.

Feeding Sponges are filter feeders that sift microscopic food particles from the water. Digestion is intracellular, meaning that it takes place inside cells. As water moves through the sponge, food particles are trapped and engulfed by choanocytes that line the body cavity. These particles are then digested or passed on to archaeocytes. The archaeocytes complete the digestive process and transport digested food throughout the sponge.

For: Structure of a Sponge activity
Visit: PHSchool.com
Web Code: cbp-8262

Form and Function in Sponges

Address Misconceptions

Students may have the misconception that a simple or primitive body plan is inferior or less than optimal. Point out that sponges and other so-called primitive animals evolved hundreds of millions of years ago and have persisted through cataclysmic environmental changes until today. Ask: **What does the longevity of the sponge say about its body plan in terms of adaptability to its environment?** *(The longevity of the sponge is evidence that it is extremely well adapted to its environment.)* L1 L2

Use Visuals

Figure 26–8 Ask: **Does this sponge exhibit symmetry?** *(It doesn't exhibit symmetry; almost all sponges are asymmetrical.)* **Through what structures does water enter a sponge?** *(Pores)* **What do choanocytes use to move a current of water through a sponge?** *(Flagella)* **Through what structure does water leave the sponge?** *(The osculum)* **Is this sponge a harder or softer sponge?** *(It is a harder sponge, because it has spicules.)* L1 L2

For: Structure of a Sponge activity
Visit: PHSchool.com
Web Code: cbe-8269
Students learn about the structure of a sponge.

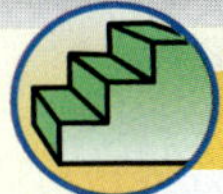

UNIVERSAL ACCESS

Inclusion/Special Needs

Display a natural sponge in its natural form. Then, have students compare it with the labeled drawing of a sponge in Figure 26–8. Call on students to relate what they see in the figure to what they observe in the natural sponge. Have students point to the osculum, central cavity, and pores in both the figure and the natural sponge. Then, touch the relevant parts of the natural sponge as you explain how water flows through it. L1

English Language Learners

Help students understand the meaning of the Vocabulary term *osculum* by explaining that the Latin word for "mouth" is *os* and that in Latin *osculum* means "little mouth." Explain that in English "to osculate" is a fancy way of saying "to kiss." Call on students to compare and contrast the form and function of a sponge's osculum with their own mouths. L1 L2

Answer to . . .

CHECKPOINT *Porifera means "pore-bearers," and sponges have pores all over their bodies.*

26–2 (continued)

Demonstration

Emphasize that sponges rely on the movement of water through their bodies for the essential functions of feeding, respiration, circulation, and excretion. Demonstrate how much water a sponge can hold by comparing the water-holding capacity of a natural sponge and a synthetic sponge of about the same mass. Measure the mass of each sponge on a scale, and record the masses on the board. Then, soak each sponge in water, and measure and record their masses again. Students should observe that the natural sponge holds more water than the synthetic sponge. L2

Build Science Skills

Applying Concepts Help students understand respiration and excretion in sponges by having them recall what they have learned about diffusion. Ask: **What is diffusion?** *(It is a process by which molecules spread through a medium—liquid, gas, or solid—from regions of high concentration to regions of low concentration.)* Reinforce the idea that diffusion occurs across cell membranes. Then, ask: **How would you describe the process of diffusion in sponge respiration?** *(Oxygen diffuses into a cell through the cell membrane from the water circulating through the sponge, because the concentration of oxygen in the water is greater than that inside the cell.)* Explain that the opposite occurs with wastes in the process of excretion. L2

Use Visuals

Figure 26–9 After students have studied the illustration of sexual reproduction in a sponge, ask: **Is a mature sponge haploid or diploid?** *(Diploid)* **What cellular process produces sperm and egg cells?** *(Meiosis)* **How do sperm reach eggs, and where does fertilization occur?** *(Sperm are released into the water, and currents carry them into the pores of other sponges. Fertilization occurs in the wall of a sponge.)* **What is the immature stage of a sponge called?** *(A larva)* L2

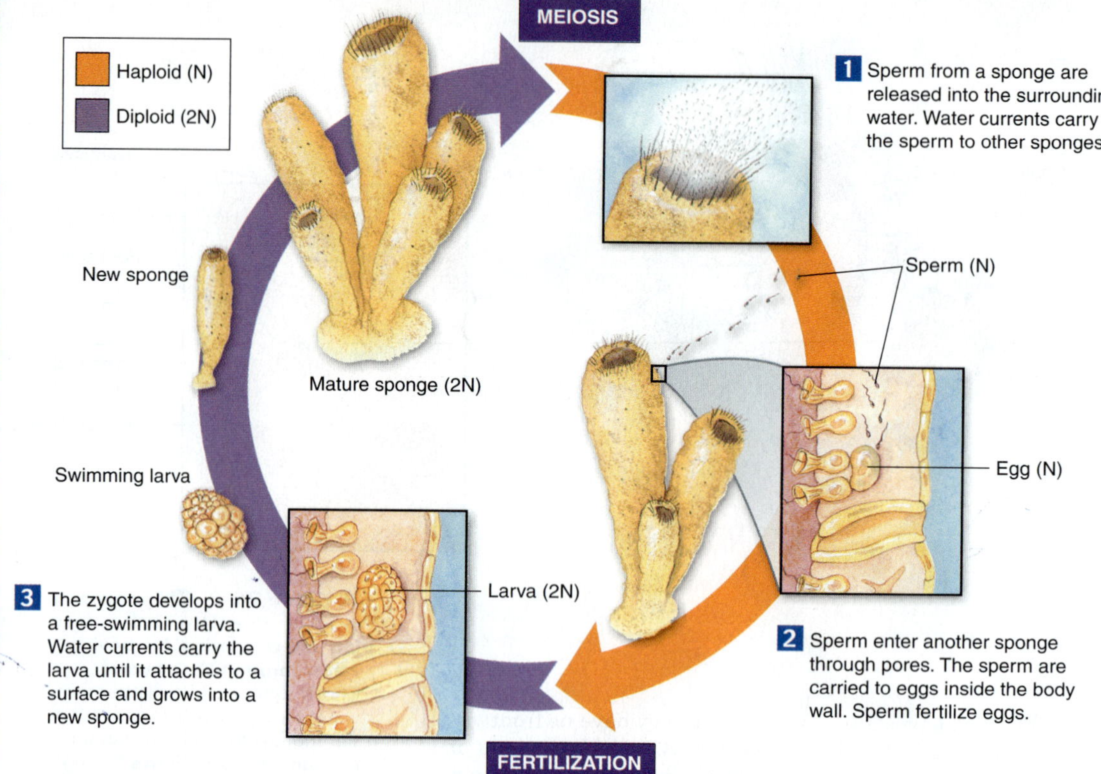

▲ **Figure 26–9** Most sponges reproduce sexually, and many have internal fertilization. **Interpreting Graphics** *Is an adult sponge haploid or diploid?*

Respiration, Circulation, and Excretion Sponges rely on the movement of water through their bodies to carry out body functions. As water moves through the body cavity, oxygen dissolved in the water diffuses into the surrounding cells. At the same time, carbon dioxide and other wastes, such as ammonia, diffuse into the water and are carried away.

Response Sponges do not have nervous systems that would allow them to respond to changes in their environment. However, many sponges protect themselves by producing toxins that make them unpalatable or poisonous to potential predators.

(a) 7 2.a

CA (a)

Reproduction Sponges can reproduce either sexually or asexually. The steps in sexual reproduction are diagrammed in **Figure 26–9.** In most sponge species, a single sponge forms both eggs and sperm by meiosis. The eggs are fertilized inside the sponge's body, in a process called **internal fertilization.** Sperm are released from one sponge and are carried by water currents until they enter the pores of another sponge. Archaeocytes carry the sperm to an egg. After fertilization, the zygote develops into a larva. A **larva** is an immature stage of an organism that looks different from the adult form. The larvae of sponges are motile and are usually carried by currents before they settle to the sea floor.

BIO INSIGHTS

HISTORY OF SCIENCE

Plant or animal?

Because sponges are sessile and asymmetric, most common observers might think that a living sponge is some kind of a plant. In fact, sponges have traditionally been thought of as plants, which is how the ancient Greeks classified them. It wasn't until naturalists in the late 1700s described the flow of water through sponges that these organisms were recognized as some kind of animal.

Throughout the 1800s, most naturalists thought sponges were related to corals and other members of the cnidarian class Anthozoa. It was thought that sponges, like anthozoans, had only a polyp stage in their life cycle. Early in the twentieth century, sponges became generally accepted as constituting a phylum of their own, separate from all other animals. Phylum Porifera now includes about 5,000 recognized species in three classes.

Sponges can reproduce asexually by budding or by producing gemmules. In budding, part of a sponge breaks off of the parent sponge, settles to the sea floor, and grows into a new sponge. When faced with difficult environmental conditions, some sponges produce **gemmules** (JEM-yoolz), which are groups of archaeocytes surrounded by a tough layer of spicules. Gemmules can survive freezing temperatures and drought. When conditions become favorable, a gemmule grows into a new sponge.

CA

a

Sexual reproduction—in sponges and other organisms—involves the joining of haploid gametes that have been produced by meiosis. Since the zygote contains genes from both parents, the new sponge is not genetically identical to either parent. Asexual reproduction, in contrast, does not involve meiosis or the joining of haploid gametes. Instead, the cells of the bud or gemmule, which are diploid, divide repeatedly by mitosis, producing growth. Asexual reproduction produces offspring that are genetically identical to the parent.

a 7 2.a

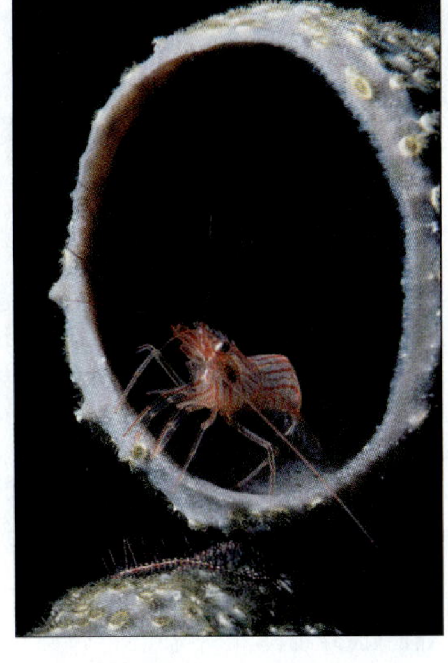

▲ **Figure 26–10** Sponges often provide habitats for other organisms. Observe how the sponge provides shelter for this snapping shrimp. **Inferring** *How might the sponge protect the shrimp from predators?*

Ecology of Sponges

Sponges are important in aquatic ecology. Sponges have irregular shapes and many are large. Therefore, they provide habitats for marine animals such as snails, sea stars, and the shrimp in **Figure 26–10.** These are examples of commensalism. Sponges also form partnerships with photosynthetic bacteria, algae, and plantlike protists. These photosynthetic organisms provide food and oxygen to the sponge, while the sponge provides a protected area where these organisms can thrive. This relationship is an example of mutualism, since both partners benefit. Sponges containing photosynthetic organisms play an important role in the ecology and primary productivity of coral reefs.

Sponges usually live attached to the sea floor, where they often receive only low levels of filtered sunlight. Recently, scientists have found clues to the mystery of how organisms within the sponge get enough light to carry out photosynthesis. The spicules of some sponges look like cross-shaped antennae. Like a lens or magnifying glass, they focus and direct incoming sunlight to cells lying below the surface of the sponge—where symbiotic organisms carry out photosynthesis. This adaptation may allow sponges to survive in a wider range of habitats.

26–2 Section Assessment

1. **Key Concept** What features do sponges share with all other animals?
2. **Key Concept** How do sponges use water to carry out essential functions?
3. Describe the different types of sponge skeletons.
4. **Critical Thinking Drawing Conclusions** Why would sponges be unable to live on land?

Focus on the BIG Idea

Interdependence in Nature

In Chapter 4, you learned about mutualism, commensalism, and other symbiotic relationships. Compare and contrast mutualism and commensalism, and explain how each is important in the life of a sponge.

26–2 Section Assessment

1. Sponges are heterotrophic, have no cell walls, and contain specialized cells.
2. The movement of water through the sponge carries needed materials, such as food and oxygen, and carries wastes away. Water also carries sperm to eggs.
3. The skeleton of many sponges is made of spiny spicules. Softer sponges have a skeleton made of flexible spongin.
4. Sponges depend on the movement of water for most functions, including feeding, respiration, circulation, excretion, and reproduction.

Ecology of Sponges

Using Visuals

Figure 26–10 Direct students' attention to the shrimp inside the sponge, and ask: **In what part of the sponge is the shrimp taking shelter?** *(The osculum)* **How does the sponge benefit from the shrimp's presence?** *(The sponge doesn't benefit.)* **Is the sponge hurt by the shrimp's presence?** *(The sponge is probably not hurt in any way.)* **What kind of symbiotic relationship is represented here?** *(Commensalism)* L2

3 ASSESS

Evaluate Understanding

Call on students at random to explain why sponges are considered animals and how sponges carry out the seven essential animal functions.

Reteach

Have students make their own drawing of Figure 26–8. Help them define each term in the labels and explain how each part of the sponge aids the organism in one of the seven essential functions.

Focus on the BIG Idea

In mutualism both species in the relationship benefit, whereas in commensalism one member benefits and the other is neither helped nor harmed. The symbiotic relationship between a sponge and an alga is an example of mutualism, in which the sponge receives food and oxygen. The symbiotic relationship between a sponge and a snapping shrimp is commensalism, in which the sponge does not benefit.

Interactive Textbook

If your class subscribes to the iText, use it to review the Key Concepts in Section 26–2.

Answers to . . .

Figure 26–9 *Diploid*

Figure 26–10 *By providing a place of concealment*

After students have read this feature, you might want to discuss one or more of the following:

- Ask students to think about how corals evolved in a way that they contain a chemical that protects them from the sun. Students should apply their knowledge of natural selection to this example.
- Have students explain why it is important that a way to produce Sunscreen 855 in the laboratory was developed. Students should infer that biologists don't want to harvest corals to extract the chemical, because coral reefs are already under high threat worldwide.
- Discuss with students the importance of bioprospecting, as well as how the prospect of products from plants and animals argues for the continued maintenance of biodiversity. Students could brainstorm a list of products they think could be derived from other animals in the wild. Suggest that they think about adaptations animals have evolved that could be exploited for helpful products.

Research and Decide

For things that the product should do, students might mention protecting against a severe sunburn and preventing skin cancer. For things that the product should not do, students might mention that the sunscreen should not cause a skin rash and should not cause some kind of systemic allergic reaction or disease. For testing the different claims, students might suggest first carrying out experiments in which animals are tested with the sunscreen and then, if there are no evident harmful effects, devising controlled studies with human volunteers.

Students can research Sunscreen 855 on the site developed by authors Ken Miller and Joe Levine.

Using Nature to Produce Sunscreen

One way of generating new medicines is to look for them in nature. Organisms of all kinds have been battling one another and their physical environment since life began. So, researchers can search for molecules that have been assembled and tested by the oldest process for generating new compounds on Earth—natural selection.

Natural UV Protection in Corals

One of these "new" molecules may be the world's first naturally produced sunscreen. Known as Sunscreen 855, this compound was discovered by researchers studying corals that live in shallow waters along Australia's Great Barrier Reef. During the low tide, these corals are exposed to the air and full sunlight. Investigators reasoned that these corals might have evolved some sort of protection against the damaging ultraviolet (UV) radiation of intense sunlight. Sure enough, their search turned up a UV-blocking compound in the tissues of these corals.

From Natural to Synthetic

After isolating and analyzing the compound in Sunscreen 855, the researchers learned that it was structurally different from the compounds used in synthetic sunscreens. They devised a way to produce it in the laboratory so that corals would not need to be harvested to make the sunscreen. Preliminary tests have shown that the sunscreen is highly efficient in absorbing radiation in the damaging UV-B region of the spectrum.

Sunscreen 855 is not sold in any drugstore—nor will it be for several years. Researchers are working with investors, lawyers, and businesspeople to test the new product for safety and effectiveness. If it passes final tests, Sunscreen 855 could be the best—and most natural—protection yet against the harmful effects of the sun.

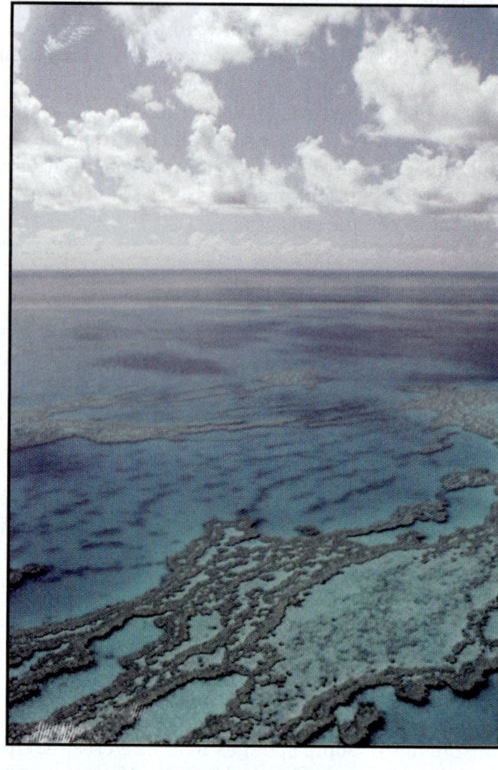

Research and Decide

Use library or Internet resources to learn more about Sunscreen 855. Then, suppose that Sunscreen 855 were made into a product that people could buy. Make a list of things that the product should do. Make another list of things it should not do (such as harmful side effects it might cause). Describe how you would test these different claims.

For: Links from the authors
Visit: PHSchool.com
Web Code: cbe-8262

FACTS AND FIGURES

Sunscreens and UV-B radiation
UV radiation makes up that part of the electromagnetic spectrum with wavelengths just shorter than those of visible light. People need some exposure to UV radiation for the production of vitamin D, which promotes healthy bones and teeth. But, excessive exposure causes skin damage and even cancer. UV radiation is divided into two regions: UV-A radiation has longer wavelengths than UV-B radiation. UV-B radiation is much more harmful, and most commercial suntan and sunscreen products absorb UV-B radiation. Sunscreen 855 has proven to be very efficient in absorbing and dissipating UV-B radiation. The development of this product is an example of bioprospecting, or biodiversity prospecting, which is the exploration of wild plants and animals for commercially valuable genetic and biochemical resources.

26–3 Cidarians

7 2.a. Students know the differences between the life cycles and reproduction methods of sexual and asexual organisms.

Imagine that you are swimming in warm, tropical waters. Far away, delicate jellyfishes float in the ocean currents. Within arm's reach, sea fans sway in the shallow currents. Brightly colored sea anemones cling to rocks, looking more like underwater flowers than animals. All these creatures are animals in the phylum Cnidaria (ny-DAYR-ee-uh), a group that includes hydras, jellyfishes, sea anemones, and corals. These fascinating animals are found in waters all over the world. Some cnidarians live as individuals. Others live in colonies composed of dozens or even thousands of connected individuals.

Guide for Reading

Key Concepts
- What is a cnidarian?
- What two body plans exist in the cnidarian life cycle?
- What are the three groups of cnidarians?

Vocabulary
cnidocyte
nematocyst
polyp
medusa
gastrovascular cavity
nerve net
hydrostatic skeleton
external fertilization

Reading Strategy: Finding Main Ideas Before you read, skim the section to identify the key concepts. Read the section carefully, and then write down the information that supports each key concept.

What Is a Cnidarian?

A few important features unite the cnidarians as a group. **Cnidarians are soft-bodied, carnivorous animals that have stinging tentacles arranged in circles around their mouths. They are the simplest animals to have body symmetry and specialized tissues.** Cnidarians get their name from the **cnidocytes** (NY-duh-syts), or stinging cells, that are located along their tentacles. **Figure 26–11** shows the structure of cnidocytes. Cnidarians use these cells for defense and to capture prey. Within each cnidocyte is a nematocyst (NEM-uh-toh-sist). A **nematocyst** is a poison-filled, stinging structure that contains a tightly coiled dart. When an unsuspecting shrimp or small fish brushes up against the tentacles, thousands of nematocysts explode into the animal, releasing enough poison to paralyze or kill the prey.

CHECKPOINT *What is the function of cnidocytes?*

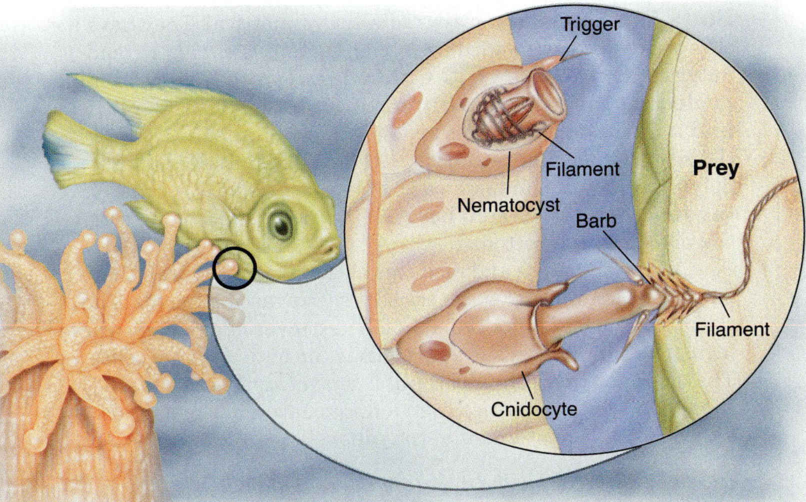

Figure 26–11 **Cnidarians are carnivorous animals that have stinging tentacles arranged around their mouths. Stinging cells called cnidocytes are used to capture and paralyze prey.** Within each cnidocyte is a stinging structure called a nematocyst. Here, a sea anemone captures a fish that has brushed the trigger of the nematocyst. When an animal touches the trigger of a nematocyst, the filament inside uncoils and shoots a barb into the animal.

SECTION RESOURCES

Print:
- ***Laboratory Manual A,*** Chapter 26 Lab
- ***Laboratory Manual B,*** Chapter 26 Lab
- ***Teaching Resources,*** Lesson Plan 26–3, Adapted Section Summary 26–3, Adapted Worksheets 26–3, Section Summary 26–3, Worksheets 26–3, Section Review 26–3, Enrichment
- ***Reading and Study Workbook A,*** Section 26–3
- ***Adapted Reading and Study Workbook B,*** Section 26–3
- ***Lab Worksheets,*** Chapter 26 Exploration

Technology:
- ***iText,*** Section 26–3
- ***Transparencies Plus,*** Section 26–3

Section 26–3

1 FOCUS

Objectives

26.3.1 ***Explain*** what a cnidarian is.
26.3.2 ***Describe*** the two body plans that exist in the cnidarian life cycle.
26.3.3 ***Describe*** how cnidarians carry out essential functions.
26.3.4 ***Identify*** the three groups of cnidarians.
26.3.5 ***Describe*** the ecology of cnidarians.

Guide for Reading

Vocabulary Preview

Explain that the name *cnidarian* is derived from Greek *knide,* which means "nettle." A nettle is a common plant with toothed leaves and stinging hairs. Point out that the first Vocabulary term, *cnidocyte,* is derived from the same Greek word.

Reading Strategy

Point out that the section's Key Concepts are in boldface type. Have students write the boldface sentences in their notebooks and find information that supports each.

2 INSTRUCT

What Is a Cnidarian?

Use Visuals

Figure 26–11 Ask: **In this figure, what part of a cnidarian is enlarged in the inset?** *(The end of a tentacle)* Point out that the inset shows two specialized cells. Ask: **What are these cells called?** *(Cnidocytes)* **What is the stinging structure inside each cnidocyte called?** *(A nematocyst)* **What is released from the nematocyst that kills or paralyzes prey?** *(A poison)*

Answer to . . .

CHECKPOINT *Cnidocytes function in defense and capturing prey.*

26–3 (continued)

Form and Function in Cidarians

Use Visuals

Figure 26–12 As students study the figure, point out that a cnidarian has only two tissue layers, the epidermis and the gastroderm. Then, ask: **What is located between those tissue layers?** *(The mesoglea, which varies from a thin, noncellular layer to a thick jelly-like material)* **In which form is the mesoglea most prominent?** *(The medusa)* Emphasize that the mesoglea is not a tissue layer made of cells. L1 L2

Build Science Skills

Using Models To reinforce the body plan of cnidarians, have students search for objects around the school that exhibit radial symmetry. Ask students to make a list of such objects, which might include an electric fan, a petri dish, a bicycle wheel, a trashcan, a basketball, a showerhead, a bowl, and a flowerpot. L2

Demonstration

Use two plastic cups, one clear and one colored, to demonstrate the difference between a cnidarian polyp and a medusa. Place the colored cup inside the clear cup, and explain that these two cups represent the two tissue layers of a cnidarian, the inside gastroderm and the outside epidermis. Then, display the double cup right side up and explain that this represents the polyp form of a cnidarian, with the mouth facing upward. Turn the double cup upside down, and explain that this represents the medusa form of a cnidarian, with mouth facing downward.

Word Origins

Cnidarian medusas have long tentacles that are something like Medusa's snakes. L2

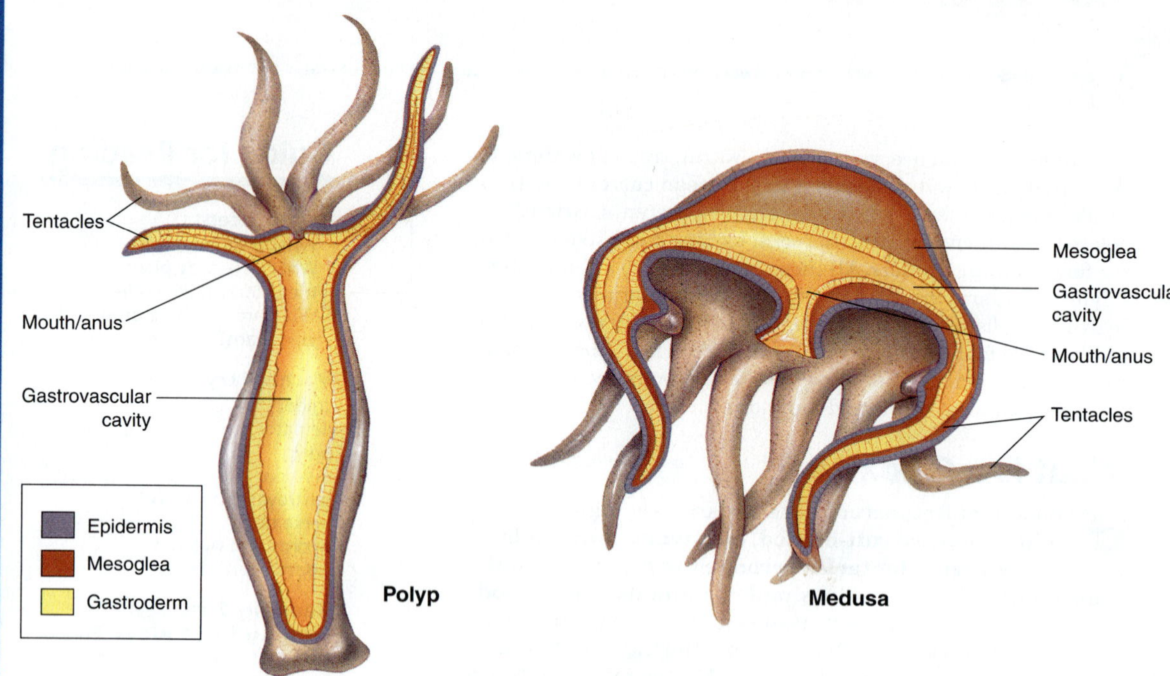

▲ **Figure 26–12** **Many cnidarians have both a polyp stage and a medusa stage.** Both stages have an outer epidermal tissue; a gastroderm tissue, which lines the gastrovascular cavity; and a mesoglea layer, which lies between the two tissues. (Note that a medusa's tentacles are much narrower than in the illustration.)

Word Origins

Medusa is the name of a monster in Greek mythology. In the myth, Medusa was once a beautiful woman, but she bragged about her beauty, causing a jealous goddess to change her into a hideous monster. Medusa had long, twisting snakes for hair. **In what way are cnidarian medusas similar to the monster named Medusa?**

Form and Function in Cnidarians

Cnidarians are only a few cells thick and have simple body systems. Most of their responses to the environment are carried out by specialized cells and tissues. These tissues function in physiological processes such as feeding and movement.

Body Plan Cnidarians are radially symmetrical. They have a central mouth surrounded by numerous tentacles that extend outward from the body.  **Cnidarians typically have a life cycle that includes two different-looking stages: a polyp and a medusa.** Both forms are shown in **Figure 26–12.** A **polyp** (PAHL-ip) is a cylindrical body with armlike tentacles. In a polyp, the mouth points upward. Polyps are usually sessile. A **medusa** (muh-DOO-suh) has a motile, bell-shaped body with the mouth on the bottom.

Cnidarian polyps and medusas each have a body wall that surrounds an internal space called a gastrovascular cavity. The gastroderm is the inner lining of the gastrovascular cavity, where digestion takes place. The epidermis is the outer layer of cells. The mesoglea (mez-uh-GLEE-uh) is a layer that lies between these two tissues. It varies from a thin, noncellular membrane to a thick, jellylike material that contains cells.

CHECKPOINT *What are the three layers in cnidarians?*

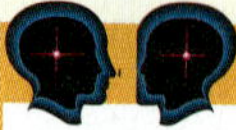

TEACHER TO TEACHER

You can use the following materials to make a model of a jellyfish: gallon-size plastic bags (not resealable), twist tie, string, tape, marker, and scissors. Ahead of time, tape in the corners of the plastic bag so your jellyfish will be round. As students watch, blow into the bag and close with twist tie. Cut the second plastic bag into long, thin strips to represent tentacles, and tape the strips onto the bag. Draw the gonads with a marker. Tape the string on to represent the nerve net. As you construct the model, talk to students about the structure of a jellyfish.

—*Beverly Cea*
Biology Teacher
Grimsley High School
Greensboro, NC

Before

After

Figure 26–13 Cidarians have nerve nets that consist of many individual nerve cells, as shown in the hydra below. Many cnidarians respond to touch by pulling their tentacles inside their bodies. This response, shown at left in cup corals, is cued by nerve cells located in the tentacles. **Formulating Hypotheses** ***How might a nerve net differ between motile and sessile cnidarians?***

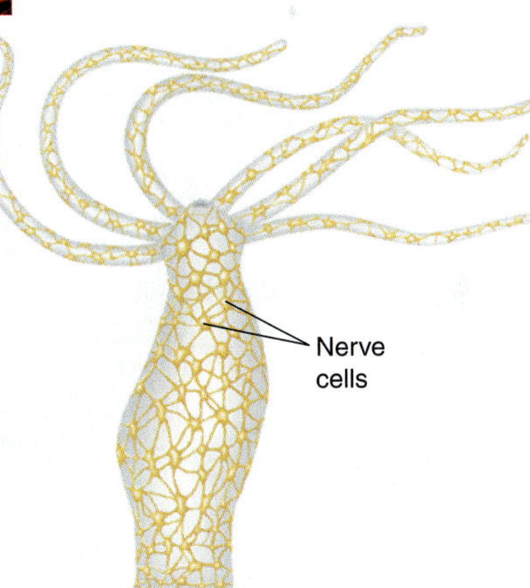

Feeding After paralyzing its prey, a cnidarian pulls the prey through its mouth and into its **gastrovascular cavity,** a digestive chamber with one opening. Food enters and wastes leave the body through that opening. Digestion—the breakdown of food—begins in the gastrovascular cavity. The digestion that occurs in the gastrovascular cavity is extracellular, meaning that it takes place outside of cells. Partially digested food is absorbed by the gastroderm. Digestion is completed intracellularly, within cells in the gastroderm. Any materials that cannot be digested are passed out of the body through the mouth.

Respiration, Circulation, and Excretion Following digestion, nutrients are usually transported throughout the body by diffusion. Cnidarians respire and eliminate the wastes of cellular metabolism by diffusion through their body walls.

Response Cnidarians gather information from their environment using specialized sensory cells. Both polyps and medusas have a nerve net, shown in **Figure 26–13.** A **nerve net** is a loosely organized network of nerve cells that together allow cnidarians to detect stimuli such as the touch of a foreign object. The nerve net is usually distributed uniformly throughout the body, although in some species it is concentrated around the mouth or in rings around the body. Cnidarians also have statocysts, which are groups of sensory cells that help determine the direction of gravity. Ocelli (oh-SEL-eye; singular: ocellus) are eyespots made of cells that detect light.

Movement Different cnidarians move in different ways. Some cnidarians, such as sea anemones, have a hydrostatic skeleton. The **hydrostatic skeleton** consists of a layer of circular muscles and a layer of longitudinal muscles that, together with the water in the gastrovascular cavity, enable the cnidarian to move. For example, if the anemone's circular muscles contract when the anemone's mouth is closed, the water inside the cavity can't escape. The pressure of the water makes the body become taller. In contrast, medusas move by jet propulsion. Muscle contractions cause the bell-shaped body to close like a folding umbrella. This action pushes water out of the bell, moving the medusa forward, as shown in **Figure 26–14.**

▲ **Figure 26–14** Jellyfishes move by means of jet propulsion. The body contracts to force water out, moving the jellyfish in the opposite direction. **Applying Concepts** ***Is the body plan of this jellyfish a medusa or a polyp?***

Build Science Skills

Comparing and Contrasting Ask students to write a paragraph that compares and contrasts sponges and cnidarians in how they carry out the seven essential functions. Students should suggest that there is great similarity between the two groups in respiration, circulation, and excretion. They should point to significant differences in feeding, response, movement, and reproduction.

Demonstration

Use familiar objects to demonstrate the difference in the ways cnidarian polyps and medusas move. For the polyp, partially fill an oblong balloon with water and tie the opening closed. Tell students that the balloon represents a cnidarian gastrovascular cavity. Then, show by squeezing parts of the balloon how it can change shape, with one part growing larger while the other shrinks. Ask: **What kind of skeleton does this represent?** *(A hydrostatic skeleton)* Next, pick up an umbrella, and tell students that it represents the bell-shaped body of a medusa. Rapidly open and close the umbrella, and explain that medusas have muscles to contract and expand their bells in a similar way. Just as the umbrella pushes air backward, a medusa's bell pushes water backward, and the organism moves in the opposite direction. L1 L2

Answers to . . .

CHECKPOINT The gastroderm is the inner lining of the gastrovascular cavity. The epidermis is the outer layer of cells. The mesoglea is a jellylike layer that lies between these two tissues.

Figure 26–13 *Students might correctly infer that the nerve net is more extensive in a motile cnidarian. In many medusas, nerve cells are complex and concentrated around the margin of the bell, which is more likely to come into contact with objects and other organisms than are other parts of the medusa.*

Figure 26–14 *A medusa*

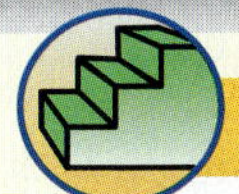

UNIVERSAL ACCESS

Less Proficient Readers
Help students relate the text to Figure 26–15 by reading the first paragraph on page 672 aloud and then asking a student to point out where the figure shows budding. Then, read the second paragraph aloud, and ask a student to point out where in the figure external fertilization is shown. L1

English Language Learners
Have students make a hierarchical graphic that shows the classification of the invertebrates discussed in Section 26–3. At the top should be phylum Cnidaria. Beneath that should be the classes Scyphozoa, Hydrozoa, and Anthozoa. Students can write examples of each class. L1 L2

Advanced Learners
After students have read about the ecology of corals, encourage interested students to prepare a report to the class about one of these aspects of coral reefs: where the world's largest reefs are found; the tremendous biodiversity associated with coral reefs; and the threat to coral reefs from human activity. L3

26–3 (continued)

Use Visuals

Figure 26–15 Have students study the figure. Then, ask: **Is the jellyfish polyp haploid or diploid?** *(Diploid)* **Is the medusa haploid or diploid?** *(It also is diploid.)* **What process occurs that ensures both are diploid organisms?** *(The polyp is diploid because it grows from a zygote produced by the joining of haploid egg and sperm. The medusa is diploid because it is produced through the process of budding by a polyp.)* **How are polyps produced?** *(Male medusas release sperm, and female medusas release eggs. Fertilization occurs in open water. The resulting zygote grows into a larva, which becomes a polyp.)* L2

Groups of Cnidarians

Build Science Skills

Classifying Give students a better understanding of how cnidarians are classified by emphasizing which form, polyp or medusa, predominates in the life of the organism. Ask students: **In which form do hydrozoans live most of their lives?** *(They live most of their lives as polyps.)* **In which form do scyphozoans live most of their lives?** *(They live most of their lives as medusas.)* **In which form do anthozoans spend their lives?** *(They have only a polyp stage in their life cycle.)* L2

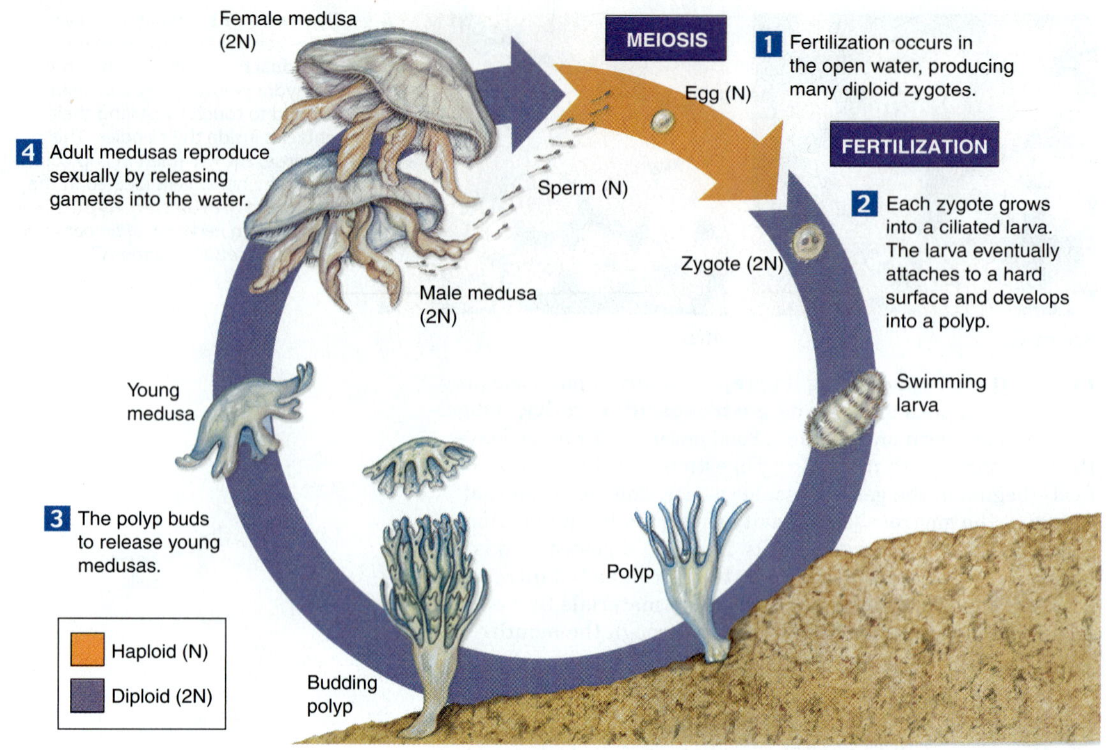

▲ **Figure 26–15** Jellyfishes reproduce sexually by producing eggs and sperm. Depending on the species, fertilization is either internal or external. In *Aurelia,* shown here, fertilization is external, occurring after eggs and sperm are released into the water. **Interpreting Graphics** *What cells are formed by the process of meiosis?*

7 2.a

Reproduction Most cnidarians reproduce both sexually and asexually. Polyps can reproduce asexually by budding. The new animal is genetically identical to the parent animal. One type of budding begins with a swelling on the side of an existing polyp. This swelling grows into a new polyp. In another type of budding, polyps produce tiny medusas that separate and become new individuals.

CA a In most cnidarians, sexual reproduction takes place with external fertilization in water. **External fertilization** takes place outside the female's body. The sexes are often separate—each individual is either male or female. The female releases eggs into the water, and the male releases sperm. The life cycle of *Aurelia,* a common jellyfish, is shown in **Figure 26–15.** Observe that the zygote grows into a free-swimming larva. The larva eventually attaches to a hard surface and develops into a polyp. Then, the polyp buds and releases a medusa that begins the cycle again.

Groups of Cnidarians

All cnidarians live under water, and nearly all live in the ocean. **Cnidarians include jellyfishes, hydras and their relatives, and sea anemones and corals.** Some of the most familiar cnidarians are the jellyfishes.

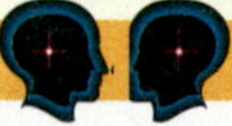

TEACHER TO TEACHER

When introducing the invertebrate phyla described in this chapter, I provide specimens of sponges and cnidarians as well as pictures, videos, or laser-disc examples. I also divide students into groups of four, and ask each group to develop questions about the various organisms. I then display these questions on the classroom walls. As students progress through the chapter, they answer the displayed questions, keeping a record of both questions and answers in their notebooks. In addition, I have the student groups make charts comparing the characteristics of sponges and cnidarians.

—Keith Orgeron
Teacher
Carencro High School
Lafayette, LA

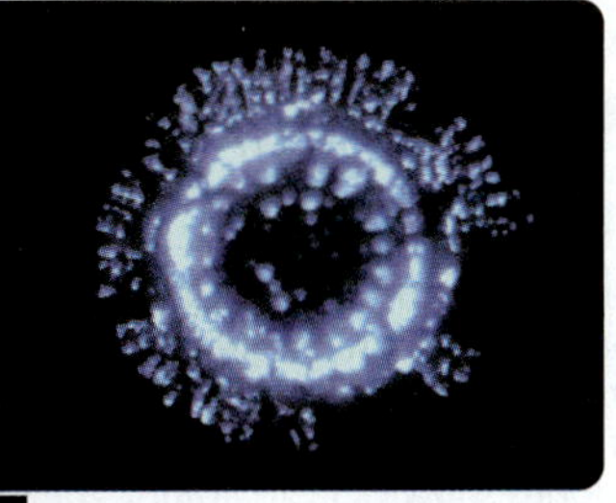

Figure 26–16 Like many marine organisms, jellyfishes use bioluminescence, or the production of light by an organism, to ward off predators. The entire body of this jellyfish becomes bioluminescent when it is threatened (inset). **Formulating Hypotheses** *How might bioluminescence discourage potential predators?*

Jellyfishes The class Scyphozoa (sy-fuh-ZOH-uh) contains the jellyfishes, such as the jellyfish shown in **Figure 26–16.** Scyphozoans, which means "cup animals," live their lives primarily as medusas. The polyp form of jellyfishes is restricted to a small larval stage, and no elaborate colonies ever form. Jellyfishes can be quite large—the largest jellyfish ever found was almost 4 meters in diameter and had tentacles more than 30 meters long. Jellyfishes reproduce sexually.

Hydras and Their Relatives The class Hydrozoa (hy-druh-ZOH-uh) contains hydras and other related animals. The polyps of most hydrozoans grow in branching colonies that sometimes extend more than a meter. Within the colony, polyps are specialized to perform different functions. In the Portuguese man-of-war, shown in **Figure 26–17,** one polyp forms a balloonlike float that keeps the entire colony afloat. Other polyps in the colony produce long tentacles that hang several meters under water and sting prey (and humans!) using nematocysts. Some polyps digest food held by the tentacles, while others make eggs and sperm.

The most common freshwater hydrozoans are hydras. Hydras differ from other cnidarians in this class because they lack a medusa stage. Instead, they live only as solitary polyps. Hydras reproduce asexually, by budding, or sexually, by producing eggs and sperm in the body wall. Many hydras get their nutrition from capturing, stinging, and digesting small prey. Some hydras, however, get their nutrition from symbiotic photosynthetic protists that live in their tissues.

How do hydras reproduce?

▶ **Figure 26–17** **Jellyfishes, hydrozoans, sea anemones, and corals are all cnidarians.** The Portuguese man-of-war, shown here, is a colonial hydrozoan that is composed of many specialized polyps. A single polyp that is enlarged and full of air helps keep the animal afloat, while other specialized polyps below water function in feeding and reproduction.

Use Visuals

Figure 26–17 Ask: **What cnidarian class does this Portuguese man-of-war represent?** *(The class Hydrozoa)* Emphasize that hydrozoans spend most of their lives as polyps. Then, ask: **Are you looking at one individual polyp or many?** *(Many, since a Portuguese man-of-war is a colonial hydrozoan)* Explain that the enlarged polyp at the top is called a float, and the colony has mechanisms that can regulate the gas in the float, which keeps the colony at a particular depth. The feeding tentacles at the bottom can be as long as 13 meters in some Atlantic species. L1 L2

Build Science Skills

Comparing and Contrasting Have students make a compare/contrast table that organizes the information they learn about the three classes of cnidarians. Column heads might include Cnidarian Class, Description, Reproduction, and Examples. After students have completed the task, divide the class into small groups, and encourage students to compare information included in their tables, revising where they think they have left out important information. L2 L3

BIO INSIGHTS — FACTS AND FIGURES

Animals with no middle tissue layer
Cnidarians only have two embryonic tissue, or germ, layers. The endoderm develops into the inner layer of the body wall, which is called the gastrodermis. The ectoderm develops into an outer layer of the body wall, called the epidermis. There is no middle germ layer, and as such, cnidarians are said to possess a diploblastic body plan, in contrast to the triploblastic body plan of more complex animals with three germ layers.

The middle layer in cnidarians is a thick, jellylike mixture called mesoglea, which usually contains some cells and fibers. In the hydrozoans, the middle layer has virtually no cells. This jellylike middle layer is more abundant in the medusa form than in the polyp form, which explains the name *jellyfish* for scyphozoan medusas. Without a middle germ layer, cnidarians never possess the complex organs of triploblastic animals.

Answers to . . .

CHECKPOINT *Hydras reproduce asexually by budding or sexually by producing sperm and eggs.*

Figure 26–15 *Sperm and egg*

Figure 26–16 *Bioluminescence makes the jellyfish seem larger and more threatening.*

26–3 (continued)

Make Connections

Chemistry Explain that the "stony" substance associated with stony corals is limestone, or calcium carbonate. To help explain the formation of a coral reef, write the formula of calcium carbonate on the board: $CaCO_3$. Point out that this compound contains the elements calcium, carbon, and oxygen. Explain that a coral animal derives the calcium from seawater that flows into its gastrovascular cavity. The carbon and oxygen are from carbon dioxide, a product of the photosynthesis carried out by algae symbionts. One of the products of a chemical reaction at the base of a coral is calcium carbonate, which precipitates. The result is a buildup of a stony exoskeleton and the coral reef. L2 L3

Ecology of Corals

Analyzing Data

 **BIIE 1.d**

Coral reefs are the "rain forests" of the ocean, a place where life is most varied and abundant. If the reefs are lost, then life on Earth will be changed dramatically. Overexploitation of marine resources includes everything from overfishing to even more destructive practices. For instance, fisheries in Indonesia sometimes use dynamite to stun reef-dwelling fish, making the take easier. Perhaps more troubling is the threat of global warming, which may eventually destroy almost all coral reefs.

L2 L3

Answers

1. The order, from greatest to least high threat, is exploitation of marine resources, inland pollution, coastal development, and marine pollution.
2. The high threat of overexploitation is almost four times greater than the high threat of coastal development.
3. A typical generalization will suggest that human activities threaten the destruction of the world's coral reefs.
4. A typical response might propose limits on the exploitation of marine resources, either by amount of catch or by restrictions on where fisheries can harvest resources.

Analyzing Data

Coral Vanishing Act

The World Resources Institute, an organization that examines global environmental problems, has announced that 58 percent of the world's coral reefs are in danger of dying. Threats to coral reefs fall into four broad categories shown in the graph. The graph indicates the percentage of reefs that are threatened by each of these categories. It also rates the threat as medium or high, based on the distance between the coral reef and the source of the threat. Use the information in the graph to answer the following questions.

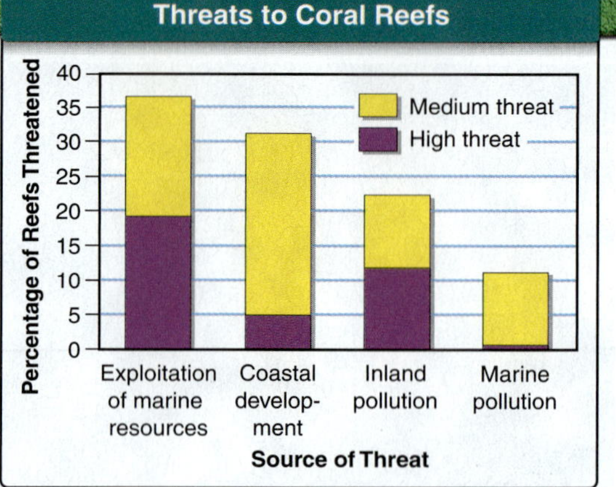

1. **Classifying** Place the four categories of risk in order from greatest high threat to least high threat.
2. **Using Tables and Graphs** Approximately how much greater is the high threat of overexploitation than the high threat of coastal development?
3. **Inferring** Based on the graph, write a generalization about the effect of human activities on the destruction of coral reefs.
4. **Making Judgments** Assume that you are a legislator drafting a law to protect coral reefs. Choose one of the threats shown in the graph, and outline a law that you would propose to counter the threat.

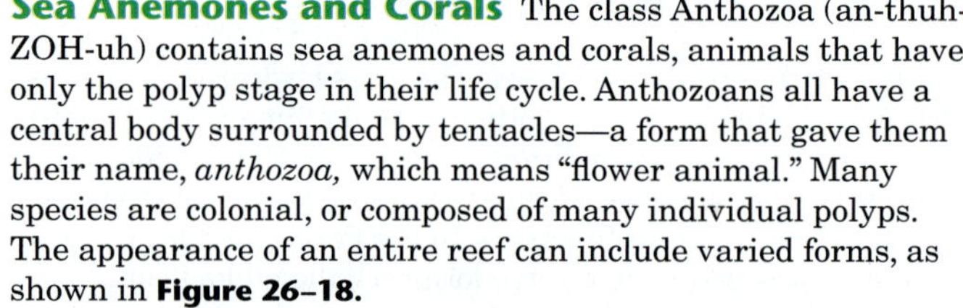

 **BIIE 1.d**

Sea Anemones and Corals The class Anthozoa (an-thuh-ZOH-uh) contains sea anemones and corals, animals that have only the polyp stage in their life cycle. Anthozoans all have a central body surrounded by tentacles—a form that gave them their name, *anthozoa,* which means "flower animal." Many species are colonial, or composed of many individual polyps. The appearance of an entire reef can include varied forms, as shown in **Figure 26–18.**

Sea anemones are solitary polyps that live at all depths of the ocean. Using nematocysts, they catch a variety of marine organisms. Many shallow-water species also depend on nutrition from photosynthetic symbionts.

Individual coral polyps look like miniature sea anemones. But most corals are colonial, and their polyps grow together in large numbers. Hard coral colonies are usually founded when a motile larva settles onto a hard surface and develops into a single polyp. New polyps are produced by budding, and as the colonies grow, they secrete an underlying skeleton of calcium carbonate, or limestone. These colonies grow slowly and may live for hundreds or even thousands of years. Many coral colonies growing near one another produce the magnificent structures known as coral reefs.

Anthozoans reproduce sexually by producing eggs and sperm that are released into the water. The zygote grows into a ciliated larva that becomes a new polyp. Some species can also reproduce asexually by budding or splitting into two halves.

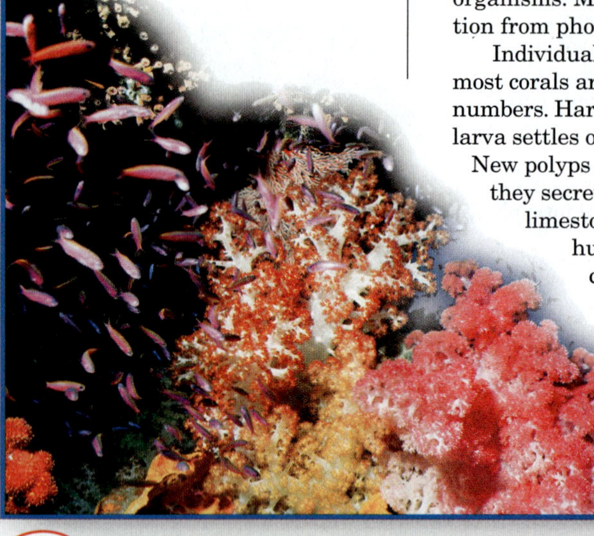

▼ **Figure 26–18** Coral reefs are home to many types of organisms. Each flowerlike form shown in this photograph is an entire colony made of thousands of individual coral polyps.

BIOLOGY UPDATE

Too late to save the world's coral reefs?
At the International Coral Reef Symposium in 2000, scientists reported that over 25 percent of the world's coral reefs have already been destroyed and warned that in the coming decades the rest might perish. Experts cited a number of causes of the destruction, including pollution, overfishing, and, most significantly, global warming, which causes bleaching. As the sea temperature rises, the symbiotic algae produce more oxygen. The corals begin to suffer from oxygen poisoning and so expel the algae. With the loss of algae, the corals lose their primary source of energy. In response to grave concerns about reef destruction, in 2000 President Clinton created the Northwestern Hawaiian Islands Coral Reef Ecosystem Reserve, the country's largest marine nature preserve. The preserve encompasses over 65 percent of coral reefs within U.S. boundary waters.

Ecology of Corals

The worldwide distribution of corals is determined by a few variables: temperature, water depth, and light intensity. The "stony" or "hard" corals that build coral reefs require high levels of light. Why should light be a requirement for an animal? Light is necessary because these corals rely on mutualistic relationships with algae that capture solar energy, recycle nutrients, and help corals lay down their calcium carbonate skeletons. Symbionts provide as much as 60 percent of the energy that corals need. This arrangement allows coral reefs to live in water that carries few nutrients.

Many coral reefs are now suffering from human activity. For example, recreational divers sometimes damage coral reefs. Silt and other sediments from logging, farming, mining, and construction can wash onto reefs and smother corals. Chemical fertilizers, insecticides, and industrial pollutants can poison the corals. Overfishing can upset the ecological balance of coral reefs. Even when human-caused problems do not kill corals, they can cause stress that makes the coral reefs susceptible to other threats.

Meanwhile, a problem called coral bleaching has become common. High temperatures can kill the algae that usually live in the tissues of corals, leaving behind only transparent cells atop ghostly white skeletons. The results of coral bleaching are shown in **Figure 26–19.** In the past, bleaching was a rare and short-term event from which many corals recovered. Over the last 20 years, however, bleaching has become more common and more severe, causing many corals to die. Researchers fear that rising ocean temperatures, produced by global warming, may be contributing to this problem. If this is the case, many reefs around the world could soon be in serious danger.

▲ **Figure 26–19** Under normal conditions, algae live within coral tissues, carrying out photosynthesis and giving the coral its green appearance. However, when stressed by pollutants or increasing temperatures, these algae can die, so only the clear cells of the coral remain. **Inferring** ***What effect might the loss of symbiotic algae have on the coral?***

26–3 Section Assessment

1. **Key Concept** Describe three characteristics that all cnidarians share.
2. **Key Concept** How do the two body plans of cnidarians differ?
3. **Key Concept** Describe the three groups of cnidarians and give an example from each.
4. Describe how the digestion and absorption of food take place in cnidarians.
5. How has human activity affected coral reefs?
6. **Critical Thinking Inferring** A medusa typically has more specialized organs for movement and response than a polyp does. Why might this be the case? *Hint:* How does the lifestyle of a medusa differ from that of most polyps?

Writing in Science

Descriptive Writing

Write a paragraph describing the body of a hydra. Assume that your readers know nothing about hydras. *Hint*: First, list all the details you want to include in your paragraph. Then, decide how you want to organize those details—for example, from the outside of the hydra to the inside.

3 ASSESS

Evaluate Understanding

Display a picture of an organism from each of the three classes of cnidarians. Ask students to identify the class of each and explain how it carries out the seven essential functions of animals.

Reteach

To help students remember the meanings of Vocabulary terms, ask them to write a story of a year in the life of a jellyfish in which they use these terms: *polyp, medusa, nerve net, nematocyst, gastrovascular cavity,* and *hydrostatic skeleton.* Students should strive to be both creative and scientifically accurate.

Writing in Science

Before students begin, you may want to allow them to observe the hydras they will use in the Exploration Lab near the end of this chapter. Then, students should use the details about hydras described on page 673. In their descriptions, students should emphasize that each hydra is an individual, solitary polyp.

If your class subscribes to the iText, use it to review the Key Concepts in Section 26–3.

26–3 Section Assessment

1. All cnidarians are soft-bodied, are carnivorous, and have stinging tentacles arranged in circles around the mouth.
2. A polyp has a cylindrical body with armlike tentacles; the mouth points upward. A medusa has a bell-shaped body with the mouth pointing downward.
3. Hydrozoans, such as hydras, spend most of their lives as polyps. Scyphozoans, such as jellyfishes, live their lives primarily as medusas. Anthozoans, such as corals, have only the polyp stage in their life cycle.
4. Extracellular digestion takes place in the gastrovascular cavity. Digestion is completed intracellularly.
5. Many coral reefs are suffering due to human activity.
6. A polyp is sessile and, thus, does not move around. A medusa is motile and, thus, needs a more complex nervous system.

Answer to . . .

Figure 26–19 *The corals might die from lack of oxygen and nutrients supplied by the algae.*

Exploration

Objectives Students will be able to
- Observe how two different kinds of hydras respond to light.
- Infer why green hydras move toward light.
- Compare and contrast the behavior of hydras with that of more complex animals. L2 L3

Skills Focus **Inferring, Drawing Conclusions**

Time 45 minutes; 10 minutes the following day

Advance Prep Order green hydras (*Chlorohydra viridissima)* and brown hydras (*Hydra littoralis* or another nongreen species) well in advance. Small *Daphnia, Cyclops,* brine shrimp (*Artemia),* or other small invertebrates can be fed to both green and brown hydras. Feed only small *Daphnia* to hydras, because large *Daphnia* may attack the hydras. Keep the green hydras in a well-lit environment. You can collect local clean pond or spring water or purchase spring water.

Safety Caution students not to drink the spring water. Advise them to handle the test tubes and the hydras carefully.

Pre-Lab Discussion Have students brainstorm a list of behaviors exhibited by large-brained animals such as mammals and small-brained animals such as insects. Have students try to explain how each behavior contributes to an animal's survival or reproduction. Have volunteers describe the cnidarian nerve net and speculate about the behavior such a simple nervous system might produce. Then, have students read the Exploration. Ask: **What are hydras?** *(Hydras are cnidarians of the class Hydrozoa.)* **From what kind of symbionts do some hydras get their nutrition?** *(Photosynthetic protists living within their tissues)* **Why do you think part of the procedure of this lab is to leave the hydras in the test tubes overnight and observe them the next day?** *(Students might infer that the purpose is to give time for the hydras to orient themselves to their environment. Students might suggest that hydras lack the complex nervous system required for direct movement toward or away from the light.)*

Exploration

Investigating the Responses of Hydras to External Stimuli

Hydras, a type of cnidarian, are some of the simplest known animals to have a nervous system. What kinds of behavior can their simple nerve nets produce? Can they detect food and move toward it? Can they detect predators and move away from them? How do they respond to light, temperature, and other external stimuli? How do these responses help them to survive? In this investigation, you will observe and try to explain the behavior of hydras.

Problem
How do hydras respond to light?

Materials
- 6 test tubes with screw caps
- test-tube rack
- green hydras
- brown hydras
- aluminum foil
- pond or spring water
- glass-marking pencil
- dropper pipette
- transparent tape

Skills
Inferring, Drawing Conclusions

Procedure

1. Make a copy of the data table shown. Number 6 test tubes 1 through 6 near the top of each tube. Fill the test tubes with pond water or spring water to within 2 cm of the top. **CAUTION:** *Handle the test tubes carefully. Do not drink the water.*
2. Use a dropper pipette to gently place 3 brown hydras in the bottoms of the test tubes labeled 1 through 3, and place 3 green hydras in the bottoms of the test tubes labeled 4 through 6.
3. Wrap the bottom half of each test tube in aluminum foil.
4. Tightly cap all 6 test tubes. Place test tubes 1 and 4 right side up in the test-tube rack and test tubes 2 and 5 upside down.
5. Label the test-tube rack with your name and place it in a brightly lit place.
6. Lay test tubes 3 and 6 on their sides next to the test-tube rack so that all 6 test tubes are equally well lit. Tape test tubes 3 and 6 in place. Place the tape over the foil and caps so that it does not block the light.
7. **Predicting** Record the time that you completed step 6. Make a prediction of how each type of hydra will respond to the external stimulus—either moving away from or toward the light. Record your prediction of any other behavior that you expect to see, along with the reasons for your predictions.

Data Table

Tube	Hydras	Source of Light	Number of Hydras		Class Total	
			In light	In dark	In light	In dark
1	brown	above				
2	brown	below				
3	brown	side				
4	green	above				
5	green	below				
6	green	side				

Sample Data Table

Tube	Hydras	Source of Light	Number of Hydras		Class Total	
			In light	In dark	In light	In dark
1	brown	above	1	2	20	40
2	brown	below	1	2	20	40
3	brown	side	1	3	20	40
4	green	above	3	0	60	0
5	green	below	3	0	60	0
6	green	side	3	0	60	0

8 Observe the test tubes. Record a description of any hydra behavior you observe. Include such information as when the behavior occurred, how many hydras you saw, what they did, and any other observations you made. Leave the test tubes overnight. Be sure to wash your hands before leaving the lab.

9 The next day, observe the test tubes and again record any hydra behavior you observe. Count the number of hydras in the light and in the dark in each test tube. Record these observations in your data table.

10 **Communicating Results** Share your observations with the class to complete the Class Total columns of your data table.

Analyze and Conclude

1. **Observing** Which type of hydra moved toward the light? Which type avoided light?
2. **Observing** How did the hydras move? Were their movements random or in a specific direction?
3. **Observing** What differences did you observe between the behavior of green and brown hydras?
4. **Inferring** Green hydras are green because of the presence of green algae in their bodies. What seems to be the relationship between the presence of algae and the behavior of green hydras?
5. **Drawing Conclusions** How might their response to light help green hydras survive?
6. **Comparing and Contrasting** The nervous system directs animal behavior. Compare the behavior of hydras to the behavior of animals with more complex nervous systems that you have observed, such as dogs and insects.
7. **SAFETY** Explain how you demonstrated safe practices as you handled the test tubes.

Go Further

Designing Experiments What are some other behaviors that hydras exhibit? For example, do they react to changes in temperature, differences in prey behavior, or the presence of predators? Can they learn? Consult scientific literature about the behavior of hydras. Then, design an experiment to investigate a specific hypothesis about hydra behavior. Formulate your hypothesis on the basis of what you have read and your own observations. Have your teacher approve your plan before you perform your experiment.

For: Data sharing
Visit: PHSchool.com
Web Code: cbd-8263

Share Your Data Online Communicate your results by entering your data on the behavior of the two types of hydra. Then, look at the data entered by other students. Based on the available data, which type of hydra moved toward the light? Which avoided light? Why might your data differ from those of other students? Does this larger set of data support your results and indicate that your conclusions are valid?

Teaching Tips

- Because hydra behavior is somewhat unpredictable, some students may observe more activity than others. Encourage students to share observations with others.
- To simplify data sharing, set up a data table on the board or overhead projector in which each student or group can enter data.
- You may want to add prey to the test tubes to allow students to observe how hydras feed. If you do, tell students that some of the prey, such as *Artemia* brine shrimp, are attracted to light. Ask students how this might affect hydra behavior and how they might design an experiment to distinguish the direct effect of light on hydra behavior from any possible tendency to migrate toward light-seeking prey.

Procedure

2. Demonstrate how to use a dropper pipette to gently place hydras in the bottom of a test tube.

3. Make sure students do not wrap more than half a test tube in foil.

7. Have students record the time they completed step 6, as well as their predictions for each of the test tubes, on a separate piece of paper.

8. Provide a well-lit place for students to leave their test tubes overnight.

Expected Outcomes

Students should observe that green hydras tend to migrate toward light, while brown hydras do not.

Go Further

Check students' experimental plans for sound design, safety, and the potential to test a clearly defined hypothesis before giving approval. A typical experiment might involve setting up a temperature differential within an environment and observing how hydras respond.

Students should see that green hydras migrate toward the light while brown hydras don't, but their results will depend on their own data and the data on the site.

Analyze and Conclude

1. Green hydras moved toward the light. Brown hydras avoided light.

2. Movement can occur in several ways. Hydras can creep, tumble, float, or sink. Green hydras move toward light. The movement of brown hydras, if it occurs, is random.

3. Green hydras moved toward the light, while brown hydras moved little, and randomly.

4. When algae are present in hydras, the hydras move toward light. This behavior provides the light the green algae need for photosynthesis. The behavior of the green hydras implies that they benefit from the algae.

5. Students should conclude that the algae provide the hydras with the oxygen or carbohydrates produced through photosynthesis.

6. Like more complex animals, hydras can respond to the environment in ways that help them to survive, though this behavior is much simpler than that of more complex animals.

7. Students should say that they handled the test tubes carefully to avoid breaking them and did not drink the water.

Chapter 26 Study Guide

Study Tip

Divide the class into small groups, and ask each group to write a review question for each Key Concept and each Vocabulary term in one of the sections. When students have completed writing their questions, have the groups place their lists in a central location. Then, ask that each group pick up a list of questions for one of the other two sections. Groups should collaborate on answering the questions.

Thinking Visually

1. Bilateral symmetry
2. Many planes of symmetry

Chapter 26 Assessment

Reviewing Content

1. c	**5.** c	**9.** a
2. c	**6.** c	**10.** b
3. a	**7.** c	
4. b	**8.** b	

Understanding Concepts

11. All members of the animal kingdom are multicellular, eukaryotic heterotrophs whose cells lack cell walls. Animals are specialized to carry out the functions of feeding, respiration, circulation, excretion, response, movement, and reproduction.

12. The epithelial cells have a thin, flat structure through which gases diffuse easily.

13. Example: When a dog becomes too hot, it pants. Panting releases heat, and body temperature decreases.

14. The terms *anterior, posterior, dorsal, lateral, ventral, bilateral symmetry,* and *motile* should be used on the drawings of a fish. The terms *radial symmetry* and *motile* should be used as titles on the jellyfish. The term *sessile* should be used to label the sponge.

15. Because cephalization involves the location of sense organs and nerve cells that process information at its anterior end, the animal can respond to the environment more quickly and in more sophisticated ways than simpler animals can.

Chapter 26 Study Guide

26–1 Introduction to the Animal Kingdom

 7 5.a

Key Concepts

- An animal is a multicellular, eukaryotic heterotroph whose cells lack cell walls.
- Animals are specialized to carry out the following essential functions: feeding, respiration, circulation, excretion, response, movement, and reproduction.
- In general, complex animals tend to have high levels of cell specialization and internal organization, bilateral body symmetry, cephalization, and a body cavity.

Vocabulary

invertebrate, p. 657
vertebrate, p. 657
feedback inhibition, p. 658
blastula, p. 661
protostome, p. 661
deuterostome, p. 661
anus, p. 661
endoderm, p. 661
mesoderm, p. 661
ectoderm, p. 661
radial symmetry, p. 662
bilateral symmetry, p. 662
cephalization, p. 663

26–2 Sponges

 7 2.a

Key Concepts

- Sponges are classified as animals because they are multicellular, heterotrophic, have no cell walls, and contain a few specialized cells.
- The movement of water through a sponge provides a simple mechanism for feeding, respiration, circulation, and excretion.

Vocabulary

choanocyte, p. 665
osculum, p. 665
spicule, p. 665
archaeocyte, p. 665
internal fertilization, p. 666
larva, p. 666
gemmule, p. 667

26–3 Cnidarians

 7 2.a

Key Concepts

- Cnidarians are soft-bodied, carnivorous animals that have stinging tentacles arranged in circles around their mouth. They are the simplest animals to have body symmetry and specialized tissues.
- Cnidarians typically have a life cycle that includes two different-looking stages, a polyp and a medusa.
- Cnidarians include jellyfishes, hydras and their relatives, and sea anemones and corals.

Vocabulary

cnidocyte, p. 669
nematocyst, p. 669
polyp, p. 670
medusa, p. 670
gastrovascular cavity, p. 671
nerve net, p. 671
hydrostatic skeleton, p. 671
external fertilization, p. 672

Thinking Visually

Complete the following concept map using information from the chapter:

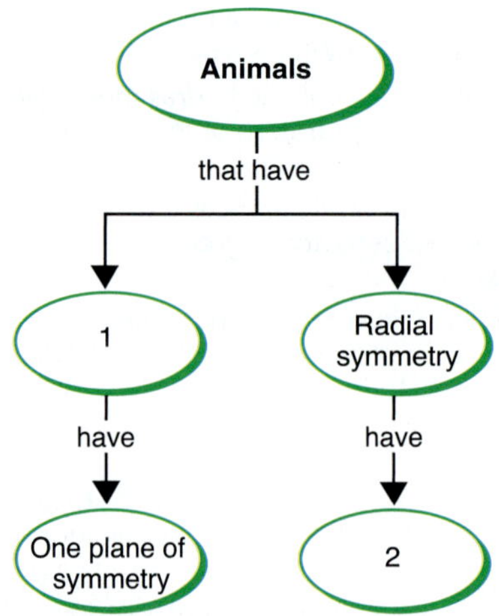

CHAPTER RESOURCES

TIME SAVER

Print:

- ***Teaching Resources,*** Chapter Vocabulary Review, Graphic Organizer, Chapter 26 Tests: Levels A and B

Technology:

- ***Computer Test Bank,*** Chapter 26 Test
- ***iText,*** Chapter 26 Assessment

Chapter 26 Assessment

Reviewing Content

Choose the letter that best answers the question or completes the statement.

1. A multicellular eukaryotic heterotroph whose cells lack cell walls is a(an)
   a. protist. c. animal.
   b. virus. d. plant.
2. The process by which animals take in oxygen and give off carbon dioxide is known as
   a. circulation. c. respiration.
   b. reproduction. d. response.
3. Animals that have a backbone, also called a vertebral column, are known as
   a. vertebrates. c. protostomes.
   b. prokaryotes. d. invertebrates.
4. Many animals have body symmetry with distinct front and back ends. This type of symmetry is
   a. radial. c. circular.
   b. bilateral. d. dorsal.
5. The developing embryo shown below is a __?__, a group that includes __?__.

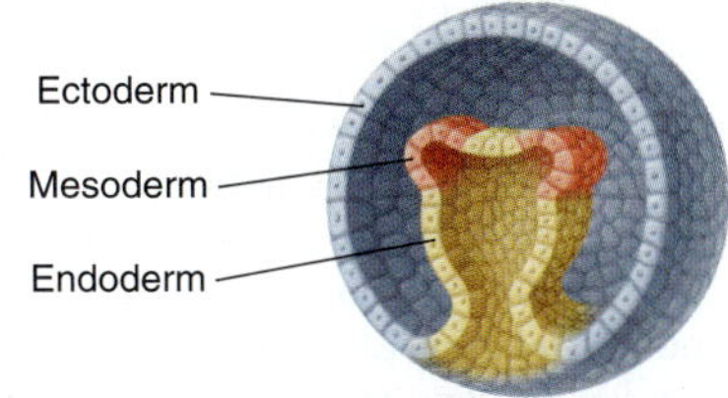

   a. protostome; simple invertebrates
   b. protostome; vertebrates
   c. deuterostome; echinoderms and chordates
   d. deuterostome; invertebrates
6. An animal whose mouth is formed from the blastopore is a
   a. deuterostome.
   b. detritivore.
   c. protostome.
   d. carnivore.
7. Animals in the phylum Porifera include
   a. chordates.
   b. sea stars.
   c. sponges.
   d. sea anemones.
8. A concentration of sense organs and nerve cells in the anterior end of the body is known as
   a. fertilization. c. symmetry.
   b. cephalization. d. anteriorization.

Interactive textbook with assessment at PHSchool.com

9. The sessile body form of a cnidarian is a
   a. polyp.
   b. medusa.
   c. planula.
   d. nematocyst.
10. A soft-bodied animal with stinging tentacles arranged around its mouth is a
   a. spicule. c. vertebrate.
   b. cnidarian. d. choanocyte.

Understanding Concepts

11. Describe the characteristics that all members of the animal kingdom share.
12. How is the structure of the epithelial cells that line an animal's lungs related to their function?
13. Describe an example of how an internal feedback mechanism helps an animal maintain homeostasis.
14. Draw a fish, a jellyfish, and a sponge. Label each drawing, using as many of the following terms as appropriate: radial symmetry, bilateral symmetry, anterior, posterior, dorsal, lateral, ventral, sessile, motile.
15. Explain the advantages that cephalization confers on an animal.
16. Distinguish between a protostome and a deuterostome.
17. During the early development of many animals, cells differentiate into three germ layers. Name these layers and give an example of a body structure that develops from each layer.
18. What are archaeocytes?
19. Briefly describe the physiological processes of nutrition, respiration, and excretion in a sponge.
20. Describe the mutually beneficial relationships that exist between many sponges and certain photosynthetic organisms.
21. What is the function of statocysts?
22. Describe the process of feeding in cnidarians.
23. Describe two ways in which budding occurs in polyps.
24. Describe the life cycle of *Aurelia*, a common jellyfish. Be sure to include how the polyp form alternates with the medusa form.

HOMEWORK GUIDE

Section:	Questions:
Section 26–1	1–6, 8, 11–17, 32
Section 26–2	7, 18–20, 25, 26, 33
Section 26–3	9, 10, 21–24, 27–31, 34

Interactive Textbook

If your class subscribes to the iText, your students can go online to access an interactive version of the Student Edition and a self-test.

(Continued from page 678)

16. A protostome is an animal whose mouth is formed from the blastopore, and a deuterostome is an animal whose anus is formed from the blastopore.
17. The endoderm is the innermost layer of tissue, which develops into the linings of the digestive tract and much of the respiratory system. The mesoderm is the middle layer of tissue, which develops into the muscular system and much of the circulatory, reproductive, and excretory systems. The ectoderm is the outermost layer of tissue, which develops into sense organs, nerves, and the outer layer of the skin.
18. Specialized cells that move around within the walls of sponges
19. Choanocytes trap and engulf food particles sifted from water that flows into the pores, and digestion is completed by archaeocytes. From water that flows inside the body cavity, oxygen diffuses into the cells, and wastes, including carbon dioxide, are carried away.
20. Many sponges have photosynthetic organisms in their tissues. These photosynthetic organisms provide food and oxygen for the sponge, and the sponge provides a protected area for the photosynthetic organisms.
21. Statocysts in cnidarians help determine the direction of gravity.
22. The cnidarian paralyzes its prey and pulls it into its gastrovascular cavity.
23. In one type, a bud grows from the side of an existing polyp. In another type, polyps produce tiny medusas that become new individuals.
24. Male and female medusas produce eggs and sperm. After external fertilization, the zygote grows into a larva that eventually becomes a polyp. The polyp buds to release young medusas.

Chapter 26 Assessment

Critical Thinking

25. **Comparing and Contrasting** Explain how sponges are similar to most other animals. How are they different?

26. **Asking Questions** The gemmules of some sponges can survive periods of severe drought or freezing. Suppose you have the opportunity to study gemmules. Write three different questions you could investigate.

27. **Inferring** Most cnidarians do not swim toward their prey. Instead, they capture prey carried by water currents. How is this behavior related to their body plan?

28. **Classifying** The comb jelly below has a body made of two layers separated by mesoglea. Its digestive system includes an anal opening through which wastes can pass. Radiating around its body are eight "combs" of cilia, which produce movement. A pair of tentacles enable it to capture food. Should this animal be classified as a cnidarian? Explain.

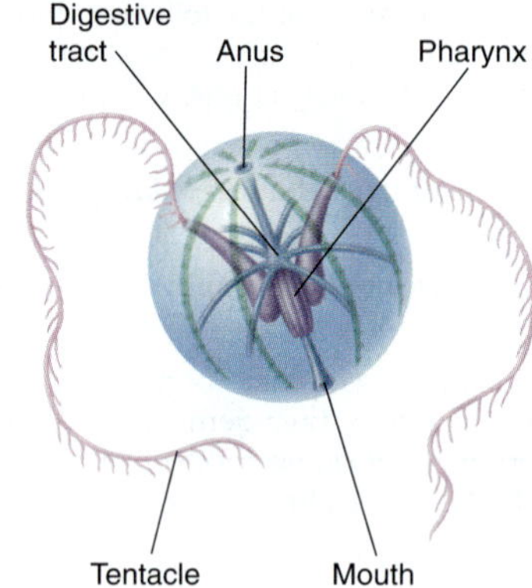

29. **Making Judgments** Choose one human activity that can harm coral reefs. Describe measures that people might take to reduce the damage. Then, evaluate the impact the measures might have on human society.

30. **Applying Concepts** Would you say that the life cycle of most cnidarians is more or less complex than the life cycle of sponges? Give details to justify your answer.

31. **Inferring** How might the nerve net of a cnidarian be related to the functioning of the cnidarian's cnidocytes?

32. **Comparing and Contrasting** An inventory clerk is a store employee who checks to make sure the store has an adequate supply of merchandise. If the supply of an item is running low, the inventory clerk orders more of the item. Explain how the job of an inventory clerk is similar to internal feedback mechanisms in an organism.

33. **Applying Concepts** How is the anatomy of a sponge's choanocytes an adaptation that enables the choanocytes to perform the physiological function of moving water through the sponge?

34. **Comparing and Contrasting** Compare a hydra to a Portuguese man-of-war. Explain how they are both similar and different.

Information and Heredity In Chapters 10 and 11, you learned about the processes of mitosis and meiosis. Compare these two processes, and explain how each is involved in the reproduction of sponges.

Writing in Science

Write a paragraph explaining the symbiotic relationship that exists between certain sponges and photosynthetic organisms. Be sure to include information about how these photosynthetic organisms obtain light. (*Hint:* After you have written a draft of your paragraph, share your draft with a friend. Ask your friend to point out any statements that are unclear. Use this information to revise your paragraph.)

Performance-Based Assessment

Making Models Construct a two- or three-dimensional model of a sponge or cnidarian. Label the organism's important structures. Explain how the organism obtains food and responds to the environment.

For: An interactive self-test
Visit: PHSchool.com
Web Code: cba-8260

Chapter 26 Assessment

Critical Thinking

25. Like other animals, sponges are multicellular, are heterotrophic, have some specialized cells, and lack cell walls. Unlike most other animals, sponges have pores all over their bodies and are sessile, and most lack symmetry.

26. Sample answers: How long can the gemmules survive without water? How long can the gemmules survive being kept in a freezer at 0°C? How long does it take gemmules that have survived drought or freezing to grow when moved to a favorable environment?

27. Cnidarians have radial symmetry. Since radially symmetrical animals lack a front end, they do not usually move forward in one direction.

28. Many of the comb jelly's characteristics are similar to those of cnidarians, but cnidarians do not have an anal opening. Therefore, the comb jelly should not be classified as a cnidarian.

29. Sample answer: Governments might pass laws that restrict the use of fertilizers and insecticides in coastal areas with coral reefs in the ocean nearby. These laws might make it difficult for farmers to make a living.

30. Sample answer: The life cycle is more complex in a cnidarian. In most cnidarian species, larvae that form as a result of fertilization develop into polyps. The polyps then reproduce asexually, forming medusas that reproduce sexually to complete the life cycle. In a sponge, there is no asexual stage in a complete life cycle, although pieces of adult sponges can reproduce asexually.

31. The nerve net enables cnidarians to detect external stimuli. Cnidocytes are activated by an external stimulus such as a brush against the cnidarian's tentacles.

32. Just as an inventory clerk maintains an even supply of merchandise, internal feedback mechanisms maintain homeostasis. When supplies run low, the clerk orders more supplies. Similarly, when the body runs low on food, for instance, an animal becomes hungry and eats. When the store's supply is adequate, the clerk stops ordering supplies. Similarly, when the body no longer needs food, hunger ceases and the animal stops eating.

33. Choanocytes are specialized cells that use flagella to move a steady current of water through the sponge.

34. Both a hydra and a Portuguese man-of-war are cnidarians of the class Hydrozoa. They differ in that a hydra lives as a solitary polyp and is found in fresh water, while a Portuguese man-of-war is a colony of polyps and is found in salt water.

Students should define both mitosis and meiosis and then explain how each is involved in sponge reproduction. In most sponge species, a single sponge forms both eggs and sperm by meiosis, and then internal fertilization occurs. The zygote then undergoes many mitotic divisions to eventually produce an adult sponge.

Standards Practice

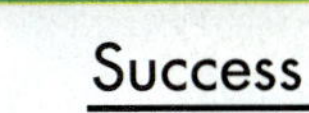

Success Tracker™
Online at PHSchool.com

Test-Taking Tip When evaluating multiple-choice answers, read all the answer choices, even if the first choice seems to be the correct one. By doing so, you can make sure that the answer you choose is the best one.

Directions: Choose the letter that best answers the question or completes the statement.

The graph below shows the growth rate of a hypothetical coral species under different conditions. Use this information to answer questions 1 and 2.

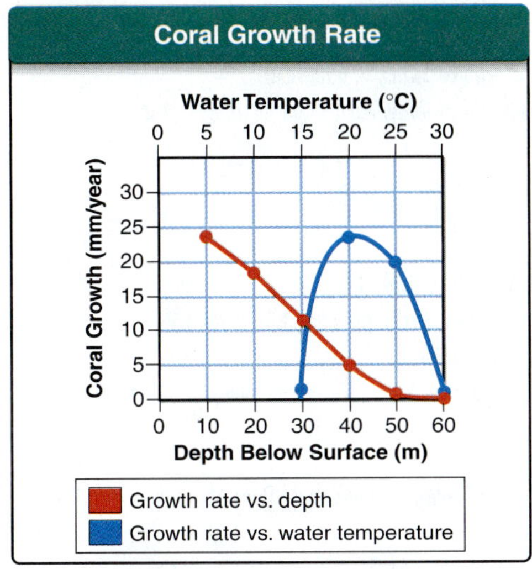

1. This coral grows best at depths of __?__ and a temperature of __?__.
   A 5–10 m; 20°C
   B less than 10 m; 15°C
   C less than 10 m; 28°C
   D more than 10 m; 21°C

2. Which of the following statements best explains the trend shown in the graph?
   A The growth rate of the coral increases as the depth below the water surface increases.
   B At temperatures of 15°C or above, the growth rate depends only on temperature.
   C Corals cannot grow below 30 m.
   D This coral grows best from 18° to 23°C.

3. Which of the following is a type of tissue that arises in most animals during development?
   I. Endoderm
   II. Mesoderm
   III. Ectoderm
   A I only
   B II only
   C I and II only
   D I, II, and III

4. An adult sponge has all of the characteristics below EXCEPT
   I. Body symmetry
   II. Ability to move from place to place
   III. Cells without cell walls
   A I only
   B II only
   C I and II only
   D II and III only

5. Which of the following is NOT a characteristic of animals?
   A the ability to make their own food
   B the ability to move
   C eukaryotic cells
   D cells that lack cell walls

6. Most animals reproduce sexually by producing **7 2.a**
   A buds.
   B spores.
   C clones.
   D haploid gametes.

7. Which of the following is a body type of a cnidarian?
   A gemmule
   B spicule
   C medusa
   D nematocyst

Questions 8–11 Each of the lettered choices below refers to the following numbered statements. Select the best lettered choice. A choice may be used once, more than once, or not at all.

A Archaeocyte
B Blastula
C Osculum
D Protostome

8. A hollow ball of cells, formed after the zygote undergoes division
9. An animal whose mouth is formed from the blastopore
10. A large hole through which water leaves a sponge
11. A specialized cell that moves around within the wall of a sponge

Standards Practice

1. A	**5.** A	**9.** D
2. D	**6.** D	**10.** C
3. D	**7.** C	**11.** A
4. C	**8.** B	

Success Tracker™
Online at PHSchool.com

Have students check their understanding of the chapter by logging onto Success Tracker.

Writing in Science

Students should identify the symbiosis as mutualism and explain that the sponge obtains food and oxygen from the photosynthetic organisms, whereas the photosynthetic organisms obtain a protected area in which to live. The spicules of the sponge direct the incoming sunlight to the photosynthetic organisms. When students have completed a draft, they might work in pairs to revise and edit their paragraphs.

Performance-Based Assessment

Labeled parts of a model of a sponge should include the osculum, central cavity, choanocytes, and flagella. Labeled parts of a model of a cnidarian should include tentacles, mouth/anus, and gastrovascular cavity. The sponge obtains food by filter feeding and may respond by producing toxins that protect it from potential predators. To feed, a cnidarian paralyzes its prey with its stinging cells and uses its tentacles to push the prey into its gastrovascular cavity. A cnidarian has a nerve net and specialized sensory cells to detect environmental stimuli. A cnidarian's responses include movement and capturing prey.

Go Online
PHSchool.com

Your students can independently test their knowledge of the chapter and print out their test results for your files.

Chapter Planner 27 Worms and Mollusks

Section and Section Objectives	Time	STANDARDS NCLB	STANDARDS Biology	Activities and Labs
27–1 Flatworms, pp. 683–688 ***27.1.1 Describe*** the defining features of flatworms. ***27.1.2 Identify*** the characteristics of the groups of flatworms.	1 period (1/2 block)			**SE:** ***Inquiry Activity,*** Does a planarian have a head?, p. 682 L2
27–2 Roundworms, pp. 689–693 ***27.2.1 Describe*** the defining features of roundworms. ***27.2.2 Describe*** form and function in roundworms. ***27.2.3 Identify*** roundworms that are important in human disease.	1 period (1/2 block)			**TE:** ***Build Science Skills,*** p. 690 L2 **SE:** ***Careers in Biology,*** Meat Inspector, p. 691 L2
27–3 Annelids, pp. 694–699 ***27.3.1 Describe*** the defining features of annelids. ***27.3.2 Identify*** the characteristics of the classes of annelids. ***27.3.3 Describe*** the ecology of annelids.	1 period (1/2 block)			**TE:** ***Use Visuals,*** p. 694 L2 **TE:** ***Build Science Skills,*** pp. 694 L1 , 696 L2 L3 , 697 L2 L3 **SE:** ***Quick Lab,*** How does an earthworm pump blood?, p. 695 L2 L3
27–4 Mollusks, pp. 701–708 ***27.4.1 Describe*** the defining features of mollusks. ***27.4.2 Describe*** form and function in mollusks. ***27.4.3 Identify*** the characteristics of the three main classes of mollusks. ***27.4.4 Describe*** the ecology of mollusks.	2 periods (1 block)			**SE:** ***Issues in Biology,*** What Can Be Done About the Zebra Mussel?, p. 700 L2 **TE:** ***Demonstration,*** pp. 702 L1 L2 , 706 L1 **TE:** ***Build Science Skills,*** pp. 703 L2 L3 , 705, 706 L2 **TE:** ***Make Connections,*** p. 704 L2 **SE:** ***Analyzing Data,*** Raising Clams, p. 707 L2 L3 **SE:** ***Exploration,*** Investigating Land Snails, p. 709 L2 **LMA:** Chapter 27 Lab L2 L3 ; **LMB:** Chapter 27 Lab L1 L2
Chapter Assessment, pp. 710–713	1 period (1/2 block)			

ACTIVITY PLANNER

SE: *Inquiry Activity*, p. 682; 10 min.; black and white paper, petri dish, planarian, spring water, rubber band

TE: *Build Science Skills*, p. 690; 15 min.; planarians, vinegar eels, pond water, petri dish, hand lens or stereo microscope, depression slide

TE: *Use Visuals*, p. 694; 15 min.; modeling clay, 3 colors; toothpicks

TE: *Build Science Skills*, p. 694; 5 min.; long sock with toe cut off

SE: *Quick Lab*, p. 695; 15 min.; earthworm, dropper pipette, nonchlorinated water, large and clear plastic straw, dissecting microscope

TE: *Build Science Skills*, p. 696; 20 min.; clear plastic box, sand, topsoil, pond water, 6–12 earthworms, clear plastic wrap

TE: *Build Science Skills*, p. 697; 15 min.; earthworm, hand lens, dish

TE: *Demonstration*, p. 702; 5 min.; rasp, scrap of wood

TE: *Build Science Skills*, p. 703; 15 min.; variety of mollusk shells

TE: *Make Connections*, p. 704; 5 min.; balloon

TE: *Build Science Skills*, p. 705; 20 min.; 20–40 liter aquarium and cover, sand, pond water, aquatic plants, pond snails, hand lens

TE: *Build Science Skills*, p. 705; 10 min.; land snail

TE: *Build Science Skills*, p. 706; 15 min.; pond water, 4 containers, 4 beakers, sieve, coffee filter, piece of screen or wire mesh, cheesecloth

TE: *Demonstration*, p. 706; 5 min.; cuttlebone

SE: *Exploration*, p. 709; 45 min.; snail, slides, dropper pipette, dissecting tray, black paper, paper towels, lamp, ruler, dissecting microscope, petri dish, clock

PLANNING KEY

Ability Levels

for students performing . . .

below grade level L1

at grade level L2

above grade level L3

Print Components

SE	Student Edition	LA	Lab Assessment
TE	Teacher's Edition	BTM	Biotechnology Manual
RSW	Reading & Study Workbook A	IDM	Issues and Decision Making
ARSW	Adapted Reading & Study Workbook B	LW	Lab Worksheets
TR	Teaching Resources	LMA	Laboratory Manual A
IF	Investigations in Forensics	LMB	Laboratory Manual B

Tech Components

CTB	Computer Test Bank
BD	BioDetectives DVD
TP	Transparencies Plus
PLM	Probeware Lab Manual
ABC	ABC DVD Library
LS	Lab Simulations
VL	Virtual Labs

Interactive textbook with assessment at PHSchool.com

Program Resources	Assessment	Media and Technology
TR: Lesson Plan 27–1, Section Summary, p. 48 L1, p. 59 L2, Worksheets, pp. 51–52 L1, pp. 61–63 L2 **RSW:** Section 27–1 L2 **ARSW:** Section 27–1 L1	**SE:** 27–1 Section Assessment, p. 688 **TR:** Section Review 27–1	**iText:** Section 27–1 **TP:** 27–1 Interest Grabber, Section Outline, Life Cycle of *Schistosoma mansoni*, Figure 27–3
TR: Lesson Plan 27–2, Section Summary, p. 48 L1, p. 59 L2, Worksheets, pp. 64–65 L2 **RSW:** Section 27–2 L2	**SE:** 27–2 Section Assessment, p. 693 **TR:** Section Review 27–2	**iText:** Section 27–2 **TP:** 27–2 Interest Grabber, Section Outline, Diseases Caused by Roundworms
TR: Lesson Plan 27–3, Section Summary, p. 49 L1, p. 59 L2, Worksheets, pp. 53–54 L1, pp. 66–68 L2, Enrichment L2 L3 **RSW:** Section 27–3 L2; **ARSW:** Section 27–3 L1 **IDM:** Issues and Decisions 28 L2 L3	**SE:** 27–3 Section Assessment, p. 699 **TR:** Section Review 27–3	**iText:** Section 27–3 **TP:** 27–3 Interest Grabber, Section Outline, Compare/Contrast Table, Figure 27–16
TR: Lesson Plan 27–4, Section Summary, p. 50 L1, p. 60 L2, Worksheets, pp. 55–57 L1, pp. 69–71 L2 **LW:** Chapter 27 Exploration L1 L2 L3 **RSW:** Section 27–4 L2 **ARSW:** Section 27–4 L1	**SE:** 27–4 Section Assessment, p. 708 **TR:** Section Review 27–4	**iText:** Section 27–4 **TP:** 27–4 Interest Grabber, Section Outline, Compare/Contrast Table, Figure 27–21, Figure 27–23 **ABC:** 35 Earthworm Anatomy
	SE: Chapter 27 Assessment, pp. 710–713 **TR:** Chapter Vocabulary Review, Graphic Organizer, Chapter 27 Test	**iText:** Chapter 27 Assessment **CTB:** Chapter 27 Test

Go Online
Students can do research, share data, and test their knowledge online.

PRESSED FOR TIME?

To Preview the Chapter

- Introduce students to all Key Concepts and Vocabulary terms.
- Assign the Reading Strategies for each section.

To Cover the Chapter Quickly

- Have students read What Is a Flatworm? and Form and Function in Flatworms in Section 27–1; What Is a Roundworm? and Form and Function in Roundworms in Section 27–2; all of Section 27–3; and What Is a Mollusk? and Form and Function in Mollusks in Section 27–4.
- Assign 27–3 Section Review; questions 1–9 and 11–20 in Chapter 27 Assessment; and Chapter 27 Standards Practice.

To Review the Chapter

- Assign Sections 27–1 through 27–4 in the Reading and Study Workbook or the Adapted Reading and Study Workbook.
- Assign Section Reviews for 27–1 through 27–4 and the Vocabulary Review for Chapter 27 in the Teaching Resources.

CHAPTER 27

ENGAGE/EXPLORE

Inquiry Activity

Objective Students will be able to draw conclusions about the structure and function of a planarian.

Skill Focus **Drawing Conclusions, Observing**

Materials black construction paper, petri dish, white sheet of paper, planarian, spring water, 4-cm piece of rubber band, pencil

Time 10 minutes

Advance Prep Cut the rubber bands into 4-cm pieces ahead of time.

Safety Have students wear disposable plastic gloves. After the activity, dispose of the gloves. Make sure students wash their hands with soap and warm water before leaving the lab.

Strategies

- You may want to place the planarians in the petri dishes for the students.
- Caution students to be gentle with the planarians, and make sure they are always covered with water.

Expected Outcomes Students should observe that the planarian's head leads as the flatworm responds to stimuli and that the planarian avoids both contact and bright light.

Think About It

1. Yes, the head end leads the planarian's movements.
2. Sample answer: A planarian's avoidance of contact and light aids in defense against predators and thus is beneficial to the organism's survival.

Assess Prior Knowledge

Call on a volunteer to list the seven essential functions of an animal. *(Feeding, respiration, circulation, excretion, response, movement, and reproduction)* Then, show students a photo of a jellyfish and another of an octopus. Ask: **In what ways is the octopus different from the jellyfish in the seven essential functions?** *(Students might suggest that an octopus has a much more complex body structure and much greater abilities in movement.)*

CHAPTER 27

Worms and Mollusks

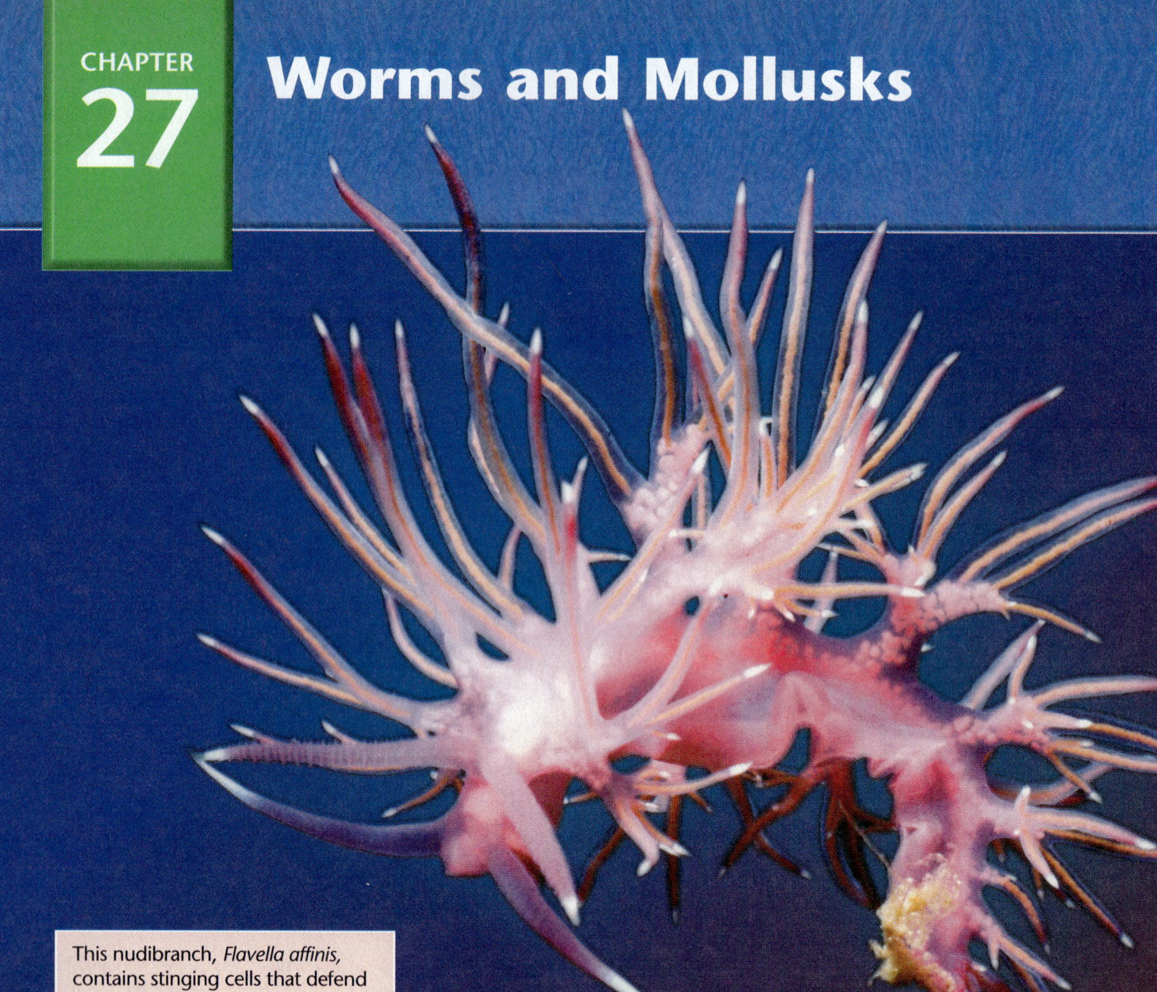

This nudibranch, *Flavella affinis*, contains stinging cells that defend against predators. A nudibranch is a kind of mollusk.

Inquiry Activity

Does a planarian have a head?

Procedure

1. Put on plastic gloves. Cover half of the outside of a petri dish with black paper. Place a white sheet of paper under the other half. Place a planarian in the center of the dish, and add spring water to keep it moist. Observe the planarian for 2 minutes. Record how long it stays on each side of the dish.
2. Where did the planarian spend more time? Hypothesize why the planarian preferred this side.
3. Tape a 4-cm piece of rubber band to a pencil so that 1 cm of the rubber band hangs freely. Use the tip of the rubber band to gently prod each end of the planarian. Observe its behavior. Wash your hands with soap and warm water before leaving the lab.

Think About It

1. **Observing** When the planarian moved, did one end always go first?
2. **Drawing Conclusions** How might the behaviors that you observed help the planarian survive?

FACTS AND FIGURES

More complexity than cnidarians

The bodies of flatworms, such as planarians, have clearly defined upper and lower surfaces, as well as clearly defined front and rear ends. These four areas of the body are most evident in more complex animals. Another important characteristic of flatworms is that they have three tissue, or germ, layers—endoderm, mesoderm, and ectoderm. All three germ tissue layers form in the flatworm embryo. This indicates that flatworms are more complex than cnidarians, which have only two tissue layers. The ectoderm is the outer tissue layer in the flatworm, and the endoderm is the inner layer. Between the two is the mesoderm, which enables cells to develop independently of the ectoderm and the endoderm. In more complex animals, the mesoderm gives rise to muscles, reproductive structures, bones, kidneys, and other internal organs and tissues.

27–1 Flatworms

When most people think of worms, they think of long, squiggly earthworms. But there are many other kinds of worms. Some are the length of your body or as thick as your arm. Others look like glowing, furry blobs. Worms can flutter and glide, or climb around with paddlelike bristles. Still others are very small and live in tubes cemented to rocks.

How is their body shape beneficial to worms? A long, slender body allows an animal to move about more rapidly than a radially symmetrical body, like that of a cnidarian. Worms can move forward in a single direction rather than remaining stationary or drifting in currents. In addition, the mouth, sense organs, and brain (if there is one) are usually located at the head, or anterior end, of the body. This arrangement allows worms to locate food and respond to stimuli as they move. Many groups of organisms have worm-shaped bodies. The familiar earthworm is a segmented worm, which you will read about later in this chapter. The unsegmented worms include flatworms and roundworms. The simplest of these are the flatworms.

Guide for Reading

Key Concepts
- What are the defining features of flatworms?
- What are the characteristics of the three groups of flatworms?

Vocabulary
acoelomate • coelom
pharynx • flame cell
ganglion • eyespot
hermaphrodite
fission • scolex
proglottid • testis

Reading Strategy: Outlining Before you read, use the headings of the section to make an outline about the characteristics of flatworms. As you read, fill in subtopics where they apply in the outline. Add phrases after each subtopic to provide key information.

What Is a Flatworm?

The phylum Platyhelminthes (plat-ih-hel-MIN-theez) consists of the flatworms. Most flatworms are no more than a few millimeters thick. **Flatworms are soft, flattened worms that have tissues and internal organ systems. They are the simplest animals to have three embryonic germ layers, bilateral symmetry, and cephalization.**

Flatworms are known as **acoelomates** (ay-SEE-luh-mayts), meaning "without coelom." A **coelom** (SEE-lum) is a fluid-filled body cavity that is lined with tissue derived from mesoderm. No coelom forms between the tissues of flatworms. **Figure 27–1** shows that the digestive cavity, which is lined with tissue derived from endoderm, is the only body cavity. Flatworms also have bilateral symmetry. This means that the animal has two well-formed sides that can be identified as left and right. Most flatworms exhibit enough cephalization to have what is called a head.

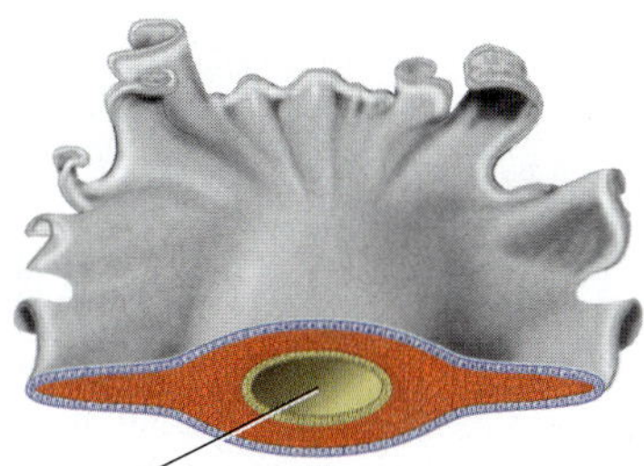

Figure 27–1 **Flatworms are the simplest animals to have three embryonic germ layers—ectoderm, endoderm, and mesoderm.** Shown here is the tropical, free-living flatworm *Pseudobiceros gloriosus.*

TIME SAVER

SECTION RESOURCES

Print:
- ***Teaching Resources,*** Lesson Plan 27–1, Adapted Section Summary 27–1, Adapted Worksheets 27–1, Section Summary 27–1, Worksheets 27–1, Section Review 27–1
- ***Reading and Study Workbook A,*** Section 27–1
- ***Adapted Reading and Study Workbook B,*** Section 27–1

Technology:
- ***iText,*** Section 27–1
- ***Transparencies Plus,*** Section 27–1

Section 27–1

1 FOCUS

Objectives

27.1.1 ***Describe*** the defining features of flatworms.

27.1.2 ***Identify*** the characteristics of the groups of flatworms.

Guide for Reading

Vocabulary Preview

Direct students' attention to the words *acoelomate* and *coelom.* Explain that *coelom* is pronounced with a long *e* and that such is often the case when a word contains the letter combination *oe.* Then, explain that *coelom* is derived from a Greek word meaning "cavity" or "hollow." A *coelomate* is an organism that has a body cavity. An *acoelomate* is an organism that lacks a body cavity, because the prefix *a-* means "without" or "not."

Reading Strategy

Advise students to use the blue headings for the first level of heads in their outlines. For the second level, they should use the green subheads, found in the longer subsections.

2 INSTRUCT

What Is a Flatworm?

Use Visuals

Figure 27–1 Review the three tissue, or germ, layers that develop in an animal embryo: the inner endoderm, the middle mesoderm, and the outer ectoderm. Then, direct students' attention to the cross section of a flatworm body. Ask: **Is there space between the three layers?** *(There is no space between the layers.)* **What is a coelom?** *(A coelom is a fluid-filled body cavity lined with tissue derived from the mesoderm.)* Emphasize that a flatworm does not have a fluid-filled body cavity lined with mesoderm. Ask: **What is an animal called that lacks a coelom?** *(An acoelomate)* L2

27–1 (continued)

Form and Function in Flatworms

Build Science Skills

Applying Concepts Flatworms are the simplest animals that exhibit bilateral symmetry. Challenge students to find objects in and around the school that also exhibit bilateral symmetry. Examples include a basketball court, a sweater, the capital letters *A* and *D,* and chairs.

Address Misconceptions

When many students think of a "worm," they automatically think of an earthworm. Point out that the familiar earthworm is actually a much more advanced animal than the worms students will study in this and the next section. Emphasize that flatworms and roundworms are unsegmented worms, meaning that their bodies are not divided into parts, or segments. Also, point out that many organisms commonly referred to as worms are not worms at all, but rather the larval stage of insects. L1

Form and Function in Flatworms

Because flatworms are thin and most of their cells are close to the external environment, materials can pass easily into and out of their bodies. All flatworms rely on diffusion for some essential body functions, such as respiration, excretion, and circulation. Other processes are carried out in different ways in different species. Free-living flatworms have organ systems for digestion, excretion, response, and reproduction.

Parasitic species of flatworms, such as the fluke in **Figure 27–2,** probably evolved from free-living ancestors. As the worms evolved into parasites, internal organs and other structures were modified or even lost. As a result, parasitic species are typically simpler in structure than their free-living relatives.

▲ **Figure 27–2** Blood flukes are parasitic flatworms that mature in the blood vessels of humans. Unlike free-living flatworms, parasitic worms take in nutrients from another organism. **Comparing and Contrasting** *How do the internal structures of parasitic flatworms compare to those of free-living flatworms?*

Feeding Free-living flatworms can be carnivores that feed on tiny aquatic animals, or they can be scavengers that feed on recently dead animals. Like cnidarians, flatworms have a digestive cavity with a single opening, or mouth, through which food and wastes pass. Near the mouth is a muscular tube called a **pharynx** (FAR-inks). Flatworms extend the pharynx out of the mouth. The pharynx then pumps food into the digestive cavity, or gut. Once inside, food is digested by cells of the gut, where digestion and nutrient absorption take place. Digested food diffuses from the digestive cavity into all other body tissues.

Parasitic worms feed on blood, tissue fluids, or pieces of cells within the host's body. Many parasitic worms obtain nutrients from foods that have already been digested by their host. Therefore, most parasitic worms do not need a complex digestive system. Many parasitic species have a digestive tract that is simpler than that of free-living forms. Some species have a pharynx that pumps food into a pair of dead-end intestinal sacs for digestion. Tapeworms, on the other hand, have no digestive tract at all. They live within the intestine of their host, such as a cow or a human, and simply absorb digested nutrients that are in their host's intestine.

Respiration, Circulation, and Excretion Because their bodies are so flat and thin, many flatworms do not need a circulatory system to transport materials. Instead, flatworms rely on diffusion to transport oxygen and nutrients to their internal tissues, and to remove carbon dioxide and other wastes from their bodies. Flatworms have no gills or other respiratory organs, and no heart, blood vessels, or blood.

Some flatworms have flame cells that function in excretion. **Flame cells** are specialized cells that remove excess water from the body. They may also filter and remove metabolic wastes such as ammonia and urea. Many flame cells are joined together to form a network of tubes that empties into the outside environment through tiny pores in the animal's skin.

What is the function of flame cells?

UNIVERSAL ACCESS

Less Proficient Readers
Relate the new term *flame cells* to students' past experience. Explain that the cells that filter and remove excess water from the body have the name "flame cells" because their action is reminiscent of the flame of a fire. Within the flame cells, tufts of cilia "flicker." When the excess tissue fluid moves into the flame cells, the flickering of the cilia drives the fluid down the tubule system to the outside of the organism. L1

Advanced Learners
Have interested students further investigate the diseases associated with flukes and tapeworms, including method of transmission, symptoms, treatment, and prevention. For flukes, have students investigate *Schistosoma.* For tapeworms, have students investigate the beef tapeworm, *Taenia saginata,* and the pork tapeworm, *Taenia solium.* L3

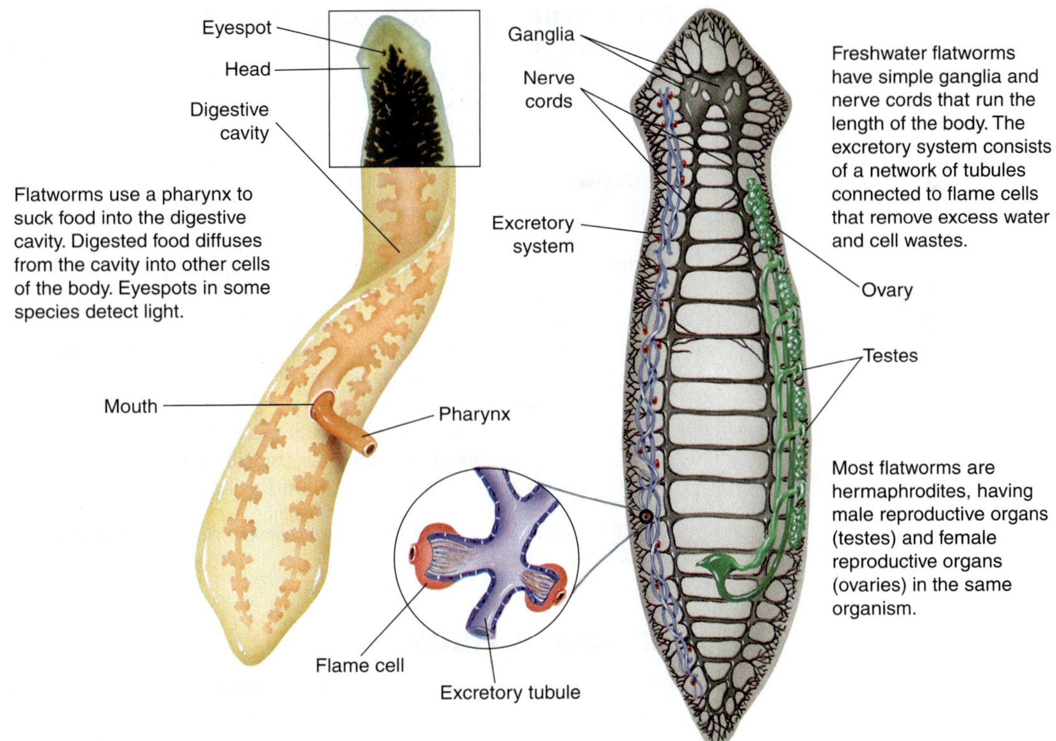

Response Most flatworms have more complex structures for detecting and responding to external stimuli than those of cnidarians or sponges. In free-living flatworms, a head encloses several **ganglia** (singular: ganglion), or groups of nerve cells, that control the nervous system. These ganglia are not complex enough to be called a brain. Two long nerve cords run from the ganglia along both sides of the body. Locate these nerve cords in **Figure 27–3.** Observe that shorter nerve cords run across the body, like the rungs of a ladder. Parasitic flatworms interact little with their external environment and typically have a less complex nervous system.

Many free-living flatworms have what look like eyes near the anterior end of their body. Each "eye" is actually an **eyespot,** or group of cells that can detect changes in the amount of light in their environment. In addition to having eyespots, most flatworms have specialized cells that detect external stimuli, such as chemicals found in food or the direction in which water is flowing. These cells are usually scattered throughout the body.

The nervous systems of free-living flatworms allow them to gather information from their environment. They use this information to locate food and to find dark hiding places beneath stones and logs during the day.

▲ **Figure 27–3** All flatworms, including this planarian, have organ systems that perform essential life functions. The digestive cavity (left) is branched throughout the body and opens to the outside through the pharynx. The diagram on the right shows the excretory system, nervous system, and reproductive system. The excretory system (in purple) consists of many flame cells (in red) that maintain water balance and may remove waste. The nervous system (in dark gray) consists of ganglia and two nerve cords that run the length of the body. The reproductive system (in green) has both testes and ovaries along both sides of the body. **Inferring** *How is a branched digestive cavity advantageous to a flatworm?*

Use Visuals

Figure 27–3 Have students list some of the important organs present in flatworms. For example, students might mention the pharynx, anterior ganglia, and nerve cords. Point out that although the flatworm does not have a respiratory system or circulatory system, it does have a digestive system and a nervous system. L2

Build Science Skills

Designing Experiments Divide the class into small groups, and ask each group to design an experiment that would investigate how sensitive a free-living flatworm's eyespot is. Advise students that they should first write a hypothesis that can be tested. A group's experiment should designate an independent variable, a dependent variable, and a control, as well as a plan to collect and evaluate data. L2 L3

BIO INSIGHTS — FACTS AND FIGURES

Getting rid of wastes with flame cells
Freshwater turbellaria have an organ system that regulates the volume and salt concentration of their body fluid. This system depends on one or more units called protonephridia. Each unit of protonephridia consists of branched tubules that extend from a pore at the body surface to many cup-shaped flame cells in the body tissues. Within the flame cells, tufts of cilia flicker—thus the name flame cells. When excess tissue fluid moves into the flame cells, the flickering of the cilia drives the fluid down the tubule system to the outside of the organism.

Answers to . . .

CHECKPOINT *Flame cells are specialized cells that remove excess water from the body. They may also function in the removal of metabolic wastes such as ammonia and urea.*

Figure 27–2 *The internal structures of parasitic flatworms are generally simpler than those of free-living flatworms.*

Figure 27–3 *The branched cavity aids in more efficient digestion because branches reduce the distance that nutrients must diffuse.*

27–1 (continued)

Groups of Flatworms

Build Science Skills

Using Tables and Graphs Have students make a compare/contrast table to organize the information they learn about groups of flatworms. The table title should be "Groups of Flatworms," and column heads could include Class, Description, Environment, and Examples. Encourage students to include as many details as possible in their table. L2

Use Visuals

Figure 27–4 Have students compare the two turbellarians shown in the figure. Ask: **How are the two species different?** *(Students might first mention color and form. Some students might also note that the two likely move differently.)* **In what sort of environments would you find these turbellarian species?** *(The species on the left lives in shallow ocean water near coral reefs, while the species on the right lives on the floor of tropical forests.)* **Would you classify either as a parasitic species?** *(No; both are free-living flatworms.)* **Are all turbellarians free-living?** *(No, but most are.)* L1 L2

Movement Free-living flatworms typically move in two ways. Cilia on their epidermal cells help them glide through the water and over the bottom of a stream or pond. Muscle cells controlled by the nervous system allow them to twist and turn so that they are able to react rapidly to environmental stimuli.

Reproduction Most free-living flatworms are hermaphrodites that reproduce sexually. A **hermaphrodite** (hur-MAF-roh-dyt) is an individual that has both male and female reproductive organs. During sexual reproduction, two worms join in a pair. The worms in the pair deliver sperm to each other. The eggs are laid in clusters and hatch within a few weeks.

Asexual reproduction is common in free-living flatworms. It takes place by **fission,** in which an organism splits in two, and each half grows new parts to become a complete organism. In some species, a worm simply "falls to pieces," and each piece grows into a new worm. Parasitic flatworms often have complex life cycles that involve both sexual and asexual reproduction.

✓CHECKPOINT *What method of asexual reproduction is common in flatworms?*

Groups of Flatworms

Flatworms are an enormously diverse group with many different forms. The three main groups of flatworms are turbellarians, flukes, and tapeworms. Most turbellarians are free-living. Most other flatworm species are parasites.

Turbellarians Free-living flatworms belong to the class Turbellaria (tur-buh-LAYR-ee-uh). **Turbellarians are free-living flatworms. Most live in marine or fresh water.** Most species are bottom dwellers, living in the sand or mud under stones and shells. The most familiar flatworms of this group are the planarians, the "cross-eyed" freshwater worms. Turbellarians can vary greatly in color, form, and size, as shown in **Figure 27–4.**

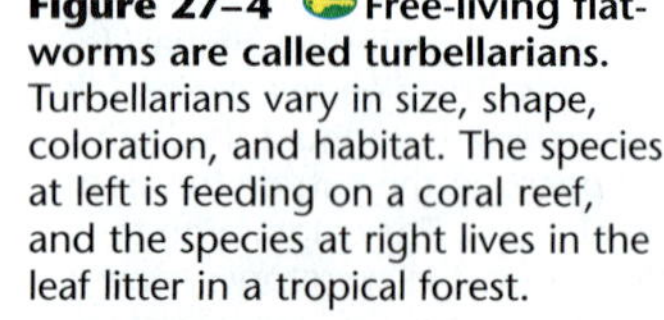

Figure 27–4 Free-living flatworms are called turbellarians. Turbellarians vary in size, shape, coloration, and habitat. The species at left is feeding on a coral reef, and the species at right lives in the leaf litter in a tropical forest.

FACTS AND FIGURES

Did flatworms evolve from cnidarians?
Scientists have discovered that the simplest turbellaria and the larval stages of flukes and tapeworms resemble the planula of the cnidarian life cycle. Planulae are formed from zygotes as part of the cnidarian reproductive process; eventually they grow into polyps. This similarity between flatworms and planulae has led some scientists to hypothesize that ancient bilateral animals evolved from ancestors that were much like planulae. This may have occurred through increased cephalization and the emergence of tissues derived from the mesoderm. If this theory is accurate, then planulalike organisms may have given rise to most groups of complex animals. So far, this theory has not been proven, but there is much evidence to support it.

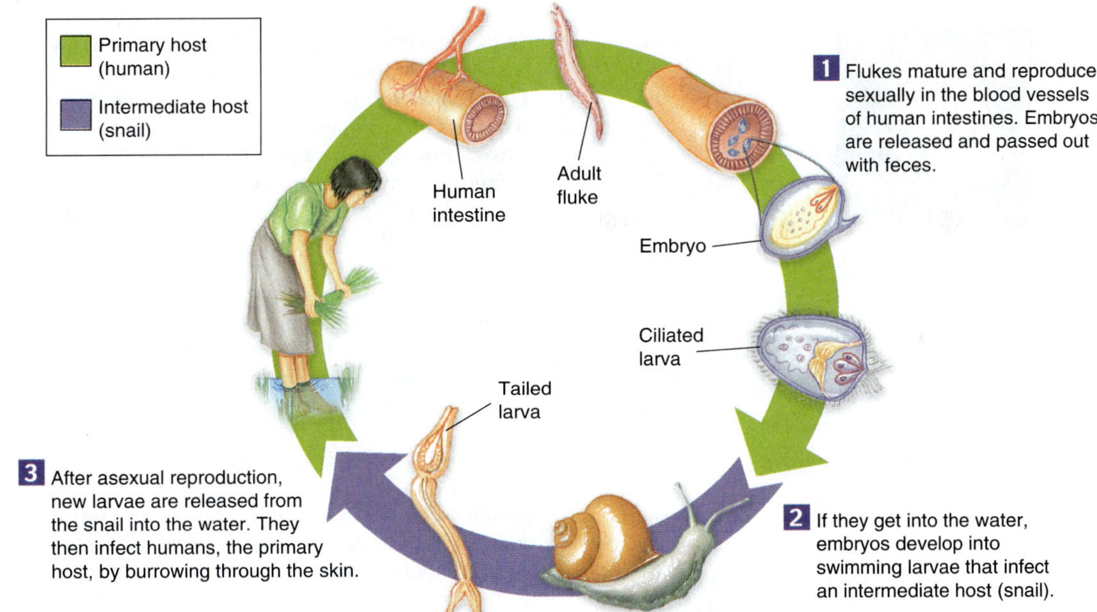

Flukes Members of the class Trematoda (trem-uh-TOH-duh) are known as flukes. **Flukes are parasitic flatworms. Most flukes infect the internal organs of their host.** They can infect the blood or virtually any internal organ of the host. Some flukes are external parasites that live on the skin, mouth, gills, or other outside parts of a host.

The blood fluke *Schistosoma mansoni* has a life cycle that is typical of parasitic flukes and of many parasites in general. As shown in **Figure 27–5**, the fluke lives in multiple hosts. Its primary host, the organism in which it reproduces sexually, is a human. Blood flukes infect humans by burrowing through exposed skin. Once inside, they are carried to the tiny blood vessels of the intestine. There, the flukes mature into adults, reproduce sexually, and release embryos into the intestine. The embryos are passed out of the body in feces.

If the embryos reach water, they develop into swimming larvae and infect freshwater snails, the intermediate host. An intermediate host is an organism in which a parasite reproduces asexually. Larvae that result from asexual reproduction are eventually released to begin the cycle again.

The *Schistosoma* fluke causes schistosomiasis (shis-tuh-soh-MY-uh-sis) in humans. Schistosomiasis is a serious disease in which the *Schistosoma* eggs clog blood vessels, causing swelling and tissue decay in the lungs, liver, spleen, or intestines. Schistosomiasis affects millions of people worldwide. It is particularly widespread in tropical areas that lack proper sewage systems, where human wastes are tossed into streams or used as fertilizer. There, the parasites are transmitted to intermediate hosts and back to humans with deadly efficiency.

▲ **Figure 27–5** **Flukes usually infect the internal organs of their host.** The life cycle of the blood fluke *Schistosoma mansoni* involves two hosts: humans and snails.

For: Links on flukes
Visit: www.SciLinks.org
Web Code: cbn-8271

Use Visuals

Figure 27–5 Ask students: **What disease is caused by the blood fluke?** *(Schistosomiasis)* **How does the life cycle of the blood fluke point to the need for effective sewage treatment?** *(The eggs are released in the feces of infected humans. Proper treatment of sewage destroys eggs before they hatch into swimming larvae and infect an intermediate host.)* **What is the difference between an intermediate host and a primary host?** *(A primary host is an organism in which the parasite reproduces sexually. An intermediate host is an organism in which the parasite reproduces asexually.)* L1 L2

Build Science Skills

Interpreting Graphics Reinforce students' understanding of the blood fluke life cycle shown in Figure 27–5 by having them sequence the following events. Write the events on the board, and ask students to rewrite them in the proper sequence, beginning with number 1.

1. Human becomes infected while standing in shallow water.
2. Fluke eggs hatch into swimming larvae.
3. Adult flukes produce eggs.
4. Snail releases tailed larvae.
5. Flukes mature in blood vessels of human intestine.
6. Human eliminates solid wastes containing fluke eggs.
7. Swimming larvae infect an intermediate host (snail).

(Proper sequence: 1, 5, 3, 6, 2, 7, 4) L1 L2

Download a worksheet on flukes for students to complete, and find additional teacher support from NSTA SciLinks.

BIO INSIGHTS — FACTS AND FIGURES

Flukes and planarians
As parasites, flukes exhibit many differences and some similarities when compared with free-living planarians. Unique to the fluke is the thick outer layer of cells called the tegument. The tegument protects flukes from being digested by their hosts. Unlike free-living worms, flukes don't have muscles or cilia for movement. Instead, they have suckers that they use to attach themselves to their hosts. Flukes also lack specialized sense organs. Flukes are similar to planarians in that they have similar excretory systems. They are also like planarians in that they are hermaphrodites.

Answer to . . .

CHECKPOINT *Fission*

27–1 (continued)

Use Visuals

Figure 27–6 Ask students: **What are proglottids?** *(The segments that make up most of a tapeworm's body)* **When a mature proglottid breaks off, what is the result?** *(Eggs are released that pass out of the host in feces.)* **In a tapeworm's life cycle, what is the primary host, and what is the secondary host?** *(The primary host is the human. The secondary host is another animal, such as a cow or fish.)* **How does a human become infected with a tapeworm?** *(A human eats incompletely cooked meat that contains a tapeworm cyst.)* L2

3 ASSESS

Evaluate Understanding

Call on students at random to explain feeding, respiration, circulation, excretion, response, movement, and reproduction in flatworms.

Reteach

Have students review the life cycle of a fluke in Figure 27–5. Then, point out that the life cycle of a tapeworm is described in the text on page 688. Help students use this description to illustrate the life cycle of a tapeworm in a way similar to that in Figure 27–5.

Writing in Science

Students should construct a Venn diagram that shows both free-living and parasitic flatworms as being unsegmented worms with the defining features listed on page 683. The Venn diagram should show that free-living flatworms have organ systems for several physiological processes (while parasitic flatworms don't), and they are typically larger than parasitic flatworms. Other differences, including how nutrients are obtained, should be noted. After constructing the Venn diagram, students should write a well-organized paragraph that describes similarities and differences.

If your class subscribes to the iText, use it to review the Key Concepts in Section 27–1.

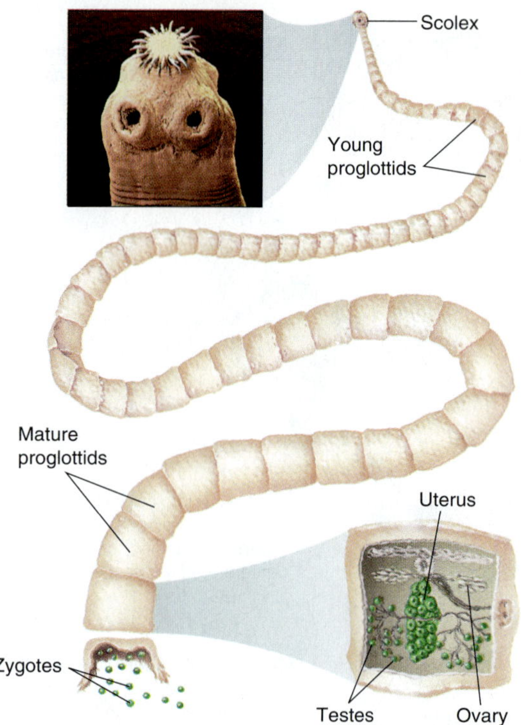

▲ **Figure 27–6** **Tapeworms are parasitic flatworms that live in the intestines of their host.** A tapeworm attaches to the host using hooks or suckers on its scolex. A single tapeworm is made of many proglottids. The youngest proglottids are at the anterior (head) end, and the largest and most mature proglottids are at the posterior (tail) end. After eggs have been fertilized, proglottids break off and release zygotes that are then passed out of the host in feces.

Tapeworms Members of the class Cestoda (ses-TOHD-uh) are called tapeworms. **Tapeworms are long, flat, parasitic worms that are adapted to life inside the intestines of their hosts.** There, they are surrounded by food that has already been digested, so it can be absorbed directly through their body walls. They have no digestive tract.

Figure 27–6 shows the structure of a tapeworm. The head of an adult tapeworm, called a **scolex** (SKOH-leks), is a structure that can contain suckers or hooks. The tapeworm uses its scolex to attach to the intestinal wall of its host, where it absorbs nutrients from the host's intestine. Behind the scolex is a narrow region that divides to produce many **proglottids** (proh-GLAHT-idz), which are the segments that make up most of the worm's body. Mature proglottids contain both male and female reproductive organs. Sperm produced by the **testes** (singular: testis), or male reproductive organs, can fertilize eggs of other tapeworms or of the same individual. After the eggs are fertilized, proglottids break off and burst to release the fertilized eggs, or zygotes. These zygotes are passed out of the host in feces.

If food or water contaminated with tapeworm zygotes is consumed by cows, fishes, or other intermediate hosts, the eggs enter the host and hatch into larvae. These larvae grow and then burrow into the muscle tissue of the intermediate host. There they form a dormant protective stage called a cyst. If a human eats incompletely cooked meat containing these cysts, the larvae become active and grow into adult worms within the human's intestines, beginning the cycle again.

27–1 Section Assessment

1. **Key Concept** What is a flatworm?
2. **Key Concept** List the three groups of flatworms and give an example of each.
3. How do the feeding methods of parasitic and free-living flatworms relate to their specific environments?
4. Describe the life cycle of the blood fluke, *Schistosoma mansoni.*
5. **Critical Thinking Applying Concepts** How do a turbellarian's nervous system and digestive system work together to provide the food that the worm's body needs?

Writing in Science

Compare-Contrast Paragraph

Write a paragraph comparing free-living and parasitic flatworms. Be sure to explain how these worms are alike as well as how they are different. *Hint:* Before you write, construct a Venn diagram to organize your ideas.

27–1 Section Assessment

1. A flatworm is a soft, flattened worm with tissues, organ systems, three germ layers, bilateral symmetry, and cephalization.
2. Turbellaria: planarian; Trematoda: fluke; Cestoda: tapeworm
3. Many parasitic flatworms obtain nutrients from their host's body. Free-living flatworms capture and digest food.
4. *S. mansoni* matures and reproduces sexually in the blood vessels of human intestines. Embryos are released with feces and hatch into swimming larvae that infect a snail, where they reproduce asexually. Larvae released from the snail into water can infect humans.
5. The nervous system allows the worm to gather information about its environment, including the location of food. The digestive system digests and absorbs the food.

27–2 Roundworms

Members of the phylum Nematoda, also known as roundworms, are among the most numerous of all animals. It is difficult to imagine how many live around us. A single rotting apple can contain as many as 90,000 roundworms. A cubic meter of garden soil can be home to more than a million!

What Is a Roundworm?

Roundworms are slender, unsegmented worms with tapering ends. They range in size from microscopic to a meter in length. Most species of roundworms are free-living, inhabiting soil, salt flats, aquatic sediments, and water, from polar regions to the tropics. Many others are parasitic and live in hosts that include almost every kind of plant and animal.

Like flatworms, roundworms develop from three germ layers. However, roundworms have a body cavity between the endoderm and mesoderm tissues. Because this cavity is lined only partially with tissue derived from the mesoderm, it is called a **pseudocoelom** (soo-doh-SEE-lum), which means "false coelom." Observe the pseudocoelom in **Figure 27–7.**

Also, unlike most flatworms, roundworms have a digestive tract with two openings. This body plan is often called a tube-within-a-tube. The inner tube is the digestive tract, and the outer tube is the body wall. This arrangement makes digestion in roundworms very different from that in flatworms because food moves in one direction through the digestive tract. Any material in the food that cannot be digested leaves through the anus. The **anus** is the posterior opening of the digestive tract. **Roundworms are unsegmented worms that have pseudocoeloms and digestive systems with two openings—a mouth and an anus.**

Guide for Reading

Key Concepts
- What are the defining features of roundworms?
- What roundworms are important in human disease?

Vocabulary
pseudocoelom
anus

Reading Strategy: Using Visuals As you read, write a statement explaining how each illustration or photograph reinforces or enhances the content of the section.

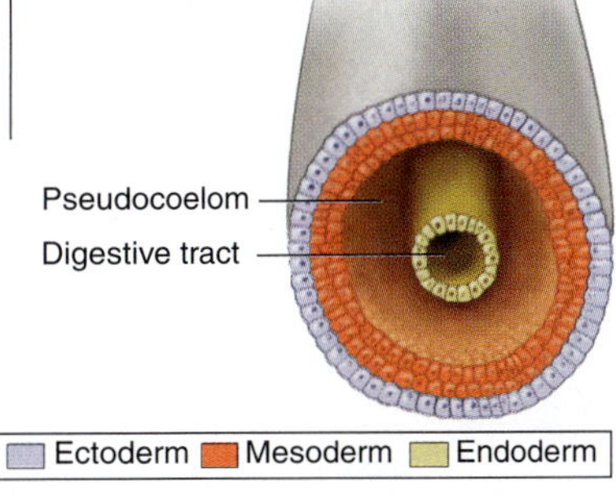

Figure 27–7 Roundworms such as hookworms are unsegmented worms that have a pseudocoelom and a digestive system with a mouth and an anus. Roundworms develop from three germ layers, and a pseudocoelom forms between the endoderm and mesoderm layers.

SECTION RESOURCES

Print:
- ***Teaching Resources,*** Lesson Plan 27–2, Adapted Section Summary 27–2, Section Summary 27–2, Worksheets 27–2, Section Review 27–2
- ***Reading and Study Workbook A,*** Section 27–2

Technology:
- ***iText,*** Section 27–2
- ***Transparencies Plus,*** Section 27–2

Section 27–2

1 FOCUS

Objectives

27.2.1 ***Describe*** the defining features of roundworms.
27.2.2 ***Describe*** form and function in roundworms.
27.2.3 ***Identify*** roundworms that are important in human disease.

Guide for Reading

Vocabulary Preview

Have students write the Vocabulary words, dividing each into its separate syllables as best they can. Remind students that each syllable usually has only one vowel sound. The correct syllabications are pseu•do•coe•lom and a•nus.

Reading Strategy

Before students read, have them skim the section to find the boldface Key Concepts. Ask students to copy the sentences onto separate sheets of paper. Then, as they read, they should make notes of details that support each Key Concept.

2 INSTRUCT

What Is a Roundworm?

Use Visuals

Figure 27–7 Direct students' attention to the cross section of a roundworm. Then, have them compare this cross section with the one shown in Figure 27–1 on page 683. Ask: **What is the main difference between the body plan of a flatworm and the body plan of the roundworm?** *(In a flatworm, there is no space between the endoderm tissue and the mesoderm tissue. In the roundworm, there is a space between those two tissues.)* Point out that this space, or body cavity, is the pseudocoelom of the roundworm. Ask: **What is "false" about a pseudocoelom?** *(A pseudocoelom is "false" because it is only partially lined with mesoderm tissue.)* **What part of the pseudocoelom is not lined with mesoderm tissue?** *(The inner boundary of the cavity)* L2 L3

27–2 (continued)

Form and Function in Roundworms

Build Science Skills

Comparing and Contrasting Set up a classroom display of live flatworms and roundworms so that students can observe and compare the two groups of animals. An appropriate flatworm is a planarian; vinegar eels are roundworms that make excellent subjects for observation. Place several planarians in a small amount of pond water or aquarium water in a petri dish. Have students use a hand lens or a stereo microscope to observe these animals move. Place a few drops of vinegar eel culture in a depression slide or on a plain microscope slide. Do not use a coverslip. Have students observe the slide under low power. Then, ask: **How would you describe the movement of the planarians?** *(They glide through the water or along the surface of the petri dish.)* **How would you describe the movement of the roundworms?** *(They move with a rapid, jerky motion.)* L2

Roundworms and Human Disease

Build Science Skills

Comparing and Contrasting Have students make a compare/contrast table to organize the information they learn about roundworms and human disease. Column heads should include Parasite, Disease, and Characteristics. L2

Figure 27–8 **Parasitic roundworms include trichinosis-causing *Trichinella* worms (top) and hookworms (inset).** *Trichinella* worms reproduce in the intestines of their host and then form cysts in the muscle tissue. Hookworms affect as many as one quarter of the world's population. They suck the host's blood from inside the intestines, weakening the host.

Form and Function in Roundworms

Roundworms have specialized tissues and organ systems that carry out essential physiological functions. In general, the body systems of free-living roundworms tend to be more complex than those of parasitic forms.

Feeding Many free-living roundworms are predators that use grasping mouthparts and spines to catch and eat other small animals. Some soil-dwelling and aquatic forms eat algae, fungi, or pieces of decaying organic matter. Others digest the bacteria and fungi that break down dead animals and plants.

Respiration, Circulation, and Excretion Like flatworms, roundworms exchange gases and excrete metabolic waste through their body walls. They have no internal transport system. Therefore, they depend on diffusion to carry nutrients and waste through their bodies.

Response Roundworms have simple nervous systems, consisting of several ganglia. Several nerves extend from ganglia in the head and run the length of the body. These nerves transmit sensory information and control movement. Roundworms have several types of sense organs. Some include simple structures that detect chemicals given off by prey or hosts.

Movement The muscles of roundworms extend the length of their bodies. Together with the fluid in the pseudocoelom, these muscles function as a hydrostatic skeleton. Aquatic roundworms contract these muscles to move like snakes through the water. Soil-dwelling roundworms simply push their way through the soil by thrashing around.

Reproduction Roundworms reproduce sexually, and most species have separate sexes—an individual is either male or female. Roundworms reproduce using internal fertilization. Usually, the male deposits sperm inside the female's reproductive tract. Parasitic roundworms often have life cycles that involve two or three different hosts or several organs within a single host.

CHECKPOINT *How do free-living roundworms that are predators obtain their food?*

Roundworms and Human Disease

Although most roundworms are free-living, the phylum is better known for species that parasitize their hosts, including humans. Parasitic roundworms, such as those in **Figure 27–8**, have been evolving relationships with other organisms for hundreds of millions of years. Unfortunately, this process has produced worms that cause a great deal of pain and suffering in humans. **Parasitic roundworms include trichinosis-causing worms, filarial worms, ascarid worms, and hookworms.**

UNIVERSAL ACCESS

Less Proficient Readers
Have students skim the subsection Roundworms and Human Disease. Then, ask them to begin a concept map about the topic by using the subsection heading as the first level and the subheadings as the second level. As they read, they should add a third level with details about the diseases. L1 L2

English Language Learners
Explain that the prefix *pseudo-* is used in a word students might come across in literature class: *pseudonym*, or "false name." Point out that authors sometimes publish under a pseudonym to protect their real identity. L1 L2

Advanced Learners
Encourage students to find out from a veterinarian whether the nematode *Dirofilaria immitis*, or dog heartworm, is a threat to dogs in your area. This parasite is spread by mosquitoes and then matures in the hearts of dogs and other animals. If untreated, infection is lethal. L3

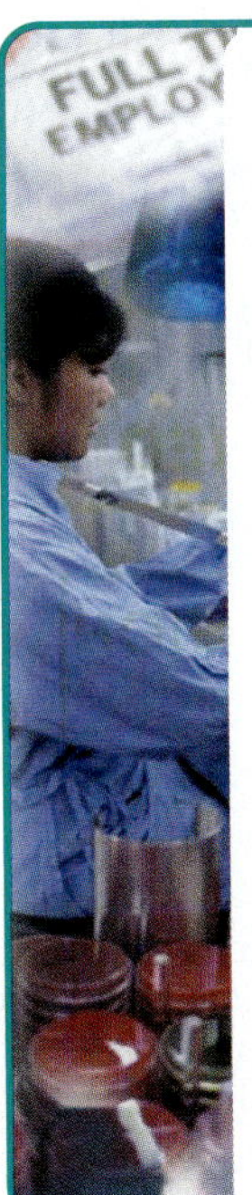

Careers in Biology

Meat Inspector

Job Description: work with farms and meat-processing plants to ensure that all meat and poultry products use healthy animals, are processed in a sanitary manner, and are labeled truthfully with no harmful ingredients added; enforce government regulations to ensure that proper safety, sanitation, preservation, disposal, and packaging procedures are followed

Education: college courses in sanitation and public health; USDA certification

Skills: knowledge of food-borne illnesses, proper sanitation practices, and regulations; public relations skills for dealing with different people in the industry; patience and communication skills for educating the public; ability to work independently and with a team

Highlights: You help protect the safety of the public by working to eliminate food-borne illnesses. You inspect farms to make sure that sanitary procedures are followed.

For: Career links
Visit: PHSchool.com
Web Code: cbb-8272

Careers in Biology

- The occupational outlook handbook for a meat inspector suggests a BA/BS in agricultural science.
- Inspections of meat and enforcement of regulations help prevent trichinosis and other diseases caused by roundworms and other organisms. L2

Resources Have students who want additional information on this career contact the U.S. Department of Agriculture's (USDA) Food Safety and Inspection Service (FSIS), which has the responsibility for ensuring that meat, poultry, and egg products are safe, wholesome, and accurately labeled.

You can have students write a more extensive job description as well as list the educational requirements for a career in this field.

Trichinosis-Causing Worms Trichinosis (trik-ih-NOH-sis) is a terrible disease caused by the roundworm *Trichinella.* Adult worms live and mate in the intestines of their hosts. Female worms carrying fertilized eggs burrow into the intestinal wall and then release larvae. These larvae travel through the bloodstream and burrow into organs and tissues, causing terrible pain for the host. The larvae form cysts and become inactive in the host's muscle tissue.

Trichinella completes its life cycle only when another animal eats muscle tissue containing these cysts. Two common hosts for *Trichinella* are rats and pigs. Humans get trichinosis almost exclusively by eating raw or incompletely cooked pork.

Filarial Worms Filarial worms, which are found primarily in tropical regions of Asia, are threadlike worms that live in the blood and lymph vessels of birds and mammals, including humans. They are transmitted from one primary host to another through biting insects, especially mosquitoes. In severe infections, large numbers of filarial worms may block the passage of fluids within the lymph vessels. This causes elephantiasis, shown in **Figure 27–9,** a condition in which the affected part of the body swells enormously.

CHECKPOINT *Describe the cause of elephantiasis.*

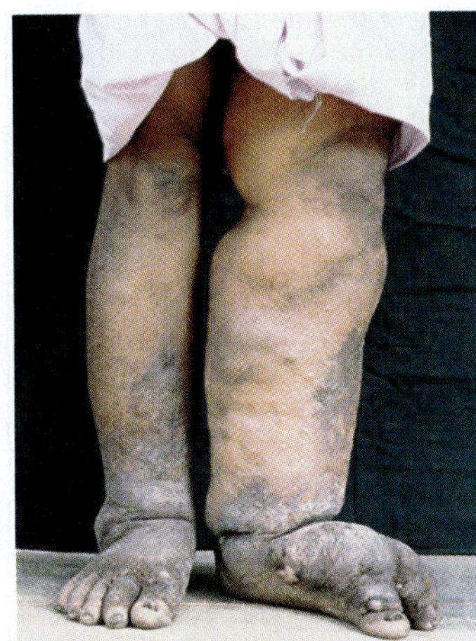

▲ **Figure 27–9** **Filarial worms are one kind of parasitic roundworm.** Elephantiasis, shown here in an advanced stage, is a disease caused by filarial worms.

TEACHER TO TEACHER

I ask a local veterinarian to come into class and talk about parasitic roundworms and flatworms found in pets and local agricultural animals. The students are more interested in roundworms and flatworms when they are discussed in terms of their parasitic impact on mammals. You might also have students examine prepared slides of parasitic worms. These slides can be obtained from a biological supply house.

—*Steve Ferguson*
Biology Teacher
Lee's Summit High School
Lee's Summit, MO

Answers to . . .

CHECKPOINT *Free-living flatworms that are predators use grasping mouthparts and spines to catch and eat small animals.*

CHECKPOINT *Elephantiasis occurs when large numbers of filarial worms block the passage of fluids within the lymph vessels of a part of the body.*

27–2 (continued)

Use Visuals

Figure 27–10 Direct students' attention to the life cycle of the ascarid worm, and ask a student to read the annotations aloud. Then, ask: **Why is this worm classified as a parasite?** *(It takes nourishment and lives at the expense of its host, such as a human. The host gains nothing from the relationship.)* **In what part of the body does the parasite do the most damage?** *(In the small intestine)* L2

Use Community Resources

Invite a representative from a local health agency to address the class about some of the diseases caused by parasitic roundworms. A public health nurse could be asked to speak about human diseases caused by roundworms. A veterinarian, or a vet student, could be asked to talk about roundworms that cause diseases in domestic animals, including pets. Before the speaker arrives, have interested students research the topic and prepare a list of questions to ask. L2 L3

Research on *C. elegans*

Use Visuals

Figure 27–11 To help students understand the significance of the research on *C. elegans*, review such basics as the composition of DNA and the definitions of *genome, chromosome,* and *base pair*. Then, ask: **What does it mean to "sequence completely" the genome of this roundworm?** *(It means to determine the exact sequence of base pairs that make up each chromosome of the roundworm's DNA.)* Point out that the photo to the right in the figure shows a method by which biochemists study that sequence. L1

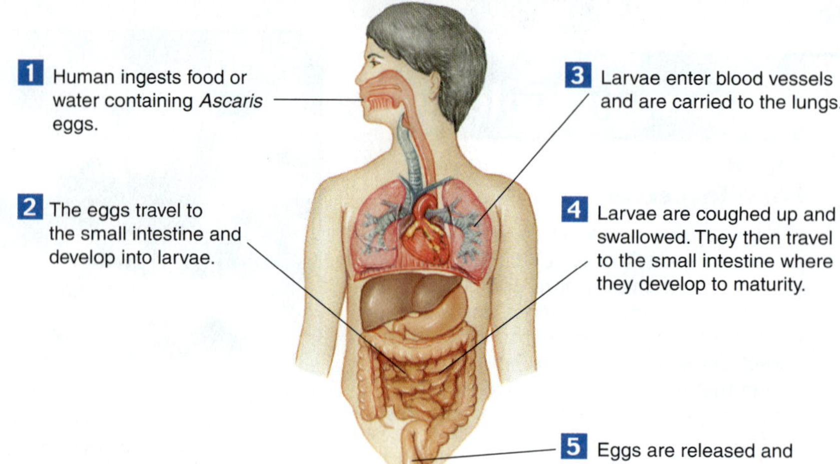

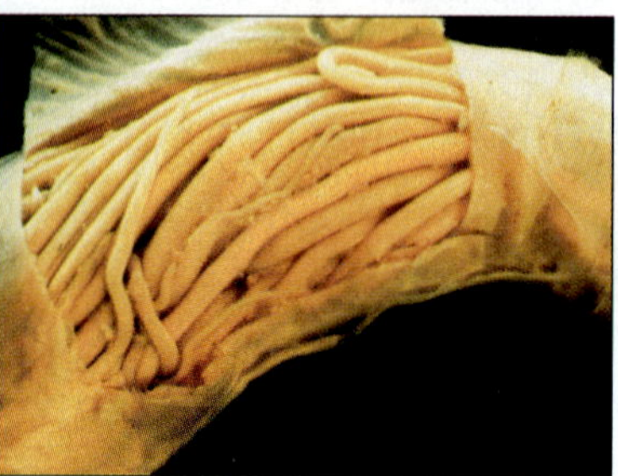

Figure 27–10 *Ascaris lumbricoides* fill the host's intestine. These worms absorb the host's digested food and can cause severe malnutrition. Blockage of the intestine can be severe enough, as shown in a pig intestine in the photograph, that it causes death. **Interpreting Graphics** *What is the sequence of organs that Ascaris travels through in humans?*

Ascarid Worms *Ascaris lumbricoides* is a serious parasite of humans and many other vertebrate animals. It causes malnutrition in more than 1 billion people worldwide. It does this by absorbing digested food from the host's small intestine. *Ascaris lumbricoides* is commonly spread by eating vegetables or other foods that are not washed properly.

The life cycle of *Ascaris* is summarized in **Figure 27–10** above. *Ascaris* matures in the intestines of its host, such as a human, and can reach a length of almost 50 cm. In the intestine, the ascarid worms produce a large number of fertilized eggs, which leave the body in the feces. If food or water contaminated with these feces is eaten by another host, then the eggs hatch in the small intestine of the new host. The young worms burrow into the walls of the intestines and enter the surrounding blood vessels. The worms are carried in the blood until they reach the lungs. There, they spread into air passages and into the throat, where they are swallowed. Carried back into the intestines, they mature, and the cycle repeats itself.

Species that are closely related to *Ascaris* affect horses, cattle, pigs, chickens, dogs, cats, and many other animals. *Ascaris* and its relatives, which are collectively known as ascarids, have life cycles that are similar to one another. One of the reasons puppies are wormed while they are young is to rid them of the ascarid worms that affect dogs.

Hookworms Today, as many as one quarter of the people in the world are infected with hookworms. Hookworm eggs hatch outside the body of the host and develop in the soil. If they find an unprotected foot, they use sharp toothlike plates and hooks to burrow into the skin and enter the bloodstream. Hookworms travel through the blood of their host to the lungs and down to the intestines. There, they suck the host's blood, causing weakness and poor growth.

FACTS AND FIGURES

A great lab animal
Caenorhabditis elegans has become such a well-established laboratory animal that more is known about its biology than that of almost any other organism. Because it is only 1 mm long when mature, *C. elegans* can be raised in small laboratory dishes. It takes only 12 hours from fertilization of the egg to hatching of the juvenile worm. In that time, successive cell divisions produce 671 cells, of which 113 are programmed to die, leaving 558 in the worm that hatches. This "programmed-to-die" characteristic is valuable to researchers studying the aging process. The precise number of 959 cells in the mature worm is adequate for studying the development of complex organ systems, but not so many that it is impossible to track the divisions of each cell. The pattern and number of cell divisions in *C. elegans* are unvarying, making it possible to study the effects of a single genetic mutation.

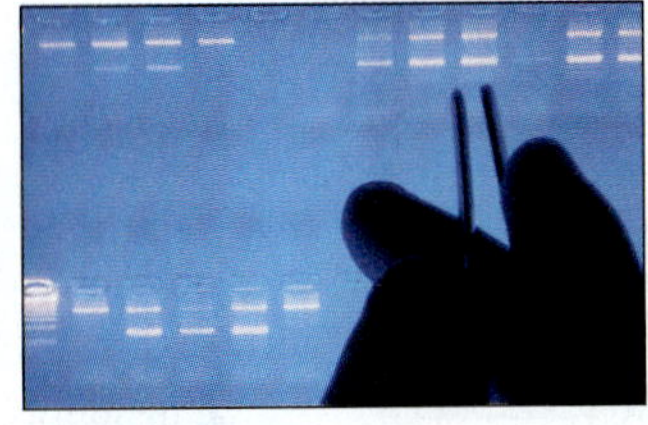

Figure 27–11 The DNA of *C. elegans,* a free-living roundworm, was the first genome of any multicellular animal to be sequenced completely. Biologists used techniques such as gel electrophoresis, shown above, to determine the exact sequence of base pairs in each chromosome. **Predicting** ***How might these results be important to our understanding of human development?***

Research on C. *elegans*

Roundworms have recently been making headlines in scientific research. The free-living roundworm *Caenorhabditis elegans*, or *C. elegans*, is shown in **Figure 27–11,** above left. This worm lives a modest existence feeding on rotting vegetation. However, this species is extraordinary because its DNA was the first of any multicellular animal's to be sequenced completely.

Scientists now have the sequence of all 97 million base pairs of *C. elegans* DNA. This is roughly one thirtieth the number of base pairs in human DNA. They have also traced the differentiation and development of each body cell of *C. elegans*, starting from a single fertilized egg. Researchers are still learning how this differentiation is controlled by the animal's DNA. This research will lead to a better understanding of how eukaryotes became multicellular. Information from *C. elegans* may also shed light on how genes make multicellular organisms both similar to and different from one another.

27–2 Section Assessment

1. **Key Concept** What is a roundworm?
2. **Key Concept** What are the parasitic roundworms?
3. Describe how humans become infected with the parasitic roundworm *Ascaris lumbricoides*.
4. How do hookworms enter the human body?
5. What have scientists already learned about *Caenorhabditis elegans*? What do they hope to learn in the future?
6. **Critical Thinking Problem Solving** What steps might individual people and governments take to reduce the spread of elephantiasis?

Thinking Visually

Creating a Poster
Choose a type of roundworm that can cause disease in humans. Design an educational poster that promotes prevention of the disease. Be sure to include information about how the roundworm infects humans.

27–2 Section Assessment

1. A roundworm is an unsegmented worm that has a pseudocoelom and a digestive system with two openings—a mouth and an anus.
2. Parasitic roundworms include trichinosis-causing worms, filarial worms, ascarid worms, and hookworms.
3. A human becomes infected by ingesting food or water containing *Ascaris* eggs.
4. Hookworms enter the human body by burrowing into the skin of a foot.
5. Students should mention basic features of the species as well as its DNA sequence. In the future, scientists hope to learn how that sequence controls differentiation.
6. Individuals could wear protective clothing and use insect repellant. Governments could implement strategies to reduce the numbers of biting insects.

3 ASSESS

Evaluate Understanding

Ask students to write a comparison of flatworms and roundworms. Tell them that they should compare both form and function, beginning with whether or not each type of invertebrate has a coelom.

Reteach

Have students write an article that might be published in the local newspaper about a person who has contracted trichinosis. Explain that they should describe the disease and how it was contracted, as well as the organism that causes the disease.

Thinking Visually

Discuss what makes an effective poster, and have students determine who their audience is, as well as the poster's objective. Posters should explain how one type of roundworm spreads to humans and how infection can be prevented.

If your class subscribes to the iText, use it to review the Key Concepts in Section 27–2.

Answers to . . .

Figure 27–10 *Mouth, small intestine, blood vessels, lungs, throat, small intestine*

Figure 27–11 *Information from* C. elegans *may shed light on how an animal's DNA controls the animal's development from a single fertilized egg to a complex multicellular organism.*

Section 27–3

1 FOCUS

Objectives

27.3.1 ***Describe*** the defining features of annelids.

27.3.2 ***Identify*** the characteristics of the classes of annelids.

27.3.3 ***Describe*** the ecology of annelids.

Guide for Reading

Vocabulary Preview

Call on volunteers to pronounce each of the Vocabulary words aloud. Correct any mispronunciations, and note any words that students with limited English proficiency have special trouble pronouncing.

Reading Strategy

Advise students to compare the labeled diagram in Figure 27–16 with that in Figure 27–3 in Section 27–1.

2 INSTRUCT

What Is an Annelid?

Use Visuals

Figure 27–12 Divide the class into pairs, and give each pair three different-colored blocks of clay. Then, ask students to make three models, beginning with one that matches the cross section of the annelid shown in this figure. After that is completed, students should make similar models of the cross sections shown in Figures 27–1 and 27–7. L2

Build Science Skills

Using Models To help students visualize a digestive tract inside a body wall, give each student or group a long sock with the toe cut off. Tell students to turn the sock halfway inside out to form a tube-within-a-tube. Explain that the inner layer of the sock represents the digestive tract, and the outer layer represents the body wall. L1

27–3 Annelids

Guide for Reading

Key Concepts

- What are the defining features of annelids?
- What are the characteristics of the three classes of annelids?

Vocabulary

septum • seta
crop • gizzard
closed circulatory system
gill • nephridium
clitellum

Reading Strategy: Using Visuals Before you read, preview **Figure 27–16.** How does this animal seem to differ from the other worms you have already studied? Briefly summarize any differences you notice.

If you have ever dug in a garden in the spring, you have probably seen earthworms wriggling through the soil. Earthworms are annelids, members of the phylum Annelida. Other annelids include exotic seafloor worms and parasitic, blood-sucking leeches. Because their bodies are long and narrow, some annelids look a bit like flatworms or roundworms. However, the annelids are a distinct group that is probably more closely related to clams and snails. One piece of evidence for this relationship is the fact that annelids, clams, and snails all share a similar larval stage.

What Is an Annelid?

The name Annelida (uh-NEL-ih-duh) is derived from the Latin word *annellus*, which means "little ring." The name refers to the ringlike appearance of annelids' body segments. The body of an annelid is divided into segments that are separated by **septa** (singular: septum), which are internal walls between each segment. Most segments are similar to one another, although they may be modified to perform special functions. Some body segments may carry one or more pairs of eyes, several pairs of antennae, and other sense organs. Other segments may be specialized for functions such as respiration. In many annelids, bristles called **setae** (SEE-tee; singular: seta) are attached to each segment.

Annelids are worms with segmented bodies. They have a true coelom that is lined with tissue derived from mesoderm. These structures are shown in **Figure 27–12.** Recall that flatworms have no coelom, whereas roundworms have a pseudocoelom. Like the roundworms, annelids have a tube-within-a-tube digestive tract that food passes through from the mouth to the anus.

CHECKPOINT *What are some functions performed by specialized segments?*

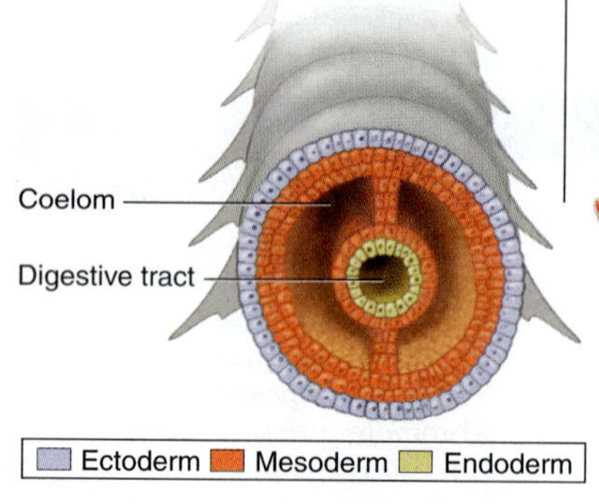

Figure 27–12 Annelids are among the simplest animals to have a true coelom that is lined with mesoderm. Annelids are also called segmented worms because the body is divided into many similar segments. The photo shows a marine annelid.

SECTION RESOURCES

Print:

- ***Teaching Resources,*** Lesson Plan 27–3, Adapted Section Summary 27–3, Adapted Worksheets 27–3, Section Summary 27–3, Worksheets 27–3, Section Review 27–3, Enrichment
- ***Reading and Study Workbook A,*** Section 27–3
- ***Adapted Reading and Study Workbook B,*** Section 27–3
- ***Issues and Decision Making,*** Issues and Decisions 28

Technology:

- ***iText,*** Section 27–3
- ***Transparencies Plus,*** Section 27–3

Quick Lab

How does an earthworm pump blood?

Materials earthworm; dropper pipette; nonchlorinated water; large, clear plastic soda straw; dissecting microscope; clock or watch with second hand

Procedure 

1. Carefully insert an earthworm into a clear plastic straw. Do not force the worm into the straw. **CAUTION:** *Handle the earthworm carefully to avoid harming it. Wash your hands after handling the worm.*
2. Use a dropper pipette to add a drop or two of nonchlorinated water into the straw.

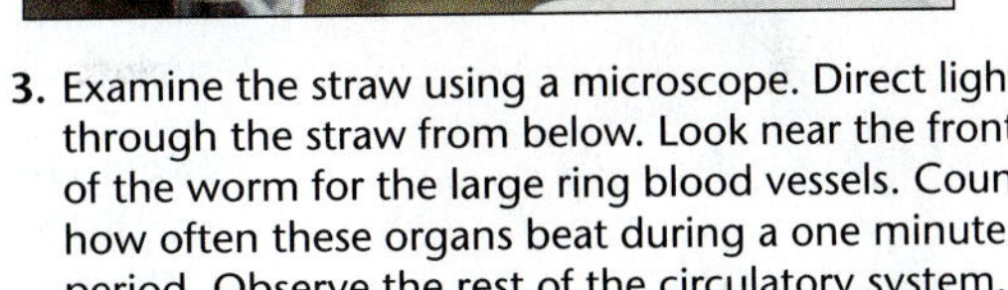

3. Examine the straw using a microscope. Direct light through the straw from below. Look near the front of the worm for the large ring blood vessels. Count how often these organs beat during a one minute period. Observe the rest of the circulatory system.

Analyze and Conclude

1. **Inferring** Did you see the worm breathing? Explain your answer. Why must the earthworm's skin be kept moist? How do your answers relate to how earthworms live in their environment?
2. **Observing** Is an earthworm's circulatory system open or closed? Explain your answer.

Form and Function in Annelids

Annelids have complex organ systems. Many of these systems are unique because of the segmented body plan of this group.

Feeding and Digestion Annelids range from filter feeders to predators. Many annelids get their food using a pharynx. In carnivorous species, such as the *Nereis* in **Figure 27–13,** the pharynx usually holds two or more sharp jaws that are used to attack prey. In annelids that feed on decaying vegetation, the pharynx is covered with sticky mucus. The worm collects food particles by extending its pharynx and pressing it against the surrounding sediments. Other annelids obtain nutrients by filter feeding. They fan water through tubelike burrows and catch food particles in a mucous bag.

In earthworms, the pharynx pumps food and soil into a tube called the esophagus. The food then moves through the **crop,** where it can be stored, and through the **gizzard,** where it is ground into smaller pieces. The food is absorbed farther along in the digestive tract, in an organ called the intestine.

Circulation Annelids typically have a **closed circulatory system,** in which blood is contained within a network of blood vessels. An earthworm's blood circulates through two major blood vessels that run from head to tail. Blood in the dorsal (top) vessel moves toward the head of the worm. Blood in the ventral (bottom) vessel runs from head to tail. In each body segment, a pair of smaller blood vessels connect the dorsal and ventral blood vessels and supply blood to the internal organs. The dorsal blood vessel functions like a heart because it contracts rhythmically and helps pump blood.

▲ **Figure 27–13** The annelid *Nereis* uses jaws to capture prey. When prey approaches, the worm lunges forward, rapidly extends its pharynx, and grabs the prey using its jaws. **Inferring** ***How is the structure of a*** **Nereis*'s*** ***jaws related to their function?***

Form and Function in Annelids

Quick Lab

Objective Students will be able to describe the structure and function of an earthworm's circulatory system.

Skill Focus **Observing, Inferring**

Materials earthworm, dropper pipette, nonchlorinated water, large and clear plastic straw, dissecting microscope

Time 15 minutes

Advance Prep Collect earthworms outdoors, or buy them from a bait shop. Pond water, aquarium water, and bottles of spring water are all acceptable forms of nonchlorinated water. Tap water can be dechlorinated by boiling and cooling overnight in an open container.

Safety Make sure students wash their hands with soap and warm water after handling the earthworms.

Strategies

- If students have trouble inserting the worm in a straw, try slitting the straw lengthwise.
- Students can also put the earthworm and a few drops of water in a petri dish cover, with the bottom of the petri dish inverted on top to hold the worm in place. Do not allow the worms to dry out.

Expected Outcomes Students should see the earthworm's dorsal vessel pulsating and that an earthworm has a closed circulatory system.

Analyze and Conclude

1. An earthworm has no breathing movements, because it exchanges gases through its skin. The earthworm's skin must be kept moist, because otherwise it will not be able to exchange gases. Earthworms live in moist soil.
2. The earthworm has a closed circulatory system, which means that blood never leaves the blood vessels.

ESL SUPPORT FOR ENGLISH LANGUAGE LEARNERS

Vocabulary: Science Glossary

Beginning Write *septum, seta, crop, gizzard* on the board. Underline the syllables as you lead the class in pronouncing each word. Define each word, and point to the corresponding structure in Figure 27–16. Have students then write the definitions of those terms in their own science glossaries. Students should draw and label their own diagrams next to the definitions. Then, in collaborative writing groups, students should write sentences using each word. L1

Intermediate Students can expand on the science-glossary activity by adding the other Vocabulary words: *closed circulatory system, gill, nephridium, clitellum.* Have the students form collaborative writing groups and write sentences for each word. Call on one student in each group to read the sentences aloud. L2

Answers to . . .

CHECKPOINT *Sample answer: sensing the environment, respiration*

Figure 27–13 *Hooks with sharp points are adapted to catch prey.*

27–3 (continued)

Build Science Skills

Observing Earthworms are among the most familiar of organisms, yet probably few students have taken the time to observe earthworms closely. To give students this opportunity, fill a clear plastic box with about 2 centimeters of sand. Place about 7 centimeters of loosely packed topsoil over the sand. Use pond water to slightly moisten the soil. (Add more water whenever the soil appears dry.) Place 6 to 12 earthworms on top of the soil. Cover the box with clear plastic wrap, and put a few air holes in the plastic wrap. Have students observe the earthworms for several days. Ask them to make labeled diagrams of the animals. Advise them to note especially how earthworms move through the soil. L2 L3

Use Community Resources

Contact a local environmental group, garden center, farming association, or garden club for a reference to a person in your area who uses earthworms to compost household organic garbage. Ask this person to speak to the class about how to set up such a system and what foods can and cannot be added to the earthworm habitat. Students might be surprised to learn that such a system can be clean and without unpleasant odors. It can not only dispose of organic wastes responsibly but also provide great soil for a garden. L2

▲ **Figure 27–14** These feather-duster worms exchange gases underwater using feathery gills. **Applying Concepts** *How do land-dwelling annelids exchange gases?*

Respiration Aquatic annelids often breathe through gills. A **gill** is an organ specialized for the exchange of gases underwater. In feather-duster worms, shown in **Figure 27–14,** feathery structures that function as gills protrude from the opening of the worm's burrow or tube. Land-dwelling annelids, such as earthworms, take in oxygen and give off carbon dioxide through their moist skin. These annelids secrete a thin protective coating of mucus, which keeps their skins moist.

Excretion Like other animals, annelids produce two kinds of waste. Digestive waste passes out through the anus at the end of the digestive tract. Cellular waste containing nitrogen is eliminated by **nephridia** (nee-FRID-ee-uh; singular: nephridium), which are excretory organs that filter fluid in the coelom.

Response Most annelids have a well-developed nervous system consisting of a brain and several nerve cords. However, the sense organs are best developed in free-living marine annelids. Many of these species have a variety of adaptations for detecting stimuli: sensory tentacles, chemical receptors, statocysts that help detect gravity, and two or more pairs of eyes.

Movement Annelids have two major groups of body muscles that function as part of a hydrostatic skeleton. Longitudinal muscles run from the front of the worm to the rear and can contract to make the worm shorter and fatter. Circular muscles wrap around each body segment and can contract to make the worm longer and thinner. The earthworm moves by alternately contracting these two sets of muscles, using its setae to prevent slipping. Burrowing annelids use their muscles to force their way through heavy sediment. Marine annelids have paddlelike appendages, or parapodia (singular: parapodium), on each segment, which they use for swimming and crawling.

Reproduction Most annelids reproduce sexually. Some species use external fertilization and have separate sexes. Other annelids are hermaphrodites. Individuals rarely fertilize their own eggs. Instead, two worms attach to each other, as shown in **Figure 27–15,** exchange sperm, and then store the sperm in special sacs. When eggs are ready for fertilization, a **clitellum** (kly-TEL-um), or band of thickened, specialized segments, secretes a mucous ring into which eggs and sperm are released. Fertilization takes place within this ring. The ring then slips off the worm's body and forms a protective cocoon. Young worms hatch weeks later.

▶ **Figure 27–15** Some annelids, including these earthworms, are hermaphrodites. Each worm produces both eggs and sperm. During mating, the worms exchange sperm, which will eventually be used to fertilize egg cells. **Applying Concepts** *When are the eggs fertilized?*

FACTS AND FIGURES

Slithering through the soil

Annelids move through soil and sediment by using the power of their muscles and the liquid inside their body segments—their hydrostatic skeleton. Each body segment is sealed off from the segment next to it, which means body fluids can't move from one segment to another. When the longitudinal muscles contract and make the worm shorter, each segment has to become wider. In a similar manner, when the circular muscles contract and make the worm longer, each segment must become narrower. When the earthworm moves forward, its first few body segments elongate while the segments just behind them hold their position. Then, the first few segments shorten and widen. Alternating contractions and elongations continue along the length of the worm's body, enabling it to move through soil or sediment.

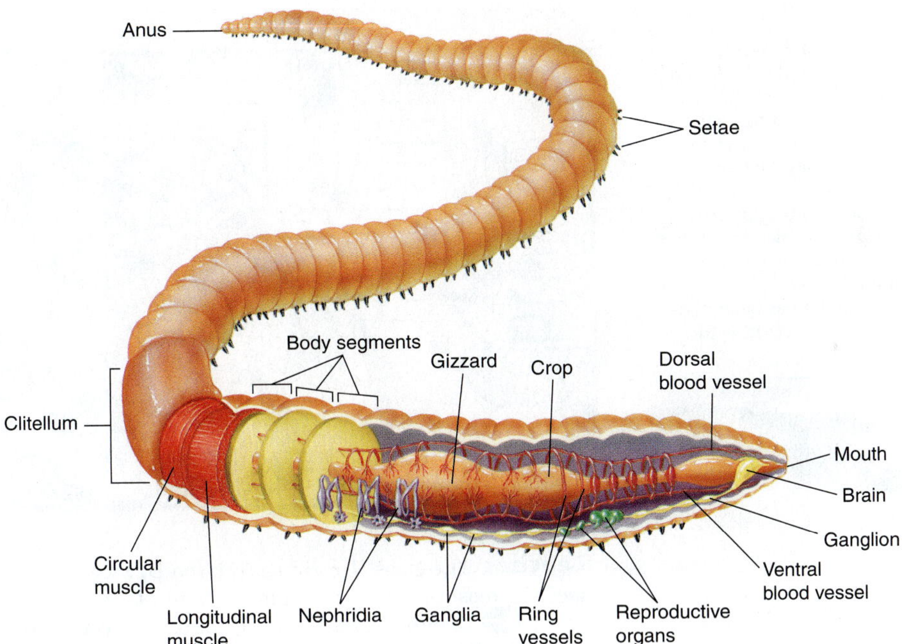

▲ **Figure 27–16 Earthworms are oligochaetes that live in soil.** Earthworms carry out essential functions using digestive, circulatory, excretory, nervous, and reproductive systems. Many organs, including nephridia and blood vessels, repeat in nearly every body segment.

Groups of Annelids

Because of their visible segmentation, all annelids show a basic similarity. Annelids are divided into three classes—oligochaetes, leeches, and polychaetes.

Oligochaetes The class Oligochaeta, or oligochaetes (AHL-ih-goh-keets), contains earthworms and their relatives. **Oligochaetes are annelids that typically have streamlined bodies and relatively few setae compared to polychaetes. Most oligochaetes live in soil or fresh water.** Earthworms, such as the one shown in **Figure 27–16,** are long, pinkish-brown worms that are common in woods, fields, and gardens. Tubifex worms—another common oligochaete—are red, threadlike aquatic worms that are sold in pet stores as food for tropical fish.

Although earthworms spend most of their lives hidden underground, you may find evidence of their presence above ground in the form of squiggles of mud known as castings. Recall that an earthworm—which swallows just about anything it can get into its mouth—uses its pharynx to suck a mixture of detritus and soil particles into its mouth. As the mixture of food and soil passes through the intestine, part of it is digested and absorbed. Sand grains, clay particles, and indigestible organic matter pass out through the anus in large quantities, producing castings. Some tropical earthworms produce enormous castings—as large as 18 centimeters long and 2 centimeters in diameter!

CHECKPOINT *What are earthworm castings?*

Word Origins

Oligochaete comes from the Greek words *oligos,* meaning "few" or "small," and *chaite,* meaning "hair." **If *poly-* means "many," what is a characteristic of the group of annelids known as polychaetes?**

Groups of Annelids

Use Visuals

Figure 27–16 Have students study the diagram of the oligochaete. Point out that this worm has body segments—annelids are worms with segmented bodies. Then, as you point out different labeled parts, call on students to describe the feeding, circulation, respiration, and response of an oligochaete. Ask: **Where does fertilization take place in an oligochaete?** *(In the clitellum)* L2

Build Science Skills

Inferring Divide the class into small groups, and provide each group with an earthworm, a type of oligochaete. Students should examine the worm with a hand lens and try to locate the setae. Have groups formulate a hypothesis to explain the function of the setae. Then, have students place the earthworm on a smooth surface, such as a glass dish or the shiny side of a piece of aluminum foil, as well as on a rougher surface, such as a damp paper towel. Students should compare the worm's movements on the two surfaces and infer the function of the setae. *(Students should infer that setae enable an earthworm to grip a surface as it moves.)* L2 L3

Word Origins

The annelids of the class Polychaeta have "many hairs." L2

TEACHER TO TEACHER

Have students in groups of four observe live earthworm movements under different conditions, such as dry, wet, cold, or warm, and on different surfaces, such as felt, glass, wood, plastic wrap, or gauze. Students record their observations, and each group reports to the class.

Students can use different tuning forks to see how earthworms react to different vibrations. Have groups decide how this information could be used to "hunt" for earthworms.

—*Keith Orgeron*
Biology Teacher
Carenero High School
Lafayette, LA

Answers to . . .

CHECKPOINT *Earthworm castings are a mixture of sand, clay, and undigested food that an earthworm expels from its anus.*

Figure 27–14 *Land-dwelling annelids exchange gases through their moist skin.*

Figure 27–15 *Eggs are fertilized after eggs and sperm are released into the mucous ring secreted by the clitellum.*

27–3 (continued)

Make Connections

Health Science Encourage interested students to contact a large, local teaching hospital and inquire about whether leeches are used in any surgical procedures at that hospital. If so, have students find out how the leeches are collected and the conditions in which they are kept while waiting for use in surgery. In addition, have students find out about the natural environment in which such leeches live and describe an artificial setup in which leeches could be kept for use in medical procedures. L3

Build Science Skills

Classifying Divide the class into small groups, and ask each group to make up 10 to 20 questions for a game called Annelid Worms—Which Class? The idea of the game is for the question to be a statement about one group of annelids. The question is answered by classifying the statement in the annelid class to which it applies. For example: "These worms spend most of their lives underground—which class?" The answer is Oligochaeta. When all groups have finished writing, pool the questions and eliminate any duplicates. Place the remaining questions in a box for students to draw at random. L2

Figure 27–17 **Most leeches are external parasites.** Medicinal leeches, such as the one below, were once used routinely to attempt to treat conditions ranging from headaches to mental illness to obesity. Doctors believed that diseases were caused by an excess of blood, so they applied leeches to the patient's skin to remove blood from the body. Here, a man who lived in the Middle Ages has become so fat that he has been confined to a room and covered with leeches.

Leeches The class Hirudinea (hir-yoo-DIN-ee-uh) contains the leeches, most of which live in moist habitats in tropical countries. **Leeches are typically external parasites that suck the blood and body fluids of their host.** Roughly one fourth of all leeches are carnivores that feed on soft-bodied invertebrates such as snails, worms, and insect larvae.

Leeches have powerful suckers at both ends of their bodies that help them cling to their hosts. The posterior sucker can also anchor a leech to rocks or leaves as it waits for a host to pass. Some leeches force a muscular extension called a proboscis (proh-BAHS-is) into the tissue of their host. Others slice into the skin with a razor-sharp pair of jaws. Once a wound has been made, the leech uses its pharynx to suck blood from the area. Some leeches also release a substance that anesthetizes the wound—keeping the host from knowing it has been bitten.

Leeches were once commonly used to treat medical conditions. Today the use of medicinal leeches is undergoing a revival of sorts. Doctors are finding that leeches can reduce swelling after surgery. After surgeries in which a body part is reattached, hungry leeches are applied to the area. These leeches can suck several milliliters of blood at a time—up to five times their own weight! They also secrete a fluid that prevents blood from clotting. This anti-clotting mechanism helps relieve pressure and congestion in the healing tissues.

▼ **Figure 27–18** **Polychaetes are marine annelids.** The bearded fireworm is a polychaete that lives in coral reefs. It is best known for its method of defense—its setae, or bristles, break off when touched and cause irritation and burning.

Polychaetes The class Polychaeta, or polychaetes (PAHL-ih-keets), contains sandworms, bloodworms, and their relatives. **Polychaetes are marine annelids that have paired, paddlelike appendages tipped with setae.** The setae are the brushlike structures on the worm shown in **Figure 27–18.** Polychaetes live in cracks and crevices in coral reefs; in sand, mud, and piles of rocks; or even out in the open water. Some burrow through or crawl over sediment.

HISTORY OF SCIENCE

Leeching to health

For centuries, the medicinal leech *Hirudo medicinalis* was used for bloodletting—a treatment thought to cure a wide range of illnesses. Shortly after the Civil War, more than 1.5 million leeches per year were used in the United States alone. When in contact with a host, the leech attaches itself and draws out blood by a pumping action. At the same time, the leech's salivary glands secrete hirudin, a substance that dilutes the host's blood, prevents blood from clotting, and acts as an anesthetic. A leech may eat up to five times its own body mass in blood before it drops off, and it may not need to feed again for 30 weeks. The leech is now scarce due to overcollecting and habitat destruction. It is still in demand, though, for hirudin, which is used as an anticoagulant for some heart patients and in some surgical procedures.

Ecology of Annelids

The importance of earthworms in nature was noted as far back as ancient Greece, when Aristotle called them "the intestines of the earth." Charles Darwin was impressed enough with earthworms that he devoted years—and an entire book—to their study. Earthworms, like the one shown in **Figure 27–19**, and many other annelids spend their lives burrowing through soil, aerating it, and mixing it to depths of 2 meters or more. Their tunnels provide passageways for plant roots and water and allow the growth of beneficial, oxygen-requiring soil bacteria. Earthworms pull plant matter down into the soil and pass it through the gut. There, they grind it, partially digest it, and mix it with bacteria that help the plant matter decompose. Worms also "mine" minerals from deeper soil layers, bringing them up to the surface. Earthworm feces (castings) are rich in nitrogen, phosphorus, potassium, micronutrients, and beneficial bacteria.

You've probably seen a bird struggling to pull an earthworm out of the ground. Earthworms are an important part of the diet of many birds, such as robins. Moles, skunks, toads, and snakes also prey on earthworms.

In the sea, annelids participate in a wide range of food chains. Many marine annelids have free-swimming larvae that are part of the animal plankton that is consumed by fishes and other plankton feeders. As adults, some marine annelids are mud-dwelling filter feeders that are common in areas where sediment is disturbed or large amounts of organic material are present. These worms are especially numerous where pollution from sewage promotes the growth of bacteria and algae. As any fisher knows, many bottom-dwelling polychaetes are important in the diets of fishes. Crustaceans, such as crabs and lobsters, also include annelids in their diets.

▲ **Figure 27–19** Some annelids, including this earthworm, burrow through soil, mixing it as they go. **Predicting** *What might happen to a garden if all the annelids in the soil were killed?*

27–3 Section Assessment

1. **Key Concept** What features distinguish annelids from roundworms?
2. **Key Concept** List the defining characteristics for each class of annelid.
3. Describe the feeding strategies of earthworms and leeches.
4. **Critical Thinking Inferring** An earthworm has more light-sensitive cells in its anterior and posterior segments than in other parts of its body. Explain how this is advantageous for the worm.

Focus on the BIG Idea

Interdependence in Nature Review what you learned about food chains in Chapter 3. Then, draw a possible food chain involving an annelid. The food chain should include at least three levels.

27–3 Section Assessment

1. Unlike roundworms, annelids have segmented bodies and a true coelom that is lined with mesoderm.
2. Oligochaetes typically have fewer setae than polychaetes and live in soil or fresh water. Leeches are typically external parasites that suck the blood and body fluids of their host. Polychaetes are marine annelids that have paired, paddlelike appendages tipped with setae.
3. Earthworms use their pharynxes to suck soil and detritus into their esophagus. Leeches suck the blood and body fluids of their host.
4. Having more light-sensitive cells in the front and back ends is advantageous, because the animal moves forward and may be attacked by a predator from the rear.

Ecology of Annelids

Make Connections

Earth Science Explain that good soil contains sediment particles, humus (organic matter), water, and air. The air is especially important, because if the soil is too compact, plants have a difficult time growing. Ask students: **How do earthworms help to mix air into soil?** *(By moving through the soil, they break up particles and make tunnels. These actions provide space for air to move throughout the soil. The movement of earthworms aerates the soil.)* L2

3 ASSESS

Evaluate Understanding

Call on students at random to provide characteristics and examples of the three classes of annelids: oligochaetes, leeches, and polychaetes.

Reteach

To help students understand and remember how annelids' bodies carry out the essential life functions, refer to Figure 27–16. As you review each function as described in the text, have students point out the organs involved in performing that function.

Focus on the BIG Idea

The details of the food chain students draw will vary. A typical food chain might include plant matter eaten by an earthworm, which is then eaten by a bird.

Interactive Textbook

If your class subscribes to the iText, use it to review the Key Concepts in Section 27–3.

Answer to . . .

Figure 27–19 *If all the annelids were killed, the soil would not be mixed and aerated, and it would lack passageways for roots, decomposed plant matter, soil bacteria, and minerals from deeper soil layers. As a result, the flowers and vegetables planted in the garden would fail to thrive.*

 BI 6.b, BIIE 1.m

After students have read the feature, lead a class discussion of the problems caused by zebra mussels and other exotic species. Then, encourage students to further investigate the zebra mussel problem and prepare a report to the class. You might divide the class into small groups and assign each group one aspect of the problem, including zebra mussels' life cycle and feeding habits, problems caused by zebra mussels to power plants and other facilities, the threat to native mussel populations and other species, and methods previously tried to eradicate the zebra mussels. After groups have reported their findings, have students discuss what they think should be done to address this problem.

Research and Decide

1. Most students will suggest that the advantage of eradication would be that the zebra mussels would no longer cause problems. The disadvantages would include cost and the possibility of harming other species by the methods used to destroy the mussels. An advantage of control and prevention might be a lower cost. A disadvantage might be a lack of effectiveness and continued damage caused by zebra mussels.
2. A thoughtful response will reflect a realistic assessment of the problem and the difficulty in finding a solution. The measures chosen by students will vary. Whichever measure is judged most effective, it should be described in detail with a reasoned assessment of its chances for success.

Students can research population growth and control of zebra mussels on the site developed by authors Ken Miller and Joe Levine.

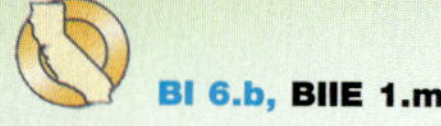 BI 6.b, BIIE 1.m

What Can Be Done About the Zebra Mussel?

Zebra mussels *(Dreissena polymorpha)* were introduced into the United States from Eastern Europe and Asia when ships from the areas emptied their ballast tanks. They were first spotted in the Great Lakes in the mid-1980s. Zebra mussels have few natural enemies here and reproduce very rapidly. They have already colonized the entire Great Lakes region and have spread to rivers in more than ten states.

Zebra mussels live attached to almost any surface—from shopping carts to fiberglass boats—and can form layers up to 20 centimeters thick. They have caused serious structural damage and have clogged water supply lines to power plants and water treatment facilities. One paper company, for example, spent over a million dollars to remove zebra mussels that were clogging its cooling pipes.

Zebra mussels also threaten the ecology of aquatic communities. They can tolerate a wide range of temperatures and light intensities. In some habitats, they have displaced native mollusks, almost making them extinct. Zebra mussels have also depleted the food of many fish species. What can be done to control zebra mussels and other exotic (nonnative) species and prevent new ones from arriving?

The Viewpoints

Control and Prevention

Many scientists believe that there is no way to remove zebra mussels and many other established exotic species. Instead, these scientists attempt to control the growth of populations and prevent the transfer of exotic species to new areas. One regulation, for example, could require boaters to filter and chemically clean all ballast water. Another approach would be to find beneficial uses for zebra mussels. Scientists are already exploring the ability of zebra mussels to filter large volumes of waste water.

Eradication

Other groups contend that zebra mussels should be eradicated. Engineers, for example, are developing robotic submarines that can remove mussels from pipelines. Chemists are testing chemicals for the potential to destroy or disrupt the life cycle of zebra mussels. Other scientists are adding chemicals to paints and plastics to prevent mussels from attaching to new surfaces.

Research and Decide

1. **Analyzing the Viewpoints** To make an informed decision, learn more about this issue by consulting library or Internet resources. Then, determine the advantages and disadvantages of each proposed solution to the problems caused by zebra mussels.
2. **Forming Your Opinion** What measures do you think would be most effective in dealing with exotic species?

For: Links from the authors
Visit: PHSchool.com
Web Code: cbe-8273

BACKGROUND

Clogged pipes cause problems

A mussel is a bivalve that permanently attaches itself to an underwater surface by means of anchor lines called byssal threads. These threads are secreted as a liquid by the byssal gland in the animal's foot. The liquid flows down a groove in the foot, sticks to the rock or other surface, and hardens. Then, the foot is withdrawn, with the thread permanently in place. In this way, zebra mussels attach themselves to the insides of water-intake pipes. A zebra mussel is only about 2 centimeters in length, and a few of them in a pipe doesn't cause concern. But Detroit Edison reported that on a single water-intake screen, there were 700,000 mussels per square meter. In the winter of 1988, ice combined with mussels blocked water intake to Detroit Edison, resulting in power outages. During the 1990s, billions of dollars were spent around the Great Lakes cleaning and refitting pipes.

27–4 Mollusks

They climb trees in tropical rain forests and float over coral reefs. They crawl into garbage cans, eat their way through farm crops, and speed through the deep ocean. Some are so small that you can hardly see them with the unaided eye, while others are 20 meters long! They are the mollusks—one of the oldest and most diverse phyla. Mollusks come in so many sizes, shapes, and forms that you might wonder why they are classified in the same phylum. To learn the answer, read on.

Guide for Reading

Key Concepts
- What are the defining features of mollusks?
- What is the basic body plan of mollusks?
- What are the characteristics of the three main classes of mollusks?

Vocabulary
trochophore • foot
mantle • shell • visceral mass
radula • siphon
open circulatory system

Reading Strategy: Building Vocabulary
As you read, make notes about the meaning of each term in the list above. After you read the section, make a table listing the different types of mollusks on the left and the vocabulary words that apply on the right.

What Is a Mollusk?

Members of the phylum Mollusca, known as mollusks, are named from the Latin word *molluscus*, which means "soft." **Mollusks are soft-bodied animals that usually have an internal or external shell.** Mollusks include snails, slugs, clams, squids, and octopi. But a snail looks very different from a squid, which looks very different from a clam. So why are these animals all placed in the same phylum? One reason is that many mollusks share similar developmental stages. Many aquatic mollusks have a free-swimming larval stage called a **trochophore** (TRAHK-oh-fawr). The trochophore larva, which is shown in **Figure 27–20,** is also characteristic of annelids, indicating that these two groups may be closely related. Molecular studies suggest that a common ancestor of annelids and mollusks lived more than 550 million years ago.

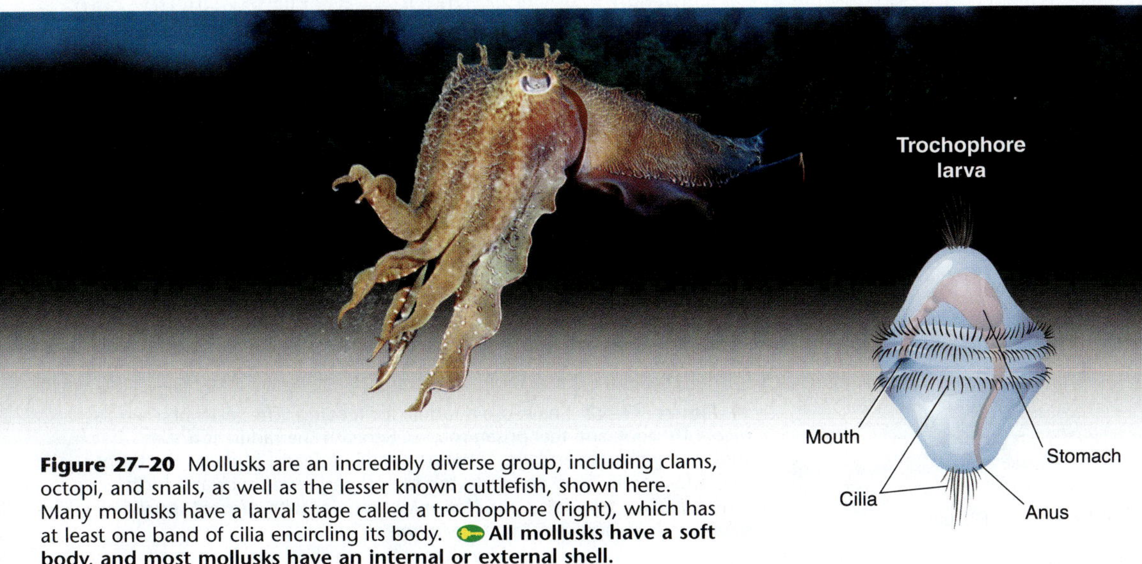

Figure 27–20 Mollusks are an incredibly diverse group, including clams, octopi, and snails, as well as the lesser known cuttlefish, shown here. Many mollusks have a larval stage called a trochophore (right), which has at least one band of cilia encircling its body. **All mollusks have a soft body, and most mollusks have an internal or external shell.**

SECTION REVIEW

Print:
- ***Laboratory Manual A,*** Chapter 27 Lab
- ***Laboratory Manual B,*** Chapter 27 Lab
- ***Teaching Resources,*** Lesson Plan 27–4, Adapted Section Summary 27–4, Adapted Worksheets 27–4, Section Summary 27–4, Worksheets 27–4, Section Review 27–4
- ***Reading and Study Workbook A,*** Section 27–4
- ***Lab Worksheets,*** Chapter 27 Exploration
- ***Adapted Reading and Study Workbook B,*** Section 27–4

Technology:
- ***iText,*** Section 27–4
- ***Animated Biological Concepts DVD,*** 35 Earthworm Anatomy
- ***Transparencies Plus,*** Section 27–4

Section 27–4

1 FOCUS

Objectives

27.4.1 ***Describe*** the defining features of mollusks.
27.4.2 ***Describe*** form and function in mollusks.
27.4.3 ***Identify*** the characteristics of the three main classes of mollusks.
27.4.4 ***Describe*** the ecology of mollusks.

Guide for Reading

Vocabulary Preview
Explain that students may use a few of the Vocabulary words in everyday speech, including *foot* and *mantle.* Caution students, especially English language learners, that they shouldn't allow the common meanings of these words to influence their understanding of the terms in the context of mollusk anatomy.

Reading Strategy
The terms *trochophore, foot, mantle, shell, visceral mass,* and *open circulatory system* apply to all mollusk groups. The term *siphon* applies only to bivalves and cephalopods. The term *radula* applies to gastropods. (You may want to point out that cephalopods also have radulae.)

2 INSTRUCT

What Is a Mollusk?

Use Visuals
Figure 27–20 Ask students: **How are the two organisms shown in the figure related?** *(The organism on the left is a mature cuttlefish, a type of mollusk. The labeled organism to the right is a trochophore, which is a free-swimming larval stage of a mollusk.)* **What defining features of mollusks can you observe in the cuttlefish?** *(It can be observed from the photo that the cuttlefish is a soft-bodied animal and does not have an external shell. Whether it has an internal shell—which it does have—cannot be determined from the image.)* L2

27–4 (continued)

Form and Function in Mollusks

Use Visuals

Figure 27–21 Point out that the three living mollusks all descended from an early mollusk, shown in the lower left. Explain that the snail, clam, and squid each represent one of the three major classes of mollusks. Then, ask: **How is the shell in the squid different from the shells in the other two mollusks shown?** *(The shell in the squid is much less prominent than the shells of the snail and the clam, and it is internal.)* Explain that a squid is a cephalopod, and most modern cephalopods have only small internal shells. L2

Demonstration

Show students a rasp, a common tool used by woodworkers. Then, use the rasp to scrape a piece of scrap wood, making a mark and producing some sawdust. Ask: **How is a snail's radula like this rasp?** *(Like the surface of a rasp, a radula has hundreds of tiny teeth that can scrape and tear up a surface.)* **Why do you think that clams and similar mollusks do not have a radula?** *(Because they are filter feeders that obtain food by straining particles from water)* L1 L2

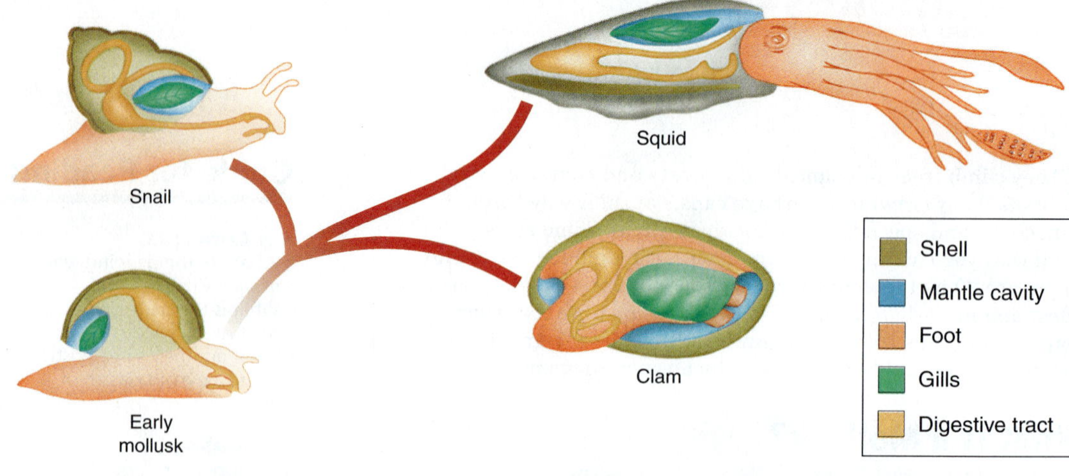

▲ **Figure 27–21** **The body plan of most mollusks includes a foot, mantle, shell, and visceral mass.** Early mollusks may have looked like the animal shown at the bottom. As they evolved, their body parts became adapted for different functions.

Form and Function in Mollusks

Like the annelids, mollusks have true coeloms surrounded by mesoderm tissue. They also have complex, interrelated organ systems that function together to maintain the body as a whole.

Body Plan The different body shapes of mollusks are variations on a single body plan, shown in **Figure 27–21.** **The body plan of most mollusks has four parts: foot, mantle, shell, and visceral mass.** The muscular **foot** takes many forms, including flat structures for crawling, spade-shaped structures for burrowing, and tentacles for capturing prey. The **mantle** is a thin layer of tissue that covers most of the mollusk's body, much like a cloak. The **shell** is made by glands in the mantle that secrete calcium carbonate. The shell has been reduced or lost in slugs and some other mollusk groups. Just beneath the mantle is the **visceral mass,** which consists of the internal organs.

Feeding Mollusks can be herbivores, carnivores, filter feeders, detritivores, or parasites. Snails and slugs feed using a flexible, tongue-shaped structure known as a **radula** (RAJ-oo-luh; plural: radulae), shown in **Figure 27–22,** to which hundreds of tiny teeth are attached. Herbivorous mollusks use their radula to scrape algae off rocks or to eat the soft tissues of plants. Carnivorous mollusks use their radula to drill through shells of other animals and to tear up and swallow the prey's soft tissue.

CHECKPOINT *How is a mollusk's shell made?*

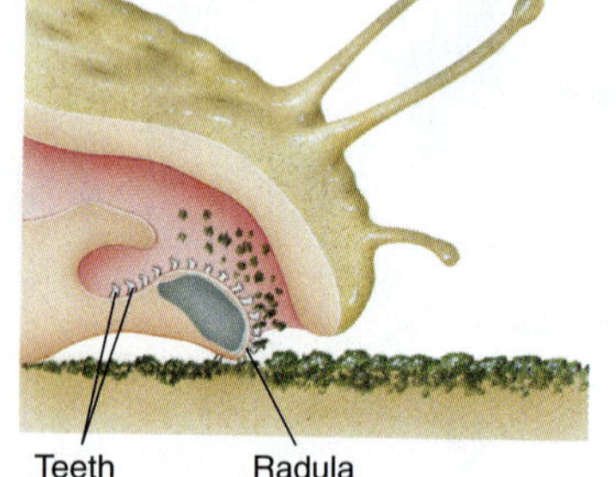

◀ **Figure 27–22** Snails use a radula for feeding. The teeth of a radula give it the look and feel of sandpaper. Beneath the radula is a stiff supporting rod of cartilage. When the mollusk feeds, it places the tip of the radula on its food and pulls the sandpapery layer back and forth. **Formulating Hypotheses** *How might radulae with different structures allow snails to inhabit different environments?*

UNIVERSAL ACCESS

Inclusion/Special Needs

Before students read the subsection Form and Function in Mollusks, preview the subsection on Groups of Mollusks by reading the names of the groups aloud. Point out that organisms in each group of mollusks will have differences in the ways they carry out the seven essential functions. Then, as students read about mollusk form and function, they should note any details that specifically apply to one or another of the groups. L1

English Language Learners

Explain that the prefix *bi-* means "two." Point out that students might be asked in math class to "bisect" a line, which means they should cut it in two by finding the midpoint of the line. Also explain that the word part *valve* means "shell" as used in the context of mollusks. Therefore, a *bivalve* is an organism with "two shells." As you explain the term *bivalve*, show students an oyster or clam shell and emphasize that two shells make up the whole. L1 L2

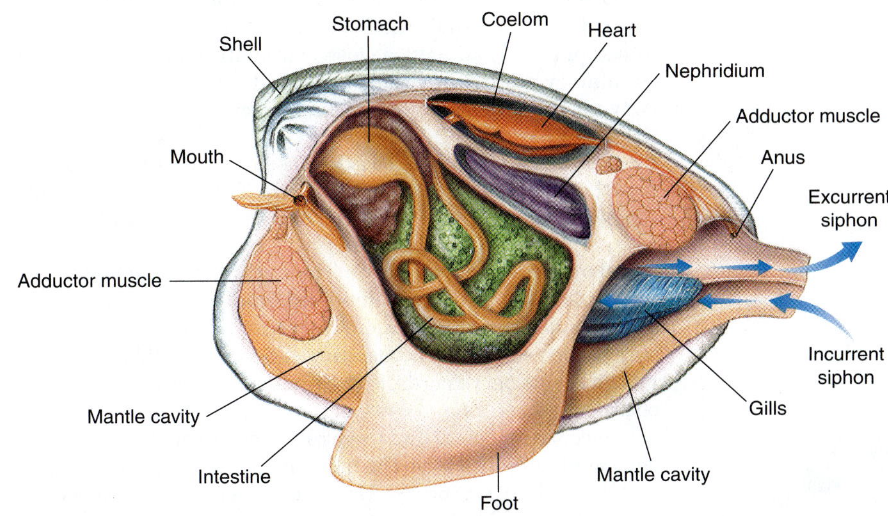

▲ **Figure 27–23** The anatomy of a clam is typical of bivalves, or two-shelled mollusks. The mantle and part of the foot have been cut away to show internal organs. The adductor muscles are used to open and shut the two exterior shells. The gills exchange oxygen and carbon dioxide between the body and the surrounding water. The arrows show the path of water over the gills. **Predicting** ***What might happen if a clam's incurrent siphon became blocked?***

Octopi and certain sea slugs use their sharp jaws to eat their prey. To subdue their prey, some octopi also produce poisons. Clams, oysters, and scallops lead a quieter existence by filter feeding using feathery gills. Food is carried by water, which enters through the incurrent siphon, shown on the right in **Figure 27–23.** A **siphon** is a tubelike structure through which water enters and leaves the body. The water flows over the gills and then leaves by the excurrent siphon. As water passes over the gills, plankton become trapped in sticky mucus. Cilia on the gills move the mixture of mucus and food into the mouth.

Respiration Aquatic mollusks such as snails, clams, and octopi typically breathe using gills inside their mantle cavity. As water passes through the mantle cavity, oxygen in the water moves into blood flowing through the gills. At the same time, carbon dioxide moves in the opposite direction—from the blood into the water. Land snails and slugs do not have gills. Instead, they respire using a mantle cavity that has a large surface area lined with blood vessels. Because this lining must be kept moist so that oxygen can diffuse across its surface, land snails and slugs typically live in moist places.

Circulation Oxygen and nutrients are carried to all parts of a mollusk's body by a circulatory system. The circulatory system of mollusks is either open or closed. "Open" does not mean that blood can spill to the outside of the animal! In an **open circulatory system,** blood is pumped through vessels by a simple heart. Blood eventually leaves the vessels and works its way through different sinuses. A sinus is a large saclike space. The blood passes from the sinuses to the gills, where oxygen and carbon dioxide are exchanged, and then back to the heart.

Build Science Skills

Classifying Display a variety of mollusk shells. These might include clam, oyster, nautilus, and snail shells. Explain that biologists think the color of shells is primarily the result of the food the mollusk has eaten. Provide students with several shell guides or other resources that they can use to identify the shells. Then, challenge students to classify each shell by which organism it belongs to. When students have completed classification, discuss their findings as a class. Have volunteers then write a caption for each shell and create a classroom display. L2 L3

Address Misconceptions

Many students associate mollusks with the term *shellfish.* Explain that *shellfish* is a common term for any marine animal with an external shell, which includes a variety of invertebrates. Point out that fish are vertebrates. Ask students: **Is a mollusk a vertebrate or an invertebrate?** *(A mollusk is an invertebrate.)* Emphasize that mollusks cannot be classified as any kind of fish, despite the common label of *shellfish.*
L1 L2

BIO INSIGHTS — FACTS AND FIGURES

Shells of all shapes and sizes
Mollusk shells occur in such a variety of shapes and sizes that they serve as the main means of identification for many mollusk species. The obvious advantage of a hard exterior shell is the protection it provides for the animal's soft body. Like the exoskeletons of arthropods, exterior shells have one major disadvantage: Because shells do not consist of living, dividing cells, mollusks outgrow them as they develop. Many mollusks, however, have evolved shell designs that allow them to build onto the shell to accommodate their increased body size. The shell is not continuously added to but is expanded periodically as needed. Another disadvantage of shells is that they reduce mobility. Most mollusks, such as snails, lumber along under the load of their heavy shells. Other mollusks, such as clams, are fairly stationary throughout their adult lives.

Answers to . . .

 CHECKPOINT *Glands in the mantle secrete the calcium carbonate of which the shell is made.*

Figure 27–22 *Depending on its structure, a radula can be used for different purposes, including scraping the algae off rocks, eating the soft tissues of plants, drilling through shells of other animals, and tearing up a prey's soft tissue. These feeding adaptations enable snails to inhabit diverse habitats, including ponds and land.*

Figure 27–23 *Since water carries food and oxygen to the clam, the clam could not obtain food or oxygen if its incurrent siphon was blocked.*

27–4 (continued)

Build Science Skills

Designing Experiments Divide the class into small groups, and challenge each group to design an experiment that would test how intelligent octopi are. Students should first write a hypothesis that they can test. Then, they should describe an experiment that has a control and a manipulated variable. Students should also indicate what sorts of data they expect the experiment would yield that could prove or disprove their hypothesis. L2 L3

Make Connections

Physics After students have read about the jet propulsion of an octopus, explain that this is an example of Sir Isaac Newton's third law of motion. The third law says that for every action, there is an equal and opposite reaction. Ask: **In this case, what is the action, and what is the reaction?** *(The action is the movement of water expelled through the siphon. The reaction is the movement of the octopus forward.)* As students watch, blow up a balloon, and then release it. Students should observe the balloon rapidly moving in the opposite direction from the air moving out of its nozzle. Ask: **How is what you have just observed similar to and different from the jet propulsion used by an octopus?** *(It is similar in that there is an action and a reaction. It is different in that there is a movement of air from the balloon, while there is a movement of water from the octopus.)* L2

Open circulatory systems work well for slow-moving mollusks such as snails and clams. Faster-moving mollusks such as octopi and squid have a closed circulatory system. A closed circulatory system can transport blood through an animal's body much more quickly than an open circulatory system.

Excretion Cells of the body release nitrogen-containing waste into the blood in the form of ammonia. Tube-shaped nephridia remove ammonia from the blood and release it outside the body.

Response The complexity of the nervous system and the ability to respond to environmental conditions vary greatly among mollusks. Clams and other two-shelled mollusks have a simple nervous system consisting of small ganglia near the mouth, a few nerve cords, and simple sense organs, such as chemical receptors and eyespots.

In contrast, octopi and their relatives are active and intelligent predators that have the most highly developed nervous system of all invertebrates. Because of their well-developed brains, these animals can remember things for long periods and may be more intelligent than some vertebrates. Octopi are capable of complex behavior, such as opening a jar to get food inside, and they have been trained to perform different tasks for a reward or to avoid punishment.

Movement Mollusks move in many different ways. Snails secrete mucus along the base of the foot, and then move over surfaces using a rippling motion of the foot. The fast-moving octopus uses a form of jet propulsion. It draws water into the mantle cavity and then forces the water out through a siphon. Water leaving the body propels the octopus in the opposite direction.

Reproduction Mollusks reproduce in a variety of ways. Many snails and two-shelled mollusks reproduce sexually by external fertilization. They release enormous numbers of eggs and sperm into the open water. The eggs are fertilized in the water and then develop into free-swimming larvae. In tentacled mollusks and certain snails, fertilization takes place inside the body of the female. Some mollusks are hermaphrodites, having both male and female reproductive organs. Individuals of these species usually fertilize eggs from another individual.

Figure 27–24 Mollusks have evolved a variety of ways of responding to potential danger. Snails (above) protect themselves by withdrawing into their shells in a matter of seconds. In some snails, a hard plate blocks the entrance to the shell, protecting the snail inside. Octopi (right) and squids squirt ink from inside their digestive tracts. The ink startles predators and may also cause temporary numbness. **Predicting** ***How might the hard plate protect snails during a period of drought?***

FACTS AND FIGURES

A chiton is a marine mollusk that has an elongated body; a large, broad foot; and a radula. Chitons eat algae, hydrozoans, and other low-growing organisms.

The dorsal shells of chitons display beautiful variations of pattern and color. The dorsal shells, which are divided into a series of eight plates, are also very practical. These plates make the shell flexible enough that the chiton can roll up into a smaller ball when it is dislodged from its attachment. Thus, it can protect itself until it can safely unroll and reattach elsewhere.

Another defense mechanism of the chiton is its ability to anchor itself to its substrate when it is disturbed or when it is exposed by a receding tide. The muscles in its foot pull the animal down tightly so that the edge of the mantle, which partly or completely covers the shell plates, can function like the rim of a suction cup. In this way, it becomes extremely difficult to dislodge the chiton.

Figure 27–25 Gastropods move by using a large, muscular foot located on the ventral side. They can be shell-less, such as the nudibranch or sea slug (top left), or have a single shell, such as the tree snail (top right). Many sea hares (bottom) have a reduced shell covered by the mantle. The sea hare defends itself by "inking"—squirting ink at potential predators.

Groups of Mollusks

Mollusks are divided into several classes according to characteristics of the foot and the shell. The three major classes of mollusks are gastropods, bivalves, and cephalopods.

Gastropods Members of the class Gastropoda, or gastropods (GAS-truh-pahdz), include pond snails, land slugs, sea butterflies, sea hares, limpets, and nudibranchs (NOO-duh-branks). **Gastropods are shell-less or single-shelled mollusks that move by using a muscular foot located on the ventral side.**

Many gastropods, such as the snails shown on the top right in **Figure 27–25,** have a single shell that protects their bodies. When threatened, they can pull completely into their coiled shells. Some snails are also protected by a hard disk on the foot that forms a solid "door" at the mouth of their shell when they withdraw.

Land slugs and nudibranchs have no shell but protect themselves in other ways. Most land slugs spend daylight hours hiding under rocks and logs, hidden from birds and other potential predators. Some sea hares, when threatened, can squirt ink into the surrounding water, producing a "smoke screen" that confuses predators.

Some nudibranchs have chemicals in their bodies that taste bad or are poisonous. When a predator bites one of these nudibranchs, the predator becomes ill. Many nudibranchs are able to recycle the nematocysts from cnidarians they eat, using them to sting predators. These "booby-trapped" nudibranchs are usually brightly colored. The bright coloring serves as a warning to potential predators.

CHECKPOINT *How do shell-less gastropods protect themselves?*

Groups of Mollusks

Build Science Skills

Observing Set up a 20-to-40 liter freshwater aquarium in the classroom. Have students add 3 to 4 centimeters of sand on the bottom. Then, have students fill the container with pond water to about 10 centimeters from the top. Add aquatic plants and several pond snails. Also, place a top over the aquarium so that the snails won't escape. Have students observe the snails, with the unaided eye and with a hand lens. They should study the shell, head, foot, and any other feature of snail anatomy they can see. Have students make drawings and write a description of what they see. L2

Build Science Skills

Observing To help students—especially those who are visually impaired—understand gastropod form and function, place a land snail in a student's hand. Once the animal acclimates itself to the surface, it will move across the hand. Tell the student to feel for the action of the snail's radula. Then, have the student use his or her other hand to feel the snail's shell. Because the snail's shell can be quite fragile, caution the student to touch the animal gently. Students should wash their hands thoroughly after touching the snail. L2

BIO INSIGHTS — FACTS AND FIGURES

How the gastropod got its twist

The coiled shell of the snail and other gastropods is the result of an internal realignment process called torsion. During a gastropod's development, the animal's visceral mass begins to grow upward. This growth is uneven on the right and left sides. The uneven growth, coupled with the contraction of certain muscles, causes the posterior mantle cavity to twist around to the right. At a critical moment, the body rotates a full 180° so that the back end of the body comes to rest just behind the head. The result is that the gastropod balances its internal organs above the rest of the body much as a human would carry a backpack. The coiled shell provides a retreat for the animal's head in times of danger. The twisted body arrangement has its drawbacks, though. The gastropod has its anus and kidney openings above the head, creating somewhat of a sanitation problem.

Answers to . . .

CHECKPOINT *Most land slugs spend the daylight hours hiding under rocks and logs. Some sea hares squirt ink into the surrounding water, confusing predators. Some nudibranchs have chemicals in their bodies that taste bad or are poisonous. Many nudibranchs recycle cnidarian nematocysts, moving the stinging cells to their own exterior.*

Figure 27–24 *By blocking the opening in the shell, the hard plate helps keep moisture inside the shell.*

27–4 (continued)

Build Science Skills

Using Models Help students understand how bivalves obtain nutrients by filter feeding through a demonstration of filtering particles from water. Divide a sample of water from a pond, lake, or ocean into several parts, pouring each into a separate container. Then, filter the water in each container into a beaker using one of these filter devices: a sieve, a coffee filter, a piece of screen or wire mesh, and a piece of cheesecloth. Have students observe the materials that remain after the water has been filtered, first with the unaided eye and then with a microscope. Ask: **Do you think any of these materials might be useful to an organism as food?** *(Answers may vary. In many cases, the correct answer is yes.)* Have students relate what they have observed to the filter-feeding mechanism of a bivalve. Point out that the gills of a bivalve are able to trap particles of exactly the right size so that the animal can obtain the type of food it needs. L2

Demonstration

Show students a cuttlebone, which can be purchased in many pet stores. Explain that cuttlebones are used by bird owners to condition and sharpen birds' beaks. After students have had a chance to examine the cuttlebone, ask: **What mollusk class includes the cuttlefish?** *(Cephalopoda)* Explain that a cuttlefish, like a nautilus, can regulate its buoyancy—and therefore its depth in the water—by altering the amount of fluid and gas in the chambers of its shell. L1

Word Origins

Pseudopod means "false foot." L2

▲ **Figure 27–26** **Bivalves are two-shelled mollusks that include clams, mussels, oysters, and scallops like the one above.** Observe the tiny blue eyespots along the open edges of the shell.

Bivalves **Members of the class Bivalvia have two shells that are held together by one or two powerful muscles.** Common bivalves include clams, oysters, mussels, and scallops. Most bivalves stay in one place for much of the time. Clams burrow in mud or sand, whereas mussels use sticky threads to attach themselves to rocks. Scallops, such as the one shown in **Figure 27–26,** are the least sedentary bivalves and can move around rapidly by flapping their shells when threatened.

Currents created by cilia on the gills circulate water through the body cavities of bivalves. Once water is inside the body, filter-feeding bivalves use mucus and cilia on their gills to trap food particles in the water. Some bivalves feed on material deposited in sand or mud. They use long, muscular extensions of tissue that surround the mouth to collect food particles from the surrounding sediments. The indigestible sand or mud particles are expelled from the mantle cavity.

CHECKPOINT *What are some common bivalves?*

Word Origins

Cephalopod comes from the Greek *kephale*, meaning "head," and *podos*, meaning "foot." **Pseudopods** are structures found in some single-celled organisms. **If *pseudo-* means "false," what does *pseudopod* mean?**

Cephalopods Cephalopods (SEF-uh-luh-pahdz)—members of the class Cephalopoda—are the most active of the mollusks. This class includes octopi, squids, cuttlefishes, and nautiluses. **Cephalopods are typically soft-bodied mollusks in which the head is attached to a single foot. The foot is divided into tentacles or arms.** Cephalopods have eight or more tentacles equipped with sucking disks that grab and hold prey. Nautiluses have many more tentacles than other cephalopods—in some cases up to 90! Their tentacles lack suckers but have a sticky, mucuslike covering.

As with some of the gastropods, most modern cephalopods have only small internal shells or no shells at all. The only present-day cephalopods with external shells are nautiluses, such as the one shown in **Figure 27–27.** These animals can control their depth in the water by regulating the amount of gas in their shells. Ancestors of the nautilus dominated the seas more then 500 million years ago.

Figure 27–27 Nautiluses like the one shown here are the most primitive group of cephalopods. **Comparing and Contrasting** *How does this nautilus differ from most cephalopods?*

FACTS AND FIGURES

A coiled shell with many chambers

The chambered nautilus is so named because of its coiled shell of many chambers. By taking in and releasing gas from chambers in its shell, a nautilus can change its buoyancy. This means that it can move from the surface down to more than 400 meters. The body of the chambered nautilus is divided into two sections. The first section is the head, which is covered by a tough tissue called the hood. The hood acts as a shield. Tentacles—of which a nautilus may have more than 90—are located in the head. Unlike tentacles of other cephalopods, the tentacles of the nautilus do not have suckers. Instead, they are covered with a sticky substance that helps to hold prey. The second section of the body consists primarily of a large sac that contains the nautilus's organs. This sac is enclosed by the mantle. Between the mantle and the sac are four large gills.

Analyzing Data

Raising Clams

Aquaculture is the growth of aquatic animals and plants for use by humans. In one example of aquaculture, hard clams are first grown in commercial hatcheries under very favorable conditions. The young clams are then removed from the hatcheries and placed into the mud beds of creeks, where they develop into adults. At that time, the size of the young clams is around 40 millimeters.

Because Georgian clams grow so quickly, they are ideal for aquaculture. Unlike the hard clams in the northeastern United States that grow only during the warm months, Georgian hard clams grow year-round. As a result, the Georgian clams grow to market size in less than half the time that the northeastern clams need to grow. The graph shows how clam shells grow over a period of 10 years.

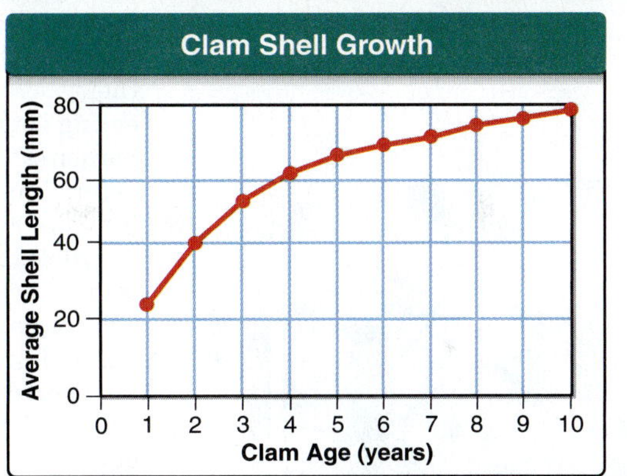

1. **Using Tables and Graphs** Approximately how many years does it take clams to reach a size at which they can be removed from hatcheries and put in creeks?
2. **Applying Concepts** How does climate affect the growth of most clams?
3. **Using Tables and Graphs** How much did the clams grow during the first 5 years? The next 5?
4. **Formulating Hypotheses** Formulate a hypothesis to explain the slower growth rate from years 5 to 10.
5. **Drawing Conclusions** What general trends do you observe about growth from the graph?

6IIE 7.c, BIIE 1.l

Cuttlefishes have small shells inside their bodies. These are the cuttlebones given to pet birds to condition their beaks. A squid's internal shell has evolved into a thin supporting rod known as a pen. Octopi have lost their shells completely.

Cephalopods also have numerous complex sense organs that help them detect and respond to external stimuli. Cephalopods distinguish shapes by sight and texture by touch. The eyes of many cephalopods, such as the squid shown in **Figure 27–28,** are as complex as those of some vertebrates, such as fishes and humans. Cephalopod eyes can be large—the size of a dinner plate in some species—and can distinguish objects as small as 0.5 centimeters from a meter away, allowing squids to locate a wide variety of prey. Though cephalopod eyes may look something like vertebrate eyes from the outside, their internal structures are quite different.

Figure 27–28 **Most cephalopods are mollusks in which the head is attached to a single foot that is divided into tentacles or arms.** They have the most complex nervous system of all the mollusks, with a highly developed brain and sense organs, such as the eye of this common squid.

Analyzing Data

6IIE 7.c, BIIE 1.l

Aquaculture is the cultivation of fish or other marine animals for food. It is a growing industry. L2 L3

Answers

1. Approximately 2 years
2. Most clams grow only during warm months.
3. The clams grew to about 68 mm during the first five years. They grew an additional 12 mm, to 80 mm, during the next five years.
4. Sample hypothesis: The older the clam, the less frequently its cells divide.
5. Clam growth is greatest in the first four or five years. Then, it levels off to a slow but steady growth.

Build Science Skills

Comparing and Contrasting

Explain to students that the cephalopod eye is similar in many ways to the eyes of vertebrates, though they are not exactly the same. The two types of eyes are often cited by biologists as a good example of convergent evolution, the process by which unrelated species independently evolve similar adaptations. Encourage interested students who need a challenge to investigate the structure and function of the cephalopod eye and draw a comparison with the human eye. Suggest that they find out how the cephalopod eye works and whether it forms images and sees colors. L3

BIO INSIGHTS — FACTS AND FIGURES

There are some giant mollusks

Biologists have described about 50,000 living mollusk species, and another 60,000 are known by their fossils. Some mollusks are quite small; the shells of some freshwater bivalves are almost never over 2 millimeters across. Yet, there are some really large mollusks. For example, the largest bivalve is the giant tropical clam, *Tridacna,* whose shells can measure more than 1.2 meters across. One species, *T. gigas,* can have a mass of over 400 kilograms. The largest octopus is the common Pacific octopus, *Octopus hongkongensis,* which can measure up to 9.7 meters from the tip of one tentacle to the tip of the opposite tentacle. The largest squid is the giant squid, *Architeuthis,* which can have a body 4 meters long with tentacles over 9 meters long.

Answers to . . .

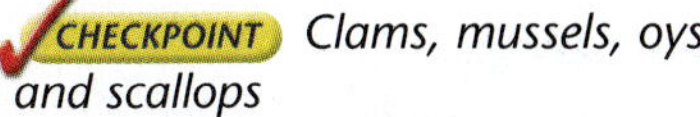
CHECKPOINT Clams, mussels, oysters, and scallops

Figure 27–27 *Unlike most cephalopods, the nautilus has an external shell.*

27–4 (continued)

Ecology of Mollusks

Use Community Resources

Students can call the state environmental protection agency and find out whether it has a program to test bivalves for pollutants. Have the students report to the class about their findings. L2 L3

3 ASSESS

Evaluate Understanding

Have students make drawings of a snail, a squid, and a clam similar to those in Figure 27–21. Then, direct their attention to the labeled drawing in Figure 27–22. Challenge students to use as many of the labels on the second figure as they can to label their drawings of the three mollusks.

Reteach

Have students make a compare/contrast table of the three major classes of mollusks. In this table, they should include the names of the classes, important characteristics of each class, and examples of each.

Focus on the BIG Idea

Students should compare the mutualism of bivalves and bacteria with the parasitism of various flatworms and roundworms, as described in the chapter. Whereas in mutualism both species benefit from the relationship, in parasitism one organism—a fluke or *Ascaris*, for instance—lives on or inside another organism and harms it.

If your class subscribes to the iText, use it to review the Key Concepts in Section 27–4.

Answer to . . .

Figure 27–29 *Mollusks feed on—and provide food for—other organisms; they filter water; they are hosts and parasites.*

▲ **Figure 27–29** These clams will find their way to many people's dinner tables. **Applying Concepts** *Besides providing food for humans and other animals, what are some other roles that mollusks play in ecosystems?*

Ecology of Mollusks

Mollusks play many different roles in living systems. For example, they feed on plants, prey on animals, and "clean up" their surroundings by filtering algae out of the water or by eating detritus. Some of them are hosts to symbiotic algae or to parasites; others are themselves parasites. In addition, mollusks are an important source of food for many organisms, including humans. **Figure 27–29** shows clams caught for human use.

Biologists' understanding of molluskan diversity and ecology is growing all the time. Recent explorations around deep-sea volcanic vents called "black smokers" have revealed a fascinating community that includes several bivalves. Researchers have discovered symbiotic bacteria within the foot-long bivalves clustered around these vents. These bacteria extract chemical energy from simple compounds released in the superheated water. From this energy, the bacteria produce food molecules that the mollusks can use. Without this mutualistic relationship with the bacteria, these mollusks would be unable to inhabit this extreme environment. Other research has discovered a similar symbiosis between related bacteria and bivalves that live in the mud of salt marshes and mangrove swamps.

Scientists have found some new uses for mollusks. Because filter-feeding bivalves concentrate dangerous pollutants and microorganisms in their tissues, they can be used to monitor water quality. Careful checks of bivalves can warn biologists and public health officials of health problems long before scientists can detect these dangers in the open water. Besides acting as environmental monitors, mollusks also serve as subjects in biological research. Some current investigations are based on the observation that snails and other mollusks never seem to develop any form of cancer. If scientists can determine what protects the cells of these animals from cancer, they will gain valuable insights into how to fight cancer in humans.

27–4 Section Assessment

1. **Key Concept** What is a mollusk?
2. **Key Concept** List and describe the four parts of the mollusk body plan.
3. **Key Concept** Describe the main characteristics of the three major classes of mollusks.
4. Why are land snails restricted to moist environments?
5. Describe how a cephalopod responds to external stimuli and explain how a cephalopod's nervous system is more complex than that of other mollusks.
6. **Critical Thinking Comparing and Contrasting** Compare open and closed circulatory systems. Why are open circulatory systems found mostly in small animals that move slowly?

Focus on the BIG Idea 

Interdependence in Nature Recall from Chapter 4 the definition of symbiosis. The mutualism that exists between bivalves and bacteria near deep-sea vents is one type of symbiosis. Describe an example of another type of symbiosis that you have read about in this chapter. How is it different from mutualism?

27–4 Section Assessment

1. A mollusk is a soft-bodied animal that usually has an internal or external shell.
2. Foot, mantle, shell, visceral mass. Descriptions should agree with information on page 702.
3. Gastropods—shell-less or one shell, ventral foot; bivalves—two shells; cephalopods—head attached to foot.
4. Land snails respire using a mantle cavity lined with blood vessels. This lining must be kept moist.
5. Cephalopods exhibit complex behavior and can locate a variety of prey. Students should describe cephalopods' complex sense organs.
6. In an open circulatory system, blood leaves the vessels and moves through sinuses. In a closed circulatory system, blood is contained within vessels. A closed circulatory system supports greater oxygen needs because blood moves quickly.

Exploration

6IIE 7.c, BIIE 1.a, BIIE 1.d

Investigating Land Snails

Although most mollusks are aquatic, some snails live on land. In this investigation, you will explore how land snails are adapted to survive in this environment.

Problem How do land snails move and react to various external stimuli?

Materials

- land snail
- glass slides
- dropper pipette
- dissecting tray
- black construction paper
- paper towels
- 40-watt desk lamp
- metric ruler
- dissecting microscope
- petri dish
- clock with second hand

Skills Observing, Calculating, Using Tables and Graphs

Procedure     

1. Using a clean pipette, put a drop of water in the center of a glass slide. Gently place the snail in the water drop. Look for the mucous trail as the snail begins to move.
2. Gently turn the slide over and place it on top of a petri dish. Place the petri dish under the dissecting microscope and observe the movement of the muscular foot under low power. Look for the radula as it scrapes the slide.
3. Copy the data table onto a separate sheet of paper.
4. Line each half of a dissecting tray with a separate piece of paper towel. Place a sheet of black construction paper above one half of the tray. Shine the desk lamp on the other half of the tray from a distance of 30 cm. **CAUTION:** *Do not touch the lamp, because it may be hot.*
5. Place the snail in the center of the tray and observe how it responds to the external stimulus of bright light. Measure and record the number of seconds in each minute that the snail spends in the dark.
6. **Calculating** Exchange data with the class and determine class averages.
7. Return the snail to its habitat, clean up your materials, and wash your hands.

Data Table

Time (minutes)	Time in Dark (seconds)	
	Group	Class Average
0–1		
1–2		
2–3		
3–4		
4–5		

Analyze and Conclude

1. **Drawing Conclusions** Describe the movement of the snail across the glass slide. Name one advantage and one limitation of this type of movement.
2. **Using Tables and Graphs** Make a bar graph of the class average data that shows the time the snails spent in the dark for each of the five minutes. What trend do you see in your data? How can you explain this result?
3. **Drawing Conclusions** Do snails prefer dark places or bright places? Refer to the class average data to explain why your conclusion is valid. Communicate your conclusion by writing a short paragraph describing your results.

For: Data sharing
Visit: PHSchool.com
Web Code: cbd-8274

Share Your Data Online Enter your data on the behavior of the land snails. Then, look at the data entered by other students. Based on the available data, do snails prefer dark places or light places? Why might your data differ from those of other students? Does this larger set of data support your results and indicate that your conclusions are valid?

Analyze and Conclude

1. The snail moves forward with its anterior end in front; the snail's foot moves in wavelike muscular contractions and leaves a trail of mucus behind. Advantages: The snail moves with its head and sense organs in front; the mucus helps the snail slide over the surface. A limitation is that the snail moves very slowly.
2. The bar graph should reflect the class averages. Although specific times will vary, the trend should be that the snail spends more time in the dark with each increasing minute. Snails will usually move into the dark, moist area within the first two minutes and remain there the rest of the time. One explanation is that the snail is less likely to be seen by predators in a dark place.
3. A snail is adapted to dark, damp places. This adaptation—including the avoidance of bright light—enables the snail both to avoid being seen by predators and to avoid dehydration.

Exploration

6IIE 7.c, BIIE 1.a, BIIE 1.d

Objective Students will be able to draw conclusions about how land snails move and react to light.

Skills Focus Using Tables and Graphs, Observing, Calculating

Time 45 minutes

Advance Prep Obtain live snails from a biological supply company. If specimens are to be observed for a period of time, keep them in a terrarium with moist soil and moss.

Alternative Materials Depending on the size of the snails and the range through which the microscope focuses, students may need to substitute a small beaker or finger bowl for the petri dish in step 2.

Safety Caution students that the lamp can become quite hot.

Teaching Tips

- Remind students that snails are living things and should be handled gently.
- Put a data table on an overhead transparency or the board for students to record their results for the class.
- Remind students to return the snails to the proper habitat upon completion of the lab.

Procedure

1. Demonstrate how to place the snail on the glass slide so that it stays on the slide long enough to be seen under the microscope.
4. Demonstrate how to place the black construction paper over half of the tray and where to position the lamp.

Expected Outcomes Students should observe that the snail leaves a trail of mucus behind it when it moves and that the snail moves away from the light to the darkness under the black construction paper.

Students should see how snails react to light, but their results will depend on their own data and the data on the site.

Chapter 27 Study Guide

Study Tip

Have students work in pairs to write questions tied to Vocabulary terms and Key Concepts and then trade questions with other pairs to answer them.

Thinking Visually

Students' concept maps should include gastropods, bivalves, and cephalopods and the characteristics of each as described in the text. Examples may include any of those mentioned in the section on mollusks.

Chapter 27 Assessment

Reviewing Content

1. d **2.** b **3.** b **4.** c **5.** b **6.** b **7.** c **8.** a **9.** d **10.** c

Understanding Concepts

11. A coelomate has a body cavity lined with mesoderm; an acoelomate does not.

12. Oxygen and nutrients are taken in through the skin and diffuse to internal cells; wastes are removed by diffusion or excreted through skin pores.

13. The pharynx takes food into the gastrovascular cavity. Inside the gut, digestion and absorption occur.

14. Flatworms have nerve ganglia, one or more long nerve cords, and short cords across the body; some have eyespots and other cells that detect and respond to stimuli. Cnidarians lack ganglia or nerve cords.

15. It causes schistosomiasis, characterized by clogged blood vessels and damage to lungs, liver, spleen, or intestines. Safe sewage disposal would limit outbreaks.

16. A tapeworm uses its scolex to attach to its host's intestinal wall; it lacks a digestive tract and absorbs nutrients from the intestine.

17. Segments called proglottids contain male and female reproductive organs. Proglottids release zygotes, which leave the host's body in feces.

18. Roundworms respire and excrete metabolic wastes through their body walls. Nutrients and wastes are transported through their bodies by diffusion.

Chapter 27 Study Guide

27–1 Flatworms

Key Concepts

- Flatworms are soft, flattened worms that have tissues and internal organ systems. They are the simplest animals to have three embryonic germ layers, bilateral symmetry, and cephalization.
- Turbellarians are free-living marine or freshwater flatworms.
- Flukes are parasitic flatworms that usually infect the internal organs of their hosts.
- Tapeworms are long, flat, parasitic worms that are adapted to life inside the intestines of their hosts.

Vocabulary

acoelomate, p. 683 • coelom, p. 683
pharynx, p. 684
flame cell, p. 684
ganglion, p. 685
eyespot, p. 685
hermaphrodite, p. 686
fission, p. 686
scolex, p. 688
proglottid, p. 688
testis, p. 688

27–2 Roundworms

Key Concepts

- Roundworms are unsegmented worms that have pseudocoeloms and digestive systems with two openings—a mouth and an anus.
- Parasitic roundworms include trichinosis-causing worms, filarial worms, ascarid worms, and hookworms.

Vocabulary

pseudocoelom, p. 689
anus, p. 689

27–3 Annelids

Key Concepts

- Annelids are worms with segmented bodies. They have a true coelom that is completely lined with mesoderm.
- Oligochaetes are annelids that typically have streamlined bodies and relatively few setae compared to polychaetes. Most oligochaetes live in soil or fresh water.
- Leeches are typically external parasites that suck the blood and body fluids of their host.
- Polychaetes are marine annelids that have paired, paddlelike appendages tipped with setae.

Vocabulary

septum, p. 694 • seta, p. 694
crop, p. 695 • gizzard, p. 695
closed circulatory system, p. 695
gill, p. 696 • nephridium, p. 696
clitellum, p. 696

27–4 Mollusks

Key Concepts

- Mollusks are soft-bodied animals that usually have an internal or external shell.
- The typical mollusk body plan has four parts: foot, mantle, shell, and visceral mass.
- Gastropods are shell-less or single-shelled mollusks that move by using a muscular foot located on the ventral side.
- Bivalves have two shells that are held together by one or two powerful muscles.
- Cephalopods are typically soft-bodied mollusks in which the head is attached to a single foot. The foot is divided into tentacles or arms.

Vocabulary

trochophore, p. 701
foot, p. 702
mantle, p. 702 • shell, p. 702
visceral mass, p. 702
radula, p. 702
siphon, p. 703
open circulatory system, p. 703

Thinking Visually

Create a concept map that shows the classes and main characteristics of mollusks. Include at least two examples of types of mollusks within each class.

CHAPTER RESOURCES

Print:

- ***Teaching Resources,*** Chapter Vocabulary Review, Graphic Organizer, Chapter 27 Tests: Levels A and B

Technology:

- ***Computer Test Bank,*** Chapter 27 Test
- ***iText,*** Chapter 27 Assessment

Chapter 27 Assessment

Reviewing Content

Choose the letter that best answers the question or completes the statement.

1. The muscular tube found near the mouth of the digestive cavity in flatworms is called a(an)
   a. proglottid. c. anus.
   b. scolex. d. pharynx.
2. The head of an adult tapeworm is called a
   a. flame cell. c. cuticle.
   b. scolex. d. mantle.
3. The body cavity of a roundworm is called a
   a. coelom. c. gizzard.
   b. pseudocoelom. d. crop.
4. What are the clusters of nerve cells in roundworms called?
   a. flame cells c. ganglia
   b. proglottids d. radulae
5. In the earthworm, waste created by cellular metabolism is eliminated by the
   a. crop. c. gizzard.
   b. nephridia. d. flame cell.
6. The digestive organ in which an earthworm stores food is number
   a. 1. c. 3.
   b. 2. d. 4.

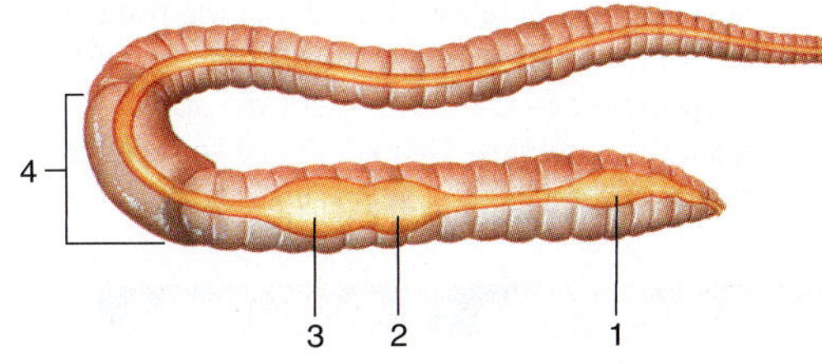

7. In earthworms, the clitellum is used in
   a. digestion. c. reproduction.
   b. excretion. d. respiration.
8. The tongue-shaped structure that some mollusks use for feeding is the
   a. radula.
   b. sinus.
   c. mantle.
   d. proglottid.
9. Mollusks eliminate nitrogen-containing wastes through simple tube-shaped organs called
   a. gills.
   b. nephrons.
   c. radulae.
   d. nephridia.

Interactive textbook with assessment at PHSchool.com

10. A mollusk with a shell consisting of two parts is a member of the class
    a. Cephalopoda. c. Bivalvia.
    b. Annelida. d. Gastropoda.

Understanding Concepts

11. Distinguish between coelomates and acoelomates.
12. Describe how respiration, circulation, and excretion are accomplished in the flatworm.
13. Explain how feeding and digestion occur in planarians.
14. How is the nervous system of a flatworm more complex than the sensory cells and nerve net of a cnidarian?
15. How does the *Schistosoma* fluke affect humans? What step can be taken to limit the number of outbreaks of schistosomiasis?
16. What adaptations do tapeworms have for their parasitic life cycle?
17. How do tapeworms reproduce?
18. Describe how respiration, circulation, and excretion are accomplished in roundworms.
19. Outline the life cycle of the *Trichinella* roundworm.
20. How does the roundworm *Ascaris* cause malnutrition?
21. Evaluate the potential impact the research on *C. elegans* will have on scientific thought.
22. List three adaptations for feeding in annelids.
23. Explain the process by which earthworms move.
24. What is a hermaphrodite? Give an example.
25. Compare respiration in aquatic and land-dwelling annelids.
26. What evidence exists to indicate that annelids and mollusks may be closely related?
27. Compare the various feeding behaviors exhibited by the three classes of mollusks.
28. Describe the path of blood in an open circulatory system.
29. Distinguish between respiration in aquatic mollusks and that in land-dwelling mollusks.
30. Explain how many two-shelled mollusks reproduce.
31. Why can mollusks be used to measure water quality?

TIME SAVER

HOMEWORK GUIDE

Section:	Questions:
Section 27–1	1, 2, 11–17
Section 27–2	3, 4, 18–21, 39, 42
Section 27–3	5–7, 22–25, 35, 40, 41
Section 27–4	8–10, 26–34, 36–38, 43

Interactive Textbook

If your class subscribes to the iText, your students can go online to access an interactive version of the Student Edition and a self-test.

(Continued from page 710)

19. Students should outline the life cycle of *Trichinella* roundworm, as detailed on page 691 of the text.

20. By absorbing the host's digested food

21. It will lead to a better understanding of how eukaryotes became multicellular and may also shed light on how genes make multicellular organisms both similar and different.

22. Sample answer: sharp jaws; pharynx covered with mucus to which food particles stick; mucous bag for catching food particles

23. By contracting longitudinal and circular muscles alternately and using its setae to prevent slipping

24. A hermaphrodite such as an earthworm is an animal that produces both sperm and eggs.

25. Aquatic annelids respire through gills. Land-dwelling annelids respire through their moist skin.

26. A free-swimming larval phase called a trochophore is characteristic of both mollusks and annelids.

27. Gastropods use a radula to eat algae and soft plant tissues or bore through the shells of prey. Cephalopods have tentacles that grab prey. Bivalves are filter feeders.

28. In an open circulatory system, blood is pumped by a simple heart through vessels, flows out of the vessels, and moves through saclike sinuses. It then goes to the gills, where gas exchange occurs, and back to the heart.

29. Aquatic mollusks respire with gills inside their mantle cavity, and land mollusks respire using a mantle cavity lined with blood vessels.

30. Sexually, by external fertilization; eggs develop into free-swimming larvae

31. Filter-feeding bivalves concentrate pollutants in their tissues; this concentration can be measured.

Chapter 27 Assessment

Critical Thinking

32. Planarians move with cilia and use muscle cells to twist and turn; earthworms move by alternately contracting longitudinal and circular muscles; and scallops move rapidly by flapping their shells. They are similar in that they all have muscle cells for movement, and different in the specific ways that they move.

33. The snail would be unable to move.

34. They both take in material—soil in the case of the earthworm and water in the case of the clam—that contains both food and substances that are not food. A clam is a filter-feeder; an earthworm is not. Food enters an earthworm's body through the mouth; it enters a clam's body through the incurrent siphon.

35. Earthworms aerate soil with their tunnels and enrich soil with their castings.

36. The siphon must remain above the seabed for respiration and feeding.

37. When an irritating grain of sand is converted into a pearl, the sand is no longer an irritant.

38. Sample hypothesis: The glands secrete a substance that promotes brooding behavior. If the surgically altered octopi are treated with chemicals from the glands, they will resume brooding and then die after brooding is finished.

39. There are fewer cells and fewer, less complex organs in a small organism than in a larger, more complex organism.

40. The earthworm would die from a lack of oxygen, which it must take in through moist skin.

41. Leeches feed by sucking blood from their hosts. The chemical keeps the blood flowing freely while a leech feeds.

42. An inspector would look for *Trichinella* cysts in the pork muscle.

43. A mollusk's respiratory system is responsible for the intake of oxygen from the environment and the expelling of carbon dioxide from the body. In aquatic mollusks, these functions are accomplished through gills; in land mollusks, these functions occur through diffusion through certain blood vessels. The circulatory system carries the oxygen to all parts of the body and carries carbon dioxide from body cells to the gills or blood vessels for diffusion into the environment.

Focus on the BIG Idea

Cross-fertilization is more likely to produce new, and possibly beneficial, combinations of genes.

Writing in Science

Students should explain that *Ascaris* is a roundworm that absorbs the digested food in a host, such as a human, and as a result can cause severe malnutrition. They also should explain that ascarid worms are spread by eating vegetables or other foods that have not been washed properly. Students' explanations should reflect an understanding of the life cycle of the parasite, as detailed in Figure 27–10.

Chapter 27 Assessment

Critical Thinking

32. **Comparing and Contrasting** Which structures are used for locomotion in the planarian, earthworm, and scallop? How are they similar? How are they different?

33. **Predicting** What would happen to a land snail if its foot stopped producing mucus?

34. **Comparing and Contrasting** In what ways are the feeding habits of the earthworm and the clam similar? In what ways are they different?

35. **Applying Concepts** Why do people purchase earthworms to put in their gardens?

36. **Inferring** Although many bivalves live buried in sand or mud, the openings to their siphons remain above the surface. Why is this important for a bivalve?

37. **Predicting** In order for an oyster to produce a pearl, a grain of sand or other irritant must get inside its shell. The mantle then secretes a substance that forms a protective covering over the irritant. Why is this an advantage for the oyster?

38. **Formulating Hypotheses** Female octopi usually die after brooding their eggs (tending and protecting eggs until they hatch). However, if certain glands near the brooding octopus's eyes are surgically removed, the octopus stops brooding, resumes feeding, and has a lifespan longer than the normal three to four years. Develop a testable hypothesis to explain what might happen if the surgically altered octopi were treated with chemicals from the glands.

39. **Inferring** Why is it easier to study cell differentiation in a small organism such as *Caenorhabditis elegans* than in larger, more complex organisms?

40. **Predicting** During heavy rains, earthworms often emerge from their burrows. What might happen to an earthworm if it did not return to its burrow when the ground dried out?

41. **Inferring** Researchers have identified a chemical in leeches that suppresses blood clotting. Why is this chemical important in leeches?

42. **Applying Concepts** Suppose you are a meat inspector. You are checking uncooked pork to see whether it is contaminated with *Trichinella*. What would you look for?

43. **Comparing and Contrasting** Compare and contrast the functions of a mollusk's respiratory and circulatory systems. Then, explain how these two systems are interrelated in the function of delivering oxygen to the body as a whole.

Focus on the BIG Idea

Interdependence in Nature The nudibranch shown below is a hermaphrodite. Hermaphrodites rarely fertilize their own eggs. Explain why fertilization of another individual is more advantageous than self-fertilization. (*Hint:* See Section 1 in Chapter 26.)

Writing in Science

Imagine that you are a healthcare worker in an area in which *Ascaris lumbricoides* infections are common. Write a short explanation of the disease that you might distribute to people in the area to help prevent new cases. Your explanation should include the cause of the disease, how the disease is transmitted, and steps that people can take to prevent the spread of the disease. (*Hint:* Review **Figure 27–10** to recall how the disease is spread.)

Performance-Based Assessment

Worm Autobiography You are a reporter for a local newspaper and are working on the children's activity section. You decide to feature different animals as if each one were writing its autobiography. The first feature is entitled "A Day in the Life of an Earthworm." Include in your autobiography how the worm performs each of the life functions, its habitat, its importance, and illustrations. The reading level of the article should be fourth or fifth grade.

For: An interactive self-test
Visit: PHSchool.com
Web Code: cba-8270

Standards Practice

Online at PHSchool.com

Test-Taking Tip For questions containing the words NOT, EXCEPT, and so on, begin by eliminating each answer choice that *does* fit the characteristic in question. After eliminating the choices, check to see that your answer is correct by confirming that it does not fit the characteristic in question.

Directions: Choose the letter that best answers the question or completes the statement.

1. All of the following are mollusks EXCEPT
A leeches. **C** octopi.
B squids. **D** clams.

2. Which invertebrates have segmented bodies?
A flatworms
B roundworms
C planarians
D annelids

3. Which are NOT parasitic roundworms?
A hookworms
B filarial worms
C ascarid worms
D tapeworms

4. The body cavity in annelids is called a(an)
A coelom.
B pseudocoelom.
C scolex.
D trochophore.

5. A scientist conducts an experiment to test the hypothesis that earthworms aid in the growth of plant roots. She grows two identical plants in pots A and B but adds earthworms only to pot B. Which of the following is true about the experiment?
A There is no control.
B There is no difference between pots A and B.
C Either pot could serve as the control.
D Pot A is the control.

6. The simplest animal to develop from three germ layers belongs in the phylum
A Mollusca. **C** Platyhelminthes.
B Annelida. **D** Nematoda.

7. Water balance is maintained in the body of a planarian by
A nephridia.
B flame cells.
C proglottids.
D scolex.

8. Which characteristics apply to flatworms?
I. Cephalization
II. Bilateral symmetry
III. Segmented bodies
A I only
B II only
C I and II only
D II and III only

Questions 9–12 Use the lettered choices below to answer questions 9–12. Select the best lettered choice. A choice may be used once, more than once, or not at all.

A Flatworms
B Roundworms
C Annelids
D Mollusks

9. Includes gastropods, bivalves, and cephalopods

10. Has internal walls, or septa, between body segments

11. Has a pseudocoelom

12. Includes turbellarians, flukes, and tapeworms

Questions 13–14

Observe that this planarian has two heads. Use your knowledge about flatworms to answer the questions that follow.

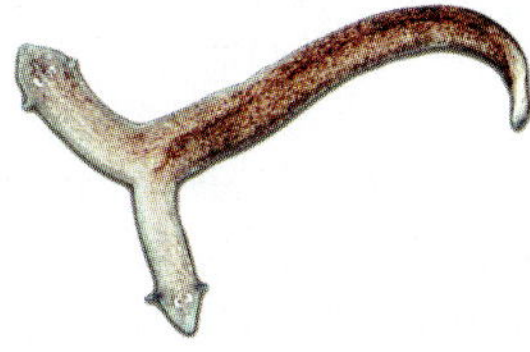

13. The process illustrated in the diagram is known as
A fission.
B sexual reproduction.
C scolex.
D hermaphroditism.

14. Two spots on the heads of the planarian are sensitive to
A heat.
B light.
C sound.
D chemicals.

Standards Practice

1. A	**5.** D	**9.** D	**13.** A
2. D	**6.** C	**10.** C	**14.** B
3. D	**7.** B	**11.** B	
4. A	**8.** C	**12.** A	

Success Tracker™

Online at PHSchool.com

Have students check their understanding of the chapter by logging onto Success Tracker.

Performance-Based Assessment

Details of students' features may vary, but each should include simple drawings of earthworms, one of which should be similar to the labeled drawing in Figure 27–16. Each feature should reflect a thorough understanding of the importance and ecology of earthworms, as explained in the text on page 699.

Go Online PHSchool.com

Your students can independently test their knowledge of the chapter and print out their test results for your files.

Chapter Planner 28 Arthropods and Echinoderms

Section and Section Objectives	Time	STANDARDS NCLB	STANDARDS Biology	Activities and Labs
28–1 Introduction to the Arthropods, pp. 715–719 **28.1.1** ***Identify*** the defining features of arthropods. **28.1.2** ***Describe*** the important trends in arthropod evolution. **28.1.3** ***Explain*** growth and development in arthropods.	1 period (1/2 block)			**SE:** ***Inquiry Activity,*** What is an arthropod?, p. 714 L2 **TE:** ***Make Connections,*** p. 716 L2 **TE:** ***Build Science Skills,*** pp. 716 L2 L3, 717 L2 L3, 719 L2 L3 **SE:** ***Quick Lab,*** Do crickets respond to odors?, p. 718 L2
28–2 Groups of Arthropods, pp. 720–725 **28.2.1** ***Explain*** how arthropods are classified. **28.2.2** ***Identify*** the distinguishing features of the three subphyla of arthropods.	2 periods (1 block)			**TE:** ***Build Science Skills,*** pp. 720 L2, 721 L2, 722 L2, 723 L2 L3, 723 L3, 723 L2 L3, 724 L1 L2 **SE:** ***Analyzing Data,*** Ticks and Lyme Disease, p. 724 L2
28–3 Insects, pp. 726–733 **28.3.1** ***Identify*** the distinguishing features of insects. **28.3.2** ***Describe*** two types of development in insects. **28.3.3** ***Explain*** what types of insects form societies.	2 periods (1 block)			**TE:** ***Build Science Skills,*** pp. 727 L2 L3, 728 L2 L3, 731 L1 L2 **SE:** ***Biology and History,*** Insect-Borne Diseases, pp. 730–731 L2 **TE:** ***Demonstration,*** pp. 731 L1, 732 L2 L3 **SE:** ***Design an Experiment,*** Observing Ant Behavior, p. 739 L2 L3 **IF:** Investigation 8 L2 L3 **LMA/B:** Chapter 28 Lab L2 L3 / L1 L2
28–4 Echinoderms, pp. 734–738 **28.4.1** ***Identify*** the distinguishing features of echinoderms. **28.4.2** ***Describe*** the functions carried out by the water vascular system of echinoderms. **28.4.3** ***Compare*** the different classes of echinoderms.	1 period (1/2 block)			**TE:** ***Demonstration,*** p. 735 L2 **TE:** ***Build Science Skills,*** p. 736 L2 L3 **TE:** ***Build Science Skills,*** p. 736 L2 L3 **TE:** ***Build Science Skills,*** p. 737 L2 **BTM:** Lab 7 L2 L3
Chapter Assessment, pp. 740–743	1 period (1/2 block)			

ACTIVITY PLANNER

SE: *Inquiry Activity*, p. 714; 10 min.; specimens or photos of arthropods, specimens or photos of other animals, hand lenses

TE: *Make Connections*, p. 716; 10 min.; fossils of trilobites

TE: *Build Science Skills*, p. 716; 20 min.; grasshopper in a small container, crayfish in a water basin, lettuce, small piece of bologna, hand lens

TE: *Build Science Skills*, p. 717; 10 min.; book, large paper clips, ruler

SE: *Quick Lab*, p. 718; 15 min.; live crickets in terrarium, wooden blocks

TE: *Build Science Skills*, p. 719; 30 min.; shovel or spade, gloves, shoebox

TE: *Build Science Skills*, p. 720; 15 min.; live lobster in a clear container

TE: *Build Science Skills*, p. 721; 15 min.; raw shrimp, hand lens, gloves

TE: *Build Science Skills*, p. 722; 15 min.; photos or slides of chelicerates

TE: *Build Science Skills*, p. 723; 30 min.; model-making materials

TE: *Build Science Skills*, p. 723; 20 min.; enamel spray paint, white construction paper, scissors

TE: *Meet Diverse Needs*, p. 724; 15 min.; specimens of uniramians

TE: *Build Science Skills*, p. 727; 30 min.; fruit flies, light source, meter stick

TE: *Build Science Skills*, p. 728; 15 min.; grasshopper, lens, gloves

TE: *Demonstration*, p. 731; 5 min.; fingernail file, index card, balloon

TE: *Demonstration*, p. 732; 20 min.; honey, spoon, sheet of paper

TE: *Demonstration*, p. 735; 15 min.; preserved sea star, gloves, goggles

TE: *Build Science Skills*, p. 736; 10 min.; small suction cup

TE: *Build Science Skills*, p. 736; 15 min.; sea star, tray, lens, gloves

SE: *Design an Experiment*, p. 739; 45 min.; ants of the same species from two colonies, ants of a second species, petri dishes with covers, hand lens, field guide, watch or clock with a second hand, disposable plastic gloves

PLANNING KEY

Ability Levels
for students performing . . .
below grade level L1
at grade level L2
above grade level L3

Print Components

SE Student Edition
TE Teacher's Edition
RSW Reading & Study Workbook A
ARSW Adapted Reading & Study Workbook B
TR Teaching Resources
IF Investigations in Forensics
LA Lab Assessment
BTM Biotechnology Manual
IDM Issues and Decision Making
LW Lab Worksheets
LMA Laboratory Manual A
LMB Laboratory Manual B

Tech Components

CTB Computer Test Bank
BD BioDetectives DVD
TP Transparencies Plus
PLM Probeware Lab Manual
ABC ABC DVD Library
LS Lab Simulations
VL Virtual Labs

Interactive textbook with assessment at PHSchool.com

Program Resources	Assessment	Media and Technology
TR: Lesson Plan 28–1, Section Summary, p. 95 L1, p. 107 L2, Worksheets, p. 98 L1, pp. 109–111 L2 **RSW:** Section 28–1 L2 **ARSW:** Section 28–1 L1	**SE:** 28–1 Section Assessment, p. 719 **TR:** Section Review 28–1	**iText:** Section 28–1 **TP:** 28–1 Interest Grabber, Section Outline, Concept Map, Figure 28–4
TR: Lesson Plan 28–2, Section Summary, p. 95 L1, p. 107 L2, Worksheets, pp. 99–101 L1, pp. 112–114 L2 **RSW:** Section 28–2 L2 **ARSW:** Section 28–2 L1	**SE:** 28–2 Section Assessment, p. 725 **TR:** Section Review 28–2	**iText:** Section 28–2 **TP:** 28–2 Interest Grabber, Section Outline, Anatomy of a Crayfish, Figure 28–9 **ABC:** 36 Crayfish Anatomy
TR: Lesson Plan 28–3, Section Summary, p. 96 L1, p. 108 L2, Worksheets, pp. 102–104 L1, pp. 115–117 L2, Enrichment L3 **LW:** Chapter 28 Experiment L1 L2 L3 **RSW:** Section 28–3 L2 **ARSW:** Section 28–3 L1	**SE:** 28–3 Section Assessment, p. 733 **TR:** Section Review 28–3	**iText:** Section 28–3 **TP:** 28–3 Interest Grabber, Section Outline, Insect Diversity, Figure 28–18 **BD:** "Insect Clues: The Smallest Witnesses"
TR: Lesson Plan 28–4, Section Summary, p. 97 L1, p. 108 L2, Worksheets, p. 105 L1, pp. 118–119 L2 **RSW:** Section 28–4 L2 **ARSW:** Section 28–4 L1 **IDM:** Issues and Decisions 30 L2 L3	**SE:** 28–4 Section Assessment, p. 738 **TR:** Section Review 28–4	**iText:** Section 28–4 **TP:** 28–4 Interest Grabber, Section Outline, Compare/Contrast Table, Figure 28–23
	SE: Chapter 28 Assessment, pp. 740–743 **TR:** Chapter Vocabulary Review, Graphic Organizer, Chapter 28 Test	**iText:** Chapter 28 Assessment **CTB:** Chapter 28 Test

Go Online
Students can do research, share data, and test their knowledge online.

PRESSED FOR TIME?

To Preview the Chapter
- Introduce students to Key Concepts and Vocabulary terms in each section.
- Assign the Reading Strategies for each section.

To Cover the Chapter Quickly
- Have students read all of Section 28–1, the introduction to Section 28–2, What Is an Insect? in Section 28–3, and all of Section 28–4.
- Assign Section Review 28–1 and Section Review 28–4, as well as questions 1–5, 8–10, 11–13, 20, 21, 23–25, and 27–35 in Chapter 28 Assessment and questions 1–10 in Chapter 28 Standards Practice.

To Review the Chapter
- Assign Sections 28–1 through 28–4 in the Reading and Study Workbook or the Adapted Reading and Study Workbook.
- Assign Section Reviews for 28–1 through 28–4 and the Chapter Vocabulary Review for Chapter 28 in the Teaching Resources.

CHAPTER 28

ENGAGE/EXPLORE

Inquiry Activity

Objective Students will be able to write an operational definition of *arthropod* in their own words. L2

Skill Focus **Forming Operational Definitions, Classifying**

Materials variety of specimens or photographs of arthropods, several specimens or photographs of animals that are not arthropods, hand lenses

Time 10 minutes

Advance Prep Collect a variety of specimens, such as an ant, a grasshopper, spider, millipede, centipede, and crayfish. Also collect other kinds of animals, such as an earthworm, a planarian, snail, and starfish. Try to supply as many actual specimens as possible.

Safety If you use actual organisms rather than photos, students should wear disposable plastic gloves. Make sure that students do not harm the animals and that they wash their hands with soap and warm water after handling them. Dispose of the plastic gloves after the activity.

Strategy
Have students use hand lenses to examine the specimens.

Expected Outcomes Students will observe the characteristics of arthropods.

Think About It
1. Accept any reasonable definition at this point. After students have read Section 28–1, have them revise their definitions on the basis of what they have learned.
2. Accept all reasonable classifications based on observable characteristics.

Assess Prior Knowledge

Point out that insects are arthropods. Ask students first to identify some insects and then to describe general characteristics of insects. Write their responses on the board. After they have read Sections 28–2 and 28–3, have students revise their ideas as necessary.

CHAPTER 28

Arthropods and Echinoderms

The zebra swallowtail butterfly is one of more than 750,000 species of arthropods—the largest phylum of animals.

Inquiry Activity

What is an arthropod?

Procedure  

1. Put on plastic gloves. Examine a variety of specimens or photographs of arthropods. Make a list of features that all of these organisms have in common.
2. Look at some animals that are not arthropods. Make a list of features that all of these organisms have in common. Compare the two lists.
3. Wash your hands with soap and warm water.

Think About It

1. **Forming Operational Definitions** Write a definition of the term *arthropod.* Include in your definition at least two characteristics that all arthropods share but most other animals do not.
2. **Classifying** Classify the arthropods you observed into two or more groups. Which characteristics did you use to distinguish the groups?

FACTS AND FIGURES

A flexible exoskeleton
The chitin that forms arthropod exoskeletons is more flexible than the calcium carbonate of which mollusk shells are made. Chitin can be molded into a variety of shapes and is less cumbersome to carry around. The chitinous exoskeleton provides the same support as a mollusk shell but does not restrict the animal's mobility. To get these advantages, however, arthropods have had to sacrifice a measure of safety. While mollusks are able to add on to their existing shells, arthropods can retain their flexibility only by molting and growing a new exoskeleton. They must do this several times during their growth and are vulnerable each time as the new exoskeleton hardens. Insect wings, such as those of butterflies, are also made of chitin. These appendages are composed of thin sheets of chitin over a framework of hollow veins.

28–1 Introduction to the Arthropods

If you have ever admired a spider's web, watched the flight of a butterfly, or eaten shrimp, you have had close encounters with members of the phylum Arthropoda (ahr-THRAHP-oh-duh). In terms of evolutionary success, which can be measured as the number of living species, arthropods are the most diverse and successful animals of all time. At least three quarters of a million species have been identified—more than three times the number of all other animal species combined!

What Is an Arthropod?

Arthropods include animals such as insects, crabs, centipedes, and spiders. **Arthropods have a segmented body, a tough exoskeleton, and jointed appendages.** Like annelids, arthropods have bodies that are divided into segments. The number of these segments varies among groups of arthropods.

Arthropods are also surrounded by a tough external covering, or **exoskeleton.** The exoskeleton is like a suit of armor that protects and supports the body. It is made from protein and a carbohydrate called **chitin** (KY-tun). Exoskeletons vary greatly in size, shape, and toughness. The exoskeletons of caterpillars are firm and leathery, whereas those of crabs and lobsters are so tough and hard that they are almost impossible to crush by hand. The exoskeletons of many terrestrial, or land-dwelling, species have a waxy covering that helps prevent the loss of body water. Terrestrial arthropods, like all animals that live entirely on land, need adaptations that hold water inside their bodies.

All arthropods have jointed appendages. **Appendages** are structures such as legs and antennae that extend from the body wall. Jointed appendages are so distinctive of arthropods that the phylum is named for them: *arthron* means "joint" in Greek, and *podos* means "foot."

Guide for Reading

Key Concepts
- What are the main features of arthropods?
- What are the important trends in arthropod evolution?
- What happens when an arthropod outgrows its exoskeleton?

Vocabulary
exoskeleton
chitin
appendage
tracheal tube
spiracle
book lung
Malpighian tubule
molting

Reading Strategy: Finding Main Ideas Before you read, skim the section to find the three boldface sentences. Copy each sentence onto a notecard. As you read, make notes of supporting details.

Figure 28–1 Arthropods such as the cave millipede have a body usually composed of segments, a tough exoskeleton, and jointed appendages. Observe the millipede's legs, which are adapted for walking.

TIME SAVER — SECTION RESOURCES

Print:
- ***Teaching Resources,*** Lesson Plan 28–1, Adapted Section Summary 28–1, Adapted Worksheets 28–1, Section Summary 28–1, Worksheets 28–1, Section Review 28–1
- ***Reading and Study Workbook A,*** Section 28–1
- ***Adapted Reading and Study Workbook B,*** Section 28–1

Technology:
- ***iText,*** Section 28–1
- ***Transparencies Plus,*** Section 28–1

Section 28–1

1 FOCUS

Objectives

28.1.1 ***Identify*** the defining features of arthropods.
28.1.2 ***Describe*** the important trends in arthropod evolution.
28.1.3 ***Explain*** growth and development of arthropods.

Guide for Reading

Vocabulary Preview

Explain that the prefix *ex-* derives from a Latin word meaning "out of." Thus, an *exoskeleton* is a skeleton that is "out of" the body, or on the outside of the body. The word *exit,* meaning a way "out of" a room, derives from the same Latin word.

Reading Strategy

Have students make an outline of the section, using the blue heads as the first level of the outline and the green heads as the second level.

2 INSTRUCT

What Is an Arthropod?

Use Visuals

Figure 28–1 Make sure students understand the meaning of the term *appendage* at this point. Explain that, basically, an appendage is an "attachment" to a body segment of an arthropod. Refer students to the photo, and point out that each pair of the millipede's legs is a pair of appendages attached to a segment. In the case of a millipede, each abdominal segment has two pairs of legs. Explain that in most arthropods, segments have fused and appendages have become modified to perform many functions other than locomotion. In a crayfish, the first two appendages are antennae. Another pair of appendages, the first pair of legs, bear large claws used for defense and to catch, pick up, crush, and cut food. L2

28–1 (continued)

Evolution of Arthropods

Make Connections

Earth Science Show students one or more fossils of trilobites, and have them observe the structure of these early arthropods. Review the process by which fossils are formed. Then, explain that trilobites became extinct at the end of the Permian Period, about 245 million years ago. Geologists and paleontologists use trilobite fossils to date rocks and correlate rock formations in different locations. Fossils that can be used in dating are called index fossils. An index fossil is a fossil that is associated with a particular span of geologic time. If a rock formation contains a trilobite fossil, it can be dated as having formed before 245 million years ago. L2

Form and Function in Arthropods

Build Science Skills

Comparing and Contrasting Divide the class into small groups, and give each group a grasshopper in a small container, a crayfish in water in a basin, lettuce, and a small piece of bologna. Have students place the lettuce in the grasshopper's container and use a hand lens to observe the grasshopper's mouthparts as it eats. Then, have students place the bologna into the basin and observe with a hand lens the crayfish's mouthparts as it eats. Ask students to make drawings of what they observe and write a comparison of the structures of these arthropods' mouthparts. L2 L3

▲ **Figure 28–2** Trilobites, such as the fossilized one shown above, were marine arthropods that were abundant more than 500 million years ago. They were divided into many body segments, each with a walking leg. Trilobites became extinct some 200 million years ago. **Living arthropods generally have fewer body segments and more specialized appendages than ancestral arthropods.**

Evolution of Arthropods

The first arthropods appeared in the sea more than 600 million years ago. Since then, arthropods have moved into all parts of the sea, most freshwater habitats, the land, and the air. **The evolution of arthropods, by natural selection and other processes, has led to fewer body segments and highly specialized appendages for feeding, movement, and other functions.**

A typical primitive arthropod was composed of many identical segments, each carrying a pair of appendages. Its body probably closely resembled that of a trilobite (TRY-loh-byt), shown in **Figure 28–2.** This early body plan was modified gradually. Body segments were lost or fused over time. Most living arthropods, such as spiders and insects, have only two or three body segments. Arthropod appendages also evolved into different forms that are adapted in ways that enable them to perform different functions. These appendages include antennae, claws, walking legs, wings, flippers, mouthparts, tails, and other specialized structures.

These gradual changes in arthropods are similar to the changes in modern cars since the Model T, the first mass-produced automobile. The Model T had all the basic components, such as an internal combustion engine, wheels, and a frame. Over time, the design and style of each component changed, producing cars as different as off-road vehicles, sedans, and sports cars. Similarly, modifications to the arthropod body plan have produced creatures as different as a tick and a lobster.

Form and Function in Arthropods

Arthropods use complex organ systems to carry out different essential functions. As with all animals, organ systems are interrelated; the functioning of one system depends on that of other systems. For example, the digestive system breaks food into nutrient molecules, which then move into blood in the circulatory system. The blood carries the nutrients to body cells.

Feeding Arthropods include herbivores, carnivores, and omnivores. There are arthropod bloodsuckers, filter feeders, detritivores, and parasites. Arthropod mouthparts have evolved in ways that enable different species to eat almost any food you can imagine. Their mouthparts range from pincers or fangs to sickle-shaped jaws that can cut through the tissues of captured prey. The mouthparts of a nut weevil are shown in **Figure 28–3.**

◀ **Figure 28–3** This photo of a nut weevil illustrates how its mouthparts are adapted in ways that enable it to bore into and eat nuts. **Applying Concepts** *Do you think a nut weevil would be able to capture and eat other arthropods? Explain your answer.*

UNIVERSAL ACCESS

Inclusion/Special Needs

Have students make a table with two columns. The left column should have the label Essential Functions. Before reading, have students list in that column the seven physiological processes animals need to carry out. The right column should have the label Arthropod Form and Function. Have students complete this column as they read the section. Explain that they should make notes about important concepts and terms in that column. L1

Less Proficient Readers

Read the subsection Form and Function in Arthropods aloud. Stop after you have read about each function and refer to Figure 28–4. Call on volunteers to read the labels on the figure that are associated with each function. For instance, after you read about feeding in arthropods, students should identify the mouth and digestive tract. After you read about respiration, students should identify the tracheal tubes and spiracles, and so on through the functions. L1 L2

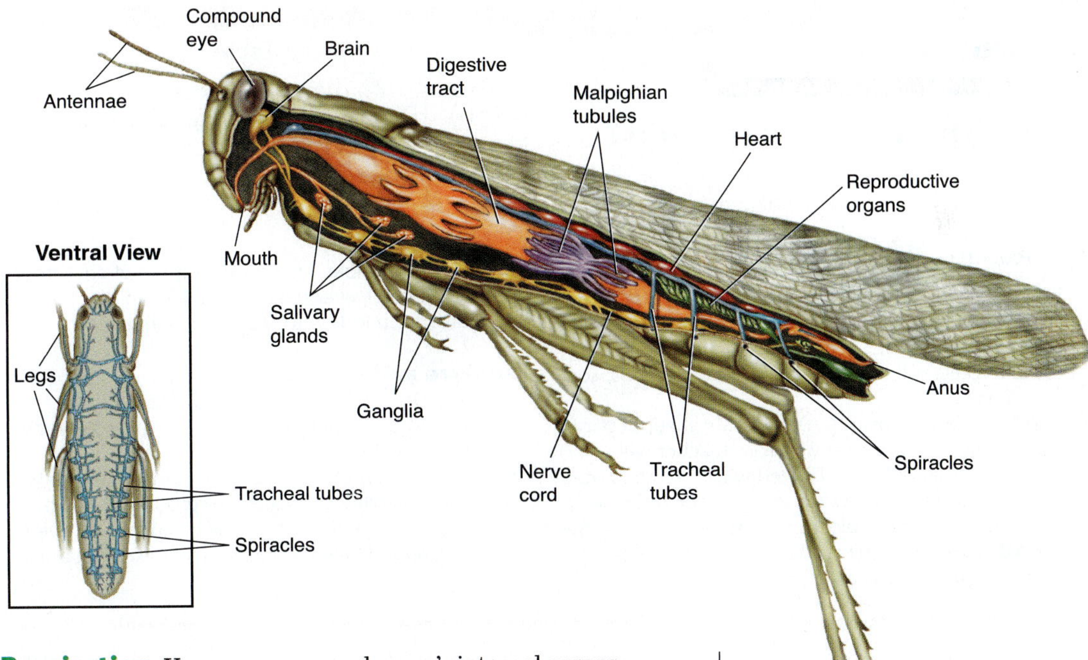

Respiration You can see a grasshopper's internal organs, including those used for respiration, in **Figure 28–4.** Most terrestrial arthropods breathe through a network of branching **tracheal** (TRAY-kee-ul) **tubes** that extend throughout the body. Air enters and leaves the tracheal tubes through **spiracles** (SPEER-uh-kulz), which are small openings located along the side of the body. Other terrestrial arthropods, such as spiders, respire using book lungs. **Book lungs** are organs that have layers of respiratory tissue stacked like the pages of a book. Most aquatic arthropods, such as lobsters and crabs, respire through featherlike gills. The horseshoe crabs, however, respire through organs called book gills.

Circulation Arthropods have an open circulatory system. A well-developed heart pumps blood through arteries that branch and enter the tissues. Blood leaves the blood vessels and moves through sinuses, or cavities. The blood then collects in a large sinus surrounding the heart. From there, it re-enters the heart and is again pumped through the body.

Excretion Most terrestrial arthropods, such as insects and spiders, dispose of nitrogenous wastes using Malpighian (mal-PIG-ee-un) tubules. **Malpighian tubules** are saclike organs that extract wastes from the blood and then add them to feces, or digestive wastes, that move through the gut. In aquatic arthropods, diffusion moves cellular wastes from the arthropod's body into the surrounding water.

CHECKPOINT *What is the function of Malpighian tubules?*

▲ **Figure 28–4** The grasshopper has organ systems typical of most arthropods. These organ systems carry out functions such as circulation, excretion, response, and movement. Arthropods have several different types of respiratory organs. In insects, tracheal tubes (inset) move air throughout the tissues of the body. **Interpreting Graphics** *Where is the grasshopper's nerve cord located?*

For: Links on arthropods
Visit: www.SciLinks.org
Web Code: cbn-8281

Use Visuals

Figure 28–4 Point out that this grasshopper is a representative arthropod and that other members of the phylum have somewhat different structures. Explain that a grasshopper, which is an insect, has three body sections. From front to back, the sections are called the head, thorax, and abdomen. Point out that all three pairs of legs, as well as the pair of wings, are attached to the grasshopper's thorax, as in all insects. Then, call on volunteers to explain the function of each of the labeled parts of this arthropod. L2

Build Science Skills

Using Models Help students understand that book lungs provide a large surface area for gas exchange, by having them compare the surface areas of an open book and a closed book. First, ask students to calculate the total surface area of the front and back covers of a book. Then, have them divide that book into 10 sections, holding the pages together with large paper clips. Ask students to calculate the total surface area of the book with the page surfaces exposed. Students will find that the total surface area of the divided book is 10 times that of the closed book.

L2 L3

Download a worksheet on arthropods for students to complete, and find additional teacher support from NSTA SciLinks.

TEACHER TO TEACHER

When introducing arthropod form and function, have students determine how different arthropods get rid of their waste products. Students should correlate the environment in which each arthropod lives to the method it uses for getting rid of wastes. Correlations should also be made for respiration, circulation, method of movement, and reproduction. This application will also help students to better understand the role the environment plays in evolution.

—*Wendy Peterson*
Biology Teacher
Velva High School
Velva, ND

Answers to . . .

CHECKPOINT *Malpighian tubules extract wastes from the blood.*

Figure 28–3 *No, because the structure of a weevil's mouthparts is adapted to drilling and piercing, not grasping and crushing.*

Figure 28–4 *The nerve cord is located in the ventral part of the grasshopper's body.*

28–1 (continued)

Quick Lab

Objective Students will be able to draw a conclusion about how responses to odor help crickets survive. L2

Skill Focus **Observing, Inferring, Drawing Conclusions**

Materials live crickets in terrarium, wooden blocks

Time 15 minutes

Advance Prep Crickets can be purchased inexpensively at a pet shop or bait shop. Place the crickets in a screen-covered aquarium or other transparent container. Rub one wooden block with fresh grass clippings or freshly chopped leaves. Rub a second block with moist soil. Soak a third block overnight in water with hair or feathers. Leave the fourth block unscented. Label each block with the name of its odor.

Safety Students should wear disposable plastic gloves if they handle the crickets. Dispose of the gloves properly after the activity. Make sure students wash their hands with soap and warm water before leaving the lab. Caution students to be careful not to injure the crickets. Some students may have allergies; check before selecting leaves and other materials for their odor.

Strategies You may want to make a data table on the chalkboard or an overhead projector so that students or groups can record data for the whole class.

Expected Outcomes Crickets will avoid blocks scented with hair or feathers and climb mostly on the one rubbed with grass clippings.

Analyze and Conclude

1. Students should observe that crickets prefer the block rubbed with grass clippings.
2. The crickets' preference for a particular block and avoidance of others indicates that they can respond to odors.
3. Odors provide clues to where foods such as grass and predators such as insect-eating mammals or birds are located. Crickets can respond to these cues by following them toward food and away from predators.

Quick Lab

Do crickets respond to odors?

Materials live crickets in terrarium, wooden blocks

Procedure  

1. **Predicting** Crickets are common in grassy areas. They eat leaves and are eaten by mice, some birds, and other animals. Record a prediction of how the crickets will respond to the odors of grass, soil, and hair.
2. Put on plastic gloves. On a separate sheet of paper, copy the data table shown. Your teacher will provide a set of blocks labeled with the odors they carry. Place the blocks in the container with the crickets so that the blocks do not touch each other. **CAUTION:** *Place the blocks in the container gently to avoid injuring the crickets.*

Data Table

Time (min)	Number of Crickets			
	Grass	Soil	Hair	Control
1				
2				

3. In your data table, record the number of crickets on each block every minute for 10 minutes.
4. Wash your hands with soap and warm water.

Analyze and Conclude

1. **Observing** Did the crickets tend to climb on some blocks more than others? If so, which blocks did they prefer?
2. **Inferring** What can you infer from these results about the ability of crickets to respond to odors?
3. **Drawing Conclusions** How could the behavior you observed help crickets survive? Explain your answer.

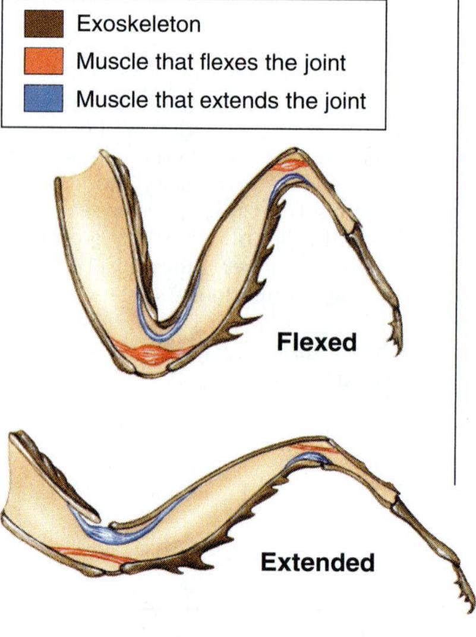

▲ **Figure 28–5** This diagrammatic representation shows how muscles attached to the exoskeleton bend and straighten the joints. (Actual muscles are much larger than those shown here.) **Applying Concepts** *How are muscles controlled and coordinated?*

Response Most arthropods have a well-developed nervous system. All arthropods have a brain. The brain serves as a central switchboard that receives incoming information and then sends outgoing instructions to muscles. Two nerves that encircle the esophagus connect the brain to a ventral nerve cord. Along this nerve cord are several ganglia, or groups of nerve cells. These ganglia coordinate the movements of individual legs and wings. Most arthropods have sophisticated sense organs, such as compound eyes for gathering information from the environment. Compound eyes may have more than 2000 separate lenses and can detect color and motion very well.

Movement Arthropods move using well-developed groups of muscles that are coordinated and controlled by the nervous system. In arthropods and other animals, muscles are made up of individual muscle cells. Muscle cells can contract, or become shorter, when stimulated by nerves. Other cells in animals' bodies do not have this ability. Muscles generate force by contracting and then pulling on the exoskeleton.

At each body joint, different muscles either flex (bend) or extend (straighten) the joint. This process is diagrammed in **Figure 28–5.** The pull of muscles against the exoskeleton allows arthropods to beat their wings against the air to fly, push their legs against the ground to walk, or beat their flippers against the water to swim.

CHECKPOINT *How do arthropods move?*

FACTS AND FIGURES

For arthropods, every decision is a no-brainer One of the great differences between animals such as arthropods and "higher" animals is the fact that the responses of arthropods depend only on the various stimuli received by their nerves. Although arthropods have a well-developed nervous system and a simple brain, it is a mistake to attribute "thought" to these animals. Unlike some animals, arthropods do not depend on "thought" or "decision making"; most behaviors are genetically programmed. Their reactions in a particular situation are almost totally predictable. Aristotle, the great observational scientist, was the first to notice that wasps can remain alive and at almost normal activity levels even when their heads have been removed.

Reproduction Terrestrial arthropods have internal fertilization. In some species, males have a reproductive organ that places sperm inside females. In other species, the males deposit a sperm packet that is picked up by the females. Aquatic arthropods may have internal or external fertilization. External fertilization takes place outside the female's body. It occurs when females release eggs into the external environment and males shed sperm around the eggs.

Growth and Development in Arthropods

An exoskeleton does not grow as the animal grows. Imagine that you are wearing a suit of armor fitted exactly to your measurements. Think of it not only as skintight but as part of your skin. What would happen when you grew taller and wider? Arthropods have this same difficulty. **When they outgrow their exoskeletons, arthropods undergo periods of molting.** During **molting,** an arthropod sheds its entire exoskeleton and manufactures a larger one to take its place. Molting is controlled by the arthropod's endocrine system. An animal's endocrine system regulates body processes by means of chemicals called hormones.

As the time for molting approaches, skin glands digest the inner part of the exoskeleton, and other glands secrete a new skeleton. When the new exoskeleton is ready, the animal pulls itself out of what remains of the original skeleton, as shown in **Figure 28–6.** This process can take several hours. While the new exoskeleton is still soft, the animal fills with air or fluids to allow room for growth before the next molting. Most arthropods molt several times between hatching and adulthood. This process is dangerous to the animal because it is vulnerable to predators while its shell is soft. To protect themselves, arthropods typically hide during the molting period or molt at night.

▲ **Figure 28–6** **When they become too large for their exoskeletons, arthropods undergo periods of molting.** This cicada has just molted and is climbing out of its old exoskeleton.

28–1 Section Assessment

1. **Key Concept** What are the main features of arthropods?
2. **Key Concept** What is the evolutionary trend for segmentation in arthropods?
3. **Key Concept** How is the process of molting related to growth in arthropods?
4. What body system controls molting?
5. How are both the circulatory and excretory systems involved in removing nitrogenous wastes from an arthropod's body?
6. **Critical Thinking** **Comparing and Contrasting** How are the muscle cells of arthropods and other animals different from other body cells? How does this difference enable movement?

Focus on the BIG Idea

Cellular Basis of Life Use what you learned about cellular respiration in Chapter 9 to explain why every cell in an arthropod's body needs oxygen. Then, describe how the respiratory system delivers the needed oxygen.

Growth and Development in Arthropods

Build Science Skills

Observing Have students investigate what types of arthropods live in soil. Take the class outdoors to a field, vacant lot, or wooded area. Divide the class into small groups, and have each group mark a 0.5-m^2 area on the ground. Have students put on disposable plastic gloves. Then, let students dig up the soil to a depth of 8–10 centimeters and examine it for living arthropods and molted exoskeletons. Caution students not to touch living arthropods. Challenge students to identify as many arthropods as they can on their own and by using field guides. L2 L3

3 ASSESS

Evaluate Understanding

Call on students to explain how arthropods carry out the seven essential functions: feeding, respiration, circulation, excretion, response, movement, and reproduction.

Reteach

Have students make their own drawing of the grasshopper shown in Figure 28–4. Then, help them to classify each label in the drawing according to which of the seven essential functions it is related to.

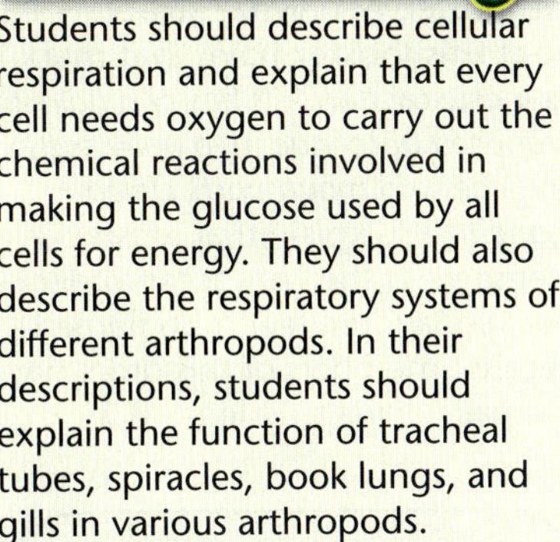

Focus on the BIG Idea

Students should describe cellular respiration and explain that every cell needs oxygen to carry out the chemical reactions involved in making the glucose used by all cells for energy. They should also describe the respiratory systems of different arthropods. In their descriptions, students should explain the function of tracheal tubes, spiracles, book lungs, and gills in various arthropods.

28–1 Section Assessment

1. Arthropods have a segmented body, a tough exoskeleton, and jointed appendages.
2. The evolution of arthropods has led to fewer body segments in some groups.
3. During molting, an arthropod sheds its entire exoskeleton and manufactures a larger one to take its place. This process creates room for growth.
4. The endocrine system
5. In most terrestrial arthropods, wastes from cells move through the circulatory system to the Malpighian tubules, which extract wastes from blood.
6. Muscle cells can contract when stimulated by nerves. Muscles generate force by contracting and then pulling on the exoskeleton.

Answers to . . .

CHECKPOINT *They use well-developed groups of muscles that generate force by pulling on the exoskeleton.*

Figure 28–5 *The nervous system controls and coordinates the action of muscles.*

Section 28–2

1 FOCUS

Objectives

28.2.1 ***Explain*** how arthropods are classified.

28.2.2 ***Identify*** the distinguishing features of the three subphyla of arthropods.

Guide for Reading

Vocabulary Preview

Pronounce each Vocabulary word, and have students repeat the pronunciation as a class. Pay special attention to words that are difficult for English language learners.

Reading Strategy

Have students preview Figures 28–8 and 28–9 and write down questions about any differences they observe. Then, as they read, they should try to answer their questions from the information in the section.

2 INSTRUCT

Crustaceans

Build Science Skills

Observing Display a live lobster in a clear container. Encourage students to examine the lobster closely and make labeled sketches of what they see. Caution students not to touch the lobster. Ask: **What structures does this lobster have that mark it as a crustacean?** *(It has two pairs of branched antennae, two body sections, and chewing mouthparts called mandibles.)* Explain that lobsters are members of the crustacean order Decapoda ("ten feet"), so named because members of this order have five pairs of walking legs. L2

Download a worksheet on crustaceans for students to complete, and find additional teacher support from NSTA SciLinks.

28–2 Groups of Arthropods

Guide for Reading

Key Concepts
- How are arthropods classified?
- What are the distinguishing features of the three major groups of arthropods?

Vocabulary
cephalothorax
thorax
abdomen
carapace
mandible
cheliped
swimmeret
chelicera
pedipalp
spinneret

Reading Strategy: Building Vocabulary
Before you read, preview new vocabulary by skimming the section and making a list of the highlighted, boldface terms. Leave space to make notes as you read.

For: Links on crustaceans
Visit: www.SciLinks.org
Web Code: cbn-8282

You are a naturalist sent to the rain forests of Brazil to bring back a representative sample of arthropods from the region. As you search the forest, your collection grows to include an astonishing array of arthropods—butterflies several centimeters across, armored wormlike animals that move about using dozens of legs, and beetles that defend themselves by shooting out a stream of poisonous liquid. You must organize your collection before you return home, but you do not know how all these arthropod species are related to one another. Where to begin?

This is the challenge that has faced biologists for many decades—how to catalogue all the world's arthropods. The diversity of arthropods is daunting to any biologist interested in understanding the relationships among organisms. As you will see, however, arthropod classification is based on a few important characteristics. **Arthropods are classified based on the number and structure of their body segments and appendages—particularly their mouthparts.** The three major groups of arthropods are crustaceans, spiders and their relatives, and insects and their relatives.

Crustaceans

Animals in subphylum Crustacea, or crustaceans (krus-TAY-shunz), are primarily aquatic. This subphylum includes organisms such as crabs, shrimps, lobsters, crayfishes, and barnacles. Crustaceans range in size from small terrestrial pill bugs to enormous spider crabs that have masses around 20 kilograms. **Crustaceans typically have two pairs of antennae, two or three body sections, and chewing mouthparts called mandibles.** An example of a crustacean is shown in **Figure 28–7.**

Figure 28–7 **Arthropods are classified based on the number and structure of their body segments and appendages.** The fiddler crab shown here is an example of a crustacean.

SECTION RESOURCES

Print:
- ***Teaching Resources,*** Lesson Plan 28–2, Adapted Section Summary 28–2, Adapted Worksheets 28–2, Section Summary 28–2, Worksheets 28–2, Section Review 28–2
- ***Reading and Study Workbook A,*** Section 28–2
- ***Adapted Reading and Study Workbook B,*** Section 28–2

Technology:
- ***iText,*** Section 28–2
- ***Animated Biological Concepts DVD,*** 36 Crayfish Anatomy
- ***Transparencies Plus,*** Section 28–2

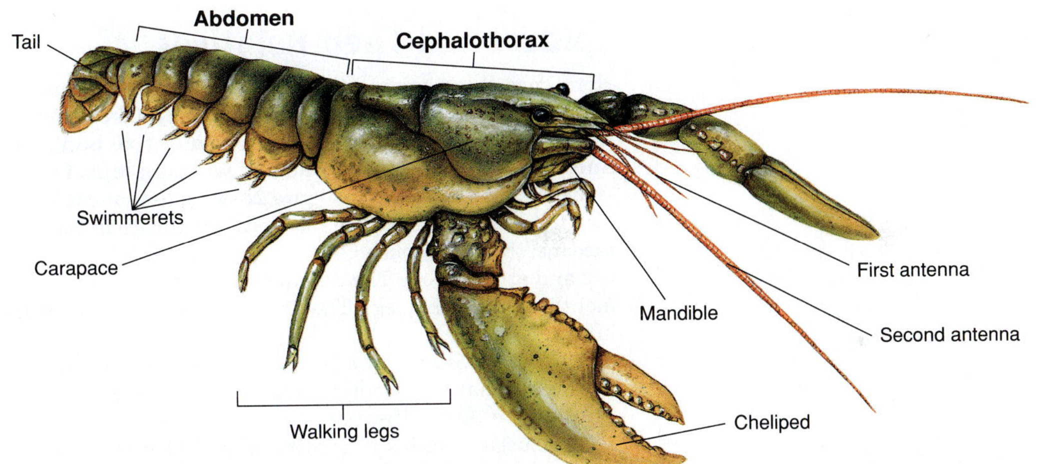

The crayfish, shown in **Figure 28–8,** has a body plan that is typical of many crustaceans. Its body is divided into a cephalothorax (sef-uh-loh-THAWR-aks) and an abdomen. The anterior **cephalothorax** is formed by fusion of the head with the **thorax,** which lies just behind the head and houses most of the internal organs. The **abdomen** is the posterior part of the body. The **carapace** is the part of the exoskeleton that covers the cephalothorax.

Crustacean appendages vary in form and function. The first two pairs of appendages are antennae, which bear many sensory hairs. In crayfish, antennae are primarily sense organs. In other crustaceans, they are used for filter feeding or swimming. The third pair of appendages are the mandibles. A **mandible** is a mouthpart adapted for biting and grinding food. Gills are attached to the appendages associated with the cephalothorax.

Crayfishes, lobsters, and crabs are members of the largest group of crustaceans: the decapods. The decapods have five pairs of legs. In crayfishes, the first pair of legs, called **chelipeds,** bear large claws that are modified to catch, pick up, crush, and cut food. Behind these legs are four pairs of walking legs. Along the abdomen are several pairs of **swimmerets,** which are flipperlike appendages used for swimming. The final abdominal segment is fused with a pair of paddlelike appendages to form a large, flat tail. When the abdominal muscles contract, the crayfish's tail snaps beneath its body. This pushes the animal backward.

The barnacles are another group of crustaceans. Unlike the decapods, barnacles are sessile, or attached to a single spot. Barnacles are crustaceans that have lost their abdominal segments and no longer use mandibles. Because of their outer shell-like coverings, barnacles were once classified as mollusks. Barnacles attach themselves to rocks along the shore and in tide pools. They even attach to the surface of marine animals such as whales. Barnacles use their appendages to capture and draw food particles into their mouths.

✓CHECKPOINT *What are the body sections of a crayfish?*

▲ **Figure 28–8** **Crustaceans typically have two pairs of antennae, two or three body sections, and chewing mouthparts called mandibles.** Notice these structures in this illustration of a crayfish, an aquatic crustacean. Each of the smaller antennae has two branches.

Word Origins

Decapod comes from the Greek word *deka,* meaning "ten," and the Greek word *podos,* meaning "foot." So, *decapod* means "ten-footed." **If *cephalo* means "head," what do you think the term *cephalopod* means?**

Use Visuals

Figure 28–8 Ask students: **What appendages does this crayfish have?** *(Antennae, chelipeds, mandibles, walking legs, and swimmerets)* Emphasize that all crustaceans have two pairs of branched antennae, as shown in the figure. **How does this aquatic arthropod respire?** *(Through featherlike gills)* **Does a crayfish have two or three body sections?** *(Two. The cephalothorax is a fusion of the head and the thorax, and the abdomen is the posterior part of the body.)* L1 L2

Build Science Skills

Observing Provide each student or pair of students with a whole unshelled, raw shrimp. (Students should wear disposable plastic gloves. Caution students not to place their hands near their face or mouth after handling the shrimp and to wash their hands with soap and warm water when they have completed their observations.) Have each student use a hand lens to observe the crustacean. Then, students should sketch the shrimp's body, note any appendages, and label all parts that can be identified. Once students have finished their sketches, ask: **From your observations, what can you infer about a shrimp's range of motion and the way it moves from place to place?** *(Students might correctly infer that a shrimp contracts its abdominal muscles and spreads its fanlike sections, so that it jerks backward in the water. It also walks and swims with its legs.)* L2

Word Origins

The term *cephalopod* means "head footed." L2

ESL SUPPORT FOR ENGLISH LANGUAGE LEARNERS

Vocabulary: Prior Knowledge

Beginning Write the word *swimmeret* on the board, and say it aloud. Have students repeat the word after you. Then, draw a box around the base word *swim.* Ask students what *swim* means. If they do not know this word, explain the definition and clarify it with pictures of swimmers. Ask students where they expect to find swimming animals (in water). Help students infer that swimmerets are structures that crustaceans use for swimming. Point out the flipperlike structure of swimmerets in Figure 28–8. Repeat this strategy for the word *spinneret* and the base word *spin.* L1

Intermediate Some students may know the word *abdomen* in relationship to human anatomy. Ask students where a crustacean's abdomen is located and how this compares with the human abdomen. L2

Answer to . . .

✓CHECKPOINT *The cephalothorax and the abdomen are the body sections of a crayfish.*

28–2 (continued)

Spiders and Their Relatives

Build Science Skills

Applying Concepts Show students photographs or slides that illustrate some of the representative kinds of chelicerates, including various spiders, ticks, scorpions, and horseshoe crabs. As you show each example, ask students to identify the organism, or tell them the name if they cannot. Then, ask: **What characteristics do all chelicerates have in common?** *(They have two pairs of appendages attached near the mouth, called chelicerae and pedipalps. Chelicerates also have two body sections and four or five pairs of legs.)* Call on volunteers to point out these characteristics in the photos or slides of chelicerates. L2

Use Visuals

Figure 28–9 Ask students: **What structures does the spider share with some other arthropods?** *(Nervous system, well-developed head with brain and sense organs such as eyes, Malpighian tubules for excretion, heart, open circulatory system, spiracles)* **What structures are characteristic of this spider and some other chelicerates?** *(Book lungs, poison gland, pedipalps and chelicerae, silk gland, four pairs of legs)*

Spiders and Their Relatives

Horseshoe crabs, spiders, ticks, and scorpions are members of subphylum Chelicerata, or chelicerates. **Chelicerates have mouthparts called chelicerae and two body sections, and nearly all have four pairs of walking legs.** Locate these structures in the spider in **Figure 28–9.** Note that chelicerates lack the antennae found on most other arthropods. As in crustaceans, the bodies of chelicerates are divided into a cephalothorax and an abdomen. The cephalothorax contains the brain, eyes, mouth, and walking legs. The abdomen contains most of the internal organs.

Chelicerates have two pairs of appendages attached near the mouth that are adapted as mouthparts. One pair, called **chelicerae** (kuh-LIS-ur-ee; singular: chelicera), contain fangs and are used to stab and paralyze prey. The other pair, called **pedipalps** (PED-ih-palps), are longer than the chelicerae and are usually modified to grab prey. Chelicerates respire using either book gills or book lungs. Horseshoe crabs, which are aquatic, move water across the membranes of book gills. In spiders, which are terrestrial, air enters through spiracles and then circulates across the surfaces of the book lung.

Chelicerates are divided into two main classes: Merostomata and Arachnida. Class Merostomata includes horseshoe crabs, and class Arachnida, or arachnids, includes spiders, mites, ticks, and scorpions.

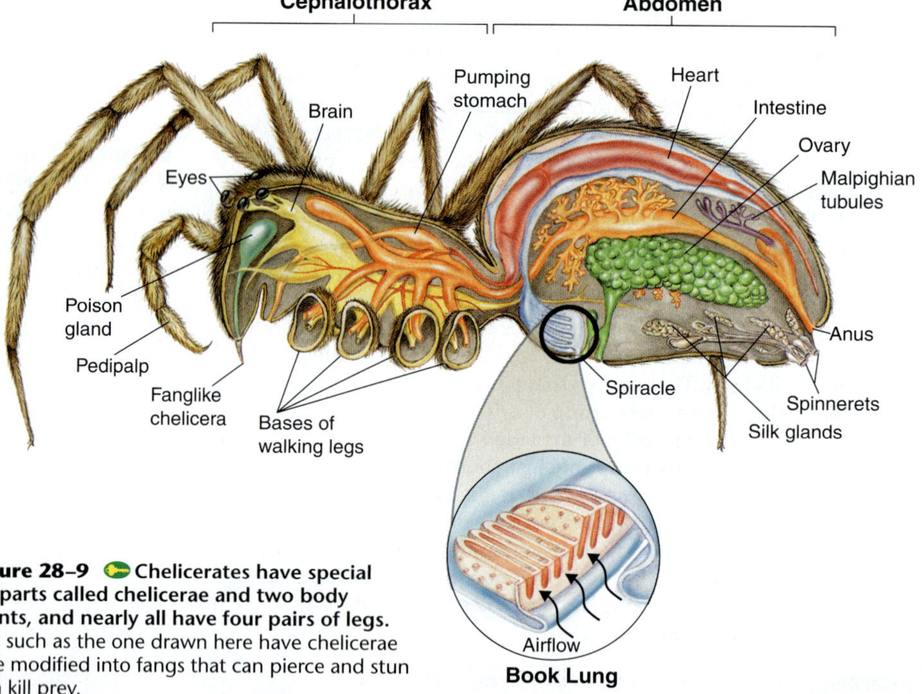

▶ **Figure 28–9** **Chelicerates have special mouthparts called chelicerae and two body segments, and nearly all have four pairs of legs.** Spiders such as the one drawn here have chelicerae that are modified into fangs that can pierce and stun or even kill prey.

FACTS AND FIGURES

Ballooning off to new territory

Female spiders usually lay eggs in a small cocoon spun from silk. In some, such as members of the genus *Theridion*, the young live on the mother's web for a month or so after hatching. When the mother captures prey, she signals to the young by strumming the web with her legs. When danger threatens, she rubs the web a different way, and the young scurry for the shelter of their cocoon.

Once they are a few weeks old, most spiders live alone. Some baby spiders leave the nest by climbing onto a tall plant and releasing a long silk thread. When a strong breeze picks up the thread, the spider lets go of its perch and sails off in the wind. This behavior, called ballooning, can carry the baby spider for hundreds of kilometers to a new, possibly less crowded, territory.

Horseshoe Crabs Horseshoe crabs, such as the one shown in **Figure 28–10**, are among the oldest living arthropods. They first appeared more than 500 million years ago and have changed little since that time. Despite their name, horseshoe crabs are not true crabs at all. They are heavily armor-plated, like crabs, but have an anatomy closer to that of spiders. They have chelicerae, five pairs of walking legs, and a long spikelike tail that is used for movement. Horseshoe crabs grow to about the size—and shape—of a large frying pan. They are common along the marshes and shallow bays of the eastern United States seacoast.

Spiders Spiders, the largest group of arachnids, capture and feed on animals ranging from other arthropods to small birds. They catch their prey in a variety of ways. Some spin webs of a strong, flexible protein called silk, which they use to catch flying prey. Others, including the tarantula shown in **Figure 28–11**, stalk and then pounce on their prey. Other spiders lie in wait beneath a camouflaged burrow, leaping out to grab insects that venture too near.

Because spiders do not have jaws for chewing, they must liquefy their food to swallow it. Once a spider captures its prey, it uses fanglike chelicerae to inject paralyzing venom into it. When the prey is paralyzed, the spider injects digestive enzymes into the wounds. These enzymes break down the prey's tissues, enabling the spider to suck the tissues into a specialized pumping stomach. The stomach forces the liquefied food through the rest of the spider's digestive system. In the digestive system, enzymes break food molecules into smaller molecules that can be absorbed.

Whether or not they spin webs, all spiders produce silk. Spider silk is much stronger than steel! Spiders spin silk into webs, cocoons for eggs, and wrappings for prey. They do this by forcing liquid silk through **spinnerets,** which are organs that contain silk glands. As the silk is pulled out of the spinnerets, it hardens into a single strand. Web-spinning spiders can spin webs almost as soon as they hatch; the complicated procedure seems to be preprogrammed behavior.

CHECKPOINT *How do chelicerates respire?*

▲ **Figure 28–10** Horseshoe crabs look a bit like true crabs, but their bodies more closely resemble those of spiders and other chelicerates. The abdomen and cephalothorax of these animals are encased in a hard shell. **Inferring** *From this photograph, what can you infer about the habitat of horseshoe crabs?*

▲ **Figure 28–11** The tarantula shown here is an example of a chelicerate. The chelicerae, or specialized mouthparts, can inject poison by way of a painful bite. **Applying Concepts** *How might this action be useful to tarantulas?*

Build Science Skills

Using Models Divide the class into pairs, and ask each pair to make a simple two- or three-dimensional model of a chelicerate's body plan. Explain that they can use materials of their choice and also choose the chelicerate they want to model. Students should use written labels or tags to name the chelicerate's body sections and major appendages. L2 L3

Build Science Skills

Classifying Challenge interested students to use a field guide or a library book about spiders to identify spider webs they find around the school or at home. Explain that each kind of spider spins a distinctive web. Some are triangular, others are dome-shaped, and so on. Ask students to make sketches of the webs they find and use books to identify the kind of spider that made each web. L3

Build Science Skills

Comparing and Contrasting Show students how they can "collect" a spider web. After finding a fresh web, spray it with enamel spray paint. Next, spray a sheet of bright white construction paper with hairspray to make it sticky. Then, push the construction paper against the spray-painted web. As one person holds the paper in place, another can use scissors to cut the strands of silk around the web. Once dry, the paper will hold the collected web. After your demonstration, divide the class into pairs and challenge each pair to find a suitable web to collect. Display the collected webs, and have students use field guides to identify the species of spiders that made the webs. L2 L3

BIO INSIGHTS

FACTS AND FIGURES

A great research animal

The horseshoe crab, *Limulus polyphemus*, can survive great changes in temperature and salinity and does not seem to be affected by doses of radiation high enough to kill humans. It can also live for almost a year without eating. For these reasons, *Limulus* has interested biologists for many years. This chelicerate is found only in the eastern part of North America, from Nova Scotia to Mexico. In the spring and summer, great numbers of *Limulus* can be seen in the shallow water of protected bays and estuaries as they prepare for mating. Biologists have studied *Limulus* reproduction extensively. The *Limulus* eye has also been invaluable to researchers who investigate vision. Because it has a relatively simple structure, it provides an excellent model for studies of the way that vision works.

Answers to . . .

CHECKPOINT *Chelicerates respire using book gills or book lungs.*

Figure 28–10 *Horseshoe crabs live in water along the seacoast.*

Figure 28–11 *The ability to inject poison enables the tarantula to capture prey and defend itself against predators.*

28–2 (continued)

Analyzing Data

The name for the disease is derived from a location—Lyme, Connecticut—near where a cluster of cases was first reported in 1975. Lyme disease is caused by the bacterial spirochete *Borrelia burgdorferi.* For the bacterium to be transferred from tick to human, the tick must remain on the human for days, and therefore prompt removal of the tick will prevent the disease. But the deer tick that carries the bacterium in the East, *Ixodus scapularis,* is so small that a person bitten by the tick may not notice it at all. A deer tick feeds three times during its life: usually on field mice as a larva and as a nymph, and then usually on a deer as an adult tick. Deer and other wild animals show no signs of being affected by the disease. In humans, antibiotics are usually effective in treating Lyme disease. L2

Answers

1. The areas where the incidence of Lyme disease is greatest are where there are the most humans.
2. One hypothesis is that climate differences are a major factor: the ticks are less abundant in the dry areas of the Southwest than in the more humid areas of the West Coast. Another hypothesis is that in the warm Southwest, the ticks prefer to feed on reptiles rather than humans.

Insects and Their Relatives

Build Science Skills

Classifying To reinforce arthropod classification, show the class photographs or specimens of a variety of uniramians, including centipedes, millipedes, and a number of different insects. Ask: **What do all these uniramians have in common?** *(All have jaws, one pair of antennae, and unbranched appendages.)* **What is the difference between a centipede and a millipede?** *(Most body segments of a centipede bear one pair of legs each. Each millipede segment bears two pairs of legs.)* L1 L2

Analyzing Data

Ticks and Lyme Disease

Lyme disease is caused by a bacterium found in two species of small ticks, the deer tick (*Ixodes scapularis*) and the western black-legged tick (*Ixodes pacificus*). Both species are most common in humid, wooded areas. They feed by sucking blood from deer, mice, birds, or humans. In warmer climates where reptiles such as lizards and snakes are most common, deer ticks prefer to feed on reptiles. The disease-causing bacteria are transmitted to the host by the bite of an infected tick. In humans the bacteria can cause a rash, fever, fatigue, joint and muscle pain, and damage to the nervous system. The bacteria do not survive well in reptiles.

The map shows the distribution of the two tick species and areas where there is a high incidence of Lyme disease. Use the map to help you answer the questions that follow.

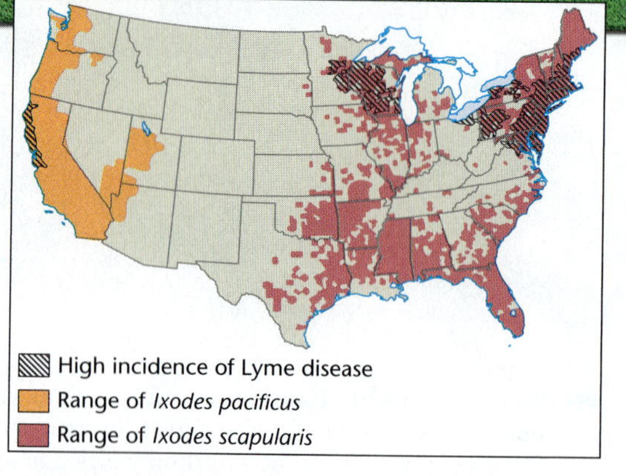

1. **Interpreting Graphics** How can you explain the differences in the incidence of Lyme disease within the range of deer ticks?
2. **Formulating Hypotheses** What are two possible reasons that Lyme disease is not common in the parts of the dry southwest where western black-legged ticks are found?

Mites and Ticks Mites and ticks are small arachnids that are often parasitic. Their chelicerae and pedipalps are specialized for digging into a host's tissues and sucking out blood or plant fluids. In many species, the chelicerae are needlelike structures that are used to pierce the skin of the host. The pedipalps are often equipped with claws for attaching to the host. These mouthparts are so strong that if a tick begins to feed on you and you try to pull it off, its cephalothorax may separate from its abdomen and remain in your skin!

Mites and ticks parasitize a variety of organisms. Spider mites damage houseplants and are major agricultural pests on crops such as cotton. Others—including chiggers, mange, and scabies mites—cause itching or painful rashes in humans and other mammals. Ticks can transmit bacteria that cause serious diseases, such as Rocky Mountain spotted fever and Lyme disease.

▼ **Figure 28–12** Scorpions are easily recognized by their clawlike pedipalps and curved abdomen that bears a stinger at its tip. Although scorpions inflict stings on humans—usually causing as much pain as a wasp sting—they typically prey on other invertebrates, such as insects. **Comparing and Contrasting** *How do scorpions and spiders capture their prey?*

Scorpions Scorpions are widespread in warm areas around the world, including the southern United States. Scorpions have pedipalps that are enlarged into claws, as shown in **Figure 28–12.** The long, segmented abdomen of a scorpion carries a venomous stinger that can kill or paralyze prey. Unlike spiders, scorpions chew their prey, using their chelicerae.

CHECKPOINT *Where are scorpions usually found?*

FACTS AND FIGURES

The sting of a scorpion

Most biologists think that scorpions have undergone little change over their history and are thus representative of the most ancient of land-dwelling arthropods. They probably moved onto land more than 300 million years ago during the Carboniferous Period. Scorpions usually spend most of the day hidden under rocks or logs. All scorpions are predators, and a scorpion first catches prey with its large front claws, or pedipalps. At the tip of a scorpion's abdomen is a stinging apparatus called the aculeus, which has a sharp, barbed point. At the base of the aculeus are venom-producing glands. When a scorpion catches prey, it stings it with the aculeus and ejects venom through the point, paralyzing the catch. Although scorpions are widely feared by people, only a few have venom that is extremely toxic to humans. *Centuroides,* which is native to the Southwest, is one scorpion whose venom can be deadly to humans.

Insects and Their Relatives

Centipedes, millipedes, and insects all belong to the subphylum Uniramia, or uniramians (yoo-nuh-RAY-mee-unz). This subphylum contains more species than all other groups of animals alive today. **Uniramians have jaws, one pair of antennae, and unbranched appendages.** They also have widely varying forms and lifestyles. Centipedes and millipedes have long, wormlike bodies composed of many leg-bearing segments, as shown in **Figure 28–13.** Insects have compact, three-part bodies, and most are adapted for flight. The insects are so diverse and important that they are discussed separately, in the next section.

Centipedes Centipedes belong to class Chilopoda. They have from a few to more than 100 pairs of legs, depending on the species. Most body segments bear one pair of legs each. Centipedes are carnivores whose mouthparts include venomous claws. They use these claws to catch and stun or kill their prey—including other arthropods, earthworms, toads, small snakes, and even mice. Centipedes usually live beneath rocks or in the soil. Their spiracles cannot close, and their exoskeleton is not waterproof. As a result, their bodies lose water easily. This characteristic restricts centipedes to moist or humid areas.

Millipedes Millipedes form class Diplopoda. Like the centipedes, millipedes have a highly segmented body. However, each millipede segment bears two, not one, pairs of legs. These two pairs of legs per segment develop from the fusion of two segments in the millipede embryo. Millipedes live under rocks and in decaying logs. They feed on dead and decaying plant material. Unlike centipedes, they are timid creatures. When disturbed, many millipedes roll up into a ball. This behavior protects their softer undersides. Millipedes may also defend themselves by secreting unpleasant or toxic chemicals.

Figure 28–13 **Uniramians such as centipedes and millipedes have jaws, one pair of antennae, and unbranched appendages.** A centipede (top) is a carnivore that feeds on earthworms and other small animals. A millipede (bottom) is a herbivore that feeds on rotting vegetation.

28–2 Section Assessment

1. **Key Concept** What characteristics are used to classify arthropods?
2. **Key Concept** How do the three largest groups of arthropods differ?
3. Describe the process of digestion in spiders.
4. What characteristic of horseshoe crabs is different from most other chelicerates?
5. Compare and contrast the body plans and feeding habits of millipedes and centipedes.
6. **Critical Thinking** **Applying Concepts** Are insects more closely related to spiders or to centipedes? Explain.

Sharpen Your Skills

Problem Solving

Use information from this section to design a new type of arthropod. Make sure that the arthropod has all the characteristics described in this section. Draw the arthropod and give it a name. Include a brief description of what it eats and where it lives.

3 ASSESS

Evaluate Understanding

Call on students at random to explain the differences in structure among the three major groups of arthropods.

Reteach

Have students make a compare/contrast table to organize the information about the three major groups of arthropods. Headings might include *Group, Characteristics*, and *Examples*. They can use this table as a study aid.

Sharpen Your Skills

Consider working with an art teacher at your school in order to provide students with more options for their drawings. Drawings should be accompanied by a name and a brief description of the fantasy arthropod, including feeding and habitat. All organisms should have a segmented body, an exoskeleton, and jointed appendages. In their drawings, students should pay special attention to the structure of the arthropod's mouthparts.

If your class subscribes to the iText, use it to review the Key Concepts in Section 28–2.

28–2 Section Assessment

1. Arthropods are classified based on the number and structure of their body segments and appendages—particularly their mouthparts.
2. Students should describe characteristics of crustaceans, chelicerates, and uniramians.
3. Spiders first inject enzymes into prey to liquefy their food, and then suck the tissues into a specialized pumping stomach, which forces the liquid through the rest of the digestive system.
4. The abdomen and cephalothorax of horseshoe crabs are encased in a hard shell, and they use a long, spikelike tail for movement.
5. Most centipede segments bear a pair of legs; each millipede segment bears two pairs of legs. Centipedes use claws on prey; millipedes feed on dead or decaying organisms.
6. Insects are more closely related to centipedes because both belong to the subphylum Uniramia, which does not include spiders.

Answers to . . .

CHECKPOINT *Scorpions are widespread in warm areas around the world.*

Figure 28–12 *Some spiders catch prey in webs. Others stalk, then pounce on their prey. Others lie in wait beneath a camouflaged burrow, leaping out to grab insects that venture too near. Scorpions use a venomous stinger that can kill or paralyze prey.*

Section 28–3

1 FOCUS

Objectives

28.3.1 ***Identify*** the distinguishing features of insects.

28.3.2 ***Describe*** two types of development in insects.

28.3.3 ***Explain*** what types of insects form societies.

Guide for Reading

Vocabulary Preview

Help students organize the section's Vocabulary words by pointing out that they fall into two general categories. The first four apply to the life cycle of insects; the last three apply to the behavior of insects and the formation by some kinds of insects of complex arrangements called societies.

Reading Strategy

Point out that in looking for the important concepts in each paragraph, students should pay attention to the headings of the section. The important concepts usually relate to the headings.

2 INSTRUCT

Use Visuals

Figure 28–14 Have students study the information contained on the pie chart. Then, ask: **What percentage of animals are insects?** *(73%)* **What percentage are vertebrates?** *(4%)* **What are some nonarthropod invertebrates you've studied?** *(These include sponges, cnidarians, worms, and mollusks.)* **What are some noninsect arthropods?** *(These include crustaceans, chelicerates, centipedes, and millipedes.)* L1 L2

28–3 Insects

Guide for Reading

Key Concepts

- What are the distinguishing features of insects?
- What two types of development can insects undergo?
- What types of insects form societies?

Vocabulary

incomplete metamorphosis
nymph
complete metamorphosis
pupa
pheromone
society
caste

Reading Strategy: Summarizing As you read, find the most important concepts in each paragraph. Then, use the important concepts to write a summary of what you have read.

What animals other than humans have the greatest impact on the activities of this planet? If you said "insects," you would be correct. From bees that flit from flower to flower to weevils that feed on crops, insects seem to be everywhere. As **Figure 28–14** shows, class Insecta contains more species than any other group of animals. Ants and termites alone account for nearly one third of all the animal biomass in the Amazon basin.

Many characteristics of insects have contributed to their evolutionary success. These include different ways of responding to stimuli; the evolution of flight, which allowed insects to disperse long distances and colonize new habitats; and a life cycle in which the young differ from adults in appearance and feeding methods. These features have allowed insects to thrive in almost every terrestrial habitat on Earth, as well as in many freshwater and some marine environments.

The insects cover an incredible variety of life forms—from stunning, iridescent beetles and butterflies to the less attractive fleas, weevils, cockroaches, and termites. Biologists sometimes disagree on how to classify insects, and the number of living orders ranges from 26 to more than 30.

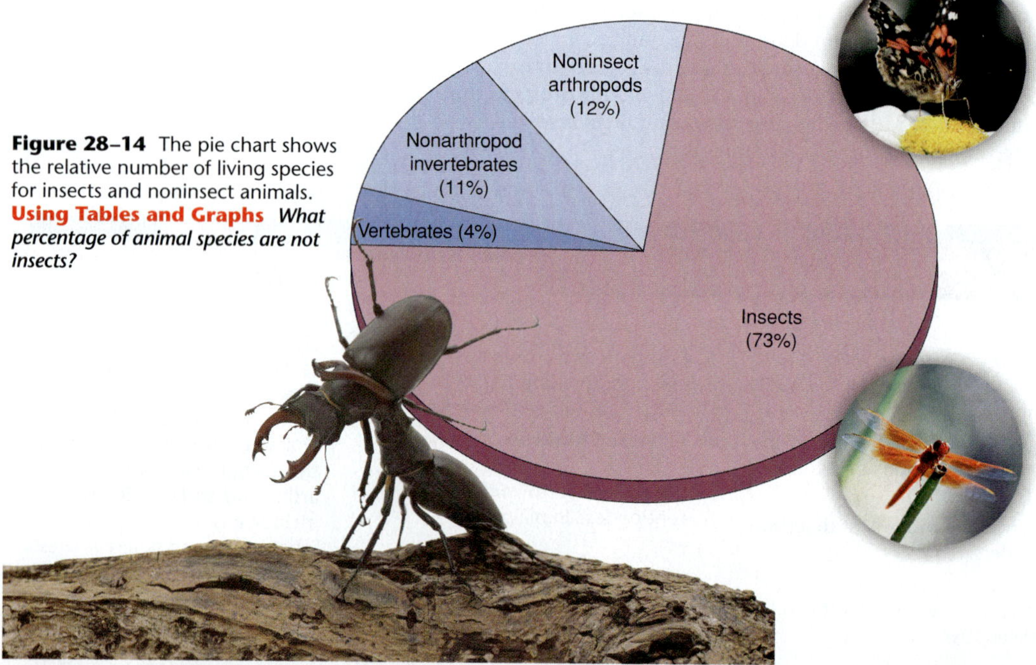

Figure 28–14 The pie chart shows the relative number of living species for insects and noninsect animals. **Using Tables and Graphs** *What percentage of animal species are not insects?*

SECTION RESOURCES

TIME SAVER

Print:

- ***Laboratory Manuals A, B,*** Chapter 28 Lab
- ***Teaching Resources,*** Lesson Plan 28–3, Adapted Section Summary 28–3, Adapted Worksheets 28–3, Section Summary 28–3, Worksheets 28–3, Section Review 28–3, Enrichment
- ***Reading and Study Workbook A,*** Section 28–3
- ***Adapted Reading and Study Workbook B,*** Section 28–3
- ***Lab Worksheets,*** Chapter 28 Design an Experiment
- ***Investigations in Forensics,*** Investigation 8

Technology:

- ***BioDetectives DVD,*** "Insect Clues: The Smallest Witnesses"
- ***iText,*** Section 28–3
- ***Transparencies Plus,*** Section 28–3

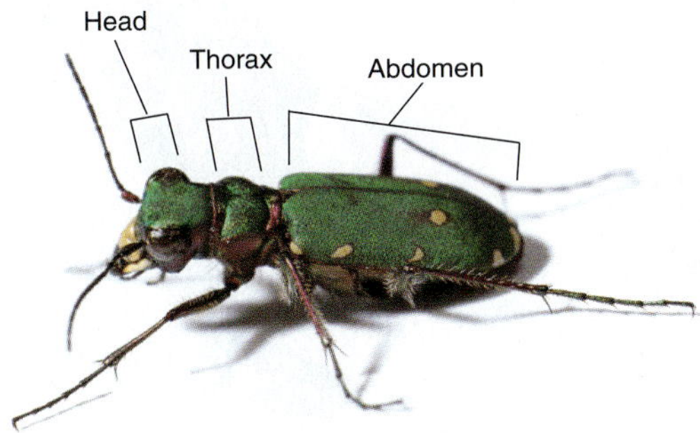

◀ **Figure 28–15 Insects have a body divided into three parts—head, thorax, and abdomen. Three pairs of legs are attached to the thorax.** In addition to these features, this green tiger beetle has other characteristics of a typical insect—wings, antennae, compound eyes, and tracheal tubes for respiration.

What Is an Insect?

Like all arthropods, insects have a segmented body, an exoskeleton, and jointed appendages. They also have several features that are specific to insects. **Insects have a body divided into three parts—head, thorax, and abdomen. Three pairs of legs are attached to the thorax.** The beetle in **Figure 28–15** exhibits these characteristics. In many insects, such as ants, the body parts are clearly separated from each other by narrow connections. In other insects, such as grasshoppers, the divisions between the three body parts are not as sharply defined. A typical insect also has a pair of antennae and a pair of compound eyes on the head, two pairs of wings on the thorax, and tracheal tubes that are used for respiration.

Insects carry out life functions in basically the same ways as other arthropods. However, insects have a variety of adaptations that deserve a closer look.

CHECKPOINT *What are the three main parts of an insect's body?*

Responses to Stimuli Insects use many sense organs to detect external stimuli. Compound eyes are made of many lenses that detect minute changes in color and movement. The brain assembles this information into a single image and directs the insect's response. Compound eyes produce an image that is less detailed than what we see. However, eyes with multiple lenses are far better at detecting movement—one reason it is so hard to swat a fly!

Insects have chemical receptors for taste and smell on their mouthparts, as might be expected, and also on their antennae and legs. When a fly steps in a drop of water, it knows immediately whether the water contains salt or sugar. Insects also have sensory hairs that detect slight movements in the surrounding air or water. As objects move toward insects, the insects can feel the movement of the displaced air or water and respond appropriately. Many insects also have well-developed ears that hear sounds far above the human range. These organs are located in what we would consider odd places—behind the legs in grasshoppers, for example.

What Is an Insect?

Use Visuals

Figure 28–15 To emphasize the differences between spiders and insects, have students study the figure and read the caption. Then, ask them to turn back to Figure 28–9 on page 722 and do the same. Ask: **What is the difference in body parts between spiders and insects?** *(Spiders have two body parts, the cephalothorax and abdomen. Insects have three body parts, the head, thorax, and abdomen.)* **What is the difference in pairs of legs?** *(Spiders have four pairs of legs, whereas insects have three pairs of legs.)* L1 L2

Build Science Skills

Designing Experiments Divide the class into small groups, and give each group these materials: a vial containing 10 fruit flies, a light source, and a meter stick. One culture tube of fruit flies should provide enough flies for an entire class. Transfer 10 adult flies to a separate vial for each group. Caution students not to open the vials. Challenge each group to formulate a hypothesis and design an experiment to investigate how fruit flies respond to light. *(In a typical experiment, students might vary the distance of the light from the flies and observe any differences in behavior.)* Have groups review their experiments with you before proceeding with the activity. L2 L3

UNIVERSAL ACCESS

Less Proficient Readers
To help students understand metamorphosis as described on page 729, make a Venn diagram on the board and then slowly read aloud the descriptions of the two processes. As you read, write important terms about incomplete and complete metamorphosis in the diagram. L1 L2

English Language Learners
Reinforce the idea of metamorphosis by explaining the meaning of the word parts in the term, which is derived from a Greek word meaning "to transform." Explain that *meta-* means "change" and that *morph* means "form." Thus, *metamorphosis* means "to change in form." L1 L2

Advanced Learners
Encourage interested students to read the short story *The Metamorphosis* by Franz Kafka, a classic of world literature. Ask readers to analyze the symbolism in the story according to both how it parallels metamorphosis in insects and how it uses the process to shed light on human development. L3

Answers to . . .

CHECKPOINT *Head, thorax, and abdomen*

Figure 28–14 *27 percent*

28–3 (continued)

Build Science Skills

Observing Have specimens of large grasshoppers serve as a representative insect for students to examine both with the unaided eye and with a hand lens. You may also want to provide students with diagrams on which they can label the various structures and their functions. If possible, have preserved specimens of other insects so that students can examine the variety of mouthparts that enable insects to obtain food from many different sources. Have students wear disposable plastic gloves and safety goggles when they examine the preserved insect. Students should wash their hands after the activity. L2 L3

Use Community Resources

Invite a local lepidopterist to address the class about collecting and preserving butterflies. You might be able to find such a collector through the biology department of a local college or by contacting an entomologist. Ask the lepidopterist to present his or her collection, explain how the insects are caught, and demonstrate how butterflies are preserved and mounted. Have students prepare for the presentation by brainstorming for a list of questions to ask. Make sure that students look for specific insect structures as they examine the mounted butterflies. L2

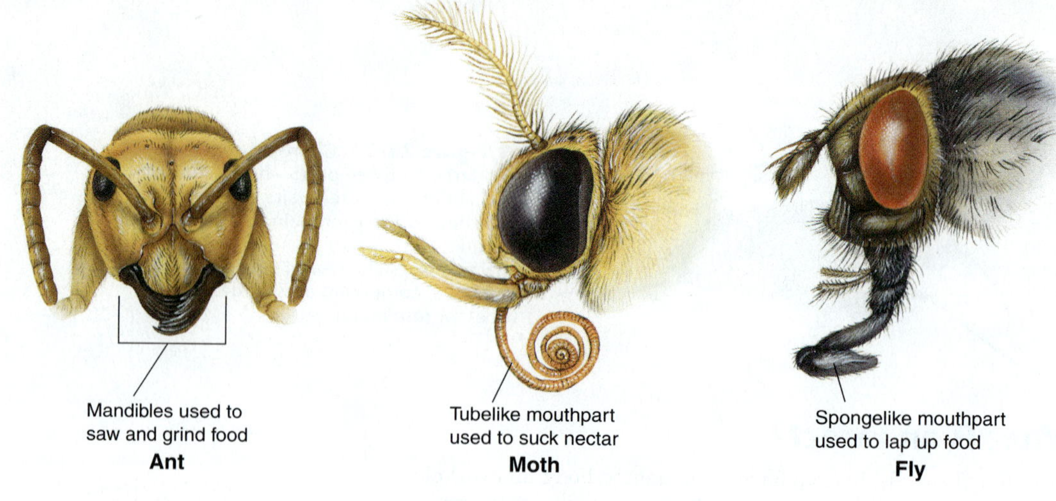

▲ **Figure 28–16** Insect mouthparts are specialized for a variety of functions. An ant's mouthparts can saw through and then grind food into a fine pulp. The mouthpart of a moth consists of a long tube that can be uncoiled to sip nectar from a flower. Flies have a spongy mouthpart that is used to stir saliva into food and then lap up the food. **Applying Concepts** *What is the function of saliva?*

Adaptations for Feeding Insects have three pairs of appendages that are used as mouthparts, including a pair of mandibles. These mouthparts can take on a variety of shapes, as shown in **Figure 28–16.**

Insect adaptations for feeding are not restricted to their mouthparts. Many insects produce saliva containing digestive enzymes that help break down food. The chemicals in bee saliva, for example, help change nectar into a more digestible form—honey. Glands on the abdomen of bees secrete wax, which is used to build storage chambers for food and other structures within a beehive.

Movement and Flight Insects have three pairs of legs, which in different species are used for walking, jumping, or capturing and holding prey. In many insects, the legs have spines and hooks that are used for grasping and defense.

Many insects can fly, as shown in **Figure 28–17.** Flying insects typically have two pairs of wings made of chitin—the same substance that makes up an insect's exoskeleton.

The evolution of flight has allowed insects to disperse long distances and to colonize a wide variety of habitats. Flying abilities and styles vary greatly among the insects. Butterflies usually fly slowly. Flies, bees, and moths, however, can hover, change direction rapidly, and dart off at great speed. Dragonflies can reach speeds of 50 kilometers per hour.

◀ **Figure 28–17** Flying insects, such as this lacewing, move their wings using two sets of muscles. The muscles contract to change the shape of the thorax, alternately pushing the wings down and lifting them up and back. In some small insects, these muscles can produce wing speeds of up to 1000 beats per second! **Drawing Conclusions** *How might the evolution of flight change an animal's habitat?*

BIO INSIGHTS — FACTS AND FIGURES

Survivability through the senses
A large measure of insects' survival ability is due to the development of their senses. The hairs that cover most insects are sensitive to touch and can detect chemicals as well. These hairs are concentrated on the head and lower legs, where they are most likely to come in contact with objects and materials in the environment. The compound eyes of insects consist of many lenses—up to 30,000 in some dragonflies. These large, multilensed eyes give insects the ability to scan a wide area at one time, allowing them to detect the motion of predators or prey. Some insects rely heavily on hearing. Mosquitoes, for example, can detect sounds with their antennae. Crickets, grasshoppers, and other insects have a membrane called a tympanum on the abdomen or legs. These structures function much like the human eardrum in sensing sound vibrations.

Metamorphosis **The growth and development of insects usually involve metamorphosis, which is a process of changing shape and form. Insects undergo either incomplete metamorphosis or complete metamorphosis.** Both complete and incomplete metamorphosis are shown in **Figure 28–18.** The immature forms of insects that undergo gradual or **incomplete metamorphosis,** such as the chinch bug, look very much like the adults. These immature forms are called **nymphs** (NIMFS). Nymphs lack functional sexual organs and other adult structures, such as wings. As they molt several times and grow, the nymphs gradually acquire adult structures. This type of development is characterized by a similar appearance throughout all stages of the life cycle.

Many insects, such as bees, moths, and beetles, undergo a more dramatic change in body form during a process called **complete metamorphosis.** These animals hatch into larvae that look and act nothing like their parents. They also feed in completely different ways from adult insects. The larvae typically feed voraciously and grow rapidly. They molt a few times and grow larger but change little in appearance. Then they undergo a final molt and change into a **pupa** (PYOO-puh; plural: pupae)—the stage in which an insect changes from larva to adult. During the pupal stage, the body is completely remodeled inside and out. The adult that emerges seems like a completely different animal. Unlike the larva, the adult typically can fly and is specialized for reproduction. **Figure 28–18** shows the complete metamorphosis of a ladybug beetle.

CHECKPOINT *What is a pupa?*

Discovery School Video To find out how insect metamorphosis plays a part in forensic science, view track 8 "Insect Clues: The Smallest Witnesses" on the *BioDetectives* DVD.

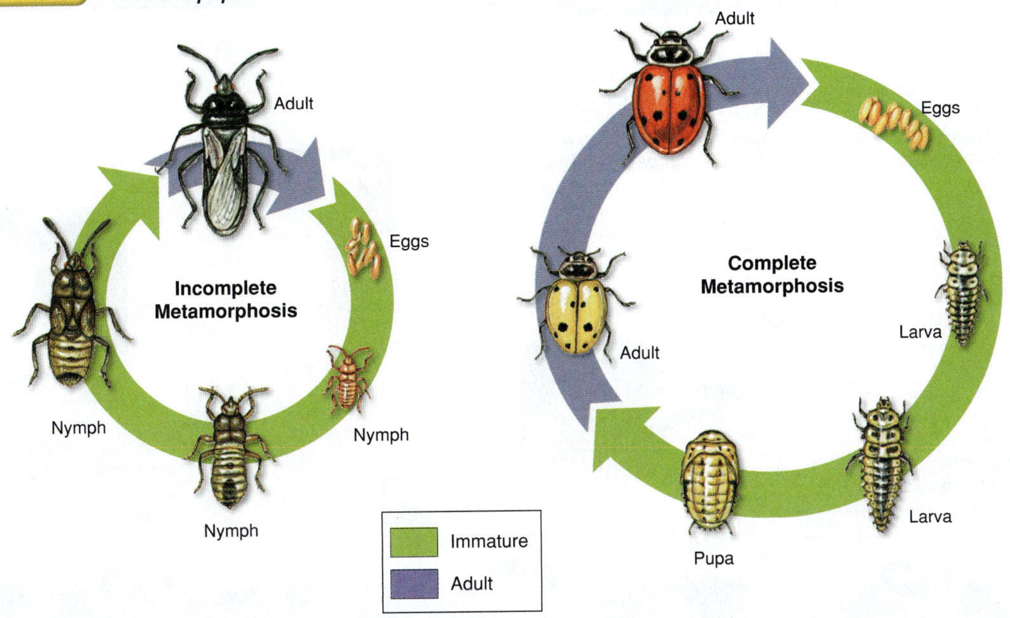

Figure 28–18 **The growth and development of insects usually involve metamorphosis, which is a process of changing shape and form.** The chinch bug (left) undergoes incomplete metamorphosis, in which the developing nymphs look similar to the adult. The ladybug (right) undergoes complete metamorphosis. During the early stages, the developing larva and pupa look completely different from the adult.

Use Visuals

Figure 28–18 Point out that the insects in the two life cycles shown are in different orders. The chinch bug is a plant bug, Order Homoptera, and it feeds on grasses. The ladybug is a type of beetle, Order Coleoptera. Then, ask: **Which type of metamorphosis includes larva and pupa stages?** *(Complete metamorphosis)* **In incomplete metamorphosis, what are the differences between the nymph and the adult?** *(Nymphs lack functional sexual organs, wings, and other adult structures.)* **In which type of metamorphosis is there a dramatic change in shape?** *(Complete metamorphosis)* L1 L2

Build Science Skills

Designing Experiments Challenge groups of students to design an experiment in which the life cycle of an insect could be observed. A typical design might involve placing food, such as an overripe banana, in an open jar for a few days until flies can be seen on the food. Then, the flies can be waved away and the jar covered with a nylon stocking. Within a few days, maggots—fly pupae—will be seen on the food. Some students may recall that in Chapter 1 they studied a similar experiment carried out by the Italian physician Francesco Redi in the 1600s. L2 L3

Quick View Video

Discovery School DVD Encourage students to view track 8 "Insect Clues: The Smallest Witnesses" on the *BioDetectives* DVD.

BIO INSIGHTS **FACTS AND FIGURES**

Studying insects from murder scenes

Insects and their larvae provide clues to forensic scientists about the circumstances of crimes—especially murders. Forensic entomologists examine the species of insects in a piece of evidence—a package of marijuana or a corpse, for example—to determine where the crime was committed. Since the larvae of many insects, such as blowflies, develop at an extremely regular rate, larvae removed from a corpse can be raised in carefully controlled conditions. The length of time it takes the larvae to develop into adults gives investigators a fairly accurate indication of when the parent fly laid her eggs on the corpse. And because the time it takes for a corpse to attract insects is also a known constant, the investigators can pinpoint the time of death.

Answers to . . .

CHECKPOINT *A pupa is the stage in which an insect changes from larva to adult.*

Figure 28–16 *Saliva contains digestive enzymes that help break down food.*

Figure 28–17 *The habitat would change from mostly on the ground to include the air and the high places previously difficult to reach.*

28–3 (continued)

Insects and Humans

Use Community Resources

Invite a local farmer to speak to the class about insect pest problems common to farms in your area. Have the farmer talk about kinds of damage insects can do to crops, specific insects that are a threat in your area, and methods commonly used to prevent insect damage. If possible, have the farmer bring to class examples of insect damage caused to crops. L2

Biology and History

After students have examined the timeline, discuss the ethics of using insecticides to eliminate disease-causing organisms. DDT, for example, proved invaluable in controlling outbreaks of malaria. But the chemical did so much damage to the environment that its use was banned in the United States. Yet, DDT is still used in other countries for disease control. Elicit students' opinions about whether the benefits of DDT use outweigh the harmful effects. L2

Writing in Science

Students might use encyclopedias, microbiology textbooks, or medical reference books on diseases to complete their research. Bubonic plague is a serious disease caused by the bacterium *Yersinia pestis.* Plague is normally a disease of rats, and the intermediate host is the rat flea, *Xenopsylla cheopis.* In the late 1800s, physicians in various parts of the world began to observe that plague outbreaks in humans were associated with large populations of rats and that diseased rats were infested with fleas that left the rats' bodies after the rats died of plague. The rat flea transmits the pathogen when it jumps from rat to rat or from rat to human. This disease is known as *bubonic* plague after the swollen lymph nodes, called buboes, that it causes. The spread of the disease can be controlled by reducing rat and flea populations.

Insects and Humans

Many insects are known for their negative effects. Termites destroy wood structures, moths eat their way through wool clothing and carpets, and bees and wasps produce painful stings. Insects such as desert locusts cause billions of dollars in damage each year to livestock and crops. Boll weevils are notorious for the trouble they cause cotton farmers in the South. Mosquitoes are annoying and have been known to spoil many a leisurely outdoor activity. Only female mosquitoes bite humans and other animals to get a blood meal for their developing eggs. Male mosquitoes, on the other hand, do not bite; they feed on nectar. Many insects, including mosquitoes, cause far more serious damage than itchy bites. Their bites can infect humans with microorganisms that cause devastating diseases such as malaria, yellow fever, and bubonic plague.

Despite their association with destruction and disease, insects also contribute enormously to the richness of human life. Agriculture would be very different without the bees, butterflies, wasps, moths, and flies that pollinate many crops. One third of the food you eat depends on plants pollinated by animals, including insects. Insects also produce commercially valuable products such as silk, wax, and honey. They are even considered a food delicacy in certain countries of Africa and Asia.

✓CHECKPOINT *How do insects affect humans negatively? Positively?*

Biology and History

Insect-Borne Diseases

For as long as humans and insects have shared planet Earth, humans have been victims of diseases carried by insects. Researchers have discovered which insects transmit specific diseases. Such discoveries have often shed light on how the diseases can be controlled.

1906
Robert Koch discovers that fleas transmit the bubonic-plague bacterium. The plague killed 25% of Europe's population between 1347 and 1351.

1909
Charles Nicolle discovers that one form of typhus, caused by a bacterium, is transmitted by the body louse.

1924
African sleeping sickness is discovered in inhabitants of central Africa. The disease is caused by a protist transmitted by tsetse flies that live in forests and areas near water.

1943
DDT, a powerful insecticide, is used for the first time during World War II to control the spread of typhus. It is also used to control outbreaks of malaria.

1900 1925 1950

FACTS AND FIGURES

Yikes—that bite itches!
Although almost everyone has been bitten by a mosquito, most people may not be aware that it is only the female that bites. Male mosquitoes cause no trouble at all, flying around and collecting pollen from flowers. The biting females use the nutrients in blood to help them produce large numbers of eggs. To prevent blood from clotting as they drink it, mosquitoes inject their saliva when they first pierce the skin. It is this saliva that can carry disease-causing organisms such as the malaria-causing protozoan, *Plasmodium falciparum.* And it is the human body's allergic reaction to this saliva that causes the itching and swelling that come with mosquito bites.

Insect Communication

Insects communicate using sound, visual, chemical, and other types of signals. Much of their communication involves finding a mate. To attract females, male crickets chirp by rubbing their forewings together, and male cicadas buzz by vibrating special membranes on the abdomen.

Visual Cues Male fireflies use visual cues to communicate with potential mates. As shown in **Figure 28–19**, a light-producing organ in the abdomen is used to produce a distinct series of flashes. When female fireflies see the signal, they flash back a signal of their own, inducing the males to fly to them. This interaction is sometimes more complicated, however, because the carnivorous females of one genus of fireflies can mimic the signal of another genus—and then lure unsuspecting males to their death!

Chemical Signals Many insects communicate using chemical signals. These chemicals are called **pheromones** (FEHR-uh-mohnz), which are specific chemical messengers that affect the behavior or development of other individuals of the same species. Some pheromones function to signal alarm or alert other insects. Other pheromones enable males and females to communicate during courtship and mating.

▲ **Figure 28–19** Fireflies use light to communicate with other individuals of their species. They are programmed to respond to specific patterns of light. **Applying Concepts** *What are some other ways in which insects communicate?*

1972
Use of DDT is severely restricted in the United States because it is found to be toxic to fishes, birds, and possibly humans.

1974
The World Health Organization begins to get rid of the black fly population of West Africa. Black flies transmit river blindness, which is caused by a roundworm.

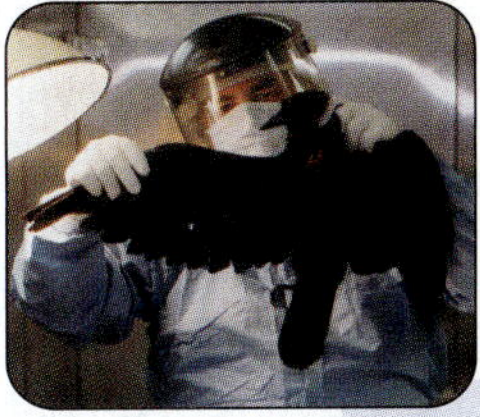

1999
An outbreak of West Nile virus occurs in New York City and its suburbs. The disease is carried by mosquitoes and can affect humans as well as birds and livestock. Officials order spraying of insecticides near bodies of water in which mosquitoes might breed.

Writing in Science

Some insect-borne diseases have an intermediate host in which the parasite reproduces asexually. Conduct research on the bubonic plague to identify its intermediate host. Write a report on how this host was discovered and how the discovery affected control of the disease.

Insect Communication

Build Science Skills

Observing If the season is right, ask volunteers to use a jar to collect fireflies one evening. Instruct students to cover the mouth of the jar with cheesecloth to allow airflow so that the insects can breathe. Have the students bring the jar of fireflies to class the next day, and encourage students to examine the organisms with a hand lens. Explain that fireflies are a type of beetle. People in primitive societies around the world have long trapped fireflies to use for light at night. Instruct students to release the insects in a field or meadow after the activity. L1 L2

Demonstration

Help students understand how insects communicate by demonstrating several ways that insects make sounds. To mimic insects such as cockroaches that produce a hissing sound, clamp your teeth together and blow air between them. To mimic insects such as grasshoppers and crickets that produce sounds by rubbing body parts together, pull a fingernail file across the edge of an index card. To mimic insects such as some moths that produce a whistling sound by blowing air through a pharynx, blow up a balloon and let the air out slowly while holding the neck of the balloon with your fingers. Challenge students to think of other insect sounds and ways to mimic those sounds. L1

Answers to . . .

CHECKPOINT *Insects affect humans negatively by destroying structures, wool clothing, and carpets; by producing painful stings; by causing billions of dollars of damage each year to crops; and by transmitting devastating diseases. Insects affect humans positively by pollinating crops; by producing commercially valuable products such as silk, wax, and honey; and by serving as food.*

Figure 28–19 *Other ways in which insects communicate include sounds, chemicals, and other types of signals.*

TEACHER TO TEACHER

When I teach students about arthropods, I try to present issues and ideas that they can relate to in their own everyday lives. A teacher should always remember that with very few exceptions the students taking high school biology will become neither biologists nor doctors. We as teachers, then, should strive to give students a handle upon which to grab life—the biology of life. For instance, I try to spend class time on spiders and their webs, as well as on the process of silk production. I also try to help students understand how and why common insects function as they do. I make a daily effort to capitalize on students' interests in order to make the study of living things relevant to their lives.

—*Dr. Chuck Campbell,*
Biology Teacher
Burbank High School
Burbank, CA

28–3 (continued)

Insect Societies

Use Visuals

Figure 28–20 Ask students: **What is the role of the queen in a tropical leaf-cutter society?** *(The queen's sole purpose is to lay eggs.)* **Which kind of ants would you likely observe outside the nest?** *(Major workers would likely be seen outside the nest, because they forage for food.)* **What kinds of insects form societies?** *(Ants, bees, termites, and some of their relatives)* L1 L2

Use Community Resources

Invite a local beekeeper to speak to the class. You might find a beekeeper by contacting an entomologist at a local university or by asking at a local store that sells beekeeping supplies. Ask the beekeeper to talk about how to start a hive, what supplies and implements are needed, how the bees behave, and what purpose the bees serve in the community. Before the speaker arrives, encourage students to make a list of questions to ask about beekeeping. L2

Demonstration

Ask students to help locate an active anthill outdoors. (Avoid stinging ants; caution students not to touch the ants.) Then, put a spoonful of honey on the ground about 1 meter away from it. Put a sheet of paper between the honey and the anthill, and have students observe the ants. The ant scouts will find the honey and establish a pheromone trail directly back to the anthill. While the ants are traveling back and forth on the trail regularly, quickly turn the paper one-quarter turn. The ants will seem confused as they search for the old trail, but eventually, they will establish a new trail to the honey. L2 L3

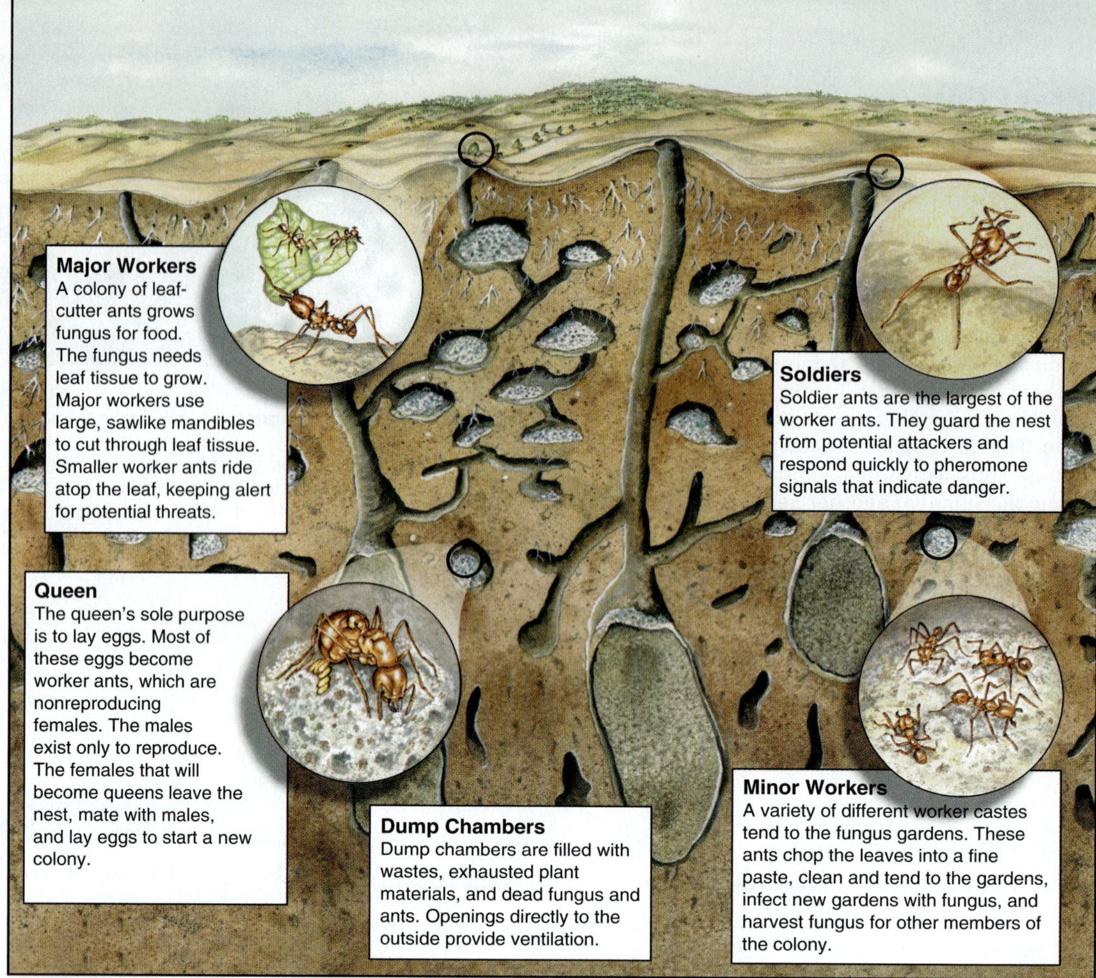

▲ **Figure 28–20** **Some insects, such as these tropical leaf-cutter ants, form societies.** In a tropical leaf-cutter society, only a single queen reproduces. The queen can produce thousands of eggs in a single day. Several different castes of leaf-cutter ants perform all other tasks within the colony. They care for the queen and her eggs and young; they grow fungus for food; and they build, maintain, and defend the colony's home. One group of workers even cultivates bacteria that produce antibiotics! These antibiotics prevent the growth of parasitic molds on the fungus that the ants use for food.

Insect Societies

Just as people form teams that work together toward a common goal, some insects live and work together in groups. Unlike people, however, insects act instinctively rather than voluntarily. **Ants, bees, termites, and some of their relatives form complex associations called societies.** A **society** is a group of closely related animals of the same species that work together for the benefit of the whole group. Insect societies may consist of more than 7 million individuals. A tropical leaf-cutter ant colony is shown in **Figure 28–20.**

Castes Within an insect society, individuals may be specialized to perform particular tasks, or roles. These are performed by groups of individuals called **castes.** Each caste has a body form specialized for its role. The basic castes are reproductive females called queens (which lay eggs), reproductive males, and workers. Most insect societies have only one queen, which is typically the largest individual in the colony.

FACTS AND FIGURES

Life in a honeybee colony

In a honeybee colony, the queen bee most of the time does little more than eat honey and lay eggs that will develop into workers. In the spring, workers build two kinds of enlarged brood cells in the honeycomb. Into one set of the cells, the queen deposits unfertilized eggs that develop into males (drones). Into the other set of enlarged cells, workers place special salivary-gland secretions that turn their honey into "royal jelly." The fertilized eggs that the queen deposits in these cells develop rapidly into large pupae that emerge as new queens. In the meantime, the workers lose interest in the old queen. Eventually, she leaves the hive with a few thousand of her daughters and a number of drones in a swarming flight to found a new colony.

Communication in Societies A sophisticated system of communication is necessary for the functioning of a society. Each species of social insect has its own "language" of visual, touch, sound, and chemical signals that convey information among members of the colony. When a worker ant finds food, for example, she leaves behind a trail of a special pheromone as she heads back to the nest. Her nest mates can then detect her trail to the food by using sensory hairs on their antennae.

Honeybees communicate with complex movements as well as with pheromones. Worker bees are able to convey information about the type, quality, direction, and distance of a food source by "dancing." As shown in **Figure 28–21**, bees have two basic dances: a round dance and a waggle dance. In the round dance, the bee that has found food circles first one way and then the other, over and over again. This dance tells the other bees that there is food within a relatively short distance from the hive. The frequency with which the dancing bee changes direction indicates the quality of the food source: The more frequent the changes in direction, the greater the energy value of the food.

In the waggle dance, the bee that has found food runs forward in a straight line while waggling her abdomen. She circles around one way, runs in a straight line again, and circles around the other way. The waggle dance tells the other bees that the food is a longer distance away. The longer the bee takes to perform the straight run and the greater the number of waggles, the farther away the food. The straight run also indicates in which direction the food is to be found. The angle of the straight run in relation to the vertical surface of the honeycomb indicates the angle of the food in relation to the sun. For example, if the dancer runs straight up the vertical part of the honeycomb, the food is in the same direction as the sun. In contrast, if the straight run is 10° to the right of the vertical, the food is 10° to the right of the sun.

▲ **Figure 28–21** Bees use dances to communicate information about food sources. The round dance indicates that food is fairly close to the hive. The waggle dance indicates that food is farther away. It also indicates the direction of the food. **Interpreting Graphics** *In what direction does the food lie, according to this bee's waggle dance?*

28–3 Section Assessment

1. **Key Concept** Describe the basic body plan of an insect.
2. **Key Concept** Compare the processes of incomplete and complete metamorphosis. Which involves a dramatic change in form?
3. **Key Concept** Describe the organization of a leaf-cutter ant society. What are the roles of the different castes?
4. What are pheromones? Identify two functions of pheromones.
5. What information is passed on by the dances of honeybees? Compare the messages of both types of dances.
6. **Critical Thinking Drawing Conclusions** The compound eyes of insects are better at detecting movement than the fine details of an image. Why might the ability to detect movement be important to insects?

Writing in Science

Explanatory Paragraph

Write a paragraph in which you briefly explain how insects communicate. *Hints:* In the first sentence in your paragraph, identify the different ways in which insects communicate. Then, in the sentences that follow, explain these ways. Use specific examples to clarify the points you make.

3 ASSESS

Evaluate Understanding

Have students turn back to the labeled drawing of a grasshopper in Figure 28–4. Ask them to explain what characteristics the grasshopper has that make it an insect and not a crustacean or a chelicerate.

Reteach

Ask students to look at one of the ants shown in Figure 28–20. Then, help them identify the structures that make up that insect and explain how those structures help the organism carry out the essential functions.

Writing in Science

Paragraphs will vary in content, though each should reflect knowledge of what the student has learned by reading the section. In the first sentence of the paragraph, students should explain that insects communicate using sound, visual, chemical, and other types of signals. Within the paragraph, students should emphasize that much of insect communication involves finding mates. Students should also explain how certain insects communicate in societies.

Interactive Textbook

If your class subscribes to the iText, use it to review the Key Concepts in Section 28–3.

28–3 Section Assessment

1. Insects have a body divided into three parts—head, thorax, and abdomen. Three pairs of legs are attached to the thorax.
2. Students' comparisons should reflect understanding of Figure 28–18 and the explanation in the text on the same page.
3. The society consists of the queen, who reproduces; males, who mate with the queen; and various castes of female workers, who perform tasks such as growing fungus.
4. Pheromones are chemical messengers that affect the behavior or development of other individuals of the same species. Two functions of pheromones are signaling alarm and communicating during courtship and mating.
5. The dances communicate the quality, distance, and direction of food. A round dance indicates that food is closer than a waggle dance.
6. Sample answer: An ability to detect motion helps insects escape from predators.

Answer to . . .

Figure 28–21 *The food lies in the direction that is 20° from the position of the sun.*

Section 28–4

1 FOCUS

Objectives

28.4.1 ***Identify*** the distinguishing features of echinoderms.
28.4.2 ***Describe*** the functions carried out by the water vascular system of echinoderms.
28.4.3 ***Compare*** the different classes of echinoderms.

Guide for Reading

Vocabulary Preview

Suggest that students preview the meaning of the Vocabulary terms in the section by skimming the text to find the highlighted, boldface words and their meanings.

Reading Strategy

Have students preview the photographs of the echinoderms shown in the section and make a list of questions they have about the form, function, and diversity of these animals. Then, as they read, they should write down the answers to their questions.

2 INSTRUCT

What Is an Echinoderm?

Use Visuals

Figure 28–22 Explain that the mouth of this brittle star is located on the underside of the animal. Similarly, the mouth of the familiar sea star, as well as other echinoderms, is also normally on the underside. Then, ask: **As you look at this photo of a brittle star, which surface are you looking at?** *(Aboral surface)* Point out that if students could touch this brittle star, its surface would feel rough. The outer covering of a lobster, which students learned about in Section 28–2, also feels rough. Ask: **Does this brittle star have an exoskeleton similar to a crustacean's?** *(No. A brittle star has an endoskeleton beneath its spiny skin.)*

28–4 Echinoderms

Guide for Reading

Key Concepts

- What are the distinguishing features of echinoderms?
- What functions are carried out by the water vascular system of echinoderms?
- What are the different classes of echinoderms?

Vocabulary
endoskeleton
water vascular system
madreporite
tube foot

Reading Strategy: Using Visuals Before you read, preview **Figure 28–23.** As you read, notice where in the sea star each function occurs.

One of the most unusual sights along the seashore might be the sea stars, sea urchins, and sand dollars that have washed up on the beach. These animals look like stars, pincushions, and coins. They are all echinoderms (ee-KY-noh-durmz), members of the phylum Echinodermata. *Echino-* means "spiny," and *dermis* means "skin." If you have ever touched a sea star, you will know why this name is appropriate. The skin of echinoderms is stretched over an internal skeleton, or **endoskeleton,** that is formed of hardened plates of calcium carbonate. These plates give the animal a bumpy and irregular texture. Echinoderms live only in the sea. Some are delicate, brightly colored, feathery-armed creatures. Others look like mud-brown half-rotten cucumbers!

What Is an Echinoderm?

The body plan of echinoderms is like no other in the animal kingdom. Adult echinoderms typically have no anterior or posterior end and lack cephalization. However, the bodies of most echinoderms are two-sided. The side in which the mouth is located is called the oral surface, and the opposite side is called the aboral surface.

Echinoderms are characterized by spiny skin, an internal skeleton, a water vascular system, and suction-cuplike structures called tube feet. Most adult echinoderms exhibit five-part radial symmetry. The body parts, which usually occur in multiples of five, are arranged around the central body like the spokes of a wheel. The brittle star in **Figure 28–22** exhibits this kind of symmetry. Although radial symmetry is characteristic of simpler animals such as cnidarians, echinoderms are actually more closely related to humans and other vertebrates. The larvae of echinoderms are bilaterally symmetrical, indicating that body symmetry evolved differently in this group than in simpler animals. Also, echinoderms are deuterostomes, animals in which the blastopore develops into an anus. This type of development is found in echinoderms and vertebrates, indicating that these groups are closely related.

Figure 28–22 **Echinoderms such as this brittle star have spiny skin, five-part radial symmetry, an internal skeleton, a water vascular system, and suction-cuplike structures called tube feet.** Observe that the brittle star has five arms. The bodies of most echinoderms are divided into parts that are multiples of five.

SECTION RESOURCES

Print:

- ***Teaching Resources,*** Lesson Plan 28–4, Adapted Section Summary 28–4, Adapted Worksheets 28–4, Section Summary 28–4, Worksheets 28–4, Section Review 28–4
- ***Reading and Study Workbook A,*** Section 28–4
- ***Adapted Reading and Study Workbook B,*** Section 28–4
- ***Issues and Decision Making,*** Issues and Decisions 30
- ***Biotechnology Manual,*** Lab 7

Technology:

- ***iText,*** Section 28–4
- ***Transparencies Plus,*** Section 28–4

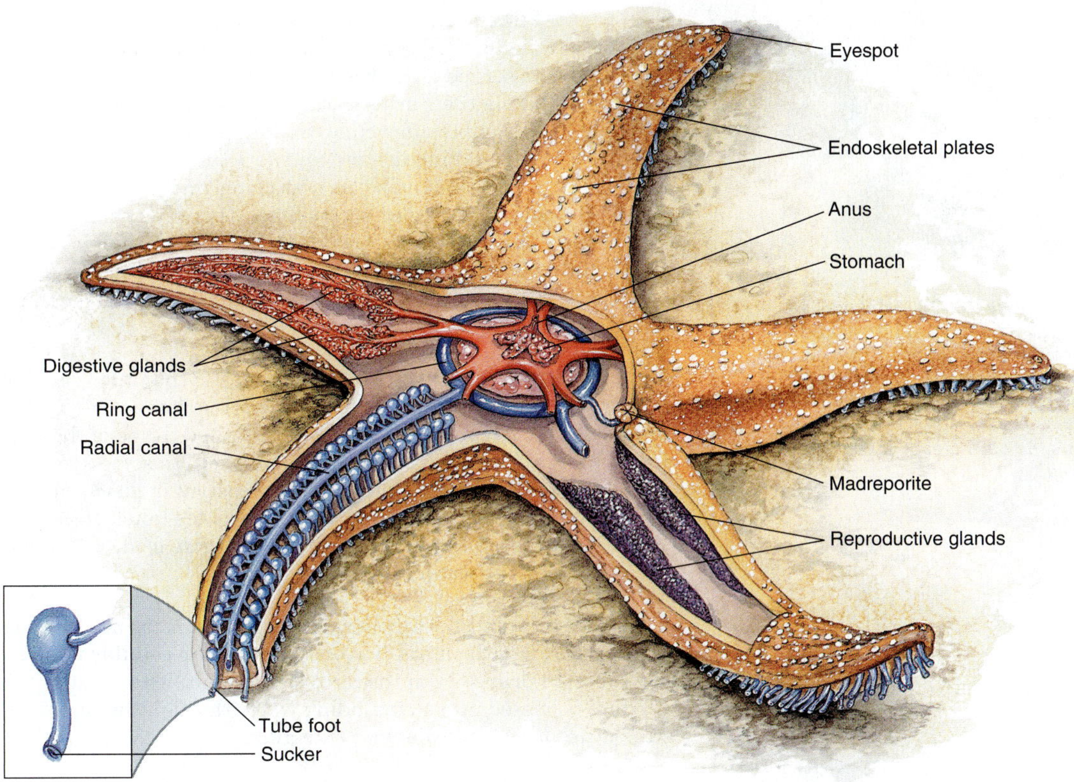

▲ **Figure 28–23** The most distinctive system of echinoderms is the water vascular system, shown here in a sea star. **The water vascular system, which extends throughout the body, functions in respiration, circulation, and movement.**

Form and Function in Echinoderms

A unique feature of echinoderms is a system of internal tubes called a **water vascular system,** which is shown in **Figure 28–23.** **The water vascular system, which is filled with fluid, carries out many essential body functions in echinoderms, including respiration, circulation, and movement.** It opens to the outside through a sievelike structure called a **madreporite** (MAD-ruh-pawr-yt). In sea stars, the madreporite connects to a ring canal that forms a circle around the animal's mouth. From the ring canal, five radial canals extend along body segments.

Attached to each radial canal are hundreds of tube feet. A **tube foot** is a structure that operates much like a suction cup. Each tube foot has a sucker on the end. Muscles pull the center of the sucker upwards, forming a cup shape. This action creates suction on the surface to which the foot is attached, so the tube foot pulls on the surface. Hundreds of tube feet acting together create enormous force, allowing echinoderms to "walk" and even to pull open shelled prey such as clams.

CHECKPOINT *What is the system of internal tubes in echinoderms?*

For: Water Vascular System activity
Visit: PHSchool.com
Web Code: cbp-8284

Form and Function in Echinoderms

Use Visuals

Figure 28–23 Ask students: **What body systems does a sea star have?** *(Digestive system, reproductive system, water vascular system, endoskeletal system, and nervous system)* **What structures are part of the water vascular system?** *(The madreporite, ring canal, radial canal, and tube feet)* **What essential body functions does the water vascular system carry out in an echinoderm?** *(Respiration, circulation, and movement)* L1 L2

Demonstration

Display a preserved sea star. (Rinse excess preservative from the specimen, and place it in a dissecting pan.) Have students put on disposable plastic gloves and safety goggles. Invite students to examine the sea star. After students have examined the sea star, ask: **What are some typical animal traits that a sea star appears not to have?** *(Answers will vary. Students might notice the absence of a head and sense organs.)* **Does the body appear to be segmented?** *(No)* Point out that the absence of segmentation is one indication that echinoderms are not close relatives of annelids and arthropods. Then, ask: **What type of symmetry does a sea star have?** *(A sea star exhibits radial symmetry.)* Review the difference between bilateral and radial symmetry, if necessary. Point out that most echinoderms, unlike cnidarians, have a five-part, or pentaradial, symmetry. L2

For: Water Vascular System activity
Visit: PHSchool.com
Web Code: cbe-8284
Students explore the water vascular system of a sea star.

UNIVERSAL ACCESS

English Language Learners
To help students understand the difference in the two sides of an echinoderm, explain that the word *oral* means "having to do with the mouth." The word often means "spoken," as in "oral instructions." In the case of echinoderms, the oral surface simply means the surface that the mouth is on. Also point out that the prefix *ab-* means "away from." Thus, the aboral surface literally means "the surface, or side, away from the mouth." L1 L2

Advanced Learners
Encourage students who need extra challenges to investigate further the threat that the crown-of-thorns poses to coral reefs, as mentioned on page 738. Suggest that students write a report on the threat using library and Internet sources. When students have finished their reports, ask them to share their findings with the class. L3

Answer to . . .

CHECKPOINT *The water vascular system*

28–4 (continued)

Build Science Skills

Using Models Divide the class into small groups, and give each group a small suction cup. Challenge students to make the suction cup adhere to a vertical surface for at least one minute. (*Through trial and error, students will discover that the surface must be smooth and that the cup will stay in place longer if it is first moistened.*) Ask groups to share their findings. Discuss how an echinoderm's tube feet are like suction cups. L2 L3

Build Science Skills

Observing Divide the class into pairs, and give each pair a preserved or live sea star and a dissecting tray. Make sure students wear goggles, disposable gloves, and lab aprons for this activity. (Caution students to keep their hands away from their faces throughout this activity and to wash their hands with soap and warm water afterward, because the preservative used to preserve the organism may cause skin and eye irritation.) Students should observe the sea star, make a sketch of what they see, and label all structures they can identify. Advise students to compare the two sides of the sea star and look especially for its tube feet. Once they have finished their sketches, ask students to explain in writing the purpose of each part they labeled in their drawings. L2 L3

Download a worksheet on echinoderms for students to complete, and find additional teacher support from NSTA SciLinks.

▲ **Figure 28–24** Echinoderms use all types of feeding methods. Sea stars, like the one shown above, are carnivores that typically feed on mussels and other bivalves. **Comparing and Contrasting** *How do other groups of echinoderms feed?*

Feeding Echinoderms have several methods of feeding. Sea urchins use five-part jawlike structures to scrape algae from rocks. Sea lilies use tube feet along their arms to capture floating plankton. Sea cucumbers move like bulldozers across the ocean floor, taking in sand and detritus. Sea stars usually feed on mollusks such as clams and mussels, as shown in **Figure 28–24.** Once the prey's shell is open, the sea star pushes its stomach out through its mouth, pours out enzymes, and digests the mollusk in its own shell. Then, the sea star pulls its stomach and the partially digested prey into its mouth.

Respiration and Circulation Other than the water vascular system, echinoderms have few adaptations to carry out respiration or circulation. In most species, the thin-walled tissue of the tube feet provides the main surface for respiration. In some species, small outgrowths called skin gills also function in gas exchange.

Circulation of needed materials and wastes takes place throughout the water vascular system. Oxygen, food, and wastes are carried by the water vascular system.

Excretion In most echinoderms, digestive wastes are released as feces through the anus. Nitrogen-containing cellular wastes are excreted primarily in the form of ammonia. This waste product is passed into surrounding water through the thin-walled tissues of tube feet and skin gills.

Response Echinoderms do not have a highly developed nervous system. Most have a nerve ring that surrounds the mouth, and radial nerves that connect the ring with the body sections. Most echinoderms also have scattered sensory cells that detect light, gravity, and chemicals released by potential prey.

Movement Most echinoderms move using tube feet. An echinoderm's mobility is determined in part by the structure of its endoskeleton. Sand dollars and sea urchins have movable spines attached to the endoskeleton. Sea stars and brittle stars have flexible joints that enable them to use their arms for locomotion. In sea cucumbers, the plates of the endoskeleton are reduced and contained inside a soft, muscular body wall. These echinoderms crawl along the ocean floor by the combined action of tube feet and the muscles of the body wall.

Reproduction Echinoderms reproduce by external fertilization. Sperm are produced in testes, and eggs are produced in ovaries. Both types of gametes are shed into open water, where fertilization takes place. The larvae, which have bilateral symmetry, swim around for some time and then swim to the ocean bottom, where they develop into adults that have radial symmetry.

For: Links on echinoderms
Visit: www.SciLinks.org
Web Code: cbn-8284

CHECKPOINT *How do echinoderms move?*

BIO INSIGHTS — FACTS AND FIGURES

Are echinoderms really invertebrates?
Although the basic nervous system and lack of a brain appear to place echinoderms among the very simple animals, they have some structures more typical of complex animals, including a unique internal skeleton. Hard nodules of calcium carbonate called ossicles are embedded in the body walls and surrounded by living tissues, providing the strength and protection of a mollusk shell. Many scientists wonder if these animals should really be classified with the invertebrates. Although echinoderms do not have backbones, their larvae appear to have much in common with a wormlike ancestor of the vertebrates. Also, the ossicles of the brittle star fit together much like the vertebrae of a backbone.

Groups of Echinoderms

There are roughly 7000 species of echinoderms—all of which live in the world's oceans. **Classes of echinoderms include sea urchins and sand dollars; brittle stars; sea cucumbers; sea stars; sea lilies and feather stars.** Some of these echinoderms are shown in **Figure 28–25**.

Sea Urchins and Sand Dollars This class includes sea urchins and disk-shaped sand dollars. These echinoderms are unique in having large, solid plates that form a box around their internal organs. Many are detritivores or grazers that eat large quantities of algae. They defend themselves in different ways. Sand dollars often burrow under layers of sand or mud. Some sea urchins wedge themselves in rock crevices during the day, whereas others defend themselves using long, sharp spines.

Brittle Stars Brittle stars are common in many parts of the sea, especially on coral reefs. They have slender, flexible arms and can scuttle around quite rapidly to escape predators. In addition to using speed for protection, brittle stars shed one or more arms when attacked. The detached arm keeps moving, distracting the predator while the brittle star escapes. Brittle stars are filter feeders and detritivores that hide by day and wander around under cover of darkness.

Sea Cucumbers Sea cucumbers look like warty, moving pickles. Most sea cucumbers are detritus feeders that move along the sea floor while sucking up organic matter and the remains of other animals and plants. Herds containing hundreds of thousands of sea cucumbers roam across the deep-sea floor.

Sea Stars Sea stars are probably the best-known group of echinoderms. They move by creeping slowly along the ocean floor. Most are carnivorous, preying on bivalves that they encounter. Many sea stars have incredible abilities to repair themselves when damaged. If a sea star is pulled into pieces, each piece will grow into a new animal, as long as it contains a portion of the central part of the body.

Figure 28–25 **Sea urchins, brittle stars, sea cucumbers, and sea stars represent different classes of echinoderms.** Observe the characteristics of these representatives of each class.

Long-Spined Sea Urchin

Brittle Star

Red-Lined Sea Cucumber

Sun Star

Groups of Echinoderms

Address Misconceptions

Explain that sea stars and starfish are different names for the same kind of echinoderm. Many students, who may have seen sea stars on a beach or in a coastal souvenir shop, may think that a sea star is some kind of fish. Point out that echinoderms are invertebrates and fishes are vertebrates, and thus a sea star cannot be classified as a fish. Similarly, some students may be misled by the echinoderm names *sea cucumber* and *sea lily.* Discuss how these animals may have gotten their names, and emphasize that they are animals, not plants. L1 L2

Build Science Skills

Classifying To reinforce understanding of echinoderm classification, show students photos or slides of a variety of different echinoderms, making sure that all classes of echinoderms are represented by at least one example. Ask volunteers to classify each echinoderm as it is shown according to the class to which it belongs. As each echinoderm class is mentioned, call on students at random to review the characteristics of members of that class, such as how they feed or move. L2

FACTS AND FIGURES

Millions of brittle stars

Brittle stars are the most abundant echinoderms, in terms of numbers both of species and of individuals. About 2000 species are found worldwide, from the seashore to depths as great as 6000 meters. In some places, millions of individuals live in clusters on the ocean floor. Brittle stars move by crawling or clinging with their flexible arms. The arms are quite flexible moving back and forth—that is, on a plane perpendicular to the line from the oral surface to the aboral surface. But the arms of a brittle star are not at all flexible moving up and down—that is, on a plane parallel to the same line. For that reason, the arms are "brittle" and break off easily.

Answers to . . .

CHECKPOINT *Most echinoderms move by using tube feet and muscle.*

Figure 28–24 *Sea urchins use five-part jaws to scrape algae from rocks. Sea lilies use tube feet along their arms to capture floating plankton. Sea cucumbers move like bulldozers across the ocean floor, taking in sand and detritus.*

28–4 (continued)

Ecology of Echinoderms

Build Science Skills

Predicting After students have read the section on the ecology of echinoderms, ask them to write a prediction of what might happen if an area of the ocean experienced a decline of sea urchins or an increase in sea stars. Students' predictions should reflect an understanding of both the ecology of echinoderms and the dynamics of a food web. L2 L3

3 ASSESS

Evaluate Understanding

Ask students to write a description of an echinoderm's water vascular system and what functions it serves.

Reteach

Have students make their own drawing of the labeled sea star in Figure 28–23. Have students also define each of the terms shown as labels.

Focus on the BIG Idea

Both a sea star and a cnidarian exhibit radial symmetry, which means that body parts extend from the center of the body. In a cnidarian, any number of imaginary planes can be drawn through the center, each dividing the body into equal halves. By contrast, most echinoderms exhibit five-part radial symmetry, which means that the bodies are divided into parts that are multiples of five.

If your class subscribes to the iText, use it to review the Key Concepts in Section 28–4.

Answer to . . .

Figure 28–26 *Sea lilies live attached to the ocean floor by a long stalk.*

Figure 28–26 Sea lilies belong to the most ancient class of echinoderms, known as crinoids. The red crinoid (top) is one of the few species of this class that are alive today. This stalked crinoid fossil (bottom) is an example of the types of crinoids that dominated Earth during the Paleozoic Era. **Comparing and Contrasting** *How are sea lilies different from other echinoderms?*

Sea Lilies and Feather Stars These filter feeders, which have long, feathery arms, make up the oldest class of echinoderms. Sea lilies and feather stars are common in tropical oceans today, and a rich fossil record shows that they were distributed widely throughout ancient seas. Like modern sea lilies, their fossilized ancestors lived attached to the ocean bottom by a long, stemlike stalk, as seen in **Figure 28–26.** Many modern feather stars live on coral reefs, where they perch on top of rocks and use their tube feet to catch floating plankton.

Ecology of Echinoderms

Echinoderms are common in a variety of marine habitats. In many areas, a sudden rise or fall in the number of echinoderms can cause major changes to populations of other marine organisms. Sea urchins help control the distribution of algae and other forms of marine life. Sea stars are important predators that help control the numbers of other organisms such as clams and corals.

A major threat to coral reefs is one kind of sea star called the crown-of-thorns. This echinoderm is named for the rows of poisonous spines located along its arms. It feeds almost exclusively on coral. In the Great Barrier Reef of Australia—one of the largest reef systems in the world—this organism has destroyed extensive areas of coral.

28–4 Section Assessment

1. **Key Concept** What is an echinoderm?
2. **Key Concept** What is the water vascular system? How is it important to echinoderms?
3. **Key Concept** List the major classes of echinoderms and describe their characteristics.
4. What are tube feet? What functions do they perform, and how do they perform them?
5. Echinoderms are deuterostomes. What does this indicate about their relationship to other animals?
6. **Critical Thinking Inferring** Why is tearing a sea star apart and throwing it back into the water an ineffective way of trying to reduce sea star populations?

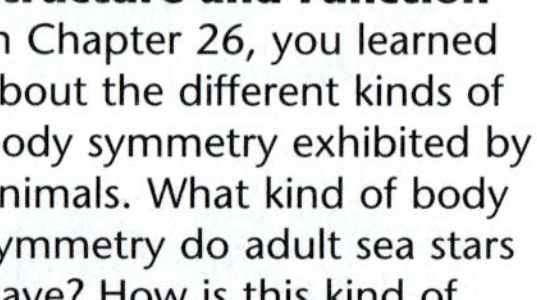

Structure and Function
In Chapter 26, you learned about the different kinds of body symmetry exhibited by animals. What kind of body symmetry do adult sea stars have? How is this kind of symmetry similar to that of a cnidarian? How is it different?

28–4 Section Assessment

1. An echinoderm has a spiny skin, an internal skeleton, and a water vascular system with tube feet. Most have five-part radial symmetry.
2. The water vascular system is a system of internal tubes. The system carries out respiration, circulation, and movement.
3. Students should list the classes and characteristics described on pages 737–738.
4. Tube feet are structures attached to the radial canal of echinoderms. Each has a sucker on the end, and muscles pull the center of the sucker upward, creating suction. Tube feet allow echinoderms to walk and to pull open shelled prey.
5. Echinoderms are more closely related to chordates than to other invertebrates, most of which are protostomes.
6. If a sea star is pulled into pieces, each piece will usually grow into a new animal.

Design an Experiment

7IIE 7.c, 8IIE 9.c, BIIE 1.a

Observing Ant Behavior

In this investigation, you will design experiments to determine how ants respond to members of other colonies and other species.

Problem How do ants respond to members of other colonies and other species?

Materials

- covered petri dish containing 10 ants of species A from the same colony (**CAUTION:** *Do not use stinging species of ants such as fire ants or harvester ants, or destructive species such as carpenter ants.*)
- hand lens or dissecting microscope
- field guide (for identifying ants)
- watch or clock with a second hand
- 3 covered petri dishes, each containing 5 ants of species A from different colonies
- covered petri dish containing 5 ants from species B (**CAUTION:** *Do not use stinging species of ants such as fire ants or harvester ants, or destructive species such as carpenter ants.*)

Skills Predicting, Drawing Conclusions

Design Your Experiment 

Part A: Observing Ants That Are Related

1. Obtain a petri dish containing 10 ants from the same colony. Look at the ants under a hand lens or dissecting microscope. Use a field guide to identify the species to which they belong.
2. For 30 seconds, count the number of ants that are fighting with one another. Record this number on a sheet of paper. If the ants are not fighting, write "0."
3. **Predicting** Record your prediction of whether ants from separate colonies of the same species will fight, and whether ants of two different species will fight.

Part B: Observing Ants That Are Not Related

4. **Designing Experiments** Design experiments to test your predictions. As you plan your investigative procedures, refer to the Lab Tips box on page 55 for information on planning safe investigations, planning wise use of materials, and selecting equipment and technology.
5. Write a hypothesis for each experiment and control all variables except the one you are testing. **CAUTION:** *Ants are delicate, and some can produce painful stings. Do not try to pick them up.* Have your teacher check your plan before you begin to perform your experiment.

Analyze and Conclude

1. **Observing** Did most of the ants fight in step 2? How would you explain the behavior you observed?
2. **Observing** What happened when you put ants from two different colonies of the same species together? When you put ants from two different species together? Were your predictions correct?
3. **Drawing Conclusions** How do you think the behavior you observed helps the ants survive?

Go Further

Asking Questions Think of some other aspects of ants and their behavior that you would like to learn about. For example, you might be curious about how different environmental conditions affect an ant colony, or which foods individual ants prefer. Write your ideas as a series of questions. Choose one of your questions and find an answer to it, either by finding information in reference materials or designing an experiment. Before performing any experiments, obtain your teacher's approval.

Analyze and Conclude

1. Most of the ants did not fight. Ants from the same colony almost never fight one another. Because they are part of the same colony, they need to cooperate, not compete, to survive.
2. Ants of the same species, but from different colonies, will usually fight. (However, Pharaoh ants from different colonies will not fight.) Ants from different species will almost always fight. Students should note whether their predictions were or were not correct.
3. Ants must compete for resources such as food. By attacking ants from other colonies or species, they reduce the number of ants that compete for the same resources.

Design an Experiment

 7IIE 7.c, 8IIE 9.c, BIIE 1.a

Objective Students will observe how ants respond to members of the same colony, other colonies, and other species. L2 L3

Skills Focus Predicting, Drawing Conclusions

Time 45 minutes

Advance Prep Collect or order ants in advance. Freshly collected wild ants are preferable. Those from supply houses have been separated from the queen and colony for so long that they have lost their identifying odors. Attract ants by putting a piece of a sugary food near cracks in a sidewalk. The pavement ant, *Tetramorium caespitum,* is a good choice for species A. It is common in the eastern United States, California, and Washington. Collect ants from two widely separated areas to ensure that they are from different colonies. Pharaoh ants, *Monomorium pharaonis,* are a good choice for species B.

Safety Students should not touch the ants. Make sure not to use stinging species such as fire ants or harvester ants, or destructive species such as carpenter ants. Check state and local regulations before obtaining ants.

Teaching Tips

- Explain that ants often communicate and identify one another by touch. Fights involve grasping with the mandibles.
- Remind students to record the number of ants fighting, not the number of fights. One fight may involve several ants.

Expected Outcomes Students should observe that ants won't fight members of their own colony but will fight members of other colonies.

Go Further

Students doing research might look for information under the following topics: ants, insects, insect societies, and animal behavior. Supervise all Internet research. If students choose to perform experiments, check and approve their plans before allowing them to begin.

Chapter 28 Study Guide

Study Tip
Divide the class into pairs, and have students quiz each other about the Vocabulary and the Key Concepts.

Thinking Visually

The diagram should begin at the top with phylum Arthropoda. On the second level should be subphylums Crustacea, Chelicerata, and Uniramia. Under Crustacea should be the decapods and the barnacles. The decapods include crayfishes, lobsters, and crabs. Under Chelicerata should be class Merostomata, the horseshoe crabs, and class Arachnida, which includes spiders, mites, ticks, and scorpions. Under Uniramia should be class Chilopoda, or the centipedes; class Diplopoda, or the millipedes; and class Insecta, the insects.

Chapter 28 Assessment

Reviewing Content

1. b	5. b	9. c
2. a	6. d	10. b
3. b	7. d	
4. b	8. d	

Understanding Concepts

11. The variety of respiratory organs among arthropods enables arthropods to live in both terrestrial and aquatic environments. Terrestrial arthropods obtain oxygen through tracheal tubes or book lungs. Aquatic arthropods use gills or book gills to remove oxygen from water.

12. Most terrestrial arthropods dispose of nitrogen-containing waste by using Malpighian tubes, which remove wastes from the blood, concentrate them, and then add them to undigested food before it leaves via the anus. In aquatic arthropods cellular wastes diffuse from the body into the water.

13. All have a brain. Two nerves that run around the esophagus connect the brain to a ventral nerve cord. Ganglia along the cord coordinate movements of the legs and wings.

14. It covers and protects the cephalothorax.

15. Decapods are motile, whereas barnacles are sessile. Barnacles have no abdominal segments and do not use mandibles.

Chapter 28 Study Guide

28–1 Introduction to the Arthropods

Key Concepts

- Arthropods have a segmented body, a tough exoskeleton, and jointed appendages.
- The evolution of arthropods, by natural selection and other evolutionary processes, has led to fewer body segments and highly specialized appendages for feeding, movement, and other functions.
- When they outgrow their exoskeletons, arthropods undergo periods of molting.

Vocabulary
exoskeleton, p. 715
chitin, p. 715
appendage, p. 715
tracheal tube, p. 717
spiracle, p. 717
book lung, p. 717
Malpighian tubule, p. 717
molting, p. 719

28–2 Groups of Arthropods

Key Concepts

- Arthropods are classified based on the number and structure of their body segments and appendages, particularly their mouthparts.
- Crustaceans typically have two pairs of antennae, two or three body sections, and chewing mouthparts called mandibles.
- Chelicerates have mouthparts called chelicerae and two body sections, and nearly all have four pairs of walking legs.
- Uniramians have jaws, one pair of antennae, and unbranched appendages.

Vocabulary
cephalothorax, p. 721
thorax, p. 721
abdomen, p. 721
carapace, p. 721
mandible, p. 721
cheliped, p. 721
swimmeret, p. 721
chelicera, p. 722
pedipalp, p. 722
spinneret, p. 723

28–3 Insects

Key Concepts

- Insects have a body divided into three parts—head, thorax, and abdomen. Three pairs of legs are attached to the thorax.
- The growth and development of insects usually involve metamorphosis, which is a process of changing shape and form. Insects undergo either incomplete metamorphosis or complete metamorphosis.
- Ants, bees, termites, and some of their relatives form complex associations called societies.

Vocabulary
incomplete metamorphosis, p. 729
nymph, p. 729
complete metamorphosis, p. 729
pupa, p. 729
pheromone, p. 731
society, p. 732
caste, p. 732

28–4 Echinoderms

Key Concepts

- Echinoderms are characterized by spiny skin, an internal skeleton, a water vascular system, and suction-cuplike structures called tube feet. Most adults have five-part radial symmetry.
- The water vascular system carries out many essential body functions in echinoderms, including respiration, circulation, and movement.
- Classes of echinoderms include sea urchins and sand dollars; brittle stars; sea cucumbers; sea stars; sea lilies and feather stars.

Vocabulary
endoskeleton, p. 734
water vascular system, p. 735
madreporite, p. 735
tube foot, p. 735

Thinking Visually
Construct a diagram that models the classification of the phylum Arthropoda. Your classification system should be based on similarities and differences. It should show a hierarchy, or the arrangement of the subgroups within the phylum. Be sure to use taxonomic nomenclature (phylum, subphylum, and so forth).

CHAPTER RESOURCES

Print:
- ***Teaching Resources,*** Chapter Vocabulary Review, Graphic Organizer, Chapter 28 Tests: Levels A and B

Technology:
- ***Computer Test Bank,*** Chapter 28 Test
- ***iText,*** Chapter 28 Assessment

Chapter 28 Assessment

Interactive textbook with assessment at PHSchool.com

Reviewing Content

Choose the letter that best answers the question or completes the statement.

1. All arthropods have
   a. gills.
   b. jointed appendages.
   c. antennae.
   d. chelicerae.

2. An arthropod's exoskeleton performs all of the following functions except
   a. production of gametes.
   b. protection of internal organs.
   c. support of the animal's body.
   d. preventing loss of body water.

3. Most terrestrial arthropods breathe using branched, air-filled structures called
   a. gills. **c.** book gills.
   b. tracheal tubes. **d.** book lungs.

4. Most arthropods have
   a. no circulatory system.
   b. an open circulatory system.
   c. a closed circulatory system.
   d. skin gills.

5. Crustaceans are the only arthropods that have
   a. three pairs of legs.
   b. two pairs of antennae.
   c. chitin in their exoskeleton.
   d. chelicerae.

6. Which of the organisms below belongs in the subphylum Chelicerata?

a.

c.

b.

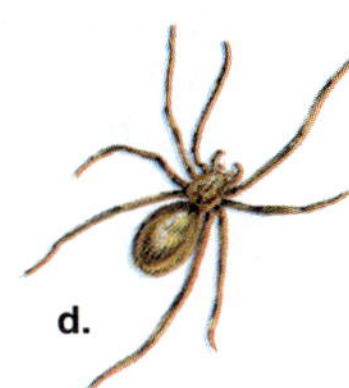
d.

7. Unlike spiders, horseshoe crabs have
   a. antennae. **c.** mandibles.
   b. a madreporite. **d.** ten legs.

8. All insects have
   a. two pairs of legs.
   b. two pairs of antennae.
   c. two pairs of wings.
   d. three body sections.

9. Most adult echinoderms show
   a. bilateral symmetry.
   b. top and bottom symmetry.
   c. radial symmetry.
   d. no symmetry.

10. Oxygen is moved around the body of a sea star in its
    a. stemlike stalk. **c.** madreporite.
    b. water vascular system. **d.** bony plates.

Understanding Concepts

11. How have the various respiratory structures found in arthropods contributed to their overall success?
12. Compare the process of excretion in terrestrial arthropods with that in aquatic arthropods.
13. Describe the structure of arthropods' nervous system.
14. What is the function of a crustacean's carapace?
15. How are barnacles different from decapods?
16. What is the function of a mandible?
17. Distinguish between chelicerae and pedipalps.
18. How are the mouthparts of mites and ticks adapted to a specific lifestyle?
19. State obvious differences in the body structure of the different groups of uniramians.
20. How have the characteristics of insects contributed to their evolutionary success?
21. Describe some of the special feeding adaptations found in insects.
22. How does the term *society* relate to ants, bees, and termites?
23. Describe how echinoderms eliminate nitrogenous wastes.
24. Briefly describe the process of sexual reproduction in sea stars.
25. How has the predation of the sea star called the crown-of-thorns affected coral reefs?

HOMEWORK GUIDE

Section:	Questions:
Section 28–1	1–4, 11–13
Section 28–2	5–7, 14–19, 27, 29, 30
Section 28–3	8, 20–22, 26, 28, 31, 33, 34
Section 28–4	9, 10, 23–25, 32

Interactive Textbook

If your class subscribes to the iText, your students can go online to access an interactive version of the Student Edition and a self-test.

(Continued from page 740)

16. It is adapted for biting and grinding food.

17. Both chelicerae and pedipalps are appendages adapted as mouthparts. Chelicerae contain fangs used to capture and paralyze prey, and pedipalps are usually modified to handle prey.

18. Ticks and mites are parasites. Their mouthparts are adapted to dig into a host's tissues and suck out fluids.

19. Centipedes have many segments, each with one pair of legs. Millipedes have many segments, each with two pairs of legs. The bodies of insects are divided into three sections—head, thorax, and abdomen—with three pairs of legs attached to the thorax.

20. The characteristics of insects have enabled them to thrive in many different habitats.

21. Insect adaptations for feeding include: mouthparts adapted to specific feeding functions, e.g., grinding or sucking; saliva containing digestive enzymes; in bees, chambers for the storage of food.

22. Ants, bees, and termites form societies in which individuals work together for the benefit of the whole group. Individuals specialize in performing specific roles or tasks.

23. In most echinoderms, nitrogen-containing cellular wastes are excreted primarily in the form of ammonia, which is passed into surrounding water through the thin-walled tissues of tube feet and skin gills.

24. The eggs and sperm of sea stars are released into open water, where fertilization occurs. Eventually the larvae, which have bilateral symmetry, swim to the ocean bottom, where they mature into adults that have radial symmetry.

25. The crown-of-thorns feeds on coral and has destroyed extensive areas of the Great Barrier Reef.

Chapter 28 Assessment

Critical Thinking

26. Applying Concepts The legs and bodies of honeybees are covered with hair that collects pollen and other materials. How is this adaptation helpful to flowering plants and honeybees?

27. Applying Concepts Blue crabs usually have hard shells. During certain times of the year some of the blue crabs have thin, papery shells. In terms of the life processes of arthropods, explain why these blue crabs have soft shells.

28. Classifying An animal is discovered that has an exoskeleton, sucking mouthparts, head fused with thorax, no wings, and four pairs of walking legs. Would you classify the animal as an insect? Explain your answer.

29. Analyzing Data Brine shrimp are small crustaceans found in salty lakes and ponds. The graph shows the effect of water temperature on the time it takes for brine shrimp eggs to hatch. Based on the graph, what can you conclude about the relationship between water temperature and hatching time? How many hours would it take for eggs to hatch at 18°C and at 25°C? Can you predict the amount of time it would take for eggs to hatch at 10°C?

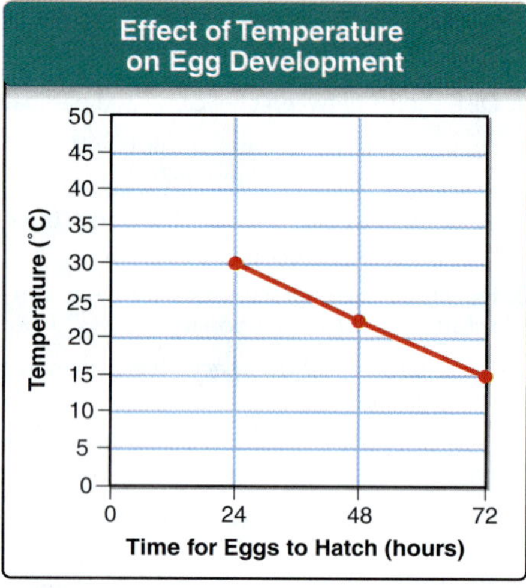

30. Inferring In a stagnant pool of water, a crayfish may spend much of its time lying with one side of its carapace near the surface of the water. In this position, it will move the walking legs on that side in a back-and-forth motion. To what external stimulus is the crayfish responding? Explain the value of this behavior.

31. Inferring In many insect species, insect adults and larvae feed on different substances. How might this characteristic help members of those species survive?

32. Comparing and Contrasting How are echinoderms structurally different from arthropods?

33. Applying Concepts What role do pheromones play in insect survival?

34. Inferring Insects today inhabit almost every environment on Earth, and they exhibit a wide variety of adaptations that enable them to survive in those environments. How might natural selection have contributed to insect diversity?

Focus on the BIG Idea

Matter and Energy Chitin is made of protein and polysaccharides. What are these two substances? You might want to review relevant concepts in Chapter 2.

Writing in Science

In your own words, write a description of how molting takes place in an arthropod, and what happens immediately after molting. Include an explanation of why it is necessary for an arthropod to undergo molting periodically. (*Hint:* Before you write, use a flowchart to organize the steps in the molting process.)

Performance-Based Assessment

Around the Neighborhood Make a photograph collection of arthropods in your neighborhood. Use field guides to identify the arthropods in your photographs. Mount the photographs in a display that indicates the major characteristics of arthropods and the various groups of arthropods.

For: An interactive self-test
Visit: PHSchool.com
Web Code: cba-8280

Chapter 28 Assessment

Critical Thinking

26. The adaptation enables honeybees to carry pollen from one flower to another, thus pollinating the flowers in the process. The adaptation also enables honeybees to collect food and carry it back to the hive.

27. Crabs have soft shells soon after they molt because the new exoskeleton has not had time to become hardened.

28. The animal is not an insect, because insects have three distinct body regions, one pair of antennae, one pair of compound eyes, three pairs of mouthparts, and three pairs of walking legs.

29. As the temperature decreases, the time for the eggs to hatch increases. It would take about 62 hours for the eggs to hatch at 18°C, and 40 hours for them to hatch at 25°C. On the basis of the trend shown on the graph, it might take 88 hours for eggs to hatch at 10°C.

30. The crayfish is responding to the greater amount of oxygen dissolved in surface water than at lower depths. In addition, the movement of the crayfish's legs can further increase the amount of oxygen dissolved in the stagnant pool and create a flow of this oxygenated water over the gills, where respiration occurs.

31. Adults and larvae do not compete with one another for food. Also, different types of food may be abundant at different times of the year, and these differences may correlate to stages in the insect's life cycle.

32. Unlike arthropods, echinoderms have spiny skin, radial symmetry, an internal skeleton, a water vascular system, and suction-cuplike structures called tube feet.

33. Pheromones warn of danger and enable males and females to communicate during courtship and mating, thus helping to ensure survival of individuals and species.

34. As insects moved into different environments over time, they evolved through natural selection adaptations that allowed them to succeed in those environments. Among these adaptations are flight, different ways of responding to stimuli, and a life cycle in which the young differ from adults in appearance and feeding methods.

Focus on the BIG Idea

Proteins are organic compounds composed of amino acids needed for the growth and repair of cells. Polysaccharides are complex carbohydrates.

Writing in Science

Students should explain that arthropods undergo periods of molting when they outgrow their exoskeletons. During molting, an arthropod sheds its entire exoskeleton and manufactures a larger one to take its place. Molting is controlled by an arthropod's endocrine system. Skin glands digest the inner part of the exoskeleton, and other glands secrete a new skeleton. To protect themselves, arthropods typically hide during the molting period or molt at night. While the new exoskeleton is soft, the animal fills with air or fluids to allow room for growth before the next molting.

Standards Practice

Success Tracker™
Online at PHSchool.com

Test-Taking Tip If you are taking a long time to answer a question, consider coming back to it later. As you answer the other questions, you may remember the information you needed to answer the skipped question.

Directions: Choose the letter that best answers the question or completes the statement.

1. Mites and ticks are examples of
   A crustaceans.
   B swimmerets.
   C arachnids.
   D chelicerae.
2. In spiders, the organs that contain the silk glands are called
   A carapaces.
   B spinnerets.
   C swimmerets.
   D madreporites.
3. Which of these is NOT a characteristic of an echinoderm?
   A five-part radial symmetry
   B a pair of antennae
   C tube feet
   D a water vascular system
4. Trilobites
   A are primarily terrestrial.
   B are extinct.
   C have highly specialized appendages.
   D communicate by "dancing."

Questions 5–8 Each of the lettered choices below refers to the following numbered statements. Select the best lettered choice. A choice may be used once, more than once, or not at all.

A Trilobites
B Pedipalps
C Arachnids
D Pheromones

5. Types of animals that have four pairs of walking legs
6. Chemical messengers that affect the behavior or development of other individuals of the same species
7. Group containing spiders, scorpions, ticks, and mites
8. Extinct group of marine arthropods that were abundant more than 500 million years ago

Questions 9–10

A biology student is investigating the relationship between cricket chirps and temperature. She catches a cricket and places it in a jar. She leaves the jar outside, and each day she measures the number of chirps during a 15-second period. At the same time, she records the outside temperature near the cricket. Her data for a 5-day period are shown below.

Relationship Between Temperature and Cricket Chirping

Day	Number of Chirps in 15 Seconds	Outside Temperature (°C)
Monday	31	23
Tuesday	20	16
Wednesday	12	11
Thursday	29	21
Friday	25	19

9. At which of the following temperatures would a cricket be most likely to chirp 9 times in 15 seconds?
   A 2°C
   B 10°C
   C 18°C
   D 0°C
10. What can the student conclude from this experiment?
   A Crickets cannot chirp more than 31 times in 15 seconds.
   B The number of chirps decreases when the temperature decreases.
   C Crickets never chirp more than 31 times every 15 seconds.
   D The number of chirps increases when the temperature decreases.

Standards Practice

1. C 2. B 3. B 4. B 5. C 6. D 7. C 8. A 9. B 10. B

Success Tracker™
Online at PHSchool.com

Have students check their understanding of the chapter by logging onto Success Tracker.

Performance-Based Assessment

Student displays should reflect an understanding of the diversity of arthropods as well as the ability to identify the characteristics that place the different groups in the same phylum.

Go Online PHSchool.com

Your students can independently test their knowledge of the chapter and print out their test results for your files.

Chapter Planner 29 Comparing Invertebrates

Section and Section Objectives	Time	STANDARDS NCLB	STANDARDS Biology	Activities and Labs
29–1 Invertebrate Evolution, pp. 745–750 **29.1.1** ***Explain*** what the Cambrian Explosion was. **29.1.2** ***Describe*** the major trends in invertebrate evolution.	2 periods (1 block)	7 3.c, BI 8.e		**SE:** ***Inquiry Activity,*** Which protective covering is better?, p. 744 L2 **TE:** ***Make Connections,*** p. 746 L2 **TE:** ***Build Science Skills,*** pp. 747 L2, 749 L2 L3 **SE:** ***Problem Solving,*** Creating an Imaginary Invertebrate, p. 750 L2 L3
29–2 Form and Function in Invertebrates, pp. 751–758 **29.2.1** ***Describe*** how the different invertebrate phyla carry out their essential life functions.	3 periods (1 1/2 blocks)	7 2.a		**TE:** ***Build Science Skills,*** pp. 751 L2 L3, 752 L1 L2 **SE:** ***Quick Lab,*** How do clams and crayfishes breathe?, p. 753 L2 L3 **TE:** ***Make Connections,*** pp. 754, 756 L2 L3 **TE:** ***Demonstration,*** p. 756 L1 L2 **SE:** ***Design an Experiment,*** Investigating Invertebrate Responses to External Stimuli, p. 759 L2 L3 **LMA:** Chapter 29 Lab L2 L3 **LMB:** Chapter 29 L1 L2 **BTM:** Lab 7 L2
Chapter Assessment, pp. 760–763	1 period (1/2 block)			

ACTIVITY PLANNER

SE: *Inquiry Activity*, p. 744; 15 min.; mollusk shells, arthropod exoskeletons

TE: *Make Connections*, p. 746; 10 min.; geologic time scale

TE: *Build Science Skills*, p. 747; 20 min.; live and preserved invertebrates, photos of invertebrates

TE: *Build Science Skills*, p. 749; 15 min.; modeling compound, 3 colors

TE: *Build Science Skills*, p. 751; 30 min. set up; aquarium; pond water, sediments, plants, and invertebrates

TE: *Build Science Skills*, p. 752; 10 min.; 1 sheet of paper towel; 1 small piece of paper towel; 2 large beakers

SE: *Quick Lab*, p. 753; 20 min.; live clam, food coloring, crayfish, small container of water

TE: *Make Connections*, p. 754; 5 min.; clear glass beaker, household ammonia

TE: *Demonstration*, p. 756; 10 min.; planarians, petri dish, water, dark paper, flashlight

TE: *Make Connections*, p. 756; 5 min.; hydraulic pump

SE: *Design an Experiment*, p. 759; 45 min.; dropper pipette, hydra culture, watch glass, dissecting microscope, blunt metal probe, planarian, petri dish, crayfish, brine shrimp, cooked egg yolk, slice of bologna

PLANNING KEY

Ability Levels

for students performing . . .

below grade level L1

at grade level L2

above grade level L3

Print Components

SE	Student Edition	LA	Lab Assessment
TE	Teacher's Edition	BTM	Biotechnology Manual
RSW	Reading & Study Workbook A	IDM	Issues and Decision Making
ARSW	Adapted Reading & Study Workbook B	LW	Lab Worksheets
TR	Teaching Resources	LMA	Laboratory Manual A
IF	Investigations in Forensics	LMB	Laboratory Manual B

Tech Components

CTB	Computer Test Bank
BD	BioDetectives DVD
TP	Transparencies Plus
PLM	Probeware Lab Manual
ABC	ABC DVD Library
LS	Lab Simulations
VL	Virtual Labs

Interactive Textbook — Interactive textbook with assessment at PHSchool.com

Program Resources	Assessment	Media and Technology
TR: Lesson Plan 29–1, Section Summary, p. 141 L1, p. 153 L2, Worksheets, pp. 144–146 L1, pp. 155–158 L2, Enrichment L2 L3 **RSW:** Section 29–1 L2 **ARSW:** Section 29–1 L1	**SE:** 29–1 Section Assessment, p. 754 **TR:** 29–1 Section Review	**iText:** Section 29–1 **TP:** 29–1 Interest Grabber, Section Outline, Compare/Contrast Table, Figure 29–4
TR: Lesson Plan 29–2, Section Summary, p. 142 L1, p. 153 L2, Worksheets, pp. 147–151 L1, pp. 159–161 L2 **LW:** Chapter 29 Design an Experiment L1 L2 L3 **RSW:** Section 29–2 L2 **ARSW:** Section 29–2 L1	**SE:** 29–2 Section Assessment, p. 762 **TR:** 29–2 Section Review	**iText:** Section 29–2 **TP:** 29–2 Interest Grabber, Section Outline, Types of Invertebrate Skeletons, Figure 29–8, Figure 29–9, Figure 29–10, Figure 29–11, Figure 29–12 **ABC:** 38 Circulatory Systems **VL:** Lab 17
	SE: Chapter 29 Assessment, pp. 760–763 **TR:** Chapter Vocabulary Review, Graphic Organizer, Chapter 29 Test **LA:** Laboratory Assessment 8	**iText:** Chapter 29 Assessment **CTB:** Chapter 29 Test **Go Online** Students can do research, share data, and test their knowledge online.

PRESSED FOR TIME?

To Preview the Chapter
- Introduce students to Key Concepts and Vocabulary terms in each section.
- Assign the Reading Strategies for each section.

To Cover the Chapter Quickly
- Have students read The Origin of the Invertebrates, Figure 29–4 and Figure 29–5 in Section 29–1, and read all of Section 29–2.
- Assign the Section Review 29–2; questions 1–10, 17–25, 26, 27, 29, 30, 35, and 37 in Chapter 29 Assessment; and questions 1–10 in Chapter 29 Standards Practice.

To Review the Chapter
- Assign Sections 29–1 and 29–2 in the Reading and Study Workbook or the Adapted Reading and Study Workbook.
- Assign Section Reviews for 29–1 and 29–2 and the Chapter Vocabulary Review for Chapter 29 in the Teaching Resources.

CHAPTER 29

ENGAGE/EXPLORE

Inquiry Activity

Objective Students will be able to draw conclusions about the biological costs and benefits of similar adaptations. L2

Skill Focus Drawing Conclusions, Predicting

Materials mollusk shells, arthropod exoskeletons, disposable plastic gloves

Time 15 minutes

Advance Prep Among the examples of arthropod exoskeletons you might collect are crab or lobster "shells" and preserved, dried insects from insect collections.

Safety Students should wear disposable plastic gloves. Dispose of them after the activity.

Strategies Check to see that students consider the costs and benefits of a number of characteristics when comparing the protective coverings. These include weight, thickness, and ability to penetrate.

Expected Outcome Students should conclude that mollusk shells provide more protection than arthropod exoskeletons but may limit movement. They should infer that this helps explain why many more arthropods are highly active and more widespread on land, where weight is more important.

Think About It

1. Mollusk shells are more difficult to penetrate because they are thicker.
2. Arthropod exoskeletons are more useful to active, motile animals because they are lighter and therefore easier to carry around.
3. A typical response might suggest that the heavier mollusk shell is better suited to the needs of slow-moving animals because fast-moving animals would have to expend too much energy to carry it around. The speed of many arthropods can make up for their thinner, weaker coverings. The heaviness of the shell makes less difference submerged than on land because of the buoyant force of water, which makes objects feel lighter.

CHAPTER 29

Comparing Invertebrates

The spotted cleaner shrimp lives among, and cleans, the tentacles of this anemone. The anemone protects the shrimp from predators.

Inquiry Activity

Which protective covering is better?

Procedure  

1. Examine some arthropod exoskeletons and mollusk shells. Observe as many differences as you can between these two types of protective coverings.
2. List the differences you observed. Next to each item, note how that difference in protective covering is adaptive to the organism in its own particular niche and habitat.

Think About It

1. **Drawing Conclusions** Which covering is more difficult for a predator to penetrate? Explain.
2. **Predicting** Animals must use energy to move. Which type of covering is more useful to an active, motile animal? Explain your answer.
3. **Drawing Conclusions** How can your observations help explain the fact that most mollusks are slow-moving animals, whereas many arthropods are more active?

FACTS AND FIGURES

The first animals

The fossils of the earliest animals appear in Precambrian rocks from about 650 to 540 million years ago. A few sites around the world contain these organisms, but the first discovered and still the most important is an area in South Australia called the Ediacara Hills. These animals are often called Ediacarans. They vary in length from less than 1 cm to more than 1 m. Most of these soft-bodied animals were either disc-shaped or leaf-shaped, much like the modern sea pen, a cnidarian. Some resemble jellyfishes, and others are like primitive arthropods. *Dickinsonia* resembles an annelid worm, though some paleontologists think it is more like a cnidarian polyp. These organisms did have some specialized cells, and one even had a primitive skeleton. Whether there is a direct link between these animals and those of the Cambrian Explosion is a matter of debate.

29–1 Invertebrate Evolution

7 3.c. Students know how independent lines of evidence from geology, fossils, and comparative anatomy provide the bases for the theory of evolution. **BI 8.e.** Students know how to analyze fossil evidence with regard to biological diversity, episodic speciation, and mass extinction.

Until recently, the origins of invertebrates were shrouded in mystery. This was because few fossils old enough to shed light on this period in Earth's history had been found. But ongoing discoveries around the world are shedding new light on the origins of invertebrates. Treasure troves of beautifully preserved invertebrate fossils, dating between 575 and 543 million years ago, have been discovered in the Ediacara Hills of Australia and in Chengjiang, China. These fossils join those known from the Burgess Shale deposits in the Canadian Rockies to show a fascinating history of early multicellular life.

Guide for Reading

Key Concept

- What are the major trends in invertebrate evolution?

Vocabulary

radial symmetry
bilateral symmetry
cephalization
coelom

Reading Strategy: Using Visuals Before you read, preview **Figure 29–4.** As you read, notice how the evolutionary trends in the cladogram are discussed in the text.

Origin of the Invertebrates

The Ediacaran fossils brought to light a strange group of ancient invertebrates. These peculiar fossils puzzled paleontologists for years because they seemed quite different from any modern invertebrates. More recently, paleontologists have identified beautifully preserved, microscopic fossils, between 610 and 570 million years old, that seem to be the developing embryos of early multicellular animals. From the same time period, they also identified what are called trace fossils. Trace fossils are tracks and burrows made by soft-bodied animals whose bodies were not fossilized.

Molecular biologists and paleontologists have also created a new field called molecular paleontology. This research uses cutting-edge studies in genetics to understand how different animal body plans evolved. DNA comparisons among living invertebrates help determine which phyla are most closely related. In addition, geneticists are studying how small changes in certain genes can cause major changes in body structures.

CA (a)

The First Multicellular Animals The Ediacaran fossils include some of the earliest and most primitive animals known. Most, like the animal shown in **Figure 29–1,** were flat and plate-shaped and lived on the bottom of shallow seas. They were made of soft tissues that absorbed nutrients from the surrounding water. Some may have had photosynthetic algae living within their bodies. These animals were segmented and had bilateral symmetry. However, they show little evidence of cell specialization or organization into a front and back end. Some of these early animals may have been related to soft-bodied invertebrates such as jellyfishes and worms. Their body plan, however, is distinct from anything alive today. Regardless of their relationships to other organisms, these animals were probably simple and had little internal specialization.

▼ **Figure 29–1** The drawing is an artist's conception of what an early invertebrate might have looked like. **Applying Concepts** *In what environment did most early invertebrates live?*

(a) BI 8.e

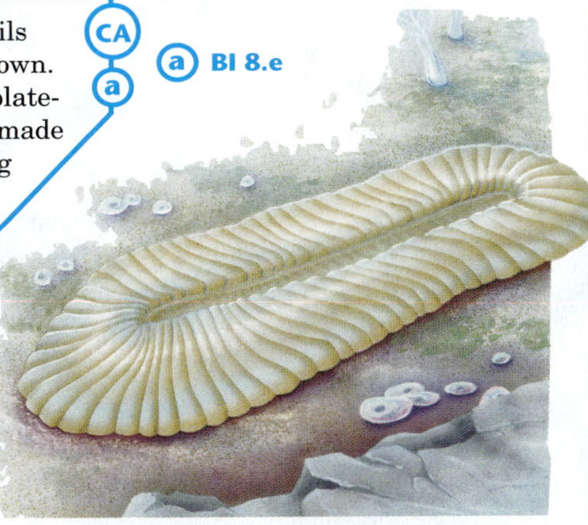

SECTION RESOURCES

Print:

- ***Teaching Resources,*** Lesson Plan 29–1, Adapted Section Summary 29–1, Adapted Worksheets 29–1, Section Summary 29–1, Worksheets 29–1, Section Review 29–1, Enrichment
- ***Reading and Study Workbook A,*** Section 29–1
- ***Adapted Reading and Study Workbook B,*** Section 29–1

Technology:

- ***iText,*** Section 29–1
- ***Transparencies Plus,*** Section 29–1

Section 29–1

7 3.c, BI 8.e

1 FOCUS

Objectives

29.1.1 ***Explain*** what the Cambrian Explosion was.
29.1.2 ***Describe*** the major trends in invertebrate evolution.

Guide for Reading

Vocabulary Preview

Suggest that students preview the meanings of the Vocabulary terms in the section by skimming the text to find the highlighted, boldface words and their definitions.

Reading Strategy

Students have already learned about specific invertebrate phyla and should remember the basics of the history of life from Chapter 17. Ask students to write a paragraph describing what they already know about the origin and evolution of invertebrates. Then, as they read the chapter, they should revise these paragraphs as needed.

2 INSTRUCT

Origin of the Invertebrates

Make Connections

Earth Science Explain that a fossil like the drawing in Figure 29–1 was probably found in a rock formation. Ask: **How would you describe the process by which this fossil might have formed?** *(Some students might correctly describe a process in which the organism died and was buried in sediment, which hardened into sedimentary rock, leaving a mold, cast, or imprint of the original organism.)* Point out that this organism had no hard body parts. **Why is it remarkable that such an organism left fossil remains?** *(Most soft tissue deteriorates more quickly than sediment hardens into rock, leaving no fossil evidence behind.)* Explain that fossils of relatively few of these earliest multicellular animals have been found because of their lack of hard parts. L2 L3

Answer to . . .

Figure 29–1 *Early invertebrates lived on the bottoms of shallow seas.*

29–1 (continued)

Use Visuals

Figure 29–3 Have students examine the illustration of Burgess Shale animals, and then direct their attention to the trilobite shown, *Olenoides.* Point out that this organism is the earliest known example of a trilobite, which students know from Chapter 28 is an ancient form of marine arthropod. Have students turn back to the subsection Evolution of Arthropods in Section 28–1 and review what they read about trilobites. Then, ask: **What can you say about this Burgess Shale trilobite in terms of body symmetry, skeleton, segmentation, cephalization, and appendages?** *(This trilobite had bilateral symmetry, an exoskeleton, many body segments, a head with compound eyes, and appendages.)* Point out that these features, or similar ones, are characteristic of living arthropods. Then, ask: **In what ways is this organism different from the animal shown in Figure 29–1?** *(Although the animal was segmented, it had no anterior and posterior end, no skeleton, and no appendages.)* Emphasize that the animals of the Burgess Shale represent the first appearance of almost all the major groups of modern animals. The illustration shows an early sponge, early arthropods, and an early annelid. L2

Make Connections

Earth Science To help students place the Burgess Shale fossils in proper context, display a geologic time scale from an encyclopedia or an Earth Science text. Note significant events in the history of life on Earth. For example, have students recall that they learned about trilobites in Chapter 28, and then point out that trilobites became extinct at the end of the Paleozoic Era. Also note the extinction of dinosaurs at the end of the Mesozoic Era. Point as well to the appearance of *Homo sapiens* in very recent time. Show students where on the scale the Cambrian Period begins, and emphasize that it was more than 500 million years ago that the Burgess Shale animals thrived. L2

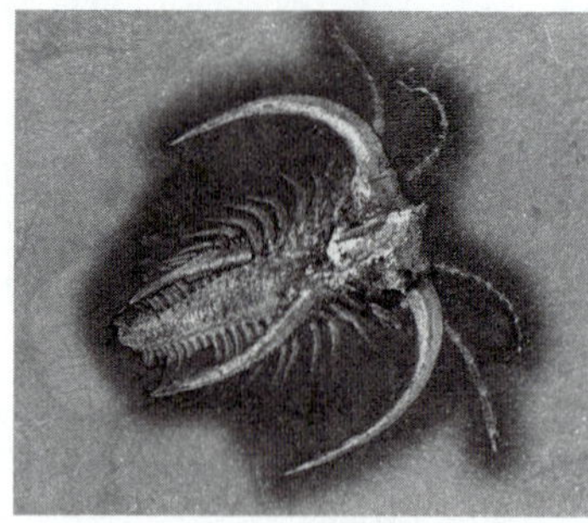

▲ **Figure 29–2** The fossilized arthropod *Marrella splendens* had body symmetry, segmentation, a skeleton, a front and a back end, and appendages adapted for many functions. **Applying Concepts** *What type of symmetry does this fossil exhibit?*

Beginnings of Invertebrate Diversity Fossils from a few million years later—a short period in geological time—paint a radically different picture of invertebrate life. The Cambrian Period, which began 544 million years ago, is marked by an abundance of different fossils. Why the difference from earlier periods? By the Cambrian Period, some animals had evolved shells, skeletons, and other hard body parts—all of which are readily preserved in fossils. Suddenly, the fossil record provided a wealth of information about animal diversity, body plans, and adaptations to life. One of the best-known sites of Cambrian fossils is the Burgess Shale of Canada. A fossil from the Burgess Shale is shown in **Figure 29–2.**

CA a You can see what some of the Burgess Shale animals may have looked like in **Figure 29–3.** Note the wide variety of body shapes and appendages. Trilobites such as *Olenoides* moved along the ocean floor. *Wiwaxia* had two rows of long, pointed spikes. The annelid *Canadia,* like many annelids today, had prominent setae. *Anomalocaris,* the largest Burgess Shale fossil, had fearsome-looking forelimbs that were probably used to grasp prey. The animals of the Burgess Shale are far more numerous and diverse than anything that lived earlier.

In just a few million years, animals had evolved complex body plans. They acquired specialized cells, tissues, and organs. Because of the extraordinary growth in animal diversity, events of the early Cambrian Period are called the Cambrian Explosion. During that time, the ancestors of most modern animal phyla first appeared in the fossil record.

▼ **Figure 29–3** This illustration shows what some of the Cambrian organisms found in the Burgess Shale may have looked like. **Observing** *What body features of these animals are similar to those of modern invertebrates?*

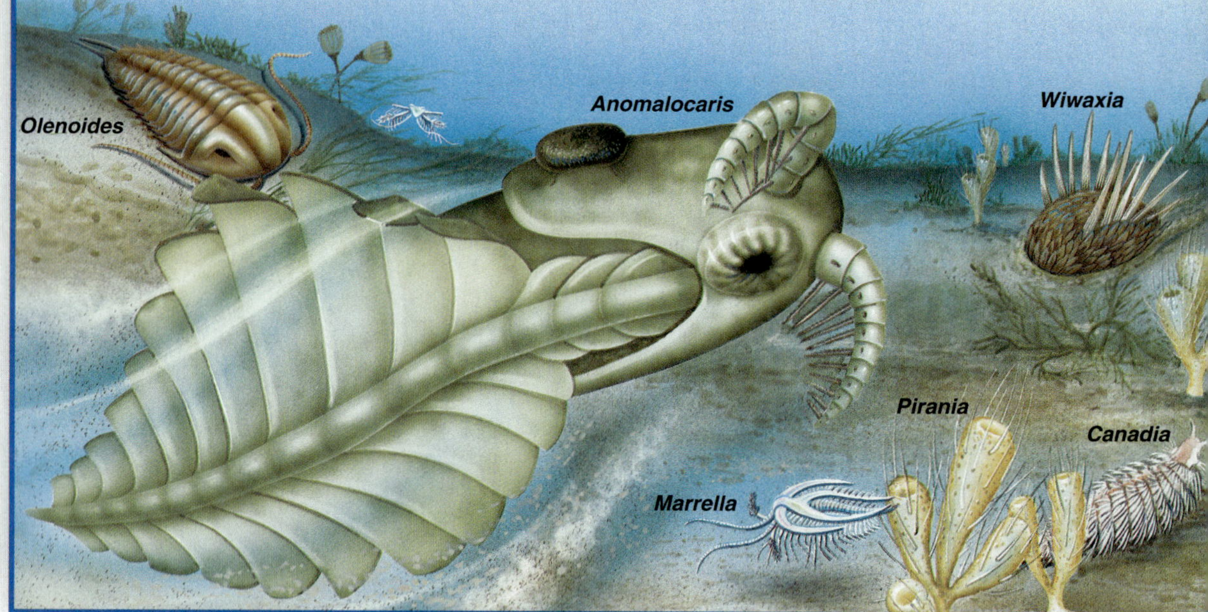

HISTORY OF SCIENCE

Creatures of the Burgess Shale

In 1909, Charles Doolittle Walcott, then secretary of the Smithsonian Institution, discovered a section of rock on the side of Mt. Stephen in British Columbia, Canada, that is possibly the most important fossil find ever. From this rock unit, about 60 m long and 2.5 m thick, Walcott collected more than 65,000 fossils. *Marrella,* a 2.5-cm-long swimming arthropod with long antennae and at least 24 pairs of legs and gills, is the most common Burgess shale organism. *Wiwaxia*, 2–5 cm long, is a bottom feeder covered by hard plates and two rows of upright spines. *Olenoides*, a bottom predator as large as 10 cm long, is the earliest example of a trilobite. *Canadia,* 2.5–5 cm long, is an annelid with two slender tentacles and a body covered with short bristles. *Pirania* is an early sponge.

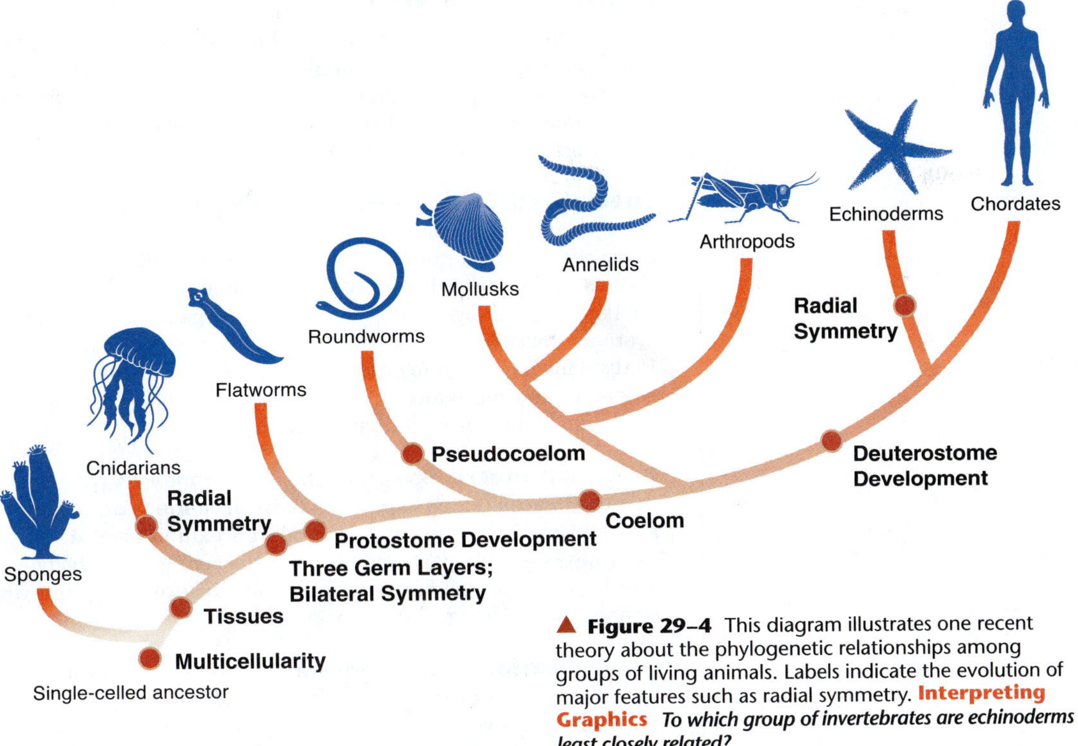

▲ **Figure 29–4** This diagram illustrates one recent theory about the phylogenetic relationships among groups of living animals. Labels indicate the evolution of major features such as radial symmetry. **Interpreting Graphics** *To which group of invertebrates are echinoderms least closely related?*

What features of the Cambrian animals made them so successful? One way of determining this is to find their common features—especially those that are present in animals today. The anatomies of Burgess Shale animals typically had body symmetry, segmentation, some type of skeleton, a front and a back end, and appendages adapted for many functions. These features are characteristic of most invertebrates living today.

Invertebrate Phylogeny

The diagram in **Figure 29–4** shows the evolutionary relationships among major groups of living invertebrates. It also indicates the sequence in which some important features evolved. These features include tissues and organs, patterns of early development, body symmetry, cephalization, segmentation, and the formation of three germ layers and a coelom. Many of these features, which have persisted up to modern times, evolved in animals of the Cambrian Period. As you review the major trends in invertebrate evolution, consider how each feature might have contributed to the evolutionary success of animals.

CA (a)

(a) 7 3.c

CHECKPOINT *What groups of animals are deuterostomes?*

Word Origins

The word *germ* in the term *germ layers* comes from the Latin word *germen,* which means "embryo" or "sprout." **If the suffix *-ate* means "to become," what happens to a seed when it germinates?**

Invertebrate Phylogeny

Build Science Skills

Inferring Construct a classroom display of as many invertebrates as possible, using photos as well as live and preserved invertebrates. Try to provide a diverse assemblage, including at least one from each of the groups studied in previous chapters. Label each animal with its common or species name. Then, ask students: **Which of these invertebrates do you think are closely related to one another?** *(Accept all reasonable responses, but challenge students to think about relationships across phylum lines.)* **What further information would you need to be sure about how closely these invertebrates are related to one another?** *(Anatomical, behavioral, and molecular information about these animals.)* L2

Go Online active art

For: Invertebrate phylogeny activity
Visit: PHSchool.com
Web Code: cbe-8299
Students build their own cladogram online.

Word Origins

When a seed germinates, it sprouts and begins growing. L2

UNIVERSAL ACCESS

Inclusion/Special Needs

Point out the heading on page 748, Evolutionary Trends. Then, discuss with students what a trend is, using examples from their everyday lives. For instance, have students identify trends in popular music, hairstyles, or fashion. Emphasize that a trend is a general movement over the course of time and that there are often exceptions to trends. Point out that *evolutionary trends* include the ways that invertebrates have evolved in general over time. L1

Advanced Learners

Encourage students to investigate further the remarkable fossils of the Burgess Shale and prepare a presentation to the class. For resources, suggest that they look for Web sites and library books on paleontology and prehistoric animals. Perhaps the best book on these fossils is *Wonderful Life: The Burgess Shale and the Nature of History* by Stephen Jay Gould (New York: Norton, 1989). L3

Answers to . . .

CHECKPOINT *Echinoderms and chordates*

Figure 29–2 *Bilateral symmetry*

Figure 29–3 *Asymmetry and pores in the spongelike animals; bilateral symmetry in the other animals; segmentation; cephalization; appendages, including antennae*

Figure 29–4 *Sponges*

29–1 (continued)

Evolutionary Trends

Address Misconceptions

Many students believe that the more-complex animals evolved from simpler animals, and thus are somehow "better" in an evolutionary sense than simpler animals. Point out that each phylum evolved as animals changed through adaptation to changing environmental conditions. Simpler animals have shown that they are quite well adapted to many environments and have persisted in much the same forms for millions and millions of years. L2

Use Visuals

Figure 29–5 Have students study the table of major characteristics, and also have them compare the table with the cladogram in Figure 29–4. Then, ask: **From the information in the table, what can you say about the differences between sponges and cnidarians?** *(Cnidarians have germ layers and body symmetry, whereas sponges have neither.)* Have students look back to the cladogram and confirm that those differences are reflected on that arrangement of phyla. Continue this strategy of providing connections between the information presented in the two figures.

Evolutionary Trends

The appearance of each phylum in the fossil record represents the evolution of a successful and unique body plan. Features of this body plan typically change over time, leading to the formation of many new traits. The major trends of invertebrate evolution are summarized in **Figure 29–5.**

Specialized Cells, Tissues, and Organs Modern sponges and cnidarians have little internal specialization. They carry out essential functions using individual cells or simple tissues. As larger and more complex animals evolved, specialized cells joined together to form tissues, organs, and organ systems that work together to carry out complex functions. Flatworms have simple organs for digestion, excretion, response, and reproduction. More complex animals, such as mollusks and arthropods, have organ systems.

Body Symmetry Sponges lack body symmetry. **All invertebrates except sponges exhibit some type of body symmetry.** Cnidarians and echinoderms exhibit **radial symmetry**—body parts extend from the center of the body. Worms, mollusks, and arthropods exhibit **bilateral symmetry,** or have mirror-image left and right sides.

Cephalization Most invertebrates with bilateral symmetry rely on movement for feeding, defense, and other important functions. The evolution of this body plan and lifestyle was accompanied by the trend toward **cephalization,** which is the concentration of sense organs and nerve cells in the front of the body. **Invertebrates with cephalization can respond to the environment in more sophisticated ways than can simpler invertebrates.** In most worms and arthropods, nerve cells are arranged in structures called ganglia. In more complex invertebrates, nerve cells form an organ called a brain.

CHECKPOINT *How does cephalization benefit an animal?*

Comparing Invertebrates

	Sponges	Cnidarians	Flatworms
Germ Layers	Absent	Two	Three
Body Symmetry	Absent	Radial	Bilateral
Cephalization	Absent	Absent	Present
Coelom	Absent	Absent	Absent
Early Development	———	———	Protostome

▶ **Figure 29–5** This table shows the major characteristics of the main groups of invertebrates. **Germ layers, body symmetry, cephalization, and development of a coelom are more common in complex invertebrates than in simple ones.** Mollusks, for example, have all of these features, but sponges have none of them.

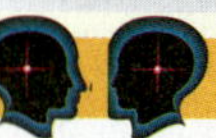

TEACHER TO TEACHER

When I introduce invertebrate evolution, I ask the students to come up with various environments in which invertebrates live. List on the board the environments (ponds, lakes, dry land, air, and so forth), and have students determine what structures are needed by invertebrates in order to survive in each particular environment. As you go over the lists, have students compare structural similarities and differences among the various groups and between the simple and complex invertebrates. This is a good start for student discussion on evolution.

—*Wendy Peterson*
Biology Teacher
Velva High School
Velva, ND

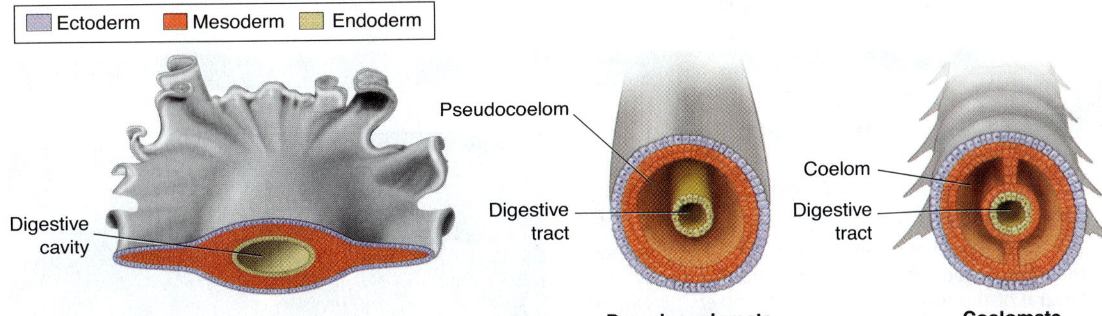

▲ **Figure 29–6** Acoelomates do not have a coelom, or body cavity, between their body wall and digestive cavity. Pseudocoelomates have body cavities that are partially lined with tissues from mesoderm. **Most complex animal phyla are coelomates, meaning that they have a true coelom that is lined completely with tissues from mesoderm.**

Segmentation Most invertebrates with bilateral symmetry also have segmented bodies. Over the course of evolution, different segments have often become specialized for specific functions. Because the same structures are repeated in each body segment, segmentation also allows an animal to increase in body size with a minimum of new genetic material.

Coelom Formation Cnidarians have a simple construction in which a jellylike layer lies between ectoderm and endoderm tissues. Other invertebrates develop from three germ layers, the endoderm, mesoderm, and ectoderm, as shown in **Figure 29–6.** Flatworms are acoelomates, meaning that no **coelom,** or body cavity, forms between the germ layers. Pseudocoelomates, such as roundworms, have a body cavity lined partially with mesoderm. **Most complex animal phyla have a true coelom that is lined completely with tissue derived from mesoderm.**

Embryological Development In most invertebrates, the zygote divides repeatedly to form a blastula—a hollow ball of cells. In protostomes, the blastopore, or the opening of the blastula, develops into a mouth. In deuterostomes, the blastopore forms an anus. Worms, arthropods, and mollusks are protostomes, and echinoderms (and chordates) are deuterostomes.

Roundworms	Annelids	Mollusks	Arthropods	Echinoderms
Three	Three	Three	Three	Three
Bilateral	Bilateral	Bilateral	Bilateral	Radial (adults)
Present	Present	Present	Present	Absent (adults)
Pseudocoelom	True coelom	True coelom	True coelom	True coelom
Protostome	Protostome	Protostome	Protostome	Deuterostome

Use Visuals

Figure 29–6 Review with students the names of the three germ layers, as discussed in Section 26–1. Then, ask: **What difference can you see between an acoelomate and a pseudocoelomate?** *(In the pseudocoelomate, there is a cavity between the gut and body wall, while in the acoelomate there is no cavity.)* **What difference can you see between the pseudocoelomate and the coelomate?** *(The cavity in the coelomate is lined completely with mesodermal tissue, while the cavity in the pseudocoelomate is only partially lined with mesodermal tissue.)* L2

Build Science Skills

Using Models Divide the class into small groups and give each group three colors of modeling compound. Then, ask each group to make models of an acoelomate, a pseudocoelomate, and a coelomate, using the illustrations in Figure 29–6 as examples of each kind of organism. L2 L3

Use Community Resources

Invite an expert to visit the classroom and speak about how scientists determine the relationships among invertebrate phyla. A university professor who has done research in molecular biology will be able to explain modern methods of biological investigation and answer questions about how molecular data can be used to confirm phylogenetic relationships. L2

BIO INSIGHTS — FACTS AND FIGURES

Advantages of a coelom

The coelom is a fluid-filled cavity between the gut or digestive tube and the outer body wall, creating a tube-within-a-tube construction. The coelom has a number of functions. This cavity serves as a buffer between the outer wall and the inner organs, cushioning them against harm. It allows for the growth of internal organs without distorting the body's outer wall. It serves as a storage place. For invertebrates with an open circulatory system, it provides a place for circulation to occur. Also, the fluid in the cavity serves as a hydrostatic skeleton for many animals. There are several theories about when and how the coelom evolved. Some zoologists think that it evolved twice, once in protostomes and again in deuterostomes. One thing is certain—there is great adaptive advantage for a crawling or burrowing organism to have a coelom.

Answer to . . .

CHECKPOINT *Because sense organs and nerve cells are concentrated in the head end, animals with cephalization can respond to the environment in more complex ways than can animals that lack cephalization.*

29–1 (continued)

Problem Solving

 BIIE 1.I

Defining the Problem Have students write a detailed description of the habitat they have chosen.

Organizing Information Make sure students consider all relevant features as they pick the body systems that would work best in the chosen environment.

Creating a Solution Advise students to write a general description of the invertebrate they create and then describe as many body systems as they can in detail.

Presenting Your Plan Have students present their "perfect invertebrates" to the class, or provide bulletin board space for students to display their plans. 

3 ASSESS

Evaluate Understanding

Call on students at random to explain the major trends of invertebrate evolution.

Reteach

Have students look at Figure 29–4. Help students write a paragraph that explains how the groups of invertebrates are related to one another, indicating what major feature appears each time the cladogram branches.

Focus on the BIG Idea

Students should compare animals such as those in Figure 29–3 with animals described on pages 745–747. Students should emphasize that many of the Burgess Shale animals had hard body parts, complex body plans, segmentation, and organ systems, whereas the earlier animals did not.

If your class subscribes to the iText, use it to review the Key Concepts in Section 29–1.

Problem Solving

Creating an Imaginary Invertebrate

 BIIE 1.I

The moth in the photo is a real animal, but you may think that it looks like a science-fiction monster. Several of the most frightening "monsters" dreamed up for the science-fiction films of the past 20 years have actually been based on bits and pieces of anatomy and behavior of real invertebrates. Now that you have studied all the invertebrate phyla, try to create the "perfect invertebrate" for a habitat of your choice.

Defining the Problem First, choose a habitat: a temperate zone desert, a tropical coral reef, or inside the body of a mammal. Depending on which habitat you chose, define the environmental challenges (such as heat, cold, or lack of water) and the biological needs (such as food and oxygen) that your organism must meet.

Organizing Information Once you have defined the problem, look back over the characteristics of all the invertebrate groups you have studied, and pick the kind of body systems that you think would work best in your chosen habitat.

Creating a Solution Assemble the body systems you have chosen into an imaginary animal. Make sure that the systems you use can work in harmony. You could not, for example, expect an animal to breathe through its skin if it had an impermeable exoskeleton covering its entire body! Make sure that you have considered all the organism's needs. Give your animal an appropriate name.

Presenting Your Plan Create external and cutaway diagrams of your animal, including any larval stages. Label the diagrams, including the name of the real-life invertebrate system that fulfills each essential function. Conclude by describing the complete life cycle of your organism.

29–1 Section Assessment

1. **Key Concept** Describe three major trends in the evolution of invertebrates.
2. Compare the first multicellular animals with those of the Burgess Shale.
3. How was the evolution of internal specialization important to invertebrate form and function?
4. Compare the body structures and other characteristics of cnidarians and mollusks.
5. **Critical Thinking Observing** Observe the fossil of *Marrella splendens* in **Figure 29–2.** What evidence does the fossil exhibit of anatomical (structural) characteristics similar to those of present-day arthropods?

Focus on the BIG Idea

Unity and Diversity
Imagine that you are one of the first paleontologists to find fossils in the Burgess Shale. Suppose that you have studied the fossils and compared them with earlier animal fossils such as the one in **Figure 29–1.** Write a report for a scientific journal about your discovery and its significance.

29–1 Section Assessment

1. Three of the following trends: specialized cells, tissues, and organs; body symmetry; cephalization; segmentation; coelom formation; and patterns of early development
2. The first multicellular animals were soft-bodied and show little evidence of cell specialization or cephalization. Animals of the Burgess Shale had hard parts as well as cephalization and specialized cells, tissues, and organ systems.
3. Specialized cells, tissues, organs, and organ systems work together to carry out complex functions.
4. Cnidarians have two germ layers and radial symmetry. Mollusks have three germ layers, bilateral symmetry, cephalization, a true coelom, and protostome development.
5. Students should mention a segmented body, an exoskeleton, jointed appendages, bilateral symmetry, and cephalization.

29–2 Form and Function in Invertebrates

7 2.a. Students know the differences between the life cycles and reproduction methods of sexual and asexual organisms.

To survive, all animals perform the same essential tasks: feeding and digestion, respiration, circulation, excretion, response, movement, and reproduction. In many ways, each animal phylum represents an "experiment" in the adaptation of body structures to carry out these tasks. The appearance of each phylum in the fossil record, therefore, represents the evolutionary development of a unique body plan. The continued history of each phylum is the story of further evolutionary changes to that plan.

Biologists can learn a great deal about the nature of life by comparing body systems among groups of living invertebrates. Body systems that perform the essential tasks of life have taken many different forms in different phyla. Each phylum has a particular type of breathing device, a certain type of body support system, and numerous variations on other physiological functions. More complicated systems are not necessarily better than simpler ones. The fact that any system is found in living animals testifies to its success in performing functions. This section reviews the basic evolutionary trends in each body system, using examples from a variety of invertebrate groups.

Guide for Reading

Key Concept
- How do different invertebrate phyla carry out life functions?

Vocabulary
intracellular digestion
extracellular digestion
open circulatory system
closed circulatory system
hydrostatic skeleton
exoskeleton
endoskeleton
external fertilization
internal fertilization

Reading Strategy: Finding Main Ideas Before you read, skim the section to identify the key ideas. Then, carefully read the section, making a list of supporting details for each main idea.

Feeding and Digestion

Invertebrates have evolved many different ways of obtaining food. The spider in **Figure 29–7**, for example, is feeding on a caterpillar after killing it with venom. Before food can be used for energy, the food must be broken down, or digested. The digested food must then be absorbed into the animal's body. Complex animals accomplish the physiological process of digestion in different ways than simpler animals.

Intracellular and Extracellular Digestion

Invertebrates have evolved different ways of digesting food. **The simplest animals break down food primarily through intracellular digestion, but more complex animals use extracellular digestion.** Sponges digest their food inside archaeocytes, which pass nutrients to other cells by diffusion. Because food is digested inside cells, this process is known as **intracellular digestion.** In contrast, mollusks, annelids, arthropods, and echinoderms rely almost entirely on extracellular digestion. In **extracellular digestion,** food is broken down outside the cells in a digestive cavity or tract and then absorbed into the body. Flatworms and cnidarians use both intracellular and extracellular digestion.

Figure 29–7 **Complex animals break down food using extracellular digestion.** The spider's venom is breaking down the tissues of the caterpillar. Later, the broken-down food molecules will be absorbed into the spider's digestive tract.

Section 29–2

7 2.a

1 FOCUS

Objective

29.2.1 ***Describe*** how the different invertebrate phyla carry out their essential life functions.

Guide for Reading

Vocabulary Preview

Before students read the section, have them locate each Vocabulary term and read its definition.

Reading Strategy

Suggest that students copy key ideas into their notebooks, leaving enough space for supporting details. Then, as they read the section, they should look for support for each key idea.

2 INSTRUCT

Feeding and Digestion

Build Science Skills

Observing Set up an aquarium in the classroom, and encourage volunteers to collect water, gravel and other sediment, plants, and invertebrates from a local freshwater pond. In the pond, students should be able to find planaria, snails, leeches, insect larvae, and hydras, which can often be found attached to rocks and stems of water plants. Ask students to make multiple trips to the pond, first building the habitat in the aquarium and then adding any invertebrates they can find. Once the aquarium contains invertebrates, encourage students to keep a daily record of what they observe about how the animals move about, feed, respond to stimuli, and defend themselves.

L2 L3

SECTION RESOURCES

TIME SAVER

Print:
- ***Teaching Resources,*** Lesson Plan 29–2, Adapted Section Summary 29–2, Adapted Worksheets 29–2, Section Summary 29–2, Worksheets 29–2, Section Review 29–2
- ***Reading and Study Workbook A,*** Section 29–2
- ***Adapted Reading and Study Workbook B,*** Section 29–2
- ***Laboratory Manuals A/B,*** Chapter 29 Lab
- ***Lab Worksheets,*** Chapter 29 Design an Experiment
- ***Biotechnology Manual,*** Lab 7

Technology:
- ***iText,*** Section 29–2
- ***Animated Biological Concepts DVD,*** 38 Circulatory Systems
- ***Transparencies Plus,*** Section 29–2
- ***Virtual Labs,*** Lab 17

29–2 (continued)

Use Visuals

Figure 29–8 After students have examined the figure, ask: **Which of the four invertebrates shown ingest food and expel waste through a single opening?** *(The cnidarian and the flatworm)* **What specialized regions can you see in the digestive tracts of any of the invertebrates?** *(The digestive tract of the cnidarian has no specialized regions, and the tract of the flatworm has only a pharynx. The one-way digestive tract of the annelid has a pharynx, crop, gizzard, intestine, and anus. The one-way digestive tract of the arthropod has a pharynx, crop, stomach and digestive glands, intestine, rectum, and anus.)* Point out that the digestive tracts shown represent the great variety of digestive systems in the invertebrate phyla. L2

Respiration

Build Science Skills

Using Analogies To help students understand that larger surface areas are more efficient at gas exchange than are smaller surfaces, compare diffusion of gases through the skin to absorption of water by paper towels. Show students two pieces of paper towel: a whole sheet and a small section cut from another sheet. Ask: **Which of these pieces will absorb more water?** *(The larger piece)* You might also provide students with two large beakers containing equal volumes of water. Have them put the small piece of paper towel in one beaker and the large piece in the other. Students can remove the paper towels and then compare the amount of water remaining in each beaker. L1 L2

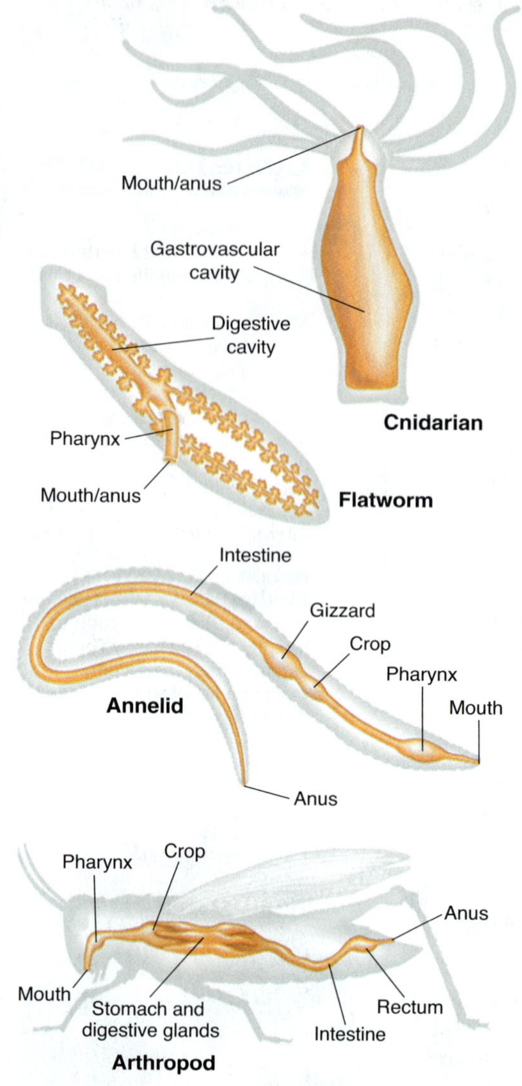

▲ **Figure 29–8** Cnidarians and flatworms have a digestive system with only one opening. In more complex animals, the digestive system has two openings. In addition, the digestive organs have become more specialized. **Interpreting Graphics** *Which of these animals has the least specialized digestive system?*

Patterns of Extracellular Digestion

Invertebrates have a variety of digestive systems, as shown in **Figure 29–8.** Simple animals such as cnidarians and most flatworms ingest food and expel wastes through a single opening. Food is digested in a cavity through both extracellular and intracellular means. Some cells of the gastrovascular cavity secrete enzymes and absorb the digested food. Other cells surround food particles and digest them in vacuoles. Digested food then diffuses to cells throughout the body.

More-complex animals digest food in a tube called the digestive tract. Food enters the body through the mouth, and wastes leave through the anus. A one-way digestive tract (which is characteristic of roundworms, annelids, mollusks, arthropods, and echinoderms) often has specialized regions, such as a stomach and intestines. Specialization of the digestive tract allows food to be processed more efficiently, because each step in the process takes place in order, at a specific place along the digestive tract.

CHECKPOINT *What is the difference between intracellular digestion and extracellular digestion?*

Respiration

All animals must exchange oxygen and carbon dioxide with the environment. The more surface area that is exposed to the environment, the greater the amount of gas exchange that can occur. In addition, gases diffuse most efficiently across a thin, moist membrane. Given these principles, all respiratory systems share two basic features. **Respiratory organs have large surface areas that are in contact with the air or water. Also, for diffusion to occur the respiratory surfaces must be moist.**

Aquatic Invertebrates Aquatic animals, such as cnidarians and some flatworms, naturally have moist respiratory surfaces. Many animals even respire through their skins. However, for most active animals larger than worms, skin respiration alone is not sufficient. Aquatic mollusks, arthropods, and many annelids exchange gases through gills. Gills are feathery structures that expose a large surface area to the water. Gills are rich in blood vessels that bring blood close to the surface for gas exchange.

ESL SUPPORT FOR ENGLISH LANGUAGE LEARNERS

Comprehension: Modified Cloze

Beginning Distribute a modified paragraph about extracellular digestion, but leave some strategic words blank. For example, "Simple animals such as _____ and most flatworms take in food and eliminate wastes through the same opening. Food is digested in the _____ cavity. Some cells that line this cavity _____ digested food." Provide students with a list of the correct answers, and have them fill in each blank with one of those words. Tell students to refer to Figure 29–8 for help. L1

Intermediate Distribute the cloze paragraph described for Beginning Level, but add two additional sentences that explore the subject in greater depth, each with a blank. To check students' comprehension, have them form collaborative groups to write a question or a response about what they have read. L2

Quick Lab

How do clams and crayfishes breathe?

Materials live clam, food coloring, crayfish, small container of water

Procedure 

1. Do not touch the clam or crayfish. Put a drop of food coloring in the water near a clam's siphons. Observe what happens to the coloring.
2. Put a drop of food coloring in the water near the middle of a crayfish's carapace. **CAUTION:** *Keep your fingers away from the crayfish's pincers.* Observe what happens to the coloring.

BIIE 1.d

Analyze and Conclude

1. **Observing** Describe what happened to the coloring in step 1. How does water move through a clam's gills?
2. **Inferring** What is the clam's main defense? How is the location of the clam's siphons related to this defense?
3. **Comparing and Contrasting** What happened in step 2? Compare the flow of water through the gills of clams and crayfish.
4. **Inferring** Why do you think the crayfish has gills rather than spiracles, as some other arthropods do?

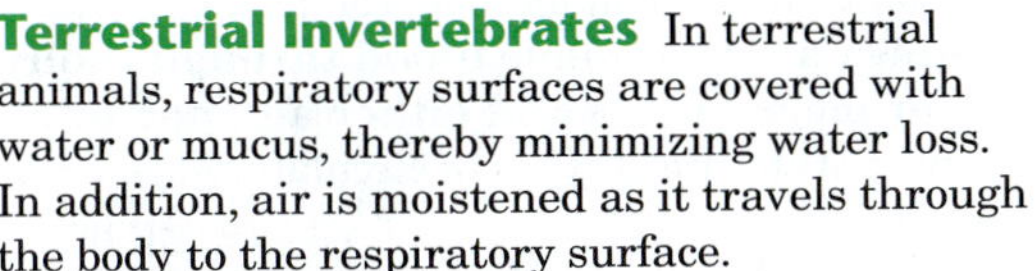

Terrestrial Invertebrates In terrestrial animals, respiratory surfaces are covered with water or mucus, thereby minimizing water loss. In addition, air is moistened as it travels through the body to the respiratory surface.

Terrestrial invertebrates have several types of respiratory surfaces. The mantle cavity of a land snail is a moist tissue that has an extensive surface area lined with blood vessels. Spiders respire using organs called book lungs, such as the one shown in **Figure 29–9.** Book lungs are made of parallel, sheetlike layers of thin tissues that contain blood vessels. In insects, air enters the body through openings called spiracles. It then enters a network of tracheal tubes, where gases diffuse in and out of surrounding body fluids.

CHECKPOINT *How does respiration in aquatic invertebrates differ from respiration in terrestrial invertebrates?*

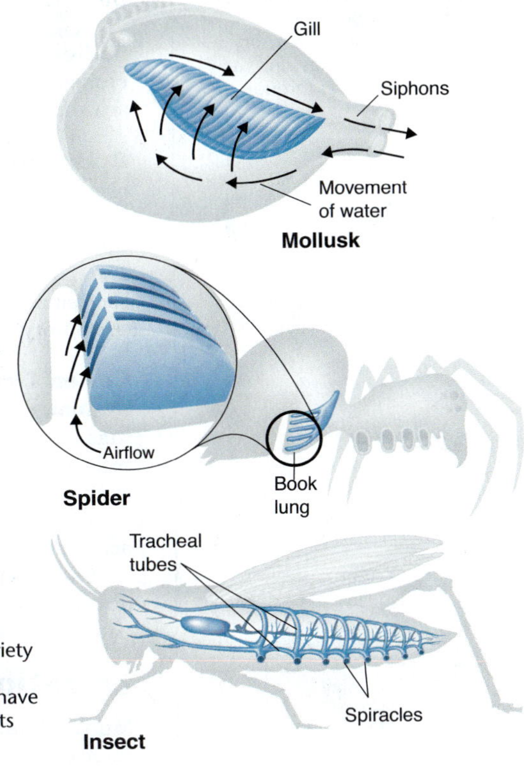

▶ **Figure 29–9** Invertebrates have a variety of respiratory structures. Clams and other aquatic mollusks have gills. Many spiders have book lungs. Grasshoppers and other insects have spiracles and tracheal tubes. **All respiratory organs have large, moist surface areas in contact with air or water.**

TEACHER TO TEACHER

When I introduce topics related to invertebrate form and function, I find that my students are almost always fascinated with the diversity of structure and process in both digestion and reproduction. To respond to this interest, I try to provide students with a great variety of examples in both areas. Then, I challenge students to explain the reasons for the success of each adaptation presented. This teaching strategy not only helps students gain some appreciation of the great diversity among invertebrates, but it also gives them an opportunity to apply their understanding of the processes involved in evolution.

—Chuck Campbell
Biology Teacher
Burbank High School
Burbank, CA

Quick Lab

 **BIIE 1.d**

Objective Students will be able to relate differences in the mechanism of gas exchange to overall adaptation in a clam and a crayfish. L2 L3

Skills Focus **Observing, Inferring, Comparing and Contrasting**

Materials live clam, food coloring, crayfish, small container of water

Time 20 minutes

Advance Prep You can keep marine clams alive for a few days in a 4% solution of sodium chloride.

Safety Make sure students do not touch the organisms.

Expected Outcome Students should observe that the food coloring enters one of the clam's siphons and exits through the other. They should also observe the turbulence around the middle of the crayfish's ventral surface, revealing the location of its gills.

Analyze and Conclude

1. The coloring entered one siphon and left through the other. Inside the clam, it flowed over the gills.
2. Its main defense is the shell. The location of the siphons allows the clam to pump water through its gills without opening its shell very wide.
3. Both clams and crayfishes draw water into the body, pass it over the gills, and then release it. A clam must open its shell to do this, whereas a crayfish has openings through which water passes in and out.
4. Spiracles do not work under water, where crayfishes live.

Answers to . . .

CHECKPOINT *In intracellular digestion, food is digested inside cells. In extracellular digestion, food is broken down outside the cells.*

CHECKPOINT *Most aquatic animals have gills for removing oxygen from water and releasing carbon dioxide. Terrestrial animals get oxygen from air; respiratory surfaces are moist.*

Figure 29–8 *The cnidarian, because its digestive system consists of only a gastrovascular cavity and one opening that serves as both mouth and anus*

29–2 (continued)

Circulation

Use Visuals

Figure 29–10 Have students use the figure to compare and contrast the two circulatory systems. Ask: **How does each type of system get blood to tissues and organs?** *(In the open circulatory system, blood is pumped to a cavity or sinus, where it comes in direct contact with tissues and organs. In a closed circulatory system, blood is pumped through vessels to tissues and organs.)* Explain that the blood in an open system aids many invertebrates in movement, acting as part of the animal's hydrostatic skeleton. Point out that although an open system may not seem as efficient as a closed system, it works well for the invertebrates that have it. L2

Excretion

Making Connections

Chemistry Explain that every amino acid contains an amino group, —NH_2. The first step in the breakdown of an amino acid, called deamination, is the removal of the amino group. With the addition of a proton, an amino group becomes ammonia, NH_3. Use a clear glass beaker to show students some household ammonia. **CAUTION:** *Do not perform this demonstration if any students are asthmatic or sensitive to ammonia fumes. Be sure the room is well ventilated and that students don't come close to the beaker.* Explain that this commercial product contains ammonia in solution with water and a detergent. Most students will know that even in this dilute solution, the ammonia can be harmful. Emphasize that both urea and uric acid are much less toxic than ammonia, which is why those compounds can be held for long periods of time and excreted by land animals without doing harm to themselves or the environment. L2 L3

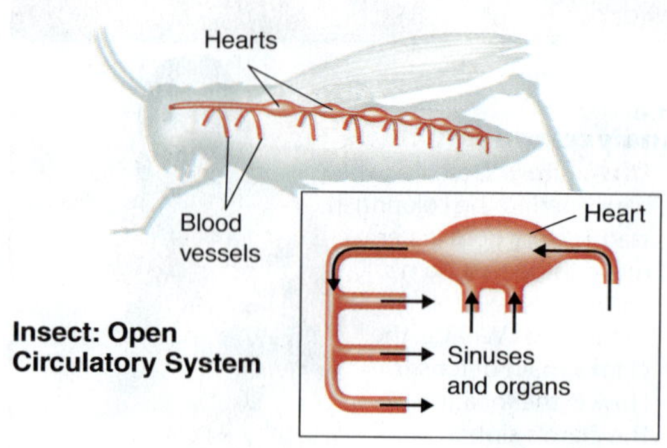

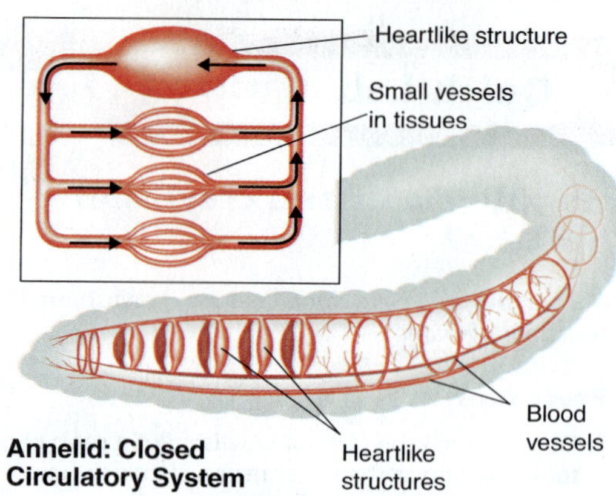

▲ **Figure 29–10** **Most complex animals have one or more hearts to move fluid through their bodies in either an open or a closed circulatory system.** An insect has an open circulatory system in which blood leaves blood vessels and then moves through sinuses, or body cavities. An annelid has a closed circulatory system in which blood stays in blood vessels as it moves through the body.

Circulation

All cells of multicellular animals require a constant supply of oxygen and nutrients, and cells must also remove metabolic wastes. The smallest and thinnest animals meet this requirement by simple diffusion between their body surface and the environment. But this system is usually insufficient for more complex animals. **Most complex animals move blood through their bodies using one or more hearts and either an open or a closed circulatory system.** Both types of circulatory systems are shown in **Figure 29–10.**

Open Circulatory Systems In an **open circulatory system,** blood is only partially contained within a system of blood vessels. Instead, one or more hearts or heartlike organs pump blood through blood vessels into a system of sinuses, or spongy cavities. The blood comes into direct contact with the tissues, collects in body sinuses, and eventually makes its way back to the heart. Open circulatory systems are found in arthropods and most mollusks.

Closed Circulatory Systems In a **closed circulatory system,** a heart or heartlike organ forces blood through vessels that extend throughout the body. The blood stays within these blood vessels. Materials reach body tissues by diffusing across the walls of the blood vessels.

Closed circulatory systems are characteristic of larger, more active animals. Because blood trapped within the blood vessels is kept at high pressure, it can be circulated more efficiently than in an open circulatory system. Among the invertebrates, closed circulatory systems are found in annelids and some mollusks.

Excretion

Multicellular animals must control the amount of water in their tissues. At the same time, all animals must get rid of ammonia. The excretory systems of invertebrates carry out these functions in a variety of ways as shown in **Figure 29–11.**

FACTS AND FIGURES

Benefits of an open circulatory system
In arthropods with an open circulatory system, the blood empties from blood vessels directly into the body cavity, where it bathes the organs. It might seem that this type of system is extremely sloppy and inefficient. Yet, the open circulatory system often has uses to the organism beyond circulation. For example, for many clams and snails, the blood in the body cavities functions as a hydrostatic skeleton, helping the animal in movement and burrowing. The blood also functions as a hydrostatic skeleton in aquatic arthropods when they molt. Many spiders are able to extend their legs by forcing the blood in the open system into the limbs. In addition, for a few insects, the open circulatory system functions as the body's thermal regulator, maintaining the body temperature within the range in which cells can function.

Most animals have an excretory system that rids the body of metabolic wastes while controlling the amount of water in the tissues.

In aquatic invertebrates, ammonia diffuses from their body tissues into the surrounding water. The water immediately dilutes the ammonia and carries it away. Flatworms use a network of flame cells to eliminate excess water. Fluid travels through execretory tubules and leaves the body through tiny pores in the animal's skin.

Terrestrial invertebrates must conserve water while removing nitrogenous wastes. To do this, many animals convert ammonia into a compound called urea. Urea is eliminated from the body in urine. Urine is highly concentrated, so little water is lost. In annelids and mollusks, urine forms in tubelike structures called nephridia. Fluid enters the nephridia through openings called nephrostomes. Urine leaves the body through excretory pores.

Some insects and arachnids have Malpighian tubules, saclike organs that convert ammonia into uric acid. Both uric acid and digestive wastes combine to form a thick paste that leaves the body through a structure called the rectum. Because the paste contains little water, this process also reduces water loss.

Figure 29–11 **Most animals dispose of wastes through excretory systems. Excretory systems also control an organism's water levels.** Flatworms excrete ammonia directly into the water and use flame cells to remove excess water. Annelids use nephridia to convert ammonia into urea and to concentrate it in urine. Some arthropods have Malpighian tubules, which convert ammonia into uric acid.

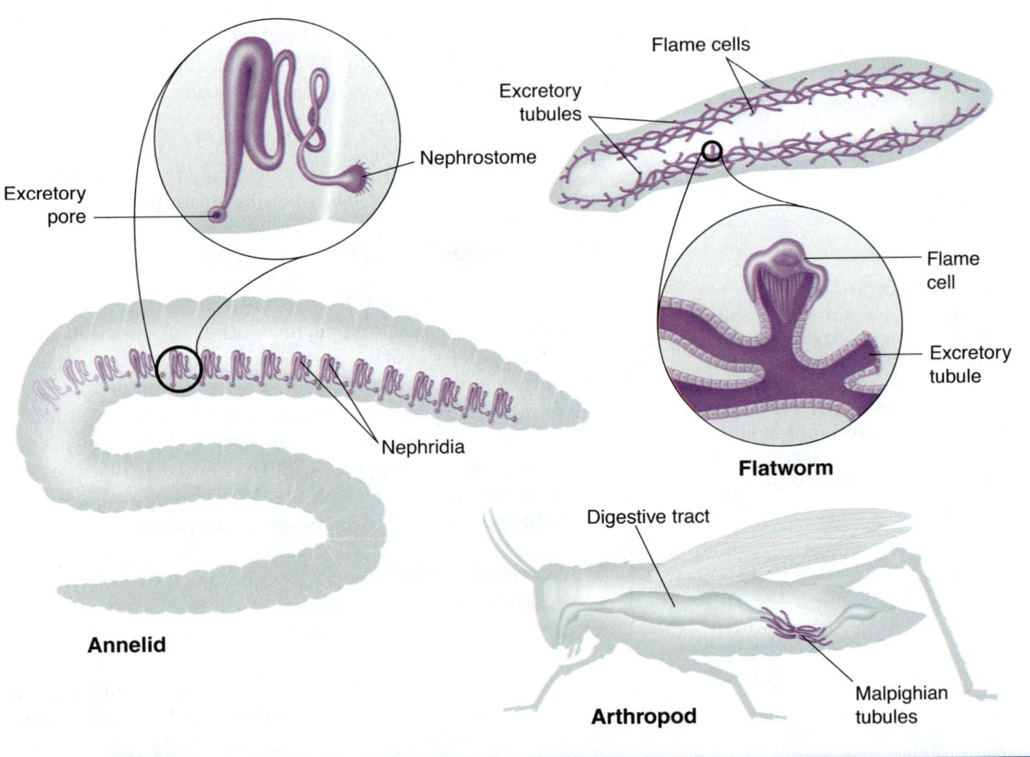

Use Visuals

Figure 29–11 Have students study the examples of the three different methods for disposing of wastes. Then, ask: **How would you compare the environments in which these three invertebrates live?** *(The flatworm lives in an aquatic environment, while the annelid and the arthropod live on land.)* **Why can the flatworm excrete ammonia directly into its environment, while the annelid and arthropod cannot?** *(When the ammonia diffuses from the flatworm's body, it is immediately diluted by the surrounding water. If the land invertebrates excreted ammonia, the ammonia would not be diluted.)* Emphasize that all land organisms must conserve water, and excreting uric acid in solid or semisolid form, as most terrestrial invertebrates do, conserves water. L2

Build Science Skills

Comparing and Contrasting Divide the class into small groups, and assign each group one of the invertebrate phyla studied in this unit. Have the members of each group work together to make a large chart on poster board that includes labeled drawings of the digestive and excretory systems used by organisms in their phylum. Once all groups have finished, have each group present its work and then display its charts on the classroom wall. L1 L2

BIO INSIGHTS — FACTS AND FIGURES

Getting rid of ammonia

Protein is an essential part of an animal's diet, and the digestion of protein in foods produces amino acids. An organism uses some of these amino acids to produce the proteins and other compounds it needs. Excess amino acids are also used in cellular respiration for energy. This use begins with the nitrogen group, forming ammonia, which is highly poisonous to the organism. The aquatic invertebrates that allow ammonia to diffuse out of their bodies are for that reason limited to aquatic environments, because water is necessary to dilute the ammonia, which would be harmful to all organisms if not diluted. Therefore, the ability to produce the relatively harmless uric acid is an important reason why invertebrates, particularly insects, have been so successful on land. Also, because uric acid is excreted in a solid or semisolid form, a land animal is able to conserve precious water.

29–2 (continued)

Response

Use Visuals

Figure 29–12 After students have compared the four examples in the figure, ask: **Which is the simplest nervous system shown, and what is it called?** *(The simplest is that shown in the cnidarian, and it is called a nerve net.)* **What controls and coordinates the nervous system in the arthropod and the mollusk?** *(The brain)* **Which of the four invertebrates exhibit cephalization?** *(The flatworm, the arthropod, and the mollusk)* L2

Demonstration

Place live planarians in a petri dish containing a small amount of chlorine-free water, and cover half the dish with a piece of dark paper. Then, shine a flashlight on the uncovered area. Have students observe that the planarians avoid the light by moving under the paper. Have students hypothesize about the selective advantage of planarians' ability to detect light and tendency to move away from light into a dark area.

Movement and Support

Make Connections

Physics Show students a hydraulic pump, such as a hydraulic car jack. Explain that when pressure is applied to a fluid in a confined area, an increase in pressure is transmitted uniformly to all parts of the fluid. This is known as Pascal's principle after the French physicist Blaise Pascal, who first described this idea. The principle is used in hydraulic pumps, as well as by various invertebrates. With a hydraulic jack, a person applies pressure by pushing down on the handle, and when the pressure is uniformly distributed, it pushes up on a piston, which raises the car. Similarly, an invertebrate applies pressure on internal fluid by contracting muscles in one part of its body and relaxing muscles in another part. As the pressure is uniformly distributed, the animal can move forward (worm), extend tube feet (echinoderm), or make any number of other movements. L2 L3

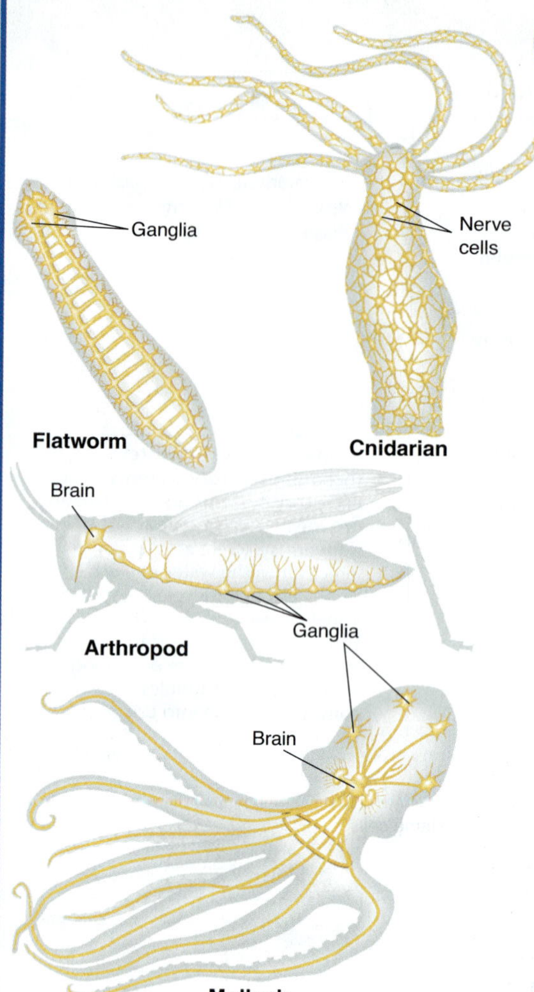

▲ **Figure 29–12** **Invertebrate nervous systems have different degrees of centralization, cephalization, and specialization.** Cnidarians have a simple nerve net. Flatworms, whose nervous systems are more centralized, have small ganglia in their heads. Arthropods and cephalopod mollusks have a centralized brain and specialized sensory organs.

Response

Nervous systems gather and process information from the environment and allow animals to respond appropriately. **Figure 29–12** shows the nervous system of four invertebrates. **Invertebrates show three trends in the evolution of the nervous system: centralization, cephalization, and specialization.** Different nervous systems have various degrees of each of these characteristics.

Centralization and Cephalization The simplest nervous systems, found in cnidarians, are called nerve nets. Nerve nets consist of individual nerve cells that form a netlike arrangement throughout the animal's body. In flatworms and roundworms, the nerve cells are more concentrated, or centralized. There are a few small clumps of nerve tissue, or ganglia, in the head. In cephalopod mollusks and arthropods, ganglia are organized into a brain that controls and coordinates the nervous system. This concentration of nerve tissue and organs in one end of the body is called cephalization.

Specialization The more complex an animal's nervous system is, the more developed its sense organs tend to be. Flatworms, for example, have simple eyespots that detect only the presence of light. More complex animals, such as insects, have eyes that detect motion and color and form images. Complex animals may have a variety of specialized sense organs that detect light, sound, chemicals, movement, and even electricity to help them discover what is happening around them.

Movement and Support

Most animals use specialized tissues called muscles to move, breathe, pump blood, and perform other life functions. Muscles work by contracting, or becoming shorter. This is the only way that muscle tissue can generate force. When they are not stimulated, muscles relax. In most animals, muscles work together with some sort of skeletal system that provides firm support. **Invertebrates have one of three main kinds of skeletal systems: hydrostatic skeletons, exoskeletons, or endoskeletons.**

Hydrostatic Skeletons Some invertebrates, such as annelids and certain cnidarians, have **hydrostatic skeletons,** shown in **Figure 29–13.** In these animals, muscles surround a fluid-filled body cavity that supports the muscles. When the muscles contract, they push against fluid in the body cavity, causing the body to change shape.

FACTS AND FIGURES

Invertebrate eyes
Almost all invertebrates have some kind of sense organ that responds to light, though light-sensing ability varies greatly. The eyespots, or ocelli, of flatworms and some other invertebrates are composed of light-sensitive cells that give the organism much information about both the intensity and the direction of light. Many arthropods, some annelids, and some mollusks have compound eyes, which are composed of many units, each with a separate nerve track that leads to a large optic nerve. The fields of vision of each unit overlap somewhat with neighboring units, giving the organism great ability for detecting movement. Some cephalopods, including squids and octopi, have complex, or camera, eyes. These eyes, which are much like vertebrate eyes, form the best images among all invertebrate eyes.

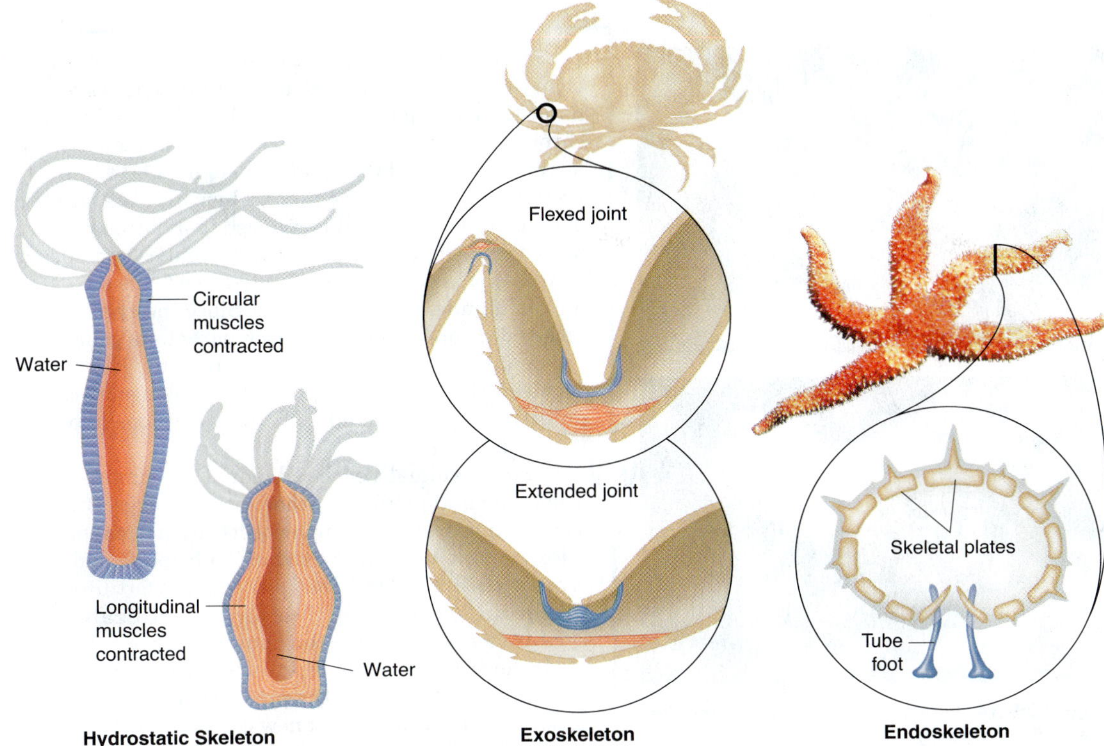

▲ **Figure 29–13** **The three main types of invertebrate skeletons are hydrostatic skeletons, exoskeletons, and endoskeletons.** In animals with hydrostatic skeletons, muscles contract against a fluid-filled body cavity. In animals with exoskeletons, the muscles pull against the insides of the exoskeleton. Echinoderms and some sponges have endoskeletons.

Exoskeletons In arthropods, the **exoskeleton,** or external skeleton, is a hard body covering made of chitin. Arthropods move by using muscles that are attached to the inside of the exoskeleton. These muscles bend and straighten different joints. The shells of some mollusks can also be considered exoskeletons. Muscles attached to the shell make it possible for snails to withdraw into their shells and for bivalves to close their shells.

Endoskeletons An **endoskeleton** is a structural support located inside the body. Sea stars and other echinoderms have an endoskeleton made of calcified plates. These plates function in support and protection, and also give these animals a bumpy and irregular texture. Vertebrates also have endoskeletons.

Sexual and Asexual Reproduction

Most invertebrates reproduce sexually during at least part of their life cycle. Depending on environmental conditions, however, many invertebrates may also reproduce asexually. Each form of reproduction has advantages and disadvantages. Asexual reproduction allows animals to reproduce rapidly and take advantage of favorable conditions in the environment. Sexual reproduction, in contrast, maintains genetic diversity in a population by creating individuals with new combinations of genes.

(a) 7 2.a

Use Visuals

Figure 29–13 Have students examine the three types of skeletons. Then, ask: **How does a hydra change its shape?** *(It contracts muscles that surround a fluid-filled body cavity.)* **Describe how an invertebrate with an exoskeleton bends and extends a limb.** *(When a limb is bent, or flexed, one muscle contracts while the other relaxes. During extension of the same limb, the opposite muscles contract and relax.)* Point out that muscles can pull but cannot push. Vertebrates, which have endoskeletons, use muscles in the same way to flex and extend limbs. L2

Sexual and Asexual Reproduction

Build Science Skills

Designing Experiments Divide the class into small groups, and ask each group to design an imaginary experiment to investigate what conditions are best for the reproduction of a specific kind of invertebrate. Tell students to imagine that they have the resources of any university biology department and an unlimited amount of time. Instruct students to write a hypothesis, identify manipulated and controlled variables, describe how they would collect data, and predict the results of the experiment. L2 L3

BIO INSIGHTS — FACTS AND FIGURES

Invertebrate hermaphrodites
In Greek myth, Hermaphroditus, the son of Hermes and Aphrodite, caught the eye of a nymph of the spring in which he was bathing. She fell in love with and clung to him, and they melded into one being—half male and half female. Likewise, a hermaphroditic animal contains both male and female organs and thus can produce both eggs and sperm. Hermaphroditism is common in invertebrates such as some worms, some gastropods, some leeches, and barnacles. During sexual reproduction, different animals pass sperm from one to the other. As a result, eggs in both organisms become fertilized. That result is an advantage of hermaphroditism, because two organisms, not one, are impregnated by each encounter. Such an event is called mutual cross-fertilization.

If your class subscribes to the iText, use it to review the Key Concepts in Section 29–2.

29–2 (continued)

Build Science Skills

Applying Concepts On the board, write groupings of related terms used in discussing invertebrate structure and function. Have students work in pairs to write short paragraphs using the terms of each group in context, comparing and contrasting kinds of invertebrates. Here are some possible groups:

- gastrovascular cavity, digestive tract
- mantle cavity, book lungs, tracheal tubes
- open circulatory system, closed circulatory system
- ammonia, urea, uric acid
- nerve net, ganglia, brain
- hydrostatic skeleton, exoskeleton, endoskeleton
- asexual reproduction, sexual reproduction L2

3 ASSESS

Evaluate Understanding

Read aloud each of the boldface sentences in the section. For each, call on a volunteer to provide a supporting detail for that key idea. Then, ask others in the class for additional supporting details. After students have provided support for the idea, ask for a volunteer to explain the importance of that idea in understanding form and function in invertebrates.

Reteach

Ask each student to choose any two organisms from two different invertebrate phyla and write a paragraph comparing the animals in terms of their feeding and digestion, respiration, circulation, excretion, response, movement and support, and reproduction.

Thinking Visually

Students' Venn diagrams should include the fact that in open systems blood comes in direct contact with tissues, whereas in closed systems blood stays within blood vessels. Open systems are characteristic of arthropods and most mollusks; closed systems are found in annelids and some mollusks.

Figure 29–14 Invertebrates may reproduce asexually or sexually. Note that the largest sea anemone in this group is undergoing asexual reproduction by splitting into two parts (top). The *Acropora* coral (bottom) is releasing brown eggs into the water. The eggs will be fertilized externally. This is an example of sexual reproduction.

a 7 2.a

Sexual reproduction is the production of offspring from the fusion of gametes. Recall that gametes are haploid, meaning that they have half the number of chromosomes found in most body cells. Gametes, such as the eggs in the lower photo in **Figure 29–14,** are produced by meiosis, the process by which the number of chromosomes per cell is reduced to half that of most body cells. When male and female gametes join during fertilization, the zygote, or fertilized egg, has the diploid number of chromosomes. Since the zygote received chromosomes from each parent, its genes are a combination of the genes of both parents. The zygote, which is one cell, grows through ongoing cell divisions, or mitosis, and eventually develops into a multicellular animal.

CA a In most animals, each individual is a single sex. The individual produces either sperm or eggs. But some animals, such as earthworms, are hermaphrodites, or individuals that produce both sperm and eggs. In **external fertilization,** eggs are fertilized outside the female's body. In **internal fertilization,** eggs are fertilized inside the female's body.

In contrast to sexual reproduction, asexual reproduction does not involve the production of gametes by meiosis or the formation of new combinations of genes. The offspring of asexual reproduction grow into multicellular organisms by mitosis of diploid cells. In asexual reproduction, all the offspring are genetically identical to the parent. Asexual reproduction sometimes occurs through budding, in which new individuals are produced by outgrowths of the body wall. Some animals reproduce asexually by dividing in two.

29–2 Section Assessment

1. **Key Concept** In your own words, describe the evolution of three different body systems of invertebrates.
2. **Key Concept** Compare asexual and sexual reproduction. What are the advantages and disadvantages of each?
3. Compare circulation in annelids and arthropods.
4. What are the three main kinds of skeletal systems in invertebrates?
5. **Critical Thinking Applying Concepts** List the three forms of nitrogenous wastes excreted by animals. How are the ways in which animals dispose of these wastes related to each animal's environment?

Thinking Visually

Creating a Venn Diagram

Create a Venn diagram that compares and contrasts open and closed circulatory systems. Be sure to include similarities as well as differences. In your Venn diagram, identify some kinds of animals that have each type of circulatory system.

29–2 Section Assessment

1. Students should describe the evolution of three body systems discussed in the section.
2. Asexual reproduction allows animals to reproduce rapidly and take advantage of favorable environments, where genetic diversity is not so important. Sexual reproduction maintains genetic diversity in a population, but it is not rapid.
3. Annelids have a closed circulatory system; arthropods have an open circulatory system.
4. Hydrostatic skeletons, exoskeletons, endoskeletons
5. Ammonia, urea, and uric acid. The method largely depends on environment: Freshwater animals generally need to get rid of excess water; terrestrial animals must conserve it.

Design an Experiment

BIIE 1.a, BIIE 1.c

Investigating Invertebrate Responses to External Stimuli

The responses of animals to external stimuli depend on their nervous systems. In this investigation, you will design experiments to test the responses of three invertebrates to touch and food.

Problem How do the responses of invertebrates to external stimuli relate to the structures of their nervous systems?

Materials

- dropper pipette
- hydra culture
- watch glass
- dissecting microscope
- blunt metal probe
- planarian
- petri dish
- crayfish
- brine shrimp
- cooked egg yolk
- slice of bologna

Skills Formulating Hypotheses, Observing

Design Your Experiment

1. Use a dropper pipette to transfer a hydra and some water to the center of a watch glass or petri dish. Do not touch the hydra.
2. Place the watch glass or petri dish on the stage of a dissecting microscope and observe the hydra's movements for a few minutes.
3. With a blunt metal probe, gently touch one of the hydra's tentacles from several directions. Observe and record the hydra's responses to this stimulus. Return the hydra to its culture.
4. Design experiments to determine how a planarian and a crayfish respond to touch. Refer to the Lab Tips box on page 55. Include touching both ends of each animal in your plan.
5. Now design another set of experiments to determine how each animal will respond to food. Hydras will consume brine shrimp, planarians will eat cooked egg yolk, and crayfish will eat small pieces of bologna.
6. **Predicting** For each experiment you plan, write your prediction of the result. After your teacher approves your plan, carry out the experiments you have designed. Wear plastic gloves while handling the animals, and handle them gently. Record your observations. Wash your hands with soap and warm water before leaving the lab.

Analyze and Conclude

1. **Comparing and Contrasting** Describe how each animal responded to touch. How were the responses of the animals related to the direction from which they were touched? What, if any, were the differences among the animals?
2. **Drawing Conclusions** Which animal displayed the most specific response to touch? Explain your answer in terms of the animals' nervous systems.
3. **Comparing and Contrasting** Describe how each animal responded to its food. Did your results support your hypothesis? How do each animal's responses relate to the structure of its nervous system?
4. **Drawing Conclusions** Which of these animals shows cephalization? Relate your answer to each animal's behavior.

Go Further

Designing Experiments Design similar experiments using other invertebrates such as sponges or earthworms. Obtain your teacher's permission before carrying out the experiments.

Analyze and Conclude

1. Students should observe that when a hydra is touched, the entire hydra contracts into a ball, whereas when a planarian or crayfish is touched, it moves away from the stimulus. The crayfish may also try to grasp with its pincers the object that touches it.
2. The crayfish demonstrated the most specific response by moving away and grasping. This can be explained by its more complex nervous system.
3. The hydra responded by waving its tentacles until one or more contacted the brine shrimp. The planarian moved toward the food. The crayfish grasped the food with its pincers and bit off small pieces. The crayfish, whose response was most complex, has the most complex nervous system.
4. The crayfish and planarian show cephalization, as reflected in their response toward or away from stimuli.

Design an Experiment

BIIE 1.a, BIIE 1.c

Objectives
Students will be able to:
- observe how different invertebrates respond to touch and food.
- draw conclusions about how the responses of invertebrates relate to the structures of their nervous systems. L2 L3

Skills Focus Formulating Hypotheses, Observing

Time 45 minutes

Advance Prep Obtain invertebrates from scientific supply houses. Planarians and hydras can also be obtained from pond water. Live brine shrimp are available at many pet stores. Don't feed animals for 24 hours before the activity. About an hour before the lab, add a suspension of carmine red powder to the shrimp culture to color them. Also, hard-boil eggs and cut up the yolks in advance.

Safety Make sure students are careful when handling the crayfish. Students should wear disposable plastic gloves and then dispose of them properly after the activity.

Teaching Tips If the planarian eats the egg yolk, students may be able to observe the egg yolk inside the digestive tract by looking at the planarian under a microscope. The yellow color will reveal the shape of the digestive system.

Expected Outcome Students should observe that different invertebrates respond differently to touch and food. They should draw the conclusion that these different responses relate to the structure of the nervous system of each kind of invertebrate.

Go Further

Students' designs will vary, though most will be similar to the experiments carried out in this activity. Review students' plans before allowing them to perform their experiments. From these further experiments, students should conclude that invertebrates with more complex nervous systems have more complex responses to external stimuli than do organisms with simpler nervous systems.

Chapter 29 Study Guide

Study Tip

Divide the class into small groups, and ask each group to brainstorm a list of challenging questions that cover all the chapter concepts. Then, have the members of each group work together to answer the questions devised by another group.

Thinking Visually

The hydra flowchart might include: food enters gastrovascular cavity through mouth; digested and absorbed in gastrovascular cavity; wastes expelled through mouth. Earthworm: food enters mouth; moves through pharynx, crop, gizzard, and intestines; wastes leave through anus.

Chapter 29 Assessment

Reviewing Content

1. b	4. a	7. b	10. b
2. a	5. d	8. c	
3. d	6. d	9. c	

Understanding Concepts

11. Specialized cells, tissues, and organ systems; body symmetry; segmentation; some type of skeleton; an anterior and posterior end; and appendages
12. Specialized cells led to the development of tissues and organ systems.
13. Sponges, or phylum Porifera
14. With cephalization, animals can respond to the environment more quickly and in more sophisticated ways. This is an advantage for feeding and defense.
15. Ectoderm, endoderm, mesoderm
16. Acoelomates have no body cavity; pseudocoelomates have a body cavity partially lined with mesoderm; coelomates have a true body cavity lined completely with mesoderm.

Chapter 29 Study Guide

29–1 Invertebrate Evolution

 **Key Concepts** 7 3.c, BI 8.e

- As animals became larger and more complex, specialized cells joined together to form tissues, organs, and organ systems that work together to carry out complex functions.
- All invertebrates except sponges exhibit some type of body symmetry—either radial symmetry or bilateral symmetry.
- Invertebrates with cephalization can respond to the environment in more sophisticated ways than can simpler invertebrates.
- Most invertebrates with bilateral symmetry also have segmented bodies. Over the course of evolution, different segments have often become specialized for specific functions.
- Most animal phyla have a true coelom that is lined completely with tissue derived from mesoderm.
- In early development, worms, arthropods, and mollusks are protostomes, and echinoderms are deuterostomes.

Vocabulary

radial symmetry, p. 748
bilateral symmetry, p. 748
cephalization, p. 748
coelom, p. 749

29–2 Form and Function in Invertebrates

 **Key Concepts**  7 2.a

- The simplest animals break down food primarily through intracellular digestion, but more complex animals use extracellular digestion.
- Respiratory organs have large surface areas that are in contact with the air or water. In order for diffusion to occur, these respiratory surfaces must be kept moist.
- Most complex animals move blood through their bodies using one or more hearts and either an open or a closed circulatory system.
- Most animals have an excretory system that rids the body of metabolic wastes and controls the amount of water in their tissues.
- Invertebrates show three trends in the evolution of the nervous system: centralization, cephalization, and specialization.
- Invertebrates have one of three main kinds of skeletal systems: hydrostatic skeletons, exoskeletons, or endoskeletons.
- Most invertebrates reproduce sexually during at least part of their life cycle. Depending on environmental conditions, however, many invertebrates also reproduce asexually.

Vocabulary

intracellular digestion, p. 751
extracellular digestion, p. 751
open circulatory system, p. 754
closed circulatory system, p. 754
hydrostatic skeleton, p. 756
exoskeleton, p. 757
endoskeleton, p. 757
external fertilization, p. 758
internal fertilization, p. 758

Thinking Visually

Create two flowcharts describing the steps in the digestion of food. One flowchart should describe digestion in a hydra. The second flowchart should describe digestion in an earthworm.

CHAPTER RESOURCES

Print:

- ***Teaching Resources,*** Chapter 29 Vocabulary Review, Graphic Organizer, Chapter 29 Tests: Levels A and B
- ***Laboratory Assessment With Scoring Guide,*** Laboratory Assessment 8

Technology:

- ***Computer Test Bank,*** Chapter 29 Test
- ***iText,*** Chapter 29 Assessment

Chapter 29 Assessment

Interactive textbook with assessment at PHSchool.com

Reviewing Content

Choose the letter that best answers the question or completes the statement.

1. The ancestors of most modern animal phyla first appeared during the
   a. Burgess Period.
   b. Cambrian Period.
   c. Precambrian Era.
   d. Ediacaran Period.
2. A cladogram shows
   a. evolutionary relationships.
   b. size relationships.
   c. symbiotic relationships.
   d. functional relationships.
3. Roundworms, which have body cavities that are partially lined with mesoderm, are classified as
   a. acoelomates.
   b. coelomates.
   c. deuterostomes.
   d. pseudocoelomates.
4. An animal that relies primarily on intracellular digestion is the
   a. sponge. c. dragonfly.
   b. clam. d. earthworm.
5. Which organ system does the diagram below illustrate?

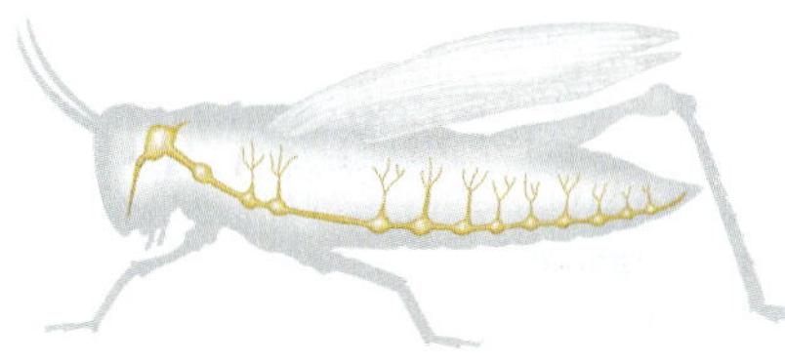

   a. digestive system
   b. circulatory system
   c. excretory system
   d. nervous system
6. In order for the exchange of oxygen and carbon dioxide to take place, an animal's respiratory surfaces must be kept
   a. cold. c. hot.
   b. dry. d. moist.
7. In a closed circulatory system, blood
   a. comes in direct contact with tissues.
   b. remains within blood vessels.
   c. empties into sinuses.
   d. does not transport oxygen.
8. Malpighian tubules convert nitrogenous wastes into
   a. urine. c. uric acid.
   b. ammonia. d. urea.
9. The simplest nervous systems are called
   a. ganglia. c. nerve nets.
   b. motor neurons. d. sensory neurons.
10. Individual animals that produce both sperm and eggs are called
    a. gametes.
    b. hermaphrodites.
    c. buds.
    d. fragments.

Understanding Concepts

11. What features of Burgess Shale animals are found in most invertebrates living today?
12. What effect did the development of specialized cells have on evolution?
13. Which invertebrate phylum does not exhibit body symmetry?
14. What is one major advantage of cephalization?
15. List the three germ layers.
16. Distinguish among the following terms: *acoelomate, pseudocoelomate,* and *coelomate.*
17. Compare the processes of intracellular digestion and extracellular digestion.
18. Why is the development of a one-way digestive system important to the evolution of animals?
19. Describe two types of respiratory structures found in terrestrial invertebrates.
20. Describe the two types of circulatory systems. Give an example of an animal that has each type.
21. What are three forms of nitrogenous wastes excreted by animals?
22. What three major trends in the evolution of the nervous system do invertebrates exhibit?
23. In the gills of aquatic animals, how do the respiratory and circulatory systems interact? How does the interaction benefit the body as a whole?
24. What is the function of an animal's heart?
25. Compare and contrast internal and external fertilization.

HOMEWORK GUIDE

Section:	Questions:
Section 29–1	1–3, 11–16, 28, 31, 33, 35
Section 29–2	4–10, 17–27, 29, 30, 32, 34, 36

Interactive Textbook

If your class subscribes to the iText, your students can go online to access an interactive version of the Student Edition and a self-test.

(Continued from page 760)

17. Intracellular digestion is the process in which food is broken down inside cells. In extracellular digestion, food is broken down outside cells in specialized structures.

18. A one-way digestive system often has specialized regions that allow food to be temporarily stored and processed in batches, like an assembly line.

19. Sample answer: the mantle cavity is moist tissue that has an extensive surface area lined with blood vessels. Book lungs are made of parallel, sheetlike layers of thin tissue that contain blood vessels. Students might also mention spiracles and tracheal tubes.

20. Open circulatory system: found in arthropods and most mollusks; does not keep blood contained within blood vessels; blood comes in direct contact with the tissues, collects in body sinuses, and makes its way back to the heart. Closed circulatory system: found in annelids and chordates; keeps the blood completely contained within blood vessels; materials diffuse from the blood to the tissue and vice versa through the walls of the blood vessels; blood kept at high pressure.

21. Ammonia, urea, uric acid

22. Centralization, cephalization, and specialization

23. The circulatory system brings carbon dioxide to the gills. Gills are rich in blood vessels that bring blood close to the surface for gas exchange, the respiratory function. The circulatory system then carries the oxygen from the gills to the cells of the body, providing the cells with the necessary oxygen to carry out cellular respiration.

24. An animal's heart moves blood through its body, either in a closed or an open circulatory system.

25. In internal fertilization, eggs are fertilized inside the female's body. In external fertilization, eggs are fertilized outside the female's body.

Chapter 29 Assessment

Critical Thinking

26. In small aquatic invertebrates, the toxic ammonia diffuses from the animal's body into the water as soon as it is produced, and before it can harm the animal.

27. The slimy coating of slugs helps prevent their bodies from drying out. The coating also aids in the absorption of oxygen and allows slugs to move across surfaces.

28. Animals with bilateral symmetry usually have specialized anterior and posterior ends as well as dorsal and ventral sides. Animals with bilateral symmetry usually move with anterior end first, so this end encounters new parts of the environment first. Sense organs are clustered at the anterior end into a head region; this is cephalization, which is advantageous for orienting, navigating, feeding, and defense.

29. Many terrestrial invertebrates convert ammonia into urea, a less toxic compound that can be concentrated to produce urine. Some terrestrial invertebrates convert ammonia into uric acid, which is concentrated into solid crystals. Both processes concentrate the waste product and therefore reduce water loss, but uric acid can be excreted as a dry, pasty solid.

30. Most respiratory structures found in invertebrates are thin and moist and have a large surface area. In aquatic invertebrates, respiratory structures are usually exposed directly to the water. The respiratory surfaces of terrestrial animals tend to be located inside the body, where they are protected from drying out.

31. Over the course of evolution, segments often became specialized for specific functions. Therefore, without segmentation, the process of specialization might have been impeded.

32. The diagrams show a hydrostatic skeleton, which consists of longitudinal and circular muscles that surround a fluid-filled cavity. When the muscles contract, they push against the fluid, causing the body to change shape.

33. Arthropods are more closely related to annelids than to cnidarians in evolutionary terms. Both arthropods and annelids have three germ layers, bilateral symmetry, cephalization, a true coelom, and protostome development. Cnidarians, in contrast, have only two germ layers and radial symmetry, no cephalization or coelom, and neither protostome nor deuterostome development.

34. If a flatworm's flame cells were damaged, its ability to remove excess water would be impaired.

35. Multicellularity, tissues, protostome development, pseudocoelom, coelom, deuterostome development

36. Both the eyespots of flatworms and the eyes of insects can detect the presence of light. That is all flatworm eyespots can detect, though. Insect eyes can also detect motion and color and form images.

Focus on the BIG Idea

Students should state the definitions of mitosis and meiosis they learned in Chapters 10 and 11. They should further explain that sexual reproduction is the production of offspring from the fusion of the haploid gametes, and gametes are produced by meiosis. Once the gametes fuse and a zygote is produced, a multicellular animal develops through mitosis. In contrast to sexual reproduction, asexual reproduction does not involve the production of gametes by meiosis. Rather, the offspring of asexual reproduction grow into multicellular organisms by mitosis of diploid cells.

Chapter 29 Assessmentt

Critical Thinking

26. Inferring The excretory systems of terrestrial invertebrates, such as earthworms, convert ammonia to less toxic components. Why is this change unnecessary in small aquatic invertebrates, such as planarians?

27. Applying Concepts The external surface of slugs is slimy. What might the adaptive advantage of this characteristic be?

28. Applying Concepts Why is bilateral symmetry an important development in the evolution of animals?

29. Applying Concepts No matter where they live, all animals need to control the amount of water within their bodies as well as get rid of ammonia—a toxic nitrogenous waste. How were invertebrates able to perform these functions, especially as they moved to terrestrial environments?

30. Comparing and Contrasting Invertebrates use a variety of structures for respiration. How are these structures similar? How are they different?

31. Inferring What might have happened to the evolution of animals if segmentation had not occurred?

32. Applying Concepts The diagrams below show a type of skeletal system found in invertebrates. What is the name for this type of skeleton? Describe how it functions.

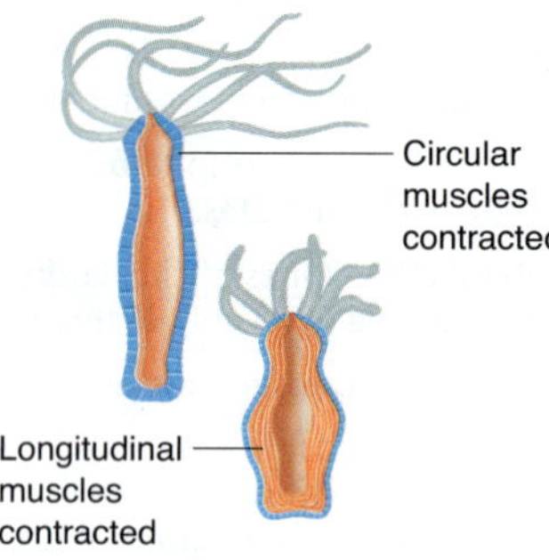

33. Comparing and Contrasting To which group—cnidarians or annelids—are arthropods more closely related in phylogenetic (evolutionary) terms? In your answer, note similarities and differences in anatomy, physiology, and embryology.

34. Predicting Predict what might happen if a flatworm's flame cells were damaged.

35. Applying Concepts Rank the following developments in the order of their appearance during evolution: pseudocoelom, tissues, deuterostome development, multicellularity, coelom, protostome development.

36. Comparing and Contrasting Compare the eyespots of flatworms to the eyes of insects. How are they similar and different?

Focus on the BIG Idea

Information and Heredity Use what you learned in Chapter 11 to compare the processes of meiosis and mitosis. Then, explain how these processes are involved in sexual and asexual reproduction.

Writing in Science

Write a paragraph in which you describe, in your own words, what the first multicellular animals were like. Begin your paragraph with a topic sentence that states the main idea of the paragraph. (*Hint:* Before you write, make a list of the characteristics of the first multicellular animals. Then, organize these characteristics in logical order.)

Performance-Based Assessment

Creative Writing Choose a kind of invertebrate, such as a cnidarian or an annelid. Imagine that you are that invertebrate and are in the process of looking for employment. Prepare a résumé that will inform a potential employer of your specialized skills.

For: An interactive self-test
Visit: PHSchool.com
Web Code: cba-8290

Standards Practice

Success Tracker™ Online at PHSchool.com

Test-Taking Tip Before taking a standardized test, it helps to become familiar with the format of the test, including the different question types. One method for this is to complete practice tests, such as this one. Even if you have practiced for a standardized test, be sure to read direction lines carefully before you begin.

Directions: Choose the letter that best answers the question or completes the statement.

1. In protostomes, the blastopore develops into the
   A ectoderm.
   B mouth.
   C anus.
   D deuterostome.
2. Which trend did NOT occur during invertebrate evolution? 7 3.c
   A specialization of cells
   B loss of a true coelom
   C segmentation of bodies
   D bilateral symmetry
3. All animals have some form of body symmetry EXCEPT
   A sponges.
   B jellyfishes.
   C worms.
   D arthropods.
4. What is a function of the excretory system?
   A to supply cells with oxygen and nutrients
   B to rid the body of metabolic wastes
   C to exchange oxygen and carbon dioxide with the environment
   D to gather information from the environment
5. Specialized tissues used to move, breathe, and pump blood are called
   A germ layers.
   B excretory systems.
   C endoderms.
   D muscles.
6. Which invertebrates have an open circulatory system?
   A most mollusks only
   B arthropods only
   C annelids only
   D arthropods and most mollusks
7. The concentration of nerve tissue and organs in one end of the body is called
   A cephalization.
   B segmentation.
   C diffusion.
   D body symmetry.
8. Which of the following do NOT have a mesoderm?
   A jellyfishes
   B earthworms
   C flatworms
   D octopi

Questions 9–10

A biology student has two samples of earthworms, as shown below. The student knows that because the worms' body temperature changes with the environment, the worms in Sample A have a higher body temperature than those in Sample B. The student uses a stereomicroscope to count the number of heartbeats per minute for three worms from each sample.

Sample A: At temperature of worms' soil environment

Sample B: In ice water

9. Look at the student's two samples. What can you conclude? 8IIE 9.c
   A Sample A is the control.
   B Sample B is the control.
   C Either sample can serve as the control.
   D This is not a controlled experiment.
10. The student finds that the worms from Sample A have a faster heart rate than the worms from Sample B. What conclusion can be drawn? 8IIE 9.c
    A The worms in Sample A are healthier than the worms in Sample B.
    B A decrease in body temperature corresponds to an increase in heart rate.
    C There is no relationship between body temperature and heart rate.
    D A decrease in body temperature corresponds to a decrease in heart rate.

Standards Practice

1. B	**5.** D	**9.** A
2. B	**6.** D	**10.** D
3. A	**7.** A	
4. B	**8.** A	

Success Tracker™ Online at PHSchool.com

Have students check their understanding of the chapter by logging onto Success Tracker.

Writing in Science

Students' paragraphs may vary. Each, though, should mention the following characteristics of most of the first multicellular animals. Most were flat, plate-shaped, made of soft tissues, and had photosynthetic algae living within their tissues. They were segmented and had bilateral symmetry, but they showed little cell specialization or cephalization. They were simple animals, with little internal specialization.

Performance-Based Assessment

Each student should identify the type of invertebrate he or she is and the kind of employment being sought. Then, the student should match that invertebrate's special functions or characteristics to the job. For instance, a student who identifies with a sponge might extol the virtues of being great at a better-than-average capacity to hold water.

Go Online PHSchool.com

Your students can independently test their knowledge of the chapter and print out their test results for your files.

UNIT 9

A great white shark leaps out of the water to catch its next meal.

Dear Colleague,

Most biologists I know have a particular group of critters of which they are especially—some would say inordinately—fond. Some of us establish that fondness early in life, and it becomes one of the reasons we choose to become professional biologists. In other cases, one or another group of critters just happens to grow on us, say sometime between freshman year in college and graduate school.

For me, the process involved both of the above. I grew up in an apartment building whose management prohibited dogs and cats. Birds were out of the question, too, because my brother and I were allergic to feathers. So, when I won a goldfish at a county fair by tossing a coin into its bowl, I started keeping fishes as pets by default. (Incidentally, it wasn't until graduate school that I learned the correct way to use the words *fish* and *fishes*. *Fish* properly refers to a single fish or to a group of individuals of the same species. *Fishes* is used when talking about several individuals of more than one species.)

My early infatuation with fishes stuck. Years later, when professors steered me away from medical school by spiriting me off to a marine biological station in the Caribbean (in January!), fishes were on my mind. Years of home aquarium keeping turned out to be useful professionally; because I could build sophisticated aquaria and maintain delicate specimens, I was able to study a number of odd and unusual species during my graduate research on the evolution of color vision.

A special familiarity with animals is part of the fun of being a biologist. I could tell stories about fishes for days without running out of material. I could also tell stories about other "fish people" who used their expertise in intriguing ways; several

ichthyologists I know employed their understanding of fish behavior to become master anglers!

Developing my own expertise was fun, but I got even more of a kick from my fellow graduate students and their "special" knowledge. If I had a question about mammals, I ran up a flight of stairs in our lab building to ask Christine or Kathleen. (Both are now professors; one of them kept a hyrax as a pet back then.) I had two other friends I could ask almost anything about amphibians or reptiles ("herps" we affectionately called them), and a whole floor of folks to bug for information on insects. (Sorry!)

But the most fun came as we compared notes about our pets and experimental subjects. Time and time again, we found useful and fascinating comparisons across the diverse animals we studied. We discussed similarities and differences in the relationship between form and function. We compared animals' sense organs, feeding habits, parental care, and adaptive radiations—in much the same way as Chapter 33 does in this unit. The more we learned, the more we realized that we had lots more yet to learn. Our subject was endless—and endlessly fascinating. To my mind, there is no better remedy for bored and blasé students than a good dose of substantive education in natural history. I'm in good company; no less a thinker than Thomas Henry Huxley agreed:

To a person uninstructed in natural history, his country or seaside stroll is a walk through a gallery filled with wonderful works of art, nine tenths of which have their faces turned to the wall.

Sincerely,

Joe Levine

Go Online PHSchool.com

Students can research chordates on the site developed by authors Ken Miller and Joe Levine.

Chapter Planner 30 Nonvertebrate Chordates, Fishes, and Amphibians

Section and Section Objectives	Time	STANDARDS NCLB	STANDARDS Biology	Activities and Labs
30–1 The Chordates, pp. 767–770 **30.1.1** ***Identify*** the characteristics that all chordates share. **30.1.2** ***Explain*** what vertebrates are. **30.1.3** ***Describe*** the two groups of nonvertebrate chordates.	1 period (1/2 block)			SE: ***Inquiry Activity,*** Is a lancelet a fish?, p. 766 L2 TE: ***Build Science Skills,*** p. 768 L1 L2 TE: ***Build Science Skills,*** p. 770 L1 L2
30–2 Fishes, pp. 771–781 **30.2.1** ***Identify*** the basic characteristics of fishes. **30.2.2** ***Summarize*** the evolution of fishes. **30.2.3** ***Explain*** how fishes are adapted for life in water. **30.2.4** ***Describe*** the three main groups of fishes.	2 periods (1 block)			TE: ***Demonstration,*** p. 773 L1 L2 TE: ***Make Connections,*** p. 773 L2 L3 SE: ***Quick Lab,*** How do fishes use gills?, p. 775 L2 TE: ***Make Connections,*** p. 776 L1 L2 TE: ***Demonstration,*** p. 777 L2 TE: ***Build Science Skills,*** pp. 778 L2, 780 L2
30–3 Amphibians, pp. 782–789 **30.3.1** ***Describe*** what an amphibian is. **30.3.2** ***Summarize*** events in the evolution of amphibians. **30.3.3** ***Explain*** how amphibians are adapted for life on land. **30.3.4** ***Describe*** essential life functions in amphibians. **30.3.5** ***Name*** the main groups of living amphibians.	2 periods (1 block)			TE: ***Build Science Skills,*** pp. 782 L2, 787 L2 TE: ***Demonstration,*** p. 784 L2 TE: ***Make Connections,*** p. 785 L2 L3 SE: ***Analyzing Data,*** Amphibian Population Trends, p. 787 L2 SE: ***Exploration,*** Investigating Homeostasis in Fishes and Amphibians, pp. 790–791 L2 LMA: Chapter 30 Lab L2 L3 LMB: Chapter 30 Lab L1 L2
Chapter Assessment, pp. 792–795	1 period (1/2 block)			

ACTIVITY PLANNER

SE: *Inquiry Activity,* p. 766; 10 min.; bony fish, hand lens, preserved lancelet, apron, safety goggles, disposable plastic gloves

TE: *Build Science Skills,* p. 768; 10 min.; skeletons of vertebrates

TE: *Build Science Skills,* p. 770; 15 min.; preserved lancelet

TE: *Demonstration,* p. 773; 10 min.; straw, various objects

TE: *Make Connections,* p. 773; 15 min.; clear tub of water, round object, square object, streamlined (spindle-shaped) object

SE: *Quick Lab,* p. 775; 10 min.; fish food, food coloring, plastic cup, dropper pipette, live fish in an aquarium

TE: *Make Connections,* p. 776; 30 min.; cucumber slices, saltwater solution, distilled water, 2 beakers or jars

TE: *Demonstration,* p. 777; 10 min.; balloon, string, screw, tub

TE: *Build Science Skills,* p. 778; 20 min.; 10–15 pictures of fishes

TE: *Build Science Skills,* p. 780; 30 min.; fish, dissecting tools

TE: *Build Science Skills,* p. 782; 15 min.; variety of live amphibians

TE: *Demonstration,* p. 784; 20 min.; preserved frog or frog model

TE: *Make Connections,* p. 785; 5 min.; balloon

TE: *Build Science Skills,* p. 787; 30 min.; materials for models

SE: *Exploration,* pp. 790 and 791; 45 min.; 5 g saltwater fish, 5 g freshwater fish, balance, 4 test tubes, test-tube rack, paper towels, 2 glass rods, 10-mL graduated cylinder, 2 funnels, 2 filter-paper circles, silver nitrate solution, 1000-mL beaker, vinegar, distilled water, string, scissors, transparent tape, blue litmus paper, sodium bicarbonate (baking soda), glass-marking pencil, apron, safety goggles, plastic gloves

PLANNING KEY

Ability Levels
for students performing . . .
below grade level L1
at grade level L2
above grade level L3

Print Components

SE	Student Edition	LA	Lab Assessment
TE	Teacher's Edition	BTM	Biotechnology Manual
RSW	Reading & Study Workbook A	IDM	Issues and Decision Making
ARSW	Adapted Reading & Study Workbook B	LW	Lab Worksheets
TR	Teaching Resources	LMA	Laboratory Manual A
IF	Investigations in Forensics	LMB	Laboratory Manual B

Tech Components

CTB	Computer Test Bank
BD	BioDetectives DVD
TP	Transparencies Plus
PLM	Probeware Lab Manual
ABC	ABC DVD Library
LS	Lab Simulations
VL	Virtual Labs

Interactive Textbook — Interactive textbook with assessment at PHSchool.com

Program Resources	Assessment	Media and Technology
TR: Lesson Plan 30–1, Section Summary, p. 4 L1, p. 16 L2, Worksheets, pp. 7–8 L1, pp. 18–19 L2 **RSW:** Section 30–1 L2 **ARSW:** Section 30–1 L1	**SE:** 30–1 Section Assessment, p. 770 **TR:** Section Review 30–1	**iText:** Section 30–1 **TP:** 30–1 Interest Grabber, Section Outline, Chordate Cladogram, Figure 30–1
TR: Lesson Plan 30–2, Section Summary, p. 4 L1, p. 16 L2, Worksheets, pp. 9–10 L1, pp. 20–23 L2, Enrichment L2 L3 **RSW:** Section 30–2 L2 **ARSW:** Section 30–2 L1 **IDM:** Issues and Decisions 37 L2 L3	**SE:** 30–2 Section Assessment, p. 781 **TR:** Section Review 30–2	**iText:** Section 30–2 **TP:** 30–2 Interest Grabber, Section Outline, Circulation in a Fish, Figure 30–11
TR: Lesson Plan 30–3, Section Summary, p. 6 L1, p. 17 L2, Worksheets, pp. 11–14 L1, pp. 24–26 L2 **LW:** Chapter 30 Exploration L1 L2 L3 **RSW:** Section 30–3 L2 **ARSW:** Section 30–3 L1 **IDM:** Issues and Decisions 33 L2 L3	**SE:** 30–3 Section Assessment, p. 789 **TR:** Section Review 30–3	**iText:** Section 30–3 **TP:** 30–3 Interest Grabber, Section Outline, Concept Map, Figure 30–26 **ABC:** 37 Frog Anatomy
	SE: Chapter 30 Assessment, pp. 792–795 **TR:** Chapter Vocabulary Review, Graphic Organizer, Chapter 30 Test	**iText:** Chapter 30 Assessment **CTB:** Chapter 30 Test

Go Online
Students can do research, share data, and test their knowledge online.

PRESSED FOR TIME?

To Preview the Chapter
- Introduce students to Key Concepts and Vocabulary terms in each section.
- Assign the Reading Strategies for each section.

To Cover the Chapter Quickly
- Have students read all of Section 30–1; read Form and Function in Fishes and Figures 30–17, 30–18, and 30–19 in Section 30–2; and read Form and Function in Amphibians and Figure 30–28 in Section 30–3.
- Assign the Section Review 30–1; questions 1, 2, 4–12, 15–20, 22–27, and 29–34 in Chapter 30 Assessment; and the Chapter 30 Standards Practice.

To Review the Chapter
- Assign Sections 30–1 through 30–3 in the Reading and Study Workbook or the Adapted Reading and Study Workbook.
- Assign Section Reviews for 30–1 through 30–3 and the Chapter Vocabulary Review for Chapter 30 in the Teaching Resources.

CHAPTER 30

ENGAGE/EXPLORE

Inquiry Activity

Objective Students will be able to explain how a lancelet differs from a fish. L2

Skill Focus **Comparing and Contrasting, Classifying**

Materials bony fish, hand lens, preserved lancelet, disposable plastic gloves

Time 10 minutes

Advance Prep Purchase bony fish from a grocery store, fish market, or scientific supply house. Purchase preserved lancelets from a scientific supply house.

Safety Students should wear disposable plastic gloves. Make sure students dispose of the gloves properly and then wash their hands thoroughly after the activity.

Strategy Partially dissect one fish and one lancelet so students can observe muscle structure and the absence of bones in the lancelet. Set this up as a demonstration or have students work in groups.

Expected Outcomes From their comparisons, students should not classify lancelets as fishes.

Think About It

1. Accept all valid comparisons. Similar: Both have a mouth, tail, gill-like structures. Different: Bony fishes have bones, eyes, jaws, scales, and fins.
2. Accept all reasonably supported answers. Lancelets are not fishes; they lack an internal skeleton, including a vertebral column (backbone).

Brain Teaser

Challenge students to compare a fish, an amphibian, a reptile, a bird, and a mammal. Name specific animals to help students focus on what they are comparing. Ask: **How are all of these animals similar?** *(Accept all logical responses, but the best answer is that all have backbones.)*

CHAPTER 30

Nonvertebrate Chordates, Fishes, and Amphibians

Many species of fish swim together in large groups called schools. This school of double-saddle butterflyfish lives in the tropical Pacific Ocean.

Inquiry Activity

Is a lancelet a fish?

Procedure  

1. Put on plastic gloves. Closely examine a fish, using a hand lens if you like. Also look at a dissected fish. List the main characteristics of fishes.
2. Now, closely examine a preserved lancelet and a dissected lancelet. List the characteristics of lancelets. Wash your hands with soap and warm water.

Think About It

1. **Comparing and Contrasting** How are the fish and the lancelet similar? How are they different from each other?
2. **Classifying** Not all fishes have jaws or scales. Given this information, do you think the lancelet is a type of fish? Explain your answer.

FACTS AND FIGURES

Chordates related to echinoderms

Even though it seems that a huge gulf of evolutionary distance separates echinoderms and chordates, the distance is actually not that great. Wormlike marine vertebrates called hemichordates bridge that gulf. Hemichordate larvae look surprisingly similar to echinoderm larvae, suggesting that hemichordates and echinoderms share a common ancestor. Hemichordates also have pharyngeal gill clefts and the suggestion of a dorsal nerve cord that relate them to chordates. And, even more compelling, all three phyla have a common pattern of early embryological development. They are all deuterostomes, meaning that during early embryonic development the mouth forms later than the anus and the body cavity.

30–1 The Chordates

At first glance, fishes, amphibians, reptiles, birds, and mammals appear to be very different from one another. Some have feathers; others have fins. Some fly; others swim or crawl. These variations are some of the characteristics that biologists use to separate these animals into different classes, yet all are members of the phylum Chordata (kawr-DAHT-uh).

What Is a Chordate?

Members of the phylum Chordata are called **chordates** (KAWR-dayts). To be classified as a chordate, an animal must have four key characteristics, although these characteristics need not be present during the entire life cycle. **A chordate is an animal that has, for at least some stage of its life, a dorsal, hollow nerve cord; a notochord; pharyngeal (fuh-RIN-jee-ul) pouches; and a tail that extends beyond the anus.** Refer to **Figure 30–1** as you read about each of these characteristics.

The hollow nerve cord runs along the dorsal (back) part of the body. Nerves branch from this cord at regular intervals and connect to internal organs, muscles, and sense organs.

The **notochord** is a long supporting rod that runs through the body just below the nerve cord. Most chordates have a notochord only when they are embryos.

Pharyngeal pouches are paired structures in the throat (pharynx) region. In some chordates—such as fishes and amphibians—slits develop that connect the pharyngeal pouches to the outside of the body. These slits may then develop gills that are used for gas exchange.

At some point in their lives, all chordates have a tail that extends beyond the anus. The tail can contain bone and muscle and is used in swimming by many aquatic species.

CHECKPOINT *What is a notochord?*

Guide for Reading

Key Concepts
- What characteristics do all chordates share?
- What are the two groups of nonvertebrate chordates?

Vocabulary
chordate
notochord
pharyngeal pouch
vertebra

Reading Strategy: Building Vocabulary
Before you read, preview new vocabulary by skimming the section and making a list of the highlighted, boldface terms. As you read, make notes next to each term.

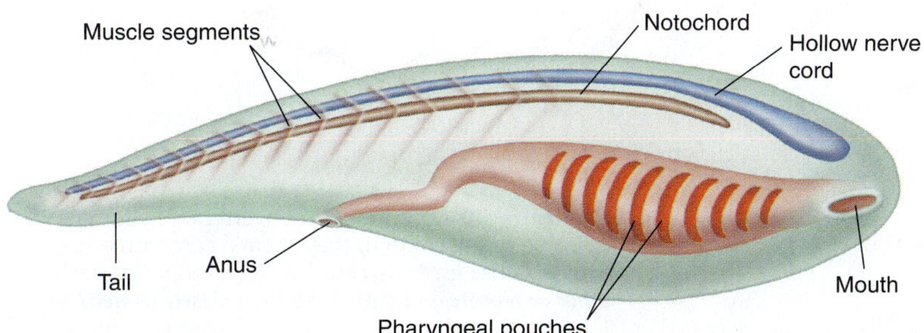

Figure 30–1 All chordates share four characteristics: a dorsal, hollow nerve cord; a notochord; pharyngeal pouches; and a tail that extends beyond the anus. Some chordates possess all these characteristics as adults; others possess them only as embryos.

SECTION RESOURCES

TIME SAVER

Print:
- ***Teaching Resources,*** Lesson Plan 30–1, Adapted Section Summary 30–1, Adapted Worksheets 30–1, Section Summary 30–1, Worksheets 30–1, Section Review 30–1
- ***Reading and Study Workbook A,*** Section 30–1
- ***Adapted Reading and Study Workbook B,*** Section 30–1

Technology:
- ***iText,*** Section 30–1
- ***Transparencies Plus,*** Section 30–1

Section 30–1

1 FOCUS

Objectives

30.1.1 ***Identify*** the characteristics that all chordates share.
30.1.2 ***Explain*** what vertebrates are.
30.1.3 ***Describe*** the two groups of nonvertebrate chordates.

Guide for Reading

Vocabulary Preview
Explain that *notochord* comes from the Greek words *noto,* meaning "back," and *chord,* meaning "string." The notochord is the structure for which chordates are named. Also explain that *pharyngeal* is an adjective used to describe objects located in the pharynx, or throat. Ask: **Where would pharyngeal pouches be located?** *(In the pharynx, or throat)*

Reading Strategy
Before students read the section, have them preview Figures 30–1, 30–3, and 30–5. Challenge them to predict how tunicates and lancelets are related. Then, as students read the section, ask them to reassess their predictions.

2 INSTRUCT

What Is a Chordate?

Build Science Skills

Applying Concepts Show students pictures of the embryos of various animals, such as humans, birds, frogs, snakes, and fishes. Invite students to identify chordate structures in each embryonic picture. Emphasize that these characteristics need not be present during the entire life cycle of a chordate. In fact, most chordates have these characteristics for only a short time during the embryonic stage. L2

Answer to . . .

CHECKPOINT *A notochord is a long supporting rod located just below the nerve cord.*

30–1 (continued)

Most Chordates Are Vertebrates

Download a worksheet on nonvertebrate chordates for students to complete, and find additional teacher support from NSTA SciLinks.

Use Visuals

Figure 30–2 As students study the evolutionary tree, remind them that chordates located on the same branch are more closely related to each other than to other chordates. Also tell them that the points of branching represent common ancestors. Ask: **Which two of these chordate groups are most closely related—birds, fishes, reptiles?** *(Birds and reptiles)* Explain that scientists determine the relationships among organisms by their similarities in structure, embryological development, and DNA sequences. Ask: **What structure do vertebrate chordates have in common?** *(Vertebral column)* L1 L2

Build Science Skills

Observing Display skeletons of various vertebrates for students to observe. If skeletons are not available, substitute pictures or diagrams. Encourage students to observe the skeletons and locate the vertebral column for each. Make sure they can also identify the vertebrae. Have students describe similarities and differences. Ask: **How are these vertebrates similar?** *(All have backbones and internal skeletons.)* Briefly discuss their differences, explaining that students will learn more about these differences in later chapters. L1 L2

For: Links on nonvertebrate chordates
Visit: www.SciLinks.org
Web Code: cbn-9301

Most Chordates Are Vertebrates

The diagram in **Figure 30–2** shows the current understanding of the phylogeny, or evolutionary relationships, of chordates. About 96 percent of all chordate species are placed in the subphylum Vertebrata and are called vertebrates. Most vertebrates have a strong supporting structure known as the vertebral column, or backbone. In vertebrates, the dorsal, hollow nerve cord is called the spinal cord. As a vertebrate embryo develops, the front end of the spinal cord grows into a brain. The backbone, which replaces the notochord in most developing vertebrates, is made of individual segments called **vertebrae** (singular: vertebra). In addition to providing support, vertebrae enclose and protect the spinal cord.

A vertebrate's backbone is part of an endoskeleton, or internal skeleton. Like an arthropod's exoskeleton, a vertebrate's endoskeleton supports and protects the animal's body and gives muscles a place to attach. However, unlike an arthropod's exoskeleton, a vertebrate's skeleton grows as the animal grows and does not need to be shed periodically. In addition, whereas an arthropod's skeleton is made entirely of nonliving material, a vertebrate's skeleton contains living cells as well as nonliving material. The cells produce the nonliving material in the skeleton.

CHECKPOINT *What is the function of the vertebral column?*

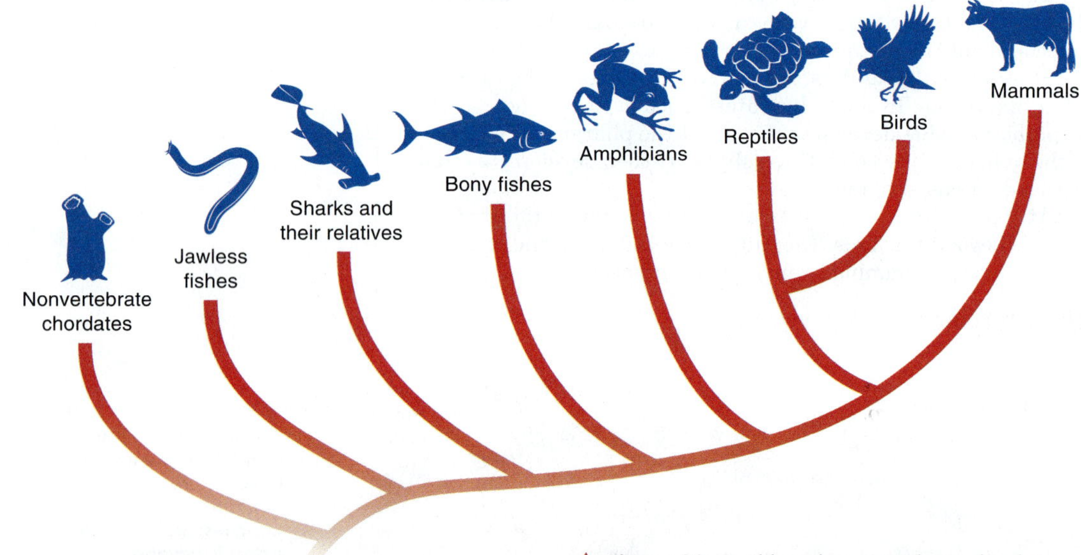

▲ **Figure 30–2** Although nonvertebrate chordates lack a vertebral column, they share a common ancestor with vertebrates. **Interpreting Graphics** *To which other vertebrate group are birds most closely related?*

UNIVERSAL ACCESS

Inclusion/Special Needs
Students with impaired vision can examine the chordate characteristics by exploring with their fingers a dissected lancelet and bony fish from the Chapter Inquiry Activity. Pair these students with others who will help them identify the structures and verbally describe their functions. Students should wear plastic gloves and wash their hands with soap and warm water afterward. L1

Less Proficient Readers
Encourage students to construct a Venn diagram that compares and contrasts tunicates and lancelets. Venn diagrams should show the characteristics specific to tunicates, those specific to lancelets, and those shared by both. Then, have students write a sentence that explains why tunicates are classified as chordates. L1

▼ **Figure 30–3** **Tunicates are one of two groups of nonvertebrate chordates.** The tadpole-shaped tunicate larva (left) has all four chordate characteristics. When most tunicate larvae grow into adults, they lose their tails and attach to a solid surface. Adult tunicates (right) look nothing like the larvae, or even like other adult chordates. Both larvae and adults are filter feeders. The blue arrows show where water enters and leaves the tunicate's body.

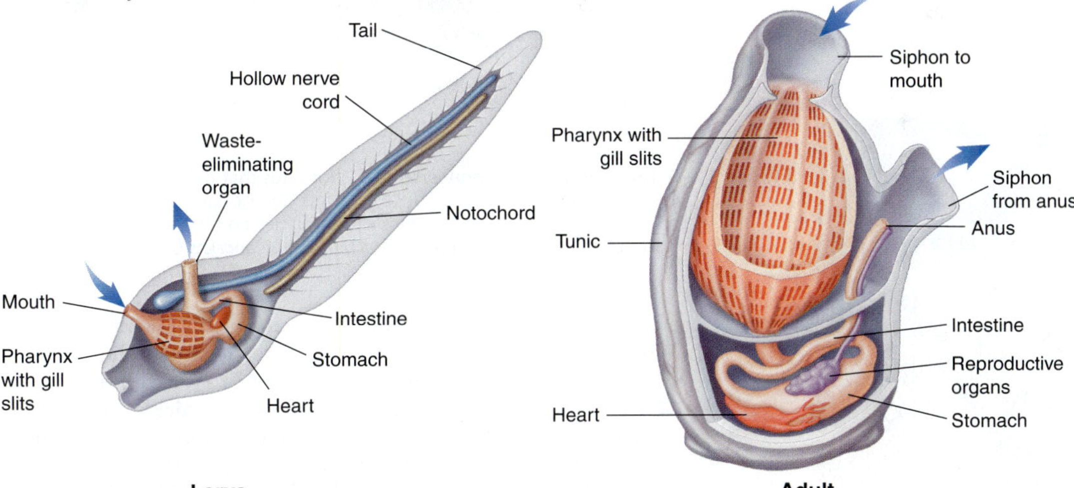

Nonvertebrate Chordates

There are two subphyla of chordates that do not have backbones. **The two groups of nonvertebrate chordates are tunicates and lancelets.** Both are soft-bodied marine organisms. Like all chordates, these animals have a hollow nerve cord, a notochord, pharyngeal pouches, and a tail at some stage of their life cycle.

In some ways, studying nonvertebrate chordates is like using a time machine to investigate the ancestors of our own subphylum, Vertebrata. Similarities in anatomy and embryological development indicate that vertebrates and nonvertebrate chordates evolved from a common ancestor. Fossil evidence from the Cambrian Period places this divergence at more than 550 million years ago. Although they seem to be simple animals, tunicates and lancelets are relatives of ours—very distant ones.

Tunicates Filter-feeding tunicates (subphylum Urochordata) certainly do not look as if they are related to us. **Figure 30–3** shows the body structure of a tunicate larva and an adult. Observe that the larval form has all of the chordate characteristics. In contrast, adult tunicates, like the ones in **Figure 30–4,** have neither a notochord nor a tail.

▲ **Figure 30–4** Tunicates get their name from the adult's body covering—the tough, nonliving tunic. Most tunicates are commonly known as sea squirts, because of the stream of water they sometimes eject. **Inferring** *In what kind of ecosystem are you likely to find tunicates?*

Make Connections

Physics Explain to students that the pull of muscles against the bones of the skeleton is responsible for most voluntary movement in vertebrates. Muscles and bones work together as levers to produce movement. A lever is a rigid object that moves around a pivot point. The fulcrum is the pivot point of a lever. The input force is the force used to move the lever. Tell students to lift their heads. Explain that the fulcrum is the joint between the topmost vertebra and the skull. Ask: **What provided the input force?** *(The muscles at the back of the neck)* L2 L3

Nonvertebrate Chordates

Build Science Skills

Formulating Hypotheses Explain that scientists have two theories that describe the chordate ancestor. In one theory, the ancestor was like a lancelet from which a sessile line evolved to become the tunicates. Another line remained motile and evolved into vertebrates. A second theory describes the ancestor as a tunicate from which lancelets and vertebrates arose from adaptations of the tadpole-shaped tunicate larva. Challenge students to hypothesize whether the chordate ancestor was like a tunicate or a lancelet. They should give reasons for their choice.  L2

Use Visuals

Figure 30–3 Ask volunteers to point out the chordate structures in the illustration of the tunicate larva. Ask: **What chordate structure is found in the adult?** *(Pharynx with gill slits)* **In what ways do tunicates differ from vertebrates?** *(The notochord is not replaced by a vertebral column.)* L1 L2

TEACHER TO TEACHER

To help my students actually see the relationship between the spinal cord and the vertebrae, I have them examine chicken necks. These are easy to obtain from the local grocery store or butcher, and I boil them prior to students' handling them. First, I encourage students to locate the vertebrae and observe how they are shaped and how they allow movement. Then, I instruct students to use dissecting probes to locate the spinal cord. I also point out that the vertebrae developed from the notochord and the spinal cord came from the dorsal, hollow nerve cord in the embryo. When they have finished examining the chicken necks, I instruct my students to draw labeled diagrams of their observations.

—*Heidi Busa*
Biology Teacher
Marcellus High School
Marcellus, NY

Answers to . . .

CHECKPOINT *To enclose and protect the spinal cord and give support*

Figure 30–2 *Reptiles*

Figure 30–4 *In the ocean*

30–1 (continued)

Build Science Skills

Classifying All students will benefit from reexamining the preserved lancelet used in the Chapter Inquiry Activity. Encourage students to draw diagrams of the lancelet anatomy and label the four chordate characteristics. Remind students that the lancelet is one of the few chordates that have all four chordate characteristics present in the adult. Ask: **Why are lancelets classified as nonvertebrates?** *(They do not have a backbone.)* L1 L2

3 ASSESS

Evaluate Understanding

Invite student volunteers to name the four chordate characteristics. Make a table on the board entitled *Nonvertebrate Chordates* with the headings *Tunicates* and *Lancelets*. Call on students to complete the table by describing their key characteristics.

Reteach

Use Figure 30–1 to reinforce some of the Vocabulary words from this section. You might have students write down the definitions of the words on a chordate diagram that they draw themselves.

Writing in Science

Students' articles should be written in the style of the typical newspaper article. Their articles should describe one of the nonvertebrate chordates discussed in this section. You might provide students with copies of *Science News* or *The New York Times* science section as examples of the style and format to use for their articles.

If your class subscribes to the iText, use it to review Section 30–1.

Answer to . . .

Figure 30–5 *All four chordate characteristics*

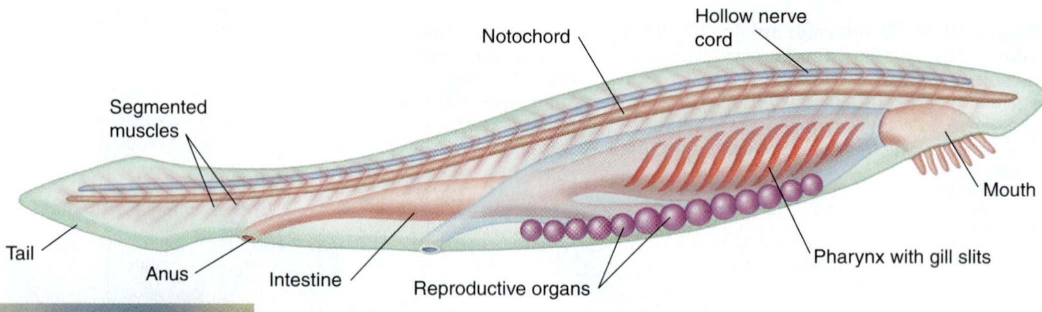

Figure 30–5 Lancelets are small nonvertebrate chordates that often live with their bodies half buried in sand. Because lancelets do not have fins or legs, they can move only by contracting the paired muscles on their bodies. **Interpreting Graphics** *Which chordate characteristics do lancelets have?*

Lancelets The small, fishlike creatures called lancelets form the subphylum Cephalochordata. Lancelets live on the sandy ocean bottom. You can see a lancelet's body structure in **Figure 30–5.** Observe that, unlike an adult tunicate, an adult lancelet has a definite head region that contains a mouth. The mouth opens into a long pharynx with up to 100 pairs of gill slits. As water passes through the pharynx, a sticky mucus catches food particles. The lancelet then swallows the mucus into the digestive tract. Lancelets use the pharynx for gas exchange. In addition, lancelets are thin enough to exchange gases through their body surface.

Lancelets have a closed circulatory system. They do not have a true heart. Instead, the walls of the major blood vessels contract to push blood through the body. The fishlike motion of lancelets results from contracting muscles that are organized into V-shaped units. The muscle units are paired on either side of the body.

30–1 Section Assessment

1. **Key Concept** Describe four characteristics of chordates.
2. **Key Concept** How do lancelets and tunicates differ?
3. What one characteristic distinguishes most vertebrates from the other chordates?
4. How is a vertebrate's skeleton similar to that of an arthropod? How is it different?
5. Describe two ways in which lancelets obtain oxygen.
6. **Critical Thinking Inferring** How would a free-swimming larval stage be an advantage for tunicates?

Writing in Science

Creative Writing

Imagine that a scientist has just discovered the existence of one of the nonvertebrate chordate groups. Write a short newspaper article describing what the scientist has discovered. *Hint:* Before you write, list the characteristics of the chordate group. Then, identify these characteristics in the article.

30–1 Section Assessment

1. Hollow nerve cord: runs along back, nerves branch from it to rest of body; notochord: long supporting rod below nerve cord; pharyngeal pouches: paired structures in the throat region; tail that extends beyond anus
2. Unlike adult tunicates, adult lancelets have a definite head region containing a mouth.
3. The vertebral column, or backbone
4. Similarities: supports and protects body, gives muscles a place to attach. Differences: does not need to be shed and contains living cells.
5. Gas exchange occurs in the pharynx and through the body surface.
6. Adult tunicates are immobile. Free-swimming larvae disperse the young throughout a wide area. This reduces competition for food and space.

30–2 Fishes

I f you think of Earth as land, then the name "Earth" is not particularly appropriate for the planet on which you live, for more than two thirds of its surface is water. And almost anywhere there is water—fresh or salt—there are fishes. At the edge of the ocean, blennies jump from rock to rock and occasionally dunk themselves in tide pools. Beneath the Arctic ice live fishes whose bodies contain a biological antifreeze that keeps them from freezing solid. In some shallow desert streams, pupfishes tolerate temperatures that would cook almost any other animal. Evolution by natural selection and other processes has resulted in a great diversity of fishes.

What Is a Fish?

You might think that with such extreme variations in habitat, fishes would be difficult to characterize. However, describing a fish is a rather simple task. **Fishes are aquatic vertebrates; most fishes have paired fins, scales, and gills.** Fins are used for movement, scales for protection, and gills for exchanging gases. You can observe most of those characteristics in **Figure 30–6.**

Fishes are so varied, however, that for almost every general statement there are exceptions. For example, some fishes, such as catfish, do not have scales. One reason for the enormous diversity among living fishes is that these chordates belong to very different classes. Thus, many fishes—sharks, lampreys, and perch, for example—are no more similar to one another than humans are to frogs!

CHECKPOINT *What are the basic functions of fins, scales, and gills?*

Guide for Reading

Key Concepts
- What are the basic characteristics of fishes?
- What were the important developments during the evolution of fishes?
- How are fishes adapted for life in water?
- What are the three main groups of fishes?

Vocabulary
cartilage • atrium • ventricle
cerebrum • cerebellum
medulla oblongata
lateral line system
swim bladder • oviparous
ovoviviparous • viviparous

Reading Strategy: Using Prior Knowledge Before you read, make a list of the things you already know about fishes. After you have finished reading, check the list. Correct any errors and add new facts.

Caudal fin
Dorsal fin
Lateral line
Scales
Eye
Mouth
Anal fin
Pelvic fin
Pectoral fin
Operculum (gill cover)

Figure 30–6 Fishes come in many shapes and sizes. **Like most fishes, this African cichlid has paired fins, scales, and gills.**

SECTION RESOURCES

Print:
- ***Teaching Resources,*** Lesson Plan 30–2, Adapted Section Summary 30–2, Adapted Worksheets 30–2, Section Summary 30–2, Worksheets 30–2, Section Review 30–2, Enrichment
- ***Reading and Study Workbook A,*** Section 30–2
- ***Adapted Reading and Study Workbook B,*** Section 30–2
- ***Issues and Decision Making,*** Issues and Decisions 37

Technology:
- ***iText,*** Section 30–2
- ***Transparencies Plus,*** Section 30–2

Section 30–2

1 FOCUS

Objectives

30.2.1 ***Identify*** the basic characteristics of fishes.
30.2.2 ***Summarize*** the evolution of fishes.
30.2.3 ***Explain*** how fishes are adapted for life in water.
30.2.4 ***Describe*** the three main groups of fishes.

Guide for Reading

Vocabulary Preview
Read aloud the Vocabulary terms so that students can hear the correct pronunciation of each word. Encourage students to use the phonetic spellings in the text to practice saying the words aloud.

Reading Strategy
Encourage students to write down the Vocabulary terms and their meanings as they read. Also encourage them to sketch some of the diagrams to help them visualize some of the body systems in fishes.

2 INSTRUCT

What Is a Fish?

Build Science Skills

Using Models Challenge students to create a model of a fish based on the defining characteristics of most fishes: aquatic vertebrate with fins, scales, and gills. Encourage students to design their model fish to have specific adaptations to survive in its particular environment. Students can simply illustrate their fish models or create a three-dimensional model. Have students present their models to the class. L1 L2

Answer to . . .

CHECKPOINT *Fins: movement; scales: protection; gills: gas exchange*

30–2 (continued)

Evolution of Fishes

Address Misconceptions

Some students might be under the impression that the fossil record for fishes is complete. Ask: **What parts of an organism fossilize well?** *(Hard parts, such as bone and teeth)* **Which parts do not?** *(Soft tissue)* Explain that many early fishes had few hard body parts (bones) and that scientists make many inferences about the gaps in the fossil record based on the structures of living organisms and fossils. L2

Use Visuals

Figure 30–7 Challenge students to infer how the various adaptations of the fishes in the illustration made them better suited to their environment. Explain that after the adaptive radiation during the Ordovician and Silurian Periods, fishes inhabited every kind of environment in the oceans. Ask: **Why do you think some of these early fishes eventually became extinct at the end of the Devonian Period?** *(They were not as efficient at moving, getting food, and protecting themselves against predators as fishes with jaws and paired fins.)* L2

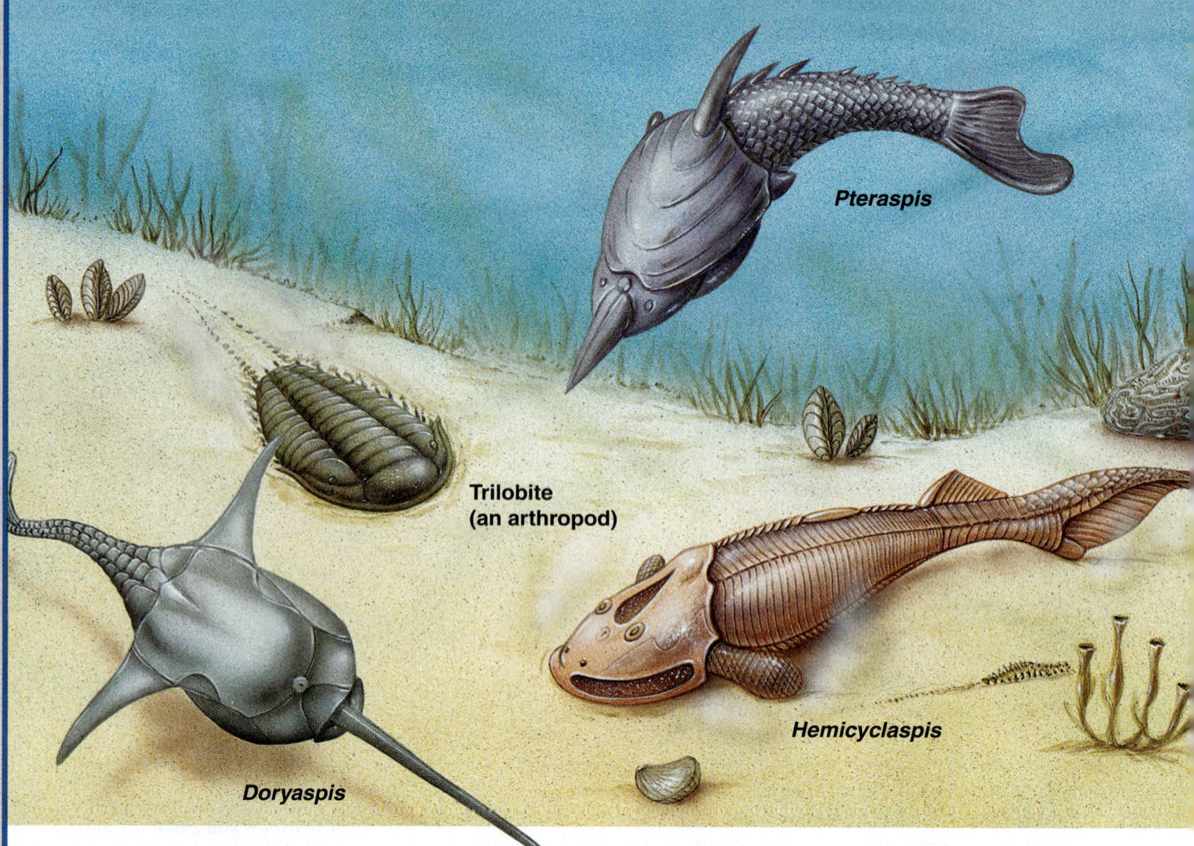

▲ **Figure 30–7** Ancient jawless fishes swam in shallow seas during the early Devonian Period, about 400 million years ago. Lacking jaws, early jawless fishes were limited in their ability to feed and to defend themselves against predators. **The evolution of paired fins, however, gave these fishes more control over their movement in the water.**

Evolution of Fishes

Fishes were the first vertebrates to evolve. They did not arise directly from tunicates or lancelets, but fishes and nonvertebrate chordates probably did evolve from common invertebrate ancestors. During the course of their evolution, fishes underwent several important changes. **The evolution of jaws and the evolution of paired fins were important developments during the rise of fishes.**

The First Fishes The earliest fishes to appear in the fossil record were odd-looking, jawless creatures whose bodies were armored with bony plates. They lived in the oceans during the late Cambrian Period, about 510 million years ago. Fishes kept this armored, jawless body plan for 100 million years.

The Age of Fishes During the Ordovician and Silurian Periods, about 505 to 410 million years ago, fishes underwent a major adaptive radiation. The species to emerge from the radiation ruled the seas during the Devonian Period, which is often called the Age of Fishes. Some of these fishes were jawless species that had very little armor. These jawless fishes were the ancestors of modern hagfishes and lampreys. Others, such as those in **Figure 30–7,** were armored and ultimately became extinct at the end of the Devonian Period, about 360 million years ago.

ESL SUPPORT FOR ENGLISH LANGUAGE LEARNERS

Comprehension: Ask Questions

Beginning To help students understand the basic characteristics of fishes, distribute a rewritten, modified version of the second paragraph on page 771. Read this paragraph aloud, and then help students construct a cluster diagram with "Characteristics of fishes" in the center and the specific characteristics listed outside. 

Intermediate Have students read the modified paragraph that you prepared for the beginning level and then read the actual text paragraph. Ask students questions that can be answered from the rewritten text. For example: For what do fishes use fins? What structure do fishes use for gas exchange? Then, ask questions that cannot be directly answered using the rewritten text, such as: What might happen to a fish that has injured fins? L2

The Arrival of Jaws and Paired Fins Still other ancient fishes kept their bony armor and possessed a feeding adaptation that would revolutionize vertebrate evolution: These fishes had jaws. Observe the powerful jaws of the ancient fish in **Figure 30–8.** Jaws are an extremely useful adaptation. Jawless fishes are limited to eating small particles of food that they filter out of the water or suck up like a vacuum cleaner. Because jaws can hold teeth and muscles, jaws make it possible for vertebrates to nibble on plants and munch on other animals. Thus, animals with jaws can eat a much wider variety of food. They can also defend themselves by biting.

The evolution of jaws in early fishes accompanied the evolution of paired pectoral (anterior) and pelvic (posterior) fins. These fins were attached to girdles—structures of cartilage or bone that support the fins. **Cartilage** is a strong tissue that supports the body and is softer and more flexible than bone. **Figure 30–9** shows the fins and fin girdles in one ancient fish species.

Paired fins gave fishes more control of body movement. In addition, tail fins and powerful muscles gave fishes greater thrust when swimming. The combination of accuracy and speed enabled fishes to move in new and varied patterns. This ability, in turn, helped fishes use their jaws in complex ways.

The Rise of Modern Fishes Although the early jawed fishes soon disappeared, they left behind two major groups that continued to evolve and still survive today. One group—the ancestors of modern sharks and rays—evolved a skeleton made of strong, resilient cartilage. The other group evolved skeletons made of true bone. A subgroup of bony fishes, called lobe-finned fishes, had fleshy fins from which the limbs of chordates would later evolve.

CHECKPOINT *Which two groups of early jawed fishes still survive today?*

▲ **Figure 30–8** This photograph shows a reconstruction of an ancient armored fish called *Dunkleosteus,* an enormous predator that lived in the inland seas of North America during the late Devonian Period. **Drawing Conclusions** *What feature made this fish a successful predator in its time?*

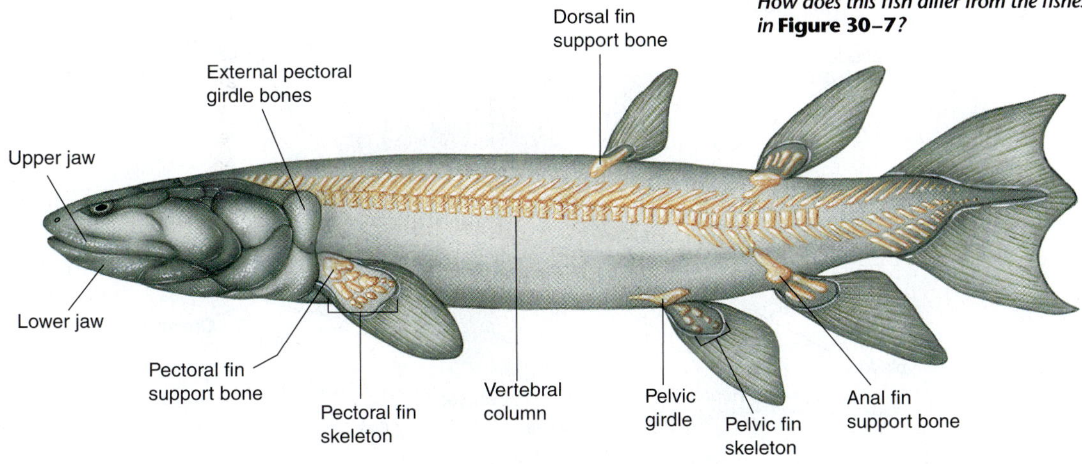

▼ **Figure 30–9** This ancient Devonian fish is called *Eusthenopteron.* Although its skeleton differs from those of most modern fishes, its basic features—vertebral column, fins, and fin girdles—have been retained in many species. **Comparing and Contrasting** *How does this fish differ from the fishes in* ***Figure 30–7****?*

BIO INSIGHTS

FACTS AND FIGURES

New tail design makes fish faster

Primitive fishes had asymmetrical tails in which the vertebral column pointed either upward or downward as it extended from the body. When the fins pushed against the water to propel the fish forward, the movement was inefficient. The forward push was unevenly distributed along the body of the fish. Such fishes did well as bottom feeders, where food consisted of stationary plant material or organic debris.

Modern fishes have tails in which two symmetrical lobes extend from the end of the vertebral column. The forward thrust provided by this tail is greater and more evenly distributed along the length of the body. Fishes with symmetrical tails swim faster. Most of the back-and-forth motion that propels the fish forward comes from the posterior end of the fish, keeping the anterior end still and better streamlined.

Demonstration

Show students how jaws enabled fishes to eat a larger variety of food by comparing a drinking straw to your hand mimicking the action of a jaw. Use the straw to try to pick up a variety of objects that represent food. Then, use your hand acting as a jaw to pick up those same objects. Ask: **What advantage did a jaw give to fishes?** *(Jaws enabled fishes to open up their mouths and close them with force in order to bite larger pieces of food from a larger variety of food sources. In addition, jaws enabled fishes to manipulate food. They also provided a means for defense—biting.)* L1 L2

Make Connections

Physics Explain that a fish must overcome inertia, or the resistance to motion, to move through water. Most of this resistance is in the form of drag, which is caused by the friction of water as it flows over the body of the fish. Drag is also caused by the backward pull of the eddies of water that form behind the fish's tail. If the fish is streamlined, the water flowing past both sides of the fish meets and blends together, producing less turbulence and, hence, less drag. Students can experiment with different body shapes moving through water to observe this phenomenon. They might compare the eddies of a round object, a square object, and a streamlined (spindle-shaped) object as they move them through water. L2 L3

Answers to . . .

CHECKPOINT *Sharks and rays and bony fishes*

Figure 30–8 *Powerful jaws*

Figure 30–9 *It has jaws.*

30–2 (continued)

Form and Function in Fishes

Use Visuals

Figure 30–11 Have students trace the path of food through the digestive system in the illustration. Ask: **Where does digestion occur?** *(Stomach, pyloric ceca, intestine)* **Where does nutrient absorption occur?** *(Pyloric ceca, intestine)* Explain that the size of the stomach and intestines varies among fishes, depending on their mode of feeding. Ask: **Would you expect herbivores or carnivores to have a longer digestive tract?** *(Herbivores; plant matter is more difficult to digest because of the cellulose in the cell walls of plant cells.)* L1 L2

Use Community Resources

Take students to a local aquarium, zoo, or fish store to give them the opportunity to observe many different fishes and their adaptations. Before going, make a class list of adaptations to look for, such as specific adaptations for getting food, attracting mates, defending against predators, and moving. When viewing the fishes, discuss their specific adaptations and how they help the fishes to survive. L2

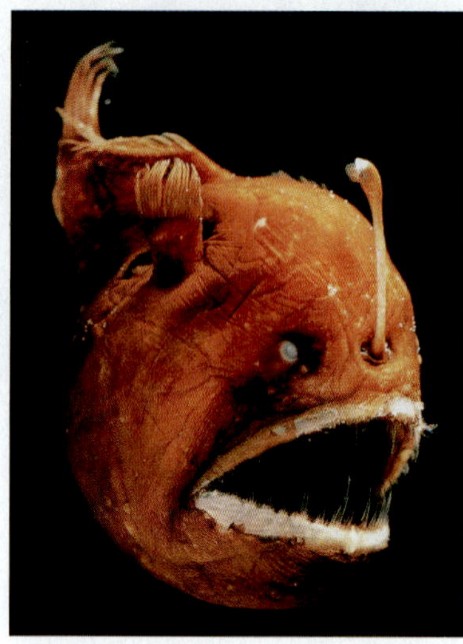

▲ **Figure 30–10** **Adaptations to aquatic life include various modes of feeding.** This deep-sea anglerfish has a built-in "fishing pole" that it uses to attract prey.

Form and Function in Fishes

Over time, fishes have evolved to survive in a tremendous range of aquatic environments. **Adaptations to aquatic life include various modes of feeding, specialized structures for gas exchange, and paired fins for locomotion.** Fishes have other types of adaptations, too, as you will learn.

Feeding Every mode of feeding is seen in fishes. There are herbivores, carnivores, parasites, filter feeders, and detritus feeders. In fact, a single fish may exhibit several modes of feeding, depending on what type of food happens to be available. Certain carp, for example, eat algae, aquatic plants, worms, mollusks, arthropods, dead fish, and detritus. Other fishes, such as barracuda, are highly specialized carnivores. A few fishes, such as some lampreys, are parasites. **Figure 30–10** shows a fish that even uses a fleshy bait to catch its meals!

Use **Figure 30–11** to locate the internal organs that are important during the fish's digestion of its food. From the fish's mouth, food passes through a short tube called the esophagus to the stomach, where it is partially broken down. In many fishes, the food is further processed in fingerlike pouches called pyloric ceca (py-LAWR-ik SEE-kuh; singular: cecum). The pyloric ceca secrete digestive enzymes and absorb nutrients from the digested food. Other organs, including the liver and pancreas, add enzymes and other digestive chemicals to the food as it moves through the digestive tract. The intestine completes the process of digestion and nutrient absorption. Any undigested material is eliminated through the anus.

▼ **Figure 30–11** The internal organs of a typical bony fish are shown here. **Applying Concepts** *What is the function of the pyloric cecum?*

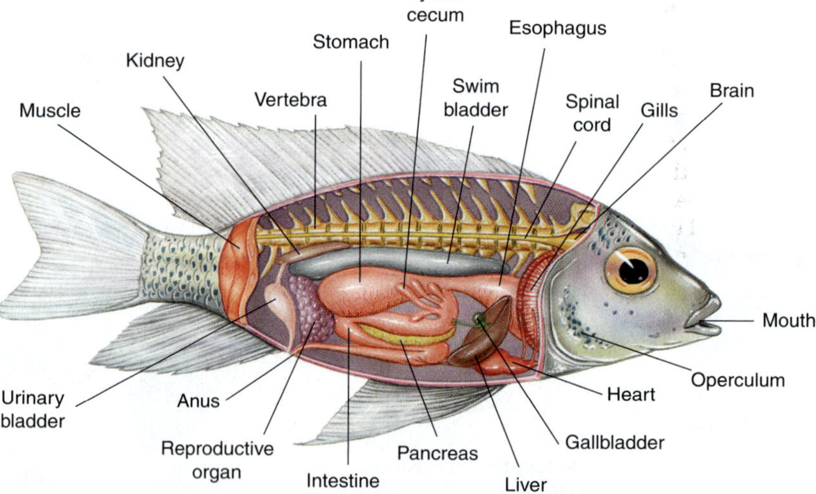

FACTS AND FIGURES

Getting a hold on food

Scientists observe as many different mouth and teeth adaptations in fishes as there are modes of feeding. Most carnivores have simple, cone-shaped teeth on the jaws and roof of the mouth and in the pharynx. The teeth in the pharynx region are commonly called throat teeth. In many carnivores, the teeth hold prey and orient it for swallowing. Such fishes have a flexible esophagus to accommodate the size of the food. Some carnivores have cutting teeth for biting chunks off their prey.

Many fishes have only throat teeth, which are used to crush or grind food. Others have no teeth at all. These fishes, often those that eat plankton, have many long, stiff rods, called gill rakers, attached to the gill bars. These rakers strain food from the water as it passes over the gills.

Quick Lab

How do fishes use gills?

Materials fish food, food coloring, plastic cup, dropper pipette, live fish in an aquarium

Procedure 

1. Mix some fish food and food coloring in a small volume of aquarium water in a plastic cup.
2. Use a dropper pipette to release the mixture near a fish in an aquarium. Release the mixture gently so that it does not scatter.
3. Observe what happens when the fish approaches the mixture. Watch the fish's gills especially closely.

Analyze and Conclude

1. **Drawing Conclusions** Describe what happened to the food coloring. What does this tell you about how water moves through a fish's body?
2. **Inferring** Why do most fishes seem to move or swallow continuously? What might happen if a fish were not able to move or stopped "swallowing"?

Respiration Most fishes exchange gases using gills located on either side of the pharynx. The gills are made up of feathery, threadlike structures called filaments. Each filament contains a network of fine capillaries that provides a large surface area for the exchange of oxygen and carbon dioxide. Fishes that exchange gases using gills do so by pulling oxygen-rich water in through their mouths, pumping it over their gill filaments, and then pushing oxygen-poor water out through openings in the sides of the pharynx.

Some fishes, such as lampreys and sharks, have several gill openings. Most fishes, however, have a single gill opening on each side of the body through which water is pumped out. This opening is hidden beneath a protective bony cover called the operculum.

A number of fishes have an adaptation that allows them to survive in oxygen-poor water or in areas where bodies of water often dry up. These fishes have specialized organs that serve as lungs. A tube brings air containing oxygen to this organ through the fish's mouth. Some lungfishes are so dependent on getting oxygen from the air that they will suffocate if prevented from reaching the surface of the water.

CHECKPOINT *What structures do fishes use for gas exchange?*

▶ **Figure 30–12** This African lungfish has a breathing adaptation that allows it to survive in shallow waters that are subject to drought. It burrows into mud, covers itself with mucus, and becomes dormant. For several months until the rains fall, the lungfish breathes through its mouth and lungs. **Drawing Conclusions** *How is it an advantage for this lungfish to cover itself with mucus?*

Quick Lab

Objective Students will be able to infer how fishes use gills. L2

Skills Focus Drawing Conclusions, Inferring

Materials fish food, food coloring, plastic cup, dropper pipette, live fish in an aquarium

Time 10 minutes

Advance Prep Do not feed the fish for 2 or 3 days before the activity.

Strategies

- For optimum visibility of the flow of food coloring, transfer the fish to any clear container with water about 4 cm deep and place the container on a white background.
- Do not operate air pumps during the activity.

Expected Outcome Students should observe the food coloring move into the fish's mouth and out through its gills.

Analyze and Conclude

1. The food coloring moved into the fish's mouth and out through its gills. This shows the path of water through a fish's body.
2. To keep water moving over the gills; it could die from lack of oxygen.

Build Science Skills

Applying Concepts Ask: **What structures increase the surface area of gills?** *(Feathery filaments)* **What advantage does this give fishes?** *(Take in more oxygen and remove more carbon dioxide in less time)* Challenge students to consider other biological processes, organisms, or objects in which an increased surface area is advantageous. *(Examples include wide leaves—getting energy from sunlight; intestinal villi—provide increased surface for absorbing nutrients; wide fan blades—moving air; ramps—moving objects.)* L2

BIO INSIGHTS FACTS AND FIGURES

Water over the gills

A shark has five to seven gill slits on both sides of its head. In order for a shark to breathe, water must continually flow across these gill slits. Like most bony fishes, the majority of sharks have a muscle-powered pumping mechanism that forces water to flow across the gills. In addition, the forward movement of some sharks contributes to gill ventilation. In this technique, called ram ventilation, the shark opens its mouth slightly as it moves forward; because of the forward motion, water enters the shark's mouth and flows over the gills.

Sharks have spiracles, which are an extra pair of gill slits located behind the eyes. These gill slits enable sharks to breathe while their mouths are full. Spiracles help bottom-dwelling sharks breathe while they are resting on the ocean floor.

Answers to . . .

CHECKPOINT *Gills or lunglike organs*

Figure 30–11 *The pyloric cecum secretes digestive enzymes and absorbs nutrients.*

Figure 30–12 *Mucus prevents the fish from drying out as water evaporates.*

30–2 (continued)

Use Visuals

Figure 30–13 Ask: **What makes the circulatory system in fishes a closed system?** *(The blood is enclosed in vessels.)* As students study the direction of blood flow in the diagram, point out that the blood travels in one loop and that the fish heart has only one atrium and one ventricle. Ask: **Does the heart pump oxygenated blood?** *(No)* **Why not?** *(The heart pumps deoxygenated blood from the body directly to the gills; from the gills, the oxygenated blood goes directly to the body tissues.)* L1 L2

Make Connections

Chemistry To review osmosis, soak cucumber slices in a saltwater solution and in salt-free distilled water for about 30 minutes. Discuss the results of the experiment, focusing on where water had the higher and lower concentrations. *(Salt water: lower concentration of water, cucumber shriveled; distilled water: higher concentration of water, cucumber swelled)* Ask: **What could happen to saltwater fishes if they did not have kidneys?** *(Shrivel up because the water concentration is less outside their bodies)* **To freshwater fishes?** *(Bloat because the water concentration is greater outside their bodies)* L1 L2

Address Misconceptions

Students might get the mistaken idea that fishes moving from salt water to fresh water can consciously adjust their kidneys to function one way or another. Relate the involuntary control fishes have over their internal organs to the involuntary control that students have over some of their own body functions, such as digesting food. L1 L2

Go Online NSTA SciLinks
Download a worksheet on fishes for students to complete, and find additional teacher support from NSTA SciLinks.

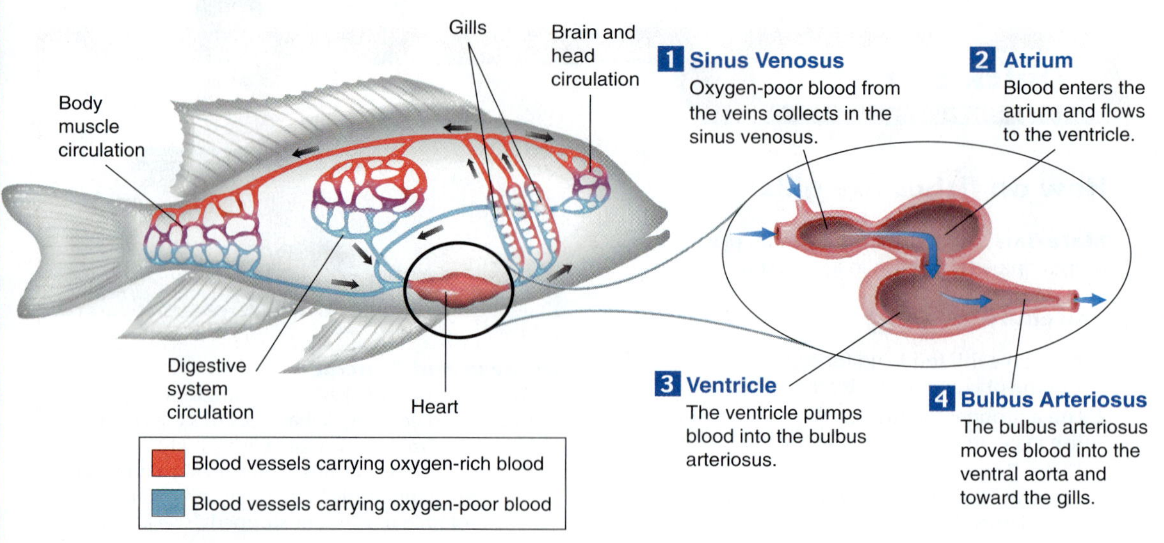

▲ **Figure 30–13** Blood circulates through a fish's body in a single loop—from the heart to the gills to the rest of the body, and then back to the heart again. (Note that in diagrams of animals' circulatory systems, blood vessels carrying oxygen-rich blood are red, while blood vessels carrying oxygen-poor blood are blue.) **Interpreting Graphics** ***Is the blood that flows from the heart to the gills oxygen-rich or oxygen-poor?***

Go Online NSTA SciLinks
For: Links on fishes
Visit: www.SciLinks.org
Web Code: cbn-9302

Circulation Fishes have closed circulatory systems with a heart that pumps blood around the body in a single loop—from the heart to the gills, from the gills to the rest of the body, and back to the heart. **Figure 30–13** shows the path of blood and the structure of the heart.

In most fishes, the heart consists of four parts: the sinus venosus (SYN-us vuh-NOH-sus), atrium, ventricle, and bulbus arteriosus (BUL-bus ahr-teer-ee-OH-sus). The sinus venosus is a thin-walled sac that collects blood from the fish's veins before it flows to the **atrium,** a large muscular chamber that serves as a one-way compartment for blood that is about to enter the ventricle. The **ventricle,** a thick-walled, muscular chamber, is the actual pumping portion of the heart. It pumps blood to a large, muscular tube called the bulbus arteriosus. At its front end, the bulbus arteriosus connects to a large blood vessel called the aorta, through which blood moves to the fish's gills.

Excretion Like many other aquatic animals, most fishes rid themselves of nitrogenous wastes in the form of ammonia. Some wastes diffuse through the gills into the surrounding water. Others are removed by kidneys, which are excretory organs that filter wastes from the blood.

Kidneys help fishes control the amount of water in their bodies. Fishes in salt water tend to lose water by osmosis. To solve this problem, the kidneys of marine fishes concentrate wastes and return as much water as possible to the body. In contrast, a great deal of water continually enters the bodies of freshwater fishes. The kidneys of freshwater fishes pump out plenty of dilute urine. Some fishes are able to move from fresh to salt water by adjusting their kidney function.

BIO INSIGHTS — FACTS AND FIGURES

Salty fish

Both saltwater fishes and freshwater fishes have an internal salt content of about one percent. With the concentration of salt in ocean water at about 3.5 percent, the body systems of saltwater fishes must work to conserve water. Most saltwater fishes drink ocean water and secrete excess salt from the gills. Sharks and rays, however, maintain a high concentration of salt within the body by storing urea in the blood. These fishes do not lose water by osmosis and do not need to drink water.

Freshwater fishes live in environments with a very low concentration of salt. Freshwater fishes do not drink water, and their kidneys serve to pump water out of their bodies in very dilute urine. Freshwater fishes still lose salt, however, and take in the dilute salts in the water with the gills.

Response Fishes have well-developed nervous systems organized around a brain, which has several parts, as shown in **Figure 30–14.** The most anterior parts of a fish's brain are the olfactory bulbs, which are involved with the sense of smell, or olfaction. They are connected to the two lobes of the cerebrum. In most vertebrates, the **cerebrum** is responsible for all voluntary activities of the body. However, in fishes, the cerebrum primarily processes the sense of smell. The optic lobes process information from the eyes. The **cerebellum** coordinates body movements. The **medulla oblongata** controls the functioning of many internal organs.

Most fishes have highly developed sense organs. Almost all fishes that are active in daylight have well-developed eyes and color vision that is at least as good as yours. Many fishes have specialized cells called chemoreceptors that are responsible for their extraordinary senses of taste and smell. Although most fishes have ears inside their head, they may not hear sounds well. Most fishes can, however, detect gentle currents and vibrations in the water with sensitive receptors that form the **lateral line system.** Fishes use this system to sense the motion of other fishes or prey swimming nearby. In addition to detecting motion, some fishes, such as catfish and sharks, have evolved sense organs that can detect low levels of electric current. Some fishes, such as the electric eel shown in **Figure 30–15,** can even generate their own electricity!

CHECKPOINT *What are the parts of a fish's brain?*

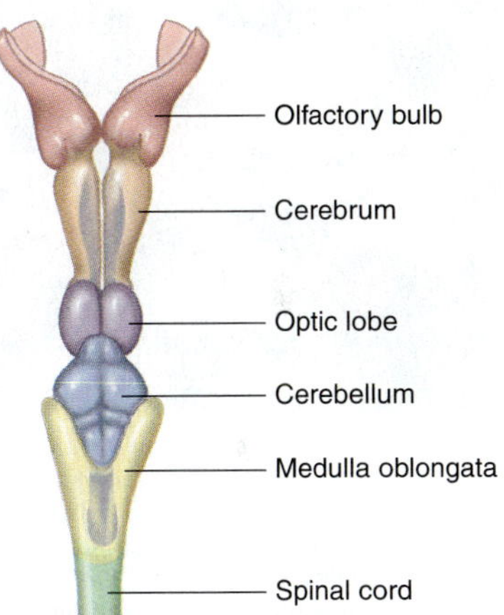

▲ **Figure 30–14** The brain of a fish, like all vertebrate brains, is situated at the anterior end of the spinal cord and has several different parts. **Inferring** *How might the size of the various parts of the brain differ in a blind cave fish that relies primarily on its sense of smell?*

Movement Most fishes move by alternately contracting paired sets of muscles on either side of the backbone. This creates a series of S-shaped curves that move down the fish's body. As each curve travels from the head toward the tail fin, it creates backward force on the surrounding water. This force, along with the action of the fins, propels the fish forward. The fins of fishes are also used in much the same way that airplanes use stabilizers, flaps, and rudders—to keep on course and adjust direction. Fins also increase the surface area of the tail, providing an extra boost of speed. The streamlined body shapes of most fishes help reduce the amount of drag (friction) as they move through the water.

Because their body tissues are more dense than the water they swim in, sinking is an issue for fishes. Many bony fishes have an internal, gas-filled organ called a **swim bladder** that adjusts their buoyancy. The swim bladder lies just beneath the backbone.

▶ **Figure 30–15** The electric eel, *Electrophorus electricus,* can produce several hundred volts of electricity in brief bursts. **Formulating Hypotheses** *What function might such powerful electric bursts serve?*

Build Science Skills

Posing Questions Challenge students to consider a fish's senses and the environment in which it lives. For example, have students consider the different environments of fishes living near the water's surface and those living along the bottom. Have small student groups work together to develop a scientific question about the senses of these two groups of fishes and how they might be similar or different. Remind students that a scientific question is very specific so that it can be answered through observation and experimentation. Discuss each group's question and possible methods of finding its answer. L2

Demonstration

Show students how a swim bladder works by tying a small screw to the neck of a deflated balloon and then putting the screw into a tub of water. Ask: **Why did the "fish" sink?** *(The "fish" weighed more than the force of the water pushing up on it.)* Then, blow up the balloon, reattach the screw, and place it into the water. Ask: **Why did the "fish" float?** *(The buoyant force of the water was greater than the weight of the "fish.")* Explain that this is similar to how a submarine works, except internal tanks are filled with water to make the submarine sink. They are emptied to make the submarine float. L2

BIO INSIGHTS

FACTS AND FIGURES

Some fishes are all "charged up"

By detecting low levels of electric current, sharks and several other fishes can detect the presence of nearby fishes or other animals. Every time an animal moves, even slightly, its muscles create a small electric current. Even a camouflaged animal that is hiding from a shark or other predator with the ability to sense electricity can be detected by the predator because the hiding animal is producing an electric current by moving the muscles required for breathing.

Fishes, such as eels, that produce their own electric current are able to detect animals as well as nonliving objects that might be in their path. The electric field that they create around the body helps them to find prey or to navigate. As an added benefit, eels use their electricity to stun or kill prey and to repel predators.

Answers to . . .

CHECKPOINT *Olfactory bulbs, cerebrum, optic lobe, cerebellum, medulla oblongata*

Figure 30–13 *Oxygen-poor*

Figure 30–14 *The brain of the cave fish might have a smaller optic lobe and a larger cerebrum and olfactory bulbs because the fish relies on its sense of smell.*

Figure 30–15 *To stun prey and deter predators*

30–2 (continued)

Groups of Fishes

Build Science Skills

Classifying Give student groups 10 to 15 pictures of different kinds of fishes. Challenge students to develop criteria for dividing the fishes into groups. Have students share their method of classification with the class. They should explain the criteria they used to categorize the fishes. Discuss the similarities and differences in the classification systems among the student groups. L2

Make Connections

Environmental Science Explain that lampreys once lived in Lake Ontario but not the other Great Lakes. They could not enter the other Great Lakes because of the natural barrier formed by Niagara Falls. In the early nineteenth century, the Welland Ship Canal was built as a shipping lane around Niagara Falls. Over the course of many years, the fish population in the inland Great Lakes began to decrease. In fact, lake trout were almost eliminated. Ask: **What might have caused the decrease in fish population?** *(Invasion of lampreys)* **How could lampreys devastate the fish population?** *(Lampreys are not indigenous to the inland Great Lakes and have few natural predators.)* L2

▲ **Figure 30–16** Some newly hatched fishes, such as these coho salmon, are nourished by yolk sacs on their bellies. **Inferring** ***What are the orange spheres at the bottom of the photograph?***

Reproduction The eggs of fishes are fertilized either externally or internally, depending on the species. In many fish species, the female lays the eggs and the embryos in the eggs develop and hatch outside her body. Fishes whose eggs hatch outside the mother's body are **oviparous** (oh-VIP-uh-rus). As the embryos of oviparous fishes develop, they obtain food from the yolk in the egg. The salmon in **Figure 30–16** are oviparous. In contrast, in **ovoviviparous** (oh-voh-vy-VIP-uh-rus) species, such as guppies, the eggs stay in the mother's body after internal fertilization. Each embryo develops inside its egg, using the yolk for nourishment. The young are then "born alive," like the young of most mammals. A few fish species, including several sharks, are viviparous. In **viviparous** (vy-VIP-uh-rus) animals, the embryos stay in the mother's body after internal fertilization, as they do in ovoviviparous species. However, these embryos obtain the substances they need from the mother's body, not from material in an egg. The young of viviparous species are also born alive.

CHECKPOINT *What are the three different modes of fish reproduction?*

Groups of Fishes

With over 24,000 living species, fishes are an extremely diverse group of chordates. These diverse species can be grouped according to body structure. **When you consider their basic internal structure, all living fishes can be classified into three groups: jawless fishes, cartilaginous fishes, and bony fishes.**

Jawless Fishes As their name implies, jawless fishes have no true teeth or jaws. Their skeletons are made of fibers and cartilage. They lack vertebrae, and instead keep their notochords as adults. Modern jawless fishes are divided into two classes: lampreys and hagfishes.

Lampreys are typically filter feeders as larvae and parasites as adults. An adult lamprey's head is taken up almost completely by a circular sucking disk with a round mouth in the center, which you can see in **Figure 30–17.** Adult lampreys attach themselves to fishes, and occasionally to whales and dolphins. There, they scrape away at the skin with small toothlike structures that surround the mouth and with a strong, rasping tongue. The lamprey then sucks up the tissues and body fluids of its host.

Hagfishes have pinkish gray, wormlike bodies and four or six short tentacles around their mouths. Hagfishes lack eyes, although they do have light-detecting sensors scattered around their bodies. They feed on dead and dying fish by using a toothed tongue to scrape a hole into the fish's side. Hagfishes have other peculiar traits: They secrete incredible amounts of slime, have six hearts, possess an open circulatory system, and regularly tie themselves into knots!

Figure 30–17 **Jawless fishes make up one of three major groups of living fishes.** Modern jawless fishes are divided into two classes: lampreys (top) and hagfishes (bottom).

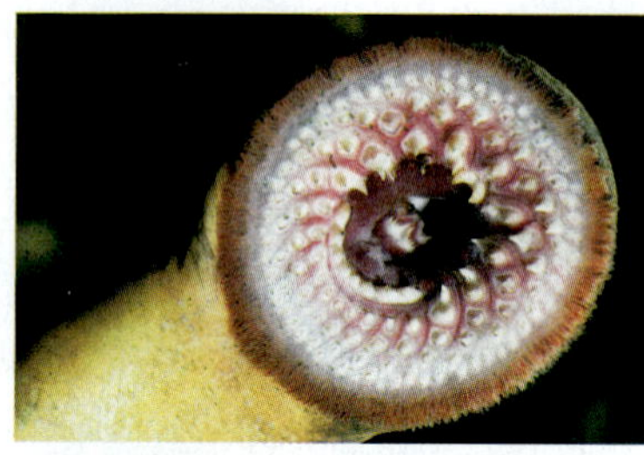

FACTS AND FIGURES

Fish mothers and fathers

Most oviparous fishes do not provide any care for their young; they simply produce hundreds, or even millions, of fertilized eggs and "let nature take its course." Most eggs do not even form into young fishes; they are often eaten or damaged.

Some oviparous fishes, however, do care for their young. Some fishes build nests to protect the fertilized eggs. Siamese fighting fish build nests of bubbles, and sticklebacks use twigs. Some cichlids hold their eggs and young in the mouth. Seahorses hold fertilized eggs in a pouch until the eggs are ready to hatch. Fishes that care for their young usually do not produce as many eggs as those that simply lay the eggs and leave.

Sharks and Their Relatives The class Chondrichthyes (kahn-DRIK-theez) contains sharks, rays, skates, and a few uncommon fishes such as sawfishes and chimaeras. Some chondrichthyes are shown in **Figure 30–18.** *Chondros* is the Greek word for cartilage, so the name of this class tells you that the skeletons of these fishes are built entirely of cartilage, not bone. The cartilage of these animals is similar to the flexible tissue that supports your nose and your external ears. Most cartilaginous fishes also have toothlike scales covering their skin. These scales make shark skin so rough that it can be used as sandpaper.

Most of the 350 or so living shark species have large curved tails, torpedo-shaped bodies, and pointed snouts with the mouth underneath. One of the most noticeable characteristics of sharks is their enormous number of teeth. Many sharks have thousands of teeth arranged in several rows. As teeth in the front rows are worn out or lost, new teeth are continually replacing them. A shark goes through about 20,000 teeth in its lifetime!

Not all sharks have such fierce-looking teeth, however. Some, like the basking shark, are filter feeders with specialized feeding structures. Their teeth are so small they are virtually useless. Other sharks have flat teeth adapted for crushing the shells of mollusks and crustaceans. Although there are a number of carnivorous sharks large enough to prey on humans, most sharks do not attack people.

Skates and rays are even more diverse in their feeding habits than their shark relatives. Some feed on bottom-dwelling invertebrates by using their mouths as powerful vacuums. However, the largest rays, like the largest sharks, are filter feeders that eat floating plankton. Skates and rays often glide through the sea with flapping motions of their large, winglike pectoral fins. When they are not feeding or swimming, many skates and rays cover themselves with a thin layer of sand and spend hours resting on the ocean floor.

▼ **Figure 30–18** Sharks and rays have skeletons that are made of cartilage. The large jaws and teeth of many sharks make them top predators in the world's oceans. **Applying Concepts** ***How is the structure of a basking shark's mouth related to its diet?***

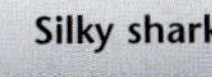

Use Visuals

Figure 30–18 Explain that shark teeth are made from bonelike material. Scientists infer that they are specialized scales. Ask: **Why is it advantageous for sharks to have teeth that are continually replaced?** *(If teeth are damaged or lost, sharks could not get food.)* Explain that most sharks are very fast swimmers. Ask: **What characteristics of the shark's body make it a fast swimmer?** *(Torpedo body shape, paired fins, strong tail)* L2

Address Misconceptions

Many students might think that sharks are very dangerous animals and should be killed on sight. Remind students that shark attacks are infrequent, but their publicity makes these attacks appear more frequent. Ask: **What role do sharks have in the environment?** *(Most are predators.)* **What might happen if sharks were hunted to the point of extinction?** *(The prey populations might increase to the point where the environment could not support them, causing ecosystem collapse by absence of a key predator.)* L2

BIOLOGY UPDATE

Where is the great white shark?
In March 2000, scientists in Australia tagged a young female great white shark with a satellite tag. This was the first shark to ever be tagged in this way. The satellite tag is an electronic tag that transmits its position by satellite to a computer at the research station. From such data, researchers should learn where a great white shark travels and how it interacts with other great white sharks. This information contributes to the knowledge of the great white's behavior and its role in the ecosystem. This knowledge can contribute to the National Recovery Plan being developed in Australia for the great white shark.

Answers to . . .

CHECKPOINT *Oviparous, ovoviviparous, and viviparous*

Figure 30–16 *Salmon eggs*

Figure 30–18 *It's a filter feeder and has specialized structures for filtering plankton.*

30–2 (continued)

Build Science Skills

Observing Allow student groups to dissect a fish obtained from a fish market or scientific supply house. Encourage students to carefully remove muscle tissue to observe the skeleton. As they examine the fish, instruct them to diagram and label the structures that are characteristic of bony fishes, such as the fin rays, swim bladder, and bony skeleton. L2

Use Visuals

Figure 30–19 Ask: **How are all the fishes shown here similar?** (*They are all bony fishes belonging to the group called ray-finned fishes. They all have ray fins.*) **What is the other group of bony fishes called?** (*Lobe-finned fishes*) **How are they different from ray-finned fishes?** (*The fleshy fins of lobe-finned fishes have more substantial support bones than the rays of ray-finned fishes. Some of these bones are jointed.*) L1 L2

Figure 30–19 Diversity of Ray-finned Fishes

Combtooth Blenny

Emperor Angelfish

Flying Fish

Peacock Flounder

Leafy Sea Dragon

Nearly all bony fishes belong to an enormous and diverse group called ray-finned fishes. These fishes have thin, bony spines that form the fins. **Observing** *What unusual adaptations do you see in each of these fishes?*

Bony Fishes Bony fishes make up the class Osteichthyes (ahs-tee-IK-theez). The skeletons of these fishes are made of hard, calcified tissue called bone. Almost all living bony fishes belong to a huge group called ray-finned fishes, some of which are shown in **Figure 30–19.** The name "ray-finned" refers to the slender bony spines, or rays, that are connected by a thin layer of skin to form the fins. The fin rays support the skin much as the thin rods in a handheld folding fan hold together the webbing of the fan.

Only seven living species of bony fishes are not classified as ray-finned fishes. These are the lobe-finned fishes, a subclass that includes lungfishes and the coelacanth (SEE-luh-kanth). Lungfishes live in fresh water, but the coelacanth lives in salt water. The fleshy fins of lobe-finned fishes have support bones that are more substantial than the rays of ray-finned fishes. Some of these bones are jointed, like the arms and legs of land vertebrates.

HISTORY OF SCIENCE

Fish tale

Perhaps the greatest American naturalist of the nineteenth century was Louis Agassiz (1807–1873), who from 1848 until his death was a professor of zoology at Harvard University. Agassiz was born in Switzerland, and his earliest scientific work was the classification of fish specimens brought to Europe from Brazil. He won worldwide attention in the 1830s for his study of fossil fishes. That fame led to a course of lectures in the United States in the 1840s. Agassiz made many contributions to science, perhaps the greatest being his revelation that Earth had ice ages in the past. But fishes remained an interest throughout his life. According to legend, he would lock a new student in a room for a day with one object, a dead fish. At day's end, the student faced an unenviable task: reporting to the professor all that he had learned by looking at that fish.

Ecology of Fishes

Most fishes spend all their lives either in fresh water or in the ocean. Most freshwater fishes cannot tolerate the high salt concentration in saltwater ecosystems, because their kidneys cannot maintain internal water balance in this environment. Since freshwater fishes cannot maintain homeostasis in salt water, they cannot survive in the ocean. In contrast, ocean fishes cannot tolerate the low salt concentration in freshwater ecosystems.

However, some fish species can move from saltwater ecosystems to fresh water, and vice versa. Lampreys, sturgeons, and salmon, for example, spend most of their lives in the ocean but migrate to fresh water to breed. Fishes with this type of behavior are called anadromous (uh-NAH-druh-mus). Salmon, for example, begin their lives in rivers or streams but soon migrate to the sea. After one to four years at sea, mature salmon return to the place of their birth to reproduce. This trip can take several months, covering as much as 3200 kilometers, and can involve incredible feats of strength, as shown in **Figure 30–20.** The adult salmon recognize their home stream using their sense of smell.

In contrast to anadromous fishes, some fishes live their lives in fresh water but migrate to the ocean to breed. These fishes are said to be catadromous (kuh-TAD-ruh-mus). European eels, for instance, live and feed in the rivers of North America and Europe. They travel up to 4800 kilometers to lay their eggs in the Sargasso Sea, in the North Atlantic Ocean. The eggs are carried by currents to shallow coastal waters. As they grow into young fish, the eels find their way to fresh water and migrate upstream.

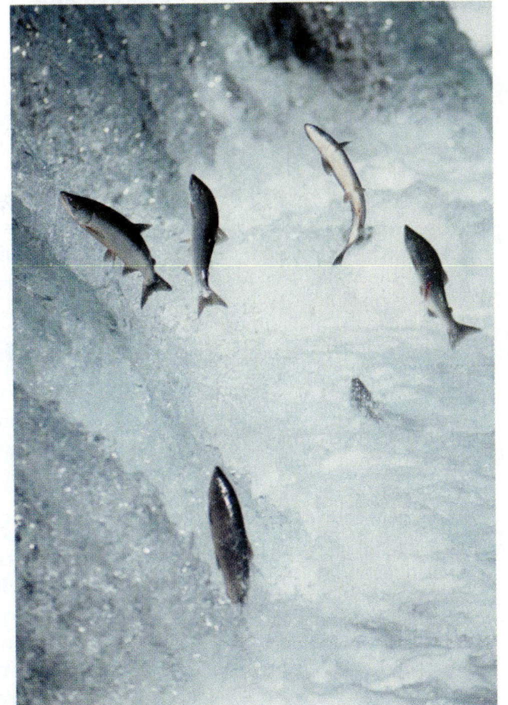

▲ **Figure 30–20** Adult salmon return from the sea to reproduce in the stream or river in which they were born. Their journey is often long and strenuous. The salmon must swim upstream against the current and may even leap up waterfalls! **Applying Concepts** ***What sense do the salmon use to find their home stream?***

30–2 Section Assessment

1. **Key Concept** Identify the main characteristics of fishes.
2. **Key Concept** What adaptive advantages do jaws and fins provide for fishes?
3. **Key Concept** List four specific ways in which fishes are adapted for aquatic life.
4. **Key Concept** Name the three main groups of fishes and give an example for each group.
5. **Critical Thinking Applying Concepts** For fishes to survive in an aquarium, the water must be kept clean and well oxygenated. Explain why water quality is so important to a fish's survival.

Focus on the BIG Idea

Structure and Function
In Chapter 27, you learned about the circulatory system of annelids. Create a Venn diagram comparing the circulatory system of an annelid with that of a fish. How are the two circulatory systems similar and different?

30–2 Section Assessment

1. Aquatic vertebrates with fins, scales, and gills
2. Jaws: defense, can manipulate materials and therefore eat a wider variety of food; fins: more controlled movements, move faster
3. Answers include various modes of feeding; gills; paired fins; kidneys that control water balance; lateral line system; and swim bladder.
4. Jawless fishes: lampreys or hagfishes; cartilaginous fishes: sharks, rays, skates, sawfishes; bony fishes: guppies, groupers, salmon, eels, lungfishes, coelacanths
5. Fish get oxygen from the water. Water that is unclean and not ventilated is low in oxygen, causing the fish to suffocate.

Ecology of Fishes

Make Connections

Environmental Science Explain that the construction of dams across many rivers in the northwestern U.S. has affected the population of salmon. Ask: **Why would dams cause a reduction in the population of salmon?** *(Dams prevent the salmon from swimming upriver to spawn.)* Explain that some dams have "fish ladders" to help salmon swim upstream of the dams. L2

3 ASSESS

Evaluate Understanding

Have students write a sentence that describes the characteristics used to classify fishes. Then, instruct them to make a table in which they list the three main groups of fishes, examples of each, and the key characteristics of each group.

Reteach

Have students create a concept map that shows at least four different ways in which fishes are adapted to live in water.

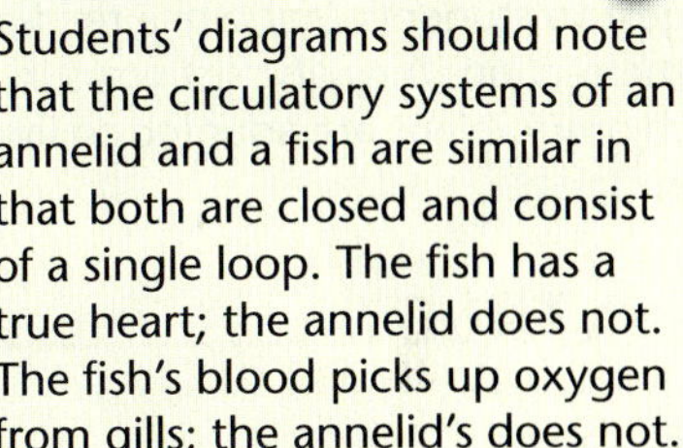

Focus on the BIG Idea

Students' diagrams should note that the circulatory systems of an annelid and a fish are similar in that both are closed and consist of a single loop. The fish has a true heart; the annelid does not. The fish's blood picks up oxygen from gills; the annelid's does not.

If your class subscribes to the iText, use it to review the Key Concepts in Section 30–2.

Answers to . . .

Figure 30–19 *Answers include color, body shape, and structure of the fins and mouth.*

Figure 30–20 *Sense of smell*

Section 30–3

1 FOCUS

Objectives

30.3.1 ***Describe*** what an amphibian is.

30.3.2 ***Summarize*** events in the evolution of amphibians.

30.3.3 ***Explain*** how amphibians are adapted for life on land.

30.3.4 ***Describe*** essential life functions in amphibians.

30.3.5 ***Name*** the main groups of living amphibians.

Guide for Reading

Vocabulary Preview

Explain that *nictitating* comes from the Latin word *nictare,* meaning "to wink." *Tympanic* comes from the Latin word *tympanum,* meaning "drum." Ask: **Where do you think the nictitating and tympanic membranes are located in an amphibian?** *(Nictitating membrane is in the eye, and tympanic membrane is in the ear.)*

Reading Strategy

Suggest to students that while reading the section, they also list ways in which amphibians are adapted to live on land.

2 INSTRUCT

What Is an Amphibian?

Build Science Skills

Observing Display a variety of live amphibians for students to observe, or take students to a zoo, an aquarium, or a pet store. As students observe the amphibians, instruct them to specifically look for ways in which the amphibians are adapted for life on land. Remind students that adaptations are not only structural but behavioral as well. Students should record all of their observations. L2

30–3 Amphibians

Guide for Reading

 **Key Concepts**

- What is an amphibian?
- How are amphibians adapted for life on land?
- What are the main groups of living amphibians?

Vocabulary

cloaca
nictitating membrane
tympanic membrane

Reading Strategy: Making Comparisons

As you read, write down similarities and differences between fishes and amphibians. Consider such characteristics as body structure, habitat, and method of reproduction.

Amphibians have survived for hundreds of millions of years, typically living in places where fresh water is plentiful. With over 4000 living species, amphibians are the only modern descendants of an ancient group that gave rise to all other land vertebrates.

What Is an Amphibian?

The word *amphibian* means "double life," emphasizing that these animals live both in water and on land. The larvae are fishlike aquatic animals that respire using gills. In contrast, the adults of most species of amphibians are terrestrial animals that respire using lungs and skin.

An amphibian is a vertebrate that, with some exceptions, lives in water as a larva and on land as an adult, breathes with lungs as an adult, has moist skin that contains mucous glands, and lacks scales and claws. In a sense, amphibians are to the animal kingdom what mosses and ferns are to the plant kingdom: They are descendants of ancestral organisms that evolved some—but not all—of the adaptations necessary for living entirely on land.

Evolution of Amphibians

The first amphibians to climb onto land probably resembled lobe-finned fishes similar to the modern coelacanth. However, the amphibians had legs, as in **Figure 30–21.** They appeared in the late Devonian Period, about 360 million years ago.

The transition from water to land involved more than just having legs and clambering out of the water. Vertebrates colonizing land habitats faced the same challenges that had to be overcome by invertebrates. Terrestrial vertebrates have to breathe air, protect themselves and their eggs from drying out, and support themselves against the pull of gravity.

◀ **Figure 30–21** Evolving in the swamplike tropical ecosystems of the Devonian Period, amphibians were the first chordates to live at least part of their lives on land. **Most amphibians live in water as larvae and on land as adults.**

SECTION RESOURCES

Print:

- ***Laboratory Manual A,*** Chapter 30 Lab
- ***Laboratory Manual B,*** Chapter 30 Lab
- ***Teaching Resources,*** Lesson Plan 30–3, Adapted Section Summary 30–3, Adapted Worksheets 30–3, Section Summary 30–3, Worksheets 30–3, Section Review 30–3
- ***Reading and Study Workbook A,*** Section 30–3
- ***Adapted Reading and Study Workbook B,*** Section 30–3
- ***Lab Worksheets,*** Chapter 30 Exploration
- ***Issues and Decision Making,*** 33

Technology:

- ***iText,*** Section 30–3
- ***Animated Biological Concepts DVD,*** 37 Frog Anatomy
- ***Transparencies Plus,*** Section 30–3

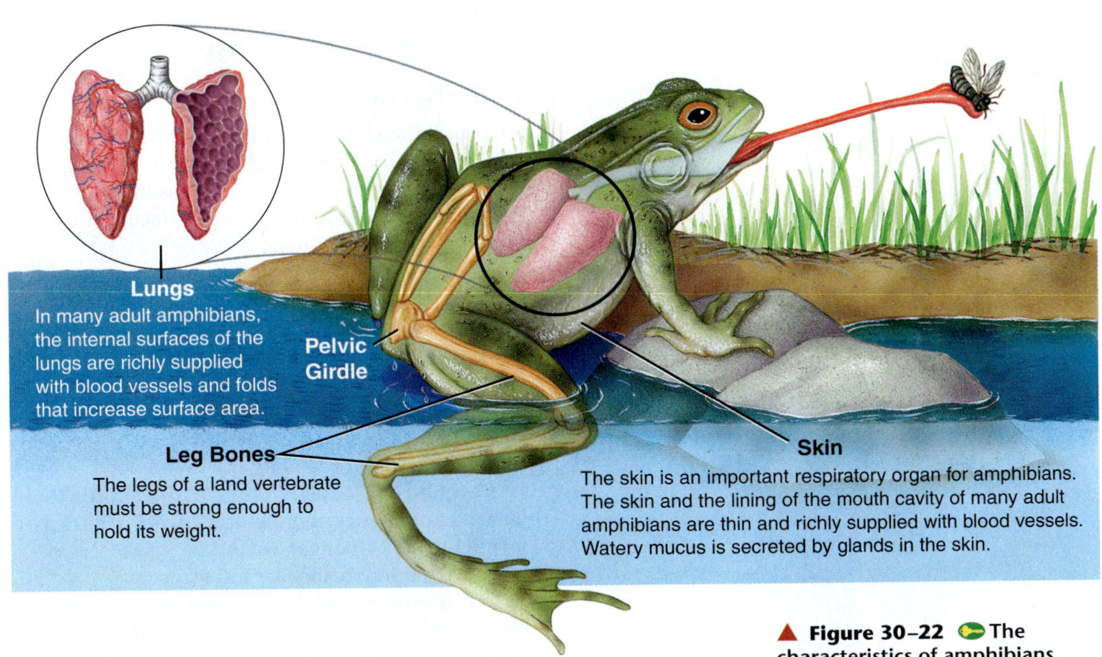

▲ **Figure 30–22** **The characteristics of amphibians include adaptations for living partially on land.** For example, lungs enable adult amphibians to obtain oxygen from air.

Early amphibians evolved several adaptations that helped them live at least part of their lives out of water. Bones in the limbs and limb girdles of amphibians became stronger, permitting more efficient movement. Lungs and breathing tubes enabled amphibians to breathe air. The sternum, or breastbone, formed a bony shield to support and protect internal organs, especially the lungs. Some of these adaptations are shown in **Figure 30–22.**

Soon after they first appeared, amphibians underwent a major adaptive radiation. Some of these ancient amphibians were huge. One early amphibian, *Eogyrinus,* is thought to have been about 5 meters long. Amphibians became the dominant form of animal life in the warm, swampy fern forests of the Carboniferous Period, about 360 to 290 million years ago. In fact, they were so numerous that the Carboniferous Period is sometimes called the Age of Amphibians. These animals gave rise to the ancestors of living amphibians and of vertebrates that live completely on land.

The great success of amphibians didn't last, however. Climate changes caused many of their low, swampy habitats to disappear. Most amphibian groups became extinct by the end of the Permian Period, about 245 million years ago. Only three orders of small amphibians survive today—frogs and toads, salamanders, and caecilians (see-SIL-ee-unz).

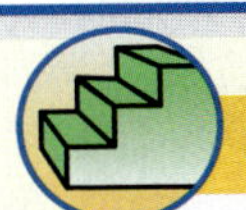
CHECKPOINT *Which geological period is called the Age of Amphibians?*

Word Origins

Carboniferous is a combination of two root words—*carbone* and *fer. Carbone* is a French word for coal; *fer* is a Latin suffix meaning "bearing or producing." *Carboniferous* is an adjective describing the coal-making period of the Paleozoic Era. **If *cone* refers to a reproductive structure of a tree, what do you think the word *coniferous* means?**

Evolution of Amphibians

Use Visuals

Figure 30–22 Have students describe how the adaptations shown in the illustration make it possible for amphibians to live successfully on land. Ask: **What is the advantage of moist skin?** *(It protects the amphibian from drying out.)* Continue in the same manner for the other adaptations shown. Then, ask: **How did these adaptations help amphibians become the dominant land vertebrate during the Carboniferous Period?** *(They were the only vertebrates adapted to live on land. They had few predators, favorable climate conditions, and plenty of food and shelter.)* L2

Word Origins

Coniferous is an adjective that describes trees that bear or produce cones. L2

UNIVERSAL ACCESS

English Language Learners
Students can use flashcards to review amphibian form and function and Vocabulary terms. Have students write the body structure on one side of the flashcard. On the other side of the flashcard, students should write its function and where it is located. Students can also explain how it helps the amphibian survive on land. L1

Advanced Learners
Students might enjoy writing an instruction manual that describes how a water-dwelling vertebrate may come to live successfully on land. They should include step-by-step instructions that explain how to overcome the special challenges of living on land, such as movement, reproduction, breathing air, supporting themselves against gravity, and protecting themselves from drying out. L3

Answer to . . .

CHECKPOINT *Carboniferous Period*

30–3 (continued)

Form and Function in Amphibians

Build Science Skills

Comparing and Contrasting As students study this subsection, encourage them to compare the form and function of amphibians with that of fishes. They might wish to organize their ideas in a Venn diagram or create a table. Challenge students to identify differences that are specific adaptations to a terrestrial environment and to an aquatic environment. *(Lungs vs. gills, nictitating membrane vs. no eyelids)* L1 L2

Demonstration

You might wish to dissect a frog so that the class can observe its internal anatomy. Point out the parts of the digestive system, the lungs, and the heart. Encourage students to draw labeled diagrams of the internal structures that they observe. As an alternative, provide a three-dimensional frog model or diagrams of frog anatomy. L2

Use Visuals

Figure 30–23 Have students trace the path of food as it travels through the frog's digestive system. Begin with the frog catching a fly with its tongue. Then, call randomly on students to tell where the food will travel next and what will happen to it there. After completing the path, ask: **How does the digestive system in a tadpole differ from an adult frog's?** *(Tadpoles have longer intestines to help digest plant material.)* L1 L2

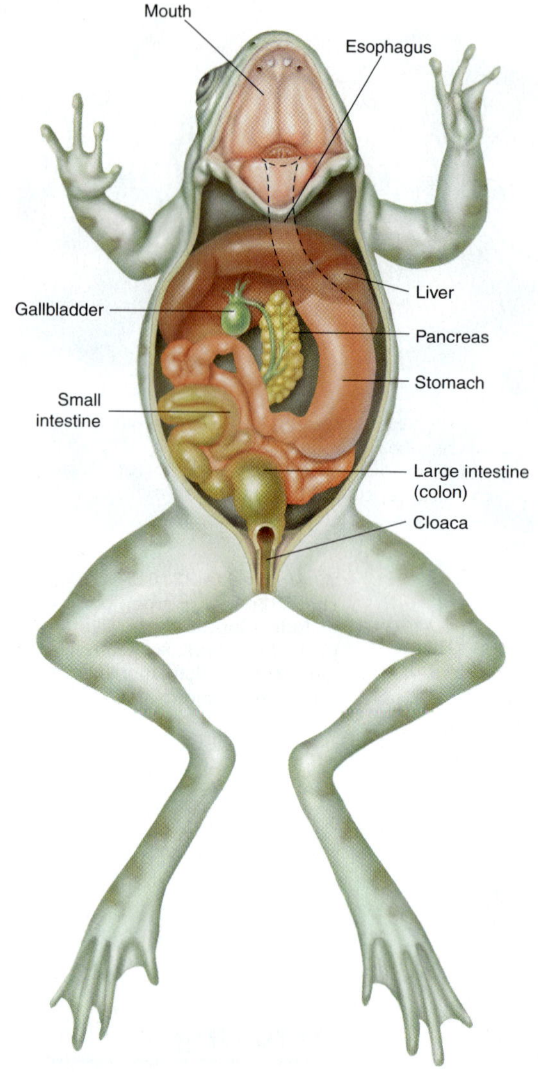

▲ **Figure 30–23** This illustration shows the organs of a frog's digestive system. **Comparing and Contrasting** *Which digestive organs are found in both frogs and fishes?*

Form and Function in Amphibians

Although the class Amphibia is relatively small, it is diverse enough to make it difficult to identify a typical species. As you examine essential life functions in amphibians, you will focus on the structures found in frogs.

Feeding The double lives of amphibians are reflected in the feeding habits of frogs. Tadpoles are typically filter feeders or herbivores that graze on algae. Like other herbivores, the tadpoles eat almost constantly. Their intestines, whose long, coiled structure helps break down hard-to-digest plant material, are usually filled with food. However, when tadpoles change into adults, their feeding apparatus and digestive tract are transformed to strictly meat-eating structures, complete with a much shorter intestine.

Adult amphibians are almost entirely carnivorous. They will eat practically anything they can catch and swallow. Legless amphibians can only snap their jaws open and shut to catch prey. In contrast, many salamanders and frogs have long, sticky tongues specialized to capture insects.

Trace the path of food in a frog's digestive system in **Figure 30–23.** From the mouth, food slides down the esophagus into the stomach. The breakdown of food begins in the stomach and continues in the small intestine, where digestive enzymes are manufactured and food is absorbed. Tubes connect the intestine with organs such as the liver, pancreas, and gallbladder that secrete substances that aid in digestion. The small intestine leads to the large intestine, or colon. At the end of the large intestine is a muscular cavity called the **cloaca** (kloh-AY-kuh), through which digestive wastes, urine, and eggs or sperm leave the body.

Respiration In most larval amphibians, gas exchange occurs through the skin as well as the gills. Lungs typically replace gills when an amphibian becomes an adult, although some gas exchange continues through the skin and the lining of the mouth cavity. In frogs, toads, and many other adult amphibians, the lungs are reasonably well developed. In other amphibians, such as salamanders, the lungs are not as well developed. In fact, many terrestrial salamanders have no lungs at all! Lungless salamanders exchange gases through the thin lining of the mouth cavity as well as through the skin.

FACTS AND FIGURES

Frogs "drink" air
Frogs are unable to inhale and exhale as we do because they do not have the musculature for it. Instead, they fill the mouth cavity with air, close the mouth, and force air back through the open glottis into the lungs. The glottis closes to keep the air inside the lungs. When its lungs are full, the frog keeps expanding and contracting the floor of its mouth. This action brings air into and out of the mouth through the nostrils. Some gas exchange occurs in the mouth tissues at this time. The continual movement of air in and out also clears any "stale" air remaining from the last breath. When the glottis and the mouth open, the lungs empty with a rush. Then, the process begins again.

Circulation In frogs and other adult amphibians, the circulatory system forms what is known as a double loop. The first loop carries oxygen-poor blood from the heart to the lungs and skin, and takes oxygen-rich blood from the lungs and skin back to the heart. The second loop transports oxygen-rich blood from the heart to the rest of the body and then carries oxygen-poor blood from the body back to the heart.

The amphibian heart, shown in **Figure 30–24,** has three separate chambers: left atrium, right atrium, and ventricle. Oxygen-poor blood circulates from the body into the right atrium. At the same time, oxygen-rich blood from the lungs and skin enters the left atrium. When the atria contract, they empty their blood into the ventricle. The ventricle then contracts, pumping blood out to a single, large blood vessel that divides and branches off into smaller blood vessels. Because of the pattern in which the blood vessels branch, most oxygen-poor blood goes to the lungs, and most oxygen-rich blood goes to the rest of the body. However, there is some mixing of oxygen-rich and oxygen-poor blood.

CHECKPOINT *How many chambers are in an amphibian's heart?*

▼ **Figure 30–24** Like all vertebrates, amphibians have a circulatory system and an excretory system. An amphibian's heart has three chambers—two atria and one ventricle. Although some wastes diffuse across the skin, kidneys remove most wastes from the bloodstream. **Applying Concepts** ***What excretory product do the kidneys produce?***

Excretion Amphibians have kidneys that filter wastes from the blood. The excretory product of the kidneys—urine—travels through tubes called ureters into the cloaca. From there, urine can be passed directly to the outside, or it may be temporarily stored in a small urinary bladder just above the cloaca.

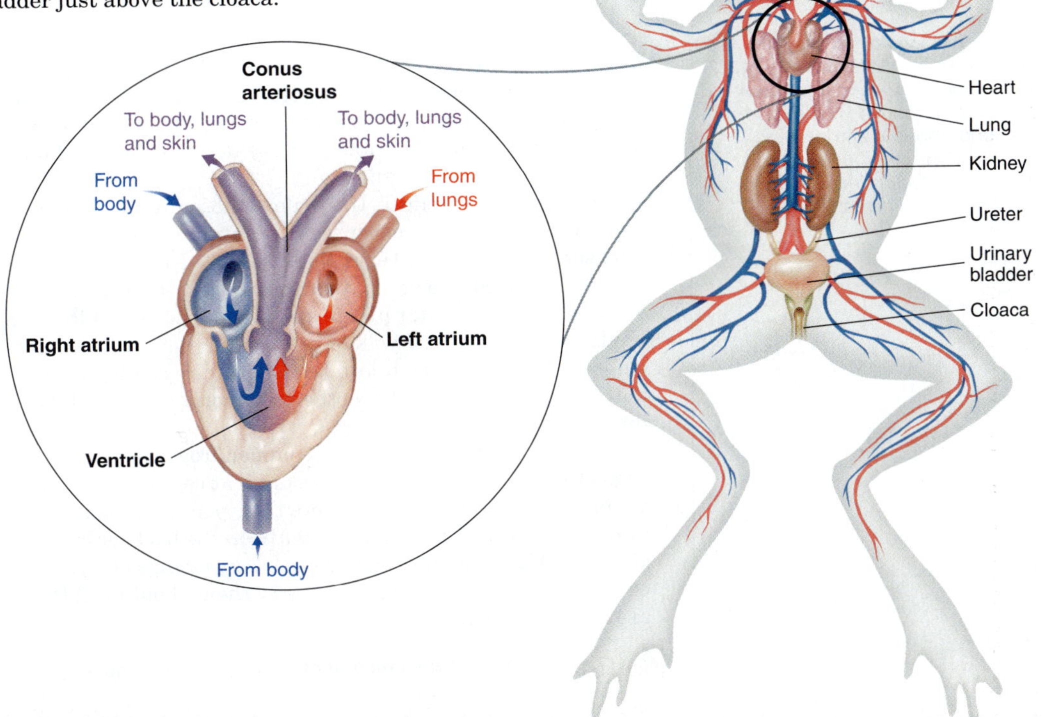

Make Connections

Physics Explain to students that changes in air pressure help to force air from the frog's mouth into the lungs. Air is a fluid and readily moves from areas of high pressure to areas of lower pressure. You can demonstrate this by blowing up a balloon. Explain that the air you push into the balloon is at a higher pressure than the air inside the balloon, causing the balloon to expand. Then, let the air out of the balloon. Ask: **Why did the air escape from the balloon?** *(The air inside the balloon was at greater pressure because the sides of the balloon were pushing it, so the air moved out.)* L2 L3

Use Visuals

Figure 30–24 Have students trace the path of blood through the frog's heart. Ask: **How many loops are in the frog's circulatory system?** *(Two; one from the heart to the lungs and back, another from the heart to the body and back)* Then, have students review the fish heart in Figure 30–13 on page 776 and compare it to the frog heart. Ask: **How many loops does the fish have?** *(One)* Explain that the tadpole heart is similar in structure and function to the fish heart. In fact, the fish heart is similar to that of most vertebrate embryos. The double-loop system is linked to the development of the lungs. Ask: **Why might the double-loop system be a better adaptation for terrestrial animals?** *(Tissues are supplied with oxygen-rich blood more efficiently because there is no loss of blood pressure. Blood pressure is lost in fishes when blood goes through the gills and then to body tissues.)* L2 L3

TEACHER TO TEACHER

Comparison of chordate circulatory systems can be used to enhance discussion of evolution. Draw on the board a two-chambered and three-chambered heart. Show the path blood takes into, through, and out of each heart. Have students determine reasons why fishes survive with only a two-chambered heart and amphibians survive with a three-chambered heart. When students read about the hearts of birds in Chapter 31, you can do the same with a four-chambered heart. Compare the number of heart chambers to the method by which each chordate obtains oxygen for respiration (gills, skin, lungs).

—*Wendy Peterson*
Biology Teacher
Velva High School
Velva, ND

Answers to . . .

CHECKPOINT *Three*

Figure 30–23 *Mouth, esophagus, liver, gallbladder, pancreas, stomach, intestine*

Figure 30–24 *Urine*

30–3 (continued)

Use Visuals

Figure 30–25 Go through the steps in the metamorphosis of a tadpole to a frog. Ask: **In what ways are tadpoles similar to fishes?** *(Both have gills, tails, lateral line systems, and live in water.)* **In what ways do tadpoles change to live on land?** *(Develop legs, lungs, carnivorous digestive system)* Tell students that tadpoles also have a heart and circulatory system similar to a fish's, but it changes to a double-loop system during metamorphosis. L2

Address Misconceptions

Some students might think that they could get warts from touching a toad. Ask: **Has anyone ever caught a toad? Did you get warts?** *(No)* Explain that although toads have bumpy skin, they do not have warts and cannot pass warts to humans. Remind students that warts are caused by viruses. L1 L2

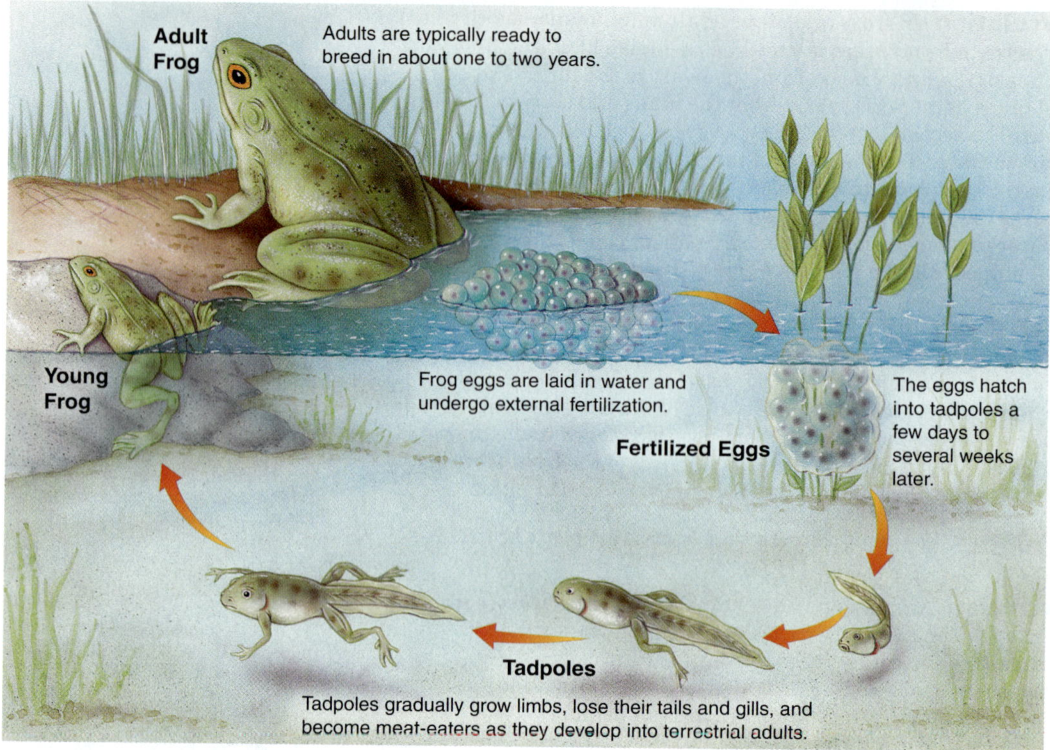

▲ **Figure 30–25** An amphibian typically begins its life in the water, then moves onto land as an adult. This diagram shows the process of metamorphosis in a frog. **Comparing and Contrasting** *How are tadpoles similar to fish? How are they different?*

Reproduction Amphibian eggs do not have shells and tend to dry out if they are not kept moist. Thus, in most species of amphibians, the female lays eggs in water, then the male fertilizes them externally. In a few species, including most salamanders, eggs are fertilized internally.

When frogs reproduce, the male climbs onto the female's back and squeezes. In response to this stimulus, the female releases as many as 200 eggs that the male then fertilizes. Frog eggs are encased in a sticky, transparent jelly that attaches the egg mass to underwater plants and makes the eggs difficult for predators to grasp. The yolk of the egg nourishes the developing embryos until they hatch into larvae that are commonly called tadpoles. **Figure 30–25** shows the metamorphosis of tadpoles into frogs.

Most amphibians, including common frogs, abandon their eggs after they lay them. A few take great care of both eggs and young. Some amphibians incubate their young in highly unusual places, such as in the mouth, on the back, or even in the stomach! Male midwife toads wrap sticky strings of fertilized eggs around their hind legs and carry them about until the eggs are ready to hatch.

What is the function of the jelly surrounding frog eggs?

FACTS AND FIGURES

Male or female?

It is difficult to tell whether a frog is a male or a female by looking at it. Sex differences in frogs are almost completely internal. Female frogs have a pair of large ovaries that produce and release eggs. The eggs pass down the oviducts into a storage area near the cloaca. Before the eggs are released, the oviduct walls surround them with a jellylike yolk.

Male frogs have a pair of testes that produce sperm. Sperm passes from the testes through a series of ducts into the cloaca. Some frogs have a seminal vesicle in which sperm are stored.

Movement Amphibian larvae often move very much like fishes, by wiggling their bodies and using a flattened tail for propulsion. Most adult amphibians, like other four-limbed vertebrates, use their front and back legs to move in a variety of ways. Adult salamanders have legs that stick out sideways. These animals walk—or, in some cases, run—by throwing their bodies into S-shaped curves and using their legs to push backward against the ground. Other amphibians, including frogs and toads, have well-developed hind limbs that enable them to jump long distances. Some amphibians, such as tree frogs, have disks on their toes that serve as suction cups for climbing.

Response The brain of an amphibian has the same basic parts as that of a fish. Like fishes, amphibians have well-developed nervous and sensory systems. **Figure 30–26** points out some sense organs in a typical frog. An amphibian's eyes are large and can move around in their sockets. The surface of the eye is protected from damage under water and kept moist on land by a transparent **nictitating** (NIK-tuh-tayt-ing) **membrane.** This movable membrane is located inside the regular eyelid, which can also be closed over the eye. Frogs have keen vision that enables them to spot and respond to moving insects. However, frogs probably do not see color as well as fishes do.

Amphibians hear through **tympanic** (tim-PAN-ik) **membranes,** or eardrums, located on each side of the head. In response to the external stimulus of sound, a tympanic membrane vibrates, sending sound waves deeper within the skull to the middle and inner ear. Many amphibian larvae and adults also have lateral line systems, like those of fishes, that detect water movement.

▼ **Figure 30–26** A frog's eyes and ears are among its most important sensory organs. Transparent eyelids called nictitating membranes protect the eyes underwater and keep them moist in air. Tympanic membranes receive sound vibrations from air as well as water. **Inferring** ***What functions does hearing serve in frogs?***

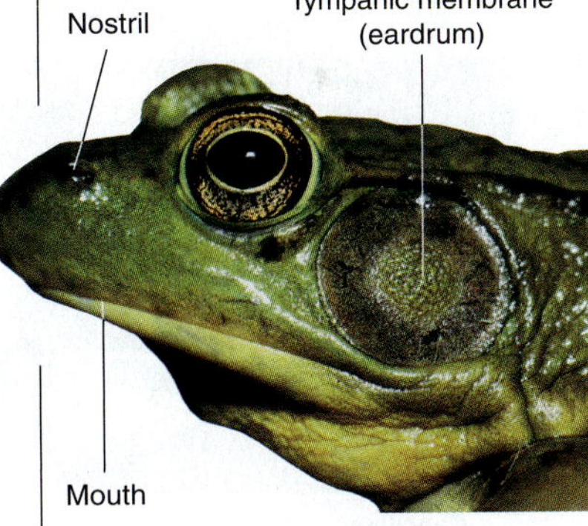

BIIE 1.d

Analyzing Data

Amphibian Population Trends

Over the past several decades, scientists have reported changes in amphibian populations worldwide. In 2000, a team of researchers analyzed data sets contributed by various amphibian population studies conducted in 37 different countries. The results of this analysis are shown in the table. Study the data table and answer the questions.

Numbers of Amphibian Populations

Region	Declining	Increasing	No Trend
Western Europe	309	248	29
North America	130	96	14
South America	31	19	1
Australia/NZ	17	6	1
Asia	10	10	1
Eastern Europe	4	5	0
Africa/Middle East	2	2	1

1. **Using Tables and Graphs** How many amphibian populations were studied?
2. **Predicting** If the trends presented in the data table continue, how do you expect amphibian populations in North America to change in the next two decades?
3. **Calculating** What percentage of worldwide amphibian populations is decreasing?
4. **Evaluating** Do you think that regional population data can be used to predict global population trends? Explain your answer.

Build Science Skills

Using Models Challenge student groups to choose one type of amphibian and model its movement. Students can use materials such as pipe cleaners, rubber bands, paper clips, straws, craft sticks, suction cups, or toothpicks to construct their models. Encourage students to do extra research to learn exactly how their amphibian moves. Groups can present their models to the class. L2

Build Science Skills

Applying Concepts Challenge students to consider how a frog's senses help to protect it from predators. Ask: **How would a frog sense a predator?** *(By sight or sound)* **How would a frog defend itself from predators?** *(By jumping or swimming away, by camouflage, or by expelling a poison)* L2

Analyzing Data

BIIE 1.d

Make sure students understand how to interpret information in the table. L2

Answers

1. 936 populations
2. Amphibian populations will decline.
3. 53.7 percent
4. Students might agree or disagree but must give reasons for their answers. Some might think that if population studies from many different regions were combined, predictions could be made about global populations. However, others might think that regions have site-specific conditions, making them unsuitable for global predictions.

FACTS AND FIGURES

Amphibians adapt to temperature extremes Like most fishes, amphibians are ectothermic animals. Unlike fishes, whose body temperature is very close to that of the water in which they live, amphibians absorb solar radiation, which causes their body temperature to be higher than the air temperature.

Amphibians living in areas that freeze during winter enter a dormant state called hibernation. Temperate-zone frogs store fat in the body to use as energy. Then, they bury themselves in the mud in stream banks or at the bottoms of ponds. Their metabolism slows until warmer temperatures arrive. Amphibians living in areas with hot, dry summers enter a dormant state called estivation to keep from drying out. During estivation, amphibians burrow into the mud and coat the inside of the burrow with mucus and dead skin. They remain in this state until the rains come.

Answers to . . .

CHECKPOINT *The jelly attaches the eggs to underwater plants and protects the eggs from predators.*

Figure 30–25 *Both have tails and gills, but tadpoles lack true fins. Also, tadpoles grow limbs and lungs as they become adults.*

Figure 30–26 *To find mates, locate prey, and escape predators*

30–3 (continued)

Groups of Amphibians

Build Science Skills

Comparing and Contrasting Have students compare and contrast the characteristics of each of the three groups of amphibians. You might ask students to construct a table or other graphic organizer, or you might discuss this orally as a class. Students should focus on the characteristics that make each group an amphibian, as well as the characteristics that define each group.

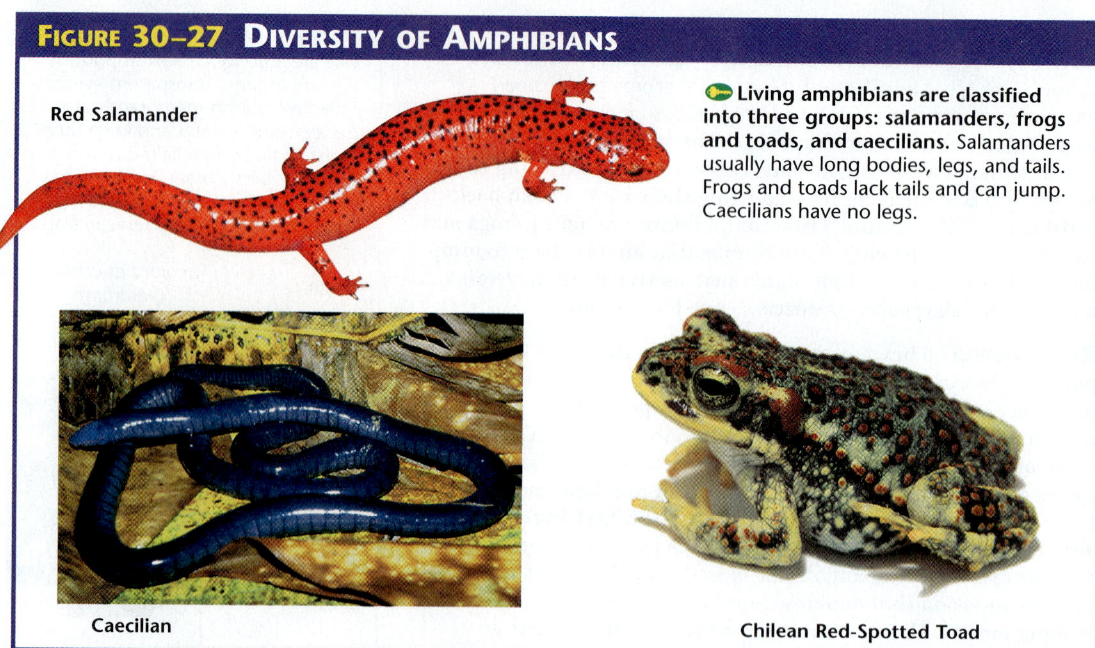

FIGURE 30–27 DIVERSITY OF AMPHIBIANS

Living amphibians are classified into three groups: salamanders, frogs and toads, and caecilians. Salamanders usually have long bodies, legs, and tails. Frogs and toads lack tails and can jump. Caecilians have no legs.

Groups of Amphibians

Modern amphibians can be classified into three categories. **The three groups of amphibians alive today are salamanders, frogs and toads, and caecilians.** Representative members are shown in **Figure 30–27.**

Salamanders Members of the order Urodela (yoor-oh-DEE-luh), including salamanders and newts, have long bodies and tails. Most also have four legs. Both adults and larvae are carnivores. The adults usually live in moist woods, where they tunnel under rocks and rotting logs. Some salamanders, such as the mud puppy, keep their gills and live in water all their lives.

Frogs and Toads The most obvious feature that members of the order Anura (uh-NOOR-uh) share is their ability to jump. Frogs tend to have long legs and make lengthy jumps, whereas the relatively short legs of toads limit them to short hops. Frogs are generally more closely tied to water—including ponds and streams—than toads, which often live in moist woods and even in deserts. Adult frogs and toads lack tails.

Caecilians The least known of the amphibians are the caecilians, members of the order Apoda (ay-POH-duh). Caecilians are legless animals that live in water or burrow in moist soil or sediment, feeding on small invertebrates such as termites. Many have fishlike scales embedded in their skin—which demonstrates that some amphibians don't fit the general definition.

BIOLOGY UPDATE

Incidence of deformed frogs rising

Since 1995, when middle-school students found many deformed frogs in a Minnesota pond, the reported number of deformed frogs has been increasing. While it is normal for about 1 percent of a population of frogs to have some deformities, these increasing numbers are alarming because frogs are bioindicators of the environment. They are more susceptible to subtle changes in the environment than are many other species.

Researchers have been working to find the cause of these deformities. Several hypotheses include chemical contamination, infection with a parasitic worm, exposure to the sun's ultraviolet rays, and physical trauma. Some researchers think that the deformities are caused by the interaction of more than one factor at the same time in a specific place.

Ecology of Amphibians

Amphibians must live near water, and they are common in moist, warm places such as tropical rain forest biomes. In contrast, because most amphibians cannot tolerate dry conditions, comparatively few live in desert biomes. Desert amphibians have adaptations that enable them to take advantage of water when it is available. For example, some toads stay inactive in sealed burrows for months, then emerge when a heavy rain falls.

Many amphibians make an ideal meal for predators such as birds and mammals. However, amphibians have adaptations that protect them from predators. For example, many species have skin colors and markings that enable them to blend in with their surroundings. Most adult amphibians, such as the toad in **Figure 30–28,** have skin glands that ooze an unpleasant-tasting and poisonous substance, or toxin.

Recently, scientists have noticed an alarming trend in amphibian populations worldwide. For the past several decades, the numbers of living species have been decreasing. The golden toad of Costa Rica, for example, seems to be extinct. In North America, the numbers of boreal toads have dwindled. Even the leopard frog and its relatives, once common worldwide, are getting harder to find.

Scientists do not yet know what is causing the global amphibian population to decline. It is possible that amphibians are susceptible to a wide variety of environmental threats, such as decreasing habitat, depletion of the ozone layer, acid rain, water pollution, fungal infections, introduced aquatic predators, and an increasing human population.

To better understand this phenomenon, biologists worldwide have been focusing their efforts and sharing data about amphibian populations. In the late 1990s, a group of scientists set up monitoring programs that cover the entire area of North America. One such program relies mostly on the efforts of volunteers, who are trained to recognize the specific call of various species such as cricket frogs, bullfrogs, or spring peepers.

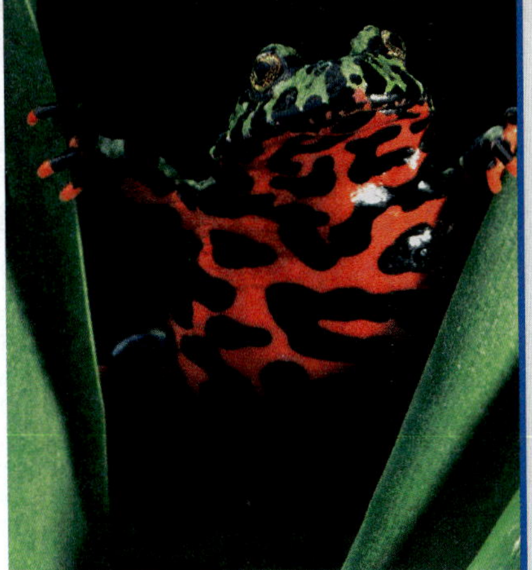

▲ **Figure 30–28** Some amphibians that release toxins, such as this European fire-bellied toad, have bodies that are brightly colored and have bold patterns. The colors and patterns serve as a warning to potential predators. **Using Analogies** *How is the underside of this frog comparable to a dog showing its teeth?*

30–3 Section Assessment

1. **Key Concept** List the characteristics of amphibians.
2. **Key Concept** What adaptations helped amphibians evolve into land animals?
3. **Key Concept** List the three groups of amphibians.
4. What characteristics usually restrict amphibian reproduction to moist environments?
5. How are scientists attempting to deal with the problem of declining amphibian populations?
6. **Critical Thinking Formulating Hypotheses** Most caecilian species are totally blind as adults. How do you think this characteristic has evolved?

Thinking Visually

Cycle Diagrams

Construct a cycle diagram that identifies and describes the stages in the life cycle of a typical amphibian. For information about cycle diagrams, see Appendix A at the back of the book.

30–3 Section Assessment

1. Vertebrates that live in water as larvae and on land as adults, breathe with lungs as adults, have moist skin with mucous glands, and lack scales and claws.
2. Strong bones; sternum that supports and protects internal organs; and lungs
3. Salamanders, frogs and toads, caecilians
4. Shell-less eggs and aquatic larvae
5. By monitoring populations of amphibians worldwide and sharing their data
6. Sample Answer: As caecilians became adapted to burrowing, those with smaller and smaller eyes suffered less damage and infection from the eyes scraping against the burrow walls. Thus, natural selection favored these variants.

Ecology of Amphibians

Make Connections

Environmental Science Explain that amphibians are good indicators of changes in the environment. Challenge students to identify amphibian characteristics that would make them susceptible to environmental changes. *(Moist skin, small body, unshelled eggs, reliance on both land and water)* L2

3 ASSESS

Evaluate Understanding

Call on students to give amphibian characteristics that are adaptations to life on land and describe how amphibians are still dependent on water.

Reteach

Give students a frog diagram and instruct them to label the adaptations that enable the frog to live on land.

Thinking Visually

Cycle diagrams should follow the life cycle diagram in Figure 30–25 on page 786. Students should include not only the stages of the life cycle—eggs, tadpoles, adults—but also a description of each stage.

Interactive Textbook

If your class subscribes to the iText, use it to review the Key Concepts in Section 30–3.

Answer to . . .

Figure 30–28 *Both are warnings to potential predators.*

Exploration

 **BIIE 1.g**

Objective Students will be able to use models to determine how fishes and amphibians maintain homeostasis. L2

Skills Focus Evaluating and Revising, Using Models

Time 45 minutes

Advance Prep
- Obtain samples of freshwater fishes (perch, walleye, catfish) and saltwater fishes (cod, halibut, mackerel) from a grocery store or fish market. Fresh fish is better than frozen.
- Precut 5-g samples of fish for students, or provide scalpels for students to cut their own.
- Prepare a 0.1 M silver nitrate solution by adding 1.7 g $AgNO_3$ to 100 mL of distilled water. **CAUTION:** *Wear an apron, safety goggles, and latex or nitrile gloves when preparing this solution.*

Alternative Materials Use clear plastic one-quart, wide-mouthed beverage jugs instead of 1000-mL beakers. Use rubber stoppers instead of folded paper towels to act as cushions in step 3.

Safety Read the safety information in the MSDS for silver nitrate before doing the lab. Silver nitrate is toxic and can be hazardous if used improperly. It will stain the skin but will wear off in about 4–7 days. Students should wear disposable plastic gloves during the activity and appropriately dispose of the gloves afterward.

Pre-Lab Discussion Review homeostasis with students. Ask: **What is homeostasis?** *(The maintenance of constant conditions in an organism)* Discuss the adaptations that saltwater fishes and freshwater fishes have for keeping the amount of water constant in the body. *(Kidneys remove extra water or keep water in the body, as needed.)* Review how amphibians get oxygen through the skin.

Teaching Tip Use qualitative filter paper. The fine pores of quantitative filter paper are easily clogged.

Exploration

 **BIIE 1.g**

Investigating Homeostasis in Fishes and Amphibians

All living organisms must maintain homeostasis, or a controlled internal environment. Fishes are adapted to avoid gaining or losing excessive amounts of water or salts due to osmosis. Amphibians need to maintain a surface that can absorb oxygen from air and release carbon dioxide. In this investigation, you will examine these adaptations.

Problem How do fishes and amphibians maintain homeostasis?

Materials

- 5 g saltwater fish
- 5 g freshwater fish
- balance
- 4 test tubes
- test tube rack
- paper towels
- 2 glass rods
- 10-mL graduated cylinder
- 2 funnels
- 2 filter-paper circles
- silver nitrate solution
- 1000-mL beaker
- vinegar
- distilled water
- string
- scissors
- transparent tape
- blue litmus paper
- sodium bicarbonate (baking soda)
- glass-marking pencil

Skills Evaluating and Revising, Using Models

Procedure     

Part A: Osmotic Homeostasis in Fishes

1. **Predicting** Predict whether saltwater fishes or freshwater fishes will have saltier flesh.
2. Put on your safety goggles, plastic gloves, and lab apron. Obtain 5-g samples of freshwater fish and saltwater fish. Label 2 test tubes "salt" and "fresh" with a glass-marking pencil. Place each sample into the corresponding test tube and add 10 mL of distilled water. Put the test tubes in the rack.
3. Fold 2 paper towels in half 3 times to make 2 cushions. Place a paper towel cushion under each test tube. To make an extract of each fish sample, gently mash the sample with a glass rod until it becomes pasty. Use a separate glass rod for each sample. **CAUTION:** *Be careful not to break the rods or the test tubes.*
4. Label 2 more test tubes "salt filtered" and "fresh filtered." Put the test tubes in a rack and place a funnel in each of these test tubes. Fold 2 filter-paper circles in half, and then in half again. Open one layer of each folded filter paper to form a cone as shown. Insert a paper cone into each funnel.

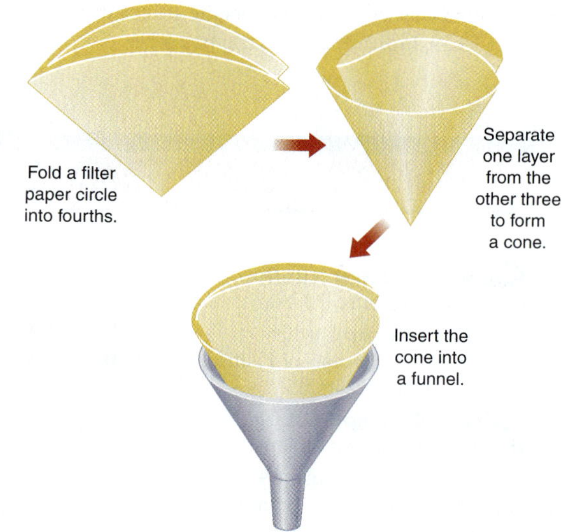

Procedure

1. Some students might predict that there is no difference. Some might predict that saltwater fishes have saltier flesh.

7. Some students might predict that gases enter a wet surface more quickly. Others might predict that gases enter a dry surface faster.

11. Wet litmus paper turns pink in about 10 seconds. Dry litmus paper turns pink in about 60 seconds.

Expected Outcomes

Students should find the salt content in freshwater fishes to be the same as in saltwater fishes. The wet litmus paper should turn pink much faster than the dry litmus paper.

5. Pour the contents of the saltwater fish test tube into the funnel in the "salt filtered" test tube. Pour the contents of the freshwater fish test tube into the funnel in the "fresh filtered" test tube. Allow the liquid to filter through, and then remove the funnels.

6. Silver nitrate is a chemical that is used to detect salt. A drop of silver nitrate turns cloudy when it is added to a solution that contains salt. **CAUTION:** *Silver nitrate is toxic and will stain your skin and clothing.* Observe each filtered sample as you add 1 drop of silver nitrate solution. Then, record your observations.

Part B: Gas Exchange in Air

7. **Predicting** Amphibians need to exchange oxygen and carbon dioxide with the air around them. Record your prediction of whether gases will enter a dry surface or a moist surface more quickly.

8. Place 100 mL of vinegar in a 1000-mL beaker. Cut a piece of paper large enough to cover the beaker and extend approximately 3 cm beyond the sides of the beaker.

9. Near the center of the paper, tape two 5-cm pieces of string approximately 3 cm apart. Then, tape a piece of blue litmus paper to the end of each string.

10. Use a drop of distilled water to moisten one of the strips of litmus paper, being sure to keep the other strip dry. The moist litmus paper is a model that represents an amphibian's skin. The color of the litmus paper will change to red in the presence of carbon dioxide gas, which acts as an acid. The reaction between vinegar and sodium bicarbonate produces this gas.

11. Add 5 g of sodium bicarbonate to the beaker of vinegar. Quickly cover the beaker with the paper lid so that the filter strips hang down into the beaker as shown in the photograph. Record the time required for each strip of litmus paper to change color.

12. Wash your hands thoroughly with soap and warm water before leaving the lab.

Analyze and Conclude

1. **Comparing and Contrasting** Compare the appearance of the saltwater and freshwater fish extracts after adding the silver nitrate.
2. **Inferring** What can you infer from this result about the ability of freshwater and saltwater fishes to maintain homeostasis?
3. **Drawing Conclusions** What must a freshwater fish do to maintain homeostasis? How would these activities differ in a saltwater fish?
4. **Inferring** What do your results in Part B indicate about the ability of gases to enter moist and dry surfaces?
5. **Inferring** Explain why it is important for amphibians to maintain a moist surface for gas exchange.

Go Further

Constructing an Alternative Model
In Part B, you created a model of how an amphibian's skin absorbs a gas. Construct an alternative model that shows a different characteristic of an amphibian's skin. (*Hint:* Recall that an amphibian's skin is thin, moist, and covered with mucus.) Analyze your new model by comparing it to the model in Part B. What does each model show that the other does not?

Analyze and Conclude

1. Both extracts appear similar.

2. Both saltwater and freshwater fishes are able to maintain osmotic homeostasis.

3. A freshwater fish excretes excess water in dilute urine because its body cells contain more salt than the water in which it lives. A saltwater fish excretes concentrated urine because its cells lose water to the salty water in which it lives.

4. The faster reaction of the moist litmus paper indicates that gases enter moist surfaces more quickly than dry surfaces.

5. Gases are exchanged more efficiently through a moist surface. If an amphibian dries out, it could suffocate.

Go Further

Students can model thin amphibian skin covered with mucus using plastic wrap to represent the skin and petroleum jelly to represent mucus. This model represents the structure and texture of the skin, whereas the model in Part B illustrates the skin's ability to act as an organ for gas exchange. This model can also illustrate how the skin acts as a barrier to protect the internal organs from damage and water loss.

Chapter 30 Study Guide

Study Tip

Students can review the chapter by rereading each section and taking notes about the Key Concepts. Students should also write definitions for each Vocabulary term.

Thinking Visually

1. Jawless fishes
2. Cartilaginous fishes
3. Bony fishes
4. Sharks and their relatives
5. Lobe-finned fishes

Chapter 30 Assessment

Reviewing Content

1. c **2.** b **3.** c **4.** a **5.** d **6.** a **7.** c **8.** a **9.** c **10.** d

Understanding Concepts

11. The backbone replaces the notochord in most developing vertebrates.

12. As water passes through the lancelet's pharynx, mucus catches food particles. The lancelet swallows the mucus into the digestive tract.

13. Cartilaginous fishes, which include sharks and rays, and bony fishes

14. Every mode of feeding is seen in fishes. They are herbivores, carnivores, parasites, filter feeders, and detritus feeders. A single fish may exhibit more than one mode of feeding, depending upon what is available.

15. Oxygen-poor blood is pumped from the body into the sinus venosus. Blood then flows into the atrium, then into the ventricle. The ventricle pumps blood into the bulbus arteriosus, which connects to the aorta, through which blood moves to the gills.

16. In the form of ammonia

17. The lateral line system is a motion-sensing organ. Fishes use the system to sense motion of other fishes, potential predators, and potential prey.

Chapter 30 Study Guide

30–1 The Chordates

Key Concepts

- A chordate is an animal that has, for at least some stage of its life, a dorsal, hollow nerve cord; a notochord; pharyngeal pouches; and a tail that extends beyond the anus.
- The two groups of nonvertebrate chordates are tunicates and lancelets.

Vocabulary

chordate, p. 767
notochord, p. 767
pharyngeal pouch, p. 767
vertebra, p. 768

30–2 Fishes

Key Concepts

- Fishes are aquatic vertebrates; most fishes have paired fins, scales, and gills.
- The evolution of jaws and the evolution of paired fins were important developments during the rise of fishes.
- Fishes' adaptations to aquatic life include various modes of feeding, specialized structures for gas exchange, and paired fins for locomotion.
- On the basis of their basic internal structure, all living fishes can be classified into three groups: jawless fishes, cartilaginous fishes, and bony fishes.

Vocabulary

cartilage, p. 773
atrium, p. 776
ventricle, p. 776
cerebrum, p. 777
cerebellum, p. 777
medulla oblongata, p. 777
lateral line system, p. 777
swim bladder, p. 777
oviparous, p. 778
ovoviviparous, p. 778
viviparous, p. 778

30–3 Amphibians

Key Concepts

- An amphibian is a vertebrate that, with some exceptions, lives in water as a larva and on land as an adult, breathes with lungs as an adult, has moist skin that contains mucous glands, and lacks scales and claws.
- Early amphibians evolved several adaptations that helped them live at least part of their lives out of water. Bones in the limbs and limb girdles of amphibians became stronger, permitting more-efficient movement. A set of lungs and breathing tubes enabled them to breathe air. Their sternum formed a bony shield that supports and protects the internal organs, especially the lungs.
- The three groups of living amphibians are salamanders, frogs and toads, and caecilians.

Vocabulary

cloaca, p. 784
nictitating membrane, p. 787
tympanic membrane, p. 787

Thinking Visually

Using information from this chapter, complete the following concept map:

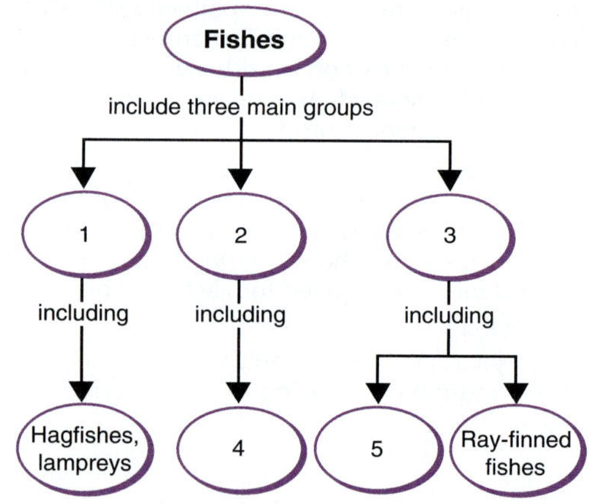

CHAPTER RESOURCES

Print:

- ***Teaching Resources,*** Chapter Vocabulary Review, Graphic Organizer, Chapter 30 Tests: Levels A and B

Technology:

- ***Computer Test Bank,*** Chapter 30 Test
- ***iText,*** Chapter 30 Assessment

Chapter 30 Assessment

Interactive textbook with assessment at PHSchool.com 

Reviewing Content

Choose the letter that best answers the question or completes the statement.

1. Which of the following is NOT characteristic of all chordates?
   a. hollow nerve cord
   b. pharyngeal pouches
   c. fins
   d. notochord
2. The term LEAST closely related to the others is
   a. chordate.
   b. cerebrum.
   c. invertebrate.
   d. lancelet.
3. The evolution of jaws and paired fins was an important development during the rise of
   a. tunicates.
   b. lancelets.
   c. fishes.
   d. amphibians.
4. Most fishes exchange gases by pumping water from their mouths
   a. over the gill filaments.
   b. through the pyloric ceca.
   c. over the atrium.
   d. through the esophagus.
5. In fishes, the part of the brain that coordinates body movements is the
   a. olfactory lobe.
   b. optic lobe.
   c. cerebrum.
   d. cerebellum.
6. A species that lays eggs that develop outside of the mother's body is
   a. oviparous.
   b. viviparous.
   c. ovoviviparous.
   d. nonviparous.
7. Examine the diagrams below. Which of these is a jawed cartilaginous fish?

8. At the end of the large intestine of a frog is a muscular cavity called the
   a. cloaca.
   b. pancreas.
   c. gallbladder.
   d. esophagus.
9. An adult amphibian's heart typically has
   a. one chamber.
   b. two chambers.
   c. three chambers.
   d. four chambers.
10. Each of the following serves as an organ of gas exchange in frogs, toads, and many salamanders EXCEPT the
    a. skin.
    b. mouth cavity.
    c. lungs.
    d. nictitating membrane.

Understanding Concepts

11. Describe what happens to the notochord in most developing vertebrates.
12. How does a lancelet obtain food?
13. Which two major groups of fishes evolved from the early jawed fishes and still survive today?
14. Identify three feeding modes that are observed in fishes.
15. Describe the flow of blood through the heart of a typical fish, naming the four structures.
16. In what form is nitrogenous waste excreted from the bodies of most fishes?
17. What is a lateral line system? What does it enable a fish to do?
18. What is the function of a fish's swim bladder?
19. How do a fish's muscles function in swimming?
20. How are lampreys and sharks similar? How are they different?
21. List some of the challenges that early vertebrates faced as they moved from water to land habitats during the course of evolution.
22. How are tadpoles and adult frogs adapted for their specific feeding behaviors?
23. What adaptation do many adult amphibians have to carry out respiration?
24. Discuss how blood flows through the heart of an adult frog.
25. Many amphibians have specialized structures that aid in movement. Describe two of these structures.
26. Why are most amphibians unable to tolerate living in desert biomes?

TIME SAVER

HOMEWORK GUIDE

Section:	Questions:
Section 30–1	1, 2, 11, 12, 32
Section 30–2	3–7, 13–20, 27, 28
Section 30–3	8–10, 21–26, 29–31

Interactive Textbook

If your class subscribes to the iText, your students can go online to access an interactive version of the Student Edition and a self-test.

(Continued from page 792)

18. The swim bladder adjusts the fish's buoyancy.

19. Paired sets of muscles on either side of the backbone are alternately contracted. This creates a series of S-shaped curves that move down the fish's body.

20. Lampreys and sharks are similar in that both are fishes with skeletons that are at least partially made of cartilage. Unlike lampreys, sharks have jaws, true teeth, paired fins, and scales.

21. Breathing air, protecting themselves and their eggs from drying out, and supporting the body against the pull of gravity

22. Tadpoles are filter feeders or herbivores that feed on algae. Their long, coiled intestines help them break down hard-to-digest plant materials. Adult amphibians are mostly carnivorous. Their feeding apparatus and digestive tract are transformed to a meat-eating structure with a much shorter intestine.

23. Lung; also, skin and mouth cavity

24. Oxygen-poor blood circulates from the body into the right atrium. At the same time, oxygen-rich blood from the lungs and skin enters the left atrium. The atria contract and blood is pumped into the ventricle. When the ventricle contracts, blood is pumped into a single vessel, which divides and distributes blood to the lungs and body. Most oxygen-poor blood goes to the lungs, and most oxygen-rich blood goes to the rest of the body.

25. Examples of structures used by amphibians for movement include tails in larvae; four legs; well-developed hind limbs for jumping long distances; and disks on their toes that serve as suction cups.

26. Amphibians require water for reproduction.

Critical Thinking

27. Many saltwater fishes could probably not survive in fresh water because their kidneys could not switch to a freshwater mode by excreting excess water and conserving salts.

28. Since dams would be an obstacle in the upstream swim of salmon, the dams would prevent some salmon from reproducing.

29. Pollutants can travel through thin, moist skin more easily than dry skin. Shell-less eggs are more vulnerable to pollutants than eggs with shells.

30. a. Devonian Period **b.** Osteichthyes; the line for amphibians originates in Osteichthyes. **c.** Jawless fishes and Osteichthyes **d.** Placoderms

31. Students need to find out what tadpoles normally eat and then alter that diet in their experiment. They would need to control the temperature, pH, and oxygen content of the water. They would have to decide whether to use increases in mass, length, or time required for metamorphosis as a measurement of development.

32. Both tunicates and lancelets have the four chordate characteristics—a dorsal, hollow nerve cord; a notochord; pharyngeal pouches; and a tail that extends beyond the anus—during some stage of their life cycle. Vertebrates are also chordates in which the notochord develops into the backbone.

Focus on the BIG Idea

Fishes with certain adaptations were able to survive in certain habitats better than others. If any new mutation gave an individual fish a selective advantage, it would be better equipped to survive in that habitat. Over time, diversity in fishes increased as they became adapted to new habitats.

Chapter 30 Assessment

Critical Thinking

27. **Applying Concepts** The kidneys of saltwater fishes are adapted to meet the needs of a marine environment. Why would it be impossible for a saltwater fish to survive in fresh water?

28. **Inferring** How might dams across rivers affect the reproduction of salmon?

29. **Inferring** The skin of amphibians is thin and moist. Amphibian eggs have no shell and must be kept moist. How might the worldwide decline of amphibian populations be related to these two characteristics?

30. **Interpreting Graphics** The chart below shows changes in five groups of vertebrates over the past 500 million years. The thickness of each band indicates changes in the relative number of species over geologic time. Use this chart to answer the questions.
    a. During which period did amphibians evolve?
    b. Did the amphibians evolve from early jawless fishes or from early bony fishes (Osteichthyes)? Explain your answer.
    c. In which groups of fishes have the number of species increased during recent times?
    d. Which group of fishes is extinct?

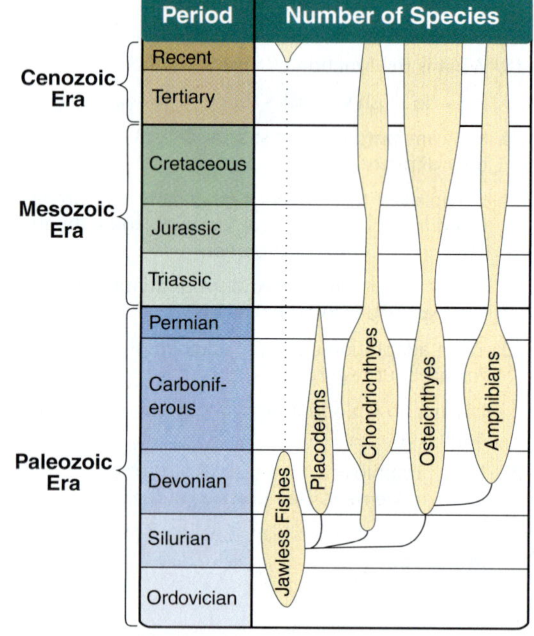

31. **Designing Experiments** Design an experiment to determine the effect of diet on the development of tadpoles. Define the variables you would need to control.

32. **Applying Concepts** Which anatomical characteristics of nonvertebrate chordates suggest that, in terms of phylogeny (evolutionary relationships), these animals are more closely related to vertebrates than to other groups of animals?

Focus on the BIG Idea

Evolution In Chapter 15, you learned about Darwin's theory of evolution by natural selection. How might natural selection have contributed to the great diversity of fishes that exists today? (*Hint*: Think of the many different kinds of aquatic environments that fishes inhabit.)

Writing in Science

Write a paragraph comparing and contrasting the characteristics of the three major groups of amphibians. Be sure to say how they are similar as well as how they are different. (*Hint:* To prepare to write, construct a compare-contrast table that compares the three groups. Characteristics for comparison might include shape of body, number of legs, and habitat.)

Performance-Based Assessment

Modeling Structure and Function Using modeling clay, paper, or other suitable materials, make a three-dimensional model of a fish or an amphibian. Identify each of the external structures described in the chapter. Attach flags or markers that describe how each of these structures is adapted to the habitat and behavior of the animal you have modeled.

For: An interactive self-test
Visit: PHSchool.com
Web Code: cba-9300

Writing in Science

In their paragraphs, students should explain how the three groups of amphibians are similar by describing how each group exhibits the general characteristics of amphibians. Then, they should explain how each group is different by describing the features that are used to classify amphibians into three groups, such as body shape, number of legs, presence of tails in adults, and method of movement.

Performance-Based Assessment

Student models will vary but should reflect the structure of the organism and how these structures are adapted to the habitat and behavior of the animal selected.

Standards Practice

Online at PHSchool.com

Test-Taking Tip If a test question seems confusing, try rephrasing it in your own words. Rephrasing a question will often allow you to better understand it.

Directions: Choose the letter that best answers the question or completes the statement.

1. Which of the following is NEVER true of oviparous fishes?
   A Their eggs are fertilized externally.
   B Their eggs hatch outside the mother's body.
   C They have paired fins.
   D The embryos receive nourishment directly from the mother's body.

2. Which of the following indicates how amphibian larvae typically feed?
   I. Filter feeders
   II. Carnivores
   III. Herbivores
   A I only
   B III only
   C I and II only
   D I and III only

3. Into which of the following groups can nonvertebrate chordates be classified?
   I. Lancelets
   II. Tunicates
   III. Fishes
   A I only
   B I and II only
   C II and III only
   D I, II, and III

4. A fish is UNLIKE an amphibian in that a fish
   A is a nonvertebrate chordate.
   B has a heart with one atrium.
   C has moist skin.
   D has a nictitating membrane.

5. Which of the following is in the order Apoda?
   A shark
   B frog
   C snake
   D caecilian

Questions 6–9 Each of the lettered choices below refers to the following numbered statements. Select the best lettered choice. A choice may be used once, more than once, or not at all.

A Tunicates
B Lancelets
C Fishes
D Caecilians

6. Legless amphibians
7. Organisms that feed through a mouth with no jaws, are thin enough to breathe through their body surface, and do not have a true heart
8. Members of the subphylum Cephalochordata
9. Aquatic vertebrates with fins, scales, and gills

Questions 10–11

An ecologist collected data about the number of frogs that inhabit a certain pond each year. In addition, he collected data about the total amount of rainfall in that area each spring. The data are shown in the table.

Rainfall and Frog Population in Pond

Year	Amount of Rainfall (centimeters)	Number of Frogs
1995	13	45
1996	20	61
1997	8	33
1998	5	20
1999	23	63

10. In what year were the most frogs observed?
    A 1996 **C** 1998
    B 1997 **D** 1999

11. Which statement is best supported by the data?
    A The number of frogs increased each year.
    B The number of frogs decreased each year.
    C The number of frogs increased or decreased based on whether it is an odd or even numbered year.
    D The number of frogs in the pond increased as the amount of rainfall increased.

Standards Practice

1. D	**5.** D	**9.** C
2. D	**6.** D	**10.** D
3. B	**7.** B	**11.** D
4. B	**8.** B	

Online at PHSchool.com

Have students check their understanding of the chapter by logging onto Success Tracker.

Your students can independently test their knowledge of the chapter and print out their test results for your files.

Chapter Planner 31 Reptiles and Birds

Section and Section Objectives	Time	STANDARDS NCLB	STANDARDS Biology	Activities and Labs
31–1 Reptiles, pp. 797–805 **31.1.1** ***Describe*** the characteristics of reptiles. **31.1.2** ***Summarize*** the evolution of reptiles. **31.1.3** ***Explain*** how reptiles are adapted to life on land. **31.1.4** ***Identify*** the four living orders of reptiles.	2 periods (1 block)			**SE:** ***Inquiry Activity,*** How are bird eggs adapted for life on land?, p. 796 L2 **SE:** ***Problem Solving,*** A Massive Controversy, p. 799 L2 **TE:** ***Demonstration,*** p. 800 L2 **TE:** ***Build Science Skills,*** p. 802 L2 **TE:** ***Build Science Skills,*** p. 804 L2 **LMA:** Chapter 31 Lab L2 L3
31–2 Birds, pp. 806–814 **31.2.1** ***Describe*** the characteristics that all birds have in common. **31.2.2** ***Summarize*** the evolution of birds. **31.2.3** ***Explain*** how birds are adapted for flight. **31.2.4** ***Describe*** the diversity of birds. **31.2.5** ***Identify*** ways in which birds interact with the environment and with humans.	2 periods (1 block)			**TE:** ***Build Science Skills,*** p. 808 L2 **TE:** ***Make Connections,*** p. 808 L2 L3 **SE:** ***Quick Lab,*** How do birds breathe?, p. 811 L2 **TE:** ***Make Connections,*** p. 812 L2 **SE:** ***Exploration,*** Examining Bird Bones, p. 815 L2 **LMB:** Chapter 31 Lab L1 L2
Chapter Assessment, pp. 816–819	1 period (1/2 block)			

ACTIVITY PLANNER

SE: *Inquiry Activity,* p. 796; 15 min.; plastic gloves, frog eggs, chicken eggs, disposable plastic or paper plates

TE: *Demonstration,* p. 800; 15 min.; 3 rocks, heat lamp, container of cool water, shady spot, 3 thermometers, tape

TE: *Build Science Skills,* p. 802; 20 min.; 3-D models, schematic diagrams, or photographs of lizards and salamanders

TE: *Build Science Skills,* p. 804; 10 min.; pictures of a snapping turtle, a sea turtle, a tortoise, and a painted turtle

TE: *Build Science Skills,* p. 808; 15 min.; 10–15 pictures of various birds, including flightless birds and excellent fliers

TE: *Make Connections,* p. 808; 20 min.; various insulating materials chosen by students, water, thermometer, jar or beaker, tape

SE: *Quick Lab,* p. 811; 15 min.; 6 round balloons, hand-powered balloon pump, measuring tape, clock with second hand

TE: *Make Connections,* p. 812; 20 min.; toy gliders or paper to make airplanes

SE: *Exploration,* p. 815; 45 min.; cut sections of bird and mammal bones, bird breastbone, hand lens, mammal bone, bird wing bone, balance, 250-mL graduated cylinder, dissecting probe, calculator, disposable plastic gloves

PLANNING KEY

Ability Levels

for students performing . . .

below grade level L1

at grade level L2

above grade level L3

Print Components

SE	Student Edition	LA	Lab Assessment
TE	Teacher's Edition	BTM	Biotechnology Manual
RSW	Reading & Study Workbook A	IDM	Issues and Decision Making
ARSW	Adapted Reading & Study Workbook B	LW	Lab Worksheets
TR	Teaching Resources	LMA	Laboratory Manual A
IF	Investigations in Forensics	LMB	Laboratory Manual B

Tech Components

CTB	Computer Test Bank
BD	BioDetectives DVD
TP	Transparencies Plus
PLM	Probeware Lab Manual
ABC	ABC DVD Library
LS	Lab Simulations
VL	Virtual Labs

Interactive textbook with assessment at PHSchool.com

Program Resources	Assessment	Media and Technology
TR: Lesson Plan 31–1, Section Summary, p. 47 L1, p. 57 L2, Worksheets, pp. 50–52 L1, pp. 59–61 L2 **RSW:** Section 31–1 L2 **ARSW:** Section 31–1 L1 **IDM:** Issues and Decisions 34 L2 L3	**SE:** 31–1 Section Assessment, p. 805 **TR:** Section Review 31–1	**iText:** Section 31–1 **TP:** TP1–1 Interest Grabber, Section Outline, Structure of a Turtle's Heart, Figure 31–8
TR: Lesson Plan 31–2, Section Summary, p. 48 L1, p. 58 L2, Worksheets, pp. 53–55 L1, pp. 62–65 L2, Enrichment L2 L3 **LW:** Chapter 31 Exploration L1 L2 L3 **RSW:** Section 31–2 L2 **ARSW:** Section 31–2 L1 **IDM:** Issues and Decisions 13 L2 L3	**SE:** 31–2 Section Assessment, p. 814 **TR:** Section Review 31–2	**iText:** Section 31–2 **TP:** 31–2 Interest Grabber, Section Outline, Concept Map, Figure 31–14, Figure 31–16
	SE: Chapter 31 Assessment, pp. 816–819 **TR:** Chapter Vocabulary Review, Graphic Organizer, Chapter 31 Test	**iText:** Chapter 31 Assessment **CTB:** Chapter 31 Test

Students can do research, share data, and test their knowledge online.

PRESSED FOR TIME?

To Preview the Chapter

- Introduce students to the Key Concepts and Vocabulary terms in each section.
- Have students examine Figures 31–4, 31–8, 31–9, 31–14, 31–16, and 31–19 and read their captions.

To Cover the Chapter Quickly

- Have students read What Is a Reptile? and Form and Function in Reptiles in Section 31–1 and What Is a Bird? and Form and Function in Birds in Section 31–2.
- Assign the Key Concept questions from 31–1 and 31–2 Section Assessments and the Chapter 31 Standards Practice.

To Review the Chapter

- Assign Sections 31–1 and 31–2 in the Reading and Study Workbook or the Adapted Reading and Study Workbook.
- Assign Section Reviews for 31–1 and 31–2 and the Chapter Vocabulary Review for Chapter 31 in the Teaching Resources.

CHAPTER 31

ENGAGE/EXPLORE

Inquiry Activity

Objective Students will be able to hypothesize how bird eggs are adapted for life on land. L2

Skill Focus **Formulating Hypotheses, Inferring**

Materials plastic gloves, frog eggs (or other amphibian or fish eggs), chicken eggs, disposable plastic or paper plates

Time 15 minutes

Safety To prevent possible exposure to *Salmonella* in raw eggs, stress the importance of keeping raw egg away from the face, wearing gloves, and washing hands well after the activity.

Strategies

- Review the environment in which frogs live and where they lay their eggs.
- Encourage students to identify parallels between their observations of frog and bird eggs. For example, the albumen of a bird's egg replicates the aquatic environment of a frog's egg.

Expected Outcomes Students should describe the frog egg as small, moist, and lacking a shell, and the bird egg as large, hard-shelled, and containing large amounts of yellow and white liquids.

Think About It

1. Moist conditions; frogs must live near water or other moist places so they have a place to lay their eggs.

2. Because bird eggs have hard protective shells that prevent the egg from drying out, birds are not restricted to living near water.

Brain Teaser

Ask students: **Which came first, the chicken or the egg?** Before accepting any answers, challenge students to think of the question in an evolutionary sense. In other words, encourage students to think of animal adaptations that enabled animals to live successfully on land without being dependent on water for part of their life cycle. Accept all reasonable, thoughtful answers.

CHAPTER 31

Reptiles and Birds

A spur-thighed tortoise hatches from its egg, ready to face life as a young reptile.

Inquiry Activity

How are bird eggs adapted for life on land?

Procedure  

1. Put on plastic gloves. Examine a frog egg. Describe the characteristics of the egg.
2. Examine a chicken egg. Carefully crack the egg, and pour the contents onto a disposable plate. Describe the structures inside. **CAUTION:** *Do not eat raw egg.*
3. Wash your hands with soap and warm water after completing this activity.

Think About It

1. **Inferring** What conditions do frog eggs require to develop? How does this affect which types of habitats these animals can live in?
2. **Formulating Hypotheses** How do the characteristics of bird eggs affect which types of habitats birds can live in?

FACTS AND FIGURES

Egg makes life on land possible

Reptiles evolved from a branch of amphibians that were already living on land. However, as the climate became drier at the end of the Carboniferous Period, the amphibians began dying out, because their life cycle required water for fertilization and embryonic development. Reptiles began to diversify and make use of the niche resources once used by amphibians.

Reptiles were more suited to living in drier areas because of internal fertilization and an amniotic egg protected by a shell. The amniotic egg is most important, because it provides the gas exchange, nourishment, and watery environment for the developing embryo. When the young reptile hatches, it looks like a small adult; the larval stage was no longer possible without a watery environment.

31–1 Reptiles

Guide for Reading

 **Key Concepts**
- What are the characteristics of reptiles?
- How are reptiles adapted to life on land?
- What are the four living orders of reptiles?

Vocabulary
ectotherm
amniotic egg
carapace
plastron

Reading Strategy: Outlining Before you read, use the headings in this section to make an outline about reptiles. As you read, add phrases or a sentence about each topic and subtopic in your outline.

Humans have always been fascinated by—and sometimes frightened of—reptiles. Some people fear snakes because of their venomous bites or the way they crawl. Explorers' encounters with lizards and crocodiles inspired images of dragons in European folk tales. Turtles, too, are the subject of many a fable. The truth about reptiles is that they are as astonishing as any creatures of human imagination.

What Is a Reptile?

The basic body plan of a reptile is typical of land vertebrates: a well-developed skull, a backbone and tail, two limb girdles, and four limbs. The iguana in **Figure 31–1** exhibits this body plan. Two types of reptiles have slightly different body plans. Snakes are mostly limbless, while turtles have hard shells that are fused to their vertebrae.

What characteristics do snakes, turtles, and other reptiles share? **A reptile is a vertebrate that has dry, scaly skin, lungs, and terrestrial eggs with several membranes.** These characteristics enable reptiles to live their entire lives out of water, unlike their amphibious relatives.

Reptilian skin is dry and often covered with thick, protective scales. These scales may be smooth or rough. A reptile's body covering helps prevent the loss of body water in dry environments. But dry, waterproof skin can also be a disadvantage to reptiles. Because the tough, scaly layer of skin does not grow when the rest of a reptile grows, it must be shed periodically as the reptile increases in size.

Today, reptiles are widely distributed on Earth. Temperate and tropical areas contain populations of reptiles that are remarkably diverse in appearance and lifestyle. The only places on Earth that most reptiles cannot live in are very cold areas. The reason for this will soon be apparent.

CHECKPOINT *What are the advantages of dry, scaly skin for reptiles?*

▶ **Figure 31–1** **Like all reptiles, this green iguana has lungs and dry, scaly skin.** These characteristics help the iguana live on land.

SECTION RESOURCES (TIME SAVER)

Print:
- ***Laboratory Manual A,*** Chapter 31 Lab
- ***Teaching Resources,*** Lesson Plan 31–1, Adapted Section Summary 31–1, Adapted Worksheets 31–1, Section Summary 31–1, Worksheets 31–1, Section Review 31–1
- ***Reading and Study Workbook A,*** Section 31–1
- ***Adapted Reading and Study Workbook B,*** Section 31–1
- ***Issues and Decision Making,*** Issues and Decisions 34

Technology:
- ***iText,*** Section 31–1
- ***Transparencies Plus,*** Section 31–1

Section 31–1

1 FOCUS

Objectives

31.1.1 ***Describe*** the characteristics of reptiles.
31.1.2 ***Summarize*** the evolution of reptiles.
31.1.3 ***Explain*** how reptiles are adapted to life on land.
31.1.4 ***Identify*** the four living orders of reptiles.

Guide for Reading

Vocabulary Preview

Explain that the term *ectotherm* comes from the Greek words *ecto*, meaning "external," and *therm* meaning "heat." Ask: **How do you think ectothermic animals maintain their body temperature?** *(By interacting with the environment; for example, moving into shade or into sunlight)*

Reading Strategy

Review the structure of an outline. Remind students to include Vocabulary terms and Key Concepts in their outlines.

2 INSTRUCT

What Is a Reptile?

Build Science Skills

Comparing and Contrasting Students can make a Venn diagram to compare the characteristics of amphibians and reptiles. Ask: **Do reptiles and amphibians have any characteristics in common?** *(Answers include lungs, backbone, limbs.)* **In what ways are reptiles better suited to live on land?** *(Scaly, waterproof skin keeps them from drying out; eggs that hatch on land do not need water.)* Encourage students to continue making comparisons between amphibians and reptiles throughout the section. L1 L2

Answer to . . .

CHECKPOINT *The skin protects the body and prevents loss of body water in dry environments.*

31–1 (continued)

Evolution of Reptiles

Word Origins

Saurian describes an animal that has the characteristics of a lizard. L2

Build Science Skills

Using Models Students can organize the sequence of events in the evolution of reptiles by making a timeline. Encourage students to customize their timelines to help them organize particular facts or events. For example, English language learners might wish to include phrases in their native languages. Advanced learners might add additional details about the time periods or the evolutionary steps that are not described in the section. Other students might illustrate their timelines with plants and animals living during the time periods. L2

Make Connections

Environmental Science Explain to students that climate changes always affect plants and animals. Ask: **Why would a change in climate cause some animal populations to decline and others to grow?** *(Animals that cannot adapt to the changes will die out. Those that are more adaptable—more genetically diverse—especially when environmental change is rapid, can better survive in the new climate and will increase in number.)* Discuss the ways in which people have changed many environments in the world. Ask: **How do these changes in the environment affect the plants and animals there?** *(Some cannot adapt to changes and become endangered or extinct. Others are able to thrive in the changes, sometimes even becoming a nuisance.)* You might wish to lead the discussion into a debate about the pros and cons of changing the environment for the benefit of people or for preserving natural habitats for other organisms. L2 L3

Word Origins

Dinosaur is a combination of two Greek words: *deinos,* meaning "terrible," and *sauros,* meaning "lizard." The suffix *-ian* is used to turn a noun into an adjective. The adjective *dinosaurian,* for example, describes a dinosaurlike animal. **What do you think the adjective *saurian* describes?**

Evolution of Reptiles

To colonize dry habitats, animals needed a way to reproduce that did not require depositing eggs into water. Reptiles, which evolved from amphibian-like ancestors, were the first vertebrates to develop this adaptation. The fossil of the first known reptile dates back to the Carboniferous Period, some 350 million years ago. As the Carboniferous Period came to a close and the Permian Period began, Earth's climate became cooler and less humid. Many lakes and swamps dried up, reducing the available habitat for water-dependent amphibians. Under these drier conditions, the first great adaptive radiation of reptiles began. These environmental pressures had a negative impact on the survival of many amphibian populations.

Mammal-like Reptiles By the end of the Permian Period, about 245 million years ago, a great variety of reptiles roamed Earth. One early group was the mammal-like reptiles, which displayed a mix of reptilian and mammalian characteristics. These chordates eventually came to dominate many land habitats. Toward the end of the Triassic Period, about 215 million years ago, another group of reptiles—the dinosaurs—became dominant.

Enter the Dinosaurs During the late Triassic and Jurassic periods, a great adaptive radiation of reptiles took place. The vast diversity and abundance of reptiles during that time are the main reasons why the Mesozoic Era is often called the Age of Reptiles. Two separate groups of large aquatic reptiles swam in the seas. Ancestors of modern turtles, crocodiles, lizards, and snakes populated many land habitats. And dinosaurs were everywhere. **Figure 31–2** shows two dinosaurs, *Plateosauras* and *Coelophysis.* The illustration also shows another kind of reptile, *Teratosaurus.*

▼ **Figure 31–2** In the Triassic Period, reptiles such as these lived in the forests. The herbivorous *Plateosaurus* (left), nibbling on leaves, was a dinosaur, as were the group of carnivorous *Coelophysis* (center). The large carnivorous *Teratosaurus* (right) was a reptile but not a dinosaur. **Observing** ***What characteristics did these reptiles have in common with modern reptiles?***

ESL SUPPORT FOR ENGLISH LANGUAGE LEARNERS

Comprehension: Key Concept

Beginning On the board, rewrite the boldface sentence (page 800) as individual sentences that each express one adaptive characteristic of reptiles, such as, "Strong limbs contributed to the success of reptiles on land." Explain each characteristic. Have students construct a concept circle with "Success of reptiles on land" in the center and the adaptive characteristics linked to the center by lines. L1

Intermediate Read aloud the boldface sentence on page 800. Ask individual students, including some ESL students, to identify characteristics that contributed to reptiles' success. Then, pair ESL students with English-proficient students. Each pair should work together to summarize the contents following one of the green headings (Body Temperature Control, etc.). L2

Problem Solving

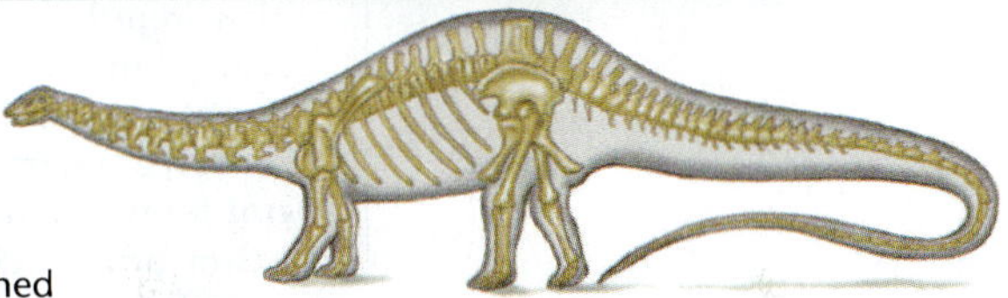

A Massive Controversy

Dinosaurs were the largest animals ever to walk on Earth. The plant-eating dinosaur *Brachiosaurus* reached lengths greater than 22 meters and had a mass of about 50,000 kilograms. It would take about 10 elephants to match the mass of one *Brachiosaurus*. How could the skeleton of such an animal support its immense mass? Imagine that you are a paleontologist searching for an answer to this question. Your job is to examine fossil skeletons of large dinosaurs for clues.

Defining the Problem Use your own words to describe the problem you face.

Organizing Information List the kinds of skeletal adaptations that would help a dinosaur support its mass.

Creating a Solution Carefully study the above illustration of a large dinosaur. Make a model of the part of the spinal column that is supported by the animal's legs. Include the legs in the model. Make another model of an alternative shape for the spinal column, one that is not curved.

Presenting Your Plan Describe what you might do to each model to discover which would support a greater mass. Show how you would test the models. Next to the models, place a card describing the steps in your test.

 **BIIE 1.d, BIIE 1.g**

Dinosaurs ranged in size from small to enormous. They ran on two legs or lumbered along on four. Some, like *Plateosaurus*, ate leafy plants. *Coelophysis* and other hunters traveled in herds. Others, such as duckbilled *Maiasaura*, lived in small family groups, caring for their eggs and young in carefully constructed nests. Certain dinosaurs may even have had feathers, which may have evolved as a means of regulating body temperature. All of the dinosaurs, however, belonged to one of two major groups: the Ornithischia (awr-nuh-THISH-ee-uh), or "bird-hipped" dinosaurs, and the Saurischia (saw-RISH-ee-uh), or "lizard-hipped" dinosaurs. From one of these two branches of dinosaurs, probably the Saurischia, came the earliest members of evolutionary lines that would lead to modern birds.

Exit the Dinosaurs At the end of the Cretaceous Period, about 65 million years ago, a mass extinction occurred worldwide. This extinction was caused by a dramatic series of natural disasters. These disasters probably included a string of massive volcanic eruptions and lava flows, the dropping of sea level, and a huge asteroid or comet smashing into what is now the Yucatán Peninsula in Mexico. The asteroid or comet collision produced major forest fires and enormous dust clouds. After these events, dinosaurs, along with many other animal and plant groups, became extinct. The disappearance of these organisms during the late Cretaceous Period provided opportunities for other kinds of organisms to evolve on land and in the seas.

CHECKPOINT *How did the extinction of the dinosaurs pave the way for modern reptiles?*

For: Links on dinosaur extinction
Visit: www.SciLinks.org
Web Code: cbn-9311

Problem Solving

 **BIIE 1.d, BIIE 1.g**

Scientists used to think that *Brachiosaurus* stayed submerged in water to help support its body weight. However, now scientists know that water pressure at the depths required to cover the body would have prevented the lungs from filling with air. *Brachiosaurus* had a strong, lightweight skeleton with broad, columnar legs that were probably strong enough to support its full weight. L2

Defining the Problem Sample answer: Determine the features of the *Brachiosaurus* skeleton that enabled it to support its mass.

Organizing Information Accept all reasonable responses. These include thick leg bones, legs placed directly under body, quadruped, lightweight vertebral column, large hip bones, and curved backbone.

Creating a Solution Display diagrams of various sauropod skeletons for students to observe. You might also display skeletons of smaller dinosaurs for the sake of comparison. Provide students with materials, such as modeling clay or toothpicks and glue, to make their models. They might also draw sketches of the skeletons instead of building a three-dimensional model.

Presenting Your Plan Most students will describe a test in which they add weight to the top of their skeleton models. Assess the testing plans for logic, clarity, comprehensiveness, and creativity.

Download a worksheet on dinosaur extinction for students to complete, and find additional teacher support from NSTA SciLinks.

BIOLOGY UPDATE

Evidence for extinction

The impact that made the Chicxulub crater in the Yucatán Peninsula is thought by some to have caused the mass extinction at the end of the Cretaceous Period. Recently, a planetary geoscientist, Peter Schultz, analyzed the Chicxulub crater and compared it to craters on the moon, Venus, and Mercury. He concluded that the asteroid hit Earth at an angle pointing toward the northwest. He theorizes that a huge cloud of hot vapor continued northwest, instantly setting fire to most of North America. This scenario helps explain why the extinction rate of plants in North America was at least triple that in the rest of the world. It also explains why land species living in North America were nine times more likely to become extinct than aquatic species. This hypothesis will require further substantiating evidence.

Answers to . . .

CHECKPOINT *The extinction provided opportunities for other kinds of organisms to evolve.*

Figure 31–2 *Backbone; lungs; dry, scaly skin; terrestrial eggs*

31–1 (continued)

Form and Function in Reptiles

Demonstration

Demonstrate how ectothermic animals control their body temperature by placing a rock under a heat lamp, a rock in cool water, and a rock in a shady spot. Have students predict the relative temperatures of the tops of the rocks in each location. Then, read the temperature of each location on a thermometer. *(The rock under the heat lamp will be warmest.)* Discuss different ways in which students keep themselves warm or cool. Then, relate their behaviors to the behaviors of ectotherms in controlling their body temperature. L2

Build Science Skills

Observing If you have a reptile as a classroom pet, give students the opportunity to observe it feeding. Invite students to point out any special adaptations the reptile has for getting and eating food. For example, snakes have fangs to deliver poison to their prey or to hold the prey while swallowing it. Challenge students to classify the reptile as a carnivore or a herbivore. Have them infer the structure of its digestive system based on its feeding mode. *(Herbivores have longer digestive tracts.)* L1 L2

Form and Function in Reptiles

Most reptiles have adapted to a fully terrestrial life. Tough, scaly skin is one adaptation to this type of life. **Well-developed lungs; a double-loop circulatory system; a water-conserving excretory system; strong limbs; internal fertilization; and shelled, terrestrial eggs are the other adaptations that have contributed to the success of reptiles on land.** In addition, reptiles can control their body temperature by moving to a different place.

Body Temperature Control The ability to control their body temperature is an enormous asset for active animals. All the animals that you have read about so far are ectotherms (EK-toh-thurmz). **Ectotherms** rely on behavior to help control body temperature. Turtles, snakes, and other modern reptiles are all ectotherms. To warm up, they bask in the sun during the day or stay under water at night. To cool down, they move to the shade, go for a swim, or take shelter in underground burrows.

▲ **Figure 31–3** The gaboon viper, like all snakes, is entirely carnivorous. It eats mice and other small mammals by stretching its jaws wide and swallowing its prey whole. **Inferring** *Besides feeding, what other function might fangs serve in snakes?*

Feeding Reptiles eat a wide range of foods. Iguanas, which are herbivores, tear plants into shreds and swallow the tough, fibrous chunks. Their long digestive systems enable them to break down plant material. Many other reptiles are carnivores. Snakes, for example, prey on small animals, bird eggs, or even other snakes, grabbing them with their jaws and swallowing them whole as shown in **Figure 31–3.** Crocodiles and alligators eat fish and even land animals when they can catch them. Most reptiles eat insects. Chameleons have sticky tongues as long as their bodies that flip out to catch insects.

Respiration The lungs of reptiles are spongy, providing more gas-exchange area than those of amphibians. This isn't surprising, because most reptiles cannot exchange gases through their skin the way many moist-skinned amphibians do. Many reptiles have muscles around their ribs that expand the chest cavity to inhale and collapse the cavity to force air out. Several species of crocodiles also have flaps of skin that can separate the mouth from the nasal passages, allowing these crocodiles to breathe through their nostrils while their mouth remains open. To exchange gases with the environment, reptiles have two efficient lungs or, in the case of certain species of snakes, one lung.

Circulation Reptiles have an efficient double-loop circulatory system. One of the loops brings blood to and from the lungs, and the other loop brings blood to and from the rest of the body. The diagram in **Figure 31–4** shows how blood flows through a turtle's heart. Reptile hearts contain two atria and either one or two ventricles. Most reptiles have a single ventricle with a partial septum, or wall, that helps separate oxygen-rich and oxygen-poor blood during the pumping cycle. Crocodiles and alligators, however, have the most developed hearts of living reptiles. The heart consists of two atria and two ventricles—an arrangement that is also found in birds and mammals.

BIO INSIGHTS **FACTS AND FIGURES**

Maintaining body temperature

All animals have a specific internal temperature at which their muscles respond best. If body temperature becomes too high, muscles tire easily and other body systems are stressed. Ectothermic animals generally have relatively low metabolic rates when they are resting. Because of this, they do not generate much internal heat and much of this heat is lost because they don't have insulation, like hair or feathers. Controlling body temperature requires heat from the environment. So, for example, a lizard might bask in the sun to warm up. Once its body reaches a certain temperature, it will move around, going about its business. The action of its muscles generates more heat. If the lizard becomes too warm, it will find a shady place to lose heat.

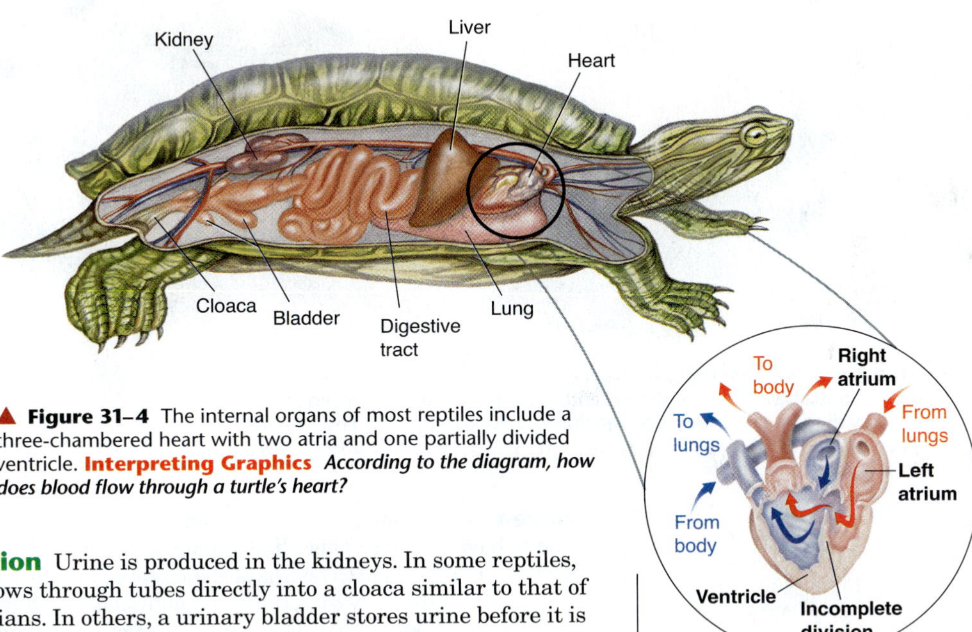

▲ **Figure 31–4** The internal organs of most reptiles include a three-chambered heart with two atria and one partially divided ventricle. **Interpreting Graphics** *According to the diagram, how does blood flow through a turtle's heart?*

Excretion Urine is produced in the kidneys. In some reptiles, urine flows through tubes directly into a cloaca similar to that of amphibians. In others, a urinary bladder stores urine before it is expelled from the cloaca.

Reptiles' urine contains either ammonia or uric acid. Reptiles that live mainly in water, such as crocodiles and alligators, excrete most of their nitrogenous wastes in the form of ammonia, a toxic compound. Crocodiles and alligators drink a large amount of water, which dilutes the ammonia in the urine and helps carry it away. In contrast, many other reptiles—especially those that live entirely on land—do not excrete ammonia directly. Instead, they convert ammonia into a compound called uric acid. Uric acid is much less toxic than ammonia, so it does not have to be diluted as much. In these reptiles, excess water is absorbed in the cloaca, reducing urine to crystals of uric acid that form a pasty white solid. By eliminating wastes that contain little water, a reptile can conserve water.

Response The basic pattern of a reptile's brain is similar to that of an amphibian, although the cerebrum and cerebellum are considerably larger compared to the rest of the brain. Reptiles that are active during the day tend to have complex eyes and can see color well. Many snakes also have an extremely good sense of smell. In addition to a pair of nostrils, most reptiles have a pair of sensory organs in the roof of the mouth that can detect chemicals when the reptiles flick their tongues. Reptiles have simple ears with an external eardrum and a single bone that conducts sound to the inner ear. Snakes can also pick up vibrations in the ground through bones in their skulls. Some snakes, such as the viper in **Figure 31–5**, have the extraordinary ability to detect the body heat of their prey.

CHECKPOINT *How does a reptile's brain compare to an amphibian's?*

▼ **Figure 31–5** The heat-sensitive pits above this eyelash viper's mouth enable it to locate prey, even in total darkness. Snakes that have these pits are commonly called pit vipers. **Inferring** *How would these organs give pit vipers an advantage over other reptiles?*

Use Visuals

Figure 31–4 Have students trace the path of blood through the heart. Make sure they understand that the circulatory system has two loops, just as the amphibian circulatory system has. Point out that oxygenated blood from the lungs and deoxygenated blood from the body go through the single ventricle at the same time. Ask: **What structure in the ventricle helps separate oxygen-rich and oxygen-poor blood?** *(Partial internal walls in the ventricle)* **Which reptiles have two ventricles instead of one?** *(Crocodiles and alligators)* L1 L2

BIO INSIGHTS — FACTS AND FIGURES

Excreting nitrogenous wastes

Excess amino acids cannot be stored or excreted. They are broken down and used as fuel for the body. Ammonia is produced when amino acids are broken down. Cells cannot survive high concentrations of ammonia. To be transported without harming cells, 1 gram of ammonia must be dissolved in 300 to 500 mL of water. In many small aquatic animals, ammonia simply diffuses from their body tissues directly into the water. Terrestrial animals, however, must conserve water. Most reptiles convert ammonia to uric acid. Uric acid is less toxic than ammonia and less soluble. One gram of uric acid needs only 10 mL of water to be transported. In the excretory system, most of the water is returned to the body, and solid crystals of uric acid are removed as a thick paste.

Answers to . . .

CHECKPOINT *It is similar, although the cerebrum and cerebellum are proportionally larger.*

Figure 31–3 *Protection from predators*

Figure 31–4 *From body to right atrium to ventricle to lungs to left atrium to ventricle to body*

Figure 31–5 *They can supplement chemical senses with an ability to sense heat from prey and thus locate prey.*

Build Science Skills

Comparing and Contrasting Give students the opportunity to compare and contrast the positions of limbs in amphibians and reptiles. Students will probably have the best success comparing lizards and salamanders. You might provide three-dimensional models of the animals, schematic diagrams, or photographs. Challenge students to develop a method to quantitate the differences by determining the angles of attachment. L2

Build Science Skills

Inferring Challenge students to make inferences about the relative survival rates of oviparous and ovoviviparous reptilian embryos. Ask: **Which embryos are more likely to survive: turtle eggs abandoned in nests or lizard eggs inside the mother's body?** *(Lizard eggs; better protected from predators)* **What adaptive advantage does an ovoviviparous reptile have over an oviparous one?** *(There is a greater chance of eggs hatching, so it can produce fewer eggs. But point out that the final result may be about the same. In both oviparous and ovoviviparous species, enough survive to perpetuate the species. The oviparous species spend energy producing eggs, whereas the ovoviviparous species spend energy protecting their young.)* L2

Figure 31–6 The shovel-snouted lizard (left) is not moving forward; rather, it lifts its feet to limit contact with the hot desert sand. The sidewinding adder propels itself forward by digging its ventral scales against the dunes while pushing its body into long curving waves. **Comparing and Contrasting** *How are the lizard's legs different from those of an amphibian?*

Movement Compared with most amphibians, reptiles with legs tend to have larger, stronger limbs that enable them to walk, run, burrow, swim, or climb. The legs of some reptiles are also rotated further under the body than those of amphibians, enabling reptiles to carry more body weight. The legs and feet of many aquatic turtles have developed into flippers. **Figure 31–6** shows some ways that reptiles can move. As with amphibians, the backbones of reptiles help accomplish much of their movement.

▼ **Figure 31–7** After a female box turtle digs a hole in the ground for her nest, she lays her eggs, dropping them one by one and gently lowering them into the hole with her hind feet. When she finishes, she will cover up her nest and leave without a backward glance. **Inferring** *Why would it be an advantage for turtles to lay a large number of eggs?*

Reproduction All reptiles reproduce by internal fertilization, in which the male deposits sperm inside the body of the female. Most male reptiles have a penislike organ that allows them to deliver sperm into the female's cloaca. After fertilization has occurred, the female's reproductive system covers the embryos with several membranes and a leathery shell.

Most reptiles are oviparous, laying eggs that develop outside the mother's body. Some species, such as the box turtle in **Figure 31–7,** lay their eggs in carefully prepared nests, then abandon them. Alligators also lay their eggs in nests, but they guard the eggs until they hatch, and provide some care after hatching. Some snakes and lizards are ovoviviparous, and the young are born alive. By carrying her eggs within her body, the female can protect the eggs and keep them warm.

Unlike an amphibian egg, which almost always needs to develop in water, the shell and membranes of a reptilian egg create a protected environment in which the embryo can develop without drying out. This type of egg is called an **amniotic** (am-nee-AHT-ik) **egg,** named after the amnion, one of the four membranes that surrounds the developing embryo. The other three membranes are the yolk sac, the chorion, and the allantois. Find each of these membranes in **Figure 31–8** and learn about their functions. The amniotic egg, also seen in birds, is one of the most important adaptations to life on land.

CHECKPOINT *What are the four membranes of an amniotic egg?*

FACTS AND FIGURES

Reptilian mothers

Surprisingly, alligators and crocodiles are very motherly reptiles. They build a nest with mud, sticks, and vegetation. This "compost pile" incubates the eggs as the vegetation breaks down. The mother stays near the nest, protecting it from predators. A large percentage of eggs hatch because of this protection. When the mother hears the babies squeaking after hatching, she uncovers the nest and picks up the babies in her mouth. Sometimes she carries the babies to water for food and protection. Baby alligators and crocodiles often stay together in groups, called pods, for their first year. During that year, they are highly susceptible to predators, but their mothers often stay nearby to provide protection.

Figure 31–8 The Amniotic Egg

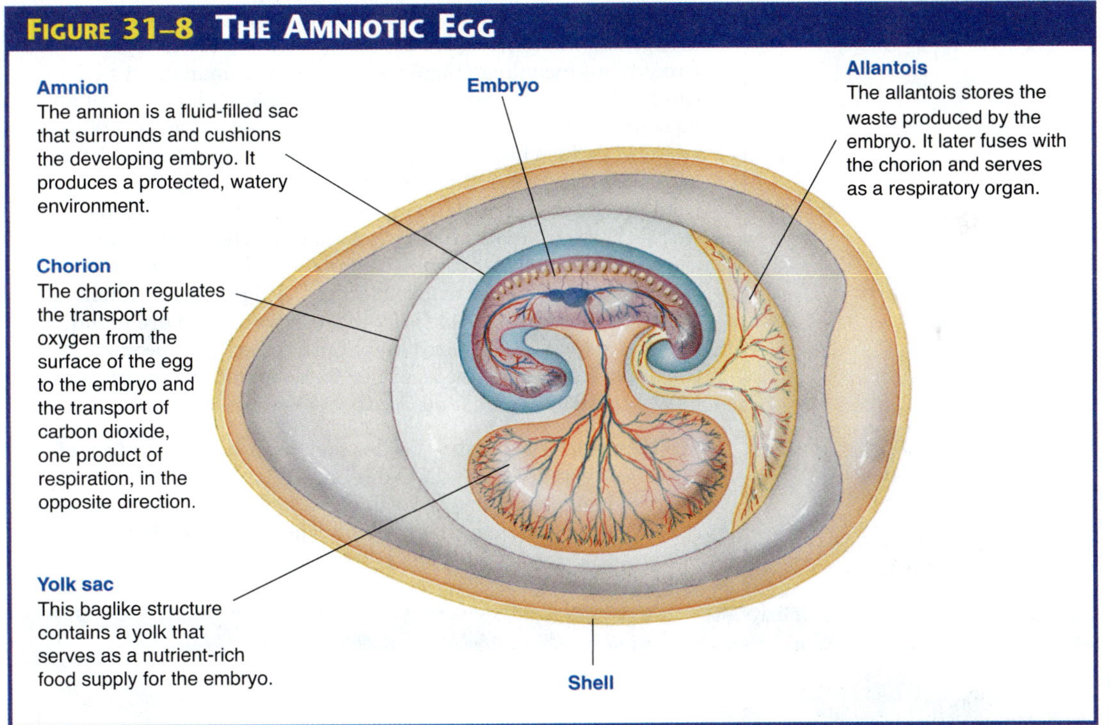

▲ An amniotic egg contains several membranes and an external shell. Although it is waterproof, the egg shell is porous, allowing gases to pass through. The shell of reptile eggs is usually soft and leathery.  **The amniotic egg is one of the most important adaptations to life on dry land.**

Groups of Reptiles

Since the dinosaurs disappeared, modern reptiles have had plenty of time and space to diversify. **The four surviving groups of reptiles are lizards and snakes, crocodilians, turtles and tortoises, and the tuatara (too-uh-TAH-ruh).**

Lizards and Snakes Modern lizards and snakes belong to the order Squamata (skwa-MAH-tuh), or scaly reptiles. Most lizards have legs, clawed toes, external ears, and movable eyelids. Some lizards have evolved into highly specialized forms. For example, Gila (HEE-luh) monsters—large, stocky lizards that live in the southwestern United States and Mexico—have glands in the lower jaw that produce venom for defense against predators.

Snakes have lost both pairs of legs during the course of their evolution. Although they are legless, snakes are highly efficient predators, even in the ocean. Some snakes are so small that they resemble earthworms. Others, such as some species of python, can grow to more than 8 meters in length. The ability of certain snakes to produce venom has caused some people to harbor an unjustified fear of all snakes. More people in the United States die from bee stings than from snakebites. In fact, snakes tend to avoid people, not confront them!

Use Visuals

Figure 31–8 Review the structure and function of the amniotic egg. Then, compare the amphibian egg to the reptilian amniotic egg. Ask: **How do the parts of the amniotic egg enable it to survive on land?** *(Shell: protects from drying out; allantois and chorion: gas exchange and waste storage; yolk sac: food for embryo; amnion: water environment to cushion embryo)* **Why are reptiles completely independent of water for reproduction?** *(Internal fertilization and amniotic egg)* L1 L2

Groups of Reptiles

Build Science Skills

Using Models When students have learned about the four groups of reptiles, challenge them to choose one reptilian order and create a model of their own reptile based on the characteristics of the group. Students can illustrate their models, or they can create models from clay or other materials. Have students present their models to the class. Challenge other students to classify each model into a group based on its characteristics. L2

BIO INSIGHTS — FACTS AND FIGURES

Color, shape, and regeneration
Lizards have many adaptations to help them survive. Geckos, for example, have pads on their toes to help them cling to trees and move across diverse terrain speedily to escape predators. Geckos can also cast off their tails if grabbed by a predator. The tailless gecko escapes, and its tail will quickly regenerate. Some lizards blend into the environment to escape predators. Anoles and chameleons change their skin color when frightened or alarmed. The change in skin color can startle a predator or enable the lizard to better blend into its environment. The frilled dragon is a lizard with a frill of skin around its neck. When startled, it extends and opens up the frill, making itself appear larger and more fearsome than it really is.

Answers to . . .

CHECKPOINT *Amnion, yolk sac, chorion, and allantois*

Figure 31–6 *The lizard's legs are stronger and larger than those of an amphibian and rotated further under the body.*

Figure 31–7 *To increase the chance that some will survive predation, because turtles do not protect their young from predators*

31–1 (continued)

Use Visuals

Figure 31–9 Have student volunteers match each reptile pictured to its order. Ask: **How do snakes differ from lizards?** *(Snakes are legless.)* **Why are tuataras in a separate order from snakes and lizards?** *(Tuataras lack external ears, have primitive scales, and have a "third eye.")* L1 L2

Build Science Skills

Classifying Display pictures of a snapping turtle, a sea turtle, a tortoise, and a painted turtle. Challenge students to identify which live on land *(tortoise)* and which live in water *(snapping turtle, painted turtle, sea turtle)*. Make sure students give reasons for their classifications by identifying the adaptations or characteristics that they used for classification. L2

Build Science Skills

Inferring Challenge students to infer why tuataras still exist. Discuss the possible causes of the mass extinction at the end of the Cretaceous Period and the location of New Zealand. Ask: **How might an island location contribute to the survival of the tuatara?** *(Tuataras were isolated from predators and from competition for resources by better adapted animals.)* L2

▼ The four orders of living reptiles are the Squamata, Crocodilia, Testudines, and Sphenodonta. **The common names of these modern reptile groups are lizards and snakes, crocodilians, turtles and tortoises, and the tuatara.**

Crocodilians Examples of crocodilians and other reptile groups are shown in **Figure 31–9.** Any member of the order Crocodilia—including alligators, crocodiles, caimans, and gavials—can easily be recognized by its long and typically broad snout and its squat appearance. Crocodilians are fierce carnivores that prey on animals such as fishes, deer, and even humans. Crocodilians are very protective of their young. The females guard their eggs from predators. After the eggs are hatched, the mother gently carries her young to a nursery area and watches over them.

Crocodilians live only in the tropics and subtropics, where the climate remains warm year-round. Alligators, and their relatives the caimans, live only in fresh water and are found almost exclusively in North and South America. Crocodiles, on the other hand, may live in either fresh or salt water and are native to Africa, India, and Southeast Asia.

Turtles and Tortoises Turtles and tortoises are members of the order Testudines (tes-TOO-dih-neez). The name *turtle* usually refers to members of this order that live in water; the name *tortoise* refers to those that live on land. A terrapin is a turtle that is found in water that is somewhat salty.

Figure 31–9 Diversity of Reptiles

BIOLOGY UPDATE

Saving sea turtles
Sea turtles have inhabited Earth's oceans for millions of years. However, their existence on Earth is threatened. Their demise has been caused by many different factors, but all of them are the result of human activity. Sea turtles are hunted directly for their meat, eggs, leather, and shells. They are harmed indirectly by their accidental capture in fishing nets, by ingestion of trash, by polluted ocean water, and by the loss of nesting sites. Many laws have been enacted to help protect sea turtles. Recently, several nations from North and South America ratified a treaty to protect sea turtles. A multinational treaty is necessary, because sea turtles have large migratory routes. Identifying these migratory routes has been made easier by tagging turtles with satellite global positioning transmitters.

Turtles and tortoises have a shell built into the skeleton, although in a few species the shell is not very hard. The shell consists of two parts: a dorsal part, or **carapace,** and a ventral part, or **plastron.** The animal's backbone forms the center of the carapace. The head, legs, and tail stick out through holes where the carapace and plastron join. Tortoises and most turtles pull into their shells to protect themselves.

Several other adaptations allow turtles and tortoises to live in a wide range of habitats—dry, wet, and in-between. Lacking teeth, these reptiles have horny ridges that cover the upper and lower jaws. The jaws are often powerful enough to deliver a damaging bite. All possess strong limbs that lift their body off the ground when walking or, in the case of sea turtles, to drag themselves across a sandy shore to lay eggs.

Tuataras The tuatara is the only surviving member of the order Sphenodonta (sfen-uh-DONT-uh). It is found only on a few small islands off the coast of New Zealand. Tuataras resemble lizards, but they differ from lizards in many ways. For example, they lack external ears and retain primitive scales. Tuataras also have a legendary "third eye," which is part of a complex organ located on top of the brain. This eye can sense the level of sunlight, but its function is unknown.

▲ **Figure 31–10** This wildlife ranger is retrieving green sea turtle eggs on Turtle Island National Park in Borneo. He will bring the eggs to an incubation station, where they can hatch safe from harm. After hatching, the young turtles will be released to the sea. **Inferring** *What might harm sea turtle eggs that are left on a beach to hatch?*

Ecology of Reptiles

Many reptiles are in danger because their habitats have been, and are being, destroyed. In addition, humans hunt reptiles for food, to sell as pets, and for their skins, from which bags, boots, and combs are made. Laws now protect some species, such as sea turtles, which were once numerous in both the Atlantic and Pacific oceans. Sea turtle recovery programs, such as the one shown in **Figure 31–10,** give many young turtles a head start on survival. Although there are many other programs in place that protect reptiles, more conservation efforts are needed worldwide to counteract their dwindling numbers.

31–1 Section Assessment

1. **Key Concept** List the main characteristics of reptiles.
2. **Key Concept** List five ways that reptiles are adapted to life on dry land.
3. **Key Concept** Name the four orders of modern reptiles and give an example of each.
4. How is excretion carried out in reptiles that live on land?
5. How does a lizard control its body temperature?
6. **Critical Thinking Predicting** What might happen to reptiles if conditions on Earth became permanently warmer and much damper?

Focus on the BIG Idea

Interdependence in Nature In Chapter 4, you learned about different biomes, including deserts. In Chapter 30, you learned about the characteristics of amphibians. Use this knowledge to explain why more reptiles than amphibians can tolerate the hot, dry climate of deserts.

31–1 Section Assessment

1. Vertebrate, scaly skin, lungs, amniotic egg
2. Any five: lungs, double-loop circulatory system, strong limbs, efficient excretory system, shelled eggs, internal fertilization
3. Squamata: lizard, snake; Crocodilia: alligator, crocodile, caiman, gavial; Testudines: turtle, tortoise; Sphenodonta: tuatara
4. They convert ammonia to uric acid.
5. By basking in the sun, moving to shade, resting under water, or moving to burrows
6. Some reptiles might colonize areas that are now too cold for them. Others might die out if they cannot successfully compete with damp-loving competitors, such as amphibians.

Ecology of Reptiles

Make Connections

Environmental Science Make sure students realize how human activity can change the environment to make it unfavorable for species living there. Ask: **How might sea turtles be affected if the beaches on which they lay their eggs become popular tourist beaches?** *(Eggs have a greater chance of being destroyed; fewer sea turtles will hatch and grow to adulthood.)* L2

3 ASSESS

Evaluate Understanding

Play a quiz game in which you give students the answers and they give you the questions. Focus on adaptations that enable reptiles to live on land and the features of the four reptile groups.

Reteach

Instruct students to draw a diagram of a typical reptile that shows the main characteristics of reptiles. They should also show how reptiles are adapted to live on land.

Focus on the BIG Idea 

Students should explain that reptiles are well adapted to live in a hot, dry desert climate because they have many water-conserving adaptations. For example, reptiles can reproduce in the absence of water because of internal fertilization and the amniotic egg. Their efficient excretory system helps to conserve water, as does their scaly skin. Well-developed lungs eliminate the need for gas exchange through moist skin.

interactive Textbook

If your class subscribes to the iText, use it to review the Key Concepts in Section 31–1.

Answer to . . .

Figure 31–10 *Predators, storms, human activities*

Section 31–2

1 FOCUS

Objectives

31.2.1 ***Describe*** the characteristics that all birds have in common.

31.2.2 ***Summarize*** the evolution of birds.

31.2.3 ***Explain*** how birds are adapted for flight.

31.2.4 ***Describe*** the diversity of birds.

31.2.5 ***Identify*** ways in which birds interact with the environment and with humans.

Guide for Reading

Vocabulary Preview

Have students compare *endotherm* to *ectotherm.* Ask: **If *endo-* means "within," how does an endotherm control its body temperature?** *(Endotherms generate their own body heat; they control body temperature from within.)*

Reading Strategy

Before students read this section, have them preview Figure 31–14. Instruct them to list characteristics common to all birds. As students read, encourage them to add or subtract characteristics to complete their list.

2 INSTRUCT

What Is a Bird?

Use Visuals

Figure 31–11 Have students compare and contrast the structure and function of contour and down feathers. Ask: **Which feathers insulate a bird's body?** *(Down)* **Which feathers help the bird to fly?** *(Contour)* Discuss how the structure of down feathers makes them good for insulation. Ask: **Would you expect a bird with only down feathers to fly?** *(No; down feathers do not give the stability needed for flight.)* L1 L2

31–2 Birds

Guide for Reading

Key Concepts

- What characteristics do all birds have in common?
- How are birds adapted for flight?

Vocabulary

feather
endotherm
crop
gizzard
air sac

Reading Strategy: Monitoring Your Understanding

As you read, make sure that you understand what you read. If you have difficulty, think of a strategy that might make the text clearer. For example, you might read the paragraph again, slowly; see whether an illustration helps you understand the printed text; or ask another student or your teacher for help.

Whether they are greeting the dawn with song or coloring the air with brilliant feathers, birds are among the most obvious and welcome of all animals. From common robins to the spectacular and rare quetzal of Central America, the nearly 10,000 modern bird species seem to live everywhere.

What Is a Bird?

In a group this diverse, it is difficult to find many characteristics that are shared by all members. But we can identify the features that most birds have in common. **Birds are reptilelike animals that maintain a constant internal body temperature. They have an outer covering of feathers; two legs that are covered with scales and are used for walking or perching; and front limbs modified into wings.** Most of these features are adaptations for flight.

The single most important characteristic that separates birds from living reptiles, and from all other living animals, is feathers. **Feathers** are made mostly of protein and develop from pits in the birds' skin. Feathers help birds fly and also keep them warm. **Figure 31–11** shows the two main types of feathers: contour feathers and down feathers. Herons and some other birds that live on or in water also have powder down, which releases a fine powder that repels water.

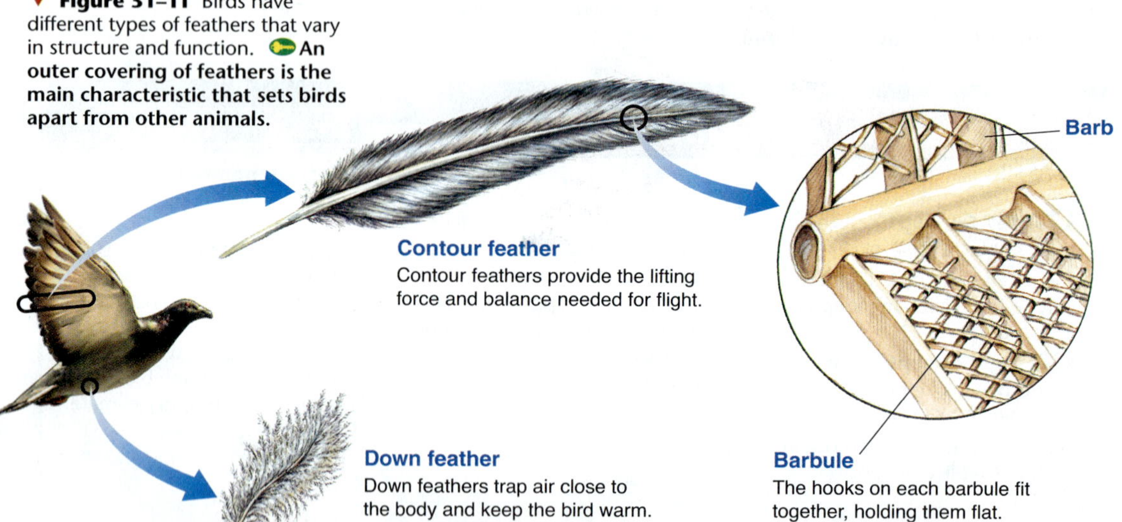

▼ **Figure 31–11** Birds have different types of feathers that vary in structure and function. **An outer covering of feathers is the main characteristic that sets birds apart from other animals.**

SECTION RESOURCES

Print:

- ***Laboratory Manual B,*** Chapter 31 Lab
- ***Teaching Resources,*** Lesson Plan 31–2, Adapted Section Summary 31–2, Adapted Worksheets 31–2, Section Summary 31–2, Worksheets 31–2, Section Review 31–2, Enrichment
- ***Reading and Study Workbook A,*** Section 31–2
- ***Adapted Reading and Study Workbook B,*** Section 31–2
- ***Lab Worksheets,*** Chapter 31 Exploration
- ***Issues and Decision Making,*** Issues and Decisions 13

Technology:

- ***iText,*** Section 31–2
- ***Transparencies Plus,*** Section 31–2

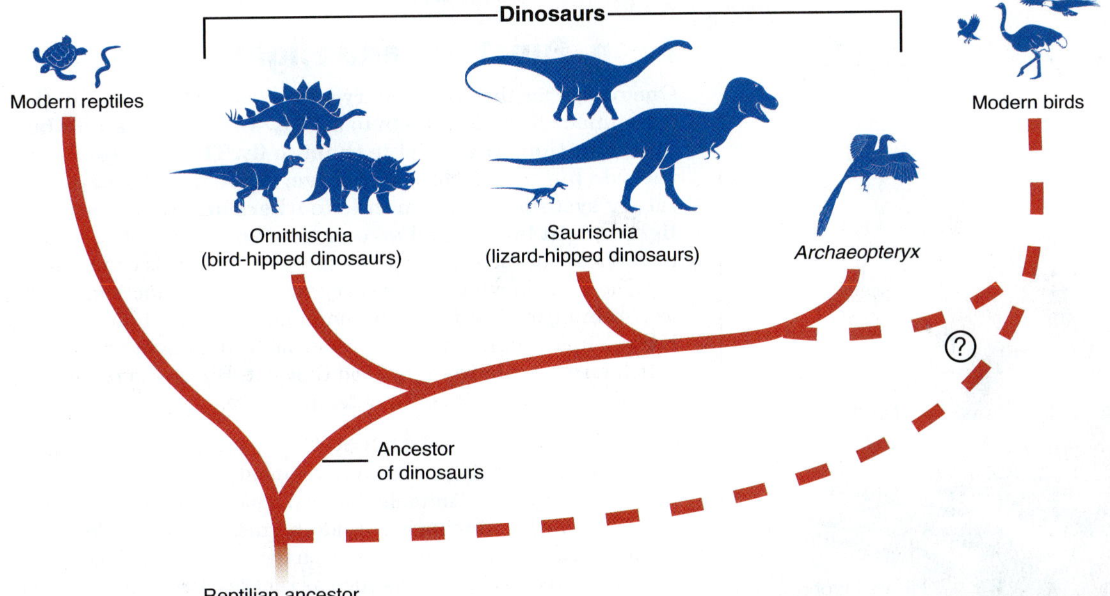

Evolution of Birds

Paleontologists agree that birds evolved from extinct reptiles. Evidence for this hypothesis is provided by many embryological, anatomical, and physiological characteristics shared by modern birds and living reptiles. For example, the embryos of birds and reptiles develop within amniotic eggs. Birds, like most reptiles, excrete nitrogenous wastes in the form of uric acid. The bones that support the front and hind limbs, and several other parts of the skeleton, are similar in both groups.

Most paleontologists think that birds evolved directly from dinosaurs. Part of the evidence consists of *Archaeopteryx* (ahr-kee-AHP-tur-iks), the first birdlike fossil discovered. This fossil dates from the late Jurassic Period, about 150 million years ago. *Archaeopteryx* looked so much like a small, running dinosaur that it would be classified as a dinosaur except for one important feature: It had well-developed feathers covering most of its body. Those feathers led to the classification of *Archaeopteryx* as an early bird. Unlike modern birds, however, this creature had teeth in its beak, a bony tail, and toes and claws on its wings. Thus, *Archaeopteryx* can be seen as a transitional species with characteristics of both dinosaurs and birds.

However, other fossil evidence leads some researchers to hypothesize that birds and dinosaurs both evolved from an earlier common ancestor. The origin of birds is still not completely resolved, as shown in the evolutionary tree in **Figure 31–12.** New fossils of ancient birds are being found all the time.

 *What is* Archaeopteryx*?*

▲ **Figure 31–12** The diagram at the top shows the evolutionary tree of modern birds. None of the animals shown are direct ancestors of modern birds. But fossils such as *Archaeopteryx* (above) do show a mixture of characteristics of birds and dinosaurs. **Interpreting Graphics** ***Based on the diagram, what are the two alternative explanations for the evolution of modern birds?***

Evolution of Birds

Use Visuals

Figure 31–12 Have students examine Figure 31–12. Ask: **In what ways was *Archaeopteryx* similar to modern birds?** *(It had feathers.)* **How was it similar to dinosaurs?** *(It had teeth in its beak, a bony tail, and toes and claws on its wings.)* **Why do you think many scientists infer that birds evolved from dinosaurs?** *(Discoveries of many birdlike dinosaur fossils, showing characteristics of both dinosaurs and birds)* L1 L2

Build Science Skills

Inferring Remind students that many researchers believe birds evolved directly from dinosaurs, based on the evidence found in fossilized species. Challenge students to infer what kind of fossilized evidence researchers would expect to find if birds and dinosaurs had instead evolved from a common ancestor. *(If birds and dinosaurs each evolved from a common ancestor, you would not expect to find any fossilized species that are intermediate between birds and dinosaurs.)* Students can write a short report that describes their inference and the evidence or background information on which they based their inference. L2 L3

UNIVERSAL ACCESS

Inclusion/Special Needs
Pair visually impaired students with other students and have them work together to make observations about the characteristics of birds. Make available different types of feathers, various avian bones and skulls, or any three-dimensional bird model. The sighted student can identify structures as the visually impaired student tactilely examines their textures and shapes. L1

Less Proficient Readers
Students can review the process of digestion in birds by making a flowchart. Students should include every part of the digestive system in which something happens to food. They should start with the mouth and end with the cloaca. 

Answers to . . .

CHECKPOINT *Birdlike species with characteristics of both dinosaurs and birds*

Figure 31–12 *Either evolved from dinosaurs or from a reptilian ancestor common to dinosaurs and birds*

31–2 (continued)

Form, Function, and Flight

Build Science Skills

Predicting Give student groups 10 to 15 pictures of various birds. Instruct groups to predict which birds fly and which do not. Next, have students predict which of the flying birds are the best fliers. After making their predictions, groups should list the characteristics they used for making their predictions. Then, tell students the answers. Encourage them to review their predictions and the criteria they used to make them. Ask groups if they would change any of the criteria they used to make their predictions and why. L2

Make Connections

Physics Let students experiment to discover how insulation helps conserve heat. Allow student groups to brainstorm for a list of materials that would be good insulators. Then, have students test these materials by observing how well they can keep a warm object warm. Students might devise a plan as simple as wrapping a jar of hot water with the material and measuring the water temperature over time to determine how much heat is lost. The better the insulator, the less heat is lost. Ask: **What quality determines the best insulators?** *(Often the best insulators trap the most air around an object.)* L2 L3

Use Community Resources

Arrange a field trip to an aviary or a display of stuffed birds at a natural history museum. Challenge students to identify the type of food each bird eats based on the shape of its bill. L2

Form, Function, and Flight

One reason for the evolutionary success of birds is found in the adaptations that allow them to fly. **Birds have a number of adaptations that enable them to fly. These adaptations include highly efficient digestive, respiratory, and circulatory systems; aerodynamic feathers and wings; strong, lightweight bones; and strong chest muscles.** Most birds have these characteristics, even though some birds cannot fly.

The ways in which birds carry out their life functions, such as obtaining food and oxygen, contribute to their ability to fly. For example, flight requires an enormous amount of energy, which birds obtain from the food they eat. Birds also require energy to maintain their body temperature.

Body Temperature Control Unlike reptiles, which must draw body warmth from their environment, birds can generate their own body heat. Animals that can generate their own body heat are called **endotherms.** Endotherms, which include birds, mammals, and some other animals, have a high rate of metabolism compared to ectotherms such as reptiles. Recall that metabolism is the sum of chemical and physical processes that go on inside the body. Metabolism produces heat. A bird's feathers insulate its body enough to conserve most of its metabolic energy, allowing the bird to warm its body more efficiently. The body temperature of most birds is about 41°C even on cold winter days.

CHECKPOINT *What is an endotherm?*

Feeding Any body heat that a bird loses must be regained by eating food. The more food a bird eats, the more heat energy its metabolism can generate. Because small birds lose heat relatively faster than large ones, small birds must eat more, relative to their body size. In fact, the phrase "eats like a bird" is quite misleading, because most birds are voracious eaters!

As you can see in **Figure 31–13**, birds' beaks, or bills, are adapted to the type of food they eat. Insect-eating birds have short, fine bills that can pick ants and other insects off leaves and branches, or can catch flying insects. Seed-eaters have short, thick bills. Carnivorous birds, such as eagles, shred their prey with strong hooked bills. Long, thin bills can be used for gathering nectar from flowers or probing soft mud for worms and shellfish. Large, long bills help birds to pick fruit from branches, while long, flat bills are used to grasp fish.

Figure 31–13 Bird bills come in a variety of shapes and sizes. You can tell a good deal about a bird's feeding habits from its bill. **Drawing Conclusions** ***Based on the size and shape of its bill, what does a roseate spoonbill feed on?***

TEACHER TO TEACHER

Teachers can use skeletal features to demonstrate the similarities between reptiles and birds. Display skeletons of a typical lizard, a pigeon, and a plaster model of *Archaeopteryx lithographica*. Lead students through a discussion of typical reptilian skeletal characteristics—toothed jaws, lizardlike tail, and so forth—and indicate where they are found in *Archaeopteryx*. Finally, show where the various characteristics persist in such modern birds as the pigeon and indicate characteristics that have been lost, such as teeth.

—William C. Alexander, Chairman
Division of Science and Mathematics
SC Governor's School for Science and Mathematics
Hartsville, SC

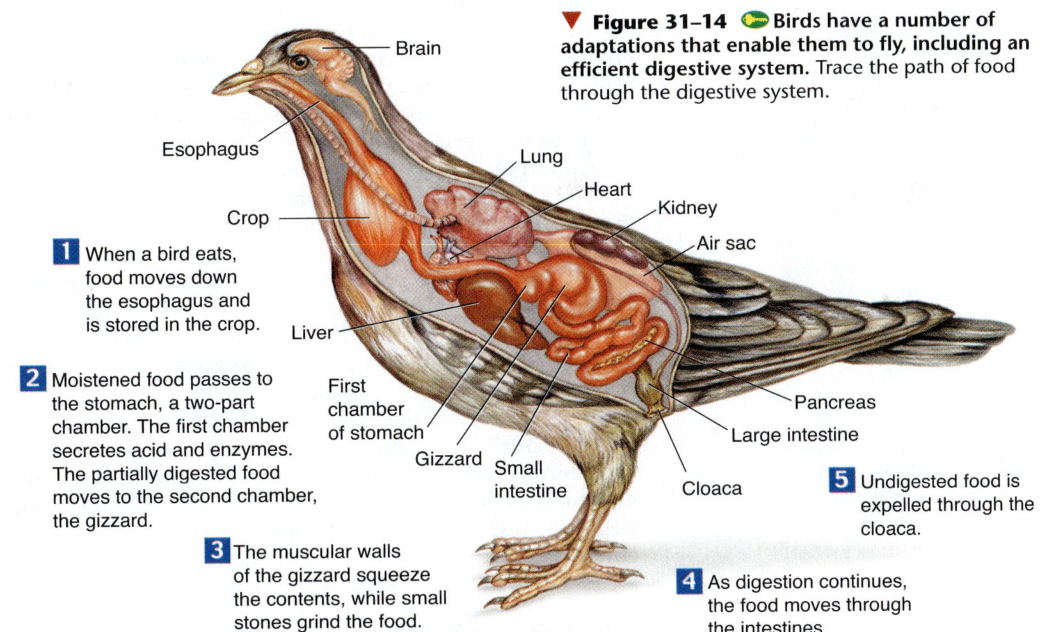

▼ **Figure 31–14** **Birds have a number of adaptations that enable them to fly, including an efficient digestive system.** Trace the path of food through the digestive system.

The digestive system of a bird is shown in **Figure 31–14.** Birds lack teeth, and therefore they cannot break down food by chewing it. However, many birds have specialized structures to help digest food. One such structure is the **crop,** which is located at the lower end of the esophagus. Food is stored and moistened in the crop before it moves further in the digestive tract.

In some birds, such as pigeons, the crop has a second function. During nesting season, the breakdown of cells in the crop produces a substance that is rich in protein and fat. Parent birds regurgitate this substance and feed their newly hatched young with it. This substance provides the young birds with materials they need to grow.

From the crop, moistened food moves into the stomach. The form that a bird's stomach takes depends on the bird's feeding habits. Birds that eat meat or fish have an expandable area in which large amounts of soft food can be stored. Birds that eat insects or seeds, however, have a muscular organ called the **gizzard** that helps in the mechanical breakdown of food by grinding it. The gizzard forms part of the stomach. In many species of bird, the gizzard contains small pieces of stone and gravel that the bird has swallowed. The thick, muscular walls of the gizzard grind the gravel and food together, crushing food particles and making them easier to digest.

Food moves from the stomach to the small intestine, where the breakdown of food is completed and food is absorbed into the body. Digestive wastes leave the body through the cloaca.

For: Links on birds
Visit: www.SciLinks.org
Web Code: cbn-9312

Address Misconceptions

Students might think birds do not eat large amounts of food. Many have heard the phrase "eats like a bird" in reference to someone who doesn't eat much food. Emphasize that because birds require energy to support their active, flying lifestyle and to maintain a constant, high body temperature, they have a very high metabolic rate. To fill their energy needs, birds eat almost constantly. L2

Use Visuals

Figure 31–14 Have students trace the path of food through the bird's digestive system. Ask: **What happens to food in the crop?** *(It's stored and moistened.)* **What is the function of the gizzard?** *(It grinds and crushes food.)* Remind students that not all birds have gizzards. Ask: **Which would be most likely to have a gizzard: insect-eating birds or fish-eating birds?** *(Insect-eating birds)* **Why do birds need the gizzard and the crop?** *(They don't have teeth. These organs help prepare food for digestion.)* L1 L2

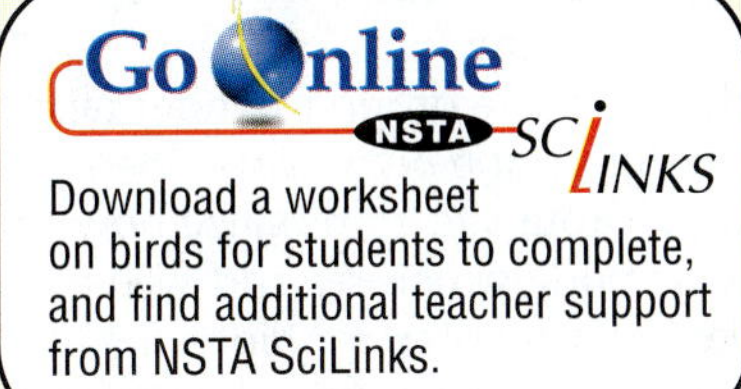

Download a worksheet on birds for students to complete, and find additional teacher support from NSTA SciLinks.

BIO INSIGHTS — FACTS AND FIGURES

Specialized digestive systems

As in other vertebrates, a bird's digestive system is slightly different depending on its diet. Birds do not have teeth and cannot chew their food into smaller pieces. Birds that eat small animals either tear off small pieces with their bills or swallow their food whole. These birds usually do not have a crop at the end of the esophagus, because the food does not have to be softened; the stomach usually has only one compartment. They do not have a gizzard. Birds that primarily eat seeds usually have a crop. The crop is required to soften the hard seeds, making them susceptible to digestive enzymes. These birds often have a two-part stomach that includes a gizzard.

Answers to . . .

 *Animal that generates its own body heat*

Figure 31–13 *Fish*

31–2 (continued)

Build Science Skills

Using Models To help all students visualize the flow of air through bird lungs, have the students act as air molecules moving through the respiratory system. Use masking tape to delineate the anterior air sacs, lungs, posterior air sacs, and trachea. Students carrying red paper circles (O_2) enter the trachea upon inhalation 1 and move into the posterior air sac. During exhalation 1, students move into lungs and exchange red circles for blue circles (CO_2). During inhalation 2, new "red" students enter the posterior air sac. The "blue" students move to the anterior air sac. During exhalation 2, the "blue" students move out into the air and the "red" students move into the lungs and exchange "gases." Continue in this manner until all students have moved through the respiratory system. **L1**

Build Science Skills

Drawing Conclusions Divide the class into small groups that represent a mixture of academic abilities. Groups should discuss what they know about the form and function of birds. Have one group member take notes during the discussion. Then, instruct groups to summarize how specific body structures and systems make birds adapted for flight. Suggest that groups also discuss what makes some birds able to fly while others cannot. Groups should summarize their conclusions and present them to the class. Compile the groups' conclusions into a table that you can update as you complete the section. **L2**

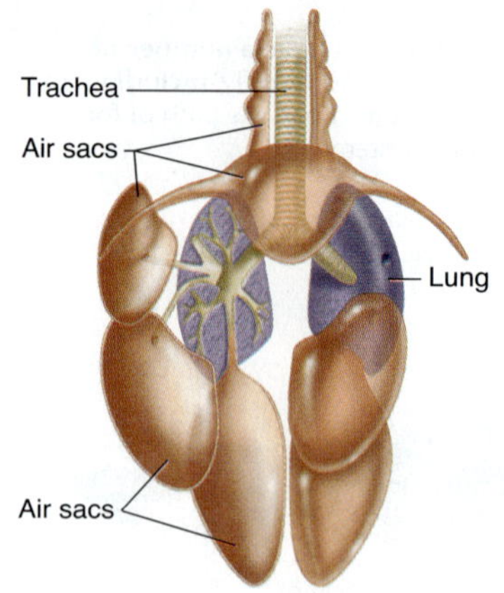

▲ **Figure 31–15** Birds have a unique respiratory system. Air sacs direct air through the lungs in an efficient, one-way flow. **Comparing and Contrasting** *How does this system differ from that of most land vertebrates?*

Respiration Birds have a unique and highly efficient way of taking in oxygen and eliminating carbon dioxide. When a bird inhales, most air first enters large posterior **air sacs** in the body cavity and bones. Observe the air sacs in **Figure 31–15.** The inhaled air then flows through the lungs. Air travels through the lungs in a series of small tubes. These tubes are lined with specialized tissue, where gas exchange takes place.

The complex system of air sacs and breathing tubes ensures that air flows into the air sacs and out through the lungs in a single direction. The one-way flow constantly exposes the lungs to oxygen-rich air. Contrast this to the system found in most land vertebrates, in which oxygen-rich air is inhaled, and oxygen-poor air is exhaled. The air travels in two directions, in and out. In an in-out system, the lungs are exposed to oxygen-rich air only during inhalation.

What advantage does the efficient respiratory system of birds provide? The constant, one-way flow of oxygen-rich air helps birds maintain their high metabolic rate. Birds need a high metabolism to maintain body temperature and provide the large amounts of energy required for flight. In addition, the efficient extraction of oxygen enables birds to fly at high altitudes where the air is thin.

✔ CHECKPOINT *How is their respiratory system advantageous to birds?*

Circulation Birds have four-chambered hearts and two separate circulatory loops. Notice in **Figure 31–16** that a bird's heart, unlike that of amphibians and most reptiles, has two separate ventricles, the right ventricle and the left ventricle. There is complete separation of oxygen-rich and oxygen-poor blood. One half of the heart receives oxygen-poor blood from the body and pumps this blood to the lungs. Oxygen-rich blood returns to the other side of the heart to be pumped to the rest of the body. This double-loop system ensures that oxygen collected by the lungs is distributed to the body tissue with maximum efficiency.

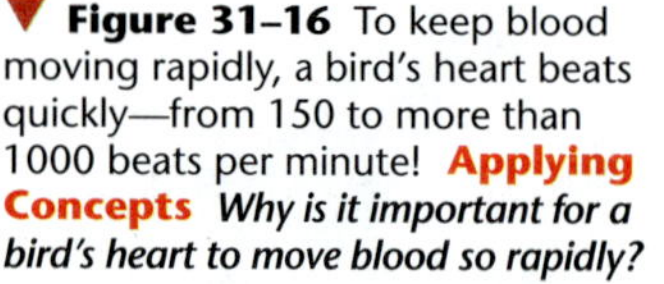

▼ **Figure 31–16** To keep blood moving rapidly, a bird's heart beats quickly—from 150 to more than 1000 beats per minute! **Applying Concepts** *Why is it important for a bird's heart to move blood so rapidly?*

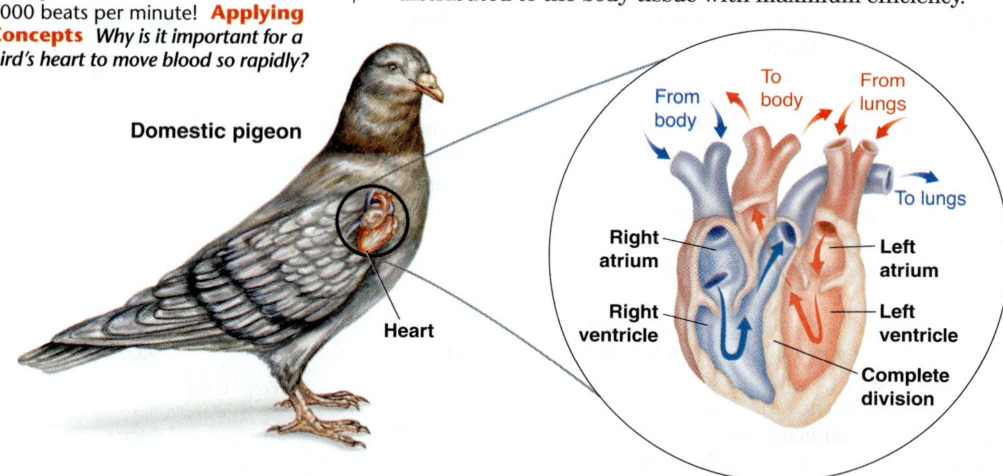

FACTS AND FIGURES

Bird sighted flying above the clouds

Some of the highest-flying birds are bar-headed geese. These geese have been observed flying over the Himalayas, which reach altitudes of over 7600 meters. Birds are able to fly at such high altitudes because of the efficiency of their lungs. In contrast, humans have difficulty climbing Mount Everest because they inhale less oxygen due to the lower air pressure.

Not only do bird lungs function efficiently at gas exchange, but the air sacs in lungs also help birds lose heat. The air sacs are located among the bird's internal organs, and they are connected to the bones. Bird bones have hollow spaces to reduce mass but also function to hold air. As air moves across the organs and through the bones during the process of respiration, it works to cool the bird's body.

Quick Lab

How do birds breathe?

Materials 6 round balloons, hand-powered balloon pump, measuring tape, clock with second hand

Procedure

1. Work in groups of three. Make a copy of the data table at right on a blank sheet of paper. One person will inflate a balloon by mouth, while a second person inflates a balloon with a hand-powered pump. The third person is the timekeeper.
2. Begin inflating both balloons at the same time. After 10 seconds, the timer will say "stop." Stop inflating the balloons and pinch the necks of the balloons to keep the air inside. **CAUTION:** *Do not try to inflate balloons by mouth if you have a condition that would make this dangerous for you.*
3. Measure and record the circumference of each balloon in your data table. **CAUTION:** *Discard all balloons that have been inflated.*

Data Table

Name	Balloon Circumference (cm)		Difference
	Mouth	Pump	
Average Difference ________			

4. Repeat Steps 1–3 until each member of your group has inflated two balloons. In your data table, record the difference in balloon diameter for each person and the average difference for the group.

Analyze and Conclude

1. **Analyzing Data** Which method was faster? Which method required more effort?
2. **Using Models** Which method worked like reptile lungs? Which method worked like bird lungs? Explain your answers.
3. **Formulating Hypotheses** How is efficient respiration especially valuable to birds?

BIIE 1.g

Excretion The excretory systems of many birds are similar to those of most living reptiles. Nitrogenous wastes are removed from the blood by the kidneys, converted to uric acid, and deposited in the cloaca. There, most of the water is reabsorbed, leaving uric acid crystals in a white, pasty form that you may recognize as bird droppings.

Response Birds have well-developed sense organs, which are adaptations that enable them to coordinate the movements required for flight. Birds also have a brain that can quickly interpret and respond to a lot of incoming signals. A bird's brain, shown in **Figure 31–17,** is relatively large for its body size. The cerebrum, which controls such behaviors as flying, nest building, care of young, courtship, and mating, is quite large. The cerebellum is also well developed, as you might expect in an animal that uses precise, coordinated movements. The medulla oblongata coordinates basic body processes, such as the heartbeat.

Birds have extraordinarily well developed eyes and sizable optic lobes in the brain. Birds see color very well—in many cases, better than humans. Most bird species can also hear quite well. The senses of taste and smell, however, are not well developed in most birds, and the olfactory bulbs in a bird's brain are small.

▼ **Figure 31–17** Compared to reptiles, birds have an enlarged cerebellum that coordinates the movements of wings and legs. **Formulating Hypotheses** ***Why would the cerebrum also be larger in birds than in reptiles?***

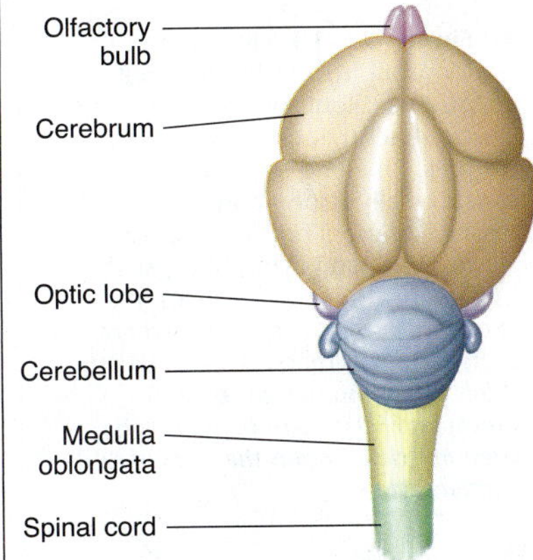

Quick Lab

BIIE 1.g

Objective Students will be able to use models to explain how birds breathe. L2

Skills Focus **Using Models, Analyzing Data, Formulating Hypotheses**

Materials 6 round balloons, hand-powered balloon pump, measuring tape, clock with second hand

Time 15 minutes

Advance Prep Inexpensive balloon pumps are available at party supply stores.

Strategies

- Discuss why birds need a more efficient way to get oxygen than do reptiles. *(Muscles require oxygen to extract energy from stored glucose; there is little oxygen at high altitudes.)* Have students compare the movements of reptiles and birds. Ask: **What do muscles need to keep working efficiently?** *(Oxygen)*

Expected Outcome Balloons are more quickly inflated with a hand pump than by mouth.

Analyze and Conclude

1. Using the pump is faster. Mouth inflation requires more effort.
2. Mouth inflation simulates the flow of air in and out of the same opening, as in reptile lungs. Air flows in one end of the pump and out the other, as in bird lungs.
3. Flight requires a high level of cellular respiration in the muscles. Also, high-altitude flight requires extra oxygen. Therefore, birds need a large oxygen supply.

FACTS AND FIGURES

Birds sing to communicate

Birds use sound to communicate with one another. Ornithologists differentiate between two kinds of bird sounds. Calls are short sounds used to warn others of danger and to communicate between members of the same species. Most calls are innate. Songs are longer vocalizations that involve many different notes. Many bird songs involve learning. Some songbirds even learn new songs each year. Birds raised in soundproof environments do not learn songs. In most cases, only males learn songs to establish and defend territories and to attract mates.

As in humans, vibrating membranes in birds produce sound. These membranes are located in the syrinx at the posterior end of the trachea. Muscles in the syrinx cause the different pitches in the calls and songs.

Answers to . . .

CHECKPOINT *It maintains a high metabolic rate and supplies the extra oxygen required for high-altitude flight.*

Figure 31–15 *Air travels in one direction only, rather than in and out.*

Figure 31–16 *To maintain high levels of oxygen in muscles*

Figure 31–17 *To control precise movements and complex behaviors*

31–2 (continued)

Make Connections

Physics Challenge student groups to experiment with different wing shapes to produce flight. Give groups toy gliders made from foam or balsa, or have them construct gliders from paper. Encourage students to change the shape of the wings and nose to improve lift. You might need to explain how air moving over the wings and the nose of the plane provides lift, the upward force. Have groups race their planes to see which fly fastest and which fly farthest. L2

Address Misconceptions

Some students might think that birds simply move their wings up and down during flight. Explain that birds move their wings in a circular motion, similar to the movement of oars when rowing. On the downstroke, feathers are held together, and the wings move down and rotate forward. This motion pushes air down and back, providing lift and propelling the bird through the air. On the upstroke, feathers are opened up to allow air to move through them, making it easier to move the wings upward. The wings bend up, moving closer to the body, and rotate backward. L2

Groups of Birds

Build Science Skills

Classifying Have students devise their own criteria for grouping the bird orders pictured in Figure 31–19. You might also give students pictures of birds from other orders that are not pictured in the figure. For their classification systems, students should describe what features they are using to define the characteristics of each order. L1 L2

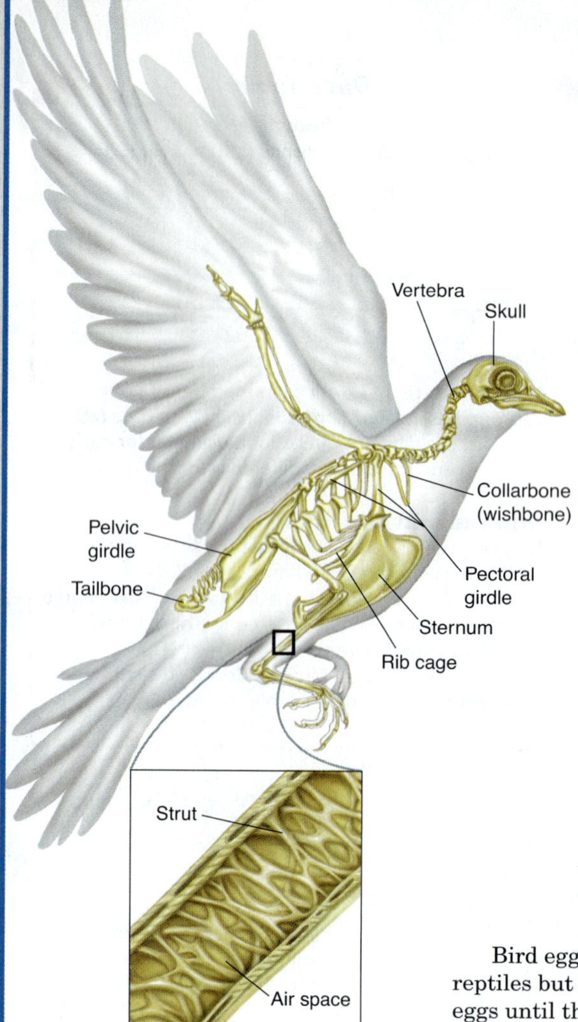

▲ **Figure 31–18** Like most of its anatomy, a bird's skeleton is well adapted for flight, providing a sturdy attachment point for muscles. The long bones are exceptionally strong and light because of cross-bracing and air spaces. In strong flying birds, such as pigeons, the chest muscles may account for as much as 30 percent of the animal's mass. **Calculating** *If this pigeon has a mass of 200 grams and 30 percent of its mass is chest muscles, what is the mass of its chest muscles?*

Movement Some birds cannot fly. Instead, they get around mainly by walking or running, like ostriches, or by swimming, like penguins. However, the vast majority of birds can fly. The skeletal and muscular systems of flying birds exhibit adaptations that enable flight.

Observe a bird's skeletal system in **Figure 31–18.** Although the bones in a bird's wings are homologous to the bones in the front limbs of other vertebrates, they have very different shapes and structures. In flying birds, many large bones, such as the collarbone, are fused together, making a bird's skeleton more rigid than a reptile's. These bones form a sturdy frame that anchors the muscles used for flight. The bones are strengthened by internal struts similar to those used in the framework of tall buildings and bridges. Air spaces make many bones lightweight. Birds also have large chest muscles that power the upward and downward wing strokes necessary for flight. The muscles attach to a long keel that runs down the front of an enlarged breastbone, or sternum.

Reproduction In birds, both male and female reproductive tracts open into the cloaca. The sex organs often shrink in size when the birds are not breeding. As birds prepare to mate, the ovaries and testes grow larger until they reach functioning size. Mating birds press their cloacas together to transfer sperm from the male to the female. Some male birds have a penis that transfers sperm to the female's cloaca.

Bird eggs are amniotic eggs. They are similar to the eggs of reptiles but have hard outer shells. Most birds incubate their eggs until the eggs hatch. When a chick is ready to hatch, it uses a small tooth on its bill to make a hole in the shell. After much pushing, poking, and prodding by the chick, the eggshell breaks open. Once the exhausted bird has hatched, it collapses for a while and allows its feathers to dry. Both parents may be kept busy providing food for their hungry offspring.

CHECKPOINT *Do birds have external or internal fertilization?*

Groups of Birds

Birds fill the woods and fields with song. Imagine how dull the world would be without the color, song, and variety of birds. With nearly 30 different orders, it is impossible to present each type of bird here. Instead, **Figure 31–19** provides an overview of some better-known groups and their adaptations. By far, the largest order of birds is the passerines (pas-uh-REENZ), or perching birds. This group includes songbirds such as larks, sparrows, and finches. There are over 5000 species of perching birds.

FACTS AND FIGURES

Air pressure "lifts" birds

Birds are able to fly because of lift. Lift is the difference in air pressure above the wing and below the wing. As birds fly, air moves across both sides of the wings. Air pressure below the wing is greater than air pressure above the wing. In effect, the air is "lifting" the wing. Moving air exerts less pressure than air that is not moving. The faster air moves, the less pressure it exerts.

Bird wings are shaped so that air moving across the top of the wings is moving faster. The top of a bird's wing is rounded, forcing the air to travel a greater distance in the same amount of time as the air moving under the wing. Because the air moving across the top of the wing has to go a greater distance in the same time span, it must move faster.

Figure 31–19 Diversity in Birds

Birds show remarkable diversity and inhabit many different environments. Some representative groups are shown below. **Applying Concepts** *Which group of birds is the largest?*

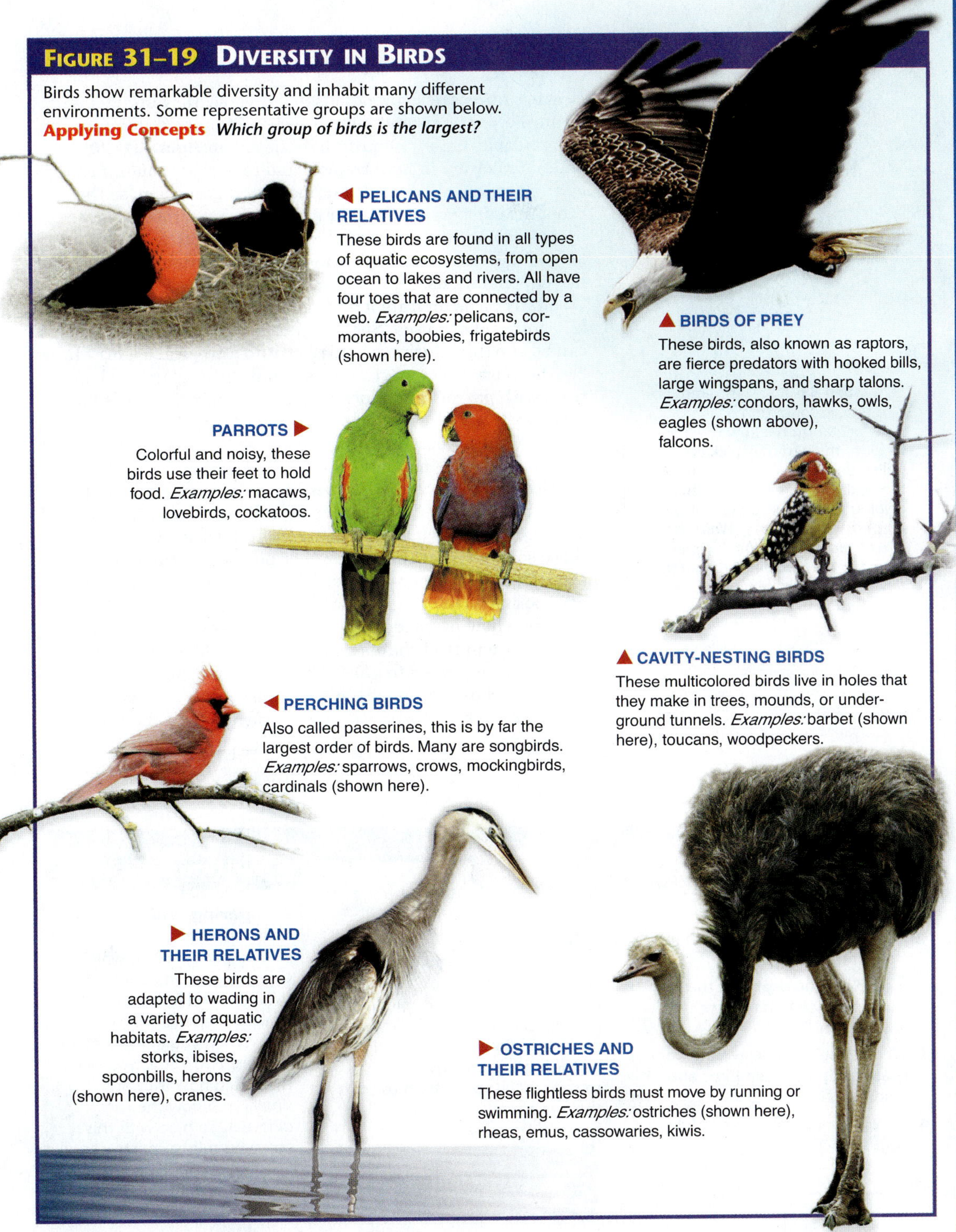

◀ Pelicans and Their Relatives
These birds are found in all types of aquatic ecosystems, from open ocean to lakes and rivers. All have four toes that are connected by a web. *Examples:* pelicans, cormorants, boobies, frigatebirds (shown here).

▲ Birds of Prey
These birds, also known as raptors, are fierce predators with hooked bills, large wingspans, and sharp talons. *Examples:* condors, hawks, owls, eagles (shown above), falcons.

Parrots ▶
Colorful and noisy, these birds use their feet to hold food. *Examples:* macaws, lovebirds, cockatoos.

▲ Cavity-Nesting Birds
These multicolored birds live in holes that they make in trees, mounds, or underground tunnels. *Examples:* barbet (shown here), toucans, woodpeckers.

◀ Perching Birds
Also called passerines, this is by far the largest order of birds. Many are songbirds. *Examples:* sparrows, crows, mockingbirds, cardinals (shown here).

▶ Herons and Their Relatives
These birds are adapted to wading in a variety of aquatic habitats. *Examples:* storks, ibises, spoonbills, herons (shown here), cranes.

▶ Ostriches and Their Relatives
These flightless birds must move by running or swimming. *Examples:* ostriches (shown here), rheas, emus, cassowaries, kiwis.

Use Visuals

Figure 31–19 Encourage students to compare and contrast the features of birds from different orders. Ask: **How are parrots different from perching birds?** *(Parrots use their feet to hold up food.)* **What features are common to birds of prey?** *(Hooked bills, large wingspans, and sharp talons)* **How are pelicans and herons similar?** *(Both live in aquatic habitats.)* L1 L2

Bio Insights: Facts and Figures

Classifying birds
Scientists group birds into more than 20 orders. To classify birds, scientists use characteristics such as bills, wings, tails, and feet. These specialized characteristics enable birds to inhabit different types of environments, move in different ways, or get different types of food. Birds with similar specialized characteristics often inhabit similar environments or have similar niches. Peacocks, for example, belong to the order Galliformes. These ground-dwelling birds have short, stout bills. Their heavy feet have short, strong claws adapted for running and scratching the ground. They have short wings and are poor fliers. Herons, as well as flamingoes and storks, belong to the order Ciconiiformes. These wading birds have long legs and necks and broad feet that are not usually webbed.

Answers to . . .

Checkpoint *Birds have internal fertilization.*

Figure 31–18 *60 grams*

Figure 31–19 *Perching birds (passerines)*

31–2 (continued)

Ecology of Birds

Make Connections

Environmental Science Have interested students read Rachel Carson's book *Silent Spring*. Then, invite the students to lead a class discussion about the book in which they explain why they think Ms. Carson wrote the book and how effective her message was. Point out that at the time, the Department of Agriculture was advocating the use of many different types of dangerous chemicals to combat insect pests. Discuss whether or not students think that Ms. Carson's book is relevant today. 

3 ASSESS

Evaluate Understanding

Call on students at random to describe the characteristics of birds. Then, call on other students to describe ways in which birds are adapted for flight.

Reteach

Have students use Figures 31–11, 31–14, and 31–19 to review the characteristics of birds and the adaptations for flight.

Writing in Science

The heart has two atria in both reptiles and birds. However, most reptiles have a three-chambered heart in which the single ventricle is partially divided. Birds have a four-chambered heart in which complete division of the ventricle prevents oxygen-rich blood from mixing with oxygen-poor blood. Some students might also mention that crocodiles and alligators have a four-chambered heart similar to that of birds.

If your class subscribes to the iText, use it to review the Key Concepts in Section 31–2.

Answer to . . .

Figure 31–20 *Mutualism*

▲ **Figure 31–20** This hummingbird uses its long, thin beak to draw nectar from a flower. While feeding, the bird may pick up pollen on its beak and carry it to the next flower it visits, thereby helping the flower to pollinate. **Applying Concepts** *Which type of ecological relationship is represented by the hummingbird and the flower: parasitism, mutualism, or commensalism?*

Ecology of Birds

Because birds are so numerous and diverse, they interact with natural ecosystems and human society in many different ways. For example, hummingbirds, like the one in **Figure 31–20**, pollinate flowers in both tropical and temperate zones. Fruit-eating birds swallow seeds but may not digest them, so their droppings disperse seeds over great distances. Insect-eating birds, such as swallows and chimney swifts, catch great numbers of mosquitoes and other insects, and therefore help control insect populations.

Many birds migrate long distances—often over hundreds of kilometers of open sea. Such migrations are usually seasonal. It can be startling during a winter visit to a tropical country to see Northern orioles or bright red cardinals flitting around banana trees with parrots and toucans! How do migrating birds find their way? Some species use stars and other celestial bodies as guides. Other species may use a combination of landmarks and cues from Earth's magnetic field.

Because birds are highly visible and are an important part of the biosphere, they can serve as indicators of environmental health. It is no accident that conservationist Rachel Carson chose songbirds for the focus of her pioneering campaign in the 1960s against the careless use of DDT and other pesticides. In her book *Silent Spring,* Carson described to the public for the first time how pesticides that stay in the environment can accumulate in food chains and cause harm to animals they were never intended to affect. Thanks to the efforts of Carson and other conservationists, many birds—especially predators such as eagles and ospreys—have returned from the brink of extinction.

31–2 Section Assessment

1. **Key Concept** Describe the characteristics of a bird.
2. **Key Concept** List three ways in which birds are well adapted for flight.
3. What is the possible evolutionary relationship between birds and dinosaurs?
4. How does a chick get out of its eggshell?
5. **Critical Thinking Applying Concepts** Crops and gizzards are especially common and well developed in seed-eating birds but less common in carnivorous birds. Explain why crops and gizzards are more advantageous to seed-eating birds than to birds that eat meat.

Writing in Science

Comparing and Contrasting

Write a paragraph in which you compare and contrast the structure and function of the hearts of reptiles and birds. *Hint:* When you compare and contrast two items, you need to explain how they are similar and how they are different. To help with this task, you might construct a Venn diagram or a compare-and-contrast table.

31–2 Section Assessment

1. Reptilelike animal, endothermic, hollow bones, feathers, two legs, wings
2. Highly efficient respiratory, digestive, and circulatory systems; aerodynamic feathers and wings; strong chest muscles; strong, lightweight skeleton
3. Birds descended either directly from dinosaurs or from a common ancestor of modern birds and dinosaurs.
4. The chick uses a small tooth on its bill to poke a hole in the shell.
5. Seeds, with their tough outer coverings, are much more difficult to digest than meat. Crops and gizzards are not advantageous to carnivorous birds, because animal tissue does not require extra softening and grinding to digest.

Exploration

BIIE 1.c

Examining Bird Bones

Birds have many adaptations that enable them to fly, including the structure and properties of their skeletons. In this investigation, you will compare bones from birds and mammals to determine how bird bones are adapted for flight.

Problem How is a bird's skeleton adapted for flight?

Materials

- cut sections of bird and mammal bones
- bird breastbone
- hand lens
- mammal bone
- bird wing bone
- balance
- 250-mL graduated cylinder
- dissecting probe
- calculator

Skills Observing, Measuring, Calculating

Procedure

Part A: Bone Structure

1. Put on plastic gloves. Use a hand lens to examine cut sections of bird and mammal bones. Look carefully at the interiors of the bones and record your observations.
2. Look at a bird breastbone (sternum). Carefully observe its structure.

Part B: Bone Density

3. Make a copy of the data table on a separate sheet of paper. Use a balance to measure the mass of a bird wing bone.
4. Put 180 mL of water in the graduated cylinder. **CAUTION:** *Handle the graduated cylinder carefully. If it breaks, tell your teacher immediately.*
5. Use a dissecting probe to hold the bird wing bone under water in the graduated cylinder. In your data table, record the water level in the cylinder. Subtract the original water volume from this value to find the volume of the bone.
6. The density of an object is equal to its mass divided by its volume (d = m/v). Calculate the density of the bone by dividing its mass by its volume. Record the density of the bird bone in your data table.
7. Repeat steps 3 to 6 to find the density of the mammal bone. Wash your hands with soap and warm water before leaving the lab.

Data Table

Source of Bone	Mass (g)	Volume (mL)			Density of Bone (g/cm^3)
		Water	Water + Bone	Bone	
Bird					
Mammal					

Analyze and Conclude

1. **Comparing and Contrasting** How are the bird and mammal bones similar? Different? How is the bird bone adapted for flight?
2. **Applying Concepts** What is the function of the muscles that attach to a bird's sternum? How is the protruding bird sternum an adaptation for flight?
3. **Drawing Conclusions** How are the densities of bird and mammal bones related to the way these animals move?
4. **Evaluating** With your teacher's permission, determine the validity of your density data by repeating Part B. Do you obtain the same results?

Go Further

Applying Concepts In addition to specialized bones, birds' adaptations to flight include several types of feathers. Use reference materials to find out how each type of feather is an adaptation.

Exploration

BIIE 1.c

Objective Students will be able to observe how a bird's skeleton is adapted for flight. L2

Skills Focus Observing, Measuring, Calculating

Time 45 minutes

Advance Prep

- Use a hacksaw or ask a butcher to cut beef or pork ribs into sections so the interior structure is visible.
- Obtain a chicken or turkey sternum and leg bones. Boil bones thoroughly to remove any meat and kill bacteria. Allow them to dry before using.
- Students should wear disposable plastic gloves. Dispose of the gloves after the activity.

Pre-Lab Discussion Begin a class discussion about a bird's adaptations for flight. Discuss how the density of bones might affect flight. Then, have students read the procedure. Answer any questions students have.

Teaching Tips

- Be prepared to review the concept of density and how it is calculated.
- If possible, use bones from a mammal and a bird of similar size, such as a squirrel and a chicken.

Procedure

1. Bird bones have more hollow spaces within them.

5. Students might need to adjust the water level or use a larger graduated cylinder if the bone is too large to be completely submerged.

7. Typical adult mammal bones have densities of about 1.7–2.0 g/mL. The densities of bird bones are less than that of mammals.

Expected Outcome Students should find that bird bones are less dense than mammal bones.

Analyze and Conclude

1. Both are hard on the outside and partly hollow inside. Bird bones have a thinner outer covering, are more hollow, and have internal struts. These features make bird bones less dense, making flight easier.
2. Muscles attached to a bird's sternum pull the wings during flight. The protruding bird sternum anchors the large flight muscles.
3. The low-density bones of birds reflect their adaptation to flight. The denser bones of mammals reflect the mammals' greater need for strong weight-bearing bones to support the body in response to the pull of gravity.
4. If students measure carefully, they should obtain the same results.

Go Further

Contour feathers give birds the strength and stability for flight. Light, fluffy down feathers insulate birds. Filoplumes sense the positions of other feathers.

Chapter 31 Study Guide

Study Tip

Students can construct a Venn diagram to show characteristics and adaptations that birds and reptiles have in common and those that are specific to each.

Thinking Visually

1. Ectotherms
2. Uric acid
3., 4. Crocodilians; Turtles and Tortoises

Chapter 31 Assessment

Reviewing Content

1. c	5. b	9. c
2. a	6. b	10. c
3. b	7. d	
4. c	8. b	

Understanding Concepts

11. The skin is shed periodically as a reptile increases in size.

12. Earth's climate became cooler and less humid. Since reptiles were better adapted than amphibians to survive in this drier climate, a great adaptive radiation of reptiles began.

13. One hypothesis asserts that at the end of the Cretaceous Period, a string of massive volcanic eruptions, lava flows, the dropping of sea level, and a huge asteroid or comet colliding into the Yucatán Peninsula in Mexico occurred. The asteroid or comet collision produced enormous dust clouds and major forest fires. Within a few million years of these events, dinosaurs, along with many other animal and plant groups, disappeared.

14. Interactions with the environment help the animal control its body temperature. When reptiles begin to cool down, they may move toward warmth, such as sunlight. When their bodies become hot, reptiles move to a cooler environment, such as shade.

Chapter 31 Study Guide

31–1 Reptiles

Key Concepts

- A reptile is a vertebrate that has scaly skin, lungs, and eggs with several membranes.
- Well-developed lungs; a double-loop circulatory system; an efficient excretory system; strong limbs; internal fertilization; and shelled, terrestrial eggs are the main adaptations that have contributed to the success of reptiles on land.
- The four surviving groups of reptiles are lizards and snakes, crocodilians, turtles and tortoises, and the tuatara.

Vocabulary

ectotherm, p. 800
amniotic egg, p. 802
carapace, p. 805
plastron, p. 805

31–2 Birds

Key Concepts

- Birds are reptilelike animals that maintain a constant internal body temperature. They have an outer covering of feathers; two legs that are covered with scales and are used for walking or perching; and front limbs modified into wings.
- Birds have a number of adaptations that enable them to fly. These adaptations include highly efficient digestive, respiratory, and circulatory systems; aerodynamic feathers and wings; strong, lightweight bones; and strong chest muscles.

Vocabulary

feather, p. 806
endotherm, p. 808
crop, p. 809
gizzard, p. 809
air sac, p. 810

Thinking Visually

Using information from this chapter, complete the following concept map:

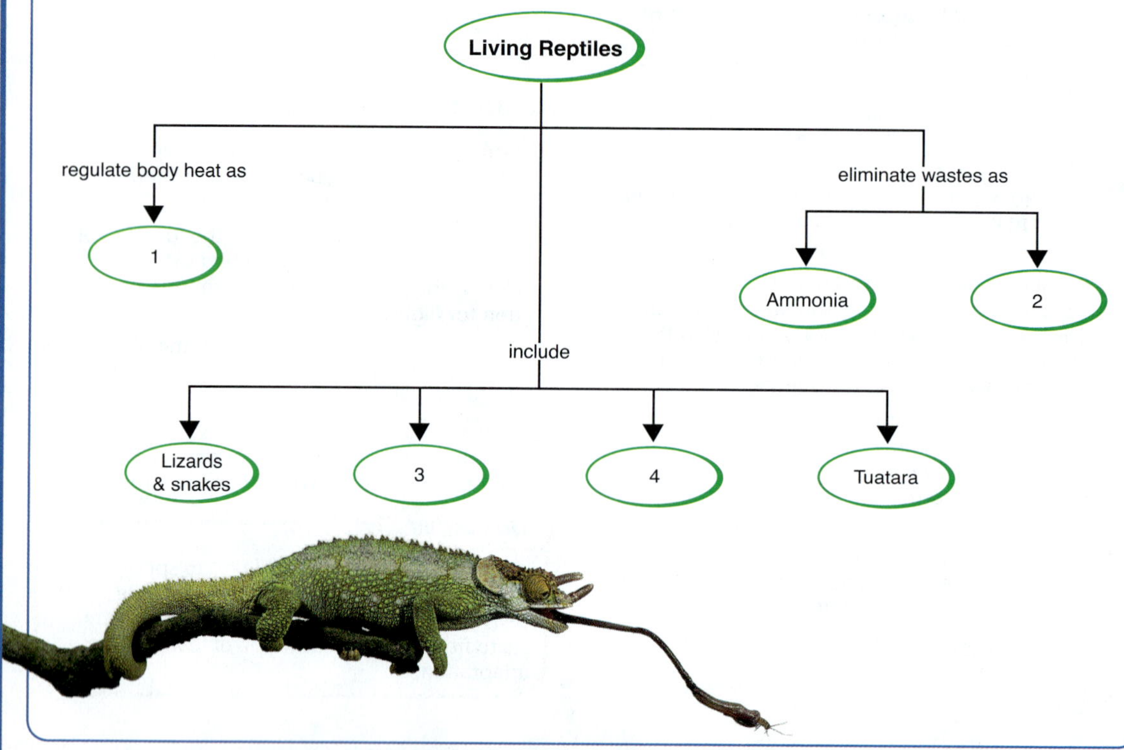

CHAPTER RESOURCES

TIME SAVER

Print:
- ***Teaching Resources,*** Chapter Vocabulary Review, Graphic Organizers, Chapter 31 Tests: Levels A and B

Technology:
- ***Computer Test Bank,*** Chapter 31 Test
- ***iText,*** Chapter 31 Assessment

Chapter 31 Assessment

Interactive textbook with assessment at PHSchool.com

Reviewing Content

Choose the letter that best answers the question or completes the statement.

1. Which adaptation is NOT characteristic of reptiles?
   a. scaly skin   c. gills
   b. amniotic egg   d. lungs
2. Dinosaurs became extinct at the end of the
   a. Cretaceous Period.   c. Carboniferous Period.
   b. Triassic Period.   d. Permian Period.
3. An animal that relies on interaction with the environment to help it control body temperature is known as a(an)
   a. endotherm.   c. flightless bird.
   b. ectotherm.   d. endoderm.
4. Which reptiles have some type of shell covering their bodies?
   a. lizards and snakes   c. turtles and tortoises
   b. crocodilians   d. tuatara
5. In the diagram below, the membrane labeled *Y* represents what part of the amniotic egg?

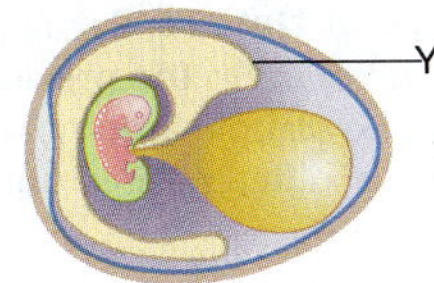

   a. amnion   c. allantois
   b. chorion   d. yolk sac
6. The single most important characteristic that separates birds from other living animals is the presence of
   a. hollow bones.   c. two legs.
   b. feathers.   d. wings.
7. Which of the following bird structures are especially adapted to support flight?
   a. cloacas   c. bills
   b. gizzards   d. chest muscles
8. The muscular part of a bird's stomach that contains gravel, which crushes food, is the
   a. cloaca.   c. crop.
   b. gizzard.   d. air sac.
9. Birds excrete nitrogenous wastes mostly in the form of
   a. urine.   c. uric acid.
   b. ammonia.   d. urea.
10. Unlike other vertebrates, birds have respiratory systems that
    a. take in oxygen and release carbon dioxide.
    b. excrete nitrogenous wastes.
    c. maintain a one-way flow of air.
    d. have modified scales.

Understanding Concepts

11. As a reptile grows, what happens to its skin?
12. What climate conditions prevailed at the end of the Carboniferous Period? How did these conditions affect the evolution of reptiles?
13. What conditions may have caused the mass extinction of the dinosaurs?
14. In what way do interactions with the environment affect the body temperatures of reptiles?
15. How is the process of respiration in reptiles adapted to life on land?
16. Why is the amniotic egg considered to be one of the most important adaptations to life on land?
17. Describe the structure of a turtle's shell.
18. How do crocodilians care for their young?
19. If a bird has a short, thick bill, what does it probably feed on?
20. How does a pigeon's crop help enable it to care for young?
21. What are air sacs? How do air sacs help ensure that a bird has an adequate supply of oxygen?
22. Describe how a bird's skeletal system is adapted in ways that enable flight.
23. Describe the structure of bird eggs, and explain what usually happens to the eggs after they are laid.
24. What adaptation enables birds to live in environments that are colder than those typically supporting reptiles?
25. What functions do the cerebrum and cerebellum control in birds?
26. Name three groups of birds, and describe some of their characteristics.
27. How do migrating birds find their way?

HOMEWORK GUIDE

Section:	Questions:
Section 31–1	1–5, 11–18, 30, 31, 37
Section 31–2	6–10, 19–29, 32–36

If your class subscribes to the iText, your students can go online to access an interactive version of the Student Edition and a self-test.

(Continued from page 816)

15. Most reptiles have two lungs composed of spongy tissue that provides a large area for gas exchange. Many reptiles have muscles around their ribs to help expand and collapse the chest cavity.

16. The shells and membranes of amniotic eggs create a protected environment in which the embryos can develop without drying out.

17. A turtle's shell is built into the skeleton. The carapace is dorsal, and the plastron is ventral.

18. Mothers guard their eggs from predators. They carry hatchlings to a nursery area and watch over them.

19. Seeds

20. During nesting season, the crop produces a substance high in protein and fat. Parent birds regurgitate this substance and feed it to their young.

21. Air sacs are part of the respiratory system that receive inhaled air and direct it through the lungs in an efficient one-way flow.

22. Fused bones provide sturdy attachments for muscles. Cross-bracing and air spaces in the bones make them strong and lightweight.

23. Bird eggs are amniotic eggs, with membranes that include the amnion, chorion, allantois, and yolk sac. They have hard outer shells. Most birds incubate their eggs until they hatch.

24. Unlike reptiles, birds are endothermic. They also have feathers, which conserve heat.

25. The cerebrum controls such behaviors as flying, nest building, caring for young, courtship, and mating. The cerebellum coordinates movement.

26. Possible answers include bird groups described in Figure 31–19.

27. Migrating birds navigate by using one or more of the following guides: stars and other celestial bodies; landmarks; Earth's magnetic field.

Chapter 31 Assessment

Critical Thinking

28. Sample hypothesis: *Archaeopteryx* used its clawed wings to glide down from trees to catch insects.

29. Sample questions: Which birds use more energy for flight? What foods are most available in each bird's habitat? Which birds are more active?

30. The snake might have moved from a cooler location to a warmer one, or the air temperature might have increased during the course of the day in a single location.

31. You would expect to find more reptiles on the tropical island, because ectotherms are more common in warmer climates.

32. The long legs of wetland birds enable the birds to wade out into the water in search of food.

33. The description closely fits that of a bird (or bat). Unlike reptiles, amphibians, and fish, birds are endothermic. The presence of modified front limbs, or wings, is a characteristic of birds.

34. The presence of a great amount of myoglobin in the chest muscles of ducks would indicate that they use these muscles for a great deal of flying. Less myoglobin in the chest muscles of chickens would indicate that these chest muscles are not used as much as those of ducks.

35. Embryos develop within amniotic eggs; adults excrete uric acid wastes; bones that support limbs are similar. Similarities indicate that these animals evolved from an earlier common ancestor.

36. Experimental plans might include repeated trials of removing a young bird from its parents and observing to which parents it returns.

37. Each student should choose a scale and use the scale to construct the diagrams. Diagrams should also include a title and a key.

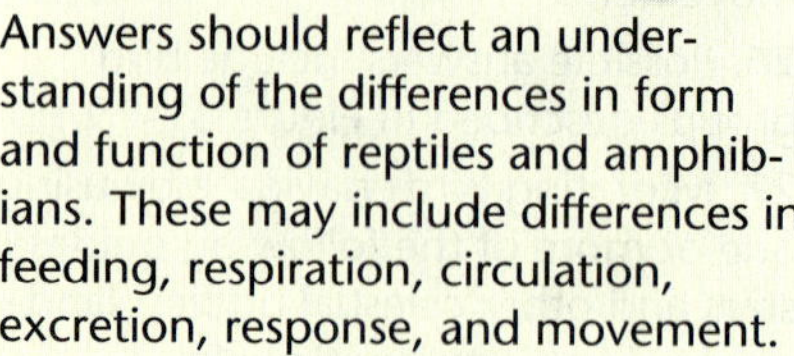

Answers should reflect an understanding of the differences in form and function of reptiles and amphibians. These may include differences in feeding, respiration, circulation, excretion, response, and movement.

Chapter 31 Assessment

Critical Thinking

28. Formulating Hypotheses From the small size of its sternum, or breastbone, scientists infer that *Archaeopteryx* was a poor flier. Propose a hypothesis to explain how *Archaeopteryx* might have used its wings.

29. Asking Questions Hummingbirds eat high-energy foods, such as nectar and fruit. Ducks eat foods that store less energy, such as grass and leaves. What are some related questions you could investigate to discover more about the birds' diets and energy needs?

30. Drawing Conclusions The body temperature of a snake was monitored every half hour for two hours. The temperature readings were 30°C, 32°C, 38°C, 39°C, 39°C. Suggest possible conditions that might explain these changes.

31. Predicting Imagine that you plan a visit to a warm tropical island followed by a visit to a much cooler island. In which of these places would you expect to find more reptiles? Explain your prediction.

32. Inferring Some wetland birds, such as storks and flamingos, have long legs. How might this adaptation help these birds obtain food?

33. Classifying You are told that an animal is endothermic, has two legs, and modified front limbs. It also has a four-chambered heart and two separate circulatory loops. What kind of an animal is it? Explain.

34. Inferring The muscles that a bird uses most often contain the greatest amount of a protein called myoglobin. The chest muscles of ducks contain more myoglobin than the chest muscles of chickens. What can you infer about the flight of these two birds?

35. Inferring Identify anatomical, physiological, and embryological characteristics shared by reptiles and birds. Explain how evolutionary biologists use these similarities as evidence that may indicate change in species.

36. Designing Experiments During breeding season, many species of sea birds nest in large colonies. At any one time, you can hear the cries of many birds in a colony. Design an experiment to determine whether young sea birds can distinguish the calls of their parents from those of other members of the colony.

37. Using Tables and Graphs Look at the information in the chart below. Using the length of each snake, construct scaled diagrams on graph paper. Develop a measurement scale (for example, 1 grid square = 2 cm). Include a key to your scale. Color each snake according to its markings.

Snake Descriptions

Snake	Length (cm)	Markings
Western coral snake	45	Black, yellow, and red rings successively from head to tail
Patch-nosed snake	92	Yellow and brown stripe down the back

Interdependence in Nature Recall what you learned about amphibians in the previous chapter. Make a table that shows how amphibians and reptiles are adapted for life in different environments.

Writing in Science

Describe the structure of down feathers and contour feathers. Explain how the structure of each type of feather is related to its function. (*Hint:* When you describe something, you tell how it looks—or sounds, tastes, smells, or feels. When you explain something, you make it understandable to your audience.)

Performance-Based Assessment

In Your Community Observe some birds that live in your area. Write descriptions of traits you notice, such as different kinds of feathers, bills, and feet. Based on your observations, what do the birds eat? What types of habitats do they prefer?

For: An interactive self-test
Visit: PHSchool.com
Web Code: cba-9310

Writing in Science

Paragraphs should include a description of down feathers (small, lack hooks, free-form arrangement of barbs) and contour feathers (long, stiff; hooks on each barbule fit together to hold it flat). They should then explain how the structure is related to function. For example, the stiff contour feathers provide the lifting force and balance needed for flight and give birds an aerodynamic shape. Soft down feathers are fluffy and trap air close to the body to keep the bird warm.

Performance-Based Assessment

Student answers should include descriptions of the birds' various traits and behaviors.

Standards Practice

Online at PHSchool.com

Test-Taking Tip When presented with questions that are related to data in a table, study each column and row of the table for information you need to answer the questions.

Directions: Choose the letter that best answers the question or completes the statement.

1. In general, reptiles can carry more body mass than amphibians because
- **A** they have a higher body temperature.
- **B** they do not live any portion of their lives in water.
- **C** their limb bones are stronger than those of amphibians.
- **D** their embryos can develop outside water.

2. Many scientists think that birds evolved from
- **A** mammal-like reptiles.
- **B** amphibians.
- **C** mammals.
- **D** dinosaurs.

3. The following animals are all reptiles EXCEPT
- **A** the tuatara.
- **B** lizards and snakes.
- **C** crocodilians.
- **D** passerines.

4. Amniotic eggs are a characteristic of
- **A** amphibians.
- **B** reptiles.
- **C** fishes.
- **D** tunicates.

5. Which of these is a characteristic of reptiles?
- **A** scaly skin
- **B** eggs that have several membranes
- **C** lungs
- **D** all of the above

6. When birds breathe, most of the inhaled air first enters the
- **A** lungs.
- **B** gizzard.
- **C** crop.
- **D** air sacs.

7. Feathers that provide lifting force and balance needed for flight are known as
- **A** down feathers.
- **B** powder feathers.
- **C** barbules.
- **D** contour feathers.

8. Which of the following is NOT a characteristic of birds' bones?
- **A** Many have air spaces.
- **B** They are strengthened by struts.
- **C** Many are fused together.
- **D** The breastbone is small.

Questions 9–10

An experiment was conducted to see how air temperature affects a snake's ability to move. The experimenter placed the snake a fixed distance away from a piece of food and recorded the air temperature. Then, she recorded the time it took for the snake to reach the food. She repeated the experiment four times. Each time, the experimenter changed the air temperature. The data are shown below.

The Effect of Temperature on Snake Movement

Temperature (°C)	Time (seconds)
4	51
10	50
15	43
21	37
27	35

9. At what air temperature did the snake reach the food the fastest?
- **A** 4°C
- **B** 10°C
- **C** 21°C
- **D** 27°C

10. What conclusion can be drawn from the data?
- **A** As the air temperature increased, the time it took for the snake to reach the food increased.
- **B** As the air temperature decreased, the time it took for the snake to reach the food increased.
- **C** Air temperature had no effect on the time it took the snake to reach the food.
- **D** Snakes are ectotherms.

Standards Practice

1. C
2. D
3. D
4. D
5. D
6. D
7. D
8. D
9. D
10. B

Success Tracker™

Online at PHSchool.com

Have students check their understanding of the chapter by logging onto Success Tracker.

Go Online PHSchool.com

Your students can independently test their knowledge of the chapter and print out their test results for your files.

Chapter Planner 32 Mammals

Section and Section Objectives	Time	STANDARDS NCLB	STANDARDS Biology	Activities and Labs
32–1 Introduction to the Mammals, pp. 821–827 **32.1.1** ***List*** the characteristics of mammals. **32.1.2** ***Tell*** when mammals evolved. **32.1.3** ***Describe*** how mammals perform essential life functions.	2 periods (1 block)	BI 9.a	*BI 9.g	**SE:** ***Inquiry Activity,*** How are teeth adapted to processing different foods?, p. 820 L2 **TE:** ***Build Science Skills,*** p. 822 L1 L2, p. 823 L1 L2 **TE:** ***Build Science Skills,*** p. 824 L2 L3, p. 826 L2 **SE:** ***Real-World Lab,*** Using Fibers as Forensic Evidence, pp. 842–843 L2 **IF:** Investigation 9 L2 L3
32–2 Diversity of Mammals, pp. 828–832 **32.2.1** ***Explain*** how the three groups of living mammals differ from one another. **32.2.2** ***Name*** the major orders of placental mammals. **32.2.3** ***Describe*** how convergent evolution caused mammals on different continents to be similar in form and function.	1 period (1/2 block)			**TE:** ***Build Science Skills,*** p. 829 L1 L2 **TE:** ***Build Science Skills,*** p. 830 L1 L2 **TE:** ***Make Connections,*** p. 831 L2
32–3 Primates and Human Origins, pp. 833–841 **32.3.1** ***Identify*** the characteristics that all primates share. **32.3.2** ***Describe*** the major evolutionary groups of primates. **32.3.3** ***Explain*** the current scientific thinking about hominid evolution.	2 periods (1 block)	7 3.c		**TE:** ***Build Science Skills,*** p. 833 L2 **SE:** ***Quick Lab,*** How is binocular vision useful?, p. 834 L2 **TE:** ***Build Science Skills,*** p. 834 L2 **SE:** ***Biology and History,*** Human-Fossil Seekers, pp. 836–837 L2 **LMA:** Chapter 32 Lab L2 L3 **LMB:** Chapter 32 Lab L1 L2
Chapter 32 Assessment, pp. 844–847	1 period (1/2 block)			

ACTIVITY PLANNER

SE: *Inquiry Activity,* p. 820; 15 min.; mammal teeth, including incisors and canines from carnivores and molars from herbivores

TE: *Build Science Skills,* p. 822; 15 min.; various animal hides

TE: *Build Science Skills,* p. 823; 15 min.; celery stick, hand mirror

TE: *Build Science Skills,* p. 824; 30 min.; sheep, cow, or pig heart, dissecting tools, dissecting tray, disposable plastic gloves, lab apron

TE: *Build Science Skills,* p. 826; 15 min.; skeletons or pictures of skeletons of various mammals

TE: *Build Science Skills,* p. 829; 30 min.; modeling clay, pipe cleaners, yarn, netting, tape, glue, photographs or diagrams of developing placental embryos

TE: *Build Science Skills,* p. 830; 15 min.; 10 pictures of mammals

TE: *Make Connections,* p. 831; 15 min.; pictures of endangered mammals

TE: *Build Science Skills,* p. 833; 10 min.; bulky mittens, small objects

SE: *Quick Lab,* p. 834; 10 min.; sheet of paper

TE: *Build Science Skills,* p. 834; 15 min.; pictures of different primates

SE: *Real-World Lab,* pp. 842 and 843; 45 min.; reference fibers, unknown fibers, microscope slides, coverslips, dropper pipette, microscope, glass-marking pencil, facial tissues, isopropyl alcohol, rubber cement, forceps, test-tube rack, 4 test tubes of biuret reagent, 4 glass stirring rods, hot water bath

PLANNING KEY

Ability Levels

for students performing . . .

below grade level L1

at grade level L2

above grade level L3

Print Components

SE	Student Edition	LA	Lab Assessment
TE	Teacher's Edition	BTM	Biotechnology Manual
RSW	Reading & Study Workbook A	IDM	Issues and Decision Making
ARSW	Adapted Reading & Study Workbook B	LW	Lab Worksheets
TR	Teaching Resources	LMA	Laboratory Manual A
IF	Investigations in Forensics	LMB	Laboratory Manual B

Tech Components

CTB	Computer Test Bank
BD	BioDetectives DVD
TP	Transparencies Plus
PLM	Probeware Lab Manual
ABC	ABC DVD Library
LS	Lab Simulations
VL	Virtual Labs

Interactive textbook with assessment at PHSchool.com

Program Resources	Assessment	Media and Technology
TR: Lesson Plan 32–1, Section Summary, p. 86 L1, p. 97 L2, Worksheets, pp. 89–91 L1, pp. 99–102 L2 **LW:** Chapter 32 Real-World Lab L1 L2 L3 **RSW:** Section 32–1 L2 **ARSW:** Section 32–1 L1	**SE:** 32–1 Section Assessment, p. 827 **TR:** Section Review 32–1	**iText:** Section 32–1 **TP:** 32–1 Interest Grabber, Section Outline, Structure of a Bear's Heart, Figure 32–4 **BD:** "Wrongly Accused: Science and Justice"
TR: Lesson Plan 32–2, Section Summary, p. 87 L1, p. 97 L2, Worksheets, p. 92 L1, pp. 103–104 L2 **RSW:** Section 32–2 L2 **ARSW:** Section 32–2 L1 **IDM:** Issues and Decisions 32 L2 L3	**SE:** 32–2 Section Assessment, p. 832 **TR:** Section Review 32–2	**iText:** Section 32–2 **TP:** 32–2 Interest Grabber, Section Outline, Compare/Contrast Table, Figure 32–13
TR: Lesson Plan 32–3, Section Summary, p. 88 L1, p. 98 L2, Worksheets, pp. 93–95 L1, pp. 105–107 L2, Enrichment L2 L3 **RSW:** Section 32–3 L2 **ARSW:** Section 32–3 L1 **IDM:** Issues and Decisions 15, 17 L2 L3	**SE:** 32–3 Section Assessment, p. 841 **TR:** Section Review 32–3	**iText:** Section 32–3 **TP:** 32–3 Interest Grabber, Section Outline, Comparison of Skulls of Human Ancestors, Figure 32–16 **BD:** "Mummies: Ties to the Past"
	SE: Chapter 32 Assessment, pp. 844–847 **TR:** Chapter Vocabulary Review, Graphic Organizer, Chapter 32 Test	**iText:** Chapter 32 Assessment **CTB:** Chapter 32 Test

Go Online

Students can do research, share data, and test their knowledge online.

TIME SAVER

PRESSED FOR TIME?

To Preview the Chapter

- Introduce students to Key Concepts and Vocabulary terms in each section.
- Have students study the illustrations and read the captions in Figures 32–4, 32–12, 32–15, and 32–16.

To Cover the Chapter Quickly

- Have students read all of Sections 32–1 and 32–2.
- Assign Section Reviews 32–1 and 32–2; questions 1–8, 11–21, 28–32, and 34–37 in the Chapter 32 Assessment; and questions 1–10 in Chapter 32 Standards Practice.

To Review the Chapter

- Review the Chapter 32 Study Guide and assign the concept map.
- Assign Section Reviews 32–1 through 32–3 in the Reading and Study Workbook or the Adapted Reading and Study Workbook.

CHAPTER 32

ENGAGE/EXPLORE

Inquiry Activity

Objectives Students will be able to infer how teeth are adapted to process different foods. L2

Skills Focus Classifying, Inferring

Materials variety of mammal teeth, including incisors and canines from carnivores and molars from herbivores, or pictures of mammal teeth

Time 15 minutes

Safety Have students wear disposable plastic gloves and dispose of them appropriately at the end of the activity.

Strategies

- Discuss why different types of teeth are required to break off and chew different types of food.
- Relate teeth to different tools that are used for similar tasks, such as scissors and incisors for cutting off grass or animal tissue.
- Give students hand mirrors to examine the shapes of their own teeth.

Expected Outcome Students should infer that sharp, tearing teeth belong to mammals that eat other animals and flat, grinding teeth belong to mammals that eat plants.

Think About It

1. Students might sort the teeth into narrow, sharp teeth and wide, flat teeth. They might also distinguish flat, slicing incisors from pointed canine (cuspid) teeth. Students should explain how they classified the teeth.
2. Accept all reasonable answers. Narrow, sharp teeth are adapted for cutting and tearing meat. Wide, flat teeth are adapted for grinding plant material.

Assess Prior Knowledge

Invite students to name as many mammals as possible. If humans have not been mentioned, ask: **Are humans mammals?** *(Yes)* Then, have students give as many characteristics of mammals as they can. List these characteristics on the board and update them as you study the chapter.

CHAPTER 32

Mammals

A collared anteater carries her young on her back. **Like all mammals, anteaters have hair, breathe air, and nurse their young with milk.**

Inquiry Activity

How are teeth adapted to processing different foods?

Procedure  

1. Put on plastic gloves. Examine a mammal tooth. Describe the shape of the tooth.
2. Based on the tooth's structure, try to infer whether the mammal ate mainly plants or other animals.
3. Repeat steps 1 and 2 for other mammal teeth.
4. Wash your hands with soap and warm water before leaving the lab.

Think About It

1. **Classifying** Sort the teeth into different groups based on their structure. Explain how you classified the teeth.
2. **Inferring** Describe what type of food you think each type of tooth is adapted to processing. Explain your reasoning.

TEACHER TO TEACHER

Have students research the DNA or amino-acid sequences of individuals of different orders of mammals. Students can then compare their findings with the DNA or amino-acid sequences of humans. Discuss how these data could provide biochemical evidence in support of established classification of mammals.

— Adam Weiss
Biology Teacher
Essex High School
Essex Junction, Vermont

32–1 Introduction to the Mammals

BI 9.a. Students know how the complementary activity of major body systems provides cells with oxygen and nutrients and removes toxic waste products such as carbon dioxide. **BI 9.g.** Students know the homeostatic role of the kidneys in the removal of nitrogenous wastes and the role of the liver in blood detoxification and glucose balance.

It is late January in the Appalachian Mountains. In a rocky den beneath the snowdrifts, a black bear has just given birth. Two tiny cubs are nursing on their mother's rich milk. It is bitterly cold outside, but the mother's dense fur and thick layer of body fat keep her and her cubs comfortably warm. When spring arrives, the hungry bears will emerge from the den. For the next two years, the cubs will follow their mother as she teaches them to search for food and defend themselves.

Bears are mammals, members of the class Mammalia. All mammals are characterized by two notable features: hair and mammary glands. In female mammals, **mammary glands**—the feature for which mammals are named—produce milk to nourish the young. **In addition to having hair and the ability to nourish their young with milk, all mammals breathe air, have four-chambered hearts, and are endotherms that generate their body heat internally.**

Guide for Reading

Key Concepts
- What are the characteristics of mammals?
- When did mammals evolve?
- How do mammals maintain homeostasis?

Vocabulary
mammary gland
subcutaneous fat
rumen
diaphragm
cerebral cortex

Reading Strategy: Asking Questions Before you read, rewrite the headings in the section as *how, why,* or *what* questions about mammals. As you read, write brief answers to these heading questions.

Evolution of Mammals

Neither mammary glands nor hair are preserved in the fossil record. But mammals have several other characteristics that help scientists to identify mammalian fossils. These characteristics include a lower jaw consisting of a large, teeth-bearing bone connected directly to the skull by a joint; complex teeth that are replaced just once in a lifetime; and distinctive features of the limbs and the backbone.

Mammals are descended from ancient reptiles. According to the fossil record, the ancestors of modern mammals diverged from ancient reptiles during the Carboniferous Period. For millions of years, various mammal-like reptiles lived alongside other reptile groups.

The first true mammals appeared during the late Triassic Period, about 220 million years ago. These mammals were very small and probably resembled modern tree shrews, like the one in **Figure 32–1.** While dinosaurs ruled the Cretaceous Period, from about 145 to 65 million years ago, mammals were generally small and remained out of sight. These mammals were probably nocturnal, or active at night.

After the disappearance of the dinosaurs at the end of the Cretaceous Period, mammals underwent a burst of adaptive radiation. They increased in size and occupied many new niches. In fact, the Cenozoic Era, which followed the Cretaceous Period, is usually called the Age of Mammals. Three major groups of mammals had evolved by the beginning of the Cenozoic Era. Surviving members of these groups include today's monotremes, marsupials, and placental mammals.

▼ **Figure 32–1** **The first mammals appeared on Earth about 220 million years ago.** They may have resembled this tree shrew from Madagascar, shown here clutching a beetle. Like this tree shrew, early mammals probably ate insects.

SECTION RESOURCES

Print:
- ***Teaching Resources,*** Lesson Plan 32–1, Adapted Section Summary 32–1, Adapted Worksheets 32–1, Section Summary 32–1, Worksheets 32–1, Section Review 32–1
- ***Reading and Study Workbook A,*** Section 32–1
- ***Adapted Reading and Study Workbook B,*** Section 32–1
- ***Investigations in Forensics,*** Investigation 9
- ***Lab Worksheets,*** Chapter 32 Real-World Lab

Technology:
- ***iText,*** Section 32–1
- ***Transparencies Plus,*** Section 32–1
- ***BioDetectives DVD,*** "Wrongly Accused: Science and Justice"

Section 32–1

1 FOCUS

Objectives

32.1.1 ***List*** the characteristics of mammals.
32.1.2 ***Tell*** when mammals evolved.
32.1.3 ***Describe*** how mammals perform essential life functions.

Guide for Reading

Vocabulary Preview

Explain that the prefix *sub-* means "under," and *cutaneous* means "having to do with the skin." Then, ask: **Where do you think subcutaneous fat is located?** *(Under the skin)*

Reading Strategy

Have students also write *how, why,* or *what* questions for the green subheadings in the section. Remind students to leave room under each question to write its answer as they read the section.

2 INSTRUCT

Evolution of Mammals

Build Science Skills

Posing Questions Challenge students to consider what types of questions a paleontologist might ask to determine whether or not a new fossil find is the remains of an early mammal. You might have groups of students work together to develop a list of questions. *(Possible question topics include presence of mammalian tooth structure, limb attachment to backbone, jaw structure, or number of limbs.)* L2

32–1 (continued)

Form and Function in Mammals

Build Science Skills

Inferring Borrow various animal hides from a zoo or natural history museum. Challenge students to make inferences about the animals' habitats based on the types of hairs in their coats. *(In general, animals in cold climates have heavy coats with two layers of hairs. Animals in warm environments have thinner coats or no hair at all. Exceptions in cold climates include dolphins, whales, and walruses, which are protected by layers of blubber.)* L1 L2

Make Connections

Environmental Science Relate the diversity of mammalian modes of feeding to the adaptive radiation of mammals in the Cenozoic Era. Ask: **Why do you think the first mammals were insectivores?** *(Possible answers: Insects provided a lot of energy to an endothermic mammal; mammals' small size restricted their predation to insects and perhaps dinosaur eggs.)* **What change in conditions opened up many new energy sources to the early mammals?** *(The extinction of dinosaurs left many niche resources open; mammals were equipped to live successfully in the changing climate, and lack of competition and predation allowed them to develop many new, diverse niches.)* Point out that the changing climate also affected plant life, and many mammals coevolved with plants. One example is grasses evolving along with mammalian herbivores in grassland ecosystems. L2 L3

▲ **Figure 32–2** **As endotherms, mammals are capable of adjusting their body heat internally.** When they get too warm, some mammals, such as this gray wolf cub, pant to rid their bodies of excess heat.

Form and Function in Mammals

The mammalian body has adapted in varied ways to a great many habitats. As a member of this class of chordates, you may be familiar with some of these adaptations.

Body Temperature Control Like birds, mammals are endotherms; their bodies can generate heat internally. Mammals and birds—especially small ones—have a much higher metabolic rate than most other chordates. The high rate of metabolism helps mammals generate body heat. Mammals also have external body hair that helps them keep warm. Hair is part of the integumentary system, which is the outer covering of the body—the skin and all structures associated with the skin. **Subcutaneous** (sub-kyoo-TAY-nee-us) **fat,** which is a layer of fat located beneath the skin, also helps conserve body heat.

Many mammals have sweat glands that help cool the body. Sweating is regulated by an internal negative feedback mechanism, which you learned about in Chapter 26. When its internal body temperature becomes too high, the mammal begins to sweat. The evaporation of the sweat then cools the body. The mammal then stops sweating. Mammals that lack sweat glands, like the wolf in **Figure 32–2,** often pant to rid themselves of excess heat. **The ability of mammals to regulate their body heat from within is an example of homeostasis.** This ability also allows mammals to move about in the cold, while most other animals would seek shelter.

Feeding Because of its high metabolic rate, a mammal must eat nearly 10 times as much food as a reptile of the same size to maintain homeostasis. Some mammals, such as rabbits and giraffes, eat only plants. Others, including cats and weasels, are meat-eaters. Bears and humans are omnivores, consuming all types of food. Certain whales, like the one in **Figure 32–3,** are filter feeders.

Early mammals ate insects. **As mammals evolved, the form and function of their jaws and teeth became adapted to eat foods other than insects.** The joint between the skull and lower jaw became stronger than that of reptiles. This joint allowed mammals to evolve larger, more powerful jaw muscles and different ways of chewing.

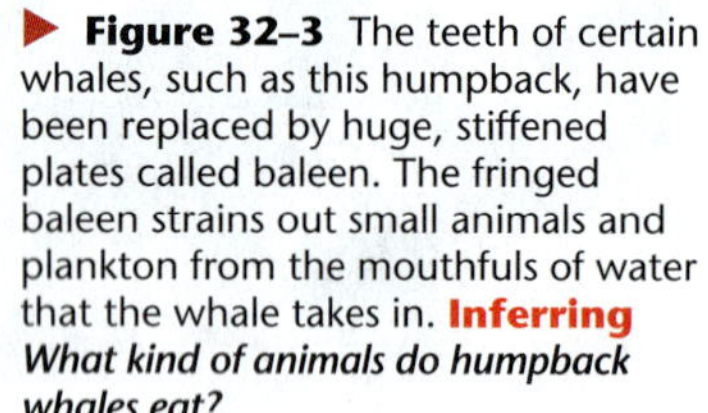

▶ **Figure 32–3** The teeth of certain whales, such as this humpback, have been replaced by huge, stiffened plates called baleen. The fringed baleen strains out small animals and plankton from the mouthfuls of water that the whale takes in. **Inferring** ***What kind of animals do humpback whales eat?***

ESL SUPPORT FOR ENGLISH LANGUAGE LEARNERS

Comprehension: Key Concept

Beginning On the board, rewrite the boldface sentence (paragraph 2, page 821) as individual sentences that each express one characteristic of mammals, e.g., "All mammals breathe air." Explain each characteristic. Then, have students construct a concept circle with "Characteristics of Mammals" in the center and the characteristics connected to the center by lines. L1

Intermediate Read aloud the boldface sentence (paragraph 2, page 821). Ask individual students, including some ESL students, to identify characteristics of mammals. Then, pair ESL students with English-proficient students. Each pair should write a summary, in their own words, of the characteristics of mammals. The student pairs should share their summaries with the class. L2

FIGURE 32–4 JAWS AND TEETH OF MAMMALS

The specialized jaws and teeth of mammals are adapted for different diets. Carnivorous mammals use sharp canines and incisors to grip and slice flesh from their prey. Their jaws usually move up and down as they chew. Herbivorous mammals use flat-edged incisors to grasp and tear vegetation, and flattened molars to grind the food. Their jaws generally move from side to side.

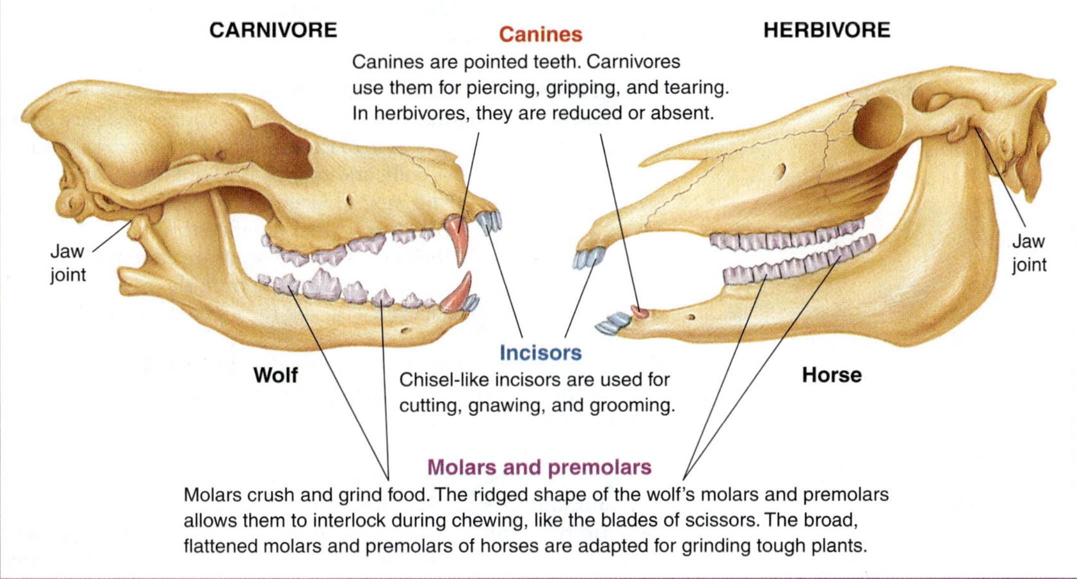

Modern mammals have specialized teeth—incisors, canines, molars, and premolars—which you can see in **Figure 32–4.** Observe that the structure of carnivores' teeth is different from that of herbivores' teeth. Mammals' teeth enable food to be processed efficiently. The more efficiently an animal can obtain and process its food, the more energy it can obtain.

A mammal's digestive tract breaks down and absorbs the type of food that it eats. Because digestive enzymes can quickly break down meat, carnivores have a relatively short intestine. Tough, fibrous plant tissues take much more time to digest, so most herbivores have a much longer intestine.

Many herbivores also have specialized digestive organs to break down plant matter. Cows and their relatives have a stomach chamber called the **rumen,** in which newly swallowed plant food is stored and processed. The rumen contains symbiotic bacteria that digest the cellulose of most plant tissues. After some time, the grazer regurgitates the food from the rumen into its mouth. The partially digested food is chewed and swallowed again. After several cycles, it moves through the rest of the stomach and into the intestines.

CHECKPOINT *What is the function of a rumen?*

Word Origins

The word **incisor** comes from the Latin word *incidere,* which means "to cut." **In surgery, what is an incision?**

Use Visuals

Figure 32–4 Have students compare and contrast the herbivore and carnivore teeth in the illustration. Make a Venn diagram on the board to note the similarities and differences. Ask: **Why do you think it is advantageous for herbivores to have flat molars?** *(The grinding motion of the teeth and jaws helps break apart tough plant fibers.)* **Could a dog successfully live on a diet of grass?** *(No)* **Why?** *(Dogs have the teeth of a carnivore; although the teeth are sharp, they could not effectively grind plant material to break it apart. The dog's digestive system is also not structured to digest and absorb all the nutrients from plant tissue.)* Point out how carnivores use their jaws differently from herbivores. Carnivores use mostly up and down motion to chew food. Herbivores use side-to-side motion to make the plant matter (usually long fibrous stems) small enough to be swallowed. L1 L2

Build Science Skills

Observing Give students a celery stick. Have them chew and swallow the celery. While they chew, challenge students to observe in a mirror how their teeth and jaws work to chew the food. Discuss students' observations, focusing on the characteristics of their teeth that enabled them to chew the food. Remind students that they are omnivores with teeth adapted for eating both plants and animals. L1 L2

Word Origins

An incision is a cut made into a tissue or an organ. L2

BIO INSIGHTS FACTS AND FIGURES

Digestion is "ruminantary"

Ruminants quickly chew grass just until it's small enough to swallow. It moves to the first chamber of the stomach, the rumen, which stores large amounts of food. It is here that simple carbohydrates, proteins, and cellulose are broken down by cellulose-digesting microorganisms. While resting, the ruminant regurgitates food from the rumen and rechews it. After the food is reswallowed, it moves into the reticulum, which screens out larger food particles, allowing smaller particles to move into the omasum. There, excess water is removed from the food by squeezing and grinding. Then, food moves into the abomasum, where acids and digestive enzymes break down protein, as in a carnivore's stomach. From there, the food enters the intestines, where digestion continues and nutrients and water are absorbed; then wastes are eliminated.

Answers to . . .

CHECKPOINT *It stores and processes newly swallowed plant food.*

Figure 32–3 *Plankton and small marine animals*

32–1 (continued)

Download a worksheet on mammals for students to complete, and find additional teacher support from NSTA SciLinks.

Use Visuals

Figure 32–5 Have students trace the path of blood through the heart. They can compare the mammalian heart in Figure 32–5 to the reptilian heart in Figure 31–4 on page 801. Remind students that mammals evolved from reptiles. Ask: **How does the mammalian heart differ from the reptilian heart?** *(The mammalian heart has two separate ventricles; most reptiles have a single ventricle.)* **Why is it advantageous to have two separate ventricles?** *(The oxygen-poor blood never mixes with the oxygen-rich blood, so the blood going to the body has the highest possible level of oxygen.)* L1 L2

Build Science Skills

Observing Some students might enjoy dissecting a mammalian heart. Obtain a cow, pig, or sheep heart from a butcher. Students also need dissecting tools and a dissecting tray. Students should wear disposable plastic gloves while dissecting the heart and wash their hands thoroughly when finished. Have students diagram the structure of the heart and label its parts. You can display the dissected hearts and the diagrams for the class to observe.

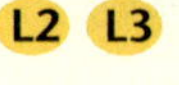

For: Links on mammals
Visit: www.SciLinks.org
Web Code: cbn-9321

Respiration All mammals, even those that live in water, use lungs to breathe. These lungs are controlled by two sets of muscles. Mammals inhale when muscles in the chest lift the rib cage up and outward, increasing the volume of the chest cavity. At the same time, a powerful muscle called the **diaphragm** (DY-uh-fram) pulls the bottom of the chest cavity downward, which further increases its volume. As a result, air is pulled into the lungs. When the chest muscles lower the rib cage and the diaphragm relaxes, the volume of the chest cavity decreases. This action pushes air out of the lungs.

Circulation The mammalian circulatory system is divided into two completely separate loops with a four-chambered heart, shown in **Figure 32–5.** The right side of the heart receives oxygen-poor blood from all over the body and pumps it to the lungs. After picking up oxygen in the lungs, blood returns to the left side of the heart. This oxygen-rich blood is then pumped through blood vessels to the rest of the body. The two separate circuits—one to and from the lungs, and the other to and from the rest of the body—efficiently transport materials throughout the body.

Excretion Mammals have highly developed kidneys that help control the composition of body fluids. Mammalian kidneys extract nitrogenous wastes from the blood in the form of urea. Urea, other wastes, and water combine to form urine. From the kidneys, urine flows to a urinary bladder, where it is stored until it is eliminated. **The kidneys of mammals help maintain homeostasis by filtering urea from the blood, as well as by excreting excess water or retaining needed water.** They also retain salts, sugars, and other compounds the body cannot afford to lose. Because they are so efficient at controlling and stabilizing the amount of water in the body, the kidneys enable mammals to live in many habitats, such as deserts, in which they could not otherwise survive.

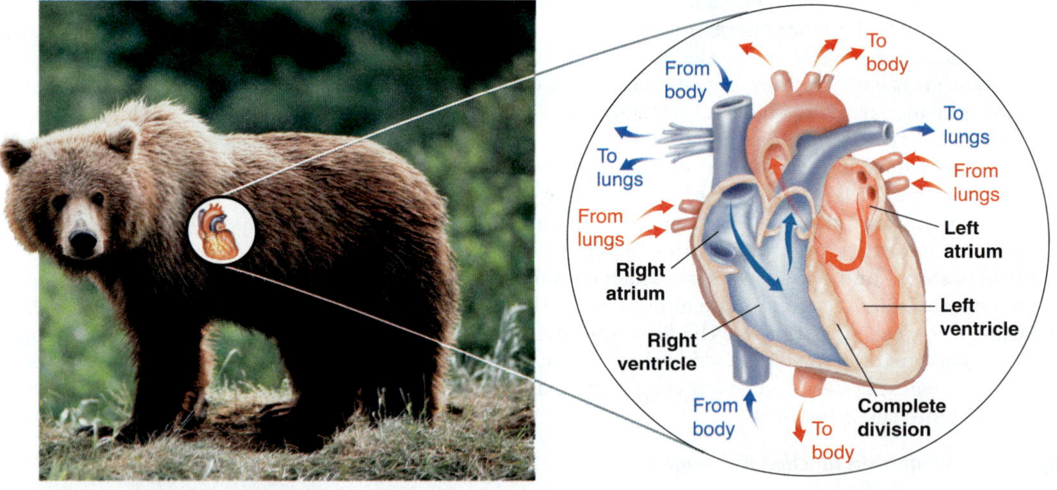

Figure 32–5 All mammals, including this brown bear, have a four-chambered heart that pumps blood in two separate circuits around the body. **Interpreting Graphics** *According to the diagram, which chamber receives blood that is low in oxygen?*

FACTS AND FIGURES

Respiratory system makes noise

Mammals make vocalizations for various reasons. Some vocalizations warn other species members of danger. Others are used to find mates or to defend territories. To make these vocalizations, mammals use the respiratory system. As air moves into the pharynx and through the trachea to the lungs, it passes through the larynx. The larynx is the location of the vocal cords. The vocal cords are a pair of folds in the cartilaginous walls of the larynx. The space between these folds is the glottis. When air is expelled from the lungs, it vibrates the vocal cords to produce a sound. The cartilage in the larynx can be highly specialized from one species to another to produce distinct sounds. Speech is produced by shaping vocal sounds into patterns using the mouth, tongue, and lips.

Response Mammals have the most highly developed brains of any animals. As you can see in **Figure 32–6,** the brain consists of three main parts: the cerebrum, the cerebellum, and the medulla oblongata. The cerebrum makes possible such complicated behaviors as thinking and learning. The cerebellum controls muscular coordination. The medulla oblongata regulates involuntary body functions, or those that are not under conscious control, such as breathing and heart rate.

A mammal's cerebrum contains a well-developed outer layer called the **cerebral cortex,** which is the center of thinking and other complex behaviors. Some activities, such as reading this textbook, are possible only with the human cerebral cortex. However, mammals other than humans also exhibit complex behaviors, such as storing food for later use.

Mammals rely on highly developed senses to detect and respond to stimuli from their external environment. Many mammals have well-developed senses of smell and hearing. You probably know, for example, that dogs can easily identify people by their particular scent. Although mammalian ears all have the same basic parts, they differ in their ability to detect sound. For example, dogs, bats, and dolphins can detect sounds at much higher frequencies than humans can. In fact, bats and dolphins can find objects in their environment using the echo of their own high-frequency sounds. Other mammals, such as elephants, can detect sounds at much lower frequencies.

Many mammals have some color-sensing structures in their eyes, yet the ability to distinguish colors may vary among different species. Color vision is most useful to diurnal animals—those that are active during daylight. Although mammals such as cats can detect color, they may not see the full range of colors that humans and some other primates can.

CHECKPOINT *What is the function of the cerebral cortex?*

Chemical Controls The nervous system is not the only system that controls body processes. Mammals, like other vertebrates, have endocrine glands that are part of an endocrine system. Endocrine glands regulate body activities by releasing chemicals called hormones that affect other organs and tissues. Hormones produced by a gland in a mammal's neck, for example, help regulate the amount of calcium in the bones. Hormones are carried by the blood to the organs that they affect.

Fighting Disease All organisms live in an environment that contains disease-causing microorganisms, or pathogens. The immune systems of mammals and other vertebrates function to protect animals from disease. When mammals do get sick, their immune systems help them recover. Mammalian immune systems consist of barriers, such as the skin, that prevent pathogens from entering the body. In addition, specialized cells and chemicals recognize and destroy pathogens.

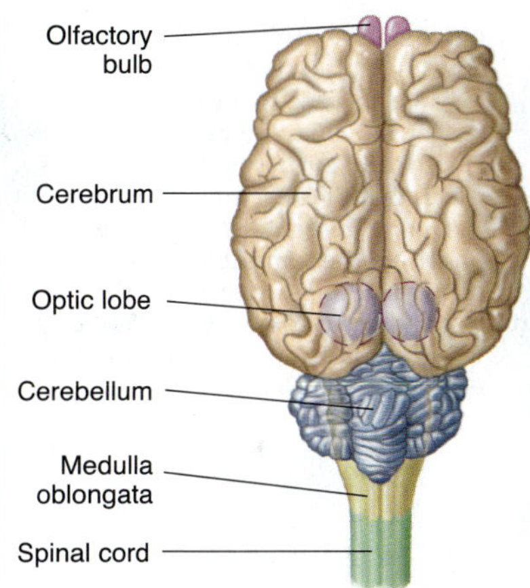

▲ **Figure 32–6** Mammals have large brains in proportion to their body size. Most of the brain is taken up by an enlarged cerebrum, which contains a well-developed cerebral cortex. **Inferring** *How would a large cerebrum be advantageous to a mammal?*

Build Science Skills

Inferring Explain that the number of rods and cones in the retina correlates with whether an animal is nocturnal or diurnal. Rods are photoreceptors that are sensitive to light but do not distinguish color. Cones are photoreceptors that do not function in night vision because they require more light to be stimulated. In daylight, cones distinguish colors. Challenge students to infer the relative compositions of rods and cones in the eyes of nocturnal and diurnal mammals. *(Nocturnal animals usually have many more rods than cones because they require sharp vision during the night when they are active. Diurnal animals have more cones, which enable them to have very sharp vision in daylight.)* L2 L3

Address Misconceptions

Emphasize to students that all vertebrates, not just mammals, have a system for fighting disease. Pathogens, such as fungi, bacteria, and viruses, infect fishes, amphibians, reptiles, and birds, as well as mammals. Explain that as in mammals, other vertebrates have barriers to pathogens that include skin and mucus secretions. Vertebrates also have white blood cells that destroy pathogens. L2

FACTS AND FIGURES

Why a larger mammalian brain?
Some scientists think the mammalian brain evolved as a result of the needs of a nocturnal animal. Many reptiles and birds are active during the day and depend substantially on eyesight to find food. Visual information, especially the three-dimensional impressions that result from binocular vision, needs little analysis and thus relatively less brain matter. A nocturnal animal, however, must also depend significantly on information from scent and sound. As the animal moves, it must compare and integrate perceptions from three senses, a process that requires a relatively more complex brain. Furthermore, an animal that could associate such information with past events—compare past to present—might have a selective advantage.

Answers to . . .

CHECKPOINT *The cerebral cortex is the center of thinking and other complex behaviors.*

Figure 32–5 *The right atrium*

Figure 32–6 *The increased ability for complex thinking increases a mammal's adaptability.*

32–1 (continued)

Use Visuals

Figure 32–7 Have students compare the mammalian limbs in Figure 32–7. Ask: **What limb characteristics are common to mammals that run?** *(Longer, less flexible, no side digits)* **How do the limbs of digging mammals differ from those of climbing mammals?** *(Climbing mammals have longer, more slender digits and limbs. Digging mammals have shorter, thicker digits and stocky limbs.)* **How are the limbs of swimming mammals similar to those of flying mammals?** *(Both have limbs and digits that are modified to support either the flipper or flaps of skin that form the wings.)* L1 L2

Build Science Skills

Classifying Provide skeletons of different mammals for students to examine. You can use diagrams if skeletons are not available. Challenge students to divide the skeletons into groups based on how the mammals move. Students should identify the characteristics of the skeletons that helped them make their classifications. Share with students the identity of each skeleton. Point out the features of the skeleton that could be used to make the correct classification. L2

Use Community Resources

Invite a zookeeper or zoologist to the class to describe the adaptive significance of maternal care in mammals. Ask the speaker to contrast the number of offspring produced by mammals with that of other vertebrates and to explain the current thinking that describes why mammals expend so much energy for maternal care. L2

Figure 32–7 The limbs and digits (fingers and toes) of many mammals are adapted to their particular way of life. Note the variety of lengths and shapes of the limb bones that different mammals use for movement. Homologous bones are the same color in all the drawings. **Applying Concepts** *Which structure shown in this figure would most closely resemble the limbs and digits of a whale?*

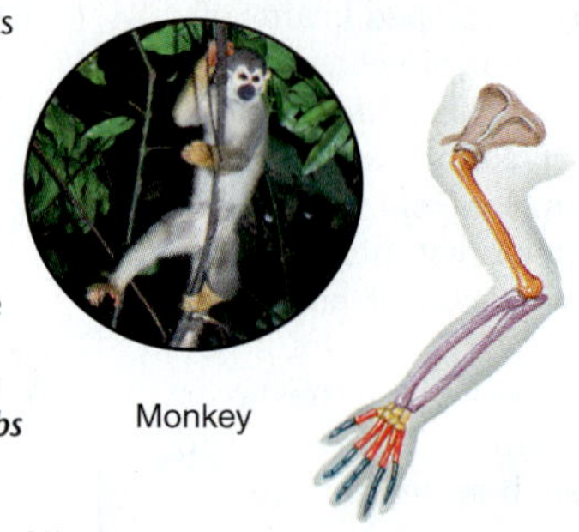

Climbers
Climbing mammals have long, flexible fingers and toes that can grasp vines and branches. They also have a flexible wrist joint.

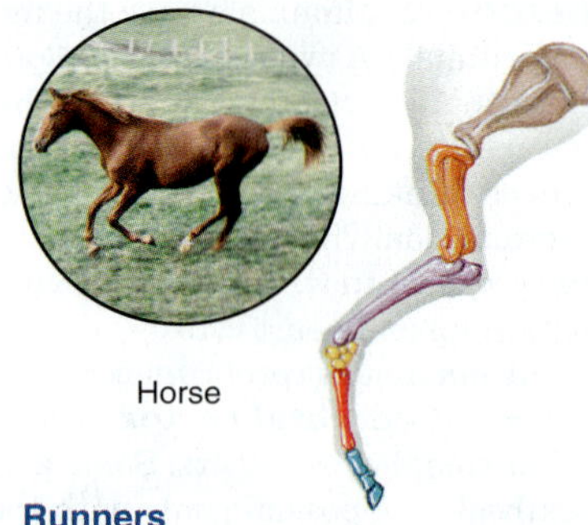

Runners
Running mammals need long limbs that can absorb shock. These animals have lost the side digits on their front and back feet. They stand on the tips of their remaining toes, which are called hooves.

Movement Mammals have evolved a variety of adaptations that aid in movement, including a backbone that flexes both vertically and side to side. This flexibility allows mammals to move with a bouncing, leaping stride. Shoulder and pelvic girdles have become more streamlined and flexible, permitting both front and hind limbs to move in a variety of ways.

Compare the adaptations of mammalian limbs shown in **Figure 32–7.** Variations in the limb bones and muscles allow mammals to run, walk, climb, burrow, hop, pounce, swing, fly, leap, and swim. Depending on their lifestyle, mammals may use any number of these methods to move about.

▼ **Figure 32–8** Still wobbly, a newborn wildebeest rises to its feet minutes after birth. Its mother will nurse and protect the calf until it is able to live on its own.

Reproduction Mammals reproduce by internal fertilization. The male deposits sperm inside the reproductive tract of the female, where fertilization occurs. As you will learn in the next section, mammals are classified into three groups, based on their modes of development and birth. Regardless of the mode of development, all newborn mammals, such as the newborn wildebeest in **Figure 32–8,** feed on their mother's milk.

Young mammals generally need care when they are born and for a long time afterward. During this period, they are cared for by one or both parents. Maternal care is an important mammalian characteristic, and the bond between mother and young is very close. Males of many species also play a role in caring for the young. Parental care helps ensure that young mammals will survive and reproduce. Mammalian parental behavior is an adaptation that is the result of natural selection and other evolutionary processes.

The duration and intensity of parental care varies among different species. Some mammals have a prolonged period when the young and the mother live together. During that period, the juvenile learns from its caregiver the behaviors it needs to survive.

BIO INSIGHTS

FACTS AND FIGURES

Elephants care about their young
Elephants have complex social interactions and behaviors associated with raising their young. The gestation period for elephants is about 22 months. Females first start mating around the age of 20 years. They will continue to have calves every two to four years until they reach about 50 years of age. Calves are highly dependent on their mothers for food for their first two years. These calves are cared for not only by their mothers but also by the other females in the herd. Older females help new mothers. Younger females play with the babies; this helps the young females prepare to become mothers. When a baby has finished weaning from its mother, it reaches an age of adolescence. Young males leave the herd, often joining bachelor herds. Young females stay with the herd and help care for other newborns.

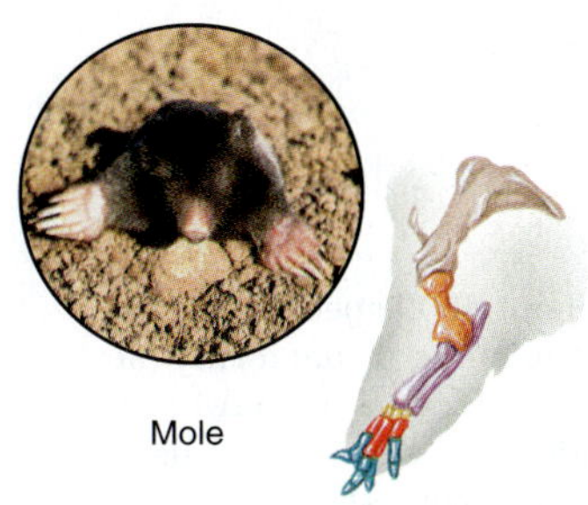

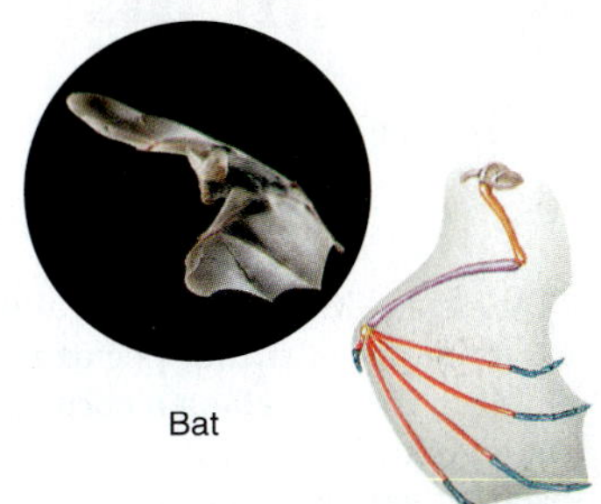

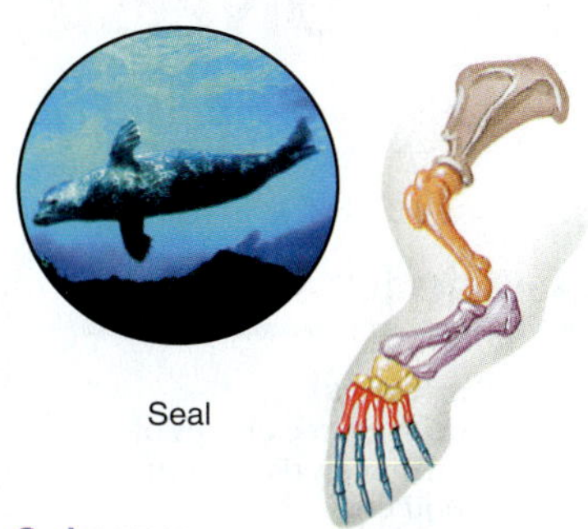

Diggers
Digging mammals have strong, thick claws, especially on their front feet. Their limbs are short and stocky, with large projections that anchor powerful muscles.

Flyers
The arms and hands of bats are modified to support flaps of skin that form wings.

Swimmers
Swimming mammals concentrate most of their movement between the arm and shoulder girdle. Their limbs are modified into broad, flat paddles, with the bones of their hands or feet extended to make a flipper.

Some mammal species, such as lions and elephants, live in groups in which the young may be cared for by adults other than the parents. Group living provides young mammals with the opportunity for complex social interaction among adults and juveniles.

Interrelationships of Organ Systems In mammals and other animals, organ systems are interdependent in order to maintain a homeostatic environment. All body systems depend on the circulatory system to transport materials. The respiratory system, for example, ensures that oxygen enters the lungs, but the blood carries oxygen to body cells. Similarly, blood carries waste products to the kidneys, which remove the waste products from the body. Nerve impulses from cells in the nervous system carry information to and from organs in every body system. The bones of the skeletal system could not grow and maintain themselves without calcium and other materials that enter the body through the digestive system. An animal's organ systems work together to meet the needs of the body as a whole.

BI 9.a

32–1 Section Assessment

1. **Key Concept** Name the characteristics that are common to all mammals.
2. **Key Concept** When did mammalian ancestors diverge from the other reptiles?
3. **Key Concept** List two ways in which mammals maintain homeostasis.
4. What is the function of the endocrine system?
5. **Critical Thinking Comparing and Contrasting** Compare the functions of the respiratory and circulatory systems. Then, explain how the structure of a mammal's heart helps these two systems work together to deliver oxygen to body cells.

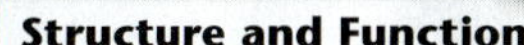
Focus on the BIG Idea

Structure and Function
Compare the structure of a mammal's brain to that of a fish, as shown in Chapter 30, **Figure 30–14.** What structures are more prominent in each animal's brain? How might these differences relate to the way the animals live?

Build Science Skills

Applying Concepts Invite students to think about eating. Ask: **What organ systems are involved in eating?** *(Nervous system: smelling, tasting, stimulating bringing food into mouth and chewing; muscular system: moving jaws for chewing, transporting food into stomach; skeletal system: jaws and teeth for chewing; digestive system: digesting food and absorbing nutrients; circulatory system: carrying nutrients to cells; excretory system: excreting wastes)* L2

3 ASSESS

Evaluate Understanding

Invite student volunteers to write on the board one characteristic of mammals. When students have exhausted all their ideas, add to the list, if necessary, to make it complete. Then, ask students to match the characteristics to the life functions that mammals perform.

Reteach

Have student pairs study the mammals pictured in this section and make a list of characteristics that mammals have in common. Students can compare their lists with the description of mammals given at the beginning of the section.

Focus on the BIG Idea

In mammals, the cerebrum is much larger, relative to the rest of the brain, than in fishes. In contrast, fishes have much larger olfactory bulbs. Mammals depend heavily on behaviors such as learning that are regulated by the cerebral cortex. Fishes are highly dependent on the sense of smell to capture prey.

32–1 Section Assessment

1. Hair, mammary glands, breathe air, have four-chambered hearts, endotherms
2. During the Carboniferous Period
3. Sample answers: regulating body heat from within, excreting or retaining liquid with the kidneys, eating a variety of foods
4. Regulates body activities by releasing hormones
5. The respiratory system brings air (oxygen) into the lungs. The circulatory system carries oxygen to the body and oxygen-poor blood to the lungs. The heart pumps blood to and from the lungs and to and from the body so that oxygen is delivered to body cells and oxygen-poor blood is delivered to the lungs.

Interactive Textbook

If your class subscribes to the iText, use it to review the Key Concepts in Section 32–1.

Answer to . . .

Figure 32–7 *The limbs of a seal, a swimming mammal*

Section 32–2

1 FOCUS

Objectives

32.2.1 ***Explain*** how the three groups of living mammals differ from one another.

32.2.2 ***Name*** the major orders of placental mammals.

32.2.3 ***Describe*** how convergent evolution caused mammals on different continents to be similar in form and function.

Guide for Reading

Vocabulary Preview

Say each Vocabulary term aloud and have students divide the word into syllables as best they can. Remind students that each syllable usually has only one vowel sound. *(mon•o•treme, mar•su•pi•al, and pla•cen•ta)*

Reading Strategy

Have students make a table with the headings *Monotreme, Marsupial,* and *Placental.* Before they read, tell students to write what they know about these mammal groups. After they read, students should add additional information and correct any misconceptions they had.

2 INSTRUCT

Monotremes and Marsupials

Build Science Skills

Comparing and Contrasting
Have students make a Venn diagram to compare and contrast the characteristics of monotremes and reptiles. In the overlap area, students should list features that monotremes and reptiles share *(cloaca, females lay soft-shelled eggs that incubate outside body).* In the separate areas of the circles, students should write characteristics specific to reptiles *(many do not care for young, ectothermic, have scales)* and those specific to monotremes *(nourish young with milk from body, endothermic, have hair).*

32–2 Diversity of Mammals

Guide for Reading

Key Concepts
- How do the three groups of living mammals differ from one another?
- How did convergent evolution cause mammals on different continents to be similar in form and function?

Vocabulary
monotreme
marsupial
placenta

Reading Strategy: Summarizing As you read, make a list of the major groups of mammals. Write several sentences describing the characteristics of each group. Then, give an example for each.

The class Mammalia contains about 4500 species, and the diversity of these species is astonishing. From a tiny mouse nibbling its way along a corncob to an African elephant uprooting a gigantic tree with its tusks and trunk, mammals have the greatest range of size of any group of vertebrates.

As you have read, tooth structure is one characteristic that scientists use to classify mammals. Mammals are also classified by the number and kinds of bones in the head. But the most important way to categorize living mammals is by the way they reproduce and develop.

The three groups of living mammals are the monotremes (MAHN-oh-treemz), the marsupials (mahr-SOO-pee-ulz), and the placentals. These three groups differ greatly in their means of reproduction and development.

Monotremes and Marsupials

Monotremes lay eggs. Marsupials bear live young, but at a very early stage of development. All monotremes are grouped in a single order, while marsupials are split into several different orders.

Monotremes Members of the **monotremes,** or egg-laying mammals, share two notable characteristics with reptiles. In monotremes, the digestive, reproductive, and urinary systems all open into a cloaca that is similar to the cloaca of reptiles. In fact, the name *monotreme* means "single opening." Reproduction in monotremes also resembles reproduction in reptiles more than other mammals. As in reptiles, a female monotreme lays soft-shelled eggs that are incubated outside her body. The eggs hatch into young animals in about ten days. Unlike young reptiles, however, young monotremes are nourished by their mother's milk, which they lick from pores on the surface of her abdomen.

Only three species of monotremes exist today: the duckbill platypus, shown in **Figure 32–9,** and two species of spiny anteaters, or echidnas. These animals are found in Australia and New Guinea.

Figure 32–9 **Like all monotremes, the platypus lays eggs that hatch outside the body but nourishes its young with milk produced in mammary glands.** The unusual snout of this duckbill platypus can sense electromagnetic signals put out by the muscles of other animals. The platypus uses its sensitive snout to locate prey, such as worms and mollusks, that burrow in the sediments.

SECTION RESOURCES

Print:
- ***Teaching Resources,*** Lesson Plan 32–2, Adapted Section Summary 32–2, Adapted Worksheets 32–2, Section Summary 32–2, Worksheets 32–2, Section Review 32–2
- ***Reading and Study Workbook A,*** Section 32–2
- ***Adapted Reading and Study Workbook B,*** Section 32–2
- ***Issues and Decision Making,*** Issues and Decisions, 32

Technology:
- ***iText,*** Section 32–2
- ***Transparencies Plus,*** Section 32–2

Marsupials Kangaroos, koalas, and wombats are examples of **marsupials**—mammals bearing live young that usually complete their development in an external pouch. When marsupials reproduce, the fertilized egg develops into an embryo inside the mother's reproductive tract. The embryo is born at a very early stage of development. It crawls across its mother's fur and attaches to a nipple. In most species of marsupials, the nipples are located in a pouch called the marsupium (mahr-SOO-pee-um) on the outside of the mother's body. Marsupials are named after this structure. Once inside the marsupium, the embryo, looking much like the one in **Figure 32–10,** spends several months attached to the nipple. It will continue to drink milk in its mother's pouch until it grows large enough to survive on its own.

CHECKPOINT *How does a marsupial differ from a monotreme?*

Figure 32–10 Most marsupials, including this wallaby, are originally from Australia and New Guinea. **Marsupials bear live young that usually complete their development in a pouch.** The pink, newborn wallaby (inset) is still an embryo but will soon grow into a "joey" that resembles a small adult.

Placental Mammals

Placental mammals are the mammals with which you are most familiar. Mice, cats, dogs, whales, elephants, humans, and the sea lions in **Figure 32–11** all fall within this category. This group gets its name from an internal structure called the **placenta,** which is formed when the embryo's tissues join with tissues from within the mother's body.

In placental mammals, nutrients, oxygen, carbon dioxide, and wastes are exchanged efficiently between embryo and mother through the placenta. The placenta allows the embryo to develop for a much longer time inside the mother—from a few weeks in mice and rats to as long as two years in elephants. After birth, most placental mammals care for their young and provide them with nourishment by nursing. **Figure 32–12,** on the following pages, describes the main orders of placental mammals.

Figure 32–11 The California sea lion is an example of a placental mammal. **In placental mammals, nutrients, oxygen, carbon dioxide, and wastes are exchanged between embryo and mother through the placenta.**

Make Connections

Environmental Science Explain to students that populations of marsupials in Australia and New Guinea are declining. This decline is caused in part by the introduction of rats, sheep, and rabbits to the continent. Ask: **These placental mammals that have been introduced are not predators. How could they cause a decline in the population of native marsupials?** *(These mammals fill many of the same niches and compete for the same resources as the native marsupials, so there are fewer resources available for the native marsupials.)* **Why do you think there are not many marsupials in other parts of the world?** *(The placental mammals outcompeted the marsupials for resources in the environment. The marsupials might also have been easier prey for predators.)* L2 L3

Placental Mammals

Build Science Skills

Using Models Challenge student groups to construct a model of a placenta with materials such as modeling clay, pipe cleaners, yarn, netting, tape, or glue. Display photographs or diagrams of a developing placental embryo as a guide. Have groups describe how the placenta works to protect the developing embryo and transfer nutrients to and wastes away from it. Ask: **How does the placenta allow an embryo to develop longer than embryos that develop inside eggs?** *(The egg has finite sources of energy for growth and a finite space for storing the wastes produced. The placenta provides an unlimited supply of energy—from the mother's food intake—and the ability to continually remove wastes via the mother's body.)* L1 L2

UNIVERSAL ACCESS

Inclusion/Special Needs
Find out what students already know about monotremes and marsupials. Many will have heard about the duck-bill platypus. Show them videos of the platypus and echidnas, as well as marsupials. As they watch the videos, encourage them to note how the animals care for their young and features that classify them as mammals. Discuss reasons why these mammals are found in Australia and New Guinea. L1

English Language Learners
Students can make a glossary for the mammalian orders. In their glossaries, they can illustrate common members of each order and write descriptions of the mammals in English and their native languages. Under the name of the order, students can also write in English and their native languages the names of animals belonging to the order. L1 L2

Answer to . . .

CHECKPOINT *Monotremes lay eggs; marsupials bear live young.*

32–2 (continued)

Use Visuals

Figure 32–12 Have students examine the photographs and read the caption for each mammalian order. Ask: **What characteristics are used to classify placental mammals?** *(Feeding habits, teeth, limbs)* **Which orders of mammals have hooves?** *(Artiodactyls and perissodactyls)* **Which order has a single pair of long, curved incisor teeth in the upper and lower jaws?** *(Rodents)* **What mammal belongs to the order Chiroptera?** *(Bats)* **To which order do you belong?** *(Primates)* L1 L2

Build Science Skills

Classifying Give students 10 pictures of different mammals. If possible, include mammals that students are not familiar with. Challenge students to use the information in Figure 32–12 to identify the order to which each mammal belongs. Students should list the characteristics of each mammal on which they based their classification. L1 L2

Use Community Resources

Take the class to the zoo. Before going, have students use the information in Figure 32–12 to create a field guide for placental mammals. Students should use their field guide at the zoo to identify the mammalian order to which each mammal belongs. L2

Figure 32–12 Orders of Placental Mammals

The 12 orders of mammals shown on these pages contain the vast majority of living placental species. **Classifying** *How are perissodactyls similar to artiodactyls? How are the two orders different?*

◀ **INSECTIVORES**
These insect eaters have long, narrow snouts and sharp claws that are well suited for digging. *Examples:* shrews, hedgehogs (shown here), moles.

◀ **CHIROPTERANS**
Winged mammals—or bats—are the only mammals capable of true flight. Bats account for about one-fifth of all mammalian species. They eat mostly insects or fruit and nectar, although three species feed on the blood of other vertebrates.

▼ **SIRENIANS**
Sirenians are herbivores that live in rivers, bays, and warm coastal waters scattered throughout most of the world. These large, slow-moving mammals lead fully aquatic lives. *Examples:* manatees, dugongs (shown here).

RODENTS ▶
Rodents have a single pair of long, curved incisor teeth in both their upper and lower jaws, which they use for gnawing wood and other tough plant material. *Examples:* mice, rats (shown here), voles, squirrels, beavers, porcupines, gophers, chipmunks, gerbils, prairie dogs, chinchillas.

▲ **PERISSODACTYLS**
This order contains hoofed animals with an odd number of toes on each foot. *Examples:* horses, tapirs, rhinoceroses, and zebras (shown here).

▼ **CETACEANS**
Like sirenians, cetaceans—the order that includes whales and dolphins—are adapted to underwater life yet must come to the surface to breathe. Most cetaceans live and breed in the ocean. *Examples:* humpback whales (shown here), narwhals, sperm whales, beluga whales, river dolphins.

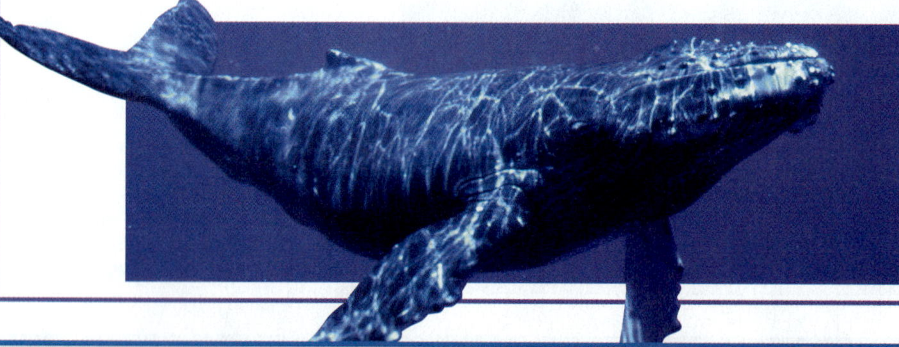

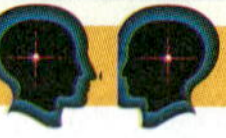

TEACHER TO TEACHER

To help my students realize how diverse mammals are, I break them into small groups and give each group a picture of a mammal that represents a particular mammalian order. First, I instruct the groups to list the characteristics of their animal that identify it as a mammal. Then, I have the groups list the characteristics that make their animal different from other mammals. Each group creates a poster of their mammalian order that describes the characteristics of mammals belonging to that order. Groups present their posters to the class. The visualization of the many mammalian orders around the room really impresses upon the students the diversity of mammals.

—Heidi Busa
Biology Teacher
Marcellus High School
Marcellus, NY

▲ **CARNIVORES**
Many mammals in this order, such as tigers and hyenas, stalk or chase their prey by running or pouncing, then kill the prey with sharp teeth and claws. Some animals in this group eat plants as well as meat. *Examples:* dogs, foxes, bears, raccoons, walruses (shown here).

▲ **XENARTHRANS**
Most of the mammals in this order have simple teeth without enamel, and a few have no teeth at all. *Examples:* sloths, anteaters, armadillos (shown here).

◀ **ARTIODACTYLS**
These hoofed mammals have an even number of toes on each foot. Like perissodactyls, this order contains mostly large, grazing animals. *Examples:* cattle, sheep, goats, pigs, ibex (shown here), giraffes, hippopotami, camels, antelope, deer, gazelles.

◀ **PRIMATES**
Members of this order are closely related to the ancient insectivores but have a highly developed cerebrum and complex behaviors. *Examples:* lemurs, tarsiers, apes, gibbons, macaques (shown here), humans.

▼ **PROBOSCIDEANS**
These are the mammals with trunks. Some time ago, this order went through an extensive adaptive radiation that produced many species, including mastodons and mammoths, which are now extinct. Only two species, the Asian elephant and this African elephant, survive today.

▲ **LAGOMORPHS**
Like rodents, members of this order are entirely herbivorous. They differ from rodents by having two pairs of incisors in the upper jaw. Most lagomorphs have hind legs that are adapted for leaping. *Examples:* Snowshoe hares (shown here), rabbits.

BIO INSIGHTS — HISTORY OF SCIENCE

Aristotle classifies animals
During the fourth century B.C., the Greek philosopher Aristotle was the first to classify animals based on their own characteristics rather than whether they were helpful or harmful to people. He published very detailed observations of the animals (and plants) that he knew. These observations led him to divide animals into two groups: those with blood and those without blood. In addition, he recognized that some animals have lungs, breathe air, are warm-blooded, and nourish their young with milk. Although he recognized that whales, dolphins, and porpoises had mammalian characteristics, he placed them in a group separate from mammals and fishes.

Address Misconceptions

Some students might think that whales are fishes, not mammals. Review the characteristics of fishes. *(Scales, gills, ectotherms, lay eggs)* Ask: **How do whales breathe?** *(They breathe air with lungs by coming to the surface of the water.)* **Do whales lay eggs or give birth to live young?** *(Give birth to live young that they nourish with their own milk)* If students do not know the answers to these questions, show them pictures of whales illustrating these behaviors, or show them a video about whales. L1 L2

Make Connections

Environmental Science Show students pictures of various endangered mammals, such as kangaroos, gorillas, cheetahs, rhinoceroses, and manatees. Discuss why the populations of these mammals are declining. Some reasons include loss of habitat, poaching, competition for resources with nonnative mammals, and accidental injury caused by increased boat traffic. Ask: **What is the ultimate cause for the decline in these mammal populations?** *(The activities of people)* L2

Answer to . . .

Figure 32–12 *Both perissodactyls and artiodactyls have feet with hoofs. Perissodactyls have an odd number of toes; artiodactyls have an even number.*

32–2 (continued)

Biogeography of Mammals

Use Visuals

Figure 32–13 Remind students that in convergent evolution, species that live in similar environments in different locations evolve similar adaptations. Ask: **What food do these mammals eat?** *(Ants and termites)* **What adaptations to eating ants do these mammals have in common?** *(Long, hairless snouts; long, sticky tongues; strong, sturdy claws for digging)* **What other adaptations do some of these mammals have?** *(Scales or spines for protection against predators)* L2

3 ASSESS

Evaluate Understanding

Call on students at random to describe the differences between monotremes, marsupials, and placental mammals. Challenge students to name the orders of placental mammals and give an example of each.

Reteach

Encourage students to use Figure 32–12 to help them construct a table that lists the name of each mammalian order, its distinguishing characteristics, and an example.

Thinking Visually

Monotremes lay eggs; marsupials bear tiny live young that complete their development in the mother's pouch; the young of placental mammals develop for a long time before birth. Similarities include all the mammalian characteristics: fur or hair, feeding young with milk, endothermy, four-chambered heart, and breathing air.

If your class subscribes to the iText, use it to review the Key Concepts in Section 32–2.

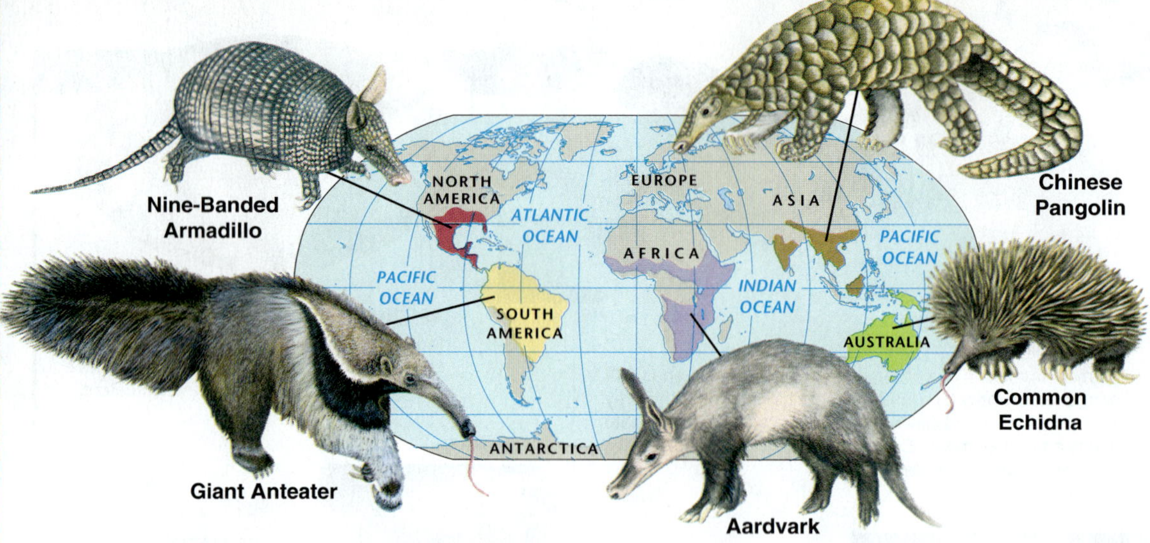

▲ **Figure 32–13** **Similar ecological opportunities on different continents have resulted in convergent evolution among these and other mammals.** Mammals that feed on ants and termites evolved not once but five times in different regions. Powerful front claws; a long, hairless snout; and a tongue covered with sticky saliva are common adaptations in these insect-eating animals.

Biogeography of Mammals

The history of Earth's geography has helped shape today's mammals. During the Paleozoic Era, the continents were one large landmass, and mammals could migrate freely across it. But as the continents drifted farther and farther apart during the Mesozoic and early Cenozoic Eras, ancestors of mammal groups were isolated from one another. Each landmass took with it a unique array of mammal groups.

Similar ecological opportunities on the different continents have produced some striking examples of convergent evolution in mammals. Thousands of kilometers apart, mammals such as those in **Figure 32–13** evolved similar adaptations in form and function. When some of the landmasses merged in the late Cenozoic Era, mammals dispersed and intermingled in new habitats. Living mammals reflect the diversity that resulted from these events.

32–2 Section Assessment

1. **Key Concept** Name the three groups of living mammals and describe the ways each develops.
2. **Key Concept** With regard to mammals, what was the result of continental drift?
3. What is the function of the placenta?
4. List the major orders of placental mammals.
5. What characteristic distinguishes lagomorphs from rodents?
6. **Critical Thinking Inferring** How are powerful front claws and sticky tongues useful adaptations in mammals that feed on ants?

Thinking Visually

Comparing and Contrasting
Create a compare-and-contrast table that describes the characteristics of monotremes, marsupials, and placental mammals. Include characteristics that they share as well as ways in which they differ.

32–2 Section Assessment

1. Monotremes: lay eggs; marsupials: immature young finish developing in marsupium; placental mammals: embryo, supported by the placenta, develops completely inside mother
2. Convergent evolution led to mammals with similar adaptations in form and function.
3. Nutrients and oxygen pass from the mother to the embryo through the placenta. Carbon dioxide and other wastes pass from the embryo to the mother through the placenta.
4. Insectivores, sirenians, cetaceans, chiropterans, rodents, perissodactyls, artiodactyls, carnivores, lagomorphs, xenarthrans, primates, proboscideans
5. Lagomorphs have two pairs of incisors; rodents have one pair.
6. Powerful front claws dig into ant colonies. Ants adhere to sticky tongues.

32–3 Primates and Human Origins

7 3.c. Students know how independent lines of evidence from geology, fossils, and comparative anatomy provide the bases for the theory of evolution.

Our own species, *Homo sapiens,* belongs to the order that also includes lemurs, monkeys, and apes. Carolus Linnaeus named our order Primates, which means "first" in Latin.

What Is a Primate?

Just what are primates "first" in? When the first primates appeared, there was little to distinguish them from other mammals besides an increased ability to use their eyes and front limbs together to perform certain tasks. As primates evolved, however, several other characteristics became distinctive.

Primates share several important adaptations, many of which are extremely useful for a life spent mainly in trees. **In general, primates have binocular vision, a well-developed cerebrum, relatively long fingers and toes, and arms that can rotate around their shoulder joints.** The gibbon in **Figure 32–14** shows many of these characteristics.

Fingers, Toes, and Shoulders Primates normally have five flexible fingers that can curl around objects. Most also have flexible toes. Flexible digits (fingers and toes) enable many primates to run along tree limbs and swing from branch to branch with ease. Primates' arms are well adapted to climbing because they can rotate in broad circles around a strong shoulder joint. In most primates, the thumb and big toe can move against the other digits. The presence of this adaptation allows many primates to hold objects firmly in their hands or feet.

Well-Developed Cerebrum The large and intricate cerebrum of primates—including a well-developed cerebral cortex—enables them to display more complex behaviors than many other mammals. For example, many primate species have elaborate social behaviors that include adoption of orphans and even warfare between rival primate troops.

Guide for Reading

Key Concepts
- What characteristics do all primates share?
- What are the major evolutionary groups of primates?
- What is the current scientific thinking about hominid evolution?

Vocabulary
binocular vision
prosimian
anthropoid
prehensile
hominoid
hominid
bipedal
opposable thumb

Reading Strategy: Finding Main Ideas Before you read, draw a line down the center of a sheet of paper. On the left side, write down the main topics about primates and human origins. On the right side, note supporting details and examples.

Figure 32–14 A white-handed gibbon displays several primate characteristics as it swings from tree to tree. **Like all primates, the gibbon has flexible fingers and toes and has arms that can rotate in broad circles around the shoulder joint.**

SECTION RESOURCES

TIME SAVER

Print:
- ***Laboratory Manual A,*** Chapter 32 Lab
- ***Laboratory Manual B,*** Chapter 32 Lab
- ***Teaching Resources,*** Lesson Plan 32–3, Adapted Section Summary 32–3, Adapted Worksheets 32–3, Section Summary 32–3, Worksheets 32–3, Section Review 32–3, Enrichment
- ***Reading and Study Workbook A,*** Section 32–3
- ***Adapted Reading and Study Workbook B,*** Section 32–3
- ***Issues and Decision Making,*** Issues and Decisions, 15, 17

Technology:
- ***BioDetectives DVD,*** "Mummies: Ties to the Past"
- ***iText,*** Section 32–3
- ***Transparencies Plus,*** Section 32–2

Section 32–3

1 FOCUS

Objectives

32.3.1 ***Identify*** the characteristics that all primates share.
32.3.2 ***Describe*** the major evolutionary groups of primates.
32.3.3 ***Explain*** the current scientific thinking about hominid evolution.

Guide for Reading

Vocabulary Preview

Help students differentiate between the words *hominoid* and *hominid.* First, say each word aloud. Then, write them on the board. Point out that the words differ only by their suffixes, *-oid* and *-id.* Explain that the suffix *-oid* comes from the Greek word *eidos,* meaning "a form or shape." Then, explain that *homo-* means "human being." Ask: **If *hominid* is the name of the family that includes only humans, what does the word *hominoid* describe?** *(It describes the family of primates that look like humans. It includes humans as well as apes.)*

Reading Strategy

While students read the section, they can write down the main topics on their sheet of paper. Remind them that they can find main ideas in boldface type, in topic sentences of paragraphs, and in headings and subheadings within the section.

2 INSTRUCT

What Is a Primate?

Build Science Skills

Applying Concepts Students probably take for granted their ability to pick up small objects. To help them sense the importance of flexible digits, challenge students to pick up small objects while wearing bulky mittens. Then, discuss how flexible digits not only help primates grasp tree branches, but also enable them to express additional behaviors, such as using tools, eating certain foods, and grooming. L2

32–3 (continued)

Quick Lab

 BIIE 1.d

Objective Students will be able to conclude how binocular vision is useful. L2

Skills Focus **Using Tables and Graphs, Drawing Conclusions**

Material sheet of paper

Time 10 minutes

Safety Make sure students have enough room to move so they don't trip over things while catching.

Strategy As an alternate activity, have students hold a pipe cleaner in one hand and a drinking straw in the other. They should extend their arms in front of them and try to insert the pipe cleaner into the straw. They should first do this with both eyes open and then repeat the procedure with one eye closed. Most students will find the procedure easier when they have both eyes open.

Expected Outcome
Students will find the ball more difficult to catch when they have one eye closed.

Analyze and Conclude
1. Graphs should show that more students are able to catch the ball with both eyes open. The combination of two perspectives with both eyes open provides depth perception.
2. Many primates move by swinging through trees. The ability to judge distances enables them to grasp branches quickly.

Evolution of Primates

Build Science Skills

Classifying Give student groups pictures of several different primates. Challenge groups to classify the primate in each picture as a prosimian or an anthropoid. Students should list characteristics of the primate that caused them to classify it as they did. L2

 BIIE 1.d

Quick Lab

Is binocular vision useful?

Material paper crumpled into a ball

Procedure
1. Throw the paper ball to your partner, who should try to catch the ball with one hand. Record whether your partner caught the ball.
2. Now have your partner close one eye. Repeat step 1.

Analyze and Conclude
1. **Using Tables and Graphs** Exchange results with other groups. Make a bar graph for the class data comparing the results with both eyes open and one eye shut.
2. **Drawing Conclusions** How is binocular vision useful to primates?

Binocular Vision Many primates have a flat face, so both eyes face forward with overlapping fields of view. This facial structure gives primates excellent binocular vision. **Binocular vision** is the ability to merge visual images from both eyes, thereby providing depth perception and a three-dimensional view of the world. This is a handy adaptation for judging the locations of tree branches, from which many primates swing.

Evolution of Primates

Humans and other primates evolved from a common ancestor that lived more than 65 million years ago. Early in their history, primates split into several groups. **Primates that evolved from two of the earliest branches look very little like typical monkeys and are called prosimians (proh-SIM-ee-unz). Members of the more familiar primate group that includes monkeys, apes, and humans are called anthropoids (AN-thruh-poydz).** Refer to **Figure 32–15** as you read about the phylogenetic relationships among these groups.

Prosimians With few exceptions, **prosimians** alive today are small, nocturnal primates with large eyes that are adapted to seeing in the dark. Many have doglike snouts. Living prosimians include the bush babies of Africa, the lemurs of Madagascar, and the lorises and tarsiers of Asia.

CHECKPOINT *What is a prosimian?*

(a) 7 3.c

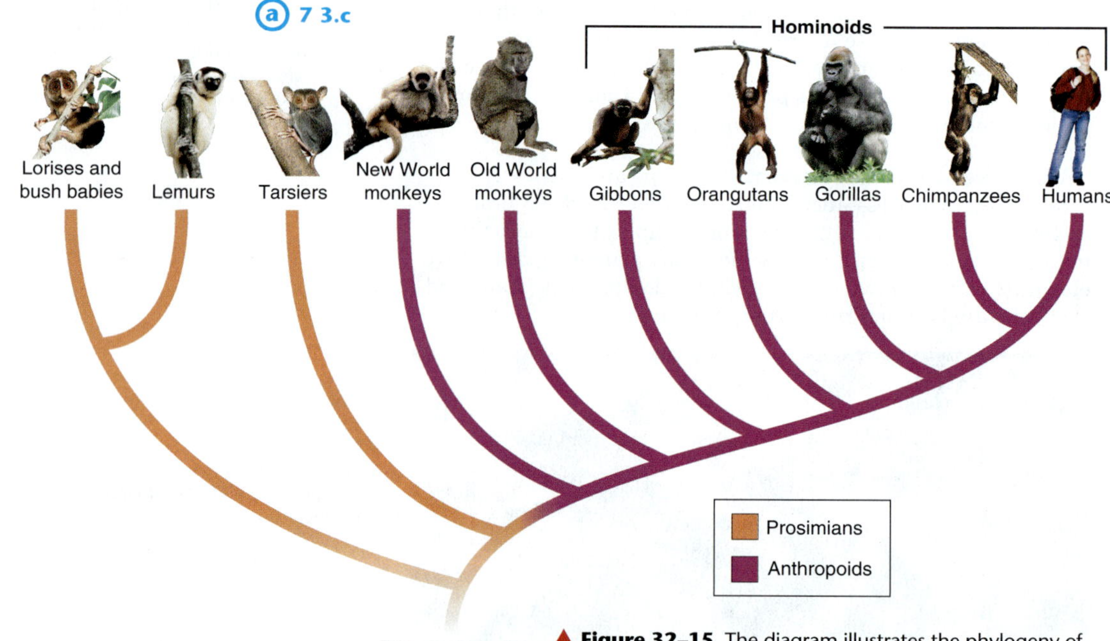

▲ **Figure 32–15** The diagram illustrates the phylogeny of modern primates. **The two main groups of primates are prosimians and anthropoids.**

FACTS AND FIGURES

Prosimians live here
The more familiar primate characteristics are less obvious in many prosimians. Some prosimians have long snouts, and their sense of smell is still very important to their survival. Others have very large eyes, probably an adaptation to nocturnal life. Prosimians are found only in the tropical forests of Africa, Southeast Asia, Madagascar, and the West Indies. Many prosimians are in danger of extinction because of habitat destruction.

Anthropoids Humans, apes, and most monkeys belong to a group called **anthropoids,** which means humanlike primates. This group split very early in its evolutionary history into two major branches. These branches became separated from each other as drifting continents moved apart. One branch, found today in Central and South America, is called the New World monkeys. (After Columbus's voyage to America, Europeans began to use the term *New World* to refer to North and South America.) New World monkeys, which include squirrel monkeys and spider monkeys, live almost entirely in trees. These monkeys have long, flexible arms that enable them to swing from branch to branch. New World monkeys also have a long, prehensile tail. A **prehensile** tail is a tail that can coil tightly enough around a branch to serve as a "fifth hand."

The other anthropoid group, which evolved in Africa and Asia, includes the Old World monkeys and great apes. Old World monkeys, such as langurs and macaques (muh-KAHKS), spend time in trees but lack prehensile tails. Great apes, also called **hominoids,** include gibbons, orangutans, gorillas, chimpanzees, and humans. Recent molecular studies confirm that chimpanzees are humans' closest relatives among the great apes. Humans and chimps share an astonishing 98 percent of their DNA!

Hominid Evolution

Between 6 and 7 million years ago, the hominoid line gave rise to a branch that ultimately led to the ancestors and closest relatives of modern humans. The **hominid** family, which includes modern humans, displayed several distinct evolutionary trends. Fossil evidence shows that as hominids evolved over millions of years, they became able to walk upright and developed thumbs adapted for grasping. They also developed large brains.

The skull, neck, spinal column, hipbones, and leg bones of early hominid species changed shape in ways that enabled later species to walk upright. **Figure 32–16** shows some ways in which the skeletons of modern humans differ from those of gorillas. The evolution of this **bipedal,** or two-foot, locomotion was very important, because it freed both hands to use tools. Meanwhile, the hominid hand evolved an **opposable thumb** that enabled grasping objects and using tools.

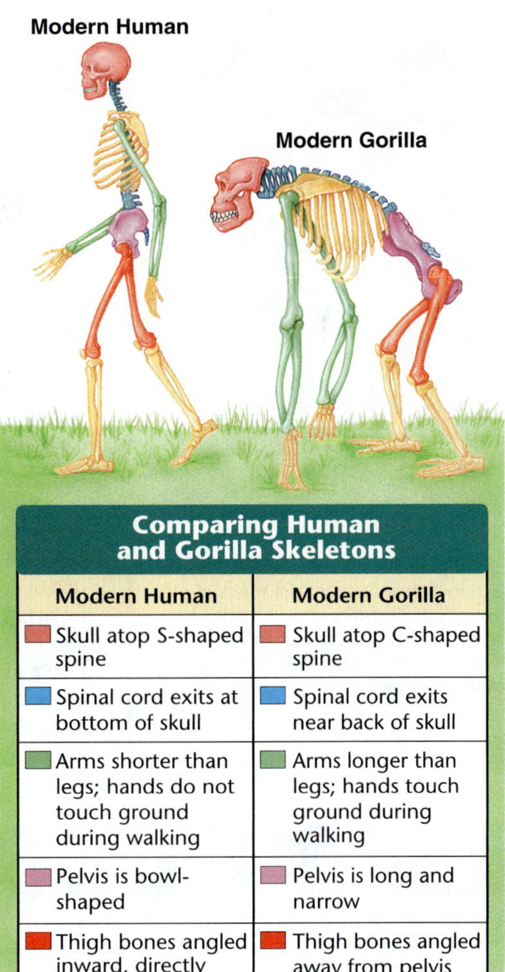

Comparing Human and Gorilla Skeletons

Modern Human	Modern Gorilla
Skull atop S-shaped spine	Skull atop C-shaped spine
Spinal cord exits at bottom of skull	Spinal cord exits near back of skull
Arms shorter than legs; hands do not touch ground during walking	Arms longer than legs; hands touch ground during walking
Pelvis is bowl-shaped	Pelvis is long and narrow
Thigh bones angled inward, directly below body	Thigh bones angled away from pelvis

▲ **Figure 32–16** Modern hominids walk upright on two legs; gorillas use all four limbs. **Comparing and Contrasting** *According to the chart and illustration, what are the other differences between humans and gorillas?*

 7 3.c

Make Connections

Earth Science On a map, show students how the eastern coast of South America fits into the western coast of Africa. Explain that primates first evolved when these two continents were connected. As the continents drifted apart, primate species were separated. Ask: **How do you think New World and Old World monkeys became different?** *(As the two groups became separated, they responded to different selection pressures—climate, food sources, environment—and evolved somewhat differently.)* Discuss the kinds of environmental changes that helped make the Old World monkeys different from New World monkeys. *(Old World monkeys adapted to an environment with fewer trees. They lost their prehensile tail, tend to sit upright, and have an opposable thumb. Most New World monkeys remain completely adapted to living in trees. Nearly all have a prehensile tail, but most lack opposable thumbs.)* L2

Hominid Evolution

Use Visuals

Figure 32–16 Explain that the S-shaped spine of the human skeleton places the center of gravity directly over the pelvis. Ask: **Why doesn't the gorilla usually walk on two legs?** *(It needs its arms to balance its body because the body leans forward.)* Have students compare the size of the human and the gorilla skulls. L2

UNIVERSAL ACCESS

Less Proficient Readers
To help students organize the main ideas and reinforce the meanings of Vocabulary terms, have them create a concept map to show the relationships and characteristics of prosimians, anthropoids, hominoids, and hominids. Make sure students know the difference between hominoids and hominids. Also point out how *anthropoid* differs from *arthropod.* L1

Advanced Learners
Students who would like an extra challenge can read Mary Leakey's autobiography entitled *Disclosing the Past.* Students who have read the book can discuss what they think about Mary Leakey's life and how they felt after reading her story. Or, you might have these students work together to prepare a class presentation about Mary Leakey's life. L3

Answers to . . .

CHECKPOINT *Most prosimians are small, nocturnal primates with large eyes.*

Figure 32–16 *Spine shape, site where spinal cord exits skull, length of arms, position of hands during walking, shape of pelvis, angle of thigh bones*

32–3 (continued)

Address Misconceptions

Some students might think that humans evolved directly from modern apes or chimpanzees. Explain that humans and apes shared a common ancestor, but humans did not directly evolve from modern apes. You can illustrate this idea by drawing a phylogenetic tree showing apes and humans diverging from a common ancestor. L1 L2

Biology and History

BIIE 1.k, 7 3.c

Discuss how theories about human ancestors have changed over time. Explain that DNA evidence, used in conjunction with fossil evidence, is also changing the way human history is interpreted. Point out the different scientific disciplines that have been involved in the study of human ancestry. Make sure students know the specialty of each scientist and understand what that specialty entails. Discuss how the knowledge of these scientists has contributed to the study of human origins.

Writing in Science

Remind students that there is no single correct answer. Challenge them to put themselves into Mary Leakey's shoes. Give them as much background information about Mary Leakey and her work as possible. As they write the journal entry, students should feel and convey the excitement that Mary Leakey felt upon making her discovery. Remind students that the journal entry should be written in the first person. Encourage them to imagine and develop any details about the day and the discovery. L2

▲ **Figure 32–17** Between 3.8 and 3.6 million years ago, members of a species of *Australopithecus* made these footprints at Laetoli in Tanzania. The footprints show that hominids walked upright millions of years ago.

Hominids also displayed a remarkable increase in brain size. Chimpanzees, our closest living relatives among the apes, have a brain size of 280 to 450 cubic centimeters. The brain of *Homo sapiens,* on the other hand, ranges in size from 1200 to 1600 cubic centimeters! Most of the difference in brain size results from an enormously expanded cerebrum—the "thinking" area of the brain.

Early Hominids Paleontologists have unearthed a treasure trove of hominid species. At present, most paleontologists agree that the hominid fossil record includes at least these genera—*Ardipithecus, Australopithecus, Paranthropus, Kenyanthropus,* and *Homo*—and as many as 20 separate species. This diverse group of hominid fossils covers roughly 6 million years. All these species are relatives of modern humans, but not all of them are human ancestors. To understand that distinction, think of your family. Your relatives may include aunts, uncles, cousins, parents, grandparents, and great-grandparents. Of these, only your parents, grandparents, and great-grandparents are your ancestors.

Almost a third of all known hominid species have been discovered in the last 20 years. This shows how rapidly knowledge of hominid fossils is growing. It also explains why hominid evolution is both fascinating and confusing. What once looked like a simple "human family tree" now looks more like a dense, branching shrub. Many questions remain about how fossil hominids are related to one another and to humans. Let's examine a few of the most important discoveries.

BIIE 1.k

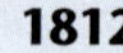

Biology and History

Human-Fossil Seekers

The study of human origins is an exciting search for our past. To piece together this complicated story requires the skills of many scientists.

1812
Georges Cuvier
Cuvier, a French zoologist, rejects the idea of evolution based on a lack of evidence in the fossil record. He is noted for saying "Fossil man does not exist!" He believed species were static and unchanging.

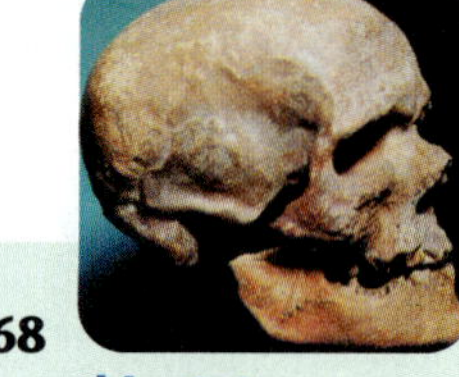

1868
Edouard Lartet
Henry Christy
French geologist Lartet and English banker Christy unearth several ancient human skeletons in a rock shelter called Cro-Magnon in France. These hominid fossils are the first to be classified as *Homo sapiens.*

1886
Marcel de Puydt
Max Lohest
De Puydt and Lohest describe two Neanderthal skeletons found in a cave in Belgium. Their detailed description of the skeletons shows that Neanderthals were an extinct human form, not an abnormal form of modern human.

1800 1850 1900

HISTORY OF SCIENCE

Edouard Lartet—Founder of Paleontology
Although Edouard Lartet was trained as a lawyer, his discovery of fossil remains at the age of 33 changed his life forever. From then on, he devoted his time to excavating caves in France. He found many examples of early tools made from bone, flint, and antlers. Many caves had colorful drawings of animals. In 1863, the English banker Henry Christy teamed up with Lartet, giving him funding to support his research. Working together, they found a mammoth bone with an image of an extinct animal carved in it. Their discoveries showed that Ice Age mammals lived at the same time as ancient humans. This idea was under great debate at the time. They also showed that the Stone Age was made up of different phases of human culture.

Australopithecus One early group of hominids, members of the genus *Australopithecus,* lived from about 4 million to a million years ago. These hominids were bipedal apes that spent at least some time in trees. The structure of their teeth suggests a diet rich in fruit. Some *Australopithecus* species seem to have been human ancestors, while others formed separate branches off the main hominid line.

The best known species is *Australopithecus afarensis*—described from a remarkably complete female skeleton, nicknamed Lucy, who stood only about 1 meter tall. The humanlike footprints shown in **Figure 32–17,** which are between 3.8 and 3.6 million years old, were probably made by members of the same species as Lucy. Since *Australopithecus* fossils have small brains, the Laetoli footprints show that hominids walked bipedally long before large brains evolved.

Paranthropus Three later species, which grew to the size of well-fed football linebackers, were originally placed in the genus *Australopithecus*. However, they are now usually placed in their own genus, *Paranthropus.* The known *Paranthropus* species had huge, grinding back teeth. Their diets probably included coarse and fibrous plant foods like those eaten by modern gorillas. Most paleontologists now place *Paranthropus* on a separate, dead-end branch of our family tree.

CHECKPOINT *What are the characteristics of* Paranthropus*?*

Quick View Video

Discovery School Video To find out more about human history, view track 6 "Mummies: Ties to the Past" on the *BioDetectives* DVD.

Writing in Science

You have found Mary Leakey's journal and noticed that the entry for her discovery of the footprints at Laetoli is missing. Write an entry for the journal as she would have, describing the events of the day and her initial reaction to the find.

1924
Raymond Dart
Dart, an Australian anatomist, finds an early hominid fossil—a nearly complete skull of a child—in South Africa. This specimen was placed in a new genus called *Australopithecus.*

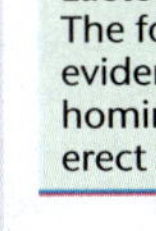

1974
Donald Johanson
An American paleontologist and his team find 40 percent of a skeleton of *Australopithecus*, which they call Lucy, in the Afar region of Ethiopia. The skeleton is about 3.2 million years old.

1978
Mary Leakey
Leakey, a British anthropologist, discovers a set of 3.6 million-year-old fossil hominid footprints at Laetoli in Tanzania. The footprints provide evidence that early hominids walked erect on two legs.

1999
Douglas Wallace
Wallace and fellow geneticists create a family tree of human evolution based on their studies of mitochondrial DNA, which is passed only from mother to child.

1900 1950 2000

Quick View Video

Discovery School DVD Encourage students to view track 6 "Mummies: Ties to the Past" on the *BioDetectives* DVD.

Build Science Skills

Using Models Students will benefit from constructing a timeline that marks the time period during which each hominid species lived. Students should realize that some hominid species lived during the same time. Help students put into perspective the large expanse of time over which these hominid ancestors lived and died. L1 L2

BIO INSIGHTS — HISTORY OF SCIENCE

The Leakey family of anthropologists
Mary Nicol Leakey was born in London in 1913, but she spent much of her life moving around Europe with her family. During her early twenties, she began working at archaeological sites, where she learned to be methodical and careful. She also became known for her abilities in illustration. In 1936, she married the anthropologist Louis Leakey, whom she met at a dinner party after a lecture. She went with him to Africa, where he was working to prove that humans originated there rather than in Asia, as was popularly thought at the time. She spent over 20 years excavating sites in the Serengeti Plains in northern Tanzania. She and her husband collected many tools and fossilized skulls of early hominids. Her greatest find, the fossilized footprints at Laetoli, came after her husband's death.

Answer to . . .

CHECKPOINT *Paranthropus* species were very large and had huge, grinding back teeth.

32–3 (continued)

Use Visuals

Figure 32–18 Point out that the skulls are arranged in order according to the age of the fossil species, with the oldest, *Sahelanthropus tchadensis,* at the top, and the most recent, *Homo erectus,* at the bottom. Have students compare and contrast the structure of the skulls. Ask: **In what ways are the skulls of *Sahelanthropus tchadensis* and *Homo erectus* similar? In what ways are they different?** *(Both have eye sockets facing forward, indicating that they have binocular vision, as do all primates. Both have relatively large brain cases. However,* H. erectus *has the larger brain.* S. tchadensis *has a flat face.)* L2

Build Science Skills

Evaluating and Revising
Deciphering early hominid evolution provides a very good example of how the scientific method works in "real-life" scientific study. Point out how the discoveries of new fossils have changed original hypotheses formed by paleontologists. Also point out how those new discoveries have led to even more questions. Work with students to put recent changes in thinking about hominid evolution into the context of the scientific method. Discuss the questions that paleontologists are asking, as well as their hypotheses. Ask: **How have paleontologists changed their hypotheses to reflect recent discoveries?** *(Instead of hominid evolution following a simple, straight-line transformation of one species into another, hominid evolution followed a series of complex adaptive radiations to produce a large number of species.)* L2

Sahelanthropus tchadensis

Kenyanthropus platyops

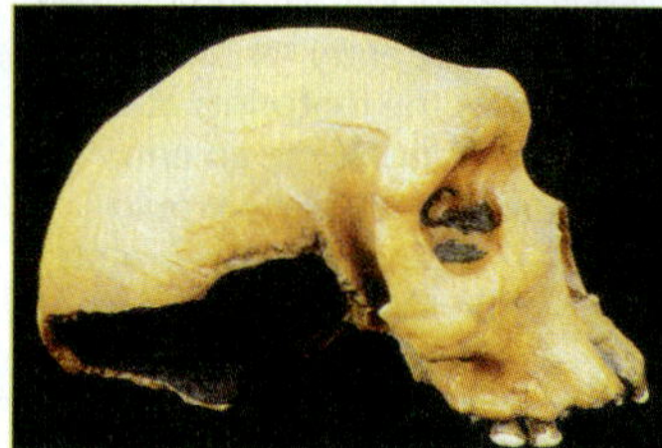

Homo erectus

▲ **Figure 32–18** Paleontologists' interpretations of hominid evolution are based on the study of fossils such as these skulls. *Sahelanthropus* may be the earliest known hominid. **Observing** *Which of these skulls most closely resembles the skull of a modern human?*

ⓐ 7 3.c

Recent Hominid Discoveries Early in 2001, a team led by paleontologist Meave Leakey announced that they had uncovered a skull in Kenya. Its ear structures resembled those of chimpanzees, and its brain was rather small. Yet some of its facial features resembled those of fossils usually placed in the genus *Homo*. Paleontologists put this skull in a new genus, *Kenyanthropus*. *Kenyanthropus* is shown in the middle in **Figure 32–18.** Evidence indicates that this species existed at the same time as *A. afarensis.*

Then, during the summer of 2002, paleontologists working in the desert in north-central Africa announced the discovery of an even more startling skull. This fossil skull, tentatively called *Sahelanthropus,* is nearly 7 million years old. If scientists agree that *Sahelanthropus* is indeed a hominid, it would be a million years older than any hominid previously known.

Sahelanthropus had a brain about the size of a modern chimp, yet its short, flat face is more like that of a human. In fact, this skull seems more humanlike in certain ways than Lucy (*A. afarensis*), who lived several million years later. While most hominid fossils have been discovered in eastern Africa, *Sahelanthropus* was discovered much farther to the west. This suggests that there may be many more fossil hominids to be found in widely separated parts of Africa.

CA ⓐ

✔CHECKPOINT *What is* Kenyanthropus platyops*?*

Rethinking Early Hominid Evolution Together with other recent fossil finds, the discovery of *Kenyanthropus* and *Sahelanthropus* has dramatically changed the way paleontologists think about hominid evolution. Researchers once thought that human evolution took place in relatively simple steps in which hominid species, over time, became gradually more humanlike. **It is now clear that hominid evolution did not proceed by the simple, straight-line transformation of one species into another. Rather, like the evolution of other mammalian groups, a series of complex adaptive radiations produced a large number of species whose relationships are difficult to determine.** Which hominids are true human ancestors? Which are just relatives? And how are all those species related to one another and to modern humans? At present, no one can answer these questions.

So what is known about hominid evolution? As shown in **Figure 32–19,** the hominid fossil record now dates back nearly 7 million years, close to the time that DNA studies suggest for the split between hominids and the ancestors of modern chimpanzees. In addition, there are many known fossil hominid species, several of which display a confusing mix of primitive and modern traits. It will probably take many years of work to more fully understand this fascinating and complex story.

FACTS AND FIGURES

Changing African climate and evolution
The climate of East Africa began changing about 10 million years ago. The air became drier, and forests gave way to grasslands. Many primates remained in the forests. But as the environment became more diverse, different primates evolved to establish new niches. These primates had characteristics that enabled them to live more successfully in open grassland. Their diet changed from being completely herbivorous to omnivorous. They began walking upright on two feet. Bipedalism enabled primates to see over the tops of grass and bushes. It enabled them to carry food or offspring in their arms. It also kept them cooler, because they received less of the sun's direct rays and could catch cool breezes above the ground. The gradual loss of body hair also helped to keep them cooler.

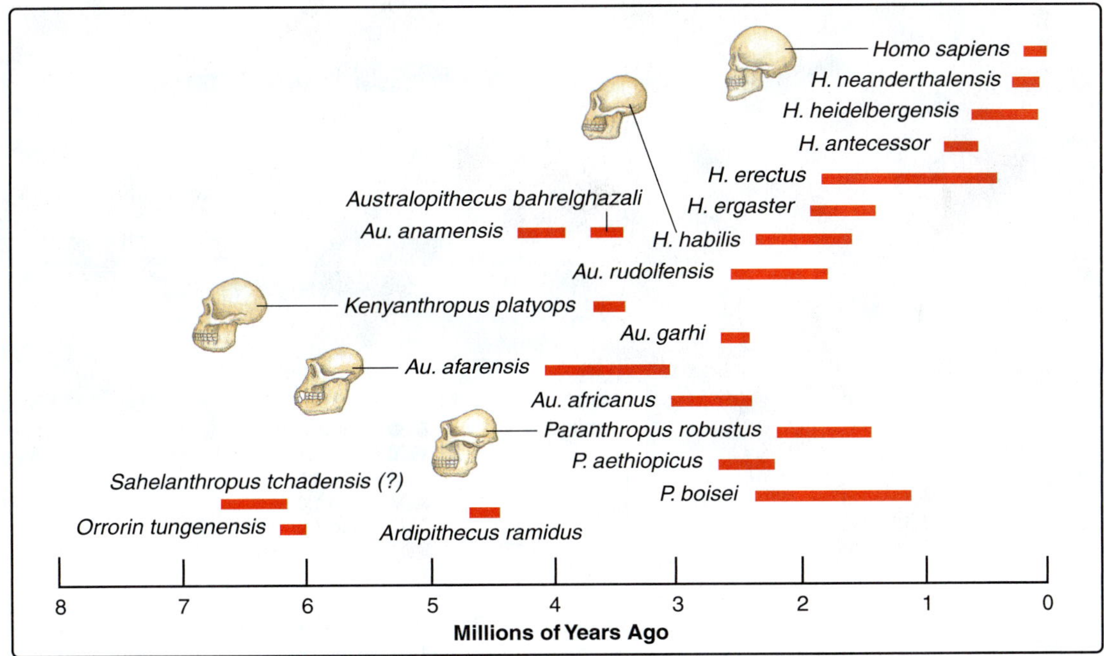

▲ **Figure 32–19** The diagram shows fossil hominids and the time ranges during which they may have existed. The time ranges are likely to change as paleontologists gather new data. The question mark after *Sahelanthropus tchadensis* indicates that scientists are not yet certain that this species is a hominid. Paleontologists do not yet have enough information to know how hominid species are related. **It is now clear that hominid evolution did not proceed by the simple, straight-line transformation of one species into another.** Current hypotheses about early stages of human evolution recognize the incompleteness of the data.

The Road to Modern Humans

The hominids that have been mentioned so far, such as *Paranthropus* and *Australopithecus,* all lived millions of years before modern humans. When did our species, *Homo sapiens,* appear? As you can see in **Figure 32–19,** other species in our genus existed before *H. sapiens,* and at least two other species in the genus *Homo* existed at the same time as early humans. As is the case with earlier hominid fossils, paleontologists still do not completely understand the history and relationships of species within our own genus.

The Genus *Homo* About 2.5 million years ago, a new kind of hominid appeared. Its fossils show that it resembled modern humans enough to be classified in the genus *Homo.* Because these fossils were found with tools made of stone and bone, researchers called the species *Homo habilis* (HAB-ih-lus), which means "handy man."

Homo habilis was the first of several species in our genus to arise in Africa. About 2 million years ago, a species larger than *H. habilis* appeared. It had a bigger brain and downward-facing nostrils that resembled those of modern humans. Today, most researchers call the African fossils of this species *Homo ergaster.* At some point, one or more species in the genus *Homo* began migrating out of Africa through what is now the Middle East. That species may have been *H. ergaster* or a closely related species named *Homo erectus.*

CA a

The Road to Modern Humans

Address Misconceptions

Some students might have the misconception that human ancestors were "dumb cave men." Address this by explaining that a large part of human evolution was developing the ability to learn and to teach. Point out that our knowledge base is large because it continues to be built on what is already known. This base of knowledge will continue to grow as new discoveries are made. If you wish, you can illustrate this concept with interlocking building blocks. Starting at the base with blocks representing simple tools made from sticks, bones, and stones, students can build a wall or other structure. Each block they add to the structure should represent some innovation or discovery that expands the knowledge base of humans. L2

Answers to . . .

CHECKPOINT Kenyanthropus platyops *is the species name given to a fossil skull discovered in Kenya by Meave Leakey's team. The skull has a flat face. It has some characteristics of chimpanzees and some characteristics of the genus* Homo.

Figure 32–18 Homo erectus

32–3 (continued)

Use Visuals

Figure 32–20 Ask: At which sites did hominids live more than 2 million years ago? *(Olduvai, Kanapoi, and Hadar)* How many times might hominids have left Africa for the Middle East? *(Four times)* When? *(2.0 to 1.5 million years ago, 1.0 to 0.5 million years ago, 0.5 to 0.1 million years ago, and less than 0.1 million years ago)* When were hominids first in what is now Beijing? *(1.0 to 0.5 million years ago)* How have scientists learned the history of human ancestors? *(By studying the fossil record and testing human DNA)* L1 L2

Build Science Skills

Making Judgments Challenge students to make a list of objects that they would include in a time capsule. Students should choose no more than ten items and give reasons for each choice. They should choose items with the idea that the time capsule will be opened 100,000 years from now. These items should give anthropologists information about what students' lives were like. L2

Build Science Skills

Applying Concepts Challenge students to make comparisons of their lifestyle to that of ancient humans. Discuss how different our lives are now, as well as how some aspects of our lives might be similar. Encourage students to make predictions about what life will be like in the future. You could have students write an essay describing their thoughts and predictions. L2

Download a worksheet on human evolution for students to complete, and find additional teacher support from NSTA SciLinks.

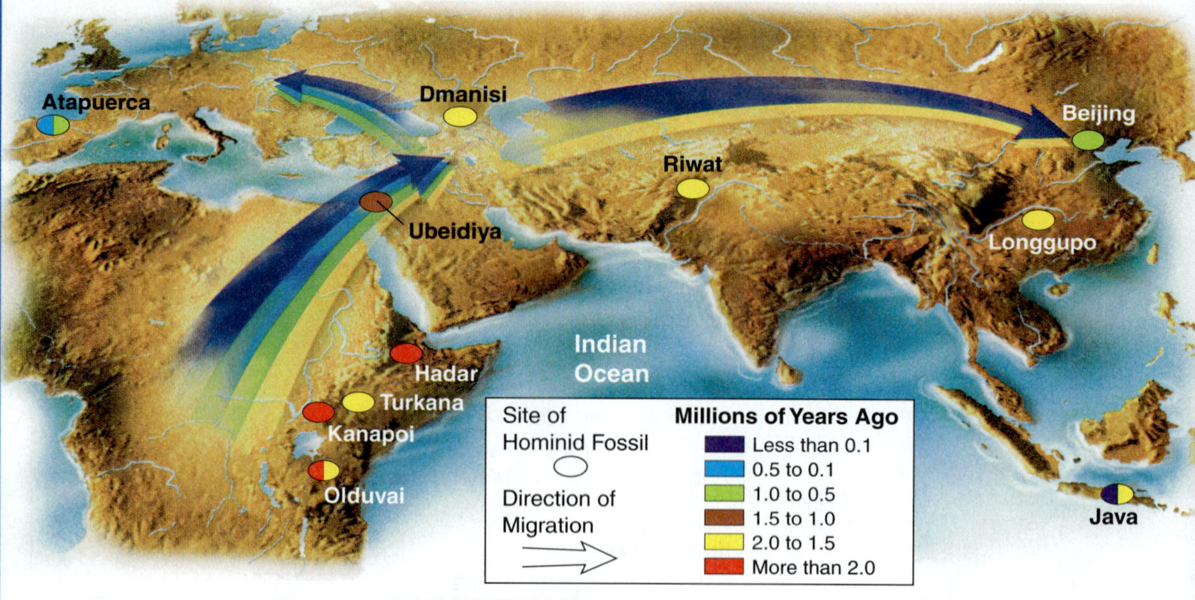

▲ **Figure 32–20** Data show that relatives and ancestors of modern humans left Africa several different times. But when did early hominids leave Africa, and how far did they travel? By comparing the mitochondrial DNA of human populations around the world and by continuing to study the fossil record, scientists hope to improve our understanding of the complex history of *Homo sapiens*.

For: Links on human evolution
Visit: www.SciLinks.org
Web Code: cbn-9323

Out of Africa—But Who and When? Researchers agree that our genus originated in Africa. But many questions remain. When did hominids first leave Africa? Did more than one species make the trip? Which of those species were human ancestors and which were merely relatives? Fossil data and molecular evidence suggest that hominids left Africa in several waves as shown in **Figure 32–20.** By a million years ago, migrants from Africa had crossed Asia and reached China and Java, and populations of *H. erectus* were living in several places across Asia.

Many researchers have hypothesized that *H. erectus* was the first of our genus to leave Africa. Two recently discovered fossil skulls may offer additional evidence that *H. erectus* did leave Africa and migrate long distances. The skulls, which strongly resemble African *H. erectus* fossils and are about 1.75 million years old, were discovered in the country of Georgia, which is north of Turkey and far from Africa.

However, other evidence makes the situation less clear. Another 1.75-million-year-old skull found in Georgia resembles 1.9 million-year-old *Homo habilis* skulls from Kenya. Does this skull indicate that *H. habilis* left Africa before *H. erectus*? The scientific jury is still evaluating the evidence.

Paleontologists are also unsure exactly where and when *Homo sapiens* arose. One hypothesis, the multi-regional model, suggests that modern humans evolved independently in several parts of the world from widely separated populations of *H. erectus*. Another hypothesis, the out-of-Africa model, proposes that modern humans evolved in Africa between 200,000 and 150,000 years ago, migrated out to colonize the world, and replaced the descendants of earlier hominid species. Scientific debate and the search for more data continue.

Modern *Homo sapiens*

▲ **Figure 32–21** This ancient cave painting from France shows the remarkable artistic abilities of Cro-Magnons. **Inferring** *How might these painted images be related to the way in which these early humans lived?*

The story of modern humans over the past 500,000 years involves two main groups. The earliest of these species is now called *Homo neanderthalensis,* named after the Neander Valley in Germany where their remains were first found. Neanderthals, as they are commonly called, flourished from Europe through western Asia between about 200,000 and 30,000 years ago. Evidence from Neanderthal sites in Europe and the Middle East suggests that they not only made stone tools but also lived in organized social groups.

The other group is anatomically modern *Homo sapiens*—in other words, people whose skeletons look like those of modern humans. These *H. sapiens,* who probably arose in Africa, appeared in the Middle East around 100,000 years ago. They joined Neanderthals who had been living in that region for at least 100,000 years. As far as anyone can tell, Neanderthals and *Homo sapiens* lived side by side in what is now Israel, Lebanon, Syria, and Turkey for around 50,000 years, using similar tools and living in remarkably similar ways.

That situation may have changed dramatically around 50,000–40,000 years ago. According to one hypothesis, that's when some populations of *H. sapiens* seem to have fundamentally changed their way of life. They used new technology to make more sophisticated stone blades, and made elaborately worked tools from bones and antlers. They produced spectacular cave paintings, such as the one in **Figure 32–21.** These *Homo sapiens* buried their dead with elaborate rituals. In other words, these people began to behave like modern humans. About 40,000 years ago, one such group, known as Cro-Magnons (kroh-MAG-nunz), appeared in Europe.

By 30,000 years ago, Neanderthals had disappeared from Europe—and from the Middle East as well. How and why they disappeared is not yet known. But since that time, our species has been Earth's only hominid.

32–3 Section Assessment

1. **Key Concept** List five anatomical characteristics that most primates share.
2. **Key Concept** Describe the major primate groups and explain how they are related phylogenetically.
3. **Key Concept** Explain the way that paleontologists currently view hominid evolution.
4. Compare and contrast hominids and other hominoids. How are they similar? Different?
5. **Critical Thinking Applying Concepts** How did the separation of the continents contribute to the development of New World and Old World monkeys?

Writing in Science

Explanatory Paragraph
Write a paragraph explaining how the structure of primates' fingers, toes, and shoulders are adaptations that help with survival. *Hint:* To prepare to write, make a table that describes the structures in the left column and then lists the advantages of those structures in the right column.

32–3 Section Assessment

1. Binocular vision, well-developed cerebrum, relatively long fingers and toes, and arms that can rotate around their shoulder joints
2. Two major groups descended from a common primate ancestor. Prosimians: small, nocturnal primates; anthropoids: humanlike primates, split into two groups: (1) New World monkeys and (2) Old World monkeys and hominoids.
3. A series of complex adaptive radiations produced a large number of species whose relationships are difficult to determine.
4. Both groups are similar in that they are anthropoids. For differences, see the chart in Figure 32–16, page 835.
5. The two groups responded to different environmental pressures and evolved differently.

Modern *Homo sapiens*

Build Science Skills

Formulating Hypotheses
Challenge students to develop a hypothesis to explain what happened to *Homo neanderthalensis*. Have students describe the type of fossilized evidence they must find that would support their hypothesis. Also have them describe what type of fossilized evidence would refute their hypothesis. L2

3 ASSESS

Evaluate Understanding

Have students make a "family tree" that shows how the primate groups (prosimians, anthropoids, hominoids, and hominids) evolved from a common ancestor. Instruct students to list the characteristics of each group.

Reteach

Have students copy the Vocabulary words from this section. For each word, students should write its meaning in their own words. For those words that describe primate groups, students should include the characteristics of primates belonging to that group.

Writing in Science

In their paragraphs, students should explain that the structure of primates' fingers, toes, and shoulders enables them to run along tree limbs and swing from branches. This behavior enables primates to find food and escape predators.

Interactive Textbook

If your class subscribes to the iText, use it to review the Key Concepts in Section 32–3.

Answer to . . .

Figure 32–21 *The paintings might show how these early humans hunted large animals.*

Real-World Lab

BIIE 1.c

Objective Students will be able to infer how forensic scientists identify unknown hairs and fibers. L2

Skills Focus **Observing, Inferring, Analyzing Data**

Time 45 minutes

Advance Prep

• Collect six reference fibers: two from people, two from animals, and two nonanimal fibers such as cotton and synthetic fibers. The four unknown fibers should include one of the human reference samples and three nonhuman fibers. Collect animal fibers directly from pets or by removing them from clothes. Collect nonanimal fibers from clothes, carpeting, or thread.

• Prepare fresh biuret reagent no more than one day in advance, and store it out of light. Make a 0.1 M solution of sodium hydroxide (NaOH) by dissolving 4 g in 1 L of water. Add 1.4 g $CuSo_4$ or 2.2 g $CuSO_4 \bullet 5\ H_2O$. To reduce the risk to students in handling this solution, dispense small test tubes containing 10 mL of biuret reagent for use in Part 2.

Safety Read the safety information in the MSDS for NaOH or biuret reagent, and for $CuSO_4$ before doing the lab. Wear plastic gloves, safety goggles, and a lab apron when handling NaOH or biuret reagent. Dispose of the gloves properly after the lab.

Pre-Lab Discussion After students read the procedure, ask: **What is hair composed of?** *(Protein)* **How could you tell whether a fiber is hair or something else?** *(By examining it with a microscope and testing it for protein)*

Teaching Tips

When cleaning up after the lab, place a screen over the sink drain and have students empty their test tubes carefully into a stream of running cold water, avoiding splashing. The screen will keep hair from clogging the drain.

Real-World Lab

BIIE 1.c

Using Fibers as Forensic Evidence

Hair and other fibers are often used by police as evidence that a suspect was at the scene of a crime such as a burglary. In this investigation, you will examine a variety of hairs and other fibers to match unknown fibers to known reference fibers. The two human hairs represent hairs from two people who are suspected of having been at the crime scene. The unknown fibers represent fibers found at the crime scene.

Discovery School Video To find out more about how scientists use forensic evidence, view track 9 "Wrongly Accused: Science and Justice" on the *BioDetectives* DVD.

Problem

How do forensic scientists identify unknown hairs and fibers?

Materials

- reference fibers
- unknown fibers
- microscope slides
- coverslips
- dropper pipette
- microscope
- glass-marking pencil
- facial tissues
- isopropyl alcohol
- rubber cement
- forceps
- test-tube rack
- 4 test tubes of biuret reagent
- 4 glass stirring rods
- hot water bath

Skills

Observing, Inferring, Analyzing Data

Procedure

Part A: Observing Fibers

1. Place one of the reference fibers on a microscope slide. **CAUTION:** *Microscopes and slides are fragile. Handle them carefully. If you break any glass, inform your teacher immediately.* Add a drop of water and a coverslip. Label the slide with the name of the fiber. On a separate sheet of paper, make a copy of the data table shown below, with 10 blank lines.
2. Place the slide on the stage of a microscope and look at it under 100× magnification. Examine the fiber carefully, looking for features such as color, shape, texture, and whether or not a hair root is attached. Record your observations in your data table. Draw and label a sketch of the fiber.
3. Repeat steps 1 and 2 for each of the reference and unknown fibers.
4. Clean one of the reference fibers by pulling it through a folded tissue moistened with a small amount of alcohol. **CAUTION:** *Alcohol is flammable. Do not use it in the presence of an open flame or sparks.*
5. Smear a thin layer of rubber cement on the middle of a glass slide. Quickly place the fiber on the surface of the rubber cement.
6. Before the cement dries, lift the fiber off the slide with forceps. You should see an imprint of the fiber on the cement. Put the slide under a microscope and observe the surface texture of the fiber. Record your observations.
7. Repeat steps 4 to 6 for each of the other fibers.

Data Table

Fiber	General Observations	Surface Texture	Biuret Test Result

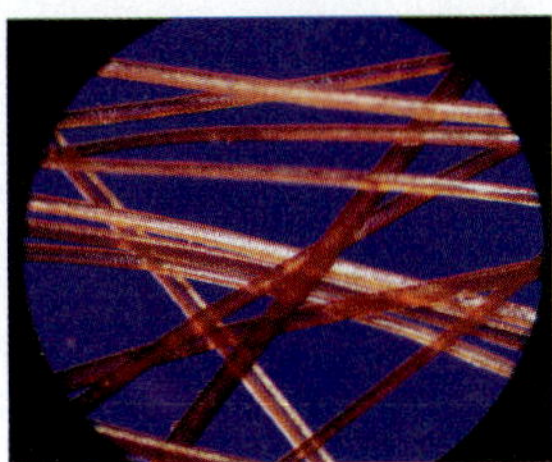
Human Hairs
(magnification: 22×)

Polyester Threads
(magnification: 70×)

Silk Fibers
(magnification: about 50×)

Part B: Testing for Protein

8. **Formulating Hypotheses** Hair contains protein. Synthetic and plant fibers do not contain protein. On the basis of the observations you have recorded in your data table, write a hypothesis about which unknown fibers contain protein. Include the reasons for your hypothesis, explaining what evidence supports your hypothesis about each fiber.

9. Label 4 test tubes of biuret reagent solution 1 through 4. **CAUTION:** *Wear safety goggles, a lab apron, and plastic gloves when working with biuret reagent solution. If any of the solution gets on your skin or clothing, wash it off immediately and inform your teacher.* Use forceps to place several strands of each unknown fiber in the test tube with the same number. Record the time.

10. Place a glass stirring rod in each test tube. Place the test tubes in the hot water bath. Stir each test tube occasionally. **CAUTION:** *Leave the stirring rods in the test tubes. Do not place the wet stirring rods on the table.*

11. Observe the color of each test tube. A change from blue to purple or reddish-brown within 5 minutes indicates the presence of protein. Add your observations to your data table. Follow your teacher's instructions for safe disposal of the biuret reagent.

Analyze and Conclude

1. **Comparing and Contrasting** How are hairs and synthetic fibers different?
2. **Observing** Did you observe any differences between human hair and other hair? If you did, describe the differences.
3. **Drawing Conclusions** Did your observations support the idea that one or both of the suspects may have been at the crime scene? Explain your answer.
4. **Evaluating** Did your observations leave room for doubt about this conclusion? If so, what other evidence would help you decide whether your conclusion is valid? Explain your answer.

Go Further

Additional Research Forensic science is the application of scientific knowledge to questions involving law. Do research to learn more about forensic science. Some topics you might investigate include the following:

- DNA evidence
- Evidence of poisoning
- Forensic dentistry
- Forensic anthropology
- Forensic pathology
- Ballistics

Analyze and Conclude

1. Hairs have a root at one end and a scaly surface. Synthetic fibers are uniformly smooth and featureless. Hairs contain protein; synthetic fibers do not.

2. Human hair is not very different from other hair. The scales of human hair are more regular than those of other hair, but the basic structure of hair is the same for all mammals.

3. Yes, one of the unknown hairs found at the crime scene matched one suspect's reference hairs.

4. Answers will vary but should suggest that the suspect's hair was similar to one found at the crime scene and that this similarity does not prove that only this person has hair that would match the hair found at the scene. Other evidence, such as matching fingerprints or DNA sequences, would make a stronger case.

Procedure

2. Students should record the color, shape, texture, and any other observations they make about the fiber.

6. Students should record the texture and pattern made by the fiber in the rubber cement.

8. Student predictions will vary. They might correctly predict that unknown fibers they believe to be hairs contain protein.

11. Test tubes with hair should change color from blue to purple or reddish-brown within five minutes.

Expected Outcome Students will distinguish hairs from nonanimal fibers on the basis of microscopic appearance and a positive biuret reaction (color change from blue to purple or reddish-brown).

Go Further

A local police laboratory or state crime laboratory might be able to provide information or direct students to useful resources on this subject.

Discovery School DVD Encourage students to view track 9 "Wrongly Accused: Science and Justice" on the *BioDetectives* DVD.

Chapter 32 Study Guide

Study Tip

Have a "Biology Bee" and ask students questions about the Vocabulary terms and Key Concepts. When a student misses a question, he or she is out. However, allow the students who are "out" to answer a missed question so they can get back "in." The game is over when all the Vocabulary terms and Key Concepts have been covered.

Thinking Visually

1. Marsupials
2. Placental mammals
3. Platypuses and echidnas

Chapter 32 Assessment

Reviewing Content

1. c	**5.** b	**9.** d
2. c	**6.** c	**10.** a
3. a	**7.** a	
4. a	**8.** b	

Understanding Concepts

11. Hair, subcutaneous fat, and a high metabolic rate

12. Regulate body activities by releasing hormones.

13. Protect animals from disease

14. Sharp teeth, such as canines and incisors, are used for biting and ripping flesh from prey. Most carnivores also have sharp molars that are used to slice meat into small pieces. Herbivores have flattened molars to grind plant food.

15. Chest muscles lift the rib cage, and the diaphragm pulls the bottom of the chest cavity downward, increasing the volume of the chest cavity. Air enters the lungs. Chest muscles then relax, lowering the rib cage. The diaphragm relaxes, and air is pushed out of the lungs.

16. Filters urea from the blood, excretes excess water or retains needed water, and retains salts, sugars, and other important molecules the body needs.

Chapter 32 Study Guide

32–1 Introduction to the Mammals

Key Concepts BI 9.a, BI 9.g

- In addition to having hair and the ability to nourish their young with milk, all mammals breathe air, have four-chambered hearts, and are endotherms that generate their body heat internally.
- The first true mammals appeared during the late Triassic Period, about 220 million years ago.
- The ability of mammals to regulate their body heat from within is an example of homeostasis.
- As mammals evolved to eat foods other than insects, the form and function of their jaws and teeth became adapted to their diets.
- The kidneys of mammals help maintain homeostasis by filtering urea from the blood, as well as excreting or retaining water.

Vocabulary
mammary gland, p. 821 • subcutaneous fat, p. 822
rumen, p. 823 • diaphragm, p. 824
cerebral cortex, p. 825

32–2 Diversity of Mammals

Key Concepts

- The three groups of living mammals are the monotremes, the marsupials, and the placentals. Marsupials bear live young, but at a very early stage of development. Monotremes lay eggs. In placental mammals, nutrients, oxygen, carbon dioxide, and wastes are exchanged between embryo and mother through the placenta.
- Similar ecological opportunities on the different continents have produced some striking examples of convergent evolution in mammals.

Vocabulary
monotreme, p. 828 • marsupial, p. 829
placenta, p. 829

32–3 Primates and Human Origins

Key Concepts 7 3.c

- In general, primates have binocular vision, a well-developed cerebrum, relatively long fingers and toes, and arms that rotate in their shoulder joints.
- Primates that evolved from two of the earliest branches look very little like typical monkeys and are called prosimians. Members of the more familiar primate group that includes monkeys, apes, and humans are called anthropoids.
- It is now clear that hominid evolution did not proceed by the simple, straight-line transformation of one species into another. Rather, like the evolution of other mammalian groups, a series of complex adaptive radiations produced a large number of species whose relationships are difficult to determine.

Vocabulary
binocular vision, p. 834
prosimian, p. 834
anthropoid, p. 835
prehensile, p. 835
hominoid, p. 835
hominid, p. 835
bipedal, p. 835
opposable thumb, p. 835

Thinking Visually

Using information from this chapter, complete the following concept map:

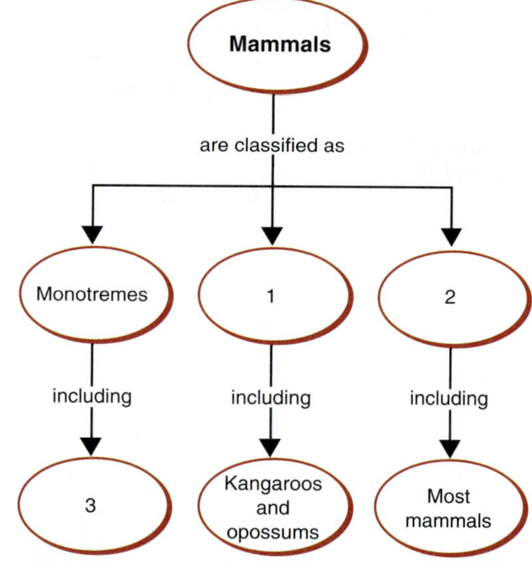

CHAPTER RESOURCES

TIME SAVER

Print:
- ***Teaching Resources,*** Chapter Vocabulary Review, Graphic Organizer, Chapter 32 Tests: Levels A and B

Technology:
- ***Computer Test Bank,*** Chapter 32 Test
- ***iText,*** Chapter 32 Assessment

Chapter 32 Assessment

Interactive textbook with assessment at PHSchool.com 

Reviewing Content

Choose the letter that best answers the question or completes the statement.

1. Which structure in female mammals produces milk to nourish young?
   a. kidney
   b. cloaca
   c. mammary gland
   d. placenta

2. The first true mammals appeared during the
   a. Permian Period.
   b. Cretaceous Period.
   c. Triassic Period.
   d. Jurassic Period.

3. Which of the animals shown below is a mammal?

a. b. c. d.

4. In mammals, the powerful muscle that aids in breathing is the
   a. diaphragm.
   b. placenta.
   c. cerebrum.
   d. kidney.

5. The composition and levels of body fluids in mammals are controlled by the
   a. lungs.
   b. kidneys.
   c. intestine.
   d. heart.

6. The reproductive system of a monotreme empties into the
   a. placenta.
   b. testes.
   c. cloaca.
   d. urinary bladder.

7. The pouch in which the young of kangaroos develop is called a
   a. marsupium.
   b. placenta.
   c. diaphragm.
   d. lagomorph.

8. Which of the following are NOT examples of placental mammals?
   a. cetaceans
   b. marsupials
   c. carnivores
   d. primates

9. Primates consist of two groups, anthropoids and
   a. monotremes.
   b. apes.
   c. hominids.
   d. prosimians.

10. How many hominid species exist today?
    a. one
    b. two
    c. nine
    d. twelve

Understanding Concepts

11. Describe three adaptations mammals have to maintain homeostasis by conserving body heat.
12. What function do endocrine glands perform?
13. What is the function of the immune system?
14. Describe how the teeth of mammals are adapted for different types of food.
15. Sequence the events that occur during mammalian breathing.
16. What functions do the kidneys of mammals carry out?
17. In general, how do the brains of mammals compare with the brains of other vertebrates? What is the significance of that difference?
18. Describe an example of a mammalian adaptation for movement.
19. Describe how the young of monotremes, marsupials, and placental mammals obtain nourishment.
20. What survival advantage does the placenta confer on mammals?
21. Describe an example of convergent evolution in mammals.
22. What anatomical characteristic allows for the binocular vision that occurs in primates?
23. Describe how various adaptations make primates successful tree dwellers.
24. List the unique characteristics of the family known as Hominidae. Give an example of a hominid.
25. What are the Laetoli footprints? What is their significance?
26. What is the earliest known species in the genus *Homo*? What does its species name mean, and why was it given that name?

HOMEWORK GUIDE

Section:	Questions:
Section 32–1:	1–5, 11–18, 29, 31, 34, 34–36
Section 32–2:	6–8, 19–21, 28, 30, 32
Section 32–3:	9, 10, 22–27, 33

Interactive Textbook

If your class subscribes to the iText, your students can go online to access an interactive version of the Student Edition and a self-test.

(Continued from page 844)

17. Mammals have larger brains than other animals in proportion to their body size. As a result, mammals are capable of complicated behaviors such as learning and social conduct.

18. Sample answers: a flexible backbone; limb bones and muscles that enable mammals to run, walk, burrow, fly, hop, swim, swing, and pounce.

19. The young of all three groups feed on milk. Monotremes lick milk from their mothers' abdomens; marsupials attach to nipples in the mother's marsupium; placental mammals obtain milk by nursing.

20. Compared to young that are hatched from eggs, the young of placental mammals are given a longer period of development during which they receive regular nourishment.

21. Mammals that feed on ants and termites evolved in different groups in different regions. They all have powerful front claws; a long, hairless snout; and a sticky tongue.

22. A flat facial structure allows both eyes to face forward, with overlapping fields of view.

23. Primates have flexible hands, and usually flexible feet. The position of the thumbs enables primates to grasp branches and other objects. Some have prehensile tails that help them grasp branches.

24. Hominids are omnivores that have bipedal locomotion, opposable thumbs, and well-developed cerebrums. Humans are an example.

25. The Laetoli footprints are fossil footprints that were probably made by a species of *Australopithecus* between 8 and 3.6 million years ago. They show that hominids were bipedal millions of years ago.

26. *Homo habilis,* which means "handy man." *H. habilis* was given this name because it apparently made and used tools.

Chapter 32 Assessment

Critical Thinking

27. The first diagram has *A. africanus* as the only immediate descendant of *Australopithecus* and in the main line to *H. sapiens.* The second diagram has both *A. africanus* and *Homo habilis* as immediate descendants, and *A. africanus* is not in the main line to *H. sapiens.*

28. The embryo of a placental mammal develops in the mother's uterus for a longer period of time than does the embryo of a marsupial. Therefore, a marsupial is born sooner and is less well developed than a placental mammal. A newborn marsupial must develop further in the mother's pouch.

29. Well-developed senses enable mammals to be aware of dangers and to find food. Well-developed brains enable mammals to react much more quickly to dangers. For example, dolphins can detect location of objects by sound, so they can find food even in poor light. Dogs can track prey by scent, so their chance of finding food is increased.

30. Monotremes have two reptile characteristics: they have a cloaca, and they lay soft-shelled eggs that are incubated outside the body.

31. Mammals have hair and produce milk to nourish the young, characteristics that bats share. Birds lay eggs and have feathers and do not nourish their young with milk, so bats are not birds, even though they fly.

32. Mammal A is a chiropteran, or member of the bat order, because it can fly. Mammal B is a rodent, such as a chipmunk, because of its diet and tooth structure. Mammal C is a cetacean, such as a whale, because it is a filter feeder and lives its entire life in water.

33. By estimating a fossil's age, paleontologists can infer when it was alive relative to other hominid species. Structural characteristics help them infer possible evolutionary relationships.

34. Parents protect developing young and may teach them ways to survive. If the parents die before the young are mature, the young may also die before mating and reproducing.

35. Endocrine system and circulatory system; endocrine glands produce hormones that travel in the blood to the organs that they affect.

Chapter 32 Assessment

Critical Thinking

27. **Interpreting Graphics** The following flowcharts show two alternative lines of descent from *Australopithecus afarensis.* Describe how the two lines of descent differ.

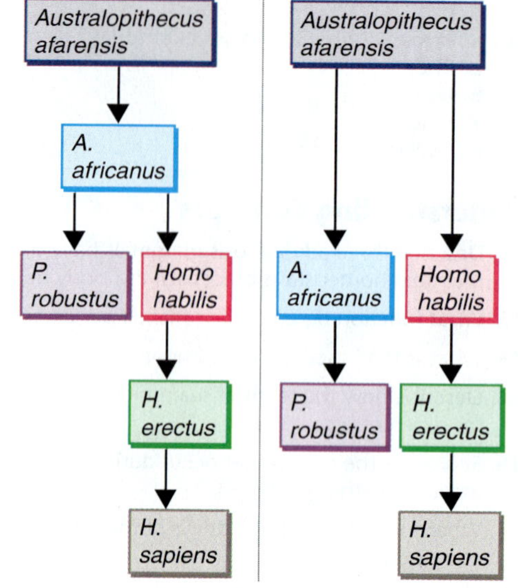

28. **Comparing and Contrasting** Describe the differences between a newborn placental mammal and a newborn marsupial.

29. **Inferring** In what ways have well-developed senses contributed to the success of specific mammals?

30. **Inferring** What evidence suggests that monotremes may have been the first mammals to evolve from reptiles?

31. **Forming Operational Definitions** Write definitions of "mammal" and "bird" that would help you explain why bats are classified as mammals even though they can fly.

32. **Classifying** You are given the following descriptions of three placental mammals: Mammal A can fly, has sharp teeth, and consumes a liquid diet. Mammal B has a single pair of sharp, curved incisor teeth and eats only plant material. Mammal C is a filter feeder, mates and bears its young in water, but comes to the surface to breathe. Place each mammal in its proper order, and explain your decision.

33. **Inferring** Why is it important for paleontologists to estimate the age of a hominid fossil as well as analyze its structural characteristics?

34. **Inferring** Many mammals care for their young for extended periods of time. This parental behavior does not help the parent survive. Why, then, might natural selection favor extended parental care?

35. **Applying Concepts** What two body systems interact to deliver hormones to the organs they affect? Describe how this interaction takes place.

36. **Inferring** How might the disappearance of the dinosaurs at the end of the Cretaceous Period have contributed to the natural selection that is partly responsible for the great diversity of mammals alive today?

Unity and Diversity In Chapter 15, you learned how adaptations contribute to the survival of a species. Name three orders of mammals. Identify two adaptations of each order, and describe the survival value of each adaptation for species in that order.

Writing in Science

Write a paragraph explaining why the process of sweating is considered to be an example of a negative feedback system. In your paragraph, explain what negative feedback is. (*Hint:* Before you write, you might list the steps in the process of sweating and then think about how they relate to negative feedback.)

Performance-Based Assessment

Expressing an Opinion Producers of a new television series want to create interesting episodes about the characteristics and diversity of mammals. They ask you whether viewers will enjoy the show more if it focuses on mammals alone or shows mammals along with other chordates. Write a memo giving your opinion. Include at least three specific examples.

Go Online PHSchool.com
For: An interactive self-test
Visit: PHSchool.com
Web Code: cba-9320

36. The disappearance of the dinosaurs opened up many new niches that could be filled by mammals. The decreased competition for resources and the removal of potential predators helped stimulate the adaptive radiation of mammals.

Sample adaptations: Carnivores have sharp teeth that make them very efficient at capturing and eating prey; insectivores have long, narrow snouts and sharp claws that enable them to dig for food; lagomorphs have hind legs adapted for leaping that help them to escape predators.

Standards Practice

Online at PHSchool.com

Test-Taking Tip Take the time to read each question completely on a standardized test, including all of the answer choices. Consider each possible choice before determining which answer is correct.

Directions: Choose the letter that best answers the question or completes the statement.

1. Which of the following is NOT a characteristic of all mammal species?
   - **A** the ability to nourish young with milk
   - **B** giving birth to live young
   - **C** having hair
   - **D** breathing air
2. Humans belong to the order
   - **A** Chiroptera.
   - **B** Carnivora.
   - **C** Sirenia.
   - **D** Primates.
3. When did the first true mammals appear?
   - **A** Cretaceous Period
   - **B** Triassic Period
   - **C** Cenozoic Era
   - **D** Permian Period
4. Which mammal is an example of a monotreme?
   - **A** elephant
   - **B** kangaroo
   - **C** duckbill platypus
   - **D** bat
5. All of the following characteristics belong to primates EXCEPT
   - **A** a well-developed cerebrum.
   - **B** binocular vision.
   - **C** flexible digits.
   - **D** a small brain in proportion to body size.
6. How are living mammals classified into groups?
   - **A** method of development
   - **B** structure of kidneys
   - **C** method of respiration
   - **D** method of regulating body temperature
7. Which is NOT an example of a placental mammal?
   - **A** whale
   - **B** rat
   - **C** kangaroo
   - **D** bat

Questions 8–10

Radioactive substances found in living things decay at a specific rate over time. The rate at which a substance decays is measured by its half-life. A half-life is the amount of time it takes for half a radioactive sample to decay. For example, the half-life of carbon-14 is 5770 years. Use the bar graph to answer the following questions.

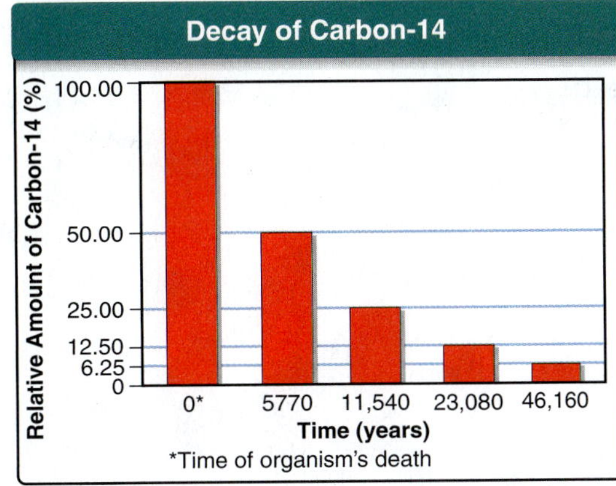

8. How much carbon-14 would remain in an 11,540-year-old fossil?
   - **A** 25 percent
   - **B** 35 percent
   - **C** 50 percent
   - **D** 60 percent
9. A paleontologist determines that a particular fossil has 1/8 of the amount of carbon-14 that was present at the time the organism died. How old is the fossil estimated to be?
   - **A** 5770 years
   - **B** 11,540 years
   - **C** 23,080 years
   - **D** 34,620 years
10. Scientists cannot accurately detect the amount of carbon-14 in a fossil when more than 1/16 of the carbon-14 has decayed. Which of these fossils could NOT be dated accurately using carbon-14?
    - **A** a 2500-year-old fossil
    - **B** a 5000-year-old fossil
    - **C** a 10,000-year-old fossil
    - **D** a 75,000-year-old fossil

Standards Practice

1. B	5. D	9. C
2. D	6. A	10. D
3. B	7. C	
4. C	8. A	

Success Tracker™

Online at PHSchool.com

Have students check their understanding of the chapter by logging onto Success Tracker.

Writing in Science

Students should explain that negative feedback is a control system in which the variable that is being monitored—body temperature, for example—triggers the control mechanism to stop. In the process of sweating, the mammal begins to sweat when body temperature becomes too high. Sweating stops when body temperature has cooled.

Performance-Based Assessment

Students should describe key mammal characteristics and examples of mammal diversity as sample topics. Some students may say that mammal diversity is so rich, it's not necessary to show other chordates; others may argue that showing how mammals compare with other chordates helps explain mammalian evolution and show distinctive mammalian characteristics.

Your students can independently test their knowledge of the chapter and print out their test results for your files.

Chapter Planner 33 Comparing Chordates

Section and Section Objectives	Time	STANDARDS NCLB	STANDARDS Biology	Activities and Labs
33–1 Chordate Evolution, pp. 849–852 ***33.1.1 Explain*** what the roots of the chordate family tree are. ***33.1.2 Summarize*** a main trend in the evolution of chordates.	1 period (1/2 block)		BI 8.f	**SE:** ***Inquiry Activity,*** What are some adaptations of vertebrae?, p. 848 L2 **TE:** ***Address Misconceptions,*** p. 851 L1 L2 **SE:** ***Issues in Biology,*** Should Marine Mammals Be Kept in Captivity?, p. 853 L2 L3 **SE:** ***Exploration,*** Comparing Chordate Family Trees, p. 865 L2
33–2 Controlling Body Temperature, pp. 854–856 ***33.2.1 Explain*** how the control of body temperature is an important aspect of vertebrate life. ***33.2.2 Contrast*** ectotherms and endotherms.	1 period (1/2 block)			**SE:** ***Analyzing Data,*** Comparing Ectotherms and Endotherms, p. 855 L2
33–3 Form and Function in Chordates, pp. 857–864 ***33.3.1 Describe*** how the organ systems of the different groups of chordates carry out essential life functions.	2 periods (1 block)	7 5.c, BI 9.a	BI 9.g	**TE:** ***Build Science Skills,*** p. 857 L2, p. 859 L2 **TE:** ***Demonstration,*** p. 858 L2, p. 859 L2 **SE:** ***Quick Lab,*** How does water affect nitrogen excretion?, p. 861 L2 **SE:** ***Careers in Biology,*** Veterinary Technician, p. 863 L2 **LMA:** Chapter 33 Lab L2 L3 **LMB:** Chapter 33 Lab L1 L2
Chapter Assessment, pp. 866–869	1 period (1/2 block)			

ACTIVITY PLANNER

SE: *Inquiry Activity,* p. 848; 15 min.; plastic gloves, chicken neck, dissecting probe, hand lens

TE: *Address Misconceptions,* p. 851; 10 min.; blocks or beads that differ only in color

TE: *Build Science Skills,* p. 857; 15 min.; 10 pictures, models, or skulls of different vertebrates whose teeth are clearly visible

TE: *Demonstration,* p. 858; 15 min.; 2 mortars and pestles; cooked piece of meat; green grass, leaves, or twigs

TE: *Build Science Skills,* p. 859; 60 min.; balloons, tubing, string, fabric, pipe cleaners, screening

TE: *Demonstration,* p. 859; 15 min.; sheet of paper, large piece of fabric or flat bed sheet

SE: *Quick Lab,* p. 861; 15 min.; 2 test tubes, 2 stoppers, test-tube rack, graduated cylinder, balance, closed glass container of ammonia, urea, uric acid, glass-marking pencil

SE: *Exploration,* p. 865; 45 min.; paper, pen or pencil

PLANNING KEY

Ability Levels

for students performing . . .

below grade level L1

at grade level L2

above grade level L3

Print Components

SE	Student Edition	LA	Lab Assessment
TE	Teacher's Edition	BTM	Biotechnology Manual
RSW	Reading & Study Workbook A	IDM	Issues and Decision Making
ARSW	Adapted Reading & Study Workbook B	LW	Lab Worksheets
TR	Teaching Resources	LMA	Laboratory Manual A
IF	Investigations in Forensics	LMB	Laboratory Manual B

Tech Components

CTB	Computer Test Bank
BD	BioDetectives DVD
TP	Transparencies Plus
PLM	Probeware Lab Manual
ABC	ABC DVD Library
LS	Lab Simulations
VL	Virtual Labs

Interactive textbook with assessment at PHSchool.com

Program Resources	Assessment	Media and Technology
TR: Lesson Plan 33–1, Section Summary, p. 129 L1, p. 139 L2, Worksheets, p. 132 L1, pp. 141–142 L2, Enrichment L2 L3 **LW:** Chapter 33 Exploration L1 L2 L3 **RSW:** Section 33–1 L2 **ARSW:** Section 33–1 L1	**SE:** 33–1 Section Assessment, p. 853 **TR:** Section Review 33–1	**iText:** Section 33–1 **TP:** 33–1 Interest Grabber, Section Outline, Concept Map, Figure 33–2, Figure 33–4
TR: Lesson Plan 33–2, Section Summary, p. 129 L1, p. 139 L2, Worksheets, p. 133 L1, pp. 143–144 L2 **RSW:** Section 33–2 L2 **ARSW:** Section 33–2 L1	**SE:** 33–2 Section Assessment, p. 856 **TR:** Section Review 33–2	**iText:** Section 33–2 **TP:** 33–2 Interest Grabber, Section Outline, Temperature Control in Chordates
TR: Lesson Plan 33–3, Section Summary, p. 130 L1, p. 139 L2, Worksheets, pp. 134–137 L1, pp. 145–147 L2 **RSW:** Section 33–3 L2 **ARSW:** Section 33–3 L1	**SE:** 33–3 Section Assessment, p. 864 **TR:** Section Review 33–3	**iText:** Section 33–3 **TP:** 33–3 Interest Grabber, Section Outline, Compare/Contrast Table, Figure 33–8, Figure 33–10, Figure 33–11 **ABC:** 38 Circulatory Systems
	SE: Chapter 33 Assessment, pp. 866–869 **TR:** Chapter Vocabulary Review, Graphic Organizer, Chapter 33 Test	**iText:** Chapter 33 Assessment **CTB:** Chapter 33 Test

Go Online
Students can do research, share data, and test their knowledge online.

PRESSED FOR TIME?

To Preview the Chapter
- Have students read the Key Concepts in each section.
- Assign the Reading Strategies for each section.

To Cover the Chapter Quickly
- Have students read Figure 33–2 in Section 33–1, Body Temperature and Homeostasis in Section 33–2, and all of Section 33–3.
- Assign the Section Review 33–3; questions 5–10, 15–25, 27, 29, 30, 32, 34, and 35 in Chapter 33 Assessment; and questions 1–10 in Chapter 33 Standards Practice.

To Review the Chapter
- Have students study Figure 33–2 in Section 33–1 and Figure 33–8 and Figures 33–10 through 33–12 in Section 33–3.
- Assign the Section Reviews for 33–1 through 33–3 and the Chapter Vocabulary Review for Chapter 33 in the Teaching Resources.
- Assign Sections 33–2 and 33–3 in the Reading and Study Workbook or the Adapted Reading and Study Workbook.

ENGAGE/EXPLORE

Inquiry Activity

Objective Students will be able to infer how the structure of vertebrae is related to their function. L2

Skill Focus **Inferring, Predicting, Drawing Conclusions**

Materials chicken neck, dissecting probe, hand lens, plastic gloves

Time 15 minutes

Advance Prep Obtain fresh chicken necks from a butcher. Soak chicken necks in bleach, and then rinse thoroughly.

Safety Make sure students wash their hands carefully after handling the chicken necks. As they observe the chicken necks, remind them not to put their hands to their faces, to prevent potential infections.

Strategies

- Make sure students try to insert the dissecting probe into the hole for the spinal cord.
- Students can use scissors to cut away the skin from the neck to better view the vertebrae.

Expected Outcome Students should infer that the structure of the vertebrae allows for a wide range of motion, as well as protection for the spinal cord.

Think About It

1. The many bones of the neck allow for a wide range of motion. The opening in the vertebrae houses and protects the spinal cord.
2. The chicken would have a rigid, inflexible body, and its spinal cord would not have any protection.
3. Larger, to support a larger skull and body

Assess Prior Knowledge

Review the characteristics of chordates. Ask: **What is a chordate?** *(An animal that has, for at least some stage of its life, a dorsal, hollow nerve cord; a notochord; pharyngeal pouches; and a muscular tail)* **Are all chordates vertebrates?** *(No; tunicates and lancelets do not have vertebral columns.)* **Which chordates are vertebrates?** *(Fishes, amphibians, reptiles, birds, and mammals)*

CHAPTER 33 Comparing Chordates

A red-billed oxpecker perches on an impala. These chordates have a mutually beneficial relationship. Oxpeckers pick ticks and other external parasites off the impala, obtaining food while ridding their host of parasites.

Inquiry Activity

What are some adaptations of vertebrae?

Procedure   

1. Put on plastic gloves. Bend a chicken neck back and forth and from side to side.
2. Insert a dissecting probe into the opening at the top of the neck. What do you observe? **CAUTION:** *Use care with sharp instruments.*

Think About It

1. **Inferring** How is the structure of the chicken's neck related to its function?
2. **Predicting** What would happen if the chicken's neck vertebrae were one bone with no central opening?
3. **Drawing Conclusions** How would you expect the vertebrae to be different in an elephant's neck? Explain your answer.

FACTS AND FIGURES

Why compare chordates?
Comparing the structure and function of various chordates ultimately leads scientists to divide them into groups based on their similarities and differences. As more and more chordate species have been identified, their classification has been changed to reflect the new knowledge. Classification systems have also been affected by the discovery of fossilized chordate species. But what is to be gained scientifically by comparing chordates? First, it increases the knowledge of how things work, for the pure sake of biology. Second, it gives scientists a sense of how organisms, chordates in particular, have evolved over time. Third, it gives scientists an idea about how chordates are related to other animal phyla.

33–1 Chordate Evolution

BI 8.f. Students know how to use comparative embryology, DNA or protein sequence comparisons, and other independent sources of data to create a branching diagram (cladogram) that shows probable evolutionary relationships.

Ever since the first chordates appeared more than 500 million years ago, they have been evolving. During this continual process, chordates developed an incredible variety of adaptations. Some of these traits—scales or hair, for example—are relatively simple. Others—such as a four-chambered heart or an amniotic egg—are far more complex. All these adaptations were tested and shaped by natural selection.

Chordate Origins

Much of what scientists know about the origins of chordates comes from studying the embryos of living organisms. Such studies suggest that the most ancient chordates were closely related to echinoderms. Do scientists know what these early chordates looked like? Surprisingly, the answer is yes.

The variety of fossilized organisms preserved in the rich Cambrian deposits of Canada's Burgess Shale includes a peculiar organism called *Pikaia* (pih-KAY-uh), shown in **Figure 33–1.** When *Pikaia* was first discovered, it was thought to be a worm. On closer inspection, scientists determined that *Pikaia* had a **notochord**—a flexible, supporting structure that is found only in chordates. *Pikaia* also had paired serial muscles that were arranged in a manner similar to those of today's nonvertebrate chordates, such as lancelets. On the basis of fossil evidence, scientists now classify *Pikaia* as an early chordate.

To better understand the early evolution of chordates, biologists study a nonvertebrate chordate that is alive today—the tunicate. The tadpolelike larvae of tunicates are the simplest living animals to have a notochord, a dorsal hollow nerve cord, a tail that extends posterior to the anus, and pharyngeal pouches—key features common to all chordates. Today, biologists are studying the genes that control the development of these features.

Guide for Reading

Key Concepts
- What are the roots of the chordate family tree?
- What is a main trend in the evolution of chordates?

Vocabulary
notochord
adaptive radiation

Reading Strategy: Asking Questions Before you read, study the cladogram in **Figure 33–2.** Make a list of questions about the cladogram. As you read, write down the answers to your questions.

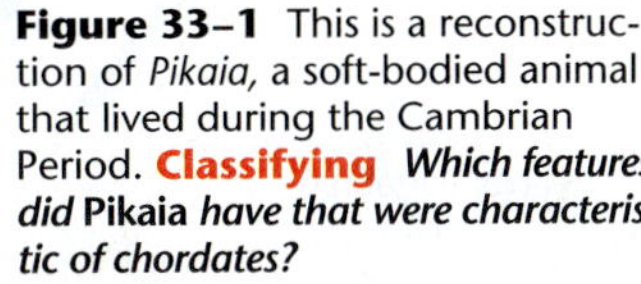

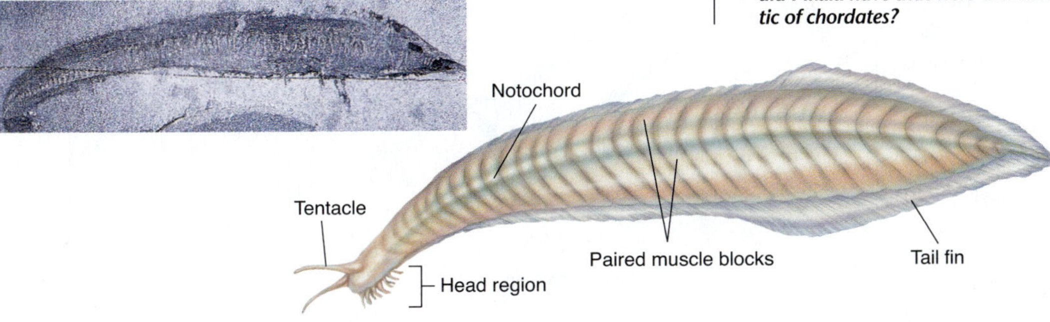

Figure 33–1 This is a reconstruction of *Pikaia,* a soft-bodied animal that lived during the Cambrian Period. **Classifying** *Which features did* Pikaia *have that were characteristic of chordates?*

SECTION RESOURCES

Print:
- ***Teaching Resources,*** Lesson Plan, 33–1, Adapted Section Summary 33–1, Adapted Worksheets 33–1, Section Summary 33–1, Worksheets 33–1, Section Review 33–1, Enrichment
- ***Reading and Study Workbook A,*** Section 33–1
- ***Adapted Reading and Study Workbook B,*** Section 33–1
- ***Lab Worksheets,*** Chapter 33 Exploration

Technology:
- ***iText,*** Section 33–1
- ***Transparencies Plus,*** Section 33–1

Section 33–1

 **BI 8.f**

1 FOCUS

Objectives

33.1.1 ***Explain*** what the roots of the chordate family tree are.

33.1.2 ***Summarize*** a main trend in the evolution of chordates.

Guide for Reading

Vocabulary Preview

Review the meanings of the terms *notochord* and *adaptive radiation.* Encourage students to draw diagrams to illustrate the meanings of these two terms.

Reading Strategy

When students study the cladogram in Figure 33–2, challenge them to explain how this diagram helps clarify the written text.

2 INSTRUCT

Chordate Origins

Make Connections

Earth Science Ask: **What part of an organism is most commonly fossilized?** *(Hard parts, such as bones, teeth, and shells)* **Why don't soft tissues fossilize?** *(They usually decay before the fossilization process is complete.)* Explain that Canada's Burgess Shale contains many fossilized organisms from the middle Cambrian Period, about 530 million years ago. These specimens are well-preserved fossils of soft-bodied organisms. Scientists think a mudslide buried the organisms, and the absence of oxygen in the mud preserved the organisms until minerals replaced the original organic material, forming hard replicas of the soft bodies. L2

Answer to . . .

Figure 33–1 *Notochord and paired muscles*

33–1 (continued)

The Chordate Family Tree

Use Visuals

Figure 33–2 Help students interpret the information illustrated in this cladogram. Be sure they realize that the chordate groups shown are only those that exist today. Extinct groups are not shown. Ask: **Which chordate group is most closely related to birds?** *(Crocodiles; they share a more recent common ancestor.)* **Why are hagfishes considered to be an older group than lungfishes?** *(Unlike lungfishes, hagfishes lack jaws and paired appendages.)* Discuss how the appearance of certain adaptations led to the adaptive radiation of different chordate groups. Ask: **What group evolved after the appearance of four limbs?** *(Amphibians)* Point out that the cladogram shows the uncertainty about when endothermy appeared. Discuss whether or not endothermy could have evolved separately in two different evolutionary lines. You may want to point out that some insects and fishes are also endotherms. L1 L2

The Chordate Family Tree

The chordate family tree has its roots in ancestors that vertebrates share with tunicates and lancelets. The cladogram in **Figure 33–2** shows chordate phylogeny—how the different groups of living chordates are related to one another and to their invertebrate ancestors. It also shows the evolution of distinctly vertebrate features, such as jaws and limbs. Notice that the fishes—from hagfishes to lungfishes—include six different groups with long and separate evolutionary histories. On the other hand, modern amphibians, reptiles, birds, and mammals share much more recent common ancestors. Where do extinct groups, such as dinosaurs, fit into the chordate phylum? The answer may be found in the fossil record.

CHECKPOINT *How many groups of fishes are alive today?*

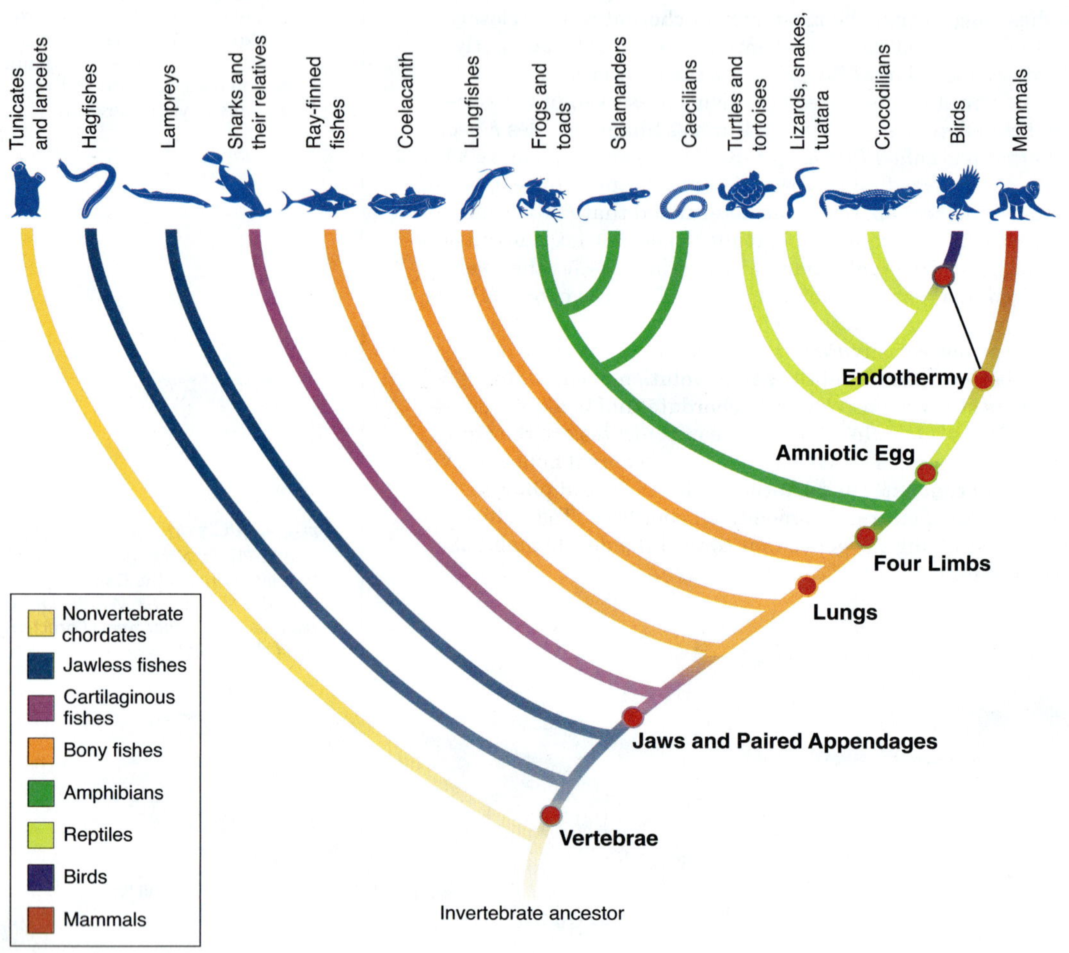

Figure 33–2 **The phylum Chordata includes both vertebrates and nonvertebrate chordates. All of these subphyla share a common invertebrate ancestor.** This cladogram shows the phylogenetic relationship of modern chordate groups to that common ancestor. The different colored lines represent the traditional groupings of these animals, as listed in the key. The red circles indicate some of the important chordate adaptations. Such adaptations are the results of evolutionary processes, including natural selection.

UNIVERSAL ACCESS

Inclusion/Special Needs

Students can develop a timeline based on the cladogram in Figure 33–2. In their timelines, have them chart the time in the geologic time scale when each vertebrate group first emerged. Encourage students to note also when vertebrate features, such as jaws and limbs, emerged.  L1

Advanced Learners

Students can investigate how chordates evolved concurrently with plants. Suggest that they start with the Geologic Time Scale and correlate a major chordate adaptation with the climate and plant life of the time. Have them consider whether plants had any influence on chordate evolution. Challenge students to infer how chordate evolution might be different if the climate had not changed. L3

Evolutionary Trends in Vertebrates

The hard body structures of many vertebrates have left behind an excellent fossil record. As a result, scientists know a great deal about vertebrates' evolutionary history. In addition, scientists infer evolutionary trends by studying the characteristics of chordates living today.

Adaptive Radiations The number of species within each chordate group has changed over geologic time. Look at the cladogram in **Figure 33–2** again. The red circles in that figure represent the origin of certain adaptive features. For example, one notable event in chordate evolution was the development of jaws. Another event was the development of paired appendages, including pectoral and pelvic fin or limb girdles. Paired appendages allowed chordates, such as the salamander in **Figure 33–3**, to move more efficiently. **Over the course of evolution, the appearance of new adaptations—such as jaws and paired appendages—has launched adaptive radiations in chordate groups.** An **adaptive radiation** is the rapid diversification of species as they adapt to new conditions.

Convergent Evolution Adaptive radiations sometimes produce species that are similar in appearance and behavior, even though they are not closely related. This trend is called convergent evolution. Convergent evolution occurred many times during chordate evolution when unrelated species encountered similar ecological conditions and evolved similar adaptations. For example, convergent evolution has produced flying vertebrates as different as birds and bats.

Chordate Diversity

Living chordates are extremely diverse, as shown in **Figure 33–4.** Yet, the species of chordates that are alive today are a small fraction of the total number of chordate species that have existed over time. Today, vertebrates make up about 96 percent of all living chordate species and account for more than 50,000 species throughout the world. The six living groups of chordates are the nonvertebrate chordates, fishes, amphibians, reptiles, birds, and mammals. Of these, the largest group by far is the fishes.

For: Links on chordates
Visit: www.SciLinks.org
Web Code: cbn-9331

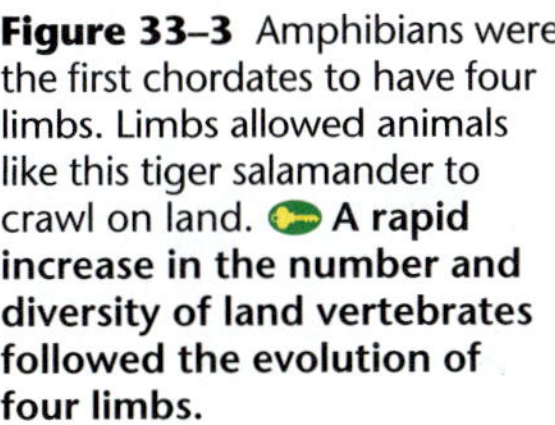

Figure 33–3 Amphibians were the first chordates to have four limbs. Limbs allowed animals like this tiger salamander to crawl on land. **A rapid increase in the number and diversity of land vertebrates followed the evolution of four limbs.**

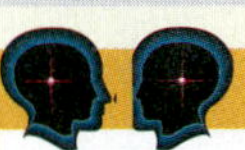

TEACHER TO TEACHER

Keep a live salamander in your classroom. Figure 33–3 takes on a new meaning for students when they can observe a salamander walking across a lab table. Better yet, have the students put on disposable plastic gloves and gently hold the salamander in their hands. Students can study the limb movements as the salamander crawls from one hand to the next. If you have fish in your classroom, have students observe the movements of the pectoral and pelvic fins to infer how ineffective fins would be on land. Use a video camera to record the movements of these animals to share with other students.

—Frank Tworek
Biology Teacher
Omaha North High School
Omaha, NE

Download a worksheet on chordates for students to complete, and find additional teacher support from NSTA SciLinks.

Evolutionary Trends in Vertebrates

Build Science Skills

Using Models Divide the class into two groups. Challenge one group to develop and perform a skit that models adaptive radiation. The other group can develop and perform a skit to model convergent evolution. Work with groups as they develop their skits to make sure their models are correct. Encourage students to use props and even scenery as space and time allow. Each group can perform its skit for the other. L2

Build Science Skills

Applying Concepts Challenge students to identify other examples of convergent evolution in the chordate family tree. One example is aquatic vertebrates, including aquatic species of reptiles (sea turtles), birds (penguins), and mammals (whales, porpoises). Have students illustrate the vertebrates, showing their similar adaptations. Students should also note the features that separate the vertebrates into different groups. L2

Chordate Diversity

Address Misconceptions

Some students might confuse diversity with numbers in a population. Demonstrate the difference in meaning with groups of colored blocks or other objects such as beads. The blocks should be similar in every way except color. Use only blocks of one color to make up the first group. Use many different-colored blocks in the second group. The first group should have more blocks than the second group. Discuss with students which group has more diversity and why. *(The second group; it has more blocks that are different from one another.)*

L1 L2

Answer to . . .

CHECKPOINT *Six*

33–1 (continued)

Use Visuals

Figure 33–4 Help students interpret the pie chart by asking the following questions: **Which chordate group in the inner circle has the most living species?** *(Fishes)* **Which group has the fewest?** *(Nonvertebrate chordates)* **Which group of amphibians has the most living species?** *(Frogs and toads)* **Which group of reptiles has the fewest living species?** *(Crocodilians)* **Of the living chordates, what percentage are birds?** *(17%)* L1 L2

3 ASSESS

Evaluate Understanding

Instruct students to draw a family tree to show the relationships among the different chordate groups. Students should show which chordates share common ancestors and where various vertebrate features, such as limbs, lungs, and jaws, arose.

Reteach

Have students develop a concept map that shows the major trends in chordate evolution. In their concept maps, students should include a definition and an example for each trend.

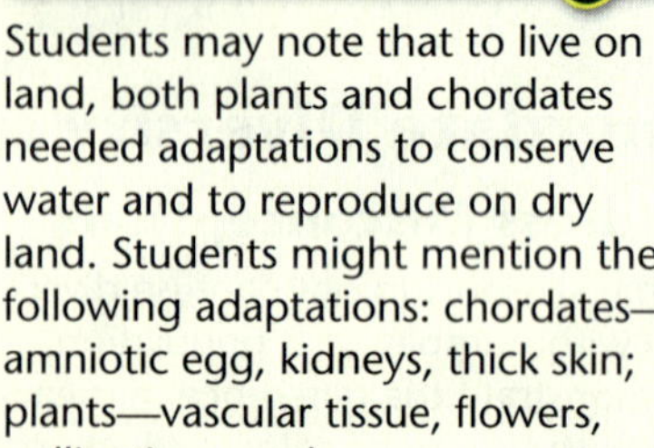

Students may note that to live on land, both plants and chordates needed adaptations to conserve water and to reproduce on dry land. Students might mention the following adaptations: chordates—amniotic egg, kidneys, thick skin; plants—vascular tissue, flowers, pollination, seeds.

If your class subscribes to the iText, use it to review the Key Concepts in Section 33–1.

Answer to . . .

Figure 33–4 *96%*

Figure 33–4 This pie chart shows the diversity of chordates. The area of each slice represents the relative number of living species in each group of chordates. The inner circle shows the six major chordate groups and gives the percentage of species contained in each. The outer circle breaks down each major group and shows the number of known species. **Calculating** ***Of the total number of fish species, what percentage is represented by the ray-finned fishes?***

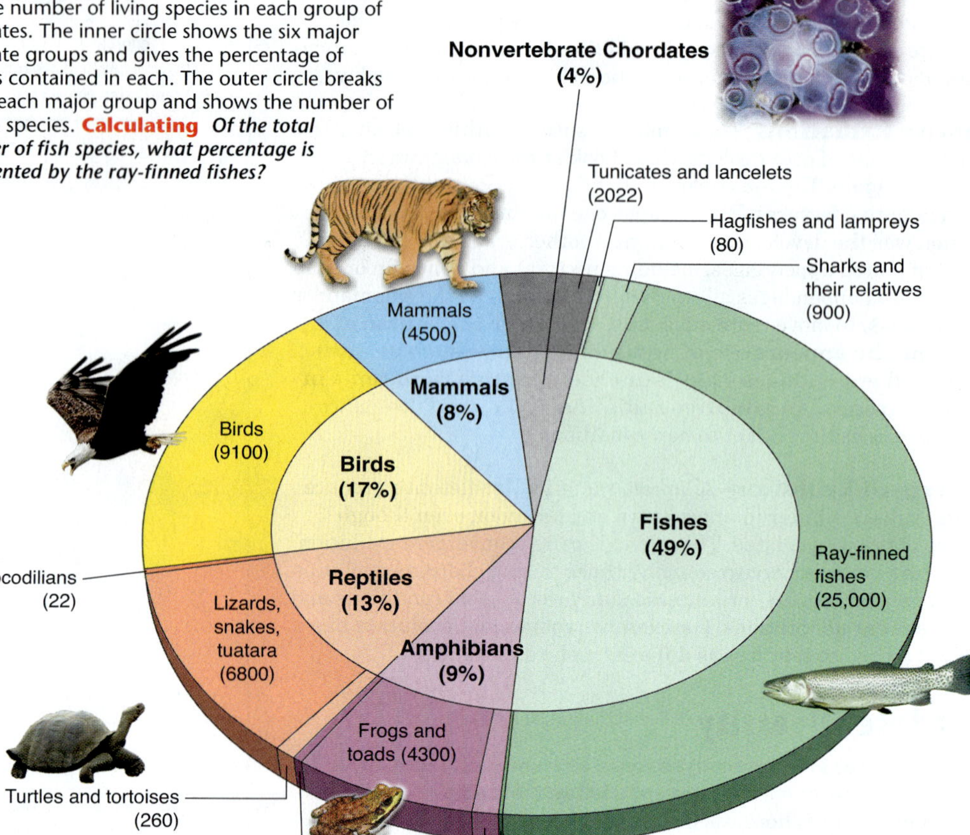

33–1 Section Assessment

1. **Key Concept** To which groups of animals are vertebrates most closely related phylogenetically?
2. **Key Concept** Describe a major trend in chordate evolution.
3. Which characteristic appeared first: four limbs or jaws?
4. What is adaptive radiation?
5. **Critical Thinking Inferring** Both frogs and ducks have webbed feet. However, ducks are more closely related to perching birds than to frogs. Explain the process that has resulted in both frogs and ducks having feet that are similar.

Focus on the BIG Idea

Evolution Recall what you learned about plant evolution in Chapter 22. In what ways are chordate adaptations to life on land similar to plant adaptations to life on land? Based on the sequence of evolutionary change illustrated in the cladograms on pages 554 and 850, identify the first adaptations in each.

33–1 Section Assessment

1. Tunicates and lancelets
2. Accept either: adaptive radiation—the rapid growth in the diversity of a group of organisms; convergent evolution—unrelated animals evolve similar body forms and habits independently
3. Jaws
4. Adaptive radiation is the rapid diversification of species as they adapt to new conditions.
5. The webbed feet are the result of convergent evolution. The adaptation helps both frogs and ducks survive in a similar environment—one that includes water.

BIIE 1.m

Should Marine Mammals Be Kept in Captivity?

Many types of marine mammals, including dolphins, killer whales, and seals, are kept in captive display for educational, entertainment, and research purposes. Yet, there is strong debate about whether public display of such animals is ethical. Should we prohibit the capture of marine mammals for public display?

The Viewpoints

Captivity Should Be Allowed

Some people believe that we have an obligation to convey knowledge of the natural world to the public by displaying animals and educating ourselves about them. Information obtained by observing captive animals may be helpful in managing their populations in the wild. Many people argue that the adverse effects of captivity are outweighed by the benefits of conservation, an enhanced human appreciation for animals, and the advancement of scientific knowledge. There is also evidence that human interactions with captive dolphins may help people with disabilities, such as autism.

Captivity Should Be Prohibited

Other people believe that because marine mammals are naturally social, with strong family bonds, they are not suited to capture or confinement. These people are concerned that the process of capture disrupts social groups.

Those opposed to the captivity of marine mammals also argue that confinement places the animals in an unnatural situation—one that is monotonous, limited, and unhealthy. In the wild, whales and dolphins travel long distances and dive much deeper than is possible in a shallow display tank. There is also a concern that human interaction with captive marine mammals increases the risk of transmitting diseases to the animals.

Research and Decide

1. **Analyzing the Viewpoints** To make an informed decision, learn more about this issue by consulting library or Internet resources. Then, list the options for education, entertainment, and research involving marine mammals. What are the benefits? The costs?
2. **Forming Your Opinion** Should marine mammals be kept in captivity? Are there some instances when captivity is a good solution and other instances when it is not? Explain.
3. **Role Playing** Suppose you are a wildlife biologist managing a declining population of wild bottlenose dolphins. You need to learn about the lifestyle of this dolphin before you can recommend any solutions. You also want to increase public awareness to help protect the population. Write a proposal on how you will do all this.

For: Links from the authors
Visit: PHSchool.com
Web Code: cbe-9334

BIIE 1.m

After students have read the feature, invite them to learn more about this issue. Students might wish to interview a zookeeper, a marine biologist, or an animal caregiver at a local marine park. After students have gathered more information, organize a class debate about this issue.

Research and Decide

1. Possible answers include the following. Captivity: General public is educated about and entertained by marine mammals. It is profitable to the companies owning the marine parks. Research is easier to conduct; however, living conditions are not natural. Captivity prohibited: General public would not be easily entertained and educated unless they go out to sea on a tour boat. Research would be more difficult to conduct, because of the difficult environment and the extreme distances and depths traveled by these mammals. However, the results would be based on observations of animals behaving in their natural environment rather than in captivity. Research would be more costly, but marine mammals would not be adversely affected.

2. Some students will think that captivity should be allowed; others will think it shouldn't be. Still others might think captivity is a good solution sometimes, but not always. In all cases, students must explain the reasoning behind their opinions.

3. Student proposals should include a plan to get the public involved in the plight of the dolphins, as well as a plan for learning about the dolphins' way of living.

BACKGROUND

Should Willy be free?

The killer whale Keiko is at the heart of the debate about captive marine mammals. Keiko, caught at the age of 2 near Iceland, was sold to an amusement park in Mexico City. When Keiko's poor health and living conditions became public in the 1993 movie *Free Willy*, the public demanded that he be freed. After millions of dollars were raised, Keiko was returned to his native waters in Iceland. In the summer of 2002, he spent nearly 60 days away from his sea pen interacting with wild whales and foraging for food. In November 2002, Keiko was moved to his new winter home — an isolated bay with deep water and protection from winter winds. Wild orcas and herring are often found there. Until his death in December 2003, his caretakers devoted their time to helping Keiko return to the wild.

Students can research marine mammals in captivity on the site developed by authors Ken Miller and Joe Levine.

Section 33–2

1 FOCUS

Objectives

33.2.1 ***Explain*** how the control of body temperature is an important aspect of vertebrate life.

33.2.2 ***Contrast*** ectotherms and endotherms.

Guide for Reading

Vocabulary Preview

Review the terms *endotherm* and *ectotherm* with students. On the board, create a list of what students already know about these terms.

Reading Strategy

As students read the section, encourage them to take notes in a compare/contrast table to help them differentiate between endothermy and ectothermy.

2 INSTRUCT

Body Temperature and Homeostasis

Use Visuals

Figure 33–5 Invite a student volunteer to identify a penguin as an endotherm or ectotherm. (*Endotherm*) Ask: **How is a penguin able to maintain homeostasis in a cold climate?** *(Generates own body heat; feathers act as insulation)* **Why is it important for a penguin to be able to maintain a constant internal temperature?** *(Essential life functions are carried out most efficiently when an animal's internal temperature stays within a certain range.)* L1 L2

33–2 Controlling Body Temperature

Guide for Reading

Key Concepts

- How is the control of body temperature an important aspect of vertebrate life?
- What is the difference between ectotherms and endotherms?

Vocabulary

ectotherm
endotherm

Reading Strategy: Finding Main Ideas Before you read, skim the section to identify the key-concept sentences about body temperature control. Then, carefully read the section, making a list of supporting details for each main idea.

On a spring morning, after a cold night, a tortoise lies on a rock basking in the sun. Nearby, a snake slides out of its burrow beneath a rotting stump. In a tree overhead, a young robin puffs up its downy feathers. As you walk out of the water after an early swim, your skin gets goose bumps and you shiver. All these activities are examples of the different ways that vertebrates control their body temperature.

Body Temperature and Homeostasis

Recall from Chapter 2 that many of the chemical reactions that are important in metabolism are influenced by temperature. For this reason, essential life functions can be carried out most efficiently when an animal's internal body temperature is within a particular "operating range." For muscles to operate quickly and efficiently, for example, their temperature can neither be too low nor too high. If muscles are too cold, they may contract slowly, making it difficult for the animal to respond quickly to events around it. If an animal gets too hot, on the other hand, its muscles may tire easily and other body systems may not function properly.

Because most chordates are vertebrates, and mechanisms for controlling body temperature are well developed among vertebrates, this section will focus exclusively on that group. **The control of body temperature is important for maintaining homeostasis in vertebrates, particularly in habitats where temperature varies widely with time of day and with season.** Vertebrates, such as the penguins in **Figure 33–5**, have a variety of ways to control their body temperature. All of these ways incorporate three important features: a source of heat for the body, a way to conserve that heat, and a method of eliminating excess heat when necessary. In terms of how they generate and control their body heat, vertebrates can be classified into two basic groups: ectotherms and endotherms.

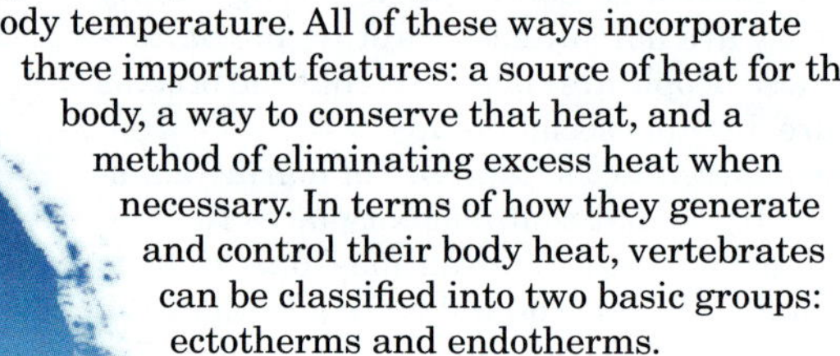

Figure 33–5 Birds and other endotherms are able to generate their own body heat. **The internal control of body temperature allows these emperor penguins to live in cold Antarctic climates, where their feathers act as insulation.**

SECTION RESOURCES

Print:

- ***Teaching Resources,*** Lesson Plan, 33–2, Adapted Section Summary 33–2, Adapted Worksheets 33–2, Section Summary 33–2, Worksheets 33–2, Section Review 33–2
- ***Reading and Study Workbook A,*** Section 33–2
- ***Adapted Reading and Study Workbook B,*** Section 33–2

Technology:

- ***iText,*** Section 33–2
- ***Transparencies Plus,*** Section 33–2

Analyzing Data

Comparing Ectotherms and Endotherms

Endotherms, such as humans, depend on their metabolism to maintain high body temperatures. Ectotherms, on the other hand, depend primarily on heat from the environment to regulate their body temperatures. The accompanying graph shows the internal body temperatures maintained by several ectotherms and endotherms at different environmental temperatures.

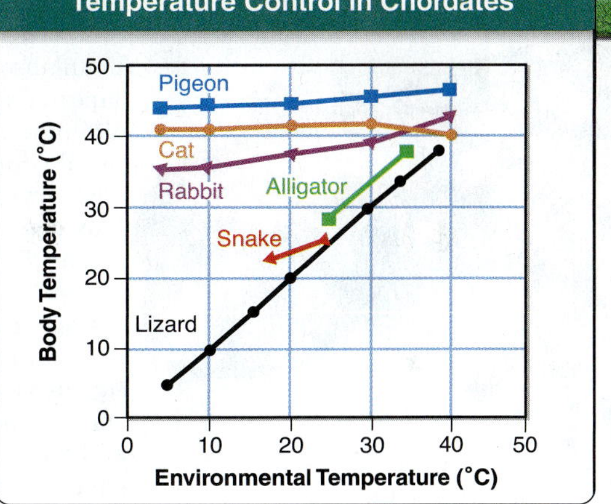

1. **Using Tables and Graphs** Which chordate has the highest body temperature when the environmental temperature is between 0° and 10°C? Which chordate has the lowest body temperature under those same conditions?
2. **Inferring** Which animals shown in the graph are ectotherms? Which are endotherms? Explain your answers.
3. **Predicting** Describe the patterns of activity you would expect for the animals shown in this graph if they lived in your local environment. Would you expect all of the animals to be equally active year-round? If not, why not?

Ectothermy On cool, sunny mornings, lizards often bask in the sun. This doesn't mean that they are lazy! A lizard is an **ectotherm,** which means that its body temperature is mainly determined by the temperature of its environment. **Most reptiles, fishes, and amphibians are ectotherms—animals whose body temperatures are controlled primarily by picking up heat from, or losing heat to, their environment.** Ectotherms often warm up by basking in the sun, and may cool down by seeking shelter in underground burrows.

Ectotherms have relatively low rates of metabolism when they are resting. Thus, their bodies do not generate much heat. When active, an ectotherm's muscles generate heat, just as your muscles do. However, because its body lacks effective insulation, the heat is lost to the environment fairly easily.

Endothermy An **endotherm** is an animal whose body temperature is controlled from within. **Birds and mammals are endotherms, which means they can generate and retain heat inside their bodies.** Endotherms have relatively high metabolic rates that generate a significant amount of heat, even when they are resting. Birds conserve body heat primarily through insulating feathers, such as down. Mammals have body fat and hair for insulation. Mammals can get rid of excess heat by panting, as dogs do, or by sweating, as humans do.

CHECKPOINT *Give an example of an ectotherm and an endotherm.*

Word Origins

Ectothermy and **endothermy** are both derived from the Greek word *therme,* meaning "heat." The prefix *endo-* is a Greek word meaning "within." Therefore, the word *endotherm* literally means "heat from within." **What do you think the prefix *ecto-* means?**

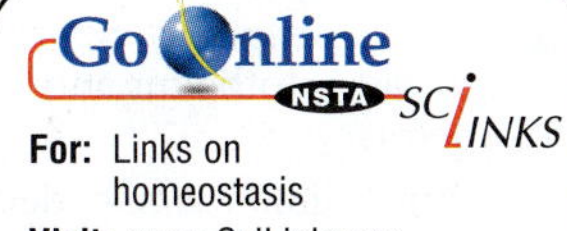

For: Links on homeostasis
Visit: www.SciLinks.org
Web Code: cbn-9332

Analyzing Data

Have student volunteers describe the line on the graph for each of the animals. Elicit descriptions in which they explain the animal's body temperature as a function of environmental temperature. For example, the body temperature of the alligator is about 3°C higher than the environmental temperature. L2

1. Highest: pigeon; lowest: lizard
2. The lizard, snake, and alligator are ectotherms. Their body temperature fluctuates based on the environmental temperature. The rabbit, cat, and pigeon are endotherms. Their body temperature remains relatively the same as the environmental temperature changes.
3. In areas with cold winters, the ectotherms would not be active during the winter. They would be active during warm months. The endotherms might be active all year, regardless of temperature changes.

Word Origins

Ecto- means "outer," "outside," or "external." L2

Download a worksheet on homeostasis for students to complete, and find additional teacher support from NSTA SciLinks.

UNIVERSAL ACCESS

Inclusion/Special Needs

Remind students that they are endotherms. Challenge them to identify behaviors that they use to conserve body heat and to eliminate excess body heat. *(Examples include wearing coats and mittens to add insulation and protect against the loss of body heat and swimming to cool off.)* L1

Advanced Learners

Challenge students to compare human characteristics with those of other endothermic vertebrates adapted to live in cold environments. Ask students to infer the type of environment to which humans are naturally adapted. *(Warm environments)* Invite students to develop a computer presentation that describes how humans have adapted to live in cold environments. L3

Answer to . . .

CHECKPOINT *Ectotherms: fishes, amphibians, and reptiles; endotherms: birds and mammals*

33–2 (continued)

Comparing Ectotherms and Endotherms

Build Science Skills

Making Judgments Conduct a mock debate on the pros and cons of ectothermy. You can either stage an entire class debate or have small groups debate each other. You might also want students to switch sides so that they have the opportunity to argue for both types of temperature control. L2

Evolution of Temperature Control

Build Science Skills

Formulating Hypotheses Challenge students to use their own ideas about evolution and the control of body temperature to devise a hypothesis to explain when endothermy first evolved. Encourage students to refer to additional resources to increase their knowledge. Students should note the evidence on which their hypothesis is based.

3 ASSESS

Evaluate Understanding

Ask students to name the three features of body temperature control. Then, have students give examples of each feature for both endotherms and ectotherms.

Reteach

Students can create a Venn diagram to compare and contrast endothermy and ectothermy.

Thinking Visually

Tables should include the six factors specified, as well as animal examples.

If your class subscribes to the iText, use it to review the Key Concepts in Section 33–2.

▲ **Figure 33–6 Unlike birds and mammals, which can regulate their body temperature from within, lizards and other ectotherms rely on their surroundings to gain or lose body heat.** The venomous gila monster, for example, makes its home in arid regions of the southwestern United States and Mexico, most often in desert and grassland biomes. To cool down, it burrows below the ground.

Comparing Ectotherms and Endotherms

In an absolute sense, neither endothermy nor ectothermy is superior. Each strategy has advantages and disadvantages in different environments. For example, endotherms move around easily during cool nights or in cold weather because they generate and conserve their own body heat. That's how musk ox live in the tundra and killer whales swim through polar seas. But the high metabolic rate that generates that heat requires a lot of fuel. The amount of food needed to keep a single cow alive would be enough to feed ten cow-sized lizards!

Ectothermic animals, like the gila monster shown in **Figure 33–6,** need much less food than similarly sized endotherms. In environments where temperatures stay warm and fairly constant most of the time, ectothermy is a more energy-efficient strategy. But large ectotherms run into trouble in habitats where temperatures get cold at night or stay cold for long periods, such as boreal forest biomes. It takes a long time for a large animal to warm up in the sun after a cold night. Most large lizards and amphibians live in warm areas such as tropical rain forest biomes.

Evolution of Temperature Control

There is little doubt that the first land vertebrates were ectotherms. But there is some doubt as to when endothermy evolved. Although modern reptiles are ectotherms, some biologists hypothesize that at least some of the dinosaurs were endotherms. Others hypothesize that endothermy evolved a long time after the appearance of the dinosaurs, so that all the dinosaurs were ectotherms. Evidence suggests that endothermy has evolved more than one time. It developed once along the evolutionary line of reptiles that led to birds and once along the evolutionary line of reptiles that led to mammals.

33–2 Section Assessment

1. **Key Concept** What important function does the control of body temperature serve in chordates?
2. **Key Concept** Compare and contrast ectotherms and endotherms.
3. What three features are needed to control an animal's body temperature?
4. How does endothermy affect an animal's need for food?
5. **Critical Thinking Inferring** Why is it unlikely that you would find a giant lizard living in the wild in North Dakota?

Thinking Visually

Comparing and Contrasting
Construct a table that compares ectothermy and endothermy. Factors you should compare include: how body temperature is controlled; relative rates of metabolism; relative amounts of food eaten; advantages; disadvantages; and examples of animals with each method of temperature regulation.

33–2 Section Assessment

1. Helps maintain homeostasis
2. Ectotherms obtain heat from outside the body and have a low metabolic rate. Endotherms can generate and retain heat inside the body and have a high metabolic rate.
3. A source of heat for the body, a way to conserve heat, and a method of eliminating excess heat
4. Endotherms need more food in order to release enough energy to generate body heat.
5. Winters in North Dakota are too cold for a giant lizard to maintain enough warmth for activity.

33–3 Form and Function in Chordates

7 5.c. Students know how bones and muscles work together to provide a structural framework for movement. **BI 9.a.** Students know how the complementary activity of major body systems provides cells with oxygen and nutrients and removes toxic waste products such as carbon dioxide. **BI 9.g.** Students know the homeostatic role of the kidneys in the removal of nitrogenous wastes and the role of the liver in blood detoxification and glucose balance.

The nonvertebrate chordates that are alive today represent a simple and ancient stage in the development of chordate body systems. However, the fact that the organ systems are simple does not mean they are inferior. After all, lancelets and tunicates have survived to the present day, so their body systems are well equipped to perform the essential functions of life.

Among vertebrates, organ systems exhibit a wider range of complexity than those of nonvertebrate chordates. Many adaptive radiations of vertebrates have produced a variety of specialized organ systems that perform essential functions and maintain homeostasis. The complexity of vertebrate organ systems can be seen in the different ways that vertebrates feed, breathe, respond, move, and reproduce.

Guide for Reading

Key Concept

- How do the organ systems of the different groups of chordates carry out essential life functions?

Vocabulary
alveolus

Reading Strategy: Using Graphic Organizers
As you read, create a table that compares and contrasts the different life functions in nonvertebrate chordates, fishes, amphibians, reptiles, birds, and mammals.

Feeding

Feeding and digestion help maintain homeostasis by providing the body with a continuing supply of needed nutrients. Most tunicates, and all lancelets, are filter feeders. These chordates remove small organisms called plankton from the water that passes through their pharynx. A few adult tunicates feed on deposited material from the surface of the sediments on which they dwell.

The skulls and teeth of vertebrates are adapted for feeding on a much wider assortment of foods, ranging from insects to large mammals, and from leaves to fruits and seeds. Some vertebrates—such as baleen whales, flamingoes, and manta rays—are filter feeders with sievelike mouth structures that enable them to strain small crustaceans and fish from the water. The long bill of the hummingbird and the narrow snout of the honey possum are both adaptations that enable them to feed on nectar. Other vertebrates, such as the crocodile in **Figure 33–7**, are adapted to eating meat. Many mammals have sharp canine teeth and incisors that they use to tear and slice their food.

▶ **Figure 33–7** The blunt, broad jaws and numerous peglike teeth of this crocodile help it catch large prey—such as zebra—even in thick vegetation. **Comparing and Contrasting** *How do the mouth structures of a filter-feeding vertebrate differ from those of a carnivore like this reptile?*

SECTION RESOURCES

Print:

- ***Laboratory Manual A,*** Chapter 33 Lab
- ***Laboratory Manual B,*** Chapter 33 Lab
- ***Teaching Resources,*** Lesson Plan 33–3, Adapted Section Summary 33–3, Adapted Worksheets 33–3, Section Summary 33–3, Worksheets 33–3, Section Review 33–3
- ***Reading and Study Workbook A,*** Section 33–3
- ***Adapted Reading and Study Workbook B,*** Section 33–3

Technology:

- ***iText,*** Section 33–3
- ***Animated Biological Concepts DVD,*** 38 Circulatory Systems
- ***Transparencies Plus,*** Section 33–3

Section 33–3

7 5.c, BI 9.a, BI 9.g

1 FOCUS

Objective

33.3.1 ***Describe*** how the organ systems of the different groups of chordates carry out essential life functions.

Guide for Reading

Vocabulary Preview

Write the words *alveolus* and *alveoli* on the board, and then pronounce them for students. Ask: **Which word is singular and which is plural?** *(Singular: alveolus; plural: alveoli)* Explain that many words in science are from Latin. Latin words that end in *-us* are usually the singular version of the word. The word is usually made plural by removing *-us* and adding *-i*. Have students make these singular words plural: *stimulus, nucleus, bronchus, ascus, villus,* and *radius.*

Reading Strategy

Before students read the section, they can set up their table using the main heads in the section as the titles for the columns. They can use the chordate groups as titles for the rows.

2 INSTRUCT

Feeding

Build Science Skills

Inferring Give students at least 10 pictures of different vertebrates whose teeth are clearly visible. Challenge students to infer what kinds of foods each vertebrate eats, based on the shape of the teeth, mouth, and skull. Ask: **What would happen to a vertebrate if its food source was unavailable, but other food sources were?** *(The vertebrate might die because its teeth and digestive system are not equipped to use the other food sources.)* L2

Answer to . . .

Figure 33–7 *Filter feeders have sievelike mouth structures. Carnivores have sharp teeth.*

33–3 (continued)

Use Visuals

Figure 33–8 As students study the digestive systems illustrated, point out that the organs are actually arranged much more compactly in live animals. Ask: **Why are structures such as the gallbladder, liver, and pancreas included as part of the digestive system?** *(These organs secrete enzymes and other substances that help to digest food.)* Help students compare and contrast the vertebrate digestive systems by asking questions like the following: **Which vertebrate has the shortest intestine?** *(Shark)* **Is a shark a herbivore or a carnivore?** *(Carnivore)* **How can you tell that a cow is a herbivore?** *(Long intestine)* **What is the purpose of the crop and gizzard in the pigeon?** *(The crop stores food, and the gizzard acts like teeth to break food down.)* **Why do birds need these organs?** *(They don't have teeth.)* L1 L2

Demonstration

Show students the difficulty of digesting plant material by using a mortar and pestle to grind a piece of cooked meat and a different mortar and pestle to grind some green grass, leaves, or stems. You might also add a little water to the contents of each mortar to make a paste. First, have student volunteers make analogies of your process to the vertebrate digestive system. Then, discuss why it took longer to grind the plant material into a mush (if at all) than it did the meat. Ask: **What characteristic of plant cells makes it more difficult to break them down?** *(Cellulose, which makes up the cell wall, gives a plant support and stability, acting as its "skeleton.")* L2

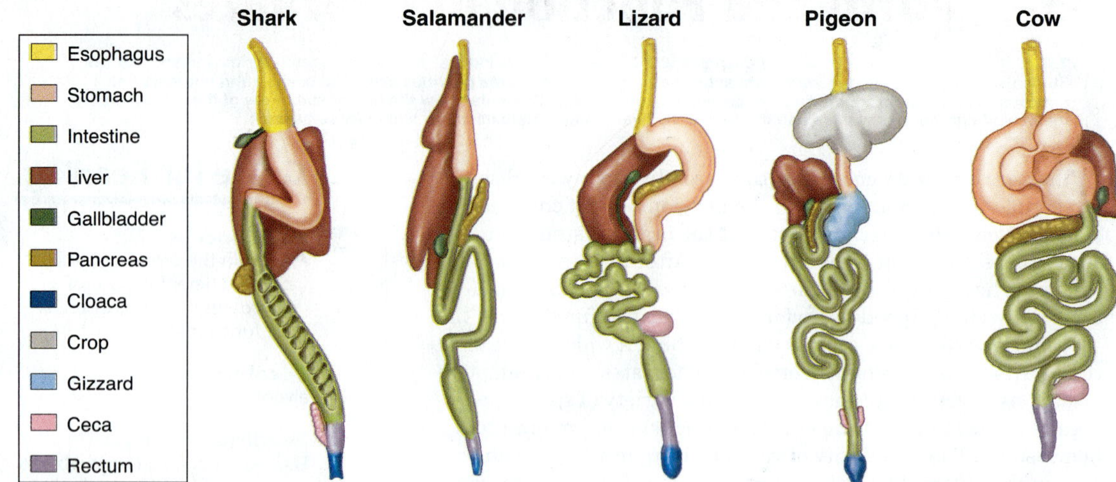

▲ **Figure 33–8** **The digestive systems of vertebrates are adapted for a variety of feeding modes.** As you can see, these systems differ in their degree of complexity.

The digestive systems of vertebrates have organs that are well adapted for different feeding habits. Such variety is shown in **Figure 33–8.** Carnivores such as sharks typically have short digestive tracts that produce fast-acting, meat-digesting enzymes. Herbivores such as cows, on the other hand, often have long intestines that harbor colonies of bacteria. These bacteria are helpful in digesting the tough cellulose fibers in plant tissues.

CHECKPOINT *Compare the digestive tracts of herbivores and carnivores.*

Respiration

Chordates typically have one of two basic structures for respiration, or gas exchange. **As a general rule, aquatic chordates—such as tunicates, fishes, and amphibian larvae—use gills for respiration. Land vertebrates, including adult amphibians, reptiles, birds, and mammals, use lungs.** However, some animals "break the rules." For example, several fishes, such as lungfishes, have both gills and lungs.

CA a BI 9.a

Some chordates have respiratory structures in addition to gills and lungs. Many bony fishes, for example, have accessory organs for respiration, such as simple air sacs, that are derived from the gut. All lancelets and some sea snakes respire by the diffusion of oxygen across their body surfaces. (Recall that diffusion is the process by which molecules move from an area of higher concentration to an area of lower concentration.) Many adult amphibians use their moist skins and the linings of their mouths and pharynxes to respire by diffusion.

Gills **Figure 33–9** shows how gills function in chordates. As water passes over the gill filaments, oxygen molecules diffuse into blood in tiny blood vessels called capillaries. At the same time, carbon dioxide diffuses from blood into the water.

ESL SUPPORT FOR ENGLISH LANGUAGE LEARNERS

Comprehension: Use Visuals

Beginning Use Figure 33–11 to help students contrast the three patterns of circulation in vertebrates. Review the terms *capillaries, atrium,* and *ventricle.* Explain that structures in red contain blood that is rich in oxygen, whereas blue structures contain oxygen-poor blood. Note that the arrows show the direction of blood flow. Students should construct flowcharts for each pattern of circulation. L1

Intermediate Have students construct a two-column table that describes the characteristics of the brains of the different classes of vertebrates. To do this, they can use both the text on page 862 and the information in Figure 33–12. The column heads should be *Part of the Brain* and *Characteristics.* The left column should list the parts of the brain indicated in the key for Figure 33–12. L2

Lungs Although the structure of the lungs varies, the basic process of breathing is the same among land vertebrates. Inhaling brings oxygen-rich air from outside the body through the trachea (TRAY-kee-uh) and into the lungs. The oxygen diffuses into the blood inside the lung capillaries. At the same time, carbon dioxide diffuses out of the capillaries into the air within the lungs. Oxygen-poor air is then exhaled.

As you move from amphibians to mammals, the surface area of the lungs increases. Observe this trend in **Figure 33–10.** The typical amphibian lung is little more than a sac with ridges. Reptilian lungs are often divided into a series of large and small chambers that increase the surface area available for gas exchange. In mammals, the lungs branch extensively, and their entire volume is filled with thousands of bubblelike structures called **alveoli** (al-VEE-uh-ly; singular: alveolus). Alveoli provide an enormous surface area for gas exchange. This lung structure enables mammals to take in the large amounts of oxygen required by their endothermic metabolism. However, because air must move in and out through the same passageways, there is always stale, oxygen-poor air trapped in the lungs of mammals and most other vertebrates.

In contrast, in the lungs of birds, air flows in only one direction. A system of tubes in a bird's lungs, plus air sacs, enables this one-way air flow. Thus, gas exchange surfaces are constantly in contact with fresh air that contains a lot of oxygen. This supply of oxygen enables birds to fly at high altitudes, where there is less oxygen in the atmosphere than at lower altitudes.

CA a

a BI 9.a

▼ **Figure 33–9** Fishes and many other aquatic chordates use gills for respiration. **Interpreting Graphics** ***Describe the path of water as it flows into and out of the fish.***

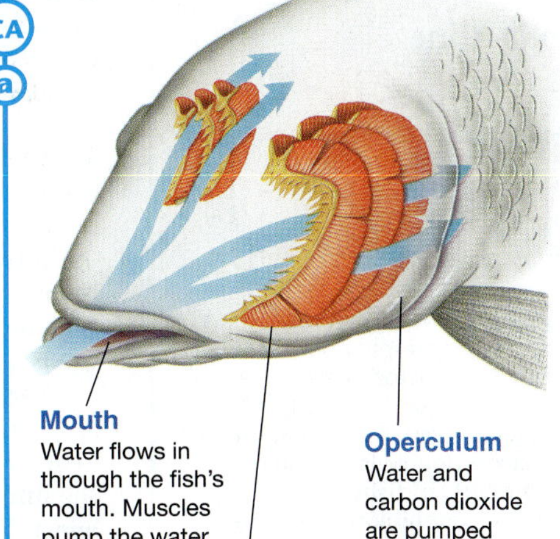

▼ **Figure 33–10** **Unlike most aquatic chordates, land vertebrates use lungs to breathe.** A few aquatic chordates, such as sea turtles and marine mammals, use lungs as well.

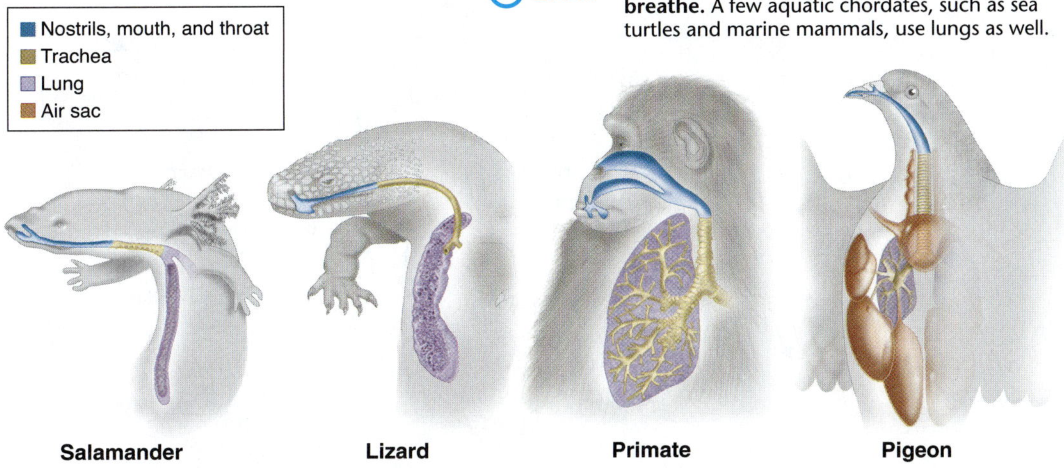

Respiration

Build Science Skills

Using Models Challenge groups of students to model the respiratory structures (lungs, gills, air sacs, and skin) of one vertebrate group. Students can use materials such as balloons, tubing, string, fabric, pipe cleaners, and screening to construct their models. Each group should present its model to the class, describing how the respiratory structures work to exchange gases efficiently. L2

Demonstration

Show students how ridges and folds increase surface area by comparing the surface area of a sheet of paper (22 cm by 28 cm) to that of a large piece of fabric that is folded up to be the same size as the paper. Have students calculate the area of the paper. Then, unfold the cloth and measure it. Have students calculate the area of the fabric. Ask: **Which has more surface area?** *(The fabric)* **Why is it advantageous to have folds, ridges, and chambers in the lungs?** *(They increase the surface area so that more gas exchange can occur without increasing the overall size of the lungs.)* **Would you expect an endotherm or an ectotherm to have more ridges and chambers in its lungs? Explain.** *(Endotherms require more oxygen to maintain their higher metabolic rate.)* L2

FACTS AND FIGURES

Complexity of lungs related to oxygen need
Amphibians have small, simple lungs. This is because they are small ectotherms and require less oxygen than endotherms. In addition, amphibians rely on the skin for gas exchange, mainly to remove carbon dioxide from the body, but also to take in oxygen, which dissolves in the skin's moist coating. In fact, some amphibians have no lungs at all.

In contrast, larger vertebrates that are completely terrestrial require larger lungs with more surface area because the skin is not available for gas exchange. The skin is thicker and covered with scales, feathers, or hair to help prevent water loss. These vertebrates also require more oxygen than amphibians because they are endothermic.

Answers to . . .

CHECKPOINT *The digestive tracts of herbivores are longer than those of carnivores and contain bacteria that aid in digesting cellulose.*

Figure 33–9 *Into mouth, across gills, out through operculum*

33–3 (continued)

Circulation

Build Science Skills

Forming Operational Definitions Challenge students to develop two or three basic rules that relate the structural complexity of the circulatory system to its function in all the chordate groups. Encourage students to think about how the structure of the circulatory system changes from lancelets and tunicates to birds and mammals. Some questions you can ask students to help them get started include: Why don't lancelets have a heart? Why do only endotherms have double-loop systems with two ventricles that are completely divided? Why do terrestrial vertebrates require a double-loop system? L2 L3

Use Visuals

Figure 33–11 Encourage students to compare and contrast the three circulatory systems by using a finger to trace the movement of blood. Ask: **Why is it important in mammals and birds that oxygen-poor blood and oxygen-rich blood do not mix?** *(Endothermic mammals and birds have a higher metabolic rate and require more oxygen for cellular respiration. These vertebrates are also more active, which requires more energy and more oxygen.)* L1 L2

For: Vertebrate Circulatory Systems activity
Visit: PHSchool.com
Web Code: cbe-9333
Students compare and contrast the circulatory systems found in fishes, typical adult amphibians, and birds.

(a) BI 9.a

Go Online active art
For: Vertebrate Circulatory Systems activity
Visit: PHSchool.com
Web Code: cbp-9333

Circulation

CA (a)

Circulatory systems maintain homeostasis by transpor materials throughout animals' bodies. The first chordate tunicates and lancelets of today, probably had simple circ systems. Tunicates have short, tubelike hearts with a simp pump but no true chambers. Lancelets have a fairly well-developed circulatory system but no specialized heart.

Single- and Double-Loop Circulation As chordates evolved, more complex organ systems and more efficient channels for internal transport developed. **Figure 33–11** shows the main transport systems in vertebrates. Those that use gills for respiration have a single-loop circulatory system. In this system, blood travels from the heart to the gills, then to the rest of the body, and back to the heart in one circuit.

Vertebrates that use lungs for respiration have a double-loop circulatory system. The first loop carries blood between the heart and lungs. Oxygen-poor blood from the heart is pumped to the lungs, while oxygen-rich blood from the lungs returns to the heart. The second loop carries blood between the heart and the body. Oxygen-rich blood from the heart is pumped to the body, while oxygen-poor blood from the body returns to the heart.

▼ **Figure 33–11** Most vertebrates that use gills for respiration have a single-loop circulatory system that forces blood around the body in one direction. Vertebrates that use lungs have a double-loop system. **The hearts of fishes have two chambers. Amphibians and most reptiles have three-chambered hearts. Crocodilians, birds, and mammals have hearts with four separate chambers.**

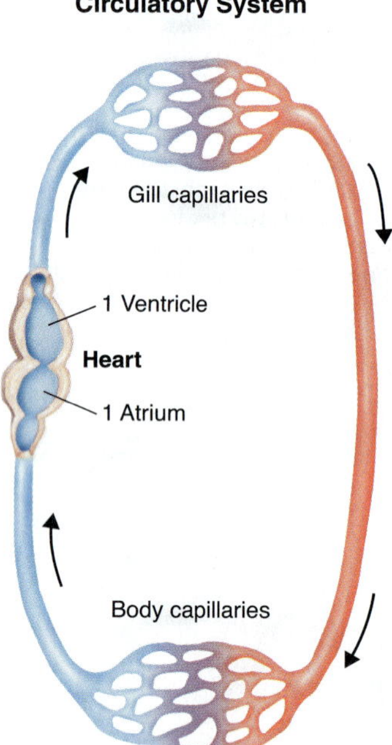

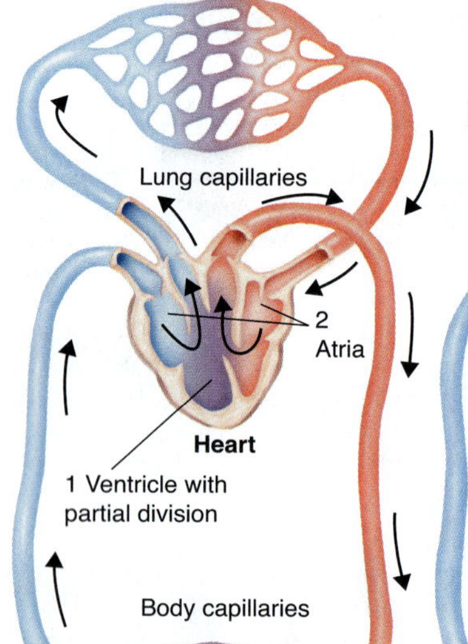

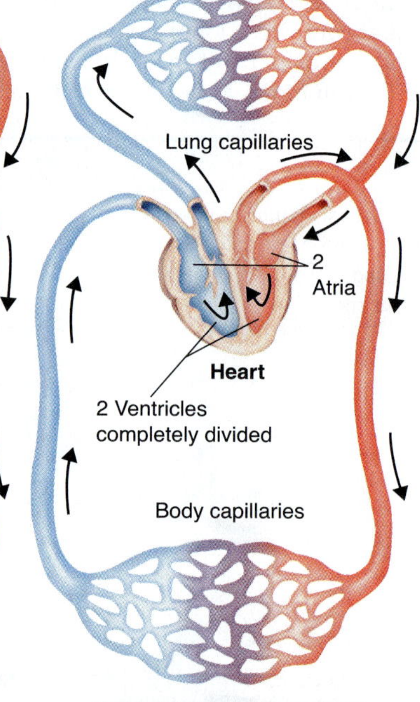

FACTS AND FIGURES

Embryonic development echoes evolution
The development of the human heart during the growth of a fetus echoes the evolutionary development of the heart from cephalochordates to mammals. In a three-week old human embryo, the heart is similar to the specialized blood vessel that serves as a heart in cephalochordates. Later, the embryo's heart develops into a line of four chambers similar to the sinus venosus, atrium, ventricle, and bulbus arteriosus in fishes. As in fishes, the sinus venosus of the human embryo serves as the pacemaker. As the human embryo continues to develop, the sinus venosus and bulbus arteriosus become incorporated into the heart and disappear. Eventually, the partitions that separate the right and left atria and the right and left ventricles grow into place. The pacemaker is finally located in the right atrium.

Heart Chambers Chordate hearts are adapted to the complexity of internal transport for each of the different groups. **During the course of chordate evolution, the heart developed chambers and partitions that help separate oxygen-rich and oxygen-poor blood traveling in the circulatory system.** In vertebrates that use gills for respiration, such as fishes and larval amphibians, the heart consists of two chambers: an atrium that receives blood from the body, and a ventricle that pumps blood to the gills and then on to the rest of the body.

The hearts of most amphibians have three chambers: two atria and one ventricle. The left atrium receives oxygen-rich blood from the lungs. The right atrium receives oxygen-poor blood from the body. Both atria empty into the ventricle. There is some mixing of oxygen-rich and oxygen-poor blood in the ventricle. However, the internal structure of the ventricle directs the flow of blood so that most oxygen-poor blood goes to the lungs, and most oxygen-rich blood goes to the rest of the body.

Most reptiles have a three-chambered heart. However, unlike amphibians, most reptiles have a partial partition in their ventricle. Because of this partition, there is even less mixing of oxygen-rich and oxygen-poor blood than there is in amphibian hearts.

Birds, mammals, and crocodilians have hearts that are completely partitioned into four chambers. This type of heart is sometimes described as a double pump. One pump moves blood through the lung loop and the other moves blood through the body loop. The two loops of the circulatory system are completely separated. There is no mixing of oxygen-rich and oxygen-poor blood.

Excretion

Excretory systems eliminate nitrogenous wastes from the body. In nonvertebrate chordates and fishes, gills and gill slits play an important role in excretion. However, most vertebrates rely on kidneys—excretory organs composed of small filtering tubes that remove wastes from the blood.

Nitrogenous wastes—formed from the breakdown of proteins—are first produced in the form of ammonia. Ammonia is a highly toxic compound that must quickly be eliminated from the body or changed into a less poisonous form. In tunicates, ammonia leaves the body through the outflow siphons. Other waste byproducts, such as uric acid, are stored within the tunicate's body and released only when the animal dies.

In vertebrates, excretion is carried out mostly by the kidneys. Aquatic amphibians and most fishes also excrete ammonia directly from the gills into the surrounding water through simple diffusion. In mammals, land amphibians, and cartilaginous fishes, ammonia is changed into urea, a less-toxic compound, before it is excreted. In most reptiles and birds, ammonia is changed into uric acid. Besides filtering wastes, vertebrate kidneys help maintain homeostasis by regulating the amounts of water, salt, and other substances dissolved in body fluids.

Quick Lab

How does water affect nitrogen excretion?

Materials 2 test tubes, 2 stoppers, test-tube rack, graduated cylinder, balance, urea, uric acid, glass-marking pencil

Procedure

1. Label one test tube "urea" and the other "uric acid." Place 2 grams of uric acid in the test tube labeled "uric acid." Place 2 grams of urea in the test tube labeled "urea."
2. Add 15 mL of water to each test tube. Stopper and shake the test tubes for 3 minutes.
3. Observe each test tube. Record your observations.

Analyze and Conclude

1. **Observing** Which substance—uric acid or urea—is most soluble? Least soluble? Explain.
2. **Inferring** Reptiles excrete nitrogenous wastes in the form of uric acid. How does this adaptation help reptiles survive on land?

Excretion

Use Community Resources

Invite a veterinarian to class to discuss comparative anatomy and physiology of vertebrates. Request that he or she bring preserved organs for students to observe. Before the visit, have students prepare questions about vertebrate form and function. 

Quick Lab

Objective Students will be able to infer how water affects nitrogen excretion. L2

Skill Focus Inferring, Observing

Materials 2 test tubes, 2 stoppers, test-tube rack, graduated cylinder, balance, urea, uric acid, glass-marking pencil

Time 15 minutes

Advance Prep Premeasure the uric acid and urea.

Safety Read the safety information in the MSDS for CH_4ON_2 and $C_5H_4O_3N_4$ before doing the lab. Make sure the students wash their hands with soap and warm water.

Strategies

- Before the lab, discuss why terrestrial animals must conserve water.
- Diagram on the board the chemical structures of urea (CH_4ON_2) and uric acid ($C_5H_4O_3N_4$). Explain that polar substances, which have a net charge, attract and separate molecules of water and effectively disperse between the water molecules to become dissolved.

Expected Outcomes Urea is more soluble than uric acid. The solution of urea should be clear.

Analyze and Conclude

1. Urea is most soluble; uric acid is least soluble.
2. To live successfully on land, reptiles must conserve water. Because uric acid crystallizes as a solid precipitate in water, it does not carry water with it when excreted from the body.

BIO INSIGHTS — FACTS AND FIGURES

Embryonic excretion and evolution
Uric acid is thought to be an adaptation for the development of the terrestrial egg. Nitrogenous wastes produced by the embryo are safely stored inside the egg as uric acid. Because uric acid is an insoluble paste, it does not require any of the limited supply of water within the egg. Mammalian embryos are not under the same constraints as reptilian and avian embryos. A mammalian mother's body safely removes wastes produced by an embryo because of the exchange of blood through the umbilical cord. For amphibian embryos, urea moves easily across the egg membrane and into the surrounding water.

33–3 (continued)

Response

Use Visuals

Figure 33–12 Have students compare and contrast the brain sizes of the different chordate groups. Ask: **How do folds in the cerebrum affect its size?** *(Increase it by increasing the surface area)* Also discuss the importance of the relative sizes of the parts of the brain and their functions in the different vertebrate groups. Ask: **Why do you think the cerebellum is best developed in birds and mammals?** *(Accept all reasonable answers. One possibility is that these more active endotherms move more quickly than ectotherms and require more brain function to coordinate the greater movement.)* L2

Address Misconceptions

Students might assume that because human brains are the most highly developed, humans also have the best-developed senses of all animals. Remind students of the superior senses of hearing and smell in dogs and cats. Also point out that fishes, some turtles, and many birds can see colors and patterns much better than humans. Encourage students to find other examples of animals with superior senses or with senses that humans don't even have, such as the "third eye" in tuataras, electrical sense of some fishes, and lateral lines in fishes. L2

Response

Compared with invertebrates, most chordates have elaborate systems that allow them to respond to stimuli in their environment. **Nonvertebrate chordates have a relatively simple nervous system with a mass of nerve cells that form a brain. Vertebrates have a more complex brain with distinct regions, each with a different function.**

Nonvertebrate chordates do not have specialized sensory organs. In tunicates, however, sensory cells in and on the siphons and other internal surfaces may help control the amount of water passing through the pharynx. Lancelets—which have a more defined head region—have a small, hollow brain with a pair of eyespots that detect light.

Vertebrates display a high degree of cephalization, or concentration of sense organs and nerve cells at the front of the body. The head contains a well-developed brain, which is situated on the anterior end of the spinal cord. The vertebrate brain is divided into several parts, including the cerebrum, cerebellum, medulla oblongata, optic lobes, and olfactory bulbs. The medulla oblongata controls the functioning of many internal organs. The optic lobes are involved in vision and the olfactory bulbs are involved in the sense of smell.

Figure 33–12 shows how the size and complexity of the cerebrum and cerebellum increase from fishes to mammals. The cerebrum is the "thinking" region of the brain. It receives, interprets, and determines the response to sensory information. The cerebrum is also involved in learning, memory, and conscious thought. In fishes, amphibians, and reptiles, the cerebrum is relatively small. In birds and mammals, especially primates, the cerebrum is greatly enlarged and may contain folds that increase its surface area. The cerebellum, which coordinates movement and controls balance, is also most developed in birds and mammals.

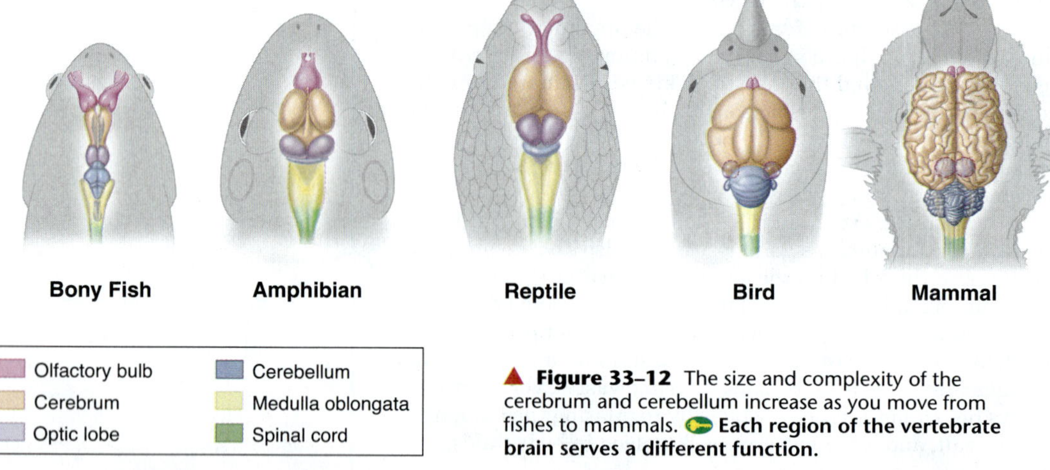

▲ **Figure 33–12** The size and complexity of the cerebrum and cerebellum increase as you move from fishes to mammals. **Each region of the vertebrate brain serves a different function.**

BIO INSIGHTS — FACTS AND FIGURES

Brainy evolution

The vertebrate brain evolved from a set of three bulges at the anterior end of the spinal cord. These regions—the forebrain, midbrain, and hindbrain—are present during embryonic development. As the brain evolved, three major trends changed these regions. First, brain size increased relative to body size. Birds and mammals have larger brains relative to body size than do fishes, amphibians, and reptiles. Second, the original three regions became divided into subregions that assumed specific control and sensory functions. Third, the cerebrum became more powerful in its ability to process information. The larger cerebrum is directly correlated with the more sophisticated behavior of birds and mammals.

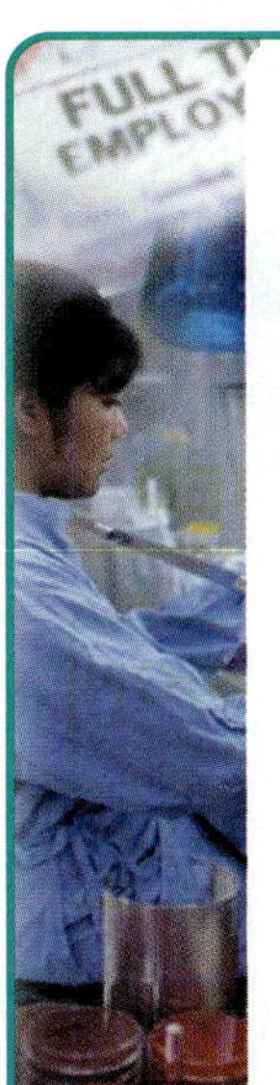

Careers in Biology

Veterinary Technician

Job Description: work in a kennel, veterinary hospital or clinic, zoo, or other setting to provide basic medical care for animals. May specialize in X-ray technology, anesthesiology, or other areas.

Education: a two-year associate or four-year bachelor's degree in Animal Health Technology. Each state has its own licensing requirements.

Skills: patient; enjoy working with animals; a good team member; effective communicator; quick thinker; excellent observer.

Highlights: You help take care of all kinds of animals in different settings. Your work can lead to medical advances that apply to humans.

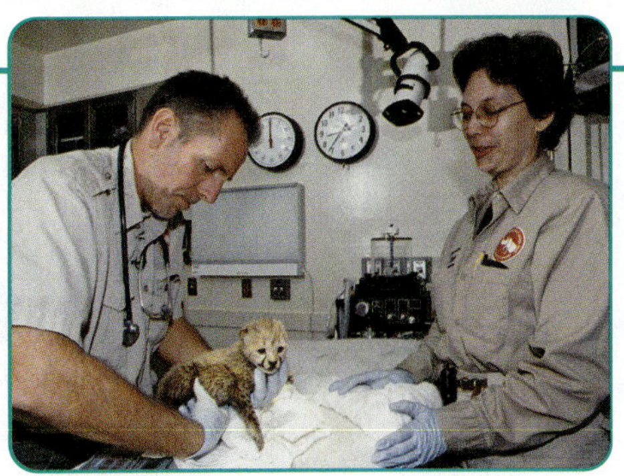

For: Career links
Visit: PHSchool.com
Web Code: cbb-9333

Movement

Unlike most other chordates, nonvertebrate chordates lack bones. They do, however, have muscles. Lancelets and larval tunicates swim with a fishlike movement of their muscular tails. Some adult tunicates use their siphons to swim by jet propulsion. However, most adult tunicates lose their tails and attach to a hard surface on the ocean floor for life.

The skeletal and muscular systems support a vertebrate's body and make it possible to control movement. Vertebrates are much more mobile than nonvertebrate chordates. With the exception of hagfishes, all vertebrates have an internal skeleton of bone—as shown in **Figure 33–13**—or, in the case of certain fishes, cartilage. The skeleton includes a backbone made up of individual bones called vertebrae. In most vertebrates, tough yet flexible tissues called ligaments connect the vertebrae and allow the backbone to bend without falling apart. Most vertebrates have fin girdles or limb girdles that support the fins or limbs.

In many fishes and snakes, the main body muscles are arranged in blocks on either side of the backbone. These muscle blocks contract in waves that make the body bend back and forth, generating forward thrust. In many amphibians and reptiles, the limbs stick out sideways from the body in a position resembling a push-up. Most mammals stand with their legs straight under them, whether they walk on two legs or on four. In this position, the legs can support the body weight efficiently.

CHECKPOINT *What three structures support a vertebrate's body and allow it to move?*

▼ **Figure 33–13** Like the skeletons of most vertebrates, this lizard's skeleton has two pairs of appendages. **Muscles and ligaments attach the appendages to the backbone and help control movement.**

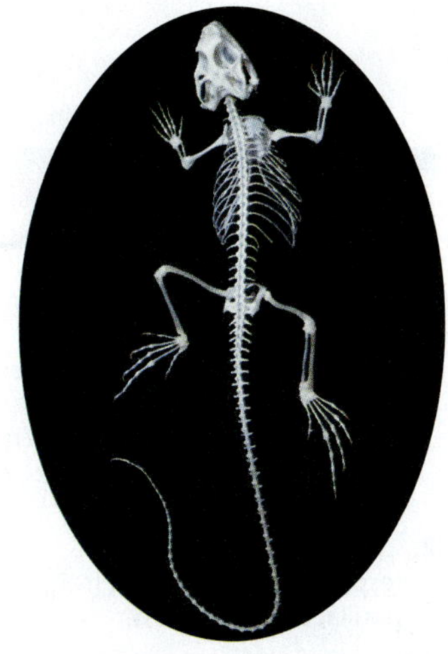

BIO INSIGHTS — FACTS AND FIGURES

Take a stand

As vertebrates adapted to terrestrial life, the position of both pairs of limbs changed. Two trends can be seen in the evolution from amphibians to mammals. First, the position of the limbs relative to the body shifts toward the center. Second, the movement of the vertebral column when the animal runs becomes up-and-down rather than side-to-side.

The positions of the pectoral and pelvic girdles and the limb bones differ among vertebrates. More primitive vertebrates, such as salamanders, have limbs that stick out from the sides of the body. The limbs of reptiles allow the body to be lifted higher off the ground. In many mammals, the limbs are positioned directly beneath the body.

Careers in Biology

- Veterinary technicians also work in biomedical research facilities, diagnostic labs, and veterinary supply companies.
- Typical duties include administering medications and vaccines, diagnostic laboratory procedures, hospital management, and surgical assistance.
- To prepare for this career, students should take college prep courses in science, math, and English. L2

Resources

Students can learn more from the National Association of Veterinary Technicians in America (NAVTA) and the American Veterinary Medical Association (AVMA). They can also contact local universities and community colleges that offer programs in veterinary technology.

Go Online PHSchool.com

You can have students write a more extensive job description as well as list the educational requirements for a career in this field.

Movement

Make Connections

Physics Diagram on the board the two types of vertebrate stances and draw in the lines of force. The lines of force for the animal's body mass point straight down, due to the force of gravity. The lines of force for the limbs point up at the angle at which they attach to the "hips." In amphibians with almost horizontal limbs, the lines of force are almost horizontal. In reptiles and mammals with vertical limbs, the lines of force point nearly straight up, almost directly opposite to the lines of force of the mass. Ask: **By looking at these lines of force, which stance can hold more mass?** *(The stance with vertical limbs)* **Why?** *(The limbs push directly upward. The weight is supported by limbs arranged vertically, the strongest way, like columns that support the roof of a building.)* L2

Answer to . . .

CHECKPOINT *Muscles, skeleton, and ligaments*

33–3 (continued)

Reproduction

Build Science Skills

Comparing and Contrasting Have students compare and contrast the amount of energy required, the number of eggs produced, and the chances of the offspring's survival for the three modes of development in vertebrates. Then, discuss the advantages and disadvantages of each mode of development. *(Viviparous development requires the most energy from the parent, fewer eggs are produced, and the chances of each offspring's survival are the highest. Oviparous development requires the least amount of energy, more eggs are produced, and the survival rate of the offspring is lowest. Ovoviviparous development is in between.)* L1 L2

3 ASSESS

Evaluate Understanding

Play a game of Jeopardy™ in which you give students the answers to questions about the seven organ systems in the six living chordate groups. Students can play as teams or individually to give the questions.

Reteach

Instruct student pairs to take turns interviewing each other about the structures and functions of the various organ systems that perform the seven essential life functions in chordates.

Writing in Science

Students should describe how carnivores, herbivores, and omnivores have specially adapted teeth and jaws to obtain food. They might also describe the special adaptations of filter feeders.

If your class subscribes to the iText, use it to review the Key Concepts in Section 33–3.

Answer to . . .

Figure 33–14 *The mountain lion*

▲ **Figure 33–14** Chordates differ enormously in the way they reproduce and develop. The male band-tailed cardinalfish (left) carries externally fertilized eggs in his mouth while the eggs incubate. Like most birds, the female emperor goose (center) actively defends her nest, which contains eggs that were internally fertilized. After bearing live young, this female mountain lion (right) nurses her cubs with milk. **Applying Concepts** *Which of these animals is viviparous?*

Reproduction

Figure 33–14 shows that chordates are diverse in the ways they reproduce and develop. Almost all chordates reproduce sexually. Vertebrate evolution shows a general trend from external to internal fertilization. The eggs of most nonvertebrate chordates—and many fishes and amphibians—are fertilized externally. The eggs of reptiles, birds, and mammals are fertilized internally.

After fertilization, the development of chordates can be oviparous, ovoviviparous, or viviparous. In oviparous species, which include most fishes and amphibians and all birds, the eggs develop outside the mother's body. In ovoviviparous animals, such as sharks, the eggs develop within the mother's body and the embryos receive nutrients from the yolk in the egg. The young of ovoviviparous species are born alive. The developing embryos of viviparous species—including most mammals—obtain nutrients directly from the mother's body. As with ovoviviparous species, the young of viviparous animals are born alive.

Some vertebrates, such as most amphibians, produce many offspring but give them little or no care. This reproductive strategy is successful in circumstances favoring populations that disperse and grow rapidly. Mammals and birds, in contrast, usually care for their young but produce few of them. This helps young survive in crowded, competitive environments.

33–3 Section Assessment

1. **Key Concept** List the organ systems that chordates use to perform life functions. How does each system vary between nonvertebrate chordates and vertebrates?
2. Compare and contrast the respiratory systems of a frog, a gorilla, and a sparrow.
3. Explain the difference between oviparous, ovoviviparous, and viviparous modes of development. Give an example of each.
4. **Critical Thinking Applying Concepts** What advantage does a three-chambered heart provide that a two-chambered heart does not?

Writing in Science

Summarizing

Write a brief summary of the ways in which chordates obtain food. Your summary should contain examples of animals that use the different methods that you describe. *Hint*: Your summary should include the words *herbivore, carnivore,* and *omnivore.*

33–3 Section Assessment

1. Digestive, respiratory, circulatory, excretory, nervous, skeletal, and reproductive; vertebrate organ systems are more complex.
2. Frog lungs: small sacs with some ridges; gorilla lungs: extensively branched and filled with thousands of alveoli; sparrow: efficient system of tubes and air sacs to ensure that lungs always contain oxygen-rich air
3. Oviparous: eggs develop outside body, birds; ovoviviparous: eggs develop internally, some fishes; viviparous: embryo receives nutrition from mother's body, mammals (Examples may vary.)
4. In a two-chambered heart, the ventricle has to pump blood with enough force so it can travel the entire loop through the body. A three-chambered heart pumps blood through two relatively shorter loops.

Exploration

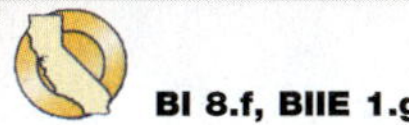

BI 8.f, BIIE 1.g

Comparing Chordate Family Trees

Differences in the amino acid sequence of a protein can indicate how long ago two or more species diverged from a common ancestor. In this investigation, you will compare cladograms of several chordate species based on their anatomy and amino acid sequences.

Problem How can you use anatomical and molecular evidence to determine the evolutionary relationships among chordates?

Animal	Amino Acid Sequence of Cytochrome C											
Human	GDVEK	GKKIF	IMKCS	QCHTV	EKGGK	HKTGP	NLHGL	FGRKT	GQAPG	YSYTA	ANKNK	GIIWG
Donkey	GDVEK	GKKIF	VQKCA	QCHTV	EKGGK	HKTGP	NLHGL	FGRKT	GQAPG	FSYTD	ANKNK	GITWK
Horse	GDVEK	GKKIF	VQKCA	QCHTV	EKGGK	HKTGP	NLHGL	FGRKT	GQAPG	FTYTD	ANKNK	GITWK
Chicken	GDIED	GKKIF	VQKCS	QCHTV	EKGGK	HKTGP	NLHGL	FGRKT	GQAEG	FSYTD	ANKNK	GITWG
Turkey	GDIEK	GKKIF	VQKCS	QCHTV	EKGGK	HKTGP	NLHGL	FGRKT	GQAEG	FSYTD	ANKNK	GITWG
Rattlesnake	GDVEK	GKKIF	TMKCS	QCHTV	EKGGK	HKTGP	NLHGL	FGRKT	GQAVG	YSYTA	ANKNK	GITWG

G=glycine, A=alanine, V=valine, L=leucine, I=isoleucine, M=methionine, F=phenylalanine, W=tryptophan, P=proline, S=serine, T=threonine, C=cysteine, Y=tyrosine, N=asparagine, Q=glutamine, D=aspartate, E=glutamate, K=lysine, R=arginine, H=histidine

Skills Using Models, Analyzing Data

Procedure

1. Use your knowledge of similarities and differences in chordate anatomy to decide how to arrange humans, donkeys, horses, chickens, turkeys, and rattlesnakes in a hierarchical classification system on a cladogram. The more closely two species are related, the shorter you should make the branches that connect them.
2. Draw your cladogram in a similar way to **Figure 33–2.**
3. Write the name of each animal at the end of the appropriate branch of the cladogram.
4. Cytochrome c is a protein found in most eukaryotic cells. The table shows the first 60 amino acids that make up this protein in each animal listed in step 1.
5. Construct a data table with the headings "Donkey," "Horse," and "Chicken." Count the number of amino acids that differ in the sequences of chicken and horse cytochrome c. Record this number in your data table.
6. Complete your data table by comparing the amino acid sequences of each pair of animals.
7. Make a cladogram based on differences among animals in cytochrome c. Use taxonomic nomenclature to label the phylum, subphylum, and class of each animal.

Analyze and Conclude

1. **Comparing and Contrasting** Did your two cladograms agree? Explain your answer.
2. **Using Models** You can think of a cladogram as a visual model that shows evolutionary relationships. With which animals do horses share the most recent ancestor? Explain.
3. **Evaluating** Could a cladogram based on anatomy differ from one based on amino acid sequences? Why or why not?

Go Further

Comparing and Contrasting What advantages would comparing the DNA base sequences have over comparing amino acid sequences?

Analyze and Conclude

1. In most cases, cladograms will differ. Molecular data and anatomical data do not always lead to similar conclusions.
2. Donkeys. Horses and donkeys differ by only one amino acid in the sequence of cytochrome c.
3. Yes. Similar anatomical traits may be the result of convergent evolution rather than a close evolutionary relationship.

Exploration

BI 8.f, BIIE 1.g

Objective Students will be able to use anatomical and molecular evidence to determine the evolutionary relationships among chordates. L2

Skills Focus **Using Models, Analyzing Data**

Time 45 minutes

Teaching Tip Point out that students need to complete only half of the table, because each pair of species appears twice.

Procedure

3. Most students will show that animals that look similar are closely related.

5. Horse and chicken differ by 6 amino acids.

6. Human-donkey: 7, human-horse: 8, human-chicken: 8, human-turkey: 7, human-rattlesnake: 3, donkey-horse: 1, donkey-chicken: 5, donkey-turkey: 4, donkey-rattlesnake: 7, horse-turkey 5, horse-rattlesnake: 8, chicken-turkey: 1, chicken-rattlesnake: 7, turkey-rattlesnake: 6

Expected Outcomes The anatomical and molecular data do not agree. The greatest anatomical difference is between humans and rattlesnakes. However, the cytochrome c sequences of these two species are very similar. Chickens and turkeys are more closely related to rattlesnakes than to mammals.

Go Further

There can be differences in the DNA sequence that do not cause differences in amino acids. Examining the DNA sequence gives a more accurate percentage of similarity.

Chapter 33 Study Guide

Study Tip

Challenge students to write a set of generalizations that describe how the form and function of the seven organ systems changed over the course of evolution from nonvertebrate chordates to mammals.

Thinking Visually

1. The animal's body
2. Ectotherms
3. Endotherms

Chapter 33 Assessment

Reviewing Content

1. d	5. b	9. b
2. a	6. c	10. b
3. b	7. c	
4. b	8. a	

Understanding Concepts

11. Notochord, dorsal hollow nerve cord, a postanal tail, and pharyngeal pouches
12. Unrelated species from different evolutionary lines evolve similar adaptations when encountering similar ecological conditions.
13. Endotherms do not need to rely on the environment for body heat, but they need to eat a lot of food to fuel a high metabolic rate. Ectotherms depend on the environment for body heat, but they eat relatively little compared to endotherms.
14. Some scientists think that endothermy evolved once along the line of reptiles that led to birds and once along the line of reptiles that led to mammals. Some think that endothermy evolved long after the appearance of dinosaurs; others think that dinosaurs were endotherms.
15. By removing small organisms from the water that passes through their pharynx
16. As water flows over gill filaments, oxygen diffuses into blood in the capillaries and carbon dioxide leaves the blood.

Chapter 33 Study Guide

33–1 Chordate Evolution

Key Concepts BI 8.f

- The chordate family tree has its roots in ancestors that vertebrates share with tunicates and lancelets.
- Over the course of evolution, the appearance of new adaptations—such as jaws and paired appendages—has launched adaptive radiations in chordate groups.

Vocabulary
notochord, p. 849
adaptive radiation, p. 851

33–2 Controlling Body Temperature

Key Concepts

- The control of body temperature is important for maintaining homeostasis in many vertebrates, particularly in habitats where temperature varies widely with time of day and with season.
- Most fishes, amphibians, and reptiles are ectotherms—organisms whose body temperatures are controlled primarily by picking up heat from, or losing heat to, their environment. Birds and mammals are endotherms, which means they can generate and retain heat inside their bodies.

Vocabulary
ectotherm, p. 855
endotherm, p. 855

33–3 Form and Function in Chordates

Key Concepts 7 5.c, BI 9.a, BI 9.g

- The digestive systems of vertebrates have organs that are well adapted for different feeding habits.
- Aquatic chordates—such as tunicates, fishes, and amphibian larvae—use gills for respiration. Land vertebrates, including adult amphibians, reptiles, birds, and mammals, use lungs.
- During the course of chordate evolution, the heart developed chambers and partitions that help separate oxygen-rich and oxygen-poor blood traveling in the circulatory system.
- Nonvertebrate chordates have a relatively simple nervous system with a mass of nerve cells that form a brain. Vertebrates have a more complex brain with distinct regions, each with a different function.
- Muscular and skeletal systems support a vertebrate's body and make it possible to control movement.

Vocabulary
alveolus, p. 859

Thinking Visually

Using information from this chapter, fill in the following concept map:

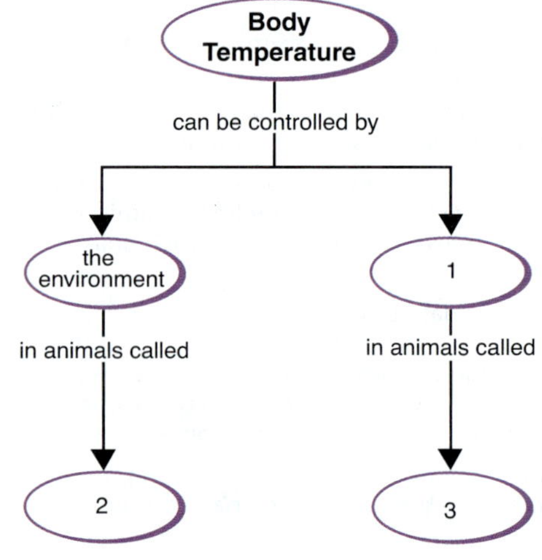

CHAPTER RESOURCES

TIME SAVER

Print:

- ***Teaching Resources,*** Chapter Vocabulary Review, Graphic Organizer, Chapter 33 Tests: Levels A and B

Technology:

- ***Computer Test Bank,*** Chapter 33 Test
- ***iText,*** Chapter 33 Assessment

Chapter 33 Assessment

Reviewing Content

Choose the letter that best answers the question or completes the statement.

1. Which characteristic is unique to chordates?
   a. ectothermy
   b. diffusion
   c. response to light
   d. a notochord
2. Which of the following has an amniotic egg?
   a. birds
   b. tunicates
   c. fishes
   d. amphibians
3. Which of the following animals does not belong with the others?

a. b. c. d.

4. The main source of heat in ectotherms is
   a. their high metabolism.
   b. the environment.
   c. their own bodies.
   d. their food.
5. A characteristic of endotherms is that they
   a. control body temperature through behavior.
   b. control body temperature from within.
   c. obtain heat from outside their bodies.
   d. have relatively low rates of metabolism.
6. Aquatic chordates such as tunicates, fishes, and amphibian larvae typically respire using
   a. lungs. c. gills.
   b. skin. d. air sacs.
7. Most chordates that use gills for respiration have a(an)
   a. double-loop circulatory system.
   b. accessory lung.
   c. single-loop circulatory system.
   d. four-chambered heart.
8. An excretory organ composed of small tubes that filter wastes from the blood is the
   a. kidney. c. cloaca.
   b. ureter. d. gill.

Interactive textbook with assessment at PHSchool.com 

9. The "thinking" region of the chordate brain is the
   a. medulla.
   b. cerebrum.
   c. cerebellum.
   d. spinal cord.
10. Most vertebrates have
    a. an inflexible backbone.
    b. a flexible backbone.
    c. a backbone made of cartilage.
    d. no backbone.

Understanding Concepts

11. What characteristics do tunicates have in common with other chordates?
12. What happens during convergent evolution?
13. Explain the advantages and disadvantages of ectothermy and endothermy.
14. Describe what scientists currently infer about the evolution of endothermy.
15. How do vertebrate filter feeders obtain food?
16. Describe how gills function.
17. How does the structure of the alveoli affect the process of gas exchange?
18. Compare single-loop circulation and double-loop circulation.
19. How do the number of heart chambers compare in a frog, a typical reptile, and a bird?
20. How do tunicates eliminate nitrogenous wastes from their bodies?
21. What are the major excretory organs in vertebrates?
22. In what way(s) do vertebrates display a high degree of cephalization?
23. Name the main parts of the vertebrate brain and describe the function of each part.
24. Describe the vertebrate backbone and explain how it enables an animal to move in complex ways.
25. What type of fertilization is characteristic of birds and mammals?

HOMEWORK GUIDE

Section:	Questions:
Section 33–1	1–3, 11, 12, 28
Section 33–2	4, 5, 13, 14, 26, 31, 33
Section 33–3	6–10, 15–25, 27, 29, 30, 32, 34, 35

Interactive Textbook

If your class subscribes to the iText, your students can go online to access an interactive version of the Student Edition and a self-test.

(Continued from page 866)

17. Alveoli provide an enormous surface area for gas exchange.

18. Single-loop circulation is found in vertebrates with gills. Blood travels in one direction, from heart to gills to body to heart. Double-loop circulation is found in vertebrates with lungs. The first loop carries blood between the lungs and the heart. The second loop carries blood between the heart and the body.

19. Frogs have two atria and one ventricle. Most reptiles have two atria and one ventricle with a partial partition. A bird has two atria and two ventricles.

20. In tunicates, ammonia leaves the body through the outflow siphons.

21. Gills and kidneys

22. There is a concentration of sense organs and nerve cells at the front of the body.

23. The cerebrum receives, interprets, and determines the response to sensory information and is also involved in learning, memory, and conscious thought; the cerebellum coordinates movement and controls balance; the medulla oblongata controls many internal organs; the optic lobes are involved in vision; and the olfactory bulbs are involved in smell.

24. The backbone is made of individual bones called vertebrae. Since the backbone consists of many small bones rather than a single bone, it is flexible and therefore enables complex movements.

25. Internal fertilization is characteristic of birds and mammals.

Chapter 33 Assessment

Critical Thinking

26. Birds and mammals (endotherms) control their body temperature internally and have structures and behaviors to retain and lose heat. Reptiles and amphibians (ectotherms) rely on the environment for heat. They are unable to generate enough body heat to live in cold biomes.

27. a. B **b.** A **c.** C

28. The similarities between fishes and whales are the result of convergent evolution; similar selective pressures result in similar body shape.

29. The legs of mammals, unlike those of amphibians and most reptiles, are positioned directly under the body. This enables them to support the weight of the body more efficiently and move better.

30. Terrestrial animals must conserve water because of the evaporative effects of air.

31. These behaviors help the duck maintain a constant body temperature by conserving body heat (sitting in the sun with wings outspread) or getting rid of excess body heat (sitting in the shade with bill open).

32. The brain is responsible for coordination of movement, so the problem may be caused by a brain injury.

33. Sample experiment: Fill two identical containers with hot water at the same temperature. Cover one with a piece of fur or a down comforter; leave the other exposed to air. After a time, measure the water temperature in both containers.

34. a. Bony fishes (amphibians acceptable if student refers to tadpoles)

b. Reptiles (specifically crocodiles)

c. Tunicates

35. The respiratory system brings in oxygen from the air that travels though the circulatory system to body cells that use oxygen to produce energy. The waste product, carbon dioxide, is removed from the body in the opposite direction.

Chapter 33 Assessment

Critical Thinking

26. Applying Concepts Birds and mammals live in both warm and cold biomes, but most reptiles and amphibians live in relatively warm biomes. Explain this difference in temperature tolerance.

27. Interpreting Graphics The diagrams below show three kinds of circulatory systems.

a. Which diagram illustrates a heart with blood containing carbon dioxide but little oxygen?
b. Which diagram shows a circulatory system with a four-chambered heart?
c. Which diagram illustrates a heart that has oxygen-rich and oxygen-poor blood in the same ventricle?

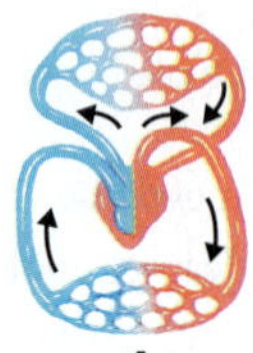
A

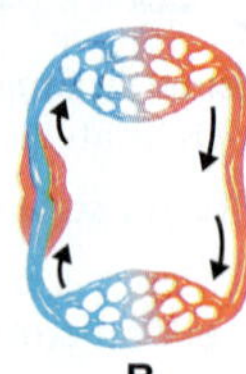
B

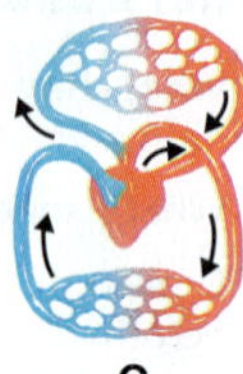
C

28. Comparing and Contrasting Fishes and whales are not closely related, but they share a number of similarities, such as overall body shape and the absence of legs. How can their similarities be explained?

29. Comparing and Contrasting How is the position of the legs of mammals different from those of amphibians and most reptiles? In what way is this characteristic an adaptive advantage?

30. Inferring Of all the nitrogenous wastes eliminated by animals, uric acid requires the least water to excrete. Why is the production of uric acid an advantage to animals that live on land?

31. Formulating Hypotheses On cool days, a student notices that a duck sits on a sunny lawn with its wings outspread. On hot days, she sees the same duck sitting in the shade of a tree with its bill open. How might each of these behaviors help maintain the duck's body temperature?

32. Applying Concepts Suppose a pet dog is having difficulty coordinating its movements. Why might a veterinary technician take an X-ray of the dog's brain?

33. Designing Experiments Design an experiment to determine how fur and feathers affect the ability of animals to retain heat in their bodies.

34. Classifying Read the following descriptions of animals and identify the chordate group to which each animal belongs.

a. Two-chambered heart; single-loop circulatory system; excretes ammonia; vertebral column
b. Four-chambered heart; feet not directly beneath the body when standing; ectotherm
c. Muscles but no bones; sensory cells on siphons

35. Applying Concepts How do a fish's respiratory and circulatory systems work together to maintain homeostasis in the body as a whole?

Evolution North American hummingbirds and Hawaiian honeycreepers have long, thin bills adapted for drinking nectar from flowers. Recall from Chapter 18 that organisms' DNA can be used to infer phylogeny, or evolutionary relationships. How could you determine whether the similarities between these two birds are the result of convergent evolution or adaptive radiation?

Writing in Science

Write a paragraph in which you compare and contrast the brain of a fish to the brain of a mammal. In your paragraph, you should identify the main parts of the brain and explain how their structures and functions are similar and different in the two animals. (*Hint:* Before you write, construct a Venn diagram that compares the brains of the two animals.)

Performance-Based Assessment

Making Models Using materials such as modeling clay, wires, or pipe cleaners, construct models of the circulatory systems of a fish, an amphibian, and a mammal. Describe whether each vertebrate has single- or double-loop circulation, and whether or not the blood flowing through the heart is rich in oxygen.

Go Online
PHSchool.com
For: An interactive self-test
Visit: PHSchool.com
Web Code: cba-9330

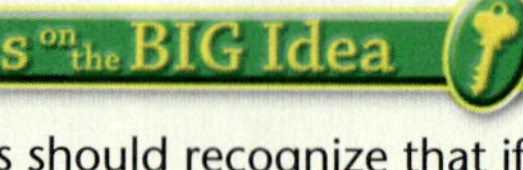

Students should recognize that if the similarities are due to convergent evolution, then the birds descended from different evolutionary lines. They could examine DNA sequences of the birds to determine how close they are.

Writing in Science

Students should explain that the brain in both fishes and mammals is composed of the cerebrum, cerebellum, medulla oblongata, optic lobes, and olfactory bulbs. The mammalian brain, however, has a much larger and more developed cerebrum and cerebellum to control thinking and learning and to coordinate more sophisticated movements in response to stimuli.

Standards Practice

Online at PHSchool.com

Test-Taking Tip Before you answer questions about a diagram, study the diagram and ask yourself what the diagram is about and what it tells you.

Directions: Choose the letter that best answers the question or completes the statement.

1. Which of the following is NOT a feature common to all chordates?
   - **A** a series of connected vertebrae
   - **B** a notochord
   - **C** pharyngeal pouches
   - **D** a dorsal hollow nerve cord
2. Which of the following helps vertebrates control their body temperature?
   - **A** a source of heat in the environment
   - **B** feathers
   - **C** panting
   - **D** all of the above
3. Which is NOT a characteristic of breathing?
   - **A** inhalation of oxygen-rich air into the lungs
   - **B** diffusion of oxygen into the blood within the lung capillaries
   - **C** diffusion of carbon dioxide out of the blood within the lung capillaries
   - **D** exhalation of oxygen-rich air
4. In chordates with four-chambered hearts, there is
   - **A** a total mixing of oxygen-rich and oxygen-poor blood.
   - **B** a partial mixing of oxygen-rich and oxygen-poor blood.
   - **C** a partial partition in the ventricle.
   - **D** no mixing of oxygen-rich and oxygen-poor blood.
5. In oviparous species, the eggs
   - **A** develop internally.
   - **B** obtain nutrients directly from the mother's body.
   - **C** obtain nutrients from the external environment.
   - **D** develop outside the body.
6. What part of a vertebrate's brain is the "thinking" region?
   - **A** olfactory bulb
   - **B** cerebrum
   - **C** cerebellum
   - **D** optic lobe
7. Most reptiles excrete wastes in the form of **BI 9.g**
   - **A** urea.
   - **B** ammonia.
   - **C** uric acid.
   - **D** salt.

Questions 8–10 Refer to the following cladogram:

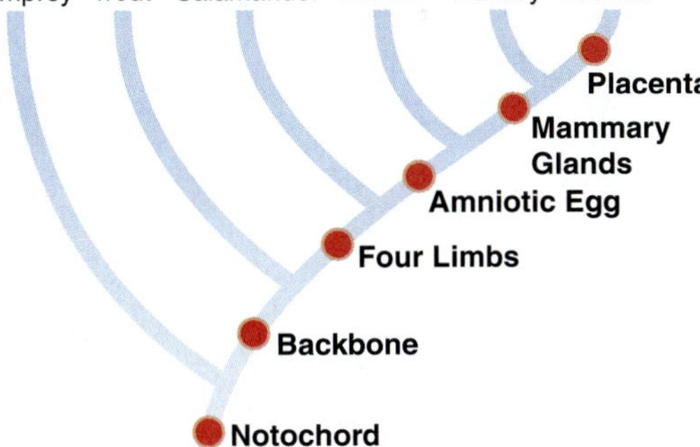

8. Which characteristic is shared by humans, wallabies, and trout? **BI 8.f**
   - **A** placenta
   - **B** notochord
   - **C** amniotic egg
   - **D** four limbs
9. Which animals in the cladogram have the closest evolutionary relationship? **BI 8.f**
   - **A** humans and wallabies
   - **B** humans and lizards
   - **C** humans and lampreys
   - **D** humans and salamanders
10. A valid conclusion from this cladogram is that **7IIE 7.c**
    - **A** salamanders, trout, and lampreys all have a backbone.
    - **B** four limbs appeared in vertebrate evolution before the notochord.
    - **C** humans and lampreys share a common ancestor.
    - **D** salamanders have amniotic eggs.

Standards Practice

1. D	**5.** D	**9.** A
2. D	**6.** B	**10.** C
3. D	**7.** C	
4. D	**8.** B	

Online at PHSchool.com

Have students check their understanding of the chapter by logging onto Success Tracker.

Performance-Based Assessment

Student models should show the correct circulatory systems and hearts with the correct number of chambers, as shown in Figure 33–11 and discussed on page 860.

Your students can independently test their knowledge of the chapter and print out their test results for your files.

Chapter Planner 34 Animal Behavior

Section and Section Objectives	Time	STANDARDS NCLB	STANDARDS Biology	Activities and Labs
34–1 Elements of Behavior, pp. 871–876 34.1.1 ***Identify*** what produces behavior in animals. 34.1.2 ***Explain*** what an innate behavior is. 34.1.3 ***Describe*** the major types of learning. 34.1.4 ***Describe*** behaviors that result from a combination of instinct and learning.	2 periods (1 block)			SE: ***Inquiry Activity,*** What is learning?, p. 870 L2 TE: ***Demonstration,*** p. 872 L2 TE: ***Build Science Skills,*** p. 873 L2 SE: ***Quick Lab,*** What kind of learning is practice?, p. 875 L2 SE: ***Technology & Society,*** Using Remote Sensing to Study Animal Behavior, p. 877 L2 LMA: Chapter 34 Lab L2 L3 LMB: Chapter 34 Lab L1 L2
34–2 Patterns of Behavior, pp. 878–882 34.2.1 ***Explain*** how environmental changes affect animal behavior. 34.2.2 ***Describe*** how courtship and social behavior increase an animal's evolutionary fitness. 34.2.3 ***Identify*** behavioral patterns used to claim and defend territories. 34.2.4 ***Summarize*** how animals communicate.	2 periods (1 block)			SE: ***Analyzing Data,*** Caring for Eggs, p. 879 L2 TE: ***Build Science Skills,*** p. 880 L2 SE: ***Design an Experiment,*** Observing Behavior in Fish, p. 883 L2
Chapter Assessment, pp. 884–887	1 period (1/2 block)			

ACTIVITY PLANNER

SE: *Inquiry Activity*, p. 870; 10 min.; coffee cans, rings and ring stands, or wooden blocks can be used as noisemakers

TE: *Demonstration*, p. 872; 15 min.; earthworms, mealworms, or sow bugs; dissecting tray or shoebox with lid; bright desk lamp

TE: *Build Science Skills*, p. 873; 10 min.; crumpled paper ball, safety goggles

SE: *Quick Lab*, p. 875; 15 min.; paper, ruler, scissors, clock with second hand

TE: *Make Connections*, p. 876; 1 1/2 hours; movie *Fly Away Home*

TE: *Build Science Skills*, p. 880; 15 min.; ant farm

SE: *Design an Experiment*, p. 883; 45 min.; male betta fish, aquarium net, clear plastic box of aquarium water, small mirror, construction paper, colored pencils or markers, transparent tape, popsicle sticks, watch with a second hand

PLANNING KEY

Ability Levels
for students performing . . .
below grade level L1
at grade level L2
above grade level L3

Print Components

SE	Student Edition	LA	Lab Assessment
TE	Teacher's Edition	BTM	Biotechnology Manual
RSW	Reading & Study Workbook A	IDM	Issues and Decision Making
ARSW	Adapted Reading & Study Workbook B	LW	Lab Worksheets
TR	Teaching Resources	LMA	Laboratory Manual A
IF	Investigations in Forensics	LMB	Laboratory Manual B

Tech Components

CTB	Computer Test Bank
BD	BioDetectives DVD
TP	Transparencies Plus
PLM	Probeware Lab Manual
ABC	ABC DVD Library
LS	Lab Simulations
VL	Virtual Labs

Interactive Textbook — Interactive textbook with assessment at PHSchool.com

Program Resources	Assessment	Media and Technology
TR: Lesson Plan 34–1, Section Summary, p. 168 L1, p. 177 L2, Worksheets, pp. 170–172 L1, pp. 179–181 L2 **RSW:** Section 34–1 L2 **ARSW:** Section 34–1 L1	**SE:** 34–1 Section Assessment, p. 876 **TR:** Section Review 34–1	**iText:** Section 34–1 **TP:** 34–1 Interest Grabber, Section Outline, Inheritance of Wing-Flipping Behavior in Moths, Figure 34–5
TR: Lesson Plan 34–2, Section Summary, p. 169 L1, p. 177 L2, Worksheets, pp. 173–175 L1, pp. 182–183 L2, Enrichment L2 L3 **LW:** Chapter 34 Design an Experiment L1 L2 L3 **RSW:** Section 34–2 L2 **ARSW:** Section 34–2 L1	**SE:** 34–2 Section Assessment, p. 882 **TR:** Section Review 34–2	**iText:** Section 34–2 **TP:** 34–2 Interest Grabber, Section Outline, Concept Map, Figure 34–8 **VL:** Lab 18, Lab 19
	SE: Chapter 34 Assessment, pp. 884–887 **TR:** Chapter Vocabulary Review, Graphic Organizer, Chapter 34 Test **LA:** Laboratory Assessment 9	**iText:** Chapter 34 Assessment **CTB:** Chapter 34 Test

Go Online
Students can do research, share data, and test their knowledge online.

PRESSED FOR TIME?

To Preview the Chapter
- Instruct students to read the Key Concepts and Vocabulary terms in each section.
- Assign the Reading Strategies for each section.

To Cover the Chapter Quickly
- Have students read all of Section 34–1 and only the captions for Figures 34–8, 34–9, 34–10, and 34–12 in Section 34–2.
- Assign the Section 34–1 Review questions; questions 1–6, 11–15, and 22–24 in Chapter 34 Assessment; and questions 1–10 in the Standards Practice.

To Review the Chapter
- Review the concept map in the Chapter 34 Study Guide.
- Assign Section Review 34–1 in the Reading and Study Workbook or the Adapted Reading and Study Workbook.

CHAPTER 34

ENGAGE/EXPLORE

Inquiry Activity

 7 7.c

Objective Students will be able to conclude how learning occurs in response to a stimulus. L2

Skill Focus Observing

Materials coffee cans, rings and ring stands, or wooden blocks can be used as noisemakers

Time 10 minutes

Advance Prep Write or select a paragraph in which the word *and* appears often and the word *an* appears at least once near the end of the paragraph.

Strategies

- Behavior during this activity may be more manageable at the end of the class period than at the beginning.
- As you read the paragraph aloud, strike the table or make a gesture such as sweeping your arm, each time you read the word *and*. Also do this when you read the word *an* near the end of the paragraph.

Expected Outcomes Students will observe that many will also respond to the word *an* when it is paired with the same gesture that accompanies the word *and*.

Think About It

1. Some students will sound their noisemakers in response to the word *an*. Some might not respond to *and*s at the beginning of the paragraph.
2. Students learned that the teacher made a gesture while reading the word *and*. Some students also sounded their noisemakers to this gesture when it was paired with the word *an*. Valid conclusions support experimental evidence.

Discrepant Event

Show students a picture of ducklings or goslings following a person. (You might find pictures of Konrad Lorenz, who studied imprinting in geese.) Ask: **Why are these birds following a human?** *(Accept reasonable answers. The birds have imprinted on the human.)* Discuss how this behavior might affect how these birds are able to survive in their environment.

CHAPTER 34

Animal Behavior

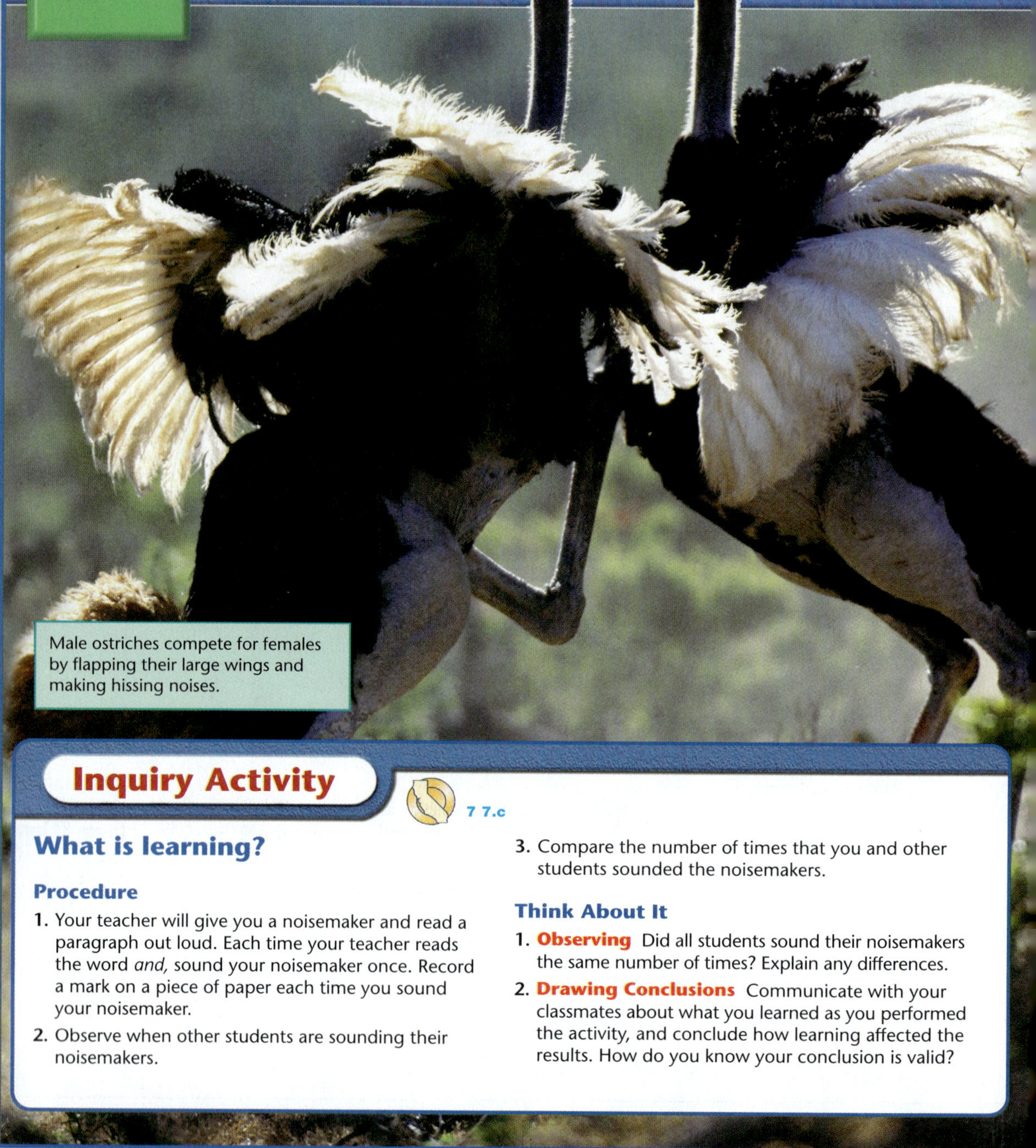

Male ostriches compete for females by flapping their large wings and making hissing noises.

Inquiry Activity

 7 7.c

What is learning?

Procedure

1. Your teacher will give you a noisemaker and read a paragraph out loud. Each time your teacher reads the word *and,* sound your noisemaker once. Record a mark on a piece of paper each time you sound your noisemaker.
2. Observe when other students are sounding their noisemakers.
3. Compare the number of times that you and other students sounded the noisemakers.

Think About It

1. **Observing** Did all students sound their noisemakers the same number of times? Explain any differences.
2. **Drawing Conclusions** Communicate with your classmates about what you learned as you performed the activity, and conclude how learning affected the results. How do you know your conclusion is valid?

FACTS AND FIGURES

Animal behavior under analysis

People have always observed how animals behave. In early times, these observations simply allowed people to survive. Only recently have scientists begun to systematically study animal behavior. Scientists approach this systematic study in different ways. Some scientists directly analyze the function of the brain and nerves. These neurophysiologists might stimulate neurons with electrodes and observe the response.

Comparative psychologists concentrate on establishing the characteristics of animal behavior based on observing how animals react to specific stimuli. Teaching a rat to move through a maze is one experiment they might conduct. Ethologists observe the behavior of animals in their natural environments. They are interested in the biological significance of behavior patterns and how these behaviors might have evolved.

34–1 Elements of Behavior

Do you wash your vegetables before you eat them? If so, you have something in common with a troop of Japanese macaque (muh-KAHK) monkeys that live on the Pacific island of Koshima. Many years ago, biologists in Koshima began leaving sweet potatoes on a sandy beach to entice the resident monkeys into the open. The monkeys ate their potatoes with sand still stuck to them. One day, a young female member of the troop dunked her potato into a nearby pool and scrubbed the sand off it with her hand. The young monkey, apparently preferring to eat a washed potato, repeated this technique each day. Soon, another monkey in the troop started to imitate her. Months later, her mother began to copy her, too. Eventually, all troop members came to wash their potatoes in the pool. To this day, the descendants of the monkeys on the island of Koshima wash their sweet potatoes before eating them.

Guide for Reading

Key Concepts
- What produces behavior in animals?
- What is an innate behavior?
- What are the major types of learning?

Vocabulary
behavior
stimulus
response
innate behavior
learning
habituation
classical conditioning
operant conditioning
insight learning
imprinting

Reading Strategy: Using Prior Knowledge Before you read, write a definition of behavior based on what you already know. After reading this section, use what you have learned to revise your definition and give examples to support it.

Stimulus and Response

The macaque monkey in **Figure 34–1** is exhibiting a learned behavior. Biologists define **behavior** as the way an organism reacts to changes in its internal condition or external environment. A behavior can be simple, such as turning your head in the direction of a noise, or complex, such as washing food. Usually, behaviors are performed when an animal reacts to a stimulus. A **stimulus** (plural: stimuli) is any kind of signal that carries information and can be detected. If you are hungry, your body is providing you with an internal stimulus that might prompt you to eat. The sound of your phone ringing on a Friday night is an external stimulus that might result in your running to answer it!

A single, specific reaction to a stimulus—such as waking up when you hear an alarm—is called a **response.** A behavior may consist of more than one response. For example, a tiger shark might respond to the movements of a potential prey by swimming toward the stimulus, attacking the source of the movement, and swallowing the prey. What stimuli are you responding to right now?

▶ **Figure 34–1** On the island of Koshima, Japanese macaques like this one rinse their sweet potatoes in water. **Inferring** *How did this monkey acquire this behavior?*

SECTION RESOURCES

Print:
- ***Laboratory Manual A,*** Chapter 34 Lab
- ***Laboratory Manual B,*** Chapter 34 Lab
- ***Teaching Resources,*** Lesson Plan 34–1, Adapted Section Summary 34–1, Adapted Worksheets 34–1, Section Summary 34–1, Worksheets 34–1, Section Review 34–1
- ***Reading and Study Workbook A,*** Section 34–1
- ***Adapted Reading and Study Workbook B,*** Section 34–1

Technology:
- ***iText,*** Section 34–1
- ***Transparencies Plus,*** Section 34–1

Section 34–1

1 FOCUS

Objectives

34.1.1 ***Identify*** what produces behavior in animals.
34.1.2 ***Explain*** what an innate behavior is.
34.1.3 ***Describe*** the major types of learning.
34.1.4 ***Describe*** behaviors that result from a combination of instinct and learning.

Guide for Reading

Vocabulary Preview

Read aloud the Vocabulary words to students. Then, instruct students to copy the words from their textbook and divide them into syllables. *(be•hav•ior, stim•u•lus, re•sponse, in•nate, learn•ing, ha•bit•u•a•tion, clas•si•cal con•di•tion•ing, op•er•ant, in•sight, im•print•ing)*

Reading Strategy

As they read, students might draw concept maps that show the relationships among the Vocabulary words. For example, four types of learning are habituation, classical conditioning, operant conditioning, and insight learning.

2 INSTRUCT

Stimulus and Response

Build Science Skills

Observing Instruct students to observe a group of people or animals for about an hour. As students observe the subjects' behaviors, they should record the stimuli and the responses that define the behaviors. Invite students to share their observations with the class. L2

Answer to . . .

Figure 34–1 *Possibly by imitating the behavior of other monkeys*

34–1 (continued)

Demonstration

Demonstrate how simple animals, such as earthworms, mealworms, or sow bugs, respond to light. Place the animals in the center of a shoebox or dissecting tray, and cover half of the box or tray. Shine a bright light over the uncovered half. The animals should move away from the light. Ask: **What is the stimulus?** *(Light)* **What is the behavior?** *(Movement away from the light)* **What body systems were involved in this response?** *(Nervous system and muscles)* **How do you think this response helps the animal to survive?** *(These animals are adapted to a dark environment. Early light-avoiding behavior was possibly favored by natural selection because it makes it harder for predators to find the animals or it helps them avoid drying conditions, or it keeps them closer to their food supply. All of these possibilities and more would need to be tested.)* L2

Behavior and Evolution

Use Visuals

Figure 34–3 Discuss how the circular pattern on the wings of the *Automeris* moth helps to protect it from predators. *(The circles look like owl eyes and scare off predators.)* Ask: **How did the wing-flipping behavior evolve in these moths?** *(Moths that did not lift their wings did not scare off predators and had a greater chance of being eaten; many did not live long enough to reproduce. Those that lifted their wings had a greater chance of scaring away predators and were able to reproduce. They passed on the genes that influenced this behavior to their offspring.)* L1 L2

▲ **Figure 34–2** **Behavior is produced by the interaction of body systems.** This frog detected a noise with its ears and is now using its brain and muscles to leap out of the water.

Types of Stimuli Animals respond to many types of external stimuli, such as light, sound, odors, and heat. However, not every animal can detect all of these stimuli. Humans perceive the world through many senses—including sight, smell, touch, taste, and hearing. Other animals have different senses and may respond to stimuli that you are not equipped to sense. The Mexican bulldog bat, for instance, uses high-pitched sounds, which humans cannot hear, to detect the ripples made by a fish breaking the surface of a lake. Some birds can detect Earth's magnetic field and use it to navigate over complex terrain.

How Animals Respond Because of the differences in animals' sensory abilities, responses can vary greatly. **When an animal responds to a stimulus, body systems—including the sense organs, nervous system, and muscles—interact to produce the resultant behavior.** Once an animal's senses have detected an external stimulus, that information is passed along nerve cells to the brain. The brain and other parts of the nervous system process the information and direct the body's response. Animals with very simple nervous systems are capable of only simple behaviors, such as moving toward a stimulus or away from it. For example, an earthworm will move away from bright light. Animals with more complex nervous systems, such as the frog in **Figure 34–2**, are better equipped to respond with more complicated and precise behaviors.

Behavior and Evolution

Animal behavior is as important to survival and reproduction as any physical characteristic, such as teeth or claws. Recall that physical traits develop according to a specific set of genetic instructions. Many behaviors are also influenced by genes. Therefore, some behaviors can be inherited by an animal's offspring. Behaviors, like physical characteristics, may evolve under the influence of natural selection. A behavior that is directed by genes may help an individual to survive and reproduce. For example, the genes that code for behavior of the moth in **Figure 34–3** may help the moth escape predators. Organisms with an adaptive behavior will survive and reproduce better than organisms that lack the behavior. After natural selection has operated for many generations, most individuals in the population will exhibit the adaptive behavior.

Figure 34–3 Moths of the genus *Automeris* normally rest with their front wings over their hind wings (left). If disturbed, the moth will move its front wings to expose a striking circular pattern on its hind wings (right). As one scientist has suggested, this behavior may scare off predators when they mistake the moth's hind-wing pattern for the eyes of predatory owls. **Inferring** ***If the scientist's hypothesis is correct, how might wing-lifting behavior in this moth illustrate the results of natural selection?***

ESL SUPPORT FOR ENGLISH LANGUAGE LEARNERS

Comprehension: Prior Knowledge

Beginning Post a card with the word *stimulus* on the left side of a bulletin board and one with *behavior* on the right, with an arrow pointing from *stimulus* to *behavior*. Under the words, post pictures of familiar stimuli and their corresponding behaviors, such as cat food and a cat eating or rain and people opening umbrellas. Use these photographs to clarify the concepts of stimulus and behavior. Have students bring in additional pictures of both concepts to post. Call attention to Figure 34–2 and ask: What is the frog's behavior? *(Jumping)* What stimulus caused the behavior? *(Noise)* L1

Intermediate Define *stimulus* and *behavior* aloud, and use Figures 34–1 and 34–2 to clarify the terms. Ask students to use their own knowledge to identify several stimulus-behavior pairs. Help them describe the stimuli and behaviors orally. L2

Innate Behavior

Why do newly hatched birds beg for food within moments after hatching? How do spiders know how to build their first web? These animals are exhibiting an **innate behavior,** also called an instinct, or inborn behavior. **Innate behaviors appear in fully functional form the first time they are performed, even though the animal may have had no previous experience with the stimuli to which it responds.** One of the simplest innate behaviors is the suckling of a newborn mammal. Other innate behaviors, such as the weaving of a spider web like the one in **Figure 34–4,** or the building of hanging nests by weaver birds, can be quite complex. All innate behaviors depend on internal mechanisms that develop as a result of complex interactions between an animal's genes and its environment. Biologists do not yet fully understand just how these kinds of interactions occur.

CHECKPOINT *What is innate behavior?*

▲ **Figure 34–4 Innate behaviors appear in fully functional form the first time they are performed.** Because web building is an innate behavior, a spider weaves a web correctly the first time it performs the behavior.

Learned Behavior

Animals often live in unpredictable environments, so their behavior must be flexible enough to deal with uncertainty and change. Many animals can alter their behavior as a result of experience. Such changes are called **learning.** Acquired behavior is another name for learning because these behaviors develop over time.

Many animals have the ability to learn. Organisms with simple nervous systems, such as most invertebrates, may learn only rarely. Among a few invertebrates, and many chordates, learning is common and occurs under a wide range of circumstances. In animals that care for their young, for example, offspring can learn behaviors from their parents or other caretakers. Scientists have identified several different ways of learning. **The four major types of learning are habituation, classical conditioning, operant conditioning, and insight learning.**

Innate Behavior

Build Science Skills

Applying Concepts Have student pairs take turns gently tossing a paper ball at each other's face. Students should wear safety goggles to protect their eyes. When students toss the paper ball, they should watch for their partner's response. *(Blink their eyes)* Explain that blinking is a reflex action—a simple innate behavior. Ask: **What is the importance of the blinking reflex?** *(Protects the eyes)* L2

Learned Behavior

Address Misconceptions

Students might attribute human feelings and motivations to animals while discussing animal behavior. Explain to students that this tendency, called anthropomorphism, is a common mistake that biologists and behaviorists must be careful not to make. Remind students that most animals behave innately in response to stimuli in their environment without premeditation. As animals react to their surroundings, they may alter certain behaviors through learning. L2

TEACHER TO TEACHER

I like to introduce animal behavior with a dramatic event. I invite a coworker to rush in and excitedly share some good news with me. My response is equally dramatic. We display as many behaviors, visual signals, sound signals, and language cues as we can. We also pretend to be completely oblivious to the class.

After my coworker leaves, I ask students to identify the stimulus and then to identify the response behaviors that they observed. I list these on the board and help students categorize these behaviors into Innate Behaviors and Learned Behaviors. Also, I have students identify the types of communication. I keep the list on the board and change it as needed while studying the chapter.

—*Susan Madden*
Biology Teacher
Chippewa Valley High School
Clinton Township, MI

Answers to . . .

CHECKPOINT *A behavior that appears in fully functional form the first time it is performed*

Figure 34–3 *Since the eyelike pattern probably discourages predators, the behavior may give these moths a greater chance of surviving and passing the genes for the trait to offspring.*

34–1 (continued)

Build Science Skills

Using Analogies Remind students of Aesop's fable about the boy who cried wolf. Ask: **What kind of learning did the villagers engage in?** *(Habituation)* Discuss why this is an example of habituation. *(The villagers stopped responding to the boy's cry of wolf because they learned to associate it with a nonthreatening, unrewarding stimulus.)* Encourage students to think of other analogies of habituation. Emphasize that habituation is the loss of a response to a stimulus, not the acquisition of a new response to a stimulus. L2 L3

Use Visuals

Figure 34–5 Ask students: **What type of learning does Pavlov's experiment model?** *(Classical conditioning)* **What is the stimulus in Pavlov's experiment?** *(The ringing bell)* **What is the reward?** *(Food)* **Why did the dogs salivate when hearing the bell, even if no food was present?** *(The dogs associated the ringing bell with food, so they salivated when they heard the bell, even in the absence of food.)* Emphasize that in classical conditioning, an animal's reflexes, or innate behaviors, are trained to respond to a stimulus.

Habituation The simplest type of learning is habituation. **Habituation** is a process by which an animal decreases or stops its response to a repetitive stimulus that neither rewards nor harms the animal. By ignoring a nonthreatening or unrewarding stimulus, animals can spend their time and energy more efficiently.

Consider the common shore ragworm. This animal lives in a sandy tube that it leaves only to feed. If a shadow passes overhead, the worm will instantly retreat to the safety of its burrow. Yet, if repeated shadows pass within a short time span, this response quickly subsides. When the worm has learned that the shadow is neither food nor threat, it will stop responding. At this point the worm has habituated to the stimulus.

Classical Conditioning When a dog sees its owner approaching with a leash, it may wag its tail and bark, eager to go for a walk. The dog has learned to associate the sight of the leash with a walk. Any time an animal makes a mental connection between a stimulus and some kind of reward or punishment, it has learned by **classical conditioning.** In the case of the dog and its owner, the stimulus of the leash is associated with a pleasant reward—a brisk walk. Now, think of what happens if a dog tries to attack a skunk. The skunk sprays the dog with a substance that stings and smells awful. In the future, that dog is likely to avoid skunks, because it associates the stimuli of the sight and scent of the skunk with the punishment of its foul spray.

The most famous example of classical conditioning is the work of the Russian physiologist Ivan Pavlov, around 1900. Pavlov was studying salivation—an innate behavior—in dogs. He discovered that if he always rang a bell at the same time he fed his dog, the dog would eventually begin to salivate whenever it heard a bell, even if no food was present. **Figure 34–5** shows how the dog in Pavlov's experiment learned to associate the bell (stimulus) with the arrival of food (reward).

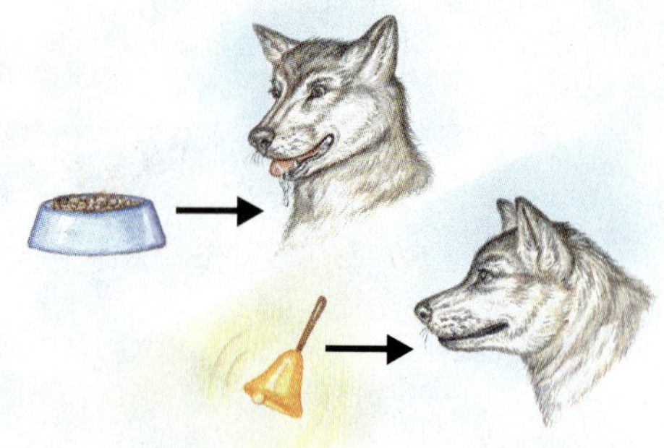

1 Before Conditioning
When a dog sees or smells food, it produces saliva. Food is the stimulus and the dog's response is salivation. Dogs do not usually salivate in response to nonfood stimuli.

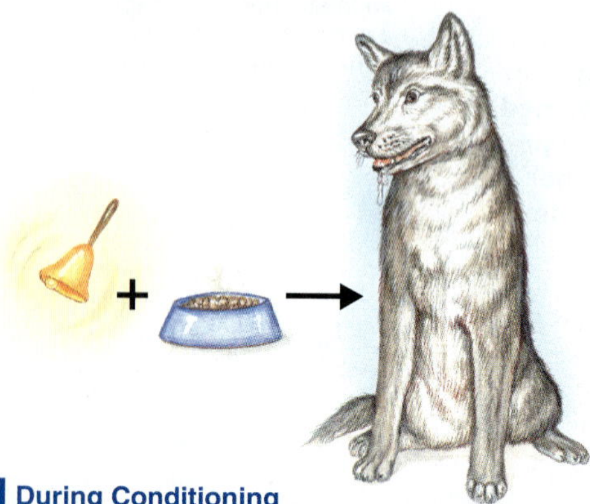

2 During Conditioning
By ringing a bell every time he fed the dog, Pavlov trained the dog to associate the sight and smell of food with the ringing bell.

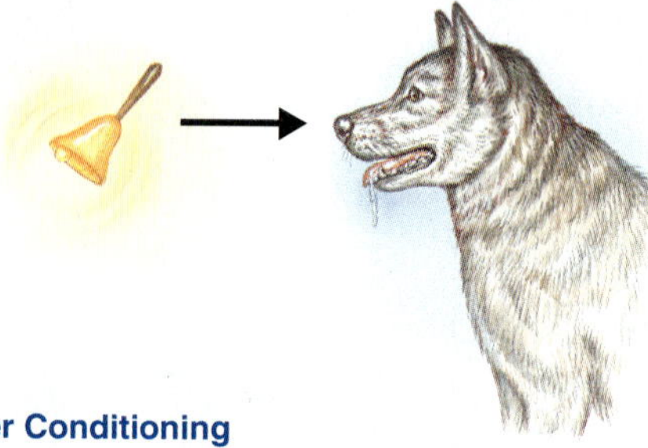

3 After Conditioning
When Pavlov rang a bell in the absence of food, the dog still salivated. The dog was conditioned to salivate in response to a stimulus that it did not normally associate with food.

Figure 34–5 Ivan Pavlov taught his dog to expect food whenever a bell was rung. **Pavlov's experiment is an example of classical conditioning, one of the four major types of learning.**

HISTORY OF SCIENCE

Pavlov's incidental discovery
Ivan Pavlov (1849–1936) was a Russian physiologist working in St. Petersburg. He pioneered studies of the digestive system and even won the Nobel Prize in Medicine in 1904 for his work on the physiology of the circulatory, digestive, and nervous systems. In his research, he measured the saliva produced when dogs, secured in harnesses, were fed. But after the dogs had been in the laboratory for a while, they would salivate as soon as they were put in a harness. This infuriated Pavlov, because it invalidated his measurements. He had begun his studies of this behavior in an attempt to eliminate it. These studies proved fascinating, though, when he discovered that he could cause dogs to salivate simply by ringing a bell or turning on a light.

Operant Conditioning Conditioning is often used to train animals. **Operant conditioning** occurs when an animal learns to behave in a certain way through repeated practice, in order to receive a reward or avoid punishment. Operant conditioning is also called trial-and-error learning because it begins with a random behavior that is rewarded in an event called a trial. Most trials result in errors, but occasionally a trial will lead to a reward or punishment.

Operant conditioning was first described in the 1940s by the American psychologist B. F. Skinner. Skinner invented a testing procedure that used a certain type of box—the "Skinner box," shown in **Figure 34–6.** A Skinner box contains a colored button or lever that, when pressed, delivers a food reward. After an animal is rewarded several times, it learns that it gets food whenever it presses the button or lever. At this point, the animal has learned by operant conditioning how to obtain food.

CHECKPOINT *What is operant conditioning?*

▲ **Figure 34–6** Notice the pigeon in the Skinner box. Sooner or later, a laboratory animal placed in a Skinner box will accidentally press a button or lever that delivers a food reward. In time, this pigeon will learn how to obtain food whenever it wants. **Applying Concepts** *Which type of learning occurs in a Skinner box?*

Insight Learning The most complicated form of learning is **insight learning,** or reasoning. Insight learning occurs when an animal applies something it has already learned to a new situation, without a period of trial and error. For instance, if you are given a new math problem on an exam, you may apply principles you have already learned in the class in order to solve the problem. Insight learning is common among humans and other primates. In one experiment, a hungry chimpanzee used insight learning to figure out how to reach a bunch of bananas hanging overhead: It stacked some boxes on top of one another and climbed to the top of the stack. In contrast, if a dog accidentally wraps its leash around a tree, the dog is usually unable to free itself.

Quick Lab

6IIE 7.c, BIIE 1.d

What kind of learning is practice?

Materials paper, ruler, scissors

Procedure

1. Draw straight lines on a piece of paper to divide it into several sections of different sizes and shapes. Then, cut the paper into sections along those lines.
2. Shuffle the pieces and then time another student as he or she tries to reassemble the pieces. Record how long it takes the student to do this task.
3. Repeat step 2 three times. Construct a graph showing how the time needed to assemble the puzzle changed with repeated practice.

Analyze and Conclude

1. **Analyzing Data** Explain the shape of your graph. How did the time needed to reassemble the pieces change with repeated trials?
2. **Drawing Conclusions** What kind of learning was displayed in this activity? Was it classical conditioning, operant conditioning, habituation, or some other kind of learning? Explain your answer.

Quick Lab

6IIE 7.c, BIIE 1.d

Objective Students will be able to draw conclusions to classify practice as a kind of learning. L2

Materials paper, ruler, scissors, clock with second hand

Time 15 minutes

Strategy
Students will get straighter cuts if they use the ruler to draw the cutting lines.

Expected Outcome The time required to assemble the puzzle will decrease with each try.

Sample Data Table

Trial	Student 1	Student 2
1	60 sec.	12 sec.
2	15 sec.	12 sec.
3	14 sec.	9 sec.

Analyze and Conclude

1. Graphs should show that the time required to assemble the puzzle decreased as students repeated the task.
2. Some students may think that the learning in this activity, practicing, is different from habituation, classical conditioning, and operant conditioning. Recognizing the shape of puzzle pieces requires conscious insight, an ability not involved in the other types of learning. Others may see this type of practicing as operant conditioning, because the first trial on the puzzle is a random effort.

BIO INSIGHTS FACTS AND FIGURES

Nature vs. nurture
The ability to learn is inherited because animals inherit their brain structures, making them capable of learning. However, knowing exactly how large an impact heredity has on learning is difficult because the environment plays such a large role in determining an animal's behavior. Most scientists agree that at some level, many learned behaviors are based on innate behaviors that have been changed by experiences in the environment.

Learning is valuable to an animal because it can improve the animal's chance for survival, thus increasing its chance of passing its genes to its offspring. Young animals learn from their parents. However, learning occurs only in animals that have the time and opportunity to learn. For example, a fawn learns many things from its mother, but a frog must rely more on instinct.

Answers to . . .

CHECKPOINT *Learning in which an animal learns a behavior through practice, in order to receive a reward or avoid punishment*

Figure 34–6 *Operant conditioning*

34–1 (continued)

Instinct and Learning Combined

Make Connections

Environmental Science Show the movie *Fly Away Home,* Columbia Pictures, 1996. Discuss the large responsibility this family accepted when they allowed the goslings to imprint on them. Help students understand the impact they have on their environment and why it's important that they take responsibility for their actions. L1 L2

3 ASSESS

Evaluate Understanding

Ask students: **What elicits a behavior?** *(Stimuli in the environment)* **How do innate behaviors and learned behaviors differ?** *(Innate—fully functional the first time it is performed; learned—developed over time in response to experience)* **Name five kinds of learning.** *(Habituation, classical conditioning, operant conditioning, insight learning, and imprinting)*

Reteach

Have students study each figure in the section and identify the type of behavior—innate or learned—that is exemplified by the figure. Students should also explain why they think it represents that behavior.

Thinking Visually

Students might construct a Venn diagram, a hierarchical map, or a concept map. The organizer should include innate behavior, learned behavior, and examples of each, including habituation, classical conditioning, operant conditioning, insight learning, and imprinting.

If your class subscribes to the iText, use it to review the Key Concepts in Section 34–1.

Answer to . . .

Figure 34–7 *They have imprinted on the aircraft.*

▲ **Figure 34–7** These young Canada geese were trained to migrate behind this ultralight aircraft in an experiment called Operation Migration. The geese followed the craft as closely as they would their own parents. This type of conditioning is now being used to help whooping cranes learn a migration route. **Inferring** *Why would these birds follow this aircraft?*

Instinct and Learning Combined

Most behaviors result from a combination of innate ability and learning. Young white-crowned sparrows, for example, have an innate ability to recognize their own species' song. To sing the complete version, however, the young birds must first hear it sung by the adults.

Some very young animals, such as ducks and geese, learn to recognize and follow the first moving object that they see during a critical time early in their lives. Usually, this object is their mother. This process is called **imprinting.** Imprinting keeps young animals close to their mother, who protects them and leads them to food sources. Once imprinting has occurred, the behavior cannot be changed.

Imprinting involves both innate and learned behavior. The young animals have an innate urge to follow the first moving object they see, but they are not born knowing what that object will look like. The young animal must learn from experience what object to follow. In fact, the object on which the young animal imprints does not have to be its mother, or even a living organism. The birds in **Figure 34–7** have imprinted on an aircraft!

Imprinting can occur through scent as well as sight. Newly hatched salmon, for example, imprint on the odor of the stream in which they hatch. Young salmon then head out to sea. Years later, when they mature, the salmon remember the odor of their home stream and return there to spawn.

34–1 Section Assessment

1. **Key Concept** Which body systems interact to produce a behavioral response?
2. **Key Concept** Compare and contrast innate and learned behavior.
3. **Key Concept** Define the four major types of learning.
4. Explain the difference between a stimulus and a response.
5. How does natural selection affect animal behavior?
6. **Critical Thinking Applying Concepts** Give an example of how humans learn through classical conditioning.

Thinking Visually

Creating a Graphic Organizer
Create a graphic organizer to compare innate behavior with the different forms of learned behavior discussed in this section. Include at least one example of each kind of behavior in your graphic organizer.

34–1 Section Assessment

1. Sense organs, nervous system, muscles
2. Innate—performed perfectly the first time; learned—changed as a result of experience
3. Habituation—decreased response to inconsequential repetitive stimuli; classical conditioning—connecting a stimulus to a reward; operant conditioning—learning a behavior through practice in order to receive reward or escape punishment; insight learning—applying knowledge to new situation
4. Stimulus—signal that carries information; response—a specific reaction to a stimulus
5. Organisms with an adaptive behavior are better able to survive and reproduce.
6. Sample answer: A baby learns to associate the sight of a juice bottle with the treat of a sweet drink.

Using Remote Sensing to Study Animal Behavior

It is difficult to study animals that travel long distances, such as elephants and blue whales. Such studies once required the capture, banding, release, and recapture of individual animals. Researchers would mark or band an animal with an identification tag. If that animal was seen again or recaptured, the identification tag would be recorded and compared to the original field notes. Using this method, scientists could get an idea of the places their subjects visited. But they had few clues to the routes that animals traveled or where they went between capture points.

Remote Sensing

Today, small radio tags or transmitters are used to track the positions of some animals as they travel. As with banding, the lightweight transmitters are attached to individual animals. Satellites that orbit Earth are programmed to locate the transmitter signal and record the position—latitude, longitude, and even depth—of the animal as it moves. Some transmitters contain computer chips that can record the animal's body temperature, rate of breathing, and other physiological characteristics. These data can be made available to researchers over periods of days, weeks, or even months. This method, called satellite telemetry (tuh-LEM-uh-tree), can be expensive, but the data it provides are extremely valuable. The data may help in efforts to protect endangered species such as elephants and sea turtles.

In the Jungle

Scientists are using remote sensing techniques to track elephants through the dense jungles of Thailand and Malaysia. Preliminary data suggest that elephants can move across long distances within a home range of almost 7000 square kilometers. Such a large area would have been impossible for researchers to cover from the ground, or even by airplane or helicopter.

In the Ocean

California researchers are also using remote sensing to study marine animals—particularly sea lions. A satellite telemetry transmitter is glued to the sea lion's back using special glue. Scientists are using the data gathered to study when and where sea lions search for food as well as record the number and length of the dives they take. The data help scientists identify important foraging areas and habitats for the sea lions.

Research and Decide

Use library or Internet resources to learn more about remote sensing in studies of animal behavior. Then, evaluate the advantages and disadvantages of this technology. (Consider factors such as kinds of information the technology does and does not provide, its probable cost, and what might be learned better by other methods.)

For: Links from the authors
Visit: PHSchool.com
Web Code: cbe-9341

After students have read this feature, you might want to discuss one or more of the following:

- What kinds of behaviors are scientists studying—innate or learned or both?
- Are the actions of the scientists affecting the behaviors of the animals they are observing? What might happen if they are?
- How do these kinds of studies help scientists protect endangered animals? What kinds of information can help save an endangered species?
- Does remote sensing tell scientists everything about the behavior of an animal? What other information does a scientist need to get the complete picture of an animal's behavior?

Research and Decide

Advantages might include tracking animal movements at all times without influencing the animal's behavior and being able to track animals in remote areas and follow migratory routes. Disadvantages might include not being able to observe the stimuli that cause an animal to move and the cost of remote sensing.

Students can research remote sensing of animals on the site developed by authors Ken Miller and Joe Levine.

Section 34–2

1 FOCUS

Objectives

34.2.1 ***Explain*** how environmental changes affect animal behavior.

34.2.2 ***Describe*** how courtship and social behavior increase an animal's evolutionary fitness.

34.2.3 ***Identify*** behavioral patterns used to claim and defend territories.

34.2.4 ***Summarize*** how animals communicate.

Guide for Reading

Vocabulary Preview

Explain that the term *circadian* comes from the Latin words *circa*, meaning "about," and *dies*, meaning "day." Therefore, *circadian* means "a period of about one day." Ask: **What is a circadian rhythm?** *(A cycle of behaviors that occurs in daily, or 24-hour, patterns)*

Reading Strategy

Before students read this section, have them preview the figures and read their captions. Then, as students read the section, remind them to write a sentence that explains how the figure relates to what they are reading.

2 INSTRUCT

Behavioral Cycles

Use Visuals

Figure 34–8 As students examine the map of the sea turtle migration, ask: **What behavioral cycle are the sea turtles engaged in?** *(Migration, an annual cycle)* **How do these sea turtles know when to leave Brazil to go to Ascension Island?** *(Accept all reasonable answers. Changes in the length of day might cause green sea turtles to migrate.)* **How is migration an adaptive advantage to green sea turtles?** *(Accept all reasonable answers. Migration has improved the fitness of green sea turtles because they feed in areas with plenty of food and lay their eggs where the young have the best chance of survival.)* L1 L2

34–2 Patterns of Behavior

Guide for Reading

Key Concepts
- How do environmental changes affect animal behavior?
- How do courtship and social behaviors increase an animal's evolutionary fitness?
- How do animals communicate?

Vocabulary
migration
circadian rhythm
courtship
territory
aggression
communication
language

Reading Strategy: Using Visuals As you read, write a sentence explaining how each diagram or photograph reinforces or enhances the content of this section.

At this very moment, somewhere in an African grassland, elephants are calling to one another. Elephants communicate with sounds that they use to locate each other across distances more than 2 kilometers away. When they are not calling long-distance, elephants may spar with each other to test their strength or greet each other by wrapping their trunks together. These behaviors are patterns that have evolved in elephants. In this section, you will investigate some common patterns of animal behavior.

Behavioral Cycles

The environment is full of natural cycles. Night follows day, seasons change, the moon has phases, the tides rise and fall. **Many animals respond to periodic changes in the environment with daily or seasonal cycles of behavior.** For example, several species of reptiles and mammals are active during warm seasons but enter into a sleeplike state, or dormancy, during cold seasons. Dormancy allows an animal to survive periods when food and other resources may not be available.

Another type of behavior that is influenced by changing seasons is **migration,** the periodic movement from one place to another and then back again. Animals that migrate include species of birds, butterflies, and whales. **Figure 34–8** shows the migratory pattern of green sea turtles. Migration usually allows animals to take advantage of favorable environmental conditions. For example, when birds fly south for the winter, they go to regions where food is more plentiful than in northern areas.

Behavioral cycles that occur in daily patterns are called **circadian** (sur-KAY-dee-un) **rhythms.** The fact that you sleep at night and attend school during the day is an example of a circadian rhythm.

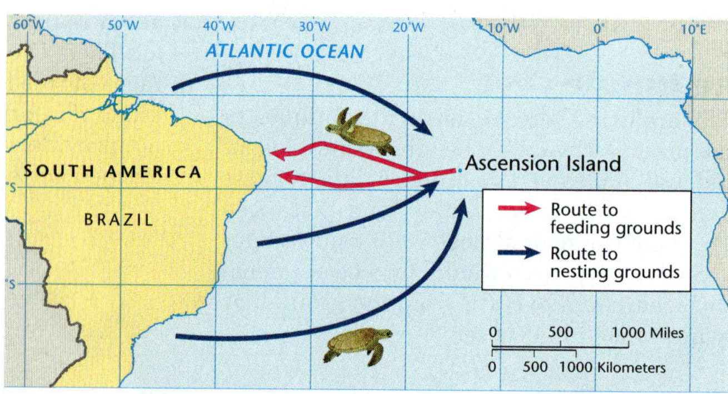

Figure 34–8 Each year, between December and June, green sea turtles migrate from their feeding grounds along the coast of Brazil to mate and nest on Ascension, a tiny island more than 2000 kilometers away. **Like many animals, sea turtles migrate in response to seasonal changes in their environment.**

TIME SAVER — SECTION RESOURCES

Print:
- ***Teaching Resources,*** Lesson Plan 34–2, Adapted Section Summary 34–2, Adapted Worksheets 34–2, Section Summary 34–2, Worksheets 34–2, Section Review 34–2, Enrichment
- ***Reading and Study Workbook A***, Section 34–2
- ***Adapted Reading and Study Workbook B***, Section 34–2
- ***Lab Worksheets***, Chapter 34 Design an Experiment

Technology:
- ***iText,*** Section 34–2
- ***Transparencies Plus,*** Section 34–2
- ***Virtual Labs,*** Lab 18, Lab 19

Analyzing Data

Caring for Eggs  BIIE 1.d

Reproduction is vital to animal survival. Humans can learn child-rearing skills. Is there evidence that other animals learn to care for their young?

The data at the right are from field studies of the short-tailed shearwater, *Puffinus tenuirostris.* Each pair of parents produces only one egg a year. If that egg breaks or if the chick dies, the egg is not replaced. The graph shows the percentage of eggs that hatch and develop into free-flying young, in relation to the number of years that the parents have been breeding.This variable is referred to as reproductive success. The purple line indicates the success rate of female parents. The green line indicates the success rate of male parents.

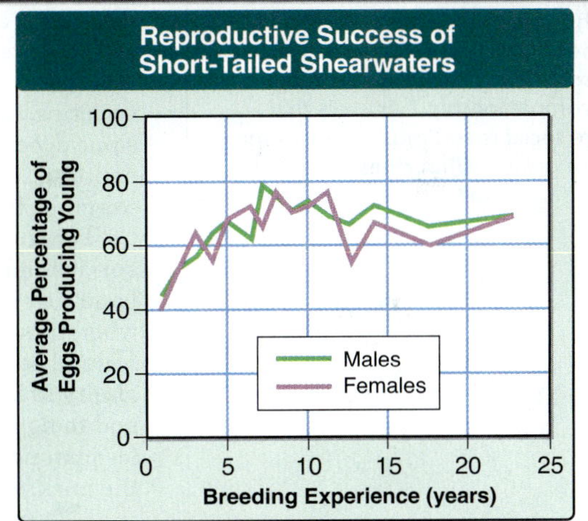

1. **Using Tables and Graphs** What is the approximate success rate of a female shearwater with 5 years of breeding experience?
2. **Using Tables and Graphs** Are there obvious differences in reproductive success between male and female shearwaters?
3. **Drawing Conclusions** Do older shearwaters have better reproductive success than younger birds? Explain your answer.
4. **Formulating Hypotheses** Do you think these birds learn to raise young more successfully over time? Is there an alternative hypothesis that could explain these data?

Courtship

Animal behavior is geared toward reproduction as well as survival. **To pass along its genes to the next generation, any animal that reproduces sexually needs to locate and mate with another member of its species at least once. Courtship behavior is part of an overall reproductive strategy that helps many animals identify healthy mates.**

In **courtship,** an individual sends out stimuli—such as sounds, visual displays, or chemicals—in order to attract a member of the opposite sex. For example, fireflies flash a distinct series of light signals to indicate their readiness to mate. The musical trill of a tree frog and the sheeplike bleat of a narrowmouth toad are among the many distinctive breeding calls of amphibians.

In some species, courtship involves an elaborate series of behaviors called rituals. A ritual is a series of behaviors performed the same way by all members of a population for the purpose of communicating. Most rituals consist of specific signals and individual responses that continue until mating occurs. For example, newly paired cranes, such as those in **Figure 34–9,** engage in intense periods of dancing before they mate.

CHECKPOINT *What is the function of courtship behavior?*

▼ **Figure 34–9** **Courtship behavior helps many animals identify healthy mates.** The courtship ritual of this pair of Japanese cranes consists of head bobbing, deep bows, leaps, grasping and tossing objects, short flights, and several other moves. If a potential mate does not perform the parts of this dance in the proper sequence, it will be rejected and must locate a different mate.

UNIVERSAL ACCESS

English Language Learners

Encourage students to make sketches that illustrate each of the behaviors described in this section. Then, have students label their sketches with the appropriate Vocabulary words. Also, allow students to label the sketches in their primary language. L1

Advanced Learners

Student groups can develop a skit showing how social behaviors help an animal society increase its evolutionary success. Groups can choose any animal and any behavior but must use accurate information and provide a bibliography. When students perform their skits for the class, the "audience" can identify how the behaviors contribute to the evolutionary success of the animals. L3

Analyzing Data

 **BIIE 1.d**

Have student volunteers explain what is measured on the vertical axis and the horizontal axis of this graph. Ask: **What does a reading of 60% at 4 years indicate?** *(That 60% of the parents with four years of breeding experience kept their chick alive until it was able to fly)* L2

Answers

1. Almost 70%

2. No

3. In general, yes. This is indicated by the rise in the graph line up until about 11 years. After 11 years, there is a slight decrease in reproductive success.

4. Most students will infer that over time, shearwaters learn to raise young more successfully. Alternative hypothesis: the fertility of shearwaters is highest between 7 and 11 years.

Courtship

Build Science Skills

Applying Concepts Invite students to research courtship behaviors of different animals. For example, they might learn about the courtship behaviors of sticklebacks, Siamese fighting fish, dance flies, fence lizards, bowerbirds, albatrosses, and rhinoceroses. Students can present their findings in a written report or storyboard. L2 L3

Answer to . . .

CHECKPOINT *Courtship behavior helps many animals identify healthy mates.*

34–2 (continued)

Social Behavior

Word Origins

A sociobiologist studies the behavior of animals as they interact with other members of their group. L2

Build Science Skills

Observing Allow students to observe the interaction of ants in an ant farm. You can purchase one ready-made from a hobby store or science supply company. Challenge students to identify the role that each ant, or group of ants, has in the colony. Students should not touch the ants. L2

Download a worksheet on animal communication for students to complete, and find additional teacher support from NSTA SciLinks.

Word Origins

The adjective **social** is related to the Latin words *socialis,* meaning "social," and *societas,* meaning "companionship." Animals that are social spend most of their time in a group. **What does a sociobiologist do?**

For: Links on animal communication
Visit: www.SciLinks.org
Web Code: cbn-9342

Social Behavior

Whenever animals interact with members of their own species, as in courtship, they are exhibiting social behavior. Many animals go beyond courtship in their social behavior and form societies. An animal society is a group of related animals of the same species that interact closely and often cooperate with one another. It takes the cooperative work of millions of termites, for example, to build a single termite mound.

For some species, membership in a society offers great survival advantages. Zebras and other grazers, for example, band together when grazing. They are safer from predators when they are part of a group rather than when they are alone. Animal societies also use strength in numbers to improve their ability to hunt, to protect their territory, to guard their young, and to fight with rivals if necessary. In wild African dog packs, for instance, adult females take turns guarding all the pups in the pack, while the other adults hunt together for prey.

Often, members of a society are closely related to one another. Related individuals share a large proportion of each other's genes. Therefore, helping a relative survive increases the chance that the genes an individual shares with that relative will be passed along to offspring. Thus, social behavior that helps a relative survive and reproduce improves an individual's evolutionary fitness.

Primates form some of the most complex animal social groups known. Macaque, baboon, and other primate societies hunt together, travel in search of new territory, and interact with neighboring societies. A great deal of what we know about primate societies comes from the work of Jane Goodall, the animal behaviorist pictured in **Figure 34–10,** who spent thousands of hours observing chimps in their natural habitat.

CHECKPOINT *What is an animal society?*

Figure 34–10 Animal societies enhance the reproductive success of individual members. The work of the British behaviorist Jane Goodall, at right, laid the foundation for modern primate studies. Goodall observed chimpanzees in their natural habitat, as shown here. Goodall's methodology and profound scientific discoveries revolutionized the field of animal behavior.

FACTS AND FIGURES

Jane in the company of chimps

Jane Goodall began her studies of chimpanzees in 1960, under the direction of anthropologist Louis Leakey. Goodall took a noninvasive approach to her studies. She quietly observed chimpanzees from a distance until they accepted her presence. Then, she quietly followed them around.

Her observations of social behavior in chimpanzees corrected many misconceptions of the time. She observed that chimpanzees have more complex social interactions and more behaviors similar to those of humans than scientists had ever imagined. For example, she learned that chimpanzees are skilled at making and using tools. Instead of vegetarians, they are omnivores and hunt and eat animals. She also witnessed a group of chimpanzees kill off another group for no obvious survival reason.

Competition and Aggression

Some animals have behaviors that help prevent others from using limited resources. Often, such patterns involve a specific area, or **territory,** that is occupied and protected by an animal or group of animals. Territories contain resources, such as food, water, nesting sites, shelter, and potential mates, that are necessary for an animal's survival and reproduction. By claiming a territory, an animal keeps others at a distance. If a rival enters a territory, the "owner" of the territory may attack the rival and drive it away. Algae-eating damselfish are notorious for making such attacks. An algae-eating damselfish can distinguish other algae-feeding species from species that do not eat algae. The damselfish chases the other algae-eaters away, but ignores the fish that do not eat algae.

When two or more animals try to claim limited resources, such as a territory or food, competition occurs. Many animals, such as the giraffes in **Figure 34–11,** use rituals and displays when they compete. During competition, animals may also show **aggression,** a threatening behavior that one animal uses to gain control over another. For instance, before a pride of lions settles down to eat, individuals may snap, claw, and snarl at one another. The most aggressive members will get to eat their fill of prey. The less aggressive lions will have to wait for their chance to feed.

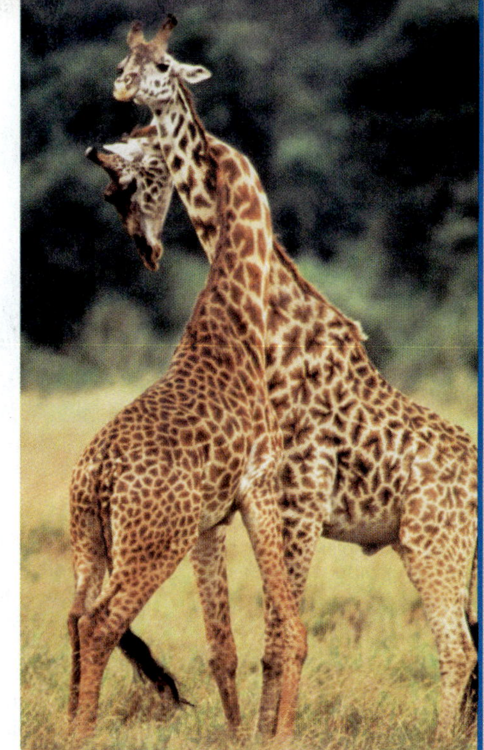

▲ **Figure 34–11** By intertwining their long necks, these two giraffes compete for resources on an African savanna. **Inferring** *What resources might these giraffes compete for?*

Communication

Often, when animal behavior involves more than one individual, some form of **communication**—the passing of information from one organism to another—is involved. **Animals may use visual, sound, touch, or chemical signals to communicate with one another.** The specific techniques that animals use depend on the types of stimuli their senses can detect.

Visual Signals Animals with good eyesight often use visual signals involving movement and color. Cuttlefish, for example, have large eyes that are as sophisticated as those of vertebrates. In a matter of seconds, a single cuttlefish, like the one in **Figure 34–12,** can undergo changes in the colors and patterns on its body. Its skin will pucker into bumps and spines, then suddenly become smooth as stone. These visual displays—as fascinating as any computer screen saver—function in defense, hunting, mating, warning, and perhaps other forms of communication that are not yet known.

▶ **Figure 34–12** **Animals use visual, sound, touch, and chemical signals to communicate.** Like many animals with good eyesight, this Pacific giant cuttlefish uses visual signals in displaying a variety of bright colors and patterns on its body.

Competition and Aggression

Build Science Skills

Formulating Hypotheses Explain that many behaviorists have observed that animals that do not face many dangers in their environment are less aggressive and lead a relatively relaxed life. However, animals that face many dangers in their environment are very aggressive, even among themselves. Challenge students to develop a hypothesis to explain these observations. L2

Communication

Demonstration

Communicate with the class without using any language. Try to get the class to perform a specific task, such as preparing to take notes or opening their books to a certain page. After students successfully complete the task, have them identify the types of signals you used to communicate with them. L2

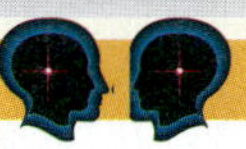

TEACHER TO TEACHER

Have students make a list of the behaviors they carry out in the course of the day to keep themselves healthy and well, such as combing hair, brushing teeth, eating, running, and resting. Then, have groups of two to four students perform a time-allocation study in the field of some common nonhuman animal, for example, a chipmunk or a squirrel. The students quickly realize that nonhuman animals go through behaviors in dealing with their environment that are similar to those of humans—for example, grooming, foraging, locomotion, and resting.

—William C. Alexander, Chairman
Division of Science and Mathematics
SC Governor's School for Science and Mathematics
Hartsville, SC

Answers to . . .

CHECKPOINT *An animal society is a group of related animals of the same species that interact closely and often cooperate with one another.*

Figure 34–11 *Food, water, mates*

34–2 (continued)

Make Connections

Chemistry Explain that pheromones are usually organic acids or alcohols that are highly volatile and can be detected in very small quantities. These chemicals work like hormones, except pheromones travel from one organism to another, rather than from one tissue to another. Like hormones, pheromones are chemical messengers that instigate a response. Certain moth sex attractants released by females stimulate male moths to follow the chemical gradient and mate with a female. Ask: **Are responses to pheromones learned behaviors or innate behaviors?** *(Innate)* L2

3 ASSESS

Evaluate Understanding

Have students write a paragraph in which they explain how animals communicate with one another in various social interactions, such as courtship or competition.

Reteach

Student pairs can develop a graphic organizer that shows the relationships among the Vocabulary words for this section.

Focus on the BIG Idea

Students should use their own words to explain that migration is the periodic movement from one place to another and then back again. Animals migrate to find more favorable environmental conditions. Students should describe the migratory behavior of at least one animal species, such as turtles, birds, butterflies, or whales.

If your class subscribes to the iText, use it to review the Key Concepts in Section 34–2.

▲ **Figure 34–13** Dolphins have fairly complex ways of communicating with one another.

Chemical Signals Animals with well-developed senses of smell, including insects, fishes, and many mammals, may communicate with chemicals. For example, some animals release pheromones (FEHR-uh-mohnz), chemical messengers that affect the behavior of other individuals of the same species, to mark a territory or to signal their readiness to mate.

Sound Signals Animals with strong vocal abilities, including crickets, toads, and birds, communicate with sound. Some animals that use sound have evolved elaborate communication systems. Dolphins, for example, rely mainly on sound signals in the dark and often murky ocean depths where vision is not very useful. Scientists have discovered that bottlenose dolphins each have their own unique "signature" whistle that is used for recognition. The dolphins' whistles function something like your signature on a letter, letting others know who is sending the communication.

Language The most complicated form of communication is language. **Language** is a system of communication that combines sounds, symbols, or gestures according to sets of rules about word order and meaning, such as grammar and syntax. Many animals, like dolphins, elephants, and gorillas, have fairly complex ways of communicating. However, outside of experiments in which they were trained by humans, none of those animals have been shown to use language. Only humans are known to use language.

34–2 Section Assessment

1. **Key Concept** Name two ways in which animal behavior is related to environmental cycles.
2. **Key Concept** Explain how an animal society can contribute to the evolutionary fitness of an individual animal.
3. **Key Concept** What are the main ways in which animals communicate with one another?
4. Define "courtship ritual," and give an example of an animal's courtship ritual.
5. How do dolphins communicate with one another?
6. **Critical Thinking Inferring** Suppose you discover a new type of animal that is very different in appearance from other animals you have seen. How could observing the sense organs of this animal help you to understand if and how it communicates?

Focus on the BIG Idea

Science as a Way of Knowing In your own words, write a paragraph explaining what migration is and the function it serves in an animal's life. As a way of clarifying and supporting your explanation, describe the migratory behavior of at least one animal species. *Hint:* You might use the information diagrammed in **Figure 34–8.**

34–2 Section Assessment

1. Migration and circadian rhythms
2. Animals within a society increase their evolutionary fitness by cooperatively performing such tasks as hunting, defense, and guarding the young.
3. By visual, sound, touch, or chemical signals
4. An elaborate series of behaviors consisting of specific signals and responses that are performed to attract a mate; example: dancing of Japanese cranes
5. With sound
6. By observing how well the animal's sense organs are developed, one can infer how it communicates. For example, if an animal has well-developed ears, it can be inferred that the animal communicates with sounds.

Design an Experiment

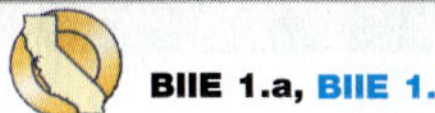

BIIE 1.a, BIIE 1.c

Observing Behavior in Fish

Animals of the same species often use aggressive behavior to signal others to retreat, but rarely do they hurt each other. In this investigation, you will examine some stimuli that provoke aggressive behavior.

Problem What triggers the aggressive behavior of male betta fish?

Materials

- male betta fish
- aquarium net
- clear plastic box of aquarium water
- small mirror
- construction paper
- colored pencils or markers
- transparent tape
- popsicle sticks
- watch with a second hand

Skills Asking Questions, Designing Experiments

Design Your Experiment

Part A: Observing Aggressive Displays

1. Use an aquarium net to transfer a male betta from the aquarium to a clear plastic box of aquarium water. **CAUTION:** *Do not touch the fish with your hands. Fish are easily injured.*
2. Observe the betta's behavior.
3. Place a mirror against the side of the box so that the fish can see its reflection. Observe and record the betta's behavior. Remove the mirror within 1 minute so that the fish does not habituate to its reflection.

Part B: Identifying the Stimulus for Aggression

4. **Formulating Hypotheses** What feature of a betta provokes aggressive behavior in other bettas? Is it color, size, movement, or something else? Record a hypothesis of what provokes aggressive displays by bettas. Base your hypothesis on your observations of bettas in Part A.
5. Design an experiment that will use paper models of bettas to test your hypothesis. You can tape the models to popsicle sticks and use colored pencils or markers to add details. Refer to the Lab Tips box on page 55. Have your teacher check your plan before you begin your experiment.
6. Carry out your experiment. Record your observations of the betta's behavior. **CAUTION:** *To avoid exhausting the betta, always allow it at least 1 minute of rest between stimuli.*
7. Wash your hands with soap and warm water before leaving the lab.

Analyze and Conclude

1. **Controlling Variables** Identify and define the manipulated and responding variables in your experiment.
2. **Observing** Did the male betta exhibit aggressive behavior? If so, how did it show aggression?
3. **Evaluating** What stimuli provoked the most aggression? Did your observations support your hypothesis?
4. **Inferring** Male bettas are more aggressive toward other males when a female betta is present. How can such behavior be an advantage to the male? How does it help the species survive?
5. **SAFETY** Explain how you demonstrated safe practices when working with live fish in this investigation.

Go Further

Designing Experiments Male bettas use aggression to defend their territory against invasion from other male bettas. Design an experiment to investigate what traits determine which male bettas will be successful in conflicts with other males.

Design an Experiment

BIIE 1.a, BIIE 1.c

Objective Students will be able to design an experiment to determine what triggers the aggressive behavior of male betta fish. L2

Skills Focus Asking Questions, Designing Experiments

Time 45 minutes

Advance Prep

- Betta fish are sold in aquarium shops as Siamese fighting fish. Do not keep male bettas together in the same tank.
- Provide white, blue, red, and green construction paper.
- Put fish in the containers a few hours before class so that the fish can acclimate.

Alternative Materials Instead of clear boxes, you can use clear 2-L bottles with the tops cut off.

Safety Touching the fish can remove their protective mucous layer, leading to infection in the fish.

Pre-Lab Discussion Discuss how aggression helps an animal to survive. Ask: **When can aggression be harmful?** *(When individuals injure or kill one another)* **How do animals benefit when individuals use only symbolic threats of aggression?** *(Individuals participate in confrontations without risking injuries.)*

Teaching Tips

- Mirrors and paper fish, and so on, should be put up to the container only from the outside.
- If the mirror is left in place for too long in step 3, the fish might become habituated to the image and fail to respond to stimuli later.
- Make sure students test only one variable in their experiment, such as color, size, or movement, and keep the other variables constant.

Expected Outcomes Fish should respond to bright color and to movement.

Go Further

Before approving proposed experiments, review them for sound design and hazards to students and fish.

Analyze and Conclude

1. Manipulated variable: paper betta models; responding variable: behavior of betta
2. Bettas show aggression by behaviors such as swimming quickly toward the mirror or model, presenting the side of the body, arching the back, lowering the head, raising the fins—especially the dorsal fin, spreading and beating the tail, extending the gill covers, or intensifying in color.
3. Bright colors and movement usually provoke the most aggression.
4. The more aggressive male is more likely to be accepted as a mate by the nearby female. The competition between the males increases the chance that only the strongest and healthiest males find mates and pass on their genes.
5. Avoided touching the fish with hands and allowed them at least 1 minute of rest between stimuli

Chapter 34 Study Guide

Study Tip

Have students make flashcards for each of the Vocabulary words and for the Key Concepts. Encourage student pairs to take turns quizzing each other with their flashcards.

Thinking Visually

1. Classical Conditioning
2. Operant Conditioning
3. Insight Learning

Chapter 34 Assessment

Reviewing Content

1. a	5. b	9. a
2. d	6. b	10. b
3. b	7. b	
4. c	8. a	

Understanding Concepts

11. Sample answer: stimulus—noise; response—frog leaps away

12. Senses detect the stimulus and pass that information to the brain. The brain interprets the information and directs the body's response.

13. Habituation enables animals to ignore irrelevant stimuli, thus conserving energy for real threats.

14. Pavlov rang a bell every time he fed a dog. After a while, he rang the bell without feeding the dog. The dog salivated in response to the bell, despite the fact that dogs normally salivate only in response to food.

15. Some animals are born with the innate ability to follow the first moving object they see. Learning is involved because the animal must learn to recognize that object during a critical period.

16. No. Migration is a periodic movement from one place to another and then back again that is related to changing seasons. The movement of these animals had nothing to do with changing seasons.

17. Sample answer: If a group searches for food, they are more likely to find it than if an individual searched; a large group is safer from predators than an individual is.

Chapter 34 Study Guide

34–1 Elements of Behavior

Key Concepts

- When an animal responds to a stimulus, body systems—including the sense organs, nervous system, and muscles—interact to produce the resultant behavior.
- Innate behaviors appear in fully functional form the first time they are performed, even though the animal may have had no previous experience with the stimuli to which it responds.
- The four major types of learning are habituation, classical conditioning, operant conditioning, and insight learning.

Vocabulary

behavior, p. 871
stimulus, p. 871
response, p. 871
innate behavior, p. 873
learning, p. 873
habituation, p. 874
classical conditioning, p. 874
operant conditioning, p. 875
insight learning, p. 875
imprinting, p. 876

34–2 Patterns of Behavior

Key Concepts

- Many animals respond to periodic changes in the environment with daily or seasonal cycles of behavior.
- To pass along its genes to the next generation, any animal that reproduces sexually needs to locate and mate with another member of its species at least once. Courtship behavior is part of an overall reproductive strategy that helps many animals identify healthy mates.
- Often, members of a society are closely related to one another. Related individuals share a large proportion of each other's genes. Therefore, helping a relative survive increases the chance that the genes an individual shares with that relative will be passed along to offspring.
- Animals may use visual, sound, touch, or chemical signals to communicate with one another.

Vocabulary

migration, p. 878
circadian rhythm, p. 878
courtship, p. 879
territory, p. 881
aggression, p. 881
communication, p. 881
language, p. 882

Thinking Visually

Using information from this chapter, complete the following concept map:

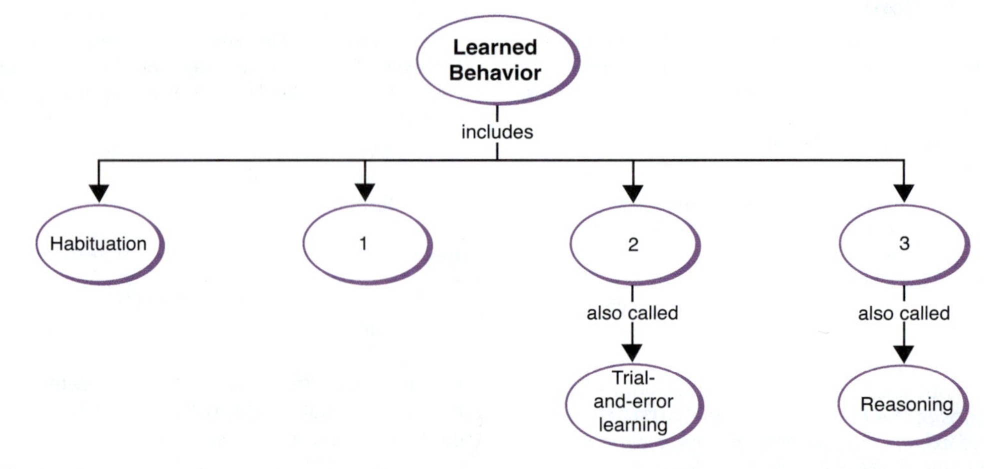

CHAPTER RESOURCES

TIME SAVER

Print:

- ***Teaching Resources,*** Chapter Vocabulary Review, Graphic Organizer, Chapter 34 Tests: Levels A and B
- ***Laboratory Assessment With Scoring Guide,*** Laboratory Assessment 9

Technology:

- ***Computer Test Bank,*** Chapter 34 Test
- ***iText,*** Chapter 34 Assessment

Chapter 34 Assessment

Reviewing Content

Choose the letter that best answers the question or completes the statement.

1. The set of reactions of an organism to changes in its internal condition or external environment is called
   a. behavior.
   b. learning.
   c. conditioning.
   d. stimuli.
2. Light, sound, and temperature are examples of
   a. responses.
   b. behaviors.
   c. circadian rhythms.
   d. external stimuli.
3. A dog learns to expect food whenever a bell is rung. This is an example of
   a. insight learning.
   b. classical conditioning.
   c. migration.
   d. instinct.
4. A decrease in response to a stimulus that neither rewards nor harms an animal is called
   a. instinct.
   b. operant conditioning.
   c. habituation.
   d. classical conditioning.
5. Insight learning is common among
   a. dogs.
   b. primates.
   c. birds and insects.
   d. birds only.
6. Study the diagram below. What type of learning is occurring?

   a. insight learning
   b. imprinting
   c. classical conditioning
   d. operant conditioning
7. The fact that you sleep at night and attend school during the day is an example of a(an)
   a. migration.
   b. circadian rhythm.
   c. aggressive behavior.
   d. social behavior.

Interactive textbook with assessment at PHSchool.com 

8. Each year, a bird called the American redstart travels from its winter home in South America to its nesting area in New York. This behavior is called
   a. migration.
   b. competition.
   c. imprinting.
   d. courtship.
9. Which of the following is NOT a type of social behavior?
   a. operant conditioning
   b. communication
   c. hunting in a pack
   d. courtship
10. A system of communication that uses meaningful sounds, symbols, or gestures according to specific rules is called
    a. behavior.
    b. language.
    c. competition.
    d. a signature.

Understanding Concepts

11. Describe an example of a stimulus and a corresponding response in animal behavior.
12. What is the brain's role in an animal's response to a stimulus?
13. How can habituation contribute to an animal's survival?
14. Describe Pavlov's experiment.
15. Explain why imprinting is a combination of innate ability and learning.
16. Because a highway has been constructed through a forest, many of the animals that once lived there have had to move to a different wooded area. Is their move an example of migration? Explain.
17. Identify two ways in which social behavior can benefit an animal.
18. What is the significance of Jane Goodall's work?
19. Explain how aggression and territorial behavior are related.
20. What are pheromones? Give an example of how they are used.
21. What animals are known to use language?

Interactive Textbook

If your class subscribes to the iText, your students can go online to access an interactive version of the Student Edition and a self-test.

(Continued from page 884)

18. Her methodology and profound scientific discoveries revolutionized the field of animal behavior.

19. Animals often use aggression or threatening behaviors to establish a territory and defend it when a rival tries to claim it.

20. Pheromones are chemical messengers that are released by an animal and affect the behavior of other animals of the same species. Sample use: marking a territory.

21. Only humans are known to use language.

TIME SAVER **HOMEWORK GUIDE**

Section:	Questions:
Section 34–1:	1–6, 11–15, 22–24
Section 34–2:	7–10, 16–21, 25–28

Chapter 34 Assessment

Critical Thinking

22. Accept all reasonable experimental designs. The only variable in students' designs should be the frequency of giving treats. Studies have shown that an occasional treat is a more effective way to train a dog than giving a treat each time a trick is completed.

23. Operant conditioning; smiling is reinforced by the reward of cuddling.

24. Horses are bred for desirable characteristics but can be conditioned, or trained, over time.

25. The three questions should address the animal's behavior. Observations might include interactions with other animals or responses to certain stimuli.

26. If allowed to live, the cubs sired by the previous male would compete with the new cubs for food and other resources. In addition, killing the cubs would hasten the females' readiness to mate, potentially increasing the new males' reproductive fitness.

27. Its body temperature fluctuates during winter months and is stable in warmer months. In winter, it is in a state of dormancy.

28. Less competition for resources, less conspicuous to predators

Focus on the BIG Idea

Plant growth and the bloom time of flowers, for example, occur at particular times of the year. The environmental conditions at these times may favor the growth of the plant as well as the activity of pollinators.

Writing in Science

Student paragraphs should give an accurate example of insight learning, which occurs when a person has applied something he or she has already learned to a new situation, without a period of trial and error.

Chapter 34 Assessment

Critical Thinking

22. Designing Experiments Some people train a dog by giving the animal a treat every single time it performs a behavior successfully. Other people reward the correct behavior on a more random schedule. Design an experiment to determine which method of training is more effective.

23. Inferring A baby smiles when her mother comes near. Often, the baby is picked up and cuddled as a result of smiling. Explain what type of learning the baby is showing.

24. Applying Concepts Explain how a racehorse's ability to win races is a combination of inherited and learned behaviors.

25. Asking Questions Choose a kind of animal with which you are familiar, such as a pet or an animal you have read about. Think of three questions about that animal's behavior that you might ask. Then, describe the observations you would need to make in order to answer the questions.

26. Inferring A pride of lions consists of several males, many females, and their offspring. About every two years, a group of new male lions drives the resident males from the pride. Often, one of the first acts of the new males is to try to kill all the young lion cubs. Explain how this behavior might give an evolutionary advantage to the new male lions.

27. Interpreting Graphics When temperatures are low and food is scarce, some mammals enter into a state of dormancy. Dormancy is an energy-saving adaptation in which metabolism decreases and, therefore, body temperature declines. The graph below tracks a ground squirrel's body temperature over the course of a year. Describe the pattern that you observe. What can you infer about the squirrel's behavior at different times of the year?

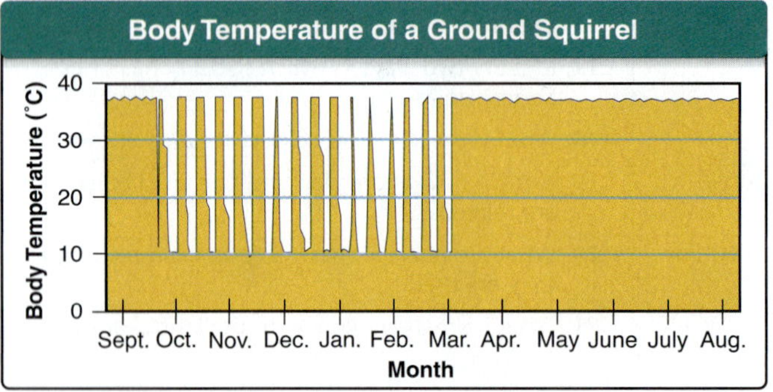

28. Formulating Hypotheses Although the members of many animal species derive benefits from living in social groups, members of other species live alone. What might be the adaptive advantage of solitary living?

Interdependence in Nature Review what you learned about plant responses in Chapter 25. Describe how some of these responses, like some animal behaviors, are related to cycles in the environment.

Writing in Science

Write a paragraph describing something you have learned by insight learning. Explain how you used past knowledge and experience in learning it. (*Hint:* In your paragraph, explain what insight learning is.)

Performance-Based Assessment

Being Social In daily life, humans demonstrate a wide variety of behaviors. Make a list of 10 social behaviors that you observe in your classmates and other people with whom you interact. Identify each type of behavior and describe how it might or might not be adaptive to the survival of humans.

For: An interactive self-test
Visit: PHSchool.com
Web Code: cba-9340

Performance-Based Assessment

Behaviors that students describe will vary. All students should include 10 different social behaviors. Examples include specific hand gestures, mannerly behaviors, flirting behaviors, aggressive behaviors, and so on. Students should identify each behavior as being learned or innate, as well as being a particular pattern of behavior, such as a behavioral cycle, courtship behavior, social behavior, competition or aggression, or communication. Students should also describe why the behavior is or is not an adaptation for human survival.

Your students can independently test their knowledge of the chapter and print out their test results for your files.

Standards Practice

Success Tracker™
Online at PHSchool.com

Test-Taking Tip When you are asked to analyze a graph showing experimental data, first look at the shape of the line. Identify the variables, and try to determine how they are related.

Questions 1–4 Each of the lettered choices below refers to the following numbered statements. Select the best lettered choice. A choice may be used once, more than once, or not at all.

A Insight learning
B Operant conditioning
C Classical conditioning
D Habituation

1. A rat learns to press a button to get food.
2. A dog always salivates at the ringing of a bell.
3. A chimpanzee stacks boxes in order to reach a banana hanging from the ceiling.
4. A bird stops responding to a repeated warning call when it is not followed by an attack.

Directions: Choose the letter that best answers the question or completes the statement.

5. Which kind of behavior does NOT involve learning?
   A habituation
   B trial and error
   C imprinting
   D instinct
6. A male three-spined stickleback fish will attack male red-bellied sticklebacks and models of fishes that have a red underside. It will not attack males or models lacking a red underside. What can you conclude from the three-spined stickleback's behavior?
   A The stimulus for an attack is a red underside.
   B The stimulus for an attack is aggression.
   C The stimulus for an attack is the presence of a fish with red fins.
   D The stimulus for an attack is the presence of a fish model.
7. Which of the following is NOT an innate behavior?
   A a dog looking for its food dish
   B a baby mammal sucking milk
   C a worm moving away from bright light
   D a spider spinning a web
8. A woman moves into a house by a railroad track. After a couple weeks, she no longer notices the sound of the train. Her reaction is an example of
   A operant conditioning.
   B habituation.
   C imprinting.
   D insight learning.

Questions 9–10

A researcher observed sedge warblers during breeding season. She charted the number of different songs a male bird sang compared to the time it took him to pair with a mate. The graph shows her data.

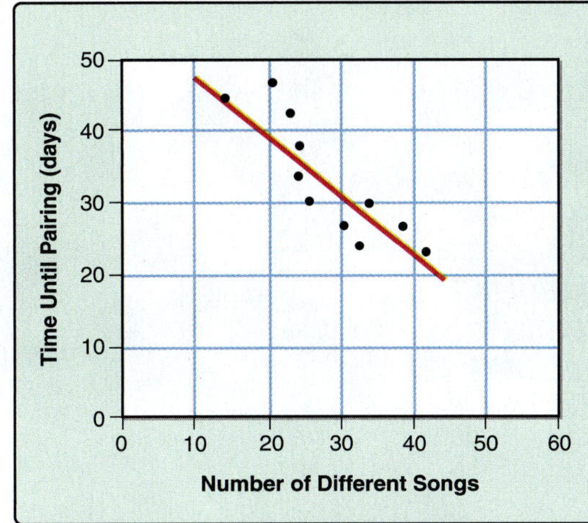

9. The researcher was trying to find out whether there is a correlation between
   A the number of a male bird's songs and the number of offspring.
   B the number of a male bird's songs and his attractiveness to females.
   C a male's age and the number of songs he sings.
   D a male's age and when he mates.
10. What can you conclude based on the graph?
   A Males prefer females that do not sing.
   B Females prefer males that do not sing.
   C Males prefer females with a large number of songs.
   D Females prefer males with a large number of songs.

Standards Practice

1. B	5. D	9. B
2. C	6. A	10. D
3. A	7. A	
4. D	8. B	

Success Tracker™
Online at PHSchool.com

Have students check their understanding of the chapter by logging onto Success Tracker.

UNIT 10

The precise coordination of the body systems keeps the bodies of these dancers in perfect working order.

Dear Colleague,

"You never appreciate what you have until it's gone." The wisdom of that old saying came back to me a couple of years ago in the midst of a very busy semester. In the spring, I teach a freshman biology class with hundreds of students, and I struggle with the challenges of keeping up with so many names and faces.

This day, however, was different. I didn't feel very hungry in the morning, so I skipped breakfast. As I prepared for my morning lecture, getting my slides and notes in order, I knew something was wrong. I felt nervous and jumpy, maybe even feverish. Perhaps I was getting a cold or a touch of the flu?

One of my teaching assistants remarked that I looked a little pale. I smiled and assured her that I was just fine. But when I bent down to pick up a notebook, I felt a pain deep in the right side of my abdomen, an unusual pain. Indigestion? No, I hadn't eaten anything at all.

I managed to sweat my way through the lecture, but when I walked back to my lab, I felt weak and very sick. Just before I called my doctor, I tried to put everything together: fever, weakness, lack of appetite, and a sharp, growing pain just below the stomach in my right side. I tried to be jovial when I spoke to my physician. "Hugh," I grinned, "I think I need a white cell count."

I had *never* felt a pain like this before, and there was only one thing I could think of: appendicitis. All the symptoms fit together, and a count of the white cells in my blood would confirm my amateur diagnosis. If my appendix was swollen and infected with bacteria, my body's immune system would have sprung into action days ago, sending millions of white blood cells into my bloodstream to fight the infection. If an

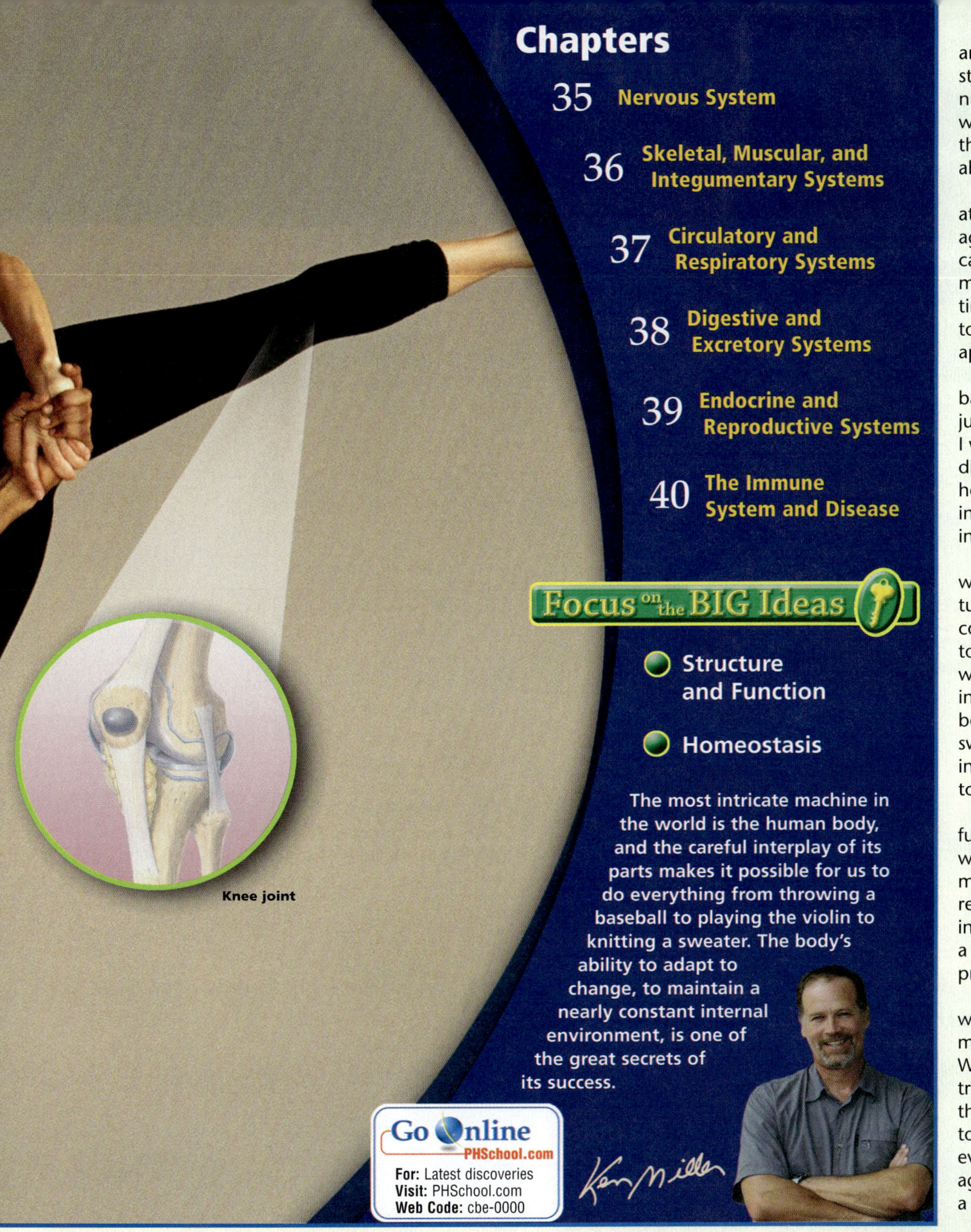

Knee joint

analysis of the cells in my bloodstream showed more than the usual number of white cells, it meant that I was fighting a serious infection. And the pain in my side left no doubt about where that infection was.

My physician laughed at my attempt to play doctor, but he agreed that a blood test was indicated. An hour later, I found out that my white cell count was nearly five times normal, and I was on my way to the hospital for an emergency appendectomy.

Recovery was quick, and I was back in the classroom and the lab in just a couple of days. Quite frankly, I was happy to be rid of that appendix. What most impressed me, however, was the number of ways in which my body reacted to that infection.

I got my first clues that something was wrong from elevated temperature and blood pressure—the body's coordinated effort to step up activity to fight infection. Unknown to me, white blood cells were being rushed into service from deep within my bones, and blood vessels were swelling around the infection, making it easier for the white blood cells to attack and subdue the bacteria.

My digestive system stopped functioning, and the hunger reflex was suppressed. My nervous system made me feel weak as more resources were directed to the site of infection, and, finally, nerves carried a sensation of pain to pinpoint the problem spot.

The separate systems of the body, which we will explore in this unit, are marvelous things in their own right. Working together, however, they are truly amazing. In my case, I was thankful that they got the message to me as quickly as they did—and even more thankful to be living in an age when modern medicine can save a life like mine as a matter of routine.

Sincerely,

Ken Miller

Go Online
PHSchool.com
Students can research the human body on the site developed by authors Ken Miller and Joe Levine.

Chapter Planner 35 Nervous System

Section and Section Objectives	Time	STANDARDS NCLB	STANDARDS Biology	Activities and Labs
35–1 Human Body Systems, pp. 891–896 ***35.1.1*** ***Describe*** how the human body is organized. ***35.1.2*** ***Explain*** homeostasis.	2 periods (1 block)	7 5.a	BI 9.c	SE: ***Inquiry Activity,*** What are the organ systems?, p. 890 L2 TE: ***Demonstration,*** p. 890 L1 L2 TE: ***Demonstration,*** p. 894 L1 L2
35–2 The Nervous System, pp. 897–900 ***35.2.1*** ***Identify*** the functions of the nervous system. ***35.2.2*** ***Describe*** how a nerve impulse is transmitted.	1 period (1/2 block)	BI 9.b	BI 9.d, BI 9.e	TE: ***Build Science Skills,*** p. 898 L2 TE: ***Demonstration,*** p. 899 L1 L2
35–3 Divisions of the Nervous System, pp. 901–905 ***35.3.1*** ***Identify*** the functions of the central nervous system. ***35.3.2*** ***Describe*** the functions of the two divisions of the peripheral nervous system.	1 period (1/2 block)	BI 9.b	BI 9.e	TE: ***Build Science Skills,*** p. 902 L2 L3 SE: ***Quick Lab,*** How do you respond to an external stimulus?, p. 903 L2 SE: ***Quick Lab,*** How do reflexes occur?, p. 905 L1 L2 TE: ***Build Science Skills,*** p. 905 L1 L2 LMA: Chapter 35 Lab L2 L3 LMB: Chapter 35 Lab L1 L2
35–4 The Senses, pp. 906–909 ***35.4.1*** ***Name*** the five types of sensory receptors. ***35.4.2*** ***Identify*** the five sense organs.	1 period (1/2 block)		BI 9.e	TE: ***Demonstration,*** p. 908 L1 L2 TE: ***Demonstration,*** p. 909 L2 SE: ***Real-World Lab,*** Modeling Corrective Lenses, p. 915 L2 L3
35–5 Drugs and the Nervous System, pp. 910–914 ***35.5.1*** ***Name*** the different classes of drugs that directly affect the nervous system. ***35.5.2*** ***Describe*** the effect of alcohol on the body.	1 period (1/2 block)			SE: ***Analyzing Data,*** Blood Alcohol Concentration, p. 913 L2 L3
Chapter Assessment, pp. 916–919	1 period (1/2 block)			

ACTIVITY PLANNER

SE: *Inquiry Activity*, p. 890; 10 min.; sheets of paper, colored pencils

TE: *Demonstration*, p. 890; 5 min.; 30-cm pieces of electrical cord

TE: *Demonstration*, p. 894; 5 min.; plastic wrap, electrical wire, roll of packaging tape

TE: *Build Science Skills*, p. 898; 15 min.; string, beads, dry pasta, modeling clay

TE: *Demonstration*, p. 899; 5 min.; dominoes

TE: *Build Science Skills*, p. 902; 10 min.; small box, newspapers, ruler

SE: *Quick Lab*, p. 903; 10 min.; scrap paper

TE: *Build Science Skills*, p. 905; 5 min.; blindfold

SE: *Quick Lab*, p. 905; 20 min.; string, packing tape, scissors, 30-cm ruler, plastic mousetraps

TE: *Demonstration*, p. 908; 5 min.; glass container, water

TE: *Demonstration*, p. 909; 10 min.; paper cups, blindfold, fruit juices

SE: *Real-World Lab*, p. 915; 45 min.; tape, cardboard photo easels, black construction paper, unruled white index card, 6-V light bulb and socket, 6-V battery and wires with alligator clips, convex lenses, modeling clay, meter sticks, concave lens

PLANNING KEY

Ability Levels

for students performing . . .

below grade level L1

at grade level L2

above grade level L3

Print Components

SE	Student Edition	**LA**	Lab Assessment
TE	Teacher's Edition	**BTM**	Biotechnology Manual
RSW	Reading & Study Workbook A	**IDM**	Issues and Decision Making
ARSW	Adapted Reading & Study Workbook B	**LW**	Lab Worksheets
TR	Teaching Resources	**LMA**	Laboratory Manual A
IF	Investigations in Forensics	**LMB**	Laboratory Manual B

Tech Components

CTB	Computer Test Bank
BD	BioDetectives DVD
TP	Transparencies Plus
PLM	Probeware Lab Manual
ABC	ABC DVD Library
LS	Lab Simulations
VL	Virtual Labs

Interactive textbook with assessment at PHSchool.com

Program Resources	Assessment	Media and Technology
TR: Lesson Plan 35–1, Section Summary, p. 6 L1, p. 18 L2, Worksheets, p. 9 L1, pp. 20–21 L2 **RSW:** Section 35–1 L2 **ARSW:** Section 35–1 L1 **IDM:** Issues and Decisions 4 L2 L3	**SE:** 35–1 Section Assessment, p. 896 **TR:** Section Review 35–1	**iText:** Section 35–1 **TP:** 35–1 Interest Grabber, Section Outline, Example of Feedback Inhibition, Figure 35–2
TR: Lesson Plan 35–2, Section Summary, p. 6 L1, p. 18 L2, Worksheets, pp. 10–12 L1, pp. 22–23 L2 **RSW:** Section 35–2 L2; **ARSW:** Section 35–2 L1	**SE:** 35–2 Section Assessment, p. 900 **TR:** Section Review 35–2	**iText:** Section 35–2 **TP:** 35–2 Interest Grabber, Section Outline, A Neuron, Figure 35–6, Figure 35–7, Figure 35–8 **ABC:** 48 Action Potential, 49 Synaptic Transmission
TR: Lesson Plan 35–3, Section Summary, p. 7 L1, p. 18 L2, Worksheets, p. 13 L1, pp. 24–25 L2 **RSW:** Section 35–3 L2 **ARSW:** Section 35–3 L1 **IDM:** Issues and Decisions 44 L2 L3	**SE:** 35–3 Section Assessment, p. 905 **TR:** Section Review 35–3	**iText:** Section 35–3 **TP:** 35–3 Interest Grabber, Section Outline, Concept Map, Figure 35–9, Cross Section of the Spinal Cord
TR: Lesson Plan 35–4, Section Summary, p. 8 L1, p. 19 L2, Worksheets, pp. 14–15 L1, pp. 26–28 L2, Enrichment L3 **RSW:** Section 35–4 L2 **ARSW:** Section 35–4 L1 **LW:** Chapter 35 Real-World Lab	**SE:** 35–4 Section Assessment, p. 909 **TR:** Section Review 35–4	**iText:** Section 35–4 **TP:** 35–4 Interest Grabber, Section Outline, Smell and Taste, Figure 35–14, Figure 35–15
TR: Lesson Plan 35–5, Section Summary, p. 8 L1, p. 19 L2, Worksheets, p. 16 L1, pp. 29–30 L2 **RSW:** Section 35–5 L2 **ARSW:** Section 35–5 L1 **IDM:** Issues and Decisions 8, 41, 42 L2 L3	**SE:** 35–5 Section Assessment, p. 914 **TR:** Section Review 35–5	**iText:** Section 35–5 **TP:** 35–5 Interest Grabber, Section Outline, Commonly Abused Drugs
	SE: Chapter 35 Assessment, pp. 916–919 **TR:** Chapter Vocabulary Review, Graphic Organizer, Chapter 35 Test	**iText:** Chapter 35 Assessment **CTB:** Chapter 35 Test

Go Online
Students can do research, share data, and test their knowledge online.

PRESSED FOR TIME?

To Preview the Chapter
- Have students read the Key Concepts for each section.
- Have students find definitions in the text for the Vocabulary terms.

To Cover the Chapter Quickly
- Have students read all of Section 35–1; the introduction to Sections 35–2, 35–3, and 35–4; and all of Section 35–5.
- Assign the Section Assessments for 35–1 and 35–5; questions 1, 2, 10–12, and 22–24 in Chapter 35 Assessment; and questions 1–11 in Chapter 35 Standards Practice.

To Review the Chapter
- Assign Sections 35–1 and 35–5 in the Reading and Study Workbook or the Adapted Reading and Study Workbook.
- Assign the Section Reviews for 35–1 and 35–5 and the Chapter Vocabulary Review for Chapter 35 in the Teaching Resources.

CHAPTER 35

ENGAGE/EXPLORE

Inquiry Activity

Objectives Students will be able to:
- identify misconceptions about the size, shape, and location of organs;
- conclude that organs can belong to more than one organ system. L2

Skills Focus **Predicting, Evaluating and Revising**

Materials large sheets of paper, colored pencils or markers

Time 10 minutes

Strategy You might want to supply outlines of the human body and have students work in groups to pool their knowledge.

Expected Outcome After interpreting the drawings, students are likely to find that their knowledge of human organs is incomplete.

Think About It

1. Yes; the mouth and pharynx are part of both the digestive system and the respiratory system. The skin is part of the excretory system and integumentary system.

2. Answers will vary. Students may be surprised at the locations of some organs, such as the stomach and kidneys, or the size of the heart in relation to the lungs.

Demonstration

Obtain two approximately 30-cm pieces of electrical cord. Remove insulation and fray one end of each cord by spreading out the wires to resemble dendrites. Touch the cut end of one cord to the frayed end of the other. Ask: **With the cords arranged in this way, could an electrical impulse travel from one cord to the other?** *(Yes)* **Why?** *(Because the ends are touching)* Then, move the two cords so they are about a centimeter apart. Ask: **Now could an electrical impulse travel from one cord to the other?** *(No)* **Why?** *(The ends are no longer touching.)* **What could serve as a link between the two cords when they are in this position?** *(Accept all reasonable answers.)* Finally, explain that nervous impulses must travel across a gap between nerve cells much like the gap between the two cords and that in this chapter students will find out how this happens.

CHAPTER 35

Nervous System

The agility and balance needed for fencing would not be possible without the coordination of the nervous system and the rest of the body.

Inquiry Activity

What are the organ systems?

Procedure

1. Draw an outline of the human body on a sheet of paper. Without referring to any illustrations, do your best to include the following organs on your outline: brain, stomach, kidneys, heart, and lungs. Pay attention to the shapes of the organs and their relative sizes, and to the specific body regions in which they are located.
2. Make a second drawing using **Figure 35–2** on pages 892 and 893 as a reference. Indicate which organs belong to which organ systems.

Think About It

1. **Predicting** Can an organ belong to more than one organ system? Explain.
2. **Evaluating and Revising** Compare your two drawings. Describe any misconceptions you had about the size, shape, or location of each organ.

HISTORY OF SCIENCE

Nervous system discoveries

In the late 1800s and early 1900s, two researchers made discoveries that revealed how the nervous system functions. The first was Santiago Ramón y Cajal, a Spanish scientist. He discovered that the nervous system is made up of billions of separate nerve cells, not a network of continuous filaments, which was the accepted view at the time. Cajal also discovered that nerve cells receive information on their cell bodies and dendrites and conduct information to distant locations through axons. The second researcher was Otto Loewi, a German scientist. He determined how nerve impulses are transmitted between neurons when he discovered the neurotransmitter acetylcholine. For their contributions to neurophysiology, both men were awarded a Nobel Prize in Physiology or Medicine, Cajal in 1906 and Loewi in 1936.

35–1 Human Body Systems

7 5.a. Students know plants and animals have levels of organization for structure and function, including cells, tissues, organs, organ systems, and the whole organization. **BI 9.c.** Students know how feedback loops in the nervous and endocrine systems regulate conditions in the body.

As the missed shot bounces high in the air, one of the defenders decides to take a chance. She breaks for the other end of the court. Another defender grabs the rebound, glances upcourt, and throws a long, arching pass toward the basket. Wide open, her teammate grabs the pass, dribbles, and leaps into the air, laying the basketball carefully off the backboard and into the unguarded basket. The buzzer goes off, and the game is over.

Guide for Reading

Key Concepts
- How is the human body organized?
- What is homeostasis?

Vocabulary
specialized cell
epithelial tissue
connective tissue
nervous tissue
muscle tissue
homeostasis
feedback inhibition

Reading Strategy: Predicting Before you read, use **Figure 35–2** to predict how many organ systems help to regulate body temperature. As you read, look for evidence to support your prediction.

Organization of the Body

Teamwork is a wonderful thing! Anyone watching the end of this game would be impressed at the way these two players worked together to make the winning play. But the real teamwork on this play involved a much larger number of players—the nearly one hundred trillion cells that make up the human body.

Every cell in the human body is both an independent unit and an interdependent part of a larger community—the entire organism. To make a winning basket, a basketball player has to use her eyes to watch the play and her brain to figure out how to score. With the support of her bones, her muscles propel her body up the court. As she sprints for a pass, her lungs absorb oxygen, which her blood carries to her cells. Her brain monitors the sensation of the ball on her fingertips and sends signals that guide her body into the air for the final play.

How does the body get so many individual cells to work together so beautifully? You can begin to answer this question by studying the organization of the human body. **The levels of organization in a multicellular organism include cells, tissues, organs, and organ systems.** Tissues are groups of similar cells that perform a single function, such as connecting a muscle to a bone. An organ is a group of tissues that work together to perform a complex function, such as sight. An organ system is a group of organs that perform closely related functions. CA a

The eleven organ systems of the human body work together to maintain homeostasis in the body as a whole. The organ systems, including their main structures and functions, are shown in **Figure 35–2** on pages 892 and 893.

a 7 5.a

▶ **Figure 35–1** Each player on a basketball team has a different role, but together the team works toward a common goal—winning the game.

Section 35–1

7 5.a, BI 9.c

1 FOCUS

Objectives

35.1.1 ***Describe*** how the human body is organized.
35.1.2 ***Explain*** homeostasis.

Guide for Reading

Vocabulary Preview

Emphasize the word *tissue*, which occurs in four of the Vocabulary terms. Remind students that a tissue is a group of similar cells that work together to perform the same function.

Reading Strategy

Point out that Figure 35–2 is a useful reference for all the chapters in this unit. Suggest that students insert a book marker on page 892 so that they can refer to the figure more easily as they study this chapter and the other chapters on the body systems.

2 INSTRUCT

Organization of the Body

Build Science Skills

Inferring Challenge students to name the organ systems they think are involved in the basketball player's actions that are described on this page. *(Students might say, for example, that the eyes and brain are used to watch the play and figure out how to score, and that they are part of the nervous system. Students also might say that muscles and bones support the body and allow movement around the basketball court, and that they are part of the muscular system and skeletal system, respectively.)* L1 L2

TIME SAVER — SECTION RESOURCES

Print:
- ***Teaching Resources,*** Lesson Plan 35–1, Adapted Section Summary 35–1, Adapted Worksheets 35–1, Section Summary 35–1, Worksheets 35–1, Section Review 35–1
- ***Reading and Study Workbook A,*** Section 35–1
- ***Adapted Reading and Study Workbook B,*** Section 35–1
- ***Issues and Decision Making,*** Issues and Decisions 4

Technology:
- ***iText,*** Section 35–1
- ***Transparencies Plus,*** Section 35–1

35–1 (continued)

Use Visuals

Figure 35–2 Review the organ systems in the figure by asking questions such as: **What is the function of the nervous system?** *(Recognizes and coordinates the body's response to external and internal changes)* **What are the structures of the integumentary system?** *(Skin, hair, nails, sweat glands, and oil glands)* **Which system makes up the body's supporting framework, allows movement, and stores mineral reserves?** *(Skeletal system)* **Which systems differ in males and females?** *(Endocrine and reproductive systems)* L1

Figure 35–2 Human Organ Systems

The levels of organization in the human body include cells, tissues, organs, and organ systems. Although each of the eleven organ systems shown here has a different set of functions, they all work together, as a whole, to maintain homeostasis.

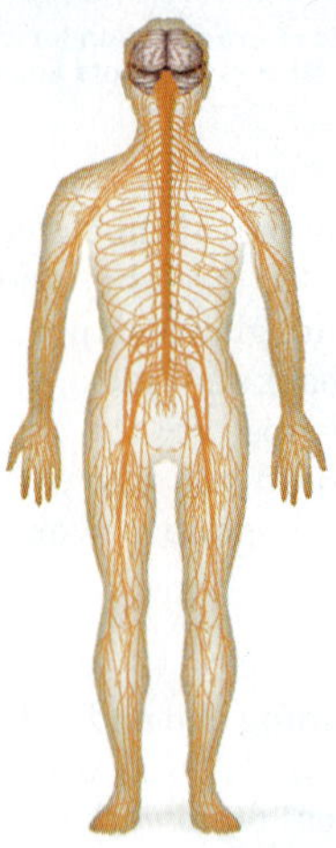

Nervous System
Structures: Brain, spinal cord, peripheral nerves
Function: Recognizes and coordinates the body's response to changes in its internal and external environments

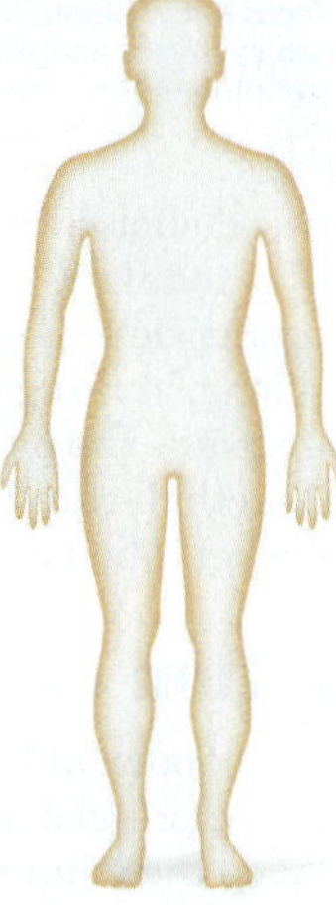

Integumentary System
Structures: Skin, hair, nails, sweat and oil glands
Function: Serves as a barrier against infection and injury; helps to regulate body temperature; provides protection against ultraviolet radiation from the sun

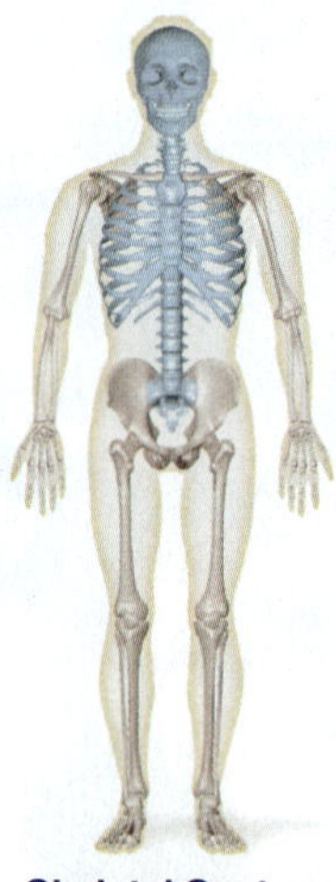

Skeletal System
Structures: Bones, cartilage, ligaments, tendons
Function: Supports the body; protects internal organs; allows movement; stores mineral reserves; provides a site for blood cell formation

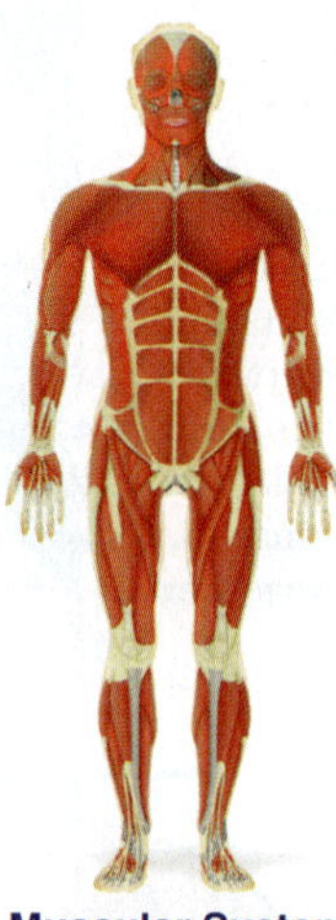

Muscular System
Structures: Skeletal muscle, smooth muscle, cardiac muscle
Function: Works with skeletal system to produce voluntary movement; helps to circulate blood and move food through the digestive system

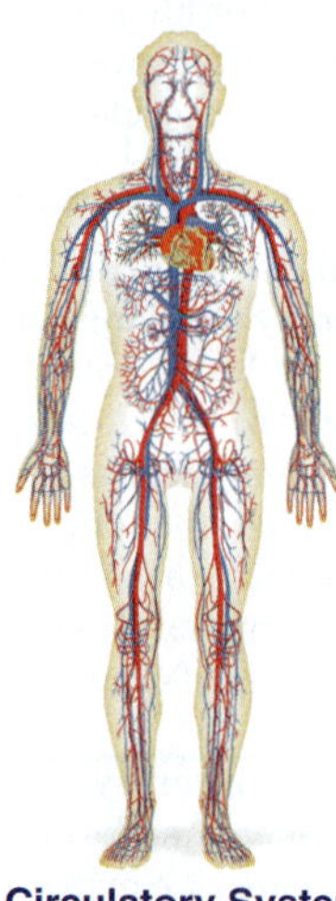

Circulatory System
Structures: Heart, blood vessels, blood
Function: Brings oxygen, nutrients, and hormones to cells; fights infection; removes cell wastes; helps to regulate body temperature

Support for English Language Learners

Comprehension: Link to Visual

Beginning Use Figure 35–2 to help students understand the levels of organization in the human body. Review the terms *cells, tissues, organs,* and *organ systems.* Have the students construct a concept circle with the name of one body system in the center and the structures and functions of that system connected to the center by lines. L1

Intermediate Pair ESL students with English-proficient students to construct a three-column table that describes the structures and functions of three body systems. To do this, they can use the information in Figure 35–2. The column heads should be *Body System, Structures,* and *Functions.* L2

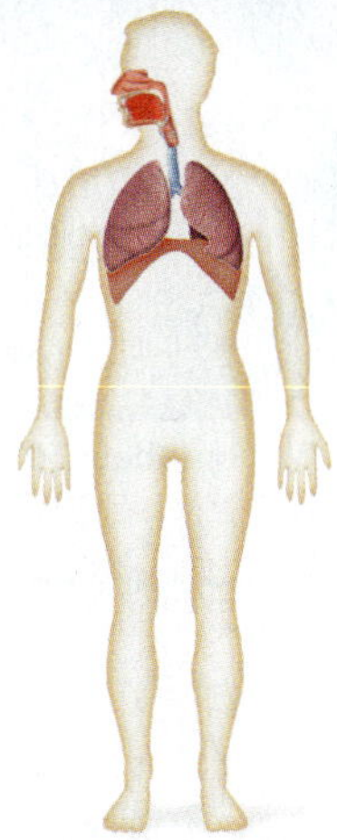

Respiratory System
Structures: Nose, pharynx, larynx, trachea, bronchi, bronchioles, lungs
Function: Provides oxygen needed for cellular respiration and removes excess carbon dioxide from the body

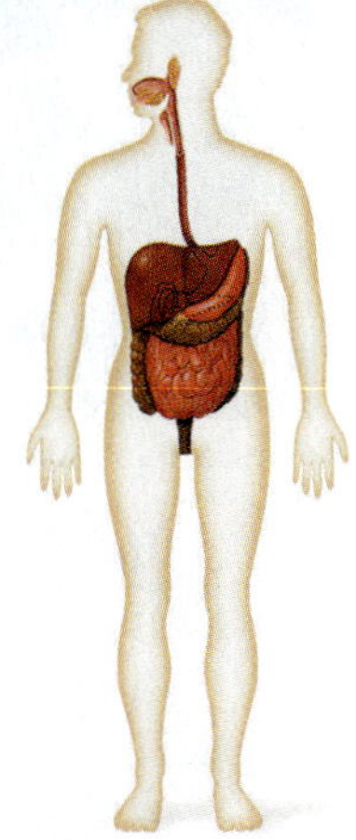

Digestive System
Structures: Mouth, pharynx, esophagus, stomach, small and large intestines, rectum
Function: Converts foods into simpler molecules that can be used by the cells of the body; absorbs food; eliminates wastes

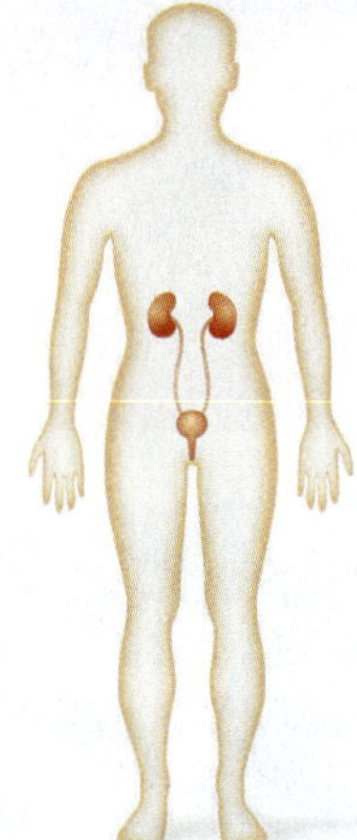

Excretory System
Structures: Skin, lungs, kidneys, ureters, urinary bladder, urethra
Function: Eliminates waste products from the body in ways that maintain homeostasis

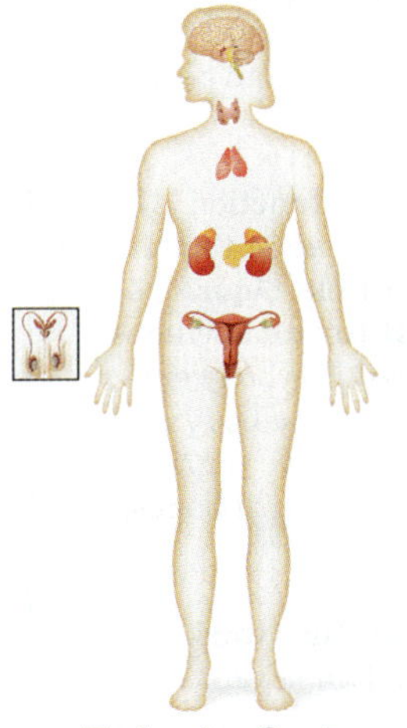

Endocrine System
Structures: Hypothalamus, pituitary, thyroid, parathyroids, adrenals, pancreas, ovaries (in females), testes (in males)
Function: Controls growth, development, and metabolism; maintains homeostasis

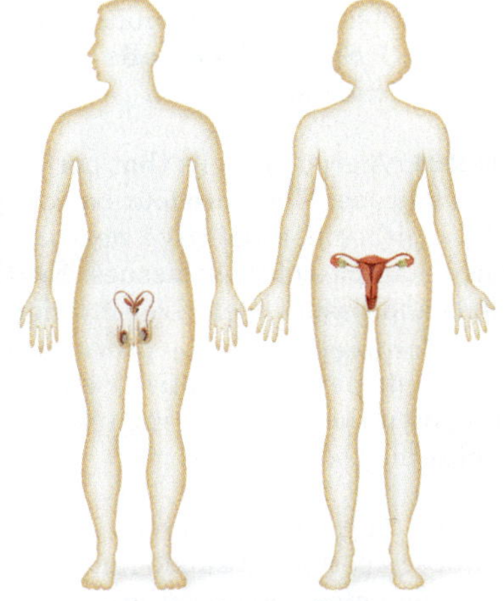

Reproductive System
Structures: Testes, epididymis, vas deferens, urethra, and penis (in males); ovaries, Fallopian tubes, uterus, vagina (in females)
Function: Produces reproductive cells; in females, nurtures and protects developing embryo

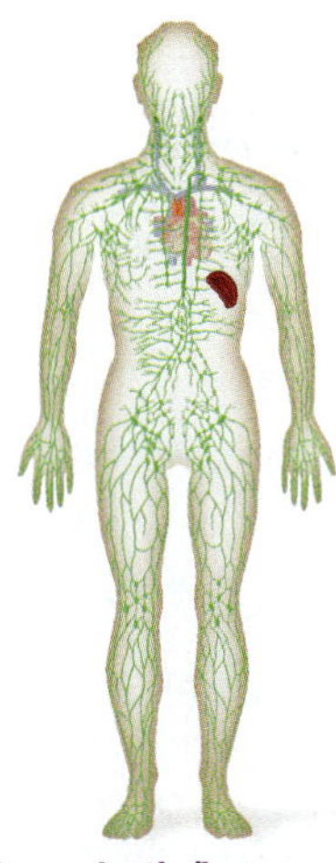

Lymphatic/Immune Systems
Structures: White blood cells, thymus, spleen, lymph nodes, lymph vessels
Function: Helps protect the body from disease; collects fluid lost from blood vessels and returns the fluid to the circulatory system

Demonstration

Use an analogy to demonstrate the importance of communication among human organ systems. Assign several students to two small groups. Have each group work to achieve the same simple goal, such as rearranging the books in a bookcase. Instruct one group to avoid any form of communication, including gestures, facial expressions, and eye contact, and to work independently toward the goal. Instruct the other group to communicate freely and to work together as a team toward the goal. Students will find that communication and teamwork make it much easier to get the job done. Point out that these concepts also apply to organ systems. L1

Build Science Skills

Using Models Encourage interested students to create an overlapping model of the human organ systems. First, students should trace or draw an outline of the human body. Next, they should trace the outlines of the different body systems on sheets of tracing paper or transparent film. Then, they should add the structures of one organ system to each sheet. Advise students to use colored pencils or markers for the different organ systems and to label the structures in each system. Allow class time for other students to examine the overlapping models so they can see how the different organ systems are positioned in the body relative to one another. L2 L3

BIO INSIGHTS — FACTS AND FIGURES

Organization of animal body plans
The general organization of animal body plans is usually taught in terms of organ systems. Students might be under the impression that all animals, or at least all vertebrates, have the same major organ systems. Although this is roughly true in most cases, there are some interesting exceptions that demonstrate that the major organ systems are not all indispensable to animal life. For example, the tube worms found at deep-sea hydrothermal vents include species in which the digestive system has virtually disappeared. These worms do not eat. Instead, their digestive tracts have been reduced to a specialized organ that houses symbiotic chemosynthetic bacteria that produce organic nutrients by reducing carbon dioxide.

35–1 (continued)

Demonstration

Display the following items: plastic wrap, electrical wire, and packaging tape. For each item, ask: **What is the purpose of this item?** *(Students might say that plastic wrap covers and protects, electrical wire transmits signals, and packaging tape binds and supports.)* Explain that three of the four types of tissues in the human body carry out similar functions. Ask: **Which type of tissue is represented by each item?** *(Epithelial tissue is represented by plastic wrap, nervous tissue by electrical wire, and connective tissue by packaging tape.)* **What could you use to represent muscle tissue?** *(Possible answers might include rubber bands or bungee cords.)* L1 L2

Build Science Skills

Using Models Have students examine their textbook to see how it is organized into units, chapters, sections, and subsections. Ask students to make a concept map to show this organization, placing the largest subdivision at the top and the smallest at the bottom. Have them compare the levels of organization in the book with those in complex organisms by asking: **Which level of organization in the book represents organ systems?** *(Units)* **Which levels in the book represent organs, tissues, and cells?** *(Chapters, sections, and subsections, respectively)* L1 L2

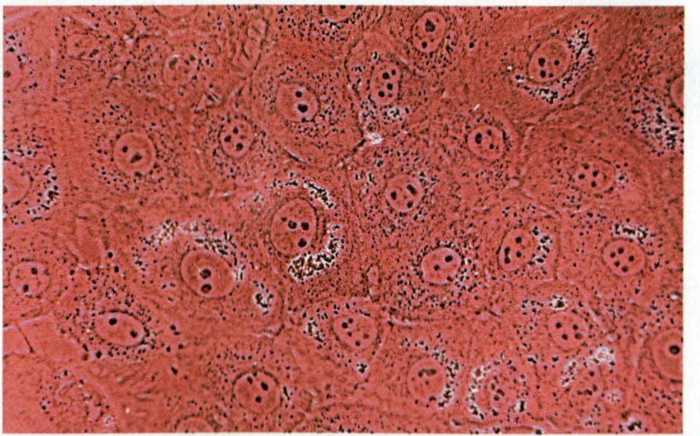

Epithelial Tissue (magnification: 6000×)

Connective Tissue (magnification: about 50×)

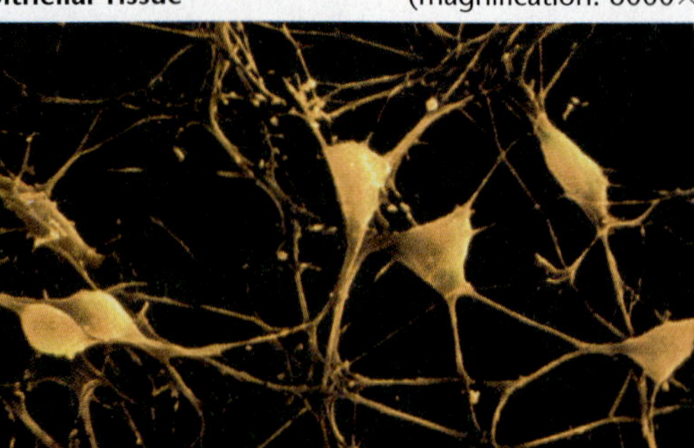

Nervous Tissue (magnification: 1100×)

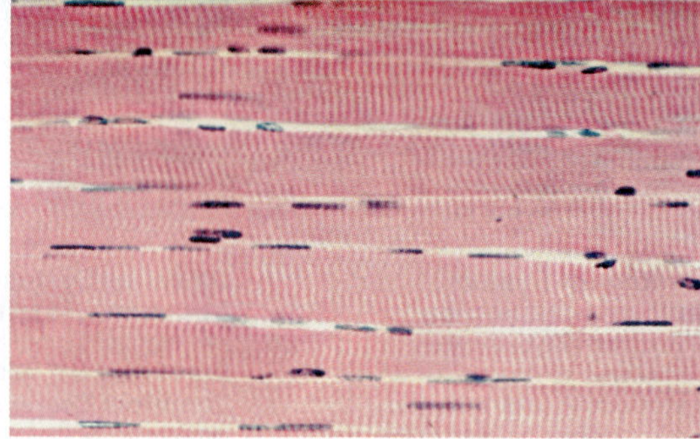

Muscle Tissue (magnification: 150×)

▲ **Figure 35–3** The four major types of tissues in the human body are epithelial tissue, connective tissue, nervous tissue, and muscle tissue. **Inferring** *What kind of tissue is bone?*

Cells A cell is the basic unit of structure and function in living things. Individual cells in multicellular organisms tend to be specialized. **Specialized cells** are uniquely suited to perform a particular function.

Tissues A group of cells that perform a single function is called a tissue. There are four basic types of tissue in the human body—epithelial, connective, nervous, and muscle. **Figure 35–3** shows examples of these tissues. **Epithelial tissue** includes glands and tissues that cover interior and exterior body surfaces. **Connective tissue** provides support for the body and connects its parts. **Nervous tissue** transmits nerve impulses throughout the body. And **muscle tissue,** along with bones, enables the body to move.

CA a

Organs A group of different types of tissues that work together to perform a single function is called an organ. The eye is an organ made up of epithelial tissue, nervous tissue, muscle tissue, and connective tissue. As different as these tissues are, they all work together for a single function—sight.

Organ Systems An organ system is a group of organs that perform closely related functions. For example, the brain is one of the organs of the nervous system, which gathers information about the outside world and coordinates the body's response.

CHECKPOINT *What is the role of nervous tissue?*

FACTS AND FIGURES

On more than one team

Many organs can be classified as belonging to more than one system. The pancreas is part of the digestive system and the endocrine system. The heart has hormone-releasing properties, making it an endocrine gland as well as the key organ of the circulatory system. Bone marrow contains tissue important to the immune system, circulatory system, and skeletal system.

Maintaining Homeostasis

You can get a glimpse of the interrelationship of your body systems when you breathe deeply after climbing a steep hill or when your blood clots to seal a cut. Behind the scenes, your organ systems are working constantly to do something that few people appreciate—maintain a controlled, stable environment. This process is called **homeostasis,** which means "keeping things in balance." **Homeostasis is the process by which organisms keep internal conditions relatively constant despite changes in external environments. Homeostasis in the body is maintained by feedback loops.**

A Nonliving Example One way to understand homeostasis is to look at a nonliving system that also keeps environmental conditions within a certain range. The heating system of a house is a perfect example. In most houses, heat is supplied by a furnace that burns oil or natural gas. When the temperature within the house drops below a set point, a sensor in a device called a thermostat switches the furnace on. Heat produced by the furnace warms the house. When the temperature rises above the set point, the thermostat switches the furnace off. Because the furnace runs only when it is needed, the temperature of the house is kept within a narrow range.

A heating system like the one described is said to be controlled by feedback inhibition. **Feedback inhibition,** or negative feedback, is the process in which a stimulus produces a response that opposes the original stimulus. **Figure 35–4** summarizes the feedback inhibition process in a home heating system. When the furnace is switched on, it produces a product (heat) that changes the environment of the house (by raising the air temperature). This environmental change then "feeds back" to "inhibit" the operation of the furnace. In other words, heat from the furnace eventually raises the temperature enough to send a feedback signal to switch the furnace off. Systems controlled by feedback inhibition are generally fully automated and very stable.

Figure 35–4 **Homeostasis is the process by which organisms keep internal conditions relatively constant despite changes in external environments.** A home heating system uses a feedback loop to maintain a stable, comfortable environment within a house.

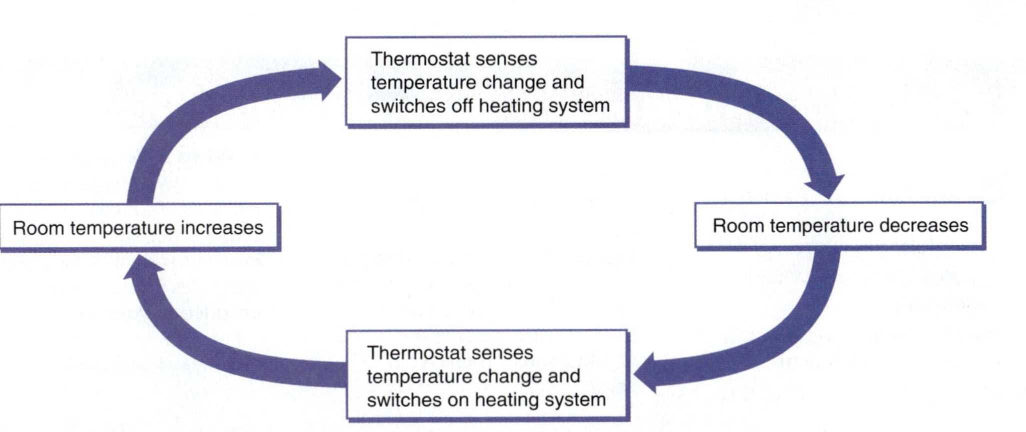

Maintaining Homeostasis

Make Connections

Chemistry Point out that chemistry is the reason we must maintain homeostasis in body temperature. Explain that most of the biochemical processes vital to life occur efficiently only within a very limited range of temperatures. Temperatures above or below these limits inhibit enzymes and thus chemical reactions; disrupt vital functions such as breathing and circulation; and, at extreme heat, can denature enzymes and other proteins. These all disrupt the body's internal chemistry. L2

FACTS AND FIGURES

Body talk

To maintain homeostasis, the body must have good internal communication. Both endocrine and nervous systems fulfill this role in humans and in many other animals. Endocrine communication depends on the release of chemicals that can travel in the blood throughout the entire body. Hours or even days may elapse between the release of a chemical by the endocrine system and the response by the cells that are sensitive to the chemical. Nervous system communication, in contrast, depends on the transmission of nerve impulses along nerve pathways, which is extremely rapid. In fact, nerve impulses can typically relay information about events in one part of the body to the brain or another organ in less than a second.

Answers to . . .

CHECKPOINT *The role of nervous tissue is to transmit nerve impulses through the body.*

Figure 35–3 *Bone is connective tissue.*

35–1 (continued)

Build Science Skills

Using Models Have students compare the regulation of body temperature in humans with the regulation of air temperature in a house. Ask: **Which structure in the human body has the same role as the thermostat in a house?** *(The hypothalamus)* You could extend the model by noting that the temperature in a house can vary with location just as body temperature varies from the core to the surface. L1 L2

Word Origins

Hypothermia means a below-normal body temperature. L2

3 ASSESS

Evaluate Understanding

Have students draw a simple diagram to show how the body regulates temperature.

Reteach

State the function of each human organ system, and challenge students to identify the system and name its structures.

Thinking Visually

Students' Venn diagrams should have a nesting structure, with concentric circles representing the four levels of organization, from smallest and simplest (cells) to largest and most complex (organ systems). Examples might include neurons for cells, nervous tissue for tissues, brain for organs, and nervous system for organ systems.

If your class subscribes to the iText, use it to review the Key Concepts in Section 35–1.

In the Body Could biological systems achieve homeostasis through feedback inhibition? Absolutely. All that is needed is a system that regulates some aspect of the cellular environment and that can respond to feedback from its own activities by switching on or off as needed.

Maintenance of homeostasis requires the integration of all organ systems at all times. One example is the maintenance of a stable body temperature. The body regulates temperature by a mechanism that is remarkably similar to that of a home heating system. A part of the brain called the hypothalamus contains nerve cells that monitor both the temperature of the skin at the surface of the body and the temperature of organs in the body's core. The temperature of the core is generally higher than the temperature of the skin.

If the nerve cells sense that the core temperature has dropped much below 37°C, the hypothalamus produces chemicals that signal cells throughout the body to speed up their activities. Heat produced by this increase in cellular activity causes a gradual rise in body temperature, which is detected by nerve cells in the hypothalamus. This feedback inhibits the production of the chemicals that speed up cellular activity and keeps body temperature from rising to a dangerous level.

Have you ever been so cold that you began to shiver? If your body temperature drops well below its normal range, the hypothalamus releases chemicals that signal muscles just below the surface of the skin to contract involuntarily—to "shiver." These muscle contractions release heat, which helps the body temperature to rise back toward the normal range.

If body temperature rises too far above 37°C, the hypothalamus slows down cellular activities, minimizing the production of heat. This is one of the main reasons you may feel tired and sluggish on a hot day. The body also responds to high temperatures by producing sweat, which helps to cool the body surface by evaporation. Because heat from the body's core is carried by the blood to the skin, evaporation at the body surface also helps to lower the temperature of the core. When this temperature returns to its set point, the body stops producing sweat.

Word Origins

Thermometer comes from the Greek words *therme,* meaning "heat," and *metron,* meaning "measure." So, thermometer means an instrument used to measure heat. **If *hypo-* is Greek for "under," what does *hypothermia* mean?**

35–1 Section Assessment

1. **Key Concept** Sequence the levels of organization in multicellular organisms.
2. **Key Concept** What is homeostasis?
3. Describe the functions of each of the eleven organ systems.
4. What are the four types of tissue?
5. **Critical Thinking Inferring** Look at the nervous tissue in **Figure 35–3.** Compare the cells of the nervous tissue to the cells of one of the other types of tissue. Which parts of an animal would contain these types of cells?

Thinking Visually

Making a Venn Diagram Draw a Venn diagram to relate the four basic levels of organization in the human body. Provide at least three examples for each level included in your diagram.

35–1 Section Assessment

1. The levels are cells, tissues, organs, and organ systems.
2. Homeostasis is the process by which organisms keep internal conditions relatively constant despite changes in external environments.
3. Students should state the functions of each of the eleven organ systems, as described in Figure 35–2.
4. The four types of tissues are epithelial, connective, nervous, and muscle.
5. Answers may vary. Cells of nervous tissue, as well as cells of each of the other types of tissues, would be found in the heart and in most other organs of an animal.

35–2 The Nervous System

BI 9.b. Students know how the nervous system mediates communication between different parts of the body and the body's interactions with the environment. **BI 9.d.** Students know the functions of the nervous system and the role of neurons in transmitting electrochemical impulses. **BI 9.e.** Students know the roles of sensory neurons, interneurons, and motor neurons in sensation, thought, and response.

Play any team sport—basketball, softball, soccer—and you will discover that communication is one of the keys to success. Coaches call plays, players signal to one another, and the very best teams communicate in a way that enables them to play as a single unit. Communication can make the difference between winning and losing.

The same is true for living organisms. Nearly all multicellular organisms have communication systems. Specialized cells carry messages from one cell to another so that communication among all body parts is smooth and efficient. In humans, these cells include those of the nervous system.  **The nervous system controls and coordinates functions throughout the body and responds to internal and external stimuli.**

CA (a)

Neurons

(a) BI 9.b

The messages carried by the nervous system are electrical signals called impulses. The cells that transmit these impulses are called **neurons.** Neurons can be classified into three types according to the direction in which an impulse travels. Sensory neurons carry impulses from the sense organs to the spinal cord and brain. Motor neurons carry impulses from the brain and the spinal cord to muscles and glands. Interneurons connect sensory and motor neurons and carry impulses between them. Although neurons come in all shapes and sizes, they have certain features in common. **Figure 35–5** shows a typical neuron. The largest part of a typical neuron is the **cell body.** The cell body contains the nucleus and much of the cytoplasm. Most of the metabolic activity of the cell takes place in the cell body.

Guide for Reading

 **Key Concepts**

- What are the functions of the nervous system?
- How is a nerve impulse transmitted?

Vocabulary

neuron
cell body
dendrite
axon
myelin sheath
resting potential
action potential
threshold
synapse
neurotransmitter

Reading Strategy: Summarizing As you read, find the main ideas for each paragraph. Write down a few key words from each main idea. Then, use the key words in your summary.

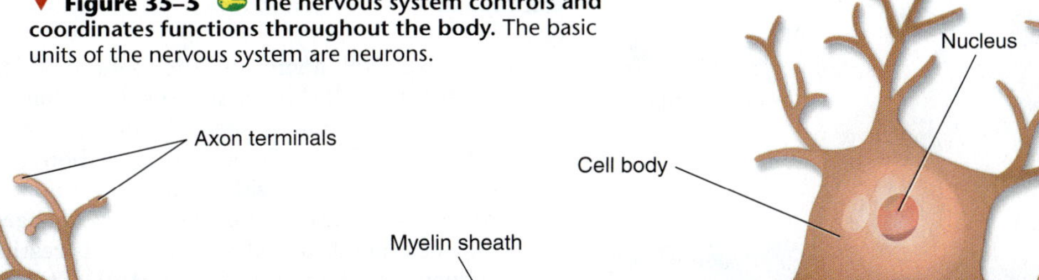

▼ **Figure 35–5** **The nervous system controls and coordinates functions throughout the body.** The basic units of the nervous system are neurons.

SECTION RESOURCES

Print:

- ***Teaching Resources,*** Lesson Plan 35–2, Adapted Section Summary 35–2, Adapted Worksheets 35–2, Section Summary 35–2, Worksheets 35–2, Section Review 35–2
- ***Reading and Study Workbook A,*** Section 35–2
- ***Adapted Reading and Study Workbook B,*** Section 35–2

Technology:

- ***iText,*** Section 35–2
- ***Animated Biological Concepts DVD,*** 48 Action Potential, 49 Synaptic Transmission
- ***Transparencies Plus,*** Section 35–2

Section 35–2

 BI 9.b, **BI 9.d, BI 9.e**

1 FOCUS

Objectives

35.2.1 ***Identify*** the functions of the nervous system.
35.2.2 ***Describe*** how a nerve impulse is transmitted.

Guide for Reading

Vocabulary Preview

Tell students that the prefix *neuro-* comes from the Greek word for nerve. Ask: **What do you think the Vocabulary terms *neuron* and *neurotransmitter* mean?** *(A neuron is a nerve cell; a neurotransmitter is a chemical that transmits messages from a neuron to another cell.)*

Reading Strategy

As students read, they should look for Vocabulary words and Key Concepts in the captions and the text. Suggest that students include the Vocabulary words and Key Concepts in their summary.

2 INSTRUCT

Demonstration

Help students appreciate how quickly the cells of the nervous system communicate. Have a volunteer repeat a movement, such as nodding the head, at irregular intervals. Have another volunteer respond to the first movement with a different movement, such as raising a finger. Challenge the class to measure the time it takes for the second volunteer's nervous system to sense, interpret, and respond to the movement made by the first volunteer. *(Students probably will find that the response time is too short to measure.)* L1 L2

Neurons

Use Visuals

Figure 35–5 Point out the nucleus in the cell body. Name each of the other parts of the neuron, and have students locate them in the figure. Urge students to refer to the figure as they read about the parts of a neuron and how they are involved in the transmission of nerve impulses.

35–2 (continued)

Download a worksheet on the nervous system for students to complete, and find additional teacher support from NSTA SciLinks.

Build Science Skills

Using Models Give interested students a chance to make a three-dimensional model of a neuron. Provide them with materials such as string, beads, dry pasta, and modeling clay. Remind students to provide a key for the parts of their model. Allow them to display their models in the classroom. L2

The Nerve Impulse

Use Visuals

Figure 35–6 Have students look at the distribution of potassium and sodium ions. Then, have them answer the question in the caption. Ask: **Why do you think the drawing has many sodium ions and one potassium ion outside the cell but one sodium ion and many potassium ions inside the cell?** *(To indicate that potassium ions diffuse across the cell membrane into the cell more easily than do sodium ions)* This difference in the ability of the positive ions to diffuse creates the difference in electrical charge across the cell membrane. L2

For: Links on the nervous system
Visit: www.SciLinks.org
Web Code: cbn-0352

Spreading out from the cell body are short, branched extensions called **dendrites.** Dendrites carry impulses from the environment or from other neurons toward the cell body. The long fiber that carries impulses away from the cell body is called the **axon.** The axon ends in a series of small swellings called axon terminals, located some distance from the cell body. Neurons may have dozens of dendrites but usually have only one axon. In most animals, axons and dendrites are clustered into bundles of fibers called nerves. Some nerves contain only a few neurons, but many others have hundreds or even thousands of neurons.

In some neurons, the axon is surrounded by an insulating membrane known as the **myelin** (MY-uh-lin) **sheath.** The myelin sheath that surrounds a single long axon leaves many gaps, called nodes, where the axon membrane is exposed. As an impulse moves along the axon, it jumps from one node to the next, which increases the speed at which the impulse can travel.

The Nerve Impulse

A nerve impulse is similar to the flow of electrical current through a metal wire. The best way to understand a nerve impulse is to first look at a neuron at rest.

The Resting Neuron When a neuron is resting (not transmitting an impulse), the outside of the cell has a net positive charge, and the inside of the cell has a net negative charge. The cell membrane is said to be electrically charged because there is a difference in electrical charge between its outer and inner surfaces. Where does this difference come from? Some of the differences come from the selective permeability of the membrane. Most of the differences, however, are the result of active transport of ions across the cell membrane.

The nerve cell membrane pumps sodium (Na^+) ions out of the cell and potassium (K^+) ions into the cell by means of active transport. The active transport mechanism that performs this pumping action is called the sodium-potassium pump, shown in **Figure 35–6.** As a result of active transport, the inside of the cell contains more K^+ ions and fewer Na^+ ions than the outside.

The neuron cell membrane allows more K^+ ions to leak across it than Na^+ ions. As a result, K^+ ions leak out of the cell to produce a negative charge on the inside of the membrane. Because of this, there is a positive charge on the outside of the membrane and a negative charge on the inside. The electrical charge across the cell membrane of a neuron in its resting state is known as the **resting potential** of the neuron. The neuron, of course, is not actually "resting," because it must produce a constant supply of ATP to fuel active transport.

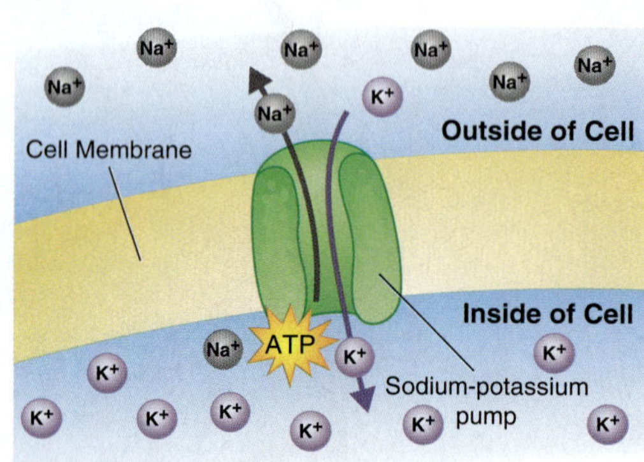

▼ **Figure 35–6** The sodium-potassium pump in the neuron cell membrane uses the energy of ATP to pump Na^+ out of the cell and, at the same time, to pump K^+ in. This ongoing process maintains resting potential. **Applying Concepts** *Is this process an example of diffusion or active transport?*

CHECKPOINT *What is resting potential?*

UNIVERSAL ACCESS

Less Proficient Readers
Provide students with a familiar way to visualize the concept of electrical potential in nerve impulses. Point out that a spring represents another type of energy potential: kinetic potential. Demonstrate by depressing and then releasing the spring. Ask: **What happens when the spring is released?** *(A burst of energy moves the spring back to its resting state.)* Explain how this is similar to a nerve impulse. L1 L2

English Language Learners
Have students compile a section glossary that includes all the highlighted, boldface terms and any technical terms used in the text or captions. Suggest that students write definitions in both English and their native language. Students also may find it helpful to illustrate their glossaries. Encourage active use of the terms by asking volunteers to share their glossaries with the rest of the class. L1 L2

The Moving Impulse A neuron remains in its resting state until it receives a stimulus large enough to start a nerve impulse. The impulse causes a movement of ions across the cell membrane. **An impulse begins when a neuron is stimulated by another neuron or by the environment.** Once it begins, the impulse travels rapidly down the axon away from the cell body and toward the axon terminals. As **Figure 35–7** shows, an impulse is a sudden reversal of the membrane potential. What causes the reversal?

The cell membrane of a neuron contains thousands of protein channels that may allow ions to pass through, depending on the state of "gates" within the channels. Generally, the gates within these channels are closed. At the leading edge of an impulse, however, gates within the sodium channels open, allowing positively charged Na^+ ions to flow inside the cell membrane. The inside of the membrane temporarily becomes more positive than the outside, reversing the resting potential. This reversal of charges, from negative to positive, is called a nerve impulse, or an **action potential.**

As the impulse passes, gates within the potassium channels open, allowing K^+ ions to flow out. This restores the resting potential so that the neuron is once again negatively charged on the inside of the cell membrane and positively charged on the outside.

A nerve impulse is self-propagating; that is, an impulse at any point on the membrane causes an impulse at the next point along the membrane. You could compare the flow of an impulse to the fall of a row of dominoes. As each domino falls, it causes the next domino to fall.

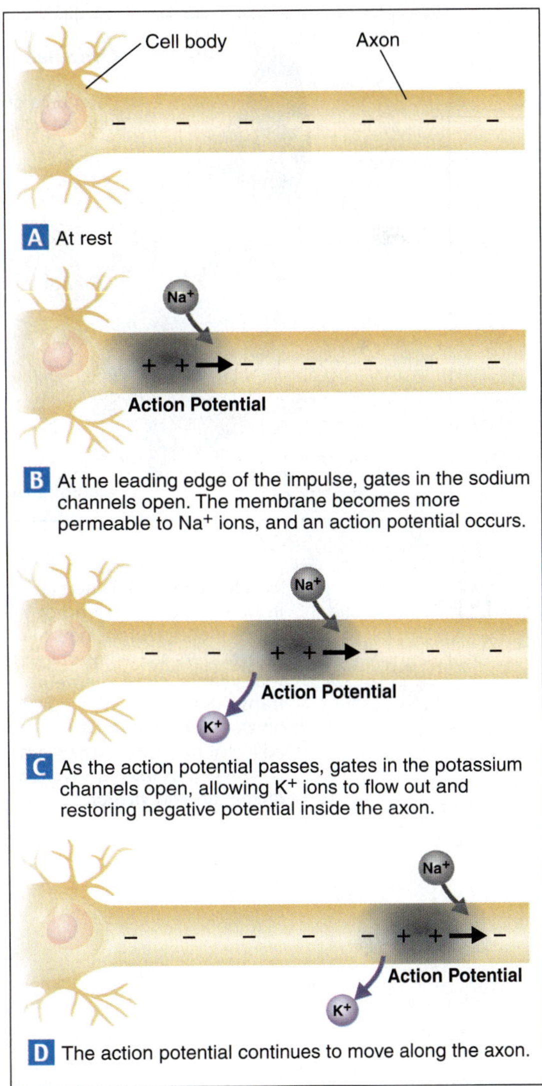

▲ **Figure 35–7** **An impulse begins when a neuron is stimulated by another neuron.**

Threshold The strength of an impulse is always the same—either there is an impulse in response to a stimulus or there is not. In other words, a stimulus must be of adequate strength to cause a neuron to transmit an impulse. The minimum level of a stimulus that is required to activate a neuron is called the **threshold.** Any stimulus that is stronger than the threshold will produce an impulse. Any stimulus that is weaker than the threshold will produce no impulse. Thus, a nerve impulse follows the all-or-none principle: Either the stimulus will produce an impulse, or it will not produce an impulse.

The all-or-none principle can be illustrated by using a row of dominoes. If you were to gently press the first domino in a row, it might not move at all. A slightly harder push might make the domino teeter back and forth but not fall. A slightly stronger push would cause the first domino to fall into the second. You have reached the threshold at which the row of dominoes would fall.

Use Visuals

Figure 35–7 Help students integrate the visuals with the text. Ask: **In part B of the figure, what causes the action potential to occur?** *(Positively charged Na^+ ions flow inside the cell membrane, causing the inside of the membrane to become more positive than the outside.)* **In part C, what causes the resting potential to occur again?** *(K^+ ions flow out of the cell membrane, causing the inside of the membrane to become negative again.)* L2

Demonstration

Use the domino analogy mentioned in the text to simulate the movement of an action potential down an axon. Arrange dominoes on end in a row, and then knock them down by giving the first one a gentle push. Ask: **Why did all the dominoes fall when only the first domino was pushed?** *(Because kinetic energy was passed from domino to domino)* **What was the source of the kinetic energy that was transmitted down the line of dominoes?** *(Some was provided by the push on the first domino, some by the position of the dominoes—standing on end, they were easily toppled by gravity when gently bumped.)* **What would you have to do in order to get the dominoes to topple again?** *(Return them to the starting position and provide an initial input of energy.)* L1 L2

For: Nerve Impulse activity
Visit: PHSchool.com
Web Code: cbe-0352
Students interact with the art online.

BACKGROUND

All or nothing
A nerve impulse usually is described as an all-or-nothing phenomenon. This means that there is a threshold level below which a stimulus cannot trigger an action potential. Any stimulus at or above the threshold level triggers exactly the same response. However, if a neuron has just fired, this picture changes. There is a period of a few milliseconds, called the absolute refractory period, during which no stimulus can produce a response, even a stimulus above the threshold level. Then, for a slightly longer period, the relative refractory period, an intense stimulus well above the threshold level is needed to provoke a response. The closer the neuron is to complete recovery, the less intense the stimulus must be to provoke a response. When the neuron is completely recovered, it responds in the all-or-nothing way once again.

Answers to . . .

CHECKPOINT *The difference in electrical charge across the cell membrane of a resting neuron*

Figure 35–6 *Active transport*

35–2 (continued)

The Synapse

Make Connections

Health Science Explain that many mental illnesses appear to be associated with abnormal levels of certain neurotransmitters. For example, depression is associated with lower-than-normal levels of serotonin and norepinephrine, and schizophrenia is associated with higher-than-normal levels of dopamine. Ask: **How do you think abnormal levels of neurotransmitters affect the functioning of the nervous system?** *(Students might say they would either decrease or increase the transmission of nerve impulses.)* L2

3 ASSESS

Evaluate Understanding

Call on students at random to define each of the Vocabulary terms. Call on other students to correct any errors.

Reteach

Provide students with copies of Figure 35–5 without the labels, and have them label each part of the neuron.

Thinking Visually

Students' flowcharts should include the following events: arrival of the nerve impulse at an axon terminal; release of neurotransmitters into the synaptic cleft; diffusion of neurotransmitters across the gap and attachment to receptors on a neighboring cell membrane; and movement of positive ions across that cell's membrane, causing stimulation of the neighboring cell.

If your class subscribes to the iText, use it to review the Key Concepts in Section 35–2.

Answer to . . .

Figure 35–8 *No; a motor neuron passes an impulse to a muscle cell.*

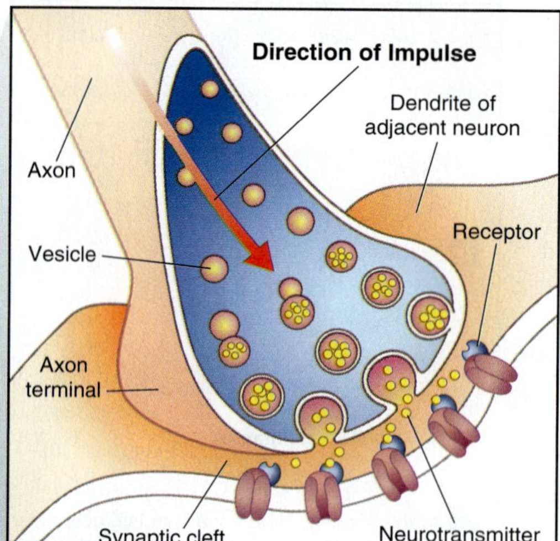

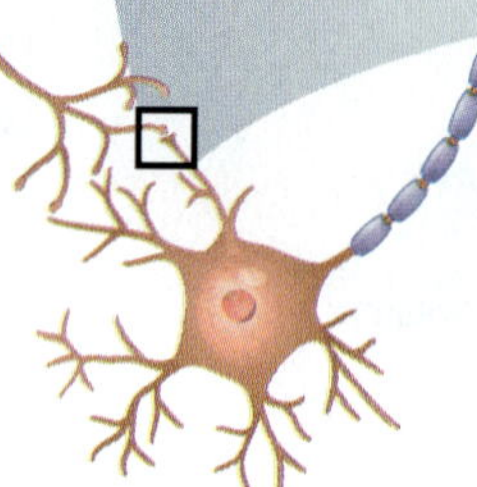

▲ **Figure 35–8** When an impulse reaches the end of the axon of one neuron, neurotransmitters are released into the synaptic cleft. The neurotransmitters bind to receptors on the membrane of an adjacent dendrite. **Applying Concepts** *Is the adjacent cell always another neuron?*

The Synapse

At the end of the neuron, the impulse reaches an axon terminal. Usually the neuron makes contact with another cell at this location. The neuron may pass the impulse along to the second cell. Motor neurons, for example, pass their impulses to muscle cells.

The location at which a neuron can transfer an impulse to another cell is called a **synapse** (SIN-aps). As shown in **Figure 35–8,** a space, called the synaptic cleft, separates the axon terminal from the dendrites of the adjacent cell, in this case a neuron. The terminals contain tiny sacs, or vesicles, filled with neurotransmitters (noo-roh-TRANZ-mit-urs). **Neurotransmitters** are chemicals used by a neuron to transmit an impulse across a synapse to another cell.

When an impulse arrives at an axon terminal, the vesicles release the neurotransmitters into the synaptic cleft. The neurotransmitter molecules diffuse across the synaptic cleft and attach themselves to receptors on the membrane of the neighboring cell. This stimulus causes positive sodium ions to rush across the cell membrane, stimulating the second cell. If the stimulation exceeds the cell's threshold, a new impulse begins.

Only a fraction of a second after binding to their receptors, the neurotransmitter molecules are released from the cell surface. They may then be broken down by enzymes, or taken up and recycled by the axon terminal.

35–2 Section Assessment

1. **Key Concept** Describe the functions of the nervous system.
2. **Key Concept** What happens when a neuron is stimulated by another neuron?
3. Name and describe the three types of neurons.
4. Describe the role of the myelin sheath.
5. **Critical Thinking Applying Concepts** How can the level of pain you feel vary if a stimulus causes an all-or-none response?

Thinking Visually

Creating a Flowchart
Create a flowchart to show the events that occur as a nerve impulse travels from one neuron to the next. Include as much detail as you can. Use your flowchart to explain the process to a classmate.

35–2 Section Assessment

1. The human nervous system controls and coordinates functions throughout the body and responds to internal and external stimuli.
2. If the stimulus is large enough, an impulse begins that travels rapidly along the axon toward the axon terminals, where the impulse is passed on to another cell.
3. Sensory neurons, motor neurons, and interneurons
4. The myelin sheath insulates the axon and greatly increases the speed of transmission of nerve impulses.
5. There are two possible factors: the number of sensory neurons activated by a stimulus and the frequency of the stimulation.

35–3 Divisions of the Nervous System

BI 9.b. Students know how the nervous system mediates communication between different parts of the body and the body's interactions with the environment. **BI 9.e. Students know the roles of sensory neurons, interneurons, and motor neurons in sensation, thought, and response.**

Neurons do not act alone. Instead, they are joined together to form a complex network—the nervous system. The human nervous system is separated into two major divisions: the central nervous system and the peripheral nervous system.

The central nervous system is the control center of the body. The functions of the central nervous system are similar to those of the central processing unit of a computer. **The central nervous system relays messages, processes information, and analyzes information.** The peripheral nervous system receives information from the environment and relays commands from the central nervous system to organs and glands.

CA a

Guide for Reading

Key Concepts

- What are the functions of the central nervous system?
- What are the functions of the two divisions of the peripheral nervous system?

Vocabulary

meninges • cerebrospinal fluid
cerebrum • cerebellum
brain stem • thalamus
hypothalamus • reflex
reflex arc

Reading Strategy: Asking Questions Before you read, rewrite the headings in the section as *how, why,* or *what* questions about the nervous system. As you read, write down the answers to your questions.

The Central Nervous System

The central nervous system consists of the brain, shown in **Figure 35–9**, and the spinal cord. The skull and vertebrae in the spinal column protect the brain and spinal cord. Both the brain and spinal cord are wrapped in three layers of connective tissue known as **meninges** (muh-NIN-jeez). Between the meninges and the central nervous system tissue is a space filled with cerebrospinal (sehr-uh-broh-SPY-nul) fluid. **Cerebrospinal fluid** bathes the brain and spinal cord and acts as a shock absorber that protects the central nervous system. The fluid also allows for the exchange of nutrients and waste products between blood and nervous tissue.

▼ **Figure 35–9** **The brain helps to relay messages, process information, and analyze information.** The brain consists of the cerebrum, cerebellum, and brain stem.

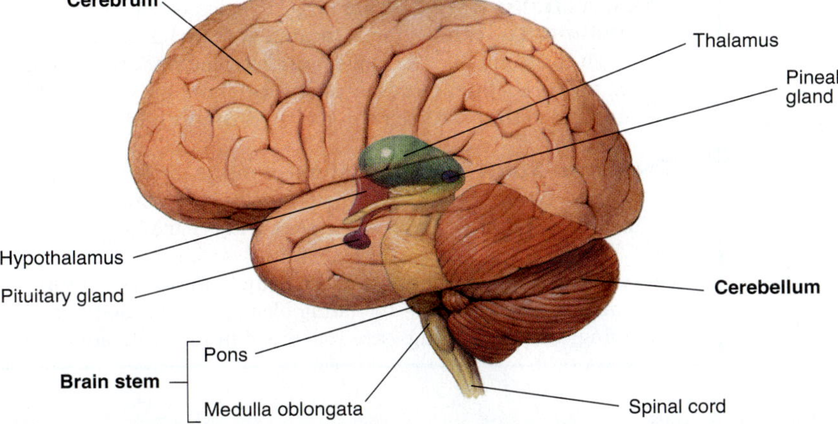

SECTION RESOURCES (TIME SAVER)

Print:

- ***Laboratory Manual A,*** Chapter 35 Lab
- ***Laboratory Manual B,*** Chapter 35 Lab
- ***Teaching Resources,*** Lesson Plan 35–3, Adapted Section Summary 35–3, Adapted Worksheets 35–3, Section Summary 35–3, Worksheets 35–3, Section Review 35–3
- ***Reading and Study Workbook A,*** Section 35–3
- ***Adapted Reading and Study Workbook B,*** Section 35–3
- ***Issues and Decision Making,*** Issues and Decisions 44

Technology:

- ***iText,*** Section 35–3
- ***Transparencies Plus,*** Section 35–3

Section 35–3

BI 9.b, BI 9.e

1 FOCUS

Objectives

35.3.1 ***Identify*** the functions of the central nervous system.

35.3.2 ***Describe*** the functions of the two divisions of the peripheral nervous system.

Guide for Reading

Vocabulary Preview

Point out that all of the Vocabulary terms refer to structures within the brain except for two terms. Ask: **Which two terms do not refer to structures in the brain?** (*Reflex and reflex arc*) Challenge students to predict what these two terms might mean, and then have them check to see if they were correct as they read the section.

Reading Strategy

Possible questions students might write include: What are the parts of the central nervous system? *(The brain and the spinal cord)* What is the role of the brain? *(It is the main switching unit of the central nervous system.)* What is the function of the spinal cord? *(It is the main communications link between the brain and the rest of the body.)* What structures make up the peripheral nervous system? *(All the nerves and associated cells that are not part of the brain and the spinal cord)*

2 INSTRUCT

The Central Nervous System

Use Visuals

Figure 35–9 Point out the location of the cerebrum and cerebellum. Explain that the brain stem is the region in front of the cerebellum that contains the pons and medulla oblongata. Ask: **Which part of the human brain is the largest part?** *(Cerebrum)* **Where in the brain are structures with endocrine function located?** *(Above the brain stem)*

35–3 (continued)

The Brain

Build Science Skills

Calculating Help students appreciate how the folds in the brain greatly increase its surface area. First, have students measure the sides of a small box, such as a cereal box or shoe box, and use the measurements to calculate its surface area. Next, have students stuff the box with folded sheets of newspaper until the box is full. Then, have students count the number of sheets of newspaper and find their total area (by multiplying the number of sheets by the area of one sheet). Students should add this number to the surface area of the box. Ask: **How much was the surface area increased by the folded sheets?** *(Exact answers will vary. Students will find that the surface area was increased greatly by the addition of the folded sheets.)* L2 L3

Use Community Resources

Invite a diagnostic imaging technician to visit the class and explain how brain injuries, tumors, and other abnormalities of the brain are diagnosed. Ask the visitor to describe MRIs and CT scans and what they reveal about the brain. If possible, have the visitor bring sample images or scans to share with students. Urge students to take notes during the talk and later use the notes to write a summary of what they learned. L2

Download a worksheet on the human brain for students to complete, and find additional teacher support from NSTA SciLinks.

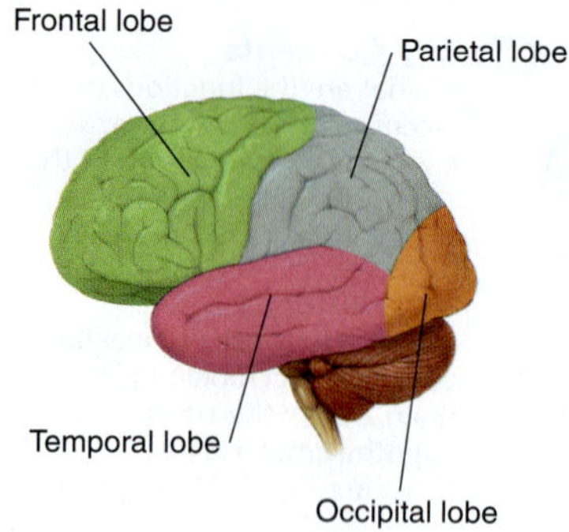

▲ **Figure 35–10** This view of the cerebrum shows the four different lobes of the brain. Different functions of the body are controlled by different lobes of the brain. **Drawing Conclusions** ***The frontal lobe controls voluntary muscle movements. What might happen if this part of the brain became injured?***

ⓐ BI 9.b

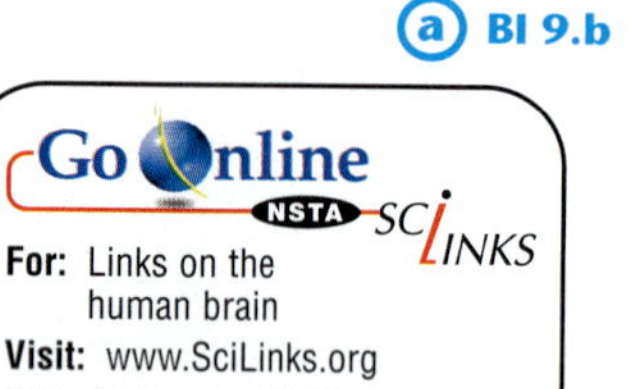

For: Links on the human brain
Visit: www.SciLinks.org
Web Code: cbn-0353

The Brain

The brain is the place to which impulses flow and from which impulses originate. The brain contains approximately 100 billion neurons, many of which are interneurons. The brain has a mass of about 1.4 kilograms.

The Cerebrum The largest and most prominent region of the human brain is the **cerebrum.** The cerebrum is responsible for the voluntary, or conscious, activities of the body. It is the site of intelligence, learning, and judgment. A deep groove divides the cerebrum into right and left hemispheres. The hemispheres are connected by a band of tissue called the corpus callosum.

Folds and grooves on the surface of each hemisphere greatly increase the surface area of the cerebrum. Each hemisphere of the cerebrum is divided into regions called lobes. The lobes are named for the skull bones that cover them. The locations of four lobes of the brain are shown in **Figure 35–10.**

Remarkably, each half of the cerebrum deals mainly with the opposite side of the body. Sensations from the left side of the body go to the right hemisphere of the cerebrum, and those from the right side of the body go to the left hemisphere. Commands to move muscles are generated in the same way. The left hemisphere controls the body's right side, and the right hemisphere controls the body's left side. Some studies have suggested that the right hemisphere may be associated with creativity and artistic ability, whereas the left hemisphere may be associated with analytical and mathematical ability.

The cerebrum consists of two layers. The outer layer of the cerebrum is called the cerebral cortex and consists of gray matter. Gray matter consists mainly of densely packed nerve cell bodies. The cerebral cortex processes information from the sense organs and controls body movements. The inner layer of the cerebrum consists of white matter, which is made up of bundles of axons with myelin sheaths. The myelin sheaths give the white matter its characteristic color. White matter connects the cerebral cortex and the brain stem.

CA ⓐ

The Cerebellum The second largest region of the brain is the **cerebellum.** The cerebellum is located at the back of the skull. Although the commands to move muscles come from the cerebral cortex, the cerebellum coordinates and balances the actions of the muscles so that the body can move gracefully and efficiently.

The Brain Stem The **brain stem** connects the brain and spinal cord. Located just below the cerebellum, the brain stem includes two regions known as the pons and the medulla oblongata. Each of these regions regulates the flow of information between the brain and the rest of the body. Some of the body's most important functions—including blood pressure, heart rate, breathing, and swallowing—are controlled in the brain stem.

UNIVERSAL ACCESS

Inclusion/Special Needs

Use a hands-on experience to help students understand the functions of the somatic and autonomic nervous systems. First, have students raise one hand over their heads. Tell them that this behavior is voluntary and controlled by the somatic nervous system. Then, have them feel their pulse to detect their heartbeat. Explain that the beating of their heart is involuntary and controlled by the autonomic nervous system. L1

Less Proficient Readers

The organization of the peripheral nervous system may be confusing to less proficient readers. Have them create a concept map to show how it is subdivided, including the sensory and motor divisions, somatic and autonomic nervous systems, and sympathetic and parasympathetic nervous systems. After they have completed their concept maps, call on students to name the function of each subdivision. L1 L2

The Thalamus and Hypothalamus The thalamus and hypothalamus are found between the brain stem and the cerebrum. The **thalamus** receives messages from all of the sensory receptors throughout the body and then relays the information to the proper region of the cerebrum for further processing. Just below the thalamus is the hypothalamus. The **hypothalamus** is the control center for recognition and analysis of hunger, thirst, fatigue, anger, and body temperature. The hypothalamus also controls the coordination of the nervous and endocrine systems. You will learn more about the endocrine system in a later chapter.

CA a

The Spinal Cord

Like a major telephone line that carries thousands of calls at once, the spinal cord is the main communications link between the brain and the rest of the body. Thirty-one pairs of spinal nerves branch out from the spinal cord, connecting the brain to all of the different parts of the body. Certain kinds of information, including some kinds of reflexes, are processed directly in the spinal cord.

A **reflex** is a quick, automatic response to a stimulus. Sneezing and blinking are two examples of reflexes. A reflex allows your body to respond to danger immediately, without spending time thinking about a response. Animals rely heavily on reflex behaviors for survival.

CHECKPOINT *What is a reflex?*

The Peripheral Nervous System

The peripheral nervous system lies outside of the central nervous system. It consists of all of the nerves and associated cells that are not part of the brain and the spinal cord. Included here are cranial nerves that pass through openings in the skull and stimulate regions of the head and neck, spinal nerves, and ganglia. Ganglia are collections of nerve cell bodies.

The peripheral nervous system can be divided into the sensory division and the motor division. **The sensory division of the peripheral nervous system transmits impulses from sense organs to the central nervous system. The motor division transmits impulses from the central nervous system to the muscles or glands.** The motor division is further divided into the somatic nervous system and the autonomic nervous system.

The Somatic Nervous System The somatic nervous system regulates activities that are under conscious control, such as the movement of the skeletal muscles. Every time you lift your finger or wiggle your toes, you are using the motor neurons of the somatic nervous system. Some somatic nerves are also involved with reflexes and can act with or without conscious control.

Quick Lab

How do you respond to an external stimulus?

Materials sheet of scrap paper

Procedure

1. Have your partner put on safety goggles.
2. Crumple up a sheet of scrap paper into a ball.
3. Watch your partner's eyes carefully as you toss the paper ball toward his or her face. Record your partner's reaction.
4. Repeat step 3, three more times.
5. Exchange roles and repeat steps 1, 3, and 4.

Analyze and Conclude

1. **Observing** What reaction did you observe when you tossed the ball at your partner's face?
2. **Observing** Was that reaction voluntary? What kind of reaction is this?
3. **Comparing and Contrasting** Did you see any change in behavior as you repeated step 3? If so, how would you describe this change?
4. **Inferring** What is the function of the blink reflex?

BI 9.e

BIO INSIGHTS — HISTORY OF SCIENCE

Broca's area
In the middle of the nineteenth century, Paul Broca, a French neurologist, discovered that a small region just above the sylvian fissure of the left frontal lobe of the cerebral cortex controls the ability to speak words correctly (rather than sounds). This area is now called Broca's area. Broca made his discovery by studying people with brain damage who had lost the ability to speak. He also studied split-brain patients—people whose hemispheres were no longer physically connected due to brain damage. Broca's discovery of this speech area was important for two reasons. It provided some of the first evidence that the left and right hemispheres of the brain have separate functions, and it was one of the first indicators that particular brain functions are localized in specific regions of the brain.

The Spinal Cord

Quick Lab

BI 9.e

Objective Students will be able to describe a common reflex and explain its function.

Skills Focus **Observing, Inferring**

Materials Sheet of scrap paper

Time 10 minutes

Safety Make sure students put on their safety goggles before the paper ball is thrown at them.

Expected Outcome Students who have the ball thrown at them should automatically blink.

Analyze and Conclude

1. The partner blinked when the paper ball was thrown at him or her.
2. The reaction happened involuntarily. Therefore, it is an automatic response, or reflex.
3. After several repetitions, the partner may not blink because he or she expects the stimulus and is able to control the response.
4. The function of the blink reflex is to help protect the eyes from injury.

Demonstration

With the help of a student volunteer, demonstrate the knee-jerk reflex. Ask students to observe how quickly the reflex occurs. Explain that this is because it is processed directly in the spinal cord and not in the brain.

The Peripheral Nervous System

Build Science Skills

Applying Concepts Challenge students to explain how a person with a healthy peripheral nervous system could lack nervous control of the leg muscles due to a spinal cord injury.

Answers to . . .

CHECKPOINT *A quick, automatic response to a stimulus that is processed in the spinal cord*

Figure 35–10 *There might be less control over voluntary muscle movements, such as walking and writing.*

Quick Lab

BI 9.e, 6IIE 7.e, 8IIE 9.b, BIIE 1.d, BIIE 1.g

Objective Students will be able to conclude that a stronger stimulus does not produce a stronger nerve impulse.

Skills Focus Drawing Conclusions, Evaluating, Applying Concepts

Materials string, packing tape, scissors, 30-cm ruler, 3 plastic mousetraps

Time 20 minutes

Safety Show students how to hold the traps open safely with one hand while using the other hand to insert a string through the bait platform.

Strategy If students are working with a partner or in groups, make sure each student has a chance to set off the trap in step 3 in order to appreciate the all-or-nothing nature of the "reflex" response.

Expected Outcome Students should find that only a tug greater than a certain threshold triggers the mousetraps.

Analyze and Conclude

1. A sufficiently strong tug is required. This level of force can be compared with the threshold level of stimulus required to activate a neuron.
2. A stronger stimulus does not produce a stronger impulse because the response of a neuron is an all-or-nothing response.
3. Answers will vary. Students may say the procedure is not an adequate model because it is slower than an actual reflex arc or because it uses mechanical instead of electrical impulses.
4. Students should say that they handled the scissors carefully and did not let the mousetrap snap on their fingers.

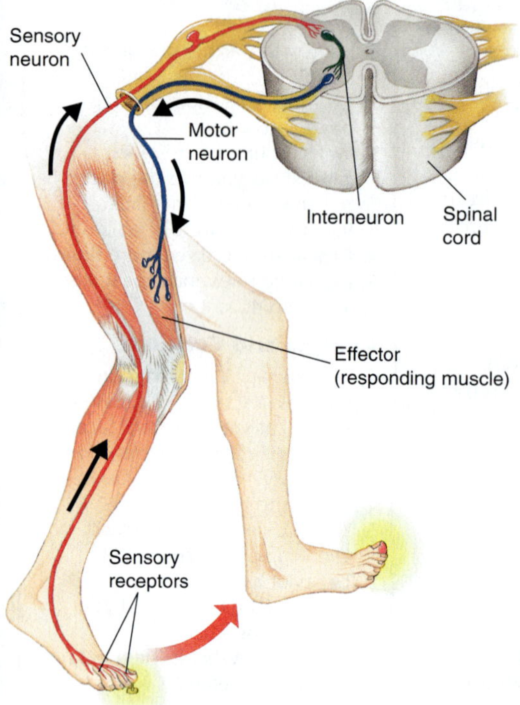

▲ **Figure 35–11** **The peripheral nervous system transmits impulses from sense organs to the central nervous system and back to muscles or glands.** When you step on a tack, sensory receptors stimulate a sensory neuron, which relays the signal to an interneuron within the spinal cord. The signal is then sent to a motor neuron, which in turn stimulates a muscle in your leg to lift your leg.

If you accidentally step on a tack with your bare foot, your leg may recoil before you are aware of the pain. This rapid response (a reflex) is possible because receptors in your skin stimulate sensory neurons, which carry the impulse to your spinal cord. Even before the information is relayed to your brain, a group of neurons in your spinal cord automatically activates the appropriate motor neurons. These motor neurons cause the muscles in your leg to contract, pulling your foot away from the tack.

The pathway that an impulse travels from your foot back to your leg is known as a reflex arc. As shown in **Figure 35–11**, a **reflex arc** includes a sensory receptor (in this case, a receptor in your toe), sensory neuron, motor neuron, and effector (leg muscle). Some reflex arcs include interneurons. In other reflex arcs, a sensory neuron communicates directly with a motor neuron.

The Autonomic Nervous System The autonomic nervous system regulates activities that are automatic, or involuntary. The nerves of the autonomic nervous system control functions of the body that are not under conscious control. The influence exerted on other body systems by the autonomic nervous system is a good example of an interrelationship that is needed between systems for the body's well-being. For instance, when you are running, the autonomic nervous system speeds up your heart rate and the blood flow to the skeletal muscles, stimulates the sweat glands and adrenal glands, and slows down the contractions of the smooth muscles in the digestive system.

The autonomic nervous system is further subdivided into two parts—the sympathetic nervous system and the parasympathetic nervous system. Most organs controlled by the autonomic nervous system are under the control of both sympathetic and parasympathetic neurons.

The sympathetic and parasympathetic nervous systems have opposite effects on the same organ system. The opposing effects of the two systems help the body maintain homeostasis. For example, heart rate is increased by the sympathetic nervous system but decreased by the parasympathetic nervous system. The process of regulating heart rate can be compared to the process of controlling the speed of a car. One system is like the gas pedal and the other is like the brake. Because there are two different sets of neurons, the autonomic nervous system can quickly speed up the activities of major organs in response to a stimulus or slam on the brakes if necessary.

CA a

a BI 9.b

TEACHER TO TEACHER

In order to test reaction time, I divide the class into pairs of students. One student should rest his or her elbow on a table and extend his or her arm over the side of the table. The second student should hold a meter stick in the air and release it unexpectedly. The first student should try to catch the meter stick between the thumb and index finger. Use the equation: Δ time = (Δ distance)/(9.8 m/s^2). After each person has calculated his or her reaction time, have students record their times in a chart on the chalkboard to see who has the best reaction time in the class. Using the meter stick and a physics equation allows the students to see the relationship between physics and biology.

—Charlotte Parnell
Biology Teacher
Lakeside High School
Hot Springs, AR

Quick Lab

BI 9.e, 6IIE 7.e, 8IIE 9.b, BIIE 1.d, BIIE 1.g

How do reflexes occur?

Materials string, scissors, 3 plastic mousetraps, packing tape, 30-cm ruler

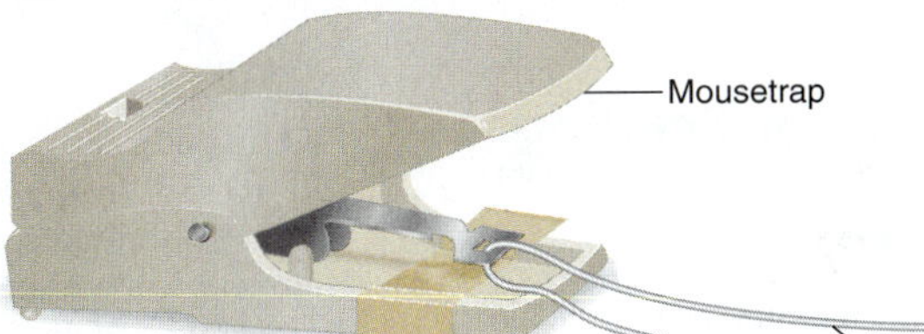

Procedure 

1. **Using Models** To model a synapse, cut a 30-cm piece of string. **CAUTION:** *Handle scissors carefully.*
2. Hold a mousetrap open. Pull the string through the bait platform as shown. **CAUTION:** *Do not let the mousetrap snap on your fingers.* Slide a piece of tape under the bait platform and tape the trap to the table as shown. Label the trap "sensory neuron."
3. Hold one end of the string in each hand. Gently pull one end without setting off the trap. Now gradually pull harder.
4. To model a reflex arc, cut two more 30-cm pieces of string. Tie one end of each piece of string to the bait platform of a separate trap.
5. Tape the 2 new traps to the table, 20 cm from the first trap. Label one new trap "motor neuron," and the other "brain."
6. Reset the first trap, and then set the new ones. Tape both ends of the strings attached to the new traps to the top of the first trap. Leave these strings slightly slack.
7. Pull the strings attached to the bait platform of the "sensory neuron."

Analyze and Conclude

1. **Drawing Conclusions** What was required for the trap to close in step 3? How does this behavior compare to the transmission of a nerve impulse?
2. **Applying Concepts** Does a stronger stimulus produce a stronger nerve impulse? Explain your answer.
3. **Evaluating** Do you consider this procedure an adequate model of a reflex arc? Explain your response by citing specific details. If not, propose an alternative model.
4. **SAFETY** Explain how you demonstrated safe practices as you carried out this investigation.

35–3 Section Assessment

1. **Key Concept** Discuss the overall function of the central nervous system.
2. **Key Concept** Describe the functions of the two divisions of the peripheral nervous system.
3. How is the central nervous system protected from injury?
4. What is the role of the hypothalamus?
5. Is a reflex part of the central nervous system, the peripheral nervous system, or both? Explain.
6. **Critical Thinking Inferring** Would you expect the cerebrum of a bird to be more or less developed relative to its size than the cerebrum of a human? Explain. (*Hint:* You may want to review Section 33–3.)

Focus on the BIG Idea

Structure and Function Using Section 34–1, decide which parts of the nervous system are most likely to be involved with innate, or inborn, behaviors. Which parts are likely to be involved with learned behaviors? Explain your reasoning.

35–3 Section Assessment

1. To relay messages and to process and analyze information
2. The sensory division transmits impulses from sense organs to the central nervous system. The motor division transmits impulses from the central nervous system to muscles.
3. It is protected by the skull and vertebrae, the meninges, and the cerebrospinal fluid.
4. It recognizes and analyzes hunger, thirst, fatigue, anger, and body temperature. It also controls the coordination of the nervous and endocrine systems.
5. Both, because it involves sensory and motor neurons of the peripheral system and is processed in the spinal cord
6. Less developed, because birds have less ability to think and learn than humans do

Build Science Skills

Observing Demonstrate the pupillary reflex, which is the automatic widening or narrowing of the pupil of the eye when the amount of light falling on it changes. Ask several volunteers to cover their eyes with a blindfold and keep their eyes closed. After a few minutes, have the volunteers uncover and open their eyes while the other students observe what happens to the size of the volunteers' pupils. Ask: **How did the size of their pupils change?** *(They were wide at first and gradually narrowed.)* **How long did the change take?** *(Several seconds)* 

3 ASSESS

Evaluate Understanding

Ask students to make a concept map of the divisions and subdivisions of the nervous system.

Reteach

Have each student create a crossword puzzle using the Vocabulary terms. Then, have students exchange and solve the puzzles.

Focus on the BIG Idea

Reflex arcs are most likely to be involved with innate behaviors, which are functional the first time they are performed. The brain plays a major role in learned behaviors, which depend on data collected through experience being processed and analyzed.

If your class subscribes to the iText, use it to review the Key Concepts in Section 35–3.

Section 35–4

BI 9.e

1 FOCUS

Objectives

35.4.1 ***Name*** the five types of sensory receptors.

35.4.2 ***Identify*** the five sense organs.

Guide for Reading

Vocabulary Preview

Ask: **Which Vocabulary terms refer to parts of the eye?** *(Pupil, lens, retina, rod, and cone)* **Which terms refer to parts of the ear?** *(Cochlea, semicircular canal)*

Reading Strategy

Have students preview the section by studying the figures and reading the captions.

2 INSTRUCT

Build Science Skills

Applying Concepts Ask students to imagine they are at a picnic on a beautiful summer day with a picnic basket full of their favorite foods. Then, ask: **How might the different categories of your sensory receptors be stimulated at the picnic?** *(Students may say, for example, that their thermoreceptors might be stimulated by holding a cold drink and their chemoreceptors by smelling and tasting food.)* L1 L2

Vision

Make Connections

Physics Explain that light is part of the electromagnetic spectrum, which includes electromagnetic waves of different wavelengths. Add that humans can see only light that falls within a very limited range of wavelengths and that light in this range is called visible light. L2 L3

35–4 The Senses

BI 9.e. Students know the roles of sensory neurons, interneurons, and motor neurons in sensation, thought, and response.

Guide for Reading

Key Concept
- What are the five types of sensory receptors?

Vocabulary
sensory receptor
pupil
lens
retina
rod
cone
cochlea
semicircular canal
taste bud

Reading Strategy: Outlining Before you read, use the headings of the section to make an outline about the five sense organs. As you read, fill in the subtopics and smaller topics. Then, add phrases or a sentence after each to provide key information.

The body contains millions of neurons that react directly to stimuli from the environment, including light, sound, motion, chemicals, pressure, and changes in temperature. These neurons, known as **sensory receptors,** react to a specific stimulus such as light or sound by sending impulses to other neurons, and eventually to the central nervous system. Sensory receptors are located throughout the body but are concentrated in the sense organs. These sense organs include the eyes, the inner ears, the nose, the mouth, and the skin. Sensory receptors within each organ enable it to respond to a particular stimulus.

There are five general categories of sensory receptors: pain receptors, thermoreceptors, mechanoreceptors, chemoreceptors, and photoreceptors. Pain receptors are located throughout the body except in the brain. Pain receptors respond to chemicals released by damaged cells. Pain is important to recognize because it usually indicates danger, injury, or disease. Thermoreceptors are located in the skin, body core, and hypothalamus. Thermoreceptors detect variations in temperature. Mechanoreceptors are found in the skin, skeletal muscles, and inner ears. They are sensitive to touch, pressure, stretching of muscles, sound, and motion. Chemoreceptors, located in the nose and taste buds, are sensitive to chemicals in the external environment. Photoreceptors, found in the eyes, are sensitive to light. **Figure 35–12** shows how photoreceptor cells appear under a scanning electron microscope.

Vision

The world around us is bathed in light. The sense organs that we use to sense light are the eyes. The structures of the eye are shown in **Figure 35–13.** Light enters the eye through the cornea, a tough transparent layer of cells. The cornea helps to focus the light, which then passes through a chamber filled with a fluid called aqueous (AY-kwee-uhs) humor. At the back of the chamber is a disklike structure called the iris. The iris is the colored part of the eye. In the middle of the iris is a small opening called the **pupil.** Tiny muscles in the iris adjust the size of the pupil to regulate the amount of light that enters the eye. In dim light, the pupil becomes larger so that more light can enter the eye. In bright light, the pupil becomes smaller so that less light enters the eye.

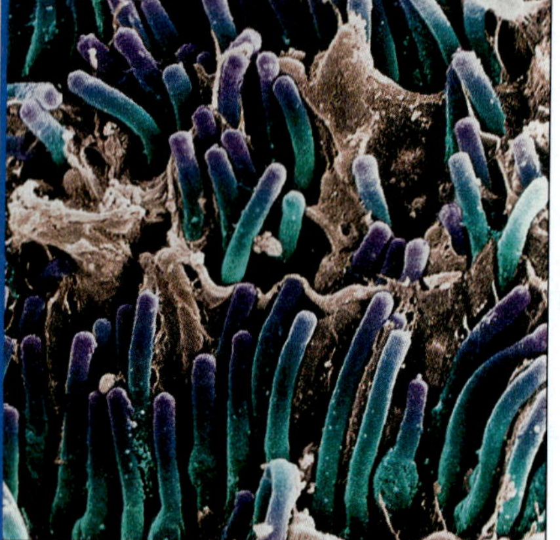

(magnification: 2000×)

Figure 35–12 **There are two types of light-sensitive photoreceptor cells in the retina—rods and cones.** This color-enhanced scanning electron micrograph shows the rod cells of an eye.

TIME SAVER — SECTION RESOURCES

Print:
- ***Teaching Resources,*** Lesson Plan 35–4, Adapted Section Summary 35–4, Adapted Worksheets 35–4, Section Summary 35–4, Worksheets 35–4, Section Review 35–4, Enrichment
- ***Reading and Study Workbook A,*** Section 35–4
- ***Adapted Reading and Study Workbook B,*** Section 35–4
- ***Lab Worksheets,*** Chapter 35 Real-World Lab

Technology:
- ***iText,*** Section 35–4
- ***Transparencies Plus,*** Section 35–4

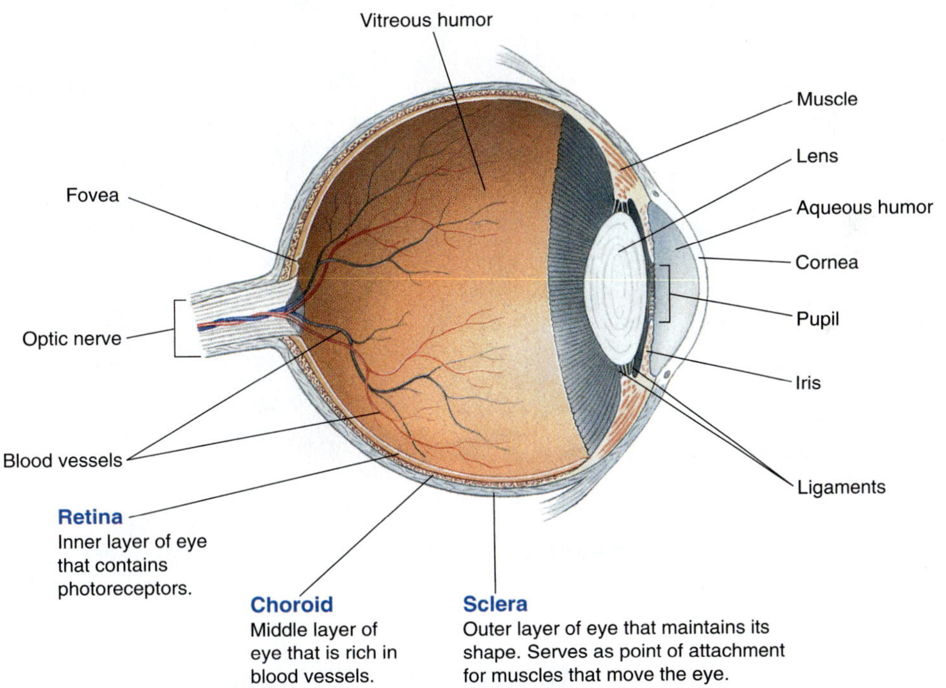

▲ **Figure 35–13** The eye is a complicated sense organ. The sclera, choroid, and retina are three layers of tissue that form the inner wall of the eyeball. **Interpreting Graphics** *What is the function of the sclera?*

Just behind the iris is the **lens.** Small muscles attached to the lens change its shape to help you adjust your eyes' focus to see near or distant objects. Behind the lens is a large chamber filled with a transparent, jellylike fluid called vitreous (VIH-tree-uhs) humor.

The lens focuses light onto the **retina.** Photoreceptors are arranged in a layer in the retina. The photoreceptors convert light energy into nerve impulses that are carried to the central nervous system. There are two types of photoreceptors: rods and cones. **Rods** are extremely sensitive to light, but they do not distinguish different colors. **Cones** are less sensitive than rods, but they do respond to light of different colors, producing color vision. Cones are concentrated in the fovea. The fovea is the site of sharpest vision. There are no photoreceptors where the optic nerve passes through the back of the eye. This place is called the blind spot.

The impulses assembled by this complicated layer of interconnected cells leave each eye by way of an optic nerve. The optic nerves then carry the impulses to the appropriate regions of the brain. The brain interprets them as visual images and provides information about the external world.

CHECKPOINT *Where are the photoreceptors located in the eye?*

For: Links on the senses
Visit: www.SciLinks.org
Web Code: cbn-0354

Use Visuals

Figure 35–13 Ask students to locate the three layers of tissue (*sclera, choroid, and retina*) that form the inner wall of the eyeball. Then, have students trace the path of light through the eye. Call on students to identify each of the structures the light passes through. Finally, ask: **What purpose do the muscles around the lens serve?** *(They change the shape of the lens to help the eye focus to see near or distant objects.)* **Where does the lens focus the light?** *(On the retina)* **What happens to the impulses after they leave the eye by way of the optic nerve?** *(They go to the appropriate regions of the brain, where the visual images are interpreted.)* L2

Build Science Skills

Using Analogies Ask: **If the lens of the eye is analogous to a projector, what part of the eye is analogous to the screen?** *(The retina)* **How is the image projected on the screen different from the image projected on the retina?** *(There are no receptors on the screen to convert the image into electrical impulses.)* L2

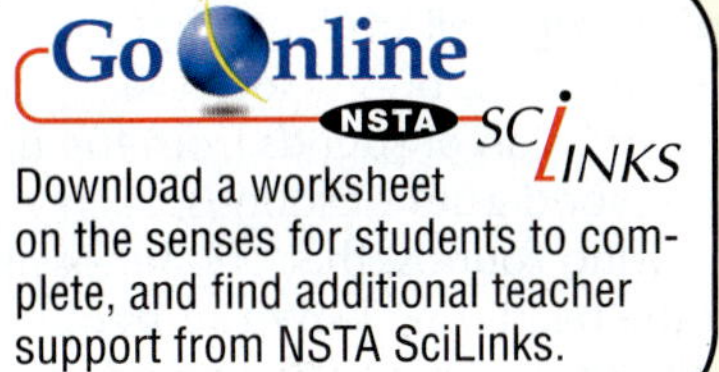

Download a worksheet on the senses for students to complete, and find additional teacher support from NSTA SciLinks.

UNIVERSAL ACCESS

Inclusion/Special Needs
Help students understand the terms for sensory receptors by writing the following prefixes on the board: *thermo-*, *mechano-*, *chemo-*, and *photo-*. Challenge students to think of words that begin with these or similar prefixes, such as *thermometer* and *mechanic*. List the words on the board. Then, ask students to define the prefixes based on the meanings of those words. L1

Advanced Learners
Give students who need an extra challenge an opportunity to investigate surgical methods for correcting vision problems, including photorefractive keratectomy (PRK) and laser in situ keratomileusis (LASIK). Encourage students to present their findings to the class in an oral report, with diagrams showing how the procedures correct specific vision problems. L3

Answers to . . .

CHECKPOINT *The retina*

Figure 35–13 *The function of the sclera is to maintain the shape of the eye and serve as a point of attachment for muscles that move the eye.*

35–4 (continued)

Hearing and Balance

Use Visuals

Figure 35–14 Name the structures that sound waves pass through after they enter the ear. As you name each structure, ask: **What role does this structure play in hearing?** *(Students might say, for example, that the auditory canal channels the sound waves to the tympanum and that the tympanum vibrates in response to the sound waves.)* L2

Make Connections

Health Science Explain that the region of the ear called the middle ear, which is the area between the tympanum and the semicircular canals, is prone to infections. This is because of the close connection between the middle ear and the eustachian tube, which originates in the throat. Viruses and bacteria in the throat can easily travel to the middle ear through the eustachian tube and cause infections, inflammation, and pain. L2

Build Science Skills

Inferring Tell students that middle-ear infections often block the transmission of sounds from the outside world but not sounds, such as chewing sounds, that originate within the head. Ask: **Why can people hear "head" sounds even when their ears are blocked because of an infection?** *(Because the sound waves are transmitted directly to the inner ear through the bones of the head)* L2

Demonstration

Half fill a glass container with water and, as students watch, slowly tilt the container from side to side. Because the water always stays parallel to the floor due to gravity, students will observe it move up and down the sides of the glass as the glass tilts. Explain that this is also how the fluid inside the semicircular canals moves as the head changes position. L1 L2

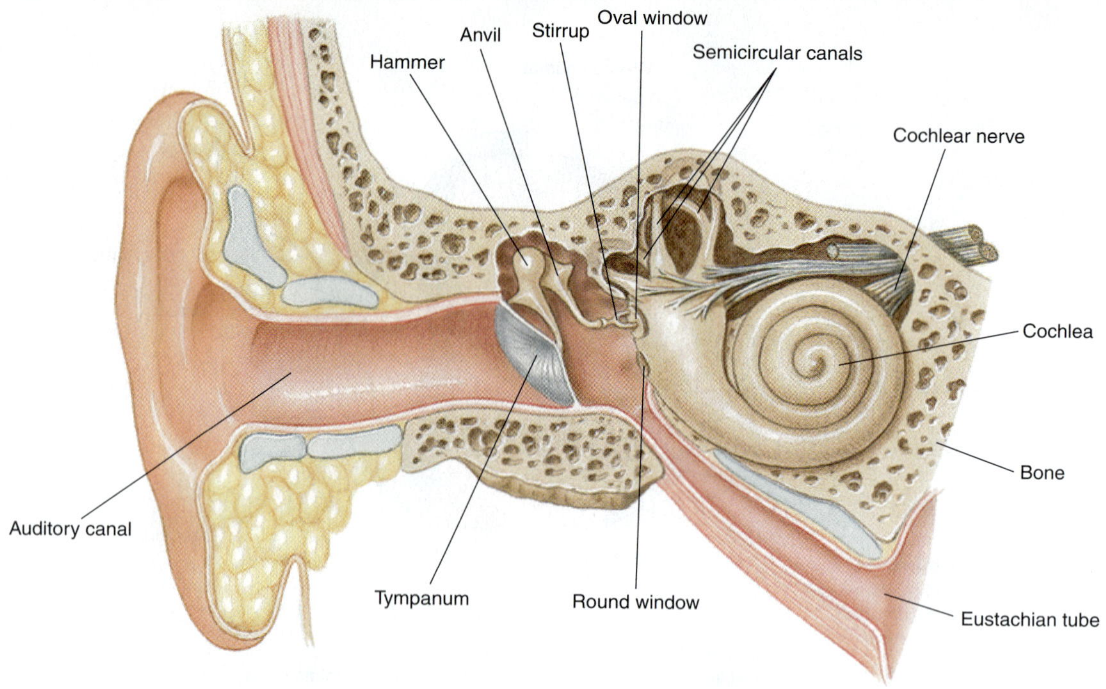

(magnification: about 3500×)

Figure 35–14 The diagram (top) shows the structures in the ear that transmit sounds. The scanning electron micrograph shows hair cells (yellow) in the inner ear. The motion of these hairs produces nerve impulses that travel to the brain through the cochlear nerve. **Predicting** *How would frequent exposure to loud noise affect a person's threshold for detecting sound?*

Hearing and Balance

The human ear has two sensory functions. One of these functions is hearing. The other function is detecting positional changes associated with movement.

Hearing Sound is nothing more than vibrations in the air around us. The ears are the sensory organs that can distinguish both the pitch and loudness of those vibrations. The structure of the ear is shown in **Figure 35–14.**

Vibrations enter the ear through the auditory canal. The vibrations cause the tympanum (TIM-puh-num), or eardrum, to vibrate. These vibrations are picked up by three tiny bones, commonly called the hammer, anvil, and stirrup. The last of these bones, the stirrup, transmits the vibrations to the oval window. Vibrations of the oval window create pressure waves in the fluid-filled **cochlea** (KAHK-lee-uh) of the inner ear.

The cochlea is lined with tiny hair cells that are pushed back and forth by these pressure waves. In response to these movements, the hair cells produce nerve impulses that are sent to the brain through the cochlear nerve.

Balance Your ears contain structures that help your central nervous system maintain your balance, or equilibrium. Within the inner ear just above the cochlea are three tiny canals at right angles to one another. They are called **semicircular canals** because each forms a half circle. The semicircular canals and the two tiny sacs located behind them monitor the position of your body, especially your head, in relation to gravity.

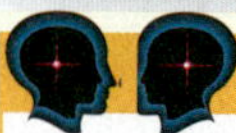

TEACHER TO TEACHER

When I teach about the senses, I give students a chance to experience sensory "fatigue." I have students rest a penny on the inside of the forearm against the skin and measure how long it takes until they can no longer sense the presence of the coin. When everyone is finished, we discuss why sensory fatigue occurs and when it is useful (for example, when you are wearing clothing). I also demonstrate sensory fatigue with the sense of smell. I ask a volunteer to come to the front of the room and hold one nostril closed while I hold a bottle of oil of wintergreen (available at pharmacies) under the other nostril. The class measures the time it takes until the volunteer can no longer distinguish the smell of wintergreen.

—Duane Nichols
Biology Teacher
Alhambra High School
Alhambra, CA

The semicircular canals and the sacs are filled with fluid and lined with hair cells. As the head changes position, the fluid in the canals also changes position. This causes the hair on the hair cells to bend. This action, in turn, sends impulses to the brain that enable it to determine body motion and position.

Smell and Taste

You may never have thought of it this way, but your sense of smell is actually an ability to detect chemicals. Chemoreceptors in the lining of the nasal passageway respond to specific chemicals and send impulses to the brain through sensory nerves.

Your sense of smell is capable of producing thousands of different sensations. In fact, much of what we commonly call the "taste" of food and drink is actually smell. To prove this to yourself, eat a few bites of food while holding your nose. You'll discover that much of the taste of food disappears until you open your nose and breathe freely.

Like the sense of smell, the sense of taste is a chemical sense. The sense organs that detect taste are the **taste buds.** Most of the taste buds are on the tongue, but a few are found at other locations in the mouth. The surface of the tongue is shown in **Figure 35–15.** The tastes detected by the taste buds are classified as salty, bitter, sweet, and sour. Sensitivity to these different categories varies on different parts of the tongue.

Touch and Related Senses

The sense of touch, unlike the other senses you have just read about, is not found in one particular place. All of the regions of the skin are sensitive to touch. In this respect, your largest sense organ is your skin. Skin contains sensory receptors that respond to temperature, touch, and pain. Not all parts of the body are equally sensitive to touch, because not all parts have the same number of receptors. The greatest density of touch receptors is found on your fingers, toes, and face.

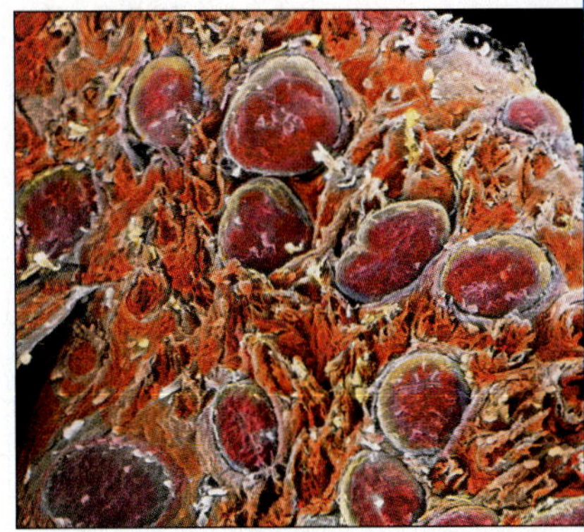

(magnification: 86×)

▲ **Figure 35–15** This color-enhanced scanning electron micrograph shows the surface of the tongue. The large pink objects are the taste buds. **Chemoreceptors found in the taste buds are sensitive to chemicals in food.**

35–4 Section Assessment

1. **Key Concept** Name the five types of sensory receptors and list where they are found in the body.
2. Identify the functions of the cornea, pupil, lens, retina, and optic nerve.
3. What are the four basic tastes detected by the tongue?
4. Explain why you can't "taste" food when you have a bad cold.
5. **Critical Thinking Applying Concepts** If you spin around for a time, the fluid in your semicircular canals also moves. When you stop suddenly, you feel as though you are still moving. Why do you think you might feel dizzy?

Writing in Science

Creative Writing

Imagine that you have to do without your sense of taste for one day. How would this influence your food choices? Write a 3- to 4-paragraph essay describing how the absence of this sense organ would affect your day.

Smell and Taste

Demonstration

Have volunteers taste and try to identify a variety of different fruit juices while wearing blindfolds and pinching their noses shut. *(Without sight cues and the sense of smell, students will find it difficult to distinguish the tastes.)* L2

Touch and Related Senses

Build Science Skills

Designing Experiments Challenge students to design an experiment to determine the distribution of heat and cold receptors in a small area of skin on the back of the hand. L2 L3

3 ASSESS

Evaluate Understanding

Provide students with copies of Figure 35–13 without the labels. Have students label each part of the eye shown in the figure.

Reteach

On the chalkboard or an overhead transparency, list five general categories of sensory receptors. Have students give examples of each category of receptors at work. *(For chemoreceptors, for example, students might say smelling a flower or tasting food.)*

Writing in Science

Answers will vary. For example, students might describe how their sense of taste is affected and how this, in turn, affects their enjoyment of food and their appetite.

35–4 Section Assessment

1. Pain receptors: everywhere except the brain; thermoreceptors: skin, body core, hypothalamus; mechanoreceptors: skin, skeletal muscles, inner ears; chemoreceptors: nose, taste buds; photoreceptors: eyes
2. Cornea: helps to focus light; pupil: controls the amount of light that enters the eye; lens: adjusts focus for near or far distances; retina: rod and cone photoreceptors convert light into electrical impulses; optic nerve: carries the electrical impulses to the brain
3. The four basic taste receptors are receptors for salty, bitter, sweet, and sour tastes.
4. Because much of the sense of taste is actually due to interaction with the sense of smell
5. Sensory receptors lag behind the rapid changes in position.

If your class subscribes to the iText, use it to review the Key Concepts in Section 35–4.

Answer to . . .

Figure 35–14 *Loud noises can damage tiny hair cells and raise the threshold for detecting sounds.*

Section 35–5

1 FOCUS

Objectives

35.5.1 ***Name*** the different classes of drugs that directly affect the nervous system.

35.5.2 ***Describe*** the effect of alcohol on the body.

Guide for Reading

Vocabulary Preview

Challenge students to predict how the Vocabulary terms *addiction* and *drug abuse* differ. As they read, they should check to see if their predictions were correct.

Reading Strategy

In their tables, students should list stimulants, depressants, cocaine, opiates, marijuana, and alcohol. They should read the Key Concepts for the effects that each drug has on the body.

2 INSTRUCT

Drugs That Affect the Synapse

Address Misconceptions

Many people do not think of alcohol and nicotine as drugs because both can be used legally. Address this misconception by pointing out that alcohol and nicotine are potentially addictive drugs that can have extremely harmful effects on the body, including liver damage and lung cancer. Alcohol and nicotine are also among the most widely used drugs, making their harmful effects more devastating. L2

Make Connections

Health Science Tell students that a number of prescription drugs also affect neurotransmitters, including antidepressant drugs, which are among the most widely prescribed medications, helping people not only with depression but also with eating disorders, drug addictions, and other mental disorders. L2

35–5 Drugs and the Nervous System

Guide for Reading

Key Concepts

- What are the different classes of drugs that directly affect the central nervous system?
- What is the effect of alcohol on the body?

Vocabulary

drug
stimulant
depressant
fetal alcohol syndrome
drug abuse
addiction

Reading Strategy: Using Graphic Organizers

As you read, create a table that lists each of the drugs in this section and the effects that each drug has on the body.

By definition, a **drug** is any substance, other than food, that changes the structure or function of the body. Some drugs, such as cocaine and heroin, are so powerful and dangerous that their possession is illegal. Other drugs, including penicillin and codeine, are prescription drugs and can be used only under the supervision of a doctor. Still other drugs, including cough and cold medicines, are sold over the counter. All drugs, both legal and illegal, have the potential to do harm if they are used improperly or abused.

Drugs differ in the ways in which they affect the body. Some drugs kill bacteria and are useful in treating disease. Other drugs affect a particular system of the body, such as the digestive or circulatory systems. Among the most powerful drugs, however, are the ones that cause changes in the nervous system, especially to the brain and the synapses between neurons.

Drugs That Affect the Synapse

The nervous system performs its regulatory functions through the transmission of information along pathways from one part of the body to another. Synapses are key relay stations along the way. The nervous system depends on neurotransmitters to bridge the gap between neurons or between a neuron and an effector. A drug that interferes with the action of neurotransmitters can disrupt the functioning of the nervous system.

Stimulants A number of drugs, called **stimulants,** increase the actions regulated by the nervous system. **Stimulants increase heart rate, blood pressure, and breathing rate. In addition, stimulants increase the release of neurotransmitters at some synapses in the brain.** This release leads to a feeling of energy and well-being. When the effects of stimulants wear off, however, the brain's supply of neurotransmitters has been depleted. The user quickly falls into fatigue and depression. Long-term use can cause circulatory problems, hallucinations, and psychological depression.

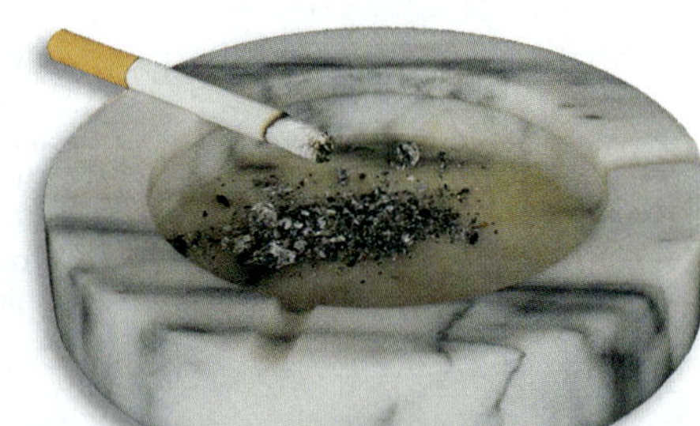

Figure 35–16 Common stimulant drugs include amphetamines, cocaine, nicotine (found in cigarettes), and caffeine (found in coffee, tea, chocolate, and cola products). **Stimulants increase heart rate, blood pressure, and breathing rate.**

TIME SAVER — SECTION RESOURCES

Print:

- ***Teaching Resources,*** Lesson Plan 35–5, Adapted Section Summary 35–5, Adapted Worksheets 35–5, Section Summary 35–5, Worksheets 35–5, Section Review 35–5
- ***Reading and Study Workbook A,*** Section 35–5
- ***Adapted Reading and Study Workbook B,*** Section 35–5
- ***Issues and Decision Making,*** Issues and Decisions 8, 41, 42

Technology:

- ***iText,*** Section 35–5
- ***Transparencies Plus,*** Section 35–5

Depressants Some drugs, called **depressants,** decrease the rate of functions regulated by the brain. **Depressants slow down heart rate and breathing rate, lower blood pressure, relax muscles, and relieve tension.** Some depressants enhance the effects of neurotransmitters that prevent some nerve cells from starting action potentials. This calms parts of the brain that sense fear and relaxes the individual. As a result, the user comes to depend on the drug to relieve the anxieties of everyday life, which may seem unbearable without the drug. When depressants are used with alcohol, the results are often fatal because that combination can depress the activity of the central nervous system until breathing stops.

CHECKPOINT *What is the general function of a depressant?*

Cocaine Even stronger effects are produced by drugs that act on neurons in what are known as the pleasure centers of the brain. The effects of cocaine are so strong that they produce an uncontrollable craving for more of the drug. Cocaine is obtained from the leaves of coca plants. **Cocaine causes the sudden release in the brain of a neurotransmitter called dopamine.** Normally, this compound is released when a basic need, such as hunger or thirst, is fulfilled. By fooling the brain into releasing dopamine, cocaine produces intense feelings of pleasure and satisfaction. So much dopamine is released when the drug is used that the supply of dopamine is depleted when the drug wears off. Users quickly discover that they feel sad and depressed without the drug. The psychological dependence that cocaine produces is difficult to break.

Cocaine also acts as a powerful stimulant, increasing heart rate and blood pressure. The stimulation can be so powerful that the heart is damaged. Sometimes, even a first-time user may experience a heart attack after using cocaine.

A particularly potent and dangerous form of cocaine is crack. Crack becomes addictive after only a few doses. The intense "high" produced by crack wears off quickly and leaves the brain with too little dopamine. As a result, the user suddenly feels sad and depressed, and quickly seeks another dose of the drug. In time, the urge to seek this drug can be so strong that it leads users to commit serious crimes and to abandon their families and children.

Opiates The opium poppy, like the one shown in **Figure 35–17,** produces a powerful class of pain-killing drugs called opiates. **Opiates mimic natural chemicals in the brain known as endorphins, which normally help to overcome sensations of pain.** The first doses of these drugs produce strong feelings of pleasure and security, but the body quickly adjusts to the higher levels of endorphins. Once this happens, the body cannot do without the drug. A user who tries to stop taking these drugs will suffer from uncontrollable pain and sickness because the body cannot produce enough of the natural endorphins.

Figure 35–17 Many illegal drugs are found in nature. Cocaine comes from the South American *Erythroxylum coca* plant (top). The centers of opium poppies (below) contain pods from which opiate drugs are derived. **Opiates mimic endorphins, which help overcome pain.** For this reason, opiates are often used medically as painkillers.

Build Science Skills

Drawing Conclusions Point out that many prescription drugs—including tranquilizers, sedatives, sleep medications, cough suppressants, and pain relievers—come with labels warning consumers to avoid the use of alcohol while taking the medications. If possible, show students examples of prescription-drug bottles with alcohol-warning labels. Then, ask: **Why is it dangerous to combine such drugs with alcohol?** *(Because both alcohol and certain drugs are nervous system depressants, and their combined effects can so depress the nervous system that breathing stops)* L2

Address Misconceptions

Students may believe that using a drug only once or a few times cannot hurt them. Explain that some drugs, such as heroin and crack cocaine, are extremely addictive and may produce a craving for the drug after only one use. In addition, illegal drugs can contain other harmful substances (contaminants) that may cause sudden death. L2

UNIVERSAL ACCESS

Less Proficient Readers
Simplify the discussion of how drugs affect the synapse. Explain that most of the drugs mentioned in the text either increase or decrease the transmission of nerve impulses across synapses and, thereby, either speed up or slow down the nervous system. Drugs that speed up the nervous system include stimulants, cocaine, and nicotine. Drugs that slow down the nervous system include depressants, opiates, and alcohol. L1 L2

Advanced Learners
Challenge students to find out more about Fetal Alcohol Syndrome (FAS). For example, students might research the incidence of FAS and how the risk of having a baby with FAS rises with the amount of alcohol that a pregnant woman consumes. Encourage students to share the results of their research with the class by writing a brochure warning pregnant women of the dangers of alcohol consumption. L3

Answer to . . .

CHECKPOINT *A depressant decreases the rate of functions regulated by the brain.*

35–5 (continued)

Use Visuals

Figure 35–18 Ask students to read about the effects on the body of the different types of commonly abused drugs. Then, guide them in applying the information by asking: **How might someone behave who is taking stimulant drugs?** *(The person might be fidgety and restless and eat very little.)* **How might someone behave who is taking depressant drugs?** *(The person might be slow moving and sleepy and speak indistinctly.)* **What particular abilities might be impaired by the two different types of drugs?** *(Stimulants might impair the ability to relax and sleep, and depressants might impair the ability to concentrate and drive.)* L2

Build Science Skills

Making Judgments Have students find and read five newspaper articles that relate to alcohol in some way. For example, they might find articles that report on a new alcohol treatment program, a teen killed by a drunk driver, or an increase in underage drinking. Challenge students to use the information provided in the articles to write a brief report summarizing some of the effects of alcohol abuse on society. L2 L3

Address Misconceptions

Many people think that black coffee or a cold shower can sober up someone who is intoxicated by alcohol. Explain that the body breaks down alcohol at a rate that depends on the person's weight and metabolism. Black coffee and a cold shower cannot increase this rate or sober up an intoxicated person more quickly. L2

Commonly Abused Drugs

Drug Type	Medical Use	Examples	Effects on the Body
Stimulants	Used to increase alertness, relieve fatigue	Amphetamines	Increases heart and respiratory rates, elevates blood pressure, dilates pupils, and decreases appetite
Depressants	Used to relieve anxiety, irritability, tension	Barbiturates Tranquilizers	Slows down the actions of the central nervous system; small amounts cause calmness and relaxation; larger amounts cause slurred speech and impaired judgment
Opiates	Used to relieve pain	Morphine Codeine	Acts as a depressant; causes drowsiness, restlessness, nausea

▲ **Figure 35–18** Legal drugs that are used for medical purposes can also be abused. **Applying Concepts** *Do you think a person can become addicted to a legal drug?*

Marijuana Statistically, the most widely abused illegal drug is marijuana. Marijuana comes from *Cannabis sativa,* a species of hemp plant. Hashish, or hash, is a potent form of marijuana made from the flowering parts of the plant. The active ingredient in all forms of marijuana is tetrahydrocannabinol (THC). Smoking or ingesting THC can produce a temporary feeling of euphoria and disorientation. Smoking marijuana is bad for the lungs. In fact, smoking marijuana is even more destructive to the lungs than smoking tobacco. Long-term use of marijuana can also result in loss of memory; inability to concentrate; and, in males, reduced levels of the hormone testosterone.

CHECKPOINT *What are the long-term effects of marijuana use?*

Alcohol One of the most dangerous and abused legal drugs is alcohol. The most immediate effects of alcohol are on the central nervous system. **Alcohol is a depressant that slows down the rate at which the central nervous system functions.** Alcohol slows down reflexes, disrupts coordination, and impairs judgment. Heavy drinking fills the blood with so much alcohol that the central nervous system cannot function properly. People who have two or three drinks in the span of an hour may feel relaxed and confident, but their blood contains as much as 0.10 percent alcohol, making them legally drunk in most states. They usually cannot walk or talk properly, and they are certainly not able to safely control an automobile, as shown in **Figure 35–19.**

The abuse of alcohol has a frightening social price. About 40 percent of the 50,000 people who die on American highways in a typical year are victims of accidents in which at least one driver had been drinking. One third of all homicides can be attributed to the effects of alcohol. When health care, property damage, and lost productivity are considered, alcohol abuse costs the U.S. economy at least $150 billion per year.

▲ **Figure 35–19** **Alcohol slows down the rate at which the central nervous system functions.** It slows down reflexes, disrupts coordination, and impairs judgment. For this reason, you should never get into a car with a driver who has been drinking.

BIO INSIGHTS — BACKGROUND

Effects of some drugs

Some drugs, such as anesthetics and certain environmental toxins, including chlorinated hydrocarbons that are found in pesticides, can make neurons more or less likely to respond to electrical impulses. Often this is because the substance affects the permeability of membranes to calcium ions. When permeability is decreased so that there is a lower-than-normal concentration of calcium ions, sodium channels may not close completely between action potentials, allowing sodium ions to cross the membrane. This makes the neurons fire more readily, and muscle spasms may result. When membrane permeability is increased and the calcium ion concentration is higher than normal, the opposite result occurs; neurons become less excitable and more difficult to fire.

But the toll of alcohol abuse does not stop there. Women who are pregnant and drink on a regular basis run the risk of having a child with fetal alcohol syndrome. **Fetal alcohol syndrome** (FAS) is a group of birth defects caused by the effects of alcohol on the fetus. Babies born with FAS can suffer from heart defects, malformed faces, delayed growth, and poor motor development. In the United States alone, more than 50,000 babies are born every year with alcohol-related birth defects, many of which are irreversible.

Alcohol and Disease People who have become addicted to alcohol suffer from a disease called alcoholism. Some alcoholics feel the need to have a drink before work or school—every day. They may drink so heavily that they black out and cannot remember what they have done while drinking. Some alcoholics, however, do not drink to the point where it is obvious that they have an alcohol-abuse problem. If a person cannot function properly without satisfying the need or craving for alcohol, that person is considered to have an alcohol-abuse problem.

Long-term alcohol use destroys cells in the liver, where alcohol is broken down. As liver cells die, the liver becomes less able to handle large amounts of alcohol. The formation of scar tissue, known as cirrhosis of the liver, occurs next. The scar tissue blocks the flow of blood through the liver and interferes with its other important functions. Eventually, a heavy drinker may die from liver failure.

Analyzing Data

Blood Alcohol Concentration

Blood alcohol concentration (BAC) is a measure of the amount of alcohol in the bloodstream per 100 mL of blood. A BAC of 0.1 percent means that one tenth of 1.0 percent of the fluid in the blood is alcohol. In some states, if a driver has a BAC of 0.08 percent, he or she is considered legally drunk. In other states, drivers with a BAC of 0.10 percent are considered drunk. The graph shows the relative risk of being involved in a fatal accident as a result of the blood alcohol concentration of the driver.

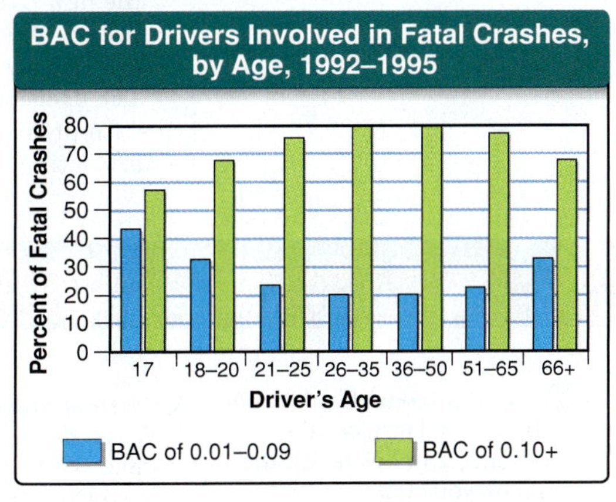

1. **Using Tables and Graphs** What trends do you see in the number of fatal crashes from age 17 to age 66+ based on the two ranges of BAC?
2. **Using Tables and Graphs** How does the consumption of alcohol affect driving risk for the average driver?
3. **Drawing Conclusions** Is the effect of alcohol consumption on driving independent of the age of the driver? Are young drivers more affected by alcohol or less affected by it than older drivers?
4. **Making Judgments** All levels of alcohol consumption affect driving skills, although the effect increases dramatically as more drinks are consumed. To minimize accidents and fatalities due to drunk driving, what should be the legal limit of blood alcohol for drivers?

Analyzing Data

Have students find out the BAC for the legal limit of blood alcohol for drivers in their state. Check students' understanding of what BAC means by asking: **If a person has a BAC of 0.1, how much alcohol is present in all 5 liters of his or her blood?** *(5 mL of alcohol)* L2 L3

Answers

1. At the higher BAC range, the percent of fatal car crashes increases from ages 17 to 35, levels off until age 50, and then starts to decline. At the lower BAC range, the percent of fatal car crashes decreases from ages 17 to 35, levels off until age 50, and then starts to rise.
2. For the average driver, there is a greater risk of fatal crashes at the higher BAC range.
3. No, the effect is not independent of the age of the driver. Young drivers are more affected by lower levels of alcohol and less affected by higher levels than older drivers are.
4. Students probably will say that the legal limit of blood alcohol should be less than 0.09 percent.

Answers to . . .

CHECKPOINT *Lung damage, loss of memory, inability to concentrate, and reduced levels of testosterone in males*

Figure 35–18 *Yes, a person can become addicted to legal drugs, including amphetamines, barbiturates, tranquilizers, morphine, and codeine.*

35–5 (continued)

Download a worksheet on drugs and drug abuse for students to complete, and find additional teacher support from NSTA SciLinks.

Drug Abuse

Use Community Resources

Encourage interested students to investigate drug abuse treatment options available in their community. Suggest that they start by looking in the Yellow Pages under *Drug Abuse and Addiction Information and Treatment Centers*. Urge students to share what they learn by creating posters called "Help for Drug Abuse and Addiction." Display their posters in the classroom. L2

3 ASSESS

Evaluate Understanding

Have students create a flowchart to show how a stimulant or depressant drug affects the synapse.

Reteach

Name each type of drug described in the text, including stimulants, depressants, cocaine, opiates, marijuana, and alcohol. Challenge students to identify one or more harmful effects of each type of drug.

Writing in Science

Students' brochures should clearly identify the negative short- and long-term effects of the drug they have chosen. These effects should be well supported with specific relevant facts from credible scientific research. The facts should be used to make a convincing argument persuading the reader to avoid taking the drug.

If your class subscribes to the iText, use it to review the Key Concepts in Section 35–5.

For: Links on drugs and drug abuse
Visit: www.SciLinks.org
Web Code: cbn-0355

As with other drugs, dealing with alcohol abuse is not simply a matter of willpower. Alcoholics often need special help and support to quit their drinking habit. Organizations such as Alcoholics Anonymous are available in most communities to help individuals and families deal with the problems created by alcohol abuse.

Drug Abuse

Each of the drugs discussed so far presents a danger to users. The misuse of either a legal or an illegal drug is a serious problem in modern society. **Drug abuse** can be defined as the intentional misuse of any drug for nonmedical purposes. With some drugs, such as cocaine, drug abuse causes serious physical damage to the body. With other drugs, such as marijuana, drug abuse produces psychological dependence that can be strong enough to disrupt family life and schoolwork.

An uncontrollable dependence on a drug is known as a drug **addiction.** Some drugs cause a strong psychological dependence. People who are psychologically dependent on a drug have a mental craving, or need, for the drug. Other drugs cause a strong physical dependence. Physical dependence occurs when the body cannot function without a constant supply of the drug. Any attempt at withdrawal, or stopping the use of the drug, will cause pain, nausea, chills, and fever.

Because many users inject drugs for maximum effect, there is another important consequence of drug use—the increased transmission of human immunodeficiency virus (HIV), the virus that causes AIDS. The virus can be spread rapidly from person to person when drug users share contaminated needles. Many of the new AIDS cases reported in the United States can be traced back to the use of injected drugs.

The best way to avoid the effects of drugs is to avoid drugs. The decision not to use drugs can be difficult when you are faced with pressure to take them. By deciding not to take drugs, you are acting to take control of your life.

35–5 Section Assessment

1. **Key Concept** Describe the effects of stimulants, cocaine, depressants, and opiates on the central nervous system.
2. **Key Concept** Explain the effects of alcohol on the body.
3. What is a drug?
4. Why is drinking and driving an extremely dangerous behavior?
5. **Critical Thinking Inferring** Which do you think is a more difficult addiction to break: one in which a person is physically dependent on a drug, or one in which a person is psychologically dependent on a drug? Explain your answer.

Writing in Science

Persuasive Writing
Research one of the drugs mentioned in this section to find out more about the short- and long-term effects of the drug on the body. Then, develop an informational brochure trying to persuade someone not to take the drug. *Hint:* Be sure to include specific facts.

35–5 Section Assessment

1. Stimulants increase the release of neurotransmitters, cocaine causes the sudden release of dopamine, depressants enhance the effects of certain neurotransmitters, and opiates mimic endorphins.
2. As a depressant, alcohol slows down the rate at which the central nervous system functions.
3. Any substance other than food that causes a change in the body
4. Because alcohol slows down reflexes, disrupts coordination, and impairs judgment
5. Some students might say a psychological dependence is more difficult to break. Others might say a physical dependence is more difficult to break. Students should support their conclusions with sound reasoning.

Real-World Lab

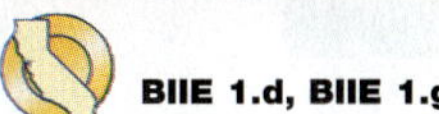
BIIE 1.d, BIIE 1.g

Modeling Corrective Lenses

The lenses of your eyes focus light on the retina. In people who are nearsighted, the lens focuses images in front of the retina, making distant objects appear blurry. In people who are farsighted, the lens focuses images behind the retina, making nearby objects difficult to see. To see more clearly, these people wear glasses or contact lenses. The shapes of these artificial lenses depend on the type of correction needed.

Problem **What types of corrective lenses are needed by nearsighted individuals and by farsighted individuals?**

Materials

- tape
- 2 cardboard photo easels
- black construction paper
- unruled white index card
- 6-V light bulb and socket
- 6-V battery and wires with alligator clips
- 2 convex lenses
- modeling clay
- meter stick
- concave lens

Skills Analyzing Data, Using Models

Procedure  

1. Set up your equipment as shown in the diagram below. Place the white index card about 50 to 60 cm in front of the bulb.
2. Place a convex lens in front of the bulb and move the lens until an image of the bulb focuses clearly on the index card. Secure the lens in this position with modeling clay or tape. The distance between the fixed lens and the index card is the focal length of the lens.
3. Move the index card about 5 to 8 cm away from the fixed lens to simulate the formation of an image in front of the retina. Observe the image and record your observations.
4. Hold the concave lens between the light bulb and the fixed lens. Try to focus the image by moving the concave lens between the light bulb and the fixed lens.
5. Repeat step 4, but this time use the second convex lens. Record your observations.
6. Move the index card about 10 to 16 cm closer to the fixed lens to simulate image formation behind the retina. Record your observations.
7. Repeat steps 4 and 5.

Analyze and Conclude

1. **Drawing Conclusions** Does the lens in your eye focus an image right side up or upside down on your retina? Why does an image appear right side up when you look at objects?
2. **Drawing Conclusions** Which lens sharpened the image that formed in front of the retina? Behind the retina?
3. **Using Models** Which condition—long-focal length or short-focal length—do you think models the problem of nearsightedness? Which condition models farsightedness? Explain your answers.

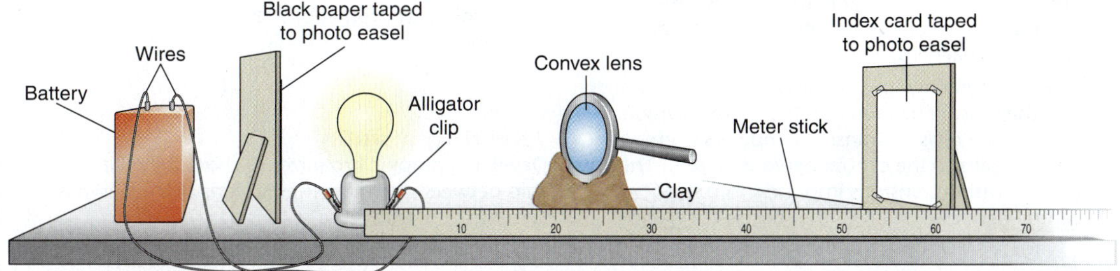

Analyze and Conclude

1. The lens in your eye focuses an image upside down on your retina. It appears right side up when you look at objects because the brain interprets the image right side up.

2. The concave lens sharpened the image that formed in front of the retina. The convex lens sharpened the image that formed behind the retina.

3. Short-focal length models the problem of nearsightedness because the image focuses in front of the "retina." Long-focal length models the problem of farsightedness because the image focuses behind the "retina."

Real-World Lab

BIIE 1.d, BIIE 1.g

Objective Students will be able to use a model to determine which types of corrective lenses are needed by nearsighted and farsighted individuals.

Skills Focus **Analyzing Data, Using Models**

Time 45 minutes

Advance Prep
- You may need to attach a piece of cardboard to the supports on the backs of the photo easels to make them stand vertically.
- An optical bench, often used in physics classes, may be used in place of the meter stick and cardboard photo easels.
- A candle can be used in place of the electric light and may give a sharper image.

Pre-Lab Discussion
Before students begin the procedure, point out that light rays can change direction when they pass from one medium (such as air) into another (such as water). You may want to put a pencil in a glass of water to illustrate this point. Explain that the water bends the light as a lens does. Have students read the procedure. Then, ask: **What does the fixed lens in the setup represent?** *(The lens of the eye)* **What does the index card in front of the fixed lens represent?** *(The retina of the eye)*

Procedure
2. Remind students to record the focal length before they move the index card in step 3.

3. Students should describe how the image becomes blurry or out of focus.

Expected Outcome Students should find that a concave lens sharpens the image when it forms in front of the retina and a convex lens sharpens the image when it forms behind the retina.

Chapter 35 Study Guide

Study Tip

Suggest that students review the chapter contents by using each of the Vocabulary terms correctly in a sentence. Check their sentences for errors. Then, have them rewrite their sentences as fill-in-the-blank questions by leaving out the Vocabulary terms. They can use the questions to quiz a classmate.

Thinking Visually

Graphic organizers should show that the nervous system consists of the central nervous system (brain and spinal cord) and the peripheral nervous system, which has sensory and motor divisions. The nervous system can also be divided into the somatic nervous system and the autonomic nervous system, the latter with its sympathetic and parasympathetic divisions.

Chapter 35 Assessment

Reviewing Content

1. c	5. a	9. b
2. b	6. c	10. a
3. a	7. b	
4. d	8. d	

Understanding Concepts

11. Cell, tissue, organ, organ system, organism

12. Unless cells of the body are kept at a temperature within a certain range, supplied with energy, bathed in fluid, and cleansed of waste—in short, unless homeostasis is maintained—permanent injury or death can occur.

13. The largest part of a typical neuron is the cell body, which contains the cell nucleus and much of the cytoplasm. The cell body is where most of the cell's metabolic activity occurs. Short, branched extensions called dendrites carry impulses from the environment or other neurons toward the cell body. The long fiber that carries impulses away from the cell body is called the axon, which ends in small swellings called axon terminals.

14. During a resting potential, potassium ions (K^+) diffuse across a neuron's cell membrane more easily than do sodium ions (Na^+), resulting in a negative charge inside the cell membrane. During an action potential, the cell membrane becomes more permeable to Na^+ ions, resulting in a reversal of charges.

Chapter 35 Study Guide

35–1 Human Body Systems

Key Concepts  7 5.a, BI 9.c

- The levels of organization in a multicellular organism include cells, tissues, organs, and organ systems.
- Homeostasis is the process by which organisms keep internal conditions relatively constant despite changes in external environments.

Vocabulary
specialized cell, p. 894
epithelial tissue, p. 894
connective tissue, p. 894
nervous tissue, p. 894
muscle tissue, p. 894
homeostasis, p. 895
feedback inhibition, p. 895

35–2 The Nervous System

 **Key Concepts**  BI 9.b, BI 9.d, BI 9.e

- The nervous system controls and coordinates functions throughout the body and responds to internal and external stimuli.
- The basic structural units of the nervous system are neurons.
- A nerve impulse begins when a neuron is stimulated by another neuron or by its environment.

Vocabulary
neuron, p. 897 • cell body, p. 897
dendrite, p. 898 • axon, p. 898
myelin sheath, p. 898
resting potential, p. 898
action potential, p. 899
threshold, p. 899 • synapse, p. 900
neurotransmitter, p. 900

35–3 Divisions of the Nervous System

Key Concepts  BI 9.b, BI 9.e

- The central nervous system relays messages, processes information, and analyzes information. The central nervous system consists of the brain and the spinal cord.
- The peripheral nervous system can be divided into the sensory division and the motor division. The sensory division transmits impulses from sense organs to the central nervous system. The motor division transmits impulses from the central nervous system to the muscles or glands.

Vocabulary
meninges, p. 901 • cerebrospinal fluid, p. 901
cerebrum, p. 902 • cerebellum, p. 902
brain stem, p. 902 • thalamus, p. 903
hypothalamus, p. 903 • reflex, p. 903
reflex arc, p. 904

35–4 The Senses

Key Concept  BI 9.e

- There are five general categories of sensory receptors: pain receptors, thermoreceptors, mechanoreceptors, chemoreceptors, and photoreceptors.

Vocabulary
sensory receptor, p. 906 • pupil, p. 906
lens, p. 907 • retina, p. 907 • rod, p. 907
cone, p. 907 • cochlea, p. 908
semicircular canal, p. 908 • taste bud, p. 909

35–5 Drugs and the Nervous System

Key Concepts

- Stimulants increase heart rate, blood pressure, and breathing rate. In addition, stimulants increase the release of neurotransmitters at some synapses in the brain.
- Depressants slow down heart rate and breathing rate, lower blood pressure, relax muscles, and relieve tension.
- Cocaine causes the sudden release of a neurotransmitter in the brain called dopamine.
- Opiates mimic natural chemicals in the brain known as endorphins, which normally help to overcome sensations of pain.
- Alcohol is a depressant that slows down the rate at which the central nervous system functions.

Vocabulary
drug, p. 910
stimulant, p. 910
depressant, p. 911
fetal alcohol syndrome, p. 913
drug abuse, p. 914
addiction, p. 914

Thinking Visually

Develop a graphic organizer to show the relationship between the different divisions of the nervous system.

TIME SAVER — CHAPTER RESOURCES

Print:

- ***Teaching Resources,*** Chapter Vocabulary Review, Graphic Organizer, Chapter 35 Tests: Levels A and B

Technology:

- ***Computer Test Bank,*** Chapter 35 Test
- ***iText,*** Chapter 35 Assessment

Chapter 35 Assessment

Reviewing Content

Choose the letter that best answers the question or completes the statement.

1. The type of tissue that covers the body, lines internal surfaces, and forms glands is
   a. muscle tissue.
   b. connective tissue.
   c. epithelial tissue.
   d. nervous tissue.
2. The process of maintaining a relatively constant internal environment despite changes in the external environment is called
   a. regulation.
   b. homeostasis.
   c. synapse.
   d. stimulation.
3. The basic units of structure and function of the nervous system are
   a. neurons.
   b. axons.
   c. dendrites.
   d. neurotransmitters.
4. In the diagram below, letter *A* is pointing to the
   a. myelin sheath.
   b. axon.
   c. dendrite.
   d. cell body.

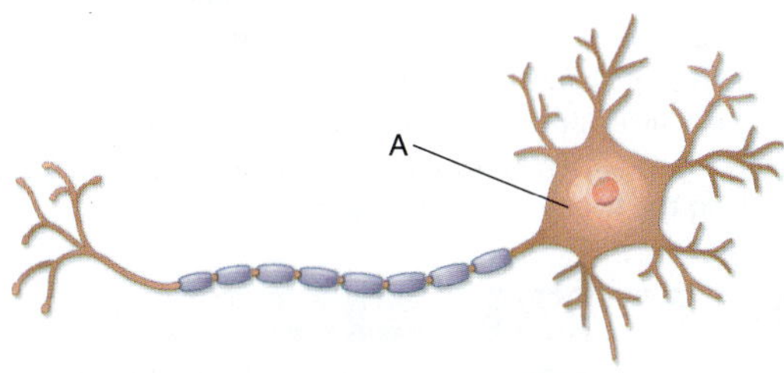

5. The place where a neuron transfers an impulse to another cell is the
   a. synapse.
   b. dendrite.
   c. myelin sheath.
   d. receptor.
6. The central nervous system consists of the
   a. sense organs.
   b. reflexes.
   c. brain and spinal cord.
   d. sensory and motor neurons.

Interactive textbook with assessment at PHSchool.com 

7. Voluntary or conscious activities of the body are controlled by the
   a. medulla oblongata. c. cerebellum.
   b. cerebrum. d. brain stem.
8. The sympathetic nervous system and the parasympathetic nervous system are divisions of the
   a. peripheral nervous system.
   b. central nervous system.
   c. somatic nervous system.
   d. autonomic nervous system.
9. The semicircular canals and the two tiny sacs located behind them help maintain
   a. night vision. c. respiratory rate.
   b. equilibrium. d. temperature.
10. Drugs that increase heart rate, blood pressure, and breathing rate are
   a. stimulants. c. opiates.
   b. depressants. d. barbiturates.

Understanding Concepts

11. Sequence the following terms from simplest to most complex: organ system, tissue, organ, organism, cell.
12. Why is it important for an organism to maintain homeostasis?
13. Describe the structure and function of a neuron.
14. What changes occur in the neuron during the resting potential? During an action potential?
15. How does the all-or-none principle relate to the transmission of a nerve impulse?
16. Describe the structure and function of the cerebrum.
17. Describe the advantage of a reflex response in the survival of an organism.
18. List the divisions of the autonomic nervous system and give the function of each.
19. Trace the path of light through the eye.
20. What are the functions of rods and cones?
21. Trace the path of sound through the ear.
22. Explain why a pregnant woman should avoid drinking alcohol.
23. Define drug abuse in your own words.
24. It has been said that no one can be cured of a drug dependence. Explain why.

TIME SAVER HOMEWORK GUIDE

Section:	Questions:
Section 35–1	1, 2, 11, 12, 34
Section 35–2	3–5, 13–15, 27, 30, 32
Section 35–3	6–8, 16–18, 25, 28
Section 35–4	9, 19–21, 26, 29, 31, 33
Section 35–5	10, 22–24

interactive Textbook

If your class subscribes to the iText, your students can go online to access an interactive version of the Student Edition and a self-test.

(Continued from page 916)

15. According to the all-or-none principle, any stimulus that is stronger than the threshold will produce an impulse and any stimulus below the threshold will not produce an impulse.

16. The cerebrum consists of two hemispheres, each divided into regions called lobes. A band of tissue known as the corpus callosum connects the two hemispheres. The cerebrum is responsible for the voluntary, or conscious, activities of the body. It is the site of intelligence, learning, and judgment.

17. A reflex allows an organism to respond to danger quickly, which is an advantage for survival.

18. The autonomic nervous system is divided into the sympathetic and parasympathetic nervous systems. The sympathetic and parasympathetic nervous systems have opposite effects on the same organ system.

19. Light enters the eye through the cornea and passes through the anterior chamber, which is filled with aqueous humor. The light then goes through the pupil, which is an opening in the iris, and through the lens into a large chamber filled with vitreous humor. The lens focuses the light on the retina, where photoreceptors convert light into impulses that are sent via the optic nerve to the brain.

20. Rods, which are extremely sensitive to light, and cones, which are less sensitive to light but can distinguish different colors, are photoreceptors in the retina. Their function is to convert light into impulses that are carried through the optic nerve to the central nervous system.

21. Sound waves, which are vibrating air molecules, enter the auditory canal and cause the tympanum to vibrate. Three tiny bones, the hammer, anvil, and stirrup, pick up the vibrations, and the stirrup transmits them to the oval window. The oval window vibrates and creates pressure waves in the fluid-filled cochlea. The pressure waves push back and forth against tiny hair cells, which respond by producing nerve impulses that are sent to the brain through the cochlear nerve.

22. She risks having a child with fetal alcohol syndrome—a set of birth defects. A child with FAS can have heart defects, a malformed face, delayed growth, and poor motor development.

23. Students may state that drug abuse is the intentional misuse of a drug, whether legal or illegal, for non-medical purposes.

24. One possible answer is: Drug dependence means that the only way a person can stop using the drug is by complete abstinence. This might be called a way to control the dependence but not a cure.

Critical Thinking

25. Students' experimental designs should include variables, controls, reasonable hypotheses, and feasible procedures. The focus should be on a simple, repetitive task.

26. The advantage relates to the thermoregulatory function of the tongue in some mammals. Mammals lose excess body heat by evaporation of water (sweating) and for many mammals, including the domestic dog, the primary organ for heat loss is the tongue.

27. If an axon is disconnected from a nerve cell body, the pathway of an outgoing nerve impulse will be disrupted.

28. The purpose of the knee-jerk reflex test is to determine whether the person's reflexes are normal. The absence of a response could indicate a disorder of one of the components of the reflex arc.

29. The slope of the graph starts to change rapidly at the age of 40 as the distance at which the person can focus clearly on nearby objects increases. Students may infer that the shape of the cornea or elasticity of the lens changes with age, affecting the focus of light entering the eyes.

30. With less myelin, nerve impulses in people with MS will travel more slowly. This will result in loss of control over motor functions, leading to paralysis, poor coordination, slurred speech, blurred vision, and tremor.

31. Constant exposure to loud noises would damage the delicate structure of the inner ear, the cochlea and the membrane covering the oval window. Hearing loss caused by damage to these structures is irreversible.

Chapter 35 Assessment

Critical Thinking

25. **Designing Experiments** Design an experiment to determine the effects of fatigue on reaction time. Formulate a hypothesis and write down your procedure. Have your teacher check your experimental plan before you begin.

26. **Applying Concepts** Heat receptors of mammals are particularly concentrated on the tongue. These receptors keep humans from burning the mouth with hot food. What advantage is it for a wild mammal that doesn't cook its food to have so many heat receptors in its tongue?

27. **Inferring** Suppose a portion of an axon is cut so that it is no longer connected to its nerve cell body. What effect would that have on the transmission of impulses?

28. **Applying Concepts** A routine examination by a doctor usually includes a knee-jerk reflex test. What is the purpose of this test? What could the absence of a response indicate?

29. **Using Tables and Graphs** The graph below compares age to the nearest distance in centimeters that many people can see an object clearly. Describe the general trend of the graph. At what age does the slope of the graph begin to change rapidly? What do you think might explain this change?

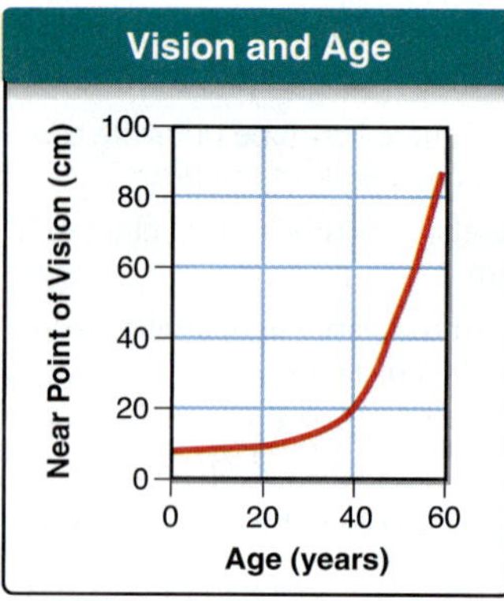

30. **Predicting** Multiple sclerosis (MS) is a disease characterized by the destruction of myelin. Based on your knowledge of neuron structure and the function of various cell parts, predict the symptoms this destruction of myelin might produce.

31. **Applying Concepts** Constant exposure to loud noises may cause loss of hearing. What parts of the ear may be damaged? Can the loss of hearing be reversed?

32. **Using Analogies** How are a neuron and an electrical extension cord similar? How are they different?

33. **Inferring** What is the advantage of having a greater concentration of touch receptors and, therefore, greater sensitivity in the fingers, toes, and face?

34. **Classifying** Would you classify blood as a cell, a tissue, or an organ? Explain your answer.

Focus on the BIG Idea

Structure and Function Compare the nervous systems of nonvertebrate chordates and the human nervous system. What is the main difference between these systems? Refer to Section 30–1 and Section 33–3.

Writing in Science

At the beginning of this chapter, you read about how the systems of the body worked together toward a common goal—winning a basketball game. Imagine that you are playing soccer. Using **Figure 35–2** as a reference, pick five body systems that are most involved in the activity, and explain how the body systems are working together. Be sure to include your reasons for picking the five body systems that you chose.

Performance-Based Assessment

Making a Collage The left and right sides of the brain are responsible for different activities. Make a collage that shows examples of some right-brain activities and some left-brain activities. Attach to your collage a paragraph outlining what learning strategies would be useful for left-brain dominant individuals and for right-brain dominant individuals.

For: An interactive self-test
Visit: PHSchool.com
Web Code: cba-0350

32. Both a neuron and an extension cord carry electrical impulses. An impulse is regenerated all along a neural pathway so that it does not lose strength. Current moving along a wire meets resistance and gradually diminishes.

33. Answers may vary. Students may say that having a greater concentration of touch receptors in the fingers, toes, and face makes these parts of the body, which are often exposed, more sensitive to pain and, therefore, better able to detect sources of potential injury, such as hot or sharp objects.

34. Blood should be classified as a tissue, because it is made up of a group of cells that perform a single function.

Focus on the BIG Idea

Nonvertebrate chordates have a relatively simple nervous system with a mass of nerve cells forming the brain. The brain does not have distinct regions, each with a specialized function, as the human brain does.

Standards Practice

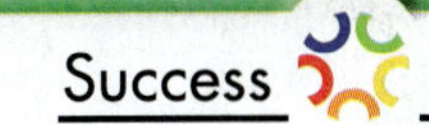

Success Tracker™
Online at PHSchool.com

Test-Taking Tip

Questions that begin with a list of lettered choices (A–D) followed by numbered statements are essentially multiple-choice questions. To solve these questions, use the same process that you use to solve standard multiple-choice questions.

Questions 1–4 Each of the lettered choices below refers to the following numbered statements. Select the best lettered choice. A choice may be used once, more than once, or not at all.

A Synapse
B Myelin sheath
C Cerebrum
D Cerebellum

1. The largest and most prominent part of the human brain
2. Carries out activities that are under voluntary control by the brain **BI 9.b**
3. Gap between two neurons
4. Insulating membrane surrounding some axons

Choose the letter that best answers the question or completes the statement.

5. The process by which organisms keep internal conditions relatively constant is called **BI 9.b**
   A resting potential.
   B positive feedback.
   C feedback inhibition.
   D homeostasis.
6. Which of the following is NOT a kind of tissue in the human body? **7 5.a**
   A epithelial
   B connective
   C neuron
   D nervous
7. The part of a neuron that carries impulses away from the cell body is called a(an) **BI 9.e**
   A axon.
   B dendrite.
   C node.
   D vesicle.
8. Which of the following is NOT a structure of the human ear?
   A tympanum
   B cochlea
   C stirrup bone
   D vitreous humor

Questions 9–11

The table below lists the blood alcohol concentration (BAC) as alcohol consumption increases. Use the information in the table to answer the questions that follow.

Blood Alcohol Concentration (Percent)

Drinks in One Hour	Body Mass					
	45 kg	54 kg	63 kg	72 kg	81 kg	90 kg
1	0.04	0.03	0.03	0.02	0.02	0.02
2	0.07	0.06	0.05	0.05	0.04	0.04
3	0.11	0.09	0.08	0.07	0.06	0.06
4	0.14	0.12	0.10	0.09	0.08	0.07
5	0.18	0.15	0.13	0.11	0.10	0.09
6	0.21	0.18	0.15	0.14	0.12	0.11
7	0.25	0.21	0.18	0.16	0.14	0.13
8	0.29	0.24	0.21	0.18	0.16	0.14
9	0.32	0.27	0.23	0.20	0.18	0.16
10	0.36	0.30	0.26	0.22	0.20	0.18

9. How many drinks in one hour would cause a 63-kg person to have a BAC percentage of 0.08?
   A 1 **C** 3
   B 2 **D** 4
10. If a 54-kg person had 3 drinks in one hour, what would his or her BAC percentage be?
   A 0.06 **C** 0.09
   B 0.08 **D** 0.11
11. If a 72-kg person had 4 drinks in two hours, what would his or her BAC percentage be?
   A 0.03 **C** 0.08
   B 0.05 **D** 0.13

Standards Practice

1. C	5. D	9. C
2. C	6. C	10. C
3. A	7. A	11. B
4. B	8. D	

Success Tracker™
Online at PHSchool.com

Have students check their understanding of the chapter by logging onto Success Tracker.

Writing in Science

Students should select five organ systems that are most closely related to playing soccer. The best choices are the nervous, skeletal, muscular, circulatory, and respiratory systems. Their explanations should reflect an understanding of the role that each system plays in the mental and physical activities associated with the game and how the systems work together.

Performance-Based Assessment

Student projects should reflect the general hypothesis that the right hemisphere of the brain is associated with creativity and artistic ability and the left hemisphere with analytical and mathematical ability.

Your students can independently test their knowledge of the chapter and print out their test results for your files.

Chapter Planner 36 Skeletal, Muscular, and Integumentary Systems

Section and Section Objectives	Time	STANDARDS NCLB	STANDARDS Biology	Activities and Labs
36–1 The Skeletal System, pp. 921–925 ***36.1.1*** ***State*** the functions of the skeletal system. ***36.1.2*** ***Describe*** the structure of a typical bone. ***36.1.3*** ***Explain*** how bones develop. ***36.1.4*** ***Identify*** the three different kinds of joints.	2 periods (1 block)	7 5.c		**SE:** ***Inquiry Activity,*** How do your joints move?, p. 920 L2 **TE:** ***Demonstration,*** p. 921 L1 L2 **TE:** ***Demonstration,*** p. 923 L1 L2 **TE:** ***Build Science Skills,*** p. 924 L1 L2 **LMA:** Chapter 36 Lab L2 L3
36–2 The Muscular System, pp. 926–931 ***36.2.1*** ***Describe*** the three types of muscle tissue. ***36.2.2*** ***Explain*** how muscles contract. ***36.2.3*** ***Explain*** why exercise is important.	2 periods (1 block)	7 5.c	BI 9.e, *BI 9.h	**TE:** ***Demonstration,*** p. 929 L1 L2 **SE:** ***Quick Lab,*** What do tendons do?, p. 930 L2 **LMB:** Chapter 36 Lab L1 L2
36–3 The Integumentary System, pp. 933–936 ***36.3.1*** ***State*** the functions of the integumentary system. ***36.3.2*** ***Describe*** the structure of hair and nails.	1 period (1/2 block)		BI 10.a	**SE:** ***Technology & Society,*** Making Artificial Skin, p. 932 L2 L3 **TE:** ***Demonstration,*** p. 933 L1 L2 **SE:** ***Analyzing Data,*** The UV Index and Sunburn, p. 935 L2 **SE:** ***Real-World Lab,*** Making a Model of a Transdermal Patch, p. 937 L2
Chapter Assessment, pp. 938–941	1 period (1/2 block)			

ACTIVITY PLANNER

SE: *Inquiry Activity,* p. 920; 10 min.; examples of hinge and ball-and-socket joints

TE: *Demonstration,* p. 921; 10 min.; human skeletal model

TE: *Demonstration,* p. 923; 5 min.; clean chicken bone, beaker, vinegar

TE: *Build Science Skills,* p. 924; 15 min.; craft sticks, toothpicks, pipe cleaners, modeling clay, glue, tacks

TE: *Demonstration,* p. 929; 5 min.; box, book

SE: *Quick Lab,* p. 930; 20 min.; plastic gloves, lab apron, raw chicken wing treated with bleach, paper towels, forceps, scissors, scalpel

TE: *Demonstration,* p. 933; 5 min.; apple, knife, plastic wrap

SE: *Real-World Lab,* p. 937; 45 min.; plastic gloves,15-cm dialysis tubing, plastic cup, phenolphthalein solution, 50-mL graduated cylinder, paper towels, scissors, metric ruler, filter paper, dropper pipette, sodium bicarbonate solution

PLANNING KEY

Ability Levels

for students performing . . .

below grade level **L1**

at grade level **L2**

above grade level **L3**

Print Components

SE	Student Edition	**LA**	Lab Assessment
TE	Teacher's Edition	**BTM**	Biotechnology Manual
RSW	Reading & Study Workbook A	**IDM**	Issues and Decision Making
ARSW	Adapted Reading & Study Workbook B	**LW**	Lab Worksheets
TR	Teaching Resources	**LMA**	Laboratory Manual A
IF	Investigations in Forensics	**LMB**	Laboratory Manual B

Tech Components

CTB	Computer Test Bank
BD	BioDetectives DVD
TP	Transparencies Plus
PLM	Probeware Lab Manual
ABC	ABC DVD Library
LS	Lab Simulations
VL	Virtual Labs

Interactive textbook with assessment at PHSchool.com

Program Resources	Assessment	Media and Technology
TR: Lesson Plan 36–1, Section Summary, p. 54 L1, p. 64 L2, Worksheets, pp. 57–58 L1, pp. 66–68 L2 **RSW:** Section 36–1 L2 **ARSW:** Section 36–1 L1 **IDM:** Issues and Decisions 38 L2 L3	**SE:** 36–1 Section Assessment, p. 925 **TR:** Section Review 36–1	**iText:** Section 36–1 **TP:** 36–1 Interest Grabber, Section Outline, The Skeletal System Figure 36–3, Figure 36–4, Figure 36–5
TR: Lesson Plan 36–2, Section Summary, p. 55 L1, p. 64 L2, Worksheets, pp. 59–61 L1, pp. 69–71 L2 **RSW:** Section 36–2 L2 **ARSW:** Section 36–2 L1	**SE:** 36–2 Section Assessment, p. 931 **TR:** Section Review 36–2	**iText:** Section 36–2 **TP:** 36–2 Interest Grabber, Section Outline, Cycle Diagram, Figure 36–7, Figure 36–8, Figure 36–11 **ABC:** 39 Muscle Contraction
TR: Lesson Plan 36–3, Section Summary, p. 56 L1, p. 65 L2, Worksheets, p. 62 L1, pp. 72–74 L2, Enrichment L3 **LW:** Chapter 36 Real-World Lab L1 L2 L3 **RSW:** Section 36–3 L2 **ARSW:** Section 36–3 L1	**SE:** 36–3 Section Assessment, p. 936 **TR:** Section Review 36–3	**iText:** Section 36–3 **TP:** 36–3 Interest Grabber, Section Outline, Concept Map, Figure 36–13
	SE: Chapter 36 Assessment, pp. 938–941 **TR:** Chapter Vocabulary Review, Graphic Organizer, Chapter 36 Test	**iText:** Chapter 36 Assessment **CTB:** Chapter 36 Test **Go Online** Students can do research, share data, and test their knowledge online.

PRESSED FOR TIME?

To Preview the Chapter

- Have students skim each section of Chapter 36 for boldface Key Concept sentences and Vocabulary terms.
- Assign the Reading Strategies for each section.

To Cover the Chapter Quickly

- Have students read The Skeleton and Types of Joints in Section 36–1, Types of Muscle Tissue and How Muscles and Bones Interact in Section 36–2, and all of Section 36–3.
- Assign questions 1–3 in Section Reviews 36–1 and 36–2 and all of the questions in Section Review 36–3. Also assign questions 6, 7, 10, 11, 16, 20–25, 30, 33–35 and the Performance-Based Assessment in Chapter 36 Assessment and questions 1–9 in Chapter 36 Standards Practice.

To Review the Chapter

- Assign the Section Reviews 36–1 through 36–3 in the Reading and Study Workbook or the Adapted Reading and Study Workbook.
- Assign Section Reviews for 36–1 through 36–3 and the Chapter Vocabulary Review for Chapter 36 in the Teaching Resources.

CHAPTER 36

ENGAGE/EXPLORE

Inquiry Activity

Objective Students will be able to classify joints based on how their bones move. L2

Skills Focus Classifying, Inferring

Materials hinge and ball-and-socket joint examples

Time 10 minutes

Advance Prep Lay out hinge and ball-and-socket joints where students can examine them. Objects with ball-and-socket joints include joysticks from computers or video games, shower-head arm mounts, and single-lever faucets.

Strategies
- Give students room to stand and move freely.
- Point out examples of other common objects that have joints, such as book covers (hinges) and ball-point pens (ball-and-socket joints).

Expected Outcome Students should be able to classify hinge and ball-and-socket joints based on the range of motion of their components.

Think About It
1. Hinge joints allow back-and-forth movement.
2. Ball-and-socket joints allow circular movement.
3. Pivot joints allow one bone to rotate around another. Saddle joints permit one bone to slide in two directions.

Assess Prior Knowledge

Guide students in organizing their prior knowledge of the three body systems covered in the chapter. Have them complete the following sentences, and then call on students at random to read their completed sentences to the class. "The skeletal system consists of . . ." *(bones, cartilage, ligaments, and tendons).* "The forces that put the skeleton into motion come from the . . ." *(skeletal muscles).* "The major function of the skin is . . ." *(to protect the body).*

CHAPTER 36

Skeletal, Muscular, and Integumentary Systems

The explosive speed needed for speed skating comes from a well-developed muscular system.

Inquiry Activity

How do your joints move?

Procedure

1. Look at the examples of a hinge joint and a ball-and-socket joint provided by your teacher. Determine how each joint moves.
2. Based on your observations, identify joints in your body that are hinge joints and joints that are ball-and-socket joints.

Think About It

1. **Classifying** What type of movement does a hinge joint allow?
2. **Classifying** What type of movement does a ball-and-socket joint allow?
3. **Inferring** Your body also has joints called pivot joints and saddle joints. Based on their names, what type of movement might these joints allow? (*Hint:* Consider how a rider might move in a saddle.)

FACTS AND FIGURES

Bones from the past

Bones are one of the most important tools paleontologists have for studying the evolution of vertebrates, including humans. Because bones are made of hard, dense material, they are more likely than other tissues, such as muscle and skin, to be preserved after an animal dies. Bones are preserved as fossils, which form when water in the ground gradually leaches away the organic material in the bones and replaces it with minerals. Paleontologists study fossils and compare them with the bones of living animals to learn more about the anatomy and way of life of extinct animals. This is much more difficult than it sounds, because complete skeletons of extinct organisms are rarely found. Instead, most fossils consist only of fragments of bone.

36–1 The Skeletal System

7 5.c. Students know how bones and muscles work together to provide a structural framework for movement.

To retain their shapes, all organisms need some type of structural support. Unicellular organisms have a cytoskeleton that provides structural support. In multicellular animals, support is provided by some form of skeleton, including the external exoskeletons of arthropods and the internal endoskeletons of vertebrates. The human skeleton is composed of a type of connective tissue called bone. Bones and other connective tissues, such as cartilage and ligaments, form the skeletal system.

Scientists can infer a lot about the behavior of extinct species by studying fossil bones and reconstructing skeletons. The human skeleton also contains important clues. The shape of your hip bones shows that you walk upright on two legs. The structure of the bones in your hands, especially your opposable thumbs, indicates that you have the ability to grasp objects. The size and shape of your skull is a clue that you have a well-developed brain.

Guide for Reading

Key Concepts
- What are the functions of the skeletal system?
- What is the structure of a typical bone?
- What are the three different kinds of joints?

Vocabulary
periosteum
Haversian canal
bone marrow
cartilage
ossification
joint
ligament

Reading Strategy: Asking Questions Before you read, rewrite the headings in this section as *how, why,* or *what* questions about the skeletal system. As you read, write brief answers to those heading questions.

The Skeleton

The skeletal system has many important functions. **The skeleton supports the body, protects internal organs, provides for movement, stores mineral reserves, and provides a site for blood cell formation.** The bones that make up the skeletal system support and shape the body much like an internal wooden frame supports a house. Just as a house could not stand without its wooden frame, the human body would collapse without its bony skeleton. Bones protect the delicate internal organs of the body. For example, the skull forms a protective shell around the brain, and the ribs form a basketlike cage that protects the heart and lungs.

(a) 7 5.c

Bones provide a system of levers on which muscles act to produce movement. Levers are rigid rods that can be moved about a fixed point. In addition, bones contain reserves of minerals, mainly calcium salts, that are important to many body processes. Finally, bones are the site of blood cell formation. Blood cells are produced in the soft marrow tissue that fills the internal cavities in some bones.

CA (a)

There are 206 bones in the adult human skeleton. As shown in **Figure 36–2** on page 922, these bones can be divided into two parts—the axial skeleton and the appendicular skeleton. The axial skeleton supports the central axis of the body. It consists of the skull, the vertebral column, and the rib cage. The bones of the arms and legs, along with the bones of the pelvis and shoulder area, form the appendicular skeleton.

Figure 36–1 **Bones provide a system of levers on which muscles act to produce movement.** Without this coordination, movement would not be possible.

Section 36–1

7 5.c

1 FOCUS

Objectives

36.1.1 ***State*** the functions of the skeletal system.
36.1.2 ***Describe*** the structure of a typical bone.
36.1.3 ***Explain*** how bones develop.
36.1.4 ***Identify*** the three different kinds of joints.

Guide for Reading

Vocabulary Preview

Tell students that words beginning with *os*, the Latin word for bone, have something to do with bone. For example, the word *ossification* means "the process of bone formation." Challenge students to find other words beginning with *os*, such as *osteocyte*, and explain each word's connection with bone.

Reading Strategy

Have students preview the material in the section by studying the figures and reading the captions. They should make note of any words they do not know and find the definitions as they read the section.

2 INSTRUCT

The Skeleton

Demonstration

Show students a three-dimensional model of the human skeleton. Challenge them to identify the bones of the axial skeleton *(skull, vertebral column, rib cage)* and the appendicular skeleton *(arms, legs, pelvic girdle, pectoral girdle)*. Allow students to manipulate the bones so that they have a better understanding of how the axial skeleton supports the body and the appendicular skeleton allows movement. L1 L2

TIME SAVER — SECTION RESOURCES

Print:
- ***Laboratory Manual A,*** Chapter 36 Lab
- ***Teaching Resources,*** Lesson Plan 36–1, Adapted Section Summary 36–1, Adapted Worksheets 36–1, Section Summary 36–1, Worksheets 36–1, Section Review 36–1
- ***Reading and Study Workbook A,*** Section 36–1
- ***Adapted Reading and Study Workbook B,*** Section 36–1
- ***Issues and Decision Making,*** Issues and Decisions 38

Technology:
- ***iText,*** Section 36–1
- ***Transparencies Plus,*** Section 36–1

36–1 (continued)

Structure of Bones

Address Misconceptions

Students may have difficulty conceiving of bone as living tissue. Ask: **Which do you think is a better model of a bone, a stick of chalk or a piece of sponge?** *(Some students may say that a stick of chalk is a better model.)* Point out that a stick of chalk may look more like a bone, but a piece of sponge is more like a bone in its structure. Both the sponge and the bone contain a network of tubes or spaces through which things can pass. Ask: **What passes through the tubes and spaces inside bone?** *(Blood vessels and nerves)* L2

Use Visuals

Figure 36–3 Make sure students understand how the two parts of the figure are related. Point out how the drawing on the right shows a cross section of a tiny piece of the bone on the left. Guide students in using the figure to distinguish between compact and spongy bone tissue. Ask: **What structures are found in compact bone?** *(Haversian canals, veins, arteries, and osteocytes)* **Where is spongy bone found?** *(Beneath compact bone at the ends of long bones and in the middle of short, flat bones)* L1 L2

Development of Bones

Build Science Skills

Comparing and Contrasting Work with the class to create a table comparing and contrasting bone and cartilage. Have a volunteer record the information in a chart on the chalkboard as the class brainstorms the similarities and differences between the two types of tissue.

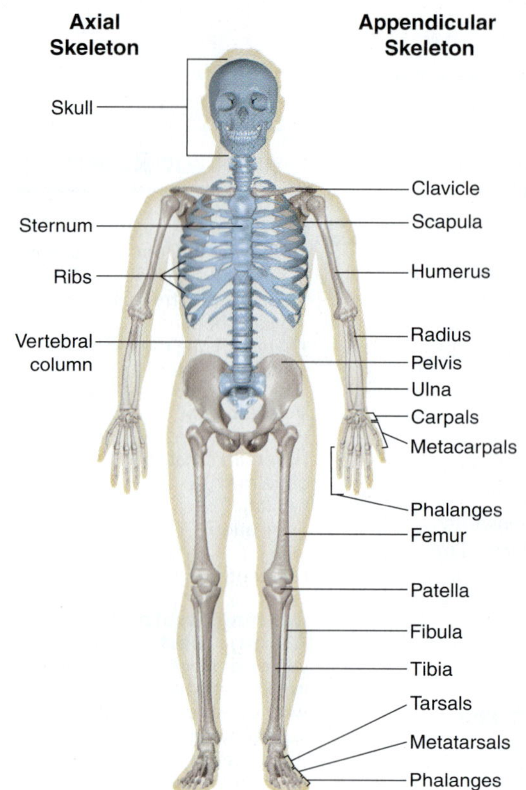

▲ **Figure 36–2** **The skeleton supports the body.** The human skeleton is divided into two parts: the axial skeleton and the appendicular skeleton.

Structure of Bones

It is easy to think of bones as nonliving. After all, most of the mass of bone is mineral salts—mainly calcium and phosphorus. However, bones are living tissue. **Bones are a solid network of living cells and protein fibers that are surrounded by deposits of calcium salts.**

Figure 36–3 shows the structure of a typical bone. The bone is surrounded by a tough layer of connective tissue called the **periosteum** (pehr-ee-AHS-tee-um). Blood vessels that pass through the periosteum carry oxygen and nutrients to the bone. Beneath the periosteum is a thick layer of compact bone. Although compact bone is dense, it is far from being solid. Running through compact bone is a network of tubes called **Haversian** (huh-VUR-zhun) **canals** that contain blood vessels and nerves.

A less dense tissue known as spongy bone is found inside the outer layer of compact bone. It is found in the ends of long bones and in the middle part of short, flat bones. Despite its name, spongy bone is not soft and spongy; it is actually quite strong. Near the ends of bones where force is applied, spongy bone is organized into structures that resemble the supporting girders in a bridge. This latticework structure of spongy bone helps to add strength to bone without adding mass.

Osteocytes, which are mature bone cells, are embedded in the bone matrix. Two other kinds of bone cells—osteoclasts (AHS-tee-oh-klasts) and osteoblasts line the Haversian canals and the surfaces of compact and spongy bone. Osteoclasts break down bone. Osteoblasts produce bone. Although we stop growing in our late teens, our bones are continuously remodeled through the activity of osteoclasts and osteoblasts.

Within bones are cavities that contain a soft tissue called **bone marrow.** There are two types of bone marrow: yellow and red. Yellow marrow is made up primarily of fat cells. Red marrow produces red blood cells, some kinds of white blood cells, and cell fragments called platelets.

Development of Bones

The skeleton of an embryo is composed almost entirely of a type of connective tissue called **cartilage.** The cells that make up cartilage are scattered in a network of protein fibers including both tough collagen and flexible elastin.

SUPPORT FOR ENGLISH LANGUAGE LEARNERS

Comprehension: Key Concept

Beginning On the board, rewrite the boldface sentence on page 921 as individual sentences that each express one function of the skeletal system. Then, pair ESL students with students who are proficient in English. Have the student pairs construct a concept circle (cluster diagram) with "Functions of the Skeletal System" in the center and the five functions connected to the center by lines. L1

Intermediate Read aloud the boldface sentence on page 921, and write it on the board. Ask individual students, including some ESL students, to identify and describe the functions of the skeletal system. Give students copies of Figure 36–2. Work with students to identify parts of the skeleton that perform specific functions, e.g., the skull protects, the femur supports. Have students label the appropriate parts with the functions. L2

Figure 36–3 Structure of a Bone

Bones are a solid network of living cells and protein fibers that are supported by deposits of calcium salts. A typical long bone such as the femur contains spongy bone and compact bone. Within compact bone are Haversian canals, which contain blood vessels.

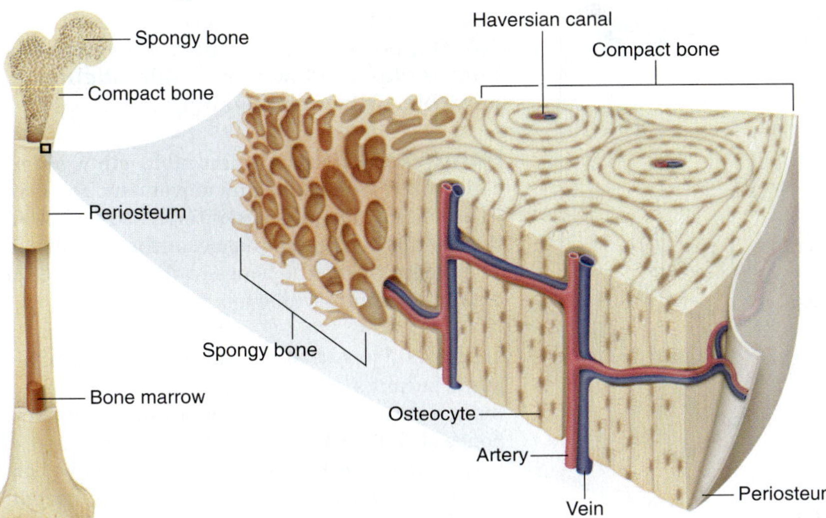

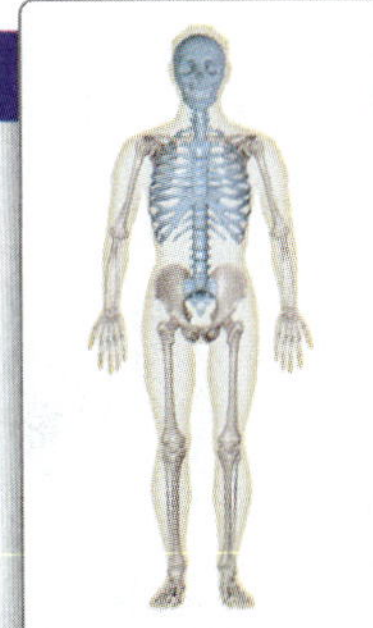

Haversian Canal
(magnification: 200×)

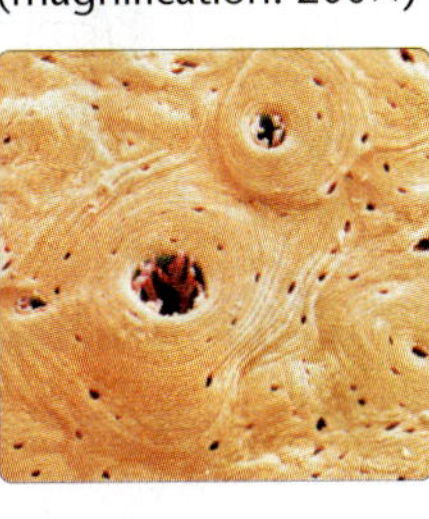

Unlike bone, cartilage does not contain blood vessels. Cartilage cells must rely on the diffusion of nutrients from the tiny blood vessels in surrounding tissues. Because cartilage is dense and fibrous, it can support weight, despite its extreme flexibility.

Cartilage is replaced by bone during the process of bone formation called **ossification** (ahs-uh-fih-KAY-shun). Ossification begins to take place up to seven months before birth. Bone tissue forms as osteoblasts secrete mineral deposits that replace the cartilage in developing bones. When the osteoblasts become surrounded by bone tissue, they mature into osteocytes.

Many long bones, including those of the arms and legs, have growth plates at either end. The growth of cartilage at these plates causes the bones to lengthen. Gradually, this new growth of cartilage is replaced by bone tissue, and the bones become larger and stronger. During late adolescence or early adulthood, the cartilage in the growth plates is replaced by bone, the bones become completely ossified, and the person "stops growing."

In adults, cartilage is found in those parts of the body that are flexible, such as the tip of the nose and the external ears. Cartilage also is found where the ribs are attached to the sternum, which allows the rib cage to move during breathing.

CHECKPOINT *What is ossification?*

Make Connections

Health Science Inform students that force must be placed on bone for ossification to occur, because it is force that stimulates the osteoblasts to secrete the minerals that replace cartilage. Ask: **What effect do you think an exercise such as walking would have on the bones of the legs?** *(It would stimulate ossification, so the bones would contain more minerals and be stronger.)* Ask: **What do you think might happen to bones that are not exposed to force, such as the bones of astronauts in zero gravity?** *(The bones would lose minerals because of lack of force exerted on them, so they would become weaker.)* L2

Demonstration

Demonstrate to students that even ossified bones contain a framework of collagen. Bring a clean chicken bone to class and, after pointing out how relatively hard and inflexible it is, place it in a beaker of vinegar to soak. After a few days, remove the bone and invite students to inspect it. They will observe that the bone has become rubbery and flexible. Explain that the vinegar dissolved the calcium (mineral) in the bone, leaving behind the collagen (protein). Ask: **What role does collagen play in an ossified bone?** *(It provides a framework for the minerals in the bone and gives the bone some flexibility.)* L1 L2

TEACHER TO TEACHER

When introducing the skeletal system, I go to a local health clinic and obtain a series of X-rays of the joints and bones that will be discussed. Technicians from local clinics are sometimes willing to visit the class and discuss the different X-rays, as well as explain the various aspects of X-ray medicine. As a class, we have also built an X-ray "skeleton" by mounting the various X-rays on a bulletin board. This "skeleton" is also a very good tool to use in reviewing the chapter.

—Bob Sprang
Biology Teacher
Mitchell Senior High School
Mitchell, South Dakota

Answer to . . .

CHECKPOINT *Ossification is the process of bone formation in which cartilage is replaced by bone.*

36–1 (continued)

Types of Joints

Build Science Skills

Using Models Provide students with materials such as craft sticks, toothpicks, pipe cleaners, modeling clay, tacks, and glue. Then, challenge them to create models of one or more types of joints shown in Figure 36–4. Invite students to demonstrate their completed models to the class. Ask: **What type of joint and what range of motion does your model illustrate?** *(Models should illustrate the range of motion of one of the four types of joints shown in the figure.)* Call on other students to name examples of that type of joint.

Demonstration

Ask a volunteer to model the movement of several different joints. As you name each joint, have the student demonstrate the range of motion permitted by the joint. In each case, challenge the rest of the class to name other joints that have the same range of motion. L1 L2

Structure of Joints

Use Community Resources

Invite a professional from the medical community to speak to the class about joints and joint problems. Possible speakers might include a radiology technician, physical therapist, chiropractor, or physician's assistant in sports medicine, rheumatology, or orthopedics. Encourage students to prepare questions for the speaker in advance. Afterward, have them write a summary of what they learned. L2

Go Online active art
For: Joint Movement activity
Visit: PHSchool.com
Web Code: cbe-0361
Students explore the skeletal and muscular systems through various joint movements.

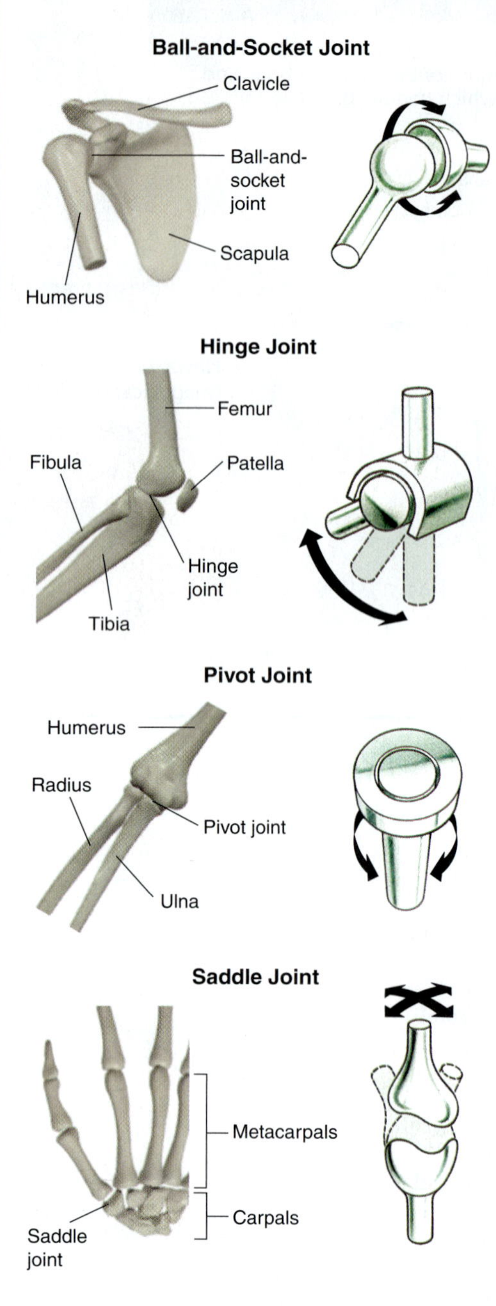

▲ **Figure 36–4** **Freely movable joints are classified by the type of movement they permit.** The joints illustrated are in the shoulder, knee, elbow, and hand.

Types of Joints

A place where one bone attaches to another bone is called a **joint.** Joints permit bones to move without damaging each other. Some joints, such as those of the shoulder, allow extensive movement. Others, like the joints of the fully developed skull, allow no movement at all. **Depending on its type of movement, a joint is classified as immovable, slightly movable, or freely movable.**

Immovable Joints Immovable joints, often called fixed joints, allow no movement. The bones at an immovable joint are interlocked and held together by connective tissue, or they are fused. The places where the bones in the skull meet are examples of immovable joints.

Slightly Movable Joints Slightly movable joints permit a small amount of restricted movement. Unlike the bones of immovable joints, the bones of slightly movable joints are separated from each other. The joints between the two bones of the lower leg and the joints between adjacent vertebrae are examples of slightly movable joints.

Freely Movable Joints Freely movable joints permit movement in one or more directions. Freely movable joints are grouped according to the shapes of the surfaces of the adjacent bones. The most common types of freely movable joints are shown in **Figure 36–4.**

Ball-and-socket joints permit movement in many directions. They allow the widest range of movement of any joint. Hinge joints permit back-and-forth motion, like the opening and closing of a door. Pivot joints allow one bone to rotate around another. Saddle joints permit one bone to slide in two directions.

CHECKPOINT *What are the four common types of freely movable joints?*

For: Joint Movement activity
Visit: PHSchool.com
Web Code: cbp-0361

BIOLOGY UPDATE

Bionic joints

Osteoarthritis plagues many older adults, causing them to have stiff, aching joints and keeping them from being as active as they would like. Replacing arthritic joints, especially the hip and knee, with artificial joints made of metal and plastic is an increasingly common solution to this problem. The major drawback has been that artificial joints tend to wear out in just 10 to 15 years. Now, a new type of polyethylene is being used to make artificial joints that last much longer. Machines that test artificial joints by putting them through a million movements a week have confirmed that the polyethylene joints should last for at least 27 years. Scientists are also researching ways to rebuild aging joints so they will not need to be replaced. For example, they are testing a type of cell that replaces damaged cartilage and a protein paste that helps repair damaged joints.

Structure of Joints

In freely movable joints, cartilage covers the surfaces where two bones come together. This protects the bones as they move against each other. The joints are also surrounded by a fibrous joint capsule that helps hold the bones together while still allowing them to move.

The joint capsule consists of two layers. One layer forms strips of tough connective tissue called **ligaments.** Ligaments, which hold bones together in a joint, are attached to the membranes that surround bones. Cells in the other layer of the joint capsule produce a substance called synovial (sin-OH-vee-ul) fluid. Synovial fluid enables the surfaces of the joint to slide over each other smoothly.

In some freely movable joints, such as the knee in **Figure 36–5,** small sacs of synovial fluid called bursae (BUR-see; singular: bursa) form. A bursa reduces the friction between the bones of a joint and also acts as a tiny shock absorber.

Skeletal System Disorders

Bones and joints can be damaged, just like any other tissue. Excessive strain on a joint may produce inflammation, a response in which excess fluid causes swelling, pain, heat, and redness. Inflammation of a bursa is called bursitis. A more serious disorder is arthritis, which involves inflammation of the joint itself.

In older people, especially women, loss of calcium in the bones can lead to a condition known as osteoporosis. Osteoporosis is a weakening of the bones that can cause serious fractures. Sound nutrition, including plenty of calcium in the diet, and weight-bearing exercise are among the best ways to prevent this serious problem.

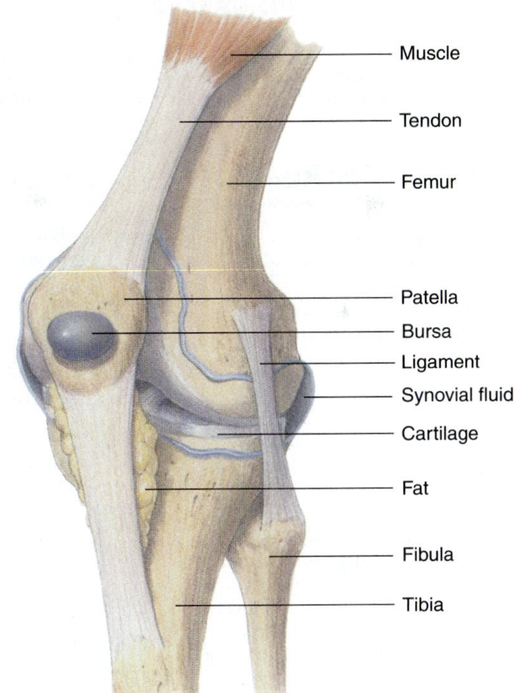

▲ **Figure 36–5** The knee joint is protected by cartilage and bursae. The ligaments hold the bones composing the knee joint—femur, patella, tibia, and fibula—together. **Inferring** ***How do the cartilage and bursae help reduce friction?***

Skeletal System Disorders

Make Connections

Health Science Point out that there are several different types of arthritis, including rheumatoid arthritis and osteoarthritis, also called degenerative joint disease. Challenge students to identify ways in which the two types differ. *(Possible answers: rheumatoid arthritis is caused by the immune system attacking joints and usually occurs by young adulthood; osteoarthritis is caused by wear and tear on joints and usually occurs after middle age.)* L2 L3

3 ASSESS

Evaluate Understanding

Read each of the Vocabulary words in the section. As you read, call on students at random to define the terms without referring to their books.

Reteach

Work with students to make a table summarizing the similarities and differences among the different types of joints. Label the columns: Type of Joint, Range of Motion, Examples.

Writing in Science

Students' advertising campaigns should make a convincing argument for milk consumption that includes information regarding the high incidence of osteoporosis at older ages, especially in women; the serious potential health consequences of osteoporosis, including broken bones; the role of dietary calcium in preventing osteoporosis; and the high calcium content of milk.

Interactive Textbook

If your class subscribes to the iText, use it to review the Key Concepts in Section 36–1.

36–1 Section Assessment

1. **Key Concept** List the different functions of the skeletal system.
2. **Key Concept** Describe the structure of a typical bone.
3. **Key Concept** What is a joint? List the three types of joints.
4. How does compact bone differ from spongy bone?
5. **Critical Thinking** **Inferring** Why do you think the amount of cartilage decreases and the amount of bone increases as a person develops?

Writing in Science

Creative Writing
Use library or Internet resources to find out more about osteoporosis. Then, develop an advertising campaign for the dairy industry based on the relationship between milk and healthy bone development.

36–1 Section Assessment

1. The skeletal system supports the body, protects internal organs, allows movement, stores mineral reserves, and provides a site for blood cell formation.
2. A typical bone has a thick layer of compact bone covered by periosteum. Haversian canals contain the blood vessels and nerves. At the ends of long bones, there is a layer of spongy bone beneath the compact bone layer.
3. A joint is a place where one bone attaches to another. Three types of joints are immovable, slightly movable, and freely movable.
4. Compact bone is denser than spongy bone. Spongy bone is found in the ends of long bones and in the middle of short, flat bones.
5. The cartilage decreases because minerals replace cartilage during ossification.

Answers to . . .

CHECKPOINT *Ball-and-socket, hinge, pivot, and saddle*

Figure 36–5 *They help reduce friction by providing a smooth, flexible surface between bones in joints.*

Section 36–2

7 5.c, BI 9.e, *BI 9.h

1 FOCUS

Objectives

36.2.1 ***Describe*** the three types of muscle tissue.

36.2.2 ***Explain*** how muscles contract.

36.2.3 ***Explain*** why exercise is important.

Guide for Reading

Vocabulary Preview

Call students' attention to the term *neuromuscular.* Point out that the term is made up of two parts, *neuro-*, which means "of or relating to the nervous system," and *muscular*, which means "of or relating to the muscular system." Ask: **What do you think the term *neuromuscular* means?** *(Of or relating to the nervous and muscular systems together)*

Reading Strategy

Before students read the section, suggest that they rewrite the headings as *how, why,* or *what* questions about the muscular system. As they read, they should write brief answers to their questions.

2 INSTRUCT

Types of Muscle Tissue

Build Science Skills

Inferring Show students a picture of a person with larger-than-average muscles, such as a wrestler or weight lifter, and then show them a picture of a person with average-sized muscles. Ask: **Would you infer that the person with larger muscles has more skeletal muscle cells?** *(Students are likely to say yes, even though the inference is incorrect.)* Explain that most people have about the same number of muscle cells, and then ask: **In what other way could muscles become larger?** *(By increasing the size of existing cells)*

L2 L3

36–2 The Muscular System

7 5.c. Students know how bones and muscles work together to provide a structural framework for movement.
BI 9.e. Students know the roles of sensory neurons, interneurons, and motor neurons in sensation, thought, and response.
***BI 9.h.** Students know the cellular and molecular basis of muscle contraction, including the roles of actin, myosin, Ca^{+2}, and ATP.

Guide for Reading

Key Concepts
- What are the three types of muscle tissue?
- How do muscles contract?
- Why is exercise important?

Vocabulary
myosin
actin
neuromuscular junction
acetylcholine
tendon

Reading Strategy: Summarizing As you read, find the main ideas for each paragraph. Write down a few key words from each main idea. Then, use the key words in your summary. Reread your summary, keeping only the most important ideas.

Despite the fantasies of Hollywood horror films, a skeleton cannot move by itself. Movement is the function of the muscular system. More than 40 percent of the mass of the average human body is muscle. The muscular system includes the large muscles displayed by some athletes. It also includes thousands of tiny muscles throughout the body that help to regulate blood pressure, move food through the digestive system, and power every movement of the body—from the blink of an eye to the hint of a smile.

Types of Muscle Tissue

Muscle tissue is found everywhere in the body—not only just beneath the skin but also deep within the body. **There are three different types of muscle tissue: skeletal, smooth, and cardiac.** Each type of muscle is specialized for a specific function in the body. Refer to **Figure 36–6** as you read about the different types of muscles.

CA a

Skeletal Muscles Skeletal muscles are usually attached to bones. Skeletal muscles are responsible for such voluntary movements as typing on a computer keyboard, dancing, or winking an eye. When viewed under a microscope at high magnification, skeletal muscle appears to have alternating light and dark bands called striations. For this reason, skeletal muscle is sometimes called striated muscle. Most skeletal muscles are consciously controlled by the central nervous system.

Skeletal muscle cells are large, have many nuclei, and vary in length from 1 millimeter to about 30 centimeters. Because skeletal muscle cells are long and slender, they are often called muscle fibers. Complete skeletal muscles consist of muscle fibers, connective tissues, blood vessels, and nerves. **Figure 36–7** shows the structure of a skeletal muscle in the leg.

Figure 36–6 **There are three types of muscle tissue: skeletal, smooth, and cardiac.** Skeletal muscle cells have striations, or stripes, and many nuclei. Smooth muscle cells are spindle-shaped and have one nucleus and no striations. Cardiac muscle cells have striations and usually only one nucleus.

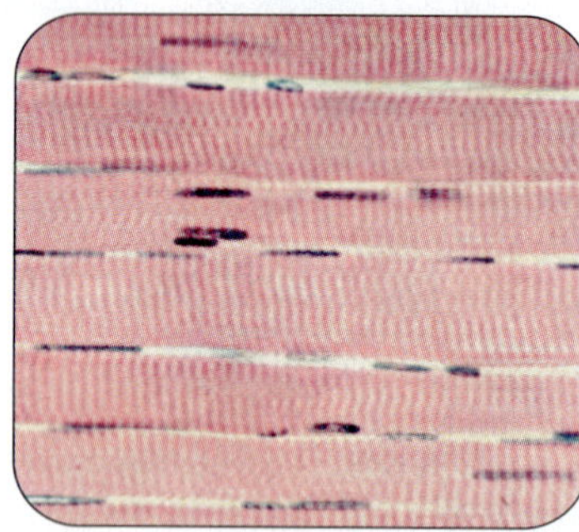

Skeletal Muscle (150×)

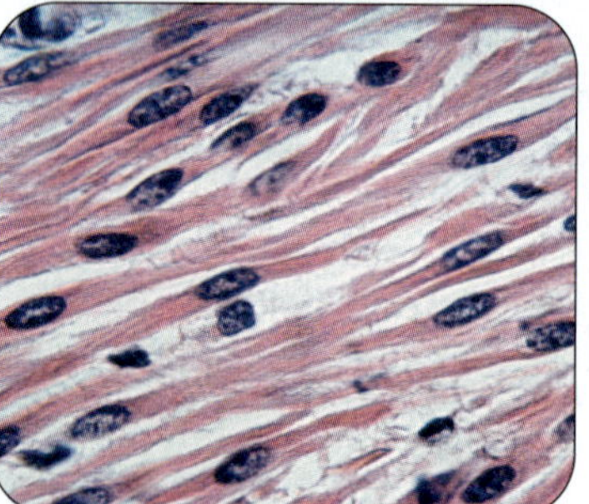

Smooth Muscle (400×)

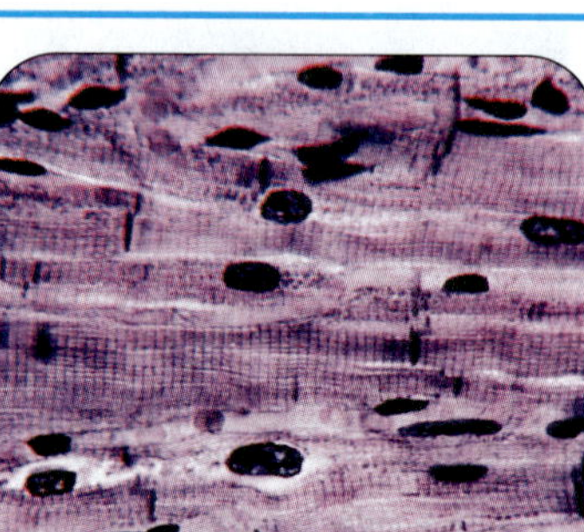

Cardiac Muscle (500×)

SECTION RESOURCES

Print:
- ***Laboratory Manual B,*** Chapter 36 Lab
- ***Teaching Resources,*** Lesson Plan 36–2, Adapted Section Summary 36–2, Adapted Worksheets 36–2, Section Summary 36–2, Worksheets 36–2, Section Review 36–2
- ***Reading and Study Workbook A,*** Section 36–2
- ***Adapted Reading and Study Workbook B,*** Section 36–2

Technology:
- ***iText,*** Section 36–2
- ***Animated Biological Concepts DVD,*** 39 Muscle Contraction
- ***Transparencies Plus,*** Section 36–2

Figure 36–7 Skeletal Muscle Structure

Skeletal muscles are made up of bundles of muscle fibers, which in turn are composed of myofibrils. Each myofibril contains thin filaments made of actin and thick filaments made of myosin. Muscle fibers are divided into functional units called sarcomeres. **Applying Concepts** *What nervous system structures carry messages to skeletal muscles?*

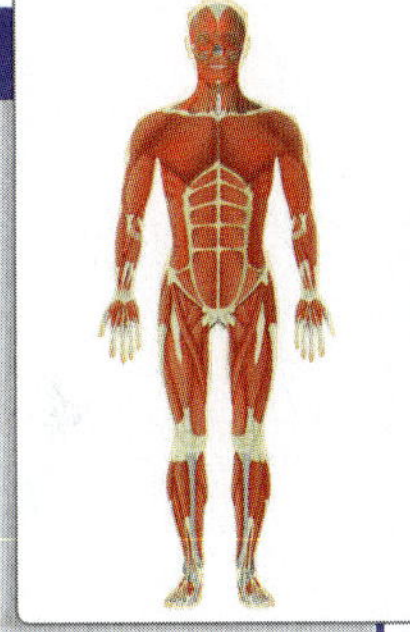

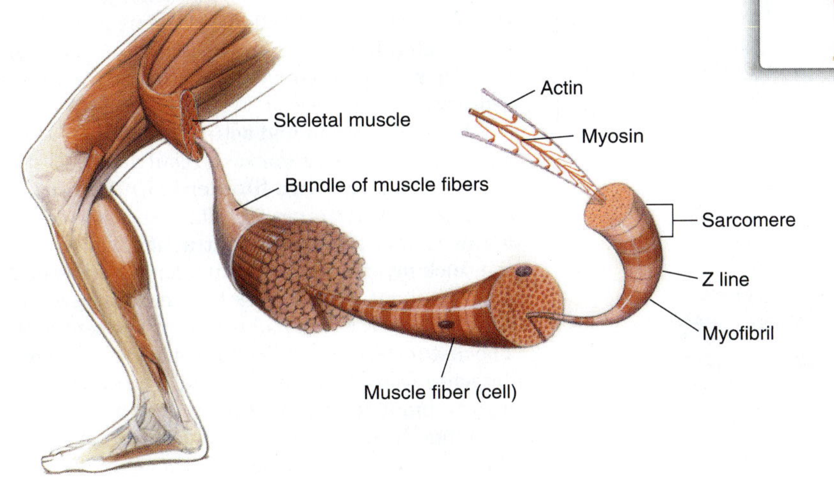

Smooth Muscles Smooth muscles are usually not under voluntary control. A smooth muscle cell is spindle-shaped, has one nucleus, and is not striated. Smooth muscles are found in the walls of hollow structures such as the stomach, blood vessels, and intestines. Smooth muscles move food through your digestive tract, control the way blood flows through your circulatory system, and decrease the size of the pupils of your eyes in bright light. Most smooth muscle cells can function without nervous stimulation. They are connected to one another by gap junctions that allow electrical impulses to travel directly from one muscle cell to a neighboring muscle cell.

Cardiac Muscle Cardiac muscle is found in just one place in the body—the heart. The prefix *cardio* comes from a Greek word meaning "heart." Cardiac muscle shares features with both skeletal muscle and smooth muscle. Cardiac muscle is striated like skeletal muscle, although its cells are smaller. Cardiac muscle cells usually have one nucleus, but they may have two. Cardiac muscle is similar to smooth muscle because it is usually not under the direct control of the central nervous system and cardiac cells are connected to their neighbors by gap junctions. You will learn more about cardiac muscle in Chapter 37.

For: Links on muscle contraction
Visit: www.SciLinks.org
Web Code: cbn-0362

CHECKPOINT *What kind of muscle tissue lines the blood vessels?*

Use Visuals

Figure 36–7 Call students' attention to the figure, which they might find confusing. Check their understanding by having them put the following terms in order from largest to smallest: myosin, muscle fiber, skeletal muscle, myofibril. *(Skeletal muscle, muscle fiber, myofibril, myosin)* Help students integrate the figure with the text by asking: **Which part of the drawing represents a single muscle cell?** *(The muscle fiber)* L1 L2

Build Science Skills

Inferring Call students' attention to the similarities between cardiac muscle and skeletal muscle and between cardiac muscle and smooth muscle. Ask: **Why is it important for cardiac muscle to share these features with the other two types of muscle?** *(The heart needs the features of skeletal muscle to perform the hard mechanical work of pumping blood throughout the body. It needs the features of smooth muscle to keep beating continuously without voluntary control.)* L2

Download a worksheet on muscle contraction for students to complete, and find additional teacher support from NSTA SciLinks.

UNIVERSAL ACCESS

Less Proficient Readers

Urge students to organize the information on types of muscle tissue in a compare/contrast matrix. Their matrices should have columns for type of tissue, how it is controlled, where it is found, whether or not it is striated, whether its cells are small or large, and whether it has one nucleus or many nuclei. Check students' completed matrices for accuracy, and advise them to save their matrices for review. L1 L2

Advanced Learners

Challenge students to research the opposing muscle groups in the human body. Using Internet or library resources, they should find the names, locations, and ranges of motion of each pair of opposing muscles. Have students create a diagram or other visual representation of what they learn and share it with the rest of the class. Allow time for questions. L3

Answers to . . .

CHECKPOINT *Smooth muscle tissue lines the blood vessels.*

Figure 36–7 *Motor neurons carry messages to skeletal muscles.*

36–2 (continued)

Muscle Contraction

Build Science Skills

Inferring Point out to students that the description of muscle contraction in the text applies specifically to skeletal muscles, which are easy to study. Guide students in inferring whether other muscles are likely to contract in a similar way. First ask: **Do you think that cardiac muscle or smooth muscles have alternating bands of thick and thin filaments as skeletal muscles do?** *(Students should infer that cardiac muscle has the filaments because it is striated like skeletal muscle, whereas smooth muscle lacks the filaments because it is not striated.)* Then, ask: **Do you think that smooth muscles or cardiac muscle contracts in a way that is similar to skeletal muscle contractions?** *(Students should infer that cardiac muscle may contract in a similar way but that smooth muscles probably do not.)* L2

Use Visuals

Figure 36–8 Make sure students understand that the three illustrations across the bottom of the figure show the sequence of events that occur during a muscle contraction. Help them integrate the top and bottom parts of the figure by asking: **What effect does the movement of the actin filament have on the distance between Z lines?** *(It shortens the distance.)* **How does this affect the muscle?** *(It causes the muscle to contract.)* L2

Muscle Contraction

The muscle fibers in skeletal muscles are composed of smaller structures called myofibrils. Each myofibril is made up of even smaller structures called filaments. The striations in skeletal muscle cells are formed by an alternating pattern of thick and thin filaments. The thick filaments contain a protein called **myosin** (MY-uh-sin). The thin filaments are made up mainly of a protein called **actin.** The filaments are arranged along the muscle fiber in units called sarcomeres, which are separated from each other by regions called Z lines. As **Figure 36–8** shows, when a muscle is relaxed, there are no thin filaments in the center of a sarcomere.

The tiny myosin and actin filaments are the force-producing engines that cause a muscle to contract. **A muscle contracts when the thin filaments in the muscle fiber slide over the thick filaments.** This process is called the sliding-filament model of muscle contraction. For a muscle to contract, the thick myosin filament must form a cross-bridge with the thin actin filament. As the cross-bridge changes shape, it pulls on the actin filament, which slides toward the center of the sarcomere. The distance between the Z lines decreases. The cross-bridge detaches from the actin filament. The cycle is repeated when the myosin binds to another site on the actin filament.

When hundreds of thousands of myosin cross-bridges change shape in a fraction of a second, the muscle fiber shortens with considerable force. The energy for muscle contraction is supplied by ATP. Because one molecule of ATP supplies the energy for one interaction between a myosin cross-bridge and an actin filament, the cell needs plenty of ATP molecules for a strong contraction. Recall that the cell can produce ATP in two ways—by cellular respiration and by fermentation.

CHECKPOINT *What is actin? What is myosin?*

Figure 36–8 During muscle contraction, the actin filaments slide over the myosin filaments, decreasing the distance between the Z lines.

Movement of Actin Filament

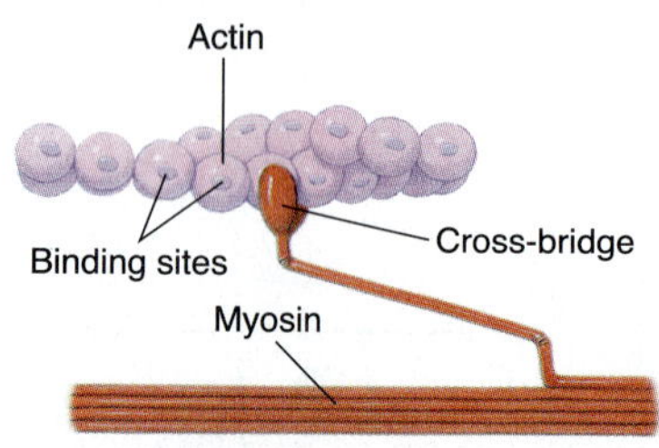

During muscle contraction, the knoblike head of a myosin filament attaches to a binding site on actin, forming a cross-bridge.

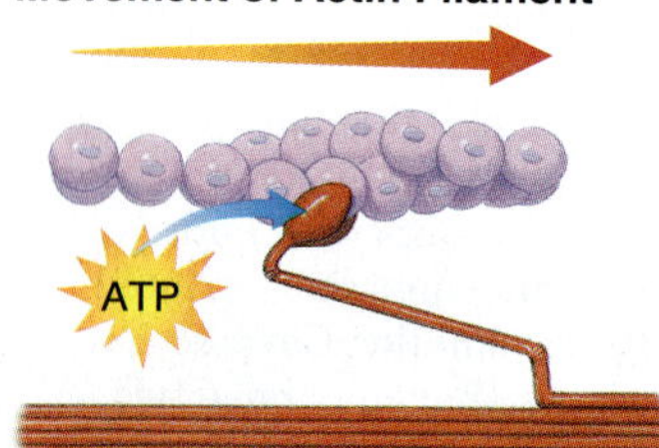

Powered by ATP, the myosin cross-bridge changes shape and pulls the actin filament toward the center of the sarcomere.

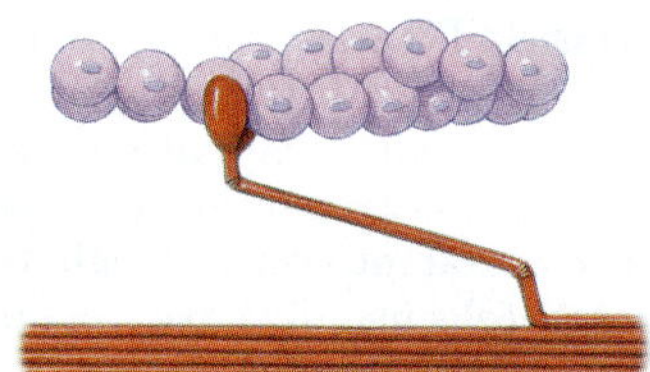

The cross-bridge is broken, the myosin binds to another site on the actin filament, and the cycle begins again.

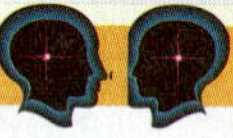

TEACHER TO TEACHER

After teaching about muscle contraction, I challenge students to defend one of two positions regarding the best way to prepare for a workout: first warm up and then stretch or first stretch and then warm up. I guide the class in concluding that warming up should precede stretching, because a cold muscle cannot be adequately stretched. I also point out that a stretched muscle can contract with greater force than a muscle that has not been stretched.

After teaching about the synapse and the enzyme cholinesterase, I ask students to predict what would happen if the enzyme were somehow inactivated. This facilitates student understanding of muscle paralysis and the actions of insecticides and nerve gases.

—*Thomas P. Rooney, Ph.D.*
Science Department Chair
Father Judge High School
Philadelphia, PA

Control of Muscle Contraction

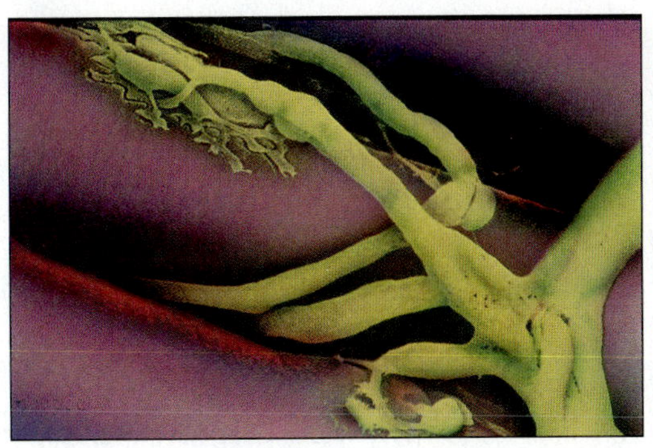

▲ **Figure 36–9** The long green axon of a motor neuron makes contact with a long pink muscle fiber at the neuromuscular junction. (Note that color has been added to this SEM.)

Skeletal muscles are useful only if they contract in a controlled fashion. Remember that motor neurons connect the central nervous system to skeletal muscle cells. Impulses from motor neurons control the contraction of skeletal muscle fibers.

Figure 36–9 shows a **neuromuscular** (noo-roh-MUS-kyoo-lur) **junction,** which is the point of contact between a motor neuron and a skeletal muscle cell. Vesicles, or pockets, in the axon terminals of the motor neuron release a neurotransmitter called **acetylcholine** (as-ih-til-KOH-leen). Acetylcholine molecules diffuse across the synapse, producing an impulse in the cell membrane of the muscle fiber. The impulse causes the release of calcium ions (Ca^{2+}) within the fiber. The calcium ions affect regulatory proteins that allow actin and myosin filaments to interact. From the time a nerve impulse reaches a muscle cell, it is only a few milliseconds before these events occur and the muscle cell contracts.

A muscle cell remains contracted until the release of acetylcholine stops and an enzyme produced at the axon terminal destroys any remaining acetylcholine. Then, the cell pumps calcium ions back into storage, the cross-bridges stop forming, and contraction ends.

What is the difference between a strong contraction and a weak contraction? Each muscle contains hundreds of cells. When you lift something light, such as a sheet of paper, your brain stimulates only a few cells in your arm muscles to contract. However, as you exert maximum effort, as the rock climber in **Figure 36–10** is doing, almost all the muscle cells in your arm are stimulated to contract.

▼ **Figure 36–10** Because this rock climber exercises regularly, her muscles are firm and have increased in size. **Predicting** ***What would happen to her muscles if she stopped exercising regularly?***

HISTORY OF SCIENCE

A painter and a poison

One of the earliest scientists to study and correctly portray the human muscular system was the Italian artist Leonardo da Vinci, who lived between 1452 and 1519. Up until da Vinci's time, knowledge of the muscular system was based as much on myth as on fact. Da Vinci's knowledge of the muscular system, in contrast, was based on dissections, and his drawings of the muscles were accurate as well as beautiful. In the mid-1800s, the role of nerves in the contraction of skeletal muscles was established by a scientist named Claude Bernard, who did experiments using a drug called curare. Curare blocks the transmission of nerve impulses, and it was used by some Amazonian Native Americans to poison the tips of their hunting arrows. Bernard injected curare into muscles and found that the muscles became paralyzed when nerve impulses were blocked by the drug.

Control of Muscle Contraction

Make Connections

Health Science Help students relate nervous control of muscles to health issues. Point out that many cases of paralysis occur as a result of spinal cord injuries. Remind students that the spinal cord carries nerve impulses from the brain to other parts of the body. Ask: **How does a spinal cord injury cause paralysis of the legs?** *(The injury interrupts the pathway of impulses from the brain to the nerves that control muscles in the legs. Without impulses from the nerves, the muscles cannot contract, and paralysis results.)* L2

Demonstration

Use a simple demonstration to emphasize the role of the central nervous system in muscle contraction. Hold a small, closed box that contains a book or other object. Tell the class that the box is empty and, therefore, very light in weight. Then, hand the box to a volunteer while the other students watch. Being prepared for a lightweight object, the volunteer is likely to nearly drop the box before realizing that it is heavy and compensating for the unexpected weight. Ask: **What would have happened if the volunteer had known the box was heavy instead of light?** *(The volunteer's central nervous system would have been prepared to stimulate more muscle cells to contract before he or she took the box.)* L1 L2

Answers to . . .

CHECKPOINT *Actin is the protein in the thin filaments of skeletal muscles. Myosin is the protein that makes up the thick filaments of skeletal muscles.*

Figure 36–10 *Her muscles would decrease in size.*

36–2 (continued)

How Muscles and Bones Interact

Quick Lab

 7 5.c

Objective Students will be able to compare and contrast movements of the tendons that control chicken wings and their own fingers. L2

Skill Focus **Applying Concepts, Comparing and Contrasting**

Materials plastic gloves, raw chicken wing treated with bleach, paper towels, forceps, scissors, scalpel

Time 20 minutes

Advance Prep Briefly soak the wings in bleach to kill any surface bacteria. Then, rinse them thoroughly in water and dry them. If you do not use the wings immediately, refrigerate them until you do.

Safety All work surfaces should be disinfected at the end of the lab. Dispose of the chicken parts properly.

Strategies

- If necessary, help students find the biceps muscle in the chicken wing.
- Students can observe the tendons that control their fingers by watching the backs of their hands as they drum their fingers on their desks.

Expected Outcomes Students should observe that pulling on the tendon in the wing causes the wing to bend and that bending their fingers causes the tendons in their hands to move.

Analyze and Conclude

1. The wing bent at the joint. In a live chicken, the biceps muscle would pull on the tendon.
2. Like the chicken's biceps muscle, muscles controlling the fingers cause the fingers to bend by pulling on tendons.

Quick Lab

What do tendons do?

 7 5.c

Biceps

Tendon

Materials raw chicken wing treated with bleach, paper towels, forceps, scissors, scalpel

Procedure   

1. Put on the plastic gloves and lab apron. **CAUTION:** *Do not touch your face with your hands during the lab. Be careful with the scissors and scalpel.*
2. Put a chicken wing on a paper towel. Peel back or cut away the skin and fat of the largest wing segment to expose the large muscle. This muscle is called the biceps. Find the tendon that attaches the biceps to the bones of the middle segment of the wing. Tendons are the tough, shiny white cords that join the muscles to the bones.
3. Use forceps to pull on the tendon of the biceps and observe what happens to the chicken wing.
4. Clean your tools and dispose of the chicken wing and gloves according to your teacher's instructions. Wash your hands with soap and warm water.
5. Next, observe the back of your hand as you move each of your fingers in turn. Compare what you see to how the chicken wing moved.

Analyze and Conclude

1. **Applying Concepts** What happened when you pulled on the tendon? In a live chicken, what structure would pull on the tendon to move the wing?
2. **Comparing and Contrasting** How is the way the wing moves similar to the way your fingers move?

How Muscles and Bones Interact

Skeletal muscles generate force and produce movement by contracting, or pulling on body parts. Individual muscles can only pull in one direction. Yet, you know from experience that your legs bend when you sit and extend when you stand up. How is this possible?

Skeletal muscles are joined to bones by tough connective tissues called **tendons.** Tendons are attached in such a way that they pull on the bones and make them work like levers. The joint functions as a fulcrum—the fixed point around which the lever moves. The muscles provide the force to move the lever. Usually, there are several muscles surrounding each joint that pull in different directions.

Most skeletal muscles work in opposing pairs. When one muscle contracts, the other relaxes. The muscles of the upper arm shown in **Figure 36–11** are a good example of this dual action. When the biceps muscle contracts, it bends, or flexes, the elbow joint. When the triceps muscle contracts, it opens, or extends, the elbow joint. A controlled movement, however, requires contraction by both muscles. To hold a tennis racket or a violin, both the biceps and triceps must contract in balance. This is why the training of athletes and musicians is so difficult. The brain must learn how to work opposing muscle groups in just the right ways to make the joint move precisely.

FACTS AND FIGURES

All about muscles

There are about 600 different muscles in the human body and an astounding 6 trillion individual muscle fibers. The largest muscle is the gluteus maximus, covering the buttocks. The smallest is the stapedius, located in the middle ear. Contrary to popular belief, muscles are not made up mostly of protein. Protein makes up only about 20 percent of muscle. Water makes up most of the rest. Muscles are surprisingly inefficient. Even under ideal conditions, more than half the total chemical energy used by muscles is lost in the form of heat. After playing squash for just 7 minutes, a 62-kilogram person produces enough heat to raise the temperature of 91 liters of water by 1°C. Although most people complete their growth in body size by age 20, muscular strength keeps increasing, usually peaking sometime between the ages of 20 and 30.

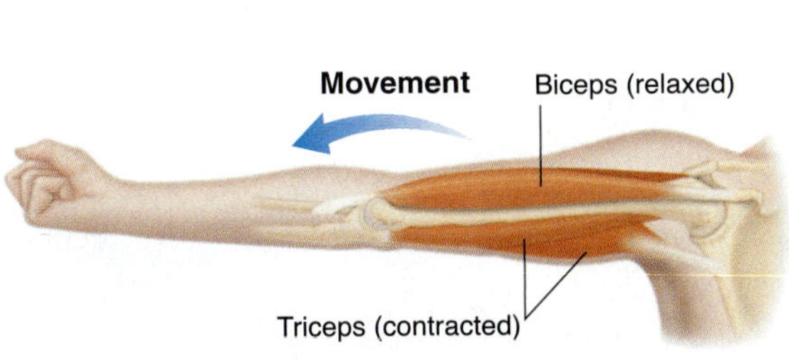

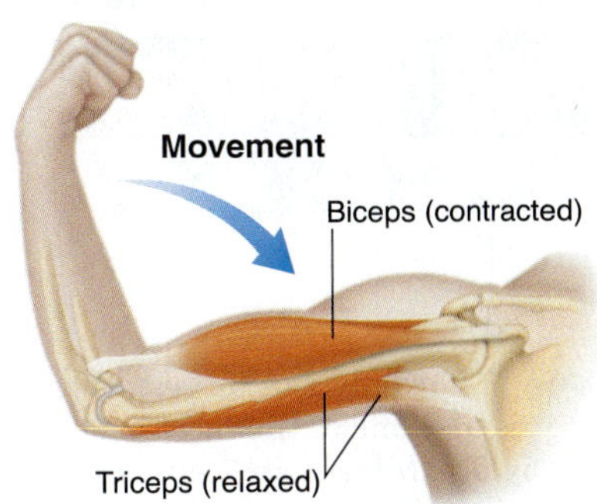

Exercise and Health

Skeletal muscles generally remain in a state of partial contraction called resting muscle tone. Muscle tone is responsible for keeping the back and legs straight and the head upright, even when you are relaxed.

Regular exercise is important in maintaining muscular strength and flexibility. Muscles that are exercised regularly stay firm and increase in size and strength by adding actin and myosin filaments. Muscles that are not used become weak and can visibly decrease in size.

Aerobic exercises—such as running and swimming—cause the body's systems to become more efficient. For example, aerobic exercise helps your heart and lungs become more efficient. This, in turn, increases physical endurance—the ability to perform an activity without fatigue. Regular exercise also strengthens your bones, making them thicker and stronger. Strong bones and muscles are less likely to become injured.

Resistance exercises, such as weight lifting, increase muscle size and strength. Resistance exercises also decrease body fat and increase muscle mass. Over time, weight-training exercises will help to maintain coordination and flexibility.

▲ **Figure 36–11** By contracting and relaxing, the triceps and biceps in the upper arm enable you to bend or straighten your elbow. **Applying Concepts** *Which skeletal muscle must contract in order for you to straighten your elbow?*

36–2 Section Assessment

1. **Key Concept** List the three types of muscle tissue and explain the function of each.
2. **Key Concept** Explain how a muscle contracts.
3. **Key Concept** Describe the importance of regular exercise.
4. What is the function of the muscular system?
5. What is the role of acetylcholine in the process of muscle contraction?
6. **Critical Thinking** **Predicting** If a muscle cell receives a second stimulus while it is contracting, will it respond to the second stimulus? Explain.

Sharpen Your Skills

Using Models

Create your own model to show how actin filaments slide over myosin filaments during a muscle contraction. Include as much detail in your model as possible.

36–2 Section Assessment

1. Skeletal, which controls voluntary movements; smooth, which controls involuntary movements; and cardiac, which controls contractions of the heart
2. Myosin cross-bridges cause the thin filaments to slide over the thick filaments, shortening the muscle.
3. It maintains muscular and skeletal strength; increases coordination, endurance, and flexibility; and decreases body fat.
4. To control body movement, help circulate blood, and help move food through the digestive system
5. Acetylcholine is a neurotransmitter. It diffuses across nerve synapses to produce impulses in muscle cell membranes.
6. No; it must relax before it can respond to a second impulse.

Exercise and Health

Use Community Resources

Invite a physical therapist, personal trainer, or other exercise specialist to speak to the class about exercising to increase and maintain muscle size and strength. Ask the speaker to tailor the message to high-school students. If possible, have the speaker demonstrate exercises to help maintain muscle tone and prevent injury. Urge students to ask questions at the end of the talk. L2

3 ASSESS

Evaluate Understanding

Have students make Venn diagrams comparing and contrasting skeletal muscle tissue, smooth muscle tissue, and cardiac muscle tissue.

Reteach

Using the chalkboard or a transparency, work with the class to make a flowchart showing how a motor neuron stimulates a muscle cell.

Sharpen Your Skills

The models should illustrate the following: A cross-bridge forms between the actin and myosin filaments. When the cross-bridge bends, the actin slides over the myosin. Then, the cross-bridge detaches, unbends, and reattaches to a new site on the actin.

If your class subscribes to the iText, use it to review the Key Concepts in Section 36–2.

Answer to . . .

Figure 36–11 *The triceps muscle must contract to straighten your elbow.*

TECHNOLOGY & SOCIETY

 BIIE 1.I

Students will get more out of the feature if they first read Section 36–3. After students have read the feature, you might want to discuss one or more of the following:

- How burns are classified based on the degree of skin damage they cause, as first-degree, second-degree, or third-degree burns, with third-degree burns being the most serious
- How burns that affect the dermis differ from burns that affect only the epidermis
- What causes burns, including matches, flammable liquids, hot water, and steam
- How students can prevent burns, for example, by following package precautions when using flammable liquids and testing bathwater before getting in

Research and Decide

Students are likely to find the most up-to-date information on artificial skin on the Internet. Useful Web sites include those of the Shriners and the National Institute of General Medical Sciences. Students' brochures should include the following steps: covering the burn to help prevent infection; elevating the hands and feet to help prevent shock; getting the victim to a hospital as soon as possible; and replacing the burned skin with a new barrier against infection, using either skin grafts or artificial skin.

Students can research artificial skin on the site developed by authors Ken Miller and Joe Levine.

TECHNOLOGY & SOCIETY

Making Artificial Skin

 BIIE 1.I

The skin is not only the largest organ in the body, it is also one of the most easily injured, especially by fire. More than 2 million Americans suffer burn injuries every year, and more than 10,000 die from such injuries. The skin is the body's most important barrier against infection, but burns can destroy that barrier, leaving tissues exposed and vulnerable.

The best way to protect badly burned tissue is to cover it with a layer of fresh skin. If the burned region is small, this can be done with skin grafts taken from other parts of the body. For larger burns, however, this isn't possible. Scientists have developed a way to help many victims of serious burns—they have developed artificial skin.

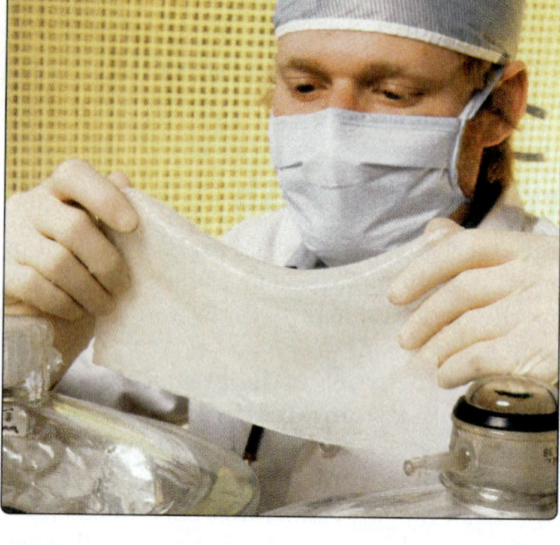

Constructing a Scaffold

Skin is a complex organ. For this reason, researchers realized that the best way to replace skin would be with an artificial skin that the body's own cells could grow into. After the outer layer of burned tissue is removed from a severely burned patient, surgeons can apply artificial skin made from a biodegradable meshwork of protein fibers similar to those in human skin. Cells from the dermis migrate upward and gradually "take over" the artificial layer, replacing the meshwork with human proteins. Thus, a new layer of dermis is produced. A very thin layer of the patient's own epidermal cells, grown in culture, is then applied to the surface of the artificial skin.

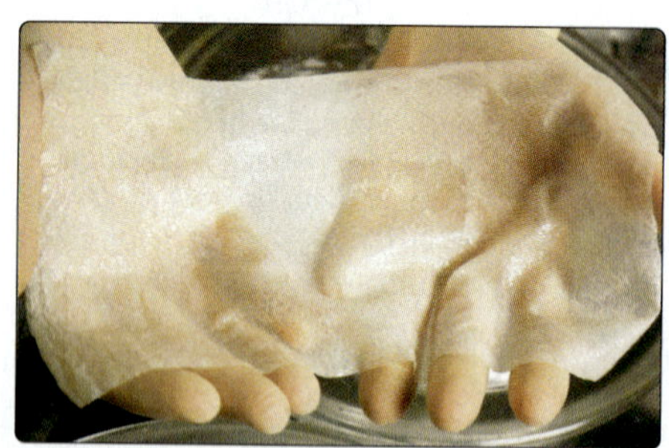

Perfecting the Technique

Artificial skin is used only in the treatment of burns so severe that normal healing is not possible. One of its main drawbacks is that the migration of cells into the artificial layer may take as long as three weeks, enough time for infection and other complications to develop. Researchers are trying to speed up the process by placing cell-growth signal chemicals in the artificial layer. If they succeed, the successful treatment of even serious burns may become routine.

Research and Decide

Use library or Internet references to learn more about artifical skin and how it is used for the treatment of serious burns. Design a brochure that explains and illustrates the steps in the treatment of third-degree burns.

For: Links from the authors
Visit: PHSchool.com
Web Code: cbe-0363

36–3 The Integumentary System

BI 10.a. Students know the role of the skin in providing nonspecific defenses against infection.

"Good fences make good neighbors," wrote the American poet Robert Frost as he explained the importance of property boundaries. Living things have their own "fences," and none is as important as the skin—the boundary that separates the human body from the outside world.

The skin, the single largest organ of the body, is part of the integumentary (in-teg-yoo-MEN-tuh-ree) system. The word *integument* comes from a Latin word that means "to cover," reflecting the fact that the skin and its related structures form a covering over the entire body. Skin and its related structures—the hair, nails, and a variety of glands—make up the integumentary system.

The Skin

The skin has many different functions, but its most important function is protection. **The integumentary system serves as a barrier against infection and injury, helps to regulate body temperature, removes waste products from the body, and provides protection against ultraviolet radiation from the sun.** Because the largest component of the integumentary system—the skin—contains several types of sensory receptors, it serves as the gateway through which sensations such as pressure, heat, cold, and pain are transmitted to the nervous system.

The skin is made up of two main layers—the epidermis and the dermis. Beneath the dermis is a subcutaneous layer of fat (the hypodermis) and loose connective tissue that help insulate the body.

Guide for Reading

Key Concept
- What are the functions of the integumentary system?

Vocabulary
epidermis
keratin
melanin
dermis
hair follicle

Reading Strategy: Building Vocabulary
Before you read, preview **Figure 36–13** to identify vocabulary with which you are unfamiliar. As you read, look for the meaning of these terms.

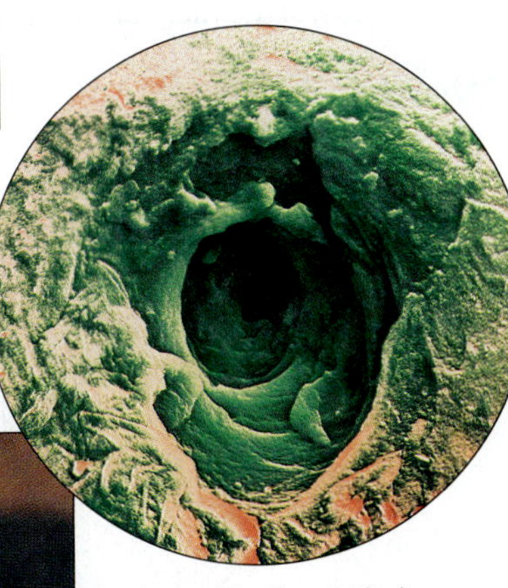

(magnification: 340×)

Figure 36–12 **After strenuous exercise, the skin produces sweat, which decreases the temperature of the body and rids the body of wastes.** Sweat is secreted by sweat glands and leaves the body through sweat pores.

SECTION RESOURCES

Print:
- ***Teaching Resources,*** Lesson Plan 36–3, Adapted Section Summary 36–3, Adapted Worksheets 36–3, Section Summary 36–3, Worksheets 36–3, Section Review 36–3, Enrichment
- ***Reading and Study Workbook A,*** Section 36–3
- ***Lab Worksheets,*** Chapter 36 Real-World Lab
- ***Adapted Reading and Study Workbook B,*** Section 36–3

Technology:
- ***iText,*** Section 36–3
- ***Transparencies Plus,*** Section 36–3

Section 36–3

BI 10.a

1 FOCUS

Objectives

36.3.1 ***State*** the functions of the integumentary system.
36.3.2 ***Describe*** the structure of hair and nails.

Guide for Reading

Vocabulary Preview
Before students read the section, suggest that they preview new Vocabulary by finding each Vocabulary word in the section and reading its definition.

Reading Strategy
Call students' attention to the Key Concept on this page that states the functions of the integumentary system. Then, when they preview Figure 36–13, have students predict which structures are involved in each function. As students read the section, they should note whether or not their predictions were correct.

2 INSTRUCT

The Skin

Demonstration
Before class begins, cut an apple in half. Tightly cover one half of the apple with plastic wrap and leave the other half exposed to the air. During class, pass the two apple halves around the room so that students can inspect them. Then, ask: **How do the two apple halves differ?** *(The cut surface of the unwrapped half has started to turn brown and dry out. The cut surface of the wrapped half is still white and moist.)* **Based on your observations, what role do you think the skin of the apple plays?** *(It protects the inside of the apple from drying out and turning brown.)* **How is the skin of an apple like human skin?** *(Both protect what is inside.)*

36–3 (continued)

Word Origins

Epiphyte means "on the outside of a plant." It is a plant that grows on another plant. L2

Use Visuals

Figure 36–13 Have students use the information in the figure to make a chart comparing and contrasting the dermis and epidermis in terms of their location and thickness and the structures they contain. *(Student charts should show that the epidermis is the thinner, outer layer of skin through which hairs and pores pass, and the dermis is the thicker, inner layer of skin containing blood vessels, nerve endings, muscles, hair follicles, and sweat and sebaceous glands.)* L1 L2

Build Science Skills

Using Models Have students sketch three simple cross-sectional models of the epidermis. Then, have them use their models to show how cells in the epidermis are replaced. They should modify the first sketch to show skin cells dividing, the second sketch to show skin cells moving upward to the skin's surface, and the third sketch to show skin cells being shed. Ask volunteers to share their completed models with the class. L2

FIGURE 36–13 STRUCTURE OF THE SKIN

The skin has an outer layer called the epidermis and an inner layer called the dermis. **Predicting** *What is the function of the dermis?*

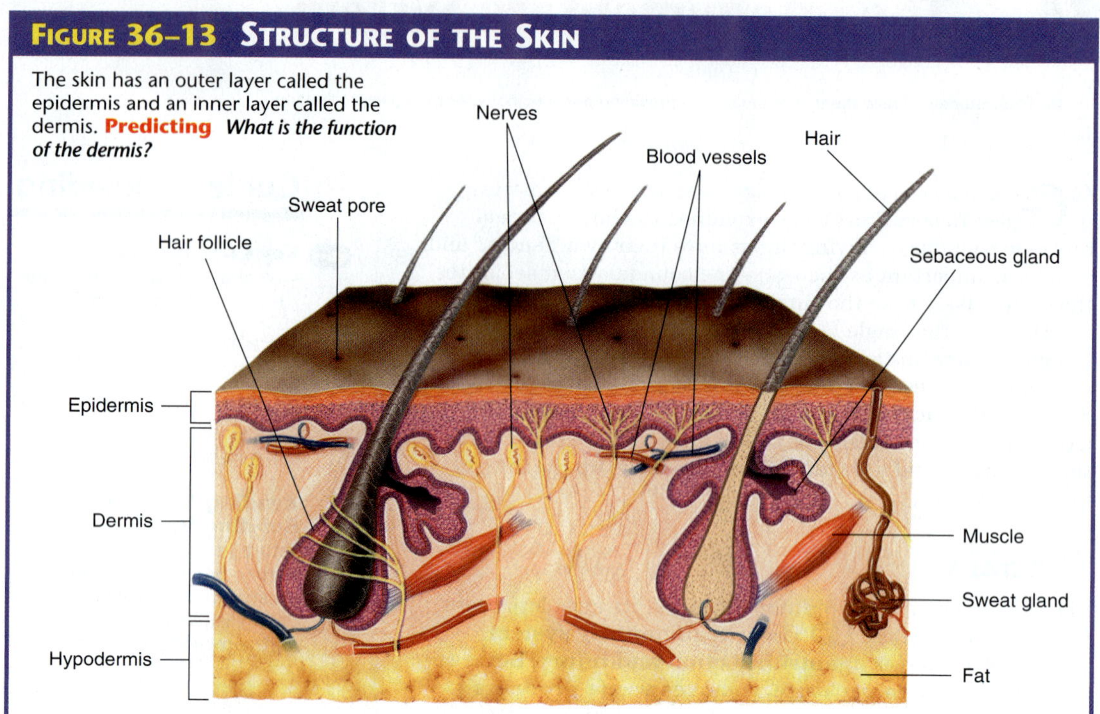

Word Origins

Epidermis comes from two Greek words: *epi,* meaning "on the outside," and *derma,* meaning "skin." **If the Greek word *phyton* means "plant," what does the term *epiphyte* mean?**

Epidermis The outer layer of the skin is the **epidermis.** The epidermis has two layers. The outside of the epidermis—the part that comes in contact with the environment—is made up of dead cells. The inner layer of the epidermis is made up of living cells.

Cells in the inner layer of the epidermis undergo rapid cell division, producing new cells that push older cells to the surface of the skin. As they move upward, the older cells become flattened and their organelles disintegrate. They also begin making **keratin,** a tough, fibrous protein.

Eventually, the keratin-producing cells die and form a tough, flexible, waterproof covering on the surface of the skin. This outer layer of dead cells is shed or washed away at a surprising rate—once every four to five weeks.

The epidermis also contains melanocytes (MEL-uh-noh-syts). Melanocytes are cells that produce **melanin,** a dark brown pigment. Melanin helps protect the skin from damage by absorbing ultraviolet rays from the sun. Although most people have roughly the same number of melanocytes in their skin, differences in skin color are caused by the different amount of melanin the melanocytes produce and where these cells are distributed.

Look closely at **Figure 36–13** and you will see that there are no blood vessels in the epidermis. This explains why a slight scratch will not cause bleeding.

What is melanin?

UNIVERSAL ACCESS

Inclusion/Special Needs

Help students appreciate the sensory abilities of the skin. Have them close their eyes and try to identify a familiar object by touch alone. Then, have students experience pressure by pushing the eraser end of a pencil against their palms. Finally, have students touch a warm object such as a heating pad and a cold object such as ice. Discuss how these sensory abilities of the skin could help protect the body from injury. L1

Advanced Learners

Challenge students to investigate the relationship between body shape and temperature regulation. *(A lean, linear body shape has more surface area of skin, relative to volume, and is better at losing heat; a short, stocky body shape has less relative surface area of skin and is better at retaining heat.)* Ask students to explain the relationship in an oral report, illustrated with pictures of people with different body shapes. L3

Dermis The inner layer of the skin is the **dermis.** The dermis lies beneath the epidermis and contains collagen fibers, blood vessels, nerve endings, glands, sensory receptors, smooth muscles, and hair follicles.

The skin interacts with other body systems to maintain homeostasis by helping to regulate body temperature. When the body needs to conserve heat on a cold day, the blood vessels in the dermis narrow, helping to limit heat loss. On hot days, the blood vessels widen, bringing heat from the body's core to the skin and increasing heat loss.

The dermis contains two major types of glands: sweat glands and sebaceous (suh-BAY-shus), or oil, glands. If your body gets too hot, sweat glands produce perspiration, or sweat. Sweat contains water, salts, and other compounds. When sweat evaporates, it takes heat away from your body. Sweat also gets rid of wastes from the blood, along with water. In this way, the skin acts as an organ of excretion. Sebaceous glands produce an oily secretion called sebum. Sebum spreads out along the surface of the skin and helps to keep the keratin-rich epidermis flexible and waterproof.

CHECKPOINT *What structures are found in the dermis?*

6IIE 7.c

Analyzing Data

The UV Index and Sunburn

Ultraviolet (UV) radiation is one type of energy from the sun. UV rays cause sunburn, some cataracts, and skin cancer. There are many factors that affect the amount of UV radiation to which you are exposed. These include the time of day, the season, the weather conditions, and your location. Recently, the National Weather Service, the Environmental Protection Agency, and the Centers for Disease Control agreed upon a national UV index. The UV index is issued daily to advise you of conditions in your region of the country. Use the information in the chart to answer the questions that follow.

1. **Interpreting Graphics** Describe the trend in the amount of time it takes to sunburn, from a minimal UV index level to a very high UV index level.
2. **Applying Concepts** Why do you think applying sunscreen is always recommended?
3. **Drawing Conclusions** Why should a hat worn as protection against UV rays have a brim?
4. **Predicting** The minutes-to-burn data apply to most people. What variable could cause the time for a particular person to burn to be shorter or to be longer?

Protection From Sunburn

UV Index Level	How to Protect Yourself	Minutes to Burn
Minimal (0–2)	Apply sunscreen Wear sunglasses near snow and water	60
Low (3–4)	Apply sunscreen Wear sunglasses and hat	45
Moderate (5–6)	Apply sunscreen Wear sunglasses and hat Apply lip balm	30
High (7–9)	Apply sunscreen Wear sunglasses and hat Seek shade from 10 AM to 4 PM	15
Very High (10+)	Apply sunscreen Wear sunglasses and hat Avoid sun from 10 AM to 4 PM	10

5. **Using Tables and Graphs** Use the data in the table to construct a bar graph. Place the UV index levels on the *x*-axis and the minutes to burn on the *y*-axis.

Address Misconceptions

Some students may think that people with dark skin do not need to protect their skin from the sun or that people who tan without burning are not damaging their skin when they get darker in the summer. Correct these misconceptions by explaining that any skin can be damaged by exposure to sunlight. Although melanin helps protect the skin from sunlight, even people with a lot of melanin in their skin can suffer sun damage. L2

Analyzing Data

6IIE 7.c

Call on students to give a definition of the term *UV index. (An indicator of the strength of UV radiation based on how long it takes skin to burn)* Suggest to students that they watch a televised weather report on a sunny day and note how the UV index is reported and what its value is. L2

Answers

1. The amount of time it takes to burn decreases.
2. Because even low levels of UV radiation can damage the skin
3. To protect the face and eyes
4. Amount of melanin in the skin
5. Graphs should have five bars of decreasing height.

BIO INSIGHTS — FACTS AND FIGURES

Evolution of human skin color
Human skin color shows a gradual geographic trend in Africa and Europe: Populations increasingly far from the equator tend to have less and less melanin in their skin. Virtually all the hypotheses that have been proposed to account for this trend assume that variation in the amount of sunlight is the ultimate cause. One widely held hypothesis states that darker skin is selected for at lower latitudes because its higher melanin content helps protect it from serious sunburn and skin cancer, which can threaten survival. Another hypothesis proposes that lighter skin is selected for at higher latitudes because it can be penetrated by sunlight, which is needed to produce vitamin D in deep layers of the skin. According to this hypothesis, the extra vitamin D produced in the skin of lighter-skinned people helps prevent rickets, which can jeopardize female fertility by causing pelvic deformities.

Answers to . . .

CHECKPOINT *Melanin is a brown pigment produced by melanocytes in the epidermis.*

CHECKPOINT *Collagen fibers, blood vessels, nerve endings, glands, sensory receptors, smooth muscles, and hair follicles*

Figure 36–13 *Based on structures located in the dermis, students may predict that the dermis produces sweat and oil, controls growth of hair, and is responsible for detecting sense stimuli such as touch.*

36–3 (continued)

Hair and Nails

Build Science Skills

Designing Experiments Point out to students that many different factors—such as age, gender, general health status, genetic background, some diseases, and certain medications—can affect the pattern and rate of hair growth. Challenge students to design an experiment to measure the effects of one particular factor on hair growth. Call on students to give a brief description of their experimental design, including the hypothesis they would test. Ask: **Which variable would you investigate and which variables would you control?** *(Students should investigate one variable, such as age or gender, and control, or hold constant, any other variables believed to affect hair growth, such as certain illnesses or medications.)* 

3 ASSESS

Evaluate Understanding

Call on several students at random to name the functions of the skin.

Reteach

Have students define or describe the function of each of the structures of the skin that are shown in Figure 36–13.

Focus on the BIG Idea

Some of the topics students might address are the outer waterproof coverings; the roles of the guard cells and sweat and oil glands; trichomes and nails; and the roles of root hair cells and human hair. Similarities include the cuticle in plants and the keratin in skin.

If your class subscribes to the iText, use it to review the Key Concepts in Section 36–3.

Answer to . . .

Figure 36–14 *The dermis contains the hair follicle.*

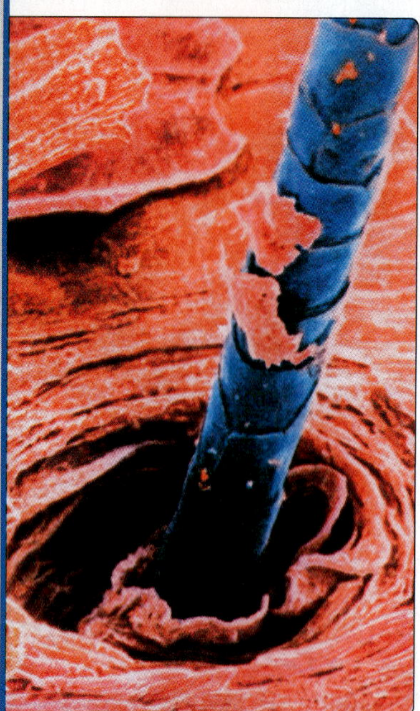

▲ **Figure 36–14** In this color-enhanced scanning electron micrograph of a hair shaft, the scalelike structures are layers of skin cells. The part of the hair that is above the skin is made up of dead cells that become filled with keratin. **Observing** *What layer of the skin contains the hair follicle?*

Skin Cancer Excessive exposure to the ultraviolet radiation in sunlight can produce skin cancer, an abnormal growth of cells in the skin. You can help protect yourself from this dangerous disease by wearing a hat, sunglasses, and protective clothing whenever you plan to spend time outside. In addition, you should always use a sunscreen with a sun protection factor (SPF) of at least 15.

Hair and Nails

The basic structure of human hair and nails is keratin. In other animals, keratin forms a variety of structures, including bull horns, reptile scales, bird feathers, and porcupine quills.

Hair Hair covers almost every exposed surface of the body and has important functions. Hair on the head protects the scalp from ultraviolet light from the sun and provides insulation from the cold. Hairs in the nostrils, external ear canals, and around the eyes (eyelashes) prevent dirt and other particles from entering the body.

Hair is produced by cells at the base of structures called hair follicles. **Hair follicles** are tubelike pockets of epidermal cells that extend into the dermis. The individual hair shown in **Figure 36–14** is actually a large column of cells that have filled with keratin and then died. Rapid cell growth at the base of the hair follicle causes the hair to grow longer. Hair follicles are in close contact with sebaceous glands. The oily secretions of these glands help maintain the condition of each individual hair.

Nails Nails grow from an area of rapidly dividing cells known as the nail root. The nail root is located near the tips of the fingers and toes. During cell division, the cells of the nail root fill with keratin and produce a tough, platelike nail that covers and protects the tips of the fingers and toes. Nails grow at an average rate of 3 millimeters per month, with fingernails growing more rapidly than toenails—about four times as fast.

36–3 Section Assessment

1. **Key Concept** List the functions of the integumentary system.
2. What organs and tissues make up the integumentary system?
3. Compare the structures of the epidermis and dermis.
4. How does the skin help maintain body temperature?
5. In what way is the growth of hair and nails similar?
6. **Critical Thinking Applying Concepts** Why does cutting your skin hurt, but cutting your hair or nails does not hurt?

Focus on the BIG Idea

Structure and Function
Compare and contrast the structure and function of the dermal tissue in plants discussed in Chapter 23 with the structures in human skin. In what ways are they similar? *Hint:* You may wish to organize your ideas in a Venn diagram.

36–3 Section Assessment

1. Serves as a barrier against infection and injury, helps regulate body temperature, removes waste products, protects against UV radiation, and allows sensory input
2. Skin, hair, nails, and glands
3. The epidermis, the outer, thinner layer, contains melanin and has a surface layer of dead cells. The dermis, the inner, thicker layer, contains blood vessels, nerves, glands, sense organs, muscles, and hair follicles.
4. Blood vessels in the dermis narrow to conserve heat and widen to increase heat loss. Evaporation of sweat also causes heat loss.
5. Both grow from an area of rapidly dividing cells at the base of the hair or nail.
6. The dermis contains nerves; hair and nails have no nerves.

Real-World Lab

BIIE 1.d, BIIE 1.g

Making a Model of a Transdermal Patch

Some medications are introduced into the body using a patch attached to the skin, rather than by mouth or by injection. This is especially useful for medications that need to be continuously released in very small quantities over an extended period of time. In this investigation, you will model how these patches, called transdermal patches, work.

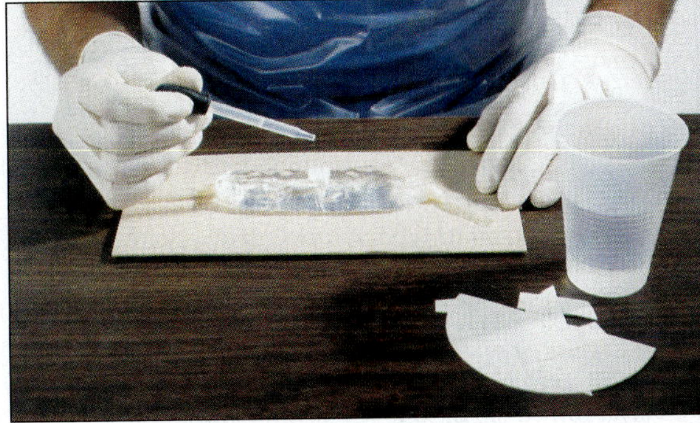

Problem How can some medications be given through the skin?

Materials

- dialysis tubing
- plastic cup
- phenolphthalein solution
- 50-mL graduated cylinder
- paper towels
- scissors
- metric ruler
- filter paper
- dropper pipette
- sodium bicarbonate solution

Skills Using Models, Observing

Procedure

1. Soak a piece of dialysis tubing in a cup of water until it is soft (about 1 minute).
2. Put on your lab apron, goggles, and plastic gloves. Tie a knot in one end of the dialysis tubing. Use a graduated cylinder to fill the tubing with phenolphthalein solution. **CAUTION:** *Phenolphthalein is toxic. Do not rub your eyes during this investigation.*
3. Squeeze as much air out of the tubing as you can, then tie a knot in the open end of the tubing to seal it off. The tubing represents the cell membrane of a skin cell.
4. Lay the model skin cell down on a paper towel. Use another paper towel to wipe dry the outside of the tubing.
5. Use the scissors to carefully cut out four 1-cm squares of filter paper. **CAUTION:** *Scissors are sharp. Handle them carefully.* Stack the filter-paper squares on top of the model skin cell. The filter paper represents a patch that will be saturated with the medication to be delivered.
6. Using a dropper pipette, carefully soak the filter paper, 1 drop at a time, with sodium bicarbonate solution. Try not to let the solution run down the sides of the tubing. The sodium bicarbonate solution represents the medication.
7. Observe the model cell for 10 to 15 minutes and record your observations.

Analyze and Conclude

1. **Observing** What happened when you added the sodium bicarbonate solution to the filter paper?
2. **Evaluating** Do you consider this procedure an adequate model of a transdermal patch? If not, propose an alternative model. Explain your response by citing specific details.
3. **Drawing Conclusions** What kinds of substances would be absorbed most easily in this way? Explain your answer.
4. **SAFETY** Explain how you demonstrated safe practices as you carried out this investigation.

Go Further

Additional Research Research transdermal patches in the library or on the Internet. Write a brief report describing at least two uses of transdermal patches. Describe the advantages and disadvantages of transdermal patches compared with injections and oral medications.

Real-World Lab

BIIE 1.d, BIIE 1.g

Objective Students will be able to draw conclusions about how some medications can be given through the skin. L2

Skills Focus Using Models, Observing

Time 45 minutes

Advance Prep
- Make the sodium bicarbonate solution by stirring baking soda into water until the solution has a pH between 8.0 and 9.0.
- You can save time by precutting the filter-paper squares.

Safety Read the safety information in the MSDS for phenolphthalein before doing the lab. Remind students to use caution when handling the toxic phenolphthalein solution.

Teaching Tips
Have students read the entire procedure for this investigation. Then, ask students the following questions:
- **How does a nicotine patch work?** *(By delivering a steady supply of nicotine that reduces the person's cravings for a cigarette)*
- **What kinds of substances can pass easily through cell membranes?** *(Water, alcohol, and small lipid molecules)*

Procedure
7. Explain that phenolphthalein turns red when exposed to basic substances such as sodium bicarbonate.

Expected Outcomes
Students will observe the phenolphthalein solution turn red after the sodium bicarbonate solution diffuses across the tubing. They should conclude that medications that can diffuse across cell membranes could be delivered with a transdermal patch.

Analyze and Conclude

1. The phenolphthalein solution near the filter-paper squares turned red.
2. Answers may vary. Accept all reasonable answers that are supported by reference to specific details of the procedure.
3. Substances with small, nonpolar molecules that are soluble in lipids because small lipid molecules can diffuse directly across cell membranes
4. Students should say that they wore aprons, goggles, and plastic gloves and were careful not to rub their eyes during the lab.

Go Further

Students should describe at least two uses of transdermal patches, such as the gradual delivery of heart medications to people with angina. An advantage of transdermal patches is that medications can be given continuously in very small quantities over an extended time. A disadvantage is that transdermal patches must be attached to the skin for extended periods and this may irritate the skin.

Chapter 36 Study Guide

Study Tip

Suggest that students review their answers to the Key Concept questions in the section assessments. Divide the class into pairs, and have students quiz each other on definitions of the Vocabulary words.

Thinking Visually

1. Ligaments
2. Protection
3. Storage of minerals
4. Flexibility
5. Connect muscle to bone

Chapter 36 Assessment

Reviewing Content

1. c	5. a	9. d
2. c	6. b	10. c
3. a	7. c	
4. d	8. b	

Understanding Concepts

11. Connective tissues including compact bone, spongy bone, cartilage, ligaments, periosteum; yellow and red bone marrow
12. Bones are a solid network of living cells and protein fibers that are surrounded by deposits of calcium salts.
13. Students' drawings should include spongy bone, compact bone, the periosteum, bone marrow, a Haversian canal, an artery, and a vein. Arteries carry oxygen and nutrients, and Haversian canals carry blood vessels and nerves.
14. Spongy bone adds strength but not mass at the point on the bone at which force is applied.
15. Red blood cells and some types of white blood cells
16. Skeletal muscles control voluntary movements; smooth muscles move food through the digestive tract, control blood flow, and decrease the size of the pupils; cardiac muscle causes the heart to contract and pump blood.

Chapter 36 Study Guide

36–1 The Skeletal System

Key Concepts  7 5.c

- The human skeleton supports the body, protects internal organs, provides for movement, stores mineral reserves, and provides a site for blood cell formation.
- Bones are a solid network of living cells and protein fibers that are surrounded by deposits of calcium salts.
- Depending on its type of movement, a joint is classified as immovable, slightly movable, or freely movable.

Vocabulary

periosteum, p. 922
Haversian canal, p. 922
bone marrow, p. 922
cartilage, p. 922
ossification, p. 923
joint, p. 924
ligament, p. 925

36–2 The Muscular System

Key Concepts  7 5.c, **BI 9.e, *BI 9.h**

- There are three different types of muscle tissue: skeletal, smooth, and cardiac.
- A muscle fiber contracts when the thin filaments in the muscle fiber slide over the thick filaments.
- Regular exercise is important in maintaining muscular strength and flexibility.

Vocabulary

myosin, p. 928
actin, p. 928
neuromuscular junction, p. 929
acetylcholine, p. 929
tendon, p. 930

36–3 The Integumentary System

Key Concept **BI 10.a**

- The integumentary system serves as a barrier against infection and injury, helps to regulate body temperature, removes waste products from the body, and provides protection against ultraviolet radiation from the sun.

Vocabulary

epidermis, p. 934
keratin, p. 934
melanin, p. 934
dermis, p. 935
hair follicle, p. 936

Thinking Visually

Using the information in this chapter, complete the following concept map:

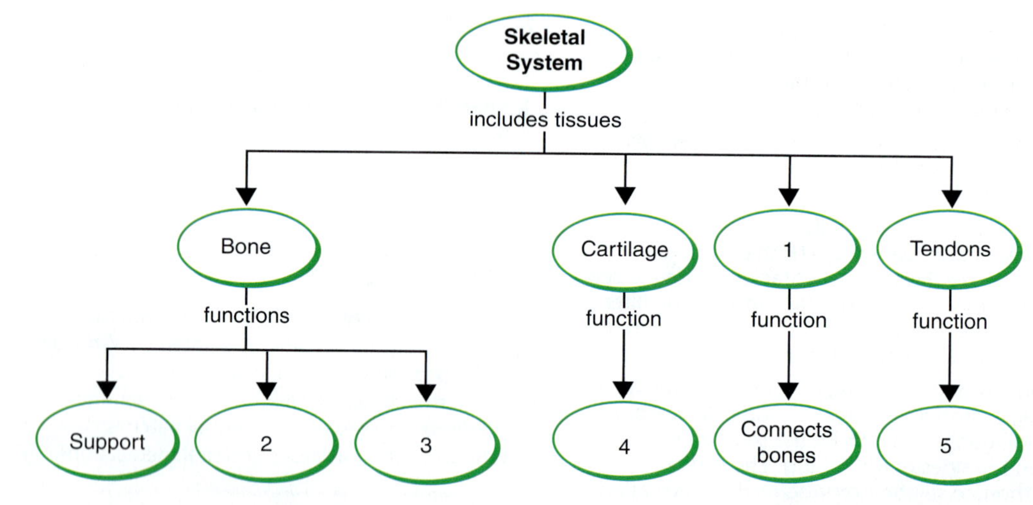

CHAPTER RESOURCES

Print:

- ***Teaching Resources***, Chapter Vocabulary Review, Graphic Organizer, Chapter 36 Tests: Levels A and B

Technology:

- ***Computer Test Bank***, Chapter 36 Test
- ***iText***, Chapter 36 Assessment

Chapter 36 Assessment

Reviewing Content

Choose the letter that best answers the question or completes the statement.

1. The tough layer of connective tissue surrounding each bone is called
   a. tendon.
   b. ligament.
   c. periosteum.
   d. cartilage.
2. The network of tubes that runs through compact bone is called the
   a. periosteum.
   b. joint.
   c. Haversian canals.
   d. marrow.
3. Cartilage is replaced by bone during the process known as
   a. ossification.
   b. calcification.
   c. photosynthesis.
   d. marrow replacement.
4. Strips of tough connective tissue that hold bones together are known as
   a. tendons.
   b. smooth muscles.
   c. striated muscles.
   d. ligaments.
5. Small sacs of synovial fluid that help reduce friction between the bones of a joint are called
   a. bursae.
   b. ligaments.
   c. tendons.
   d. striations.
6. Joints that allow for circular movement are
   a. gliding joints.
   b. ball-and-socket joints.
   c. hinge joints.
   d. pivot joints.
7. Which figure shows smooth muscle tissue?

a. 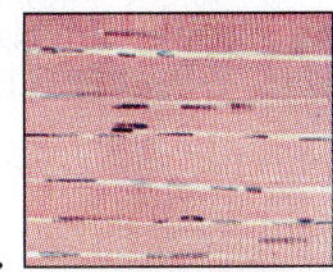

c. 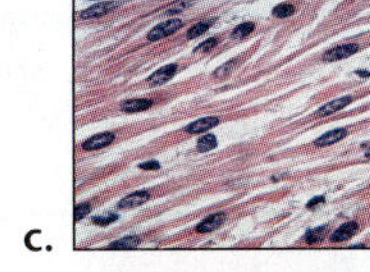

b. 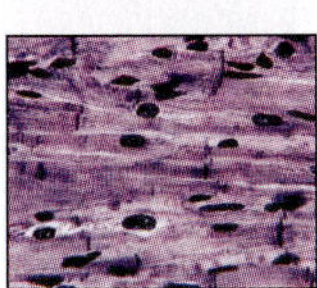

d. 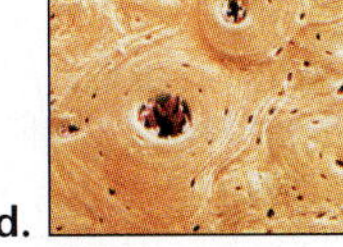

Interactive textbook with assessment at PHSchool.com 

8. Two proteins that are involved in the contraction of muscle are
   a. sarcomere and myofibril.
   b. actin and myosin.
   c. periosteum and cartilage.
   d. ATP and acetylcholine.
9. The point of contact between a motor neuron and a skeletal muscle cell is called a
   a. cross-bridge site.
   b. periosteum.
   c. tendon.
   d. neuromuscular junction.
10. The outer layer of the skin is called the
    a. dermis.
    b. keratin.
    c. epidermis.
    d. melanin.

Understanding Concepts

11. What types of tissues make up the skeletal system?
12. What are bones?
13. Draw a diagram of a long bone and label the structures. Identify which structures carry oxygen and nutrients, and identify which carry blood vessels and nerves.
14. What is the advantage of spongy bone tissue in the ends of long bones?
15. Which cells are produced in red bone marrow?
16. Describe the primary function of the three types of muscle.
17. Use the sliding filament model to describe how skeletal muscles work.
18. Describe how the release of acetylcholine from a motor neuron affects a muscle cell.
19. Compare a ligament with a tendon.
20. Explain the statement: "Most skeletal muscles work in opposing pairs."
21. What is the most important function of the integumentary system? Describe three ways it performs that function.
22. Compare the outer and inner layers of the skin.
23. How does melanin affect the color of skin?
24. How does the skin help maintain homeostasis?
25. How do fingernails and toenails grow?

HOMEWORK GUIDE

Section:	Questions:
Section 36–1	1–6, 11–15, 26, 28–32, 35
Section 36–2	7–9, 16–20, 27, 33
Section 36–3	10, 21–25, 34

Interactive Textbook

If your class subscribes to the iText, your students can go online to access an interactive version of the Student Edition and a self-test.

(Continued from page 938)

17. One end of the myosin filament forms a cross-bridge with the actin filament. Using energy supplied by ATP, the cross-bridge changes shape, pulling the actin filament along. The cross-bridge then detaches from the actin filament, snaps back to its original shape, and binds to another site on the actin filament.

18. It produces an impulse in the cell membrane of the muscle cell, which causes the release of calcium ions that affect regulatory proteins and allow actin and myosin to interact.

19. A ligament is connective tissue that holds bones together. A tendon is connective tissue that attaches skeletal muscles to bones.

20. Individual muscles can pull bones in only one direction by contracting. By working in opposing pairs, muscles allow movement in more than one direction around a joint.

21. The most important function is protection. It performs this function by serving as a barrier against infection and injury, helping to regulate body temperature, removing waste products from the body, and providing protection against ultraviolet radiation from the sun.

22. The outer layer serves as a barrier against injury and infection. It contains sweat pores and cells that produce melanin. The inner layer contains hair follicles, blood vessels, sensory receptors, sweat glands, and oil glands.

23. Melanin, a brown pigment, gives color to the skin. The color produced depends on the amount of melanin present and the way it is distributed.

24. The skin helps to regulate body temperature. It also gets rid of water and wastes from the blood.

25. Nails grow from a nail root, an area of rapidly dividing cells. Cells of the nail root fill with keratin and produce tough, platelike nails at the tips of fingers and toes.

Chapter 36 Assessment

Critical Thinking

26. These disks serve to protect and cushion the bones.

27. Because without acetylcholine from motor neurons, muscles cannot contract, including muscles that control swallowing and breathing

28. The hand on the left, which has the largest clear areas between the shaft and the knobs of the individual bones, belongs to the youngest person because bones are less ossified in younger people.

29. Eating calcium-rich foods can help prevent osteoporosis because it provides the body with a supply of calcium to replace calcium that is lost from bones.

30. Student answers might include the fact that the elbow is where the humerus, radius, and ulna meet, and that it is both a pivot joint and a hinge joint.

31. Students might explain that the repeated pressure on the elbow caused the bursa in the joint to swell in order to protect the joint from injury.

32. Injured ligaments might heal more slowly because they have less oxygen and fewer nutrients available to them.

33. Adverse effects of overexercising include too little body fat, joint injuries, and cessation of menstruation in females.

34. Experimental designs may vary. One possible design is to have volunteers expose small patches of protected and unprotected skin to sunlight for measured periods of time to determine how well the sunscreens work.

35. People often get calluses on their feet because the skin is repeatedly rubbed by their shoes.

Focus on the BIG Idea

One possible example is to compare the forelimbs of animals that climb, such as monkeys, with the forelimbs of animals that walk on four legs, such as horses. The forelimbs of monkeys have joints that allow a wider range of movement.

Chapter 36 Assessment

Critical Thinking

26. Inferring Disks of rubbery cartilage are found between the individual bones in the spinal column. What function do you think these disks serve?

27. Applying Concepts Certain bacteria produce a toxin that prevents the release of acetylcholine from the motor neurons. Explain why this can result in a fatal loss of muscle movement.

28. Interpreting Graphics Because cartilage does not appear on X-ray film, it is seen as a clear area between the shaft and the ends of the individual bones. Examine the X-rays below. Which hand belongs to the youngest person? How do you know?

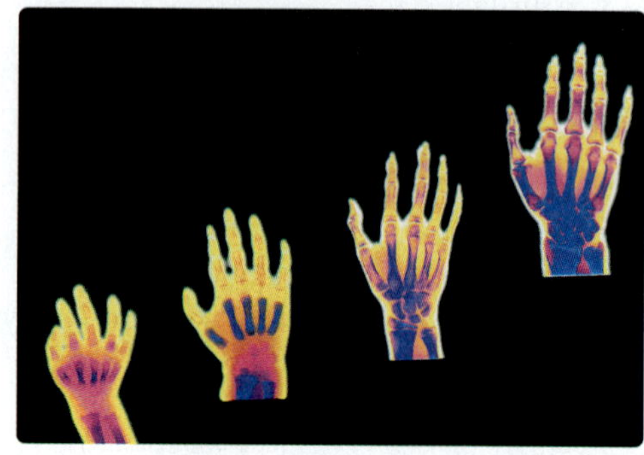

29. Applying Concepts Osteoporosis is a disease that usually occurs in older women. It involves a loss and weakening of bone tissue. Doctors recommend that all women eat more calcium-rich foods. How might this be helpful in preventing osteoporosis?

30. Using Models Suppose that you want to build a robotic arm that works the way the human elbow works. Describe or sketch three facts about the elbow that you could use in your planning.

31. Formulating Hypotheses Assume you have a habit of leaning on your elbow while reading. One day, you notice that you have developed a painful swelling on your elbow. Formulate a hypothesis to explain what might have caused this.

32. Predicting Blood vessels bring oxygen and nutrients to all parts of the body. Ligaments contain fewer blood vessels than some other kinds of tissues. How might this situation affect the rate of healing in injured ligaments? Explain.

33. Applying Concepts Although exercising can increase your strength and endurance, overexercising can have some adverse effects on the body. Use resources in the library or on the Internet to find out what these adverse effects are. Summarize your findings in a brief report.

34. Designing Experiments Ultraviolet rays from the sun can cause sunburn. Sunscreens have been advertised as effective protection against sunburns. Design an experiment to determine whether the advertising claims are accurate.

35. Inferring A skin callus is a thickening of the epidermis caused by repeated rubbing. Why do people often get calluses on their feet?

Focus on the BIG Idea

Structure and Function Recall what you learned about the bones of fishes, amphibians, reptiles, birds, and mammals. Compare examples of specific skeletal parts, such as backbones or forelimbs. Relate the bones to the way the animal moves.

Writing in Science

Support and movement are the basic functions of the skeletal, muscular, and integumentary systems. In a paragraph, compare these three body systems with similar structures of a building. For example, which body system has the same function as the girders of a building? Of the walls? How are they similar? How are they different? (*Hint:* To get started, you may want to list shared characteristics.)

Performance-Based Assessment

Demonstrating Bone Movement With one or more partners, prepare a safe demonstration showing the location of some immovable, slightly movable, and freely movable joints. Show examples of different types of movable joints.

For: An interactive self-test
Visit: PHSchool.com
Web Code: cba-0360

Writing in Science

Students should choose building structures that are similar in function to each of the three body systems. For example, they might compare and contrast the skeletal system with the girders that form the supporting framework of a building. The most important assessment criterion is demonstration of correct knowledge of the features and functions of the three body systems.

Performance-Based Assessment

Examples of immovable joints are the joints of the skull; slightly movable joints include the joints of the vertebrae; freely movable joints include ball-and-socket joints such as the shoulder, hinge joints such as the knee and elbow, pivot joints such as the elbow, and saddle joints such as the wrist.

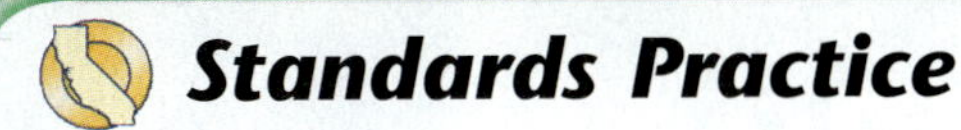

Standards Practice

Success Tracker™
Online at PHSchool.com

Test-Taking Tip When evaluating multiple-choice answers, be sure to read all the choices, even if the first choice seems to be correct. When you consider all the choices, you are more likely to choose the best one.

Directions: Choose the letter that best answers the question or completes the statement.

1. What determines differences in skin color among individuals?
   A number of melanocytes in the skin
   B amount of melanin produced by each melanocyte
   C amount of keratin in the skin
   D amount of sebum produced
2. Smooth muscle is found in the
   A walls of blood vessels.
   B heart.
   C appendicular skeleton.
   D skeletal muscles.
3. All of the following are important roles of the skeletal system EXCEPT **7 5.c**
   A protection of internal organs.
   B facilitation of movement.
   C storage of mineral reserves.
   D regulation of body temperature.

Questions 4–7 Select the best lettered choice for each of the following numbered statements. A choice may be used once, more than once, or not at all.

A Myosin
B ATP
C Acetylcholine
D Ligament

4. Supplies the energy required for muscle contraction ***BI 9.h**
5. Is released by the motor neuron at the neuromuscular junction **BI 9.e**
6. Protein that composes the thick filaments ***BI 9.h**
7. Connective tissue that holds bones together in a joint **7 5.c**

Questions 8–9

Osteoporosis is a disease characterized by the loss and weakening of bone tissue. One possible explanation for this condition is that as people age, the mineral content of their bones decreases. To assess this hypothesis, the bone mineral content of 250 men and 250 women was measured. The data are shown below.

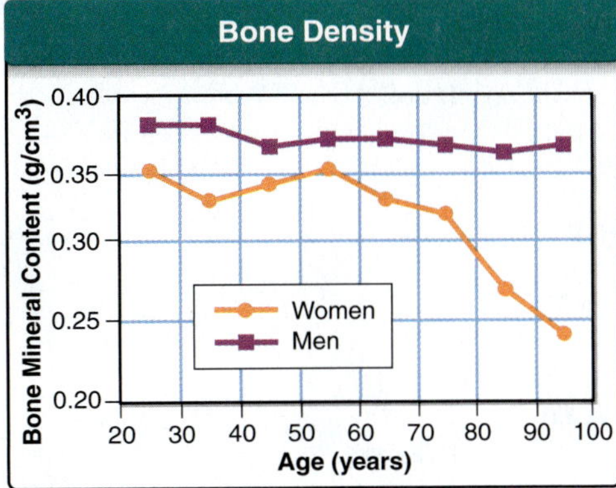

8. At which age do women show the lowest bone mineral content?
   A 50–59 years
   B 60–69 years
   C 80–89 years
   D 90–95 years
9. A valid conclusion that can be drawn from this graph is that, on average,
   A women lose more bone mineral content as they age than men do.
   B men lose more bone mineral content as they age than women do.
   C women and men lose the same bone mineral content as they age.
   D women gain bone mineral content as they age.

Standards Practice

1. B	**5.** C	**9.** A
2. A	**6.** A	
3. D	**7.** D	
4. B	**8.** D	

Success Tracker™
Online at PHSchool.com

Have students check their understanding of the chapter by logging onto Success Tracker.

Go Online
PHSchool.com

Your students can independently test their knowledge of the chapter and print out their test results for your files.

Chapter Planner 37 Circulatory and Respiratory Systems

Section and Section Objectives	Time	STANDARDS NCLB	STANDARDS Biology	Activities and Labs
37–1 The Circulatory System, pp. 943–950 37.1.1 ***Identify*** the functions of the human circulatory system. 37.1.2 ***Describe*** the structures of the circulatory system. 37.1.3 ***Name*** the three types of blood vessels in the circulatory system. 37.1.4 ***Describe*** blood pressure.	2 periods (1 block)	7 6.j, BI 9.b	*BI 9.i	SE: ***Inquiry Activity,*** What factors affect heart rate?, p. 942 L2 TE: ***Demonstration,*** p. 944 L1 L2 SE: ***Biology and History,*** Cardiovascular Advances, pp. 948–949 L2 TE: ***Demonstration,*** p. 949 L1 L2 LMB: Chapter 37 Lab L1 L2 PLM: What factors affect heart rate? L1 L2 L3
37–2 Blood and the Lymphatic System, pp. 951–955 37.2.1 ***Describe*** blood plasma. 37.2.2 ***Explain*** the functions of red blood cells, white blood cells, and platelets. 37.2.3 ***Describe*** the role of the lymphatic system.	1 period (1/2 block)		*BI 10.f	TE: ***Demonstration,*** p. 953 L1 L2 SE: ***Analyzing Data,*** Blood Transfusions, p. 954 L2 L3 IF: Investigation 10 L1 L2 L3
37–3 The Respiratory System, pp. 956–963 37.3.1 ***Describe*** respiration. 37.3.2 ***Identify*** the function of the respiratory system. 37.3.3 ***Describe*** gas exchange and breathing. 37.3.4 ***Explain*** how smoking affects the respiratory system.	2 periods (1 block)	BI 9.b		TE: ***Demonstration,*** pp. 958, 961 L1 L2 SE: ***Careers in Biology,*** Respiratory Care Practitioner, p. 959 L2 TE: ***Build Science Skills,*** p. 959 L2 L3 SE: ***Quick Lab,*** How does your body respond to increases in carbon dioxide?, p. 960 L2 SE: ***Design an Experiment,*** Modeling Breathing, pp. 964–965 L2 L3 LMA: Chapter 37 Lab L2 L3
Chapter Assessment, pp. 966–969	1 period (1/2 block)			

ACTIVITY PLANNER

SE: *Inquiry Activity,* p. 942; 10 min.; stopwatch or watch with second hand

TE: *Demonstration,* p. 944; 5 min.; three-dimensional model of the heart

TE: *Demonstration,* p. 949; 5 min.; bicycle pump, rubber tubing

TE: *Demonstration,* p. 953; 10 min.; microprojector, prepared slides of red and white blood cells and platelets

TE: *Demonstration,* p. 958; 10 min.; clear glass container, calcium hydroxide, water, straw

TE: *Build Science Skills,* p. 959; 10 min.; large round balloon, tape measure

SE: *Quick Lab,* p. 960; 10 min.; seltzer tablet, plastic cup or 250-mL beaker, water

TE: *Demonstration,* p. 961; 5 min.; tobacco, water, hot plate, paper towel, beaker, spray bottle, plant with aphids

SE: *Design an Experiment,* pp. 964–965; 45 min.; small clear plastic bottle, large round balloon, small round balloon, one-hole rubber stopper, scissors

PLANNING KEY

Ability Levels

for students performing . . .

below grade level L1

at grade level L2

above grade level L3

Print Components

SE	Student Edition	LA	Lab Assessment
TE	Teacher's Edition	BTM	Biotechnology Manual
RSW	Reading & Study Workbook A	IDM	Issues and Decision Making
ARSW	Adapted Reading & Study Workbook B	LW	Lab Worksheets
TR	Teaching Resources	LMA	Laboratory Manual A
IF	Investigations in Forensics	LMB	Laboratory Manual B

Tech Components

CTB	Computer Test Bank
BD	BioDetectives DVD
TP	Transparencies Plus
PLM	Probeware Lab Manual
ABC	ABC DVD Library
LS	Lab Simulations
VL	Virtual Labs

Interactive textbook with assessment at PHSchool.com

Program Resources	Assessment	Media and Technology
TR: Lesson Plan 37–1, Section Summary, p. 96 L1, p. 107 L2, Worksheets, pp. 99–101 L1, pp. 109–111 L2, Enrichment L3 **RSW:** Section 37–1 L2 **ARSW:** Section 37–1 L1	**SE:** 37–1 Section Assessment, p. 950 **TR:** Section Review 37–1	**iText:** Section 37–1 **TP:** 37–1 Interest Grabber, Section Outline, The Sinoatrial Node, Figure 37–2, Figure 37–3, Figure 37–5 **ABC:** 43 Human Circulation **Lab Simulations CD-ROM:** Cardiovascular 1: The Beating Heart **VL:** Lab 20
TR: Lesson Plan 37–2, Section Summary, p. 97 L1, p. 107 L2, Worksheets, pp. 102–103 L1, pp. 112–113 L2 **RSW:** Section 37–2 L2 **ARSW:** Section 37–2 L1	**SE:** 37–2 Section Assessment, p. 955 **TR:** Section Review 37–2	**iText:** Section 37–2 **TP:** 37–2 Interest Grabber, Section Outline, Blood Transfusions, Figure 37–7, Figure 37–10, Figure 37–11, Types of White Blood Cells
TR: Lesson Plan 37–3, Section Summary, p. 98 L1, p. 108 L2, Worksheets, pp. 104–105 L1, pp. 114–117 L2 **LW:** Chapter 37 Design an Experiment L1 L2 L3 **RSW:** Section 37–3 L2 **ARSW:** Section 37–3 L1 **IDM:** Issues and Decisions 41 L2 L3	**SE:** 37–3 Section Assessment, p. 963 **TR:** Section Review 37–3	**iText:** Section 37–3 **TP:** 37–3 Interest Grabber, Section Outline, Flowchart, Figure 37–13, Figure 37–14, Figure 37–15 **ABC:** 42 Human Respiration
	SE: Chapter 37 Assessment, pp. 966–969 **TR:** Chapter Vocabulary Review, Graphic Organizer, Chapter 37 Test	**iText:** Chapter 37 Assessment **CTB:** Chapter 37 Test

Go Online
Students can do research, share data, and test their knowledge online.

PRESSED FOR TIME?

To Preview the Chapter

- Have students read the boldface Key Concept statements in each section.
- Have students find the highlighted, boldface Vocabulary terms in the text and read their definitions.

To Cover the Chapter Quickly

- In Section 37–1, have students read Functions of the Circulatory System; in Section 37–2, have them read the introduction; and in Section 37–3, have them read The Human Respiratory System and Tobacco and the Respiratory System.
- Assign the Key Concept questions in Section Assessment 37–3; questions 1, 8, 9, 11, 24, and 25 in Chapter 37 Assessment; and questions 1–10 in Chapter 37 Standards Practice.

To Review the Chapter

- Assign the Sections for 37–1 through 37–3 in the Reading and Study Workbook or the Adapted Reading and Study Workbook.
- Assign the Section Reviews for 37–1 through 37–3 and the Chapter Vocabulary Review for Chapter 37 in the Teaching Resources.

CHAPTER 37

ENGAGE/EXPLORE

Inquiry Activity

 **BIIE 1.a**

Objective Students will be able to formulate hypotheses to explain the difference between sitting and standing heart rates. L2

Skill Focus Formulating Hypotheses

Materials stopwatch or watch with second hand

Time 10 minutes

Advance Prep If you are using probeware in this activity, use the instructions in the *Probeware Lab Manual.*

Strategies

- If students cannot find the radial pulse in the wrist, suggest that they try to find the carotid pulse in the neck under the jaw, where the pulse is usually stronger.
- You may want to have students predict and test how the heart rate is affected by other factors, for example, by lying down or running in place before taking the pulse.

Expected Outcome Students should find that the heart rate is faster when they are standing than when they are sitting.

Think About It The correct explanation is that the heart has to do more work to raise the blood higher.

Brain Teaser

Point out that Chapter 37 covers both the circulatory and respiratory systems. Ask: **How are these two systems related?** *(The respiratory system brings oxygen into the body and expels carbon dioxide from the body. The circulatory system transports these two gases throughout the body.)*

CHAPTER 37 Circulatory and Respiratory Systems

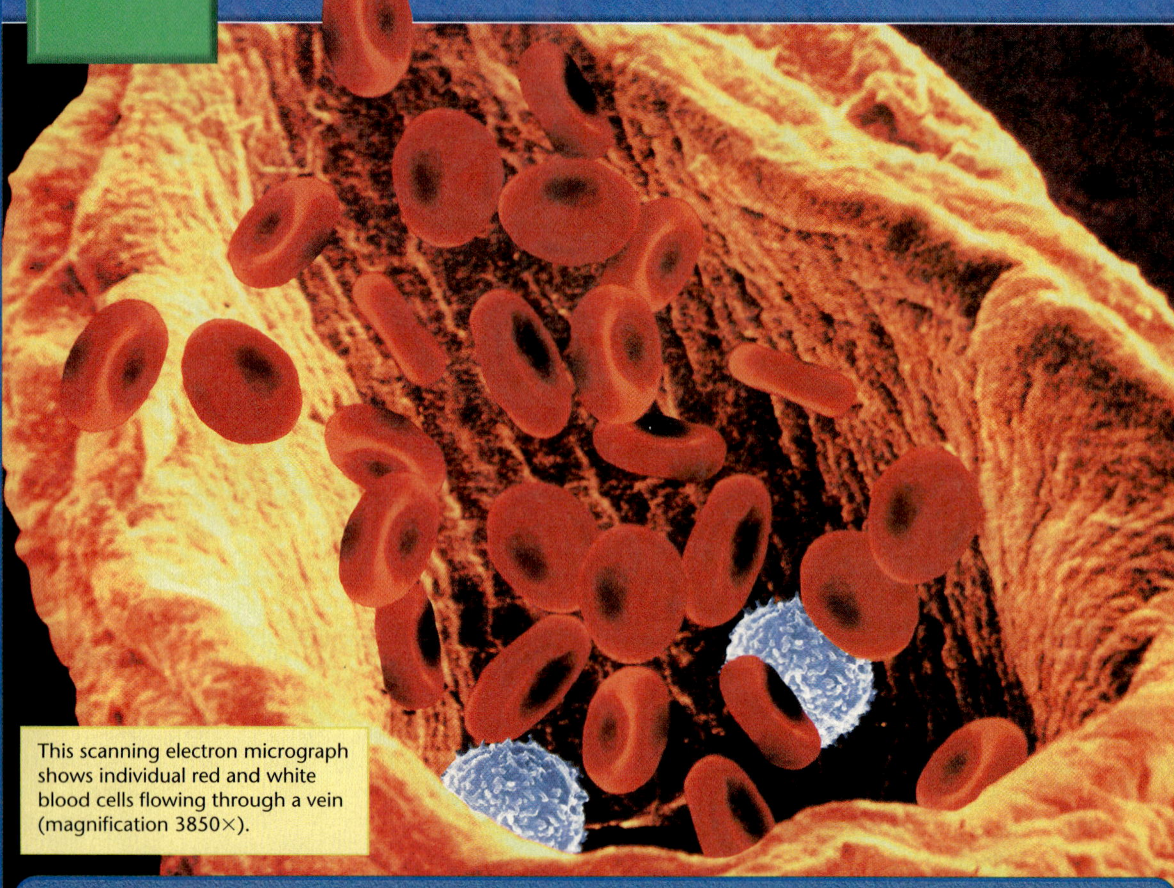

This scanning electron micrograph shows individual red and white blood cells flowing through a vein (magnification 3850×).

Inquiry Activity

 **BIIE 1.a**

What factors affect heart rate?

Procedure

1.  If you are using a heart-rate sensor, see your teacher for instructions.
2. While sitting still, measure your heart rate. To do this, find the pulse in one of your wrists using the first two fingers of your other hand.
3. Count the number of beats you feel in 15 seconds and multiply this number by 4. This will give you the number of beats per minute.
4. What do you think would happen if you stood up? Would your heart rate decrease, increase, or stay the same? Stand up and measure your heart rate to find out.

Think About It

Formulating Hypotheses Propose an explanation for any difference between your sitting heart rate and your standing heart rate.

TEACHER TO TEACHER

When I teach about the circulatory system, I give students a chance to see how various drugs affect the heart rate by having them observe *Daphnia.* I have students compare the resting heart rate with the heart rate after the application of drugs in products such as tobacco, coffee, tea, soft drinks, alcohol, sleeping pills, and antihistamines. When I teach about blood, I challenge students to use their knowledge of blood groups to solve a simulated crime. Students must type simulated blood in order to solve the crime.

—*Sheila Smith*
Biology Teacher
Terry High School
Terry, MS

37–1 The Circulatory System

7 6.j. Students know that contractions of the heart generate blood pressure and that heart valves prevent backflow of blood in the circulatory system. **BI 9.b.** Students know how the nervous system mediates communication between different parts of the body and the body's interactions with the environment. ***BI 9.i.** Students know how hormones (including digestive, reproductive, osmoregulatory) provide internal feedback mechanisms for homeostasis at the cellular level and in whole organisms.

Your heartbeat is a sign of life itself. Even when you drift off to sleep, your heart continues to beat at a steady rhythm. Why is this process so important that it must keep going even when you sleep?

Each breath you take brings air into your respiratory system. The oxygen in that air is needed by the trillions of cells in your body. Your heart is essential in delivering that oxygen. Its beating produces the force to move oxygen-rich blood through the circulatory system. Interrelationships between the circulatory and respiratory systems supply cells throughout the body with the nutrients and oxygen they need to stay alive.

Guide for Reading

Key Concepts
- What are the structures of the circulatory system?
- What are the three types of blood vessels in the circulatory system?

Vocabulary
myocardium
atrium
ventricle
pulmonary circulation
systemic circulation
valve
pacemaker
aorta
artery
capillary
vein
atherosclerosis

Reading Strategy: Using Visuals Before you read, preview **Figure 37–3.** Make a list of questions about the illustration. As you read, write down the answers to the questions.

Functions of the Circulatory System

Organisms composed of a small number of cells do not need a circulatory system. Most cells in such organisms are in direct contact with the environment. Oxygen, nutrients, and waste products can easily diffuse back and forth across cell membranes.

Larger organisms, however, cannot rely on diffusion. Most of their cells are not in direct contact with the environment, and substances made in one part of the organism may be needed in another part. In a way, this same problem is faced by the millions of people living in a large city. Cities have transportation systems that move people, goods, and waste material from one place to another. The transportation system of a city is its streets, highways, and rail lines. The transportation system of a living organism is its circulatory system.

Humans and other vertebrates have closed circulatory systems. This means that a circulating fluid called blood is contained within a system of vessels. **The human circulatory system consists of the heart, a series of blood vessels, and the blood that flows through them.**

◀ **Figure 37–1** These roads form a transportation system. **Using Analogies** *How is the human circulatory system like the streets and highways of a large city?*

Section Resources

Print:
- ***Laboratory Manual B,*** Chapter 37 Lab
- ***Teaching Resources,*** Lesson Plan 37–1, Adapted Section Summary 37–1, Adapted Worksheets 37–1, Section Summary 37–1, Worksheets 37–1, Section Review 37–1, Enrichment
- ***Reading and Study Workbook A,*** Section 37–1
- ***Adapted Reading and Study Workbook B,*** Section 37–1
- ***Probeware Lab Manual,*** What factors affect heart rate?

Technology:
- ***iText,*** Section 37–1
- ***Animated Biological Concepts DVD,*** 43 Human Circulation
- ***Transparencies Plus,*** Section 37–1
- ***Lab Simulations CD-ROM,*** Cardiovascular 1: The Beating Heart
- ***Virtual Labs,*** Lab 20

Section 37–1

7 6.j, BI 9.b, *BI 9.i

1 FOCUS

Objectives

37.1.1 ***Identify*** the functions of the human circulatory system.
37.1.2 ***Describe*** the structures of the circulatory system.
37.1.3 ***Name*** the three types of blood vessels in the circulatory system.
37.1.4 ***Describe*** blood pressure.

Guide for Reading

Vocabulary Preview

Explain that the circulatory system consists of the heart and blood vessels. Then, call students' attention to the vocabulary words and ask: **Which words refer to structures of the heart, and which words refer to types of blood vessels?** *(Myocardium, atrium, ventricle, valve, aorta, and pacemaker refer to structures of the heart. Artery, capillary, and vein refer to types of blood vessels.)*

Reading Strategy

Have students write the headings and subheadings in outline form. As they read, have them fill in the outline with enough details to make each topic clear and informative.

2 INSTRUCT

Functions of the Circulatory System

Build Science Skills

Calculating Help students appreciate how much blood is pumped through the circulatory system. Tell them that the heart pumps an average of about 5 L of blood per minute. Ask: **How many liters of blood are pumped through the circulatory system in an average lifespan of 75 years?** *(Almost 200,000,000 L)* L2

Answer to . . .

Figure 37–1 *Blood vessels are like the streets and highways that carry materials to each part of a city.*

37–1 (continued)

The Heart

Demonstration

Display a three-dimensional model of the heart that can be taken apart to show the inside. Call on students to identify each part of the heart described in the text, including the septum, atria, and ventricles. Have students trace the route of blood through the heart. Point out the valves, and explain how they let blood flow in only one direction.

Use Visuals

Figure 37–2 Help students understand how blood flows through the heart. Explain that blood always leaves the heart through arteries and always returns to the heart through veins. Check students' understanding of how the heart pumps blood by asking: **Where is blood pumped by the atria?** *(To the ventricles)* **Where is blood pumped by the ventricles?** *(To the lungs and the rest of the body)* L1

For: The Heart activity
Visit: PHSchool.com
Web Code: cbe-0371
Students learn the parts of the heart and see the flow of blood through the heart.

Structures of the Heart

Figure 37–2 The circulatory system consists of the heart, a series of blood vessels, and the blood. Notice the valves between the atria and ventricles and those between the ventricles and the blood vessels leaving the heart. The valves prevent blood from flowing backward.

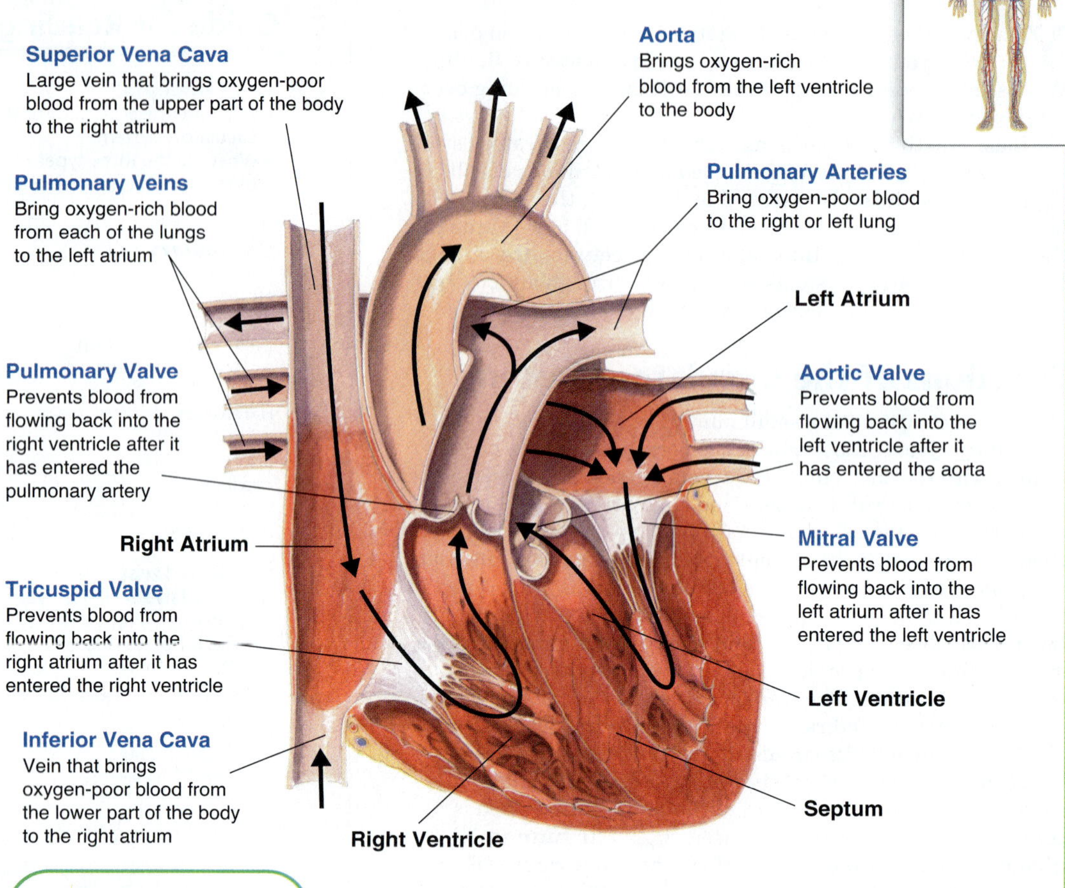

Go Online active art
For: The Heart activity
Visit: PHSchool.com
Web Code: cbp-0371

The Heart

As you can feel with your hand, your heart is located near the center of your chest. The heart, shown in **Figure 37–2**, which is composed almost entirely of muscle, is a hollow organ that is about the size of your clenched fist. The heart is enclosed in a protective sac of tissue called the pericardium (pehr-ih-KAHR-dee-um). In the walls of the heart, there are two thin layers of epithelial and connective tissue that form a sandwich around a thick layer of muscle called the **myocardium.** The powerful contractions of the myocardium pump blood through the circulatory system.

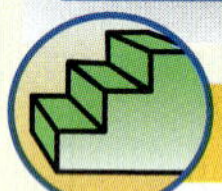

UNIVERSAL ACCESS

Inclusion/Special Needs

Use a hands-on experience to help students appreciate the work of the heart. Have them squeeze a tennis ball once per second for two minutes without stopping. As they do, explain that this is how hard the heart works. Stress that the heart continues to work this way nonstop for life. L1

Less Proficient Readers

Help students understand the different types of blood vessels by having them make a graphic organizer, such as a compare/contrast table or Venn diagram, to summarize the similarities and differences among the three types.

Advanced Learners

Have students who need an extra challenge learn about heart valve defects. They should investigate types of defects and their causes, how they affect health, and whether they can be repaired surgically. Urge students to share what they learn in an oral report.

The heart muscle contracts on average 72 times a minute, pumping about 70 milliliters of blood with each contraction. This means that during one year, an average person's heart pumps more than enough blood to fill an Olympic-sized swimming pool. (An Olympic-sized swimming pool is about 2,000,000 liters: 0.07 liters × 4320 beats per hour × 24 hours × 365 days = 2,649,024 liters.)

Dividing the right side of the heart from the left side of the heart is the septum. The septum prevents the mixing of oxygen-poor and oxygen-rich blood. On each side of the septum are two chambers. The upper chamber, which receives the blood, is the **atrium** (plural: atria). The lower chamber, which pumps blood out of the heart, is the **ventricle.** The heart has four chambers in total—two atria and two ventricles.

Circulation Through the Body The heart functions as two separate pumps. **Figure 37–3** shows the circulation of blood through the body. The right side of the heart pumps blood from the heart to the lungs. This pathway is known as **pulmonary circulation.** In the lungs, carbon dioxide leaves the blood and oxygen is absorbed. The oxygen-rich blood then flows into the left side of the heart and is pumped to the rest of the body. This pathway is called **systemic circulation.** Blood that returns to the right side of the heart is oxygen-poor because cells have absorbed much of the oxygen and loaded the blood with carbon dioxide. At this point, it is ready for another trip to the lungs.

▼ **Figure 37–3** The circulatory system is divided into two pathways. Pulmonary circulation carries blood between the heart and the lungs. Systemic circulation carries blood between the heart and the rest of the body. **Observing** *What kind of blood—oxygen-rich or oxygen-poor—leaves the lungs and returns to the heart?*

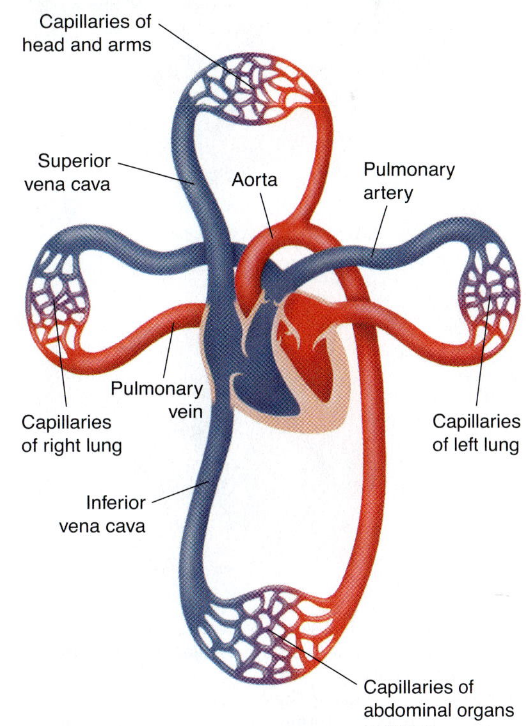

Circulation Through the Heart Blood enters the heart through the right and left atria. As the heart contracts, blood flows into the ventricles and then out from the ventricles to either the body or the lungs. There are flaps of connective tissue called **valves** between the atria and the ventricles. Blood moving from the atria holds the valves open. When the ventricles contract, the valves close, which prevents blood from flowing back into the atria.

At the exits from the right and left ventricles, there are valves that prevent blood that flows out of the heart from flowing back in. This system of valves keeps blood moving through the heart in one direction, like traffic on a one-way street. The one-way flow increases the pumping efficiency of the heart. The valves are so important to heart function that surgeons often attempt to repair or replace a valve that has been damaged due to disease.

CA (a)

(a) 7 6.j

CHECKPOINT *What is the function of the heart valves?*

Use Visuals

Figure 37–3 Explain that the red-colored blood vessels carry oxygen-rich blood and the blue-colored blood vessels carry oxygen-poor blood. Add that most of the oxygen-rich blood is carried in the arteries and most of the oxygen-poor blood is carried in the veins. The only exceptions are the pulmonary artery and vein. Ask: **Why are the pulmonary artery and vein exceptions in this way?** *(Because they carry blood to and from the lungs, where the blood picks up oxygen)* Remind students that the red and blue color scheme is a convention that makes it easier to follow the flow of blood through the circulatory system, but the blue does not represent the actual color of oxygen-poor blood. L1 L2

Build Science Skills

Using Models Point out that a good model of a heart valve is an automatic door that opens in only one direction, like the doors typically found in supermarkets. Ask: **How is a heart valve like a one-way door?** *(Like a one-way door, the heart valve allows only one-way flow through an opening.)* L2

Use Community Resources

Invite a nurse or technician who administers electrocardiograms, or ECGs, to speak to the class. Suggest that the speaker explain how ECGs are performed and what they measure. If possible, have the speaker bring a sample ECG printout to class and use it to explain to students how ECGs are interpreted. Have students write a paragraph summarizing what they learn. L2

BIO INSIGHTS

HISTORY OF SCIENCE

William Harvey's contributions

One scientist is known above all others for his contributions to our understanding of the human circulatory system. That scientist is William Harvey, the English physician whose 1628 book on the circulation of blood was a landmark publication. Until Harvey's time, there were many misconceptions about the blood and circulation. For example, it was believed that blood formed in the liver, that it moved very sluggishly if at all, and that pulmonary and systemic blood were not connected. Harvey dissected cadavers and studied living patients to prove many of these beliefs wrong. He determined that blood is forced by the pumping of the heart in a circular pathway throughout the body, leaving the heart via the arteries and returning to the heart through the veins. Harvey also explained how the valves in the heart and veins keep blood flowing in just one direction.

Answers to . . .

CHECKPOINT *The function of the heart valves is to prevent any backflow of blood from the ventricles to the atria and from the aorta and pulmonary artery to the ventricles.*

Figure 37–3 *Oxygen-rich blood leaves the lungs and returns to the heart.*

37–1 (continued)

Make Connections

Health Science Point out that artificial pacemakers are implanted in people whose hearts need help maintaining a normal rate of contractions. The battery-operated pacemaker sends electrical impulses to the heart whenever it starts to beat abnormally. For example, if the heart starts to beat too slowly, the pacemaker sends electrical impulses that stimulate the heart to beat faster. Ask: **Based on how the artificial pacemaker works, how do you think the heart's natural pacemaker works to control the heart?** *(By sending out electrical impulses)* L2

Blood Vessels

Demonstration

Show students the direction in which blood travels in veins using a demonstration originally designed by William Harvey. Select a student volunteer who has obvious veins in the forearms. Press down with your fingers on one of the more prominent veins near the wrist. While continuing to press down on the vein, run a fingertip along the same vein toward the elbow. The vein will disappear and blood will not flow back into the vein until you release the pressure near the wrist. Ask: **In which direction is blood flowing in the vein?** *(From the wrist to the elbow)* **What prevented the blood from flowing back into the vein after it was pushed toward the elbow?** *(One-way valves in the vein)* L2

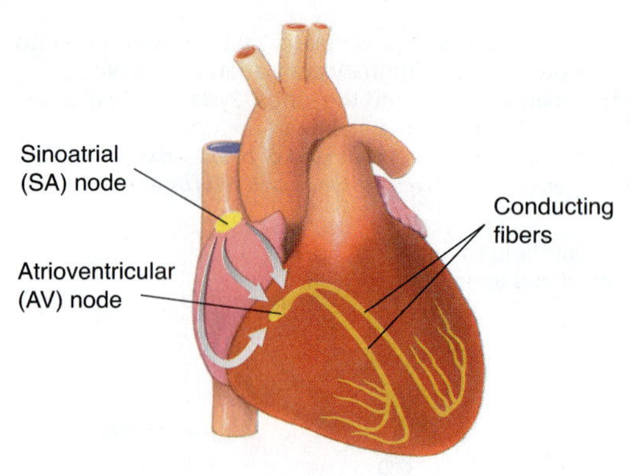

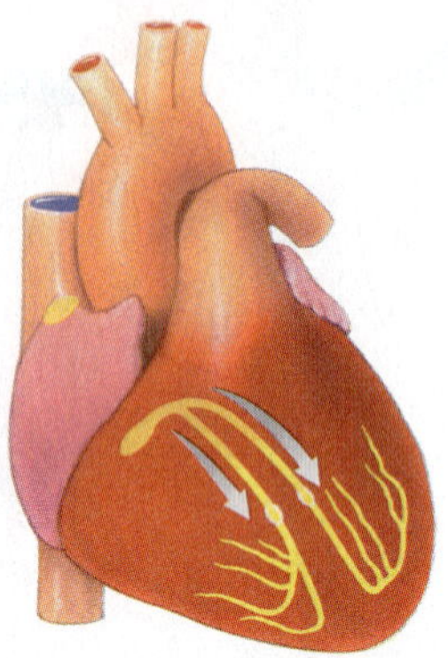

▲ **Figure 37–4** The signal to contract spreads from the sinoatrial node to the cardiac muscle cells of the atria, causing the atria to contract. The impulse is picked up by the atrioventricular node, which transmits the impulse to muscle fibers in the ventricles, causing the ventricles to contract. **Predicting** *In times of stress, does the heart beat faster or slower?*

Heartbeat There are two networks of muscle fibers in the heart, one in the atria and one in the ventricles. When a single fiber in either network is stimulated, all the fibers are stimulated and the network contracts as a unit. Each contraction begins in a small group of cardiac muscle cells—the sinoatrial node—located in the right atrium. Because these cells "set the pace" for the heart as a whole by starting the wave of muscle contraction through the heart, they are also called the **pacemaker.**

As shown in **Figure 37–4,** the impulse spreads from the pacemaker (SA node) to the network of fibers in the atria. It is picked up by a bundle of fibers called the atrioventricular node and carried to the network of fibers in the ventricles. When the network in the atria contracts, blood in the atria flows into the ventricles. When the muscles in the ventricles contract, blood flows out of the heart. This two-step pattern of contraction makes the heart a more efficient pump.

Your heart can beat faster or more slowly, depending on your body's need for oxygen-rich blood. During vigorous exercise, your heart rate may increase to about 200 beats per minute. Although the heartbeat is not directly controlled by the nervous system, the autonomic nervous system does influence heart rate. Neurotransmitters released by the sympathetic nervous system increase heart rate. Those released by the parasympathetic nervous system decrease heart rate.

Blood Vessels

Blood leaving the left side of the heart is loaded with oxygen from the lungs. When it leaves the left ventricle, the blood passes into a large blood vessel known as the **aorta.** The aorta is the first of a series of blood vessels that carry the blood on its round trip through the body and back to the heart. **As blood flows through the circulatory system, it moves through three types of blood vessels—arteries, capillaries, and veins.**

Arteries Large vessels that carry blood from the heart to the tissues of the body are called **arteries.** Arteries are the superhighways of the circulatory system. Except for the pulmonary arteries, all arteries carry oxygen-rich blood. Arteries have thick walls that help them withstand the powerful pressure produced when the heart contracts and pushes blood into the arteries.

FACTS AND FIGURES

All about the heart

The nervous system influences the heart rate, but does not directly control contractions of cardiac muscle. In fact, the heart may keep beating for several minutes after it is removed from the body. The "lub-dub" sound of the heartbeat is produced by vibrations in the walls of the heart when the heart valves snap shut. The heart of a newborn beats about twice as fast as the heart of an adult, at about 140 beats per minute compared with about 70 beats per minute. Throughout a lifetime, the average person's heart beats about 3 billion times. To do all this work, cardiac muscle requires a lot of oxygen. Heart tissue uses about 80 percent of the oxygen supplied to it, while most other tissues use about 25 percent of the oxygen supplied to them.

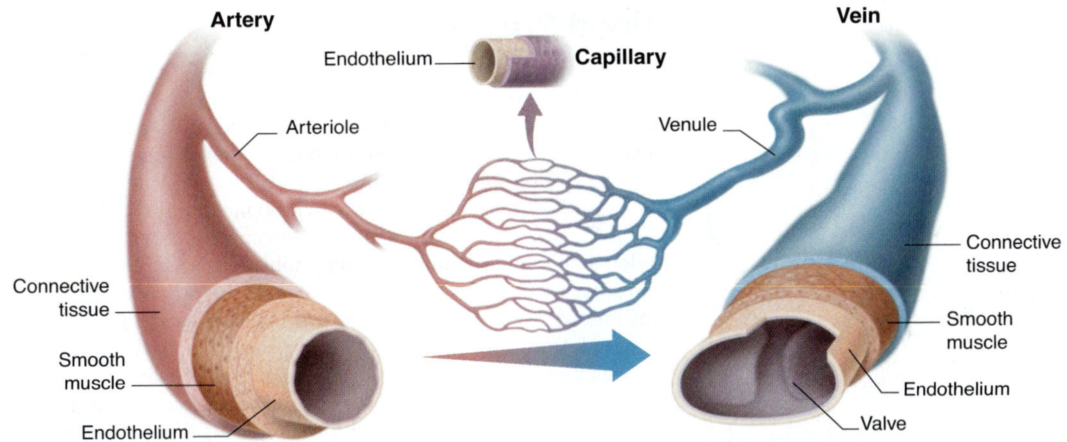

▲ **Figure 37–5** **In the circulatory system, there are three types of blood vessels—arteries, capillaries, and veins.** The walls of these vessels contain connective tissue, smooth muscle, and endothelium.

Figure 37–5 shows that the walls contain connective tissue, smooth muscle, and endothelium. The elastic connective tissue allows an artery to expand under pressure. Contractions of the smooth muscle regulate the diameter of an artery.

Capillaries The smallest of the blood vessels are the **capillaries.** Capillaries are the side streets and alleys of the circulatory system. The walls of capillaries are only one cell thick, and most are so narrow that blood cells must pass through them in single file. The real work of the circulatory system—bringing nutrients and oxygen to the tissues and absorbing carbon dioxide and other waste products from them—is done in the capillaries.

Veins Once blood has passed through the capillary system, it must be returned to the heart. This is the job of the **veins.** As with arteries, the walls of veins contain connective tissue and smooth muscle. Large veins, such as those shown in the leg in **Figure 37–6,** contain valves that keep blood moving toward the heart. Many veins are located near and between skeletal muscles. When you exercise, contracting these muscles helps force blood through the veins. Blood flow through the veins of the arms and legs often occurs against the force of gravity. Exercise helps to keep blood from accumulating in the limbs and stretching the veins out of shape. If the walls around the veins weaken from lack of activity, the valves can weaken. This causes blood to pool in the veins, producing a condition known as varicose veins.

CHECKPOINT *What happens in the capillaries?*

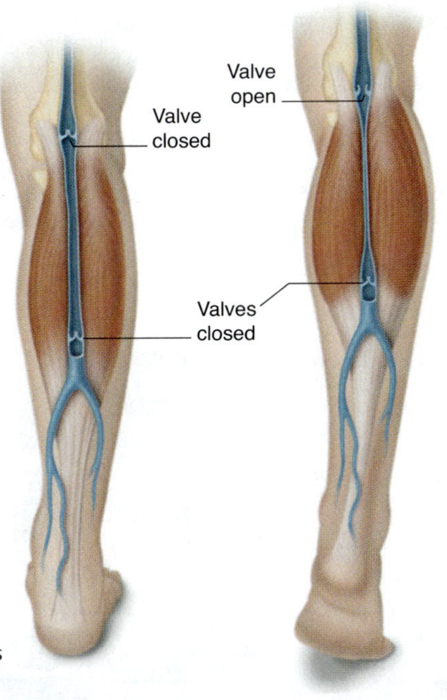

▶ **Figure 37–6** Contraction of skeletal muscles helps move blood in veins toward the heart. **Drawing Conclusions** *What role do valves play in large veins?*

Use Visuals

Figure 37–5 Point out the horizontal arrow in the figure, and explain that it shows the direction of blood flow through the blood vessels. Check students' understanding of the different types of blood vessels by having them complete the analogy: arterioles are to arteries as venules are to ______. *(veins)* Challenge students to identify how the drawings of the vein and artery differ. *(The vein has a valve; the artery does not. The artery has a thicker layer of smooth muscle than the vein does.)* L1 L2

Build Science Skills

Inferring Students are likely to be aware that they can monitor the beating of the heart by feeling a pulse in the wrist. Ask: **Why can you feel a pulse in your wrist every time your heart beats?** *(Arteries are somewhat elastic, so they expand slightly each time the heart pumps blood into the aorta. This expansion can be felt as a pulse in arteries that are close to the surface of the body, such as those in the wrist.)* L2

BIO INSIGHTS **FACTS AND FIGURES**

Aorta, CEO of arteries

The aorta has been called the CEO of the arterial blood circulation system. It is the principal artery in the body, from which almost all other arteries divide and subdivide, down to the tiniest arteriole. At its maximum diameter, where it begins at the left ventricle, the aorta is almost 3 cm in diameter. From there, it arches back and down through the chest and diaphragm to the abdomen. Some of the major branches of the aorta as it travels through the body are the coronary arteries, which supply blood to the heart; the innominate, subclavian, and carotid arteries, which supply blood to the head, neck, and arms; and the right and left iliac arteries, which supply blood to the legs. The aorta can develop atherosclerosis, or fat deposits on the walls. Without treatment, this can contribute to high blood pressure and potentially fatal bulges in the aortic wall called aneurysms.

Answers to . . .

CHECKPOINT *Nutrients and oxygen are delivered to the tissues, and carbon dioxide and other waste products are absorbed by the blood.*

Figure 37–4 *It beats faster.*

Figure 37–6 *They keep blood flowing toward the heart.*

37–1 (continued)

Blood Pressure

Address Misconceptions

Many people think that it is natural for blood pressure to increase significantly with age. Explain that this is a myth. It is based on the tendency of older people to have high blood pressure because of years of high-fat diets and other behaviors that increase the chances of developing high blood pressure. Emphasize that high blood pressure is unhealthy at any age. Also, point out that young people can develop high blood pressure, especially if they are overweight, do not exercise, or have certain illnesses. L1 L2

Use Community Resources

Invite a school nurse or other health professional to bring a sphygmomanometer to class and show students how it is used to measure blood pressure. Encourage the health professional to explain how both systolic and diastolic pressures are read and what each measures. If possible, after the demonstration, give interested students a chance to use the sphygmomanometer to take each other's blood pressure while being supervised. L1 L2

ⓐ 7 6.j

ⓑ BI 9.b

Blood Pressure

Like any pump, the heart produces pressure. When the heart contracts, it produces a wave of fluid pressure in the arteries. The force of the blood on the arteries' walls is known as blood pressure. Blood pressure decreases when the heart relaxes, but the system still remains under pressure. It's a good thing, too. Without that pressure, blood would stop flowing through the body.

CA ⓐ Medical workers can measure blood pressure with a device called a sphygmomanometer (sfig-moh-muh-NAHM-uh-tur). A cuff is wrapped around the upper arm. Air is pumped into the cuff until blood flow through an artery is blocked. As the pressure is released, the worker listens to the pulse with a stethoscope and records two numbers from a pressure gauge. The first number is the systolic pressure—the force felt in the arteries when the ventricles contract. The second number is the diastolic pressure—the force of the blood felt in the arteries when the ventricles relax. A typical blood pressure reading for a healthy person is 120/80.

CA ⓑ The body normally regulates blood pressure in two ways. Sensory receptors at several places in the body detect the level of blood pressure, sending impulses to the medulla oblongata region of the brain stem. When blood pressure is too high, the autonomic nervous system releases neurotransmitters that cause the smooth muscles in blood vessel walls to relax, lowering blood pressure. When blood pressure is too low, neurotransmitters are released that elevate blood pressure by causing these smooth muscles to contract.

Biology and History

Cardiovascular Advances

William Harvey correctly described the role of the heart in the circulation of blood more than three centuries ago. Since then, advances in this area have improved the lives of many people with heart disease.

1902
Alexis Carrel
Carrel paves the way for organ transplantation by developing techniques for rejoining severed blood vessels.

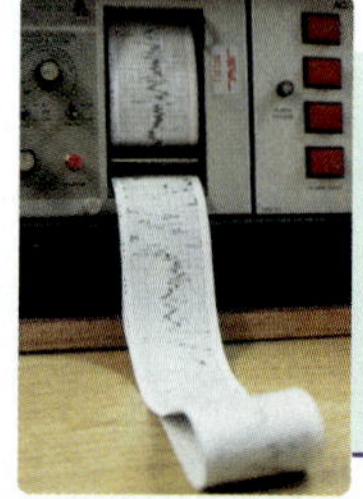

1924
Willem Einthoven
Einthoven wins a Nobel Prize for his invention of the electrocardiograph (EKG), a device used to measure tiny electric currents produced by the heart.

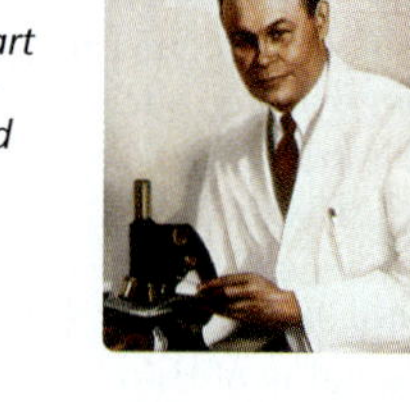

1939
Charles R. Drew
Drew develops a method to process and preserve blood plasma so that it can be stored and shipped.

1948
Dwight Harken
Charles Bailey
Harken and Bailey independently perform operations to open up closed heart valves in patients. Twelve years later, Harken replaces a heart valve with an artificial valve.

1900 — 1920 — 1940

FACTS AND FIGURES

Blood pressure's ups and downs

Blood pressure rises and falls throughout life and even throughout the day. Babies and children usually have much lower blood pressure than adults, and blood pressure is generally lowest during sleep and highest during the morning. Blood pressure also rises during exercise and periods of emotional excitement. Weight gain is usually associated with an increase in blood pressure. Regulation of blood pressure's ups and downs is complex. When blood pressure falls, it causes the release of the kidney enzyme renin. Renin, in turn, activates the hormone angiotensin, which causes the arterioles to constrict. Constriction of the arterioles leads to an increase in blood pressure. Angiotensin also stimulates the adrenal gland to release aldosterone, which causes the kidney to retain salt. This leads to an increase in water in the blood, and the greater blood volume causes an increase in blood pressure.

The kidneys, which remove water from the blood, also help to regulate blood pressure. Hormones produced by the heart and other organs cause the kidneys to remove more water from the blood when blood pressure is high. This action reduces blood volume, thereby lowering the blood pressure.

CHECKPOINT *What instrument measures blood pressure?*

Diseases of the Circulatory System

Unfortunately, diseases of the circulatory system are all too common. Cardiovascular diseases—especially heart disease and stroke—are among the leading causes of death and disability in the United States. High blood pressure and a condition known as atherosclerosis (ath-ur-oh-skluh-ROH-sis) are two of the main causes of cardiovascular disease. **Atherosclerosis** is a condition in which fatty deposits called plaque build up on the inner walls of the arteries.

High Blood Pressure High blood pressure, or hypertension, is defined as a sustained elevated blood pressure of 140/90 or higher. The heart is forced to pump against increased resistance, which enlarges the myocardium. This forces the heart to work harder, which may weaken or damage the heart muscle and blood vessels. People with high blood pressure are more likely to develop coronary heart disease and to suffer from other diseases of the circulatory system. Hypertension increases the risk of heart attack and stroke.

1958
Wilson Greatbatch
Greatbatch invents the implantable pacemaker. The mechanical device emits electrical signals that keep the heart beating normally.

1977
Andreas Gruentzig
Gruentzig performs the first angioplasty by inserting a hollow tube containing a tiny uninflated balloon into a patient's coronary artery. The balloon is inflated, opening up the blocked area and restoring blood flow to the heart.

1982
William DeVries
DeVries leads a team of doctors to implant the Jarvik-7 artificial heart in a patient, who lives for 112 days.

2001
Laman Gray
Robert Dowling
Gray and Dowling implant the first completely self-contained artificial heart into a patient.

1960 1980 2000

Writing in Science

Use the Internet or a library to find out more about the research conducted by one of these scientists. Then, write a summary of the contributions of the scientist to the field of medicine.

BIO INSIGHTS — HISTORY OF SCIENCE

Other cardiovascular advances
The first American surgeon to perform a human heart transplant was Dr. Norman E. Shumway. In 1968, just one year after the first human heart transplant was performed by Christiaan Barnard, Shumway transplanted a heart into a 54-year-old man whose own heart had been injured by a viral infection. Although this patient survived for only 15 days following transplant surgery, Shumway went on to perform many successful heart transplant surgeries. Shumway also made other achievements in heart surgery, including the transplantation of heart valves. One of the reasons early heart transplants failed was because the donor heart was rejected by the patient's immune system. The development of effective immuno-suppressant drugs greatly increased the success rate of transplantation.

Diseases of the Circulatory System

Demonstration

Give students a hands-on demonstration of how atherosclerosis increases blood pressure and the work the heart has to do to pump blood. Obtain a bicycle pump and a piece of rubber tubing that fits over the air nozzle of the pump. Give several volunteers a chance first to pump air through the open tube, and then to pump air through the tube when you squeeze it almost closed. Urge students to describe to the class the difference in the amount of work required when the tube was open and when it was almost closed. Conclude by saying that this is similar to the way athero-sclerosis narrows the arteries, causing the heart to work harder and blood pressure to increase. L1 L2

Biology and History

Explain to students that thousands of heart transplants have been performed since the first heart transplant was performed by Christiaan Barnard in 1967. By 1995, heart transplants had a 90 percent success rate. However, heart transplants are still usually reserved for patients who have the most serious types of heart disease that cannot be treated with drugs or other types of surgery.

Writing in Science

Encourage students to select different scientists so that all of the scientists are covered. After students have completed their summaries, call on volunteers to read about each of the scientists in the timeline in chronological order. Ask students which scientist they think made the most valuable contribution. Have them explain their choices. L2

Answer to . . .

CHECKPOINT *A sphygmomanometer measures blood pressure.*

37–1 (continued)

Download a worksheet on the cardiovascular system for students to complete, and find additional teacher support from NSTA SciLinks.

Build Science Skills

Using Tables and Graphs Challenge students to use library sources to find data tables and graphs that relate behavioral variables such as smoking, sedentary lifestyle, and high-fat diet to the risk of circulatory disorders such as high blood pressure, heart attack, and stroke. Call on volunteers to explain their tables and graphs to the class by summarizing in words what the data show in numbers. L2 L3

3 ASSESS

Evaluate Understanding

Call on students at random to define each of the Vocabulary terms. Call on other students to correct any errors.

Reteach

Have students trace the path of blood through the heart in Figure 37–3 and name each of the structures through which the blood passes.

Writing in Science

Make sure students use reliable sources, especially on the Internet. The American Heart Association and National Institutes of Health are good Internet sources for additional information. Students' commentaries should contain only accurate, relevant information and be written in a succinct, journalistic style.

If your class subscribes to the iText, use it to review the Key Concepts in Section 37–1.

For: Links on the cardiovascular system
Visit: www.SciLinks.org
Web Code: cbn-0371

Consequences of Atherosclerosis Atherosclerosis is particularly dangerous in the coronary arteries, which bring oxygen and nutrients to the heart muscle itself. If one of these arteries becomes blocked, part of the heart muscle may begin to die from a lack of oxygen. If enough heart muscle is damaged, a condition known as a heart attack occurs.

The symptoms of a heart attack include nausea, shortness of breath, and severe, crushing chest pain. People who show these symptoms need immediate medical attention. New drugs are available that can increase blood flow enough to save the heart, but they must be given in the early stages of a heart attack to save the heart muscle and prevent death.

Blood clots that can form as a result of atherosclerosis may break free and get stuck in one of the blood vessels leading to a part of the brain. This condition is known as a stroke. Brain cells served by the particular blood vessel gradually die from a lack of oxygen, and brain function in that region may be lost. Depending on what part of the brain they affect, strokes may cause paralysis, loss of the ability to speak, and death.

Circulatory System Health Like other diseases, cardiovascular diseases are easier to prevent than to cure. Some of the ways of avoiding cardiovascular disease include getting regular exercise, eating a balanced diet, and avoiding smoking. Exercise makes your heart muscle stronger and more efficient. It also helps control your weight, reduces body fat, and reduces stress.

A diet low in saturated fat and cholesterol can reduce your risk of developing heart disease as well. High levels of fat and cholesterol in the blood increase the likelihood that it will be deposited onto the artery walls. This process begins in childhood and worsens as you get older. For this reason, you should limit your intake of foods with saturated fat. A low-fat diet will also help control your weight. Being overweight enlarges the circulatory system, causing the heart to pump harder to force blood through it. The cardiovascular system is also damaged by smoking. You will learn more about the effects of smoking later in this chapter.

37–1 Section Assessment

1. **Key Concept** List the structures of the circulatory system.
2. **Key Concept** Compare the functions of the three types of blood vessels in the circulatory system.
3. Describe the path of blood circulation through the body.
4. What is the role of the nervous system in heartbeat regulation?
5. **Critical Thinking Inferring** If you were standing, would you expect the blood pressure to be higher in your arm or in your leg? Explain your answer.

Writing in Science

Cause and Effect
Use library or Internet resources to research the connection between a high-fat diet and cardiovascular disease. Write a short commentary that could be used on a television news program that explains the connection. *Hint:* Prepare a cause-and-effect diagram to organize your ideas.

37–1 Section Assessment

1. Heart, blood vessels, and blood
2. Arteries carry blood from the heart to the tissues; capillaries bring food and oxygen to the tissues and absorb carbon dioxide and waste products; veins carry blood back to the heart from the rest of the body.
3. The right side of the heart pumps blood from the heart to the lungs. Oxygen-rich blood from the lungs returns to the left side of the heart, where it is pumped to the rest of the body. The veins return oxygen-poor blood to the right side of the heart.
4. Neurotransmitters released by the sympathetic nervous system increase heartbeat. Those released by the parasympathetic nervous system decrease heartbeat.
5. It would be higher in your arm because your arms are physically closer to your heart. Blood pressure decreases as you move farther from the heart.

37–2 Blood and the Lymphatic System

*BI 10.f. Students know the roles of phagocytes, B-lymphocytes, and T-lymphocytes in the immune system.

Just as a plumbing system carries water through a series of pipes to different parts of a house, the circulatory system carries blood through a series of blood vessels to different parts of the body. Blood is a type of connective tissue containing both dissolved substances and specialized cells. Blood collects oxygen from the lungs, nutrients from the digestive tract, and waste products from tissues. Blood helps to regulate factors in the body's internal environment, such as body temperature. In addition, components in blood help to fight infections. Blood can even form clots to repair damaged blood vessels.

Guide for Reading

Key Concepts
- What is the function of each type of blood cell?
- What is the function of the lymphatic system?

Vocabulary
plasma
hemoglobin
lymphocyte
platelet
lymph

Reading Strategy: Asking Questions Before you read, rewrite the headings in the sections as *how, why,* or *what* questions about blood and the lymphatic system. As you read, write brief answers to the heading questions.

Blood Plasma

The human body contains 4 to 6 liters of blood, which is about 8 percent of the total mass of the body. As **Figure 37–7** shows, about 45 percent of the volume of blood consists of cells, which are suspended in the other 55 percent—a straw-colored fluid called **plasma.** Plasma is about 90 percent water and 10 percent dissolved gases, salts, nutrients, enzymes, hormones, waste products, and proteins called plasma proteins.

Plasma proteins, which perform a variety of functions, are divided into three groups: albumins, globulins, and fibrinogen. Albumins and globulins transport substances such as fatty acids, hormones, and vitamins. Albumins also help to regulate osmotic pressure and blood volume. Some globulins fight viral and bacterial infections. Fibrinogen is the protein responsible for the ability of blood to clot.

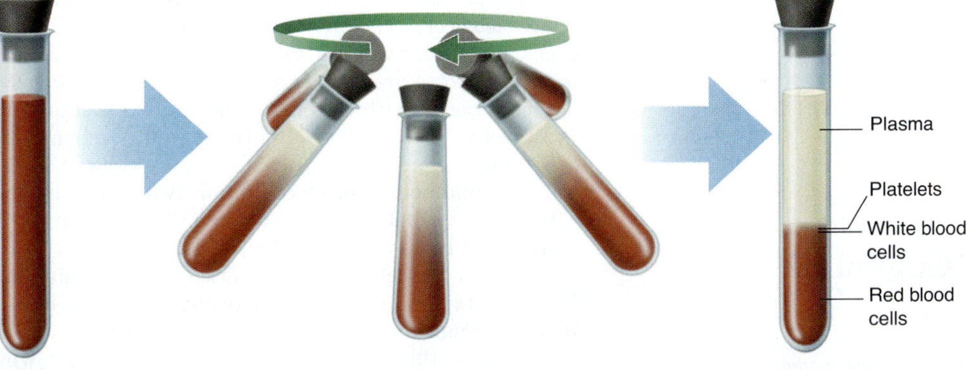

▼ **Figure 37–7** Blood consists of plasma, blood cells, nutrients, hormones, waste products, and plasma proteins. **Interpreting Graphics** *When a whole blood sample is placed in a centrifuge, as shown below, what is the result?*

Section 37–2

*BI 10.f

1 FOCUS

Objectives

37.2.1 ***Describe*** blood plasma.
37.2.2 ***Explain*** the functions of red blood cells, white blood cells, and platelets.
37.2.3 ***Describe*** the role of the lymphatic system.

Guide for Reading

Vocabulary Preview

Have students preview new vocabulary by skimming the section and listing the highlighted, boldface terms. They should leave space to make notes as they read the section.

Reading Strategy

Suggest that students preview section content by studying the figures and reading the captions. They should write down any unfamiliar terms and try to find the meanings as they read.

2 INSTRUCT

Blood Plasma

Use Community Resources

Have students contact their local chapter of the American Red Cross to learn about blood banks and blood drives in their community. Suggest that they try to find out who can and cannot donate blood, how donations are made, and what happens to the donated blood. Urge students to share what they learn with the class.

SECTION RESOURCES

Print:
- ***Teaching Resources,*** Lesson Plan 37–2, Adapted Section Summary 37–2, Adapted Worksheets 37–2, Section Summary 37–2, Worksheets 37–2, Section Review 37–2
- ***Reading and Study Workbook A,*** Section 37–2
- ***Adapted Reading and Study Workbook B,*** Section 37–2
- ***Investigations in Forensics,*** Investigation 10

Technology:
- ***iText,*** Section 37–2
- ***Transparencies Plus,*** Section 37–2

Answer to . . .

Figure 37–7 *The cellular portion and the plasma portion of blood separate.*

Blood Cells

Build Science Skills

Calculating Help students appreciate the relative proportions of red and white cells in blood. Point out that a milliliter of blood contains about 5 million red blood cells (about 5.2 million cells in males and about 4.7 million cells in females) and that red blood cells outnumber white blood cells about 1000 to 1. Ask: **How many white blood cells are there in a milliliter of blood?** *(About 7000)* **If a milliliter of blood was found to have 20,000 white blood cells, what might explain this increase?** *(An infection)* L2 L3

Use Community Resources

Arrange for interested students to visit a clinic or hospital laboratory where they can observe blood counts being performed. If possible, have a lab technician or supervisor explain why blood counts are performed and what can be learned from them. Other topics the technician or supervisor might address include the importance of accuracy in blood counts and the safety precautions that must be taken when handling blood samples. Have students report to the class on what they learn. L2

Download a worksheet on blood cells for students to complete, and find additional teacher support from NSTA SciLinks.

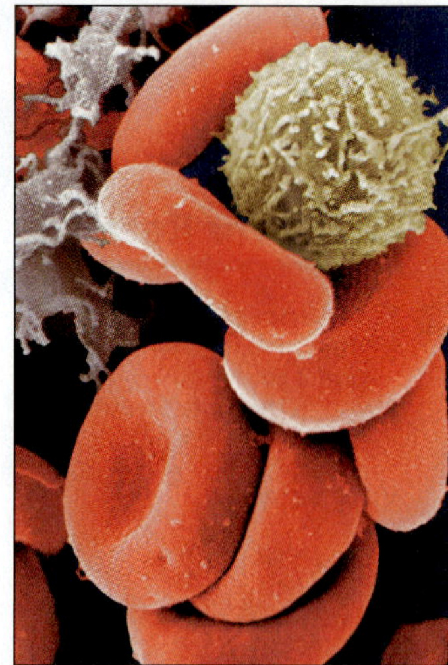

(magnification: 2342×)

▲ **Figure 37–8** **Red blood cells transport oxygen. White blood cells fight invasions of foreign substances, cells, and organisms.** Red blood cells and a single white blood cell are shown in this scanning electron micrograph.

For: Links on blood cells
Visit: www.SciLinks.org
Web Code: cbn-0372

Blood Cells

The cellular portion of blood consists of red blood cells, white blood cells, and platelets. Red blood cells transport oxygen, white blood cells perform a variety of protective functions, and platelets help in the clotting process. Platelets are actually fragments of cells derived from larger cells in bone marrow.

Red Blood Cells The most numerous cells in the blood are the red blood cells, or erythrocytes (eh-RITH-roh-syts). **Red blood cells transport oxygen.** They get their color from hemoglobin. **Hemoglobin** is the iron-containing protein that binds to oxygen in the lungs and transports it to tissues throughout the body where the oxygen is released.

Red blood cells, like those shown in **Figure 37–8,** are shaped like disks that are thinner in the center than along the edges. These cells are produced from cells in red bone marrow. As these cells gradually become filled with hemoglobin, their nuclei and other organelles are forced out. Thus, mature red blood cells do not have nuclei. Red blood cells circulate for an average of 120 days before they are worn out from squeezing through narrow capillaries. Old red blood cells are destroyed in the liver and spleen.

White Blood Cells White blood cells, or leukocytes (LOO-koh-syts), do not contain hemoglobin. They are much less common than red cells, which outnumber them almost 1000 to 1. Both white and red blood cells are produced from the same population of blood-forming stem cells found in the bone marrow. Unlike red blood cells, however, white blood cells contain nuclei. They may live for days, months, or even years.

White blood cells are the "army" of the circulatory system—they guard against infection, fight parasites, and attack bacteria. There are many types of white blood cells, and they perform a wide variety of important functions. Some protect the body by acting as phagocytes, or "eating cells," that engulf and digest bacteria and other disease-causing microorganisms. Some white blood cells react to foreign substances by releasing chemicals known as histamines. These chemicals increase blood flow into the affected area, producing redness and swelling that are often associated with allergies. Other white blood cells, known as **lymphocytes,** are involved in the immune response. B lymphocytes produce antibodies. Antibodies are essential to fighting infection and help to produce immunity to many diseases. T lymphocytes help fight tumors and viruses. You will learn more about lymphocytes in Chapter 40.

White blood cells are not confined to the circulatory system. Many white blood cells are able to slip out of capillary walls, travel through the lymphatic system, and attack invading organisms in the tissues of the body. In many ways, white blood cells are the first lines of defense when the body is invaded by disease-causing organisms.

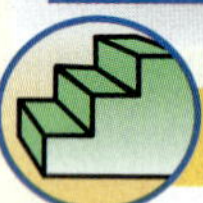

UNIVERSAL ACCESS

Inclusion/Special Needs

Help students grasp the material on blood cells by helping them organize the details in a compare/contrast table. Use headings for type of blood cell, number, size, shape, functions, presence/absence of nucleus, source, and life span. Then, call on volunteers to fill in the table with a row for red blood cells and a row for white blood cells. Have students save their tables to use as study guides. L1

Advanced Learners

Challenge students to find out how hemophilia is inherited and why it occurs primarily in males. Have them focus on hemophilia in the family of Queen Victoria of England. They should find a family tree showing which of Victoria's descendants had the disease or carried the defective gene. Ask volunteers to explain to the class how hemophilia is inherited, using the family tree to illustrate their explanation. L3

Like an army with units in reserve, the body is able to increase the number of white blood cells dramatically when a "battle" is underway. A sudden increase in the white blood cell count is one of the ways in which physicians can tell that the body is fighting a serious infection.

Platelets and Blood Clotting Blood is essential to life. An injury can cause the body to lose this essential fluid. Fortunately, blood has an internal mechanism to slow bleeding and begin healing. A minor cut or scrape may bleed for a few seconds or minutes, but then it stops. Clean it up with soap and water, cover it with a bandage, and it begins to heal. Have you ever wondered why the bleeding stops?

The answer is that blood has the ability to form a clot. **Figure 37–9** summarizes the process. **Blood clotting is made possible by plasma proteins and cell fragments called platelets.** There are certain large cells in bone marrow that can break into thousands of small pieces. Each fragment of cytoplasm is enclosed in a piece of cell membrane and released into the bloodstream as a **platelet.**

When platelets come into contact with the edges of a broken blood vessel, their surfaces become very sticky, and a cluster of platelets develops around the wound. These platelets then release proteins called clotting factors. The clotting factors start a series of chemical reactions that are quite complicated. In one reaction, a clotting factor called thromboplastin (thrahm-boh-PLAS-tin) converts prothrombin, which is found in blood plasma, into thrombin. Thrombin is an enzyme that helps convert the soluble plasma protein fibrinogen into a sticky mesh of fibrin filaments. These filaments stop the bleeding by producing a clot. **Figure 37–10** shows the tangle of microscopic fibers in an actual blood clot.

CHECKPOINT *What are platelets?*

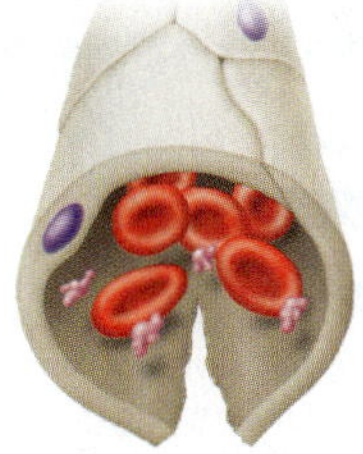

Break in Capillary Wall

Blood vessels injured.

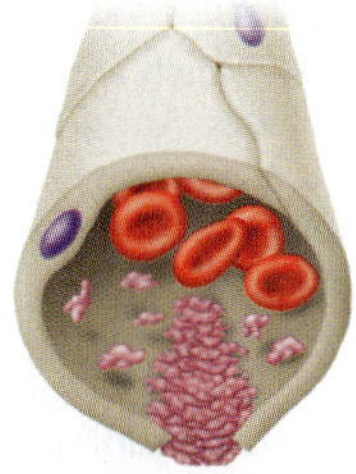

Clumping of Platelets

Platelets clump at the site and release thromboplastin. Thromboplastin converts prothrombin into thrombin.

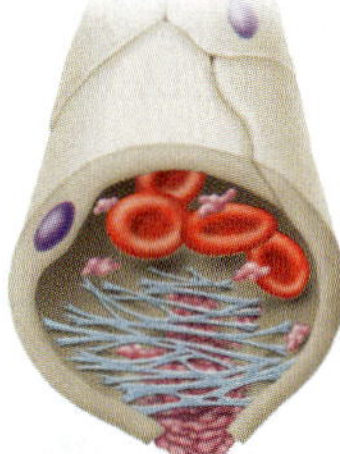

Clot Forms

Thrombin converts fibrinogen into fibrin, which causes a clot. The clot prevents further loss of blood.

▲ **Figure 37–9** **Blood clotting is made possible by a number of plasma proteins and cell fragments called platelets.** Calcium and vitamin K aid in converting prothrombin into thrombin.

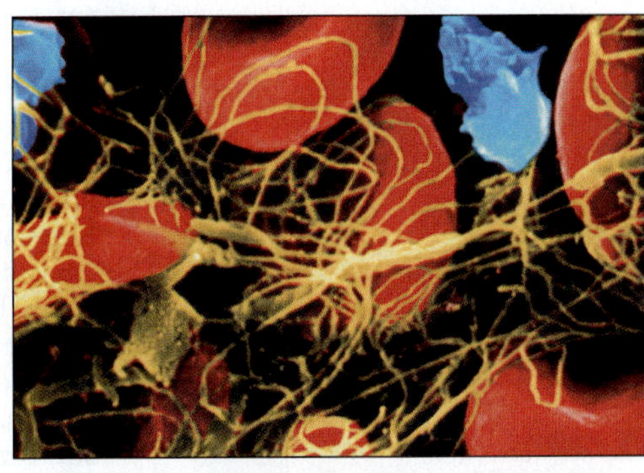

(magnification: 3000×)

▶ **Figure 37–10** Strands of fibrin trap blood cells, forming a net that prevents blood from leaving a damaged blood vessel. **Using Analogies** *How is a blood clot similar to a screened-in porch?*

Demonstration

Use a microprojector to display prepared slides of red blood cells, white blood cells, and platelets. Have students make a sketch of each structure. Then, call on students to describe the size, shape, and general appearance of each structure.

Use Visuals

Figure 37–9 Check students' comprehension of the figure by having them identify each of the following in the drawings: red blood cells (red), platelets (pink), and fibrin filaments (blue). Then, ask: **What is the main role of platelets in blood clotting?** *(The production of clotting factors such as thromboplastin)* **What role do calcium and vitamin K play in blood clotting?** *(They help convert prothrombin to thrombin.)* L1 L2

FACTS AND FIGURES

Red blood cell shapes

Normal red blood cells are disk-shaped, but some people have red blood cells with abnormal shapes, such as spherical, oval, or sickle shapes. People with spherical red blood cells have an inherited disorder called spherocytosis. Because of their shape, the red cells become trapped and destroyed by the spleen, leading to anemia. Treatment may include removal of the spleen, which corrects the anemia but not the abnormal shape of the red cells. People with oval red blood cells have the inherited disorder elliptocytosis. This sometimes causes mild anemia but usually requires no treatment. People with sickle-shaped red blood cells have sickle cell disease, another inherited disorder and the most serious of the three disorders. Sickle cell disease can cause severe anemia, organ damage, deformities, and even death.

Answers to . . .

CHECKPOINT *Platelets are cell fragments that form a cluster around a wound and release clotting factors.*

Figure 37–10 *It is similar in forming a mesh barrier that prevents blood from leaving a damaged vessel (or that keeps insects out).*

Analyzing Data

Tell students that the first successful blood transfusions were performed in the early 1800s by a British physician named James Blundell. At least half of Blundell's patients benefited from the transfusions, but many others had severe reactions to the transfused blood, and most of these died. In 1900, an Austrian physician, Karl Landsteiner, discovered the ABO blood group. Knowledge of ABO blood types explained Blundell's results and, in general, why some transfusions are successful and others are not. L2 L3

Answers

1. Type O is sometimes referred to as the "universal donor." Type AB is sometimes referred to as the "universal recipient."
2. Yes, because people with type A blood can safely receive type O blood, but people with type O blood cannot safely receive type A blood.
3. Student answers should reflect an understanding of blood groups and genetics. Suggested answer: People who have type O blood do not produce blood antigens and therefore can donate blood to any of the other blood groups safely. Because the alleles for type A and B are codominant, people with type AB blood can receive blood from all groups.

The Lymphatic System

Build Science Skills

Applying Concepts Tell students that both malaria and sickle cell anemia are diseases that damage red blood cells. Ask: **Why do people with malaria or sickle cell anemia often have enlarged spleens?** *(Damaged red blood cells are removed by the spleen. It becomes enlarged when there are many damaged cells.)*

Analyzing Data

Blood Transfusions

Although the first successful transfusions of human blood were carried out in the 1820s, many recipients had severe reactions to the transfused blood, and several died. Today we know why. We inherit one of four blood types—A, B, AB, or O—which are determined by antigens on our blood cells. Antigens are substances that trigger an immune response. People with blood type A have A antigens on their cells, those with type B have B antigens, those with AB blood have both A and B, and those with type O have neither A nor B antigens.

When blood types match, the transfusion is successful. However, transfusions are successful in some cases even when the blood types of the donor and the recipient do not match. Use the table to answer the questions that follow.

Blood Transfusions

Blood Type of Donor	Blood Type of Recipient			
	A	B	AB	O
A	✓	X	✓	X
B	X	✓	✓	X
AB	X	X	✓	X
O	✓	✓	✓	✓

X = Unsuccessful transfusion ✓ = Successful transfusion

1. **Drawing Conclusions** Which blood type is sometimes referred to as the "universal donor"? Which is known as the "universal recipient"?
2. **Drawing Conclusions** In a transfusion involving the A and O blood types, does it make a difference which blood type belongs to the recipient and which to the donor?
3. **Applying Concepts** Write a brief explanation for the results in the chart using information about phenotypes and genotypes in blood group genes. (*Hint:* Review Section 14–1 if needed.)

Blood Clotting Problems If the wound is small, within a few minutes the mesh of platelets and fibrin seals the wound, and bleeding stops. Most of the time, this clotting reaction works so well that we take it for granted. However, if one of the clotting factors is missing or defective, the clotting process does not work well. Hemophilia is a genetic disorder that results from a defective protein in the clotting pathway. People with hemophilia cannot produce blood clots that are firm enough to stop even minor bleeding. They must take great care to avoid injury. Fortunately, hemophilia can be treated by injecting extracts containing the missing clotting factor.

The Lymphatic System

As blood circulates, some fluid leaks from the blood into the surrounding tissues. This isn't an altogether bad thing. A steady flow of fluid helps to maintain an efficient movement of nutrients and salts from the blood into the tissues. However, more than 3 liters of fluid leak from the circulatory system into surrounding tissues every day! If this leakage continued unchecked, the body would begin to swell with fluid—not a very pleasant prospect.

Fortunately, the interrelationship between two body systems does not allow this to happen. **A network of vessels, nodes, and organs called the lymphatic system collects the fluid that is lost by the blood and returns it back to the circulatory system.** The fluid is known as **lymph** (LIMF).

FACTS AND FIGURES

Lymphatic System Facts

The thymus is the primary lymphoid organ and the site where lymphocytes acquire their antigen receptors. It attains its full size by age two, then decreases in size until puberty, after which it almost disappears. Secondary lymphoid organs include the spleen and tonsils. Most antibodies are made in the spleen. It consists of white pulp, where T cells are stimulated by antigen, and red pulp, where old red blood cells are removed. The red pulp also manufactures new red blood cells when too many are lost during illness. Tonsils are small pieces of lymphatic tissue in the throat. Their primary role is to trap and destroy bacteria that enter the respiratory tract. One set of tonsils protrudes from each side of the pharynx behind the mouth. Another set, commonly called adenoids, is located higher up in the pharynx behind the nose.

Lymph collects in lymphatic capillaries and slowly flows into larger and larger lymph vessels. Like large veins, lymph vessels contain valves that prevent lymph from flowing backward. Ducts collect the lymph and return it to the circulatory system through two openings in the superior vena cava. The openings are under the left and right clavicle bones just below the shoulders. **Figure 37–11** shows the lymphatic system.

Along the length of the lymph vessels are small bean-shaped enlargements called lymph nodes. Lymph nodes act as filters, trapping bacteria and other microorganisms that cause disease. When large numbers of microorganisms are trapped in the lymph nodes, the nodes become enlarged. If you have ever had "swollen glands," you actually had swollen lymph nodes.

Lymph vessels do not merely return excess fluid to the circulation. They also play a very important role in nutrient absorption. Lymph vessels lie near the cells that line the intestines, where they absorb fats and fat-soluble vitamins from the digestive tract and carry them to the blood. Lymph moves through the lymphatic system under osmotic pressure from the blood and is pushed along by the contractions of nearby skeletal muscles. It is important that there is a steady flow of lymph. Edema, a swelling of the tissues due to the accumulation of excess fluid, can occur when lymphatic vessels are blocked due to injury or disease.

In addition to the lymph vessels and lymph nodes, the thymus and spleen also have important roles in the lymphatic system. The thymus is located beneath the sternum. Certain lymphocytes called T cells mature in the thymus before they can function in the immune system. T cells are the cells that recognize foreign "invaders" in the body. The spleen helps to cleanse the blood and removes damaged blood cells from the circulatory system. The spleen also harbors phagocytes that engulf and destroy bacteria and other microorganisms.

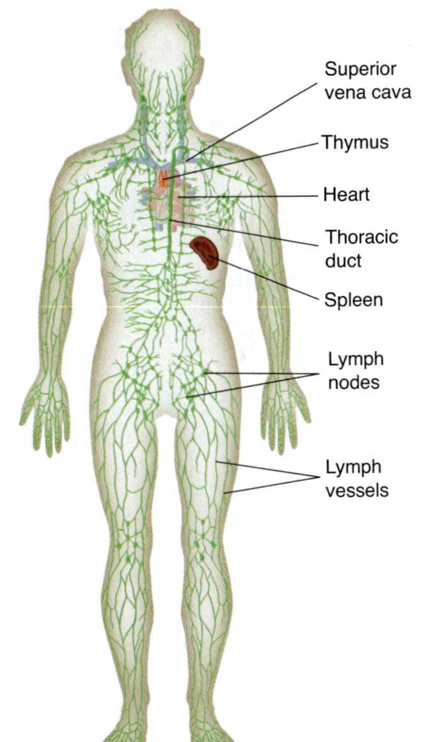

▲ **Figure 37–11 The lymphatic system collects and returns fluid that leaks from blood vessels.** The spleen is an organ whose main function is to destroy damaged red blood cells and platelets. Certain white blood cells called T lymphocytes, or T cells, mature in the thymus gland, which produces hormones that promote their development.

Use Visuals

Figure 37–11 Have students compare the distribution of lymphatic vessels with the distribution of blood vessels, shown in Figure 37–3. Then, ask: **How are the lymphatic and circulatory systems related?** *(The lymphatic system collects fluid that seeps into the tissues from blood and returns it to the circulatory system.)* Point out that the vein where this fluid is returned to the blood is called the superior vena cava. Have students find the superior vena cava in the figure. Also have them locate the clusters of lymph nodes. Ask: **If you have a sore throat because of an infection, which lymph nodes might become swollen?** *(The lymph nodes in the neck)* L2

37–2 Section Assessment

1. **Key Concept** List the main function of red blood cells, white blood cells, and platelets.
2. **Key Concept** Describe the role of the lymphatic system.
3. What types of materials are dissolved in plasma?
4. Explain how blood clots.
5. **Critical Thinking Inferring** Sometimes lymph nodes must be surgically removed. Although more lymph vessels eventually grow, what result would you expect to see immediately after surgery?

Thinking Visually

Constructing a Concept Map
Construct a concept map that shows the components of blood. Include information about the functions of the different components. (Be sure to include the different types of white blood cells.)

37–2 Section Assessment

1. Red blood cells carry oxygen; white blood cells fight infection; platelets help blood to clot.
2. Its role is to collect fluid lost by blood and return it to the circulatory system.
3. Gases, salts, nutrients, enzymes, hormones, waste products, and plasma proteins
4. When platelets come in contact with the broken edges of a blood vessel, their surfaces become sticky. A cluster of platelets develops around the wound. The platelets release clotting factors, which start reactions that produce a blood clot.
5. Areas without lymph nodes and vessels would retain excess fluid and become swollen immediately after surgery.

3 ASSESS

Evaluate Understanding

Call on students at random to name each component of the blood. Call on other students to describe the function of each component.

Reteach

Using the chalkboard or a transparency, work with students to create a concept map of the functions of blood based on information in the opening paragraph of the section. Then, have students identify the parts of the blood involved in each function.

Thinking Visually

Students' concept maps should show that blood consists of plasma, platelets, red blood cells, and white blood cells, of which there are five main types: neutrophils, eosinophils, basophils, monocytes, and lymphoctyes.

If your class subscribes to the iText, use it to review the Key Concepts in Section 37–2.

Section 37–3

BI 9.b

1 FOCUS

Objectives

37.3.1 ***Describe*** respiration.
37.3.2 ***Identify*** the function of the respiratory system.
37.3.3 ***Describe*** gas exchange and breathing.
37.3.4 ***Explain*** how smoking affects the respiratory system.

Guide for Reading

Vocabulary Preview

Call students' attention to the Vocabulary terms. Ask: **Which term refers to a respiratory disease?** *(Emphysema)* **Which term refers to a toxic chemical in tobacco smoke?** *(Nicotine)* Point out that all the rest of the words are structures of the respiratory system.

Reading Strategy

Before students read the section, have them predict how respiration, gas exchange, and breathing are related. As they read, they should check to see if their predictions were correct.

2 INSTRUCT

What Is Respiration?

Address Misconceptions

Students may have the misconception that breathing is the same as respiration. Remind students that respiration is the exchange of gases that takes place in the alveoli of the lungs. Breathing is the movement of air into and out of the lungs. Ask: **How is breathing related to respiration?** *(Inhaling provides a fresh supply of oxygen to the lungs; exhaling removes excess carbon dioxide from the lungs.)* L1 L2

37–3 The Respiratory System

BI 9.b. Students know how the nervous system mediates communication between different parts of the body and the body's interactions with the environment.

Guide for Reading

Key Concepts
- What is the function of the respiratory system?
- How does smoking affect the respiratory system?

Vocabulary
pharynx
trachea
larynx
bronchus
alveolus
diaphragm
nicotine
emphysema

Reading Strategy: Monitoring Your Understanding Make a table with three columns labeled K, W, and L. Before you read, write what you know about respiration in column K and what you want to learn in column W. After you read, write what you have learned in column L.

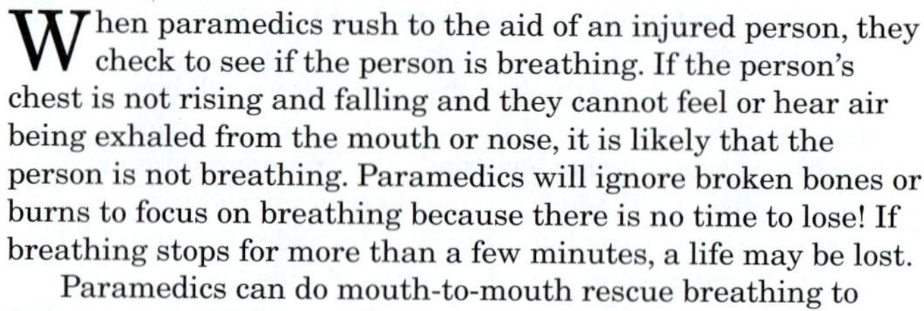

When paramedics rush to the aid of an injured person, they check to see if the person is breathing. If the person's chest is not rising and falling and they cannot feel or hear air being exhaled from the mouth or nose, it is likely that the person is not breathing. Paramedics will ignore broken bones or burns to focus on breathing because there is no time to lose! If breathing stops for more than a few minutes, a life may be lost.

Paramedics can do mouth-to-mouth rescue breathing to force air into the lungs. They can do chest compressions to keep the blood circulating. Cardiopulmonary resuscitation, or CPR, is rescue breathing combined with chest compressions.

What Is Respiration?

In biology, the word *respiration* is used in two slightly different ways. Cellular respiration, which takes place in mitochondria, is the release of energy from the breakdown of food molecules in the presence of oxygen. Without oxygen, cells lose much of their ability to produce ATP. Without ATP, cells cannot synthesize new molecules, pump ions, or carry nerve impulses.

The blood carries oxygen from the lungs to the body's tissues, and carries carbon dioxide—a waste product of cellular respiration—in the opposite direction. At the level of the organism, respiration means the process of gas exchange—the release of carbon dioxide and the uptake of oxygen between the lungs and the environment.

The Human Respiratory System

The basic function performed by the human respiratory system is remarkably simple—to bring about the exchange of oxygen and carbon dioxide between the blood, the air, and tissues. With each breath, air enters the body through the air passageways and fills the lungs, where gas exchange takes place. The respiratory system consists of the nose, pharynx, larynx, trachea, bronchi, and lungs.

Figure 37–13 shows the structures of the respiratory system. Air moves through the nose to a tube at the back of the mouth called the pharynx, or throat. The **pharynx** serves as a passageway for both air and food. Air moves from the pharynx into the **trachea,** or windpipe. A flap of tissue called the epiglottis covers the entrance to the trachea when you swallow.

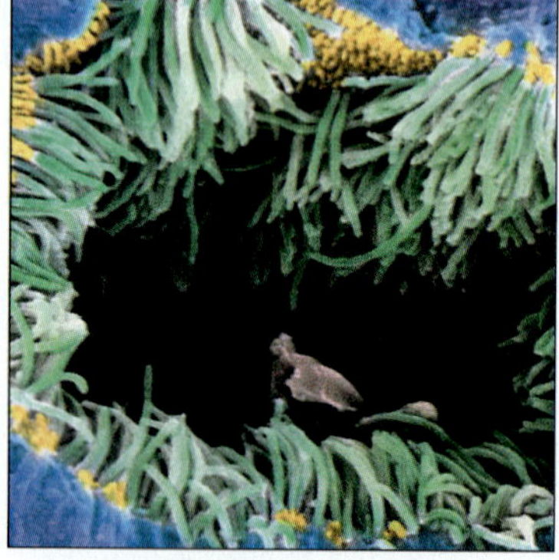

(magnification: 5600×)

Figure 37–12 In this cross section of the trachea, the cilia have been colored green. **Inferring** *What is the role of cilia in the respiratory system?*

SECTION RESOURCES

Print:
- ***Laboratory Manual A,*** Chapter 37 Lab
- ***Teaching Resources,*** Lesson Plan 37–3, Adapted Section Summary 37–3, Adapted Worksheets 37–3, Section Summary 37–3, Worksheets 37–3, Section Review 37–3
- ***Reading and Study Workbook A,*** Section 37–3
- ***Adapted Reading and Study Workbook B,*** Section 37–3
- ***Issues and Decision Making,*** Issues and Decisions 41
- ***Lab Worksheets,*** Chapter 37 Design an Experiment

Technology:
- ***iText,*** Section 37–3
- ***Animated Biological Concepts DVD,*** 42 Human Respiration
- ***Transparencies Plus,*** Section 37–3

FIGURE 37–13 THE RESPIRATORY SYSTEM

The respiratory system is responsible for the exchange of oxygen and carbon dioxide. Air moves through the nose, pharynx, larynx, trachea, and lungs. After reaching the lungs, the trachea branches into smaller and smaller tubes called bronchioles, which end in alveoli, or air sacs.

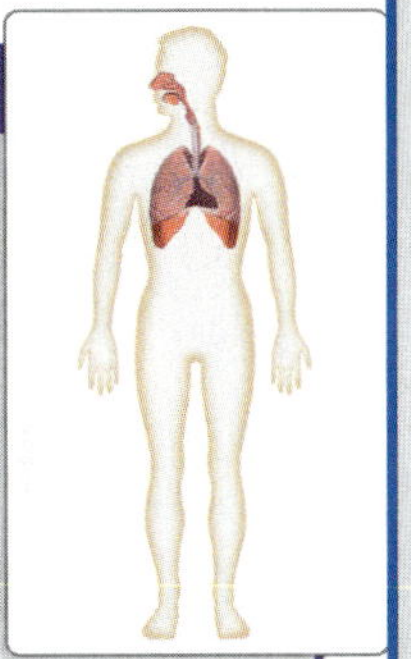

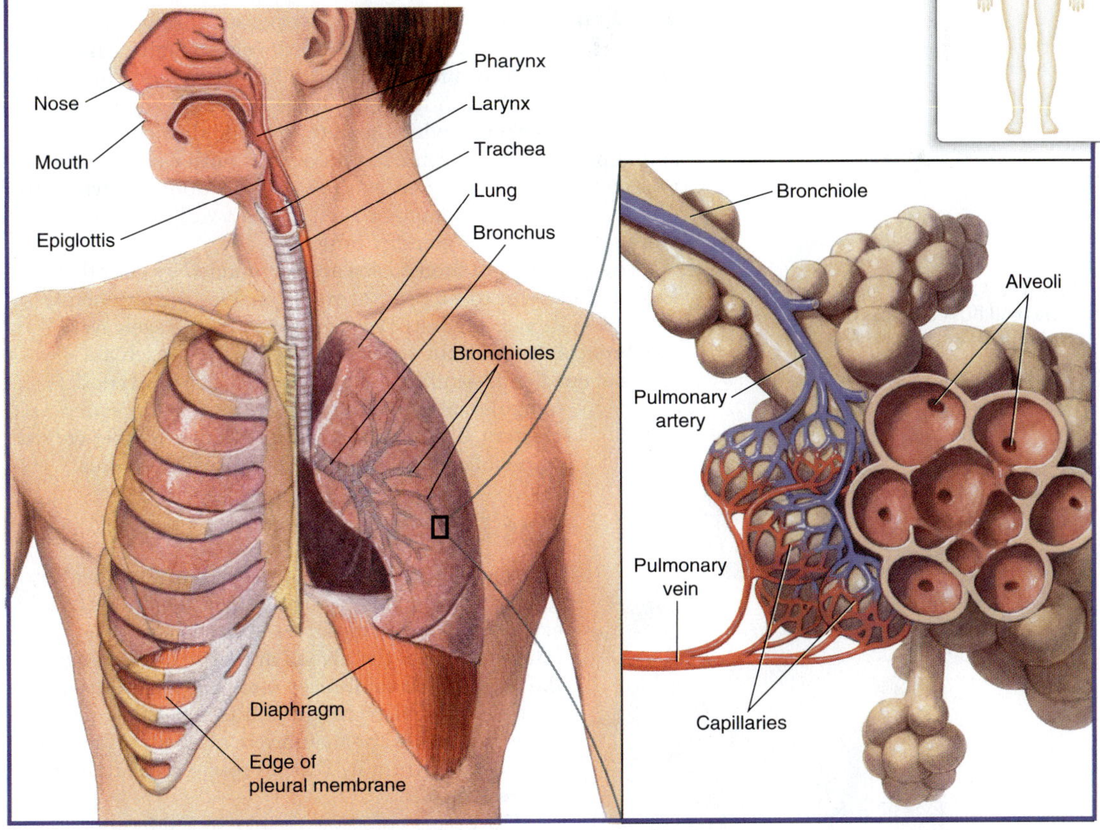

Cilia and Mucus The respiratory passageways allow air to pass directly into some of the most delicate tissues in the body. To keep the lung tissue healthy, air entering the respiratory system must be warmed, moistened, and filtered. Large dust particles get trapped by the hairs lining the entrance to the nasal cavity. Some of the cells that line the respiratory system produce a thin layer of mucus. The mucus moistens the air and traps inhaled particles of dust or smoke. Cilia sweep the trapped particles and mucus away from the lungs toward the pharynx. The mucus and trapped particles are either swallowed or spit out. These protective measures help keep the lungs clean and open for the important work of gas exchange.

CHECKPOINT *What is the pharynx?*

The Human Respiratory System

Use Visuals

Figure 37–13 Make sure students understand how the drawing on the right relates to the drawing on the left. Have students use the drawings to trace the pathway of air through the respiratory system as they read about it in the text. They should identify each of the structures through which the air passes, starting with the nose and ending with the alveoli. L1

Use Community Resources

Invite a paramedic to demonstrate to the class rescue breathing (mouth-to-mouth) and chest compressions. Before the paramedic arrives, tell students that people sometimes stop breathing in cases of drowning, electric shock, or smoke inhalation and that rescue breathing helps keep them alive until they begin breathing again on their own. Also explain how choking occurs because of the role of the pharynx in both the digestive and respiratory systems. Suggest that students prepare questions in advance for the paramedic to address. L1 L2

ESL SUPPORT FOR ENGLISH LANGUAGE LEARNERS

Vocabulary: Link to Visual

Beginning Use Figure 37–13 to help students visualize the meaning of the terms *pharynx, trachea, larynx, bronchus,* and *diaphragm.* Point out each of the structures as you model the proper pronunciation of each term. Then, distribute an unlabeled diagram similar to Figure 37–13, and have students label the pharynx, trachea, larynx, bronchus, and diaphragm. Post these terms on a word wall with other vocabulary terms from the chapter. L1

Intermediate Students should start by doing the beginning-level activity. Then, pair the ESL students with English-proficient students to write five sentences describing the functions of the pharynx, trachea, larynx, bronchus, and diaphragm in their own words. Ask for volunteers to read their sentences. L2

Answers to . . .

CHECKPOINT *The pharynx is a tube at the back of the mouth that serves as a passageway for both air and food.*

Figure 37–12 *Cilia sweep mucus and trapped particles away from the lungs toward the pharynx.*

37–3 (continued)

Gas Exchange

Build Science Skills

Inferring Explain how exhaled air is used in rescue breathing. Point out that exhaled air has already gone through the gas exchange process in the lungs. Ask: **How can rescue breathing provide the person receiving the "second-hand" air with enough oxygen to survive?** *(Exhaled air contains about 75 percent of the oxygen of inhaled air—more than enough to keep a person alive.)* L2

Demonstration

Make limewater in a clear glass container by adding calcium hydroxide to water until the solution is saturated. Tell students that when carbon dioxide reacts with limewater, it causes the limewater to turn cloudy. Have a student volunteer exhale through a straw into the limewater. (Caution the student not to suck any of the limewater through the straw.) While the student exhales, have other students observe what happens. *(The limewater turns cloudy.)* Ask: **Why did the limewater turn cloudy?** *(The exhaled breath contained carbon dioxide.)* L1 L2

Breathing

Build Science Skills

Measuring Students can measure their lung capacity. (Advise any with respiratory illnesses, such as asthma or bronchitis, to avoid participating.) Give each student a large round balloon and, with students working in pairs, tell one student to inhale as large a breath as possible and then to exhale it as completely as possible into the balloon. Students should hold the balloons shut until their partner measures the circumference with a tape measure. Then, repeat the steps for the other partner. Students can calculate their lung capacity by finding the volume of the inflated balloon, using the formula $V = 4/3\pi r^3$, where r is the radius of the inflated balloon. The radius can be found from the circumference, using the formula $c = 2\pi r$.

L2 L3

The Larynx At the top of the trachea is the larynx. The **larynx** contains two highly elastic folds of tissue known as the vocal cords. When muscles pull the vocal cords together, the air moving between them causes the cords to vibrate and produce sounds. Your ability to speak, shout, and sing comes from these tissues.

The Bronchi From the larynx, air passes through the trachea into two large passageways in the chest cavity called **bronchi** (singular: bronchus). Each bronchus leads into one of the lungs. Within each lung, the large bronchus subdivides into smaller bronchi, which lead to even smaller passageways called bronchioles. Air moving along this path can be compared to a motorist who takes an exit off an eight-lane highway onto a four-lane highway, makes a turn onto a two-lane road, and ends up on a narrow country lane.

The bronchi and bronchioles are surrounded by smooth muscle that helps to support them and enables the autonomic nervous system to regulate the size of the air passageways. The bronchioles continue to subdivide until they reach a series of dead ends—millions of tiny air sacs called **alveoli** (singular: alveolus). Alveoli are grouped in little clusters, like bunches of grapes. A delicate network of thin-walled capillaries surrounds each alveolus.

▼ Figure 37–14 Gas exchange occurs by diffusion across the membrane of an alveolus and a capillary. **Drawing Conclusions** ***Where is oxygen more concentrated, in an alveolus or in a capillary?***

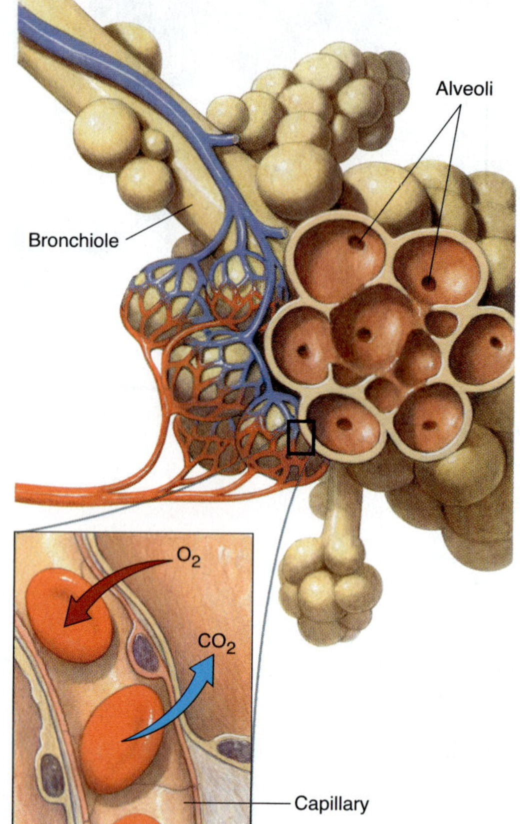

Gas Exchange

There are about 150 million alveoli in each healthy lung, providing an enormous surface area for gas exchange. Oxygen dissolves in the moisture on the inner surface of the alveoli and then diffuses across the thin-walled capillaries into the blood. Carbon dioxide in the bloodstream diffuses in the opposite direction, across the membrane of an alveolus and into the air within it. This process is illustrated in **Figure 37–14.**

The process of gas exchange in the lungs is very efficient. The air that you inhale usually contains 21 percent oxygen and 0.04 percent carbon dioxide. Exhaled air usually contains less than 15 percent oxygen and 4 percent carbon dioxide. The lungs remove about one fourth of the oxygen in the air that you inhale and increase the carbon dioxide content of that air by a factor of 100.

Because oxygen dissolves easily, you may wonder why hemoglobin, the oxygen-carrying protein in blood, is needed at all. The reason is efficiency. Hemoglobin binds with so much oxygen that it increases the oxygen-carrying capacity of the blood more than 60 times. Without hemoglobin to carry the oxygen that it uses, your body might need as much as 300 liters of blood to get the same result!

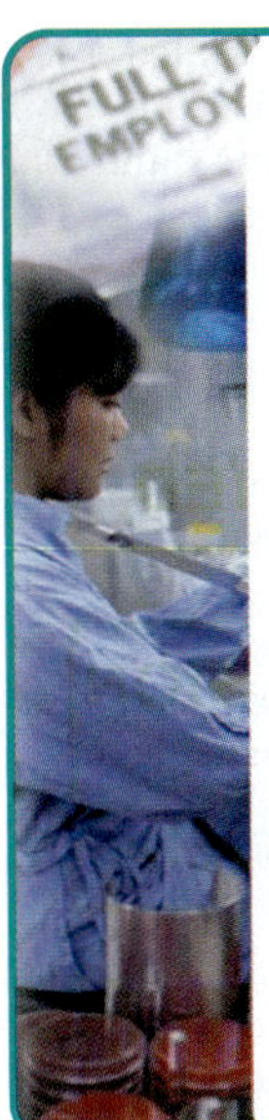

Careers in Biology

Respiratory Care Practitioner

Job Description: provide care for patients with respiratory problems in hospitals, clinics, nursing homes, schools, and at home

Education: a two-year or four-year training program; certification exams; individual states have additional licensing requirements

Skills: good communication skills; enjoy working with people; capable of working independently; good decision-making skills; knowledge of anatomy, physiology, microbiology

Highlights: You provide quick responses in emergency situations. You work as a member of a team.

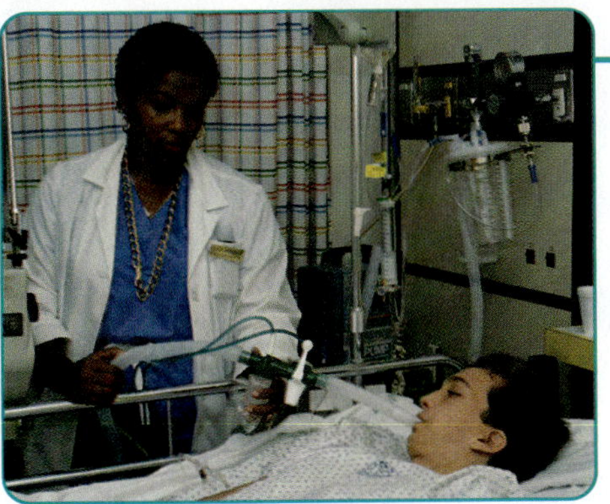

For: Career links
Visit: PHSchool.com
Web Code: cbb-0373

Breathing

Breathing is the movement of air into and out of the lungs. Surprisingly, there are no muscles connected to the lungs. The force that drives air into the lungs comes from ordinary air pressure. How does the body use this force to inflate the lungs? The lungs are sealed in two sacs, called the pleural membranes, inside the chest cavity. At the bottom of the cavity is a large, flat muscle known as the **diaphragm.**

As **Figure 37–15** shows, when you breathe in, or inhale, the diaphragm contracts and the rib cage rises up. This expands the volume of the chest cavity. Because the chest cavity is tightly sealed, this creates a partial vacuum inside the cavity. Atmospheric pressure does the rest, filling the lungs as air rushes into the breathing passages.

Most of the time, exhaling is a passive event. When the rib cage lowers and the diaphragm muscle relaxes, the pressure in the chest cavity becomes greater than atmospheric pressure. Air rushes back out of the lungs. To blow out a candle, you need a greater force. Muscles surrounding the chest cavity provide that extra force, contracting vigorously just as the diaphragm relaxes.

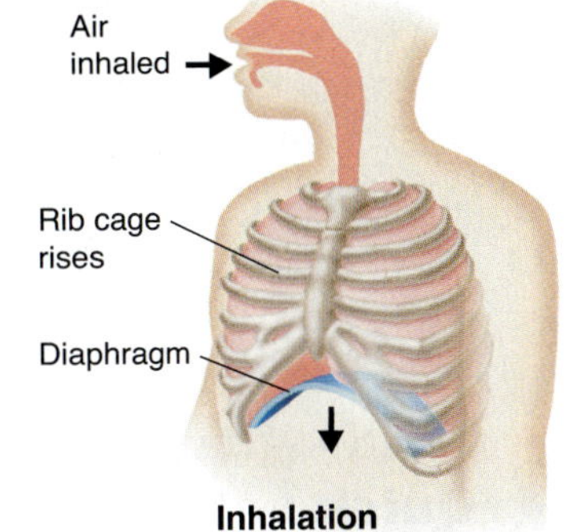

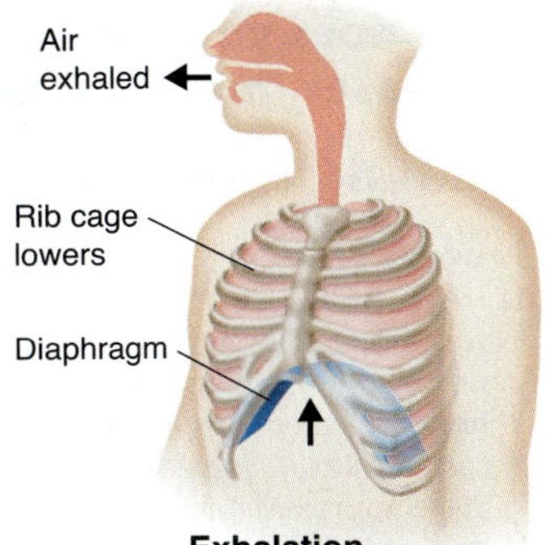

▶ **Figure 37–15** During inhalation the rib cage rises and the diaphragm contracts, increasing the size of the chest cavity. **Interpreting Graphics** *What happens as the diaphragm relaxes?*

Go Online **active art**

For: The Process of Breathing activity
Visit: PHSchool.com
Web Code: cbp-0373

Careers in Biology

- Explain that most respiratory care practitioners work in hospitals and that many hospitals have separate respiratory care departments.
- Describe some of the specific job duties of respiratory care practitioners, including maintaining and operating various kinds of breathing equipment, leading aerobic exercise classes, and conducting smoking cessation programs. L2

Resources For additional information on this career, students can contact the National Board for Respiratory Care or the American Association for Respiratory Care, or they can contact the respiratory care department of a local hospital.

You can have students write a more extensive job description as well as list the educational requirements for a career in this field.

For: The Process of Breathing activity
Visit: PHSchool.com
Web Code: cbe-0373
Students explore the events involved during the breathing process.

TEACHER TO TEACHER

To impress on the students the surface area of the human lungs, I give them this "Gee Whiz" fact. The surface area of the 300 million alveoli in the human lungs would cover 70 square meters. That's about the size of an average classroom (measuring 25 feet by 25 feet). I also describe to the class the role of the surfactant cells in the alveoli that help keep the alveoli from collapsing. I tell them that the absence of surfactant in premature babies can cause breathing problems. To illustrate collapsed alveoli, I use plastic bags like the ones you get in the produce section of the grocery store that are so hard to open!

—*Betsy Halpern*
Biology Teacher
South Eugene High School
Eugene, Oregon

Answers to . . .

Figure 37–14 *In an alveolus*

Figure 37–15 *As the diaphragm relaxes, the pressure in the chest cavity becomes greater than atmospheric pressure, so air rushes out of the lungs.*

37–3 (continued)

How Breathing Is Controlled

Quick Lab

 7IIE 7.c

Objective Students will be able to formulate a hypothesis about how breathing is affected by carbon dioxide. L2

Skills Focus Drawing Conclusions, Inferring, Observing

Materials seltzer tablet, plastic cup or 250-mL beaker, water

Time 10 minutes

Safety Get parental permission before doing this lab. Students who have breathing problems should not perform this lab. Students should remain seated while doing this lab.

Strategies

- For best results use straight-sided plastic cups or beakers.
- Room-temperature water will produce more carbon dioxide.

Expected Outcome Students should observe that inhaling carbon dioxide makes them feel short of breath and in need of more air.

Analyze and Conclude

1. Students may say they felt short of breath or as if they needed more air.
2. If students hypothesized that they would feel out of breath, their hypothesis was supported.
3. The stimulus of increased carbon dioxide indicates that gases are not being exchanged in the lungs and, therefore, that the body is not receiving enough oxygen. The increase in carbon dioxide stimulated breathing, which both removes carbon dioxide and brings in oxygen.

Build Science Skills

Inferring Explain that extremely rapid or deep breathing, which is called hyperventilation, is caused by lower-than-normal levels of carbon dioxide in the blood. Point out that breathing into a paper bag for a few minutes can stop hyperventilation. Ask: **Why does breathing into a paper bag stop hyperventilation?** *(It leads to a normal level of carbon dioxide in the blood, and this slows down the rate of breathing.)* L2

The system works only because the chest cavity is sealed. A puncture wound to the chest—even if it does not affect the lungs directly—may allow air to leak into the chest cavity and make breathing impossible. This is one of the reasons chest wounds are always serious.

How Breathing Is Controlled

You can control your breathing almost anytime you want, whether it's to blow up a balloon or to play a musical instrument. But this doesn't mean that breathing is purely voluntary. If you hold your breath for a minute or so, you'll see what happens. Your chest begins to feel tight, your throat begins to burn, and the muscles in your mouth and throat struggle to keep from breathing. Eventually your body takes over. It "forces" you to breathe!

ⓐ BI 9.b

Breathing is such an important function that your nervous system will not let you have complete control over it. The part of the brain that controls breathing is the medulla oblongata. Autonomic nerves from the medulla oblongata to the diaphragm and chest muscles produce the cycles of contraction that bring air into the lungs. How does the medulla oblongata "know" when it's time to breathe? Cells in its breathing center monitor the amount of carbon dioxide in the blood. As the carbon dioxide level rises, nerve impulses from the breathing center cause the diaphragm to contract, bringing air into the lungs. The higher the carbon dioxide level, the stronger the impulses. If the carbon dioxide level reaches a critical point, the impulses become so powerful that you cannot keep from breathing.

Quick Lab

 7IIE 7.c

How does your body respond to increases in carbon dioxide?

Materials seltzer tablet, plastic cup

Procedure

1. **Formulating Hypotheses** Carbon dioxide is a waste material synthesized during the cellular process of respiration. Write a hypothesis about how your breathing will be affected if the level of carbon dioxide increases.
2. Place approximately 100 mL of water in the cup and add a seltzer tablet. The bubbles in the water are carbon dioxide. Bring the cup up to your face and inhale deeply.

Analyze and Conclude

1. **Observing** Describe what happened when you inhaled the carbon dioxide.
2. **Drawing Conclusions** Did your results support your hypothesis or not? Explain your answer.
3. **Inferring** Why is it important for your body to respond to the stimulus of increased carbon dioxide?

BIOLOGY UPDATE

Asthma on the rise

Asthma is a potentially fatal respiratory illness characterized by repeated asthmatic attacks, during which muscles surrounding the air passages that lead to the lungs contract. Constriction of the air passages makes it difficult to get enough air. It can also cause death in severe attacks. An estimated 5 to 10 percent of high-school students suffer from asthma. That number is higher than ever before and is still on the rise. Some scientists think that the increase in asthma may be partly due to air pollution. Laws regulating smokestack emissions and the use of coal have led to a reduction in industrial air pollution. However, air pollution from motor-vehicle exhaust contains many substances that are harmful to the respiratory system, including carbon monoxide, carbon dioxide, nitrogen oxides, sulfur oxides, lead, and hydrocarbons.

▲ **Figure 37–16** This pilot must use an oxygen mask because there is not enough oxygen available in the air at high altitudes. **Applying Concepts** ***How would a mountain climber decide when to carry a supply of oxygen?***

That the breathing center responds primarily to carbon dioxide can have dangerous consequences. Consider a plane flying at high altitude. Although the amount of oxygen in the air decreases as the altitude increases, the passengers do not need oxygen masks because the cabin is pressurized. Oxygen is available for use in an emergency, but the passengers often have to be told to begin breathing the oxygen. Although their bodies may be starving for oxygen, they have no more carbon dioxide in their blood than usual, so the breathing center does not sense a problem. The pilot in **Figure 37–16** is not in a pressurized cabin and must use an oxygen mask at high altitudes.

 *What does the breathing center in the brain do?*

Tobacco and the Respiratory System

The upper part of the respiratory system is generally able to filter out dust and foreign particles that could damage the lungs. Millions of people engage in an activity—smoking tobacco—that damages and eventually destroys this protective system.

Substances in Tobacco Tobacco smoke contains many substances that affect the body. Three of the most dangerous substances are nicotine, carbon monoxide, and tar. **Nicotine** is a stimulant drug that increases the heart rate and blood pressure. Carbon monoxide is a poisonous gas that blocks the transport of oxygen by hemoglobin in the blood. It decreases the blood's ability to supply oxygen to its tissues, depriving the heart and other organs of the oxygen they need to function. Tar contains a number of compounds that have been shown to cause cancer.

Tobacco and the Respiratory System

Demonstration

Demonstrate to students how toxic tobacco is. Before class, make a tobacco solution by boiling tobacco in water for 15 minutes and then straining the solution through a paper towel. Allow the solution to cool. During class, spray the solution on a plant that is infested with aphids, and have students observe what happens. (The aphids die.) Ask: **What do you think killed the aphids?** *(Something in the tobacco)* Conclude by telling students that the nicotine in tobacco is so toxic that it is actually used as a pesticide. 

Make Connections

Chemistry Elaborate on how carbon monoxide in tobacco smoke blocks the transport of oxygen by the blood. Remind students that oxygen normally binds with the iron in hemoglobin molecules. Explain that when carbon monoxide is present in the blood, it binds with hemoglobin at the same site, but much more strongly, so the oxygen is not released to the cells where it is needed. Ask: **Besides tobacco smoke, what are some other sources of carbon monoxide?** *(Possible answers include car exhausts and faulty fireplaces, gas furnaces, and other gas appliances.)* L2

BIO INSIGHTS — FACTS AND FIGURES

Smoking, cancer, and death

A person who smokes cigarettes is 10 to 15 times more likely to develop lung cancer than a nonsmoker. The more cigarettes one smokes, the greater the chances of developing lung cancer and the more likely one is to die from lung cancer. If a person smokes two or more packs of cigarettes a day, he or she is 20 to 25 times more likely to die from lung cancer than a nonsmoker. Three of every four deaths from lung cancer in women are caused by smoking. Cancer is not the only risk that smokers face. Smokers are also three times more likely to die from a heart attack than nonsmokers. Men in their thirties who smoke can expect to lose about eight years of life if they do not quit smoking.

Answers to . . .

CHECKPOINT *The breathing center monitors the amount of carbon dioxide in the blood. As the level rises, nerve impulses from the breathing center cause the diaphragm to contract.*

Figure 37–16 *The mountain climber would base the decision on the altitude of the mountain.*

37–3 (continued)

Use Community Resources

Invite a respiratory care practitioner or other knowledgeable health professional to address the class on diseases of the respiratory system caused by smoking. Ask the speaker to describe symptoms of such diseases as chronic bronchitis and emphysema and how the diseases limit the activity and quality of life of people who have them. Also ask the speaker to describe how respiratory therapy is used to help treat the symptoms of the diseases.  L1 L2

Make Connections

Health Science Explain that lung cancer is often fatal because there is no easy way to detect it at an early stage before it has spread. New X-ray techniques now allow doctors to detect very small lung tumors, but determining whether they are cancerous requires a lung biopsy. This is a major surgical procedure with potentially serious risks, and it is not undertaken lightly. Ask: **If a simple, nonsurgical technique were discovered to detect lung cancer at an early stage, how would this affect treatment of the disease?** *(Being able to detect lung cancer early would allow doctors to treat the cancer or remove the tumor surgically before cancer cells spread to other parts of the body.)* L2

Build Science Skills

Designing Experiments Challenge small groups of students to design an experiment to determine the effects of a smoking-education class on teen smoking attitudes and habits. Students should describe the subject content of the class and how teen smoking attitudes and habits would be measured, both before and after the subjects attended the class. Ask groups to share their experimental designs with the class. L2 L3

Effects on Respiratory System Smoking tobacco brings nicotine and carbon monoxide into the upper respiratory system. These compounds paralyze the cilia. With the cilia out of action, the inhaled particles stick to the walls of the respiratory tract or enter the lungs.

Without cilia to sweep it along, smoke-laden mucus becomes trapped along the airways. This explains why smokers often cough. Irritation from the accumulated mucus triggers a cough that helps to clear the airways. Smoking also causes the lining of the respiratory tract to swell, which reduces the air flow to the alveoli.

Diseases Caused by Smoking Only 30 percent of male smokers live to age 80, but 55 percent of male nonsmokers live to that age. Clearly, smoking reduces life expectancy. **Smoking can cause such respiratory diseases as chronic bronchitis, emphysema, and lung cancer.** In chronic bronchitis, the bronchi become swollen and clogged with mucus. Even smoking a moderate number of cigarettes on a regular basis can produce chronic bronchitis. Affected people often find simple activities, such as climbing stairs, difficult.

Long-term smoking can also cause a respiratory disease called emphysema (em-fuh-SEE-muh). **Emphysema** is the loss of elasticity in the tissues of the lungs. This condition makes breathing very difficult. People who have emphysema cannot get enough oxygen to the body tissues or rid the body of excess carbon dioxide.

Smoking is an important, but preventable, cause of lung cancer. **Figure 37–17** shows the effects of smoking on the lungs. Lung cancer is particularly deadly because its cells can spread to other locations. By the time lung cancer is detected, it usually has spread to dozens of other places. About 160,000 people in the United States are diagnosed with lung cancer each year. Few will survive for five years after the diagnosis.

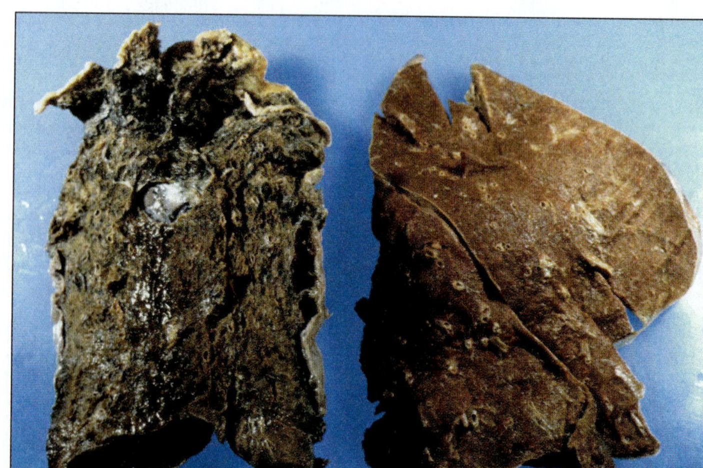

Figure 37–17 Smoking can cause respiratory diseases such as chronic bronchitis, emphysema, and lung cancer. The lung on the left is from a smoker. The lung on the right is from a nonsmoker.

HISTORY OF SCIENCE

Doll's doctors

It is common knowledge today that cigarette smoking is the major cause of lung cancer and a contributing factor to a number of other serious health problems. However, as recently as 1950, doctors were unaware of the health risks of tobacco use. All that changed in the 1950s with the innovative research of Sir Richard Doll. Doll used epidemiological methods to establish a link between cigarette smoking and many serious illnesses, including lung cancer and heart disease. His approach was to follow a large sample of people over many years to establish correlations between suspected risk factors and the development of disease. Ironically, the sample Doll followed to establish the link between smoking and lung cancer was a group of British doctors. Doll later used the same method to study the effects of other risk factors on cancer development, including the effects of asbestos on the development of a certain type of lung cancer.

Smoking is also a major cause of heart disease. Smoking constricts, or narrows, the blood vessels. This causes blood pressure to rise and makes the heart work harder. The effects of smoking on the circulatory system can be seen in **Figure 37–18.** There is a drastic change in body temperature and in circulation immediately after smoking a cigarette. Smoking doubles the risk of death from heart disease for men between 45 and 65. Moreover, for men and women of all ages, the risk of death from heart disease is greater among smokers than among nonsmokers.

Smoking and the Nonsmoker In recent years, evidence has shown that tobacco smoke is damaging to anyone who inhales it, not just the smoker. For this reason, many states have restricted smoking in restaurants and other public places.

Passive smoking, or inhaling the smoke of others, is particularly damaging to young children because their lungs are still developing. Studies now indicate that the children of smokers are twice as likely as children of nonsmokers to develop respiratory problems, such as asthma.

Dealing With Tobacco Whatever the age of a smoker, and no matter how long that person has smoked, his or her health can be improved by quitting. Nicotine is a powerful drug with strong addictive qualities that make it very difficult to quit smoking. Thus, considering the cost, the medical dangers, and the powerful addiction, the best solution is not to begin smoking.

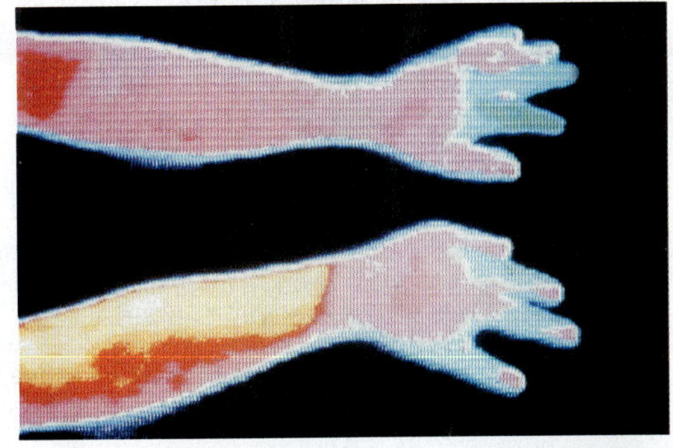

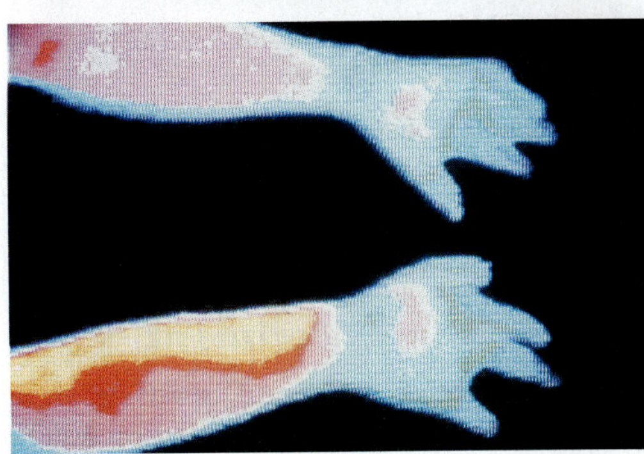

▲ **Figure 37–18** These thermograms provide a color-coded map of temperature distribution over the body surface (blue = cold; pink = hot). The top thermogram shows the forearm and hand area prior to smoking a cigarette. The bottom thermogram shows the same area after smoking. **Interpreting Graphics** ***Do you think circulation is increased or decreased after smoking?***

37–3 Section Assessment

1. **Key Concept** Interpret the function of the respiratory system by stating what it does.
2. **Key Concept** Describe some of the health problems caused by smoking tobacco.
3. Explain the process of gas exchange in the lungs.
4. Describe how breathing is controlled.
5. **Critical Thinking Inferring** As you have read, the breathing center in the brain responds to the level of carbon dioxide in the blood—not the level of oxygen. What consequences does this have for people at high altitudes?

Focus on the BIG Idea

Structure and Function

Compare what you learned in Units 8 and 9 about respiration in terrestrial arthropods, fish, and flatworms with human respiration. Relate the method of respiration to the type of environment the organism inhabits. What do these methods have in common? How do they differ?

Use Community Resources

Have interested students contact their local chapter of the American Lung Association to find out about programs available to people who want to quit smoking, such as the Great American Smokeout. Students should request copies of pamphlets, brochures, and other written materials that are available free of charge from the association. Ask students to share these materials with the class. 

3 ASSESS

Evaluate Understanding

Write the following words on the chalkboard: *nose, larynx, pharynx, trachea, lung, bronchus, alveolus.* Call on students at random to describe the function of each structure.

Reteach

Work with students to create a simple schematic diagram showing what occurs during the process of gas exchange in the alveoli.

Focus on the BIG Idea

Students might note that flatworms, which do not have respiratory organs, use diffusion to transport and excrete materials. Students can compare tracheal tubes and book lungs of terrestrial arthropods with human respiratory structures, or the removal of oxygen from water in gills with the removal of oxygen from air in alveoli.

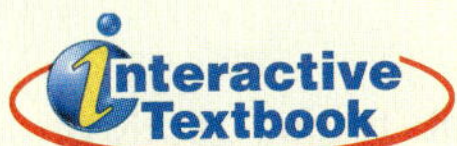

If your class subscribes to the iText, use it to review the Key Concepts in Section 37–3.

37–3 Section Assessment

1. It brings about the exchange of oxygen and carbon dioxide between the blood, the air, and tissues.
2. Chronic bronchitis: bronchi become swollen and clogged with mucus; emphysema: loss of elasticity in lungs; lung cancer: deadly disease that spreads to other parts of body
3. Oxygen diffuses from alveoli into the blood across capillary walls, and carbon dioxide diffuses from blood into air in the alveoli.
4. When the level of carbon dioxide rises in the blood, the breathing center sends out nerve impulses that cause the diaphragm to contract and bring air into the lungs.
5. The level of carbon dioxide in their blood is normal, so their breathing center does not increase the rate of breathing. As a result, they do not get enough oxygen.

Answer to . . .

Figure 37–18 *Circulation is decreased after smoking. This explains why the hand in the bottom photograph is colder after smoking.*

Design an Experiment

BIIE 1.b, BIIE 1.g

Objective Students will be able to use a model to determine how muscle contractions move air in and out of the lungs. L2 L3

Skills Focus Using Models

Time 45 minutes

Advance Prep

- You may want to have each student bring in a plastic bottle, such as a 16-oz drink bottle, to use for the lab.
- Make sure the bottles are clean before students use them.
- You can save time and reduce risk of injury by cutting off the bottoms of the plastic bottles before class.
- A number 2 rubber stopper will fit a 16-oz plastic drink bottle.

Safety Advise students to be careful when they use the scissors to puncture the plastic bottle, because the plastic is tough and may cause the scissors to slip.

Teaching Tips After students have read the entire procedure, ask:

- **What do the different parts of the model represent?** *(The bottle represents the chest or chest wall, the large balloon represents the diaphragm, the small balloon represents a lung, and the hole in the stopper represents the air passages leading to the lung.)*
- **What do you predict will happen when you pull down on the large balloon?** *(Students may or may not correctly predict that the small balloon will fill with air and expand when they pull down on the large balloon.)*
- Caution students to pull gently on the large balloon so that it does not slip off the plastic bottle.
- If students have difficulty deciding how to modify the model to represent a punctured chest, review what each part of the model represents. Students should describe puncturing the plastic bottle to model a punctured chest. Students may or may not predict correctly that puncturing the bottle will cause the small balloon to no longer be affected by the pulling down or pressing up on the large balloon.

Design an Experiment

BIIE 1.b, BIIE 1.g

Modeling Breathing

As you breathe, your body moves air into and out of your lungs. All body movements depend on muscles, which work only by contracting. How does your body use muscles to cause air to flow into and out of your lungs? In this investigation, you will make a working model of human lungs that will help you answer this question.

Problem

How do muscle contractions move air into and out of the lungs?

Materials

- small, clear plastic bottle
- large round balloon
- small round balloon
- one-hole rubber stopper
- scissors

Skills

Using Models

Design Your Experiment

Part A: A Model of Normal Lungs

1. Place a clear plastic bottle on its side. Press one point of a pair of scissors through the side of the bottle about 1 cm from the bottom.
2. Using the scissors, cut off the bottom of the bottle by cutting all the way around. Trim off any rough spots from the edge.
3. Stretch a small balloon, and blow it up several times to make it pliable.
4. Pull the opening of the small balloon over the bottom of a one-hole rubber stopper.
5. Insert the balloon through the mouth of the bottle. Press the stopper tightly into the bottle so that it holds the lip of the balloon in place.

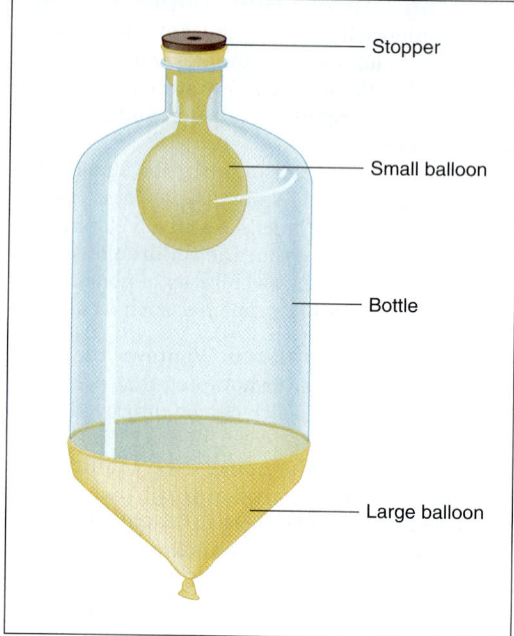

6. Stretch a large balloon, and blow it up several times to make it pliable.
7. Using the scissors, cut off about 1 cm from the rounded, closed end of the large balloon. Tie the other end closed.
8. Stretch the large balloon far enough over the cut end of the bottle to keep the balloon from slipping off, as shown in the diagram.
9. As you watch the small balloon, pull down on the knot of the large balloon. Then, still watching the small balloon, press up on the large balloon.

Expected Outcomes

- In Part A, students should observe that pulling down on the large balloon causes the small balloon to inflate and that pressing up on the large balloon causes the small balloon to deflate.
- In Part B, students should puncture the bottle and then observe that the small balloon no longer inflates or deflates as the large balloon is pulled down or pressed up.

Part B: A Model of a Chest Injury

10 **Formulating Hypotheses** If a person receives an injury that punctures the skin and muscles of the chest, outside air can come into direct contact with the outer surfaces of the lungs. How would such an event affect a person's ability to breathe? Record your hypothesis.

11 Think of a way you could modify your model of human lungs to represent the lungs in a person with a punctured chest. Write a description of your plan, including your prediction of how the alternative model will behave and how the model will test your hypothesis.

12 Show your plan to your teacher. If your teacher approves, make a model of a punctured chest. Use your model to test your hypothesis.

Analyze and Conclude

1. **Observing** In Part A, what happened to the small balloon in your model when you pulled down on the large balloon?
2. **Observing** What happened to the small balloon when you pressed up on the large balloon?
3. **Inferring** What happened to the pressure inside the bottle when you moved the large balloon up and down?
4. **Formulating Hypotheses** What caused the small balloon in Part A to expand and contract?
5. **Using Models** Do you consider the model you made in Part A an adequate representation of the human respiratory system? Explain.
6. **Drawing Conclusions** In Part B, how did your alternative model represent a chest injury? What does that model show about the role of the chest wall in breathing?
7. **Evaluating** In Part B, was your prediction correct? Did the behavior of your second model support your hypothesis? Explain your answer.
8. **Drawing Conclusions** How do muscles cause air to flow into and out of human lungs?
9. **SAFETY** Explain how you demonstrated safe practices as you used sharp objects such as scissors.

Go Further

Making Models Obtain information from a hospital, doctor's office, or county health department about the mechanics of breathing and diseases such as asthma and emphysema that make breathing difficult. Find out what causes these diseases, how they affect breathing, and how they are prevented and treated. Then, make a new model that demonstrates the effects of one of these diseases. Be prepared to explain how well your model represents that disease.

Go Further

Students will learn that asthma is caused by the narrowing of air passageways leading to the lungs, often due to allergic reactions. They will also learn that emphysema is caused by loss of elasticity in the lungs, often due to cigarette smoking. Students might model asthma by narrowing the hole in the stopper with modeling clay, tape, or some other material so that air movement into and out of the small balloon is restricted. Students might model emphysema by replacing the small balloon with a new balloon that has not been blown up or stretched out to make it pliable. In each case, there would be less inflation or deflation of the small balloon as the large balloon is pulled down or pressed up.

Analyze and Conclude

1. The small balloon inflated.
2. The small balloon deflated.
3. When the large balloon was pulled down, the pressure decreased. When the large balloon was pressed up, the pressure increased.
4. Decreased pressure in the bottle allowed air to fill the small balloon. Increased pressure in the bottle pushed the air out of the small balloon.
5. Sample answer: It shows how a lung functions, but only one lung is represented.
6. The model represents a chest injury in which a puncture allows air to enter the chest. It shows that the chest wall must be intact for breathing to occur.
7. If the chest wall is punctured, changes in pressure needed for breathing cannot occur.
8. When the diaphragm contracts, it pulls down, allowing air to enter the lungs. When the diaphragm relaxes, it pushes up, forcing air out of the lungs.
9. Students should say that they handled scissors carefully to avoid cutting themselves.

Chapter 37 Study Guide

Study Tip

Have students choose partners and quiz each other on the Key Concept questions in the Section Assessments. Also, have students make flashcards for the Vocabulary terms and use them to quiz each other.

Thinking Visually

1. Atrium
2. Pumps blood to lungs
3. Pulmonary arteries
4. Pulmonary veins
5. Receives blood from lungs
6. Left ventricle
7. Brings blood from left ventricle to body

Chapter 37 Assessment

Reviewing Content

1. c	5. b	9. a
2. d	6. a	10. c
3. a	7. c	
4. d	8. a	

Understanding Concepts

11. In a closed circulatory system, blood always remains within the blood vessels.

12. Pulmonary circulation carries blood between the heart and the lungs. Systemic circulation carries blood between the heart and the rest of the body.

13. Blood enters the heart through the atria. As the heart contracts, blood is forced first into the ventricles and then out from the ventricles into the circulation.

14. A valve in the heart prevents any backflow of blood. Valves are also found in veins.

15. The function of the pacemaker is to control the heart rate.

16. From the sinoatrial node to a network of fibers in the atria, to the atrioventricular node, to muscle fibers in the ventricles

17. Arteries are wide vessels with thick walls. Capillaries are narrow vessels with walls only one cell in thickness. Veins are wide vessels with walls that are thicker than capillaries but thinner than arteries.

Chapter 37 Study Guide

37–1 The Circulatory System

Key Concepts 7 6.j, BI 9.b, *BI 9.i

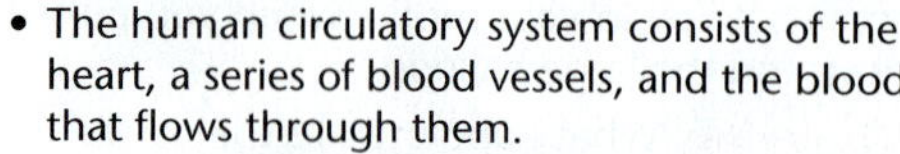

- The human circulatory system consists of the heart, a series of blood vessels, and the blood that flows through them.
- As the blood flows through the circulatory system, it moves through three types of blood vessels—arteries, capillaries, and veins.

Vocabulary

myocardium, p. 944
atrium, p. 944
ventricle, p. 944
pulmonary circulation, p. 944
systemic circulation, p. 944
valve, p. 945
pacemaker, p. 946
aorta, p. 946
artery, p. 946
capillary, p. 947
vein, p. 947
atherosclerosis, p. 949

37–2 Blood and the Lymphatic System

Key Concepts *BI 10.f

- Red blood cells transport oxygen.
- White blood cells guard against infection, fight parasites, and attack bacteria.
- Blood clotting is made possible by plasma proteins and cell fragments called platelets.
- A network of vessels, nodes, and organs called the lymphatic system collects the fluid that is lost by the blood and returns it to the circulatory system.

Vocabulary

plasma, p. 951
hemoglobin, p. 952
lymphocyte, p. 952
platelet, p. 953
lymph, p. 954

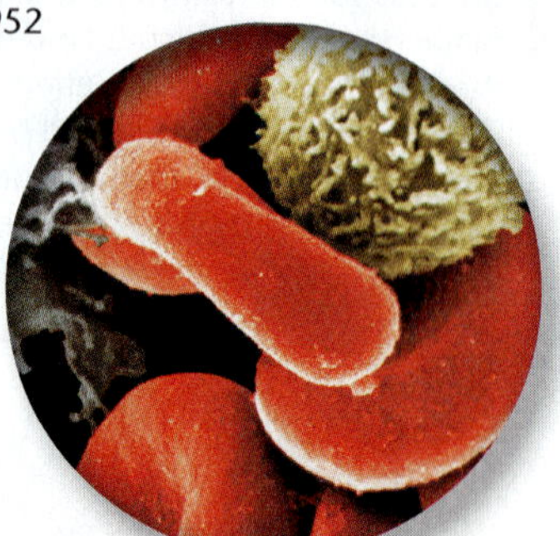

37–3 The Respiratory System

Key Concepts BI 9.b

- The basic function of the human respiratory system is to bring about the exchange of oxygen and carbon dioxide between the blood, the air, and tissues.
- Smoking can cause such respiratory diseases as chronic bronchitis, emphysema, and lung cancer.

Vocabulary

pharynx, p. 956
trachea, p. 956
larynx, p. 958
bronchus, p. 958
alveolus, p. 958
diaphragm, p. 959
nicotine, p. 961
emphysema, p. 962

Thinking Visually

On a separate sheet of paper, make a copy of the chart below. Then, fill in the missing structures and functions.

Structures and Functions of the Circulatory System

Structure	Function
1	Chamber where blood enters heart from the body
Right ventricle	2
3	Carry blood from the heart to the lungs
4	Carry blood back to the heart from the lungs
Left atrium	5
6	Chamber that pumps blood to the body
Aorta	7

TIME SAVER CHAPTER RESOURCES

Print:

- ***Teaching Resources,*** Chapter Vocabulary Review, Graphic Organizer, Chapter 37 Tests: Levels A and B

Technology:

- ***Computer Test Bank,*** Chapter 37 Test
- ***iText,*** Chapter 37 Assessment

Chapter 37 Assessment

Reviewing Content

Choose the letter that best answers the question or completes the statement.

1. The circulatory system is composed of the
   a. lung, heart, and brain.
   b. lung, blood vessels, and heart.
   c. heart, blood, and blood vessels.
   d. heart, arteries, and veins.
2. The upper chambers of the heart are the
   a. ventricles.
   b. septa.
   c. myocardia.
   d. atria.
3. Blood leaving the heart for the body passes through a large blood vessel known as the
   a. aorta.
   b. vena cava.
   c. pulmonary vein.
   d. pulmonary artery.
4. Which cells are able to protect the body by engulfing foreign cells or producing antibodies?
   a. red blood cells
   b. plasma cells
   c. platelets
   d. white blood cells
5. Exchange of nutrients and wastes with the body cells takes place by diffusion through the walls of
   a. veins.
   b. capillaries.
   c. arteries.
   d. atria.
6. Which substance is the iron-containing protein found in red blood cells?
   a. hemoglobin
   b. fibrinogen
   c. prothrombin
   d. thrombin
7. The process shown below is made possible by a number of plasma proteins and cell fragments called
   a. fibrins.
   b. thrombins.
   c. platelets.
   d. lymphocytes.

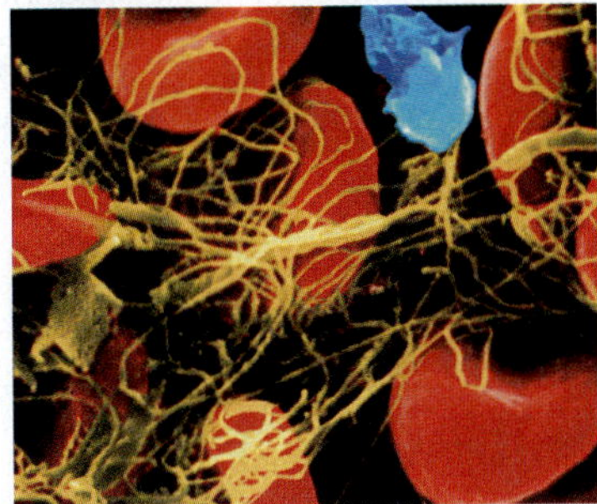

8. The tiny hollow air sacs where oxygen exchange takes place are the
   a. alveoli.
   b. lymph nodes.
   c. capillaries.
   d. bronchioles.

Interactive textbook with assessment at PHSchool.com 

9. Two highly elastic folds of tissue known as the vocal cords can be found in the
   a. larynx.
   b. pharynx.
   c. trachea.
   d. bronchi.
10. The large, flat muscle that moves up and down to alter the volume of the chest cavity is the
    a. trachea.
    b. epiglottis.
    c. diaphragm.
    d. larynx.

Understanding Concepts

11. What is a closed circulatory system?
12. Compare pulmonary circulation and systemic circulation.
13. Trace the flow of blood through the heart.
14. What is the major function of a valve in the heart? Where else in the circulatory system are valves found?
15. Describe the function of the pacemaker.
16. How are impulses transmitted through the heart?
17. Compare the wall thickness and diameter of the three different types of blood vessels.
18. Distinguish between systolic pressure and diastolic pressure.
19. How does exercise help to prevent circulatory system disorders?
20. What are the major components of blood? List the functions of each component.
21. Explain why people with hemophilia need to avoid injury.
22. What are the primary functions of the lymphatic system?
23. What part of the brain controls involuntary breathing?
24. What are three of the most dangerous substances in tobacco smoke? Describe how each affects the body.
25. How does emphysema affect the respiratory system?

HOMEWORK GUIDE

Section:	Questions:
Section 37–1	1–3, 5, 11–19, 26, 27, 30, 31
Section 37–2	4, 6, 7, 20–22, 28, 29, 33, 34
Section 37–3	8–10, 23–25, 32

Interactive Textbook

If your class subscribes to the iText, your students can go online to access an interactive version of the Student Edition and a self-test.

(Continued from page 966)

18. Systolic pressure is the force of the blood felt in the arteries when the ventricles contract. Diastolic pressure is the force of the blood felt in the arteries when the ventricles relax.

19. Exercise helps to prevent circulatory system disorders by increasing the respiratory system's efficiency, controlling weight, reducing body fat, reducing stress, and strengthening the heart muscle.

20. The major components of blood are plasma, platelets, white blood cells, and red blood cells. Plasma provides the fluid that carries the other blood components. It also contains proteins that are involved in several important functions, including immune reactions and blood clotting. Platelets cluster around a wound and release proteins that start a series of chemical reactions resulting in a clot. White blood cells attack foreign substances and organisms. Red blood cells transport oxygen.

21. Because people with hemophilia have a defective or absent clotting element, they cannot produce blood clots that are firm enough to stop even relatively minor bleeding.

22. The primary functions of the lymphatic system are to collect fluid lost by the blood and return it to the circulatory system; filter bacteria and other microorganisms from the fluid; house white blood cells, called lymphocytes, that help fight infection; and absorb fat and fat-soluble vitamins from the digestive tract and carry them to the circulatory system.

23. Involuntary breathing is controlled by centers in the pons and medulla oblongata, parts of the brain located just above the spinal cord.

Chapter 37 Assessment

24. Three of the most dangerous substances in tobacco smoke are nicotine, carbon monoxide, and tar. Nicotine increases the heart rate and blood pressure. Carbon monoxide blocks the transport of oxygen by hemoglobin in the blood. Tar contains compounds that cause cancer.

25. Emphysema is a loss of elasticity in lung tissues. It makes breathing difficult and prevents the tissues from getting the oxygen they need or eliminating excess carbon dioxide.

Critical Thinking

26. The most likely experimental design is to measure each subject's heart rate at rest to determine the normal heart rate and then again at frequent timed intervals after the subject has exercised, until the heart rate returns to the normal rate.

27. If a blood clot lodges in a major blood vessel, it might block the flow of blood, deprive tissues of needed oxygen, and cause tissue damage.

28. A person with a low red blood cell count has fewer red blood cells to transport oxygen to cells. Without adequate oxygen, the production of energy from cellular respiration is reduced.

29. Patients who have had a stroke take aspirin because it makes platelets less sticky.

30. The powerful pressure produced when the heart contracts pushes blood into and through arteries.

31. All the blood flows through the lungs to pick up oxygen. During exercise, much more blood flows through the skeletal muscles to fuel the production of energy needed for muscle contraction.

32. A respiratory care practitioner might use his or her knowledge by helping the person with asthma understand the cause of the disease as well as how to avoid triggering asthma attacks and how to bring attacks under control.

33. Removal of the lymph nodes would lessen the body's ability to fight disease. The lymph nodes filter bacteria and other disease-causing microorganisms from the lymph before it is returned to the circulatory system. The lymph nodes also house white blood cells, called lymphocytes, which help fight infection.

Chapter 37 Assessment

Critical Thinking

26. Designing Experiments Design an experiment that determines the amount of time needed for a person's heart rate to return to normal after exercise.

27. Predicting What might happen if a blood clot forms inside the circulatory system and lodges in a major blood vessel?

28. Applying Concepts Explain why a person with a low red blood cell count is likely to experience fatigue.

29. Inferring Aspirin reduces the clot-forming ability of the blood. Why do you think some doctors prescribe aspirin for patients who have had a stroke?

30. Drawing Conclusions Large veins contain one-way valves, which keep the blood flowing in one direction. Why don't large arteries need similar valves?

31. Analyzing Data The following table shows the relative blood flow through various organs in the human body—that is, the fraction of blood that flows through a given human organ. Through which organ(s) does all of the blood flow? Explain the reason for the differences indicated in blood flow to skeletal muscles (normal versus during exercise).

Blood Flow Through Human Organs

Organ	Percentage of Total Flow
Brain	14%
Heart	5%
Kidneys	22%
Liver	13%
Lungs	100%
Skeletal muscles	18%
Skeletal muscles during exercise	75%

32. Applying Concepts How might a respiratory care practitioner use his or her knowledge of anatomy, physiology, and microbiology to help a person with asthma?

33. Predicting How would the removal of a person's lymph nodes affect the body's ability to fight disease?

34. Applying Concepts Hemophilia is a genetic disorder in which a defective gene for blood clotting is present. How would injections of normal clotting proteins help a hemophiliac?

Focus on the BIG Idea

Cellular Basis of Life As you may remember from Chapter 9, the term *respiration* may be used to describe two different biological processes. How are these two processes similar? How are they different?

Writing in Science

Make a list of the things you do that affect your circulatory and respiratory systems. After completing your list, place a check mark next to those that are harmful. Pick one harmful habit and write a paragraph explaining how you will change or eliminate that habit.

Performance-Based Assessment

Making a Model Construct a simple stethoscope out of rubber tubing and a metal funnel. Listen for the sounds of air rushing into and out of your lungs as you inhale and exhale. Record a description of the sounds while you are inhaling and exhaling. How does the sound change when you cough? What do you think it would sound like if you had a cold? Bronchitis? Prepare a brief report of your findings and present it to the class.

For: An interactive self-test
Visit: PHSchool.com
Web Code: cba-0370

34. Injections of normal clotting proteins would help a hemophiliac by providing missing proteins needed for normal blood clotting. With the injections, the hemophiliac's blood would clot in case of an injury.

Focus on the BIG Idea

One process, called cellular respiration, involves the chemical breakdown of foods and making of ATP in cells throughout the body. Respiration, the other process, involves gas exchange in the lungs and active tissues. Oxygen, taken up by the blood in the lungs, is delivered to the tissues, where carbon dioxide is picked up by the blood and delivered to the lungs, where it is released.

Standards Practice

Online at PHSchool.com

Test-Taking Tip

When you are asked questions about structures in a diagram, first identify each structure. Then, try to answer the questions

Directions: Choose the letter that best answers the question or completes the statement.

1. Which of the following protects the human body by destroying pathogens? ***BI 10.f**
   - **A** red blood cells
   - **B** platelets
   - **C** lymphocytes
   - **D** hemoglobin
2. Which statement best describes an interaction between the circulatory and respiratory systems that helps maintain homeostasis?
   - **A** Blood plasma transports salts, sugars, fats, and dissolved proteins through the body to keep it healthy.
   - **B** The diaphragm and rib cage work together to move air into and out of the lungs.
   - **C** The lymphatic system contains nodes that act as filters to remove bacteria that could otherwise cause disease.
   - **D** Blood cells pick up and carry oxygen from the lungs to the body's cells.
3. Where does gas exchange occur in the human respiratory system?
   - **A** vocal cords
   - **B** bronchi
   - **C** aveoli
   - **D** trachea
4. Human blood is composed of all of the following EXCEPT
   - **A** plasma.
   - **B** mucus.
   - **C** phagocytes.
   - **D** hemoglobin.
5. Nicotine in tobacco
   - **A** is not addictive.
   - **B** decreases blood pressure.
   - **C** decreases the heart rate.
   - **D** paralyzes cilia.
6. Antibodies are produced by
   - **A** red blood cells.
   - **B** platelets.
   - **C** lymphocytes.
   - **D** fibrinogen.

Questions 7–10 Use the diagram below to answer the questions that follow.

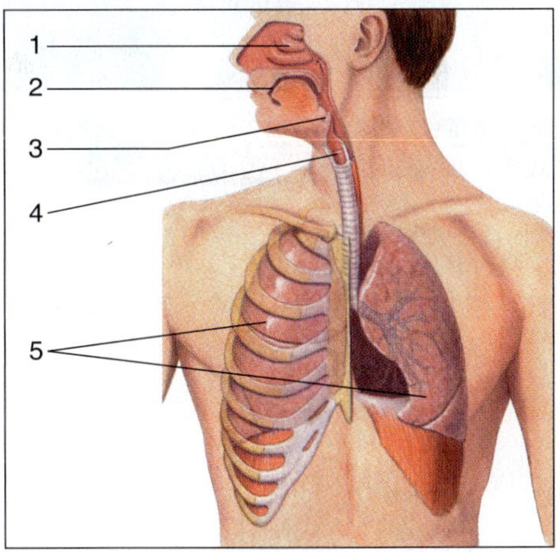

7. Which structure's primary function is to warm and moisten the air?
   - **A** 1
   - **B** 2
   - **C** 3
   - **D** 4
8. Which structure contains the vocal cords?
   - **A** 1
   - **B** 2
   - **C** 3
   - **D** 4
9. Which structure is altered by emphysema?
   - **A** 1
   - **B** 2
   - **C** 4
   - **D** 5
10. Which structure contains aveoli?
    - **A** 1
    - **B** 2
    - **C** 3
    - **D** 5

Standards Practice

1. C	**5.** D	**9.** D
2. D	**6.** C	**10.** D
3. C	**7.** A	
4. B	**8.** D	

Success Tracker™

Online at PHSchool.com

Have students check their understanding of the chapter by logging onto Success Tracker.

Writing in Science

Answers will vary. Students might list smoking and not exercising regularly as things they do that are harmful to their circulatory and respiratory systems. They might explain how they will quit smoking by joining a smoking cessation class or how they will increase their level of exercise by joining a sports team.

Performance-Based Assessment

Students might say that normal breathing sounds like a muffled roar, which changes to a loud, sharp, rushing sound when they cough. With a cold, they would be likely to hear normal breathing sounds because a cold causes symptoms primarily in the upper part of the respiratory tract, such as the nose and larynx. With bronchitis, students might expect to hear wheezing sounds because of mucus in the large air passages in the chest.

PHSchool.com

Your students can independently test their knowledge of the chapter and print out their test results for your files.

Chapter Planner 38 Digestive and Excretory Systems

Section and Section Objectives	Time	STANDARDS NCLB	STANDARDS Biology	Activities and Labs
38–1 Food and Nutrition, pp. 971–977 ***38.1.1*** ***Explain*** how food provides energy. ***38.1.2*** ***Describe*** the nutrients your body needs. ***38.1.3*** ***State*** why water is such an important nutrient. ***38.1.4*** ***Explain*** how to use the food pyramid.	2 periods (1 block)			**SE:** ***Inquiry Activity,*** What's in a chip?, p. 970 L2 **TE:** ***Demonstration,*** p. 972 L1 L2 **SE:** ***Analyzing Data,*** Evaluating Food Labels, p. 977 L2
38–2 The Process of Digestion, pp. 978–984 ***38.2.1*** ***Identify*** the organs of the digestive system. ***38.2.2*** ***Describe*** the function of the digestive system.	2 periods (1 block)		*BI 9.f	**TE:** ***Demonstration,*** p. 978, p. 979, p. 980 L1 L2 **TE:** ***Make Connections,*** p. 981 L2 **SE:** ***Quick Lab,*** How do villi help the small intestine absorb nutrients?, p. 982 L2 **TE:** ***Demonstration,*** p. 983 L1 **SE:** ***Design an Experiment,*** Investigating the Effects of Enzymes on Food Molecules, pp. 990–991 L2 L3 **LMB:** Chapter 38 Lab L1 L2
38–3 The Excretory System, pp. 985–989 ***38.3.1*** ***Identify*** the functions of the kidneys. ***38.3.2*** ***Explain*** how blood is filtered.	1 period (1/2 block)		*BI 9.g	**TE:** ***Demonstration,*** p. 985 L1 L2 **TE:** ***Build Science Skills,*** p. 986 L1 L2 **TE:** ***Demonstration,*** p. 987 L2 **LMA:** Chapter 38 Lab L2 L3
Chapter Assessment, pp. 992–995	1 period (1/2 block)			

ACTIVITY PLANNER

SE: ***Inquiry Activity,*** p. 970; 10 min.; ordinary potato chips, baked potato chips, brown paper bags, shallow metal or glass container, matches, potato chip package labels

TE: ***Demonstration,*** p. 972; 5 min., 5 min. a few days later; apple slice, potato slice, slice of bread, cracker, balance, paper plates

TE: ***Demonstration,*** p. 978; 10 min.; raw egg, bowl, fork, pan of boiling water

TE: ***Demonstration,*** p. 979; 10 min.; soda crackers

TE: ***Demonstration,*** p. 980; 5 min.; 25- to 30-cm length of flexible plastic or rubber tubing, marble

TE: ***Make Connections,*** p. 981; 5 min.; 100 mL 0.5% hydrochloric acid, beaker, pH paper, sodium bicarbonate solution

SE: ***Quick Lab,*** p. 982; 20 min.; paper towels, scissors, cardboard tubes, metric rulers, 30-mL graduated cylinders, plastic cups

TE: ***Demonstration,*** p. 983; 5 min.; piece of velvet fabric

TE: ***Demonstration,*** p. 985; 5 min.; balloon, water

TE: ***Build Science Skills,*** p. 986; 5 min.; water, food coloring, sand, silt, paper coffee filter

TE: ***Demonstration,*** p. 987; 10 min.; beef or lamb kidney, scalpel or sharp knife

SE: ***Design an Experiment,*** pp. 990–991; 45 min. first day, 15 min. two days later; Benedict's solution, boiling water bath, cooked egg white, scalpel or single-edged razor blade, metric ruler, 6 large test tubes with stoppers, glass-marking pencil, test-tube rack, 10-mL graduated cylinder, 1% pepsin solution, 0.2% hydrochloric acid, cooked potato, 1% amylase solution, test-tube holder, heat-resistant gloves

PLANNING KEY

Ability Levels

for students performing . . .

below grade level L1

at grade level L2

above grade level L3

Print Components

SE	Student Edition	LA	Lab Assessment
TE	Teacher's Edition	BTM	Biotechnology Manual
RSW	Reading & Study Workbook A	IDM	Issues and Decision Making
ARSW	Adapted Reading & Study Workbook B	LW	Lab Worksheets
TR	Teaching Resources	LMA	Laboratory Manual A
IF	Investigations in Forensics	LMB	Laboratory Manual B

Tech Components

CTB	Computer Test Bank
BD	BioDetectives DVD
TP	Transparencies Plus
PLM	Probeware Lab Manual
ABC	ABC DVD Library
LS	Lab Simulations
VL	Virtual Labs

Interactive Textbook — Interactive textbook with assessment at PHSchool.com

Program Resources	Assessment	Media and Technology
TR: Lesson Plan 38–1, Section Summary, p. 139 L1, p. 147 L2, Worksheets, pp. 142–143 L1, pp. 149–151 L2 **RSW:** Section 38–1 L2 **ARSW:** Section 38–1 L1 **IDM:** Issues and Decisions 5, 35, 39, 49 L2 L3	**SE:** 38–1 Section Assessment, p. 977 **TR:** Section Review 38–1	**iText:** Section 38–1 **TP:** 38–1 Interest Grabber, Section Outline, Concept Map, Figure 38–6, Figure 38–7, Figure 38–8
TR: Lesson Plan 38–2, Section Summary, p. 140 L1, p. 147 L2, Worksheets, pp. 144–145 L1, pp. 152–155 L2, Enrichment L3 **LW:** Chapter 38 Design an Experiment L1 L2 L3 **RSW:** Section 38–2 L2 **ARSW:** Section 38–2 L1	**SE:** 38–2 Section Assessment, p. 984 **TR:** Section Review 38–2	**iText:** Section 38–2 **TP:** 38–2 Interest Grabber, Section Outline, Digestive Enzymes, Figure 38–10, Figure 38–13, Figure 38–14 **ABC:** 40 Human Digestion
TR: Lesson Plan 38–3, Section Summary, p. 141 L1, p. 148 L2, Worksheets, pp. 156–157 L2 **RSW:** Section 38–3 L2 **ARSW:** Section 38–3 L1 **IDM:** Issues and Decisions 40 L2 L3	**SE:** 38–3 Section Assessment, p. 989 **TR:** Section Review 38–3	**iText:** Section 38–3 **TP:** 38–3 Interest Grabber, Section Outline, Urinary System, Figure 38–17, Figure 38–19, The Nephron **ABC:** 41 Kidney Function
	SE: Chapter 38 Assessment, pp. 992–995 **TR:** Chapter Vocabulary Review, Graphic Organizer, Chapter 38 Test	**iText:** Chapter 38 Assessment **CTB:** Chapter 38 Test

Go Online

Students can do research, share data, and test their knowledge online.

PRESSED FOR TIME?

To Preview the Chapter

- Introduce students to the Vocabulary terms in Section 38–1 and to the organs of the digestive and excretory systems in Sections 38–2 and 38–3.
- Have students read the boldface sentences in each section.

To Cover the Chapter Quickly

- Have students read Section 38–1, the introduction to Section 38–2, Figures 38–10 and 38–17, and Functions of the Excretory System and Control of Kidney Function in Section 38–3.
- Assign the Section Review 38–1; questions 1 and 2 in Section Reviews 38–2 and 38–3; questions 1–3, 11–14, 27, 30, and 34 in Chapter 38 Assessment; and questions 1–8 in Chapter 38 Standards Practice.

To Review the Chapter

- Assign the Section Reviews 38–1 through 38–3 in the Reading and Study Workbook or the Adapted Reading and Study Workbook.
- Assign the Section Reviews for 38–1 through 38–3 and the Chapter Vocabulary Review for Chapter 38 in the Teaching Resources.

CHAPTER 38

ENGAGE/EXPLORE

Inquiry Activity

Objective Students will be able to infer which of two potato chips has more stored chemical energy based on the fat content of the chips. L2

Skills Focus **Inferring, Drawing Conclusions, Observing**

Materials 1 ordinary potato chip, 1 baked potato chip, 2 brown paper bags, shallow metal or glass container, matches, potato chip package labels

Time 10 minutes

Advance Prep Make copies for each student of the nutrition facts labels from the two packages of potato chips.

Strategy Suggest that students label each paper bag with the type of potato chip that was crushed in it.

Expected Outcome Students should infer that the ordinary potato chip contains more stored chemical energy.

Think About It

1. The ordinary potato chip
2. The ordinary potato chip
3. The ordinary chip leaves a larger grease spot and burns longer because it has more fat and more stored chemical energy.

Brain Teaser

Ask students whether each of the following commonly believed statements is true or false: **Only foods containing sugar give you energy.** *(False, because any kind of food that contains Calories can be broken down by the body and converted into energy)* **Fats have no place in a healthy diet.** *(False, because small quantities of fats are essential for good health)*

CHAPTER 38

Digestive and Excretory Systems

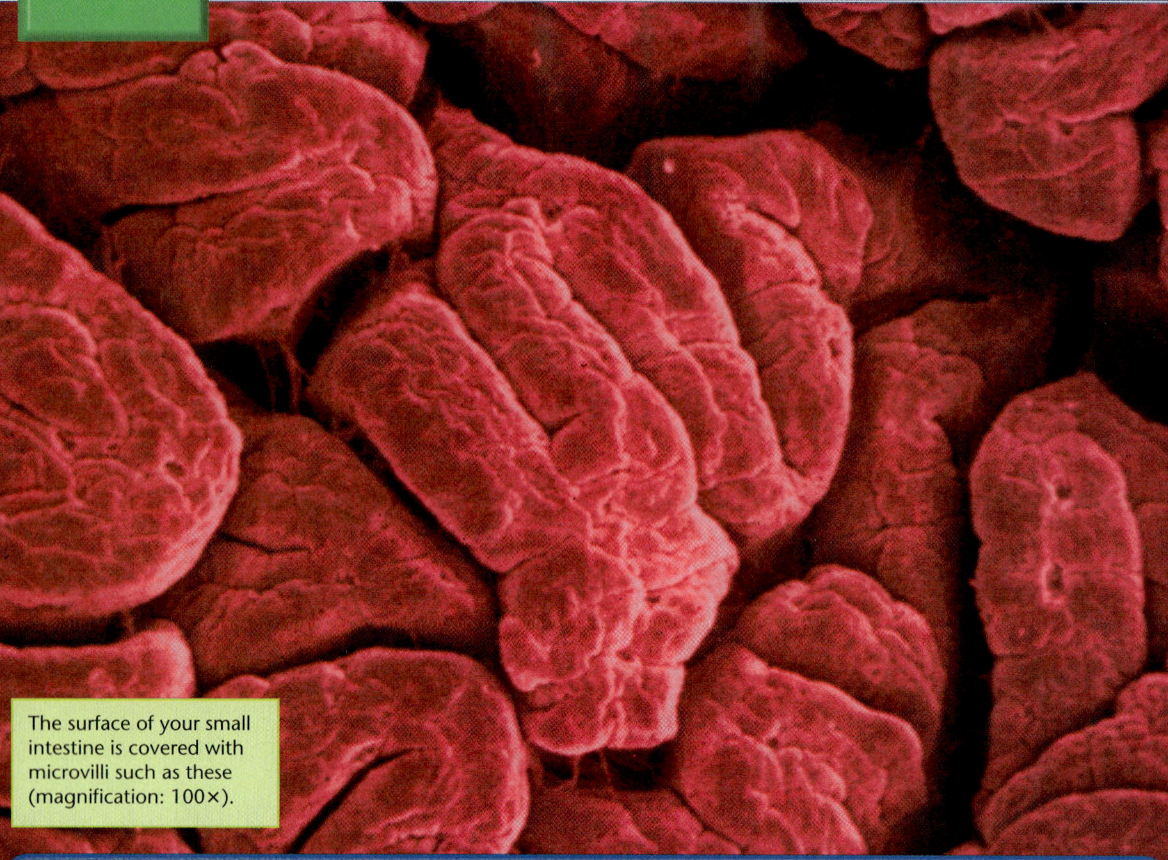

The surface of your small intestine is covered with microvilli such as these (magnification: 100×).

Inquiry Activity

What's in a chip?

Procedure 

1. Place an ordinary potato chip on a brown paper bag, and fold the bag over the chip. Repeat, using a similarly sized, baked potato chip and another paper bag. **CAUTION:** *Do not eat the potato chips.*
2. Press down on the bags for 1 minute, and then unfold them. Hold the bags up to the light. A bright spot indicates the presence of fat.
3. Observe as your teacher burns the potato chips.

Think About It

1. **Observing** Which type of potato chip contains more fat?
2. **Inferring** Which potato chip has more stored chemical energy?
3. **Drawing Conclusions** How are the results from burning the potato chips related to the fat and Calorie contents listed on their package labels?

TEACHER TO TEACHER

When I teach nutrition, I have each student bring in 10 labels from food packages. The labels should contain the name of the product, the ingredients list, and the nutrition facts table. I have students attach each label to a sheet of paper and beside the label write the serving size and the amount of Calories, fat, and sodium one serving of the food contains. When we discuss the labels, students usually say they are surprised to learn how small serving sizes are and how much fat many foods contain. We discuss how the ingredients are always listed in order from most to least common. Students are surprised to learn that what they thought they purchased is not always the first-listed ingredient.

—Duane Nichols
Biology Teacher
Alhambra High School
Alhambra, CA

38–1 Food and Nutrition

How important is food in your life? Before you answer, think of two American holidays: Independence Day and Thanksgiving Day. What comes to mind? No matter where you live, chances are that meals are the centerpieces of those special days. To most of us, food is more than just nourishment—it is an important part of our culture. Human societies throughout the world organize meetings and family gatherings around food.

Guide for Reading

Key Concepts
- What are the nutrients your body needs?
- Why is water such an important nutrient?

Vocabulary
Calorie
carbohydrate
fat
protein
vitamin
mineral

Reading Strategy: Finding Main Ideas Before you read, skim the section to identify the key ideas. Then, carefully read the section, making a list of supporting details for each main idea.

Food and Energy

Have you ever wondered why you need to eat food? The most obvious answer is to obtain energy. You need energy to climb stairs, lift books, run, and even to think. Just as a car needs gasoline, your body needs fuel for all that work, and food is your fuel. Cells convert the chemical energy stored in the sugar glucose and other molecules into ATP.

The energy available in food can be measured in a surprisingly simple way—by burning the food! When food is burned, the energy content of the food is converted to heat, which is measured in terms of calories. The amount of heat needed to raise the temperature of 1 gram of water by 1 degree Celsius is 1 calorie. Scientists refer to the energy stored in food as dietary Calories with a capital *C*. One **Calorie** is equal to 1000 calories, or 1 kilocalorie (kcal).

The energy needs of an average-sized teenager are about 2200 Calories per day for females and about 2800 Calories per day for males. If you engage in vigorous physical activity, however, your energy needs may be higher.

Chemical pathways in your body's cells can extract energy from almost any type of food. Why then does it matter which foods you eat? Although most of the food you eat is used as fuel, a certain amount of the food you eat has other important functions. Food supplies the raw materials used to build and repair body tissues. Some of these raw materials are used to manufacture new biomolecules. These include the proteins that regulate cellular reactions, the phospholipids in cell membranes, and DNA—your genetic material. Food also contains at least 45 substances that the body needs but cannot manufacture.

The science of nutrition—the study of food and its effects on the body—tries to determine how food helps the body meet all of its various needs. Based on their research, nutritionists recommend balanced diets that include many different types of food. They also plan diets for people with particular needs, such as diabetics.

▼ **Figure 38–1** Holidays and other celebrations often center around food.

Section 38–1

1 FOCUS

Objectives

38.1.1 ***Explain*** how food provides energy.
38.1.2 ***Describe*** the nutrients your body needs.
38.1.3 ***State*** why water is such an important nutrient.
38.1.4 ***Explain*** how to use the food pyramid.

Guide for Reading

Vocabulary Preview

Point out that five of the Vocabulary terms are nutrients, or substances in food that the body needs, and that the other term is a measure of the amount of energy in food. Ask: **Which term refers to the amount of energy in food?** *(Calorie)*

Reading Strategy

Suggest that students create a table as they read to compare and contrast the nutrients that the body needs. Possible column headings might include: *Type of Nutrient, Foods in Which It Is Found,* and *Role It Plays in the Body.* Advise students to save their tables for study guides.

2 INSTRUCT

Food and Energy

Make Connections

Chemistry Remind students that ATP stands for adenosine triphosphate and that each molecule of ATP contains one ribose molecule and three phosphate molecules. Ask: **How is the energy in ATP released so that cells can use it?** *(Energy is released when chemical bonds are broken and ATP loses phosphate groups to become, first, ADP, or adenosine diphosphate, and then AMP, or adenosine monophosphate.)* L2

TIME SAVER — SECTION RESOURCES

Print:
- ***Teaching Resources,*** Lesson Plan 38–1, Adapted Section Summary 38–1, Adapted Worksheets 38–1, Section Summary 38–1, Worksheets 38–1, Section Review 38–1
- ***Reading and Study Workbook A,*** Section 38–1
- ***Adapted Reading and Study Workbook B,*** Section 38–1
- ***Issues and Decision Making,*** Issues and Decisions 5, 35, 39, 49

Technology:
- ***iText,*** Section 38–1
- ***Transparencies Plus,*** Section 38–1

38–1 (continued)

Nutrients

Demonstration

Ask: **What are the sources of water in our diets?** *(Students are likely to mention drinking water and other beverages, but they might not mention the water contained in food.)* Explain that some foods are mostly water, whereas other foods contain almost no water. Demonstrate how much water is contained in a variety of foods, such as a slice of apple, a slice of potato, a slice of bread, and a cracker. Measure the masses of the foods when they are fresh. Then, leave the foods out to dry on paper plates for a few days and measure their masses again. Have students compare the dry masses with the fresh masses and infer which food contained the most water and which contained the least. L1 L2

Build Science Skills

Designing Experiments Relate that populations with high-fiber diets have been found to have low rates of colon cancer. Add that people who eat high-fiber diets usually also have low-fat diets, which are known to lower colon cancer rates. Thus, it is not clear if fiber alone lowers colon cancer rates. Challenge students to design an experiment to help resolve this issue. *(Students should say they would compare colon cancer rates in people on high-fiber, low-fat diets with the rates in people on low-fiber, low-fat diets.)* L3

▲ **Figure 38–2** **Every cell in the body needs water because many of the body's processes take place in water.** On hot days or when you exercise, you need to drink more water to replace the water that is lost in sweat.

▲ **Figure 38–3** Breads, pastas, and cereals are foods rich in carbohydrates. Simple carbohydrates do not have to be digested or broken down. Complex carbohydrates must be broken down before they can be used by the body. **Inferring** *Which type of carbohydrate—simple or complex—provides the body with quick energy?*

Nutrients

Nutrients are substances in food that supply the energy and raw materials your body uses for growth, repair, and maintenance. **The nutrients that the body needs are water, carbohydrates, fats, proteins, vitamins, and minerals.**

Water The most important nutrient is water. **Every cell in the human body needs water because many of the body's processes, including chemical reactions, take place in water.** Water makes up the bulk of blood, lymph, and other bodily fluids. On hot days or when you take part in strenuous exercise, sweat glands remove water from your tissues and release it as sweat on the surface of your body. As the water in sweat evaporates, it cools the body. In this way, sweating helps maintain homeostasis. Water vapor is also lost from the body with every breath you exhale and in urine.

Humans need to drink at least 1 liter of water each day. If enough water is not taken in to replace what is lost, dehydration can result. This condition leads to problems with the circulatory, respiratory, and nervous systems. Drinking plenty of clean water, as the woman is doing in **Figure 38–2**, is one of the best things you can do to help keep your body healthy.

✓CHECKPOINT *How does sweat help to maintain homeostasis?*

Carbohydrates Simple and complex **carbohydrates** are the main source of energy for the body. **Figure 38–3** shows some of the foods that contain carbohydrates. The sugars found in fruits, honey, and sugar cane are simple carbohydrates, or monosaccharides and disaccharides. The starches found in grains, potatoes, and vegetables are complex carbohydrates, or polysaccharides. Starches are broken down by the digestive system into simple sugars. These molecules are absorbed into the bloodstream and carried to cells throughout the body. Sugars that are not immediately used to supply energy are converted into the complex carbohydrate glycogen, which is stored in the liver and in skeletal muscles.

Many foods contain the complex carbohydrate cellulose, often called fiber. Although the human digestive system cannot break down cellulose, you need fiber in your diet. The bulk supplied by fiber helps muscles to keep food and wastes moving through your digestive and excretory systems. Foods such as whole-grain breads, bran, and many fruits and vegetables are rich in fiber.

Fats Fats, or lipids, are an important part of a healthy diet. **Fats** are formed from fatty acids and glycerol. Your body needs certain fatty acids, called essential fatty acids, to produce cell membranes, myelin sheaths, and certain hormones. Fatty acids also help the body absorb fat-soluble vitamins. When a person eats more food than is needed, the body stores the extra energy as fat. Deposits of fat protect body organs and insulate the body.

ESL SUPPORT FOR ENGLISH LANGUAGE LEARNERS

Vocabulary: Science Glossary

Beginning Write the following Vocabulary terms on the board: *carbohydrate, fat, protein, vitamin,* and *mineral.* Underline the syllables as you model the pronunciation of the terms. Write a short definition of each term on the board. Provide appropriate pictures from newspapers or magazines to add a visual component to the definitions (for example, a picture of bread to be placed with the definition of *carbohydrate*). L1

Intermediate Have the students complete the science glossary activity described for beginning students. Then, with an English-proficient student, each student should write sentences using his or her choice of three of the Vocabulary terms. A volunteer from each pair should read the sentences out loud. Post these terms on a word wall with other Vocabulary terms from the chapter. L2

Figure 38–4  **Fats and proteins are two of the six nutrients the body needs.** The foods on the left contain essential fatty acids. The foods below are good sources of proteins.

Based on the structure of their fatty acid chains, fats are classified as saturated or unsaturated. When there are only single bonds between the carbon atoms in the fatty acids, each carbon atom has the maximum number of hydrogen atoms and the fat is said to be saturated. Most saturated fats are solids at room temperature—including butter and other animal fats.

Unsaturated fats have at least one double bond in a fatty acid chain. Unsaturated fats are usually liquids at room temperature. Because many vegetable oils contain more than one double bond, they are called polyunsaturated. **Figure 38–4** shows foods containing both saturated and unsaturated fats.

People often consume more fat than they actually need. The American Heart Association recommends a diet with a maximum of 30 percent of Calories from fat, of which only 10 percent should be from saturated fats. The health consequences of a diet high in fat are serious. They include an increased risk of high blood pressure, heart disease, obesity, and diabetes.

Proteins Proteins have a wide variety of roles in the body. **Proteins** supply raw materials for growth and repair of structures such as skin and muscle. Proteins have regulatory and transport functions. For example, the hormone insulin is a protein that regulates the level of sugar in the blood. Hemoglobin, a protein found in red blood cells, helps the blood transport oxygen.

Proteins are polymers of amino acids. The body is able to synthesize only 12 of the 20 amino acids used to make proteins. The other 8, which are listed in **Figure 38–5**, are called essential amino acids. Essential amino acids must be obtained from the foods that you eat. Meat, fish, eggs, and milk generally contain all 8 essential amino acids. Foods derived from plants, such as grains and beans, do not. People who don't eat animal products must eat a combination of plant foods, such as beans and rice, to obtain all of the essential amino acids.

▼ **Figure 38–5** When plant foods are eaten in the right combination, they provide all of the essential amino acids. **Interpreting Graphics** *Which amino acids are found in both grains and legumes?*

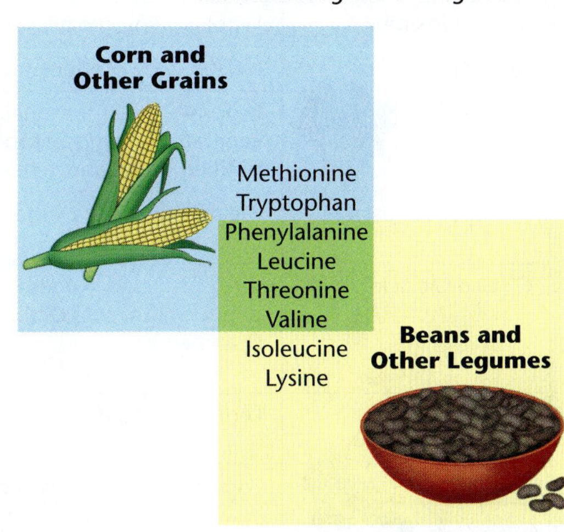

Make Connections

Mathematics Point out that no more than 30 percent of the Calories in the diet should come from fat. Ask: **If you eat 2000 Calories a day, what is the maximum number of Calories that should come from fat?** *(600 Calories)* Urge students to read nutrition labels to find the total fat content of foods they might eat in a typical day. L2

Build Science Skills

Applying Concepts Explain the concept of complementary proteins, that is, proteins that individually lack one or more essential amino acids but together contain all eight. Point out that the amino acids in grains, such as corn, rice, and wheat, complement the amino acids in legumes, such as beans, peas, and peanuts. Challenge students to apply the concept of complementary proteins by planning a meatless meal that contains all eight essential amino acids. *(Possible meals might include beans with rice or peanut butter with bread.)* L2 L3

Use Visuals

Figure 38–5 Check that students understand how to interpret the figure. Point out that it is actually a Venn diagram. Ask: **How can you find out which amino acids are found in particular foods?** *(Students might think, incorrectly, that the information is included on nutrition facts labels.)* Tell them that the amino acid content of foods can be found on several Internet Web sites, including the U.S. Food and Drug Administration Web site. L1 L2

FACTS AND FIGURES

How sweet it is

Because milk does not taste sweet, some people are surprised to learn that it contains sugar. In fact, 8 oz of milk contains 11 g of sugar, or more than half the sugar in the same amount of orange juice. Most of the sugar in milk is in the form of lactose, which is broken down into simpler sugars in the digestive tract by the enzyme lactase. Most human infants produce lactase and can digest lactose. Many adult humans, on the other hand, no longer produce lactase. Therefore, they cannot digest lactose. When some of these people drink milk, the lactose ferments in their intestines and causes gas, cramps, and diarrhea. Fortunately, there are special milk products available that lactose-intolerant people can digest because the products contain lactase-producing bacteria.

Answers to . . .

CHECKPOINT *When sweat evaporates from the body surface, it carries heat away, which cools the body.*

Figure 38–3 *Simple carbohydrates provide the body with quick energy.*

Figure 38–5 *Phenylalanine, leucine, threonine, and valine*

38–1 (continued)

Build Science Skills

Inferring Review the basic roles in the body that are played by carbohydrates, fats, and proteins. Ask: **What do you think would happen if you did not eat enough carbohydrates?** *(You might feel tired because you would not have enough immediate energy, and you would lose weight because your body would need to use stored reserves of energy. Your digestive system might not function properly due to lack of fiber.)* **What do you think would happen if you did not eat enough fat?** *(Your supply of fat-soluble vitamins might be depleted, which would affect functions such as blood clotting, vision, or bone growth. Because fats are needed for myelin sheaths, the function of the nervous system could be impaired.)* **What do you think would happen if you did not eat enough proteins?** *(Almost every body function could be affected because enzymes [proteins] make biochemical reactions efficient. You might feel tired because the body could not produce the hemoglobin needed to carry the oxygen that cells use for cellular respiration.)* L2

Use Visuals

Figure 38–6 Point out the column for sources of vitamins and ask: **Which types of food seem to be rich in many different vitamins?** *(Vegetables, whole grains, and dairy products)* Next, call students' attention to the column for function of vitamins and ask: **Which body systems need vitamins to function properly?** *(Virtually all body systems)* Have students compare the functions of the B vitamins in particular. Then, ask: **What general function do all the B vitamins have in common?** *(Metabolism)* Remind students that metabolism refers to all the chemical reactions that build up or break down substances in the body. L1 L2

Vitamins If you think of carbohydrates, fats, and proteins as the fuel of an automobile, then vitamins are the ignition. **Vitamins** are organic molecules that help regulate body processes, often working with enzymes. As you can see in **Figure 38–6,** most vitamins must be obtained from food. However, the bacteria that live in the digestive tract are able to synthesize vitamin K. The skin is able to synthesize vitamin D when exposed to sunlight. A diet lacking certain vitamins can have serious, even fatal, consequences.

There are two types of vitamins: fat-soluble and water-soluble. The fat-soluble vitamins A, D, E, and K can be stored in the fatty tissues of the body. The body can build up small stores of these vitamins for future use.

▼ **Figure 38–6** This table lists the food sources and functions of 14 essential vitamins. The fat-soluble vitamins are listed in the blue rows, and the water-soluble vitamins in the white rows. **Using Tables and Graphs** *What is the function of vitamin K?*

Vitamins

Vitamin	Sources	Function
A (retinol)	Yellow, orange, and dark green vegetables; dairy products	Important for growth of skin cells; important for night vision
D (calciferol)	Fish oils, eggs; made by skin when exposed to sunlight; added to dairy products	Promotes bone growth; increases calcium and phosphorus absorption
E (tocopherol)	Green leafy vegetables, seeds, vegetable oils	Antioxidant; prevents cellular damage
K	Green leafy vegetables; made by bacteria that live in human intestine	Needed for normal blood clotting
B_1 (thiamine)	Whole grains, pork, legumes, milk	Normal metabolism of carbohydrates
B_2 (riboflavin)	Dairy products, meats, vegetables, whole-grain cereal	Normal growth; part of electron transport chain; energy metabolism
Niacin	Liver, milk, whole grains, nuts, meats, legumes	Important in energy metabolism
B_6 (pyridoxine)	Whole grains, meats, vegetables	Important for amino acid metabolism
Pantothenic acid	Meats, dairy products, whole grains	Needed for energy metabolism
Folic acid	Legumes, nuts, green leafy vegetables, oranges, broccoli, peas, fortified bread and cereal	Coenzyme involved in nucleic acid metabolism; prevents neural-tube defects in developing fetuses
B_{12} (cyanocobalamin)	Meats, eggs, dairy products, enriched cereals	Coenzyme in nucleic acid metabolism; maturation of red blood cells
C (ascorbic acid)	Citrus fruits, tomatoes, red or green peppers, broccoli, cabbage, strawberries	Maintenance of cartilage and bone; antioxidant; improves iron absorption; important for healthy gums, tissue repair, and wound healing
Biotin	Legumes, vegetables, meat	Coenzyme in synthesis of fat; glycogen formation; amino acid metabolism
Choline	Egg yolk, liver, grains, legumes	Required for phospholipids and neurotransmitters

HISTORY OF SCIENCE

How vitamins were named

In the 1800s, sailors in the Japanese navy developed a nervous disorder named beriberi when they were fed a mostly white-rice diet. The sailors became extremely weak and suffered uncontrollable muscle spasms. Toward the end of the 1800s, a Dutch doctor noticed that prisoners who were fed mostly white rice also developed beriberi, whereas prisoners who were fed ordinary brown rice did not. The doctor inferred that some factor in the hull of the rice, which was removed when brown rice was converted to white, was needed by the body to prevent beriberi. A short time later, a Polish chemist isolated the factor and named it "vital amine," because it was so important to life and because he thought its chemical structure was that of an amine compound. He was incorrect with regard to the latter, but the name stuck and gave birth to the term *vitamin.*

Important Minerals

Mineral	Sources	Function
Calcium 	Dairy products, salmon, sardines, kale, tofu, collard greens, legumes	Bone and tooth formation; blood clotting; nerve and muscle function
Phosphorus	Dairy products, meats, poultry, grains	Bone and tooth formation; acid-base balance
Potassium 	Meats, dairy products, many fruits and vegetables, grains	Acid-base balance; body water balance; nerve function; muscle function
Chlorine	Table salt, processed foods	Acid-base balance; formation of gastric juice
Sodium 	Table salt, processed foods	Acid-base balance; body water balance; nerve function; muscle function
Magnesium	Whole grains, green leafy vegetables	Activation of enzymes in protein synthesis
Iron 	Meats, eggs, legumes, whole grains, green leafy vegetables, dried fruit	Component of hemoglobin and of electron carriers used in energy metabolism
Fluorine	Fluoridated drinking water, tea, seafood	Maintenance of tooth structure; maintenance of bone structure
Iodine	Seafood, dairy products, iodized salt	Component of thyroid hormones
Zinc 	Meats, seafood, grains	Component of certain digestive enzymes

▲ **Figure 38–7** Minerals are sometimes called trace elements because they are needed by the body in such small amounts. **Inferring** *Why do you think some cities and towns add fluoride to their water supplies?*

The water-soluble vitamins, which include vitamin C and the B vitamins, dissolve in water and cannot be stored in the body. Therefore, they should be included in the foods you eat each day. Eating a diet containing a variety of foods will supply the daily vitamin needs of nearly everyone.

Food stores and pharmacies sell vitamin supplements. Taking extra-large doses of vitamin supplements does not benefit the body; and, in some cases, it may cause real harm. Excessive amounts of vitamins A, D, E, and K can be toxic.

CHECKPOINT *Why is it important not to take more than the recommended amount of certain vitamins?*

Minerals Inorganic nutrients that the body needs, usually in small amounts, are called **minerals.** Some examples of minerals are calcium, iron, and magnesium. Calcium is a major component of bones and teeth; and iron is needed to make hemoglobin, the oxygen-carrying protein in red blood cells. Calcium, sodium, and potassium are required for normal functioning of nerves. **Figure 38–7** lists some of the minerals needed by the body.

Although the body does not metabolize the minerals it takes in, it does lose many of them in sweat, urine, and other waste products. How are these important chemicals replaced? Many of these elements are found in the living tissues of plants and other animals. By eating a variety of foods, you can meet your daily requirement of minerals.

For: Links on nutrition
Visit: www.SciLinks.org
Web Code: cbn-0381

Address Misconceptions

Ask students: **Can taking a daily vitamin pill make up for a lack of vegetables, whole grains, dairy products, or other vitamin-rich foods in the diet?** *(Some students might say "Yes.")* Explain that foods such as these are rich not only in vitamins but in other nutrients as well. Ask: **What other nutrients do whole grains, vegetables, and dairy products provide?** *(Vegetables and whole grains provide carbohydrates, vitamins, and minerals. Dairy products provide proteins, fats, and minerals.)* L2

Use Visuals

Figure 38–7 Guide students in analyzing the information presented in the table by asking: **Which minerals are needed for healthy bones and teeth?** *(Calcium, phosphorus, and fluorine)* **Which mineral is needed for normal blood clotting?** *(Calcium)* **Which minerals are found in meats?** *(Phosphorus, potassium, iron, and zinc)* **Which minerals are found in grains?** *(Phosphorus, potassium, magnesium, iron, and zinc)* **What one type of food could you eat to increase the amount of fluorine, iodine, and zinc in your diet?** *(Seafood)* L1 L2

Download a worksheet on nutrition for students to complete, and find additional teacher support from NSTA SciLinks.

BIOLOGY UPDATE

Please pass the selenium

Scientists continue to discover new substances in food that play important roles in the body. For example, in 1996 researchers at the Arizona Cancer Center found that patients who received 200 µg per day of the trace mineral selenium had a 50 to 60 percent lower risk of dying from lung, prostate, or colorectal cancer. Scientists still do not understand why selenium seems to protect against cancer, and not all scientists are convinced of its cancer-fighting abilities. Nonetheless, the results of the Arizona study have sparked further research to test selenium for its effect on specific cancers. Selenium is found in foods such as grain, meat, and fish, and most people in the United States eat enough of these foods to receive the recommended dietary allowance of 55 to 70 µg per day. However, this may not be enough selenium for an anticancer effect.

Answers to . . .

CHECKPOINT *They can be stored in the fatty tissues of the body and may reach toxic levels.*

Figure 38–6 *Vitamin K is needed for normal blood clotting.*

Figure 38–7 *To prevent cavities in children's teeth*

38–1 (continued)

Nutrition and a Balanced Diet

Use Visuals

Figure 38–8 Arrange to give students access to the Internet so that they can develop a personal eating plan based on MyPyramid. Challenge students to plan one day of meals and snacks that altogether contain the correct number of servings from each food group. Call on a few students to share their meal plans with the class. Note that individual eating plans will vary based on the student's age, gender, and activity level. L2

Make Connections

Environmental Science Point out that if you follow the food pyramid, most of the food you eat will come from the grains, vegetables, and fruits groups. Ask: **Where are grains and plants always found in a food chain, and what role do they fill?** *(They are always found on the bottom, and they fill the role of producer.)* Explain that only 10 percent of the energy at one level of a food chain is passed on to the next level. Conclude by saying that people can get far more energy from plants by eating plants directly than by eating animals that eat plants. L2

For: Food Pyramid activity
Visit: PHSchool.com
Web Code: cbe-0381
Students learn about the food groups and how they can be combined to form a healthy diet.

For: Food Pyramid activity
Visit: PHSchool.com
Web Code: cbp-0381

▼ **Figure 38–8** MyPyramid illustrates the main characteristics of a balanced diet. **Interpreting Graphics** *Why do you think nutritionists recommend that you limit your intake of fats, oils, and sweets?*

Nutrition and a Balanced Diet

It's no easy task to figure out the best balance of nutrients for the human diet, but nutritionists have tried to do exactly that. The result is MyPyramid shown in **Figure 38–8.**

The new food pyramid—MyPyramid—classifies foods into six categories: grains; vegetables; fruits; milk; meat and beans; and fats, sugars, and salts. Each color in the pyramid represents a different food category. The narrow yellow bar represents fats, sugars, and salt; those should be used sparingly. The large orange bar represents the grains, especially whole grains, which should make up the largest part of your diet. The figure climbing up the side of the pyramid represents exercise. You should try and get at least 30 minutes of exercise each day. A personalized eating plan, based on your age, gender, and activity level can be found at **www.mypyramid.gov**.

Food labels can also be used to choose healthful foods. A food label provides some general information about nutrition, listing the Daily Values and the Calories per gram for protein, carbohydrates, and fats. The daily value shows you how the particular food fits into the overall daily diet. Daily values are based on a 2000-Calorie diet, and nutrient needs are affected by age, gender, and lifestyle. Rapidly growing adolescents and other groups of people need more nutrients than the daily values indicate.

When choosing foods, you should use the information on food labels to compare similar foods on the basis of their proportion of nutrients to Calories. When you choose a food, it should be high in nutrition and low in Calories.

FACTS AND FIGURES

Eating bugs

Although eating bugs sounds disgusting to most Americans, in many other cultures bugs are considered to be an excellent food source. For example, in Mexico worms are served on tortillas, and in Colombia ground-up ants are spread on bread. Hundreds of other examples could be given. Why are bugs so appealing? Most insects are not only cheap sources of complete protein, but they are far cleaner and much lower in fat than other sources. Insects can also be very tasty. Deep-fried larvae and grubs, for example, are said to be delicious. Although most Americans do not deliberately eat bugs, they still get a lot of bugs in their diet—in fact, a whopping pound or two per person a year. Microscopic pieces of insects are found in many processed foods, including jam, peanut butter, tomato sauce, and frozen vegetables. In some foods, the addition of insects can actually increase the nutritional content.

Analyzing Data

Evaluating Food Labels

Federal regulations require that labels on packaged foods display the nutrients each food contains and the percentage of daily value each nutrient represents for a person, as well as serving size, number of servings per container, and Calories per serving. Carefully examine the nutritional information on the cereal label shown. Based on the information on the label, answer the questions that follow.

1. **Calculating** If you ate 2 cups of this product, how many grams of fat would you eat? How many grams of protein?
2. **Interpreting Graphics** How many Calories are in a gram of fat? Of protein? Of carbohydrate?
3. **Interpreting Graphics** On a 2000-Calorie diet, what is the Daily Value for total fat? For sodium? For fiber?
4. **Evaluating** Advertising claims for this product say that it is a good source of iron. Is this promotional claim true?
5. **Going Further** People with hypertension, or high blood pressure, often are advised to restrict their intake of sodium. Visit a local food store and look at the labels on 5 types of packaged foods. From this information, recommend which of the foods would be healthful for people who have hypertension.

Nutrition Facts

Serving Size 1 cup (30g)
Servings Per Container About 10

Amount Per Serving	
Calories 110	Calories from Fat 15
	% Daily Value*
Total Fat 2g	3%
Saturated Fat 0g	0%
Cholesterol 0mg	0%
Sodium 280mg	12%
Total Carbohydrate 22g	7%
Dietary Fiber 3g	12%
Sugars 1g	
Protein 3g	

Vitamin A 10%	• Vitamin C 20%
Calcium 4%	• Iron 45%

* Percent Daily Values are based on a 2,000 Calorie diet. Your daily values may be higher or lower depending on your caloric needs:

	Calories	2,000	2,500
Total Fat	Less than	65g	80g
Sat. Fat	Less than	20g	25g
Cholesterol	Less than	300mg	300mg
Sodium	Less than	2,400mg	2,400mg
Total Carbohydrate		300g	375g
Fiber		25g	30g

Calories per gram:
Fat 9 • Carbohydrate 4 • Protein 4

Ingredients: Whole grain oats, sugar, salt, milled corn, oat fiber, dried whey, hon... almonds, d...

38–1 Section Assessment

1. **Key Concept** List the six nutrients needed by the body.
2. **Key Concept** What is the importance of water in the body?
3. Why is fiber an important part of your diet?
4. How are vitamins and minerals similar? How are they different?
5. **Critical Thinking Using Tables and Graphs** Which vitamins and minerals promote healthy bones? (*Hint*: See **Figure 38–6** and **Figure 38–7**.)

Writing in Science

Designing a Brochure
Design and create a brochure that explains how the body uses the six nutrients necessary for normal function. Use images from magazines or from the Internet to illustrate your brochure.

38–1 Section Assessment

1. Water, carbohydrates, fats, proteins, vitamins, and minerals
2. Some body tissues, such as blood, are mostly water, and water is needed for many vital body processes, including chemical reactions, elimination of wastes, and keeping the body cool through evaporation.
3. Fiber adds bulk to the material moving through the digestive system, helping it to process food more effectively.
4. Both vitamins and minerals are nutrients that are needed in small amounts for good health, but vitamins are organic molecules, whereas minerals are inorganic.
5. Vitamins C and D, calcium, phosphorus, and fluorine

Analyzing Data

Make sure students understand that the daily values on the nutrition label depend on the total Calories in the diet. Active teens may need 2500 or more Calories a day instead of the 2000 Calories that are used for calculating the percent daily values. L2

Answers

1. 4 g of fat and 6 g of protein
2. A gram of fat has 9 Calories. Protein and carbohydrate each have 4 Calories per gram.
3. Total fat: less than 65 g; sodium: less than 2400 mg; fiber: 25 g
4. Yes; it supplies 45% of the daily value of iron.
5. Students should recommend foods that are low in sodium.

3 ASSESS

Evaluate Understanding

Call on students to name the six types of nutrients and to describe their roles in the body.

Reteach

Have students review the food pyramid. Then, have them name the nutrients that foods in each group are rich in. *(For example, the vegetable food group is rich in carbohydrates, vitamins, and minerals.)*

Writing in Science

Brochures should demonstrate an understanding of the most important functions of each of the six types of nutrients.

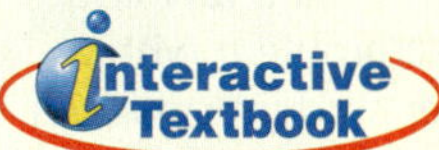

If your class subscribes to the iText, use it to review the Key Concepts in Section 38–1.

Section 38–2

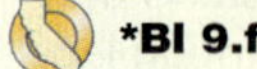 *BI 9.f

1 FOCUS

Objectives

38.2.1 ***Identify*** the organs of the digestive system.

38.2.2 ***Describe*** the function of the digestive system.

Guide for Reading

Vocabulary Preview

If students have difficulty pronouncing any of the Vocabulary words, it may interfere with their comprehension. Read each of the words to the class and have students repeat them after you. Point out that *villus* is singular and the plural is *villi*.

Reading Strategy

Before they read, have students draw a line down the center of a piece of paper. On the left side they should write down the organs of the digestive system. Then, as they read the section, they should record important details about each organ on the right side of the paper, including the organ's location, structure, and function.

2 INSTRUCT

The Mouth

Demonstration

Help students understand the difference between the mechanical and chemical digestion that take place in the mouth by having them observe mechanical and chemical processes. Have one student break a raw egg into a bowl and scramble it with a fork. Have another student pour the scrambled raw egg into a pan of boiling water. Have students watch as the egg solidifies in the boiling water. Ask: **Which process was mechanical, and which was chemical?** *(Breaking and scrambling the raw egg was mechanical. Cooking the raw egg was chemical.)* L1 L2

38–2 The Process of Digestion

***BI 9.f.** Students know the individual functions and sites of secretions of digestive enzymes (amylases, proteases, nucleases, lipases), stomach acid, and bile salts.

Guide for Reading

Key Concepts
- What are the organs of the digestive system?
- What is the function of the digestive system?

Vocabulary
amylase
esophagus
peristalsis
stomach
chyme
small intestine
pancreas
liver
villus
large intestine

Reading Strategy: Asking Questions Before you read, rewrite the seven blue heads in the section as *how, why,* or *what* questions. As you read, write brief answers to your questions.

Food presents every chordate with at least two challenges. The first is how to obtain it. Once a chordate has caught, or gathered its food, it faces a new challenge—how to break that food down into small molecules that can be passed to the cells that need them. In humans and many other chordates, this is the job of the digestive system. As food passes through the digestive system, it gets disassembled, distributing its nutrient value to the body along the way.

The human digestive system, like those of other chordates, is built around an alimentary canal—a one-way tube that passes through the body. **The digestive system includes the mouth, pharynx, esophagus, stomach, small intestine, and large intestine. Several major accessory structures, including the salivary glands, the pancreas, and the liver, add secretions to the digestive system.**

The Mouth

As you take a forkful of food into your mouth, the work of the digestive system begins. The teeth, shown in **Figure 38–9,** tear and crush the food into a fine paste until it is ready to be swallowed. Chewing begins the process of mechanical digestion. Mechanical digestion is the physical breakdown of large pieces of food into smaller pieces. But there is a great deal more to it than that. As you chew your food, digestive enzymes begin the breakdown of carbohydrates into smaller molecules. This process is called chemical digestion. During chemical digestion, large food molecules are broken down into smaller food molecules. **The function of the digestive system is to help convert foods into simpler molecules that can be absorbed and used by the cells of the body.** The organs of the digestive system are shown in **Figure 38–10.**

Teeth The teeth are anchored in the bones of the jaw. The surfaces of the teeth are protected by a coating of mineralized enamel. Teeth do much of the mechanical work of digestion by cutting, tearing, and crushing food into small fragments.

 *What do the teeth do?*

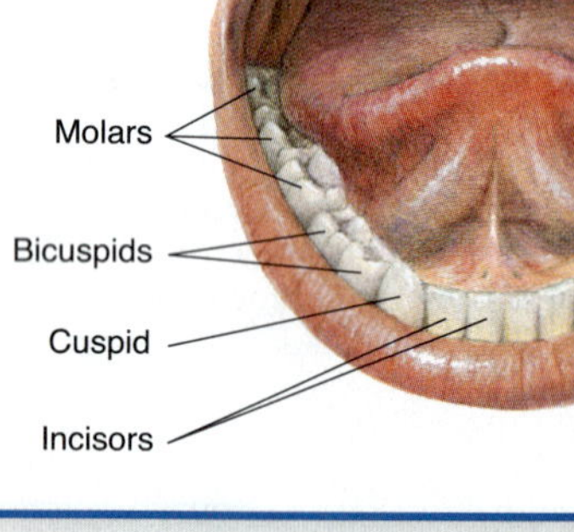

Figure 38–9 Human teeth include sharp incisors; cuspids and bicuspids, which grasp and tear food; and large, flat molars. **Inferring** *How do human teeth reflect an omnivorous diet?*

SECTION RESOURCES

Print:
- ***Laboratory Manual B,*** Chapter 38 Lab
- ***Teaching Resources,*** Lesson Plan 38–2, Adapted Section Summary 38–2, Adapted Worksheets 38–2, Section Summary 38–2, Worksheets 38–2, Section Review 38–2, Enrichment
- ***Reading and Study Workbook A,*** Section 38–2
- ***Adapted Reading and Study Workbook B,*** Section 38–2
- ***Lab Worksheets,*** Chapter 38 Design an Experiment

Technology:
- ***iText,*** Section 38–2
- ***Animated Biological Concepts DVD,*** 40 Human Digestion
- ***Transparencies Plus,*** Section 38–2

FIGURE 38–10 THE DIGESTIVE SYSTEM

The digestive system includes the mouth, pharynx, esophagus, stomach, small intestine, and large intestine. Because the pancreas and most of the gallbladder are behind other organs, their locations are indicated by dotted lines.

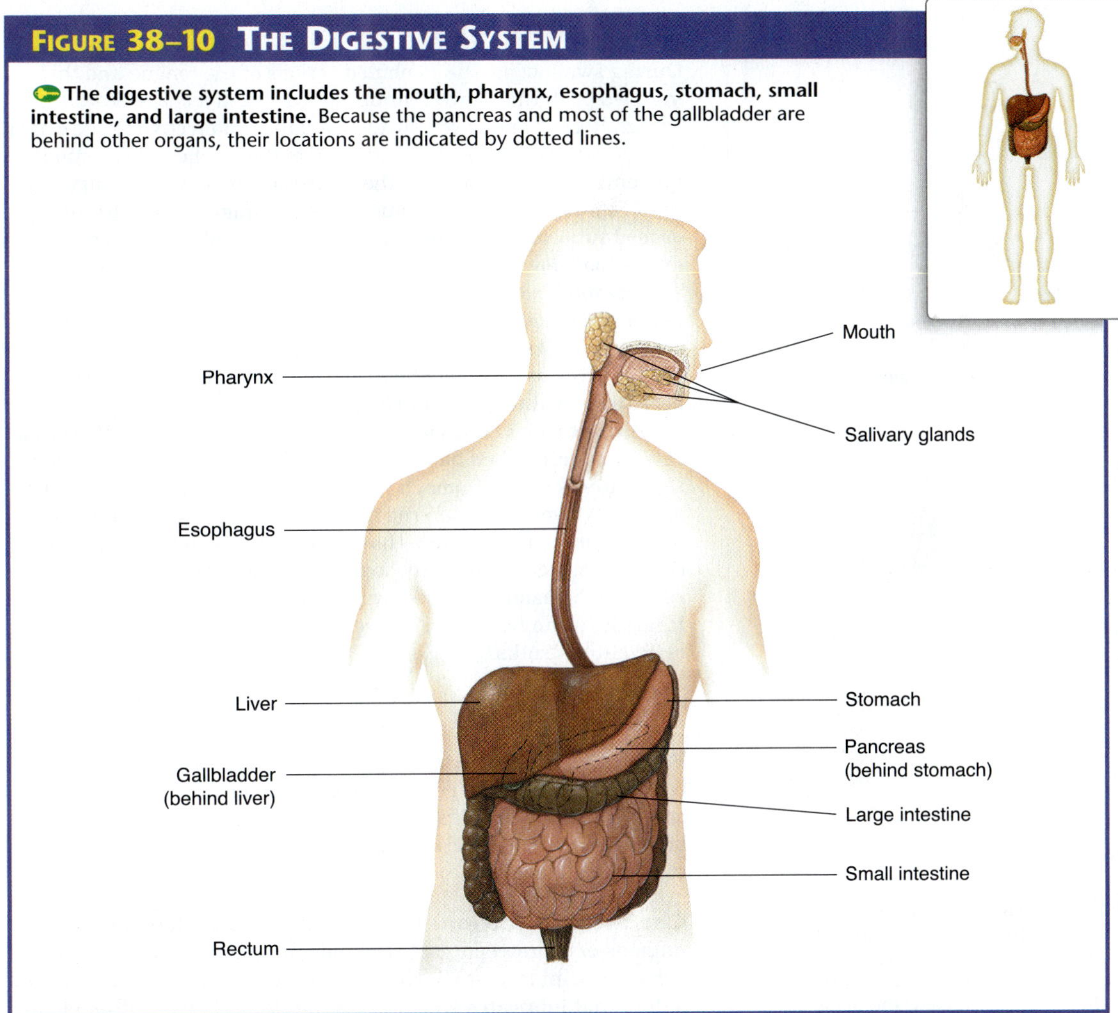

Saliva As the teeth cut and grind the food, the salivary glands secrete saliva, which helps to moisten the food and make it easier to chew. The release of saliva is under the control of the nervous system and can be triggered by the scent of food—especially when you are hungry!

Saliva not only helps ease the passage of food through the digestive system but also begins the process of chemical digestion. Saliva contains an enzyme called **amylase** that breaks the chemical bonds in starches and releases sugars. If you chew on a starchy food like a cracker long enough, it will begin to taste sweet. This sweet taste is a sign that sugar has been released from starch by the action of amylase. Saliva also contains lysozyme, an enzyme that fights infection by digesting the cell walls of many bacteria that may enter the mouth with food.

For: Links on digestion
Visit: www.SciLinks.org
Web Code: cbn-0382

Build Science Skills

Using Models Point out that different types of teeth have different mechanical functions: incisors cut, canines tear, and molars crush. Ask: **Can you think of tools that perform similar mechanical functions?** *(Scissors cut like incisors, tweezers tear like canines, and mallets crush like molars.)* L2

Demonstration

Demonstrate how the amylase in saliva chemically breaks down food. Give each student a soda cracker. Have students chew the cracker for five seconds and record how it tastes. Have them continue chewing the cracker for five minutes and again record how it tastes. Ask: **How and why did the taste of the cracker change?** *(The cracker became sweeter as amylase broke down some of the starches into sugars.)* L1 L2

Use Visuals

Figure 38–10 Name each of the digestive organs. As you name each organ, have students locate it in the figure. Tell students that the liver and pancreas secrete substances that help break down food but that food does not actually pass through them. L1 L2

Download a worksheet on digestion for students to complete, and find additional teacher support from NSTA SciLinks.

UNIVERSAL ACCESS

Inclusion/Special Needs
Help students master the main points about the digestive process by creating a flowchart showing the organs that food passes through as it is digested, starting with the mouth and ending with the large intestine. Students should read the corresponding subsection in the text to determine what happens to food as it passes through each organ and then illustrate each step in the flowchart with a sketch. L1

English Language Learners
Review the pronunciation and meaning of the Vocabulary terms with nonnative speakers and other students who tend to have difficulty with technical terminology. Suggest that each student translate the terms into his or her own language and write them on index cards, with the term in English on one side and in his or her own language on the other side. L1 L2

Answers to . . .

CHECKPOINT *The teeth cut, tear, and crush food into smaller fragments.*

Figure 38–9 *The different types and functions of human teeth make them well suited for eating the variety of foods in an omnivorous diet.*

38–2 (continued)

The Esophagus

Demonstration

Demonstrate with a simple model how peristalsis pushes food through the esophagus. Place a marble inside one end of a 25- to 30-cm length of flexible plastic or rubber tubing. With a squeezing motion of your hands, move the marble down and out the other end of the tube. Ask: **If this is a model of the esophagus, what does the tube represent and what does the marble represent?** *(The tube represents the esophagus, and the marble represents the bolus of food that is being swallowed.)* **How is peristalsis modeled?** *(By the squeezing of your hand along the tube from one end to the other)* L1 L2

The Stomach

Build Science Skills

Inferring Ask students: **How do you know when you are hungry?** *(Students probably will say that their stomach growls or hurts.)* Explain that these feelings of hunger are controlled by a center in the hypothalamus at the base of the brain, called the hunger center. The hunger center senses when blood levels of nutrients are low, and sends out nerve impulses that lead to stomach contractions. Ask: **What do you think causes the feelings of hunger to stop once you have eaten?** *(Students may infer that increasing levels of nutrients in the blood stimulate the hunger center to send out nerve impulses that stop the stomach contractions.)* You may wish to tell students, however, that satiety is tied to fat intake. L2

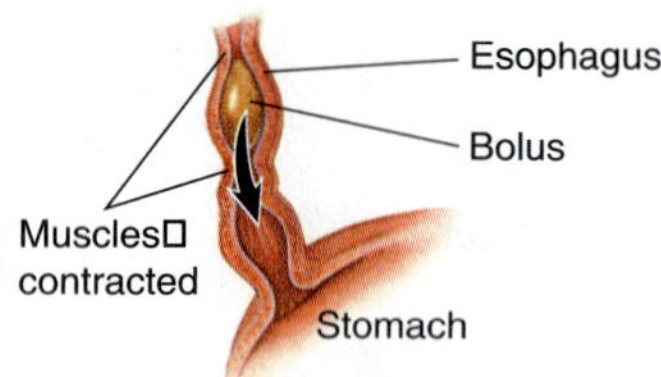

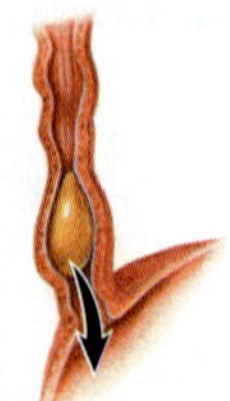

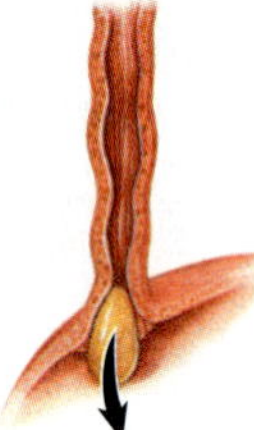

▲ **Figure 38–11** Muscles in the walls of the esophagus contract in waves. Each wave pushes the chewed clump of food, or bolus, in front of it. Eventually, the bolus is pushed into the stomach. **Applying Concepts** *What kind of muscle surrounds the esophagus?*

The Esophagus

During swallowing, the combined actions of the tongue and throat muscles push the chewed clump of food, called a bolus, down the throat. Recall that as you swallow, a flap of connective tissue called the epiglottis closes over the opening to the trachea. This action prevents food from blocking the air passageways to the lungs.

From the throat, the bolus passes through the **esophagus,** or food tube, into the stomach. You might think that gravity draws food down through the esophagus, but this is not correct. The reason food travels through the esophagus into the stomach is that it is moved along by contractions of smooth muscle. These contractions, known as **peristalsis** (pehr-uh-STAL-sis), squeeze the food through the esophagus into the stomach. The process of peristalsis is illustrated in **Figure 38–11.**

A thick ring of muscle, called the cardiac sphincter, closes the esophagus after food has passed into the stomach and prevents the contents of the stomach from moving back up into the esophagus. Have you ever suffered from "heartburn"? Heartburn is a painful, burning sensation that feels as if it is coming from the center of the chest (by your heart), just above the stomach. The sensation is usually caused by a backflow of stomach acid. Heartburn can be caused by overeating or drinking an excess of caffeinated drinks.

The Stomach

Food from the esophagus empties into a large muscular sac called the **stomach.** The stomach continues the mechanical and chemical digestion of food. Alternating contractions of the stomach's three smooth muscle layers thoroughly churn and mix the food you swallow.

Chemical Digestion The lining of the stomach contains millions of microscopic gastric glands that release a number of substances into the stomach. Some of these glands produce mucus, a fluid that lubricates and protects the stomach wall. Other glands produce hydrochloric acid, which makes the contents of the stomach very acidic. The acid activates pepsin, an enzyme that begins the digestion of protein and is secreted by a third set of stomach glands. Pepsin works best under the acidic conditions present in the stomach. The combination of pepsin and hydrochloric acid begins the complex process of protein digestion. Pepsin breaks proteins into smaller polypeptide fragments. While pepsin requires the acidic environment of the stomach in order to function, other enzymes such as amalyse are denatured by the stomach acid. As a result, chemical digestion of carbohydrates stops when food enters the stomach and does not resume until the food passes into the small intestine. Not all enzymes that aid in digestion are released by the stomach. Other enzymes that help in digestion are shown in **Figure 38–12.**

✓CHECKPOINT *What is the role of pepsin?*

FACTS AND FIGURES

Not just heartburn

Most people have experienced heartburn, the burning sensation in the chest that is caused by stomach acids entering the esophagus. In about 25 to 35 percent of people, heartburn becomes chronic and signals a more serious disorder, called gastroesophageal reflux disease, or GERD. In addition to heartburn, symptoms of GERD may include regurgitation and difficulty swallowing. There is no single cause of GERD, but factors such as defects in the lower esophageal sphincter, slower-than-normal emptying of the stomach, and decreased secretion of bicarbonate by the esophagus may all play a role. Complications of GERD include esophagitis, or inflammation of the esophagus, and Barrett's esophagus, a precancerous condition in which abnormal cells replace normal cells in the esophagus. Treatment of GERD includes lifestyle changes, medications to control stomach acids, and, in severe cases, surgery.

Mechanical Digestion As digestion proceeds, stomach muscles contract to churn and mix stomach fluids and food, gradually producing a mixture known as **chyme** (KYM). After an hour or two, the pyloric valve, which is located between the stomach and small intestine, opens and chyme begins to flow into the small intestine.

The Small Intestine

As chyme is pushed through the pyloric valve, it enters the duodenum (doo-oh-DEE-num). The duodenum is the first of three parts of the **small intestine,** and it is where almost all of the digestive enzymes enter the intestine. Most of the chemical digestion and absorption of the food you eat occurs in the small intestine. As chyme enters the duodenum from the stomach, it mixes with enzymes and digestive fluids from the pancreas, the liver, and even the lining of the duodenum itself. The pancreas and liver are shown in **Figure 38–13.**

Effects of Digestive Enzymes

Active Site	Enzyme	Effect on Food
Mouth	Salivary amylase	Breaks down starches into disaccharides
Stomach	Pepsin	Breaks down proteins into large peptides
Small intestine (from pancreas)	Amylase	Continues the breakdown of starch
	Trypsin	Continues the breakdown of protein
	Lipase	Breaks down fat
Small intestine	Maltase, sucrase, lactase	Breaks down remaining disaccharides into monosaccharides
	Peptidase	Breaks down dipeptides into amino acids

▲ **Figure 38–12** Di esti e enzymes break down foods and make n trients a ailable to the body. **Using Tables and Graphs** ***Where in the body does the digestion of carbohydrates begin?***

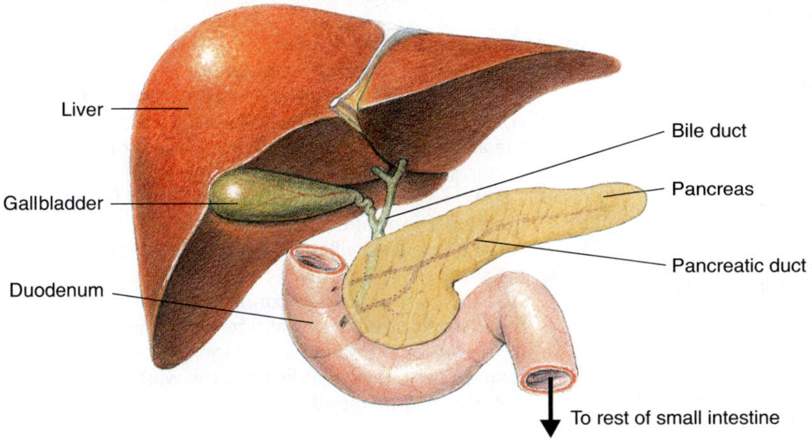

Accessory Structures of Digestion Just behind the stomach is the **pancreas.** The pancreas is a gland that serves three important functions. One function is to produce hormones that regulate blood sugar levels. Within the digestive system, the pancreas plays two key roles. It produces enzymes that break down carbohydrates, proteins, lipids, and nucleic acids. The pancreas also produces sodium bicarbonate, a base that neutralizes stomach acid so that these enzymes can be effective. Why is this neutralization necessary? Recall that enzymes are proteins. Stomach acid can change the shapes of protein molecules. If the shape of an enzyme's active site does not match the shape of its substrate, the enzyme will not be effective.

Liver
Gallbladder
Duodenum
Bile duct
Pancreas
Pancreatic duct
To rest of small intestine

◀ **Figure 38–13** **Accessory structures, including the liver and pancreas, add secretions to the digestive system.** The pancreas secretes enzymes that help break down carbohydrates, proteins, and fats.

Use Visuals

Figure 38–12 Guide students in interpreting the information in the table. Remind them that food passes through each of the organs listed in the table and that the pancreas is a gland that secretes digestive enzymes into the small intestine. Ask: **Which enzymes break down proteins?** *(Pepsin, trypsin, and peptidase)* **Where are these enzymes found?** *(Pepsin is found in the stomach; trypsin and peptidase are found in the small intestine.)* **Where does the breakdown of starch into simpler carbohydrates take place?** *(The mouth and small intestine)* **Which nutrients do enzymes secreted by the pancreas help digest?** *(Starch, protein, and fat)* L1

The Small Intestine

Use Visuals

Figure 38–13 Point out in Figure 38–13 where the liver and pancreas are located. Explain that the role of the gallbladder is to store bile produced in the liver. Ask: **Where does the bile go after it leaves the gallbladder?** *(To the small intestine)*

Make Connections

Chemistry Pour 100 mL of 0.5 percent hydrochloric acid into a beaker and measure its acidity with pH paper. Then, stir 2 mL of sodium bicarbonate solution into the acid and test the pH again. Continue adding small amounts of sodium bicarbonate as needed until the solution has a neutral pH of 7. Ask: **Where in the digestive system is sodium bicarbonate produced?** *(In the pancreas and secreted into the small intestine)* **What is the result of its production?** *(It neutralizes hydrochloric acid so that it will not break down pancreatic digestive enzymes.)* L2

BIO INSIGHTS **HISTORY OF SCIENCE**

Watching as the stomach churns

In 1822, a U.S. army surgeon named William Beaumont was called upon to treat a gunshot wound in the stomach of a Canadian fur trapper. The wound eventually healed, but it left a permanent hole to the outside in the man's stomach. Beaumont saw this as a rare opportunity to study the role of the stomach in digestion. With his patient's reluctant permission, Beaumont inserted bits of food tied to strings into the stomach through the hole. Then, he withdrew them periodically to see the extent of digestion. Beaumont also siphoned off gastric secretions and had their chemical composition analyzed. He learned that digestion is primarily a chemical process and that gastric secretions consist mostly of hydrochloric acid. These and other results of Beaumont's innovative research still remain valid today.

Answers to . . .

CHECKPOINT *To break proteins into smaller polypeptide fragments*

Figure 38–11 *Smooth muscle*

Figure 38–12 *In the mouth*

38–2 (continued)

Absorption in the Small Intestine

Quick Lab

BIIE 1.g

Objective Students will be able to apply the concept that folding increases surface area. L2

Skills Focus **Applying Concepts, Inferring, Calculating**

Materials 2 paper towels, scissors, 3 cardboard tubes, metric ruler, 30-mL graduated cylinder, 2 plastic cups

Time 20 minutes

Advance Prep Ask students to bring in cardboard tubes from rolls of paper towels, aluminum foil, or plastic wrap to use for the lab.

Strategy You may wish to calculate class averages for the data before students answer the questions so that all the students are working with the same numbers.

Expected Outcome Students should observe that the tubes containing folded paper towels retain more water.

Analyze and Conclude

1. Students' calculations will vary; however, the folded model (step 4) will have a far greater surface area than the flat model (step 2).
2. The folded paper towel in tube 3 has more surface area, which enables it to absorb more water. Students may have predicted correctly that the folded towel would absorb more water.
3. Folds and projections increase the area of the surface and its ability to absorb substances. Villi increase the surface area of the small intestine, which increases its ability to absorb nutrients.
4. Dividing the flow of blood among many small structures increases the surface area through which wastes can be removed.

Assisting the pancreas is the **liver,** a large organ located just above and to the right of the stomach. The liver produces bile, a fluid loaded with lipids and salts. Bile acts like a detergent, dissolving and dispersing the droplets of fat found in fatty foods. This action makes it possible for enzymes to reach the smaller fat molecules and break them down. Bile is stored in a small, pouchlike organ called the gallbladder.

CHECKPOINT *What is bile?*

Absorption in the Small Intestine

The duodenum is much shorter than the remaining parts of the small intestine—the jejunum and the ileum, which together average about 6 meters long. By the time chyme enters these parts of the small intestine, much of the chemical digestion has been completed. The chyme is now a rich mixture of medium and small nutrient molecules.

The small intestine is specially adapted for the absorption of nutrients. The folded surfaces of the small intestine are covered with fingerlike projections called **villi** (VIL-eye; singular: villus).

BIIE 1.g

Quick Lab

How do villi help the small intestine absorb nutrients?

Materials 2 paper towel sheets, scissors, 3 cardboard tubes, metric ruler, 30-mL graduated cylinder, 2 plastic cups

Procedure 

1. Cut cardboard tube 1 lengthwise, and flatten it. **CAUTION:** *Scissors are sharp.* Lay paper towel sheet 1 over the flattened cardboard. Cut sheet 1 to the same size as the cardboard tube.
2. Determine the area of the flattened sheet with a ruler (area = width x length). Record the measurements.
3. Roll sheet 1 lengthwise until the sides meet but do not overlap. Insert rolled sheet 1 inside tube 2. The tube represents the small intestine, and the sheet represents an intestinal lining without villi.
4. Fold uncut sheet 2 back and forth in a zigzag pattern, as for a fan. Determine the area of sheet 2 and record the measurement. Roll sheet 2 until the sides meet, and insert it in tube 3. The folds represent an intestinal lining with villi.

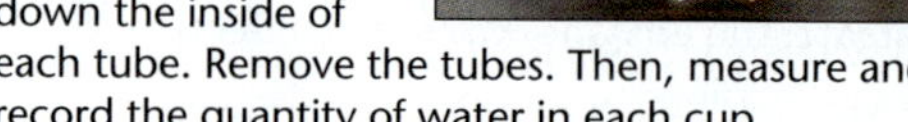

5. **Predicting** Predict which model will absorb more water.
6. Stand each tube in a plastic cup. Slowly pour 30 mL of water down the inside of each tube. Remove the tubes. Then, measure and record the quantity of water in each cup.

Analyze and Conclude

1. **Calculating** Use your calculations in steps 2 and 4 to show which model had more surface area.
2. **Applying Concepts** How does surface area affect the ability to absorb substances? Was your prediction in step 5 correct?
3. **Applying Concepts** How do folds and fingerlike projections affect the area of an absorbing surface? How do villi help the intestine absorb nutrients?
4. **Inferring** Your kidneys contain about 1 million microscopic structures that filter waste products from your blood. What advantage does this arrangement have over filtering the waste products out of one large blood vessel?

FACTS AND FIGURES

The gallbladder examined

Located just beneath the liver, the gallbladder is a pear-shaped sack about 9 cm long that concentrates and stores liver bile until it is needed to help digest fats. The gallbladder can store up to 50 mL of concentrated bile. When the bile is needed for digestion, it travels from the gallbladder to the small intestine through the bile duct, which also transports digestive enzymes from the pancreas to the small intestine. In some people, mineral salts in the gallbladder harden to form gallstones. Some of these may lodge in the bile duct and block it, causing pain as well as preventing the bile duct from transporting bile and pancreatic enzymes to the small intestine. Ultrasound is often used to break up the stones so that they can pass out of the body, although in severe cases removal of the gallbladder may be necessary.

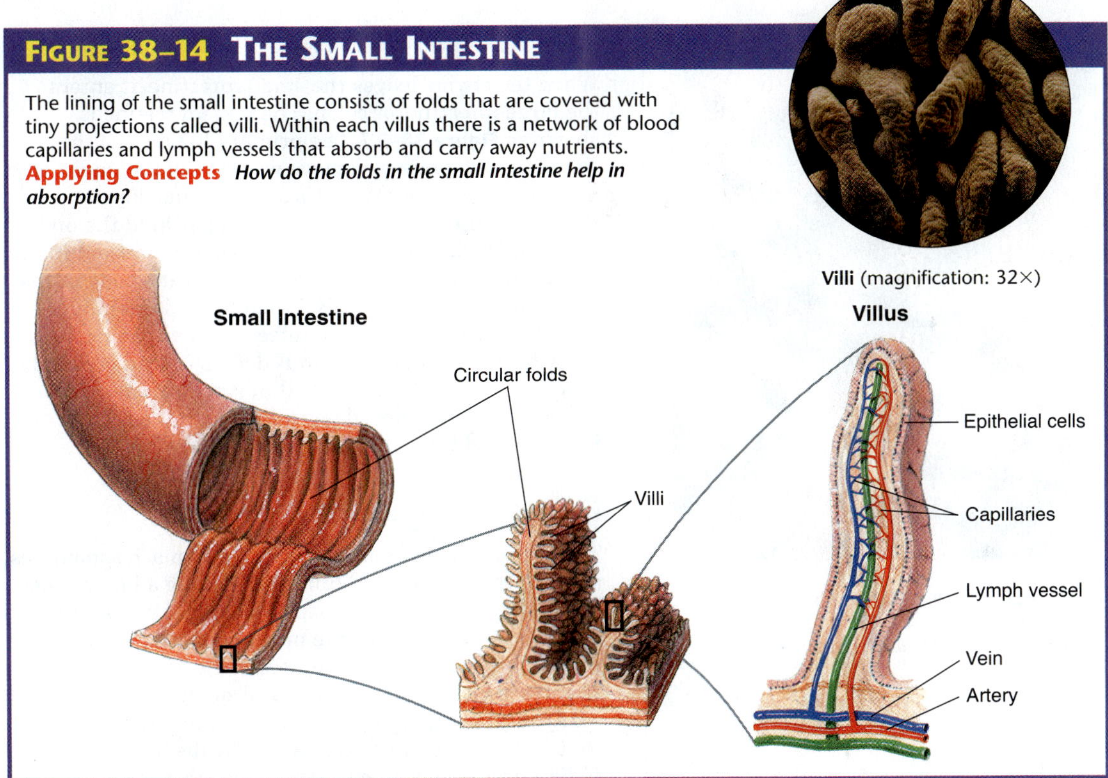

FIGURE 38–14 THE SMALL INTESTINE

The lining of the small intestine consists of folds that are covered with tiny projections called villi. Within each villus there is a network of blood capillaries and lymph vessels that absorb and carry away nutrients. **Applying Concepts** *How do the folds in the small intestine help in absorption?*

The villi are illustrated in **Figure 38–14.** The surfaces of the cells of the villi are covered with thousands of fingerlike projections known as microvilli. These folds and projections provide an enormous surface area for the absorption of nutrient molecules. Slow, wavelike contractions of smooth muscles move the chyme along this surface.

Nutrient molecules are rapidly absorbed into the cells lining the small intestine. Most of the products of carbohydrate and protein digestion are absorbed into the capillaries in the villi. Molecules of undigested fat and some fatty acids are absorbed by lymph vessels.

By the time food is ready to leave the small intestine, it is basically nutrient-free. The complex organic molecules have been digested and absorbed, leaving only water, cellulose, and other undigestible substances behind.

As the water, cellulose, and other undigestible substances leave the small intestine and enter the large intestine, they pass by a small saclike organ called the appendix. In humans, the appendix appears to do little to promote digestion. In other mammals, the appendix is used to store cellulose and other materials that the digestive enzymes cannot break down. The only time you may pay attention to the appendix is when it becomes clogged and inflamed, causing appendicitis. The only remedy for appendicitis is to remove the infected organ by surgery—as quickly as possible.

Address Misconceptions

Students may have the mistaken impression that the duodenum is the most important part of the small intestine because the bulk of chemical digestion takes place there. Point out that about 3 meters of the small intestine are devoted to absorption, whereas only about 25 centimeters are involved in digestion. Ask: **What percentage of the small intestine is involved in absorbing nutrients?** *(About 92 percent)* **What is the value of its length?** *(The small intestine's great length adds more absorbing surface area, which is critical to digestion and absorption.)* L2

Use Visuals

Figure 38–14 Make sure students understand how the different parts of the figure are related. Call attention to the many capillaries in each villus, and describe their role in the absorption of nutrients. Also, help students relate the figure to the information in the text by asking them to complete the following analogy: **Villi are to the small intestine as ________ are to villi.** *(Microvilli)* L1 L2

Demonstration

Give students an opportunity to feel how small and densely distributed villi are. Pass a piece of velvet fabric around the room, and have students run their hands over the napped surface. Tell them that the tiny projections on the surface of the cloth are similar in size and density to the villi lining the small intestine. L1

BIO INSIGHTS — FACTS AND FIGURES

Beneficial bacteria

There are enough bacteria in your large intestine to fill a soup can. The relationship between you and the bacteria is mutualistic because both of you benefit: The bacteria provide you with vitamins and help your digestion, while you provide the bacteria with a warm, moist environment and plenty of nutrients. The environment is also a safe one for the bacteria—unless you take antibiotics for an infection. Antibiotics kill beneficial as well as harmful bacteria. If too many beneficial bacteria are killed, you may develop vitamin deficiencies and form light-colored stools, both caused by the absence of bacteria.

Answers to . . .

CHECKPOINT *Bile is a fluid produced by the liver that dissolves and disperses the droplets of fat found in fatty foods.*

Figure 38–14 *The folds increase the surface area for the absorption of nutrients.*

38–2 (continued)

The Large Intestine

Make Connections

Mathematics Challenge students to estimate the surface area of the large intestine based on its diameter (6 cm) and length (150 cm), using the formula for the area of a cylinder: $2\pi r(r+h)$. *(The surface area is about 2800 cm².)* Explain that, because of villi, the surface area of the small intestine is far greater, at about 8,000,000 cm². L2 L3

Digestive System Disorders

Build Science Skills

Applying Concepts Ask students: **Why do disorders of the large intestine often cause diarrhea?** *(The main function of the large intestine is to remove water from waste. If the large intestine is not working properly because of illness, too little water may be removed, causing diarrhea.)*

3 ASSESS

Evaluate Understanding

Have students make a table with the headings: *Mouth, Stomach, Small Intestine, Pancreas.* Have them list the enzymes found in or produced by each organ and the nutrients that the enzymes help break down.

Reteach

Describe the functions of the digestive organs, and have students identify them from their functions.

Focus on the BIG Idea

Students should explain that the rate of digestion would decrease, because enzymes speed up the rate of chemical reactions.

If your class subscribes to the iText, use it to review the Key Concepts in Section 38–2.

Answer to . . .

Figure 38–15 *To remove water from undigested material*

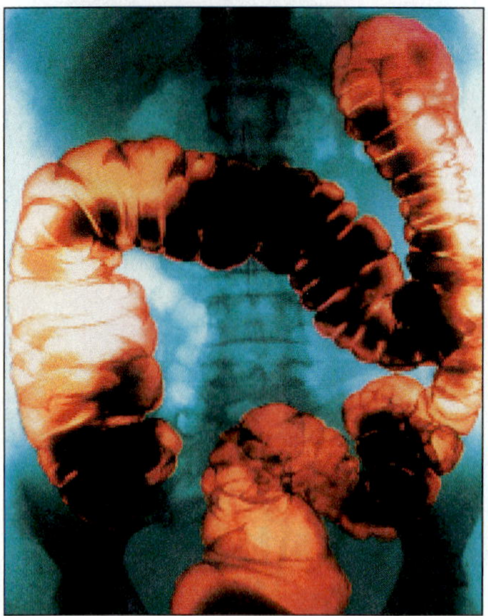

▲ **Figure 38–15** This barium X-ray shows the large intestine. **Applying Concepts** *What is the role of the large intestine?*

The Large Intestine

When the chyme leaves the small intestine, it enters the large intestine, or colon. The large intestine is shown in **Figure 38–15.** The primary function of the **large intestine** is to remove water from the undigested material that is left. Water is absorbed quickly across the wall of the large intestine, leaving behind the undigested materials. Rich colonies of bacteria present in the large intestine produce compounds that the body is able to use, including vitamin K. When large doses of antibiotics are given to fight an infection, they can destroy these bacteria and a vitamin K deficiency can occur. The concentrated waste material that remains after the water has been removed passes through the rectum and is eliminated from the body.

Digestive System Disorders

The powerful acids released into the stomach sometimes damage the organ's own lining, producing a hole in the stomach wall known as a peptic ulcer. For years, physicians hypothesized that the primary cause of ulcers was too much stomach acid. They prescribed drugs that suppressed acid production and recommended bland, easily digested diets. Scientists have since discovered that most peptic ulcers are caused by the bacterium *Helicobacter pylori*. Doctors now know that many peptic ulcers are caused by an infectious disease that can be cured. Thanks to powerful antibiotics, cure rates for peptic ulcers are as high as 90 percent.

Other digestive system disorders include diarrhea and constipation. When something happens that interferes with the removal of water by the large intestine, you usually become aware of it right away. If not enough water is absorbed, a condition known as diarrhea occurs. If too much water is absorbed from the undigested materials, a condition known as constipation occurs.

38–2 Section Assessment

1. **Key Concept** List the organs of the digestive system and give the function of each.
2. **Key Concept** Explain the function of the digestive system.
3. How do mechanical and chemical digestion work together to break down foods?
4. How does bile help in the digestion of fats?
5. **Critical Thinking Inferring** What can you infer about the diet of an animal that has a large appendix?

Focus on the BIG Idea

Matter and Energy
How would the rate of digestion be affected if enzymes were not released by the various organs and glands? You may wish to refer to Chapter 2 for a review of enzyme action.

38–2 Section Assessment

1. Mouth: begins mechanical digestion, begins chemical digestion of starch; esophagus: moves food to stomach; stomach: continues mechanical digestion, begins chemical digestion of protein; small intestine: completes chemical digestion of starch and protein, chemical digestion of fats; large intestine: removes water from undigested food
2. To help convert foods into simple molecules that can be absorbed and used by cells
3. Mechanical digestion physically breaks down food into smaller pieces, which makes it easier for enzymes to chemically break down large food molecules into smaller molecules.
4. Bile dissolves and disperses fat droplets, making it easier for enzymes to reach and further break down fats.
5. The diet probably contains a lot of cellulose.

38–3 The Excretory System

***BI 9.g.** Students know the homeostatic role of the kidneys in the removal of nitrogenous wastes and the role of the liver in blood detoxification and glucose balance.

The chemistry of the human body is a marvelous thing. An intricate system of checks and balances controls everything from your blood pressure to your body temperature. Nutrients are absorbed, stored, and carefully released when they are needed. However, every living system, including the human body, produces chemical waste products that are not useful to the body. In fact, some waste products are so toxic that they will cause death if they are not eliminated.

Guide for Reading

Key Concepts

- What are the functions of the kidneys?
- How is blood filtered?

Vocabulary

kidney
ureter
urinary bladder
nephron
filtration
glomerulus
Bowman's capsule
reabsorption
loop of Henle
urethra

Reading Strategy: Building Vocabulary

Before you read, preview **Figure 38–17** to identify vocabulary with which you are unfamiliar. Look for the meanings of these terms as you read.

Functions of the Excretory System

You might think that homeostasis involves the body's efforts to respond only to changes in the external environment. However, homeostasis also requires the body to deal with internal processes that might upset the internal cellular environment. For example, as a normal consequence of being alive, every cell in the body produces metabolic wastes, such as excess salts, carbon dioxide, and urea. Urea is a toxic compound that is produced when amino acids are used for energy. The process by which these metabolic wastes are eliminated is called excretion. Excretion is one part of the many processes that maintain homeostasis.

You have already learned about two organs of excretion—the skin and the lungs. The skin excretes excess water and salts, as well as a small amount of urea, in the form of sweat. The lungs excrete carbon dioxide, a gas produced when energy is captured from compounds in foods.

The liver, which we normally think of as a digestive organ, also plays a number of important roles in excretion. When cells of the body break down proteins, excess amino acids are released into the bloodstream. The liver takes up these amino acids and converts them into other useful compounds, producing nitrogen wastes in the process. The liver quickly converts these potentially poisonous nitrogen compounds into urea. Urea, in turn, is removed from the bloodstream along with other metabolic wastes by the body's principal organs of excretion, the kidneys. **The kidneys play an important role in maintaining homeostasis. They remove waste products from the blood; maintain blood pH; and regulate the water content of the blood and, therefore, blood volume.**

▶ **Figure 38–16** As part of the excretory system, the skin excretes water, salts, and urea in sweat.

SECTION RESOURCES

Print:

- ***Laboratory Manual A,*** Chapter 38 Lab
- ***Teaching Resources,*** Lesson Plan 38–3, Adapted Section Summary 38–3, Section Summary 38–3, Worksheets 38–3, Section Review 38–3
- ***Reading and Study Workbook A,*** Section 38–3
- ***Adapted Reading and Study Workbook B,*** Section 38–3
- ***Issues and Decision Making,*** Issues and Decisions 40

Technology:

- ***iText,*** Section 38–3
- ***Animated Biological Concepts DVD,*** 41 Kidney Function
- ***Transparencies Plus,*** Section 38–3

Section 38–3

1 FOCUS

Objectives

38.3.1 ***Identify*** the functions of the kidneys.
38.3.2 ***Explain*** how blood is filtered.

Guide for Reading

Vocabulary Preview

Point out that all but two of the Vocabulary terms are parts of the excretory system. The other two terms refer to processes of the excretory system. Ask: **Which two terms refer to processes?** *(Filtration and reabsorption)* Have students predict what these two terms mean and check to see if they were correct after they read the section.

Reading Strategy

Suggest that students outline the section by first writing the headings and subheadings on a separate sheet of paper and then filling in important details as they read.

2 INSTRUCT

Functions of the Excretory System

Demonstration

Before chemical wastes are excreted from the body, they must be removed from individual cells. Demonstrate the importance of this process by modeling a cell with a balloon. Attach the balloon to a faucet, and gradually add water. As the balloon fills up, explain that this is what would happen to a cell if it could not eliminate its waste products. Ask: **What would happen to the cell if the amount of waste products continued to increase?** *(The cell would swell until it burst.)*

38–3 (continued)

The Kidneys

Use Visuals

Figure 38–17 Explain that each nephron is about 3 cm long and only 0.03 mm in diameter, so it is too thin to be seen with the unaided eye. Also, explain that each kidney is about 10 cm long and 6 cm in diameter and contains about a million nephrons. Ask: **How do the sizes of the kidney and nephron in the figure compare with their actual sizes?** *(The kidney in the drawing is somewhat smaller than its actual size. The nephron in the drawing is much larger than its actual size.)* Suggest that students locate each part of the kidney and nephron in the figure as they read about it in the text. L2

Build Science Skills

Using Models Explain that the function of the kidney is to filter out wastes and other substances from the blood. Model how the kidney works by pouring water mixed with food coloring, sand, and silt through a paper coffee filter. Invite students to examine the contents of the coffee filter and the colored water that emerges from it. Ask: **How are kidneys and coffee filters similar?** *(Both filter out substances from a fluid.)* **How are they different?** *(The kidneys filter out water and dissolved materials, whereas the coffee filter filters out only solids. The kidneys also return some of the filtered materials to the fluid.)* L1 L2

FIGURE 38–17 STRUCTURE OF THE KIDNEYS

Kidneys are made up of nephrons. **Blood enters the nephron, where impurities are filtered out and emptied into the collecting duct. The purified blood leaves the nephron through the renal vein.**

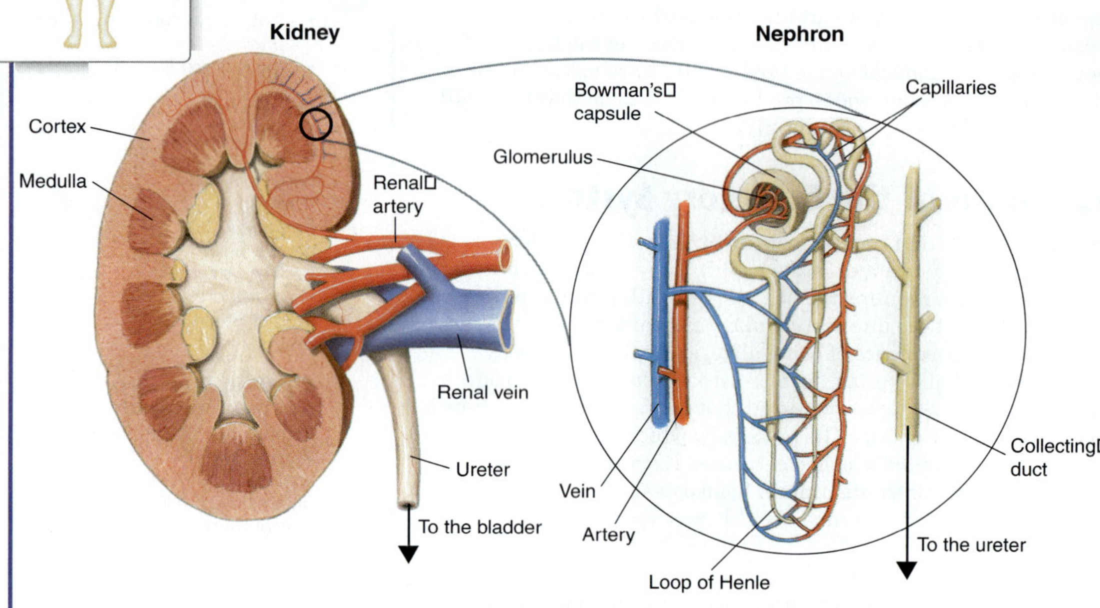

The Kidneys

The **kidneys** are located on either side of the spinal column near the lower back. A tube, called the **ureter** (yoo-REET-ur), leaves each kidney, carrying urine to the urinary bladder. The **urinary bladder** is a saclike organ where urine is stored before being excreted. The structures of the kidney are shown in **Figure 38–17.**

What does a kidney do? As waste-laden blood enters the kidney through the renal artery, the kidney removes urea, excess water, and other waste products and passes them to the ureter. The clean, filtered blood leaves the kidney through the renal vein and returns to circulation.

Kidney Structure If a kidney is cut in half, two distinct regions can be seen. The inner part is called the renal medulla. The outer part is called the renal cortex. The functional units of the kidney are called **nephrons** (NEF-rahnz). Each nephron is a small, independent processing unit. Nephrons are located in the renal cortex, except for their loops of Henle, which descend into the renal medulla.

UNIVERSAL ACCESS

Inclusion/Special Needs

Have students construct a three-dimensional model of the excretory system, including the kidneys, renal blood vessels, ureter, and urinary bladder. They can use dry pasta, legumes, cereal, clay, string, or other suitable materials to represent the different parts of the system. Ask students to explain what each part of their completed model represents. L1

English Language Learners

Help students interpret Figure 38–17 so that they will not need to rely on the text as much to understand the kidney. Point out the parts of the kidney. Then, have students trace the path through the nephron as you describe how blood enters through the artery; impurities are filtered out in the glomerulus, pass through the loop of Henle, and empty into the collecting duct; purified blood exits through the vein.

Each nephron has its own blood supply: an arteriole, a venule, and a network of capillaries connecting them. In addition, each nephron releases fluids to a collecting duct, which leads to the ureter. **As blood enters a nephron through the arteriole, impurities are filtered out and emptied into the collecting duct. The purified blood exits the nephron through the venule.** The mechanism of blood purification involves two distinct processes: filtration and reabsorption.

CHECKPOINT *What are the two parts of a kidney?*

Filtration Passing a liquid or gas through a filter to remove wastes is called **filtration.** The filtration of blood mainly takes place in the glomerulus (gloh-MUR-yoo-lus). The **glomerulus** is a small network of capillaries encased in the upper end of the nephron by a hollow, cup-shaped structure called **Bowman's capsule.** A glomerulus is shown in **Figure 38–18.**

Because the blood is under pressure and the walls of the capillaries and Bowman's capsule are permeable, much of the fluid from the blood flows into Bowman's capsule. The materials that are filtered from the blood are collectively called the filtrate. The filtrate contains water, urea, glucose, salts, amino acids, and some vitamins. Because plasma proteins, cells, and platelets are too large to pass through the capillary walls, they remain in the blood.

Reabsorption The kidneys filter all the blood in the body approximately every 45 minutes. Needless to say, not all of the filtrate is excreted. Most of the material removed from the blood at Bowman's capsule makes its way back into the blood. The process in which liquid is taken back into a vessel is called **reabsorption.**

A number of materials, including amino acids, fats, and glucose, are removed from the filtrate by active transport and reabsorbed by the capillaries. Because water follows these materials by osmosis, almost 99 percent of the water that enters Bowman's capsule is reabsorbed into the blood. When the filtrate drains in the collecting ducts, most of the water and nutrients have been reabsorbed into the blood.

Urine Formation The material that remains, called urine, is emptied into a collecting duct. Urine, which contains urea, excess salts, and water, among other substances, is primarily concentrated in the loop of Henle. The **loop of Henle** is a section of the nephron tubule in which water is conserved and the volume of urine minimized.

As the kidney works, purified blood is returned to circulation while urine is collected in the urinary bladder. Urine is stored in the urinary bladder until it can be released from the body through a tube called the **urethra** (yoo-REE-thruh).

▼ **Figure 38–18** Blood enters each nephron through a ball of capillaries called a glomerulus. **The glomerulus is where filtration takes place.**

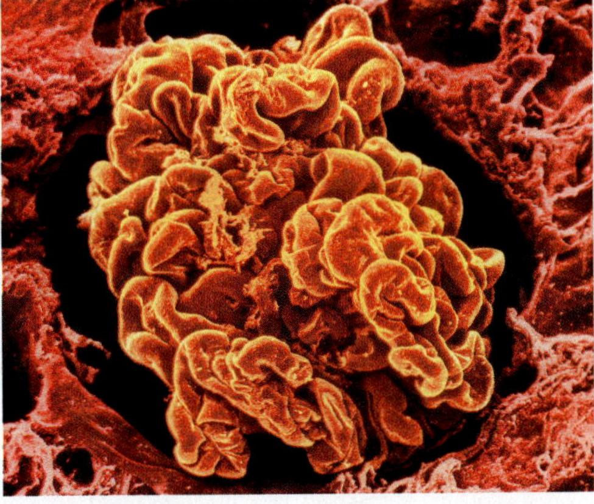

(magnification: 185×)

Demonstration

Obtain a beef or lamb kidney from a butcher and display it to the class. Ask: **How might this kidney be different from a human kidney?** *(It might be different in size, depending on the animal it came from, but its structure and function should be similar to those of a human kidney.)* Point out the renal artery, renal vein, and ureter. Ask: **What roles do these structures play?** *(The renal artery carries blood with impurities to the kidney, the renal vein carries purified blood away from the kidney, and the ureter carries urine from the kidney to the bladder.)* Cut the kidney lengthwise and point out the renal medulla and renal cortex. Ask: **Where are the nephrons located?** *(In the renal cortex, except for their loops of Henle)* L2

Build Science Skills

Inferring Ask students: **Why is so much of the material that is filtered from blood returned to the blood?** *(Because it consists of substances such as nutrients and water that the body needs)* L2

BIO INSIGHTS

FACTS AND FIGURES

Maple syrup urine and other diseases

Some people have urine that smells like maple syrup. Others have urine that turns black when it is exposed to air. The reason? They have disorders of protein metabolism—maple syrup urine disease or alkaptonuria, respectively—that result in the kidneys excreting substances that are not normally found in the urine. Diagnosing diseases by analyzing urine is called urinalysis. It involves examination of the urine chemically, physically, and microscopically. Urinalysis is one of the most commonly performed medical laboratory procedures because the composition of the urine reflects the status of many different body functions. For example, in diabetes mellitus there often is sugar in the urine because the excess sugar in the blood is filtered out by the kidneys and excreted in the urine.

Answer to . . .

CHECKPOINT *The renal medulla, which is the inner part, and the renal cortex, which is the outer part*

38–3 (continued)

Download a worksheet on the excretory system for students to complete, and find additional teacher support from NSTA SciLinks.

Control of Kidney Function

Build Science Skills

Inferring Help students build inferring skills and increase their understanding of how the kidneys maintain homeostasis. Ask: **Why is your urine lighter in color after you drink a lot of fluids?** *(The kidneys remove the excess water from the blood and excrete it in the urine, making the urine less concentrated and lighter in color.)* **Why might your urine be darker in color after you have been sweating a lot?** *(The kidneys remove less water from the blood to compensate for the water lost in sweat, making the urine more concentrated and darker in color.)* L2

Make Connections

Health Science Relate the kidneys' ability to maintain homeostasis to health issues. Tell students that the role of the kidneys is essential to life, yet people can live long, healthy lives with just one kidney. Ask: **Why can someone function normally with just one kidney?** *(Students should infer that the one kidney can accommodate the greater workload placed on it by filtering out more substances from the blood.)* L2 L3

For: Links on the excretory system
Visit: www.SciLinks.org
Web Code: cbn-0383

Urine Testing When blood is filtered through the kidneys, small molecules, including salts, amino acids, sugars, and many drugs, are removed from the circulation. Although many of these are reabsorbed into the bloodstream, drugs generally remain in the filtrate and are eliminated in the urine. This is one of the principal reasons why the effects of many drugs, including antibiotics, wear off over time. This also means that drugs, legal and illegal, become concentrated in the urine, providing a quick and easy way to test for their presence. Urine testing is now done routinely to check for the presence of prohibited drugs in athletes. It has also become common for employers to use such tests to screen job applicants for illegal drug use.

Kidney Stones Sometimes substances such as calcium, magnesium, or uric acid salts in the urine crystallize and form kidney stones. When kidney stones block the ureter, they cause great pain. Kidney stones are often treated using ultrasound waves. The sound waves pulverize the stones into smaller fragments, which are eliminated with the urine.

Control of Kidney Function

To a large extent, the activity of the kidneys is controlled by the composition of blood itself. In addition, regulatory hormones are released in response to the composition of blood. These mechanisms combine to ensure that the kidneys will maintain the proper composition of blood.

When you drink glass after glass of liquid, the liquid is quickly absorbed into the blood through the digestive system. As a result, the concentration of water in the blood increases. If it were not for your kidneys, this increased concentration of water in the blood would force water into cells and tissues by osmosis, causing your body to swell.

As the amount of water in the blood increases, the rate of water reabsorption in the kidneys decreases. Less water is returned to the blood, and the excess water is sent to the urinary bladder to be excreted as urine.

If you eat salty food, your kidneys will respond to the increased level of salt in your blood. When your kidneys detect an increase in salt, they respond by returning less salt to the blood by reabsorption. The excess salt the kidneys retain is excreted in urine, thus maintaining the composition of the blood.

Homeostasis by Machine

The kidneys are the master chemists of the blood supply. If anything goes wrong with the kidneys, serious medical problems soon follow. Fortunately, humans have two kidneys and can survive with only one. If both kidneys are damaged by disease or injury, however, there are only two ways to keep an individual alive. The first way is to transplant a healthy kidney from a compatible donor to the person in need of the kidney.

HISTORY OF SCIENCE

Bright's disease and Bowman's capsule
The first person to use urinalysis to diagnose disease was an English physician named Richard Bright. In 1829, Bright discovered that people who suffer from "dropsy," or what we now call edema, have a substance in their urine that coagulates, just as egg white does, when the urine is boiled. The substance is now known to be serum albumin, and it does not normally appear in the urine. When it does, it is a sign that the patient has nephritis, or inflammation of the kidneys. Because of Bright's hallmark work, nephritis is still sometimes referred to as Bright's disease. Another nineteenth-century English physician, Sir William Bowman, discovered the capsules in the kidney that were subsequently named after him. Bowman also discovered how urine is produced by filtration.

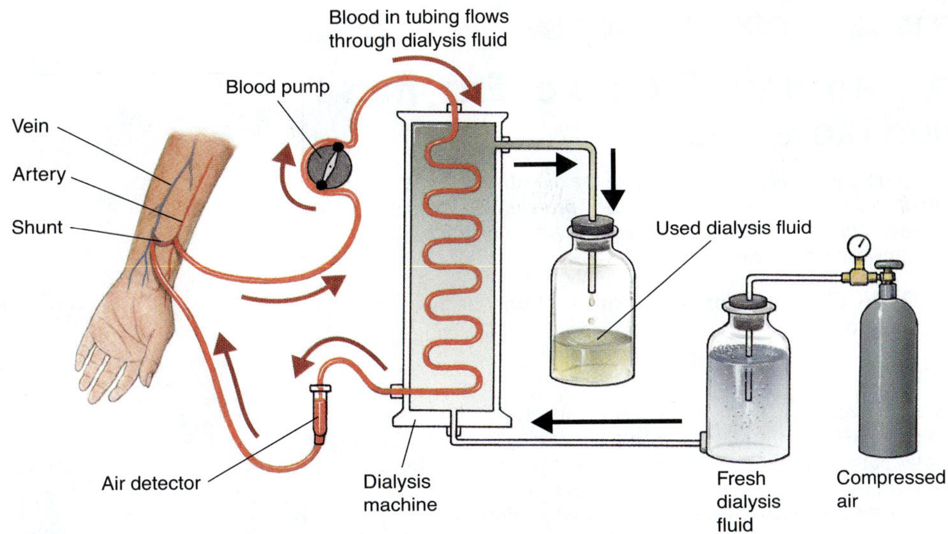

A second way is used when a donor is not available or surgery is not advisable. In these instances, a kidney dialysis machine becomes a lifesaver. In a common form of dialysis, blood is removed from the body through a tube inserted in the arm and pumped through special tubing that acts like nephrons. Tiny pores in the tubing allow salts and small molecules, including nitrogen wastes, to pass through. Wastes—urea and excess salts—diffuse out of the blood into the fluid-filled chamber, allowing purified blood to be returned to the body. This process of dialysis is shown in **Figure 38–19.** Dialysis is not only expensive, but it also is time-consuming, occupying several hours a day as often as three times a week. The ideal solution, assuming a kidney transplant is not possible, would be the implantation of an artificial kidney. Medical science is working toward developing such an artificial kidney.

▲ **Figure 38–19** For people with damaged kidneys, dialysis machines can perform many of the functions of the kidneys. **Applying Concepts** *Why is dialysis such an important lifesaving technique?*

38–3 Section Assessment

1. **Key Concept** What are the functions of the kidneys?
2. **Key Concept** Describe how blood is purified.
3. Describe the structures of a kidney.
4. What is the role of the skin in excretion?
5. **Critical Thinking Inferring** When there is too much fluid in the blood, the heart must pump harder. Diuretics are substances that stimulate the kidneys to remove more fluid from the body. Why do you think diuretics are often prescribed as a treatment for high blood pressure?

Thinking Visually

Constructing a Flowchart
Construct a flowchart that illustrates how wastes are removed by the kidneys. Be sure to include the terms *Bowman's capsule, loop of Henle, capillaries, collecting duct,* and *ureter.*

38–3 Section Assessment

1. Kidneys remove waste products from blood, maintain blood pH, and regulate water content and volume of blood.
2. Blood enters a nephron through the arteriole; impurities are filtered out and emptied into the collecting duct; purified blood exits through the venule.
3. Renal medulla: inner part of kidney; renal cortex: outer part of kidney; nephron: functional unit of kidney; renal artery and vein: blood vessels entering and leaving kidney; glomerulus: small network of capillaries in nephron; Bowman's capsule: hollow, cup-shaped structure in nephron; loop of Henle: section of nephron tubule; collecting duct: tube for transferring waste
4. The skin excretes water, salts, and urea in sweat.
5. Because diuretics reduce the volume of blood and, thereby, lower blood pressure

Homeostasis by Machine

Use Community Resources

Invite a dialysis technician or nurse to speak to the class about dialysis. Suggest that the speaker address such issues as how effective dialysis is compared with normal kidney function, who needs dialysis and why, and what it is like to receive dialysis treatments. Have students take notes during the presentation and later use them to write a summary of what they learned. L2

3 ASSESS

Evaluate Understanding

Call on students at random to state the functions of the different parts of the kidney and nephron that are highlighted in the text. Call on other students to correct any errors.

Reteach

Have students use Figure 38–17 to trace the path of blood into and out of the kidney and to trace the path of urine from the kidney to the urethra.

Thinking Visually

Provide students with large sheets of paper and colored pens or markers. Flowcharts should demonstrate an understanding of how the kidney removes wastes such as urea from blood.

If your class subscribes to the iText, use it to review the Key Concepts in Section 38–3.

Answer to . . .

Figure 38–19 *Without dialysis, wastes in the blood would soon reach toxic levels, and the person could die.*

Design an Experiment

*BI 9.f, 8IIE 9.c

Objective Students will be able to design experiments to test their predictions about the specificity of digestive enzymes. L2 L3

Skills Focus **Formulating Hypotheses, Controlling Variables, Forming Operational Definitions**

Time 45 minutes one day; 15 minutes two days later

Advance Prep

- Cook the eggs and potatoes in advance. The potatoes need to be boiled or microwaved only for a few minutes. Eggs can be microwaved in a container of water.
- To prepare 1 L of 0.2 percent hydrochloric acid, add 2 mL of concentrated hydrochloric acid to 998 mL of water.

Safety

- Read the safety information on the MSDS for Benedict's solution and hydrochloric acid before doing the lab.
- Remind students to add the acid to the water, not the water to the acid. Remind them that the concentrated acid is extremely corrosive.
- Caution students to be careful handling the boiling water.

Teaching Tips

- Before students begin the procedure, you might want to have them test the egg white and potato for starch and protein.
- Ask: **What is the purpose of this investigation?** *(To determine whether digestive enzymes act only on specific compounds)*
- Ask: **What is the purpose of test tubes 1 and 2?** *(They are controls; they show that nothing happens to the egg white without pepsin.)*
- Ask: **What do you think would happen to egg white in a test tube of pepsin and water?** *(Students should infer that the pepsin would not be able to break down the egg white because it needs an acidic environment to work effectively.)*

Design an Experiment

*BI 9.f, 8IIE 9.c

Investigating the Effects of Enzymes on Food Molecules

In this investigation, you will test the ability of the digestive enzyme pepsin to break down egg white, which is mostly protein. You will also design your own experiments to test the effect of pepsin on starch, and the effects of amylase on proteins and starch.

Problem **Do different digestive enzymes act only on specific types of compounds?**

Materials

- heat-resistant gloves
- Benedict's solution
- boiling water bath
- cooked egg white
- scalpel or single-edged razor blade
- metric ruler
- 6 large test tubes
- 6 stoppers for test tubes
- glass-marking pencil
- test-tube rack
- 10-mL graduated cylinder
- 1% pepsin solution
- 0.2% hydrochloric acid
- cooked potato
- 1% amylase solution
- test-tube holder

Skills Formulating Hypotheses, Controlling Variables, Forming Operational Definitions

Design Your Experiment

Part A: The Basic Procedure

1. **Predicting** Predict whether pepsin can break down protein.
2. Put on an apron and safety goggles. Label three test tubes 1, 2, and 3; and put them in a test-tube rack. Cut three 5-mm cubes of cooked egg white and add one to each test tube.
3. Put on plastic gloves. Use a graduated cylinder to add 6 mL of water to test tube 1, and 3 mL of water and 3 mL 0.2% hydrochloric acid to test tube 2. **CAUTION:** *Hydrochloric acid can damage skin and clothing. If hydrochloric acid spills, notify your teacher at once. Wash the affected area with large amounts of cool water for 10 to 15 minutes.* Carefully rinse the graduated cylinder.
4. To test tube 3, add 3 mL 1% pepsin solution and 3 mL 0.2% hydrochloric acid. Carefully rinse the graduated cylinder.
5. Put a stopper in each test tube, and gently turn the tubes upside down several times to mix the contents. Put the tubes back in the test-tube rack. Set your test-tube rack where it will not be disturbed. Make a copy of the data table (on page 991).
6. After 2 days, examine the contents of each test tube. Record your observations in your copy of the data table.

Part B: Design Your Own Experiments

7. **Formulating Hypotheses** Do you think pepsin will digest potato, which is rich in starch? Use the observations you just made and your knowledge of enzymes to form a hypothesis about the way digestive enzymes work. Record your hypothesis.
8. Design an experiment to test your hypothesis. You can use the test for sugars described in Part C to determine whether starch has been broken down.
9. As you plan your investigative procedures, refer to the Lab Tips box on page 55 for information on demonstrating safe practices, making wise choices in the use of materials, selecting equipment and technology, and evaluating your experimental design.

Design Your Experiment

1. Students should predict that pepsin can break down protein in the presence of an acid.

6. Students should observe that the egg white broke down in test tube 3 (pepsin and hydrochloric acid) but not in the other two test tubes.

7. Students should predict that pepsin will not digest potato. They can test it by following steps 2 through 6, but using potato instead of egg white, and then following steps 14 through 16 to test for the presence of sugar.

11. Students should design an experiment based on Part A of the procedure, but they should test amylase instead of pepsin and omit the hydrochloric acid. They should test egg white in one experiment and potato in the other experiment. A test tube of water should be used as a control.

13. Students should observe that the amylase broke down the starch but not the protein.

Data Table			
Test Tube	Compound Tested	Liquid(s) Added	Observations
1	protein (egg white)	6 mL water	
2	protein (egg white)	3 mL water, 3 mL hydrochloric acid	
3	protein (egg white)	3 mL pepsin, 3 mL hydrochloric acid	

10. Write down your procedure. What is your manipulated variable? Your responding variable? Make sure to control all other variables. **CAUTION:** *Before you perform your experiment, have your teacher approve your procedure.*
11. Design two experiments to test whether amylase can digest protein or starch. Make sure to develop a hypothesis and to control your variables. Develop a data table similar to the one above. Record in your data table what you put in each test tube. **CAUTION:** *Before you perform your experiments, have your teacher approve your procedures.*
12. Set your test-tube rack aside where it will not be disturbed for 2 days.
13. After 2 days, examine each test tube. Record your observations in your data table.

Part C: Testing for Sugar

14. To test for the presence of sugar in the liquid in the tubes that contain potato: Put 1 mL of the liquid in a test tube. Add 2 mL of water and mix.
15. Add 3 mL Benedict's solution to the same tube.
16. Your teacher will provide a boiling water bath. Put on the heat-resistant gloves and use a test-tube holder to put the test tubes from step 14 in the boiling water bath. **CAUTION:** *Be careful when working with boiling water.* Observe the test tube for about 5 minutes. A change in color from blue to yellow (or green, or orange, or red) is a positive test for sugar. Record your observations in your data table.

Analyze and Conclude

1. **Applying Concepts** Why was hydrochloric acid included with the pepsin in step 4? Did you add hydrochloric acid to the amylase solution? Why or why not?
2. **Observing** What effect did pepsin have on the egg white? Was your prediction correct? Explain your answer.
3. **Observing** What effect did water, and water with hydrochloric acid, have on the egg white? What was the purpose of including these tests?
4. **Drawing Conclusions** Describe the results of the experiments you designed. Do the enzymes you tested act only on specific compounds? Explain your answer.
5. **SAFETY** Explain how you demonstrated safe practices when working with hydrochloric acid.

Go Further

Designing Experiments What factors affect the rates of the reactions you tested? How could you increase these rates? Design one or more experiments to test the effects of changing one of these factors. Remember to write a prediction and to control variables. After obtaining approval from your teacher, carry out your experiment(s).

Analyze and Conclude

1. Pepsin works in the acidic environment of the stomach. Students should not have added hydrochloric acid to the amylase solution, because amylase works in the more neutral environment of the mouth.
2. Pepsin breaks down the protein in the egg white in the presence of hydrochloric acid because it needs an acidic environment to work effectively.
3. They had no effect. They were included as controls.
4. Students should find that amylase can digest starch but not protein.
5. Students should say that they wore aprons, goggles, and plastic gloves and that they notified their teacher and washed the affected area with large amounts of cool water if they spilled any hydrochloric acid.

Go Further

Possible factors to test include temperature, pH, and surface area. Increasing the temperature to 37°C, decreasing the pH (for pepsin), and chopping the foods finer to increase surface area all will increase the reaction rate.

Chapter 38 Study Guide

Study Tip

Divide the class into pairs, and have members of each pair quiz each other by making up questions on the Vocabulary terms and Key Concepts. Have students make flashcards for any questions they cannot answer correctly.

Thinking Visually

Flowcharts should include all the digestive organs in sequence, including the mouth, esophagus, stomach, small intestine, and large intestine. Organs should be correctly labeled, and arrows should indicate the direction of food through the system.

Chapter 38 Assessment

Reviewing Content

1. c **2.** c **3.** b **4.** c **5.** c **6.** b **7.** c **8.** d **9.** a **10.** c

Understanding Concepts

11. The body uses food for energy and as building blocks to make or repair body tissues.

12. Carbohydrates and fats provide the body with energy.

13. Proteins provide the raw materials for growth and repair. They have regulatory and transport functions. The enzymes that make biochemical reactions efficient are proteins.

14. The food pyramid gives you specific information based on your age, gender, and activity level. The pyramid also supplies you with the number of servings of different types of food that should be included each day in a balanced diet.

15. A flap of tissue known as the epiglottis is forced over the opening to the air passageways as swallowing occurs.

16. Enzymes chemically break down large food molecules into smaller molecules that can be absorbed and used by the cells of the body.

17. Mechanical digestion is a physical process. Chemical digestion involves the breaking of bonds.

Chapter 38 Study Guide

38–1 Food and Nutrition

Key Concepts

- The nutrients that the body needs are water, carbohydrates, fats, proteins, vitamins, and minerals.
- Every cell in the human body needs water because many of the body's processes, including chemical reactions, take place in water.

Vocabulary

Calorie, p. 971
carbohydrate, p. 972
fat, p. 972
protein, p. 973
vitamin, p. 974
mineral, p. 975

38–2 The Process of Digestion

Key Concepts

*BI 9.f

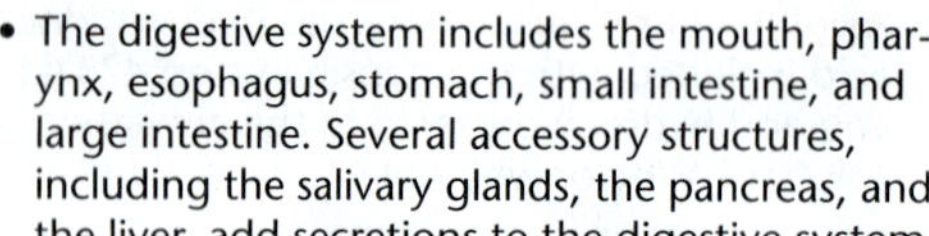

- The digestive system includes the mouth, pharynx, esophagus, stomach, small intestine, and large intestine. Several accessory structures, including the salivary glands, the pancreas, and the liver, add secretions to the digestive system.
- The function of the digestive system is to help convert foods into simpler molecules that can be absorbed and used by the cells of the body.

Vocabulary

amylase, p. 979
esophagus, p. 980
peristalsis, p. 980
stomach, p. 980
chyme, p. 981
small intestine, p. 981
pancreas, p. 981
liver, p. 982
villus, p. 982
large intestine, p. 984

38–3 The Excretory System

Key Concepts

*BI 9.g

- The kidneys play an important role in maintaining homeostasis. They regulate the water content of the blood and, therefore, blood volume; maintain blood pH; and remove waste products from the blood.
- As blood enters a nephron through the arteriole, impurities are filtered out and emptied into the collecting duct. The purified blood exits the nephron through the venule.

Vocabulary

kidney, p. 986
ureter, p. 986
urinary bladder, p. 986
nephron, p. 986
filtration, p. 987
glomerulus, p. 987
Bowman's capsule, p. 987
reabsorption, p. 987
loop of Henle, p. 987
urethra, p. 987

Thinking Visually

Create a flowchart that shows the path of food through the organs of the digestive system.

CHAPTER RESOURCES

Print:

- ***Teaching Resources,*** Chapter Vocabulary Review, Graphic Organizer, Chapter 38 Tests: Levels A and B

Technology:

- ***Computer Test Bank,*** Chapter 38 Test
- ***iText,*** Chapter 38 Assessment

Chapter 38 Assessment

Interactive textbook with assessment at PHSchool.com

Reviewing Content

Choose the letter that best answers the question or completes the statement.

1. The amount of energy in foods is measured in
   a. ATP. c. Calories.
   b. carbohydrates. d. disaccharides.
2. The nutrients that are the main source of energy for the body are
   a. proteins. c. carbohydrates.
   b. fats. d. vitamins.
3. Inorganic nutrients that your body needs, usually in small amounts, are called
   a. vitamins. c. proteins.
   b. minerals. d. amino acids.
4. Much of mechanical digestion takes place in the
   a. esophagus. c. mouth.
   b. large intestine. d. small intestine.
5. An enzyme in saliva that breaks the chemical bonds in starch, releasing sugar, is
   a. pepsin. c. amylase.
   b. bile. d. chyme.
6. Muscle contractions that help to squeeze food through the esophagus are known as
   a. chemical digestion. c. chyme.
   b. peristalsis. d. microvilli.
7. Going without food affects the amount of urea in the urine. The graph shows that the amount of urea excreted in urine
   a. increases steadily during 14 days of fasting.
   b. decreases steadily during 14 days of fasting.
   c. increases for the first few days of fasting.
   d. will be 6 grams after 16 days of fasting.

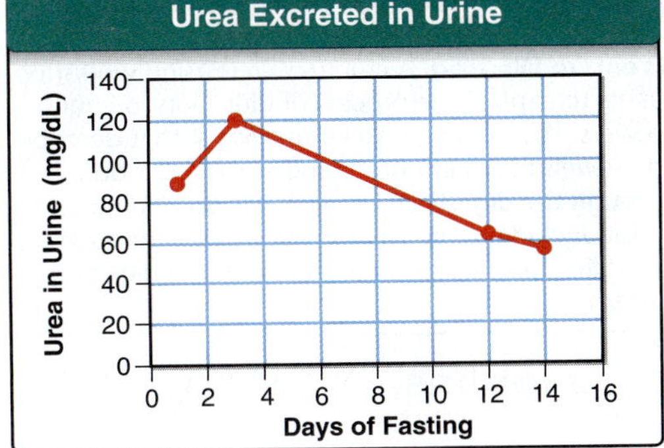

8. Most absorption of the end products of digestion into the circulatory system occurs
   a. in the mouth.
   b. through the lining of the esophagus.
   c. in the stomach.
   d. through the villi of the small intestine.
9. The basic functional unit of the kidney is the
   a. nephron.
   b. Bowman's capsule.
   c. glomerulus.
   d. loop of Henle.
10. Urine is excreted from the body through the
   a. ureter.
   b. urinary bladder.
   c. urethra.
   d. renal vein.

Understanding Concepts

11. What are the two primary functions of food in the body?
12. Which nutrients provide the body with energy?
13. What three ways are proteins important to the body?
14. What information is given in the new food pyramid?
15. Explain why swallowed food does not usually enter the airway leading to the lungs.
16. What role do enzymes play during digestion?
17. How do mechanical digestion and chemical digestion differ?
18. Describe the functions of hydrochloric acid and pepsin in the stomach.
19. Describe the functions of the pancreas.
20. How is the structure of the villi adapted to their function?
21. What is the primary function of the large intestine?
22. What causes peptic ulcers?
23. What materials are filtered from the blood in the kidney? What materials remain in the blood?
24. What kinds of filtered materials are reabsorbed by the blood in the kidney?
25. How is the activity of the kidney controlled?

HOMEWORK GUIDE

Section:	Questions:
Section 38–1	1–3, 11–14, 27, 30
Section 38–2	4–6, 8, 15–22, 26, 28, 29, 31, 32
Section 38–3	7, 9, 10, 23–25, 33

Interactive Textbook

If your class subscribes to the iText, your students can go online to access an interactive version of the Student Edition and a self-test.

(Continued from page 992)

18. Hydrochloric acid activates the enzyme pepsin, which begins the complex process of protein digestion by breaking proteins into smaller polypeptide fragments.

19. The pancreas produces hormones that regulate blood sugar; enzymes that break down carbohydrates, proteins, lipids, and nucleic acids; and sodium bicarbonate, a base that neutralizes stomach acid, allowing these enzymes to work effectively.

20. The villi contain a network of capillaries and lymph vessels that absorb nutrients from the small intestine. Each villus is covered with fingerlike projections called microvilli. These projections greatly increase the surface area available for absorption of nutrients.

21. The primary function of the large intestine is to remove water from undigested food before this material is eliminated from the body.

22. Prior to 1980, doctors thought peptic ulcers were caused by too much stomach acid. Since 1980, doctors have known that many, if not all, peptic ulcers are caused by bacterial infections.

23. Water, urea, glucose, salts, amino acids, and some vitamins are filtered from the blood in the kidney. Plasma proteins, cells, and platelets remain in the blood.

24. Most of the water and nutrients are reabsorbed by the blood in the kidney.

25. The activity of the kidney is controlled by the composition of blood itself and by the action of hormones that are released in response to the composition of blood.

Chapter 38 Assessment

Critical Thinking

26. Individuals can survive without a stomach if they are given predigested foods. However, they could not survive without a small intestine, which is needed for nutrient absorption.

27. Diets with a limited variety of foods may be unhealthy because they may not provide all the vitamins, minerals, and other nutrients needed for good health.

28. a. Hydrochloric acid, protein, and fat **b.** The amounts of bicarbonate and digestive enzymes secreted are equal. **c.** The amount of bicarbonate secreted decreases and the amount of digestive enzymes secreted increases.

29. One experimental design is to have subjects chew soda crackers until they start to taste sweet. Because starches are broken down into sugars when they are digested, the sweet taste is an indication that starch digestion begins in the mouth.

30. They might be healthier because their high-carbohydrate, low-protein, low-fat diets are closer to the balanced diet represented by the food pyramid.

31. An antibiotic that killed all the bacteria in your body would destroy the beneficial bacteria in the large intestine that normally help remove water from waste. As a result, you could develop vitamin deficiencies. You may also be subject to bacterial infections from pathogens that are normally held in check by the usual populations of harmless bacteria.

32. Prolonged chewing would result in more chemical digestion of starches in the mouth. It would also aid in the mechanical digestion of both carbohydrates and proteins, which in turn would promote chemical digestion of these nutrients.

33. Kidney failure can be fatal because, without the kidneys to filter wastes and excess water from the blood, these substances would accumulate to toxic levels.

Focus on the BIG Idea

The kidneys play a role in homeostasis by regulating the water content of blood, volume of blood, and blood pH and by removing chemical waste products from blood.

Chapter 38 Assessment

Critical Thinking

26. **Inferring** Individuals who have had part, or even all, of their stomachs removed can survive if fed predigested food. Do you think the same individuals could survive without a small intestine? Explain your answer.

27. **Applying Concepts** Fad diets that boast of rapid weight loss often become popular. Many of these diets involve eating only a limited variety of foods. Explain why these diets are an unhealthy way to lose weight.

28. **Using Tables and Graphs** Pancreatic juice contains sodium bicarbonate and digestive enzymes. The juice is secreted by the pancreas in response to the specific composition of chyme in the upper portion of the small intestine. The graph below shows the secretions of the pancreas in response to the presence of three different substances.
    - a. Each pair of bar graphs represents the response of the pancreas to a different variable. What are the three variables?
    - b. How does the presence of protein affect the amounts of bicarbonate and digestive enzymes secreted?
    - c. How does the presence of fat affect the composition of pancreatic juice?

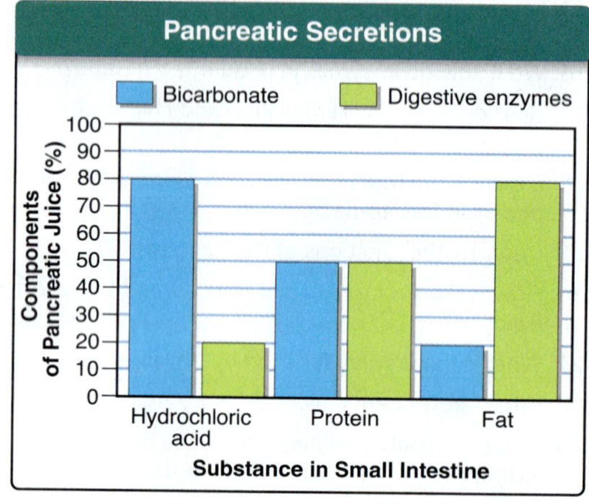

29. **Designing Experiments** Your friend tells you that the digestion of starches begins in the stomach. You suggest that starch digestion begins in the mouth. Design an experiment to show that your hypothesis is correct.

30. **Applying Concepts** In some countries, people have diets that contain more complex carbohydrates and fewer fats and proteins than the typical American diet. What are two reasons such diets might be healthier than the typical American diet?

31. **Inferring** Suppose your doctor prescribed an antibiotic that killed all the bacteria in your body. What effect would this have on your digestive system?

32. **Formulating Hypotheses** How would prolonged chewing affect the digestion of carbohydrates and proteins?

33. **Applying Concepts** Explain why kidney failure can be a fatal condition.

Homeostasis In Chapter 1, you learned that an organism maintains an internal stability called homeostasis. Explain how the kidneys play a role in this process.

Writing in Science

Imagine you are a nutritionist and someone has come to you wanting your advice on taking vitamin and mineral supplements. Using **Figure 38–6** and **Figure 38–7**, recommend a one-day food plan that the person could follow to meet his or her vitamin and mineral needs without taking supplements.

Performance-Based Assessment

Creative Writing A children's television workshop wants to explain the process of digestion to young viewers. You are asked to write a script that describes the travels of a hamburger and hamburger bun through the digestive system. Write an outline of your script, including information about what happens to the different nutrients in each part of the digestive system.

For: An interactive self-test
Visit: PHSchool.com
Web Code: cba-0380

Writing in Science

Students' food plans may vary. Assess the plans on the basis of their vitamin and mineral content in comparison with percent daily values. In general, a diet containing green leafy vegetables, grains, legumes, and dairy products will provide adequate amounts of most vitamins and minerals.

Performance-Based Assessment

Students might write a script that describes a trip through the digestive system for nutrients in the hamburger (fats and proteins) and in the bun (carbohydrates). The script should show that students understand how and where each nutrient is digested, as summarized in Figure 38–12.

Standards Practice

Success Tracker™

Online at PHSchool.com

Test-Taking Tip When you answer a question based on experimental data, read the description of the experiment carefully to determine the steps followed. Then, try to see if there are any trends in the data. For example, "if x increases, what happens to y?"

Directions: Choose the letter that best answers the question or completes the statement.

1. Each of the following aids in the process of digestion EXCEPT
   A teeth.
   B kidney.
   C stomach.
   D small intestine.

2. What moves food through the esophagus?
   A gravity
   B the cardiac sphincter
   C muscle contractions
   D the epiglottis

3. In the human body, hydrochloric acid is responsible for the low pH of the contents of the ***BI 9.f**
   A kidney.
   B gallbladder.
   C liver.
   D stomach.

4. Which is NOT a function of the kidneys?
   A removal of waste products from the blood
   B maintenance of blood pH
   C regulation of water content of the blood
   D excretion of carbon dioxide

5. The main function of the digestive system is to
   A break down large, insoluble molecules into smaller, soluble molecules.
   B excrete oxygen and carbon dioxide.
   C synthesize minerals and vitamins needed for a healthy body.
   D add essential vitamins to blood.

6. In the kidneys, both useful substances and wastes are removed from the blood by ***BI 9.g**
   A reabsorption.
   B excretion.
   C dialysis.
   D filtration.

Questions 7–8 Use the data in the table to answer the questions that follow.

A student is studying the effect of temperature on the action of an enzyme in stomach fluid. The enzyme digests protein. An investigation was set up using five identical test tubes, each containing 40 mL of stomach fluid and 20 mm of glass tubing filled with gelatin. After 48 hours, the amount of gelatin digested in each tube was measured in millimeters. The results for the five test tubes are shown in the table.

Effect of Temperature on Enzyme Action

Test Tube	Temperature (°C)	Amount of Digestion After 48 Hours
1	2	0.0 mm
2	10	3.0 mm
3	22	4.5 mm
4	37	8.0 mm
5	100	0.0 mm

7. Which is the manipulated (independent) variable in this investigation? **8IIE 9.c**
   A gastric fluid
   B length of glass tubing
   C temperature
   D time

8. An additional test tube was set up that was identical to the other test tubes and placed at a temperature of 15°C for 48 hours. What amount of digestion would you expect to occur in this test tube?
   A less than 3.0 mm
   B between 3.0 and 4.5 mm
   C between 4.5 mm and 8.0 mm
   D more than 8.0 mm

Standards Practice

1. B 2. C 3. D 4. D 5. A 6. D 7. C 8. B

Success Tracker™

Online at PHSchool.com

Have students check their understanding of the chapter by logging onto Success Tracker.

Go Online PHSchool.com

Your students can independently test their knowledge of the chapter and print out their test results for your files.

Chapter Planner 39 Endocrine and Reproductive Systems

Section and Section Objectives	Time	STANDARDS NCLB	STANDARDS Biology	Activities and Labs
39–1 The Endocrine System, pp. 997–1002 **39.1.1** ***State*** the function of the endocrine system. **39.1.2** ***Describe*** hormones and glands. **39.1.3** ***Explain*** how the endocrine system maintains homeostasis.	2 periods (1 block)		BI 9.c, *BI 9.i	SE: ***Inquiry Activity,*** Where in cells do hormones go?, p. 996 L2 TE: ***Demonstration,*** p. 998 L1 L2
39–2 Human Endocrine Glands, pp. 1003–1008 **39.2.1** ***Identify*** the functions of the major endocrine glands.	2 periods (1 block)	BI 9.b	*BI 9.i	TE: ***Demonstration,*** p. 1007 L1 L2 SE: ***Exploration,*** Modeling Blood Glucose Regulation, p. 1025 L2
39–3 The Reproductive System, pp. 1009–1015 **39.3.1** ***Describe*** sexual development. **39.3.2** ***Explain*** the functions of the male and female reproductive systems. **39.3.3** ***Identify*** the four phases of the menstrual cycle.	2 periods (1 block)	BI 2.b	*BI 9.i	TE: ***Demonstration,*** p. 1010 L1 L2 LMA: Chapter 39 Lab L2 L3 LMB: Chapter 39 Lab L1 L2
39–4 Fertilization and Development, pp. 1016–1024 **39.4.1** ***Describe*** fertilization. **39.4.2** ***Identify*** the stages of early development. **39.4.3** ***Describe*** the function of the placenta. **39.4.4** ***Outline*** the life cycle after birth.	3 periods (1 1/2 blocks)			TE: ***Build Science Skills,*** p. 1017 L1 L2 TE: ***Demonstration,*** p. 1019 L1 L2 SE: ***Quick Lab,*** How do embryos develop?, p. 1022 L2
Chapter Assessment, pp. 1026–1029	1 period (1/2 block)			

ACTIVITY PLANNER

SE: *Inquiry Activity,* p. 996; 10 min.; 2 test tubes with stoppers, 2 droppers, water, vegetable oil, food coloring, annatto coloring

TE: *Demonstration,* p. 998; 10 min.; empty egg carton, scissors, water

TE: *Demonstration,* p. 1007; 5 min.; glucose test strips, paper cup, water, yellow food coloring, sugar

TE: *Demonstration,* p. 1010; 10 min.; prepared slide of sperm cell, microscope

TE: *Build Science Skills,* p. 1017; 15 min.; modeling clay

TE: *Demonstration,* p. 1019; 5 min.; raw egg, resealable gallon-size storage bag, water

SE: *Quick Lab,* p. 1022; 20 min.; dropper pipette, early-stage frog embryos, depression slide, dissecting microscope, prepared slides of frog embryos

SE: *Exploration,* p. 1025; 40 min.; construction paper of three different colors, scissors

PLANNING KEY

Ability Levels

for students performing . . .

below grade level L1

at grade level L2

above grade level L3

Print Components

SE	Student Edition	LA	Lab Assessment
TE	Teacher's Edition	BTM	Biotechnology Manual
RSW	Reading & Study Workbook A	IDM	Issues and Decision Making
ARSW	Adapted Reading & Study Workbook B	LW	Lab Worksheets
TR	Teaching Resources	LMA	Laboratory Manual A
IF	Investigations in Forensics	LMB	Laboratory Manual B

Tech Components

CTB	Computer Test Bank
BD	BioDetectives DVD
TP	Transparencies Plus
PLM	Probeware Lab Manual
ABC	ABC DVD Library
LS	Lab Simulations
VL	Virtual Labs

Interactive Textbook — Interactive textbook with assessment at PHSchool.com

Program Resources	Assessment	Media and Technology
TR: Lesson Plan 39–1, Section Summary, p. 180 L1, p. 191 L2, Worksheets, pp. 183–185 L1, pp. 193–195 L2 **RSW:** Section 39–1 L2 **ARSW:** Section 39–1 L1	**SE:** 39–1 Section Assessment, p. 1002 **TR:** Section Review 39–1	**iText:** Section 39–1 **TP:** 39–1 Interest Grabber, Section Outline, Hormone Action, Figure 39–2
TR: Lesson Plan 39–2, Section Summary, p. 180 L1, p. 191 L2, Worksheets, pp. 186 L1, pp. 196–198 L2 **LW:** Chapter 39 Exploration L1 L2 L3 **RSW:** Section 39–2 L2 **ARSW:** Section 39–2 L1 **IDM:** Issues and Decisions 43 L2 L3	**SE:** 39–2 Section Assessment, p. 1008 **TR:** Section Review 39–2	**iText:** Section 39–2 **TP:** 39–2 Interest Grabber, Section Outline, Concept Map, Actions of Insulin and Glucagon **ABC:** 47 Regulation of Blood Sugar
TR: Lesson Plan 39–3, Section Summary, p. 181 L1, p. 191 L2, Worksheets, pp. 187–188 L1, pp. 199–201 L2 **RSW:** Section 39–3 L2 **ARSW:** Section 39–3 L1	**SE:** 39–3 Section Assessment, p. 1015 **TR:** Section Review 39–3	**iText:** Section 39–3 **TP:** 39–3 Interest Grabber, Section Outline, Menstrual Cycle, Figure 39–12, Figure 39–14
TR: Lesson Plan 39–4, Section Summary, p. 182 L1, p. 192 L2, Worksheets, p. 189 L1, p. 202–203 L2, Enrichment L2 L3 **RSW:** Section 39–4 L2 **ARSW:** Section 39–4 L1 **IDM:** Issues and Decisions 6, 45 L2 L3	**SE:** 39–4 Section Assessment, p. 1024 **TR:** Section Review 39–4	**iText:** Section 39–4 **TP:** 39–4 Interest Grabber, Section Outline, Fertilization and Implantation, Figure 39–22
	SE: Chapter 39 Assessment, pp. 1026–1029 **TR:** Chapter Vocabulary Review, Graphic Organizer, Chapter 39 Test	**iText:** Chapter 39 Assessment **CTB:** Chapter 39 Test

Go Online

Students can do research, share data, and test their knowledge online.

TIME SAVER — PRESSED FOR TIME?

To Preview the Chapter

- Introduce students to Key Concepts and Vocabulary terms in each section.
- Assign the Reading Strategies for each section.

To Cover the Chapter Quickly

- Have students read all of Sections 39–1 and 39–2, and in Section 39–3, have them read Sexual Development and Figures 39–12 and 39–14.
- Assign the Section Review 39–1; questions 1–7, 11–14, 18, 30, 32, and 36 in Chapter 39 Assessment; and questions 1–11 in the Chapter 39 Standards Practice.

To Review the Chapter

- Assign the Section Reviews 39–1 and 39–3 in the Reading and Study Workbook or the Adapted Reading and Study Workbook.
- Assign the Section Reviews for 39–1 and 39–3 and the Chapter Vocabulary Review for Chapter 39 in the Teaching Resources.

CHAPTER 39

ENGAGE/EXPLORE

Inquiry Activity

Objective Students will be able to infer that substances can pass through cell membranes if they are soluble in oil.

Skill Focus Observing, Inferring

Materials 2 test tubes with stoppers, 2 droppers, water, vegetable oil, food coloring, annatto coloring (Annatto coloring is used to color butter and cheese. It comes from the pulp around the seeds of a tropical dicotyledonous tree.)

Time 10 minutes

Advance Prep You can substitute turmeric for annatto.

Safety Remind students to handle the test tubes carefully.

Strategy Relate the activity to hormone action. Tell students that some hormones can cross the cell membrane and work inside the cell, whereas other hormones cannot cross the cell membrane and must work at the cell surface.

Expected Outcome Students should observe that food coloring dissolves in water and annatto coloring dissolves in oil.

Think About It

1. The food coloring dissolves in water. The annatto coloring dissolves in oil.
2. Food coloring cannot pass through cell membranes. Annatto coloring can pass through cell membranes.

Assess Prior Knowledge

Have students recall a time when they were startled by something frightening, such as someone jumping unexpectedly out of the shadows. Ask: **What did it feel like to be startled?** *(Students are likely to mention such physiological reactions to fear as rapid heart rate, shortness of breath, and sweaty palms.)* Explain to students that these physical changes are due to nerve and hormone action. Students will learn about hormones in this chapter.

CHAPTER 39

Endocrine and Reproductive Systems

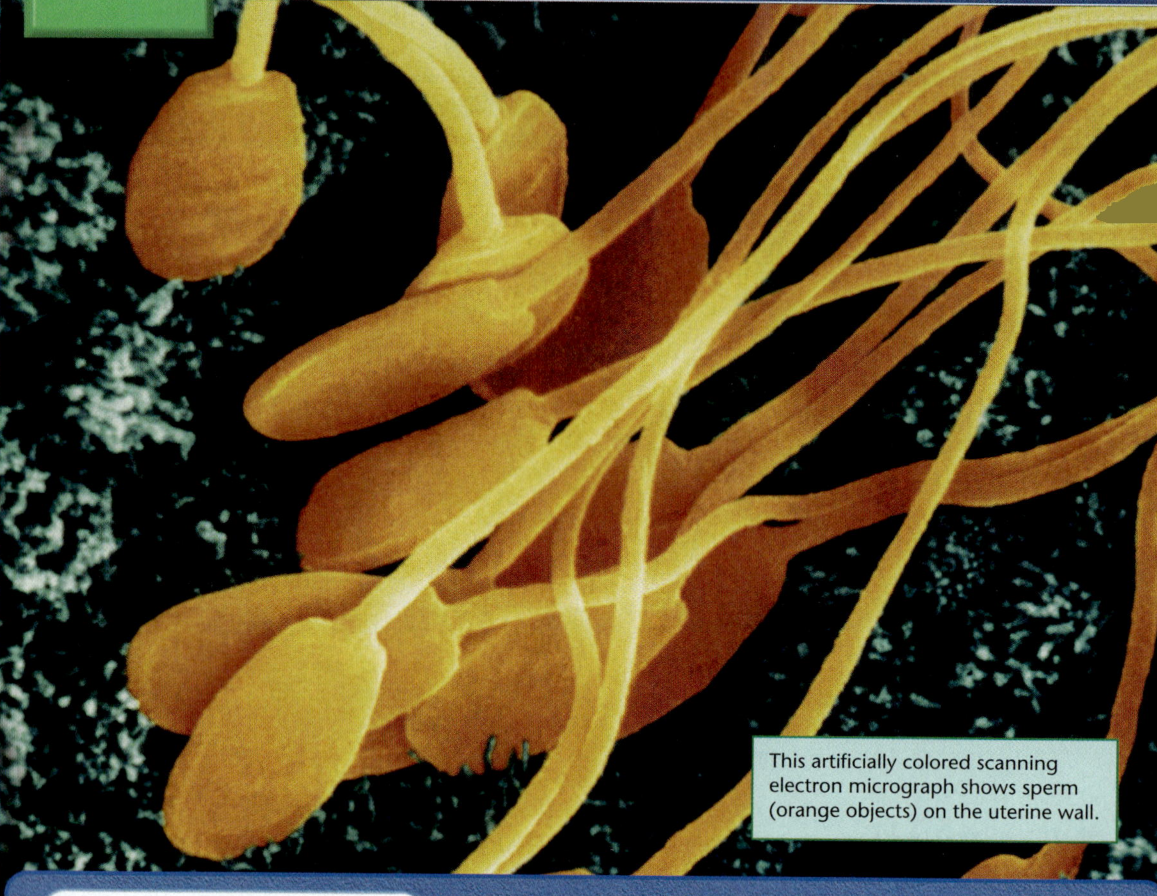

This artificially colored scanning electron micrograph shows sperm (orange objects) on the uterine wall.

Inquiry Activity

Where in cells do hormones go?

Procedure 

1. Fill 2 test tubes one third full of water. Add the same amount of vegetable oil (a lipid) to each test tube.
2. Add a few drops of food coloring to one of the test tubes. Stopper the test tube and turn it upside down to mix the contents.
3. Repeat step 2 using a drop of annatto coloring and the second test tube.

Think About It

1. **Observing** Did the food coloring dissolve in water or oil? Did the annatto coloring dissolve in water or oil?
2. **Inferring** Do you think food coloring can pass through cell membranes? (*Hint:* Cell membranes are composed of lipids.) Do you think annatto coloring can pass through cell membranes?

FACTS AND FIGURES

Plants have hormones, too

Humans and other animals are not the only organisms that depend on hormones to regulate functions within the organism. Plants have hormones, too. In fact, plants may depend on hormones even more than animals do. Unlike animals, plants do not have a nervous system to communicate messages from one part of the organism to another. As a result, plants must depend solely on hormones for such internal communication. Specific plant hormones regulate many important life cycle functions, including rates of growth, flowering, and seed production. Even the structure of plant leaves is controlled by hormones.

39–1 The Endocrine System

BI 9.c. Students know how feedback loops in the nervous and endocrine systems regulate conditions in the body.
***BI 9.i. Students know how hormones (including digestive, reproductive, osmoregulatory) provide internal feedback mechanisms for homeostasis at the cellular level and in whole organisms.**

If you had to get a message to just one or two of your friends, what would you do? You might use the telephone. Wires running from your house to theirs would carry the message almost instantaneously. The telephone is a good way to reach a small number of people, but what if you wanted to get that same message to thousands of people? You might decide to broadcast it on the radio, sending the message in a way that made it possible to contact thousands of people at once.

Your nervous system works much like the telephone: Many impulses move swiftly over a system of wirelike neurons that carry specific messages from one cell to another. But another system, the endocrine system, does what the nervous system generally cannot.  **The endocrine system is made up of glands that release their products into the bloodstream. These products deliver messages throughout the body.** In the same way that a radio broadcast can reach thousands or even millions of people in a large city, the chemicals released by the endocrine system can affect almost every cell in the body. In fact, the chemicals released by the endocrine system affect so many cells and tissues that the interrelationships of other organ systems to one another cannot be understood without taking the endocrine system into account.

Guide for Reading

Key Concepts
- What is the function of the endocrine system?
- How does the endocrine system maintain homeostasis?

Vocabulary
hormone
target cell
exocrine gland
endocrine gland
prostaglandin

Reading Strategy: Making Comparisons
As you read, list the differences and similarities between types of glands, and between types of hormones.

Hormones

The chemicals that "broadcast" messages from the endocrine system are called hormones. **Hormones** are chemicals released in one part of the body that travel through the bloodstream and affect the activities of cells in other parts of the body. Hormones do this by binding to specific chemical receptors on those cells. Cells that have receptors for a particular hormone are called **target cells.** If a cell does not have receptors or the receptors do not respond to a particular hormone, the hormone has no effect on it.

In general, the body's responses to hormones are slower and longer-lasting than the responses to nerve impulses. It may take several minutes, several hours, or even several days for a hormone to have its full effect on its target cells. A nerve impulse, on the other hand, may take only a fraction of a second to reach and affect its target cells.

▶ **Figure 39–1** **The endocrine system releases hormones that affect the activities of other cells.** Much of the increase in heart rate and breathing that the people are experiencing on this ride is due to the actions of hormones.

SECTION RESOURCES

Print:
- ***Teaching Resources,*** Lesson Plan 39–1, Adapted Section Summary 39–1, Adapted Worksheets 39–1, Section Summary 39–1, Worksheets 39–1, Section Review 39–1
- ***Reading and Study Workbook A,*** Section 39–1
- ***Adapted Reading and Study Workbook B,*** Section 39–1

Technology:
- ***iText,*** Section 39–1
- ***Transparencies Plus,*** Section 39–1

Section 39–1

BI 9.c, *BI 9.i

1 FOCUS

Objectives

39.1.1 ***State*** the function of the endocrine system.
39.1.2 ***Describe*** hormones and glands.
39.1.3 ***Explain*** how the endocrine system maintains homeostasis.

Guide for Reading

Reading Strategy

Explain to students that the prefix *endo-* means "within" and that endocrine glands are glands that secrete substances into the bloodstream within the body. Ask: **If *exo-* means "outside," what do you think exocrine glands are?** *(Glands that secrete substances to the outside)* These substances pass out of the glands into ducts, which lead either directly to the outside of the body (sweat or milk ducts) or into internal structures (saliva and digestive enzymes).

Reading Strategy

Have students study the figures and read the captions to preview the material in the section. Suggest that they write down any questions they have about the material based on the figures and then try to find the answers as they read the section.

2 INSTRUCT

Hormones

Build Science Skills

Using Analogies Help students understand the endocrine system by comparing it with familiar human relationships in which one person directs the actions of others—such as coach and team, conductor and orchestra members, traffic officer and motorists, and movie director and actors. Ask: **How are these relationships similar to those of the endocrine system?** *(An endocrine gland is like a director, the hormones are like verbal or visual directions, and cells are like the people being directed.)* L1

39–1 (continued)

Demonstration

Demonstrate hormone-target cell interactions with a model. Have students use an empty egg carton to model a tissue. First, they should create "target cells" by cutting small holes in the top of the carton over a few of the sections. Then, they should pour water over the egg carton to model a circulating hormone. Ask: **Which cells in your model contain hormone?** *(Just the target cells)* **What effect did the hormone have on the other cells?** *(none)* L1 L2

Glands

Build Science Skills

Inferring Call on students at random to compare and contrast endocrine and exocrine glands. *(Endocrine glands release their hormones into the bloodstream; exocrine glands release their products through ducts into open spaces.)* Then, ask: **Based on how they release their hormones, what can you infer about the effects on the body of hormones released by endocrine glands and products released by exocrine glands?** *(Hormones released by endocrine glands can affect cells throughout the body, whereas products released by exocrine glands tend to have local effects.)* L2

Use Visuals

Figure 39–2 Call students' attention to the figure. Make sure they understand that the ovaries are found only in females and the testes only in males. Name several different glands, and have students locate them in the figure. As students locate each gland, ask: **What hormones does the gland produce, and what roles do the hormones play in the body?** *(Students should identify the hormones and roles of the glands by reading the appropriate labels in the figure.)* L1

Glands

A gland is an organ that produces and releases a substance, or secretion. **Exocrine glands** release their secretions, through tubelike structures called ducts, directly to the organs that use them. Exocrine glands include those that release sweat, tears, and digestive juices. Unlike exocrine glands, **endocrine glands** release their secretions (hormones) directly into the bloodstream. **Figure 39–2** shows the location of the major endocrine glands in the human body.

CHECKPOINT *What are exocrine glands?*

▼ **Figure 39–2** Endocrine glands produce hormones that affect many parts of the body. **Interpreting Graphics** *What is the function of the pituitary gland?*

Hypothalamus The hypothalamus makes hormones that control the pituitary gland. In addition, it makes hormones that are stored in the pituitary gland.

Pituitary gland The pituitary gland produces hormones that regulate many of the other endocrine glands.

Parathyroid glands These four glands release parathyroid hormone, which regulates the level of calcium in the blood.

Thymus During childhood, the thymus releases thymosin, which stimulates T cell development and proper immune response.

Adrenal glands The adrenal glands release epinephrine and norepinephrine, which help the body respond to stress.

Pineal gland The pineal gland releases melatonin, which is involved in rhythmic activities, such as daily sleep-wake cycles.

Thyroid The thyroid produces thyroxine, which regulates metabolism throughout the body.

Pancreas The pancreas produces insulin and glucagon, which regulate the level of glucose in the blood.

Ovary Ovaries produce estrogen and progesterone. Estrogen is required for the development of female secondary sex characteristics and for the development of eggs. Progesterone prepares the uterus for a fertilized egg.

Testis The testes produce testosterone, which is responsible for sperm production and the development of male secondary sex characteristics.

UNIVERSAL ACCESS

Inclusion/Special Needs

Help students understand hormone action. First, guide them in creating two parallel flowcharts, one showing how a steroid hormone interacts with a target cell and the other showing how a nonsteroid hormone interacts with a target cell. Then, after the flowcharts are completed, have students identify differences between the two types of hormone action by comparing the flowcharts, step by step. L1

Advanced Learners

Challenge students to learn more about prostaglandins. Ask them to find out how prostaglandins were discovered, how they differ from other hormones, and the roles played by specific prostaglandins, such as those in the uterus, blood vessels, or bronchioles. Urge students to share what they learn with the class in a PowerPoint® presentation. L3

Hormone Action

Hormones may be classified as belonging to two general groups—steroid hormones and nonsteroid hormones. Steroid hormones are produced from a lipid called cholesterol. Nonsteroid hormones include proteins, small peptides, and modified amino acids. The two basic patterns of hormone action are shown in **Figure 39–3.**

Steroid Hormones Because they are lipids, steroid hormones can cross cell membranes easily, passing directly into the cytoplasm and even into the nuclei of target cells.

1. A steroid hormone enters a cell by passing directly across its cell membrane.
2. Once inside, it binds to a steroid receptor protein (found only in its target cells) to form a hormone-receptor complex.
3. The hormone-receptor complex enters the nucleus of the cell, where it binds to a DNA control sequence.
4. This binding initiates the transcription of specific genes to messenger RNA (mRNA).
5. The mRNA moves into the cytoplasm and directs protein synthesis.

Hormone-receptor complexes work as regulators of gene expression—they can turn on or turn off whole sets of genes. Because steroid hormones affect gene expression directly, they can produce dramatic changes in cell and organism activity.

Nonsteroid Hormones Nonsteroid hormones generally cannot pass through the cell membrane of their target cells.

1. A nonsteroid hormone binds to receptors on the cell membrane.
2. The binding of the hormone activates an enzyme on the inner surface of the cell membrane.
3. This enzyme activates secondary messengers that carry the message of the hormone inside the cell. Calcium ions, cAMP (cyclic adenosine monophosphate), nucleotides, and even fatty acids can serve as second messengers.
4. These second messengers can activate or inhibit a wide range of other cell activities.

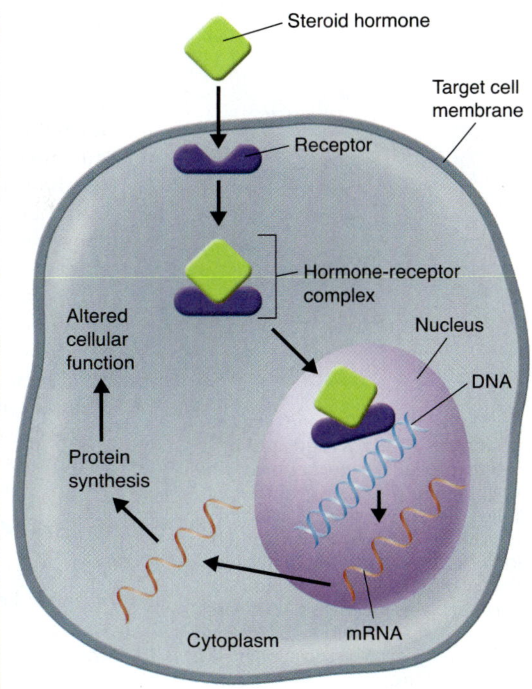

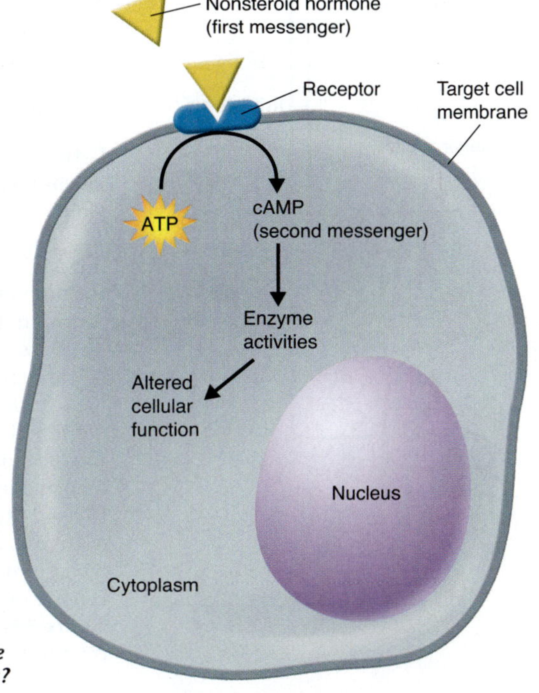

Figure 39–3 The two main types of hormones are steroid hormones (top) and nonsteroid hormones (bottom). **Comparing and Contrasting** *How are steroid hormones different from nonsteroid hormones?*

Hormone Action

Build Science Skills

Comparing and Contrasting
Work with the class to compare and contrast the two types of hormone action. On the board or an overhead projector, make a two-column table called Hormone Action, with one column headed Steroid Hormones and the other headed Nonsteroid Hormones. Then, challenge students to brainstorm similarities and differences between the two types of hormones. *(Examples of similarities include: both bind to receptors; both affect the activity of the receptor cell. Examples of differences include: steroid hormones are lipids, whereas nonsteroid hormones are proteins; steroid hormones enter cells and go to the cell nucleus, whereas nonsteroid hormones stay outside of the cell and work via a secondary messenger.)* As the similarities and differences are identified, record them in the table. Suggest that students copy the table into their class notes. L1 L2

Use Visuals

Figure 39–3 Ask: **Why does the green hormone enter the top cell whereas the yellow hormone stays outside the bottom cell?** *(The green hormone is a steroid hormone, and it can cross cell membranes. The yellow hormone is a nonsteroid hormone, so it cannot cross cell membranes.)* **Why does the steroid hormone exert a greater influence on cell activity?** *(It enters the nucleus of the cell, where it regulates gene expression directly.)*

TEACHER TO TEACHER

To demonstrate the second messenger mechanism, I use a model. Prior to class, I arrange for another teacher to send a student from his or her class to my class with a message, such as "turn out the lights." The message is placed in an envelope with my name on it and the name of a student in my class. The student from the other class enters my classroom and hands the envelope to me. I hand the envelope to my student whose name is also on the envelope. This student opens the envelope and responds to the message. Then, I challenge students to tell me who represented the first messenger *(the student from the other class)*, the receptor *(me)*, and the second messenger *(my student)*.

*—Sheila Smith
Biology Teacher
Terry High School
Terry, MS*

Answers to . . .

CHECKPOINT *Glands that release their secretions into local tissues through ducts*

Figure 39–2 *The pituitary produces hormones that regulate the activity of many other endocrine glands.*

Figure 39–3 *Steroid hormones can cross cell membranes. Nonsteroid hormones generally cannot cross cell membranes.*

39–1 (continued)

Prostaglandins

Build Science Skills

Inferring Point out that prostaglandins are called "local hormones" because they affect only nearby cells and tissues. Ask: **What advantage might this give prostaglandins over endocrine hormones?** *(Prostaglandins might work more quickly because they do not have to travel to another part of the body and the response is localized.)* L2

Control of the Endocrine System

Use Visuals

Figure 39–4 Check students' comprehension of the inhibition mechanism in the figure. Have them find the arrows that connect TSH and thyroxine to the hypothalamus. Then, ask: **How do TSH and thyroxine affect the hypothalamus?** *(Increased levels of TSH and thyroxine inhibit TRH secretion by the hypothalamus.)* L1 L2

Build Science Skills

Using Analogies Help students better understand the feedback mechanisms that control the endocrine system by extending the thermostat analogy in the text. Ask: **How does a thermostat control a furnace?** *(When the temperature falls below a set point, a sensor in the thermostat signals the furnace to switch on and produce heat; when the temperature rises above a set point, the sensor signals the furnace to switch off.)* Tell students that the thyroid gland is like a furnace because it can increase or decrease its output of the hormone thyroxine, which changes the rate of metabolism and, consequently, core body temperature. Ask: **If the thyroid is a furnace, what is the thermostat?** *(The hypothalamus, because it senses changes in the level of thyroxine or changes in internal body temperature and signals the anterior pituitary to release TSH)* L1 L2

▼ **Figure 39–4 One way the endocrine system is regulated by internal feedback mechanisms is by maintaining the rate of metabolism.** When the hypothalamus senses that the level of thyroxine in the blood is low, it secretes TRH. TRH stimulates the anterior pituitary to secrete TSH. TSH stimulates the thyroid to release thyroxine. Increased levels of TSH and thyroxine inhibit TRH secretion by the hypothalamus.

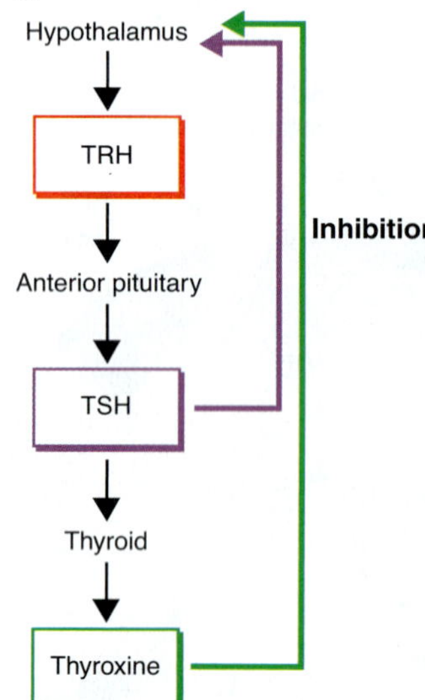

Prostaglandins

Until recently, the glands of the endocrine system were thought to be the only organs that produced hormones. However, except for red blood cells, all cells have been shown to produce small amounts of hormonelike substances called **prostaglandins** (prahs-tuh-GLAN-dinz). Prostaglandins get their name from a gland in the male reproductive system, the prostate, in which they were first discovered. Prostaglandins are modified fatty acids that are produced by a wide range of cells. They generally affect only nearby cells and tissues, and thus are known as "local hormones."

Some prostaglandins cause smooth muscles, such as those in the uterus, bronchioles, and blood vessels, to contract. One group of prostaglandins causes the sensation of pain in most headaches. Aspirin helps to stop the pain of a headache because it inhibits the synthesis of these prostaglandins.

Control of the Endocrine System

As powerful as they are, hormones are monitored by the body in order to keep the functions of different organs in balance. Even though the endocrine system is one of the master regulators of the body, it too must be controlled. **Like most systems of the body, the endocrine system is regulated by feedback mechanisms that function to maintain homeostasis.**

Recall that feedback inhibition occurs when an increase in any substance "feeds back" to inhibit the process that produced the substance in the first place. Heating and cooling systems, controlled by thermostats, are examples of mechanical feedback loops. The hormones of the endocrine system are biological examples of the same type of process.

Controlling Metabolism To see how an internal feedback mechanism regulates the activity of the endocrine system, let's look at the thyroid gland and its principal hormone, thyroxine. Thyroxine affects the activity of cells throughout the body, increasing their rate of metabolism. Recall that metabolism is the sum of all of the chemical reactions that occur in the body. A drop in thyroxine decreases the metabolic activity of cells.

Does the thyroid gland determine how much thyroxine to release on its own? No, instead the activity of the thyroid gland is controlled by the hypothalamus and the anterior pituitary gland. When the hypothalamus senses that the thyroxine level in the blood is low, it secretes thyrotropin-releasing hormone (TRH), a hormone that stimulates the anterior pituitary to secrete thyroid-stimulating hormone (TSH). TSH stimulates the release of thyroxine by the thyroid gland. High levels of thyroxine in the blood inhibit the secretion of TRH and TSH, which stops the release of additional thyroxine. This feedback loop, shown in **Figure 39–4,** keeps the level of thyroxine in the blood relatively constant.

FACTS AND FIGURES

Fast-acting hormones
In humans and most other animals, endocrine hormones bring about relatively slow changes, sometimes taking hours or even days to achieve their full effects. In some small animals, however, certain hormones produce a more immediate change. Examples are the hormones that cause vertebrates such as chameleons to change their color and pattern so they are camouflaged in their environment. The hormones that lead to such color changes usually produce their full effects in a matter of seconds. The effects are brought about by special color-containing cells in the skin, which change in size to produce a different color pattern. The color-containing cells are controlled by endocrine hormones that are produced in response to light patterns entering the eye of the animal.

Recall that the hypothalamus is also sensitive to temperature. When the core body temperature begins to drop, even if the level of thyroxine is normal, the hypothalamus produces extra TRH. The release of TRH stimulates the release of TSH, which stimulates the release of additional thyroxine. Thyroxine increases oxygen consumption and cellular metabolism. The increase in metabolic activity that results helps the body maintain its core temperature despite lower temperatures.

CHECKPOINT *What process does thyroxine control?*

Maintaining Water Balance Homeostatic mechanisms regulate the levels of a wide variety of materials dissolved in the blood and in extracellular fluids. These include minerals such as sodium, potassium, and calcium, and soluble proteins such as serum albumin, which is found in blood plasma. Most of the time, homeostatic systems operate so smoothly that we are scarcely aware of their existence. However, that is not the case with one of the most important homeostatic processes, the one that regulates the amount of water in the body.

When you exercise strenuously, you lose water as you sweat. If this water loss continued, your body would soon become dehydrated. Generally, that doesn't happen because your body's homeostatic mechanisms swing into action.

The hypothalamus contains cells that are sensitive to the concentration of water in the blood. As you lose water, the concentration of dissolved materials in the blood rises. The hypothalamus responds in two ways. First, the hypothalamus signals the pituitary gland to release a hormone called antidiuretic hormone (ADH). ADH molecules are carried by the bloodstream to the kidneys, where the removal of water from the blood is quickly slowed down. Later, you experience a sensation of thirst, a signal that you should take a drink to restore lost water.

When you finally get around to taking that drink, you might take in as much as 1 or 2 liters of fluid. Most of that water is quickly absorbed into the bloodstream. But this volume of water added to the blood would dilute it so much that the equilibrium between the blood and the cells of the body would be disturbed. Large amounts of water would diffuse across blood vessel walls into the tissues. The cells of the body would swell with the excess water.

Needless to say, this doesn't happen, because the same homeostatic mechanism intervenes. When the water content of the blood rises, the pituitary releases less ADH. In response to lower ADH levels, the kidneys remove water from the bloodstream, restoring the blood to its original concentration. This homeostatic system sets both upper and lower limits for blood water content: A water deficit stimulates the release of ADH, causing the kidneys to conserve water; an oversupply of water causes the kidneys to eliminate the excess water as a component of urine.

▼ **Figure 39–5** When exercising on a hot day, it is important to replenish lost liquid. **Applying Concepts** ***Explain why people who are exercising should drink fluids before they are thirsty.***

Demonstration

Remind students of the discussion of feedback inhibition in Section 35–1. Point out that the endocrine system is regulated by feedback inhibition mechanisms and that feedback inhibition is sometimes referred to as negative feedback. Demonstrate the difference between a positive- and a negative-feedback mechanism by dividing the class into two groups. Tell members of one group to take turns saying the word *positive*, with each student saying it louder than the previous person. Then, instruct members of the other group to take turns saying the word *negative*, with students alternating between saying it louder and saying it softer than the previous person. Conclude by asking: **How did negative feedback affect the volume?** *(It kept the volume more or less constant.)* **How did positive feedback affect the volume?** *(It steadily increased the volume.)* **When would a positive-feedback mechanism be useful?** *(Positive feedback intensifies a response until the condition that stimulated the response is under control. For example, the signal for formation of a blood clot will be amplified until the bleeding is under control and the signal is no longer produced.)* L1 L2

Build Science Skills

Using Models To help students understand how the body maintains water balance, create two flowcharts on the chalkboard, one illustrating a water deficit and one illustrating an oversupply of water. Call on students to fill in the steps for each flowchart. *(Deficit: hypothalamus signals pituitary → pituitary releases ADH → blood carries ADH to kidneys → kidneys decrease removal of water. Oversupply: water content of blood rises → pituitary releases less ADH → kidneys increase removal of water from blood)* L1 L2

BIO INSIGHTS — FACTS AND FIGURES

The power of hormones

The endocrine glands, despite their tremendous importance in the body, are amazingly small. The pituitary gland, which produces nine different hormones and controls most of the other endocrine glands, is only as large as a pea. All of the body's endocrine tissues combined would fit in the palm of one hand. The quantity of hormones produced by this small amount of glandular tissue is also slight. For example, the average woman produces only about 5 mL, or a teaspoonful, of the steroid hormone estrogen in her entire lifetime. Obviously, to have the far-reaching effects on the body that they do, hormones must be very powerful. In fact, most hormones are so potent that they are effective at concentrations as low as one part per million.

Answers to . . .

CHECKPOINT *Thyroxine controls the level of metabolic activity in cells.*

Figure 39–5 *They could become dehydrated before they experience a sensation of thirst.*

39–1 (continued)

Download a worksheet on the endocrine system for students to complete, and find additional teacher support from NSTA SciLinks.

Complementary Hormone Action

Build Science Skills

Applying Concepts Help students understand how hormones regulate calcium concentration. Ask: **What causes the parathyroid glands to produce PTH?** *(A decrease in the level of calcium in the blood)* **What does PTH do?** *(Stimulates the intestines to absorb more calcium, the kidneys to retain more calcium, and the bones to release calcium)* **What causes the thyroid gland to produce calcitonin?** *(An increase in the level of calcium in the blood)* **What does calcitonin do?** *(Stimulates the bones and kidneys to take up calcium and the intestines not to take up calcium)*

3 ASSESS

Evaluate Understanding

Have some students compare steroid and nonsteroid hormones, and have others name examples of each.

Reteach

Guide students in making two Venn diagrams, comparing and contrasting (1) exocrine and endocrine glands and (2) hormones and prostaglandins.

Focus on the BIG Idea

Steroid hormones are lipids, so they can pass through the cell membrane and enter cells. Nonsteroid hormones are not lipids, so they cannot pass through the cell membrane and must act from outside cells.

If your class subscribes to the iText, use it to review the Key Concepts in Section 39–1.

For: Links on the endocrine system
Visit: www.SciLinks.org
Web Code: cbn-0391

Complementary Hormone Action

Sometimes two hormones with opposite effects act to regulate part of the body's internal environment. One way to think about how the endocrine system functions is to think about driving a car. A good driver might be able to control a car on an open highway by using only the accelerator pedal. But driving around town, even a good driver would get into trouble using just the accelerator. There are too many situations in which the brake is needed to slow the car down.

In the same way, many endocrine functions depend on the complementary effects of two opposing hormones. Such a complementary system regulates the level of calcium ions in the bloodstream. The level of calcium dissolved in the bloodstream is kept within a narrow range. The two hormones that regulate calcium concentration are calcitonin, from the thyroid gland, and parathyroid hormone (PTH), from the parathyroid glands. Calcitonin decreases the level of calcium in the blood, while PTH increases it.

When blood calcium levels are too high, the thyroid secretes calcitonin. Calcitonin signals the kidneys to reabsorb less calcium as they form urine. Calcitonin also reduces the amount of calcium absorbed in the intestines and stimulates calcium deposition in the bones.

If calcium levels drop too low, PTH is released by the parathyroids. PTH, together with vitamin D, stimulates the intestine to absorb more calcium from food. PTH also causes the kidneys to retain more calcium, and it stimulates bone cells to release some of the calcium stored in bone tissue into the bloodstream.

You may be surprised that the body regulates calcium levels so carefully. This adaptation has evolved because calcium is one of the most important minerals in the body. If calcium levels drop below their normal range, blood cannot clot, muscles cannot contract, and the transport of materials across cell membranes may fail.

39–1 Section Assessment

1. **Key Concept** Describe the function of the endocrine system in the body.
2. **Key Concept** Explain how the endocrine system helps maintain homeostasis.
3. Compare endocrine glands and exocrine glands.
4. What are prostaglandins and why are they called "local hormones"?
5. **Critical Thinking Applying Concepts** What are the advantages of having both a nervous system and an endocrine system?

Focus on the BIG Idea

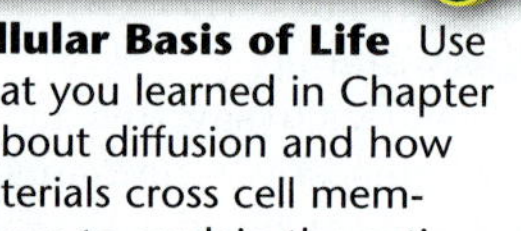

Cellular Basis of Life Use what you learned in Chapter 7 about diffusion and how materials cross cell membranes to explain the actions of steroid hormones and nonsteroid hormones.

39–1 Section Assessment

1. To produce hormones that affect the activities of cells throughout the body
2. The endocrine system, along with the autonomic nervous system, continually adjusts many body activities, helping the body maintain relatively constant internal conditions.
3. Endocrine glands secrete hormones directly into the bloodstream. Exocrine glands release their secretions through ducts.
4. All cells produce hormonelike substances called prostaglandins, which are called "local hormones" because they affect only nearby cells or tissues.
5. The nervous system broadcasts specific messages quickly to a limited number of cells, whereas the endocrine system broadcasts messages slowly to target cells throughout the body.

39–2 Human Endocrine Glands

BI 9.b. Students know how the nervous system mediates communication between different parts of the body and the body's interaction with the environment. ***BI 9.i.** Students know how hormones (including digestive, reproductive, osmoregulatory) provide internal feedback mechanisms for homeostasis at the cellular level and in whole organisms.**

The endocrine glands are scattered throughout the body. Generally, they do not have direct connections to one another. Like signals that are beamed throughout the country from a broadcast station, the hormones released from the endocrine glands into the bloodstream travel throughout the body, reaching almost every cell.

The human endocrine system regulates a wide variety of activities. Any improper functioning of an endocrine gland may result in a disease or a disorder. The major glands of the endocrine system include the pituitary gland, the hypothalamus, the thyroid gland, the parathyroid glands, the adrenal glands, the pancreas, and the reproductive glands.

Pituitary Gland

The **pituitary gland** is a bean-sized structure that dangles on a slender stalk of tissue at the base of the skull. As you can see in **Figure 39–6,** the gland is divided into two parts: the anterior pituitary and the posterior pituitary. **The pituitary gland secretes nine hormones that directly regulate many body functions and controls the actions of several other endocrine glands.**

Normal function of the pituitary gland is essential to good health. For example, if the pituitary gland produces too much growth hormone (GH) during childhood, the body grows too quickly and a condition called gigantism results. Too little GH during childhood causes a condition known as pituitary dwarfism, which can be treated by administering growth hormone. Growth hormone used to be in short supply. Today, however, genetically engineered bacteria are able to produce GH in large quantities.

Guide for Reading

Key Concept
- What are the functions of the major endocrine glands?

Vocabulary
pituitary gland
diabetes mellitus
ovary
testis

Reading Strategy: Finding Main Ideas Before you read, skim the text paragraphs in this section to find the boldface key sentences. Copy each sentence onto a notecard. As you read, note supporting details on the cards.

▼ **Figure 39–6 The pituitary gland, which controls many other endocrine glands, is located below the hypothalamus in the brain.** The pituitary gland has two lobes: an anterior lobe and a posterior lobe.

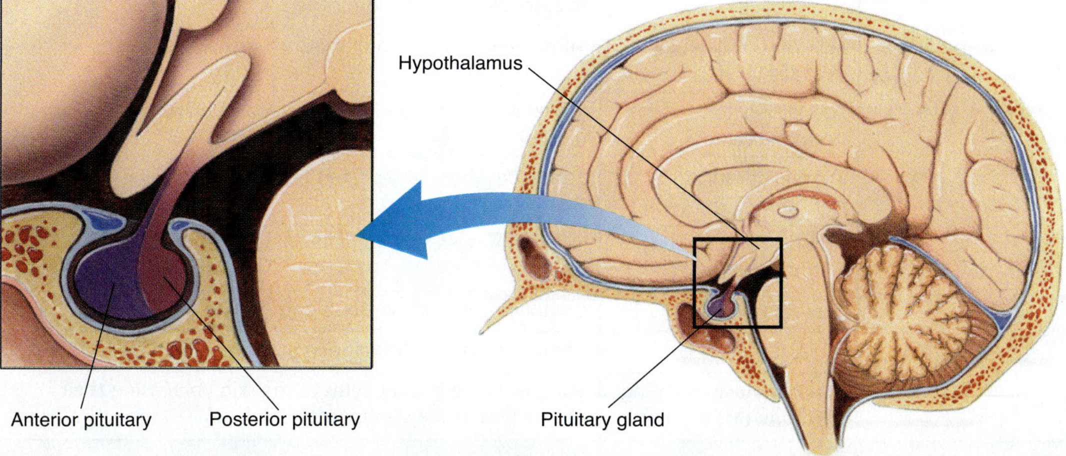

SECTION RESOURCES

Print:
- ***Teaching Resources,*** Lesson Plan 39–2, Adapted Section Summary 39–2, Adapted Worksheets 39–2, Section Summary 39–2, Worksheets 39–2, Section Review 39–2
- ***Reading and Study Workbook A,*** Section 39–2
- ***Adapted Reading and Study Workbook B,*** Section 39–2
- ***Issues and Decision Making,*** Issues and Decisions 43
- ***Lab Worksheets,*** Chapter 39 Exploration

Technology:
- ***iText,*** Section 39–2
- ***Animated Biological Concepts DVD,*** 47 Regulation of Blood Sugar
- ***Transparencies Plus,*** Section 39–2

Section 39–2

BI 9.b, *BI 9.i

1 FOCUS

Objective

39.2.1 ***Identify*** the functions of the major endocrine glands.

Guide for Reading

Vocabulary Preview

Before students read the section, have them preview new Vocabulary by skimming the section and making a list of the highlighted, boldface terms. They should leave spaces after the terms to write the definitions as they read the section.

Reading Strategy

Have students make a table with the headings *Endocrine Gland, Location, Hormones, and Functions.* As students read the section, they should fill in the table for each of the endocrine glands.

2 INSTRUCT

Pituitary Gland

Use Visuals

Figure 39–6 Explain to students that the close-up drawing on the left is greatly enlarged and that the pituitary gland is actually smaller than the tip of the little finger. Point out the close spatial relationship between the hypothalamus and pituitary, and relate it to control of the pituitary by the hypothalamus. Have students locate the anterior and posterior pituitary in the drawing on the left. Tell them that the word *anterior* means "toward the front." Ask: **What do you think the word *posterior* means?** *(Toward the back)* Relate Figure 39–6 to Figure 39–7 by asking: **Which pituitary hormones are produced by the anterior pituitary, and which are produced by the posterior pituitary?** *(FSH, LH, TSH, ACTH, GH, prolactin, and MSH are produced by the anterior pituitary. ADH and oxytocin are produced by the posterior pituitary.)* L1 L2

39–2 (continued)

Download a worksheet on glands for students to complete, and find additional teacher support from NSTA SciLinks.

Hypothalamus

Address Misconceptions

Students may have heard the pituitary gland referred to as the body's "master gland," because the pituitary's hormones control so many other glands and organs. Explain that scientists no longer refer to the pituitary gland in this way, because it is now known that the hypothalamus controls the pituitary. Ask: **What are the two mechanisms by which the hypothalamus controls the pituitary gland?** *(The hypothalamus manufactures ADH and oxytocin, releasing them directly into storage cells of the posterior pituitary and later stimulating their release directly into the bloodstream.)* L2

Build Science Skills

Applying Concepts Point out that the hypothalamus responds to stress as well as to sensory input, providing one route by which stress can affect health. Ask: **How could stress, by affecting the hypothalamus, indirectly affect health?** *(Stress could cause the hypothalamus to stimulate the pituitary to produce more or less of its hormones and, indirectly, stimulate the thyroid and other glands controlled by the pituitary to produce more or less of their hormones. These hormonal imbalances, in turn, could cause health problems.)* L2

For: Links on glands
Visit: www.SciLinks.org
Web Code: cbn-0392

ⓐ BI 9.b

Hypothalamus

The hypothalamus is the part of the brain above and attached to the posterior pituitary. **The hypothalamus controls the secretions of the pituitary gland.** The activity of the hypothalamus is influenced by the levels of hormones in the blood and by sensory information collected by other parts of the central nervous system. Interactions between the nervous system and the endocrine system take place at the hypothalamus.

The posterior pituitary is made up of axons belonging to cells called neurosecretory cells, whose cell bodies are in the hypothalamus. When these cell bodies are stimulated, the axons in the posterior pituitary release their hormones into the bloodstream. In a way, the posterior pituitary is an extension of the hypothalamus.

In contrast, the hypothalamus has indirect control of the anterior pituitary. The hypothalamus produces small amounts of chemicals called releasing hormones, which are secreted directly into blood vessels. The releasing hormones are carried by the circulatory system to the anterior pituitary, where they control the production and release of hormones.

The close connection between the hypothalamus and the pituitary gland means that the nervous and endocrine systems can act together to help coordinate body activities. Hormones released by the pituitary gland are listed in **Figure 39–7**.

CHECKPOINT *What is the role of releasing hormones?*

▼ **Figure 39–7** **The hypothalamus controls the secretions of the pituitary gland.** Notice the effect that each hormone produced by the pituitary gland has on the body.

Pituitary Gland Hormones

Pituitary Gland	Hormone	Action
Posterior pituitary	Antidiuretic hormone (ADH)	Stimulates the kidneys to reabsorb water from the collecting tubules
	Oxytocin	Stimulates contractions of uterus during childbirth; releases milk in nursing mothers
Anterior pituitary	Follicle-stimulating hormone (FSH)	Stimulates production of mature eggs and sperm
	Luteinizing hormone (LH)	Stimulates ovaries and testes; prepares uterus for implantation of fertilized egg
	Thyroid-stimulating hormone (TSH)	Stimulates the synthesis and release of thyroxine from the thyroid gland
	Adreno-corticotropic hormone (ACTH)	Stimulates release of some hormones from the adrenal cortex
	Growth hormone (GH)	Stimulates protein synthesis and growth in cells
	Prolactin	Stimulates milk production in nursing mothers
	Melanocyte-stimulating hormone (MSH)	Stimulates the melanocytes of the skin, increasing their production of the skin pigment melanin

ESL SUPPORT FOR ENGLISH LANGUAGE LEARNERS

Comprehension: Key Concepts

Beginning Prepare a two-column graphic organizer that lists the major endocrine glands in the left column and the function of each gland in the right column. Correctly pronounce each term. Then, ask questions that can be answered directly from the information in the graphic organizer, for example, "Which endocrine gland helps the body deal with stress?" L1

Intermediate Prepare a graphic organizer similar to the one described for beginning students, but leave the left column (the names of the endocrine glands) blank. Fill in the right column with the functions of the endocrine glands, using wording similar to that used in the boldface sentences found on pages 1003–1008. Then, direct the students to use the boldface sentences to find the information they need to complete the graphic organizer. L2

Thyroid Gland

If you look at **Figure 39–8,** you can see that the thyroid gland is located at the base of the neck and wraps around the upper part of the trachea. **The thyroid gland has the major role in regulating the body's metabolism.** Cells in the thyroid gland produce thyroxine, which is made up of the amino acid tyrosine and the mineral iodine. Remember that thyroxine affects nearly all of the cells of the body by regulating their metabolic rates. Thyroxine increases the rate of protein, carbohydrate, and fat metabolism as well as the rate of cellular respiration, which means that the cells release more heat and energy. Decreased levels of thyroxine can decrease the rate of cellular respiration and the amount of heat and energy released.

The homeostatic activities of the thyroid gland are so well controlled that you may never become aware of them. However, if the thyroid gland produces too much thyroxine, a condition called hyperthyroidism occurs. Hyperthyroidism results in nervousness, elevated body temperature, increased metabolic rate, increased blood pressure, and weight loss. Too little thyroxine causes a condition called hypothyroidism. Lower metabolic rates and body temperature, lack of energy, and weight gain are characteristics of this condition. In some cases, hypothyroidism can cause a goiter, an enlargement of the thyroid gland.

The importance of proper thyroid activity can be seen in parts of the world where food lacks enough iodine for the thyroid to produce normal amounts of thyroxine. Unable to produce the thyroxine needed for normal development, iodine-deficient infants suffer from a condition called cretinism (KREE-tuh-niz-um), in which neither the skeletal system nor the nervous system develops properly. Two effects of cretinism are dwarfism and severe mental retardation. Cretinism usually can be prevented by the addition of small amounts of iodine to table salt or other items in the food supply.

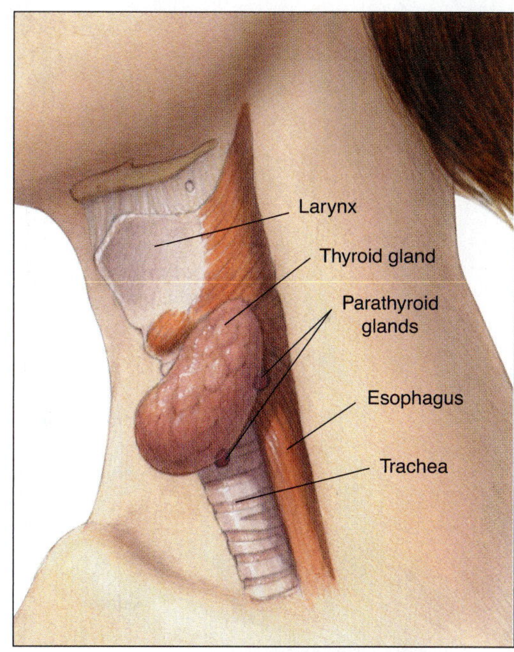

▲ **Figure 39–8 Hormones produced by the thyroid gland and the parathyroid glands maintain the level of calcium in the blood.** The thyroid gland wraps around the trachea.

Parathyroid Glands

The four parathyroid glands are found on the back surface of the thyroid gland. **Hormones from the thyroid gland and the parathyroid glands act to maintain homeostasis of calcium levels in the blood.** Parathyroid glands secrete parathyroid hormone (PTH). Recall that PTH and calcitonin have opposite effects on the body. PTH regulates the calcium levels in the blood by increasing the reabsorption of calcium in the kidneys and by increasing the uptake of calcium from the digestive system. Parathyroid hormone also affects other organ systems, promoting proper nerve and muscle function and bone structure.

Thyroid Gland

Make Connections

Health Science Explain that low levels of iodine in the diet may cause the thyroid gland to compensate by increasing in size and producing a noticeable swelling in the throat called a goiter. If possible, show students pictures of people with goiters. Also explain that lack of thyroxine in adults does not produce cretinism but a condition called myxedema, which is characterized by lethargy, puffiness, and mental dullness. Point out that people with myxedema can recover from the condition with no lasting effects. Ask: **Why are the effects of iodine deficiency permanent in young children but not in adults?** *(The effects are permanent in children because the hormone deficiency interferes with normal development, leaving the child with abnormal brain and body conditions when growth is complete.)* L2

Parathyroid Glands

Build Science Skills

Applying Concepts Challenge students to apply the concept of homeostasis to the parathyroid glands. Have them create a simple diagram, similar to the one in Figure 39–4 on page 1000, to show how the parathyroid glands regulate the calcium level in the blood. Their diagrams should show that a high blood calcium level leads to the secretion of parathyroid hormone, or PTH, which, in turn, stimulates the kidneys to reabsorb more calcium and the digestive system to take up more calcium. L1 L2

FACTS AND FIGURES

Effects of a faulty thyroid

Iodine deficiencies severe enough to cause thyroid problems once occurred largely in mountainous inland regions, such as the Alps or Andes. However, iodine deficiency is not the only cause of abnormal thyroid activity. Two autoimmune diseases, both more common in females than in males, also cause thyroid problems. One disease is Hashimoto's disease, which is the second most common cause of hypothyroidism, or underproduction of thyroid hormones. Some of the signs and symptoms of hypothyroidism are enlarged thyroid gland, slow heart rate, dry skin, fatigue, and weight gain. The other disease is Graves' disease. It causes hyperthyroidism, or overproduction of thyroid hormone. Symptoms of hyperthyroidism include enlarged thyroid gland, rapid heart rate, bulging eyes, hand tremor, and weight loss.

Answer to . . .

✓CHECKPOINT *Releasing hormones are chemical messengers from the hypothalamus that prompt the anterior pituitary to release its hormones.*

39–2 (continued)

Adrenal Glands

Use Visuals

Figure 39–9 Point out the adrenal glands' location on top of the kidneys. Have students find the kidneys in Figure 39–2 if they do not know where they are located. Then, have students find the two parts of the adrenal gland in Figure 39–9. Tell them that the term *cortex* refers to the outer part of an organ or gland. Ask: **What do you think the term *medulla* refers to?** *(The inner part of an organ or gland)* **Besides location, what relationship is there between the kidneys and the adrenal glands?** *(The adrenal cortex secretes aldosterone, which regulates the reabsorption of sodium ions and the excretion of potassium ions by the kidneys.)* L1 L2

Make Connections

Health Science Explain to students that when someone is under constant stress, the adrenal medulla may be continually stimulated to produce its "fight or flight" hormones. Ask: **What effect do you think this might have on the body over the long run?** *(The increased heart rate and blood pressure and other responses to epinephrine and norepinephrine would put wear and tear on the body and could lead to illness.)* L2

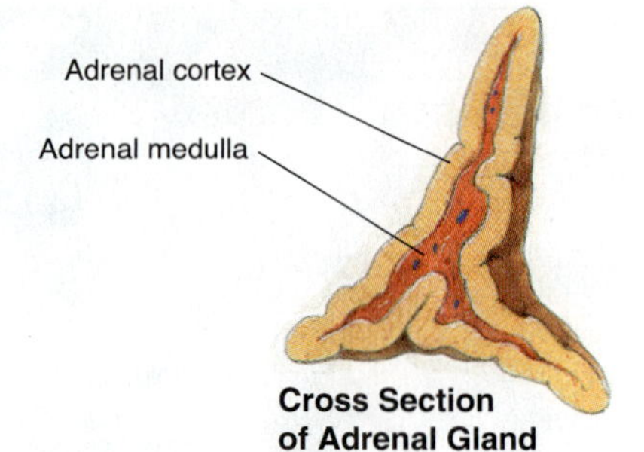

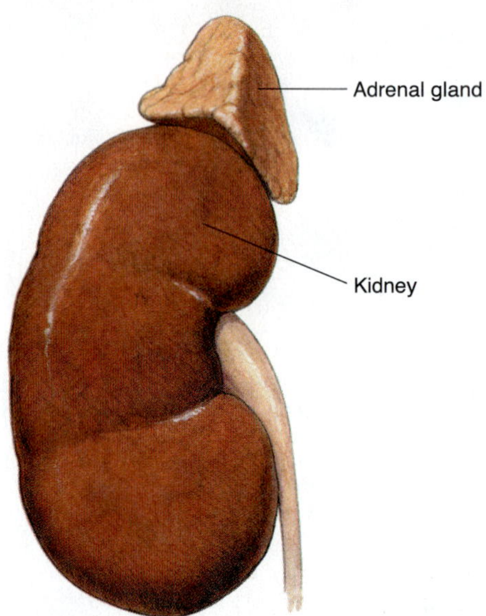

▲ **Figure 39–9** **The adrenal glands release hormones that help the body prepare for and deal with stress.** Each adrenal gland is divided into two structural parts: the adrenal cortex and the adrenal medulla.

Adrenal Glands

The adrenal glands are two pyramid-shaped structures that sit on top of the kidneys, one gland on each kidney, as shown in **Figure 39–9.** **The adrenal glands release hormones that help the body prepare for and deal with stress.** An adrenal gland has an outer part called the adrenal cortex and an inner part called the adrenal medulla. These parts contain different types of tissues.

Adrenal Cortex About 80 percent of an adrenal gland is its adrenal cortex. The adrenal cortex produces more than two dozen steriod hormones called corticosteroids (kawr-tih-koh-STEER-oydz). One of these hormones, aldosterone (al-DAHS-tuh-rohn), regulates the reabsorption of sodium ions and the excretion of potassium ions by the kidneys. Another hormone, called cortisol, helps control the rate of metabolism of carbohydrates, fats, and proteins.

Adrenal Medulla The release of hormones from the adrenal medulla is regulated by the sympathetic nervous system. The sympathetic nervous system prepares the body for energy-intense activities. The two hormones released by the adrenal medulla are epinephrine and norepinephrine. Epinephrine, which is more powerful than norepinephrine, makes up about 80 percent of the total secretions of the adrenal medulla.

The adrenal medulla produces the "fight or flight" response to stress. This response is the feeling you get when you are excited or frightened. Nerve impulses from the sympathetic nervous system stimulate cells of the adrenal medulla. This stimulation causes the cells to release large amounts of epinephrine and norepinephrine. These hormones increase heart rate, blood pressure, and blood flow to the muscles. They cause air passageways to open wider, allowing for an increase in the intake of oxygen. They also stimulate the release of extra glucose into the blood to help produce a sudden burst of energy. The result of all these actions is a general increase in body activity, which can serve as preparation for intense physical activity. If your heart rate speeds up and your hands begin to perspire when you take a test, you are feeling the effects of your adrenal medulla!

CHECKPOINT *Which hormones are released from the adrenal cortex? From the adrenal medulla?*

HISTORY OF SCIENCE

From dog urine to crystals

In 1889, scientists removed the pancreas from laboratory dogs and found, by chance, that the dogs' urine attracted bees. The scientists inferred that the urine contained sugar, which was also known to be true of the urine of people with diabetes mellitus. The scientists concluded that the pancreas must produce a substance that was involved somehow in the disease. The substance was named insulin after *insula*, the Latin word for "island," because it was thought to be produced by the islets of Langerhans. In 1922, insulin was isolated and identified by Sir Frederick Banting and Charles Best. Banting received a Nobel prize for the discovery the following year. Banting and Best also determined insulin's role in carbohydrate metabolism and diabetes mellitus. In 1969, the English chemist Dorothy Crowfoot Hodgkin used crystallography to determine insulin's crystal structure.

Pancreas

The pancreas is an unusual gland that has both exocrine and endocrine functions. Recall that the pancreas is a digestive gland whose enzyme secretions help to break down food. These secretions are released into the pancreatic duct and flow into the small intestine. This makes the pancreas an exocrine gland. However, different cells in the pancreas release hormones into the blood, making the pancreas an endocrine gland as well.

The hormone-producing portion of the pancreas consists of clusters of cells that resemble islands. These clusters of cells are called islets of Langerhans after their discoverer, the German anatomist Paul Langerhans. Each islet includes beta cells, which secrete a hormone called insulin, and alpha cells, which secrete another hormone called glucagon. **Insulin and glucagon help to keep the level of glucose in the blood stable.** Insulin stimulates cells in the liver and muscles to remove sugar from the blood and store it as glycogen or fat. Glucagon stimulates the liver to break down glycogen and release glucose back into the blood. It also stimulates the release of fatty acids from stored fats.

Maintaining Blood Sugar Levels When blood glucose levels rise after eating, the pancreas releases insulin. Insulin stimulates cells throughout the body to take glucose out of the bloodstream. Insulin's major target cells are found in the liver, skeletal muscles, and fat (adipose) tissue. Glucose taken out of circulation is stored as glycogen in the liver and skeletal muscles. In fat tissue, glucose molecules are converted to lipids. Insulin prevents the level of glucose in the blood from rising too rapidly and ensures that excess glucose is stored for future use.

Within one or two hours after eating, when the level of blood glucose drops, glucagon is released from the pancreas. Glucagon stimulates the cells of the liver and skeletal muscles to break down glycogen and increase glucose levels in the blood. Glucagon also causes fat cells to break down fats so that they can be used for the production of carbohydrates. These actions make more chemical energy available to the body and help raise the blood glucose level back to normal.

Diabetes Mellitus When the pancreas fails to produce or properly use insulin, a condition known as **diabetes mellitus** occurs. In diabetes mellitus, the amount of glucose in the blood may rise so high that the kidneys actually excrete glucose in the urine. Very high blood glucose levels can damage almost every system and cell in the body, including the coronary artery, shown in **Figure 39–10.**

There are two types of diabetes mellitus. Type I diabetes is an autoimmune disorder that usually develops in people before the age of 15. In this type of diabetes, there is little or no secretion of insulin. People with this type of diabetes must follow a strict diet and get daily injections of insulin to keep their blood glucose levels under control.

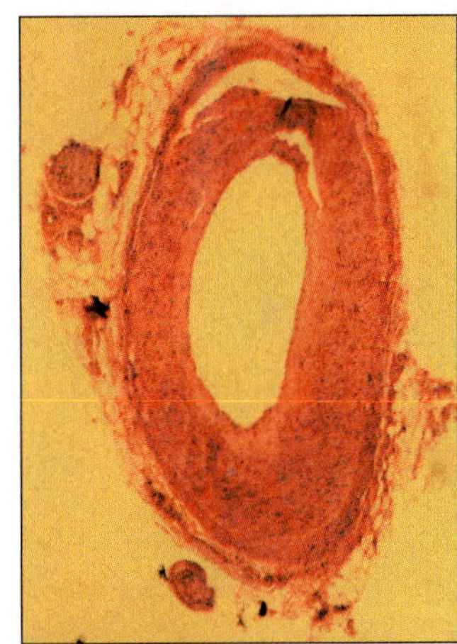

Normal Coronary Artery

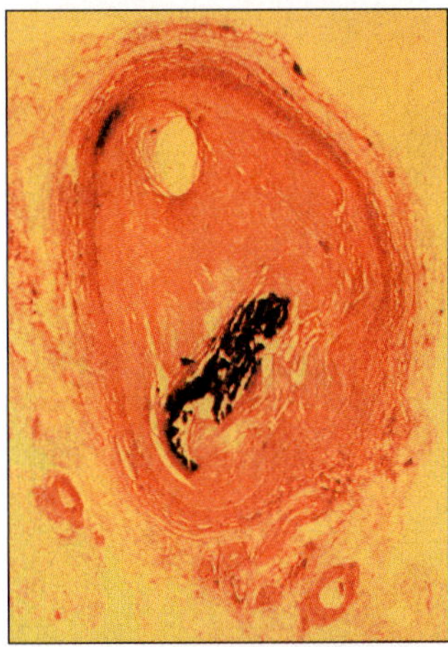

Coronary Artery Totally Blocked

▲ **Figure 39–10** Type II diabetes promotes atherosclerosis, which reduces the elasticity of arteries. **Applying Concepts** ***What effect do blocked arteries have on blood pressure?***

Pancreas

Address Misconceptions

Students are likely to have heard diabetes mellitus referred to simply as "diabetes." Point out that the term *diabetes* actually refers to any disease that is characterized by excessive urination and thirst and that there is more than one type of diabetes. For example, diabetes insipidus is a type of diabetes caused by lack of the pituitary hormone ADH and not by lack of insulin. Ask: **If diabetes mellitus is controlled by insulin injections, how do you think diabetes insipidus could be controlled?** *(By ADH injections)* L2

Demonstration

Tell students that diabetes mellitus sometimes is diagnosed by detecting sugar in the urine. Give students glucose test strips and explain how they are used. Then, have students use the test strips to test either a mixture of water, yellow food coloring, and sugar or a mixture of water and yellow food coloring alone. Ask: **Did your "urine" specimen contain sugar?** *(Answers will depend on which mixture was tested.)* Check that students have correctly interpreted their test results. L1 L2

Use Community Resources

Ask a nurse or other medical professional who is knowledgeable about diabetes mellitus to visit your class. Have the visitor explain why and when people with insulin-dependent diabetes mellitus must measure their blood glucose and why and when insulin must be taken. If possible, have the visitor demonstrate how a glucometer and an insulin kit are used. Urge students to prepare a list of questions in advance, such as: What dietary restrictions must diabetics follow? Is diabetes mellitus inherited? L2

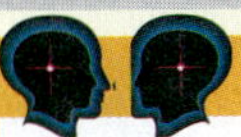

TEACHER TO TEACHER

After students have read about the endocrine hormones, I check their comprehension by showing them pictures of situations in which a particular hormone is needed. Then, I have students identify the hormone and explain why it is produced. For example, if I show students a picture of someone eating candy, they should respond that insulin produced by the pancreas helps control increased blood sugar levels. If I show them a picture of someone shivering on a winter day, they should respond that TSH produced by the pituitary stimulates the thyroid to release thyroxine to increase body metabolism.

—*Ruth Gleicher*
Biology Teacher
Niles West High School
Skokie, IL

Answers to . . .

CHECKPOINT *Corticosteroid hormones, such as aldosterone and cortisol, are released from the adrenal cortex. Epinephrine and norepinephrine are released from the adrenal medulla.*

Figure 39–10 *Blocked arteries increase blood pressure.*

39–2 (continued)

Reproductive Glands

Address Misconceptions

Students are likely to think that testosterone is produced only by males and estrogen only by females. Tell students that the adrenal glands produce small amounts of estrogen and testosterone in both females and males. Ask: **Why do you think males do not show the effects of adrenal estrogen or females the effects of adrenal testosterone?** *(The amounts of hormones produced by the adrenal glands are small compared with the amounts produced by the gonads.)* L2

3 ASSESS

Evaluate Understanding

Call on students to identify hormones produced by each endocrine gland. Call on other students to describe the function of each hormone.

Reteach

Divide the class into two teams. Play a quiz game in which you act as moderator and require students on alternating teams to identify hormones based on a description.

Writing in Science

Students' brochures should be assessed on the basis of both content and format. Check that the facts they list are accurate and that all of the relevant information is incorporated, including risk factors, treatment, and prevention. Students should use a brochure format with eye-catching illustrations. Encourage them to use a computer software program that creates brochures.

If your class subscribes to the iText, use it to review the Key Concepts in Section 39–2.

The second type of diabetes, Type II, most commonly develops in people after the age of 40. People with Type II diabetes produce low to normal amounts of insulin. However, their cells are unable to properly respond to the hormone because the interaction of the insulin receptors and the insulin is inefficient. In its early stages, Type II diabetes can often be controlled through diet and exercise. A diet high in complex carbohydrates and low in saturated fat and sugar can prevent blood sugar fluctuations.

Unfortunately, many people with Type II diabetes eventually require medication, as well. If the body stops producing insulin, the person will also need to have daily insulin injections.

Reproductive Glands

The gonads are the body's reproductive glands. **The gonads serve two important functions: the production of gametes and the secretion of sex hormones.** The female gonads—the **ovaries**—produce eggs (ova; singular: ovum). The male gonads—the **testes** (singular: testis)—produce sperm. The gonads also produce sex hormones.

The ovaries produce the female sex hormones, estrogen and progesterone. Estrogen is required for the development of eggs and for the formation of the physical characteristics associated with the female body. These characteristics include the development of the female reproductive system, widening of the hips, and development of the breasts. Progesterone prepares the uterus for the arrival of a developing embryo.

The testes produce testosterone (tes-TAHS-tuh-rohn). Testosterone is required for normal sperm production and the development of physical characteristics associated with the male body. These characteristics include the growth of facial hair, increase in body size, and deepening of the voice. You will read more about these hormones in the next section.

39–2 Section Assessment

1. **Key Concept** Describe the role of each major endocrine gland.
2. Why is the hypothalamus an important part of both the nervous system and the endocrine system?
3. What endocrine gland goes to work when you are surprised with a pop quiz?
4. What are the two types of diabetes mellitus?
5. **Critical Thinking Predicting** Suppose the secretion of a certain hormone causes an increase in the concentration of substance X in the blood. A low concentration of X causes the hormone to be released. What is the effect on the rate of hormone secretion if an abnormal condition causes the level of X in the blood to remain very low?

Writing in Science

Creating an Informational Brochure

Create a brochure that describes both types of diabetes. You may wish to include information on risk factors, treatment, and preventive measures that can be taken. Use images from magazines or the Internet to illustrate your brochure. *Hint:* Be sure to choose some high-interest images to make your brochure visually appealing.

39–2 Section Assessment

1. Pituitary: regulates functions such as growth and actions of other glands; hypothalamus: controls the pituitary gland; parathyroids and thyroid: metabolism and level of calcium in blood; adrenals: metabolism, salt excretion, and response to stress; pancreas: level of blood glucose; ovaries and testes: production of gametes and secretion of sex hormones
2. It monitors sensory input from the nervous system and uses it to control the endocrine system via the pituitary gland.
3. The adrenal gland
4. Type I (little or no secretion of insulin) and Type II (low or normal levels of insulin but cell response to insulin is inefficient)
5. The rate of hormone secretion remains high.

39–3 The Reproductive System

BI 2.b. Students know only certain cells in a multicellular organism undergo meiosis. *BI 9.i. Students know how hormones (including digestive, reproductive, osmoregulatory) provide internal feedback mechanisms for homeostasis at the cellular level and in whole organisms.

Reproduction is the formation of new individuals. This makes the reproductive system unique among the systems of the body. If any other body system, such as the nervous or circulatory system, failed to function, the result would be fatal in most animals. This is not the case for the reproductive system because an individual can lead a healthy life without reproducing. However, the reproductive system could be thought of as the single most important system for the continuation of a species—without it, no species could produce another generation.

In humans, as in other vertebrates, the reproductive system produces, stores, and releases specialized sex cells known as gametes. These cells are released in ways that make possible the fusion of sperm and egg to form a zygote, the single cell from which all cells of the human body develop.

Guide for Reading

Key Concepts
- What are the main functions of the male and female reproductive systems?
- What are the four phases of the menstrual cycle?

Vocabulary
puberty • scrotum
seminiferous tubule
epididymis • vas deferens
urethra • penis • follicle
ovulation • Fallopian tube
uterus • vagina
menstrual cycle
corpus luteum • menstruation
sexually transmitted disease

Reading Strategy: Outlining Before you read, use the headings in this section to make an outline about the reproductive system. As you read, fill in subtopics. Then, add phrases or a sentence after each subtopic to provide key information showing how the reproductive system is important.

Sexual Development

For the first six weeks of development, human male and female embryos are identical in appearance. Then, during the seventh week, major changes occur. The primary reproductive organs—the testes in males and the ovaries in females—begin to develop. The testes begin to produce testosterone. Tissues of the embryo respond to this hormone by developing into the male reproductive organs. If the embryo is female, the ovaries produce estrogen. In response to this hormone, the tissues of the embryo develop into the female reproductive organs. These hormones determine whether the embryo will develop physically into a male or female.

After birth, the gonads produce small amounts of sex hormones that continue to influence the development of the reproductive organs. However, neither the testes nor the ovaries are capable of producing active reproductive cells until puberty. **Puberty** is a period of rapid growth and sexual maturation during which the reproductive system becomes fully functional. At the completion of puberty, the male and female reproductive organs are fully developed. The onset of puberty varies considerably among individuals. It usually occurs any time between the ages of 9 and 15, and, on average, begins about one year earlier in females than in males.

Puberty begins when the hypothalamus signals the pituitary to produce increased levels of two hormones that affect the gonads. These hormones are follicle-stimulating hormone (FSH) and luteinizing hormone (LH).

▼ **Figure 39–11** Many changes in your life—both social and physical—are dependent on your age.

Section 39–3

1 FOCUS

Objectives

39.3.1 ***Describe*** sexual development.

39.3.2 ***Explain*** the functions of the male and female reproductive systems.

39.3.3 ***Identify*** the four phases of the menstrual cycle.

Guide for Reading

Vocabulary Preview

Tell students that all the Vocabulary words, except *puberty* and *sexually transmitted disease,* refer to either the male or the female reproductive system. Challenge students to identify which words refer to each system. They should check to see if they were right as they read the section.

Reading Strategy

Before students read the section, have them find and rewrite each boldface sentence in a question-and-answer format. After students read the section, they should check their comprehension by trying to answer the questions.

2 INSTRUCT

Sexual Development

Make Connections

Environmental Science Tell students that many compounds released into the environment by human activities mimic estrogen if they enter the body through contaminated water or food. Ask: **What effect do you think these "environmental estrogens" might have on the development of males?** *(Students might speculate that the estrogens could cause male embryos to develop into females or, at puberty, males to develop female traits such as enlarged breasts.)* L2

SECTION RESOURCES

Print:
- ***Laboratory Manual A,*** Chapter 39 Lab
- ***Laboratory Manual B,*** Chapter 39 Lab
- ***Teaching Resources,*** Lesson Plan 39–3, Adapted Section Summary 39–3, Adapted Worksheets 39–3, Section Summary 39–3, Worksheets 39–3, Section Review 39–3
- ***Reading and Study Workbook A,*** Section 39–3
- ***Adapted Reading and Study Workbook B,*** Section 39–3

Technology:
- ***iText,*** Section 39–3
- ***Transparencies Plus,*** Section 39–3

39–3 (continued)

The Male Reproductive System

Demonstration

Obtain a prepared slide of a sperm cell. Focus the slide under the microscope and invite students to take turns viewing it, or use a microprojector. Have students locate the three main parts of the sperm cell *(Head, midpiece, and tail)* and draw a sketch of the cell with the three parts labeled. Ask: **Why do you think the sperm cell has a tail?** *(To help the sperm "swim" through the female reproductive tract)* L1 L2

Use Visuals

Figure 39–12 Have students study the figure and read the caption. Then, ask: **Where are sperm produced?** *(In the testis)* **Where are sperm stored?** *(In the epididymis)* **How do sperm get from the epididymis to the urethra?** *(Through the vas deferens)* **Which other reproductive organs or glands must sperm pass by or through to reach the urethra?** *(Seminal vesicle, prostate gland, and bulbourethral gland)* L1 L2

The Male Reproductive System

The release of FSH and LH stimulates cells in the testes to produce testosterone. FSH and testosterone stimulate the development of sperm. Once large numbers of sperm have been produced in the testes, the developmental process of puberty is completed. The reproductive system is now functional, meaning that the male can produce and release active sperm. **The main function of the male reproductive system is to produce and deliver sperm.**

Figure 39–12 shows the structures of the male reproductive system. The primary male reproductive organs, the testes, develop within the abdominal cavity. Just before birth (and sometimes just after) the testes descend through a canal into an external sac called the **scrotum.** The testes remain in the scrotum, outside the body cavity, where the temperature is about one to three degrees lower than the normal temperature of the body (37°C). The lower temperature is important for proper sperm development. Within each testis are clusters of hundreds of tiny tubules called **seminiferous** (sem-uh-NIF-ur-us) **tubules.** The seminiferous tubules are tightly coiled and twisted together. Sperm are produced in the seminiferous tubules.

What is the role of the seminiferous tubules?

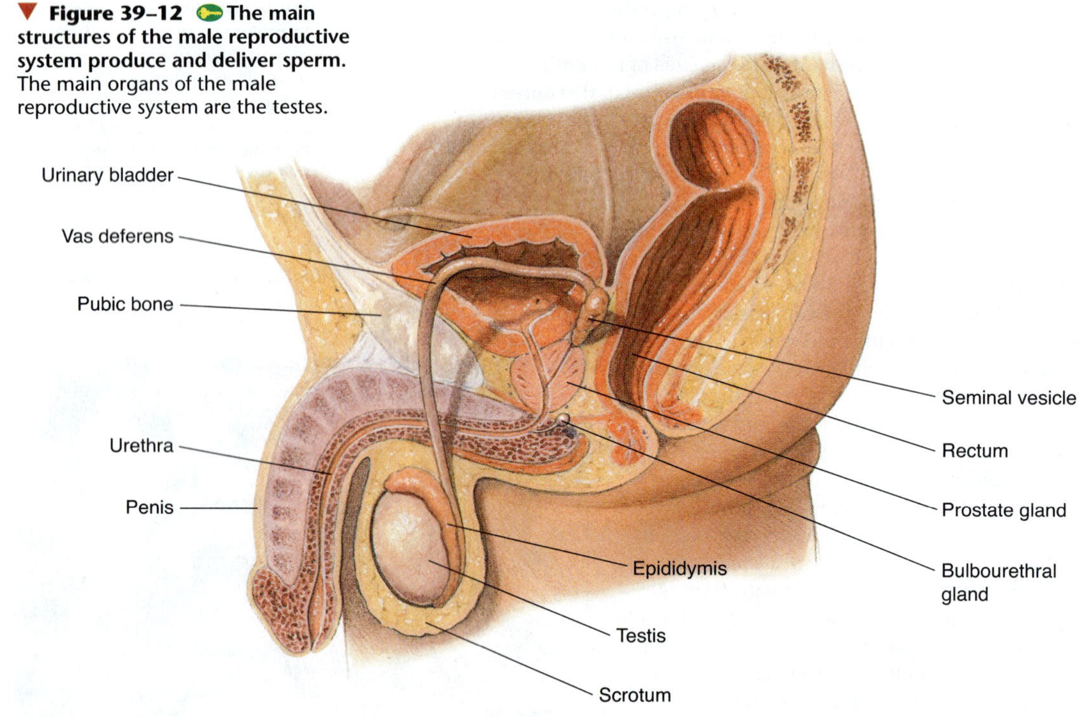

Figure 39–12 **The main structures of the male reproductive system produce and deliver sperm.** The main organs of the male reproductive system are the testes.

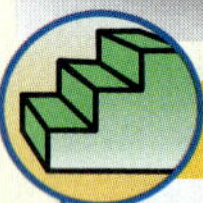

UNIVERSAL ACCESS

Inclusion/Special Needs

Reinforce section content for students who benefit from hands-on learning. Give each student a simple, unlabeled drawing of the male reproductive system. Then, using a large anatomical chart or model, point out each of the male reproductive organs and describe its function. Have students find each organ on their drawing and label it with the name and function. Suggest that students save their drawings for study guides. L1

English Language Learners

The detailed text on the menstrual cycle may be difficult for some students to comprehend. Have students summarize the material by creating a cycle diagram of the four phases. Students' diagrams should show the name and sequence of each phase, its relative length, and the major events that occur in that phase. Display students' completed diagrams in the classroom.  

Sperm Development Sperm are derived from specialized cells in the testes that undergo the process of meiosis to form the haploid nuclei of mature sperm. Recall that a haploid cell contains only a single set of chromosomes.

A sperm cell is illustrated in **Figure 39–13.** A sperm cell consists of a head, which contains a highly condensed nucleus; a midpiece, which is packed with energy-releasing mitochondria; and a tail, or flagellum, which propels the cell forward. At the tip of the head is a small cap that contains an enzyme vital to the process of fertilization.

Sperm produced in the seminiferous tubules are moved into the **epididymis** (ep-uh-DID-ih-mis). This is the structure in which sperm fully mature and are stored. From the epididymis, some sperm are moved into a tube called the **vas deferens.** The vas deferens extends upward from the scrotum into the abdominal cavity. Eventually, the vas deferens merges with the **urethra,** the tube that leads to the outside of the body through the **penis.**

Glands lining the reproductive tract—including the seminal vesicles, the prostate, and the bulbourethral (bul-boh-yoo-REE-thrul) glands—produce a nutrient-rich fluid called seminal fluid. The seminal fluid nourishes the sperm and protects them from the acidity of the female reproductive tract. The combination of sperm and seminal fluid is known as semen. The number of sperm present in even a few drops of semen is astonishing. Between 50 and 130 million sperm are present in 1 milliliter of semen. That's about 2.5 million sperm per drop!

Sperm Release When the male is sexually aroused, the autonomic nervous system prepares the male organs to deliver sperm. Sperm are ejected from the penis by the contractions of smooth muscles lining the glands in the reproductive tract. This process is called ejaculation. Because ejaculation is regulated by the autonomic nervous system, it is not completely voluntary. About 2 to 6 milliliters of semen are released in an average ejaculation. If these sperm are released in the reproductive tract of a female, the chances of a single sperm fertilizing an egg, if one is available, are quite good.

The Female Reproductive System

The primary reproductive organs in the female are the ovaries. The ovaries are located in the abdominal cavity. As in males, puberty in females starts when the hypothalamus signals the pituitary gland to release FSH and LH. FSH stimulates cells within the ovaries to produce estrogen.

The main function of the female reproductive system is to produce ova. In addition, the female reproductive system prepares the female's body to nourish a developing embryo. In contrast to the millions of sperm produced each day in the male reproductive system, the ovaries usually produce only one mature ovum (plural: ova), or egg, each month.

(a) BI 2.b

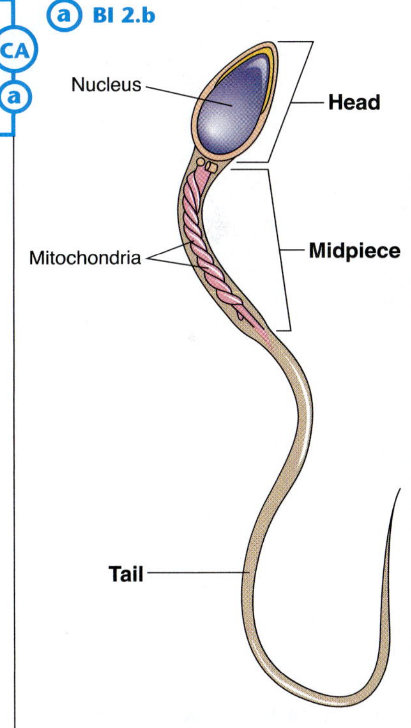

Figure 39–13 The sperm is the male gamete, or sex cell. **Interpreting Graphics** *What are the three sections of a sperm cell?*

For: Links on gametes
Visit: www.SciLinks.org
Web Code: cbn-0393

Build Science Skills

Inferring Point out the huge number of sperm present in each milliliter of semen. Then, ask: **What is the value of producing so many sperm?** *(To increase the chances that one will be able to reach the egg and fertilize it)* L2

The Female Reproductive System

Address Misconceptions

Students may have the misconception that a female is able to reproduce from the time she has her first menstrual period at menarche until she has her last menstrual period at menopause. Inform students that menstrual cycles, especially at both ends of the reproductive period, may occur without the release of an egg. Cycles that do not produce eggs can also occur at other times, for example, at times of stress or illness. L2

Download a worksheet on gametes for students to complete, and find additional teacher support from NSTA SciLinks.

BIO INSIGHTS — FACTS AND FIGURES

Not too hot, not too cold

Testes do not always descend into the scrotum at birth. When they remain undescended, the condition is called cryptorchidism. It can be corrected with surgery or hormones administered before puberty. If the condition is not corrected, infertility or sterility is likely to result because sperm need the cooler temperatures outside the body to develop. Even in males with both testes descended, hot baths or tight clothing may increase the temperature of the testes enough to inhibit sperm production and cause temporary infertility. Sperm production may also be inhibited if the temperature of the testes becomes too cold. This is why, in cold weather, involuntary muscular contractions move the testes closer to the body. Sperm are among the smallest human cells. For a clump of sperm to be visible with the unaided eye, it would have to contain about 100,000 cells.

Answers to . . .

CHECKPOINT *Seminiferous tubules produce sperm.*

Figure 39–13 *Head, midpiece, and tail*

39–3 (continued)

Use Visuals

Figure 39–14 Explain that the drawing in the figure is a side view. Point out the fingerlike projections, called fimbriae, at the ends of the Fallopian tubes nearest the ovaries. Explain how the fimbriae move in a beckoning motion that helps draw eggs into the Fallopian tubes. Ask: **What happens to an egg after it enters a Fallopian tube?** *(It travels through the Fallopian tube to the uterus.)* L1 L2

Make Connections

Mathematics Have students use mathematics to improve their understanding of female reproduction. Ask: **If a female begins producing mature eggs at age 13 and continues uninterrupted until age 48, about how many mature eggs does she produce in a lifetime?** *(About one egg per month for 35 years, or a total of about 420 eggs)* **About how many eggs never mature?** *(The two ovaries together have about 800,000 immature eggs at birth, of which about 799,580 never mature.)* L2 L3

Demonstration

Draw a simple diagram on the chalkboard to demonstrate how an immature egg undergoes meiosis to form a single large mature egg and three small polar bodies. Include at least one pair of chromosomes in your diagram to show how meiosis produces haploid cells. Ask: **Why is the mature egg called a haploid cell?** *(Because it contains half the usual number of chromosomes)* **What cells in males are haploid cells?** *(Sperm cells)* **Why must eggs and sperm both be haploid cells?** *(So that when they join together at fertilization, they produce a cell with the diploid number of chromosomes)* Add to your diagram to illustrate fertilization and how it affects chromosome number. L2

Egg Development Each ovary contains about 400,000 primary **follicles,** which are clusters of cells surrounding a single egg. The function of a follicle is to help an egg mature for release into the reproductive tract, where it can be fertilized. Eggs develop within their follicles.

CA a

Although a female is born with thousands of immature eggs (primary follicles), only about 400 eggs will actually be released. Approximately every 28 days, under the influence of FSH, a follicle gets larger and completes the first meiotic cell division. When meiosis is complete, a single large haploid egg and three smaller cells called polar bodies are produced. The polar bodies have very little cytoplasm and soon disintegrate.

Egg Release When a follicle has completely matured, its egg is released in a process called **ovulation.** The follicle breaks open, and the egg is swept from the surface of the ovary into the opening of one of the two **Fallopian tubes.** The egg moves through the fluid-filled Fallopian tube, pushed along by microscopic cilia lining the walls of the tube. During its journey through the Fallopian tube, an egg can be fertilized. After a few days, the egg passes from the Fallopian tube into the cavity of an organ known as the **uterus.** The lining of the uterus is ready to receive a fertilized egg, if fertilization has occurred. The outer end of the uterus is called the cervix. Beyond the cervix is a canal—the **vagina**—that leads to the outside of the body. The structures of the female reproductive system are shown in **Figure 39–14.**

▼ **Figure 39–14** **The main function of the female reproductive system is to produce ova.** The ovaries are the main organs of the female reproductive system.

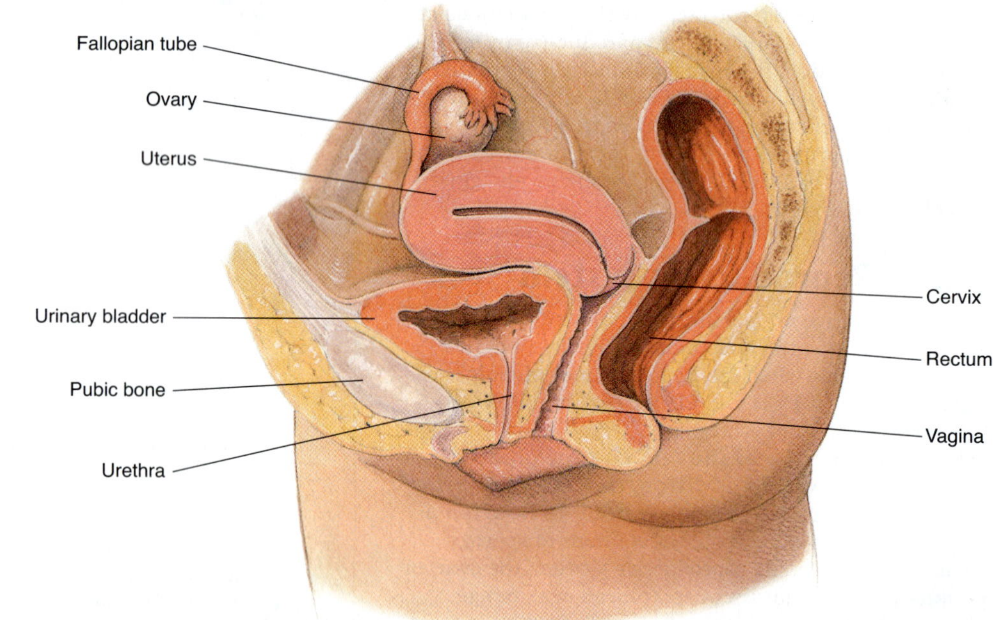

BIO INSIGHTS FACTS AND FIGURES

Treating female infertility
Female infertility is usually due to failure of the ovaries to release mature eggs or to blockage of the Fallopian tubes, which prevents eggs from being fertilized and reaching the uterus. Scientists have developed techniques that address each of these problems. Human menopausal gonadotropins can be injected to stimulate the follicles to develop, and drugs such as clomiphene can be given to promote ovulation. To bypass blocked Fallopian tubes, eggs can be harvested as they are ovulated, fertilized with sperm in a test tube, and placed in the uterus, a procedure that is called *in vitro fertilization*, or *IVF*. In a similar procedure, called *gamete intrafallopian tube transfer*, or *GIFT*, the sperm and unfertilized egg are placed in a Fallopian tube. GIFT is used for women who ovulate and have normal Fallopian tubes but who still fail to conceive.

The Menstrual Cycle

After puberty, the interaction of the reproductive system and the endocrine system in females takes the form of a complex series of periodic events called the menstrual cycle. The cycle takes an average of about 28 days. The word *menstrual* comes from the Latin word *mensis,* meaning "month." The menstrual cycle is regulated by hormones made by the hypothalamus, pituitary gland, and ovaries; and it is controlled by internal feedback mechanisms.

The menstrual cycle begins at puberty and continues until a female is in her mid-forties. At this time, the production of estrogen declines, and ovulation and menstruation stop. The permanent stopping of the menstrual cycle is called menopause. The average age for menopause is about 51, but it can occur anytime between the late thirties and late fifties.

During the **menstrual cycle,** an egg develops and is released from an ovary. In addition, the uterus is prepared to receive a fertilized egg. If the egg is fertilized, it is implanted in the uterus and embryonic development begins. If an egg is not fertilized, it is discharged, along with the lining of the uterus. **The menstrual cycle has four phases: follicular phase, ovulation, luteal phase, and menstruation.** Refer to **Figure 39–16** on page 1014 as you read about what happens during each phase.

Follicular Phase The follicular phase begins when the level of estrogen in the blood is relatively low. The hypothalamus reacts to low estrogen levels by producing a releasing hormone that stimulates the anterior pituitary to secrete FSH and LH. These two hormones travel through the circulatory system to the ovaries, where they cause a follicle to develop to maturity. Generally, just a single follicle develops, but sometimes two or even three mature during the same cycle.

As the follicle develops, the cells surrounding the egg enlarge and begin to produce increased amounts of estrogen. As the follicle produces more and more of the hormone, the estrogen level in the blood rises dramatically. Estrogen causes the lining of the uterus to thicken in preparation for receiving a fertilized egg. The development of an egg in this stage of the cycle takes about 10 days.

What happens during the follicular phase?

Ovulation This phase is the shortest in the cycle. It occurs about midway through the cycle and lasts three to four days. During this phase, the hypothalamus sends a large amount of releasing hormone to the pituitary gland. This causes the pituitary gland to produce FSH and LH. The release of these hormones has a dramatic effect on the follicle: It ruptures, and a mature egg is released into one of the Fallopian tubes.

▼ **Figure 39–15** This photomicrograph shows an ovum (white object) being released from an ovary. **Applying Concepts** *What is this process called?*

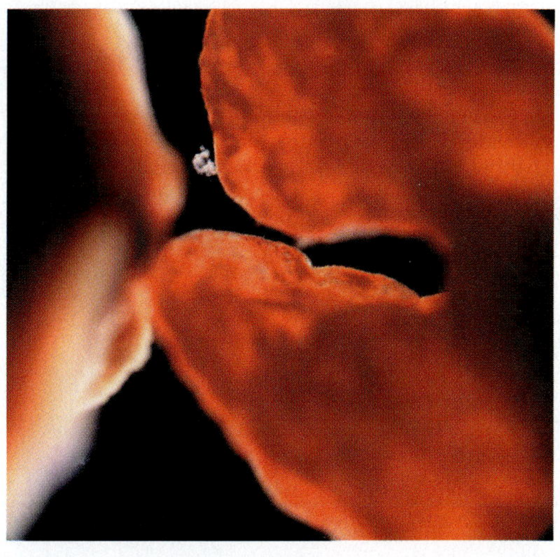

The Menstrual Cycle

Build Science Skills

Using Models Challenge students to create a diagram to model the feedback inhibition mechanisms that regulate the menstrual cycle when the egg is not fertilized. Students' diagrams should show how levels of LH, FSH, estrogen, and progesterone change during the cycle and how they affect target organs and glands. Call on volunteers to share their diagrams with the class. Ask: **What would happen to hormone levels if the egg were fertilized?** *(The corpus luteum would continue to produce estrogen and progesterone, but the pituitary would not produce LH and FSH because of the high estrogen level.)* L2

Make Connections

Health Science Inform students that symptoms such as weight gain, irritability, and depression commonly occur during the menstrual cycle. The symptoms typically start about one week before the onset of menstruation and decline once the menstrual period begins. This is why the condition is referred to as premenstrual syndrome, or PMS. Ask: **During which phase of the menstrual cycle does PMS occur?** *(The luteal phase)* L1 L2

BIO INSIGHTS **BIOLOGY UPDATE**

Mice grow human eggs

Women facing the prospect of infertility due to disease or surgery used to have only one option if they eventually wanted to have children. They could arrange to have their mature eggs frozen and later thawed, fertilized, and implanted, using in vitro fertilization. Unfortunately, this option is not very satisfactory, because mature, unfertilized eggs are often damaged by the low temperatures needed to preserve them. To overcome this problem, scientists recently transplanted small pieces of previously frozen ovarian tissue into the backs of mice. The mice were then injected with FSH to promote growth of ovarian follicles. Later, the mice were injected with human chorionic gonadotropin to stimulate ovulation, so that the eggs could be retrieved for further maturation in the lab. The scientists hope eventually to bypass the mice and mature the eggs using only lab equipment.

Answers to . . .

CHECKPOINT *A follicle develops.*

Figure 39–15 *The process is called ovulation.*

39–3 (continued)

Use Visuals

Figure 39–16 Guide students in interpreting the chart by asking: **On which days of the menstrual cycle does menstruation occur?** *(Days 0 to 7)* **What happens to the uterine lining between days 5 and 21?** *(It increases.)* **On what day of the cycle is the egg released from the follicle?** *(Around day 14)* **When is the level of estrogen highest?** *(Around day 12, just before ovulation)* **When does the level of progesterone peak?** *(Around day 24, toward the end of the luteal phase)* L1 L2

Address Misconceptions

Students may have the misconception that the average length of the menstrual cycle, which is 28 days, is also the normal length and that shorter or longer cycles are abnormal. Explain the difference between average and normal. Point out that normal cycles can range from 20 to 36 days and normal menstrual periods from 3 to 6 days. L1 L2

Build Science Skills

Predicting Challenge students to predict what would happen to the hormonal, follicular, and uterine cycles shown in Figure 39–16 if the egg produced on day 14 were fertilized. *(Students may or may not correctly predict that the progesterone level would remain high instead of decreasing and that both the corpus luteum and uterine lining would remain intact and start functioning instead of declining.)* L2

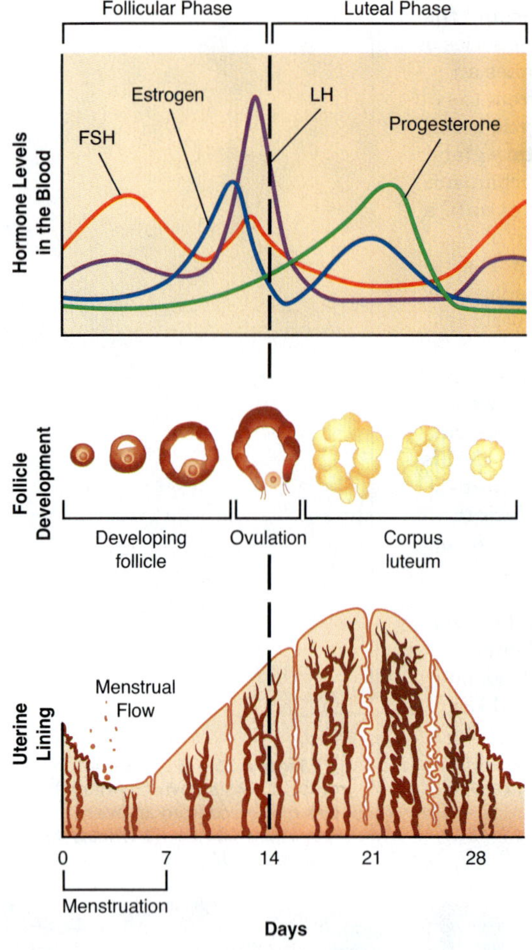

▲ **Figure 39–16** **The menstrual cycle is divided into four phases.** Notice the changes in hormone levels in the blood, the development of the follicle, and the changes in the uterine lining during the menstrual cycle.

Luteal Phase The luteal phase begins after the egg is released. As the egg moves through the Fallopian tube, the cells of the ruptured follicle undergo a change. The follicle turns yellow and is now known as the **corpus luteum** (KAWR-pus LOOT-ee-um), which means "yellow body" in Latin. The corpus luteum continues to release estrogen but also begins to release progesterone. During the first 14 days of the cycle, rising estrogen levels stimulate cell growth and tissue development in the lining of the uterus. Progesterone adds the finishing touches by stimulating the growth and development of the blood supply and surrounding tissue.

During the first two days of the luteal phase, immediately following ovulation, the chances that an egg will be fertilized are the greatest. This is usually from 10 to 14 days after the completion of the last menstrual cycle. If an egg is fertilized by a sperm, the fertilized egg will start to divide by the process of cell division known as mitosis. After several divisions, a ball of cells will form and implant itself in the lining of the uterus. The embryo continues to grow by repeated mitotic divisions. Within a few days of implantation, the uterus and the growing embryo will release hormones that keep the corpus luteum functioning for several weeks. This allows the lining of the uterus to nourish and protect the developing embryo.

Menstruation What happens if fertilization does not occur? Within two to three days of ovulation, the egg will pass through the uterus without implantation. The corpus luteum will begin to disintegrate. As the old follicle breaks down, it releases less estrogen and less progesterone. The result is a decrease in the level of these hormones in the blood.

When the level of estrogen falls below a certain point, the lining of the uterus begins to detach from the uterine wall. This tissue, along with blood and the unfertilized egg, are discharged through the vagina. This phase of the cycle is called **menstruation.** Menstruation lasts about three to seven days on average. A new cycle begins with the first day of menstruation.

A few days after menstruation ends, levels of estrogen in the blood are once again low enough to stimulate the hypothalamus. The hypothalamus produces a releasing hormone that acts on the pituitary gland, which then starts to secrete FSH and LH, and the menstrual cycle begins again.

BIOLOGY UPDATE

Solving the puzzle of menstruation

Scientists have long puzzled over the occurrence of menstruation in human females. The occurrence of menstruation seems to fly in the face of natural selection, because it limits the amount of time available to a female for reproduction and also costs her blood and energy. If anything, menstruation seems to be wasteful and even potentially dangerous. An answer to this puzzling situation was recently suggested by University of California professor Margie Profet, who hypothesized that menstruation might help the uterus rid itself of bacteria and viruses introduced during sexual intercourse. Profet's hypothesis has not been tested, but it does offer a reason that menstruation could be a benefit and not just a drawback and, therefore, why it might be favored by natural selection.

Sexually Transmitted Diseases

Diseases that are spread from one person to another during sexual contact are known as **sexually transmitted diseases (STDs).** STDs are a serious health problem in the United States, infecting millions of people each year and accounting for thousands of deaths.

Unfortunately, public information about many STDs has not kept pace with the rate of infection. For example, one might think that the name of the most commonly reported infectious disease in the United States would be a household word, but it isn't. That disease is chlamydia. The Centers for Disease Control estimates that more than three million cases of chlamydia occur in the United States every year. Chlamydia is caused by a bacterium (shown in **Figure 39–17**) that is passed from person to person by sexual contact. Females between the ages of 15 and 19 show the highest incidence of chlamydia infection of any age group. Chlamydia puts them at risk of infertility due to the damage this disease can cause in the reproductive system.

Other STDs caused by bacteria include syphilis, which can be fatal, and gonorrhea, a serious infection that is easily spread during intercourse. Viruses can also cause STDs. Viral STDs include hepatitis B, genital herpes, genital warts, and AIDS. AIDS, a result of human immunodeficiency virus (HIV) infection, causes tens of thousands of deaths in the United States alone. Millions of deaths around the world can also be attributed to AIDS. Unlike the bacterial STDs, these viral infections cannot be treated with antibiotics.

Like other infectious diseases, STDs can be avoided. Any sexual contact carries with it the chance of infection. The safest course to follow is to abstain from sexual contact before marriage and for both partners in a committed relationship to remain faithful. The next safest course is to use a latex condom, but even a latex condom does not provide 100 percent protection.

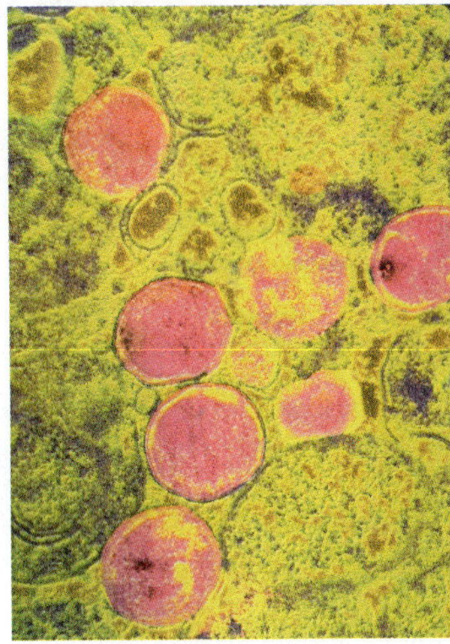

▲ **Figure 39–17** The red spherical objects in this micrograph show *Chlamydia trachomatis,* the bacterium that causes chlamydia.

39–3 Section Assessment

1. **Key Concept** Describe the functions of the male and female reproductive systems.
2. **Key Concept** What happens during each of the four phases of the menstrual cycle?
3. What is puberty?
4. Name two STDs caused by bacteria and two caused by viruses.
5. **Critical Thinking Using Tables and Graphs** Which hormone is at its peak during ovulation? (*Hint:* You may wish to refer to **Figure 39–16.**)

Focus on the BIG Idea

Information and Heredity
How many chromosomes are there in a human egg cell or in a sperm cell? How many are there in a fertilized egg? You may wish to refer back to Section 14–1.

Sexually Transmitted Diseases

Build Science Skills

Inferring State that most sexually transmitted diseases are caused by either viruses or bacteria. Point out that the most common sexually transmitted disease is chlamydia. Ask: **What causes chlamydia?** *(A bacterium,* Chlamydia trachomatis*)* Then, ask: **How would you infer that chlamydia is treated?** *(With antibiotics, because it is caused by a bacterium)* L2

3 ASSESS

Evaluate Understanding

Call on students at random to define each of the Vocabulary words. Call on other students to correct any errors.

Reteach

Have students use Figure 39–12 to trace the path of sperm through the male reproductive system and Figure 39–14 to trace the path of an egg through the female reproductive system.

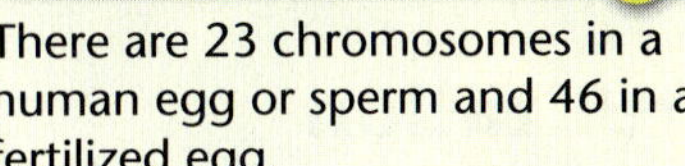

There are 23 chromosomes in a human egg or sperm and 46 in a fertilized egg.

If your class subscribes to the iText, use it to review the Key Concepts in Section 39–3.

39–3 Section Assessment

1. To produce, store, and release gametes; The female reproductive system also prepares the female's body to nourish a developing embryo.
2. Follicular phase: egg develops; ovulation: egg is released; luteal phase: egg travels through Fallopian tube, where it may be fertilized, to the uterus; menstruation: lining of uterus, blood, and egg are discharged through vagina
3. Puberty is a period of rapid growth and sexual maturation.
4. Bacterial STDs include chlamydia, syphilis, and gonorrhea. Viral STDs include hepatitis B, genital herpes, genital warts, and AIDS.
5. Luteinizing hormone, or LH

39–4 (continued)

1 FOCUS

Objectives

39.4.1 ***Describe*** fertilization.
39.4.2 ***Identify*** the stages of early development.
39.4.3 ***Describe*** the function of the placenta.
39.4.4 ***Outline*** the life cycle after birth.

Guide for Reading

Vocabulary Preview

Challenge students to predict what the Vocabulary words mean by writing a definition for each word. As they read the section, students should check their predictions and revise their definitions as needed.

Reading Strategy

Before they read the section, have students use the headings and subheadings to make an outline. Then, as they read, they should fill in phrases under the headings and subheadings to provide key information.

2 INSTRUCT

Fertilization

Use Community Resources

Invite a medical professional from the community to address the class about fertility problems. Good choices of speakers include specialists in obstetrics or endocrinology. Suggest that the speaker address both causes and treatments of infertility. Other relevant topics might include the emotional and financial costs of infertility problems and treatments. Urge students to ask questions after the presentation. L2

39–4 Fertilization and Development

Guide for Reading

Key Concepts
- What is fertilization?
- What are the stages of early development?
- What is the function of the placenta?

Vocabulary
zygote
implantation
differentiation
gastrulation
neurulation
placenta
fetus

Reading Strategy: Using Graphic Organizers As you read, draw a flowchart that shows the steps from fertilized egg to newborn baby.

When an egg is fertilized, the remarkable process of human development begins. In this process, a single cell no larger than the period at the end of this sentence undergoes a series of cell divisions that results in the formation of a new human being.

Fertilization

If an egg is to become fertilized, sperm must be present in the female reproductive tract—usually, in a Fallopian tube. During sexual intercourse, sperm are released when semen is ejaculated through the penis into the vagina. The penis generally enters the vagina to a point just below the cervix, which is the opening that connects the vagina to the uterus. Sperm swim actively through the uterus into the Fallopian tubes. Hundreds of millions of sperm are released during an ejaculation, so that if an egg is present in one of the Fallopian tubes, its chances of being fertilized are good.

The egg is surrounded by a protective layer that contains binding sites to which sperm can attach. When a sperm attaches to a binding site, a sac in the sperm head releases powerful enzymes that break down the protective layer of the egg. The sperm nucleus then enters the egg, and chromosomes from the sperm and egg are brought together. **The process of a sperm joining an egg is called fertilization.** After the two haploid (N) nuclei (one from the sperm and one from the egg) fuse, a single diploid (2N) nucleus is formed. A diploid cell contains a set of chromosomes from each parent cell. The fertilized egg is called a **zygote.**

Figure 39–18 **The process by which a sperm joins an egg is called fertilization.** Ernest Everett Just (left) discovered that once the sperm nucleus enters the egg, the egg's cell membrane changes, preventing other sperm from entering.

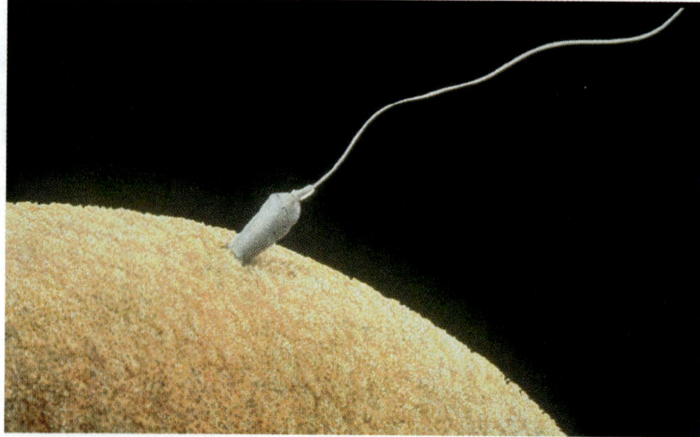

SECTION RESOURCES

Print:
- ***Teaching Resources,*** Lesson Plan 39–4, Adapted Section Summary 39–4, Adapted Worksheets 39–4, Section Summary 39–4, Worksheets 39–4, Section Review 39–4, Enrichment
- ***Reading and Study Workbook A,*** Section 39–4
- ***Adapted Reading and Study Workbook B,*** Section 39–4
- ***Issues and Decision Making,*** Issues and Decisions 6, 45

Technology:
- ***iText,*** Section 39–4
- ***Transparencies Plus,*** Section 39–4

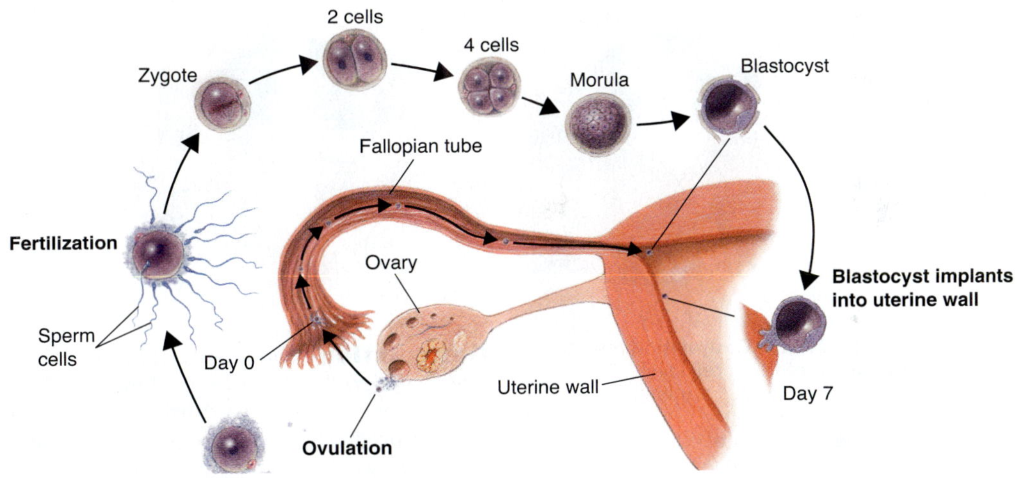

▲ **Figure 39–19** If an egg is fertilized, a zygote forms and begins to undergo cell division (mitosis) as it travels to the uterus. (The egg in this illustration has been greatly enlarged.) **Interpreting Graphics** *How much time passes before the blastocyst is attached to the uterine wall?*

What prevents more than one sperm from fertilizing an egg? Early in the twentieth century, cell biologist Ernest Everett Just, shown in **Figure 39–18,** found the answer. The egg cell contains a series of granules just beneath its outer surface. When a single sperm enters the egg, the egg reacts by releasing the contents of these granules outside the cell. The material in the granules coats the surface of the egg, forming a barrier that prevents other sperm from attaching to and entering the egg.

Early Development

While still in the Fallopian tube, the zygote begins to undergo mitosis, as shown in **Figure 39–19.** Cell division continues. As each cell divides, the number of cells doubles. Four days after fertilization, the embryo is a solid ball of about 64 cells called a morula (MAWR-yoo-luh). **The stages of early development include implantation, gastrulation, and neurulation.**

Implantation As the morula grows, a cavity forms in the center. This transforms the morula into a hollow structure with an inner cavity called a blastocyst. About six or seven days after fertilization, the blastocyst attaches itself to the wall of the uterus. The embryo secretes enzymes that digest a path into the soft tissue. This process is known as **implantation.**

At this point, cells in the blastocyst begin to specialize as a result of the activation of genes. This specialization process, called **differentiation,** is responsible for the development of the various types of tissue in the body. A cluster of cells, known as the inner cell mass, develops within the inner cavity of the blastocyst. The embryo itself will develop from these cells, while the other cells of the blastocyst will differentiate into the tissues that surround the embryo.

Early Development

Build Science Skills

Using Models Challenge students to use illustrations in reference books to create three-dimensional clay models of the zygote, morula, and blastocyst stages. Have students show their models to the class. Ask: **What changes have occurred at each stage?** *(From the single-celled zygote to the morula stage, cell divisions have produced a solid mass of cells. By the blastocyst stage, the mass of cells has become a hollow, fluid-filled ball.)* L1 L2

Use Visuals

Figure 39–19 Ask: **Where does fertilization usually occur?** *(In the Fallopian tube)* **How does the zygote differ from the egg that has just been released from the ovary?** *(It has been fertilized by a sperm, making it a diploid cell.)* **What happens to the zygote before it reaches the uterus?** *(It undergoes many cell divisions.)* **At what stage does implantation occur?** *(At the blastocyst stage)* L1 L2

Make Connections

Health Science Tell students that in about one percent of pregnancies, the blastocyst implants in the Fallopian tube or abdominal cavity instead of in the wall of the uterus. When this occurs, it is called ectopic pregnancy. It poses serious risks for both fetus and mother. Diagnosis of an ectopic pregnancy can be made with an ultrasound examination. L2

UNIVERSAL ACCESS

English Language Learners
The technical terms in this section may be difficult for students to master. Give them extra practice by having them write each word and its definition on opposite sides of an index card. They should write the definitions in both English and their native language. For more reinforcement, have pairs of students use the cards to quiz each other on the spelling, pronunciation, and meaning of each term. L1 L2

Advanced Learners
Give students an extra challenge by having them research dangers to the embryo during weeks four through nine of gestation. Students should find out which substances are toxic and how they affect the embryo during each week of development. *(Students may find out, for example, that infectious agents can cause heart defects in week five and blindness in week six.)* L3

Answer to . . .

Figure 39–19 *7 days*

39–4 (continued)

Build Science Skills

Classifying Have students classify organs of the body according to the primary germ layers from which they originate. This will help them appreciate the significance of the germ layers. First, write the terms *Ectoderm, Mesoderm,* and *Endoderm* on the board. Then, name several different organs—for example, uterus, small intestine, skin, heart, stomach, and brain—and challenge students to list each organ under the correct germ layer. *(For the examples given, students should list uterus and heart under* Mesoderm, *skin and brain under* Ectoderm, *and stomach and small intestine under* Endoderm.*)* L1 L2

Use Visuals

Figure 39–21 Help students appreciate the details of the central nervous system formation shown in the figure by challenging them to find everything that differs from one drawing to the next in the sequence. Also, call on students to identify the three cell layers—ectoderm, mesoderm, and endoderm—in each drawing. L1 L2

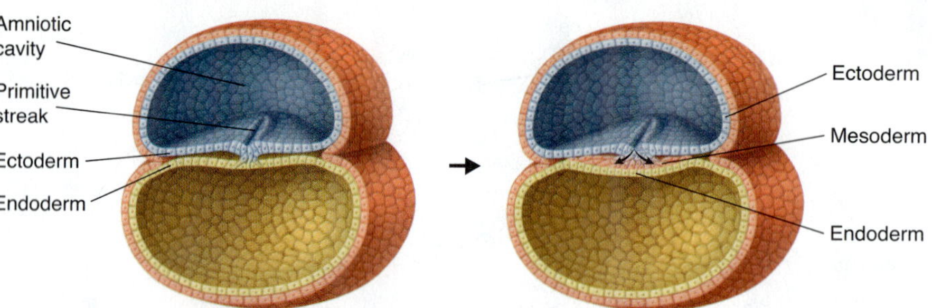

▲ **Figure 39–20** **Gastrulation results in the formation of three cell layers.** The diagram on the left shows the primitive streak, a line that forms in the center of the blastocyst. The movement of cells away from the primitive streak, shown in the diagram on the right, forms the mesoderm.

Gastrulation The inner cell mass of the blastocyst gradually sorts itself into two layers, which then give rise to a third layer. The third layer is produced by a process of cell migration known as **gastrulation** (gas-troo-LAY-shun), shown in **Figure 39–20.** The result of gastrulation is the formation of three cell layers: ectoderm, mesoderm, and endoderm. These three layers are referred to as the primary germ layers, because all of the organs and tissues of the embryo will be formed from them. The ectoderm will develop into the skin and the nervous system. The endoderm forms the lining of the digestive system and many of the digestive organs. Mesoderm cells differentiate to form many of the body's internal tissues and organs.

Neurulation Gastrulation is followed by an important step in human development, neurulation (NUR-uh-lay-shun). **Neurulation** is the development of the nervous system. Shortly after gastrulation is complete, a block of mesodermal tissue begins to differentiate into the notochord. Recall that all chordates possess a notochord at some stage of development. As the notochord develops, the neural groove changes shape, producing a pair of ridges, or neural folds, as shown in **Figure 39–21.** Gradually, these folds move together to create a neural tube from which the spinal cord and the rest of the nervous system, including the brain, develop.

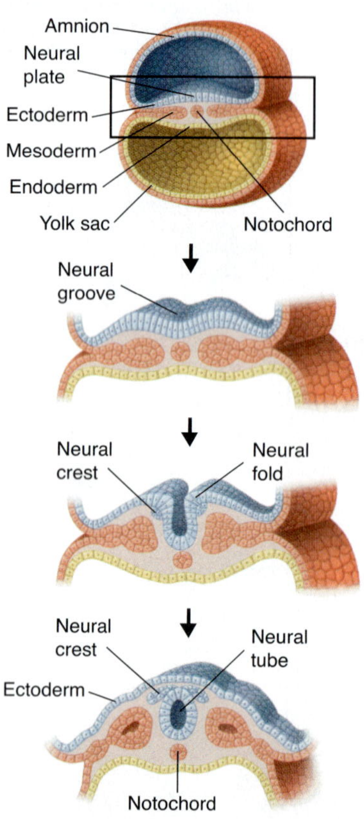

◀ **Figure 39–21** **Neurulation is the formation of the central nervous system.** The ectoderm near the notochord thickens and forms the neural plate. The raised edges of the neural plate form neural folds. The neural folds gradually move together and fuse to form the neural tube. One end of the neural tube will develop into the brain; the other end develops into the spinal cord. Cells of the neural crest migrate to other locations and develop into nerves.

HISTORY OF SCIENCE

Observing fertilization

Scientists of antiquity could not observe fertilization, so they had no direct evidence for how it occurs. Aristotle thought that semen was a seed that gave rise to a new individual and that the female body was simply the place where the seed was nourished. In the mid-1600s, when microscopes were invented, scientists were able to see human sperm for the first time. Even then, however, some claimed they saw a tiny human, which they named homunculus, within each sperm. Scientists of the 1700s and 1800s studied frog eggs, because amphibian eggs are large enough to be seen with a magnifying glass. They were able to see how fertilized eggs developed from zygote to morula and blastocyst stages. Human eggs were first viewed in the early 1900s, but it was not until the 1940s that the fertilization of human eggs was observed directly.

Extraembryonic Membranes As the embryo develops, membranes form to protect and nourish the embryo. Two of these membranes are the amnion and the chorion. The amnion develops into a fluid-filled amniotic sac, which cushions and protects the developing embryo within the uterus. By the end of the third week of development, the chorion—the outermost of the extraembryonic membranes—has formed. Small, fingerlike projections called chorionic villi form on the outer surface of the chorion and extend into the uterine lining.

The chorionic villi and uterine lining form a vital organ called the **placenta.** The placenta is the connection between mother and developing embryo. The developing embryo needs a supply of nutrients and oxygen. It also needs a means of eliminating carbon dioxide and metabolic wastes. Nutrients and oxygen in the blood of the mother diffuse into the embryo's blood in the chorionic villi. Wastes diffuse from the embryo's blood into the mother's blood.

In actuality, the blood of the mother and that of the embryo flow past each other, but they do not mix. They are separated by the placenta. Across this thin barrier, gases exchange, and food and waste products diffuse. **The placenta is the embryo's organ of respiration, nourishment, and excretion.** The placenta allows the embryo to make use of the mother's organ systems while its own are developing. **Figure 39–22** shows a portion of the placenta.

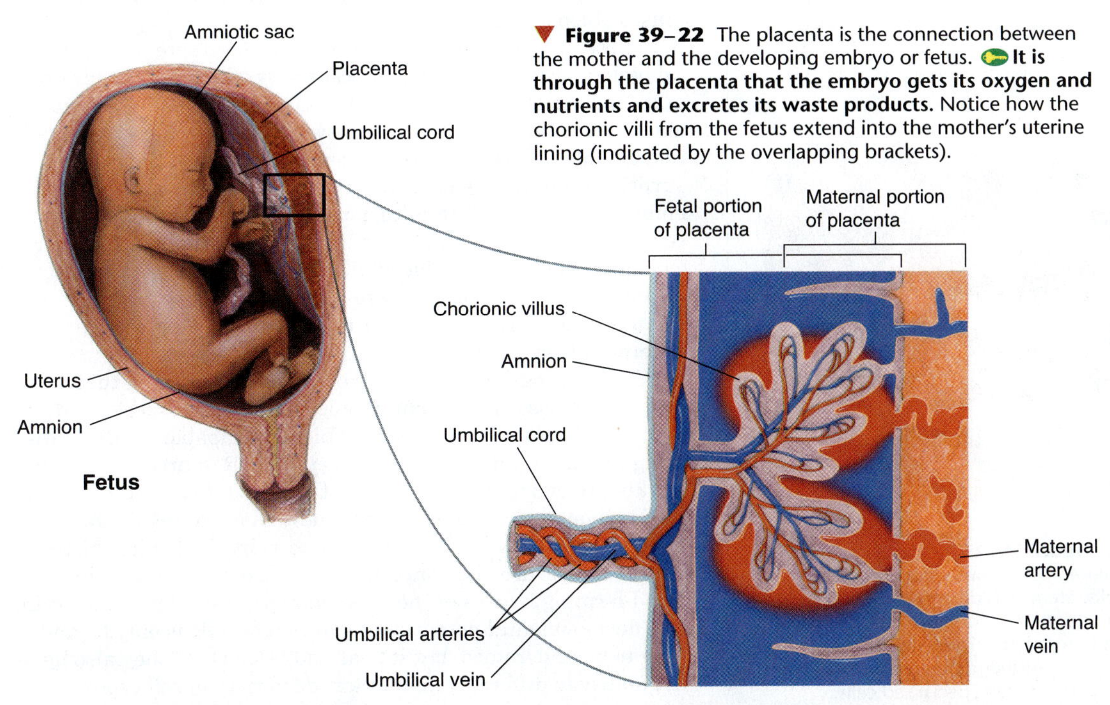

▼ **Figure 39–22** The placenta is the connection between the mother and the developing embryo or fetus. **It is through the placenta that the embryo gets its oxygen and nutrients and excretes its waste products.** Notice how the chorionic villi from the fetus extend into the mother's uterine lining (indicated by the overlapping brackets).

Demonstration

Demonstrate the important role played by the amnion. Put a raw egg inside a gallon-size resealable plastic storage bag, fill the bag with water, and seal it shut. Challenge one or more students to try to break the egg without removing the egg or water from the bag. Then, ask: **If the amnion is like the storage bag, what role does it play in fetal development?** *(It cushions the developing fetus from outside injuries.)* **When might this be important?** *(Possible answers might include in case the mother falls or is in an automobile accident.)* L1 L2

Make Connections

Health Science Point out that the mother's antibodies may cross the placenta, which helps protect the child if the antibodies are specific to foreign invaders, such as viruses and bacteria. However, if the antibodies are specific to the child's own blood cells, it can lead to fatal complications for the fetus. This can occur if the mother is Rh negative and the fetus is Rh positive, meaning that the fetal blood cells carry the Rh antigen. Explain that the presence of the Rh antigen in the fetal blood stimulates the mother to produce antibodies against it. Conclude by saying that drugs to suppress the formation of antibodies against the Rh antigen can be given to the mother to prevent problems for the Rh-positive fetus. L2

BIO INSIGHTS

BIOLOGY UPDATE

Fetal surgery for spina bifida

About 1 in every 1000 children is born with spina bifida, a condition in which some of the vertebrae do not develop normally, leaving part of the spinal cord exposed to damage from amniotic fluid before birth and from infection and injury during and after birth. Symptoms of spina bifida depend on the extent to which the spinal cord is exposed and damaged. In severe cases, the condition may cause hydrocephalus (water on the brain), mental retardation, abnormalities of the kidneys and bladder, and physical deformities. In the mid-1990s, doctors performed the first successful human fetal surgery to help correct spina bifida in utero. Since then, many more fetal surgeries for spina bifida have been performed with good results. Spina bifida babies who have fetal surgery require fewer postnatal shunt procedures to control hydrocephalus, and they are less likely to develop malformations of the hindbrain.

Download a worksheet on human growth and development for students to complete, and find additional teacher support from NSTA SciLinks.

Use Community Resources

Ask a physician's assistant, nurse, or technician who assists with or performs pregnancy ultrasound scans to speak to the class about the procedure. Suggest that the speaker address such topics as why and when ultrasound scans are performed during pregnancy and what can be learned from them. If possible, have the speaker bring sample ultrasound scans of fetuses at different stages of development to show the class. Ask students to write a brief summary of what they learn. **L2**

Control of Development

Build Science Skills

Making Judgments After students have read about the role of stem cells in fetal development, have them go online to find information on the use of stem cells in scientific research. Encourage students to make a judgment, based on what they learn, about whether the advantages of stem cell research outweigh any potential disadvantages. Call on volunteers to share their judgments with the class. **L2** **L3**

For: Links on human growth and development
Visit: www.SciLinks.org
Web Code: cbn-0394

Importance of Development This early period of development is particularly important because a number of external factors can disrupt development at this time. The placenta acts as a barrier to some harmful or disease-causing agents. Other disease-causing agents, including the ones that cause AIDS and German measles, can penetrate the placenta and affect development. So can drugs—including alcohol, medications, and addictive substances.

After eight weeks of development, the embryo is called a **fetus.** By the end of three months of development, most of the major organs and tissues of the fetus are fully formed. During this time, the umbilical cord also forms. The umbilical cord, which contains two arteries and one vein, connects the fetus to the placenta. The muscular system of the fetus is by now well developed, and the fetus may begin to move and show signs of reflexes. The fetus is about 8 centimeters long and has a mass of about 28 grams.

CHECKPOINT *What is the function of the umbilical cord?*

Control of Development

As you have read, over just a few weeks of development, a single zygote cell differentiates into the many complex cells and tissues of a human fetus. How does this happen? Is the fate of each cell in the embryo predetermined? Is there a master control switch that decides whether a cell will become skin, muscle, blood, or bone?

These are the kinds of questions that fascinate developmental biologists, who study the processes by which organisms grow and develop. Although many of the most important questions about development are still unanswered, researchers have made remarkable progress in the last few years. One of their most surprising findings is that the fates of many cells in the early embryo are not fixed. In mice, for example, researchers can mix cells from the inner cell mass of two different embryos. Rather than growing into a jumble of disorganized tissues, a perfectly normal mouse develops. This suggests that embryonic cells communicate with one another to regulate development and differentiation.

This finding is confirmed by experiments showing that the inner cell mass contains embryonic stem cells, unspecialized cells like those in **Figure 39–23,** which are capable of differentiating into nearly any specialized cell type. Researchers are now working to learn the mechanisms that control stem cell differentiation, hoping eventually to grow new tissue to repair the damage caused by injury or disease to individuals after birth.

Stem cells are also found in adult tissues, including the blood-forming tissues of the bone marrow, and even in the brain. The developmental potential of adult stem cells is only beginning to be understood, but it is already clear that they also have the ability to differentiate into a wide variety of cell types.

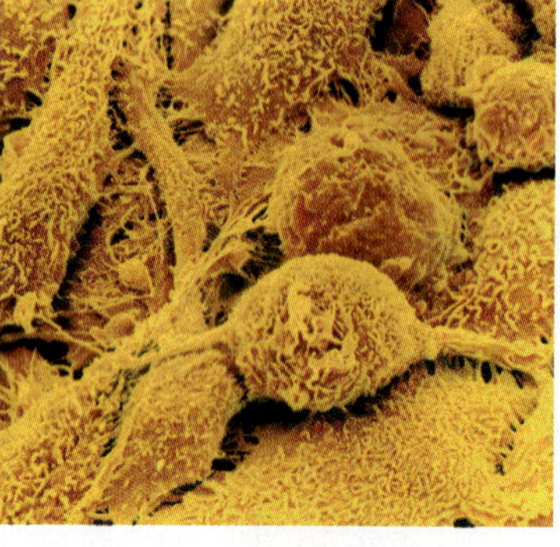

▲ **Figure 39–23** This artificially colored SEM shows embryonic stem cells. Stem cells differentiate into cells that form the endoderm, ectoderm, and mesoderm. These cells then undergo further differentiation to form all of the body's specialized cells.

Later Development

During the fourth, fifth, and sixth months after fertilization, the tissues of the fetus become more complex and specialized, and begin to function. The fetal heart becomes large enough so that it can be heard with a stethoscope. Bone continues to replace the cartilage that forms the early skeleton. A layer of soft hair grows over the fetus's skin. As the fetus increases in size, the mother's abdomen swells to accommodate it. The mother can begin to feel the fetus moving.

During the last three months, the organ systems mature, and the fetus grows in size and mass. The fetus doubles in mass, and the lungs and other organs undergo a series of changes that prepare them for life outside the uterus. The fetus is now able to regulate its body temperature. In addition, the central nervous system and lungs complete their development. **Figure 39–24** shows an embryo and a fetus at different stages of development.

On average, it takes nine months for a fetus to fully develop. Babies born before eight months of development, called premature babies, often have severe breathing problems because of incomplete lung development.

CHECKPOINT *What happens in a fetus during the last three months of development?*

Figure 39–24 At 7 weeks, most of the organs have begun to form. The heart—the large, dark rounded structure—is beating. By 14 weeks, the hands, feet, and legs have reached their birth proportions. The eyes, ears, and nose are well developed. When the fetus is full-term, it is fully developed and capable of living on its own. **Interpreting Graphics** *What significant changes do you see from 7 weeks to 14 weeks?*

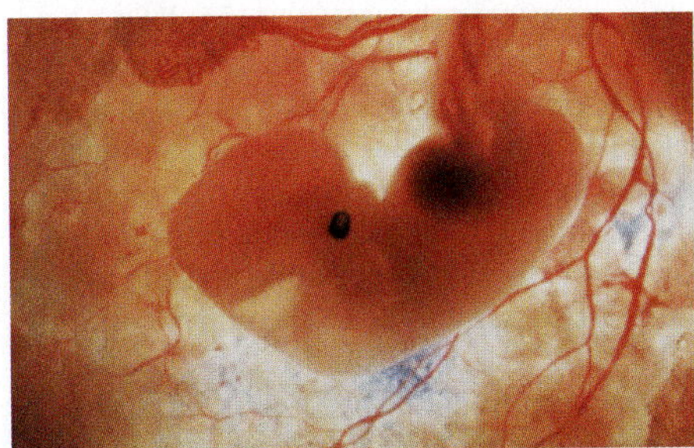

Embryo at 7 Weeks

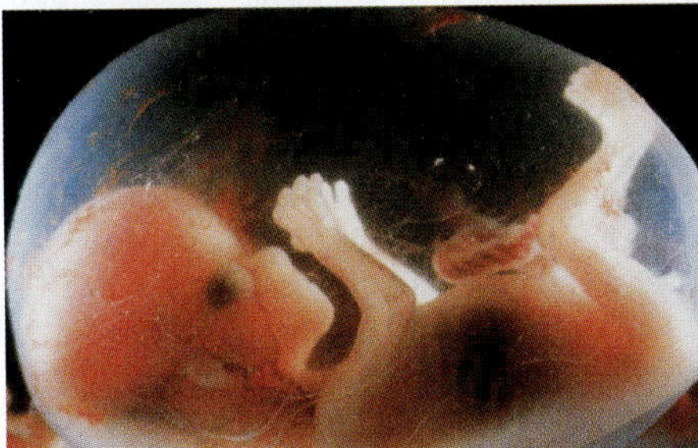

Fetus at 14 Weeks

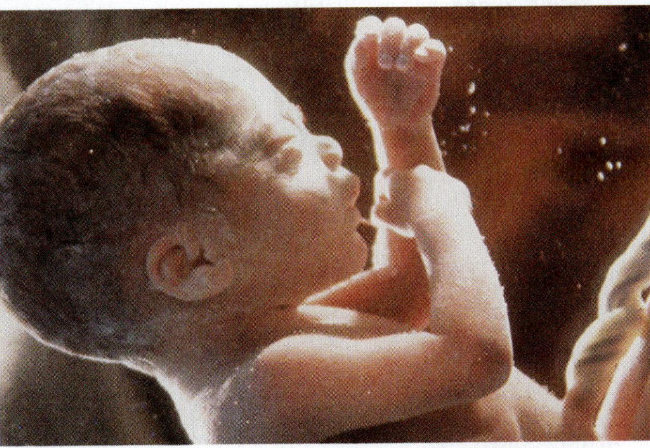

Fetus at Full Term

Later Development

Make Connections

Mathematics Guide students in using mathematics to appreciate how quickly a fetus grows. Draw a small dot on the chalkboard, and tell students that the dot represents a fertilized egg. Point out that an actual human egg is smaller, about 0.1 mm in diameter and barely visible with the unaided eye. Then, show students a baby doll that is about the same size as a newborn, or about 50 cm in length. Ask: **How fast must the fetus grow to change from the size of an egg to the size of a newborn in nine months of gestation?** *(About 56 mm per month)* Ask: **How tall would the individual be by age 15 if growth continued at that rate?** *(About 10 meters tall)* L2

Answers to . . .

CHECKPOINT *The umbilical cord connects the fetus to the placenta.*

CHECKPOINT *During the last three months of development, the organ systems mature and the fetus grows in size and mass.*

Figure 39–24 *The hands, feet, and legs have reached their birth proportions, and the eyes, ears, and nose are visible.*

39–4 (continued)

Quick Lab

Objective Students will be able to observe at which stage frog embryos start to show developmental changes.

Skills Focus **Observing, Drawing Conclusions**

Materials dropper pipette, early-stage frog embryos, depression slide, dissecting microscope, prepared slides of frog embryos

Time 20 minutes

Advance Prep Order frog eggs so that they arrive just before you need them, because they develop into tadpoles within a week.

Safety Remind students to handle microscope slides carefully.

Strategy Guide students in looking for visible differences such as cell size and shape.

Expected Outcome
After observing cells, students should conclude that frog embryos start to show developmental changes in the late gastrula or early neurula stage.

Analyze and Conclude

1. Differences in cell size are visible at the gastrula stage.
2. The body plan becomes visible after neurulation, as the embryo elongates and the head and tail become recognizable.
3. Organ formation is first visible at the neurula stage, as the neural tube takes shape.

Childbirth

Make Connections

Health Science Tell students that the health status of a newborn is assessed at one minute after birth with a procedure called the Apgar test. The infant is given a score of 0, 1, or 2 on each of the following five items: heart rate, respiration, muscle tone, response to stimuli, and color. The maximum score is 10, and a score of 7 to 10 is generally considered normal. Infants with lower scores need immediate medical attention. Ask: **Which body systems are assessed with the Apgar test?** *(Cardiovascular, respiratory, muscular, and nervous systems)* L2

Quick Lab

How do embryos develop?

Materials dropper pipette, early-stage frog embryos, depression slide, dissecting microscope, prepared slides of frog embryos

Procedure 

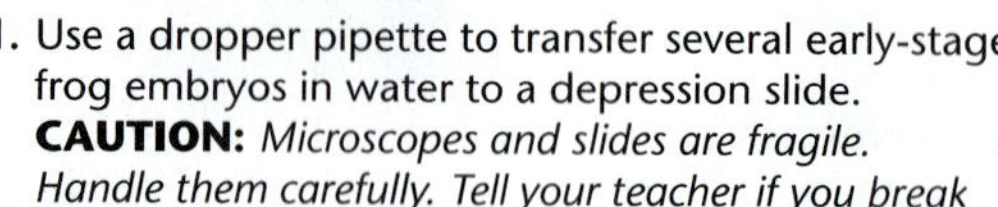

1. Use a dropper pipette to transfer several early-stage frog embryos in water to a depression slide. **CAUTION:** *Microscopes and slides are fragile. Handle them carefully. Tell your teacher if you break any glass.*
2. Look at the embryos under the dissecting microscope at low power. Sketch what you see.
3. Look at prepared slides of the early embryonic stages of a frog. Make sketches of what you see.

Frog Embryos

Analyze and Conclude

1. **Observing** Describe any differences you saw among the cells. At what stage is cell differentiation visible?
2. **Observing** Were you able to see a distinct body plan? At what stage did the body plan become visible?
3. **Drawing Conclusions** Describe any organs you saw. At what stage did specific organs form?

▼ **Figure 39–25** A newborn baby takes its first breath of air.

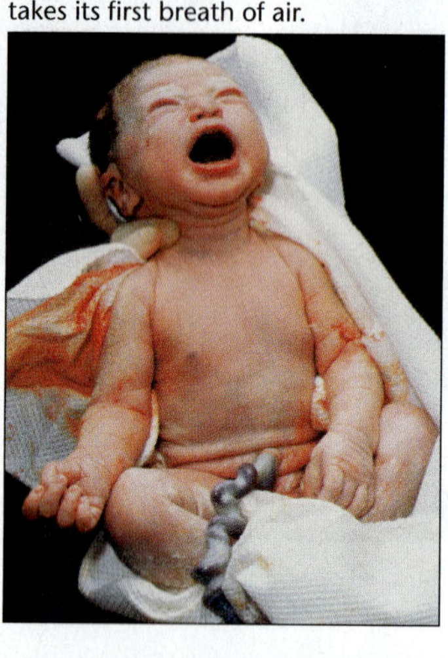

Childbirth

About nine months after fertilization, the fetus is ready for birth. A complex set of factors affects the onset of childbirth. One factor is the release of the hormone oxytocin from the mother's posterior pituitary gland. Oxytocin affects a group of large involuntary muscles in the uterine wall. As these muscles are stimulated, they begin a series of rhythmic contractions known as labor. The contractions become more frequent and more powerful. The opening of the cervix expands until it is large enough for the head of the baby to pass through it. At some point, the amniotic sac breaks, and the fluid it contains rushes out of the vagina. Contractions of the uterus force the baby, usually head first, out through the vagina.

As the baby meets the outside world, he or she may begin to cough or cry, a process that rids the lungs of fluid. Breathing starts almost immediately, and the blood supply to the placenta begins to dry up. The umbilical cord is clamped and cut, leaving a small piece attached to the baby. This piece will soon dry and fall off, leaving a scar known as the navel—or in its more familiar term, the belly button. In a final series of uterine contractions, the placenta itself and the now-empty amniotic sac are expelled from the uterus as the afterbirth.

The baby now begins an independent existence. Most newborn babies are remarkably hardy. Their systems quickly switch over to life outside the uterus, supplying their own oxygen, excreting wastes on their own, and maintaining their own body temperatures.

HISTORY OF SCIENCE

Caesarean section
Caesarean section is an operation in which a baby is removed from a mother's body through incisions in her abdominal wall and uterus. It is a procedure that is referred to in folklore from around the world. The name may have come from a Roman law, under Julius Caesar, that required all women dying in childbirth to undergo the procedure in order to save their offspring. The law may have been part of an imperialistic effort to increase the Roman population. Until the development of anesthetics, antibiotics, and modern surgical procedures over the past two centuries, caesarean sections were extremely painful and had a high risk of death for both mother and infant. Therefore, a caesarean section was almost always a last resort, performed only when the mother was dead or dying and for the sole purpose of trying to save her infant's life.

The interaction of the mother's reproductive and endocrine systems does not end at childbirth. Within a few hours after birth, the pituitary hormone prolactin stimulates the production of milk in the breast tissues of the mother. The nutrients present in that milk contain everything the baby needs for growth and development during the first few months of life.

Multiple Births

Sometimes more than one baby develops during a pregnancy. For example, if two eggs are released during the same cycle and fertilized by two different sperm, fraternal twins result. Fraternal twins are not identical in appearance because each has been formed by the fusion of a different sperm and egg cell. Fraternal twins may or may not be the same sex.

Sometimes a single zygote splits apart to produce two embryos. These two embryos are called identical twins. Identical siblings are formed by the fusion of the same sperm and egg cell; therefore, they are genetically identical. Identical twins are always the same sex.

✓CHECKPOINT ***What are the differences between identical twins and fraternal twins?***

Figure 39–26 During infancy, an infant learns to stand, walk, speak a few words, and imitate others. From ages 5 to 12, children grow to about 70 percent of their adult height and weight.

Early Years

Although the most spectacular changes of the human body occur before birth, development is a continuing process—it lasts throughout the life of an individual. In the first weeks of a baby's life, the systems that developed before birth now move into high gear, supporting rapid growth that generally triples a baby's birth weight within 12 months.

Infancy The first two years of life are known as infancy. Infancy is a period of rapid growth and development. The nervous system develops coordinated body movements as the infant begins to crawl and then to walk. A baby's first teeth appear, and the baby begins to understand and use language. Growth in the skeletal and muscular systems is especially rapid, demanding good nutrition to support proper development.

Childhood Childhood lasts from infancy until the onset of puberty, typically at an age of 12 or 13. Children become more active and independent. Language is acquired, motor coordination is perfected, permanent teeth begin to appear, and the long bones of the skeletal system reach 80 percent of their adult length. The key elements of personality and human social skills are developed, and reasoning skills are developed to a high level.

FACTS AND FIGURES

Multiple births

Multiple births occur normally in many species of mammals, but they are relatively uncommon in humans. Human twins are born in one out of about 90 births, triplets in one out of about 8000 births, and quadruplets in one out of about 750,000 births. Approximately 70 percent of twins are dizygotic, or two-egg, twins. The chances of having dizygotic twins are greater in women who take the fertility drug clomiphene, which stimulates the ovaries to produce eggs. The chances are also greater in women who have a family history of multiple births, are in their later childbearing years, or are of African ancestry. The chances of having monozygotic, or one-egg, twins, in contrast, appear to be the same in most women, regardless of family history, age, or race.

Use Community Resources

Arrange for a Lamaze instructor to visit the class to demonstrate the Lamaze method for helping women cope with the pain of childbirth. Have the instructor explain the philosophy behind the Lamaze method and describe what else is taught in Lamaze classes. After the visit, ask students: **Under what other circumstances might the Lamaze method be useful?** *(Whenever a person has to cope with severe stress or pain)* L2

Multiple Births

Build Science Skills

Applying Concepts Tell students that some fertility treatments increase the chances of multiple births by causing more than one egg to be released during ovulation. Ask: **Which type of twins, identical or fraternal, would be produced in such cases?** *(Fraternal twins, because they result from the fertilization of two eggs)* L1 L2

Early Years

Demonstration

Have students bring in photographs of themselves when they were less than two years of age. Display the unlabeled photos in the classroom, and challenge students to identify as many of their classmates as they can. Then, ask: **In what ways do people change physically between infancy and adolescence?** *(People change in body size and proportions. Their facial features also become larger and more mature looking.)* **What are some of the features that remain constant enough that we can use them for identification?** *(Students might mention skin or eye color or the shape of certain distinctive facial features, such as the nose, chin, or eyes.)* Point out that features such as eye color and skin tone can change during infancy. L1

Answer to . . .

✓CHECKPOINT *Identical twins are genetically identical; fraternal twins are not.*

39–4 (continued)

Adulthood

Use Community Resources

Suggest that students consult local libraries, senior centers, and government agencies to find out what services are available in their area for seniors. (Services might include meal delivery, social programs, transportation, and nursing care.) Ask: **What needs of seniors are met by these services?** *(Students might mention help for people with disabling health problems or physical limitations and the need for social interaction.)* L2

3 ASSESS

Evaluate Understanding

Call on students at random to name the stages of development of the embryo and fetus. Call on other students to describe the features of the embryo or fetus at each stage.

Reteach

Using the chalkboard, work with students to develop a timeline of important events from fertilization to birth.

Thinking Visually

The timelines should show that students can recognize important developmental milestones, such as walking, talking, learning to read, first permanent tooth, learning to share, and the first signs of puberty.

If your class subscribes to the iText, use it to review the Key Concepts in Section 39–4.

Answer to . . .

Figure 39–27 *Factors include a well-balanced, low-fat diet, and regular exercise.*

▲ **Figure 39–27** By maintaining a healthy lifestyle, you may be able to slow the aging process. **Applying Concepts** *What factors contribute to a healthy lifestyle?*

Adolescence Adolescence begins with puberty and ends with adulthood. The surge in sex hormones that starts at puberty produces a growth spurt that will conclude in mid-adolescence as the long bones of the arms and legs stop growing and complete their ossification. The continuing development of intellectual skills combines with personality changes that are associated with adult maturity.

Adulthood

Development continues during adulthood. By most measures, adults reach their highest levels of physical strength and development between the ages of 25 and 35. During these years most individuals assume the responsibilities of adulthood.

In most individuals, the first signs of physiological aging appear in their thirties. Joints begin to lose some of their flexibility, muscle strength starts to decrease, and several body systems show slight declines in efficiency. By age 50, these changes, although generally still minor, are apparent to most individuals. In women, menopause greatly reduces estrogen levels. After menopause, follicle development no longer occurs and ovulation stops. At around age 65, most systems of the body become less efficient, making homeostasis more difficult to maintain.

Although there are some changes in mental functioning during older adulthood, these changes usually have little effect on thinking, learning, or long-term memory. The brain remains open to change and to learning. In fact, evidence suggests that the aging process can be slowed by keeping the mind active and challenged. Most older adults are fully capable of continuing stimulating intellectual work. By practicing the habits of good health and regular exercise, as the woman in **Figure 39–27** is doing, every person can hope to be happy and productive at every stage of human development.

39–4 Section Assessment

1. **Key Concept** Describe the process of fertilization.
2. **Key Concept** Describe the role of the placenta.
3. **Key Concept** Describe the three stages of early development.
4. What are the three germ layers that result from gastrulation?
5. What is oxytocin, and what is its role in childbirth?
6. **Critical Thinking Applying Concepts** Why do you think doctors recommend that women avoid most medications and alcohol during pregnancy?

Thinking Visually

Creating a Timeline
Starting with your birth date, create a timeline of physical and social developmental milestones. As resources, you can use interviews, photographs, and memories.

39–4 Section Assessment

1. Sperm attaches to a binding site and releases enzymes that attack the egg's protective layer; egg and sperm nuclei merge.
2. The placenta is the embryo's organ of respiration, nourishment, and excretion.
3. Implantation: blastocyst attaches itself to the wall of the uterus; gastrulation: three cell layers form; neurulation: the nervous system develops
4. Ectoderm, mesoderm, and endoderm
5. Oxytocin is a hormone that stimulates labor.
6. Because these substances may cross the placenta and harm the embryo or fetus

Exploration

BI 9.c, BI 9.g, *BI 9.i, BIIE 1.g

Modeling Blood Glucose Regulation

Regulating the level of blood glucose is one of the body's most important jobs. Two hormones, insulin and glucagon, help to regulate the level of glucose in blood. Because these two hormones have opposite effects, it is important that a proper balance between them is maintained. In this investigation, you will simulate how this regulatory mechanism works.

Problem How does the body regulate blood glucose levels?

Materials

- 3 pieces of construction paper of different colors
- scissors

Skills Using Models, Asking Questions

Procedure

1. Work in groups of three students. Give each member of the group a number from 1 to 3.
2. Cut 15 cards out of construction paper of one color. On each card, print "10 mg glucose/100 mL blood" on the front and "glycogen" on the back. These are your glucose cards. Turning over a glucose card represents converting glucose into glycogen, or vice versa.
3. Cut out 2 cards of a second color. On each of these cards print "insulin." Each of these insulin cards can convert 1 glucose card into glycogen.
4. Cut out 2 more cards of a third color. On each of these cards print "glucagon." One glucagon card can convert 1 glucose card from glycogen into glucose.
5. Place 9 glucose cards face up on the table. This represents the normal level of glucose in blood (90 mg glucose/100 mL blood). Student 1 should keep 2 more glucose cards face up.
6. Student 2 should keep the insulin and glucagon cards. Student 3 should keep the remaining 4 glucose cards face down, to represent stored glycogen.
7. To simulate the effect of a meal, student 1 should add a glucose card to the 9 on the table. Discuss how the body responds to this change.
8. Students 2 and 3 should use the cards to model how the body restores the normal blood glucose level after a meal.
9. To simulate the effect of exercise, student 1 should remove a glucose card from the 9 on the table. Repeat step 8.
10. To simulate what happens when a person has Type I diabetes, repeat steps 7 and 8 without using the insulin cards.

Analyze and Conclude

1. **Applying Concepts** What organ does student 2 represent? Explain your answer.
2. **Using Models** How did students 2 and 3 respond in step 8? In step 9? In step 10? Describe what happens in the body in each situation.
3. **Applying Concepts** How does this activity model homeostasis in the body?
4. **Predicting** What would happen if a person with Type I diabetes ate a large amount of sugar?

Go Further

Using Models What do you think would happen if the body did not produce enough glucagon? Use your cards to model what would happen in this situation.

Exploration

BI 9.c, BI 9.g, *BI 9.i, BIIE 1.g

Objective
Students will be able to use a model to gain an understanding of blood glucose regulation.

Skills Focus **Using Models, Asking Questions**

Time 40 minutes

Advance Prep You can save time by cutting out the cards before class or by using colored index cards instead of cards cut from colored paper.

Teaching Tip Before students follow the procedure, review how blood glucose is regulated by insulin and glucagon. (See page 1007.)

Procedure
9. You may need to help students reason through the effects of exercise on blood glucose levels.

Expected Outcome Students should observe how the insulin and glucagon in their model regulate blood glucose.

Go Further

If the body did not produce enough glucagon, it would not be able to convert glycogen into glucose. After exercise or several hours without food, the body's blood glucose level might become too low.

Analyze and Conclude

1. The pancreas, because the pancreas produces and releases insulin and glucagon

2. In step 8, student 2 placed an insulin card on the table and student 3 turned over one of the glucose cards. In the body, insulin is released, causing glucose to be converted into glycogen. In step 9, student 2 placed a glucagon card on the table and student 3 turned over one of the glycogen cards. In the body, glucagon is released, causing glycogen to be converted into glucose. In step 10, students 2 and 3 did not respond. In the body, insulin is not released and glucose increases instead of being converted to glycogen and lipids.

3. In this activity, the cards labeled "glucagon" and "insulin" were used to model how the body maintains homeostasis in blood glucose level. As blood glucose levels changed, people responded by placing the appropriate cards (hormones) on the table.

4. His or her blood glucose level would rise.

Chapter 39 Study Guide

Study Tip

Have students work in pairs to make flashcards for the Vocabulary terms and Key Concept questions and use the cards to quiz each other on the chapter.

Thinking Visually

Students' charts should include the following: pituitary gland (ADH, oxytocin, FSH, LH, TSH, ACTH, GH, prolactin, MSH), parathyroid glands (parathyroid hormone), thyroid gland (thyroxine, calcitonin), adrenal glands (epinephrine, norepinephrine, aldosterone, cortisol), pancreas (insulin, glucagon), ovary (estrogen, progesterone), and testis (testosterone).

Chapter 39 Assessment

Reviewing Content

1. b **5.** c **9.** c
2. b **6.** a **10.** c
3. b **7.** b
4. d **8.** c

Understanding Concepts

11. A hormone binds to a specific chemical receptor on a target cell or to receptors inside the cell. For example, progesterone binds to a receptor site inside a uterine cell.
12. Prostaglandins are hormonelike substances that affect only nearby cells or tissues.
13. When the level of a hormone increases in the blood, it "feeds back" to inhibit the gland that produced it.
14. The pituitary gland
15. Epinephrine increases heart rate, blood pressure, and blood flow to the muscles. It also causes air passageways to widen and stimulates the release of extra glucose into the blood to help produce a sudden burst of energy. These actions result in a general increase in body activity, which can serve as preparation for intense physical activity.
16. Diabetes mellitus may occur. Very high blood glucose levels can cause serious complications or death.
17. A period of rapid growth and sexual maturation during which the reproductive system becomes fully functional
18. Follicle-stimulating hormone (FSH) and luteinizing hormone (LH)

Chapter 39 Study Guide

39–1 The Endocrine System

Key Concepts  BI 9.c, *BI 9.i

- The endocrine system is made up of glands that release their products—hormones—into the bloodstream. Hormones travel through the bloodstream and affect the activities of other cells.
- The endocrine system is regulated by feedback mechanisms that function to maintain homeostasis.

Vocabulary
hormone, p. 997
target cell, p. 997
exocrine gland, p. 998
endocrine gland, p. 998
prostaglandin, p. 1000

39–2 Human Endocrine Glands

Key Concepts  BI 9.b, *BI 9.i

- The pituitary gland secretes nine hormones that directly regulate many body functions and controls the actions of several other endocrine glands.
- The hypothalamus controls the secretions of the pituitary gland and helps coordinate the interactions of the nervous and endocrine systems.
- The thyroid gland secretes hormones that help to regulate the body's metabolism.
- Hormones from the thyroid gland and the parathyroid glands act to maintain homeostasis of calcium levels in the blood.
- The adrenal glands release hormones that help the body prepare for and deal with stress.
- The pancreas secretes insulin and glucagon, which help to keep the level of glucose in the blood stable.
- The gonads—the ovaries and testes—serve two important functions: the production of gametes and the secretion of sex hormones.

Vocabulary
pituitary gland, p. 1003
diabetes mellitus, p. 1007
ovary, p. 1008
testis, p. 1008

39–3 The Reproductive System

Key Concepts BI 2.b, *BI 9.i

- The main function of the male reproductive system is to produce and deliver sperm.
- The main function of the female reproductive system is to produce ova. In addition, the female reproductive system prepares the female's body to nourish a developing embryo.
- The menstrual cycle has four phases: follicular phase, ovulation, luteal phase, and menstruation.

Vocabulary
puberty, p. 1009 • scrotum, p. 1010
seminiferous tubule, p. 1010
epididymis, p. 1011 • vas deferens, p. 1011
urethra, p. 1011 • penis, p. 1011
follicle, p. 1012 • ovulation, p. 1012
Fallopian tube, p. 1012 • uterus, p. 1012
vagina, p. 1012 • menstrual cycle, p. 1013
corpus luteum, p. 1014 • menstruation, p. 1014
sexually transmitted disease, p. 1015

39–4 Fertilization and Development

Key Concepts

- The process of a sperm joining with an egg is called fertilization.
- The stages of early development include implantation, gastrulation, and neurulation.
- The placenta is the embryo's organ of respiration, nourishment, and excretion.

Vocabulary
zygote, p. 1016
implantation, p. 1017
differentiation, p. 1017
gastrulation, p. 1018
neurulation, p. 1018
placenta, p. 1019
fetus, p. 1020

Thinking Visually

Use the information in this chapter to construct a chart listing the actions of each hormone discussed. Your chart should include three headings: Endocrine Gland, Hormone, and Action of Hormone.

TIME SAVER — CHAPTER RESOURCES

Print:
- ***Teaching Resources,*** Chapter Vocabulary Review, Graphic Organizer, Chapter 39 Tests: Levels A and B

Technology:
- ***Computer Test Bank,*** Chapter 39 Test
- ***iText,*** Chapter 39 Assessment

Chapter 39 Assessment

Reviewing Content

Choose the letter that best answers the question or completes the statement.

1. Glands that release hormones into the blood are part of the
   a. digestive system.
   b. endocrine system.
   c. circulatory system.
   d. nervous system.
2. Hormones produced from cholesterol are called
   a. protein hormones.
   b. steroid hormones.
   c. nonsteroid hormones.
   d. peptide hormones.
3. Hormonelike substances produced by nearly all cells are called
   a. thyroxines.
   b. prostaglandins.
   c. steroids.
   d. androgens.
4. Hormones that help regulate blood calcium levels are produced by the
   a. adrenal gland.
   b. thymus gland.
   c. pancreas.
   d. parathyroid gland.
5. The rate of metabolism is regulated by
   a. PTH.
   b. aldosterone.
   c. thyroxine.
   d. calcitonin.
6. The diagram shows the female reproductive system. Which structure is indicated by the X?

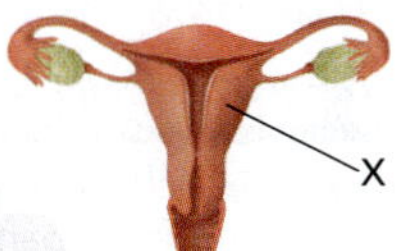

   a. uterus c. ovary
   b. Fallopian tube d. cervix
7. The principal male sex hormone is
   a. FSH. c. estrogen.
   b. testosterone. d. insulin.
8. Another name for a fertilized egg is a
   a. gastrula.
   b. placenta.
   c. zygote.
   d. fetus.

Interactive textbook with assessment at PHSchool.com 

9. Fertilization usually occurs in the
   a. uterus.
   b. vagina.
   c. Fallopian tube.
   d. ovary.
10. After the eighth week of development, the human embryo is known as a(an)
   a. zygote.
   b. infant.
   c. fetus.
   d. morula.

Understanding Concepts

11. What is the relationship between a hormone and a target cell? Use a specific example to explain your answer.
12. What are prostaglandins?
13. How does a feedback mechanism regulate the activity of the endocrine system?
14. What endocrine gland produces growth hormone?
15. How does the secretion of epinephrine prepare the body for emergencies?
16. What happens if blood glucose levels are not kept stable?
17. What is puberty?
18. What are the two hormones that stimulate the gonads to produce their hormones?
19. List the secondary sex characteristics that appear in males at puberty.
20. Describe the structure of a sperm.
21. Trace the path of sperm from a testis until it leaves the body.
22. What are the functions of estrogen?
23. Trace the path of an unfertilized egg from a follicle until it leaves the body.
24. Explain why the menstrual cycle is an example of a feedback mechanism.
25. Trace the development of a zygote from fertilization through implantation.
26. Explain the importance of the primary germ layers.
27. What is the function of the placenta?
28. Describe what happens during childbirth.

TIME SAVER HOMEWORK GUIDE

Section:	Questions:
Section 39–1	1–3, 11–13, 30, 36
Section 39–2	4, 5, 14–16, 29, 31
Section 39–3	6, 7, 17–24, 34, 35, 37, 38
Section 39–4	8–10, 25–28, 32, 33

Interactive Textbook

If your class subscribes to the iText, your students can go online to access an interactive version of the Student Edition and a self-test.

(Continued from page 1026)

19. Growth of facial and body hair, increase in body size, and deepening of the voice

20. A sperm cell consists of a head containing a highly condensed nucleus, a midpiece packed with mitochondria, and a flagellum that propels it forward.

21. Sperm travel from the seminiferous tubules in the testes into the epididymis, where they mature and are stored. Sperm then are moved into the vas deferens, where fluids from the seminal vesicle, prostate gland, and bulbourethral gland are added to form semen. The semen is ejected from the penis through the urethra.

22. Development of the reproductive system and female secondary sex characteristics, regulation of the menstrual cycle, and preparation of the uterus for implantation

23. It passes through a Fallopian tube and the uterus and if unfertilized is discharged from the body through the vagina.

24. The menstrual cycle is regulated by hormones that are controlled by feedback inhibition mechanisms. For example, the hypothalamus reacts to low estrogen levels in the blood by producing a releasing hormone that acts on the pituitary gland. In response, the pituitary releases FSH and LH.

25. A zygote undergoes cell division as it passes through the Fallopian tube from a two-celled embryo on day 2 to a solid, 50-cell morula on day 4. As the embryo grows, a fluid-filled cavity forms in the center, transforming it into a hollow blastocyst. About six or seven days after fertilization, the blastocyst implants into the wall of the uterus.

26. All organs of the embryo form from the primary germ layers.

27. The placenta, which contains maternal and fetal tissues, can be thought of as the fetus's organ of respiration, nutrition, and excretion.

(Continued from page 1027)

28. Childbirth begins when the pituitary gland releases oxytocin, which stimulates contractions. The contractions cause the opening of the cervix to expand enough for the baby to pass through it. The amniotic sac breaks, and contractions of the uterus force the baby out through the vagina.

Critical Thinking

29. The red line represents a person with diabetes, and the blue line represents a person who does not have diabetes. The person with diabetes has a high level of blood glucose for a longer period of time following a meal due to lack of insulin to help remove glucose from the blood.

30. Students' drawings should show that the level of thyroxine in the blood stimulates the hypothalamus and then the pituitary gland to produce more or less thyroid-stimulating hormone, which, in turn, leads to the production of more or less thyroxine by the thyroid gland.

31. The heartbeat increases before a meet because nervousness or excitement leads to the production of "fight or flight" hormones by the adrenal gland. During the meet, the heartbeat increases due to oxygen demand by muscles.

32. The placenta is made up of two layers, the fetal portion and the maternal portion. This two-layered structure allows the blood of the mother and the embryo to flow past each other but not to mix.

33. Because the Fallopian tube does not provide the fetus with enough room to grow and the tube would eventually rupture

34. This keeps sperm at a cooler temperature than internal body temperature, which is needed for normal development.

35. Insufficient amounts of FSH and LH would cause follicles to fail to develop to maturity and release mature eggs. Further, without a rise in estrogen and progesterone, the uterine lining would not be maintained.

36. Traffic reports are similar to hormones because they broadcast messages that affect the activities of motorists. They act as a feedback control by inhibiting motorists from moving toward areas of traffic congestion.

Chapter 39 Assessment

Critical Thinking

29. Using Tables and Graphs The graph below shows the levels of glucose in the blood of two people during a 5-hour period immediately following the ingestion of a typical meal. Which line represents a person with diabetes? Which line represents a person who does not have diabetes? Explain your answers.

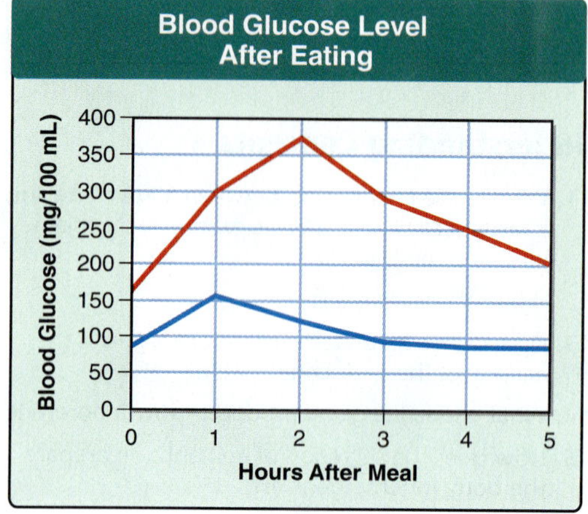

30. Using Models Make a diagram of a negative-feedback mechanism involving the hormones that regulate the production of thyroxine.

31. Applying Concepts The heartbeat of a swimmer was found to increase significantly both before and during a swim meet. Explain why this happens.

32. Applying Concepts The placenta develops from tissues produced by both the embryo and the uterus. How does the structure of the placenta prevent the mother's blood from mixing with the blood of the developing embryo?

33. Inferring Occasionally, a zygote does not move into the uterus but attaches to the wall of a Fallopian tube instead. Why might this be a very dangerous situation for the mother?

34. Formulating Hypotheses Sperm are stored in the epididymis, which is located in the scrotum. Why is it advantageous for sperm to be stored in the scrotum?

35. Predicting Predict the effects that insufficient amounts of FSH and LH will have on the menstrual cycle.

36. Using Analogies In many areas during rush hour, radio stations broadcast traffic reports. How are traffic reports similar to hormones? How do the reports act as a feedback control mechanism to control the flow of traffic?

37. Applying Concepts Describe how each of the following represents an adaptation that helps to ensure successful fertilization: seminal fluid; production and release of millions of sperm; cilia lining the Fallopian tubes; long tail of a sperm.

38. Drawing Conclusions The menstrual cycle is suppressed during pregnancy. Explain why this is important to the success of a full-term pregnancy.

Focus on the BIG Idea

Cellular Basis of Life Sperm cells contain numerous mitochondria. Use what you learned about mitochondria in Chapter 7 to explain how mitochondria might affect sperm activity.

Writing in Science

Anabolic steroids are synthetic versions of the hormone testosterone. Although anabolic steroids have important medical uses, they can damage the body if abused. Use library or Internet resources to find more information about anabolic steroids. Then, write an article for your school newspaper informing people of the harmful effects of these substances. (*Hint:* Be sure to support your main idea with specific details.)

Performance-Based Assessment

In the Community Research the topic of fetal alcohol syndrome. Then, design a pamphlet to be used in a clinic informing women of the dangers of drinking alcohol during pregnancy. Your pamphlet must have a title, illustrations, and brief facts about fetal alcohol syndrome.

For: An interactive self-test
Visit: PHSchool.com
Web Code: cba-0390

37. Seminal fluid provides a nutrient-rich medium in which sperm are nourished and transported. The production and release of millions of sperm help ensure that at least one sperm will reach and fertilize the egg. Cilia lining the Fallopian tubes push eggs, which are not motile, toward the uterus. The long tail of a sperm helps it travel to the egg.

38. During pregnancy, an embryo is implanted into the uterine lining. If the menstrual cycle continued as usual and a new egg cell was not fertilized, the corpus luteum could start to disintegrate, and the embryo could be discharged from the uterus.

Mitochondria release energy, providing sperm cells with the energy needed to reach an egg.

Standards Practice

Test-Taking Tip For questions containing words such as NOT or EXCEPT, first rule out any choice that fits the characteristic in question. Use this approach to eliminate four out of five choices. To check if your answer is correct, confirm that it does not fit the characteristic in question.

Directions: Choose the letter that best answers the question or completes the statement.

1. Which sequence correctly describes the route sperm take through the human male reproductive system?
   A vas deferens, urethra, epididymis
   B epididymis, vas deferens, urethra
   C vas deferens, epididymis, urethra
   D urethra, epididymis, vas deferens

2. Each of these terms refers to a stage in the human menstrual cycle EXCEPT
   A ovulation
   B luteal phase
   C corpus phase
   D follicular phase

3. Which of the following is NOT an endocrine gland?
   A thyroid gland
   B pituitary gland
   C parathyroid gland
   D sweat gland

Questions 4–7 Each of the lettered choices below refers to the following numbered statements. Select the best lettered choice. A choice may be used once, more than once, or not at all.

A Ovary
B Follicle
C Hypothalamus
D Epididymis

4. Cluster of cells surrounding an egg that prepares it for release into the human female reproductive tract
5. Produces estrogen and progesterone
6. Controls the secretions of the pituitary gland
7. Stores sperm in the human male reproductive system

Questions 8–11 The diagram below shows the human endocrine system. Use the diagram to answer the questions.

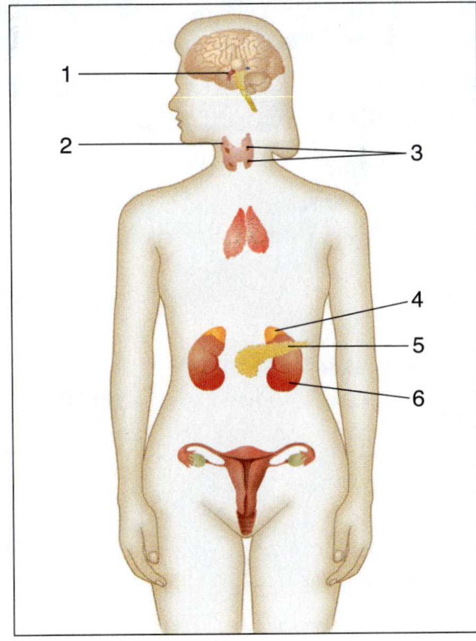

8. Which gland helps the body prepare for and deal with stress?
   A 1 **C** 4
   B 2 **D** 5

9. Which gland is both an endocrine and an exocrine gland?
   A 2 **C** 4
   B 3 **D** 5

10. Which gland secretes growth hormone?
   A 1 **C** 3
   B 2 **D** 4

11. Which gland secretes thyroxine?
   A 1 **C** 3
   B 2 **D** 4

Standards Practice

1. B	**5.** A	**9.** D
2. C	**6.** C	**10.** A
3. D	**7.** D	**11.** B
4. B	**8.** C	

Success Tracker™
Online at PHSchool.com

Have students check their understanding of the chapter by logging onto Success Tracker.

Writing in Science

Because of the many Web sites promoting anabolic steroids for bodybuilding, check to make sure that students are finding accurate, unbiased information supported by empirical studies. Stress that they should research both physical and emotional problems associated with anabolic steroid abuse. Their articles should include specific details in support of each main idea.

Performance-Based Assessment

Students' pamphlets should indicate that fetal alcohol syndrome refers to birth defects—including low birth weight, facial abnormalities, heart defects, and lower-than-normal intelligence—caused by ingestion of alcohol during pregnancy. Pamphlets should make it clear that there is no safe level of alcohol consumption during pregnancy.

Your students can independently test their knowledge of the chapter and print out their test results for your files.

Chapter Planner 40 The Immune System and Disease

Section and Section Objectives	Time	STANDARDS NCLB	STANDARDS Biology	Activities and Labs
40–1 Infectious Disease, pp. 1031–1035 **40.1.1** ***Identify*** the causes of disease. **40.1.2** ***Explain*** how infectious diseases are transmitted. **40.1.3** ***Describe*** how antibiotics fight infection.	1 period (1/2 block)	BI 10.d		**SE:** ***Inquiry Activity,*** How do diseases spread?, p. 1030 L2 **TE:** ***Demonstration,*** p. 1032 L2 **LMA:** Chapter 40 Lab L2 L3 **BTM:** Lab 16 L2
40–2 The Immune System, pp. 1036–1042 **40.2.1** ***Identify*** the body's nonspecific defenses against invading pathogens. **40.2.2** ***Describe*** the function of the immune system.	2 periods (1 block)	BI 10.b, BI 10.c	BI 10.a, *BI 10.f	**TE:** ***Demonstration,*** p. 1037 L1 L2, p. 1038 L1 **SE:** ***Quick Lab,*** How does cell-mediated immunity work?, p. 1041 L1 L2 **SE:** ***Real-World Lab,*** Testing the Specificity of Antibodies, p. 1055 L2 L3 **LMB:** Chapter 40 Lab L1 L2
40–3 Immune System Disorders, pp. 1043–1047 **40.3.1** ***State*** what happens when the immune system overreacts. **40.3.2** ***Explain*** what an autoimmune disease is. **40.3.3** ***Describe*** how HIV is transmitted and affects the immune system.	2 periods (1 block)		BI 10.e	**SE:** ***Issues in Biology,*** Slowing a Worldwide Epidemic, p. 1048 L2
40–4 The Environment and Your Health, pp. 1049–1054 **40.4.1** ***Identify*** environmental factors that affect your health. **40.4.2** ***Describe*** how you can maintain your health.	1 period (1/2 block)			**TE:** ***Demonstration,*** p. 1053 L2 **SE:** ***Analyzing Data,*** Cancer Mortality p. 1053 L2 **BTM:** Lab 13 L2
Chapter Assessment, pp. 1056–1059	1 period (1/2 block)			

ACTIVITY PLANNER

SE: *Inquiry Activity,* p. 1030; 10 min.; Glo Germ™ oil or dilute fluorescein solution, ultraviolet lamp

TE: *Demonstration,* p. 1032; 5 min., 5 min.; bacterial culture, wire loop, 2 sterile petri dishes with nutrient agar, Bunsen burner

TE: *Demonstration,* p. 1037; 10 min.; microprojector, drop of pond water on slide

TE: *Demonstration,* p. 1038; 15 min.; poster board, string, scissors, markers

SE: *Quick Lab,* p. 1041; 15 min.; 3 red balloons; 3 yellow balloons; 3 light-blue balloons; red, purple, and light-blue adhesive notes; toothpick

TE: *Demonstration,* p. 1053; 5 min.; microprojector, slides of normal and cancerous cells

SE: *Real-World Lab,* p. 1055; 45 min.; Strep A diagnostic kits with control samples for three tests, sterile water, plastic gloves

PLANNING KEY

Ability Levels

for students performing . . .

below grade level L1

at grade level L2

above grade level L3

Print Components

SE	Student Edition	LA	Lab Assessment
TE	Teacher's Edition	BTM	Biotechnology Manual
RSW	Reading & Study Workbook A	IDM	Issues and Decision Making
ARSW	Adapted Reading & Study Workbook B	LW	Lab Worksheets
TR	Teaching Resources	LMA	Laboratory Manual A
IF	Investigations in Forensics	LMB	Laboratory Manual B

Tech Components

CTB	Computer Test Bank
BD	BioDetectives DVD
TP	Transparencies Plus
PLM	Probeware Lab Manual
ABC	ABC DVD Library
LS	Lab Simulations
VL	Virtual Labs

Interactive textbook with assessment at PHSchool.com

Program Resources	Assessment	Media and Technology
TR: Lesson Plan 40–1, Section Summary, p. 227 L1, p. 235 L2, Worksheets, pp. 237–238 L2 **RSW:** Section 40–1 L2	**SE:** 40–1 Section Assessment, p. 1035 **TR:** Section Review 40–1	**iText:** Section 40–1 **TP:** 40–1 Interest Grabber, Section Outline, Koch's Postulates, Figure 40–3 **BD:** "Influenza: Tracking a Virus" "Hantavirus: A Tale of Mice and People"
TR: Lesson Plans 40–2, Section Summary, p. 227 L1, p. 235 L2, Worksheets, pp. 230–232 L1, pp. 239–241 L2 **LW:** Chapter 40 Real-World Lab L1 L2 L3 **RSW:** Section 40–2 L2 **ARSW:** Section 40–2 L1	**SE:** 40–2 Section Assessment, p. 1042 **TR:** Section Review 40–2	**iText:** Section 40–2 **TP:** 40–2 Interest Grabber, Section Outline, Primary and Secondary Responses, Figure 40–7, Figure 40–8, Figure 40–9, Figure 40–10 **ABC:** 44 Inflammatory Response, 45 Humoral Immunity, 46 Cell-Mediated Immunity
TR: Lesson Plan 40–3, Section Summary, p. 228 L1, p. 236 L2, Worksheets, pp. 242–243 L2 **RSW:** Section 40–3 L2	**SE:** 40–3 Section Assessment, p. 1047 **TR:** Section Review 40–3	**iText:** Section 40–3 **TP:** 40–3 Interest Grabber, Section Outline, Stages of HIV Infection
TR: Lesson Plans 40–4, Section Summary, p. 229 L1, p. 236 L2, Worksheets, p. 233 L1, pp. 244–245 L2, Enrichment L2 L3 **RSW:** Section 40–4 L2 **ARSW:** Section 40–4 L1	**SE:** 40–4 Section Assessment, p. 1054 **TR:** Section Review 40–4	**iText:** Section 40–4 **TP:** 40–4 Interest Grabber, Section Outline, Concept Map
	SE: Chapter 40 Assessment, pp. 1056–1059 **TR:** Chapter Vocabulary Review, Graphic Organizer, Chapter 40 Test **LA:** Laboratory Assessment 10	**iText:** Chapter 40 Assessment **CTB:** Chapter 40 Test

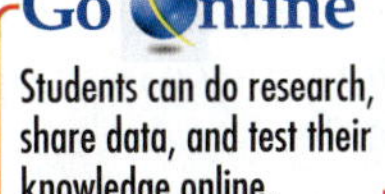

Students can do research, share data, and test their knowledge online.

PRESSED FOR TIME?

To Preview the Chapter

- Have students study the figures in Sections 40–1 and 40–2 and read the captions.
- Have students scan Sections 40–1 and 40–2 for highlighted, boldface Vocabulary terms and read the definitions.

To Cover the Chapter Quickly

- Have students read all of Sections 40–1 and 40–2 and the introductions to Sections 40–3 and 40–4.
- Assign the Section Assessments 40–1 and 40–2; questions 1–9, 11–22, 27, 30, 32, 33, and 36 in Chapter 40 Assessment; and questions 1–10 in Chapter 40 Standards Practice.

To Review the Chapter

- Assign Sections 40–1 and 40–2 in the Reading and Study Workbook or the Adapted Reading and Study Workbook.
- Assign the Section Reviews for 40–1 and 40–2 and the Chapter Vocabulary Review for Chapter 40 in the Teaching Resources.

CHAPTER 40

ENGAGE/EXPLORE

Inquiry Activity

Objectives Students will be able to
- infer how a virus spreads;
- conclude that thorough hand washing helps prevent the spread of diseases.

Skills Focus **Inferring, Drawing Conclusions**

Materials Glo Germ™ oil or dilute fluorescein solution, ultraviolet lamp

Time 10 minutes

Advance Prep Apply the Glo Germ™ oil no more than 10 minutes before students arrive.

Safety Caution students to avoid getting the fluorescent substance in their eyes or mouths.

Strategy You can make sure the "virus" spreads to students' hands by applying the fluorescent substance to the classroom doorknob and any other objects in the classroom that students are likely to touch.

Expected Outcomes
- Students should observe the "virus" in various areas of the classroom and on their hands.
- Students should find that thorough hand washing removes the "virus" from their hands.

Think About It

1. The "virus" spread by contact as students moved around the room and touched objects.
2. Thorough hand washing helps prevent the spread of diseases by removing disease-causing agents before they can be spread to other people.

Quick View Video

Discovery School DVD Encourage students to view track 10 "Influenza: Tracking a Virus" on the *BioDetectives* DVD.

CHAPTER 40

The Immune System and Disease

White blood cells help protect the body from disease. Here, one type of white blood cell—a macrophage—engulfs a parasite (magnification: 1950×).

Quick View Video

Discovery School Video To find out more about the transmission of a virus, view track 10 "Influenza: Tracking a Virus" on the *BioDetectives* DVD.

Inquiry Activity

How do diseases spread?

Procedure 

1. Your teacher has placed a fluorescent material in the classroom to simulate a virus. The material glows when exposed to ultraviolet (UV) radiation. Use a UV lamp to check for the "virus" on your hands and objects you touched since entering the classroom. **CAUTION:** *Ultraviolet light can harm your eyes. Do not look directly at the ultraviolet light.*
2. Exchange results with your classmates to determine how the "virus" spread through the classroom. Wash your hands with soap and warm water.

Think About It

1. **Inferring** What can you infer about how the "virus" spread through the classroom?
2. **Drawing Conclusions** How does thorough hand washing help prevent the spread of diseases?

HISTORY OF SCIENCE

Koch and his postulates

Robert Koch was a German surgeon born in 1843. Today, he is considered to be one of the founders of modern bacteriology, but when he developed his postulates he was just a country doctor. During a local anthrax epidemic, Koch tried to identify the cause of the disease. He isolated the pathogen from infected cattle, transferred it to mice, and recovered the same pathogen from the mice. Although Koch's postulates still guide bacteriology and epidemiology, there are some important exceptions to their use. For example, many pathogens, such as the pathogens that cause syphilis and AIDS, cannot yet be grown in culture. This makes it impossible to fulfill the second of Koch's postulates in linking these pathogens with a disease. In cases such as these, scientists must depend on circumstantial evidence, such as the presence of the organism in every individual diagnosed with the disease.

40–1 Infectious Disease

BI 10.d. Students know there are important differences between bacteria and viruses with respect to their requirements for growth and replication, the body's primary defenses against bacterial and viral infections, and effective treatments of these infections.

Good health is something that you might take for granted—until you or someone close to you gets sick. Then, the value of good health becomes all too obvious. Why do you get sick? How do you get better? What is the best way for you to avoid getting sick in the first place? These are questions that people have been asking for centuries. Today, in most cases, these questions can be answered.

A **disease** is any change, other than an injury, that disrupts the normal functions of the body.  **Some diseases are produced by agents, such as bacteria, viruses, and fungi. Others are caused by materials in the environment, such as cigarette smoke. Still others, such as hemophilia, are inherited.** Disease-causing agents are called **pathogens,** which means "sickness-makers." Diseases caused by pathogens are generally called infectious diseases.

Guide for Reading

Key Concepts
- What causes disease?
- How are infectious diseases transmitted?

Vocabulary
disease
pathogen
germ theory of disease
Koch's postulates
vector
antibiotic

Reading Strategy: Using Prior Knowledge Before you read, make a list of some of the diseases that you have had. As you read, determine which pathogen might have caused each disease.

The Germ Theory of Disease

For thousands of years, people believed that diseases were caused by curses, evil spirits, or night vapors. In the mid-nineteenth century, a new explanation was put forth based on the work of the French chemist Louis Pasteur and the German bacteriologist Robert Koch. The observations of Pasteur and Koch led them to conclude that infectious diseases were caused by microorganisms of different types, commonly called germs. This idea is now known as the **germ theory of disease.**

The world is filled with microorganisms of every shape and description. How can scientists be sure that a particular organism causes a certain disease? In 1975, Allen Steere of Yale University had a chance to ask that question. In a small area of Connecticut, Steere found 39 children and several adults suffering from pain and joint inflammation. Their symptoms looked like a rare form of childhood arthritis. However, Steere thought that there were far too many cases of arthritis for such a small population. He looked for another explanation. The rural location of the outbreak and the fact that most of the cases had started in summer or early fall made Steere suspect, at first, that this could be an infectious disease carried by an insect.

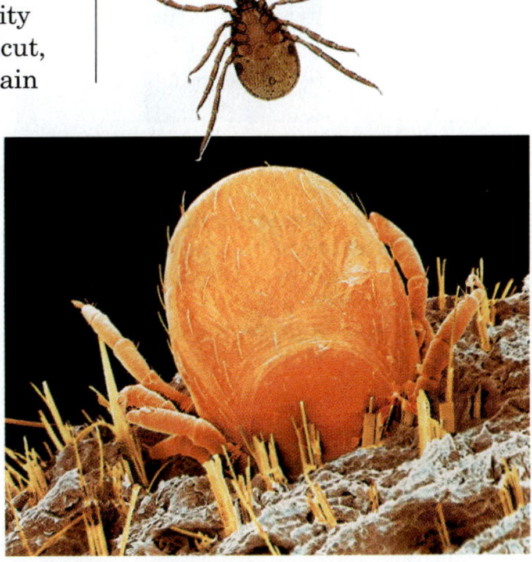

Figure 40–1 **Diseases can be inherited, caused by materials in the environment, or produced by pathogens.** Certain species of ticks often carry bacteria or viruses that are transmitted when they bite a host.

(magnification: about 30×)

SECTION RESOURCES

Print:
- ***Laboratory Manual A,*** Chapter 40 Lab
- ***Teaching Resources,*** Lesson Plan 40–1, Adapted Section Summary 40–1, Section Summary 40–1, Worksheets 40–1, Section Review 40–1
- ***Reading and Study Workbook A,*** Section 40–1
- ***Adapted Reading and Study Workbook B,*** Section 40–1
- ***Biotechnology Manual,*** Lab 16

Technology:
- ***iText,*** Section 40–1
- ***BioDetectives DVD,*** "Influenza: Tracking a Virus"; "Hantavirus: A Tale of Mice and People"
- ***Transparencies Plus,*** Section 40–1

Section 40–1

1 FOCUS

Objectives

40.1.1 ***Identify*** the causes of disease.
40.1.2 ***Explain*** how infectious diseases are transmitted.
40.1.3 ***Describe*** how antibiotics fight infection.

Guide for Reading

Vocabulary Preview

Tell students that the term *pathogen* refers to an agent that causes disease. Ask: **How do you think the term *pathogen* is related to the germ theory of disease?** *(Germ is another term for pathogen. According to the theory, germs, or pathogens, cause disease.)*

Reading Strategy

Students are likely to list respiratory infections such as colds and flu and gastrointestinal infections that cause stomachaches and diarrhea. They should determine which pathogen might have caused each disease.

2 INSTRUCT

Address Misconceptions

Explain that some diseases have multiple causes. For example, some types of cancer, such as lung cancer, are caused by environmental factors, for example, cigarette smoke. Other types of cancer, such as cervical cancer, are caused by pathogens (for cervical cancer, human papilloma virus). L1 L2

The Germ Theory of Disease

Demonstration

Help students appreciate the importance of the germ theory of disease by showing them death rates by cause of death in the United States population for the late 1800s and also for a recent year. Then, ask: **How did the number of deaths caused by infectious diseases change?** *(It fell dramatically.)* Add that identifying germs as the cause of infectious diseases was the first step in bringing these diseases under control. L2

40–1 (continued)

Koch's Postulates

Demonstration

Demonstrate the importance of using sterile techniques when applying Koch's second postulate. Hold a wire loop in the flame of a Bunsen burner for a few seconds. Allow the loop to cool, dip it in a bacterial culture, and run it over sterile agar in a petri dish. (**CAUTION:** Use a safe strain of bacteria, such as *E. coli,* from a scientific supply company, and apply sterile techniques to the handling of the bacterial culture.) Sterilize the loop again, let it cool, and run it over sterile agar in a second petri dish. Incubate both dishes at 37°C for 24 hours, and then have students observe the differences in the agar. (*Bacteria should be visible growing in the first petri dish but not the second.*) Ask: **Which step of the demonstration caused the different outcomes in the two petri dishes?** *(The resterilization of the wire loop)* **How does this demonstration relate to Koch's second postulate?** *(If you had been trying to isolate and grow a pathogen in the petri dishes, only the second dish would produce a pure culture. The first petri dish would have produced bacteria in addition to the pathogen.)* L2

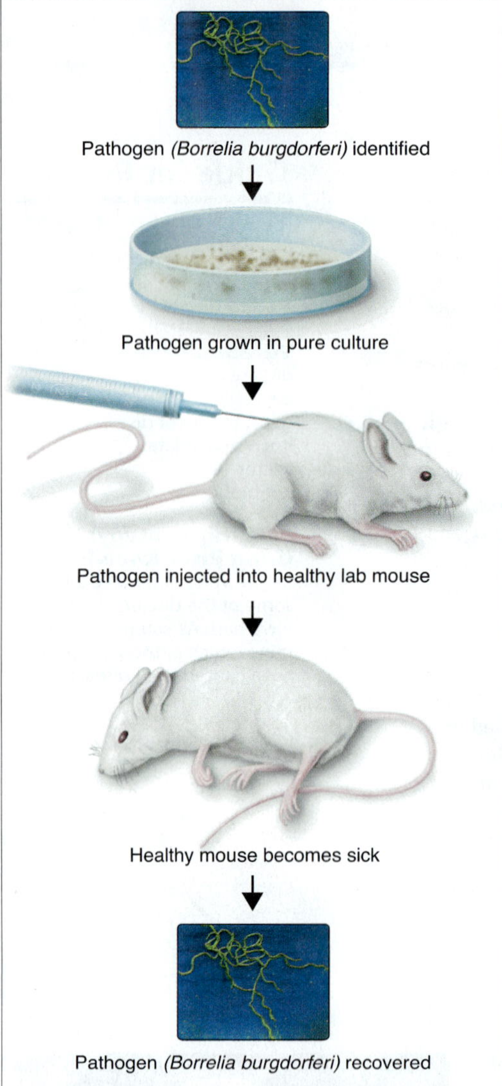

▲ **Figure 40–2** Allen Steere followed Koch's postulates to test his theory that the bacterium *Borrelia burgdorferi* caused Lyme disease. **Inferring** ***Why must the pathogen be grown in a pure culture?***

Sure enough, many of the children reported that their problems began with what they thought was an insect bite. The bite was followed by an expanding skin rash. Steere called the infection Lyme disease after the town of Lyme, Connecticut, where it was first discovered.

Steere and his colleagues were able to link the skin rash to the bite of the tiny deer tick *(Ixodes scapularis).* One of Steere's colleagues, Dr. Willy Burgdorfer, found an unusual spiral-shaped bacterium *(Borrelia burgdorferi)* in the ticks. Steere found the same bacterium in patients with Lyme disease. Could this bacterium be the cause of Lyme disease?

For ethical reasons, Steere did not try to infect healthy children with the bacterium. However, when the bacterium was injected into laboratory mice, they developed arthritis and other symptoms, just as the children had. From the sick mice, Steere recovered the bacteria, which were then injected into healthy mice. The healthy mice then developed the disease. Steere and his colleagues had found the organism that caused Lyme disease. The process Steere used is shown in **Figure 40–2.**

Koch's Postulates

The groundwork for Allen Steere's work with Lyme disease was actually laid more than a hundred years earlier by Robert Koch. From his studies with various bacteria, Koch developed a series of rules still used today to identify the microorganism that causes a specific disease. These rules are known as **Koch's postulates.** Koch's postulates can be stated as follows:

1. The pathogen should always be found in the body of a sick organism and should not be found in a healthy one.
2. The pathogen must be isolated and grown in the laboratory in pure culture.
3. When the cultured pathogens are placed in a new host, they should cause the same disease that infected the original host.
4. The injected pathogen should be isolated from the second host. It should be identical to the original pathogen.

Why are these rules important? Because identifying pathogens that cause disease is the first step toward preventing or curing the ailments they produce.

UNIVERSAL ACCESS

Less Proficient Readers

Reinforce the material for less proficient readers by having them make posters that show ways infectious diseases can be spread and also how their spread can be prevented. For example, students might use a picture of two people shaking hands to illustrate the spread of diseases through physical contact and beside it a picture of someone washing hands to prevent the spread of diseases in this way. L1 L2

Advanced Learners

Have students who need extra challenges learn more about Lyme disease. Students might investigate the current distribution of the disease in the United States, the number of people who are infected, how the disease is treated, and whether it can be transmitted by other vectors. Students should share what they learn in an oral report illustrated with visuals, such as a map showing the distribution of Lyme disease. L3

Agents of Disease

For many pathogens, the human body provides just the right conditions for growth—a suitable body temperature, a watery environment, and an abundance of nutrients. The large intestine, for example, harbors dense colonies of bacteria that help in the process of digestion. Bacteria and yeast are also found in the mouth and throat. Fortunately, most of these organisms are harmless, and many are actually beneficial.

If this is true, then exactly how do pathogens cause disease? Some pathogens, including viruses and some bacteria, destroy cells as they grow. Other bacteria release toxins that harm an organism. Still others, especially parasitic worms, produce sickness when they block the flow of blood, remove nutrients from the digestive system, and disrupt other bodily functions. The *Ascaris* worm in **Figure 40–3** is a parasitic worm.

Viruses Viruses are tiny particles that invade and replicate within living cells. Viruses attach to the surface of a cell, insert their genetic material in the form of RNA or DNA, and take over many of the functions of the host cell. Viruses can infect nearly every type of organism—including plants, animals, and bacteria. Diseases caused by viruses include the common cold, influenza, smallpox, and warts.

Bacteria Most bacteria are harmless to humans. Unfortunately, the few that are pathogens cause serious diseases. Bacteria cause disease in one of two ways—either by breaking down the tissues of the infected organism for food or by releasing toxins that harm the body. Bacterial diseases include streptococcus infections, diphtheria, botulism, and anthrax.

Protists You may not associate protists with disease, but a protist causes what may be the single most damaging infectious disease afflicting humans—malaria. Malaria is caused by *Plasmodium*, a protist that is spread from person to person by mosquitoes. Insects also spread another protist known as *Trypanosoma*. *Trypanosoma* protists live in the bloodstreams of vertebrate animals. The protist feeds off the nutrients in the host organism's blood. *Trypanosoma* causes African sleeping sickness. Contaminated water supplies are responsible for amebic dysentery, a serious infection caused by the protist *Entamoeba*.

Worms Flatworms and roundworms are also responsible for a number of serious human diseases. People in many tropical regions of the world can become infected by a parasitic flatworm known as *Schistosoma*. These flatworms live part of their lives in snails and then leave the snails to enter the fresh water of streams and rice paddies. *Schistosoma* worms frequently infect people working in rice fields. Other parasitic worms that infect humans include tapeworms and hookworms.

CHECKPOINT *What are three diseases caused by protists?*

Quick View Video

Discovery School Video To see how scientists test a hypothesis about how a disease is caused and transmitted, view track 7 "Hantavirus: A Tale of Mice and People" on the *BioDetectives* DVD.

Figure 40–3 Protists and worms often cause disease in humans and other animals. The protist *Trypanosoma* (purple objects) causes African sleeping sickness. The *Ascaris* worm matures in the intestine and causes severe malnutrition in its hosts.

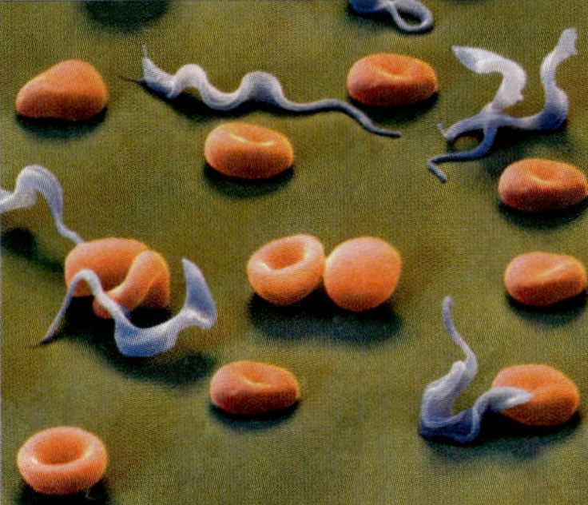

Trypanosoma **Among Red Blood Cells**

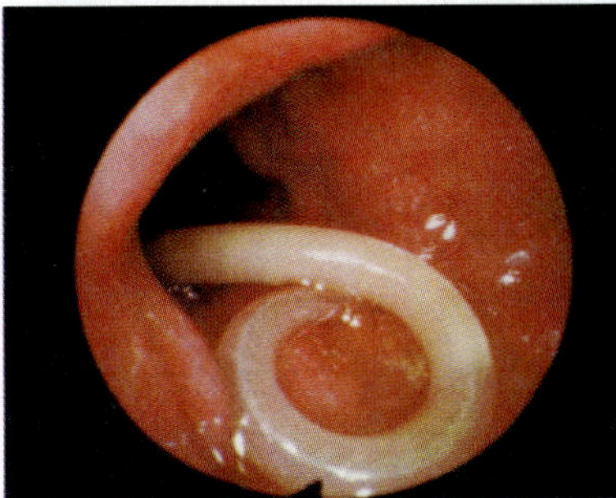

Ascaris **Worm in Intestine**

Agents of Disease

Quick View Video

Discovery School DVD Encourage students to view track 7 "Hantavirus: A Tale of Mice and People" on the *BioDetectives* DVD.

Build Science Skills

Drawing Conclusions Assign students to research an example of each of the types of pathogens described on this page. Students should find out how the pathogen causes disease and report back to the class. *(Findings will vary depending on the pathogen. For example, the bacterium that causes tetanus produces a toxin that causes involuntary muscle spasms, especially of the jaw.)* After all the students have reported, ask: **Based on these findings, what conclusions can you draw about different types of pathogens and how they cause disease?** *(Students might conclude, for example, that worms cause disease by removing nutrients from the digestive system or by injuring tissues.)* L2

Address Misconceptions

Explain that symptoms of infectious diseases are sometimes due to the response of the immune system to the presence of a pathogen. For example, the sneezing and runny nose associated with a cold are due to the production of histamines in response to the presence of the cold virus. Students may think that all infectious diseases are contagious. Explain that contagious diseases are spread from person to person by direct or indirect contact. Measles and influenza are contagious; tetanus is not. L1 L2

FACTS AND FIGURES

All about tetanus

Although tetanus was described by Hippocrates 2400 years ago, its prevalence has been masked because it strikes individuals and does not cause epidemics. The organism that causes tetanus, the bacillus *Clostridium tetani*, is found mainly in soil. It can enter the body through any break in the skin, from a superficial scratch to a puncture wound. Because *C. tetani* is anaerobic, it grows best in deeper tissues, so puncture wounds are especially prone to developing tetanus infections. The bacterium produces one of the most powerful toxins known. It affects the nervous system and causes painful muscle contractions, especially in the muscles of the neck, jaw, and thorax. It frequently leads to death. Fortunately, tetanus can be prevented with a vaccine.

Answers to . . .

CHECKPOINT *Malaria, African sleeping sickness, and amebic dysentery*

Figure 40–2 *To make sure that only the suspected pathogen has been transferred to the new host*

40–1 (continued)

Download a worksheet on diseases for students to complete, and find additional teacher support from NSTA SciLinks.

How Diseases Are Spread

Build Science Skills

Designing Experiments Challenge students to design an experiment to measure the effects of frequent hand-washing on the transmission of infectious diseases such as the common cold. Each experimental design should include a clearly stated research question, a description of the variables to be tested and how they will be measured, and an explanation of how other variables will be controlled. L2 L3

Make Connections

Environmental Science List some vector-borne diseases found in the United States and the vectors that spread them, such as Rocky Mountain spotted fever, which is spread by ticks, and encephalitis, which is spread by mosquitoes. Ask: **What are some ways you could reduce the spread of these diseases?** *(Students are likely to say by eliminating the vectors, for example, by spraying with pesticides, or by avoiding contact with the vectors, for example, by wearing protective clothing.)* **Are there any drawbacks to these approaches?** *(Unless pesticides are pathogen-specific, they can harm other organisms.)* L2

For: Links on diseases
Visit: www.SciLinks.org
Web Code: cbn-0401

▲ **Figure 40–4** **Some infectious diseases are spread from person to person by sneezing.** Thousands of pathogen particles can be released by a sneeze.

Fungi Most fungi are harmless, but a few are capable of causing serious problems. One genus of fungi, *Tinea,* is particularly adept at penetrating the outer layers of skin. When it attacks the skin between the toes it produces the infection known as athlete's foot. The same fungus can infect the scalp, where it results in rough, scaly patches known as ringworm. Other types of fungi infect the mouth, the throat, and even the fingernails and toenails.

How Diseases Are Spread

Infectious diseases can be transmitted in a number of ways. **Some infectious diseases are spread from one person to another through coughing, sneezing, or physical contact. Other infectious diseases are spread through contaminated water or food. Still others are spread by infected animals.**

Physical Contact Some infectious diseases can be spread by direct physical contact. For example, a disease may be transmitted when a healthy person touches a person with a disease. Some of the most dangerous pathogens are spread from one person to another by sexual contact.

Most diseases are spread by indirect contact. For example, some pathogens can be carried through the air. If a person with a cold or virus coughs or sneezes, thousands of droplets are released, as shown in **Figure 40–4.** The pathogens can also settle on objects. If you touch those objects, the pathogens can be transferred to your hands, and you can infect yourself by touching your mouth or nose.

Some behaviors can help to control transmission of diseases spread by physical contact. Simple measures, such as covering your mouth with a tissue when you cough, can limit the spread of infection. Washing your hands thoroughly and often also helps to prevent the spread of many pathogens.

Contaminated Food and Water Have you ever had food poisoning? Food poisoning is caused by eating food that contains pathogens. Bacteria are always present in uncooked meat. Bacteria also grow quickly in warm, partially cooked food. If food is cooked thoroughly, the risk of food poisoning due to contamination may be reduced. Contaminated water also causes disease, especially in parts of the world with poor sanitation and untreated sewage.

Infected Animals Animals, such as the mosquito shown in **Figure 40–5,** also spread infectious disease. Animals that carry pathogens from person to person are called **vectors.** Malaria, Lyme disease, West Nile virus, and rabies are diseases carried by vectors. Avoiding tall grass and wooded areas where deer and field mice dwell will limit your exposure to ticks that carry Lyme disease. Staying away from wild animals can reduce your risk of being bitten by a rabid animal.

HISTORY OF SCIENCE

The black death
Bubonic plague—or the black death, as it was referred to in the Middle Ages—is caused by a bacillus, *Yersinia pestis,* that is transmitted by fleas. *Y. pestis* is usually spread among wild rodent populations, but it can also spread to other mammals, including humans. Huge epidemics of bubonic plague have afflicted human populations throughout history. For example, in the mid-1300s, bubonic plague swept across Europe and killed roughly a quarter of the human population. Between 1890 and 1930, more than 13 million people worldwide died of plague. Most people are surprised to learn that plague is still present today in wild rodent populations in many areas of the world, including some parts of the United States, and that local outbreaks of plague occasionally occur in human populations. Fortunately, the disease now can be treated successfully with antibiotics.

Fighting Infectious Diseases

Because prevention isn't always possible, drugs have been developed for use against some types of pathogens. Antibiotics are perhaps the most useful single class of infection-fighting drugs. **Antibiotics** are compounds that kill bacteria without harming the cells of the human or animal hosts. Antibiotics work by interfering with the cellular processes of microorganisms.

Discovery of Antibiotics Many antibiotics are produced naturally by living organisms. Other antibiotics are synthetic. One antibiotic, penicillin, was discovered accidentally in 1928 by the Scottish bacteriologist Alexander Fleming. Fleming had been growing *Staphylococcus* bacteria in a culture dish. One day, he noticed that the culture of bacteria had been contaminated by a species of green mold called *Penicillium notatum.* On closer observation, Fleming saw something surprising. The bacteria were not growing near the mold. Something produced by the mold was apparently inhibiting their growth. Later, researchers discovered that penicillin—the name Fleming gave the antibiotic—interferes with the growth of bacteria.

Antibiotics have no effect on viruses. However, antiviral drugs have been developed to fight certain viral diseases. These drugs generally inhibit the ability of viruses to invade cells and to multiply once inside cells.

Over-the-Counter Drugs You probably know that you can buy many medicines without a prescription. These medicines, called over-the-counter drugs, treat only the symptoms of the disease—including cough, congestion, and fever. These medicines help you feel better, but they do not actually treat the cause of the infection. The best treatment for most infections includes rest, a well-balanced diet, and plenty of fluids.

▲ **Figure 40–5** **Some infectious diseases are spread by insects.** This *Anopheles* mosquito may be a carrier of the protist that causes malaria.

CA a

a BI 10.d

40–1 Section Assessment

1. **Key Concept** Describe some of the causes of disease.
2. **Key Concept** What are the ways in which infectious diseases are spread?
3. How do vectors spread disease?
4. What are antibiotics?
5. **Critical Thinking Inferring** Why did Koch require all four steps in determining the cause of an infectious disease? Could you eliminate one of the steps? Explain your answer.

Writing in Science

Descriptive Writing

Describe how Allen Steere used Koch's postulates to discover the cause of Lyme disease. You may want to start by listing the postulates in one column of a table and, in another column, listing the steps used by Steere.

Fighting Infectious Diseases

Make Connections

Health Science Introduce the concept of bacterial resistance to antibiotics. Explain that it occurs when people fail to take antibiotics long enough to kill all the bacteria that are causing an infection. Ask: **Why does this lead to the bacteria's developing resistance to the antibiotic?** *(The remaining bacteria are those that have some resistance to the antibiotic. Through time, repeated selection in this way for the most resistant bacteria leads to bacteria that are almost completely resistant to a particular antibiotic.)* L2

3 ASSESS

Evaluate Understanding

Call on students at random to name the agents of disease. Call on other students to give an example of each agent.

Reteach

Have students write each of Koch's postulates, unnumbered, on an index card. Then, have students shuffle the cards and try to put them back in the correct order.

Writing in Science

Students' explanations should include the information described in the text on pp. 1031–1032.

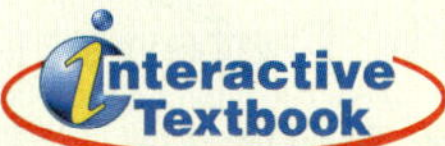

If your class subscribes to the iText, use it to review the Key Concepts in Section 40–1.

40–1 Section Assessment

1. Inherited factors, materials in the environment, and pathogens
2. By coughing, sneezing, or physical contact; contaminated water and food; and infected animals
3. By carrying pathogens from person to person
4. Compounds that kill bacteria without harming human or animal cells
5. Answers will vary. Most students will say that you could not eliminate one of Koch's steps. However, accept all logical answers that have an adequate explanation.

Section 40–2

BI 10.a, BI 10.b, BI 10.c, *BI 10.f

1 FOCUS

Objectives

40.2.1 ***Identify*** the body's nonspecific defenses against invading pathogens.

40.2.2 ***Describe*** the function of the immune system.

Guide for Reading

Vocabulary Preview

Explain that immunity means resistance to infection. Then, challenge students to fill in the blanks in the following statements with the correct Vocabulary terms containing the word *immunity*. **Immune response outside cells, involving antibodies, is called _____ immunity.** *(humoral)* **Immunity involving killer T cells is called _____ immunity.** *(cell-mediated)* **When the body is injected with antibodies, it is called _____ immunity.** *(passive)* **When the body makes antibodies in response to an antigen, it is called _____ immunity.** *(active)* After students read the section, they should check to see if their answers were correct.

Reading Strategy

Have students preview the section by studying the figures and reading the captions.

2 INSTRUCT

Nonspecific Defenses

Build Science Skills

Applying Concepts Ask: **If you eat food that contains bacteria, which nonspecific defenses will help protect your body from illness?** *(Lysozyme in saliva and stomach acid and digestive enzymes in the stomach)*

40–2 The Immune System

BI 10.a. Students know the role of the skin in providing nonspecific defenses against infection. **BI 10.b.** Students know the role of antibodies in the body's response to infection. **BI 10.c.** Students know how vaccination protects an individual from infectious diseases. **BI 10.f.** Students know the roles of phagocytes, B-lymphocytes, and T-lymphocytes in the immune system.

Guide for Reading

Key Concepts

- What is the function of the immune system?
- What are the body's nonspecific defenses against invading pathogens?

Vocabulary

immunity
inflammatory response
fever
interferon
immune response
antigen
humoral immunity
cell-mediated immunity
antibody
vaccination
active immunity
passive immunity

Reading Strategy: Finding Main Ideas Before you read, skim the section to identify the key ideas. Then, carefully read the section, making a list of supporting details for each main idea.

With pathogens all around us, it might seem like a miracle that you aren't sick all of the time. There's a reason, of course, why most of us enjoy good health. Our bodies have a protective system—a series of defenses that guard against disease.

The immune system is the body's main defense against pathogens. The immune system recognizes, attacks, destroys, and "remembers" each type of pathogen that enters the body. It does this by producing specialized cells that inactivate pathogens. For each kind of pathogen, the immune system produces cells that are specific to that pathogen. **The function of the immune system is to fight infection through the production of cells that inactivate foreign substances or cells.** This process is called **immunity.**

The immune system includes two general categories of defense mechanisms against infection: nonspecific defenses and specific defenses. Nonspecific defenses are like the fortress walls of the system. They guard against infections by keeping most things out of the body. Specific defenses work like security guards. They track down harmful pathogens that have managed to break through the body's nonspecific defenses.

Nonspecific Defenses

Nonspecific defenses do not discriminate between one threat and another. These defenses include physical and chemical barriers.

First Line of Defense The function of the first line of defense is to keep pathogens out of the body. This role is carried out by skin, mucus, sweat, and tears. **Your body's most important nonspecific defense is the skin.** Very few pathogens can penetrate the layers of dead cells at the skin's surface. The importance of the skin as a barrier against infection becomes obvious as soon as the skin is broken. When that happens, pathogens can enter your body and multiply. As they grow, they cause the symptoms of an infection, such as swelling, redness, and pain.

Many secretions of the body, including mucus, saliva, and tears, contain lysozyme, an enzyme that breaks down the cell walls of many bacteria. In addition, oil and sweat glands in the skin produce an acidic environment that kills many bacteria.

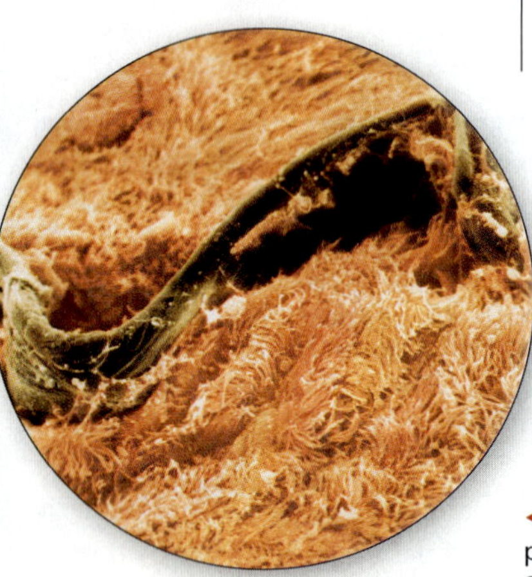

(magnification: 1100×)

Figure 40–6 **The immune system fights infection.** The production of mucus is one of your body's defenses. Pathogens can get trapped in mucus the way the long brown strand of dirt shown in the micrograph is trapped.

SECTION RESOURCES

Print:

- ***Laboratory Manual B,*** Chapter 40 Lab
- ***Teaching Resources,*** Lesson Plan 40–2, Adapted Section Summary 40–2, Adapted Worksheets 40–2, Section Summary 40–2, Worksheets 40–2, Section Review 40–2
- ***Reading and Study Workbook A,*** Section 40–2
- ***Adapted Reading and Study Workbook B,*** Section 40–2
- ***Lab Worksheets,*** Chapter 40 Real-World Lab

Technology:

- ***iText,*** Section 40–2
- ***Animated Biological Concepts DVD,*** 44 Inflammatory Response, 45 Humoral Immunity, 46 Cell-Mediated Immunity
- ***Transparencies Plus,*** Section 40–2

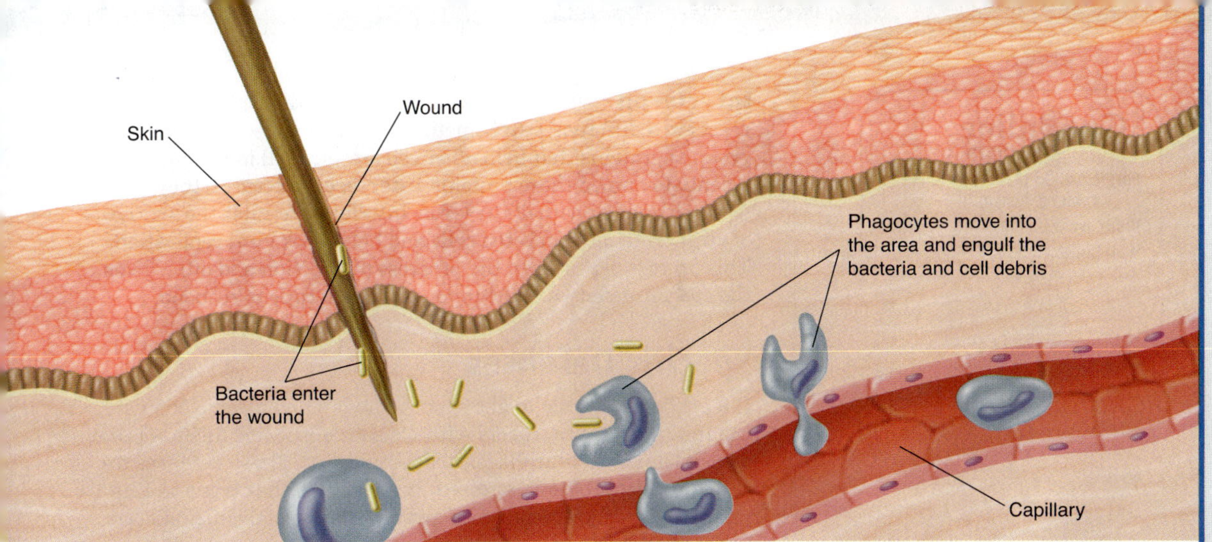

Pathogens can also enter your body through other body openings, including your mouth and nose. Your body has other nonspecific defenses that protect these openings. Mucus in your nose and throat helps to trap pathogens. The cilia that line your nose and throat help to push pathogens away from your lungs. Stomach acid and digestive enzymes destroy many pathogens that make their way to your stomach.

Second Line of Defense If pathogens do manage to enter your body, they may multiply quickly, releasing toxins into your tissues. When this happens, the **inflammatory response**—a second line of defense—is activated. **The inflammatory response is a nonspecific defense reaction to tissue damage caused by injury or infection.** When pathogens are detected, the immune system produces millions of white blood cells, which fight the infection. Blood vessels near the wound expand, and white blood cells move from the vessels to enter the infected tissues. Many of these white blood cells are phagocytes, which engulf and destroy bacteria. The infected tissue may become swollen and painful. The inflammatory response is summarized in **Figure 40–7.**

The immune system also releases chemicals that increase the core body temperature. You may have experienced this elevated body temperature, called a **fever.** The increased body temperature is advantageous because many pathogens can survive only within a narrow temperature range. An elevated temperature slows down or stops the growth of such pathogens. The higher body temperature also increases the heart rate so that the white blood cells get to the site of infection faster. Physicians know that a fever and an increased number of white blood cells are two indications that the body is hard at work fighting infection.

CHECKPOINT *What is the role of phagocytes in the inflammatory response?*

▲ **Figure 40–7**  **The inflammatory response is a nonspecific defense reaction to tissue damage caused by injury or infection.** When pathogens enter the body, phagocytes move into the area and engulf the pathogens. In addition, platelets and clotting factors leak from the capillaries.

Word Origins

Phagocyte comes from the Greek *phag*, meaning "eat," and *kutos*, meaning "cell." Thus, a phagocyte is a cell that eats or engulfs. **If the Greek prefix *macro-* means "large," what might the word *macrophage* mean?**

Demonstration

Use a microprojector and a drop of pond water on a slide to show students how amoebas feed. Point out the amoebas on the slide. As students watch their activity, ask: **What do amoebas do to consume their prey?** *(They engulf, or surround, their prey.)* Explain that phagocytes engulf bacteria and other pathogens in the same way. L1 L2

Make Connections

Health Science Explain that since interferons were discovered in 1957, doctors have been excited about the possibility of using them to prevent disease. In 1980, an interferon became the first biopharmaceutical to be successfully mass-produced using genetic engineering. Mass production made interferons available for research and clinical purposes. Challenge interested students to find out the results of interferon research since 1980 and report to the class on what they learn. *(Students will find that interferons show promise against many viral diseases and some cancers.)* L2 L3

Word Origins

Macrophage means a large cell that eats or engulfs. L2

UNIVERSAL ACCESS

Inclusion/Special Needs
The material in this section may be difficult for some students to understand. Encourage them to focus mainly on the figures and captions. Name the processes that are illustrated in Figures 40–7 through 40–10. For each figure, describe the process, and have students follow through the diagram and read the labels as you do. Urge students to ask questions about each process as you describe it. L1

Advanced Learners
Have students who are gifted writers create a story about nonspecific defenses. Their stories should take the point of view of a pathogen and correctly portray the action and order of the nonspecific defenses the pathogen must overcome when it enters the body. Urge students to read their work to the class. Have other students identify the nonspecific defenses as they are described in the stories. L3

Answer to . . .

CHECKPOINT *Phagocytes engulf and destroy bacteria.*

Download a worksheet on the immune system for students to complete, and find additional teacher support from NSTA SciLinks.

Specific Defenses

Use Visuals

Figure 40–8 Point out that the drawings are greatly simplified abstractions of what are in reality complex molecules. Make sure students realize that the drawing on the right is just an enlargement of the drawing on the left with the antigens removed, making the antigen-binding sites easier to see. L1

Demonstration

Demonstrate to students how the immune system responds to specific pathogens. Select ten student volunteers. Have the students use poster board, string, scissors, and markers to make five signs (attached to string so they can be worn around the neck) labeled: Whooping Cough, Strep Throat, Bacterial Pneumonia, Diphtheria, and Tetanus. Also have the students cut five squares of poster board in half, each one in a different way so that it forms two unique pieces that fit together like pieces of a jigsaw puzzle but that do not fit with any of the other pieces. Then, assign five of the students to wear the signs and play the roles of bacteria. Give each of them one half of a puzzle, and have them line up at the back of the room. Assign the remaining five students to be B cells, give them the other halves of the puzzles, and have them line up at the front of the room. Finally, tell the bacteria to "invade" the room and the B cells to "attack" the bacterium that has the matching puzzle piece. When a B cell finds the bacterium that is its match, both should sit down. After the last pair sits down, ask: **What do the puzzle pieces carried by the "bacteria" represent?** *(Antigens)* **What do the puzzle pieces carried by the "B cells" represent?** *(Antibodies)* L1

For: Links on the immune system
Visit: www.SciLinks.org
Web Code: cbn-0402

Interferon When viruses enter the body, the body sometimes reacts in a different way. Sometimes, virus-infected cells produce a group of proteins that help other cells resist viral infection. Scientists named these proteins **interferons** because they "interfere" with the growth of the virus. Interferons inhibit the synthesis of viral proteins in infected cells and help block viral replication. This process slows down the progress of infection and often gives the specific defenses of the immune system time to respond.

Specific Defenses

If a pathogen is able to get past the body's nonspecific defenses, the immune system reacts with a series of specific defenses that attack the particular disease-causing agent. These defenses are called the **immune response.** A substance that triggers this response is known as an **antigen.** Viruses, bacteria, and other pathogens may serve as antigens.

The cells of the immune system that recognize specific antigens are two types of lymphocytes: B lymphocytes (B cells) and T lymphocytes (T cells). B cells provide immunity against antigens and pathogens in the body fluids. This process is called **humoral immunity.** T cells provide a defense against abnormal cells and pathogens inside living cells. This process is called **cell-mediated immunity.**

(a) BI 10.b

CA (a)

Humoral Immunity When a pathogen invades the body, its antigens are recognized by a small fraction of the body's B cells. These B cells grow and divide rapidly, producing large numbers of plasma cells and memory B cells.

Plasma cells release antibodies. **Antibodies** are proteins that recognize and bind to antigens. The antibodies are carried in the bloodstream to attack the pathogen that is causing the infection. As the antibodies overcome the infection, the plasma cells die out and stop producing antibodies.

Once the body has been exposed to a pathogen, millions of memory B cells remain capable of producing antibodies specific to that pathogen. These memory B cells greatly reduce the chance that the disease could develop a second time. If the same antigen enters the body a second time, a secondary response occurs. The memory B cells divide rapidly, forming new plasma cells. The plasma cells produce the specific antibodies needed to destroy the pathogen.

Antibody Structure As shown in **Figure 40–8,** an antibody is shaped like the letter Y and has two identical antigen-binding sites. Small differences in the amino acids affect the shapes of the binding sites. The shape of the binding site makes it possible for the antibody to recognize a specific antigen with a complementary shape. The different shapes give antibodies the ability to recognize a large variety of antigens. It is estimated that a healthy adult can produce about 100 million different types of antibodies.

▼ **Figure 40–8** An antibody molecule has two identical antigen-binding sites. It is at these sites that one or two specific antigens bind to the antibody. **Applying Concepts** *How do antibodies help in the immune response?*

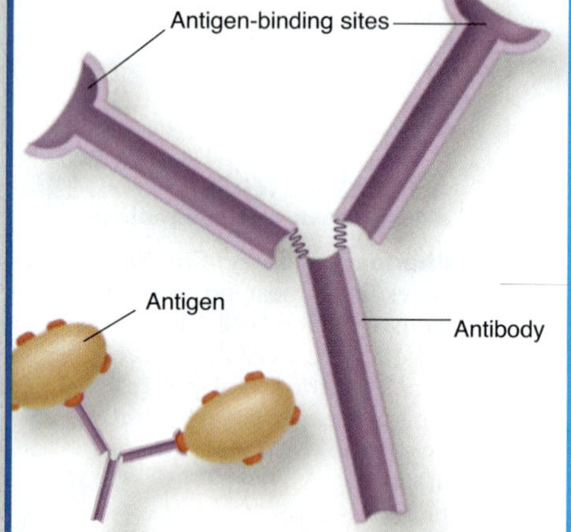

TEACHER TO TEACHER

After students have learned about nonspecific defenses and before they read about specific defenses, I challenge them to design a cell or cells to attack a particular pathogen. I have students work in groups and use a cold virus as the pathogen. Then, I have each group share its results by listing the cell specifications on the board and explaining them to the class. After the activity, as students read about specific defenses, they can see how their design compares with the "real thing." This activity helps students anticipate the complexity of specific defense cells before they actually read about them.

—*Ruth Gleicher*
Biology Teacher
Niles West High School
Skokie, IL

Figure 40–9 Humoral Immunity

Once the body has been exposed to a pathogen, it remains capable of producing specific antibodies to attack that pathogen. The reaction to a second infection by the same pathogen is much faster.

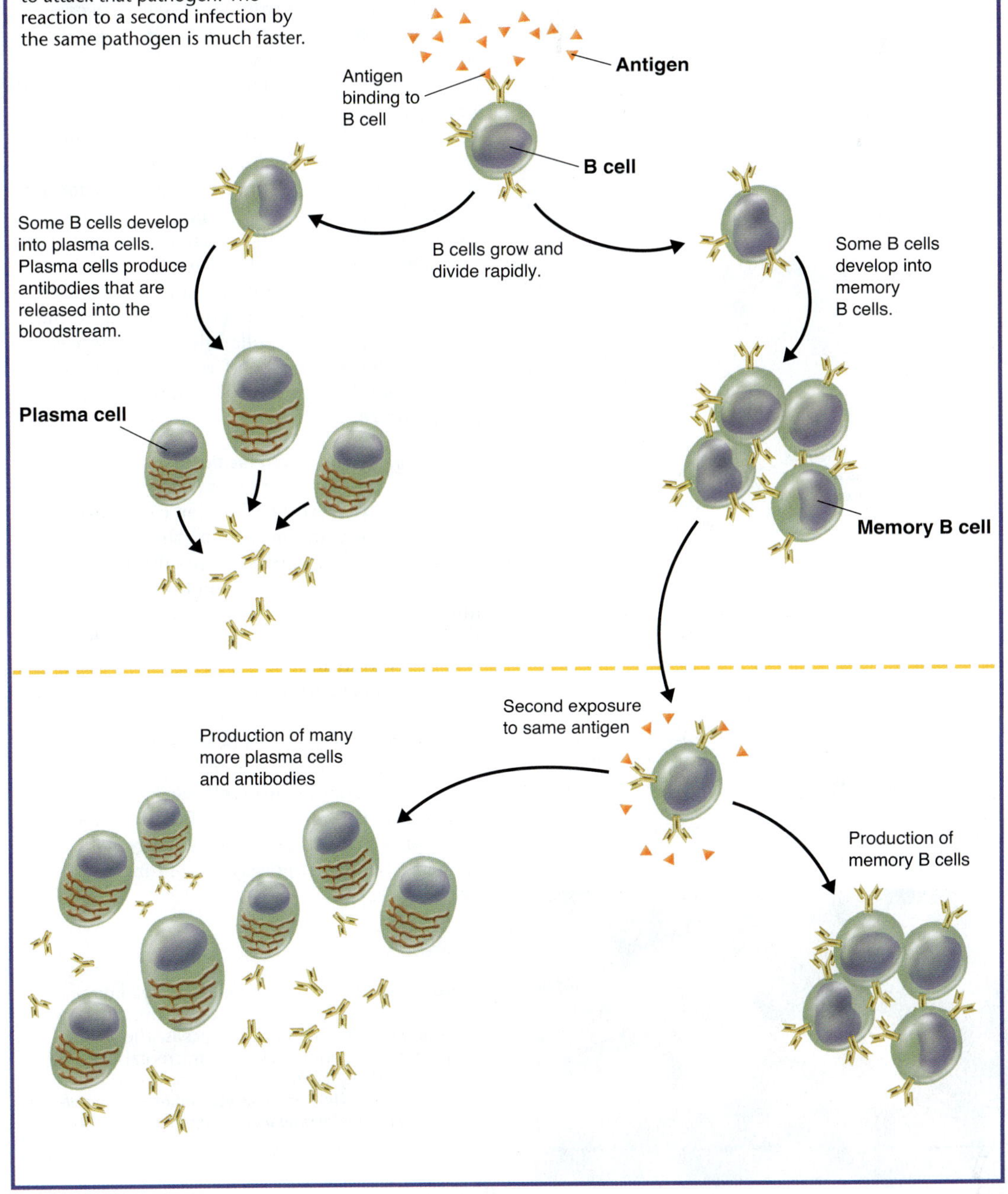

Antigen

Antigen binding to B cell

B cell

B cells grow and divide rapidly.

Some B cells develop into plasma cells. Plasma cells produce antibodies that are released into the bloodstream.

Plasma cell

Some B cells develop into memory B cells.

Memory B cell

Second exposure to same antigen

Production of many more plasma cells and antibodies

Production of memory B cells

Make Connections

Chemistry Explain that the stem of each Y-shaped antibody is essentially the same but the end of each arm has a region that is unique. In this area, two polypeptide chains are folded to form a groovelike cavity that is complementary to the contour and electric charge of a particular antigen. Ask: **How do these differences in the antigen-binding sites of antibodies occur?** *(The genes that code for the two polypeptide chains rearrange themselves in slightly different ways in each B cell.)* L2 L3

Use Visuals

Figure 40–9 Have students follow the flowchart as you read the captions, starting with the first step and ending with the last. Make sure students can identify the cells involved in each step. L1 L2

FACTS AND FIGURES

Phagocyte power

Phagocytes develop from stem cells in bone marrow. Types of phagocytes include neutrophils, eosinophils, and monocytes, which mature into macrophages. Phagocytes are drawn by altered chemical gradients into an area of damaged or invaded tissues. There, they engulf and destroy pathogens and other foreign substances by endocytosis. In endocytosis, the plasma membrane of the phagocyte encloses the pathogen at or near the cell surface of the phagocyte. Then, the membrane pinches off to form a closed endocytic vesicle around the pathogen. The endocytic vesicle provides a "traveling compartment" that enables the pathogen to be transported into the cytoplasm of the phagocyte. Once inside the cytoplasm, the endocytic vesicle fuses with lysosomes, and the pathogen is destroyed.

Answer to . . .

Figure 40–8 *By binding to antigens on the surfaces of pathogens and linking pathogens together in a large mass, which attracts phagocytes and makes engulfment easier*

40–2 (continued)

Use Visuals

Figure 40–10 Check students' comprehension of the flowchart by asking: **What causes a T cell to become a helper T cell?** *(Activation by a macrophage)* **What causes a killer T cell to attack the infected cell?** *(Activation by a helper T cell)*

Build Science Skills

Applying Concepts Point out that cell-mediated immunity is particularly important for diseases caused by eukaryotic pathogens. Ask: **Which pathogens are eukaryotic, and what are some of the diseases they cause?** *(Protists, fungi, and worms are eukaryotic pathogens. Some of the diseases they cause include malaria, beef tapeworm, and athlete's foot.)* L2

Cell-Mediated Immunity The body's primary defense against its own cells when they have become cancerous or infected by viruses is known as cell-mediated immunity. Cell-mediated immunity is also important in fighting infection caused by fungi and protists. When viruses or other pathogens get inside living cells, antibodies alone cannot destroy them.

During cell-mediated immunity, T cells divide and differentiate into killer T cells (cytotoxic T cells), helper T cells, suppressor T cells, and memory T cells. Killer T cells track down and destroy the bacteria, fungi, protozoan, or foreign tissue that contains the antigen. Helper T cells produce memory T cells. The memory T cells, like the memory B cells, will cause a secondary response if the same antigen enters the body again. As the pathogenic cells are brought under control, suppressor T cells release substances that shut down the killer T cells. The process of cell-mediated immunity is summarized in **Figure 40–10**.

CHECKPOINT *What is cell-mediated immunity?*

Transplants Although killer T cells are helpful in the immune system, they make the acceptance of organ transplants difficult. Body cells have marker proteins on their surfaces that allow the immune system to recognize the cells. If an organ was going to be transplanted into your body, your immune system would recognize the transported organ as foreign and attack it. Your immune system damages and destroys the transplanted organ. This process is known as rejection. To prevent organ rejection, doctors search for a donor whose cell markers are nearly identical to the cell markers of the recipient. Recipients must take drugs—usually for the rest of their lives—to suppress the cell-mediated immune response.

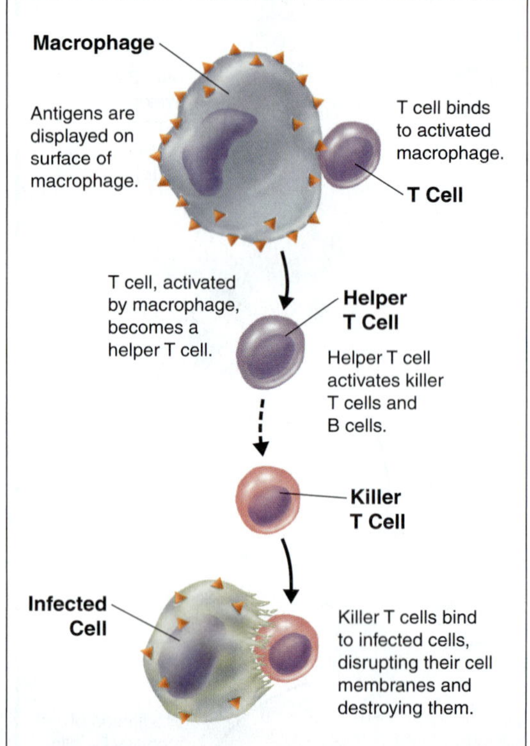

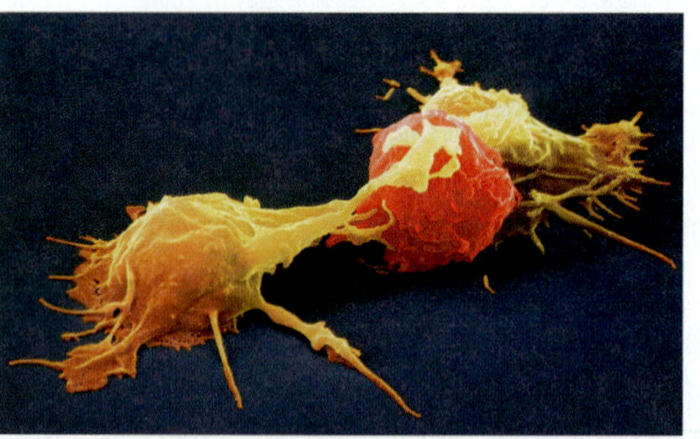

Figure 40–10 During the cell-mediated immune response, T cells provide defense against abnormal cells and pathogens inside living cells. The yellow objects in the scanning electron micrograph are killer T cells attacking a cancer cell. **Comparing and Contrasting** *How are humoral immunity and cell-mediated immunity similar? How are they different?*

HISTORY OF SCIENCE

Cells that eat cells

A significant step in understanding the immune system came in 1883 with the work of Elie Metchnikoff. The Russian biologist was researching the cause of inflammation in animals, using sea star larvae as research subjects because they have transparent bodies that allow for clear observation of internal processes. Wondering how the organism's cells would react to a foreign body, Metchnikoff plucked a thorn from one of the roses in his rose garden and plunged it into a larva. A day later, he noticed the thorn was surrounded by a swarm of cells. Through further study, he identified similar cells in humans, specifically the white blood cells in pus. He recognized that these cells are able to digest foreign particles, and he named the cells phagocytes, from the Greek words meaning "to eat" and "cells."

Quick Lab

How does cell-mediated immunity work?

BI 10.d

Materials 3 red balloons; 3 yellow balloons; 3 light-blue balloons; red, purple, and light-blue adhesive notes; toothpick

Procedure

1. Partially inflate and tie the balloons. The balloons represent pathogens. The different colors represent different surface antigens. Put the inflated balloons on the table.
2. The adhesive notes represent antibodies that can bind to antigens on the surface of a pathogen of the same color. Use the adhesive notes to model the binding of antibodies to antigens on pathogens.
3. The toothpick represents a killer T cell. Use the toothpick to burst any balloons marked by adhesive notes.

Analyze and Conclude

1. **Using Models** How did you model the binding of antibodies to matching antigens in step 2?
2. **Using Models** What signals a killer T cell to attack a pathogen?
3. **Using Models** What do the yellow balloons and purple adhesive notes represent in the model?

Acquired Immunity

More than 200 years ago, the English physician Edward Jenner wondered if it might be possible to produce immunity against one of the deadliest diseases of the day—smallpox. Jenner knew that a mild disease called cowpox was often contracted by milkmaids. Jenner observed that the milkmaids who contracted cowpox developed an immunity to smallpox. Was there a way, he wondered, to deliberately infect people with cowpox and thus protect them from getting the more serious disease of smallpox?

To answer this question, Jenner took fluid from one of the sores of a cowpox patient and put the fluid into a small cut that he made on the arm of a young farm boy named Jamie Phipps. As expected, Jamie developed a mild cowpox infection. Two months later, Jenner performed a daring experiment. He injected Jamie with fluid from a smallpox infection. Fortunately for Jamie, the experiment was a success—the boy did not develop smallpox. His cowpox infection had made him immune to smallpox.

Active Immunity The injection of a weakened form of a pathogen to produce immunity is known as a **vaccination.** *Vacca* is the Latin word for "cow," reflecting the history of Jenner's first vaccination experiment. Today, more than 20 serious human diseases can be prevented by vaccination. Like early vaccines, modern vaccines stimulate the immune system to create millions of plasma cells ready to produce specific types of antibodies.

BI 10.c

BIO INSIGHTS — FACTS AND FIGURES

So many flu strains, so little time

Influenza, or flu, is caused by an airborne virus. It occurs in periodic epidemics, which sometimes have a high death toll. For example, a 1968 flu epidemic killed almost 700,000 people worldwide in just six weeks. Scientists have developed fairly effective flu vaccines, but it takes at least six months to prepare a vaccine once the particular strain of flu virus is isolated. Mutations occur frequently in the flu virus, and new strains appear every couple of years, so scientists cannot predict for certain which strain of flu virus will strike in a given year. Therefore, a vaccine that is effective against one year's strain of flu virus may prove useless against the next year's strain.

Quick Lab

BI 10.d

Objective Students will be able to use a model to determine how cell-mediated immunity works.

Skill Focus **Using Models**

Materials 3 red balloons; 3 yellow balloons; 3 light-blue balloons; red, purple, and light-blue adhesive notes; toothpick

Time 15 minutes

Advance Prep To save time, you can inflate the balloons before class.

Strategy You might want to have students work in pairs on this lab. If you do, make sure each student individually answers the Analyze and Conclude questions.

Expected Outcome Students should break only the red and light-blue balloons.

Analyze and Conclude

1. The binding of antibodies to matching antigens was modeled by attaching colored adhesive notes to balloons of the same color.
2. An antibody bound to an antigen on the surface of a pathogen signals a killer T cell to attack the pathogen.
3. In the model, the yellow balloons represent pathogens for which there are no antibodies, and the purple adhesive notes represent antibodies for which there are no pathogens.

Acquired Immunity

Use Community Resources

Have students contact their local health department to obtain a schedule of recommended vaccinations from birth to adulthood. Then, have students create a poster to convey the information in an eye-catching way. If possible, arrange to have their posters displayed at a location in the community where families with young children are likely to see them, for example, at a public library or preschool. L1 L2

Answers to . . .

CHECKPOINT *Immunity in which killer T cells destroy infected cells*

Figure 40–10 *Both are specific defenses. In humoral immunity, B cells produce antibodies against the pathogen. In cell-mediated immunity, killer T cells attack infected cells.*

40–2 (continued)

Build Science Skills

Inferring Ask: **Why does passive immunity last for only a few weeks or months?** *(Passive immunity occurs when antibodies are injected into the blood or ingested in milk. Because antigens are not included with the antibodies, the immune system does not "learn" how to make the antibody. Once the antibodies are destroyed, the person is no longer immune.)* L2

3 ASSESS

Evaluate Understanding

Have students make a concept map entitled "Defenses Against Pathogens," using the following terms: *nonspecific defenses, specific defenses, humoral immunity, cell-mediated immunity, first-line defenses,* and *second-line defenses.*

Reteach

Play a quiz game in which you read definitions of the Vocabulary terms and student contestants try to identify the terms from the definitions.

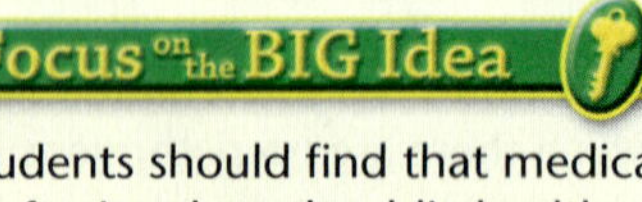

Students should find that medical professionals and public health officials strongly support vaccinations because they prevent epidemic outbreaks of disease and prevent deaths. However, vaccinations cause side effects in a number of people. For this reason, some people do not think vaccinations should be mandatory. Assign several students to represent each viewpoint. Assign a moderator and a timekeeper to ensure that each side has the same amount of time to present its views.

If your class subscribes to the iText, use it to review the Key Concepts in Section 40–2.

Answer to . . .

Figure 40–11 *Active immunity*

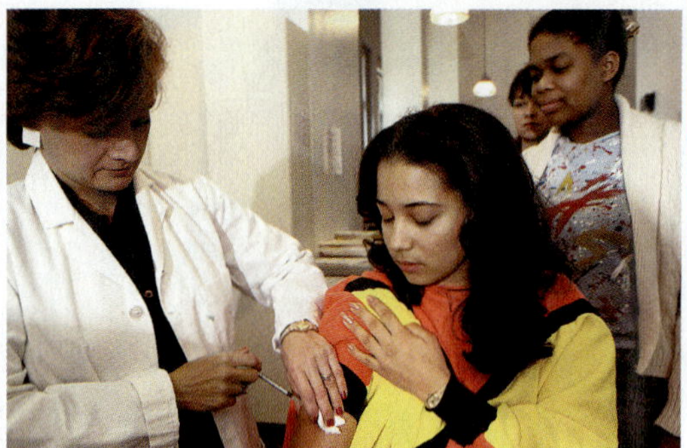

▲ **Figure 40–11** Vaccines stimulate the immune system to produce plasma cells. **Applying Concepts** *What type of immunity do vaccines produce?*

The type of immunity produced by the body's reaction to a vaccine is known as **active immunity.** Active immunity appears after exposure to an antigen, as a result of the immune response. Active immunity may develop as a result of natural exposure to an antigen (fighting an infection) or from deliberate exposure to the antigen (through a vaccine). CA a

Passive Immunity In active immunity, the body makes its own antibodies in response to an antigen. The body can also be temporarily protected from disease in another way. If antibodies produced by other animals against a pathogen are injected into the bloodstream, the antibodies produce a **passive immunity** against the pathogen. Passive immunity lasts only a short time because eventually the body destroys the foreign antibodies.

Like active immunity, passive immunity can develop naturally or by deliberate exposure. One kind of natural immunity occurs when antibodies produced by the mother are passed to the fetus during development (across the placenta) or in early infancy through breast milk. This immunity protects a child against most infectious diseases for the first few months of its life, or longer if the infant is breast-fed.

Sometimes, antibodies are administered to fight infection or prevent disease. For example, travelers to certain regions of the world are given vaccines before leaving home. These vaccines may contain antibodies against tropical diseases, such as malaria. People who have been bitten by rabid animals are injected with antibodies that attack the rabies virus. This is another example of passive immunization.

40–2 Section Assessment

1. **Key Concept** Describe the body's nonspecific defenses against pathogens.
2. **Key Concept** Describe the function of the immune system.
3. How do interferons protect the body against viruses?
4. How are antigens related to antibodies?
5. **Critical Thinking Comparing and Contrasting** How are active and passive immunity similar? How are they different?

Focus on the BIG Idea

Science, Technology, and Society Getting vaccinated is much safer than getting the disease that the vaccine prevents. However, like any drug, vaccines are capable of causing serious problems. Interview five people about their thoughts on vaccinations. As a class, arrange a debate that addresses both the benefits and risks of vaccinations.

40–2 Section Assessment

1. Unbroken skin is a barrier to pathogens. If pathogens penetrate the skin, they cause an inflammatory response. Pathogens that enter through the mouth or nose are trapped in mucus, or attacked by lysozyme, digestive enzymes, and stomach acid. Viruses trigger the production of interferons.
2. To protect the body against pathogens
3. Interferons inhibit the progress of viral infections, which may give specific defenses time to respond.
4. An antigen is a substance on the surface of a pathogen that triggers an immune response. Antibodies are molecules that are custom-made to bind to specific antigens.
5. They both provide antibodies against a specific pathogen. Active immunity is often permanent; passive immunity is temporary.

40–3 Immune System Disorders

BI 10.e. Students know why an individual with a compromised immune system (for example, a person with AIDS) may be unable to fight off and survive infections by microorganisms that are usually benign.

Although the immune system defends the body from a wide range of pathogens, sometimes disorders occur in the immune system itself. There are three different types of disorders. These disorders include allergies, autoimmune diseases, and immunodeficiency diseases.

Guide for Reading

Key Concepts
- What is an autoimmune disease?
- How can AIDS be prevented?

Vocabulary
allergy
histamine
asthma

Reading Strategy: Using Prior Knowledge Do you or someone you know have allergies? As you read this section, use what you learn to explain the causes and symptoms of allergies.

Allergies

The most common overreactions of the immune system to antigens are known as **allergies.** Common allergies include those to pollen, dust, mold, and bee stings. Antigens that cause allergic reactions are called allergens. Some common allergens are shown in **Figure 40–12.**

When allergy-causing antigens enter the body, they attach themselves to mast cells. Mast cells are specialized immune system cells that initiate the inflammatory response. The activated mast cells release chemicals known as **histamines.** Histamines increase the flow of blood and fluids to the surrounding area. They also increase mucous production in the respiratory system. The increased mucous production brings on the sneezing, watery eyes, runny nose, and other irritations that make a person with allergies so uncomfortable. If you have allergies, you may have taken *anti*histamines. Antihistamines are drugs that are used to counteract the effects of histamines.

Figure 40–12 Common allergens include ragweed pollen, dust, and dust mites. In the SEM of the dust ball, notice the insect parts, gray spider webbing, and other dirt. Dust mites live in furniture, mattresses, and even pillows. **Inferring** *Why do you think it is recommended that people wash their bed coverings in hot water?*

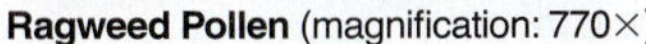

Ragweed Pollen (magnification: 770×)

Dust Ball (magnification: 760×)

Dust Mite (magnification: 900×)

SECTION RESOURCES

Print:
- ***Teaching Resources,*** Lesson Plan 40–3, Adapted Section Summary 40–3, Section Summary 40–3, Worksheets 40–3, Section Review 40–3
- ***Reading and Study Workbook A,*** Section 40–3
- ***Adapted Reading and Study Workbook B,*** Section 40–3

Technology:
- ***iText,*** Section 40–3
- ***Transparencies Plus,*** Section 40–3

Section 40–3

BI 10.e

1 FOCUS

Objectives

40.3.1 ***State*** what happens when the immune system overreacts.
40.3.2 ***Explain*** what an autoimmune disease is.
40.3.3 ***Describe*** how HIV is transmitted and affects the immune system.

Guide for Reading

Vocabulary Preview

Suggest that students scan the section for the highlighted, boldface Vocabulary terms and write a definition for each term based on the information in the text.

Reading Strategy

Have students read the figure captions and find the terms *allergens, autoimmune disease*, and *retrovirus*. Challenge students to define the terms based on the information in the captions.

2 INSTRUCT

Allergies

Build Science Skills

Using Tables and Graphs Have students design a simple allergy questionnaire that includes questions on whether the subject has allergies and which allergens are known or thought to be responsible. Then, have each student administer the questionnaire to at least five people, such as family members and neighbors, and summarize the results in a table that shows the number of people with allergies and the number allergic to each allergen. Assign a few students to pool the results for the whole class, and use the data to create a bar graph showing the proportion of the total sample affected by the top three allergens. L2 L3

Answer to . . .

Figure 40–12 *To kill dust mites that can cause allergies*

40–3 (continued)

Asthma

Use Community Resources

Arrange to have a nurse, physician's assistant, or other medical professional visit the class. Ask the visitor to explain the various causes of asthma as well as the different types of medications used to treat asthma. Encourage students to ask any questions they might have. L2

Autoimmune Diseases

Make Connections

Health Science Point out that there are many autoimmune diseases in addition to those listed in the text. Another relatively common example is systemic lupus erythematosus (SLE). In this disease, the immune system attacks normal connective tissue, and this leads to inflammation and pain in the joints, among other symptoms. L2

Asthma

Some allergic reactions can create a dangerous condition called asthma. **Asthma** is a chronic respiratory disease in which the air passages become narrower than normal. This narrowing of the air passages causes wheezing, coughing, and difficulty in breathing. Many factors, including both heredity and environment, play a role in the onset of the symptoms of asthma.

Asthma is a leading cause of serious illness among children, and can be a life-threatening disease. If treatment is not started early enough or if medications are not taken properly, asthma can lead to permanent damage or destruction of lung tissue.

Asthma attacks can be triggered by respiratory infections, exercise, emotional stress, and certain medications. Other triggers include cold air, pollen, dust, tobacco smoke, pollution, molds, and pet dander.

There is no cure for asthma; however, people who have asthma can sometimes control the condition. If the attacks are caused by an allergy, a series of tests can identify what substances cause the problem. Medications are sometimes used to relieve the symptoms of asthma. Often, these medications relax the smooth muscles around the airways, making breathing easier.

CHECKPOINT *What happens in the lungs during an asthma attack?*

▼ Figure 40–13 **When the immune system makes a mistake and attacks the body's own cells, it produces an autoimmune disease.** Multiple sclerosis is one example of an autoimmune disease in which axons in the optic nerve, brain, or spinal cord are affected. Symptoms of multiple sclerosis include problems with balance and motor coordination.

Autoimmune Diseases

The immune system could not defend your body against a host of invading pathogens unless it was able to distinguish those pathogens from the cells and tissues that are part of your body. In other words, the immune system usually has the ability to distinguish "self" from "nonself." **When the immune system makes a mistake and attacks the body's own cells, it produces an autoimmune disease.** In an autoimmune disease, the immune system produces "antiself" antibodies.

Some examples of autoimmune diseases include Type I diabetes, rheumatoid arthritis, myasthenia gravis, and multiple sclerosis (MS). In Type I diabetes, antibodies attack the insulin-producing cells of the pancreas. In rheumatoid arthritis, antibodies attack connective tissues around the joints. In myasthenia gravis, antibodies attack neuromuscular junctions. Multiple sclerosis is an autoimmune disease in which antibodies destroy the functions of the neurons in the brain and spinal cord.

Some autoimmune diseases are treated with medications that alleviate specific symptoms. For example, people who have Type I diabetes can be given insulin injections. Other autoimmune diseases are treated with medications that suppress the immune response. However, these medications also affect the normal immune response against pathogens, so this type of therapy is not used often or is carefully monitored. As researchers find out more about autoimmune diseases, they hope to develop more effective treatments.

SUPPORT FOR ENGLISH LANGUAGE LEARNERS

Vocabulary: Word Analysis

Beginning Write *disease* and *antibiotic* on the board. Then, rewrite each word as a separate prefix and base, i.e., *dis-* and *ease*, and *anti-* and *biotic*. Explain that the two prefixes, *dis-* and *anti-*, can have similar meanings; they can mean "against," or "opposing." Explain that *ease* can mean "comfort" or "wellness," and that *disease* is the opposite of comfort or wellness. Similarly, *biotic* comes from a word meaning "life," and an antibiotic acts against harmful living things, specifically bacteria. Discuss other words with these prefixes, such as *disagree, discomfort,* and *antifreeze.* L1

Intermediate After the beginning-level activity, have the students form a collaborative writing group to write sentences using each term. Have a volunteer from the group read the sentences. L2

AIDS, an Immunodeficiency Disease

Another type of immune system disorder is immunodeficiency disease. In one type of immunodeficiency disease, the immune system fails to develop normally. A second type of immunodeficiency disease is AIDS. AIDS results from a viral infection that destroys helper T cells. As the number of helper T cells declines, the normal immune response breaks down.

During the late 1970s, some physicians in Europe and the United States were bewildered. Some of their patients were dying from infections produced by benign microorganisms that didn't normally cause disease. Previously healthy people began to suffer from unusual illnesses such as *Pneumocystis carinii* (a kind of pneumonia), Kaposi's sarcoma (a rare form of skin cancer), and severe fungal infections of the mouth and throat. Normally, such infections are prevented by the immune system. Individual doctors realized that the symptoms were a signal that the immune systems of their patients had been weakened.

Some doctors recognized that these illnesses were actually symptoms of a new disease. Doctors in Los Angeles suggested the name AIDS—for acquired immune deficiency syndrome. As more cases appeared, researchers realized that this "syndrome" was actually an infectious disease caused by a pathogen that was unknown to the scientific community.

The Virus That Causes AIDS In 1983, researchers identified the cause of AIDS—a virus that they named HIV for human immunodeficiency virus. HIV is a retrovirus—a virus that carries its genetic information in RNA, rather than DNA. HIV turned out to be a deadly and efficient virus for two reasons. First, HIV evades the defenses of the immune system. Second, HIV attacks key cells in the immune system, destroying the body's defenses and leaving the body with no protection against other pathogens.

Among HIV's main targets are the helper T cells. When the HIV virus attacks a helper T cell, it attaches to receptor molecules on the cell membrane. This allows the virus to enter the cell, as shown in **Figure 40–14.** Once the viral core is inside the cell, it forces the host cell to make DNA copies of the virus's RNA. Some of those copies insert themselves into host cell DNA and stay there permanently. Other copies remain in the cytoplasm. The viral DNA may remain inactive in the host cell for varying periods of time. When activated, it directs the production of viral RNA and proteins that are assembled into new virus particles. These viruses eventually leave the infected cell and infect new cells. The immune system produces antibodies for HIV. Unfortunately, these antibodies are not effective in stopping the progression of the disease.

Despite the production of antibodies, HIV destroys ever-increasing numbers of T cells, crippling the immune system. By counting the number of the helper T cells, the progression of HIV infection can be monitored. The fewer helper T cells, the more advanced the disease.

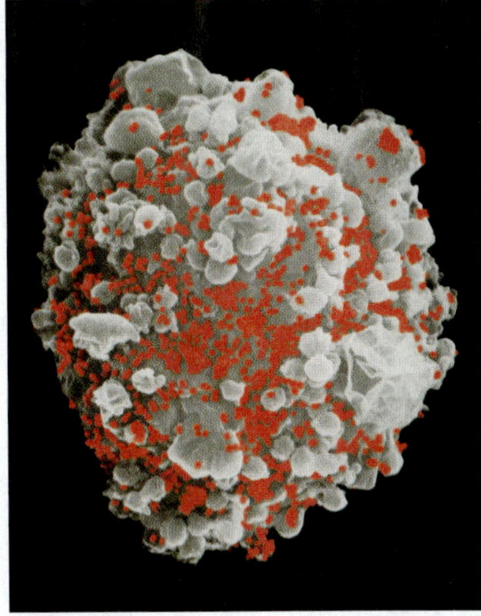

(magnification: about 5000×)

▲ **Figure 40–14** HIV is an example of a retrovirus, which contains RNA as its genetic material. Retroviruses get their name because their genetic information is first copied backward from RNA to DNA. **Interpreting Graphics** *In the micrograph, what type of blood cell are the red HIV particles attacking?*

AIDS, an Immunodeficiency Disease

Address Misconceptions

Point out that the terms HIV infection and AIDS are often used interchangeably. Explain that a person with an HIV infection may or may not have symptoms of the disease AIDS. In fact, an infected person may have no idea that he or she is even infected. Add that a person is diagnosed with AIDS only after the HIV infection has caused immune system damage leading to specific unusual infections, such as fungal infections in the mouth and rare forms of skin cancer. The clinical definition of AIDS includes a helper T cell count of 200/mm³ of blood or lower. L1 L2

Build Science Skills

Applying Concepts Check students' comprehension of the way HIV causes disease. Ask: **How does HIV "trick" helper T cells into making new copies of HIV?** *(HIV forces host T cells to make DNA copies of viral RNA. The DNA, in turn, directs the production of new viral RNA and proteins that are assembled into new virus particles.)* Ask: **How does HIV enter the central nervous system?** *(By hiding inside certain blood cells)* L1 L2

Make Connections

Health Science Emphasize the point that the symptoms of AIDS are not caused directly by HIV but rather by the damage HIV does to the immune system. Explain that similar symptoms are produced by other causes of immune system damage or dysfunction, including immunosuppressant drugs, which are given to people who have organ transplants. L1 L2

Answer to . . .

Smooth muscle contractions reduce the size of air passageways in the lungs and make breathing very difficult.

Figure 40–14 *White blood cell*

40–3 (continued)

Make Connections

Health Science Explain that HIV infections can be detected with a blood test for the presence of antibodies to HIV. A positive test indicates that the antibodies are present, and a negative test indicates that the antibodies are not present. Ask: **What do you think a false negative result indicates?** *(That antibodies are present but not detected by the test)* Point out that someone who was very recently infected with HIV might have a false negative result because the immune system has not yet produced enough antibodies to be detected in the blood. L2

Use Community Resources

Invite a professional who works with people with AIDS to speak to the class about the medical, emotional, and financial consequences of living with AIDS. Possible speakers might include a public-health nurse, home healthcare provider, or social worker. Urge students to ask questions at the end of the presentation. L1 L2

FIGURE 40–15 HIV Infection

HIV travels through the bloodstream, where it binds to receptors on helper T cells. Once inside the cell, the virus directs the cell to produce many new viruses. These new viruses are quickly released back into the bloodstream, where they travel to new cells and destroy them.

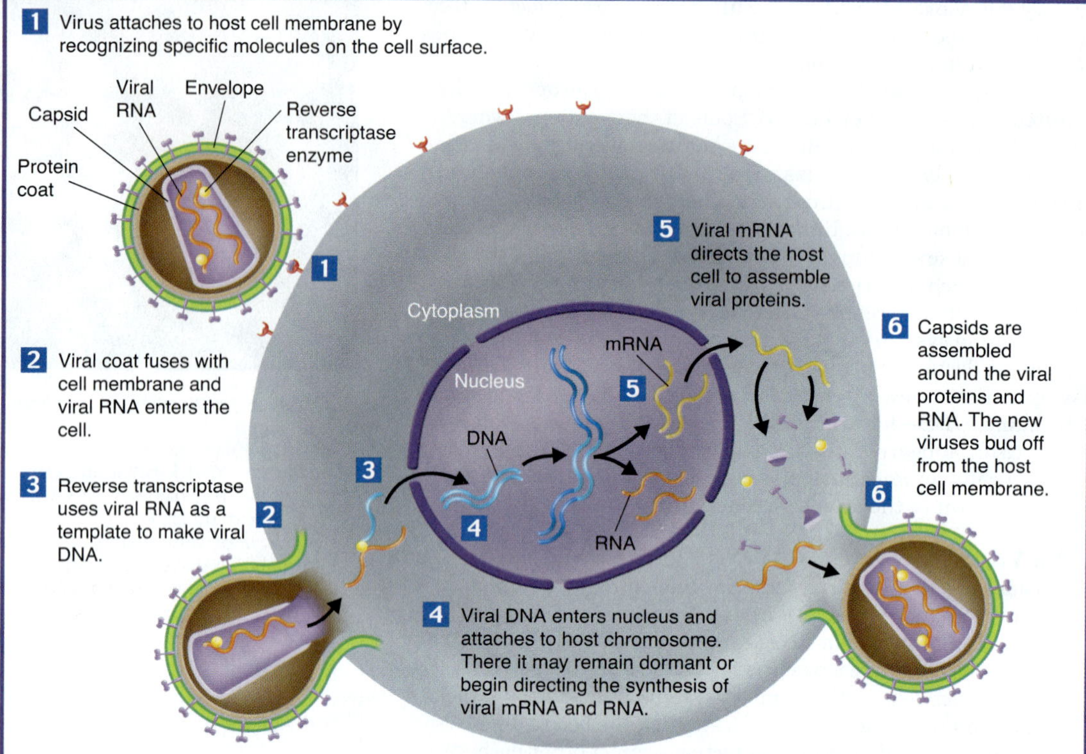

As the number of helper T cells decreases, the body becomes more and more susceptible to other diseases. The diseases that attack a person with a weakened immune system are called opportunistic diseases.

Transmission of HIV Although HIV is a deadly disease, it is not easily transmitted. It is not transmitted through casual contact. HIV can only be transmitted through the exchange of blood, semen, vaginal secretions, or breast milk.

There are four main ways that HIV can be transmitted:

- through any form of sexual intercourse with an infected person;
- through shared needles or syringes that are contaminated with the blood of an infected person;
- through contact with blood or blood products of an infected person; and
- from an infected mother to child, either during pregnancy, during birth, or during breast-feeding.

FACTS AND FIGURES

HIV and helper T cells

Two types of HIV virus are known: HIV–1 and HIV–2. In both types, each viral particle consists of a protein core that surrounds its RNA and several copies of the enzyme reverse transcriptase. When the virus attaches to a helper T cell, the protein core becomes wrapped in a lipid envelope derived from the T cell's plasma membrane. The virus progresses from the surface of the T cell to the cell interior. Once the virus is inside the T cell, the reverse transcriptase uses the viral RNA as a template for making DNA. This DNA is then inserted into a chromosome of the helper T cell. When the helper T cell is activated, it transcribes the HIV DNA along with portions of its own DNA, thus inadvertently producing copies of viral RNA. The viral RNA is translated into viral proteins, which assemble to form new viruses that go on to infect and destroy more helper T cells.

Preventing HIV Infection Fortunately you can choose behaviors that will help you reduce your risk of becoming infected with HIV. **The only no-risk behavior with respect to HIV and AIDS is abstinence.** Within a committed sexual relationship such as marriage, sexual fidelity between two uninfected partners presents the least risk of becoming infected with HIV.

Avoiding drug use is also important for reducing the risk of HIV infection. People who share contaminated needles to inject themselves with drugs are at a high risk for contracting HIV. People who have sex with drug abusers are also at high risk.

Before 1985, HIV was transmitted to some hemophiliacs and surgical patients through transfusions of infected blood or blood products. Such cases have been nearly eliminated by screening the blood supply for HIV antibodies and by discouraging potentially infected individuals from donating blood.

Can AIDS Be Cured? At present, there is no cure for AIDS. However, progress has been made in developing drugs that make it possible to survive HIV infection for years. Unfortunately, HIV mutates and evolves very rapidly. For this reason, the virus has been able to evolve into many different strains that are resistant to virtually all drugs used against them. Because HIV evolves so rapidly, no one has developed a vaccine that offers protection for any length of time.

At present, the only way to control the virus is to use expensive multidrug and multivitamin "cocktails" that fight the virus in several ways. Thanks to these drugs, more HIV-infected people are now living with HIV rather than dying from it.

Unfortunately, the knowledge that HIV can be treated (though not cured) has given people the idea that HIV infection is not as serious as it was a decade ago. In one year, more than 5 million people around the world became infected with HIV, including roughly 800,000 people under the age of 15. That same year, more than 3 million people around the world died of AIDS, bringing the total number of deaths worldwide to more than 20 million people.

40–3 Section Assessment

1. **Key Concept** What happens in an autoimmune disease?
2. **Key Concept** Describe the various ways HIV is transmitted from person to person.
3. What are the two main types of immune system disorders?
4. Why is it difficult for a person with HIV to fight off infections?
5. **Critical Thinking** **Applying Concepts** In treating asthma, the first thing many physicians do is ask patients to list times and places they have experienced asthmatic reactions. Why do you think doctors do this?

Focus on the BIG Idea

Structure and Function
Compare the process of HIV replication with that of other viruses. You may wish to review **Figure 40–14** as well as Chapter 19.

3 ASSESS

Evaluate Understanding

Have students write a concise, informative paragraph correctly using each of the Vocabulary terms.

Reteach

On the chalkboard or an overhead transparency, make a concept map with the following terms: *immune system disorders, allergies, autoimmune diseases,* and *AIDS*. Call on students to describe or give an example of each type of disorder listed in the concept map.

Focus on the BIG Idea

As a retrovirus, HIV transcribes DNA from an RNA template, which is the opposite of how most other viruses replicate.

If your class subscribes to the iText, use it to review the Key Concepts in Section 40–3.

40–3 Section Assessment

1. In an autoimmune disease, the immune system attacks the body's own cells.
2. Answers should include the four bulleted items on page 1046.
3. Autoimmune diseases, and immunodeficiency diseases
4. HIV kills off most of the helper T cells, which greatly reduces the immune system's response to infection.
5. Doctors ask asthmatic patients where and when their asthmatic reactions occur in order to identify the antigens that trigger the asthma attacks.

 **BIIE 1.m**

Have students role-play a conference about the issues. Assign students to play the following roles: representative of an American pharmaceutical company that manufactures anti-HIV drugs; minister of health of an African country; president of the World Health Organization; and an expert consultant on AIDS-prevention education. Students should research the issues and then take one of the viewpoints presented in the feature. In their role-playing, students should present logical arguments, based on their research, in support of the viewpoint they have chosen.

Research and Decide

1. Students should list the options in this feature as well as any additional options they find through their research.
2. Answers will vary depending on how individuals choose to allocate the money. Student answers should include appropriate reasons and explanations for their choices.

Students can research the AIDS epidemic on the site developed by authors Ken Miller and Joe Levine.

 **BIIE 1.m**

Slowing a Worldwide Epidemic

AIDS is a threat on every continent in the world, but nowhere has its effect been more devastating than in Africa. Thirty million of the world's 42 million people infected with HIV live in Africa. In some African countries, the HIV-infection rate is as high as one in three people. Leaders from around the world disagree on how the AIDS epidemic should be handled. Some argue that generic drugs should be made available. Others argue that the focus should be on AIDS prevention and education. Still others think that some money needs to be spent on the millions of AIDS orphans.

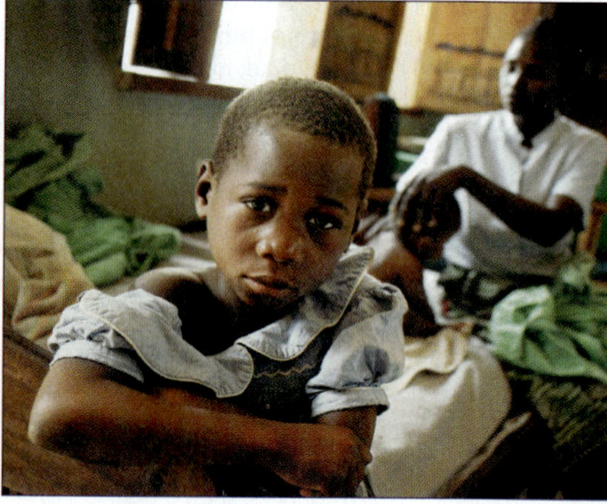

The Viewpoints

Make Drugs More Affordable

AIDS workers in Africa believe that more affordable drugs should be the top priority. HIV-infected people in Africa do not have access to the advanced medicines that people have in the United States. In Africa, the use of antiviral drugs is not common. Although the antiviral drugs do not cure AIDS, they help prolong life as long as they are taken on a regular basis. To increase access to these drugs, activists are looking for generic drugs, which would be lower in cost. Large pharmaceutical companies, however, don't like this idea because they say that generic drugs violate the companies' patents on such antiviral drugs.

Spend Money for Prevention

Many people in HIV-infected populations do not have basic knowledge about AIDS, including how HIV is spread. Thus, what is needed is an intensive program of public health education to stop the spread of the virus. If prevention programs including education and counseling were available, the incidence of new HIV infections could be reduced.

Spend Money on AIDS Orphans

More than 11 million children have lost parents to AIDS. Orphanages are overflowing with children who have no one to look after them. It is expected in Ethiopia—the country with the fastest-growing HIV-infection rate—that the number of orphans could increase about 150 percent over the next ten years. Because of this growing problem, a number of people feel that some of the money used to fight AIDS should be given to care for these orphans.

Research and Decide

1. **Analyzing the Viewpoints** To make an informed decision, learn more about this issue by consulting library or Internet resources. Then, list the key arguments for each of the viewpoints.
2. **Forming Your Opinion** Given limited resources to fight HIV, how would you decide the allocation of those resources? Would you spend all of the money on one area, or would you split it up among the different areas? What are the reasons for your decision?

For: Links from the authors
Visit: PHSchool.com
Web Code: cbe-0403

BACKGROUND

Putting HIV and AIDS in context

No one knows why HIV appeared suddenly in the late 1970s, although most scientists believe it originated in Africa. It could have been a virus in monkeys that mutated and infected humans, but it has never been isolated from any animal source. In the United States and Europe, HIV has been transmitted most often among male homosexuals and intravenous drug users. In Africa, it has been transmitted almost solely among heterosexuals. Heterosexual transmission is also on the rise in Latin America. Besides education and treatment, a third way to possibly slow the AIDS epidemic is through vaccination. Scientists have been working for years on a vaccine to prevent HIV infection, but developing a vaccine has been difficult because HIV mutates rapidly. Nonetheless, a vaccine may be available in the near future.

40–4 The Environment and Your Health

Staying healthy involves more than the battles against pathogens. You interact constantly with both living and nonliving parts of your environment. Aspects of your environment that are important to health include the buildings in which you live, the people with whom you share those spaces, the air you breathe, the water you drink, and the food you eat.

Factors that have the potential to affect health in a negative way are called risk factors. A **risk factor** is anything that increases the chance of disease or injury. Both heredity (the genes you carry) and environmental factors can affect your health.  **Environmental factors that can affect your health include air and water quality, poisonous wastes in landfills, and exposure to solar radiation.**

Guide for Reading

Key Concepts
- What environmental factors affect your health?
- How can you maintain your health?

Vocabulary
risk factor
tumor
carcinogen

Reading Strategy: Hypothesizing Before you read, hypothesize about how the environment can affect your health. As you read, list evidence that supports or rejects your hypothesis.

Air Quality

The air you breathe comes into very close contact with your delicate lung tissue and blood. It shouldn't be surprising, therefore, that the quality of the air is very important to your health. But what is meant by "air quality"? Air quality refers to the number and concentrations of various gases present, as well as the nature and amount of tiny particles suspended in the air. Gases that are important to air quality include carbon monoxide and ozone. Particles in the air include dust, pollen, or particulates produced by cars and trucks or the burning of coal. If the concentration of these impurities gets too high, they can become risk factors for various health problems.

Carbon Monoxide Carbon monoxide (CO) is an odorless gas produced when certain compounds are burned. Carbon monoxide is found in automobile exhaust and cigarette smoke. Carbon monoxide also can be produced by the furnace of a heating system or by space heaters that burn fuel.

Recall that hemoglobin in red blood cells usually helps carry oxygen to the cells of your body. If you inhale carbon monoxide, that gas binds to hemoglobin, preventing it from carrying oxygen. As a result, the body does not receive the oxygen it needs. Overexposure to carbon monoxide can be fatal.

Ozone Ozone (O_3), a highly reactive form of oxygen, is another gas found in the air that is a potential risk factor when it occurs at ground level. Ozone is produced by vehicle exhaust and factory emissions. When the air is stagnant, ozone accumulates. When ozone levels are high, you should limit your time outdoors as much as possible, especially if you have a respiratory condition such as asthma, bronchitis, or emphysema.

Figure 40–16 **Poor air quality can affect your health.** Smog is a mixture of chemicals that appears in the atmosphere as a gray-brown haze. Smog is particularly dangerous for people with respiratory conditions.

TIME SAVER — SECTION RESOURCES

Print:
- ***Teaching Resources,*** Lesson Plan 40–4, Adapted Section Summary 40–4, Adapted Worksheets 40–4, Section Summary 40–4, Worksheets 40–4, Section Review 40–4, Enrichment
- ***Reading and Study Workbook A,*** Section 40–4
- ***Adapted Reading and Study Workbook B,*** Section 40–4
- ***Biotechnology Manual,*** Lab 13

Technology:
- ***iText,*** Section 40–4
- ***Transparencies Plus,*** Section 40–4

Section 40–4

1 FOCUS

Objectives

40.4.1 ***Identify*** environmental factors that affect your health.

40.4.2 ***Describe*** how you can maintain your health.

Guide for Reading

Vocabulary Preview

Call students' attention to the section Vocabulary. Point out that risk factors sometimes, but not always, involve risky behaviors. Call on students to give examples of both types of risk factors. *(Possible examples include smoking cigarettes and sex or gender.)*

Reading Strategy

Challenge students to predict what each of the terms means before they look for them in the section. Have visual learners preview the section by studying the figures and reading the captions.

2 INSTRUCT

Build Science Skills

Applying Concepts Challenge students to identify ways that plants, animals, and other people in their environment might affect their health. *(Possible answers: Plants and plant pollens may cause allergies; animals are vectors of Lyme disease and other illnesses; and people may behave violently and injure or even kill other people.)* L1 L2

Air Quality

Make Connections

Health Science Point out that carbon monoxide is a relatively common danger in the home. It is especially dangerous because it is odorless and colorless. As a result, people may breathe it in and succumb to its effects without ever realizing they are in danger. Explain that one of the best ways to prevent carbon monoxide poisoning is by using carbon monoxide detectors in the home. You might want to bring a carbon monoxide detector to class and explain how it works. L2

40–4 (continued)

Make Connections

Health Science Tell students that some particulates known to cause human diseases are found in high concentrations in the air in certain occupations. Describe the example of coal dust. It causes a deadly lung disease called "black lung" in long-term coal miners. Also, describe the example of hemp fibers. They can cause a lung disease referred to as "brown lung" in people who work with hemp. L2

Water Quality

Use Community Resources

Arrange for students to visit a water treatment plant to see how water is processed to make it safe for human use in their community. After the visit, have students make a diagram showing the sequence of steps through which water passes in the treatment plant. Ask: **What is removed from water in each phase of treatment?** *(Students should name the particulate matter, biological pollutants, and other pollutants that are removed from water during the phases of treatment.)* L2

Airborne Particulates Airborne particulates of many different kinds can also be risk factors. Tiny dust mites, pollen, mold spores, and animal dander can trigger allergic reactions that can lead to respiratory problems or make existing health problems worse. Some potential sources of airborne particulates that can be found indoors are shown in **Figure 40–17.**

Another type of particulate that can cause serious harm is the metal lead. Lead can poison the liver, kidneys, and nervous system. Lead poisoning in babies and young children can also result in slow mental development.

Lead became a serious problem because for many years it was added to gasoline to improve the performance of engines. When that gas was burned, tiny particulates of lead were released into the air. People inhaled lead particulates as they breathed. Many more lead particulates were washed into rivers and streams. When research revealed the health problems that resulted, leaded gasoline was phased out and replaced with unleaded gasoline. Within a few years, levels of lead in surface waters dropped dramatically.

Another particulate that can be carried in air is asbestos, which was commonly used for insulation. Asbestos can fragment into tiny fibers that are small enough to remain suspended in air for some time. When inhaled repeatedly, asbestos fibers can cause lung cancer.

Water Quality

Water, like air, can carry biological and chemical pollution. Biological pollutants in water, such as human and animal wastes, can contain bacteria or viruses that can cause cramps, vomiting, diarrhea, or diseases such as hepatitis or cholera.

Some chemical pollutants can cause organ damage. Others interfere with the development of organs and tissues, causing birth defects. Still others can damage DNA, causing normal cells to become cancerous.

▼ **Figure 40–17** Air pollution can occur indoors as well as outdoors. Indoor air pollutants include fumes and vapors given off by carpets, paints, and household cleaning products.

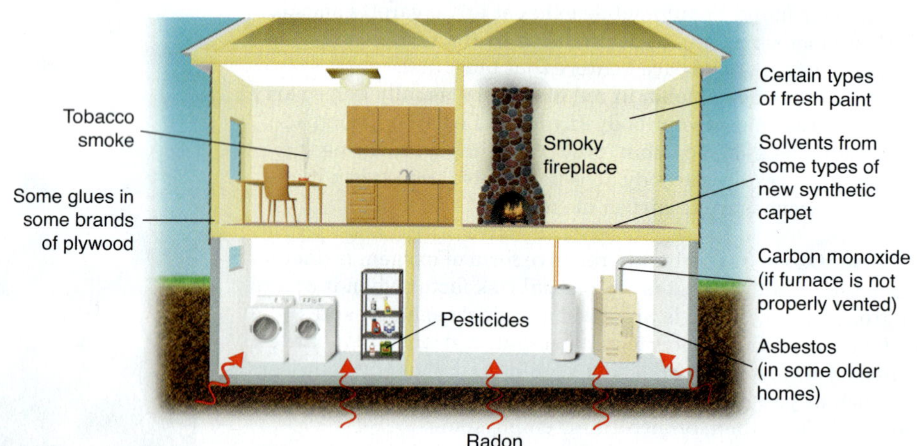

UNIVERSAL ACCESS

Inclusion/Special Needs

On the board or an overhead transparency, work with at-risk students to create a concept map that incorporates the headings and subheadings in the section. After the concept map is completed, have students add examples to it. For example, under radiation, they could add UV radiation, X-rays, or radon. Tell students to copy the completed concept map into their class notebook and use it as a study guide. L1

Less Proficient Readers

Guide students who need extra help in organizing the material in the section. Have them draw a line down the middle of a sheet of paper. Then, as they read, have them fill in the left side of the paper with a list of environmental factors that adversely affect health. They should fill in the right side of the paper with a list of steps they can take to maintain their health. Advise them to save the paper as a study guide. L1 L2

◀ **Figure 40–18** Many cities and towns have sewage-treatment plants that process household waste water. In huge outdoor tanks, water is treated with chemicals and microorganisms and then aerated. **Applying Concepts** *What is the role of microorganisms in treating waste water?*

Fortunately, regulations requiring proper treatment of residential and industrial sewage, for example, have led to significant decreases in the amount of sewage-related bacteria in drinking-water supplies across the nation. In the United States, for example, public water systems supply clean, safe drinking water to cities and many towns. Providing safe drinking water has probably been the single most important factor in nearly doubling human life expectancy over the last century or so.

Bioterrorism

In recent years, bioterrorism has become a new health threat. Bioterrorism is the intentional use of biological agents to disable or kill individuals. Bioterrorism can involve the intentional release of infectious agents—viruses (such as smallpox) or bacteria (such as anthrax)—or the spread of toxic compounds (such as botulinus toxin) extracted from living organisms.

Some forms of bioterrorism pose risks in part because research and public health measures have been so successful in the past. For example, worldwide vaccination programs eliminated smallpox around the world years ago. As a result, almost no one has been vaccinated against the virus for decades. Thus, the release of smallpox virus could cause serious problems.

Other forms of bioterrorism involve treating pathogens to maximize their ability to infect and cause disease. Anthrax is a disease that is common in cattle-ranching areas, but it is usually present in a form that either is not easily transmitted or is not life-threatening. The spores of anthrax bacteria, however, can be treated to make them light and fine enough to be spread through the air and inhaled—which produces a possibly fatal infection. Medical, research, and military establishments are still in the process of performing research and evaluating the best ways to minimize the risks of bioterrorism.

Bioterrorism

Build Science Skills

Drawing Conclusions Point out that methods of bioterrorism are also often referred to as "weapons of mass destruction." Ask: **Why are infectious diseases, such as smallpox and anthrax, potentially so deadly?** *(Because they can be fatal and, being infectious, can easily infect huge numbers of people)* L2

FACTS AND FIGURES

Not just anthrax and smallpox

Media attention has made the public aware of the potential threat of bioterrorism with the smallpox virus and anthrax bacterium. However, other pathogens are also potential agents of bioterrorism, including the bacterium that causes tularemia and the virus that causes hemorrhagic fever. Both have been studied in germ warfare laboratories for decades. In addition, the hemorrhagic fever virus has been weaponized by the United States and Russia, and the tularemia bacterium may already have been used as a weapon by the former Soviet Union in World War II. Both pathogens are normally found in nonhuman animal populations. When introduced to human populations, they cause potentially fatal, flulike illnesses. Aerosol dispersal could result in hundreds of thousands of people being infected and thousands of lives being lost.

Answer to . . .

Figure 40–18 *Microorganisms break down complex compounds in waste water to produce simpler ones. The process produces water, carbon dioxide, nitrogen gas, and compounds that can be used as fertilizer.*

40–4 (continued)

Cancer

Make Connections

Environmental Science Explain how destruction of the ozone layer in Earth's atmosphere has increased the amount of ultraviolet radiation to which people are potentially exposed. Ask: **How is this likely to affect rates of skin cancer?** *(The rates are likely to increase.)* Add that skin cancer rates have in fact increased since the late 1900s. L2

Demonstration

Point out that tumors can often be detected by physical exam or X-ray but determining whether a tumor is cancerous usually requires a biopsy. Explain that a biopsy is the surgical removal of a small mass of tissue of a tumor so it can be examined under a microscope for evidence of cancer. Use a microprojector and show students slides of normal and cancerous cells. Alternatively, you can show students pictures of normal and cancerous cells from histology textbooks or Internet sites. Ask: **How do the normal and cancerous cells appear to differ?** *(Cancer cells are often small, mitotically active cells with little sign of cell differentiation.)* L2

Download a worksheet on cancer for students to complete, and find additional teacher support from NSTA SciLinks.

For: Links on cancer cells
Visit: www.SciLinks.org
Web Code: cbn-0404

Cancer

Cancer is a life-threatening disease in which cells multiply uncontrollably and destroy healthy tissue. Cancer is a unique disease because the cells that cause it are not foreign cells but rather the body's own cells. This fact has made cancer difficult to treat and to understand.

All forms of cancer are ultimately caused by harmful mutations in genes that control cell growth and development. Sometimes, cancer arises almost entirely because some factor in the environment damages DNA. An increased likelihood of developing some cancers can be inherited.

Cancers begin when something goes wrong with the controls that normally regulate cell growth and reproduction. A single cell or a group of cells begin to grow and divide uncontrollably, often resulting in the formation of a mass of growing tissue known as a **tumor.** However, not all tumors are cancerous. Some tumors are benign, or noncancerous. A benign tumor does not spread to surrounding healthy tissue or to other parts of the body. Cancerous tumors, on the other hand, are malignant, which means that they can invade and destroy surrounding healthy tissue.

As the cancer cells spread, they absorb the nutrients needed by other cells, block nerve connections, and prevent the organs they invade from functioning properly. Soon, the delicate balances that exist in the body are disrupted, and life-threatening illness results.

▼ **Figure 40–19** The body recognizes cancer cells as foreign and tries to destroy them. In this color-enhanced SEM, a killer T cell (orange) is attacking a cancer cell (purple).

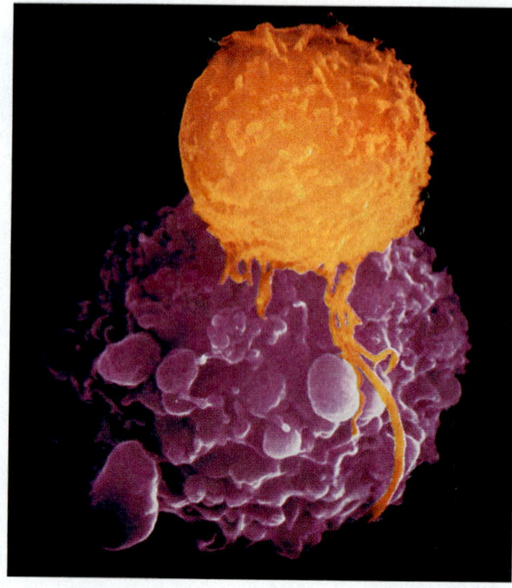

(magnification: about 3000×)

Causes of Cancer Cancers are caused by defects in the genes that regulate cell growth and division. There are several sources of such defects. They may be inherited, be caused by viruses, or may result from mutations in DNA that occur spontaneously or are produced by chemicals or radiation.

Chemical compounds cause cancer by triggering mutations in the DNA of normal cells. Chemical compounds that are known to cause cancer are called **carcinogens.** Some carcinogens are produced in nature. One of these, aflatoxin, is produced by molds that grow on peanuts. Others, such as chloroform and benzene, are synthetic compounds. Some of the most powerful chemical carcinogens are found in tobacco smoke. In the United States, cigarette smoking is responsible for nearly half the cancers that occur.

Most forms of radiation—including sunlight, X-rays, and nuclear radiation—cause cancer by producing mutations in DNA. If mutations occur in genes that control cell growth, a normal cell may be transformed into a cancer cell. Most cases of skin cancer, for example, are caused by the ultraviolet radiation in sunlight. For this reason, it is important to avoid prolonged exposure to the sun.

Analyzing Data

6IIE 7.c, 7IIE 7.c

Cancer Mortality

Cancer is a disease that is easier to treat if it is detected early. There are also things you can do to decrease your risk of cancer, such as eating a diet high in fruits, vegetables, and fiber; staying out of the sun; and not smoking. The data in the table show the 5-year mortality rates of five different types of cancer since 1950. Use the data to answer the questions.

1. **Using Tables and Graphs** Construct a line graph of the data in the table.
2. **Using Tables and Graphs** Which type of cancer has shown the greatest increase in mortality rate?
3. **Inferring** What can you infer about the use of tobacco in men over the last 50 years? In women?
4. **Predicting** Given the trend in melanoma cancer deaths over the past 50 years, predict the incidence in 1995–1998 in both men and women.
5. **Inferring** Why do you think the incidence of death from breast cancer has stayed relatively stable over the last 50 years?

Cancer Mortality Rates (per 100,000 people)

Year	Lung		Colon		Melanoma		Breast	Prostate
	Male	Female	Male	Female	Male	Female	Female	Male
1950–54	25.51	4.98	16.94	18.49	1.20	0.92	26.42	20.85
1960–64	42.15	6.39	17.86	17.48	1.67	1.19	26.22	19.78
1970–74	60.79	12.80	19.49	16.43	2.18	1.40	26.92	20.05
1980–84	71.30	23.33	21.22	15.52	2.95	1.64	26.90	21.29
1990–94	71.71	33.43	18.79	12.85	3.49	1.69	26.19	24.37
1995–98	68.00	34.30	20.50	14.10	?	?	24.20	23.70

Radon is another source of radiation. Radon is a radioactive gas that is found naturally in some rocks and that sometimes leaks into the foundations of buildings. If your home is located in an area where radon is present, it can be tested for the presence of radon.

Treating Cancer As with other diseases, prevention is the best defense. The best way to fight cancer is by protecting your DNA from agents that cause cancer. For example, you can dramatically reduce your risk of developing lung cancer by not smoking. In addition, regular exercise and a balanced diet with plenty of fruits and vegetables can help to lower your cancer risk.

Physicians also stress that if a cancer is detected early the chances of treating it successfully may be as high as 90 percent. Regular checkups and tests are an important preventive measure. Recommended tests depend on a person's age, gender, and family history. Self-examinations for skin, breast, or testicular cancer are also helpful when combined with regular checkups. Your doctor can give you instructions for performing these self-examinations.

Analyzing Data

6IIE 7.c, 7IIE 7.c

You may wish to point out to students that breast cancer can occur in males, although it is very rare. Also point out that the values are for 5-year time spans, except the last row, which is only four years. L2

Answers

1. Check students' line graphs to make sure that they have plotted the data correctly.
2. Lung cancer for both men and women
3. Tobacco use in both sexes has increased dramatically.
4. Accept all logical responses. Male rate may be around 4.0; female rate may be around 1.8–1.9.
5. Self-exams have helped in early detection of cancers, increasing the rate of survival. Also, there are a variety of treatments available to breast cancer patients.

BIO INSIGHTS FACTS AND FIGURES

Radon and cancer

The invisible, odorless, radioactive gas radon is released through the decay of uranium in soil and rocks. When uranium decays, it emits tiny radioactive particles that can damage the cells lining the lungs, and long-term exposure can lead to lung cancer. Radon's link with lung cancer was first discovered when scientists discovered that underground uranium miners died of lung cancer at far-higher-than-expected rates. Although everyone breathes in some radon every day, it is usually at very low levels that have little if any health risks. However, radon can reach dangerously high levels in well-insulated homes and other buildings. As a result, it is estimated to be responsible for about 10 percent of annual lung cancer cases in the United States, making radon second only to cigarette smoking as a cause of lung cancer.

40–4 (continued)

Maintaining Health

Build Science Skills

Applying Concepts Ask students to think of at least one specific way that they can maintain their health for each of the four general ways that are presented in the section: healthful diet, exercise and rest, abstaining from harmful activities, and regular checkups. *(Possible ways include avoiding high-fat foods; working out three or more times a week; saying no to drugs, alcohol, and sex; and getting regular checkups.)* L1

Make Connections

Health Science Review some of the regular screening tests recommended for most adults, including testicular and breast self-exams, mammograms, Pap smears, and colonoscopies. Discuss the role of screening in early detection and successful treatment of the diseases. L2

3 ASSESS

Evaluate Understanding

Ask students to make a concept map of environmental factors that affect health.

Reteach

Using the chalkboard or an overhead transparency, work with students to make an outline of the section by writing the section headings and subheadings as outline topics and subtopics and calling on students to fill in important details.

Focus on the BIG Idea 

Cells would be most vulnerable to damage from radiation during the S phase of the cell cycle, when DNA is being replicated. Cancer cells would be especially vulnerable to radiation because cancer is characterized by rapid cell division.

If your class subscribes to the iText, use it to review the Key Concepts in Section 40–4.

▲ **Figure 40–20 Getting regular exercise is one way to maintain your health.** You should try to get a minimum of 30 minutes of aerobic exercise each day.

Maintaining Health

To keep your immune system working efficiently, you can practice behaviors that reduce your exposure to pathogens and maintain overall good health. **Healthful behaviors include eating a healthful diet, getting plenty of exercise and rest, abstaining from harmful activities, and having regular checkups.**

Healthful Diet Food provides the nutrients and energy your cells need to function properly. To help all your body systems work at their best, it is important to eat a balanced diet that provides essential nutrients. Eating foods that are low in saturated fat and cholesterol may help prevent obesity. Eating plenty of fruits, vegetables, and whole grains will also help protect you from certain cancers, especially colon and rectal cancers.

Exercise and Rest Regular exercise helps move blood throughout the body and maintains cardiovascular fitness. Exercise also helps maintain an appropriate body weight, which helps prevent certain kinds of heart disease. Adequate rest is important for keeping your body functioning well. For most people, adequate rest means getting about eight hours of sleep each night.

Abstaining From Harmful Activities Drugs, including alcohol and tobacco products, can have harmful effects on the body. Many types of drugs, including alcohol, can slow or suppress the immune system. Smoking and tobacco products also cause a variety of respiratory conditions as well as certain cancers, including cancers of the lung, mouth, and throat.

Some diseases can be spread through sexual contact with an infected person. These sexually transmitted diseases (STDs) include HIV, chlamydia, and gonorrhea. The only way to absolutely prevent exposure to sexually transmitted diseases is to abstain from all sexual activity.

Regular Checkups It usually is easier to treat a disease if it is discovered early. You can perform regular self-examinations for skin cancer, breast cancer, and testicular cancer. By getting regular checkups, you can help maintain your health.

40–4 Section Assessment

1. **Key Concept** Describe the environmental factors that affect your health.
2. **Key Concept** Name three things you can do to maintain your health.
3. List some of the causes of cancer.
4. Why are regular medical checkups and self-examinations important?
5. **Critical Thinking Classifying** Should cancer be considered an infectious disease? Explain your answer.

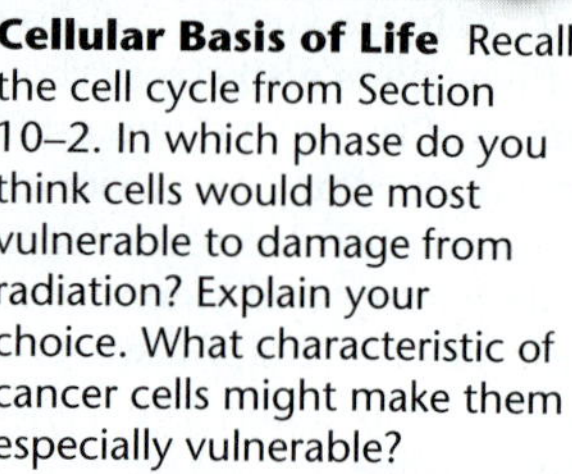

Cellular Basis of Life Recall the cell cycle from Section 10–2. In which phase do you think cells would be most vulnerable to damage from radiation? Explain your choice. What characteristic of cancer cells might make them especially vulnerable?

40–4 Section Assessment

1. Students should describe air and water quality, poisonous wastes in landfills, and exposure to solar radiation.
2. Any three of the following: eating a healthful diet, getting enough exercise and rest, abstaining from harmful activities, and having regular checkups
3. Cancers are caused by defects in the genes that regulate cell growth and division. These defects may be inherited or caused by viruses, or they may result from mutations in DNA produced by radiation or chemicals.
4. Regular medical checkups and self-examinations are important for detecting problems early so that there is a better chance of treating them successfully.
5. Most cases of cancer are not infectious. However, cancer-causing viruses can be passed from person to person.

Real-World Lab

7IIE 7.c, BIIE 1.d

Testing the Specificity of Antibodies

Antibodies are very selective. They will bind only to specific antigens. An antibody that binds strongly to a certain protein or carbohydrate may not bind at all to another molecule that has a very similar structure. In this investigation, you will determine the specificity of an antibody.

Problem

How specific is the binding of antibodies to antigens?

Materials

- Strep A diagnostic kits with control samples (materials for three tests)
- sterile water

Skills

Predicting, Evaluating, Drawing Conclusions

Procedure

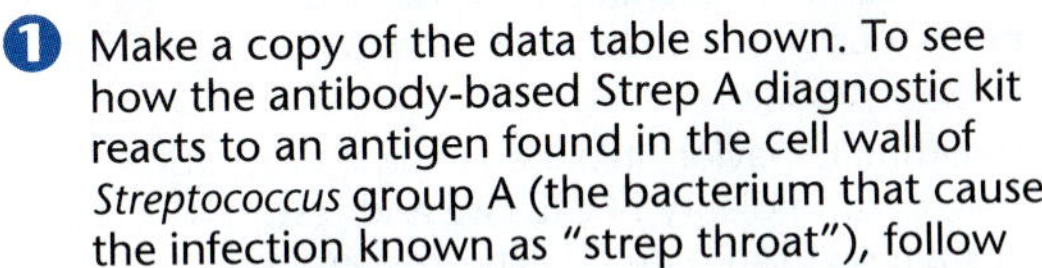

1. Make a copy of the data table shown. To see how the antibody-based Strep A diagnostic kit reacts to an antigen found in the cell wall of *Streptococcus* group A (the bacterium that causes the infection known as "strep throat"), follow the instructions in the kit to test the positive control sample. Record the result of this test.
2. **Predicting** *Streptococcus* group C is closely related to *Streptococcus* group A but does not cause disease. Record your prediction of how the diagnostic kit will react to antigens from the cell wall of *Streptococcus* group C.
3. Test the *Streptococcus* group C sample as you did the *Streptococcus* group A sample in step 1. Record the result of this test.
4. **Predicting** Record your prediction of whether *Streptococcus* group A is present on the tabletops in your lab.
5. Use sterile water to moisten the tip of one of the test swabs supplied with your diagnostic kit and rub it on the tabletop. Then, test the sample on the swab and record your results.
6. Wash your hands with soap and warm water before leaving the classroom.

Data Table

Sample	Result (Positive or Negative)
Streptococcus Group A	
Streptococcus Group C	
Tabletop Swab	

Analyze and Conclude

1. **Observing** Did the antibody-based test react to the antigen of *Streptococcus* group A? To the antigen of group C?
2. **Analyzing Data** Did your results support the idea that an antibody can be used to distinguish between two similar antigens, such as those of *Streptococcus* group A and group C?
3. **Evaluating** Assess the quality and appropriateness of the data from steps 1 through 3 by stating whether the results enable you to answer the Problem question. Did your data enable you to determine whether *Streptococcus* group A was present on the tabletop? Explain your reasoning.
4. **Drawing Conclusions** Use what you have learned about the specificity of antibodies to explain what happens in autoimmune diseases such as multiple sclerosis.

Go Further

Interviewing a Professional Interview a health professional to find out how antibody-based tests are used to determine blood types and to diagnose diseases.

Real-World Lab

7IIE 7.c, BIIE 1.d

Objective Students will be able to make and test predictions about the specificity of the Strep A antibody.

Skills Focus **Predicting, Evaluating, Drawing Conclusions**

Time 45 minutes

Advance Prep You can obtain Strep A diagnostic kits from a pharmacy or a pharmaceutical distributor without a prescription. Before the activity, carefully read the instructions enclosed with the test kits.

Safety Students should wear disposable plastic gloves when working with the diagnostic kits. Be sure to collect and properly dispose of the gloves after the lab. Make sure students wash their hands with soap and warm water before leaving the lab.

Teaching Tip Have students read the entire procedure. Then, ask: **What does it mean when a sample "tests positive" with the Strep A diagnostic kit?** *(A positive test result means that the sample is Strep A.)* **What causes the positive reaction to occur when Strep A is tested?** *(Strep A antibodies in the diagnostic kit bind with Strep A antigens in the sample.)*

Procedure

5. Students may not know that *Streptococcus* group A is not normally found on tabletops. Explain that it is more likely to be found in warm, dark, moist places like the human throat.

Expected Outcome Students should find that the antibody-based Strep A diagnostic kit tests positive for Strep A but not Strep C.

Analyze and Conclude

1. The antibody-based test reacted to the antigen of *Streptococcus* group A but not to the antigen of *Streptococcus* group C.
2. Yes, the results supported the idea that an antibody can distinguish between two similar antigens.
3. It is unlikely that the diagnostic kit detected any *Streptococcus* group A on the tabletop. The ability of the diagnostic kit to distinguish between *Streptococcus* group A and *Streptococcus* group C in steps 1 through 3 supported the idea that this is a reliable result.
4. In autoimmune diseases such as multiple sclerosis, the antibodies that form to fight a pathogen cannot distinguish between the pathogen's antigens and some of the body's own proteins. As a result, the antibodies attack body cells as well as the pathogen.

Go Further

Students might interview a laboratory technician or clinical nurse. Students will learn that antibody-based tests are used to help diagnose many different diseases, including AIDS, and to determine ABO and Rh blood groups. In tests for blood types, the antibodies to the blood group antigens cause the red blood cells in the sample to clump together, or agglutinate.

Chapter 40 Study Guide

Study Tip

Have students review the chapter by rereading all the boldface sentences. Suggest that pairs of students quiz each other on the Vocabulary terms.

Thinking Visually

1. Nonspecific defenses
2. Inflammatory response
3. Interferons
4. Cell-mediated immunity

Chapter 40 Assessment

Reviewing Content

1. a	5. a	9. b
2. c	6. d	10. c
3. b	7. a	
4. d	8. a	

Understanding Concepts

11. The germ theory of disease states that infectious diseases are caused by microorganisms or germs. (Viruses can also cause infectious diseases.)

12. Koch's postulates can be used to identify the pathogen that causes a specific infectious disease.

13. The five types of pathogens are viruses, bacteria, fungi, worms, and protists. Examples are given on page 1033.

14. Animals that carry pathogens from person to person

15. The spread of disease can be stopped by such habits as hand washing and covering the mouth when sneezing or coughing; by cooking food thoroughly; and by avoiding vectors.

16. Antibiotics interfere with the cellular processes of bacteria, thereby killing them.

17. A fever slows down or stops the growth of many pathogens; increases heart rate so that white blood cells get to the site of an infection faster; and speeds up the activity of white blood cells and the reactions that help repair damaged tissues.

18. Antibodies are proteins that help destroy pathogens. They are produced by plasma cells.

Chapter 40 Study Guide

40–1 Infectious Disease

Key Concepts  BI 10.d

- Some diseases are produced by pathogens. Others are caused by materials in the environment. Still others are inherited.
- Some infectious diseases are spread from one person to another through coughing, sneezing, or physical contact. Other infectious diseases are spread through contaminated water or food. Still others are spread by infected animals.

Vocabulary
disease, p. 1031 • pathogen, p. 1031
germ theory of disease, p. 1031
Koch's postulates, p. 1032
vector, p. 1034 • antibiotic, p. 1035

40–2 The Immune System

Key Concepts  BI 10.a, BI 10.b, BI 10.c, BI 10.f

- The function of the immune system is to fight infection through the activation of specific defenses.
- Your body's most important nonspecific defense is the skin.
- The inflammatory response is a nonspecific defense reaction to tissue damage caused by injury or infection.

Vocabulary
immunity, p. 1036
inflammatory response, p.1037 • fever, p. 1037
interferon, p. 1038 • immune response, p.1038
antigen, p. 1038 • humoral immunity, p. 1038
cell-mediated immunity, p. 1038
antibody, p. 1038 • vaccination, p. 1041
active immunity, p. 1042
passive immunity, p. 1042

40–3 Immune System Disorders

Key Concepts 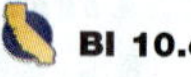 BI 10.e

- When the immune system makes a mistake and attacks the body's own cells, it produces an autoimmune disease.
- The only no-risk behavior with respect to HIV and AIDS is abstinence.

Vocabulary
allergy, p. 1043 • histamine, p. 1043
asthma, p. 1044

40–4 The Environment and Your Health

Key Concepts

- Environmental factors that can affect your health include air and water quality, poisonous wastes in landfills, and exposure to solar radiation.
- Healthful behaviors include eating a healthful diet, getting plenty of exercise and rest, abstaining from harmful activities, and having regular checkups.

Vocabulary
risk factor, p. 1049
tumor, p. 1052
carcinogen, p. 1052

Thinking Visually

Using the information in this chapter, complete the following concept map:

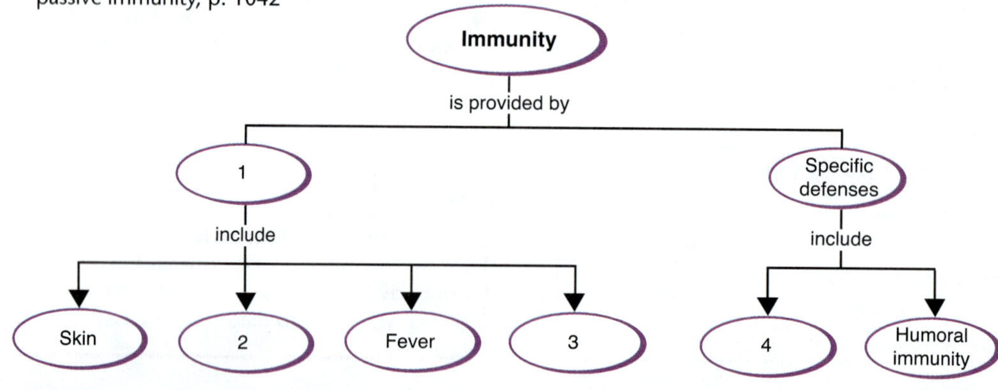

CHAPTER RESOURCES

Print:

- ***Teaching Resources,*** Chapter Vocabulary Review, Graphic Organizer, Chapter 40 Tests: Levels A and B
- ***Laboratory Assessment,*** Laboratory Assessment 10

Technology:

- ***Computer Test Bank,*** Chapter 40 Test
- ***iText,*** Chapter 40 Assessment

Chapter 40 Assessment

Reviewing Content

Choose the letter that best answers the question or completes the statement.

1. Any change, other than an injury, that disrupts the normal functions of a person's body is a
   a. disease. c. toxin.
   b. pathogen. d. vector.
2. Disease-causing agents such as viruses, bacteria, and fungi are known as
   a. antibodies. c. pathogens.
   b. antigens. d. toxins.
3. The germ theory of disease was established by
   a. Steere. c. Hooke.
   b. Koch. d. Salk.
4. The body's most important nonspecific defense against pathogens is
   a. tears. c. saliva.
   b. mucus. d. skin.
5. A nonspecific defense reaction to tissue damage caused by injury or infection is known as
   a. the inflammatory response.
   b. active immunity.
   c. cell-mediated immunity.
   d. passive immunity.
6. The swelling and pain associated with inflammation are caused by the
   a. secretion of antibodies.
   b. expansion of local blood vessels.
   c. secretion of antigens.
   d. destruction of bacteria by white blood cells.
7. A protein that helps other cells resist viral infection is
   a. interferon.
   b. penicillin.
   c. prednisone.
   d. histamine.
8. In the illustration below, label X is pointing to the

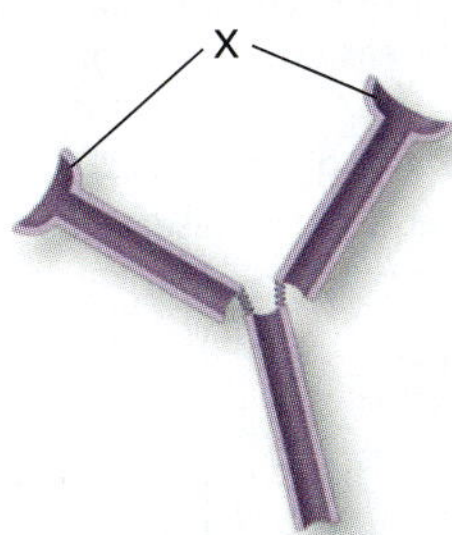

   a. antigen-binding sites. c. antibodies.
   b. antigens. d. interferons.

Interactive textbook with assessment at PHSchool.com 

9. A substance that triggers an immune response is a(an)
   a. antibody.
   b. antigen.
   c. B cell.
   d. pathogen.
10. Mast cells release chemicals known as
    a. antibodies.
    b. antigens.
    c. histamines.
    d. pathogens.

Understanding Concepts

11. What is the germ theory of disease?
12. What purpose do Koch's postulates serve?
13. List the five types of pathogens that are responsible for the spread of infectious disease. Give an example of a disease that each specific pathogen may cause.
14. What are vectors?
15. What are some ways by which the spread of disease can be stopped?
16. Describe how antibiotics work.
17. How might a fever be beneficial to a person who is sick?
18. What are antibodies? Describe how they are formed.
19. Describe the roles of helper T cells and killer T cells.
20. Distinguish between humoral immunity and cell-mediated immunity.
21. How did people acquire immunity to a disease before the development of vaccines?
22. Describe how passive immunity to a disease is obtained and why it lasts for only a short period of time.
23. Explain why allergies are not classified as autoimmune diseases.
24. Describe the specific action of HIV that makes the body unable to cope with other infections.
25. What is air quality?
26. What are three sources of radiation?

HOMEWORK GUIDE

Section:	Questions:
Section 40–1	1–3, 11–15, 27
Section 40–2	4–9, 16–22, 28, 30, 32, 33
Section 40–3	10, 23, 24, 31, 34, 35
Section 40–4	25, 26, 29, 36

Interactive Textbook

If your class subscribes to the iText, your students can go online to assess an interactive version of the Student Edition and a self-test.

(Continued from page 1056)

19. Helper T cells help activated B cells to develop into antibody-producing plasma cells and activate cytotoxic T cells, which attack infected cells.
20. In humoral immunity, B cells secrete antibodies that bind to antigens. In cell-mediated immunity, killer T cells rupture infected cells.
21. Before vaccines, people acquired immunity to a disease by contracting the disease and surviving.
22. Passive immunity is short-lived because the body destroys the borrowed antibodies.
23. In an autoimmune disease, the immune system attacks the body's own cells. The allergens that cause allergies are foreign materials.
24. HIV penetrates and destroys helper T cells, causing the body to lose much of its ability to efficiently fight infections that are normally prevented by the immune system.
25. Air quality is the number and concentrations of various gases present, as well as the nature and amount of tiny particles suspended in the air.
26. Accept any three of the following: sunlight, X-rays, nuclear radiation, radon.

Chapter 40 Assessment

Critical Thinking

27. Students should suggest that if the same pathogen causing a disease in the original host is not isolated from the second host, there is no way to verify that the same pathogen caused illness in both host organisms.

28. Responses should reflect an understanding of vaccines and immunity.

29. As of 1995, prostate cancer has the highest survival rate, slightly higher than the rate for breast cancer. Lung cancer has the worst survival rate. Survival rates have increased due to the development of better treatments.

30. A slight fever means that the body is probably fighting an infection. The slight fever may be beneficial if it makes the body temperature too high for pathogens to survive.

31. Once HIV enters the body, it attaches to receptors on the surface of helper T cells and invades the cells. HIV replicates within the T cells and eventually kills the cells.

32. Benefits would include developing permanent active immunity naturally. Risks would include developing a serious, possibly deadly, illness.

33. Both B cells and T cells are involved in specific immunity. B cells are lymphocytes that produce antibodies. Helper T cells help stimulate the development of activated B cells. T cells are also involved in cell-mediated immunity. Killer T cells attack and destroy infected cells.

34. When people who are sensitive to bee venom are stung, they produce antibodies that bind to mast cells. When venom from a second sting attaches to the antibodies, the mast cells release histamines and other chemicals, which produce a systemic reaction called anaphylactic shock.

35. It could increase the number of T cells because T cells are made in the bone marrow. The new T cells could be rejected.

36. Several environmental factors can cause mutations in DNA which can lead to cancer. These factors include sunlight, nuclear radiation, radon, and tobacco smoke.

Chapter 40 Assessment

Critical Thinking

27. Inferring Why is the fourth step of Koch's postulates necessary to prove that a disease is caused by a specific pathogen?

28. Making Judgments Edward Jenner developed his smallpox vaccine in 1796. Jenner tested his immunization theory on a young boy. Do you think Jenner was justified in using the child as an experimental test subject? Support your answer.

29. Interpreting Graphics The chart below shows the relative 5-year cancer survival rates in the United States. Which type of cancer has the highest survival rate? The lowest? Why do you think the 5-year survival rates increased over the years shown in the chart?

Relative 5-Year Cancer Survival Rates (in %)

Site	1974–76	1983–85	1992–97
All sites	50	52	62
Brain	22	27	32
Breast (female)	75	78	86
Colon	50	58	61
Lung and bronchus	12	14	15
Leukemia	34	41	45
Prostate	67	75	96

30. Inferring Many people become alarmed if they have a slight fever. Why might a slight fever be considered beneficial, assuming it lasts for just a few days?

31. Applying Concepts The blood of a person with HIV often shows decreasing numbers of helper T cells. How do you explain this decrease?

32. Problem Solving Suggest some risks and benefits associated with gaining immunity to a disease by intentionally exposing yourself to it.

33. Comparing and Contrasting Compare the roles of B cells and T cells in the immune response.

34. Applying Concepts Why is a second bee sting more dangerous than the first for a person who is allergic to bee stings?

35. Predicting Bone marrow transplants are a method of treatment being considered for some AIDS patients. How might a bone marrow transplant benefit some AIDS patients? What might be some problems with this treatment?

36. Applying Concepts Cancer results from errors in the genetic information that regulates cell division. Explain the connection between cancer and the environment.

Focus on the BIG Idea

Homeostasis Use what you learned about homeostasis in Section 1–3 to explain how the immune system works to maintain homeostasis in the human body. Give a specific example.

Writing in Science

The ability of bacteria to resist antibiotics has become an increasing public health problem. This problem is due to the overuse and misuse of antibiotics. Suppose that one of your friends always takes antibiotics when sick. Write a letter to your friend explaining the problem of antibiotic resistance.

Performance-Based Assessment

Oral Presentation Prepare a radio broadcast in which you explain how a specific infectious disease invades the body. Describe how the body's immune system responds to the infectious disease. Your broadcast must include the following:

- How the pathogen comes in contact with the body.
- A description of the first symptom of the disease and the first defense response of the body.
- A description of further symptoms and immune responses as the disease moves to different sites within the body.
- The final results of the disease conflict.
- Any long-term effects of the disease on the body.

For: An interactive self-test
Visit: PHSchool.com
Web Code: cba-0400

Focus on the BIG Idea

The immune system helps maintain homeostasis by protecting the body from disease-causing pathogens. Pathogens can disrupt homeostasis by releasing toxins or removing nutrients from the digestive system.

Writing in Science

Student letters will vary but should convey an understanding of antibiotic resistance. Overuse of antibiotics, as well as not following a prescription properly, can increase the problem of antibiotic resistance.

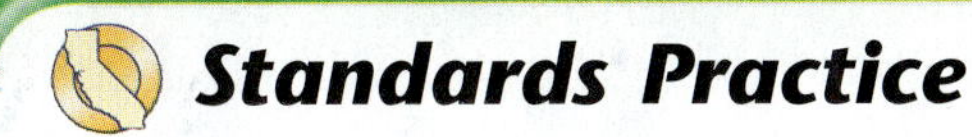

Standards Practice

Online at PHSchool.com

Test-Taking Tip When evaluating multiple-choice answers, be sure to read all of the answer choices, even if the first answer choice seems to be the correct one. By doing so, you can make sure that the answer you chose is the best one.

Directions: Choose the letter that best answers the question or completes the statement.

1. All of the following prevent pathogens from entering the human body EXCEPT
- **A** red blood cells.
- **B** tears.
- **C** mucus.
- **D** skin.

2. Which of the following is NOT a symptom of the inflammatory response?
- **A** White blood cells rush to infected tissues.
- **B** Blood vessels near the wound shrink.
- **C** Phagocytes engulf and destroy pathogens.
- **D** The wound becomes swollen.

3. What is one effect of a fever?
- **A** It speeds up the growth of pathogens.
- **B** It decreases the heart rate.
- **C** It decreases the rate of chemical reactions.
- **D** It increases the heart rate.

Questions 4–7 Each of the lettered choices below refers to the following numbered statements. Select the best lettered choice. A choice may be used once, more than once, or not at all.
- **A** Antibody
- **B** B cells
- **C** T cells
- **D** Phagocytes

4. White blood cells that produce antibodies

5. White blood cells that activate plasma cells

6. Proteins that bind to surface antigens **BI 10.b**

7. White blood cells that can engulf pathogens **BI 10.f**

Questions 8–10

A researcher measured the concentrations of HIV and T cells in 120 HIV-infected patients over a period of 10 years. Her data are summarized in the graph.

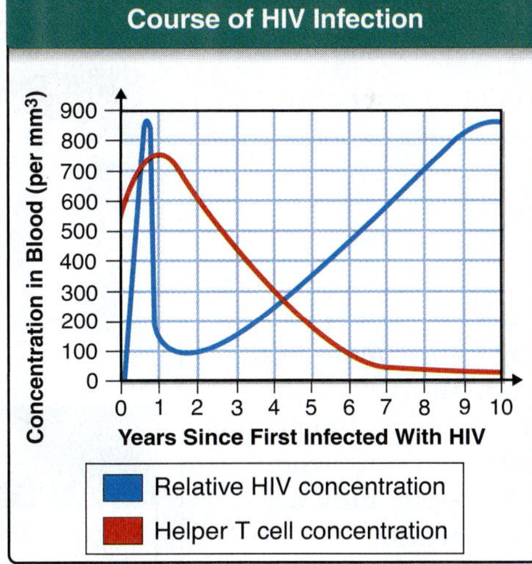

8. Why does the T cell concentration decrease after two years? **BI 10.e**
- **A** HIV dies off after two years.
- **B** HIV destroys T cells.
- **C** T cells produce toxins.
- **D** An inflammatory response occurs.

9. What happened to the HIV concentration over years 2 through 9? **BI 10.e**
- **A** It stayed about the same, and then suddenly increased.
- **B** It stayed about the same, and then suddenly decreased.
- **C** It steadily increased.
- **D** It steadily decreased.

10. What is probably responsible for the change in HIV concentration during the first year? **BI 10.e**
- **A** immune response
- **B** inflammatory response
- **C** passive immunity
- **D** HIV vaccination

Performance-Based Assessment

Students' presentations should reflect an understanding of pathogens and how the immune system responds to them.

Go Online PHSchool.com

Your students can independently test their knowledge of the chapter and print out their test results for your files.

Standards Practice

1. A	**5.** D	**9.** C
2. B	**6.** A	**10.** A
3. D	**7.** D	
4. C	**8.** B	

Online at PHSchool.com

Have students check their understanding of the chapter by logging onto Success Tracker.

Appendix A — SCIENCE SKILLS

Basic Process Skills

During a biology course, you often carry out short lab activities as well as lengthier experiments. Here are some skills that you will use.

Observing

In every science activity, you make a variety of observations. Observing is using one or more of the five senses to gather information. Many observations involve the senses of sight, hearing, touch, and smell. On rare occasions in a lab—but only when explicitly directed by your teacher—you may use the sense of taste to make an observation.

Sometimes you will use tools that increase the power of your senses or make observations more precise. For example, hand lenses and microscopes enable you to see things in greater detail. Rulers, balances, and thermometers help you measure key variables. Besides expanding the senses or making observations more accurate, tools may help eliminate personal opinions or preferences.

In science, it is customary to record your observations at the time they are made, usually by writing or drawing in a notebook. You may also make records by using computers, cameras, videotapes, and other tools. As a rule, scientists keep complete accounts of their observations, often using tables to organize their observations.

Inferring

In science, as in daily life, observations are usually followed by inferences. Inferring is interpreting an observation or statement based on prior knowledge. For example, suppose you're on a mountain hike and you see footprints like the ones illustrated in the next column. Based on their size and shape, you might infer that a large mammal had passed by. In making that inference, you would use your knowledge about the shape of animals' feet. Someone who knew much more about mammals might infer that a bear left the footprints. You can compare examples of observations and inferences in the table.

Notice that an inference is an act of reasoning, not a fact. An inference may be logical but not true. It is often necessary to gather further information before you can be confident that an inference is correct. For scientists, that information may come from further observations or from research done by others.

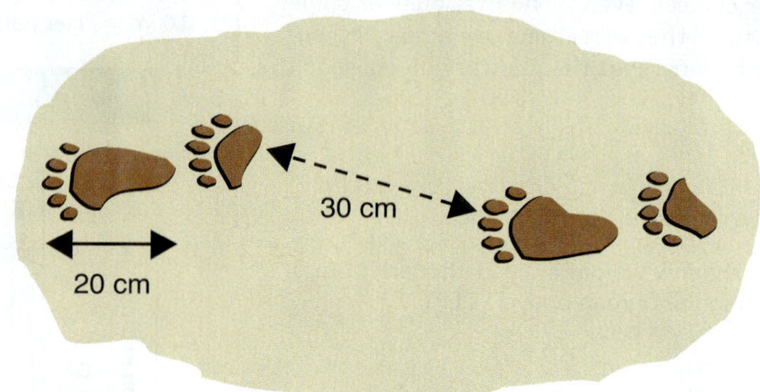

Comparing Observations and Inferences

Sample Observations	Sample Inferences
The footprints in the soil each have five toes.	An animal made the footprints.
The larger footprints are about 20 cm long.	A bear made the footprints.
The space between each pair of footprints is about 30 cm.	The animal was walking, not running.

As you study biology, you may make different types of inferences. For example, you may generalize about all cases based on information about some cases: *All the plant roots I've observed grow downward, so I infer that all roots grow downward.* You may determine that one factor or event was caused by another factor or event: *The bacteria died after I applied bleach, so I infer that bleach kills bacteria.* Predictions may be another type of inference.

Predicting

People often make predictions, but their statements about the future could be either guesses or inferences. In science, a prediction is an inference about a future event based on evidence, experience, or knowledge. For example, you can say, *On the first day next month, it will be sunny.* If your statement is based on evidence of weather patterns in the area, then the prediction is scientific. If the statement was made without considering any evidence, it's just a guess.

Predictions play a major role in science because they provide a way to test ideas. If scientists understand an event or the properties of a particular object, they should be able to make accurate predictions about that event or object. Some predictions can be tested simply by making observations. At other times, carefully designed experiments are needed. You'll read more about the relationship between predictions and experiments on the next two pages.

Classifying

If you have ever heard people debate whether a tomato is a fruit or a vegetable, you've heard an argument about classification. Classifying is the process of grouping items that are alike according to some organizing idea or system. Classifying occurs in every branch of science, but it is especially important in biology because living things are so numerous and diverse.

You may have the chance to practice classifying in different ways. Sometimes you will place objects into groups using an established system. At other times, you may create a system of your own by examining a variety of objects and identifying their properties.

Classification can have different purposes. Sometimes it's done just to keep things organized, for example, to make lab supplies easy to find. More likely, though, classification helps scientists understand living things better and discover relationships among them. For example, one way biologists determine how groups of vertebrates are related is to compare their bones. Biologists classify certain animal parts as bone or muscle and then investigate how they work together.

Using Models

Some cities refuse to approve any new buildings that could cast shadows on a popular park. As architects plan buildings in such locations, they use models that can show where a proposed building's shadow will fall at any time of day at any season of the year. A model is a mental or physical representation of an object, process, or event. In science, models are usually made to help people understand natural objects and processes.

Model of a Glucose Molecule

CH_2OH, C, O, H, OH, C, H, C, OH, HO, C, H, C, H, OH

Models can be varied. Mental models, such as mathematical equations, can represent some kinds of ideas or processes. For example, the equation for the surface area of a sphere can model the surface of Earth, enabling scientists to determine its size. Physical models can be made of a huge variety of materials; they can be two-dimensional (flat) or three-dimensional (having depth). In biology, a drawing of a molecule or a cell is a typical two-dimensional model. Common three-dimensional models include a representation of a DNA molecule and a plastic skeleton of an animal.

Physical models can also be made "to scale," which means they are in proportion to the actual object. Something very large, such as an area of land being studied, can be shown at 1/100 of its actual size. A tiny organism can be shown at 100 times its size.

Appendix A Science Skills

Conducting an Experiment

A science experiment is a procedure designed to test a prediction. Some types of experiments are fairly simple to design. Others may require ingenious problem solving.

Starting With Questions or Problems

A gardener collected seeds from a favorite plant at the end of the summer, stored them indoors for the winter, then planted them the following spring. None of the stored seeds developed into plants, yet uncollected seeds from the original plant germinated in the normal way. The gardener wondered: *Why didn't the collected seeds germinate?*

An experiment may have its beginning when someone asks a specific question or wants to solve a particular problem. Sometimes the original question leads directly to an experiment, but often researchers must restate the problem before they can design an appropriate experiment. The gardener's question about the seeds, for example, is too broad to be tested by an experiment, because there are so many possible answers. To narrow the topic, the gardener might think about related questions: *Were the seeds I collected different from the uncollected seeds? Did I try to germinate them in poor soil or with insufficient light or water? Did storing the seeds indoors ruin them in some way?*

Developing a Hypothesis

In science, a question about an object or event is answered by developing a possible explanation called a **hypothesis.** The hypothesis may be developed after long thought and research, or it may come to a scientist "in a flash." How a hypothesis is formed doesn't matter; it can be useful as long as it leads to predictions that can be tested.

The gardener decided to focus on the fact that the nongerminating seeds were stored in the warm conditions of a heated house. That led the person to propose this hypothesis: *Seeds require a period of low temperatures in order to germinate.* The next step is to make a prediction based on the hypothesis, for example: *If seeds are stored indoors in cold conditions, they will germinate in the same way as seeds left outdoors during the winter.* Notice that the prediction suggests the basic idea for an experiment.

Designing an Experiment

A carefully designed experiment can test a prediction in a reliable way, ruling out other possible explanations. As scientists plan their experimental procedures, they pay particular attention to the factors that must be controlled.

The gardener decided to study three groups of seeds: (1) some that would be left outdoors throughout the winter, (2) some that would be brought indoors and kept at room temperature, and (3) some that would be brought indoors and kept cold.

Controlling Variables

As researchers design an experiment, they identify the **variables,** factors that can change. Some common variables include mass, volume, time, temperature, light, and the presence or absence of specific materials. An experiment involves three categories of variables. The factor that scientists purposely change is called the **manipulated variable.** A manipulated variable is also known as an **independent variable.** The factor that may change because of the manipulated variable and that scientists want to observe is called the **responding variable.** A responding variable is also known as a **dependent variable.** Factors that scientists purposely keep the same are called **controlled variables.** Controlling variables enables researchers to conclude that the changes in the responding variable are due exclusively to changes in the manipulated variable.

What Is a Control Group?

When you read about certain experiments, you may come across references to a control group (or "a control") and the experimental groups. All the groups in an experiment are treated exactly the same except for the manipulated variable. In the experimental group, the manipulated variable is being changed. The control group is used as a standard of comparison. It may consist of objects that are not changed in any way or objects that are being treated in the usual way. For example, in the gardener's experiment, the seeds left outdoors would be the control group, because they reveal what happens under natural conditions.

For the gardener, the manipulated variable is whether the seeds were exposed to cold conditions. The responding variable is whether or not the seeds germinate. Among the variables that must be controlled are whether the seeds remain dry during storage, when the seeds are planted, the amount of water the seeds receive, and the type of soil used.

Forming Operational Definitions

In an experiment, it is often necessary to define one or more variables explicitly so that any researcher could measure or control the variable in exactly the same way. An **operational definition** describes how a particular variable is to be measured or how a term is to be defined. ("Operational" means "describing what to do.")

The gardener, for example, had to decide exactly what the indoor "cold" conditions of the experiment would involve. Since winter temperatures often fell below freezing, the gardener decided that "cold" would mean keeping the seeds in a freezer.

Interpreting Data

The observations and measurements that are made in an experiment are called **data.** Scientists usually record data in an orderly way. When an experiment is finished, the researcher analyzes the data for trends or patterns, often by doing calculations or making graphs, to determine whether the results support the hypothesis.

For example, after planting the seeds in the spring, the gardener counted the seeds that germinated and found these results: None of the seeds kept at room temperature germinated, 80 percent of the seeds kept in the freezer germinated, and 85 percent of the seeds left outdoors during the winter germinated. The trend was clear: The gardener's prediction appeared to be correct.

To be sure that the results of an experiment are correct, scientists review their data critically, looking for possible sources of error. Here, "error" refers to differences between the observed results and the true values. Experimental error can result from human mistakes or problems with equipment. It can also occur when the small group of objects studied does not accurately represent the whole group. For example, if some of the gardener's seeds had been exposed to a herbicide, the data might not reflect the true seed germination pattern.

Drawing Conclusions

If researchers are confident that their data are reliable, they make a final statement summarizing their results. That statement—called the conclusion of the experiment—indicates whether the data support or refute the hypothesis. The gardener's conclusion was: *Some seeds must undergo a period of freezing in order to germinate.* A conclusion is considered valid if it is a logical interpretation of reliable data.

Following Up an Experiment

When an experiment has been completed, one or more events often follow. Researchers may repeat the experiment to verify the results. They may publish the experiment so that others can evaluate and replicate their procedures. They may compare their conclusion with the discoveries made by other scientists. And they may raise new questions that lead to new experiments. For example, *Are the spores of fungi affected by temperature as these seeds were?*

Researching other discoveries about seeds would show that some other types of plants in temperate zones require periods of freezing before they germinate. Biologists infer that this pattern makes it less likely the seeds will germinate before winter, thus increasing the chances that the young plants will survive.

Organizing Information

When you study or want to communicate facts and ideas, you may find it helpful to organize information visually. Here are some common graphic organizers you can use. Notice that each type of organizer is useful for specific types of information.

Concept Maps

Concept maps can help you organize a broad topic having many subtopics. A concept map begins with a main idea and shows how it can be broken down into specific topics. It makes the ideas easier to understand by presenting their relationships visually.

You construct a concept map by placing the concept words (usually nouns) in ovals and connecting the ovals with linking words. The most general concept usually is placed at the top of the map or in the center. The content of the other ovals becomes more specific as you move away from the main concept. The linking words, which describe the relationship between the linked concepts, are written on a line between two ovals. If you follow any string of concepts and linking words down through a map, they should sound approximately like a sentence.

Some concept maps may also include linking words that connect a concept in one branch to another branch. Such connections, called cross-linkages, show more complex interrelationships.

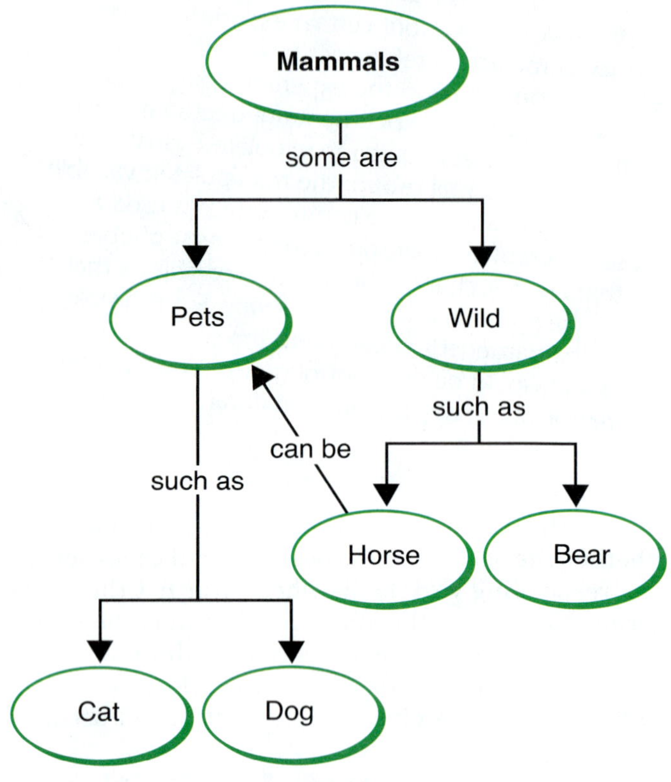

Compare-and-Contrast Tables

Compare-and-contrast tables are useful for showing the similarities and differences between two or more objects or processes. The table provides an organized framework for making comparisons based on specific characteristics.

To create a compare-and-contrast table, list the items to be compared across the top of the table. List the characteristics that will form the basis of your comparison in the column on the left. Complete the table by filling in information for each item.

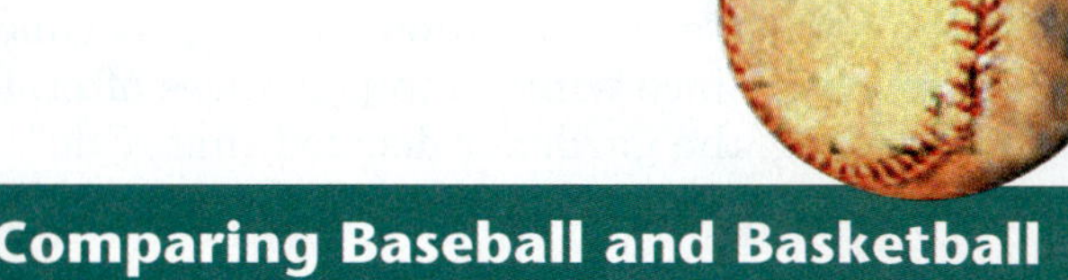

Comparing Baseball and Basketball

Characteristic	Baseball	Basketball
Number of Players	9	5
Playing Field	Baseball diamond	Basketball court
Equipment	Bat, baseball, mitts	Basket, basketball

Venn Diagrams

Another way to show similarities and differences between items is with a Venn diagram. A Venn diagram consists of two or more circles or ovals that partially overlap. Each circle or oval represents a particular object or idea. Characteristics that the objects share are written in the area of overlap. Differences or unique characteristics are written in the areas that do not overlap.

To create a Venn diagram, draw two overlapping circles or ovals. Label them with the names of the objects or the ideas they represent. Write the unique characteristics in the part of each circle or oval that does not overlap. Write the shared characteristics within the area of overlap.

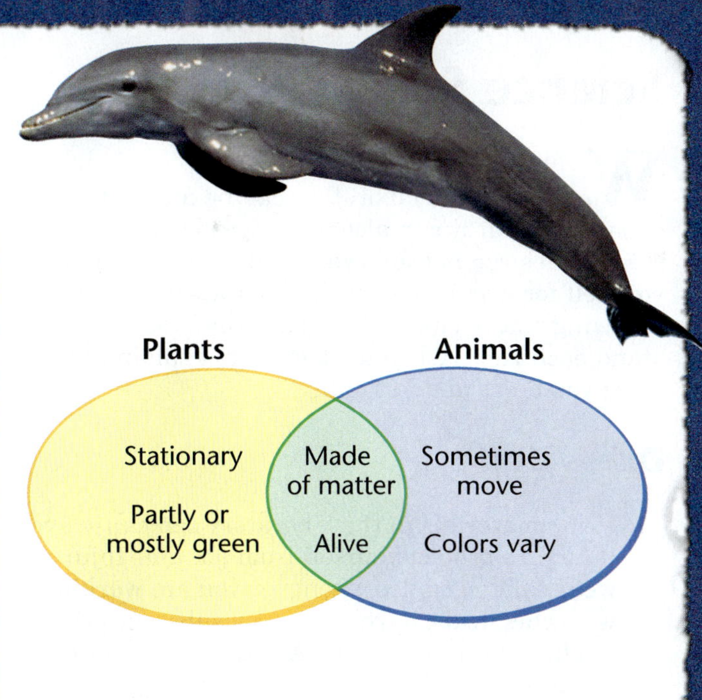

Flowcharts

A flowchart can help you represent the order in which a set of events has occurred or should occur. Flowcharts are useful for outlining the steps in a procedure or stages in a process with a definite beginning and end.

To make a flowchart, list the steps in the process you want to represent and count the steps. Then, create the appropriate number of boxes, starting at the top of a page or on the left. Write a brief description of the first event in the first box, then fill in the other steps, box by box. Link each box to the next event in the process with an arrow. Then, add a title to the flowchart.

Preparing Pasta

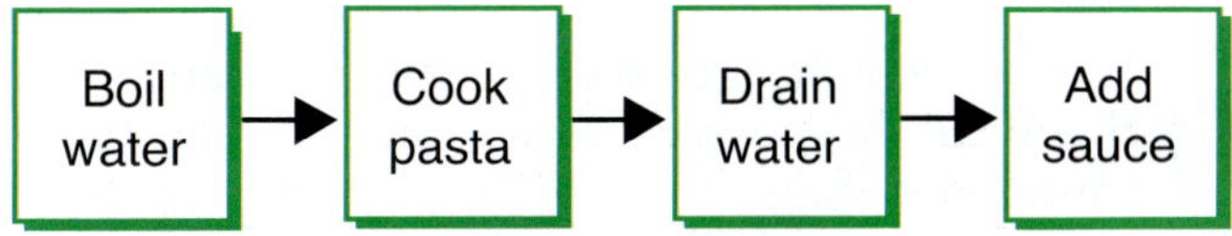

Cycle Diagrams

A cycle diagram shows a sequence of events that is continuous, or cyclical. A continuous sequence does not have a beginning or an end; instead, each event in the process leads to another event. The diagram shows the order of the events.

To create a cycle diagram, list the events in the process and count them. Draw one box for each event, placing the boxes around an imaginary circle. Write one of the events in a box, and then draw an arrow to the next box, moving clockwise. Continue to fill in the boxes and link them with arrows until the descriptions form a continuous circle. Then, add a title.

The Moon as Seen From Earth

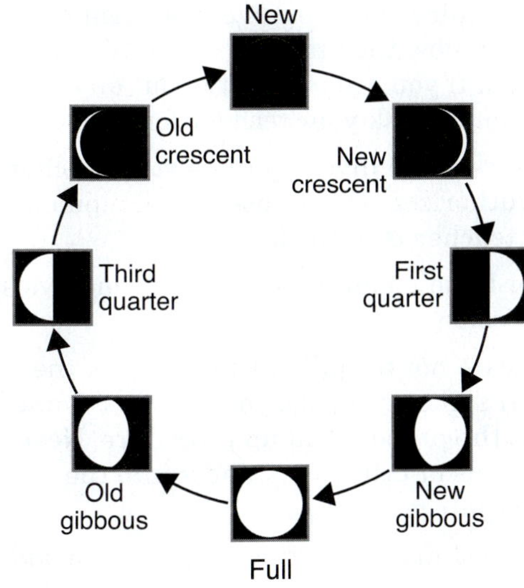

Science Safety Rules

Working in the laboratory can be an exciting experience, but it can also be dangerous if proper safety rules are not followed at all times. To prepare yourself for a safe year in the laboratory, read the following safety rules. Make sure that you understand each rule. Ask your teacher to explain any rules you don't understand.

Dress Code

1. Many materials in the laboratory can cause eye injury. To protect yourself from possible injury, wear safety goggles whenever you are working with chemicals, burners, or any substance that might get into your eyes. Avoid wearing contact lenses in the laboratory. Tell your teacher if you need to wear contact lenses to see clearly, and ask if there are any safety precautions you should observe.
2. Wear a laboratory apron or coat whenever you are working with chemicals or heated substances.
3. Tie back long hair to keep it away from any chemicals, burners, candles, or other laboratory equipment.
4. Before working in the laboratory, remove or tie back any article of clothing or jewelry that can hang down and touch chemicals and flames.

General Safety Rules and First Aid

5. Read all directions for an experiment several times. Follow the directions exactly as they are written. If you are in doubt about any part of the experiment, ask your teacher for assistance.
6. Never perform investigations your teacher has not authorized. Do not use any equipment unless your teacher is in the lab.
7. Never handle equipment unless you have specific permission.
8. Take care not to spill any material in the laboratory. If spills occur, ask your teacher immediately about the proper cleanup procedure. Never pour chemicals or other substances into the sink or trash container.
9. Never eat, drink, or bring food into the laboratory.
10. Immediately report all accidents, no matter how minor, to your teacher.
11. Learn what to do in case of specific accidents, such as getting acid in your eyes or on your skin. (Rinse acids off your body with lots of water.)
12. Be aware of the location of the first-aid kit. Your teacher should administer any required first aid due to injury. Your teacher may send you to the school nurse or call a physician.
13. Know where and how to report an accident or fire. Find out the location of the fire extinguisher, fire alarm, and phone. Report any fires to your teacher at once.

Heating and Fire Safety

14. Never use a heat source such as a candle or burner without wearing safety goggles.
15. Never heat a chemical you are not instructed to heat. A chemical that is harmless when cool can be dangerous when heated.
16. Maintain a clean work area and keep all materials away from flames. Be sure that there are no open containers of flammable liquids in the laboratory when flames are being used.
17. Never reach across a flame.
18. Make sure you know how to light a Bunsen burner. (Your teacher will demonstrate the proper procedure for lighting a burner.) If the flame leaps out of a burner toward you, turn the gas off immediately. Do not touch the burner. It may be hot. Never leave a lighted burner unattended!
19. When you are heating a test tube or bottle, point the opening away from yourself and others. Chemicals can splash or boil out of a heated test tube.
20. Never heat a closed container. The expanding hot air, vapors, or other gases inside may blow the container apart, causing it to injure you or others.
21. Never pick up a container that has been heated without first holding the back of your hand near it. If you can feel the heat on the back of your hand, the container may be too hot to handle. Use a clamp or tongs when handling hot containers or wear heat-resistant gloves if appropriate.

Using Chemicals Safely

22. Never mix chemicals for "the fun of it." You might produce a dangerous, possibly explosive substance.

23. Many chemicals are poisonous. Never touch, taste, or smell a chemical that you do not know for certain is harmless. If you are instructed to smell fumes in an experiment, gently wave your hand over the opening of the container and direct the fumes toward your nose. Do not inhale the fumes directly from the container.

24. Use only those chemicals needed in the investigation. Keep all container lids closed when a chemical is not being used. Notify your teacher whenever chemicals are spilled.

25. Dispose of all chemicals as instructed by your teacher. To avoid contamination, never return chemicals to their original containers.

26. Be extra careful when working with acids or bases. Pour such chemicals from one container to another over the sink, not over your work area.

27. When diluting an acid, pour the acid into water. Never pour water into the acid.

28. If any acids or bases get on your skin or clothing, rinse them with water. Immediately notify your teacher of any acid or base spill.

Using Glassware Safely

29. Never heat glassware that is not thoroughly dry. Use a wire screen to protect glassware from any flame.

30. Keep in mind that hot glassware will not appear hot. Never pick up glassware without first checking to see if it is hot.

31. Never use broken or chipped glassware. If glassware breaks, notify your teacher and dispose of the glassware in the proper trash container.

32. Never eat or drink from laboratory glassware. Thoroughly clean glassware before putting it away.

Using Sharp Instruments

33. Handle scalpels or razor blades with extreme care. Never cut material toward you; cut away from you.

34. Notify your teacher immediately if you cut yourself when in the laboratory.

Working With Live Organisms

35. No experiments that will cause pain, discomfort, or harm to animals should be done in the classroom or at home.

36. Your teacher will instruct you how to handle each species that is brought into the classroom. Animals should be handled only if necessary. Special handling is required if an animal is excited or frightened, pregnant, feeding, or with its young.

37. Clean your hands thoroughly after handling any organisms or materials, including animals or cages containing animals.

End-of-Experiment Rules

38. When an experiment is completed, clean up your work area and return all equipment to its proper place.

39. Wash your hands before and after every experiment.

40. Turn off all burners before leaving the laboratory. Check that the gas line leading to the burner is off as well.

Appendix  SCIENCE SAFETY

Safety Symbols

These symbols appear in laboratory activities to alert you to possible dangers and to remind you to work carefully.

Safety Goggles Always wear safety goggles to protect your eyes during any activity involving chemicals, flames or heating, or the possibility of flying objects, particles, or substances.

Lab Apron Wear a laboratory apron to protect your skin and clothing from injury.

Breakage Handle breakable materials such as thermometers and glassware with care. Do not touch broken glass.

Heat-Resistant Gloves Use an oven mitt or other hand protection when handling hot materials. Heating plates, hot water, and glassware can cause burns. Never touch hot objects with your bare hands.

Plastic Gloves Wear disposable plastic gloves to protect yourself from contact with chemicals or organisms that could be harmful. Keep your hands away from your face, and dispose of the gloves according to your teacher's instructions at the end of the activity.

Heating Use a clamp or tongs to hold hot objects. Do not touch hot objects with your bare hands.

Sharp Object Scissors, scalpels, pins, and knives are sharp. They can cut or puncture your skin. Always direct sharp edges and points away from yourself and others. Use sharp instruments only as directed.

Electric Shock Avoid the possibility of electric shock. Never use electrical equipment around water or when the equipment or your hands are wet. Be sure cords are untangled and cannot trip anyone. Disconnect equipment when it is not in use.

Corrosive Chemical This symbol indicates the presence of an acid or other corrosive chemical. Avoid getting the chemical on your skin or clothing, or in your eyes. Do not inhale the vapors. Wash your hands when you are finished with the activity.

Poison Do not let any poisonous chemical get on your skin, and do not inhale its vapor. Wash your hands when you are finished with the activity.

Physical Safety This activity involves physical movement. Use caution to avoid injuring yourself or others. Follow instructions from your teacher. Alert your teacher if there is any reason that you should not participate in the activity.

Animal Safety Treat live animals with care to avoid injuring the animals or yourself. Working with animal parts or preserved animals may also require caution. Wash your hands when you are finished with the activity.

Plant Safety Handle plants only as your teacher directs. If you are allergic to any plants used in an activity, tell your teacher before the activity begins. Avoid touching poisonous plants and plants with thorns.

Flames Tie back loose hair and clothing, and put on safety goggles before working with fire. Follow instructions from your teacher about lighting and extinguishing flames.

No Flames Flammable materials may be present. Make sure there are no flames, sparks, or exposed sources of heat present.

Fumes Poisonous or unpleasant vapors may be produced. Work in a ventilated area or, if available, in a fume hood. Avoid inhaling a vapor directly. Test an odor only when directed to do so by your teacher, using a wafting motion to direct the vapor toward your nose.

Disposal Chemicals and other materials used in the activity must be disposed of safely. Follow the instructions from your teacher.

Hand Washing Wash your hands thoroughly when finished with the activity. Use antibacterial soap and warm water. Lather both sides of your hands and between your fingers. Rinse well.

General Safety Awareness You may see this symbol when none of the symbols described earlier applies. In this case, follow the specific instructions provided. You may also see this symbol when you are asked to design your own experiment. Do not start your experiment until your teacher has approved your plan.

The Metric System

The metric system of measurement is used by scientists throughout the world. It is based on units of 10. Each unit is 10 times larger or 10 times smaller than the next unit. The most commonly used units of the metric system are given below. After you have finished reading about the metric system, try to put it to use. How tall are you in meters? What is your mass? What is your normal body temperature in degrees Celsius?

Commonly Used Metric Units

Length The distance from one point to another

meter (m)	A meter is slightly longer than a yard.
	1 meter = 1000 millimeters (mm)
	1 meter = 100 centimeters (cm)
	1000 meters = 1 kilometer (km)

Volume The amount of space an object takes up

liter (L)	A liter is slightly more than a quart.
	1 liter = 1000 milliliters (mL)

Mass The amount of matter in an object

gram (g)	A paper clip has a mass equal to about one gram.
	1000 grams = 1 kilogram (kg)

Temperature The measure of hotness or coldness

degrees Celsius (°C)	0°C = freezing point of water
	100°C = boiling point of water

Metric–English Equivalents

2.54 centimeters (cm) = 1 inch (in.)
1 meter (m) = 39.37 inches (in.)
1 kilometer (km) = 0.62 miles (mi)
1 liter (L) = 1.06 quarts (qt)
236 milliliters (mL) = 1 cup (c)
1 kilogram (kg) = 2.2 pounds (lb)
28.3 grams (g) = 1 ounce (oz)
°C = 5/9 × (°F–32)

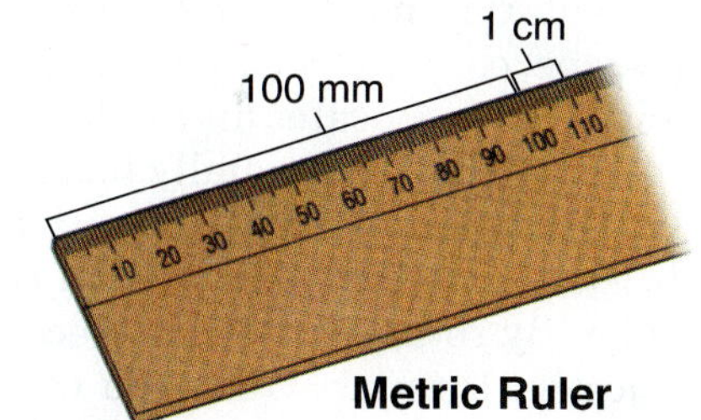

Metric Ruler

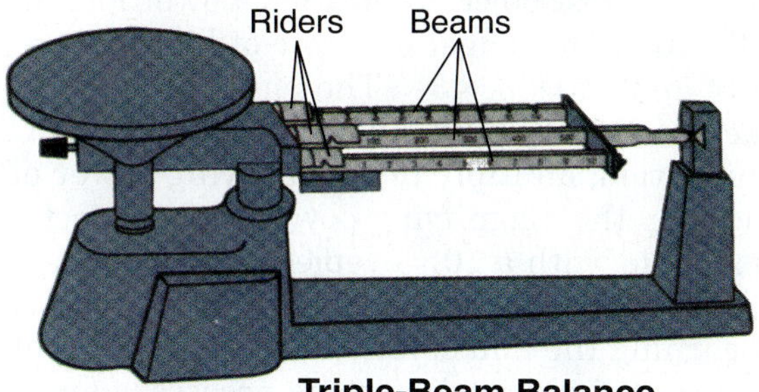

Triple-Beam Balance

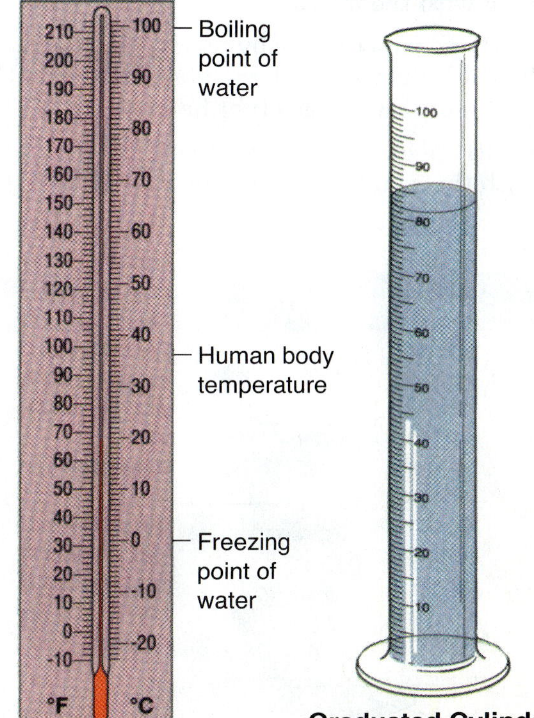

Thermometer

Graduated Cylinder

Appendix D USE OF THE MICROSCOPE

The Compound Microscope

The microscope used in most biology classes, the compound microscope, contains a combination of lenses. The eyepiece lens is located in the top portion of the microscope. This lens usually has a magnification of 10×. Other lenses, called objective lenses, are at the bottom of the body tube on the revolving nosepiece. By rotating the nosepiece, you can select the objective through which you will view your specimen.

The shortest objective is a low-power magnifier, usually 10×. The longer ones are of high power, usually up to 40× or 43×. The magnification is marked on the objective. To determine the total magnification, multiply the magnifying power of the eyepiece by the magnifying power of the objective. For example, with a 10× eyepiece and a 40× objective, the total magnification is 10 × 40 = 400×.

Learning the name, function, and location of each of the microscope's parts is necessary for proper use. Use the following procedures when working with the microscope.

1. Carry the microscope by placing one hand beneath the base and grasping the arm of the microscope with the other hand.
2. Gently place the microscope on the lab table with the arm facing you. The microscope's base should be resting evenly on the table, approximately 10 cm from the table's edge.
3. Raise the body tube by turning the coarse adjustment knob until the objective lens is about 2 cm above the opening of the stage.
4. Rotate the nosepiece so that the low-power objective (10×) is directly in line with the body tube. A click indicates that the lens is in line with the opening of the stage.
5. Look through the eyepiece and switch on the lamp or adjust the mirror so that a circle of light can be seen. This is the field of view. Moving the lever of the diaphragm permits a greater or smaller amount of light to come through the opening of the stage.
6. Place a prepared slide on the stage so that the specimen is over the center of the opening. Use the stage clips to hold the slide in place.
7. Look at the microscope from the side. Carefully turn the coarse adjustment knob to lower the body tube until the low-power objective almost touches the slide or until the body tube can no longer be moved. Do not allow the objective to touch the slide.

PARTS OF THE MICROSCOPE AND THEIR FUNCTION

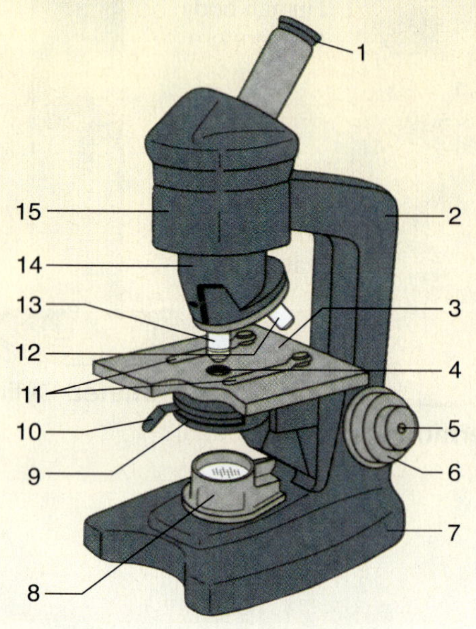

1. **Eyepiece** Contains a magnifying lens
2. **Arm** Supports the body tube
3. **Stage** Supports the slide being observed
4. **Opening of the stage** Permits light to pass up to the eyepiece
5. **Fine adjustment knob** Moves the body tube slightly to sharpen the image
6. **Coarse adjustment knob** Moves the body tube to focus the image
7. **Base** Supports the microscope
8. **Illuminator** Produces light or reflects light up toward the eyepiece
9. **Diaphragm** Regulates the amount of light passing up toward the eyepiece
10. **Diaphragm lever** Opens and closes the diaphragm
11. **Stage clips** Hold the slide in place
12. **Low-power objective** Provides a magnification of 10× and is the shortest objective
13. **High-power objective** Provides a magnification of 40× and is the longest objective
14. **Nosepiece** Holds the objectives and can be rotated to change the magnification
15. **Body tube** Maintains the proper distance between the eyepiece and the objectives

8. Look through the eyepiece and observe the specimen. If the field of view is out of focus, use the coarse adjustment knob to raise the body tube while looking through the eyepiece. **CAUTION:** *To prevent damage to the slide and the objective, do not lower the body tube using the coarse adjustment while looking through the eyepiece.* Focus the image as best you can with the coarse adjustment knob. Then, use the fine adjustment knob to focus the image more sharply. Keep both eyes open when viewing a specimen. This helps prevent eyestrain.
9. Adjust the lever of the diaphragm to allow the right amount of light to enter.
10. To change the magnification, rotate the nosepiece until the desired objective is in line with the body tube and clicks into place.
11. Look through the eyepiece and use the fine adjustment knob to bring the image into focus.
12. After every use, remove the slide. Return the low-power objective into place in line with the body tube. Clean the stage of the microscope and the lenses with lens paper. Do not use other types of paper to clean the lenses; they may scratch the lenses.

Preparing a Wet-Mount Slide

1. Obtain a clean microscope slide and a coverslip. A coverslip is very thin, permitting the objective lens to be lowered very close to the specimen.
2. Place the specimen in the middle of the microscope slide. The specimen must be thin enough for light to pass through it.

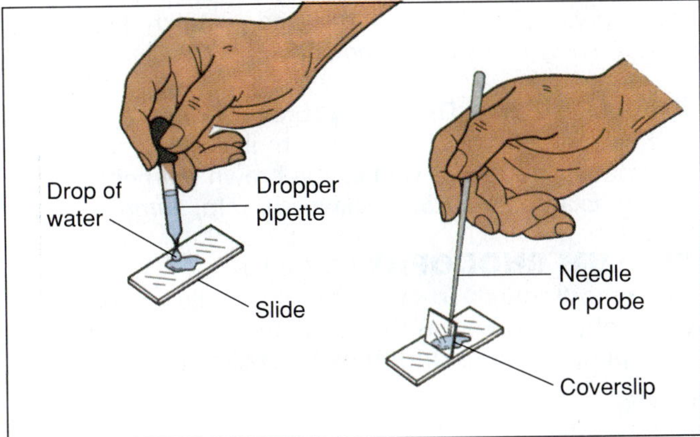

3. Using a dropper pipette, place a drop of water on the specimen.
4. Lower one edge of the coverslip so that it touches the side of the drop of water at about a 45° angle. The water will spread evenly along the edge of the coverslip. Using a dissecting needle or probe, slowly lower the coverslip over the specimen and water as shown in the drawing. Try not to trap any air bubbles under the coverslip. If air bubbles are present, gently tap the surface of the coverslip over the air bubble with a pencil eraser.
5. Remove any excess water at the edge of the coverslip with a paper towel. If the specimen begins to dry out, add a drop of water at the edge of the coverslip.

Staining Techniques

1. Obtain a clean microscope slide and coverslip.
2. Place the specimen in the middle of the microscope slide.
3. Using a dropper pipette, place a drop of water on the specimen. Place the coverslip so that its edge touches the drop of water at a 45° angle. After the water spreads along the edge of the coverslip, use a dissecting needle or probe to lower the coverslip over the specimen.

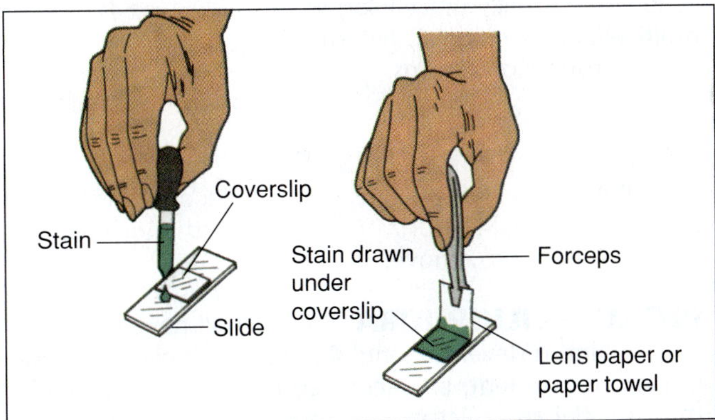

4. Add a drop of stain at the edge of the coverslip. Using forceps, touch a small piece of lens paper or paper towel to the opposite edge of the coverslip, as shown in the drawing. The paper causes the stain to be drawn under the coverslip and to stain the cells in the specimen.

Appendix E Classification

DOMAIN ARCHAEA
Kingdom Archaebacteria

Unicellular prokaryotic organisms that lack peptidoglycan cell walls and have distinctive ribosomal RNA sequences.

The Archaebacteria include methanogens (organisms that produce methane gas, such as *Methanobacterium*), salt-loving bacteria (*Halococcus*), and thermoacidophilic bacteria (*Thermoplasma*), which grow in extremely high temperatures.

DOMAIN BACTERIA
Kingdom Eubacteria

Unicellular prokaryotic organisms; most have peptidoglycan cell walls. Sometimes form colonies of clumps or filaments.

The Eubacteria include the blue-green bacteria (cyanobacteria such as *Anabaena*), chemoautotrophs (*Nitrobacter*), spirochetes (*Treponema*), prochlorobacteria (*Prochloron*), spore-forming bacteria (*Bacillus*), and obligate internal parasites, such as the rickettsiae (*Rickettsia*).

DOMAIN EUKARYA
Kingdom Protista

Eukaryotic; usually unicellular; some multicellular or colonial; heterotrophic or autotrophic organisms.

ANIMAL-LIKE PROTISTS

Unicellular; heterotrophic; usually motile; also known as protozoa. Animal-like protists are classified into phyla based on how they move.

PHYLUM CILIOPHORA (ciliates) All have cilia at some point in development; almost all use cilia for feeding and movement; characterized by two types of nuclei: macronuclei and micronuclei; most have a sexual process known as conjugation. Examples: *Paramecium, Didinium, Stentor.*

PHYLUM ZOOMASTIGINA (zooflagellates) Possess one or more flagella that are used for movement; most reproduce asexually by mitosis. Examples: *Trichomonas, Trichonympha.*

PHYLUM SPOROZOA Nonmotile parasites; produce small infective cells called sporozoites; life cycles usually complex, involving more than one host species; cause a number of diseases, including malaria. Example: *Plasmodium.*

PHYLUM SARCODINA Sarcodines use pseudopods for feeding and movement; some produce elaborate shells that contain silica or calcium carbonate; most free-living; a few parasitic; some involved in formation of sedimentary rock. Examples: *Amoeba*, foraminiferans.

PLANTLIKE PROTISTS

Photosynthetic autotrophs that have characteristics similar to those of plants. Some are unicellular; others are multicellular.

PHYLUM EUGLENOPHYTA (euglenophytes) Primarily photosynthetic; unicellular; most live in fresh water; possess two unequal flagella; lack cell walls. Example: *Euglena.*

PHYLUM PYRROPHYTA (dinoflagellates) Two flagella; about half live in salt water, are photosynthetic, and have rigid cell walls that contain cellulose; other half are heterotrophs; some are luminescent; unicellular; many are symbiotic. Examples: *Gonyaulux, Noctilucans scintillans.*

PHYLUM CHRYSOPHYTA (chrysophytes) Mostly photosynthetic; aquatic; mostly unicellular; contain bright yellow pigments. Example: *Thallasiosira.*

PHYLUM BACILLARIOPHYTA (diatoms) Photosynthetic; live in fresh and salt water; have unique glasslike cell walls; among the most abundant organisms on Earth. Example: *Navicula.*

PHYLUM CHLOROPHYTA (green algae) Live in fresh water and salt water; unicellular or multicellular; chlorophylls and accessory pigments similar to those in vascular plants; food stored as starch. Examples: *Ulva, Chlamydomonas, Spirogyra.*

PHYLUM PHAEOPHYTA (brown algae) Live almost entirely in salt water; multicellular; contain chlorophyll *a* and *c* as well as the brown pigment fucoxanthin. Examples: *Fucus* (rockweed), kelp, *Sargassum.*

PHYLUM RHODOPHYTA (red algae) Live almost entirely in salt water; multicellular; contain chlorophyll *a* as well as the red pigment phycobilin. Examples: *Chondrus* (Irish moss), coralline algae.

FUNGUSLIKE PROTISTS

Heterotrophs that have some characteristics similar to those of fungi, though they have centrioles and lack cell walls of chitin.

PHYLUM ACRASIOMYCOTA (cellular slime molds) Spores develop into independent free-living amoeba-like cells that may come together to form a multicellular structure; this structure forms a fruiting body that produces spores. Example: *Dictyostelium*.

PHYLUM MYXOMYCOTA (acellular slime molds) Spores develop into haploid cells that can switch between flagellated and amoeba-like forms; these haploid cells fuse to form a zygote that grows into a plasmodium, which ultimately forms spore-producing fruiting bodies. Example: *Physarum*.

PHYLUM OOMYCOTA (water molds) Unicellular or multicellular; mostly aquatic; cell walls contain cellulose. Example: *Phytophthora infestans*.

Kingdom Fungi

Eukaryotic; heterotrophic; unicellular or multicellular; cell walls typically contain chitin; mostly decomposers; some parasites; some commensal or mutualistic symbionts; asexual reproduction by spore formation, budding, or fragmentation; sexual reproduction involving mating types; classified according to structure and method of reproduction.

PHYLUM ZYGOMYCOTA (common molds) Cell walls of chitin; hyphae generally lack cross walls; sexual reproduction by conjugation produces diploid zygospores; asexual reproduction produces haploid spores; most parasites; some decomposers. Example: *Rhizopus stolonifer* (black bread mold).

PHYLUM ASCOMYCOTA (sac fungi) Cell walls of chitin; hyphae have perforated cross walls; most multicellular; yeasts unicellular; sexual reproduction produces ascospores; asexual reproduction by spore formation or budding; some cause plant diseases such as chestnut blight and Dutch elm disease. Examples: *Neurospora* (red bread mold), baker's yeast, morels, truffles.

PHYLUM BASIDIOMYCOTA (club fungi) Cell walls of chitin; hyphae have cross walls; sexual reproduction involves basidiospores, which are borne on club-shaped basidia; asexual reproduction by spore formation. Examples: mushrooms, puffballs, shelf fungi, rusts.

PHYLUM DEUTEROMYCOTA (imperfect fungi) Cell walls of chitin; sexual phase of life cycle never observed; members resemble ascomycetes, basidiomycetes, or zygomycetes. Example: *Penicillium*.

Kingdom Plantae

Eukaryotic; multicellular and nonmotile; photosynthetic autotrophs; possess chlorophylls *a* and *b* and other pigments in organelles called chloroplasts; cell walls contain cellulose; food stored as starch; reproduce sexually; alternate haploid (gametophyte) and diploid (sporophyte) generations.

PHYLUM BRYOPHYTA (mosses) Generally small; multicellular plants; live on land in moist habitats; lack vascular tissue; lack true roots, leaves, and stems; gametophyte dominant; water required for reproduction.

PHYLUM HEPATICOPHYTA (liverworts) Generally small, flat, lobe-shaped; multicellular plants; live on land in moist habitats; lack vascular tissue and true roots, leaves, and stems; gametophyte dominant; water required for reproduction.

PHYLUM ANTHCEROPHYTA (hornworts) Generally small; multicellular plants; live on land in moist habitats; lack vascular tissue and true roots, leaves, and stems; gametophyte dominant; named for horn-shaped sporophyte; water required for reproduction.

PHYLUM LYCOPHYTA (club mosses) Primitive vascular plants; usually small; sporophyte dominant; possess roots, stems, and leaves; water required for reproduction. Examples: club moss, quillwort.

PHYLUM ARTHROPHYTA (horsetails) Primitive vascular plants; stems comprise most of mature plants and contain silica; produce only one kind of spore; motile sperm must swim in water. Only one living genus. Example: *Equisetum*.

PHYLUM PTEROPHYTA (ferns) Vascular plants well adapted to live in predominantly damp or seasonally wet environments; sporophyte dominant and well adapted to terrestrial life; gametophyte inconspicuous; reproduction still dependent on water for free-swimming gametes. Examples: cinnamon fern, Boston fern, tree fern, maidenhair fern.

Appendix  Classification

PHYLUM CYCADOPHYTA (cycads) Evergreen, slow-growing, tropical and subtropical shrubs; many resemble small palm trees; palmlike or fernlike compound leaves; sexes are separate—individuals have either male pollen-producing cones or female seed-producing cones.

PHYLUM GINKGOPHYTA (ginkgoes) Deciduous trees with fan-shaped leaves; sexes separate; outer skin of ovule develops into a fleshy, fruitlike covering. Only one living species: *Ginkgo biloba* (ginkgo).

PHYLUM GNETOPHYTA (gnetophytes) Few species; reproductive scales are clustered into cones. Examples: *Welwitschia*, Mormon tea (*Ephedra*).

PHYLUM CONIFEROPHYTA (conifers) Seeds born on cones; predominantly wind-pollinated; most are evergreen; most are temperate and subarctic shrubs and trees; many have needlelike leaves; in most species, sexes are not separate. Examples: pine, spruce, cedar, cypress, yew, fir, larch, sequoia.

PHYLUM ANTHOPHYTA (angiosperms: flowering plants) Seeds develop enclosed within ovaries; leaves modified into flowers; flowers pollinated by wind or by animals, including insects, birds, and bats; occur in many different forms; found in most land and freshwater habitats; a few species found in shallow saltwater and estuarine areas.

Class Monocotyledonae (monocots) Embryo with a single cotyledon; leaves with predominantly parallel venation; flower parts in multiples of three; vascular bundles scattered throughout stem. Examples: lily, corn, grasses, iris, palm, tulip.

Class Dicotyledonae (dicots) Embryo with two cotyledons; leaves with venation in netlike patterns; flower parts in multiples of fours or fives; vascular bundles arranged in rings in stem. Examples: rose, maple, oak, daisy, apple.

Kingdom Animalia

Multicellular; eukaryotic; typically heterotrophs that ingest their food; lack cell walls; in most phyla, cells are organized into tissues that make up organs; most reproduce sexually; development involves formation of a hollow ball of cells called a blastula.

PHYLUM PORIFERA (sponges) Aquatic; lack true tissues and organs; motile larvae and sessile adults; filter feeders; internal skeleton made up of spongin and/or spicules of calcium carbonate or silica. Examples: Venus' flower basket, bath sponge, tube sponge.

PHYLUM CNIDARIA (cnidarians) Previously known as coelenterates; aquatic; mostly carnivorous; two layers of true tissues; radial symmetry; tentacles bear stinging nematocysts; many alternate between polyp and medusa body forms; gastrovascular cavity.

Class Hydrozoa Spend most of their time as polyps; colonial or solitary; reproduce asexually by budding or sexually by producing eggs and sperm. Examples: hydra, Portuguese man-of-war.

Class Scyphozoa Spend most of their time as medusas; some species bypass polyp stage; reproduce sexually. Examples: lion's mane jellyfish, moon jelly, sea wasp.

Class Anthozoa Colonial or solitary polyps; no medusa stage; have central body surrounded by tentacles; reproduce sexually or asexually. Examples: reef coral, sea anemone, sea pen, sea fan.

PHYLUM PLATYHELMINTHES (flatworms) Three layers of tissues (endoderm, mesoderm, ectoderm); bilateral symmetry; some cephalization; acoelomate; free-living or parasitic.

Class Turbellaria (turbellarians) Free-living carnivores and scavengers; live in fresh water, in salt water, or on land; move with cilia. Example: planarians.

Class Trematoda (flukes) Parasites; life cycle typically involves more than one host. Examples: *Schistosoma*, liver fluke.

Class Cestoda (tapeworms) Internal parasites; lack digestive tract; body composed of many repeating sections (proglottids). Example: tapeworms.

PHYLUM NEMATODA (roundworms) Unsegmented worms; digestive system has two openings—a mouth and an anus; pseudocoelomates. Examples: *Ascaris lumbricoides*, hookworms, *Trichinella*.

PHYLUM ANNELIDA (segmented worms) Body composed of segments separated by internal partitions; digestive system has two openings; coelomate; closed circulatory system.

Class Polychaeta (polychaetes) Live in salt water; pair of bristly, fleshy appendages on each segment. Examples: sandworm, fanworm, feather-duster worm.

Class Oligochaeta (oligochaetes) Lack appendages; few setae; live in soil or fresh water. Examples: *Tubifex*, earthworm.

Class Hirudinea (leeches) Lack appendages; carnivores or blood-sucking external parasites; most live in fresh water. Example: medicinal leech (*Hirudo medicinalis*).

PHYLUM MOLLUSCA (mollusks) Soft-bodied; often possess a hard, calcified shell secreted by a mantle; muscular foot; digestive system with two openings; coelomates.

Class Bivalvia (bivalves) Two-part hinged shell; wedge-shaped foot; typically sessile as adults; primarily aquatic; some burrow in mud or sand. Examples: clam, oyster, scallop, mussel.

Class Gastropoda (gastropods) Use broad, muscular foot in movement; most have spiral, chambered shell; some lack shell; distinct head; some terrestrial, others aquatic; many are cross-fertilizing hermaphrodites. Examples: snail, slug, nudibranch, sea hare, sea butterfly.

Class Cephalopoda (cephalopods) Head is attached to a single foot; foot is divided into tentacles; live in salt water; closed circulatory system; highly developed brain and sense organs. Examples: octopus, squid, nautilus, cuttlefish.

PHYLUM ARTHROPODA (arthropods) Exoskeleton of chitin; jointed appendages; segmented body; many undergo metamorphosis during development; open circulatory system; largest animal phylum; classified based on the number and structure of body segments and appendages.

Subphylum Trilobita (trilobites) Two furrows running from head to tail divide body into three lobes; one pair of unspecialized appendages on each body segment; each appendage divided into two branches—a gill and a walking leg; all extinct.

Subphylum Chelicerata (chelicerates) First pair of appendages specialized as feeding structures called chelicerae; body composed of two parts—cephalothorax and abdomen; lack antennae; most terrestrial. Examples: horseshoe crab, tick, mite, spider, scorpion.

Subphylum Crustacea (crustaceans) Most aquatic; most live in salt water; two pairs of antennae; two or three body sections and chewing mouthparts called mandibles; many have a carapace that covers part or all of the body. Examples: crab, crayfish, pill bug, water flea, barnacle.

Subphylum Uniramia Almost all terrestrial; one pair of antennae; mandibles; unbranched appendages.

Class Chilopoda (centipedes) Long body consisting of many segments; one pair of legs per segment; poison claws for feeding; carnivorous.

Class Diplopoda (millipedes) Long body consisting of many segments; two pairs of legs per segment; mostly herbivorous.

Class Insecta (insects) Body divided into three parts—head, thorax, and abdomen; three pairs of legs and usually one or two pairs of wings attached to thorax; some undergo complete metamorphosis. Examples: termite, ant, beetle, dragonfly, fly, moth, grasshopper.

PHYLUM ECHINODERMATA (echinoderms) Live in salt water; adults typically have radial symmetry; endoskeleton; tube feet; water vascular system used in respiration, excretion, feeding, and locomotion; deuterostomes.

Class Crinoidea (crinoids) Filter feeders; feathery arms; mouth and anus on upper surface of body disk; some sessile. Examples: sea lily, feather star.

Appendix  Classification

Class Asteroidea (sea stars) Star-shaped; carnivorous; bottom dwellers; mouth on lower surface. Examples: crown-of-thorns sea star, sunstar.

Class Ophiuroidea Small body disk; long armored arms; most have only five arms; lack an anus; most are filter feeders or detritus feeders. Examples: brittle star, basket star.

Class Echinoidea Lack arms; body encased in rigid, box-like covering; covered with spines; most grazing herbivores or detritus feeders. Examples: sea urchin, sand dollar, sea biscuit.

Class Holothuroidea (sea cucumbers) Cylindrical body with feeding tentacles on one end; lie on their side; mostly detritus or filter feeders; endoskeleton greatly reduced.

PHYLUM CHORDATA (chordates) Dorsal hollow nerve cord, notochord, pharyngeal pouches, and a muscular tail during at least part of development.

Subphylum Urochordata (tunicates) Live in salt water; tough outer covering; display chordate features during larval stages; many adults sessile, some free-swimming. Examples: sea squirt, sea peach, salp.

Subphylum Cephalochordata (lancelets) Fishlike; live in salt water; filter feeders; no internal skeleton. Example: Branchiostoma.

Subphylum Vertebrata Most possess a vertebral column (backbone) that supports and protects dorsal nerve chord; endoskeleton; distinct head with a skull and brain.

Class Myxini (hagfishes) Jawless; mostly scavengers; lack eyes; short tentacles around mouth; rasping tongue; extremely slimy; open circulatory system.

Class Cephalaspidomorphi (lampreys) Jawless; larvae filter feeders; adults are parasites whose circular mouth is lined with rasping toothlike structures.

Class Chondrichthyes (cartilaginous fishes) Have jaws, fins, and endoskeleton of cartilage; most live in salt water; typically several gill slits; tough small scales with spines; ectothermic; two-chambered heart; males possess structures for internal fertilization. Examples: shark, ray, skate, chimaera, sawfish.

Class Osteichthyes (bony fishes) Bony endoskeleton; aquatic; ectothermic; well-developed respiratory system, usually involving gills; possess swim bladder; paired fins; divided into two groups—ray-finned fishes, which include most living species, and lobe-finned fishes, which include lungfishes and the coelacanth. Examples: salmon, perch, sturgeon, tuna, goldfish, eel.

Class Amphibia (amphibians) Adapted primarily to life in wet places; ectothermic; most carnivorous; smooth, moist skin; typically lay eggs that develop in water; usually have gilled larvae; most have three-chambered heart; adults either aquatic or terrestrial; terrestrial forms respire using lungs, skin, and/or lining of the mouth.

Order Urodela (salamanders) Possess tail as adults; carnivorous; usually have four legs; usually aquatic as larvae and terrestrial as adults.

Order Anura (frogs and toads) Adults in almost all species lack tail; aquatic larvae called tadpoles; well-developed hind legs adapted for jumping.

Order Apoda (legless amphibians) Wormlike; lack legs; carnivorous; terrestrial burrowers; some viviparous. Example: caecilians.

Class Reptilia (reptiles) As a group, adapted to fully terrestrial life, some live in water; dry, scale-covered skin; lungs; ectothermic; most have three-chambered hearts; internal fertilization; amniotic eggs typically laid on land; extinct forms include dinosaurs and flying reptiles.

Order Sphenodonta (tuataras) Lack internal ears; primitive scales; found only in New Zealand; carnivorous. One species: *Sphenodon punctatus*.

Order Squamata (lizards and snakes) Most carnivorous; majority terrestrial; lizards typically have legs; snakes lack legs. Examples: iguana, gecko, skink, cobra, python, boa.

Order Crocodilia (crocodilians) Carnivorous; aquatic or semiaquatic; four-chambered heart. Examples: alligator, crocodile, caiman, gavial.

Order Testudines (turtles and tortoises) Bony shell; ribs and vertebrae fused to upper part of shell; some terrestrial, others semiaquatic or aquatic; all lay eggs on land. Examples: snapping turtle, tortoise, hawksbill turtle, box turtle.

Class Aves (birds) Endothermic; feathered over much of body surface; scales on legs and feet; bones hollow and lightweight in flying species; four-chambered heart; well-developed lungs and air sacs for efficient air exchange. Examples: owl, eagle, duck, chicken, pigeon, penguin, sparrow, stork.

Class Mammalia (mammals) Endothermic; subcutaneous fat; hair; most viviparous; suckle young with milk produced in mammary glands; four-chambered heart; use lungs for respiration.

Order Monotremata (monotremes) Exhibit features of both mammals and reptiles; possess a cloaca; lay eggs that hatch externally; produce milk from primitive nipple-like structures. Examples: duckbill platypus, short-beaked echidna.

Order Marsupialia (marsupials) Bear live young that complete their development in external pouch. Examples: opossum, kangaroo, koala.

Order Insectivora (insectivores) Placental mammals; have long, narrow snouts and sharp claws for digging. Examples: shrew, mole, hedgehog.

Order Chiroptera (bats) Placental mammals; flying mammals, with forelimbs adapted for flight; most nocturnal; most navigate by echolocation; most species feed on insects, nectar, or fruits; some species feed on blood. Examples: fruit bat, flying fox, vampire bat.

Order Primates (primates) Placental mammals; highly developed brain and complex social behavior; excellent binocular vision; quadrupedal or bipedal locomotion; five digits on hands and feet. Examples: lemur, monkey, chimpanzee, human.

Order Xenarthra (xenarthrans) Placental mammals; teeth reduced or absent; feed primarily on social insects, such as termites and ants. Examples: anteater, armadillo.

Order Lagomorpha (lagomorphs) Placental mammals; small herbivores with chisel-shaped front teeth; generally adapted to running and jumping. Examples: rabbit, pika, hare.

Order Rodentia (rodents) Placental mammals; mostly herbivorous but some omnivorous; sharp front teeth. Examples: rat, beaver, guinea pig, hamster, gerbil, squirrel.

Order Cetacea (cetaceans) Placental mammals; fully adapted to aquatic existence; feed, breed, and give birth in water; forelimbs specialized as flippers; external hindlimbs absent; many species capable of long, deep dives; some use echolocation to navigate; communicate using complex auditory signals. Examples: whale, porpoise, dolphin.

Order Carnivora (carnivores) Placental mammals; mostly carnivorous; live in salt water or on land; aquatic species must return to land to breed. Examples: seal, bear, raccoon, weasel, skunk.

Order Proboscidea (elephants) Placental mammals; herbivorous; have trunks; largest land animal. Examples: Asian elephant, African elephant.

Order Sirenia (sirenians) Placental mammals; aquatic herbivores; slow-moving; forelimbs modified as flippers; hindlimbs absent; little body hair. Examples: manatee, sea cow.

Order Perissodactyla (odd-toed ungulates) Placental mammals; hoofed herbivores; odd number of digits on each foot; teeth, jaw, and digestive system adapted to plant material. Examples: horse, donkey, rhinoceros, tapir.

Order Artiodactyla (even-toed ungulates) Placental mammals; hoofed herbivores; hoofs derived from two digits on each foot; digestive system adapted to thoroughly process tough plant material. Examples: sheep, cow, hippopotamus, antelope, camel, giraffe, pig.

Advance Prep
- Become familiar with local laws and regulations regarding the collection of specimens.
- Scout a suitable locale and become familiar with the organisms and terrain. Look out for potential hazards, such as poisonous plants, wasp nests, or difficult terrain.
- Obtain permissions from parents and school authorities.
- In addition to the materials specified, obtain the following items to take on the trip: a first-aid kit; insect repellent; sunscreen; disposable, premoistened cleansing tissues; and trash bags for refuse.

Safety Check students' written plans in advance of the trip for safety considerations. Bring a first-aid kit on the trip. Point out to students any known hazards in the locale to which you will be taking them. Familiarize students with the appearance of poisonous plants, amphibians, or reptiles indigenous to the area. Establish rules ahead of time to ensure that you are always in contact with your students. Caution students not to touch living things unless necessary for making observations or obtaining specimens. Also caution students to keep their hands away from their eyes and mouths and not to eat during the activity. Remind students that they should wash their hands with soap and warm water at the earliest opportunity after the field activity.

Pretrip Discussion
- Describe the type of area you will be visiting. Discuss the types of organisms students might find and how they might best observe them. Instruct students to disturb the area as little as possible.
- Advise students about what they are—and are not—permitted to collect.

Tips for Successful Field Trips

Biology field trips can have different purposes and take place in a variety of environments. The steps you take and the observations you make can vary greatly. However, field trips often involve common elements, such as the way you plan the event and what you do at the site. If you plan well and organize your activities thoughtfully, your field trips will be more productive and enjoyable. Here are some suggestions to consider.

Planning the Trip

1. Discuss with your teacher and classmates the type of area you will visit and decide what you are likely to gather. This will help determine the materials needed to collect specimens.
2. When you go on a field trip, you will encounter some living things you can collect and some you cannot.
   - For things you can't collect, such as most animals and large plants or plants on other people's property, take a photograph or make a sketch.
   - For things you can collect, such as water samples, soil samples, small plants, flowers, pine cones, fungi, and insects, take containers such as prelabeled plastic bags and jars with lids. Some jar lids should contain air holes. You may also need tools for collecting, such as a small trowel or garden spade for soil and an aquarium net for small water organisms.
3. List the materials you will need, including the following items:
   - data table and blank sheets of paper in a firm notebook or on a clipboard
   - a camera
   - marking pens and writing utensils
   - a magnifying glass
4. Write the steps in your plan. Have your teacher check it for practicality and safety.

During the Trip

1. Before leaving for the site, make sure you have all the materials listed in your plan.
2. Wear sturdy shoes, long sleeves, and long pants. Depending upon the time of year and the site itself, you should also consider wearing insect repellent and sunscreen.
3. Work in the groups that your teacher has assigned.
4. When you collect samples to bring back to the classroom, make sure you follow these rules:
   - Observe all local laws, and respect other people's property.
   - Avoid contact with poisonous plants and animals. Bright colors and highly contrasting colors may indicate that an animal is dangerous.
   - When turning over logs and stones, use a long stick in case stinging insects or snakes are underneath.
   - Do not collect any animals without the permission of your teacher.
   - Remember that all animals must be treated humanely. All vertebrates collected for study, such as small fish or tadpoles, must be returned to their environment unharmed.
   - As soon as possible after you have finished, wash your hands thoroughly with soap and warm water.

After the Trip

Make sure that the samples you bring back to the classroom for observation are stored under the appropriate conditions. Generally, samples should have access to air (either put holes in the lids of the containers or keep them loosely covered). Do not leave any samples completely uncovered, because they might dry out. Keep the samples cool and *do not* store in direct sunlight.

How Do Living Things Interact?

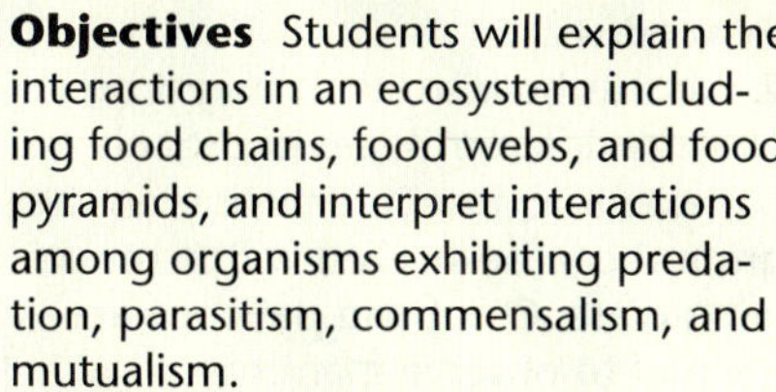

Living things spend a lot of time obtaining nutrients. How they do this influences their relationships with other organisms. In this activity, you will discover those relationships.

Problem **What interactions exist among organisms in an ecosystem?**

Materials

- containers (plastic bags and jars with lids)
- camera (optional)
- magnifying glass
- microscope
- glass slides
- coverslips
- dropper pipette
- field guides

Skills Observing, Inferring, Analyzing Data, Drawing Conclusions

Procedure

Part A: Preparing for the Field Trip

1. Your goal is to observe and identify as many organisms as you can in the area you are visiting so that you can construct an accurate picture of the food webs in that ecosystem. During the field trip itself, you will identify each organism or trace of an organism you observe by name or with a description and a picture.
2. Discuss with your teacher and classmates the type of area you will visit to help you plan for what you might observe.
3. Review classification at the kingdom level on pages 457–461, if necessary. Identifying the kingdom is a useful step in determining how an organism gets food.
4. Gather enough descriptive information about the organisms you expect to observe so that you can identify them with a field guide. This will enable you to research which step in the food chain the organism occupies.
5. Just because you don't see an organism doesn't mean it leaves no traces of its existence and interactions with its surroundings. Spider webs, for example, mean there are spiders eating insects. This kind of indirect evidence enables you to identify a consumer and infer where it is in the food chain. Other indirect evidence can include nests, burrows, and paw prints. Plan to sketch or photograph these traces.
6. Familiarize yourself with the biomes and ecosystems described on pages 99–112. Different plants grow in different biomes. The types of plants in an area determine the type of community.
7. Physical characteristics of an area determine the kinds of producers and ultimately the type of ecosystem. Find out as much as you can about the biome and ecosystem you will be visiting.
8. Some of your observations will be made in the field, and some will be made in the classroom. Prepare a data table similar to the one on the next page to record your observations.
9. Have your teacher check your written plan and review all safety considerations.

Part B: Working at the Site

10. On the day of your trip, bring along all the materials listed in your plan.
11. Describe the location in which you are making observations. Observe a sufficient number of plants to help determine the nature of the ecosystem. If it is a land ecosystem, examine the soil for moisture and texture.
12. If you are visiting an aquatic ecosystem, collect some water samples. The organisms at or near the bottom of the water food chains are often microscopic.
13. Describe, sketch, and photograph any organisms or traces of organisms (tracks, nests, burrows, for example) that you see.
14. The best way to get close to larger animals is to wait patiently and quietly, hiding where you will not be seen. While you are waiting you can observe the surrounding plants and the behavior of smaller animals. Use a magnifying glass. Watch the skies for birds as well.

Objectives Students will explain the interactions in an ecosystem including food chains, food webs, and food pyramids, and interpret interactions among organisms exhibiting predation, parasitism, commensalism, and mutualism.

Skills Focus Observing, Inferring, Analyzing Data, Drawing Conclusions

Time 45 minutes for days 1 and 3; 2–4 hours for day 2

Advance Prep

- See page 1078 for general suggestions regarding advance preparation for field trips.
- Work with your school librarian and/or local libraries to obtain a selection of field guides for identifying organisms, including some that identify animal tracks. The National Audubon Society publishes a number of field guides.
- Try out suggested Internet searches in advance, and then suggest appropriate search criteria to students. "Nature guide" works better than "field guide."

Safety Check students' written plans in advance. Bring a first-aid kit. Point out any known hazards in the locale to which you will be taking students. Familiarize students with the appearance of poisonous plants, amphibians, or reptiles indigenous to the area. Set up plans and rules ahead of time to ensure that you are always in contact with your students. Caution students to keep their hands away from their eyes and mouths, and not to eat during the activity. Remind students that they should wash their hands with soap and warm water at the earliest opportunity after the field activity.

Pretrip Discussion

- See page 1078 for general suggestions for discussion to precede field trips.
- Review the following terms: *population, community, ecosystem, biome, food chain, food web, producer, primary consumer, secondary consumer, decomposer,* and *symbiosis*. Give students a hypothetical list of organisms to arrange into several food chains and food webs, for which they should identify trophic levels.

Procedure

2. Discuss how students might best observe different types of organisms. For example, insects crawling on the ground can be studied with a magnifying glass. Quiet and patience are needed to observe mammals.

11. Students should check to see whether the soil is dry or sandy. Sand holds less moisture than other soils. As a result, sandy soil would probably have coniferous trees in a region that otherwise might have a deciduous forest.

13. To collect water samples, students should dip jars into the water without getting their fingers wet.

16. The observations in this step help identify the trophic level. For example, hiding and burrowing are more typical of prey than predators.

18. Remind students how to prepare a wet mount. Larger organisms such as hydra will require a depression slide.

Analyze and Conclude

1. Typical interactions include stalking, hunting, evading, hiding, eating, etc.

2. Answers will depend on organisms observed. All food chains should begin with a producer.

3. Food webs should be consistent with the food chains described in question 2.

4. Answers will depend on observations. Pollination, spreading seeds by gathering fruit, or eating parasites off a larger host are examples of mutualism. Hitching a ride either by a smaller animal or by seeds is commensalism. Blood-sucking behavior is parasitism. Students should note whether relationships are based on food-gathering or other factors.

5. Answers will depend on observations. See pages 100–104 for descriptions of biomes.

6. Students should describe what safety precautions they took.

Go Further

On the Internet, students can use a search phrase including the name of the biome and the phrase "food chain," such as "desert food chain."

How Do Living Things Interact? (continued)

Data Table

Number	Location	Organism or Trace	Feeding Behavior (Producer, herbivore, carnivore, decomposer)	Other Behavior	Other	Identity of Organism
1						
2						
3						

15. When you see an animal, pay careful attention to the placement of the eyes. Predators often have their eyes in the front of their heads. Animals that are preyed upon often have eyes at the sides of their heads.

16. Watch for behavior. Observe what an animal eats and how it eats. This tells you something about where it is on the food chain. Describe any other animal behavior you observe, such as hiding, burrowing, or nesting.

17. Record any other observations that you think might help to identify the role of the organism in its community. As soon as possible after you have finished, wash your hands with soap and warm water.

Part C: Following the Field Trip

18. If you collected any water samples, prepare wet mounts of samples from the top, middle, and bottom of the container. Examine the slides for the presence of organisms. Fill in the required observations on the data table. Note whether the organisms have chlorophyll or not. Watch for feeding behavior. Wash your hands with soap and warm water when you have finished.

19. Try to identify the organisms you have observed and the organisms that produced the traces you have observed, using field guides or the Internet. It is not necessary to know the species of each organism. You need to know only enough to learn how the organism obtains nutrients and what its predators are. For example, identifying a bird as an owl, a hawk, or a pigeon is sufficient for finding out what it eats. Write your conclusion in your data table.

20. If necessary, after you identify the organisms you observed, research in the library or on the Internet how the organisms obtain nutrients and which other organisms interact with them.

Analyze and Conclude

1. **Classifying** What were some of the interactions you observed between organisms? Describe at least one example of predation.
2. **Analyzing Data** Based on your observations and research, draw one or more food chains from the organisms in the community you visited. Identify the trophic levels in each food chain (producer, primary consumer, secondary consumer, decomposer).
3. **Analyzing Data** Based on the food chains you drew, draw a food web for the community you visited.
4. **Drawing Conclusions** Give one or more examples of symbiosis that you observed. Explain whether each relationship is based on food-getting or on other factors, such as living space.
5. **Drawing Conclusions** Based on the climate and types of organisms found in the community you observed, in what biome is it found? Support your conclusion with evidence and reasoning.
6. **SAFETY** How did you demonstrate safe practices during this investigation?

Go Further

Comparing and Contrasting Select a biome different from the one you visited. Do research to determine what organisms are present in a community located in that biome and what ecological relationships exist among them. Write a plan describing how you would gather data in that biome and what you might observe. Describe some possible food chains and food webs in that biome. How is it different from the one you observed? How is it similar?

Which Kingdoms Live in Your Neighborhood?

Much of the life around you goes unnoticed because it is either hidden or so familiar that you take it for granted. In this activity, you will observe the life-forms in your neighborhood in sufficient detail to classify them into their proper kingdoms.

Problem

How can you collect and classify organisms at the kingdom level?

Materials

- camera (optional)
- containers (plastic bags and jars with lids)
- small trowel or garden spade
- aquarium net
- unrefrigerated food
- large plastic cup
- marking pens
- rubber tubing
- large funnel
- hose clamp
- iron ring and ring stand
- cheesecloth
- white paper
- dissecting tray
- magnifying glass
- coverslips
- petroleum jelly
- dropper pipette
- depression slides
- microscope
- glass slides

Skills

Observing, Classifying, Comparing and Contrasting

Procedure

Part A: Preparing for the Field Trip

1. As you plan for your trip, follow the guidelines in the Lab Tips box on page 55 and the field trip tips on page 1078.
2. You will make observations in the field and in the classroom. Prepare a data table similar to the one below to record observations.
3. Make sure you are familiar with the six-kingdom classification system explained in Section 18–3.
4. Write a plan that describes a procedure for your field trip. Have your teacher review the plan for practicality and safety.
5. At home, select some food items to bring to class just before your field trip. These will be left unrefrigerated to speed growth of microorganisms.
6. Before going on the trip, set aside the food items you brought in a place designated by your teacher. Dry foods such as beans or bread should be placed in a container with some moisture. Also, set aside a large plastic cup of water.

Part B: Working at the Site

7. At the site, look in a variety of places with different characteristics to find the largest variety of organisms. Look in sunny areas, in the shade, in the water, in the air, behind plants, between the blades of grass, within a forest, at the edge of a forest, and so on. When you locate an organism, record your observations in your data table.

Data Table

Number	Size (microscopic or macroscopic)	Movement (yes or no)	Color	Description	Kingdom
1					
2					
3					

Objective Students will collect and classify organisms at the kingdom level.

Time 45 minutes for days 1, 3, and 4; 2–4 hours for day 2

Skills Focus Observing, Classifying, Comparing and Contrasting

Advance Prep

- See page 1078 for general suggestions for advance preparation for field trips.
- Set up lab groups prior to beginning so students can work together in the planning stages as well as in the field.

Safety

- Checks students' written plans in advance. Bring a first-aid kit. Point out any known hazards in the field-trip locale, such as poisonous plants, amphibians, or reptiles. Set up plans and rules ahead of time to ensure that you are always in contact with your students. Caution students to keep their hands away from their eyes and mouths, and not to eat during the activity. Remind students that they should wash their hands with soap and warm water at the earliest opportunity after the field activity.
- Students with mold allergies should not perform the part of the activity that involves examining food samples for mold and bacterial cultures. After the food samples have been exposed to the air for awhile, they should be covered lightly with plastic to prevent spore dispersal. Students should avoid touching the exposed food samples or any fluids, and they should wash their hands with warm, soapy water immediately after the activity.

Teaching Tips Have students practice using a dichotomous key—for example, by doing the leaf-classification lab in Chapter 18. Make sure that students understand the contrasting nature of the statements in a dichotomous key. Have them review the key on page 1083 prior to going into the field in order to focus the types of observations they make. Students who cannot participate in the actual field trip can use the key to classify photos of organisms.

Pretrip Discussion
- See page 1078 for general suggestions for discussion to precede field trips.
- Review the six-kingdom classification system. Ask students to compare the criteria in the dichotomous key (page 1083) to the characteristics of each kingdom.

Procedure

1. Discuss any limitations on what may be collected.

4. Suggest specific food items for students to bring in. Bread without preservatives is good for growing mold. Bean infusions made from dried beans and water are good for culturing bacteria. Milk and plain yogurt are good for bacterial observation. Rotting citrus fruits are good for mold. Prepare food items before leaving for the field trip to increase the chances that there will be bacterial and mold growth to observe on the last day of the activity.

5. The water will be used later to prepare a leaf infusion. It must be preconditioned by setting it aside overnight; otherwise, the chlorine will kill any microorganisms.

11. This apparatus is designed to concentrate soil roundworms. They collect just above the hose clamp.

15. Even if the water has been preconditioned as described in step 5, it may take several days for quantities of microorganisms to become sufficient for observation.

Which Kingdoms Live in Your Neighborhood? (continued)

8. Supplement your observations with drawings or photographs. Keep in mind that when you take photographs outside, using a flash may sometimes be necessary. Place the row number from your data table on each drawing, photograph, or container to help keep your observations organized.

9. Here are some hints for filling in your data table:
   - The organisms you see in the field will all be macroscopic (able to be seen without a microscope). This usually tells you that the organism is multicellular.
   - When you look for locomotion, you are looking for movement by an animal, not motion because of wind or other objects.
   - As you examine an organism's color, look for signs of the green pigment chlorophyll and note if it is present. The presence of chlorophyll is typical of plants and some protists.
   - In your description, include information such as where the organism is found. If the organism is found on another living thing, for example, it may be using it for food, as fungi do.
   - Indicate whether the organism has appendages. Animals may remain still when you look at them, but the presence of wings or legs is a sign they can move.
   - Note if the organism is anchored. Plants and fungi are generally anchored, but some animals such as sponges or barnacles are anchored, too. Look for an opening it uses for taking in food.

10. Try to collect the following samples to bring back to the classroom: water from ponds, lakes, streams, oceans, or puddles; soil and sand; natural mulch or leaves; and small plants or parts of plants. Wash your hands with soap and warm water.

Part C: Following the Field Trip, Day 1

11. If you collected moist soil, set up the apparatus shown above, right, to collect roundworms and other tiny animals. Put a piece of rubber tubing on the end of a large funnel. Place a hose clamp on the rubber tubing. Hang the funnel through an iron ring on a ring stand.

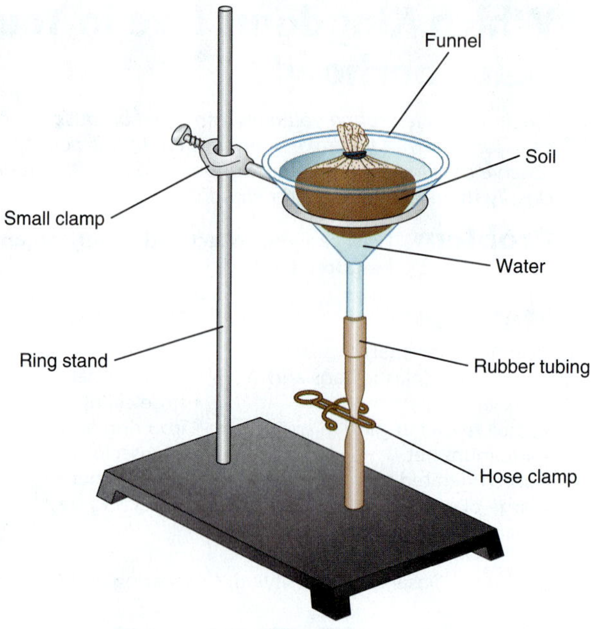

12. Double a piece of cheesecloth and place a sample of soil in the middle. Then, tie it closed to make a small sack. Put the sack in the funnel. Then, pour enough water into the funnel to fill it almost to the top. Leave the sack in the water for 24 hours.

13. If you collected sand or dry soil, place a sheet of white paper in a dissecting tray and spread a thin layer of the sand or soil on the paper. Examine the thin layer of soil with a magnifying glass. Look for signs of life. If you find any organisms, record your observations in your data table and draw diagrams or take a photograph of what you find.

14. If you collected mulch or leaves, place a clean piece of white paper in a dissecting tray and repeat the procedure you used in step 13 with a portion of the leaves or mulch.

15. Fallen leaves and mulch often contain microorganisms that can be rinsed off for study. Take some moist leaves or mulch from the bottom of the pile and place them in the cup of water you set aside in step 6. Leave them overnight.

16 To examine water samples you collected, prepare a slide as follows: Using a dropper pipette, withdraw water from the top of the water sample. Place a drop in the center of a clean slide. Then, cover the drop with a coverslip. If you pick up any macroscopic organisms with your dropper pipette, use a depression slide rather than a plain glass slide.

17 Prepare two more slides with water from the middle and bottom of the sample.

18 Examine the slides under low power. If necessary, switch to higher power for a closer look. Record your observations in your data table and draw diagrams of what you find. Wash your hands with soap and warm water.

Part D: Following the Field Trip, Day 2

19 Examine the food substances from step 5 for the presence of organisms. Look for fuzzy growth on the surface of the food. Examine the fluid surrounding the food using the process in steps 16–18. Record your observations in your data table and draw diagrams of what you find.

20 Examine the water in the funnel you set up in steps 11 and 12. Look for the presence of soil organisms as follows. Place a beaker under the rubber tubing and open the hose clamp for an instant to release some water.

21 Using a dropper pipette, put a few drops of the water onto a depression slide. Cover the slide with a coverslip. Locate some organisms under low power. Then, switch to high power. Record your observations in your data table and draw diagrams of what you find.

22 Prepare a slide from the beaker of water containing leaves or mulch from step 15. Using a dropper pipette, put a drop of the water onto a glass slide. Cover the slide with a coverslip.

23 Locate some organisms under low power with a microscope. Then, switch to higher power. If you don't find any organisms, make new slides each day for a week. As the organisms reproduce, your chance of finding them will improve. Record your observations in your data table and draw diagrams of what you find. Wash your hands with soap and warm water.

24 Classify each kind of organism you observed, using the dichotomous key above, right. Note any problems with the key as you work. Record the kingdom in your data table.

Dichotomous Key for Kingdoms

1. Microscopic or macroscopic
   1a) Microscopic (often unicellular) ....go to step 2
   1b) Macroscopic (multicellular) ....go to step 4
2. Presence or absence of nucleus
   2a) No nucleus (cell is also very small) ....Eubacteria or Archaebacteria
   2b) Nucleus (organelles will also be visible) ....go to step 3
3. Presence or absence of cell walls
   3a) Cell walls but no chloroplasts ....Fungi
   3b) May have or lack cell walls; may have chloroplasts..........Protista
4. Presence or absence of chloroplasts
   4a) Chloroplasts (some green color) ....Plantae
   4b) No chloroplasts (lack of green color) ....go to step 5
5. Mobile or anchored
   5a) Anchored to food source; absorbs food ....Fungi
   5b) Moves (or has appendages) and/or eats food ....Animalia

Analyze and Conclude

1. **Classifying** How did you determine the kingdoms of the various organisms?
2. **Evaluating and Revising** Did you detect any problems with the dichotomous key you used? How could you improve it? What difficulties might arise as you try to improve it?
3. **Inferring** Modern classification is based on evolutionary relationships. Does the dichotomous key you used reflect those relationships? Explain your answer.
4. **SAFETY** How did you demonstrate safe practices during this investigation?

Go Further

Classifying Select one kingdom you just investigated. Develop a dichotomous key to group those organisms into phyla. Review your key with classmates to see if it is workable. Then, classify the organisms.

19. If no signs of life are seen, tell students to set the samples aside and continue observations each day until organisms are seen.
20. Students should open the clamp only briefly, as the largest concentration of roundworms is directly above the clamp.
23. If no signs of life are seen, tell students to set the samples aside and continue observations each day until organisms are seen.
24. Use of the key can sometimes be misleading. Macroscopic examination of organisms doesn't always show the presence or absence of chloroplasts because of masking pigments. It is not obvious that fungi grow on their food source. Mushrooms often look anchored in the ground like plants. Filter feeders such as sponges cannot be easily observed eating.

Analyze and Conclude

1. Students should use the characteristics in the dichotomous key.
2. Some organisms may not have fit the criteria described in the key; for example, sponges are animals, but they do not move.
3. The key does not distinguish between eubacteria and archaebacteria; otherwise, the key reflects current understanding of evolutionary relationships.
4. Students should describe what safety precautions they took.

Go Further

Students may want to try classifying vertebrates or arthropods into classes in addition or as an alternative to classifying organisms in a kingdom into phyla. Sample classification keys can be found online using search terms such as *animals dichotomous key, chordates dichotomous key,* and *arthropods dichotomous key.*

BIIE 1.h

How to Read a Topographic Map

A map is a model that shows all or part of Earth's surface on a flat surface such as a sheet of paper. There are many different types of maps. A topographic map is a map that shows the elevation of different points on Earth's surface. It also shows many other features on Earth's surface, including water, roads, and buildings.

Direction on Maps

Most maps are drawn so that north is at the top of the map and south is at the bottom. East is on the right side, and west is on the left. Most topographic maps have a small drawing called a compass rose that shows the different directions. The compass rose also shows magnetic north, which is the direction a compass points. An example of a compass rose is shown in the key of the topographic map in Figure 1.

Contour Lines

Look at the brown lines on the right-hand map in Figure 1. Each line connects points that are at the same elevation. For example, the brown contour line in the bottom right of the map is marked "1200." This means that all points on this line are 1200 feet above sea level. In the United States, most topographic maps give contour intervals in feet rather than in meters. The thicker contour lines are called index contours.

The difference in elevation between contour lines is called the contour interval. The contour interval for a given map is always the same. In Figure 1, the contour interval is 200 feet. The thin brown line just west of the 1200 contour is at 1400 feet. If you were to walk north from one contour line to the next, you would gain 200 feet in elevation.

The closer together contour lines are, the steeper the terrain is. Near Dublin Lake, there are only a few contour lines, which indicates that the land is almost flat. Look at the area marked Summit, to the south of the lake. The contour lines there are very close together, which indicates a steep rock face.

Horizontal Distance

You have seen that vertical distances on maps are indicated using contour lines. Horizontal distances are indicated using a scale. Look at the scale on the map.

Figure 1

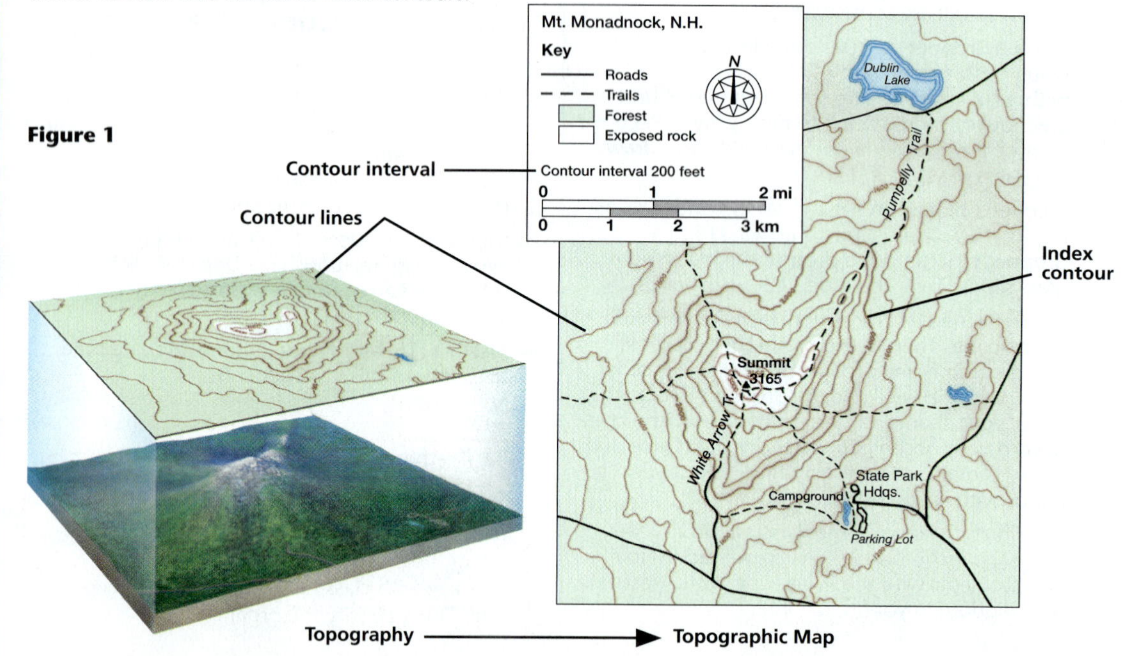

Figure 2

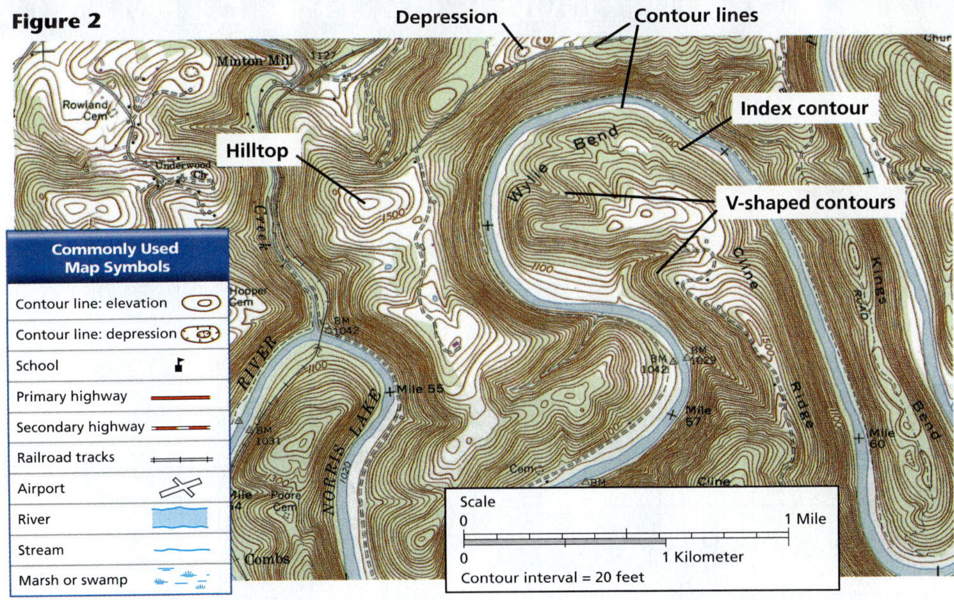

A scale indicates how much distance on a map is equivalent to a certain distance on Earth's surface. Most topographic maps in the United States are at a scale of 1 : 24,000. This means that one inch on the map equals 24,000 inches on the ground (about 2000 feet).

In the scale in Figure 1, the scale reads 1 inch = 1 mile. Topographic maps often also use a bar to show the scale of the map. To find a distance on a map, measure the distance using a ruler. Then, convert using the scale. For example, if the distance on the map is 4 inches, the distance on Earth's surface would be 4 miles.

Colors on Maps

Different colors are used to indicate various features on topographic maps. As you have seen, brown lines are used to indicate elevation. Look near the Summit in Figure 1. Most of the area is white, which indicates an area with no trees. White areas can be open fields or bare rock. Much of the map is green, which indicates that the green areas are forested. The color blue indicates water. In Figure 1, this is Dublin Lake. Creeks, ponds, lakes, and oceans are also shown in blue on topographic maps. Red and black are used for artificial structures. For example, red and black are used to indicate roads. Trails are shown as dashed black lines. Densely populated areas are shown in either gray or red.

Symbols on Topographic Maps

Topographic maps use a wide variety of symbols that represent different features. For example, a contour line that forms a closed loop with dashes indicates a depression, or hollow, in the ground. The shape of the contour lines also can help to show ridges or valleys (see Figure 2). V-shaped contour lines pointing downhill indicate a ridgeline. V-shaped contour lines pointing uphill indicate a valley. Other common symbols used on topographic maps are shown on the map in Figure 2.

Assessment

Use the topographic maps shown to answer these questions.

1. From Dublin Lake, in what direction would you walk to get to the State Park Headquarters?
2. Is the area marked Summit flat or steep? How do you know?
3. What is the approximate elevation of the parking lot?
4. How far is it from Dublin Lake to the Summit?
5. Is the campground located in open or forested land? How do you know?
6. How might hikers make use of topographic maps?

Assessment

1. South
2. Steep; the contour lines are close together.
3. 1200 feet
4. About 3 miles (close to 5 km)
5. Forested land; it's located on a green area on the map.
6. Hikers could check conditions of the land where they are hiking (i.e. Is the land flat or does it have steep slopes? Is it forested or open land?)

Appendix H Periodic Table of the Elements

Periodic Table of the Elements

	Nonmetals	Metals	Metalloids
Solid	C	Li	B
Liquid	Br	Hg	
Gas	H		
Not found in nature		Tc	

Atomic number — 6
Element symbol — C
Element name — Carbon
Atomic mass — 12.011

1 1A	2 2A	3 3B	4 4B	5 5B	6 6B	7 7B	8 8B	9	10	11 1B	12 2B	13 3A	14 4A	15 5A	16 6A	17 7A	18 8A
1 H Hydrogen 1.0079																	2 He Helium 4.0026
3 Li Lithium 6.941	4 Be Beryllium 9.0122											5 B Boron 10.81	6 C Carbon 12.011	7 N Nitrogen 14.007	8 O Oxygen 15.999	9 F Fluorine 18.998	10 Ne Neon 20.179
11 Na Sodium 22.990	12 Mg Magnesium 24.305											13 Al Aluminum 26.982	14 Si Silicon 28.086	15 P Phosphorus 30.974	16 S Sulfur 32.06	17 Cl Chlorine 35.453	18 Ar Argon 39.948
19 K Potassium 39.098	20 Ca Calcium 40.08	21 Sc Scandium 44.956	22 Ti Titanium 47.90	23 V Vanadium 50.941	24 Cr Chromium 51.996	25 Mn Manganese 54.938	26 Fe Iron 55.847	27 Co Cobalt 58.933	28 Ni Nickel 58.71	29 Cu Copper 63.546	30 Zn Zinc 65.38	31 Ga Gallium 69.72	32 Ge Germanium 72.59	33 As Arsenic 74.922	34 Se Selenium 78.96	35 Br Bromine 79.904	36 Kr Krypton 83.80
37 Rb Rubidium 85.468	38 Sr Strontium 87.62	39 Y Yttrium 88.906	40 Zr Zirconium 91.22	41 Nb Niobium 92.906	42 Mo Molybdenum 95.94	43 Tc Technetium (98)	44 Ru Ruthenium 101.07	45 Rh Rhodium 102.91	46 Pd Palladium 106.4	47 Ag Silver 107.87	48 Cd Cadmium 112.41	49 In Indium 114.82	50 Sn Tin 118.69	51 Sb Antimony 121.75	52 Te Tellurium 127.60	53 I Iodine 126.90	54 Xe Xenon 131.30
55 Cs Cesium 132.91	56 Ba Barium 137.33	71 Lu Lutetium 174.97	72 Hf Hafnium 178.49	73 Ta Tantalum 180.95	74 W Tungsten 183.85	75 Re Rhenium 186.21	76 Os Osmium 190.2	77 Ir Iridium 192.22	78 Pt Platinum 195.09	79 Au Gold 196.97	80 Hg Mercury 200.59	81 Tl Thallium 204.37	82 Pb Lead 207.2	83 Bi Bismuth 208.98	84 Po Polonium (209)	85 At Astatine (210)	86 Rn Radon (222)
87 Fr Francium (223)	88 Ra Radium (226)	103 Lr Lawrencium (262)	104 Rf Rutherfordium (261)	105 Db Dubnium (262)	106 Sg Seaborgium (263)	107 Bh Bohrium (264)	108 Hs Hassium (265)	109 Mt Meitnerium (268)	110 *Uun Ununnilium (269)	111 *Uuu Unununium (272)	112 *Uub Ununbium (277)		114 *Uuq Ununquadium				

*Name not officially assigned.

Lanthanide Series

57 La Lanthanum 138.91	58 Ce Cerium 140.12	59 Pr Praseodymium 140.91	60 Nd Neodymium 144.24	61 Pm Promethium (145)	62 Sm Samarium 150.4	63 Eu Europium 151.96	64 Gd Gadolinium 157.25	65 Tb Terbium 158.93	66 Dy Dysprosium 162.50	67 Ho Holmium 164.93	68 Er Erbium 167.26	69 Tm Thulium 168.93	70 Yb Ytterbium 173.04

Actinide Series

89 Ac Actinium (227)	90 Th Thorium 232.04	91 Pa Protactinium 231.04	92 U Uranium 238.03	93 Np Neptunium (237)	94 Pu Plutonium (244)	95 Am Americium (243)	96 Cm Curium (247)	97 Bk Berkelium (247)	98 Cf Californium (251)	99 Es Einsteinium (252)	100 Fm Fermium (257)	101 Md Mendelevium (258)	102 No Nobelium (259)

GLOSSARY

abdomen posterior part of an arthropod's body (p. 721)

abiotic factor physical, or nonliving, factor that shapes an ecosystem (p. 90)

abscission layer layer of cells at the petiole that seals off a leaf from the vascular system (p. 642)

accessory pigment compound other than chlorophyll that absorbs light at different wavelengths than chlorophyll (p. 506)

acellular slime mold slime mold that passes through a stage in which its cells fuse to form large cells with many nuclei (p. 516)

acetylcholine neurotransmitter that diffuses across a synapse and produces an impulse in the cell membrane of a muscle cell (p. 929)

acid compound that forms hydrogen ions (H^+) in solution (p. 43)

acid rain rain containing nitric and sulfuric acids (p. 148)

acoelomate animal lacking a coelom, or body cavity (p. 683)

actin protein that mainly makes up the thin filaments in striations in skeletal muscle cells (p. 928)

action potential reversal of charges across the cell membrane of a neuron; also called a nerve impulse (p. 899)

activation energy energy needed to get a reaction started (p. 50)

active immunity immunity produced by exposure to an antigen, as a result of the immune response (p. 1042)

active transport energy-requiring process that moves material across a cell membrane against a concentration difference (p. 188)

adaptation inherited characteristic that increases an organism's chance of survival (p. 380)

adaptive radiation process by which a single species or small group of species evolves into several different forms that live in different ways; rapid growth in the diversity of a group of organisms (pp. 436, 851)

addiction uncontrollable dependence on a drug (p. 914)

adenosine triphosphate (ATP) one of the principal chemical compounds that living things use to store and release energy (p. 202)

adhesion attraction between molecules of different substances; in plants, attraction between unlike molecules (pp. 41, 599)

aerobic process that requires oxygen (p. 226)

age-structure diagram graph of the numbers of males and females within different age groups of a population (p. 131)

aggression threatening behavior that one animal uses to gain control over another (p. 881)

agriculture the practice of farming (p. 141)

air sac one of several sacs attached to a bird's lungs into which air moves when a bird inhales; allows for the one-way flow of air through the respiratory system (p. 810)

algal bloom an immediate increase in the amount of algae and other producers that results from a large input of a limiting nutrient (p. 80)

allele one of a number of different forms of a gene (p. 265)

allergy overreaction of the immune system to antigens (p. 1043)

alternation of generations process in which many algae switch back and forth between haploid and diploid stages of their life cycles (p. 512)

alveolus tiny air sac at the end of a bronchiole in the lungs that provides surface area for gas exchange to occur (pp. 859, 958)

amino acid compound with an amino group ($—NH_2$) on one end and a carboxyl group ($—COOH$) on the other end (p. 47)

amniotic egg egg composed of shell and membranes that create a protected environment in which the embryo can develop out of the water (p. 802)

amoeboid movement type of locomotion used by amoebas (p. 500)

amphibian vertebrate that, with some exceptions, lives in water as a larva and on land as an adult, breathes with lungs as an adult, has moist skin that contains mucous glands, and lacks scales and claws (p. 782)

amylase enzyme in saliva that breaks the chemical bonds in starches (p. 979)

anaerobic process that does not require oxygen (p. 224)

anal pore region of the cell membrane of a ciliate where waste-containing food vacuoles fuse and are then emptied into the environment (p. 502)

anaphase the third phase of mitosis, during which the chromosome pairs separate and move toward opposite poles (p. 248)

angiosperm flowering plant; bears its seeds within a layer of tissue that protects the seed (p. 564)

Animalia kingdom of multicellular eukaryotic heterotrophs whose cells do not have cell walls (p. 461)

annual flowering plant that completes a life cycle within one growing season (p. 572)

anther flower structure in which haploid male gametophytes are produced (p. 612)

antheridium male reproductive structure in some algae and plants (pp. 519, 559)

anthropoid primate group made up of humans, apes, and most monkeys (p. 835)

antibiotic compound that blocks the growth and reproduction of bacteria (pp. 486, 1035)

antibody protein that helps destroy pathogens (p. 1038)

anticodon group of three bases on a tRNA molecule that are complementary to an mRNA codon (p. 304)

antigen substance that triggers an immune response (p. 1038)

anus opening through which wastes leave the digestive tract (pp. 661, 689)

aorta large blood vessel in mammals through which blood travels after it leaves the left ventricle (p. 946)

Glossary

aphotic zone permanently dark layer of the oceans below the photic zone (p. 109)

apical dominance phenomenon in which the closer a bud is to the stem's tip, the more its growth is inhibited (p. 636)

apical meristem group of undifferentiated cells that divide to produce increased length of stems and roots (p. 582)

appendage structure, such as a leg or antenna, that extends from the body wall (p. 715)

aquaculture the raising of aquatic organisms for human consumption (p. 147)

Archaea domain of unicellular prokaryotes that have cell walls that do not contain peptidoglycan (p. 459)

Archaebacteria kingdom of unicellular prokaryotes whose cell walls do not contain peptidoglycan (p. 459)

archaeocyte specialized cell in a sponge that makes spicules (p. 665)

archegonium female reproductive structure in some plants, including mosses and liverworts (p. 559)

artery large blood vessel that carries blood from the heart to the tissues of the body (p. 946)

artificial selection selection by humans for breeding of useful traits from the natural variation among different organisms (p. 379)

ascospore haploid spore produced within the ascus of ascomycetes (p. 532)

ascus structure within the fruiting body of an ascomycete in which two nuclei of different mating types fuse (p. 532)

asexual reproduction process by which a single parent reproduces by itself (p. 17)

asthma chronic respiratory disease in which the air passageways become narrower than normal (p. 1044)

atherosclerosis condition in which fatty deposits called plaque build up on the inner walls of the arteries (p. 949)

atom basic unit of matter (p. 35)

ATP synthase large protein that uses energy from H^+ ions to bind ADP and a phosphate group together to produce ATP (p. 210)

atrium upper chamber of the heart that receives and holds blood that is about to enter the ventricle (pp. 776, 945)

autosome chromosome that is not a sex chromosome (p. 341)

autotroph organism that can capture energy from sunlight or chemicals and use it to produce its own food from inorganic compounds; also called a producer (pp. 67, 201)

auxin substance produced in the tip of a seedling that stimulates cell elongation (p. 635)

axon long fiber that carries impulses away from the cell body of a neuron (p. 898)

bacillus rod-shaped prokaryote (p. 473)

Bacteria domain of unicellular prokaryotes that have cell walls containing peptidoglycan (p. 459)

bacteriophage virus that infects bacteria (pp. 289, 479)

bark tree structure that includes all tissues outside the vascular cambium, including phloem, the cork cambium, and cork (p. 593)

base compound that produces hydroxide ions (OH^+) in solution (p. 43)

base pairing principle that bonds in DNA can form only between adenine and thymine and between guanine and cytosine (p. 294)

basidiospore spore in basidiomycetes that germinates to produce haploid primary mycelia (p. 535)

basidium spore-bearing structure of a basidiomycete (p. 534)

behavior the way an organism reacts to changes in its internal condition or external environment (p. 871)

behavioral isolation form of reproductive isolation in which two populations have differences in courtship rituals or other types of behavior that prevent them from interbreeding (p. 404)

benthos organisms that live attached to or near the ocean floor (p. 112)

biennial flowering plant that completes its life cycle in two years (p. 572)

bilateral symmetry body plan in which only a single, imaginary line can divide the body into two equal halves; characteristic of worms, arthropods, and chordates (pp. 662, 748)

binary fission type of asexual reproduction in which an organism replicates its DNA and divides in half, producing two identical daughter cells (p. 475)

binocular vision ability to merge visual images from both eyes, which provides depth perception and a three-dimensional view of the world (p. 834)

binomial nomenclature classification system in which each species is assigned a two-part scientific name (p. 448)

biodiversity biological diversity; the sum total of the variety of organisms in the biosphere (p. 150)

biogeochemical cycle process in which elements, chemical compounds, and other forms of matter are passed from one organism to another and from one part of the biosphere to another (p. 74)

biological magnification increasing concentration of a harmful substance in organisms at higher trophic levels in a food chain or food web (p. 152)

biology science that seeks to understand the living world (p. 15)

biomass total amount of living tissue within a given trophic level (p. 72)

biome group of ecosystems that have the same climate and dominant communities (pp. 64, 98)

biosphere part of Earth in which life exists including land, water, and air or atmosphere (p. 63)

biotic factor biological influence on organisms within an ecosystem (p. 90)

bipedal term used to refer to two-footed locomotion (p. 835)

bird endothermic animal that has an outer covering of feathers, two legs covered with scales that are used for walking or perching, and front limbs modified into wings (p. 806)

blade thin, flattened section of a plant leaf that collects sunlight (p. 595)

blastula hollow ball of cells formed when a zygote undergoes a series of divisions (p. 661)

bone marrow soft tissue inside the cavities within bones (p. 922)

book lung organ that has layers of respiratory tissue that is used by some terrestrial arthropods for the exchange of gases (p. 717)

Bowman's capsule cup-shaped structure in the upper end of a nephron that encases the glomerulus (p. 987)

brain stem structure that connects the brain and spinal cord; includes the medulla oblongata and the pons (p. 902)

bronchus passageway leading from the trachea to a lung (p. 958)

bryophyte nonvascular plant; examples are mosses and their relatives (p. 556)

bud plant structure containing undeveloped tissue that can produce new stems and leaves (p. 589)

budding asexual process by which yeasts increase in number; process of attaching a bud to a plant to produce a new branch (pp. 533, 623)

buffer weak acid or base that can react with strong acids or bases to help prevent sharp, sudden changes in pH (p. 43)

calorie amount of energy needed to raise the temperature of 1 gram of water by 1 degree Celsius (p. 221)

Calorie term used by scientists to measure the energy stored in foods; 1000 calories (p. 971)

Calvin cycle reactions of photosynthesis in which energy from ATP and NADPH is used to build high-energy compounds such as sugars (p. 212)

cancer disorder in which some of the body's own cells lose the ability to control growth (p. 252)

canopy dense covering formed by the leafy tops of tall rain forest trees (p. 100)

capillary smallest blood vessel; brings nutrients and oxygen to the tissues and absorbs carbon dioxide and waste products (p. 947)

capillary action tendency of water to rise in a thin tube (p. 599)

capsid outer protein coat of a virus (p. 479)

carapace in crustaceans, the part of the exoskeleton that covers the cephalothorax; in turtles and tortoises, the dorsal part of the shell (pp. 721, 805)

carbohydrate compound made up of carbon, hydrogen, and oxygen atoms; major source of energy for the human body (pp. 45, 972)

carcinogen chemical compound known to cause cancer (p. 1052)

carnivore organism that obtains energy by eating animals (p. 69)

carpel innermost part of a flower that produces the female gametophytes (p. 612)

carrying capacity largest number of individuals of a population that a given environment can support (p. 122)

cartilage strong connective tissue that supports the body and is softer and more flexible than bone (pp. 773, 922)

Casparian strip waterproof strip that surrounds plant endodermis cells (p. 587)

caste group of individual insects specialized to perform particular tasks, or roles (p. 732)

catalyst substance that speeds up the rate of a chemical reaction (p. 51)

cell collection of living matter enclosed by a barrier that separates the cell from its surroundings; basic unit of all forms of life (pp. 16, 170)

cell body largest part of a typical neuron; contains the nucleus and much of the cytoplasm (p. 897)

cell culture group of cells grown in a nutrient solution from a single original cell (p. 27)

cell cycle series of events that cells go through as they grow and divide (p. 245)

cell division process by which a cell divides into two new daughter cells (p. 243)

cell fractionation technique in which cells are broken into pieces and the different cell parts are separated (p. 27)

cell-mediated immunity immunity against abnormal cells and pathogens inside living cells (p. 1038)

cell membrane thin, flexible barrier around a cell; regulates what enters and leaves the cell (p. 182)

cell specialization the process in which cells develop in different ways to perform different tasks (p. 190)

cell theory idea that all living things are composed of cells, cells are the basic units of structure and function in living things, and new cells are produced from existing cells (p. 170)

cell wall strong supporting layer around the cell membrane in plants, algae, and some bacteria (p. 182)

cellular respiration process that releases energy by breaking down glucose and other food molecules in the presence of oxygen (p. 222)

cellular slime mold slime mold whose individual cells remain separated during every phase of the mold's life cycle (p. 516)

centriole one of two tiny structures located in the cytoplasm of animal cells near the nuclear envelope (pp. 181, 246)

centromere area where the chromatids of a chromosome are attached (p. 245)

cephalization concentration of sense organs and nerve cells at the front of an animal's body (pp. 663, 748)

cephalothorax region of a crustacean formed by the fusion of the head with the thorax (p. 721)

GLOSSARY

cerebellum region of the brain that coordinates body movements (pp. 777, 902)

cerebral cortex outer layer of the cerebrum of a mammal's brain; center of thinking and other complex behaviors (p. 825)

cerebrospinal fluid fluid in the space between the meninges that acts as a shock absorber that protects the central nervous system (p. 901)

cerebrum area of the brain responsible for all voluntary activities of the body (pp. 777, 902)

chelicerae pair of mouthparts in chelicerates that contain fangs and are used to stab and paralyze prey (p. 722)

cheliped one of the first pair of legs of decapods (p. 721)

chemical reaction process that changes one set of chemicals into another set of chemicals (p. 49)

chemoautotroph organism that makes organic carbon molecules from carbon dioxide using energy from chemical reactions (p. 474)

chemoheterotroph organism that must take in organic molecules for both energy and carbon (p. 473)

chemosynthesis process by which some organisms, such as certain bacteria, use chemical energy to produce carbohydrates (p. 68)

chitin complex carbohydrate that makes up the cell walls of fungi; also found in the external skeletons of arthropods (pp. 527, 715)

chlorophyll principal pigment of plants and other photosynthetic organisms; captures light energy (p. 207)

chloroplast organelle found in cells of plants and some other organisms that captures the energy from sunlight and converts it into chemical energy (p. 180)

choanocyte specialized cell in sponges that uses a flagellum to move a steady current of water through the sponge (p. 665)

chordate member of the phylum Chordata; animal that has, for at least some stage of its life, a dorsal hollow nerve cord, a notochord, pharyngeal pouches, and a muscular tail (p. 767)

chromatid one of two identical "sister" parts of a duplicated chromosome (p. 244)

chromatin granular material visible within the nucleus; consists of DNA tightly coiled around proteins (pp. 176, 296)

chromosome threadlike structure within the nucleus containing the genetic information that is passed from one generation of cells to the next (p. 176)

chyme mixture of stomach fluids and food produced in the stomach by contracting stomach muscles (p. 981)

cilium short hairlike projection similar to a flagellum; produces movement in many cells (p. 501)

circadian rhythm behavioral cycle that occurs in a daily pattern (p. 878)

cladogram diagram that shows the evolutionary relationships among a group of organisms (p. 453)

class group of similar orders (p. 449)

classical conditioning learning process in which an animal makes a mental connection between a stimulus and some kind of reward or punishment (p. 874)

climate average, year-after-year conditions of temperature and precipitation in a particular region (p. 87)

clitellum band of thickened, specialized segments in annelids that secretes a mucous ring into which eggs and sperm are released (p. 696)

cloaca a muscular cavity at the end of the large intestine through which digestive wastes, urine, and eggs or sperm leave the body (p. 748)

clone member of a population of genetically identical cells produced from a single cell (p. 333)

closed circulatory system system in which blood is contained within a network of blood vessels (pp. 695, 754)

cnidocyte stinging cell of cnidarians; used for defense and to capture prey (p. 669)

coastal ocean marine zone that extends from the low-tide mark to the end of the continental shelf (p. 110)

coccus spherical prokaryote (p. 473)

cochlea fluid-filled part of the inner ear; sends nerve impulses to the brain through the cochlear nerve (p. 908)

codominance situation in which both alleles of a gene contribute to the phenotype of the organism (p. 272)

codon three-nucleotide sequence on messenger RNA that codes for a single amino acid (p. 302)

coelom fluid-filled body cavity lined with mesoderm (pp. 683, 749)

coevolution process by which two species evolve in response to changes in each other (p. 437)

cohesion attraction between molecules of the same substance (p. 41)

collenchyma type of ground tissue cell with a strong, flexible cell wall; helps support larger plants (p. 582)

commensalism symbiotic relationship in which one member of the association benefits and the other is neither helped nor harmed (p. 93)

common descent principle that all living things were derived from common ancestors (p. 382)

communication passing of information from one organism to another (p. 881)

community assemblage of different populations that live together in a defined area (p. 64)

companion cell phloem cell that surrounds sieve tube elements (p. 581)

competitive exclusion principle ecological rule that states that no two species can occupy the same exact niche in the same habitat at the same time (p. 92)

complete metamorphosis type of insect development in which the larvae look and act nothing like their parents and also feed in completely different ways (p. 729)

compound substance formed by the chemical combination of two or more elements in definite proportions (p. 37)

compound light microscope microscope that allows light to pass through a specimen and uses two lenses to form an image (p. 26)

concentration the mass of solute in a given volume of solution, or mass/volume (p. 183)

cone in gymnosperms, a seed-bearing structure; in the retina of the eye, a photoreceptor that responds to light of different colors, producing color vision (pp. 564, 907)

conidium tiny fungal spore that forms at the tips of specialized hyphae in ascomycetes (p. 532)

coniferous term used to refer to trees that produce seed-bearing cones and have thin leaves shaped like needles (p. 103)

conjugation form of sexual reproduction in which paramecia and some prokaryotes exchange genetic information (pp. 475, 502)

connective tissue tissue that holds organs in place and binds different parts of the body together (p. 894)

conservation wise management of natural resources, including the preservation of habitats and wildlife (p. 154)

consumer organism that relies on other organisms for its energy and food supply; also called a heterotroph (p. 68)

contractile vacuole cavity in the cytoplasm of some protists that collects water and discharges it from the cell (p. 502)

controlled experiment a test of the effect of a single variable by changing it while keeping all other variables the same (p. 9)

controlled variable factor in an experiment that a scientist purposely keeps the same (p. 1062)

convergent evolution process by which unrelated organisms independently evolve similarities when adapting to similar environments (p. 437)

coral reef diverse and productive environment named for the coral animals that make up its primary structure (p. 111)

cork cambium lateral meristematic tissue that produces the outer covering of stems (p. 591)

corpus luteum name given to a follicle after ovulation because of its yellow color (p. 1014)

cortex spongy layer of ground tissue just inside the epidermis of a root (p. 585)

cotyledon first leaf or first pair of leaves produced by the embryo of a seed plant (p. 570)

courtship type of behavior in which an animal sends out stimuli in order to attract a member of the opposite sex (p. 879)

covalent bond bond formed by the sharing of electrons between atoms (p. 38)

crop in earthworms, part of the digestive system in which food can be stored; in birds, structure at the lower end of the esophagus in which food is stored and moistened (pp. 695, 809)

crossing-over process in which homologous chromosomes exchange portions of their chromatids during meiosis (p. 277)

cyclin one of a family of closely related proteins that regulate the cell cycle in eukaryotic cells (p. 251)

cytokinesis division of the cytoplasm during cell division (p. 244)

cytokinin plant hormone produced in growing roots and in developing fruits and seeds (p. 636)

cytoplasm material inside the cell membrane—not including the nucleus (p. 174)

cytoskeleton network of protein filaments within some cells that helps the cell maintain its shape and is involved in many forms of cell movement (p. 181)

data evidence; information gathered from observations (pp. 4, 1057)

deciduous term used to refer to a tree that sheds its leaves during a particular season each year (p. 100)

decomposer organism that breaks down and obtains energy from dead organic matter (p. 69)

deforestation destruction of forests (p. 146)

demographic transition change in a population from high birth and death rates to low birth and death rates (p. 130)

demography scientific study of human populations (p. 130)

dendrite extension of the cell body of a neuron that carries impulses from the environment or from other neurons toward the cell body (p. 898)

denitrification conversion of nitrates into nitrogen gas (p. 78)

density-dependent limiting factor limiting factor that depends on population size (p. 125)

density-independent limiting factor limiting factor that affects all populations in similar ways, regardless of population size (p. 127)

deoxyribonucleic acid (DNA) nucleic acid that contains the sugar deoxyribose (p. 47)

dependent variable factor in an experiment that a scientist wants to observe, which may change because of the manipulated variable; also known as a responding variable (p. 1062)

depressant drug that decreases the rate of functions regulated by the brain (p. 911)

derived character characteristic that appears in recent parts of a lineage, but not in its older members (p. 453)

dermis inner layer of the skin (p. 935)

descent with modification principle that each living species has descended, with changes, from other species over time (p. 381)

desertification in areas with dry climates, a process caused by a combination of poor farming practices, overgrazing, and drought that turns productive land into desert (p. 145)

detritivore organism that feeds on plant and animal remains and other dead matter (p. 69)

detritus particles of organic material that provide food for organisms at the base of an estuary's food web (p. 108)

GLOSSARY

deuterostome animal whose anus is formed from the blastopore of a blastula (p. 661)

diabetes mellitus condition that occurs when the pancreas produces too little insulin, resulting in an increase in the level of blood glucose (p. 1007)

diaphragm large, flat muscle at the bottom of the chest cavity that helps with breathing (pp. 824, 959)

dicot angiosperm whose seeds have two cotyledons (p. 570)

differentiation process in which cells become specialized in structure and function (pp. 312, 583, 1017)

diffusion process by which molecules tend to move from an area where they are more concentrated to an area where they are less concentrated (p. 184)

diploid term used to refer to a cell that contains both sets of homologous chromosomes (p. 275)

directional selection form of natural selection in which the entire curve moves; occurs when individuals at one end of a distribution curve have higher fitness than individuals in the middle or at the other end of the curve (p. 398)

disease any change, other than an injury, that disrupts the normal functions of the body (p. 1031)

disruptive selection form of natural selection in which a single curve splits into two; occurs when individuals at the upper and lower ends of a distribution curve have higher fitness than individuals near the middle (p. 399)

DNA fingerprinting analysis of sections of DNA that have little or no known function, but vary widely from one individual to another, in order to identify individuals (p. 357)

DNA polymerase enzyme involved in DNA replication that joins individual nucleotides to produce a DNA molecule (p. 299)

domain most inclusive taxonomic category; larger than a kingdom (p. 458)

dormancy period of time during which a plant embryo is alive but not growing (pp. 620, 641)

double fertilization fertilization in angiosperms, in which two distinct fertilization events take place between the male and female gametophytes (p. 616)

drug any substance, other than food, that causes a change in the structure or function of the body (p. 910)

drug abuse intentional misuse of any drug for nonmedical purposes (p. 914)

E

ecological pyramid diagram that shows the relative amounts of energy or matter within each trophic level in a food chain or food web (p. 72)

ecological succession gradual change in living communities that follows a disturbance (p. 94)

ecology scientific study of interactions among organisms and between organisms and their environment (p. 63)

ecosystem collection of all the organisms that live in a particular place, together with their nonliving environment (p. 64)

ecosystem diversity variety of habitats, living communities, and ecological processes in the living world (p. 150)

ectoderm outermost germ layer of most animals; gives rise to outer layer of the skin, sense organs, and nerves (p. 661)

ectotherm animal that relies on interactions with the environment to help it control body temperature (pp. 800, 855)

electron negatively charged particle; located outside the atomic nucleus (p. 35)

electron microscope microscope that forms an image by focusing beams of electrons onto a specimen (p. 26)

electron transport chain a series of proteins in which the high-energy electrons from the Krebs cycle are used to convert ADP into ATP (p. 228)

element substance consisting entirely of one type of atom (p. 36)

embryo organism in its early stage of development (p. 565)

embryo sac female gametophyte within the ovule of a flowering plant (p. 615)

emigration movement of individuals out of an area (p. 120)

emphysema disease in which the tissues of the lungs lose elasticity, making breathing very difficult (p. 962)

endangered species species whose population size is rapidly declining and will become extinct if the trend continues (p. 151)

endocrine gland gland that releases its secretions directly into the bloodstream (p. 998)

endocytosis process by which a cell takes material into the cell by infolding of the cell membrane (p. 189)

endoderm innermost germ layer of most animals; develops into the linings of the digestive tract and much of the respiratory system (p. 661)

endodermis layer of cells that completely encloses vascular tissue (p. 585)

endoplasmic reticulum internal membrane system in cells in which lipid components of the cell membrane are assembled and some proteins are modified (p. 177)

endoskeleton structural support located inside the body of an animal (pp. 734, 757)

endosperm food-rich tissue that nourishes a seedling as it grows (p. 616)

endospore type of spore formed when a bacterium produces a thick internal wall that encloses its DNA and a portion of its cytoplasm (p. 475)

endosymbiotic theory theory that eukaryotic cells formed from a symbiosis among several different prokaryotic organisms (p. 427)

endotherm animal that generates its own body heat and controls its body temperature from within (pp. 808, 855)

enzyme protein that acts as a biological catalyst (p. 51)

epidermal cell cell that makes up the dermal tissue, which is the outer covering of a plant (p. 580)

epidermis outer layer of the skin (p. 934)

epididymis structure in the male reproductive system in which sperm fully mature and are stored (p. 1011)

epiphyte plant that is not rooted in soil but instead grows directly on the body of another plant (p. 645)

epithelial tissue tissue that covers the surface of the body and lines internal organs (p. 894)

equilibrium when the concentration of a solute is the same throughout a solution (p. 184)

era one of several subdivisions of the time between the Precambrian and the present (p. 421)

esophagus food tube connecting the mouth to the stomach (p. 980)

estuary wetlands formed where rivers meet the ocean (p. 108)

ethylene plant hormone that stimulates fruits to ripen (p. 638)

Eubacteria kingdom of unicellular prokaryotes whose cell walls are made up of peptidoglycan (p. 459)

Eukarya domain of all organisms whose cells have nuclei, including protists, plants, fungi, and animals (p. 460)

eukaryote organism whose cells contain nuclei (p. 173)

evaporation process by which water changes from a liquid into an atmospheric gas (p. 75)

evolution change in a kind of organism over time; process by which modern organisms have descended from ancient organisms (pp. 20, 369)

evolutionary classification method of grouping organisms together according to their evolutionary history (p. 452)

exocrine gland gland that releases its secretions through tubelike structures called ducts (p. 998)

exocytosis process by which a cell releases large amounts of material (p. 189)

exon expressed sequence of DNA; codes for a protein (p. 302)

exoskeleton external skeleton; tough external covering that protects and supports the body of many invertebrates (pp. 715, 757)

exponential growth growth pattern in which the individuals in a population reproduce at a constant rate (p. 121)

external fertilization process in which eggs are fertilized outside the female's body (pp. 672, 758)

extinct term used to refer to a species that has died out (p. 417)

extinction disappearance of a species from all parts of its geographical range (p. 151)

extracellular digestion process in which food is broken down outside the cells in a digestive tract (p. 751)

eyespot group of cells that can detect changes in the amount of light in the environment (pp. 507, 685)

facilitated diffusion movement of specific molecules across cell membranes through protein channels (p. 187)

facultative anaerobe organism that can survive with or without oxygen (p. 474)

Fallopian tube one of two fluid-filled tubes in human females through which an egg passes after its release from an ovary (p. 1012)

family group of genera that share many characteristics (p. 449)

fat lipid; made up of fatty acids and glycerol; protects body organs, insulates body, and stores energy in the body (p. 972)

feather structure made mostly of protein that develops from a pit in a bird's skin (p. 806)

feedback inhibition process in which the product or result stops or limits the process (pp. 658, 895)

fermentation process by which cells release energy in the absence of oxygen (p. 224)

fertilization process in sexual reproduction in which male and female reproductive cells join to form a new cell (p. 263)

fetal alcohol syndrome group of birth defects caused by the effects of alcohol on a fetus (p. 913)

fetus name given to a human embryo after eight weeks of development (p. 1020)

fever elevated body temperature that occurs in response to infection (p. 1037)

fibrous root part of a root system in which roots branch to such an extent that no single root grows larger than the rest (p. 584)

filament in algae, a long threadlike colony formed by many green algae; in plants, a long, thin structure that supports an anther (pp. 512, 612)

filtration process by which a liquid or gas passes through a filter to remove wastes (p. 987)

fish aquatic vertebrate characterized by paired fins, scales, and gills (p. 771)

fission form of asexual reproduction in which an organism splits into two, and each half grows new parts to become a complete organism (p. 686)

fitness ability of an organism to survive and reproduce in its environment (p. 380)

flame cell specialized cell that filters and removes excess water from the body of a flatworm (p. 684)

flower seed-bearing structure of an angiosperm (p. 564)

follicle cluster of cells surrounding a single egg in the human female reproductive system (p. 1012)

food chain series of steps in an ecosystem in which organisms transfer energy by eating and being eaten (p. 69)

food vacuole small cavity in the cytoplasm of protists that temporarily stores food (p. 500)

food web network of complex interactions formed by the feeding relationships among the various organisms in an ecosystem (p. 70)

foot muscular part of a mollusk (p. 702)

fossil preserved remains or evidence of an ancient organism (p. 371)

fossil record information about past life, including the structure of organisms, what they ate, what ate them, in what environment they lived, and the order in which they lived (p. 417)

founder effect change in allele frequencies as a result of the migration of a small subgroup of a population (p. 400)

frameshift mutation mutation that shifts the "reading" frame of the genetic message by inserting or deleting a nucleotide (p. 307)

frond large leaf of a fern (p. 562)

fruit wall of tissue surrounding an angiosperm seed (p. 569)

fruiting body slender reproductive structure that produces spores and is found in some funguslike protists; reproductive structure of fungus that develops from a mycelium (pp. 516, 528)

Fungi kingdom composed of heterotrophs; many obtain energy and nutrients from dead organic matter (p. 460)

gametangium gamete-producing structure found in mold (p. 530)

gamete specialized cell involved in sexual reproduction (p. 266)

gametophyte haploid, or gamete-producing, phase of an organism (pp. 514, 552)

ganglion group of nerve cells (p. 685)

gastrovascular cavity digestive chamber with a single opening, in which cnidarians, flatworms, and echinoderms digest food (p. 671)

gastrulation process of cell migration by which a third layer of cells is formed within the cavity of a blastocyst (p. 1018)

gel electrophoresis procedure used to separate and analyze DNA fragments by placing a mixture of DNA fragments at one end of a porous gel and applying an electrical voltage to the gel (p. 323)

gemma small cup-shaped structure in liverworts that contains many haploid cells; used for asexual reproduction (p. 557)

gemmule group of archaeocytes surrounded by a tough layer of spicules; produced by some sponges (p. 667)

gene sequence of DNA that codes for a protein and thus determines a trait (pp. 265, 300)

gene map diagram showing the relative locations of each known gene on a particular chromosome (p. 280)

gene pool combined genetic information of all the members of a particular population (p. 394)

genetic diversity sum total of all the different forms of genetic information carried by all organisms living on Earth today (p. 150)

genetic drift random change in allele frequencies that occurs in small populations (p. 400)

genetic engineering process of making changes in the DNA code of living organisms (p. 322)

genetic equilibrium situation in which allele frequencies remain constant (p. 401)

genetic marker gene that makes it possible to distinguish bacteria that carry a plasmid with foreign DNA from those that don't (p. 328)

genetics scientific study of heredity (p. 263)

genotype genetic makeup of an organism (p. 268)

genus group of closely related species, and the first part of the scientific name in binomial nomenclature (p. 448)

geographic isolation form of reproductive isolation in which two populations are separated physically by geographic barriers such as rivers, mountains, or stretches of water (p. 405)

geologic time scale scale used by paleontologists to represent evolutionary time (p. 421)

germ theory of disease idea that infectious diseases are caused by microorganisms, or germs (p. 1031)

germination early growth stage of a plant embryo (p. 621)

gibberellin growth-promoting substance produced by plants (p. 637)

gill filamentous organ in aquatic animals specialized for the exchange of gases with water (p. 696)

gizzard in earthworms, part of the digestive system in which food is ground into smaller pieces; in birds, a muscular organ that helps in the mechanical breakdown of food (pp. 695, 809)

global warming increase in the average temperatures on Earth (p. 159)

glomerulus small network of capillaries encased in the upper end of a nephron; where the filtration of blood takes place (p. 987)

glycolysis first step in releasing the energy of glucose, in which a molecule of glucose is broken into two molecules of pyruvic acid (p. 221)

Golgi apparatus stack of membranes in the cell that modifies, sorts, and packages proteins from the endoplasmic reticulum (p. 178)

grafting use of a stem as a scion (p. 623)

gravitropism response of a plant to the force of gravity (p. 635)

greenhouse effect natural situation in which heat is retained in Earth's atmosphere by carbon dioxide, methane, water vapor, and other gases (p. 87)

green revolution the development of highly productive crop strains and the use of modern agricultural techniques to increase yields of food crops (p. 142)

guard cell specialized cell in the epidermis of plants that controls the opening and closing of stomata by responding to changes in water pressure (p. 596)

gullet indentation in one side of a ciliate that allows food to enter the cell (p. 502)

gymnosperm seed plant that bears its seeds directly on the surfaces of cones (p. 564)

habitat the area where an organism lives, including the biotic and abiotic factors that affect it (p. 90)

habitat fragmentation splitting of ecosystems into small fragments (p. 151)

habituation learning process by which an animal decreases or stops its response to a repetitive stimulus that neither rewards nor harms it (p. 874)

hair follicle tubelike pocket of epidermal cells that extends into the dermis; cells at the base of hair follicles produce hair (p. 936)

half-life length of time required for half of the radioactive atoms in a sample to decay (p. 420)

haploid term used to refer to a cell that contains only a single set of chromosomes and therefore only a single set of genes (p. 275)

Hardy-Weinberg principle principle that allele frequencies in a population will remain constant unless one or more factors cause the frequencies to change (p. 400)

Haversian canal one of a network of tubes running through compact bone that contains blood vessels and nerves (p. 922)

heartwood older xylem near the center of a woody stem that no longer conducts water (p. 592)

hemoglobin iron-containing protein in red blood cells that transports oxygen from the lungs to the tissues of the body (p. 952)

herbicide compound that is toxic to plants (p. 636)

herbivore organism that obtains energy by eating only plants (p. 69)

hermaphrodite individual that has both male and female reproductive organs (p. 686)

heterotroph organism that obtains energy from the foods it consumes; also called a consumer (pp. 68, 201)

heterozygous term used to refer to an organism that has two different alleles for the same trait (p. 268)

histamine chemical released by activated mast cells that increases the flow of blood and fluids to the surrounding area (p. 1043)

histone protein molecule around which DNA is tightly coiled in chromatin (p. 296)

homeostasis process by which organisms maintain a relatively stable internal environment (pp. 16, 895)

hominid primate that walks upright, has opposable thumbs, and possesses a large brain; only living members are humans (p. 835)

hominoid anthropoid group that includes apes and humans (p. 835)

homologous term used to refer to chromosomes that each have a corresponding chromosome from the opposite-sex parent (p. 275)

homologous structures structures that have different mature forms in different organisms but develop from the same embryonic tissues (p. 384)

homozygous term used to refer to an organism that has two identical alleles for a particular trait (p. 268)

hormone substance produced in one part of an organism that affects another part of the same organism (pp. 634, 997)

hox genes series of genes that controls the differentiation of cells and tissues in an embryo (p. 312)

humoral immunity immunity against antigens and pathogens in the body fluids (p. 1038)

humus material formed from decaying leaves and other organic matter (p. 103)

hybrid offspring of crosses between parents with different traits (p. 264)

hybridization breeding technique that involves crossing dissimilar individuals to bring together the best traits of both organisms (p. 319)

hydrostatic skeleton layers of circular and longitudinal muscles, together with the water in the gastrovascular cavity, that enable movement (pp. 671, 756)

hypertonic when comparing two solutions, the solution with the greater concentration of solutes (p. 185)

hypha tiny filament that makes up a multicellular fungus or a water mold (pp. 518, 527)

hypothalamus brain structure that acts as a control center for recognition and analysis of hunger, thirst, fatigue, anger, and body temperature (p. 903)

hypothesis possible explanation for a set of observations or possible answer to a scientific question (pp. 5, 1062)

hypotonic when comparing two solutions, the solution with the lesser concentration of solutes (p. 185)

immigration movement of individuals into an area occupied by an existing population (p. 120)

immune response the body's specific defenses that attack a disease-causing agent (p. 1038)

immunity ability of the body to resist a specific pathogen (p. 1036)

implantation process in which a blastocyst attaches itself to the wall of the uterus (p. 1017)

imprinting learning based on early experience; once imprinting has occurred, the behavior cannot be changed (p. 876)

inbreeding continued breeding of individuals with similar characteristics to maintain the desired characteristics of a line of organisms (p. 320)

incomplete dominance situation in which one allele is not completely dominant over another (p. 272)

incomplete metamorphosis type of insect development characterized by a similar appearance throughout all stages of the life cycle (p. 729)

independent assortment independent segregation of genes during the formation of gametes (p. 271)

independent variable factor in an experiment that a scientist purposely changes; also known as a manipulated variable (p. 1062)

index fossil distinctive fossil used to compare the relative ages of fossils (p. 419)

inference logical interpretation based on prior knowledge and experience (p. 4)

inflammatory response nonspecific defense reaction to tissue damage caused by injury or infection (p. 1037)

innate behavior instinct, or inborn behavior; behavior that appears in a fully functional form the first time it is performed (p. 873)

Glossary

insight learning also called reasoning; learning process in which an animal applies something it has already learned to a new situation without a period of trial and error (p. 875)

interferon one of a group of proteins that help cells resist viral infection (p. 1038)

internal fertilization process in which eggs are fertilized inside the female's body (pp. 666, 758)

internode region between nodes on plant stems (p. 589)

interphase period of the cell cycle between cell divisions (p. 245)

intracellular digestion process in which food is digested inside cells (p. 751)

intron sequence of DNA that is not involved in coding for a protein (p. 302)

invasive species plants and animals that have migrated to places where they are not native (p. 153)

invertebrate animal that does not have a backbone, or vertebral column (p. 657)

ion atom that has a positive or negative charge (p. 38)

ionic bond bond formed when one or more electrons are transferred from one atom to another (p. 38)

isotonic when the concentration of two solutions is the same (p. 185)

isotope atom of an element that has a number of neutrons different from that of other atoms of the same element (p. 36)

joint place where one bone attaches to another (p. 924)

karyotype photograph of chromosomes grouped in order in pairs (p. 341)

kelp forest coastal ocean community named for its dominant organism—kelp, a giant brown alga (p. 110)

keratin tough, fibrous protein found in skin (p. 934)

kidney organ that removes urea, excess water, and other waste products from the blood (p. 986)

kingdom large taxonomic group, consisting of closely related phyla (p. 449)

Koch's postulates series of guidelines used to identify the microorganism that causes a specific disease (p. 1032)

Krebs cycle second stage of cellular respiration, in which pyruvic acid is broken down into carbon dioxide in a series of energy-extracting reactions (p. 226)

language system of communication that combines sounds, symbols, or gestures according to a set of rules about word order and meaning (p. 882)

large intestine colon; organ that removes water from the undigested materials that pass through it (p. 984)

larva immature stage of an organism that looks different from the adult form (p. 666)

larynx structure in the throat containing the vocal cords (p. 958)

lateral bud meristematic area on the side of a stem that gives rise to side branches (p. 636)

lateral line system sensitive receptor system that enables fish to detect gentle currents and vibrations in the water (p. 777)

leaf photosynthetic organ that contains one or more bundles of vascular tissue (p. 561)

learning alterations in behavior as a result of experience; also called acquired behavior (p. 873)

lens transparent object behind the iris that changes shape to help adjust the eye's focus to see near or distant objects (p. 907)

lichen symbiotic association between a fungus and a photosynthetic organism (p. 540)

ligament strip of tough connective tissue that holds bones together at a joint (p. 925)

light-dependent reactions reactions of photosynthesis that use energy from light to produce ATP and NADPH (p. 210)

lignin substance in vascular plants that makes cell walls rigid (p. 560)

limiting factor factor that causes the growth of a population to decrease (p. 124)

limiting nutrient single nutrient that either is scarce or cycles very slowly, limiting the growth of organisms in an ecosystem (p. 80)

lipid macromolecule made mainly from carbon and hydrogen atoms; includes fats, oils, and waxes (p. 46)

lipid bilayer double-layered sheet that forms the core of nearly all cell membranes (p. 182)

liver large organ just above the stomach that produces bile (p. 982)

logistic growth growth pattern in which a population's growth rate slows or stops following a period of exponential growth (p. 122)

long-day plant plant that flowers when days are long (p. 641)

loop of Henle section of the nephron tubule that conserves water and minimizes the volume of urine (p. 987)

lymph fluid lost by the blood into surrounding tissue (p. 954)

lymphocyte type of white blood cell that produces antibodies that help destroy pathogens (p. 952)

lysogenic infection process by which a virus embeds its DNA into the DNA of the host cell and is replicated along with the host cell's DNA (p. 480)

lysosome cell organelle filled with enzymes needed to break down certain materials in the cell (p. 179)

lytic infection process in which a virus enters a cell, makes a copy of itself, and causes the cell to burst (p. 480)

macroevolution large-scale evolutionary changes that take place over long periods of time (p. 435)

macronucleus the larger of a ciliate's two nuclei, contains multiple copies of most of the genes that the cell needs in its day-to-day existence (p. 501)

madreporite sievelike structure through which the water vascular system of an echinoderm opens to the outside (p. 735)

Malpighian tubule saclike organ in most terrestrial arthropods that extracts wastes from the blood, adding them to feces that move through the gut (p. 717)

mammary gland gland in mammals that produces milk to nourish the young (p. 821)

mandible mouthpart adapted for biting and grinding food (p. 721)

mangrove swamp coastal wetland dominated by mangroves, salt-tolerant woody plants (p. 108)

manipulated variable factor in an experiment that a scientist purposely changes; also known as independent variable (pp. 9, 1062)

mantle thin layer of tissue that covers most of a mollusk's body (p. 702)

marsupial mammal which bears live young that complete their development in an external pouch (p. 829)

mass extinction event in which many types of living things become extinct at the same time (p. 431)

medulla oblongata area of the brain that controls the functioning of many internal organs (p. 777)

medusa motile stage of the life cycle of a cnidarian that has a bell-shaped body (p. 670)

meiosis process by which the number of chromosomes per cell is cut in half through the separation of homologous chromosomes in a diploid cell (p. 276)

melanin dark-brown pigment found in skin (p. 934)

meninges three layers of connective tissue in which the brain and spinal cord are wrapped (p. 901)

menstrual cycle cycle during which an egg develops and is released from an ovary and the uterus is prepared to receive a fertilized egg (p. 1013)

menstruation phase of the menstrual cycle during which the lining of the uterus, along with blood and the unfertilized egg, is discharged through the vagina (p. 1014)

meristem cluster of tissue that is responsible for continuing growth throughout a plant's lifetime (p. 582)

meristematic tissue plant tissue found only in the tips of shoots and roots; responsible for plant growth (p. 582)

mesoderm middle germ layer of most animals; gives rise to muscles and much of the circulatory, reproductive, and excretory systems (p. 661)

mesophyll specialized ground tissue that makes up the bulk of most leaves; performs most of a plant's photosynthesis (p. 596)

messenger RNA (mRNA) RNA molecule that carries copies of instructions for the assembly of amino acids into proteins from DNA to the rest of the cell (p. 301)

metabolism set of chemical reactions through which an organism builds up or breaks down materials as it carries out its life processes (p. 17)

metaphase second phase of mitosis, during which the chromosomes line up across the center of the cell (p. 248)

metric system decimal system of measurement based on certain physical standards and scaled on multiples of 10 (p. 24)

microclimate climate within a small area that differs significantly from the climate of the surrounding area (p. 98)

microfossil microscopic fossil (p. 426)

micronucleus the smaller of a ciliate's two nuclei; contains a "reserve copy" of all of the cell's genes (p. 501)

microscope device that produces magnified images of structures that are too small to see with the unaided eye (p. 25)

migration periodic movement and return of animals from one place to another (p. 878)

mineral inorganic nutrient the body needs, usually in small amounts (p. 975)

mitochondrion cell organelle that converts the chemical energy stored in food into compounds that are more convenient for the cell to use (p. 179)

mitosis part of eukaryotic cell division during which the cell nucleus divides (p. 244)

mixture material composed of two or more elements or compounds that are physically mixed together but not chemically combined (p. 41)

molecular clock model that uses DNA comparisons to estimate the length of time that two species have been evolving independently (p. 455)

molecule smallest unit of most compounds (p. 38)

molting process in which an arthropod sheds its exoskeleton and manufactures a larger one to take its place (p. 719)

monocot angiosperm whose seeds have one cotyledon (p. 570)

monoculture farming strategy in which large fields are planted with a single crop, year after year (p. 141)

monomer small unit that can join together with other small units to form polymers (p. 45)

monosaccharide single sugar molecule (p. 46)

monotreme egg-laying mammal (p. 828)

multiple alleles three or more alleles of the same gene (p. 273)

muscle tissue tissue that controls the internal movement of materials in the body, as well as external movement (p. 894)

mutation change in a DNA sequence that affects genetic information (p. 307)

mutualism symbiotic relationship in which both species benefit from the relationship (p. 93)

mycelium many hyphae tangled together into a thick mass; comprises the bodies of multicellular fungi (p. 528)

mycorrhiza symbiotic association of plant roots and fungi (p. 541)

myelin sheath insulating membrane surrounding the axon in some neurons (p. 898)

myocardium thick middle muscle layer of the heart; pumps blood through the circulatory system (p. 944)

myosin protein that makes up the thick filaments in striations in skeletal muscle cells (p. 928)

NAD$^+$ (nicotinamide adenine dinucleotide) electron carrier involved in glycolysis (p. 223)

NADP$^+$ (nicotinamide adenine dinucleotide phosphate) one of the carrier molecules that transfers high-energy electrons from chlorophyll to other molecules (p. 209)

natural selection process by which individuals that are better suited to their environment survive and reproduce most successfully; also called survival of the fittest (p. 381)

nematocyst stinging structure within each cnidocyte of a cnidarian that is used to poison or kill prey (p. 669)

nephridium excretory organ of an annelid that filters fluid in the coelom (p. 696)

nephron blood-filtering unit in the renal cortex of the kidney (p. 986)

nerve net loosely organized network of nerve cells that together allow cnidarians to detect stimuli (p. 671)

nervous tissue tissue that receives messages from the body's external and internal environment, analyzes the data, and directs the response (p. 894)

neuromuscular junction point of contact between a motor neuron and a skeletal muscle cell (p. 929)

neuron cell that carries messages throughout the nervous system (p. 897)

neurotransmitter chemical used by a neuron to transmit an impulse across a synapse to another cell (p. 900)

neurulation development of the nervous system (p. 1018)

niche full range of physical and biological conditions in which an organism lives and the way in which the organism uses those conditions (p. 91)

nicotine stimulant drug in tobacco that increases heart rate and blood pressure (p. 961)

nictitating membrane movable transparent membrane in amphibians located inside the regular eyelid; protects the surface of the eye from damage under water and keeps it moist on land (p. 787)

nitrogen fixation process of converting nitrogen gas into ammonia (pp. 78, 477)

node point on a stem where a leaf is attached (p. 589)

nondisjunction error in meiosis in which homologous chromosomes fail to separate (p. 352)

nonrenewable resource resource that cannot be replenished by natural processes (p. 144)

notochord long supporting rod that runs through a chordate's body just below the nerve cord (pp. 767, 849)

nuclear envelope layer of two membranes that surrounds the nucleus of a cell (p. 176)

nucleic acid macromolecule containing hydrogen, oxygen, nitrogen, carbon, and phosphorus (p. 47)

nucleolus small, dense region within most nuclei in which the assembly of proteins begins (p. 176)

nucleotide monomer of nucleic acids made up of a 5-carbon sugar, a phosphate group, and a nitrogenous base (pp. 47, 291)

nucleus the center of the atom which contains the protons and neutrons; in cells, structure that contains the cell's genetic material (DNA) and controls the cell's activities (pp. 35, 173)

nutrient chemical substance that an organism requires to live (p. 76)

nymph immature form that lacks functional sex organs and other adult structures (p. 729)

obligate aerobe organism that requires a constant supply of oxygen in order to live (p. 474)

obligate anaerobe organism that cannot live in the presence of oxygen (p. 474)

observation use of one or more of the senses—sight, hearing, touch, smell, and sometimes taste—to gather information (p. 4)

omnivore organism that obtains energy by eating both plants and animals (p. 69)

oogonium specialized structure formed by hyphae that produces female nuclei (p. 519)

open circulatory system system in which blood is not always contained within a network of blood vessels (pp. 703, 754)

operant conditioning learning process in which an animal learns to behave in a certain way through repeated practice, in order to receive a reward or avoid punishment; also called trial-and-error learning (p. 875)

operational definition description of how a particular variable is to be measured or how a term is to be defined (p. 1063)

operator region of chromosome in an operon to which the repressor binds when the operon is "turned off" (p. 310)

operon group of genes operating together (p. 309)

opposable thumb thumb that enables grasping objects and using tools (p. 835)

order group of similar families (p. 449)

organ group of tissues that work together to perform closely related functions (p. 193)

organ system group of organs that work together to perform a specific function (p. 193)

organelle specialized structure that performs important cellular functions within a eukaryotic cell (p. 174)

osculum large hole at the top of the sponge through which water leaves the sponge (p. 665)

osmosis diffusion of water through a selectively permeable membrane (p. 185)

ossification process of bone formation, during which cartilage is replaced by bone (p. 923)

ovary in plants, a flower structure that contains one or more ovules from which female gametophytes are produced; in animals, the female gonad that produces eggs (pp. 612, 1008)

oviparous term used to refer to animals whose eggs hatch outside the mother's body (p. 778)

ovoviviparous term used to refer to animals whose young are born alive after developing in eggs inside the mother's body (p. 778)

ovulation process in which an egg is released from the ovary (p. 1012)

ovule structure in seed cones in which female gametophytes develop (p. 610)

ozone layer atmospheric layer in which ozone gas is relatively concentrated (p. 157)

pacemaker small group of cardiac muscle cells in the right atrium that "set the pace" for the heart as a whole; also known as the sinoatrial node (p. 946)

paleontologist scientist who studies fossils (p. 417)

palisade mesophyll layer of tall, column-shaped mesophyll cells just under the upper epidermis of a leaf (p. 596)

pancreas gland that produces hormones that regulate blood sugar; produces enzymes that break down carbohydrates, proteins, lipids, and nucleic acids; and produces sodium bicarbonate, a base that neutralizes stomach acid (p. 981)

parasitism symbiotic relationship in which one organism lives in or on another organism (the host) and consequently harms it (p. 93)

parenchyma type of ground-tissue cell with a thin cell wall and large central vacuole (p. 582)

passive immunity short-term immunity caused when antibodies produced by other animals for a pathogen are injected into the body (p. 1042)

pathogen disease-causing agent (pp. 485, 1031)

pedigree chart that shows the relationships within a family (p. 342)

pedipalps pair of mouthparts in chelicerates that are usually modified to grab prey (p. 722)

pellicle cell membrane in euglenas (p. 507)

penis external male reproductive organ (p. 1011)

perennial flowering plant that lives for more than two years (p. 572)

period unit of time into which eras are subdivided (p. 422)

periosteum tough layer of connective tissue surrounding a bone (p. 922)

peristalsis rhythmic muscular contractions that squeeze food through the esophagus into the stomach (p. 980)

permafrost layer of permanently frozen subsoil in the tundra (p. 104)

petal brightly colored structure just inside the sepals; attracts insects and other pollinators to a flower (p. 612)

petiole thin stalk by which a leaf blade is attached to a stem (p. 595)

pH scale measurement system used to indicate the concentration of hydrogen ions (H^+) in solution; ranges from 0 to 14 (p. 43)

phagocytosis process in which extensions of cytoplasm surround and engulf large particles and take them into the cell (p. 189)

pharyngeal pouch one of a pair of structures in the throat (pharynx) region of a chordate (p. 767)

pharynx muscular tube at the end of the gastrovascular cavity, or throat, that connects the mouth with the rest of the digestive tract and serves as a passageway for air and food (pp. 684, 956)

phenotype physical characteristics of an organism (p. 268)

pheromone specific chemical messenger that affects the behavior or development of other individuals of the same species (p. 731)

phloem vascular tissue responsible for the transport of nutrients and the carbohydrates produced by photosynthesis (p. 560)

photic zone well-lit upper layer of the oceans (p. 109)

photoautotroph organism that uses energy from sunlight to convert carbon dioxide and water to carbon compounds (p. 474)

photoheterotroph organism that is photosynthetic but needs organic compounds as a carbon source (p. 473)

photoperiodism response of plants to periods of light and darkness (p. 641)

photosynthesis process by which plants and some other organisms use light energy to convert water and carbon dioxide into oxygen and high-energy carbohydrates such as sugars and starches (pp. 68, 204)

photosystem light-collecting units of the chloroplast (p. 208)

phototropism tendency of plants to grow toward a source of light (p. 634)

phycobilin accessory pigment found in red algae that is especially good at absorbing blue light (p. 510)

phylogeny the study of evolutionary relationships among organisms (p. 452)

phylum group of closely related classes (p. 449)

phytochrome plant pigment responsible for photoperiodism (p. 641)

phytoplankton population of algae and other small, photosynthetic organisms found near the surface of the ocean and forming part of plankton (pp. 107, 509)

pigment light-absorbing molecule (p. 207)

pinocytosis process by which a cell takes in liquid from the surrounding environment (p. 189)

pioneer species first species to populate an area during primary succession (p. 94)

pith parenchyma cells inside the ring of vascular tissue in dicot stems (p. 590)

pituitary gland gland in the base of the skull that secretes nine hormones that directly regulate many body functions and control the actions of several other endocrine glands (p. 1003)

placenta organ in placental mammals through which nutrients, oxygen, carbon dioxide, and wastes are exchanged between embryo and mother (pp. 829, 1019)

plankton tiny, free-floating organisms that occur in aquatic environments (p. 107)

Plantae kingdom of multicellular photosynthetic autotrophs that have cell walls containing cellulose (p. 461)

plasma straw-colored fluid that makes up about 55 percent of blood (p. 951)

plasmid small circular piece of DNA (p. 327)

plasmodium structure with many nuclei formed by acellular slime molds (p. 518)

plastron ventral part of a turtle's or tortoise's shell (p. 805)

platelet cell fragment released by bone marrow that helps in blood clotting (p. 953)

point mutation gene mutation involving changes in one or a few nucleotides (p. 307)

polar zone cold climate zone where the sun's rays strike Earth at a very low angle (p. 88)

pollen cone cone in gymnosperms that produces male gametophytes in the form of pollen grains (p. 610)

pollen grain male gametophyte in seed plants (p. 565)

pollen tube structure grown by a pollen grain; contains two haploid sperm nuclei (p. 611)

pollination transfer of pollen from the male reproductive structure to the female reproductive structure (p. 565)

pollutant harmful material that can enter the biosphere through the land, air, or water (p. 148)

polygenic trait trait controlled by two or more genes (pp. 273, 396)

polymer large compound formed from combinations of many monomers (p. 45)

polymerase chain reaction (PCR) technique that allows molecular biologists to make many copies of a particular gene (p. 325)

polyp usually sessile stage of the life cycle of a cnidarian that has a cylindrical body with armlike tentacles (p. 670)

polyploidy condition in which an organism has extra sets of chromosomes (p. 308)

polysaccharide large macromolecule formed from monosaccharides (p. 46)

population group of individuals of the same species that live in the same area (p. 64)

population density number of individuals per unit of area (p. 119)

predation interaction in which one organism captures and feeds on another organism (p. 93)

predator-prey relationship mechanism of population control in which a population is regulated by predation (p. 126)

prehensile term used to refer to a long tail that can grasp branches (p. 835)

pressure-flow hypothesis hypothesis that considers plants in terms of where they produce and use materials from photosynthesis (p. 602)

primary growth type of plant growth that occurs at the tips of roots and shoots (p. 590)

primary productivity rate at which organic matter is created by producers in an ecosystem (p. 80)

primary succession succession that occurs on surfaces where no soil exists (p. 94)

prion infectious particle made up of protein rather than RNA or DNA (p. 490)

probability likelihood that a particular event will occur (p. 267)

producer organism that can capture energy from sunlight or chemicals and use it to produce food from inorganic compounds; also called an autotroph (p. 67)

product element or compound produced by a chemical reaction (p. 49)

proglottid one of the segments that make up most of a tapeworm's body (p. 688)

prokaryote unicellular organism lacking a nucleus (pp. 173, 471)

promoter region of DNA that indicates to an enzyme where to bind to make RNA (p. 301)

prophage the viral DNA that is embedded in the host cell's DNA (p. 480)

prophase first and longest phase of mitosis, during which the chromosomes become visible and the centrioles separate and take up positions on the opposite sides of the nucleus (p. 246)

prosimian small, nocturnal primate that has large eyes for seeing in the dark (p. 834)

prostaglandin hormonelike modified fatty acid produced by a wide range of cells; generally affects only nearby cells and tissues (p. 1000)

protein macromolecule that contains carbon, hydrogen, oxygen, and nitrogen; needed by the body for growth and repair and to make up enzymes (pp. 47, 973)

proteinoid microsphere tiny bubble, formed of large organic molecules, that has some characteristics of a cell (p. 425)

protist any eukaryote that is not a plant, an animal, or a fungus (p. 497)

Protista kingdom composed of eukaryotes that are not classified as plants, animals, or fungi (p. 460)

protonema mass of tangled green filaments in mosses that forms during germination (p. 558)

protostome animal whose mouth is formed from its blastopore (p. 661)

pseudocoelom body cavity between the endoderm and mesoderm tissues that is partially lined with mesoderm tissue (p. 689)

pseudopod temporary projection of cytoplasm, or a "false foot," used by some protists for feeding or movement (p. 500)

puberty period of rapid growth and sexual maturation during which the reproductive system becomes fully functional (p. 1009)

pulmonary circulation pathway of circulation between the heart and the lungs (p. 945)

punctuated equilibrium pattern of evolution in which long stable periods are interrupted by brief periods of more rapid change (p. 439)

Punnett square diagram showing the gene combinations that might result from a genetic cross (p. 268)

pupa stage of metamorphosis in which an insect changes from a larva into an adult (p. 729)

pupil small opening in the middle of the iris through which light enters the eye (p. 906)

radial symmetry body plan in which body parts repeat around the center of the body; characteristic of sea anemones and sea stars (pp. 662, 748)

radioactive dating technique in which scientists calculate the age of a sample based on the amount of remaining radioactive isotopes it contains (p. 420)

radula tongue-shaped structure used for feeding by snails and slugs (p. 702)

reabsorption process in which liquid is taken back into a vessel (p. 987)

reactant element or compound that enters into a chemical reaction (p. 49)

recombinant DNA DNA produced by combining DNA from different sources (p. 324)

reflex quick automatic response to a stimulus (p. 903)

reflex arc sensory receptor, sensory neuron, motor neuron, and effector that are involved in a quick response to a stimulus (p. 904)

relative dating method of determining the age of a fossil by comparing its placement with that of fossils in other layers of rock (p. 419)

relative frequency number of times an allele occurs in a gene pool compared with the number of times other alleles occur (p. 394)

renewable resource resource that can regenerate quickly and that is replaceable (p. 144)

replication copying process by which a cell duplicates its DNA (p. 299)

reproductive isolation separation of species or populations so that they cannot interbreed and produce fertile offspring (p. 404)

reptile any vertebrate that has dry scaly skin, lungs, and terrestrial eggs with several protective membranes (p. 797)

resource any necessity of life, such as water, nutrients, light, food, or space (p. 92)

responding variable factor in an experiment that a scientist wants to observe, which may change in response to the manipulated variable; also known as a dependent variable (pp. 9, 1062)

response single, specific reaction to a stimulus (p. 871)

resting potential electrical charge across the cell membrane of a resting neuron (p. 898)

restriction enzyme enzyme that cuts DNA at a specific sequence of nucleotides (p. 323)

retina innermost layer of the eye; contains photoreceptors (p. 907)

retrovirus virus that contains RNA as its genetic information (p. 482)

rhizoid in fungi, a rootlike hypha that penetrates the surface of an object; in mosses, a long, thin cell that anchors the moss to the ground and absorbs water and minerals from the surrounding soil (pp. 530, 557)

rhizome creeping or underground stem in ferns (p. 562)

ribonucleic acid (RNA) single-stranded nucleic acid that contains the sugar ribose (p. 47)

ribosomal RNA (rRNA) type of RNA that makes up the major part of ribosomes (p. 301)

ribosome small particle in the cell on which proteins are assembled; made of RNA and protein (p. 177)

risk factor anything that increases the chance of disease or injury (p. 1049)

RNA polymerase enzyme similar to DNA polymerase that binds to DNA and separates the DNA strands during transcription (p. 301)

rod photoreceptor in eye that is sensitive to light but not to colors (p. 907)

root underground organ in plants that absorbs water and minerals (p. 561)

root cap tough structure that protects a root as it forces its way through the soil (p. 585)

root hair tiny projection from the outer surface, or epidermis, of a root (p. 585)

rumen stomach chamber in cows and related animals in which newly swallowed plant food is stored and processed (p. 823)

salt marsh temperate-zone estuary dominated by salt-tolerant grasses above the low-tide line and by seagrasses under water (p. 108)

saprobe organism that obtains food from decaying organic matter (p. 537)

sapwood area in plants that surrounds heartwood and is active in fluid transport (p. 592)

science organized way of using evidence to learn about the natural world; also, the body of knowledge that scientists have built up after years of using this process (p. 3)

sclerenchyma type of ground-tissue cell with an extremely thick, rigid cell wall that makes ground tissue tough and strong (p. 582)

scolex head of an adult tapeworm; can contain suckers or hooks (p. 688)

scrotum external sac containing the testes (p. 1010)

secondary growth pattern of plant growth in which stems increase in width (p. 591)

secondary succession succession following a disturbance that destroys a community without destroying the soil (p. 95)

seed embryo of a living plant that is encased in a protective covering and surrounded by a food supply (p. 565)

seed coat structure that surrounds and protects a plant embryo and keeps it from drying out (p. 565)

seed cone cone that produces female gametophytes (p. 610)

GLOSSARY

segregation separation of alleles during gamete formation (p. 266)

selective breeding method of breeding that allows only those individual organisms with desired characteristics to produce the next generation (p. 319)

semicircular canal one of three structures within the inner ear that help monitor the position of the body (p. 908)

seminiferous tubule one of hundreds of tiny tubules in the testes in which sperm are produced (p. 1010)

sensory receptor neuron that reacts to a specific stimulus, such as light or sound, by sending impulses to other neurons and eventually to the central nervous system (p. 906)

sepal outermost circle of flower parts that encloses a bud before it opens and protects the flower while it is developing (p. 612)

septum internal wall between the segments of an annelid's body (p. 694)

seta bristle attached to the segments of many annelids (p. 694)

sex chromosome one of two chromosomes that determine an individual's sex (p. 341)

sex-linked gene gene located on the X or Y chromosome (p. 350)

sexual reproduction process by which cells from two different parents unite to produce the first cell of a new organism (p. 17)

sexually transmitted disease (STD) disease spread from one person to another during sexual contact (p. 1015)

shell structure in mollusks made by glands in the mantle that secrete calcium carbonate (p. 702)

short-day plant plant that flowers when daylight is short (p. 641)

sieve tube element phloem cell that is joined end-to-end to similar cells to form sieve tubes (p. 581)

single-gene trait trait controlled by a single gene that has two alleles (p. 395)

siphon tubelike structure through which water enters and leaves a mollusk's body (p. 703)

small intestine digestive organ in which most chemical digestion takes place (p. 981)

smog mixture of chemicals that occurs as a gray-brown haze in the atmosphere (p. 148)

society group of closely related animals of the same species that work together for the benefit of the group (p. 732)

soil erosion wearing away of surface soil by water and wind (p. 145)

solute substance that is dissolved in a solvent to make a solution (p. 42)

solution mixture of two or more substances in which the molecules of the substances are evenly distributed (p. 42)

solvent substance in which a solute is dissolved to form a solution (p. 42)

sorus cluster of sporangia on the underside of a fern frond (p. 562)

specialized cell cell that is uniquely suited to performing a particular function (p. 894)

speciation formation of new species (p. 404)

species group of similar organisms that can breed and produce fertile offspring (p. 64)

species diversity number of different species in the biosphere (p. 150)

spicule spike-shaped structure that makes up the skeletons of harder sponges; made of either calcium carbonate or silica (p. 665)

spindle fanlike microtubule structure that helps separate the chromosomes during mitosis (p. 247)

spinneret organ in spiders that contains silk glands (p. 723)

spiracle small opening located along the side of the body through which air enters and leaves the body of many terrestrial arthropods (p. 717)

spirillum spiral or corkscrew-shaped prokaryote (p. 473)

spongy mesophyll loose tissue beneath the palisade layer of a leaf (p. 596)

spontaneous generation hypothesis (disproven) stating that life could arise from nonliving matter (p. 8)

sporangiophore specialized hyphae where sporangia are found (p. 528)

sporangium structure in ferns and some fungi that contains spores (pp. 528, 562)

spore haploid reproductive cell (p. 514)

sporophyte diploid, or spore-producing, phase of an organism (pp. 514, 552)

stabilizing selection form of natural selection by which the center of the curve remains in its current position; occurs when individuals near the center of a distribution curve have higher fitness than individuals at either end (p. 399)

stamen male part of the flower; made up of an anther and a filament (p. 612)

stem supporting structure that connects roots and leaves and carries water and nutrients between them (p. 561)

stigma sticky portion at the top of the style where pollen grains frequently land (p. 612)

stimulant drug that increases the actions regulated by the nervous system (p. 910)

stimulus a signal to which an organism responds (pp. 17, 871)

stolon in fungi, a stemlike hypha that runs along the surface of an object; in plants, a long, trailing stem that produces roots when it touches the ground (pp. 530, 622)

stoma opening in the underside of a leaf that allows carbon dioxide and oxygen to diffuse into and out of the leaf (p. 596)

stomach large muscular sac that continues the mechanical and chemical digestion of food (p. 980)

stroma region outside the thylakoid membranes in chloroplasts (p. 208)

struggle for existence competition among members of a species for food, living space, and the other necessities of life (p. 380)

style narrow stalk of the carpel in a flower (p. 612)

subcutaneous fat layer of fat cells beneath the skin that helps conserve body heat (p. 822)

substrate reactant of an enzyme-catalyzed reaction (p. 52)

survival of the fittest process by which individuals that are better suited to their environment survive and reproduce most successfully; also called natural selection (p. 381)

suspension mixture of water and nondissolved materials (p. 42)

sustainable development using natural resources at a rate that does not deplete them (p. 145)

swim bladder internal gas-filled organ in many bony fishes that adjusts their buoyancy (p. 777)

swimmerets flipperlike appendages used by decapods for swimming (p. 721)

symbiosis relationship in which two species live closely together (p. 93)

synapse location at which a neuron can transfer an impulse to another cell (p. 900)

systemic circulation pathway of circulation between the heart and the rest of the body except the lungs (p. 945)

taiga biome in which the winters are cold but summers are mild enough to allow the ground to thaw (p. 104)

taproot primary root found in some plants that grows longer and thicker than other roots (p. 584)

target cell cell that has a receptor for a particular hormone (pp. 634, 997)

taste bud sense organ that detects the flavor of a substance (p. 909)

taxon group or level of organization into which organisms are classified (p. 449)

taxonomy discipline of classifying organisms and assigning each organism a universally accepted name (p. 447)

telophase fourth and final phase of mitosis, during which the chromosomes begin to disperse into a tangle of dense material (p. 248)

temperate zone moderate climate zone between the polar zones and the tropics (p. 88)

temporal isolation form of reproductive isolation in which two populations reproduce at different times (p. 405)

tendon tough connective tissue that joins skeletal muscles to bones (p. 930)

territory specific area occupied and protected by an animal or group of animals (p. 881)

testis male reproductive organ that produces sperm (pp. 688, 1008)

tetrad structure containing 4 chromatids that forms during meiosis (p. 276)

thalamus brain structure that receives messages from the sense organs and relays the information to the proper region of the cerebrum for further processing (p. 903)

theory well-tested explanation that unifies a broad range of observations (pp. 13, 369)

thigmotropism response of plants to touch (p. 639)

thorax body part of a crustacean that lies just behind the head and houses most of the internal organs (p. 721)

threshold minimum level of a stimulus required to activate a neuron (p. 899)

thylakoid saclike photosynthetic membrane found in chloroplasts (p. 208)

tissue group of similar cells that perform a particular function (p. 192)

tolerance organism's capacity to grow or thrive when subjected to an unfavorable environmental factor (p. 98)

trachea windpipe; tube through which air moves (p. 956)

tracheal tube one of many branching, air-filled tubes that extend throughout the bodies of many terrestrial arthropods (p. 717)

tracheid hollow plant cell in xylem tissue with thick cell walls that resist pressure (p. 560)

trait specific characteristic that varies from one individual to another (p. 264)

transcription process in which part of the nucleotide sequence of DNA is copied into a complementary sequence in RNA (p. 301)

transfer RNA (tRNA) type of RNA molecule that transfers amino acids to ribosomes during protein synthesis (p. 301)

transformation process in which one strain of bacteria is changed by a gene or genes from another strain of bacteria (p. 288)

transgenic term used to refer to an organism that contains genes from other organisms (p. 331)

translation decoding of a mRNA message into a polypeptide chain (p. 304)

transpiration loss of water from a plant through its leaves (pp. 75, 596)

trichocyst small, bottle-shaped structure used for defense by paramecia (p. 501)

trochophore free-swimming larval stage of an aquatic mollusk (p. 701)

trophic level step in a food chain or food web (p. 70)

tropical zone warm climate zone that receives direct or nearly direct sunlight year round (p. 88)

tropism response of a plant to an external stimulus (p. 639)

true-breeding term used to describe organisms that produce offspring identical to themselves if allowed to self-pollinate (p. 263)

tube foot suction-cuplike structure attached to radial canals of echinoderms; used to walk and to open shells (p. 735)

tumor mass of growing tissue (p. 1052)

tympanic membrane eardrum of amphibians inside the skull; vibrates in response to sound, allowing hearing (p. 787)

understory layer in a rain forest formed by shorter trees and vines (p. 100)

ureter tube that carries urine from the kidney to the urinary bladder (p. 986)

urethra tube that carries urine from the bladder and releases it from the body; in males, tube through which semen is released from the body (pp. 987, 1011)

urinary bladder saclike organ in which urine is stored before being excreted (p. 986)

uterus organ of the female reproductive system in which a fertilized egg can develop (p. 1012)

vaccination injection of a weakened or mild form of a pathogen to produce immunity (p. 1041)

vaccine a preparation of weakened or killed pathogens (p. 486)

vacuole cell organelle that stores materials such as water, salts, proteins, and carbohydrates (p. 179)

vagina in the human female reproductive system, a canal that leads from the uterus to the outside of the body (p. 1012)

valve flap of connective tissue between an atrium and a ventricle, or in a vein, that prevents backflow of blood (p. 945)

van der Waals forces a slight attraction that develops between the oppositely charged regions of nearby molecules (p. 39)

variable factor in an experiment that can change (p. 1062)

vas deferens tube that carries sperm from the epididymis to the urethra (p. 1011)

vascular bundle plant stem structure that contains xylem and phloem tissue (p. 590)

vascular cambium lateral meristematic tissue that produces vascular tissues and increases the thickness of the stem over time (p. 591)

vascular cylinder central region of a root that includes the vascular tissue—xylem and phloem (p. 585)

vascular tissue type of plant tissue specialized to conduct water and nutrients throughout a plant (p. 560)

vector animal that carries pathogens from person to person (p. 1034)

vegetative reproduction method of asexual reproduction used by many flowering plants (p. 622)

vein in plants, a cluster of vascular tissue in leaves; in animals, a blood vessel that returns blood to the heart (pp. 561, 947)

ventricle lower chamber of the heart that pumps blood out of the heart (pp. 776, 945)

vertebra individual segment of the backbone; encloses and protects the spinal cord (p. 768)

vertebrate animal that has a vertebral column, or backbone (p. 657)

vessel element in angiosperms, xylem cell that forms part of a continuous tube through which water can move (p. 581)

vestigial organ organ that serves no useful function in an organism (p. 384)

villus folded projection that increases the surface area of the walls of the small intestine (p. 982)

viroid single-stranded RNA molecule that has no surrounding capsids (p. 490)

virus particle made up of nucleic acid, protein, and in some cases lipids that can replicate only by infecting living cells (p. 478)

visceral mass area beneath the mantle of a mollusk that contains the internal organs (p. 702)

vitamin organic molecule that helps regulate body processes (p. 974)

viviparous term used to refer to animals that bear live young that are nourished directly by the mother's body as they develop (p. 778)

water vascular system system of internal tubes in echinoderms that carries out essential functions such as feeding, respiration, circulation, and movement (p. 735)

weather condition of Earth's atmosphere at a particular time and place (p. 87)

wetland ecosystem in which water either covers the soil or is present at or near the surface of the soil for at least part of the year (p. 107)

xerophyte plant that lives in the desert biome (p. 644)

xylem vascular tissue that carries water upward from the roots to every part of a plant (p. 560)

zonation prominent horizontal banding of organisms that live in a particular habitat (p. 110)

zooplankton tiny animals that form part of the plankton (p. 107)

zoosporangium spore case (p. 518)

zygospore resting spore that contains zygotes formed during the sexual phase of a mold's life cycle (p. 530)

zygote fertilized egg (p. 1016)

Spanish Glossary

abdomen/abdomen parte posterior del cuerpo de un artrópodo (pág. 721)

abiotic factor/factor abiótico factor físico, o sin vida, que da forma a un ecosistema (pág. 90)

abscission layer/capa de absición capa de células en el pecíolo que separa una hoja del sistema vascular (pág. 642)

accessory pigment/pigmento accesorio compuesto diferente a la clorofila que absorbe luz de diferentes longitudes de onda que la clorofila (pág. 506)

acellular slime mold/moho mucilaginoso acelular moho mucilaginoso que pasa por una etapa en la que sus células se unen para formar células más grandes con muchos núcleos (pág. 516)

acetylcholine/acetilcolina neurotransmisor que se difunde a través de una sinapsis y produce un impulso en la membrana celular de una célula muscular (pág. 929)

acid/ácido compuesto que forma iones de hidrógeno (H^+) en una solución (pág. 43)

acid rain/lluvia ácida lluvia que contiene ácidos nítrico y sulfúrico (pág. 148)

acoelomate/acelomado animal que carece de celoma o cavidad corporal (pág. 683)

actin/actina proteína que compone principalmente los finos filamentos en las estrías de células musculares esqueléticas (pág. 928)

action potential/potencial de acción inversión de cargas a través de la membrana celular de una neurona; también llamada impulso nervioso (pág. 899)

activation energy/energía de activación energía que se necesita para conseguir que comience una reacción (pág. 50)

active immunity/inmunidad activa inmunidad producida por la exposición a un antígeno, como resultado de una respuesta inmune (pág. 1042)

active transport/transporte activo proceso que necesita energía para mover material a través de una membrana celular contra una diferencia en concentración (pág. 188)

adaptation/adaptación característica heredada que aumenta la probabilidad de supervivencia de un organismo (pág. 380)

adaptive radiation/radiación adaptiva proceso en el cual una especie única o un grupo pequeño de especies evoluciona y cambia a varias formas diferentes que viven de diferentes maneras; crecimiento rápido en la diversidad de un grupo de organismos (págs. 436, 851)

addiction/adicción dependencia incontrolable de una droga (pág. 914)

adenosine triphosphate (ATP)/trifosfato de adenosina (ATP) uno de los principales compuestos químicos que los seres vivos usan para almacenar y desprender energía (pág. 202)

adhesion/adhesión atracción entre moléculas de diferentes sustancias; en plantas: atracción entre moléculas diferentes (págs. 41, 599)

aerobic/aeróbico proceso que requiere oxígeno (pág. 226)

age-structure diagram/diagrama de estructura por edades gráfica del número de hombres y mujeres en diferentes grupos de edades de una población (pág. 131)

aggression/agresión comportamiento amenazador que un animal usa para ejercer control sobre otro (pág. 881)

agriculture/agricultura práctica del cultivo (pág. 141)

air sac/saco aéreo uno de muchos sacos que se encuentran en los pulmones de las aves en los que fluye el aire cuando el ave aspira; permite el flujo de aire en una dirección a través del sistema respiratorio (pág. 810)

algal bloom/floración de algas un aumento inmediato en la cantidad de algas y otros productores que resulta de un aporte significativo de un nutriente limitante (pág. 80)

allele/alelo una de las diferentes formas de un gen (pág. 265)

allergy/alergia reacción exagerada del sistema inmune a los antígenos (pág. 103)

alternation of generations/alternación de generaciones proceso en el cual muchas algas alternan entre las etapas de haploide y diploide en sus ciclos de vida (pág. 512)

alveolus/alvéolo saco de aire diminuto al final de un bronquiolo en los pulmones que provee área de superficie para que ocurra el intercambio de gases (págs. 859, 958)

amino acid/aminoácido compuesto con un grupo de aminos ($-NH_2$) en un extremo y un grupo de carboxilo ($-COOH$) en el otro (pág. 47)

amniotic egg/huevo amniótico huevo compuesto de una cáscara y membranas que crean un ambiente protegido en el cual el embrión puede desarrollarse fuera del agua (pág. 802)

amoeboid movement/movimiento ameboide tipo de movimiento que usan las amebas (pág. 500)

amphibian/anfibio vertebrado que, con algunas excepciones, vive en el agua de larva y en la tierra de adulto, respira con pulmones de adulto, tiene piel húmeda que contiene glándulas mucosas, y no tiene escamas ni garras (pág. 782)

amylase/amilasa enzima de la saliva que rompe los enlaces químicos de los almidones (pág. 979)

anaerobic/anaeróbico proceso que no necesita oxígeno (pág. 224)

anal pore/poro anal región de la membrana celular de un ciliado donde se fusionan las vacuolas alimentarias que contienen desechos de alimentos y se vacían al exterior (pág. 502)

anaphase/anafase tercera fase de la mitosis durante la cual las parejas de cromosomas se separan y se mueven hacia polos opuestos (pág. 248)

angiosperm/angiosperma planta con flores; porta sus semillas dentro de una capa de tejido que las protege (pág. 564)

Animalia/*Animalia* reino de eucariotas heterótrofos multicelulares cuyas células no tienen pared celular (pág. 461)

annual/anual planta con flores que completa un ciclo de vida durante una estación de crecimiento (pág. 572)

anther/antera estructura de la flor en la que se producen gametofitos haploides masculinos (pág. 612)

antheridium/anteridio estructura reproductora masculina de algunas plantas y algas (págs. 519, 559)

anthropoid/antropoideo grupo de primates compuesto por humanos y la mayoría de los monos (pág. 835)

antibiotic/antibiótico compuesto que bloquea el crecimiento y la reproducción de una bacteria (págs. 486, 1035)

antibody/anticuerpo proteína que ayuda a destruir a los patógenos (pág. 1038)

anticodon/anticodón grupo de tres bases en una molécula de tARN que son complementarias a un codón de mARN (pág. 304)

antigen/antígeno sustancia que provoca una respuesta inmunológica (pág. 1038)

anus/ano orificio por donde las sustancias de desecho salen del tracto digestivo (págs. 661, 689)

aorta/aorta arteria de los mamíferos a través de la cual viaja la sangre después de salir del ventrículo izquierdo (pág. 946)

aphotic zone/zona afótica capa permanentemente oscura de los océanos que se encuentra debajo de la zona fótica (pág. 109)

apical dominance/dominancia apical fenómeno en el cual cuanto más cerca está una yema de la punta del tallo, más inhibido es su crecimiento (pág. 636)

apical meristem/meristemo apical grupo de células no diferenciadas que se dividen para producir mayor longitud en tallos y raíces (pág. 582)

appendage/apéndice estructura, como una pata o una antena, que se extiende desde la cubierta del cuerpo (pág. 715)

aquaculture/acuicultura cría de organismos acuáticos para el consumo humano (pág. 147)

Archaea/*Archaea* dominio de procariotas unicelulares cuyas paredes celulares que no contienen peptidoglicano (pág. 459)

Archaebacteria/*Archaebacteria* reino de procariotas unicelulares cuyas paredes celulares no contienen peptidoglicano (pág. 459)

archaeocyte/arqueocito célula especializada en una esponja que crea espículas (pág. 665)

archegonium/arquegonio estructura reproductora femenina en algunas plantas, incluidas musgos y hepáticas (pág. 559)

artery/arteria vaso sanguíneo grande que lleva la sangre desde el corazón a los tejidos del cuerpo (pág. 946)

artificial selection/selección artificial selección por parte de los humanos para reproducir rasgos útiles provenientes de la variación natural en diferentes organismos (pág. 379)

ascospore/ascospora espora haploide producida en el asca de los ascomicetos (pág. 532)

ascus/asca estructura dentro de un cuerpo frutal de un ascomiceto en el cual se unen dos núcleos de diferentes tipos de reproducción (pág. 532)

asexual reproduction/reproducción asexual proceso por el cual un solo individuo se reproduce por sí mismo (pág. 17)

asthma/asma enfermedad respiratoria crónica en la cual se reduce el tamaño de las vías respiratorias más de lo normal (pág. 1044)

atherosclerosis/arteriosclerosis condición en la que depósitos de grasa, llamados placas, se forman en las paredes interiores de las arterias (pág. 949)

atom/átomo unidad básica de la materia (pág. 35)

ATP synthase/ATP sintetasa proteína grande que usa energía de los iones H^+ para unirse al ADP y a un grupo fosfato para producir ATP (pág. 210)

atrium/atrio cámara superior del corazón que recibe y mantiene la sangre que está a punto de entrar al ventrículo (págs. 776, 945)

autosome/autosoma cromosoma que no es un cromosoma sexual (pág. 341)

autotroph/autótrofo organismo que capta energía de la luz solar o de sustancias químicas y la usa para producir su propia alimentación de compuestos inorgánicos; también se le llama productor (págs. 67, 201)

auxin/auxina sustancia producida en la punta de una plántula que estimula la elongación celular (pág. 635)

axon/axón fibra larga que lleva los impulsos del cuerpo celular de una neurona (pág. 898)

bacillus/bacilo procariota con forma de bastoncillo (pág. 473)

Bacteria/Bacteria dominio de procariotas unicelulares cuyas paredes celulares contienen peptidoglicano (pág. 459)

bacteriophage/bacteriófago virus que infecta a una bacteria (págs. 289, 479)

bark/corteza estructura del árbol que incluye todos los tejidos fuera del cámbium vascular, incluido el floema, el felógeno y el corcho (pág. 593)

base/base compuesto que produce iones de hidróxido (OH^+) en una solución (pág. 43)

base pairing/pares de bases principio que dice que los enlaces del ADN pueden formarse sólo entre adenina y tiamina y entre guanina y citosina (pág. 294)

basidiospore/basidiospora espora en los basidiomicetos que germina para producir un micelio primario haploide (pág. 535)

basidium/basidio estructura que contiene las esporas de un basidiomiceto (pág. 534)

behavior/comportamiento manera en que un organismo reacciona a los cambios en sus condiciones internas o en el ambiente exterior (pág. 871)

behavioral isolation/aislamiento de comportamiento forma de aislamiento reproductivo en la cual dos poblaciones tienen diferencias en rituales de cortejo u otros tipos de comportamiento que previene su apareamiento (pág. 404)

benthos/bentos organismos que viven pegados o cerca del suelo oceánico (pág. 112)

biennal/bienal planta con flores que completa su ciclo de vida en dos años (pág. 572)

bilateral symmetry/simetría bilateral conformación corporal en el cual una sola línea imaginaria puede dividir el cuerpo en dos mitades exactas; característica de gusanos, artrópodos y cordados (págs. 662, 748)

binary fission/fisión binaria tipo de reproducción asexual en la cual un organismo replica su ADN y se divide por la mitad, produciendo dos células hijas idénticas (pág. 475)

binocular vision/visión binocular capacidad de fusionar imágenes visuales de los dos ojos, que provee una percepción profunda y tridimensional del mundo (pág. 834)

binomial nomenclature/nomenclatura binaria sistema de clasificación en el que se le asigna a cada especie un nombre científico de dos partes (pág. 448)

biodiversity/biodiversidad diversidad biológica; la suma total de la variedad de organismos en la biosfera (pág. 150)

biogeochemical cycle/ciclo biogeoquímico proceso en el cual elementos, compuestos químicos y otras formas de materia pasan de un organismo a otro y de una parte de la biosfera a otra (pág. 74)

biological magnification/magnificación biológica incremento en la concentración de una sustancia dañina en organismos a niveles tróficos más altos en una cadena o trama alimentaria (pág. 152)

biology/biología ciencia que busca entender el mundo de los seres vivos (pág. 15)

biomass/biomasa cantidad total de tejido vivo en un nivel trófico dado (pág. 72)

biome/bioma grupo de ecosistemas que tienen el mismo clima y comunidades dominantes semejantes (págs. 64, 98)

biosphere/biosfera parte de la tierra en la que la vida existe y que incluye la tierra, el agua y el aire o la atmósfera (pág. 63)

biotic factor/factor biótico influencia biológica en organismos de un ecosistema (pág. 90)

bipedal/bípedo término usado para referirse a la locomoción en dos extremidades (pág. 835)

bird/ave animal endotérmico que tiene una cubierta externa de plumas, dos patas cubiertas con escamas que usa para caminar o posarse y extremidades delanteras transformadas en alas (pág. 806)

blade/limbo sección delgada y plana de la hoja de una planta que recoge la luz solar (pág. 595)

blastula/blástula esfera hueca de células formada cuando el cigoto sufre una serie de divisiones (pág. 661)

bone marrow/médula ósea tejido suave dentro de las cavidades de los huesos (pág. 922)

book lung/pulmón laminar órgano que tiene capas de tejido respiratorio usadas por algunos artrópodos terrestres para intercambiar gases (pág. 717)

Bowman's capsule/cápsula de Bowman estructura en forma de taza en la parte superior de una nefrona que encierra al glomérulo (pág. 987)

brain stem/tronco cerebral estructura que conecta el cerebro y la espina dorsal; incluye el bulbo raquídeo y la protuberancia anular (pág. 902)

bronchus/bronquio vía que conecta la tráquea con los pulmones (pág. 958)

bryophyte/briofita planta no vascular; por ejemplo el musgo y sus parientes (pág. 556)

bud/yema estructura de la planta que contiene tejidos no desarrollados que pueden producir nuevos tallos y hojas (pág. 589)

budding/gemación proceso asexual por el cual las levaduras aumentan en número; proceso de unir una yema a una planta para producir nuevas ramas (págs. 533, 623)

buffer/disolución amortiguadora ácido o base débil que puede reaccionar con ácidos o bases fuertes para ayudar a prevenir cambios fuertes y repentinos en el pH (pág. 43)

calorie/caloría cantidad de energía necesaria para elevar la temperatura de 1 gramo de agua 1 grado Celsius (pág. 221)

Calorie/Caloría término usado por los científicos para medir la energía almacenada en los alimentos; 1000 calorías (pág. 971)

Calvin cycle/ciclo de Calvin reacciones de fotosíntesis en las cuales la energía de ATP y NADPH se usa para crear componentes de alta energía, como los azúcares (pág. 212)

cancer/cáncer desorden por el que algunas de las células del cuerpo pierden la capacidad de controlar su crecimiento (pág. 252)

canopy/bóveda arbórea cubierta densa formada por las cimas hojeadas de los árboles altos en los bosques lluviosos (pág. 100)

capillary/capilar el vaso sanguíneo más pequeño; trae nutrientes y oxígeno a los tejidos y absorbe el dióxido de carbono y los productos de desecho (pág. 947)

capillary action/acción capilar tendencia del agua a subir por un tubo delgado (pág. 599)

capsid/cápside cubierta externa de proteína de un virus (pág. 479)

carapace/caparazón en los crustáceos, la parte del exoesqueleto que cubre el cefalotórax; en las tortugas, la parte dorsal de la coraza (pág. 721)

carapace/carapacho parte dorsal del caparazón (pág. 805)

carbohydrate/carbohidrato compuesto formado por carbono, hidrógeno y átomos de oxígeno; fuente principal de energía para el cuerpo humano (págs. 45, 972)

carcinogen/carcinógeno compuesto químico que causa cáncer (pág. 1052)

carnivore/carnívoro organismo que obtiene energía de comer otros animales (pág. 69)

carpel/carpelo parte más interna de una flor que produce los gametofitos femeninos (pág. 612)

carrying capacity/capacidad de carga mayor número de individuos que puede sustentar un medio ambiente dado (pág. 122)

cartilage/cartílago tejido de conexión fuerte que sostiene el cuerpo y es más suave y más flexible que el hueso (págs. 773, 922)

Casparian strip/banda de Caspary banda a prueba de agua que rodea las células de la endodermis de las plantas (pág. 587)

caste/casta grupo de insectos especializados para realizar tareas o asumir papeles particulares (pág. 732)

catalyst/catalizador sustancia que acelera la velocidad de una reacción química (pág. 51)

cell/célula colección de materia viva rodeada por una barrera que separa la célula de su alrededor; unidad básica en todas las formas de vida (págs. 16, 170)

cell body/cuerpo celular parte más grande de una neurona típica; contiene el núcleo y la mayoría del citoplasma (pág. 897)

cell culture/cultivo celular grupo de células que crecen en una solución de nutrientes a partir de una célula única (pág. 27)

cell cycle/ciclo celular serie de sucesos que sufren las células a medida que crecen y se dividen (pág. 245)

cell division/división celular proceso por el cual una célula se divide en dos células hijas nuevas (pág. 243)

cell fractionation/fraccionamiento celular técnica en la cual se rompen las células en pedazos y se separan las diferentes partes de las células (pág. 27)

cell-mediated immunity/inmunidad celular inmunidad contra células anormales y patógenos dentro de células vivas (pág. 1038)

cell membrane/membrana celular barrera delgada y flexible alrededor de la célula; regula lo que entra y sale de la célula (pág. 182)

cell specialization/especialización celular proceso por el que se desarrollan las células de diferentes maneras para realizar tareas distintas (pág. 190)

cell theory/teoría celular idea que propone que todos los seres vivos están compuestos de células, las células son la unidad básica de la estructura y función en los seres vivos y las células existentes producen nuevas células (pág. 170)

cell wall/pared celular capa fuerte de apoyo alrededor de la membrana celular en plantas, algas y algunas bacterias (pág. 182)

cellular respiration/respiración celular proceso que libera energía al romper glucosa y otras moléculas de alimentos en presencia de oxígeno (pág. 222)

cellular slime mold/moho mucilaginoso celular moho mucilaginoso cuyas células permanecen separadas durante todas las fases del ciclo de vida del moho (pág. 516)

centriole/centriolo una de dos estructuras diminutas localizadas en el citoplasma de las células animales cerca de la membrana nuclear (págs. 181, 246)

centromere/centrómero área donde se unen las cromátidas de un cromosoma (pág. 245)

cephalization/cefalización concentración de los órganos de los sentidos y las células nerviosas en la parte frontal del cuerpo de un animal (págs. 663, 748)

cephalothorax/cefalotórax región de un crustáceo formado por la fusión de la cabeza con el tórax (pág. 721)

cerebellum/cerebelo región del cerebro que coordina los movimientos del cuerpo (págs. 777, 902)

cerebral cortex/corteza cerebral capa externa del cerebro de un mamífero; centro de pensamiento y otros comportamientos complejos (pág. 825)

cerebrospinal fluid/líquido cefalorraquídeo líquido en el espacio entre las meninges que actúa como un absorbente de golpes que protege el sistema nervioso central (pág. 901)

cerebrum/cerebro área responsable de las actividades voluntarias del cuerpo (págs. 777, 902)

chelicerae/quelíceros par de colmillos en la boca de los quelicerados que usan para clavar y paralizar a la presa (pág. 722)

cheliped/quelipedo cada una del par de patas anteriores de los decápodos (pág. 721)

chemical reaction/reacción química proceso que transforma un conjunto de sustancias químicas en otro conjunto de sustancias químicas (pág. 49)

chemoautotroph/quimioautótrofo organismo que fabrica moléculas de carbono orgánico a partir del dióxido de carbono usando la energía de una reacción química (pág. 474)

chemoheterotroph/quimioheterótrofo organismo que debe consumir moléculas orgánicas tanto para la energía como para el carbono (pág. 473)

chemosynthesis/quimiosíntesis proceso por el cual algunos organismos usan la energía química para producir carbohidratos (pág. 68)

chitin/quitina carbohidrato complejo que conforma la pared celular de los hongos; también se encuentra en el esqueleto externo de los artrópodos (págs. 527, 715)

chlorophyll/clorofila pigmento principal de las plantas y otros organismos fotosintetizadores; absorbe energía de la luz (pág. 207)

chloroplast/cloroplasto organelo que se encuentra en las células de las plantas y otros organismos que capta la energía de la luz solar y la convierte en energía química (pág. 180)

choanocyte/coanocito célula especializada de las esponjas que usa un flagelo para mover una corriente de agua continua a través de la esponja (pág. 665)

chordate/cordado miembro del fílum Chordata; animal que tiene, durante al menos algunas etapas de su vida, un cordón nervioso hueco, notocordio, sacos faríngeos y una cola musculosa (pág. 767)

chromatid/cromátida una de dos partes "hermanas" idénticas de un cromosoma duplicado (pág. 244)

chromatin/cromatina material granular visible del núcleo; consiste de ADN enrollado fuertemente alrededor de las proteínas (págs. 176, 296)

chromosome/cromosoma estructura filamentosa en el núcleo que contiene la información genética que se pasa de una generación de células a la siguiente (pág. 176)

chyme/quimo mezcla de líquidos y alimento producida en el estómago al contraerse los músculos estomacales (pág. 981)

cilium/cilio estructura parecida a un pelo y similar a un flagelo, que muchas células usan para moverse (pág. 501)

circadian rhythm/ritmo circadiano ciclo de comportamiento que ocurre en un patrón diario (pág. 878)

cladogram/cladograma diagrama que muestra las relaciones evolutivas entre un grupo de organismos (pág. 453)

class/clase grupo de órdenes similares (pág. 449)

classical conditioning/condicionamiento clásico proceso de aprendizaje en el cual un animal hace una conexión mental entre un estímulo y algún tipo de recompensa o castigo (pág. 874)

climate/clima media de las condiciones de temperatura y precipitación año tras año en una región particular (pág. 87)

clitellum/clitelio en los anélidos, banda de segmentos especializados y gruesos que secreta un anillo mucoso en el que se liberan los huevos y el esperma (pág. 696)

cloaca/cloaca cavidad muscular al final del intestino grueso a través de la cual los desechos de la digestión, la orina, los huevos o el esperma abandonan el cuerpo (pág. 784)

clone/clon miembro de una población de células genéticamente idénticas producidas por una única célula (pág. 333)

closed circulatory system/sistema circulatorio cerrado sistema en el cual la sangre se mueve por una red de vasos sanguíneos (págs. 695, 754)

cnidocyte/cnidocito célula urticante de los cnidarios; la usan para defenderse y para capturar a la presa (pág. 669)

coastal ocean/océano continental zona marina que se extiende desde la marea baja hasta el final de la costa continental (pág. 110)

coccus/coco procariota esférico (pág. 473)

cochlea/caracol parte del oído interno lleno de fluido; envía impulsos nerviosos al cerebro mediante el nervio acústico (pág. 908)

codominance/codominancia situación en la que ambos alelos de un gen contribuyen al fenotipo de un organismo (pág. 272)

codon/codón secuencia triple de nucleótidos en el ARN mensajero que codifica un aminoácido específico (pág. 302)

coelom/celoma cavidad corporal llena de fluidos envuelta con mesodermo (págs. 683, 749)

coevolution/coevolución proceso por el cual dos especies evolucionan en respuesta a cambios en uno o en el otro (pág. 437)

cohesion/cohesión atracción entre moléculas de la misma sustancia (pág. 41)

collenchyma/colénquima tipo de célula de tejido fundamental con una pared celular fuerte y flexible; ayuda al soporte de plantas grandes (pág. 582)

commensalism/comensalismo relación simbiótica en la cual un miembro de la asociación se beneficia y al otro ni se le ayuda ni se le perjudica (pág. 93)

common descent/descendencia común principio que enuncia que todos los seres vivos vienen de antepasados comunes (pág. 382)

communication/comunicación pasar información de un organismo a otro (pág. 881)

community/comunidad ensamblaje de diferentes poblaciones que viven juntas en un área específica (pág. 64)

companion cell/célula acompañante célula floema que rodea el tubo criboso (pág. 581)

competitive exclusion principle/principio de la exclusión competitiva norma ecológica que enuncia que dos especies no pueden ocupar el mismo nicho ecológico en el mismo hábitat al mismo tiempo (pág. 92)

complete metamorphosis/metamorfosis completa tipo de desarrollo en los insectos en el que la larva no se parece ni actúa como sus padres y también se alimenta de forma diferente (pág. 729)

compound/compuesto sustancia formada por una combinación química de dos o más elementos en proporciones definidas (pág. 37)

compound light microscope/microscopio óptico compuesto microscopio que permite que la luz pase a través de un espécimen y usa dos lentes para formar una imagen (pág. 26)

concentration/concentración masa de un soluto en un volumen dado de solución; o masa/volumen (pág. 183)

cone/cono en las gimnospermas, estructura que porta las semillas; en la retina del ojo, un fotoreceptor que responde a la luz de diferentes colores produciendo visión de color (págs. 564, 907)

conidium/conidio espora diminuta de un hongo que se forma en la punta de una hifa especializada en los ascomicetos (pág. 532)

coniferous/conífera término usado para referirse a los árboles que producen conos que portan semillas y tienen hojas delgadas en forma de agujas (pág. 103)

conjugation/conjugación forma de reproducción sexual en la cual los paramecios y algunos procariotes intercambian información genética (págs. 475, 502)

connective tissue/tejido conectivo tejido que mantiene los órganos en su lugar y une diferentes partes del cuerpo (pág. 894)

conservation/conservación administración sensata de los recursos naturales, que incluye la preservación de hábitats y de la vida silvestre (pág. 154)

consumer/consumidor organismo que depende de otros organismos para energía y alimentación; también se le conoce como heterótrofo (pág. 68)

contractile vacuole/vacuola contráctil cavidad en el citoplasma de algunos protistas que recoge el agua de la célula y la elimina (pág. 502)

controlled experiment/experimento controlado prueba del efecto de una variable única al cambiarla, mientras el resto de las variables se mantienen fijas (pág. 9)

controlled variable/variable controlada factor en un experimento que un científico mantiene fijo a propósito (pág. 1062)

convergent evolution/evolución convergente proceso por el cual organismos no relacionados que evolucionan independientemente desarrollan semejanzas cuando se adaptan a medio ambientes similares (pág. 437)

coral reef/arrecife de coral medio ambiente diverso y productivo, nombrado así por los corales que forman su estructura primaria (pág. 111)

cork cambium/felógeno tejido merismático lateral que produce la cubierta externa de los tallos (pág. 591)

corpus luteum/cuerpo luteal nombre dado a un folículo después de la ovulación debido a su color amarillo (pág. 1014)

cortex/parénquima cortical capa esponjosa de tejido fundamental que se encuentra dentro de la epidermis de una raíz (pág. 585)

cotyledon/cotiledón primera hoja o par de hojas producidas por el embrión de una plántula (pág. 570)

courtship/cortejo tipo de comportamiento en el cual un animal produce estímulos para atraer a un miembro del sexo opuesto (pág. 879)

covalent bond/enlace covalente enlace formado entre átomos al compartir electrones (pág. 38)

crop/buche en los gusanos, parte del sistema digestivo en el que se almacena la comida; en los pájaros, estructura en la parte inferior del esófago en que la comida se almacena y se humedece (págs. 595, 809)

crossing-over/cruzamiento proceso en el cual los cromosomas homólogos intercambian porciones de cromátidas durante la meiosis (pág. 277)

cyclin/ciclina de una familia de proteínas muy relacionadas que regula el ciclo celular en las células eucarióticas (pág. 581)

cytokinesis/citocinesis división del citoplasma durante la división de la célula (pág. 244)

cytokinin/citocinina hormonas vegetales que se producen en las raíces, frutos y semillas en desarrollo (pág. 636)

cytoplasm/citoplasma material dentro de la membrana celular, sin incluir el núcleo (pág. 174)

cytoskeleton/citoesqueleto red de filamentos de proteína dentro de algunas células que ayuda a que la célula mantenga su forma y que participa en muchas formas del movimiento de la célula (pág. 181)

D

data/datos evidencia; información reunida a partir de observaciones (págs. 4, 1057)

deciduous/caducifolio término usado para referirse a un árbol que muda sus hojas durante una estación específica cada año (pág. 100)

decomposer/descomponedor organismo que deshace y obtiene energía de materia orgánica muerta (pág. 69)

deforestation/deforestación destrucción de bosques (pág. 146)

demographic transition/transición demográfica cambio en una población de altos a bajos índices de natalidad y mortandad (pág. 130)

demography/demografía estudio científico de poblaciones humanas (pág. 130)

dendrite/dendrita extensión de la célula de una neurona que lleva impulsos desde el medio ambiente o desde otras neuronas hacia el cuerpo celular (pág. 898)

denitrification/desnitrificación conversión de nitratos en gas nitrógeno (pág. 78)

density-dependent limiting factor/factor limitante dependiente de la densidad factor limitante que depende del tamaño de la población (pág. 125)

density-independent limiting factor/factor limitante independiente de la densidad factor limitante que afecta todas las poblaciones de manera similar, sin importar el tamaño de la población (pág. 127)

deoxyribonucleic acid (DNA)/ácido desoxirribonucleico (ADN) ácido nucleico que contiene el azúcar desoxirribosa (pág. 47)

dependent variable/variable dependiente factor en un experimento que un científico quiere observar, el cual puede cambiar debido a la variable manipulada; también conocido como variable respuesta (pág. 1062)

depressant/depresivo droga que reduce la velocidad de las funciones reguladas por el cerebro (pág. 911)

derived character/rasgo derivado característica que aparece en partes recientes de un linaje, pero que no tienen los miembros más viejos (pág. 453)

dermis/dermis capa interna de la piel (pág. 935)

descent with modification/descendencia con modificación principio que dice que todos los seres vivos han descendido, con cambios, de otras especies con el tiempo (pág. 381)

desertification/desertificación en áreas con clima seco, proceso causado por la combinación de prácticas inadecuadas de agricultura, pastoreo excesivo y sequía que convierte la tierra productiva en desértica (pág. 145)

detritivore/detritívoro organismo que se alimenta de restos de animales y plantas y otra materia muerta (pág. 69)

detritus/detrito partículas de material orgánico que proveen alimento para los organismos en la base de una trama alimentaria de un estuario (pág. 108)

deuterosome/deuterostomo animal cuyo ano se forma a partir de la blastopora de una blástula (pág. 661)

diabetes mellitus/diabetes mellitus condición que ocurre cuando el páncreas produce muy poca insulina, resultando en un aumento en la cantidad de glucosa en la sangre (pág. 1007)

diaphragm/diafragma músculo plano y grande bajo la cavidad pectoral que ayuda a la respiración (págs. 824, 959)

dicot/dicotiledónea angiosperma cuyas semillas tienen dos cotiledóneas (pág. 570)

differentiation/diferenciación proceso en el cual las células se especializan en estructura y función (págs. 312, 583, 1017)

diffusion/difusión proceso por el cual las moléculas tienden a moverse desde un área donde están más concentradas a un área donde están menos concentradas (pág. 184)

diploid/diploide término usado para referirse a una célula que contiene los dos conjuntos de cromosomas homólogos (pág. 275)

directional selection/selección direccional forma de selección natural en la cual se mueve la curva completa; ocurre cuando los individuos a un extremo de una curva de distribución son más aptos que los individuos en el medio o en el otro extremo de la curva (pág. 398)

disease/enfermedad cualquier cambio, diferente a una herida, que interrumpe las funciones normales del cuerpo (pág. 1031)

disruptive selection/selección disruptiva forma de selección natural en la cual una única curva se divide en dos; ocurre cuando los individuos en los extremos más alto y más bajo de una curva de distribución son más aptos que los individuos en el medio (pág. 399)

DNA fingerprinting/huellas de ADN análisis de secciones de ADN que tienen una función poco o nada conocida, pero que varía notablemente de un individuo a otro; se usa para identificar individuos (pág. 357)

DNA polymerase/polimerasa de ADN enzima que participa en la replicación del ADN al unir nucleótidos individuales para producir una molécula de ADN (pág. 299)

domain/dominio categoría taxonómica más inclusiva; más grande que un reino (pág. 458)

dormancy/dormición periodo durante el cual el embrión de una planta está vivo pero no crece (págs. 620, 641)

double fertilization/doble fertilización fertilización de angiospermas, en la que dos sucesos distintivos de fertilización tienen lugar entre los gametofitos masculino y femenino (pág. 616)

drug/droga cualquier sustancia, diferente a los alimentos, que causa un cambio en la estructura o función del cuerpo (pág. 910)

drug abuse/toxicomanía mal uso intencionado de cualquier droga para propósitos no médicos (pág. 914)

ecological pyramid/pirámide ecológica diagrama que muestra las cantidades de energía o materia relativas en cada nivel trófico en la cadena o trama alimentaria (pág. 72)

ecological succession/sucesión ecológica cambio gradual en comunidades vivas que sigue a una alteración (pág. 94)

ecology/ecología estudio científico de interacciones entre organismos y entre organismos y su medio ambiente (pág. 63)

ecosystem/ecosistema colección de todos los organismos que viven en un lugar particular, junto con su medio ambiente no vivo (pág. 64)

ecosystem diversity/diversidad de ecosistemas variedad de hábitats, comunidades vivas y procesos ecológicos en el mundo vivo (pág. 150)

ectoderm/ectodermo capa embrionaria más externa de la mayoría de los animales; origina la capa externa de la piel, órganos sensoriales y nervios (pág. 661)

ectotherm/ectotérmico animal que depende de las interacciones con el medio ambiente para ayudarse a controlar la temperatura del cuerpo (págs. 800, 855)

electron/electrón partícula cargada negativamente; localizado fuera del núcleo del átomo (pág. 35)

electron microscope/microscopio electrónico microscopio que forma una imagen al centrar un haz de electrones en un espécimen (pág. 26)

electron transport chain/cadena de transporte de electrones serie de proteínas en las que se usan los electrones de alta energía del ciclo de Krebs para convertir ADP en ATP (pág. 228)

element/elemento sustancia que consiste enteramente de un tipo de átomo (pág. 36)

embryo/embrión organismo en su primera etapa de desarrollo (pág. 565)

embryo sac/saco embrionario gametofito femenino en el óvulo de una planta con flores (pág. 615)

emigration/emigración movimiento de individuos fuera de un área (pág. 120)

emphysema/enfisema enfermedad en la cual los tejidos de los pulmones pierden elasticidad, lo que dificulta la respiración (pág. 962)

endangered species/especies en vías de extinción especies cuyo tamaño poblacional está disminuyendo rápidamente y se extinguiría si continúa la tendencia (pág. 151)

endocrine gland/glándula endocrina glándula que libera sus secreciones directamente en la corriente sanguínea (pág. 998)

endocytosis/endocitosis proceso por el cual una célula introduce material en la célula por doblamiento de la membrana celular (pág. 189)

endoderm/endodermo capa embrionaria más interna de la mayoría de los animales; se convierte en las paredes del tracto digestivo y de la mayoría del sistema respiratorio (pág. 661)

endodermis/endodermis capa de células que encierra completamente el tejido vascular (pág. 585)

endoplasmic reticulum/retículo endoplasmático sistema de membranas internas en las células en la que se forman los componentes lípidos de la membrana celular y se modifican algunas proteínas (pág. 177)

endoskeleton/endoesqueleto soporte estructural localizado dentro del cuerpo de un animal (págs. 734, 757)

endosperm/endosperma tejido rico en alimento que nutre a la semilla mientras crece (pág. 616)

endospore/endospora tipo de espora formada cuando una bacteria produce una pared interna gruesa que encierra su ADN y una porción de su citoplasma (pág. 475)

endosymbiotic theory/teoría endosimbiótica teoría que enuncia que las células eucarióticas se formaron por una simbiosis entre varios organismos procarióticos diferentes (pág. 427)

endotherm/endotérmico animal que genera su propio calor y controla la temperatura de su cuerpo internamente (págs. 808, 855)

enzyme/enzima proteína que actúa como catalizador biológico (pág. 51)

epidermal cell/célula epidérmica célula que crea el tejido dermal, que es la cubierta externa de la planta (pág. 580)

epidermis/epidermis capa externa de la piel (pág. 934)

epididymis/epidídimio estructura del sistema reproductor masculino en donde el esperma madura completamente y es almacenado (pág. 1011)

epiphyte/epífito planta que no está arraigada al suelo, sino que crece directamente en el cuerpo de otra planta (pág. 645)

epithelial tissue/tejido epitelial tejido que cubre la superficie del cuerpo y las paredes de los órganos internos (pág. 894)

equilibrium/equilibrio cuando la concentración de un soluto es igual en toda la solución (pág. 184)

era/era una de las muchas subdivisiones temporales entre el Precámbrico y el presente (pág. 421)

esophagus/esófago tubo para el alimento que conecta la boca con el estómago (pág. 980)

estuary/estuario humedal formado donde los ríos se encuentran con el océano (pág. 108)

ethylene/etileno hormona de la planta que estimula la maduración de los frutos (pág. 638)

Eubacteria/*Eubacteria* reino de procariotas unicelulares cuyas paredes celulares están hechas de peptidoglicano (pág. 459)

Eukarya/*Eukarya* dominio de todos los organismos cuyas células tienen núcleo, incluyen los protistas, plantas, hongos y animales (pág. 460)

eukaryote/eucariota organismo cuyas células contienen núcleo (pág. 173)

evaporation/evaporación proceso en el cual el agua cambia de líquido a gas atmosférico (pág. 75)

evolution/evolución cambio de una clase de organismo con el tiempo; proceso por el cual los organismos modernos descienden de organismos antiguos (pág. 369)

evolutionary classification/clasificación evolutiva método de agrupación de organismos según su historia evolutiva (pág. 452)

evolve/evolucionar cambiar con el paso del tiempo (pág. 20)

exocrine gland/glándula exocrina glándula que libera sus secreciones a través de estructuras tubulares llamadas conductos (pág. 998)

exocytosis/exocitosis proceso en el cual una célula libera grandes cantidades de material (pág. 189)

exon/exón secuencia expresada de ADN; codifica una proteína (pág. 302)

exoskeleton/exoesqueleto esqueleto externo; cubierta externa resistente que protege y soporta el cuerpo de muchos invertebrados (págs. 715, 757)

exponential growth/crecimiento exponencial patrón de crecimiento en el que los individuos en una población se reproducen a una razón constante (pág. 121)

external fertilization/fertilización externa proceso en el cual los huevos se fertilizan fuera del cuerpo femenino (págs. 672, 758)

extinct/extinto término usado para referirse a una especie que ha desaparecido (pág. 417)

extinction/extinción desaparición de una especie de toda su zona de distribución geográfica (pág. 151)

extracellular digestion/digestión extracelular proceso en el que los alimentos se descomponen fuera de las células del tracto digestivo (pág. 751)

eyespot/mancha ocular grupo de células que pueden detectar cambios en la cantidad de luz en el ambiente (págs. 509, 685)

facilitated diffusion/difusión facilitada movimiento de moléculas específicas a lo largo de las membranas celulares a través de canales de proteínas (pág. 187)

facultative anaerobe/anaerobio facultativo organismo que puede sobrevivir con o sin oxígeno (pág. 474)

Fallopian tube/trompa de falopio uno de dos tubos llenos de fluido en las mujeres a través de los que pasa un óvulo después de su liberación del ovario (pág. 1012)

family/familia grupo de géneros que tienen muchas características en común (pág. 449)

fat/grasa lípido; formada por ácidos grasos y glicerina; protege los órganos corporales, aisla el cuerpo y almacena energía para el cuerpo (pág. 972)

feather/pluma estructura compuesta principalmente de proteína que se desarrolla en la superficie de la piel del pájaro (pág. 806)

feedback inhibition/retroinhibición proceso por el cual el producto o resultado para o limita el proceso (págs. 658, 895)

fermentation/fermentación proceso por el cual las células liberan energía en la ausencia de oxígeno (pág. 224)

fertilization/fertilización proceso en la reproducción sexual en el cual células reproductoras masculinas y femeninas se unen para formar una nueva célula (pág. 263)

fetal alcohol syndrome/síndrome alcohólico fetal grupo de defectos de nacimiento causados por los efectos del alcohol en un feto (pág. 913)

fetus/feto nombre dado al embrión humano después de ocho semanas de desarrollo (pág. 1020)

fever/fiebre temperatura corporal elevada que ocurre como respuesta a una infección (pág. 1037)

fibrous root/raíz fibrosa parte de un sistema de raíces en la cual las raíces se ramifican a tal grado que ninguna raíz crece más que el resto (pág. 584)

filament/filamento en las algas, na colonia larga en forma de hilos formada por muchas algas verdes; en las plantas, estructura larga y fina que soporta una antera (págs. 512, 612)

filtration/filtración proceso por el cual un líquido o gas pasa a través de un filtro para eliminar desperdicios (pág. 987)

fish/pez vertebrado acuático caracterizado por tener un par de aletas, escamas y branquias (pág. 771)

fission/fisión forma de reproducción asexual en la que un organismo se divide en dos, y cada mitad genera nuevas partes hasta convertirse en un organismo completo (pág. 686)

fitness/eficacia biológica capacidad de un organismo de sobrevivir y reproducirse en su medio ambiente (pág. 380)

flame cell/célula flamígera célula especializada que filtra y elimina el exceso de agua del cuerpo de un gusano plano (pág. 684)

flower/flor estructura portadora de semillas de una angiosperma (pág. 564)

follicle/folículo grupo de células que rodean a un solo óvulo en el sistema reproductor de la mujer (pág. 1012)

food chain/cadena alimentaria serie de pasos en el ecosistema en el que los organismos transfieren energía al comer y ser comidos (pág. 69)

food vacuole/vacuola alimentaria cavidad pequeña en el citoplasma de los protistas que almacena comida temporalmente (pág. 500)

food web/trama alimentaria red de interacciones complejas formada por las relaciones de alimentación entre varios organismos en un ecosistema (pág. 70)

foot/pie parte muscular de un molusco (pág. 702)

fossil/fósil restos o evidencias preservadas de un organismo antiguo (pág. 371)

fossil record/registro fósil información sobre la vida del pasado que incluye la estructura de organismos, lo que comían, sus predadores, el ambiente en que vivían y el orden en el que vivieron (pág. 417)

founder effect/efecto fundador cambio en las frecuencias alélicas como resultado de la migración de un pequeño subgrupo de una población (pág. 400)

frameshift mutation/cambio de pauta mutación que cambia el marco de lectura del mensaje genético al insertar o borrar un nucleótido (pág. 307)

frond/fronda hoja grande de un helecho (pág. 562)

fruit/fruto pared de tejido que rodea a la semilla de una angiosperma (pág. 569)

fruiting body/cuerpo fructífero estructura reproductora fina que produce esporas y que se halla en algunos protistas de tipo hongo; estructura reproductora de un hongo que se desarrolla de un micelio (págs. 516, 528)

Fungi/*Fungi* reino compuesto de heterótrofos; muchos obtienen la energía y los nutrientes de materia orgánica muerta (pág. 460)

gametangium/gametangio estructura productora de gametos, que se halla en el moho (pág. 529)

gamete/gameto célula especializada que participa en la reproducción sexual (pág. 266)

gametophyte/gametofito fase haploide o productora de gametos de un organismo (págs. 514, 552)

ganglion/ganglio grupo de células nerviosas (pág. 685)

gastrovascular cavity/cavidad gastrovascular espacio hueco digestivo con una abertura única, en la que los cnidarios, gusanos y equinodermos digieren la comida (pág. 671)

gastrulation/gastrulación proceso de migración celular por el cual una tercera capa de células se forma en la cavidad de un blastocisto (pág. 1018)

gel electrophoresis/electroforesis de gel procedimiento usado para separar y analizar fragmentos de ADN, colocando una mezcla de los fragmentos de ADN en un extremo de un gel poroso y aplicando un voltaje eléctrico al gel (pág. 323)

gemma/cápsula estructura pequeña en forma de taza en las hepáticas que contiene muchas células haploides; se usa en la reproducción asexual (pág. 557)

gemmule/gémula grupo de arqueocitos rodeados por una capa resistente de espículas; producida por algunas esponjas (pág. 667)

gene/gen secuencia de ADN que codifica una proteína y por ende determina un rasgo (págs. 265, 300)

gene map/mapa génico diagrama que muestra las ubicaciones relativas de cada gen conocido en un cromosoma particular (pág. 280)

gene pool/reservorio génico información genética combinada de todos los miembros de una población en particular (pág. 394)

genetic diversity/diversidad genética suma total de todas las diferentes formas de información genética llevada por todos los organismos que viven en la Tierra en la actualidad (pág. 150)

genetic drift/deriva genética cambio aleatorio en frecuencias alélicas que ocurre en poblaciones pequeñas (pág. 400)

genetic engineering/ingeniería genética proceso que consiste en hacer cambios en el código de ADN de organismos vivos (pág. 322)

genetic equilibrium/equilibrio genético situación en la que las frecuencias alélicas se mantienen constantes (pág. 401)

genetic marker/marcador genético gene que hace posible distinguir la bacteria que lleva un plásmido con un ADN extraño de las que no lo llevan (pág. 328)

genetics/genética estudio científico de la herencia (pág. 263)

genotype/genotipo formación genética de un organismo (pág. 268)

genus/género grupo de especies muy relacionadas, primera parte del nombre científico en la nomenclatura binomial (pág. 448)

geographic isolation/aislamiento geográfico forma de aislamiento reproductivo en la cual dos poblaciones están separadas físicamente por barreras geográficas como ríos, montañas o extensiones de agua (pág. 405)

geologic time scale/escala de cronología geológica escala usada por los paleontólogos para representar el tiempo evolutivo (pág. 421)

germ theory of disease/teoría germinal de las enfermedades idea de que las enfermedades infecciosas son causadas por microorganismos o gérmenes (pág. 1031)

germination/germinación etapa del crecimiento temprano del embrión de una planta (pág. 621)

gibberellin/giberelina sustancia producida por las plantas que ayuda al crecimiento (pág. 637)

gill/branquia órgano filamentoso en animales acuáticos especializado en el intercambio de gases en el agua (pág. 696)

gizzard/molleja en lombrices de tierra, parte del sistema digestivo en el que el alimento es despedazado en pedazos más pequeños; en pájaros, un órgano muscular que ayuda a la descomposición mecánica del alimento (págs. 695, 809)

global warming/calentamiento global aumento del promedio de temperatura en la tierra (pág. 159)

glomerulus/glomérulo pequeña red de capilares encerrados en el extremo superior de una nefrona; donde ocurre la filtración de la sangre (pág. 987)

glycolysis/glucólisis primer paso en la liberación de energía de la glucosa, en el cual una molécula de glucosa se divide en dos moléculas de ácido pirúvico (pág. 221)

Golgi apparatus/aparato de Golgi pila de membranas en la célula que modifica, clasifica y empaqueta proteínas del retículo endoplasmático (pág. 178)

grafting/injerto uso de un tallo como esqueje (pág. 623)

gravitropism/gravitropismo respuesta de una planta a la fuerza de la gravedad (pág. 635)

greenhouse effect/efecto invernadero ocurrencia natural en la que el calor es retenido en la atmósfera de la Tierra por el dióxido de carbono, el metano, el vapor de agua y otros gases (pág. 87)

green revolution/revolución verde desarrollo de variedades de cultivo altamente productivas y la introducción de técnicas de agricultura modernas para aumentar el rendimiento de los cultivos alimenticios (pág. 142)

guard cell/célula oclusiva célula especializada en la epidermis de las plantas que controla la apertura y cierre de los estomas como respuesta a cambios en la presión del agua (pág. 596)

gullet/cavidad bucal abertura en un lado de un ciliado que permite la entrada de alimento a la célula (pág. 502)

gymnosperm/gimnosperma planta con semillas que porta sus semillas directamente en la superficie de sus conos (pág. 564)

habitat/hábitat área donde vive un organismo, incluyendo los factores bióticos y abióticos que afectan al organismo (pág. 90)

habitat fragmentation/fragmentación del hábitat segmentación de ecosistemas en pequeños fragmentos (pág. 151)

habituation/habituación proceso de aprendizaje mediante el cual un animal disminuye o detiene su respuesta a un estímulo repetitivo que ni lo premia ni lo castiga (pág. 874)

hair follicle/folículo piloso saco en forma de tubo de las células de la epidermis que se extiende hasta la dermis; células en la base de los folículos pilosos que producen pelo (pág. 936)

half-life/vida media periodo requerido para que la mitad de los átomos radioactivos de una muestra se descompongan (pág. 420)

haploid/haploide término usado para referirse a una célula que contiene un único juego de cromosomas y, por lo tanto, un único juego de genes (pág. 275)

Hardy-Weinberg principle/principio de Hardy-Weinberg principio que enuncia que las frecuencias de los alelos en una población se mantendrán constantes, a menos que uno o más factores causen cambios en las frecuencias (pág. 400)

Haversian canal/conducto de Havers tubo perteneciente a una red de tubos que recorren el hueso compacto y que contienen vasos sanguíneos y nervios (pág. 922)

heartwood/duramen xilema más viejo situado cerca del centro de un tallo leñoso que ya no conduce agua (pág. 592)

hemoglobin/hemoglobina proteína en los glóbulos rojos que contiene hierro y que transporta el oxígeno de los pulmones a los tejidos del cuerpo (pág. 952)

herbicide/herbicida compuesto que es tóxico para las plantas (pág. 636)

herbivore/herbívoro organismo que obtiene energía alimentándose únicamente de plantas (pág. 69)

hermaphrodite/hermafrodita organismo que tiene órganos reproductores masculinos y femeninos (pág. 686)

heterotroph/heterótrofo organismo que obtiene energía de los alimentos que consume; también se le llama consumidor (págs. 68, 201)

heterozygous/heterocigoto término usado para referirse a un organismo que tiene dos alelos diferentes para el mismo rasgo (pág. 268)

histamine/histamina sustancia química liberada por las células madre activas, que incrementa el flujo de la sangre y los fluidos a la zona circundante (pág. 1043)

histone/histona proteína globular alrededor de la cual el ADN se enrolla estrechamente en la cromatina (pág. 296)

homeostasis/homeostasis proceso por el cual los organismos mantienen un ambiente interno relativamente estable (págs. 16, 895)

hominid/homínido primate que camina en dos patas, tiene pulgares oponibles y posee un cerebro grande; los humanos son los únicos miembros sobrevivientes (pág. 835)

hominoid/hominoideo grupo de antropoides que incluye los monos y los humanos (pág. 835)

homologous/homólogo término usado para referirse a los cromosomas que tienen por cada cromosoma correspondiente al progenitor de un sexo, otro correspondiente al progenitor del otro sexo (pág. 275)

homologous structures/estructuras homólogas estructuras que tienen diferentes formas en diferentes organismos pero que se desarrollan a partir de los mismos tejidos embriónicos (pág. 384)

homozygous/homocigoto término usado para referirse a un organismo que tiene dos alelos idénticos para un rasgo particular (pág. 268)

hormone/hormona sustancia producida en una parte de un organismo que afecta otra parte del mismo organismo (págs. 634, 997)

hox genes/genes HOX serie de genes que controla la diferenciación de células y tejido en un embrión (pág. 312)

humoral immunity/inmunidad humoral inmunidad contra patógenos en los fluidos del cuerpo (pág. 1038)

humus/humus material formado por hojas en descomposición y otra materia orgánica (pág. 103)

hybrid/híbrido descendencia de cruzamientos entre padres con diferentes rasgos (pág. 264)

hybridization/hibridación técnica de crianza que incluye el cruce de individuos distintos para reunir los mejores rasgos de ambos organismos (pág. 319)

hydrostatic skeleton/esqueleto hidrostático capas de músculos circulares y longitudinales que junto con el agua de la cavidad gastrovascular, permiten el movimiento (págs. 671, 756)

hypertonic/hipertónico cuando se comparan dos soluciones, la solución que tiene la mayor concentración de solutos (pág. 185)

hypha/hifa filamento diminuto que conforma un hongo multicelular o un moho de agua (págs. 518, 527)

hypothalamus/hipotálamo estructura del cerebro que actúa como un centro de control para el reconocimiento y el análisis del hambre, la sed, la fatiga, el enojo y la temperatura del cuerpo (pág. 903)

hypothesis/hipótesis explicación posible a un grupo de observaciones o respuesta posible a una pregunta científica (págs. 5, 1062)

hypotonic/hipotónico cuando se comparan dos soluciones, la solucion con la menor concentración de solutos (pag. 185)

immigration/inmigración movimiento de individuos hacia un área que ya tiene población (pág. 120)

immune response/respuesta inmunológica defensas específicas del cuerpo que atacan al agente causante de una enfermedad (pág. 1038)

immunity/inmunidad capacidad del cuerpo de resistir un patógeno específico (pág. 1036)

implantation/implantación proceso en el cual un blastocisto se pega a la pared del útero (pág. 1017)

imprinting/impronta aprendizaje basado en la experiencia temprana; una vez que sucede la impronta, no se puede cambiar el comportamiento (pág. 876)

inbreeding/endogamia reproducción continua de individuos con características similares para mantener las características deseadas en una generación de organismos (pág. 320)

incomplete dominance/dominancia incompleta situación en la cual un alelo no es completamente dominante sobre el otro (pág. 272)

incomplete metamorphosis/metamorfosis incompleta tipo de desarrollo en los insectos caracterizado por una apariencia similar a través de todas las etapas del ciclo de vida (pág. 729)

independent assortment/transmisión independiente segregación independiente de genes durante la formación de gametos (pág. 271)

independent variable/variable independiente factor en un experimento que un científico cambia a propósito; también conocida como variable respuesta (pág. 1062)

index fossil/fósil índice fósil distintivo usado para comparar las edades relativas de los fósiles (pág. 419)

inference/inferencia interpretación lógica basada en conocimiento previo y en experiencia (pág. 4)

inflammatory response/respuesta inflamatoria reacción de defensa no específica a un daño de los tejidos causada por una lesión o infección (pág. 1037)

innate behavior/comportamiento innato comportamiento instintivo o de nacimiento; comportamiento que aparece de forma completamente funcional la primera vez que se realiza (pág. 873)

insight learning/aprendizaje por discernimiento también se llama razonamiento; proceso de aprendizaje en el cual un animal aplica algo que ya ha aprendido a una nueva situación sin un periodo de ensayo y error (pág. 875)

interferon/interferón una de un grupo de proteínas que ayuda a las células a resistir las infecciones virales (pág. 1038)

internal fertilization/fertilización interna proceso en el cual los huevos son fertilizados dentro del cuerpo de la madre (págs. 666, 758)

internode/entrenudo región entre los nudos en el tallo de una planta (pág. 589)

interphase/interfase periodo en el ciclo de una célula entre las divisiones celulares (pág. 245)

intracellular digestion/digestión intracelular proceso en el cual el alimento se digiere dentro de las células (pág. 751)

intron/intrón secuencia de ADN que no participa en la codificación de una proteína (pág. 302)

invasive species/especie invasora plantas y animales que han emigrado a lugares de donde no son nativas (pág. 153)

invertebrate/invertebrado animal que no tiene columna vertebral o espina dorsal (pág. 657)

ion/ion átomo que tiene una carga positiva o negativa (pág. 38)

ionic bond/enlace iónico enlace formado cuando uno o más electrones se transfieren de un átomo a otro (pág. 38)

isotonic/isotónico cuando la concentración de dos soluciones es igual (pág. 185)

isotope/isótopo átomo de un elemento que tiene un número de neutrones diferente a los otros átomos del mismo elemento (pág. 36)

joint/articulación lugar donde un hueso se une a otro (pág. 924)

karyotype/cariotipo fotografía de cromosomas agrupados en orden en pares (pág. 341)

kelp forest/bosque de laminarias comunidad del litoral marítimo nombrada así por su comunidad dominante, el quelpo, un alga marrón gigante (pág. 110)

keratin/queratina proteína resistente y fibrosa que se encuentra en la piel (pág. 934)

kidney/riñón órgano que remueve la urea, el exceso de agua y otros productos de desecho de la sangre (pág. 986)

kingdom/reino grupo taxonómico grande que consiste de los fílums cercanos (pág. 449)

Koch's postulates/postulados de Koch serie de directrices usadas para identificar el microorganismo que causa una enfermedad específica (pág. 1032)

Krebs cycle/ciclo de Krebs segunda etapa de la respiración celular en la cual el ácido pirúvico es descompuesto en dióxido de carbono en una serie de reacciones de extracción de energía (pág. 226)

language/lenguaje sistema de comunicación que combina sonidos, símbolos o gestos según un conjunto de reglas sobre el orden y significado de las palabras (pág. 882)

large intestine/intestino grueso colon, órgano que remueve el agua de los materiales no digeridos que pasan a través de él (pág. 984)

larva/larva etapa inmadura de un organismo que tienen una apariencia diferente a la forma adulta (pág. 666)

larynx/laringe estructura en la garganta que contiene las cuerdas vocales (pág. 958)

lateral bud/brote lateral área meristemática en el lado de un tallo que origina las ramas laterales (pág. 636)

lateral line system/sistema lineal lateral sistema receptor sensible que permite a un pez detectar corrientes suaves y vibraciones en el agua (pág. 777)

leaf/hoja órgano fotosintetizador que contiene uno o más fajos de tejido vascular (pág. 561)

learning/aprendizaje alteraciones en el comportamiento como resultado de la experiencia; también se llama comportamiento aprendido (pág. 873)

lens/cristalino objeto transparente detrás del iris que cambia de forma para que el ojo enfoque y pueda ver objetos cercanos y lejanos (pág. 907)

lichen/liquen asociación simbiótica entre un hongo y un organismo fotosintetizador (pág. 540)

ligament/ligamento tira de tejido conectivo resistente que mantiene los huesos unidos en una articulación (pág. 925)

light-dependent reactions/reacciones dependientes de la luz reacciones de fotosíntesis que usan la energía de la luz para producir ATP y NADPH (pág. 210)

lignin/lignina sustancia en las plantas vasculares que hace que las paredes celulares sean rígidas (pág. 560)

limiting factor/factor limitante factor que causa la disminución del crecimiento de una población (pág. 124)

limiting nutrient/nutriente limitante nutriente único que es escaso o tienen un ciclo muy lento, limitando así el crecimiento de organismos en un ecosistema (pág. 80)

lipid/lípido macromolécula formada principalmente por átomos de carbono e hidrógeno; incluye las grasas, los aceites y las ceras (pág. 46)

lipid bilayer/bicapa lípida lámina de doble capa que forma la base de casi todas las membranas celulares (pág. 182)

liver/hígado órgano grande justo encima del estómago que produce bilis (pág. 982)

logistic growth/crecimiento logístico patrón de crecimiento en el cual la tasa de crecimiento de una población baja o se detiene después de un periodo de crecimiento exponencial (pág. 122)

long-day plant/planta de día largo planta que florece cuando los días son largos (pág. 641)

loop of Henle/asa de Henle sección del túbulo de la nefrona que conserva agua y minimiza el volumen de orina (pág. 987)

lymph/linfa fluido perdido por la sangre al tejido circundante (pág. 954)

lymphocyte/linfocito tipo de célula blanca que produce anticuerpos que ayudan a destruir los patógenos (pág. 952)

lysogenic infection/infección lisogénica proceso en el cual un virus introduce su ADN en el ADN de una célula huésped y es replicado junto con el ADN de la célula huésped (pág. 480)

lysosome/lisosoma organelo de la célula lleno de enzimas necesarias para descomponer ciertos materiales de la célula (pág. 179)

lytic infection/infección lítica proceso en el cual un virus entra una célula, hace una copia de sí mismo y causa que la célula se reviente (pág. 480)

M

macroevolution/macroevolución cambios evolutivos a gran escala que tienen lugar durante largos periodos (pág. 435)

macronucleus/macronúcleo el núcleo más grande de los dos núcleos de un ciliado, contiene copias múltiples de la mayoría de los genes que la célula necesita para su existencia diaria (pág. 501)

madreporite/madreporita estructura parecida a un colador a través de la cual el sistema vascular acuoso de un equinodermo se abre al exterior (pág. 735)

Malpighian tubule/túbulo de Malpigio órgano en forma de saco que tienen la mayoría de los artrópodos terrestres, que extrae los desechos de la sangre y los añade a las heces que pasan por la tripa (pág. 717)

mammary gland/glándula mamaria glándula en los mamíferos que produce leche para alimentar a las crías (pág. 821)

mandible/mandíbula parte de la boca adaptada para morder y triturar alimentos (pág. 721)

mangrove swamp/manglar humedal costero dominado por mangles, plantas leñosas que toleran la sal (pág. 108)

manipulated variable/variable manipulada factor en un experimento que un científico cambia a propósito; también conocida como variable independiente (págs. 9, 1062)

mantle/manto capa fina de tejido que cubre la mayor parte del cuerpo de un molusco (pág. 702)

marsupial/marsupial mamífero que engendra crías vivas que completan su desarrollo en una bolsa externa (pág. 829)

mass extinction/extinción masiva suceso en el cual muchos tipos de seres vivos se extinguen al mismo tiempo (pág. 431)

medulla oblongata/bulbo raquídeo área del cerebro que controla el funcionamiento de muchos órganos internos (pág. 777)

medusa/medusa etapa móvil del ciclo de vida de un cnidario en que el cuerpo tiene forma de campana (pág. 670)

meiosis/meiosis en una célula diploide, proceso por el cual el número de cromosomas por célula se corta a la mitad a través de la separación de cromosomas homólogos (pág. 276)

melanin/melanina pigmento marrón oscuro que se encuentra en la piel (pág. 934)

meninges/meninges tres capas de tejido conectivo que envuelven el cerebro y la espina dorsal (pág. 901)

menstrual cycle/ciclo menstrual ciclo durante el cual un óvulo se desarrolla y sale del ovario y el útero se prepara para recibir el óvulo fertilizado (pág. 1013)

menstruation/menstruación fase del ciclo menstrual durante la cual el revestimiento del útero, junto con sangre y el óvulo sin fertilizar, salen por la vagina (pág. 1014)

meristem/meristemo grupo de tejido que es responsable del crecimiento continuo de una planta a lo largo de su vida (pág. 582)

meristematic tissue/tejido meristemático tejido de las plantas que se encuentra sólo en la punta de los brotes y de las raíces; es responsable del crecimiento de las plantas (pág. 582)

mesoderm/mesodermo capa embrionaria media de la mayoría de los animales; da origen a los músculos y una gran parte de los sistemas circulatorio, reproductor y excretor (pág. 661)

mesophyll/mesofilo tejido fundamental especializado que forma la mayor parte de casi todas las hojas; realiza la mayoría de la fotosíntesis de la planta (pág. 596)

messenger RNA (mRNA)/ARN mensajero (mARN) molécula de ARN que lleva copias de instrucciones para la transformación de aminoácidos a proteínas, del ADN al resto de la célula (pág. 301)

metabolism/metabolismo conjunto de reacciones químicas mediante las cuales un organismo construye o descompone materia mientras realiza sus procesos vitales (pág. 17)

metaphase/metafase segunda fase de la mitosis durante la cual los cromosomas se alinean a través del centro de la célula (pág. 248)

metric system/sistema métrico sistema decimal de medida basado en ciertos estándares físicos y que mide en múltiplos de 10 (pág. 24)

microclimate/microclima clima dentro de un área pequeña que difiere significativamente del clima del área de alrededor (pág. 98)

microfossil/microfósil fósil microscópico (pág. 426)

micronucleus/micronúcleo el núcleo más pequeño de los dos núcleos de un ciliado; contiene una "copia de reserva" de todos los genes de la célula (pág. 501)

microscope/microscopio aparato que produce imágenes ampliadas de estructuras que son demasiado pequeñas para verlas a simple vista (pág. 25)

migration/migración desplazamiento periódico y regreso de animales de un lugar a otro (pág. 878)

mineral/mineral nutriente inorgánico que el cuerpo necesita, normalmente en pequeñas cantidades (pág. 975)

mitochondrion/mitocondria organelo de la célula que convierte la energía química almacenada en el alimento en compuestos que la célula puede usar más cómodamente (pág. 179)

mitosis/mitosis parte de la división celular eucariota durante la cual se divide el núcleo (pág. 245)

mixture/mezcla material compuesto por dos o más elementos o compuestos que están mezclados físicamente pero no están combinados químicamente (pág. 41)

molecular clock/reloj molecular modelo que usa comparaciones de ADN para estimar el tiempo que dos especies han evolucionado independientemente (pág. 455)

molecule/molécula unidad más pequeña de la mayoría de los compuestos (pág. 38)

molting/mudar cubierta proceso en el cual un artrópodo pierde el exoesqueleto y fabrica uno más grande que ocupa su lugar (pág. 719)

monocot/monocotiledónea angiosperma cuyas semillas tienen un cotiledón (pág. 570)

monoculture/monocultivo estrategia de cultivo en la cual campos grandes se siembran con un solo cultivo (pág. 141)

monomer/monómero unidad pequeña que se puede unir a otras unidades pequeñas para formar polímeros (pág. 45)

monosaccharide/monosacárido molécula de azúcar única (pág. 46)

monotreme/monotrema mamífero que pone huevos (pág. 828)

multiple alleles/alelos múltiples tres o más alelos del mismo gen (pág. 273)

muscle tissue/tejido muscular tejido que controla el movimiento interno de materiales en el cuerpo, y el movimiento externo (pág. 894)

mutation/mutación cambio en una secuencia del ADN que afecta la información genética (pág. 307)

mutualism/mutualismo relación simbiótica en la que dos especies se benefician de la relación (pág. 93)

mycelium/micelio muchas hifas unidas juntas que forman una masa gruesa; comprende los cuerpos de los hongos multicelulares (pág. 528)

mycorrhiza/micorriza asociación simbiótica de raíces de plantas y hongos (pág. 541)

myelin sheath/vaina de mielina membrana aislante que rodea el axón de algunas neuronas (pág. 898)

myocardium/miocardio capa media de músculo grueso del corazón; bombea la sangre a través del sistema circulatorio (pág. 944)

myosin/miosina proteína que forma los filamentos gruesos en las estriaciones de las células del músculo esquelético (pág. 928)

NAD^+ (nicotinamide adenine dinucleotide)/NAD^+ (dinucleótido de adenina y nicotinamida) portador de electrones que participa en la glucólisis (pág. 223)

$NADP^+$ (nicotinamide adenine dinucleotide phosphate)/$NADP^+$ (fosfato de dinucleótido de adenina y nicotinamida) una de las moléculas portadoras que transfiere los electrones de alta energía de la clorofila a las otras moléculas (pág. 209)

natural selection/selección natural proceso por el cual los individuos que se adaptan mejor a su medio ambiente sobreviven y se reproducen con más éxito; también se le llama supervivencia del más apto (pág. 381)

nematocyst/nematocisto estructura urticante en cada cnidocito de un cnidario que usa para envenenar o matar a la presa (pág. 669)

nephridium/nefridio órgano excretor de un anélido que filtra fluido en el celoma (pág. 696)

nephron/nefrona unidad de filtración de sangre en la corteza renal de un riñón (pág. 986)

nerve net/plexo nervioso red de células nerviosas vagamente organizadas que juntas permiten a los cnidarios detectar estímulos (pág. 671)

nervous tissue/tejido nervioso tejido que recibe mensajes del medio ambiente interno y externo del cuerpo, analiza la información y dirige la respuesta (pág. 894)

neuromuscular junction/unión neuromuscular punto de contacto entre una neurona motora y una célula muscular esquelética (pág. 929)

neuron/neurona célula que lleva mensajes a través del sistema nervioso (pág. 897)

neurotransmitter/neurotransmisor sustancia química usada por una neurona para transmitir un impulso a otra célula mediante una sinapsis (pág. 900)

neurulation/neurulación desarrollo del sistema nervioso (pág. 1018)

niche/nicho gama completa de todas las condiciones físicas y biológicas en las que un organismo vive y la que manera en la que el organismo usa esas condiciones (pág. 91)

nicotine/nicotina droga estimulante en el tabaco que acelera el pulso y aumenta la presión sanguínea (pág. 961)

nictitating membrane/membrana nictitante en los anfibios, membrana transparente movible localizada dentro del párpado regular; protege la superficie del ojo de daños bajo el agua y lo mantiene húmedo en la tierra (pág. 787)

nitrogen fixation/fijación del nitrógeno proceso de conversión del gas nitrógeno en amoniaco (págs. 78, 477)

node/nudo punto de un tallo donde una hoja se une al tallo (pág. 589)

nondisjunction/no disyunción error en la meiosis en la que los cromosomas homólogos no se separan (pág. 352)

nonrenewable resource/recurso no renovable recurso que no puede ser reemplazado por procesos naturales (pág. 144)

notochord/notocordio varilla larga de sostén que atraviesa el cuerpo de un cordado justo debajo del cordón nervioso (pág. 849)

nuclear envelope/membrana nuclear capa de dos membranas que rodea el núcleo de una célula (pág. 176)

nucleic acid/ácido nucleico macromolécula que contiene hidrógeno, oxígeno, nitrógeno, carbono y fósforo (pág. 47)

nucleolus/nucléolo región pequeña y densa dentro de la mayoría de los núcleos en la que empieza la formación de los proteínas (pág. 176)

nucleotide/nucleótido monómero de ácidos nucleicos formado por un azúcar de 5 carbonos, un grupo fosfato y una base nitrogenada (págs. 47, 291)

nucleus/núcleo centro de un átomo que contiene los protones y neutrones; en las células, estructura que contiene el material genético (ADN) y controla las actividades de la célula (págs. 35, 173)

nutrient/nutriente sustancia química que necesita un organismo para vivir (pág. 76)

nymph/ninfa forma inmadura que no tiene órganos sexuales funcionales ni ninguna otra estructura adulta (pág. 729)

obligate aerobe/aerobio obligado organismo que requiere suministro constante de oxígeno para vivir (pág. 474)

obligate anaerobe/anaerobio obligado organismo que no puede vivir en presencia de oxígeno (pág. 474)

observation/observación uso de uno o más de los sentidos (vista, oído, tacto, olfato y, a veces, gusto) para reunir información (pág. 4)

omnivore/omnívoro organismo que obtiene energía al comer tanto animales como plantas (pág. 69)

oogonium/oogonio estructura especializada formada por hifas que produce núcleos femeninos (pág. 519)

open circulatory system/sistema circulatorio abierto sistema en el cual la sangre no está siempre contenida en una red de vasos sanguíneos (págs. 703, 754)

operant conditioning/condicionamiento operante proceso de aprendizaje en el cual un animal aprende a comportarse de una cierta manera por medio de una práctica repetida, para recibir un premio o evitar un castigo; también se le llama aprendizaje de ensayo y error (pág. 875)

operational definition/definición operacional descripción de cómo una variable particular se puede medir o de cómo un término se puede definir (pág. 1063)

operator/operador región del cromosoma en un operón en el que el represor se une cuando el operón es desactivado (pág. 310)

operon/operón grupo de genes que operan juntos (pág. 309)

opposable thumb/pulgar oponible pulgar que permite agarrar objetos y usar herramientas (pág. 835)

order/orden grupo de familias similares (pág. 449)

organ/órgano grupo de tejidos que trabajan juntos para realizar funciones que están muy relacionadas (pág. 193)

organ system/sistema de órganos grupo de órganos que trabajan juntos para realizar una función específica (pág. 193)

organelle/organelo estructura especializada que realiza importantes funciones celulares dentro de una célula eucariótica (pág. 174)

osculum/ósculo gran orifico en la parte superior de la esponja a través del cual la esponja expulsa el agua (pág. 665)

osmosis/osmosis difusión de agua a través de una membrana permeable selectiva (pág. 185)

ossification/osificación proceso de formación de huesos, durante el cual el cartílago es reemplazado por hueso (pág. 923)

ovary/ovario en las plantas, una estructura de la flor que contiene uno o más óvulos en los que se producen los gametofitos femeninos; en los animales, la gónada femenina que produce los óvulos (págs. 612, 1008)

oviparous/ovíparo término usado para referirse a los animales cuyos huevos se desarrollan fuera del cuerpo de la madre (pág. 778)

ovoviviparous/ovovivíparo término usado para referirse a los animales cuyas crías nacen vivas después de desarrollarse en huevos dentro del cuerpo de la madre (pág. 778)

ovulation/ovulación proceso en el cual el óvulo es liberado por el ovario (pág. 1012)

ovule/óvulo estructura en conos de semillas en el que se desarrollan los gametofitos femeninos (pág. 610)

ozone layer/capa de ozono capa en la atmósfera en la que el gas ozono está relativamente concentrado (pág. 157)

pacemaker/marcapasos grupo pequeño de células musculares cardiacas en el atrio derecho que "marcan el paso" para el corazón como un todo; también conocido como nodo sinoatrial (pág. 946)

paleontologist/paleontólogo científico que estudia los fósiles (pág. 417)

palisade mesophyll/mesofilo en empalizada capa de células mesófilas en forma de columna altas justo debajo de la epidermis superior de una hoja (pág. 596)

pancreas/páncreas glándula que produce hormonas que regulan el azúcar de la sangre; produce enzimas que descomponen carbohidratos, proteínas, lípidos y ácidos nucleicos; y produce bicarbonato sódico, una base que neutraliza el ácido del estómago (pág. 982)

parasitism/parasitismo relación simbiótica en la cual un organismo vive dentro o sobre otro organismo (el anfitrión) y como consecuencia lo daña (pág. 93)

parenchyma/parénquima tipo de célula de tejido fundamental con una pared celular fina y una vacuola central grande (pág. 582)

passive immunity/inmunidad pasiva inmunidad de corto plazo causada cuando los anticuerpos de otros animales producidos para un patógeno, son inyectados en el cuerpo (pág. 1042)

pathogen/patógeno agente causante de enfermedades (págs. 485, 1031)

pedigree/genealogía gráfica que muestra las relaciones en una familia (pág. 342)

pedipalps/pedipalpo en los quelicerados, par de partes de la boca que generalmente están adaptadas para atrapar a las presas (pág. 722)

pellicle/cutícula membrana celular en las euglenas (pág. 507)

penis/pene órgano reproductor masculino externo (pág. 1011)

perennial/perenne planta con flores que vive durante más de dos años (pág. 572)

period/periodo unidad de tiempo en las que están subdivididas las eras (pág. 422)

periosteum/periostio capa resistente de tejido conectivo que cubre hueso (pág. 922)

peristalsis/peristaltismo contracciones musculares rítmicas que hacen pasar el alimento del esófago al estómago (pág. 980)

permafrost/permagélido capa de subsuelo permanentemente congelada en la tundra (pág. 104)

petal/pétalo estructura de color reluciente que se encuentra justo dentro de los sépalos; atrae insectos y otros polinizadores a la flor (pág. 612)

petiole/pecíolo estructura fina que une la hoja al tallo (pág. 595)

pH scale/escala pH sistema de medida usado para indicar la concentración de iones de hidrógeno (H^+) en una solución; el rango va del 0 al 14 (pág. 43)

phagocytosis/fagocitosis proceso en el cual extensiones del citoplasma rodean y atrapan partículas grandes y las llevan a la célula (pág. 189)

pharyngeal pouch/saco faríngeo una de las dos estructuras en la región de la garganta (faringe) de un cordado (pág. 767)

pharynx/faringe tubo muscular al final de la cavidad gastrovascular, o garganta, que une la boca con el resto del tracto digestivo y que sirve como vía para el aire y el alimento (págs. 684, 956)

phenotype/fenotipo características físicas de un organismo (pág. 268)

pheromone/feromona mensajero químico específico que afecta el comportamiento o el desarrollo de otros individuos de la misma especie (pág. 731)

phloem/floema tejido vascular responsable del transporte de los nutrientes y carbohidratos producidos por la fotosíntesis (pág. 560)

photic zone/zona fótica capa superior bien iluminada de los océanos (pág. 109)

photoautotroph/fotoautótrofo organismo que usa la energía del sol para convertir dióxido de carbono y agua en componentes de carbono (pág. 474)

photoheterotroph/fotoheterótrofo organismo que es fotosintetizador pero que también necesita compuestos orgánicos como fuente de carbono (pág. 474)

photoperiodism/fotoperiodicidad respuesta de las plantas a los periodos de luz y oscuridad (pág. 641)

photosynthesis/fotosíntesis proceso por el cual las plantas y algunos otros organismos usan la energía de la luz para convertir el agua y el dióxido de carbono en oxígeno y en carbohidratos de alta energía, como azúcares y almidones (págs. 68, 204)

photosystem/fotosistema unidades recolectoras de luz del cloroplasto (pág. 208)

phototropism/fototropismo tendencia de las plantas a crecer hacia una fuente de luz (pág. 634)

phycobilin/ficobilina pigmento accesorio que se encuentra en las algas rojas y que es especialmente bueno en la absorción de luz azul (pág. 510)

phylogeny/filogenia el estudio de las relaciones evolutivas entre organismos (pág. 452)

phylum/fílum grupo de clases muy relacionadas (pág. 449)

phytochrome/fitocromo pigmento de la planta responsable de la fotoperiodicidad (pág. 641)

phytoplankton/fitoplancton población de algas y otros pequeños organismos fotosintetizadores que se encuentran cerca de la superficie del mar y que forman parte del plancton (págs. 107, 509)

pigment/pigmento molécula que absorbe la luz (pág. 207)

pinocytosis/pinocitosis proceso por el cual una célula absorbe líquido del ambiente que la rodea (pág. 189)

pioneer species/especie pionera primera especie que puebla un área durante la sucesión primaria (pág. 94)

pith/médula conjunto de células parénquimas dentro del anillo de tejido vascular en el tallo de las dicotiledóneas (pág. 590)

pituitary gland/glándula pituitaria glándula en la base del cráneo que secreta nueve hormonas que regulan directamente muchas funciones del cuerpo y controlan las acciones de otras glándulas endocrinas (pág. 1003)

placenta/placenta órgano en los mamíferos placentarios a través del cual nutrientes, oxígeno, dióxido de carbono y desechos son intercambiados entre el embrión y la madre (págs. 829, 1019)

plankton/plancton organismos diminutos de flotación libre que viven en medios acuáticos (pág. 107)

Plantae/*Plantae* reino de autótrofos multicelulares fotosintetizadores que tienen pared celular que contiene celulosa (pág. 461)

plasma/plasma fluido de color amarillo claro que compone el 55 por ciento de la sangre (pág. 951)

plasmid/plásmido pequeña pieza circular de ADN (pág. 327)

plasmodium/plasmodio estructura con muchos núcleos formada por mohos mucilagenosos acelulares (pág. 518)

plastron/plastrón parte ventral de la coraza de una tortuga (pág. 805)

platelet/plaqueta fragmento celular liberado por la médula ósea que ayuda a la coagulación de la sangre (pág. 953)

point mutation/mutación puntual mutación genética que provoca cambios en uno o pocos nucleótidos (pág. 307)

polar zone/zona polar zona de clima frío donde los rayos de sol llegan a la Tierra a un ángulo muy bajo (pág. 88)

pollen cone/cono de polen cono en las gimnospermas que produce gametofitos masculinos en forma de granos de polen (pág. 610)

pollen grain/grano de polen gametofito masculino en las plantas con semillas (pág. 565)

pollen tube/tubo polínico estructura que crece en el grano de polen; contiene dos núcleos espermáticos haploides (pág. 611)

pollination/polinización transporte del polen de la estructura reproductora masculina a la estructura reproductora femenina (pág. 565)

pollutant/contaminante sustancia dañina que puede entrar en la biosfera a través de la tierra, aire o agua (pág. 148)

polygenic trait/rasgo poligénico rasgo controlado por dos o más genes (págs. 273, 396)

polymer/polímero compuesto grande formado por combinaciones de muchos monómeros (pág. 45)

polymerase chain reaction (PCR)/reacción en cadena de la polimerasa (PCR) técnica que permite a los biólogos moleculares hacer muchas copias de un gen en particular (pág. 325)

polyp/pólipo etapa normalmente sésil del ciclo de vida de un cnidario en la que tiene el cuerpo cilíndrico y tentáculos que parecen brazos (pág. 670)

polyploidy/poliploidía condición en la que un organismo tiene grupos extra de cromosomas (pág. 308)

polysaccharide/polisacárido macromolécula grande formada por monosacáridos (pág. 46)

population/población grupo de individuos de la misma especie que vive en la misma área (pág. 64)

population density/densidad de población número de individuos por unidad de área (pág. 119)

predation/depredación interacción en la cual un organismo captura a otro organismo y se alimenta de él (pág. 93)

predator-prey relationship/relación entre depredador-y presa mecanismo de control de población en la cual una población es regulada por la depredación (pág. 126)

prehensile/prensil término usado para referirse a una cola larga que puede agarrarse de las ramas (pág. 835)

pressure-flow hyphothesis/hipótesis de flujo por presión hipótesis que considera las plantas en términos de dónde producen y usan los materiales de la fotosíntesis (pág. 602)

primary growth/crecimiento primario en las plantas, tipo de crecimiento que ocurre en las puntas de las raíces y brotes (pág. 590)

primary productivity/productividad primaria tasa a la que la materia orgánica es producida por los productores en un ecosistema (pág. 80)

primary succession/sucesión primaria sucesión que ocurre en las superficies donde no existe el suelo (pág. 94)

prion/prión partícula infecciosa compuesta de proteína en vez de ARN o ADN (pág. 490)

probability/probabilidad posibilidad de que ocurra un suceso en particular (pág. 267)

producer/productor organismo que puede captar la energía de la luz solar o de las sustancias químicas y usarla para producir alimento de compuestos inorgánicos; también se le llama autótrofo (pág. 67)

product/producto elemento o compuesto producido por una reacción química (pág. 49)

proglottid/proglótide uno de los segmentos que forman la mayoría del cuerpo de la tenia (pág. 688)

prokaryote/procariota organismos unicelulares que carecen de núcleo (págs. 173, 471)

promoter/promotor región del ADN que le indica a una enzima adónde debe enlazarse para formar ARN (pág. 301)

prophage/prófago el ADN vírico que está incrustado en el ADN de la célula anfitriona (pág. 480)

prophase/profase fase primera y más larga de la mitosis, durante la cual los cromosomas se hacen visibles y los centríolos se separan y toman posiciones en lados opuestos del núcleo (pág. 246)

prosimian/prosimio primate pequeño y nocturno que tiene ojos grandes que le permiten ver en la oscuridad (pág. 834)

prostaglandin/prostaglandina ácido graso modificado parecido a una hormona y producido por una gran variedad de células; generalmente afecta sólo células y tejidos cercanos (pág. 1000)

protein/proteína macromolécula que contiene carbono, hidrógeno, oxígeno y nitrógeno; necesitada por el cuerpo para el crecimiento y la reparación y para fabricar enzimas (págs. 47, 973)

proteinoid microsphere/microsfera proteinoide burbuja diminuta formada por grandes moléculas orgánicas, que tiene algunas de las mismas características de la célula (pág. 425)

protist/protista cualquier eucariota que no es una planta, un animal o un hongo (pág. 497)

Protista/*Protista* reino compuesto de eucariotas que no están clasificados como plantas, animales u hongos (pág. 460)

protonema/protonema masa de filamentos verdes entrelazados en los musgos, que se forma durante la germinación (pág. 558)

protostome/protostomo animal cuya boca se forma de su blastoporo (pág. 661)

pseudocoelom/seudoceloma cavidad corporal entre los tejidos endodermo y mesodermo que está parcialmente recubierta de mesodermo (pág. 689)

pseudopod/seudópodo proyección temporal del citoplasma, o un "pie falso", que usan algunos protistas para alimentarse o moverse (pág. 500)

puberty/pubertad periodo de crecimiento rápido y maduración sexual durante el cual el sistema reproductor se hace totalmente funcional (pág. 1009)

pulmonary circulation/circulación pulmonar vía circulatoria entre el corazón y los pulmones (pág. 945)

punctuated equilibrium/equilibrio puntual patrón de evolución en el cual los periodos estables largos son interrumpidos por breves periodos de cambio rápido (pág. 439)

Punnett square/cuadro de Punnett diagrama que muestra las combinaciones de genes que podría resultar de un cruce genético (pág. 268)

pupa/pupa etapa de la metamorfosis en la cual un insecto cambia de larva a adulto (pág. 729)

pupil/pupila pequeña abertura en el centro del iris a través de la cual entra la luz al ojo (pág. 906)

radial symmetry/simetría radial conformación corporal en la cual las partes del cuerpo se repiten alrededor del centro del cuerpo; característica de las anémonas y las estrellas de mar (págs. 662, 748)

radioactive dating/datación radioactiva técnica en la que los científicos calculan la edad de una muestra basándose en la cantidad residual de isótopos radiactivos que contiene (pág. 420)

radula/rádula estructura en forma de lengua usada por los caracoles y babosas para alimentarse (pág. 702)

reabsorption/reabsorción proceso en el cual se recupera el líquido en un vaso (pág. 987)

reactant/reaccionante elemento o compuesto que entra en una reacción química (pág. 49)

recombinant DNA/ADN recombinante ADN producido por la combinación de ADN de diferentes fuentes (pág. 324)

reflex/reflejo respuesta rápida y automática a un estímulo (pág. 903)

reflex arc/arco reflejo receptor sensorial, neurona sensorial, neurona motriz y catalizador que están involucrados en una respuesta rápida a un estímulo (pág. 904)

relative dating/datación relativa método para determinar la edad de un fósil al comparar su ubicación con los fósiles que están en otras capas de la roca (pág. 419)

relative frequency/frecuencia relativa número de veces que ocurre un alelo en un reservorio génico comparado con el número de veces que ocurren otros alelos (pág. 394)

renewable resource/recurso renovable recurso que se puede regenerar rápidamente y que es reemplazable (pág. 144)

replication/replicación proceso de copia por el cual una célula duplica su ADN (pág. 299)

reproductive isolation/aislamiento reproductivo separación de especies o poblaciones tal que no pueden cruzarse ni tener descendencia fértil (pág. 404)

reptile/reptil cualquier vertebrado que tiene piel seca escamada, pulmones y se reproduce en tierra por huevos que tienen varias membranas protectoras (pág. 797)

resource/recurso cualquier necesidad vital, como el agua, nutrientes, luz, alimento o espacio (pág. 92)

responding variable/variable respuesta factor en un experimento que un científico quiere observar, el cual puede cambiar en respuesta a una variable manipulada; también se conoce como variable dependiente (págs. 9, 1062)

response/respuesta reacción única y específica a un estímulo (pág. 871)

resting potential/potencial de reposo carga eléctrica en toda la membrana celular de una neurona en reposo (pág. 898)

restriction enzyme/enzima de restricción enzima que corta el ADN en una secuencia específica de nucleótidos (pág. 323)

retina/retina capa más interna del ojo; contiene fotoreceptores (pág. 907)

retrovirus/retrovirus virus que contiene ARN como su información genética (pág. 482)

rhizoid/rizoide en los hongos, una hifa parecida a una raíz que penetra la superficie de un objeto; en los musgos, una célula larga y delgada que sujeta el musgo a la tierra y absorbe el agua y los minerales del suelo que le rodea (págs. 530, 557)

rhizome/rizoma tallo trepador o subterráneo de los helechos (pág. 562)

ribonucleic acid (RNA)/ácido ribonucleico (ARN) hebra única de ácido nucleico que contiene el azúcar ribosa (pág. 47)

ribosomal RNA (rRNA)/ARN ribosómico (rARN) tipo de ARN que conforma principalmente a los ribosomas (pág. 301)

ribosome/ribosoma partícula pequeña en la célula en la que se fabrican las proteínas; está hecho de ARN y proteína (pág. 177)

risk factor/factor de riesgo cualquier elemento que aumenta las posibilidades de enfermedad o lesión (pág. 1049)

RNA polymerase/polimerasa de ARN enzima similar al ADN polimerasa que se une al ADN y separa las hebras de ADN durante la transcripción (pág. 301)

rod/bastoncillo fotoreceptor en el ojo que es sensible a la luz, pero no a los colores (pág. 907)

root/raíz órgano subterráneo en las plantas que absorbe agua y minerales (pág. 561)

root cap/caliptra estructura resistente que protege la raíz a medida que ésta penetra en la tierra (pág. 585)

root hair/pelos radicales proyecciones diminutas de la superficie externa, o epidermis, de una raíz (pág. 585)

rumen/rumen cavidad estomacal en los vacunos y animales relacionados en la que se almacenan y procesan las plantas recién tragadas (pág. 823)

salt marsh/marisma estuario de zona templada dominado por pastos que toleran la sal, por encima del nivel de la marea baja, y por algas, bajo el agua (pág. 108)

saprobe/saprófito organismo que obtiene los alimentos de materia orgánica en descomposición (pág. 537)

sapwood/albura área en las plantas que rodea el duramen y es activa en el transporte de fluidos (pág. 592)

science/ciencia manera organizada de usar la evidencia para aprender sobre el mundo natural; también el conjunto de conocimientos que los científicos han desarrollado después de años de usar este proceso (pág. 3)

sclerenchyma/esclerénquima tipo de célula del tejido fundamental con una pared celular extremadamente rígida y gruesa que hace que el tejido fundamental sea resistente y fuerte (pág. 582)

scolex/escólex cabeza de un tenia adulta; puede tener ventosas o ganchos (pág. 688)

scrotum/escroto saco externo que contiene los testículos (pág. 1010)

secondary growth/crecimiento secundario patrón del crecimiento de una planta en la cual el tallo aumenta su grosor (pág. 591)

secondary succession/sucesión secundaria sucesión que sigue a una alteración que destruye una comunidad sin destruir el suelo (pág. 95)

seed/semilla embrión de una planta viva que está en una cápsula protectora y rodeado de su fuente de alimento (pág. 565)

seed coat/tegumento seminal estructura que rodea y protege el embrión de una planta y evita que se seque (pág. 565)

seed cone/cono de semillas cono que produce gametofitos femeninos (pág. 610)

segregation/segregación separación de alelos durante la formación de gametos (pág. 266)

selective breeding/cruzamiento dirigido método de cruzamiento que permite que sólo aquellos organismos con las características deseadas produzcan la siguiente generación (pág. 319)

semicircular canal/conducto semicircular una de las tres estructuras en el oído interno que ayudan a mantener la posición del cuerpo (pág. 908)

seminiferous tubule/tubo seminífero uno de los cientos de túbulos diminutos en los testículos en donde se produce el semen (pág. 1010)

sensory receptor/receptor sensorial neurona que reacciona a un estímulo concreto, como la luz o el sonido, enviando impulsos a otras neuronas y con el tiempo al sistema nervioso central (pág. 906)

sepal/sépalo círculo externo de las flores que encierra un brote antes de que se abra y que protege la flor mientras se desarrolla (pág. 612)

septum/septo pared interna entre los segmentos del cuerpo de un anélido (pág. 694)

seta/queta cilio pegado a los segmentos de muchos anélidos (pág. 694)

sex chromosome/cromosoma sexual uno de los dos cromosomas que determinan el sexo de un individuo (pág. 341)

Kuhn Photography **205** t.r. ©Bettmann/CORBIS **208** b.l. ©John Durham/Science Photo Library/Photo Researchers, Inc. **208** b.r. ©Newcomb & Wegin/Stone **208** t.l. ©Clyde H. Smith/Peter Arnold, Inc. **210** ©David Muench 2000 **214** b. ©PhotoDisc, Inc., 2001 **214** t. ©Larry Brownstein/Rainbow/PictureQuest **215** Pearson Education/PH School **216** ©David Muench 2000 **218** ©Ken Wagner/Phototake/PictureQuest **220** Duomo Photography, Inc. **221** l. ©Bob Gurr/DRK Photo **221** m.b. ©John Durham/Science Photo Library/Photo Researchers, Inc. **221** m.t. ©Ron Boardman/Stone **221** r. ©Keith Porter/Photo Researchers, Inc. **224** ©Becky Luigart-Stayner/CORBIS **226** ©Science Photo Library/Photo Researchers, Inc. **230** ©Allsport/Ross Kinnaird **231** Pearson Education/PH School **233** l. ©Najlah Feanny/CORBIS **233** r. Getty Images-Photodisc **234** Pearson Education/PH School **235** Pearson Education/PH School **236** ©Allsport/Ross Kinnaird **236** b. ©Bob Gurr/DRK Photo **240** ©CAMR/A.B. Dowsett/Science Photo Library/Photo Researchers, Inc. **241** ©Kevin Summers/Stone **242** Pearson Education/PH School **244** ©Gunther F. Bahr/AFIP/Stone **246** b. ©Ed Reschke/Peter Arnold, Inc. **246** m. ©Ed Reschke/Peter Arnold, Inc. **246** t. ©Ed Reschke/Peter Arnold, Inc. **247** b.l. ©Ed Reschke/Peter Arnold, Inc. **247** b.r. ©Ed Reschke/Peter Arnold, Inc. **247** t. ©Ed Reschke/Peter Arnold, Inc. **248** ©R. Calentine/Visuals Unlimited **252** ©Dr. Gopal Murti/Science Photo Library/Photo Researchers, Inc. **253** b.l. ©Stan Flegler/Visuals Unlimited **253** b.r. ©Professor P.M. Motta & E. Vizza/Science Photo Library/Photo Researchers, Inc. **253** t.l. ©CAMR/A.B. Dowsett/Science Photo Library/Photo Researchers, Inc. **253** t.r. ©Dr. Dennis Kunkel/Phototake **254** ©Ed Reschke/Peter Arnold, Inc. **255** Pearson Education/PH School **256** ©Dr. Gopal Murti/Science Photo Library/Photo Researchers, Inc. **166-167** ©Dr. Brian Eyden/Science Photo Library/Photo Researchers, Inc. **260–261** ©MAXIMILIAN STOCK LTD./Animals Animals Enterprises **260** b.l. Adrian Warren, Lastrefuge.co.uk **261** b. Courtesy of Ken Miller **262** W. Perry Conway/CORBIS **263** ©CORBIS **267** ©Al Francekevich/The Stock Market **270** ©James W. Richardson/Visuals Unlimited **271** Runk/Schoenberger/Grant Heilman Photography **273** b.l. ©Jane Burton/Bruce Coleman, Inc. **273** b.r. ©Hans Reinhard/Bruce Coleman, Inc. **273** t.l. ©John Gerlach/Visuals Unlimited **273** t.r. Animals Animals/©Richard Kolar **274** Kim Taylor/Bruce Coleman, Inc. **279** Animals Animals/©George Bernard **281** Pearson Education/PH School **284** ©S. Nielsen/DRK Photo **286** Jacob Halaska/Index Stock Imagery, Inc. **287** ©Klaus Guldbrandsen/Science Photo Library/Photo Researchers, Inc. **289** ©Lee D. Simon/Science Source/Photo Researchers, Inc. **292** b. ©Bettmann/CORBIS **292** l.m. ©Science Source/Photo Researchers, Inc. **292** t.r. ©Cold Spring Harbor Laboratory Archives/Peter Arnold, Inc. **293** b.l. ©A. Barrington/Photo Researchers, Inc. **293** b.r. Jane Reed/Harvard University **293** t. ©2000 Kay Chernush/Howard Hughes Medical Institute **294** Jacob Halaska/Index Stock Imagery, Inc. **296** Science Photo Library/Custom Medical Stock Photo, Inc. **298** ©Dr. Gopal Murti/Science Photo Library/Photo Researchers, Inc. **301** From J. Frank, American Scientist 86 (2000), 428–439, Courtesy of Joachim Frank, All Rights Reserved. **313** Pearson Education/PH School **318** ©Anup Shah/Dembinsky Photo Associates **319** ©Darrell Gulin/DRK Photo **320** b. ©Manfred Kage/Peter Arnold, Inc. **320** t. ©Mitsuaki Iwago/Minden Pictures, Inc. **321** Runk/Schoenberger/Grant Heilman Photography **326** Pearson Education/PH School **330** N. Cobbing. ©Still Pictures/Peter Arnold, Inc. **331** ©Keith V. Wood/Visuals Unlimited **333** "PA" News **335** Pearson Education/PH School **336** "PA" News **340** Richard Hutchings/Photo Researchers, Inc. **341** ©CNRI/Science Photo Library/Photo Researchers, Inc. **343** ©Craig Farraway **344** ©The Stock Market/Charles Gupton **346** ©Simon Fraser/RVI, Newcastle-Upon Tyne/Science Photo Library/Photo Researchers, Inc. **347** ©Omikron/Photo Researchers, Inc. **352** ©PhotoDisc, Inc., 2001 **353** t.l. ©Lawrence Migdale **353** t.r. ©Dr. Dennis Kunkel/CNRI/Phototake **354** AP/Wide World Photos **355** b. AP/Wide World Photos **355** t. ©James King-Holmes/Science Photo Library/Photo Researchers, Inc. **356** l. ©Leonard Lessin/Peter Arnold, Inc. **356** r. ©D. VoTrung/Phototake **357** Paul Hosefros/NYT Permissions **359** t.l. ©PhotoDisc, Inc., 2001 **359** t.r. ©Peter Hvizdak/The Image Works **362** ©CNRI/Science Photo Library/Photo Researchers, Inc. **364** ©ISM/Phototake **367** b. Russ Lappa/PH School **368** Art Wolfe Incorporated **370** l. Syndics of Cambridge University Library **370** r. ©Joe McDonald/Bruce Coleman, Inc./PictureQuest **371** b. ©D. Cavagnaro/DRK Photo **371** m. ©David Cavagnaro/DRK Photo **371** t. ©D. Cavagnaro/DRK Photo **372** ©Frans Lanting/Photo Researchers, Inc. **373** Bibliotheque des Arts Decoratifs, Paris, France/Archives Charmet/Bridgeman Art Library **374** b. Stock Montage, Inc. **374** m. The Granger Collection, New York **374** t. ©Tom and Susan Bean/DRK Photo **375** b. ©2000 North Wind Picture Archives **375** t.l. The Granger Collection, New York **375** t.r. Brown Brothers **377** Archiv für Kunst und Geschichte, Berlin **378** Mark Downey/Index Stock Photography, Inc. **380** ©J. Sneesby/B. Wilkins/Stone **381** ©Ron Austing/Photo Researchers, Inc. **382** Neil Fletcher/©Dorling Kindersley **385** b. Prof. Dr. Michael K. Richardson **385** b.l. ©George Whiteley/Photo Researchers, Inc. **385** b.r. ©David Spears/Science Photo Library/Photo Researchers, Inc. **385** m.b. Animals Animals/©Keith Gillett **385** m.b. Ann Campbell Burke/Wesleyan University/Journal of Morphology. **385** t. Harry Taylor/©Dorling Kindersley **386** ©ARCHIV/Photo Researchers, Inc. **390** b. ©D. Cavagnaro/DRK Photo **390** t. ©David Cavagnaro/DRK Photo **392** ©MURRAY, PATTI/Animals Animals Enterprises **393** ©Melanie Carr/Zephyr Photos **395** ©David Young-Wolff/PhotoEdit/PictureQuest **396** New York Public Library, (Rare Book Division or Print Collection. Miriam and Ira D. Wallach Division of Art, Prints and Photographs); Astor, Lenox and Tilden Foundations **397** ©Charlie Ott/Photo Researchers, Inc. **399** ©Melanie Carr/Zephyr Photos **401** Pearson Education/PH School **402** ©Lee F. Snyder/Photo Researchers, Inc. **403** ©David R. Frazier/Photo Researchers, Inc. **404** l. ©Harold Hoffman/Photo Researchers, Inc. **404** r. ©Steve Kaufman/DRK Photo **405** inset: l. Animals Animals/©Breck P. Kent **405** inset: r. ©Tom & Pat Leeson/DRK Photo **405** t. ©Danny Lehman/CORBIS **407** b. Photograph by P.R. Grant **407** t. Photograph by B.R. Grant **410** David Sanders/DS Photography **411** Pearson Education/PH School **416** Jackie Beckett/American Museum of Natural History **417** Ira Block/National Geographic Society **419** l. ©David Hanson/Stone **419** r. ©CORBIS **425** ©Sidney Fox/Visuals Unlimited **426** ©Fred Bavendam/Peter Arnold, Inc. **428** British Museum of Natural History, London **429** ©D.W. Miller **430** British Museum of Natural History, London/J. Sibbick **431** b. Grant Heilman Photography **431** t. Field Museum of Natural History **432** 1989 Mark Hallett **433** b.l. ©PhotoDisc, Inc., 2001 **433** b.r. Ira Block **433** t. The Natural History Museum London/M. Long **434** ©Douglas Henderson **435** ©D. Van Ravenswaay/Science Photo Library/Photo Researchers, Inc. **437** b. Mike Bacon/Tom Stack & Associates **437** m. ©Wayne Lynch/DRK Photo **437** t. ©PhotoDisc, Inc., 2001 **438** b. ©Charles Marden Fitch **438** t. The Natural History Museum, London **439** Sean Milne/©Dorling Kindersley **441** Pearson Education/PH School **446** ©Gary Randall/Visuals Unlimited **447** ©Jeff Lepore/Photo Researchers, Inc. **448** ©Kenneth W. Fink/Photo Researchers, Inc. **449** b.r. Daniel J. Cox/naturalexposures.com **449** m.b. Animals Animals/©Norbert Rosing **449** m.l. ©Art Wolfe/Photo Researchers, Inc. **449** t. ©Bettmann/CORBIS **451** b.l. ©Peter Howorth/Mo Yung Productions/www.norbertwu.com **451** b.r. ©Nancy Sefton/Photo Researchers, Inc. **451** t.l. Animals Animals/©Rudolf Ingo Riepl **454** b. ©D. Parer & E. Parer-Cook/Auscape International Photo Library **454** m. ©PhotoDisc, Inc., 2001 **454** t. ©Barbara Gerlach/DRK Photo **456** ©Marie Selby Botanical Gardens **457** l. ©Michael Abbey/Photo Researchers, Inc. **457** r. ©CNRI/Phototake **463** Matthew Ward/©Dorling Kindersley **463** cw-1 Matthew Ward/©Dorling Kindersley **463** cw-2 ©Dorling Kindersley **463** cw-3 ©Dorling Kindersley **463** cw-4 ©Dorling Kindersley **463** cw-6 Matthew Ward/©Dorling Kindersley **463** m. Matthew Ward/©Dorling Kindersley **468–469** Biophoto Associates/Photo Researchers, Inc. **469** b. Courtesy of Ken Miller **470** Michael T. Sedam/CORBIS **471** Esther R. Angert, Harvard University **472** ©M. Wurtz/Biozentrum, University of Basel/Science Photo Library/Photo Researchers, Inc. **473** b. ©Scott Camazine/Photo Researchers, Inc. **473** m. ©David M. Phillips/Visuals Unlimited **473** t. ©David Scharf/Peter Arnold, Inc. **474** ©Fred McConnaughey/Science Source/Photo Researchers, Inc. **475** l. ©Dr. Dennis Kunkel/Phototake **475** m. ©Dr. Dennis Kunkel/Phototake **475** r. ©A. B. Dowsett/Science Photo Library/Photo Researchers, Inc. **476** ©Michael P. Gadomski/Photo Researchers, Inc. **477** ©Richard L. Carlton/Visuals Unlimited **478** ©Norm Thomas/Photo Researchers, Inc. **479** l. ©M. Wurtz/Biozentrum, University of Basel/Science Photo Library/Photo Researchers, Inc. **479** m. ©Dr. O. Bradfute/Peter Arnold, Inc. **479** r. ©National Institute for Biological Standards and Control, England/Photo Researchers, Inc. **482** Pearson Education/PH School **484** ©Kim Kulish/CORBIS **485** ©A. Wolf/Explorer/Photo Researchers, Inc. **486** Mary Evans Picture Library R.W.J. Short **487** m. Chris Ware/Liaison Agency **487** l. Courtesy of Historical Collections & Services, Claude Moore Health Sciences Library, University of Virginia. **487** r. ©Bettmann/CORBIS **487** t.r. CDC/PHIL/CORBIS **489** l. ©PhotoDisc, Inc., 2001 **490** Sinclair Stammers/Science Photo Library/Photo Researchers, Inc. **492** t. ©M. Wurtz/Biozentrum, University of Basel/Science Photo Library/Photo Researchers, Inc. **493** b.l. ©David Scharf/Peter Arnold, Inc. **493** b.r. ©Scott Camazine/Photo Researchers, Inc. **493** t.l. ©M. Wurtz/Biozentrum, University of Basel/Science Photo Library/Photo Researchers, Inc. **493** t.r. ©David M. Phillips/Visuals Unlimited **496** Andrew Syred/Science Photo Library/Photo Researchers, Inc. **497** l. ©Manfred Kage/Peter Arnold, Inc. **497** m. ©Manfred Kage/Peter Arnold, Inc. **497** r. ©M.I. Walker/Photo Researchers, Inc. **498** ©T.E. Adams/Visuals Unlimited **499** l. ©Michael Abbey/Photo Researchers, Inc. **499** r. ©Oliver Meckes/Photo Researchers, Inc. **500** Runk/Schoenberger/Grant Heilman Photography **501** ©Eric V. Grave/Photo Researchers, Inc. **503** ©Oliver Meckes/Photo Researchers, Inc. **504** ©Robert Brons/Biological Photo Service **505** l. ©Dr. Dennis Kunkel/Phototake **505** r. ©Eric Grave/Science Source/Photo Researchers, Inc. **506** ©A. Flowers & L. Newman/Photo Researchers, Inc. **507** b. ©Dr. Dennis Kunkel/Phototake **508** ©Dr. Dennis Kunkel/Phototake **509** inset ©David M. Phillips/Visuals Unlimited **509** t. ©Bill Bachman/Photo Researchers, Inc. **510** ©G. Robinson/Visuals Unlimited **512** b. ©Laurie Campbell/NHPA **512** m. ©James W. Richardson/Visuals Unlimited **512** t. Biophoto Assoc./Photo Researchers, Inc. **515** b. DeSanto/StockFood **515** t. Eising/StockFood **516** ©L. West/Photo Researchers, Inc. **517** ©Matt Meadows/Peter Arnold, Inc. **518** ©Dr. Dennis Kunkel/Phototake **520** b.l. ©E. Webber/Visuals Unlimited **520** b.r. ©Holt Studios Int./Photo Researchers, Inc. **520** t. The Granger Collection, New York **521** Pearson Education/PH School **526** ©D. Cavagnaro/DRK Photo **528** b. Robert & Linda Mitchell Photography **528** t. ©Sarah J. Frankling/Stone **529** ©Jeff Lepore/Photo Researchers, Inc. **532** Lee Rentz/Bruce Coleman, Inc. **535** b.l. ©Michael Fogden/DRK Photo **535** b.r. ©Ed Reschke/Peter Arnold, Inc. **535** m.b. ©Michael Fogden/DRK Photo **535** m.t. ©Robert W. Domm/Visuals Unlimited **535** t.l. ©Jeff Lepore/Photo Researchers, Inc. **535** t.r. ©Laurie Campbell/Stone **536** b. ©David Scharf/Peter Arnold, Inc. **536** t. ©Jack M. Bostrack/Visuals Unlimited **537** D. Redecker (B-E), R. Kodner (A); ©Science, 2000 **538** ©Stephen G. Maka/DRK Photo **539** b. ©Michael Fogden/DRK Photo **539** m.t. ©Holt Studios International/Nigel Cattlin/Photo Researchers, Inc. **539** t.l. ©Astrid & Hanns-Frieder Michler/Science Photo Library/Photo Researchers, Inc. **539** t.r. ©Dr. P. Marazzi/Photo Researchers, Inc. **540** b. ©L. West/Photo Researchers, Inc. **540** m. ©Jack Dermid **540** t. ©Courtney Milne **541** Mark Richards/PhotoEdit **542** b. Runk/Schoenberger/Grant Heilman Photography **542** t. ©John D. Cunningham/Visuals Unlimited **543** Richard Haynes Photography/Pearson Education/PH School **548–549** ©Royalty-Free/Corbis **549** b. Courtesy of Ken Miller **550** Terry Donnelly/Dembinsky Photo Associates **551** Runk/Schoenberger/Grant Heilman Photography **552** ©Russell D. Curtis/Photo Researchers, Inc. **553** b. Animals Animals/©Joyce & Frank Burek **553** t. Jane Grushow/Grant Heilman Photography **554** Hans Steur, The Netherlands **555** cw: 1 ©Dorling Kindersley **555** cw: 2 ©Ed Reschke/Peter Arnold, Inc. **555** cw: 3 ©Ed Reschke/Peter Arnold, Inc. **555** cw: 4 ©Pat Lynch/Photo Researchers, Inc. **556** ©Terry Donnelly/Stone **557** l. ©Alvin E. Staffan/National Audubon Society/Photo Researchers, Inc. **557** r. Robert & Linda Mitchell Photography **559** ©Farrell Greham/Photo Researchers, Inc. **560** b. ©Brad Mogen/Visuals Unlimited **560** t. ©Dorling Kindersley **561** l. ©Gary W. Carter/Visuals Unlimited **561** r. ©Ed Reschke/Peter Arnold, Inc. **562** b.l. ©Biophoto Associates/Photo Researchers, Inc. **562** b.r. ©Ed Reschke/Peter Arnold, Inc. **562** t. ©Peter Chadwick/Dorling Kindersley **564** Animals Animals/©Erwin & Peggy Bauer **565** b. CORBIS Digital Stock **566** b. Peter Chadwick/©Dorling Kindersley **566** t. Dr. E.R. Degginger **567** b. ©Walter H. Hodge/Peter Arnold, Inc. **567** t.l. ©Biophoto Associates/Photo Researchers, Inc. **567** t.r. ©Gerald & Buff Corsi/Visuals Unlimited **568** l. ©Stephen G. Maka/DRK Photo **568** r. Larry Lefever/Grant Heilman Photography **569** l. Hans Reinhard/Bruce Coleman, Inc. **569** r. ©PhotoDisc, Inc., 2001 **571** r. Alana Van Rensselaer **571** l. ©PhotoDisc, Inc., 2001 **572** l. Joy Spurr/Bruce Coleman, Inc. **572** m. Jonathan Buckley/©Dorling Kindersley **572** r. Larry Lefever/Grant Heilman Photography **573** ©Fritz Polking/Visuals Unlimited **574** ©Dorling Kindersley **576** Brian Parker/Tom Stack & Associates **578** Getty Images **580** b. ©Andrew Syred/Science Photo Library/Photo Researchers, Inc. **581** Ray F. Evert, University of Wisconsin **582** l. ©Ed Reschke/Peter Arnold, Inc. **582** m. ©Ed Reschke/Peter Arnold, Inc. **582** r. ©George Wilder/Visuals Unlimited **583** Ray F. Evert, University of Wisconsin **590** ©Ed Reschke/Peter Arnold, Inc. **592** ©Manfred Kage/Peter Arnold, Inc. **594** b.l. ©Geoff Dann/Dorling Kindersley **594** b.r. ©Dorling Kindersley **594** t.l. Barry L. Runk/Grant Heilman Photography **594** t.r. ©Dorling Kindersley **597** ©Dr. Jeremy Burgess/Science Photo Library/Photo Researchers, Inc. **598** b.r. ©Kjell B. Sandved/Visuals Unlimited **598** l. ©Kjell B. Sandved/Visuals Unlimited **598** m. ©Doug Sokell/Visuals Unlimited **598** t.r. ©Brian P. Foss/Visuals Unlimited **600** ©Jack M. Bostrack/Visuals Unlimited **601** Richard Haynes Photography/Pearson Education/PH School **608** ©Carl R. Sams II/Peter Arnold, Inc. **610** b.l. ©Martha Cooper/Peter Arnold, Inc. **610** b.r. ©Manfred Kage/Peter Arnold, Inc. **610** t. ©Walter H. Hodge/Peter Arnold, Inc. **612** l. ©Nigel Cattlin/H.S.I./Photo Researchers, Inc. **612** r. ©Rod Planck/Photo Researchers, Inc. **613** b.l. Geoff Dann©Dorling Kindersley **613** t. Pearson Education/PH School **615** b.l. Animals Animals/©Carroll W. Perkins **615** b.r. ©M. H. Sharp/Photo Researchers, Inc. **615** t.r. ©Geoff Bryant/Photo Researchers, Inc. **617** Florigene Limited **618** ©Dorling Kindersley **619** b. ©Stephen J. Krasemann/Photo Researchers, Inc. **619** t. ©Gregory K. Scott/Photo Researchers, Inc. **620** ©L. Linkhart/Visuals Unlimited **622** Runk/Schoenberger/Grant Heilman Photography **623** b. ©Holt Studios Int./Photo Researchers, Inc. **623** t. ©Michael P. Gadomski/Photo Researchers, Inc. **624** b.l. ©Werner H. Muller/Peter Arnold, Inc. **624** b.r. ©Keren Su/CORBIS **624** m.l. ©PhotoDisc, Inc., 2001 **624** m.r. SBG **624** t. ©Wolfgang Kaehler/CORBIS **625** b. ©PhotoDisc, Inc., 2001 **625** t.l. ©Holt Studios Int./Nigel Cattlin/Photo Researchers, Inc. **625** t.r. ©David Cavagnaro/Peter Arnold, Inc. **626** ©Michael P. Gadomski/Photo Researchers, Inc. **632** ©Dr. Paul A. Zahl/Photo Researchers, Inc. **633** Animals Animals/©Dani/Jeske **635** Dr. E.R. Degginger **637** ©Sylvan Wittwer/Visuals Unlimited **638** Courtesy of Stephen Gladfelter, Stanford University **639** ©Charles D. Winters/Photo Researchers, Inc. **640** ©Ed. Reschke/Peter Arnold, Inc. **642** ©Ed. Reschke/Peter Arnold, Inc. **643** ©Paul A. Souders/CORBIS **644** ©Doug Sokell/Visuals Unlimited **645** b. ©Ray Pfortner/Peter Arnold, Inc. **645** t. Sean Morris/©Oxford Scientific Films **646** l. ©Bill Ivy/Stone **646** r. ©Rod Planck/Photo Researchers, Inc. **647** Richard Haynes Photography/Pearson

Credits

Education/PH School **648** ©Jack Bostrack/Visuals Unlimited **654–655** ©Dwight Kuhn **655** b. Russ Lappa/PH School **656** Fred McConnaughey/Photo Researchers, Inc. **657** ©Ken Highfill/Photo Researchers, Inc. **658** b.l. ©BIOS (F. Marquez)/Peter Arnold, Inc. **658** b.r. ©Roger Eriksson **658** m.l. Francisco Cruz/SuperStock **658** t.l. ©John Cancalosi/ DRK Photo **659** b. ©Tom & Pat Leeson/Photo Researchers, Inc. **659** l. ©Anthony Bannister/Photo Researchers, Inc. **659** r. ©Kevin Schafer/Stone **661** ©Carolina Biological Supply/Phototake **663** F. Rauschenbach/Natural Selection Stock Photography, Inc. **664** l. ©Mary Beth Angelo/Photo Researchers, Inc. **664** r. ©Charles V. Angelo/Photo Researchers, Inc. **667** ©Fred McConnaughey/Photo Researchers, Inc. **668** ©Larry Dunmire/Photo Network/PictureQuest **671** l. Jeffrey L. Rotman **671** r. ©Mary Beth Angelo/Photo Researchers, Inc. **673** b. ©2001 Norbert Wu/www.norbertwu.com **673** t.l. Copyright ©2000 Harbor Branch Oceanographic/E. Widder **673** t.r. Copyright ©2000 Harbor Branch Oceanographic **674** ©Doug Perrine/Innerspace Visions **675** ©2001 Norbert Wu/www.norbertwu.com **677** Pearson Education/PH School **682** ©Jeffrey L. Rotman **683** ©Fred McConnaughey/Photo Researchers, Inc. **684** ©Drs. Kessel and Shih/Peter Arnold, Inc. **685** ©Carolina Biological Supply Company/Phototake **686** l. ©Jeffrey L. Rotman/Peter Arnold, Inc. **686** r. ©Brian Rogers/Visuals Unlimited **688** ©Oliver Meckes/Photo Researchers, Inc. **689** ©Cabisco/Visuals Unlimited **690** b. ©David Scharf/Peter Arnold, Inc. **690** t. ©Oliver Meckes/Photo Researchers, Inc. **691** b. ©R. Umesh Chandran, TDR, WHO/Science Photo Library/Photo Researchers, Inc. **691** t.l. ©PhotoDisc, Inc., 2001 **691** t.r. Jim Foster/Pearson Education/PH School **692** ©C. James Webb/Phototake NYC **693** l. ©Sinclair Stammers/Science Photo Library/Photo Researchers, Inc. **693** r. ©Fernand Ivaldi/Stone **694** ©Kjell B. Sandved/Visuals Unlimited **695** b. Animals Animals/©Raymond A. Mendez **695** t. Pearson Education/PH School **696** b. Bruce Coleman, Ltd. **696** t. ©Aldo Brando/Peter Arnold, Inc. **698** b. ©Hal Beral/Visuals Unlimited **698** t.l. ©C.P. Hickman/Visuals Unlimited **698** t.r. National Archives **699** ©Robert Pickett/CORBIS **700** James F. Lubner, University of Wisconsin Sea Grant Institute **701** ©Kelvin Aitken/Peter Arnold, Inc. **704** b. ©Fred Bavendam/Peter Arnold, Inc. **704** ©Jane Burton/Dorling Kindersley **705** b.r. ©Alexandra Edwards/Peter Arnold, Inc. **705** t.l. ©A. Flowers and L. Newman/Photo Researchers, Inc. **705** t.r. ©William J. Weber/Visuals Unlimited **706** b. ©Dave B. Fleetham/Visuals Unlimited **706** t. ©Fred Bavendam/Peter Arnold, Inc. **707** ©Frank Greenway/Dorling Kindersley **708** ©Heather R. Davidson **710** ©Jeffrey L. Rotman/Peter Arnold, Inc. **712** ©Marty Snyderman/Visuals Unlimited **713** ©T.E. Adams/Visuals Unlimited **714** ©Skip Moody/Dembinsky Photo Associates **715** ©Carolina Biological Supply/Phototake **716** b. ©Dorling Kindersley **716** t. ©John Cancalosi/DRK Photo **719** Barry L. Runk/Grant Heilman Photography **720** ©Rod Planck/Photo Researchers, Inc. **723** b. ©Dorling Kindersley **723** t. ©Franz Lanting/ Minden Pictures, Inc. **724** b. ©BIOS (X. Eichaker)/Peter Arnold, Inc. **724** t. ©R. Calentine/ Visuals Unlimited **725** b. ©Michael & Patricia Fogden/DRK Photo **725** t. ©Tom McHugh/ Photo Researchers, Inc. **726** b.l. ©Dorling Kindersley **726** b.r. ©M.C. Chamberlain/DRK Photo **726** t. Wolfgang Kaehler Photography **727** ©Dorling Kindersley **728** ©Stephen Dalton/Photo Researchers, Inc. **730** b.l. ©David Scharf/Peter Arnold, Inc. **730** b.r. ©Galen Rowell/CORBIS **730** t. ©Martin Dohrn/Science Photo Library/Photo Researchers, Inc. **731** b. AP/Wide World Photos/David Jennings **731** t. ©E. R. Degginger/Photo Researchers, Inc. **734** ©Glenn M. Oliver/Visuals Unlimited **736** ©Dorling Kindersley **737** b.l. ©Fred Bavendam/Peter Arnold, Inc. **737** b.r. ©Andrew J. Martinez/Photo Researchers, Inc. **737** m. Animals Animals/©Clay Wiseman **737** t. ©Charles V. Angelo/Photo Researchers, Inc. **738** b. ©James Amos/Photo Researchers, Inc. **738** t. ©M.C. Chamberlain/DRK Photo **739** Raymond A Mendez/Animals Animals **744** ©Brandon Cole/Visuals Unlimited **746** Chip Clark/National Museum of Natural History, Smithsonian **750** Runk/Schoenberger/ Grant Heilman Photography **751** ©Ray Coleman/Photo Researchers, Inc. **753** Pearson Education/PH School **757** ©Lawrence Naylor/Photo Researchers, Inc. **758** b. ©Kelvin Aitken/Peter Arnold, Inc. **758** t. ©Brandon D. Cole **759** Pearson Education/PH School **764–765** Steve Bloom Images **765** b. Russ Lappa/PH School **766** ©Art Wolfe/Stone **769** Animals Animals/©W. Gregory Brown **770** Runk/Schoenberger/Grant Heilman Photography **771** ©Labat-Lanceau/AUSCAPE International **773** Dr. Michael E. Williams/Cleveland Museum of Natural History **774** www.norbertwu.com **775** b. Animals Animals/©A. Root **775** t. Pearson Education/PH School **777** ©Richard T. Nowitz/ Photo Researchers, Inc. **778** b. ©Brian Parker/Tom Stack & Associates **778** m. Animals Animals/©Zig Leszczynski **778** t. ©Natalie Fobes/Stone **779** b. ©Stephen Frink/Stone **779** m. Animals Animals/©Herb Segars **779** t. Howard Hall Productions **780** m.l. ©2001 Stephen Frink/Waterhouse Stock **780** m.r. Howard Hall Productions **780** m.t. ©Fred Bavendam/Minden Pictures, Inc. **780** t.l. ©Fred Bavendam/Minden Pictures, Inc. **780** t.r. ©Norbert Wu/DRK Photo **781** ©Ralph A. Clevenger/CORBIS **787** Animals Animals/ ©Bill Beatty **788** b.l. Animals Animals/©Juan Manuel Renjifo **788** b.r. ©Dorling Kindersley **788** t.l. ©William Leonard/DRK Photo **789** Animals Animals/©Stephen Dalton **791** Pearson Education/PH School **792** b. ©Labat-Lanceau/AUSCAPE International **792** t. ©William Leonard/DRK Photo **796** ©Bruce Coleman, Ltd./Natural Selection **797** ©David A. Northcott/CORBIS **800** ©Joe McDonald/Natural Selection **801** ©Michael Fogden/DRK Photo **802** b. ©E.R. Degginger/Photo Researchers, Inc. **802** t.l. ©Michael Fogden/DRK Photo **802** t.r. ©Michael Fogden/DRK Photo **804** b.l. ©John Cancalosi/Peter Arnold, Inc. **804** b.r. ©Gary Retherford/Photo Researchers, Inc. **804** m. Michael & Patricia Fogden/CORBIS **804** t.l. ©Dorling Kindersley **804** t.r. ©Anup & Manoj Shah/DRK Photo **805** ©Gerry Ellis/gerryellis.com **806** AP/Wide World Photos **807** ©Sinclair Stammers/Science Photo Library/Photo Researchers, Inc. **808** t-b:1 ©Steve Gettle/gerryellis.com **808** t-b:2 ©Joe McDonald/DRK Photo **808** t-b:3 ©Gerry Ellis/ gerryellis.com **808** t-b:4 ©Michael Fogden/DRK Photo **808** t-b:5 © McDonald Wildlife Photo., Inc./DRK Photo **808** t-b:6 ©Frans Lanting/Minden Pictures, Inc. **813** cw: 1 ©Stephen J. Krasemann/DRK Photo **813** cw: 2 Michael Gore/Frank Lane Picture Agency/CORBIS **813** cw: 3 ©Tim Davis/Photo Researchers, Inc. **813** cw: 4 ©M.H. Sharp/ Photo Researchers, Inc. **813** cw: 5 ©PhotoDisc, Inc., 2001 **813** cw: 6 Seldon Jr., W. Lynn/Omni-Photo Communications, Inc. **813** m.l. ©2000, Gail Shumway/FPG International LLC **814** ©Wayne Lankinen/DRK Photo **815** AP/Wide World Photos **816** ©Dorling Kindersley **820** ©Zefa (RM)/M. Botzek/Masterfile **821** ©Frans Lanting/ Minden Pictures, Inc. **822** b. ©Flip Nicklin/Minden Pictures, Inc. **822** t. Daniel J. Cox/ naturalexposures.com **824** ©The Stock Market/Keenan Ward **826** b. ©Thomas Mangelsen/ Minden Pictures, Inc. **826** t.l. ©Jany Sauvanet/Photo Researchers, Inc. **826** t.r. ©Mitsuaki Iwago/Minden Pictures, Inc. **827** l. ©Manfred Danegger/OKAPIA/Photo Researchers, Inc. **827** m. ©Stephen Dalton/Photo Researchers, Inc. **827** r. ©Gregory Ochocki/Photo Researchers, Inc. **828** ©Tom McHugh/Photo Researchers, Inc. **829** b. Nicole Galeazzi/Omni-Photo Communications, Inc. **829** m. ©D. Parer and E. Parer-Cook/Stone **829** t.r. ©Art Wolfe/ Stone **830** cw: 1 ©Merlin D. Tuttle/Bat Conservation International/Photo Researchers, Inc. **830** cw: 2 ©Wayne Lawler/Photo Researchers, Inc. **830** cw: 3 ©Stone **830** cw: 4 Graeme Ellis-Ursus/Ursus Photography, Vancouver **830** cw: 5 ©Doug Perrine/Innerspace Visions **830** cw: 6 ©Anthony Mercieca/Photo Researchers, Inc. **831** b.l. ©Thomas Kitchin/Natural Selection **831** b.r. ©Frans Lanting/Minden Pictures, Inc. **831** m.l. Animals Animals/ ©Michael Dick **831** m.r. Daniel J. Cox/naturalexposures.com **831** t.l. ©Tui De Roy/Minden Pictures, Inc. **831** t.r. Daniel J. Cox/naturalexposures.com **833** ©Gerry Ellis/Minden Pictures, Inc. **834** l-r #1 ©Mitsuaki Iwago/Minden Pictures, Inc. **834** l-r #2 ©Frans Lanting/ Minden Pictures, Inc. **834** l-r #3 ©Tom McHugh/Photo Researchers, Inc. **834** l-r #4 Kevin Schafer **834** l-r #5 Daniel J. Cox/naturalexposures.com **834** l-r #6 ©Tim Davis/Photo Researchers, Inc. **834** l-r #7 ©Mark Newman/Photo Researchers, Inc. **834** l-r #8 ©Fra Lanting/Minden Pictures, Inc. **834** l-r #9 ©Tim Davis/Photo Researchers, Inc. **834** l-r # ©PhotoDisc, Inc., 2001 **836** b. ©Science Photo Library/Photo Researchers, Inc. **836** m. ©Archivo Iconograpico, S.A./CORBIS **836** t. ©John Reader/Science Photo Library/Photo Researchers, Inc. **837** b.l. ©David L. Brill Photography **837** b.r. ©John Reader/Photo Researchers, Inc. **837** t. Institute of Human Origins **838** b. Animals Animals/©E. R. Degginger **838** m. Fred Spoor, copyright National Museums of Kenya **838** t. copyright M.P.F.T **840** Laurie Grace & Janna Brenning/Scientific American Magazine **841** ©De Sazo/Photo Researchers, Inc. **843** l. Runk/Schoenberger/Grant Heilman Photography **843** m. Dwight Kuhn Photography, ©1986 **843** r. Runk/Schoenberger/Grant Heilman Photography **844** ©The Stock Market/Keenan Ward **848** Nigel J. Dennis/Photo Researchers, Inc. **849** S. Conway Morris, University of Cambridge **851** ©Dorling Kindersley **852** CW 1 ©Hal Beral/Visuals Unlimited **852** CW 2 ©Tom & Pat Leeson/Photo Researchers, Inc. **852** CW 3 ©Roger Treadwell/Visuals Unlimited **852** CW 4 Nicole Galeazzi/Omni-Photo Communications, Inc. **852** CW 5 ©Stephen J. Krasemann/DRK Photo **852** CW 6 ©Tom McHugh/Photo Researchers, Inc. **853** ©CORBIS **854** ©Frans Lanting/Minden Pictures, Inc. **856** Animals Animals/©Marian Bacon **857** ©Art Wolfe/Photo Researchers, Inc. **863** The Zoological Society of San Diego **863** b. ©E.R. Degginger/Photo Researchers, Inc. **863** t.l. ©PhotoDisc, Inc., 2001 **864** t.l. ©Fred Bavendam/Minden Pictures, Inc. **864** t.m. ©Stephen J. Krasemann/Photo Researchers, Inc. **864** t.r. Daniel J. Cox/naturalexposures.com **866** b. Daniel J. Cox/naturalexposures.com **866** t. Animals Animals/©Marian Bacon **870** ©OSF/LILLIE, PETER/Animals Animals Enterprises **871** ©Heather Angel/Biofotos **872** b.l. ©Rod Planck/Photo Researchers, Inc. **872** t. ©Joe McDonald/DRK Photo **873** Courtesy of Wolfgang Kaehler **876** William Lishman & Associates Limited **877** Carey Kuhn/Long Marine Lab, Santa Cruz, CA **879** Courtesy of Wolfgang Kaehler **880** Michael K. Nichols/ National Geographic Society **881** b. ©Fred McConnaughey/Photo Researchers, Inc. **881** t. ©Gregory Dimijian/Photo Researchers, Inc. **882** ©Francois Gohier/Photo Researchers, Inc. **882** Philip Gould/CORBIS **883** Anne et Jacques Six **884** ©Francois Gohier/Photo Researchers, Inc. **888–889** ©Allen Birnbach/Masterfile **889** b. Courtesy of Ken Miller **891** l. Corel Professional Photos CD-ROM™ **891** r. ©Jim Cummins/FPG International LLC **894** b.l. ©Dr. Dennis Kunkel/Phototake **894** b.r. Quest/Science Photo Library/Photo Researchers, Inc. **894** t.l. ©David M. Phillips/Visuals Unlimited **894** t.r. ©Michael Abbey/Photo Researchers, Inc. **895** David Mager/Pearson Learning Group **906** Quest/ Science Photo Library/Photo Researchers, Inc. **908** ©Prof. P. Motta, Dept. of Anatomy, University La Sapienza, Rome/Science Photo Library/Photo Researchers, Inc. **909** ©Prof. P. Motta/Dept. of Anatomy, University La Sapienza, Rome/Science Photo Library/Photo Researchers, Inc. **910** l. Pearson Education Corporate Digital Archive **910** r. ©PhotoDisc, Inc., 2001 **911** b. Dr. E.R. Degginger **911** t. ©Dr. Morley Read/Science Photo Library/Photo Researchers, Inc. **912** ©David Young-Wolff/PhotoEdit/PictureQuest **920** ©Getty Images **921** Manny Millan/Sports Illustrated **923** t. ©Andrew Syred/Science Photo Library/ Photo Researchers, Inc. **926** l. ©Eric Graves/Phototake **926** m. ©Biophoto Associates/ Photo Researchers, Inc. **926** r. ©John D. Cunningham/Visuals Unlimited **929** b. ©James Balog/Stone **929** t. Don W. Fawcett/Photo Researchers, Inc. **932** ©Dan McCoy/Rainbow **933** b. ©1996 Jim Cummins/FPG International LLC **933** t. ©Dr. Jeremy Burgess/Science Photo Library/Photo Researchers, Inc. **936** ©Quest/Science Photo Library/Photo Researchers, Inc. **937** Pearson Education/PH School **939** b.l. ©John D. Cunningham/ Visuals Unlimited **939** b.r. ©Andrew Syred/Science Photo Library/Photo Researchers, Inc. **939** t.l. ©Eric Graves/Phototake **939** t.r. ©Biophoto Associates/Photo Researchers, Inc. **940** ©Salisbury District Hospital/Science Photo Library/Photo Researchers, Inc. **942** ©Image Shop/Phototake **943** ©Will & Deni McIntyre/Photo Researchers, Inc. **948** b. ©Joseph Nettis/Photo Researchers, Inc. **948** t. The Granger Collection, New York **949** b.r. ©Hank Morgan/Science Source/Photo Researchers, Inc. **949** t.l. AP/Wide World Photos **949** t.r. ABIOMED, Inc **952** ©Yorgos Nikas/Stone **953** ©Dr. Dennis Kunkel/Phototake **956** ©Prof. Motta, Correr & Nottola/University La Sapienza, Rome/Science Photo Library/Photo Researchers, Inc. **959** l. ©PhotoDisc, Inc., 2001 **959** r. Custom Medical Stock Photo **960** Pearson Education/PH School **961** ©George Hall/Check Six/ PictureQuest **962** ©A. Glauberman/Photo Researchers, Inc. **963** b. ©Science Photo Library/Photo Researchers, Inc. **963** t. ©Science Photo Library/Photo Researchers, Inc. **965** Pearson Education/PH School **966** ©Yorgos Nikas/Stone **967** ©Dr. Dennis Kunkel/ Phototake **970** ©Fred Hossler/Visuals Unlimited **971** b. Bob Daemmrich/Stock, Boston **972** b. ©Don & Pat Valenti/DRK Photo **972** t. ©Chris Harvey/Stone **973** t.l. Grant Heilman Photography **973** t.r. United States Department of Agriculture **982** b. Pearson Education/PH School **983** t.r. ©David Scharf/Peter Arnold, Inc. **984** ©Sovereign/ Phototake **985** John McDonough/Sports Illustrated **987** ©Lennart Nilsson/The Incredible Machine, Albert Bonniers Forlag AB **990** Pearson Education/PH School **992** b. ©David Scharf/Peter Arnold, Inc. **992** t. Bob Daemmrich/Stock, Boston **996** ©David M. Phillips/Photo Researchers, Inc. **997** ©Jeff Greenberg/Visuals Unlimited **1001** David Young-Wolff/PhotoEdit **1007** ©Sloop-Ober/Visuals Unlimited **1009** Florian Franke/ SuperStock **1013** Lennart Nilsson/Albert Bonnier Förlag AB, A CHILD IS BORN, Dell Publishing Company **1015** ©CNRI/Photo Researchers, Inc. **1016** l. The Granger Collection, New York **1016** r. ©Leroy Francis/Photo Researchers, Inc. **1020** ©Dr. Yorgas Nikas/Photo Researchers, Inc. **1021** ©Petit Format/Nestle/Science Source/Photo Researchers, Inc. **1022** b. Keith/Custom Medical Stock Photo **1022** t. ©T. Wiewandt/DRK Photo **1023** b. ©William Campbell/DRK Photo **1023** t. ©Jose Luis Pelaez, Inc./The Stock Market **1024** ©Bob Daemmrich/Stock, Boston/PictureQuest **1025** Pearson Education/PH School **1030** © Juergen Berger/Max-Plank Institute/Science Photo Library/Photo Researchers, Inc. **1031** b. ©Volker Steger/Science Photo Library/Photo Researchers, Inc. **1031** t. ©Carolina Biological Supply/Phototake **1032** ©Microworks/Phototake **1033** b. Fuessl, NEJM.331:301, (1994) **1033** t. ©Oliver Meckes/Photo Researchers, Inc. **1034** ©Mednet/Phototake **1035** ©Oliver Meckes/Photo Researchers, Inc. **1036** Lennart Nilsson/Albert Bonniers Forlag **1040** ©Eye of Science/Photo Researchers, Inc. **1041** Richard Haynes Photography/ Pearson Education/PH School **1042** ©Zeva Oelbaum/Peter Arnold, Inc. **1043** l. ©David Scharf/Peter Arnold, Inc. **1043** m. ©David Scharf/Peter Arnold, Inc. **1043** r. ©Oliver Meckes/ Ottawa/Photo Researchers, Inc. **1044** ©Rodolfo Gonzalez/Denver Rocky Mountain News/ CORBIS Sygma **1045** ©National Institute for Biological Standards and Control, England/ Science Photo Library/Photo Researchers, Inc. **1048** Andy Nelson/The Christian Science Monitor **1049** Getty Images, Inc./Liaison Agency **1051** ©David Smart/DRK Photo **1052** ©Dr. Andrejs Liepins/Science Photo Library/Photo Researchers, Inc. **1054** ©Michael Newman/PhotoEdit **1055** Pearson Education/PH School **1061** ©E.R. Degginger/Photo Researchers, Inc. **1062** ©Mark Moffett/Minden Pictures, Inc. **1063** t. ©Nigel Cattlin/Holt Studios Int'l/Photo Researchers, Inc. **1064** l. ©Dan Smith/Stone **1064** r. ©PhotoDisc, Inc., 2001 **1065** ©Francois Gohier/Photo Researchers, Inc. **1067** Pearson Education/PH School **1072** b. ©Manfred Kage/Peter Arnold, Inc. **1072** m. ©David Scharf/Peter Arnold, Inc. **1072** t. ©Fr. Westall/Eurelios/Phototake **1073** l. Lee Rentz/Bruce Coleman, Inc. **1073** r. ©Ed Reschke/Peter Arnold, Inc. **1074** l. Geoff Dann/©Dorling Kindersley **1074** r. ©Charles V. Angelo/Photo Researchers, Inc. **1075** l. ©R. Calentine/Visuals Unlimited **1075** r. ©John Cancalosi/DRK Photo **1076** b.l. Animals Animals/©Marian Bacon **1076** b.r. ©William Leonard/DRK Photo **1076** t. ©Labat/Jacana/Photo Researchers, Inc. **1077** b Kevin Schafer **1077** t. Merlin D. Tuttle/Bat Conservation International **1078** Animals Animals/©Jennifer Loomis **1079** ©Sarah J. Frankling/Stone **1081** ©Gerry Ellis/Minden Pictures, Inc. **1084** Animals Animals/©Carroll W. Perkins

Periodic Table of the Elements

Nonmetals	Metals	Metalloids	
C	Li	B	Solid
Br	Hg		Liquid
H			Gas
	Tc		Not found in nature

1 1A	2 2A	3 3B	4 4B	5 5B	6 6B	7 7B	8 8B	9 8B
1 **H** Hydrogen 1.0079								
3 **Li** Lithium 6.941	4 **Be** Beryllium 9.0122							
11 **Na** Sodium 22.990	12 **Mg** Magnesium 24.305							
19 **K** Potassium 39.098	20 **Ca** Calcium 40.08	21 **Sc** Scandium 44.956	22 **Ti** Titanium 47.90	23 **V** Vanadium 50.941	24 **Cr** Chromium 51.996	25 **Mn** Manganese 54.938	26 **Fe** Iron 55.847	27 **Co** Cobalt 58.933
37 **Rb** Rubidium 85.468	38 **Sr** Strontium 87.62	39 **Y** Yttrium 88.906	40 **Zr** Zirconium 91.22	41 **Nb** Niobium 92.906	42 **Mo** Molybdenum 95.94	43 **Tc** Technetium (98)	44 **Ru** Ruthenium 101.07	45 **Rh** Rhodium 102.91
55 **Cs** Cesium 132.91	56 **Ba** Barium 137.33	71 **Lu** Lutetium 174.97	72 **Hf** Hafnium 178.49	73 **Ta** Tantalum 180.95	74 **W** Tungsten 183.85	75 **Re** Rhenium 186.21	76 **Os** Osmium 190.2	77 **Ir** Iridium 192.22
87 **Fr** Francium (223)	88 **Ra** Radium (226)	103 **Lr** Lawrencium (262)	104 **Rf** Rutherfordium (261)	105 **Db** Dubnium (262)	106 **Sg** Seaborgium (263)	107 **Bh** Bohrium (264)	108 **Hs** Hassium (265)	109 **Mt** Meitnerium (268)

Lanthanide Series

57 **La** Lanthanum 138.91	58 **Ce** Cerium 140.12	59 **Pr** Praseodymium 140.91	60 **Nd** Neodymium 144.24	61 **Pm** Promethium (145)	62 **Sm** Samarium 150.4

Actinide Series

89 **Ac** Actinium (227)	90 **Th** Thorium 232.04	91 **Pa** Protactinium 231.04	92 **U** Uranium 238.03	93 **Np** Neptunium (237)	94 **Pu** Plutonium (244)